THE LAW OF HUMAN RIGHTS

VOLUME 1

THE LAW OF HUMAN RIGHTS

by

Richard Clayton
Barrister, Devereux Chambers, London

Hugh Tomlinson
Barrister, Matrix Chambers, London

with

Carol George
Solicitor and Lecturer in International Economic Law, London School of Economics

and with the assistance of

Vina Shukla
Barrister, 4 Stone Buildings, London

OXFORD
UNIVERSITY PRESS

OXFORD
UNIVERSITY PRESS

Great Clarendon Street, Oxford OX2 6DP

Oxford University Press is a department of the University of Oxford.
It furthers the University's objective of excellence in research, scholarship,
and education by publishing worldwide in

Oxford New York

Athens Auckland Bangkok Bogotá Buenos Aires Calcutta
Cape Town Chennai Dar es Salaam Delhi Florence Hong Kong Istanbul
Karachi Kuala Lumpur Madrid Melbourne Mexico City Mumbai
Nairobi Paris São Paulo Shanghai Singapore Taipei Tokyo Toronto Warsaw

with associated companies in Berlin Ibadan

Oxford is a registered trade mark of Oxford University Press
in the UK and in certain other countries

Published in the United States
by Oxford University Press Inc., New York

First published 2000

British Library Cataloguing in Publication Data
Data available

Library of Congress Cataloging in Publication Data
Data available

ISBN 0–19–826223–X (set)

ISBN 0–19–924360–3 (Vol. 1)

ISBN 0–19–924361–1 (Vol. 2)

3 5 7 9 10 8 6 4 2

Typeset in Garamond by
Cambrian Typesetters, Frimley, Surrey

Printed in Great Britain
on acid-free paper by
The Bath Press, Bath

FOREWORD

The implementation of the Human Rights Act 1998 has assumed something of the character of a religious event: an event eagerly-sought and long-awaited but arousing feelings of apprehension as well as expectation, the uncertainty that accompanies any new and testing experience. St. Luke's advice is no doubt apposite:

> Let your loins be girded about, and your lights burning. And be yourselves like unto men that wait for their lord, when he will return from the wedding; that when he cometh and knocketh, they may open unto him immediately.

The authors of this book have done all that the evangelist could have wished. They have studied the provisions of the Act. They have mastered the steadily growing body of literature on it. They have read the Strasbourg decisions. They have considered the human rights experience of countries such as Canada, New Zealand, South Africa and the United States and drawn conclusions which may be of value to us here in the United Kingdom when our turn comes.

This is a valuable book, thoughtful and well-researched. And it is thought and careful research which will, in particular, be needed if the British courts are to be guided towards sound and sensible decisions, recognising the important values which infuse the Act but recognising also the strengths of our own native traditions, idiosyncratic though some of them doubtless are. The reader of this book will have his light burning, and will be ready to open when the knock comes.

Tom Bingham
10 January 2000

PREFACE

The early 1990s saw a revival of the 'Bill of Rights' debate which Lord Scarman had prompted in his 1974 Hamlyn Lectures.[1] In 1991, Liberty had published its own, radical, proposal for a bill of rights,[2] and in 1993 the Labour Party announced its conversion to the idea of incorporating the European Convention on Human Rights into the law of the United Kingdom.[3] The supporters of the incorporation of the Convention had prevailed and it seemed likely that, if a Labour Government were to be elected, there would be some form of 'Bill of Rights'.

This was the context in which the idea for the present book began to form in 1994. Our first joint project, *Civil Actions Against the Police*,[4] had dealt with the vindication of rights in a specific area. Discussions with Oxford University Press led to us to propose a more general book dealing with how the English law might develop if the European Convention on Human Rights was, in fact, incorporated. Our original proposal was entitled 'The Bill of Rights in English Law'. It set out to answer two questions: first, to what extent would a Bill of Rights alter the substantive English law of 'rights'; and secondly, if the Convention did become part of English law, how would the English courts interpret it by reference to the English, Strasbourg and Commonwealth authorities.

With these aims in mind we initially told Oxford University Press that our book would be about 350 pages. One academic referee thought it would be twice that amount and even that forecast has been substantially exceeded. Instead of writing a short, freestanding, book about the impact of a possible Bill of Rights, we have found ourselves writing a very long one which forms part of what has become a steady stream of books analysing the effect of the Human Rights Act 1998.

A central theme of our book is that, in approaching human rights questions, the English courts should consider human rights issues from three perspectives: domestic, European and international. Human rights issues cannot be approached solely by reference to Strasbourg case law or decisions in other jurisdictions. We believe that a different approach is necessary. The full implications of introducing Convention rights into our domestic law cannot be appreciated without first

---

[1] L Scarman, *English Law—The New Dimension* (Stevens, 1974).

[2] Liberty, *A People's Charter* (National Council for Civil Liberties, 1991).

[3] For the debate during this period see M Zander, *A Bill of Rights?* (4th edn, Sweet & Maxwell, 1997) 27–39 and see generally para 1.47ff.

[4] 2nd edn, Sweet & Maxwell, 1992.

examining domestic law before the Human Rights Act. The case law of the European Commission and Court of Human Rights is obviously an essential consideration. But consideration must then be given to the international jurisprudence of human rights law, particularly the case law of common law jurisdictions such as Canada, New Zealand and South Africa where human rights instruments were adopted in 1982, 1990 and 1996 respectively. The Court of Appeal and House of Lords in recent years have drawn on principles developed in other jurisdictions when considering human rights issues like freedom of expression[5] and rights to fair trial;[6] and this approach will be equally valuable when formulating and developing new legal principles under the Human Rights Act.

The title we have chosen reflects the broad subject that we have tried to address. We are conscious that no book could fully meet the expectations implicit in the title. It has been necessary to cover an enormous range of domestic legal issues, while the body of international human rights law is immense and continually expanding. For these reasons we do not claim to be comprehensive. What we have tried to do is to draw attention to some of the themes which are important both domestically and internationally. In particular, international case law will provide important and often illuminating source material for the English courts as they confront the challenge of 'putting human rights into practice'. For further details of the approach we have adopted see the Introduction below, from para In.13.

Our own relationship goes back many years. We first met and collaborated in Oxford in 1973. We then took rather different routes which led us to the law and to undertaking various projects together. Over the years we have jointly written *Civil Actions Against the Police*,[7] *Judicial Review Procedure*[8] and *Police Actions: A Practical Guide*.[9] Our shared efforts mean that many (including from time to time the Legal Aid Board) insist that we are, in reality, one and the same person. *The Law of Human Rights* examines a number of themes which we have discussed in our earlier books. To some extent it is a further contribution to the wider project we identified in the Preface to *Civil Actions Against the Police* as one of that book's objectives: an examination of the legal remedies available to the citizen against abuses of power by public authorities.

It is impossible to write a book of this length and complexity without the help and encouragement of many others. We are enormously indebted to Carol George who combines strong academic skills with the practical experience of having been a practising lawyer in Canada. Her diligence and energy led her to shoulder the

[5] *Derbyshire County Council v Times Newspapers* [1993] AC 534 and *Reynolds v Times Newspapers* [1999] 3 WLR 1010.
[6] *R v DPP, ex p Kebilene* [1999] 3 WLR 972.
[7] 2nd edn, Sweet & Maxwell, 1992.
[8] 2nd edn, Chancery Wiley Law Publications, 1996.
[9] 2nd edn, Hart Publishing, Aug 1997.

initial work on the Convention, Canadian and New Zealand case law. Vina Shukla became involved at a later stage; but her expertise in international human rights law (particularly, in South Africa) has greatly contributed to the appendices on the case law in other human rights jurisdictions. Frederic Reynold QC undertook the immense task of reading and commenting on the manuscript; his enthusiasm and counsel has hugely helped us to maintain our momentum in a project which has seemed never ending. Antony Shaw reviewed all the Appendices relating to the New Zealand Bill of Rights Act and gave us the benefit of his unrivalled experience and knowledge in this area.

We have benefited from the generous advice or assistance of a large number of individuals whom we wish to thank: Ben Adamson, John Bowers QC, David Bean QC, Michael Beloff QC, Dr Robin Benians, Keith Bryant, Jeffrey Burke QC, Andrew Burns, Tim Corner, David Craig, Professor Paul Craig QC, Andrew Davies, Richard Drabble QC, James Goudie QC, Robert Griffiths QC, Richard Harrison, Lisa Harvey, Charles Howard QC, Natasha Joffe, Alan Levy QC, Clive Lewis, Ken Macdonald QC, Suzanne McKie, John McLinden, Professor Gillian Morris, Akash Nawbatt, Estelle Overs, Heather Rogers, Liz Shurdom, Ingrid Simler, Alison Padfield, Rabinder Singh, Nicholas Randall, James Taylor, John Wadham, Rob Weir and Susan Willcox. We have each given many talks on the implications of the Human Rights Act; and have benefited from debating specific points with many other individuals whom we also wish to thank.

We are particularly grateful to Lord Bingham for finding the time, amongst his many commitments, to look at the manuscript and to write the generous Foreword. We hope that this book will serve to temper the evangelism of those who see the implementation of the Human Rights Act as a religious event.

We would also like to thank those at Oxford University Press who have been associated with this project. The book is not only substantially longer than intended, but our timing has not been very accurate. Had we been involved in the determination of civil rights and obligations, there would have been a clear breach of Article 6. The first deadline we missed for submitting the manuscript was in January 1998. There have been many others. Chris Rycroft has been a consistent support in trying to lighten our burden. Rebecca Allen has displayed great patience in chasing the recalcitrant authors.

Attempting to combine writing this book with full time practice has put our families under considerable (and often unfair) strain. We are very grateful to Anne and Caroline for the good humour and tolerance which they have succeeded in retaining; and would like to thank our children, Ben and Jack and Georgia, Felix and Fred for the patience they have shown.

The breadth of the material covered in this book has stretched us to the full. We have tried to survey very disparate areas of English law and to understand the human rights and constitutional principles of many different jurisdictions. Furthermore, our predictions about the impact of the Human Rights Act on English law are inevitably speculative and incomplete. There are increasing numbers of statutory amendments designed to ensure that English law is consistent with the Convention.[10] We have tried to incorporate as many of these as possible but the pace of change is such that we may not have caught every development in this area. The responsibility for errors and omissions is entirely our own.

We have attempted to cover the law up to 1 May 2000 but we have been able to include some later material. Regular cumulative supplements will be issued to keep the book updated between editions.

Richard Clayton
Devereux Chambers
Devereux Court
London WC2R 3JJ

Hugh Tomlinson
Matrix Chambers
Gray's Inn
London WC1R 5LN

15 May 2000

[10] See eg Youth Justice and Criminal Evidence Act 1999, s 58 (inferences from silence) and s 59 and Sch 3 (restrictions on answers obtained by compulsion) and the Regulation of Investigatory Powers Act 2000.

CONTENTS—SUMMARY

VOLUME 1

CONTENTS

VOLUME 1

VOLUME 2

APPENDICES

TABLES OF CASES

A. Alphabetical—All Cases

A (Application for Leave), Re [1998] 1 FLR 1, CA 11.365
A (A Minor), Re [1992] 3 Med L Rev 303 .... 7.07
A *v* A (Shared Residence Order) [1994] 1 FLR 669 .... 13.23
A *v* France (Application 17262/90) (1991) 68 DR 319, ECommHR 22.41
A *v* France Series A No 277-B, (1993) 17 EHRR 462, ECtHR 6.130, 12.91, 12.105, 12.119, 12.126
A *v* Spain (Application 13750/88) (1990) 66 DR 188, ECommHR 16.67
A *v* Switzerland (Application 10248/83) (1984) 38 DR 219, ECommHR 9.30
A *v* United Kingdom (Application 3625/67) (1970) 13 YB 340; (1970) 36 CD 1 ECommHR 20.22
A *v* United Kingdom (Application 6840/74) (1980) 20 DR 5; (1980) 3 EHRR 131, ECommHR 8.47, 8.68
A *v* United Kingdom (Application 25599/94) (1998) 27 EHRR 611; RJD 1998-VI 2692; (1998) 5 BHRC 137; [1998] 3 FCR 597; [1998] 2 FLR 959; [1998] Fam Law 733; [1998] Crim LR 892, ECtHR 3.82, 5.10, 8.15, 8.20, 8.27, 8.61, 8.66, 13.02, 21.47, 21.166
A and A *v* Netherlands (Application 14501/89) (1992) 72 DR 118, ECommHR 13.96
A and others *v* Denmark (Application 20826/92) (1996) 22 EHRR 458; RJD 1996-I 85, ECtHR 22.25
A Association *v* Austria (Application 9905/82) (1984) 36 DR 187, ECommHR 22.22
A B *v* South West Water Services Ltd [1992] 4 All ER 574; [1993] QB 507; [1993] 2 WLR 507; [1993] 1 All ER 609, CA 21.69, 21.71, 21.74
A, B and Company AS *v* Germany (Application 7742/76) (1978) 14 DR 146, ECommHR 18.35, 18.37
A, B, C, D *v* United Kingdom (Application 8531/79) (1981) 23 DR 203 ECommHR 18.75, 18.91
ABBM Printing and Publishing (Pty) Ltd *v* Transnet Ltd 1997 (10) BCLR 1429; 1998 (2) SA 109 (SA) 6.158
ADT *v* United Kingdom (Application 35765/97), 16 March 1999, ECtHR 12.152, 12.159, 17.130, 17.148
AGOSI *v* United Kingdom. *see* Allgemeine Gold- und Silverscheideanstalt (AGOSI) *v* United Kingdom
APB Ltd, APP and AEB *v* United Kingdom (Application 30552/96) (1998) 25 EHRR CD 141, ECommHR 11.177, 11.199, 11.329, 11.331
ARM Chappell (Application 12587/86) (1987) 53 DR 241, ECommHR 22.25
ARW Transformers *v* Cupples [1977] IRLR 228 .... 17.44

Strickland *v* Ermel (1992) 91 DLR (4th) 694, Sask QB; [1994] 1 WWR 417, Sask CA Can) 16.128, 16.130
Stubbings *v* Webb [1992] QB 197; [1991] 3 WLR 383; [1991] 3 All ER 949, CA; [1993] AC 498; [1993] 2 WLR 120, HL 11.277
Stubbings and others *v* United Kingdom (Applications 22083/93 and 22095/93) (1996) 23 EHRR 213; RJD 1996-IV 1487; [1997] 3 FCR 157, [1997] 1 FLR 105, ECtHR 5.83, 6.118, 11.192A, 11.277, 17.89, 17.139, 21.155
Student Representative Council of Molepolole College of Education *v* Attorney-General of Botswana *see* Molepolole College Student Representative Council *v* Attorney-General of Botswana
Subash Kumar *v* Bihar AIR 1991 SC 420 (SC Ind) 7.94
Subramanien *v* Government of Mauritius [1995] 4 LRC 320 (Maur) 18.138-18.139
Sudath Silva *v* Kodituwakku (1987) 2 Sri LR 119 (Sri L) 8.128
Sugarman *v* Dougall (1973) 413 US 634 (SC US) 17.207
Sulak *v* Turkey (Application 24515/94) (1996) 84-A DR 98, ECommHR 19.37, 19.48
Sumayyah Mohamed (A Minor) *v* Lucia Moraine [1996] 3 LRC 475 (HC Trin & Tob) 14.132
Sunday Times case *see* Attorney-General *v* Times Newspapers Ltd.
Sunday Times *v* United Kingdom Series A No 30, (1979) 2 EHRR 245, ECtHR . 6.18-6.19, 6.36, 6.43, 6.45, 6.52, 6.73, 6.128-6.129, 6.132-6.134, 6.147, 10.125, 10.193, 12.127, 15.48, 15.149, 15.154, 15.176, 15.187-15.189, 15.191, 15.196, 15.212-15.213, 15.218, 15.226, 22.22, 22.25
Sunday Times *v* United Kingdom (No 2) Series A No 217, (1991) 14 EHRR 229, ECtHR 2.08, 15.155, 17.118, 17.134, 23.74
Sunday trading cases *see* R *v* Stoke on Trent Council, *ex p* B & Q
Sunil Batra *v* Delhi Administration (No 1) AIR 1978 SC 597 (SC Ind) 8.114
Sunil Batra *v* Delhi Administration (No 2) AIR 1980 SC 1579 (SC Ind) 8.114, 15.196, 15.218, 15.230
Suraj *v* State of MP AIR 1960 MP 303 (Ind) 9.44
Suraj Mall *v* ITI Commissioner AIR 1954 SC 545 (SC Ind) 17.218
Surek *v* Turkey (No 1) (Application 26682/95), 8 July 1999, ECtHR 15.198
Surek *v* Turkey (No 2) (Application 24122/94), 8 July 1999, ECtHR 15.198
Surek *v* Turkey (No 4) (Application 24762/94), 8 July 1999, ECtHR 15.198
Sullivan *v* New York Times (1964) 376 US 254 (SC US) 15.36
Surrey County Council *v* Minister of Education [1953] 1 WLR 516; [1953] 1 All ER 705 .... 19.30
Sutcliffe *v* Pressdram Ltd [1991] QB 153; [1990] 2 WLR 271; [1990] 1 All ER 269, CA 15.38
Sutherland *v* United Kingdom (Application 25186/94) [1997] EHRLR 117, ECommHR 12.159, 17.125, 17.130, 17.148, 17.161
Suthipong Smittachartch, Re [1993] 1 HKLR 93 (HK) 11.469
Sutter *v* Switzerland (Application 8209/78) (1979) 16 DR 166, ECommHR 11.224
Sutter *v* Switzerland Series A No 74, (1984) 6 EHRR 272, ECtHR 11.232
Svenska Managementgruppen *v* Sweden (Application 11036/84) (1985) 45 DR 211, ECommHR 18.75
Swami Motor Transport (P) Ltd *v* Sankaraswamigal Mutt 1963 Supp (1) SCR 282 (Ind) 18.127
Swann *v* Charlotte-Mecklenburg Board of Education (1971) 402 US 1 (SC US) 19.100, 21.153
Swaptronics, Re, 31 July 1998, *The Times*, 17 August 1998 .... 3.40, 11.48
Swedish Engine Driver's Union *v* Sweden Series A No 20, (1976) 1 EHRR 617, ECtHR 5.10, 5.32, 6.27, 16.75-16.76
Swinney *v* Chief Constable of Northumbria Police Force [1997] QB 464; [1996] 3 WLR 968; [1996] 3 All ER 449, CA 11.45
Sybron Corporation *v* Barclays Bank plc [1985] Ch 299; [1984] 3 WLR 1055 .... 12.33
Szrabjer and Clarke *v* United Kingdom (Applications 27004/95 and 27011/95) [1988] EHRLR 230, ECommHR 18.39, 18.93, 18.109

T (Adult: Refusal of Treatment), *In re* [1993] Fam 95; [1992] 3 WLR 782; [1992] 4 All ER 649, CA 7.19

B. Chronological and Numerical

1. European Commission of Human Rights

1956

1978

1979

1983

1984

1985

1994

2. European Court of Justice

3. Court of First Instance

TABLES OF LEGISLATION AND TREATIES

A. UK Statutes

Abortion Act 1967 ....17.162
s 1 ....7.11
Access to Health Records Act 1990 ....12.48
Access to Justice Act 1999 ....11.52
s 1 ....11.52
s 5 ....11.52
s 10 ....11.53
s 12 ....11.52
s 17(1) 11.95
(2) 11.95
(3) 11.95
Pt I 11.95
Sch 2 ....11.52
Sch 3
para 2 11.95
para 5(1) 11.95
(2) 11.95
(4) 11.95
Access to Medical Reports Act 1988 ....12.48
Access to Personal Files Act 1987 ....12.47
Acquisition of Land Act 1981 ....18.18
Acquisition of Land (Assessment of Compensation) Act 1919 ....1.67
Act of Settlement 1700 ....1.89, 11.10
s 2 ....14.17
s 3 ....14.17, 20.07
Administration of Justice Act 1960
s 12 ....11.79, 11.83
s 14(2) 10.12
Administration of Justice Act 1970
s 8 ....18.99
s 36 ....11.318, 18.99
Adoption Act 1976
s 6 ....13.45, 13.47
s 12(6) 13.47
s 13(1)-(2) 13.46
s 16(1)(b) 13.46
s 24(2) 13.47
s 39 ....13.44, 13.57
s 40 ....13.52
s 72 ....17.158
Air Force Act 1955
s 29A 16.45
ss 31-39 ....16.45
Arbitration Act 1996 ....11.21
s 12(3) 11.317A
Armed Forces Act 1996
Sch I 11.65
Pt III 11.65
Army Act 1955 ....10.31, 11.296
s 29A 16.45
ss 31-39 ....16.45
Army Act 1996 ....11.141
Asylum and Immigration Act 1995 ....10.52-10.53
Asylum and Immigration Appeals Act 1993 ....3.86, 5.106, 10.52

Bail Act 1976 ....10.177
s 3(6) 10.58
s 3A 10.58
(1) 10.47
s 4(1) 10.57
(8A) 10.60
s 5(3) 10.57
s 7 ....10.178
Sch 1
para 2 ....10.57
para 2A 10.178
para 3 ....10.57
para 4 ....10.57
paras 6-7 ....10.57
para 6 ....10.178
para 8 ....10.58

B. UK Statutory Instruments

C. National Legislation from other Jurisdictions

D. Treaties and Conventions

E. EC Legislation

Regulations

Directives

LIST OF ABBREVIATIONS

Ad & EL	Adolphus and Ellis' Reports
A-G	Attorney General
AG	Advocate General (EC)
AIR	All India Reporter
AJCL	American Journal of Comparative Law
ALJ	Australian Law Journal
All ER	All England Reports
ALR	Australian Law Reports
Alta	Alberta
Ant & Bar	Antigua and Barbuda
AR	Alberta Reports
Auck	Auckland
Aus	Australia
B & C	Barnewall & Creswell
BCC	British Company Cases
BCCA	British Columbia Court of Appeal
BCLR	Butterworths Constitutional Law Reports
BCSC	British Columbia Supreme Court
Berm	Bermuda
BHRC	Butterworths Human Rights Cases
BMLR	Butterworths Medico-Legal Reports
Botsw	Botswana
BYIL	British Yearbook of International Law
CA	Court of Appeal
Can	Canada
CC	Constitutional Court
CC	County Court
CCA	Court of Criminal Appeal
CCC	Central Criminal Court (Canada)
CFI	Court of First Instance
ChD	Chancery Division, High Court
CHRD	Commonwealth Human Rights Digest
CLC	Commercial Law Cases
CLJ	Cambridge Law Journal
CLP	Current Legal Problems
CLR	Commonwealth Law Reports (Australia)
CMLR	Common Market Law Reports
Co Rep	Coke's King's Bench Reports
COD	Crown Office Digest

Col	Colorado
Coll	Collection of Decisions of ECommHR before 1975
CPD	Cape Provincial Division (South Africa)
CR	Criminal Reports (Canada)
Crim	Criminal
Crim LR	Criminal Law Review
DC	Divisional Court, High Court
Div Ct	Divisional Court
DLR	Dominion Law Reports
DPP	Director of Public Prosecutions
DR	Decisions and Reports of the ECommHR from 1975 onwards
East	East's Term Reports, King's Bench
EAT	Employment Appeal Tribunal
ECJ	European Court of Justice
ECommHR	European Commission of Human Rights
ECR	European Court Reports
ECtHR	European Court of Human Rights
EHRLR	European Human Rights Law Review
EHRR	European Human Rights Reports
EJIL	European Journal of International Law
EMLR	Entertainment and Media Law Reports
Env LR	Environmental Law Reports
Eur	European
Fam Div	Family Division, High Court
Fam Law	Family Law
FC	Federal Court
FCR	Family Court Reporter
Fed	Federal
FLR	Family Law Reports
FSR	Fleet Street Reports
Gam	Gambia
Guj	Gujerat
GWD	Green's Weekly Digest (Scotland)
H & N	Hurlstone and Norman's Exchequer Reports
HC	High Court
HCJ	High Court Justiciary
HK	Hong Kong
HKLR	Hong Kong Law Reports
HL	House of Lords
HLR	Housing Law Reports
Hob	Hobart's Reports (Common Pleas and King's Bench)
HRNZ	Human Rights Reports of New Zealand
ICLQ	International and Comparative Law Quarterly
ICR	Industrial Case Reports
ILJ	Industrial Law Journal

Ill	Illinois
ILR	International Law Reports
ILRM	Irish Law Reports Monthly
Imm AR	Immigration Appeal Reports
Ind	India
Intl	International
IR	Irish Reports
Ire	Ireland
IRLR	Industrial Relations Law Reports
J	Journal
Jam	Jamaica
JP	Justice of the Peace Reports
JPL	Journal of Planning and Environment Law
JR	Judicial Review
Ken	Kenya
L S Gaz R	Law Society Gazette Reports
LD Raym	Lord Raymond's King's Bench Reports
Les	Lesotho
LGR	Local Government Reports
Lloyd's Rep	Lloyd's Law Reports
LQR	Law Quarterly Review
LRC	Law Reports of the Commonwealth
LT	LawTimes
M & W	Meeson and Welsby's Exchequer Reports
Man	Manitoba
Maur	Mauritius
McGill LJ	McGill Law Journal
Med L Rev	Medical Law Review
Mel U L Rev	Melbourne University Law Review
MLR	Modern Law Review
Nam	Namibia
NBQB	New Brunswick Queen's Bench
NBR	New Brunswick Reports
Nfld	Newfoundland
NI	Northern Ireland
Nig	Nigeria
NIJB	Northern Ireland Judgment Bulletin
NLJ	New Law Journal
NLJR	New Law Journal Reports
NLR	New Law Reports (Sri Lanka)
NSR	Nova Scotia Reports
NWTCA	North West Territories Court of Appeal
NWTR	North West Territories Reports
NWTSC	North West Territories Supreme Court
NZ	New Zealand

NZLJ	New Zealand Law Journal
NZLR	New Zealand Law Reports
OJLS	Oxford Journal of Legal Studies
Ont CA	Ontario Court of Appeal
Ont Dist Ct	Ontario District Court
Ont Gen Div	Ontario General Division
Ont HCJ	Ontario High Court Justiciary
OR	Ontario Reports
P	Probate, Divorce and Admiralty (Law Reports, 1891—)
PAD	Planning Appeal Decisions
Pak	Pakistan
Papua NG	Papua New Guinea
PC	Privy Council
PL	Public Law
PLR	Planning Law Reports
Prov Ct	Provincial Court
Q	Quarterly
QB	Queen's Bench Division, High Court
Que	Quebec
R	Reports
R & IT	Rating and Income Tax Reports
RA	Rating Appeals
Rev	Review
RJD	Reports of Judgments and Decisions of the ECtHR from 1996 onwards
RPC	Reports of Patent, Design and Trade Mark Cases
RTR	Road Traffic Reports
RVR	Rating and Valuation Reporter
S Aus	South Australia
SA	South Africa
Sask	Saskatchewan
Sask R	Saskatchewan Reports
SC	Supreme Court
SC Can	Supreme Court, Canada
SC NS	Supreme Court, Nova Scotia
SC US	Supreme Court, United States of America
SCC	Supreme Court Cases
Sc/Scot	Scotland
SCR	Supreme Court Reports (Canada)
Series A	Official report of all judgments of the ECtHR up to 1995
Sing	Singapore
SLR	Scottish Law Reporter (1865—1925)
Sol Is	Solomon Islands
Sol Jo	Solicitor's Journal
Sri L	Sri Lanka
St C, N & A	St Christopher, Nevis and Anguilla

State Tr	State Trials
Statute LR	Statute Law Review
STC	Simon's Tax Cases
Tanz	Tanzania
TLR	Times Law Reports
Trin & Tob	Trinidad and Tobago
U	University
UNHRC	Human Rights Committee
US	United States of America
VR	Victorian Reports (Australia, 1875—1956)
Web JCL	Web Journal of Current Legal Issues
WIR	West Indian Reports
WLR	Weekly Law Reports
WN	Weekly Notes
WWR	Western Weekly Reports (Canada)
YB	Yearbook of European Convention on Human Rights
Ybk	Yearbook
YEL	Yearbook of European Law
YT CA	Yukon Territory Court of Appeal
Zam	Zambia
Zim	Zimbabwe
ZLR	Zimbabwe Law Reports

INTRODUCTION

A. The English Law and Human Rights

In writing this book we have set out to provide a practitioner's textbook on the law of human rights in England and Wales following the implementation of the Human Rights Act 1998. A textbook on the English law of human rights is not a straightforward undertaking. Even a decade ago, such a book would have been greeted with surprise: the law of human rights was something for other jurisdictions. In this introduction we briefly consider the development of this new area of law and, in particular, the influence of international jurisprudence. We will then describe the structure of the book and map out some possible future developments. The book has been written at a turning point in legal history: at the time when international human rights law begins to be woven into the fabric of the common law. At this stage, the new framework can only be sketched in barest outline. Its shape and content remain to be formed. As a result, the book must face two ways: back to the past and forward to the future. It is both descriptive and indicative. **In.01**

We begin with a brief description of the history of human rights in English law.[1] Although the rights of individuals lie at the heart of the common law they are not 'human rights' in the modern sense:[2] in constitutional law, the individual is a subject of the Crown, not a bearer of rights.[3] English lawyers have, traditionally, been suspicious of 'fundamental rights', preferring an 'incremental approach'.[4] In the **In.02**

[1] For more detail, see para 1.20ff.

[2] For a detailed discussion of issues concerning the nature and scope of rights, see para 1.04ff.

[3] See generally, *Halsbury's Laws of England* Vol 8(2) 'Constitutional Law and Human Rights' (4th edn, Reissue, Butterworths, 1996) para 26ff.

[4] S de Smith, 'Fundamental Rights in the New Commonwealth' (1961) 10 ICLQ 83.

eighteenth century, Blackstone provided a classification of the absolute rights of persons 'founded on nature and reason': personal security, personal liberty and property.[5] But, as Dicey made clear, these rights did not derive from higher principles, rather:

> the rules which in foreign countries naturally form part of a constitutional code, are not the source but the consequence of the rights of individuals, as defined and enforced by the Courts.[6]

The 'private law' basis of citizen's rights discouraged the English law from developing any general approach to rights issues. Sceptical views were still being expressed as late as 1958 when Sir Ivor Jennings wrote:

> in Britain we have no Bill of Rights; we merely have liberty, according to the law; and we think—truly, I believe—that we do the job better than any country which has a Bill of Rights or a Declaration of the Rights of Man.[7]

In.03 This standpoint meant that no provisions for the protection of fundamental rights were included in the independence constitutions of Ceylon in 1946 and of Ghana in 1957. There was, however, a change of attitude in the late 1950s because of the perceived need to protect white minorities when African countries were granted independence. In December 1959, Nigeria became the first former British colony to have a constitutional bill of rights; and 37 others followed over the next 30 years.[8] These provisions were substantially based on the European Convention on Human Rights which English lawyers had helped to draft and which the United Kingdom had ratified in 1951.[9]

In.04 In the 1960s a 'rights centred' approach began to emerge under the influence of developments in other jurisdictions. 'Rights based' analysis first made its appearance, under the influence of American case law, in the form of 'civil liberties'. The first book dealing with this area in England and Wales was not published until 1963[10] and, despite a small number of student texts, it remains the case that there is no practitioner's textbook devoted to civil liberties. The Privy Council, as the court of final appeal for many Commonwealth countries, was often called upon to interpret constitutional 'rights instruments' and did so with increasing creativity, particularly in a series of 'death row' cases.[11] In 1983, Oxford University Press

[5] W Blackstone, *Commentaries on the Laws of England* (1st edn, Oxford, 1765) Chap 1 (Facsimile Edition, University of Chicago Press, 1979).

[6] A V Dicey, *An Introduction to the Study of the Law of the Constitution* (8th edn, Macmillan, 1915) (Liberty Fund, 1982) 121.

[7] W I Jennings, *The Approach to Self Governance* (Cambridge University Press, 1958) 20.

[8] See generally, N Jayawickrama, 'The Bill of Rights' in R Wacks (ed), *Human Rights in Hong Kong* (Oxford University Press, 1992).

[9] For the United Kingdom and the Convention, see A Lester, 'Fundamental Rights: The United Kingdom Isolated' [1984] PL 47.

[10] H Street, *Freedom, the Individual and the Law* (Penguin, 1963).

[11] Beginning with *Pratt v A-G for Jamaica* [1994] 2 AC 1, see generally para 3.08ff.

published Paul Sieghart's seminal *The International Law of Human Rights*[12] which provided a masterly summary of international human rights jurisprudence under the treaties and conventions which were then in force.

Nevertheless, until recently, 'human rights law' has only had a spectral presence in domestic English law. The first book centrally concerned with human rights in English law was not published until 1997.[13] In the same year the definitive practitioner's text, *Halsbury's Laws of England*, issued a volume which, for the first time, dealt with 'Constitutional Law and Human Rights'.[14] The pace then began to increase and the late 1990s saw a steady stream of new books on 'human rights'.[15] At the same time, the awareness of human rights issues and conventions amongst practitioners and judges has increased exponentially. In.05

B. International Human Rights Law

An important catalyst for this shift of approach has been the development of international human rights law[16] in the aftermath of the Second World War: as part of the new international order designed to ensure that the atrocities which had been experienced could never recur.[17] Human rights played a prominent role in the United Nations Charter signed on 26 June 1945 and resulted in the establishment of a Commission on Human Rights. The Commission, chaired by Eleanor Roosevelt, took responsibility for drafting the Universal Declaration of Human Rights[18] which was adopted by 48 members of the General Assembly on 10 December 1948. Shortly afterwards, the Council of Europe began to frame a human rights instrument for Europe, based on the Universal Declaration.[19] After a difficult drafting process the European Convention on Human Rights was opened for signature in November 1950. The United Kingdom was an initial party to both the Universal Declaration and the European Convention.[20] In.06

[12] Clarendon Press, 1983.

[13] M Hunt, *Using Human Rights Law in English Courts* (Hart Publishing, 1997); this was four years after David Feldman's magisterial work *Civil Liberties and Human Rights in England and Wales* (Clarendon Press, 1993): however, as is clear from its title, the latter was primarily devoted to 'civil liberties' issues and it did not deal with human rights issues such as fair trial rights.

[14] Vol 8(2), also published as a separate work: Lord Lester and D Oliver (eds), *Constitutional Law and Human Rights* (Butterworths, 1997).

[15] See Note on Materials in Vol 2.

[16] For a general account, see G Robertson, *Crimes Against Humanity* (Allen Lane, 1999) in particular, Chaps 1–3.

[17] Two books merit special mention: H G Wells, *H G Wells on the Rights of Man* (Penguin Press, 1940) and H Lauterpacht, *An International Bill of the Rights of Man* (Columbia University Press, 1945).

[18] See generally, A Robertson and J Merrills, *Human Rights in the World*, (4th edn, Manchester University Press, 1996) Chap 2.

[19] See generally, A Robertson and J Merrills, *Human Rights in Europe: A Study of the European Convention on Human Rights*, (3rd edn, Manchester University Press, 1993) 5–14.

[20] It was the first country to ratify the Convention: for the history, see Robertson and Merrills, ibid, Chap 1; for some of these international conventions see Apps H to N in Vol 2.

In.07 The next 50 years saw the adoption of a large number of human rights treaties and conventions under the umbrella of the United Nations and other bodies.[21] Human rights law has become increasingly international[22] and a number of human rights are now recognised by customary international law.[23] These include the rights to be free from torture,[24] slavery, prolonged arbitrary detention and the principle of non-discrimination on the ground of race or sex.[25] Most importantly, the recognition of the right of individual petition under a number of human rights treaties has meant that international human rights tribunals can now decide cases brought by individuals against states.[26] The first acknowledgement of such a right was under the European Convention on Human Rights.[27] The Court did not become operative until September 1958 when eight countries accepted its compulsory jurisdiction. The right to individual petition and the compulsory jurisdiction of the Court were not accepted by the United Kingdom until 14 January 1966.[28]

In.08 The right of individual petition is also available under the Optional Protocol of the International Covenant on Civil and Political Rights.[29] The Human Rights Committee has received over 850 individual complaints and has given views on 300 cases. The United Kingdom is considering ratification of this Optional Protocol. The Committee for the Elimination of Racial Discrimination and the Committee on Torture can receive communications from individuals subject to the jurisdiction of states which have accepted the competence of the Committee to receive such communications. Only a small number of individual communications have been considered.[30]

In.09 The most important tribunal, both in relation to the United Kingdom and from the point of view of international human rights jurisprudence, has been the European Court of Human Rights. This court has taken on an increasing caseload

---

21 See R Clayton, H Tomlinson and V Shukla, *Human Rights Handbook* (Hart Publishing, 2000).

22 For a general account of the public international law of human rights see I Brownlie, *The Principles of Public International Law* (5th edn, Clarendon Press, 1998) Chap XXV.

23 *Restatement (Third) The Foreign Relations Law of the United States* (American Law Institute, 1987) §702.

24 *R v Bow Street Metropolitan Stipendiary Magistrate, ex p Pinochet Ugarte (No 3)* [1999] 2 WLR 827, 841; and see *Filartiga v Peña-Irala* (1980) 630 F 2d 876.

25 See Brownlie (n 22 above) 602–603.

26 For a discussion of these tribunals, see P Sands, R Mackenzie and Y Shany (eds), *Manual on International Courts and Tribunals* (Butterworths, 1999) Part D.

27 Sweden accepted the right in 1953 and the procedure became operative in Jul 1955 after six acceptances.

28 See generally, Lord Lester, 'UK Acceptance of the Strasbourg Jurisdiction: What really went on in Whitehall in 1965' [1998] PL 237.

29 See App J in Vol 2; and see generally, P Ghandi, *The Human Rights Committee and the Right of Individual Communication* (Dartmouth, 1998).

30 The Committee for the Elimination of Racial Discrimination has considered eight and the Committee on Torture 133.

over four decades. In the first 20 years of its existence, 1961 to 1981, it determined an average of just over two cases a year. In the next decade, this figure rose to nearly 23 per annum. By the end of 1999, the total number of cases decided by the Court had reached one thousand, with 177 admissible cases being disposed of in 1999.

The European Convention on Human Rights itself has had an increasing impact on the development of the English law. The first United Kingdom case decided by the European Court of Human Rights was *Golder* in 1975.[31] The United Kingdom has come before the Court in admissible cases on 115 occasions[32] and has been found to be in violation of Convention rights in 72 cases. Following findings of violation, the United Kingdom has made substantial changes in domestic law, including at least 11 changes in primary legislation.[33] Provisions such as the Contempt of Court Act 1981, the Mental Health Act 1983 and the Children Act 1989 have been, in part, responses to adverse findings by the European Court of Human Rights. **In.10**

C. The Human Rights Act

The steady stream of United Kingdom cases in Strasbourg has been a potent force for change, encouraging the idea of 'bringing rights home'.[34] The Labour Government elected in 1997 indicated that it would legislate to make the European Convention on Human Rights part of English law. A White Paper, *Rights Brought Home: The Human Rights Bill*[35] and draft Bill were published in October 1997. After extensive parliamentary debate, the Human Rights Act 1998 received royal assent on 9 November 1998 and comes into force in its entirety on 2 October 2000. It will, for the first time, make human rights issues justiciable in the English courts. It will be unlawful for public authorities to act in a way which is incompatible with Convention rights.[36] English judges will, for the first time, be required to consider 'rights issues' in the full range of their decision-making. The present book is organised around the Act and the rights which it introduces into English law. **In.11**

The Convention is not, however, a modern human rights instrument. It was designed in the late 1940s to meet specific historical circumstances. Its inspiration **In.12**

[31] (1975) 1 EHRR 524; see para 11.185ff.

[32] To end of Jun 2000; for details see 'Table of Admissible UK Cases before the European Court of Human Rights' in Vol 2.

[33] For a detailed discussion see para 2–06ff.

[34] In Dec 1996 the Labour Party published a consultation paper, *Bringing Rights Home: Labour's Plans to Incorporate the European Convention on Human Rights into United Kingdom Law* (Labour Party, 1996): reproduced in J Wadham and H Mountfield, *The Human Rights Act 1998* (Blackstone Press, 1999) App 2, 173–183.

[35] Cm 3882 (HMSO, 1997), the text is reproduced at App B in Vol 2.

[36] See para 5.120ff.

was the desire to protect Western European democracies against fascism. In essence, it protects traditional civil and political rights. It contains no freestanding anti-discrimination provision but guarantees a right to property and to education; and it therefore only indirectly applies to social and economic issues. As a result, the Convention rights which are to be enforceable in the English courts are limited in range. It is instructive to compare the restricted nature of the rights created by the Convention with those in Chapter 2 of the 1996 South African Constitution. This contains amongst other rights: a right for the individual to choose his occupation, a right to fair labour practices including the right to strike, the right to an environment which is not harmful to health or well being, extensive property rights, a right to adequate housing and a right of access to health care, social security and emergency medical treatment and the right to administrative action that is lawful, reasonable and procedurally fair.[37] Although the Labour Party retains a theoretical commitment to a 'modern bill of rights',[38] it is unlikely that any further steps will be taken in this direction for many years. The proposed EU Charter of Fundamental Rights contains a number of social and economic rights as well as rights of access to medical care and environmntal rights.[38a] However, it appears that this charter will be not legally enforceable in the courts. As a result, the Convention is likely to provide the template for human rights in England and Wales for the foreseeable future.

D. The Purpose and Structure of the Book

In.13 A wide range of books on the Human Rights Act have been published over the past three years.[39] A number of these have provided comprehensive coverage of the Act and the jurisprudence of the European Convention on Human Rights. Others have set out to analyse the possible impact of the Act on different areas of the law. We have approached the law of human rights from a perspective which is different in two respects.

In.14 First, this is a book about the *English* law of human rights. Our starting point is an exposition of the English law before the Human Rights Act takes effect in the areas covered by Convention rights[40] such as the right to life, the right to a fair trial, the right to respect for private life and freedom of expression. In some areas—for example, liberty and privacy—the relevant English law has been extensively

[37] Contained in ss 22–27 and s 33 respectively; the text is reproduced at App S in Vol 2.

[38] See para 1.48.

[38a] See generally, S Fredman, C McCrudden and M Freedland, 'An EU Charter of Fundamental Rights' [2000] PL 178.

[39] There are at least 14 at the time of writing, see Note on Materials, Section 4 'Textbooks' in Vol 2.

[40] For this term, see para 3.43.

covered by first rate textbooks.[41] In others—such as the right to fair trial—we have provided an overview of the relevant law for the first time.

Secondly, we have frequently referred to the case law in other common law jurisdictions. Substantial assistance can be obtained from these cases when considering Convention rights. Many of the 'independence constitutions' of Commonwealth countries contain 'human rights provisions' closely modelled on the Convention. Furthermore, in many Commonwealth jurisdictions, the judges have long approached human rights cases from a 'comparative perspective'. It is not unusual to find a point on constitutional interpretation being approached via a detailed consideration of case law from Canada, England, India and the United States. Many of the points which will arise under the Human Rights Act have already been extensively analysed in other jurisdictions.[42] The English lawyer will often find the approach of common law judges more familiar and congenial than the delphic style of the European Court of Human Rights. The fact that human rights instruments have been introduced in jurisdictions such as Canada, New Zealand and South Africa[43] in the relatively recent past means that their case law is of particular value. **In.15**

It is also worth reiterating that until 10 years ago, comparatively few cases had been decided by the European Court of Human Rights. There will be many instances where it will be more fruitful to examine the decisions in other common law jurisdictions: either because they have considered problems which have not been addressed in Strasbourg or because the principles are more fully developed than the approach taken by the Commission or Court. For example, in *R v DPP, ex p Kebilene*,[44] the very first case in which the House of Lords considered the Human Rights Act, Canadian and South African as well as Strasbourg decisions were considered when deciding the proper approach to a reverse onus provision.[45] **In.16**

In recent years, the higher courts have often approached questions of legal principle by examining the authorities in other jurisdictions. For example, in *White v Jones*[46] Lord Goff found it of assistance to discuss the position under German law[47] when considering the proper scope of a duty of care in relation to a disappointed beneficiary under a will. In *Derbyshire County Council v Times Newspapers*[48] the House of Lords decided the question of whether the ability of a local authority to sue in defamation would be an undesirable restriction on exposing a **In.17**

41 See Note on Materials in Vol 2.
42 See eg the discussion of 'reverse onus' clauses in criminal cases, para 11.115ff.
43 For the relevant provisions see Apps R, S and T in Vol 2.
44 [1999] 3 WLR 972.
45 See generally, para 11.119.
46 [1995] AC 207.
47 Ibid 262–264.
48 [1993] AC 534.

democratically elected government to uninhibited public criticism by examining cases from the United States and South Africa as well as from Strasbourg. The House of Lords addressed the controversial issue of whether qualified privilege should provide a public figure defence in defamation actions in *Reynolds v Times Newspapers*[49] by looking in detail at the principles developed in the United States, Canada, India, Australia, South Africa and New Zealand in addition to Convention case law.[50]

In.18 Practitioners should, however, exercise restraint when referring to international human rights law. Used carefully and appropriately, it can be of immense benefit. As the Chief Justice of Zimbabwe recently observed:

> a judicial decision has greater legitimacy and will command more respect if it accords with international norms that have been accepted by many jurisdictions than if it is based upon the parochial experience or foibles of a particular judge or court.[51]

Nevertheless, transplanting legal principles from one jurisdiction to another is not always straightforward: the differences in legal values may be so extreme as to render virtually meaningless the discovery that systems have the same or a different rule.[52] As a consequence, advocates would do well to exercise some moderation when relying on international human rights case law. As Mummery LJ stressed in *Williams v Cowell*:[53]

> when human rights points are taken, there is a temptation to impress (and to oppress) the court with bulk and to turn a judicial hearing into an international human rights seminar. This temptation should be resisted . . . It is not necessary to include all the treaty, convention, legislative, judicial and periodical material which has been uncovered. In the interests of saving the legal costs of the parties and the time of the court, as well as for the preservation of the environment, self-restraint should be exercised to select what is reasonably required.

A similar point was made by Auld LJ in *R v North West Lancashire Health Authority, ex p A*[54] when he complained that counsel had:

> indicated that the purpose of his fairly detailed submissions and references to Strasbourg jurisprudence was merely to show that transsexualism is a sufficiently serious condition 'to raise human rights problems'. Such an unfocused recourse to that jurisdiction, whether before or after the statutory absorption of part of the Convention into the law of England and Wales, is not helpful to the Court. Indeed, it is positively unhelpful, cluttering up its consideration of adequate and more precise domestic principles and authorities governing the issues in play.

---

[49] [1999] 3 WLR 1010.

[50] See generally, para 15.36.

[51] A Gubbay, 'Foreword' in (1996) 1 CHRLD at i.

[52] A Watson, *Legal Transplants in Comparative Law* (2nd edn, University of Georgia Press, 1993) 5.

[53] [2000] 1 WLR 187, 198.

[54] *The Times*, 24 Aug 1999.

The book is divided into four sections. Part I deals with the background to the Human Rights Act: the constitutional protection of human rights and the impact of human rights treaties prior to the Act. Part II deals with general principles under the Human Rights Act: this begins with the structure of the Act and its interpretation, and then analyses its impact on statute law and its effect on public authorities. **In.19**

Part III is the central section of the book. The first chapter of this section deals with the general principles applicable to the interpretation and application of the Convention. The next 14 chapters deal with the specific rights covered by Articles 3 to 12, 14 and the First Protocol of the Convention. Each of these chapters has the same structure: after an introduction dealing with the background to the right, the next two sections set out to describe the present state of the law of human rights in England and Wales, and then the jurisprudence under the Convention. The fourth section of each chapter deals with the impact of the Human Rights Act in relation to the particular right covered by the chapter. Each chapter has three Appendices: the first two providing a summary of the case law under the relevant provision of the Canadian Charter and the New Zealand Bill of Rights Act and the last dealing with some of the human rights case law in other jurisdictions. Part IV of the book deals with Remedies and Procedure: both in the English courts and under the Convention. **In.20**

A word of caution is necessary in relation to the Appendices to Chapters 7 to 20 inclusive. In relation to the substantive sections of the Chapters, the book seeks to provide an accurate and up to date exposition of the English and Convention law. The position in relation to the Appendices is rather different. We cannot claim any specific expertise in the law of Canada, New Zealand or any of the other jurisdictions covered by the Appendices. We have relied heavily on a number of excellent textbooks.[55] The purpose of these Appendices is not to provide comprehensive coverage of human rights law in any of the 42 jurisdictions mentioned but simply to provide some initial direction to the English lawyer in respect of what we believe is a valuable body of case law. **In.21**

The richest body of human rights jurisprudence in the common law world is to be found in the decisions of the courts in the United States. We have not provided a specific section in the Appendices dealing with this case law. There are a number of reasons for this. First, despite the increasing 'internationalisation' of human rights law over recent decades, the American courts have paid almost no regard to international human rights instruments or case law from other jurisdictions. They have instead developed a strong indigenous tradition over 200 years which has become insulated from developments elsewhere. Secondly, the American Bill of **In.22**

[55] See Note on Materials in Vol 2.

Rights is, in substance, an eighteenth century document which has a very different structure from twentieth century human rights instruments (such as the Convention or the Canadian Charter). In the most well known example, the First Amendment simply provides that 'Congress shall make no law . . . prohibiting the free exercise of religion' or 'abridging the freedom of speech, or of the press'. In contrast, instruments such as the Convention or the Canadian Charter make express provision for limiting rights such as freedom of religion or expression in the general interest. It is inevitable that the jurisprudence dealing with rights expressed in such 'absolute' terms will take a very different direction to that which begins with the recognition of express limitations to rights. Thirdly, the very different political and social culture of the United States may make it inappropriate to implement their legal principles into English law.[56] Fourthly, the US case law on human rights issues has been very strongly marked by political controversy. The consistent division of the Supreme Court on political lines in recent decades has generated jurisprudence which is often only of local significance. Finally, and more pragmatically, the vast body of US case law defies any simple summary. More than 500 volumes of Supreme Court reports are supplemented by tens of thousands of federal and state court decisions bearing on human rights issues.

In.23 Nevertheless, the American jurisprudence cannot be ignored by human rights lawyers. Many of the most profound and difficult problems were first examined and developed by American judges. Questions concerning the nature of speech, religion and property have been more comprehensively analysed in the United States than in any other jurisdiction. We have, therefore, provided some reference to the American material in the introductions to the Appendices on Human Rights Cases in Other Jurisdictions and in the course of the discussion of English law and impact issues.

E. The Impact of the Human Rights Act

In.24 Although the Human Rights Act will have an immediate impact on English criminal and public law, it is unlikely to have such a dramatic initial effect in other areas. While there are a few examples of plain incompatibility, it seems likely that most of these will have been removed by 2 October 2000.[57] Nevertheless, there are

[56] See eg Sir Stephen Sedley, 'The First Amendment: a Case for Import Controls?' in I Loveland (ed), *Importing the First Amendment* (Hart Publishing, 1998) where he argues that the right to freedom of expression should not be developed in line with American law.

[57] See eg Youth Justice and Criminal Evidence Act 1999, s 58 (inferences from silence) and s 59 and Sch 3 (restrictions on answers obtained by compulsion) and the Regulation of Investigatory Powers Act 2000 (dealing with powers of surveillance).

a number of specific areas in which the present English law may not be compatible with Convention rights. In the context of the present work we have discussed this impact with reference to each Article of the Convention rather than considering the relevant areas of law in isolation.

Before turning to the areas we have identified, it is important to express some diffidence about the exercise we have undertaken. The process of anticipating the impact of the Act is inevitably speculative and partial: we have no doubt that legal ingenuity and imagination will lead to developments in many unexpected directions. Although it provided us with the stimulus for writing the book and we have benefited enormously from discussions with colleagues, friends and many others, the suggestions we make are no more than that. We cannot claim to be comprehensive, and doubtless many of our predictions as to future developments will turn out to be incorrect. Our principal objective is to prompt debate about how Convention rights will be translated into English law. **In.25**

We have discussed the potential impact of the Human Rights Act in 15 areas of law, as follows: **In.26**

Commercial Law: Chapters 11, 12, 15, 18
Criminal Law: Chapters 8, 9, 10, 11, 12, 13, 14, 15, 16, 17
Education: Chapters 11, 12, 14, 15, 17, 19
Employment & Discrimination: Chapters 9, 11, 12, 13, 14, 15, 17
Family: Chapters 11, 12, 13, 14, 15, 17
Healthcare: Chapters 7, 11, 12, 17
Housing: Chapters 11, 12, 13, 17
Immigration: Chapters 7, 8, 10, 11, 12, 13, 17
Local Government Law: Chapters 10, 11, 12, 13, 15, 17, 18
Media Law: Chapters 12, 15
Mental Health Law: Chapters 8, 10, 11, 12
Planning & Environment Law: Chapters 7, 11, 12, 14, 18
Police Law: Chapters 7, 8, 10, 11, 12, 14, 17
Prison Law: Chapters 8, 10, 11, 12, 13, 14, 15, 17
Social Security Law: Chapters 11, 17, 18, 19

The areas we have chosen are not intended to be definitive and, doubtless, other selections could have been made. Our classifications reflect what appear to be the major areas of impact. In some chapters, we have dealt with general areas of impact in more detail, in particular, the following discussions are to be found in the chapters mentioned:

Chapter 11 (Article 6, Fair Trial Rights): access to the court and immunities, impact on civil proceedings, impact on judicial review proceedings

Chapter 12 (Article 8, Rights to Respect for Home, Private Life and Correspondence): Privacy and common law, impact on civil procedure, right to personal information
Chapter 15 (Article 10, Freedom of Expression): Section 12 of the Human Rights Act, defamation and freedom of information
Chapter 16 (Article 11, Freedom of Assembly and Association): Impact on law relating to assembly, trade unions
Chapter 17 (Article 14, Freedom from Discrimination): Sexual orientation discrimination and religious discrimination
Chapter 18 (Article 1, First Protocol, Enjoyment of Possessions): Property litigation
Chapter 20 (Article 3, First Protocol, Elections): Impact on electoral law

F. Future Developments

In.27 The long term impact of the Human Rights Act is difficult to predict. However, in the short term it is likely to generate considerable uncertainty. There are a number of reasons for this. First, the language of Convention Articles is broad, so that the opposite conclusions on the same facts may be equally arguable. For example, the question whether, on a particular set of facts, the right to privacy is a disproportionate interference with freedom of expression is an issue about which reasonable men or women can (and will) differ. Secondly, there are many questions that are not definitively answered by the Act. These include the following questions: to what extent the Human Rights Act applies 'horizontally' to disputes between private persons;[58] what the dividing line is between a standard public authority and a body which is a public authority by virtue of the fact it carries out public functions;[59] whether employees of such functional public authorities are outside the scope of the Human Rights Act because contracts of employment involve an 'act of a private nature';[60] and whether a local authority is able to bring proceedings under the Act either because it is a 'victim'[61] or because it can seek a declaration on an issue of statutory construction under section 3 of the Act.[62] Thirdly, the Act does not provide firm guidance about the extent to which the English courts should apply or follow decisions of the European Court of Human Rights or, indeed, an authority from Canada, New Zealand, South Africa or elsewhere. Different judges will take divergent approaches and it will often be difficult to predict in advance which line of authority will be the most persuasive.

[58] See para 5.38ff.
[59] See para 5.03ff.
[60] See para 5.31ff.
[61] See para 22.26ff.
[62] See para 22.47ff.

Nevertheless, the 'rights based' reasoning required by the Act will, over time, produce a fundamental shift of attitude on the part of English judges in cases where human rights are in play. In other common law jurisdictions the impact of bills of rights has taken very different forms: from the activist approaches of the Canadian[63] and South African[64] courts, through the more cautious approach of the Courts in New Zealand,[65] to the extremely limited impact of the Hong Kong Bill of Rights Ordinance.[66] **In.28**

The impact in England is likely to be somewhere between Canada and New Zealand. The repercussions will be less marked than in Canada because the Human Rights Act does not allow judges to 'strike down' statutes but has been designed to preserve the doctrine of parliamentary sovereignty.[67] At the same time, the consequences are likely to be more extensive than in New Zealand not least because the Act has excited enormous interest among judges and practitioners which is likely to bear fruit in several respects. We believe that the Act is a constitutional instrument[68] of profound importance for the development of the English legal system. It is likely to lead to a fundamental shift of emphasis in English constitutional law. The Act is not intended to result in judges remaking the decisions of public authorities. It will, however, ensure that more rigorous standards will prevail where, for example, central or local government interfere with a person's human rights. **In.29**

The Act will have an even broader impact on our political, social and legal culture. It will require a different starting point for decision makers who are public authorities. Individuals will have the benefit of positive rights guarantees which a public authority must respect; and a public authority must acknowledge these rights unless and until it can formulate a substantial basis in fact and law for **In.30**

---

[63] A number of commentators argue that the Charter has been a success; see eg R Penner, 'The Canadian experience with the Charter of Rights: Are there Lessons for the United Kingdom' [1996] PL 104; T Ison, 'A Constitutional Bill or Bills—The Canadian Experience' (1997) 60 MLR 499; D Beatty, 'The Canadian Charter of Rights: Lessons and Laments' (1997) 60 LQR 481. For a more critical view, see, for example, A Petter, 'Canada's Charter Flight: Soaring Backwards into the Future' (1989) 16 Journal of Law and Society 151; J Bakan 'Constitutional Arguments: Interpretation and Legitimacy in Canadian Constitutional Thought' (1989) 27 Osgoode Hall LJ 123.

[64] Cf H Corder, 'South Africa's Transitional Constitution: Its Design and Implementation' [1996] PL 291 and see also S Kentridge, 'Lessons from South Africa' in B Markesinis (ed), *The Impact of the Human Rights Bill on English Law* (Oxford University Press, 1999).

[65] See eg M Taggart, 'Tugging on Superman's Cape: Lessons from the Experience with the New Zealand Bill of Rights' [1998] PL 266; A Butler, 'The Bill of Rights Debate: why the New Zealand Bill of Rights is a bad model for Britain' [1997] OJLS 332; H Schwartz, 'The Short Happy Life and the Tragic Death of the New Zealand Bill of Rights Act' [1998] NZLR 259.

[66] See eg R Swede, 'One Territory—Three Systems? the Hong Kong Bill of Rights' [1995] 44 ICLQ 360; Y Ghai, 'Sentinels of Liberty or sheep in Woolf's clothing? Judicial politics and the Hong Kong Bill of Rights' [1997] 60 MLR 459; A Byrnes, 'And Some Have Bills of Rights Thrust Upon Them: The Experience of Hong Kong's Bill of Rights', in P Alston (ed), *Promoting Human Rights Through Bills of Rights* (Oxford University Press, 1999).

[67] See para 1.82ff.

[68] See paras 1.90 and 3.06ff.

overriding them. The implications of English law moving from the traditional view that an individual can do whatever he likes provided there is not a law against it[69] to positive rights guarantees will therefore be immense.

In.31 The 'limited incorporation' of the Convention is not the final word. The United Kingdom has ratified a large number of international human rights in diverse areas such as discrimination and the rights of the child.[70] These treaties are not directly enforceable in the English courts.[71] Nevertheless, they are increasingly likely to inspire new and unpredictable developments as human rights permeate the entire legal system.[72]

In.32 However, the most important long term effect of the Human Rights Act will be the development of a distinctive indigenous human rights jurisprudence which is shaped by and reflects our domestic norms and our political and social culture. As the courts formulate and evolve new principles, they might bear in mind some remarks of Harold Lasky:

> vigilance is necessary in the realm of what Cromwell called fundamentals. Bills of rights are quite undoubtedly a check upon possible excesses in the Government of the day. They warn us that certain popular powers have had to be fought over and may have to be fought over again. The solemnity they embody serves to set the people on their guard. It acts as a rallying point in the State for all who care deeply for the ideals of freedom.[73]

[69] The perspective traditionally associated with Dicey is discussed at para 1.21ff below.
[70] A number of these treaties are set out in Apps H to N in Vol 2.
[71] See generally, Chap 2.
[72] See eg para 21.138 where we consider the possibility of the court making declarations of incompatibility with international human rights instruments.
[73] H Lasky, *Liberty and the Modern State* (Penguin, 1948) 75.

Part I

THE BACKGROUND TO THE HUMAN RIGHTS ACT

1

THE CONSTITUTIONAL PROTECTION OF HUMAN RIGHTS

A. Introduction

In English constitutional law there is a clear and well-established boundary between the province of the courts and that of the executive: **1.01**

> The proper constitutional relationship of the executive with the courts is that the courts will respect all acts of the executive which are within its lawful province, and that the executive will respect all decisions of the courts as to what its lawful province is.[1]

[1] *Per* Nolan LJ in *M v the Home Office* [1992] QB 270, 314, 315 (affirmed at [1994] AC 377); Sir Stephen Sedley argues that the independent role of the courts in interpreting, applying and supplementing the law laid down by Parliament is the constitutional function of the common law: 'The Common Law and the Constitution' in M Nolan and S Sedley, *The Making and Remaking of the British Constitution* (Blackstone, 1997).

However, the balance to be struck in the constitutional relationship of the executive, legislature and the judiciary will be radically altered by the Human Rights Act. The Act will provide positive guarantees of the rights and freedoms established as Convention rights[2] and the scope for judicial intervention will significantly increase. As the Lord Chancellor, Lord Irvine, said during the Third Reading of the Bill[3] 'Convention rights are the magnetic north and the needle of judicial interpretation will swing towards it.'

1.02 Under the Human Rights Act the approach of the courts towards statutory construction will change profoundly. Where legislation conflicts with Convention rights, the court will have to comply with a strong interpretative obligation to read and give effect to the legislation, as far as it is possible to do so, in order to ensure that the legislation is compatible with Convention rights.[4] The courts will, accordingly, read into the exercise of broad statutory discretions[5] the obligation of a public authority[6] to adhere to Convention rights. If the conflict between a statutory provision and the Convention cannot be overcome, the court will have the power to make a declaration of incompatibility.[7] Individuals or companies who are victims[8] of the act of a public authority which is incompatible with Convention rights[9] will be able to apply to the court to have a decision struck down. As the court is itself a public authority[10] which must abide by Convention rights, the common law will develop in line with Convention principles.[11]

1.03 The Human Rights Act therefore has important implications for the constitutional framework within which the courts operate. To appreciate the ramifications of the Act, it is important to examine a number of issues at the outset. This opening chapter will examine the nature of rights, the status of rights in English law, the arguments that led to the enactment of the Human Rights Act, the repercussions of the Act for parliamentary sovereignty, and, finally, the legislation's impact in terms of the constitutional safeguards it will provide for the rights of the citizen.

---

[2] See para 3.43ff.

[3] *Hansard*, HL col 840 (5 Feb1998).

[4] s 3(1) of the Human Rights Act: para 4.04ff.

[5] The Human Rights Act will reverse the effect of the House of Lords decision in *R v Secretary of State for the Home Department, ex p Brind* [1991] 1 AC 696 which held that there is no presumption that a public body would exercise a statutory discretion in a manner which does not contravene the European Convention: see para 4.04ff below.

[6] s 6 of the Human Rights Act: see para 5.120ff below.

[7] s 19 of the Human Rights Act: see para 4.43ff below.

[8] s 7(1), (3) and (7) of the Human Rights Act: see para 22.14ff below.

[9] s 6 of the Human Rights Act: see para 5.120ff below.

[10] s 6(3) of the Human Rights Act: see para 5.38ff below.

[11] See para 5.88ff.

B. The Nature of Rights

(1) Introduction

The vocabulary of rights has in recent times become debased through over usage. Since their emergence in the twelfth century,[12] rights have come to take a central place in political debate. The doctrine of natural rights is said to have inspired the Glorious Revolution of 1688 as well as the American and French Revolutions. Rights often form a vital element of the constitutional arrangements of the modern state. They provide the moral justification for assertions and counter assertions in a wide variety of political debates. Rights are claimed, for instance, on behalf of unborn children, animals and the environment. Rights are used both to defend the position of minorities against the majority and to justify the majority prevailing over the minority, to justify obedience to (and defiance of) the law and to defend and attack the free market and the welfare state. **1.04**

Even though it is widely recognised that human rights are of fundamental significance in the legal process, there is little unanimity about their content. International rights instruments such as the Universal Declaration of Human Rights,[12a] the International Covenant on Civil and Political Rights[12b] and the International Covenant on Economic, Social and Cultural Rights,[12c] the European Convention on Human Rights,[12d] the American Convention on Human Rights and the African Charter on Human and People's Rights differ significantly in terms of the protection they afford. What follows in paragraphs 1.06 to 1.15 is an attempt to sketch some of the debates and thinking that can be used to explain and justify the notion of 'rights' at all. It is, by necessity, a brief survey of the subject, intended to give practitioners some background to the theory of rights. **1.05**

(2) Forms of rights

A right confers an entitlement. In his classic analysis,[13] Hohfeld identified four different types of legal relations which might be described as entitlements: a *claim* right, where one person asserts he has a claim on another; a *liberty* right, which authorises a person to do as he pleases by, for example, smoking; a *power*, by which a **1.06**

[12] For a history, see R. Tuck, *Natural Rights Theories: their Origin and Development* (Cambridge University Press, 1979).

[12a] The text is reproduced at App H in Vol 2.

[12b] The text is reproduced at App J in Vol 2.

[12c] The text is reproduced at App K in Vol 2.

[12d] The text is reproduced at App E in Vol 2.

[13] W Hohfeld, *Fundamental Legal Conceptions as applied in Judicial Reasoning* (Yale University Press, 1919); and see also N McCormick 'Rights in Legislation', in P Hacker and J Raz, *Law Morality and Society* (Clarendon Press, 1977); A Halpin, 'Hohfeld's conceptions: from eight to two' (1985) 44 CLJ 435; M J Kramer, 'Rights Without Trimmings', in M J Kramer, N E Simmonds and H Steiner, *A Debate over Rights* (Clarendon Press, 1998).

person is enabled or empowered, for example, to vote; and an *immunity*, which protects a person from the power of another, as in the case of an entrenched constitution which precludes the legislature from overriding constitutional rights.

1.07 Hohfeld took the view that the term 'right' in the strict sense should be confined to a claim right. He also argued that claim rights impose correlative duties or obligations, in other words that where, for example, a person claims a right to freedom of expression, this claim creates a duty on another to uphold that right. Thus, the possession of a claim right consists of being legally protected against another's interference. By contrast, a liberty right imposes no corresponding duty upon another: having a liberty to engage in a particular action like smoking means that an individual is free from any duty to refrain from smoking. Nevertheless, extensive (if imperfect) protection for individual rights can be based on a liberty right even though a liberty right does not place restrictions on anyone. Thus, the liberty right to freedom of expression makes it permissible to interfere with the freedom of speech of another by, for instance, obstructing or ridiculing the speaker, provided the interference does not interfere with his other rights such as his right not to be physically assaulted or not to be defamed.

1.08 The analysis of different forms of rights does not, of course, throw any light on the content of rights. A very substantial literature has developed about the relationship of legal rights and moral rights. At one end of the spectrum are the legal positivists who argue that there is no necessary connection between law and morality;[14] at the other lie the natural rights theorists.[15] However, it is not necessary to examine these debates when addressing one of the central issues in human rights debates: what priority should be given to rights where they conflict with other claims?

(3) The status of rights

1.09 When it is said that a person has 'rights', this normally means something more than saying that he or she deserves to be treated (or would like to be treated) in a particular way. A right is a moral entitlement. As Dworkin pointed out in describing a right 'in a strong sense',[16] the status of a right therefore entails that a person both is entitled to stand on his own right *and* to require others to be duty bound to respect it. It means, for example, that when a person asserts his right to privacy, he has a claim right which others are duty bound to respect; and also that

[14] See in particular, H L A Hart, *The Concept of Law* (Clarendon Press, 1961) and *Essays in Jurisprudence and Philosophy* (Clarendon Press, 1983) Chaps 1 and 2; R Dworkin, *Taking Rights Seriously* (Duckworth, 1978) Chaps 2 and 3; R Sartorius, 'Hart's Concept of Law', in R Summers (ed), *More Essays in Legal Philosophy* (1971).

[15] See J Finnis, *Natural Law and Natural Rights* (Clarendon Press, 1980); R Tuck, *Natural Rights Theories: their Origin and Development* (Cambridge University Press, 1979); R P George (ed), *Natural Law Theory* (Clarendon Press, 1992).

[16] R Dworkin, *Taking Rights Seriously* (n14 above) 188–192.

he has a liberty right to privacy which entitles him to insist on an entitlement to be let alone.

Nonetheless, the special status which is said to attach to such moral rights has been hard to justify. In particular, it is difficult to demonstrate that rights matter in the context of consequentialist moral theories, in other words, those moral theories which define themselves in terms of achieving goals (such as utilitarianism).[17] In fact, the relationship between rights and utilitarianism is especially problematic. If society aims to maximise utility or to achieve the greatest happiness for the greatest number, then rights of particular individuals can be ignored if they conflict with maximising utility for society as a whole; it is therefore morally acceptable to feed Christians to the lions if this results in greater happiness for the spectators who are watching. As a result 'act utilitarianism' (the idea that to do right a person should do whatever in the circumstances maximises the utility of humanity) provides an inadequate framework for moral decision making or, indeed, for recognising an individual's rights. It once seemed that 'rule utilitarianism'[18] might yield a more satisfactory account of rights: if a person's moral behaviour was governed by rules which themselves were justified by reference to utility (as opposed to calculating whether every individual act would maximise utility), then it might be possible to uphold rights within a utilitarian framework. However, rule utilitarianism has recently fallen out of favour, not least because it is difficult to justify attaching significance to rules if the fundamental rationale of the particular moral theory in question is to promote utility. In reality, rule utilitarianism leads to the paradox that whilst the underlying principle is utilitarian, the rule utilitarianism nevertheless requires compliance with rules despite the fact they do not maximise utility. A more subtle attempt to reconcile rights with utilitarianism has been put forward by Hare.[19] His version of indirect utilitarianism distinguishes between critical morality and intuitive morality and argues that whilst rights may on an intuitive level appear to outweigh utility, they ultimately (like all intuitive principles) must be justified in terms of utility. **1.10**

Dworkin, on the other hand, has suggested the idea of rights as trumps.[20] He does not argue that rights should have an absolute status but merely that they should make a difference to the way social and political decisions should be made: by requiring a justification which is over and above showing that a particular decision **1.11**

[17] See J J C Smart and B Williams, *Utilitarianism: For and Against* (Cambridge University Press, 1973); A M Quinton, *Utilitarian Ethics* (Duckworth, 1973); D Regan, *Utilitarianism and Co-operation* (1980); A Sen and B Williams (eds), *Utilitarianism and Beyond* (Cambridge University Press, 1982); S Scheffler (ed), *Consequentialism and its Critics* (Cambridge University Press, 1988).

[18] D Lyons, *Forms and Limits of Utilitarianism* (Clarendon Press, 1965).

[19] R M Hare, *Moral Thinking: Its Levels, Methods and Point* (Clarendon Press, 1981)

[20] R Dworkin, *Taking Rights Seriously* (n14 above) 90–94, 364–368; *A Matter of Principle* (Clarendon Press, 1985) 335–372 and see M Cohen (ed), *Ronald Dworkin and Contemporary Jurisprudence* (Duckworth, 1984); A Hunt, *Reading Dworkin Critically* (Bury Publishers, 1992); S Guest, *Ronald Dworkin* (2nd edn, Edinburgh University Press, 1992).

is likely to produce an overall benefit to the community. It is permissible in a given situation to interfere with a right if the values it protects are not really at stake, if there are competing rights or if exercising the right poses a real risk to society.[21] This leads him to argue[22] that constitutional rights can be given effect through a 'moral reading' of human rights instruments. The contention is that such instruments should be interpreted and applied on the understanding that they invoke moral principles about political decency and justice. A human rights instrument should be interpreted by the judiciary to reflect the historical intention of its drafters and with constitutional integrity to ensure that moral judgments are consistent in principle with the instrument itself. Dworkin goes on to deny there is a duty that these moral rights should defer to the will of the majority. He argues that democracy does not compel the majoritarian premise that it is always unfair when a political majority is not allowed to have its way. He formulates a constitutional conception of democracy, the idea that the aim of democracy is to produce collective decisions whose structure, composition and practices treat all members of the community, as individuals, with equal respect and concern.[23]

1.12 These arguments may be contrasted with those of two other leading contemporary writers. Nozick[24] puts forward a very different basis for giving priority to rights in support of his theory that liberty and equality are inherently incompatible. He suggests that rights are 'side constraints' which place moral limits on goals which may be pursued in the sense that whatever we may do, we must not violate the rights of others. He argues that every individual has exclusive rights in himself and no rights in anyone else; which therefore implies that individuals have rights to liberty and property. In contrast, Raz[25] asserts that rights take effect by generating exclusionary reasons which displace the ordinary rules of conduct; thus, if someone has a right, others must conform to it because the right provides reasons for conduct which preempt or exclude (rather than outweigh) the utilitarian reasons for making a particular decision.

(4) Justifying rights

1.13 The notion of rights itself was once said to be derived from 'natural rights' which individuals possessed in a 'state of nature'. Thus, Locke[26] regarded it as a fundamental

---

[21] R Dworkin, *Taking Rights Seriously* (n 14 above) 200.

[22] See 'The Moral Reading and the Majoritarian Premise', in *Freedom's Law* (Clarendon Press, 1996).

[23] Although the right to equal concern and respect is fundamental to Dworkin's views (see *Taking Rights Seriously* (n 14 above) 272–278) the right may be so vague as to be meaningless: see J Raz, 'Professor Dworkin's Theory of Rights' 26 Political Studies 123.

[24] R Nozick, *Anarchy State and Utopia* (Blackwell, 1974); and see J Paul, *Reading Nozick* (Blackwell, 1981); R Wolff, *Robert Nozick: Property Justice and the Minimal State* (Polity, 1991).

[25] *The Morality of Freedom* (Clarendon Press, 1986).

[26] *Two Treatises on Government* P Laslett (ed), (Cambridge University Press, 1960) Book II, s 6; for natural rights generally, see n 15 above.

law of nature that 'no one ought to harm another in his Life, Health, Liberty or Possessions' so that when individuals consented to having political authority imposed on them, they nevertheless retained their natural rights. Both the American Declaration of Independence[27] and the French Declaration of the Rights of Man and the Citizen[28] assume that the role of government is to safeguard natural rights; and that where the state violates natural rights, it loses its right to rule and might be legitimately overthrown.

The idea of deriving rights from a social contract was revived by Rawls[29] who suggested that if hypothetical individuals were devising a structure for future society where they were ignorant of what sort of individuals they were or what positions in society they would occupy, those individuals would agree that each person should have an equal right to the most extensive total system of equal basic rights which are compatible with a similar system of liberty for all. Rawls' first principle of justice protects only certain conventional civil liberties such as freedom of speech, freedom from arbitrary arrest, freedom of conscience and freedom to hold private property. He argues that rational individuals would choose this particular package of liberties: the only safe decision in a state of ignorance is to choose a principle which protects the individual from the oppressive effect of others. However, in the final analysis his choice of particular civil liberties is difficult to justify objectively. It merely reflects his own views about the value of particular liberties he favours. **1.14**

In recent times it is more often asserted that rights are possessed by human beings simply by virtue of their being human. For example, Dworkin derives rights from the premise that the state owes duties to treat its citizens with equal concern and respect.[30] The International Covenant on Civil and Political Rights[30a] states that human rights derive from the inherent dignity of the human person. Human rights are therefore 'general' rights rather than 'specific' rights: they are universal to all humanity.[31] This means that there is no obvious way of identifying what particular **1.15**

---

[27] The Declaration of Independence states that 'We hold these truths to be self evident. That all men are created equal. That they are endowed by their creator with certain inalienable rights. That among them are life, liberty and the pursuit of happiness. That to secure these rights, governments are instituted by men, deriving their just powers from the consent of the governed. That whenever any form of government becomes destructive of those ends, it shall be the right of the people to alter or abolish it, and to institute new government, laying its foundations upon such powers in such forms, as shall seem to them most likely to effect their safety and happiness.'

[28] Cf *Matadeen v Pointu* [1999] AC 98 on the application of this document in the law of Mauritius.

[29] J Rawls, *A Theory of Justice* (Clarendon Press, 1971); and see B Barry, *The Liberal Theory of Justice* (Clarendon Press, 1973); N Daniels, *Reading Rawls* (1975); R Wolf, *Understanding Rawls* (1977); B Barry, *Theories of Justice* (University of California Press, 1989).

[30] R Dworkin, *Taking Rights Seriously* (n 14 above) 272–278.

[30a] The text is reproduced at App J in Vol 2.

[31] H L A Hart, 'Are there any natural rights', in A Quinton (ed) *Political Philosophy* (Oxford University Press, 1967).

rights come within the scope of 'human rights': for example, the right to social security might arise from a right possessed from being a citizen in a particular type of society as opposed to an individual's humanity as such.[32] Indeed, MacIntyre has argued that there are no such things as human rights, which he likens to a belief in witches and unicorns.[33]

(5) **Civil rights and economic rights**

1.16 The Universal Declaration of Human Rights[33a] recognises that there are economic, social and cultural rights as well as political and civil ones. The rights and freedoms protected by the European Convention of Human Rights (and, consequently, those given further effect by the Human Rights Act as Convention rights)[34] are designed to protect a number of traditional civil and political rights: although the right to the protection of property[35] and the right to education[36] can more properly be characterised as an economic or social right. The current debate about a new constitutional framework for the United Kingdom has therefore seriously neglected the issues arising from social and economic rights.[37]

1.17 The appearance of social and economic rights in human rights instruments can probably be traced back to the International Labour Organisation. When the UN Charter was being drafted in the 1940s, various proposals were made to include the maintenance of full employment as a commitment to be undertaken by member states.[38] This resulted in the Universal Declaration containing the rights to social security, the right to work, the right to rest and leisure, the right to an adequate standard of living, the right to education and the right to participate in cultural life.[39]

1.18 In 1966 the General Assembly of the United Nations adopted the International Covenant on Economic, Social and Cultural Rights which entered into force in 1977. Part III of the Covenant[40] recognises the rights: to work, to enjoy just and favourable conditions of work, to rest and leisure, to form and join trade unions, to strike, to social security, to special protection for the family, mothers and chil-

---

[32] A Melden, *Rights and Persons* (Blackwell, 1967) 179–184.
[33] A MacIntyre, *After Virtue* (Duckworth, 1981).
[33a] The text is reproduced at App H in Vol 2.
[34] See para 6.86ff below.
[35] The right to enjoyment of possessions under Art 1 to the First Protocol is discussed at para 18.26ff below.
[36] Under Art 2 of Protocol 1: see para 19.34ff below.
[37] See K Ewing, 'Social Rights and Constitutional Law' [1999] PL 104.
[38] See generally, R Russell and J Muther, *History of the United Nations Charter: the role of the United States 1940–45* (1958) 786.
[39] See Arts 22–28 of the Universal Declaration.
[40] The text is reproduced at App K in Vol 2.

dren, to an adequate standard of living including food, clothing and housing, physical and mental health, to education and to scientific and cultural life. Unlike the International Covenant on Civil and Political Rights, the International Covenant on Economic, Social and Cultural Rights is subject to the availability of resources and the obligations are to be progressively realised.[41]

However, very real doubts exist about whether socio-economic rights can qualify in principle as 'human rights'. Cranston has suggested that social and economic rights do not amount to human rights because they do not meet the test of practicability, universality and of being of paramount importance.[42] Even if socio-economic rights can properly be asserted on behalf of all human beings,[43] they do not give rise to *universal* human rights: since the extent to which a society can provide economic goods for its members must depend on the availability of resources within that society. If, for example, the citizens of Europe have more and better welfare rights than citizens in a third world country, then it is difficult to see how all of those welfare rights can be seen as 'human' rights. **1.19**

C. The Status of Rights in English Common Law Prior to the Human Rights Act

(1) Introduction

English lawyers have traditionally been sceptical about rights. The conventional view was described by Dicey:[44] **1.20**

> most foreign constitution makers have begun with declarations of rights. For this they have often been in no way to blame . . . On the other hand, there remains through the English constitution that inseparable connection between the means of enforcing a right and the right to be enforced which is the strength of judicial legislation. The law

[41] See Art 2(1).

[42] M Cranston, *What are Human Rights* (Bodley Head, 1973); and see R Plant, H Lesser and P Taylor-Gooby, *Political Philosophy and Social Welfare* (Routledge, 1980); J Donnelly, *The Concept of Human Rights* (Croom Helm, 1985).

[43] See Plant, Lesser and Taylor-Gooby, (n 42 above) 73–82.

[44] A Dicey, *An Introduction to the Study of The Law and the Constitution* (Macmillan, 1965) 198–199. This approach also coloured views about the value of the Convention: see, for example, the remarks of Lord Denning MR in *R v Chief Immigration Officer, Heathrow Airport, Salamit Bibi* [1976] 1 WLR 979, 985:

> The [European] Convention is drafted in a style very different from the way in which we are used to in legislation. It contains wide statements of principle. They are apt to lead to much difficulty in application: because they give rise to much uncertainty. They are not the sort of thing which we can easily digest. Article 8 [the right to privacy] is an example. It is so wide as to be incapable of practicable application. So it is much better to stick to our principles and only to look at the Convention for guidance in case of doubt.

> *ubi jus ubi remedium* . . . means that the Englishmen whose labours gradually framed the completed set of laws and institutions which we call the Constitution, fixed their minds more intently on providing the remedies for the enforcement of particular rights . . . than upon any declaration of the Rights of Man or of Englishmen.

In his *Commentaries on the Laws of England*[45] Blackstone identified three rights in English law 'founded on nature and reason': the right to personal security, the right to personal liberty and the right to private property. Dicey demonstrated that rights were to be derived from the rule of law by discussing the right to personal freedom,[46] freedom of discussion[47] and the right to assembly.[48] However, the development of a more rights based approach to public law[49] enabled Fordham[50] to catalogue a rather larger number of fundamental rights including access to the court,[51] the right to be at liberty unless detention is authorised by law,[52] freedom of expression,[53] privacy,[54] the right to silence,[55] freedom of association,[56] the right to a jury trial,[57] parental rights,[58] access to information,[59] the right of self determination,[60] the right to life,[61] the fundamental human need for

[45] R Kerr (ed) (4th edn, John Murray, 1876) Vol 1, 100–110.

[46] 'the right not to be subjected to imprisonment, arrest or other physical coercion in a way which does not admit of legal justification', Dicey (n 44 above) Chap 5, 208.

[47] Ibid Chap 6, ('little else than the right to write or say anything which a jury consisting of twelve shopkeepers thinks expedient and should be said or written', 246).

[48] Ibid 271.

[49] See T Allan, *Law, Liberty and Justice* (Oxford University Press, 1993).

[50] M Fordham, *Judicial Review Handbook* (2nd edn, John Wiley, 1997) paras 9.1–9.3.

[51] See *R v Secretary of State for the Home Department, ex p Leech (No 2)* [1994] QB 198 *per* Steyn LJ at 210; *Raymond v Honey* [1983] 1 AC 1 *per* Lord Wilberforce at 13; the position in English Law before the Human Rights Act comes into force is discussed at para 11.15ff.

[52] See eg *In Re S-C (Mental Patient: Habeas Corpus)* [1996] QB 599 *per* Sir Thomas Bingham MR at 603; *Spicer v Holt* [1977] AC 987 ('the important constitutional right of personal liberty'); the liberty rights in English law prior to the Human Rights Act are discussed at para 10.04ff below.

[53] See eg, *R v Secretary of State for the Home Department, ex p Brind* [1991] 1 AC 696 *per* Lord Ackner at 757; for a discussion of the position before the Human Rights Act comes into force, see para 15.06ff below.

[54] See *R v Inland Revenue Commissioners, ex p Rossminster Ltd* [1980] AC 952, 1021 *per* Lord Scarman, see para 12.06ff below.

[55] See the analysis of Lord Mustill in *R v Director of Serious Fraud Squad, ex p Smith* [1993] AC 1, 30–44, see para 11.101ff below.

[56] See eg *McEldowney v Forde* [1971] AC 632, see para 16.06ff.

[57] See *R v Islington North Juvenile Court, ex p Daley* [1983] 1 AC 347 *per* Lord Diplock at 364, see para 11.12ff below.

[58] See *Gillick v West Norfolk and Wisbech Area Health Authority* [1986] AC 112.

[59] See *R v Mid-Glamorgan Family Health Services Authority, ex p Martin* [1995] 1 WLR 110; *R v British Coal Corporation, ex p Ibstock Building Products* [1995] Env LR 277.

[60] *R v Secretary of State for Home Department, ex p Robb* [1995] Fam 127.

[61] *R v Cambridge Area Health Authority, ex p B* [1995] 1 FLR 1055 (reversed on appeal at [1995] 1 WLR 898); the obligation to protect life under English law before the Human Rights Act comes into force is discussed at para 7.08ff below.

shelter,[62] freedom of religion,[63] the right to vote,[64] to sexual orientation,[65] freedom from destitution,[66] property rights[67] and the right to livelihood.[68]

(2) The concept of residual rights

1.21 The traditional doctrine in English law is that Parliament is sovereign.[69] However, individuals may say or do whatever they please provided they do not transgress the substantive law or infringe the legal rights of others. Furthermore, public authorities including the Crown may do nothing but that which they are authorised to do by some rule of common law (including the royal prerogative) or statute and, in particular, may not interfere with the liberties of individuals without statutory authority. Where public authorities are not authorised to interfere with the individual, the individual has liberties. It is in this sense that such liberties are residual rather than fundamental and positive in their nature: they consist of what remains after taking account of all the legal restraints that impinge upon an individual. The classical statement by Lord Camden CJ in *Entick v Carrington*[70] about the nature of negative rights stressed that:

> The great end, for which men entered into society was to secure their property. That right is preserved sacred and incommunicable in all instances, where it has not been taken away or abridged by some public law for the good of the whole.

1.22 The fact that these rights (before the enactment of the Human Rights Act) were residual was often said to be an advantage.[71] Dicey argued that in England the constitution was pervaded by the rule of law because general constitutional principles (such as the right to personal liberty or the right of public meeting) were the result of judicial decisions determining the rights of private individuals whereas under foreign constitutions the security ('such as it is') given to individual rights

62 *R v Lincolnshire County Council and Wealden District Council, ex p Atkinson* (1996) 8 Admin LR 529, 535, 536.

63 See *R v Secretary of State for the Home Department, ex p Moon* (1996) 8 Admin LR 477, 480; the religious rights recognized in English law prior to the Human Rights Act are discussed at para 14.03ff.

64 *Hibberton v Newbory District Electoral Officer* [1985] QB 1060.

65 See *R v Ministry of Defence, ex p Smith* [1996] QB 517; until the Human Rights Act comes into force, sexual orientation discrimination is not unlawful: see para 17.20 below.

66 See *R v Secretary of State for Social Security, ex p Joint Council for the Welfare of Immigrants* [1997] 1 WLR 275, 292.

67 See eg *R v Secretary of State for Transport, ex p Rothschild* [1989] 1 All ER 933 *per* Slade LJ at 939; the protection of property rights in English law before the Human Rights Act comes into force is discused at para 18.09ff below.

68 See *R v Herrod, ex p Leeds City Council* [1978] AC 403.

69 See eg *Halsbury's Laws of England* (4th edn), Vol 8(2), para 101.

70 (1765) 2 Wils 275, 19 State Tr 1029, 1066.

71 Sir Ivor Jennings, for example, wrote 'in Britain we have no Bill of Rights; we merely have liberty according to the law; and we think—truly, I believe—that we do the job better than any country which has a Bill of Rights or Declaration of the Rights of Man' *The Approach to Self Governance* (Cambridge University Press, 1958) 20.

resulted from general principles of the constitution.[72] In *A-G v Guardian Newspapers Ltd (No 2)*[73] Lord Goff took the view, when comparing freedom of expression in English law and that under the European Convention, that:

> I can see no inconsistency between English law on this subject and Article 10 of the [European Convention] . . . The only difference is that whereas Article 10 . . . proceeds to state a fundamental right and then to qualify it, we in this country (where everybody is free to do anything, subject only to the provisions of the law) proceed rather upon the assumption of free speech, and turn to the law to discover the exceptions to it.

1.23 However, the fact that common law rights were residual had at least three important consequences for the protection of fundamental human rights. First, the doctrine of Parliamentary sovereignty meant that Parliament could always legislate fundamental rights out of existence by, for example, removing citizenship rights from 200,000 East African Asians (by enacting by the Commonwealth Immigrants Act 1968) or restricting freedom of assembly (by creating new criminal offences like trespassory assembly under the Criminal Justice and Public Order Act 1994).[74] Secondly, even at common law the judiciary could override civil rights as in *Elias v Pasmore*[75] where it was held that 'the interests of the State must excuse the seizure of documents which seizure would otherwise be unlawful'. The inadequacies of this approach were trenchantly criticised by Lord Bridge in his dissenting judgment in *A-G v Guardian Newspapers*[76] where interlocutory injunctions were granted to prevent publication of alleged wrongdoing by the security forces in *Spycatcher* until the trial of the breach of confidence proceedings brought against the *Guardian* and the *Observer*:

> Having no written constitution, we have no equivalent of the First Amendment to the Constitution of the United States of America. Some think that puts freedom of speech on too lofty a pedestal. We have not adopted as part of our law the European Convention for the Protection of Human Rights and Fundamental Freedoms to which this country is a signatory. Many think that we should. I have hitherto not been of that persuasion, in large part because I have had confidence in the capacity of the common law to safeguard fundamental freedoms essential to a free society including the right to freedom of expression which is specifically safeguarded by article 10 of the convention. My confidence is seriously undermined by your Lordships' judgment . . .
>
> Freedom of speech is always the first casualty under a totalitarian regime. Such a regime cannot afford to allow the free circulation of information and ideas among its citizens. Censorship is the indispensable tool to regulate what the public may and what they may not know. The present attempt to insulate the public in this country from information which is freely available elsewhere is a significant step down a very

72 Dicey (n 44 above) 195–196.
73 [1990] 1 AC 109, 283.
74 See para 16.28 below.
75 [1934] 2 KB 164, 173.
76 [1987] 1 WLR 1248, 1286.

dangerous road. The maintenance of the ban as more and more copies of the book *Spycatcher* enter this country and circulate here will seem more and more ridiculous. If the Government are determined to fight to maintain the ban to the end, they face inevitable condemnation and humiliation by the European Court of Human Rights in Strasbourg.[77] Long before that they will have been condemned at the bar of opinion in the free world.

Thirdly, it was not generally possible for judges to provide common law protection of a human right by fashioning a new cause of action. Thus, in *Malone v Metropolitan Police Commissioner*[78] Sir Robert Megarry VC rejected a claim that telephone tapping breached the 'right to privacy' in these terms:

it is no function of the courts to legislate in a new field. The extension of the existing laws and principles is one thing, the creation of an altogether new right is another. At times judges must, and do, legislate; but as Holmes J once said, they do so only interstitially, and with molecular rather than molar motion: see *Southern Pacific Co v Jensen*,[78a] in a dissenting judgment. Anything beyond that must be left for legislation. No new right in law, fully-fledged with all the appropriate safeguards, can spring from the head of a judge deciding a particular case; only Parliament can create such a right.

(3) Fundamental rights and statutory construction

The critical question which arose in relation to negative rights was how and to what extent they could be effective where they conflicted with legislation. Precisely because there was no limitation to Parliament's power to legislate so as to remove human rights,[79] the courts took the view that legislation did not abrogate fundamental rights unless a statute expressly said so in clear words.[80] The basic principle of construction was described by Lord Browne-Wilkinson in *R v Secretary of State for the Home Department, ex p Pierson*:[81] **1.24**

---

[77] The prediction proved to be correct when the European Court in *The Observer and The Guardian v United Kingdom* (1991) 14 EHRR 153 took the view that once *Spycatcher* was published abroad, there were insufficient reasons to justify maintaining the interlocutory injunctions: see para 15.19ff below for a discussion of the way the *Spycatcher* litigation developed.

[78] [1979] Ch 344, 372; see also *Kaye v Robertson* [1991] FSR 62.

[78a] (1917) 244 US 205, 221.

[79] Lord Irvine, 'Judge and Decision-Makers: The Theory and Practice of Wednesbury Review' [1996] PL 59, 76–78 (commenting on the views of Lord Woolf in 'Droit Public—English style' [1995] PL 57, 67–71; Sir John Laws 'Law and Democracy' [1995] PL 72, 81–93; Sir Stephen Sedley 'Human Rights: a Twenty-First Century Agenda' [1995] PL 386 and see Cooke P in *New Zealand Drivers Association v New Zealand Road Carrier* [1982] 1 NZLR 374, 390, *Fraser v State Services Commission* [1984] 1 NZLR 116, 121; *Taylor v New Zealand Poultry* [1984] 1 NZLR 394, 398; *Te Runganga v Wharekauri* [1993] 2 NZLR 301 and R Cooke, 'Fundamentals' (1988) NZLR 158; and see para 1.38 below.

[80] *Per* Viscount Simonds in *Pyx Granite Co Ltd v Ministry of Housing and Local Government* [1960] AC 260, 286.

[81] [1998] AC 539, 575; see generally, F Bennion, *Statutory Interpretation* (3rd edn, Butterworths, 1997) Pt XVII, 637ff.

> a power conferred by Parliament in general terms is not to be taken to authorise the doing of acts by the donee of the power which adversely affects the legal rights of the citizen or the basic principles on which the law of the United Kingdom is based unless the statute conferring the power makes it clear that such was the intention of Parliament.

Thus, Parliament was presumed not to enact legislation which interfered with the liberty of the subject without making it clear that this was its intention.[82] Unless there was clear authority of law, it was presumed that there should be no interference with the life[83] or health,[84] family rights,[85] freedom of assembly and association[86] or freedom of speech.[87]

1.25 The basis for this approach to statutory construction was said to be that the principle of doubtful penalisation required strict construction of penal statutes (which was not limited to criminal statutes but extended to any form of detriment).[88] It was also said that the rules derived from a general presumption against unclear changes in the law.[89] Lord Devlin suggested that the rationale for the rule of construction was the refusal of judges to act on the ordinary meaning of words: by looking behind a statute to find a Victorian Bill of Rights favouring (subject to the observance of the accepted standards of morality), the liberty of the individual, the freedom of contract, the sacredness of property and which was highly suspicious of taxation.[90] More recently, Lord Hoffmann in *R v Secretary of State for the Home Department, ex p Simms*[91] explained that:

> Parliamentary sovereignty means that Parliament can, if it chooses, legislate contrary to fundamental principles of human rights. The Human Rights Act 1998 will not detract from this power. The constraints upon its exercise by Parliament are ultimately political, not legal. But the principle of legality means that Parliament must squarely confront what it is doing and accept the political cost. Fundamental rights cannot be overridden by general or ambiguous words. This is because there is

[82] *R v Hallstrom, ex p W (No 2)* [1986] QB 1090, 1104 *per* McCullough J; Bennion (n 81 above) s 273, p 645.

[83] See *Bugdaycay v Secretary of State for the Home Department* [1987] AC 514; M Fordham 'What is "Anxious Scrutiny" ', [1996] JR 81, see Bennion, (n 81 above) s 272, p 640.

[84] See eg *R v Eastbourne (Inhabitants)* (1803) 4 East 103 where Lord Ellenborough CJ said that 'the law of humanity which is anterior to all positive laws, obliges us to afford them relief, to save them from starving; and [the poor laws] were only passed to fix the obligation more certainly and to point out distinctly in what manner it should be borne'; and see *R v Hammersmith & Fulham London Borough Council, ex p Joint Council for the Welfare of Immigrants* [1996] 4 All ER 385; see Bennion (n 81 above) s 273, p 641.

[85] See eg *Lewisham London Borough Council v Lewisham Juvenile Court Justices* [1980] AC 273, 307 *per* Lord Scarman, see Bennion (n 81 above) s 274, p 648.

[86] See *Beatty v Gillbanks* (1882) 9 QBD 308, and see Bennion, s 276, p 650.

[87] *Re X (A Minor) (Wardship: Jurisdiction)* [1975] Fam 47; see Bennion (n 81 above) s 277, p 651.

[88] Bennion (n 81 above) s 271.

[89] R Cross, *Statutory Interpretation* (3rd edn, Butterworths, 1995) 167–170.

[90] P Devlin, *The Judge* (Oxford University Press, 1979) 15.

[91] [1999] 3 All ER 400, 412.

> too great a risk that the full implications of their unqualified meaning may have passed unnoticed in the democratic process. In the absence of express language or necessary implication to the contrary, the courts therefore presume that even the most general words were intended to be subject to the basic rights of the individual. In this way the courts of the United Kingdom though acknowledging the sovereignty of Parliament, apply principles of constitutionality little different from those which exist in countries where the power of the legislature is expressly limited by a constitutional document.

Lord Browne-Wilkinson has similarly argued that these rules of statutory construction meant that for most practical purposes the English common law provided protection to the individual at least equal to that given by the European Convention.[92]

In *R v Lord Chancellor, ex p Witham*[93] Laws J described the rule of construction as creating constitutional rights: **1.26**

> The common law does not generally speak in the language of constitutional rights, for the good reason that in the absence of a sovereign text, a written constitution which is logically and legally prior to the power of the legislature, executive and judiciary alike, there is on the face of it no hierarchy of rights such that any one of them is more entrenched by the law than any other. And if the concept of a constitutional right is to have any meaning, it must surely sound in the protection the law affords it. Where a written constitution guarantees a right, there is no conceptual difficulty. The state authorities must give way, save to the extent that the constitution allows them to deny it . . .
>
> In the unwritten legal order of the British State, at a time when the common law continues to accord legislative supremacy to Parliament, the notion of a constitutional right can in my judgment inhere only in this proposition, that the right in question cannot be abrogated by statute save by the specific provision in an Act of Parliament or by regulations whose vires are in the main legislation specifically confers the power to abrogate. General words would not suffice. And any such rights would be the creatures of the common law, since their existence would not be the consequence of the democratic political process but would be logically prior to it.

He went on to hold that the power of the Lord Chancellor to prescribe court fees did not entitle him to preclude the right of access to the courts by preventing an applicant on income support from issuing proceedings for defamation. However, the limitations of this approach were illustrated by the decision in *R v Lord Chancellor, ex p Lightfoot*[94] where the Court of Appeal held that the minimum fee on presenting a debtor's petition for bankruptcy did not curtail the constitutional right to access.

[92] Lord Browne-Wilkinson 'The Infiltration of a Bill of Rights' [1992] PL 397.

[93] [1998] QB 575, 585–586; see also the classic statement in the dissenting judgment by Browne-Wilkinson LJ in *Wheeler v Leicester City Council* [1985] AC 1054, 1065.

[94] [2000] 2 WLR 318 affirming the decision of Laws J at [1998] 4 All ER 764; see M Elliott, 'Lightfoot: Tracing the Perimeter of Constitutional Rights' [1998] JR 217 which discussed the approach taken at first instance.

1.27 The impact of deriving rights from rules of construction was illuminated in a series of cases where prisoners alleged that the prison authorities were interfering with their fundamental civil rights: the issue in dispute was whether the power to manage prisoners under section 47 of the Prison Act 1952 was wide enough to entitle the authorities to interfere with fundamental human rights.[95] In *Raymond v Honey*[96] Lord Wilberforce stated that a prisoner retained all his civil rights which were not taken away expressly or by necessary implication; the House of Lords went on to hold that section 47 was not sufficient to authorise the restriction on a prisoner's fundamental right of access to the courts. In *R v Secretary of State for the Home Department, ex p Anderson*[97] the Divisional Court extended the principle by concluding that it was unlawful to impede a prisoner's right to legal advice which was inseparable from his right of access to the courts. In *R v Secretary of the Home Department, ex p Leech (No 2)*[98] the Court of Appeal considered whether the right of access was restricted by necessary implication; and took the view that this depended on showing there was a self evident and pressing need for the interference which was the minimum necessary to ensure that the need was met. In *R v Secretary of State for the Home Department, ex p Simms*[99] the House of Lords decided that it was unlawful to deprive a prisoner of his fundamental right to exercise freedom of expression: by seeking to persuade a journalist at an oral interview to investigate his conviction to gain access to the courts as a miscarriage of justice. By comparison, in *R v Secretary of State for the Home Department, ex p O'Dhuibhir*[100] the Court of Appeal held that no fundamental rights were at issue because closed visits were *intra vires* the Prison Rules.

1.28 The doctrine of fundamental human rights also arises under European Union law[101] since 'respect for human rights is a condition of the lawfulness of Community acts'.[102] This general principle of Community law has been inspired by national constitutional traditions[103] as well as by international rights treaties[104]

[95] See T Owen, 'Prisoners and Fundamental Rights' [1997] JR 81; and see S Livingstone and T Owen, *Prison Law* (Oxford University Press, 1999), para 1.34ff.

[96] [1983] 1 AC 1, 10

[97] [1984] 1 QB 778.

[98] [1994] QB 198.

[99] [1999] 3 All ER 400.

[100] [1997] COD 315.

[101] For a fuller treatment see eg N Neuwahl and A Rosas, *The European Union and Human Rights* (Kluwer, 1995); L Betten and N Grief, *EU Law and Human Rights* (Longman, 1998); E Guild and G Lesieur, *The European Court of Justice on the European Convention on Human Rights* (Kluwer, 1998) G de Burca, 'Fundamental Rights and the Reach of EC Law' (1993) 13 OJLS 283; J H H Weiler and N H S Lockhart, 'Taking Rights Seriously: The European Court and its Fundamental Rights Jurisprudence' (1995) 32 CML Rev 51 and 579; the relationship between European Community law and European Convention law is discussed at para 2.26ff below.

[102] Opinion 2/94 *Accession by the Community to the Convention for the protection of Human Rights and Fundamental Freedoms* [1996] ECR I–1759.

[103] See eg *Internationale Handelsgesellschaft mbH v Einfur- und Vorratsstelle für Getreide und Futtermittel* [1970] ECR 1125.

[104] See eg *Nold AG (Firma) v Commission* [1974] ECR 491.

(including the European Convention itself).[105] The doctrine, although non justiciable, is now embodied in Article F(2)(6)(2) of the Treaty on European Union:

> The Union shall respect fundamental rights, as guaranteed by the European Convention for the Protection of Human Rights and Fundamental Freedoms signed in Rome on 4 November 1950 and as they result from the constitutional traditions common to the Member States as general principles of Community law.

The doctrine of fundamental rights is normally invoked when interpreting or striking down Community measures and developed from the decision of the European Court of Justice in *Stauder v City of Ulm*[106] where it was argued that a Community scheme to provide cheap butter to recipients of welfare benefits breached Community rights. For example, in *Hauer v Land Rheinland-Pfalz*[107] the European Court of Justice had to rule on whether a Community regulation banning the planting of new vines contravened the right to property and the right to pursue a trade or profession. The Court accepted that fundamental rights formed an integral part of the 'general principles of law, the observance of which it ensures'. It went on to hold that the measure criticised did not entail any 'undue limitation upon exercise of the right to property' and was valid. In addition, the doctrine requires Member States to respect fundamental rights. It is used to interpret provisions in the Treaties or Community legislation by, for example, extending the scope of anti discrimination measures to transsexuals[108] but not to homosexuals.[109] National measures which come within the scope of Community law[110] must comply with its human rights standards, so that the Divisional Court in *R v Secretary of State for the Home Department, ex p Adams*[111] had to assess whether an exclusion order imposed under the Prevention of Terrorism Act was a proportionate restriction under Article 10 of the European Convention. Where Community provisions grant rights to individuals which are subject to derogation on grounds such as public policy, any derogation made by a national government must not violate the Community concept of fundamental rights.[112] Furthermore, if Member States implement Community rules by enacting domestic legislation, **1.29**

[105] See eg *Rutili v Minister for the Interior* [1975] ECR 1219; *Hauer v Land Rheinland-Pfaltz* [1979] ECR 3727.

[106] [1969] ECR 419.

[107] [1979] ECR 3727.

[108] *P v S and Cornwall County Council* [1996] ECR I–1191.

[109] *Grant v South-West Trains* [1998] ECR I-621.

[110] See *R v Ministry of Agriculture, Fisheries and Food, ex p First City Trading* [1997] 1 CMLR 250 where Laws J took the view that the general principles of law articulated by the European Court of Justice have a narrower application than those contained in the Treaty itself. However, his reasoning is open to question (see L Betten and N Grief, *EU Law and Human Rights* n 101 above 80); and cannot be derived from the case law of the Court of Justice (S Boyron 'General Principles of Law and national courts: apply a jus commune' (1998) 23 ELR 171).

[111] [1995] All ER (EC) 177.

[112] See eg *Ellinki Radiophonia Tileorassi AE v Dimotiki Etairia Plitoforris and Storious Kouvelas* [1991] ECR I–2925.

Member States must so far as possible apply the rules in accordance with fundamental rights.[113]

(4) Civil rights and administrative law decisions

1.30 Even where there was no scope for applying the statutory presumption that legislation would not be construed as interfering with fundamental human rights in the absence of clear words,[114] English law prior to the Human Rights Act still protected human rights as part of general administrative law principles. Unfortunately, however, the test of *Wednesbury* unreasonableness provided only a pragmatic (and uncertain) measure of protection.[115] Sir John Laws in his seminal article 'Is the High Court the Guardian of Fundamental Constitutional Rights'[116] proposed that where fundamental constitutional rights were in issue, the courts should develop different standards of substantive principles of judicial review. He argued that if a decision overrode a fundamental right without sufficient objective justification, it should be struck down on grounds of proportionality,[117] that cases involving fundamental human rights required decision-makers to give reasons[118] and that statutes should be construed so that interference with fundamental rights would only be justified if the policy of the legislation permitted such an interference. These suggestions were further developed by Sedley J in *R v Secretary of State for the Home Department, ex p McQuillan*[119] when he remarked that:

> Once it is accepted that the standards articulated in the [European] convention are standards which march with those of the common law and inform the jurisprudence of the European Union, it becomes unreal and potentially unjust to continue to develop English public law without reference to it.

1.31 In reality, however, the courts did not apply such radical principles when assessing the lawfulness of administrative decision-making. In *Bugdaycay v Secretary of State for the Home Department*[120] Lord Bridge stated that:

---

113 *Wachauf v Germany* [1989] ECR 2609; *R v Ministry of Agriculture, Fisheries and Food, ex p Bostock* [1994] ECR I–955

114 See para 1.24ff above.

115 See eg J Jowell and A Lester, '*Beyond Wednesbury: Substantive Principles of Administrative Law*' [1987] PL 368.

116 [1993] PL 59.

117 The approach of Laws J is epitomised by the right to life case, *R v Cambridge Health Authority, ex p B* [1995] 1 FLR 1055 where he quashed the refusal of the authority to provide medical health treatment to a child with leukaemia and held that where the life of a ten year old child might be saved by however slim a chance, the health authority must do more than 'toll the bell of tight resources' (his decision was reversed on appeal [1995] 1 WLR 898); see generally, para 6.44ff below.

118 See eg *R v Secretary of State for the Home Department, ex p Doody* [1994] 1 AC 531, 565 *per* Lord Mustill; *R v Higher Education Funding Council, ex p Institute of Dental Surgery* [1994] 1 WLR 421 where the Divisional Court held that there was an implied duty to provide reasons for a decision where the subject matter is of an interest so highly regarded by the law (for example, personal liberty) that fairness requires reasons as of right; and *R v Mayor of City of London, ex p Matson* [1996] 8 Admin LR 49; *Stefan v General Medical Council* [1999] 1 WLR 1293, PC; and see D Toube, 'Requiring Reasons at Common Law' [1997] JR 68.

119 [1995] 4 All ER 400, 422.

120 [1987] AC 514, 531.

> The Court must, I think, be entitled to subject an administrative decision to the more rigorous examination, to ensure that it is in no way flawed, according to the gravity of the issue which the decision determines. The most fundamental of all human rights is the individual's right to life and when an administrative decision under challenge is said to be one which may put the applicant's life at risk, the basis for the decision must call for the most anxious scrutiny.

Although the doctrine of 'anxious scrutiny' dictated that in cases involving fundamental rights, the grounds for judicial review should be applied especially rigorously and that the onus fell on the respondent to show the legal propriety of the action in question,[121] its practical effect was open to question. Thus, in *R v Ministry of Defence, ex p Smith*[122] the Court of Appeal while accepting that the more substantial the interference with human rights, the more the court would require by way of justification before it was satisfied that the decision was *Wednesbury* reasonable, went on to decide that it was lawful to dismiss servicemen on the ground that they were homosexual.[122a] On the other hand, in *R v Lord Saville, ex p A*[123] the Court of Appeal took the view that the Bloody Sunday inquiry failed to attach sufficient significance to the right to life (which it described as the most fundamental of all human rights) in holding that the inquiry had acted irrationally by refusing to grant anonymity to witnesses who were to appear before it.

Singh[124] has argued that when considering fundamental rights in the context of broad discretionary powers, the following propositions had become established: **1.32**

- There are certain fundamental rights which enjoy a pre-eminent status within the common law (such as the right to life, freedom of expression, freedom of movement and the right of respect for privacy and family life).
- A public body will be required to take the relevant right into account.
- A public body will be required to balance the impact of the decision concerned on the fundamental right against whatever public interests militate in favour of making that decision.
- A primary judgment concerning whether the balance has been struck in the right place is for the public body on whom the power has been conferred. However, the court will perform a secondary judgment to assess the rationality of the decision taken.

[121] M Fordham, 'What is "Anxious Scrutiny" ' [1996] JR 81.

[122] [1996] QB 517.

[122a] The very restrictive *Wednesbury* approach resulted in the Court of Human Rights in *Smith and Grady v United Kingdom* [1999] IRLR 734 deciding that the applicants had been denied an effective remedy in breach of Art 13: see para 21.178 below.

[123] [1999] 4 All ER 860.

[124] R Singh, *The Future of Human Rights in the United Kingdom* (Hart Publishing, 1998) Chap 1.

- In assessing the rationality of the decision, the court will require greater justification (by way of countervailing public interests) for the decision taken, depending on the importance of the fundamental right and the breadth or gravity of the interference with that right.
- The court will not be satisfied by a simple incantation of a ritual mantra, to the effect that the public body has taken into account the fundamental right at stake. The court will scrutinise the decision closely, and most anxiously, where the right to life is at stake.
- The court is unlikely to take a benevolent view of any defect in the decision-making process, for example, by refusing relief in the exercise of its discretion, as it might do if the case did not involve human rights.

However, the application of these propositions has been uneven in the case law prior to the Human Rights Act coming into force.

(5) 'Common law' rights

1.33 The common law is antecedent law: it provides the ultimate foundation of the constitution in English law.[125] Consequently, it is sometimes claimed that it is possible to locate in the common law *positive* (as opposed to residual) rights which have substantive content. Thus, Allan[126] has argued that common law constitutional rights are the product of two interacting facets of the rule of law: freedom of expression exists, for example, both as the outcome of a residual liberty and as a manifestation of the court's attachment to the value of free speech as a principle. As a result, the common law could be the source of important individual rights, reflecting moral judgments about basic values which justice seems to support. He argues that the weight given to rights in a particular case cannot ultimately be determined by the language of a bill of rights; but depends on the value the rights are *accorded* by the judge in that case. Consequently, he favours a communitarian conception of the rule of law,[127] which subjects public power to principles of justice and fairness, reflecting the community's commitment to fundamental values embodied within the common law. He criticises the traditional majoritarian view that legislation should be relatively immune from judicial review because it carries the authority of the majority of elected representatives; and rejects its corollary that the scope of judicial review

[125] Sir Owen Dixon, 'The Common Law as an Ultimate Constitutional Foundation' (1957) 31 ALJ 240.

[126] T Allan, *Constitutional Rights and the Common Law*: *Law, Liberty and Justice* (Clarendon Press, 1993), Chap 6.

[127] T Allan, 'Fairness, Equality, Rationality' in C Forsyth and I Hare (eds), *The Golden Metwand and the Crooked Cord* (Clarendon Press, 1998).

should be confined to a narrow doctrine of *ultra vires*[128] and *Wednesbury*[129] principles.

1.34 Sir John Laws elaborated his views about how constitutional principles could be derived from the common law itself.[130] He identified two first order constitutional principles:

- the common law rule that private individuals can do everything which is not forbidden and
- the general principle forbidding a public body from doing anything which is not allowed.[131]

He went on to suggest that common law presumptions (like the presumption that rights cannot be removed by Parliament except by express words) operated as second order constitutional principles. A third order constitutional principle came into play where a right was potentially infringed by the use of a discretionary power granted by statute in express terms (thereby overriding the presumption contained in the second order principle); in that circumstance the decision-maker would nevertheless have to offer a compelling public interest justification for the power's use.[132]

1.35 Nevertheless, defining the content of positive common law rights raised difficult questions. In 'Is the High Court the Guardian of Fundamental Constitutional Rights'[133] Sir John Laws maintained that Convention law was capable of informing the common law; and his views attracted support in subsequent cases.

[128] The coherence of *ultra vires* as general justification for judicial review has been much criticised: see eg D Oliver, 'Is the Ultra Vires rule the basis of judicial review' [1987] PL 543; P Craig, *Administrative Law* (3rd edn, Sweet & Maxwell, 1994), Chaps 10 and 16; Lord Woolf, 'Droit Public—English style' [1995] PL 57; Sir John Laws 'Illegality: the problem of jurisdiction' in M Supperstone and J Goudie (eds) *Judicial Review* (2nd edn, Butterworths, 1997); Sir Stephen Sedley, 'The common law and the constitution' in Lord Nolan and Sir Stephen Sedley, *The Making and Remaking of the British Constitution* (Blackstone, 1997); P Craig, 'Ultra vires and the Foundations of Judicial Review' [1998] 58 CLJ 63; J Jowell, 'Of Vires and Vacuums: The Constitutional Context of Judicial Review' [1999] PL 448; and contrast the view of eg C Forsyth, 'Of Fig Leaves and Fairy Tales: the Ultra Vires Doctrine, the Sovereignty of Parliament and Judicial Review' (1995) 55 CLJ 122; H Wade, 'Habeas Corpus and Judicial Review' (1997) 113 LQR 55; M Elliott, 'The Ultra Vires Doctrine in a Constitutional Setting: Still the Central Problem in Administrative Law' (1999) 59 CLJ 129; M Elliott, 'The Demise of Parliamentary Sovereignty? The Implications for Justifying Judicial Review' (1999) 115 LQR 119.

[129] See eg Lord Irvine, 'Judge and Decision-Makers: The Theory and Practice of Wednesbury Review' [1996] PL 59; Sir Robert Carnwath, 'The Reasonable Limits of Local Authority Power' [1996] PL 244; and contrast the views of Sir John Laws ,'Wednesbury' in Forsyth and Hare (eds), (n 127 above).

[130] Sir John Laws, 'Meiklejohn, the First Amendment and Free Speech in English Law' in I Loveland (ed), *Importing the First Amendment* (Hart Publishing, 1998).

[131] As he expressed in *R v Somerset County Council, ex p Fewings* [1995] 1 All ER 513, 524.

[132] See the views of Lord Bridge in *R v Secretary of State for the Home Department, ex p Brind* [1991] 1 AC 696, 748, 749.

[133] [1993] PL 59; in 'Judicial Remedies and the Constitution' (1994) 57 MLR 213 he argued that nothing prevents the judges from regarding the Convention not as a source of given law but as a source from which they may derive the law.

For instance, it was suggested that the right of access to the courts,[134] the right to legal advice,[135] the right to freedom of religion,[136] the right to freedom of expression[137] and the right of assembly[138] all broadly resembled Convention law. Beloff and Mountfield argued that the use made by the courts of Convention law had infused the substance of Convention law into English law if not achieving the back-door incorporation of its text.[139] Hunt contended that such developments were nothing short of a common law human rights jurisdiction, showing a judicial willingness to develop the common law in a way which provided recognition for and greater protection of fundamental human rights.[140] Klug and Starmer suggested that the increased profile of the Convention reflected the determination of some senior judges to provide a more substantial foundation for the protection of fundamental rights already protected by the common law.[141] In fact, this elision of common law rights with rights under the Convention was criticised since it impliedly left it open to the English courts to ignore Convention jurisprudence on the relevant issues.[142] More importantly, an assertion, for example, that there was a common law right to freedom of expression which is equivalent to Article 10 was so vague as a matter of analysis that it failed to produce legal certainty where the courts sought to apply the principle to a particular case.

1.36 The real significance of positive common law rights was the potential impact that they might have in cases where they conflicted with the terms of a statute. A rule of construction in favour of fundamental rights[143] would not, of course, prevent Parliament from legislating in terms to override them in the appropriate language. If, instead, there were positive rights in the common law, it would not be open for Parliament to trump fundamental rights. At an early stage in the development of the common law, it appeared that natural law might place limits on what Parliament would be able to enact. Thus, in *Dr Bonham's Case*[144] Coke CJ stated that:

---

[134] See eg *Raymond v Honey* [1983] AC 1; *R v Lord Chancellor, ex p Witham* [1998] QB 575.

[135] *R v Secretary of State for the Home Department, ex p Anderson* [1984] 778; *R v Chief Constable of South Wales, ex p Merrick* [1994] 1 WLR 663.

[136] *R v Secretary of State for the Home Department, ex p Moon* (1996) 8 Admin LR 477, 480; *R v Salisbury District Council, ex p Pendragon*, unreported, 9 Jun 1995 (Laws J).

[137] *A-G v Guardian Newspapers Ltd (No 2)* [1990] 1 AC 109 *per* Lord Goff at 283; *Derbyshire County Council v Times Newspapers Ltd* [1993] AC 534; *Rantzen v Mirror Group Newspapers (1986) Ltd* [1994] QB 670.

[138] *R v Salisbury District Council, ex p Pendragon* unreported, 9 Jun 1995.

[139] M Beloff and H Mountfield 'Unconventional Behaviour? Judicial Uses of the European Convention in England and Wales' [1996] EHRLR 467.

[140] M Hunt, *Using Human Rights in the English Courts* (Hart Publishing, 1997) 205.

[141] F Klug and K Starmer, 'Incorporation Through the Backdoor' [1997] PL 223.

[142] Hunt, (n 140 above) 303–308.

[143] See para 1.24ff above.

[144] (1610) 8 Co Rep 107, 108; there is considerable debate about whether Coke CJ was expressing an unusual view about statutory construction (see T Plucknett, 'Dr Bonham's Case and judicial review' (1926) 40 Harv L Rev 35; S Thorne, 'Dr Bonham's Case' (1938) LQR 543) or something more: see C Dike, 'The case against Parliamentary sovereignty' [1976] PL 283.

> When an act of parliament is against the common right and reason or repugnant, or impossible to be performed, the common law will control it, and adjudge such act to be void.

In *Day v Savadge*[145] Hobart CJ said that:

> even an Act of Parliament made against natural equity, as to make a man judge in his own cause, is void in itself.

However, these notions became obsolete when the supremacy of Parliament was established by the Glorious Revolution of 1688.[146]

In the last few years a number of judges have suggested that the courts could refuse to recognise legislation which violated fundamental rights.[147] Lord Woolf said that the courts might refuse to recognise legislation which removed the power of judicial review.[148] Sir John Laws claimed that the concept of a higher order law might justify the courts refusing to acknowledge legislation abolishing fundamental freedoms.[149] Sir Stephen Sedley also argued that parliamentary sovereignty might be overridden by the courts.[150] For example, in *R v Secretary of State for the Home Department, ex p Pierson*[151] Lord Steyn stated that Parliament must be presumed not to legislate contrary to the rule of law; and that the rule of law included an obligation to meet a minimum standard of substantive fairness.[152] He therefore concluded that the Home Secretary had acted unlawfully in increasing the tariff period of imprisonment (which a life prisoner had to serve) on the ground that he had breached substantive fairness because a prison sentence which is lawfully passed cannot be retrospectively increased. **1.37**

However, the idea that parliamentary sovereignty must give way to fundamental rights was particularly associated with the former President of the New Zealand Court of Appeal, Lord Cooke of Thorndon.[153] In *L v M*[154] he doubted whether Parliament could constitutionally confer on a body other than the courts a power to determine conclusively whether actions in courts could be barred. In *New* **1.38**

145 (1614) Hob 85.

146 *Pickin v British Railways Board* [1974] AC 765 *per* Lord Reid at 782.

147 See also T Allan, 'The Limits of Parliamentary Sovereignty' [1985] PL 614; and see S Lee, 'Comment' [1985] PL 632.

148 Lord Woolf, 'Droit Public—English style' [1995] PL 57, 67–71.

149 Sir John Laws, 'Law and Democracy' [1995] PL 72, 81–93.

150 Sir Stephen Sedley, 'Human Rights: a Twenty-First Century Agenda' [1995] PL 386.

151 [1998] AC 539, 591.

152 See also eg J Jowell, 'The Rule of Law today', in J Jowell and D Oliver (eds), *The Changing Constitution* (3rd edn, Clarendon Press, 1994); P Craig, 'Formal and Substantive Conceptions of the Rule of Law' [1997] PL 467.

153 See eg Sir Robin Cooke, 'Fundamentals' (1988) NZLR 158; and see also P Rishworth, 'Lord Cooke and the Bill of Rights' and M Kirby, 'Lord Cooke and Fundamental Rights' in P Rishworth (ed), *The Struggle for Simplicity in the Law* (Butterworths, 1997).

154 [1979] 2 NZLR 519, 527 dissenting.

Zealand Drivers Association v New Zealand Road Carrier[155] he questioned whether legislation could take away rights of access to the courts for the determination of rights. He observed in *Fraser v State Services Commission*[156] and again in *Taylor v New Zealand Poultry Board*[157] that some common law rights lie presumably so deep that even Parliament cannot override them. In *Te Runganga v Wharekauri*[158] Cooke P took the view that the implied right to freedom of expression in public and political affairs necessarily exists in a system of representative government.

1.39 The notion of fundamental common law rights has had the greatest impact in Australia.[159] The Commonwealth of Australia Constitution Act 1900 contains a number of express rights;[160] and the courts have to a limited extent implied rights from certain specific constitutional provisions.[161] More importantly, the limitations on the exercise of governmental power have been derived from the constitutional text and the political system it established; they are said to exist in the structure of the constitution and are to be revealed or uncovered by judicial exegesis.[162] In a series of cases Murphy J attempted to imply fundamental rights from the Constitution Act and asserted that legislation would be invalid if it contravened these implied rights.[163] This approach was adopted by the High Court of Australia in *Australian Capital Television Pty Ltd v The Commonwealth of*

[155] [1982] 1 NZLR 374, 390 *per* Cooke, McMullin and Ongley JJ.

[156] [1984] 1 NZLR 116, 121.

[157] [1984] 1 NZLR 394, 398.

[158] [1993] 2 NZLR 301, 308.

[159] See generally, H Lee, 'The Australian High Court and Implied Fundamental Guarantees' [1993] PL 606; and J Doyle and B Wells, 'How Far can the Common Law Go Towards Protecting Human Rights' in P Alston (ed), *Promoting Human Rights Through Bills of Rights* (Oxford University Presss, 1999); G Williams, *Human Rights under the Australian Constitution* (Oxford University Press, 1999) Chaps 7 and 8 and see also G Winterton, 'Extra-Constitutional Notions in Australian Constitutional Law' [1986] 16 FLR 223; D Smallbone, 'Recent Suggestions of an Implied "Bill of Rights" in the Constitution Considered as Part of a General Trend of Constitutional Interpretation' (1993) 22 FLR 254; L Zines, 'A Judicially Created Bill of Rights' (1994) 16 SLR 166.

[160] 'Just terms' for the acquisition of property (s 51(xxxi)); trial by jury for indictable offences (s 80); free exercise of religion (s 116); protection from discrimination by States on grounds of residence (s 117).

[161] See generally, G Kennett, 'Individual Rights, the High Court and the Constitution' (1995) 19 Mel U L Rev No 3.

[162] *McGinty v State of Western Australia* (1996) 186 CLR 140 *per* Brennan CJ; *Lange v Australian Broadcasting Corporation* (1997) 189 CLR 520, 556, 557.

[163] See eg *R v Director General of Social Welfare for Victoria, ex p Henry* (1975) CLR 369, 388 (slavery, serfdom, self determination); *Buck v Bavone* (1976) 135 CLR 110, 137 (travel); *Ansett Transport Industries v Commonwealth* (1977) 139 CLR 54, 87, 88 (travel, speech and communication); *Seaman's Union of Australia v Utah Developments* (1978) 144 CLR 120, 157 (serfdom); *McGraw–Hinds (Australia) v Smith* (1979) 144 CLR 633, 668– 670 (slavery, serfdom, rule of law, freedom of movement and communication); *Ansett Transport Industries v Wardley* (1980) 142 CLR 237, 267 (sexual discrimination); *Uebergang v Australia Wheat Board* (1980) 145 CLR 266, 311, 312 (freedom of speech, assembly, communication and travel); *Sillery v R* (1981) 35 ALR 227, 233, 234 (cruel and unusual punishment); *Miller v TCN Channel Nine Pty* (1986) 67 ALR 321, 336, 338 (freedom of speech, communication and travel).

Australia[164] which relied on an implied common law right to freedom of information on political matters in striking down legislation which restricted political advertising before elections and referenda. It has also been suggested that the fundamental right to a fair trial can be implied from the constitution.[165]

Nevertheless, the legitimacy of the judiciary (as opposed to Parliament or a constitutional convention) quarrying in the common law to find rights must remain open to question; and the notion of fundamental common law rights which override statute faces a number of serious objections. Lord Irvine, in particular, has severely criticised the notion of judicial supremacism,[166] arguing that it is contrary to the established law and constitution of the United Kingdom.[167] He contends that the claim by judges to negate parliamentary decisions is inconsistent with the fundamental tenets of a free democracy. Secondly, it is has been pointed out that the pragmatic development of the common law rights is a reactive and potentially deeply conservative process of law-making.[168] Furthermore, the scope and content of any fundamental right that is found may be entirely subjective: depending on little else than the individual opinion of the judge hearing the particular case.[169] **1.40**

D. The Bill of Rights Debate

(1) The campaign for a Bill of Rights

The difficulties in arriving at any generally acceptable notion of 'common law rights' led an increasing number of influential legal and political figures to campaign for the enactment of a statutory 'Bill of Rights'. Most of the debate centred on whether or not the United Kingdom should 'incorporate' the European Con- **1.41**

---

164 (1992) 177 CLR 106; *Nationwide News v Wills* (1992) 177 CLR 1; *Lange v Australian Broadcasting* (n 162 above); *Levy v Victoria* (1997) 146 ALR 248; for a discussion of the Australian cases on freedom of expression, see para 15.351ff.

165 *Dietrich v R* (1992) 177 CLR 292 *per* Deane J at 328, Gaudron J at 364; for a discussion of fair trial rights in Australia, see para 11.463ff below.

166 Lord Irvine, 'Judges and Decision-Makers: the Theory and Practice of Wednesbury Review' [1996] PL 59; and see also 'Principle and Pragmatism: the Development of English Public Law Under the Separation of Powers' Lecture at High Court in Hong Kong 18 Sep 1998 where Lord Irvine argues that if the theoretical basis for judicial review ignores the *ultra vires* doctrine and entitles judges to enforce automonous principles of good administration that bear no relation to the intention of Parliament, then the judiciary are contradicting the legislature and the constitutional order is undermined; but contrast R Singh, *The Future of Human Rights in the United Kingdom* (Hart Publishing, 1997) Chap 3.

167 See eg *Liversidge v Anderson* [1942] AC 206, 260, 261 *per* Lord Wright; *Malzaimbamuto v Lardner-Burke* [1969] 1 AC 645, 723 *per* Lord Reid.

168 See F Donson, 'Civil Liberties and Judicial Review: Can the Common Law Really Protect Rights?' in P Leyland and T Woods (eds), *Administrative Law Facing the Future: Old Constraints and New Horizons* (Blackstone, 1997).

169 See eg K Ewing, 'New Constitutional Constraints in Australia' [1993] PL 256.

vention on Human Rights into domestic law. The Convention was adopted by the Council of Europe in 1950. The United Kingdom played a major role in drafting the Convention itself; the actual draftsman of the Convention was the former senior legal advisor in the Home Office, Sir Oscar Dowson, and a prominent role was played in the process by Sir David Maxwell-Fife (who later became the Lord Chancellor, Lord Kilmuir).[170] The United Kingdom was also the first state to ratify the Convention on 8 March 1951 and it came into force on 3 September 1953.[171]

1.42 However, there were objections to the individuals' right to petition the European Commission of Human Rights directly and the United Kingdom did not introduce the right to petition until December 1965. It appears[172] that the timing of that decision was strongly influenced by the wish to prevent an application under the European Convention by Burmah Oil to challenge the lawfulness of the War Damage Act 1965 on the basis that it retrospectively overruled the House of Lords decision[173] that Burmah Oil was entitled to compensation for war time damage in Burma.

1.43 Lord Scarman is widely recognised as the first eminent legal figure to support a Bill of Rights in England. In 1974 Lord Scarman argued for an entrenched Bill of Rights in his Hamlyn lectures.[174] However, there were a number of earlier attempts to enact Bills of Rights. In 1969 Lord Lambton introduced a 10-minute rule bill to preserve the rights of the individual[175] as did Mr Emlyn Hooson QC MP.[176] In 1970 Lord Annan proposed[177] and then withdrew a bill which was modelled on the Canadian Bill of Rights of 1960. In 1971 Sam Silkin QC MP moved the second reading of the Protection of Human Rights Act[178] which proposed that the United Kingdom Commission on Human Rights be set up but his bill was counted out because of a lack of members. Following the 1974 election there was a renewed interest in a Bill of Rights. The Ulster Unionist MP, James Kelfedder, put forward a motion in July 1975 to set up a Royal Commission to investigate and report on a Bill of Rights for the United Kingdom.[179] Shortly afterwards the Liberals supported a Bill of Rights Bill which was introduced by Alan Beith MP.[180] The Labour Party also took up the issue of incorporating the European Convention

[170] A Lester, 'Fundamental Rights: The United Kingdom Isolated?' [1984] PL 47.

[171] G Marston, 'The United Kingdom's Part in the Preparation of the European Convention on Human Rights' (1993) 43 ICLQ 819.

[172] See Lord Lester, 'UK Acceptance of the Strasbourg Jurisdiction: What Really Went On in Whitehall in 1965' [1998] PL 237.

[173] *Burmah Oil Co Ltd v Lord Advocate* [1965] AC 75.

[174] Sir Leslie Scarman, *English Law—The New Dimension* (Stevens, 1974).

[175] *Hansard*, HC vol 782, col 474.

[176] *Hansard*, HC vol 787, col 1519.

[177] *Hansard*, HL vol 313, col 243.

[178] *Hansard*, HC vol 814, col 1854.

[179] *Hansard*, HC vol 894, col 32.

[180] *Hansard*, HC vol 895, col 1270.

at this time. The Human Rights Sub-Committee of Labour's National Executive Committee, chaired by Shirley Williams MP, issued a discussion document arguing for a Charter of Human Rights.

In March 1976 the Standing Advisory Committee on Human Rights in Northern Ireland published a discussion paper on a Bill of Rights. Lord Wade then moved a debate to incorporate the European Convention into English law[181] and the bill was given an unopposed second reading. In June 1976 the Home Office issued a Green Paper[182] which discussed three main options: keeping the status quo, incorporating the European Convention or drafting a new Bill of Rights. **1.44**

Indeed, the Conservative Party at this time also appeared to favour incorporation[183]. In February 1977 Leon Brittain MP, the Shadow spokesman on devolution, proposed an amendment to the Scotland Bill at the committee stage which would have incorporated the European Convention in Scotland;[184] the proposal was defeated by 251 votes to 227. In February 1977 Lord Wade again introduced a debate[185] which resulted in the establishment of the Select Committee on a Bill of Rights. The Select Committee reported in 1978.[186] The Report indicated that it was required to consider two issues: whether a Bill of Rights was desirable and if so, what form it should take. The Select Committee was unanimous that the bill should be based on the European Convention but found it impossible to agree whether such a bill would be desirable.[187] When the Report was debated in the House of Lords in November 1978, Lord Wade[188] persuaded the House of Lords to vote in favour of introducing a bill to incorporate the Convention. **1.45**

Lord Wade continued to press for incorporation after the 1979 election. In 1979 he introduced a bill which was passed by the House of Lords and sent to the House of Commons. In 1981 Lord Wade again succeeded in putting forward a bill which passed through the House of Lords and was debated in the House of Commons where it was defeated in a second reading.[189] Various further attempts were made to enact legislation but without success. In 1983 Robert Maclennan MP introduced a European Human Rights Convention Bill[190] under the 10-minutes rule but the bill lapsed. In 1985 the Conservative peer, Lord Broxbourne[191] introduced the Human Rights and Fundamental Freedoms Bill to incorporate the Convention **1.46**

[181] *Hansard*, HL vol 369, col 775.
[182] *Legislation on Human Rights: with particular reference to the European Convention.*
[183] See eg the Society of Conservative Lawyer's *Another Bill of Rights?*
[184] *Hansard*, HC vol 943, col 491.
[185] *Hansard*, HL vol 389, col 973.
[186] *Report of the Select Committee of the House of Lords on a Bill of Rights* (HL Paper No 176).
[187] See para 1.50ff below.
[188] *Hansard*, HL vol 396, col 1308.
[189] *Hansard*, HC (Series 6) vol 4, cols 419–457.
[190] *Hansard*, HC (Series 6) vol 50, col 852.
[191] *Hansard*, HL vol 469, col 156.

and that bill was given a third reading in the House of Lords and was introduced to the House of Commons by Sir Edward Gardiner QC MP where it fell on its second reading.

1.47 However, support for a Bill of Rights was beginning to broaden and a number of pressure groups campaigned for a Bill of Rights. In November 1988 Charter 88[192] published its proposals in the *Guardian* newspaper to establish a new constitutional settlement which included creating a Bill of Rights which would enshrine the right to peaceful assembly, freedom of association, freedom from discrimination, freedom from detention without trial, the right to trial by jury, the right to privacy and the right to freedom of expression. A number of Conservatives also argued for incorporation.[193] In October 1991 Liberty (formerly the National Council of Civil Liberties) published *A People's Charter—Liberty's Bill of Rights.*[194] Liberty drew on a variety of human rights instruments like the International Covenant on Civil and Political Rights, the International Labour Organisation Convention on the Right to Organise and Collective Bargaining, the European Social Charter and the Canadian Charter of Rights and Freedoms. Its detailed and complex proposals were designed to minimise the impact of judicial interpretation. Liberty also proposed a new parliamentary committee which would scrutinise legislation to ensure conformity with the Bill of Rights both before and after review by the courts. The Institute for Public Policy Research also published 'A British Bill of Rights' in December 1991 as the first part of a proposed written constitution for the United Kingdom. The Institute drafted its own Bill of Rights based on the Convention and the International Covenant on Civil and Political Rights.

1.48 The Labour Party's position again began to shift, this time in favour of incorporation. On 1 March 1993 the then leader of the Labour Party, John Smith delivered a lecture calling for the incorporation of the Convention into English law. In September 1993 the Labour Party published *A New Agenda for Change: Labour's Proposals for Constitutional Reform* arguing for a Human Rights Bill which would incorporate the European Convention. The legislation was designed to trump primary legislation. The Labour Party would introduce a 'notwithstanding' clause so that subsequent legislation could only override the

[192] See also eg A Lester, *A Bill of Rights for England* (Charter 88, 1991); F Mount, *The Recovery of the Constitution* (Charter 88, 1992); A Lester, *The Crisis Facing Human Rights in Europe; Does the British Government Really Care?* (Charter 88, 1993); F Klug, *Reinventing the Community: The Rights and Responsibilities Debate* (Charter 88, 1996).

[193] See eg F Vilbert, *Constitutional Reform in the United Kingdom—An Incremental Agenda* (Institute of Economic Affairs, 1990) and F Mount, *The British Constitution Now: Recovery or Decline* ? (Charter 88, 1992).

[194] See F Klug and K Wadham, 'The "democratic entrenchment" of a Bill of Rights: Liberty's Proposals' [1993] PL 579.

Human Rights Bill if it expressly said so (modelled on the Canadian Charter of Rights).[194a] The Human Rights Act would in terms apply to (and prevail over) existing legislation. The legislation would only apply to individuals and would be enforced in the ordinary courts. Furthermore, the Labour Party indicated that incorporating the Convention would only represent the first stage. Because the European Convention does not, for example, cover freedom of information, data protection, the rights of the disabled or social and economic rights, the Labour Party proposed that an all party commission should draft a new Bill of Rights within a prescribed period. Many of the Labour Party's proposals were included in the Human Rights Bill introduced by Graham Allen MP (which he had prepared with assistance from Liberty). The bill would both have incorporated the European Convention and appointed a Bill of Rights Commission which was charged with preparing a draft Bill of Rights relating to civil, political, economic and social rights. Although Graham Allen's bill received a first reading in January 1994, it did not proceed further.

The Human Rights Bill proposed by Lord Lester in November 1994 received more detailed consideration from Parliament. The original bill proposed that the Convention should have similar status to that of European Union law and was modelled on section 2 of the European Communities Act 1972; but was amended to take effect as a rule of construction in the same way as the New Zealand Bill of Rights Act 1990.[195] Although the bill received support from a number of senior judges including Lords Ackner, Browne-Wilkinson, Scarman, Lloyd, Simon, Slynn, Taylor and Woolf as well as from Sir Thomas Bingham MR, the Bill failed in the House of Commons due to lack of time. The Human Rights Bill that Lord Lester proposed in 1996[196] was again closely modelled on the New Zealand legislation. It was introduced with the support of Lord Woolf and other senior members of the judiciary and was given an unopposed second reading in the House of Lords. **1.49**

(2) The debate over the Bill of Rights

The 1978 House of Lords Select Committee on a Bill of Rights considered the arguments for and against legislation to incorporate the European Convention on Human Rights.[197] It identified the most important arguments in favour of a Bill of Rights as being the following: **1.50**

- An individual would be better off if the Convention were made part of UK law

194a s 33; the Charter is reproduced at App O in Vol 2.

195 See generally, Lord Lester, 'The Mouse That Roared: The Human Rights Bill 1995' [1995] PL 198.

196 *Hansard*, HL, cols 1725–1730 (5 Feb 1997).

197 Report of the *Select Committee of the House of Lords on a Bill of Rights* (HL Paper No 176) 30–34.

because, where there was a conflict, whichever was more favourable would prevail.

- Embodying the Convention in domestic law would provide the citizen with a positive and public declaration of guaranteed rights at a time when many individuals and groups felt impotent in the face of the size and complexity of public authorities.
- Experience had shown that domestic law sometimes provided no remedy for breaches of Convention rights.
- There was no reason to suppose that the English courts were not equally capable of adjudicating on rights as the European Commission or European Court of Human Rights.
- Incorporation of the Convention would complement other human rights legislation and 'freshen up' the common law.
- Membership of the European Community made it all the more important for the British legal system to develop as part of the Community rather than in splendid isolation.
- A Bill of Rights would provide a framework of human rights guaranteed throughout the United Kingdom; this would have special value if devolved assemblies were established in Scotland and Wales.
- The Convention would have a far more practical effect on legislators, administrators, the executive, the judiciary and individual citizens if it became an integral part of UK law.

The Select Committee then summarised the most important arguments against a Bill of Rights:

- Incorporation of the Convention would open up wide areas of legislative policy such as freedom of expression, privacy, education and race relations and effectively hand them over to the judiciary.
- Under a Bill of Rights the courts would cease to develop legal principles slowly and empirically as they did under the common law; they would start with principles of the widest generality and have a free hand to decide how those principles operated in the cases before them.
- The broad and general terms of the Convention would introduce uncertainty into the law and result in a great extension of litigation.
- Incorporating the Convention would give judges a role which went far beyond those played by the judges at Strasbourg.
- The existing situation in the United Kingdom most accorded with the original philosophy of the European Convention.
- Even on the most unfavourable view of the extent to which UK law falls short of Convention standards, incorporation would only bestow a remedy in a few marginal situations such as in the areas of privacy and the conduct of prisons.

In the light of these conflicting arguments the Select Committee could not reach a conclusion about whether or not it was desirable in principle to enact a Bill of Rights. However, by the early 1990s, establishment opinion had moved decisively towards the incorporation of the Convention into English law.[198] It has now become difficult to disentangle the various arguments which were the most persuasive.[199] **1.51**

The fact that Britain lagged behind the rest of the world by failing to enact human rights legislation was a potent force for change. English lawyers played an important part in drafting the European Convention on Human Rights[200] and the UK Government went on to ensure that the Nigerian Constitution of 1960 contained fundamental human rights similar to the European Convention.[201] Thereafter, the United Kingdom was instrumental in ensuring that 24 Commonwealth countries now contain such fundamental rights. Nevertheless, despite the enactment of human rights legislation in, for example, Canada,[202] Israel,[203] Hong Kong,[204] New Zealand[205] and most recently, South Africa,[206] the United Kingdom **1.52**

---

198 See eg A Ryan, 'The British, the Americans and Rights' in M Lacey and K Haakonssen (eds), *A Culture of Rights* (Cambridge University Press, 1991); R Dworkin, 'Does Britain Need a Bill of Rights?' in *Freedom's Law* (Oxford University Press, 1996); Lord Lester, 'Taking Human Rights Seriously' in R Gordon and R Willmot-Smith (eds), *Human Rights in the United Kingdom* (Oxford University Press, 1996).

199 For an excellent summary of arguments for and against introducing a bill of rights, see M Zander, *A Bill of Rights?* (4th edn, Sweet & Maxwell, 1997).

200 See generally, A Lester, 'Fundamental Rights: the United Kingdom Isolated' [1984] PL 47.

201 In fact, the approach taken towards Nigeria represented a fundamental change. The early Commonwealth constitutions such as Canada, Australia, South Africa and Ireland did not contain any comprehensive statement of fundamental rights. Lord Simons' *Report of the Joint Parliamentary Committee on Indian Constitutional Reform* (HL 6 and HL 5 1933/34) rejected the suggestion that the Indian guarantee should contain guarantees of the right of respect for religion and equal rights. When Sir Ivor Jennings acted as the constitutional advisor to Ceylon, he advised against introducing a comprehensive guarantee of human rights into the draft constitution; the Ceylon (Constitutional) Order in Council in 1946 simply prohibited legislative action which interfered with the free exercise of religion or which discriminated against a community or religious group. The British Government also rejected a draft constitution for the West African colony of the Gold Coast which contained seven articles protecting human rights and adopted the Ceylon model. The dramatic change in attitude towards constitutional bills of rights manifested itself in the decision in Nov 1959 to provide Nigeria with a constitutional bill of rights and the constitutional conference in 1960 which preceded Kenyan independence where the British Government insisted on the constitutional protection of human rights; it was prompted by various international developments such as the Universal Declaration of Human Rights in 1949, the ratification of the European Convention in 1951 (and its application to 42 dependent territories in 1954), the statement of fundamental rights introduced into the constitutions of India in 1949, Pakistan in 1956, Malaysia in 1957 and Ceylon in 1959: see generally, N Jayawickrama, 'The Bill of Rights' in R Wacks (ed), *Human Rights in Hong Kong* (Oxford University Press, 1992).

202 The Canadian Bill of Rights in 1960 and the Canadian Charter of Rights and Freedoms in 1992; the text of the Charter is reproduced at App O in Vol 2.

203 Basic Law: Human Dignity and Freedom.

204 The Bill of Rights Ordinance 1991.

205 The New Zealand Bill of Rights Act 1990; the text is reproduced at App R in Vol 2.

206 Chap 2 of the Constitution Act; the text is reproduced at App S in Vol 2.

was slow to follow their initiative. Indeed, until the Human Rights Act came into force, the United Kingdom was the only Western member of the Council of Europe in which the Convention was not part of domestic law.

1.53 The Government presented its case for incorporating the Convention law in very practical terms in its White Paper, *Rights brought Home: the Human Rights Bill*[207] (which was published when the Human Rights Bill was introduced in October 1997): the cost[208] and time taken[209] in waiting for an adjudication from the European Court of Human Rights was unjustified, particularly against a background where the United Kingdom has been one of the states most frequently charged with Convention violations.

1.54 There were a range of other arguments which were used by advocates of a Bill of Rights. Perhaps the most important of these was the educational impact of a Bill of Rights in terms of creating a 'culture of rights', although it was unclear whether the objective was to create a culture of rights among ordinary citizens who internalise fundamental norms, or among politicians, opinion formers and other members of the political élite or whether the purpose was to create a rights culture that was to be absorbed into institutional arrangements which provide constitutional safeguards.[210]

1.55 One of the most noticeable features of the debate about a Bill of Rights in recent years was that senior British judges explicitly participated in the process. The attitude of the senior judiciary towards parliamentary sovereignty significantly affected the shape of the Human Rights Act. Thus, Lord Browne-Wilkinson[211] suggested a bill of rights should be formulated as a rule of construction presuming, in the absence of clear and precise statutory words to the contrary, that Parliament did not intend to infringe fundamental rights. He emphasised the protection given to human rights from membership of the European Union[212] and from the common law;[213] and justified incorporation of the Convention in terms of raising judicial consciousness: by reminding the judicial mind of fundamental rights so that they would uphold rights even where 'the merits' of the particular case did not encourage such a conclusion.[214] Lord Woolf also favoured a

[207] Cm 3782.

[208] In *Rights brought Home: The Human Rights Bill* (1997) Cm 3782 it is estimated that the average case costs £30,000: see para 1.14. The text is reproduced at App B in Vol 2.

[209] The Council of Europe has said that it takes five years before a case is finally decided before the European Court or Council of Ministers: see Council of Europe *Protocol 11 to the European Convention on Human Rights and Explanatory Report* May 1994 (H (94 5) 19 para 21).

[210] D Barnum, J Sullivan and M Sunkin, 'Constitutional and Cultural Underpinning of Political Freedom in Britain and the United States' (1992) 12 OJLS 362.

[211] 'The Infiltration of a Bill of Rights' [1992] PL 397.

[212] See para 1.28ff above.

[213] See para 1.33ff above.

[214] See also Lord Browne-Wilkinson, 'The Impact on Judicial Reasoning' in B Markesinis (ed), *The Impact of the Human Rights Bill on English Law* (Clarendon Press, 1998).

form of incorporation which did not threaten parliamentary sovereignty. He supported incorporation of the Convention along the lines of the New Zealand Bill of Rights.[215] On the other hand, Lord Bingham[216] suggested that the statute of incorporation should provide that, subject to express abrogation or derogation in any later statute, rights specified in the Convention should be fully recognised and enforced in the United Kingdom. He was sceptical of the claim that Convention rights were already protected by the common law, pointing out that if that were right, it was surprising that the United Kingdom's record as a litigant in Strasbourg was not more favourable. He also took the view that the positive case for incorporation was so clear that the burden lay on its opponents to make good their grounds of opposition.

Those who opposed a Bill of Rights often put forward arguments which were the mirror image of those deployed by the other side to the controversy: for instance, that a Bill of Rights was unnecessary because the common law provided sufficient protection, that a Bill of Rights would politicise the judges or that it would generate frivolous litigation. To some extent opposition to a Bill of Rights reflected a general antipathy towards lawyers. As Lord Bingham pointed out,[217] the idea that law was the ultimate guarantor of the rights and liberties of the citizen was not universally shared.[218] Lawyers were, for example, banned from Sir Thomas More's Utopia,[219] would have been forbidden in Gerrard Winstanley's ideal commonwealth[220] and were in fact forbidden to practice in Massachusetts in the early days of the colony.[221] **1.56**

Perhaps the most compelling objection to human rights legislation was that its broad language might result in a transfer of political power from politicians to the judiciary which could be characterised as 'undemocratic'.[222] The Lord Chancellor, Lord Mackay,[223] expressed concerns in 1996 that: **1.57**

[215] 'Droit Public—English Style' [1995] PL 57.

[216] Lord Bingham, 'The European Convention on Human Rights: Time to Incorporate' in R Gordon and R Wilmot-Smith (eds), *Human Rights in the United Kingdom* (Clarendon Press, 1996).

[217] Lord Bingham 'The Way We Live Now: Human Rights in the New Millennium' (1998) 1 Web JCL 1, Earl Grey Memorial Lecture, 29 January 1998.

[218] C Hill, *Liberty against the Law* (Allen Lane, 1996).

[219] Ibid 264.

[220] Ibid 268.

[221] Ibid 268.

[222] See eg J A G Griffiths, *The Politics of the Judiciary* (5th edn, Fontana, 1997); K Ewing and C Gearty, *Democracy or a Bill of Rights* (Society of Labour Lawyers, 1991) and *Freedom under Thatcher: Civil Liberties in Modern Britain* (Oxford University Press, 1990) 262–275; and 'Rocky Foundations for Labour's New Rights' [1997] EHRLR 146.

[223] 'Parliament and the Judges—A Constitutional Challenge' lecture to the Citizenship Foundation 8 Jul 1996; see also Sir Nicholas Lyell 'Whither Strasbourg? Why Britain Should Think Long and Hard Before Incorporating the European Convention on Human Rights' [1997] EHRLR 132.

> Incorporation of the European Convention or a Bill of Rights as the yardstick by which Acts of Parliament are to be measured would inevitably draw judges into making decisions of a far more political nature, measuring policy against abstract principles with possible implications for the development of broad social and economic policy which has been accepted by the judiciary to be properly the preserve of Parliament. The question which would then be asked, and to which an answer could not be postponed indefinitely, is whether the introduction of such a political element into the judicial function would require a change in the criteria for appointing judges, making the political stance of each candidate a matter of importance as much as his or her ability to decide cases on their individual facts and the law applicable to those facts. Following on from that is the question of how confidence in judicial independence and impartiality can be maintained, and whether their appointment should be subjected to political scrutiny of the sort recently seen in the United States.

On the other hand, it was suggested that the role of the judiciary would still remain a distinctive one: because judicial power would guarantee that the framework of fundamental democratic principles was ultimately vindicated in the sense that it would ensure that the Government operated within the framework of fundamental democratic principles.[224] The rationale for this approach was powerfully stated by the American Supreme Court in *Virginia State Board of Education v Barnette*:[225]

> The very purpose of a Bill of Rights was to withdraw certain subjects from the vicissitudes of political controversy to place them beyond the reach of majorities and officials and to establish them as legal principles to be applied by the courts. One's right to life, liberty and property, to free speech, a free press, freedom of worship and assembly, and other fundamental rights may not be submitted to the vote; they depend on the outcome of no elections.

Nevertheless, difficult questions remain concerning the legitimacy of judges being drawn into controversial positions on substantive issues of policy.

1.58 Judicial decisions concerning human rights legislation are not necessarily predictable; nor do they invariably attract a broad political consensus. For example, the Supreme Court of Canada decided that a provision which protects a complainant in a sexual assault or rape case from being cross examined about her past sexual activity was unconstitutional under the Canadian Charter of Rights because it deprived the accused of the right to make full answer and defence.[226]

1.59 Furthermore, the broad language of human rights legislation inevitably provokes

[224] See eg R Dworkin, 'The Moral Reading and the Majoritarian Premise' in *Freedom's Law* (Oxford University Press, 1996); Sir John Laws 'Law and Democracy' [1995] PL 72; contrast Lord Devlin, 'The Law and Lawmakers' (1976) 39 MLR 1; and see the debate between Sir John Laws, 'The Constitution: Morals and Rights' [1996] PL 623 and Lord Irvine, 'Response to Sir John Laws 1996' [1996] PL 636.

[225] (1943) 319 US 624 *per* Jackson J.

[226] *R v Seaboyer* [1991] 2 SCR 577.

diametrically opposed viewpoints which may be equally well reasoned and justified, making the proper interpretation of human rights instruments inherently controversial. The vigorous debate in the United States in relation to interpreting the American Bill of Rights is fundamentally an issue about the legitimacy of judicial intervention in the democratic process. As that most distinguished of American judges, Learned Hand, pointed out 'it would be most irksome to be ruled by a bevy of Platonic Guardians, even if I knew how to choose them, which I assuredly did not'.[227] At one extreme, it is argued that judicial review of legislation should be confined to the language of the constitution and its original intent.[228] At the other, non-intepretivism asserts that the vague and indeterminate nature of the constitutional text permits a variety of standards and values: the moral values of the judge, the moral values of society or, perhaps, some form of natural law such as a theory of justice, democracy or morality.[229] The unsatisfactory nature of these approaches has led Ely[230] to argue that the purpose of a Bill of Rights is to protect the *process* of decision-making, limiting judicial decisions to issues of fair process instead of broader substantive issues.

Even so, concerns arising from judicial intervention in policy questions are likely to play a significant role in interpreting the Human Rights Act itself. Where the court scrutinises the justification for an interference with a qualified Convention right[231] such as the right to respect for privacy or freedom of expression, it is likely to attach weight to the views of the decision-maker himself, particularly where it considers political judgments or issues of policy.[232] **1.60**

E. Parliamentary Sovereignty and the Entrenchment of a Bill of Rights

(1) The incorporation issue

Whenever the question of enacting a bill of rights into English law was discussed, its proponents faced the difficulty that the doctrine of parliamentary sovereignty enabled Parliament to legislate human rights out of existence. They frequently argued **1.61**

[227] Learned Hand, *The Bill of Rights* (Harvard University Press, 1958) 73; and see generally, G Gunther, *Learned Hand the Man and the Judge* (Harvard University Press, 1994).

[228] See eg R Bork, *The Tempting of America: the Political Seduction of the Law* (MacMillan, 1990); R Berger, *Government by Judiciary* (Harvard University Press, 1971); and contrast the views of R Dworkin in *Freedom's Law* (Oxford U niversity Press, 1996) Chaps 12 and 14.

[229] The wide range of approaches are discussed by W Fisher, 'The Development of Modern American Legal Theory and the Judicial Interpretation of the Bill of Rights' in M Lacey and K Haakonssen (eds), *A Culture of Rights* (Cambridge University Press, 1991) and also J Ely, *Democracy and Distrust* (Harvard University Press, 1980) Chap 3.

[230] Ely (n 229 above), but see eg L Tribe ,'The Puzzling Persistence of Process-Based Constitutional Theory' (1980) 89 Yale LJ 1063.

[231] See para 6.90ff below.

[232] See para 5.125ff below.

that a bill of rights should be enacted in a way which preserved its special constitutional status: by ensuring that a bill of rights could not be repealed by ordinary legislation. As a result there has been a continuing debate about the nature of parliamentary sovereignty and whether it is technically feasible to entrench a bill of rights.

1.62 The way in which other countries within the Council of Europe have incorporated the Convention into their domestic law has varied considerably.[233] Some countries such as Austria have expressly incorporated the Convention into constitutional law so that no statute or secondary legislation is valid if it contravenes Convention rights. In the great majority of countries, such as France[234] for example, international treaties in general, and the European Convention in particular, occupy an intermediate status as a result of ratification: they have a higher rank than normal legislation but have a lower status than the constitution, and thus the Convention will prevail over ordinary legislation. In some states, however, the Convention is part of domestic law and has the same status as normal legislation. For example, in Germany,[235] Holland[236] and Sweden[237] the Convention will take precedence over existing laws and will prevail over legislation. In practice, however, the Convention is usually regarded as supreme unless a later statute is clearly intended to override the Convention.[237a]

1.63 The Home Office Green Paper in 1976 considered a variety of methods of entrenchment to protect a bill of rights against actions by a temporary majority. These included enacting legislation which imposed specific requirements for its alteration (such as a two thirds majority of both Houses) or a statute to be enacted by a constituent assembly or a new constitutional settlement. However, the Green Paper concluded that it was doubtful that such an attempt could be wholly effective.[238] In 1980 Jaconelli[239] comprehensively analysed the legal difficulties in enacting a bill of rights and proposed a draft bill that would have entitled a court to

[233] See generally, R Bernhardt, 'The Convention and Domestic Law' in R St J Macdonald, F Matscher and H Petzold (eds), *The European System for the Protection of Human Rights* (Nijhoff, 1993); J Gardiner (ed), *Aspects of Incorporation of the European Convention into Domestic Law* (1993); C A Gearty (ed), *European Civil Liberties and the European Convention on Human Rights* (Kluwer, 1997); for a survey of the position as it appears to the Committee of Ministers of the Council of Europe at Strasbourg, see F Sundleberg, 'Status of the ECHR in the Member States' in L Betten (ed), *The Human Rights Act 1998 What it Means* (Nijhoff, 1999).

[234] E Steiner, 'France' in Gearty (n 233 above).

[235] E Voss, 'Germany' in Gearty (n 233 above).

[236] See eg Y Klerk and E de Jonge, 'The Netherlands' in Gearty (n 233 above); S Martens, 'Incorporating the European Convention: the role of the judiciary' [1998] EHRLR 5.

[237] I Cameron, 'The Swedish Experience of the European Convention on Human Rights Since Incorporation' (1999) 48 ICLQ 20.

[237a] R Bernhardt, 'The Convention and Domestic Law' in R St J Macdonald, F Matscher and H Petzold (eds) *The European System for the Protection of Human Rights* (n 233, above).

[238] *Legislation on Human Rights: with particular reference to the European Convention.*

[239] J Jaconelli, *Enacting a Bill of Rights* (Clarendon Press, 1980).

strike down legislation which was inconsistent with fundamental rights and freedoms. These issues again came to the fore after Tony Blair became leader of the Labour Party in 1994 and reiterated the Labour Party's commitment to incorporating the Convention. The shadow Lord Chancellor, Lord Irvine QC, at that time argued in favour of incorporation on the Canadian model and in favour of confining the scope of any legislation to individuals (rather than to companies or organisations).[240]

The debate concerning the form of incorporation then moved on. When Lord Lester took soundings from the senior judiciary in relation to his first Human Rights Bill in 1994, he concluded that many had no enthusiasm for new powers which would put them directly at odds with the elected branch of parliamentary government and modified his approach from one modelled on the European Communities Act to one based on the New Zealand Bill of Rights.[241] In February 1997 the Labour Party published its consultative paper, *Bringing Rights Home: Labour's Plans to Incorporate the European Convention in UK law.*[242] The consultative paper itself accepted the traditional theory of parliamentary sovereignty[243] and took the view that the Convention could not be entrenched into domestic law.[244] The Labour Party appeared to be leaning away from introducing a form of incorporation which might disturb the balance of the separation of powers between the judiciary, Parliament and the executive.[245] Nevertheless, many still favoured a form of entrenchment along the lines of the European Communities Act[246] or the Canadian Charter of Rights.[247] **1.64**

240 Lord Irvine, 'The Legal System and Law Reform Under Labour' in D Bean (ed), *Law Reform for All* (Blackstone, 1996).

241 Lord Lester, 'The Mouse That Roared: the Human Rights Act 1995' [1995] PL 198; see also Lord Woolf 'Droit Public—English style' [1995] PL 57.

242 [1997] EHRLR 71.

243 See para 1.66ff below.

244 Contrast the earlier position of the Labour Party in 1993 in *A New Agenda for Change: Labour's Proposals for constitutional reform* when it favoured legislation enacted on the Canadian model.

245 Lord Irvine, 'Constitutional Reform and a Bill of Rights' [1997] EHRLR 483; the Labour Party itself seemed to be moving in favour of the New Zealand approach (see para 1.81 below.) despite the notorious drafting of the New Zealand legislation: see A Butler, 'The Bill of Rights Debate: Why the New Zealand Bill of Rights Act 1990 is a Bad Model for Britain' (1997) 17 OJLS 323.

246 See eg S Kentridge, 'Parliamentary Supremacy and the Judiciary under a Bill of Rights: some lessons from the Commonwealth' [1997] PL 96 who pointed out that taking the New Zealand approach would negate the real purpose of incorporating the Convention, giving British judges the same powers as the judges of the European Court of Human Rights; see also B Emmerson, 'This year's model—the options for incorporation' [1997] EHRLR 313.

247 See eg The Constitution Unit, *Human Rights Legislation* (1996) Chap 2; Liberty, *Response to Labour's Plans to Incorporate the European Convention on Human Rights in UK Law* (Mar 1997); the Institute for Public Policy Research, *Labour's plans to incorporate the European Convention on Human Rights into UK Law: Response to the Consultation Paper from the Institute for Public Policy Research* (Mar 1997); Sir William Wade, *'Human Rights and the Judiciary'* [1998] EHRLR 520; the form of entrenchment under the Canadian Charter of Rights is outlined at para 1.79 below.

1.65 The Government introduced the Human Rights Bill in October 1997 accompanied by a white paper, *Rights Brought Home: the Human Rights Bill.*[248] In a preface to the White Paper the Prime Minister described the Human Rights Bill as a major step in the Government's programme of reform, whose elements include Scottish and Welsh devolution, reform of the House of Lords, an elected Mayor for London and a freedom of information bill.[249] However, the Human Rights Act was designed to preserve parliamentary sovereignty[250] by requiring the courts to apply the European Convention as an *interpretative* tool.[251] Most of the technical problems which are raised by attempting to reconcile the entrenchment of a human rights instrument with the doctrine of parliamentary sovereignty therefore do not, at present, arise. Nevertheless, it is still helpful to survey the issues central to the debate over incorporation and parliamentary sovereignty, not least because arguments will be raised about the effect of the Human Rights Act which will compel the courts to consider how and to what extent the Act achieves its purpose.

(2) The doctrine of parliamentary sovereignty

1.66 The nature of parliamentary sovereignty is an inherently contested idea and is conventionally debated between proponents of the traditional theory and the new theory of sovereignty.[252] The traditional theory of 'continuing' parliamentary sovereignty has been vigorously upheld by Sir William Wade;[253] he has summarised his position in these terms:

> An orthodox English lawyer, brought up consciously or unconsciously on the doctrine of parliamentary sovereignty stated by Coke and Blackstone and enlarged upon by Dicey, could explain it in these terms. He would say that it meant that no act of the sovereign legislature (comprising the Queen, the Lords and Commons) could be invalid in the eyes of the courts; that it is always open to the legislature, so constituted, to repeal any legislature whatsoever; that therefore no Parliament could bind its successors; and that the legislature only had one process for enacting legislation, whereby it was declared to be a joint Act of the Crown, the Lords and the Commons in Parliament assembled. He would probably add that it is an invariable rule that in the case of conflict between two Acts of Parliament, the later repeals the earlier. If he were then asked whether it would be possible for the United Kingdom to 'entrench' legislation—for example, if it should wish to adopt a Bill of Rights

248 (1997) Cm 3782 which is reproduced at App B in Vol 2.

249 See eg R Hazell, 'Reinventing the Constitution: Can the State Survive?' [1999] PL 84.

250 See eg *Rights brought Home: the Human Rights Bill* paras 2.10 to 2.16 which is reproduced at App B in Vol 2; *Hansard,* HL col 1229 (3 Nov1997); HC cols 771, 782, 790, 858 (16 Feb 1998); Lord Irvine, 'Keynote address' in J Beatson, C Forsythe and I Hare (ed), *Constitutional Reform in the United Kingdom: Practice and Principles* (Hart Publishing, 1998).

251 N Bamforth, 'Parliamentary sovereignty and the Human Rights Act 1998' [1998] PL 572.

252 For a survey of the debate see G Winterton, 'The British Grundnorm: Parliamentary Sovereignty Re-examined' (1976) 92 LQR 591.

253 H Wade, 'The Basis of Legal Sovereignty' [1955] CLJ 172, 174.

> which would be repealable only by some specially safeguarded process—he would answer that under English law this is a legal impossibility: it is easy enough to pass such legislation but since such legislation, like all other legislation, would be repealable by any ordinary Act of Parliament the special safeguards would be futile . . . It follows therefore that there is one, and only one, limit to Parliament's legal power: it cannot detract from its continuing sovereignty.

Wade relies on three cases in arguing that later legislation must impliedly repeal an earlier statute. The first two arose out of the Acquisition of Land (Assessment of Compensation) Act 1919. The 1919 Act stated that the provisions of any Act which authorised the acquisition of land and which were inconsistent with the 1919 Act 'shall cease to have or shall have no effect'. Because certain provisions of the Housing Act 1925 were inconsistent with the 1919 Act, it was argued that these later inconsistent provisions could be ignored. However, this contention was rejected in *Vauxhall Estates v Liverpool Corporation*[254] and *Ellen Street Estates v Minister of Health*.[255] Similar views about the doctrine of implied repeal were expressed by the Privy Council in *British Coal Corporation v The King*[256] when Lord Sankey LC suggested that, in theory, Parliament could repeal section 4 of the Statute of Westminster and once again enact legislation for the Dominions. **1.67**

However, it is clear that the doctrine of parliamentary sovereignty must in the final analysis derive from the common law[257] in the sense that no statute is capable of conferring the power on Parliament: that assumes the very power that is to be conferred in the first place.[258] However, Wade claims that the doctrine of parliamentary sovereignty is a political (rather then legal) fact which is the ultimate rule of recognition;[259] it is the law because those who operate the system accept that it is the law. **1.68**

By comparison, supporters[260] of the new theory of sovereignty argue that sovereignty is 'self embracing'[261] and that Parliament can enact legislation which alters its manner and form without detracting from its sovereignty. The exercise of ascertaining whether Parliament has complied with procedural rules (and has thereby enacted valid legislation) is *logically prior* to determining any question **1.69**

---

254 [1932] 1 KB 733.

255 [1934] 1 KB 590; Maugham LJ at 597 took the view 'the legislature cannot, according to our constitution, bind itself as to the form of subsequent legislation, and it is impossible for Parliament to enact that in a subsequent statute dealing with the same matter, there can be no implied repeal. If in a subsequent Act Parliament chooses to make it plain that the earlier statute is to some extent repealed, effect must be given to that intention just because it is the will of the legislature.'

256 [1935] AC 500.

257 I Jennings, *The Law and the Constitution* (5th edn, University of London Press, 1967) Chap 4.

258 J Salmon, *Jurisprudence* (10th edn, Stevens, 1957) 155.

259 H L A Hart, *The Concept of Law*, (Clarendon Press, 1961) Chap 6.

260 See eg I Jennings (n 257 above) Chap 4, R F V Heuston, *Essays in Constitutional Law* (Stevens, 1964) Chap 1; G Marshall, *Constitutional Theory* (Oxford University Press, 1971) Chap 3.

261 Hart (n 259 above) 146.

concerning sovereignty as such. Thus, in *Attorney-General for New South Wales v Trethowan*[262] the Privy Council held that the legislature of New South Wales could not enact legislation in 1931 without holding a referendum in accordance with legislation enacted in 1929 because section 5 of the Colonial Laws Validity Act 1865 expressly required that any amendment to a colonial constitution must be in the manner and form of existing legislation. Similarly, in *Harris v Minister of Interior*[263] the Supreme Court of South Africa decided that the Separate Representation of Voters Act 1951 which created a separate roll for coloured voters was invalid as the legislation had been enacted in breach of the procedural requirements of the South Africa Act 1909. The extent to which analogies can be drawn from these cases about parliamentary sovereignty in English law is unclear. Unlike the British Parliament, the New South Wales legislature was not 'sovereign'. Even though the South African legislature was 'sovereign', it was constituted by a written instrument whereas in English law these issues must be addressed by reference to the common law. Furthermore, the readiness of the courts to scrutinise parliamentary procedures when considering the validity of legislation is also not certain,[264] despite the well established rule that the court will only look to the parliamentary roll when examining whether legislation is validly enacted.[265]

1.70 There is a more fundamental logical problem about the new theory of sovereignty. A provision altering the form and manner in which legislation is enacted may be so draconian (for example, requiring approval by 90% of the electorate in a referendum) that it effectively amounts to a fetter on the substantive power of Parliament to legislate: in other words Parliament may be purporting to abdicate its own sovereignty.[266]

1.71 The debate about the nature of sovereignty has acquired a much sharper focus as a result of the impact of European Union law.[267] European Union law was given direct effect into English law by section 2(1) of the European Communities Act 1972 which (so far as is relevant) states:

> All such rights . . . from time to time created or arising by or under the Treaties . . . as in accordance with the Treaties are without further enactment to be given

[262] [1932] AC 526.

[263] 1952 (2) SA 428.

[264] *Manuel v A-G* [1983] Ch 77; compare *Bribery Commissioners v Ranasinghe* [1965] AC 172.

[265] *Edinburgh and Dalkeith Railway v Wauchope* (1842) 8 Cl & Fin 710; *Lee v Bude and Torrington Junction Railway Co* (1871) LR 6 CP 576, 582 *per* Willes J; *British Railways Board v Pickin* [1974] AC 765.

[266] Although Dicey appears to have accepted that Parliament could abdicate its sovereignty (see G Winterton, 'The British Grundnorm: Parliamentary Sovereignty Re-examined' (1976) 92 LQR 591, 600–604), Heuston, for example, made it clear that there could be no restriction on the area or ambit of the power of Parliament: see *Essays in Constitutional Law* (n 260 above) 6–16.

[267] It has created comparable difficulties for other member states in adjusting their constitutional systems: see eg J P Warner, 'The Relationship between European Community Law and the National Laws of Member States' (1977) 93 LQR 349.

> legal effect . . . in the United Kingdom [and] shall be recognised . . . in law, and be enforced . . . accordingly . . .

Section 2(4) of the European Communities Act appears to be addressed to the issue of parliamentary sovereignty and (so far as is relevant) states:

> . . . any enactment passed or to be passed . . . shall be construed and have effect subject to the foregoing provisions of this section.

The repercussions of European Union law on parliamentary sovereignty were exposed in the *Factortame* litigation. The applicants were UK sea fishing companies where the majority directors and shareholders were Spanish. The statutory regime affecting sea fishing was fundamentally changed by the Merchant Shipping Act 1988 which discriminated against citizens of other member states because ships could only register to fly the British flag if they were 75% owned by those who were British citizens, or were owned by those domiciled or resident in the United Kingdom. Proceedings were brought complaining that the 1988 Act was in breach of European Union law and, in particular, the prohibition against discrimination on grounds of nationality. The constitutional issue raised by the litigation was whether, contrary to the principle of implied repeal,[268] the inconsistency created by the *later* UK legislation had to be resolved in favour of the earlier European Communities Act. At every stage the English courts agreed that a reference should be made to the European Court of Justice under Article 177[268a] and the critical issue was whether the applicants were entitled to an interim injunction pending the reference. The House of Lords in *R v Secretary of State for Transport, ex p Factortame Ltd*[269] rejected the claim for an interim injunction, holding that the presumption that an Act of Parliament was valid could not be displaced and that there was no jurisdiction under English law to grant an interim injunction against the Crown.[270] However, in the course of giving the judgment, Lord Bridge said[271] that section 2(4) of the European Communities Act: **1.72**

> . . . has precisely the same effect as if a section were incorporated in Part II of the 1988 Act which in terms enacted that the provisions with respect to registration of British fishing vessels were to be without prejudice to the Community right of nationals of any Member State of the EC.

The European Court of Justice[272] went on to decide in favour of the applicants and held that directly applicable Community laws must be fully and uniformly applied to the laws of Member States and that they rendered any conflicting **1.73**

[268] The principle is discussed at para 4.33 below.

[268a] Now Art 234.

[269] [1990] 2 AC 85.

[270] A view which the House of Lords declined to follow in *M v Home Office* [1994] 1 AC 377.

[271] n 269 above, 140.

[272] *R v Secretary of State for Transport, ex p Factortame Ltd (No 2)* [1990] ECR I–2433 relying on *Amministrazione delle Finanze dellor Stato v Simmenthal SpA* [1978] ECR 629.

domestic law automatically inapplicable. The European Court concluded that full effectiveness of Community law required that interim relief be granted. The case then returned to the House of Lords for reconsideration in the light of the European Court's preliminary ruling. The House of Lords now decided that they had power to grant interim relief to the applicants and did so on the facts of the particular case. However, Lord Bridge also expressed views on the more general question of sovereignty;[273]

> If the supremacy . . . of Community law over the national law of member states was not always inherent in the EEC Treaty, it was certainly well established in the jurisprudence of the Court of Justice long before the United Kingdom joined the Community. Thus, whatever limitation of its sovereignty Parliament accepted when it enacted the European Communities Act was entirely voluntary.

The rationale is essentially that the United Kingdom knew what it was getting into when it joined and must be taken to have contracted on those terms.

1.74 Nevertheless, controversy remains about the precise basis for asserting that European Union law takes precedence over UK legislation. The most straightforward approach is to regard section 2(4) of the European Communities Act as establishing a rule of construction that later statutes have to be read as being subject to it.[274] That was favoured when the European Communities Act was passed[275] and has been adopted by a number of judges subsequently.[276] As Craig points out, it preserves the formal veneer of Diceyian orthodoxy whilst undermining its substance and has the advantage of making Parliament rather than the courts responsible for making a 'political choice' at the 'boundary of the legal system'.[277] However, the construction view assumes[278] that legislation in 1972 succeeded in enacting restrictions on Parliament in 1988 contrary to the doctrine of implied repeal[279] and the traditional theory of sovereignty.[280] In other words, the construction view breaks down because it involves more than questions of construction; and begs the question of whether it is open to Parliament to restrict its sovereignty in this way.

1.75 The new theory of sovereignty also provides an unsatisfactory explanation for

[273] *R v Secretary of State for Transport, ex p Factortame Ltd (No 2)* [1991] 1 AC 603, 658, 659.

[274] See eg T Hartley, *The Foundations of European Community Law* (4th edn, Oxford University Press, 1998) 254–257; A W Bradley, 'The Sovereignty of Parliament—in Perpetuity?' in J Jowell and D Oliver (eds), *The Changing Constitution* (3rd edn, Clarendon Press, 1994); Sir John Laws, 'Law and Democracy' [1995] PL 72.

[275] See eg the views of Lord Colville *Hansard,* HL, cols 1026–1027 (8 Aug 1972); and Lord Diplock, col 1029.

[276] *McCarthy's Ltd v Smith* [1981] 1 QB 180 *per* Lord Denning MR at 200; *Garland v British Rail Engineering Ltd* [1983] 2 AC 751 *per* Lord Diplock at 751.

[277] P Craig, 'Sovereignty of the United Kingdom Parliament after Factortame' [1991] Yearbook of European Law 221, 251, 252.

[278] Sir William Wade, 'Supremacy: Revolution or Evolution' (1996) 112 LQR 568, 570.

[279] The principle is discussed at para 4.33 below.

[280] See para 1.66ff above.

changes to the legal regime effected by accession to the European Community. The supremacy of European Union law restricts the substantive power of Parliament to enact legislation; it therefore goes well beyond altering the manner and form of parliamentary procedures (which is permitted by the new theory of sovereignty): unless its adherents maintain the view that it is ultimately possible for the United Kingdom to withdraw from the European Union. Wade has argued that accession to the European Community has resulted in a legal revolution[281] by adopting a new rule of recognition about the validity and effect of Acts of Parliament,[282] although this may rather oversimplify the position.[283]

It is submitted that the better view is to regard the basis of sovereignty and the changes effected by the European Communities as being a common law development, an evolution of the judiciary's sense of its own constitutional obligations.[284] As Allan[285] contends, the scope of sovereignty and its implications for constitutional change cannot be settled except by analysis of the political authority from which it derives its authority. Controversial questions of constitutional authority are moral questions requiring attention to political traditions and values which constitute the polity. No single characterisation of the rule enjoining judicial obedience to statute can supply the answers in advance. **1.76**

(3) Methods of entrenchment

There are a number of different ways of implementing human rights instruments into domestic law: by full entrenchment, by limited entrenchment and by a rule of construction. The approach taken in the Human Rights Act was to introduce a strong rule of construction under section 3;[286] and the various alternatives that the Government rejected need only be summarised. **1.77**

Where a human rights instrument is fully entrenched, the courts have the ultimate power to strike down legislation which violates human rights. The strongest means of achieving this status is where judicial powers are derived from a constitutional instrument which has superior status over ordinary legislation. Thus, in **1.78**

[281] But see J Eekelaar, 'The Death of Parliamentary Sovereignty—a Comment' (1997) 113 LQR 185.

[282] W Wade 'Sovereignty and the European Communities' (1972) 88 LQR 1; 'What has Happened to the Sovereignty of Parliament' (1991) 107 LQR 1.

[283] See T Allan 'Parliamentary Sovereignty: Law, Politics and Revolution' (1997) 113 LQR 443.

[284] Sir Owen Dixon, 'The Common Law as the Ultimate Constitutional Foundation' (1957) 31 ALJ 240; for full discussion, see M Hunt, *Using Human Rights in the English Courts* (Hart Publishing, 1997) Chaps 2 and 3.

[285] T Allan, *Law Liberty and Justice* (Clarendon Press, 1993) Chap 11 'Legislative Supremacy'.

[286] See para 4.04ff below.

the famous case of *Marbury v Madison*[287] Marshall CJ held that 'it is emphatically the province and duty of the judicial department to say what the law is' with the result that the United States Supreme Court had the ultimate responsibility to interpret the constitution. Germany also exemplifies the judicial entrenchment of constitutional rights. The constitutions in numerous new Commonwealth countries contain a statutory provision which states that its constitution is the supreme law and that any other law, to the extent it is inconsistent, is void. These constitutions also include Bills of Rights enabling the courts to strike down legislation and they have done so, notably in India[287a] and Zimbabwe.[287b]

1.79 A form of limited entrenchment which provides scope for legislative supremacy is the 'notwithstanding' provision of the Canadian Charter of Rights and Freedoms.[288] Under section 33 of the Canadian Charter the federal or provincial Parliament can expressly declare that a statutory provision is operative notwithstanding that it contravenes the Charter.[289] Section 52 of the Canadian Charter allows the courts to make a variety of different orders where legislation is inconsistent with the Charter and has no effect,[290] whereas under section 24 of the Charter the court may award any remedy it considers appropriate and just in the circumstances where the Charter has been infringed.[291] It has been argued[292] that the Charter of Rights has been a considerable success in providing a shield to protect basic political, legal minority and equality rights as well as enhancing the culture of liberty although this is not uncontroversial.[293]

---

[287] (1803) 5 US 137 at 177; this power of judicial review was foreshadowed in the Federalist Papers 'The interpretation of the laws is the proper and peculiar province of the courts. A Constitution is, in fact, and must be regarded by the judges as, a fundamental law . . . Nor does this conclusion by any means suppose a superiority of the judicial to the legislative power. It only supposes that the power of the people is superior to both, and that where the will of the legislature, declared by its statutes, stands in opposition to that of the people, declared in the Constitution, the judges ought to be governed by the latter rather than the former. They ought to regulate their decisions by the fundamental laws rather than by those which are not fundamental': see J Madison, A Hamilton and J Jay, *The Federalist Papers* (Penguin, 1987) No 78, 439.

[287a] The text is reproduced at App P in Vol 2.

[287b] The text is reproduced at App U in Vol 2.

[288] See eg J Black-Branch 'Entrenching Human Rights under Constitutional Law: the Canadian Charter of Rights and Freedoms' [1998] EHRLR 312.

[289] P W Hogg, *Constitutional Law of Canada* (4th edn, Carswell, 1997) Chap 36.

[290] The court has the option of nullification, temporary invalidity, severance, reading in, reading down or constitutional exemption: see the analysis of Lamer CJ in *Schachter v Canada* [1992] 2 SCR 679, 695–719.

[291] P W Hogg (n 289 above) Chap 37.

[292] R Penner, 'The Canadian experience with the Charter of Rights: are there lessons for the United Kingdom' [1996] PL 104; T Ison, 'A constitutional bill or bills—the Canadian experience' (1997) 60 MLR 499; D Beatty, 'The Canadian Charter of Rights: lessons and laments' (1997) 60 LQR 481.

[293] See eg A Petter, 'Canada's Charter Flight: Soaring Backwards into the Future' (1989) 16 Journal of Law and Society 151; J Bakan, 'Constitutional Arguments: interpretation and legitimacy in Canadian constitutional thought' (1989) 27 Osgoode Hall LJ 123.

A different way of achieving limited entrenchment was used in the Hong Kong Bill of Rights Ordinance 1990 which sharply distinguished between legislation passed before or after the Bill of Rights.[294] If legislation had been enacted earlier, legislation had to be interpreted consistently with the Bill of Rights; if no such interpretation was possible, the courts could declare that the legislation was of no effect. On the other hand, where legislation was passed after the Bill of Rights came into force, the court remained under a duty to interpret it consistently with the Bill of Rights; however, if no such interpretation was possible, then the court had no power to declare the legislation ineffective but was obliged to apply it.[295] **1.80**

The use of a human rights instrument as a rule of construction is exemplified by the New Zealand Bill of Rights.[296] The Bill of Rights was originally drafted along the lines of the Canadian Charter of Rights but opposition to judicial review of the validity of legislation meant that it became enacted as ordinary legislation.[297] Under section 6 the court is obliged wherever an enactment can be given a meaning that is consistent with the rights and freedoms contained in the Bill of Rights, to prefer that meaning to any other meaning.[298] Although a bill of rights instrument which has the status of ordinary legislation could be viewed as no more than a symbolic gesture, this ultimately depends on the attitude taken by the judiciary; and the approach of the judiciary to the New Zealand Bill of Rights shows that, even as an interpretative aid, it can have a considerable impact on the general law.[299] **1.81**

(4) Parliamentary sovereignty under the Human Rights Act

The Human Rights Act has been designed to square the circle of maintaining parliamentary sovereignty while entrenching human rights. The Act has adopted a rule of construction weaker than that in the Hong Kong Bill of Rights Ordinance[300] but gives the higher courts[301] the power to grant a declaration of **1.82**

---

[294] See ss 3 and 4

[295] See R Wacks, *Human Rights in Hong Kong* (Oxford University Press, 1992); and eg R Swede, 'One Territory—Three Systems? the Hong Kong Bill of Rights' (1995) 44 ICLQ 360; Y Ghai, 'Sentinels of Liberty or Sheep in Woolf's Clothing? Judicial Politics and the Hong Kong Bill of Rights' (1997) 60 MLR 459; A Byrnes, 'And Some Have Bills of Rights Thrust Upon Them: The Experience of Hong Kong's Bill of Rights' in P Alston (ed), *Promoting Human Rights Through Bills of Rights* (Oxford University Press, 1999).

[296] See ss 4, 5 and 6.

[297] See generally, M Taggart, 'Tugging on Superman's Cape: lessons from the experience with the New Zealand Bill of Rights' [1998] PL 266; and see also A Butler, 'The Bill of Rights Debate: Why the New Zealand Bill of Rights is a Bad Model for Britain' [1997] OJLS 332; H Schwartz, 'The Short Happy Life and the Tragic Death of the New Zealand Bill of Rights Act' [1998] NZLR 259.

[298] The interpretation of s 6 is discussed at para 4.23ff below.

[299] See generally, M Taggart (n 297 above).

[300] See para 1.80 above.

[301] See para 4.53ff below.

incompatibility.[302] If there is an irreconcilable conflict between a statute and the Human Rights Act, the legislation will prevail. Although the court may make a declaration of incompatibility,[303] section 4(6) of the Act[304] states that the declaration does not affect the validity, continuing operation or enforcement of the provision nor will it be binding on the parties in the proceedings. It will, however, give Parliament the option of using the fast track procedure to amend the offending legislation.[305]

1.83 Lord Irvine, when opening the debate on the second reading of the Human Rights Bill,[306] described the approach in these terms:

> The design of the Bill is to give the courts as much space as possible to protect human rights, short of a power to set aside or ignore Acts of Parliament. In very rare cases where the higher courts will find it impossible to read and give effect to any statute in a way which is compatible with convention rights, they will make a declaration of incompatibility. Then it will be for Parliament to decide whether there should be remedial legislation. Parliament may, not must, and generally will, legislate. If a Minister's prior assessment of compatibility (under [section] 19) is subsequently found by a declaration of incompatibility by the courts to have been mistaken, it is hard to see how a Minister could withhold remedial action. But the remedial action will not retrospectively make unlawful an act which is a lawful act—lawful since sanctioned by the statute. This is the logic of the Bill. It maximises the protection of human rights without trespassing on parliamentary sovereignty.

The way in which the Act enhances human rights within the traditional framework of parliamentary sovereignty has attracted widespread praise. Lord Lester has described the Act as 'an ingenious and successful reconciliation of the principles of parliamentary sovereignty and the need for effective remedies'.[307] Kentridge regards the declaration of incompatibility procedure as a subtle compromise between parliamentary sovereignty and fundamental rights.[308] Ewing, on the other hand, argues that the Act represents an unprecedented transfer of political power from the executive and legislature to the judiciary.[309]

1.84 The Human Rights Act also ensures that legislation enacted both before and after the Act comes into force are subject to a strong interpretative obligation.

---

[302] See para 4.46ff below.

[303] See para 4.43ff below.

[304] See para 4.55ff below.

[305] See para 4.57ff below.

[306] *Hansard,* HL col 1228 (3 Nov 1997); see also speech of the Home Secretary, Jack Straw MP, when introducing the Bill in the House of Commons at the second reading: *Hansard,* HC col 772 (16 Feb1998); see also *Rights Brought Home: the Human Rights Bill* (1997) Cm 3782 para 2.8–2.12 which is reproduced at App B in Vol 2.

[307] *Hansard,* HL col 521 (18 Nov 1997).

[308] J Kentridge, 'The Incorporation of the European Convention on Human Rights' in J Beatson, C Forsyth and I Hare (eds), *Constitutional Reform in the United Kingdom: Practice and Principles* (Hart Publishing, 1998).

[309] K Ewing, 'The Human Rights Act and Parliamentary Democracy' (1999) 62 MLR 79.

Section 3 of the Human Rights Act[310] provides that so far as it is possible to do so, primary and subordinate legislation must be read and given effect in a way which is compatible with Convention rights.[311]

At the Committee stage of the Human Rights Bill Lord Simon[312] indicated that the Human Rights Act breaches the doctrine of implied repeal: since section 4(6) seems to contemplate the simultaneous existence of Convention rights and legislation which has been declared incompatible with it during the period between the issue of a declaration of incompatibility and any remedial action under section 10[313] which the Government takes to amend the offending statutory provision. It is submitted that section 4(6) does not have this effect. As Bamforth[314] observes, the Human Rights Act protects Convention rights only to the extent that interpreting a statutory provision in accordance with section 3 of the Human Rights Act resolves that apparent divergence; where the court issues a declaration of incompatibility, the conflicting legislation falls *outside* the protection that section 3 affords to Convention rights. **1.85**

F. The Nature of Rights Protection Under the Human Rights Act

(1) Introduction

In many common law jurisdictions human rights have a protected status in constitutional law because they are derived from a written constitutional instrument. In the United Kingdom, by comparison, constitutional law consists of piecemeal legislation, common law doctrines and constitutional conventions which are binding in a political rather than legal sense.[315] The absence of a written constitutional document also means that it is difficult to identify what is meant by the British Constitution: other than to say it describes the rules for determining the creation and operation of governmental institutions.[316] The term 'unconstitutional', therefore, has no defined legal content in English law. As a Canadian writer put it: **1.86**

> for the American, anything unconstitutional is illegal, however it may seem: for the British, anything unconstitutional is wrong, however legal it may be.[317]

---

310 See para 4.04ff below.
311 See para 5.03ff below.
312 *Hansard,* HL col 510 (18 Nov 1998).
313 See para 4.57ff below.
314 N Bamforth, 'Parliamentary Sovereignty and the Human Rights Act' [1998] PL 572.
315 *Halsbury's Laws* (4th edn, reissue, Butterworths, 1996) Vol 8(2), para 1.
316 Sir Ivor Jennings, *The Law of the Constitution* (5th edn, University of London Press, 1958) 36.
317 J R B Mallory, *The Structure of Canadian Government*, quoted in A Bradley and K Ewing, *Constitutional and Administrative Law* (12th edn, Longmans, 1997) 27.

Nevertheless, the Human Rights Act will profoundly alter the constitutional basis for the rights of the citizen. Sir Stephen Sedley[318] has remarked that there can come a point even in an organic constitution at which change has to be acknowledged to be contrary to the ground rules and—if it is to be legitimised—addressed and debated as such.

(2) The constitutional protection of human rights

1.87 The way in which the common law provides constitutional protection to human rights was described by Dicey:[319]

> The 'rule of law' lastly may be used as a formula expressing the fact that with us the law of the constitution, the rules which in foreign countries naturally form part of a constitutional code, are not the source but the consequence of the rights of individuals as defined and enforced by the courts; that in short, the principles of private law have with us been the action of the courts and Parliament so extended as to determine the position of the Crown and of its servants; thus, the constitution is the result of the ordinary law of the land.

The effectiveness of the common law in safeguarding human rights is limited. Parliament can always legislate civil rights out of existence, it is open to the judiciary to override 'common law rights' and it is not possible for judges to protect human rights by using the common law to create a new cause of action at common law.[320]

1.88 In particular, common law does not always[321] confer special status upon human rights. For example, in the controversial decision[322] in *Duncan v Jones*[323] Lord Hewart CJ observed:[324]

[318] Sir Stephen Sedley, 'Law and Public Life' in M Nolan and S Sedley, *The Making and Remaking of the British Constitution* (Blackstone, 1997).

[319] A Dicey, *An Introduction to the Study of the Law of the Constitution* (10th edn, McMillan, 1965); see also J Jowell, 'The Rule of Law today' in J Jowell and D Oliver, *The Changing Constitution* (3rd edn, Clarendon Press, 1994).

[320] See para 5.95ff below.

[321] But see, in particular, the views of Sir John Laws who argues that the common law can develop such a constitutional role: see eg *R v Lord Chancellor, ex p Witham* [1998] QB 575; and the development of his position in 'The Ghost in the Machine: Principle in Public Law' [1989] PL 27; 'Is the High Court the Guardian of Fundamental Constitutional Rights' [1993] PL 59; 'Judicial Remedies and the Constitution' (1994) 57 MLR 213; 'Law and Democracy' [1996] PL 72; 'The Constitution: Morals and Rights' [1996] PL 636; 'Meikeljohn, the First Amendment and Free Speech in English Law' in I Loveland (ed), *Importing the First Amendment* (Hart Publishing, 1998).

[322] In *R v Coventry City Council, ex p Phoenix* [1995] 3 All ER 37, 59 Simon Brown LJ took the view that the decision did not involve 'any penetrating analysis of the legal principles in play'; and see T Daintith, 'Disobeying a constable: a fresh look at Duncan v Jones' [1966] PL 248; M Supperstone, *Brownlie's Law of Public Order and National Security* (2nd edn, Butterworths, 1981), 111–113; G Robertson, *Freedom the Individual and the Law* (7th edn, Penguin, 1993) 87 describes it as a miserable decision for civil liberties, all the more so because the judges purported to find no difficulty in principle in achieving the result.

[323] [1936] 1 KB 218.

[324] Ibid 221, 222.

> There appear to have been moments during the argument in this case when it appeared to be suggested that the Court had to do with a grave case involving what is called the right to a public meeting. I say 'called' because English law does not recognise any special right of public meeting for political or other purposes. The 'right of assembly' as Professor Dicey puts it, is nothing more than a view taken by the Court of the individual liberty of the subject.

As Lord Scarman pointed out in *Secretary for Defence v Guardian Newspapers Ltd*[325] when counsel claimed that section 10 of the Contempt of Court Act[326] was:

> introducing into the law 'a constitutional right'. There being no written constitution, his words will sound strange to some. But they may more accurately prophesy the direction in which English law has to move and under the compulsions to which it is now subject than many are yet prepared to accept. The section, it is important to note in this connection, bears a striking similarity to the way in which many of the articles of the European Convention for the Protection of Human Rights and Fundamental Freedoms (1953) (Cmnd 8969) which formulate the fundamental rights and freedoms protected by that Convention are framed: namely a general rule subject to carefully drawn and limited exceptions . . .

In fact, the English law now recognises a wide variety of constitutional rights including: a constitutional right of access to the courts,[327] a constitutional right of free speech[328] (which encompasses the right of speech in Parliament which should not to be impeached or questioned elsewhere),[329] a constitutional right to personal liberty,[330] a constitutional right to a fair trial,[331] a constitutional right to trial by jury,[332] a constitutional right of a citizen to bring a private prosecution[333] and a **1.89**

[325] [1985] AC 339, 361.

[326] See para 15.73ff below.

[327] See eg the views of Lord Diplock in *A-G v Guardian Newspapers* [1974] AC 373, 310 and again in *Bremer Vulkan Schiffbau und Maschinenfabrik v South India Shipping Corporation Ltd* [1981] AC 909, 977; see also *R v Secretary of State for Home Department, ex p Leech (No 2)* [1994] QB 198 *per* Steyn LJ at 210; *R v Lord Chancellor, ex p Witham* [1998] QB 575 *per* Laws J at 585, 586; *R v Lord Chancellor, ex p Lightfoot* [1998] 4 All ER 764 *per* Laws J at 773.

[328] E.g. *Cassell and Co Ltd v Broome* [1972] AC 1027 *per* Lord Kilbrandon at 1133; *Secretary of State for Defence v Guardian Newspapers Ltd* [1985] AC 339 *per* Lord Fraser at 359; *Verrall v Greater Yarmouth Borough Council* [1981] 1 QB 202 *per* Cumming Bruce LJ at 849.

[329] See *per* Lord Browne-Wilkinson, *Pepper v Hart* [1993] 1 AC 593, 638D.

[330] *Spicer v Holt* [1977] AC 987 *per* Lord Fraser at 1013.

[331] *Per* Steyn LJ, *R v Brown (Winston)* [1994] 1 WLR 1599, 1606E; see generally, Lord Steyn, 'The Role of the Bar, the Judge and the Jury', [1999] PL 51, 55; and also *Dodd v Chief Constable of Cheshire*, unreported, 22 Oct 1997 'the plaintiff's constitutional right is for a fair trial . . .'; in *Bray v Ford* [1896] AC 44 Lord Watson at 49 expressed the view that there was a constitutional right to have a case fairly submitted for consideration to a tribunal.

[332] See *R v Islington North Juvenile Court, ex p Daley* [1983] AC 347; *R v Hayden* [1975] 1 WLR 852 *per* Lord Widgery CJ; and see Lord Diplock in *Gouriet v A-G* [1978] AC 435, 499 where he stated that there was a constitutional right, at a trial by jury, to have guilt established by reference to the criminal standard of proof; Lord Denning MR remarked in *Rothermere v Times Newspapers Ltd* [1973] 1 WLR 448, 452, that 'Every defendant has a constitutional right to have his guilt or innocence determined by a jury' (said in the context of defamation proceedings) and he expressed the same view in *Associated Newspapers Ltd v Dingle* [1964] AC 371, 408; see also *Morey v Woodfield (No 2)* [1964] 1 WLR 16 *per* Harman LJ at 21.

[333] *R v Leeds Magistrates' Court, ex p Serif Systems Ltd* 9 Oct 1997, Div Ct.

constitutional right to equal protection under the law.[334] There are also a number of historic statutes such as the Magna Carta 1215, the Bill of Rights 1689 and the Act of Settlement 1701 which should be regarded as constitutional legislation:[335] they embody and set forth constitutional principles and confer constitutional rights which cannot be displaced except by clear words.[336]

1.90 Even so, the enactment of the Human Rights Act marks a turning point in the United Kingdom's legal and constitutional history.[337] The Act provides the English courts with a unique opportunity to develop their own approach to the interplay of human rights with the decisions of public authorities.[338] Indeed, the Act goes further: for the first time it enables the adjudication of human rights to be made by reference to specific and defined constitutional principles. Whereas the human rights protection achieved by judicial review has its jurisdictional basis in the incremental common law development of administrative law principles,[339] the Human Rights Act provides explicit constitutional underpinning for the fundamental rights of the citizen.[340] Convention rights[341] will be expressly guaranteed within a statutory framework which prescribes and limits the exercise of public power over private individuals. Like the Interpretation Act, the Human Rights Act will contribute to a framework which shapes the interpretation and implementation of other legislation; and the substantive values imbued in the Act endow it with a distinctive constitutional status.[342] The enactment of the Convention gives effect in English law to what the European Court of Human Rights has described as the 'constitutional instrument of European public order'.[343] As a result, the Human Rights Act can

---

334 *Fitzpatrick v Sterling Housing Association Ltd* [1998] 2 WLR 225 *per* Ward LJ at 256.

335 F Bennion, *Statutory Interpretation* (3rd edn, Butterworths, 1997) 126; he argues that modern legislation which amends or adds to these Acts such as the Parliament Acts 1911 and 1949 should also be regarded as a constitutional act.

336 Thus, in *Antrim's (Earl) Petition* [1967] 1 AC 991 Lord Wilberforce at 724 said 'I confess to some reluctance to holding that an Act of such constitutional significance as the Union with Ireland Act is subject to the doctrine of implied repeal': *Re Parliamentary Privilege Act 1770* [1958] AC 331, 350 *per* Viscount Simmonds; *Kariapper v Wijesinha* [1968] AC 717.

337 Cf Lord Lester, 'The Impact of the Human Rights Act on Public Law' in J Beatson, C Forsyth and I Hare (eds), *Constitutional Reform in the United Kingdom: Practice and Principles* (Hart Publishing, 1998).

338 See para 5.03ff below.

339 See para 1.33ff above.

340 R Gordon, 'Why We Need a Constitutional Court' in R Gordon and R Wilmot-Smith (eds), *Human Rights in the United Kingdom* (Oxford University Press, 1996).

341 See para 6.86ff below.

342 D Feldman, 'The Human Rights Act 1998 and Constitutional Principles' [1999] Legal Studies 165: Feldman argues that Arts 2, 3, 4, 8, 9, 10, 11, 12 and Arts 2 and 3 of the First Protocol provide the necessary conditions for automony, dignity and respect whereas Arts 5, 6, 7, 8, Art 1 of the First Protocol and the Sixth Protocol are particularly concerned with security, especially legal security. He also suggests that the Human Rights Act will encourage the judiciary to impose higher and more rigorous standards on public authorities when they interfere with human rights.

343 *Loizidou v Turkey (Preliminary Objections)* (1995) 20 EHRR 99 para 75.

properly be characterised as a constitutional instrument;[344] and is subject to special principles of construction.[345]

As legal principles evolve under the Human Rights Act, the courts will therefore acquire a new constitutional role. In the final analysis, it is the courts and the courts alone which will be the decisive arbiters of the conflicts between human rights and public authorities.[346] A former Chief Justice of the United States Supreme Court[347] once remarked that 'a constitution is what the judges say it is': and Sir Stephen Sedley has pointed out that 'the reverse is true as well: if the judges are not prepared to speak for it, a constitution is nothing'.[348] The challenge the courts must confront in interpreting fundamental human rights as identified by the Lord Chancellor, Lord Irvine[349] is to balance activism and restraint. Their responsibility will be of prime importance: to give effect to the purpose and function of a constitution by articulating and preserving society's fundamental moral principles.[350] In discharging this duty it will be open to the courts, in their adjudication of cases under the Human Rights Act, to adopt a moral reading[351] of the Act through interpreting the statutory language in abstract moral terms as restrictions on the power of public authorities. Thus, Lord Irvine has argued[352] that the: **1.91**

> court decisions made in relation to the Human Rights Act will be based on a more overtly principled and, perhaps, moral basis. The Court will look at the positive right. It will only accept an interference with that right where a justification allowed under the Convention is made out. The scrutiny will not be limited to seeing if the *words* of an exception can be satisfied. The Court will need to be satisfied that the *spirit* of this exception is made out. It will need to be satisfied that the interference with the protected right *is* justified in the public interest in a free and democratic society. Moreover, the courts in this area will have to apply the Convention principle of proportionality. This means that the Court will look *substantively* at that question. It will not be limited to a secondary review of the decision making process but

344 Cf Lord Browne-Wilkinson's reference to Art 9 of the Bill of Rights as a provision of the highest constitutional importance which ought not to be narrowly construed, *Pepper v Hart* [1993] 1 AC 593, 638D; cf Lord Lester and D. Pannick, *Human Rights Law and Practice* (Butterworths, 1999) Chap 3 'Principles of Interpretation' para 3.1 (where this position is asserted without argument).

345 The special principles of construction are discussed at para 3.06ff below.

346 See para 5.03ff below.

347 Former Chief Justice Hughes speaking when he was Governor of New York; quoted E Corwin, *The Constitution and what it means today* (14th edn, Princeton University Press, 1978) xiv.

348 Sir Stephen Sedley, 'The Sounds of Silence: Constitutional Law Without a Constitution' (1994) 110 LQR 270.

349 Lord Irvine, 'Activism and Restraint: Human Rights and the Interpretative Process' [1999] EHRLR 350.

350 I Loveland, *Constitutional Law a Critical Introduction* (Butterworths, 1996) 2.

351 R Dworkin, 'The Moral Reading and the Majoritarian premise' in *Freedom's Law* (Oxford University Press, 1996).

352 See 'The Development of Human Rights in Britain Under an Incorporated Convention on Human Rights' [1998] PL 221, 229.

> at the primary question of the merits of the decision itself. In reaching its judgment, therefore, the Court will need to expand and explain its own view of whether the conduct is legitimate. It will produce in short a decision on the *morality* of the conduct and not simply its compliance with the bare letter of the law.

The impact of the Human Rights Act is uncertain[353] but potentially immense. It has been described by Lord Bingham[354] in these terms:

> It would be naive to suppose that incorporation of the Convention would usher in a new Jerusalem. As on the morrow of a general election, however glamorous the promises of the campaign, the world will not at once feel very different. But the change would over time stifle the insidious and damaging belief that it is necessary to go abroad to obtain justice. It would restore our country to its former place as an international standard-bearer of liberty and justice. It would help to reinvigorate the faith, which our eighteenth and nineteenth century forbears would not for an instant have doubted, that these were fields in which Britain was the world's teacher, not its pupil. And it would enable the judges more effectively to honour their ancient and sacred undertaking to do right to all manner of people after the laws and usages of their realm, without fear or favour, affection or ill will.

[353] A T H Smith, 'The Human Rights Act and the Criminal Lawyer: The Constitutional Context' [1999] Crim L Rev 231.

[354] 'The European Convention on Human Rights: Time to Incorporate' in R Gordon and R Wilmot-Smith (eds), *Human Rights in the United Kingdom* (Clarendon Press, 1996).

2

THE IMPACT OF UNINCORPORATED HUMAN RIGHTS TREATIES

A. Introduction

2.01 The United Kingdom is a party to a large number of multilateral instruments and treaties relating to the protection of human rights. These include the Universal Declaration of Human Rights (1948), the European Convention on Human Rights (1950), the International Covenant on Civil and Political Rights (1966), the International Covenant on Economic, Social and Cultural Rights (1966), and the European Social Charter (1965).[1] These treaties guarantee the rights contained in them: this means that the UK Government is obliged, as a matter of international law, to secure in domestic law the protected rights and freedoms and to provide effective remedies before national authorities for breaches of the treaty provisions.

[1] See generally, P Sieghart, *The International Law of Human Rights* (Clarendon Press, 1983); and for a fuller list see Lord Lester and D Oliver, *Constitutional Law and Human Rights* (Butterworths, 1997) para 103.

2.02 However, the European Convention on Human Rights is the only human rights treaty which has given individual UK citizens a right of petition in respect of alleged violations. The International Covenant on Civil and Political Rights permits an individual petition under the First Optional Protocol but this has not been accepted by the United Kingdom. During the drafting of the Covenant by the UN Human Rights Commission in 1949, a proposal that individuals and groups of individuals should have a right of petition to an international conciliation body divided the Commission evenly, and was rejected.[2] Similar proposals put forward at subsequent drafting sessions were consistently declined, as was a request by the General Assembly of the United Nations that the Commission consider inserting in the draft Covenant provisions for receipt and examination of petitions from individuals. Until the late 1960s, the Commission took the position that it had no jurisdiction to hear individual human rights petitions. The Human Rights Committee was established to hear inter-state complaints but not complaints from individuals or non-governmental organisations. Even though, under the Optional Protocol, nationals of states party to the Protocol may now have their 'communications' heard before the Committee,[3] the Committee has no judicial mandate. As a result, the 'views' of the Committee on the merits of the communication are not legally binding, but mere recommendations.

2.03 Prior to the enactment of the Human Rights Act, human rights treaties were capable of affecting domestic law in the United Kingdom in two ways. First, they might have an impact as a consequence of a parliamentary or governmental decision to change the law in response to adverse findings of the international bodies responsible for adjudicating on treaty violations. Adverse decisions of the European Court of Human Rights have led to a number of changes in United Kingdom law over the past 25 years.[4] Secondly, human rights treaties have had a 'direct' impact on domestic law where the judiciary have considered their provisions when formulating or applying domestic law. Once again, the Convention has been the most important human rights treaty in this area but much of the case law discussed below in respect of the unincorporated Convention is potentially of equal application to the other unincorporated treaties.

2.04 In this chapter, we will consider both types of impact. An assessment of the changes resulting from governmental action illuminates the areas which the Human Rights Act might affect in the future. An examination of changes that have come about through the courts will provide guidance on the principles to be

[2] At its fifth drafting session in 1949, the Human Rights Commission voted eight for and eight against the proposal.

[3] See generally, P Ghandi, *The Human Rights Committee and the Right of Individual Communication: Law and Practice*, (Dartmouth, 1998).

[4] See para 2.05ff below.

applied to the Human Rights Act; and will remain relevant to English law because of the repercussions of human rights treaties apart from the Convention.

B. The Convention and Changes to Domestic Law

As at 30 June 2000, the United Kingdom had appeared as a respondent before the European Court of Human Rights in 115 concluded admissible cases. In 72 of these cases the Court had found a violation of at least one Article of the Convention.[5] Once a judgment of the European Court of Human Rights is given, it is transmitted to the Committee of Ministers which 'supervises its execution'. If a violation of the Convention has been found, the Committee will invite the respondent government to inform it of the measures which have been taken in response to the judgment. When a satisfactory response has been received, the Committee declares by resolution that its function under Article 54 has been exercised. **2.05**

A number of changes in domestic law have been made in response to adverse rulings by the European Commission and Court of Human Rights. Fifty-nine of the 'violation' cases have been the subject of resolution by the Committee of Ministers under Article 54. The violations have been dealt with in a number of different ways. Almost half the cases have required the enactment of primary legislation; the other cases which required state action have been dealt with by administrative measures of various kinds.[6] **2.06**

For example, in 11 cases, findings of violations have led to parliamentary enactment or amendment of primary legislation. The first *Sunday Times* case[7] was an important factor in the reform of the law of contempt by the Contempt of Court Act 1981.[8] Section 2 of the Employment Act 1982, bringing to an end the closed shop, was the result of the decision in *Young, James & Webster v United Kingdom.*[9] The decision in *X v United Kingdom*[10] led to the amendment of the legislation relating to Mental Health Review Tribunals.[11] The finding of the European Court of Human Rights in *Malone v United Kingdom,*[12] that the non-statutory system of telephone tapping was in breach of Article 8, led to the enactment of the **2.07**

[5] For a complete list and further details of the cases in question, see 'Table of Admissible UK cases before the European Court of Human Rights' in Vol 2; see also F Klug, K Starmer and S Weir, *The Three Pillars of Liberty* (Routledge, 1997) 48–54 and C Gearty, 'The United Kingdom', in C Gearty (ed), *European Civil Liberties and the European Convention on Human Rights* (Nijhoff, 1997), 100–101.

[6] See generally, R Churchill and J Young, 'Compliance with Judgments of the European Court of Human Rights and Decisions of the Committee of Ministers: The Experience of the United Kingdom, 1975–1987' [1991] British Ybk of Intl L, 283.

[7] *Sunday Times v United Kingdom (No 1)* (1979) 2 EHRR 524.

[8] See generally, *Arlidge, Eady and Smith on Contempt* (2nd edn, Sweet & Maxwell, 1999) paras 1-103–1-114.

[9] (1981) 4 EHRR 38.

[10] (1981) 4 EHRR 188; *cf R v Canons Park Mental Health Review Tribunal, ex p A* [1995] QB 60.

[11] Mental Health (Amendment) Act 1982; see Pt V, Mental Health Act 1983.

[12] (1984) 7 EHRR 14.

Interception of Communications Act 1985. The series of decisions of 1987 which found the United Kingdom public child care procedures to be in breach of the Convention,[13] was a factor in the enactment of the Children Act 1989. The decisions in *Weeks v United Kingdom*[14] and *Thynne Wilson and Gunnell v United Kingdom*[15] concerning 'discretionary lifers' were dealt with by section 34 of the Criminal Justice Act 1991. The decision of the European Court of Human Rights in *Campbell and Cosans v United Kingdom*[16] led to the statutory abolition of corporal punishment in state schools by the Education (No 2) Act 1986.

2.08 In eight cases, substantive changes were made to English law without the need for primary legislation. In three cases a practice note or circular was sent out.[17] In five cases new subordinate legislation was passed.[18] In eight cases, the Committee of Ministers decided that no changes in UK law were required because:

- action had already been taken;[19]
- all that was required was an assurance that a violation would be avoided or discontinued;[20]
- the payment of compensation was sufficient compliance with the ruling of the European Court of Human Rights.[21]

In *Brogan v United Kingdom*,[22] the finding of infringement resulted in a derogation from the terms of the Convention.

C. The Impact of the Convention in the English Courts Prior to the Human Rights Act

(1) Introduction

2.09 The status in domestic law of international human rights instruments (including

[13] *W v United Kingdom* (1987) 10 EHRR 29; *R v United Kingdom* (1987) 10 EHRR 74, *B v United Kingdom* (1987) 10 EHRR 87, *H v United Kingdom* (1987) 10 EHRR 95.

[14] (1987) 10 EHRR 293.

[15] (1990) 13 EHRR 666.

[16] (1982) 4 EHRR 293.

[17] *Campbell and Fell v United Kingdom* (1985) 7 EHRR 165; *Granger v United Kingdom* (1990) 12 EHRR 469; *Tyrer v United Kingdom* (1980) 2 EHRR 1.

[18] *Golder v United Kingdom* (1975) 1 EHRR 524; *Dudgeon v United Kingdom* (1981) 4 EHRR 149; *Silver v United Kingdom* (1983) 5 EHRR 347; *Abdulaziz v United Kingdom* (1985) 7 EHRR 471; *Campbell v United Kingdom* (1992) 15 EHRR 137.

[19] *Fox, Campbell and Hartley v United Kingdom* (1990) 13 EHRR 157; *McCallum v United Kingdom* (1990) 13 EHRR 596.

[20] *Boyle and Rice v United Kingdom* (1988) 10 EHRR 425; *Soering v United Kingdom* (1989) 11 EHRR 439: the UK Government sent a diplomatic note to the effect that extradition would be refused if the penalty might include the death penalty; *Ireland v United Kingdom* (1978) 2 EHRR 25: an assurance was accepted that the unlawful administrative practice would not continue.

[21] *Gillow v United Kingdom* (1986) 11 EHRR 335; *The Observer and The Guardian v United Kingdom* (1991) 14 EHRR 153; *Sunday Times v United Kingdom (No 2)* (1991) 14 EHRR 229; *Darnell v United Kingdom* (1993) 18 EHRR 205.

[22] (1989) 13 EHRR 439.

the Convention, prior to the Human Rights Act) has never been wholly clear.[23] In some countries the ratification of international treaties means that they immediately become part of the domestic law.[24] However, this is not the case in the United Kingdom. The alternative, 'dualist', view of the relationship between international and domestic law is that a treaty is not a *direct* source of rights or duties in domestic law. This is because:

> the making of a treaty is an executive act, while the performance of its obligations, if they entail alteration of the existing domestic law, requires legislative action.[25]

The dualist approach has been subjected to powerful and persuasive academic criticism,[26] including the argument that it allows the executive a freedom to ignore its obligations under international instruments. Nevertheless, dualism remains the dominant view in the Commonwealth. In defence of this position, the judiciary in New Zealand[27] and Australia[28] have expressly rejected the implication that states which operate on the dualist model may be irresponsible with respect to their international obligations. Cooke P said of the notion:

> That is an unattractive argument, apparently implying that New Zealand's adherence to the international instruments has been at least partly window-dressing.[29]

However, the 'dualist' view also continues to prevail in England. As Lord Oliver **2.10**
said in the leading case:

> Treaties, as it is sometimes expressed, are not self-executing. Quite simply, a treaty is not part of English law unless and until it has been incorporated into the law by legislation. So far as individuals are concerned, it is *res inter alios acta* from which they cannot derive rights and by which they cannot be deprived of rights or subjected to obligations; and it is outside the purview of the court not only because it is made in the conduct of foreign relations, which are a prerogative of the Crown, but also because, as a source of rights and obligations, it is irrelevant.[30]

---

[23] For general discussions see the excellent treatment in M Hunt, *Using Human Rights Law in English Courts* (Hart Publishing, 1997) and see also A Clapham, *Human Rights in the Private Sphere*, (Clarendon Press, 1993), A Drzemczewski, *The European Convention in Domestic Law: A Comparative Study* (Oxford University Press, 1983); A Cunningham, 'ECHR, Customary law the Constitution' (1994) 43 ICLQ 537; D Beyleveld, 'The Concept of Human Rights and the Incorporation of the ECHR' [1995] PL 577; M Beloff and H Mountfield, 'Unconventional Behaviour? Judicial Uses of the European Convention in England and Wales', [1996] EHRLR 467.

[24] See para 1.62 above.

[25] *Per* Lord Atkin, *(A-G) for Canada v (A-G) for Ontario* [1937] AC 326, 347–348; see *The Parlement Belge* (1879) 4 PD 129, 154.

[26] D Beyleveld, 'The Concept of a Human Right and Incorporation of the European Convention on Human Rights', [1995] PL 577; and see also the comprehensive discussion in Hunt, n 23 above, Chap 1.

[27] See *Tavita v Minister of Immigration* [1994] 2 NZLR 257.

[28] See *Ministry for Immigration and Ethnic Affairs v Teoh* (1995) 128 ALR 353; see generally, Hunt, n 23 above, 242–59.

[29] *Tavita* (n 27 above) 266, lines 1–2.

[30] *J H Rayner (Mincing Lane) v Department of Trade and Industry* [1990] 2 AC 418, 500, *per* Lord Oliver.

The same view was taken by the House of Lords when the issue was raised in relation to the Convention in *R v Secretary of State for the Home Department, ex p Brind*.[31] The qualification was expressed, however, that a non-incorporated treaty ought to be given consideration wherever there are two courses of action that are open to the Court and:

> one would lead to a decision inconsistent with Her Majesty's international obligations under the convention while the other would lead to a result consistent with those obligations. If statutory words have to be construed or a legal principle formulated in an area of law where Her Majesty has accepted international obligations, our Courts—who of course take notice of the acts of Her Majesty done in the exercise of her sovereign power—will have regard to the convention as part of the full content or background of the law. Such a convention, especially a multilateral one, should then be considered by Courts even though no statute expressly or impliedly incorporates it into our law.[32]

Unincorporated treaties can also have effect in domestic law where they supplement and become subsumed within the common law. Thus, the Privy Council in *Thomas v Baptiste*[32a] took the view that litigants had a general right not to have the outcome of legal processes pre-empted by executive action. The government of the Bahamas, by ratifying an international treaty which provided access to an international body, the Inter-American Court of Human Rights, had made that process part of its domestic criminal justice system and at least temporarily extended the scope of its constitutional due process clause.[32b]

2.11 The Convention began to influence domestic law in the 1970s. Following a number of setbacks in the 1980s, this influence grew considerably thereafter.[33] Citations of the Convention have been identified in 473 cases decided up to the end of 1996.[34] Nevertheless, the practical impact of the Convention on domestic case law prior to the Human Rights Act was not great. In a study carried out by the Democratic Audit of all cases on a database between 1972 and 1993, it was found

[31] [1991] AC 696, 762, *per* Lord Ackner.

[32] *Pan-American World Airways Inc v Department of Trade* [1976] 1 Lloyd's Rep 257, 261, *per* Scarman LJ.

[32a] [1999] 3 WLR 249, 260–262, *per* Lord Millett; and see also, the Privy Council decision in *Higgs v Minister of National Security*, unreported, 14 Dec 1999; *cf Briggs v Baptiste* [2000] 2 WLR 575 where the Privy Council held that the fact that a treaty was unincorporated entitled the national courts themselves to interpret its provisions.

[32b] The approach taken by the Privy Council in *Thomas v Baptiste* (n 32a above) was not based on the doctrine of legitimate expectation which it held did not assist the appellants: see 262, 263 *per* Lord Millett; this doctrine on unratified treaties is considered at para 2.39ff below.

[33] For an analysis of three phases of judicial reactions to the Convention (Phase I—mid 1970s, judicial activism; Phase II—late 1970s to late 1980s—judicial conservatism, Phase III—late 1980s to date, increasing use of the Convention), see Hunt (n 26 above) 129–30 and generally Chaps 4 and 5.

[34] See Hunt (n 23 above) App I. This Table is not complete as it relies on the cases on the LEXIS database which does not include all first instance High Court decisions.

that the Convention had only been mentioned in 0.2% of them. The Audit concluded that the Convention influenced the reasoning of the court in only 24 cases and affected the outcome in only three.[35]

Although the domestic courts were not able to grant a declaration of violation of Convention rights,[36] it became widely recognised that the Convention could be taken into account in English law in a number of situations.[37] These included the following:[38] 2.12

- where the terms of a statute or secondary legislation were ambiguous or if the case involved the construction of a statute intended to implement Convention obligations;
- where the common law was uncertain, unclear or incomplete;
- where the courts were required to exercise a discretion;
- where the courts considered matters of public policy;
- where the Convention formed part of Community law;
- in a limited range of cases in which the lawfulness of the exercise of administrative discretion was being considered.

The use made of the Convention in these situations is considered in the remainder of this section.

(2) The Convention as an aid to construing statutes

It is a 'principle of legal policy' that domestic law should conform to public international law.[39] As Diplock LJ put it: 2.13

> there is a prima facie presumption that Parliament does not intend to act in breach of international law, including therein specified treaty obligations; and if one of the meanings that can reasonably be attributed to the legislation is consonant with the treaty obligations and another or others are not, the meaning which is so consonant is to be preferred.[40]

In other words, if a statute is ambiguous, the court will adopt the construction

[35] See Klug, Starmer, and Weir (n 5 above) 106; also F Klug and K Starmer, 'Incorporation Through the Back Door?' [1997] PL 223.

[36] See *Malone v Metropolitan Police Commissioner* [1979] Ch 344.

[37] Different commentators have made slightly different classifications; see eg M Beloff and H Mountfield, 'Unconventional Behaviour? Judicial uses of the European Convention in England and Wales', [1996] EHRLR 467; A Lester, 'Impact of European Human Rights Law', [1996] JR 21; A Cunningham, 'ECHR, Customary law the Constitution' (1994) 43 ICLQ 537; A Clapham, *Human Rights in the Private Sphere* (Clarendon Press, 1993) Chap 1. In his maiden speech in the House of Lords Lord Bingham suggested that the Convention influenced domestic practice in six respects: see *Hansard*, HL cols 1465, 1466 (3 Jul 1996). However, the most comprehensive discussion is in Hunt (n 26 above) Chaps 4–8.

[38] Cf *R v Secretary of State for the Environment, ex p NALGO* [1993] 5 Admin LR 785, 795–8.

[39] F Bennion, *Statutory Interpretation* (3rd edn, Butterworths, 1997) 630.

[40] *Salomon v Commissioners of Customs & Excise* [1967] 2 QB 116, 143.

which is consistent with treaty obligations. This is a 'mere canon of construction which involves no importation of international law into the domestic field'.[41]

2.14 It is clear that this approach is applicable in relation to the human rights treaties: if two or more meanings are available, the court will prefer that which is consistent with the relevant treaty. As Lord Denning MR said in *R v Chief Immigration Officer, Heathrow Airport ex p Bibi*:[42]

> The position as I understand it is that if there is any ambiguity in our statutes, or uncertainty in our law then these courts can look to the Convention as an aid to clear up ambiguity and uncertainty . . .

This analysis applies to both primary and secondary legislation.[43] It has been applied in relation to the Convention in a number of cases. For example, in *Waddington v Miah*[44] the House of Lords, in deciding whether penal legislation had retrospective effect, referred to the provisions of Article 7 of the Convention and Article 11(2) of the Universal Declaration prohibiting retrospective penal legislation.

2.15 There has been considerable debate as to whether the human rights treaties can be taken into account in construction even when the statute is not 'ambiguous' in the ordinary sense. Much reliance has been placed on a *dictum* of Lord Diplock in *Garland v British Rail Engineering Ltd*[45] in which he said:

> it is a principle of construction of United Kingdom statutes . . . that the words of a statute passed after the Treaty has been signed and dealing with the subject matter of the international obligation of the United Kingdom, are to be construed, *if they are reasonably capable of bearing such a meaning*, as intended to carry out the obligation, and not to be inconsistent with it (emphasis added).

Hunt has forcefully argued that this represents an approach which goes far beyond the 'ambiguity requirement'.[46] De Smith, Woolf and Jowell have described this broader approach as 'orthodox'.[47] However, when the point was argued in the *Brind* case Lord Ackner saw no distinction between the approach of Lord Diplock in *Garland* and the traditional 'ambiguity' requirement.[48] In another case, the House of Lords appeared to treat the approaches as identical. It was said:

> While English Courts will strive when they can to interpret statutes as conforming with the obligations of the United Kingdom under the Convention they are nevertheless

[41] *R v Secretary of State for the Home Department, ex p Brind* [1991] 1 AC 696, 748.
[42] [1976] 1 WLR 979, 984.
[43] *R v Secretary of State for the Home Department, ex p Brind* [1991] 1 AC 696, 760G.
[44] [1974] 1 WLR 683, 694B–E.
[45] [1983] 2 AC 751, 771.
[46] Hunt (n 26 above) Chap 1, 18–21.
[47] Lord Woolf and J Jowell, *De Smith, Woolf and Jowell, Judicial Review of Administrative Action* (5th edn, Sweet & Maxwell, 1995), para 6-052; however, Bennion takes the opposite view (n 39 above) 632.
[48] *R v Secretary of State for the Home Department, ex p Brind* [1991] 1 AC 696, 760F.

> bound to give effect to statutes which are free from ambiguity in accordance with their terms.[49]

The weight of authority seemed, therefore, to require that 'ambiguity' exist before the courts could rely on the Convention as an aid to construction.[50] This meant that if an unambiguous statutory provision was contrary to a human rights treaty, the statute must prevail. Thus, in *Taylor v Co-operative Retail Services Ltd*,[51] the Court of Appeal accepted that although the dismissal of the applicant for failing to join a union was contrary to his rights under the Convention, it was, by English statute, required to be treated as fair.[52]

The presumption that Parliament intended to legislate in accordance with the Convention could, of course, be rebutted by reference to *Hansard* in accordance with the principle in *Pepper v Hart*.[53] It was suggested that if both *Hansard* and the Convention were relevant to a point of statutory interpretation, the Convention must yield if *Hansard* disclosed a clear intention to take a course which was contrary to it.[54] **2.16**

The approach to construction was, however, different if the statute in question was intended by Parliament to fulfil the United Kingdom's treaty obligations.[55] Thus, when considering the interpretation of the Contempt of Court Act 1981,[56] the House of Lords commented that: **2.17**

> on any point on which any doubt arises as to its construction, [Parliament] may be presumed to have been intended to avoid future conflicts between the law of contempt of court in the United Kingdom and the obligations of the United Kingdom under the . . . Convention.[57]

This suggested that the 'implementing' statute ought to be interpreted, whenever possible, so as to be in conformity with the Convention. Such an approach was applied in the case of *ex p Guardian Newspapers*[58] in which the court considered the

49 *Re M and H (Minors)* [1990] 1 AC 686, 721G, *per* Lord Brandon; and see also *R v Kelly* [1999] 2 All ER 13, 20.

50 But see *R v Radio Authority, ex p Bull* [1997] 2 All ER 561, 570d–j, where the Court of Appeal referred to Art 10 in applying a 'restrictive construction' of words restricting freedom of communication.

51 [1982] ICR 600.

52 See also *Re M and H (Minors)* [1990] 1 AC 686; *R v Morrisey* (1997) 2 Cr App R 426 (no power to exclude 'compelled' evidence, despite the fact that the provision was incompatible with Art 6 of the Convention).

53 [1993] 1 AC 593: for a discussion of the doctrine, see para 4.35ff below.

54 See *R v Broadcasting Complaints Commission, ex p Barclay* (1997) 9 Admin LR 265, *per* Sedley J.

55 See *Fothergill v Monarch Airlines Ltd* [1981] AC 251; and see generally, Bennion (n 39 above) s 221, p 523ff.

56 The principles to be applied for statutory construction are discussed at para 2.13ff above.

57 *Re Lonrho plc* [1990] 2 AC 154, 208H–209A.

58 [1999] 1 All ER 65.

construction of the rules governing appeals from orders restricting publicity which had been enacted in response to an application under the Convention.[59] The court took a 'purposive' approach:

> It appears to us that we ought to interpret the relevant rules purposively in order, if possible, to comply with the clear intention of Parliament that our national law and procedures should be altered in order to bring them in line with the [Convention].

(3) The Convention as an aid to the common law

2.18 The Convention also influenced the development of the common law.[60] In the *Spycatcher* case, Lord Goff expressed the view that there was no inconsistency between English law on freedom of expression and Article 10. He went on to say:

> I conceive it to be my duty, when I am free to do so to interpret the law in accordance with the obligations of the Crown under this treaty.[61]

Thus, the courts were 'free' to interpret the law in accordance with the Convention whenever the common law or equity was incomplete or uncertain.[62]

2.19 The possibility that the Convention could be taken into account in the development of the common law was considered in a number of cases. In *Derbyshire County Council v Times Newspapers Ltd*,[63] the court had to consider whether a local authority could bring an action for libel. There were conflicting earlier decisions on the point, but no relevant decision of the Court of Appeal or the House of Lords. As a result, the Court of Appeal took the view that, as the law of England was uncertain, Article 10 of the Convention could be taken into account. Balcombe LJ put the point in this way:

> In my judgment . . . where the law is uncertain, it must be right for the court to approach the issue before it with a predilection to ensure that our law should not involve a breach of article 10.[64]

Ralph Gibson LJ said:

> If . . . it is not clear by established principles of our law that the council has the right to sue in libel . . . then, as is not in dispute, this court must, in so deciding,

[59] Following *R v Central Criminal Court, ex p Crook, The Times*, 8 Nov, 1984; see para 15.60 below.

[60] Cf *R v Secretary of State for the Home Department, ex p Launder* [1997] 1 WLR 839, 867C.

[61] *A-G v Guardian Newspapers Ltd (No 2)* [1990] 1 AC 109, 283.

[62] See *R v Secretary of State for the Environment, ex p NALGO* [1993] 5 Admin LR 785, 795; the position of the House of Lords was unclear: although it was and is free to alter the common law or principles of equity whenever it appears right to do so (see *Practice Statement (Judicial Precedent)* [1966] 1 WLR 1234) it seems unlikely that it would have overturned settled principles of law on the sole ground that they were inconsistent with treaty obligations as this would have involved the 'backdoor incorporation' disapproved in *R v Secretary of State for the Home Department, ex p Brind* [1991] AC 696.

[63] [1992] 1 QB 770, CA; [1993] AC 534, HL.

[64] Ibid 813B.

> have regard to the principles stated in the Convention and, in particular, in Article 10.[65]

According to Butler-Sloss LJ:

> where there is an ambiguity, or the law is otherwise unclear or so far undeclared by an appellate court, the English court is not only entitled but in my judgment obliged to consider the implications of Article 10.[66]

Taking Article 10 into account, the Court of Appeal held that a local authority had no right to sue for libel.

The *Derbyshire* decision was upheld by the House of Lords on the basis of the common law, without reliance upon the Convention. The dicta of the Court of Appeal on this point were, however, not disapproved. Lord Keith commented: **2.20**

> Lord Goff of Chieveley in *A-G v Guardian Newspapers (No 2)* [1990] 1 AC 109, 283–284, expressed the opinion that in the field of freedom of speech there was no difference in principle between English law on the subject and article 10 of the Convention. I agree and can only add that I find it satisfactory to be able to conclude that the common law of England is consistent with the obligations assumed by the Crown under the Treaty in this particular field.[67]

In a number of other cases, the conclusions reached as to the common law were 'reinforced and buttressed' by the Convention.[68] In *R v Secretary of State for the Home Department, ex p Leech,*[69] conclusions of the Court of Appeal as to the rights of a prisoner to access to the courts were 'reinforced' by a decision made under the Convention.[70] In *R v Mid-Glamorgan Family Health Services Authority, ex p Martin,*[71] Evans LJ accepted that the principles of the Convention inform the content of the common law.[72] In *DPP* v. *Jones*[73] Lord Irvine LC accepted that, in cases where the common law was uncertain and developing, regard should be had to the Convention in resolving the uncertainty and determining how it should develop.

However, as a matter of strict analysis the claim that the Convention was a legitimate tool for the development of the common law where it was otherwise ambiguous was open to question. The same point could be made in relation to the **2.21**

[65] Ibid 819.

[66] Ibid 830A–B.

[67] [1993] AC 534, 553F.

[68] See eg *John v MGN Ltd* [1997] 2 QB 586.

[69] [1994] QB 198.

[70] *R v Secretary of State for the Home Department, ex p Anderson* [1984] 1 QB 778; see also *R v Lord Chancellor, ex p Witham* [1998] QB 575 in relation to the right of access to the courts.

[71] [1995] 1 WLR 110.

[72] See also *R v Secretary of State for the Home Department, ex p McNeill*, *The Times*, 26 May 1994; *R v Secretary of State for the Home Department, ex p Hickey* [1995] QB 43; *R v Radio Authority, ex p Bull* [1996] QB 169, Div Ct; [1998] QB 294, CA; *R v Mayor and Commonalty and Citizens of the City of London, ex p Matson* [1996] 8 Admin LR 49.

[73] [1999] 2 WLR 625, 634E.

idea that the common law was subject to a strong interpretative obligation[74] to construe in a manner consistent with international human rights norms. As Sir John Laws pointed out,[75] a definitive text such as a statute might be ambiguous because of the particular form of words used. By comparison, where the common law was uncertain, the question was not what is the meaning as a matter of language of the previous texts: it was, rather, which way should the common law go. In other words, the elaboration and development of the common law was a wholly different process from that of statutory construction; and it was a category error to equate the two.

2.22 It was also suggested that, even where the common law had, hitherto, been certain, the principles of the Convention might lead to its revision. Some support for this approach could be found in the case of *R v Chief Metropolitan Stipendiary Magistrate, ex p Choudhury*,[76] in which the Divisional Court said:

> [Counsel] maintained the common law of blasphemy is without doubt certain; accordingly it is not necessary to pay any regard to the Convention. Nevertheless, he thought it necessary, and we agreed, in the context of this case, to attempt to satisfy us that the United Kingdom is not in any event in breach of the Convention . . .

However, there does not appear to have been any decided case in which the common law was so revised.

(4) The Convention and judicial discretion

2.23 The Convention was also taken into account during deliberations of the court about how to exercise a discretion or a statutory power.[77] Thus, in *R v Advertising Standards Authority Ltd, ex p Vernons Organisation Ltd*[78] Article 10 was taken into account in a decision to refuse interim relief to restrain publication of information. Similarly, Article 10 was taken into account during an exercise of discretion as to whether to grant an injunction involving a restriction of free speech: the court had to consider whether the suggested restraint was necessary.[79]

2.24 In *Rantzen v Mirror Group Newspapers (1986) Ltd*,[80] the Court of Appeal considered that its power to substitute its own award of damages for a jury award it considered excessive or inadequate[81] should be exercised in such a way as to give

---

[74] M Hunt, *Using Human Rights in the English Courts* (Hart Publishing, 1997) 298; see para 5.76ff.

[75] Sir John Laws, 'Is the High Court the Guardian of Fundamental Constitutional Rights?' [1993] PL 59.

[76] [1991] 1 QB 429, 449.

[77] See *A-G v Guardian Newspapers Ltd (No 1)* [1987] 1 WLR 1248, 1296–7; and *R v Secretary of State for the Environment, ex p NALGO* [1993] 5 Admin LR 785, 795; but see B Bix and A Tomkins, 'Unconventional Use of the Convention' [1992] MLR 721.

[78] [1992] 1 WLR 1289.

[79] *Middlebrook Mushrooms Ltd v Transport and General Workers' Union* [1993] IRLR 232, 235.

[80] [1994] QB 670.

[81] Under the Courts and Legal Services Act 1990, s 8, and CPR 52.10(3).

proper weight to Article 10 of the Convention. It was held that the previous practice of giving no guidelines to juries which assess defamation damages 'conflicts with the principle enshrined in the second paragraph of article 10 that restrictions on the exercise of freedom of expression should be prescribed by law'.[82] The Convention was also on occasion considered relevant to the exercise of discretion in criminal cases. A breach of the Convention, for example, was taken into consideration in the exercise of a discretion to exclude evidence under section 78 of the Police and Criminal Evidence Act 1984[83] or the judicial discretion on sentencing.[84]

(5) The Convention as a guide to public policy

The English courts also had regard to the provisions of the Convention as a source of principles or standards of public policy. As Lord Wilberforce said in *Blathwayt v Baron Cawley*:[85] **2.25**

> I do not doubt that conceptions of public policy should move with the times and that widely accepted treaties . . . may point the direction in which such conceptions, as applied by the courts, ought to move.

This was because it was 'part of the public policy of this country that our courts should give effect to clearly established rules of international law'.[86] It was said, on a number of occasions, that 'in matters of legal policy regard should be had to this country's international obligations to observe the treaty as interpreted by the European Court of Human Rights'.[87]

(6) The Convention and Community law

The European Community is not a party to the Convention.[88] It has long been recognised, however, that 'respect for fundamental rights forms an integral part of the general principles of Community law protected by the Court of Justice'.[89] Thus, although the European Court of Justice is not bound by the Convention, 'the principles on which that Convention is based must be taken into consideration **2.26**

---

[82] *Rantzen v Mirror Group Newspapers (1986) Ltd* [1994] QB 670, 693G–694C.

[83] *R v Khan* [1997] AC 558.

[84] *R v Turner* [1999] All ER (D) 134.

[85] [1976] AC 397.

[86] *Oppenheimer* v *Cattermole* [1976] AC 249, 278.

[87] *Cheall v Association of Professional Executive Clerical and Computer Staff* [1983] 1 QB 127, 146, *per* Donaldson LJ; see also *Schering Chemicals Ltd v Falkman Ltd* [1982] 1 QB 1; see generally, Hunt (n 74 above) 139–140.

[88] It is not competent to accede without amendment to the EC Treaty: Opinion 2/94 [1996] ECR I–1759; see generally S O'Leary, 'Accession by the European Community to the European Convention on Human Rights—The Opinion of the ECJ' [1996] EHRLR 362.

[89] *Internationale Handelsgesellschaft mbH v Einfuhr-und-Vorratsstelle für Getreide und Futtermittel* [1970] ECR 1125; see also *Nold AG (Firma) v Commission* [1974] ECR 491.

in Community law'.[90] The European Court of Justice has used the Convention as an aid to determining the validity of Community acts[91] and the actions of member states.[92] As a result, it is clear that there has been a degree of 'indirect incorporation' of the Convention into English domestic law via European Community law.[93]

2.27 The Convention has been taken into account by the European Court of Justice in a number of United Kingdom cases. In *R v Kent Kirk,*[94] a Danish fisherman was prosecuted for fishing in UK coastal waters. It was held that a Council Regulation validating the UK ban on such fishing could not have retrospective effect:

> The principle that penal provisions may not have retroactive effect is one which is common to all legal orders of the Member States and is enshrined in Article 7 of . . . [the Convention]; it takes its place among the general principles of law whose observance is ensured by the Court of Justice.[95]

Similarly, in *Johnston v Chief Constable of the Royal Ulster Constabulary,*[96] the European Court of Justice took Articles 6 and 13 of the Convention into account in determining that the applicant did not have an effective remedy. The relevant legislation provided for a certificate of 'conclusive evidence' which, in effect, excluded the exercise of a power of review by the courts.

2.28 Where national legislation falls within the field of application of Community law, the European Court of Justice:

> must give the national court all the guidance as to interpretation necessary to enable it to assess the compatibility of that legislation with the fundamental rights—as laid down in particular in the Convention—whose observance the Court ensures.[97]

Nevertheless, the European Court of Justice cannot give interpretative guidance

---

[90] *Johnston v Chief Constable of the Royal Ulster Constabulary* [1987] QB 129, 147H.

[91] See eg *Prais v Council* [1976] ECR 1589 (Art 9); *Hauer v Land Rheinland-Pfalz* [1979] ECR 3727 (Art 1 of Protocol 1); *National Panasonic (UK) Ltd v Commission* [1980] ECR 2033 (Art 8(2)); *Orkem SA v Commission* [1989] ECR 3283 (Art 6); *R v Ministry of Agriculture, Fisheries and Food, ex p Fédération Européene de la Santé Animale* [1990] 1 ECR I–4023 (Art 7).

[92] *Rulti v Minister for the Interior* [1975] ECR 1219, right of free movement, Arts 8–11 and Art 2 of Protocol 4; *Society for the Protection of Unborn Children Ireland Ltd v Grogan* [1991] ECR I-4685.

[93] See A Drzemczewski, *The European Human Rights Convention in Domestic Law: A Comparative Study,* (Clarendon Press, 1983), Chap 9; Grief, 'The Domestic Impact of the European Convention on Human Rights as Mediated Through Community Law', [1991] PL 555; F Klug, K Starmer and S Weir, *The Three Pillars of Liberty* (Routledge, 1996) 107–9; and Hunt (n 74 above) Chap 7.

[94] [1985] 1 All ER 453.

[95] Ibid 462.

[96] [1987] QB 129.

[97] See *Society for the Protection of Unborn Children Ireland Ltd v Grogan* [1991] ECR I–4685, para 31.

for determining whether national legislation which lies outside the scope of Community law is in conformity with the Convention.[98]

The result of these decisions of the European Court of Justice was that the principles of the Convention have informed European law and hence, where European law applies, English law. This means that 'the principles and standards set out in the Convention can certainly be said to be matter of which the law of this country now takes notice in setting its own standard'.[99] As Lord Browne-Wilkinson put it, writing extra-judicially: **2.29**

> The European Court, although not tying itself to the ECHR as the only source of the law of fundamental human rights, in practice tests such cases by reference to the Convention. There is no case in which the European Court has upheld the validity of actions which conflicted with the ECHR. It seems, therefore, that in those areas affected by the EEC Treaties, the ECHR is already indirectly incorporated into English domestic law. The principles of the Convention form an integral part of EEC law and English domestic law is subject to EEC law. United Kingdom legislation must comply with directly applicable EEC legislation which itself falls to be construed so as to give effect the ECHR.[100]

(7) The Convention and administrative discretion

A fundamental issue concerning direct impact was the extent to which a public body was obliged to act in accordance with the United Kingdom's obligations under international human rights treaties.[101] In a number of cases in the 1970s it was argued that, in exercising administrative discretions, public officials were obliged to have regard to the Convention. At first this argument seemed to gain some ground,[102] but it was decisively rejected by the Court of Appeal in *R v Chief Immigration Officer, Heathrow Airport, ex p Salamat Bibi.*[103] Lord Denning MR thought that it was too much to expect immigration officers to know or apply the Convention. This pragmatic argument was subsequently extended to one of principle: it was held that the Secretary of State was not under an obligation to take the Convention into account in his determination as to whether or not to suspend a deportation order.[104] **2.30**

---

[98] *Kremzow v Austria* [1997] ECR I–2629

[99] *R v Secretary of State for the Home Department, ex p McQuillan* [1995] 4 All ER 400, 422e–g, *per* Sedley J.

[100] Lord Browne-Wilkinson, 'The Infiltration of a Bill of Rights' [1992] PL 397, 401; see also Lord Bingham, 'The European Convention on Human Rights: Time to Incorporate', in R Gordon and R Wilmot-Smith (eds), *Human Rights in the United Kingdom* (Clarendon Press, 1996) 1–11.

[101] See generally, N Blake, 'Judicial Review of Discretion in Human Rights Cases' [1997] EHRLR 391.

[102] See eg *R v Secretary of State for the Home Department, ex p Bhajan Singh* [1976] QB 198.

[103] [1976] QB 198.

[104] *Fernandes v Secretary of State for the Home Department* [1981] Imm AR 1; see also *R v Secretary of State for the Home Department, ex p Kirkwood* [1984] 1 WLR 913; and generally, M Hunt, *Using Human Rights in the English Courts* (Hart Publishing, 1997), Chap 4, 140ff.

2.31 The rigour of this approach was, however, mitigated somewhat by the decision of the House of Lords in *R v Secretary of State for the Home Department, ex p Bugdaycay*.[105] The applicant in that case was an asylum seeker from Uganda. The Home Secretary had ordered that he be removed to Kenya, the 'safe country' from which he had arrived. The applicant contended that he was unlikely to be allowed back into Kenya but would be removed to Uganda where he feared his life was in danger. The applicant invoked the 'right to life'. Lord Bridge said:

> The Court must, I think be entitled to subject an administrative decision to the more rigorous examination, to ensure that it is in no way flawed, according to the gravity of the issue which the decision determines. The most fundamental of all human rights is the individual's right to life and when an administrative decision under challenge is said to be one which may put the applicant's life at risk, the basis of the decision must surely call for the most anxious scrutiny.[106]

The House of Lords quashed the decision of the Home Secretary. The necessity of 'anxious scrutiny' in an administrative decision involves an 'enhancement' of the *Wednesbury* test for irrationality in public law.[107] It became recognised that such 'anxious scrutiny' was appropriate whenever 'fundamental rights are in play'.[108] The rights mentioned in the cases as attracting such scrutiny included: the right to life,[109] the right of free speech,[110] the right to home and family life[111] and the right to private life.[112]

2.32 The extent to which the Convention was to be taken into account in the exercise of discretion was raised directly in the leading case of *R v Secretary of State for the Home Department, ex p Brind*.[113] This concerned a directive issued by the Home Secretary requiring the broadcasting authorities to refrain from broadcasting the spoken words of persons representing proscribed terrorist organisations. The Home Secretary had a broad power to require the broadcasting authority to refrain from broadcasting any specified matter.[114] It was argued that, when a statute conferred a discretion which was capable of infringing a basic human right protected by the Convention, it should be presumed that the

---

[105] [1987] AC 514.

[106] Ibid 531E–g.

[107] See Lord Woolf and J Jowell, *De Smith, Woolf and Jowell, Judicial Review of Administrative Action* (5th edn, Sweet & Maxwell, 1995) para 13-060; Hunt (n 104 above) 182–185; and see para 1.30ff above.

[108] See generally M Fordham, 'What is "Anxious Scrutiny"'? [1996] JR 81; and for a discussion of the doctrine, see para 1.31 above.

[109] As in the *Bugdaycay* case (n 105, above).

[110] See *R v Secretary of State for the Home Department, ex p Brind* [1991] 1 AC 696.

[111] See *R v Secretary of State for Transport, ex p Richmond-upon-Thames Borough Council (No 4)* [1996] 1 WLR 1460, 1481.

[112] *R v Ministry of Defence, ex p Smith* [1996] QB 517.

[113] [1991] 1 AC 696.

[114] Broadcasting Act 1990, s 29(3), and clause 13(4) of the Licence and Agreement between the BBC and the Secretary of State.

discretion was to be exercised within the limits which the Convention imposed. As a result, it was contended, the directives were *ultra vires* because they contravened Article 10. This argument was unanimously rejected by the House of Lords.

Lord Bridge (with whom Lord Roskill agreed), took the view that to presume that an administrative discretion was to be exercised within Convention limits would have been to import the Convention into domestic administrative law and would therefore have been a 'judicial usurpation of the legislative function'.[115] He went on to say, however, that in deciding whether the imposition by the Secretary of State of the restriction on broadcasting organisations was reasonable in the exercise of his discretion, the court could start from the premise that any restriction of the right to freedom of expression required justification. Further, he stated that nothing less than an important competing public interest would have been sufficient grounds for such justification.[116] Lord Ackner (with whom Lord Lowry agreed), took the strict 'dualist' view: an incorporated treaty could only be relevant if the statute was ambiguous. As the relevant statutory provision was not ambiguous, the Convention was not relevant. If the Secretary of State had been obliged to have regard to the Convention in exercising his discretion 'this would inevitably result in incorporating the Convention into English domestic law by the back door'.[117] Although in agreement with the result, Lord Templeman's approach was somewhat different. In his view: **2.33**

> The courts cannot escape from asking themselves whether a reasonable Secretary of State, on the material before him, could reasonably conclude that the interference with freedom of expression which he determined to impose was justifiable. In terms of the Convention, as construed by the European Court, the interference with freedom of expression must be necessary and proportionate to the damage which the restriction is designed to prevent.[118]

On the evidence, he could not conclude that the Home Secretary had abused or exceeded his powers.

The *Brind* case was subject to severe criticism from a number of commentators. Extra judicial criticism of the decision was made by Lords Browne-Wilkinson[119] and Woolf.[120] There was considerable debate as to the extent to which the case allowed 'human rights' considerations to be taken into account in judicial review applications. In *R v Secretary of State for the Environment, ex p NALGO*,[121] Neill LJ suggested that the following principles applied: **2.34**

---

115 At 748B–F.
116 At 748F–749B.
117 At 760A–762D.
118 At 751E.
119 'The Infiltration of the Bill of Rights' [1992] PL 406.
120 Lord Woolf and J Jowell, *De Smith, Woolf and Jowell, Judicial Review of Administrative Action* (5th edn, Sweet & Maxwell, 1995) para 6-052.
121 (1993) 5 Admin LR 785, 798.

> (1) Article 10 is not part of English domestic law. It is therefore not necessary for the Minister when exercising an administrative discretion conferred on him by Parliament to exercise that discretion in accordance with the provisions of Art 10. Nor will a court when reviewing the decision of the Minister interfere with it on the ground that he did not have regard to the provisions of Art 10 . . .
>
> (2) Nevertheless, where fundamental human rights including freedom of expression are being restricted the Minister will need to show that there is an important competing public interest which is sufficient to justify that restriction.
>
> (3) The primary judgement as to whether the competing public interest justifies the particular restriction is for the Minister. The court is only entitled to exercise a secondary judgment by asking whether a reasonable Minister, on the material before him, could reasonably make that primary judgment . . .

In *R v Ministry of Defence, ex p Smith,*[122] the following formulation of counsel was accepted as an 'accurate distillation' of the principles laid down in *Brind* and *Bugdaycay*:

> The court may not interfere with the exercise of an administrative discretion on substantive grounds save where the court is satisfied that the decision is unreasonable in the sense that it is beyond the range of responses open to a reasonable decision-maker. But in judging whether the decision-maker has exceeded this margin of appreciation the human rights context is important. The more substantial the interference with human rights, the more the court will require by way of justification before it is satisfied that the decision is reasonable in the sense outlined above.

In other words, the greater the interference with human rights, the more anxious the scrutiny and the closer the courts would come to applying a 'proportionality' test in judicial review.[123]

2.35 There were, however, a limited number of situations in which the court did take the Convention into account when considering the lawfulness of the exercise of an administrative discretion. The court referred to the Convention when reviewing an exercise of discretion:

- under a statute intended to bring English law into line with the Convention;
- the effect of which was to bring the human rights of the applicant directly into issue;
- in circumstances in which the decision-maker was required to take the Convention into account; and
- in circumstances in which the applicant had a legitimate expectation that the Convention would be taken into account.

2.36 The first type of case was exemplified by *R v Secretary of State for the Home*

[122] [1996] QB 517, 554E: the formulation was by Mr David Pannick QC.

[123] See generally, Lord Woolf and J Jowell, *De Smith, Woolf and Jowell, Judicial Review of Administrative Action* (5th edn, Sweet & Maxwell, 1995) para 13–070ff.

Department, ex p Norney.[124] In issue there was the lawfulness of the policy of the Home Secretary, whereby he declined to refer cases of prisoners serving discretionary life sentences to the Parole Board until the 'tariff' had expired. The discretion in question was conferred on the Home Secretary by the Criminal Justice Act 1991, which had been passed in response to a decision of the European Court of Human Rights[125] with the intention of bringing English law into line with the requirements of the Convention. It was argued that, following *Brind*, the legality of the exercise of an administrative discretion could not be impugned on the basis that the provisions of the Convention had not been taken into account. This argument was rejected by Dyson J who said:

> I accept that as a general rule, the lawfulness of the exercise of executive discretion is not measured by asking whether it involves an infringement of Convention rights. But where it is clear that the statutory provision which creates the discretion was passed in order to bring the domestic law into line with the Convention, it would in my judgment be perverse to hold that, when considering the lawfulness of the exercise of the discretion, the court must ignore the relevant provisions of the Convention.[126]

He went on to hold that the policy of the Home Secretary was unlawful.

Secondly, the Convention was taken into account where the impugned exercise of discretion unavoidably raised the issue of fundamental human rights. Such was the case in *R v Secretary of State for the Home Department, ex p Launder*,[127] which involved judicial review of an exercise of discretion in the extradition context. The applicant there sought to resist extradition to Hong Kong, on the ground, *inter alia*, that he would not receive a fair trial after the transfer of sovereignty to the People's Republic of China. The applicant had made representations to the Secretary of State that, if he were returned to Hong Kong, his rights under the Convention, and in particular his rights to life, to liberty, to a fair trial and to protection from degrading and inhuman treatment, would be at risk. The House of Lords decided, on the evidence, that the Home Secretary had had proper regard for these rights in arriving at his decision. **2.37**

Thirdly, the Convention was considered during judicial review of exercises of discretion which themselves required the original decision-maker to consider the Convention. The matter arose in connection with the lawfulness of some immigration decisions in the United Kingdom. Home Office Policy DP/2/93,[128] for example, provided guidance on immigration cases involving marriage and children **2.38**

[124] (1995) 7 Admin LR 861, *per* Dyson J.

[125] *Thynne, Wilson and Gunnell v United Kingdom* (1990) 13 EHRR 666.

[126] *R v Secretary of State for the Home Department, ex p Norney*, 871C–D.

[127] [1997] 1 WLR 839.

[128] See M Hunt, *Using Human Rights in the English Courts* (Hart Publishing, 1997) App VI, 415.

and directed attention specifically to Article 8 of the Convention. In effect, immigration officers were required to act within the general terms[129] of the policy guidelines, with the result that a demonstrated disregard of the guidance in terms of Article 8 could be a valid basis on which to assert that the decision was wrongly made.[130]

2.39 Finally, judicial review proceedings could consider the Convention in circumstances in which there was created a legitimate expectation that the decision-maker would, in his exercise of discretion, adhere to the Convention. The High Court of Australia had held that the ratification of a treaty created a legitimate expectation that the executive would act in accordance with it.[131] The position in English law is considered below.[132]

2.40 It has been argued that the UK Government created a legitimate expectation that it would comply with its obligations under international human rights treaties by the publication of the *Questions of Procedure for Ministers*, the Civil Service Code and recent answers to parliamentary questions.[133] The Government made it clear, however, that its duty to comply with the treaties was an international obligation. Furthermore, in order for an applicant to have a legitimate expectation that the Convention would be taken into account, there would have had to have been a clear and unambiguous[134] representation to that effect, whether expressly[135] or by conduct.[136] The representation must have been to particular individuals, corporations or associations, rather than to the public at large.[137] As a result, the doctrine of legitimate expectation only leads to an obligation to take the Convention into account in a very limited class of cases.[137a] In *R v Director of Public Prosecutions, ex p Kebilene*[138] Lord Bingham CJ expressed the view that:

> It was generally assumed at the time that ratification would have no practical effect

[129] See *R v Secretary of State for the Home Department, ex p Jordan Abiodun Iye* [1994] Imm AR 63, 66.

[130] See also *R v Secretary of State for the Home Department, ex p Amankwah* [1994] Imm AR 240; and generally, Hunt (n 128 above) 234–238.

[131] See *Minister for Immigration and Ethnic Affairs v Teoh* (1995) 69 ALR 353.

[132] At para 2.66 below.

[133] See A Lester, 'Government Compliance with International Human Rights Law: A New Year's Legitimate Expectation', [1996] PL 187; relying on the Australian case of *Minister for Immigration and Ethnic Affairs v Teoh* (1995) 128 ALR 353, 365 (see also, *R v Secretary of State for the Home Department, ex p Ahmed, The Times*, 15 Oct 1998, approving this passage).

[134] See *R v Inland Revenue Commissioners, ex p MFK Underwriting Agents Ltd* [1990] 1 WLR 1545.

[135] See eg *R v Secretary of State for the Home Department, ex p Khan* [1984] 1 WLR 1337; *R v Ministry of Agriculture, Fisheries and Food, ex p Hamble (Offshore) Fisheries Ltd* [1995] 2 All ER 714; *R v Secretary of State for the Home Department, ex p Hargreaves* [1997] 1 WLR 906.

[136] See eg *R v Inland Revenue Commissioners, ex p Unilever plc* [1996] 68 TC 205.

[137] *R v Secretary of State for the Home Department, ex p Fire Brigades Union* [1995] 2 AC 513, 545H.

[137a] See also para 2.66 below.

[138] [1999] 3 WLR 175.

> on British law or practice, as proved for many years to be the case. It cannot plausibly be said that ratification so long ago gives rise to any legitimate expectation today

The enactment of the Human Rights Act 1998 did not, of itself, form the basis for a legitimate expectation that public authorities would immediately act in accordance with the Convention. This was because section 22(3) provided that the Act would come into force on such day as the Secretary of State may, by order, appoint, and:

> It would . . . fly in the face of the clear legislative intention of Parliament if the central provisions of the Act were to be treated . . . as having immediate effect when the Act itself provides that they shall not.[139]

D. The Impact of Other Human Rights Treaties

(1) Introduction

By comparison with the Convention the other human rights treaties to which the United Kingdom is a party are not well known. While MPs, journalists, judges, non govermental organisations and the public are aware in broad terms of the Convention, there is a much greater level of ignorance in regard to other human rights treaties.[140] Many of these human rights treaties have been promulgated under the aegis of the United Nations. To date, these human rights treaties have had a very limited impact on legislation and on the courts although the Human Rights Act may change the perspective of the English courts. It has recently been suggested that the Human Rights Act could provide a template for other international treaties such as the European Social Charter:[141] however, there is no indication that the government intends to take this course. For present purposes we will consider: the Universal Declaration on Human Rights, the International Covenant on Civil and Political Rights, the United Nations Convention on the Rights of the Child, the treaties prohibiting torture and discrimination and the treaties dealing with economic and social rights. There is no reason in principle why any of these treaties should not be invoked in appropriate cases in accordance with the principles set out above.[142] **2.41**

The enactment of the Human Rights Act has encouraged the Government to **2.41A**

[139] *Per* Lord Bingham CJ, *R v DPP, ex p Kebilene* [1999] 3 WLR 175, 185.

[140] See comments by R Higgins in D Harris and S Joseph (eds), *International Covenant on Civil and Political Rights and United Kingdom Law* (Oxford University Press, 1995), Foreword, xv; for a list of all the cases in which international human rights treaties were referred to by the English courts up to the end of 1996, see Hunt (n 128 above) App I.

[141] K Ewing, 'Social Rights and Constitutional Law' [1999] PL 104, 122.

[142] The various ways in which the courts make use of unincorporated treaties are summarised at para 2.12 above; and see also para 2.61ff below.

re-examine the question whether it should ratify other human rights instruments. The Government's views concerning unratified protocols of the European Convention are discussed in Chapter 3.[142a] However, the review also considered the position in relation to the International Covenant on Civil and Political Rights, the Convention against Torture, the Convention on the Rights of the Child, the Convention on the Elimination of all Forms of Discrimination against Women, the International Covenant on Economic and Social Rights and the discrimination and minimum age conventions of the International Labour Organisation.[142b] The Government has stated, in particular, that following the implementation of the Human Rights Act, it will reconsider granting the right of individual petition under the International Covenant on Civil and Political Rights and under the Convention against Torture.

(2) The Universal Declaration of Human Rights

2.42 The Universal Declaration of Human Rights[143] was adopted on 10 December 1948 by the General Assembly. It is not a legally binding instrument as such, but some of its provisions constitute 'general principles of law' and it is an authoritative guide to the interpretation of the United Nations Charter.[144] Although it has now been in force for over 50 years, it has rarely been considered in the case law. The earliest reference appears to be that in *Waddington v Miah*[145] where the House of Lords referred to the provision against retrospective penal offences in Article 11(2). In *Kiam v Neill*[146] the Court of Appeal invoked the right to protection of the law against attacks on honour and reputation in Article 12 in defence of the English law of libel:

> The European Convention on Human Rights does not stand alone as a declaration of human rights. Under the United Nations Universal Declaration Article 8 and Article 12 everyone has a right to the protection of the law against attacks upon his honour and reputation no less than the right of others under Article 19 to freedom of opinion and expression and to impart information and ideas through the media. The right to protection of the law against attacks on honour and reputation are as important in a democratic society as the right to freedom of the press.

2.43 The courts have been referred to the Universal Declaration more often in recent years. The Articles referred to have included: Article 3 (the right to life),[147] Article

[142a] See para 3.83.

[142b] *Home Office Review of Human Rights Instruments (Amended)*, 26 Aug 1999.

[143] UN Doc A/811; the text is reproduced at App H in Vol 2.

[144] See generally, I Brownlie, *Principles of Public International Law* (5th edn, Oxford University Press, 1998) 573ff.

[145] [1974] 1 WLR 683, 690H–691A; see also *R v Secretary of State for the Home Department, ex p Findlay*, *The Times*, 23 May 1984.

[146] [1994] EMLR 1.

[147] *R v Secretary of State for the Home Department, ex p McQuillan* [1995] 4 All ER 400.

5 (the prohibition on torture),[148] Articles 10 and 11(1) (the right to a fair trial and the presumption of innocence),[149] Article 12 (the right to privacy),[150] Article 14 (the right to asylum)[151] and Article 23(1) (the right to work).[152] However, the Universal Declaration has not played a decisive role in any of these cases.

(3) The International Covenant on Civil and Political Rights

The International Covenant on Civil and Political Rights[153] is not well known to the legal profession or the judiciary in the United Kingdom, and has accordingly had little direct impact on the development and interpretation of statutory and common law. In 1984, the UK Government's representative to the UN Human Rights Committee was unable to identify even one case in which the British courts had made reference to the Covenant. Since then, although the courts have referred to the Covenant in a few cases, with one exception, it has had little impact. **2.44**

The one area in which the Covenant has had an important impact on the English law concerns the right to compensation for miscarriages of justice in Article 14(6).[154] In order to comply with the United Kingdom's obligations under this provision, the Government first introduced a non-statutory scheme for compensation[155] and then enacted section 133 of the Criminal Justice Act 1988 which provides that: **2.45**

> when a person has by a final decision been convicted of a criminal offence and when subsequently his conviction has been reversed, or he has been pardoned, on the ground that a new or newly discovered fact shows beyond reasonable doubt that there has been a miscarriage of justice, the Secretary of State shall pay compensation for miscarriage of justice to the person who has suffered punishment as a result of such conviction . . . unless the non-disclosure of the unknown fact was wholly or partly attributable to the person convicted.

The courts have, in considering both the non-statutory scheme and the provisions

---

148 *Al-Adjani v Goverment of Kuwait, The Times*, 29 Mar 1996; *R v Secretary of State for the Home Department, ex p Singh*, [1999] Imm AR 445.

149 *R v Khan* [1997] AC 558.

150 *R v Secretary of State for the Home Department, ex p Ruddock* [1987] 1 WLR 1482, 1493F–H; *Hunter v Canary Wharf* [1997] AC 655, *per* Lord Cooke, dissenting.

151 *R v Secretary of State for the Home Department, ex p Khahil Yassine* [1990] Imm AR 354.

152 *R v Secretary of State for the Home Department, ex p Ouanes The Times*, 26 Nov 1997; *Stefan v General Medical Council* [1999] 1 WLR 1293.

153 For the text of the Covenant, see App J in Vol 2; and see generally, D Harris and S Joseph (eds), *International Covenant on Civil and Political Rights and United Kingdom Law* (Clarendon Press, 1995); D McGoldrick, *The Human Rights Committee* (Clarendon Press, 1994); P Ghandi, *The Human Rights Committee and the Right of Individual Communication: Law and Practice* (Dartmouth, 1998).

154 See para 11.138ff below.

155 See Written Answer, 29 Nov 1985, *Hansard*, HC vol 87, col 689.

of section 133, made a number of references to Article 14(6).[156] In *R v Secretary of State for the Home Department, ex p Atlantic Commercial Ltd*[157] Popplewell J used the Covenant as an aid to construe the word 'person' in section 133. As a result, he concluded that the section only applied to natural persons.

2.46 The Covenant has been cited in a number of other cases but usually in passing and in conjunction with reference to the Covention. The Articles referred to have included: Article 6 (right to life),[158] Article 7 (prohibition of torture),[159] Article 14(1) (right to a fair and public hearing),[160] Article 19 (freedom of expression)[161] and Article 26 (right to equal protection of the law).[162]

2.47 The Covenant is likely to become more important in English law after the Human Rights Act comes into force because it contains a number of rights which are not included in the Convention. Attention is drawn to the following:

- the rights of aliens to be expelled only in accordance with the law, with reasons and a review of the decision;[163]
- the right to appeal and the prohibition of double jeopardy;[164]
- the right of a child to 'such measures of protection as are required by his status as a minor';[165]
- the rights of every citizen to take part in public affairs and to have 'access on general terms of equality, to public service';[166]
- the free standing right to equal protection of the law and prohibition of discrimination;[167]
- rights of ethnic, religious or linguistic minorities 'to enjoy their own culture, to profess and practice their own religion, or to use their own language'.[168]

[156] See eg *R v Secretary of State for the Home Department, ex p Batemann, The Times*, 1 Jul 1994; *R v Secretary of State for the Home Department, ex p Ogunbusola*, unreported, 6 Mar 1996; *R v Secretary of State for the Home Department, ex p Sheffield*, unreported, 7 Oct 1997; *R v Secretary of State for the Home Department, ex p Garner*, unreported, 19 Apr 1999.

[157] *The Times*, 10 Mar 1997.

[158] *Airedale NHS Trust v Bland* [1993] AC 789.

[159] *R v Secretary of State for the Home Department, ex p Chahal* [1995] 1 WLR 526; *Al-Adjani v Government of Kuwait, The Times*, 29 Mar 1996.

[160] *Connelly v RTZ Corporation plc* [1996] QB 361.

[161] *Derbyshire County Council v Times Newspapers Ltd* [1992] 1 QB 770, CA; not mentioned in the House of Lords [1993] AC 534.

[162] *Fitzpatrick v Sterling Housing Association Ltd* [1998] Ch 304, *per* Ward LJ dissenting, the decision of the Court of Appeal was overruled by the House of Lords [1999] 3 WLR 1113.

[163] Art 13; the text is reproduced at App J in Vol 2.

[164] Art 14(5) and (6).

[165] Art 24.1.

[166] Art 25.

[167] Art 26.

[168] Art 27.

(4) The United Nations Convention on the Rights of the Child

The United Nations Convention on the Rights of the Child ('the Child Convention')[169] confers a comprehensive range of civil, political, social, economic, cultural, recreational and humanitarian rights upon children. The aim of the Convention is to prevent harm to children, to protect them against discrimination, to provide them with assistance for their basic needs and to allow children to participate in decisions which affect their destiny.[170] The Child Convention was ratified by the United Kingdom on 16 December 1991. It is enforced through the Committee on the Rights of the Child which considers reports submitted by the United Kingdom every five years[171] and comments on the United Kingdom's performance. **2.48**

The Child Convention has been considered in a number of English cases. For example, in *Re H (A Minor) (Blood Tests: Paternity Rights)*[172] the Court of Appeal had regard to the child's right to know his parents under Article 7. In *R v Accrington Youth Court, ex p Flood*[173] the court attached significance to the child's right to be accommodated separately from adults under Article 37(c) in considering the unlawfulness of the Home Secretary committing a young offender to an adult prison. In *R v Secretary of State for the Home Department, ex p Venables and Thompson*[174] Lord Browne-Wilkinson relied on Articles 3(1) and 40(1) of the Convention when considering the proper approach the Home Secretary should take towards deciding the length of detention which was appropriate for a child murderer being held at Her Majesty's pleasure; he took the view that it was legitimate to assume that Parliament had not maintained a statutory power which was capable of being exercised in a manner inconsistent with the United Kingdom's treaty obligations. **2.49**

The Child Convention applies to every child below 18.[175] The United Kingdom is required to respect and ensure that the rights are extended to all children within its jurisdiction without discrimination of any kind, irrespective of the child, his parent or his guardian's race, colour, sex, language, religion, political or other opinions, national, ethnic or social origin, property, disability, birth or **2.50**

[169] The text is reproduced at App N in Vol 2. See, generally, D McGoldrick, 'The United Nations Convention on the Rights of the Child' (1991) 5 IJLF 132; B Walsh, 'The United Nations Convention on the Rights of the Child: A British View' (1991) 5 IJLF 170; P Alston, S Parker and J Seymour, *Children Rights and the Law* (Oxford University Press, 1992); G Van Bueren, *The International Law on the Rights of the Child* (Nijhoff, 1995).

[170] G Van Bueren, 'The UN Convention on the Rights of the Child' (1991) 3 JCL 63.

[171] Art 44.

[172] [1997] Fam 89.

[173] [1998] 1 WLR 156.

[174] [1988] AC 407, 499.

[175] Art 1.

other status.[176] Article 3 obliges the United Kingdom to undertake to ensure the child such protection and care as is necessary for his well being, taking into account the rights and duties of his parents, legal guardians or other individuals legally responsible for him, and to this end, to take all appropriate legislative and administrative measures; however, this obligation is qualified by the specific duties and obligations owed to parents and other carers under Article 5.

2.51 The Child Convention confers a number of rights on children including the following:

- the inherent right to life and to survival and development to the maximum extent possible;[177]
- the right to an identity comprising the right to be registered immediately after birth and the right from birth to a name, the right to acquire a nationality and, as far as possible, the right to know and be cared for by his parents[178] and the obligation on the state to preserve his identity including his nationality, name and family relations as recognised by law without unlawful interference;[179]
- the obligation on the state to ensure that a child shall not be separated from his parents against his will, except where a competent authority, subject to judicial review, determines in accordance with applicable law and procedures, that such separation is necessary for the best interests of the child;[180]
- the obligation on the state to assure that the child who is capable of forming his own views has the right to express those views freely in all matters affecting the child, the view of the child being given due weight in accordance with the age and maturity of the child;[181]
- various civil rights of the child such as the right to freedom of expression (subject to certain qualifications),[182] the obligation on the state to respect the right of the child to freedom of thought, conscience and religion subject to the rights and duties of the parent to give directions to the child,[183] the right of the child to freedom of association and freedom of peaceful assembly,[184] the protection of the child against interference with his privacy, family, home or correspondence[185] and the right of the child to access to information, especially material aimed at promoting his social, spiritual and moral well being and his physical and mental health;[186]

---

176 Art 2(1).
177 Art 6.
178 Art 7(1.)
179 Art 8.
180 Art 9.
181 Art 12(1).
182 Art 13.
183 Art 14.
184 Art 15.
185 Art 16.
186 Art 17.

- the obligation on the state to use its best endeavours to ensure recognition of the principle that parents have common responsibilities for the upbringing and development of the child and recognition that parents (or guardians) have the prime responsibility for the upbringing and development of the child;[187]
- child protection rights such as the obligation on the state to take all appropriate legislation, administrative, social and educational measures to protect the child from all forms of physical or mental violence, injury or abuse, neglect or negligent treatment, maltreatment or exploitation (including sexual abuse) while in the care of a parent, guardian or other carer,[188] the right where temporarily or permanently deprived of his family environment to special protection and assistance,[189] detailed regulation of adoption[190] and the protection of a child's health;[191]
- the right of the child to receive social welfare entitlements such as the right to social security,[192] the right to an adequate standard of living,[193] education,[194] the right to belong to and enjoy minority rights[195] and the obligation on the state to uphold recreational rights;[196] and
- the right of the child to protection from various forms of exploitation such as economic exploitation,[197] protection against narcotics,[198] sexual exploitation and sexual abuse,[199] trafficking in children[200] and protecting the child from torture and other cruel, inhuman or degrading treatment or punishment.[201]

(5) The prevention of torture

The right contained in Article 7 of the International Covenant on Civil and Political Rights[202] not to be subjected to torture or to cruel, inhuman or degrading treatment or punishment has been supplemented by the Convention against Torture and Other Cruel, Inhuman or Degrading Treatment or Punishment ('the Torture Convention').[203] The Torture Convention was ratified by the United **2.52**

187 Art 18(1).
188 Art 19.
189 Art 20.
190 Art 21.
191 Art 24.
192 Art 26.
193 Art 27.
194 Arts 28 and 29.
195 Art 30.
196 Art 31.
197 Art 32.
198 Art 33.
199 Art 34.
200 Art 35.
201 Art 37.
202 The text is reproduced at App J in Vol 2.
203 See generally N Rodley, *The Treatment of Prisoners under International Law* (2nd edn, Oxford University Press, 1999).

Kingdom on 8 December 1988. The United Kingdom submits a report every four years[204] to the Committee Against Torture which monitors its performance. The United Kingdom has accepted the Committee's jurisdiction to receive inter state complaints[205] but has declined to recognise its competence to receive complaints from individuals.[206]

2.53 The Torture Convention confers a number of rights and obligations in relation to torture:[207]

- the obligation on the state to take effective legislative, administrative, judicial or any other measures to prevent acts of torture in any territory under its jurisdiction;[208]
- the prohibition against a state expelling, returning or extraditing a person to another state where there are substantial grounds for believing that he would be in danger of being subjected to torture;[209]
- the obligation on the state to ensure that all acts of torture are offences under its criminal law under Article 4 (together with a number of ancillary obligations: the obligation[210] to take such measures as may be necessary to establish its jurisdiction under Article 4, an obligation,[211] after examining the information available to it, to take into its custody any person alleged to have committed an offence, an obligation[212] to prosecute, if it does not extradite him and an obligation[213] to afford to other states the greatest measure of assistance in connection with an Article 4 offence).

2.54 The United Kingdom is also subject to the European Convention for the Prevention of Torture and Inhuman Treatment or Punishment[214] which was ratified in June 1988. This is intended to prevent breaches of Article 3 of the European Convention[215] by obliging a state to permit visits to places of detention. The European Committee for the Prevention of Torture and Inhuman Treatment or Punishment submits a report of its visits (including any findings of facts and recommendations for action) to which the United Kingdom must respond in writing.

---

[204] Art 19.
[205] Under Art 21.
[206] Under Art 22.
[207] Which is widely defined in Art 1.
[208] Art 2.
[209] Art 3.
[210] Art 5.
[211] Art 6.
[212] Art 7.
[213] Art 10.
[214] See generally, Council of Europe, *Yearbook of the European Convention for the Prevention of Torture and Inhuman or Degrading Treatment or Punishment* Vol 1 (1989–1992) and Vol 2 (1993); and M Evans and R Morgan, *Preventing Torture: A Study of the European Convention for the Prevention of Torture* (Oxford University Press, 1998).
[215] See para 8.13ff below.

(6) The prevention of discrimination

The International Convention on the Elimination of All Forms of Racial Discrimination[216] was ratified by the United Kingdom in March 1969. The United Kingdom is obliged to submit reports to the Committee on the Elimination of Racial Discrimination every two years on the legislative, judicial and administrative measures it has adopted and which give effect to the provision of the Convention.[217] The inter states complaints procedure is obligatory[218] and the United Kingdom has not accepted the right to individual petition.[219] Racial discrimination is broadly defined in Article 1. The Convention imposes a number of obligations on the state not to discriminate,[220] requires it to condemn all racial propaganda and organisations,[221] to prevent race discrimination in relation to a wide range of civil, political, economic and social rights[222] and to take immediate and effective measures, particularly in the fields of teaching, education, culture and information to combat prejudice leading to racial discrimination.[223] **2.55**

The Convention on the Elimination of All Forms of Discrimination against Women[223a] was ratified by the United Kingdom in April 1986. The Committee on the Elimination of All Forms of Discrimination against Women considers reports which the United Kingdom submits every four years[224] and makes General Recommendations which provide guidelines on the Articles of the Convention.[225] Discrimination against women is broadly defined in Article 1. This Convention imposes comprehensive obligations on the state to eliminate discrimination[226] as well as specific obligations to take measures to eliminate discrimination in the fields of education,[227] employment,[228] health care,[229] economic and social life[230] and in marriage and family relations.[231] **2.56**

---

[216] The text is reproduced at App L in Vol 2. See generally, M Banton, *International Action against Racial Discrimination* (Clarendon Press, 1996).

[217] Art 9.

[218] Under Art 11.

[219] Under Art 14.

[220] Art 2.

[221] Art 4.

[222] Art 5.

[223] Art 7.

[223a] The text is reproduced at App M in Vol 2.

[224] Art 18.

[225] *General Recommendations No 1 to 20*, IHRR Vol 1, No 1 [1994] 15; *General Recommendations 22 and 23*, IHRR Vol 5, No 1 [1998] 6.

[226] See Arts 2 to 9.

[227] Art 10.

[228] Art 11.

[229] Art 12.

[230] Art 13.

[231] Art 16.

(7) Treaties dealing with social and economic rights

2.57 The United Kingdom is party to two important international human rights treaties dealing with social and economic rights:[232] the International Covenant on Economic Social and Cultural Rights (1966)[233] and the European Social Charter (1965).[234] These two treaties recognise a wide range of rights which are not established in English law. These include:

- the right to work;[235]
- the right to just conditions of work, including fair wages and equal pay for equal work, a decent living, safe and healthy working conditiions, equal opportunity to be promoted and rest, leisure and reasonable limitation of working hours and paid holidays;[236]
- the right to social security;[237]
- the right to form trade unions and the right to strike;[238]
- the right to an adequate standard of living for himself and for his family, including food, clothing, housing and to the continuous improvement of living conditions;[239]
- the right to everyone to the enjoyment of the highest attainable standard of physical and mental health.[240]

These, and similar rights are recognised by the constitutions of a number of European and Commonwealth countries[241] and are justiciable in a number of jurisdictions.

2.58 The United Kingdom has also agreed to provide various social and economic rights through the International Labour Organisation. The ILO was founded in 1919 by the Treaty of Versailles[242] and is now a specialist agency of the United Nations. The United Kingdom must submit periodic reports on the measures it has adopted to give effect to ILO Conventions which are examined by a Committee of Experts. If an association of employers or workers wishes to complain that a state has failed to

[232] See generally, K Ewing, 'Social Rights and Constitutional Law' [1999] PL 104.

[233] The text is reproduced at App K in Vol 2, and see M Craven, *The International Covenant on Economic, Social and Cultural Rights* (Revised edn, Clarendon Press, 1998).

[234] The text is reproduced at App G in Vol 2, and see D Gomien, D Harris and L Zwaak, *Law and Practice of the European Convention on Human Rights and the European Social Charter* (Council of Europe Publishing, 1996).

[235] ESC, Art 1; ICESC, Art 6(1); see Universal Declaration, Art 23(1).

[236] ESC, Arts 2, 3 and 4; ICESC, Art 7; see Universal Declaration, Art 23.

[237] ESC, Art 12; ICESC, Art 9.

[238] ESC, Arts 5 and 6; ICESC, Art 8.

[239] ICESC, Art 11(1); Universal Declaration, Art 25(1).

[240] ESC, Art 11; ICESC, Art 12.

[241] See eg the South African Constitution, s 23 (right to form unions and to strike), s 26 (right to housing), s 27 (right of access to health care services, food and water and social security).

[242] See eg A Alcock, *The History of the International Labour Organisation* (Macmillan, 1971)

observe a Convention, the Governing Body of the ILO may communicate the complaint to the state and arrange a hearing before a special committee which then reports back to the Governing Body.

The General Council of the ILO adopted a Declaration of Aims and Purposes in 1944,[243] stating that labour is not to be regarded as a commodity; that freedom of expression and association are essential to sustained progress; that all human beings have the right to pursue both material well-being and spiritual development in conditions of freedom and dignity, economic security and equal opportunity, without discrimination on the grounds of race, creed or sex. The objectives of the ILO oblige it to further programmes to include achieving full employment, a minimum living wage, a basic income for all in need and a just share in the fruits of progress for all, recognition of right to free collective bargaining, adequate protection for the life and health of all workers, child welfare and maternity protection. **2.59**

The ILO has adopted 181 Conventions and 189 Recommendations. However, the United Kingdom has ratified only 80 Conventions and denounced a number in the 1980s.[244] ILO Conventions cover issues such as trade union rights and collective bargaining[245] and equal opportunities and discrimination.[246] Although it has sometimes been argued that ILO Conventions are relevant in employment disputes in the English courts,[247] they have yet to have any effect on the decision reached. **2.60**

E. The Limits of Applicability of Unincorporated Treaties

The impact of the international human rights treaties prior to the enactment of the Human Rights Act, both indirectly and in the English courts, led certain legal commentators to argue that there existed, even in the absence of incorporation, a 'common law Bill of Rights'. Hunt has presented a powerful case for the thesis that: **2.61**

---

243 E Lee, 'The Declaration of Philidelphia: Retrospect and Prospect' (1994) 133 Intl Lab Rev 467.

244 K Widdows, 'The Denunciation of International Labour Conventions' (1994) 33 ICLQ 1052.

245 Freedom of Association and the Protection of the Right to Organise Convention 1948 (Convention 87), Right to Organise and Collective Bargaining Convention 1949 (Convention 98), Workers Representatives Convention 1971 (Convention 135), Labour Relations (Public Service) Convention 1978 (Convention 151).

246 See eg Discrimination (Employment and Occupation) Convention 1958 (Convention 111), Equal Remuneration Convention 1951 (Convention 100) and Workers with Family Responsibilities Convention 1981 (Convention 156).

247 See eg *Williams v National Theatre Board Ltd* [1981] ICR 248; *Blackpool and the Fylde College v National Association of Teachers in Further and Higher Education* [1994] ICR 648.

> In more recent years . . . we have witnessed in the United Kingdom the emergence of a common law human rights jurisdiction . . . whereby the judiciary have contrived to provide a degree of protection for the rights and freedoms typically contained in international human rights treaties.[248]

He argued that international human rights law had thus achieved a status in domestic law higher than that of unincorporated treaties generally, although still falling short of the impact of fully incorporated international obligations. He contended further that this imposed on the English courts a strong 'interpretive obligation' to construe domestic law in a manner consistent with international human rights norms.

2.62 There are powerful arguments in favour of the first of these points. There has been increased judicial protection in domestic law of those human rights that are typically protected by international treaties.[249] This has, to some extent, produced very similar norms in the corpus of the common law. However 'contrived' this process might be, once they have emerged, common law human rights principles will certainly be more highly regarded in English law than if they had remained outside its remit altogether.

2.63 However, Hunt's contention that a 'common law human rights jurisdiction' imposes on the courts an obligation to interpret *all* of domestic law in accordance with international human rights standards, is more difficult to sustain.[250] There is much to be said for this approach, which would give proper recognition to international human rights instruments. Nevertheless, a 'strong interpretive obligation' to construe not only common law principles but also statute and exercises of administrative discretion in accordance with unincorporated international law is, on the current state of the authorities, difficult to support. Hunt argues that recognition of a common law foundation for judicial review has rendered unsustainable the distinction between the role of international law in the interpretation of statutes and its role in the development of the common law. In his view, the fact that human rights standards have been increasingly reflected in government policy documents and in guidance to civil servants has led the judiciary to consider themselves under a duty to interpret statutory law, as well as the common law, in conformity with international human rights standards. It has, he says, become difficult for the courts to maintain a dualist stance.

---

[248] M Hunt, *Using Human Rights in the English Courts* (Hart Publishing, 1997) 298; see also R Higgins' Foreword to D Harris and S Joseph (eds), *The ICCPR in UK Law* (Clarendon Press, 1995) xvi, where she noted that the common law was prior to incorporation frequently regarded as the same as European Convention law, that the ECHR had been the back-drop to that interpretation of the common law and that this seemed to be the way forward in the absence of incorporation.

[249] See para 1.35 above.

[250] The claim that the common law should be 'interpreted' in this way is open to question: see para 2.21 above.

The question turns on whether ambiguity in the domestic law is a precondition for consideration of a relevant human rights treaty provision, or whether the interpretive obligation of the courts requires them to resort to legal fiction. In the absence of any ambiguity in the language of a statute, an obligation to 'construe legislation so as to be in conformity with international law',[251] requires the court to disregard the clear intention of the legislature to the contrary. The orthodox view is, of course, that the Crown cannot legislate by treaty; that domestic enactment is the prerogative of Parliament. Where the treaty in question confers rights directly upon citizens,[252] however, the merits of this constitutional perspective are diminished. The refusal of parliament to accept that it is bound to act in accordance with the provisions of the treaty does make the international commitments of the United Kingdom look like 'window dressing'. **2.64**

There has nevertheless been considerable judicial reluctance to rely on the human rights treaties as an aid to statutory interpretation where to do so would contradict English law. Where prior to the Human Rights Act the Convention provisions were considered, for instance, there was a peculiar tendency to treat them as being identical to the common law. The various cases involving Article 10 contain repeated assertions of 'consistency' between common law and Convention without analysis of the Convention jurisprudence. This can be seen in other fields where the courts identified common law 'constitutional rights' mirroring those in the Convention.[253] In the few cases in which the Convention appears to have been influential, subsequent decisions seem to have downplayed its role in the outcome and reasserted the importance of the common law.[254] This phenomenon will have undesirable consequences for the development of English human rights law: **2.65**

> There is a danger that the 'rediscovery' of the common law's constitutional dimension will serve only to marginalise international human rights norms and the jurisprudence interpreting them, instead of according them a central role in the development of the common law . . .[255]

When formulating common law human rights principles, there is no doubt that, faced with clearly conflicting decisions of a higher English court and an unincorporated human rights treaty, a court is obliged to follow the former, in the absence of incorporation of the relevant treaty. Unless there is an ambiguity in the law itself, no 'interpretive obligation' will assist it to overcome this hurdle. This point **2.66**

[251] *Per* Lord Denning, *Corocraft Ltd v Pan American Airways Inc* [1968] 3 WLR 1273, 1281.

[252] See Hunt (n 248 above) Chap 1.

[253] See eg *R v Lord Chancellor, ex p Witham* [1998] QB 575 in relation to a right of access to the courts.

[254] See eg *Derbyshire County Council v Times Newspapers Ltd* [1992] 1 QB 770; [1993] AC 534: the House of Lords decided the case on the basis of the common law rather than the Convention.

[255] Hunt (n 248 above) 303.

was made before the Human Rights Act came into force in the case of *Camelot Group v Centaur Communications Ltd*[256] in which it was held that the question as to whether a publisher should be required to disclose the source of published information was to be determined in accordance with English law.[257] As the English law was clear and unambiguous, it was not necessary to apply the decision of the European Court of Human Rights on the same facts.[258] A similar approach was taken in the criminal case of *R v Morrisey,*[259] again prior to the Act coming into force. It was held that, despite the finding of the European Court of Human Rights in *Saunders v United Kingdom*[260] that the use of evidence obtained under powers of compulsion was incompatible with Article 6 of the Convention, the English courts would receive such evidence in a criminal trial.[261]

2.67 The result of the Human Rights Act is that it will be unlawful for the courts to act in a way which is incompatible with Convention rights.[262] Although decisions of the European Court of Human Rights will not be binding on the English courts[263] they are likely, in practice, to follow those decisions in most cases. However, the strict position in relation to breaches of *other* human rights treaties will be unaffected: in cases of conflict, the English courts will follow statute or precedent rather than international treaties. It remains to be seen whether the new 'culture of rights' under the Human Rights Act[264] will lead to any change of attitude in relation to unincorporated human rights treaties.

2.68 Nevertheless, an unincorporated treaty can create a legitimate expectation that the executive will act in accordance with it.[265] Such a legitimate expectatation can only give 'procedural' and not substantive protection of the rights found in an unincorporated treaty;[266] the executive can depart from the expected course of conduct if it has given notice that it intends to do so and gives the person affected the

[256] *The Times*, 5 Jul 1997 *per* Maurice Kay J.

[257] Contempt of Court Act 1981, s 10, as interpreted in *X Ltd v Morgan-Grampian (Publishers) Ltd* [1991] 1 AC 1.

[258] *Goodwin v United Kingdom* (1996) 22 EHRR 123; however, the judge went on to hold that, in any event, it was unlikely that the application of the Convention in the *Goodwin* case would make any difference.

[259] [1997] 2 Cr App R 426; see para 11.105 below.

[260] (1996) 23 EHRR 313.

[261] The Attorney-General subsequently made it clear to prosecuting authorities that such evidence should not be used, see para 11.107 below, and the law has now been brought into line with the Convention by statute, see Youth Justice and Criminal Evidence Act 1999, s 59 and Sch 3.

[262] s 6(1) of the Act: see para 5.120ff below.

[263] s 2(1) requires the court to take account of Convention case law: see para 3.46ff below.

[264] See para 1.54 above.

[265] *R v Secretary of State for the Home Department, ex p Ahmed and Patel* [1999] Imm AR 22.

[266] *Thomas v Baptiste* [1999] 3 WLR 249, 262–263.

opportunity to make representations.[267] A decision-maker may therefore act inconsistently with a legitimate expectation which he has created in relation to an unincorporated treaty provided that he gives those who are affected an opportunity to state their case.[268]

[267] *Thomas v Baptiste* (n 266 above) 261, 262 *per* Lord Millett; see also *Higgs v Ministry of National Security*, unreported, 14 Dec 1999.

[268] *Fisher v Minister of Public Safety (No 2)* [1999] 2 WLR 349, 356D.

Part II

GENERAL PRINCIPLES UNDER THE HUMAN RIGHTS ACT

3

THE HUMAN RIGHTS ACT: INTERPRETATION AND SYNOPSIS

A. Introduction

The Human Rights Act 1998 received royal assent on 9 November 1998. Its main provisions are brought into effect on 2 October 2000.[1] The purpose of the Act is, **3.01**

[1] But note that s 18 (Appointment to the Court of Human Rights); s 20 (Power to make orders under the Act); s 21(5) (removal of death penalty for military offences); and s 22 came into effect immediately. The power to allow ministers to make statements of incompatibility in relation to new

in the words of the long title, 'to give further effect to the rights and freedoms guaranteed under the European Convention on Human Rights'. It is designed to make Convention rights enforceable in the courts of the United Kingdom.[2] The way in which this is done is complex. The Act does not take the immediately obvious course of making the Convention a statutory United Kingdom Bill of Rights but makes it justiciable in the courts by the indirect route of making it unlawful for public authorities[3] to act in a way which is incompatible[4] with a Convention right.[5]

3.02 The reason for this 'indirect incorporation' was the Government's concern for parliamentary sovereignty and the perceived political dangers of giving the courts the power to strike down legislation which was inconsistent with Convention rights. The Labour Party's proposal in 1993[6] to incorporate the Convention was based upon the Canadian legislation and permitted the courts to override primary legislation.[7] However, the Human Rights Act takes a different approach. The Government decided that the courts should not have power to set aside primary legislation, either past or future, on the grounds of incompatibility with the Convention. This decision was explained in the White Paper as being based on:

> the importance which the Government attaches to Parliamentary sovereignty . . . In enacting legislation, Parliament is making decisions about important matters of public policy. The authority to make those decisions derives from a democratic mandate . . . To make a provision in the Bill for the courts to set aside Acts of Parliament would confer on the judiciary a general power over the decisions of Parliament which, under our present constitutional arrangements they do not possess and would be likely on occasions to draw the judiciary into serious conflict with Parliament.[8]

3.03 The result of this decision is that the Human Rights Act has no special legislative status: it is not 'entrenched'. If a statute is inconsistent with Convention rights, the statute must prevail (although the court has the power to make a declaration

---

legislation and to make provision for pensions for judges of the European Court came into force on 24 Nov 1998: see The Human Rights Act (Commencement) Order 1998, SI 1998/2882. The impact of the Human Rights Act before it comes into effect is discussed at para 3.75 below.

[2] For the general aims of the Act, see the White Paper, *Rights Brought Home* (1997) Cm 3782 which is reproduced at App B in Vol 2; and see Lord Irvine LC, *Hansard*,HL cols 1227–1238 (3 Nov 1997) (introducing the Bill in the House of Lords); The Home Secretary (Jack Straw), *Hansard*, HC cols 769–782 (16 Feb 1998); Under Secretary of State (Mike O'Brien) *Hansard*, HC cols 858–861 (16 Feb 1998).

[3] For the meaning of these words in the Act, see para 5.03ff below.

[4] For the meaning of this word in the Act, see para 5.120ff below.

[5] The rights created under the Act are defined as Convention rights by s 1: see para 3.43ff below.

[6] See para 1.43 above.

[7] See para 1.79 above.

[8] *Rights Brought Home* (1997) Cm 3782, para 2.13.

of incompatibility).[9] Furthermore, the Convention has not been made part of English law: it is not an English statute directly justiciable in the courts.[10] The intention appears to be that the doctrine of 'implied repeal' does not apply in relation to earlier legislation.[11]

The absence of entrenchment does not mean that the Human Rights Act must, in all respects, be approached as an ordinary statute. The Act forms part of a 'comprehensive programme of constitutional reform' by the Government.[12] Furthermore, it gives effect to 'fundamental rights and freedoms'. Although the notion of 'constitutional rights' in English law is generally confined to common law rights whose 'constitutional status' makes them immune to 'implied abrogation'[13] certain statutes have always been recognised as having a special status. These include the Magna Carta, the Bill of Rights and the Statute of Westminster.[14] Statutes with 'constitutional status' have no special immunity from repeal but a different approach to their construction may be adopted by the courts. It is submitted that the Human Rights Act has the special status of a 'constitutional Act'[15] and should, therefore, be subject to special principles of construction.[16] This would apply both to the Act itself and to the interpretation of Convention rights themselves. These principles are discussed in the next section of this chapter. **3.04**

The chapter then goes on to outline the provisions of the Human Rights Act. The two most important elements of the Act concern statutory interpretation[17] and the position of public authorities under the Act;[18] these require fuller discussion and are dealt with in Chapters 4 and 5 respectively. In the final section of the chapter the weaknesses of the Human Rights Act are examined in terms of whether it can be described as a modern human rights instrument which reflects contemporary conditions and attitudes. **3.05**

---

[9] See para 4.43ff below.

[10] Cf Lord Irvine's comments at the Report Stage, *Hansard*, HL 29 Jan 1998, cols 421–422 (quoted at para 3.89 below).

[11] See para 4.33ff below.

[12] *Rights Brought Home* (1997) Cm 3782, Preface by the Prime Minister; and see Lord Irvine LC, *Hansard*, HL, col 1227 (3 Nov 1997).

[13] See *R v Lord Chancellor, ex p Witham* [1998] QB 575; *R v Lord Chancellor, ex p Lightfoot* [1999] 2 WLR 1114; and see para 1.26 above.

[14] See *Halsbury's Statutes*, (4th edn, Butterworths, 1985) Vol 10 for these and others.

[15] See F. Bennion, *Statutory Interpretation* (3rd edn, Butterworths, 1997) 126; and for a discussion concerning the constitutional status of the Human Rights Act, see para 1.90ff above.

[16] See para 3.06ff above.

[17] s 3.

[18] s 6.

B. The Construction of Constitutional Instruments

(1) Introduction

3.06 It was earlier suggested that the Human Rights Act is a constitutional statute which is subject to special principles of construction.[19] It is the first modern constitutional English enactment dealing with 'fundamental rights'. Nevertheless, the principles of construction applicable to such instruments have been the subject of extensive consideration in many other common law jurisdictions.[20] Senior English judges have made a substantial contribution through the work of the Privy Council in construing provisions relating to fundamental rights when considering appeals from Commonwealth countries. All but one of these countries[21] have written constitutions containing 'rights provisions'. These 'rights provisions' take different forms and each has to be construed in the context of the constitutional instrument in which it appears.

3.07 The Privy Council has drawn attention to the fact that 'Constitutions are formulated in different terms and must each be read within its own particular context and framework'.[22] Nevertheless, many of the 'human rights instruments' considered by the Privy Council are closely modelled on the Convention. The Privy Council has often examined the general principles which apply to interpreting such 'rights': and their views will provide important guidance as to the likely approach of the English courts to similar issues.[23]

(2) General principles

(a) Introduction

3.08 It has long been recognised that constitutional provisions must be approached in a flexible manner so that they can be adapted to changing conditions. Thus the American jurist, Benjamin Cardozo[23a] identified the distinctive feature of a constitutional instrument by stressing that:

> Statutes are designed to meet the fugitive exigencies of the hour. Amendment is easy as the exigencies change. In such cases, the meaning once construed tends legitimately to stereotype itself in the form first cast. A *constitution* states or ought to state not rules for the passing hour, but principles for an expanding future. In so far as it

[19] See paras 1.90 and 3.04 above.

[20] For a recent comprehensive discussion see Lord Irvine LC, 'Activism and Restraint: Human Rights and the Interpretative Process' [1999] EHRLR 350.

[21] The exception is New Zealand.

[22] *Matadeen v Pointu* [1998] 3 WLR 18, 28H. The quotation is from *Union of Campement Site Owners and Lessees v Government of Mauritius* [1984] MR 100, 107.

[23] For a recent general discussion see L Blom-Cooper and C Gelber, 'The Privy Council and the Death Penalty in the Caribbean: A Study in Constitutional Change' [1998] EHRLR 386.

[23a] B Cardozo, *The Nature of the Judicial Process* (Yale University Press, 1991) 83–85.

> deviates from that standard and descends into details and particulars, it loses its flexibility, the scope of interpretation contracts, the meaning hardens. While it is true to its function, it maintains its power of adaption, its suppleness, its play . . . there are jurists, at any rate abroad, who maintain that the meaning of today is not the meaning of tomorrow . . . 'We do not inquire' [M Ballot-Beaupre][23b] said, 'what a legislator willed a century ago, but what he would have willed if he had known what our present conditions would be.' . . . I have no doubt that [this method of interpretation] has been applied in the past and with increasing frequency will be applied in the future, to fix the scope and meaning of the broad precepts and immunities in state and national constitutions. I see no reason why it may not be applied to statutes framed upon lines similarly general.

This approach has given rise to the doctrine of 'progressive interpretation', in which a constitutional instrument is seen as a 'living tree capable of growth and expansion within its natural limits'.[24]

3.09 The starting point for consideration of the approach of the Privy Council to rights instruments is the well-known case of *Minister of Home Affairs v Fisher*,[25] which concerned the determination of the status of an illegitimate child under the Constitution of Bermuda. Lord Wilberforce said that international conventions on human rights required:

> a generous interpretation, avoiding what has been called 'the austerity of tabulated legalism', suitable to give to individuals the full measure of the fundamental rights and freedoms referred to.[26]

He distinguished the Constitution of Bermuda from *ordinary* Acts of Parliament dealing with specific subjects, on the basis of its special characteristics: first, its broad and ample drafting style which lays down principles of width and generality; secondly, the antecedents to,[27] and form of, Chapter I of that Constitution dealing with Protection of Fundamental Rights and Freedoms of the Individual;[28] and thirdly, the provision of Section 11, such that Chapter I is to have effect for the protection of rights and freedoms, subject only to the limitations contained therein, which are designed to ensure that the enjoyment of the rights does not prejudice the public interest. Lord Wilberforce said that a constitution ought not to be construed simply as if it were an Act of Parliament with allowance for interpreting it with 'less rigidity or greater generosity'. Rather, he

---

23b Munroe Smith *Jurisprudence*, 29, 30.

24 The most quoted use of this phrase is in *Edwards v A-G of Canada* [1930] AC 114, 136, *per* Lord Sankey; see also *British Coal Corporation v The King* [1935] AC 500, 518 and *(A-G) of Ontario v (A-G) of Canada* [1947] AC 127, 154; a similar approach has been taken to the construction of the Convention as a 'living instrument', see para 6.23ff below.

25 [1980] AC 319.

26 Ibid 328.

27 Chap I was greatly influenced by the European Convention on Human Rights and Fundamental Freedoms (1953).

28 Ibid 328.

preferred a more 'radical approach: a constitutional instrument should be treated as *sui generis*, calling for principles of construction of its own without necessary acceptance of all the presumptions that are relevant to legislation of private law'.[29] He went on to say that:

> This is in no way to say that there are no rules of law which should apply to the interpretation of a constitution. A constitution is a legal instrument giving rise, amongst other things, to individual rights capable of enforcement in a court of law. Respect must be paid to the language which has been used and to the traditions and the usages which have given meaning to that language. It is quite consistent with this, and with the recognition that rules of interpretation may apply, to take as a point of departure for the process of interpretation a recognition of the character and origin of the instrument, and to be guided by the principle of giving full recognition and effect to those fundamental rights and freedoms with a statement of which the constitution commences.[30]

3.10 The issue which the Privy Council had to consider was whether an illegitimate child was a 'child' for the purposes of the protection of its right to freedom of movement (which was confined to 'persons not belonging to Bermuda'). Lord Wilberforce considered the objectives of the Constitution of Bermuda as a whole, noting that the stated rights applied, *prima facie*, to 'every person in Bermuda'; and that, in contrast to Bermuda's immigration legislation, the Constitution made no reference to legitimacy or illegitimacy anywhere in its provisions. The Privy Council therefore held that the statutory presumption applicable to property, succession and citizen that a 'child' meant 'legitimate child' did *not* apply. The language of the Constitution recognised the unity of the family as a group with the result that the word 'child' should not be given a restrictive meaning.

3.11 The Privy Council have considered the proper approach to the construction of rights instruments in a number of subsequent cases. Although *Minister of Home Affairs v Fisher* has often been quoted with approval, analysis of the case law suggests that a number of different, overlapping, approaches have been taken. Three of these can be distinguished:

- a 'generous approach', involving the development of new principles of construction, different from those developed in relation to ordinary statutes;
- a 'purposive approach', in which the court seeks to discern the purpose of the right granted and to give effect to it;
- a 'realistic approach', in which ordinary principles of construction are applied but in a more 'flexible' manner with a view to achieving a 'realistic' construction of the right in question.

[29] This approach was pre-figured in *Hinds* v *R* [1977] AC 195, 211H.
[30] Ibid 328–9.

(b) The 'generous approach'

A number of cases have emphasised the need for the courts to develop new principles of interpretation when dealing with human rights instruments. Thus, in *Ong Ah Chuan v Public Prosecutor; Koh Chai Cheng v Public Prosecutor*[31] the Privy Council said that: **3.12**

> the way to interpret a constitution on the Westminster model is to treat it not as if it were an Act of Parliament but 'as *sui generis*, calling for principles of interpretation of its own, suitable to its character . . . without necessary acceptance of all the presumptions that are relevant to legislation of private law'.

The defendant claimed he had been wrongly convicted of trafficking in illegal drugs because a rebuttable presumption that possession constituted trafficking was unconstitutional. The issue that arose was the meaning of 'law' for the purposes of the constitutional protection of rights such as the right not to be deprived of life or liberty except in accordance with 'law', and the right to equality before 'the law'. The Public Prosecutor had argued that the constitutional definition of 'law' comprised any written law in force in Singapore, which implied that limitations on constitutional freedoms would be in conformity with the constitution if they were set out in an Act of Parliament, no matter how arbitrary or contrary to fundamental rules of natural justice the provisions of such Act might be. However, the Privy Council held that the 'law' in the relevant provisions referred to a whole 'system of law' that had incorporated the rules of natural justice of the common law and provided assurances that the fundamental freedoms of citizens would not be flouted. On the facts, the Privy Council concluded that no rule of natural justice had been violated and the statutory presumption was therefore constitutional.

In *Riley v A-G of Jamaica*[32] the majority of the Privy Council decided that 'death row' delays of over six years could afford no ground for holding that the execution was 'degrading and inhuman'. Lords Scarman and Brightman dissented from the 'austere legalism' of the majority, preferring the 'generous interpretation' advocated in *Fisher*. They took the view that prolonged and unnecessary delay may render it degrading and inhuman to execute the condemned man. Ten years later this approach was accepted by the Privy Council in the seminal 'death row' case of *Pratt v A-G for Jamaica*.[33] **3.13**

In *Huntley v A-G for Jamaica*[34] the Privy Council had to determine the effect of the Constitution of Jamaica and the common law requirements of fairness on the re-classification of the criminal offence of murder into the two offences of capital **3.14**

[31] [1981] AC 648.
[32] [1983] AC 719.
[33] [1994] 2 AC 1; *Fisher* was cited but was not mentioned in the Opinion of the Board.
[34] [1995] 2 AC 1.

and non-capital murder.[35] The appellant was a prisoner on death row who contested the reclassification of his crime as a capital murder, which precluded the commutation of his sentence to life imprisonment, on grounds that it constituted a violation of the prohibition on 'retrospective penalties' in the Constitution.[36] His argument was that the death sentence lapsed when the new legislation came into effect; and that the reclassification of his offence as capital murder involved him being found guilty of a criminal offence which at the time it took place did not constitute 'such an offence'. In seeking to apply the constitutional provisions of section 20 and the common law requirements of fairness to the decision of the Court of Appeal, the Privy Council deprecated the 'technical approach' of the appellant as one which focused on form rather than on substance, and affirmed the 'generous approach'. It was held that this approach meant that the court should not be 'over-concerned with technicalities' but would look at the 'substance and reality' of what was involved. Applying that approach, the Privy Council decided on the facts to dismiss the appeal.[37]

3.14A There are some recent *dicta* supporting the application of the 'generous approach' to the Human Rights Act. Thus, in *R v DPP, ex p Kebilene* [37a] Lord Hope dealt with the interpretation of the Act in the following terms:

> In *Attorney-General of Hong Kong v Lee Kwong-kut* [37b] Lord Woolf referred to the generous approach to the interpretation of constitutions and bills of rights indicated in previous decisions of the Board which he said were equally applicable to the Hong Kong Bill of Rights Ordinance 1991. He mentioned Lord Wilberforce's observation in *Minister of Home Affairs v Fisher*[37c] that instruments of this nature call for a generous interpretation suitable to give individuals the full measure of the fundamental rights and freedoms referred to, and Lord Diplock's comments in *A-G of the Gambia v Momodou Jobe*[37d] that a generous and purposive construction is to be given to that part of a constitution which protects and entrenches fundamental rights and freedoms to which all persons in the state are to be entitled. The same approach will now have to be applied in this country when issues are raised under the

[35] The (Jamaican) Offences Against the Person (Amendment) Act 1992 repealed s 2 of the Offences Against the Person Act 1864 and substituted a new s 2 that established two separate categories of murder: capital murder and non-capital murder. The new s 3 provided that capital murder should result in a death sentence and that the sentence for non-capital murder was to be life imprisonment. The process of reclassification included a notice requirement and a right of review of the decision.

[36] s 20 of the Jamaican Constitution sets out the rights of a person charged with an offence, and in particular s 20(7) provides that: 'No person shall be held to be guilty of a criminal offence on account of any act or omission which did not, at the time it took place, constitute such an offence, and no penalty shall be imposed for any criminal offence which is severer in degree or description than the maximum penalty which might have been imposed for that offence at the time when it was committed'; the equivalent provision in the Convention is Art 7, see para 11.257ff below.

[37] At 14D–E.

[37a] [1999] 3 WLR 972, 988.

[37b] [1993] AC 951, 966.

[37c] [1980] AC 319, 328.

[37d] [1984] AC 689, 700.

Act of 1998 about the compatibility of domestic legislation and of the acts of public authorities with the fundamental rights and freedoms which are enshrined in the Convention.

(c) The 'broad and purposive approach'

3.15 In other cases the Privy Council has used different language to describe the approach to be taken in the construction of constitutional instruments. As Lord Diplock said in *A-G of The Gambia v Momodou Jobe*:[38]

> a constitution, and in particular that part of it which protects and entrenches fundamental rights and freedoms to which all persons in the state are to be entitled, is to be given a generous and purposive construction.[39]

This echoed the language of earlier Privy Council case law.[40]

3.16 In *A-G of Trinidad and Tobago v Whiteman*[41] the Privy Council described the correct approach as a 'broad and purposive' one, stating that:

> the language of a Constitution falls to be construed, not in a narrow and legalistic way, but broadly and purposively, so as to give effect to its spirit, and this is particularly true of those provisions which are concerned with the protection of human rights.

The issue in that case was the constitutional requirement that Parliament must not deprive a person of the right to 'procedural provisions' for the purpose of giving effect and protection to the other stated rights and freedoms. It was argued for the Attorney-General that mere procedures could not be the subject of constitutional rights and that therefore the term 'provisions' must refer to some specific rules of procedure, such as rules of court. Nevertheless, it was held that there were no grounds for giving a restrictive meaning to the words 'procedural provisions'. As a result, the Judges' Rules, which included the right of a person in custody to be informed orally of the rights and facilities available to him, and to communicate with a legal adviser, were such 'procedural provisions'.

(d) The 'realistic approach'

3.17 In a number of cases the Privy Council have approached issues of construction on the basis of what might be called a 'realistic approach'. This involves treating a constitution as being like an ordinary statute whose language is expressed in broad terms: it needs to be 'construed with less rigidity and more generosity than other Acts'.[42] This does not involve any special, *sui generis*, principles of interpretation.

[38] n 37d above.

[39] See also, *Société United Docks v Government of Mauritius* [1985] 1 AC 585; and dissenting judges in *Robinson v The Queen* [1985] 1 AC 956.

[40] See eg *Edwards v A-G of Canada* [1930] AC 124: 'a large and liberal interpretation'.

[41] [1991] 2 AC 240, 247.

[42] *A-G of St Christopher, Nevis and Anguilla v Reynolds* [1980] AC 637.

Such an approach goes hand in hand with a 'realistic approach' to construction: when construing rights instruments the court must take into account other policy objectives of the legislature as expressed by the statutes under challenge. This approach can be illustrated by three Privy Council cases.

3.18 In *Robinson v The Queen*[42a] the question was whether the trial judge had 'permitted' the defendant a legal representative of his own choice, when he refused to grant an adjournment to enable the defendant to instruct counsel in place of those who had withdrawn from the case. The majority[43] found no breach of the right, in light of the fact that the judge had invited counsel to act on legal aid before proceeding with the trial,[44] and of the repeated adjournments in the past. On that basis, the refusal to adjourn did not constitute a failure to meet the constitutional obligation. The minority[45] construed the relevant constitutional provisions 'generously' and held that the word 'permit' should include a negative obligation on the part of the judge not to prevent the accused from choosing to be defended by a legal representative.[46]

3.19 In *A-G of Hong Kong v Lee Kwong-kut*[47] the Privy Council considered the Hong Kong Bill of Rights Ordinance 1991. The Hong Kong courts had held that two statutory provisions placing burdens of proof on criminal defendants were inconsistent with the presumption of innocence in the Hong Kong Bill of Rights. In allowing the appeal of the Attorney-General in one case, Lord Woolf, made a number of general observations about the construction of human rights instruments. He expressed concern about the need to balance the rights of the individual and society and said that:

> While the Hong Kong judiciary should be zealous in upholding an individual's rights under the Hong Kong Bill, it is also necessary to ensure that disputes as to the effect of the Bill are not allowed to get out of hand. The issues involving the Hong Kong Bill should be approached with realism and good sense and kept in proportion. If this is not done the Bill will become a source of injustice rather than justice and it will be debased in the eyes of the public. In order to maintain the balance between the individual and the society as a whole, rigid and inflexible standards should not be imposed on the legislature's attempts to resolve the difficult and intransigent problems with which society is faced when seeking to deal with serious crime. It must be remembered that questions of policy remain primarily the responsibility of the legislature.[48]

3.20 In the case of *Matadeen v Pointu*[49] the Privy Council had to consider the effect of

---

[42a] n 39, above.
[43] Lords Keith, Roskill and Templeman.
[44] The invitation was refused.
[45] Lords Scarman and Edmund-Davies.
[46] See also, *Dunkley v R* [1995] 1 AC 419, in which *Robinson* was approved.
[47] [1993] AC 951.
[48] Ibid 975B–C.
[49] [1998] 3 WLR 18.

anti-discrimination provisions in the Constitution of Mauritius. The Supreme Court had held that human rights were to be regarded as a global and universal concept and the principle of 'equal protection of the law' was implicit in the Constitution. This led them to hold that certain educational provisions did not meet the test of 'equal treatment' for all those similarly situated[50] and the Privy Council allowed the defendants' appeal. In the course of his opinion Lord Hoffman[51] took the opportunity to make a statement of general principles about the proper approach towards construing constitutional instruments:

> constitutions are not to be construed as commercial documents. This is because every utterance must be construed in its proper context, taking into account the historical background and purpose for which the utterance was made. The context and purpose of a commercial contract is very different from that of a constitution. The background of a constitution is an attempt at a particular moment in history, to lay down an enduring scheme of government in accordance with certain moral and political values. Interpretation must take these purposes into account. They may expressly state moral and political principles to which judges are required to give effect in accordance with their own conscientiously held views of what such principles entail. It is however a mistake to suppose that these considerations release judges from the task of interpreting the statutory language and enable them to give free reign to whatever they consider should have been the moral and political views of the framers of the constitution. What the interpretation of commercial documents and constitutions have in common is in each case the court is concerned with the meaning of the language which has been used. As Kentridge AJ said in giving the judgment of the South African Constitutional Court in *State v Zuma*:[52] 'if the language used by the lawgiver is ignored in favour of a general resort to values, the result is not interpretation but divination'.

The Privy Council went on to construe the Constitution of Mauritius narrowly, finding that it contained no generally justiciable principle of equal protection.

(e) Comparing the approaches

It is submitted that the 'realistic approach' favoured in some of the cases does not do justice to the unique status of constitutional instruments. In construing such an instrument, the court must go beyond the ordinary 'interpretative' process of discerning the 'true meaning' of a document towards one which seeks to give 'the fullest weight and effect' to the rights which are guaranteed consistent with the language used.[53] **3.21**

The 'generous approach' and the 'broad and purposive approach' more accurately reflect the unique nature of this process of construction. The two approaches are **3.22**

[50] See the note of the case: *Pointu v Minister of Education* [1996] 1 CHRD 39.

[51] Ibid 25.

[52] 1995 4 BCLR 401, 142.

[53] Cf Lord Steyn's discussion in his dissenting opinion in *Fisher v Minister of Public Safety and Immigration* [1998] AC 673.

often used interchangeably or cumulatively to convey that the court will not be restricted in its treatment of constitutions to the conventional approach to statutory construction. However, the view that the terms are synonymous has been powerfully criticised by Hogg. Commenting on the approach taken by the Canadian Supreme Court he says:

> The Court has generally assumed that a 'purposive' approach and a 'generous' approach are one and the same thing—or at least are not inconsistent. . . . In the case of some rights that is correct: a purposive interpretation will yield a broad scope for the right. In the case of most rights, however, the widest possible reading of the right, which is the most generous interpretation, will 'overshoot' the purpose of the right, by including behaviour that is outside the purpose and unworthy of constitutional protection. The effect of a purposive approach is normally going to be to narrow the scope of the right. Generosity is a helpful idea as long as it is subordinate to purpose. Obviously, the Courts in interpreting the Charter should avoid narrow, legalistic interpretations that might be appropriate to a detailed statute. But if the goal of generosity is set free from the limiting framework of purpose, the results of a generous interpretation will normally be inconsistent with the purposive approach.[54]

3.23 It is submitted that under the Human Rights Act the court must first decide the purpose of the right being protected by a particular provision. This purpose is not ascertained by 'formal' interpretative techniques and the court should take a generous rather than a 'literal' approach. There are a number of matters which can be taken into account[55] when ascertaining the purpose of the right including:

- the nature of the right, and, in particular, whether it is qualified or unqualified;[56]
- the language of the instrument and the context in which the right is expressed;
- the case law interpreting the right in the context of the instrument under consideration and similar rights in other jurisdictions.

One of the important aspects of the purpose will be to ensure that the right is 'practical and effective'.[57] Once the 'purpose' has been ascertained, then the language of the instrument can be construed so as to give effect to it. Throughout this process, the courts will also bear in mind what Lord Irvine has recently described as their 'overarching goal':

> securing respect for individual's rights in a manner which is sensitive to the broader framework of the separation of powers.[58]

---

[54] P W Hogg, *Constitutional Law of Canada*, (4th edn, Carswell, 1997) 625–6; see also R Edwards, 'Generosity and the Human Rights Act: The Right Interpretation' [1999] PL 400.

[55] Cf P W Hogg (n 54 above) 625.

[56] See para 6.86ff below.

[57] See the Convention jurisprudence discussed at para 6.28ff below.

[58] See Lord Irvine LC, 'Activism and Restraint: Human Rights and the Interpretative Process' [1999] EHRLR 350.

(3) The effect of prior law and practice

Constitutional rights and freedoms have to be considered in the context of the pre-existing common law. In a number of cases, the Privy Council has looked to the prior law and practice in order to obtain assistance with the definition of acceptable limitations on the stated rights and freedoms. It was said in *Maharaj v A-G of Trinidad and Tobago (No 2)*[59] that the lack of all specificity in the descriptions of the rights and freedoms protected: 3.24

> may make it necessary sometimes to resort to an examination of the law as it was at the commencement of the Constitution in order to determine what limits upon freedoms that are expressed in absolute and unlimited terms were nevertheless intended to be preserved in the interests of the people as a whole and the orderly development of the nation; for the declaration that the rights and freedoms protected by that section already existed at that date may make the *existing law as it was then administered in practice* a relevant aid to the ascertainment of what kind of executive or judicial act was intended to be prohibited by the wide and vague words used in those paragraphs.

However, this will not be appropriate when the limitations are themselves particularised in the relevant constitutional provisions. The Privy Council in *Maharaj v A-G of Trinidad and Tobago (No 2)*[60] went on to say that:

> . . . this external aid to construction is neither necessary nor permissible where the treatment complained of is specifically described in the constitution as a particular example of treatment of an individual by the executive or judiciary which would infringe those rights.

Where the existing statutory or common law does not speak directly to the constitutional freedom in question, the court may also consider the existing legal practice in effect prior to the Constitution coming into force. Thus, in *Pratt v A-G for Jamaica*[61] the Privy Council assessed the constitutional provisions against the 'pre-existing common law practice' that execution followed as soon as was practicable after sentencing. It found that where the Constitution required that a death sentence be referred by the Attorney-General to the Privy Council, the reference and the consequent advice of the Privy Council were to be carried out as soon as practicable. This was a departure from *Riley v A-G for Jamaica*[62] which had, when considering whether a lengthy delay between death sentence and execution was inhuman and degrading, construed the death penalty for murder to be constitutional,[63] no matter how long the delay between the passing of the sentence 3.25

59 [1979] AC 385.

60 Ibid.

61 [1994] 2 AC 1.

62 [1983] AC 719.

63 s 17(2), following the prohibition of torture and inhuman or degrading punishment or other treatment in s 17(1) provides that: 'Nothing contained in or done under the authority of any law

and the execution. Disagreeing with the view in *Riley* that the legality of a delay in execution could never have been questioned before independence, the Privy Council was satisfied that an excessively delayed execution could have been stayed as an abuse of process: to carry out a sentence in those circumstances amounted to a breach of the prohibition on inhuman and degrading treatment.

3.26 In *Bell v DPP*[64] it was held that when determining whether the applicant had been afforded a fair hearing within a reasonable time by an independent and impartial court established by law, the practice and procedure of the courts established by law prior to the Constitution must be respected. In *Grant v DPP*[65] the applicants argued that as a result of an invalid indictment, their constitutional right to freedom from detention, except upon reasonable suspicion of having committed a criminal offence, had been violated; they claimed that it had been the 'invariable practice' of the Director of Public Prosecutions to prefer indictments only after a preliminary examination had been held, and that they had a constitutional right to the continuance of that practice in their case. The Privy Council found that the Criminal Justice Act clearly conferred upon the Director the right to prefer an indictment without the necessity for a preliminary examination of the accused before a magistrate. It distinguished the case of *Thornhill v A-G of Trinidad and Tobago*,[66] on the basis that the relevant right,[67] had not been regulated by statute prior to the Constitution coming into effect; but was enjoyed only as a matter of settled administrative practice. In contrast, the preferment of indictments in Jamaica was regulated by statute, which empowered the Director of Public Prosecutions to prefer an indictment without preliminary examination and he could not amend the statute by adopting a settled practice to the contrary.

(4) Taking account of jurisprudence from other jurisdictions

3.27 The Privy Council has consistently looked to the jurisprudence of other common law jurisdictions for guidance in the construction and application of human rights and fundamental freedoms. The case of *A-G of Hong Kong v Lee Kwong-kut*[68] illustrates the willingness of the Privy Council to weigh the approaches of various other jurisdictions and to improvise upon them as appropriate in the

shall be held to be inconsistent with or in contravention of this section to the extent that the law in question authorizes the infliction of any description of punishment which was lawful in Jamaica immediately before the appointed day.'

64 [1985] 1 AC 937; relying on *Abbott v A-G of Trinidad and Tobago* [1979] 1 WLR 1342.

65 [1982] AC 190.

66 [1981] AC 61.

67 The right to a reasonable opportunity to consult a lawyer.

68 [1993] AC 951.

situation before it. As this was the Privy Council's first opportunity to consider the Hong Kong Bill of Rights Ordinance, it considered earlier constitutional orders containing similar provisions, and referred to the decision of the Court of Appeal in relation to one of the defendants,[69] and the common law jurisprudence that the Appeal Court had sought to rely upon. Lord Woolf[70] expressed caution in relation to the use of decisions from other jurisdictions:

> Such decisions can give valuable guidance as to the proper approach to the interpretation of the Hong Kong Bill, particularly in relation to an article in the same or substantially the same terms as that contained in the equivalent provision of the Hong Kong Bill. However, it must not be forgotten that decisions in other jurisdictions are persuasive and not binding authority and that the situations in those jurisdictions may not necessarily be identical to that in Hong Kong.

In fact, Lord Woolf went on to analyse the approach of the Canadian courts, which the Hong Kong Court of Appeal had found of great assistance, at some length. Ultimately, the Privy Council found that although the Canadian jurisprudence might be helpful in difficult cases, the majority of Hong Kong cases could be decided without reference to the complex two-step process established by the Canadian courts, as necessitated by the limitation provision in the Charter.[70a]

Other cases have demonstrated a similar pattern in their consideration of the ju- **3.28**
risprudence of other jurisdictions. If the provisions are very similar or identical, the jurisprudence in relation to the comparable right or freedom is referred to and applied freely.[71] In relation to the Constitution of Singapore,[72] the Privy Council found that the decisions of the courts of India ought to be applied with caution, because provisions of the Indian Constitution differed considerably from those of Singapore; decisions out of the United States were said to be of little help in construing the provisions of the Constitution of Singapore or other modern Commonwealth constitutions which follow broadly the Westminster model.[73] American judgments are often cited though, as they were at length in *Francis v Chief of Police,*[74] for principles and policy considerations going to the issue at hand, but are unlikely to be of assistance in dealing with issues of construction.[75]

[69] *R v Sin Yau-ming* [1992] 1 HKCLR 127.

[70] Ibid 966.

[70a] The structure of the Canadian Charter of Rights is discussed at para 6.62ff below.

[71] For example, the relationship between the Constitutions of Trinidad and Tobago and Jamaica has been examined on several occasions: *Riley v A-G of Jamaica* [1983] AC 719.

[72] *Ong Ah Chuan v Public Prosecutor* [1981] AC 648.

[73] Ibid 669.

[74] *Francis v Chief of Police* [1973] AC 761, 770.

[75] See *Ong Ah Chuan v Public Prosecutor* [1981] AC 648, 669.

(5) Interpretation of rights instruments in other common law jurisdictions

3.29 The appropriate approach to the construction of rights instruments has been considered in the cases of many different common law jurisdictions. There has been a high degree of cross-fertilisation between them. The jurisprudence of the European Court on Human Rights has also been influential. Although the language varies among the many human rights instruments, there are clear patterns of similarity of drafting and these have been taken into account by the courts in the interpretation of particular provisions. Problems such as the 'balancing' of different rights, the construction of 'justifiable limitations' and the interpretation of provisions relating to the onus of proof in criminal proceedings have arisen in similar forms in many jurisdictions.

(a) Canada

3.30 The Canadian courts have adopted a 'flexible' and 'progressive' interpretation of the Charter of Rights.[76] It has been said on many occasions that the interpretation should be 'large and liberal' or 'generous'.[77] However, in recent years more emphasis has been given to the need for 'purposive construction'. In *R v Big M Drug Mart Ltd,*[78] it was said that:

> The meaning of a right or freedom guaranteed by the Charter was to be ascertained by an analysis of the purpose of such a guarantee; it was to be understood, in other words, in the light of the interests it was meant to protect. In my view this analysis is to be undertaken, and the purpose of the right or freedom in question is to be sought by reference to the character and larger objects of the Charter itself, to the language chosen to articulate the specific right or freedom, to the historical origins of the concept enshrined, and where applicable, to the meaning and purpose of the other specific rights and freedoms with which it is associated within the text of the Charter. The interpretation should be . . . a generous rather than legalistic one, aimed at fulfilling the purpose of a guarantee and the securing for individuals of the full benefit of the Charter's protection.

It has been pointed out, however, that an interpretation of guaranteed rights that is too broad can be counter-productive from the point of view of rights protection. This is due to the fact that, in order to counter balance rights which have been too broadly formulated, the Canadian courts feel bound to uphold the legislation by a broad interpretation of the 'limitation' clause in section 1 of the Char-

---

[76] See generally, P W Hogg, *Constitutional Law of Canada*, (4th edn, Carswell, 1996) s 33.7, 620–630; the Canadian Courts draw on international human rights case law, including that under the Convention, ibid, s 33.8, 631ff; see generally, W Schabas, *International Human Rights Law and the Canadian Charter* (Carswell, 1991).

[77] The classic statement being in *Edwards v A-G of Canada* [1930] AC 124, 136; *A-G of Quebec v Blaikie* [1979] 2 SCR 1016, 1029–1030; *Hunter v Southam* [1984] 2 SCR 145, 156.

[78] (1985) 18 DLR (4th) 321, 395–6.

ter.[79] It has been suggested that it is preferable to give a narrower, more 'purposive' interpretation of Charter rights and maintain strict standards of justification. This is because:

> . . . if the scope of the guaranteed rights is wide and the standard of justification is relaxed, a large number of Charter challenges will come before the courts and will fall to be balanced under s 1. Since s 1 requires that the policy of the legislation be balanced against the policy of the Charter, and since it is difficult to maintain meaningful standards to constrain the balancing process, judicial review will become even more unpredictable . . .[80]

(b) Hong Kong

The Bill of Rights Ordinance in Hong Kong incorporates the International Covenant on Civil and Political Rights into domestic law. The Court of Appeal in *Sin Yau-ming*[81] referred to the approach of the Privy Council to the construction of constitutions[82] and to the decisions of other common law jurisdictions, including the United States of America, Canada and the European Court of Human Rights. It was said that particular provisions must be interpreted: **3.31**

> in the light of the context of the Covenant and its aims and objects, with a bias towards the interests of the individual.[83]

However, the Hong Kong Courts have sometimes expressed concern about the wholesale importation of material from other jurisdictions, particularly from Canada.[84] As mentioned above, the decision of the Privy Council in *A-G of Hong Kong v Lee Kwong-kut*[85] demonstrated a more conservative approach to interpretation of the Bill of Rights Ordinance and a new willingness to put the 'interests of society' above those of the individual. More recently, it has been emphasised that a 'literal, technical, rigid or narrow approach' should not be adopted, but that the courts should 'give a generous interpretation to the . . . constitutional guarantees' in the Basic Law.[86]

---

[79] See P W Hogg, 'Interpreting the Charter of Rights: Generosity and Justification' (1990) 28 Osgoode Hall LJ 817.

[80] See P W Hogg, *Constitutional Law of Canada* (4th edn, Carswell, 1996) 624–5; what is being advocated is more 'definitional balancing' and less 'ad hoc balancing': see S Peck 'An Analytical Framework for the Application of the Charter' (1987) 25 Osgoode Hall LJ 1.

[81] *R v Sin Yau-ming* [1992] 1 HKCLR 127 (the decision in this case was 'intended to provide guidance to the Hong Kong courts as to the proper approach to the application of Art 11(1) of the Hong Kong Bill').

[82] *Minister of Home Affairs v Fisher* [1980] AC 319; *A-G of The Gambia v Momodou Jobe* [1984] AC 689.

[83] *R v Sin Yau-ming* [1992] 1 HKCLR 127, 145; *R v Fun Yan* [1992] 2 HKCLR 59, 68.

[84] See eg *Ex p Lee Kwok Hung* [1993] 2 HKLR 51, 56; and see *Kwan Kong Co Ltd v Town Planning Board* [1995] HKC Lexis 715, 31 Jul 1995: 'only in very exceptional circumstances, would the court be much assisted by looking at the foreign jurisprudence': this judgment contains an unorthodox full-scale critique of 'constitutional construction' of the Bill of Rights Ordinance.

[85] [1993] AC 951; see para 3.27 above.

[86] *Ng Ka Ling v Director of Immigration* [1999] 1 HKLRD 315, 340, *per* Li CJ.

(c) Ireland

3.32 The Irish courts have, since 1922, taken a series of different, often inconsistent, approaches to constitutional interpretation. The leading textbook identifies no less than five different approaches to constitutional interpretation: literal interpretation, the 'broad approach', the doctrine of harmonious interpretation, the historical approach and the natural law approach.[87] The 'broad approach' has been favoured in recent times. The broad approach is one which 'would look at the whole text of the Constitution and identify its purpose and objective in protecting human rights'.[88] This is allied to the attempt to achieve a 'harmonious interpretation'. This is an interpretation:

> which requires where possible the relevant constitutional provisions to be construed and applied so that each will be given due weight in the circumstances of the case.[89]

The Irish courts have acknowledged the existence of a hierarchy of constitutional rights which must be taken into account in interpreting the Constitution. Thus, in *The People v Shaw*[90] it was said:

> There is a hierarchy of constitutional rights, and when a conflict arises between them, that which ranks higher must prevail.

For example, it has been claimed that the right to life is clearly superior to the right to liberty, but the right to fair procedures is not.[91] However, the notion of hierarchy has caused difficulties, particularly in relation to the well known 'rape victim abortion' cases.[92]

(d) New Zealand

3.33 In New Zealand the courts have also drawn on the jurisprudence of other common law countries. The fact that the language of some provisions of the New Zealand Bill of Rights Act clearly reflects the Canadian Charter has led to particular importance being given to Canadian decisions. In general, the New Zealand courts have emphasised:

> the need for a generous interpretation of the Bill of Rights suitable to give individuals the full measure of the fundamental rights and freedoms it affirms.[93]

---

[87] J M Kelly, *The Irish Constitution*, (3rd edn, Butterworths, 1994) xcviii; the discussion which follows is drawn from this book.

[88] See *Murray v Ireland* [1985] IR 532.

[89] *Dillane v Ireland* [1980] IRLM 167; see Kelly, (n 87 above) ci–cix.

[90] [1982] IR 1: a case in which a murder suspect had been held in detention with the hope of saving the life of the suspected victim.

[91] *Murray v Ireland* [1985] IR 532.

[92] See *A-G v X* [1992] IR 1: right to life of foetus to take precedence over right to free movement of mother; see Kelly, (n 87 above) cvii.

[93] *Quilter v A-G of New Zealand* (1997) 3 BHRC 461, 502h–i, 512d; and see *Ministry of Transport v Noort* [1992] 3 NZLR 260, 268, 277.

The interpretation must be 'liberal and purposive' rather than being of a technical kind.[94]

(e) South Africa

The South African Constitutional Court has expressed caution about taking the 'generous approach' too far: **3.34**

> While we must always be conscious of the values underlying the Constitution, it is nonetheless our task to interpret a written instrument. I am well aware of the fallacy of supposing that general language must have a single 'objective' meaning. Nor is it easy to avoid the influence of one's personal intellectual and moral preconceptions. But it cannot be too strongly stressed that the Constitution does not mean whatever we might wish it to mean.
>
> We must heed Lord Wilberforce's reminder that even a constitution is a legal instrument, the language of which must be respected. If the language used by the lawgiver is ignored in favour of a general resort to 'values' the result is not interpretation but divination.[95]

However, the ordinary common law rules and presumptions should not be ignored when interpreting the Bill of Rights.[96]

C. The Provisions of the Human Rights Act

(1) Introduction

The fact that the Human Rights Act is not, in any way, 'entrenched' and the failure to provide for any 'direct' incorporation of the Convention might, on first impression, suggest that the Act involves an extremely weak form of 'indirect incorporation'. This impression is misleading because indirect incorporation is greatly strengthened by three provisions of the Act: **3.35**

- The requirement under section 6 that all public authorities should exercise their powers in a way which is compatible with the Convention[97] unless it could not have acted differently as a result of a statutory provision;[98]
- The enactment of a 'rule of construction' under section 3 that other legislation is to be interpreted 'so far as possible' so as to be compatible with the Convention[99] but not affecting the validity of primary legislation;

---

[94] *Quilter v A-G of New Zealand* (1997) 3 BHRC 461, 513h.

[95] *State v Zuma* 1995 (4) BCLR 401, paras 17 and 18, *per* Kentridge AJ; the last sentence was quoted with approval in *Matadeen v Pointu* [1998] 3 WLR 18, 26A.

[96] *Phato v Eastern Cape* 1994 (5) BCLR 99, 112; and see G Marcus, 'Interpreting the Chapter on Fundamental Rights' (1994) 10 SAJHR 92, 99.

[97] *Rights Brought Home: The Human Rights Bill* (1987) Cm 3782 para 2.2; Human Rights Act 1998, s 6, see para 5.120ff.

[98] s 6(2).

[99] *Rights Brought Home* para 2.7–2.8; Human Rights Act 1998, s 3(1) and (2); the principle of statutory construction is discussed at para 4.04ff below.

- The provision for making 'declarations of incompatibility' if legislation cannot be made compatible with the Convention and a 'fast track' amendment mechanism by way of 'remedial order'.[100]

3.36 The actions of a public authority which are incompatible with Convention rights will be unlawful unless one of the two 'exceptions' in section 6(2) are made out. The public authority must show either:

- that, as a result of a provision of primary legislation, it could not have acted differently;[100a] or
- that it was acting so as to 'give effect to or enforce' a statutory provision which cannot be read in a way which is compatible with Convention rights.[100b]

The occasions on which the first exception will apply are likely to be rare: most statutes confer powers on public authorities but do not compel them to act in a particular way. In relation to the second exception, it is suggested that the court must approach the matter in three stages:[100c]

- is the public authority acting to 'give effect to' or 'enforce' a particular statutory provision? if so,
- can this provision, on an ordinary construction, be given effect to or enforced in a manner which is compatible with Convention rights? if not,
- can the provision be read and given effect to in a manner which is compatible with Convention rights?

Only if the provision cannot be so read or given effect, will section 6(1) fall to be disapplied under section 6(2). It is likely that, bearing in mind the strong interpretative obligation in section 3,[100d] that the occasions on which the public authority will be entitled to rely on section 6(2) will be relatively rare.

(2) The Human Rights Act before commencement

3.37 The main provisions of the Human Rights Act are not in force at the time of writing. The Secretary of State is under no legally enforceable duty to bring these provisions into force. He must consider when it is appropriate for him to do so and does not enjoy an absolute and unfettered discretion not to do so.[101] Although section

[100] *Rights Brought Home* para 2.9; Declarations of incompatibility can be made under s 5 and are discussed at para 4.43ff below. The procedure used for remedial orders is discussed at para 4.57ff below.

[100a] Human Rights Act 1998, s 6(2)(a).

[100b] Ibid s 6(2)(b).

[100c] Cf *Brown v Procurator Fiscal*, unreported, 4 Feb 2000, High Court of Justiciary, *per* Lord Justice General.

[100d] See para 4.04 below.

[101] See *R v Secretary of State for the Home Department, ex p Fire Brigades Union* [1995] 2 AC 513, 550H, 570H, 575E.

22(4) of the Act introduces an element of retrospectivity on which victims of acts made unlawful by the Convention might rely when section 7(1)(b) is brought into force, this does not give rise to a legitimate expectation that public authorities will exercise their discretion in a way which is compatible with Convention rights. Such an expectation was contradicted by the express terms of the Act. If Parliament had intended the whole Act to take effect upon its receiving the Royal Assent, it would have so provided. [102]

Thus, until the main provisions of the Act are in force, the general principle is that a court should not consider their possible effect as they may never pass into law.[103] As a result, an application to stay an action pending the coming into force of the Human Rights Act (to allow the respondent to take Convention points) was refused.[104] **3.38**

Nevertheless, in *R v Director of Public Prosecutions, ex p Kebilene* the court was asked to consider whether prosecutions could proceed even though the Human Rights Act was not in force. The defendants alleged that the prosecution was based on a reverse onus provision contravening the presumption of innocence. The Divisional Court[105] granted a declaration that the decision of the Director of Public Prosecutions to continue prosecutions for offences under sections 16A and 16B of the Prevention of Terrorism (Temporary Provisions) Act 1989 was unlawful because these provisions were incompatible with Article 6(2) of the Convention. The Director had obtained advice as to compatibility before proceeding with the prosecution and it was, therefore, appropriate for the court to review the soundness of this advice.[106] It was held that the advice was unsound and, as a result, the Director's decision to proceed was unlawful. The Director then successfully appealed to the House of Lords[106a] which declined to decide the case on the broad basis taken by the Divisional Court, holding that the application should be refused because the challenges should be made at trial or on appeal rather than in collateral proceedings for judicial review. However, Lord Hope discussed a number of the issues addressed by the Divisional Court obiter[106b] and expressed the view that the question of whether a criminal offence is compatible with Convention rights should await decision after the criminal trial had concluded.[106c] **3.39**

[102] See *R v DPP, ex p Kebilene* [1999] 3 WLR 972.

[103] See *Willow Wren Canal Carrying Company Ltd v British Transport Commission* [1956] 1 WLR 213.

[104] *Hinchliffe v Secretary of State for Trade* [1999] BCC 226.

[105] n 102, above.

[106] Relying on the approach of the House of Lords in *R v Secretary of State for the Home Department, ex p Launder* [1997] 1 WLR 839, 867.

[106a] n 102, above.

[106b] Lord Hope examined at length the proper approach to be taken when construing a statutory provision so as to read it compatibly with Convention rights: see para 4.04ff below.

[106c] *R v DPP, ex p Kebilene*, n 102 above, at 1000.

3.40 Even before the Act comes into force judges can take the Convention into account in exercising discretion in both civil and criminal cases[107] and this has become a much more important factor because the Act will soon be in force. Thus, it has recently been taken into account in deciding whether to exercise the power to strike out a Statement of Case in civil proceedings. A case in which the Human Rights Act might alter the result will not be 'plain and obvious' for the purposes of striking out.[108] The Convention has been extensively considered in criminal cases in relation to the exercise of judicial discretion.[109]

3.41 Furthermore, the fact that prior to the enactment of the Human Rights Act, the Convention was a source of 'public policy'[110] may affect the way in which the courts approach Convention issues between enactment and coming into force. The Act demonstrates Parliament's view that the Convention is a powerful source of policy and, it is submitted, Convention rights should be directly taken into account when policy issues are being considered.

(3) Synopsis of the Human Rights Act

3.42 The Human Rights Act can conveniently be divided in accordance with its nine sub-headings:

Introduction: The 'Convention rights' are defined in section 1[111] and section 2 deals with the interpretation of Convention rights.[112]

Legislation: One of the most important provisions of the Act is the 'interpretative obligation' in section 3. This places the courts under an obligation, 'so far as it possible to do so' to 'read and give effect' to legislation in a way which is compatible with the Convention rights.[113] Section 4 introduces a 'declaration of incompatibility' procedure under which the higher courts may declare that primary legislation is incompatible with the Convention.[114] Section 5 gives the Crown the right to intervene when declarations of incompatibility are being considered.[115]

---

[107] See para 2.22ff above.

[108] Cf *Barret v London Borough of Enfield*, [1999] 3 WLR 79, *per* Lord Browne-Wilkinson; see also *Re Swaptronics*, *The Times*, 17 Aug 1999 (refusing to hear contemnor).

[109] See eg *R v Gokal* [1997] 2 Cr App R 266 and *R v Thomas* [1998] Crim LR 887 (discretion to receive hearsay evidence); *R v Stratford Justices, ex p Imbert* (1999) 2 Cr App R 276 (fairness of trial and disclosure of evidence); *R v Richards*, 15 Dec 1998 (exclusion of public from a trial); *R v Bowden* [1999] 1 WLR 823 (right to silence and waiver of privilege; *R v Kirk* [1999] 4 All ER 698 (admission of confessions) see generally, para 11.69ff below.

[110] See para 2.25ff above.

[111] See para 3.43ff below; the Act is reproduced in full at App A below.

[112] See para 3.46ff below.

[113] See para 4.04ff below.

[114] See para 4.43ff below.

[115] See para 22.73ff below.

Public authorities: The central operative provision of the Act is in section 6 which makes it unlawful for public authorities to act in a way which is incompatible with a Convention right. This does not apply where the public authority 'could not have acted differently' as the result of a provision of primary legislation, or where the public authority is enacting to give effect to or enforce such a provision. Section 6 also provides a partial definition of 'public authority'.[116] Section 7 makes provision in relation to the bringing of proceedings against public authorities under the Act.[117] Section 8 deals with the remedies which can be made in relation to unlawful acts of public authorities.[118] Section 9 provides 'judicial acts' with some protection from proceedings under the Act.

Remedial action: Section 10 gives ministers the power to take 'remedial action', amending by order[119] legislation which has been found to be incompatible with Convention rights. Remedial orders involve, in effect, the amendment of secondary or primary legislation by secondary legislation.[120]

Other rights and freedoms: Section 11 contains a safeguard for existing rights.[121] Sections 12 and 13 make limited special provision in relation to 'freedom of expression' and 'freedom of thought, conscience and religion'.[122]

Derogations and reservations: Sections 14 to 17 preserve the United Kingdom derogation and reservation from the Convention.[123] Provision is made as to the period for which derogations and reservations are to have effect and for the periodic review of reservations.[124]

Judges of the European Court of Human Rights: Section 18 makes provision for the appointment of English judges to the European Court of Human Rights.

Parliamentary procedure: Section 19 places a duty on the Minister in charge of a Bill to make a statement that it is compatible with the Convention rights or a statement to the effect that, despite the absence of compatibility, the Government wishes the House to proceed.[125]

Supplemental: Section 20 makes provision for orders under the Act, section 21 is the interpretation section and section 22 deals with short title, commencement, application and extent.

[116] See para 5.03ff below.
[117] See para 22.50ff below.
[118] See para 21.01ff below.
[119] In accordance with Sch 2.
[120] See generally, para 4.57ff below.
[121] See para 3.57 below.
[122] See para 14.75ff below.
[123] The derogation from Art 5(3) in relation to the Prevention of Terrorism legislation is discussed at para 10.63 below and the reservation to the right to education under Art 2 of the First Protocol is discussed at para 19.70 below.
[124] The position concerning derogations is discussed at para 3.64ff below and for reservations at para 3.69ff below.
[125] See para 4.39ff below.

The issues arising in relation to legislation and public authorities are dealt with in the next two chapters. The impact of enacting each of the Convention rights is discussed in Part 3 of the book. Remedies and procedure are dealt with in Part 4. The remaining issues concerning the provisions of the Act are dealt with in the sections immediately below.

(4) **Section 1: The scope of the rights**

3.43 Section 1 of the Human Rights Act identifies the particular rights and freedoms which the Act has introduced into domestic law. Section 1(1) states that 'Convention rights' mean the rights and fundamental freedoms contained in Articles 2 to 12 and 14 of the Convention and Articles 1 to 3 of the First Protocol and Articles 1 and 2 of the Sixth Protocol. The Convention Articles which have been enacted are set out in Schedule 1 of the Act.[126] Section 1(2) requires that these Convention rights are to be read subject to Articles 16,[127] 17[128] and 18[129] of the Convention[130] and have effect subject to any designated derogation (under section 14[131] of the Human Rights Act) or reservation (under section 15[132] of the Human Rights Act). A significant omission from the Human Rights Act is that it does not enact the right to an effective remedy under Article 13[133] of the Convention on Human Rights.

3.44 The Secretary of State has the power[134] to amend section 1 or Schedule 1 of the Human Rights Act by an order[135] 'as he considers it appropriate' to reflect a protocol which the United Kingdom has ratified or which it has signed with a view to ratification.[136]

3.45 The following 'rights and fundamental freedoms' are encompassed by the Human Rights Act:

- the right to life (Article 2 of the Convention);[137]

[126] See s 1(3) of the Human Rights Act; the Act is reproduced in full at App A below.
[127] The restrictions in Art 16 on the activities of aliens are discussed at para 6.107ff below.
[128] The restriction in Art 17 on activities aimed at the destruction of Convention rights is discussed at para 6.111ff below.
[129] The prohibition in Art 18 on using restrictions in the Convention for an improper purpose are discussed at para 6.113ff below.
[130] See s 1(1) of the Human Rights Act.
[131] Ibid.
[132] Ibid.
[133] The principles that have been developed in the case law concerning Art 13 are discussed at para 21.156ff below.
[134] Under s 1(4) of the Human Rights Act.
[135] See s 20 of the Human Rights Act.
[136] See s 1(5) of the Human Rights Act; however, no amendment may be made which comes into force before the protocol concerned is in force in relation to the United Kingdom: see s 1(6).
[137] See Sch 1; and para 7.30ff below.

- the prohibition of torture (Article 3 of the Convention);[138]
- the prohibition of slavery and forced labour (Article 4 of the Convention);[139]
- the right to liberty and security (Article 5 of the Convention);[140]
- the right to a fair trial (Article 6 of the Convention);[141]
- no punishment without law (Article 7 of the Convention);[142]
- the right to respect for private and family life, the home and correspondence (Article 8 of the Convention);[143]
- the right to thought, conscience and religion (Article 9 of the Convention;[144]
- freedom of expression (Article 10 of the Convention);[145]
- freedom of assembly and association (Article 11 of the Convention);[146]
- the right to marry (Article 12 of the Convention);[147]
- the prohibition of discrimination (Article 14 of the Convention);[148]
- the protection of property (Article 1 of the First Protocol to the Convention);[149]
- the right to education (Article 2 of the First Protocol to the Convention);[150]
- the right to free elections (Article 3 of the First Protocol to the Convention);[151] and
- the abolition of the death penalty (Articles 1 and 2 of the Sixth Protocol).[152]

(5) Section 2: Taking account of Convention jurisprudence

(a) The approach to be taken

The approach to be taken towards the case law of the European Commission of Human Rights, the European Court of Human Rights or the decisions of the Committee of Ministers is set out in section 2. This provides that: **3.46**

> (1) A court or tribunal determining a question which has arisen under this Act in connection with a Convention right must take account of any—
> (a) judgment, decision, declaration or advisory opinion of the Court,
> (b) opinion of the Committee given in a report adopted under Article 31 of the Convention,

138 See Sch 1; and para 8.13ff below.
139 See Sch 1; and para 9.09ff below.
140 See Sch 1; and para 10.80ff below.
141 See Sch 1; and para 11.150ff below.
142 See Sch 1; and para 11.144ff below.
143 See Sch 1; the rights to private life, the home and correspondence are discussed at para 12.81ff below and the right to family life at para 13.70ff below.
144 See Sch 1; and para 14.36 below.
145 See Sch 1; and para 15.137ff below.
146 See Sch 1; and para 16.56ff below.
147 See Sch 1; and para 13.74ff below.
148 See Sch 1; and para 17.79ff below.
149 See Sch 1; and para 18.26ff below.
150 See Sch 1; and para 19.34ff below.
151 See Sch 1; and para 20.19ff below.
152 See para 7.31 below.

(c) decision of the Commission in connection with Article 26 or Article 27(2) of the Convention, or
(d) decision of the Committee of Ministers taken under Article 46 of the Convention,

whenever made or given, so far as, in the opinion of the court or tribunal, it is relevant to the proceedings in which that question has arisen.

(2) Evidence of any judgment, decision, declaration or opinion of which account may have to be taken into account under this section is to be given in proceedings before any court or tribunal in such a manner as may be provided by rules.[153]

3.47 It should be noted that the procedure for deciding applications under the European Convention radically altered on 1 November 1998 when Protocol 11 of the Convention was implemented.[154] The decisions and opinions that the court will examine under section 2(1) which were made before 1 November 1998 were made under a procedure which can be summarised as follows. When an application was submitted alleging violations of Convention rights, the European Commission of Human Rights would then decide whether or not the complaint was admissible. If the Commission concluded that the complaint was admissible, the parties could reach a friendly settlement. Where no friendly settlement took place and the complaint had not been struck out for any other reason (such as where the parties had reached a private agreement or where the applicant was not willing to pursue his complaint), the Commission prepared an opinion on the merits under Article 31.[154a] The final decision about the application was made by the Court or the Committee of Ministers.[154b] If no friendly settlement was reached, either the Commission or the state could refer the complaint to the Committee of Ministers of the Council of Europe under Article 44 of the Convention. More frequently, however, the complaint was heard before the Court.

3.47A It is important to appreciate that different *weight* should be attached to the various types of decisions identified in section 2(1) and account taken of the date when they were decided. Differentiating between the various decision-makers is vital. The question of whether a complaint is admissible was considered by the Commission until its abolition and thereafter by committees or chambers of the new Court. Admissibility decisions[154c] are often summary in form and frequently

[153] That is, rules of court made for the purpose of s 2, see s 2(3), and App C in Vol 2.

[154] In particular, Protocol 11 abolished the role of the European Commission of Human Rights; the new procedure for making complaints to Strasbourg is discussed at para 23.32ff below.

[154a] Under the new procedure there is only one decision on the merits of an application by a chamber of the Court: see para 23.66 below. However, a case may now be referred to a Grand Chamber if a chamber relinquishes it or if a party under Art 43 requests that the case is referred to the Grand Chamber: see para 23.69ff below.

[154b] Under the new procedure the jurisdiction of the Committee of Ministers is confined by Art 46 to supervising the execution of the Court's judgments.

[154c] See generally, para 23.32 below.

in standard terms. They are unlikely to be of significant jurisprudential value to the English courts. Once a complaint is ruled admissible, the Commission ascertained the facts and gave an opinion on the merits of the application. The opinion of the Commission was reached after submissions both by the applicant and the respondent government; it was not uncommon for the Commission's opinions to differ from the ultimate conclusions of the Court and it will be open to an English court to prefer its reasoning to that of the Court. However, judgments of the Court[154d] are likely to be treated as authorities which have the greatest weight, although judgments of the plenary[154e] or Grand Chamber[154f] may take precedence over those of a chamber.[154g] By comparison, decisions of the Committee of Ministers[154h] are unlikely to be persuasive since the applicant has no right to address the Committee, is not aware of the any communications or submissions of the respondent government and the Committee itself does not give reasons for its decisions. Similarly, the reference to advisory opinions of the Court is not of the first importance as the Court has never given an advisory opinion. Furthermore, it is often important to examine the date a decision was made because of the principle that the Convention is a living instrument.[154i] The Court and Commission have therefore attached greater weight to more recent authorities when deciding cases before them; and it is submitted that a similar approach should be taken in the Human Rights Act.

(b) The construction of section 2

Section 2(1) states that a court or tribunal 'must take account' of the various decisions made by the European Commission and Court of Human Rights. According to Government spokesmen, there were three reasons for drafting section 2 in terms of 'taking account' of Convention jurisprudence (rather than being 'bound' by it): **3.48**

- that Convention law has no strict rule of precedence;[154j]
- that the only instance where the United Kingdom is strictly bound by the Court is where the application in question came from the United Kingdom; and
- that it was important for the English courts to have scope to develop their own human rights law.[155]

This approach can be contrasted with that under the European Communities Act 1972, section 3(1) which states:

[154d] See para 23.66ff below.
[154e] See para 23.13 below.
[154f] See para 23.14 below.
[154g] See para 23.16 below.
[154h] See para 23.20 below.
[154i] See para 6.23ff below.
[154j] See D Feldman, 'Precedent and the European Court of Human Rights' in Law Commission, *Bail and the Human Rights Act* Consultation Paper No 157, (The Stationery Office, 1999), App C, 112–124; and see para 23.09A below.
[155] See Lord Irvine LC, *Hansard* HL col 1270 (19 Jan 1988).

> For the purpose of all legal proceedings any question as to the effect of any of the Treaties or as to the validity, meaning or effect of any Community instrument, shall be treated as a question of law (and, if not referred to the European Court, be treated for determination as such in accordance with the principles laid down by and by any relevant decision [of the European Court of Justice or any court attached thereto]).

Consequently, the case law of the European Court of Justice is *binding* on United Kingdom courts and tribunals. Preliminary rulings made by the European Court of Justice under Article 234 of the Treaty of European Union are binding not only on the court or tribunal which makes the reference[156] but on all the courts and tribunals of Member States before which the point arises.

3.49 Nevertheless, section 2(1) of the Human Rights Act creates a kind of duty in relation to Convention decisions: since a court or tribunal *must take account of* decisions made by the Commission or the Court. However, some may seek to argue that section 2(1) imposes a more onerous obligation, that it requires a court or tribunal to give particular *weight* to Convention decisions. It is therefore helpful to compare the language of section 2 with that used in other statutory contexts where it has been held that discretion must be exercised in accordance with particular guidelines. For example, in the community care field, section 7(1) of the Local Authority Social Services Act 1970 states local authorities 'shall in the exercise . . . functions . . . act under the general guidance of the Secretary of State'. In *R v Islington LBC, ex p Rixon*[157] Sedley J took the view that:

> Parliament, in enacting section 7(1), did not intend local authorities to whom ministerial guidance has been given to be free, having considered it, to take it or leave it. Such a construction would put this kind of statutory guidance on a par with many forms of non statutory guidance issued by departments of state. While guidance and directions are semantically and legally different things, and while 'guidance does not compel a particular decision' (*Laker Airways Ltd v Department of Trade)*[158] especially when prefaced by the word 'general', in my view Parliament by s 7(1), has required local authorities to follow the path charted by the Secretary of State's guidance, with liberty to deviate from it where the local authority judges, on admissible grounds, that there is a good reason to do so, but without freedom to take a substantially different course.

3.50 It is submitted that on a true construction section 2(1):

- imposes a *duty* on the court to take as a starting point relevant Convention case law and
- imposes a duty to *consider* the relevant case law for the purposes of making its adjudication.

156 *Wünsche Handelsgesellschaft v Germany* [1986] ECR 947.
157 (1996) 32 BMLR 136, 140; see also *R v Sutton LBC, ex p Tucker* [1996] COD 144.
158 [1977] QB 643, 714 *per* Roskill LJ.

However, the terms of section 2(1) do not provide any assistance on the extent to which the court should follow or depart from Convention case law. It is submitted that it will be open to the court to take account of other 'human rights' jurisprudence, for example, the case law that has developed in other jurisdictions (such as Canada, New Zealand, South Africa or elsewhere) when construing their human rights legislation. Furthermore, it may also be relevant to consider the terms of other international human rights instruments which the United Kingdom has ratified (and any jurisprudence that has evolved in consequence). This has been the approach of the Privy Council[158a] and is the approach of the English courts in other areas of law. The English courts have in recent years derived valuable assistance from examining the case law in other jurisdictions, particularly in human rights cases.[158b] It is submitted that the English courts will not be confined to considering that case law which the Court of Human Rights would have been likely to consider if it were dealing with the case:[158c] such an approach would not be consistent with the Government's stated intention of producing a 'creative dialogue' between the judges in the United Kingdom and the European Court of Human Rights.[158d]

(c) Proving a relevant Convention decision

Section 2(2) and (3) of the Human Rights Act provides for the rules of court or tribunal rules to prove the judgment, decision, declaration or opinion in question. In fact, many decisions made under the Convention are readily available.[159] Draft rules have been published under this section.[159a] These provide that, where a party intends to cite a Strasbourg authority at a hearing: **3.51**

- this should be cited from an authoritative and complete report;[159b]
- the party should give the court and any other party a list of authorities it intends to cite along with copies not more than seven days nor less than three days before the hearing.

[158a] See para 3.22 above.

[158b] See eg *Derbyshire County Council v Times Newspapers* [1993] AC 534; *Reynolds v Times Newspapers* [1999] 3 WLR 1010 and, in relation to the Human Rights Act, *R v DPP, ex p Kebilene* [1999] 3 WLR 972.

[158c] As suggested by Rt Hon Lord Justice Buxton, 'The Convention and the English Law of Evidence' in J Beatson, C Forsyth and I Hare, *The Human Rights Act and the Criminal Justice and Regulatory Process* (Hart Publishing, 1999) 54–55.

[158d] See *Rights Brought Home: The Human Rights Bill* (Cm 3782) para 1.18, App B in Vol 2.

[159] See Note on Materials in Vol 2.

[159a] The text of which is reproduced at App C in Vol 2.

[159b] The Official Reports in paper form or from the Courts Website (see Note on Materials in Vol 2), the EHRR, the BHRC and the full text reports from Lawtel, Eurolaw, JUSTIS, LEXIS or Westlaw.

(6) Sections 3 to 5 and 19: Legislation

3.52 Section 3(1) of the Human Rights Act provides that:

> So far as it is possible to do so, primary legislation and subordinate legislation must be read and given effect in a way which is compatible with Convention rights.

This introduces a new rule of construction, allowing 'strained constructions' in order to preserve compatibility with Convention rights.[160] The rule does not, however, affect the 'validity, continuing operation or enforcement' of incompatible legislation.[161] In the rare cases[162] in which legislation is found to be incompatible, the higher courts[163] may make a 'declaration of incompatibility'. Where a court is considering whether to make such a declaration, the Crown is entitled to notice and to be joined.[164]

(7) Sections 6 to 9: Public authorities

3.53 The central operative provision of the Human Rights Act is section 6(1) which provides that:

> It is unlawful for a public authority to act in a way which is incompatible with a Convention right.[165]

No exhaustive definition of 'public authority' is given but it includes 'standard authorities' such as government departments, local authorities and the police. It also includes 'a court or tribunal'[166] and any person 'certain of whose functions are of a public nature'.[167] The fact that the court is a public authority means that the Human Rights Act will have an impact on litigation between *private* individuals.[168]

3.54 A person who claims that a public authority has acted in a way which is unlawful under section 6, may only bring proceedings in the appropriate court or rely on the Convention rights in any legal proceedings if he is a 'victim' of the unlawful act.[169] The court has the power to grant such relief or remedy within its powers as it considers 'just and appropriate'.[170] An award of damages can only be made if the

[160] See para 4.04ff below.
[161] See s 3(2)(c).
[162] The rule of construction under the Human Rights Act is a strong one: see generally, para 4.27ff below.
[163] The Crown Court, county court and magistrates' court are not included, s 4(5); and see para 4.53ff below.
[164] s 5; see para 22.73ff below.
[165] See generally, para 5.01ff below.
[166] s 6(3)(a); for the potentially far reaching consequences of this inclusion, see para 5.38ff below.
[167] s 6(3)(b); see para 5.16ff below.
[168] See para 5.38ff below.
[169] s 7; see para 22.14ff below.
[170] s 8(1); see para 21.01ff below.

court is satisfied that this is necessary 'to afford just satisfaction to the person in whose favour it is made'.[171]

The Human Rights Act does not impose any *criminal* liability on those who breach the Act. Section 7(8) of the Act states that nothing in the Act creates a criminal offence; and Schedule 2, paragraph 4 states that no person shall be guilty of a criminal offence solely as the result of the retrospective effect of a remedial order.[172] **3.55**

(8) Section 10: Remedial action

If a court has made a declaration of incompatibility the Minister may, by order, make such amendments to the legislation as he considers necessary to remove the incompatibility.[173] The procedure is set out in Schedule 2 to the Act. **3.56**

(9) Sections 11 to 13: Other rights and proceedings

The Human Rights Act is designed to provide a *minimum* standard of human rights protection and will not affect any additional rights an individual might have. Section 11 of the Act states: **3.57**

> A person's reliance on a Convention right does not restrict—
> (a) any other right or freedom conferred on him or by him or under the law having effect in any part of the United Kingdom; or
> (b) his right to make any claim or bring any proceedings which he could make or bring apart from section 7 to 9.

Lord Irvine, LC, described the purpose of the section:

> convention rights are, as it were, a floor of rights: and if there are different or superior rights or freedoms conferred by or under any law having effect in the United Kingdom, this is a Bill which only gives and does not take away.

The Act will therefore not affect an individual's fundamental rights at common law[174] or any rights he might have under European Union law.

Section 12 makes special provision in relation to freedom of expression. It was introduced following concerns expressed by the media as to the impact of the privacy rights in Article 8 on press freedom and was designed to: **3.58**

---

171 The power of the court under s 8 of the Act to award compensation is discussed at para 21.10ff.

172 The fast track procedure for amending legislation following a declaration of incompatibility under s 4 is discussed at para 4.57ff below.

173 s 10; see para 4.57ff below.

174 See para 1.24ff above.

> enhance press freedom in a wider way than would arise simply from the incorporation of the Convention.[175]

Its provisions are considered in detail in the context of freedom of expression.[176]

3.59 The effect of the Human Rights Act on religious activities was the subject of vigorous debate when the Bill was considered in Parliament. Indeed, section 2 of the Human Rights Act was significantly amended by the House of Lords to permit a statutory defence where a person was acting in pursuance of a manifestation of religious belief. As a result section 13 was enacted.[177] The section provides:

> (1) If a court's determination of any question arising under this Act might affect the exercise by a religious organisation (itself or its members collectively) of the Convention right to freedom of thought, conscience and religion, it must have particular regard to the importance of that right.
> (2) In this section, 'court' includes a tribunal.

3.60 However, despite the controversies over religious bodies during the passage of the Act, it is very doubtful that the Human Rights Act will have the impact that many religious groups feared. It seems that the decisions of religious leaders are not themselves justiciable.[178] Even though religious bodies such as church schools or religious charities would be public authorities, these bodies would be entitled to justify the activities by relying on the Convention right entitling them to freedom of religion.[179]

(10) Sections 14 to 17: Derogations and reservations

3.61 Section 1(2) of the Human Rights Act states that Convention rights[180] take effect subject to any designated derogation or reservation. Section 14 of the Act defines the power to designate derogations and section 15 of the Act defines the power to designate reservations.

3.62 Under Article 15[181] of the Convention the United Kingdom has the right to derogate from its obligations in exceptional and prescribed circumstances. Section 14

---

[175] See the statement of the Home Secretary on its introduction: *Hansard*, HC col 535 (2 Jul 1998).

[176] See para 15.237ff below.

[177] See the statement of the Home Secretary on its introduction: *Hansard*, HC col 1020 (20 May 1998) and see, generally, P Cumper 'The Protection of Religious Rights under section 13 of the Human Rights Act 1998' [2000] PL 254.

[178] See eg *R v Chief Rabbi of the United Hebrew Congregation of Great Britain and the Commonwealth, ex p Wachman* [1992] 1 WLR 1036; *R v Inman, ex p Sulamman Ali* [1994] COD 142; *ex p Williamson, The Times*, 9 Mar 1994; *R v Ecclesiastical Committee of Both Houses of Parliament, ex p Church Society* (1994) 6 Admin LR 670, 672; *Williamson v Archbishop of Canterbury, The Times*, 25 Nov1994.

[179] Art 9: see para 14.36ff below.

[180] See para 3.43 above.

[181] For a fuller discussion, see para 6.92ff.

of the Human Rights Act preserves this right of derogation in domestic law to ensure consistency with the United Kingdom's derogations under international law.

Section 14(1)(a) expressly maintains the right to derogate from Article 5(3) in relation to the Prevention of Terrorism legislation.[182] However, the Government indicated in the White Paper introducing the Human Rights Act,[183] that it was considering the enactment of primary legislation which might remove the need for this derogation. In any event, section 16(1) of the Human Rights Act states that the derogation will cease after five years of the Human Rights Act being in force unless both Houses of Parliament approve a statutory instrument which extends the notice of derogation.[184] **3.63**

Section 14(1)(b) of the Human Rights Act enables the Secretary of State to designate a new derogation by making an order; and provides that these further derogations will cease within five years of being designated unless both Houses of Parliament approve a statutory instrument which extends the notice of derogation.[185] **3.64**

The powers under section 14 enable: **3.65**

- a designated derogation to cease where it is amended or replaced;[186]
- the Secretary of State to exercise a fresh designation order in respect of the Article concerned;[187]
- the Secretary of State to make by order any amendments to the derogations set out in the Act[188] as he considers appropriate to reflect any designation order and the effect of the amendment or replacement of such an order.[189]

Under Article 57[190] of the Convention the United Kingdom has the right in prescribed circumstances to enter a reservation in relation to its Convention obligations. Section 15 of the Act ensures that these reservations apply to domestic law to ensure consistency with the United Kingdom's reservations under international law. **3.66**

At present the United Kingdom has entered one reservation to the Convention. The right to education under Article 2 of the First Protocol[191] ensures that: **3.67**

[182] See s 14(1)(a); s 14(2) and Pt 1 Sch 3 of the Human Rights Act.
[183] See *Rights Brought Home: The Human Rights Bill* (1997) Cm 3782 para 4.3.
[184] See s 20 of the Human Rights Act.
[185] See ss 16 and 20 of the Human Rights Act; an order for a new derogation ceases to have effect at the end of the 40-day period for consideration under s 16(3) unless a resolution is passed by both Houses of Parliament approving the order.
[186] s 14(3) of the Human Rights Act.
[187] s 14(4) of the Human Rights Act; a fresh order would need to be made under s 14(1)(b).
[188] In Pt I of Sch 3.
[189] s 14(5) of the Human Rights Act.
[190] For a fuller discussion, see para 6.94ff below.
[191] See para 19.34ff below.

> No person shall be denied the right to education. In the exercise of any functions which it assumes in relation to education and to teaching, the State shall respect the right of parents to ensure such education and teaching in conformity with their own religion and philosophical convictions.

Article 2 of the First Protocol therefore conflicts with a fundamental principle of education law (now contained in section 9 of the Education Act 1996)[192] which requires:

> that pupils are to be educated in accordance with the wishes of their parents so far as that is compatible with the provision of efficient instruction and training and the avoidance of unreasonable public expenditure.

3.68 Section 15(1) of the Human Rights Act expressly maintains the reservation in relation to Article 2 of the First Protocol. Section 15(2) preserves the power to create further reservations from the Convention by order which then take effect in domestic law.

3.69 The powers under section 15 enable:

- a designated reservation to cease where it is amended or replaced;[193]
- the Secretary of State to exercise a fresh designation order in respect of the Article concerned;[194]
- the Secretary of State to make by order any amendments to the reservations to set out in the Act[195] as he considers appropriate to reflect any designation order and the effect of the amendment or replacement of such an order.[196]

3.70 Section 16 of the Act reflects the temporary and exceptional nature of derogation orders by ensuring that they cease to have effect under the Act unless extended by Parliament. The current derogation in relation to Article 5(3) will cease five years after the Human Rights Act comes into effect;[197] any future derogation order will also cease after five years.[198] However, before the five year period expires, the Secretary of State has the power to extend the derogation.[199]

3.71 Section 17 provides a similar procedure in relation to reservations. Reservations cease to have effect under the Act unless extended by Parliament. The appropriate Minister[200] is required to review the current reservation to the right to education

---

[192] Originally enacted in the Education Act 1944.
[193] s 15(3) of the Human Rights Act.
[194] s 15(4) of the Human Rights Act; a fresh order would need to be made under s 15(1)(b).
[195] In Pt II of Sch 3.
[196] s 15(5) of the Human Rights Act.
[197] s 16(1)(a) of the Human Rights Act.
[198] s 16(1)(b) of the Human Rights Act.
[199] s 16(2) of the Human Rights Act; he may exercise the power by a statutory instrument under s 20(1) which is subject to the affirmative resolution procedure.
[200] As defined by s 21(1) of the Human Rights Act.

within five years of the Act coming into force.[201] The appropriate Minister is also obliged to review any future designated reservation within five years of it coming into force.[202]

(11) Sections 20 to 22: Supplemental matters

Section 20 confers powers on Ministers to make orders under the Human Rights Act. As Ministers are 'public authorities', it follows from section 6 that it will be unlawful to exercise such powers in a way which is incompatible with Convention rights. **3.72**

Section 21 deals with interpretation. It is expressly provided that Acts of the Scottish Parliament[203] and the Northern Ireland Assembly[204] and Orders in Council other than those made under the Royal Prerogative[205] are subordinate legislation. Measures made by the National Assembly of Wales will also be subordinate legislation. They will, therefore, be of no effect if incompatible with the Convention. This is consistent with the primary legislation which provides that the National Assembly of Wales[206] and the Scottish Parliament[207] have no power to make confirm or approve any subordinate legislation incompatible with any Convention right. No similar express provision is made in relation to the powers of the Northern Ireland Assembly[208] but the Northern Ireland Act 1998 provides a number of ways in which the compatibility of Assembly legislation with Convention rights can be checked.[209] **3.73**

Section 22(2) of the Human Rights Act states that three specific provisions came into force when the Act received its royal assent on 9 November 1998: the power to make appointments to the European Court of Human Rights under section 18, the power to make orders under section 20 of the Act and the replacement of the death penalty.[210] In every other respect the Human Rights Act was to be brought into force by statutory instrument by the Home Secretary.[211] Section 19[212] which **3.74**

---

[201] s 17(1)(a) of the Human Rights Act; if the designated reservation is still in force, he is required under s 17(1)(b) to review it within five years of the last report before Parliament.

[202] s 17(2)(a) of the Human Rights Act; if the designated reservation is still in force, he is required under s 17(2)(b) to review it within five years of the last report before Parliament.

[203] s 21(1)(b).

[204] s 21(1)(e).

[205] And under the Northern Ireland Constitution Act 1973, s 38(1)(a) or the corresponding provision of the Northern Ireland Act 1998 or orders amending primary legislation.

[206] Government of Wales Act 1998, s 107(1).

[207] Scotland Act 1998, s 29(2)(b).

[208] The Act extends to Northern Ireland, s 22(6).

[209] See Lord Lester and D Pannick, *Human Rights Law and Practice* (Butterworths, 1999) para 6.22ff.

[210] s 22(5) of the Human Rights Act.

[211] s 20(1), (2), and (3) of the Human Rights Act.

[212] See para 4.39ff below.

allows a minister to make a statement of compatibility[213] in relation to new legislation was brought into force on 24 November 1998;[214] and the power to make provision for pensions for a judge appointed to the European Court of Human Rights was brought into force on 7 December 1998.[215] The Act will be brought into force in its entirety on 2 October 2000. However, in Scotland and Wales the Act was implemented on a limited basis on 1 July 1999. Under the Scotland Act 1998 legislation passed by the Scottish Parliament is outside its legislative competence if it is incompatible with Convention rights.[215a] Furthermore, a member of the Scottish executive has no power to make any subordinate legislation or to do any act which is incompatible with Convention rights.[215b] Until the Human Rights Act comes into force, these provisions have effect in the same way as they will once the Human Rights Act is fully in force.[215c] This means that, in practice, the Act has been in full force in Scotland since 1 July 1999 in relation to devolved matters. The Welsh Assembly has no equivalent legislative powers but it has no power to make, confirm or approve any subordinate legislation or do any act where the subordinate legislation or act is incompatible with Convention rights.[215d]

3.75 In general, the Act applies to any acts[216] committed after the relevant provisions of the legislation have come into force. However, section 22(4) has introduced an element of *retrospectivity* and came into force on 9 November 1998. Section 22(4) provides:

> Paragraph (b) of subsection (1) of section 7 applies to proceedings brought by or at the instigation of a public authority whenever the act in question took place; but otherwise that subsection shall not apply to an act taking place before the coming into force of that section.

Once the right to rely on Convention rights in proceedings[217] comes into force, a defendant can rely on a Convention right[218] even though the act in question took place *before* the Act itself came into force. However, the effect of section 22(4) is obscure.[218a] Until the Act comes into force, it is *not* unlawful for a public authority to act in a way which is incompatible with a Convention right under section 6(1). As a result any failure to comply with section 6(1) at that point in time is not

[213] See para 4.43ff below.
[214] The Human Rights Act 1998 (Commencement) Order 1998, SI 1998/2882.
[215] The Judicial Pensions (European Court of Human Rights) Order 1998, SI 1998/2768.
[215a] Scotland Act 1998, s 29(1), (2)(d) and s 126(1).
[215b] Ibid s 57(2).
[215c] Ibid s 129(2).
[215d] Government of Wales Act 1998, s 107(1).
[216] See para 5.120ff below.
[217] Under s 7(1)(b) of the Human Rights Act; see para 22.89ff below.
[218] Ibid.
[218a] See the analysis of Lord Hobhouse in *R v DPP, ex p Kebilene* [1999] 3 WLR 972, 1008.

unlawful under section 7(1)(b). Nevertheless, the government appears to take the view that section 22(4), by necessary implication, ensures that after 2 October 2000 section 6(1) is treated as having been in force before commencement.[219]

Legal proceedings are defined for the purposes of section 22(4) to include an appeal against the decision of a court or tribunal.[219a] It therefore contemplates that a defendant may be able to rely on Convention rights when he is appealing a decision which was taken before the Human Rights Act came into effect. In *R v DPP, ex p Kebilene*[219b] Lord Steyn expressly rejected the argument put forward by the Director of Public Prosecutions that section 22(4) only extended the Act retrospectively to trials, but not to appeals: **3.75A**

> a construction which treats the trial and the appeal as parts of one process is more in keeping with the purpose of the Convention and the Act of 1998. It is a sensible and just construction.

It will therefore be possible for defendants in criminal proceedings to institute appeals after 2 October 2000 based on the retrospective effect of the Human Rights Act.[219c]

D. The Weaknesses of the Human Rights Act

(1) Introduction

The Human Rights Act received widespread and enthusiastic support during its passage through Parliament. Lord Scarman described the way in which the Act reconciles right guarantees with parliamentary sovereignty as brilliant[220] and Lord Donaldson thought the bill was very cleverly crafted.[221] There have, however, been some dissenting voices. For example, Fredman[222] has argued that the Human Rights Act has not been fashioned to ensure there are effective democratic constraints on the judiciary: unlike Canada or South Africa the Act did not emerge through a public debate to develop a 'home grown' set of rights. She points out that the Act has done little to strengthen the accountability of judges by creating a constitutional court whose system of appointment is transparent and that no attempt has been made to adapt the traditional model of adversarial litigation to one more suited to human rights litigation (by permitting class actions, institutional litigators or Brandeis briefs).[223] **3.76**

[219] See F Bennion, 'A Human Rights Act Provision Now in Force' (1999) 163 JP 164.
[219a] Human Rights Act 1998, s 7(6)(b).
[219b] [1999] 3 WLR 972, 982.
[219c] See generally, K Kerrigan, 'Unlocking the Human Rights Floodgates' [2000] Crim LR 71.
[220] *Hansard*, HL col 1256, (3 Nov 1997).
[221] *Hansard*, HL col 1292, (3 Nov 1997).
[222] S Fredman, 'Bringing Rights Home' (1998) 114 LQR 538.
[223] For a discussion of Brandeis briefs, see para 22.106ff below.

3.77 It should also be remembered that the Labour Party in 1993[224] envisaged incorporation of the European Convention on Human Rights as being the first stage of a process; and that an all party commission should draft a new Bill of Rights within a prescribed period. There are limitations both within the European Convention on Human Rights and the Human Rights Act itself which are discussed below. Powerful reasons exist for arguing that the current legislation should be seen as a staging post towards achieving a more comprehensive and effective human rights protection in English law.

(2) The limitations of the European Convention model

3.78 The European Convention on Human Rights was drafted in the aftermath of the Second World War when a very different climate of opinion prevailed. Many critics have suggested that human rights legislation which becomes fully effective in 2000[225] should be drafted to reflect contemporary conditions.[226] Thus, Sir Stephen Sedley has pointed out that the Convention enshrines the Enlightenment's values of possessive individualism deriving from a historical paradigm where the natural enemy is the state and where the maximum personal liberty provides the maximum benefit for society.[227]

3.79 One of the most articulate exponents of the view that the Convention provides an inadequate framework for a domestic bill of rights is the current Director of Liberty, John Wadham. He has identified a number of deficiencies in the Convention:[228] it does not contain the right to freedom of information; it does not provide for rights of due process or fair trial in the extradition system or before deportation; its anti-discrimination provision is very restrictive since it does not expressly prohibit discrimination on grounds of sexual orientation[228a] or disability and only applies where another Convention right has been violated;[229] it does not contain an absolute prohibition against compelling a criminal defendant to testify against himself or confess guilt[230] nor does it guarantee a right of trial before

---

[224] *A New Agenda for Change: Labour's Proposals for constitutional reform.*

[225] Although the main provisions of the Act will come into force in Oct 2000, a number of its provisions come into force earlier: see para 3.74ff above.

[226] See for example Liberty's *Manifesto for Human Rights* (National Council of Civil Liberties, 1997).

[227] Sir Stephen Sedley, 'Human Rights: a Twenty-First Century Agenda' [1995] PL 386.

[228] See eg J Wadham, 'A Bill of Rights' in D Bean (ed), *Law Reform for All* (Blackstone, 1996); 'Why incorporation of the European Convention on Human Rights is Not Enough' in R Gordon and R Wilmott-Smith, *Human Rights in the United Kingdom* (Oxford University Press, 1996).

[228a] Discrimination on these grounds may breach Art 8: see, in particular, the cases arising from the dismissal of homosexual servicemen, *Lustig-Prean v United Kingdom* (1999) 7 BHRC 65 and *Smith v United Kingdom* [1999] IRLR 734; and see generally, para 12.92ff below.

[229] Unlike eg the United Nations International Covenant on Civil and Political Rights, Art 26.

[230] Unlike the International Covenant on Civil and Political Rights, Art 14(3)(g).

a jury;[231] there are no minimum conditions for detention outside Article 3 nor do detainees have any positive rights such as right of access to a lawyer; its privacy rights do not provide for due process rights such as requiring an independent tribunal to adjudicate about whether to authorise a restriction of privacy rights; and the Convention does not contain any specific rights for children.[231a] Furthermore, a number of rights contained in the Fourth[232] and Seventh[233] Convention protocols have not been ratified by the United Kingdom, such as freedom from imprisonment for breach of contract, freedom of movement and residence, the right to appeal following conviction and the right of compensation for those who are wrongly convicted, the prohibition from double jeopardy in criminal trials and equality of rights between spouses. In addition, the state has a widely drawn entitlement to restrict rights under the European Convention, for example, the phrase 'national security' is notoriously vague, as are 'the prevention of disorder' or the 'protection of health or morals'. Ewing and Gearty voice a more fundamental objection about the terms of the Convention.[234] They argue that the Convention is a deeply ideological document and that its incorporation guarantees supremacy of its narrowly individualistic view of society, representing a triumph of liberalism which has now been embodied in the constitution over socialism.

There is, without doubt, an important problem[235] about using the Convention model for the Human Rights Act. The Convention gives very limited protection to social and economic rights,[236] being confined to protecting traditional civil and political rights (with the exception of the right to protect property[237] and the right to education).[238] Nevertheless, Lord Irvine argued the case for incorporating the Convention on the basis that the rights and freedoms of citizens should be put centre stage as part of their fundamental protection from the overweening state;[239] and that the notion of citizenship embraces civil, political and economic rights.[240] **3.80**

[231] Compare the Sixth Article of the American Bill of Rights.

[231a] See eg J Fortin, 'Rights Brought Home for Children' [1999] 62 MLR 350.

[232] The text of the Convention including the Fourth Protocol is reproduced at App E in Vol 2.

[233] The text of the Convention including the Seventh Protocol is also reproduced at App E in Vol 2.

[234] K Ewing and C Gearty, 'Rocky Foundations of Labour's New Rights' [1997] EHRLR 146.

[235] Cf K Ewing, 'Social Rights and Constitutional Law' [1999] PL 104.

[236] See para 1.16ff above.

[237] Under Art 1 of the First Protocol; see para 18.26ff below.

[238] Under Art 2 of the first Protocol; see para 19.34ff below.

[239] Lord Irvine, 'The Legal System and Law Reform Under Labour', in D Bean (ed), *Law Reform for All* (Blackstone, 1996).

[240] T H Marshall *Citizenship and Social Class* (Cambridge University Press, 1950); Greenwood, *Class Citizenship and Social Development* (1973); but see eg M Anthony, M Bulmer, A Rees and A Smith, *Citizenship today: the contemporary relevance of T H Marshall* (UCL Press, 1998); K Faulks, *Citizenship in Modern Britain* (Edinburgh University Press, 1998); and see also R Plant, 'Citizenship Rights and Welfare' in A Coote (ed), *The Welfare of Citizens* (Rivers Oram, 1992); R Lister, 'Welfare Rights and the Constitution' in A Barnett, C Ellis and P Hirst (eds), *Debating the Constitution* (Polity, 1993).

However, it is illuminating to compare the limited nature of the rights created by the Convention with those in Chapter 2 of the South African Constitution Act[241] which contains: a right for the individual to choose his occupation,[242] a right to fair labour practices including the right to strike,[243] the right to an environment which is not harmful to health or well being and to have protection to prevent pollution and ecological degradation,[244] extensive property rights,[245] a right to adequate housing[246] and a right of access to health care, social security and emergency medical treatment.[247]

(3) The limitations of the Human Rights Act

3.81 In addition to the broad criticism about the value of using the Convention as the model for enacting the Human Rights Act, there are several other substantial concerns about the drafting of the Act. The failure to enact various rights contained in the Convention and its protocols has been rightly criticised.[248] The Human Rights Act only requires that public authorities must act in accordance with Articles 2 to 12 and Article 14 of the Convention, Articles 1 to 3 of the First Protocol and Articles 1 and 2 of the Sixth Protocol. It also permits derogations from the Convention; and specifically enacts the one derogation of the Convention made by the United Kingdom in relation to Article 5(3).[249] The Human Rights Act also permits reservations to be made such as the reservation made in relation to the right to education[250] under the Education Act 1996.[251]

3.82 The Human Rights Act fails to incorporate Article 1 of the Convention which obliges the High Contracting Parties to secure to everyone within its jurisdiction the rights and freedoms set out in Articles 2 to 18 of the Convention. Article 1 has not played a significant role in Convention case law. However, the Court relied on Article 1 in *Young James and Webster v United Kingdom*[251a] in holding that the state was responsible for breaches of the right of association under Article 11[251b] where employees were dismissed as a result of the closed-shop legislation; and again in

[241] The text is reproduced at App S in Vol 2.
[242] s 22
[243] s 23
[244] s 24
[245] s 25
[246] s 26
[247] s 27
[248] The failure to incorporate Arts 1 and 13 is discussed in para 3.82 below and the failure to include the Fourth and Seventh Protocols is discussed in para 3.83 below.
[249] See para 6.93 below.
[250] Under Art 2 of the First Protocol; see para 19.34ff below.
[251] See para 19.70ff below.
[251a] (1981) 4 EHRR 38 para 49.
[251b] See para 16.66ff below.

A v United Kingdom[251c] in deciding that the failure of the state to ensure that individuals were not subjected to inhuman treatment contrary to Article 3[251d] made it liable because the defence of reasonable chastisement to a charge of assaulting a child gave inadequate protection to children. Its omission from the Human Rights Act reflects the fact that the Act is a domestic human rights instrument. More significantly, the Act specifically omits to incorporate Article 13 of the Convention. Article 13 states:

> Everyone whose rights and freedoms as set forth in this Convention are violated shall have an effective remedy before a national authority notwithstanding that the violation has been committed by persons acting in an official capacity.

In fact, Article 13 has played a part in a number of English decisions where Convention points have been argued[252] as well as several significant cases before the European Court of Human Rights.[253] Its omission from the Human Rights Bill attracted criticism since the Convention jurisprudence on Article 13 may be ignored even where it is relevant to issues considered under the Act.[253a] In particular, the failure to incorporate Article 13 confirms that relief in judicial review cases under the Human Rights Act remains discretionary.[253b] However, the Lord Chancellor, Lord Irvine justified the decision against incorporating Article 13 in Committee on the basis that:[254]

> We have set out in the Bill a scheme to provide remedies for the violation of Convention rights. We also believe it is undesirable to provide for Articles 1 and 13 in the Bill. . . . The courts would be bound to ask what was intended beyond the existing scheme of remedies set out in the Act. It might lead them to fashion remedies other than [section] 8 remedies, which we regard as sufficient and clear. We believe that [section] 8 provides effective remedies before our courts.

Consequently, Feldman[255] suggests that courts or tribunals would be entitled to interpret the remedial provisions of the Human Rights Act in a way that meets the requirements of Article 13 by relying on these remarks under the doctrine of *Pepper v Hart.*[256] However, it is submitted that the views expressed by the Home

---

[251c] (1988) 27 EHRR 611 para 22.

[251d] See para 8.13ff below.

[252] See eg *Rantzen v Mirror Group Newspapers (1986) Ltd* [1994] QB 670; *John v MGN* [1997] QB 586; *R v Khan* [1997] AC 558.

[253] See eg *Chahal v United Kingdom* (1996) 23 EHRR 413; *Aksoy v Turkey* (1996) 23 EHRR 553; *Aydin v Turkey* (1997) 25 EHRR 251.

[253a] But see S Grosz, J Beatson and P Duffy, *Human Rights: The 1998 Act and the European Convention* (Sweet & Maxwell, 2000) para 1–06.

[253b] See para 21.109 below.

[254] *Hansard*, HL col 475 (18 Nov 1997).

[255] D Feldman 'Remedies for violations of Convention rights under the Human Rights Act' [1998] EHRLR 691.

[256] [1993] 1 AC 593; see para 4.35ff below.

Secretary, Jack Straw MP, in Committee[257] about the omission of Article 13 do not satisfy the requirement under *Pepper v Hart*[258] that statements of the minister about the meaning of the Act must be sufficiently clear.

3.83 In addition, the Human Rights Act does not incorporate rights contained in two Convention protocols which the United Kingdom has not ratified: the Fourth Protocol and the Seventh Protocol. The Human Rights Bill was originally drafted to exclude the Sixth Protocol[259] as well but this was subsequently inserted into the Act.[260] The Fourth Protocol contains a prohibition against deprivation of liberty on the ground of an inability to fulfil a contractual obligation, a right to freedom of movement, a right of non expulsion from a home state, a right of entry to the state of which a person is a national and a prohibition from the collective expulsions of aliens. In *Rights Brought Home: the Human Rights Bill*[261] the Government explained that the Fourth Protocol has not been ratified because of concerns about the exact nature of the obligation regarding rights of entry and indicated that there were no immediate plans to ratify it. The Seventh Protocol contains a prohibition on expulsion of aliens without a decision in accordance with the law or opportunities for a review, a right to a review of conviction or sentence after criminal conviction, a right to compensation following a miscarriage of justice, a prohibition on double jeopardy in criminal cases and a right of equality between spouses. In *Rights Brought Home: the Human Rights Bill*[262] the Government stated that it proposed to remove certain inconsistencies between the Protocol and domestic law (such as in relation to the property rights of spouses) and would then ratify the Protocol. The Government has again reviewed the question about ratification of these Protocols.[262a] In relation to Protocol 4, it takes the view that difficulties arise about rights conferred in relation to passports under Article 2 and a right of abode for British nationals under Article 3 because of their impact on those who do not currently enjoy such rights. The Government is therefore considering whether it would be possible to draft a reservation to enable the United Kingdom to ratify the protocol or whether fresh immigration legislation is required. On the other hand, it proposes to ratify the Seventh Protocol by enacting legislation which

[257] *Hansard*, HC cols 979–980 (20 May 1998), 'If we were to include art 13 in the Bill in addition to the remedies provided the question would inevitably arise what the courts would make of the amendment which, on the face of it, contains nothing new. I suggest that the amendment would either cause confusion or prompt the courts to act in ways not intended by the Bill'.

[258] Ibid.

[259] The provisions concerning the abolition of the death penalty are discussed at para 7.31 below.

[260] [1998] EHRLR 517; for a discussion of the constitutional implications of Parliament binding its successors by enacting the Sixth Protocol, see D Judge, '*Capital Punishment: Burke and Dicey Meet the European Convention on Human Rights*' [1999] PL 6.

[261] (1997) Cm 3782, paras 4.10–4.11.

[262] Ibid. paras 4.14–4.15.

[262a] See *Home Office Review of Human Rights Instruments (Amended)*, 26 Aug 1999.

changes some existing family law principles.[262b] It will also enter a reservation concerning the right of review of an alien who is lawfully resident in the United Kingdom.

During the passage of the bill there was considerable disquiet about the restrictive definition of standing under the Human Rights Act. In order to bring proceedings under the Act a claimant must show under section 7 that he is a *victim*,[263] because the Government decided to adopt the same requirement for standing under the Human Rights Act as that contained in Article 34 of the Convention. However, the rationale for the Government's approach is not persuasive. Although it is strongly arguable that a supra-national human rights court should not intervene in domestic decision-making unless the complainant is directly affected, this principle has no direct application to a domestic rights instrument. **3.84**

By comparison, in judicial review cases an applicant is normally required to establish that he has a 'sufficient interest';[264] a threshold requirement which has been given a generous interpretation by the courts, both in relation to individual applicants[265] and pressure groups.[266] In this context it is helpful to distinguish between different types of 'representational standing':[267] public interest standing (where an individual or group represents the 'public interest', such as an organisation like Greenpeace),[268] associational standing (where an association represents a group of interested parties such as the application launched by the Fleet Street casuals),[269] and surrogate standing (where an individual or association acts as a nominal plaintiff to protect the interests of another individual because of their age or mental capacity). It is likely that, as a result of the narrow definition of standing, a public interest representative will not obtain a remedy under the Human Rights Act. **3.85**

[262b] The Government proposes to abolish: the common law rule that a husband has a duty to maintain his wife but not vice versa, the principles applying to household allowances under the Married Woman's Act 1964, s 1, and the principle of advancement which applies to husbands and not wives.

[263] See para 22.14ff below.

[264] See the Supreme Court Act 1981, s 31(3); CPR R53.3(7).

[265] See eg *R v Felixstowe Justices, ex p Leigh* [1987] QB 582; *R v Secretary of State for Foreign and Commonwealth Affairs, ex p Rees-Mogg* [1994] QB 552; *R v Somerset County Council, ex p Dixon* [1997] COD 323.

[266] See eg *R v Inspectorate of Pollution, ex p Greenpeace Ltd (No 2)* [1994] 4 All ER 329; *R v Secretary of State for Foreign and Commonwealth Affairs, ex p World Development Movement Ltd* [1995] 1 WLR 386; *R v Secretary of State for Employment, ex p Equal Opportunities Commission* [1995] 1 AC 1; and for the jurisdiction to grant protective costs orders in relation to public interest representatives, see *R v Lord Chancellor, ex p Child Poverty Action Group* [1999] 1 WLR 347.

[267] P Cane, 'Standing up for the Public' [1995] PL 276; and P Cane 'Standing Representation and the Environment' in I Loveland (ed), *A Special Relationship: American influences on public law in the UK* (Oxford University Press, 1995).

[268] *R v Inspectorate of Pollution, ex p Greenpeace (No 2)* [1994] 4 All ER 329.

[269] *R v Inland Revenue Commissioners, ex p Federation of the Self Employed and Small Businesses Ltd* [1982] AC 617.

Liberty[270] argued that this restrictive criterion of victim would mean that the Equal Opportunities Commission would have standing in judicial review proceedings to raise arguments about fundamental human rights in the context of challenging the *vires* of legislation or its compatibility with European Community law but could not do so in relation to breaches of the Human Rights Act. Nevertheless, the Government declined at the third reading to support the necessary amendment to the bill which had been proposed by Lord Lester and supported by Lord Slynn, Lord Simon and Lord Ackner.[271]

3.86 The restrictive approach towards standing under the Act is difficult to understand. The Under-Secretary of State, Mike O'Brien MP, said at the Committee stage in the House of Commons:[271]

> As a government, our aim is to grant access to victims. It is not to create opportunities to allow interest groups from SPUC to Liberty . . . to venture into frolics of their own in the courts. The aim is to confer access to rights, not to licence interest groups to clog up the courts with test cases, which will delay access to the courts.

However, requiring the courts to apply a test for standing under the Human Rights Act which is different from the general one used in judicial review will cause needless complexity, particularly where judicial review is sought on more than one ground.[272] It may also provide insufficient access to justice to meet the basic objectives of the Human Rights Act.[273] Section 7(3)[274] of the Human Rights Act prohibits judicial review proceedings where a public authority is alleged to have acted incompatibly with Convention rights only if the applicant is a victim. It has been convincingly argued[275] that a pressure group (or public body) could nevertheless obtain declaratory relief under the Human Rights Act outside the scope of section 7. A pressure group could seek a declaration on conventional administrative law principles that an immigration rule or some other form of subordinate legislation is *ultra vires* the primary legislation under which it is enacted as being incompatible with a Convention right; thus, in *R v Secretary of State for Social Security, ex p Joint council for the Welfare of Immigrants* [276] the Court of Appeal decided that regulations excluding asylum seekers from obtaining income

[270] Liberty, *Parliamentary Briefing on the Human Rights Bill,* Oct 1997, para 5.1.
[271] *Hansard*, HC col 1086, (24 Jun, 1997).
[272] But see J Marriott and D Nichol, 'The Human Rights Act, Representative Standing and the Victim Culture' [1998] EHRLR 730.
[273] J Miles, 'Standing Under the Human Rights Act 1998: Theories of Rights Enforcement and the Nature of Public Law Adjudication' [2000] 59 Cam LJ 133.
[274] See para 22.14ff below.
[275] S Grosz, J Beatson and P Duffy, *Human Rights: The 1998 Act and the European Convention* (Sweet & Maxwell, 2000) para 4–42ff; but see D Feldman, 'Remedies for Violations of Convention rights under the Human Rights Act' [1998] EHRLR 691.
[276] [1997] 1 WLR 275; the case is discussed further at para 5.106 below.

support was *ultra vires* the Asylm and Immigration Appeals Act 1993. A representative group or public group may also seek a declaration under section 3 of the Act[277] that the legislation must be given a particular interpretation[278] or is incompatible with the Human Rights Act.[279]

Nevertheless, any public interest applicant may consider it prudent to bring an application for judicial review *both* on behalf of itself and an individual applicant, as the Equal Opportunities Commission chose to do in *R v Secretary of State for Employment, ex p Equal Opportunities Commission.*[280] The most serious difficulty of utilising the victim test of the Convention for standing under the Human Rights Act may be that, in borderline cases, courts or tribunals will be obliged to scrutinise decisions of the European Commission on Human Rights which were often inconsistent and sometimes unreported. **3.87**

Views were also sought in *Rights Brought Home: the Human Rights Bill*[281] on whether to establish a Human Rights Commission which might perform a comparable role to the Equal Opportunities Commission or Commission for Racial Equality. A number of commentators argued strongly for the creation of a Commission.[282] Although the Government has not ruled out a Commission for the future, there are no immediate plans to establish one.[283] However, the Government has supported the establishment of a parliamentary committee on human rights.[284] Nevertheless, the rationale for establishing a Human Rights Commission is compelling: it would have a role promoting good practices among public authorities, promoting awareness of human rights principles among the public, scrutinising draft legislation and advising government and Parliament on whether there are potential conflicts with international rights instruments, providing advice and assistance to individuals and providing legal representation for selected cases, having powers to investigate human rights abuses as well as having a limited international role.[285] **3.88**

---

[277] See para 4.04ff below.

[278] The limits of the interpretative obligation under s 3 are discussed at para 4.27ff below.

[279] See para 4.43ff below.

[280] [1995] 1 AC 1

[281] (1997) Cm 3782 pp 14–15.

[282] See eg Institute for Public Policy Research, *A Human Rights Commission: the options* (1997); Justice, *Human Rights Bill: Justice briefing for the second reading in the House of Lords.*

[283] See Lord Irvine at the second reading (*Hansard,* HL col 1233 (3 Nov 1997)) and the Parliamentary Under Secretary to the Home Department, Mr Mike O'Brien, MP in Committee (*Hansard,* HC col 1088 (24 Jun 1998)).

[284] See R Blackburn, 'Current topic: a Human Rights Committee for the UK Parliament—the options' [1998] EHRLR 534; on 14 Dec 1998 the Leader of the House of Commons, Margaret Beckett MP announced that both the House of Commons and House of Lords would be asked to set up a Committee before the Human Rights Act came into force, and the Joint Select Committee on Human Rights is due to start in autumn 2000.

[285] S Spencer and I Bynoe, *A Human Rights Commission: The options for Britain and Northern Ireland* (Institute for Public Policy Research, 1998).

3.89 Another issue that provoked considerable debate during the passage of the Human Rights Bill was the extent to which it achieved its declared purpose of bringing Convention rights home.[286] The long title of the Human Rights Bill states that it is 'an Act to give *further effect* to rights and freedoms guaranteed under the Convention'; and in Committee the Lord Chancellor, Lord Irvine indicated that:[287]

> convention rights will not . . . in themselves become part of the substantive domestic law.

The position was further explained in an exchange between Lord Irvine and Lord Lester when the Bill was at the Report Stage:[288]

> **Lord Irvine:** . . . I have to make this point absolutely plain. The European Convention on Human Rights under this Bill is not made part of our law. The Bill gives the European Convention on Human Rights a special relationship which will mean that the courts will give effect to the interpretative provisions . . . but it does not make the convention directly justiciable as it would be if it were part of our law. I want there to be no ambiguity about that.
>
> **Lord Lester:** My Lords, I am extremely grateful to the Lord Chancellor; but I wonder whether he would mind explaining the difference between requiring our court (as a public authority) to give effect to the convention, requiring our courts where possible to interpret Acts of Parliament to comply with the convention, requiring our courts to develop the common law to have regard to the convention rights, and requiring our courts to give effective remedies where there is a breach of those rights. What is the difference between all of that and incorporating the convention? What else would be needed over and above all that in order to incorporate the convention.
>
> **Lord Irvine:** My Lords, this is fast becoming something of a theological dispute and I should like to bring it to a conclusion as quickly as I may. The short point is that if the convention were incorporated into our law, it would be directly justiciable and would be enforced by our courts. If the courts found it impossible to construe primary legislation in a way which is compatible with the convention rights, the primary legislation remains in full force and effect. All that the courts can do is make a declaration of incompatibility.

The point appears to be that although the courts are under the 'interpretive obligation'[289] and it is unlawful for public authorities to act in a way which is incompatible[290] with Convention rights,[291] the Convention itself does not have the force of a UK statute: it does not, therefore, impliedly repeal other statutes.[292]

---

286 See eg J Straw and P Boateng, 'Bringing Rights Home: Labour's Plans to Incorporate the European Convention on Human Rights into UK Law' [1997] EHRLR 71; *Rights Brought Home: The Human Rights Bill* (1997) Cm 3782; but see G Marshall 'Patriating Rights—Without Reservations—the Human Rights Bill 1998' in J Beatson, C Forsyth and I Hare (eds), *Constitutional Reform in the United Kingdom: Practice and Procedure* (Hart Publishing, 1998).

287 *Hansard*, HL col 508 (18 Nov 1997).

288 *Hansard*, HL cols 421, 422 (29 Jan 1998).

289 Under s 3(1) of the Human Rights Act; see, generally, para 4.04ff below.

290 Under s 6(1) of the Human Rights Act; see generally, para 5.120ff below.

291 As defined by s 1(1) of the Human Rights Act; see generally, para 3.43ff above.

292 For a discussion of the impact of the doctrine of implied repeal on the Human Rights Act , see para 4.33ff below.

4

THE HUMAN RIGHTS ACT AND STATUTE LAW

A. Introduction

The relationship between the Human Rights Act and other legislation was central to the debates which led to its enactment. The compromise solution, designed to preserve parliamentary sovereignty,[1] involved a 'strong rule of construction' allied to a procedure for obtaining 'declarations of incompatibility'.[2] This 'rule of construction' appears to represent a fundamental new direction in statutory construction and it is likely that the English courts will draw on interpretive principles applicable to European Union law and to 'constitutional provisions' in other jurisdictions. The desire of the Government to ensure the compatibility of legislation with Convention rights is underscored by the 'statement of compatibility' procedure in relation to new legislation. **4.01**

[1] For a discussion of the doctrine, see para 1.66ff above.

[2] See generally, para 4.43ff below.

4.02 If the courts are driven to make a 'declaration of incompatibility' then the Government will have to consider whether or not to make a 'remedial order' to bring the legislation into line with the Convention. Such orders are a constitutional innovation and are likely to give rise to legal and political controversy in some cases.

4.03 The next two sections of this Chapter deal with the effect of the rule of statutory construction in section 3 of the Human Rights Act and the 'statement of compatibility' procedure in section 19 of the Act. The last two sections deal with the 'declaration of incompatibility' procedure and the power to make remedial orders in respect of incompatible legislation.

B. The Rule of Construction

(1) Introduction: the scope of section 3(1)

4.04 The 'rule of construction' is set out in section 3(1) of the Human Rights Act which provides that:

> (1) So far as it is possible to do so, primary legislation and subordinate legislation must be read and given effect in a way which is compatible with Convention rights.[3]

There can be no doubt that this places a strong 'interpretative obligation' on the courts. The requirement to construe legislation so that it is 'compatible' with Convention rights means that the court must undertake an exercise similar to that it uses when considering whether a public authority has acted in a way which is 'incompatible' with Convention rights.[4] Nevertheless, the language of section 3(1) is not familiar and the statute itself provides no further guidance as to the way in which this 'rule of construction' should be applied.

4.05 The meaning of section 3(1) itself has become clearer as a result of a number of statements made by the Government about the intended effect of the rule. According to the White Paper:

> This goes far beyond the present rule which enables the courts to take the Convention into account in resolving any ambiguity in a legislative provision. The courts will be required to interpret legislation so as to uphold the Convention rights unless the legislation itself is so clearly incompatible with the Convention that it is impossible to do so.[5]

When introducing the bill at the second reading, the Lord Chancellor, Lord Irvine, stated[6] that section 3:

---

[3] As defined in s 1(1).

[4] Under s 6(1) of the Human Rights Act: see generally, para 5.120ff below.

[5] *Rights Brought Home: The Human Rights Bill* (1997) Cm 3782, para 2.7.

[6] *Hansard*, HL col 1230 (3 Nov 1997).

> will ensure that, if it is possible to interpret a statute two ways—one compatible with the convention and one not—the courts will always choose the interpretation that is compatible. In practice, this is a strong form of incorporation.

At the Committee stage Lord Irvine[7] said (echoing the White Paper):

> We want the courts to strive to find an interpretation of legislation which is consistent with Convention rights so far as the language of the legislation allows, and only in the last resort to conclude that the legislation is so clearly incompatible with the Convention that it is impossible to do so.

Lord Irvine[8] has argued that under section 3, the courts will interpret so as to be consistent with Convention rights not only statutory provisions which are ambiguous (in the sense that the language used is capable of two different meanings)[9] but also those where there is *no* ambiguity in language: unless a *clear* limitation on Convention rights is stated in terms.[10]

Nevertheless, the precise effect of the 'rule of construction' in section 3 has given **4.06**
rise to considerable parliamentary and academic debate.[11] The difficulty is how far the 'possible' meanings of a statutory provision can be taken. It has been suggested

[7] *Hansard*, HL col 535 (18 Nov 1997); it is noteworthy that at the Third Reading he predicted that: 'in 99% of the cases that arise, there will be no need for judicial declarations of incompatibility' (*Hansard*, HL, col 840 (5 Feb 1998)); and Jack Straw MP, said at the Committee stage that: 'We expect that, in almost all cases, the courts will be able to interpret legislation compatibly with the Convention' (*Hansard*, HC, cols 421, 422 (3 Jun 1998)). Sir Anthony Hooper regards as authoritative (on the basis of *Pepper v Hart* [1993] 1 AC 593; see para 4.35ff below) the views expressed in Parliament about the very strong likelihood of interpreting legislation as being compatible with the Convention: see Sir Anthony Hooper, 'The Impact of the Human Rights Act on Judicial Decision Making' [1998] EHRLR 676.

[8] Lord Irvine, 'The Development of Human Rights in Britain under an Incorporated Convention on Human Rights' [1998] PL 221, 228.

[9] As it now does: see para 2.13ff.

[10] At the report stage of the Bill, Lord Lester quoted a number of passages from Lord Irvine's article (*Hansard*, HL cols 1291, 1292 (19 Jan 1998)), no doubt because the views of the Bill's promoter might be seen as relevant under the *Pepper v Hart* doctrine when construing s 3. However, in the debate Lord Irvine declined to add to or repeat the views he had earlier expressed (*Hansard*, HL col 1294 (19 Jan1998)).

[11] The literature discussing the impact of s 3 is now extensive: see eg G Marshall, 'Interpreting Interpretation in the Human Rights Act' [1998] PL 167; 'Patriating Rights—With Reservations—the Human Rights Bill 1998' in J Beatson, C Forsyth and I Hare (eds), *Constitutional Reform in the United Kingdom: Practice and Principles* (Hart Publishing, 1998) and 'Two Kinds of Compatibility: More About s 3 of the Human Rights Act 1998' [1999] PL 377; Lord Lester, 'The Art of the Possible—Interpreting Statutes Under the Human Rights Act' [1998] EHRLR 665; Sir William Wade, 'Human Rights and the Judiciary' [1998] EHRLR 520; Lord Steyn, 'Incorporation and Devolution—A Few Reflections on the Challenging Scene' [1998] EHRLR 153; Lord Irvine, 'The Development of Human Rights in Britain Under an Incorporated Convention on Human Rights' [1998] PL 221; Lord Cooke, 'The British Embracement of Human Rights' [1999] EHRLR 243; M Beloff, 'What Does It All Mean? Interpreting the Human Rights Act 1998' in L Betten(ed), *The Human Rights Act 1998 What It Means* (Nijhoff, 1999); F Bennion, 'What Interpretation is 'Possible' Under Section 3(1) of the Human Rights Act 1998' [2000] PL 77; S Grosz, J Beatson andP Duffy, *Human Rights The 1998 Act and the European Convention* (Sweet & Maxwell, 2000) Chap 3.

that the court can apply a meaning which is 'fairly possible'[12] or 'reasonably possible'.[13] However, it is to be noted that the Government opposed an amendment which would have required the courts to adopt a 'reasonable', rather than a 'possible' interpretation because it would have meant that 'the courts would not go so far down the road of interpreting legislation'.[14] Some commentators[15] have argued that the search for meaning under section 3 of the Human Rights Act will not be for the 'true meaning' of a particular statutory provision; but for the meaning which best accords with Convention rights. As Lord Steyn has suggested:

> The questions will be: (1) What meanings are the words capable of yielding? (2) And, critically, can the words yield a meaning consistent with Convention rights? In practical effect there will be a rebuttable presumption in favour of an interpretation consistent with Convention rights.

4.07 Although the English courts have not previously had to deal with any 'rule of construction' in the terms of section 3, it is suggested that assistance as to the approach which is likely to be taken can be obtained by considering four areas in which the courts have gone beyond 'literal construction' of statutes:

- the doctrine of 'purposive construction';
- the rules relating to the construction of statutes in European Community law;
- the doctrines of 'reading in' and 'reading down'; and
- the rule of construction in New Zealand.

These will be considered in the next four sections.

(2) Purposive construction

4.08 The English courts are willing, in limited circumstances, to engage in the 'purposive construction' of statutes. Two conditions have to be fulfilled:

> First, it [must be] . . . possible to determine from a consideration of the provisions of the Act read as a whole precisely what the mischief was that it was the purpose of the Act to remedy; secondly, it [must be] . . . apparent that the draftsman and Parliament had by inadvertence overlooked and so omitted to deal with, an eventuality that required to be dealt with if the purpose of the Act was to be achieved.[16]

[12] Lord Cooke of Thorndon, *Hansard*, HL col 583 (18 Nov 1997).

[13] Lord Simon, ibid col 536.

[14] *Hansard*, HC col 421 (3 Jun 1998) (Committee Stage).

[15] See eg Sir William Wade, 'Human Rights and the Judiciary' [1998] EHRLR 520; Lord Cooke, 'The British Embracement of Human Rights' [1999] EHRLR 243 and in *R v DPP, ex p Kebiline* [1999] 3 WLR 972, 987 Lord Cooke described s 3 as 'a strong adjuration'; Lord Steyn, 'Incorporation and Devolution—A Few Reflections on the Challenging Scene' [1998] EHRLR 153.

[16] Per Lord Diplock, Carter v Bradbeer [1975] 1 WLR 1204, 1206, 1207; he suggests a third condition (it must be 'possible to state with certainty what were the additional words that would have been inserted by the draftsman and approved by Parliament had their attention been drawn to the omission before the Bill passed into law'), but this does not appear to be consistent with authority;

The analogy between section 3 and 'purposive construction' is not exact: the section does not require the courts to treat previous statutes as if their purpose were to give effect to Convention rights. Nevertheless, the 'purposive construction' cases illustrate the approach taken by the courts when required to 'strain' the literal meaning of a statute in the light of wider considerations.

The cases provide a number of examples of 'purposive construction' in which the courts have been prepared to add or remove words from a statute in order to achieve the perceived legislative purpose. Thus, in *Liversidge v Anderson*[17] the House of Lords construed the wartime power of the Home Secretary to intern individuals if he had 'reasonable cause to believe' certain matters; the House of Lords took the view that the purpose of an emergency regulation to ensure public safety would be frustrated unless the regulation was construed as meaning in effect that the Home Secretary *thinks* he has reasonable cause to believe[18]. Similarly, in *Wills v Bowley*[19] the House of Lords construed a power of arrest exercisable only when an offence 'was being committed' as extending to the situation where a police officer had reasonable grounds to suspect that an offence was being committed.[20] The House of Lords recently analysed the limits of applying a purposive construction in *Clarke v General Accident Fire and Life Assurance Corporation plc.*[21] Lord Clyde said: **4.09**

> It may be perfectly proper to adopt even a strained construction to enable the object and purpose of the legislation to be fulfilled. But it cannot be taken to the length of applying unnatural meanings to familiar words or of so stretching the language that its former shape is transformed into something which is not only significantly different but has a name of its own. This must be particularly so where the language has no evident ambiguity or uncertainty about it.

The impact of 'purposive construction' is illustrated by the approach taken in *Ex p Guardian Newspapers.*[22] Defendants in criminal proceedings intended to apply for a stay of proceedings as an abuse of process; and sought an order that the hearing be held in private which was opposed by a newspaper. The difficulty that arose was whether the relevant words in the Crown Court Rules,[23] 'all or part of **4.10**

see generally, F Bennion, Statutory Interpretation (3rd edn, Butterworths, 1997) s 304: he describes this approach as 'purposive-strained construction'; and for a recent example, see the decision of the House of Lords in Inco Europe v First Choice Distribution [2000] 1 WLR 586.

17 [1942] AC 206.

18 Ibid; see the famous dissenting judgment of Lord Atkin at 245 where he suggests that the only authority to justify the proposed construction is the discussion between Alice and Humpty Dumpty in *Through the Looking Glass.*

19 [1983] 1 AC 57.

20 See also *DPP v McKeown* [1997] 1 All ER 737, 743.

21 [1998] 1 WLR 1647, 1658 (when examining the meaning of the word 'road' under the Road Traffic Act 1988, s 192).

22 [1999] 1 All ER 65.

23 Rules 16B and 24A(1).

the trial', could be extended to cover an interlocutory pre-trial application. The Court of Appeal construed the rule so that it extended to all or part of the trial process. Brooke LJ explained[24] that:

> The statutory scheme of which [the rules] form an integral part was introduced in 1989 in order that this country could comply with its international obligations under the European Convention on Human Rights. The mischief the scheme was introduced to combat was obvious and the right it was seeking to protect—the right of the news media to have an effective remedy against an order preventing them from exercising their Article 10 rights to receive information from court proceedings (and see also Article 6(1))—is an important one. In our judgment it is incumbent on us to interpret this rule purposively,[25] and to presume that the rule-maker did not intend an unworkable or inconvenient result when he was intent on ensuring that this country fulfils its international obligations in matters affecting freedom of expression.

(3) The construction of statutes in European Community law

4.11 The most distinctive feature of European Community jurisprudence on statutory interpretation is that the courts apply a broad goal-oriented or teleological method of construction. The courts will search for the purpose of a provision so as to ensure that it achieves the general effect intended by the legislator. However, the crucial technique of construction is the integrative approach of blending together a systematic and goal orientated interpretation.[26] This approach towards purposive construction was described by Lord Denning[27] as follows:

> [European judges] adopt a method which they call in English by strange words—at any rate they are strange to me—the 'schematic and teleological' method of interpretation. It is not really so alarming as it sounds. All it means is that the judges do not go by the literal meaning of the words or by the grammatical structure of the sentence. They go by the design or purpose . . . behind it. When they come to a situation which is to their minds within the spirit—but not the letter—of the legislation, they solve the problem by looking at the design and purpose of legislature—at the effect it was sought to achieve. They then interpret the legislation so as to produce the desired effect. This means they fill in the gaps, quite unashamedly, without hesitation. They simply ask: what is the sensible way of dealing with this situation so as to give effect to the presumed purpose of the legislature? They lay down the law accordingly.

4.12 The importance of the European Community law in this context is reinforced by the decision in *Marleasing*.[28] In that case, the European Court of Justice laid down

---

[24] Rules 16B and 24A(1) 73.

[25] See the cases cited in n 5 to para 1475 of Vol 44(1) of *Halsbury's Laws*.

[26] See J Schwarze, *European Administrative Law* (Sweet & Maxwell, 1992) 257–258; L Brown and T Kennedy, *The Court of Justice of the European Communities* (Sweet & Maxwell, 1994) Chap 14.

[27] *James Buchanan and Company Ltd v Babco Forwarding and Shipping (UK) Ltd* [1977] QB 208, 213.

[28] *Marleasing SA v La Comercial Internacionale de Alimentación SA* [1990] ECR I-4135.

a rule of construction in relation to the interpretation of domestic legislation in the light of European Directives to the effect that:

> in applying national law, whether the provisions in question were adopted before or after the Directive, the national court called upon to interpret it is required to do, so far as it is possible, in the light of the wording and purpose of the directive in order to achieve the result pursued by the latter.

The Court of Justice uses the language which was taken up in section 3 of the Human Rights Act; and it seems likely that the statutory wording was derived from the *Marleasing* case.[29]

This approach is applied by the English courts when testing the validity of legislation against European Directives. In such cases: **4.13**

> it is proper to strain to give effect to the design and purpose behind the legislation, and to give weight to the spirit rather than the letter. . . . But even in this context the exercise must still be one of construction and it should not exceed the limits of what is reasonable.[30]

The *Marleasing* approach has been applied in a number of English cases. For example, in *Webb v Emo Air Cargo (UK) Ltd (No 2)*[31] the House of Lords interpreted the Sex Discrimination Act in line with the Equal Treatment Directive;[32] but it did so in very different terms from the 'conventional' statutory construction it had adopted before the European Court of Justice ruled on the point.[33] However, the principles are confined to interpretation and no more;[34] if the court instead were to impose a meaning *regardless* of whether the words of the statute could reasonably bear that meaning, then the court would in reality be giving direct effect to the Directive. As the Employment Appeal Tribunal emphasised in *Chessington World of Adventures Ltd v Reed*,[35] legislation must be interpreted consistently with a Directive without doing impermissible violence to language; the court cannot, in the guise of interpretation, distort the language of a statute and clear language will *exclude* any possibility[36] of giving a broad purposive construction.

A stronger principle of construction is found in cases in which UK legislation is **4.14**

---

29 Beloff argues that the interpretative obligation under s 3(1) of the Human Rights Act is closely analogous to the *Marleasing* approach: see M Beloff, 'What Does it All Mean? Interpreting the Human Rights Act 1998' in L Betten (ed), *The Human Rights Act 1998 What it Means* (Nijhoff, 1999).

30 *Per* Lord Clyde, *Clarke v General Accident Fire and Life Assurance* [1998] 1 WLR 1647, 1656.

31 [1995] 1 WLR 1454.

32 Council Directive (EEC) 76/207.

33 See *Webb v Emo Air Cargo (UK) Ltd* [1993] 1 WLR 49.

34 Ibid, 60 *per* Lord Keith; *Faccini Dori v Recreb Srl* [1994] ECR I–3325 at para 26.

35 [1998] ICR 97.

36 See eg *Duke v Reliance Systems Ltd* [1988] AC 618 and *MacMillan v Edinburgh Voluntary Organisation Council* [1995] IRLR 536.

designed to give effect to a Directive. In such cases the courts will adopt a purposive approach to construction to avoid a potential conflict between the legislation and the Directive. If necessary, the court will add words to make the two compatible. This approach is illustrated by two House of Lords cases. In *Litster v Forth Dry Dock and Engineering Company Ltd*[37] it was necessary to construe the Transfer of Undertakings Regulations[38] in the light of decisions of the European Court of Justice concerning the effect of the European Directive which the Regulations purported to implement. The issue was whether the Regulations (which were limited to those employed by the business 'immediately before the transfer') could nevertheless be extended to employees who had been unfairly dismissed *before* the transfer. The applicants had been dismissed one hour before the business had been transferred so as to avoid liability under the Regulations. The applicants therefore had plainly not been employed 'immediately before the transfer' (in the way that regulation was normally interpreted).[39] Furthermore, the statutory language set out in the Regulations was not ambiguous. Nonetheless, the House of Lords interpreted the Regulations by adding or reading in the words 'or would have been so employed if they had not been unfairly dismissed [by reason of the transfer]'.

4.15 A similar approach was taken in *Pickstone v Freemans plc*[40] where the House of Lords had to consider the true construction of an amendment to the Equal Pay Act. The statutory amendment resulted from the decision of the European Court of Justice[41] that the United Kingdom was in breach of European Community Treaty obligations by failing to implement a Directive;[42] the existing legislation failed to ensure that a woman received equal pay for work of equal value. However, the amended legislation only conferred a right to equal pay if an employee was outside the scope of the pre-existing legislation. The difficulty that then arose was that a woman wished to rely on the new amended provision although her case was also in fact covered by the pre-existing legislation. It was therefore apparent that despite introducing an amendment to plug a loophole identified by the European Court of Justice, the new legislation had failed to achieve its purpose. The employer argued that the female employee could not rely on the amended

[37] [1990] 1 AC 546.

[38] 1981, SI 1981/1794.

[39] However, the European Court of Justice had recently interpreted the European Community Directive which had inspired the Regulations (the Acquired Rights Directive (EEC) 77/187) as meaning that workers should be regarded as still being employed by the transferor if the only reason for their dismissal was the projected transfer: see Case 101/78 *P Bork International A/S v Forensingen af Arbejdsledere i Danmark* [1988] ECR 3057.

[40] [1989] AC 66.

[41] *Commission v United Kingdom* [1982] ECR 2601.

[42] The Equal Pay Directive (EEC) 75/117.

legislation because she fell within the pre-existing statute and succeeded at the Employment Appeal Tribunal[43] and in the Court of Appeal.[44] However, when the case was heard by the House of Lords,[45] they adopted a broad purposive construction which modified and extended the literal wording of the legislation.

4.16 It has been argued that this broad goal-orientated approach to construction should be utilised when applying section 3(1) to a potential conflict between a statutory provision and a Convention right by reading in, reading down or giving effect to the provision in a way which is compatible with Convention rights. Lord Irvine, for example, has said that the interpretative techniques used in European Community cases provide useful guidance to the courts in developing a strong interpretive approach to section 3.[46]

(4) The doctrines of 'reading in' and 'reading down'

4.17 The doctrine of 'reading in' is a well established principle of constitutional law which permits a court to imply words into a statute in order to uphold its validity where it is inconsistent with the Constitution. In *Schachter v Canada*[47] the Supreme Court of Canada had to consider whether the legislation for paternity benefits breached the equality provisions of the Canadian Charter of Rights[48] by discriminating between natural parents and adoptive parents. As Lamer CJ put it[49] when describing how the approach of 'reading in' operates in relation to the Canadian Charter of Rights:

> a court [must] define carefully the extent of the inconsistency between the statute in question and the requirements of the Constitution . . . In the case of reading down the inconsistency is defined as what the statute wrongly *excludes* . . . [and] the inconsistency may be to include the excluded group within the statutory scheme. This has the effect of extending the reach of the statute by way of reading in rather than reading down.

4.18 The doctrine of 'reading in' has played a limited role in cases decided under the Canadian Charter of Rights, and the principles evolved by the Canadian courts must be treated with caution, since the Canadian courts have much

---

43 [1986] ICR 886.

44 [1989] AC 66.

45 Ibid.

46 Lord Irvine, 'The Development of Human Rights in Britain Under an Incorporated Convention on Human Rights' [1998] PL 221, 228.

47 [1992] 2 SCR 679.

48 Under Art 15.

49 Ibid 697, 698.

wider powers[50] to remedy conflicts between the Charter and primary legislation (including a variety of ways in which to strike down the statute). By comparison, under the Human Rights Act the court can only choose between ensuring compatibility with Convention rights by interpreting legislation under section 3(1) or making a declaration of incompatibility. The different remedies available to the Canadian courts mean that they may be reluctant to make a declaration which reads in words to a statute when they could instead defer to the legislature by using a more appropriate remedy.

4.19 The remedy of reading in has created particular controversy in Canada in relation to 'underinclusive' legislation, in other words legislation which confers benefits on some types of claimants but fails to include others, who then claim they have been unlawfully discriminated against.[51] As Lamer CJ pointed out in *Schachter v Canada*:[52]

> A statute may be worded in such a way that it gives a benefit or right to one group (inclusive wording) or it may be worded to give a right or benefit to everyone except a certain group (exclusive wording). It would be an arbitrary distinction to treat inclusively and exclusively worded statutes differently. To do so would create a situation where the style of drafting would be the single critical factor in the determination of a remedy. This is entirely inappropriate.

Consequently, in *Haig v Canada*[53] the Ontario Court of Appeal held that the legislation prohibiting discrimination in employment was unconstitutional[54] because it did not include sexual orientation as a ground for discrimination; and went on to order[55] that the legislation be 'interpreted, applied and administered as though it contained "sexual orientation" as prohibited ground of discrimination'. Similarly, in *Miron v Trudel*[56] the Supreme Court of Canada remedied unconstitutional[57] legislation requiring compulsory insurance (including benefits payable

[50] Section 52 of the Constitution Act states that 'any law which is inconsistent with the provisions of the Constitution is, to the extent of the inconsistency, of no force and effect'. In *Schachter v Canada* [1992] 2 SCR 679 the Supreme Court discussed the various choices available to the court:

1. nullification, declaring a statute invalid;
2. temporary validity, ie suspending a declaration of invalidity on a temporary basis;
3. severance, striking down the invalid part of a statute, severing it from the remainder;
4. reading in, ie adding words;
5. reading down ie interpreting the statute so that it becomes consistent with the Constitution;
6. constitutional exemption, ie excluding from the statute the application which is inconsistent with the Constitution.

[51] Under s 15 of the Charter of Rights.

[52] [1992] 2 SCR 679, 698.

[53] (1992) 9 OR (3d) 495.

[54] As a denial of equality rights under s 15 of the Charter.

[55] (1992) 9 OR (3d) 495, 508.

[56] [1995] 2 SCR 418.

[57] Since discrimination on marital status breached equality rights under s 15.

to the spouse of the insured person) by reading in words so as to extend the benefits to common law spouses. The Supreme Court again deployed the doctrine of 'reading in' in *Vriend v Alberta* when it overruled a contentious decision of the Alberta Court of Appeal[58] which had upheld the failure of the provincial anti-discrimination legislation to extend to discrimination on grounds of sexual orientation. The Supreme Court[59], on the other hand, concluded that the legislation breached the Charter of Rights; and went on to decide that discrimination on grounds of sexual orientation should be read into the legislation.

It is submitted that the technique of 'reading in' will provide an effective means of ensuring that 'so far as it is possible to do so, primary legislation and subordinate legislation must be read and given effect in a way which is compatible with Convention rights' under section 3(1). The most obvious examples will arise where the court will read in or imply Convention rights into broad statutory discretions. Thus, the decision in *R v Secretary of the Home Department, ex p Brind*[60] will be reversed so that it will become necessary for public authorities to exercise their discretion so as not to act incompatibly with Convention rights.[61] **4.20**

The doctrine of 'reading down' is also a well recognised principle of constitutional law; where statutory language will bear two meanings, the court will apply the *narrow* interpretation in order to ensure that the legislation remains valid. Thus, 'reading down' permits the court to interpret a statute which is actually inconsistent with constitutional rights to be interpreted *as if* it were consistent with them. The Privy Council has recently echoed the concerns expressed in the Canadian cases in *De Freitas v Permanent Secretary of Ministry of Agriculture Fisheries, Lands and Housing*[62] where it declined to 'read down' a statutory provision restricting the freedom of expression of civil servants to confine it only to situations where the forbearance of particular civil servants from publication was reasonably required for the proper performance of their official functions. Lord Clyde expressed the view that: **4.21**

> the deficiency of the proposed solution can be found in the principle that an enactment construed by severing, reading down or making implications into what the legislature actually said should take the form that it could reasonably be supposed that Parliament had intended to enact. The proposed solution requires the subsection to be applied on a case by case basis, amounting for all practical purposes to a

[58] (1996) 132 DLR (4th ed) 595.

[59] (1998) 156 DLR (4th ed) 385; see also M Childs, 'Constitutional Review and Underinclusive Legislation' [1998] PL 647.

[60] [1991] 1 AC 696; for a discussion of the case see para 2.31ff above.

[61] See para 6.86ff below.

[62] [1998] 3 WLR 675.

retrospective imposition of liability on those civil servants considered by the court to have fallen on the wrong side of the line. That would be an altogether different provision from that which Parliament enacted. In this context reference may usefully be made to the observations of Sopinka J, giving the judgment of the majority of the Supreme Court of Canada in *Osborne v Canada (Treasury Board)*.[63] In that case the Canadian Supreme Court held unconstitutional a statute which prohibited public servants from 'engaging in work' for or against a political party or candidate. It will be noticed that the statute did not prohibit freedom of expression as such and so would probably not have attracted the principle of overbreadth applied by the United States Supreme Court to First Amendment rights: see *Broadrick v Oklahoma*.[64] Nevertheless, the Supreme Court held the entire provision unconstitutional on the principle of 'reading down'. Sopinka J said:[65]

> 'The language of [the section] is so inclusive that [the trial judge] declined to provide any definition of its scope but rather preferred to deal with the activities of each of the plaintiffs individually in measuring the restriction imposed by the section against the Charter. The number of instances in which the operation of the section would otherwise have been in breach of . . . the Charter is extensive. On this basis there is little doubt that in future other instances will arise which will require similar reading down of the section. In the final analysis, a law that is invalid in so many of its applications will, as a result of wholesale reading down, bear little resemblance to the law that Parliament passed and a strong inference arises that it is invalid as a whole . . . In my opinion, it is Parliament that should determine how the section should be redrafted and not the court. Apart from impracticability of a determination of the constitutionality of the section on a case-by-case basis, Parliament will have available to it information and expertise that is not available to the court.'

It is precisely the same considerations which in the view of their Lordships apply to the solution proposed by the Court of Appeal and render it inadequate to save the validity of the provision in question.

4.22 Nevertheless, the technique of 'reading down' legislation is likely to have a significant impact under the Human Rights Act, enabling the court to adopt a narrow construction of statutory words so as to render it compatible with Convention rights. This approach to statutory construction has already been important in cases under the Act.[65a]

(5) The rule of construction in New Zealand

4.23 Like the Human Rights Act the New Zealand Bill of Rights Act is an ordinary act of parliament. The New Zealand courts must in cases of conflict apply rules of construction to ascertain which legislation prevails. The approach taken in New

[63] (1991) 82 DLR (4th) 321.
[64] (1973) 413 US 601.
[65] n 63, above, at 347.
[65a] See para 4.28A below.

Zealand[66] can, therefore, throw light on the issues of statutory construction that will arise under the Human Rights Act. Section 6 of the New Zealand Bill of Rights Act states that:

> Whenever an enactment can be given a meaning which is consistent with the rights and freedoms contained in this Bill of Rights, this meaning should be preferred to any other meaning.

On the first occasion when the New Zealand Court of Appeal had to consider section 6, it took a bold view of its impact. The issue in *Flickinger v Hong Kong*[67] was whether a long standing interpretation of section 66 of the Judicature Act which prevented an unsuccessful applicant for habeas corpus from appealing to the Court of Appeal continued to prevail after the enactment of the Bill of Rights Act. Cooke P in giving the majority judgment took the view that the right in section 23(1)(c) of the Bill of Rights Act to have the validity of detention determined by habeas corpus was to be 'construed generously' so as to give to individuals 'the full measure of the fundamental rights and freedoms referred to'. As a result, he was prepared to give the relevant statutory provisions 'a wider interpretation than has prevailed hitherto'. However, in subsequent cases a more restrictive view has been taken about the impact of section 6. In *Ministry of Transport v Noort* [68] Cooke P said: **4.24**

> The rights and freedoms in Part II are not constitutionally entrenched and may be overridden by an ordinary enactment, but in interpreting an enactment a consistent meaning is to be preferred to any other meaning. The preference will come into play only when the enactment can be given a meaning consistent with the rights and freedoms. This must mean, I think, can reasonably be given such a meaning. A strained interpretation will not be enough.

This approach was clarified in *R v Philips*[69] where Cooke P rejected a complaint that a reverse onus presumption in the Misuse of Drugs Act contravened the Bill of Rights Act:

> we are not persuaded that the ordinary and natural meaning of the word 'proof' is capable of extending so far. To suggest that section 6(6) of the Misuse of Drugs Act can be read in the sense contended for is, in our view, a strained and unnatural interpretation

[66] See eg A Butler, 'The Bill of Rights Debate: Why the New Zealand Bill of Rights Act 1990 is a Bad Model for Britain' (1997) 17 OJLS 323; Lord Cooke, 'Mechanisms for Entrenchment and Protection of a Bill of Rights: The New Zealand Experience' [1997] EHRLR 490; M Taggart, 'Tugging on Superman's Cape: Lessons from Experience with the New Zealand Bill of Rights Act 1990' [1998] PL 266; H Schwartz, 'The Short Happy Life and the Tragic Death of the New Zealand Bill of Rights Act' [1998] NZLR 259; P Rishworth, 'Reflections on the Bill of Rights After *Quilter v Attorney-General*' [1998] NZLR 683.

[67] [1991] NZLR 439.

[68] [1992] 3 NZLR 260, 272.

[69] [1991] 3 NZLR 175, 177; see also *Simpson v A-G* [1994] 3 NZLR 667, 674 in which Cooke P said in relation to section 6: 'I accept that this legislative injunction does not extend to a strained meaning'.

> which, even with the aid of the New Zealand Bill of Rights Act, this Court would not be justified in adopting.

4.25 Where there is a clear conflict of language between the Bill of Rights Act and another statute, there is no scope for the rule of construction enacted by section 6. The Bill of Rights Act must give way. Thus, in *R v Bennett*[70] the High Court rejected a prisoner's claim to vote in the general election. The statutory disqualification on prisoners voting prevailed over the right to vote under the Bill of Rights Act[71] because Greig J said the conflict was 'so plain as to give no room for any argument'. The question that arose in *Jones v Police*[72] was whether an amendment to a criminal charge could be made after all the evidence had been heard and judgment had been reserved. The New Zealand Bill of Rights creates the right to a fair trial[73] and requires that a defendant is informed promptly and in detail about the nature and cause of the charge.[74] Nevertheless, the Court of Appeal robustly rejected the claim that the power to make a late amendment conflicted with the Bill of Rights, on the ground that the safeguards in the procedure precluded any possibile conflict with the Bill of Rights Act.

4.26 In *Quilter v A-G of New Zealand*[75] the issue was whether the Marriage Act allowed marriage between persons of the same sex. It was accepted that when the legislation was drafted marriage carried its traditional common law meaning and included only marriages between persons of the opposite sex. However, the applicant contended that the prohibition against discrimination in the Bill of Rights Act[76] required a modern interpretation to be placed on the Marriage Act and marriage: since the Bill of Rights Act signalled that discrimination on grounds of sexual orientation was not to be sanctioned by the courts. Nevertheless, the Court of Appeal concluded that the Bill of Rights Act did not have the effect of making a fundamental change to the concept of marriage. In the course of the judgments a variety of views were also expressed about the proper construction to be given to section 6 of the Bill of Rights Act. Tipping J[77] said that the fundamental question:

> which arises under section 6 of the Bill of Rights Act is whether the Marriage Act

[70] (1993) 2 Human Rights Reports of New Zealand 358.
[71] Under s 12.
[72] [1998] 1 NZLR 447.
[73] s 25(a).
[74] s 24(a).
[75] [1998] 1 NZLR 523; see A Butler, 'Same Sex Marriage and Freedom From Discrimination in New Zealand' [1998] PL 396; P Rishworth, 'Reflections on the Bill of Rights after *Quilter v Attorney-General*' [1998] NZLR 683 where he considers whether it would be desirable for the New Zealand courts to grant declarations of incompatibility as they can under the Human Rights Act: see para 4.43ff below.
[76] s 19 of the Act.
[77] n 75, above, 581.

> can properly be given the meaning for which the appellants contend. . . . By 'properly' I mean by a legitimate process of construction. I have come to the conclusion that the meaning for which the appellants contend cannot properly be given . . .

Thomas J dissented from the majority on the question of whether, but for the clear meaning of the Marriage Act, there would have been a breach of the discrimination provision under the Bill of Rights Act. However, he discussed the correct approach to section 6 in these terms:[78]

> where a breach of a fundamental right or freedom enshrined in the Bill of Rights is found to exist in any statute, the Court should conscientiously strive to arrive at a meaning that will avoid that breach . . . Even adopting that approach in the present case, I am unable to interpret the Marriage Act in the manner sought by the appellants. The legislative history of the Bill of Rights Act is well known. Parliament expressly rejected a Bill of Rights which would enable the Courts to strike legislation down as invalid on the ground it is contrary to the Bill of Rights. Parliament or legislative supremacy was deliberately retained by the legislature. This Court has an interpretative role and while it must, in accordance with Parliament's directive prefer a meaning which is consistent with the Bill of Rights, it cannot adopt a meaning which is clearly contrary to Parliament's intent . . .
>
> Declining to strain the meaning of the Act does not mean that this Court is shirking its responsibilities to apply section 6. That section does not authorise the Court to legislate. Even if a meaning is theoretically possible, it must be rejected if it is clearly contrary to what Parliament intended . . .

Section 6 of the New Zealand Bill of Rights therefore places significant restrictions on the court in holding that legislation breaches the Bill of Rights Act.[79]

(6) The effect and the limits of the 'rule of construction'[79a]

It is submitted that the proper approach to section 3 is to bear in mind the conventional rule that when interpreting a statute, the courts are seeking to determine the 'intention of the legislature', so that: **4.27**

> the object of all judicial interpretation of [statute law] is to determine what intention is either expressly or by implication conveyed by the language used, so far as necessary for the purpose of determining whether a particular case or state of facts which is presented to the interpreter falls within it.[80]

We suggest that, in all cases in which Convention rights are in play, the effect of section 3 is equivalent to requiring the courts to act on a presumuption that the intention of the legislature was to enact a provision compatible with Convention

[78] Ibid 541, 542.

[79] J Coppel, *The Human Rights Act 1998: Enforcing the European Convention in the Domestic Courts* (John Wiley & Sons, 1999) paras 2.61–2.66.

[79a] See generally, F Bennion, 'What Interpretation is "Possible" Under Section 3(1) of the Human Rights Act 1998' [2000] PL 77.

[80] P Maxwell, *The Interpretation of Statutes* (1st edn, 1875) 1; quoted in F. Bennion, *Statutory Interpretation* (3rd edn, Butterworths, 1997), pp.8–9.

rights. In relation to statutes passed before the Human Rights Act, section 3 can be read as, in effect, adding a statement to the effect that the statute is intended to be read in a way which is compatible with Convention rights. In the case of statutes passed after the Human Rights Act, this will be made clear by the 'statement of compatibility' with Convention rights.[81]

4.28 In the light of this 'statutory intention', the courts will be able to construe legislation in a way which is compatible with the Convention rights by using techniques such as the following:

- adopting a 'strained' or non-literal construction to make the statute compatible (provided that 'unnatural meanings' are not imposed) in order to give full effect to fundamental rights;
- 'reading in' words the addition of which would render the statute compatible; and
- 'reading down' words to adopt a narrow construction of statutory words so as to render it compatible with Convention rights.

In adopting such a construction, the courts will not be bound by previous authority as to the interpretation of a particular statutory provision.[82]

4.28A It is already apparent from decisions under the Human Rights Act that the doctrine of 'reading down' will have a significant impact where a public authority argues that a statutory provision is incompatible with Convention rights. Thus, in *R v DPP, ex p Kebilene* the Divisional Court took the view that a reverse onus provision in the Prevention of Terrorism Act was plainly incompatible[82a] with the presumption of innocence under Article 6(2).[82b] However, in the House of Lords, Lord Cooke suggested[82c] that the words 'unless the contrary is proved' could be 'read down' to mean 'unless sufficient evidence is given to the contrary' and that the statute could be satisfied by evidence which a reasonable jury could take to support the defence. In the Scots case of *Brown v Procurator Fiscal*[82d] the High Court of Justiciary had to consider whether the power of the police to *compel* information from a driver under section 172 of the Road Traffic Act 1988 was incompatible with the presumption of innocence. The prosecution wished to adduce evidence that the driver said 'it was me' when questioned under section 172. The defence argued that section 172 was incompatible with Article 6(2) and

---

[81] See para 4.39ff below.

[82] Cf the *Notes on Clauses* on cl 3 of the Bill: 'the Bill may well require an interpretation which differs from one previously adopted by a United Kingdom court'.

[82a] Lord Bingham CJ said at [1999] 3 WLR 175, 190 that the sections 'underlined, in a blatant and obvious way, the presumption of innocence'; Laws LT at 201 agreed.

[82b] See para 11.236ff below.

[82c] [1999] 3 WLR 972, 987C–G; see also Lord Steyn at 985E–H.

[82d] 4 Feb 2000.

the prosecution countered by saying that the only option the court had was to make a declaration of incompatibility.[82e] However, the Court decided that since the section does not say expressly that the Crown could use the information in a prosecution, it would read the section down as simply permitting the police officer to require the keeper to give the information and not as permitting the Crown to use the information to incriminate the keeper at any subsequent trial.

Difficult questions will also arise about the proper approach under section 3(1) towards traditional aids to statutory construction. When examining if a particular construction is possible as a matter of language, it is uncertain whether the courts should disregard conventional rules of construction such as the impact of relevant related enactments or the need to avoid absurd results.[83] In particular, it may be highly pertinent to look at the views expressed in *Hansard*, and the Human Rights Act is likely to encourage a re-examination of *Pepper v Hart*.[84] **4.29**

It is submitted that the only occasions on which a court will be unable to construe legislation in a way which is compatible with Convention rights is where the statute uses clear and specific words which have the effect of restricting the Convention right in question.[85] An example of this sort of provision was section 25 of the Criminal Justice and Public Order Act 1994[85a] which stated that a person charged with murder, attempted murder, manslaughter, rape or attempted rape 'shall not be granted bail'. In relation to future legislation where there has been a statement of compatibility[86] it seems highly unlikely that the courts will be prepared to adopt a construction incompatible with Convention rights.[87] Nevertheless, the precise limits of the section 3 rule of construction remain controversial. It could be argued that section 3 ensures that Convention rights cannot be overriden unless the statute *expressly* derogates from such rights. A principle framed in this way is more properly characterised as a rule of priority than a rule of construction since it does not direct attention to interpretation of the language of the statute. We would submit that in the final analysis the limits of section 3 cannot extend beyond an obligation to interpret the legislative wording. **4.30**

[82e] See para 4.43ff below.

[83] For a discussion of these issues in the context of s 6 of the New Zealand Bill of Rights and the decision in *Quilter v A-G* [1998] 1 NZLR 523 see A Butler, 'Same Sex Marriage and Freedom From Discrimination in New Zealand' [1998] PL 396, 403, 404

[84] [1993] 1 AC 593; for a discussion of the doctrine, see para 4.35ff below.

[85] Cf Lord Irvine, 'The Development of Human Rights in Britain Under an Incorporated Convention on Human Rights' [1998] PL 221, 228.

[85a] Now amended by the Crime and Disorder Act 1998, s 56.

[86] See para 4.39ff below.

[87] Cf Lord Lester and D Pannick, *Human Rights Law and Practice* (Butterworths, 1999) para 2.3.4, n 2, 25 (expressing a similar view).

(7) The provisions of section 3(2)

4.31 Section 3(2) of the Human Rights Act provides that:

> This section—
>
> (a) applies to primary legislation and subordinate legislation whenever enacted;
> (b) does not affect the validity, continuing operation or enforcement of any incompatible primary legislation; and
> (c) does not affect the validity, continuing operation or enforcement of any incompatible subordinate legislation if (disregarding any possibility of revocation) primary legislation prevents removal of incompatibility.

The meaning of section 3(2)(a) appears clear: the 'rule of construction' applies to all statutes which are enacted before or after the Human Rights Act. The rule could, however, presumably be displaced by express subsequent statutory provision: either enacting a new 'rule of construction' or specifically disapplying section 3.

4.32 The meaning of section 3(2)(b) and (c) is somewhat obscure. It is difficult to see how a 'rule of construction' could affect the validity, continuing operation or enforcement of a statute. It might be thought that it went without saying that a statute which could not be 'read and given effect to' in a way which was compatible with Convention rights would remain 'valid' and 'effective'. Nevertheless, these provisions could be read as being an answer, 'for the avoidance of doubt', to the question 'what if a statute cannot be read and given effect to in a way which is compatible with Convention rights'.

4.33 It has, however, been suggested that section 3(2) has a wider purpose: the disapplication of the doctrine of 'implied repeal'. This is a common law doctrine of statutory interpretation whereby the provisions of an earlier statute which are contrary to those of a later one are repealed by implication.[88] Thus, according to the *Notes on Clauses* on the Bill

> It is not intended that the so-called doctrine of 'implied repeal' in relation to pre-Bill legislation should apply (hence the use of the phrase 'whenever enacted').

The Lord Chancellor, Lord Irvine, also said when introducing the Bill at the second reading[89] that the Government:

> did not wish to incorporate the Convention rights, and then, in reliance on the doctrine of implied repeal, allow the Courts to strike down Acts of Parliament.

If the object was to ensure that the Human Rights Act did not 'impliedly repeal'

---

[88] In accordance with the maxim 'later laws abrogate earlier contrary laws' (*leges posteriores priores contrarias abrogant*), see generally, Bennion (n 80 above) s 87ff; for a discussion of the doctrine of implied repeal, see para 1.67 above.

[89] *Hansard*, HL col 522 (18 Nov 1998).

any inconsistent previous legislation, this has plainly not been achieved by section 3(2). It applies only to section 3 ('This section . . .') and cannot affect the operation of the rest of the Act. It could, therefore, be argued that, for example, section 9(3) of the Human Rights Act impliedly repeals the statutory immunity conferred on magistrates for *ultra vires* acts.[89a]

Nevertheless, it is unlikely that such an argument would be successful. There is, in general, a presumption against implied repeal.[90] This presumption is greatly strengthened by express provisions for 'declarations of incompatibility'[91] and the repeated insistence by the Government that the Act is not intended to allow judges to set aside primary legislation.[92] The White Paper deals explicitly with the 'implied repeal' point: **4.34**

> It has been suggested that the courts should be able to uphold the rights in the Human Rights Bill in preference to any provisions of earlier legislation which are incompatible with those rights. This is on the basis that a later Act of Parliament takes precedence over an earlier Act if there is a conflict [the doctrine of implied repeal] But the Human Rights Bill is intended to provide a new basis for judicial interpretation of all legislation, not a basis for striking down any part of it.[93]

As a result, it is most unlikely that a statutory provision enacted before the Human Rights Act which is found to be incompatible with it (and incapable of being construed to be compatible) will be held to have been impliedly repealed.

(8) The doctrine of *Pepper v Hart*

A particular feature of the parliamentary debates concerning the Human Rights Bill was the numerous attempts to draw out Government spokesmen about the meaning of the Bill; and *Hansard* is likely to be a rich source of material[94] which may assist the true construction of the Act. **4.35**

The traditional rule of statutory construction prohibited the use of parliamentary material as an interpretative aid;[95] but this approach has been significantly eroded **4.36**

89a Justices of the Peace Act 1997, s 52: see para 10.175A below.

90 See eg *R* v *Governor of Holloway Prison, ex p Jennings* [1982] 1 WLR 949; and generally, Bennion (n 80 above) 225–6.

91 See para 4.43ff below.

92 See eg Lord Irvine LC, *Hansard*, HL col 1230 (3 Nov 1997); Jack Straw *Hansard*, HC col 780 (16 Feb 1998).

93 *Rights Brought Home: The Human Rights Bill* (1997) Cm 3782 para 2.14.

94 See eg F Klug, 'The Human Rights Act, *Pepper v Hart* and All That' [1999] PL 246.

95 *Beswick v Beswick* [1968] AC 58 *per* Lord Reid at 74; *Davis v Johnson* [1979] AC 264 *per* Viscount Dilhorne at 337 and Lord Scarman at 349, 350; *Hadmor Productions Ltd v Hamilton* [1983] AC 191 *per* Lord Diplock at 232, 233.

in recent years.[96] In *Pepper v Hart*[97] the House of Lords modified the rule;[98] Lord Browne-Wilkinson stated[99] that the courts could examine *Hansard* as an aid to statutory construction *provided*:

- the legislation in question was ambiguous, obscure or led to absurdity;
- the material relied on consisted of statements by a Minister (or the promoter of the bill); and
- the statements must disclose the mischief aimed at by the enactment or the legislative intention and must be clear.

The rationale he gave was that:[100]

> Statute law consists of the words that Parliament has enacted. It is for the courts to construe those words and it is the court's duty in doing so to give effect to the intention of Parliament in using those words. It is an inescapable fact that, despite all the care in passing legislation, some statutory provisions when applied to the circumstances under consideration in any specific case are found to be ambiguous. One of the reasons for such ambiguity is that the members of the legislature in enacting the statutory provision may have been told what result those words are intended to achieve. Faced with a given set of words which are capable of conveying that meaning, it is not surprising that the words are accepted as having that meaning. Contrast that with the position of the courts. The courts are faced simply with a set of words which are in fact capable of bearing two meanings. The courts are ignorant of the underlying Parliamentary purpose. Unless something in other parts of the legislation discloses such purpose, the courts are forced to adopt one of the two possible meanings using highly technical rules of construction. In many, I suspect most, cases references to Parliamentary materials will not throw any light on the matter. But in a few cases it may emerge that the very question was considered by Parliament in enacting the legislation. Why in such a case should the courts blind themselves to a clear indication of what Parliament intended in using those words? The courts cannot attach a meaning to words which those words cannot bear, but if

[96] In *Black-Clawson International Ltd v Papierwerke Waldhof-Aschaffenburg AG* [1975] AC 591 the House of Lords admitted in evidence a Committee report (on which the Foreign Judgments (Reciprocal Enforcement) Act 1933 was based) so it could identify the mischief which the statute was intended to cure, although the material was inadmissible for the purpose of ascertaining the meaning of the words used by Parliament to effect that cure; in *Pickstone v Freemans Plc* [1989] AC 66 the House of Lords referred to speeches by the Minister when construing a statutory instrument which purported to carry into effect obligations under European Community law; and the House of Lords in *R v Secretary of State for Transport, ex p Factortame Ltd* [1990] 2 AC 85 examined a Law Commission report: not merely to identify the mischief but also to draw an inference about Parliament's intention from the fact that Parliament had not expressly implemented one of the Commission's recommendations.

[97] [1993] 1 AC 593.

[98] For a discussion of the reasons for the change in judicial attitude see, for example, Lord Lester, 'Pepper v Hart Revisited' (1994) 15 Statute L Rev 10; and see generally, Bennion (n 80, above) s 217, 472–487.

[99] *Pepper v Hart* (n 97, above), 640.

[100] Ibid 634–635.

the words are capable of bearing more than one meaning, why should not Parliament's true intention be enforced rather than thwarted?

Nevertheless, reference should only be made to *Hansard* if clear statements were made by ministers on the *very point* in question in the litigation. In *Melluish v BMI Ltd (No 3)*[101] Lord Browne-Wilkinson criticised the Revenue for introducing statements made by ministers into the appeal which related to a different statutory provision and another problem, emphasising that judges should be astute to check misuse of the rule in *Pepper v Hart*[102] by making wasted costs orders. **4.37**

If *Hansard* is to be referred to in court,[103] the party who proposes to do so must serve on all the other parties and on the court both the extract and a summary of the argument in support of the application not less than five clear working days in advance. One survey[104] indicated that there have been very few cases[105] where statements in *Hansard* have assisted on questions of statutory construction. This reflects the very strict pre-conditions which must be satisfied before recourse can be had to *Hansard*. However, the Human Rights Act is likely to encourage greater use of *Hansard*, in relation to the statement of compatibility procedure[106] as well as Parliamentary debates concerning potentially incompatible statutory provisions. The Act is likely to encourage a re-examination of *Pepper v Hart*[107] itself. **4.38**

C. Statements of Compatibility

Section 19 of the Human Rights Act has created a special procedure to be used when new legislation is to be enacted. Under section 19 the Minister in charge of the bill must make a statement before the second reading stating either that the bill is compatible with Convention rights[108] or that, although the Government wishes the bill to proceed, he is unable to make a statement of compatibility. Section 19 states: **4.39**

(1) A Minister of the Crown in charge of a Bill in either House of Parliament must, before the Second Reading of the Bill—

(a) make a statement to the effect that in his view the provisions of the Bill are compatible with the Convention rights ('a statement of compatibility'); or

---

101 [1995] 3 WLR 631, 645.

102 See n 97 above.

103 *Practice Direction (Hansard: Citation)* [1995] 1 WLR 192.

104 R Clayton, 'Life after Pepper v Hart' [1996] JR 77.

105 See eg *R v Warwickshire County Council, ex p Johnson* [1993] AC 583; *Chief Adjudication Officer v Foster* [1993] AC 754; *R v Secretary of State for the Home Department, ex p Mehari* [1994] QB 474; *Restick v Crickmore* [1994] 1 WLR 420; *R v Hampshire* [1996] QB 1.

106 See para 4.39ff below.

107 See n 97 above.

108 See para 5.120ff.

(b) make a statement to the effect that although he is unable to make a statement of incompatibility the government nevertheless wishes the House to proceed with the Bill.

(2) The statement must be in writing and be published in such a manner as the Minister making it considers it appropriate.

The obligation to make a statement of compatibility came into force on 24 November 1998.[109]

4.40 The Act does not provide for any independent element in assessing the compatibility of proposed legislation with the Convention. It has been pointed out that this appears to be little improvement on the pre-existing inadequate arrangements for ensuring that legislation complies with the Convention.[110] Under the comparable provision in New Zealand the Attorney-General is required to bring any apparent incompatibilities to the attention of Parliament.[111] Even with this additional scrutiny it appears that infringing legislation has been introduced without comment and the standard of legal advice has been criticised.[112] The level of scrutiny which will be exercised in England is not at present clear.

4.41 It seems likely that, in making a statement of compatibility, the Minister will be exercising a function in connection with proceedings in Parliament and will not, therefore, be subject to the Human Rights Act itself.[113] Furthermore, the obligation under section 19 is probably not justiciable in the courts due to the provisions of Article 9 of the Bill of Rights 1688 which confers immunity on 'proceedings in Parliament'.[114] This view has been taken by the New Zealand courts in relation to similar provisions in the New Zealand Bill of Rights Act 1990.[115]

4.42 The importance that the courts will attach to statements of compatibility when construing the legislation in accordance with section 3(1)[116] is unclear. Under the doctrine in *Pepper v Hart*[117] it is only appropriate to examine *Hansard* as an aid to statutory construction where the legislation in question is ambiguous, obscure or leads to absurdity. However, it is submitted that the courts are likely to give some weight to statements of compatibility when construing legislation in accordance

[109] The Human Rights Act 1998 (Commencement) Order 1998, SI 1998/2882.

[110] M Taggart, 'Tugging on Superman's Cape: Lessons from Experience with the New Zealand Bill of Rights Act 1990' [1998] PL 266, 272–3.

[111] New Zealand Bill of Rights Act 1990, s 7.

[112] See generally, M Taggart (n 110 above) 273–274.

[113] s 6(3); see generally, para 5.05ff below.

[114] For a discussion as to whether the obligation under s 19 to make a statement of compatibility is judicially enforceable, see N Bamforth, 'Parliamentary Sovereignty and the Human Rights Act 1998' [1998] PL 572; for a discussion of parliamentary privilege, see generally, para 15.330 below.

[115] The obligation is in s 7; see *Mangawaro Enterprises Ltd v A-G* [1994] 2 NZLR 451.

[116] See para 4.27ff.

[117] [1993] 1 AC 593; para 4.35ff.

with section 3(1)[118] of the Human Rights Act. The Lord Chancellor, Lord Irvine[119] has expressed the view that:

> it should be clear from the Parliamentary history, and in particular the Ministerial statement of compatibility which will be required by the Act, that Parliament will not intend to cut across a Convention right. Ministerial statements of compatibility will inevitably be a strong spur to the courts to find the means of construing statutes compatibly with the Convention.

D. Declarations of Incompatibility

(1) Introduction

The Human Rights Act has introduced the constitutional innovation of permitting the courts to identify a conflict between Convention rights[120] and other statutory provisions while at the same time deferring to the doctrine of Parliamentary sovereignty.[121] The Act therefore represents a refinement of the possibilities available when the Government was considering whether to incorporate the European Convention along the lines of the Canadian[122] or New Zealand[123] models. **4.43**

The Human Rights Act treats primary legislation passed by the Westminster Parliament rather differently from legislation enacted by the Scottish Parliament, the Welsh Assembly or the Northern Ireland Assembly. Legislation by Westminster is defined as primary legislation under section 21 whereas that emanating from Scotland, Northern Ireland[123a] and Wales[123b] is regarded as secondary legislation, and as secondary legislation the courts will have wider powers[124] to interpret the legislation so as to render it compatible with Convention rights. **4.44**

However, the Act has introduced some important limitations into the declaration of incompatibility procedure. Section 4(5) of the Act restricts the power to make declarations to the High Court and above.[125] Where such a declaration is being considered, the Crown has a *right* under section 5 to be given notice of the proceedings in question.[126] Even if a declaration is granted, section 4(6) states that it **4.45**

---

[118] See para 4.27ff above.

[119] Lord Irvine, 'The Development of Human Rights in Britain Under an Incorporated Convention on Human Rights' [1998] PL 221.

[120] See para 3.43 above.

[121] See para 1.66ff above.

[122] See para 1.79 above.

[123] See para 1.81 above.

[123a] Under s 21 legislation made in Scotland or Northern Ireland is defined as subordinate legislation.

[123b] Government of Wales Act 1998, s 107(1).

[124] See para 4.52 below.

[125] See para 4.54 below.

[126] See para 22.73 below.

does not affect the continuing validity, operation or enforcement of the statutory provision nor does it bind the parties in the proceedings themselves.[127] A declaration of incompatibility gives the Minister of State a *power* under section 10 to make a remedial order[128] although he is not obliged to do so. Nevertheless, a failure to remedy a breach of Convention rights following a declaration of incompatibility would provide powerful support to an application made to the European Court of Human Rights.[129]

(2) The power to make a declaration of incompatibility

4.46 Sub-sections 4(1) and (2) allow the court to make a declaration of incompatibility in relation to primary legislation and state that:

> (1) Subsection (2) applies to any proceedings in which a court determines whether a provision of primary legislation is compatible with a Convention right.
> (2) If the court is satisfied that the provision is incompatible with a Convention right, it may make a declaration of that incompatibility.

Where the court is considering subordinate legislation, sub-sections 4(3) and (4) state:

> (3) Subsection (4) applies to any proceedings in which a court determines whether a provision of subordinate legislation, made in the exercise of a power conferred by primary legislation, is incompatible with a Convention right.
> (4) If the court is satisfied—
> (a) that the provision is incompatible with a Convention right and
> (b) that (disregarding any possibility of revocation) the primary legislation concerned prevents the removal of incompatibility
> it may make a declaration of that incompatibility.

4.47 The burden of satisfying the court[130] that a statutory provision is incompatible with Convention rights will lie on the applicant. However, the public authority will have the burden of showing that a statutory provision cannot be construed under section 3 to make it compatible with Convention rights and that a declaration of incompatibility should be made. Where a court is considering making a declaration of incompatibility, the Crown is entitled under section 5 of the Human Rights Act to be given notice[131] and to be joined as a party to the proceedings.[132] For the purposes of proving that a statutory provision is incompatible with Convention rights, the word 'incompatible' is to be given its natural and ordinary meaning.[133]

---

[127] See para 4.56 below.
[128] See para 4.57ff below.
[129] For the procedure see para 23.08 below.
[130] See para 6.101ff below.
[131] See para 22.75 in relation to civil proceedings and para 22.78 in relation to criminal proceedings.
[132] See s 5(2) and see para 22.74ff.
[133] See generally, para 5.120ff below.

Primary legislation is defined by section 21 of the Human Rights Act, which states that: **4.48**

> 'primary legislation' means any—
> (a) public general Act;
> (b) local and personal Act;
> (c) private Act;
> (d) Measure of Church Assembly;
> (e) Measure of the General Synod of the Church of England;
> (f) Order in Council made under section 38(1)(a) of the Northern Ireland Constitution Act 1973;
> (g) Order in Council made in exercise of Her Majesty's Royal Prerogative;
>
> and includes an order or other instrument made (other than by the National Assembly for Wales or a member of the Scottish Executive) under primary legislation to the extent to which it operates to bring one or more provisions of that legislation into force or amends any primary legislation.

Although Orders in Council are defined as primary legislation under section 21 (and must be interpreted in accordance with section 3(1) of the Act), it is nevertheless submitted that when *making* such Order, the Privy Council is subject to section 6 of the Act. As a result, a declaration could be made that making the order is incompatible with Convention rights. **4.49**

Subordinate legislation is also defined by section 21 of the Human Rights Act, which states that: **4.50**

> 'subordinate' legislation, means any—
> (a) Order in Council other than one made in exercise of Her Majesty's Royal Prerogative or under section 38(1)(a) of the Northern Ireland Constitution Act 1973;
> (b) Act of the Scottish Parliament;
> (c) Act of the Parliament of Northern Ireland;
> (d) Measure of the Northern Ireland Assembly;
> (e) order, rules, regulations, scheme, warrant, byelaw or other instrument made under primary legislation (except to the extent that it operates to bring one or more provisions of that legislation into force or amends any primary legislation);
> (f) order, rules, regulations, scheme, warrant, byelaw or other instrument made under legislation mentioned in paragraph (b), (c), (d) or made under an Order in Council applying only to Northern Ireland.

The position concerning primary legislation is straightforward: provided it can be demonstrated that it cannot be interpreted compatibly with Convention rights under section 3(1) of the Human Rights Act,[134] it will then be appropriate to make a declaration of incompatibility. A statutory provision will be incompatible **4.51**

[134] See para 4.04ff above.

with Convention rights *either* because the statutory language is framed in terms which give no scope for a public authority to act differently or because the public authority is giving effect to or enforcing a statutory provision which is incompatible with Convention rights.[135]

4.52 Where subordinate legislation is at issue, the court must satisfy itself on two questions: first, whether the legislation is incompatible with Convention rights[136] and secondly whether *primary* legislation prevents the removal of the incompatibility. Because the primary legislation under which subordinate legislation is made is so often expressed in very broad language, the court will rarely be obliged to make a declaration of incompatibility in relation to subordinate legislation.

(3) Jurisdiction to make declarations of incompatibility

4.53 Section 4(5) defines the court for the purposes of making declarations of incompatibility and states that:

> (5) In this section 'court' means—
> (a) the House of Lords;
> (b) the Judicial Committee of the Privy Council;
> (c) the Courts-Martial Appeal Court;
> (d) in Scotland, the High Court of the Justiciary sitting otherwise than as a trial court or the Court of Session;
> (e) in England and Wales or Northern Ireland, the High Court or Court of Appeal.

The Human Rights Act does not entitle the lower courts to make declarations of incompatibility. It therefore will not be possible for the magistrates' court or Crown Court[137] to make declarations of incompatibility in the course of criminal proceedings. The county court has no power to make such declarations; nor will the power extend to tribunals such as employment tribunals or the Social Security Commissioners.

4.54 It is also clear that the Employment Appeals Tribunal will not have jurisdiction to grant declarations of incompatibility. Whereas the general jurisdiction of the High Court is conferred by section 19 of the Supreme Court Act 1981, the Employment Appeals Tribunal has a specific statutory jurisdiction[138] and is not a part of the High Court.

---

[135] See para 5.104ff below.

[136] See generally, para 5.120ff below.

[137] However, in *R v DPP, ex p Kebilene* [1999] 3 WLR 972 the Crown Court decided that anti-terrorist legislation was incompatible with Art 6(2) of the European Convention. The DPP was then asked to reconsider his consent to bringing the prosecution; and when he maintained that view, it was challenged in judicial review proceedings.

[138] Under the Employment Protection Act 1975 and now continued by virtue of s 20 of the Industrial Tribunals Act 1996. The appellate jurisdiction of the Employment Appeals Tribunal is derived from s 21 of the Industrial Tribunals Act and from s 9(1)(2) and (4), s 95, s 104 and s 126(1)

(4) The impact of a declaration of incompatibility

Section 4(6) states that: **4.55**

> A declaration made under this section ('a declaration of incompatibility')—
> (a) does not affect the validity, continuing operation or enforcement of the provision in respect of which it is given; and
> (b) is not binding on the parties to the proceedings in which it is made.

Thus, a declaration of incompatibility has no direct effect on the legislation under scrutiny nor, indeed, any practical consequences for the litigation in which it is made. The declaration merely creates a power to allow the Government to take remedial action[139] where the court has identified a conflict between a statutory provision and Convention rights.[140] However, the Government has no duty to take remedial action and a declaration of incompatibility may simply be the first step in an application to the European Court of Human Rights.[141]

It has been argued[142] that a declaration of incompatibility will not alter the liability for costs because the losing party is not affected by the declaration being made. However, the applicant may save himself by seeking a stay; if this is granted and is followed by a remedial order with retrospective effect,[143] then the court 'second time round' may decide to apply the legislation as remedied and award costs in his favour. It could also be argued that the normal costs rules do not apply to claims under the Human Rights Act because of their chilling effect.[144] **4.56**

E. Remedial Orders

(1) Introduction

If a declaration of incompatibility is made, the Government may use a fast track procedure to remove the incompatibility by laying a draft remedial order before Parliament under the affirmative resolution procedure. However, the Government has a discretion whether or not to lay such a resolution and the failure to take remedial action cannot itself be challenged in the courts.[145] **4.57**

---

and (3) of the Trade Union and Labour Relations (Consolidation) Act 1992 and its original jurisdiction is derived from s 67(2) and s 176(2) of the Trade Union and Labour Relations (Consolidation) Act 1992.

139 See para 4.59 below.
140 See para 3.43 above.
141 See para 23.08 below.
142 Sir Gavin Lightman and J Bowers, 'Incorporation of the ECHR and its Impact on Employment Law' [1998] EHRLR 560; and see S Grosz, J Beatson and P Duffy, *Human Rights: the 1998 Act and the European Convention* (Sweet & Maxwell, 2000), para 3-50.
143 See para 4.45 above.
144 See generally, para 22.113ff below.
145 See para 5.103 below.

4.58 When the bill was being enacted, the fast track procedure was the subject of substantial criticism from the Select Committee of Delegated Powers and Deregulation of the House of Lords.[146] The Committee, in particular, expressed concern that orders could be made which change sensitive and important areas of existing law and drew attention to the views of the Lord Chancellor, Lord Irvine,[147] when introducing the bill:

> the power to make a remedial order may be used only to remove an incompatibility or possible incompatibility between legislation and the Convention. It may therefore be used only to protect human rights, not to infringe them. And the Bill also specifically provides that no person is guilty of a criminal offence solely as a result of any retrospective effect of a remedial order.

The Committee also commented on the fact that the affirmative resolution procedure did not allow Parliament to amend an order and suggested that it might be appropriate to develop a new procedure which allowed the opportunity for amendments to be proposed.

(2) The power to take remedial action

4.59 The power to take remedial action under section 10 of the Human Rights Act arises in two different circumstances: either if a declaration of incompatibility has been made[148] or if the European Court of Human Rights has made an adverse finding against the United Kingdom in proceedings before it. Section 10(1) of the Act states:

> (1) This section applies if—
> (a) a provision of legislation has been declared under section 4 to be incompatible with a Convention right and, if an appeal lies—
> (i) all persons who may appeal have stated in writing that they do not intend to do so;
> (ii) the time for bringing an appeal has expired and no appeal has been brought within that time; or
> (iii) an appeal brought within that time has been determined or abandoned; or
> (b) it appears to the Minister of the Crown or to Her Majesty in Council that, having regard to a finding in the European Court of Human Rights made after the coming into force of this section in proceedings against the United Kingdom, a provision of legislation is incompatible with an obligation of the United Kingdom arising under the Convention.

The person responsible for exercising the power to make a remedial order[149] is a Minister of the Crown. The term 'Minister of the Crown' will have the same

[146] Sixth Report, 5 Nov 1997.
[147] *Hansard*, HL col 1231 (3 Nov 1997).
[148] See para 4.43ff above.
[149] A remedial order means an order made under s 10: see s 21 of the Human Rights Act.

meaning as in the Ministers of the Crown Act 1975.[150] Section 8 of that Act defines a Minister of the Crown as

> the holder of an office in Her Majesty's Government in the United Kingdom, and includes the Treasury, the Board of Trade and the Defence Council.

The Minister of the Crown may make a remedial order in three situations. In relation to primary[151] legislation section 10(2) states that: **4.60**

> If a Minister of the Crown considers there are compelling reasons for proceeding under this section, he may by order make such amendments to the legislation as he considers necessary to remove that incompatibility.

The Minister has two additional powers allowing him to take remedial action concerning subordinate[152] legislation.[153] First, if there are compelling reasons for doing so, the Minister may make a remedial order under section 10(3) which states:

> If, in the case of subordinate legislation, a Minister of the Crown considers—
> (a) that it is necessary to amend the primary legislation under which the subordinate legislation in question was made, in order to enable the incompatibility to be removed, and
> (b) that there are compelling reasons for proceedings under this section,
>
> he may by an order make such amendments to the primary legislation as he considers necessary.

Secondly, the Minister may make a remedial order under section 10(4) in relation to subordinate legislation where he wishes to use the urgent procedure[154] for making a remedial order. Section 10(4) states:

> This section also applies where the provision in question is in the subordinate legislation and has been quashed or declared invalid, by reason of incompatibility with a Convention right and the Minister proposes to proceed under paragraph 2(b) of schedule 2.

The procedures for making remedial orders are contained in Schedule 2 of the Human Rights Act.[155] However, if the legislation is an Order in Council, the powers to make a remedial order are to be exercised by Her Majesty in Council.[156] The procedure for taking remedial action does not apply to measures of the Church Assembly or General Synod of the Church of England.[157] **4.61**

---

150 s 21 of the Human Rights Act.

151 Although primary legislation is defined in s 21 of the Human Rights Act (see para 4.48 above), s 10(6) of the Act makes it clear that no remedial order may be made in relation to a Measure of the Church Assembly or the General Synod of the Church of England.

152 Defined in s 21, see para 4.50 above.

153 The circumstances where subordinate legislation will be incompatible with Convention rights are discussed at para 4.52 above.

154 See para 4.66ff below.

155 See s 10(7).

156 See s 10(5).

157 s 10(6).

4.62 Section 6(6)(b) of the Human Rights Act provides that the failure of a Minister to make a remedial order where the court has made a declaration of incompatibility is not an 'act of a public authority' for the purposes of section 6. It does not prohibit challenges to such a failure under general administrative law principles. However, it is most unlikely that such a challenge would be successful.

(3) The scope of a remedial order

4.63 Schedule 2, paragraph 1 of the Human Rights Act confers very broad powers on the Minister in making a remedial order and states:

> (1) A remedial order may—
>
> (a) contain such incidental, supplemental, consequential or transitional provision as the person making it considers appropriate;
> (b) be made so as to have effect from a date earlier than that on which it is made;
> (c) make provision for the delegation of specific functions;
> (d) make different provision for different cases.
>
> (2) The power conferred by sub-paragraph (1)(a) includes—
>
> (a) power to amend or repeal primary legislation (including primary legislation other than that which contains the incompatible provision); and
> (b) power to amend or repeal subordinate legislation (including subordinate legislation other than that which contains the incompatible provision)
>
> (3) A remedial order may be made so as to have the same extent as the legislation that it affects.

However, no person will be guilty of an offence solely as a result of the retrospective effect of a remedial order.[158]

(4) The procedure for making remedial orders

4.64 The procedure for making a remedial order is contained in Schedule 2 of the Human Rights Act. Whereas the procedure for making a remedial order for an Order in Council is exercised by Her Majesty in Council,[159] in every other case it is necessary to lay an order before Parliament. Schedule 2 prescribes the ordinary procedure to be used as well as one to be utilised in urgent cases.

4.65 The normal procedure requires the Minister[160] to lay a draft before Parliament. In the first instance the Minister must place the draft order before Parliament for a period of 60[161] days[162] together with[163] the required information[164] (containing an explanation of the incompatibility which the order seeks to remove,

158 Sch 2, para 1(4) of the Human Rights Act.
159 See s 10(5).
160 As defined by para 4.59 above.
161 Calculating the period in accordance with Sch 2, para 6 .
162 Under Sch 2 para 3(1)(a).
163 Sch 2, para 3(1)(b).
164 Defined in Sch 2, para 5 .

particulars of the relevant declaration, finding or order and a statement of his reasons for proceeding under section 10 and for making a remedial order in those terms). If any representations[165] are made during this 60-day period, the draft order that is laid before Parliament must contain a summary of the representations and of any details of changes (if the proposed order has been changed).[166] The draft order must then be approved by a resolution of each House of Parliament within 60[167] days of the draft being laid.[168]

Under section 10(4) of the Human Rights Act the Minister169 is entitled in relation to subordinate legislation170 to use a special procedure for urgent cases. In such circumstances he must lay an order before Parliament which declares that because of the urgency of the matter, it is necessary to make the remedial order without a draft first being approved by both Houses.171 However, the remedial order will cease to have effect if after 120172 days of the original or replacement order being made, a resolution is not passed by both Houses of Parliament approving the order.173 Even though the remedial order will then cease to have effect, this will not affect anything done previously under a remedial order nor will it affect the power of the Minister to make a fresh remedial order.[174] **4.66**

When initiating the special procedure, the Minister must lay before Parliament the order together with the required information[175] (containing an explanation of the incompatibility which the order seeks to remove, particulars of the relevant declaration, finding or order and a statement of his reasons for proceeding under section 10 and for making a remedial order in those terms).[176] If representations[177] are made during the period of 60[178] days from the original order being made, the Minister must at the end of the period lay a statement before Parliament containing a summary of the representations and, if he considers it appropriate to change **4.67**

[165] Which are defined under Sch 2, para 5 as representations about a remedial order (or proposed remedial order) made to the person making (or proposing to make) it and includes any relevant Parliamentary report or resolution.

[166] See Sch 2, para 3(2).

[167] Calculating the period in accordance with Sch 2, para 6 .

[168] See Sch 2, para 2(a).

[169] See para 4.59 above.

[170] See para 4.50 above.

[171] Under Sch 2, para 2(b).

[172] Calculating the period in accordance with Sch 2 para 6 .

[173] Under Sch 2 para 4(4).

[174] Under Sch 2, para 4(4).

[175] Defined in Sch 2, para 5.

[176] Under Sch 2, para 4(1).

[177] Which are defined under Sch 2, para 5 as representations about a remedial order (or proposed remedial order) made to the person making (or proposing to make) it and include any relevant Parliamentary report or resolution.

[178] Calculating the period in accordance with Sch 2, para 6 .

the original order, details of the changes.[179] Where the Minister decides to change the drafting of the order, he must make a further remedial order and lay it before Parliament.[180]

[179] Under Sch 2, para 4(2).
[180] Under Sch 2, para 4(3).

5

HUMAN RIGHTS AND PUBLIC AUTHORITIES

A. Introduction

5.01 Section 6 is the key provision in the Human Rights Act. When enacting the legislation, the Government decided against the straightforward approach of incorporating the European Convention. Instead the Act gives effect to Convention rights by imposing a statutory duty on public authorities. The fundamental principle of the Act is that it is unlawful under section 6(1) of the Act for a public authority to act incompatibly with Convention rights.[1] This obligation expressly binds public authorities but does not directly regulate relations between private individuals.[2] However, because section 6 defines courts and tribunals as public authorities, the Act will *indirectly* affect litigation between private parties; the extent it will do so is one of the most difficult issues that arises under the Act.[3]

5.02 Several distinct issues must be addressed when considering whether there has been a breach of section 6(1):

- is the body involved a 'public authority'[4] in the first place; and if so
- has the public authority 'acted'[5] (as defined by section 6); and if so
- is the act of the public authority 'incompatible'[6] with a Convention right or rights.

These questions are considered in sections B to D, E and F respectively of this chapter. The final topic covered in section G considers whether (and to what extent) 'judicial deference' to the views of public authorities is appropriate under the Human Rights Act.

B. The Definition of Public Authorities Under the Act

(1) The nature of a public authority

5.03 Section 6 of the Human Rights Act places obligations upon 'public authorities'. When the Lord Chancellor, Lord Irvine, moved the Human Rights Bill at the second reading,[7] he justified focusing the Act on public authorities in these terms:

> I should say something about our approach to the application of this Bill to public authorities. We decided, first of all, that a provision of this kind should apply only to public authorities, however defined, and not to private individuals. That reflects the arrangements for taking cases to the convention institutions in Strasbourg. The

[1] The meaning of incompatibility is discussed at para 5.120ff below.
[2] See para 5.38ff below.
[3] Our conclusions concerning the horizontal impact of the Act are set out in para 5.99 below.
[4] See para 5.03ff below.
[5] See para 5.100ff below.
[6] See para 5.120ff below.
[7] *Hansard*, HL cols 1231, 1232 (3 Nov 1997).

> convention had its origins in a desire to protect people from misuse of power by the state, rather than from the actions of private individuals. Someone who takes a case to Strasbourg is proceeding against the United Kingdom Government, rather than a private individual. We have also decided that we should apply the Bill to a wide rather than a narrow range of public authorities so as to provide as much protection as possible to those who claim their rights have been infringed.
>
> [Section] 6 is designed to apply not only to obvious public authorities such as government departments and the police, but also to bodies which are public in certain respects but not others. Organisations of this kind will also be liable under [section 6] . . . for any of their acts, unless the act is of a private nature. Finally, [section 6] . . . does not impose liability on organisations which have no public functions at all.

The explanation given for the approach taken towards public authorities in section 6 by the Home Secretary, Jack Straw MP,[8] was that:

> We decided the best approach would be by reference to the concept of a public function . . . [section] 6 accordingly provides that a public authority includes a court or tribunal and 'any person certain of whose functions are functions of a public nature'. The effect of that is to create three categories, the first of which contains organisations which might be termed 'obvious' public authorities, all of whose functions are public. The clearest examples are Government Departments, local authorities and the police. . . . The second category contains organisations with a mix of public and private function. One of the things with which we had to wrestle was the fact that many bodies, especially over the last 20 years, have performed public functions which are private, partly as a result of privatisation and partly as a result of contracting out. . . . The third category is organisations with no public functions—accordingly, they fall outside the scope of [section] 6 . . . it will be for the courts to determine whether an organisation is a public body. . . . The courts will consider the nature of the body and the activities in question.

The White Paper which accompanied the Bill[9] gave examples of the sort of individuals or organisations whose acts (or omissions) might be challenged under the Human Rights Act. These included: central government (including the executive agencies), local government, the police, immigration officers, prisons, courts and tribunals and, to the extent that they are carrying out public functions, companies responsible for areas of activity which were previously within the public sector such as privatised utilities. The Human Rights Act is therefore not intended to regulate relationships between private individuals. However, although the general intention and effect of section 6 of the Act is clear, its impact may be wider than the Government envisaged. Because the courts themselves are public authorities, they must not act incompatibly with Convention rights[10] when adjudicating in disputes between private individuals[11]. **5.04**

[8] *Hansard*, HC cols 409, 410 (17 Jun 1998).

[9] *Rights Brought Home: The Human Rights Bill* (1997) Cm 3782 para 2.2; see App B in Vol 2.

[10] The meaning of incompatibility is considered at para 5.120ff below.

[11] This is the result of the court being a public authority which is obliged to act in accordance with Convention rights: see generally, para 5.32ff below.

(2) Types of public authorities

5.05 The Human Rights Act does not provide an exhaustive definition of 'public authorities'. Section 6(3) states:

> In this section 'public authority' includes—
>
> (a) a court;
>
> (b) a tribunal which exercises functions in relation to legal proceedings, and
>
> (c) any person certain of whose functions are functions of a public nature,
>
> but does not include either House of Parliament or a person exercising functions in connection with proceedings in Parliament.

5.06 This is an 'enlarging definition',[12] designed to make clear that the term includes a matter which otherwise would (or might) be taken to be outside it. In other words, 'public authority' bears its ordinary meaning but also 'includes' courts, tribunals and persons exercising public functions. The *Notes on Clauses* on the Human Rights Bill commented on the definition of 'public authorities' in section 6(3) by stating that:

> The need to look at the detailed provisions which appear in paragraphs (a) [and] (b) . . . only arises if the person or body in which one is interested is not clearly recognisable as a public authority (*e.g.* a Government department, minister of the Crown or local authority). In other words, the Clause proceeds on the basis that some authorities are so obviously public authorities that it is not necessary to define them expressly . . .

5.07 There is, therefore, no substance to the argument that public bodies are to be regarded as public authorities either because they are a court or tribunal or because certain of their functions are functions of a public nature but not otherwise.[13] If this construction were correct, *all* public authorities would fall within section 6(3) because they have functions of a public nature, and all would be outside the scope of the Act if the nature of the act complained of was of a private nature under section 6(5).[14] This is clearly not the intention of Parliament: as is plain from parliamentary statements made by the Secretary of State, Lord Williams of Mostyn,[15] and by the Home Secretary, Jack Straw MP.[16]

---

[12] See F Bennion, *Statutory Interpretation* (3rd edn, Butterworths, 1997) 441.

[13] Cf T Linden, 'Bodies Which are Bound by the Human Rights Act (1)' Lecture 6 Nov 1998 *The Human Rights Act and Public Law* (JUSTICE).

[14] See para 5.28ff below.

[15] 'When the Bill is enacted, one will be dealing with two types of public authority—those which everyone would recognise as being plainly public authorities in the exercise of their functions and those public authorities which are public authorities because in part of their functions they carry out what would be regarded as public functions.' *Hansard*, HL cols 758–759 (24 Nov 1997).

[16] 'It is not practicable to list all the bodies to which the Bill's provisions should apply. Nor would it be wise to do so. What was needed instead was a statement of principle to which the courts should give effect. Clause 6 therefore adopts a non exhaustive definition of a public authority. Obvious public authorities, such as central government and the police, are caught in respect of everything they do. Public—but not private—acts of bodies which have a mix of public and private functions are also covered.' *Hansard*, HC col 775 (16 Feb 1998).

In other words, the Human Rights Act envisages *three* different types of public authorities: **5.08**

- public bodies which are obviously public authorities (and which might be described as *standard* public authorities);[17]
- public authorities defined as such under the Human Rights Act by virtue of carrying out some public functions[18] (which might be described as *functional* public authorities);[19] and
- courts and tribunals.[20]

The distinction between 'standard public authorities' and 'functional public authorities' is an important one. A standard public authority is obliged to act in accordance with Convention rights in relation to all its activities. By comparison, a functional public authority is not acting unlawfully under section 6(5)[21] where the particular act being challenged is 'of a private nature'. Consequently, anomalies between these two types of public authorities will arise which will be difficult to justify. For example, the Human Rights Act may result in employees of a local authority acquiring Convention rights whereas employees of a local authority trading company may not.

(3) The primary approach for identifying public authorities

Section 6 of the Act gives no specific guidance about the proper approach to be taken for identifying a public authority or for distinguishing between a standard authority and a functional authority. **5.09**

Convention jurisprudence[22] also provides very little assistance when attempting to ascertain or classify public authorities under the Human Rights Act. Under Article 1 of the Convention it is the obligation of the Contracting Parties to secure that everyone within its jurisdiction enjoys its rights and freedoms. Complaints about breaches of the Convention can therefore only be brought against the state or state bodies such as the courts or security forces and not against private bodies such as newspapers or lawyers. Unfortunately, however, the case law is sometimes obscure. This issue is normally decided at the stage that a complaint is ruled admissible[23] and was until 1 November 1998[24] determined by the Commission. **5.10**

[17] See para 5.14ff below.

[18] See para 5.23ff below for a discussion of the test for identifying public functions.

[19] See para 5.16ff below.

[20] See para 5.38ff below.

[21] See para 5.28ff below.

[22] The scope of state responsibility is an important issue in public international law generally; for a comprehensive survey, see I Brownlie, *System of the Law of Nations: State Responsibility, Part I* (Clarendon Press, 1983) and *Principles of International Law* (5th edn, Clarendon Press, 1998), Chap 21.

[23] See para 23.32 below.

[24] The Eleventh Protocol of the European Convention came into effect on 1 Nov 1998. The Protocol has abolished the Commission and fundamentally changed the procedure for making complaints to the European Court of Human Rights: see generally, para 23.08ff below.

Nevertheless, it is well established that the Convention imposes obligations on the state as employers in relation to its employees.[25] The state will also be liable where it has in effect delegated its duties under the Convention and remains responsible, for example, for the arrangements of the legal profession to compel lawyers to act for poor clients[26] or to regulate its members,[27] for a failure to provide a defendant in criminal proceedings effective legal representation[28] and for the state's delegation of educational responsibilities to private schools.[29] The more difficult question of whether the state has responsibility for the acts of *other* public bodies has not received a definitive answer.[30] To some extent the importance of resolving this question has been superseded by the development of the jurisprudence imposing a positive duty on the state to secure certain Convention rights such as the right to life,[31] the right to privacy,[32] freedom of expression[33] and freedom of association.[34]

5.11 Furthermore, it seems that helpful analogies cannot be drawn from the case law which indicates when private individuals can directly rely on European Community directives to enforce Community rights. In European Community law, claims can be brought against the state or emanations of the state (which include the police).[35] In *Foster v British Gas plc*[36] the House of Lords took the view that British Gas before privatisation was an emanation of the state because it was an organisation made responsible for a measure adopted by the state for providing a public service under the control of the state and for that purpose had special powers beyond the normal rules applicable to individuals. This factor of state control is therefore not the decisive factor.[37] In *National Union of Teachers v Governing*

---

[25] *Swedish Engine Driver's Union v Sweden* (1976) 1 EHRR 617 para 37; *Schmidt and Dalström v Sweden* (1976) 1 EHRR 632; see generally, G Morris, 'The Human Rights Act and the Public/Private Divide in Employment Law' (1998) 27 ILJ 293.

[26] *Van de Mussele v Belgium* (1983) 6 EHRR 163; *Martins Moreira v Portugal* (1988) 13 EHRR 517; *Moreira de Azevedo v Portugal* (1991) 14 EHRR 113.

[27] *Casada Coca v Spain* (1994) 18 EHRR 1.

[28] *Goddi v Italy* (1984) 6 EHRR 457 31.

[29] eg *Kjeldsen, Busk, Madsen & Pedersen v Denmark* (1976) 1 EHRR 711; *Costello-Roberts v United Kingdom* (1993) 19 EHRR 112; *A v United Kingdom* (1998) 27 EHRR 611.

[30] See eg *Hilton v United Kingdom* (1988) 57 DR 108, 117–118 where the European Commission declined to consider whether United Kingdom was responsible for the BBC; and see also *British Broadcasting Corporation v United Kingdom* (1996) 21 EHRR CD 93; *Young James and Webster v United Kingdom* (1981) 4 EHRR 38 paras 48–49 where the European Court took the view that the United Kingdom was responsible for dismissals for refusing to join a closed shop by enacting the legislation in the first place.

[31] See para 7.35ff below.

[32] See para 12.106ff below.

[33] See para 15.183 below.

[34] See para 16.83ff below.

[35] See *Johnston v Chief Constable of the Royal Ulster Constabulary* [1987] QB 129.

[36] [1991] 2 AC 306.

[37] *Doughty v Rolls Royce* [1992] ICR 538.

Body of St Mary's Church of England (Aided) Junior School[38] the Court of Appeal indicated that the test formulated in *Foster v British Gas*[39] is not definitive. It now seems that the court will take a broad view of emanation of the state, particularly where it is considering the status of a non commercial organisation.

An 'emanation of the state' may therefore have a broader application[40] than a standard public authority[41] under the Human Rights Act. This means that employees of a public body which is an emanation of the state for the purposes of European Community Directives may have the benefit of Convention rights in the exercise of their European Community rights (such as where they complain of sex discrimination);[42] but have no Convention rights derived from the Human Rights Act, because they are employed by a functional public authority[43] which (as an employer) is performing a function of a private nature.[44] **5.12**

It is submitted that a more useful starting point in identifying a public authority under the Human Rights Act will be to draw on the principles that have evolved concerning whether a particular decision-maker is a 'public body' which is amenable to judicial review proceedings.[45] **5.13**

(4) Standard public authorities

A standard public authority will be acting unlawfully if it acts in a way which is incompatible with Convention rights across the *whole range* of its activities.[45a] The White Paper which accompanied the Human Rights Bill[46] said that central government (including the executive agencies), local government, the police, immigration officers and prisons will be public authorities. Unfortunately, the wording of section 6 of the Human Rights Act does not itself help to identify which public bodies should be treated as standard public authorities and which as functional authorities. **5.14**

The only public bodies that seem certain to be treated as standard public authorities under the Human Rights Act are those that are obviously *governmental* in character such as central government (and their next step agencies), local government and the police. However, it is submitted that bodies whose functions are **5.15**

---

[38] [1997] ICR 334 *per* Schiemann LJ at 350.

[39] [1991] 2 AC 306, 350.

[40] Cf *Griffin v South West Waters Services* [1995] IRLR 15.

[41] See para 5.14ff below.

[42] See eg *Johnston v Chief Constable of the Royal Ulster Constabulary* [1986] ECR 1651 where the employees could rely on Art 6 and Art 13 (breach of the right to an effective remedy.

[43] See para 5.16ff below.

[44] See para 5.28ff below.

[45] For a discussion of the relevant principles, see para 5.22ff below.

[45a] For detailed consideration of this point, see S Grosz, J Beatson and P Duffy, *Human Rights: The 1998 Act and the European Convention* (Sweet & Maxwell, 2000) para 4–10ff.

[46] *Rights Brought Home: The Human Rights Bill* (1997) Cm 3782 para 2.2.

largely or predominantly of a public nature should also be treated as 'standard' public authorities for the purposes of section 6.[47] Such an approach would reflect the need to give a generous interpretation to human rights instruments,[48] since a functional authority is under fewer obligations to act in a way which is compatible with Convention rights than a standard authority as result of section 6(5).[49]

C. Functional Public Authorities

(1) The definition of functional authorities

5.16 As indicated earlier,[50] the approach of section 6(3) of the Human Rights Act is to provide an enlarging definition of public authorities.[51] Section 6(3)(c) of the Human Rights Act expressly includes as public authorities all bodies which carry out public functions. It then identifies two sets of circumstances which result in a public authority no longer remaining within the scope of the Act. Section 6 provides that:

> (3) In this section 'public authority' includes—
>
> . . .
>
> (c) any person certain of whose functions are functions of a public nature, but does not include either House of Parliament or a person exercising functions in connection with proceedings in Parliament.
>
> (4) In subsection (3) 'Parliament' does not include the House of Lords in its judicial capacity.
>
> (5) In relation to a particular act, a person is not a public authority by virtue only of subsection (3)(c) if the nature of the act is private.

5.17 The definition in section 6(3)(c) of 'any person' means that a public authority in question is an identifiable natural person or a corporation. Consequently, it seems that the Human Rights Act excludes an unincorporated body from being a public authority. However, it will be open to a claimant under the Human Rights Act to identify the particular individuals whose decision adversely affected him and bring proceedings against them in a representative capacity.[52]

5.18 The Government's approach was that some bodies were obviously public bodies,[53] but it has expressed the view that functional authorities include: the privatised

[47] Cf J Coppel, *The Human Rights Act 1998: Enforcing the European Convention in Domestic Courts* (John Wiley, 1999) paras 2.28–2.30.

[48] See para 3.12ff above.

[49] See para 5.28ff below.

[50] See para 5.06 above.

[51] See F Bennion, *Statutory Interpretation* (3rd ed, Butterworths, 1997) 441.

[52] CPR Sch 2, RSC Ord 15, r 12.

[53] For a discussion of standard public authorities, see para 5.05ff above and, particularly 5.14–5.15.

utilities,[54] Railtrack, the National Society for the Prevention of Cruelty to Children, private security firms managing contracted out prisons, doctors in general practice,[55] the BBC, the Independent Television Commission (but not the independent television companies),[56] the Jockey Club,[57] the water companies, the Takeover Panel,[58] the British Board of Film Classification[59] and the Press Complaints Commission.[60]

However, it may be difficult in practice to predict whether a particular public body will be found to be a standard authority or a functional authority. The absence of any definition of a standard authority complicates the position. During the Committee stage of the Bill Lord Irvine, LC[61] explained that section 6 applied: **5.19**

> in the first place to bodies which are quite plainly public authorities, such as government departments; and secondly, to other bodies whose functions include functions of a public nature, and therefore the focus should be on their functions and not on the nature of their authority.

It is submitted that, where the status of a public body is so uncertain that it becomes necessary to examine whether its functions are public or private, then it should be regarded as a functional authority. It may also be of value to distinguish between bodies performing governmental functions which have been privatised (which should probably be regarded as standard authorities) and regulatory bodies which are private bodies regulating private organisations (which are likely to be regarded as functional public authorities). The principle that human rights instruments should be given a generous interpretation[62] will be relevant when construing the scope of section 6; section 6(5)[63] ensures that functional authorities are not obliged to act in a way which is compatible with Convention rights in relation to their private functions whereas a standard authority must do so in relation to all of its activities. **5.20**

It is clear that the court must begin, when considering the phrase 'functions of a public nature' under section 6(3)(c), by examining the person's functions. The more difficult issue is identifying the *public* nature of those functions. A number **5.21**

[54] *Rights Brought Home: The Human Rights Bill* (1997) Cm 3782 para 2.2.

[55] The Lord Chancellor, Lord Irvine, *Hansard*, HL cols 796, 811 (24 Nov 1997).

[56] The Secretary of State, Lord Williams, *Hansard*, HL cols 1309, 1310 (3 Nov 1997); the Home Secretary, Jack Straw MP, *Hansard*, HC col 778 (16 Feb 1998).

[57] The Home Secretary, Jack Straw MP, *Hansard*, HC col 1018 (20 May 1998).

[58] The Home Secretary, Jack Straw MP, *Hansard*, HC cols 409, 410 (17 Jun 1998).

[59] The Home Secretary, Jack Straw MP, *Hansard*, HC col 413 (17 Jun 1998).

[60] The Home Secretary, Jack Straw MP, expressed the view that 'it will ultimately be a matter for the courts, but our considered view is that the Press Complaints Commission undertake public functions but the press do not.': see *Hansard*, HC col 414 (17 Jun 1998).

[61] *Hansard*, HL col 797 (24 Nov 1997).

[62] See para 3.12ff above.

[63] See para 5.28ff below.

of approaches have been suggested by commentators on the Act.[64] It is submitted that the question of whether a body is one which performs 'public functions' should be answered primarily by reference to the principles which determine whether a decision-maker is a 'public body' amenable to judicial review.[65] This was the view expressed by the Home Secretary, Jack Straw MP, at the Committee Stage of the Bill. He said that:

> As a matter of practice, we think that there is much guidance to be gained from the way in which British domestic courts have developed the concept of judicial review. . . . We wanted to ensure that, when courts were already saying that a body's activities in a particular respect were a public function for the purposes of judicial review, other things being equal, that would be the basis for action under the Bill. . . . The most valuable asset that we have to hand was the jurisprudence relating to judicial review.[66]

He went on to say:

> we could not directly replicate in the Bill the definition of public authorities used in Strasbourg because, of course, the respondent in any application to the Strasbourg Court is the United Kingdom, as the state. We have, therefore, tried to do the best we can in terms of replication by taking account whether the body is sufficiently public to engage the responsibilities of the state . . . As we are dealing with public functions and with an evolving situation, we believe the test must relate to the substance and nature of the act, not to the form and legal personality.[67]

5.22 The traditional test for deciding whether a particular body was a 'public body' which was subject to judicial review was to examine the source of its power.[68] Wade has argued that judicial review is designed to prevent excesses and abuses of

[64] For example, J Coppel, *The Human Rights Act 1998: Enforcing the European Convention in Domestic Courts* (John Wiley & Sons, 1999) para 2.21 argues that the notion of 'functions of a public nature' has been borrowed from s 3 of the New Zealand Bill of Rights Act and, as a result, it is fundamental to the analysis of a public function that it is conferred by or pursuant to law. Lord Lester and D Pannick, *Human Rights Law and Practice* (Butterworths, 1999) para 2.6.3 suggest that assistance can be obtained from European Convention law, judicial review cases, the authorities under the Public Authorities Protection Act 1893 and the meaning of 'public body' under s 2 of the Prevention from Corruption Act 1916. Grosz, Beatson and Duffy argue that the law on the scope of judicial review will not be definitive: first, because the English courts will have to take account of the Strasbourg jurisprudence which differs from the judicial review case law and is automonous (for a discussion of the principle, see para 6.17 below and in relation to the automonous approach of the Court to public bodies, see *Chassagnou v France*, Judgment of 29 Apr 1999 para 100); and secondly, because the case law on judicial review is itself not altogether consistent: see S Grosz, J Beatson and P Duffy, *Human Rights: The 1998 Act and the European Convention* (Sweet & Maxwell, 2000) para 4-04.

[65] See Lord Woolf and J Jowell, *De Smith, Woolf and Jowell, Judicial Review of Administrative Action* (5th edn, Sweet & Maxwell, 1995) para 3-023ff; and see N Bamforth, 'The Application of the Human Rights Act 1998 to Public Authorities and Public Bodies' (1999) 58 CLJ 159.

[66] *Hansard*, HC cols 408, 409 (17 Jun 1998).

[67] *Hansard*, HC col 433 (17 Jun 1998).

[68] *R v Panel of Take-Overs and Mergers, ex p Datafin* [1987] QB 815, 847 *per* Lloyd LJ; *Council of Civil Service Unions v Minister for the Civil Service* [1985] AC 374, 409 *per* Lord Diplock.

power so that a clear test for determining the limits of the court's jurisdiction can be identified: 'power' means legal power conferred by Act of Parliament.[69] Thus, the classical statement of Atkin LJ in *R v Electricity Commissioners, ex p London Electricity Joint Committee Company (1920) Ltd*[70] described the scope of prerogative remedies as being:

> Wherever any body of persons having legal authority to determine questions affecting the rights of subjects, and having the duty to act judicially, act in excess of their legal authority, they are subject to the controlling jurisdiction of the King's Bench Division exercised in these writs.

It follows that whenever a individual or organisation exercises a statutory power, the court has power to review its exercise.[71] As a result of the *GCHQ*[72] case, judicial review also extends to the exercise of prerogative powers although there are some prerogative powers which are not justiciable and remain outside the scope of judicial review.[73]

The question of identifying 'public functions' for the purpose of judicial review was first fully explored in *R v Panel of Take-Overs and Mergers, ex p Datafin*.[74] In that case the Take Over Panel, a self-regulatory body which devises, promulgates, amends and interprets the City Code on Take-Overs and Mergers, was held to be susceptible to judicial review as it carried out public functions. This decision radically extended the scope of judicial review.[75] The courts now attach little significance to the source of a body's power when deciding whether or not it is a public body.[76] As Sir John Donaldson MR suggested:[77] **5.23**

> Possibly the only essential elements giving rise to the exercise of the supervisory jurisdiction of the court are what can be described as a public element, which can take many different forms.

[69] H Wade and C Forsyth, *Administrative Law* (7th Edn, Clarendon Press, 1994) 659.

[70] [1924] 1 KB 171, 205.

[71] See eg *R v National Joint Council for the Craft of Dental Technicians (Disputes Committee), ex p Neave* [1953] 1 QB 704, 706 *per* Lord Goddard CJ; *Council for the Civil Service Unions v Minister for Civil Service* [1985] AC 374, 409 *per* Lord Diplock; *Leech v Deputy Governor of Parkhurst Prison* [1988] AC 533, 561 *per* Lord Bridge

[72] *Council of Civil Service Unions v Minister for the Civil Service* [1985] AC 374.

[73] The question of whether prerogative powers are justiciable may also arise under the Human Rights Act: see para 5.116ff below.

[74] [1987] QB 815.

[75] See eg C Forsyth, 'The Scope of Judicial Review: "Public Duty" not "Public Source" ' [1987] PL 356; M Beloff ,'Pitch, Pool, Rink . . . Court? Judicial Review in the Sporting World' [1989] PL 95; D Pannick ,'Who is Subject to Judicial Review and in Respect of What?' [1992] PL 1; N Bamforth, 'The Scope of Judicial Review: Still Uncertain' [1993] PL 239.

[76] See *R v Royal Life Savings Society, ex p Heather Rose Marie Howe* [1990] COD 440 where the Court of Appeal thought the source of the Society's power as a body incorporated by royal charter was a factor of very little, if any weight and *R v Secretary of State for the Environment, ex p British Telecom* [1991] RA 307 where it was held that the fact a body was established under statute was not sufficient to bring the claim within the jurisdiction of judicial review.

[77] [1987] QB 815, at 838.

Even if a public body is amenable to review, it does not follow that it will be reviewable in all its functions.[78] The critical issue in each case is whether the decision being challenged affects some public law right.[79]

5.24 First, the court considers the '*but for*' test: whether, but for the existence of the non-statutory body, the Government itself almost inevitably would have intervened to regulate the activity in question.[80] As Glidewell LJ put it in *R v Advertising Standards Authority, ex p Insurance Service*,[81] in the absence of a self-regulatory body, the functions of the Authority would undoubtedly be exercised by the Director General of Fair Trading. This approach was also adopted in *R v Football Association Ltd, ex p Football League Ltd*[82] where Rose J concluded that the Football Association was not a public body, partly influenced by the absence of any evidence showing that if the Association did not exist, the state would have intervened to create a public body to perform its functions. By comparison, evidence showing that governments outside the United Kingdom regulated horse racing was not regarded as significant in concluding that the Jockey Club was not a public body in *R v Disciplinary Committee of the Jockey Club, ex p Aga Khan*.[83] Although Sir Thomas Bingham MR took the view that if the Jockey Club did not regulate horse racing, the Government would have done so[84] he went on to hold that the Jockey Club was not in origin, history, constitution or membership a public body.

5.25 Secondly, an important factor is whether there are indicia of governmental support for the decision-maker. The question as posed by Sir Thomas Bingham MR in *R v Disciplinary Committee of the Jockey Club, ex p Aga Khan*[85] was whether the Jockey Club was woven into a system of governmental control. However, the mere fact that the decision-maker is recognised by legislation is not significant[86] in terms of showing there are sufficient indications of governmental support to justify concluding

[78] *R v Jockey Club, ex p RAM Racecourses Ltd* [1993] 2 All ER 225, 246 *per* Simon Brown J.

[79] *R v Disciplinary Committee of the Jockey Club, ex p Massingberd-Mundy* [1993] 2 All ER 207, 220 *per* Neild LJ; *R v Jockey Club, ex p RAM Racecourses Ltd* [1993] 2 All ER 225, 247 *per* Simon Brown J.

[80] *R v Chief Rabbi of the United Hebrew Congregation of Great Britain and the Commonwealth, ex p Wachman* [1992] 1 WLR 1036, 1041 *per* Simon Brown LJ.

[81] (1990) 2 Admin LR 77, 86.

[82] [1993] 2 All ER 833, 848.

[83] [1993] 1 WLR 909.

[84] Ibid 923; unlike Farquarson and Hoffman LJJ, at 930, 932.

[85] Ibid 921.

[86] See eg *R v Chief Rabbi of the United Hebrew Congregation of Great Britain and the Commonwealth, ex p Wachman* [1992] 1 WLR 1036 (where the existence and some of the functions of the Chief Rabbi were recognised by the United Synagogues Act 1870 and the Slaughter Houses Act 1974); *R v Insurance Ombudsman, ex p Aegon Life Assurance* [1994] CLC 88 (where LAUTRO is recognised by the Secretary of State as a self-regulating body under the Financial Services Act 1986; *R v Football Association Ltd, ex p Football League Ltd* [1993] 2 All ER 833, (where the Football Association is recognised under the Football Spectators Act 1989, s 4).

that it is a public body. Even though a decision-maker exercises monopolistic powers, this factor in itself will not be sufficient to make it a public body.[87] Furthermore, the fact that a decision is of great interest to the public does not mean that the decision-maker is a public body.[88]

The development of the functional approach to public bodies has greatly increased the scope of judicial review.[89] The bodies which are now subject to judicial review include: **5.26**

- media regulators such as the Broadcasting Standards Commission,[90] the Independent Broadcasting Authority,[91] probably the Press Complaints Authority[92] and the Advertising Standards Authority;[93]
- city regulators such as the Stock Exchange,[94] the Bank of England,[95] the Director-General of Fair Trading,[96] the Monopolies and Mergers Commission,[97] the Take Over and Merger Panel,[98] regulatory bodies under the Financial Services Act 1986 (such as the Life Assurance and Unit Trust Regulatory Organisation,[99] the Financial Intermediaries Managers and Brokers Regulatory Association,[100] the Investment Management Regulatory Organisation,[101] the Securities and Investment Board[102] and the Investor's Compensation Scheme);[103]
- health service bodies such as NHS authorities,[104] the Code of Practice

---

[87] See for example *R v Football Association Ltd, ex p Football League Ltd* (n 86 above) 848; *R v Disciplinary Committee of the Jockey Club, ex p Aga Khan* [1993] 1 WLR 909, and contrast *Mercury Energy v Electricity Corp of New Zealand Ltd* [1994] 1 WLR 521.

[88] See eg *R v Chief Rabbi of the United Hebrew Congregation of Great Britain and the Commonwealth, ex p Wachman* (n 86 above) 1036; *R v Disciplinary Committee of the Jockey Club, ex p Aga Khan* (n 87 above) 932, 933 *per* Hoffman LJ.

[89] See J Black, 'Constitutionalising Self-Regulation' (1996) 59 MLR 24; M Taggart (ed), *The Province of Administrative Law* (Hart Publishing, 1997); J Alder, 'Obsolescence and Renewal: Judicial Review in the Private Sector' in P Leyland and T Woods (eds), *Administrative Law Facing the Future: Old Constraints and New Horizons* (Blackstone, 1997).

[90] *R v Broadcasting Complaints Commission, ex p Owen* [1985] QB 1153.

[91] *R v Independent Broadcasting Authority, ex p Whitehouse, The Times*, 4 Apr 1985.

[92] *R v Press Complaints Authority, ex p Stewart Brady* (1997) 9 Admin LR 274.

[93] *R v Advertising Standards Authority Ltd, ex p The Insurance Service* (1990) 2 Admin LR 77.

[94] *R v International Stock Exchange of the United Kingdom and the Republic of Ireland, ex p Else* [1993] QB 534.

[95] *R v Bank of England, ex p Mellstrom* [1995] CLC 232.

[96] *R v Director General of Fair Trading, ex p Southdown Motor Services, The Times*, 24 Apr 1995.

[97] *R v Monopolies and Mergers Commission, ex p Argyll Group plc* [1986] 1 WLR 763.

[98] *R v Panel of Take-Overs and Mergers, ex p Datafin* [1987] QB 815.

[99] *R v Life Assurance Unit Trust Regulation Organization Ltd, ex p Ross* [1993] QB 17.

[100] *R v FIMBRA, ex p Cochrane* [1990] COD 33.

[101] *Bank of Scotland v IMRO* [1989] SLT 432.

[102] *R v Securities and Investment Board, ex p Independent Financial Advisor's Association, The Times*, 18 May 1995; *R v Securities and Investment Board, ex p Sun Life Assurance, The Times*, 9 Oct 1995.

[103] *R v Investor's Compensation Scheme Ltd, ex p Bowden* [1996] AC 261.

[104] *In re Walker's application, The Times*, 26 Nov 987.

Committee of the British Pharmaceutical Industry,[105] the Human Fertilisation and Embryology Authority[106] or a hospital's Infertility Services Ethical Committee;[107]

- educational bodies such as city technology colleges,[108] University Visitors[109] and Universities with no Visitor;[110] and
- professional bodies such as the General Medical Council,[110a] the Law Society[110b] and the Bar Council.[110c]

5.27 The principles the courts will apply in identifying functional public authorities under the Human Rights Act are likely to be as follows:

- A body which is subject to judicial review is almost certainly a functional authority (assuming it is not a standard public authority);[110d] the principle that human rights instruments should be given a generous interpretation[111] would not justify any other conclusion.
- Some public bodies which are not currently amenable to judicial review may nevertheless be functional authorities because they perform public functions. These may include regulatory bodies which have a contractual relationship with their members such as the Jockey Club,[112] the Institute of Chartered Accountants[112a] or the Insurance Ombudsman,[112b] housing associations (or socially registered landlords),[112c] universities with visitors[112d] and private schools.[112e]

---

[105] *R v Code of Practice Committee of the British Pharmaceutical Industry, ex p Professional Counselling Aids* (1990) 3 Admin LR 697.

[106] *R v Human Fertilisation and Embryology Authority, ex p Blood* [1997] 2 WLR 806.

[107] *R v Infertility Services Ethical Committee of St Mary's Hospital, ex p H* [1988] 1 FLR 512.

[108] *R v Governors of Haberdashers' Aske's Hatcham College, ex p T* [1995] ELR 350.

[109] *R v Hull University Visitor, ex p Page* [1993] AC 682.

[110] *R v Manchester Metropolitan University, ex p Nolan* [1994] ELR 380.

[110a] *R v General Medical Council, ex p Coleman* [1990] 1 All ER 489.

[110b] See eg *R v Law Society, ex p Mortgage Express* [1997] 2 All ER 348.

[110c] *R v General Council of the Bar, ex p Percival* [1991] 2 QB 212.

[110d] See paras 5.14–5.15 above.

[111] See para 3.12ff above.

[112] See *R v Disciplinary Committee of the Jockey Club, ex p Aga Khan* [1993] 1 WLR 909; and for a discussion about the position of sporting bodies in general, see para 5.36 ff below.

[112a] *Andreov v Institute of Chartered Accountants* [1998] 1 All ER 489.

[112b] *R v Insurance Ombudsman, ex p Aeyon Life Assurance* [1994] CLC 88.

[112c] See *Peabody Housing Association Green* (1978) P & CR 644; and see C Hunter and A Dymond, 'Housing Law' in C Baker (ed), *The Human Rights Act 1998: A Practitioner's Guide* (Sweet & Maxwell, 1998) and *R v Servite Houses, ex p Goldsmith*, 12 May 2000 (Unreported).

[112d] The limitations on judicial review arise because the university visitor has exclusive jurisdiction over certain matters: see *Thomas v University of Bradford* [1987] AC 795; and in relation to judicial review of the visitor, see *Page v University of Hull Visitor* [1993] AC 682 .

[112e] Judicial review is not normally available against private schools because they have a contractual relationship with pupils (see, *R v Fernhill Motor Public School, ex p A* [1993] 1 FLR 620) or against a non maintained school: see *R v Mutham House School, ex p R, The Times*, 16 Jan 2000; however, judicial review can be obtained where private schools perform public functions such as a city technology college (see *R v Governors of Haberdashers' Aske's Hatcham College, ex p T* [1995] ELR 350) or where a private school purported to withdraw an assisted place (see *R v Cobham Hall School, ex p S* [1998] ELR 389).

It is therefore submitted that the class of functional public authorities will extend to any person which (not being a standard public authority)[112f] either undertakes a governmental activity or performs a regulatory function.

(2) The exclusion of private acts of functional public authorities

Section 6(5) of the Human Rights Act provides that: **5.28**

> In relation to a particular act, a person is not a public authority by virtue only of subsection (3)(c) if the nature of the act is private.

The Human Rights Act therefore excludes from its scope the activities of *some* public authorities where the act being challenged is of a private nature. However, the impact of section 6(5) is limited. Where an act of a 'private' nature is performed by a standard public authority[113] (such as a government department or local authority), it is subject to the Human Rights Act irrespective of the nature of the act itself. For instance, public employers will have to act in a way which is compatible with Convention rights in their treatment of public employees. But when the meaning of public authority is extended under section 6(3) (because the person in question carries out public functions), section 6(5) states that a decision-maker will not be treated as a public authority in respect of private acts.

At the Committee stage of the Bill, Lord Irvine gave examples of three situations **5.29** where public authorities are performing private acts:[114] Railtrack plc exercises public functions in its role as a safety regulator but is acting privately in its role as a property developer; a private security firm would be exercising public functions when managing a contracted out prison but not when acting privately by guarding commercial premises; and doctors in general practice would be public authorities in relation to their National Health Service functions but not in relation to their private patients.

When the court is considering whether the nature of an act is 'private', it may as- **5.30** sist to look at the principles concerning the distinction between public law and private law activities for the purposes of applying for judicial review. As a general rule, once[115] a public body enters into a contractual relationship, the obligations it owes are contractual unless some additional element exists which creates a public law obligation.[116] The distinction between public law and private law activities

[112f] See paras 5.14–5.15 above.

[113] See para 5.14ff above.

[114] *Hansard*, HL col 811 (24 Nov 1997).

[115] A decision of a public body about whether or not to *enter* into a contract is normally a public function and may be subject to judicial review where it is alleged that the public body has acted for an improper purpose: see, for example, *Wheeler v Leicester City Council* [1985] AC 1054; *R v Lewisham London Borough Council, ex p Shell UK Ltd* [1988] 1 All ER 938; *R v Ealing LBC, ex p Times Newspapers Ltd* (1986) 85 LGR 316; *R v Lambeth LBC, ex p Thompson* [1996] COD 217.

[116] See generally, M Freedland, 'Government by Contract and Public Law' [1994] PL 86.

has been most closely examined in the field of public employment. The basic principles were canvassed in *R v East Berkshire Health Authority, ex p Walsh*[117] where Sir John Donaldson MR refused to equate public law with the interest of the public:

> If the public through Parliament gives effect to [the public] interest by means of statutory provisions, that is quite different but the interest of the public *per se* is not sufficient.

A breach of contract claim will therefore be treated as a private law claim[118] *unless* there is some public element injected into the employment such as statutory underpinning[119]. Thus, in *R v British Coal, ex p Vardy*[120] the Divisional Court took the view that where a consultation procedure had statutory underpinning, the managerial decision to close down coal collieries was subject to judicial review. Sir Thomas Bingham MR identified another kind of public law element in the employment relationship in *R v Crown Prosecution Service, ex p Hogg*;[121] he took the view that a complaint concerning disciplinary action against a Crown Prosecutor which affected his independence would properly fall within the scope of judicial review.

5.31 In *McClaren v Home Office*[122] Woolf LJ, in summarising the relevant principles permitting employees to bring judicial review proceedings against a public employer, pointed out that an employee of a public body would be entitled to challenge his employer's decision in judicial review proceedings if he was adversely affected by a decision of *general* application. Thus, in the *GCHQ* case[123] it was appropriate to challenge in judicial review proceedings a decision to vary terms and conditions of staff on grounds of national security so that employees could no longer belong to trade unions, because the issue affected employees generally.[124] The difficulty in maintaining that a case involving a group of employees is 'public' whereas a case involving a single employee is 'private' is in

---

[117] [1985] QB 152, 164.

[118] See eg *R v East Berkshire Health Authority, ex p Walsh* (n 117, above); *R v Derbyshire County Council, ex p Noble* [1990] ICR 808; *McClaren v Home Office* [1990] ICR 824; *Doyle v Northumbria Probation Committee* [1991] 1 WLR 1340; *R v Lord Chancellor, ex parte Hibbert and Saunders* [1993] COD 326; *R v Crown Prosecution Service, ex p Hogg* (1994) 6 Admin LR 778; *R v Independent Broadcasting Authority, ex p Rank Organisation, The Times*, 14 Mar 1996.

[119] See eg *R v Secretary of State for the Home Department, ex p Benwell* [1985] QB 554.

[120] [1993] ICR 720 *per* Glidewell LJ at 751 disapproving of *R v National Coal Board, ex p National Union of Mine Workers* [1986] ICR 791, 795 where Macpherson J took the view that an executive, business or managerial decision was in the same category as a decision in similar circumstances made by a public company.

[121] (1994) 6 Admin LR 778.

[122] [1990] ICR 824, 900.

[123] *Council of Civil Service Unions v Minister for the Civil Service* [1985] AC 374.

[124] See eg *R v Hillingdon Health Authority, ex p Goodwin* [1984] ICR 800; *R v Liverpool City Council, ex p Ferguson and Ferguson* [1985] IRLR 501; *R v London Borough of Hammersmith, ex p NALGO* [1991] IRLR 249.

identifying where the line should be drawn and what the essential difference is.[125] However, De Smith[126] argues that the critical distinction is not simply the number of employees affected or involved, but this factor *together* with the decision being one of significance or interest by itself to the public at large, meaning that the decision is of a public nature and not merely a dispute between an employer and an employee. Unfortunately, the underlying principles remain obscure; and it is difficult to see how this approach can be readily applied to section 6(5) of the Human Rights Act in relation to contracts other than contracts of employment.

If section 6(5) is interpreted in line with the public law/ private law jurisprudence, it will mean that most employees of 'functional public authorities' will *not* have Convention rights in relation to their employers.[127] Employees of standard public authorities will have Convention rights since the Convention is binding on the state as employer.[128] Those employed by functional public authorities, in general, and by private employers will not. This was the view put forward by Lord Irvine at the Committee stage[128a] **5.32**

> In relation to employment matters, for example, I do not see a distinction between a private security company which has a contracted-out prison in its portfolio and one that does not. There is no reason to make the first company liable under [section] 6 in respect of its private acts and the second one not liable simply because the first company is also responsible for the management of a prison.

Some, however, take a rather narrower view of the impact of section 6(5) on employment issues. Thus, Hepple[129] suggests that where a recently privatised body is required to contract on special employment terms prescribed by statute or to set up a particular machinery for consultation with employees or to act under government directives, this may involve the exercise of functions of a public nature which confers Convention rights on employees. Wadham and Mountfield[130] argue that where a functional authority is dealing with an employment issue which relates to its public functions (such as being disciplined **5.33**

[125] S Fredman and G Morris, 'Public or Private: State Employees and Judicial Review' (1991) 107 LQR 298.

[126] Lord Woolf and J Jowell, *De Smith, Woolf and Jowell, Judicial Review of Administrative Action* (5th edn, Sweet & Maxwell, 1995) para 3-065, n 72.

[127] See generally, G Morris, 'The Human Rights Act and the Public/Private Divide in Employment Law' (1998) 27 ILJ 293.

[128] *Swedish Engine Driver's Union v Sweden* (1976) 1 EHHR 617, para 37; *Schmidt and Dalström v Sweden* (1976) 1 EHRR 632.

[128a] *Hansard*, HL col 812 (24 Nov 1997).

[129] B Hepple, 'The Impact on Labour Law' in B Markesinis (ed), *The Impact of the Human Rights Bill on English Law* (Oxford University Press, 1998).

[130] J Wadham and H Mountfield, *Blackstone's Guide to the Human Rights Act 1998* (Blackstone, 1999) para 5.3.

for whistle blowing), this sort of activity might be outside the scope of an act of a private nature for the purposes of section 6(5). Morris[131] contends that the mere fact that a public body has been entrusted with the performance of a public function affords the necessary public element, even if the numbers affected are not great. She points out that it is open to the courts under the Human Rights Act to depart from the jurisprudence that has developed in relation to judicial review. The argument is that the Human Rights Act should be interpreted so that all bodies performing public functions are liable for breaches of Convention rights in relation to all employees who are performing public functions. Morris suggests that this approach is supported by Convention case law and the principles that European Union law has developed towards emanations of the state.

5.34 It is submitted that a critical factor in deciding whether a public authority is performing acts of a 'private nature' under section 6(5) of the Human Rights Act will be whether there is statutory underpinning for the particular activity in question. One example of such statutory underpinning is the privatised prison service where prison custody officers are subject to a highly regulated statutory regime.[132] It will also be relevant to consider whether the act of the public authority adversely affects a number of individuals on an issue which is significant to the public in general. When applying section 6(5), it will be necessary to examine a number of issues such as the nature of the function being performed, why the authority is performing it, whether there is a statutory obligation to do so, whether it is in the nature of a business and whether it is touched by issues of public policy.[133] It is, however, submitted that, in general, employees of functional authorities will not have the benefit of Convention rights.

(3) Sporting bodies

5.35 Sporting bodies typically have a contractual relationship with those over whom they exercise jurisdiction; thus, in *Laws v National Greyhound Racing Club*[134] the Court of Appeal held that any proceedings against the sporting body must be brought as a breach of contract claim. That decision has been followed in a number of unsuccessful judicial review applications against both the Jockey Club[135]

---

[131] G Morris, 'The Human Rights Act and the Public/Private Divide in Employment Law' (1998) 27 ILJ 293.

[132] Criminal Justice Act 1991; Lord Irvine, however, took a different view about the position of prison officers in contracted out prisons at the Committee stage of the Bill; see para 5.32 above.

[133] Cf J Carter, 'Employment and Labour Relations Law' in C Baker (ed), *Human Rights Act 1998: A Practical Guide* (Sweet & Maxwell, 1998) para 13–52.

[134] [1983] 1 WLR 1302.

[135] *R v Disciplinary Committee of the Jockey Club, ex p Aga Khan* [1993] 1 WLR 909; *R v Disciplinary Committee of the Jockey Club, ex p Massingbird-Mundy* [1993] 2 All ER 207; and *R v Jockey Club, ex p RAM Racecourses Ltd* [1993] 2 All ER 225.

and the Football League.[136] On the other hand, in Scotland,[137] New Zealand[138] and Australia[139] sporting authorities have been held to be amenable to judicial review. It is strongly arguable that sports bodies are in substance regulators whose decisions ought to be amenable to judicial review.[140] In applying section 6(3)(b) the courts are not bound by the judicial review authorities. The Home Secretary expressed the view during the passage of the Human Rights Bill that the Jockey Club was a functional authority under the Act;[141] and it may well transpire that some sporting bodies will be treated as public authorities which are obliged under the Human Rights Act to act in ways compatible with Convention rights.[142]

(4) **Religious bodies**

The impact of the Human Rights Act on religious bodies provoked real controversy during the passage of the Bill, and resulted in the enactment of section 13[143] which requires the court to have particular regard to freedom of thought, conscience and religion where its decision might affect their exercise by a religious organisation (itself or its members collectively). It seems that the decisions of religious leaders are not themselves justiciable.[144] Furthermore, public authorities such as church schools or religious charities would be entitled to justify their activities in accordance with the Convention right to freedom of religion.[145] The right of religious bodies to appoint appropriate staff will also be unaffected by the Human Rights Act since such conduct does not appear to infringe any Convention rights. **5.36**

[136] *R v Football Association Ltd, ex p Football League Ltd* [1993] 2 All ER 833; see also *R v Football Association of Wales, ex p Flint Town United Football Club* [1991] COD 44.

[137] See eg, *St Johnson Football Club v Scottish Football Association* (1965) SLT 171; *West v Secretary of State for Scotland* (1992) SLT 171.

[138] *Finnigen v New Zealand Rugby Football Union* [1985] NZLR 159.

[139] See eg *Forbes v New South Wales Trotting Club* (1979) 143 CLR 242; *Victoria v Master Builders Association* [1995] 2 VR 121.

[140] See *R v Disciplinary Committee of Jockey Club, ex p Massingberd-Mundy* [1993] 2 All ER 207 where Neill LJ at 219 and Roch J at 222 said that had the issue been free from authority, they would have held that the Jockey Club was susceptible to judicial review; and see the remarks of Simon Brown J in *R v Jockey Club, ex p RAM Racecourses Ltd* [1993] 2 All ER 225, at 247, 248 also see D Pannick, 'Judicial Review of Sporting Bodies' [1997] JR 150; D Griffith Jones, *Law and Business of Sport* (Butterworths, 1997), 51–57.

[141] *Hansard*, HC col 1018 (20 May 1998).

[142] See para 3.43ff above.

[143] See P Cumper 'The Protection of Religious Rights under section 13 of the Human Rights Act' [2000] PL 254; and see generally, para 14.75ff below.

[144] See eg, *R v Chief Rabbi of the United Hebrew Congregation of Great Britain and the Commonwealth, ex p Wachman* [1992] 1 WLR 1036; *R v Inman, ex p Sulamman Ali* [1994] COD 142; *Ex p Williamson, The Times*, 9 Mar 1994; *R v Ecclesiastical Committee of Both Houses of Parliament, ex p Church Society* (1994) 6 Admin LR 670, 672; *Williamson v Archbishop of Canterbury, The Times*, 25 Nov 1994.

[145] Art 9: see para 14.36 below.

(5) The parliamentary exclusion

5.37 Section 6 of the Human Rights Act excludes from the definition of public authority:

> (3) . . . either House of Parliament or a person exercising functions in connection with proceedings in Parliament.
>
> (4) In subsection (3) 'Parliament' does not include the House of Lords in its judicial capacity.

The section is deliberately drafted in wide terms. But it then excludes from the ambit of the legislation any acts or omissions of the legislature itself as well as any person exercising 'functions in connection with proceedings in Parliament'. The courts are likely to interpret the scope of the Parliamentary exception broadly; as Lord Browne-Wilkinson stated in *Prebble v Television New Zealand*[146] when examining whether defamation proceedings contravened Article 9 of the Bill of Rights 1689:

> there is a long line of authority which supports the broad principle, of which article 9 is merely one manifestation, *viz.* that the courts and Parliament are both astute to recognise their respective constitutional roles. So far as the courts are concerned, they will not allow any challenge to be made to what is said or done within the walls of Parliament in performance of its legislative function and the protection of its established privileges . . . As Blackstone said in his *Commentaries on the Laws of England*:
>
>> 'The whole of the law and custom of Parliament has its original from this one maxim, "that whatever matter arises concerning either House of Parliament, ought to be examined, discussed and adjudged in that House to which it relates and not elsewhere." '

This principle means, for example, that the Parliamentary Commissioner for Standards is not subject to judicial review;[147] and he is also likely to be excluded from the scope of the Human Rights Act.

D. The Human Rights Act and the Courts

(1) Introduction

5.38 Section 6(3)(a) expressly provides that courts and tribunals are public authorities. Courts or tribunals will, therefore, be acting unlawfully under section 6(1) if they act[148] in a way which is incompatible[149] with Convention rights.[150] The fact

[146] [1995] 1 AC 321, 332; see generally, para 15.33 below.
[147] *R v Parliamentary Commissioner for Standards, ex p Al Fayed* [1998] 1 WLR 669.
[148] An Act as defined by s 6(6) is considered at para 5.100ff below.
[149] The meaning of 'incompatibility' is considered at para 5.120ff below.
[150] Convention rights as defined by s 1(1) are discussed at para 3.43 above.

that courts and tribunals are public authorities has a potential impact in three areas:

(1) *Administrative functions*: like a standard public authority,[150a] courts and tribunals may be acting unlawfully if they, for example, breach the Convention rights of their own employees.[151]
(2) *Convention Due Process Rights*: some Convention rights directly concern the operation of the courts such as an individual's right to have the lawfulness of his detention decided speedily by the courts under Article 5[152] and, more particularly, those rights contained in Article 6.[153] The courts themselves will be acting unlawfully if they do not give effect to such rights.
(3) *Private litigation*: although the legislation was designed to ensure that public authorities comply with Convention rights, the court when adjudicating in litigation between private parties may *itself* be acting unlawfully if it acts (or fails to act) in a way which is incompatible with one or more of the Convention rights, so that relationships between private individuals will, potentially, be affected by the Human Rights Act.

The first two areas are unlikely to present serious analytical difficulties. However, **5.39** the third involves one of the most important (and uncertain) questions which arises under the Human Rights Act. The approach taken to section 6(3) will therefore determine whether the Human Rights Act has only *vertical* application (only applying to the relationship between individuals and the state)[154] or whether it also has *horizontal* application (extending to the regulation of relations *between private* individuals or bodies, allowing Convention rights to be invoked by them in private law disputes). English courts are already familiar through European Community law with arguments about whether a provision has direct effect vertically or also has direct effect horizontally. It is well established, for example, that Treaty provisions[155] and Community regulations[156] confer rights and impose obligations on private individuals whereas directives do not have such horizontal direct effect[157] on private individuals. The question of horizontality has also been

[150a] See para 5.14ff.

[151] Under the Canadian Charter of Rights a union which was lawfully on strike was then issued with an injunction by the Chief Justice of British Columbia to prohibit picketing of the court. The union succeeded in its claim that the court order was subject to the Charter and breached its freedom of expression; but the Supreme Court of Canada went on to hold that the breach of the Charter was justified: see *British Columbia Government Employees v British Columbia* [1988] 2 SCR 214.

[152] See para 10.155ff below.

[153] See Chap 11 below.

[154] In the same way that a Directive in European Community law only has direct effect on the emanation of the state: see *Marshall v Southampton and South-West Hampshire Area Health Authority* [1986] QB 401; *Foster v British Gas plc* [1991] 2 AC 306.

[155] *Defrenne v Sabena* [1976] ECR 455.

[156] Under Art 249 of the Treaty (formerly Art 189).

[157] See *Marshall v Southampton and South West Hampshire Area Health Authority* [1986] QB 401.

analysed in terms of the concept of *drittwirkung*, a principle most fully developed in German law,[157a] which permits an individual to bring a claim against a private individual based on the bill of rights.[157b]

5.40 The debate over whether the Human Rights Act has horizontal (as well as vertical) effect reflects different philosophical conceptions about the nature of the state. Proponents of a vertical only application of human rights assert that there is an essential distinction between the public and private sphere; and that the proper protection of human rights should be confined to coercive intrusion from the state. Those favouring horizontal application argue that no principled distinction can be made between the public and private power: because all private activities ultimately depend on acquiescence by the state, even private activities are derived from the state.[158] However, conducting a debate in terms of a vertical/horizontal dichotomy oversimplifies the position.[159] In reality, such a hard and fast distinction cannot be drawn, not least because of the difficulties in delineating the boundaries prescribing what activities should properly fall within the public law sphere.[160] In order to examine the position under the Human Rights Act, it is useful to make a further distinction between two different types of horizontality:

- 'direct horizontality' arises because private bodies are placed under a direct obligation not to interfere with human rights;
- 'indirect horizontality' arises where private bodies are prevented from interfering with human rights by some indirect mechanism, for example, the refusal of the court to provide a remedy which would involve such an interference.[160a]

5.41 The crucial question is to identify where the Human Rights Act will lie in the

---

[157a] See, generally, K Lewin, 'The Significance of Constitutional Rights for Private Law: Theory and Practice in West Germany' (1968) 17 ICQR 572; P Quint, 'Free Speech and Private Law in German Constitutional Theory' (1989) 48 Maryland Law Review 247; and B Markesinis, 'Privacy, Freedom of Expression and the Horizontal Effect of the Human Rights Bill: Lessons from Germany' (1999) 115 LQR 47.

[157b] This is the principle of 'direct drittwirkung'.

[158] See eg A Clapham, *Human Rights in the Private Sphere* (Clarendon Press, 1993) and by the same author 'The Privatisation of Human Rights' [1996] EHRLR 20; A Petter and P Monahan, 'Developments in Constitutional Theory: The Decision in Dolphin Delivery' in R F Devlin (ed), *Constitutional Interpretation* (Edmond Montgomery, 1991); A Butler, 'Constitutional Rights in Private Litigation: A Critique and Comparative Analysis' (1993) 22 Anglo-American L Rev 1; Lord Justice Sedley, 'Public Power and Private Power' in *Freedom, Law and Justice* (Sweet & Maxwell 1999).

[159] See *Du Plessis v De Klerk* 1996 (3) SA 850 *per* Kentridge AJ at 871; *per* Kriegler J at 909. South African jurists have used the term 'diagonality' to describe a position between the two.

[160] Compare eg the views of J Allison in *A Continental Distinction in the Common Law: A Historical and Comparative Perspective on English Public Law* (Clarendon Press, 1996); T Allan, *Law Liberty and Justice: The Legal Foundation of British Constitutionalism* (Clarendon Press, 1993); P McAuslan, *The Ideologies of Planning Law* (Pergamon, 1980); M Loughlin *Public Law and Political Theory* (Clarendon Press, 1992); C Harlow, 'Back to Basics: Reinventing Administrative Law' [1997] PL 245.

[160a] G Phillipson, 'The Human Rights Act, "Horizontal effect" and the Common Law: a Bang or a Whimper?' (1999) 62 MLR 824.

continuum between the vertical and the vertical *plus* horizontal application of human rights. Before directly addressing the impact of section 6(3), it is helpful to consider the approaches taken in other jurisdictions. They show a wide variety of perspectives: from a modified vertical approach (as in the United States), through indirect horizontality (as it has been developed in Canada, New Zealand, South Africa under its interim constitution and Germany) to direct horizontality (as in Ireland and South Africa under the Constitution Act 1996). These divergent viewpoints demonstrate that the extent to which private litigation is subject to the 1998 Act requires a more complex approach than posing the question in terms of a stark choice between the purely vertical on the one hand and the vertical plus fully horizontal application of human rights on the other. However, the first question that requires consideration is the meaning to be given to given to 'courts and tribunals'.

(2) Courts and tribunals

The Human Rights Act does not itself define a 'court'. It can be defined as individuals who exercise judicial functions either directly or indirectly from the Sovereign and exercise their jurisdiction by reason of the sanctity of the law and not because of voluntary submission to its jurisdiction.[161] It is submitted that religious courts and tribunals are not within the scope of section 6(3) since they do not adjudicate on legal rights or obligations and are concerned with essentially private matters.[162] **5.42**

A 'tribunal' is defined in section 21(1) of the Human Rights Act as: **5.43**

> any tribunal in which legal proceedings may be brought.

The word 'tribunal' does not have an ascertainable meaning in English law.[163] However, the critical issue under section 6(3) is the scope of the words 'legal proceedings', a phrase which is not defined in section 6.[164] Some assistance can be gained from section 19 of the Contempt of Court Act 1981[165] which provides that:

---

[161] *Halsbury's Laws of England* (4th edn) Vol 10, para 701.

[162] It is well established that religious courts and tribunals are not public bodies for the purpose of judicial review; see eg *R v Chief Rabbi of the United Hebrew Congregation of Great Britain and the Commonwealth, ex p Wachman* [1992] 1 WLR 1036; *R Inman, ex p Sulamman Ali* [1994] COD 142; *R v London Beth Din (Court of the Chief Rabbi), ex p Michael Bloom* [1998] COD 131.

[163] *Royal Aquarium and Summer and Winter Garden Society Ltd v Parkinson* [1892] 1 QB 431, 466 *per* Fry LJ.

[164] It is defined for the purposes of s 7 in s 7(6):

'In subsection (1)(b) 'legal proceedings' includes—

(a) proceedings brought by or at the instigation of a public authority, and
(b) an appeal against a decision of a court or tribunal.'

[165] See generally, *Arlidge, Eady and Smith on Contempt* (2nd edn, Sweet & Maxwell, 1999), Chap 13.

'court' includes any tribunal or body exercising the judicial power of the State,[166] and 'legal proceedings' shall be construed accordingly.

It has been held that mental health review tribunals[167] and employment tribunals[168] are 'courts' within this definition but that the General Medical Council is not.[169] It seems likely that all the tribunals listed in Schedule 1 of the Tribunals and Inquiries Act 1992 will be public authorities for the purposes of the Human Rights Act. As the Parliamentary Under-Secretary for the Home Department, Mike O'Brien MP, stressed at the Committee stage of the Bill:

> We shall ensure that individuals can rely on their convention rights and have access to them at the earliest possible opportunity. . . . Furthermore, in a significant proportion of such cases a tribunal, not a court, will be the forum in which a case is brought. Social security, employment, housing and immigration are but a few of the many areas where tribunals handle the bulk of cases.

It is therefore unlikely that the 'domestic tribunals' such as those constituted by trade unions for dealing with disciplinary disputes fall within the scope of section 6(3). However, it is plain that a hearing held under an arbitration agreement will not be regarded as a hearing before a 'court' or 'tribunal' under the Human Rights Act.

(3) The application of human rights provisions in the United States: a modified vertical approach

(a) Introduction

5.44 The protection of constitutional rights in the United States illustrates a human rights instrument which exclusively focuses on the rights of private persons against the state. However, the development of 'state action' doctrine shows that even where the constitutional rights are defined in vertical terms, the courts will extend constitutional guarantees to some relationships between private individuals.

5.45 The United States Constitution defines how governmental powers are structured and applied.[170] Interference with individual rights is only prohibited where it arises from the activities of the state or federal government[171] (with the exception of slavery).[172]

---

[166] These words appear to come from Lord Scarman's speech in *A-G v British Broadcasting Corporation* [1981] AC 303, 359.

[167] *P v Liverpool Daily Post and Echo Newspapers plc* [1991] 2 AC 370.

[168] *Peach Grey & Co v Sommers* [1995] 2 All ER 513, 519ff.

[169] *General Medical Council v British Broadcasting Corporation* [1998] 3 All ER 426.

[170] L Tribe, 'Refocusing the State Action Inquiry' in *Constitutional Choices* (Harvard University Press, 1985).

[171] The First to Eighth Amendments restrict the federal government, the Fourteenth Amendment's due process and equal protection clause only apply to state action and the guarantees of the Fifteenth, Nineteenth, Twenty-Fourth and Twenty-Sixth Amendments restrain both federal and state governmental action.

[172] The Thirteenth Amendment prohibition of slavery applies to private action.

This means that constitutional rights can only be infringed where a complaint is made about governmental action. Normally, the issue is straightforward. If, for example, a challenge is made to the validity of a state or federal statute[173] or to a decision of the state courts,[174] this amounts to state action[175] which can be judicially reviewed. Even though the Constitution defines rights exclusively against the state, the courts have developed a more expansive approach; and have taken the view that private individuals too may be obliged to conform to constitutional norms. **5.46**

(b) General principles

The application of constitutional rights to private conduct first required close consideration after the American Civil War. At that time Congress passed a series of statutes designed to protect blacks against the actions of state officials and private individuals which were subsequently challenged in the courts. In 1875 the Congress enacted the Civil Rights Act which made it illegal to exclude blacks from private hotels, railways and theatres on grounds of race. When individuals were charged with breaching the legislation, they claimed that the Act was unconstitutional because the Act went beyond the constitutional powers of the Congress in enacting legislation. The Government responded by various arguments including the contention that the Act was passed in accordance with Congress' powers under the Fourteenth Amendment, the relevant part of which states: **5.47**

> No State shall make or enforce any law which shall abridge the privileges and immunities of citizens of the United States; nor shall any State deprive any person of life, liberty or property without due process of law; nor deny to any person within its jurisdiction the equal protection of the law.
>
> . . . The Congress shall have the power to enforce, by appropriate legislation, the provisions of this Article.

However, the Supreme Court in the *Civil Rights Cases*[176] decided that the Civil Rights Act was unconstitutional: the Fourteenth Amendment applied only to 'state action' and did not permit Congress to prohibit discrimination between private persons. As Bradley J[177] put it:

---

[173] See eg *Brown v Board of Education of Topeka* (1954) 347 US 483.

[174] See eg *New York Times v Sullivan* (1964) 376 US 254 where the state ruled that publishers of untrue statements were liable in defamation; see para 5.54 below.

[175] See H J Abraham and B A Perry, *Freedom and the Court* (7th edn, Oxford University Press, 1998) 389–410; L Tribe, *American Constitutional Law* (2nd edn, Foundation Press, 1988) Chap 18; and for useful surveys of the 'state action' doctrine see H C Strickland, 'The State Action Doctrine and the Rehnquist Court' (1991) 18 Hastings Const LQ 577; G S Buchanan, 'A Conceptual History of the State Action Doctrine: the Search for Governmental Responsibility' (1997) 34 Houston L Rev 333, 665.

[176] (1883) 109 US 3: see generally, H Abraham and B A Perry (n 175, above) Chap 7.

[177] *Civil Rights Cases*, n 176 above 11.

> It is State action of a particular character that is prohibited. Individual invasion of individual rights is not the subject matter of the amendment.

5.48 The 'state action' doctrine which has evolved subsequently has been described by Black as a 'conceptual disaster area';[178] and it is difficult to discern coherent principles from the case law.[179] Indeed, Tribe has argued that the boundaries of state action depend more on the type of constitutional right or value at stake in each case than on the type of body that made the decision being challenged.[180] Nevertheless, in *Edmonson v Leesville Concrete*[181] Kennedy J set out some general principles:

> We ask first whether the claimed constitutional deprivation resulted from the exercise of a right or privilege having its source in state authority [*Lugar v Edmonson Oil*],[181a] and second, whether the private party charged with the deprivation [can] be described in all fairness as a state actor[181b] . . . Our precedents establish that in determining whether a particular action or course of conduct is governmental in character, it is relevant to examine the following: the extent to which the actor relies on governmental assistance and benefits, see *Tulsa Professional Collection Services v Pope*;[182] *Burton v Willington Parking Authority,*[188] whether the actor is performing a traditional governmental function, see *Terry v Adams*;[184] *Marsh v Alabama*;[185] cf *San Francisco Arts and Athletics v United States Olympics,*[186] and whether the injury caused is aggravated in a unique way by the incidents of governmental authority, see *Shelley v Kraemer.*[187]

In fact, issues concerning the state action doctrine arise in two rather different contexts: whether the activities of a private individual can be properly *characterised* as state action poses different problems from those raised by whether the state has *authorised* a private individual's violation of another's constitutional rights.

5.49 In deciding whether the activities of a private person amount to 'state action' the Supreme Court has often used a public function test. The principles were first

---

[178] H Black, 'The Supreme Court, 1966 Term—Foreword: State Action, Equal Protection and California's Proposition' 81 Harv L Rev 69, 95; despite this difficulty the underlying rationale for such a doctrine remains: see for example M J Phillips, 'The Inevitable Incoherence of Modern State Action Doctrine' [1984] St Louis ULJ 683; K Cole, 'Federal and State "State Action": the Undercritical Embrace of a Hypercritical Doctrine' (1990) 24 Georgia L Rev 224.

[179] For a contrary view see L Tribe, *Constitutional Choices* (Harvard University Press, 1985) 248.

[180] L Tribe, *American Constitutional Law* (2nd edn, Foundation Press, 1988) 1699–1703.

[181] (1991) 500 US 614, 621, 622 giving the opinion of the court.

[181a] (1982) 457 US 922, 939–941.

[181b] Ibid 941–942.

[182] (1988) 485 US 478

[183] (1961) 365 US 715

[184] (1953) 345 US 461

[185] (1946) 326 US 501.

[186] (1987) 483 US 522.

[187] (1948) 334 US 1.

developed in a series of cases[188] where the Supreme Court held that the political process itself was state action: when deciding that the state of Texas was acting unconstitutionally in excluding blacks from participating in the primary elections of the Democratic Party through increasingly more convoluted schemes. The Supreme Court also applied the public functions analysis in deciding that restricting free speech in a privately owned company town was unconstitutional;[189] and then stretched the principles to privately owned shopping centres[190] before concluding that it was not unconstitutional for shopping centres to prohibit demonstrators from distributing leaflets[191] or to prohibit union members from picketing.[192] In the 1970s and 1980s the Supreme Court significantly restricted the scope of the public functions approach; it took the view that state action is limited to the exercise of powers which are exclusively reserved to the state by private entities.[193] However, more recently, the Supreme Court has said that the controlling test is whether the action in question involves the performance of a traditional function of government.[194]

The Supreme Court has also identified state action by asking whether the private individual is a joint participant with the state in the challenged activity,[195] in other words whether there is a symbiotic relationship between the two.[196] In *Jackson v Metropolitan Edison*[197]Rehnquist J suggested that: **5.50**

> the inquiry must be whether there is a sufficiently close nexus between the State and the challenged activity of the regulated entity so that the action of the latter can be fairly treated as that of the State.

The Supreme Court therefore held in *Burton v Wilmington Park Authority*[198] that a refusal to serve a black customer, in a restaurant located in a government owned and operated buildings, was unconstitutional . By contrast, in *Moose Lodge No 107 v Irvis*[199] the Supreme Court ruled that a refusal to serve alcohol to a black guest at a private club did not amount to state action; the fact that the state licensing board had issued the private club with a licence was not sufficient to implicate the state in

188 *Nixon v Herndon* (1927) 273 US 536; *Nixon v Condon* (1932) 286 US 73; *Smith v Allwright* (1944) 321 US 649; *Terry v Adams* (1953) 345 US 461.

189 *Marsh v Alabama* (1946) 326 US 501.

190 *Amalgamated Foot Employees Union v Logan Valley Plaza* 391 US 308.

191 *Lloyd Corp v Tanner* (1972) 407 US 551.

192 *Hudgens v National Labor Relations Board* (1976) 424 US 507 overruling *Amalgamated Foot Employees Union v Logan Valley Plaza* (1968) 391 US 308.

193 See *Jackson v Metropolitan Edison* (1974) 419 US 345; *Flagg Bros v Brooks* (1978) 436 US 149; *Rendall-Baker v Kohn* (1982) 457 US 830; *Blum v Yaretsky* (1982) 457 US 991; *San Francisco Arts and Athletics v United States Olympic Committee* (1987) 483 US 522.

194 See eg *Edmonson v Leesville Concrete* (1991) 500 US 614; *Georgia v McCallum* (1992) 505 US 42.

195 *Burton v Willington Parking Authority* (1961) 365 US 715 at 725.

196 *Moose Lodge No 107 v Irvis* (1972) 407 US 163.

197 (1974) 419 US 345, at 351.

198 (1961) 365 US 715.

199 (1972) 407 US 163.

the discriminatory policy of the club. The Supreme Court has also applied the state nexus approach in cases about the rights of creditors and debtors.[200] In the 1960s[201] the Supreme Court approached the state nexus question by sifting through all the facts to weigh up all the circumstances. By the 1970s and 1980s the Supreme Court approached the exercise by examining each factor in isolation.[202] In the last few years, however, the Supreme Court has reverted to considering all the factors cumulatively.[203]

5.51 The question of whether the state has authorised unconstitutional behaviour by private individuals has been examined almost exclusively in the context of race discrimination cases. The state will normally be held liable for a private decision where it has exercised coercive power; or where it has provided such significant encouragement (either overt or covert) that the choice must in law be deemed to be that of the state.[204] Thus, in *Peterson v City of Greenville*[205] the Supreme Court held where the state legislature required a restaurant to serve food on a racially segregated basis, the actions of the restaurant owners amounted to state action. Similarly, in *Lombard v Louisiana*[206] the convictions of demonstrators were quashed on the basis that city officials had officially encouraged store owners to use the state trespass laws in a discriminatory way. In 1967 the Supreme Court in *Reitman v Mulkey*[207] held that a constitutional amendment in California which prohibited property owners from disposing of their property at their absolute discretion was unconstitutional on the ground that the amendment authorised racial discrimination in the sale or rental of housing. However, the principles underlying state authorisation have not been discussed by the Supreme Court since 1970[208] which Buchanan has described as a 'conspiracy of silence'.[209]

(c) The role of the court within the 'state action' doctrine

5.52 When considering whether there is 'state action',[210] the American courts have

[200] *Sniadach v Family Finance* (1969) 395 US 337; *Fuentes v Shevin* (1972) 407 US 67; *Flagg Bros v Brooks* (1978) 436 US 149; *Lugar v Edmondson Oil* (1982) 457 US 922; *Tulsa Professional Collection Services v Pope* (1988) 485 US 478.

[201] *Burton v Wilmington Park Authority* (1961) 365 US 715, at 722; *Evans v Newton* (1966) 382 US 296.

[202] *Moose Lodge No 107 v Irvis* (1972) 407 US 163; *Jackson v Metropolitan Edison* (1974) 419 US 345; *Rendall-Baker v Kohn* (1982) 457 US 830; *Blum v Yaretsky* (1982) 457 US 991; *San Francisco Arts & Athletics v United States Olympic Committee* (1987) 483 US 522; but see *NCCA v Tarkanian* 488 US 179.

[203] *Edmondson v Leesville Concrete* (1991) 500 US 614; *Georgia v McCollum* (1992) 505 US 42; *Lebron v National RR Passenger Corp* (1995) 115 S Ct 961.

[204] *Blum v Yaretsky* (1982) 457 US 991, 1004.

[205] (1963) 373 US 244.

[206] (1963) 373 US 267.

[207] (1967) 387 US 369.

[208] By Brennan J in his dissenting judgment in *Evans v Abney* (1970) 396 US 435, 456, 457.

[209] G S Buchanan, 'A Conceptual History of the State Action Doctrine: the Search for Governmental Responsibility' (1997) 34 Houston LR 665, 699.

[210] See para 5.47ff above.

specifically examined issues arising from the court *itself* being a public authority. It is well established that the decisions of a court amount to state action. The principles that have evolved illuminate the position under the Human Rights Act.

Where a court grants relief in civil proceedings, it is forcibly intervening in a dispute between litigants, either to award compensation or to regulate conduct. Even if no relief is granted, the court has still affected the activities of private citizens. Thus, a state court has been held to have denied constitutional rights when applying common law principles: by initiating contempt proceedings which threatened freedom of expression;[211] by granting an injunction to an employer in an industrial dispute which was alleged to interfere with freedom of expression;[212] and by convicting a Jehovah's witness who was selling religious literature of breach of the peace.[213] **5.53**

The well known case of *New York Times v Sullivan*[214] illustrates the principle. The plaintiff was an elected official in Alabama who brought proceedings because he was libelled in the *New York Times*. Some of the statements made in the newspaper were false and the trial court held that they were libellous *per se* so that the jury could (and did) award damages without proof of pecuniary loss or malice. After the judgment was upheld by the Alabama Supreme Court, the newspaper appealed to the United States Supreme Court. The argument that the application of a rule of law in civil proceedings was not state action for the purposes of the Fourteenth Amendment was rejected by Brennan J giving the opinion on behalf of the court in these terms:[215] **5.54**

> We may dispose at the outset of two grounds asserted to insulate the judgment of Alabama courts from constitutional scrutiny. The first is the proposition relied on by the State Supreme Court—that 'The Fourteenth Amendment is directed against State Action and not private action'. Although this is a civil lawsuit between private parties, the Alabama courts have applied a state rule of law which the petitioners claim to impose invalid restrictions on their constitutional rights of speech and press. It matters not that the law has been applied in civil proceedings and that it is common law only, though supplemented by statute.[215a] The test is not the form in which the state power has been applied but, whatever the form, whether such power has in fact been exercised. See *Ex parte Virginia*;[216] *American Federation of Labor v Swing*.[217]

The court will therefore scrutinise whether principles of the *substantive* law **5.55**

[211] *Bridges v California* 314 US 252.
[212] *American Federation of Labor v Swing* (1941) 312 US 321.
[213] *Cantwell v Connecticut* (1940) 310 US 296.
[214] (1964) 376 US 254.
[215] Ibid 265.
[215a] See eg Alabama Code Tit 7 #908–917.
[216] (1879) 100 US 339, 346–347.
[217] (1941) 312 US 321.

(which have developed at common law) are compatible with constitutional guarantees. The Fourteenth Amendment will only be violated if the application of a common law principle denies a citizen property or liberty without due process of law or denies him equal protection of the law. Thus, in *New York Times v Sullivan*[218] the Supreme Court took the view[219] that the imposition of liability in defamation for the negligent (as opposed to intentional or reckless) publication of a false statement would deter 'would-be critics of official conduct . . . from voicing their criticism, even though it is believed to be true and even though it is in fact true, because of a doubt whether it can be proved in court or the fear of the expense of doing so'.

5.56 However, the reach of constitutional guarantees was significantly extended in *Shelley v Kraemer*[220] where the Supreme Court had to consider whether the state courts were in breach of the equal protection clause of the Fourteenth Amendment by granting an injunction to enforce restrictive covenants which prohibited a property owner selling to a black.[221] As Vinson CJ put it:[222]

> The undisputed facts disclose that the petitioners were willing purchasers of properties upon which they desired to build homes. The owners of the properties were willing sellers; and contracts of sale were accordingly consummated. It is clear that but for the active intervention of the state courts, supported by the full panoply of state power, the petitioners would have been free to occupy the properties in question without restraint.
>
> These are not cases, as has been suggested, in which the States have merely abstained from action, leaving private individuals free to impose discrimination as they see fit. Rather, these are cases in which the States have made available to such individuals the full coercive power of government to deny the petitioners, on grounds of race or colour, the enjoyment of property rights in premises which the petitioners are willing and financially able to acquire and which the grantors are willing to sell. The difference between judicial enforcement and nonenforcement of the restrictive covenants is the difference between being denied rights of property available to other members of the community and being accorded full enjoyment of those rights on an equal footing.
>
> The enforcement of the restrictive agreements by the state courts in these cases was directed pursuant to the common law policy of the States . . . the [Fourteenth] Amendment [is] not ineffective simply because the particular pattern of discrimination, which the State enforced, was defined initially by the terms of a private agreement. State action, as the phrase is understood for the purposes of the Fourteenth Amendment, refers to the exertion of the state in all forms. And when the ef-

[218] (1964) 376 US 254.

[219] Ibid 264, 265

[220] (1948) 334 US 1; and see eg A Higginbotham Jr, 'Race, Sex, Education and Missouri Jurisprudence: Shelley v Kraemer in Historical Perspective' [1989] 67 Wash U LQ 673; F Allen, 'Remembering Shelley v Kraemer: of Public and Private Worlds' (1989) 67 Wash U LQ 709.

[221] See M Tushnet, 'Shelley v Kraemer and Theories of Equality' 33 New York School of Law Rev 383.

[222] (1948) 334 US 1, 19, 20.

fect of that action is to deny rights subject to the protection of the Fourteenth Amendment, it is the obligation of this Court to enforce the constitutional commands.

We hold that in granting judicial enforcement of the restrictive agreements in these cases, the States have denied the petitioners the equal protection of the laws and that, therefore, the action of the state courts cannot stand.

The Supreme Court appears to have decided that any decision of a court which has the effect of breaching constitutional rights is therefore unlawful and unconstitutional.[223]

The approach taken in *Shelley v Kraemer* marks a new departure. The conventional approach in American constitutional jurisprudence is to assess if a court's decision (whether at common law or construing a statute) breaches constitutional rights. However, in *Shelley v Kraemer* the Supreme Court appears to have conflated the process: by holding that the *mere* fact that the court exercised a discretion in favour of discrimination in and of *itself* rendered the court's action unconstitutional. In other words, the Supreme Court assumed that the application of neutral legal principles in favour of discrimination was unlawful under the Fourteenth Amendment without making explicit its second stage inquiry into whether the principles the court applied were themselves unconstitutional. **5.57**

The decision in *Shelley v Kraemer* has been severely criticised.[224] Weschler has described the decision as 'unprincipled', pointing out that it is not obvious from the Supreme Court's reasoning how the state can be liable for discrimination when it does no more than give effect to an agreement which private individuals are entirely free to make.[225] **5.58**

Furthermore, the decision suggests that constitutional rights apply to *all* dealings by private individuals: since in principle *any* claim can be litigated in court (which would then be obliged to give effect to the constitutional guarantees). The logic of *Shelley v Kraemer* therefore goes further than prohibiting all contracts which conflict with constitutional values; the reasoning also, for example, makes unenforceable a **5.59**

[223] Tribe has sought to suggest an alternative explanation for the broad reasoning of the Supreme Court. He points out that Supreme Court decisions such as *Washington v Davis* (1976) 426 US 229 have decided that disparate adverse impact on a racial minority is not sufficient to make an apparently neutral law unconstitutional or even suspect. Tribe argues that because Missouri treats restrictive covenants as being unenforceable unless the substance of the covenant is reasonable and consistent with public policy, the state was breaching constitutional rights by automatically enforcing restrictive covenants which discriminate against blacks while in general regarding such restrictive covenants as unlawful and unenforceable: see L Tribe, *Constitutional Choices* (Harvard University Press, 1985) 259–264.

[224] See eg M Horowitz, 'The Misleading Search for State Action under the Fourteenth Amendment' 30 S Cal Rev 208; W Van Alstyne and K Karst, 'State Action' 14 Stan L Rev 3; L Henkin, 'Shelley v Kraemer: Notes for a Revised Opinion' 110 U Pa L Rev 473; L Alexander, 'Cutting the Gordian Knot: State Action and Self-help Repossession' 2 Hastings Const LQ 893.

[225] See H Weschler, 'Towards Neutral Principles of Constitutional Law' 73 Harv L Rev 1, 29–31.

testator's capricious bequest in a will or a refusal to welcome an intruder into the home who wishes to enter to deliver a political speech. Thus, the principle in *Shelley v Kraemer* ultimately means that all private acts are inseparable from governmental action so long as the state provides courts which can enforce a right to do those private acts.[226] However, it is questionable whether courts should treat the motives or conduct of a private person as if he *were* the state. There is a difference of principle between the state, on the one hand, and a private landowner, on the other, who refuses to allow black neighbours onto his land.[227]

5.60 It may be, however, that the decision in *Shelley v Kraemer*[228] can be justified and explained on a much *narrower* ground. It is arguable that the principle in the case is that where a court takes positive action in granting a *remedy* like an injunction, then the court must itself act in accordance with constitutional norms. An obligation on the court to adhere to constitutional principles when awarding a remedy does not entail a further requirement on the court that it must create *causes of action* between private individuals where it is alleged that constitutional rights are infringed.

5.61 Nevertheless, it is striking that the Supreme Court has failed to extend[229] the application of *Shelley v Kraemer*. Although the case has been considered in the context of state action on many occasions, the Supreme Court has in fact only applied the decision once. In 1953 in *Barrows v Jackson*[230] the Supreme Court merely extended the holding in *Shelley v Kraemer* where it found that state courts had acted unlawfully in awarding damages where property had been sold in breach of restrictive covenants which discriminate on grounds of race. By the 1960s the Supreme Court was ignoring *Shelley v Kraemer* even though the principles of the decision were obviously relevant. For example, the Supreme Court quashed a number of trespass convictions[231] arising from civil rights 'sit-ins' on the basis that there were sufficient indications of state involvement (using the state nexus doctrine):[232] instead of taking the more straightforward route of relying on *Shelley v*

[226] See M Schwarzchild, 'Value Pluralism and the Constitution: in Defense of the State Action Doctrine' (1988) 5 Supreme Court Rev 129.

[227] T McCoy, 'Current State Action Theories, the Jackson Nexus Requirement and Employee Discharge by Semi-Public and State Aided Institutions' 31 Vand L Rev 785.

[228] (1948) 334 US 1.

[229] G Gunther and K Sullivan, *Constitutional Law* (13th edn, Foundation Press, 1997) 1002–1006; T McCoy, 'Current State Action Theories' 31 Vand L Rev 785; R Schneider, 'State Action—Making Sense out of Chaos—an Historical Approach' 37 U Fla L Rev 737.

[230] (1953) 346 US 249.

[231] See eg *Peterson v City of Greenville* (1963) 373 US 244, 246–248 (relying on a city ordinance requiring segregated dining); *Lombard v Louisiana* (1963) 373 US 267, 270–274 (statements by city officials that police were ready to enforce local laws); *Griffin v Maryland* (1964) 378 US 130, 135–137 (reliance on the role of a deputy sheriff); *Robinson v Florida* (1964) 378 US 153, 155–157 (reliance on city ordinance).

[232] See para 5.50 above.

Kraemer to hold that it was unlawful for the court to enforce a claim that property owners were entitled to prohibit access to their property on grounds of race.

(4) The application of human rights provisions in Ireland: a direct horizontal approach

It is often assumed that human rights instruments cannot extend to regulating private individuals in their dealings with one other. However, in Ireland it is well established that constitutional guarantees have direct horizontal application to litigation between private individuals, in other words, the Irish constitution *itself* directly imposes obligations on private individuals to respect the constitutional rights of other private individuals.[233] **5.62**

The general principles were discussed by Walsh J in *Meskell v Coras Iompair Eireann*:[234] **5.63**

> It has been said on a number of occasions by this Court, and most notably in the decision in *Byrne v Ireland*[235] that a right guaranteed by the Constitution or granted by the Constitution can be protected by action or enforced by action even though such action may not fit into any of the ordinary forms of action in either the common law or equity and that the constitutional right carries with it its own right to a remedy for the enforcement of it. Therefore, if a person has suffered damages by virtue of a breach of a constitutional right or the infringement of an unconstitutional right, that person is entitled to seek redress against the person or persons who infringed that right.

Thus, in *Lovett v Gogan*[236] an individual who was licensed under the Road Transport Act to operate particular passenger services relied on his constitutional right to earn a living[237] in seeking an injunction to prevent another private individual who did not hold a licence from running a similar service. The Irish Supreme Court ruled that there was no breach of statutory duty but nevertheless held that the plaintiff was entitled to an injunction to protect his constitutional rights. In *Glover v BLN*[237a] it was held that the constitutional principles of natural justice were enforceable against a private body. The application of this doctrine means that exemplary damages could be awarded against a private individual who

[233] See J M Kelly, *The Irish Constitution* (3rd edn, Dublin, Butterworths, 1994) 696–697; A Butler, 'Constitutional Rights in Private Litigation: a Critique and Comparative Analysis' (1993) 22 Anglo-American L Rev1; S Mullally, 'Equity Guarantees in Irish Constitutional Law—The Myth of Constitutionalism and the "Neutral" State', in T Murphy and P Twomey (eds), *Ireland's Evolving Constitution* (Hart Publishing, 1998).

[234] [1973] IR 121, 132, 133.

[235] [1972] IR 241.

[236] [1995] IRLM 12; see also *Parson v Kavanagh* [1990] IRLM 560.

[237] Which is one of the 'unenumerated rights' guaranteed by the Irish Constitution: see eg *Murphy v Stewart* [1973] IR 97; see also *Murtagh Properties v Cleary* [1972] IR 330 (trade union secretary had a duty to respect implied constitutional right to earn a livelihood).

[237a] [1973] IR 388.

breached a constitutional right.[237b] However, the Irish courts have refused to apply the principles to purely commercial relationships.[237c]

(5) Indirect horizontal application of human rights

(a) Canada

5.64 The way that Canadian Charter of Rights and Freedoms has treated disputes between private individuals represents another possibility in the continuum between vertical and vertical *plus* horizontal applications of human rights instruments. The Charter of Rights defines the public bodies to which the Charter applies. Although the Charter does not require the 'court' to adhere to the Charter when determining litigation between private bodies or individuals, the Canadian case law has extended the scope of the Charter indirectly: by requiring the courts to apply Charter 'values' in interpreting the common law when determining such disputes.

5.65 Section 32 of the Charter provides:

> (1) This Charter applies:
>
> (a) to the Parliament and government of Canada in respect of all matters within the authority of Parliament . . .
> (b) to the legislature and government of each province in respect of all matters within the authority of the legislature of each province.

The Charter therefore does not include the court as a public body to which the Charter applies.

5.66 The implications of this statutory omission were considered in the *Dolphin Delivery* case.[238] Dolphin Delivery sought an injunction against a union on the basis that it was not part of the dispute with the employer and the picketing of its premises constituted 'secondary picketing'. An injunction was granted to prevent picketing on the ground that the union was inducing a breach of contract and the union argued before the Supreme Court of Canada that the injunction should be set aside because it interfered with the Charter guarantee of freedom of expression. The Supreme Court held that a court order could not amount to governmental action (as defined by section 32) and that the injunction was therefore not subject to the Charter. As McIntyre J put it:[239]

[237b] *Conway v Irish National Teachers Organisation* [1991] IRLM 497 (right to free primary education).

[237c] *Carna Foods v Eagle Star Insurance* [1995] 1 IR 526 (no constitutional duty on an insurance company to give reasons for decisions relating to non-renewal of policies).

[238] *Retail, Wholesale and Department Store Union v Dolphin Delivery* [1986] 2 SCR 573.

[239] Ibid, 600.

> To regard a court order as an element of governmental intervention necessary to invoke the Charter would, it seems to me, widen the Charter application to virtually all private litigation.

However, the rationale for this approach is section 32 itself; as La Forest J later explained in *McKinney v University of Guelph*:[240]

> The exclusion of private activity from the *Charter* was . . . a deliberate choice which must be respected. . . . Government is the body that can enact and enforce rules and authoritatively impinges on individual freedom. Only the government requires to be shackled to preserve the rights of the individual.

The impact of *Dolphin Delivery*[241] is confined to litigation between *private* parties. If, on the other hand, a case involves a public body (such as criminal prosecution)[242] or is governed by statute law or the Court of its own motion issues an order for a public purpose,[243] then there will be a sufficient element of governmental action to make the court proceedings subject to the Charter. This will apply even if the Government's activities are contractual or commercial in nature.[244] **5.67**

Although the Charter does not apply directly to disputes between private parties, it does affect private litigation *indirectly*. Section 52(1) states: **5.68**

> The Constitution of Canada is the supreme law of Canada, and any law that is inconsistent with the provisions of the Constitution is, to the extent of the inconsistency, of no force and effect.

Thus, in *Dolphin Delivery*[245] McIntyre J relied on section 52(1) in holding that the Charter applied to the common law; and went on to say obiter:[246]

> the judiciary ought to apply and develop the principles of the common law in a manner consistent with the fundamental values enshrined in the Constitution . . . in this sense, then, the Charter is far from irrelevant to private litigants whose disputes fall to be considered at common law.

This suggestion was taken up in *Dagenais v Canadian Broadcasting Corporation*[247] where the Supreme Court reformulated the common law principles of contempt because the common law gave insufficient weight to the Charter value of freedom of expression; the Supreme Court therefore struck down an

---

240 [1990] 3 SCR 229, 262.
241 [1986] 2 SCR 573.
242 See eg *R v Rahey* [1987] 1 SCR 588.
243 Such as issuing an injunction to prohibit picketing of the courts: see *British Columbia Governmental Employees Union v British Columbia* [1988] SCR 214.
244 *Lavigne v Ontario Public Service Employees Union* (1986) 29 DLR (4th) 321 (the use by a Union of subscriptions under a collective agreement with the government).
245 [1986] 2 SCR 573, 593.
246 Ibid, 603.
247 [1994] 3 SCR 835.

order prohibiting a television broadcast which might prejudice an impending criminal trial.

5.69 More recently, in *Hill v Church of Scientology*[248] the Supreme Court examined the question of whether the common law of defamation required modification to allow a public figure defence[249] in order to be consistent with Charter values. The proper approach to be taken was described by Cory J as follows:[250]

> It is clear from *Dolphin Delivery*[251] that the common law must be interpreted in a manner which is consistent with Charter principles. This obligation is simply a manifestation of the inherent jurisdiction of the court to modify or extend the common law in order to comply with prevailing social conditions and values. As was said in *Salituro*:[252]
>
> > The courts are the custodians of the common law and it is their duty to see that the common law reflects the emerging needs and values of society.
>
> Historically, the common law evolved as a result of the courts making those incremental changes which were necessary in order to make the law comply with current societal values. The Charter represents a restatement of the fundamental values which guide and shape our democratic society and our legal system. It follows that it is appropriate to make such incremental revisions to the common law as may be necessary to have it comply with the Charter.
>
> When determining how the Charter applies to the common law, it is important to distinguish between those cases where the constitutionality of government action is challenged and those in which there is no governmental action involved. It is important not to import into private litigation the analysis which applies in cases involving governmental action . . .
>
> Private parties owe each other no such constitutional duties and cannot found their cause of action upon a Charter right. The party challenging the common law cannot allege that the common law violates a Charter right because, quite simply, Charter rights do not exist in the absence of state action. The most a private litigant can do is to argue that the common law is inconsistent with Charter values. It is very important to draw this distinction between Charter rights and Charter values. Care must be taken not to expand the application of the Charter beyond that established by section 32(1), either by creating new causes of action or subjecting all court orders to Charter scrutiny. Therefore, in the context of civil litigation involving only private parties, the Charter will 'apply' to the common law only to the extent that the common law is found to be inconsistent with Charter values.
>
> Courts have traditionally been cautious regarding the extent to which they will amend the common law. Similarly, they must not go further than is necessary when taking Charter values into account. Far-reaching changes to the common law must be left to the legislature.

---

[248] [1995] 2 SCR 1130.

[249] The position in various jurisdictions is summarised at para 15.248 below.

[250] [1995] 2 SCR 1130, 1169–1171.

[251] [1986] 2 SCR 573.

[252] *R v Salituro* [1991] 3 SCR 654, 678.

> When the common law is in conflict with Charter values, how should the competing principles be balanced . . . the balancing must be more flexible than the traditional section 1 analysis undertaken in cases involving governmental action cases. Charter values, framed in general terms, should be weighed against the principles which underlie the common law. The Charter values will then provide the guidelines for any modification to the common law which the court feels is necessary.
>
> Finally, the division of the onus of proof which normally operates in a Charter challenge to governmental action should not be applicable in a private litigation Charter 'challenge' to the common law. This is not a situation in which one party must prove a *prima facie* violation of a right while the other bears the onus of defending it. Rather, the party who is alleging that the common law is inconsistent with the Charter should bear the onus of proving both that the common law fails to comply with Charter values and that, when these values are balanced, the common law should be modified.

(b) New Zealand

Under section 3(a) of the New Zealand Bill of Rights the rights and freedoms of **5.70** the Bill of Rights apply to acts of the judiciary. The New Zealand courts have said on a number of occasions[253] that common law rules or principles will be set aside where they conflict with the Bill of Rights but the issue has not been definitively resolved. The Bill of Rights has strengthened the common law's rule against granting an injunction to restrain a defamatory broadcast;[254] and provided the reason against striking out an injunction in defamation proceedings requiring a broadcaster to issue a retraction or right of reply.[255] In *R v H*[256] the New Zealand Court of Appeal gave an extended meaning to governmental action so as to bring information which was repeatedly passed by an accountant to the police within the protection from unreasonable search and seizure provision,[257] so that it could be excluded as unlawfully obtained evidence. In *Lange v Atkinson*[258] the New Zealand Court of Appeal considered the impact of the right to freedom of expression[259] on the public figure defence[260] in libel proceedings; since it was conceded that the Bill of Rights Act was the guiding principle for the development of the common law, it seems that the approach taken should be characterised as indirect horizontality.[261]

---

[253] See *R v H* [1994] 2 NZLR 143, 147; *Solicitor General v Radio New Zealand* [1994] 1 NZLR 45, 48; *Duff v Communicado Ltd* (1995) 2 HRNZ 370, 382.

[254] *Auckland Area Health Board v A-G* [1992] 2 NZLR 406, 407 *per* Cooke P.

[255] *TV3 Network v Eveready NZ* [1993] 1 NZLR 435, 441 *per* Cooke P.

[256] [1994] 2 NZLR 143.

[257] s 21 of the New Zealand Bill of Rights.

[258] [1997] 2 NZLR 22.

[259] Under s 14 of the New Zealand Bill of Rights.

[260] The present position in various jurisdictions is summarised at para 15.248 below.

[261] Indirect horizontality as distinguished from direct horizontality at para 5.40 above.

(c) South Africa

5.71 A similar approach was taken in South Africa in relation to the provisions of the Interim Constitution. In *Du Plessis v De Klerk*[262] the Constitutional Court sharply divided on the question of whether Chapter 3 of the Constitution (Fundamental Rights) had horizontal as well as vertical application. Kentridge AJ in giving the leading judgment stressed the fact that, by section 7(1) the Interim Constitution provided that the Bill of Rights:

> shall bind all legislative and executive organs of state at all levels of government.

but did not refer to the judiciary and therefore precluded direct horizontality.[263] However, he went on to say:[264]

> Fortunately, the Constitution allows for the development of the common law and customary law by the Supreme Court in accordance with the objects of Chapter 3. This was provided for in section 35(3) . . . I have no doubt that this subsection introduces the *indirect* application of the fundamental rights provision to private law.

Kentride AJ relied on the approach of the Canadian Supreme Court in *Dolphin Delivery*[265] and summarised the position in the following terms:

> (a) Constitutional rights under Chapter 3 may be invoked against an organ of government but not by one private litigant against another.
> (b) In private litigation any litigant may nonetheless contend that a statute (or executive act) relied on by the other party is invalid as being inconsistent with the limitations placed on legislature and executive under Chapter 3.
> (c) As Chapter 3 applies to common law, governmental acts or omissions in reliance on the common law may be attacked by a private litigant as being inconsistent with Chapter 3 in any dispute with an organ of government.[266]

5.72 The position in South Africa is now different under the 1996 Constitution. Section 8 provides that:

> (1) The Bill of Rights applies to all law and binds the legislature, the executive, the judiciary, and all organs of state.
> (2) A provision of the Bill of Rights binds natural and juristic persons if, and to the extent that, it is applicable, taking into account the nature of the right and of any duty imposed by the right.
> (3) In applying the provisions of the Bill of Rights to natural and juristic persons in terms of subsection (2), a court—
> (a) in order to give effect to a right in the Bill, must apply, or where necessary, develop, the common law to the extent that legislation does not give effect to that right; and

262 1996 (3) SA 850.
263 Ibid 877.
264 1996 (3) SA 850, 885.
265 See para 5.66 above.
266 Ibid para 49.

(b) may develop rules of the common law to limit the right, provided that the limitation is in accordance with section 36(1).[267]

When this section was considered by the Constitutional Court on the certification of the Constitution it was recognised and accepted that this would give rise to 'horizontal application' of the Constitution.[268]

(d) Germany

The German Constitutional Court has also considered the issue of the indirect horizontal application of basic rights.[269] The rights of individuals entrenched in the Basic Law do not directly apply to private law disputes. However, the values embodied in the Basic Law do affect the rules of private law which regulate legal relations between individuals, as the German courts develop and interpret private law in the light of applicable constitutional norms. Constitutionally protected interests have to be balanced against each other and against established private law rights. Markesinis has suggested that the experience of the German courts may provide useful lessons about the horizontal application of human rights. He draws on this tradition to suggest that the Human Rights Act should be regarded as containing an objective set of values which has a superior moral, if not legal, content and that where courts are adjudicating private law disputes, they must ensure that beyond a certain point the application of private law principles does not offend the basic values of the Human Rights Act.[270] **5.73**

(6) The court as a public authority under the Human Rights Act

(a) Introduction

The Human Rights Act aims to give 'further effect to the rights and freedoms guaranteed' under the Convention. The orthodox view is that the Convention confers rights which are exercisable *exclusively* against the state[271] (although the Convention may extend to the conduct of private individuals where there are **5.74**

---

[267] See also, s 39(2).

[268] See *In Re 1996 Certification of the Constitution of the Republic of South Africa* 1996 (4) SA 744 para 53ff; but see *Fedics Group (Pty) Ltd v Matus* 1997 (9) BCLR 1199 and *Amod v Multilateral Motor Vehicle Accident Fund* 1997 (12) BCLR 1716.

[269] See generally, K. Lewin, 'The Significance of Constitutional Rights for Private Law: Theory and Practice in West Germany' (1968) 17 ICQR 572; P Quint, 'Free Speech and Private Law in German Constitutional Theory' (1989) 48 Maryland L Rev 247–346; and B Markesinis, 'Privacy, Freedom of Expression and the Horizontal Effect of the Human Rights Bill: Lessons from Germany' (1999) 115 LQR 47.

[270] See Markesinis (n 269 above).

[271] See eg P van Dijk and G van Hoof, *Theory and Practice of the European Convention on Human Rights* (3rd edn, Kluwer, 1998) 15–20; but see Clapham's powerful arguments to the contrary (A Clapham, *Human Rights in the Private Sphere* (Clarendon Press, 1993), and 'The Privatisation of Human Rights' [1995] EHRLR 20.

positive obligations on the state to secure particular Convention rights).[272] The position under the Human Rights Act is less straightforward as a result of the provisions of section 6 that:

> (1) It is unlawful for a public authority to act in a way which is incompatible with one or more of the Convention rights. . . .
> (3) In this section 'public authority' includes—
> (a) a court;
> (b) a tribunal which exercises functions in relation to legal proceedings.

In other words, the court as a public authority is under a duty not to act in a way which is incompatible with Convention rights and so it seems that the Act must have some 'horizontal' application. The issue as to the extent of the horizonal application of Convention rights is fundamental to the whole operation of the Human Rights Act.

5.75 When the Human Rights Bill was before Parliament, amendments were proposed in Committee to prevent the courts from using Convention rights to develop a common law right to privacy. In opposing those amendments Lord Irvine LC,[273] expressed his views about the effect of section 6(3) as follows:

> it is right as a matter of principle for the courts to have the duty of acting compatibly with the convention not only in cases involving other public authorities but also in developing the common law in deciding cases between individuals. Why should they not? In preparing this Bill, we have taken the view that it is the other course, that of excluding the convention altogether from cases between individuals which would have to be justifiable; nor indeed, do we think it would be practicable . . . the courts already bring convention considerations to bear and I have no doubt that they shall continue to do so in developing the common law . . . the judges are free to develop the common law in their own independent judicial sphere . . . In my opinion, the court is not obliged to remedy the failure by legislating via the common law either where a convention right is infringed by incompatible legislation or where, because of the absence of legislation—say, privacy legislation—a convention right is left unprotected. In my view, the courts may not act as legislators and grant new remedies for infringement of convention rights unless the common law itself enables them to develop new rights or remedies. I believe that the true view is that the courts will be able to adapt and develop the common law by relying on existing domestic principles in the laws of trespass, nuisance, copyright, confidence and the like, to fashion a common law right to privacy.

However, in his final speech at the Third Reading, Lord Irvine[274] stressed that:

> we have not provided for the Convention rights to be directly justiciable between private individuals. We have sought to protect the human rights of individuals against the abuse of power by the state, broadly defined, rather than to protect them against each other.

[272] See para 5.87 below.
[273] *Hansard*, HL cols 783–785 (24 Nov 1997).
[274] *Hansard*, HL col 1231 (3 Nov 1998).

(b) Views concerning the effect of section 6(3)

There is a wide spectrum of opinion about how section 6(3)(a) will operate. On the one hand, it might be argued that this section is intended simply to confirm the current position[275] that the court in the exercise of its *judicial* functions should take account of Convention rights. It might be said, for example, that the court must have regard to freedom of expression when deciding whether in its discretion to grant an injunction.[276] This approach would mean that the Human Rights Act had only vertical application and is exclusively limited to disputes between individuals and the state. It has been argued that section 6(3) means only that the court *in its own sphere* must give effect to fundamental rights such as the right to a fair trial.[276a] However, the terms of section 6 do not support such a narrow construction. Section 6(3) does not distinguish between the different functions that the court (or tribunal) is undertaking; and therefore there is no justification for suggesting that the court is a public authority in some contexts but not others. Nor does the language of section 6(3) suggest that the court when acting as a public authority has a more limited obligation than other public authorities when complying with Convention rights. It is therefore submitted that on a proper construction section 6(3) is not confined to requiring the court to exercise its judicial functions in a way which is compatible with Convention rights. **5.76**

At the other extreme Wade[277] has argued that the Human Rights Act may have horizontal application to *all* disputes between private parties. He suggests that although the Act does not give effect to Article 13 of the Convention,[278] the court will nevertheless take its statutory duty under section 6(1) of the Act as sufficient warrant to award remedies in accordance with Strasbourg practice. There are a number of difficulties in justifying this view, not least that the Convention itself distinguishes between public and private bodies for the purpose of bringing applications.[279] The reasons why the Human Rights Act does not result in total horizontal application are discussed below.[280] **5.77**

A number of writers have suggested various intermediate positions. Lester and **5.78**

[275] See para 2.23ff above.

[276] See eg *R v Advertising Standards Authority, ex p Vernon* [1992] 1 WLR 1289; *Middlebrook Mushroom v TGWU* [1993] IRLR 232, 235.

[276a] S Kentridge, 'The Incorporation of the European Convention' in J Beatson, C Forsyth and I Hare, *Constitutional Reform in the UK: Practice and Procedure* (Hart Publishing, 1998).

[277] Sir William Wade, 'The United Kingdom's Bill of Rights' in J Beatson, C Forsyth and I Hare (eds), *Constitutional Reform in the United Kingdom: Practice and Principles* (Hart Publishing, 1998); 'Human Rights and the Judiciary' [1998] EHRLR 520; and 'Horizons of Horizontality' (2000) 116 LQR 217.

[278] See para 21.156ff below.

[279] Only applications can be made against the state; the circumstances in which a state is liable under the European Convention are considered at para 5.10 above.

[280] See para 5.95ff below.

Pannick[281] argue that the Human Rights Act will have a powerful but *indirect* impact on private law rights and obligations. Grosz, Beatson and Duffy also suggest that there is likely to be a substantial indirect effect.[281a] Sir Richard Buxton, on the other hand, argues that the Act will only have a 'tangential' impact on private law litigation.[281b] Hunt[282] has suggested a more complex analysis of section 6(3) which he describes as the 'application to all law model'. He maintains that the effect of section 6(3) goes further than the current position that allows English courts to take the Convention into account when interpreting or developing the common law or exercising judicial discretion;[283] or the Canadian (and German) approach of indirect horizontality which obliges the Court to take account of human rights 'values' in interpreting the common law.[284] He suggests that the Convention will be regarded as applying to all law[285] and is therefore relevant in proceedings between private parties but will fall short of being directly horizontal because it does not confer any new private causes of action against individuals in respect of breaches of Convention rights. Thus, he argues that if an all male golf club refused to allow women into its bar, the Human Rights Act would not confer any new cause of action on the women who wished to complain about the violation of their rights to freedom of association[286] without discrimination.[287] On the other hand, he suggests that if a woman were physically ejected from the bar and sued for assault, the Court would reject the club's defence of justification because, in putting forward its defence, the club was enlisting the assistance of the state (in the form of the courts) in preserving its present freedom to discriminate which is something which section 6 of the Human Rights Act would not permit the courts to do.

5.79 In an important article, Leigh[288] has suggested a number of different ways in which the Human Rights Act could potentially have horizontal effect:

---

[281] Lord Lester and D Pannick, *Human Rights Law and Practice* (Butterworths, 1999) para 2.6.3 relying on the Canadian case law (see para 5.64ff above) and *Du Plessis v De Klerk* 1996 (3) SA 850: for a discussion of the case, see para 5.71 above.

[281a] S Grosz, J Beatson and P Duffy, *Human Rights: The 1998 Act and the European Convention* (Sweet & Maxwell, 2000) para 4–45ff.

[281b] Sir Richard Buxton, 'The Human Rights Act and Private Law' (2000) 116 LQR 48.

[282] M Hunt, 'The "Horizontal Effect" of the Human Rights Act' [1998] PL 423.

[283] See paras 2.18ff and 2.23 above respectively.

[284] See paras 5.64ff and 5.73 above respectively.

[285] Hunt favours the approach taken by Kriegler J in his dissenting judgment in *Du Plessis v De Klerk* 1996 (3) SA 850, 914, 915 where he accepts that private individuals are at liberty to conduct their affairs exactly as they please so far as fundamental rights and freedoms are concerned *unless and until* they resort to law; however, Mahmomed DP at 894 rejected the stance taken by Kreiger J on the basis that *all* acts performed by private individuals are acts performed in terms of what the common law will allow.

[286] See para 16.66ff below.

[287] See para 17.79ff below.

[288] I Leigh, 'Horizontal Rights, the Human Rights Act and Privacy: Lessons from the Commonwealth' (1999) 48 ICLQ 57.

- *Direct statutory horizontality*: where statutes applying between private individuals are interpreted under section 3[289] of the Human Rights Act to give effect wherever possible to Convention rights;
- *Public liability horizontality*: where public bodies for which the state would not be liable under the European Convention[290] are treated as 'public authorities' under the Human Rights Act because of the extended meaning given to this phrase under section 6(3);
- *Intermediate horizontality*: where public authorities have power to protect a person against infringements of Convention rights from another private person, a public authority may be compelled to intervene;
- *Remedial horizontality*: where the courts as public authorities consider the impact on private parties' Convention rights when granting or withholding of remedies;
- *Common law horizontality*:[290a] where courts as public authorities influence the general development of the common law as it applies between private parties;
- *Full horizontality*: where the inclusion of the courts as public authorities is treated as giving effect to Convention rights in all private common law litigation.

He argues that 'public liability horizontality' and 'remedial horizontality' are well established under the Convention jurisprudence and that there is little reason for the UK courts to depart from this approach in applying the Human Rights Act. He suggests that 'direct statutory horizontality', 'intermediate horizontality' and 'common law horizontality' are readily supportable either as a clear reading of the Human Rights Act or on pre-existing authority. Leigh concludes, however, that the drafting of the Act, the scheme of the Convention and the constitutional principles developed in other jurisdictions do not justify the Human Rights Act conferring full or 'direct' horizontality.

In another important article, Phillipson[290b] distinguishes between *weak* indirect horizontally (where the court applies and develops the law in the light of *values* derived from constitutional rights)[290c] and *strong* indirect horizontally (where the court is under an obligation to ensure that existing laws are compatible with Convention rights themselves). Phillipson argues that the Human Rights Act results in a weak indirect horizontality for a number of reasons. First, the Act does not **5.79A**

[289] See generally, para 4.04ff above.

[290] The extent to which the meaning of public authority has been extended under the Act by functional authorities is examined at para 5.16ff above.

[290a] Referred to by Leigh as 'indirect horizontality', a term we use in a broader sense, see para 5.40 above.

[290b] G Phillipson, 'The Human Rights Act, "Horizontal Effect" and the Common Law: a Bang or a Whimper' (1999) 62 MLR 824.

[290c] As in Canada (see para 5.64ff above), South Africa under the interim constitution (see para 5.71 above) and Germany (see para 5.73 above).

state that all UK citizens have the rights set out in the Convention.[290d] Since the Act does not *expressly* state that Convention rights are part of domestic law, a claimant has no right to be upheld when the court act as a public authority under section 6. Secondly, he argues that the failure to incorporate the right to an effective remedy under Article 13[290e] means that private litigants have no right to redress if the courts fail to develop existing causes of action in line with Convention rights. Thirdly, he points out that if the courts were always required to make the common law compatible with Convention rights, then they would *always* override the common law; and this approach would prevent the common law developing organically by reference to its own doctrines and principles. Fourthly, he suggests that the Parliamentary debates do not provide a mandate for imposing liability on private bodies. Finally, he contends that an unqualified duty to make all private law claims compatible with Convention rights would, in reality, make the outcome of most cases depend on judicial discretion. There are a number of difficulties with this analysis. It is strongly arguable that the omission of Articles 1 and 13 of the Convention do not have the consequences suggested.[290f] Furthermore, it is important to recognise that section 6(1) is negative in terms; and does not impose a positive duty on the court to make the common law compatible with Convention rights.[290g]

(c) Analysis of the effect of section 6(3)

5.80 It may be helpful to consider some of the less controversial issues concerning horizontality under the Human Rights Act before turning to the difficult question of the impact of section 6(3) on the development of the common law.

5.81 **Procedural horizontality.** Section 6(3) requires the court to act in a way which is not incompatible with Convention rights. This means that the court will be obliged to regulate its own procedures to act in conformity with Convention rights. For example, the court must not act incompatibly with Convention rights when deciding whether to impose an order banning the publication of a defendant's name which potentially breaches Article 10[291] or whether to publish evidence to the public potentially in breach of Article 8.[292] It may in family cases require the court to consider the rights of the Article 8 rights[293] of grandparents who are not parties to the proceedings.

[290d] The Act does not incorporate Art 1 of the Convention (see para 3.82 above) and therefore contains no provisions like the South African Interim Constitution, s 7 or the Canadian Charter or Rights and Freedoms which states in ss 7–15 that 'everyone has a right to'.

[290e] See para 21.156ff below.

[290f] See para 3.82 above.

[290g] See para 5.93 below.

[291] See para 15.137ff below.

[292] *Z v Finland* (1997) 25 EHRR 371.

[293] See generally, para 13.113ff below.

Remedial horizontality. The court will also be obliged to modify remedies to ensure that they comply with Convention rights. This principle of remedial horizontality is illustrated by the decision of the United States Supreme Court in *Shelley v Kraemer*,[294] where the Court refused to grant an injunction to enforce restrictive covenants which discriminated on grounds of race because it would breach constitutional rights. Remedial horizontality under the Human Rights Act requires that damages in defamation cases should not be so excessive as to violate the right to freedom of expression.[295] Furthermore, when granting an injunction the court must ensure, for example, that a seizure order[296] does not breach the right to privacy[297] or that an interim injunction does not offend the right to freedom of expression under Article 10[298] (as in the *Spycatcher* case).[299] In other words, the court must not interfere with a private litigant's right to privacy, freedom of expression or freedom of assembly without proper justification. **5.82**

However, the nature of the justification for the interference will be rather *different* when it is an interference by the court (as opposed to a private litigant). For example, the enforcement of a restrictive covenant on grounds of religion may not amount to discrimination if ordered by the court (even though the claimant himself is guilty of discrimination); the reasonable and objective justification given for a difference in treatment would not be the same. When anticipating the sort of considerations the court might accept as justifying interferences with Convention rights, it may be helpful to look at the case law in which the European Court of Human Rights has developed the principle that the right of access to the court is subject to 'inherent limitations'.[300] For example, the court has justified a denial of access so as to permit an order for security for costs,[301] to prevent unfair harassment by litigation,[302] to prevent the multiplicity of proceedings[303] or to ensure legal certainty.[304] **5.83**

Direct statutory horizontality. Less straightforward is the question whether the Human Rights Act will create direct statutory horizontality. The Canadian Charter of Rights extends to litigation between private individuals where a question arises about the compatibility of a statute with the Charter;[305] in *Re Blaney and* **5.84**

[294] (1948) 334 US 1: the case is discussed at para 5.56.
[295] *Tolstoy Miloslavsky v United Kingdom* (1995) 20 EHRR 442, paras 48–51.
[296] CPR Pt 25 (formerly, an Anton Piller Order).
[297] *Chappell v United Kingdom* (1990) 12 EHRR 1; for search orders, see CPR 25.7.
[298] *The Observer and the Guardian v United Kingdom* (1992) 14 EHRR 153, paras 66–71.
[299] Ibid.
[300] See para 6.114ff below.
[301] *Tolstoy Miloslavsky v United Kingdom* (1995) 20 EHRR 442, paras 62–67.
[302] *Ashingdane v United Kingdom* (1985) 7 EHRR 528, para 58.
[303] In *Lithgow v United Kingdom* (1986) 8 EHHR 329, para 197.
[304] *Stubbings v United Kingdom* (1996) 23 EHRR 213, para 50–57.
[305] For a discussion of horizontality in Canada, see generally, para 5.64ff above.

Ontario Hockey Association[306] the Ontario Court of Appeal held that a statutory exception in discrimination legislation in favour of a boys-only sports team was incompatible with the Charter of Rights. The Human Rights Act may also affect disputes between private individuals where a statutory provision is in issue: because of the obligation under section 3(1)[307] to read and give effect to legislation so far as possible in a way which is compatible with Convention rights. For example, section 3(1) may entitle an employee of a private employer who belongs to a religious group which cannot establish it is a racial group under the Race Relations Act (such as a Rastafarian)[308] to make a claim under the Race Relations Act on the basis that the court should read in discrimination (or give effect) to discrimination on grounds of religion when construing[309] the definition of race discrimination in section 3(1) of the 1976 Act.

5.85 However, two difficult issues arise when a litigant seeks to rely on 'direct statutory horizontality'. First, it might be argued that section 3(1) does not come into play *at all* when the dispute is one between private litigants. It could be said that, because private litigants do not have 'Convention rights' as against *each other*, there is no obligation to 'read and give effect' to statutes in a way which is compatible with Convention rights: the obligation to construe legislation in accordance with section 3(1) does not arise in the first place. Thus, because a private individual has no 'right to private life' as against another individual, there can be no question of construing the Protection from Harassment Act 1997 in a way which is compatible with this right. It therefore seems that an obligation to construe statutes in private litigation in accordance with section 3(1) *cannot* be spelt out of section 3(1) itself. On the other hand, section 6[310] makes it unlawful for a court to act in a way which is incompatible with Convention rights. It is arguable that section 6(1) *requires* a court undertaking the 'act' of statutory construction to do so in accordance with section 3(1) and that, as a result, this produces 'direct statutory horizontality'.

5.86 Secondly, in each case it will be necessary to consider whether or not the Human Rights Act can be construed to take away fundamental rights which are vested in private individuals. Such arguments will not apply in many cases of 'direct statutory horizontality'; but they are likely to arise in relation to statutes which restrict

306 (1986) 26 DLR (4th) 728; the reasoning for extending the Charter of Rights to provincial legislation was because s 32(1)(b) of the Charter makes provincial legislation subject to the Charter: *per* Durban JA at 521. The decision itself was approved in the *Dolphin Delivery* case (1984) 10 DLR (4th) 198.

307 See para 4.04ff above.

308 *Crown Suppliers (Property Services Agency) v Dawkins* [1993] ICR 517: see generally, para 14.18 above.

309 The Race Relations Act is an example of underinclusive legislation where the courts will have ample scope to read in Convention rights: see, generally, para 4.19 above.

310 Our views on the impact of s 6(3) are discussed at para 5.99ff below.

the use of property, or affect rights such as freedom of expression. On ordinary principles of statutory construction, property rights cannot be taken away by implication, but only by clearly expressed provisions.[311] Any attempt to restrict rights by the 'back door' of direct statutory horizontality will therefore attract counter-arguments based on the existence of such fundamental rights. For example, it might be said (as in *Fitzpatrick v Sterling Housing Association Ltd*)[312] that the inability of a homosexual to exercise a statutory right to succession to a Rent Act tenancy is in breach of Convention rights.[313] On the other hand, it might be objected that normal statutory presumption requiring clear words to remove the property rights of landlords should prevail over the obligation under section 3(1) of the Human Rights Act to construe statutes in conformity with Convention rights. It is submitted that the strong interpretative obligation in section 3(1) is sufficient to override such fundamental rights. The precise effect will, nevertheless, depend on whether the Convention right in question is a qualified or an unqualified right.[313a] If the Convention right is unqualified, it will trump the common law fundamental right. If, on the other hand, the right is qualified, it is likely that the fundamental right will become an important factor to be taken into account when justifying the interference with the qualified right.

Positive rights horizontality. There are also a number of situations in which the Convention case law imposes a *positive* obligation[314] on the state to secure compliance with Convention rights (such as the right to life,[315] freedom from inhuman treatment,[315a] the right to respect for privacy[316] or family life,[317] freedom of expression,[318] freedom of assembly[318a] and freedom of association).[319] For example, it is arguable that where a private employer engages in hazardous activities with hidden consequences for health, it will have an effective and accessible **5.87**

[311] See generally, F Bennion, *Statutory Interpretation* (3rd edn, Butterworths, 1997) ss 271–282; and para 1.24ff above. Section 11 of the Human Rights Act would have no relevance in this context because it only applies where a person is *relying* on Convention rights: see para 3.57 above.

[312] [1999] 3 WLR 1113.

[313] In fact, on current Convention jurisprudence it would be difficult to sustain such an argument that a right to succession to a tenancy should be extended to those in a homosexual relationship. The right of respect for family life does not extend to homosexual relationships (see para 13.107 below). However, the treatment of homosexuals may constitute a breach of the right of respect for private life (see para 12.92 below) and, possibly a breach of Art 14 as discrimination on grounds of sexual orientation (see para 17.129ff below) within the ambit (see para 17.86ff below) of the right of respect for the peaceful enjoyment of property (see para 18.26ff below).

[313a] See para 6.86ff.

[314] See para 6.97ff below.

[315] See para 7.35ff below.

[315a] See para 8.19ff below.

[316] See para 12.106ff below.

[317] See para 14.52ff below.

[318] See para 15.183 below.

[318a] See para 16.64ff below.

[319] See para 16.83ff below.

procedure to ensure that all relevant and appropriate information is available to any employees exposed to those activities. Such a duty might arise as a consequence of the positive duty on the state to secure compliance with Article 8;[320] and the court could evolve a cause of action permitting employees in the private sector access based on this principle. It is therefore submitted that where there is a positive obligation to secure Convention rights, the court will have some scope to create new causes of action.[320a] Because there is a positive duty on the court to act, the court would be breaching section 6(1) of the Act if it failed to do so.

5.88 **The development of the common law.** The final area of potential 'horizontal impact' of the Human Rights Act concerns the development of the common law. It is submitted that section 6(3) of the Act will create a duty on the court which extends beyond the exercise of judicial discretion.[321] The critical issue to be resolved is whether the Act creates a weak or strong horizontal effect[322] in litigation between private individuals. In fact, the Human Rights Act does not *expressly* state whether it applies to the common law.[323] However, it is well established that the American Bill of Rights[324] and New Zealand Bill of Rights[325] affect substantive common law principles *even though* the legislation is silent on this question and a similar approach is likely to be applied under the Human Rights Act.

5.89 Several commentators[326] argue that the Human Rights Act will have a *weak* indirect effect on the common law along the lines of the Canadian Charter of Rights[327] or the approach taken by the South African Constitutional Court in *Du Plessis v De Klerk*[328] to the South African Interim Constitution. This obligation on the court to develop the common law in line with the values of the Human Rights Act does not arise under any *specific* statutory provision of the Act. Instead, the principle of common law horizontality reflects a public policy commitment to inform the common

[320] See *McGinley and Egan v United Kingdom* (1998) 27 EHRR 1: the extent of the positive obligations under Art 8 are discussed at para 12.111ff below.

[320a] Grosz, Beatson and Duffy deal with a number of counterarguments to positive rights horizontality: see S Grosz, J Beatson and P Duffy, *Human Rights: The 1998 Act and the European Convention* (Sweet & Maxwell, 2000) para 4.49ff below.

[321] See para 5.76 above.

[322] This distinction is explained at para 5.79A above.

[323] The fact that s 6(3) binds the court but does not define the scope of the obligation it creates results in the uncertainty about its effect on the common law: see para 5.76ff above.

[324] See para 5.52ff above.

[325] See 5.70ff above.

[326] See eg Lord Lester and D Pannick, *Human Rights Law and Practice* (Butterworths, 1999) para 2.6.3; I Leigh, 'Horizontal Rights, the Human Rights Act and Privacy: Lessons from the Commonwealth' (1999) 48 ICLQ 57; G Phillipson, 'The Human Rights Act, "Horizontal effect" and the Common Law: a Bang or a Whimper' [1999] 62 MLR 824; S Grosz, J Beatson and P Duffy, *Human Rights: The 1998 Act and the European Convention* (Sweet & Maxwell, 2000) para 4-45ff.

[327] See para 5.64ff above.

[328] 1996 (3) SA 850; the case is discussed at para 5.71 above.

law with the constitutional principles[329] inherent in the Human Rights Act. The rationale for this approach is similar to that which justified the Convention influencing the development of the common law prior[330] to the enactment of the Human Rights Act (although the impact of common law horizontality after enactment is likely to be more significant).

There are, however, a number of reasons for questioning this view. First, it should be emphasised that the Canadian cases[331] and *Du Plessis v De Klerk*[332] were decided within a fundamentally *different* statutory framework. Section 32(1) of the Canadian Charter of Rights states: **5.90**

> This Charter applies
> (a) to the Parliament and government of Canada in respect of all matters within the authority of Parliament including all matters relating to the Yukon Territory and Northwest Territory; and
> (b) to the legislature and the government of each province in respect of all matter within the authority of the legislature of each province.

Section 7 of the South African Interim Constitution provided:

> Application
> (1) This Chapter shall bind all legislative and executive organs of the state at all levels of government.
> (2) This Chapter shall apply to all law in force and all administrative decisions taken and acts performed during the period of the operation of the Constitution.[333]

Neither of these provisions apply to 'judicial' decisions;[334] this exclusion necessarily means that any impact of the human rights legislation on private litigation must be indirect. The legislative exclusion of 'judicial' decisions means that the Canadian Charter[334a] and Interim Constitution require a specific statutory provision to extend their scope to the common law. Thus, in *Du Plessis v De Klerk*[335] Kentridge AJ said:

> Fortunately, the Constitution allows for the development of the common law and customary law by the Supreme Court in accordance with the objects of Chapter 3. This was provided for in section 35(3) . . . I have no doubt that this subsection introduces the *indirect* application of the fundamental rights provision to private law.[336]

329 See para 1.87ff above.
330 See para 2.18ff above.
331 See para 5.64ff above.
332 1996 (3) SA 850; the decision is discussed at para 5.71 above.
333 In contrast, s 8 of the final Constitution makes it clear that the Bill of Rights binds the judiciary: see generally, M Chaskalson, *Constitutional Law of South Africa* (Juta, 1996) 10.57ff.
334 Contrast the position in New Zealand where s 3(a) provides that the New Bill of Rights Act 1990 extends to acts by 'the judicial branch' of Government: see generally, P Joseph, 'New Zealands's Bill of Rights Experience' in P Alston (ed), *Promoting Human Rights Through Bills of Rights: Comparative Perspectives* (Oxford University Press, 1999) 297–298.
334a s 52.
335 n 32 above.
336 Ibid 885.

The Human Rights Act, by comparison, sets out a more straightforward statutory regime by enacting that the court as a public authority would be acting unlawfully if it acted in a way which is incompatible with Convention rights. Furthermore, the precise limits and effect of the doctrine of 'indirect horizontality' are obscure. The difference between developing the common law in line with constitutional 'values' (as opposed to constitutional 'rights') is somewhat elusive; and the doctrine gives no clear guidance in difficult cases about when and to what extent the common law must bow to constitutional values.

5.91 It is submitted that an obligation on the court to develop the common law in a way which is not incompatible with Convention rights can be derived from section 6(3) itself.[337] Such a broad construction of section 6(3) does not conflict with any other statutory provisions within the Human Rights Act. Under section 7(1)(b) a victim[338] who claims that a court is proposing to act in a way which is incompatible with Convention rights can rely on the Convention right in any[339] legal proceedings including proceedings between private individuals.[340] Nor does the Act contain any restriction that *limits* the scope of section 6(3).

5.92 It is also submitted that the purpose of including the court as a public authority under section 6(3) is to ensure that the general obligation on public authorities not to act in a way which is incompatible with Convention rights extends to the court when it carries out one of its most distinctive function: the application and development of the common law when adjudicating on cases between private individuals.

5.93 On this construction of section 6(3), the court would be subject to a *negative* obligation forbidding it from developing common law principles in a way which is incompatible with Convention rights.[340a] Section 6(3) would thus require the courts to ensure that substantive common law doctrines do not *conflict* with Convention rights by, for instance, ensuring that the law of defamation does not violate Article 10 by modifying the defence of qualified privilege;[341] and by ensuring that its determination of actions in negligence do not breach the right of access to the courts as a result of the policy immunity protecting public authorities.[342] Such a reading of section 6(3) means that the impact of the Human Rights Act on the

[337] Cf Lord Irvine LC, 'it is right as a matter of principle for the courts to have the duty of acting compatibly with the convention not only in cases involving other public authorities but also *in developing the common law* in deciding cases between individuals' (emphasis added) (*Hansard*, HL col 783, 24 Nov1997).

[338] The victim requirement is examined at para 22.20ff below.

[339] The restrictions on taking proceedings in relation to judicial acts in s 9(1) of the Human Rights Act only apply where a victim brings proceedings against the authority under the Act in accordance with s 7(1)(a).

[340] Cf s 7(6).

[340a] Cf Sir Richard Buxton, 'The Human Rights Act and Private Law' (2000) 116 LQR 48.

[341] See generally, para 15.34ff below.

[342] See generally, para 11.40ff below.

development of the common law will be profound. An illuminating example of its repercussions occurred in *Hunter v Canary Wharf*[343] where the House of Lords held that only a person who had an interest in the land could sue for private nuisance. However, Lord Cooke in a dissenting judgment took the view that any member of the household should be entitled to sue in nuisance, drawing in part[344] on Article 16 of the United Nations Convention on the Rights of the Child (which declares that no child should be subject to unlawful interference with his home and that the child has the right to protection of the law against such interference) and on Article 12 of the Universal Declaration of Human Rights and Article 8 of the European Convention which are aimed in part at protecting the home and are construed to give protection against nuisances.[345]

Section 6(3), therefore, does not go as far as imposing a *positive* obligation on the court to act in a way which is compatible with Convention rights. The court is not *compelled* to develop the common law in line with Convention rights wherever it has the opportunity to do so: section 6(3) is a *prohibition* which enjoins the court from acting in a way which is inconsistent with Convention rights. **5.94**

There are a number of other issues which could influence the willingness of the court to decide that the common law is incompatible with Convention rights. These could include: **5.94A**

- whether the claimant has chosen to acquiese in the interference to the right at some earlier stage;[345a]
- whether the harm caused by the private body is comparable to that caused by the state;
- the status of the common law rule in question (whether, for example, it is based on public policy which can no longer be sustained); and
- whether the issue involves complex social and ethical problems which might be left to Parliament.[345b]

Even if a court holds that a common law right is incompatible with Convention rights, the court has a discretion under section 8 of the Act to decline to grant a remedy.[345c]

[343] [1997] AC 655.

[344] Ibid 713, 714.

[345] Lord Cooke relied on *Arrondelle v United Kingdom* (1982) 26 DR 5, EComm HR (aircraft noise); *Lopez Ostra v Spain* (1994) 20 EHRR 277 (fumes and smells from a waste protection plant); D Harris, M O'Boyle and C Warbrick, *Law of the European Convention on Human Rights* (Butterworths, 1995) 319.

[345a] G Phillipson in 'The Human Rights Act: "Horizontal Effect" and the Common Law: a Bang or a Whimper?' (1999) 62 MLR 824 argues that this issue of autonomy is central to the German approach to horizontality.

[345b] S Grosz, J Beatson and P Duffy, *Human Rights: The 1998 Act and the European Convention* (Sweet & Maxwell, 2000) para 4-65ff.

[345c] See para 21.01ff below.

5.95 **New causes of action in *private law*.** However, it is clear that section 6(3) does not impose an obligation on the court to create new *causes of action* between private individuals: this would mean that the Human Rights Act regulated all relationships between private individuals through achieving full horizontality.

5.96 There are a number of reasons for this conclusion.[345d] First, as a matter of construction, it is most unlikely that extending the definition of a public authority through section 6(3) to the court was intended to override the basic principle in section 6(1)[346] by making it unlawful for *all* persons to act in a way which is incompatible with the Convention. Such construction would make the fundamental principle in section 6(1) otiose by making the exception in section 6(3) take precedence over the general rule contained in section 6(1). Secondly, the obscurities in section 6 would entitle the court to examine on *Pepper v Hart*[347] principles the Parliamentary debates concerning the Human Rights Act. The views of the Bill's promoters[348] make it plain beyond argument that full direct horizontality was not intended.

5.97 Thirdly, it must be borne in mind that under section 6, the actions (or failures to act) under consideration are those of the *court*. The fact that a private litigant has acted in a way which (if he were a public authority) would constitute a breach of Convention rights does not, of itself, involve any action by the court which is incompatible with the Convention. Whether or not the Court violates the Convention depends on what the court does in response to a claim by the private litigant. On the one hand, if the court grants (or fails to grant)[349] a remedy which results in an interference with the other party's Convention rights[350] the court itself will have 'acted in a way which is incompatible with Convention rights'. The party's rights will have been violated by the exercise of the 'judicial power of the state'. On the other hand, if the court refuses to recognise a right to damages to a private litigant by rejecting the idea that a private individual can base a private law cause of action on a breach of Convention rights,[351] the court will not *itself* have violated those rights. In other words, the court is not under an obligation to act in accordance with Convention rights when deciding cases between private parties unless

[345d] See also Sir Richard Buxton, 'The Human Rights Act and Private Law' (2000) 116 LQR 48, 57 where he suggests that the structure of the Act itself supports this conclusion.

[346] That 'it is unlawful for a *public authority* to act in a way which is incompatible' with Convention rights.

[347] [1993] 1 AC 593: see generally, para 4.35ff above.

[348] See, in particular the views of Lord Irvine, LC in Committee (see *Hansard*, HL cols 783–785 (24 Nov 1997) and his final speech at the Third Reading (see *Hansard*, HL col 1231 (3 Nov 1998) which is quoted at para 5.75 above).

[349] Act includes the failure to act under s 6(6): see generally, para 5.100ff below.

[350] For example, restricting his freedom of expression or discriminating against him on the grounds of religion.

[351] For example, someone who claims that his right to privacy has been violated by the gathering of information by a private sector employer.

it is under a *specific duty to act*: because, for example, a public authority has breached Convention rights, or because it is obliged to construe a statute which must be interpreted so as to be compatible with Convention rights.[352] In short, the mere fact that the court must adjudicate in a dispute where one private individual claims that another is acting in breach of the rights and freedoms of the Convention does not in and of itself place the court under a duty to find in favour of the litigant who claims his rights are being violated. Fourthly, the sophisticated American case law[353] on 'state action' concerning the court as a public authority shows that an obligation on the court to act in accordance with constitutional rights does not involve the further step of requiring the court to fashion constitutional rights that bind private individuals.

It follows that the Human Rights Act does not permit the court in general to *create* new causes of action such as a general right of privacy which one private individual can rely on against another private individual. Section 6 does not entitle the court to formulate a new cause of action because there is no duty on the court to intervene in cases between private individuals to protect Convention rights (although the position may be different if a public authority is under a specific positive duty to secure Convention rights).[354] **5.98**

(d) Conclusion

In summary, it is submitted that the Human Rights Act is likely to have 'horizontal' impact on disputes between private litigants in the following areas:[355] **5.99**

- *Procedural horizontality*: which arises where the court as a public authority exercises discretionary powers to control the procedure in private litigation;[356]
- *Remedial horizontality*: which arises where the court as a public authority considers the impact on private parties' Convention rights of the granting or withholding of remedies in the context of private litigation;[357]
- *Direct statutory horizontality*: which arises where statutes applying between private individuals[358] are interpreted under section 3[359] of the Human Rights Act

[352] See para 4.04ff above.

[353] See para 5.52ff above.

[354] The scope for positive rights horizontality is considered at para 5.87 above.

[355] Drawing on Leigh's classification, see para 5.79 above: see I Leigh, 'Horizontal Rights, the Human Rights Act and Privacy: Lessons from the Commonwealth' [1999] 48 ICLQ 57.

[356] See para 5.81 above. For example, in relation to the admission of evidence obtained in breach of Art 8 or issues as to whether parties should be prevented from pursuing cases due to procedural defaults (see para 11.185 below).

[357] See para 5.82ff above. For example, the granting of an injunction to enforce a covenant which discriminates on the ground of religion or which restricts freedom of speech.

[358] See para 5.84ff above. For example, the Data Protection Act 1998 or s 3 of the Protection from Harassment Act 1997, s 3 which creates a civil remedy for someone who is the victim of harassment.

[359] The interprative obligation under s 3 is discussed at para 4.04ff.

(in conjunction with section 6) to give effect wherever possible to Convention rights;

- *Positive rights horizontality*: which arises where the court as a public authority is under a positive duty to protect a person against infringements of Convention rights from another private person, compelling it to intervene;[360]
- *Common law horizontality*: which arises where the court as a public authority develops the common law as it applies between private parties in a way which is not incompatible with Convention rights.[361]

However, the Human Rights Act will not produce 'full' or 'direct' horizontality[361a] as now exists in Ireland[361b] and South Africa.[362] Private litigants will not be able to sue each other for breaches of Convention rights.

E. The Acts of a Public Authority

(1) The 'act' of a public authority

5.100 The Human Rights Act does not expressly define the term 'act' but gives an 'enlarging definition'[363] in section 6(6) to the effect that:

> 'An act' includes a failure to act.

Because a *failure* to act constitutes an 'act', it will be unnecessary to examine some of the complex issues that can arise in judicial review cases about whether there is a decision at all or whether a public law claim is either premature or too late.[364]

5.101 It seems likely that 'act' will cover any 'decision' by a public authority which could have been challenged in judicial review proceedings. It is clear that such a decision need not be binding and conclusive. It may simply be:

- a recommendation (such as a recommendation for deportation);[365]
- a preliminary decision (such as the proposals made by a local authority for school closures which are put before the Secretary of State for his approval);[366]

[360] See para 5.87ff above.
[361] The meaning of incompatibility is discussed at para 5.120ff below.
[361a] See para 5.89ff above.
[361b] See para 5.62ff above.
[362] See para 5.71ff above.
[363] See F Bennion, *Statutory Interpretation* (3rd edn, Butterworths, 1997) 441.
[364] See eg *R v Secretary of State for Trade, ex p Greenpeace* [1998] Env LR 414 and generally, J Beatson, 'Prematurity and Ripeness for Review' in C Forsyth and I Hare (eds), *The Golden Metwand and the Crooked Cord* (Clarendon Press, 1998).
[365] *R v Secretary of State for the Home Department, ex p Santillo* [1981] QB 778.
[366] See eg *R v Brent London Borough Council, ex p Gunning* (1985) 84 LGR 168.

- advice (even general advice, such as advice to doctors concerning contraception for 16 year old girls);[367]
- a report (such as a report by the local government ombudsman).[368]

The effect of section 6(6) is that judicial review proceedings can be instituted under the Human Rights Act seeking a declaration despite the fact that there is no actual decision under challenge.[369] The Human Rights Act can be invoked if a public authority does nothing to rectify a potential breach of the Convention, for example, a failure to establish a legal framework for non-intrusive surveillance.[370] Furthermore, the fact that section 6(6) extends to a failure to act indicates that it will be unlawful where a public authority[371] fails to comply with its *positive* obligations. It will be unlawful, for example, for a public authority to fail to secure respect for Convention rights (such as the right to life,[372] freedom from inhuman treatment,[372a] the right to privacy[373] or family life,[374] freedom of expression[375] and freedom of assembly[375a] and association),[376] just as much as when it acts in a way which interferes with Convention rights. **5.102**

(2) The exclusion of liability for failing to take legislative acts

The parliamentary exemption under section 6(6) is consistent with the general tenor of the Human Rights Act which maintains the doctrine of parliamentary sovereignty[377] and will exclude the courts from examining questions about whether Parliament has acted in accordance in Convention rights. Section 6(6) states that: **5.103**

> 'An act' includes a failure to act, but does not include a failure to—
> (a) introduce in, or lay before Parliament a proposal for legislation; or
> (b) make any primary legislation or remedial order.

The provision ensures that the courts will not be entitled in the future to remedy any omissions by Parliament to respond to or rectify the consequences of adverse judicial decisions under the Human Rights Act; and, in particular, excludes the

367 As in *Gillick v West Norfolk and Wisbech Area Health Authority* [1986] AC 112.
368 *R v Commissioner for Local Administration, ex p Croydon London Borough Council* [1989] 1 All ER 1033.
369 See *R v Secretary of State for Employment, ex p Equal Opportunities Commission* [1995] 1 AC 1 *per* Lord Browne-Wilkinson at 36.
370 See para 12.128ff below.
371 See para 5.03ff above.
372 See para 7.35ff below.
372a See para 8.19ff below.
373 See para 12.106ff below.
374 See para 14.52ff below.
375 See para 15.183 below.
375a See para 16.64ff below.
376 See para 16.83ff below.
377 See para 1.66ff above.

possiblity of any Human Rights Act challenge based on a failure to legislate where a declaration of incompatibility[378] has been made, holding that there is a clear breach of Convention rights.

(3) The exclusion of liability for acts required by primary or delegated legislation

5.104 Section 6(1) of the Human Rights Act provides that, in general, public authorities are under a duty not to act in a way which is incompatible with Convention Rights. However, there will be many situations in which a public authority will claim that it is obliged to breach a Convention right because it must comply with a conflicting statutory provision.

5.105 Section 3(1)[379] of the Human Rights Act sets out the basic approach that the court must take when adjudicating between the Human Rights Act and competing legislation and requires that:

> So far as it is possible to do so, primary legislation and subordinate legislation must be read and given effect in a way which is compatible with Convention rights.

Nonetheless, the primary obligation on a public authority to comply with Convention rights in section 6(1) may be displaced by section 6(2) which states that:

> Subsection (1) does not apply to an act if—
> (a) as a result of one or more provisions of primary legislation, the authority could not have acted differently; or
> (b) in the case of one or more provisions of, or made under, primary legislation which cannot be read or given effect to in a way which is compatible with Convention rights, the authority was acting so as to give effect to or enforce those provisions.

The exemption in section 6(2) dovetails with the rule of construction contained in section 3 of the Human Rights Act. The purport of section 6(2) is that a public authority will not be acting unlawfully if there is conflicting primary legislation.

5.105A Section 6(2)(a) is designed to cover a statutory provision which gives a public authority *no alternative* but to breach a Convention right. It is submitted that section 6(2) is to be given a narrow construction. This approach is required by the principle that a 'generous approach' should be taken to the interpretation of the Act[379a] and is consistent with the construction given by the House of Lords to a comparable provision in the Race Relations Act.[379b] Section 6(1)(a) is unlikely to

---

[378] See para 4.43ff above.
[379] See generally, para 4.04ff above.
[379a] See *R v DPP, ex p Kebeline* [1999] 3 WLR 972; and see para 3.14A above.
[379b] Race Relations Act 1976, s 41; see *Hampson v Department of Education and Science* [1991] 1 AC 171.

be important in practice since it is rare for a statutory duty to be so tightly and unequivocally defined that it cannot be 'read in' or 'read down' so that it is compatible with Convention rights.[379c] One example of this sort of provision was section 25 of the Criminal Justice and Public Order Act 1994[379d] which stated that a person charged with murder, attempted murder, manslaughter, rape or attempted rape 'shall not be granted bail'.

Section 6(2)(b) applies where a public authority is acting to give effect to or enforce a statutory provision which cannot be read or given effect to in a way which is compatible with Convention rights. It appears, therefore, to extend to the situation where a public authority seeks to rely on a discretionary power where an exercise of the power will mean that the authority is acting in a way which is incompatible with a Convention right. For example, section 6(2)(b) would allow a police constable to exercise his stop and search powers even if these powers are incompatible with Article 5.[379e] This construction of section 6(2)(b) is consistent with the general thrust of the Human Rights Act in terms of preserving Parliamentary sovereignty; and it is consistent with the general administrative law principle that a public body cannot effectively surrender its discretion.[379f] In the Scots case of *Brown v Procurator Fiscal*[379g] the Lord Justice General suggested that the proper approach to section 6(2)(b) was to consider: **5.105B**

- is the public authority acting to 'give effect to' or 'enforce' a particular statutory provision? If so,
- can this provision, on an ordinary construction, be given effect to or enforced in a manner which is compatible with Convention rights? if not
- can the provision be read and given effect to in a manner which is compatible with Convention rights?

As a result, the court read down the discretionary power to stop motor cars under section 172 of the Road Traffic Act so as to make it compatible with the presumption of innocence under Article 6(2). The court robustly rejected the Crown's claim that the statutory discretion was preserved under section 6(2)(b) of the Human Rights Act.

The position regarding delegated legislation is more complex. Under general administrative law principles delegated legislation must be *intra vires* the **5.106**

[379c] The doctrines of 'reading down' and 'reading in' are discussed at para 4.17ff above.

[379d] Now amended by Crime and Disorder Act 1998, s 56.

[379e] The question of whether these powers are compatible with Art 5 is considered at para 10.189ff below.

[379f] *R v Port of London, ex p Kynoch* [1919] 1 KB 176, *per* Banks LJ at 184; *R v Secretary of State for the Home Department, ex p Fire Brigades Union* [1995] 2 AC 513, *per* Lord Browne-Wilkinson at 551D/G, *per* Lord Lloyd at 527A/D, *per* Lord Nichols at 575F.

[379g] Unreported, 4 Feb 2000.

primary legislation which implemented it. The impact of fundamental human rights in terms of the *vires* of delegated legislation was strikingly illustrated in *R v Secretary of State for Social Security, ex p Joint Council for the Welfare of Immigrants*.[380] Judicial review proceedings were brought because the Secretary of State had introduced regulations under the social security legislation which excluded those claiming asylum status from obtaining income support. The purpose of the regulations was to discourage asylum claims by economic migrants. However, the applicants argued that the social security regulations conflicted with the rights conferred on asylum seekers by the Asylum and Immigration Appeals Act 1993. Although the applicants succeeded before the Court of Appeal, they did so on rather different grounds. Simon Brown LJ took the view that:[381]

> the fact that asylum seekers have hitherto enjoyed benefit payments appears to me to be not entirely irrelevant. After all, the 1993 Act confers on asylum seekers fuller rights than they have ever previously enjoyed, the right to asylum in particular. And yet these regulations for some genuine asylum seekers at least, must now be regarded as rendering these rights nugatory. Either that or the 1996 regulations necessarily contemplate for some a life which is so destitute that, to my mind, no civilised nation can tolerate it. So basic are the human rights here at issue, that it cannot be necessary to resort to the Convention . . . to take note of their violation. Nearly 200 years ago Lord Ellenborough CJ in *R v Eastbourne (Inhabitants)*[381a] said:
>
>> As to there being no obligation for maintaining poor foreigners before the statutes ascertaining the different methods of acquiring settlements, the law of humanity, which is anterior to all positive law, obliges us to afford them relief, to save them from starving. . .
>
> True, no obligation arises under article 24 of the 1951 convention until asylum seekers are recognised as refugees. But that is not to say that up to that point their fundamental needs can properly be ignored. I do not accept that they can. Rather, I would hold it unlawful to alter the benefit regime so drastically as must inevitably not merely prejudice, but on occasion defeat, the statutory right of asylum seekers to claim refugee status.

Similarly, in *R v Secretary of State for the Home Department, ex p Simms*[381b] the House of Lords took the view that delegated legislation in the form of the Prison Rules could be *ultra vires* as the right to freedom of expression could not be overriden except by clear words.

5.107 The extent to which delegated legislation can lawfully breach Convention rights under the Human Rights Act depends on the operation of section 6(2)(b). In order to escape liability, a public authority must show that the *enabling* legislation

[380] [1997] 1 WLR 275.
[381] Ibid 401.
[381a] (1803) 4 East at 103.
[381b] [1999] 3 WLR 328 *per* Lord Hoffman at 342.

deprives it of any discretion about how it can act.[382] Thus, the public authority will have a complete defence under the Human Rights Act if it is acting to give effect to or enforce a provision made under primary legislation which 'cannot be read or given effect to in a way which is compatible with Convention rights'. Because the enabling legislation is often drafted in very broad terms, breaches of Convention rights in delegated legislation will rarely be justified under section 6(2)(b). In particular, violations of Convention rights in delegated legislation made under Henry VIII clauses[383] (which permit ministers to amend primary legislation, whether through the parent Act or another statute such as the Deregulation and Contracting Out Act 1994) cannot be successfully defended under section 6(2)(b) since the language of the enabling legislation is expressed in wide discretionary terms.

(4) Administrative acts

The conventional principles of administrative law provide limited protection for fundamental human rights when public bodies make discretionary decisions.[384] However, in *R v Secretary of State for the Home Department, ex p Brind*[385] it was argued that there was an obligation to exercise discretionary powers in accordance with freedom of expression (as defined by Article 10[386] of the Convention). The Home Secretary had issued a directive under the Broadcasting Act 1981 which prohibited the television and radio authorities from broadcasting the spoken words of certain proscribed Northern Ireland organisations. A number of journalists then commenced judicial review proceedings to challenge the ban; and lost at every stage (including before the European Commission of Human Rights).[387] In the domestic courts the journalists argued that Parliament must be presumed not to have intended to confer power on the Home Secretary which unnecessarily conflicted either with freedom of expression or with international treaty obligations under the Convention. However, the House of Lords rejected these contentions, taking the view that they amounted to an attempt to incorporate the Convention by the backdoor.[388] **5.108**

The Human Rights Act will make a significant difference to such administrative **5.109**

[382] It might be argued that s 6(2)(b) is also applicable where only the *secondary* legislation cannot be read or given effect to in a way which is compatible with Convention rights: on the basis that the 'provision' in question cannot be interpreted so as to accord with Convention rights. This would mean, for example, that Prison Rules could be made which were incompatible with Convention rights but could nevertheless be justified under s 6(2)(b). It is submitted, however, that this construction of s 6(2)(b) cannot be sustained since it involves an unnatural reading of grammar and punctuation.

[383] It seems that the nickname derives from the reputation Henry VIII had as an autocrat.

[384] See para 1.30ff above.

[385] [1991] 1 AC 696.

[386] See para 15.137ff below.

[387] *Brind v United Kingdom* (1994) 77-A DR 42.

[388] *Ex p Brind* (n 382 above) *per* Lord Bridge at 748, Lord Ackner at 762

decisions in the future. The Act will oblige public authorities to exercise administrative discretion in a way which is not incompatible with Convention rights. In future, it will be necessary for public authorities to ensure that they meet the obligations imposed, for example, by Article 8[389] where they interfere with the right to private life or the home.

(5) Judicial acts

5.110 Section 9 of the Human Rights Act imposes restrictions on instituting proceedings which relate to 'judicial' acts. First, section 9(1) defines the types of proceedings in which judicial acts can be challenged . Secondly, section 9(3) of the Act ensures that, in general, damages cannot be awarded in respect of a judicial act which is done in good faith.[390] However, damages may be available under the Act if a court is not acting in good faith or to the extent that they are required under Article 5(5) of the Convention.[391] The right to damages that will arise in English law as a result of Article 5(5) is discussed in Chapter 10.[392] Section 9 states:

> (1) Proceedings under section 7(1)(a)[393] in respect of a judicial act may be brought only—
>
> (a) by exercising a right of appeal;
> (b) on an application (in Scotland a petition) for judicial review; or
> (c) in such other forum as may be prescribed by the rules.
>
> (2) That does not affect any rule of law which prevents the court from being the subject of judicial review.
>
> (3) In proceedings under this Act in respect of a judicial act done in good faith, damages may not be awarded otherwise than to compensate a person to the extent required by Article 5(5) of the Convention.
>
> (4) An award of damages permitted by subsection (3) is to be made against the Crown; but no award may be made unless the appropriate person, if not a party to the proceedings, is joined.
>
> (5) In this section—
>
> 'appropriate person' means the Minister responsible for the court concerned, or a person or government department nominated by him;
> 'court' includes a tribunal;
> 'judge' includes a member of a tribunal, a justice of the peace and a clerk or other officer entitled to exercise the jurisdiction of the court;
> 'judicial act' means a judicial act of the court and includes an act done on the instructions, or on behalf, of a judge; and
> 'rules' has the same meaning as in section 7(9)

[389] See para 12.81ff below.
[390] See para 21.26ff below.
[391] See generally, para 10.159ff below.
[392] See para 10.175ff below.
[393] Where a person claims that a public authority has acted or proposes to act in a way which is unlawful under s 6(1) of the Human Rights Act.

The purpose of section 9 is to ensure that decisions of courts and tribunals can only be challenged by an appeal, by judicial review or by some other forum as prescribed by the rules; section 7(9) of the Act defines rules in England and Wales as: **5.111**

> (a) in relation to proceedings before a court or tribunal outside Scotland, rules made by the Lord Chancellor or the Secretary of State for the purpose of this section or rules of court. . . .

The rules which apply are discussed in Chapter 22.[394]

The Human Rights Act does not create any new means by which judicial decisions can be challenged. Nor does it affect any rule of law which prevents a court from being the subject of judicial review. Proceedings in superior courts such as the High Court cannot be subject to judicial review but can only be reviewed through the appellate procedure.[395] Although the Crown Court is a superior court, section 29(3) of the Supreme Court Act 1981 allows judicial review, but only in respect of matters relating to 'trial on indictment'.[396] **5.112**

The procedure for challenging a failure of a court or tribunal to act in a way which is not incompatible with Convention rights therefore treats its decision as an error of law. Where a right of appeal exists, this will be the appropriate venue; and, if no other means of testing the decision is available, it will be necessary to apply for judicial review.[397] **5.113**

(6) The impact on the common law and the rules of precedence

The inclusion of the court as a public authority under section 6(3) of the Human Rights Act places the court under a duty to ensure that the common law is not developed incompatibly with Convention rights[398] and is likely to have the following effects: **5.114**

- substantive principles of law will not develop incompatibly with Convention rights[399] so as to ensure that, for example, the law of defamation complies with freedom of expression;
- in general, section 6(3) does not entitle a court to create a new cause of action in proceedings between private individuals because there is no general *duty*[400]

[394] See para 22.116ff below.
[395] e.g. *Murrell v British Leyland Trustees* [1989] COD 389.
[396] See eg *Re Smalley* [1985] AC 622; *Re Sampson* [1987] 1 WLR 194.
[397] Bamforth has observed that the procedure for remedying a breach of s 6(1) is less clear than it might be, compared to that used where other public authorities breach s 6(1): N Bamforth, 'The Application of the Human Rights Act 1998 to public authorities and public bodies' [1999] 58 CLJ 159.
[398] The identity and nature of Convention rights are considered at para 6.86ff below.
[399] See n 398.
[400] See para 5.95ff above.

on the court to act; however, it is arguable that the court may be entitled to formulate new causes of action where a public authority is under a specific positive duty[401] to secure Convention rights;[402]

- the court will also modify its approach to remedies[403] and procedure[404] so that it is in line with Convention rights; and
- wherever a public authority is exercising a common law duty or power, it will be under a duty to act in a way which is compatible with Convention rights so that for example, decisions of the Civil Service Appeal Board in dismissing civil servants[405] might be unlawful if they fail to comply with Article 6.[406]

5.115 However, the most striking effect of the Human Rights Act is that it will radically affect the law of precedent. The Act comprehensively affects most areas of the English law; and will mean that current case law will need to be re-examined in the light of new principles. It will therefore be open to a court to refuse to follow authority on the basis that those decisions are not compatible with Convention rights. Consequently, a magistrates' court may decline to follow a relevant decision of the House of Lords on the ground that the House of Lords decision cannot stand as a result of the Human Rights Act. Furthermore, the exercise of re-evaluating existing case law will be part of a dynamic process. Because the Convention is to be regarded as a living instrument,[407] the court is entitled to reverse a previous decision in order to reflect changing standards and social attitudes.

(7) Are there non-justiciable acts under the Human Rights Act?

5.116 For the purposes of judicial review proceedings, there is still uncertainty about whether there are unreviewable discretions[408] which are not amenable to the supervisory jurisdiction of the court. It is likely that similar arguments will be put forward to claim that some governmental acts are not justiciable under the Human Rights Act. At one time the court rejected the idea that it could judicially review prerogative powers[409] (that is, those powers which come within the scope

[401] See para 6.97ff below.

[402] See n 398 above.

[403] See para 5.82ff above.

[404] See para 5.81 above.

[405] e.g. *R v Civil Service Appeal Board, ex p Bruce* [1989] ICR 171; *R v Civil Service Appeal Board, ex p Cunningham* [1992] ICR 816.

[406] See para 11.359ff below.

[407] See para 6.23 above.

[408] See eg Lord Woolf and J Jowell, *De Smith, Woolf and Jowell, Judicial Review of Administrative Action* (5th edn, Sweet & Maxwell, 1995) paras 6-014–6-035; P Wallington, 'Discretionary Powers—the limits of legality' in M Supperstone and J Goudie (eds), *Judicial Review* (2nd edn, Butterworths, 1997), paras 5.9–5.14.

[409] e.g. *Musgrove v Chun Teeong Toy* [1918] AC 272 (exclusion of an alien); *Chandler v DPP* [1964] AC 763, 790–92 *per* Lord Reid (disposition of forces); *Hanratty v Lord Butler* (1971) 115 SJ 386 (the prerogative of mercy); *Blackburn v A-G* [1971] 1 WLR 1037 (treaty-making powers).

of the Crown's residual discretionary powers).[410] However, in *R v Criminal Injuries Compensation Board, ex p Lain*[411] the Court of Appeal quashed a decision of the Criminal Injuries Compensation Board even though it was exercising prerogative power;[412] and in the *GCHQ* case[413] the House of Lords held that judicial review extended to prerogative powers. Nevertheless, in the course of his judgment in the *GCHQ* case,[414] Lord Roskill also suggested that some prerogative powers would not be amenable to judicial review.

The vital issue in the subsequent case law has been whether the decision under challenge is *justiciable*.[415] Some questions of 'high policy' have remained outside the scope of judicial review[416] such as the making of treaties;[417] the defence of the realm;[418] the granting of honours; the dissolution of Parliament; the appointment of Ministers; and decisions of the Attorney-General.[419] On the other hand, the Divisional Court upheld a challenge to the prerogative of mercy in *R v Secretary of State for the Home Department, ex p Bentley*.[420] At the other end of the spectrum judicial review has been available in relation to lower level administrative decisions such as the power to issue passports,[421] the residual prerogative power to depart from the Immigration Rules,[422] a Home Secretary's warrant to intercept telephone communications,[423] the power to store riot equipment under the prerogative powers for maintaining law and order,[424] awards of the Civil Service Appeal **5.117**

[410] See the definition given by A Dicey in *An Introduction to the Study of the Law of the Constitution* (8th edn, Macmillan 1915) which was approved in *A-G v de Keyser's Royal Hotel Ltd* [1920] AC 508, 526 and in *Council of Civil Service Unions v Minister for the Civil Service* [1985] AC 374.

[411] [1967] 2 QB 864.

[412] *R v Criminal Injuries Compensation Board, ex p Lain* [1967] 2 QB 864.

[413] *Council of Civil Service Unions v Minister for the Civil Service* (n 410 above); *R v Secretary of State for the Home Department, ex p Fire Brigades Union* [1995] 2 AC 513.

[414] *Council of Civil Service Unions v Minister for the Civil Service* (n 410 above) 418.

[415] See D Pollard, 'Judicial Review of Prerogative Power in the United Kingdom and France' in P Leyland and T Woods, *Administrative Law Facing the Future: Old Constraints and New Horizons* (Blackstone Press, 1997); P Craig, 'Prerogative, Precedent and Power' in C Forsyth and I Hare (eds), *The Golden Metwand and the Crooked Cord* (Clarendon Press, 1998).

[416] See C Neenan, 'Reviewing Prerogative Powers: Roskill's List Revisited' [1998] JR 36.

[417] *R v Secretary of State for Foreign and Commonwealth Affairs, ex p Rees-Mogg* [1994] QB 552.

[418] But see the decision of the Divisional Court in *R v Ministry of Defence, ex p Smith* [1996] QB 517 where it rejected the argument; at 539 Simon Brown LJ said that only the rarest cases would now be beyond the purview of the court (such as cases involving national security and where the court lacks expertise or material to form a judgment); and see Curtis J at 545.

[419] *R v A-G, ex p Taylor* (1996) 8 Admin LR 206; however, when the Attorney-General performs statutory functions under the Coroners Act, he is also immune from judicial review: see *R v A-G, ex p Ferrante* [1995] COD 18.

[420] [1994] QB 349; but see *Reckley v Minister of Public Safety and Immigration (No 2)* [1996] 1 AC 527 which regarded *ex p Bentley* as exceptional.

[421] *R v Secretary of State for Foreign and Commonwealth Affairs, ex p Everett* [1989] QB 811.

[422] *R v Secretary of State for Home Department, ex p Beedasee* [1989] COD 525.

[423] *R v Secretary of State for the Home Department, ex p Ruddock* [1987] 1 WLR 1482.

[424] *R v Secretary of State for the Home Department, ex p Northumbria Police Authority* [1989] QB 26.

Board,[425] the discretion of the Crown Prosecution Service to refuse to bring[426] or continue criminal proceedings[427] and the discretion of the police to issue a caution.[428]

5.118 It is submitted that arguments to the effect that there are non-justiciable decisions of public authorities under the Human Rights Act will fail. The Act binds the Crown[429] and the obligation on public authorities to comply with Convention rights under section 6(1) is expressed in unqualified terms. The Human Rights Act does not give the court a discretion to refuse in principle to review the acts of a public authority.

5.119 The approach taken towards the Canadian Charter of Rights supports this view that there are no decisions of public authorities which will be outside the scope of the Human Rights Act on the ground that they are not justiciable. In *Operation Dismantle Inc v The Queen*[430] proceedings were brought by a peace organisation alleging that the government's decision to allow the United States to test cruise missiles violated the Charter. Although the claim itself failed, the Supreme Court rejected the suggestion that an issue might become non-justiciable because it was too political to be decided by the courts.[431]

F. Acts Which are 'Incompatible' With Convention Rights

(1) The meaning of 'incompatible'

5.120 Section 6(1) is the central provision by which the Human Rights Act makes Convention rights enforceable in English law. The Government declined to incorporate the European Convention into domestic law directly.[431a] and Convention rights do not take direct effect in the same way as European Union law.[431b] Instead the Act imposes statutory restrictions on the actions of public authorities.[431c] Section 6(1) makes it unlawful for a public authority to act in a way which is 'incompatible' with Convention rights. The meaning of this provision is not straightforward. In order to assess whether the actions of the public authority are unlawful, it is necessary to go through a two-stage process:

[425] eg *R v Civil Service Appeal Board, ex p Bruce* [1989] ICR 171; *R v Civil Service Appeal Board, ex p Cunningham* [1992] ICR 816.

[426] *R v DPP, ex p C* (1995) 7 Admin LR 385.

[427] *R v Chief Constable of Kent, ex p L* [1993] 1 All ER 756.

[428] *R v Commissioner of Police for the Metropolis, ex p P* (1996) Admin LR 6; *R v Commissioner of Police of the Metropolis, ex p Thompson* [1997] 1 WLR 1519.

[429] See s 22(5).

[430] [1985] 1 SCR 441.

[431] Ibid *per* Wilson J at 472; Dickson J concurred at 459.

[431a] See para 3.89 above.

[431b] See para 1.76ff above.

[431c] The principles for identifying public authorities are discussed at para 5.03ff above.

- the identification of the 'Convention rights' relevant to the action in question;
- the assessment as to whether the acts of the public authority are 'compatible' with those rights.

In relation to the first issue, the court can be guided by the Strasbourg jurisprudence in accordance with section 2(1) of the, Human Rights Act 1998[432] but must, ultimately, make its own assessment. In relation to the second, 'incompatible' in this context must mean 'inconsistent'.[433] It is submitted that an act will be 'inconsistent' with a Convention right if it constitutes a 'violation' of that right but not otherwise.

To some extent the exercise the courts must carry out under the Human Rights Act is comparable to that which is undertaken when the courts have to assess whether domestic law is compatible with European Union law. For example, in the *Factortame* litigation[434] the domestic courts have had to grapple with the implications of the Merchant Shipping Act breaching Article 6 of the EC Treaty which prohibits any discrimination on grounds of nationality. Similarly, in *R v Secretary of State for Employment, ex p Equal Opportunities Commission*[435] the House of Lords made a declaration that limited employment protection rights given to part time workers were incompatible with European Union law on grounds of indirect sex discrimination. **5.121**

Nevertheless, ascertaining whether a public authority has acted inconsistently with Convention rights is not a straightforward process. Where it is said that the public authority has acted incompatibly with an unqualified right[435a] (such as the right to life or a liberty right), the court must decide whether the unqualified right is in play; if so, the unqualified right will prevail if the action is, indeed, incompatible. A more complex approach is necessary where the court is examining a qualified right[435b] (such as the right to privacy or freedom of expression). Assessing whether a public authority has acted incompatibly with a qualified right involves a two stage exercise: first, is there an interference with the right; and if so, is the interference justified as being prescribed by law, for a legitimate purpose and necessary in a democratic society?[435c] The difficulty of this exercise is demonstrated by *R v DPP,* **5.121A**

[432] See para 3.46ff above.

[433] The *Oxford English Dictionary* defines compatible as 'mutually tolerant; capable of being admitted together, or of existing together in the same subject; accordant; consistent; congruous; agreeable': see (Clarendon; 1989) Vol III.

[434] See *R v Secretary of State for Transport, ex p Factortame* [1990] 2 AC 85; *R v Secretary of State for Transport, ex p Factortame (No 2)* [1991] 1 AC 603; *Brasserie du Pêcheur SA v Germany* Case C-46/93 [1996] ECR I-1029; *R v Secretary of State for Transport, ex p Factortame (No 4)* [1996] ECR I-1029; *R v Secretary of State for Transport, ex p Factortame (note)* [1998] 1 All ER 736.

[435] [1995] 1 AC 1.

[435a] See para 6.86ff below.

[435b] See para 6.90ff below.

[435c] See generally, para 6.91 below.

ex p Kebeline which considered whether a reverse onus provision in the Prevention of Terrorism Act breached the presumption of innocence in Article 6(2).[435d] Whereas the Divisional Court took the view that the incompatibility was plain.[435e] Lord Hope in the House of Lords carried out a much more elaborate analysis, ultimately deciding that the issue depended on striking a fair balance between the demands of the general interests of the community and the protection of the fundamental rights of the individual.[435f]

(2) The need to make a primary judgment

5.122 When the court has to decide whether a public authority has acted incompatibly with Convention rights, it will be making a *primary* judgment, a point of critical significance which was accepted by Simon Brown LJ in *R v Ministry of Defence, ex p Smith*:[436]

> If the Convention . . . were part of our law and we were accordingly entitled to ask whether the policy answers a pressing social need and whether the restriction on human rights can be shown to be proportionate to the restriction on human rights involved, then clearly the primary judgment (subject only to a limited 'margin of appreciation') should be for us and not for others; the constitutional balance would shift.

In other words, under the Human Rights Act the court is faced with the stark choice of deciding whether or not a public authority has acted in a way which is incompatible with a Convention right.[437]

5.123 As a result, the court will be required to carry out a fundamentally different exercise from that used when considering whether a public body has acted in a way which is '*Wednesbury* unreasonable' when it considers an administrative law decision affecting human rights.[438] In the *Wednesbury* context the court is always involved in a 'review' exercise: it has to make a secondary judgment about the reasonableness of the decision-maker's primary judgment. As Lord Bridge emphasised in *R v Secretary of State for the Home Department, ex p Brind*[439] when considering a judicial review challenge concerning whether a broadcasting ban breached freedom of expression:

> In exercising the power of judicial review . . . we are . . . perfectly entitled to start from the premise that any restriction requires to be justified and that nothing less

435d See generally, para 11.236ff below.

435d Lord Bingham CJ said at [1999] 3 WLR 175, 190 that the sections 'undermined, in a blatant and obvious way, the presumption of innocence'; Laws LJ at 201 agreed.

435f [1999] 3 WLR 972, 996–999.

436 [1996] QB 517, 541.

437 The meaning of 'incompatibility' is considered at para 5.120ff above.

438 See para 1.31 above.

439 [1991] 1 AC 696, 748, 749.

> than an important competing concern would be sufficient to justify it. The primary judgment as to whether a particular competing public interest justifies the particular restriction imposed falls on the Secretary of State to whom Parliament has entrusted the discretion. But we are entitled to exercise a secondary judgment by asking whether the reasonable Secretary of State on the material before him could reasonably make the primary judgment.

Under the Human Rights Act, the 'primary judgment' will be for the court. In the case of 'unqualified rights'[440] the only issue is whether there has been a violation of the right. In the case of 'qualified rights'[441] the exercise for the court is more complex: first it must consider whether there was an interference with the right, secondly, whether the interference was justified.[442] However, it is submitted that even in relation to 'qualified rights' the court cannot confine itself to a 'secondary judgment' but must, itself, make a 'primary judgment' about whether the interference with the right is justified. **5.124**

G. 'Judicial Deference' and the Human Rights Act

(1) Introduction

When the court is making a primary judgment about whether a public authority has acted unlawfully by acting incompatibly[443] with Convention rights, it will often be obliged to apply the doctrine of proportionality.[444] A critical question under the Human Rights Act will be the extent to which the court defers to the judgment of the public authority itself when assessing whether that public authority has violated a Convention right. On the one hand, if the court adopts an excessively deferential approach to the views of the public authority, this could undermine the purpose of the Human Rights Act in the first place. On the other hand, an extreme form of judicial activism would involve the courts in making decisions which are outside its area of expertise and would breach the constitutional doctrine of separation of powers. The ability of the courts to find a proper balance between judicial restraint and judicial activism will be one of the most important challenges it faces under the Human Rights Act.[445] **5.125**

---

[440] Such as life or freedom from torture, see generally, para 6.86ff below.

[441] Such as privacy, freedom of religion, freedom of expression, freedom of assembly and association, see generally, para 6.90ff below.

[442] The three requirements that must be overcome to justify an interference with a qualified right are discussed at para 6.123ff below.

[443] See para 5.120ff below.

[444] See para 6.75ff below.

[445] Lord Irvine, 'Activism and Restraint: Human Rights and the Interpretative Process' [1999] EHRLR 350.

(2) Proportionality and *Wednesbury* unreasonableness

5.126 The fundamental basis for reviewing public authorities under the Human Rights Act will be the principle of proportionality.[446] A crucial question under the Act will be whether the court regards proportionality merely as a *Wednesbury* irrationality issue, in other words whether, as some public authorities will argue, the Court should merely ask, *could* a decision-maker acting *reasonably* have reached its decision.[447] The *Wednesbury* doctrine[448] in fact conceals two distinct propositions: first, that the Court is exercising a secondary judgment about the reasonableness of a decision-maker's primary judgment[449] and secondly, that the appropriate test of reasonableness is the very stringent one of posing the question 'is the decision so absurd that no sensible person could ever dream it lay within the powers of the decision-maker';[450] 'is the decision so wrong that no reasonable person could sensibly take that view';[451] or 'is the decision so outrageous in its defiance of logic or of accepted moral standards that no sensible person who applied his mind to the question to be decided could have arrived at it'.[452]

5.127 It is sometimes argued that, in practice, the principle of proportionality is no different from the doctrine of *Wednesbury* irrationality.[453] However, it is submitted that the two approaches are different. First, proportionality requires the court to test the 'necessity'[454] of interfering with human rights. The 'necessity' requirement imposes a much more onerous obligation on a public authority to satisfy than the *Wednesbury* standard. The very high threshold an applicant must overcome in proving *Wednesbury* irrationality is demonstrated by *R v Ministry of Defence ex p Smith*.[454a] In that case the Court of Appeal held that that the more substantial the interference with human rights, the more the Court will require by way of justification before it is persuaded that the decision is *Wednesbury* reasonable; however, it went on to decide that it was lawful to dismiss servicemen on the ground that they were homosexual. As a result the European Court of Human Rights concluded in *Smith and*

---

[446] For a discussion of proportionality as it will apply under the Human Rights Act, see para 6.75ff below.

[447] See, in particular, the remarks of Lord Cooke in *R v Chief Constable of Sussex, ex p International Trader's Ferry* [1998] 3 WLR 1260, 1288, 1289; and for a helpful review of the case law see *R v Secretary of State for the Home Department, ex p Brind* [1991] 1 AC 696 *per* Lord Lowry at 764, 765.

[448] The *Wednesbury* principles as applied to human rights cases are considered at para 1.31.

[449] Unlike the position under the Human Rights Act: see para 5.122ff above.

[450] *Associated Provincial Picture Houses v Wednesbury Corporation* [1948] 1 KB 223, 764.

[451] *Secretary of State for Education and Science v Thameside Metropolitan Borough Council* [1977] AC 1014, 1026 *per* Lord Denning MR.

[452] *Council of Civil Service Unions v Minister for the Civil Service* [1985] AC 374, 410 *per* Lord Diplock.

[453] See, in particular, Lord Hoffman, 'The influence of the European principle of proportionality' in E Ellis (ed), *The Principle of Proportionality in the Laws of Europe* (Hart Publishing 1999).

[454] See para 6.146ff below.

[454a] [1996] QB 517.

Grady v United Kingdom[454b] that the applicants had been denied an effective remedy in breach of Article 13. Secondly, there is a difference in approach between the proportionality and *Wednesbury* doctrines when addressing the question of whether a public body has manifestly imbalanced the relationship between ends and means. For the purposes of proportionality, reasonableness must be *explicitly* related to the objective in question so that the balancing exercise required is more clearly articulated.[455] As Laws J said in *R v Ministry of Agriculture, Fisheries and Food, ex p First City Trading*:[456]

> It is not enough merely to set out the problem, and assert that within his discretion the Minister chose this or that solution constrained only by the requirement that his decision must be a reasonable one which a reasonable Minister might make. Rather the Court will test the solution arrived at, and pass it only if substantial factual considerations are put forward in its justification: considerations which are relevant, reasonable and proportionate to the aim in view.

Nonetheless, the courts would in effect be applying a *Wednesbury* test under the Human Rights Act if they relied on Convention case law; and dealt with proportionality by asking whether a public authority had breached Convention rights by exceeding its margin of appreciation.[457] **5.128**

In a number of English cases the judges have assumed that where Convention law is examined, the decision-maker himself has a 'margin of appreciation or discretion' that must be respected.[458] Thus, in *Lamuratu Mbatube v Secretary of State for the Home Department*[459] Hirst LJ suggested that the Secretary of State: **5.129**

> must be allowed quite a large margin of discretion in performing their obligations when breaches of the Convention are alleged.

Numerous judicial review cases have suggested that *Wednesbury* irrationality is equivalent to holding that the decision maker has acted outside his margin of appreciation.[460] For example, in *R v Somerset County Council, ex p Fewings*[461] Simon

[454b] [1999] IRLR 734; and see para 21.178 below.

[455] F Jacobs, 'Public Law—The Impact of Europe' [1999] PL 232.

[456] [1997] 1 CMLR 250, 279.

[457] For a discussion of the role of the margin of appreciation under Convention jurisprudence: see para 6.34ff below. The relationship between proportionality and the margin of appreciation under the Human Rights Act is discussed at para 6.82ff below.

[458] See eg *R v Secretary of State for the Home Department, ex p Brind* [1991] 1 AC 696 *per* Lord Templeman at 751, *per* Lord Ackner at 762.

[459] [1996] Imm AR 184, 189 where the Court of Appeal approved *R v Secretary of State for the Home Department, ex p Bina Patel* [1995] Imm AR 223.

[460] eg *R v Monopolies and Mergers Commission, ex p Elders IXL Ltd* [1987] 1 WLR 1221; *R v Secretary of State for the Home Department, ex p Brind* [1991] 1 AC 696; *R v Solihull Metropolitan Borough Council Housing Benefit Review Board, ex p Simpson* (1993) 26 HLR 370; *R v Commissioner of Police for the Metropolis, ex p P* (1996) 8 Admin LR 6, 14; *R v Ministry of Defence, ex p Smith* [1996] QB 517, 554 *per* Sir Thomas Bingham MR; *R v Chief Constable of Sussex, ex p International Trader's Ferry Ltd* [1999] 1 All ER 129.

[461] [1995] 1 WLR 1037, 1049.

Brown LJ examined the question of whether a decision-maker had taken account of irrelevant considerations and took the view there are considerations:

> to which a decision maker may have regard if in his judgment and discretion he thinks it right to do so. There is, in short, a margin of appreciation within which the decision maker must decide just what sort of considerations should play a part in his reasoning process.

5.130 It is, however, submitted that there is no justification[462] for introducing the concept of margin of appreciation into the doctrine of the proportionality.[463] Furthermore, the Human Rights Act does not provide any support for a reasonableness test when the court assesses whether a public authority has breached Convention rights. In particular, the Human Rights Act does not provide for any 'general limitation' of rights on the grounds of reasonableness. As a result, it differs significantly from the Canadian Charter of Rights and the New Zealand Bill of Rights: both of which provide that restrictions can be justified if they are *reasonable* ones. Thus, section 1 of the Canadian Charter of Rights states:

> The Canadian Charter of Rights and Freedoms guarantees the rights and freedoms set out in it subject only to such *reasonable* limits prescribed by law as can be demonstrably justified in a free and democratic society.

Similarly, section 5 of the New Zealand Bill of Rights states:

> . . . the rights and freedoms contained in this Bill of Rights may be subject only to such *reasonable* limits prescribed by law as can be demonstrably justified in a free and democratic society.

It would therefore be wrong in principle to claim that the Human Rights Act gives a public authority a margin of appreciation which had to be exceeded in order to show that the authority had acted in a way which was incompatible with Convention rights.

5.131 At the same time, it is clear that the courts will defer to the judgment of public authorities where they are making discretionary judgments on policy issues where the legislature, executive and public bodies are better placed than the judiciary to decide.[464] Judicial deference or restraint is fundamental to the approach towards proportionality taken by Convention,[465] European Union[466] and Canadian case law,[467] as it has been where the English courts apply *Wednesbury*[468] or proportionality[469] principles.

---

462 See para 6.82ff below.
463 See para 6.75ff below.
464 D Pannick, 'Principles of Interpretation of Convention Rights Under the Human Rights Act and Discretionary Areas of Judgment' [1998] PL 545.
465 See para 6.42ff below.
466 See para 6.56ff below.
467 See para 6.62ff below.
468 See para 5.126 above.
469 See para 6.54ff below.

(3) The views of a public authority

A more difficult question is what *weight* to attach to the public authority's *own* view about whether a particular restriction is necessary in the interests of a democratic society. The language of the European Convention is very broad; and as Lord Mustill stressed in *R v Monopolies and Mergers Commission, ex p South Yorkshire Transport Ltd*[470] a phrase: 5.132

> may be so imprecise that different decision-makers, each acting rationally may reach differing conclusions when applying it to the facts of a given case. In such a case the court is entitled to substitute its own opinion for that of the person to whom the decision was entrusted only if the decision is so aberrant that it cannot be classed as rational.

Lord Woolf MR expressed comparable views in *R v Radio Authority, ex p Bull*,[471] holding that a public authority has a margin of appreciation when it has to direct itself to a statutory duty which is expressed in wide terms:

> (a) The authority is a regulatory body consisting of lay members which is intended to take a broadbrush approach to its task. . . .
> (b) The onus is on [the applicant] to show that the authority transgressed. . . .
> (c) From an examination of the different elements of [the statutory provision][472] it is apparent that it is difficult to identify with precision the parameters of the paragraph. The language of the provision therefore allows the authority a reasonable degree of tolerance in its application.
> (d) Because of its lay nature and the terms of the [statutory provision], the court should be prepared to allow the authority a margin of appreciation and only interfere with its decisions where there is a manifest breach of the principles applied on judicial review.

However, it is submitted that the views of a public authority itself will not be the decisive factor. First, under the Human Rights Act the court is making a primary[473] judgment; and must be satisfied that it is not *itself* acting incompatibly with Convention rights[474] when making an adjudication under the Act. Secondly, the standard or intensity of review will depend on the *context*. It may be appropriate to defer to a public authority's views on issues of political, economic or social policy, or when legislative choices are under consideration, since the court should defer to policy judgments made through the democratic process. It may also be fitting to attach weight to a public authority's views where it is making an expert judgment. However, these factors will not be significant when considering 5.133

[470] [1993] 1 WLR 23, 32; see also *R v Ministry of Defence, ex p Walker*, *The Times*, 11 Feb 1999.
[471] [1997] 2 WLR 1094, 1106; see also *R v Broadcasting Standards Authority, ex p British Broadcasting Corporation*, *The Times*, 12 Apr 2000.
[472] Broadcasting Act 1990, s 92(1).
[473] See para 5.122ff above.
[474] Under s 6(1): see para 5.120ff above.

routine administrative decisions; in this context strict scrutiny is more appropriate. As Lord Hope stressed in *R v DPP, ex p Kebeline*[474a] when considering the position under the Human Rights Act where it was alleged a reverse onus provision in the Prevention of Terrorism Act was incompatible with the presumption of innocence:

> difficult choices may need to be made by the executive or the legislature between the rights of the individual and the needs of society. In some circumstances it will be appropriate for the courts to recognise that there is an area of judgment within which the judiciary will defer, on democratic grounds, to the considered opinion of the elected body or person whose act or decision is said to be in compatible with the Convention . . . It will be easier for such an area of judgement to be recognised where the Convention itself requires a balance to be struck, much less so where the right is stated in terms which are unqualified. It will be easier for it to be recognised where the issues involve questions of social or economic policy, much less so where the rights are of high constitutional importance or are of a kind where the courts are especially well placed to assess the need for protection. But even where the right is stated in terms which are unqualified the courts will need to bear in mind the jurisprudence of the European Court which recognises that due account should be taken of the special nature of terrorist crime and the threat which it poses to a democratic society.[474b]

(4) 'Judicial deference under the Act': conclusion

5.134 When the court is applying proportionality principles under the Human Rights Act,[475] it will be obliged to consider whether and to what extent it is appropriate to defer to the views of the public authority. It is submitted that the court will take account of the following factors when scrutinising the judgment of a public authority which is restricting Convention rights:[476]

- the *importance* of the rights at stake: some rights are of particular importance and will require a high degree of constitutional protection: for example, access to the courts,[477] freedom of expression (particularly, political expression)[478] and intimate aspects of private life such as an individual's sexuality;[479]
- the *extent* of the interference with the right and, in particular, whether the interference impairs the very essence of the right;
- whether the reason for interfering with the right is sufficiently important to *justify* the interference;[480]

[474a] [1999] 3 WLR 972, 994.

[474b] *Murray v United Kingdom* (1994) 19 EHRR 22 para 47.

[475] See para 6.72ff below.

[476] See para 6.86ff below.

[477] The right of access in English Law is discussed at para 11.15ff below; the relevant Convention case law is considered at para 11.185ff below.

[478] The relevant Convention case law is discussed at para 15.163ff below.

[479] Breach of confidence is considered at para 12.27ff below and the relevant Convention case law is discussed at para 12.92ff below.

[480] It is submitted that this requirement is in fact part of the proportionality principle: see para 6.75ff below.

- the *context* within which the public authority is operating: the court is likely to defer to discretionary judgements which require consideration of social, economic or political policy at one end of the spectrum, but will be disinclined to do so when considering routine administrative decisions;
- the degree of specialist *expertise* involved: there are some areas where the court has a particular expertise (for example, in relation to the criminal law) and others where it is appropriate to defer to the specialist expertise of the decision maker.

However, the court is making a primary judgment about whether the decision or action of the public authority is compatible with Convention rights; and in making that primary judgment, the court must satisfy the obligation that it *itself* owes as a public authority not to act incompatibly with Convention rights.

Part III

THE CONVENTION RIGHTS

6

GENERAL PRINCIPLES UNDER THE CONVENTION

A. Introduction

6.01 The European Convention on Human Rights is an international treaty which must be interpreted in accordance with the established rules of public international law. In addition, the European Commission and Court of Human Rights have developed a substantial jurisprudence dealing with the interpretation of the Convention itself. The principles of interpretation applicable to the Convention must be taken into account by the English courts when applying the Human Rights Act.[1] They are, potentially, of very considerable importance in enabling English judges to understand the nature of the rights created by the Convention. The interpretation of the Convention is considered in the next section of this chapter.

6.02 When interpreting the Convention, the Court and the Commission have been sensitive to the fact they are supervising the application of an international human rights instrument. They recognise that the domestic states may in the first instance be best placed to assess whether human rights violations have taken place in their jurisdiction. The principles of margin of appreciation and proportionality have evolved to ensure effective rights protection which reflects the Convention's international character. They are fundamental to Convention case law; and their role and scope under the Human Rights Act is likely to be controversial. We discuss the margin of appreciation and proportionality in sections C and D of this chapter.

6.03 The Convention contains 59 Articles and has seven protocols.[2] Only 12 of the

[1] See s 2(1) of the Human Rights Act 1998; for the 'common law principles' applying to the construction of constitutional instruments see para 3.06ff above.

[2] These are the First Protocol (ratified by the Council of Europe on 20 Feb 1952); the Fourth Protocol (ratified on 16 Sept 1963), the Sixth Protocol (ratified on 28 Apr 1983), the Seventh Protocol (ratified on 22 Nov 1984), the Ninth Protocol (ratified on 6 Nov 1990), the Tenth Protocol (ratified on 25 Mar 1992) and the Eleventh Protocol (ratified on 11 May 1994). The United Kingdom has ratified the First, Sixth, Ninth, Tenth and Eleventh Protocols. (The remaining Protocols have amended the enforcement machinery (the Third, Fifth, Eighth, Ninth and Tenth) or given the Court power to give advisory opinions (the Second).

Articles confer substantive rights (which have been enacted under the Human Rights Act):[3]

- the right to life (Article 2 of the Convention);[4]
- the prohibition of torture (Article 3 of the Convention);[5]
- the prohibition of slavery and forced labour (Article 4 of the Convention);[6]
- the right to liberty and security (Article 5 of the Convention);[7]
- the right to a fair trial (Article 6 of the Convention);[8]
- no punishment without law (Article 7 of the Convention);[9]
- the right to respect for private and family life (Article 8 of the Convention);[10]
- the right to thought, conscience and religion (Article 9 of the Convention;[11]
- freedom of expression (Article 10 of the Convention);[12]
- freedom of assembly and association (Article 11 of the Convention);[13]
- the right to marry (Article 12 of the Convention);[14]
- the prohibition of discrimination (Article 14 of the Convention).[15]

There are also substantive rights which are contained in protocols ratified by the United Kingdom (and which have been enacted under the Human Rights Act):[16]

- the protection of property (Article 1 of the First Protocol to the Convention);[17]
- the right to education (Article 2 of the First Protocol to the Convention);[18]
- the right to free elections (Article 3 of the First Protocol to the Convention);[19]
- the abolition of the death penalty (Articles 1 and 2 of the Sixth Protocol).[20]

These rights fall into two distinct groups: unqualified and qualified.[21]A number 6.04
of other issues also arise about the nature of the Convention rights: the ability of the United Kingdom to derogate and make reservations in relation to rights, the type of obligations that they impose (negative and positive) and the burden of proof that must be satisfied in proving a breach of a Convention right. These are discussed in section E of the chapter.

[3] Under s 1(1): see Sch 1 of the Human Right Act.
[4] See Chap 7 below.
[5] See Chap 8 below.
[6] See Chap 9 below.
[7] See Chap 10 below.
[8] See Chap 11 below.
[9] See Chap 11 below.
[10] See Chaps 12 and 13 below.
[11] See Chap 14 below.
[12] See Chap 15 below.
[13] See Chap 16 below.
[14] See Chap 13 below.
[15] See Chap 14 below.
[16] Under s 1(1).
[17] See Chap 18 below.
[18] See Chap 19 below.
[19] See Chap 20 below.
[20] See Chap 7 below.
[21] See para 6.86ff below.

6.05 Articles 15,[22] 16,[23] 17[24] and 18[25] of the Convention apply general restrictions on Convention rights. In addition, a number of 'implied limitations' have been developed in the case law. These restrictions on Convention rights are analysed in Section F below.

6.06 The next topic discussed in this chapter concerns the operation of the restrictions laid down by the Convention in the case of 'qualified' rights. These rights, contained in Articles 8 to 11 of the Convention, are some of the most important: respect for private and family life, freedom of religion, freedom of expression and freedom of assembly and association. In each case, the relevant Article of the Convention makes express provision as to the basis on which interference with such rights is permissible. Section G deals with the issues which are common to the operation of all these qualified rights. It is also possible for individuals to waive their Convention rghts. The scope of this doctrine is considered in section H.

B. The Interpretation of the Convention

(1) Principles of treaty interpretation in international law

(a) Vienna Convention on the Law of Treaties

6.07 As stated above, the European Convention on Human Rights is an international treaty and must, therefore, be interpreted in accordance with principles of public international law.[26] The primary source of international law for the interpretation of treaties is the Vienna Convention on the Law of Treaties 1969.[27] Article 31 of the Vienna Convention establishes the general rule of interpretation. Article 31(1) provides that:

> A treaty shall be interpreted in good faith in accordance with the ordinary meaning to be given to the terms of the treaty in their context and in the light of its object and purpose.

For the purpose of interpretation of a treaty, 'context' includes, in addition to the text, the preamble[28] and annexes, any agreement between all of the parties, and

---

[22] Derogation in times of emergency.

[23] Political rights of aliens.

[24] Restrictions on activities aimed at the destruction of Convention rights.

[25] Using restrictions for an improper purpose.

[26] See generally, I Brownlie, *Principles of Public International Law* (5th edn, Clarendon Press, 1998) 631–638; see also J Merrills, *The Development of International Law by the European Court of Human Rights* (2nd edn, Manchester University Press, 1995) 69–97; D Harris, M O'Boyle and C Warbrick, *Law of the European Convention on Human Rights* (Butterworths, 1995) 55–8; F Jacobs and R White, *The European Convention on Human Rights* (2nd edn, Clarendon Press, 1996) 26–38.

[27] The 'Vienna Convention': (1980) Cmnd 7964; In particular, Arts 31–33: see the *Commentary of the International Law Commission on the Final Draft Articles of the Vienna Convention* YBILC (1966), ii 172.

[28] See G Fitzmaurice 'The Law and Procedure of the International Court of Justice 1951–4: Treaty Interpretation and Other Treaty Points' 33 BYIL 227–8.

any instrument made by one or more parties, in connection with the conclusion of the treaty.[29]

Article 31(3) of the Vienna Convention requires that other elements be taken into account, together with the context, in the interpretation of a treaty. Any subsequent agreement between the parties,[30] and any subsequent practice which establishes such agreement,[31] in relation to the interpretation and application of the provisions of the treaty, must be considered.[32] Importantly, any relevant rule of international law applicable in the relations between the parties must also be taken into account.[33] Finally, the general rule of interpretation provides that a special meaning shall be given to a term 'if it is established that the parties so intended'.[34] **6.08**

If the application of Article 31 leaves the meaning of a treaty ambiguous or obscure, or leads to a manifestly absurd or unreasonable result, recourse may be had to supplementary means of interpretation. These supplementary aids include the preparatory work of the treaty and the circumstances of its conclusion.[35] Moreover, such recourse may be had to verify or confirm a meaning that emerges as a result of the textual approach.[36] **6.09**

Where a treaty has been authenticated in two or more languages, the text is equally authoritative in each language unless the treaty provides, or the parties have agreed, otherwise.[37] The terms of the treaty are presumed to have the same meaning in each authentic text.[38] The Convention is authenticated in both English and French and each version is, therefore, equally authoritative. However: **6.10**

> where a comparison of the authentic texts discloses a difference in meaning which the application of Articles 31 and 32 does not remove, the meaning which best reconciles the texts, having regard to the object and purpose of the treaty, shall be adopted.[39]

(b) The teleological approach

Although the Vienna Convention establishes an essentially textual approach to **6.11**

---

[29] Art 31(2); see also the *Young Loan Arbitration* [1980]59 ILR 495.

[30] Art 31(3)(a).

[31] Art 31(3)(b).

[32] See *Air Transport Services Agreement Arbitration* (1963) 38 ILR 182; *Air Transport Services Agreement Arbitration* (1965) RIAA xvi 75; *Young Loan Arbitration* [1980] 59 ILR 495; G Fitzmaurice (n 28 above).

[33] Art 31(3)(c).

[34] Art 31(4).

[35] R Jennings, 'General Course on Principles of International Law' 121 Hague Recueil 550–2; *Young Loan Arbitration* 59 ILR 495; *Fothergill v Monarch Airlines Ltd* [1981] AC 251; *Commonwealth of Australia v State of Tasmania* (1983) 46 ALR 625, ILR 68, 266.

[36] Art 32.

[37] Art 33(1).

[38] Art 33(3).

[39] Art 33(4).

interpretation, it requires that the terms of a treaty are to be construed in context, and in the light of the objects and purposes of the treaty. The reference to objects and purposes in Article 31(1) of the Vienna Convention permits a teleological approach, by which the interpreter seeks to realise the objects and purposes of the treaty. This method first determines what the purposes are, and then any ambiguity of meaning may be resolved by importing the substance 'necessary' to the realisation of the objects and purposes.

(c) 'Living principles'

6.12 It follows from the teleological emphasis on objects and purposes that a treaty may be given a 'dynamic' or 'evolving' interpretation. As a result, the teleological approach may involve judicial implementation of purposes in a manner not entirely contemplated by the parties.

6.13 The traditional approach to international law has always found expression in the formulation of living principles, rather than a positivist insistence on strict proof of the consent of states to particular formulations of specific rules.[40] Furthermore, some international lawyers argue that 'international law is a decision-making process in which the judge must exercise policy-making options by weighing the conflicting interests of the parties in the context of the interests of the world community as a whole'.[41] An innovative interpretation may not, in practice, depart drastically from the textual method, which often leaves the interpreter to choose from a number of potential meanings, a decision that is invariably influenced by policy considerations.

(2) Construing the Convention

(a) Construing the Convention as a treaty

6.14 Although the Vienna Convention was not in force when the European Convention on Human Rights was concluded,[42] the European Court of Human Rights in *Golder v UK*[43] confirmed that the terms of the Vienna Convention are applicable to the European Convention because they enunciate in essence 'generally accepted principles of international law'.[44]

6.15 The jurisprudence of the Court provides numerous examples of its application of

---

[40] C W Jenks, *Orthodoxy and Innovation in the Law of Nations* (The Proceedings of the British Academy, Vol LVII, 1971) 6.

[41] R Higgins, 'Policy Considerations and the International Judicial Process' (1968) 17 ICLQ 58. Note the divergence between this and the current view of many British international lawyers, who accept that international law is a set of neutral rules which it is the task of the judge to apply objectively to the facts before him: Jenks (n 40 above) 6.

[42] The Vienna Convention is not retroactively effective.

[43] (1975) 1 EHRR 524, para 14; see also *Johnstonv Ireland* (1986) 9 EHRR 203 para 51.

[44] *Golder* (n 43 above), para 29.

the Vienna Convention principles.[45] These may be conveniently considered under the headings of 'ordinary meaning', 'special meaning', 'object and purpose', 'comparing the authoritative texts' and the 'use of the *travaux préparatoires*'.

Ordinary meaning. The Court has often considered the 'ordinary meanings' of words in particular Articles. In an appropriate case, the Court will look at the dictionary meaning of words or phrases in both the French and English text.[46] **6.16**

Special meaning. Some terms are given 'special' or 'autonomous' meanings in accordance with Article 31(4) of the Vienna Convention. A number of key concepts in the Convention have a meaning which: **6.17**

> is 'autonomous' in relation to their meaning in domestic law. The Court will 'look behind the appearances and investigate the realities of the procedure in question'.[47]

Thus, 'criminal charge',[48] 'civil rights and obligations',[49] 'tribunal'[50] and 'witness'[51] have each been given an autonomous meaning in the context of Article 6. The concept of 'penalty' in Article 7 is also an autonomous Convention concept.[52]

Object and purpose. The Court has used the object and purpose of the Convention[53] as an aid to interpretation on many occasions. In essence, the purpose of the Convention is to 'protect the fundamental rights of individual human beings from infringement by any of the High Contracting Parties'.[54] For this reason, limitations or qualifications of the rights granted by the Convention are to be narrowly construed.[55] The Court will try to: **6.18**

> seek the interpretation that is most appropriate in order to realise the aim and achieve the object of the treaty, not that which would restrict to the greatest possible degree the obligations undertaken by the parties.[56]

When the question is whether a particular Article is applicable, the fact that there

---

[45] For an application of the general rule, see *Luedicke, Belkacem and Koc v Germany* (1978) 2 EHRR 149 para 46.

[46] See eg *Leudicke, Belkacem and Koc v Germany* (n 45 above), para 46 in relation to the words 'gratuitement' and 'free' in Art 6(3)(a), referring to the 'free assistance of an interpreter'.

[47] See R Ryssdall, 'The Coming of Age of the European Convention on Human Rights' (1996) 1 EHRLR 18, 23; the quotation is from *Deweer v Belgium* (1980) 2 EHRR 439 para 44.

[48] *Engel and others v Netherlands (No 2)* (1976) 1 EHRR 706 para 81; and see para 11.174ff below.

[49] *König v Germany* (1978) 2 EHRR 170 para 88.

[50] *Belilos v Switzerland* (1988) 10 EHRR 466 para 64.

[51] D Harris, M O'Boyle and C Warbrick, *Law of the European Convention on Human Rights* (Butterworths, 1995) 267.

[52] See *Welch v United Kingdom* (1995) 20 EHRR 247 para 27.

[53] The 'object and purpose' of the Convention can be found in its Preamble: *Wemhoff v Germany* (1968) 1 EHRR 55.

[54] *Austria v Italy* (1961) 4 YB 116, 138 EComm HR.

[55] See eg *Klass v Germany* (1978) 2 EHRR 214 para 42 (Art 8(2); *Sunday Times v United Kingdom* (1979) 2 EHRR 245 para 65 (Art 10(2)).

[56] *Wemhoff v Germany* (1968) 1 EHRR 55 para 8.

is another Article dealing with the same topic is not a conclusive objection.[57] But the Court will not permit one Article to be used in a way which neutralises another. Furthermore, if a right has been omitted from one Article, it will not be read into another.[58]

6.19 **Authoritative text.** In cases in which the English and French texts appear to bear different meanings, the Court has sought to reach an interpretation which best reconciles them, bearing in mind the object and purpose of the Convention. Thus, the phrase 'in the public interest' in Article 1 of the First Protocol was given a broad construction as best reconciling the two authentic texts 'having regard to the object and purpose' of Article 1, namely guarding against arbitrary confiscation of property.[59]

6.20 **'*Travaux préparatoires*'.** The Court has considered the '*travaux*' in a number of cases, although they have rarely influenced the result. The '*travaux préparatoires*' are generally regarded as being of limited assistance in the construction of the Convention, largely because the Convention is considered to be a 'living instrument', towards which the Court has adopted a 'dynamic interpretation'.[60] In the *Loizidou* case[61] it was said that the Convention:

> cannot be interpreted solely in accordance with the intentions of their authors as expressed more than forty years ago . . . at a time when a minority of the present Contracting Parties adopted the Convention.

In *Lawless v Ireland (No 2)*,[62] the Court refused to resort to the preparatory work to assist in the interpretation of Article 5(1)(c), because it found the provision to be clear and unequivocal. In *Young, James & Webster v United Kingdom*,[63] reference was made to the '*travaux préparatoires*' in support of the contention that the right not to join an association had been deliberately omitted from Article 11, but ultimately the Court found that there had been a violation.[64] The '*travaux*' were, however, important in *James v United Kingdom*,[65] in which they supported the finding of the Court that Article 1 of the First Protocol does not include a right to compensation in cases of expropriation.

57 *Guzzardi v Italy* (1980) 3 EHRR 333.
58 *Johnston v Ireland* (1986) 9 EHRR 203 para 57: right to divorce was omitted from Art 12 and could not be read into Art 8.
59 *James v United Kingdom* (1986) 8 EHRR 123 para 42; see also *Sunday Times v United Kingdom* (1979) 2 EHRR 245 para 48.
60 See para 6.23ff below.
61 *Loizidou v Turkey (Preliminary Objections)* (1995) 20 EHRR 99 para 71.
62 (1961) 1 EHRR 13 para 11.
63 (1981) 4 EHRR 38, para 51.
64 And see *Sigurjonsson v Iceland* (1993) 16 EHRR 462.
65 (1986) 8 EHRR 123 para 64.

(b) The Convention as a 'constitutional instrument'

Although the Convention is a treaty, it is, nevertheless, a treaty of a special kind. It has been said that: **6.21**

> the Convention comprises more than mere reciprocal engagements between contracting States. It creates, over and above a network of mutual, bilateral undertakings, objective obligations which, in the words of the Preamble, benefit from a 'collective enforcement'.[66]

The Convention has a special character as a 'constitutional instrument of European public order.'[67] The special character of the Convention is reflected in the interpretation of its provisions. As the Court said in the *Soering* case:

> In interpreting the Convention, regard must be had to its special character as a treaty for the collective enforcement of human rights and fundamental freedoms . . . the object and purpose of the Convention as an instrument for the protection of individual human beings require that its provisions be interpreted and applied so as to makes its safeguards practical and effective.[68]

In addition, any interpretation of the rights and freedoms guaranteed must be consistent with the

> general spirit of the Convention, an instrument designed to maintain and promote the ideals and values of a democratic society.[69]

Democracy involves 'pluralism, tolerance and broadmindedness'.[70] It is underpinned by the fundamental principles of the rule of law and free expression.[71]

As discussed below, the special status of the Convention has led to the development of a number of principles of construction[72] which extend beyond the traditional principles applied to treaties. These principles have a great deal in common with the 'common law' approach to the construction of constitutional instruments which are discussed in Chapter 3.[73] **6.22**

(c) The Convention as a 'living instrument'

A 'dynamic interpretation' of the Convention recognises that the standards by which Convention rights are assessed are not static. The principle is comparable to the doctrine of progressive interpretation which is applied to constitutional **6.23**

---

66 *Ireland v United Kingdom* (1978) 2 EHRR 25 para 23.

67 *Loizidou v Turkey (Preliminary Objections)* (1995) 20 EHRR 99 para 75.

68 *Soering v United Kingdom* (1989) 11 EHRR 439 para 34.

69 *Kjeldsen, Busk, Madsen and Pedersen v Denmark* (1976) 1 EHRR 711 para 53.

70 *Handyside v United Kingdom* (1976) 1 EHRR 737 para 49.

71 See J Merrills, *The Development of International Law by the European Court of Human Rights* (2nd edn, University of Manchester Press, 1995) Chap 6.

72 See P van Dijk and G van Hoof, *Theory and Practice of the European Convention on Human Rights* (3rd edn, Kluwer, 1998) 74–80; Merrills (n 71 above) Chaps 5 and 6.

73 See para 3.06ff above.

instruments.[73a] The Convention is 'a living instrument which . . . must be interpreted in the light of present day conditions'.[74] The Court 'cannot but be influenced by the developments and commonly accepted standards' of the state parties in the particular field. This approach:

> is closely linked to a search for common European standards on the basis of domestic law and practice in the Member States of the Council of Europe, of other international or European instruments and the case law of the Court itself.[75]

6.24 There are several examples of the 'growth' of the Convention to accommodate changing social attitudes. The *Tyrer*[76] case considered whether the birching of juveniles constituted 'degrading punishment'. The Court held that, in the light of present conditions, such punishment was a violation of Article 3.[77] Other issues which have been addressed in a similar fashion include the definition of 'persons of unsound mind' in Article 5(1)(e),[78] the distinction between 'legitimate' and 'illegitimate' children[79] and criminal prohibitions on homosexual activity.[80]

6.25 There are, however, limits to this technique of 'dynamic interpretation'. It must be applied carefully and in accordance with generally accepted changes in standards. While distinct changes have been recognised in relation to matters such as corporal punishment and homosexuality, developments in other areas are less well-defined. The Court has, on a number of occasions, considered the legal position of transsexuals. Although it has acknowledged scientific and legal developments in relation to the treatment of transsexuals, it has not been satisfied that these:

> establish the existence of any common European approach to the problems created by the recognition in law of post-operative gender status . . . it continues to be the case that transsexualism raises complex scientific, legal, moral and social issues, in respect of which there is no generally shared approach among the Contracting States.[81]

As a result, the 'growth' of the Convention has not been sufficient to recognise rights of transsexuals. A similar approach has been taken in relation to the law of blasphemy.[82] Furthermore, it appears that this technique of interpretation can merely adapt the standards of the Convention to new situations. It 'cannot . . . extend the catalogue of protected rights'.[83] It might, however, be argued that

[73a] See para 3.08ff above.

[74] *Tyrer v United Kingdom* (1978) 2 EHRR 1 para 16; and see *Loizidou v Turkey (Preliminary Objections)* (1995) 20 EHRR 99 para 71.

[75] van Dijk and van Hoof (n 72 above) 78.

[76] See n 74 above.

[77] Ibid.

[78] *Winterwerp v Netherlands* (1979) 2 EHRR 387 para 37.

[79] *Marckx v Belgium* (1979) 2 EHRR 330 para 41.

[80] *Dudgeon v United Kingdom* (1981) 4 EHRR 149 para 60.

[81] *Sheffield and Horsham v United Kingdom* (1998) 27 EHRR 163 paras 57–58.

[82] See *Wingrove v United Kingdom* (1996) 24 EHRR 1 para 57.

[83] See R Ryssdall, 'The Coming of Age of the European Convention on Human Rights' (1996) 1 EHRLR 18, 24.

'dynamic interpretation' would allow the Court to imply new rights which are ancillary to those already recognised.

On some occasions, the Court has been prepared to go as far as implying positive rights into the Convention which are not expressly recognised in the text. Perhaps the most striking example is the 'implied right of access to the courts' recognised in *Golder v United Kingdom*.[84] That case concerned the refusal of the Home Secretary to permit a prisoner to write to his solicitor in relation to proposed libel proceedings against a prison officer. The majority held that this was in violation of an implied Convention right of access to the courts. This was found to be: **6.26**

> an element which is inherent in the right stated by Article 6(1). This is an extensive interpretation forcing new obligations on the Contracting States: it is based on the very terms of the first sentence of Article 6(1) read in its context and having regard to the object and purpose of the Convention, a lawmaking treaty . . . and to general principles of law.[85]

This has been described as 'one of the most creative steps taken by the Court in its interpretation of any Article of the Convention'.[86]

In general, the Court has taken a cautious approach to the 'implication' of Convention rights. For example, while it has been accepted that the right to form and to join trade unions in Article 11(1) includes an implied right to represent its members,[87] there is no implied right to be consulted[88] or to make collective agreements.[89] In some cases, Convention rights stated in general terms have been said to be subject to implied limitations.[90] In the *Golder* case, the Court recognised that the right of access to the courts was itself subject to implied limitations.[91] However, the Court has rejected the argument that qualified rights are subject to implied limitations. The limitations affecting those rights are themselves set out in the relevant Article of the Convention. Thus, the right of correspondence in Article 8 is not subject to 'implied limitations' in relation to prisoners because the words of Article 8(2)[92] leave no room for such a concept.[93] **6.27**

---

84 (1975) 1 EHRR 524.

85 Ibid para 36.

86 D Harris, M O'Boyle and C Warbrick, *Law of the European Convention on Human Rights* (Butterworths, 1995) 196; but has also been subject to criticism, see Merrills (n 71 above) 85–87. For a discussion of the doctrine of positive rights see para 6.97ff below.

87 *National Union of Belgian Police v Belgium* (1975) 1 EHRR 578 para 39.

88 Ibid para 40.

89 *Swedish Engine Drivers' Union* case (1976) 1 EHRR 617 para 40; see generally, Merrills (n 71 above) 86–7.

90 See *Belgian Linguistics (No 2)* case (1968) 1 EHRR 252 para 5; and see *Mathieu-Mohin and Clerfayt v Belgium* (1987) 10 EHRR 1 para 52 and see generally, para 6.114ff below.

91 (1975) 1 EHRR 524 paras 37–40.

92 'There shall be no interference . . . except such as . . .'.

93 Ibid para 44; see also *De Wilde, Ooms and Versyp v Belgium (No 1)* (1971) 1 EHRR 373 para 93.

(d) The principle of effectiveness

6.28 The principle of 'effectiveness'[94] is a fundamental principle of interpretation because:

> the object and purpose of the Convention as an instrument for the protection of individual human beings requires that its provisions be interpreted and applied so as to make its safeguards practical and effective.[95]

This means that when considering an alleged violation of a Convention right, the Court must focus on the realities of the situation. The Convention is not intended to guarantee rights that are 'theoretical or illusory but rights that are practical and effective'.[96] It is 'designed to safeguard the individual in a real and practical way as regards those areas with which it deals'.[97]

6.29 The application of the 'effectiveness' principle led the Court to hold, in the *Airey* case,[97a] that the 'right to a fair trial' under Article 6 included a right to civil legal aid. The applicant was a married woman who wished to obtain a decree of judicial separation but could not afford a lawyer. There was no civil legal aid available in Ireland. It was held that the applicant did not enjoy an effective right of access to the court and that, as a result, Article 6 had been breached.[98]

6.30 The principle of effectiveness has led the Court to impose positive obligations on states in a number of instances.[99] The right to family life in Article 8, for example, includes positive obligations to ensure that the domestic law integrates the illegitimate child into the family[100] and requires the state to establish an authority to handle access to child care records.[101] In order to be effective, the right to freedom of assembly may, similarly, require positive measures by the state:

> Genuine, effective freedom of peaceful assembly cannot . . . be reduced to a mere duty on the part of the State not to interfere: a purely negative conception would not be compatible with the object and purpose of Article 11. Like Article 8, Article 11 sometimes requires positive measures to be taken, even in the sphere of relations between individuals.[102]

In the *Plattform* case, there was a violation of Article 11 because the state had failed to provide sufficient protection for anti-abortion demonstrations which had been disrupted by counter-demonstrations. The principle of effectiveness also means

[94] See Merrills (n 71 above) 98–124.
[95] See *Loizidou v Turkey (Preliminary Objections)* (1995) 20 EHRR 99 para 72.
[96] See *Artico v Italy* (1980) 3 EHRR 1 para 33.
[97] *Airey v Ireland* (1979) 2 EHRR 305 para 26.
[97a] Ibid.
[98] Ibid paras 26–28.
[99] See generally, Merrills, (n 71 above) 102–6.
[100] *Marckx v Belgium* (1979) 2 EHRR 330 para 31.
[101] *Gaskin v United Kingdom* (1989) 12 EHRR 36 para 49.
[102] *Plattform 'Artzte für das Leben' v Austria* (1988) 13 EHRR 204 para 32.

that, in relation to qualified rights, the exceptions will be narrowly interpreted. Thus, it has been held that the exceptions to the right to liberty,[103] the right to private life[104] and freedom of expression[105] must be construed narrowly.

C The Doctrine of 'Margin of Appreciation'

(1) Introduction

The concept of a 'margin of appreciation' can be traced back in French administrative law to the Conseil d'Etat.[106] However, under the Convention the margin of appreciation[107] refers to the latitude allowed to Member States in their observance of the Convention. Because there is a distribution of powers between the institutions of the Convention and the national authorities, and a shared responsibility for its enforcement, the dividing line between the two is reflected in the 'margin of appreciation'.[108] The doctrine has therefore been defined as the line at which international supervision should give way to the state's discretion in enacting or enforcing its laws.[109] However, it is also a principle of judicial review which governs the extent to which the Commission (or Court) should scrutinise the complaint that has been made;[110] and reflects the principle of subsidiarity.[111] 6.31

[103] *Guzzardi v Italy* (1980) 3 EHRR 333.

[104] *Klass v Germany* (1978) 2 EHRR 214 para 21.

[105] *The Observer and The Guardian v United Kingdom* (1991) 14 EHRR 153, 191.

[106] The term 'margin of appreciation' is a (poor) translation of the French 'marge d'appreciation'; a better translation would be 'margin of judgement'. The concept is drawn from the mode of review used by the continental systems of administrative law which are modelled on the French Conseil d'Etat: see F Jacobs, *The European Convention on Human Rights* (1st edn, Oxford University Press, 1975) 201; see also J Kokott, *The Burden of Proof in Comparative and International Human Rights Law* (Kluwer Law International, 1998) 218ff.

[107] See eg R St J Macdonald, 'The Margin of Appreciation' in R St J Macdonald, F Matscher and H Petzold (eds), *The European System for the Protection of Human Rights* (Kluwer, 1983); T O'Donnell, 'The Margin of Appreciation Doctrine: Standards in the Jurisprudence of the Court' (1982) 4 HRQ 474; P Mahoney, 'Judicial Activism and Judicial Self-Restraint in the Court: Two Sides of the Same Coin' [1990] HRLJ 57; P Mahoney, 'Marvellous Riches of Diversity or Invidious Cultural Relativism' 19 HRLJ 1; and other contributors discussing 'The Doctrine of the Margin of Appreciation Under the European Convention on Human Rights: Its Legitimacy in Theory and Application in Practice' 6–36 of the same volume; and for a general survey see H Yourow, *The Margin of Appreciation Doctrine in the Dynamics of European Human Rights Jurisprudence* (Kluwer, 1996).

[108] P Mahoney, 'Judicial Activism and Judicial Self Restraint in the Court: Two Sides of the Same Coin' [1990] HRLJ 57, 81.

[109] W Wong, 'The Sunday Times Case: Freedom of Expression vs English Contempt of Court Laws in the Court' 17 New York University J of Intl L and Politics 35, 58.

[110] T O'Donnell, 'The Margin of Appreciation Doctrine: Standards in the Jurisprudence of the Court' (1982) 4 HQR 474, 475.

[111] H Petzold, 'The Convention and the Principle of Subsidiarity' in R St J Macdonald, F Matscher and H Petzold (eds), *The European System for the Protection of Human Rights* (Nijhoff, 1993).

Thus, Merrills[112] argues that the doctrine is a way of recognising that international human rights and sovereign freedom of action are not contradictory but complementary.

6.32 In fact, the margin of appreciation performs two quite different roles in Convention jurisprudence;[113] and it is helpful to distinguish between them. The margin of appreciation is:

- an *interpretative obligation to respect* domestic cultural traditions and values when considering the meaning and scope of human rights; and
- a *standard of judicial review* to be used when enforcing human rights protection.

The importance that Convention institutions attach to the domestic context when interpreting rights (and the impact this will have on the Human Rights Act) is discussed in what follows in this section. In section D below we examine the more difficult question of how the margin of appreciation operates as a standard of judicial review in Convention case law[114] as part of the principle of proportionality. We argue that the doctrine has no role to play under the Human Rights Act when applying the proportionality principle.[115]

6.33 The margin of appreciation arises out of the interaction of Article 1 with Article 19 of the Convention. Article 1 of the Convention states:

> The High Contracting Parties shall secure to everyone within their jurisdiction the rights and freedoms defined in Section 1 of the Convention.

Article 19 of the Convention, on the other hand, now[116] states:

> To ensure the observance of the engagements undertaken by the High Contracting Parties in the Convention and the Protocols thereto, there shall be set up a European Court of Human Rights, hereinafter referred to as 'the Court'. It shall function on a permanent basis.

The Court must therefore supervise the activities of the High Contracting Parties to ensure their observance of Article 1, ie to ensure that they secure the relevant rights and freedoms.

---

112 J Merrills *The Development of International Law by the European Court of Human Rights* (2nd edn, Manchester University Press, 1995), Chap 7.

113 See also the discussion in S Grosz, J Beatson and P Duffy, *Human Rights: The 1998 Act and the European Convention* (Sweet & Maxwell, 2000) para 5–16.

114 See para 6.49ff below.

115 See para 6.82ff below.

116 Until amended by Protocol 11 on 1 Nov 1998 Art 19 stated:

> To ensure the observance of the engagements undertaken by the High Contracting Parties in the present Convention, there shall be set up:
> (a) a European Commission of Human Rights . . .;
> (b) a European Court of Human Rights . . .

(2) The Convention case law

The notion of a margin of appreciation was initially developed[117] by the Commission as a means of ensuring that national governments had a certain freedom of action when derogating from the Convention under Article 15.[118] Thus, in *Lawless v Ireland*[119] the Commission took the view that it: 6.34

> does recognise that the question of whether or not to employ the exceptional powers under Article 15 involves problems of appreciation and timing for a Government which may be most difficult, and especially difficult in a democracy . . . where governments are susceptible to the impact of public opinion. It also recognises that the Government has to balance the ills involved in a temporary restriction of fundamental rights against even worse consequences then for the people and perhaps larger dislocations then of fundamental rights and freedoms, if it is to put the situation right again.
>
> The concept behind [margin of appreciation] is that Article 15 has to be read in the context of the rather special subject area with which it deals: the responsibilities of a government for maintaining law and order in times of war or other public emergency threatening the life of the nation. The concept of margin of appreciation is that a Government's discharge of these responsibilities is essentially a delicate problem of appreciating complex factors and balancing conflicting considerations in the public interest; and once the Commission or Court is satisfied that the Government's appreciation is at least on the margin of the powers conferred by Article 15, then the interest which the public itself has in effective government and in the maintenance of order justifies and requires a decision in favour of the legality of the Government's appreciation.

The margin of appreciation was first discussed by the Court in the *Handyside* case[120] when considering whether the forfeiture of the *Little Red Schoolbook* on grounds of obscenity violated freedom of expression. The Court said: 6.35

> According to the Government and the majority of the Commission, the Court has only to ensure that the English courts acted reasonably, in good faith and within the limits of the margin of appreciation left to the Contracting States by Article 10(2). On the other hand, the minority of the Commission sees the Court's task as being not to review the Inner London Quarter Session's judgment but to examine the Schoolbook directly in the light of nothing but the Convention . . .
>
> The Court points out that the machinery of protection established by the Convention is subsidiary to the national system safeguarding human rights.[121] The Convention leaves to each Contracting State, in the first place, the task of securing the rights and liberties it enshrines. The institutions created by it make their own contribution to this task but they only become involved through contentious proceedings and once all domestic remedies have been exhausted . . .

[117] See *Greece v United Kingdom* (1956) 2 YB 174, EComm HR; and generally, C C Morrison, 'The Margin of Appreciation in European Human Rights Law' (1970) 6 HRJ 263.

[118] Art 15 permits the state to derogate from certain Convention rights 'in time of war or other emergency threatening the life of the nation'; see para 6.92 below.

[119] Application 332/57 A 61.501 48–49.

[120] *Handyside v United Kingdom* (1976) 1 EHRR 737.

[121] *Belgian Linguistic Case (No 2)* (1968) 1 EHRR 252 para 10.

> By reason of their direct and continuous contact with the vital forces of their countries, state authorities are in principle in a better position than the international judge to give an opinion on the . . . 'necessity' of a 'restriction' or 'penalty' . . . it is for the national authorities to make the initial assessment of the reality of the pressing social need implied by the notion of 'necessity' in this context.
>
> Consequently, Article 10(2) leaves to the contracting states a margin of appreciation. This margin is given both to the domestic legislator ('prescribed by law') and to the bodies, judicial among others, that are called upon to interpret and apply the laws in force.
>
> Nevertheless, Article 10(2) does not give the contracting states an unlimited power of appreciation. The Court which, with the Commission, is responsible for ensuring the observance of those State's engagements (Article 19), is empowered to give the final ruling on whether 'restriction' or 'penalty' is reconcilable with freedom of expression. The domestic margin of appreciation thus goes hand in hand with European supervision. Such supervision concerns both the aim of the measure challenged and its 'necessity'; it covers not only the basic legislation but also the decision applying it, even one given by an independent court.[122]

6.36 The doctrine has been applied to cases involving the right to liberty[123] under Article 5,[124] the right to a fair trial[125] under Article 6,[126] the right of respect for family[127] or private life[128] under Article 8,[129] freedom of expression[130] under Article 10,[131] the prohibition from discrimination[132] under Article 14, the right to derogate from the Convention[133] and the right to peaceful enjoyment of possessions[134] under the First Protocol.[135] However, there is no reason in principle why the doctrine of margin of appreciation could not be applied to *all* of the Articles of the Convention.[136]

---

[122] Ibid paras 47–49.

[123] See eg *Weeks v United Kingdom* (1987) 10 EHRR 293; *Brogan v United Kingdom* (1988) 11 EHRR 117.

[124] See para 10.80 below.

[125] See eg *Le Compte v Belgium* (1981) 4 EHRR 1.

[126] See para 11.150 below.

[127] See eg *Johnston v Ireland* (1986) 9 EHRR 203; *Eriksson v Sweden* (1989) 12 EHRR 183.

[128] See eg *Rees v United Kingdom* (1986) 9 EHRR 56; *Leander v Sweden* (1987) 9 EHRR 433.

[129] See para 12.81ff below.

[130] See eg *Sunday Times v United Kingdom (No 1)* (1979) 2 EHRR 245; *Lingens v Austria* (1986) 8 EHRR 103; *Müller v Austria* (1988) 13 EHRR 212; *Marks v Belgium* (1989) Series A No 165 ECtHR.

[131] See para 15.137ff below.

[132] See eg *Engel and others v Netherlands (No.2)* (1976) 1 EHRR 706; *Marckx v Belgium* (1979) 2 EHRR 330.

[133] See eg *Lawless v Ireland (No 3)* (1961) 1 EHRR 15.

[134] See eg *Sporrong and Lönnroth v Sweden* (1982) 5 EHRR 35; *Lithgow v United Kingdom* (1986) 8 EHRR 329.

[135] See para 18.26ff below.

[136] See T O'Donnell, 'The Margin of Appreciation Doctrine: Standards of Jurisprudence of the Court' (1982) 4 HRQ 474, 477.

(3) Margin of appreciation and the Human Rights Act

Convention rights are expressed in broad and open textured[137] language. This means that when construing the Human Rights Act, it will be both appropriate and inevitable that the English courts should put these broad concepts in context: by reflecting domestic legal and cultural values and traditions. Precisely because the Commission and the Court recognise an interpretative obligation to respect the primacy of domestic states in interpreting the scope and content of rights, the English courts will be afforded a margin of appreciation in developing a human rights jurisprudence to meet domestic conditions. Buxton LJ described the position in *R v Stratford Justices, ex p Imbert*[138] as follows: **6.37**

> The rights recognised by the Convention . . . have been interpreted by the Strasbourg Court subject to the doctrine developed by the Court of the 'margin of appreciation'; see, for instance, *Handyside v United Kingdom*[139] . . . The application of the doctrine of margin of appreciation would appear to be solely a matter for the Strasbourg Court. By appealing to the doctrine that court recognised that the detailed content of at least some Convention obligations are more appropriately determined in the light of national conditions . . . that approach is necessarily translated into a view of the meaning and reach of the detailed provisions of the Convention that is flexible or, according to the observer's point of view, relativist.[140]
>
> The English judge cannot therefore himself apply or have recourse to the doctrine of the margin of appreciation as implemented by the Strasbourg Court. He must, however, recognise the impact of that decision upon the Strasbourg Court's analysis of the meaning and implication of the broad terms of the Convention provisions.

The idea of a 'margin of appreciation' in this very *general* sense must be distinguished from the controversial role it plays in the Convention jurisprudence as part of the doctrine of proportionality.[141] The role that the margin of appreciation has *vis à vis* proportionality under the Human Rights Act and the conceptual problems it has caused is discussed below,[142] where it is submitted that the doctrine has no application to the principle of proportionality. **6.38**

There is, however, one specific type of situation in which the English courts may have to consider directly applying the margin of appreciation or some analogous doctrine. Where it is said that a public authority has breached a positive obligation[143] (such as the positive obligation to respect privacy), it seems that the public **6.39**

---

[137] H L A Hart, *The Concept of Law* (2nd Edn, Clarendon Press, 1994) 127–136.

[138] (1999) 2 Cr App R 276, 286–287.

[139] (1976) 1 EHRR 737.

[140] See the remarks of Judge de Meyer in a dissenting judgment disapproving of the use and effect of the doctrine that is noted in *Z v Finland* (1997) 25 EHRR 371, 415, 416.

[141] See para 6.42ff below.

[142] See para 6.82ff below.

[143] See para 6.97ff below.

authority cannot attempt to justify the breach as being in accordance with the 'legitimate aim' specified in a particular Article in question. In those circumstances the Court has sometimes used the doctrine of the margin of appreciation to limit the scope of the positive obligation. Thus, in *Rees v United Kingdom*[143a] the Court took the view that a wide margin of appreciation was necessary where there was a diversity of practices within the Contracting States and very little common ground (as was the case where transexuals wanted the option of changing their personal status to their post operative identity); and a similar approach was taken in *Lopez Ostra v Spain*.[143b] However, in other cases such as *Gaskin v United Kingdom*[143c] and *B v France*[143d] the Court made no reference to the need for a wide margin of appreciation. It is therefore arguable that the margin of appreciation may have some application when the court decides where to strike the fair balance between general interests of the community and the rights of the individual.[143e]

D. The Doctrine of Proportionality

(1) Introduction

6.40 The principle of proportionality requires that there be a reasonable relationship between a particular objective to be achieved and the means used to achieve that objective.[144] Proportionality plays an important role in Convention jurisprudence since it is the test which is normally used to assess whether there is a violation of Convention rights. The doctrine itself originated in Prussia in the nineteenth century.[145] It developed as a means of limiting the discretionary powers of the police on the basis that the state requires special permission where it infringes a citizen's civil liberties. Proportionality continues to have an important impact on administrative law in many European countries such as Germany and France.[146] The standard principles[147] of the well developed German case law require:

143a (1987) 9 EHRR 56 para 37.

143b (1994) 20 EHRR 27 para 51.

143c (1990) 12 EHRR 36.

143d (1993) 16 EHRR 1.

143e See generally, para 6.97ff below.

144 *Halsbury's Laws of England* (4th edn reissue, Butterworths) Vol 1(1) para 78.

145 The principle of 'Verhaltnismassigkeit' developed to restrict the discretionary powers of police authorities: see M P Singh, *German Administrative Law: A Common Lawyer's View* (Springer-Verlag, 1985) 81–101.

146 For a survey of the role of proportionality both generally and in relation to Germany and France see J Schwarze, *European Administrative Law* (Sweet & Maxwell, 1992) Chap 5; P Walker, 'Unreasonableness and Proportionality' in M Supperstone and J Goudie (eds), *Judicial Review* (2nd edn, Butterworths 1997).

147 J Schwarze (n 146 above) 687.

- *suitability*: an administrative or legal power must be exercised in a way which is suited to achieve the purpose intended and for which the power was conferred;
- *necessity*: the exercise of the power must be necessary to achieve the relevant purpose; and
- *proportionality in the narrow sense*: the exercise of the power must not impose burdens or cause harm to other legitimate interests which are disproportionate to the importance of the object achieved.

Kentridge[148] suggests that the most difficult and important problem facing the English courts under the Human Rights Act will be to develop (or rather invent) a coherent and defensible jurisprudence of proportionality. The starting point will be the complex jurisprudence of the Convention.[149] However, English courts have themselves considered proportionality in several contexts: as a possible free standing ground for challenging decision making in judicial review proceedings and, more routinely, as a fundamental principle in European Union law. Proportionality has also played a significant role in interpreting the Canadian Charter of Rights, the New Zealand Bill of Rights and the South African Constitution Act. It is therefore likely that the courts will draw on all of these sources in developing a doctrine of proportionality under the Human Rights Act. **6.41**

(2) Proportionality under the Convention

(a) Introduction

Although the word 'proportionality' is not to be found in the Convention, the principle applies to a wide variety of situations[150] including: **6.42**

- where the Court[151] assesses whether a state is entitled to derogate from the Convention in a time of war or other public emergency under Article 15;
- where the Court assesses whether interference with a qualified right[152] can be justified as being 'necessary in a democratic society';[153]
- where the Convention expressly allows a public authority to restrict Convention

[148] S Kentridge, 'The incorporation of the European Convention' in J Beatson, C Forsyth and I Hare (eds), *Constitutional Reform in the United Kingdom: Practice and Principles* (Hart Publishing, 1998).

[149] s 2(1) of the Human Rights Act; see generally, para 3.46ff above.

[150] For a general survey see for example M Eissen, 'The Principle of Proportionality in the Case Law of the Court' in R St J Macdonald, F Matscher and H Petzold (eds), *The European System for the Protection of Human Rights* (Nijhoff, 1993); J McBride, 'Proportionality and the European Convention on Human Rights' in E Ellis (ed), *The Principle of Proportionality in the Laws of Europe* (Hart Publishing, 1999).

[151] See eg *Lawless v Ireland (No 3)* (1961) 1 EHRR 15; *Ireland v United Kingdom* (1978) 2 EHRR 25; the term proportionality is not in fact used but the approach taken towards the margin of appreciation is effectively the same.

[152] See para 6.123ff below.

[153] This is the context in which the doctrine is most frequently used; see para 6.146ff below.

rights such as justifying continued detention under Article 5(3)[154] on the basis of relevant and sufficient grounds,[155] justifying[156] restrictions on marriage under Article 12,[157] justifying[158] a deprivation of property under Article 1 of Protocol 1,[159] or justifying[160] state control of the use of property under the same Article;[161]

- where the doctrine of 'inherent limitations'[162] applies;
- where proportionality has defined the limits[163] of positive obligations[164] under Convention rights;
- where there is a finding of discrimination contrary to Article 14[165] because there is no reasonable relationship between the means employed and the aim to be realised.[166]

Lester and Pannick suggest[167] that the doctrine is central to the principle of 'fair balance' between the general interest of the community and the interests of the individual, the search for which is often said to be 'inherent in the whole of the Convention'.[168]

(b) The principle of proportionality

6.43 When applying the principle of proportionality the Court sometimes confines itself to asking whether an interference is justifiable in principle and proportionate,[169] and whether there is a reasonable relationship between the interference and the legitimate aim pursued.[170] More frequently, however, the Court has applied a

[154] See para 10.133ff below.
[155] See eg *Wemhoff v Germany* (1968) 1 EHRR 55 paras 12–17; *Stögmüller v Austria* (1969) 1 EHRR 155 paras 13–16; *Ringeisen v Austria (No 3)* (1972) 1 EHRR 513 paras 104–109; *Letellier v France* (1991) 14 EHRR 83 paras 35–53.
[156] See eg *F v Switzerland* (1987) 10 EHRR 411 paras 30–40.
[157] See para 13.74ff below.
[158] See eg *James v United Kingdom* (1986) 8 EHRR 123 paras 68–79; *Lithgow v United Kingdom* (1986) EHRR 329 paras 120–175.
[159] See para 18.43ff below.
[160] See eg *Agosi v United Kingdom* (1986) 9 EHRR 1 paras 52–62; *Tre Traktörer Aktiebolag v Sweden* (1991) 13 EHRR 309 paras 59–62.
[161] See para 18.46ff below.
[162] See para 6.114ff below.
[163] See eg *Soering v United Kingdom* (1989) 11 EHRR 439 paras 100 and 104–111; *Van der Mussele v Belgium* (1983) 6 EHRR 163 paras 38–40.
[164] See para 6.97 below.
[165] See para 17.79ff below.
[166] See eg *Belgium Linguistics Case (No 2)* (1967) 1 EHRR 252 paras 32; *Abdulaziz, Cabales and Balkandali v United Kingdom* (1985) 7 EHRR 471 paras 77–83.
[167] See Lord Lester and D Pannick, *Human Rights Law and Practice* (Butterworths, 1999) paras 3.09–3.10.
[168] *Rees v United Kingdom* (1986) 9 EHHR 56 para 37; *Gaskin v United Kingdom* (1989) 12 EHRR 36 para 42.
[169] See eg *Kokkinakis v Greece* (1993) 17 EHRR 397 para 21; *Casado Coca v Spain* (1994) 18 EHRR 1 para 20.
[170] See eg *Hadjianastassiou v Greece* (1992) 16 EHRR 219 para 19; *Chorherr v Austria* (1993) 17 EHRR 358 para 37.

more rigorous approach, particularly in the context of Article 10[171] where it takes the view that interferences with freedom of expression must be narrowly interpreted and the necessity for any restrictions must be convincingly established.[172] Thus, in *Sunday Times v United Kingdom*[173] the Court applied a three-fold test:[174]

- whether the interference complained of corresponded to a 'pressing social need';
- whether it was 'proportionate to the legitimate aim pursued'; and
- whether the reasons given by the national authority to justify it were 'relevant and sufficient'.

The strictness of the test for proving that a justification was *relevant and sufficient* is illustrated by the approach taken to the criminalisation of homosexual activity in *Dudgeon v United Kingdom*.[175] The Court took the view that the case involved a most intimate aspect of private life[176] and that there was no pressing need[177] to make homosexual acts criminal: **6.44**

> Although members of the public who regard homosexuality as immoral may be shocked, offended or disturbed by the commission by others of private homosexual acts, this cannot on its own warrant the application of penal sanctions when it is consenting adults alone who are involved.

Similarly, in *Goodwin v United Kingdom*[178] the Court held that an order requiring a journalist to disclose his source was a disproportionate restriction on his freedom of expression. The Court decided[179] that the justification for ordering disclosure was not sufficient because an injunction had already prevented dissemination of confidential information and, to the extent that the order reinforced the injunction, the additional restriction was not supported by sufficient reasons. The Court also concluded[180] that, where a party seeks disclosure of a source because he cannot otherwise exercise his legal rights, the balance of competing interests favours

[171] See eg *Sunday Times v United Kingdom (No 1)* (1979) 2 EHRR 245; *Lingens v Austria* (1986) 8 EHRR 103.

[172] See eg *The Observer and Guardian v United Kingdom* (1991) 14 EHRR 153 para 59.

[173] (1979) 2 EHRR 245 para 62; applied for example in *Dudgeon v United Kingdom* (1981) 4 EHRR 149 paras 52–54; *Barthold v Germany* (1985) 7 EHRR 383 para 55; *Muller v Switzerland* (1988) 13 EHRR 212 para 32; *The Observer and The Guardian v United Kingdom* (1991) 14 EHRR 153 para 59; *Olsson v Sweden (No 2)* (1992) 17 EHRR 134 para 87; *Jersild v Denmark* (1994) 19 EHRR 1 para 30; *Vogt v Germany* (1995) 21 EHRR 205 para 52; *Goodwin v United Kingdom* (1996) 22 EHRR 123 para 40; *Wingrove v United Kingdom* (1996) 24 EHRR 1 para 58.

[174] Derived from *Handyside v United Kingdom* (1976) 1 EHRR 737 paras 48–50.

[175] (1981) 4 EHRR 149; see also the approach taken by the Court to the investigation and dismissal of homosexuals from the armed forces in *Lustig-Prean v United Kingdom* (1999) 7 BHRC 65 and *Smith v United Kingdom* [1999] IRLR 747.

[176] *Dudgeon v United Kingdom* (1981) 4 EHRR 149 para 52.

[177] Ibid para 60.

[178] (1996) 22 EHRR 123.

[179] Ibid para 42.

[180] Ibid para 44.

the interests in a democratic society of securing a free press. In contrast, the Court in *Wingrove v United Kingdom*[181] considered that a refusal to grant a classification licence for a cinema to show an erotic video which was offensive to Christians was an acceptable restriction on freedom of expression; the government succeeded in proving that there were relevant and sufficient reasons. The high threshold of profanity embodied in the offence of blasphemy, fell within a state's margin of appreciation when regulating matters which offended intimate personal moral and religious convictions.

6.45 The various versions of the proportionality test appear to reflect varying standards of review in different contexts. The strict approach set out in *Sunday Times v United Kingdom (No 1)*[182] is appropriate where fundamental rights are at stake (such as freedom of expression[183] or intimate aspects of private life).[184] Where property rights are at issue,[185] the Court uses the looser formulation of a reasonable relationship between the means and the aim sought to be realised or a fair balance between the general and individual interests at stake. Furthermore, it has been held that the possible existence of alternative solutions does not make legislation unlawful under the right to property; and that it is not for the Court to consider whether legislation represents the best way of dealing with the problem or whether the legislative discretion should have been exercised in another way.[186]

6.46 In practice, the Court appears to take account of a number of factors when deciding whether an interference with Convention rights is proportionate. The extent to which the interference restricts the right is important. The Court will regard an interference as disproportionate if it impairs the very essence of the right.[186a] The Court will also reject an interference with a Convention right as being disproportionate if the justification for the interference cannot be proved. For example, in *Vereinigung Demokratischer Soldaten Österreichs and Gubi v Austria*[187] the Court decided that prohibiting the distribution of a journal to soldiers was disproportionate because the contents of the articles were not a serious threat to military discipline (even though they were critical of military life).

6.47 Convention case law does not *explicitly* recognise the 'least restrictive means' test

[181] (1996) 24 EHRR 1 para 60.
[182] (1979) 2 EHRR 245.
[183] See eg *Handyside v United Kingdom* (1976) 1 EHRR 737; *Lingens v Austria* (1986) 8 EHRR 103.
[184] *Dudgeon v United Kingdom* (1981) 4 EHRR 149.
[185] See eg *Sporrong and Lönnroth v Sweden* (1982) 5 EHRR 35; *James v United Kingdom* (1986) 8 EHRR 123; *AGOSI v United Kingdom* (1986) 9 EHRR 1.
[186] *James v United Kingdom* (1986) 8 EHRR 123 para 51; *Mellacher v Austria* (1989) 12 EHRR 391 para 53.
[186a] See eg *Belgian Linguistic* Case (1968) 1 EHRR 252, 281 para 5.
[187] (1994) 20 EHRR 55.

as an aspect of proportionality (although this is a well recognised part of the doctrine in, for example, European Community[188] and Canadian law).[189] Nevertheless, the Court has often in practice decided the question of proportionality by asking whether a particular measure could be achieved by a less restrictive means. For example, in *Campbell v United Kingdom*[190] the Court rejected the justification for opening and reading all correspondence between prisoners and their solicitors, pointing out that the Prison Service could open (but not read) correspondence to see if they contained illicit enclosures, and that suitable guarantees could be put in place to prevent reading the correspondence such as opening the letter in the prisoner's presence. Similarly, in *Open Door Counselling and Dublin Well Woman v Ireland*[191] the Court took the view that the permanent injunction granted by the Irish Supreme Court to restrain the provision of information to pregnant women about abortion facilities abroad, regardless of age, the state of health or reasons for seeking termination of their pregnancy, was over broad and disproportionate. In the recent case of *Ahmed v United Kingdom*[192] the Court expressly considered the question of proportionality by examining whether the aim of legislation restricting the political activities of local government officers was pursued with the least impairment to their right to freedom of expression.

In several cases where it has been alleged that court procedures fail to respect Convention rights, the Court has indicated that minimum *procedural* standards must be met in order to show that an interference is proportionate. Thus, in *McMichael v United Kingdom*[193] the Court stated: **6.48**

> Whilst Article 8 contains no explicit procedural requirements, the decision making process leading to measures of interference must be fair and such as to afford due respect for the interests safeguarded by Article 8:
>
> > [W]hat . . . has to be determined is whether, having regard to the particular circumstances of the case and notably the serious nature of the decisions to be taken, the parents have been involved in the decision making process as a whole, to a degree sufficient to provide them with the requisite protection of their interests. If they have not, there will be a failure to respect their family life and the interference resulting from the decision will not be capable of being regarded as 'necessary' within the meaning of Article 8.[194]

Similarly, in *Johansen v Norway*[195] the Court examined the fairness of the decision-making process to see if it involved the applicant sufficiently to protect her

[188] See para 6.59 below.
[189] See para 6.54ff below.
[190] (1992) 15 EHRR 137 para 48.
[191] (1992) 15 EHRR 244 paras 73, 74.
[192] [1999] IRLR 188 para 62.
[193] (1995) 20 EHRR 205 para 87.
[194] *W v United Kingdom* (1987) 10 EHRR 29, paras 62 and 64.
[195] (1996) 23 EHRR 33 para 66.

interests. The principle was extended to breaches of the right to freedom of expression in *Tolstoy Miloslavksy v United Kingdom*,[196] where the Court concluded that the latitude given to juries when directing them on damages for defamation failed to provide adequate and effective safeguards against a disproportionately large award.

(c) Proportionality and the margin of appreciation

6.49 The value of distinguishing between the role of the margin of appreciation as an interpretative obligation (requiring respect for domestic values and traditions) and its role as a standard of judicial review has already been emphasised.[197] The primary ground of judicial review used by the Court and Commission when examining alleged breaches of human rights is to assess whether an interference with human rights is disproportionate; and the Commission and Court have frequently emphasised that the Contracting Parties to the Convention have a margin of appreciation[198] when the question of proportionality comes to be evaluated. As the Court made clear in *Handyside v United Kingdom*:[199]

> By reason of their direct and continuous contact with the vital forces of their countries, state authorities are in principle in a better position than the international judge to give an opinion on the . . . 'necessity' of a 'restriction' or 'penalty' . . . it is for the national authorities to make the initial assessment of the reality of the pressing social need implied by the notion of 'necessity' in this context.
>
> Consequently, Article 10(2) leaves to the contracting states a margin of appreciation. This margin is given both to the domestic legislator ('prescribed by law') and to the bodies, judicial among others, that are called upon to interpret and apply the laws in force.
>
> Nevertheless, Article 10(2) does not give the contracting states an unlimited power of appreciation. The Court which, with the Commission is responsible for ensuring the observance of the states' engagements, is empowered to give the final ruling on whether 'restriction' or 'penalty' is reconcilable with freedom of expression. The domestic margin of appreciation thus goes hand in hand with European supervision. Such supervision concerns both the aim of the measure challenged and its 'necessity'; it covers not only the basic legislation but also the decision applying it, even one given by an independent court.

6.50 The basic principle is that the margin of appreciation is used to justify why a low standard of judicial review is applied in a particular case.[200] However, the relationship of the margin of appreciation with the proportionality principle raises real dif-

[196] Series A No 316–B (1995) para 50.

[197] See para 6.32 below. The impact of the margin of appreciation as an interpretative obligation is discussed at para 6.82ff below.

[198] For a discussion of the doctrine, see generally, para 6.31ff above.

[199] (1976) 1 EHRR 737 paras 48–49.

[200] J Kokott, T*he Burden of Proof in Comparative and International Human Rights Law* (Kluwer, 1999) 144 where she argues that the margin of appreciation is utilised as the functional equivalent of the deferential rational basis test in American constitutional law.

ficulties in the Court's analysis. There is an obvious tension between *subsidiarity*, on the one hand, (the notion that the state should itself decide democratically what is appropriate for *itself*) which requires judicial restraint and *universality* (the idea of insisting on the same European protection for everyone, whatever the national community in question, by the development of *common standards*).[201] Unfortunately, however, attempts to rationalise[202] the jurisprudence fail to identify any discernable principle which can explain inconsistencies.[203] These difficulties are compounded by the Court's opaque reasoning. As Judge McDonald points out, the terse style of the Court's judgments often means that it is unclear whether it has rejected an application on the basis that the complaint (i) should not be reviewed *in principle* or (ii) that the particular restriction in question is a *justifiable* interference with rights.[204] Furthermore, the term 'margin of appreciation' is not used consistently. For example, it seems that the Court has used three different perspectives on the margin of appreciation when evaluating freedom of expression under Article 10.[205] In addition, a lack of clarity in the reasoning obscures the process of identifying a *principled* basis for explaining the impact of the margin of appreciation in the proportionality test. It is therefore impossible to predict *how* the margin of appreciation will affect the outcome in any particular case: in other words, whether the Court will apply a high standard of judicial review and a strict approach towards proportionality; or whether it will utilise a low standard of review where great weight is attached to the domestic state's margin of appreciation.

The Court's approach has consequently been described as 'elusive';[206] and the development of the doctrine has been likened to spreading disease.[207] Lord Lester has commented that the concept of the margin of appreciation has become as slippery and as elusive as an eel and that the Court has used the doctrine as a substitute for coherent analysis of the issues at stake.[208] **6.51**

Nevertheless, when the interrelationship between proportionality and the margin of appreciation comes to be considered the following factors appear to be important: **6.52**

- the significance of the right in question—the Court has stated that some

[201] S Martens, 'Incorporating the European Convention: The Role of the Judiciary' [1998] EHRLR 5.

[202] See eg P Mahoney, 'Universality versus Subsidiarity in the Strasbourg Case Law on Free Speech: Explaining Some Recent Judgments' [1997] EHRLR 364.

[203] See A Lester, 'Universality versus Subsidiarity: A Reply' [1998] EHRLR 73.

[204] R St J Macdonald, 'The Margin of Appreciation' in R St J Macdonald, F Matzer and H Petzold (eds), *The European System for the Protection of Human Rights* (Kluwer, 1983) 84–85.

[205] N Lavender, 'The problem of the Margin of Appreciation' [1997] EHRLR 380.

[206] T O'Donnell, 'The Margin of Appreciation: Standards in the Jurisprudence of the Court' (1982) HRQ 474, 495.

[207] P van Dijk and G van Hoof, *Theory and Practice of the European Convention on Human Rights* (3rd edn, Kluwer, 1998) 604 .

[208] *Proceedings of the 8th International Colloquy on the Convention on Human Rights* 227–240, 236.

Convention rights have been characterised as fundamental (such as the right to a fair trial[209] or to private life[210] or freedom of expression);[211]

- the objectivity of the restriction in question—in *Sunday Times v United Kingdom (No 1)*[212] the Court distinguished between the objective nature of maintaining the authority of the judiciary (which left a narrower margin of appreciation for the state) and the subjective nature of the protection of morals, where the Court should defer to domestic views;[213]
- whether there is a consensus in law and practice among the member states—for example, in *Marckx v Belgium*[214] the Court acknowledged an emerging consensus about the legal treatment of illegitimate children and struck down inheritance laws which discriminated against them.

6.53 It is submitted that the nature of the doctrine is clarified once it is *explicitly* acknowledged that the 'margin of appreciation' is an application of the principle of subsidiarity: a principle which is implicit in the Convention, inherent in the system of protection it has established and has been confirmed by Convention case law.[215] This means that the margin of appreciation has no obvious application when interpreting domestic human rights instruments.[216] In any event, the lack of analytical rigour in Convention cases about the precise relationship between proportionality and the margin of appreciation raises real doubts about the wisdom of attempting to apply that jurisprudence to the Human Rights Act.[217] It is more useful to consider the development of the doctrine of proportionality in other jurisdictions.

(3) Proportionality in English administrative law

6.54 Although Lord Diplock suggested in 1984[218] that proportionality might be adopted as a free standing ground for judicial review, the English courts have tended to regard it as simply an aspect of *Wednesbury* irrationality.[219] However,

---

[209] See eg *Delcourt v Belgium* (1970) 1 EHRR 355.

[210] See eg *Dudgeon v United Kingdom* (1981) 4 EHRR 149; *Eriksson v Sweden* (1989) 12 EHRR 183.

[211] See eg *Handyside v United Kingdom* (1976) 1 EHRR 737; *Lingens v Austria* (1986) 8 EHRR 103; *Weber v Switzerland* (1990) 12 EHRR 508.

[212] (1979) 2 EHRR 245.

[213] See eg *Müller v Switzerland* (1988) 13 EHRR 212.

[214] (1979) 2 EHRR 330.

[215] H Petzold, 'The Convention and the Principle of Subsidiarity' in R St J Macdonald, F Matscher and H Petzold (eds), *The European System for the Protection of Human Rights* (Nijhoff, 1993).

[216] See para 6.84 below.

[217] The application of the margin of appreciation doctrine to proportionality under the Human Rights Act is discussed at para 6.82ff below.

[218] In *Council of the Civil Service Unions v Minister for the Civil Service* [1985] AC 374, 410.

[219] See eg *R v Brent, London Borough Council, ex p Assegai* (1987) 151 LG Rev 891; but see *R v Secretary of State for Transport, ex p Pegasus Holdings (London) Ltd* [1988] 1 WLR 991; *R v Barnsley Metropolitan Borough Council, ex p Hook* [1976] 1 WLR 1052, 1057, 1062.

when applying the *Wednesbury* test, the courts have sometimes approached the issues as if they were considering a proportionality test. For example, it has been held that a decision is *Wednesbury* irrational in the following situations:

- where the decision-maker has manifestly failed to balance the relevant considerations;[220]
- where the impact of a decision is oppressive in the sense that it subjects complainants to excessive hardship;[221]
- where disproportionate penalties have been imposed;[222]
- where the decision-maker has failed to take the least harmful means when there are more than one available means of achieving an objective.[223]

Furthermore, in considering irrationality the courts use a sliding scale of intensity of review ranging from *super Wednesbury* managerial decisions where there is a high degree of deference to the decision-maker (such as decisions involving the allocation of resources or policy)[224] to cases involving human rights where (as the Court of Appeal emphasised in *R v Ministry of Defence, ex p Smith*)[225] the more substantial the interference with human rights, the more the court will require by way of justification before it is satisfied that the decision is reasonable. This is a similar approach to that used when considering proportionality.

Nevertheless, when the House of Lords considered an administrative law challenge which directly addressed the principle of proportionality in *R v Secretary of State for the Home Department, ex p Brind*,[226] the doctrine was rejected.[227] The **6.55**

---

[220] See eg *R v Secretary of State for Home Department, ex p Benson* [1989] COD 329; *Tesco Stores Ltd v Secretary of State for the Environment* [1995] 1 WLR 759.

[221] As in *R v Secretary of State for the Home Department, ex p Leech (No 2)* [1994] QB 198 where the Court of Appeal held that prison regulations wrongfully infringed a prisoner's constitutional rights and there was no self evident and pressing need for the exercise of power; see also *R v Secretary of State for the Home Department, ex p Handscomb* (1987) 86 Cr App R 59 (where the review of a life prisoner's sentence was unreasonable); *R v Secretary of State for the Home Department, ex p Norney* [1995] 7 Admin LR 861.

[222] See eg *R v Brent London Borough Council, ex p Assagai* (1987) 151 LG Rev 891; *R v Highbury Corner Magistrates Court, ex p Uchendu* [1994] RA 51.

[223] See eg *Hall and Company Ltd v Shoreham-by-Sea Urban District Council* [1964] 1 WLR 240.

[224] See *R v Secretary of State for the Environment, ex p Nottinghamshire County Council* [1986] AC 240; *R v Secretary of State for the Environment, ex p Hammersmith and Fulham London Borough Council* [1991] AC 521.

[225] [1996] QB 517.

[226] [1991] 1 AC 696.

[227] Although Lords Bridge, Roskill and Templeman left open its possible recognition as an independent ground of judicial review, ibid 749, 750, 751; but see Neill LJ in *R v Secretary of State for the Environment, ex p NALGO* (1992) 5 Admin LR 785, 800, 801 where he took the view that the House of Lords rejected the doctrine of proportionality in *Brind*; and contrast the views of on the one hand Hoffman LJ in *R v Plymouth City Council, ex p Plymouth and South Devon Cooperative Society* [1993] PLR 75, 88 where he said that the status of this principle as an instrument of English judicial review was to say the least uncertain and on the other hand Sedley J in *R v Manchester Metropolitan University, ex p Nolan* [1994] ELR 380, 395 where he said that proportionality was potentially available today as a discrete head of challenge in appropriate cases.

future development of proportionality in English administrative law continues to attract considerable debate[228] and De Smith[229] argues that proportionality should be specifically adopted in English law as a separate ground for judicial review.

(4) Proportionality in European Community law

6.56 In European Community law the principle of proportionality[230] is applied as a 'general principle of law' in the same way as the principles of legal certainty and equality. The first occasion[231] upon which the European Court of Justice gave detailed consideration to the impact of proportionality on European Community law was in *Internationale Handelsgesellschaft mbH v Einfuhr-und Vorratsstelle für Getreide und Futtermittel*.[232] The rationale for proportionality was explained by the European Court of Justice in *Firma Nold KG v Commission*:[233]

> As the Court has already stated, fundamental rights form an integral part of the general principles of law, the observance of which it ensures. In safeguarding these rights the Court is bound to draw inspiration from the constitutional traditions common to the Member States.
>
> If rights of ownership are protected by the constitutional laws of the Member States, and if similar guarantees are given in respect of their rights freely to choose and practice their trade or profession, the rights thereby guaranteed, far from constituting unfettered prerogatives, must be viewed in the light of the social function of property and activities protected thereunder. For this reason, rights of this nature are protected by law subject always to limitations laid down in accordance with the public interest.
>
> Within the Community legal order, it likewise seems legitimate that these rights should, if necessary, be subject to certain limits justified by the overall objectives pursued by the Community, on condition that the substance of these rights is left untouched.

Although proportionality first became incorporated into Community law through decisions of the European Court of Justice, the principle has now been

228 See eg Lord Irvine, 'Judges and Decision Makers: the Theory and Practice of Wednesbury Review' [1996] PL 59; J Jowell, 'In the Shadow of Wednesbury' [1997] JR 75; Sir John Laws, 'Wednesbury' in C Forsyth and I Hare (eds), *The Golden Metwand and the Crooked Cord* (Oxford University Press, 1998).

229 Lord Woolf and J Jowell, *De Smith, Woolf and Jowell: Judicial Review of Administrative Action* (5th edn, Sweet & Maxwell, 1995) 411–421.

230 For a general survey see eg G de Burca, 'The Principle of Proportionality and its Application in EC Law' (1993) 13 YEL 105; N Emiliou, *The Principle of Proportionality in European Law* (Kluwer, 1996); F Jacobs, 'Recent Developments in the Principle of Proportionality in EC Law', W van Gervin, 'The Effect of Proportionality on Actions of Member States of the European Community: National Viewpoints from Continental Europe' and T Tridimas, 'Proportionality in Community Law: Searching for the Appropriate Standard of Scrutiny' in E Ellis (ed), *The Principle of Proportionality in the Laws of Europe* (Hart Publishing, 1999).

231 But see eg *Fédération Charbonnière de Belgique v High Authority* [1956] ECR 245, 299.

232 [1970] ECR 1125.

233 [1974] ECR 491, 507.

embodied in the Treaty as a result of the Maastricht Agreement. Article 3b of the EC Treaty states that:

> Any action by the Community shall not go beyond what is necessary to achieve the objectives of this Treaty.

The application of the principle of proportionality appears to involve considera- **6.57** tion of three elements: first, whether the measure in question was a useful, suitable or effective means of achieving a legitimate aim or objective; secondly, whether there were means of achieving the aim which were less restrictive of the applicant's interest; and thirdly, even if there were a no less restrictive means of achieving the aim available, whether the measure has an excessive or disproportionate effect on the applicant's interest.[234] In practice, however, the question of proportionality tends to be tested in two ways:

- by the *balancing* test (in other words, balancing the objectives which a decision attempts to achieve against the means applied to achieve it) and
- by the *necessity* test (in other words, where a particular objective can be attained by more than one available means, the least harmful of these means must be adopted).

(a) The balancing test

Lord Diplock encapsulated the balancing test in *R v Goldstein*[235] in saying: 'You **6.58** must not use a steam hammer to crack a nut'. The forfeiture cases show how the balancing test is used to strike down administrative measures. For example, in *Buitoni SA v Fonds d'Orientation et de Régularisation des Marchés Agricoles*[236] the European Court of Justice held that a fixed penalty for infringing import and export licences was disproportionate in terms of achieving the objectives of administrative efficiency in running the scheme.

(b) The necessity test

The approach taken when applying the necessity test is illustrated by the **6.59** *Skimmed-Milk Powder* case[237] where the European Commission attempted to reduce the surplus of skimmed-milk powder by forcing animal feed producers to use it instead of soya despite the fact that it was three times more expensive. The European Court of Justice concluded that the scheme was discriminatory and went on to hold:[238]

[234] See eg the opinion of Advocate General Van Gerven in *Society for the Protection of Unborn Children Ireland Ltd v Grogan* [1991] ECR I–4685 para 27; *R v Ministry of Agriculture, Fisheries and Food, ex p Fédération Européenne de la Santé Animale* [1990] ECR I–4023 para 13.

[235] [1983] 1 WLR 151, 155.

[236] Case 122/78 [1979] ECR 677, 685; and see *Atlanta Amsterdam BV v Produktschap voor Vee en Vlees* [1979] ECR 2137; *Fa Man v IBAP* [1985] ECR 2890.

[237] *Bela-Mühle Joseph Bergman KG v Grows-Farm GmbH* [1977] ECR 1211.

[238] Ibid 1221.

> Nor, moreover, was such an obligation necessary in order to attain the objective in view, namely the disposal of stocks of skimmed-milk power. It could not therefore be justified for the purpose of attaining the Common Agricultural Policy.

Similarly, where the British Government imposed restrictions on importing milk and cream which had undergone UHT treatment partly to prevent foot and mouth disease, the European Court of Justice took the view that:[239]

> whilst the protection of health of animals is one of the matters justifying the application of Article 36,[239a] it must nonetheless be ascertained whether the machinery employed in the present case by the United Kingdom constitutes a measure which is disproportionate in relation to the objective pursued, on the ground that the same result may be achieved by means of less restrictive measures, or whether, on the other hand, regard had to be had to the technical constraints already mentioned and hence it was justified under Article 36.

The European Court of Justice held that the restrictions were disproportionate because the UK authorities could have achieved their desired objective by abandoning a licence requirement and instead requiring importers to provide information, accompanied if necessary by appropriate certificates.

6.60 Lord Hoffman has argued that the standard of review implicit in the doctrine of proportionality is much the same as that of *Wednesbury* irrationality.[240] However, the European Court of Justice will in certain contexts use a much stricter test than *Wednesbury* reasonableness; and has not applied the principle of proportionality as a *uniform* standard. The intensity of review is higher if the dispute involves a breach of a fundamental norm.[241] Thus, when a national measure contravenes a fundamental provision of the Treaty, it will be scrutinised very carefully. In *Rutili v Minister for the Interior*[242] the European Court of Justice held that interference with freedom of movement can only be justified by 'a genuine and sufficiently serious threat to public policy necessary for the protection of those interests in a democratic society.' By contrast, where the dispute concerns a breach of a less

[239] *Commission v United Kingdom* [1983] ECR 203, 236.

[239a] Now Art 30 of the Treaty of European Union.

[240] Lord Hoffman, 'A Sense of Proportion' in M Andenas and F Jacobs (eds), *European Community Law in the English Courts* (Clarendon Press, 1998); when applying the principle of proportionality in the Sunday trading cases (*R v Stoke on Trent Council, ex p B & Q* [1990] 3 CMLR 31 para 47) Hoffman J (as he then was) expressed the view: 'it is not my function to carry out the balancing exercise or to form my own view on whether the legislative objective could be achieved by other means. These questions involve compromises between competing interests which in a democratic society must be resolved by the legislator. The duty of the Court is only to inquire whether the compromise adopted by the United Kingdom Parliament, so far as it affects Community trade, is one which a reasonable legislator could have reached. The function of the Court is to review the acts of legislatures but not to substitute its policies or values.'

[241] See G de Burca, 'The Principle of Proportionality and its application to EC Law' (1993) 13 YB 105.

[242] [1975] ECR 1219.

fundamental provision, the European Court of Justice has given the decision-maker a wide discretion.[243]

6.61 Where the European Court of Justice is considering a broad discretionary power, it will often approach the issue by asking whether a measure was a manifestly inappropriate way of achieving the aim intended. In the economic[244] or political field, the European Court of Justice applies a more deferential approach to proportionality than in other areas. For example, in *R v Ministry of Agriculture, Fisheries and Food, ex p Fédération Européenne de la Santé Animale*[245] the European Court of Justice said:

> The Court has consistently held that the principle of proportionality is one of the general principles of Community law. By virtue of that principle, the lawfulness of the prohibition of economic activity is subject to the conditions that the prohibitory measures are appropriate and necessary in order to achieve the objectives legitimately pursued by the legislation in question; when there is a choice between several appropriate measures recourse must be had to the least onerous and the disadvantages caused must not be disproportionate to the aims pursued.
>
> However, with regard to judicial review of compliance with those conditions, it must be stated that in matters concerning the common agricultural policy, the Community has a discretionary power which corresponds with the political responsibilities given to it by Articles 40[245a] and 43[245b] of the Treaty. Consequently, the legality of a measure adopted in this sphere can be affected only if the measure is manifestly inappropriate, having regard to the objective which the competent institution is seeking to pursue.[246]

More recently, in the challenge by the United Kingdom to the Working Time Directive[247] in *United Kingdom v Council*[248] the European Court of Justice stressed:

> the Council must be allowed a wide discretion in an area which, as here, involves the legislature in making social policy choices and requires it to carry out complex assessments. Judicial review of the exercise of that discretion must therefore be limited to examining whether it has been vitiated by manifest error or misuse of power or whether the institution concerned has manifestly exceeded the limits of its discretion.

Thus, the House of Lords in *R v Chief Constable of Sussex, ex p International*

[243] See eg *Germany v Council (Bananas)* [1994] ECR I–4973.

[244] In particular, in the agricultural sphere see eg *Balkin Import-Export GmbH v Hauptzollamt Berlin-Packhof* Case 5/73 [1973] ECR 1091; *Walzmuble* [1981] ECR 3211; *Zardi (Vincento) v Consorzio Agrario Provinciale di Ferrera* [1990] ECR I–2525.

[245] [1990] ECR I–4023.

[245a] Now Art 34 of the Treaty of European Union.

[245b] Now Art 37 of the Treaty of European Union.

[246] See, in particular, the judgment in Case 265/87 *Schrader H S Kraftfutter GmbH & Company KG v Hauptzollamt Gronau* [1989] ECR 2237 paras 21 and 22.

[247] Council Directive (EC) 934/104 concerning certain aspects of the organisation of working time.

[248] [1996] ECR 1–5755.

Trader's Ferry[249] took the view that there was no real difference between the proportionality test and *Wednesbury* irrationality when deciding if a decision of the Chief Constable to provide limited policing of animal rights protesters could be justified on public policy grounds under Article 34.[249a] One reason for applying what is in effect a *Wednesbury* irrationality test in these circumstances is that, where Community institutions with discretionary powers have to balance a number of conflicting variables, a more intensive standard of review would result in numerous challenges, on the basis that the variables in question should have been balanced in some other way.[250]

(5) Proportionality under the Canadian Charter of Rights

6.62 Section 1 of the Canadian Charter of Rights states:

> The Canadian Charter of Rights and Freedoms guarantees the rights and freedoms set out in it subject only to such reasonable limits prescribed by law as can be demonstrably justified in a free and democratic society.

The standard interpretation of section 1 remains that of the Supreme Court in *R v Oakes*[251] where Dickson CJ set out the general principles to be applied :

> To establish that a limit is reasonable and demonstrably justified, two central criteria must be satisfied. First, the objective, which the measures responsible for a limit on a Charter right or freedom are designed to serve, must be of 'sufficient importance to warrant overriding a constitutionally protected right or freedom' . . . The standard must be high in order to ensure that objectives which are trivial or discordant with the principles integral to a free and democratic society do not gain section 1 protection. It is necessary, at a minimum, that the objective relate to concerns which are pressing and substantial in a free and democratic society before it can be characterised as sufficiently important.
>
> Second, once a sufficiently significant objective is recognised, then the party invoking section 1 must show that the means chosen are reasonable and demonstrably justified. This involves a form of proportionality test. . . . Although the nature of the proportionality test will vary depending on the circumstances, in each case courts will be required to balance the interests of society with those of individuals and groups. There are, in my view, three important components of a proportionality test. First, the measures adopted must be carefully designed to meet the objective in question. They must not be arbitrary, unfair or based on irrational considerations. In short, they must be rationally connected to the objective. Second, the means, even if rationally connected to the objective in the first sense, should impair 'as little as possible' the rights or freedoms in question . . . Third, there must be a proportionality between the *effects* of the measures which are responsible for limiting the Charter's right or freedom and the objective which has been identified as of 'sufficient importance'.

[249] [1999] 2 AC 418 (applying *Commission v French Republic* [1997] ECR-I 6959.
[249a] Now Art 30 of the Treaty of European Union.
[250] P Craig, *Administrative Law* (3rd edn, Sweet & Maxwell, 1994) 420.
[251] [1986] 1 SCR 103, 137, 138; see also *R v Chaulk* [1990] 3 SCR 1303.

There has only been one case where the Supreme Court has ruled that a legislative objective is not sufficiently important to override a Charter right. In *R v Big M Drug Mart*[251a] it held that the Sunday closing law which compelled observance of the Christian sabbath was not a sufficently important purpose to justify infringing the right to freedom of religion. By contrast, it has not been difficult to prove a rational connection between the law in question and its objective. The Supreme Court in *R v Oakes*[252] itself concluded that there was a failure to prove a rational connection[253] between a reverse onus provision and the presumption of innocence; the Supreme Court decided that the possession of a small amount of controlled drugs did not justify the inference of drug trafficking. In *Benner v Canada*[253a] the Supreme Court took the view that a provision which discriminated between mothers and fathers for the purposes of immigration legislation had no rational connection with the purported objective of screening out dangerous people. **6.63**

By contrast, the critical issue in most cases under the Charter is the application of the 'least drastic means' test. For example, the Canadian Supreme Court has ruled that the prohibition of English in commercial signs in Quebec was too drastic a means of protecting the French language[254] and that it was illegal to regulate professional standards by prohibiting Albertan lawyers from forming partnerships with non-resident lawyers[255] or by prohibiting advertising by dentists.[256] **6.64**

However, the Supreme Court has mitigated the rigour of the 'least drastic means' test. In *R v Edwards Books and Art*[257] it held that a Sunday closing law which applied to retail shops infringed the right to religion and went on to consider whether the restriction could be justified. In particular, the question arose as to whether the law satisfied the least drastic means test: there was an exemption for retailers who observed Saturday as the sabbath, but the exemption was limited to small retailers. Nevertheless, the Court concluded that the limitation on the exemption to small retailers was lawful. Dickson CJ took the view that the law abridged freedom of religion of Saturday observers 'as little as **6.65**

[251a] [1985] 1 SCR 295.

[252] [1986] 1 SCR 103.

[253] A reverse onus provision that possession of an illegal drug raised a presumption that the accused was in possession for the purpose of supplying drugs failed the rational connection test because possession of a negligible quantity of drugs could not support an inference of supplying drugs.

[253a] [1997] 1 SCR 358.

[254] *Ford v Quebec* [1988] 2 SCR 712; but contrast *Devine v Quebec* [1988] 2 SCR 790 where it was held that requiring the use of French was acceptable.

[255] *Black v Law Society of Alberta* (1986) 27 DLR (4th) 527.

[256] *Rocket v Royal College of Dental Surgeons* [1990] 2 SCR 232.

[257] [1986] 2 SCR 713.

possible'[258] and that the legislation in question was 'one that was reasonable for the legislature to impose'.[259] Thus, the Supreme Court recognised a margin of appreciation which would tolerate a variety of different Sunday closing laws.

6.66 Since *R v Edwards Books and Art*[260] the Canadian courts have taken a more flexible approach towards the least means test. Indeed, in *Irwin Toy v Quebec (A-G)*[261] the Supreme Court used the phrase 'margin of appreciation' to describe its perspective. In a succession of cases[262] the Canadian Supreme Court has deferred to legislative choice on the ground that the choice fell inside a range within which reasonable legislators could disagree. The Supreme Court re-stated the principles to be applied in *Libman v A-G of Quebec*[263] where it said:

> In [*RJR-McDonald Inc v Canada (A-G)*[264]] McLachlin J explained the minimum impairment test as follows,[265]
>
> > [T]he government must show that the measures at issue impair the right of free expression as little as reasonably possible in order to achieve the legislative objective. The impairment must be 'minimal', that is the law must be carefully tailored so that rights are impaired no more than necessary. The tailoring process seldom admits of perfection and the courts must accord some leeway to the legislator. If the law falls within a range of reasonable alternatives, the court will not find it over broad because they can conceive of an alternative which may better tailor the objective to infringement . . .
>
> This Court has pointed out on a number of occasions that in the social, economic and political spheres, where the legislature must reconcile competing interests in choosing one policy among several that might be acceptable, the courts must accord great deference to the legislature's choice because it is in the best position to make such a choice. On the other hand, the courts will judge the legislature's choice more harshly in areas where the government plays the role of the 'singular antagonist of the individual'—primarily in criminal matters owing to their expertise in this area (*Irwin Toy,*[266] *McKinney v University of Guelph,*[267] *Stoffman v Vancouver-General Hospital,*[268] *RJR-McDonald*).[269]
>
> La Forest J's comment on the subject in RJR-McDonald[270] is perfectly apposite:

[258] Ibid 772.
[259] Ibid 781–782.
[260] [1986] 2 SCR 713.
[261] [1989] 1 SCR 927, 999.
[262] See eg *R v Whyte* [1988] 2 SCR 3; *British Columbia Government Employees Union v Attorney-General of British Columbia* [1988] 2 SCR 214; *Re ss 193 and 195.1 of the Criminal Code* [1990] 2 SCR 1123; *Harvey v New Brunswick* [1996] 2 SCR 876.
[263] (1997) 151 DLR (4th) 385, 415, 416.
[264] (1995) 127 DLR (4th) 1.
[265] Ibid 342.
[266] [1989] 1 SCR 927, 993, 994.
[267] [1990] 3 SCR 299, 304, 305.
[268] [1990] 3 SCR 483, 521.
[269] (1995) 127 DLR (4th) 1, 279 and 331–332.
[270] Ibid 277.

> Courts are specialists in the protection of liberty and the interpretation of legislation and are, accordingly, well placed to subject criminal justice legislation to careful scrutiny. However, courts are not specialists in the realm of policy making, nor should they be. This is a role properly assigned to the elected representatives of the people, who have at their disposal the necessary institutional resources to enable them to compile and assess social science evidence, to mediate between competing social interests and protect vulnerable groups.

The Supreme Court went on to hold that a restriction on spending by individuals on referendum campaigns (other than through authorised committees) was not a proportionate means of preventing the most affluent members of society from dominating such campaigns by their spending. Similarly, in *Thompson Newspapers v Canada*[270a] the Supreme Court decided that prohibiting the publication of opinion polls in the last three days of an election campaign was too drastic a means of protecting the voters from inaccurate information.

The third element of the proportionality test (as described in *R v Oakes*)[271] was modified by the Canadian Supreme Court in *Dagenais v Canadian Broadcasting Corporation*[272] where it decided that there must be proportionality both between the objective and the deleterious effects of the restriction and between the deleterious and salutary effects of the restriction. However, the process of balancing the objective sought by the law against the infringement of civil liberties has not to date been a significant factor when the Canadian Supreme Court has considered limitations of Charter rights. **6.67**

(6) Proportionality under the New Zealand Bill of Rights Act

Section 5 of the New Zealand Bill of Rights Act permits limitations of its rights and freedoms; section 5 states: **6.68**

> . . . the rights and freedoms contained in this Bill of Rights may be subject only to such reasonable limits prescribed by law as can be demonstrably justified in a free and democratic society.

However, it is not possible to distil any principles from the cases about section 5.[273]

[270a] [1998] 1 SCR 877.

[271] [1986] 1 SCR 103; see para 6.62 above.

[272] [1994] 3 SCR 835.

[273] This question has been clouded because there are divergent views concerning purpose and effect of s 5 when seen in the context of the so-called 'sections 4–5–6 puzzle'; that is, how these three sections relate to each other: see M Taggart, 'Tugging on Superman's Cape' [1998] PL 266. For a penetrating discussion of the unnecessary complexity of the statutory provisions, see A Butler ,'The Bill of Rights Debate: Why the New Zealand Bill of Rights Act 1990 is a Bad Model for Britain' (1997) 17 OJLS 323.

6.69 In *Ministry of Transport v Noort*[274] Richardson J took the view that restrictions on rights could be justified if the court applied the relevant principles of the Canadian Charter of Rights,[275] the balancing exercise was carried out by the court in *Solicitor General v Radio New Zealand*[276] by taking a more broad brush approach. In *Duff v Communications*[277] the principles were summarised as follows:

> In the end it is a matter of weighing:
>
> (1) the significance in the particular case of the values underlying the Bill of Rights Act;
> (2) the importance in the public interest of the intrusion on the particular right protected by the Bill of Rights Act;
> (3) the limits sought to be placed on the application of the common law in the particular case; and
> (4) the effectiveness of the intrusion in protecting the interests put forward to justify those limits.

(7) Proportionality under the South African Constitution

6.70 Part II of the South African Constitution Act 1996 sets out various fundamental rights and freedoms. Restrictions on these rights can be justified on a general basis in a similar way to section 1 of the Canadian Charter of Rights.[278] Section 35(1) of the Constitution Act states:

> The rights in the Bill of Rights may be limited only in terms of laws of general application to the extent that the limitation is reasonable and justifiable in an open and democratic society based on human dignity, equality and freedom, having regard to all relevant factors including—
>
> (a) the nature of the right;
> (b) the importance of the purpose of the limitation;
> (c) the nature and extent of the limitation;
> (d) the relationship between the limitation and its purpose; and
> (e) less restrictive means to achieve the purpose.

6.71 This provision closely follows the leading case on proportionality decided under the Interim Constitution, *State v Makwanyane*.[279] In that case, the Constitutional Court decided that the death sentence was unlawful because it breached the Constitution. In the course of his judgment Chaskalson P examined the principle of proportionality in Canada, Germany and under the Convention, and expressed the view[280] that:

---

274 [1992] 3 NZLR 260 at 283; McKay J concurring.
275 See para 6.62ff above.
276 [1994] 1 NZLR 48.
277 [1996] 2 NZLR 89, citing Richardson J in *Noort*.
278 See para 6.62ff above.
279 1995 (3) SA 391.
280 Ibid 436.

> The limitation of constitutional rights for a purpose that is reasonable and necessary in a democratic society involves the weighing up of competing values, and ultimately an assessment of proportionality. This is implicit in the provisions of section 33(1). The fact that different rights have different implications for democracy, and in the case of our Constitution, for 'an open and democratic society based on freedom and equality', means that there is no absolute standard which can be laid down for determining the reasonableness and necessity. Principles can be established, but the application of those principles to particular circumstances can only be done on a case by case basis. This is inherent to the requirement of proportionality, which calls for the balancing of different interests. In the balancing process, the relevant considerations will include the nature of the right that is limited, and its importance to an open and democratic society based on freedom and equality, the purpose for which the right is limited and the importance of that purpose to such a society, the extent of the limitation, its efficacy, and particularly, where the limitation has to be necessary, whether its desired end could be reasonably achieved through other means less damaging to the right in question. In the process regard must be had to the provisions of section 33(1) and the underlying values of the Constitution, bearing in mind that, as a Canadian Judge has said 'the role of the Court is not to second-guess the wisdom of policy choices made by legislators'.[281]

(8) Proportionality under the Human Rights Act

(a) Introduction

Until the Human Rights Act comes into force, the English courts have only been able to examine Convention case law in limited circumstances.[282] Nevertheless, the doctrine of proportionality in the Convention context has attracted considerable interest. For example, in *Attorney-General v Guardian (No 2)*[283] Lord Goff said that: **6.72**

> It was established in the jurisprudence of the Court that . . . interference with freedom of expression should be no more than is proportionate to the legitimate aim pursued. I have no reason to believe that English law, as applied in the courts, leads to any different conclusion.

English Courts have attached weight to Convention jurisprudence on proportionality on several other occasions.[284]

Some assistance as to the approach towards proportionality to be taken under the Human Rights Act can be obtained from the decided cases construing section 10 of the Contempt of Court Act 1981.[285] Section 10 provides that a journalist cannot be compelled to disclose his sources unless it is established: **6.73**

281 *Reference re ss 193 and 195(1)(c) of the Criminal Code of Manitoba* (1990) 48 CRR 1, 62.

282 See para 2.09ff above.

283 [1990] 1 AC 109, 283.

284 See eg *Derbyshire County Council v Times Newspaper* [1992] QB 770 *per* Balcombe LJ at 817 and Butler Sloss LJ at 834 (affirmed on other grounds): [1993] AC 534; *Rantzen v Mirror Group Newspapers (1986) Ltd* [1994] QB 670, 692.

285 Which was enacted following the decision in *Sunday Times v United Kingdom (No 1)* (1979) 2 EHRR 245; see generally, para 15.74ff below.

> that disclosure is necessary in the interests of justice or national security or for the prevention of disorder or crime.

It has been said that:

> 'Necessary' is a word in common usage in everyday speech with which everyone is familiar. Like all words, it will take colour from its context . . . I doubt if it is possible to go further than to say that 'necessary' has a meaning that lies somewhere between 'indispensable' on the one hand, and 'useful' or 'expedient' on the other and to leave it to the judge to decide in any case toward which end of the scale of meaning he will place it on the facts of any particular case. The nearest paraphrase I can suggest is 'really needed'.[286]

6.74 More recently, the Privy Council in *de Freitas v Permanent Secretary of Ministry of Agriculture, Fisheries, Lands and Housing*[287] examined the phrase 'reasonably justifiable in a democratic society' and, drawing on Canadian case law concerning the Charter of Rights,[288] held that it is satisfied where:

- the legislative object is sufficiently important to justify limiting a fundamental right;
- the measures designed to meet the legislative object are rationally connected to it; and
- the means used to impair the right or freedom are no more than is reasonably necessary to accomplish the objective.

(b) The proportionality principle

6.75 It is submitted that under the Human Rights Act, the courts will apply a proportionality test drawing on the Convention, European Community and Canadian jurisprudence. As a result, a public authority seeking to show that an interference is proportionate will have to satisfy four conditions:

- the objective of restricting the right must be so pressing and substantial that it is *sufficiently important* to justify interfering with a fundamental right;
- the restriction must be *suitable*: it must be rationally connected to the objective in mind so that the limitation is not arbitrary, unfair or based on irrational considerations;
- the restriction must be *necessary* to accomplish the objective intended: the public authority must adopt the least drastic means of attaining the objective in mind provided the means suggested are not fanciful; and
- the restriction must *not* be *disproportionate*: the restriction must not impose burdens or cause harm which is excessive when compared to the importance of the objective to be achieved.

---

[286] *In re An Inquiry under the Company Securities (Insider Dealing) Act 1985* [1988] AC 660, 704, *per* Lord Griffiths.

[287] [1998] 3 WLR 675, 684.

[288] See para 6.62ff above.

The first requirement, that the objective of restricting a right must be sufficiently important, is a principle which is derived from Convention[288a] and Canadian case law[289] and was applied by the Privy Council in *de Freitas v Permanent Secretary of Ministry of Agriculture, Fisheries, Lands and Housing.*[290] It reflects the emphasis in the Convention jurisprudence that only a pressing social need justifies interfering with a Convention right.[291] **6.76**

The second condition that a restriction must be suitable is an element in the European Union[292] and Canadian cases.[293] **6.77**

The third requirement, the necessity test, is derived from the language used in Convention rights to justify qualified rights;[294] and the least drastic means test is applied in Convention[295] and European Community[296] cases as well as in cases concerning the Canadian Charter of Rights.[297] The principle of least restrictive alternative is also well established in American constitutional law. The American Supreme Court in *Shelton v Tucker*[298] took the view that if a legislative purpose is a legitimate one involving substantial government interference: **6.78**

> that purpose cannot be pursued by means that broadly stifle fundamental personal liberties when the end can be more narrowly achieved. The breadth of legislative abridgment must be viewed in the light of less drastic means for achieving the basis purpose.

Although the least restrictive means test has been applied to such issues as the state regulation affecting inter state commerce,[299] the doctrine has had its greatest impact on the free speech area.[300]

However, it is submitted that where it is claimed that a public authority has failed to use the least restrictive means, the means suggested must not be *fanciful.* As Blackmun J pointed out in *Illinois Elections v Socialist Workers Party*:[301] **6.79**

> a judge would be unimaginative indeed if he could not come up with something a little less 'drastic' or a little less 'restrictive' in almost any situation and thereby enable himself to strike legislation down.

[288a] See para 6.43 ff above.
[289] See para 6.62ff above.
[290] [1998] 3 WLR 675, 684.
[291] See para 6.43 above.
[292] See para 6.57 above.
[293] See para 6.63 above.
[294] For a discussion of qualified rights see para 6.86ff below.
[295] See para 6.47 above.
[296] See para 6.59ff above.
[297] See para 6.64ff above.
[298] (1960) 364 US 581, 582.
[299] See eg *Dean Milk v Madison* (1951) 340 US 349.
[300] See eg *Shelton v Tucker* 364 US 581; *Virginia State Board of Pharmacy v Virginia Citizens Consumer Council* (1976) 425 US 748; see generally, L H Tribe, *American Constitutional Law* (2nd edn, Foundation Press, 1988) para 12–33.
[301] (1979) 440 US 173, 188, 189.

The approach taken by the Canadian courts to the least drastic means test[302] shows that this test must be tempered with common sense and requires a close examination of the particular context in which it is applied.

6.80 Nevertheless, the 'least drastic means' test is likely to be an important element of the necessity test under the Human Rights Act. As De Smith[303] points out in relation to ordinary administrative law principles, the court may do well in human rights cases to use the necessity test, demanding that the infringement of a human right be the least restrictive alternative. It is therefore submitted that the question of whether a public authority has used the least drastic means of imposing a restriction on Convention rights gives useful guidance to whether or not the restriction is necessary provided (i) that any least drastic means suggested are not fanciful and (ii) that (as in Canada) some significance is attached to the particular context so that some latitude is permitted to the public authority in relation to *legislation* which involve issues of political, economic or social policy.

6.81 The final requirement of ensuring that the restriction is not disproportionate or excessive in the narrow sense is well established in all jurisdictions which utilise a proportionality principle.

(c) Proportionality and the margin of appreciation

6.82 One of the critical issues to be decided under the Human Rights Act is whether the doctrine of the margin of appreciation[304] has any role to play when the court applies the principle of proportionality. In other words, whether the court will approach proportionality by asking whether the public authority had exceeded its margin of appreciation in making a decision in relation to Convention rights. The Court and Commission use the phrase 'margin of appreciation' in cases where they apply a low level of scrutiny when reviewing interferences with human rights.[305] Some English cases already assume that where Convention law is examined, the decision-maker himself has a margin of appreciation that must be respected;[306] and there have also been numerous judicial review cases that have discussed *Wednesbury* irrationality in terms of the decision-maker having a margin of appreciation.[307]

[302] See para 6.64ff above.

[303] Lord Woolf and J Jowell, *De Smith, Woolf and Jowell, Judicial Review of Administrative Action* (5th edn, Sweet & Maxwell, 1995) para 13–085.

[304] See para 6.31ff above.

[305] See para 6.32 above.

[306] See eg *R v Secretary of State for the Home Department, ex p Brind* [1991] 1 AC 696 *per* Lord Templeman at 751, *per* Lord Ackner at 762; *Lamuratu Mbatube v Secretary of State for the Home Department* [1996] Imm AR 184, 189.

[307] See eg *R v Monopolies and Mergers Commission, ex p Elders IXL Ltd* [1987] 1 WLR 1221; *R v Secretary of State for the Home Department, ex p Brind* [1991] 1 AC 696; *R v Solihull Metropolitan Borough Council Housing Benefit Review Board, ex p Simpson* (1993) 26 HLR 370; *R v Somerset*

Nevertheless, it is submitted there is no justification for introducing the concept of margin of appreciation into the doctrine of proportionality. The margin of appreciation does not originate from the actual *language* of the Convention itself. It has developed as a doctrine of judicial review which evinces judicial restraint: because supra national courts are obliged to ensure that the Contracting Parties to the Convention retain some degree of autonomy over domestic decision making.[308] As Lord Woolf pointed out in *Kong v Lee Kwong-but*[309] the court: 6.83

> is not concerned directly with the validity of domestic legislation but whether, in relation to a particular complaint, a state has in its domestic jurisdiction infringed the rights of the complainant under the European Convention.

It would be wrong in principle to claim that the Human Rights Act gives a public authority[310] a margin of appreciation which has to be exceeded in order to show that the authority has acted in a way which is incompatible with Convention rights. The doctrine reflects the fact that the European Convention has a supra national function in regulating human rights in the domestic context and has no place to play in purely domestic arrangements for protecting human rights. Commentators on the Human Rights Act have provided overwhelming support[311] for the view that the doctrine of margin of appreciation has *no* 6.84

County Council, ex p Fewings [1995] 1 WLR 1037, 1049; *R v Commissioner of Police for the Metropolis, ex p P* (1996) 8 Admin LR 6, 14; *R v Ministry of Defence, ex p Smith* [1996] QB 517, 554 *per* Sir Thomas Bingham MR; *R v Chief Constable of Sussex, ex p International Trader's Ferry Ltd* [1999] 2 AC 418.

308 See para 6.31ff above.

309 [1993] AC 951, 966.

310 See generally, para 5.03ff above.

311 See eg T H Jones, 'The Devaluation of Human Rights Under the European Convention' [1995] PL 430; J Stevens and D Feldman, 'Broadcasting Advertisements by Bodies with Political Objects, Judicial Review and the Influence of Charities Law' [1997] PL 615; J Kentridge, 'The Incorporation of the European Convention on Human Rights' and Lord Lester, 'The Impact of the Human Rights Act on Public Law' in J Beatson, C Forsyth and I Hare (eds), *Constitutional Reform in the United Kingdom: Practice and Principles* (Hart Publishing, 1998); Sir John Laws, 'The Limitation of Human Rights' [1998] PL 254; K Starmer, 'Reviewing The Margin of Appreciation in the Dynamics of the European Human Rights Jurisprudence' [1998] EHRLR 357; Sir Gavin Lightman and J Bowers, 'Incorporation of the ECHR and its Impact on Employment Law' [1998] EHRLR 560; Sir Anthony Hooper, 'The Impact of the Human Rights Act on Judicial Decision Making' [1998] EHRLR 676; D Pannick, 'Principles of Interpretation of Convention Rights Under the Human Rights Act and Discretionary Areas of Judgment' [1998] PL 545 (and see also Lester and Pannick, *Human Rights Law and Practice* (Butterworths, 1999) para 3.21); J Wadham and H Mountfield, *Blackstone's Guide to the Human Rights Act 1998* (Blackstone, 1999) para 2.5; S Singh, M Hunt and M Demetriou, 'Is There a Role for the "Margin of Appreciation" in National Law after the Human Rights Act?' [1999] EHRLR 15; D Feldman, 'Proportionality and the Human Rights Act 1998' in E Ellis (ed), *The Principles of Proportionality in the Laws of Europe* (Hart Publishing, 1999); Rt Hon Lord Justice Laws, 'Overview' in J Beatson, C Forsyth and I Hare, *The Human Rights Act and the Criminal Justice and Regulatory Process* (Hart Publishing, 1999); S Grosz, J Beatson and P Duffy, *Human Rights: The 1998 Act and the European Convention* (Sweet & Maxwell, 2000) para 2–05.

role[312] to play when considering the doctrine of proportionality under the Human Rights Act. As Buxton LJ put it *R v Stratford Justices, ex p Imbert*:[313]

> The rights recognised by the Convention . . . have been interpreted by the Strasbourg Court subject to the doctrine developed by that Court of the 'margin of appreciation'; see, for instance, *Handyside v United Kingdom*[314] . . . The application of the doctrine of margin of appreciation would appear to be solely a matter for the Strasbourg Court. By appealing to the doctrine that court recognised that the detailed content of at least some Convention obligations are more appropriately determined in the light of national conditions. . . that approach is necessarily translated into a view of the meaning and reach of the detailed provisions of the Convention that is flexible or, according to the observer's point of view, relativist.[315]
>
> The English judge cannot therefore himself apply or have recourse to the doctrine of the margin of appreciation as implemented by the Strasbourg Court. He must, however, recognise the impact of that decision upon the Strasbourg Court's analysis of the meaning and implication of the broad terms of the Convention provisions.

The same point about the margin of appreciation was made by Lord Hope in *R v DPP, ex p Kebeline*:[315a]

> This doctrine is an integral part of the supervisory jurisdiction which is exercised over state conduct by an international court. By conceding a margin of appreciation to each national system, the court has recognised that the Convention, as a living system, does not need to be applied uniformly to all states but may vary in application according to local needs and conditions. This technique is not available to the national courts when they are considering Convention issues arising within their own countries.

6.85 At the same time it is also plain that the courts will more readily defer to the views of public authorities where they are exercising discretionary areas of judgment in relation to policy issues where the legislature, executive and public bodies are better placed than the judiciary to decide.[316] Judicial restraint is fundamental to the approach taken towards proportionality in Convention,[317] European Union[318]

---

312 Contrast those who argue that the margin of appreciation should be applied as a doctrine of judicial restraint and may have application to the Human Rights Act, eg D O'Sullivan, 'The Allocation of Scarce Resources and the Right to Life Under the European Convention on Human Rights' [1998] PL 389; J Coppel, *The Human Rights Act Enforcing the European Convention in the Domestic Courts* (Wiley Chancery Law, 1999) paras 2.109–2.112, R Gordon 'Editorial Review' [1999] COD 1.

313 (1999) 2 Cr App R 276, 286–287.

314 (1976) 1 EHRR 737.

315 See the remarks of Judge de Meyer in a dissenting judgment disapproving of the use and effect of the doctrine that is noted in *Z v Finland* (1997) 25 EHRR 371, 415, 416.

315a [1999] 3 WLR 972, 993, 994.

316 D Pannick, 'Principles of Interpretation of Convention Rights Under the Human Rights Act and Discretionary Areas of Judgment' [1998] PL 545.

317 See para 6.42ff above.

318 See para 6.56ff above.

and Canadian case law,[319] as it has been where the English courts apply *Wednesbury*[320] or proportionality[321] principles.

E. The Nature of Convention Rights

(1) Unqualified and qualified rights

(a) Unqualified rights

Convention rights can be divided into two types: unqualified and qualified. Most Convention rights fall into the first category. The unqualified Convention rights comprise: **6.86**

- the right to life (Article 2 of the Convention);[322]
- the prohibition of torture (Article 3);[323]
- the prohibition of slavery and forced labour (Article 4);[324]
- the right to liberty and security (Article 5);[325]
- the express rights to a fair trial (Article 6);[326]
- no punishment without law (Article 7);[327]
- the right to marry (Article 12);[328]
- the prohibition of discrimination (Article 14);[329]
- the right to education (Article 2 of the First Protocol to the Convention);[330] and
- the right to free elections (Article 3 of the First Protocol);[331]
- the abolition of the death penalty (Articles 1 and 2 of the Sixth Protocol).[332]

First, it should be stressed that some unqualified rights are *absolute* in the sense that the State cannot opt out or derogate from them. Article 15(2)[333] prohibits the State from derogating in times of war or other public emergencies from: **6.87**

- the right to life[334] (except in respect of deaths resulting from lawful acts of war);

319 See para 6.62ff above.
320 See para 5.126ff above.
321 See para 6.54ff above.
322 See Chap 7.
323 See Chap 8.
324 See Chap 9.
325 See Chap 10.
326 See Chap 11.
327 See Chap 11.
328 See Chap 13.
329 See Chap 14.
330 See Chap 19.
331 See Chap 20.
332 See Chap 7.
333 See para 6.92 below.
334 Under Art 2.

- the prohibition from torture;[335]
- the right not to be held in slavery or servitude;[336] and
- the right not to be held liable for a criminal offence on the ground that the act or omission was not criminal at the time it took place.[337]

6.88 Whether or not an absolute right, when a particular Convention right is *unqualified*, a breach of the right will be established if the claimant can satisfy the burden of proving on the balance of probabilities[338] that the public authority has failed to comply with the terms of that particular right. There is no obligation upon the court to examine whether the interference of the Convention right can be *justified* by the public authority. Furthermore, the question which the court must address is whether or not the public authority has interfered with the relevant Convention right; in other words, the court is making a *primary* judgment[339] (and not a secondary assessment on *Wednesbury* grounds[340] about whether the public authority's primary judgment was lawful). It may, however, be necessary to consider whether the right is subject to the doctrine of 'inherent limitations'.[341]

6.89 The impact of unqualified rights is illustrated by *Chahal v United Kingdom.*[342] In that case the applicant had brought judicial review proceedings in England to challenge the decision to refuse him refugee status and then to deport him. The Home Secretary had a duty to balance the interests of the applicant against those of natural security; and the Court of Appeal concluded that the balancing decision he made was not *Wednesbury* irrational.[343] When the applicant claimed there had been a breach of the Convention, the Government argued that in expulsion cases there was an inherent limitation[344] on the right not to be tortured so that even where there was a real risk of ill treatment on removal, he could still be deported if this was required on national security grounds. The Court rejected the Government's argument in these terms:[345]

> Article 3 [the prohibition against torture][346] enshrines one of the fundamental values of a democratic society. The Court is well aware of the immense difficulties faced by States in modern times in protecting the community from terrorist violence. However, even in these circumstances, the Convention prohibits in absolute terms torture or inhuman or degrading treatment or punishment irrespective of the victim's con-

[335] Under Art 3.
[336] The first sentence of Art 4.
[337] Under Art 7.
[338] See 6.101ff below.
[339] See para 5.122 above.
[340] See para 5.126ff above.
[341] See para 6.114ff below.
[342] (1996) 23 EHHR 413.
[343] *R v Secretary of State for the Home Department, ex p Chahal* [1995] 1 WLR 526.
[344] See para 6.114ff below.
[345] (1996) 23 EHHR 413, paras 79 and 80.
[346] See Chap 8 below.

duct. Unlike most of the substantive clauses of the Convention and of Protocols Nos 1 and 4, Article 3 makes no provision for exceptions and no derogation from it is permissable under Article 15 even in the event of a public emergency threatening the life of the nation.

The prohibition provided by Article 3 against ill treatment is equally absolute in expulsion cases. Thus, whenever substantial grounds have been shown for believing that an individual would face a real risk of being subjected to treatment contrary to Article 3 if removed to another State, the responsibility of the Contracting State to safeguard him or her against such treatment is engaged in the event of expulsion. In these circumstances the activities of the individual, however undesirable or dangerous, cannot be a material consideration.

This reasoning will apply in any case in which a public authority acts in a way which is incompatible with an unqualified Convention right.

(b) Qualified rights

Many of the most important rights under the Convention are 'qualified'. As a result, the state is entitled to justify what is a *prima facie* interference with the right. Those Convention rights which are qualified are: **6.90**

- the right to respect for private and family life, home and correspondence (Article 8 of the Convention);[347]
- the right to freedom of thought, conscience and religion (Article 9);[348]
- freedom of expression (Article 10);[349]
- freedom of assembly and association (Article 11);[350]
- the right to the enjoyment of possessions (Article 1 of the First Protocol to the Convention);[351] and
- the right to education (Article 2 of the First Protocol)[352] to the extent of the reservation made by the United Kingdom to reflect the provision now contained in section 9 of the Education Act 1996.[353]

Articles 8 to 11 *entitle* a public authority[354] to interfere with Convention rights in broadly similar terms. The first issue[355] is whether the claimant can satisfy the burden of proving on the balance of probabilities that there is a *prima facie* breach of the right. The court will be making a primary judgment[356] about whether or not the right in question has been breached. However, once it is **6.91**

---

347 See Chap 13.
348 See Chap 14.
349 See Chap 15.
350 See Chap 16.
351 See Chap 18.
352 See Chap 19.
353 See Chap 19.
354 See s 6 of the Human Rights Act; and para 5.03ff above.
355 See para 6.101 below.
356 See s 6; and para 5.122ff below.

demonstrated that there has been a breach, a public authority has the burden of proving on the balance of probabilities[357] that it is entitled to restrict the qualified right by showing (these requirements are *cumulative*):

- that it has acted in a manner 'prescribed by law';[358]
- that the aim of the restriction in question is one of those identified in the particular Convention right as being a 'legitimate' restriction; and
- that the restriction on the right is 'necessary in a democratic society'.[359]

The Court has adopted a similar approach when considering the 'inherent limitations' on unqualified rights.[359a]

(2) **Derogations from Convention rights**

6.92 Article 15 of the Convention permits a state to derogate from certain Convention Articles in time of war or other public emergency threatening the life of the nation. Article 15 states that:

> (1) In time of war or other public emergency threatening the life of the nation, any High Contracting Party may take measures derogating from its obligations under this Convention to the extent strictly required to meet the exigencies of the situation, provided that such measures are not inconsistent with its other obligations under international law.
>
> (2) No derogation from Article 2,[360] except in respect of deaths resulting from lawful acts of war or from Articles 3,[361] 4 (paragraph 1)[362] and 7[363] shall be made under this provision.
>
> (3) Any High Contracting Party availing itself of this right of derogation shall keep the Secretary General of the Council of Europe fully informed of the measures which it has taken and the reasons therefor. It shall also inform the Secretary General of the Council of Europe when such measures have ceased to operate and the provisions of the Convention are again being fully executed.

6.93 At present the United Kingdom has one derogation in place: in relation to Article 5(3) of the Convention. In *Brogan v United Kingdom*[364] several individuals were arrested under the Prevention of Terrorism legislation and detained from four to six days; because they were never brought before a court, the Court held there was a breach of the obligation under Article 5(3) to bring an arrested person 'promptly before a judge or other officer authorised by law to exercise judicial power'. The

[357] See para 6.101ff below.
[358] See para 6.142ff below.
[359] See para 6.149ff below.
[359a] See para 6.114ff below.
[360] The right to life: see Chap 7 below.
[361] The prohibition of torture: see Chap 8 below.
[362] The prohibition of slavery: see Chap 9 below.
[363] No punishment without law: see Chap 11 below.
[364] (1988) 11 EHHR 117.

United Kingdom had in fact withdrawn a notice of derogation before the incident in question. It therefore responded to the adverse adjudication in 1988 by entering a new derogation in order to preserve the Secretary of State's power to extend the period of detention for individuals suspected of terrorism connected with Northern Ireland for up to seven days. The United Kingdom entered a further derogation in 1989 (which is still in force); and the validity of that derogation was upheld by the Court in *Brannigan and McBride v United Kingdom.*[365] The general right of derogation and this particular derogation are expressly preserved by the Human Rights Act.[366]

(3) Reservations from Convention rights

Article 57[367] of the Convention allows a state to enter a reservation where a national law in force at the time of signing (or ratification) is not in conformity with a provision in the Convention. Article 57 states that: **6.94**

> (1) Any State may, when signing this Convention or when depositing its instrument of ratification, make a reservation in respect of any particular provision of the Convention to the extent that any law then in force in its territory is not in conformity with this provision. Reservations of a general character shall not be permitted under this article.
>
> (2) Any reservation made under this article shall contain a brief statement of the law concerned.

The United Kingdom's reservation in relation to the right to education under Article 2 of the First Protocol (which is now contained in section 9 of the Education Act 1996)[368] is expressly preserved by the Human Rights Act.[369]

(4) Negative obligations imposed by Convention rights

Most Convention rights impose negative obligations in the sense that the state is required to *abstain* from interfering with a specific human right. For example, the state must refrain from torture or depriving individuals of their liberty or imposing impermissible restrictions on freedom of expression. The obligation not to interfere with human rights reflects the traditional preoccupation of civil and political rights with negative liberty.[370] Nevertheless, the Court has developed the principle that Convention rights also give rise to positive obligations. **6.95**

---

[365] (1993) 17 EHRR 539.

[366] s 14; see para 3.61ff above.

[367] Until Nov 1998 when the Eleventh Protocol came into force this was Art 64.

[368] See para 19.15 below.

[369] See s 15; and see generally, para 3.68ff above.

[370] See eg I Berlin, 'Two Concepts of Liberty' in H Hardy and R Hausheer (eds), *Isaiah Berlin The Proper Study of Mankind* (Chatto & Windus, 1997); Sir John Laws, 'The Constitution: Morals and Rights' [1996] PL 622 and Lord Irvine, 'Response to Sir John Laws 1996' [1996] PL 636.

6.96 It is not difficult in practice to prove an 'interference' with Convention rights. As the Court stressed when considering the refusal of the Home Secretary to allow a prisoner to consult with a solicitor in *Golder v United Kingdom*:[371]

> By forbidding Golder to make such contact, the Home Secretary actually impeded the launching of the contemplated action. Without formally denying Golder his right to institute proceedings before a court, the Home Secretary did in fact prevent him from commencing an action at that time, 1970. Hindrance in fact can contravene the Convention just as much as a legal impediment.
>
> It is true that—as the Government has emphasised—on obtaining his release Golder would have been in a position to have recourse to the courts at will, but in March and April 1970 this was rather remote and hindering the effective exercise of such a right may amount to a breach of that right, even if the hindrance is of temporary character.

(5) Positive obligations imposed by Convention rights

6.97 There are a number of positive obligations which arise from the express words of the Convention itself, for example: the obligation to protect the right to life;[372] the obligation to provide prison conditions which are not inhuman;[373] in relation to the right to fair trial,[374] the obligation to provide courts, legal aid and translators; and the obligation to hold free elections.[375]

6.98 However, the Court has, in addition, interpreted Convention rights to create positive obligations. The principles were developed in *Marckx v Belgium*[376] where the Court had to consider Belgian family law which did not recognise an illegitimate child as a member of the mother's family; and, thus, prevented mother and child from leading a normal family life. The Court[377] stressed that:

> By proclaiming in paragraph 1 the right to respect for family life, Article 8 signifies first that the State cannot interfere with the exercise of that right otherwise than in accordance with the strict conditions set out in paragraph 2. As the Court stated in the *Belgian Linguistic* case, the object of the Article is 'essentially' that of protecting the individual from arbitrary interference by the public authorities.[378] Nevertheless, it does not merely compel the State to abstain from such interference: in addition to this primarily negative undertaking, there may be positive obligations inherent in an effective 'respect' for family life.
>
> This means, amongst other things, that when the State determines in its domestic legal system the regime applicable to certain family ties such as between an

[371] (1975) 1 EHRR 524 para 26.

[372] Art 2(1) states that 'Everbody's right to life shall be protected by law'; see, generally, para 7.35ff below.

[373] Under Art 3; see para 8.13ff below.

[374] Under Art 6; see para 11.235ff below.

[375] Art 3 of the First Protocol; see para 19.40ff below.

[376] (1979) 2 EHRR 330.

[377] Ibid para 31.

[378] *Belgian Linguistic (No 2)* (1968) 1 EHRR 252 para 7.

> unmarried mother and her child, it must act in a manner calculated to allow those concerned to lead a normal family life. As envisaged by Article 8, respect for family life implies in particular, in the Court's view, the existence in domestic law of legal safeguards that render possible as from the moment of birth the child's integration into his family. In this connection, the State has a choice of various means, but a law that fails to satisfy this requirement violates paragraph 1 of Article 8 without there being a call to examine it under paragraph 2.

The Court has extended the range of Convention articles that entail positive obligations to include: the right to life,[379] the prohibition from inhuman treatment,[380] the right to respect for private[381] and family[381a] life, the right to freedom of religion, thought and conscience,[382] the right to freedom of expression,[383] freedom of assembly[384] and association,[384a] the right to possession of property[385] and the right to education.[386] The positive obligations accepted by the Court fall into three categories:[387] **6.99**

- the obligation to change a law or administrative practice;[388]
- the obligation to provide financial assistance;[389] and
- the obligation to intervene in the relationship between individuals in order to prevent 'private' violations of rights protected by the Convention.[390]

The existence of a positive right depends upon a fair balance being struck between the general interests of the community and the interests of the individual. The question of fair balance involves applying the proportionality principle.[390a] In some cases such as *Rees v United Kingdom*[390b] and *Lopez Ostra v Spain*[390c] the Court has also taken into account the need for a wide margin of appreciation.[390d]

---

379 See para 7.35ff below.
380 See para 8.19ff below.
381 See para 12.106ff below.
381a See para 13.115ff below.
382 See para 14.52ff below.
383 See para 15.183 below.
384 See para 16.64ff below.
384a See para 16.83ff below.
385 See para 18.40ff below.
386 See para 19.42 below.
387 R Lawson and H Schermers, *Leading Cases of the Court of Human Rights* (Ars Aequi Libri, 1997) 82.
388 See eg *Marckx v Belgium* (1979) 2 EHRR 330; *Rees v United Kingdom* (1986) 9 EHRR 56; *Gaskin v United Kingdom* (1989) 12 EHRR 36; *B v France* (1992) 16 EHRR 1.
389 See eg *Airey v Ireland* (1979) 2 EHRR 305; *Lopez Ostra v Spain* (1994) 20 EHRR 277; *Vereinigung Demokratischer Soldaten v Austria Österreichs and Gubi* (1994) 20 EHRR 55.
390 See eg *X and Y v Netherlands* (1985) 8 EHRR 235; *Plattform Ärzte für das Leben v Austria* (1988) 13 EHRR 204.
390a See para 6.42ff above for the Convention case law.
390b (1987) 9 EHRR 56 para 37.
390c (1994) 20 EHRR 27 para 51.
390d See generally, para 6.14ff above.

However, in other cases such as *Gaskin v United Kingdom*[390e] and *B v France*[390f] the Court made no reference to this doctrine.

6.100 The approach taken in *Marckx v Belgium*[391] suggested that where there was a breach of a positive obligation, a public authority was *not* entitled to justify its conduct by relying on the grounds set out in Convention rights which permit interferences in respect of negative obligations. The failure to comply with a positive obligation did not amount to an *interference* with a Convention right.[392] Thus, in *Rees v United Kingdom*:[393]

> In determining whether or not a positive obligation exists, regard must be had to the fair balance that has to be struck between the general interest of the community and the interests of the individual, the search for which is inherent in the whole of the Convention.[394] In striking this balance the aim mentioned in the second paragraph of Article 8 may be of a certain relevance, although this provision refers only in terms to 'interferences' with the right protected by the first paragraph—in other words is concerned with the negative obligations flowing therefrom.[395]

More recently, however, the Court[396] has been reluctant to draw a sharp distinction between negative and positive obligations; and in *Lopez Ostra v Spain*[397] the Court considered whether noxious smells violated Article 8 in these terms:

> Whether the question is analysed in terms of a positive duty on the State—to take reasonable and appropriate measures to secure the applicant's wishes under paragraph 1 of Article 8—, as the applicant wishes in her case, or in terms of an 'interference by a public authority' to be justified in accordance with paragraph 2, the broad principles are broadly similar. In both contexts regard must be had to the fair balance that has to be struck between competing interests of the individual and of the community as a whole, and in any case the State enjoys a certain margin of appreciation. Furthermore, even in relation to the positive obligations flowing from the first paragraph of Article 8, in striking the required balance the aims mentioned in the second paragraph may be of a certain relevance.

(6) The burden of proof

6.101 There is no developed case law in relation to the burden of proving violations of

---

390e (1990) 12 EHRR 36.
390f (1993) 16 EHRR 1.
391 (1979) 2 EHRR 330 para 31.
392 Under Art 8(2), 9(2), 10(2) and 11(2).
393 (1986) 9 EHHR 56 para 37; *Gaskin v United Kingdom* (1989) 12 EHRR 36 para 42.
394 See *James v United Kingdom* (1986) 8 EHRR 123 para 50; *Sporrong and Lönnroth v Sweden* (1982) 5 EHRR 35.
395 See *Marckx v Belgium* (1979) 2 EHRR 330 para 31.
396 See eg *Powell and Rayner v United Kingdom* (1990) 12 EHRR 288 para 41; *Keegan v Ireland* (1994) 18 EHRR 342 paras 49–52; *Stjerna v Finland* (1994) 24 EHRR 194 para 38; *Gül v Switzerland* (1996) 22 EHRR 93 para 38; *Ahmut v Netherlands* (1996) 24 EHRR 62 para 63.
397 (1994) 20 EHRR 277 para 51.

convention rights either under international law or under the Convention.[398] It appears that, at the admissibility stage, the applicant only needs to present facts which show that his contentions are not completely groundless.[399] At the merits stage, there is strictly speaking no burden on the applicant as the Court has a duty to 'pursue the examination of the case' and 'if need be, undertake an investigation'.[400] The Court has therefore accepted that it is under a duty to examine all the material and to investigate a complaint on its own initiative, rather than relying on the concept of the burden of proof.[401]

Under the Human Rights Act the Court is likely to take a different approach, requiring a victim[402] to prove a breach of a Convention right on the conventional principle that he who asserts must prove. **6.102**

Where a dispute arises concerning a qualified right[403] and the victim proves there is a *prima facie* interference with that right, the burden will shift to the public authority to prove the justification for the interference. The burden of justifying interference with a right has been extensively considered in the cases concerning the Canadian Charter of Rights. In the leading case of *R v Oakes*[404] Dickson CJ dealt with the question of proving that a restriction was justified: **6.103**

> The onus of proving that a limit on a right or freedom guaranteed by the Charter is reasonably and demonstrably justified in a free and democratic society rests upon the party seeking to uphold the limitation. It is clear from the text of section 1 that limits on the rights and freedoms enumerated in the Charter are exceptions to their general guarantee. The presumption is that the rights and freedoms are guaranteed unless the party invoking section 1 can bring itself within the exceptional criteria that justify their being limited. This is further substantiated by the use of the word 'demonstrably' which clearly indicates that the onus of justification is on the party seeking to limit: *Hunter v Southam Inc.*[405]
>
> The standard of proof under section 1 is the civil standard, namely proof by a preponderance of probability. The alternative criminal standard, proof beyond reasonable doubt, would in my view, be unduly onerous on the party seeking to limit. Concepts such as 'reasonableness', 'justifiability' and 'free and democratic society' are simply not amenable to such a standard. Nevertheless, the preponderance of

398 For the general issues, see J Kokott, *The Burden of Proof in Comparative and International Human Rights Law* (Kluwer, 1998); she points out that principles which have developed in the framework of adversarial proceedings do not work easily when applied to the investigative or inquisitorial methods used under international human rights instruments when protecting rights (at 1).

399 See D Harris, M O'Boyle and C Warbrick, *Law of the European Convention on Human Rights* (Butterworths, 1995) 598.

400 Art 38(1)(a); this was formerly the function of the Commission, see Harris, O'Boyle and Warbrick (n 399 above) 598.

401 *Artico v Italy* (1980) 3 EHRR 1 para 30.

402 See para 22.14ff below.

403 See para 6.90ff above.

404 Ibid [1986] 1 SCR 103, 137–138.

405 [1984] 2 SCR 145.

probability test must be applied rigorously. Indeed, the phrase 'demonstrably justified' in section 1 supports this conclusion. . . . As Lord Denning explained in *Bater v Bater*:[406]

> The case may be proved by the preponderance of probability, but there may be degrees of probability within that standard. The degree depends on the subject matter. A civil court when considering a charge of fraud will naturally require a higher degree of probability than that it would require if considering whether negligence was established. It does not adopt so high a degree as the criminal court, even when considering a charge of a criminal nature, but it does require a degree of probability which is commensurate with the occasion.

. . . Having regard to the fact that section 1 is being invoked for the purpose of justifying a violation of constitutional rights and freedoms the Charter was designed to protect, a very high degree of probability will be . . ., in the words of Lord Denning, 'commensurate with the occasion'. When evidence is required in order to prove the constituent elements of a section 1 inquiry, and this will generally be the case, it should be cogent and persuasive and make clear to the Court the consequences of imposing or not imposing the limit: see *Law Society of Upper Canada v Skapinker*;[407] *Singh v Canada (Minister of Employment and Immigration).*[408] A Court will also need to know what alternative measures for implementing the objective were available to legislators when they made their decision. I should also add that there may be cases where certain elements of the section 1 analysis are obvious or self evident.

6.104 Although the Canadian Supreme Court has applied the standard of proof as the balance of probabilities, it has accepted that this may be established by the application of common sense to what is known, even though what is known may be deficient from a scientific point of view.[409] Consequently, when assessing questions that fall within the realm of social science (such as whether restrictions on expenditure on referendum campaigns are justified under section 1 of the Charter), the Supreme Court has taken the view that such questions do not lend themselves to precise proof.[410]

F. General Restrictions and Limitations on Convention Rights

(1) Introduction

6.105 The rights contained in the Convention are subject to a number of limitations. The Convention itself contains express restrictions in three specific areas:

- Article 16 (restrictions on the political activities of aliens);

---

406 [1950] 2 All ER 458, 459.
407 [1984] 1 SCR 357, 384.
408 [1985] 1 SCR 177, 217.
409 *RJR-MacDonald Inc v Canada (A-G)* [1995] 3 SCR 199, 333.
410 *Libman v A-G of Quebec* (1997) 151 DLR (4th Ed) 385, 407.

- Article 17 (restrictions on activities aimed at the destruction of Convention rights); and
- Article 18 (prohibition on using Convention restrictions for an improper purpose).

Section 1(1) of the Human Rights Act requires that *all* Convention rights[411] are read with Articles 16 to 18 of the Convention.

In addition, the case law has developed 'implied restrictions' in some areas. Furthermore, all qualified rights allow a public authority to impose restrictions on interferences with such rights, which will enable them to justify what would otherwise be a breach of Convention rights. The limitations on qualified rights are discussed in section G below. **6.106**

(2) Restrictions on the political activities of aliens

Article 16 states: **6.107**

> Nothing in Articles 10, 11 and 14 shall be regarded as preventing the High Contracting Parties from imposing restrictions on the political activities of aliens.

Aliens include stateless persons.[412] In *Piermont v France*[413] the term was given a restrictive meaning by the Commission who regarded the provision as outdated and took the view that it should be narrowly construed.[414]

Article 16 applies to those who do not have a right of residence in the United Kingdom. The Court of Appeal has held that nationals of other European Union countries cannot rely on Article 8a of the EC Treaty to establish a right of residence in the United Kingdom[415] and, as result, restrictions can be imposed on the political activities of these nationals. **6.108**

Article 16 expressly authorises restrictions on the political activities of aliens even though they interfere with freedom of expression under Article 10[416] or freedom of assembly and association under Article 11.[417] Article 16 also entitles the State to discriminate against aliens in their rights under Article 3 of the First Protocol to the Convention[418] including the right to vote.[419] Although the Convention does **6.109**

411 As enacted under the Act under s 1.

412 See the explanatory reports on the Fourth Protocol (H(71)11(1971) at 50. Explanatory reports provide guidance and are not binding on the Court.

413 (1995) 20 EHRR 301.

414 Ibid Com Rep paras 59–69.

415 *R v Secretary of State for the Home Department, ex p Phull* [1996] Imm AR 72; *R v Secretary of State for the Home Department, ex p Vitale* [1996] Imm AR 275.

416 See para 15.137ff below.

417 See paras 16.57ff and 16.66ff below respectively.

418 See para 20.19ff below.

419 *Mathieu-Mohin and Clerfayt v Belgium* (1987) 10 EHRR 1 para 54.

not grant privileged status to aliens who are nationals of member states of the Council of Europe (unlike the way in which European Union law treats nationals of its members),[420] the Court in *Piermont v France*[421] took the view that the applicant's possession of German nationality (in addition to her status as a member of the European Parliament) excluded the operation of Article 16 in relation to her activities in France.

6.110 The Parliamentary Assembly has called for the deletion of Article 16.[422] However, the Article must be seen against the background that the state has the ultimate sanction of deporting an alien whom it regards as objectionable. The Convention does not directly restrict the power of deportation[423] but it may *indirectly* do so if deportation interferes with the right to life under Article 2,[424] the prohibition from torture under Article 3[425] or because it breaches Article 8 through its impact on family ties.[426]

(3) Restrictions on activities aimed at the destruction of Convention rights

6.111 Article 17 states:

> Nothing in this Convention may be interpreted as implying for any state, group or person any right to engage in any activity or perform any act aimed at the destruction of any of the rights and freedoms set forth herein or at their limitation to any greater extent than is provided for in the Convention.

Article 17 is an unusual Convention right because it can be used both by an individual against the state and the state against an individual.

6.112 It seems that the state is entitled to rely on Article 17 to safeguard itself against a threat of totalitarianism. Under Article 17 the Commission has held that banning the German Communist Party was justified under Article 17[427] and that individuals convicted for distributing racist pamphlets could be excluded from participating in an election on a racist platform.[428] Although the State can invoke Article 17 against an individual, the fact that the individual aims to destroy or restrict the

[420] See para 13.53 below.
[421] n 413 above para 24.
[422] Recommendation 799 (1977) on the Political Rights and Positions of Aliens, CE Parl Ass, 28th Ord sess, 3rd Pt, Texts Adopted, see also P van Dijk and G van Hoof, *Theory and Practice of the European Convention on Human Rights* (3rd edn, Kluwer, 1998) 750 who describe the provision as a 'dead letter to be abolished'.
[423] So that it can deport an alien on account of his political activities: see Agee *v United Kingdom* (1976) 7 DR 164, EComm HR.
[424] See para 7.30ff below.
[425] See para 8.13ff below.
[426] See generally, para 13.111ff below.
[427] *K P D v Germany* (1957) 1 YB 222, EComm HR; it is very doubtful that this case would now be followed: see *United Communist Party of Turkey v Turkey* 1998 RJD–I; *Socialist Party v Turkey* (1998) 27 EHRR 51; *Freedom and Democratic Party v Turkey*, Judgment of 8 Dec 1999.
[428] *Glimmerveen v Netherlands* (1979) 18 DR 187, EComm HR.

fundamental rights of others does not mean that he may be deprived of all Convention rights. Article 17 only applies to the rights which are abused for this aim. Thus, in *Lawless v Ireland*[429] the Court decided that the state was not entitled to deprive the applicant of rights to liberty under Articles 5 and fair trial rights under Article 6, merely because he was accused of being a member of a terrorist organisation.

(4) The prohibition on using restrictions for an improper purpose

Article 18 states: **6.113**

> The restrictions permitted under this Convention to the said rights and freedoms shall not be applied for any purpose other than those for which they have been prescribed.

An allegation of breach of Article 18 must be made in conjunction with a complaint about an infringement of some other provision of the Convention.[430] The Court has held that it is not essential to examine an alleged violation of Article 18 where it has concluded that the right in question has not been breached[431] and even when the other right has been violated.[432] In practice, applications concerning breaches of Article 18 have failed because they amount to allegations of bad faith. However, the Commission held that a breach of Article 18 was established where a government had derogated from the Convention under Article 15 after the emergency in question had passed;[433] the Commission also accepted that the French police had abused their power where it was applying a judgment of the Court[434] to that effect.[435]

(5) Implied restrictions on Convention rights: the 'inherent limitations' doctrine

The Commission and the Court have developed principles which impliedly restrict Convention rights. The well established doctrine of 'inherent limitations' does not originate from the express language of the Convention and there is considerable uncertainty about whether and to what extent these principles will play a role under the Human Rights Act. **6.114**

[429] *Lawless v Ireland (No 3)* (1961) 1 EHRR 15 para 22; see van Dijk and van Hoof (n 422 above) 753.
[430] See eg *Kamma v Netherlands* (1975) YB 300, 316; *Sporrong and Lönnroth v Sweden* (1982) 5 EHRR 535.
[431] *Engel and others v Netherlands (No 1)* (1976) 1 EHRR 647 para 104.
[432] Ibid para 93.
[433] *De Becker v Belgium* (1958) 2 YB 214, EComm HR (although the point was conceded by the Government).
[434] *Bozano v France* (1986) 9 EHRR 297.
[435] *Bozano v France* (1984) 39 DR 119, 141, EComm HR.

6.115 At one time the Commission took the view that particular classes of individuals by virtue of their status (such as prisoners, psychiatric patients, soldiers and civil servants) had more limited rights and freedoms than others.[436] For example, the Commission held that the inherent limitations of being imprisoned resulted in detained individuals having fewer rights to family life[437] and correspondence.[438]

6.116 However, the Court has rejected the notion that limitations can be implied in relation to qualified Convention rights.[439] Thus, in the course of a prisoner case, *Golder v United Kingdom*[440] the Court said:

> In the submission of the Government the right to respect for correspondence is subject, apart from interference covered by paragraph 2 of Article 8,[441] to implied limitations resulting, inter alia from the terms of Article 5(1): a sentence of imprisonment passed after conviction by a competent court inevitably entails consequences affecting the operation of other Articles of the Convention, including Article 8.
>
> As the Commissioners have emphasised, the submission is not in keeping with the manner in which the Court dealt with the issue raised by Article 8 in the Vagrancy Cases.[442] In addition and more particularly, the submission conflicts with the explicit text of Article 8. The restrictive formula used at paragraph 2 ('There is no interference . . . except such as . . .') leaves no room for the concept of implied limitations.

Nevertheless, a person's status may be taken into account where the restrictions themselves have to be considered. Consequently, in *Schönenberger and Durmaz v Switzerland*[443] the Court referred to earlier case law (to the effect that in the case of a prisoner, the pursuit of the objective of the prevention of disorder or crime may justify wider measures of interference than in the case of a person at liberty) in holding that the same reasoning applied to persons on remand.

6.117 In contrast, where unqualified rights are at issue, the Court has adopted the doctrine of 'inherent limitations'. In *Golder v United Kingdom*[444] the Court was obliged to consider whether a requirement on a prisoner to obtain permission from the Home Secretary before consulting a solicitor breached his right of access to the court under Article 6(1)[445] and said:

---

[436] See generally, F Jacobs and R White, *The European Convention on Human Rights* (2nd edn, (Clarendon Press, 1996) 297–300.

[437] See *X v Austria* (1967) 23 CD 31, EComm HR.

[438] *X v Germany* (1967) 22 CD 45, EComm HR; *Kenneth Hugh de Courcy v United Kingdom* 2749/66, YB X 388.

[439] See para 6.90ff above.

[440] (1975) 1 EHRR 524 para 45.

[441] See generally, para 12.118ff below.

[442] *De Wilde, Ooms and Versyp v Belgium* (1971) 1 EHRR 373 para 93.

[443] (1988) 11 EHRR 202.

[444] (1975) 1 EHRR 524 paras 38, 39.

[445] See generally, para 11.185 below.

> The Court considers, accepting the views of the Commission and the alternative views of the Government, that the right of access to the courts is not absolute. As this is a right which the Convention set forth (see Articles 13, 14, 17 and 25) without, in the narrower sense of the term, defining it, there is room, apart from the bounds delimiting the very content of any right, for limitations permitted by implication. . . . The Court and the Commission have cited examples of regulations and especially of limitations which are to be found in the national law of states in matters of access to the courts, for instance regulations relating to minors and persons of unsound mind. Although it is of a less frequent kind, the restriction complained of by *Golder* constitutes a further example of such a limitation.

However, the Court went on to hold that the restriction in question did indeed breach the right of access to the courts.

The doctrine of inherent limitations has been most extensively developed in cases concerning the right of access to the court.[446] The right of access is not subject to implied restrictions if the type of restriction in question is not for a legitimate purpose and there is no reasonable relationship of proportionality between the means employed and the aim sought to be achieved.[447] The Court therefore held that the right of access had been breached in *De Geouffre de la Pradelle v France*[448] where the applicant did not have a clear practical and effective opportunity to challenge an administrative act which directly interfered with his right to property.[449] On the other hand, the Court has held that an interference with access to the court has been proportionate and for a legitimate aim in a wide variety of situations: **6.118**

- in *Ashingdane v United Kingdom*[450] in order to protect those responsible for caring for the mentally ill from being unfairly harassed by litigation;
- in *Lithgow v United Kingdom*[451] to prevent a multiplicity of claims and proceedings by individual shareholders (in relation to disputes arising from nationalisation);
- in *Fayed v United Kingdom*[452] to further the public interest in ensuring the proper conduct of the affairs of public companies and to ensure that the inspectors could make their report with courage and frankness;
- in *Tolstoy Miloslavsky v United Kingdom*[453] where the Court took the view that an order for security for costs was not disproportionate;

[446] See para 11.185 below.

[447] *Ashingdane v United Kingdom* (1985) 7 EHRR 528 para 57; *Lithgow v United Kingdom* (1986) 8 EHHR 329 para 194; *Tolstoy Miloslavsky v United Kingdom* (1995) 20 EHRR 442 para 59; and see generally, para 11.190ff below.

[448] (1992) Series A No 253–B para 34.

[449] See also *Bellet v France* (1995) Series A No 333–B.

[450] (1985) 7 EHRR 528 paragraph 58.

[451] (1986) 8 EHRR 329 para 197.

[452] (1994) 18 EHRR 393 paras 67–70.

[453] (1995) 20 EHRR 442 paras 62–67.

- in *Stubbings v United Kingdom*[454] where it held that the time limits applied in the English courts to sex abuse cases served a legitimate aim (that is, legal certainty); and
- in *Osman v United Kingdom*[455] where the Court accepted that the immunity of police investigations from a negligence claim served a legitimate aim, since it was directed to maintaining an effective police force, and therefore prevented disorder and crime.

6.119 It also seems that the right to vote and stand for election under Article 3 of Protocol 1[456] is subject to certain 'inherent limitations'. In *Mathieu-Mohin and Clerfayt v Belgium*[457] the Court said:

> The rights in question are not absolute. Since Article 3 recognises them without setting them forth in express terms, let alone defining them, there is room for implied limitations . . . In their internal orders the Contracting States make the rights to vote and to stand for election subject to the conditions which are not in principle precluded under Article 3 . . . They have a wide margin of appreciation in this sphere but it is for the Court to determine in the last resort whether the requirements of Protocol 1 have been complied with; it has to satisfy itself that the conditions do not curtail the rights in question to such an extent as to impair their very essence and deprive them of their effectiveness; they are imposed in pursuit of a legitimate aim and the means employed are not disproportionate.

6.120 However, the Court has expressed reservations about the impact of the doctrine on the mentally handicapped. In *Winterwerp v Netherlands*[458] when considering a complaint that the applicant had been confined in a psychiatric hospital without being heard by a competent court in breach of Article 5(4)[459] it said:

> The judicial proceedings referred to in Article 5(4) need not, it is true, always be attended by the same guarantees as those required under Article 6(1) for criminal or civil litigation (see [*The Vagrancy* cases]).[460] Nonetheless, it is essential that the person concerned should have access to the court and the opportunity to be heard either in person or, where necessary, through some form of representation, failing which he will not have been afforded 'the fundamental guarantees of procedure applied in matters of deprivation of liberty' (see [*The Vagrancy* cases]).[461] Mental illness may entail restricting or modifying the manner of such a right (see, as regards Article 6(1), *Golder v United Kingdom*),[462] but it cannot justify impairing the very essence of the right.
>
> Indeed, special procedural safeguards may prove to be called for in order to protect the interests of persons who, on account of their mental disabilities, are not fully capable of acting for themselves.

[454] (1996) 23 EHRR 213 paras 50–57.
[455] (1998) 5 BHRC 293 para 150.
[456] See para 20.19ff below.
[457] (1987) 10 EHRR 1 para 52.
[458] (1979) 2 EHRR 387 para 60.
[459] See para 10.145ff below.
[460] (1971) 1 EHRR 373 para 78.
[461] Ibid para 76.
[462] (1975) 1 EHRR 524.

The Court have also rejected the suggestion that there are implied limitations to the prohibition against ill treatment under Article 3. In *Chahal v United Kingdom*[463] the Commission expressly refused to accept that there were implied limitations entitling the State to expel a person because of the requirements of national security;[464] the Court also held that Article 3 was absolute in expulsion cases.[465]

There are powerful arguments to be made against the principle of 'inherent limitations' on express Convention rights.[466] First, Article 1 of the Convention[467] obliges the High Contracting States to secure to *everyone* the rights and freedoms defined in the Convention. Secondly, the language of the Articles themselves militates against differentiating between individuals on the basis of their status. If the drafters of the Convention had wished to permit special restrictions for particular categories of persons, they could have done so in relation to each individual article: as they did by exempting the armed forces, police and state administration from freedom of assembly and association under Article 11[468] or limiting the scope of 'forced or compulsory labour' under Articles 4(3)(a) and 4(3)(b).[469] Thirdly, Article 18[470] of the Convention also suggests that the doctrine of 'inherent limitations' is unjustified. This states that the restrictions permitted under the Convention shall not be applied for any purpose other than those for which they have been prescribed.[471] Since no implicit purposes for restrictions are permissible, it follows that no inherent limitations on express rights should be allowed. The doctrine is, however, less objectionable in relation to 'implied rights': the above objections have no application in relation to rights which were not expressly granted by the Convention. As has been shown above, the most important area in which 'inherent limitations' have been allowed is that of 'access to the courts' under Article 6. The effect of these limitations has been to develop what is, in substance a 'qualified right' of access to the court subject to the same limitations as expressly imposed in Articles 8 to 11. **6.121**

Nevertheless, it is likely that the doctrine of 'inherent limitations' will have some application to the Human Rights Act. It is submitted, in particular, that the implied right of access to the court will be subject to implied limitations when it is applied by the English courts.[472] **6.122**

463 (1996) 23 EHRR 413.
464 Ibid para 102 Com Rep.
465 Ibid paras 76–80.
466 See eg van Dijk and van Hoof (n 422 above) 576–577.
467 Which was not enacted into domestic law by the Human Rights Act.
468 See para 16.82 below.
469 See para 9.21ff below.
470 Art 18 has been made part of domestic law under the s 1(1) of the Human Rights Act: see para 3.43ff.
471 See para 6.113 above.
472 See generally, para 11.185ff below.

G. Interference with Qualified Rights

(1) Introduction

6.123 The most important express restrictions on Convention rights are those that apply to qualified rights.[473] The right to private life, the home, correspondence and family life under Article 8,[474] freedom of thought under Article 9,[475] freedom of expression under Article 10[476] and freedom of association under Article 11[477] all entitle a public authority to *justify* a *prima facie* restriction on Convention rights by identifying specific objectives which make the restriction legitimate (such as the protection of public order or the interests of national security).

6.124 The central difficulty in relation to qualified rights is balancing two opposing aims: the protection of a democratic society, on the one hand, and the full respect for the fundamental rights of the individual on the other.[477a] Normally, these two interests coincide and mutually reinforce one another, so that the Court has described freedom of expression,[478] freedom of thought, conscience and religion[479] and the right to the fair administration of justice[480] as comprising essential foundations of a democratic society. Furthermore, the mere fact that minority interests clash with those of the majority is not decisive. As the Court said in respect of the complaint concerning legislation enforcing the closed shop, *Young, James and Webster v United Kingdom*:[481]

> pluralism, tolerance and broad mindedness are the hallmarks of a 'democratic society'.[482] Although individual interests must on occasion be subordinated to those of a group, democracy does not simply mean that the views of the majority must always prevail: a balance must be achieved which ensures the fair and proper treatment of minorities and avoids the abuse of a dominant position. Accordingly, the mere fact that the applicants' standpoint was adopted by very few of their colleagues is again not conclusive of the issue now before the Court.

---

[473] See para 6.90ff above.

[474] See para 12.118ff below; but in relation to family life see para 13.128ff below.

[475] See para 14.54ff below.

[476] See para 15.177ff below.

[477] See paras 16.59ff and 16.79 respectively.

[477a] It has been suggested that it would be preferable under the Human Rights Act to adopt a more rigorous analysis than the pragmatic approach used by the Court: see A McHarg, 'Reconciling Human Rights and the Public Interest: Conceptual Problems and Doctrinal Uncertainty in the Jurisprudence of the European Court of Human Rights' [1999] 62 MLR 671.

[478] *Handyside v United Kingdom* (1976) 1 EHRR 737 para 49; *Lingens v Austria* (1986) 8 EHRR 103 para 41.

[479] *Kokkinakis v Greece* (1993) 17 EHRR 397.

[480] *Delacourt v Belgium* (1970) 1 EHRR 355 para 25; *Kostovski v Netherlands* (1989) 12 EHRR 434.

[481] (1981) 4 EHRR 38 para 63.

[482] *Handyside v United Kingdom* (1976) 1 EHRR 737 para 49.

However, where there is a conflict between human rights and democracy as in *Klaas v Germany*[483] (a case concerning secret surveillance), the Court has expressed the view that:

> some compromise between the requirements for defending democratic society and individual rights is inherent in the system of the Convention (see *mutatis mutandis* [the *Belgian Linguistic* case]).[484] As the Preamble to the Convention states: 'Fundamental Freedoms . . . are best maintained on the one hand by an effective political democracy and on the other by a common understanding and observance of the Human Rights upon which (the Contracting States) depend.' In the context of Article 8, this means a balance must be sought between the exercise by the individual of the rights guaranteed to him under paragraph 1 and the necessity under paragraph 2 to impose secret surveillance for the protection of democratic society as a whole.

The concept of a 'democratic society' has played an important role in a number of recent cases.[484a] As the Court stressed in *Socialist Party v Turkey*:[484b] **6.124A**

> It is of the essence of democracy to allow diverse political programmes to be proposed and debated, even those that call into question the way a State is currently organised, provided they do not harm democracy itself.

Nonetheless, the right to effective democracy may justify imposing restrictions, for example on government employees in order to safeguard the rights of others.[484c]

Where a public authority seeks to justify a restriction on a qualified right, it is necessary for it to prove on the balance of probabilities:[485] **6.125**

- that it has acted in a manner 'prescribed by law';
- that the restriction in question has a 'legitimate aim' (ie that it is designed to achieve one of the prescribed objectives set out in the Article); and
- that the restriction is 'necessary in a democratic society'.

The meaning of 'prescribed by law'[486] and 'necessary in a democratic society'[487] are discussed below. In practice, it is usually straightforward to show that the restriction in question has a 'legitimate aim' in accordance with the very broadly worded objective specified in the particular Article.

---

[483] (1993) 18 EHHR 305 para 59; see, in relation to a similar compromise in the context of anti-terrorist legislation, *Murray v United Kingdom* (1994) 19 EHRR 193.

[484] *Belgian Linguistic Case (No 2)* (1968) 1 EHRR 252 para 5.

[484a] For a survey, see S Marks, 'The European Convention on Human Rights and its "Democratic Society" ' (1995) British Yearbook of International Law 209; A Mowbray, 'The role of the European Court of Human Rights in the Promotion of Democracy' [1999] PL 703.

[484b] (1998) 27 EHRR 51 para 47.

[484c] *Ahmed v United Kingdom* (1998) 5 BHRC 111 para 52; *Rekvényi v Hungary* (1996) 6 BHRC 554 paras 41, 48, 49.

[485] See para 6.104 above.

[486] See para 6.126ff below.

[487] See para 6.146ff below.

(2) 'Prescribed by law'

(a) Introduction

6.126 Several of the qualified Convention rights[488] entitle a public authority to justify interfering with Convention rights provided it can show that it has acted in a manner 'prescribed by law' or 'in accordance with the law'. The right to respect for private or family life[489] entitles a public authority to interfere with the right if it has acted 'in accordance with the law'; the right to freedom of thought, conscience and religion[490] allows limitations which are 'prescribed by law'; the right to freedom of expression[491] is 'subject to such formalities, conditions, restrictions or penalties as are prescribed by law'; and the right to freedom of assembly and association[492] is subject to restrictions which are 'prescribed by law'.

6.127 These Convention Articles therefore reverse the approach of Megarry J in *Malone v Commissioner of Police for the Metropolis*[492a] when he held that public authorities are permitted to do anything which is not unlawful. The principle that underlies the idea of being 'prescribed by law' or 'in accordance with the law' is that restrictions on rights must comply with the rule of law by satisfying the requirement of *legal certainty*.[493] It is striking that the justification for restricting rights under the Canadian Charter of Rights and the New Zealand Bill of Rights Act also requires public authorities to prove that the restriction is 'prescribed by law' (even though the relevant provisions are very differently framed from the European Convention).

(b) The Convention approach

6.128 In *Sunday Times v United Kingdom*[494] the Court took the view that, despite the differences in language between the relevant Articles, the various phrases such as 'prescribed by law' or 'in accordance with law' should be interpreted in the same way. In fact, the French text of the Convention uses the phrase 'prevue par la loi' both for 'prescribed by law' and 'in accordance with the law'.

6.129 In a trilogy of cases, *Sunday Times v United Kingdom*,[495] *Silver v United*

---

[488] See para 6.90ff above.

[489] See para 12.125ff below.

[490] See para 14.56 below.

[491] See para 15.186ff below.

[492] See paras 16.59 and 16.79 below respectively.

[492a] [1979] Ch 344; cf the approach taken by Laws J in *R v Somerset County Council, ex p Fewings* [1995] 1 All ER 513 where he observed that the rule of law that applied to private and public persons were wholly different: whereas a private person can do whatever he likes unless the law prohibits it, a public body has no rights and any action it takes must be justified by positive law.

[493] See, in particular, *de Freitas v Permanent Secretary of Ministry of Agriculture, Fisheries, Lands and Housing* [1998] 3 WLR 675, 681 *per* Lord Clyde: see para 6.142 below.

[494] (1979) 2 EHRR 245 para 48; see also *Silver v United Kingdom* (1983) 5 EHRR 347 para 85.

[495] (1979) 2 EHRR 245.

Kingdom[496] and *Malone v United Kingdom*,[497] the Court has ruled that the phrase 'prescribed by law' and/or 'in accordance with the law' creates three requirements:

- the interference in question must have some basis in domestic law;
- the law must be adequately accessible; and
- the law must be formulated so that it is sufficiently foreseeable.

The basis in domestic law. The first requirement is that the restriction in question must have *some* basis in domestic law.[498] The role of the Court in reviewing domestic law is therefore relatively limited.[499] To be 'prescribed by law' refers to national law[500] (which includes statute law,[501] other non-statutory regulations[502] and common law);[503] the Court has always understood the term 'law' in its substantive rather than its formal sense.[504] The concept of 'prescribed by law' does not, however, merely refer back to domestic law; it refers to the *quality* of the law, requiring it to be compatible with the rule of law, a principle which is expressly mentioned in the preamble to the Convention.[505] Because the inquiry of the court is limited to establishing whether measures are rooted in national law, the Court has said on several occasions that its role is not to interpret and apply domestic law: this question is primarily the task of the national courts.[506] **6.130**

'Prescribed by law' implies that the interfering measures must be accompanied by adequate and effective safeguards in the domestic law to protect against arbitrary **6.131**

[496] (1983) 5 EHRR 347.

[497] (1984) 7 EHRR 14.

[498] *Leander v Sweden* (1987) 9 EHRR 433 para 50; *Chappell v United Kingdom* (1989) 12 EHRR 1 para 52; *Andersson v Sweden* (1992) 14 EHRR 615; *A v France* (1993) 17 EHRR 462 para 38; *Murray v United Kingdom* (1994) 19 EHRR 193 para 88.

[499] *Eriksson v Sweden* (1989) 12 EHRR 183 para 62.

[500] *Campbell v United Kingdom* (1992) 15 EHRR 137 para 37.

[501] See *Norris v Ireland* (1988) 13 EHRR 186 para 40: the interference was plainly 'in accordance with the law' since it arose from the very existence of the impugned legislation.

[502] *De Wilde, Ooms and Versyp v Belgium* (1971) 1 EHRR 373 para 93; *Golder v United Kingdom* (1975) 1 EHRR 524 para 45 (involving Prison Rules 1964).

[503] See: *Dudgeon v United Kingdom* (1981) 4 EHRR 149 para 44; *Kruslin v France* (1990) 12 EHRR 547 para 29; *Huvig v France* (1990) 12 EHRR 528 para 28; *Herczegfalvy v Austria* (1992) 15 EHRR 437 para 91: the provisions in question did not offer the minimum degree of protection against arbitrariness required by the rule of law and there was no case-law to remedy the situation; *Murray v United Kingdom* (1994) 19 EHRR 193: the taking and retention of a photograph of the applicant without her consent had no statutory basis but were lawful under the common law.

[504] *Kruslin v France* (1990) 12 EHRR 547 para 29; *Huvig v France* (1990) 12 EHRR 528 para 28.

[505] *Malone v United Kingdom* (1984) 7 EHRR 14 para 67; *Silver v United Kingdom* (1983) 5 EHRR 347 para 90; *Golder v United Kingdom* (1975) 1 EHRR 524 para 34.

[506] *Olsson v Sweden (No 2)* (1992) 17 EHRR 134 para 79; *Andersson v Sweden* (1992) 14 EHRR 615 para 82; *Kruslin v France* (1990) 12 EHRR 547 para 29; *Eriksson v Sweden* (1989) 12 EHRR 183 para 62; *Chappell v United Kingdom* (1989) 12 EHRR 1 para 54; *Campbell v United Kingdom* (1992) 15 EHRR 137 para 37: it is not for the Court to examine the validity of secondary legislation.

interferences by authorities with the rights guaranteed by Article 1.[507] For example, the failure of domestic law to provide *any* regulation of interceptions of telephone calls outside the public network (where the applicant complained about telephoning tapping at her workplace) led the Court to hold that the interference was not 'prescribed by law' in *Halford v United Kingdom.*[508]

6.132 **Accessibility.** The accessibility requirement was described in *Sunday Times v United Kingdom*[509] in the following terms:

> the law must be adequately accessible: the citizen must have an indication which is adequate in the circumstances of the legal rules which are applicable to the given case.

The Court therefore ruled in *Silver v United Kingdom*[510] that certain prison rules restricting the right of prisoners to correspondence failed to meet the obligation of accessibility because the relevant internal orders and instructions were not published or otherwise made known to prisoners.

6.133 **Foreseeability.** The third requirement, of 'foreseeability', has raised the most difficult issues. In *Sunday Times v United Kingdom*[511] it was said that:

> a norm cannot be regarded as the law unless it is formulated with sufficient precision to enable the citizen to regulate his conduct: he must be able—if need be with appropriate advice—to foresee, to a degree that is reasonable in the circumstances, the consequences which a given action will entail. These consequences need not be foreseeable with absolute certainty: experience shows that is unattainable. Again, while certainty is highly desirable, it may bring in its train excessive rigidity and the law must be able to keep pace with changing circumstances. Accordingly, many laws are inevitably couched in terms which to a greater or lesser extent, are vague and whose interpretation and application are questions of practice.

Nevertheless, in *Silver v United Kingdom*[512] the Court emphasised that 'a law which confers a discretion must indicate the scope of that discretion'. In deciding whether this criterion of foreseeability has been met, the court must take into account that absolute precision is unattainable and that, in order to avoid excessive

[507] *Malone v United Kingdom* (1984) 7 EHRR 14 para 67; *Herczegfalvy v Austria* (1992) 15 EHRR 437 para 91; *Rieme v Sweden* (1992) 16 EHRR 155 para 60: although a basis in Swedish law was undisputed, the applicant argued (unsuccessfully) that the law in question did not afford him adequate protection against arbitrary interference; *Chappell v United Kingdom* (1989) 12 EHRR 1, para 56 discusses *Anton Piller* orders in UK law and their associated dangers which necessitate accompanying provisions safeguarding against arbitrary interference and abuse; see also *Eriksson v Sweden* (1989) 12 EHRR 183 para 60 and *Olsson v Sweden (No 1)* (1988) 11 EHRR 259 para 62, which discuss safeguards in relation to taking children into public care: 'preparatory work' providing guidance as to the exercise of the discretion conferred, and administrative review at several levels.

[508] (1997) 24 EHRR 523 paras 51, 52.

[509] (1979) 2 EHRR 245 para 49.

[510] (1983) 5 EHRR 347.

[511] n 509 above; see also *Wingrove v United Kingdom* (1996) 24 EHRR 1 para 40.

[512] (1983) 5 EHRR 347 para 33.

rigidity and to keep pace with changing circumstances, many laws will inevitably be couched in terms which are to some extent vague.[513] The degree of precision required of the 'law' will depend upon the particular subject matter[514] as well as the content of the instrument concerned, the field it was designed to cover and the number and status of those to whom it is addressed.[515] Although the scope of the discretion must be indicated in the law, it is not necessary that the detailed procedures and conditions to be observed in its implementation be contained in rules of substantive law. Thus, the administrative directives concerning prisoners' correspondence in *Silver v United Kingdom*[516] did not have the force of law; but nonetheless satisfied the requirement of foreseeability since the directives constituted an established practice that was to be followed save in exceptional circumstances, rather than one that varied with each individual case.

In applying the 'foreseeability' principle, the Court has tended to interpret the requirement generously. In *Sunday Times v United Kingdom (No 1)*[517] the Court addressed the inherent unpredictability of the development of common law principles[518] and concluded that it was sufficient if there was some *adequate* indication that in the circumstances a particular common law development was foreseeable. The common law must therefore be sufficiently clear and unambiguous to enable a citizen to know the precise extent of his legal entitlement without the necessity of extrapolation.[519] The Court again stressed in *Goodwin v United Kingdom*[520] that a certain degree of flexibility may be desirable to enable the national courts to develop the law in the light of their assessment of what measures are necessary in the interests of justice. A similar approach was taken in *Olssen v Sweden (No 1)*[521] where the Court ruled that legislation about taking children into care could be framed in very broad terms while nevertheless being 'prescribed by law'. **6.134**

513 *Silver v United Kingdom* (1983) 5 EHRR 347 para 88; *Olsson v Sweden (No 1)* (1988) 11 EHRR 259; see also *Sunday Times v United Kingdom (No 1)* (1979) 2 EHRR 245 para 49.

514 *Sunday Times v United Kingdom* (n 513 above) para 49; *Malone v United Kingdom* (1984) 7 EHRR 14 para 67.

515 *Chorherr v Austria* (1993) 17 EHRR 358 paras 35, 36; *Vereinigung Demokratischer Soldaten Österreichs and Gubi v Austria* (1994) 20 EHRR 55 paras 15, 16.

516 (1983) 5 EHRR 347 para 33.

517 (1979) 2 EHRR 245; but see *Harman v United Kingdom* (1984) 38 DR 53, EComm HR where the Commission declared admissible a complaint that the English courts had created a new category of contempt in *Harman v Secretary of State for the Home Department* [1983] 1 AC 280; however, the application was then settled.

518 Whereas in *A-G v Times Newspapers* [1973] QB 710 the Divisional Court applied the principle that a deliberate attempt to influence the settlement of pending proceedings by bringing public pressure to bear on a party amounted to a contempt of court, the House of Lords seemed to prefer the view that it is a contempt to publish material which prejudges pending litigation: see [1974] AC 273.

519 *Huvig v France* (1990) 12 EHRR 528.

520 (1996) 22 EHRR 123 para 33.

521 (1988) 11 EHRR 259 para 61; see also *Eriksson v Sweden* (1989) 12 EHRR 183 paras 59, 60.

6.135 More recently, in *Vogt v Germany*[522] the Court rejected the applicant's case commenting on a divergence of view on the law between the Administrative Court and the Federal Labour Court by holding:

> the mere fact that a legal provision is capable of more than one construction does not mean that it does not meet the requirement implied in the notion of 'prescribed by law'.

In *Steel v United Kingdom*[523] the Court took the view that the English law on the concept of breach of the peace provided sufficient guidance and was formulated with sufficient precision despite the notorious difficulties in the case law in defining the offence.[524] By contrast, in *Hashman and Harrup v United Kingdom*[524a] the Court took the view that a bind over to be of good behaviour[524b] was too imprecise to be 'prescribed by law'.

6.136 However, where it is dealing with secret measures (such as secret surveillance), the Court has held that the law itself must indicate the scope of discretion with sufficient clarity.[525] The Convention requirement of foreseeability in relation to laws authorising interception of communications for the purposes of police investigation cannot be exactly the same as it is in relation to a law that seeks to restrict the conduct of individuals. Obviously it cannot require that the applicant have advance warning of the surveillance: it is enough that he know whether he might be subject to telephone monitoring. Even so, the right to respect for private life in Article 8[526] requires that the law must be sufficiently clear in its terms to

> give citizens an adequate indication as to the circumstances in which and the conditions on which public authorities are empowered to resort to this secret and potentially dangerous interference with the right to respect for private life and correspondence.[527]

There must be detailed provisions dealing with matters such as: the parties that are subject to surveillance; the period for which a telephone-tap may remain in place; the purposes for which the information obtained might be used; the period for which tapes will be retained and any rights of access by the applicant.[528]

---

[522] (1995) 21 EHRR 205 para 48.
[523] (1998) 28 EHRR 603.
[524] Ibid paras 25–28 and 55.
[524a] Judgment of 25 Nov 1999 paras 29–41.
[524b] The obligation of behaviour not being *contra bonos mores* has been described as 'conduct which has the property of being wrong rather than right in the judgment of the majority of contemporary fellow citizens': *per* Glidewell LJ in *Hughes v Holley* (1988) 86 Crim App R 130.
[525] See eg *Leander v Sweden* (1987) 9 EHRR 433; *Kruslin v France* (1990) 12 EHRR 547; *Huvig v France* (1990) 12 EHRR 528.
[526] For a discussion of the requirements of proving that an interference is 'prescribed by law' for the purposes of secret surveillance, see para 12.128ff below.
[527] *Malone v United Kingdom* (1984) 7 EHRR 14 para 67.
[528] *Kruslin v France* (1990) 12 EHRR 547 para 17.

Thus, in *Malone v United Kingdom*[529] the Court decided that the law in relation to telephone-tapping was not sufficiently foreseeable because: 6.137

> on the evidence before the Court it cannot be said with any reasonable certainty what elements of the powers to intercept are incorporated into legal rules and what elements remain within the discretion of the executive. In view of the attendant obscurity and uncertainty as to the state of the law in this essential respect, . . . [the Court concluded] that the law of England and Wales does not indicate with reasonable clarity the scope and manner of exercise of the relevant discretion conferred on public authorities.

In *Hewitt and Harman v United Kingdom*[530] it was also held that an unpublished non-statutory directive from a Department of State (which was not legally binding) was incapable of satisfying the requirements of accessibility or precision.

In *Kruslin v France*[531] the Court held that a legal requirement that 'the investigating judge shall, in accordance with the law, take all investigative measures which he deems useful for establishing the truth',[532] and case law indicating that such measures included telephone-tapping did not provide sufficient safeguards against abuse of the power to render it 'in accordance with law' under Article 8. The law of telephone-tapping in Luxembourg, on the other hand, exhibited the necessary detail and provision for control of the use of the discretion so as to be 'in accordance with law'.[533] 6.138

(c) The Canadian approach

The rights and freedoms of the Canadian Charter of Rights are subject to the limitations created by section 1 which states: 6.139

> The Canadian Charter of Rights and Freedoms guarantees the rights and freedoms set out in it subject only to such reasonable limits prescribed by law as can be demonstrably justified in a free and democratic society.

The phrase 'prescribed by law' in section 1 has not yet been examined in detail by the Canadian Supreme Court. However, the Canadian decisions are consistent with the requirement that the law must be (i) accessible and (ii) foreseeable. Thus, in *R v Thomsen*[534] Le Dain J when giving the judgment of the Supreme Court said:

> The limit will be prescribed by law within the meaning of section 1 if it is expressly provided for by statute or regulation, or results by necessary implication from the

[529] (1984) 7 EHRR 14 para 36.
[530] (1991) 14 EHRR 657.
[531] (1990) 12 EHRR 547.
[532] Code of Criminal Procedure, Art 81.
[533] *Mersch v Luxembourg* (1985) 43 DR 34, 94, 114 EComm HR; the Commission acknowledged the presence of the ultimate safeguard: the Convention was directly applicable in Luxembourg law.
[534] [1988] 1 SCR 613, 645.

terms of a statute or regulation or from its operating requirements. The limit may also result from the application of a common law rule.

6.140 A law which confers a discretion will not be 'prescribed by law' if the discretion is not constrained by legal standards. In *Ontario Film and Video Appreciation Society v Ontario Board of Censors*[535] the Ontario Court of Appeal decided that a statute authorising film censorship failed to comply with section 1 of the Charter of Rights and Freedoms because the censor board was given an unfettered discretion to ban or cut films for public exhibition. Although the censor board had developed its own criteria which were publicly available, the Court of Appeal nevertheless held that the criteria were not sufficient because they were not binding on the board. On the other hand, the Supreme Court has on several occasions taken the view that random stops are 'prescribed by law' where the police are exercising powers which give unfettered discretion to stop vehicles[536] or individuals on the street.[537] In *Slaight Communications v Davidson*[537a] Lamer CJ distinguished between two types of discretion: a statute which expressly or by necessary implication authorises a decision which breaches Charter rights (such as the *Ontario Film* and stop and search cases) and a discretion where the language was broad enough to encompass a violation of the Charter but it did not expressly or impliedly authorise such an infringement. In this second class of case it is the decision and not the statute which must satisfy the requirement of being prescribed by law. Thus, in *Eldridge v British Columbia*[537b] the Supreme Court held that a discretionary decision to deny sign language interpretation to deaf people using medical services was unlawful. In *Irwin Toy v Quebec (A-G)*[538] the Supreme Court considered a challenge to provincial legislation prohibiting commercial advertisements directed at individuals who were under 13. The legislation in question identified three specific factors which would be considered in determining whether the advertisements were directed at those under 13, but the scope of the advertisements which were prohibited remained very uncertain. The Supreme Court held that it was not practicable to seek 'absolute precision' in a statute and that it would only fail to be 'prescribed by law' under section 1 'where there is no intelligible standard and where the legislation has given a plenary discretion to whatever seems best in a wide set of circumstances'.[539]

(d) The New Zealand approach

6.141 Under the New Zealand Bill of Rights it may be lawful to restrict the rights set out in the Bill. Section 5 states that:

---

[535] (1984) 45 OR (2d) 80.
[536] *R v Hufsky* [1988] 1 SCR 621.
[537] *R v Ladouceur* [1990] 1 SCR 1257.
[537a] [1989] SCR 1038, 1077, 1080.
[537b] [1997] 3 SCR 624.
[538] [1989] 1 SCR 927.
[539] Ibid 983.

> the rights and freedoms contained in this Bill of Rights may be subject only to such reasonable limits prescribed by law as can be demonstrably justified in a free and democratic society.

The requirement of 'prescribed by law' has not been closely studied in any New Zealand decisions. However, in the leading case of *Ministry of Transport v Noort*[540] the Court of Appeal appeared to take the view that the phrase should be interpreted in the same way as it has been under the Convention and in Canada.[541]

(3) 'Prescribed by law' under the Human Rights Act

Since the phrase has been interpreted in several jurisdictions in virtually the same terms, it is submitted that the courts are likely to follow the Convention principles when interpreting 'prescribed by law' and 'in accordance with law'. Furthermore, the Privy Council recently considered the scope of this obligation in *de Freitas v Permanent Secretary of Ministry of Agriculture, Fisheries, Lands and Housing*,[542] and applied Convention principles. A civil servant was deprived of his constitutional right to freedom of assembly and expression because of a statutory provision which prohibited him from publishing or broadcasting any information or expressions of opinion on matters of national or international controversy. The Court of Appeal had implied a limitation on the statutory provision by restricting it to such constraints as were reasonably required for the better performance of his duties. Lord Clyde[543] said that the implied limitation failed: **6.142**

> One principle which has to be observed is that of legal certainty. This was succinctly expressed in *G v Germany*[544] where it was stated that 'legal provisions which interfere with individual rights must be . . . formulated with sufficient precision to enable the citizen to regulate his conduct'. The critical question then is whether the prohibition in [the statutory provision] as qualified by the Court of Appeal produces a rule sufficiently precise to enable any given civil servant to regulate his conduct.
>
> The rule applies to all civil servants without distinction so that it is left to the individual in any given situation to decide whether he is or is not complying with the rule. Their Lordships are not persuaded that the guidance given is sufficiently precise to secure the validity of the provision. It is to be noticed that the provision is fenced around with a possible criminal sanction . . . and it is necessary that in that context a degree of precision is required so that the individual will be able to know with some confidence where the boundaries of legality lie. It cannot be that all expressions critical of the conduct of a politician are forbidden. It is a fundamental principle of a democratic society that citizens should be entitled to express their

540 [1992] 3 NZLR 260.

541 Ibid *per* Cooke P at 272; *per* Richardson J at 283 (with whom McKay J concurred); and *per* Gault J at 295.

542 [1998] 3 WLR 675.

543 Ibid 681.

544 (1989) 60 DR 256, 261, EComm HR.

opinions about politicians, and while there may be legitimate restraints upon their freedom in the case of some civil servants, that restraint cannot be made absolute and universal. But where the line is to be drawn is a matter which cannot in fairness be left to the hazard of individual decision. Even under the formulation of the Court of Appeal the civil servant is left with no clear guidance as to the exercise of his constitutional rights.

6.143 A public authority[545] will therefore succeed in demonstrating that it has acted in a manner which is 'prescribed by the law' or 'in accordance with the law' under the Human Rights Act if it can show *all* of the following:

- that the interference in question has some basis in domestic law;
- that the law is adequately accessible; and
- that the law is formulated so that its requirements are sufficiently foreseeable.

The relevant Convention case law has been discussed above.[546]

(4) Legitimate aims

6.144 The Articles of the Convention which confer 'qualified rights' each list the 'legitimate aims' for the promotion of which the state may interfere with the rights. The state must be acting:

- in the interest of national security;[547]
- in the interest of public safety;[548]
- in the interest of the economic well being of the country;[549]
- to prevent disorder or crime;[550]
- to protect health or morals;[551]
- to protect the rights and freedoms of others;[552]
- to protect public order;[553]
- to protect territorial integrity;[554]
- to protect the reputation or rights of others;[555]
- to prevent the disclosure of information received in confidence;[556]
- to maintain the authority and impartiality of the judiciary.[557]

545 See generally, para 5.03ff above.
546 See para 6.128ff above.
547 Art 8(2), Art 10(2), Art 11(2).
548 Art 8(2); Art 9(2), Art 10(2), Art 11(2).
549 Art 8(2).
550 Art 8(2), Art 10(2), Art 11(2).
551 Art 8(2), Art 9(2), Art 10(2), Art 11(2).
552 Art 8(2), Art 9(2), Art 11(2).
553 Art 9(2).
554 Art 10(2).
555 Art 10(2).
556 Art 10(2).
557 Art 10(2).

In accordance with general principles of Convention interpretation these aims should be narrowly interpreted.[558] However, the 'legitimate aims' are expressed in broad terms and the state is usually able to establish that an interference was for a proper purpose.[558a] **6.145**

(5) 'Necessary in a democratic society'

The most complex issue raised by qualified rights is whether or not an interference is 'necessary in a democratic society'. The meaning of 'necessary' was extensively analysed in *Handyside v United Kingdom*[559] where the Court had to consider whether the forfeiture of the *Little Red Schoolbook* on obscenity grounds[559a] breached Article 10(2) of the Convention. It was held that: **6.146**

> whilst the adjective 'necessary' within the meaning of Article 10(2) is not synonymous with 'indispensable' (cf in Article 2(2) and 6(1), the words 'absolutely necessary' and 'strictly necessary' and in Article 15(1), the phrase 'to the extent strictly required by the exigencies of the situation'), neither has it the flexibility of such expressions as 'admissible', 'ordinary' (cf Article 4(3)), 'useful' (cf the French text of the first paragraph of Article 1 of Protocol 1), 'reasonable' (cf Articles 5(3) and 6(1)) or desirable. Nevertheless, it is for the national authorities to make the initial assessment of the reality of the pressing social need implied by the notion of 'necessity' in this context.

Furthermore, as already discussed[559b] it may also be essential to examine what is meant by the interests of 'democracy' in order to justify an interference with qualified rights.

The most important test to be applied in assessing whether an interference is necessary is the principle of proportionality.[560] The Commission and the Court have developed the doctrine as the *means* of assessing whether a particular measure can be justified as being 'necessary in a democratic society'. The Court applies a 'three fold test':[561] **6.147**

- did the interference complained of correspond to a 'pressing social need';
- was it 'proportionate to the legitimate aim pursued'; and
- were the reasons given by the national authority to justify it 'relevant and sufficient'?

[558] See para 6.30 above.
[558a] See D Harris, M O'Boyle and C Warbrick, *Law of the European Convention on Human Rights* (Butterworths, 1995) 290.
[559] (1976) 1 EHRR 737 paras 47, 48.
[559a] Following a conviction under the Obscene Publications Act 1964: see para 15.81.
[559b] See para 6.124ff above.
[560] See para 6.43ff above.
[561] See *Sunday Times v United Kingdom (No 1)* (1979) 2 EHRR 245 para 62, for a full discussion, see para 6.43ff above.

The elements of the proportionality principle under the Human Rights Act are likely to be refinements of the Convention standards. We earlier examined how the doctrine has been formulated in general administrative law, European Community law and in Canada, New Zealand and South Africa;[561a] and it is possible to discern a number of common features. The English courts will also obtain assistance by examining the authorities under section 10 of the Contempt of Court Act 1981 which permits disclosure of journalistic sources where it is 'necessary':

- in the interests of justice;
- in the interests of national security;
- for the prevention of disorder; or
- for the prvention of crime.[561b]

In this context it has been held that the word 'necessary' has a meaning somewhere between 'indispensable' and 'useful' or expedient, the nearest paraphrase being 'really needed'.[561c]

6.147A It is submitted that a public authority seeking to show that an interference is 'necessary in a democratic society' will have to satisfy the *four* conditions identified in paragraph 6.75 above.

H. 'Waiver' of Convention Rights

(1) Introduction

6.148 An important issue under the Convention is the extent to which it is possible to 'waive' Convention rights. The issue of 'waiver' can arise in a number of different areas but is of particular importance in two contexts. First, arguments can arise about whether an applicant has waived his fair trial rights under Article 6.[562] Secondly, public authorities may seek to persuade employees to contract out of Convention rights such as the right to freedom of expression or privacy. These issues have been addressed in Convention case law as well as in other jurisdictions.

(2) The Convention case law

6.149 It is well established that Convention rights can be waived.[563] However, the waiver

[561a] See para 6.54ff above for general administrative law, para 6.56ff above for European Union law, para 6.62ff above for Canadian law, para 6.68ff above for New Zealand law and para 6.70 above for South African law.
[561b] See para 15.74 below.
[561c] *In re An inquiry under the Company Securities (Insider Dealing) Act 1985* [1988] AC 660, 704.
[562] See generally, Chap 11.
[563] For a general discussion, see R Lawson and H Schermers (eds), *Leading Cases of the European Court of Human Rights* (Ars Aequi Libri, 1997) 637–638.

of a Convention right is only effective if it is established in an unequivocal manner[564] and is attended by the minimum safeguards commensurate with its importance.[565] Thus, in *Deweer v Belgium*[566] a butcher, who had breached price regulations, was subject to an order which provisionally closed his shop; he was then offered a friendly settlement by paying a modest fine. He complained that he had been deprived of his right of access to the court under Article 6,[567] and the Court had to consider whether a settlement waived the right of access to the court. It expressed the view that:[568]

> In the Contracting States' domestic legal system a waiver of this kind is frequently encountered in both civil matters, notably in the shape of arbitration clauses in contracts, and in criminal matters, in the shape inter alia, of fines paid by way of composition. The waiver, which has undeniable advantages for the individual concerned as well as for the administration of justice, does not in principle offend against the Convention . . . Nevertheless, in a democratic society too great an importance attaches to the 'right to a court' . . . for its benefit to be forfeited solely by reason of the fact that an individual is party to a settlement reached in the course of a procedure ancillary to court proceedings. In an area concerned with the public order of the member states of the Council of Europe, any measure or decision alleged to be in breach of Article 6 calls for a particularly careful review[569]. . . At least the same degree of vigilance would appear to be indispensable when someone formerly 'charged with a criminal offence' challenges a settlement that has barred criminal proceedings. Absence of constraint is in all events one of the conditions to be satisfied; this much is dictated by an international instrument founded on freedom and the rule of law.[570]

The Court went on to decide that the settlement reached was tainted by constraint on the basis that he was threatened with the closure of his shop.[571] Where a settlement is alleged, the Court has said that a thorough analysis is required in determining whether a friendly settlement has been reached.[572] Thus, a written

[564] See eg *Neumeister v Austria (No 2)* (1974) 1 EHRR 136 para 36; *Le Compte, Van Leuven and De Meyere v Belgium* (1981) 4 EHRR 1 para 43; *Albert and Le Compte v Belgium* (1983) 5 EHHR 533 para 35; *Colozza v Italy* (1985) 7 EHRR 516 para 28; *Barberà Messegué and Jabardo v Spain* (1988) 11 EHRR 360 para 82; *Håkansson and Sturesson v Sweden* (1990) 13 EHRR 1 para 67; *Oberschlick v Austria (No 1)* (1991) 19 EHRR 389 para 51; *Schuler-Zgraggen v Switzerland* (1993) 16 EHRR 405 para 58; *Zumtobel v Austria* (1993) 17 EHRR 116 para 34; *Pauger v Austria* (1997) 25 EHRR 105 para 60.

[565] See eg *Pfeifer and Plankl v Austria* (1992) 14 EHRR 692 para 37; *Imbrioscia v Switzerland* (1993) 17 EHRR 441 para 31.

[566] (1980) 2 EHRR 439.

[567] See generally, para 11.185ff below.

[568] n 566 above para 49.

[569] See, for Art 5(5) the *Vagrancy* cases (1978) 1 EHRR 373 para 65.

[570] *Golder v United Kingdom* (1975) 1 EHRR 524 para 34.

[571] See also eg *Luedicke Belkacem & Koç v Germany* (1978) 2 EHRR 149 para 36.

[572] See *Pailot v France RJD* 1998–II 787 paras 49–53; *Richard v France RJD* 1998–II 809 paras 46–50.

agreement in and of itself is not sufficient to prove that an individual has waived Convention rights; the issue is determined by examining the surrounding circumstances in which the agreement was made.

6.150 In *Vereinigung Rechtswinkels Utrecht v Netherlands*[573] an agency established in a prison with the agreement of its director to advise on prisoners' rights complained that its right to freedom of expression had been breached. At the request of prisoners, the agency had published a press statement blaming a prisoner's suicide on the prison authorities. The prison director then terminated the agreement. The Commission rejected the application on the ground that the termination of the agreement did not hinder the agency from expressing its opinions to the press any further than the applicant had accepted in entering the agreement in the first place. It is submitted that this decision was incorrect and should not be followed. First, the Commission failed to take account of the Convention principle that Convention guaranteed rights should not be theoretical or illusionary but practical and effective.[573a] Secondly, the Commission's approach cannot be reconciled with its decision in *Rommelfanger*.

6.151 In *Rommelfanger v Germany*[574] the Commission decided that the contractual relationship between employer and employee is not sufficient of itself to result in a waiver of Convention rights. A doctor at a Catholic hospital was dismissed after writing a letter about abortion which was published in the weekly magazine, 'Stern'. His contract of employment contained a clause imposing duties of loyalty towards the Catholic church. The Commission rejected the argument that the doctor had waived his right to freedom of expression *as such* by assuming certain duties of loyalty although, in principle, individuals could freely make such an agreement.

6.152 In fact, most of the Convention cases which have addressed the issue of waiver have concerned fair trial rights under Article 6 and, in particular, the right to a public hearing.[575] Although the public character of a court hearing is a fundamental principle under Article 6(1), neither the letter nor the spirit of the provision prevents a person waiving of his own free will (whether expressly or by implication) the right to have his case heard in public.[576] In particular, the Court suggested in *Schuler-Zgraggen v Switzerland*[577] that where a dispute raised no issues of public importance and considered only highly technical and private

---

[573] (1986) 46 DR 200, EComm HR.
[573a] See para 6.28ff above.
[574] (1989) 62 DR 151.
[575] The rights guaranteed by Art 6(1) are summarised at para 11.183 below.
[576] See eg *Le Compte, Van Leuven and De Meyere v Belgium* (1981) 4 EHRR 1 para 59; *H v Belgium* (1987) 10 EHRR 339 para 54.
[577] (1993) 16 EHRR 405 para 58.

questions of a medical nature, the failure to hold a public hearing (following a failure by the applicant to request one) did not violate Article 6(1). The breach of the right to a public hearing cannot be cured if the court which subsequently hears the case is not permitted to deal with the merits of the case.[578]

Furthermore, as the Court emphasised in *Håkansson and Sturesson v Sweden*,[579] a waiver must be made in an unequivocal manner and must not run counter to any important public interest. A failure to request a public hearing where the court has a power to grant one is an unequivocal waiver.[580] However, if, in practice, there never are any public hearings in the proceedings in question, the applicant cannot be faulted for failing to make an application which had no prospect of success.[581] **6.153**

In *Bulut v Austria*[582] the applicant lawyer expressly waived the right to challenge the impartiality of the investigating judge at a preliminary hearing; and the domestic court decided that such a waiver could lawfully be made. The Court took the view that it had no reason to question the resolution of the issue by the domestic court;[583] and went on to hold that the applicant was not entitled to complain that he had legitimate reasons to doubt the impartiality of the judiciary under Article 6(1)[584] where he had failed to make a challenge before the domestic court. **6.154**

(3) Waiver in other jurisdictions

The courts in other common law jurisdictions have adopted different approaches to the question of waiver of constitutional rights. The US Supreme Court has held that the accused may waive the right to trial by jury.[585] In *Adams v United States, ex rel McCann*[586] Frankfurter J said that to deny an accused in the exercise of his free choice the right to dispense with some of the safeguards provided by the Constitution: **6.155**

> and to base such denial on an arbitrary rule that a man cannot choose to conduct his defense before a judge rather than a jury unless, against his will, he has a lawyer to advise him, although he reasonably deems himself the best advisor for his own needs, is to imprison a man in his privileges and call it the Constitution.

---

578 See eg *Le Compte, Van Leuven and De Meyere* (n 576 above).
579 (1990) 13 EHRR 1 para 66.
580 Ibid para 67; *Schuler-Zgraggen v Switzerland* (1993) 16 EHRR 405 para 58; *Zumtobel v Austria* (1993) 17 EHRR 116 para 34; *Pauger v Austria* (1997) 25 EHRR 105 para 60.
581 *Werner v Austria* (1997) 26 EHRR 310 para 48.
582 (1996) 24 EHRR 84.
583 Ibid para 29.
584 See generally, para 11.226ff below.
585 See *Patton v United States* (1930) 281 US 276.
586 (1942) 317 US 269; see also *Singer v United States* (1965) 380 US 24 and *Brookhart v Janis* (1966) 384 US 1.

It has been held that the right to counsel,[587] the privilege against self-incrimination,[588] the protection against double jeopardy[589] and the benefits of the prohibition against unreasonable search and seizure[590] can all be waived.

6.155A On the other hand, the US Supreme Court has consistently held that a person taking up public employment cannot be required to surrender constitutional rights such as the right to freedom of expression.[590a] Thus, the Supreme Court has decided that it is unconstitutional to make appointments to the civil service on condition that no political statements may be made or that the political policies of the government will be supported.[590b] It has also been held to be unconstitutional to award unemployment benefit on the condition that the recipient must work on his religious holidays.[590c]

6.156 The Canadian approach to due process rights has been similar to the US Supreme Court. The general principles used by the Supreme Court were described by Sopinka J in *R v Morin*[591] as follows:

> This Court has clearly stated that in order for an accused to waive his or her rights under s 11(b) [the right to a speedy trial], such waiver must be clear and unequivocal, with full knowledge of the rights the procedure is enacted to protect and of the effect that waiver will have on those rights (*Kopornay v Attorney-General*;[592] see also *Clarkson v Queen*;[593] *Askoy v Queen*).[594] Waiver can be explicit or implicit. If the waiver is said to be implicit, the conduct of the accused must comply with the stringent test for waiver set out above. As Cory J described it in *Askoy*:[595]
>
> > . . . there must be something in the conduct of the accused that is sufficient to give rise to an inference that the accused has understood that he or she had a s 11(b) guarantee, understood its nature and has waived the right provided by that guarantee.
>
> Waiver requires advertence to the release rather than mere inadvertence. If the mind of the accused or his or her counsel is not turned to the issue of waiver and is not aware of what his or her conduct signifies, then this conduct does not constitute waiver . . . consent to a trial date can give rise to an inference of waiver. This will not be so if the consent to the date amounts to mere acquiescence to the inevitable.

---

[587] *Johnson v Zerbst* (1938) 304 US 458; *Bute v Illinois* (1948) 333 US 640.

[588] *Escobedo v Illinois* (1964) 378 US 478.

[589] *Haddad v United States* (1965) 349 F 2d 511.

[590] *Zap v United States* (1946) 328 US 624.

[590a] See *Keyishian v Board of Regents of University of the State of New York* (1967) 385 US 589; *Perry v Sindermann* (1972) 408 US 593.

[590b] *Elrod v Burns* (1976) 427 US 347; *Pickering v Board of Education* (1968) 391 US 563.

[590c] *Hobbie v Unemployment Appeals Commission* (1987) US 136; *Thomas v Review Board of the Industrial Unemployment Security Division* (1981) 450 US 707; *Sherbert v Verner* (1963) US 398.

[591] [1992] 1 SCR 771, 790.

[592] [1982] 1 SCR 41, 49.

[593] [1986] 1 SCR 383, 394, 396.

[594] [1990] 2 SCR 1199, 1228, 1229.

[595] Ibid 1228.

Waiver in this sense has also been applied to the right to counsel[596] and the right to a jury trial.[597] However, the threshold to be overcome in proving clear and unequivocal waiver with full knowledge of the consequences depends on the specific right; and a very high threshold applies to the right to be assisted by an interpreter.[598] In *McKinney v University of Guelph*[599] doubts were expressed as to whether the right to equality could be waived. The New Zealand Court of Appeal has also taken the same view. In *Police v Kohler*[599a] Cooke P stated that:

> a valid waiver requires a conscious choice that is both informed and voluntary and . . . a vaild waiver cannot be implied from silence . . . It is also entirely clear that a mere failure to request rights cannot of itself be a waiver.

In some jurisdictions the courts have been more reluctant to allow waiver. Thus, a majority of the High Court of Australia held that a constitutional provision requiring trial by jury cannot be waived by the accused.[600] Although the case turned on a point of statutory construction, Dawson J relied on a more general point: **6.157**

> the administration of criminal justice . . . is regarded in our system of law as being of public rather than private concern. Its standards are consistently maintained and are not relaxed, even with the consent of the parties or either of them, in an individual or particular case.[601]

The Supreme Court of India has held that there could be no waiver of the fundamental right to equality.[602] In *Tellis v Bombay Municipal Corp*[603] it was held that a person could not be deprived of fundamental rights by operation of the doctrine of estoppel. The Supreme Court went on to say: **6.158**

> Fundamental rights are undoubtedly conferred by the Constitution upon individuals which have to be asserted and enforced by them, if those rights are violated. But, the high purpose which the Constitution seeks to achieve by conferment of fundamental rights is not only to benefit individuals but to secure the larger interests of the community . . . No individual can barter away the freedoms conferred upon him by the Constitution.[604]

596 *R v Clarkson* [1986] 1 SCR 383, 394; *R v Smith* [1991] 1 SCR 714, 727.
597 *R v Lee* [1989] 1 SCR 1384, 1411.
598 *R v Tran* [1994] 2 SCR 951.
599 [1990] 3 SCR 229, 406 (*per* Wilson J, in dissent).
599a [1993] 3 NZLR 129, 133.
600 *Brown v The Queen* (1986) 160 CLR 171 (the minority took the view that the right could be waived by the accused as it was a 'privilege' rather than an absolute right).
601 Para 5, relying on a passage in *R v Bertrand* (1867) LR 1 PC 520, 534.
602 See *Basheshar Nath v Commissioner of Income Tax* [1959] 1 SCR 528 (two members were prepared to go further, adding that there could not be a waiver of any of the fundamental rights guaranteed by the Constitution).
603 (1987) LRC (Const) 351.
604 Ibid 366h–367b.

The point has not been definitively considered in South Africa but there are dicta in a number of cases expressing doubts as to whether constitutional rights can be waived.[605]

(4) Waiver under the Human Rights Act

6.159 The principle that an individual can waive rights is well established in English law. For example, an applicant may waive a breach of the rules of natural justice made by an administrative decision-maker.[606]

6.160 It is submitted that the doctrine of waiver will also be applied to the Human Rights Act. Thus, in *Clancy v Caird*[606a] the Court of Session (Inner House) in Scotland decided that the failure of the claimant to protest at a temporary judge hearing his case waived any right he had afterwards to complain that the appointment breached Article 6.[606b] However, the doctrine may be limited to Convention rights which are 'personal rights and privileges'; so it will be necessary to examine each Convention right *separately* to determine whether its central focus is a personal privilege belonging to an individual such as fair trial rights or whether the provision is aimed at the general benefit of the public (so that public policy would prevent a private individual from waiving the right in question).[607]

6.161 Furthermore, before a public authority can establish waiver, it is likely that a number of conditions will have to be satisfied. The waiver will have to be:

- 'clear and unequivocal';
- made in the absence of constraint;
- made in 'full knowledge' of the nature and extent of the right.

In other words, it is a necessary (but *not* sufficient) condition in order to establish contracting out of a Convention right for a public authority to prove that the claimant unequivocally chose to waive his right.

6.162 The possibility of waiving the right to a public hearing by creating an administrative practice which places the onus on the applicant to request a public hearing has wide implications for public authorities exercising regulatory functions. Such a waiver may not, however, be established in the case of unrepresented applicants who have not expressly indicated their agreement to a private hearing.

---

[605] See *S v Shaba* 1998 (2) BCLR 220; *ABBM Printing and Publishing (Pty) Ltd v Transnet Ltd* 1997 (10) BCLR 1429, 1437.

[606] See eg *R v Comptroller-General of Patents and Designs, ex p Parke Davies and Company* [1953] 1 All ER 862; *R v British Broadcasting Corporation, ex p Lavelle* [1983] 1 WLR 23, 39.

[606a] *The Times*, 9 May 2000.

[606b] See generally, para 11.309ff below.

[607] *McKinney v University of Guelph* [1990] 3 SCR 229, 406; *Brown v The Queen* (1986) 160 CLR 171.

It is also likely that public authorities as employers will seek to persuade their employees to contract out of their Convention rights (such as privacy rights). Such a waiver will not be effective unless the employee is expressly made aware of the relevant provision and of the extent of his rights before agreeing to it. Furthermore, where a public authority employer effectively forces the workforce to contract out of Convention rights (such as by dismissing and then re-engaging employees), the process itself amounts to an interference with Convention rights, and would entitle the employees to bring proceedings under the Act. **6.163**

7

THE RIGHT TO LIFE AND THE ABOLITION OF THE DEATH PENALTY

A. The Nature of the Right to Life

7.01 The right to life is often said to be the most fundamental of all human rights, the basic precondition of the enjoyment of other rights.[1] The earliest express protection

[1] See Human Rights Committee, General Comment 14, (1994) 1 IHRR 15–16; see also *State v Makwanyane* 1995 5 BCLR 665, para 144.

for the right was the Fifth Amendment to the US Constitution which provided that no person shall 'be deprived of life . . . without due process of law'. Article 3 of the Universal Declaration of Human Rights states that:

> Everyone has the right to life, liberty and security of the person.

Although there were extensive debates on the point,[2] the final draft made no reference to the circumstances in which life might lawfully be taken. An attempt was made to deal with these issues when the International Covenant on Civil and Political Rights was being drafted.[3] Article 6(1) was the product of 11 years' debate. It states that:

> (1) Every human being has the inherent right to life. This right shall be protected by law. No one shall be arbitrarily deprived of his life.

The remainder of the Article deals with the death penalty. Article 6(5) prescribes that sentence of death:

> shall not be imposed for crimes committed by persons below eighteen years of age and shall not be carried out on pregnant women.

Article 6(6) makes it clear that nothing in the Article is to be invoked to delay or prevent the abolition of capital punishment.[4]

7.02 Like the International Covenant on Civil and Political Rights, a number of human rights instruments declare the 'death penalty' to be an exception to the right to life.[5] Some make provision for the abolition of the death penalty.[6] In jurisdictions which provide for the retention of the death penalty, the case law has focused not on the right to life but on the question as to whether particular ways of carrying the death sentence out are 'inhuman and degrading'.[7]

---

[2] For discussion see W Schabas, *The Abolition of the Death Penalty in International Law* (2nd edn, Cambridge University Press, 1997), Chap 1 'The Universal Declaration of Human Rights and the Recognition of the Right to Life'.

[3] Ibid Chap 2 'The International Covenant on Civil and Political Rights: Drafting, Ratification and Reservation'.

[4] The Second Optional Protocol, which entered into force on 11 Jul 1991, provides for the abolition of the death penalty in the territory of state parties, see ibid, Chap 4 'Towards Abolition: The Second Optional Protocol and Other Developments'.

[5] See eg Art 4, American Convention on Human Rights; and the constitutional provisions in Commonwealth Caribbean constitutions summarised in M Demerieux, *Fundamental Rights in Commonwealth Carribbean Constitutions* (Faculty of Law Library, University of West Indies, 1992) 124 (all except Trinidad and Tobago provide for a right to life 'save in the execution of the sentence of the court' in differently defined circumstances, Trinidad and Tobago provides for the right not to be deprived of life 'save by due process of law').

[6] See eg Art 102 of the German Constitution, 1949 which provides that 'Capital punishment is abolished'.

[7] See eg in relation to Caribbean countries, L Blom-Cooper and C Gelber, 'The Privy Council and the Death Penalty in the Caribbean: A Study in Constitutional Change' [1998] EHRLR 386; and see generally, para 8.10 below.

In general, those who draft human rights instruments have avoided trying to define the limits of the right to life in areas beyond the 'death penalty'. Issues concerning abortion, euthanasia and the extent of the state's positive obligations to protect life have been among the most controversial in human rights law. The right to life has played varying roles in the case law dealing with these fundamental issues. On the one hand, in many jurisdictions the courts have often chosen to approach 'right to life' issues indirectly. For example, abortion regulation has been dealt with on the basis of the right to 'privacy'[8] or 'liberty'[9] of the mother and euthanasia has been considered in the context of 'fundamental justice'[10] or 'due process'.[11] On the other hand, in some jurisdictions, most notably India,[12] the courts have taken an expansive view of the 'right to life' itself, extending it to the means of living a healthy and fulfilling life. This approach puts into sharp focus the relationship between 'civil and political' and 'economic and social' rights.[13] **7.03**

The protection of the right to life by a general prohibition of the intentional taking of life by non-judicial bodies is not controversial. However, complex issues arise in at least three areas: **7.04**

(1) *The scope of the right*: The most important issue under this head concerns the identity of those who should enjoy the right. Whether or not a foetus enjoys a 'right to life' is one of the most fiercely contested of all human rights questions, requiring examination of what constitutes a human being and how to balance the rights to life of foetus and mother.
(2) *The obligation to protect life*: The second contentious area concerns the extent to which the 'right to life' involves the imposing of positive duties on other individuals or on the state. At one end of the spectrum, the right to life is seen as involving only a 'negative' right: preventing the intentional killing of individuals except in very strictly defined circumstances. At the other the right could include the obligation to take positive 'life preserving' steps, placing 'social welfare' duties on the state and 'life saving' duties on individuals. It also means looking at the circumstances in which it is permissible to allow a person to die by the cessation or withholding of medical treatment.
(3) *Exceptions to the prohibition from taking life*: The third set of problems surround the circumstances in which individuals might be lawfully deprived of life, raising questions such as: whether judicial killing is ever justified, whether force should be used to preserve the life of others and whether it is

[8] *Roe v Wade* (1973) 410 US 113.
[9] *R v Morgentaler (No 2)* (1988) 44 DLR (4th) 385.
[10] *Rodriguez v British Columbia (A-G)* (1993) 107 DLR (4th) 342.
[11] *Washington v Glucksberg* (1997) 2 BHRC 539.
[12] See para 7.93ff below.
[13] See generally, para 1.16 above.

justifiable to kill an individual to protect others? This topic requires consideration of the powers of the police and army to use lethal force against criminals or terrorists. Finally, it is necessary to examine the circumstances in which an individual can lawfully assist another in terminating his own life.

B. The Right in English Law Before the Human Rights Act

(1) The scope of the right

7.05 The common law has always recognised the fundamental importance of human life. It is the first of what Blackstone describes as the three absolute rights of the people of England:

> Life is the immediate gift of God, a right inherent by nature in every individual . . . of such high value . . . that it pardons even homicide if committed *de defendendo* . . . The law not only regards life and member, and protects every man in the enjoyment of them, but also furnishes him with everything necessary for their support.[14]

7.06 Life begins when the whole body of a child has emerged into the world and its existence is no longer dependent upon that of its mother. It is not clear, however, whether this means that the child must simply be able to breathe on its own;[15] or also requires that the circulation of the child be independent of that of its mother.[16] Since embryonic independent circulation occurs within one or two months of conception, a child appears to be 'capable of being born alive' when it is able to breathe without dependence on its mother;[17] the umbilical cord need not have been severed.

7.07 The end of life was, historically, determined as a matter of common observation.[18] However, the development of 'life support systems' has meant that deciding when life ends now gives rise to considerable legal difficulties.[19] In *Re A (A Minor)*[20] two consultants had concluded that a two-year-old child was 'brain stem dead'. The judge held that the child was legally dead and declared that it would not be unlawful to disconnect him from the ventilator. In the important 'life support' case of *Airedale NHS Trust v Bland*,[21] the point was not argued, but Lords Keith, Goff

---

[14] R Kerr (ed), *Blackstone's Commentaries on the Laws of England* (4th edn, John Murray, 1876) Vol I, 101.

[15] *R v Handley* (1874) 13 Cox 79; cf *R v Brain* (1834) 6 C & P 349.

[16] *R v Enoch* (1833) 5 C & P 539; *R v Wright* (1841) 9 C & P 754.

[17] *Rance v Mid-Downs Health Authority* [1991] 1 QB 587; also *C v S* [1987] 2 WLR 1108.

[18] See I Kennedy and A Grubb (eds), *Principles of Medical Law* (Oxford University Press, 1998) para 17.01.

[19] For a general discussion see I Kennedy and A Grubb (n 18, above) Chap 17 'Death' and M Brazier, *Medicine, Patients and the Law* (Penguin Books, 1992) Chap 20 'Defining Death'.

[20] [1992] 3 Med L Rev 303; see generally, I Kennedy and A Grubb (n 18, above) para 17.15.

[21] [1993] AC 789.

and Browne-Wilkinson took the view that 'brain stem death' is the legal definition of death in English law.[22]

(2) The obligation to protect life

(a) Introduction

The obligation to protect life can be seen in the various criminal offences which are committed by one person killing another. The taking of human life with 'malice aforethought' constitutes the common law crime of murder.[23] A person will be guilty of murder if they intend to kill or cause really serious harm.[24] A person who causes death by a lesser unlawful act, or by gross negligence[25] is guilty of manslaughter. If a woman kills a child under 12 months when 'the balance of her mind is disturbed by reason of not having fully recovered from the effect of giving birth', she will be guilty of infanticide.[26] There are also a number of criminal offences involving the destruction of unborn children. These are dealt with in the next section. **7.08**

(b) The protection of life and the unborn child

The destruction of an unborn child is not, in itself, a crime. The destruction of a child capable of being born alive may, however, amount to child destruction; and the intentional procuring of a miscarriage of a child capable of being born alive may amount to the crime of abortion.[27] If a child is born alive, and dies because of ante-natal injuries which were intentionally inflicted, the person responsible is guilty of murder[28] or manslaughter,[29] depending on the state of mind with which he acted.[30] **7.09**

A number of statutes create criminal offences in order to protect the life of a foetus. The Offences Against the Person Act 1861 made abortions illegal. A pregnant woman who, with intent to procure her own miscarriage, unlawfully administers to herself any poison or other noxious thing, or uses an instrument or other means to the same end, is guilty of an offence; as is anyone who administers drugs or uses **7.10**

---

[22] See also *Re A* (A Minor) [1992] 3 Med LR 303.

[23] See generally, *Blackstone's Commentaries* (n 14 above, B1.1ff; a person over 21 convicted of this offence must be sentenced to life imprisonment (see s 1(1), Murder (Abolition of Death Penalty) Act 1965) whereas if he was under 18 when the offence was committed the sentence is one of indefinite detention, 'during Her Majesty's Pleasure': see s 53(1), Children and Young Persons Act, 1933.

[24] *DPP v Smith* [1961] AC 290; see generally, R Kerr (n 14 above), B1.11.

[25] See *R v Adomako* [1995] 1 AC 171.

[26] s 1, Infanticide Act 1938; this will not usually attract custodial sentence, see *R v Sainsbury* (1989) 11 Cr App R (S) 533.

[27] See para 7.10 below.

[28] *R v West* (1848) 2 Car & Kir 784.

[29] *R v Senior* (1832) 1 Mood CC 346.

[30] The law set out above is substantially repeated in the draft Criminal Code Bill, cl 53: Law Commission, *A Criminal Code for England and Wales* (Law Com No 177, 1989) para 3.21.

an instrument or other means with the intent to procure the miscarriage of any woman, whether or not she is pregnant.[31] A person who supplies any poison, noxious thing, instrument, or anything else, knowing it is intended to be used to procure a miscarriage, also commits an offence.[32] In addition, the Infant Life (Preservation) Act 1929 ensured that a person could be successfully prosecuted for destroying the life of a child 'capable of being born alive'; this protected the child who was in the midst of the birth process but not yet completely separated from its mother.[33]

7.11 However, section 1 of the Abortion Act 1967[34] permits an abortion if it is initiated by a registered medical practitioner and one of four prescribed conditions is met. The issue of abortion and the 'right to life debate' have therefore largely been removed from the courts and responsibility for determining the legality of abortion has been placed firmly in the control of the medical profession.

7.12 Although English law prior to the Human Rights Act acknowledges that the foetus has *interests* worthy of protection,[35] it does not regard the foetus as having any legal *rights*. A child is not even within the jurisdiction of the English courts until it is born. Consequently, when deciding whether doctors should intervene to protect a foetus by authorising a Caesarian section without the consent of the mother, the court is not entitled to take into account the interests of the unborn child.[36] Similarly, an unborn child cannot be made a ward of the court[37] or sue for prenatal injuries;[38] and a father cannot even sue as the next friend of the unborn child for an injunction restraining the mother or a doctor from procuring an abortion.[39] Where an injury is deliberately inflicted on a mother carrying a child *in utero* so that the child is born alive but is so premature that it subsequently dies, the assailant will not be guilty of murder. The assault will, however, amount to manslaughter if the assailant intended to injure the mother.[40]

---

[31] Offences Against the Person Act 1861, s 58.

[32] Offences Against the Person Act 1861, s 59.

[33] *Rance v Mid-Downs Health Authority* [1991] 1 QB 587.

[34] As amended by the Human Fertilisation and Embryology Act 1990, s 37.

[35] See D Feldman, *Civil Liberties and Human Rights in England and Wales* (Clarendon Press, 1993) 106.

[36] *Re M B (Caesarian Section) The Times*, 18 Apr 1997; see also *St George's Healthcare NHS Trust v S* [1999] Fam 26, in which a pregnant woman of sound mind was detained under the Mental Health Act 1983 and subjected to treatment, including Caesarean section, against her consent. The Court found that when the proposed treatment raises a conflict between the interests of mother and foetus, the unborn child's need for medical help cannot override the right of the mother to refuse invasive treatment, however repugnant her decision might seem in moral terms. As her capacity to consent had not been reduced, she was found to have been wrongfully detained.

[37] *Re F (In Utero)* [1988] Fam 122.

[38] Congenital Disabilities (Civil Liability) Act 1976; *Burton v Islington Health Authority* [1993] QB 204.

[39] *Paton v British Pregnancy Advisory Service Trustees* [1979] QB 276; the position is the same in Scotland: see *Kelly v Kelly The Times*, 5 Jun 1997.

[40] See *A-G's Reference (No 3 of 1994)* [1998] AC 245.

Nonetheless, where a foetus is viable it has been accorded some legal protection, particularly in connection with medical treatment of the mother. Whether or not she can provide rational reasons for doing so, the mother is presumed to have the necessary capacity to decide to forego medical intervention. The critical issue is therefore whether the presumption of capacity can be rebutted. Lack of capacity will result only from an impairment or disturbance of mental function (such as a phobia), which would make the individual incapable of making a decision.[41] Furthermore, the Court of Appeal has rejected the argument that a live foetus with severe abnormalities is worse off than one having no life at all.[42] Damages may be awarded to a mother for the distress, pain and suffering, and the costs of maintenance from having such a severely handicapped child as a result of negligence[43] but not for the costs of caring for and bringing up a healthy child who is born after his father had undergone a vasectomy operation.[43a] **7.13**

(c) Euthanasia

'Euthanasia' is the inducing of an 'easy death', a 'mercy killing' of a terminally ill person, or a person who does not wish to continue living.[44] Commentators distinguish two forms: 'involuntary euthanasia' (ie the mercy killing of a person in order to relieve pain and suffering) and 'voluntary euthanasia', (the killing of a person with their consent). However, in English law the motive for a killing (as opposed to the intention to kill) is not relevant to its lawfulness: 'euthanasia is not lawful at common law'.[45] **7.14**

A positive act which causes a person's death is murder. Thus, in *R v Cox*[46] a consultant rheumatologist gave a terminally ill patient an injection of potassium chloride. The patient died shortly afterwards and the doctor was convicted of attempted murder (on the basis that it was not clear whether the patient would have died anyway).[47] The position is different, however, when death is caused by an omission or if the primary purpose of the act complained of was not to cause death.[48] **7.15**

---

[41] *Re M B (Caesarian Section) The Times*, 18 Apr 1997.

[42] *McKay v Essex Area Health Authority* [1982] QB 1166.

[43] *Re J (A Minor) Wardship: Medical Treatment* [1991] Fam 33.

[43a] *McFarlane v Tayside Health Board* [1999] 3 WLR 1301.

[44] For general discussions see I Kennedy and A Grubb (eds), *Principles of Medical Law* (Oxford University Press, 1998) Chap 16 'Ending Life' and M Brazier, *Medicine, Patients and the Law* (Penguin Books, 1992) Chap 21 'Death, Dying and the Medical Practitioner'.

[45] *Per* Lord Goff, *Airedale NHS Trust v Bland* [1993] AC 789, 865; and see generally, B Hale, *From the Test Tube to the Coffin*, Hamlyn Lectures (Sweet & Maxwell, 1996) 92ff.

[46] (1992) 12 BMLR 38.

[47] The doctor received a suspended sentence: see R Harper, *Medical Treatment and the Law* (Family Law, 1999) para 10.5.1, cf the reference to this case in *Airedale NHS Trust v Bland* [1993] AC 789, 865.

[48] See para 7.20 below.

7.16 The fact that a person consents to their own death is no defence to a charge of murder. Nor is consent, in general, a defence to a charge of causing serious injury[49] or death. At common law, suicide was a crime although this was abrogated by statute.[50] However it remains an offence to aid, abet, counsel or procure the suicide of another.[51] Consequently, people who are capable of taking their own lives may do so legally, while those who procure the assistance of others place the helper at risk of criminal liability. The offence will be committed when a person assists a terminally ill patient to die by, for example, providing lethal drugs.[52] The offence can be committed even if the other person does not in fact kill or attempt to kill himself.[53] Distributing a booklet advising those who are contemplating taking their own life on the best way to do so also will involve the commission of this offence.[54]

(d) The duties of medical practitioners

7.17 There is a strong presumption that medical practitioners should take all steps capable of preserving human life.[55] However:

> The doctor who is caring for . . . a patient cannot . . . be under an absolute obligation to prolong his life by any means available to him, regardless of the quality of the patient's life.[56]

7.18 Any treatment administered by a doctor without the consent of a competent patient is a trespass to the person.[57] This means that, unless a terminally ill patient provides consent, the doctor has no other option but to withhold potentially life-saving treatment. On the other hand, a doctor may treat a patient who is incapable of giving consent, provided that such treatment is in the patient's best interests.[58]

7.19 An adult patient is entitled to refuse consent irrespective of the wisdom of the decision. However, such a refusal will be effective *only* if doctors are satisfied that the capacity of the patient has not been diminished by illness, medication, false assumptions or misinformation, that his will has not been overborne by another and that he has directed his attention to the relevant situation.[59] The strength of this

---

49 *R v Brown* [1994] 1 AC 212; but the case law defies rational analysis, see Law Commission, *Consent and Offences Against the Person* (Law Com No 134, 1994).

50 Suicide Act 1969, s 1.

51 Suicide Act 1961, s 2.

52 See eg *R v Hough* (1984) 6 Cr App R (S) 406 (the sentence was nine months' imprisonment).

53 *R v McShane* (1977) 66 Cr App R 97.

54 *A-G v Able* [1984] QB 795, 812D–E.

55 See R Harper, *Medical Treatment and the Law* (Family Law, 1999) para 2.4, 12; I Kennedy and A Grubb (eds), *Principles of Medical Law* (Oxford University Press, 1998) para 4.196.

56 *Airedale NHS Trust v Bland* [1993] AC 789, 867; see also *Re J (A Minor)(Wardship: Medical Treatment)* [1991] Fam 33.

57 *Re F (Sterilisation) Mental Patients* [1990] 2 AC 1, 55; see generally, Harper (n 55 above) Chap 1.

58 *Re F* (n 57 above) see Harper (n 55 above) 23–24.

59 *In re T: Adult Refusal of Treatment* [1993] Fam 95.

principle is illustrated by the case of *St George's Healthcare NHS Trust v S*[60] in which it was held that a woman who was 36 weeks' pregnant and was suffering from pre-eclampsia could not be forced to submit to treatment against her will, despite the serious risks to her own life and to her unborn child. Similarly, the Home Office is not under a duty to 'force feed' a prisoner on hunger strike as long as he retains the capacity to refuse food and drink.[61]

The duty to preserve life is also circumvented by the doctrine of double effect. Under this doctrine a doctor, with the consent of the patient, is able to prescribe a course of treatment which is likely to shorten the life of the patient. Such treatments are often prescribed to improve the quality of life for terminally ill patients who are suffering severe pain as a result of their illness. However, in pursuing this course of treatment the doctor must act in accordance with the respected medical opinion at the time. If he fails to do so, he can be charged with murder. **7.20**

By comparison, where a child is born with very severe handicaps, neither parents nor doctors have the right to decide to withhold treatment or to take active steps to terminate its life. Although the wishes of the parents and the opinion of the medical profession will be given some weight, the court must decide what is in the best interests of the child. Continuance of life has generally been viewed as in its best interest unless there is compelling evidence to the contrary.[62] **7.21**

No court can authorise a doctor to take *active* steps to terminate the life of a patient.[63] In *Re J*[64] the Court of Appeal distinguished the absolute duty not to kill from the much more circumscribed duty to maintain life; it went on to decide that in the exceptional circumstances of the case, it might be in the best interests of the child not to have life prolonged. Similarly, in *Airedale NHS Trust v Bland,*[65] the House of Lords upheld the view of the doctors that it would not be unlawful to stop feeding a patient in a persistent vegetative state; and decided that it was lawful to withhold treatment so that the patient would end his life with dignity and with the least possible suffering. However, *Bland* was a relatively clear case. Where the position is less certain, the House of Lords have favoured the *Bolam* test:[66] the doctors must reach a view which is supported by a responsible and competent **7.22**

[60] [1999] Fam 26; see generally, Harper (n 55 above) 61–63.

[61] *Secretary of State for the Home Department v Robb* [1995] Fam 127; contrast *Leigh v Gladstone* (1909) 26 TLR 139 (in which the jury were directed that the prison authorities had a duty to preserve the health of prisoners and this included force feeding, decided at a time when suicide was a crime).

[62] *Re B (A Minor) (Wardship: Medical Treatment)* [1981] 1 WLR 1421.

[63] *Re C (A Minor) (Wardship: Medical Treatment)* [1990] Fam 26.

[64] *Re J (A Minor) (Wardship: Medical Treatment)* [1991] Fam 33 see also *A National Health Service Trust v D, The Times* 19 Jul 2000 (declaration that, in the event of cardiac failure doctors had leave to administer treatment excluding resuscitation through artificial ventilation).

[65] [1993] AC 789.

[66] *Bolam v Friern Hospital Management Committee* [1957] 1 WLR 582.

body of relevant medical opinion, preferably with guidance from the British Medical Association. There are, however, strong reservations about applying such a test to matters which are ethical rather than medical, and which involve the criminal law of murder and manslaughter rather than civil liability for negligence.[67] Nevertheless, where there is a lack of independent evidence, the role of the court remains one of review: the most that it can do is to scrutinise the medical evidence carefully to assess whether the decision of the doctors is in the best interests of the patient.[68]

(e) The right to life in administrative law

7.23 In recent years the courts have explicitly recognised a 'right to life' which public bodies must take into account in their decision-making. Thus, in *Bugdaycay v Secretary of State for the Home Department*[69] Lord Bridge said that:

> The most fundamental of all human rights is the individual's right to life and when an administrative decision under challenge is said to be one which may put the applicant's life at risk, the basis of the decision must surely call for the most anxious scrutiny.[70]

Thus, where there is a threat to life resulting from deportation or a refusal of asylum this must be given careful consideration, even where considerations of 'public good' or 'national security' favour the applicant's removal.[71]

7.24 It has been suggested at first instance that the right to life is a fundamental right and that Parliament must be presumed to legislate in accordance with it,[72] but the Court of Appeal rejected this approach.[73] The issue arose directly in *R v Cambridgeshire Health Authority, ex p B*. The health authority had refused to fund speculative specialist treatment for a young leukaemia patient. Laws J[74] held that the authority was under a positive duty to sustain life if there was a chance of survival, however small. However, the Court of Appeal[75] decided that the health authority

[67] D Feldman, *Civil Liberties and Human Rights in England and Wales* (Clarendon Press, 1993) 122. Note also that Lords Mustill and Browne-Wilkinson were reluctant parties to the Bland decision (see n 65) for these reasons.

[68] *Franchy Healthcare NHS Trust v S* [1994] 1 WLR 601; the relevant application procedure is set out in *Practice Note (Persistent Vegetative State: Withdrawal of Treatment)* [1996] 4 All ER 766.

[69] [1987] AC 514, 531.

[70] On this point see M Fordham, 'What is "Anxious Scrutiny"?' [1996] JR 81. Cases considering and following *Bugdaycay* include *R v Secretary of State for the Home Department, ex p Launder* [1997] 1 WLR 839; *R v Secretary of State for the Home Department and another, ex p Canbolat* [1998] 1 All ER 161.

[71] *R v Secretary of State for the Home Department, ex p Chahal* [1995] 1 WLR 526; *R v Secretary of State for the Home Department, ex p McQuillan* [1995] 4 All ER 400.

[72] *R v Hammersmith and Fulham London Borough Council, ex p M* (1997) 30 HLR 10 *per* Collins J.

[73] (1998) 30 HLR 10.

[74] [1995] 1 FLR 1055.

[75] [1995] 1 WLR 898; see also D O'Sullivan, 'The Allocation of Scarce Resources and the Right to Life Under the European Convention on Human Rights' [1998] PL 389.

had properly taken account of all the relevant considerations, including lack of resources.

The right to life was also considered in a case involving the deportation of an illegal immigrant who suffered from AIDS and sought benefits under the National Assistance Act.[76] Finding that the overstayer was not able to undertake a journey out of the United Kingdom without risk to his life or serious injury to his health, Moses J held that the duty of every civilised nation to safeguard life and health could in exceptional cases override the general principle that an applicant cannot take advantage of his own wrongdoing. A similar approach was taken in *R v Secretary of State for the Home Department, ex p M*[76a] where the deportation of the applicant who was terminally ill with AIDS was quashed on the ground that the medical treatment in Uganda might arguably interfere with Article 2 of the Convention. The importance of the right to life led to the quashing of a decision concerning the anonymity of soldiers who were called as witnesses at the 'Bloody Sunday' inquiry.[77] It was held that the failure of a tribunal consisting of three distinguished judges to give sufficient weight to potential threats to the lives of the soldiers and their families meant that their decision to refuse anonymity was flawed. **7.25**

(3) Exceptions to the prohibition from taking life

(a) The death penalty

The death penalty for murder was abolished in the United Kingdom in 1965.[78] However, it was retained for certain specific crimes in relation to which it has now been abolished: treason, piracy with violence[79] and military offences.[80] No execution has taken place in England since 1964.[81] **7.26**

(b) Duress and self-defence

English law does not recognise duress as a defence to murder.[82] Thus, a civilian who kills another individual will be liable for murder even though the killing was carried out at the direction of a captor, while held at gunpoint and under threat of loss of life and those of family members. **7.27**

76 *R v Brent LBC, ex p D* (1998) 1 CCLR 234.

76a (1999) Imm AR 548.

77 *R v Lord Saville , ex p. A* [1999] 4 All ER 860 CA and *The Times*, 15 Apr 1999, Div Ct.

78 Murder (Abolition of Death Penalty) Act 1965.

79 Crime and Disorder Act 1998, s 36, with effect from 30 Sept1998.

80 Human Rights Act 1998, s 21(5), with effect from 9 Nov 1998.

81 There were two executions for murder in 1964 and three in 1963. There has been no execution for treason since 1946.

82 See *Abbott v R* [1977] AC 755, PC; *R v Howe* [1987] AC 417, HL overruling *Lynch v DPP for Northern Ireland* [1975] AC 653, HL. This principle has been severely criticised, see I Dennis, 'Duress, Murder and Criminal Responsibility' [1980] LQR 208.

7.28 On the other hand, force may be used by citizens (or members of the police and armed forces) to take the life of another if it is done in self-defence. The degree of force used in civilian situations must, however, be reasonable in relation to the threat. That means that a person who uses excessive force to defend himself or fails to retreat when that option is available will, should the attacker be killed, be liable for murder or manslaughter. In assessing the reasonableness of the force used by persons acting in self-defence, the courts have, however, been very willing to take into account the subjective views held by the accused as to the threat they were facing and the magnitude of response required to protect themselves at the time of the attack.[83]

(c) Arrest and preventing escape

7.29 Section 3 of the Criminal Law Act 1967 and section 117 of the Police and Criminal Evidence Act 1984 prescribe the force which is legally permissible in making a lawful arrest or preventing the escape of a lawfully detained person. Under the Criminal law Act 1967, force must be used only when 'necessary' and the amount used 'reasonable'. Where a criminal is deemed to be dangerous the courts have taken a liberal interpretation of 'necessary'.[84] Thus, it has been held to be reasonable for a soldier to shoot an escaping suspect in the back who he reasonably believed to be involved in terrorist activities.[85]

C. The Law Under the European Convention

(1) The scope of the right

7.30 Article 2 of the European Convention on Human Rights states:

> (1) Everyone's right to life shall be protected by law. No one shall be deprived of his life intentionally, save in the execution of a sentence of a court following his conviction of a crime for which this penalty is provided by law.
> (2) Deprivation of life shall not be regarded as inflicted in contravention of this Article when it results from the use of force which is no more than absolutely necessary:
> (a) in defence of any person from unlawful violence;
> (b) in order to effect a lawful arrest or to prevent the escape of a person lawfully detained;
> (c) in action lawfully taken for the purpose of quelling a riot or insurrection.

[83] See *Palmer v The Queen* [1971] AC 814; *R v Shannon* (1980) 71 Cr App R 192; *R v Whyte* [1987] 3 All ER 416; thus, in *R v Scarlett* [1993] 4 All ER 629, Bedlam LJ could see no reason for distinguishing between a mistaken belief as to the necessity of force and as to the appropriate amount of force to be used; he applied the requirement of an honest belief to both circumstances.
[84] See eg *Farrell (formerly McLaughlin) v Secretary of State for Defence* [1980] 1 WLR 172 HL.
[85] *R v McNaughton* [1975] NI 203.

The right to life is one of the most fundamental provisions of the Convention and enshrines one of the basic values of democratic societies.[86]

The second sentence of Article 2(1) recognises the continued existence of the death penalty. However, the Sixth Protocol to the Convention provides for the abolition of the death penalty in the following terms: **7.31**

> (1) The death penalty shall be abolished. No one shall be condemned to such penalty or executed.
>
> (2) A State may make provision in its law for the death penalty in respect of acts committed in time of war or imminent threat of war; such penalty shall be applied only in the instances laid down in the law and in accordance with its provisions. The State shall communicate to the Secretary-General of the Council of Europe the relevant provision of that law.

Article 2 comprises two separate provisions: a positive duty on states to protect the right to life by law; and an obligation on public authorities to refrain from the taking of human life, except in very limited circumstances. As the European Court of Human Rights said in *LCB v United Kingdom*:[87] **7.32**

> the first sentence of art 2(1) enjoins the state not only to refrain from the intentional and unlawful taking of life, but also to take appropriate steps to safeguard the lives of those within its jurisdiction.

What the Convention protects is not *life* itself, but the *right to life*.[88] Thus, neither aspect of Article 2 indicates that the right to life is absolute: on the contrary, it confirms that persons may be deprived of life in accordance with conditions prescribed by law. Nevertheless, Article 2 is one of the few Convention Articles from which no derogation is permitted in times of war or emergency.[89] Article 2 imposes liability on the state for acts of its public officials such as police officers,[90] soldiers[91] and prison officers.[92] However, it does not make a state liable for the taking of life by individual persons. The obligation on the state is therefore confined to the provision of legal protection in accordance with the first sentence of Article 2(1).[93] **7.33**

Article 2 applies not only to cases of intentional taking of life, but to unintentional killings as well.[94] A state might also be liable under Article 2 for extradition or deportation of an individual where 'substantial grounds have been shown for **7.34**

---

[86] *Andronicou and Constantiou v Cyprus* (1997) 25 EHRR 491 para 171.

[87] (1998) 27 EHRR 212 para 36.

[88] P Sieghart, *The International Law of Human Rights* (Oxford University Press, 1983) 130–31; compare with the language of Art 6(1) of the International Covenant on Civil and Political Rights which affirms an 'inherent right to life'.

[89] Save in respect of deaths resulting from lawful acts of war themselves, Art 15(2).

[90] *McCann v United Kingdom* (1995) 21 EHRR 97; *X v Belgium* (1969) 12 YB 174, EComm HR.

[91] *Stewart v United Kingdom* (1984) 39 DR 162, EComm HR.

[92] *X v United Kingdom* (1970) 34 CD 48.

[93] See *Stewart v United Kingdom* (1984) 39 DR 162, 169, EComm HR.

[94] See *Stewart v United Kingdom* (1984) 39 DR 162, EComm HR.

believing that the person faces a real risk'[95] of being killed, on his return. This was the test adopted in the *Soering*[96] case; and which was applied to potential breaches of Article 3 where the fugitive faced the death row phenomenon as a result of capital punishment. It has been argued that it should also apply to a real risk of *any* breach of Article 2 following deportation and not merely to a breach involving the death penalty.[97]

(2) The obligation to protect life

(a) Introduction

7.35 Article 2(1) requires that 'everyone's right to life shall be protected by law'. This establishes a positive duty on states to ensure that there are in effect suitable laws for the protection of human life and to provide the necessary means of enforcing those laws. In order to satisfy this obligation, the state must put in place effective criminal law provisions to deter the commission of offences against the person, 'backed up by law-enforcement machinery for the prevention, suppression and sanctioning of breaches of such provisions'.[98] But the nature and extent of liability for violation of the law and rules for its enforcement are left to be determined by the individual state.[99]

7.36 A state is not required to make every taking of a life illegal. However, the unequivocal exceptions to the general rule are relatively few; and include capital punishment, killings in self-defence committed by private persons,[100] accidental sporting deaths and causing death by omission.

(b) Positive duty to protect life

7.37 It is clear that Article 2 places a positive obligation on the State 'to take preventive operational measures to protect an individual whose life is at risk from the criminal acts of another individual'.[101] There will be a violation of Article 2 if:

> the authorities did not do all that could be reasonably expected of them to avoid a real and immediate risk to life of which they have or ought to have knowledge.[102]

---

[95] *Lynas v Switzerland* (1976) 6 DR 141, EComm HR.

[96] *Soering v United Kingdom* (1989) 11 EHRR 439.

[97] See D Harris, M O'Boyle and C Warbrick, *Law of the European Convention on Human Rights* (Butterworths, 1995) 45.

[98] See *Osman v United Kingdom* (1998) 5 BHRC 293, para 115; and generally, Harris, O'Boyle and Warbrick (n 97 above) 38.

[99] See *McCann v United Kingdom* (1995) 21 EHRR 97 para 151ff; and see Harris, O'Boyle and Warbrick (n 97 above) 38.

[100] Art 2(2) applies to state authorities, so that the exception does not benefit private persons; most European states make the defence of 'self-defence' a part of their criminal law.

[101] See *Osman v United Kingdom* (1998) 5 BHRC 293 para 115.

[102] Ibid para 116. The Court rejected the Government's submission that it was necessary to show 'gross negligence' or wilful disregard of the duty to protect life.

The reasonable protection of the public against acts of terrorists and others that place the lives of individuals at risk does not require that 'any possible violence' against the person must be completely excluded.[103] Thus, in *W v United Kingdom*[104] the European Commission of Human Rights considered the number of armed and security forces in place, but not the appropriateness and efficiency of the preventive measures, before finding that there had not been a breach of the Convention. In *X v Ireland*[105] the application was rejected because Article 2:

> could not be interpreted as imposing a duty on a state to give protection of this nature, at least not for an indefinite period.

It is not inconsistent with Article 2 to provide an amnesty for persons convicted or suspected of murder so long as it reflects a proper balance between the interests of the state in the particular circumstances and the general need to enforce the law to protect the right to life.[106]

7.38 The obligation to protect the right to life by law also 'requires that there should be some form of effective official investigation when individuals have been killed as a result of the use of force by, *inter alios*, agents of the State'.[107] Proper investigation of deaths includes inquiry into deaths that occur in custody, as well as disappearances of individuals in circumstances that may suggest death. In *McCann v United Kingdom*[108] three members of the IRA had been killed by security forces in Gibraltar. One of the complaints was that the requirement of an effective investigation had not been satisfied by the inquest procedure. The Court found it unnecessary to decide what form the investigation should take, as a public inquest had taken place at which the applicants had been legally represented and there had been a 'thorough, impartial and careful examination of the circumstances surrounding the killings'.[109]

7.39 The extent to which the positive obligation on the state includes protection against detrimental circumstances (such as lack of food or medical attention, unsafe roads or workplaces and environmental pollution) is unclear. It has been recognised in a number of cases that the right to life requires the state 'to take appropriate steps to safeguard life'.[110] In *Association X v United Kingdom*[111] an application arose out of

[103] See *W v United Kingdom* (1983) 32 DR 190, 200, EComm HR.

[104] Ibid; cf (1985) 8 EHRR 49 and *M v United Kingdom and Ireland* (1986) 47 DR 27, EComm HR.

[105] *X v Ireland* (173) 16 YB 388, 392, EComm HR.

[106] *Dujardin v France* (1992) 72 DR 236, EComm HR.

[107] *McCann v United Kingdom* (1995) 21 EHRR 97 para 161; *Kaya v Turkey* (1998) 28 EHRR 1 para 86; *Gülec v Turkey* (1999) 28 EHRR 121 para 78.

[108] n 107 above.

[109] Ibid para 164.

[110] See *LCB v United Kingdom* (1998) 27 EHRR 212 para 36; cf *Tavares v France* Application 16593/90, (1991) unreported (the wife of the applicant had died during childbirth, application refused on the basis that the hospital had followed its established procedures).

[111] (1978) 14 DR 31, 32, EComm HR; see also *X v Ireland* (1976) 7 DR 78, EComm HR.

an incident in which young children died in connection with a voluntary public vaccination scheme. The Commission found that Article 2(1):

> enjoins the state not only to refrain from taking life intentionally, but, further, to take appropriate steps to safeguard life.

This suggests that the state is under an obligation to provide for its citizens food, shelter, medical care and education, and to establish adequate working conditions and environmental standards.[112] In the event, the Commission found the case to be inadmissible on the facts because 'appropriate steps' had been taken with a view to the safe administration of the scheme. In *LCB v United Kingdom*[113] the applicant, whose father had been present during British nuclear tests, had contracted leukaemia. She complained of a breach of Article 2 in relation to the Government's failure to advise her parents to monitor her health. The Court considered that its task was to determine whether, in the circumstances:

> the State did all that could have been required of it to prevent the applicant's life from being avoidably put at risk.[114]

On the facts, bearing in mind the information available to the state at the relevant time, there was no breach.

7.40 The development of a positive obligation to take 'life protecting' measures involves the partial transformation of Article 2 into a 'social right'[115] and the Court has proceeded cautiously.[116] Thus, in a number of cases in which 'the positive right to protect life' has been invoked, the Court has preferred to decide the cases on the basis of violations of other rights and has declined to express a view on the 'right to life' issue.[117] This approach can be contrasted with the liberal interpretation of the right to life taken by the Human Rights Committee towards the International Covenant on Civil and Political Rights (ICCPR).[118]

7.41 There are, however, some signs of development in the Court's thinking on this

[112] See D Harris, M O'Boyle and C Warbrick, *Law of the European Convention on Human Rights* (Butterworths, 1995) 40–41.

[113] (1998) 27 EHRR 212.

[114] Ibid para 36.

[115] See para 1.16ff above and also para 2.57ff above; there would be an overlap with Art 11 of the European Social Charter (right to protection of health, see D Gomien, D Harris and L Zwaak, *Law and Practice of the European Convention on Human Rights and the European Social Charter* (Council of Europe Publishing, 1996) 397–398.

[116] See generally, Harris, O'Boyle and Warbrick (n 112 above) 41.

[117] See eg *D v United Kingdom* (1997) 24 EHRR 423 para 55ff (no view on the submission that the removal of a terminally ill patient to a country lacking medical facilities would be a breach of the positive obligation to safeguard life, see also para 8.28 below); and *Guerra v Italy* (1998) 26 EHRR 357 para 61ff (no view on the submission that the failure to provide information in relation to a factory producing toxic emissions infringed Art 2).

[118] See para 7.91ff below.

point. In both *LCB*[119] and *Osman*[120] the Court appeared to acknowledge a wider duty of 'life protection'. In *Scialacqua v Italy*[120a] the Commission was prepared to assume that Article 2 could be interpreted as imposing on states the obligation to cover the costs of medical treatments or medicines essential to save life. It has also been said that the positive obligation to protect life 'includes the requirement for hospitals to have regulations for the protection of their patients' lives'.[120b] In his concurring opinion in *Guerra v Italy*[121] Judge Jambrek expressed the view that the 'protection of health and physical integrity' was closely associated with the 'right to life'. He took the view that:

> It may . . . be time for the court's case law on art 2 . . . to start evolving, to develop the respective implied rights, articulate situations of real and serious risk to life, or different aspects of the right to life.[122]

In that case, Judge Jambrek and Judge Walsh were prepared to find a violation of Article 2 in a situation in which 150 people had suffered arsenic poisoning after an accident at a chemical factory. The Commission has rejected a complaint under Article 2 in relation to the transportation of nuclear waste on the basis that this was carried out in accordance with national and international norms.[123]

(c) Abortion

It is not clear whether the right to life in Article 2 extends to unborn children.[124] **7.42**
In *Paton v United Kingdom*[125] the Commission left the question open; but held that if such a right does exist from conception, that right is not absolute but must be subject to limitations in certain circumstances. It found that because the life of the foetus is intimately connected with, and cannot be regarded in isolation from, the life of the pregnant woman, an absolute right to life of the foetus would require prohibition of abortion even when continuance of the pregnancy would involve serious risk to the life of the pregnant woman, and would in effect give the life of the foetus higher value than that of the mother, 'a person already born' or a life in being. Examining the term 'everyone' as it appears in Article 2 and elsewhere in the Convention, the Commission observed:

---

119 *LCB v United Kingdom* (1998) 27 EHRR 212.
120 *Osman v United Kingdom* (1998) 5 BHRC 293.
120a (1998) 26 EHRR CD 164.
120b *Erikson v Italy* Application 37900/97, 26 Oct 1999.
121 (1998) 26 EHRR 357.
122 Ibid 387.
123 *L M and R v Switzerland* (1996) 22 EHRR CD 130.
124 See Harris, O'Boyle and Warbrick (n 112 above) 41–44; P van Dijk and G van Hoof, *Theory and Practice of the European Convention on Human Rights* (3rd edn, Kluwer, 1998) 300–302; Lord Lester and D Pannick, *Human Rights Law and Practice* (Butterworths, 1999) paras 4.2.21–4.2.23; for the Canadian cases, see para 7.74 below.
125 (1981) 3 EHRR 408, EComm HR (the English case was *Paton v British Pregnancy Advisory Service Trustees* [1979] QB 276 see para 7.12 above); and see *Brüggemann and Scheuten v Germany* (1978) 10 DR 100, EComm HR.

> In nearly all these instances the use of the word is such that it can apply only post-natally. None indicates clearly that it has any possible prenatal application, although such application in a rare case cannot be entirely excluded. All of the limitations contained in Article 2 by their nature concern persons already born and cannot be applied to the foetus. Thus, both the general usage of the term 'everyone' ('toute personne') of the Convention and the context in which this term is employed in Article 2 tend to support the view that it does not include the unborn.

The Commission therefore decided that the abortion of a 10-week old foetus under English law did not violate Article 2 where it was performed in order to protect the physical or mental health of the mother. To similar effect in *H v Norway*[126] the Commission did not exclude the possibility that in certain circumstances (which it did not elaborate), Article 2 protection might be available to the unborn child; but went on to uphold the lawful abortion of a 14-week old foetus on the social grounds that 'pregnancy, birth or care for the child may place the woman in a difficult situation of life'.[127] The Commission also emphasised that in such a delicate area states have a margin of appreciation.

(d) Euthanasia

7.43 The right to life is relevant to euthanasia. Euthanasia may be conducted in either an active or passive fashion: by administering a lethal drug or by refusing to continue life saving treatment. It seems clear that an active termination of a person's life by medical authorities will be a *prima facie* breach of Article 2.[128] However, if a patient consents, then it may be that active euthanasia would not be a breach of the Article.[129] It seems that suicide is outside the scope of Article 2 and allowing a hunger striker to die rather than force feeding him will not be a breach.[130] In relation to 'passive euthanasia', the Commission has decided that this is not prohibited by Article 2: where death is assisted through the omission of medical care or

---

[126] (1992) 73 DR 155, EComm HR; the Commission noted that the German Federal Constitutional Court had held that Art 2(2) includes unborn human beings but that the Austrian Constitutional Court had taken the opposite view.

[127] Norwegian statutory law provided that, between 12 and 18 weeks, abortion required medical authorisation based on several criteria.

[128] Cf Lord Lester and D Pannick (n 124 above) para 4.2.22; see also Harris, O'Boyle and Warbrick (n 112 above) 38.

[129] Robertson suggests that unless the right to life is to be regarded as inalienable, it is difficult to see how euthanasia carried out with the consent of the subject should be considered a contravention of the right to life: see *Human Rights in Europe* (2nd edn, Manchester University Press, 1977) 34; but see *De Wilde, Ooms and Versyp v Belgium (No 1)* (1971) 1 EHRR 373 (right to liberty cannot be lost by agreement to detention)).

[130] See T Opsahl, 'The Right to Life', in R St J Macdonald, F Matscher and H Petzold (eds), *The European System for the Protection of Human Rights* (Nijhoff, 1993).

treatment, the Convention does not require such an omission to be criminalised.[131]

(c) Deaths in custody

When a person dies in custody, whilst under the control of police or prison officers, the state is under an obligation to provide a plausible explanation as to the cause of death.[132] Furthermore, it is arguable that the state owes a positive duty to take adequate and appropriate measures to secure effective protection of the life of a person in custody.[133] This is the position under Article 6 of the ICCPR.[134] **7.44**

(3) Exceptions to the right to life

(a) The death penalty

The first exception to the prohibition against taking of life is capital punishment, which is expressly permitted under Article 2(1) as a sentence of a court following conviction for any 'crime'[135] for which the penalty is prescribed by law. This exclusion was included because, at the time of the drafting of the Convention, the domestic law of the majority of state parties made provision for the death penalty; since then the existence and implementation of the death penalty has become the exception. **7.45**

The Sixth Protocol prohibits the death penalty in times of peace. It came into force on 1 March 1985 and was ratified by the United Kingdom on 27 January 1999.[136] This has the effect that any state which becomes a party to the Protocol has to remove the death penalty from its law. In addition, every individual has a right not to be condemned to the death penalty or to be executed. It will be a breach of the Sixth Protocol to extradite a person to a state where there is a real risk **7.46**

---

[131] In *Widmer v Switzerland* (1993) (Application 20527/92), EComm HR, it was sufficient that Swiss law provided criminal liability for negligent medical treatment causing death. The termination of treatment previously administered to a patient, such as the disconnection of a life support system, will probably not be considered a positive act, but as part of a series of steps which together constitute a passive withholding of treatment to the individual: see *Airedale NHS Trust v Bland* [1993] AC 789; for the position in Canada, see para 7.78 below.

[132] Cf *Ribitsch v Austria* (1995) 21 EHRR 573 para 34 and *Aksoy v Turkey* (1996) 23 EHRR 553 para 61 (making the same point in relation to ill-treatment in custody).

[133] See the admissibility decision of *Keenan v United Kingdom* (1998) 26 EHRR CD 64, 72.

[134] See *Dermit Barbato v Uruguay* (1981) Doc A/38/40; and generally, D McGoldrick, *The Human Rights Committee* (Clarendon Press, 1994) para 8.16, 337–338. The text of Art 6 is reproduced at para 7.01 above.

[135] With the application of the principle of proportionality, the death penalty should apply to only the 'most serious crimes', as is the case under the ICCPR Art 6, and the American Convention on Human Rights, Art 4; it is also prohibited for 'political offences or other related common crimes' under the ACHR.

[136] For the history of the drafting of the Protocol see W Schabas, *The Abolition of the Death Penalty in International Law* (2nd edn, Cambridge University Press, 1997) 238ff.

that the death penalty will be imposed.[137] This Protocol is non-derogable[138] and no reservation can be made in relation to it.[139]

(b) The exceptions in Article 2(2)

7.47 Article 2(2) describes the situations in which it is permitted to 'use force' which may result, as an unintended outcome, in taking life.[140] Where such use of force is absolutely necessary in the circumstances, the deprivation of life by the state shall not breach the right to life:

- during self-defence or defence of another;
- during the apprehension of an individual to prevent an escape or effect a lawful arrest;
- to quell a riot or insurrection.

These exceptions are to be considered exhaustive and must be narrowly interpreted.[141]

7.48 Article 2(2)(a) allows the use of force by the state in self-defence or the defence of another, but does not permit it in defence of property. The only real issue in relation to the self-defence exception is whether the force used was 'absolutely necessary' for the specified purpose.[142]

7.49 Article 2(2)(b) permits the state to take life to quell a riot or insurrection. There is little jurisprudence dealing with taking life by a use of force for these purposes. No case of the Commission or the Court defines either term.[143] However, *Stewart v United Kingdom*[144] suggests the two can be taken to have different meanings under the Convention. This case also establishes that there is no obligation on police or security forces to retreat when quelling a riot.[145] Nevertheless, like all the Article 2(2) exceptions, a strict interpretation of the requirement that the use of force must be 'absolutely necessary' will be important: to ensure caution on the part of law enforcement officers. In *X v Belgium*,[146] a claim that Article 2(2)(c) justified

[137] *Aylor-Davis v France* (1994) 76-A DR 164, EComm HR; see also *Raidl v Austria* (1995) 82-A DR 134, EComm HR.

[138] Sixth Protocol, Art 3.

[139] Sixth Protocol, Art 4.

[140] *Ergi v Turkey* RJD 1998–IV 1751 para 79.

[141] *Stewart v United Kingdom* (1984) 39 DR 162, 169, EComm HR.

[142] Contrast the unsuccessful claims in *Wolfgram v Germany* (1986) 49 DR 213, EComm HR and *Díaz Ruano v Spain* (1994) 19 EHRR 555, with the decision of the Court in *McCann v United Kingdom* (1995) 21 EHRR 97; and see para 7.51ff below.

[143] The Commission in *Stewart v United Kingdom* (1984) 39 DR 162, EComm HR decided on the facts that 'an assembly of 150 people throwing missiles at a patrol of soldiers to the point that they risked serious injury must be considered, by any standard, to constitute a riot'.

[144] Ibid.

[145] (1984) 39 DR 162.

[146] (1969) 12 YB 174, EComm HR; declared inadmissible on other grounds.

the shooting of an innocent bystander by a policeman attempting to quell a riot was rejected; the officer had failed to obtain the required authorisation for his firearms and their use was not 'lawful' under Belgian law.

Article 2(2)(c) permits the state to take life to effect an arrest or to prevent an escape. Deadly force was considered 'absolutely necessary' in *Wolfgram v Germany*[147] to effect a lawful arrest under Article 2(2)(b) of the Convention. In *Farrell v United Kingdom*[148] the question was whether a finding under English law that soldiers had used 'reasonable' force meant that such force was lawful under Article 2. However, the issue was not tested because the case was subject to a friendly settlement after the Commission had ruled the application admissible. In *Kelly v United Kingdom*[149] the applicant's son was a joy rider who was shot at a police check point in Northern Ireland. The Commission found that the use of force was justified under Article 2(2)(b) to effect an arrest, despite the fact that there was no power of arrest under domestic law;[150] and the application was dismissed as manifestly ill-founded. The decision is difficult to understand, has been the subject of considerable criticism[151] and is unlikely to be followed. In *Gülec v Turkey*[152] there was a breach of Article 2 when gendarmes fired into a crowd to disperse demonstrators. The Court described the unavailability of less forceful means of crowd control such as truncheons, riot shields, water cannon, rubber bullets or tear gas as 'incomprehensible and unacceptable'. **7.50**

(c) 'No more than absolutely necessary'

The three situations in which taking life by the state is justified under Article 2(2) require that the force used is 'no more than absolutely necessary'. This is a strict requirement: **7.51**

> the use of the term 'absolutely necessary' in Article 2(2) indicates that a stricter and more compelling test of necessity must be employed from that normally applicable when determining whether state action is 'necessary in a democratic society' under paragraphs 2 of Articles 8 to 11 of the Convention. In particular, the force used must be strictly proportionate to the achievement of the aims set out in sub-paragraphs 2(a), (b) and (c) of Article 2.[153]

The standard is stricter than a provision that the use of force must be 'reasonably

[147] (1986) 49 DR 213, EComm HR.

[148] *Farrell v United Kingdom* (1982) 30 DR 96 (admissibility); (1984) 38 DR 44, EComm HR.

[149] (1993) 16 EHRR CD 20.

[150] The Judge in Northern Ireland had held that the force was justified for the 'prevention of crime' which does not appear in Art 2(2).

[151] See D Harris, M O'Boyle and C Warbrick, *Law of the European Convention on Human Rights* (Butterworths, 1995) 51–53.

[152] (1999) 28 EHRR 121.

[153] *Andronicou and Constantinou v Cyprus* (1997) 25 EHRR 491 para 171; see also *McCann v United Kingdom* (1995) 21 EHRR 97 para 148; and *Stewart v United Kingdom* (1984) 39 DR 162, EComm HR.

justifiable'.[154] The force may be justified where it is based on reasonably held honest belief which turns out to be mistaken.[155]

7.52 In *McCann v United Kingdom*[156] the complaint concerned the killing of three members of the IRA by SAS soldiers in Gibraltar. The majority of 10–9 took the view that the Court had to consider not only whether the force used by the soldiers was proportionate but also:

> whether the anti-terrorist operation was planned and controlled by the authorities so as to minimise, to the greatest extent possible, the recourse to lethal force.[157]

The Court examined the background to the killings and concluded that 'having regard to the decision not to prevent the suspects from travelling into Gibraltar, to the failure of the authorities to make sufficient allowance for the possibility that their intelligence assessments might, in some respects at least, be erroneous and to the automatic recourse to lethal force when the soldiers opened fire',[158] it was not persuaded that the killing of the three terrorists 'constituted the use of force which was no more than absolutely necessary' within Article 2(2)(a). However, there was a strong dissenting judgment by the minority[159] which emphasised the seriousness of the allegation being made against the State and concluded that there was no failing in the organisation and control of the operation. It is by no means clear that the decision would be followed in the future.

7.53 More recently, the Turkish Government has been found to be in breach of Article 2 on a number of occasions arising out of the activities of its security forces in relation to Kurdish demonstrators. Thus, in *Ergi v Turkey*[160] the applicant's sister had been killed during armed action by the security forces against the Workers Party of Kurdistan (PKK). It was held that:

> In the light of the failure of the authorities of the respondent State to adduce direct evidence on the planning and conduct of the ambush operation, the Court, in agreement with the Commission, finds that it can reasonably be inferred that insufficient precautions had been taken to protect the lives of the civilian population.

A similar conclusion was reached following the death of a demonstrator in the case of *Gülec v Turkey*.[161]

---

[154] See *McCann v United Kingdom* (n 153 above) para 154.
[155] Ibid para 200.
[156] (1995) 21 EHRR 97.
[157] Ibid para 194.
[158] Ibid para 213.
[159] Which included Judges Ryssdal and Bernhardt.
[160] RJD 1998–IV 1751.
[161] (1999) 28 EHRR 121, see para 7.50 above.

D. The Impact of the Human Rights Act

(1) Introduction

Although English law is broadly consistent with Article 2, the positive and absolute nature of the Convention obligations to protect the right to life means that incorporation may have significant impact in several areas, particularly if the courts adopt a broad interpretation of the right to life.[162] The Human Rights Act is likely to affect the law in relation to health care, immigration, planning and the enviroment and police law. 7.54

(2) UK cases prior to the Human Rights Act

There have been over 30 United Kingdom applications which have directly addressed issues under Article 2. However, only a small number of cases have been declared admissible by the Commission and the Court has found a violation in only one case.[162a] The Commission has rejected, as being manifestly ill-founded, an application involving UK abortion law. In *Paton v United Kingdom*,[163] a father contended that the UK law, pursuant to which he had been refused an injunction to prevent his estranged wife from obtaining an abortion, contravened the Convention. Even though it was acknowledged that the father was a 'victim', the application was manifestly ill-founded because of an implied limitation, in favour of the life and health of the mother, over the 'right to life' of the foetus. 7.55

In *Taylor, Crampton, Gibson, King v United Kingdom*[164] the parents of four children who were murdered by a nurse in a children's ward of a hospital claimed that the state was responsible for failing to prevent such incidents: by employing a person such as the nurse in question, by failing to respond adequately and effectively to sudden collapses of several children in one ward and by failing to conduct a sufficient public and independent inquiry into the procedural mechanisms used to deal with the incidents. The Commission found no indication that the case had not been sufficiently investigated; nor that there had been a failure to provide a mechanism whereby those with criminal or civil responsibility would be held answerable. 7.56

Other cases before the Commission and Court have addressed the actions of the armed forces, the police or prison officers who have in some way been involved in the death of a person. The case of *Stewart v United Kingdom*[165] involved a claim 7.57

[162] The Human Rights Committee have taken a broad view of the right to life in the International Covenant of Civil and Political Rights, suggesting that it requires states to adopt to take all positive measures to reduce infant mortality and to increase life expectancy: see para 7.91ff below.

[162a] *McCann v United Kingdom* (1996) 21 EHRR 97.

[163] (1980) 19 DR 244, EComm HR.

[164] (1994) 79-A DR 127.

[165] (1984) 39 DR 162, EComm HR.

by a mother in regard to the death of her child by a plastic bullet fired by a British soldier in Northern Ireland. The Commission found that the force used was no more than was 'absolutely necessary' in action lawfully taken to quell a riot under Article 2(2)(c). Similarly, soldiers who shot one of four youths who were joy riding in Belfast when they sought to evade a road block were found to have reasonably believed the occupants of the stolen car to be terrorists; the use of force was found to be justified under Article 2(2) of the Convention.[166]

7.58 In *McCann v United Kingdom*[167] three Provisional IRA members were shot dead in Gibraltar by members of the SAS in circumstances which had raised suspicions of a planned terrorist attack. On the question of the proportionality of the response of the state to the perceived threat, the Court, contrary to the conclusion of the Commission, found that the United Kingdom had breached Article 2 of the Convention. While rejecting allegations that there had been a premeditated plot to kill the suspects, it found that the anti-terrorist plan had involved the communication of hypotheses which, when conveyed to soldiers as certainties, made the use of lethal force almost unavoidable. The Coroner found that all four soldiers had shot with intention to kill the suspects and there was no indication that they had been instructed to assess whether the use of firearms to wound the suspects might have been warranted. The majority of the Court was not convinced that the killing of the three terrorists constituted a use of force that was 'no more than absolutely necessary' in defence of persons from unlawful violence within the meaning of Article 2(2)(a) of the Convention.

7.59 In *Osman v United Kingdom*[168] the complaint concerned a failure by the police to take proper measures to prevent murder taking place. Although it was accepted that the authorities were under a positive obligation to protect the right to life by suppressing offences against the person, the obligation had to be interpreted 'in a way which does not impose an impossible or disproportionate burden on the authorities'.[169] It was held that, on the facts, there was no violation of Article 2.[170]

7.60 In *LCB v United Kingdom*[171] the Court rejected a claim where the applicant alleged that her leukemia was caused by the state's failure to monitor her father's exposure to radiation when stationed at Christmas Island during nuclear tests.

---

[166] *Kelly v United Kingdom* (1993) 74 DR 139, EComm HR.

[167] (1995) 21 EHRR 97; see para 7.52 above.

[168] (1998) 5 BHRC 293; for a fuller discussion, see para 11.95ff below.

[169] Ibid para 116.

[170] Judges de Meyer, Lopes Rocha and Casadevall dissented on this point, Ibid, 336–338; see also *Bromiley v United Kingdom* Application 33747/96, 23 Nov 1996 (no breach by release on home leave of a violent prisoner who committed a murder).

[171] (1998) 27 EHRR 212.

(3) General impact issues

(a) Introduction

When examining the lawfulness of any administrative decision under the Human Rights Act when the right to life is engaged, the court will be making a primary judgment[172] about whether the right to life has been breached.[173] It will no longer be confined to making a secondary judgment as to the lawfulness of the decision on *Wednesbury* grounds.[174] Article 2 will have important implications for health care, particularly where the court considers cases where medical treatment engages the right to life. Article 2 will also affect immigration, planning and environment and police law. **7.61**

(b) Health care

The absolute protection afforded to the right to life could affect the provision of medical treatment to those suffering from life-threatening illnesses. It could be argued that the absolute nature of the right casts doubt on the balancing exercise endorsed by the Court of Appeal in *R v Cambridge Health Authority, ex p B*[175] in such cases. If Article 2 places states under a positive duty to provide treatment where there is a *real risk* to life, as opposed to an obligation to sustain life *however small* the chance of survival,[176] it would follow that the court must intervene to ensure that treatment is provided or continued.[177] Nevertheless, in view of the impact of such arguments on complex political issues concerning the allocation of health service resources, it seems unlikely that they will be accepted by the English courts.[178] It can be argued that the positive right does not extend to this situation because it is not justified in terms of the need to strike a fair balance between the general interest of the community and the interests of the individual.[178a] The courts may, however, take the view that when life is at stake, the policy choices involved in health care rationing should be explained and justified.[179] **7.62**

[172] See generally, para 5.122ff above.

[173] For example, in the case of an exclusion order under the Prevention of Terrorism Act, reversing the effect of *R v Secretary of State for the Home Department, ex p McQuillan* [1995] 4 All ER 400.

[174] For the present position, see para 7.23ff above.

[175] [1995] 1 WLR 898; see generally, R James and D Longley, 'Judicial Review and Tragic Choices' [1995] PL 367; and see para 7.24 above.

[176] [1995] 1 FLR 1055 *per* Laws J.

[177] See D O'Sullivan, 'The Allocation of Scarce Resources and the Right to Life Under the European Convention on Human Rights' [1998] PL 389; R Owen, S Lambert and C Neenan, 'Clinical Negligence and Personal Injury Litigation' in R English and P Havers (eds), *An Introduction to Human Rights and the Common Law* (Hart Publishing, 2000), 139.

[178] Cf *Soobramoney v Minister of Health (KwaZulu-Natal)* (1998) 4 BHRC 308 discussed at para 7.105 below.

[178a] In determining whether a positive obligation exists, it is well established that a fair balance must be struck: see, eg, *Rees v United Kingdom* (1986) 9 EHRR 56 para 37; and see generally, para 6.100 above.

[179] See James and Longley (n 175 above) 372–373.

7.63 The position may, however, be different in relation to emergency treatment for life threatening conditions. If an accident victim was refused treatment because, for example, of a lack of hospital beds it might be argued that there was a breach of the positive duty to preserve life under Article 2.[180]

7.64 The positive right to life will raise new and important arguments where the court considers medical treatment. The doctrine of double effect[181] where the treatment hastens death appears to breach Article 2; and the same argument can be made where it is said that the court should authorise the termination of life because of a patient's poor quality of life. It also seems that the prohibition against patient assisted suicide contained in section 2 of the Suicide Act is compatible with Convention rights.[181a] Article 2 may require the court to take a more interventionist approach in cases where children need medical treatment to which their parents strongly object.[182] On the other hand, anticipatory decisions[183] (such as an individual deciding against medical treatment for senile dementia which will result in his death) are likely to be treated as a waiver[184] of the right to life. In *A National Health Service Trust v D*[184a] it was held that a declaration that a severely disabled child did not have to be given artificial ventilation did not breach the child's Article 2 rights.

7.65 It has also been suggested that a 'positive right to life' might be invoked in other situations:

- to challenge the closure of a residential home which results in the relocation of vulnerable elderly people who have lived there for many years;[185]
- to expand the duties of public authorities in relation to health and safety when employees are involved in tasks which might endanger life;[186]
- to expand the liability of public authorities in clinical negligence cases on the basis that the duty to preserve life is not discharged simply by taking reasonable care.[187]

---

[180] Cf the decision of the Supreme Court of India in *Paschim Banga Khet Mazdoor Samity v State of West Bengal* 1996 4 SCC 37 (failure of Government hospitals to treat a person suffering from serious head injuries was violation of right to life), see para 7.95 below; and see Art 27 of the South African Constitution which provides a qualified right to access to health care services but provides that 'No one may be refused emergency medical treatment'.

[181] See para 7.20 above.

[181a] See generally, M Freeman, 'Death, Dying and the Human Rights Act 1998' [1999] CLP 218.

[182] Reversing *In re T (A Minor)(Wardship: Medical Treatment)* [1997] 1 WLR 242.

[183] See eg *F v West Berkshire Health Authority* [1989] 2 All ER 545.

[184] See generally para 6.148ff above.

[184a] The Times, 19 Jul 2000.

[185] See L Clements, *Community Care and the Law* (Legal Action Group, 1996) 86–7; cf *R v North and East Devon Health Authority, ex p Coughlan* (1999) 51 BMLR 1 (in which it was held that the closure of a residential home was a breach of Art 8).

[186] Cf R Owen (n 177 above) 141–142.

[187] See R Owen (n 177 above) 141.

Such arguments could be supported by reliance on the United Kingdom's treaty obligations to take steps necessary to prevent, treat and control disease[188] and to protect health.[189] Nevertheless, it is likely that the English courts will follow the Strasbourg authorities in proceedings cautiously;[190] and that any positive duty recognised under this head will be strictly limited.

(c) Right to life and abortion

It is also likely that the rights of the unborn child will be re-examined under Article 2. It is doubtful that Article 2 would enable a father to object to a termination by the mother.[191] However, where a woman declines medical treatment (such as an enforced Caesarean section) which would save the life of her unborn foetus,[192] it could be argued that the foetus in those circumstances has a right to life.[193] **7.66**

(4) Specific areas of impact

(a) Immigration

The 'right to life' is an unqualified right and, where it arises, it will take precedence over all other considerations. Thus, the domestic courts are likely to approach 'right to life' cases in the same manner as did the European Court of Human Rights in *Chahal v United Kingdom*.[194] In that case, the Court held that a real risk of being subjected to inhuman or degrading treatment was a breach of Article 3, with the effect that it was *irrelevant* whether Mr Chahal posed a threat to national security.[195] **7.67**

Following the decision in *Chahal v United Kingdom*[196] the Home Office changed its policy so that it will not seek to expel or return an asylum seeker to his country of origin if he can satisfy the Home Secretary that there are substantial grounds for believing that there is a danger, *inter alia*, of loss of life. However, the Human Rights Act will require the English courts to decide if there has been a breach of the right to life, rather than reviewing the rationality of the Home Secretary's decision. **7.68**

The Human Rights Act may also affect the position of refugees. To qualify for refugee status, it is necessary that a claimant meet the requirements of the Geneva Convention and Protocol on the Status of Refugees[197] and prove, for example, **7.69**

---

188 Art 12, International Covenant on Economic, Social and Cultural Rights, 1966.

189 Art 11, European Social Charter, 1965.

190 See generally, para 7.37ff above.

191 *Paton v British Pregnancy Advisory Service* [1979] QB 276.

192 See eg *St George's Healthcare Trust v S* [1999] Fam 26.

193 P Havers and N Sheldon, 'The Impact of the Convention on Medical Law' in R English and P Havers (eds), n 177 above.

194 (1996) 23 EHRR 413.

195 Cf *R v Secretary of State for the Home Department, ex p Chahal* [1995] 1 WLR 526.

196 Ibid.

197 1951 Cmnd 9171 and 1967 Cmnd 3906.

membership of a 'particular social group'. Although this requirement has been given a liberal interpretation[198] there will be some refugees who will not be able to establish membership of such a group. Similarly, in *Adan v Secretary of State for the Home Department*[199] the House of Lords decided that an asylum seeker could not show a well founded fear of being persecuted if he was at no greater risk of killing or torture than any other member of his clan as a result of the civil war in Somalia. Article 2 could now provide an alternative basis for relief: if a claimant can show a 'real risk' to his life on return, he might be able to rely directly upon a breach of Article 2 to justify remaining in the United Kingdom.

(b) Planning and environment

7.70 It is arguable that Article 2 places positive duties on public authorities to ensure a safe environment.[200] This argument has succeeded before the Human Rights Committee and in the courts of India.[201] However, it is unlikely to do so under Article 2 unless the 'life threatening' nature of the environmental hazard is clear. Environmental issues are more likely to be dealt with under Article 8 of the Convention.[202] In any event, it is unlikely that a breach of Article 2 would be found if steps had been taken to assure safety in compliance with international environmental norms.[203]

(c) Police law

7.71 Article 2 could have a significant impact in cases in which the state is expressly *permitted* to take life. At common law and under statute, police officers or soldiers may use 'reasonable force' either in self-defence or to prevent crime. In appropriate circumstances, this force may be lethal. However, under Article 2(2) the force used must be 'no more than absolutely necessary'; and can only be used for the limited purposes set out. These standards are stricter than those at common law.[204] The police will, therefore, have to satisfy a stricter test in order to justify deaths which result from the use of force against suspects. This will apply not only to the force used by police officers but also to the planning and control of the operation. The courts are likely to have to consider issues as to the adequacy of the training of police officers in dealing with life-threatening situations.[205]

---

[198] See eg *R v Immigration Appeal Tribunal, ex p Shah* [1999] 2 All ER 545 (women could constitute a particular social group if they lived in a society which discriminated against them on grounds of sex).

[199] [1998] 2 WLR 702.

[200] See generally, N Grief, 'Convention Rights and the Environment' in L Betten (ed), *The Human Rights Act 1998: What it Means* (Kluwer, 1999) 143–146.

[201] See para 7.93ff below.

[202] As in *Guerra v Italy* (1998) 26 EHRR 357; see para 12.99 below.

[203] See para 7.41 above.

[204] Cf *McCann v United Kingdom* (1995) 21 EHRR 97 para 154.

[205] See J Wadham and H Mountfield, *Blackstone's Guide to the Human Rights Act 1998* (Blackstone, 1999) 65.

Deaths in police custody may give rise to a number of issues under Article 2. First, there will be a duty to conduct an 'effective official investigation' as to the circumstances of the death.[206] It is arguable that the inquest procedure, with its limited rights of representation for the deceased's family, may not be sufficient to satisfy this requirement.[207] Secondly, there will be a burden on the police to prove that such deaths were not their responsibility.[208] Thirdly, the police may be under a positive duty to take steps to protect the health and life of those held in custody. However, this duty does not appear to be any stronger than the common law 'duty of care' towards those held in police custody.[209] 7.72

Appendix 1: The Canadian Charter of Rights

(1) The scope of the right

Section 7 of the Charter provides: 7.73

> Everyone has the right to life, liberty and security of the person and the right not to be deprived thereof except in accordance with the principles of fundamental justice.

The grammatical structure of section 7 suggests that two separate rights might be protected. It would seem that there is first, a right to life, liberty and security which is absolute, subject to the general limitation under section 1 that the freedoms are subject to such reasonable limits prescribed by law as can be demonstrably justified in a free and democratic society. Secondly, there would appear to be a right not to be deprived of life except in accordance with principles of fundamental justice. However, this construction would result in a breach every time there was a deprivation of life irrespective of whether the principles of fundamental justice had been infringed. Therefore, the 'single right' interpretation is more acceptable: there is no violation of section 7 unless principles of fundamental justice have been denied.[210]

The benefit of the section is for 'everyone' which, contrary to the usual interpretation of that word, does not include artificial persons such as corporations.[211] Neither does 7.74

---

[206] See para 7.38 above.

[207] P Havers and N Sheldon, n 193 above, 129–130.

[208] See para 7.44 above.

[209] See most recently, *Reeves v Commissioner of Police for the Metropolis* [1999] 3 WLR 363.

[210] *Chiarelli v Canada* [1992] 1 SCR 711 stated that a denial of liberty in accordance with fundamental justice was not a breach of s 7; see, though, the positions of Lamer J and Wilson J in *Re BC Motor Vehicle Act* [1985] 2 SCR 486. Lamer J presented an elaborate discussion of the principles of fundamental justice, which would be unnecessary if every deprivation of life were an infringement of the section; he then, at 500, expressly left open the issue. Wilson J, contrary to what she had earlier suggested in *Operation Dismantle Inc v Canada* [1985] 1 SCR 441, 487, said that even if fundamental justice were satisfied, s 1 would also have to be satisfied, apparently adopting the 'two rights' interpretation.

[211] *Irwin Toy v Quebec (A-G)* [1989] 1 SCR 927; *Dywidag Systems v Zutphen Bros* [1990] 1 SCR 705, 709; nevertheless, a corporation might benefit from the fact that the law would be a violation of s 7 if applied to an individual. In *R v Wholesale Travel Group Inc* [1991] 3 SCR 154, the Supreme Court of Canada rejected the argument that a law could be unconstitutional for individuals but constitutional for corporations.

'everyone' include the unborn child, as the interest of a foetus in life is not constitutionally protected until birth.[212] The Supreme Court of Canada has in fact used section 7 to uphold liberal abortion laws on the basis that the restrictions deprived the mother of her right to liberty or security of the person.[213] 'Everyone' does, however, include illegal immigrants because section 7 rights 'may be asserted by every human being physically present in Canada and by virtue of such presence amenable to Canadian law'.[214]

7.75 The definition of the term 'life' in section 7 has not given rise to the sort of difficult issues associated with questions of justification for deprivation of life. 'Life', which implies the right to preservation and continuation of the human self, begins at birth[215] and is the essential condition from which all other freedoms under the Charter flow.

(2) 'Fundamental justice'

7.76 Section 7 protects everyone's right to life, liberty and security of the person, subject to deprivations sanctioned by the 'principles of fundamental justice'.[216] In contrast to Article 2 of the European Convention, section 7 of the Charter does not define those situations in which deprivation of life might be justified as an exception to the rights provided for,[217] but expresses only the general requirement that any deprivations must be 'in accordance with principles of fundamental justice'. It is therefore left to the courts to define the limits of the justifiable exceptions; in doing so, they have necessarily focused on the concept of fundamental justice rather than on distinctions between life, liberty and security. Furthermore, much of the jurisprudence under section 7 has arisen, not in the context of a deprivation of life, but in relation to purported infringements of liberty or security of the person.[218]

(3) The obligation to protect life

7.77 As the law does not consider a foetus to be a person until it is born, it does not have the right to life that benefits 'everyone' under section 7.[219] For the purposes of Charter rights,

---

[212] *Borowski v A-G of Canada* (1987) 39 DLR (4th) 731, Sask CA; see also *Tremblay v Daigle* [1989] 2 SCR 530 (no private law basis for injunction by father of unborn child to restrain abortion, court refrained from dealing with question as to whether 'everyone' included a foetus).

[213] *R v Morgentaler (No 2)* (1988) 44 DLR (4th) 385.

[214] Wilson J, in *Singh v Canada (Minister of Employment and Immigration)* [1985] 1 SCR 177, 202 explained that she meant that any illegal immigrant who claimed to be a refugee was entitled to have the matter determined before an authorised tribunal; she rejected the argument that such a procedure would make it impossible to handle applications expeditiously given the number of refugee claimants arriving in the country, as an 'inadmissible administrative or utilitarian concern' that could not be permitted to vitiate individual rights.

[215] *Borowski v A-G of Canada* (1987) 39 DLR (4th) 731, Sask CA.

[216] See generally, para 11.388ff below.

[217] Art 2 of the Convention preserves the legitimacy of capital punishment, which has since been prohibited by the Sixth Protocol, to which some states, including the United Kingdom, have yet failed to subscribe. Art 2 also justifies the taking of life by the use of force, to the extent necessary, in defence of self or others, to effect a lawful arrest or prevent an escape, and in quelling a riot or insurrection.

[218] See para 10.206ff below.

[219] *Borowski v A-G of Canada* (1987) 39 DLR (4th) 731, Sask CA; however, the issue arises in relation to the security of the mother: see para 7.74 above.

abortion does not involve deprivation of life.[220] The ability of the mother to procure an abortion is based in her right to security of the person.

7.78 Questions concerning the administration or termination of medical treatment causing death, such as euthanasia, have not been addressed in any extensive way under section 7 of the Charter. As in England[221] and New Zealand,[222] the withdrawal of life support or the withholding of life-sustaining treatment in Canada is not considered to be a potentially culpable taking of life by public authorities, but as the right of an individual to die; the security of the person guaranteed by section 7 arguably enables the individual to maintain dignity and control over such events in the death process.[223]

7.79 In *Rodriguez v British Columbia (A-G)*[224] the Supreme Court of Canada considered a request for physician-assisted suicide by a terminally ill patient; and held a Criminal Code prohibition on aiding and abetting suicide was not unconstitutional, but constituted a justifiable limitation on the right of the individual to autonomy over his person, under section 1. The Supreme Court rejected the argument that the prohibition against assisting suicide infringed the right to life, liberty and security of the person.

7.80 The relationship between the right to life of the child and the liberty of parents to make decisions for his benefit[225] has been considered in several cases dealing with the provision of medical treatment to a child contrary to the wishes and religious beliefs of its parents. The right of the child has taken precedence over the competing right of the parents to be free from state intervention in the raising of their children.[226] Legislation providing for the appointment of an official legal guardian, and authorisation of medical treatment for a child did not violate section 7, because the purpose of the statute was to protect, rather than to deprive, the child of his right to life.[227]

7.81 In *B(R) v Children's Aid Society of Metropolitan Toronto*[228] the Supreme Court of Canada found that, while the provisions of the Child Welfare Act did infringe the right of the parents to choose medical treatment for their infant contrary to section 7 of the Charter, such a deprivation of parental 'liberty' was made in accordance with the principles of fundamental justice. The Court also affirmed the common law recognition of the *parens patriae* jurisdiction of the state to intervene to protect children whose lives are in jeopardy.

(4) Prohibition against the taking of life

7.82 In 1976 the Canadian Parliament abolished the death penalty for virtually all offences.

---

[220] See para 7.74 above.

[221] See para 7.22 above.

[222] See para 7.85 below.

[223] See J Gilmour, 'Withholding and Withdrawing Life Support From Adults at Common Law' (1993) 31 Osgoode Hall LJ 473.

[224] (1993) 107 DLR (4th) 342; see 10.125, under 'security of the person'; see also the US Supreme Court's decision in *Washington v Glucksberg* (1997) 2 BHRC 539.

[225] N Bala and J D Redfearn, 'Family Law and the "Liberty Interest": Section 7 of the Canadian Charter of Rights' (1983) 15 Ottawa L Rev 274; E Colvin, 'Section Seven of the Canadian Charter of Rights and Freedoms' (1989) 68 Canadian Bar Rev 560.

[226] *T v Catholic Children's Aid Society (Metropolitan Toronto)* (1984) 46 OR (2d) 347.

[227] *REDM and ERM v Alberta Director of Child Welfare* (1987) 47 Alta LR (2d) 380, quashing 88 AR 346.

[228] *B(R) v Children's Aid Society of Metropolitan Toronto* [1995] 1 SCR 315.

However, there is still scope for asking whether the death penalty constitutes a violation of the right to life capable of contravening section 7 of the Charter. In a pre-Charter case decided under the Canadian Bill of Rights, *Miller and Cockriell v The Queen*,[229] the Supreme Court of Canada decided that it could not be the intention of Parliament to 'create anew the absolute right not to be deprived of life under any circumstances'. However, questions concerning the death penalty must now be examined in the context of the protection afforded the right to life in section 7, and subjected to the test contained in section 1.

Appendix 2: The New Zealand Bill of Rights Act

(1) Introduction

7.83 Section 8 of the New Zealand Bill of Rights Act provides:

> **Right not to be deprived of life**
>
> No one shall be deprived of life except on such grounds as are established by law and are consistent with the principles of fundamental justice.

The language of section 8 appears to be taken from section 7 of the Canadian Charter. Although one might therefore expect the use of the phrase 'fundamental justice' to give rise to difficulties[230] similar to those addressed in the Canadian jurisprudence, these have not yet been considered by the courts in New Zealand.

(2) The case law

7.84 In the case of *Lawson v Housing New Zealand*[231] the High Court of Auckland had to assess whether the scope of the right to life under the Bill of Rights extended to economic rights. Between 1991 and 1994 the Government implemented a new housing policy in order to remedy the nature of differences in state assistance for low income earners based on their tenancy. Tenants in state houses received three times the assistance provided to tenants in private sector rental accommodation. The Government transferred houses to Housing New Zealand, increased rents in stages to market rates, and provided an accommodation benefit to all low income earners. When Housing New Zealand sought to terminate the plaintiff's tenancy, she brought proceedings for judicial review, claiming that the increase in her rent to market rates breached her right to life under the Bill of Rights Act, by depriving her of adequate and affordable shelter. The High Court disagreed. Although the 1990 Act had to be interpreted liberally and with regard to international rights norms, it would be to place undue strain on the construction of the provision to include in the 'right not to be deprived of life' a right not to be charged market rent. There were also strong policy considerations for excluding such a right, since an economic role for section 8 would submit all elements of the welfare state to judicial review.

7.85 In *Auckland Health Board v A-G*[232] the High Court of Auckland considered the lawfulness of the withdrawal of life-giving artificial ventilatory support from a patient in circumstances

[229] [1977] 2 SCR 680, 704, *per* Ritchie J.
[230] See para 11.390 below.
[231] [1997] 2 NZLR 475.
[232] [1993] 1 NZLR 235.

in which the support could not be medically justified. Thomas J considered the impact of the right to life in section 8. He pointed out that it cannot be said that:

> the sanctity of life represents an absolute value. Few, if any, values can be stated in absolute terms. The qualification in s 8 itself confirms that to be the case.[233]

He went on to point out that human dignity and personal privacy belong to every person, whether living or dying.[234] However, the central issue in the case was not the right to life but the question as to whether a doctor was obliged to continue medical treatment which had no medical value. He held that a doctor, acting in good faith and in accordance with good medical practice, is not under a duty to supply the support necessary to prolong life if that provision, in his or her judgment, is contrary to the best interests of the patient.

In the more difficult case of *Shortland v Northland Health Ltd*,[235] health authorities refused a kidney transplant to a man with a fatal kidney condition and terminated his otherwise interim dialysis treatment, because his moderate dementia was considered a clinical impediment to the high level of cooperation that the dialysis treatment would require of him. The Court of Appeal dismissed the claims of the family of the patient, finding that the decision to discontinue dialysis was consistent with the requirements of good medical practice referred to in *Auckland Health Board v A-G*[236] and was not a deprivation of life contrary to section 8 of the New Zealand Bill of Rights Act 1990. The health authority had acted in good faith and carefully conformed with prevailing medical standards, practices and procedures; there was widespread consultation with specialists; renal physicians unanimously concluded that the patient was unsuitable for long-term dialysis; and it was unnecessary for the authorities to consult with an ethical body, because the issue was one of clinical rather than ethical judgment. **7.86**

The relationship between the right to life and the right to manifest religion and belief under section 15 was considered in a case where Jehovah Witnesses refused to consent to a blood transfusion for their child.[237] Ellis J held that: **7.87**

> A child's right to life under section 8 overrides the parents' right to freedom of religion and belief and their otherwise general power to decide upon the child's medical treatment.[238]

This approach was supported by the Court of Appeal which adopted the approach of 'definitional balancing' of rights, holding that the rights of the parents under section 15 were to be construed as being subject to the child's rights under section 8.[239]

Appendix 3: Human Rights Cases in Other Jurisdictions

(1) Introduction

Issues arising in relation to the right to life have been among the most controversial in **7.88**

233 Ibid 244 line 54 to 245, line 1.
234 Referring to *Nancy B v Hotel-Dieu de Quebec* (1992) 86 DLR (4th) 385.
235 [1998] 1 NZLR 433.
236 [1993] 1 NZLR 235.
237 *Re* J [1995] 3 NZLR 73; *Re J, B and B v Director-General of Social Welfare* [1996] 2 NZLR 134.
238 [1995] 3 NZLR 73, 82 line 2.
239 [1996] 2 NZLR 134, 146 line 32ff.

human rights law over recent decades. In particular, the debates surrounding the abolition of the death penalty[240] abortion and euthanasia[241] have taken centre stage.

7.89 The US Supreme Court has made it clear that the state has an 'unqualified interest in the preservation of human life'.[242] However, the only protection for the 'right to life' in the US Constitution is the 'due process' clauses of the Fifth and Fourteenth Amendments. In the 1970s and early 1980s the US Supreme Court placed severe restrictions on the availability of the death penalty on the ground that it constituted cruel and unusual punishment.[243] In the deeply contentious case of *Roe v Wade*[244] the Supreme Court held that a foetus was not a 'person' having due process rights under the Fourteenth Amendment.[245] It went on to recognise the right to abortion as an aspect of the implied constitutional right of privacy.[246] In the cases that followed,[247] the right to abortion has been reaffirmed, but with restricted protection for limitations on the availability of abortions.

7.90 Although the due process clause appears to protect the 'traditional right to refuse unwanted lifesaving medical treatment'[248] it does not extend to a 'right' to euthanasia.[249] The state interest in the 'sanctity of life' commands 'maximum protection of every individual's interest in remaining alive' but it will not always outweigh the interests of a person who, because of pain or incapacity, finds life intolerable.[250]

(2) Human Rights Committee

7.91 Article 6 of the International Covenant on Civil and Political Rights provides that:[251]

> (1) Every human being has the inherent right to life. This right shall be protected by law. No one shall be arbitrarily deprived of his life.

Article 6 goes on to make detailed provision in relation to the death penalty.[252] The right to life has been described as the 'supreme right'.[253] The Human Rights Committee has made it clear that the protection of this right:

> requires that States adopt positive measures. In this connexion the Committee considers that

---

[240] For a general discussion see W Schabas, *The Abolition of the Death Penalty in International Law* (2nd edn, Cambridge University Press, 1997).

[241] See generally, R Dworkin, *Life's Dominion* (HarperCollins, 1993).

[242] *Cruzan v Director, Missouri Department of Health* (1990) 497 US 261, 282.

[243] For a short summary, see J Nowak and R Rotunda, *Constitutional Law*, (5th edn, West Publishing, 1995) para 13.3; see also para 8.105 below.

[244] (1973) 410 US 113.

[245] See generally, Nowak and Rotunda (n 243 above) para 13.3.

[246] See generally, Nowak and Rotunda (n 243 above) para 14.29 and L Tribe, *American Constitutional Law* (2nd edn, Foundation Press, 1988) para 15–10.

[247] Most recently, *Planned Parenthood v Casey* (1992) 505 US 833; *Sternberg v Carhart* 28 Jun 2000.

[248] *Cruzan v Director, Missouri Department of Health* (1990) 497 US 261, 278–279.

[249] *Washington v Glucksberg* (1997) 2 BHRC 539; *Vacco v Quill* (1997) 117 S Ct 2293.

[250] See *Washington v Glucksberg* (n 249 above) Stevens J (concurring), 563–564.

[251] For the full text, see App J in Vol 2.

[252] Ibid.

[253] General Comment 6(16), Doc A/37/40; for general discussions see D McGoldrick, *The Human Rights Committee* (Clarendon Press, 1996) Chap 8, 328–361; D Harris and S Joseph, *The International Covenant on Civil and Political Rights and United Kingdom Law* (Clarendon Press, 1995) Chap 5, 'The Right to Life', 155–183.

> it would be desirable for States parties to take all possible measures to reduce infant mortality and to increase life expectancy, especially in adopting measures to eliminate malnutrition and epidemics.[254]

Most communications under the Optional Protocol have dealt with disappearances of persons in state custody or killings by the security forces. In *Barbato v Uruguay*[255] the Government claimed that the person in custody had committed suicide. The Human Rights Committee could not arrive at a definite finding about the cause of death, concluding that: **7.92**

> in all the circumstances the Uruguayan authorities either by act or by omission were responsible for not taking adequate measures to protect his life, as required by article 6(1) of the Covenant.

In *Herrera Rubio v Colombia*[256] the applicant's parents had been taken away by force and found dead a week later. It was alleged that the military authorities were responsible but no conclusive evidence was produced. The Human Rights Committee reiterated its general comment that:

> the State parties should take specific and effective measures to prevent the disappearance of individuals and establish effective facilities and procedures to investigate thoroughly, by an appropriate impartial body, cases of missing and disappeared persons in circumstances which may involve a violation of the right to life.

On this basis, the Committee expressed the view that there had been a violation of Article 6.

(3) India

Article 21 of the Indian Constitution provides that: **7.93**

> No person shall be deprived of his life or personal liberty except according to procedure established by law.[257]

In *Rathinam v Union of India*[258] the offence of attempted suicide was struck down as being in violation of the constitution on grounds that the right to life extends also to the right *not* to live. However, this case was not followed in *Gian Kaur (Smt) v State of Punjab*.[259] The court rejected the argument that the offence of abetting suicide was assistance constituting the furtherance or enforcement of the right to life of the individual. The Constitution Bench held that it was constitutionally permissible to penalise both attempted suicide, and abetting suicide. In *Kewal Pati v State of UP*[260] the widow of a prisoner who had been killed by a fellow convict was held to be entitled to recover compensation for the breach of the prisoner's right to life.

The right in Article 21 has been given a broad interpretation by the Supreme Court of **7.94**

254 GC 6(16), Doc A/37/40, quoted in D McGoldrick (n 253 above) 329.

255 Case 84/1981, Doc A/38/40, 124, UNHRC.

256 Doc A/43/40, 190, UNHRC; see also *Miango v Zaire* Doc A43/40, 218 and *Laureano Atachahua v Peru* (1997) 1 BHRC 338, 345f–g para 8.3.

257 See generally, S Mahajan, *Constitutional Law of India* (7th edn, 1991).

258 (1994) 3 SCC 394.

259 [1996] 2 LRC 264.

260 [1995] 3 SCR 207. See also *Nilabeti v State of Orissa* 1993 2 SCR 581.

India. Thus, where a chemical industrial plant had been established without the requisite permission and clearances and was then run in blatant disregard of the law to the detriment of the life and liberty of citizens living in the vicinity, the court had power to intervene in order to protect those fundamental rights protected under Article 21 of the Constitution.[261] As was said in *T Damodhar Rao v Municipal Corp of Hyderabad*:[262]

> The slow poisoning by the polluted atmosphere caused by environmental pollution and spoilation should also be treated as amounting to violation of Art 21 of the Constitution

Works that cause pollution may be closed down by the courts even if such closure leads to economic disadvantage and loss of jobs.[263] In the Ganga water pollution case, *M C Mehta v Union of India*[264] the Supreme Court ordered the owners of tanneries which were polluting the river to establish treatment plants.

7.95 The right to life also includes the right to earn a livelihood because:

> no person can live without the means of living, that is, the means of livelihood. If the right to livelihood is not treated as part of the Constitutional right to life, the easiest way of depriving a person of his right to life would be to deprive him of his means of livelihood to the point of abrogation. Such deprivation would not only denude the life of its effective content and meaningfulness but it would make life impossible to live.[265]

In *Narendra Kumar Chandla v State of Haryana*[266] the Supreme Court of India stated that the right to a livelihood meant that where an employee could no longer continue with his employment because of disability, the employer must make every endeavour to re-deploy him to a post in which the employee would be suitable to discharge his duties.

7.95A In *Paschim Banga Khet Mazdoor Samity v State of West Bengal*[267] a breach of the right was found when a person who had sustained serious head injuries and a brain haemorrhage was refused treatment at six successive State hospitals because the hospitals either had inadequate medical facilities or did not have a vacant bed at the time. It was said that:

> Article 21 imposes an obligation on the State to safeguard the right to life of every person. Preservation of human life is thus of paramount importance. The Government hospitals run by the State and medical officers employed therein are duty bound to extend medical assistance for preserving human life. Failure on the part of a Government hospital to provide timely medical treatment to a person in need of such treatment results in violation of his right to life guaranteed under Article 21.

---

[261] *Indian Council for Enviro-Legal Action v Union of India* [1996] 2 LRC 226. See also *Consumer Education and Research Centre v Union of India* [1995] 1 SCR 626 (directions issued in relation to asbestos); *Koolwal v Rajasthan* AIR 1988 Raj 2 (petition to enforce sanitation measures received favourable disposition based in part on right to life argument); *M C Mehta v Union of India* AIR 1987 SC 1086 (escape of oleum gas which led to immediate injury was breach of right to life); *Subash Kumar v Bihar* AIR 1991 SC 420 (action lies to court for pollution which endangers or impairs the quality of life in derogation of laws).

[262] AIR 1987 AP 171, 181.

[263] *Abhilash Textile v Rajkot Municipal Corp* AIR 1988 Guj 57.

[264] AIR 1987 SC 965.

[265] *Tellis v Bombay Municipal Corporation* (1987) LRC (Const) 351; see also *Madhu Kishwar v State of Bihar* (1996) 5 SCC 125; but see *Delhi Development Horticulture Employees' Union v Delhi Administration, Delhi et al* [1993] 4 LRC 182 (right to life does not include the right to work and the right to livelihood, as country lacks economic capacity to honour such guarantees; right to livelihood is part of chapter on 'directive principles' where it is appropriately qualified).

[266] [1994] 1 SCR 657.

[267] 1996 4 SCC 37.

More generally, the right to life includes the right to the bare necessities of life such as adequate nutrition, clothing and shelter, and facilities for reading and writing, and the freedom to mingle with others.[268] It also includes the right to education because 'the dignity of the individual cannot be assured unless it is accompanied by the right to education'.[269] **7.96**

Furthermore, in *Vishaka v State of Rajasthan*,[270] the Supreme Court of India affirmed that the right to life implies a life with dignity and, as a result, laid down guidelines to require employers to take steps to deter sexual harassment. The Supreme Court said that although the primary responsibility for ensuring the availability of a safe working environment[271] and dignity of life was through suitable legislation, in the absence of such legislation the courts must lay down appropriate guidelines. Such guidelines were to be treated as constitutional law and strictly observed at all workplaces for the preservation and enforcement of the right to gender equality for working women.[272] **7.97**

(4) Ireland

Article 40.3 of the Irish Constitution provides that: **7.98**

> (1) The State guarantees in its law to respect, and, as far as practicable by its laws to defend and vindicate the personal rights of the citizen.
> (2) The State shall, in particular, by its laws protect as best it may from unjust attack and, in the case of injustice done, vindicate the life, person, good name and property rights of every citizen.

The right to life has not received extensive consideration in the Irish courts.[273] However, in *G v An Bord Uchtála*[274] it was held that the right to life necessarily implies the right to be born and the right to have life preserved and defended.

Following a referendum in 1983, an additional paragraph was inserted into Article 40.3: **7.99**

> The State acknowledges the right to life of the unborn and, with due regard to the equal right to life of the mother, guarantees in its laws to respect, and as far as practicable, by its laws to defend and vindicate that right.

This amendment produced considerable legal and political debate in Ireland. In *The Society*

[268] *Mullin v Administrator, Union Territory of Delhi* AIR 1981 SC 746; see also *Tellis v Bombay Municipal Corporation* (1987) LRC (Const) 351 and *State of HP v Umed Ram Sharma* AIR 1986 SC 847 (right to life may include right to roads; obligation to residents of remote hilly areas to provide roads to enable communication). The Supreme Court in the *Francis Corali* case applied the decision of *Kharak Singh v State of UP* AIR 1963 SC 1295. *Kharak Singh* relied on the old US case of *Munn v Illinois* (1876) 94 US 113, in which the US Supreme Court observed that 'life' means not merely continuance of the animal existence of a person, but a right to the possession of each of his organs and limbs as well.

[269] *Mohini Jain v State of Karnataka* (1992) 3 SCC 666, 679–680; see also *Unni Krishnan v State of AP* (1993) 1 SCC 645 (limiting right to education to 14 years).

[270] (1998) 3 BHRC 261, SC (India).

[271] The Supreme Court referred also to the fundamental right to carry on a trade, occupation or profession secured by the Convention on the Elimination of all Forms of Discrimination against Women 1979.

[272] See also *Apparel Export Promotion Council v A K Chopra*, [2000] 2 LRC 563.

[273] See generally, J M Kelly, *The Irish Constitution* (3rd edn, Butterworths, 1994) 749–50.

[274] [1980] IR 32, 69.

for the Protection of Unborn Children Ireland Ltd v Grogan[275] the Society obtained an injunction restraining the distribution of information in relation to abortion services outside Ireland. However, the Commission on Human Rights reluctantly held that this was contrary to Article 10 of the Convention.[276] In *Attorney-General v X*,[277] Costello J granted an injunction to prevent a 14 year old rape victim from travelling to the United Kingdom to have an abortion. The injunction was discharged by the Supreme Court. This case led to a further referendum in 1992 which approved the insertion of an additional paragraph in Article 40.3.3:

> This subsection shall not limit freedom to travel between the State and another state. This subsection shall not limit freedom to obtain or make available, in the State, subject to such conditions as may be laid down by law, information relating to services lawfully available in another state.

7.100 In *Burke v Central Independent Television*,[278] the High Court reduced the scope of discovery in a libel action, on the basis that disclosure of certain documents would endanger the lives of persons named therein. The High Court noted that the constitutional rights to life and bodily integrity of necessity took precedence over the right to the protection and vindication of one's good name.

(5) Nigeria

7.101 Section 30 of the 1979 Constitution provides that every person has a right to life, and no one shall be deprived intentionally of his life, save in execution of the sentence of a court in respect of a criminal offence of which he has been found guilty. In *Ezeadukwa v Maduka*[279] the Court of Appeal stated that a mere oral threat to kill was not enough to sustain the action for breach of the right to life. The threat should be backed up with some overt act of an attempt to kill or exhibition of weapons or materials capable of effecting the murder or killing.

(6) Pakistan

7.102 The Supreme Court of Pakistan has decided that the guarantee of the right to life extends to the protection of quality and enjoyment of life. In *Shehla Zia v WAPDA*[280] four petitioners who were resident in an area in which a proposed power station was to be built claimed that the high voltage transmission lines would pose a health hazard to residents of such severity as to infringe their constitutional right to life. The Supreme Court appointed a Commissioner to further examine and report on the likelihood of a hazard resulting from the scheme, finding that the word 'life' cannot be restricted to vegetative or animal life or to a mere period of biological existence. It found that 'life' includes all such amenities and facilities that a person born in a free country is entitled to enjoy legally and constitutionally, with dignity. The Supreme Court noted that although the term had not been defined in either of the Constitutions of Pakistan or India, the Supreme Court of India had decided that

[275] [1991] ECR I-4685.
[276] (1992) 14 EHRR 131, EComm HR; subsequently upheld by the European Court of Human Rights in *Open Door Counselling and Dublin Well Woman Centre Ltd v Ireland* (1992) 15 EHRR 244.
[277] [1992] IR 1.
[278] [1994] 2 ILRM 161.
[279] [1997] 8 NWLR 635.
[280] PLD 1994 SC 693.

the right to life included the right to live with human dignity and all that goes along with it, namely adequate nutrition, clothing, shelter and facilities for reading and writing.[281]

(7) South Africa

Section 11 of the 1996 Constitution provides that: **7.103**

> Everyone has the right to life.[282]

Although this right is unqualified, it is subject to the general limitation clause in section 36.[283] The Constitutional Court has described this right as the most important of all human rights.[284] The right does not extend to the unborn foetus and the statutory provisions allowing for abortion were not unconstitutional.[285] The taking of another person's life in self-defence is not unconstitutional. Where a choice is to be made between the lives of two people, 'the life of the innocent is given preference over the life of the aggressor'.[286]

In *State v Makwanyane*[287] after comprehensive consideration of the case law from the United States, the Human Rights Committee and other jurisdictions[288] the Constitutional Court held that the 'clear and convincing case' that was required to justify the death sentence as a penalty for murder under the general limitation clause had not been made out. As a result, the imposition of the death penalty was unconstitutional. **7.104**

In *Soobramoney v Minister of Health*[289] the Constitutional Court rejected an application by a terminally ill patient for an order directing a hospital to provide him with dialysis treatment. It was held that the right to medical treatment did not have to be inferred from the right to life because it was dealt with expressly by section 27 of the Constitution. This section placed the state under an obligation to take 'reasonable legislative and other measures, within its available resources, to achieve the progressive realisation' of, *inter alia*, the right to access to health care services.[290] As there were insufficient funds to provide patients such as the applicant with treatment, the failure to provide dialysis was not a breach of Constitutional rights.[291] The arguments based on the right to life were rejected. As Sachs J said: **7.105**

> However the right to life may come to be defined in South Africa, there is in reality no meaningful way in which it can constitutionally be extended to encompass the right indefinitely to evade death.[292]

---

281 *Mullin v Administrator, Union Territory of Delhi*, AIR 1981 SC 746. See also *Sajida Bibi v Incharge, Chouki (No 2)* (1997); 2 CHRLD 60 (right to life of married couple violated when they were compelled to live separately against their wishes).

282 See generally, M Chaskalson, J Kentridge, J Klaaren, G Marcus, D Spitz and S Woolman (eds), *Constitutional Law of South Africa* (Juta, 1996) Chap 15.

283 See App S in Vol 2.

284 *State v Makwanyane* 1995 (4) BCLR 665 para 144.

285 *Christian Lawyers Association of SA v The Minister of Health* 1998 (11) BCLR 1434.

286 Ibid para 138.

287 1995 (4) BCLR 665.

288 See in particular the Judgment of Chaskalson P.

289 (1997) 4 BHRC 308.

290 It also provides, by s 27(3), that 'No one may be refused emergency medical treatment'.

291 Citing *R v Cambridge Health Authority, ex p B* [1995] 1 WLR 898.

292 (1997) 4 BHRC 308.

(8) Tanzania

7.106 Article 14 of the Constitution of Tanzania provides that:

> Every person has a right to life and to receive from society the protection of his life, in accordance with the law.[293]

In *Mbushuu v Republic of Tanzania*[294] the Court of Appeal held that this right is not absolute but qualified and subject to due process of law. Although the death penalty was inherently cruel, inhuman and degrading punishment and infringed the right to dignity, it was saved by Article 30(2) of the Constitution which provided for derogation from fundamental rights in the public interest. The death penalty was not arbitrary and it was for society, through the legislative process, to decide whether, in the absence of conclusive evidence regarding its effectiveness, the death penalty was 'reasonably necessary' for the protection of the right to life.

[293] This is a translation of the Swahili, the English version being misleading, see *Mbushuu v Republic of Tanzania* [1995] 1 LRC 216, 225g–h.
[294] n 293 above.

8

RIGHT NOT TO BE SUBJECT TO TORTURE OR INHUMAN OR DEGRADING TREATMENT

A. The Nature of the Rights

The first clear acceptance of the right to 'physical' or 'bodily' integrity was the prohibition on 'cruel and unusual punishment' in Article 10 of the Bill of Rights of 1688.[1] More recently, the importance of the right to protection from torture has 8.01

[1] Reproduced in the Eighth Amendment to the US Constitution see App T in Vol 2.

been recognised and the right universally accepted.[2] The right to freedom from inhuman or degrading treatment or punishment is now acknowledged by all comprehensive human rights instruments. These rights are, for example, dealt with using slightly different wording, in Article 5 of the Universal Declaration, Article 7 of the International Covenant and Article 3 of the European Convention of Human Rights. Specific conventions have been entered into to strengthen such general provisions. These include the United Nations 'Convention Against Torture and Other Cruel, Inhuman or Degrading Treatment or Punishment' 1984[3] and the European Convention for the Prevention of Torture and Inhuman and Degrading Treatment or Punishment 1987 ('the Torture Convention').[4]

8.02 Although the 'core' of these rights is easily identified, the limits of the conduct which infringes them are harder to define. Difficult issues arise in at least three areas:

(1) *Judicial punishment*: The extent to which punishments laid down by the courts can properly be characterised as 'inhuman' or 'degrading' can be problematic. In many jurisdictions the courts have been concerned with matters such as the 'degrading and inhuman' nature of corporal punishment,[5] delays in the carrying out of death sentences[6] and the death sentence itself.[7] In relation to English law, the relevant areas are those concerning prison conditions and long sentences of imprisonment.
(2) *Extradition and deportation*: Torture continues to be practised in a number of states. The deportation of a person to such a state may, itself, constitute a breach of his rights under this head. Issues arise as to the extent to which the risk of torture or degrading and inhuman treatment has to be taken into account when deportation decisions are made.
(3) *Child discipline*: A third area concerns the extent to which the corporal punishment of children is 'degrading and inhuman'. Although the imposition of corporal punishment by court order is now considered unacceptable, different views have been taken as to whether or not such punishment should be allowed in the school or the home.

[2] Torture is a crime under international law; see generally, *R v Bow Street Metropolitan Stipendiary Magistrate, ex p Pinochet Ugarte (No 3)* [1999] 2 WLR 827.

[3] (1985) Cmnd 9593; ratified by 113 states; this came into force on 26 Jun 1987 and was ratified by the United Kingdom in Dec 1988; see para 2.51 above; the text is reproduced at App H in Vol 2.

[4] (1991) Cm 1634, ratified in by the United Kingdom in Jun 1988; see para 2.53 above.

[5] See, in particular, *Ncube v State* [1988] LRC (Const) 442 and see para 8.133 below.

[6] See, in particular, *Pratt v A-G for Jamaica* [1994] 2 AC 1 and generally, para 8.116 below.

[7] See, in particular, *State v Makwanyane* [1995] 1 LRC 269; see para 8.124 below.

B. The Rights in English Law Before the Human Rights Act

(1) Introduction

The common law recognises the 'fundamental principle, plain and incontestable . . . that every person's body is inviolate'.[8] Any interference with that right will, *prima facie*, constitute the crime and tort of assault or battery.[9] Battery is the intentional and direct application of force to another person, whereas assault is an act of the defendant which causes the claimant reasonable apprehension of the infliction of a battery on him by the defendant.[10] **8.03**

There are, however, a number of circumstances in which the law regards an assault or a battery as 'justified'. A 'touching' will not be unlawful if the person who is touched consents. However, under the criminal law a person cannot lawfully consent to actual bodily harm. Thus, in *R v Brown (Anthony)*[11] it was held that consent to sado-masochistic activity is no defence to a charge of causing actual bodily harm.[12] Exceptions are made only for activities such as properly conducted games and sports, lawful chastisement or correction, reasonable surgical interference and dangerous exhibitions.[13] **8.04**

The concept of 'degrading and inhuman treatment' has been considered by the Privy Council in a number of cases. It has been pointed out that the prohibition on such treatment is absolute and unqualified and no express or implied derogation by the state is permitted. Breaches cannot be justified by a lack of resources or the need to fight terrorism or violent crime. It is therefore an absolute and unqualified guarantee which provides no scope for cultural relativism.[13a] **8.04A**

(2) Use of reasonable force

The use of reasonable force will be justified in self-defence, the prevention of crime or a breach of the peace and in the lawful exercise of police powers. The force used in self-defence or when effecting an arrest should be proportionate to the mischief it is intended to prevent. Therefore, arms may be fired only as a last resort to preserve **8.05**

[8] *Collins v Willcock* [1984] 1 WLR 1172, 1177.

[9] For the criminal law, see generally, *Blackstone's Criminal Practice* (Blackstone Press, 1999) Part B2; for the civil law see M Brazier (ed), *Clerk and Lindsell on Torts* (18th edn, Sweet & Maxwell, 1998) Chap 12, s 2 and 3.

[10] *Clerk and Lindsell* (n 9 above) para 12–01.

[11] [1994] 1 AC 212.

[12] This decision was endorsed by the European Court of Human Rights, *Laskey, Jaggard and Brown v United Kingdom* (1997) 24 EHRR 39.

[13] See *A-G's Reference (No 6 of 1980)* [1981] QB 715; *R v Wilson (Alan)* [1997] QB 47 and *R v Emmett, The Times* 15 Oct 1999.

[13a] See the dissents of Lord Steyn in *Fisher v Minister of Public Safety and Immigration* [1998] AC 673, 688, 689 and *Higgs v Minister of National Security* [2000] 2 WLR 1368.

life.[14] There will be no justification for doing so if no reasonable man with the knowledge of the facts known or which reasonably ought to have been known to the police officer in the circumstances, could think that the prevention of harm if a suspect escaped justified exposing him to the risk of harm.[15] It has been held to be reasonable for a soldier to shoot an escaping suspect in the back when he reasonably believed the escapee to be involved in terrorist activities.[16]

(3) Child discipline

8.06 A person who has 'parental responsibility' for a child[17] is entitled to do acts in relation to the child which would otherwise be batteries. In particular, a person with parental responsibility has the right to administer moderate and reasonable punishment to the child. If the force used is reasonable, the parent will have a defence to a charge of assault and battery.[18] However, if corporal punishment is unreasonable or excessive it will constitute an actionable battery.[19]

8.07 Corporal punishment has now been abolished in all schools, both state funded and private.[20] Giving 'corporal punishment' to a child (that is, any person under the age of 18) means:

> doing anything for the purpose of punishing that child (whether or not there are other reasons for doing it) which, apart from any justification, would constitute battery.[21]

However, corporal punishment will not be taken to have been given by virtue of anything done to avert an immediate danger of personal injury or property.[22] Corporal punishment as a penalty imposed by the criminal courts was abolished in England and Wales by the Criminal Justice Act 1948 and corporal punishment in prisons was abolished by the Criminal Justice Act 1967.

(4) Inhuman and degrading treatment and punishment

8.08 The Bill of Rights of 1688 provided that 'cruell and unusuall punishments' should not be inflicted. If Government servants are in breach of this provision their actions

---

14 *Lynch v Fitzgerald* [1938] IR 382.

15 *A-G for Northern Ireland's Reference (No 1 of 1975)* [1977] AC 105.

16 See *R v McNaughton* [1975] NI 203; see also *Carey and Ficken v Commissioner of Police for the Metropolis* (unreported, 11 Jul 1989, Waller J) in which it was held that police officers were justified in shooting two unarmed men in circumstances where they honestly believed that an armed robbery was taking place and that they were being attacked.

17 Which is defined as all rights, duties, powers, responsibility and authority which by law a parent of a child has in relation to the child and his property: see Children Act 1989, s 3(1).

18 See *R v Hopley* (1860) 2 F&F 202; *R v Mackie* (1973) 57 Cr App R 453.

19 See *R v Derrivière* (1969) 53 Cr App R 637.

20 Education Act 1996, s 548, as substituted by School Standards and Framework Act 1998, s 131.

21 Ibid s 548(4).

22 Ibid s 548(5).

will be unlawful and an action for damages will lie if the conduct is otherwise tortious.[23] It has been held that, in the context of the Bill of Rights 1688, the words 'cruel' and 'unusual' must be read conjunctively.[24]

The meaning of the phrase 'inhuman or degrading punishment or other treatment' has only infrequently been considered by the English courts, generally in regard to applications for asylum. In *Akdag v Secretary of State for the Home Department*,[25] the court found that deportation itself cannot amount to inhuman or degrading treatment even if it causes mental or physical distress. However, the court in *M v Secretary of State for the Home Department*[26] held that to return to a country of origin a person who, while not a refugee, would be in danger of torture, loss of life or inhuman or degrading treatment, would breach Article 3 of the European Convention on Human Rights. The Court of Appeal in *R v Secretary of State for the Home Department, ex p I*[27] found that the return of an HIV positive mother and child to Uganda was neither irrational nor contrary to Article 3 of the Convention, given that there were medical facilities in Uganda and the position of the applicant and her daughter was shared by many. However, in *R v Secretary of State for the Home Department, ex p M*[27a] the order for the deportation of the applicant who was terminally ill with AIDS was quashed on the ground that the medical treatment in Uganda was so poor that deportation amounted to inhuman and degrading treatment. It is now accepted that, if there is a real risk of a person being subjected to degrading or inhuman treatment in a particular country then he cannot be deported, irrespective of the victim's conduct or good faith.[27b] **8.09**

The meaning of 'inhuman or degrading punishment or other treatment' has been considered by the Privy Council when dealing with appeals from Commonwealth countries. In the important case of *Pratt v A-G for Jamaica*[28] the Privy Council held that in any case in which execution is to take place more than five years after sentence, there will be strong grounds for believing that this delay will constitute 'inhuman or degrading punishment or other treatment'. In reaching this conclusion, **8.10**

[23] See *Williams v Home Office (No 2)* [1981] 1 All ER 1211; see also *R v Secretary of State for the Home Department, ex p Herbage (No 2)* [1987] QB 1077 (these appear to be the only modern cases in which this provision has been considered); and see generally, S Livingstone and T Owen, *Prison Law*, (2nd edn, Oxford University Press, 1999) para 5.61ff.

[24] See *Williams (No 2)* (n 23 above) 1242; this approach is controversial in US law, see eg A Goldberg and A Derschowitz, 'Declaring the Death Penalty Unconstitutional' (1970) 83 Harv L Rev 1773.

[25] [1993] Imm AR 172.

[26] [1996] 1 WLR 507, 514H.

[27] [1997] Imm AR (29) 172.

[27a] [1999] Imm AR 548.

[27b] See *Danian v Secretary of State for the Home Department* [2000] Imm AR 96 CA, applying *Chahal v United Kingdom* (1996) 23 EHRR 413, see para 8.58 below.

[28] [1994] 2 AC 1.

the Privy Council placed reliance on the Convention case of *Soering v United Kingdom*[29] in which the European Court of Human Rights held that a long period of delay could constitute 'degrading and inhuman treatment'. The reasoning in the *Pratt* case has been applied by the Privy Council in appeals from a number of other jurisdictions.[30]

(5) Torture

8.11 Torture is a crime under English law. Section 134(1) of the Criminal Justice Act 1988 provides:

> A public official or person acting in an official capacity, whatever his nationality, commits the offence of torture if in the United Kingdom or elsewhere he intentionally inflicts severe pain or suffering on another in the performance or purported performance of his official duties.

It is immaterial whether the pain or suffering is physical or mental and whether it is caused by acts or omissions.[31] It is, however, a defence for a person charged to show that he had 'lawful authority, justification or excuse'.[32] The consent of the Attorney-General is required for a prosecution under this section.

8.12 In *Treadaway v Chief Constable of West Midlands*[33] the defendant was awarded exemplary damages when it was held that police had engaged in conduct which amounted to torture and that their violence had been a serious abuse of authority.

C. The Law Under the European Convention

(1) Introduction

8.13 Article 3 of the Convention provides that:

> No one shall be subjected to torture or to inhuman or degrading treatment or punishment.

Except for the omission of any reference to 'cruel' treatment or punishment, the language of Article 3 is identical to that of Article 5 of the Universal Declaration of Human Rights[34] and the first sentence of Article 7 of the International

---

[29] (1989) 11 EHRR 439, see para 8.55 below.

[30] See *Bradshaw v A-G of Barbados* [1995] 1 WLR 936; *Guerra v Baptiste* [1996] AC 397; *Henfield v A-G of the Commonwealth of The Bahamas* [1997] AC 413 (in the context of a system where the target period for appeals was two years, a lapse of three-and-a-half years was sufficient to render execution inhuman punishment).

[31] s 134(3).

[32] s 134(4), (5).

[33] *Independent*, 23 Jul 1994.

[34] Cf 1 *Travaux Préparatoires* 206, which refers to 'torture or cruel, inhuman or degrading treatment or punishment'.

Covenant on Civil and Political Rights. Article 3 of the European Convention is supplemented by the Torture Convention[35] which has been ratified by 29 parties, all of which are parties to the Convention. This has established an independent Committee of experts with access to places of public detention, enabling it to produce confidential national reports and make recommendations for the protection of detainees.

The Court has made it clear on many occasions that Article 3 enshrines one of the fundamental values of a democratic society.[36] The prohibition against torture and inhuman and degrading treatment is in absolute terms and no derogation is permissible even in the event of a public emergency threatening the life of the nation.[37] However, the Article only applies to a natural person, not to other 'legal persons' such as a company.[38] **8.14**

Article 3 provides protection against only the most serious ill-treatment: the treatment must attain a minimum level of severity before there is a violation. The assessment of this minimum is relative: **8.15**

> it depends on all the circumstances of the case, such as the nature and context of the treatment, its duration, its physical or mental effects and, in some instances, the sex, age and state of health of the victim.[39]

It has been held that the suffering produced by three strokes with a gym shoe,[40] corporal punishment in schools[41] and 'rough treatment consisting of only slaps or blows of the hand on the head or face'[42] did not constitute violations of Article 3. However, as the protection of human rights improves, standards are becoming stricter and some of these earlier decisions may need to be reassessed.[43]

Although Article 3 of the Convention does not prevent lesser forms of maltreatment the protection it affords is (subject to a few recognised exceptions),[44] unqualified. As a result, ill-treatment which breaches Article 3 is never justifiable for any reason, even that of the highest public interest. So, for example, neither violations **8.16**

---

35 (1991) Cm 1634; see para 2.53 above.

36 See eg *Soering v United Kingdom* (1989) 11 EHRR 439 para 88; *Chahal v United Kingdom* (1996) 23 EHRR 413 para 79.

37 See Art 15(2) and eg *Aksoy v Turkey* (1996) 23 EHRR 553.

38 *Kontakt-Information-Therapie and Hagen v Austria* (1988) 57 DR 81, EComm HR.

39 See *A v United Kingdom* (1998) 27 EHRR 611 para 20; the formulation derives from *Ireland v United Kingdom* (1978) 2 EHRR 25 para 162).

40 *Costello Roberts v United Kingdom* (1993) 19 EHRR 112; contrast *Tyrer v United Kingdom* (1978) 2 EHRR 1 (birching of teenage boy degrading punishment).

41 *Campbell and Cosans v United Kingdom* (1982) 4 EHRR 293.

42 The *Greek case* (1969) 12 YB1, EComm HR.

43 See *Selmouni v France* (2000) 29 EHRR 403 para 101, see para 8.26 below.

44 It has been found that inhuman conditions of detention and treatment may be justified in instances where a prisoner may be attempting to escape or commit suicide (see *Kröcher and Möller v Switzerland* (1982) 34 DR 25, EComm HR).

of physical integrity[45] nor the use of various techniques of psychological interrogation causing suffering above the threshold of Article 3[46] can be justified on grounds that they are necessary in order to combat terrorism or for national security.[47] However, it appears that free and informed consent will be a defence to a claim of violation in the case of medical treatment.[48]

8.17 In general, it is unnecessary to distinguish between the various categories of ill-treatment set out in Article 3: a finding of any one of them will result in a violation, and there is a close inter-relationship between inhuman and degrading treatment and punishment. The distinction between torture and other forms of ill-treatment is, however, relevant with respect to compensation to be awarded under Article 50[49] and to a state's reputation. The Court and Commission have 'commonly but not always'[50] sought to distinguish between the various categories where the facts of a case warrant it.

8.18 A claim under Article 3 may also raise issues under other Articles of the Convention. This has arisen in practice largely in connection with the Article 8 rights to respect for family and private life, where the emphasis has been placed primarily on the Article 8 claim.[51] If there is no infringement of Article 8, it is unlikely that there will be a breach of Article 3.[52]

(2) State liability

8.19 Under Article 3 states are 'strictly liable' for the conduct of their servants or agents: 'they are under a duty to impose their will on subordinates and cannot shelter behind their inability to ensure that it is respected'.[53] It seems likely, however, that a state would not be responsible if it had taken proper measures to ensure that its subordinates did not violate Article 3, had investigated complaints and had disci-

[45] *Tomasi v France* (1992) 15 EHRR 1 para 115.

[46] The threshold, beyond which ill-treatment is prohibited under Art 3, is a relative one depending on 'all the circumstances of the case, such as the duration of the treatment, its physical or mental effects and, in some cases, the sex, age and state of health of the victim, etc.' (*Ireland v United Kingdom* (1978) 2 EHRR 25).

[47] See the recent decisions in *Chahal v United Kingdom* (1996) 23 EHRR 413; *Ahmed v Austria* (1996) 24 EHRR 278.

[48] See *X v Denmark* (1983) 32 DR 282, EComm HR.

[49] And to damages under the Human Rights Act; see generally, para 21.10ff below.

[50] D Harris, M O'Boyle and C Warbrick, *Law of the European Convention on Human Rights* (Butterworths, 1995) 56, n 14, citing *Soering v United Kingdom* (1989) 11 EHRR 439 as a case in which the distinction between 'treatment' and 'punishment' was not considered.

[51] See *Marckx v Belgium* (1979) 2 EHRR 330 and *X and Y v Netherlands* (1985) 8 EHRR 235.

[52] See eg *Olsson v Sweden (No 1)* (1988) 11 EHRR 259; cf *Hendriks v Netherlands* (1982) 29 DR 5, EComm HR.

[53] *Ireland v United Kingdom* (1978) 2 EHRR 25 para 159; see also *Cyprus v Turkey* (1976) 4 EHRR 482, 537, EComm HR (Turkey responsible for acts of rape committed by its soldiers because adequate steps were not taken to prevent such conduct nor to punish those who had perpetrated the acts).

plined those responsible. However, the state is under a positive obligation to carry out a prompt, impartial and effective investigation into allegations of breaches of Article 3. Such an investigation must be capable of leading to the identification and punishment of those responsible. The failure to undertake such an investigation will breach Article 3.[53a]

The state can also be held responsible for failure to provide positive legal protection for citizens subjected to ill-treatment at the hands of private persons. In *Costello-Roberts v United Kingdom*,[54] which dealt with corporal punishment in private schools, the Court found that Article 3 imposes a positive obligation on parties to the Convention to ensure a legal system which provides adequate protection of the physical and emotional integrity of children. The same result was reached in *A v United Kingdom*[55] in respect of corporal punishment carried out by the applicant's step-father. The Court held that states are required to take measures designed to ensure that individuals within their jurisdiction are not subjected to torture or inhuman or degrading treatment or punishment, including such ill-treatment administered by private individuals. **8.20**

The obligation of the state to carry out a thorough and effective investigation capable of leading to the identification and punishment of those responsible is of particular importance when claims of mistreatment in state custody are made.[56] Where an individual is taken into police custody in good health but is found to be injured at the time of release, it is incumbent on the state to provide a plausible explanation of how those injuries were caused, failing which a clear issue arises under Article 3 of the Convention.[57] **8.21**

(3) Torture

The Convention distinguishes between 'torture' and other forms of degrading and inhuman treatment in order to attach a special stigma to deliberate inhuman treatment causing very serious and cruel suffering.[58] The Court has distinguished torture from inhuman and degrading treatment in two respects. First, torture causes a greater or more intense degree of suffering than other actions that are considered inhuman or degrading treatment.[59] Secondly, the suffering is **8.22**

[53a] *Askoy v Turkey* (1997) 23 EHRR 533 paras 98, 99; *Aydin v Turkey* (1998) 25 EHRR 251 paras 88–98; *Assenov v Bulgaria* (1998) 28 EHRR 652 para 102; *Selmouni v France* (2000) 29 EHRR 403, para 79; *Caloc v France*, Judgment 20 Jul 2000.

[54] *Costello-Roberts v United Kingdom* (1993) 19 EHRR 112.

[55] (1998) 27 EHRR 611, see para 8.26 below.

[56] See n 53a above; and see Art 12 of the UN Convention Against Torture (1985) Cmnd 9593.

[57] See para 8.79 below.

[58] *Ireland v United Kingdom* (1978) 2 EHRR 25 para 167.

[59] Torture is defined in *Ireland v United Kingdom* (1978) 2 EHRR 25 para 16 as '. . . inhuman treatment causing very serious and cruel suffering'; the Court also cited the definition of torture in the 1975 UN Declaration on Torture (UN GA Resolution 3452): 'torture constitutes an aggravated and deliberate form of cruel, inhuman or degrading treatment or punishment'.

inflicted intentionally.[60] Because the Court in *Ireland v United Kingdom* pointed out that the ill treatment in question had been used to obtain confessions (and other information), that decision has been interpreted to mean that torture involves the infliction of suffering for an intended purpose (in contrast to inhuman treatment or punishment). The Commission took this approach in the *Greek* case,[61] but Judge Fitzmaurice in his separate opinion in *Ireland v United Kingdom* firmly rejected any such requirement. In view of the absolute nature of Article 3, it seems unlikely that this makes any difference in practice; if treatment amounts to very serious and cruel suffering it will be found to be torture, whether or not there is 'intent'.

8.23 States have been found responsible for the infliction of torture on only a limited number of occasions. In the *Greek* case,[62] the Commission investigated 30 instances of alleged torture of political detainees and found that the treatment in 11 of them constituted torture: in particular, beating of all parts of the body including the genitals, electric shock treatment, mock executions, head vice squeezing and sleep deprivation through water-dripping on the head and intense noise. The findings of the Commission in that case were confirmed, as a matter of final decision, by the Committee of Ministers.

8.24 The finding of torture by the Commission in the *Ireland v United Kingdom*[63] case was, surprisingly, overturned by the Court. While the Commission unanimously held that the application of the 'five techniques'[64] as an aid to police interrogation of 14 persons amounted to torture, the Court found that the pain and suffering that they caused, while constituting inhuman treatment, did not amount to torture. The decision in *Ireland* may be accounted for by the fact that the Commission had considered evidence of weight loss, mental disorientation and acute *psychiatric* symptoms in some of the 14 subjects during interrogation while the Court's finding of inhuman treatment was based on the *physical* assaults perpetrated against the detainees. It has been suggested that this may indicate a

[60] The Court in *Ireland v United Kingdom* (n 59 above) said that torture was 'deliberate' inhuman treatment causing very serious and cruel suffering; the difference between deliberate and reckless or negligent conduct has not yet been considered.

[61] (1969) 12 YB 1, EComm HR; the Commission found that torture is an aggravated form of inhuman treatment 'which has a purpose, such as the obtaining of information or confession, of the infliction of punishment'.

[62] Ibid.

[63] *Ireland v United Kingdom* (1978) 2 EHRR 25.

[64] The 'five techniques' described in *Ireland v United Kingdom* (n 63 above) para 96, consist of: (1) *wall standing*: forcing the detainees to remain for hours in a 'stress position', spread-eagled against the wall, standing on their toes with the weight of the body mainly on the fingers; (2) *hooding*: keeping a black or navy coloured bag over the detainees' heads except during interrogation; (3) *subjection to noise*: confining detainees, pending interrogation, in a room in which a continuous loud, hissing noise could be heard; (4) *deprivation of sleep*: pending interrogations, depriving the detainees of sleep; (5) *deprivation of food and drink*: subjecting detainees to a reduced diet during their containment and pending interrogations.

reticence on the part of the Court to consider the psychological impact of treatment; but it is implicit in the case that mental anguish, in the absence of physical injury, may, if the suffering is sufficiently serious, amount to torture.[65]

8.25 There have been a number of recent findings of torture in cases involving Turkey. In *Aksoy v Turkey*[66] the applicant had been subjected to 'Palestinian hanging': he had been stripped naked, with his arms tied together behind his back and suspended by his arms. The Court considered that this treatment was of 'such a serious and cruel nature that it can only be described as torture'. The case of *Aydin v Turkey*[67] concerned the rape and ill-treatment of a 17-year old female detainee by a Turkish military official during disturbances between security forces and members of the Workers' Party of Kurdistan in South-East Turkey. The girl was isolated from her father and sister-in-law, blindfolded, stripped of her clothes, put into a car tyre and spun round and round, beaten and sprayed with cold water from high pressure jets. She was raped, left in pain and covered in blood, and was later beaten for an hour by several persons who warned her not to report what they had done to her. Although previous incidents of rape and assaults on persons detained in a similar context had been found to be examples of inhuman treatment,[68] the Commission and the Court agreed that the rape, being an especially grave and abhorrent form of ill-treatment, and the other forms of physical and mental suffering to which the applicant had been subjected, were sufficiently severe and humiliating to give rise to separate violations of Article 3, both of which could be characterised as torture. Findings of torture have also been made in cases involving beatings with sticks and rifle butts in police custody.[68a]

8.26 The standard of 'severity' required to establish torture depends on all the circumstances of the case, such as the duration of the treatment, its physical or mental effects and, in some cases, the sex, age and state of health of the victim.[69] The standards to be applied are becoming stricter. Thus, in the case of *Selmouni v France*[70] the Court had to decide whether a large number of blows and humiliations inflicted on a person in custody on suspicion of drug offences over a number of days was of sufficient severity to constitute torture. It held that:

---

[65] See *dicta* in *Ireland v United Kingdom* (1978) 2 EHRR 25 para 162 (in which it is said that the assessment of a minimum level of ill-treatment depends on 'all the circumstances of the case, such as the duration of the treatment, its physical or *mental* effects, and, in some cases, the sex, age and state of health of the victim'; in the *Greek* case (1969) 12 YB 1, EComm HR the Commission referred to 'non-physical torture' which it described as 'the infliction of mental suffering by creating a state of anguish and stress by means other than bodily assault'); see also *Tyrer v United Kingdom* (1978) 2 EHRR 1; *Campbell and Cosans v United Kingdom* (1982) 4 EHRR 293; and *Soering v United Kingdom* (1989) 11 EHRR 439.

[66] (1996) 23 EHRR 553.

[67] (1997) 25 EHRR 251; see also *Mejia Egocheaga v Peru* (1996) 1 BHRC 229 (Inter American Commission, rape of applicant was torture).

[68] *Cyprus v Turkey* (1976) 4 EHRR 482, EComm HR.

[68a] *Salman v Turkey*, Judgment 27 Jun 2000; *Ihlan v Turkey*, Judgment 27 Jun 2000.

[69] *Selmouni v France* (2000) 29 EHRR 403 para 100.

[70] Ibid.

> having regard to the fact that the Convention is a 'living instrument which must be interpreted in the light of present-day conditions' . . . certain acts which were classified in the past as 'inhuman and degrading treatment' as opposed to 'torture' could be classified differently in future . . . the increasingly high standard being required in the area of the protection of human rights and fundamental liberties correspondingly and inevitably requires greater firmness in assessing breaches of the fundamental values of democratic societies.[71]

On the facts, the Court was satisfied that the physical and mental violence, considered as a whole, committed against the applicant's person caused 'severe' pain and suffering, was particularly serious and cruel and should, therefore, be regarded as acts of torture.[72]

(4) Degrading and inhuman treatment and punishment

(a) Inhuman treatment

8.27 Ill-treatment 'must attain a minimum level of severity' if it is to amount to inhuman treatment contrary to Article 3.[73] Whether or not it must also be deliberate is not entirely clear. Although the Court in *Ireland v United Kingdom* found that treatment need not be intentional to be inhuman,[74] it noted in *Soering v United Kingdom*[75] that its finding of inhuman treatment in *Ireland* had been based on the premeditation of the perpetration of intense suffering. It appears:

> The question whether the purpose of the treatment was to humiliate or debase the victim is a further factor to be taken into account . . . but the absence of any such purpose cannot conclusively rule out a finding of violation of Article 3.[76]

8.28 Inhuman treatment may take the form of mental suffering resulting from a 'sufficiently real and immediate' threat of torture,[77] conduct in the form of physical assault, the use of psychological interrogation techniques,[78] detention in inhuman conditions[79] or the deportation or extradition of a person to face the real risk of inhuman treatment in another country,[80] including the lack of proper medical care for a serious illness.[81] The destruction of personal property[82] and a parent's 'uncertainty,

[71] *Selmouni v France* (2000) 29 EHRR 403 para 101.
[72] Ibid para 105; damages of FRF500,000 were awarded for 'personal injury'.
[73] See eg *A v United Kingdom* (1998) 27 EHRR 611 para 20.
[74] *Ireland v United Kingdom* (1978) 2 EHRR 25 para 167; see also paras 8.40 and 8.43.
[75] (1989) 11 EHRR 439.
[76] *Labita v Italy* Judgment of 6 Apr 2000 para 120.
[77] *Campbell and Cosans v United Kingdom* (1982) 4 EHRR 293.
[78] *Ireland v United Kingdom* (1978) 2 EHRR 25 para 167.
[79] *Greek* case (1969) 12 YB 1 EComm HR *Cyprus v Turkey* (1976) 4 EHRR 482, EComm HR.
[80] *Soering v United Kingdom* (1989) 11 EHRR 439; *Cruz Varas v Sweden* (1991) 14 EHRR 1 paras 69–70; *Vilvarajah and others v United Kingdom* (1991) 14 EHRR 248 paras 102–116; see also *Altun v Germany* (1983) 36 DR 209, EComm HR; *Kirkwood v United Kingdom* (1984) 37 DR 158.
[81] *Hurtado v Switzerland* (1994) Series A No 280-A; *D v United Kingdom* (1997) 24 EHRR 423.
[82] *Selcuk and Asker v Turkey* (1998) 26 EHRR 477 para 78.

doubt and apprehension' suffered by the applicant following the disappearance of her son after being taken into military custody[83] have also been found to cause suffering of sufficient severity to be categorised as inhuman treatment.

(b) Inhuman punishment

In assessing whether a punishment is inhuman, regard must be had to the physical or mental suffering, which must reach the level which a person of normal sensibilities, given factors such as the applicant's sex, age and health, would, in the circumstances, consider to be inhuman. This threshold was not surpassed in the *Tyrer* case,[84] in which a 15-year-old boy convicted of assault was sentenced by a juvenile court to three strokes of the birch which were administered at the local police station. There, the Court stated that, in reaching its decision its 'assessment' was 'relative' in that 'it depend[ed] on all the circumstances of the case and, in particular, on the nature and context of the punishment itself and the manner and method of its execution'.[85] **8.29**

However, the case of *D v United Kingdom*[86] illustrates the absolute nature of the rights under Article 3. The applicant was a citizen of St Kitts who had illegally entered the United Kingdom and had been convicted of drug smuggling and was found to be suffering from AIDS. Directions were given for his removal to St Kitts. The Court held that the rights in Article 3 were so fundamental that they could not be limited to intentionally inflicted acts but had to extend to situations in which the risk of infringement came from sources for which the public authorities were not directly or indirectly responsible. The deportation of the applicant to St Kitts where he would not receive adequate medical treatment or support would expose him to a real risk of dying under distressing circumstances and amounted, therefore, to inhuman treatment. **8.30**

A disproportionately severe sentence of imprisonment could constitute 'inhuman punishment'.[87] If there is a risk that criminal proceedings abroad could lead to 'an unjustified or disproportionate sentence', a deportation may be a breach of Article 3.[88] **8.31**

[83] *Kurt v Turkey* (1998) 27 EHRR 373 paras 130–134; relying on the decision of the Human Rights Committee in *Quinteros v Uruguay* (1983) A/38/40, UNHRC and see C Jones, 'Human Rights: Rights of Relatives of Victims—Views of the Human Rights Committee in the Quinteros Communication' (1984) 25 Harv I LJ 470; and see *Timurtas v Turkey*, Judgment 13 Jun 2000.

[84] (1978) 2 EHRR 1.

[85] Ibid para 30 (although this punishment did not amount to inhuman treatment it was considered to breach Art 3 as it constituted degrading punishment, see para 8.36 below).

[86] (1997) 24 EHRR 423.

[87] See *Weeks v United Kingdom* (1987) 10 EHRR 293 para 47, see also *Hussain v United Kingdom* (1996) 22 EHRR 1 para 53.

[88] See *Altun v Germany* (1983) 36 DR 209, EComm HR.

(c) Degrading treatment

8.32 Degrading treatment is treatment that humiliates or debases. Here too, a minimum threshold must be exceeded before a breach of Article 3 will be found. The conduct that results in such a breach must be of a type that 'grossly humiliates'.[89] The question to be asked, therefore, is whether a person of normal sensibilities in the circumstances of the applicant, including his or her sex, age, health etc., would, in the circumstances, consider the conduct to be degrading. The same treatment may be both degrading and inhuman[90] but not all degrading treatment or punishment is necessarily inhuman.[91] Torture is always inhuman and degrading treatment.[92]

8.33 Racial discrimination can also provide the grounds for a finding of degrading treatment. In the *East African Asians* case[93] 25 East African Asians who had retained their UK citizenship were refused admission to the United Kingdom following the passing of legislation which denied the right of entry to UK citizens who lacked ancestral or 'place of birth' connections. The Commission ruled that such legislation was discriminatory and that the subjection of the applicants to it constituted an affront to their dignity substantial enough to be considered degrading treatment in breach of Article 3. The Commission confirmed its *East African Asians* decision in *Abdulaziz, Cabales and Balkandali v United Kingdom*[94] when it stated that 'the state's discretion in immigration matters is not of an unfettered character, for a state may not implement policies of a purely racist nature, such as a policy prohibiting the entry of any person of a particular skin colour'. In *Hilton v United Kingdom*[95] the Commission considered allegations of racial abuse of a prisoner by prison officers sufficient grounds upon which to raise an issue under Article 3.

8.34 Other forms of discrimination, apart from racial, have also been considered by the Commission. In *Marckx v Belgium*[96] legislation discriminating against illegitimate children and their parents was found not to violate Article 3. However, such discrimination has been found to violate Article 14 of the Convention which, amongst other things, prohibits discrimination on grounds of 'birth'.[97]

---

[89] The *Greek* case (1969) 12 YB 1, 186; see also *Smith and Grady v United Kingdom* [1999] IRLR 747 (interrogation of homosexual servicemen about private life, not degrading treatment).

[90] See eg *Ireland v United Kingdom* (1978) 2 EHRR 25; *Tomasi v France* (1992) 15 EHRR 1; see also *Tekin v Turkey* RJD 1998-IV 53.

[91] *Tyrer v United Kingdom* (1978) 2 EHRR 1.

[92] The *Greek* case (1969) 12 YB 1, 186.

[93] (1981) 3 EHRR 76, EComm HR.

[94] (1985) 7 EHRR 471, Com Rep para 113.

[95] (1976) 4 DR 177, EComm HR.

[96] (1979) 2 EHRR 330 para 66.

[97] See para 17.79ff below.

(d) Degrading punishment

8.35 The term 'degrading' when used in relation to 'punishment' has the same meaning as it does in connection with 'treatment'. Thus, a punishment may be degrading where it constitutes 'an assault on a person's dignity and physical integrity'.[98] The level of humiliation required for a breach of Article 3 to occur must be:

> other than that usual element of humiliation . . . (. . . which follows from the very fact of being convicted and punished by a court). The assessment is, in the nature of things, relative: it depends on all the circumstances of the case and, in particular, on the nature and context of the punishment itself and the manner and method of its execution.[99]

8.36 In *Tyrer v United Kingdom*[100] the applicant, a 15-year-old boy, was convicted of assault by a juvenile court on the Isle of Man and was sentenced to receive three strokes of the birch. The sentence was carried out three weeks later by a police officer at the local station while two other officers (to hold the boy), a doctor and the father of the boy were present. The Court found in favour of the applicant on his claim of degrading punishment under Article 3. In reaching its decision the Court noted that a punishment may be degrading even though it does not outrage public opinion, is an effective deterrent, is administered in private, inflicts no lasting injury and is imposed for crimes of violence.

8.37 In *Tyrer* the Court adopted a 'dynamic' approach to the interpretation of Article 3. It stated that the Convention is 'a living instrument which, as the Commission rightly stressed, must be interpreted in the light of present day conditions'.[101] As such, it considered the 'nature and context'[102] of corporal punishment, stating that 'the Court cannot but be influenced by the developments and commonly accepted standards in the penal policy of the member States of the Council of Europe in this field'.[103]

8.38 The issue of corporal punishment has also been dealt with in relation to discipline in schools.[104] In *Costello-Roberts v United Kingdom*[105] a seven-year-old boy had been given three smacks through his trousers with the rubber sole of a gym shoe. No one else was present and the beating left no physical marks. In rejecting the

---

98 *Tyrer v United Kingdom* (1978) 2 EHRR 1 para 33.

99 Ibid para 30; see also *T v United Kingdom* (2000) 7 BHRC 659 para 69.

100 (1978) 2 EHRR 1.

101 (1978) 2 EHRR 1, 31.

102 Ibid para 30.

103 Ibid para 31.

104 See eg *Costello-Roberts v United Kingdom* (1993) 19 EHRR 112; cf *Warwick v United Kingdom* (1986) 60 DR 5 Com Rep; CM Res DH (89) 5, EComm HR; *X v United Kingdom* No 7907/77, (1981) 24 YB 420, EComm HR; and, *Y v United Kingdom* (1992) 17 EHRR 238 see also *Campbell and Cosans v United Kingdom* (1982) 4 EHRR 293 (where the threat of corporal punishment was found not to cause sufficient degradation to be regarded as a violation of Art 3).

105 (1993) 19 EHRR 112.

application, the Court noted that the applicant had been a boarder at a private school and was therefore subject to 'the disciplinary rules in force within the school'.[106] It found that the punishment meted out had not attained the minimum level of severity necessary to find a breach of Article 3. In *Warwick v United Kingdom*[107] a sixteen-year-old girl caught smoking at a state school was given one stroke of a cane on her hand, leaving a bruise. Although the caning was administered by the headmaster in his office with the deputy headmaster and another student present, the Commission was of the opinion that Article 3 had been breached. In *Y v United Kingdom*[108] a headmaster administered, in private, four strokes of a cane through the trousers of a 15-year-old boy for defacing the file of another student. The caning left heavy bruising. Upon a friendly settlement, the United Kingdom Government paid £8,000 plus costs and the case was withdrawn.

(5) **Individuals in detention**

(a) Assaults

8.39 When a person is in custody, force which has not been made strictly necessary by his own conduct diminishes human dignity and is, in principle, an infringement of Article 3.[109] In *Hurtado v Switzerland*[110] the Court applied a test of proportionality to assess the degree of force used to effect an arrest, finding on the facts of that case that a fractured rib and bruises was not disproportionate where the applicant arrested was a potentially violent suspected drug trafficker.

8.40 Where an individual is taken into police custody in good health but is found to be injured at the time of release, it is incumbent on the state to provide a plausible explanation of how those injuries were caused.[111] In *Ireland v United Kingdom*[112] the Court held that the cuts and bruises received by four detainees were the result of severe beatings during the course of their interrogation by the security forces in Northern Ireland. It was established that those four instances of inhuman treatment were part of an administrative practice contrary to Article 3. However, the Court also referred to other assaults that occurred while in transit or interrogation that 'must have been individual violations of Article 3'.[113]

8.41 In *Tomasi v France*,[114] the applicant, arrested on suspicion of terrorism, successfully

[106] Ibid para 31.
[107] (1986) 60 DR 5, EComm HR.
[108] (1992) 17 EHRR 238.
[109] See *Ribitsch v Austria* (1995) 21 EHRR 573 para 38, *Tekin v Turkey* RJD 1998–IV 53.
[110] (1994) Series A No 280-A.
[111] *Tomasi v France* (1992) 15 EHRR 1 para 108–111; *Ribitsch v Austria* (1995) 21 EHRR 573 para 34.
[112] (1978) 2 EHRR 25.
[113] Ibid para 182.
[114] (1992) 15 EHRR 1; see also *Ribitsch v Austria* (1995) 21 EHRR 573 (Government failed to establish that bruises suffered by applicant were not the result of inhuman treatment by police).

claimed that he had been subjected to inhuman treatment while in police custody. Given medical evidence of 'the large number of blows inflicted upon Mr Tomasi and their intensity'[115] and the absence of an alternative explanation from the Government sufficient to discharge the burden of proof on it, the Court found that the marks on the applicant's body had been caused by agents of the defendant Government. Similarly, in *Tekin v Turkey*,[116] the wounds and bruises on the body of the applicant supported a finding of inhuman treatment of the applicant while held in police custody.[117]

These cases may be contrasted with the decision in *Klaas v Germany*.[118] In a civil claim for compensation a German court was faced with conflicting evidence from a woman alleging assault during the course of an arrest for a blood alcohol test, and state evidence that the woman had injured herself while resisting the arrest. The German court found for the state, because the woman had not discharged the civil burden of proof on her to show that the injuries were a result of excessive police force. The Court accepted the findings of the national court and distinguished *Tomasi* on the basis that 'while in that case certain inferences could be drawn from the fact that Mr Tomasi had sustained unexplained injuries during forty-eight hours spent in police custody', in the *Klaas* case, no 'cogent elements have been provided which could lead the Court to depart from the findings of fact of the national courts'.[119] The decision has been criticised on the basis that German law placed the burden on the applicant to prove that the injuries sustained by persons in custody are the responsibility of the state.[120] **8.42**

(b) Interrogation and other treatment

In addition to physical assaults, the interrogation of persons in detention in connection with acts of terrorism in *Ireland v United Kingdom* involved 'five techniques'[121] causing intense psychological suffering. The Court found such treatment to be inhuman because: **8.43**

> applied in combination, with premeditation and for hours at a stretch, they caused, if not actual bodily injury, at least intense physical and mental suffering to the persons subjected thereto and also led to acute psychiatric disturbances during interrogation.[122]

[115] Ibid para 115.

[116] RJD 1998-IV 53.

[117] In that case, the conditions of detention were such as to result in a finding of degrading as well as inhuman treatment.

[118] (1993) 18 EHRR 305.

[119] Ibid para 30.

[120] Judge Walsh argues in his dissenting opinion that the burden of proof under Art 3 should always be placed on the police in respect of persons under arrest. Others make the distinction that the burden should be on the police only where the injuries occur to an arrested person while out of sight in a police station and not when they result from an 'on the street' incident.

[121] See n 64 above.

[122] (1978) 2 EHRR 25 para 167.

8.44 Findings of degrading treatment have also been made in cases involving detention. In *Hurtado v Switzerland*[123] the applicant was prohibited from changing his trousers until the next day after he had defecated in them because of the shock caused by the use of a stun grenade in effecting his arrest. This was held to constitute degrading treatment. In *McFeeley v United Kingdom*[124] the Commission held that neither public presentation of a convicted terrorist prisoner in handcuffs and uniform nor intimate body searches[125] constituted the sort of humiliation contemplated under degrading treatment in Article 3. In *Raninen v Finland*[126] the unnecessary handcuffing of a person in wrongful detention was not a breach of Article 3. The Court said that:

> handcuffing does not normally give rise to an issue under Art 3 of the Convention where the measure has been imposed in connection with a lawful arrest or detention and does not entail the use of force or public exposure, exceeding what is reasonably considered necessary in the circumstances.[127]

The mandatory drug testing of prisoners by requiring the production of urine samples in the presence of a supervisor does not attain the minimum level of severity in order to fall within Article 3.[127a]

(c) Conditions of detention

8.45 The conditions to which persons are subjected while in detention may be such as to amount to inhuman treatment.[128] Several factors have been considered by the Commission and Court in various combinations. In the *Greek* case, the Commission referred to the lack of hygiene, lack of natural light, overcrowding, lack of access to elementary sanitary facilities, deprivation of food while detained in solitary confinement, lack of beds or bedding, insufficient medical care, lack of contact with the outside world and lack of recreation and exercise, particularly for those

[123] (1994) Series A No 280-A; cf *B v United Kingdom* (1981) 32 DR 5, EComm HR, where findings of poor sanitary conditions and overcrowding were not felt to constitute degrading treatment; cf *Ireland v United Kingdom* (1978) 2 EHRR 25 para 181, where conditions described as 'discreditable and reprehensible' did not amount to a violation of Art 3.

[124] (1980) 20 DR 44, EComm HR.

[125] It is not clear whether intimate body searches would violate Art 3 in the case of a non-terrorist detainee. As was said in *Hilton v United Kingdom* (1978) 3 EHRR 104, EComm HR, degrading treatment contrary to Art 3 may be shown by reference to particular incidents or the general regime of treatment to which prisoners are subjected. See also D Harris, M O'Boyle and C Warbrick, *Law of the European Convention on Human Rights* (Butterworths, 1995) 84.

[126] (1997) 26 EHRR 563.

[127] Ibid para 56.

[127a] *Galloway v United Kingdom* [1999] EHRLR 119; *Peters v Netherlands* (1994) 77–A DR 75.

[128] See generally, S Livingstone and T Owen, *Prison Law* (2nd edn, Oxford University Press, 1999) para 10.61ff.

held in solitary confinement cells as amounting to inhuman treatment.[129] The same types of deficiencies were found in *Ireland v United Kingdom,*[130] *Cyprus v Turkey*[131] and *Tekin v Turkey*[132] in varying degrees.

However, where degrading conditions of detention are self-imposed there will be no breach of Article 3. Thus, in *McFeeley v United Kingdom,*[133] inmates at a prison went on a 'dirty protest' campaign, defiling their cells with waste food, urine and faeces, and refusing to wear prison uniforms. The Commission said that the resulting cell conditions would have been inhuman if caused by the state, but found that the state is not responsible for 'self-imposed conditions of detention'.[134] It also established in that case that account must be taken of the cumulative effect of conditions and not simply specific allegations.[135] **8.46**

Cases alleging inhuman conditions have arisen in relation to mental hospitals as well as prisons. In *B v United Kingdom*[136] the Commission visited Broadmoor Hospital and noted 'deplorable overcrowding' and less than satisfactory sanitary conditions, concluding that facilities were 'extremely unsatisfactory'. However, it does not appear to have considered the cumulative effect of the issues raised, and declined to find that there was inhuman treatment contrary to Article 3. In another Broadmoor case,[137] the United Kingdom agreed to pay compensation in order to make the necessary improvements in the conditions of detention of segregated patients. A friendly settlement was also agreed in *Simon-Herold v Austria*[138] in which a remand prisoner was transferred for a physical examination to a hospital where he was kept for over a week in a closed ward with violent, mentally ill patients, several of whom died in his presence. By the terms of the settlement, Austria conceded that the transfer to such a ward of a prisoner who was not suspected of mental illness might be inhuman treatment, and indicated that it had taken steps to prevent such transfers in future.[139] **8.47**

[129] (1969) 12 YB 1, EComm HR.
[130] (1978) 2 EHRR 25 para 182.
[131] (1976) 4 EHRR 482, 541, EComm HR (inadequate supply of food and drinking water and medical treatment was found to breach Art 3 under grounds of inhuman treatment).
[132] RJD 1998-IV 53.
[133] *McFeeley v United Kingdom* (1980) 20 DR 44, EComm HR.
[134] Cf *McQuiston v United Kingdom* (1986) 46 DR 182, EComm HR.
[135] (1980) 20 DR 44, 83.
[136] (1981) 32 DR 5, EComm HR.
[137] *A v United Kingdom* (1980) 3 EHRR 131, EComm HR.
[138] (1971) 14 YB 352, EComm HR.
[139] Harris, O'Boyle and Warbrick (n 125 above) 67–68.

(d) Medical treatment of detainees

8.48 States are obliged to provide medical care for those persons in their detention.[140] Medical attention must be made available to detainees, even if this requires their temporary release, if failure to treat would result in injury to their health.[141] However, detention incompatible with a prisoner's health, does not constitute a breach of Article 3 unless it can be found that other appropriate punishments were available.[142]

8.49 The obligation to provide medical treatment extends, at the very least, to that which is in accordance with the 'standards accepted by medical science' where necessary to prevent death or serious injury.[143] Such treatment may be administered forcefully if the detainee is suffering from a mental disorder such as would make him incapable of making rational decisions for himself.[144] In cases where the detainee is of sound mind, it is not clear whether forced medical treatment would constitute inhuman or degrading treatment under Article 3. Accepting the requirement for treatment of the minimum standard, the forced feeding of hunger strikers and the administration of drugs to seriously ill detainees would not be inhuman or degrading, although it could be construed as humiliating.[145]

8.50 In *Chartier v Italy*,[146] a French national charged with murder claimed he was suffering from a hereditary illness causing obesity which could not be treated in the Italian centre for the physically handicapped in which he was detained. The Commission accepted that detention for M Chartier was a 'particularly painful experience' and, without finding a breach of Article 3, suggested that the Italian

[140] See the *Greek* case (1969) 12 YB 1, EComm HR; *Cyprus v Turkey* (1976) 4 EHRR 482, EComm HR; *Hurtado v Switzerland* (1994) Series A No 280-A, in which a person forcibly arrested was, despite his request, not given an X-ray for six days, which when given revealed a fractured rib; *McFeeley v United Kingdom* (1980) 20 DR 44, 67, EComm HR which says that states are generally obligated to review detention arrangements for detainees' health and well-being continuously; cf *Estelle v Gamble* (1976) 429 US 97, (deliberate indifference to medical needs of prisoners 'cruel and unusual punishment').

[141] *Bonnechaux v Switzerland* (1979) 18 DR 100, EComm HR, in which it was found that a detainee in his seventies had received adequate medical treatment for cardio-vascular troubles and diabetes throughout his three years on remand; *Chartier v Italy* (1982) 33 DR 41, EComm HR.

[142] *X v Germany* (1983) 6 EHRR 110, EComm HR.

[143] See *Herczegfalvy v Austria* (1992) 15 EHRR 437 para 242 (Comm Rep).

[144] See eg *Herczegfalvy v Austria* (1992) 15 EHRR 437 para 83. Cf *X v Germany* (1980) 20 DR 193, EComm HR.

[145] In *X v Germany* (1984) 7 EHRR 152, the Commission held that the state's obligation to secure the right to life of detainees under Art 2 overrides any claim a detainee might have under Art 3 regarding the application of medical treatment for the prevention of injury to his health or to prevent his death. It should be noted that the administration of medical treatment in the absence of consent does not extend to experimental medical treatment, *X v Denmark* (1983) 32 DR 282, EComm HR, and cannot include sterilisation, 1 *Travaux Préparatoires* 116–7.

[146] (1982) 33 DR 41, EComm HR.

authorities might take measures to either attenuate the effects of, or terminate, the applicant's detention.[147]

(e) Solitary confinement[148]

Solitary confinement cases fall into two categories: those in which the detainee is subjected to total social and sensory isolation and those in which a detainee is removed from association with other prisoners for reasons of the administration of justice,[149] security,[150] protection[151] or discipline. In order to determine whether breach of Article 3 has occurred, it is necessary to have 'regard for the surrounding circumstances, including the particular conditions, the stringency of the measure, its duration, the objective pursued and its effects on the person concerned'.[152] **8.51**

None of the arrangements for the solitary confinement of remand or convicted criminals that have been challenged have been found to be in breach of Article 3. Segregation from other prisoners for periods of up to six years have been found to be justified.[153] Article 3 can, however, be infringed when social isolation is coupled with 'complete sensory isolation'.[154] So far such 'complete' sensory isolation has not been found to exist in the cases which have appeared before the Commission and Court. **8.52**

In *Kröcher and Möller v Switzerland*[155] two West Germans were detained on remand in Switzerland on charges of attempted murder arising out of terrorist activities. In order to prevent their suicide or escape, the applicants were detained in separate, isolated cells. The windows were frosted over and lights burnt continuously in their cells. They were placed under constant television surveillance and allowed 20 minutes' exercise a day outside of their cells on weekdays only. **8.53**

---

[147] For other cases where it was said that failure to provide adequate medical care may violate Art 3 see *Kotälla v The Netherlands* (1978) 14 DR 238, EComm HR; *B v United Kingdom* (1981) 33 DR 5, EComm HR; *Herczegfalvy v Austria*, (1992) 15 EHRR 437 para 242.

[148] See generally, S Livingstone and T Owen, *Prison Law* (2nd edn, Oxford University Press, 1999) para 10.61ff.

[149] *Ensslin, Baader and Raspe v Germany* (1978) 14 DR 64, 109, EComm HR; *R v Denmark*, (1985) 41 DR 149; *Kröcher and Möller v Switzerland* (1982) 34 DR 25, 57, EComm HR; *Treholdt v Norway* (1991) 71 DR 168, EComm HR.

[150] *X v United Kingdom* (1980) 21 DR 95, EComm HR; *X v United Kingdom* (1984) 7 EHRR 140, EComm HR.

[151] *Ensslin, Baader and Raspe v Germany* (1978) 14 DR 64, EComm HR.

[152] Ibid; see also *McFeeley v United Kingdom* (1980) 20 DR 44, EComm HR; *Kröcher and Möller v Switzerland* (1982) 34 DR 25 at 57; *E v Norway* (1990) 17 EHRR 30.

[153] *Ensslin, Baader and Raspe v Germany* (1978) 14 DR 64, EComm HR, (the security risks of an attack by terrorist to secure the release of the applicants, who were members of that group, was seen as justification for the segregation of the applicants from other prisoners for almost three years); *M v United Kingdom* (1983) 35 DR 130, EComm HR in which a prisoner who killed two fellow detainees was segregated for six years.

[154] See generally, *Ensslin, Baader and Raspe v Germany* (1978) 14 DR 64, 109, EComm HR.

[155] (1982) 34 DR 25, EComm HR.

Newspapers, radio and television were prohibited and the applicants' watches and diaries were removed. They were not allowed contact with each other, with other prisoners or with lawyers. These conditions prevailed for a month; some of them were relaxed during the next five months of detention on remand. The Commission was of the opinion that because of (i) the gradual relaxation of the conditions of sensory and social isolation and the medical evidence as to their effect and (ii) their refusal to take advantage of certain opportunities for outside contact, the applicants had not been 'subjected to a form of physical or moral suffering designed to punish them, destroy their personality or break their resistance' in breach of Article 3.[156]

(6) Extradition and deportation

8.54 Extradition or deportation will be inhuman or degrading treatment in breach of Article 3 if it results in severe suffering to an ill person,[157] the separation of a mother from her child,[158] the removal of stateless persons who will not be received elsewhere[159] or a real risk to the applicant of ill-treatment or death by either private groups or the state.[160]

8.55 It is the last of these circumstances which has produced the most important decisions of the Court in this area. The case of *Soering v United Kingdom*[161] was the first concerned with a claim that extradition from a contracting State to a non-Contracting State would result in the applicant being subjected to torture or inhuman or degrading treatment. The Home Secretary signed a warrant for the extradition of a West German to Virginia, USA, where he faced murder charges. The Court found that if Mr Soering was returned he would almost certainly be found guilty of the charges, having confessed to his crime, and would face a real risk of being sentenced to death. This, of itself, would not have amounted to a breach of Article 3[162] but the Court held that a breach would occur:

---

156 See D Harris, M O'Boyle and C Warbrick, *Law of the European Convention on Human Rights* (Butterworths, 1995) 69–70.

157 *Bulus v Sweden* (1984) 35 DR 57; (1984) 39 DR 75, EComm HR (mental illness); *X v Belgium* (1961) 6 CD 39, EComm HR; *X v Switzerland* (1980) 24 DR 205, EComm HR; *D v United Kingdom* (1997) 24 EHRR 423 (deportation of AIDS sufferer to St Kitts where there was no adequate medical treatment).

158 Although this is more likely to raise a claim under Art 8, see *Berrehab v Netherlands* (1988) 11 EHRR 322; *Moustaquim v Belgium* (1991) 13 EHRR 802; *Beldjoudi v France* (1992) 14 EHRR 801.

159 See eg *Harabi v Netherlands* (1986) 46 DR 112, EComm HR; *Giama v Belgium* (1980) 21 DR 73, EComm HR.

160 See eg *Amekrane v United Kingdom* (1973) 16 YB 356, EComm HR; *Altun v Germany*, (1983) 36 DR 209, EComm HR; *Soering v United Kingdom* (1989) 11 EHRR 439; *Vilvarajah v United Kingdom* (1991) 14 EHRR 248.

161 (1989) 11 EHRR 439.

162 Although Art 2 protects the right to life, it allows states to maintain the death penalty.

where *substantial grounds* have been shown for believing that the person concerned, if extradited, faces a real risk of being subjected to torture or to inhuman or degrading treatment or punishment in the requesting country. (emphasis added)[163]

Such grounds were found to include 'the manner in which [the death penalty] is imposed or executed, the personal circumstances of the condemned person and a disproportionality to the gravity of the crime committed, as well as the conditions of detention awaiting execution'.[164] The key factor was the likely delay of six to eight years between sentencing and execution, known as the 'death row' phenomenon, which the Court held would constitute inhuman treatment or punishment in violation of Article 3.[165]

The Court applied the 'substantial grounds' test again in *Cruz Varas v Sweden*.[166] In that case a Chilean applicant had unsuccessfully[167] challenged a deportation order claiming that he would face political persecution, including the possibility of torture or even death, if his family was deported to Chile. The Court found that the testimony given in support of the claim was unconvincing, and in the light of the more liberal political climate in Chile, could not find probable inhuman treatment. As a result, the deportation order was upheld. However, the case extended the 'substantial grounds' standard to deportation cases. **8.56**

In *Vilvarajah v United Kingdom*[168] five Tamils were expelled to Sri Lanka despite their claims that they would be subject to inhuman treatment if they were returned to Sri Lanka. Three of the applicants suffered beatings and torture upon their return. Despite this, the Court upheld the decision to expel the applicants which could only be made 'with reference to those facts which were known to the Contracting State at the time of the expulsion'. Upon reviewing those facts[169] the Court found that only a 'mere possibility' rather than a 'real risk' of inhuman treatment had existed at the time of the decision. **8.57**

The absolute nature of the Article 3 right means that, if there is a real risk of violation on deportation, there can be no question of balancing the interests of the individual against those of the deporting state:[170] **8.58**

the national interests of the State could not be invoked to override the interests of

[163] (1989) 11 EHRR 439.

[164] Ibid para 104.

[165] For other 'death row' cases see para 8.62 below.

[166] (1991) 14 EHRR 1 para 100.

[167] The case arose after the Commission had requested the respondent state not to deport the applicant.

[168] (1991) 14 EHRR 248.

[169] At the time the situation in Sri Lanka vis-à-vis the Government violence against the Tamil liberation movement and the Tamil population in general had improved to the point that large numbers of Tamils who had left Sri Lanka during the violence were returning of their own volition.

[170] *Chahal v United Kingdom* (1996) 23 EHRR 413; *Ahmed v Austria* (1996) 24 EHRR 278.

> the individual where substantial grounds had been shown for believing that he would be subjected to ill-treatment if expelled.[171]

The activities of the threatened individual in the expelling state cannot be a material consideration, however undesirable or dangerous. As a result, in the *Chahal* case[172] deportation would have been a violation of Article 3, despite the fact that the Home Secretary had certified that his continued presence in the United Kingdom was not conducive to the public good for reasons of national security.[173]

D. The Impact of the Human Rights Act

(1) Introduction

8.59 In accordance with its general approach, the English law does not provide any positive right to be free from torture or degrading and inhuman treatment. There are, however a number of specific rights in this area, protected by a combination of the civil and criminal law. However, there are a number of areas in which English law may be in conflict with the Convention.[174] Article 3 is likely to have a significant impact in the fields of criminal law, immigration law, prison law and police law. In addition, there may be some impact on the present criminal law relating to torture.

8.60 In general, the positive obligation on each Convention party to ensure that its legal system provides adequate protection of the right to freedom from degrading and inhuman treatment[175] has potentially far-reaching implications. It might lead to a finding of breach if, for example, the legal system does not provide adequate means of controlling domestic violence, racial discrimination in the work place, or ill-treatment in private prisons or the armed forces.

(2) United Kingdom cases prior to the Human Rights Act

(a) Introduction

8.61 Prior to the Human Rights Act, the United Kingdom cases which came before the Commission and the Court concerned treatment of individuals upon deportation or extradition, corporal punishment and conditions afforded to prisoners

171 *Chahal*, n 170 above, para 78.

172 Ibid.

173 For the decision of the English court, to the opposite effect, see *R v Secretary of State for the Home Department, ex p Chahal* [1994] Imm AR 107.

174 See generally, F Klug, K Starmer and S Weir, *The Three Pillars of Liberty* (Routledge, 1996), 259–265.

175 See *Costello-Roberts v United Kingdom* (1993) 19 EHRR 112; and see para 8.38 above.

and other detainees. The United Kingdom has been found to be in breach of Article 3 in six cases: one relating to the interrogation of IRA suspects in Northern Ireland;[175a] two relating to the corporal punishment of minors[175b] and three relating to deportation and extradition.[175c]

(b) Deportation and extradition

Although entry, residence and expulsion of aliens is essentially the prerogative of the nation state, an Article 3 issue may arise under the Convention where there are substantial grounds for believing that the individual faces a real risk of torture or inhuman or degrading treatment or punishment. For example, the decision of the Court in *Vilvarajah and others v United Kingdom*[176] concerned the expulsion of Tamil refugees who had been expelled to Cyprus claimed that Article 3 had been violated. However, the anticipated ill-treatment was indistinguishable from that which every non-combatant in the region might have expected at that time and the Court found there was no breach of Article 3. In *Soering v United Kingdom*,[177] on the other hand, it was held that the extradition of the applicant to the United States, where he was likely to be convicted of murder and face a death sentence, would have resulted in a breach of Article 3. It was not the potential punishment itself, but the 'death row phenomenon' of intense anguish during the delay between imposition and execution of sentence, in conditions of incarceration, that elevated the risk of ill-treatment beyond the threshold of Article 3. **8.62**

The case of *Chahal v United Kingdom*[178] established that the right to be free from torture or degrading and inhuman treatment is absolute: the existence of a 'real risk' of inhuman or degrading treatment contrary to Article 3 will take priority over other considerations, including national security. Mr Chahal, who had been given indefinite leave to remain in the United Kingdom, was tortured by the Indian police for political activity, on a visit to the Punjab, and upon his return to Britain his role as a leading figure among British Sikhs led the UK Government to seek to deport him on grounds of national security. The Court held that the possibility of ill-treatment of the applicant was of paramount concern, in spite of importance of the fight against terrorism. In light of the risk of torture, it was irrelevant whether Mr Chahal posed a threat to national security.[179] **8.63**

[175a] *Ireland v United Kingdom* (1978) 2 EHRR 25.
[175b] *Tyrer v United Kingdom* (1979) 2 EHRR 1; *A v United Kingdom* (1998) 27 EHRR 611.
[175c] *Soering v United Kingdom* (1989) 11 EHRR 439; *Chahal v United Kingdom* (1996) 23 EHRR 413; *D v United Kingdom* (1997) 24 EHRR 423.
[176] (1991) 14 EHRR 248.
[177] (1989) 11 EHRR 439.
[178] (1996) 23 EHRR 413.
[179] Cf *R v Secretary of State for the Home Department, ex p Chahal* [1995] 1 WLR 526.

8.64 In *East African Asians v United Kingdom*[180] the Commission found that differential treatment of immigrants on the basis of race might constitute a special form of affront to human dignity and thus degrading treatment, depending on the legislation applied in each case. The Commonwealth Immigrants Acts 1962 and 1968 and the Immigration Appeals Act 1969 were found to discriminate against aliens on the ground of race or colour, which in the circumstances amounted to 'degrading treatment'. 'British protected persons', however, did not suffer such discrimination, as the legislation did not distinguish between different groups of them on the basis of race or colour.

(c) Corporal punishment

8.65 In *Tyrer v United Kingdom*[181] the Court held that the sentence, imposed by a juvenile court, of three strokes of the birch over the bare posterior of a 15-year-old was neither torture nor inhuman treatment, but did amount to degrading punishment within the meaning of Article 3. However, no violation was established in *Costello-Roberts v United Kingdom*,[182] where a school head master gave a seven-year-old three strokes with a soft-soled gym shoe on his backside, through his gym shorts, causing no visible injury. In *Campbell and Cosans v United Kingdom*[183] the Court made it clear that the threat of physical chastisement associated with the attendance of students at a school which provides for such a disciplinary regime does not itself constitute degrading treatment.

8.66 In *A v United Kingdom*[184] the applicant was a nine-year-old child who had been beaten by his stepfather with a cane. The stepfather was acquitted on a charge of assault occasioning actual bodily harm. The Court held that the beating had reached the necessary level of severity to engage Article 3. States were under a duty to take measures designed to ensure that individuals within their jurisdiction were not subjected to degrading and inhuman treatment. The fact that English law had required the prosecution to prove beyond reasonable doubt that the assault went beyond the limits of lawful punishment meant that there was violation of Article 3.

(d) Conditions of detention

8.67 The UK's treatment of prisoners and other detainees such as mental patients has been raised before the Commission on a number of occasions.[185] In *Hilton v United Kingdom*[186] the applicant complained of harassment and victimisation

---

[180] (1994) 78-A DR 5, EComm HR.
[181] (1978) 2 EHRR 1.
[182] (1993) 19 EHRR 112.
[183] (1982) 4 EHRR 293.
[184] (1998) 27 EHRR 611.
[185] See generally, S Livingstone and T Owen, *Prison Law* (2nd edn, Oxford University Press, 1999) para 5.69ff.
[186] (1976) 4 DR 177, EComm HR; see para 8.33 above.

aggravated by racial prejudice expressed by prison staff. He also relied on a failure to protect him from other prisoners by removing him from association with them, personal escort or transfer to another prison; lack of exercise; abusive and threatening language against him; and abuse of disciplinary measures, including searches, by prison staff. The case of *McFeeley v United Kingdom*[187] involved complaints about the disciplinary regime of continuous and cumulative sanctions, the imposition of 'isolation' punishment, restricted diets and the conditions of detention.

On the other hand, solitary confinement of a mentally ill patient in *A v United Kingdom*,[188] together with deprivation of adequate furnishings and clothing, resulted in a friendly settlement between the UK Government and the applicant. Although not admitting liability, the United Kingdom published new guidelines on the use of seclusion at Broadmoor. **8.68**

(e) Other cases

In *Ireland v United Kingdom*[188a] police officers used five 'sensory deprivation' techniques when interrogating internees in Northern Ireland. The Court found that these techniques constituted inhuman and degrading treatment, but not torture. In *T v United Kingdom*[188b] the Court held that the trial of an 11-year-old in the Crown Court and the sentence of detention at Her Majesty's pleasure did not breach Article 3. **8.68A**

(3) Potential impact

(a) General

Under the Human Rights Act the examination of the lawfulness of any administrative decision of a domestic court will require the court to make a primary judgment[189] about whether Article 3 determination as to whether the Convention right to be free from subjection to inhuman or degrading treatment has been breached. The court will no longer be confined to making a secondary judgment as to whether or not the decision was taken in accordance with the principles established in *Wednesbury*.[190] This fundamental change of approach will have a potential impact in a number of areas of law, particularly in immigration law. **8.69**

---

187 (1980) 20 DR 44, EComm HR; see para 8.44 above.
188 (1980) 20 DR 5, EComm HR.
188a (1978) 2 EHRR 25.
188b (2000) 7 BHRC 659.
189 See generally, para 5.122ff above.
190 For the present position, see para 2.30ff above.

(b) Criminal law

8.70 The English criminal law in relation to torture is arguably incompatible with the Convention. Although the definition of 'torture' in section 134 of the Criminal Justice Act 1988 appears to be wider than that adopted under the Convention, the section does not recognise the absolute nature of the right to be free from torture;[191] rather it provides for a defence of 'lawful authority, justification or excuse',[192] in direct contradiction to Article 3.

8.71 Section 2 of the Crime (Sentences) Act 1997 provides for 'automatic life sentences' for persons convicted of a second 'serious offence'.[193] It is possible that such sentences will constitute 'degrading and inhuman treatment'.[194] The courts will have to consider whether, in a particular case, the automatic sentence is 'grossly disproportionate' to the offence committed. If so, it is possible that a declaration of incompatibility could be made.

(c) Immigration

8.72 There are a number of areas in which the Convention may have an impact on English immigration law.[195] The right to be free from torture or degrading and inhuman treatment is an absolute right and takes priority over other considerations. As a result, the domestic courts will have to take the same approach to these cases as that used by the Court in *Chahal v United Kingdom*.[196] There, the Court held that a real risk of being subjected to inhuman or degrading treatment was a breach of Article 3, so that it became irrelevant whether Mr Chahal posed a threat to national security.[197] It will no longer be lawful, therefore, to balance the right to freedom from inhuman or degrading treatment against national security considerations, either in asylum cases[198] or where an exclusion order is made under the Prevention of Terrorism Act.[199]

8.73 The shift in the function of the court in the examination of administrative decisions, from a secondary review on the basis of *Wednesbury*[200] to a primary

---

[191] See, most recently, *Aksoy v Turkey* (1996) 23 EHRR 553.

[192] See D Feldman, *Civil Liberties and Human Rights in England and Wales* (Clarendon Press, 1993) 130; F Klug, K Starmer, S Weir, *The Three Pillars of Liberty* (Routledge, 1996) 260.

[193] See generally, *Blackstone's Criminal Practice* (Blackstone Press, 1999) E1.22, 1727–1728.

[194] See the Canadian case of *R v Smith* [1987] 1 SCR 1045, para 8.85ff below and for the position in Namibia and South Africa see paras 8.120 and 8.124 below.

[195] For a detailed discussion, see I Macdonald and N Blake, *Immigration Law and Practice in the United Kingdom* (4th edn, Butterworths, 1995) 439ff.

[196] (1996) 23 EHRR 413.

[197] Cf *R v Secretary of State for the Home Department, ex p Chahal* [1995] 1 WLR 526.

[198] In other words, reversing the effect of *R v Secretary of State for the Home Department, ex p Chahal* [1995] 1 WLR 526.

[199] In other words, reversing the effect of *R v Secretary of State for the Home Department, ex p McQuillan* [1995] 4 All ER 400.

[200] For the present position, see para 2.30ff above.

determination as to conformity with the Convention, also has a potential impact on several aspects of immigration law. For example, it is Home Office policy not to expel or return an asylum seeker to his country of origin if he can satisfy the Home Secretary that there are substantial grounds for believing that there is a danger, *inter alia*, of torture. Prior to incorporation, a threat of torture obliged the unsuccessful asylum seeker to argue that the Home Secretary had acted irrationally in rejecting his claim; the court would review the decision for lawfulness in accordance with the legislation which purportedly authorised it.[201] By contrast, after the Human Rights Act comes into force the court will need to determine whether the decision, in the context of its governing legislation, is a direct breach of Article 3 of the Convention.

The extradition or expulsion of a person to a place where he is likely to be subjected to degrading or inhuman treatment will also be unlawful under Article 3.[202] It must, however, be shown that there is a real risk of injury which is serious enough to constitute torture, or inhuman or degrading treatment. **8.74**

Article 3 will widen the entitlement for refugees who wish to remain in the United Kingdom because they face inhuman or degrading treatment if returned to their place of origin. In order to qualify for refugee status, it is necessary for a claimant to meet the requirements imposed by the Geneva Convention and Protocol on the Status of Refugees.[203] A person must have a well-founded fear of persecution for reasons of 'race, religion, nationality, membership of a particular social group or political opinion.'[204] Article 3, however, provides an alternative basis for seeking leave to remain in the United Kingdom. **8.75**

Furthermore, it is possible that Article 3 will have an impact on decisions relating to entry into the United Kingdom. The case law shows that refusal of entry on grounds which are racially discriminatory may be considered to be degrading or inhuman treatment. This was the view of the Commission in the *East African Asians* case.[205] Generally though, such a finding will be appropriate only where special circumstances, such as a deprivation of livelihood, are present.[206] **8.76**

---

[201] See eg *R v Secretary of State for the Home Department, ex p Bugdaycay* [1987] AC 514.

[202] *Soering v United Kingdom* (1989) 11 EHRR 439; see also *R v Secretary of State for the Home Department, ex p M* [1999] Imm AR 548 and *Danian v Secretary of State for the Home Department* [2000] Imm AR 96, CA which are discussed at para 8.09 above.

[203] (1951) Cmnd 9171 the text of which is reproduced at App I in Vol 2 and (1967) Cmnd 3906.

[204] Ibid, Art 1A(2): cf *Islam v Secretary of State for the Home Department* [1999] 2 WLR 1015 (Pakistani women constituted a 'particular social group').

[205] (1981) 3 EHRR 76, EComm HR.

[206] Thus, there was no breach of Art 3 in a case in which the applicants had work and a place to live (*X and Y v United Kingdom* (1974) CD 29, EComm HR).

(d) Mental health law

8.77 The high 'minimum threshold' for 'inhuman or degrading treatment'[207] means that, in order to breach Article 3, mistreatment must be very serious. As a result, it appears that well regulated and monitored mental health practice, even at the extremes of treatment, will rarely, if ever, breach Article 3.[208]

(e) Police law

8.78 Under the Police and Criminal Evidence Act 1984 ('PACE'), the police have a power to carry out 'intimate searches' of suspects in police custody without the person's consent. An 'intimate search' is a search which consists of the physical examination of the bodily orifices of a person.[209] An intimate search may be made if an officer, of at least the rank of superintendent, has reasonable grounds for believing that the arrested suspect may have:

- concealed on his person anything he could use to cause physical injury to himself or others during detention or in court custody; or
- concealed on himself a Class A drug which he held with an intent to supply to another or to export with an intent to evade a prohibition or restriction.[210]

A Class A drug search may be conducted only at a hospital, doctor's surgery or other place used for medical purposes and must be conducted by a suitably qualified person.[211] It is arguable that an 'intimate search' of this nature constitutes 'inhuman or degrading treatment' under Article 3:[212] such a search is likely to be humiliating and there is an obvious risk of injury. As a result, it is arguable that any attempt by the police officer to exercise the discretion to conduct such a search would be rendered unlawful by section 6 of the Human Rights Act.[213]

8.79 In some circumstances the unlawful use of force by the police may be sufficiently severe to constitute a violation of Article 3. If a person is unreasonably handcuffed in connection with a wrongful arrest or detention and in public this may be 'degrading or inhuman treatment'.[214] If a prisoner is severely beaten or threatened and humiliated by police officers in order to obtain a confession, this may be suffi-

---

207 See para 8.15 above.
208 See O Thorold, 'Implications of the Convention for United Kingdom Mental Health Legislation' [1996] EHRLR 619, 620.
209 PACE, s 118(1).
210 PACE, s 55(1).
211 PACE, s 55(4).
212 See the discussion in D Feldman, *Civil Liberties and Human Rights in England and Wales* (Clarendon Press, 1993) 261–264.
213 See para 5.122ff above.
214 Cf *Raninen v Finland* (1997) 26 EHRR 563 para 56.

ciently severe to constitute 'torture'.[215] If a person is injured whilst in custody, there will be a clear burden on the police to provide an explanation as to how the injuries were caused.[216] A failure by the police properly to investigate mistreatment of a person in custody may itself be a breach of Article 3.[217] An investigation by the Police Complaints Authority is unlikely to satisfy the requirements of Article 8 because it is not sufficiently independent of the police and the Home Secretary.[217a]

(f) Prison law

The Strasbourg case law suggests that a breach of Article 3 will only be found in relation to the most serious complaints about conditions of detention.[218] Nevertheless, standards are becoming stricter[219] and Article 3 may have an important impact on the conditions in which prisoners can be lawfully detained.[220] It is arguable that the cumulative effect of overcrowding and lack of proper sanitation in some British prisons constitutes a breach of Article 3.[221] The Human Rights Committee has held that such conditions of detention amount to inhumanity.[222] It is also arguable that the denial of appropriate medical care to prisoners would constitute a breach of Article 3.[223] **8.80**

In addition, the systematic use of 'strip searches' in prisons could constitute 'degrading treatment' in breach of Article 3. Such searches may not, at present, be tortious in English law.[224] The effect of incorporation is that, in the absence of clear lawful statutory justification, such searches will be unlawful if the treatment can be shown to cross the high 'minimum threshold' for 'inhuman or degrading treatment'.[225] **8.81**

---

[215] *Selmouni v France* (2000) 29 EHRR 403; see para 8.26 above, and cf *Treadaway v Chief Constable of West Midlands Independent*, 23 Jul 1994 (McKinnon J).

[216] See para 8.41 above.

[217] See para 8.19 above.

[217a] On the lack of independence of the PCA see *Govell v United Kingdom* [1999] EHRLR 121 (EComm HR, Merits) and *Khan v United Kingdom*, *The Times* 23 May 2000.

[218] See para 8.15 above.

[219] See *Selmouni v France* (2000) 29 EHRR 403 para 101.

[220] See generally, S Livingstone and T Owen, *Prison Law* (2nd edn, Oxford University Press, 1999) para 5.58ff and see D Cheney, L Dickson, J Fitzpatrick and S Uglow, *Criminal Justice and the Human Rights Act 1998* (Jordans, 1999) 156ff.

[221] See *Report to the United Kingdom Government on the Visit to the United Kingdom carried out by the Committee for the Prevention of Torture and Inhuman or Degrading Treatment or Punishment*, adopted by the Committee, 21 Mar 1991, see D Feldman (n 212 above) 271ff.

[222] *Estrella v Uruguay* Application 79/1980, UNHRC.

[223] D Feldman (n 212 above) 167; Cheney (n 220 above) 157–158.

[224] But see *Bayliss v Home Secretary*, Legal Action, Feb 1993, 16 which suggests that there may be a tort of 'unlawfully inducing a person to remove his/her clothes'.

[225] See para 8.15 above.

Appendix 1: The Canadian Charter of Rights

(1) Introduction

8.82 Section 12 of the Charter provides that:

> Everyone has the right not to be subjected to any cruel and unusual treatment or punishment.

In contrast to Article 7 of the International Covenant on Civil and Political Rights,[226] section 12 of the Canadian Charter of Rights and Freedoms omits any reference to the act of torture and the adjective 'unusual' is used instead of 'inhuman or degrading' to describe the categories of treatment and punishment prohibited. 'Cruel'[227] punishment or treatment is also prohibited, and in this additional detail the section differs from Article 3 of the European Convention on Human Rights. Section 2(b) of the Canadian Bill of Rights also prohibits any 'cruel and unusual treatment or punishment'.[228]

(2) Treatment or punishment

8.83 Unless a particular sanction amounts to a 'treatment or punishment', it is not prohibited by the application of section 12. A civil sanction such as the automatic suspension of a driver's licence is neither 'treatment' nor 'punishment',[229] while deportation of a non-citizen criminal is not a 'punishment'.[230] Section 12 also applies to the actual conditions in which offenders are confined.[231] Oppressive conditions or severe disciplinary measures in penitentiaries or prisons could amount to cruel and unusual punishment.[232]

(3) 'Cruel and unusual'

(a) Introduction

8.84 The Canadian courts have not yet provided a clear definition of 'cruel and unusual' as used

---

[226] Art 7 of the ICCPR, states: 'No one shall be subjected to torture or to cruel, inhuman or degrading treatment or punishment. In particular, no one shall be subjected without his free consent to medical or scientific experimentation' see App J in Vol 2.

[227] s 12 adopts the traditional Anglo-American expression, 'cruel and unusual', derived from the English Bill of Rights 1688 and used in the Eighth Amendment of the United States Constitution.

[228] For commentary on s 2(b) of the Canadian Bill of Rights, see W S Tarnopolsky, 'Just Deserts or Cruel and Unusual Treatment or Punishment? Where Do We Look For Guidance?' (1978) 10 Ottawa LR 1; Berger, 'The Application of the Cruel and Unusual Punishment Clause under the Canadian Bill of Rights' (1978) 24 McGill LJ 161.

[229] *R v Miller* (1988) 65 OR (2d) 746, CA; cf *Re Bulmer* (1987) 36 DLR (4th) 688, Alta QB.

[230] The Supreme Court in *Chiarelli v Canada* [1992] 1 SCR 711 said that it might be 'treatment', but found it unnecessary to determine the issue, because deportation was not in any event, 'cruel and unusual'.

[231] P W Hogg, *Constitutional Law of Canada*, (4th edn, Carswell, 1997), s 50.6.

[232] See *McCann v The Queen* [1976] 1 FC 570, TD: conditions in solitary confinement were held to be cruel and unusual under s 2(b) of the Canadian Bill of Rights; *Collin v Kaplan* [1983] 1 FC 496: double-celling was not considered cruel and unusual under s 12 of the Charter; *R v Olson* (1987) 62 OR (2d) 321, CA: segregation of prisoner from other inmates for his protection was held not to be cruel and unusual; *R v McC(T)* (1991) 4 OR (3d) 203, Ont Prov Ct: dirty, overcrowded holding cells for young offenders was found to be cruel and unusual.

in the Charter. The first question is whether the two terms are to be read conjunctively, so that a treatment or punishment will only be a violation if it is both cruel and unusual, or disjunctively, meaning that treatment or punishment, that is one or the other, but not both, breaches section 12. The Supreme Court in *R v Miller*,[233] referring to the Canadian Bill of Rights, seemed to accept the conjunctive alternative, saying that the words 'cruel and unusual' are 'interacting expressions colouring each other, so to speak, and hence to be considered together as a compendious description of a norm'.[234] It also stated that the test for 'cruel and unusual punishment' is whether the prescribed sanction is 'so excessive as to outrage standards of decency'.[235]

In the Charter case of *R v Smith*[236] the Supreme Court accepted that the bases for analysis of treatment and punishment, synthesised by Professor Tarnopolsky in 1978 from case law under the Canadian Bill of Rights,[237] provided a solid foundation on which to assess a challenge to treatment or punishment under section 12. The nine tests suggested are as follows: **8.85**

- Does the punishment go beyond what is necessary to achieve a legitimate penal aim?
- Are there adequate alternatives?
- Is it unacceptable to a large segment of the population?
- Can it be applied upon a rational basis in accordance with ascertained or ascertainable standards?
- Is it arbitrarily imposed?
- Does it have value in the form of some social purpose such as reformation, rehabilitation, deterrence or retribution?
- Does it accord with public standards of decency and propriety?
- Is it shocking to the general conscience or intolerable in fundamental fairness?
- Is it unusually severe and hence degrading to human dignity and worth?

Against this backdrop, the case of *R v Smith* established that the phrase 'cruel and unusual' includes two types of treatment or punishment: those that are barbaric in themselves and those which are grossly disproportionate to the offence.

(b) Intrinsically barbaric

The first group comprises punishments or treatments that would be cruel and unusual in and of themselves, regardless of the heinousness of the offence or the nature of the offender. In *R v Smith*[238] Lamer J suggested that corporal punishment such as the lash, the lobotomisation of dangerous offenders and the castration of sexual offenders were examples in this category. **8.86**

There has also been some speculation as to whether capital punishment may be considered 'cruel and unusual' under section 12 of the Charter. The death penalty has now been **8.87**

---

[233] [1977] 2 SCR 680.

[234] *Dictum* of Laskin CJ in ibid 690; accepted by the court in *R v Smith* [1987] 1 SCR 1045, 1072, 1088, 1109.

[235] Although this was also asserted with reference to the Canadian Bill of Rights, it too was accepted by the court in *R v Smith* [1987] 1 SCR 1045, 1072, 1089, 1109.

[236] *R v Smith* [1987] 1 SCR 1045, SCC.

[237] See W S Tarnopolsky, 'Just Deserts or Cruel and Unusual Treatment or Punishment? Where Do We Look for Guidance?' [1978] 10 Ottawa LR 1.

[238] *R v Smith* [1987] 1 SCR 1045, 1074.

abolished in Canada except in relation to the National Defence Act offences of espionage and mutiny with violence,[239] and for war crimes under the War Crimes Act.[240] Before its abolition in 1977, the death penalty for murder was unanimously upheld by the Supreme Court of Canada in *R v Miller*[241] in a case under the Canadian Bill of Rights. It has, however, been suggested that the result would be different under the Charter and that the death penalty would be held to be cruel and unusual.[242]

(c) Grossly disproportionate

8.88 In relation to the second category of cases of 'cruel and unusual treatment or punishment', the courts have focused on the imposition of mandatory minimum sentences: for in relation to a 'most innocent offender', even a minimum sentence may be so grossly inappropriate as to be considered to be cruel and unusual.

8.89 **Mandatory minimum sentences.** The 'most innocent offender' principle started with the case of *R v Smith*.[243] In that case it was held that a minimum sentence of seven-years' imprisonment for the importation of narcotics was 'cruel and unusual' because, if it were imposed upon a young person returning to Canada from a vacation with his or her 'first joint of grass', it would be grossly out of proportion to the offence committed.[244] The Supreme Court held the requirement of a minimum sentence to be invalid despite the importance of deterrence and regardless of the fact that the minimum sentence may be appropriate, or too low, for the actual offender before the court. In *R v Netser*[245] it was held that, in the circumstances, a mandatory firearms prohibition was grossly disproportionate and in breach of section 12. It has also been held that imprisonment for non-payment of parking fines was disproportionate and so excessive as to outrage standards of decency.[246]

8.90 In *R v Goltz*[247] the Supreme Court examined a minimum sentence of seven-days imprisonment for driving a motor vehicle while prohibited, the lower courts using the 'good samaritan' hypothetical as the most innocent offender imaginable. They suggested that if a person whose licence has been suspended had driven a vehicle whose driver had become disabled in an accident a few feet off the highway in order to permit other cars to get by, the minimum penalty would surely be grossly disproportionate, and both the trial court and the Court of Appeal found the seven day minimum sentence cruel and unusual. Even though the decision illustrated that no minimum sentence could withstand the 'most innocent offender' principle, the Supreme Court of Canada, in a decision split five judges to three, overturned the lower courts and held that the minimum sentence was not cruel and unusual. While the minority was in favour of individualised sentencing, Gonthier J, for the majority, although agreeing that the proportionality of the sentence must be tested in

239 RSC 1985, C N-4, ss 78 and 79.
240 SC 1946, C 73, s 11.
241 [1977] 2 SCR 680.
242 P W Hogg, *Constitutional Law of Canada* (4th edn, Carswell, 1997) s 50.7.
243 [1987] 1 SCR 1045.
244 *Per* Lamer J, ibid 1053.
245 (1992) 70 CCC (3d) 477; but see *R v Sawyer* [1992] 3 SCR 809.
246 *R v Joe* [1994] 1 WWR 1.
247 [1991] 3 SCR 485; see also *R v Bowen* [1991] 1 WWR 466; *R v Lefevre* (1992) 72 CCC (3d) 162, (person convicted of murdering a police officer not eligible for parole for 25 years, no violation of s 12).

relation to a hypothetical example, said that the example must be reasonable and not far-fetched. He restricted the standard to 'imaginable circumstances which could commonly arise in day-to-day life',[248] and accordingly found that the high threshold of gross disproportionality had not been crossed.

8.91 In *R v Latimer*[249] the majority of the Supreme Court of Canada refused to strike down the mandatory minimum penalty for murder of life imprisonment without eligibility for parole for 10 years. Although the accused had carried out a 'mercy killing' he was not entitled to take the law into his own hands. The statutory penalties for murder were fashioned to meet the broad objectives of the criminal law and it was not for the court to pass judgment on the wisdom of Parliament in respect of the range of penalties for those found guilty of murder. Other minimum sentences which have held to be acceptable under section 12 have included: four-years' imprisonment for robbery involving the use of a firearm,[250] one-year's imprisonment for use of a firearm in the commission of an indictable offence,[251] 12-months's imprisonment for a second offence of unlawful importation of goods under the Customs Act[252] and 90-days' imprisonment for a third conviction for driving while over the alcohol limit.[253]

8.92 The current position is therefore that the court will continue to assess the proportionality of a minimum sentence in relation to reasonable hypothetical situations rather than limiting its consideration to the individual case before it. What is unreasonable or far-fetched will presumably include those sorts of cases that would not normally result in a charge or prosecution.[254]

8.93 **Indeterminate sentences.** Prior to 1977, when the 'habitual criminal' provisions of the Criminal Code were amended, an offender who had been convicted of an indictable offence at least three times and was 'leading persistently a criminal life' could be sentenced to imprisonment for an indeterminate term. Such sentence was found to be 'cruel and unusual' under section 12 of the Charter where the offender was not dangerous, but merely a 'social nuisance',[255] and the 'habitual criminal' provisions were amended. Now the indeterminate sentence is only authorised with respect to an offender who has committed a serious personal injury offence and been classified as a 'dangerous offender'. The National Parole Board must review the terms of detention three years after classification and every two years thereafter, and may release the offender when it is satisfied that he is no longer an undue risk to society. The case of *R v Lyons*[256] made it clear that the new provisions did not violate section 12, and that detention of an indefinite duration was not disproportionate to the offence as a result of its preventive purpose and the Parole Board review requirement. La Forest J stated that 'gross disproportionality' was not an 'exacting' standard and did not require 'punishments to be perfectly suited to accommodate the moral nuances of every crime and every offender'.[257]

---

248 [1991] 3 SCR 485, 515–516.
249 [1997] 1 SCR 217.
250 *R v McDonald* (1998) 127 CCC (3d) 57.
251 *R v Brown* [1994] 3 SCR 749; and see *R v Morrissey* (1998) 124 CCC (3d) 38 and *R v McDonald* (1998) 127 CCC (3d) 57.
252 *R v Slaney* [1985] 22 CCC (3d) 240.
253 *Parsons v R* [1988] 40 CCC (3d) 128, Nfld TD.
254 P W Hogg, *Constitutional Law of Canada* (4th edn, Carswell, 1997), s 50.4.
255 *R v Mitchell* (1983) 6 CCC (3d) 193.
256 [1987] 2 SCR 309.
257 Ibid 344–345.

However, the continued detention of an offender has been found to be cruel and unusual where a decision of the National Parole Board not to release him was found to be erroneous.[258] On the other hand, in *R v Milne,*[259] the Supreme Court of Canada held that the continuing status of dangerous offender was warranted even though the offence for which the convicted persons had been classified as such was subsequently deleted from the list of Criminal Code offences which could give rise to the designation.

(d) Other circumstances

8.94 Not every case of 'cruel and unusual' treatment can be easily characterised as 'barbaric' or 'grossly disproportionate', terms which more aptly describe forms of punishment than treatments. In particular, there may be other treatments administered by public authorities which are nonetheless cruel and unusual.

8.95 **Medical treatment.** A provincial court order awarding custody of a severely handicapped child to a Government authority in order to facilitate the replacement of a brain shunt was found to be cruel and unusual treatment of the child where the surgical intervention was 'extraordinary' and 'unnecessary'.[260] Psychiatric treatment administered by an agent of the Government without the consent and against the will of the patient was 'grossly intrusive' and thus 'cruel and unusual' treatment, even though the statutory provisions enabling the Government authority to determine who has mental competence to consent to the treatment did not offend section 12.[261] However, in *Rodriguez v British Columbia (A-G),*[262] a criminal prohibition on physician-assisted suicide did not, by reason of the circumstances of the terminally ill appellant, constitute cruel and unusual treatment at the hands of the state.

8.96 **Treatment on arrest or while detained.** The use of a knife by police officers to remove a snowsuit from the accused immediately upon his arrest was held to be cruel and unusual treatment,[263] as was the detention of a boy for three consecutive days pending trial in a segregation unit reserved for female prisoners.[264] But, segregation pending trial does not in general offend section 12. This is demonstrated by the case of *R v Olson*[265] where the full-time segregation of a convicted serial murderer, with the exception of one hour of exercise per day, was not cruel and unusual treatment where its purpose was to protect the lives of both the staff and offender. The detention of a violent offender in a 'strip cell' with limited access to proper hygiene was not so excessive to outrage standards of decency.[265a]

8.97 Other examples of treatment found to be acceptable under section 12 include: fingerprinting someone charged with an indictable offence[266] in the absence of special circumstances;[267] compelling a murder suspect to testify at a coroner's inquest;[268] double-bunking

[258] *Steele v Mountain Institution* (Warden) [1990] 2 SCR 1385.
[259] [1987] 2 SCR 512.
[260] *Re S D* [1983] 3 WWR 597.
[261] *Howlett v Karunaratne* (1984) 64 OR (2d) 418, 435, Ontario District Ct.
[262] (1993) 107 DLR (4th) 342.
[263] *R v Hudye* [1983] 7 CRR 363.
[264] *R v Ferguson* (1985) 20 CCC (3d) 256.
[265] (1987) 62 OR (2d) 321, affirmed by the SCC No 20640, 24 Jan 1989.
[265a] *Carlson v Canada* (1998) 80 ACWS (3d) 316, FCTD.
[266] *R v McGregor* (1983) 3 CCC (3d) 200, Ont HC.
[267] *Re M H and R* [1984] 17 CCC (3d) 443.
[268] *Michaud v New Brunswick (Minister of Justice)* (1983) 3 CCC (3d) 325.

of inmates in a prison cell meant for one;[269] treatment of remand prisoners including limitation of visits, imposition of intimate body searches and delousing with pesticides;[270] the use of handcuffs and shackles in escorting remand prisoners;[271] opening of prisoners' mail;[272] revocation of mandatory supervision under the Parole Act;[273] detention 'at the pleasure of the Lieutenant Governor' of an accused found not guilty by reason of insanity;[274] a five-year delay in imprisoning the accused after his conviction was confirmed on appeal, even though the delay was through no fault of his own[275] and proceeding to trial a third time, after two previous trials had ended in jury disagreements.[276]

Administrative decisions. In a number of cases decisions of public authorities have been challenged under section 12. The courts have rejected the following section 12 challenges: requiring the appearance of an individual before a human rights inquiry body;[277] prohibition of the release of documentation in connection with an adoption application, except upon court order or authorisation of the Director of Child Welfare;[278] removal of children from their mother under the provisions of the Family Services Act;[279] denial of access to an abortion in accordance with the Criminal Code provisions;[280] execution of a deportation order on the basis of evidence as to conditions in Guyana;[281] and the extradition of a fugitive to another country, even where it would severely affect his mental health.[282] **8.98**

Appendix 2: The New Zealand Bill of Rights Act

By section 9, the New Zealand Bill of Rights Act 1990 provides: **8.99**

> Everyone has the right not to be subjected to torture or to cruel, degrading or disproportionately severe treatment or punishment.

Section 10 provides that:

> Every person has the right not to be subjected to medical or scientific experimentation without that person's consent.

---

269 *Piche v Solicitor-General Canada* [1984] 17 CCC (3d) 1, Fed TD.

270 *Soenen v Thomas* [1983] 8 CCC (3d) 224, Alta QB; cf *Weatherall v Can (A-G)* [1988] 59 CR (3d) 247 where it was held that strip searches of male inmates in the presence of female guards is cruel and unusual treatment that violates s 12 in the absence of an emergency. *Soenen* was distinguished on the basis that it did not involve cross-gender body searches.

271 *Maltby v Saskatchewan (A-G)* (1982) 13 CCC (3d) 308.

272 *Henry v Canada (Commissioner of Penitentiaries)* [1987] 3 FC 420.

273 *R v Belliveau* (1984) 13 CCC (3d) 138.

274 *R v Swain* (1991) 24 CCC (3d) 385.

275 *Leblanc v R* unreported, 21 Oct 1982.

276 *R v Mailman* [1982] 41 NBR (2d) 369.

277 *Mehta v MacKinnon* (1985) 67 NSR (2d) 112, affirmed 19 DLR (4th) 148, leave to appeal to SCC refused.

278 *Ferguson v Director of Child Welfare* [1983] 3DLR (4th) 178.

279 *Shingoose v Minister of Social Services* [1983] 149 DLR (3d) 400.

280 *R v Morgentaler* (1984) 16 CCC (3d) 1.

281 *R v Gittens* (1982) 137 DLR (3d) 687.

282 *R v Larabie* [1988] 42 CCC (3d) 385.

8.100 These provisions have received very little judicial attention in New Zealand. The case of *Hawkins v Sturt*[283] concerned the question as to whether a spouse could be compelled to give evidence against the other spouse. It was held that the fundamental common law principle of non-compellability could only be overturned by clear positive enactment. It was also argued that to compel the spouse to give evidence would be 'cruel treatment' under section 9. The Judge rejected this argument, holding that:

> The word 'cruel' in the context of that section, is intended to relate to treatment of a kind altogether different from and harsher than that requiring a spouse to answer such questions.[284]

8.101 In *R v P*[284a] the High Court held that the words 'disproportionately severe' in section 9 encompassed punishment which was not, in itself, cruel and unusual but became so because it was disproportionately severe in the particular circumstances. A mentally retarded rapist was not sentenced to a term of imprisonment as this would have been 'disproportionately severe'. The case of *R v Leitch*[285] addressed section 9 in relation to the appropriateness of a sentence of 'preventive detention' for a 'persistent predator' who had pleaded guilty to nine counts of indecent assault. The indeterminate sentence would have required the offender to serve at least 10 years prior to eligibility for release on parole and possible subsequent recall into custody. Although the Court found the sentence manifestly excessive on other grounds, it dealt with the argument that the sentence was in breach of section 9 as being 'disproportionately severe treatment or punishment' and contrary to the International Covenant on Civil and Political Rights. The detainee would not be provided with treatment until near the end of a 10-year period, his position is not regularly reviewed during the 10-year period and the sentence thus incorporates punishment for possible future offending. The Crown asserted, in response, that punishment does not breach section 9 unless it is so excessive as to outrage standards of decency[286] and that the central issue for the Court was the appropriateness of the sentence imposed in terms of domestic law, in light of New Zealand's international obligations. The sentence of preventive detention was quashed and replaced by a finite sentence of eight years.

8.102 In *R v Roulston*[287] the defendant had placed a small package in his mouth during a lawful strip search and police officers had attempted to remove it. In fact, due to the defendant's resistance the officers did not place their fingers or any instrument in his mouth. The Court of Appeal described that argument that this constituted 'cruel and degrading treatment' as 'far fetched'.

Appendix 3: Human Rights Cases in Other Jurisdictions

(1) Introduction

8.103 The prohibition on 'cruel and unusual punishments' in Article 10 of the Bill of Rights of

[283] [1992] 3 NZLR 602.
[284] Ibid 610.
[284a] (1993) 1 HRNZ 417.
[285] [1998] 1 NZLR 420.
[286] On the basis of the Canadian case of *Smith v The Queen* (1987) 40 DLR (4th) 435, see para 8.85 above.
[287] [1998] 2 NZLR 468.

1688 was taken up in the Eighth Amendment to the United States Constitution. The case law under this provision has been influential in other jurisdictions.

The United States Supreme Court has said that the words 'cruel and unusual punishment' should be interpreted 'in a flexible and dynamic manner' as covering more than just the physically barbarous punishments which the drafters had in mind when the Amendment was ratified.[288] The Eighth Amendment draws its meaning 'from the evolving standards of decency that mark the progress of a maturing society'[289] and incorporates 'broad and idealistic concepts of dignity, civilised standards, humanity and decency'.[290] **8.104**

There has been considerable debate as to the extent to which the Eighth Amendment strikes down penalties on the ground that they are disproportionate to the offences for which they may be imposed. In some cases, penalties have been struck down as 'disproportionate'.[291] Although the death penalty is not inherently cruel or unusual[292] death penalty statutes have been struck down as being 'cruel and unusual' in a series of cases.[293] However, more recently the United States Supreme Court has consistently upheld the death penalty.[294] In *Harmelin v Michigan*[295] the Supreme Court held that a mandatory term of life imprisonment, without the possibility of parole, imposed for possession of 650 gms or more of cocaine, constituted 'cruel and unusual punishment'. Some doubt was expressed as to whether the Eighth Amendment included any 'proportionality review' in non-capital cases although a majority took the view that an 'extreme sentence' which was 'grossly disproportionate' to the crime would be 'cruel and unusual'. **8.105**

The conditions in which prisoners are detained or the way in which they are treated may give rise to breaches of the Eighth Amendment.[296] However, it must be shown that the prison officials were aware of and disregarded excessive risk to inmate health or safety.[297] Deliberate indifference by prison personnel to a prisoner's serious illness or injury constitutes cruel and unusual punishment.[298] **8.106**

(2) The Bahamas

In *Henfield v A-G of the Commonwealth of the Bahamas, Farrington v Minister of Public* **8.107**

[288] See *Gregg v Georgia* (1976) 428 US 153, 171.

[289] *Trop v Dulles* (1958) 356 US 86, 101.

[290] *Estelle v Gamble* (1976) 429 US 97, 102.

[291] See eg *Robinson v California* (1962) 370 US 660 (a California statute making it a crime 'to be addicted to narcotics' was a 'cruel and unusual punishment' as it did not require proof of purchase or use of the drugs).

[292] *Gregg v Georgia* (1976) 428 US 513.

[293] *Roberts v Louisiana* (1976) 428 US 335 (mandatory death penalty for defendants convicted of one of five categories of murder); *Coker v Georgia* (1977) 433 US 584 (death penalty for rape); *Thomson v Oklahoma* (1988) 487 US 815 (execution of a 15-year-old).

[294] *Stanford v Kentucky* (1989) 492 US 361 (16- and 17-year-olds); *Penry v Lynaugh* (1989) 492 US 302 (mentally retarded rapist); *Tison v Arizona* (1987) 481 US 137 (accomplices).

[295] (1991) 501 US 957.

[296] *Bell v Wolfish* (1979) 441 US 520; *Rhodes v Chapman* (1981) 452 US 337.

[297] *Farmer v Brennan* (1994) 511 US 825.

[298] *Estelle v Gamble* (1976) 429 US 97; see generally, J Palmer and S Palmer, *The Constitutional Rights of Prisoners* (6th edn, Anderson Publishing, 1999) 228ff.

Safety and Immigration[299] the Privy Council re-examined the approach it took in its earlier view in *Pratt v A-G for Jamaica*,[300] where it held that in any case in which execution was to take place more than five years after sentence, there would be strong grounds for believing that execution after such delay was inhuman punishment. The Privy Council noted that the five-year period was not a fixed limit applicable in all cases, but was rather a norm from which the court may depart in appropriate circumstances. That norm was departed from in *Farrington's* case, in which the delay was three years four months. Furthermore, the conditions of imprisonment after the sentence of death could be relevant factors in deciding whether the sentence of death was inhuman.

8.108 In *Reckley v Minister of Public Safety and Immigration*,[301] the appellant argued that the execution of the sentence of death after four and a half years on death row would be a contravention of his right under Article 17(1) of the Constitution of the Commonwealth of the Bahamas not to be subjected to inhuman or degrading punishment or treatment. The Privy Council found that no blame attached to either the legal system or the Government for any delay and that the process of exhausting the domestic rights of appeal had been completed in 14 months.[302] Referral of the matter to the advisory committee had been postponed pending a separate decision of the Privy Council as to the legality of the death penalty in the Bahamas; and, in any event, did not exceed the five-year period envisaged by *Pratt*. In *Fisher v Ministry of Public Safety (No 2)*[302a] the Privy Council rejected the argument that the applicant had a legitimate expectation created by an unratified treaty; and that his case would be considered by the Inter-American Commission on Human Rights before the death penalty was carried out. Pre-trial delays are not to be counted for the purposes of assessing the delay in executing the death penalty. As explained by Lord Goff in *Fisher v Minister of Public Safety and Immigration*[303] the Privy Council could:

> see no basis for simply extending the *Pratt* principle to take into account delay which occurred before trial. This would involve consideration of two different types of period,part of the period awaiting trial and the whole of the period from sentence to the date fixed for execution; and, quite apart from the fundamental objection that the state of mind of the man in question is different during the two periods, it is difficult to see on what basis a norm could be established which would accommodate both these periods. In truth, as the Court of Appeal recognised, the principle in *Pratt's* case was established in response to the fact that, in some Caribbean countries, men sentenced to death were being held on death row for wholly unacceptable periods of time, and was specifically fashioned to meet the problem. It does not admit to being extended, in the manner contended for on behalf of the appellant, to address the wholly different problem of pre-trial delay.[304]

---

[299] [1997] AC 413. The decision in *Henfield* was corrected by *Fisher v Minister of Public Safety and Immigration* [1998] AC 673 in that the Government recognised the power of the Inter-American Commission on Human Rights to receive communications from citizens complaining of violations of their human rights.

[300] [1994] 2 AC 1.

[301] [1995] 2 AC 491, Judicial Committee of the Privy Council.

[302] The Court relied on *Pratt v A-G for Jamaica* [1993] 2 LRC 349, [1994] 2 AC 1 which envisaged a two-year target for exhaustion of domestic remedies and completion of the whole appeals process within five.

[302a] [1999] 2 WLR 349.

[303] [1998] AC 673, Lord Steyn dissenting.

[304] Ibid 680.

Pre-trial detention in a tiny cell with no bed or toilet facilities was found to constitute inhuman and degrading treatment in *Beneby v The Commissioner of Police*.[305]

(3) Barbados

In *Bradshaw v A-G*[306] a period of more than five years had elapsed between the imposition of the death sentence and intended execution. The Privy Council held that such a delay amounted to a presumption of inhuman or degrading punishment or other treatment; the death penalties were quashed and sentences of life imprisonment substituted. The right approach was to take the whole period of delay and then deduct those periods due entirely to the fault of the accused, which he was not entitled to take advantage of. The Privy Council did not deduct a delay between the dismissal of the appeal by the Court of Appeal and abandonment of the appeal to the Privy Council, nor the time taken to pursue a petition to the UNHRC.[307] **8.109**

(4) Bermuda

Section 3 of the Bermuda Constitution is in the same terms as Article 3 of the Convention. In *Shorter v R*[308] the Court of Appeal considered the argument that mandatory sentencing provisions relating to firearms offences[309] were in breach of section 3. It was held that the relevant provision did not 'cast the net unduly wide'. It was difficult to imagine a situation in which the mandatory sentence imposed was 'brutal, barbarous or cruel'. As a result, there was no breach of section 3.[310] **8.110**

(5) Belize

The case of *Lauriano v A-G*[311] dealt with the constitutionality of capital punishment. The Court of Appeal held that the sentence of death by execution did not constitute degrading and inhuman punishment or treatment as contemplated by section 7(6) of the Belize Constitution, having regard to the saving provision of section 4, which provides that a person shall not be deprived of his life intentionally save in execution of the sentence of a court following conviction of a criminal offence. **8.111**

(6) Botswana

The Court of Appeal of Botswana has held that the Penal Code provisions prescribing the death penalty are not *ultra vires* the provisions of the Constitution of Botswana which prohibit torture and inhuman or degrading punishment.[312] In spite of international and United Nations sentiment in favour of the abolition of capital punishment, the Constitution makes express preservation of the death penalty as a competent punishment under the Penal Code and an exception to the right to life. **8.112**

[305] [1996] 1 CHRD 28.
[306] [1995] 1 WLR 936, PC.
[307] *Harewood v A-G* (1997) 2 CHRLD 15.
[308] [1989] LRC (Crim) 440.
[309] Firearms Act 1973, s 30(1A) (Bermuda).
[310] [1989] LRC (Crim) 440, 522–523.
[311] [1996] 2 LRC 96.
[312] *State v Ntesang* [1995] 2 LRC 338.

(7) India

8.113 The Constitution of India contains no provision prescribing torture or inhuman or degrading treatment. However, in *Mullin v Administrator, Union Territory of Delhi*[313] the Supreme Court held that the right to life guaranteed by Article 21 included a right to live with basic human dignity which, itself, included the right not be subjected to torture or to cruel, inhuman or degrading punishment or treatment.[314]

8.114 The Supreme Court has held that solitary confinement in prison has a degrading and dehumanising effect and could only be imposed in exceptional cases.[315] It has been held that the use of fetters[316] and handcuffs[317] is inhuman and is unjustified save where safe custody was otherwise impossible. The death sentence, even if justifiably imposed, cannot be executed if supervening events make its execution harsh, unjust or unfair.[318] It has, however, been held that the only delay which could be considered was from the date when the judicial process came to an end.[319]

(8) Ireland

8.115 The right to bodily integrity is not specifically protected by the Irish Constitution. However, in *Ryan v A-G,*[320] the Supreme Court decided that one of the unenumerated rights protected by Article 40.3 was the right to bodily integrity. In *State v John Frawley*[321] it was held that the principle of the right to bodily integrity operated to prevent an act or omission of the executive which, without justification, would expose the health of a person to risk or danger. The judge went on to hold that restraints used on a prisoner to eliminate the possibility of his harming himself could not constitute torture, inhuman or degrading treatment and punishment as that concept must be construed 'as being not only evil in its consequences but evil in its purpose as well'.[322] If prison conditions in Ireland pose a health risk to prisoners, the court may order their improvement.[323]

(9) Israel

8.115A The rules governing interrogation by the security services were considered by the Supreme Court of Israel in the case of *Public Committee against Torture in Israel v Israel.*[323a] It was pointed out that in formulating such rules there was a clash between, on the one hand, the

---

313 AIR 1981 SC 746.

314 See generally, N Jaswal, *Role of the Supreme Court with Regard to Life and Personal Liberty* (Ashish, 1990).

315 *Sunil Batra v Delhi Administration (No 1)* AIR 1978 SC 597; *Kishore Singh Ravinder Dev v State of Rajasthan* AIR 1981 SC 625.

316 *Sunil Batra v Delhi Administration (No 2)* AIR 1980 SC 1579.

317 *Prem Shankar v Delhi Administration* AIR 1980 SC 1535.

318 See *Vatheeswaran v State of Tamil Naud* AIR 1983 SC 361; *Sher Singh v State of Punjab* [1983] 2 SCR 583.

319 *Triveniben v State of Gujurat* [1992] LRC (Const) 425; *Madhu Mehta v India* [1989] 3 SCR 775.

320 [1965] IR 294.

321 [1976] IR 365.

322 Ibid 374.

323 *State (Richardson) v Governor, Mountjoy Prison* [1980] ILRM 82.

323a (1999) 7 BHRC 31.

public interest in exposing and preventing crime and, on the other, the protection of the dignity and liberty of the suspect. Although the resolution of this clash had to be dealt with on the facts of each case, the Court identified some general principles:

> First, a reasonable investigation is necessarily one which is free of torture, free of cruel, inhuman treatment of the subject and free of any degrading handling whatsoever . . . These provisions are 'absolute'. There are no exceptions to them and there is no room for balancing. Indeed, violence directed at a suspect's body or spirit does not constitute a reasonable investigation practice. Second, a reasonable investigation is likely to cause discomfort; it may result in insufficient sleep; the conditions under which it is conducted risk being unpleasant.[323b]

As a result, the Court held that the security service did not have authority to use methods of interrogation involving placing opaque sacks over the suspect's head, powerfully loud music, forcing suspects to crouch on the tips of their toes, excessive tightening of cuffs and excessive sleep deprivation.

(10) Jamaica

Section 17 of the Jamaica Constitution provides: **8.116**

> (1) No person shall be subjected to torture or to inhuman or degrading punishment or other treatment.
>
> (2) Nothing contained in or done under the authority of any law shall be held to be inconsistent with or in contravention of this section to the extent that the law in question authorises the infliction of any description of punishment which was lawful in Jamaica immediately before the appointed day.

In *Pratt v A-G for Jamaica*,[324] the Privy Council accepted that delays in the execution of the death penalty could amount to inhuman and degrading treatment. As stated by Lord Griffiths:

> In their Lordships' view a state that wishes to retain capital punishment must accept the responsibility of ensuring that execution follows as swiftly as practicable after sentence, allowing a reasonable time for appeal and consideration of reprieve.[325]

The Privy Council added that the entire domestic appeal process in Jamaica should be carried out in two years. Further:

> In any case in which execution is to take place more than five years after sentence there will be strong grounds for believing that the delay is such as to constitute 'inhuman or degrading punishment or other treatment'.[326]

(11) Namibia

Article 8 of the Constitution of Namibia provides that: **8.117**

> (1) The dignity of all persons shall be inviolable.
>
> (2) (a) In any judicial proceedings or in other proceedings before any organ of the

[323b] Ibid 45g–46a.
[324] [1994] 2 AC 1.
[325] Ibid 33.
[326] Ibid 35.

State and during the enforcement of a penalty, respect for human dignity shall be guaranteed.

(b) No person shall be subject to torture or to cruel, inhuman or degrading treatment or punishment.

8.118 In response to a constitutional question initiated by the Attorney-General, the Namibian Supreme Court has declared that any sentence of corporal punishment by a judicial or quasi-judicial authority or corporal punishment in Government schools is unlawful.[327] It confirmed that all corporal punishment is degrading and inhuman punishment under Article 8(2)(b) of the Constitution for a number of reasons: the physical assaults were generally administered by a stranger and based, at least in part, on irrationality, retribution and insensitivity to the individual punished; the quality and intensity of the punishment was dependent on the idiosyncrasies of the punisher and therefore inherently arbitrary; such assault and the attendant pain and suffering causes humiliation which violates the dignity and self-respect of the individual; the systematic public planning of such assaults demeans society and reduces it to the level of the offender.

8.119 In *State v Tcoeib*[328] it was argued that the sentence of life imprisonment was unconstitutional, *inter alia*, because it constituted cruel, inhuman and degrading treatment. Mahomed CJ held that such a sentence was not constitutionally sustainable:

> if it effectively amounts to an order throwing the prisoner into a cell for the rest of the prisoner's natural life as if he was a 'thing' instead of a person without any continuing duty to respect his dignity (which would include his right not to live in despair and helplessness and without any hope of release, regardless of the circumstances).[329]

However, life imprisonment included the prospect of release, via parole, probation, and the granting of executive pardons. The hope of release had to constitute a sufficiently concrete and fundamentally realisable expectation adequate to protect the prisoner's right to dignity. That would not exist if the system of parole and probation depended on the entirely capricious exercise of the discretion of the prison and executive authorities. The imposition of life imprisonment could nevertheless be unconstitutional if it was so grossly disproportionate to the severity of the crime committed that it constituted cruel, inhuman or degrading punishment or impermissibly invaded the dignity of the accused.[330]

8.120 The constitutionality of statutory minimum sentence provisions was considered in *State v Vries*.[331] The High Court held that such a provision was not in breach of Article 8 provided that the sentences were appropriate in all the circumstances. However, if the mandatory sentence was grossly disproportionate it would constitute cruel, inhuman or degrading punishment under Article 8 and would be unconstitutional.[332] The statute under consideration provided that, on a second or subsequent conviction for stock theft the minimum sentence was three years. The accused had stolen a goat and had a previous conviction for stealing a sheep in 1969. The High Court declared the relevant statutory provision

[327] *Ex p A-G of Namibia, In re Corporal Punishment by Organs of State* [1992] LRC (Const) 515.

[328] [1997] 1 LRC 90.

[329] Ibid 101f–g.

[330] Ibid 105b–e; relying on *Gregg v Georgia* (1976) 428 US 153; *Rummel v Estelle* (1980) 445 US 263, US Sup Ct.

[331] [1997] 4 LRC 1.

[332] Ibid 7c–10g.

unconstitutional and imposed a sentence of six months' imprisonment. In *State v Likuwa*[332a] the High Court declared a provision imposing a minimum sentence of 10 years for the possession of armaments to be unconstitutional.

(12) Papua New Guinea

Section 36(1) of the Constitution of Papua New Guinea provides that: **8.121**

> No person shall be submitted to torture (whether physical or mental), or to treatment or punishment that is cruel or otherwise inhuman, or is inconsistent with respect for the inherent dignity of the human person.

An argument that legislation prescribing minimum penalties for criminal offences based on the US authorities was rejected by the Supreme Court.[333]Although a penalty could, by its very length, be inconsistent with respect for human dignity and cruel, the penalties imposed by the statute under consideration were not excessive.

(13) Singapore

Singapore is one of several jurisdictions that has addressed the constitutionality of a delay in execution of a death sentence. In *Jabar v Public Prosecutor*[334] the Court of Appeal held that the mental anguish suffered by prisoners awaiting execution did not amount to a contravention of their constitutional rights. The decision was in part a result of the fact that, in the absence of a prohibition of 'inhuman or degrading treatment'[335] the appellants could rely solely on Article 9(1) of the Constitution of Singapore which provides that 'no person shall be deprived of his life or liberty save *in accordance with law*'. The Court of Appeal rejected arguments that the provision was comparable to that found in the Constitution of India, and that Indian precedents, to the effect that the procedure used in the deprivation of life must be just, fair and reasonable,[336] were applicable. It distinguished the situation in Singapore on two grounds: it noted that the Indian Constitution provided for deprivation of life in accordance with *procedure* established by law rather than law alone. In Singapore, any law providing for the deprivation of a person's life or personal liberty was binding if validly passed by Parliament. The court was not concerned with whether the law was also fair and reasonable. Secondly, the Indian courts had jurisdiction to address whether events after the judicial process had ended amounted to an infringement of the prisoner's constitutional rights, whereas the courts in Singapore did not. In Singapore, capital cases carried a mandatory death sentence and the power to order a stay of execution or respite of the sentence lay exclusively with the President, to whom the prisoner must petition for clemency. **8.122**

(14) The Solomon Islands

Section 7 of the Constitution of the Solomon Islands prohibits torture, inhuman or **8.123**

[332a] [2000] 1 LRC 600.

[333] *Constitutional Reference by the Morobe Provincial Government* [1985] LRC (Const) 642.

[334] [1995] 2 LRC 349.

[335] The Court considered *Pratt v A-G for Jamaica* [1994] 2 AC 1; and *Riley v A-G of Jamaica* [1983] AC 719 neither of which it found applicable, as there was no equivalent of s 17(1) of the Constitution of Jamaica in the Constitution of Singapore.

[336] See *Maneka Gandhi v Union of India* AIR 1978 SC 597.

degrading treatment or punishment. In *Osifelo v R*[337] the Court of Appeal found that police interrogation techniques did not amount to inhuman or degrading treatment. After six days in police custody, the appellants underwent about 12 hours of general and cautioned interrogation between 1.20pm and 11.20am during which they were deprived of sleep, food, cigarettes and betel-nut. The Court of Appeal found that while it is possible that such conditions might amount to 'inhuman' treatment, the conduct in that case did not reach the level of barbarity, brutality or cruelty which 'inhuman' ordinarily imports.

(15) South Africa

8.124 The Constitutional Court of South Africa has declared that capital punishment is cruel, inhuman and degrading punishment and that a sentence of death for the offences of murder, aggravated robbery, kidnapping, child-stealing and rape was contrary to Section 11(2) of the Constitution.[338] The sentence of juvenile whipping for certain offences was also declared to be inhuman and degrading treatment.[339] However, the taking of the accused's fingerprints was not degrading and was constitutional.[340] A sentence of life imprisonment without any prospect of release would be 'inhuman and degrading punishment' but an expectation of release is inherent in the legislation dealing with life sentences.[341]

(16) Sri Lanka

8.125 Article 11 of the 1978 Sri Lankan Constitution provides that:

> No person shall be subject to torture or to cruel, inhuman or degrading treatment or punishment.

Article 16(2) provides that the infliction of punishment under a law which existed at the time of the commencement of the Constitution cannot be challenged as being cruel, inhuman or degrading treatment.

8.126 The Supreme Court surveyed the literature and jurisprudence concerning torture and inhuman and degrading treatment in *Channa Pieris v A-G.*[342] The Supreme Court stated that, having regard to the nature and gravity of the issue, a high degree of certainty was required before the balance of probability might be said to tilt in favour of a petitioner alleging torture, or inhuman or degrading treatment. Although the Supreme Court was conscious of the difficulties in the proof of allegations of torture, it concluded that the treatment meted out to detainees in that case did not amount to inhuman or degrading treatment. The Supreme Court noted the lack of medical corroborating evidence, and the evidence of collusion between the detainees.

8.127 The Sri Lankan courts have found the mandatory punishments in the Essential Public Services Bill 1979 to constitute degrading punishment. That Bill provided that a person convicted of any offence under it would be liable to imprisonment, and/or a fine. In

337 [1995] 3 LRC 602.
338 *State v Makwanyane* [1995] 1 LRC 269.
339 *S v Williams* 1995 (3) SA 632.
340 *S v Huma* 1996 (1) SA 232.
341 See *S v De Kock* 1997 (2) SACR 171.
342 [1994] 1 Sri LR 1.

addition, it was mandatory that all movable and immovable property of the offender be forfeited and in the event that the offender were a registered practitioner under any law for practising his profession or vocation, his name would be removed from such register. The Supreme Court held that the mandatory punishments were excessive, and therefore contrary to Article 11 of the Constitution.[343]

A breach of Article 11 was also found in *Kumarasena v Sub-Inspector Shriyantha*.[344] The petitioner in that case was a young girl who had been arrested without reasonable grounds and detained for about six hours at a police station. She was sexually harassed during that time. Police misconduct was also in issue in *Thadchanamoorthi v A-G*,[345] in which police officers were alleged to have tortured the petitioner. It was stated by a superior officer that the alleged acts were never authorised by him or his own superior officers. The Supreme Court stated that, in the absence of an 'administrative practice' of adopting or tolerating acts of torture, the state would not be liable for such acts. However, recent cases have retreated from that position, holding that the state is liable for the acts of its officers providing that those acts were done under the colour of office.[346] Once it is established that injuries were received while in the custody of state officers, the state is liable for the injuries in the absence of evidence that they were inflicted in the course of arrest, were self-inflicted or were inflicted by some other person.[347] **8.128**

The Supreme Court made a finding of degrading treatment in *Faiz v A-G*,[348] where police connived at the petitioner's assault by private individuals whilst in police custody. However, the Supreme Court declined to make a finding of degrading treatment in *Mrs W M K De Silva v Chairman, Ceylon Fertilizer Corporation*.[349] The petitioner was treated badly at work after she refused to alter some minutes. She was not allowed the use of her cubicle or allocated any work. She was made to sit in the verandah at a broken table on a broken chair, and even locked out. Life in the office became humiliating and conditions intolerable. The Supreme Court held that while the treatment meted out to the petitioner was a grossly unfair labour practice, it did not constitute 'torture, or cruel, inhuman or degrading treatment or punishment'. **8.129**

(17) Tanzania

In *Mbushuu v Republic*[350] the Court of Appeal agreed with the High Court[350a] that the death penalty had elements of torture and was a cruel, inhuman and degrading punishment. However, the Court of Appeal overturned the judge's decision that the death penalty was unconstitutional. Society had decided that the death penalty was reasonably necessary to protect the right to life of potential murder victims and, as a result, it was a permissible derogation from fundamental rights in the pubic interest. **8.130**

---

343 Decisions of the Supreme Court on Parliamentary Bills, Vol 1 (1979–1983) 63, see J Wickramaratne, *Fundamental Rights in Sri Lanka* (Navrang, 1996) 140.

344 SC Application 257/93, SC Minutes of 23.05.94; see *Channa Pierris v A-G* (n 342 above) 106–107.

345 FRD (1) 129, see Wickramaratne (n 343 above) 120.

346 *Mariyadas Raj v A-G* (1997), FRD (2) 397; *Vivienne Goonewardena v Perera* (1997) FRD (2) 426.

347 *Sudath Silva v Kodituwakku* (1987) 2 Sri LR 119.

348 [1996] 1 CHRD.

349 (1989) 2 Sri LR 393.

350 [1995] 1 LRC 216.

350a *Republic v Mbushuu* [1994] 2 LRC 335.

(18) Trinidad and Tobago

8.131 The case of *Guerra v Baptiste* concerned the issue of delay in carrying out the death sentence.[351] The Privy Council allowed the appeal and commuted the sentence of death to one of life imprisonment. In assessing what was a reasonable time for appeal, great importance was to be attached to ensuring that delay did not occur, but the Privy Council rebutted any notion of a rule that completion of the appellate procedure within a five-year period would guarantee 'reasonableness'. The Privy Council asserted that, in the legal conditions prevailing in Trinidad and Tobago, the goal should be to decide an appeal within 12 months and a further appeal to the Privy Council within another 12 months, so that the whole process could be completed within two years of conviction. In *Thomas v Baptiste*[351a] the Privy Council held that by ratifying a treaty, the Government had extended the scope of domestic constitutional rights and the criminal justice system; as a result it was prevented from taking executive action which would pre-empt an application to the Inter-American Commission on Human Rights. However, the Privy Council decided in *Briggs v Baptiste*[351b] that the question of whether there were issues to be determined by the Commission could be decided by the domestic courts.

(19) Zimbabwe

8.132 Section 15(1) of the Constitution of Zimbabwe prohibits torture, and inhuman or degrading punishment or other such treatment.[352] It has been said that:

> The *raison d'etre* underlying section 15(1) is nothing less than the dignity of man. It is a provision that embodies broad and idealistic notions of dignity, humanity and decency, against which penal measures should be evaluated.[353]

The Supreme Court has rejected the argument that the words 'inhuman or degrading punishment' were to be restricted to types of punishment which were themselves inhuman and degrading but held that the inhumanity or degrading nature of the punishment depended on the context and the reasons for its imposition.[354]

8.133 It has been held that sentences of whipping an adult person[355] and of corporal punishment on juveniles[356] are inhuman and degrading. The punishment of solitary confinement with a 'spare diet' has been held to amount to torture and degrading and inhuman punishment.[357] In *Chinamora v Angwa Furnishers (Private) Ltd*[358] the Supreme Court rejected the argument that imprisonment of a recalcitrant debtor was 'degrading' treatment, noting that such imprisonment was remedial in nature, the debtor being able to end it by paying

---

[351] [1996] 1 AC 397, PC; appeal from *Wallen v Baptiste* [1994] 2 LRC 62, CA.

[351a] [1999] 3 WLR 249.

[351b] [2000] 2 WLR 574.

[352] See The Zimbabwe Constitution Order (1979) 3 EHRR 418, 422; see generally, J Hatchard, *Individual Freedoms and State Security in the African Context: The Case of Zimbabwe* (James Currey, 1993) Chap 8.

[353] *Per* Gubbay JA, *Ncube v State* [1988] LRC (Const) 442, 460h–461a.

[354] Ibid 459–460, not following *Runyowa v R* [1967] 1 AC 26.

[355] *Ncube v State* [1988] LRC (Const) 442, after a survey of the law relating to corporal punishment in South Africa, England, Canada, Australia and the USA, see 450–457.

[356] *S v Juvenile* 1990 (4) SA 151.

[357] *S v Masitere* 1990 (2) ZLR 289.

[358] (1997) 1 BHRC 460.

his debt. In *Blanchard v Minister of Justice*[358a] the Supreme Court held that imprisonment of unconvicted prisoners in solitary confinement, in prison clothes, with a light burning constantly and with no food from outside constituted inhuman and degrading treatment.

In *Catholic Commission for Justice and Peace in Zimbabwe v Attorney-General*[359] the Supreme Court considered the question of delay in the carrying out of the death penalty. It was held that intervening events, such as inordinate delay between sentencing and execution, could convert a sentence of death to an inhuman and degrading punishment. Following consideration of the case law in India, the United States, the West Indies and the Human Rights Committee it held that the proper test was the likely effect of the delay on the prisoner, rather than its cause, and that in the case of the death penalty the cause of delay was irrelevant. Since the appeal against the death penalty was automatic, the period which the prisoner spent in the condemned cell had to be taken to start with the imposition of the death sentence.[360] The Supreme Court decided that delays of 52 months and 72 months were impermissible and set aside the death sentences, substituting instead sentences of life imprisonment. Section 15 was subsequently amended to provide that delay after the sentence of death 'shall not be held' to be a contravention of section 15(1). It has been held that this provision did not have retrospective effect.[361] Section 15 was also amended to provide that, once a sentence had been imposed, that sentence could not be stayed, altered or remitted on the ground that, since the sentence had been imposed, there had been a contravention of section 15(1).[362] This provision is expressed to have retrospective effect and it has been strictly construed as having no application to 'death sentence' cases.[363] **8.134**

In *Arab v The State*[364] the Supreme Court rejected the argument that a three-year minimum sentence for unlicensed dealing in precious stones constituted degrading or inhuman punishment. The Supreme Court was heavily influenced by the fact that the statute allowed a lesser sentence if the court found there to be special reasons. **8.135**

[358a] [2000] 1 LRC 671.
[359] [1993] 2 LRC 279.
[360] Ibid 311.
[361] s 15(5); *State v Nkomo* 1994 (3) SA 34.
[362] s 15(6).
[363] *State v Nkomo*, n 361 above 42–43 (as these are expressly dealt with in s 15(5)).
[364] [1990] LRC (Crim) 40.

9

FREEDOM FROM SLAVERY, SERVITUDE AND FORCED LABOUR

A. The Nature of the Rights

The right to freedom from slavery has a special status in human rights law as the first human right to be protected by international treaty.[1] The Berlin Treaty of 1885 acknowledged that 'trading in slaves is forbidden in conformity with international law'. The Slavery Convention of 1926 defined slavery as: 9.01

[1] See P Sieghart, *The International Law of Human Rights* (Clarendon Press, 1983) 229; A Robertson and J Merrills, *Human Rights in the World* (4th edn, Manchester University Press, 1996) 15ff; see also D Feldman, *Civil Liberties and Human Rights in England and Wales* (Clarendon Press, 1993) 36.

> the status or condition of a person over whom any or all of the powers attaching to the right of ownership are exercised.[2]

The states which were party to this Convention undertook to 'prevent and suppress the slave trade' and 'to bring about, progressively and as soon as possible, the abolition of slavery in all its forms'.[3] Numerous international treaties and a widespread and uniform state practice have crystallised into a rule of customary international law prohibiting slavery and the slave trade.[4]

9.02 In addition to a person having rights of ownership over another, there are a range of other situations in which private individuals exercise a level of control over others which approaches ownership; this is covered by the term 'servitude'. Both slavery and servitude are prohibited absolutely by all human rights instruments. Thus, Article 4 of the Universal Declaration provides that:

> No one shall be held in slavery or servitude: slavery and the slave trade shall be prohibited in all their forms.[5]

9.03 Closely related to 'servitude' is the condition of 'forced labour': where a person is made to work under the threat of a penalty. Freedom from forced labour is also well-established in international law being addressed in international treaties[6] and the conventions and resolutions of the International Labour Organisation.[7] A United Nations Ad Hoc Committee on Slavery in 1951 concerned itself solely with forms of servitude such as debt bondage, persons 'sold' into marriage, and sham adoptions of children. The Supplementary Convention on the Abolition of Slavery, the Slave Trade and Institutions and Practices Similar to Slavery[8] defined institutions and practices similar to slavery as:

> (1) debt bondage, that is the status or condition arising from a pledge by a debtor of his personal services or of those of a person under his control as security for a debt, if the value of those services as reasonably assessed is not applied towards the liquidation of the debt or the length or nature of those services are not respectively limited and defined;

---

[2] (1926) Cmnd 2910, Art 1 (25 parties to the European Convention, including the United Kingdom, are parties to this Convention).

[3] Ibid Art 2.

[4] See Robertson and Merrills (n 1 above) 47; however, the trade in slaves is not, by international law, piracy or a crime, except by treaty (*Buron v Denman* (1848) 2 Exch 167).

[5] See also International Covenant on Civil and Political Rights, Art 8.

[6] The prohibition of forced or compulsory labour is not found in the Universal Declaration of Human Rights, but is present in the International Covenant on Civil and Political Rights. Art 4(3), which sets out four types of work or service that are not 'forced or compulsory labour' is reproduced almost exactly in Art 8(3) of the International Covenant on Civil and Political Rights. The text of the Universal Declaration is reproduced at App H; the text of the International Covenant is reproduced at App J.

[7] See, in particular, Forced Labour Convention (ILO Convention 29) 1930, 39 LNTS 55, 134 BFSP 449, Cmd 3693; and the supplementary Abolition of Forced Labour Convention (ILO Convention 105) 1957, 320 UNTS 291, Cmnd 328.

[8] (1956) Cmnd 257.

> (2) serfdom, that is the condition or status of a tenant who is by law, custom or agreement bound to live and labour on land belonging to another person and to render some determinate service to such person, whether for reward or not, and is not free to change his status;
>
> (3) any institution or practice whereby:
>
> (a) a woman without the right to refuse, is promised or given in marriage on payment of a consideration in money or in kind to her parents, guardians, family or any other person or group; or
>
> (b) the husband of a woman, his family or his clan has the right to transfer her to another person for value received or otherwise; or
>
> (c) a woman on the death of her husband is liable to be inherited by another person;
>
> (4) any institution or practice whereby a child or young person under the age of 18 years is delivered by either or both of his natural parents or by his guardian to another person, whether for reward or not, with a view to the exploitation of the child or young person or of his labour.[9]

The prohibition of slavery and servitude is not controversial. The disputes which have arisen concern the right to freedom from 'forced labour'. The disputes usually arise from the state (or some other institution) having the right to compel an individual to work for a specified period of time, whether as a form of punishment or as a form of 'community service' or apprenticeship. **9.04**

B. The Rights in English Law Before the Human Rights Act

(1) Introduction

The common law recognised the state of 'villeinage' but this was extinguished at the beginning of the seventeenth century.[10] However, as late as 1694 the English courts accepted that a slave was a 'chattel'.[11] Nevertheless, in *Smith v Brown and Cooper*[12] Holt CJ said that 'as soon as a negro comes to England' he becomes free; and in the well-known case of *Somersett v Stewart*[13] Lord Mansfield expressed the view that: **9.05**

> The state of slavery is of such a nature, that it is incapable of being introduced on any reasons moral or political, but only by positive law . . . It is so odious, that nothing can be suffered to support it, but positive law.

[9] Ibid Art 7.

[10] See the argument in *Somersett v Stewart* (1772) 20 St Tr 1.

[11] *Gelly v Cleve* (1694) 1 Ld Raym 147 (as a result, an action for trover was available to slave owner); for a discusssion of the approach taken by the common law to slavery, see Sir Stephen Sedley 'Law and Public Life' in M Nolan and S Sedley, *Making and Remaking the British Constitution* (Blackstone, 1997).

[12] 2 Salk 666.

[13] (1772) 20 St Tr 1.

Slavery was abolished in the British dominions by the Slavery Abolition Act 1833. There are no legal relationships now recognised by English law which are likely to be regarded as equivalent to 'slavery' or 'servitude'.

(2) Forced and compulsory labour

9.06 The English courts have long been reluctant to force a person to work. Thus, it is well established that the court will not compel a person to carry out a 'contract of service'.[14] This is because:

> the right to choose for himself whom he would serve constitutes the main difference between a servant and a serf.[15]

9.07 The English law does, nonetheless, permit forced or compulsory labour in very limited circumstances. The Crown still has a theoretical power to compel persons of a seafaring character into naval service by force, known as 'impressment' or 'press ganging'.[16] Although this power has been in abeyance since the early nineteenth century it has never been specifically removed by statute. There have been a number of statutory provisions concerning compulsory service in the armed forces[17] but none are presently in force.

9.08 Prisoners can be compelled to work whilst serving their sentences. By Prison Rule 31(1),[18] all convicted prisoners are required to work a maximum of ten hours' useful work per day. It is an offence against discipline intentionally to fail to work properly or, being required to work, to refuse to do so.[19] The work is often repetitive and low-skilled and the conditions may be in breach of non-binding international standards for the treatment of prisoners.[20]

C. The Law Under the European Convention

(1) Introduction

9.09 Article 4 of the European Convention on Human Rights provides:

---

[14] This is the basis for the rule that the court will not order the specific performance of a contract of employment: see Trade Union and Labour Relations (Consolidation) Act 1992 s 236.

[15] *Nokes v Doncaster Amalgamated Collieries Ltd* [1940] AC 1014, 1026. However, the position on transfer of employees where there is a transfer of the undertaking is now governed by the Transfer of Undertakings Regulations 1981, SI 1981/1794 as amended and the Acquired Rights Directive (EEC) 77/187.

[16] See *Halsbury's Laws of England* (4th edn, Butterworths, 1997) Vol 41, 'Royal Forces', para 152.

[17] eg the National Service Act 1948.

[18] Prison Rules 1999, SI 1999/728.

[19] Ibid r 47(18), SI 1989/330.

[20] See generally, S Livingstone and T Owen, *Prison Law* (2nd edn, Oxford University Press, 1999) para 5.24, 160ff.

> (1) No one shall be held in slavery or servitude.
> (2) No one shall be required to perform forced or compulsory labour.
> (3) For the purpose of this Article the term 'forced or compulsory labour' shall not include:
> (a) any work required to be done in the ordinary course of detention imposed according to the provisions of Article 5 of the Convention or during conditional release from such detention;
> (b) any service of a military character or, in the case of conscientious objectors in countries where they are recognised, service exacted instead of compulsory military service;
> (c) any service exacted in case of an emergency or calamity threatening the life or well-being of the community;
> (d) any work or service which forms part of normal civic obligations.

Article 4(1) is absolute and is not subject to derogation in time of war or public emergency.[21] In contrast, the prohibition on forced or compulsory labour in Article 4(2) is qualified by the exceptions in Article 4(3). Article 4 does not merely impose a negative obligation upon a state to refrain from putting individuals into a condition of slavery, servitude or compulsory labour. It also creates a positive obligation to ensure that its laws prevent individuals from imposing such conditions upon others.[22] **9.10**

(2) Slavery and servitude

Article 4(1) provides that no one shall be held in slavery or servitude. 'Slavery' involves being in the legal ownership of another.[23] In practice, issues concerning slavery have not arisen under the Convention because legally sanctioned slavery does not exist in any of the states which are parties to it. **9.11**

'Servitude' also embraces the totality of the status or condition of a person. However, it is distinguishable from slavery in that servitude does not involve ownership, but concerns less extensive forms of restraint. Servitude can also be differentiated from forced labour. In the *Van Droogenbroeck*[24] case, the Commission stated that: **9.12**

> in addition to the obligation to provide another with certain services the concept of servitude includes the obligation on the part of the 'serf' to live on another's property and the impossibility of changing his condition.[25]

The Commission went on to hold that a person who was convicted of a criminal

[21] Art 15(2).
[22] See eg *X v Netherlands* (1983) 5 EHRR 598 para 2, EComm HR.
[23] See para 9.01, n 1 above.
[24] *Van Droogenbroeck v Belgium* (1980) B 44, Com Rep para 79.
[25] The decision of the Commission was based on the definition of serfdom in the Supplementary Convention on the Abolition of Slavery etc. 1956, Art 1, 266 UNTS 3, UKTS 59 (1957), Cmnd 257.

offence had not been subjected to servitude when the court ordered him to be placed at the disposal of the state for a number of years following completion of his prison sentence. It took into consideration the limited period of time involved, the fact that any decision to recall was subject to judicial review and that the applicant's detention was accordance with Article 5[26] of the Convention.[27]

9.13 Servitude also overlaps with 'forced or compulsory labour' to the extent that the work or service required by servitude in breach of Article 4(1) may also be forced or compulsory labour contrary to Article 4(2). This overlap is limited, however, because there are types of work that may amount to servitude that are excluded from the definition of forced labour under Article 4(3).[28]

(3) Freedom from forced or compulsory labour

9.14 Article 4(2) states that no one shall be required to perform forced or compulsory labour law. Forced labour connotes direct compulsion whereas compulsory labour impliedly includes *indirect* forms of compulsion as well. In the drafting of the 1930 ILO Convention[29] a suggestion to reduce the terminology to 'compulsory labour' was rejected because the original phrase, which had made its first international appearance in the League of Nations Mandates, had become generalised in studies, recommendations and conventions under the League, the ILO, the UN and in national legislation:

> It is not always possible to distinguish between law and practice as regards forced labour in the strict sense and practice with regard to various forms of compulsion to labour.[30]

In most cases the distinction between the two is unnecessary.[31]

9.15 The Strasbourg authorities have looked to ILO Conventions to establish the meaning of the phrase 'forced or compulsory labour'. In *X and Y v Germany*[32] the

[26] See para 10.80ff below.

[27] It should be noted that a failure to observe Art 5(4) did not automatically mean that there was a failure to observe Art 4 (see *Van Droogenbroeck v Belgium* (1982) 4 EHRR 443 para 59).

[28] See *W, X, Y and Z v United Kingdom* (the 'Boy Soldiers' cases) (1968) 28 CD 109, EComm HR, in which the Commission, even though it found that the applicants' military service could not be forced labour because it was excluded by Art 4(3), also considered and rejected the argument that such labour constituted servitude.

[29] Forced Labour Convention (ILO Convention 29) 1930, 39 LNTS 55, 134 BFSP 449, Cmd 3693.

[30] *Report of the Committee of Experts on the Application of Conventions and Recommendations* (1962) paras 34, 81, 82.

[31] J Fawcett, *The Application of the European Convention on Human Rights* (2nd edn, Clarendon Press, 1987) 57.

[32] (1978) 10 DR 224, EComm HR.

Commission referred to five categories of forced labour set out in ILO Convention No 105:[33]

- political coercion or education as a punishment for holding or expressing political views or views ideologically opposed to the established political, social, or economic system;
- mobilising and using labour for purposes of economic development;
- labour discipline;
- punishment for having participated in strikes;
- racial, social or religious discrimination.

As a result, 'labour' extends beyond physical work to all kinds of work or service;[34] and 'forced or compulsory' labour comprises two elements: involuntariness and an unjustifiable or oppressive character.[35]

In *Iversen v Norway*[36] the Commission ruled as inadmissible an application by a dentist who, upon qualification, was required under Norwegian law, subject to a criminal sanction, to take paid work for a year in the public dental sector in a part of the country in which dentists were in demand. Four of six members of the majority of the Commission found that the facts did not amount to forced labour because the service was required for a limited time period, was properly remunerated, was in keeping with the profession of the applicant, and the law had not been arbitrarily applied to him. Two of the majority felt that the Norwegian measures were not 'forced labour' but fell under Article 4(3)(c) as an 'emergency or calamity threatening the life or well-being of the community'. The minority said that the circumstances did not exclude the possibility of 'forced labour', but that the question of the application of the third paragraph called for further examination. **9.16**

It has been held that consent, once given, deprives the work of its compulsory character. In *W, X, Y and Z v United Kingdom* (the *Boy Soldiers* case),[37] four young men, aged 15 and 16, had joined the Navy on nine-year contracts and sought discharge, *inter alia*, on the ground that there was a breach of Article 4. They claimed that their age in the service constituted servitude; however, the Commission **9.17**

[33] Ibid.

[34] In *Van der Mussele v Belgium* (1983) 6 EHRR 163, the voluntary legal aid services required to be provided by a trainee advocate were considered 'labour' in the sense of Art 4(2).

[35] *X v Germany* (1974) 17 YBHR 148; *X v Germany* (1980) 18 DR 216, EComm HR; *X v Netherlands* (1983) 32 DR 180, EComm HR; *Reitmayr v Austria* [1995] 20 EHRR CD 98; in *Van der Mussele v Belgium* (1983) 6 EHRR 163, the Court adopted as a starting point the ILO Forced Labour Convention (ILO Convention 29) 1930 definition of 'forced or compulsory labour' as follows: 'all work or service which is exacted from any person under the menace of any penalty and for which the said person has not offered himself voluntarily'.

[36] (1963) 6 YB 278, EComm HR.

[37] (1968) 11 YB 562, EComm HR.

treated as conclusive the fact that their parents had given the consent in accordance with the relevant law. Because the military service was excluded from 'forced or compulsory labour' under Article 4(2) (as opposed to being an exception under Article 4(1)), the complaint was dismissed as manifestly unfounded.

9.18 However, this restrictive approach was not followed in *Van der Mussele v Belgium.*[38] The applicant was a trainee advocate who was compelled by the regulations of the Order of Advocates to represent clients without payment if so directed by the Order. The fact that the applicant had given his prior consent to provide free legal aid services when he had become a trainee advocate was not conclusive. The Court said that:

> a considerable and unreasonable imbalance between the aim pursued—to qualify as an *avocat*—and the obligations undertaken in order to achieve that aim would alone be capable of warranting the conclusion that the service exacted of Mr Van der Mussele in relation to legal aid were compulsory despite his consent.[39]

Nevertheless, it was held that, on the facts, no such imbalance was disclosed. The Court looked at all of the circumstances of the case, including: the fact that the service was not unconnected with the profession; that the advocate received certain advantages, such as exclusive right of audience in the courts, in return; that the work contributed to the professional training of the trainee advocate; that the work related to a right guaranteed in the Convention (the right to legal aid under Article 6(3)(c)), and was similar to the 'normal civic obligations' exception allowed by Article 4(3)(d); and that the burden of the required nonremunerative services did not leave the applicant with insufficient time for paid work.

9.19 It has been argued that the Court's approach in *Van der Mussele* was incorrect because, even if a person has voluntarily entered into a labour contract or agreed to perform certain services, circumstances may change or obligations may become so onerous (particularly for engagements for a long period) that Article 4(2) is violated.[40] The Court placed less emphasis on the second element of 'forced or compulsory' than it did on voluntariness. It held that although a refusal of a trainee to act as free legal aid lawyer was not punishable by any criminal sanction, there was a 'menace of any penalty' since by such a refusal the applicant risked being struck off the rolls of trainees or having his application for registration as an advocate rejected.[41]

9.20 No finding of forced or compulsory labour has been made under Article 4(2). It has been decided that the following situations do not amount to forced or com-

[38] (1983) 6 EHRR 163.

[39] Ibid para 40.

[40] P van Dijk and G van Hoof, *Theory and Practice of the European Convention on Human Rights* (3rd edn, Kluwer, 1998) 340.

[41] *Van der Mussele v Belgium* (1983) 6 EHRR 163 para 35.

pulsory labour: an obligation on notaries to work for non-profit organisations, such as churches, at lower rates than those charged other clients;[42] making deductions of social security payments or income tax from an employee's salary;[43] and a requirement that an unemployed person accept a job offer or lose his unemployment benefit.[44]

(4) Permitted work or services

(a) Introduction

Article 4(3) identifies certain activities which are not included in the definition of forced or compulsory labour in Article 4(2). The areas of work or service described in Article 4(3) are not 'justifiable exceptions' to the prohibition against forced labour or restrictions on the exercise of the right protected by Article 4(2). They are work or services that are excluded *entirely* from 'forced labour' in the first instance. Thus, Article 4(3) is not intended to 'limit' the exercise of the right guaranteed by Article 4(2), but to define the very content of the right. It forms a whole with Article 4(2) and indicates what the term 'forced or compulsory labour does not include'.[45] As a result, Article 4(3) serves as an aid to construction of Article 4(2): **9.21**

> The four sub-paragraphs of [Art 4(3)] notwithstanding their diversity, are grounded on the governing idea of the general interest, social solidarity and what is normal in the ordinary course of affairs.[46]

However, the exclusions in Article 4(3) may be subject to a finding of discrimination under Article 14.[47] Thus, any type of work which, but for Article 4(3), would be 'forced labour' loses its permissible character if it is imposed on a discriminatory basis.[48] **9.22**

(b) Work during detention or conditional release (Article 4(3)(a))

Article 4(3)(a) excludes from forced labour 'work required to be done in the ordinary course of detention imposed according to the provisions of Article 5' or 'during conditional release from such detention'.[49] **9.23**

---

[42] *X v Germany* (1979) 18 DR 216, EComm HR.

[43] *Four Companies v Austria* (1976) 7 DR 148, EComm HR. The question of whether Art 4 could protect a company was left open.

[44] *X v Netherlands* (1976) 7 DR 161, EComm HR; see D Harris, M O'Boyle and C Warbrick, *Law of the European Convention on Human Rights* (Butterworths, 1995) 93.

[45] *Schmidt v Germany* (1994) 18 EHRR 513 para 22.

[46] Ibid.

[47] See para 17.79ff below.

[48] See P van Dijk and G van Hoof, *Theory and Practice of the European Convention on Human Rights* (3rd edn, Kluwer, 1998) 343.

[49] This includes not only work done in prison but work done by a convicted prisoner for a private enterprise: *Twenty-one Detained Persons v Germany* (1968) 11 YB 528, EComm HR.

9.24 The detention during which the work takes place must be in accordance with Article 5(1).[50] Because lawful detention is *not* limited to detention following conviction by a court of law, Article 4(3)(a) is not aimed exclusively at work done by convicted prisoners[51] or those detained by judicial order.[52] It also applies to work required of a detained minor[53] or a vagrant.[54] In other words, it will apply to work or services performed in *any* situation which constitutes a lawful deprivation of liberty under Article 5(1).

9.25 However, a violation of Article 5(4)[55] does not necessarily imply a breach of Article 4. The fact that a person, lawfully detained under Article 5(1), is denied the opportunity to challenge the legality of his detention, contrary to Article 5(4), does not render any labour required of him during detention 'forced or compulsory' contrary to Article 4.[56]

9.26 Whether the work is required in 'the ordinary course' of detention is measured not only against the usual requirements of the state concerned, but also in relation to the comparable practice of other members of the Council of Europe, based on the nature, purpose and extent of the services.[57] Thus, in *X v Switzerland*[58] the Court examined whether the work required of a detained minor was:

> abnormally long or arduous in view of the applicant's age or was of no educational value.

In the *Vagrancy* cases,[59] work in a vagrancy centre was not offensive to Article 4(3)(a) because it was directed at the rehabilitation of the prisoner and was not out of keeping with European standards.[60]

9.27 The Commission has held that there was no breach of Article 4(2) where prisoners were obliged to work in prison for insufficient pay and without social security benefits;[61] where they undertake compulsory work in a forced labour institution;[62] and where they are hired out to work for private enterprise.[63]

---

[50] See para 10.92ff below.
[51] Cf ILO Convention No 29.
[52] Cf Art 8 of the International Covenant on Civil and Political Rights.
[53] *X v Switzerland* (1979) 18 DR 238, EComm HR.
[54] *X v Germany* (1960) 6 CD 1, EComm HR.
[55] See para 10.145ff below.
[56] In *De Wilde, Ooms, and Versyp v Belgium (Vagrancy cases)* (1971) 1 EHRR 373 the Commission held that a contravention of Art 5(4) precluded the authorities from relying on Art 4(3)(a) to protect them from a finding of 'forced labour', but the Court did not adopt the same position.
[57] Cf Harris, O'Boyle and Warbrick (n 44 above) 95.
[58] *X v Switzerland* (1979) 18 DR 238, EComm HR.
[59] *De Wilde, Ooms, and Versyp v Belgium (Vagrancy cases)* (1971) 1 EHRR 373.
[60] The *Vagrancy* cases, (n 59 above); *X v Switzerland* (1979) 18 DR 238, EComm HR.
[61] *X v Austria* (1960) 3 YB 428, EComm HR; *X v Germany* (1966) 23 CD 1, EComm HR.
[62] *X v Germany* (1960) 6 CD 1, EComm HR; *X v Austria* (1966) 9 YB 550, EComm HR.
[63] *Twenty One Detained Persons v Germany* (1968) 11 YB 528, EComm HR.

(c) Service of a military character (Article 4(3)(b))

Under Article 4(3)(b) 'service of a military character . . .' does not come within the definition of forced or compulsory labour. Article 4(3)(b) differs from the provisions of Article 2(2)(a) of ILO Convention 29 which refers to 'any work or service exacted in virtue of "compulsory" military service laws for work of a purely military character'. Since Article 4 is not confined to 'compulsory military service', the Commission has decided that 'service of a military character' was intended to cover both voluntary enlistment and compulsory military service.[64] Van Dijk and van Hoof suggest that the rationale of the exception indicates that the application to voluntary military service is only justified where this replaces compulsory military service.[65] **9.28**

Although several European states retain compulsory military service,[66] there has not yet been a case in which the length or conditions of compulsory military service have been considered. **9.29**

(d) Work of conscientious objectors (Article 4(3)(b))

In countries where conscientious objectors are recognised, 'service exacted instead of compulsory military service' is also excluded from 'forced or compulsory labour'. The significance of this provision is three-fold. First, a conscientious objector may be required to do work as a substitute for military service without it being considered 'forced labour'. Secondly, the conscientious objector does not have a Convention right to perform civil work as an alternative to compulsory military service. The acknowledgement that he may be required to do alternative civil work is limited by the fact that the alternative work is only excluded from 'forced labour' in those countries where conscientious objectors are 'recognised'.[67] **9.30**

It is clear that conscientious objectors cannot claim that substitute service is a violation of their freedom of conscience under Article 9.[68] Article 4(3)(b) means that sanctions, such as detention for the period of military service, may be imposed for non-compliance, to ensure that the alternative service is performed.[69] **9.31**

---

64 *W, X, Y and Z v United Kingdom* (1968) 28 CD 109, EComm HR.

65 See P van Dijk and G van Hoof, *Theory and Practice of the European Convention on Human Rights* (3rd edn, Kluwer, 1998) 342 (the authors suggest that because the section excludes service required of conscientious objectors as an alternative to compulsory military activity, so voluntary military service should only be excluded from 'forced or compulsory labour' where it is rendered as an alternative to compulsory military service).

66 A majority of Council of Europe members retain conscription: CM Rec R (87) 8.

67 Nevertheless, failure of a state to recognise such a right for conscientious objectors may be reviewed for its conformity with Art 9: *A v Switzerland*, (1984) 38 DR 219, EComm HR.

68 *Grandrath v Germany* (1967) 10 YB 626, EComm HR.

69 *Johansen v Norway* (1985) 44 DR 155; *Grandrath v Germany* (1967) 10 YB 626, EComm HR.

(e) Community service in emergency or calamity (Article 4(3)(c))

9.32 Article 4(3)(c) excludes 'any service exacted in case of an emergency or calamity threatening the life or well-being of the community'. This allows a government to mobilise its population to cope with an emergency without the need to make a formal derogation under Article 15.[70] The requirement that there be an 'emergency or calamity threatening the life or "well-being" of the community' is a less stringent test than that under Article 15,[71] which refers to 'time of war or other emergency threatening the "life" of the community'. In the *Iversen*[72] case two members of the Commission took the view that there were reasonable grounds for the judgment of the Norwegian government that a shortage in the supply of volunteer dentists was an emergency threatening the well-being of a northern Norwegian community. In *S v Germany*,[73] the requirement that a person holding shooting rights over land should implement measures to control rabies in foxes on the property was also found to comply with Article 4(3)(c). The exception is of most obvious application in cases of 'acute emergencies with a temporal character'.[74]

(f) Normal civic obligations (Article 4(3)(d))

9.33 Article 4(3)(d) excludes from the prohibition in Article 4(2) 'any work or service which forms part of normal civic obligations', thus allowing governments to maintain various community obligations without the necessity of proving the existence of an emergency or calamity. The work and services permissible under this section remain restricted to those required by the state in the general interest.

9.34 The term 'normal' in Article 4(3)(d) describes the obligations customarily accepted in a particular community; and will, accordingly, vary with the needs and traditions of the place concerned. However, the concept of 'normal' also includes what would be required in the particular circumstances by a specific individual and might, therefore, include special duties required of professionals in the public interest.[75] However, it is arguable that the normal obligations in the course of

[70] A Robertson and J Merrills, *Human Rights in Europe* (3rd edn, Manchester University Press, 1993) 50–51.

[71] See Chap 15 below.

[72] *Iversen v Norway* (1963) 6 YB 278, EComm HR.

[73] (1984) 39 DR 90, EComm HR.

[74] P van Dijk and G van Hoof suggest that these include services such as aid in extinguishing a fire, urgent repairs of transport systems and dams, supply of water and food in case of a sudden shortage, transport of wounded persons or the evacuation of persons threatened by some danger, and similar incidental services which can be required of everyone in the public interest depending on their capabilities (see *Theory and Practice of the European Convention on Human Rights* (3rd edn, Kluwer, 1998) 342).

[75] For example, free legal aid; in *Van der Mussele v Belgium* (1983) 6 EHRR 163 the decision of the Court that the provision of unpaid legal aid services by a trainee advocate did not amount to forced labour was based on other grounds and it therefore found it unnecessary to decide whether such work constituted 'normal civic obligations'.

a profession are not within Article 4(3)(d) since there is no real compulsion: a person is free not to take the job. Normal civic obligations include compulsory fire services,[76] the obligation of a person enjoying shooting rights to participate in the gassing of fox holes[77] or any financial contribution paid in lieu of such services.[78]

D. The Impact of the Human Rights Act

(1) Introduction

The English law has long recognised the fundamental right to be free from 'slavery' and 'servitude'. There are few areas in which English law provides for 'forced labour' and these all appear to fall within the permitted exceptions in Article 4(3). As a result, the Human Rights Act is unlikely to have any substantial impact on the law in this area. **9.35**

(2) Cases prior to the Human Rights Act

There have been very few United Kingdom applications under Article 4 and no findings of violation by the Court. The most important United Kingdom case on Article 4 is the *Boy Soldiers* case.[79] In that case, four young men, aged 15 and 16, had joined the Navy on nine-year contracts and sought discharge, *inter alia*, on the ground that there was a breach of Article 4. The Commission held that it was an essential feature of servitude that a person had been forced to work against his will. In that case, the requisite consent by the parents of the minors had been given in accordance with the relevant law. Because the military service was excluded from 'forced or compulsory labour' under the second section but did not form an exception to the first, the complaint was dismissed as manifestly unfounded. In *Harper v United Kingdom*[80] it was held that a change in the compulsory retirement age did not constitute a breach of Article 4. A complaint about compulsory labour in prison was dismissed by the Commission.[81] **9.36**

(3) Potential impact

(a) Introduction

It seems unlikely that Article 4 will have a significant effect on English law. Two specific areas of impact can be considered: criminal law and employment law. **9.37**

[76] *Schmidt v Germany* (1994) 18 EHRR 513 para 23.
[77] *S v Germany* (1984) 39 DR 90, EComm HR.
[78] *Schmidt v Germany* (1994) 18 EHHR 513.
[79] *W, X, Y & Z v United Kingdom* (1968) 11 YB 562, EComm HR.
[80] (1986) 9 EHRR 235, EComm HR.
[81] *X v United Kingdom* (1969) 12 YB 288, EComm HR.

(b) Criminal law

9.38 It has been argued[82] that imposing a community service order without consent[83] is incompatible with Article 4(2) as forced or compulsory labour. The only relevant exception which might justify the position is Article 4(3)(a) which permits work done in the course of detention.[84] However, a community service order is a community order[85] and not a custodial sentence[86] nor a form of conditional release from custody. The fact that no 'detention' is involved means that it is difficult to apply Article 4(3)(a). It is possible, therefore, that the requirement for consent to community service orders will have to be reintroduced.

(c) Employment and discrimination

9.39 Article 4 will not be breached where employees complain that they are working unduly long or unsocial contractual hours since the obligation is unlikely to be disproportionate.[86a] One possible area of impact concerns 'workfare' schemes under which the payment of welfare benefits is made conditional on taking a place on an approved 'work scheme'. Hepple has suggested[87] that welfare legislation which allows benefits to be withdrawn if a claimant refuses a job[88] could lead to breaches of Article 4(2). However, the Commission has taken the view that a requirement that an unemployed person to accept a job offer or lose welfare benefit was not a breach of Article 4.[89] As a result, it seems unlikely that Article 4 will have any impact in this area.

Appendix 1: The Canadian Charter of Rights

9.40 There is no provision of the Charter comparable to Article 4 of the Convention.

[82] See A Ashworth, 'The Impact on Criminal Justice' in B Markesenis (ed), *The Impact of the Human Rights Bill in English Law* (Oxford University Press, 1998) and D Thomas, 'Incorporating the European Convention on Human Rights: its Impact on Sentencing Law' in J Beatson, C Forsyth and I Hare (eds), *The Human Rights Act and the Criminal Justice and Regulatory Process* (Hart Publishing, 1999).

[83] The requirement of consent was abolished by Criminal (Sentences) Act 1997, s 38.

[84] See para 10.90ff below.

[85] Criminal Justice Act 1991, s 6.

[86] Criminal Justice Act 1991, s 31.

[86a] Cf *Van der Mussele v Belgium* (1983) 6 EHRRR 163, see para 9.18ff above.

[87] See B Hepple, 'Impact on Labour Law', in B Markesinis (ed), *The Impact of the Human Rights Bill on English Law* (Clarendon Press, 1998) 64.

[88] For example, the Jobseeker's Act 1996, s 19(5)(b) provides that jobseeker's allowance is not payable where a claimant has, without good cause, refused or failed to carry out a reasonable jobseeker's direction.

[89] *X v Netherlands* (1976) 7 DR 161, EComm HR; *Talmon v Netherlands* [1997] EHRLR 448.

Appendix 2: The New Zealand Bill of Rights Act

There is no provision of the New Zealand Bill of Rights Act comparable to Article 4 of the Convention. By section 98(1) of the Crimes Act (New Zealand), 'dealing in slaves' is a crime. This provision was considered in *R v Decha-Iamsakun*,[90] in which it was held that a sufficient definition of the word 'slave' was 'a person held as property'. **9.41**

Appendix 3: Human Rights Cases in Other Jurisdictions

(1) Introduction

Prohibitions on slavery, servitude and forced labour feature in many constitutional human rights provisions.[91] Perhaps the most well known is the Thirteenth Amendment to the United States Constitution which provides that: **9.42**

> Neither slavery nor involuntary servitude, except as a punishment for a crime whereof the party shall have been duly convicted, shall exist within the United States, or any place subject to their jurisdiction.

It has been said that the plain intention of this amendment was: **9.43**

> to abolish slavery of whatever name and form and all its badges and incidents; to render impossible any state of bondage, to make labour free, by prohibiting that control by which the personal service of one man is disposed of or coerced for another's benefit which is of the essence of involuntary servitude.[92]

It does not, however, prevent enforcement of duties owed by the individual to the state, such as services in the army,[93] juries or requirements to carry out public works.[94] The granting of injunctions in industrial disputes does not breach this provision.[95] The state cannot require individuals to engage in forced labour to pay a civil debt.[96]

(2) India

Article 23 of the Indian Constitution prohibits traffic in human beings and forced labour and provides that: **9.44**

> (1) Traffic in human beings and begar and other similar forms of forced labour are prohibited and any contravention of this provision shall be an offence punishable in accordance with law.
>
> (2) Nothing in this article shall prevent the State from imposing compulsory service for public purposes, and in imposing such service the State shall not make any discrimination on ground only of religion, race, caste or class or any of them.

---

[90] [1993] 4 LRC 746.

[91] For European provisions see eg German Constitution 1948, Art 12; Italian Constitution 1947, Art 23.

[92] *Bailey v Alabama* (1911) 219 US 207.

[93] *Arver v United States* (1918) 245 US 366.

[94] *Butler v Perry* (1916) 240 US 328 (state statute requiring able bodied males to work on public roads or make payment in lieu upheld).

[95] *International Union UAWA v Wisconsin Employment Relations Board* (1949) 336 US 245.

[96] *Peonage Cases* (1903) 123 Fed 671.

'*Begar*' means labour or service exacted by the Government or a person in power without remuneration.[97] Labour may be 'forced' not only in terms of physical force, but also on account of a legal provision such as imprisonment or fine where the employee fails to provide the service, and also owing to hunger and poverty which compels him to accept employment for remuneration which is less than the statutory minimum wage.[98] A contract for personal service enforceable under penal law is within the prohibition of Article 23.[99] The result is the same where the penalty for default in rendering the service is founded on custom,[100] administrative fiat[101] or in repayment of an alleged debt.[102] Where a person provides labour or service for remuneration less than the minimum wage prescribed by statute this is 'forced labour' under Article 23(1).[103]

(3) South Africa

9.45 Section 12 of the Final Constitution provides that:

> No person shall be subject to servitude or forced labour.

This provision does not appear to have been considered by the South African courts. It has been suggested that it may prevent the conscription of labour for state purposes, including the deployment of conscripts in Government offices.[104]

---

[97] *Vasudevan v Mittal* A 1962 Bom 53 (67); *Suraj v State of MP* A 1960 MP 303.

[98] *People's Union of Democratic Rights v Union of India* (1983) 1 SCR 456; *Sanjit v State of Rajasthan* A 1983 SC 328.

[99] *People's Union* (n 98 above).

[100] *Kahaosan v Simirei* A 1961 Mani 1.

[101] *Chandra v State of Rajasthan* A 1956 Raj 188.

[102] *People's Union* (n 98 above); *Bandhua Mukti Mascha v Union of India* AIR 1984 SC 802.

[103] *People's Union* (n 98 above).

[104] M Chaskalson, J Kentridge, J Klaaren, G Marcus, D Spitz and S Woolman (eds), *Constitutional Law of South Africa* (Juta, 1996) para 30.2(b).

10

THE RIGHT TO LIBERTY

A. The Nature of the Rights

10.01 The right to personal liberty and freedom from arbitrary arrest and detention is very well established as a fundamental human right. The Magna Carta provided that:

> no freeman shall be taken or imprisoned . . . but . . . by the law of the land.

The right was recognised in the Fifth Amendment to the United States Constitution under the terms of which:

> No person shall be . . . deprived of life, liberty, or property, without due process of law.[1]

Similar provision was made by the *Declaration of the Rights of Man* of 1789.[2] The right is protected by Article 9 of the Universal Declaration of Human Rights which provides that:

> No one shall be subjected to arbitrary arrest, detention or exile.

and is protected by the International Covenant on Civil and Political Rights[3] and by all other general rights instruments.[4]

10.02 The right to liberty, is, of course, not an absolute one. The freedom is from *arbitrary* arrest and detention: this implies the common (and correlative) provision that a person should be deprived of liberty only in accordance with the law. However, modern human rights instruments recognise a number of important rights which arise out of the basic 'right to liberty'. The 'right to liberty' comprises the following elements:[5]

- the freedom from arbitrary arrest and detention;[6]
- the right to suffer deprivation of liberty only when this is 'in accordance with the law';[7]
- the right to be informed of the reasons for arrest;[8]
- the right to judicial control of arrest and detention;[9]

[1] See also Fourteenth Amendment, applying to the States; see generally, L Tribe, *American Constitutional Law* (2nd edn, Foundation Press, 1988) Chap 11.

[2] Art 7: 'no one shall be accused, arrested or imprisoned, save in the cases determined by law, and according to the forms which it has prescribed'.

[3] Art 9(1), 'Everyone has the right to liberty and security of person. No one shall be subjected to arbitrary arrest or detention. No one shall be deprived of his liberty except on grounds and in accordance with such procedure as are established by law'.

[4] For a list see P Sieghart, *The International Law of Human Rights* (Clarendon Press, 1983) para 14.2.1, 135–138.

[5] See generally, Sieghart (n 4 above), para 14.2.3, 139–140.

[6] UDHR, Art 9; ICCPR, Art 9(1).

[7] All instruments except the UDHR make express provision to this effect.

[8] ICCPR, Art 9(2); Convention, Art 5(2).

[9] All instruments except the UDHR make express provision to this effect.

- the right to an opportunity to test the legality of arrest or detention;[10]
- compensation for unlawful arrest and detention.[11]

A number of complex legal issues arise in relation to the 'right to liberty' including: **10.03**

Rights before being brought before the court: After a person is arrested and before he is brought before the court, he may be held in police detention for a considerable period. It is generally thought that the right to liberty involves rights of access to lawyers and the availability of procedures for reviewing detention should be available. Particular difficulties have arisen in terrorism cases.

Rights to bail: After an arrested person is brought before the court but before conviction, there is generally understood to be a right to bail. The circumstances in which this right can be limited or removed continue to be vigorously debated.

Judicial control over detention: The right to liberty is only effective if those in detention can have speedy recourse to the courts. The circumstances in which such recourse should be available and the nature of the 'review' exercise undertaken by the courts have given rise to continuing disputes in a number of jurisdictions.

Other powers of detention: While international human rights instruments contemplate the existence of powers of detention outside the criminal process, the precise extent of these powers and the circumstances in which they can be exercised remain contentious.

B. The Rights in English Law Before the Human Rights Act

(1) Introduction

The right of a freeman not to be imprisoned save by the law of the land was recognised by the Magna Carta. The right to personal liberty of individuals is described by Blackstone as an 'absolute right inherent in every Englishman'.[12] He defines the right as consisting in: **10.04**

> the power of locomotion, of changing situation or removing one's person to whatsoever place one's own inclination may direct; without imprisonment or restraint, unless by due course of law.[13]

[10] ICCPR, Art 9(4), Convention, Art 5(4).
[11] ICCPR, Art 9(5); Convention, Art 5(5).
[12] R Kerr (ed), *Blackstone's Commentaries on the Laws of England* (4th edn, John Murray, 1876) 100.
[13] Ibid 105.

Lord Bingham CJ recently put the point in these terms:

> no adult citizen of the United Kingdom is liable to be confined in any institution against his will, save by the authority of the law. That is a fundamental constitutional principle, traceable back to Ch 29 of Magna Carta 1297 (25 Edw 1 c 1) and before that to Ch 39 of Magna Carta (1215). There are, of course, situations in which the law sanctions detention. The most obvious is in the case of those suspected or convicted of crime. Powers then exist to arrest and detain. But the conditions in which those powers may be exercised are very closely prescribed by statute and the common law.[14]

10.05 In English law this right has, traditionally, been protected in three ways. First, any person who is restrained by state authorities can seek the writ of *habeas corpus*, to bring his body before the court to determine whether his imprisonment is lawful.[15] Secondly, it is a criminal offence to interfere with a person's liberty without proper justification. Thirdly, any 'total restraint' of a person's movement gives rise to a claim in the tort of false imprisonment.

10.06 However, the English law also recognises a number of 'lawful justifications' for the infringement of personal liberty:

- there are extensive powers of arrest and detention both at common law and under statute in relation to those suspected of criminal offences;
- a person can be detained pursuant to an order of the criminal courts both before and after sentence;
- the civil courts can make orders for the detention of persons found to be in contempt of court;
- there are a number of other common law and statutory powers of detention exercisable by public officials or the court in relation to special categories of person, such as those suffering from mental disorder or persons entering the United Kingdom.

Because of the importance placed on the right to liberty these powers are narrowly construed by the courts.

(2) Habeas corpus

(a) Introduction

10.07 'Habeas corpus ad subjiciendum'[16] is a prerogative writ by which the courts can inquire into the reasons for the imprisonment of any person. The purpose of the

[14] *In Re S-C (Mental Patient: Habeas Corpus)* [1996] QB 599, 603.

[15] *Blackstone's Commentaries on the Laws of England* (n 12 above) 106.

[16] For a fuller treatment, see eg Lord Woolf and J Jowell, *De Smith, Woolf and Jowell, Judicial Review of Administrative Action* (5th edn, Sweet & Maxwell, 1995) paras 15-036–15-057; R Gordon, *Judicial Review and Crown Office Practice* (Sweet & Maxwell, 1999) Pt 4.

writ is to order the production of the body of the imprisoned person before the court so that inquiries into the reasons for the imprisonment can be made and release from unlawful detention can be secured. The writ will, in general, not be issued in respect of a detention which has been discontinued.[17] It has been said that the writ of habeas corpus[18] is the foundation stone of the liberties of the subject.[19] The modern limitations on the writ mean that this statement sounds somewhat exaggerated today; and Sir Simon Brown has recently argued that the remedy of habeas corpus should now be incorporated within the jurisdiction of judicial review.[19a] Nevertheless, in extreme cases, it does serve as a remedy for those in detention and the threat of an application may be sufficient to secure the early release of detained persons.

(b) Availability of the writ

Habeas corpus is available in any case where a citizen has been wrongfully deprived of his liberty. Once a person has been convicted by a competent criminal court (whether on indictment[20] or by a court of summary jurisdiction),[21] habeas corpus will not be granted. The appropriate means of redress is an appeal.[22] In general, habeas corpus is, like all 'administrative law' remedies, simply concerned with the question of whether the order for detention was made with jurisdiction, not whether it was correct on the merits. Difficult judgments may be involved in deciding whether in a particular set of circumstances habeas corpus or judicial review is the more appropriate remedy.[23] **10.08**

The more recent cases[24] suggest that a distinction must be drawn between: **10.09**

- an allegation that the detention has been made without jurisdiction where the prisoner disputes the existence of some precedent fact; and
- an application based on challenging the prior underlying administrative decision.

The implication is that habeas corpus is not available in this second situation. The justification for this appears to be that:

> as judicial review has developed into an ever more flexible and responsive jurisdiction,

[17] *Barnardo v Ford* [1892] AC 326.
[18] For a fuller treatment, see eg *De Smith, Woolf and Jowell* (n 16 above) paras 15-036–15-057.
[19] See *R v Batcheldor* (1839) 1 Per & Dav 516, 567.
[19a] The Rt Hon Sir Simon Brown, 'Habeas Corpus—A New Chapter' [2000] PL 31.
[20] *Ex p Lees* (1858) EB & E 828.
[21] *Re Corke* [1954] 1 WLR 899.
[22] See *Ex p Hinds* [1961] 1 WLR 325.
[23] See eg O Davies, 'Habeas Corpus or Judicial Review?' [1997] JR 11.
[24] See *R v Secretary of State for the Home Department, ex p Muboyayi* [1992] QB 244; *R v Secretary of State for the Home Department, ex p Cheblak* [1991] 1 WLR 890.

the need for a parallel, blunter remedy by way of habeas corpus has diminished.[25]

This approach has been criticised as being unduly technical and fraught with complexities.[26] It also appears to be inconsistent with binding authority.[27]

(c) Procedure

10.10 An application for a writ of habeas corpus is made without notice to the Divisional Court of the Queen's Bench Division or, if no such court is sitting, to a single judge in court or, if no court is sitting, 'otherwise than in court', in other words, at home or wherever a judge can be found.[28] The application should be supported by a witness statement or affidavit by the person restrained[29] or, if he is unable to make a witness statement or affidavit, by someone acting on his behalf.[30] The witness statement or affidavit should set out the nature of the restraint.[31] The application need not be in the name of the person detained but may be made by any person at his instance, or by a relative or friend on his behalf. The witness statement or affidavit should set out the reasons why the person detained is not making the application.[32] A mere stranger acting without authority will not be allowed to apply.[33] The old cases indicate that applications should be made by counsel and this will not be departed from 'unless some sufficient ground is shown'.[34]

10.11 An application which is not made to the Divisional Court may be ordered to be adjourned to the Divisional Court.[35] At the without notice stage, the court can either issue the writ immediately or adjourn the application so that notice can be given to the respondent.[36] In practice, the writ will only be issued immediately in exceptional cases.[37] If notice is given, a hearing with notice will take place, with the respondent serving an affidavit setting out the justification for the detention. At such a hearing the court may order that the person restrained be released.[38]

---

[25] *Per* Simon Brown LJ, *R v Oldham Justices, ex p Cawley* [1996] 2 WLR 681; see also *R v Secretary of State for the Home Department, ex p Muboyayi* [1992] QB 244; *R v Secretary of State for the Home Department, ex p Rahman* [1996] 4 All ER 945 (affirmed [1997] 1 All ER 796).

[26] See *De Smith, Woolf and Jowell* (n 16 above) 15-051 but see The Rt Hon Sir Simon Brown, 'Habeas Corpus—A New Chapter' [2000] PL 31.

[27] See *R v Governor of Brixton Prison, ex p Armah* [1968] AC 192; *R v Secretary of State for the Home Department, ex p Khawaja* [1984] AC 74; and generally, W Wade, 'Habeas Corpus and Judicial Review' (1997) 113 LQR 55.

[28] CPR Sch 1 Ord 54, r 1(1).

[29] CPR Sch 1 Ord 54 r 1(2).

[30] CPR Sch 1 Ord 54, r 1(3).

[31] CPR Sch 1 Ord 54, r 1(2).

[32] CPR Sch 1 Ord 54, r 1(3).

[33] *Ex p Child* (1854) 15 CB 238.

[34] *Re Greene* (1941) 57 TLR 533; see eg *Ex p Hinds* [1961] 1 WLR 325, in which the applicant's wife was heard.

[35] CPR Sch 1 Ord 54, r 2(1).

[36] CPR Sch 1 Ord 54, r 2.

[37] See Supreme Court Practice, 1999, 54/2/1.

[38] CPR Sch 1 Ord 54, r 4.

An application cannot be renewed in respect of the same person on the same grounds unless there is fresh evidence in support.[39] Raising late an argument previously open to an applicant will not necessarily amount to an abuse of the process.[40] However, even where, technically, the applicant can identify some fresh evidence or fresh ground, the court retains its jurisdiction to strike out the application in an appropriate case.[41] Where an applicant in extradition proceedings makes a second application for habeas corpus, it is necessary to consider the test used in asylum cases for deciding whether the second application is an abuse of process; the court must compare the new claim with the earlier one rejected and, excluding material on which the claimant might reasonably have been expected to rely in the earlier application, decide if the new claim is sufficiently different to give it a realistic prospect of success despite the earlier unfavourable conclusion.[42] **10.12**

In a civil matter an appeal against a refusal to grant a writ lies to the Court of Appeal. In a criminal matter appeal lies to the House of Lords. **10.13**

If a writ of habeas corpus is issued it is usually served personally on the person to whom it is directed.[43] The return to the writ must state 'all the causes of the detainer of the person restrained'.[44] If the return on its face shows that there is a valid authority for the detention the onus is then on the applicant to show that the detention is illegal. As Ashworth J put it in *R v Governor of Brixton Prison, ex p Ahsan*:[45] **10.14**

> I accept entirely the principle that the custodian is called upon to justify the detention, but he does so by making a return which is valid on the face of it . . . it is then for the person detained to place evidence before the court showing that what appears to be a valid return is in fact invalid.

If the detention is unlawful the writ is granted 'as of right'.[46] Although it may be refused where there is another remedy available whereby the validity of the detention may be questioned, the court has no discretion to refuse it if the detention is unlawful and no other remedy is available.[47]

---

39 Administration of Justice Act 1960, s 14(2); this represents the common law position, see *Re Hastings (No 2)* [1959] 1 QB 358.

40 *R v Governor of Brixton Prison, ex p Osman (No 3)* [1992] 1 WLR 36.

41 *R v Governor of Brixton Prison, ex p Osman (No 4)* [1992] 1 All ER 579.

42 *Re Debs* 12 Nov1999 applying *R v Secretary of State for the Home Department, ex p Onibiyo* [1996] QB 768.

43 CPR Sch 1 Ord 54, r 6.

44 CPR Sch 1 Ord 54, r 7.

45 [1969] 2 QB 222, 237; see also *R v Governor of Risley Remand Centre, ex p Hassan* [1976] 1 WLR 971.

46 *Re Corke* [1954] 1 WLR 899; *R v Pentonville Prison Governor, ex p Azam* [1974] AC 18, 32.

47 *Greene v Secretary of State for Home Office* [1942] AC 284, 302.

10.15 When terms of a statute afford the executive a discretion, whether wide or narrow, the review of the discretion in habeas corpus proceedings is limited to considering the conformity of the exercise with the empowering statute. The court cannot consider the lawfulness of the exercise of the discretion itself.[48]

(3) Criminal offences involving interference with liberty

10.16 The state protects liberty by making it a criminal offence to interfere with the liberty of a person without proper justification. The two most important offences are false imprisonment and kidnapping.[49] Both are common law offences which have not been defined by statute.

10.17 The offence of false imprisonment is committed by unlawfully subjecting a person to a total restraint of liberty or compelling him to go to a particular place. Every confinement of the person is an imprisonment, whether it is in a common prison or a private house, or even by forcibly detaining a person in the streets.[50] The offence is committed where a person unlawfully and intentionally or recklessly restrains the victim's freedom of movement from a particular place.[51]

10.18 It is also an offence at common law to kidnap a person. The elements of this offence are as follows:[52]

- the taking and carrying away of one person by another;
- by force or fraud;
- without the consent of the person carried away;
- without lawful excuse.

The offence can be committed against a child under the age of 14, by a parent against an unmarried child who is still a minor and by a husband against his wife.[53]

10.19 The Taking of Hostages Act 1982 creates a statutory offence which is committed by anyone who detains another and, in order to compel any state, international governmental organisation or person to do or abstain from doing any act, threatens to kill, injure or continue to detain the hostage. The Child Abduction Act 1984 creates two statutory offences involving the abduction of children under 16.[54]

---

48 See *De Smith, Woolf and Jowell* (n 16 above) 15-037.

49 For a fuller treatment, see *Archbold: Criminal Pleading, Evidence and Practice* (Sweet & Maxwell, 2000); para 19.331ff.

50 2 Co Inst 482, 589.

51 See *R v Rahman* (1985) 81 Cr App R 349, 353; and see *R v Hutchins* [1988] Crim LR 379.

52 See *R v D* [1984] AC 778.

53 See *R v Reid* [1973] QB 299.

54 Ss 1 and 2 as amended by the Children Act 1989.

(4) False imprisonment

The right to liberty is also protected by the law of tort. The tort of 'false imprisonment'[55] is committed by someone who intentionally subjects another to total restraint of movement either by actively causing his confinement or preventing him from exercising his privilege of leaving the place where he is.[56] Any interference with liberty is unlawful unless the person responsible for the imprisonment can show that it is justified.[57] It is therefore irrelevant that the person responsible is not at fault for detaining the claimant.[57a] **10.20**

Confinement in any form may be false imprisonment. This means that an individual may be confined in a house,[58] in a car driven at such speed that he cannot alight[59] or even in a large area within which he is free to move.[60] It is necessary, however, that there is *in fact* a complete deprivation or restraint on a person's liberty.[61] The person who is detained does not have to be aware of the fact in order to have a claim for false imprisonment.[62] However, the area of confinement must be fixed by the defendant and must constitute a total rather than partial restraint on his liberty. Consequently, it is not a false imprisonment to prevent someone from moving in a particular direction and forcing him to turn back; he is not imprisoned if he is free to go in some directions but not others.[63] **10.21**

The constraint on the claimant that will amount to false imprisonment may be actual physical force, but also includes the assertion of legal authority to confine him[64] or dissuading him from leaving confinement[65] or restraining him through the desire of the claimant to avoid public embarrassment.[66] Merely making a charge against the claimant without actually confining him does not constitute false imprisonment.[67] **10.22**

---

55 For a fuller treatment see eg R Clayton and H Tomlinson, *Civil Actions Against the Police* (3rd edn, Sweet & Maxwell, 2001) Chap 4.

56 See the discussions in *R v Deputy Governor of Parkhurst, ex p Hague* [1992] 1 AC 58.

57 *Allen v Wright* (1835) 8 C & P 522.

57a *R v Governor of Brockhill Prison, ex p Evans (No 2)* [1999] 2 WLR 103.

58 *Warner v Ruddiford* (1858) 4 CB(NS) 180.

59 *Burton v Davies* [1953] QSR 26.

60 *Kuchenmeister v Home Office* [1958] 1 QB 496; the plaintiff was prevented from proceeding from the airport to an aeroplane by immigration officers who were not authorised to prescribe the area within which he had to remain.

61 *R v Bournewood Community and Mental Health NHS Trust, ex p L* [1998] 3 WLR 107, 117 *per* Lord Goff.

62 See *Murray v Ministry of Defence* [1988] 1 WLR 692, 701–702; in such a situation the damages for wrongful detention would be nominal: see *R v Bournewood NHS Trust, ex p L* [1998] 2 WLR 764, CA.

63 *Bird v Jones* (1845) 7 QB 742.

64 *Warner v Riddiford* (1858) 4 CB(NS) 180, 204.

65 *Harnett v Bond* [1925] AC 669.

66 *Conn v David Spencer* (1930) 1 DLR 805.

67 *Simpson v Hill* (1795) Esp 431.

10.23 The tort can also be committed if an individual is initially lawfully detained but his detention, for some reason, becomes unlawful later. At common law a constable could only detain a felon, arrested without warrant, for a reasonable time;[68] after this time had elapsed the detention would become unlawful. These common law powers have now been replaced, however, by the provisions of the Police and Criminal Evidence Act 1984 ('PACE'). An initially lawful detention will become unlawful if the relevant provisions of PACE are not complied with.[69] However, where a person arrested by the police is brought before the magistrates and is subsequently detained as a result of a court order, any claim for false imprisonment must be made against the magistrates rather than the police.[69a]

(5) **Powers of arrest and detention**

(a) Introduction

10.24 The police and other public officers have numerous statutory powers of arrest and a number of powers of detention.[70] If an arrest is carried out in conformity with such a power, this will provide a defence to an action for false imprisonment by the person arrested. However, statutory words giving powers of arrest and detention are construed strictly, so that:

> if the statutory words relied upon as authorising the acts are ambiguous or obscure, a construction should be placed upon them that is least restrictive of individual rights which would otherwise enjoy the protection of the common law.[71]

There are a number of grounds on which a deprivation of liberty can be justified. In this section we will consider deprivation of liberty by police officers prior to the making of court orders: powers of arrest and detention.

10.25 In general, police officers and other public officials have no power to detain someone for questioning without making an arrest.[72] A person who attends voluntarily at a police station without being arrested is, therefore, entitled to leave at will.[73] If the police pressurise him to stay they will be guilty of false imprisonment. There is, however, a power to detain if this is necessary for the exercise of any other police power such as the execution of a search warrant.[74]

---

68 See *Wright v Court* (1825) 4 B&C 596; *John Lewis and Company Ltd v Tims* [1952] AC 676, 682.

69 See *Roberts v Chief Constable of Cheshire* [1999] 1 WLR 662.

69a *Austin v Dowling* (1870) LR 5 CP 534, 540 *per* Willes J; the liability of magistrates for false imprisonment is discussed at para 10.78 below and the impact of the Human Rights Act is considered at para 10.75ff below.

70 For a fuller treatment, see eg R Clayton & H Tomlinson, *Civil Actions against the Police* (3rd edn, Sweet & Maxwell, 2001) Chap 5.

71 *Inland Revenue Commissioners v Rossminster Ltd* [1980] AC 952, 1008 *per* Lord Diplock; and see *Hill v Chief Constable of South Yorkshire* [1990] 1 WLR 946, 952 *per* Purchas LJ.

72 *Kenlin v Gardner* [1967] 2 QB 510.

73 PACE, s 29.

74 See *Parry v Sharples*, CA, unreported, 17 Jul 1991.

(b) Stop and search powers

The police have a number of statutory powers of detention short of arrest. First, there is a general power of stop and search under section 1 of PACE. The power to search is exercisable if the police have 'reasonable grounds to believe' that they will find stolen or prohibited articles.[75] The police also have a power to carry out a 'drug search' under section 23(2) of the Misuse of Drugs Act 1971. This includes a power to take a person to a place were search can properly be carried out.[76] This power can only be exercised if the constable has reasonable grounds to suspect that the person is in possession of a controlled drug. **10.26**

Under the Criminal Justice and Public Order Act 1994, if a police officer of the rank of superintendent, or higher, reasonably believes that 'incidents involving serious violence may take place' he may, if it is expedient to do so, authorise the use of special powers to stop and search within that locality for up to 24 hours.[77] A constable is thereby granted a power to stop and search pedestrians or vehicles for 'offensive weapons or dangerous instruments'.[78] Under this power: **10.27**

> A constable may . . . stop any person or vehicle and make any search he thinks fit whether or not he has any grounds for suspecting that the person or vehicle is carrying weapons or articles of that kind.[79]

If a person fails to stop when required to do so then he commits an offence punishable by imprisonment of up to one month.[80] By section 13A of the Prevention of Terrorism (Temporary Provisions) Act 1989[81] where it appears expedient to a police officer of the rank of commander or assistant chief constable 'in order to prevent acts of terrorism'[82] he may authorise any police officer in uniform:

> (a) to stop any vehicle;
> (b) to search any vehicle, its driver or any passenger for articles of a kind which could be used for a purpose connected with the preparation or instigation of acts of terrorism.[83]

These powers are exercisable at any place within the authorising officers area or a specified locality within that area for a specified period not exceeding 28 days.[84] It is expressly provided that a constable may exercise his powers 'whether or not he has any grounds for suspecting the presence' of such articles.[85] There is a

[75] PACE, s 1(3).
[76] See *Farrow v Tunnicliffe* [1976] Crim LR 126.
[77] s 60(1).
[78] s 60(4).
[79] s 60(5).
[80] s 60(8).
[81] Inserted by Criminal Justice and Public Order Act 1994, s 32.
[82] As defined by s 13A(2).
[83] s 13A(3).
[84] s 13A(1).
[85] s 13A(4).

similar power to authorise officers to stop and search pedestrians within a specified area.[86]

(c) Arrest

10.28 **Introduction.** Police officers have three general powers of arrest. They may arrest:

- under an arrest warrant;
- if they have reasonable grounds to suspect that a person is committing or is guilty of an arrestable offence;[87]
- if they have reasonable grounds to suspect that a non-arrestable offence has been committed and one of the 'general arrest conditions' is fulfilled.[88]

In addition, police officers have one remaining common law power of arrest: to prevent an actual or apprehended breach of the peace and a number of specific statutory powers of arrest.

10.29 The lawfulness of the arrest depends on the existence of the power to arrest. An honest belief in the existence of such a power will be insufficient.[89] Difficulties have arisen, however, where an individual has been arrested or detained on the basis of a legal power which is *subsequently* held to be unlawful. In *Percy v Hall*[90] the Court of Appeal took the view that the police could justify arrests for breaching certain byelaws when defending a false imprisonment claim by showing that they reasonably believed an offence had been committed *even though* the byelaws were subsequently held to be unlawful. The Court of Appeal explained in *R v Governor of Brockhill Prison, ex p Evans (No 2)*[91] that this case had limited application: the fact that an executive or administrative decision like a byelaw may be valid for some purposes until set aside does not enable a defendant in a false imprisonment case to argue that a court decision which is overruled nevertheless provides a legal justification for detaining the claimant.

10.30 However, a lawful arrest will not be rendered unlawful by the use of undue force in the course of the arrest.[92]

10.31 **Arrest with warrant.** A warrant is an authority to do something which would otherwise be unlawful. An arrest warrant gives the person to whom it is directed authority to deprive the named person of his liberty. Most arrest warrants are issued by magistrates. Upon an information being laid before a justice that any

86 s 13B; added by the Prevention of Terrorism (Additional Powers) Act 1996.
87 PACE, s 24.
88 PACE, s 25.
89 See *Wershof v Commissioner of Police for the Metropolis* [1978] 3 All ER 540.
90 [1997] QB 924.
91 [1999] 2 WLR 103.
92 *Simpson v Chief Constable of South Yorkshire Police, The Independent*, 27 Feb 1991.

person is suspected of committing an offence, the justice may issue a summons or a warrant.[93] A warrant cannot be issued unless the information is in writing and substantiated on oath. There are numerous other statutes empowering the issue of arrest warrants.[94]

Police constables are given protection for acts done in obedience to warrants issued without jurisdiction by the Constables Protection Act 1750. A constable who acts in obedience to a warrant is protected from an action in tort even though the warrant is unlawful[95] if he has acted strictly in obedience to its terms.[96] As a result, a person making an arrest under the terms of a warrant will only be liable in the tort of false imprisonment in a limited number of situations.[97] **10.32**

Arrest without warrant. The most common type of arrest in the course of ordinary police activity is arrest 'without warrant for an arrestable offence under the provisions of section 24 of PACE'. Section 24(6) provides that: **10.33**

> Where a constable has reasonable grounds for suspecting that an arrestable offence has been committed he may arrest without warrant anyone whom he has reasonable grounds for suspecting to be guilty of the offence.[98]

Any consideration of the lawfulness of an arrest under this power must first determine whether it was an arrest 'for an arrestable offence'. Generally, an 'arrestable offence' is defined as 'an offence for which a person could be sentenced to a term of imprisonment of five years or more'.[99] A number of offences are also specifically designated as being 'arrestable'.[100] It should be noted that an arrest by a private citizen will only be lawful if the offence has actually been committed.[101]

Once it is clear that a suspect was, indeed, arrested for an arrestable offence, three questions arise:[102] **10.34**

1. Did the arresting officer suspect that the person who was arrested was guilty of the offence? The answer to this question depends entirely on the findings of fact as to the state of mind of the officer.
2. Assuming that the officer had the necessary suspicion, was there reasonable

[93] Magistrates' Court Act 1980, s 1; see also Supreme Court Act 1981, s 81.
[94] See eg the Army Act 1955, the Insolvency Act 1986 and the Extradition Act 1870; see generally, L Leigh, *Police Powers in England and Wales* (2nd edn, Butterworths, 1985), 91ff.
[95] See *Atkins v Kilby* (1840) 11 Ad & El 777.
[96] See *Hoye v Bush* (1840) 1 Man & G 775.
[97] For a fuller discussion, see R Clayton and H Tomlinson, *Civil Actions Against the Police*, (3rd edn, Sweet & Maxwell, 2001) Chap 5.
[98] See also s 24(4), (5) and (7).
[99] See PACE, s 24.
[100] See PACE, s 24(2).
[101] *Walters v W H Smith* [1914] 1 KB 595.
[102] For the first two, see *King v Gardner* (1979) 71 Cr App R 13.

cause for that suspicion? This is a purely objective requirement to be determined by the judge, if necessary, on facts found by the jury.

3. If the answers to the first two questions are in the affirmative, then the officer may, in his discretion, make an arrest. Whether that discretion has been properly exercised may be determined in accordance with the [*Wednesbury*] principles.[103]

In cases of arrest without warrant, the burden of proof is upon the defendant to show that the arresting officer had the necessary suspicion and that there were reasonable grounds for the arrest.[104] The burden of showing that the discretionary power to arrest has been exercised improperly is on the claimant.

10.35 The concept of 'reasonable grounds for suspicion' is an elusive one. A comprehensive definition has not been attempted in any case or statute. Reasonable grounds will only be present if a reasonable man, in the position of the officer at the time of the arrest, would have thought that the suspect was probably guilty of the offence.[105] This is a question of fact to be determined on the basis of all of the circumstances. It is for the judge to make the decision on the basis of the jury's findings of fact as to what happened and what the officers believed. The standard is objective but is not a high one. Thus, it has been said that in the context of section 24:

> 'reasonable' qualifies suspicion only to the extent that the suspicion must not be fanciful but must be based upon reasonable, i.e. rational, grounds.[106]

Although information provided by an informant can constitute 'reasonable grounds', it should be treated with 'very considerable reserve' and a police officer 'should hesitate before regarding such information, without more, as a basis for reasonable suspicion'.[107] Information provided by another police officer will, on the other hand, often be sufficient to provide an arresting officer with reasonable grounds for suspicion.[108]

10.36 There is some doubt as to the extent to which a police officer is under a duty to inquire before concluding that he has reasonable grounds to suspect a person of the commission of an offence. In one case it was held that 'courses of inquiry which may or may not be taken by an investigating police officer before arrest are not relevant to the consideration whether, on the information available to him at the time of the arrest he had reasonable cause for suspicion'.[109]

---

[103] *Per* Woolf LJ, *Castorina v Chief Constable of Surrey* [1988] NLJ Rep 180.

[104] *Allen v Wright* (1835) 8 C & P 522.

[105] See *Dallison v Caffrey* [1965] 1 QB 348, 371 and *Wiltshire v Barrett* [1966] 1 QB 312, 322.

[106] *James v Chief Constable of South Wales Police The Daily Telegraph*, 3 May 1991, *per* Lord Donaldson MR; see also *Mulvaney v Chief Constable of Cheshire*, CA, unreported, 8 Mar 1990.

[107] *James v Chief Constable of South Wales Police, The Daily Telegraph*, 3 May 1991.

[108] *O'Hara v Chief Constable of the Royal Ulster Constabulary* [1997] AC 286.

[109] *Castorina v Chief Constable of Surrey* [1988] NLJ Rep 180; but see *Dumbell v Roberts* [1944] 1 All ER 326, 329 *per* Scott LJ; *McArdle v Egan* (1934) 150 TLR 412, 413; *McCarrick v Oxford* [1983] RTR 117.

Over and above the existence of reasonable grounds for suspecting that the plaintiff has committed an arrestable offence, the lawfulness of the arrest will depend upon the lawfulness, in public law, of the exercise of the discretion to arrest.[110] Provided that there is a power of arrest, it is lawful to arrest an individual in order to question him.[111] However, the discretion will not have been lawfully exercised if it can be shown that, at the time of the arrest, the arresting officer knew that there was no possibility of a charge being made.[112] **10.37**

Special provisions govern the arrest of those suspected of involvement in terrorism. Under the Prevention of Terrorism (Temporary Provisions) Act 1989, there is a power to arrest those who are reasonably suspected of various terrorist offences.[113] There is also a power to arrest a person who a constable suspects, on reasonable grounds, is: **10.38**

> a person who is or has been concerned in the commission, preparation or instigation of acts of terrorism . . .[114]

This applies to acts of terrorism connected with the affairs of Northern Ireland or to others, except acts connected solely with the affairs of the United Kingdom other than Northern Ireland.[115]

General power of arrest. By section 25 of PACE a police constable is authorised to make an arrest for any offence, however minor, provided that one of the general arrest conditions is satisfied and the service of a summons is impracticable or inappropriate. PACE gives the police a power of arrest without warrant when a person has failed to comply with a requirement that he attend a police station in order that his fingerprints be taken.[116] **10.39**

Other powers of arrest. All citizens have a power of arrest and detention in cases of breach of the peace. A breach of the peace must involve actual or threatened harm to person or property.[117] 'Public alarm and excitement', 'noise alone' or 'being a nuisance and keeping one's neighbours awake' has been found not to constitute a breach of the peace.[118] Such a breach can take place on private premises.[119] Any citizen has a power of arrest for breach of the peace in three situations: **10.40**

---

110 *Mohammed-Holgate v Duke* [1984] AC 437.
111 Ibid.
112 *Plange v Chief Constable of South Humberside Police The Times*, 23 Mar 1992.
113 s 14(1)(a).
114 s 14(1)(b).
115 s 14(2).
116 PACE, s 27(3).
117 *R v Howell (Errol)* [1982] QB 416.
118 *Lewis v Chief Constable of Greater Manchester The Times*, 22 Oct 1991.
119 *McConnell v Chief Constable of Greater Manchester Police* [1990] 1 WLR 364.

- where the breach is committed in his presence;
- where the arrestor reasonably believes that such a breach will be committed in the immediate future by the person arrested, even though at the time of the arrest, no breach had been committed;
- where a breach of the peace had been committed and it was reasonably believed that a renewal of it was threatened.[120]

A police officer is entitled to rely on information from another to provide 'reasonable grounds' for his belief.[121]

10.41 Finally, although section 26(1) of PACE repeals all previous statutory powers of arrest, section 26(2) expressly preserves those contained in Schedule 2 to the Act. These powers concern, primarily the arrest of persons unlawfully at large, offences relating to animals, terrorist offences and immigration offences. In addition, a number of powers of arrest have been conferred by post-PACE statutes, including the Public Order Act 1986.

10.42 **Reasons on arrest.** An arrest is unlawful unless the person arrested is informed of the ground for the arrest at the time of, or as soon as is practicable after, the arrest.[122] This applies whether or not the ground for the arrest is obvious.[123] The giving of reasons on arrest is 'of the utmost constitutional significance'.[124] An arrest which is unlawful on this basis will, however, become lawful from the moment that the proper information is given.[125] The statement of the reasons for the arrest does not have to be in 'technical language' or identify a particular offence.[126] However, the reasons should be stated in sufficient detail for the suspect to be able to give a convincing denial.[127] For example, a suspect must be informed of the date and place of an alleged burglary for which he is being arrested.[128]

(d) Detention by the police

10.43 **Introduction.** When a person is arrested for an offence, his detention will only be lawful if it is accordance with Part IV of PACE.[129] The police must justify detention on a minute-by-minute basis.[130] Part IV does not apply to cases in which a person is not 'arrested for an offence'. These include persons detained 'in order

[120] See *R v Howell (Errol)* [1982] QB 416, 426.
[121] *Timothy v Simpson* (1835) 1 CM & R 755, 761–3.
[122] PACE, s 28(3).
[123] PACE, s 28(4).
[124] *Edwards v DPP* (1993) 97 Cr App R 301.
[125] *Lewis v Chief Constable of South Wales Constabulary* [1991] 1 All ER 206.
[126] *Abbassy v Commissioner of Police of the Metropolis* [1990] 1 WLR 385.
[127] *R v Telfer* [1976] Crim LR 562.
[128] *Murphy v Oxford* 15 Feb 1985, CA, unreported.
[129] See s 34: see eg *Hill v Chief Constable of South Yorkshire* [1990] 1 WLR 946; *Roberts v Chief Constable of Cheshire Police* [1999] 1 WLR 662.
[130] *Mercer v Chief Constable of the Lancashire Constabulary* [1991] 1 WLR 367.

to prevent a breach of the peace' or for a 'drug search'.[131] In practice, police forces create custody records for such detainees.

Authorisation of police detention. On arrival at the police station, a custody record is opened by the custody officer who must decide whether there is sufficient evidence to charge the suspect. If there is sufficient evidence to charge, the custody officer is under a duty to charge or release.[132] If the custody officer fails to charge the suspect when there is sufficient evidence to do so,[133] any subsequent detention will be unlawful. If there is not sufficient evidence to charge, the suspect must be released unless the custody officer has reasonable grounds for believing that it is nevertheless necessary to detain the person: 10.44

> to secure or preserve evidence relating to an offence for which he is under arrest or to obtain such evidence by questioning.[134]

In such circumstances, authorisation of detention for any other reason is unlawful and any subsequent detention will be a false imprisonment. Where a custody officer authorises detention without charge, a written record must be made of the grounds.[135] A failure to make such a written record renders the subsequent detention unlawful. If the custody officer becomes aware that the grounds for detention have ceased to apply he is under a duty to release the suspect.[136] 10.45

A person may be detained without charge for up to 24 hours.[137] After six hours the detention must be 'reviewed'. The review officer must again decide whether there is sufficient evidence to charge the suspect.[138] Detention after the review can only be authorised on the same grounds as the original detention could have been authorised. The review officer must give the suspect or his solicitor an opportunity to make representations about the detention.[139] A police officer of the rank of at least superintendent can authorise detention for a further 12 hours.[140] This can only be done in the case of a 'serious arrestable offence'[141] and if the investigation is being conducted 'diligently and expeditiously'.[142] Detention for a further period of up to a total of 60 hours can be authorised by a magistrates' court.[143] 10.46

[131] Misuse of Drugs Act 1971, s 23(2).
[132] PACE, s 37(7).
[133] See *R v Holmes, ex p Sherman* [1981] 2 All ER 612.
[134] PACE, s 37(2).
[135] Ibid s 37(4).
[136] Ibid s 34(2).
[137] Ibid s 41(1).
[138] Ibid s 40. The review must be made in face-to-face confrontations between the review officer and the suspect and cannot be made by video link: see *R v Chief Constable of Kent Constabulary, ex p Kent Police Federation Joint Branch Board The Times*, 1 Dec 1999.
[139] Ibid s 40(12).
[140] Ibid s 42.
[141] Ibid s 116.
[142] Ibid s 42(1).
[143] Ibid s 43; magistrates can only authorise 36 hours at a time.

10.47 Once a person has been charged, the custody officer is under a duty to order his release with or without bail unless, in case of an adult, one of the conditions in subsection 38(1)(a) is fulfilled. The custody officer must record the reason for detention after charge.[144] Failure to do so will render the detention unlawful unless and until a magistrates' court orders remand in custody. Where the suspect is both charged and kept in detention he must be brought before the magistrates' court, in the petty sessional division where the police station is situated, as soon as is practicable. The police are obliged to bring him before the court no later than the first sitting after he is charged.[145] If no sitting is scheduled for the day of the charge or the one following, the custody officer must inform the clerk to the justices of the situation[146] and he must arrange for a court to sit no later than the day next following the relevant day.[147] The custody officer has the power to release a person on conditional bail.[147a]

10.48 **Detention to prevent a breach of the peace.** A police officer may detain someone in police custody 'to prevent an imminent breach of the peace' under the common law.[148] In addition, it has been suggested that a police officer is entitled, or perhaps even under a duty, to detain a person arrested for breach of the peace until the next sitting of the magistrates' court.[149] This power existed at common law to ensure that a person was brought before the justices to apply for an order that he be bound over.[150] The power to bind over can, however, now be exercised by order on 'complaint'[151] and it appears that the entire common law procedure for binding over, including the power of detention, has been superseded.

(e) Detention of suspected terrorists

10.49 A person arrested under section 14 of the Prevention of Terrorism (Temporary Provisions) Act 1989[152] can be detained for up to 48 hours.[153] This period can be extended by the Secretary of State by further periods not exceeding five days in all.[154] There are special provisions for the review of detention by a 'review officer'.[155]

10.50 When a person arrives in or is seeking to leave Great Britain, he may be examined

[144] Ibid s 38(3).
[145] Ibid s 46(1) and (2).
[146] Ibid s 46(3).
[147] Ibid s 46(6).
[147a] Bail Act 1976, s 3A(1), inserted by the Criminal Justice and Public Order Act 1994, s 27(3).
[148] *Albert v Lavin* [1982] AC 546 (this power is available to any citizen).
[149] See *Marsh v Chief Constable*, unreported, 5 Nov 1992, Poole county court.
[150] See *Timothy v Simpson* (1835) 1 CM&R 757, 761.
[151] See Magistrates' Court Act 1980, s 115; see para 10.61 below.
[152] See para 10.42 above.
[153] s 14(4).
[154] s 14(5).
[155] Sch 3.

by an examining officer for the purpose of determining whether he appears to be concerned in the commission, preparation or instigation of acts of terrorism or is subject to an exclusion order.[156] A person who is to be examined may be detained on the authority of an examining officer. The period of examination may exceed 12 hours if there are reasonable grounds for suspecting that the person examined is concerned with terrorism.[157] The examining officer may authorise a period of examination which exceeds 24 hours, pending conclusion of this examination or decisions as to exclusion or prosecution.[158] The maximum period of detention that an examining officer may authorise is 48 hours[159] but the Secretary of State may extend this period by up to five days.[160]

(f) Other powers of detention

Detention under the Immigration Acts. When a person arrives in the United Kingdom, he may be examined by an immigration officer to determine whether or not he is a British citizen, whether he is entitled to enter the United Kingdom without leave and, if not, whether he should be given leave and for what period and on what conditions.[161] A person required to submit to such an examination: **10.51**

> may be detained under the authority of an immigration officer pending his examination and pending a decision to give or refuse him leave to enter.[162]

There is no time limit on the period of examination.[163] Anyone liable to be so detained can be arrested without warrant by an immigration officer or a police officer.[164]

Individuals in respect of whom directions for removal may be given may be detained under the authority of an immigration officer pending the giving of directions or the removal.[165] Such persons include anyone who has entered in breach of a deportation order or of the immigration laws. There is a duty upon entrants not to make statements known or believed to be false[166] and a person who has entered by deception is an illegal entrant. Detention and removal will also apply to an asylum seeker who is appealing against a decision to remove or exclude him from the United Kingdom.[167] **10.52**

---

[156] s 16 and Sch 5.
[157] Sch 5, para 2(4).
[158] Sch 5, para 6(1).
[159] Sch 5, para 6(2).
[160] Sch 5, para 6(3).
[161] Immigration Act 1971, Sch 2, para 2(1).
[162] Ibid Sch 2, para 16(1).
[163] *R v Secretary of State for Home Department, ex p Thirukumar* [1989] Imm AR 270.
[164] Immigration Act 1971, Sch 2, para 17.
[165] Ibid Sch 2, para 16(2).
[166] See *R v Secretary of State for the Home Department, ex p Khawaja* [1984] AC 74.
[167] See generally, Asylum and Immigration Appeals Act 1993 and Asylum and Immigration Act 1996.

10.53 After five consecutive days' detention, the detention must be either at a prison, remand centre, approved hospital, place of safety (for children) or one of the four 'authorised detention centres'.[168] A person who has been detained pending examination or the giving of directions may be released on bail by a chief immigration officer or an adjudicator.[169] The right to bail does not arise until seven days after arrival.[170] The person must enter a recognisance and may be subject to sureties.[171]

10.54 **Detention of persons in need of care and attention.** The National Assistance Act 1948 provides local authorities with a power to apply to a court of summary jurisdiction for the removal of certain persons 'to a suitable hospital or other place' and for their 'detention and maintenance therein'. Such an application can be made in relation to persons who:

(a) are suffering from grave chronic disease or, being aged, infirm or physically incapacitated, are living in unsanitary conditions; and
(b) are unable to devote to themselves, and are not receiving from other persons, proper care and attention.[172]

The application can only be made if the proper officer certifies that it is necessary to remove the person from the premises in which he is residing, either in the interests of the individual or 'for preventing injury to the health of, or serious nuisance to, other persons'.[173] The detention order may be issued for a period of up to three months but can be extended, from time to time, for a further period, not exceeding three months.[174]

10.55 **Detention of those suffering from infectious diseases.** Under the provisions of the Public Health (Control of Diseases) Act 1984 the Secretary of State for Health can order the hospitalisation and, if necessary, detention in quarantine of people who have infectious diseases to prevent the spread of the disease.[175] Furthermore, a magistrate has power to order detention in hospital of a person suffering from a notifiable disease.[176]

---

[168] See Immigration (Places of Detention) Direction 1996.
[169] See Immigration Act 1971, Sch 2, para 22, as amended by Asylum and Immigration Act 1996.
[170] Immigration Act 1971, Sch 2, para 22.1 and 1(B).
[171] See generally, M Supperstone and D O'Dempsey, *Supperstone and O'Dempsey on Immigration and Asylum* (4th edn, Sweet & Maxwell, 1996), 289–291.
[172] s 47(1).
[173] s 47(2).
[174] s 47(4).
[175] See Public Health (Infectious Diseases) Regulations 1985, SI 1985/434.
[176] Public Health (Control of Diseases) Act 1984, s 39; see generally, D Feldman *Civil Liberties and Human Rights in England and Wales* (Clarendon Press, 1993) 299.

(6) Deprivation of liberty by court order

(a) Introduction

The English law provides for the deprivation of liberty by court order in a number of situations. First, when a person who has been arrested and charged is brought before the magistrates' court, the court can decide to order his detention pending trial. Secondly, a person can be deprived of his liberty following conviction by a criminal court. Thirdly, the civil courts have wide powers to order the detention of persons found to be in contempt of court. Fourthly, persons suffering or appearing to suffer from mental disorder may be detained under the provisions of the Mental Health Act 1983. **10.56**

(b) Detention pending trial

When an arrested person is brought before the court in custody, he has the right to apply for release on bail.[177] The right to liberty is recognised by the presumption that a person who applies 'shall be granted bail' unless certain exceptions apply.[178] Bail may only be refused if there are 'substantial grounds for believing' that the accused would fail to answer to bail, commit further offences on bail or interfere with witnesses or otherwise obstruct the course of justice.[179] In addition, an accused need not be granted bail if the court is satisfied that he should be kept in custody for his own protection or, in the case of a child or young person, his own welfare,[180] or if the accused is already in custody as a result of prison sentence.[181] The court can also refuse bail where there is insufficient time to gather information in relation to the bail decision or if the accused has breached the conditions of bail in the same proceedings[182] or if, where the case has been adjourned for reports or inquiries, it is impracticable to gain the necessary information without remanding the accused in custody.[183] The court must give reasons for withholding bail or for imposing or varying bail conditions.[184] The procedure for making repeated applications for bail is now governed by Part IIA of Schedule 1 to the Bail Act 1976. At the first hearing after that at which the court decided not to grant bail a 'full bail application' may be made. At subsequent hearings the **10.57**

[177] For a fuller treatment, see, P Murphy (ed), *Blackstone's Criminal Practice 1999* (Blackstone Press, 1999) D5.

[178] Bail Act 1976, s 4(1); there are 19 separate statutory provisions providing for powers, rights and duties relating to bail: see the notes to s 25, Criminal Justice and Public Order Act 1994 in *Halsburys Statutes* (4th edn, Butterworths, 1994) Vol 12 and see generally, Law Commission, *Bail and the Human Rights Act* Consultation Paper No 157 (The Stationery Office, 1999) Pt II.

[179] Bail Act 1976, Sch 1, para 2.

[180] Sch 1, para 3.

[181] Sch 1, para 4.

[182] Sch 1, para 6.

[183] Sch 1, para 7.

[184] s 5(3).

court need not hear arguments as to fact or law which it has heard previously. Where a magistrates' court has heard full argument and refused bail, the defendant may apply to the Crown Court or to the High Court for bail.[184a]

10.58 The court is entitled to impose conditions on the grant of bail if they are necessary in order to prevent the accused absconding, committing offences or interfering with witnesses, obstructing the course of justice and to ensure that he makes himself available for the purpose of inquiries or reports.[185] Commonly imposed conditions included residence, curfew, reporting at a police station, non-association with particular persons or non-engagement in particular activities. Conditions may be in force for many months while a person is awaiting trial. During the 1984 miners' strike, those accused of public order offences relating to the strike were subjected to bail conditions which had the effect of preventing the accused from taking any further part in the protest. In *R v Mansfield Justices, ex p Sharkey* the Divisional Court rejected the contention that the regular imposition of these conditions was unlawful.[186] Such conditions may be imposed even where the accused is charged with an non-imprisonable offence.[187]

10.59 The Criminal Justice and Public Order Act 1994 removed the right to bail in certain circumstances. Section 25 applies the grant of bail to a person who in any proceedings has been charged with murder, attempted murder, manslaughter, rape or attempted rape. The section states that if that person has been:

> previously convicted by or before a court in any part of the United Kingdom of any such offence or of culpable homicide and, in the case of a previous conviction of manslaughter or of culpable homicide, if he was then sentenced to imprisonment or, if he was then a child or young person, to long-term detention under any of the relevant enactments.[188]

then he 'shall not be granted bail'.[189] This provision has now been amended by the Crime and Disorder Act 1998 to provide for bail if there are exceptional circumstances to justify it.[190] By section 26 of the Criminal Justice and Public Order Act 1994[191] a person accused or convicted of committing offences whilst on bail 'need not be granted bail'.

10.60 The Prosecution of Offences Act 1985 provides for 'custody time limits'[192] for

---

184a Supreme Court Act 1981, s 81(1)(g) and Criminal Justice Act 1967, s 22(1).

185 Bail Act 1976, s 3(6), s 3A and Sch 1, para 8.

186 [1985] QB 613.

187 See *R v Bournemouth Justices, ex p Cross* (1989) 89 Cr App R 90 (hunt saboteur charged with a minor public order offence, bailed on condition that he did not attend any hunts).

188 s 25(3).

189 s 25(1).

190 s 56.

191 Which amends the Bail Act 1976, Sch 1, Pt I.

192 For a fuller treatment, see P Murphy (ed), *Blackstone's Criminal Practice 1999* (Blackstone Press, 1999) D10.4.

those accused of indictable offences. The maximum period of custody between the first appearance of the accused and the time when the court decides whether or not to commit the accused to the Crown Court for trial is 70 days.[193] The maximum period of custody between committal and trial is 112 days. [194] However, the appropriate court may, at any time before the expiry of a time limit imposed by the regulations, extend, or further extend, that limit if it is satisfied:

- that there is good and sufficient cause for doing so; and
- that the prosecution has acted with 'all due expedition'.[195]

The Act and the Regulations made under it have three overriding purposes:

> (1) to ensure that the periods for which unconvicted defendants are held in custody awaiting trial are as short as reasonably and practically possible; (2) to oblige the prosecution to prepare cases for trial with all due diligence and expedition; and (3) to invest the court with a power and duty to control any extension of the maximum period under the regulations for which any person may be held in custody awaiting trial.[196]

When considering applications for extensions, the court will bear in mind that the periods laid down are maxima, not targets.[197] The fact that the offence is serious[198] and the need to protect the public,[199] cannot be 'good and sufficient cause'. Although the unavailability of a suitable judge or courtroom within the maximum period specified may, in special cases, amount to good and sufficient cause, this should be approached with great caution.[200] Applications for the extension of custody time limits call for careful consideration and many call for rigorous scrutiny and the reasons for granting or refusing extensions should be given.[201] Once the time limit has expired the defendant must be released on bail.[201a]

(c) Binding over to keep the peace

The power to impose a bind over does not, strictly speaking, result in the deprivation of liberty; it can, however, significantly restrict an individual's ability to participate in activities where he wishes to exercise the right to freedom of expression or peaceful assembly. The power to bind over to keep the peace derives partly from **10.61**

193 The Prosecution of Offences (Custody Time Limits) Regulations 1987, SI 1987/299, reg 4.
194 Ibid reg 5(3).
195 Prosecution of Offences Act 1985, s 22(3).
196 *R v Crown Court at Manchester, ex p McDonald* [1999] 1 All ER 805, 807.
197 Ibid 808.
198 *R v Governor of Winchester Prison, ex p Roddie* [1991] 1 WLR 303, 306.
199 *R v Central Criminal Court, ex p Abu-Wardeh* [1998] 1 WLR 1083, 1088.
200 *R v Crown Court at Manchester, ex p McDonald* (n 196 above) 809–812; referring to the Convention case law.
201 Ibid 812.
201a Bail Act 1976, s 4(8A), inserted by the Prosecution of Offences (Custody Time Limits) Regulations 1987, SI 1987/299, reg 8.

statute[202] and partly from the common law.[203] A bind over may be made after a complaint is made under the Magistrates' Court Act[204] which is probably decided on the criminal standard of proof;[205] or may be made where the court binds over a person who is appearing before it as a party or a witness[206] in proceedings. The court can decide to bind an individual over to keep the peace generally or to be of good behaviour to a particular person.

10.62 Normally a person who is about to be bound over will be allowed to make representations.[207] The person bound over must acknowledge his indebtedness to the sovereign in the sum of the recognizance which means that the court cannot unilaterally impose a bind over.[208] Before making a bind over the court should be satisfied that there is material before it which justifies the conclusion that there is a risk of a breach of the peace unless action is taken to prevent it, that a sufficient indication has been given so representations can be made, that there is a means inquiry before fixing the recognizance and that the bind over is for a finite period.[209]

(d) Imprisonment and other orders on conviction

10.63 **General.** The criminal courts have extensive powers to impose sentences which involve convicted offenders being deprived of their liberty.[210] Once a person is sentenced to a term of imprisonment, he is deprived of his liberty for all purposes. Thus,

> a prisoner at any time has no liberty to be in any place other than where the regime permits . . . An alteration of his conditions therefore deprives him of no liberty because he has none already.[211]

10.64 The importance of the right to liberty is demonstrated by the fact that the extensive judicial powers of deprivation of liberty in the criminal sentencing process are subject to a number of statutory restrictions. A court must not pass a custodial sentence unless it is of the opinion that the offence was so serious that no other type of sentence would suffice or if, where the offence is a violent or sexual offence, a custodial sentence would alone be adequate to protect the public from serious harm.[212] The court must obtain and consider a pre-sentence report before forming such an opinion.[213]

202 Justice of the Peace Act 1391.
203 *Lansbury v Riley* [1914] 3 KB 229.
204 Magistrates' Court Act 1980, ss 115 and 116.
205 *Percy v DPP* [1995] 1 WLR 1382.
206 *R v Wilkins* [1907] 2 KB 380.
207 *Sheldon v Broomfield Justices* [1964] QB 573.
208 *Veater v G* [1981] 1 WLR 567.
209 *R v Lincolnshire Crown Court, ex p Jude* [1998] 1 WLR 24.
210 For imprisonment, see Powers of the Criminal Courts Act 1973, s 18(1).
211 *R v Deputy Governor of Parkhurst Prison, ex p Hague* [1992] 1 AC 58, 177 *per* Lord Jauncey; see also at 139, *per* Lord Bridge.
212 Criminal Justice Act 1991, s 1(2).
213 Ibid, s 3.

A court cannot impose a sentence of imprisonment on a person under 21 years of age.[214] However, in the case of offenders between 15 and 21 years of age, it is open to the court to pass a sentence of detention in an institution for young offenders.[215] The criminal courts have power to impose 'curfew orders' on convicted offenders. Such orders require the offender to remain at a specified place at specified times[216] and may include requirements for securing the electronic monitoring of the whereabouts of the offender during the curfew periods.[217] In relation to an offender under 21 years of age, the court may order him to attend at an attendance centre for a specified number of hours.[218] **10.65**

The liability of prison governors for false imprisonment where a prisoner is detained without lawful authority has been considered in a number of recent cases. In *Olotu v Home Office*[218a] the Court of Appeal struck out a claim by a prisoner who had been detained after the expiry of the custody time limits;[218b] although the defendant had a right to apply to the court to be released on bail, the governor had no authority to release the plaintiff without an order of the court. This decision was distinguished by the Court of Appeal in *R v Governor of Brockhill Prison, ex p Evans (No 2)*[218c] where the prison governor was held to be liable for false imprisonment for incorrectly computing the period of custody a prisoner should serve. **10.65A**

Parole. Under the Criminal Justice Act 1967, the Home Secretary was empowered to appoint a 'Parole Board' to advise on the suitability of prisoners for early release on licence. The position is now governed by the Criminal Justice Act 1991.[219] This places duties on the Home Secretary to release prisoners depending on the length of their sentences. The Act provides that: **10.66**

- prisoners sentenced to less than 12 months are to be released unconditionally after serving half their sentence;[220]
- short-term prisoners, sentenced to up to four-years' imprisonment, are to be released on parole after half their sentences;[221] and
- long-term prisoners, sentenced to four years' or more, may be released after serving two thirds of their sentences.[222]

---

214 Criminal Justice Act 1982, s 1.
215 Ibid s 1A.
216 Ibid s 12.
217 Ibid s 13.
218 Ibid s 17.
218a [1997] 1 WLR 328.
218b See generally, para 10.60 above.
218c [1999] 2 WLR 103.
219 For a fuller treatment, see S Livingstone and T Owen, *Prison Law* (2nd edn, Oxford University Press, 1999) paras 12.21–12.59.
220 s 33(1)(a).
221 s 33(1)(b).
222 s 33(2).

10.67 The position of prisoners serving life sentences has given rise to a number of problems concerning the circumstances of release. Such prisoners are divided into two categories: 'mandatory' and 'discretionary'. In the first category are those convicted of murder, in the second category are those given life sentences for other offences such as manslaughter, rape or arson. In a series of cases, starting in the late 1980s, the courts identified a number of rights arising from the special position of discretionary lifers.[223] It was decided that the 'tariff' should be fixed at the outset of the period of custody,[224] that the test for deciding whether further detention was justified after the expiry of the tariff was whether the prisoner was dangerous,[225] and that the discretionary lifer had a right of access to reports being considered by the Parole Board.[226]

10.68 The requirements for proper procedures to determine whether or not discretionary lifers should be released were confirmed by the decisions of the European Court of Human Rights in *Weeks*[227] and *Thynne, Wilson and Gunnell.*[228] These decisions led to the enactment of section 34 of the Criminal Justice Act 1991 which, in substance, provides that the sentencing judge can specify the mandatory period of punishment.[229] When the specified part of the sentence has been served, the discretionary lifer may require the Home Secretary to refer his case to the Parole Board.[230] If the Parole Board directs that the prisoner is to be released, the Home Secretary is under a duty to release him.[231] Release can be directed if the Board is satisfied that confinement is no longer necessary for the protection of the public.[232] The reviews are conducted by three-person panels of the Parole Board, known as 'Discretionary Life Panels', which hold oral hearings. The prisoner has the right to see all the reports on which the panel is relying.[233] If, however, a discretionary lifer is transferred to a mental hospital, consideration of his discharge will be governed by the applicable Mental Health Act procedures, rather than by those procedures applicable solely to discretionary lifers.[234]

10.69 Mandatory lifers are treated differently.[235] A distinction has been drawn between

---

[223] For a fuller treatment, see Livingstone and Owen (n 219 above) paras 14.36–14.74.

[224] *R v Secretary of State for the Home Department, ex p Handscomb* (1987) 86 Cr App R 59.

[225] *R v Home Secretary, ex p Benson The Times*, 21 Nov1988; *R v Parole Board, ex p Bradley* [1991] 1 WLR 134.

[226] *R v Parole Board, ex p Wilson* [1992] QB 740.

[227] *Weeks v United Kingdom* (1987) 10 EHRR 293.

[228] *Thynne, Wilson and Gunnell v United Kingdom* (1990) 13 EHRR 666.

[229] s 34(2); and see *Practice Direction (Crime: Life Sentences)* [1993] 1 WLR 223.

[230] s 34(5).

[231] s 34(3).

[232] See s 34(2).

[233] See Livingstone and Owen (n 219 above) paras 14.38–14.74; D Feldman *Civil Liberties and Human Rights in England and Wales* (Clarendon Press, 1993) 292–298.

[234] See *R v Secretary of State for the Home Department, ex p H* [1995] QB 43.

[235] Release on licence is governed by the Criminal Justice Act 1991, s 35(2). For a fuller treatment, see, Livingstone and Owen (n 219 above) paras 13.34–13.32.

the essentially punitive nature of mandatory life sentences and the partially protective nature of discretionary life sentences.[236] The Home Secretary has a broad discretion as to whether and when to release a mandatory life prisoner and is not bound by judicial advice as to the tariff period which reflects the minimum period to be served in the interests of deterrence and retribution.[237] There is no reason in principle why a crime of sufficient heinousness should not attract life long imprisonment for purpose of punishment.[238] The tariff period established at the commencement of a mandatory life sentence is only a preliminary decision, and, in exceptional circumstances, may be revised.[239] The tariff cannot, however, be increased retrospectively by the Home Secretary, in the absence of exceptional circumstances.[240] Once the tariff period has been completed the Home Secretary will consider fixing further periods of imprisonment to reflect the risk to the public and to maintain the public's confidence in the criminal justice system. However, his discretion is not limited by the principle that an offender's detention should correspond with the crime he committed and not the risk of future non-violent offences; and the Secretary of State is entitled to make decisions concerning mandatory life prisoners by considering broader public issues than those relevant to releasing discretionary life prisoners.[241]

When a young person is sentenced to detention for life 'at Her Majesty's pleasure'[242] the Home Secretary is under a duty to decide from time to time, whether the detention is still justified. As a result, it is unlawful for the Home Secretary to adopt a policy which treats as irrelevant the progress and development of the child.[243] However, as the sentence does contain a punitive element, the Home Secretary has a discretion to set a provisional and reviewable tariff for a child given such a sentence. This tariff should generally be one half rather than two thirds of the appropriate determinate sentence.[244] **10.70**

(e) Detention of mental patients

Powers of detention. There are a number of powers of detention under English law in relation to 'a person who is or appears to be suffering from mental disorder'.[245] These powers are contained in the Mental Health Act 1983. The House of **10.71**

[236] This distinction was accepted by the European Court of Human Rights in *Wynne v United Kingdom* (1994) 19 EHRR 333.

[237] See *R v Secretary of State for the Home Department, ex p Doody* [1994] 1 AC 531, 559 A–D.

[238] *R v Secretary of State for the Home Department, ex p Hindley* [2000] 2 WLR 730, 735 *per* Lord Steyn approving the *dictum* of Lord Bingham CJ at [1998] QB 751, 769.

[239] Policy Statement, 27 Jul 1993.

[240] *Pierson v Home Secretary* [1998] AC 539.

[241] *R v Secretary of State for the Home Department, ex p Stafford* [1998] 3 WLR 372.

[242] Children and Young Persons Act 1993, s 53(2).

[243] *R v Secretary of State for the Home Department, ex p Venables* [1998] AC 407.

[244] *R v Secretary of State for the Home Department, ex p Furber* [1998] 1 All ER 23.

[245] 'Mental disorder' is defined in s 1(2) as mental illness, arrested or incomplete development of mind, psychopathic disorder and any other disorder or disability of mind.

Lords held in *R v Bournewood Community and Mental Health NHS Trust, ex p L*[246] that the Act recognised that those who were treated for mental disorder as in patients at a hospital fell into two categories: those who were compulsorily and formally admitted[247] and those who were informally admitted[248] either as consenting patients or as those who, without capacity to consent, did not object. The common law doctrine of necessity entitled the hospital to care for and treat compliant incapacitated patients.

10.72 The Mental Health Act is based on the principle that, whenever possible, patients should be admitted on an informal basis.[249] Once a patient is informally detained, there is a power to detain pending an application for compulsory admission.[250] The Mental Health Act provides for six powers of compulsory 'civil' admission.[251] They authorise admission:

- for assessment in cases of emergency;[252]
- for patients detained by the police in public places;[253]
- for patients detained under a warrant following an information on oath by a social worker;[254]
- for assessment in a hospital;[255]
- for treatment in a hospital;[256] and
- following reception into guardianship.[257]

10.73 There are also a number of powers of compulsory admission in relation to those charged with or convicted of criminal offences. A person found to be unfit to plead under section 4 of the Criminal Procedure (Insanity) Act 1964 may be detained for the purposes of the preparation of a psychiatric report[258] and subsequently for treatment.[259] A convicted person suffering from mental illness, psychopathic disorder, severe mental impairment or mental impairment may be made the subject of a number of different detention orders:

246 [1998] 3 WLR 107.
247 Under ss 2–5 of the 1983 Act.
248 Under s 131(1) of the 1983 Act.
249 See s 131.
250 s 5(2) and (4).
251 For a fuller treatment see eg A Eldergill, *Mental Health Review Tribunals Law and Practice* (Sweet & Maxwell, 1997) Chaps 4 and 6.
252 s 4.
253 s 136(1).
254 s 135(1).
255 s 2.
256 s 3.
257 s 7.
258 s 35.
259 s 36.

- an interim hospital order for 12 weeks, renewable for 28-day periods, up to a maximum of six months;[260]
- a hospital order for six months, renewable for a further six months and then for periods of one year at a time;[261]
- a guardianship order for six months, renewable for a further six months and then for periods of one year at a time;[262]
- a restriction order which is without limit of time or for a period fixed by the court.[263]

The restriction order is the most serious form of detention order. It can only be made by a Crown Court where a hospital order exists and, having regard to the nature of the offence, the antecedents of the offender and the risk of his committing further offences if set at large, restriction is necessary to protect the public from serious harm. A patient subject to a restriction order can only be discharged by the Home Secretary[264] or a Mental Health Review Tribunal.[265] A patient who is not restricted can be discharged by the hospital managers or the health authority.[266] Hospital managers are under a duty to give information to patients so that they understand which provisions of the Mental Health Act they are detained under and can identify their rights of application to Mental Health Review Tribunals.[267] **10.74**

Review of detention. Patients who have been admitted to hospital have statutory rights to apply to Mental Health Review Tribunals.[268] Where patients do not exercise their rights to apply to tribunals, the hospital managers are under a duty to refer their cases.[269] The tribunal has a power to discharge the patient if he is no longer suffering from mental disorder or his detention is no longer justified in the interests of his own health or safety or with a view to the protection of others.[270] **10.75**

Common law powers. At common law, there is a power to detain persons who are a danger to themselves or others insofar as this is shown to be necessary. Two conditions must be fulfilled: **10.76**

- there must be a 'necessity to act when it is not practicable to communicate with the assisted person';

[260] s 38.
[261] s 37.
[262] s 37.
[263] s 41.
[264] s 42.
[265] s 73.
[266] s 23.
[267] s 132.
[268] s 66(1).
[269] s 68.
[270] s 72. The law was amended following the decision of the European Court of Human Rights in *X v United Kingdom* (1981) 4 EHRR 188, para 61, that tribunals with advisory powers did not comply with Art 5(4) of the Convention; see para 10.164 below.

- 'the action taken must be such as a reasonable person would in all circumstances take, acting in the best interests of the assisted person'.[271]

It is now clear that this common law principle was not affected by the provisions of section 131 of the Mental Health Act 1983.[272]

(7) Compensation for unlawful detention

10.77 There is no general right to compensation which arises where a person is unlawfully detained. Damages are available where a person is falsely imprisoned[273] and where he was in custody as a result of being maliciously prosecuted;[274] but not if an individual was negligently prosecuted.[275]

10.78 Where a person is imprisoned by a court order, he will not be entitled to damages even if the order is subsequently quashed.[276] Those who are imprisoned under court orders which are made without jurisdiction have a right to compensation in only very limited circumstances. There is a long established common law rule that judges are immune from suit for their judicial acts.[277] If a judge of the Supreme Court (which can include judges of the Crown Court)[277a] makes an order without jurisdiction for the detention of a person, the judge will not be liable in damages so long as he has acted in good faith in the purported performance of his duties.[278] On the other hand, in *Re McC (A Minor)*[279] the House of Lords made it clear that *magistrates* would be liable in damages if they made detention orders without jurisdiction. The position was then reversed by statute.[280] Thus, a magistrate is not liable for any act or omission in the execution of his duty with respect to any matter within his jurisdiction and nor shall he be liable for any act or omission in the purported exercise of his duty with respect to a matter which is outside his jurisdiction unless it is proved that he acted in bad faith.

---

[271] See *Re F (Mental Patient: Sterilisation)* [1990] 2 AC 1, 75H; cf D Feldman, *Civil Liberties and Human Rights in England and Wales* (Clarendon Press, 1993),149–50.

[272] *R v Bournewood Community and Mental Health NHS Trust, ex p L* [1998] 3 WLR 107.

[273] See para 10.20ff above.

[274] See generally, R Clayton and H Tomlinson, *Civil Actions against the Police* (3rd edn, Sweet & Maxwell, 2001) Chap 8.

[275] *Elguzouli-Daf v Commissioner of Police of the Metropolis* [1995] QB 335; *Kumar v Metropolitan Police Commissioner*, 31 Jan 1995.

[276] See *R v Governor of Brockhill Prison, ex p Evans (No 2)* [1999] 2 WLR 103, 127 *per* Judge LJ.

[277] See generally, Feldman (n 271 above) 274–276; A Olowofoyeku, *Suing Judges: A Study of Judicial Immunity* (Clarendon Press, 1993) and 'State Liability for the Exercise of Judicial Power' [1998] PL 444.

[277a] The Crown Court is a superior court of record by virtue of the Supreme Court Act 1981, s 45(1); it seems that a Crown Court is a superior court when dealing with trials on indictment and an inferior court when acting on appeals from Magistrates: see *Sirros v Moore* [1975] QB 118, 143, 149; *Re McC* [1985] AC 528, 550.

[278] *Sirros v Moore* [1975] QB 118.

[279] [1985] AC 528.

[280] Justices of the Peace Act 1997, ss 51 and 52.

Furthermore, the Home Secretary has the power to award compensation for victims of a miscarriage of justice.[281] However, in *R v Secretary of State for the Home Department, ex p Chahal (No 2)*[282] the Divisional Court held that a decision to refuse compensation to a person detained on national security grounds whose deportation was held to be in breach of the European Convention[283] was not irrational. **10.79**

C. The Law Under the European Convention

(1) Introduction

Article 5 of the Convention provides: **10.80**

> (1) Everyone has the right to liberty and security of the person. No one shall be deprived of his liberty save in the following cases and in accordance with a procedure prescribed by law:
>
> (a) the lawful detention of a person after conviction by a competent court;
> (b) the lawful arrest or detention of a person for non-compliance with the lawful order of a court or in order to secure the fulfilment of any obligation prescribed by law;
> (c) the lawful arrest or detention of a person effected for the purpose of bringing him before the competent legal authority on reasonable suspicion of having committed an offence or when it is reasonably considered necessary to prevent his committing an offence or fleeing after having done so;
> (d) the detention of a minor by lawful order for the purpose of educational supervision or his lawful detention for the purpose of bringing him before the competent legal authority;
> (e) the lawful detention of persons for the prevention of the spreading of infectious diseases, of persons of unsound mind, alcoholics or drug addicts or vagrants;
> (f) the lawful arrest or detention of a person to prevent his effecting an unauthorised entry into the country or of a person against whom action is being taken with a view to deportation or extradition;
>
> (2) Everyone who is arrested shall be informed promptly, in a language which he understands, of the reasons for his arrest and of any charge against him.
>
> (3) Everyone arrested or detained in accordance with the provisions of paragraph 1(c) of this Article shall be brought promptly before a judge or other officer authorised by law to exercise judicial power and shall be entitled to trial within a reasonable time or to release pending trial. Release may be conditioned by guarantees to appear for trial.
>
> (4) Everyone who is deprived of his liberty by arrest or detention shall be entitled to take proceedings by which the lawfulness of his detention shall be decided speedily by a court and his release ordered if the detention is not lawful.

[281] See para 11.138ff below.
[282] *The Times*, 10 Nov 1999.
[283] *Chahal v United Kingdom* (1996) 23 EHRR 413; see generally, para 8.58 above.

(5) Everyone who has been the victim of arrest or detention in contravention of the provisions of this Article shall have an enforceable right to compensation.

10.81 This Article guarantees to the individual the right to liberty[284] and the security of the person, a right that is at the heart of all political systems that purport to abide by the rule of law.[285] The purpose of Article 5 is to protect the individual from arbitrary arrest and detention.[286] Article 5 enshrines the fundamental human right of protecting the individual against arbitrary interferences by the state with the right of liberty: as the Court emphasised in *Brogan v United Kingdom*[287] judicial control of such interferences is implied by the rule of law and is one of the fundamental principles of a democratic society. It proclaims the right of individual liberty, defines the range of situations in which the right might be curtailed, and lays down the essential conditions which must be observed if that power is to be controlled by law. It also provides a person in detention with a remedy by which he can challenge the legality of the detention and obtain compensation if it is not lawful.

10.82 The right to physical liberty is not absolute. It must give way where vital community interests are at stake. Accordingly, a person may be deprived of his or her liberty, but only if the exercise of powers of arrest and detention by state authorities is governed by due process of law and consistent with recognised standards. Issues concerning arrest and detention arise frequently and account for a large proportion of the jurisprudence in the Commission and the Court.[288] The emphasis in Article 5 on due process of law in relation to the deprivation of liberty overlaps with the more general and comprehensive protection for procedural due process granted by Article 6.[289] These provisions cannot be examined in isolation.

10.83 Article 5 relates only to the fact of detention; it has no application to the conditions in which a person is detained. Treatment of detainees is governed specifically by Article 3 which protects against 'torture or inhuman or degrading treatment or

[284] By 'liberty' is meant physical liberty: see *Engel and others v Netherlands (No 1)* (1976) 1 EHRR 647 para 58.

[285] See *Winterwerp v Netherlands* (1979) 2 EHRR 387 para 37.

[286] *Engel and others v Netherlands (No 1)* (1976) 1 EHRR 647 para 58; *Bozano v France* (1986) 9 EHRR 297 para 54.

[287] (1988) 11 EHRR 117 para 58.

[288] For statistics on the frequency and incidence of the invocation of Arts 5 and 6 of the European Convention to 1980, see S Trechsel, 'The Right to Liberty and Security of the Person—Article 5 of the European Convention on Human Rights in the Strasbourg Case Law' (1980) 1 HRLJ 88, 88.

[289] Especially Art 5(3): the right to be brought promptly before a judge and the right to trial within a reasonable period of time; and Art 6(1): the right of an accused person to a trial of his or her case within a reasonable time.

punishment'.[290] Article 5 applies to an arrest or detention by the State whether within its own territory or abroad.[291] If, however, a person is received in custody from a non-Convention country, he cannot claim breach of Article 5 even though the return is in contravention of the law of the returning country or of the Convention itself.[292]

(2) The substance of the guarantees

'Personal liberty' under the Convention means simply the freedom of physical movement of persons from one place to another.[293] The notion has not been extended to include the integrity of the person. **10.84**

At one time there was some uncertainty as to whether 'liberty and security' involved two autonomous concepts. However, the case law has not ascribed any separate meaning to 'security of the person' in Article 5.[294] This is to be understood in the context of physical liberty,[295] and does not refer to such matters as a right to social security[296] or the ability to submit a civil claim to a court.[297] The concept cannot, therefore, be extended to underpin civil and political rights.[298] The Court in *Bozano v France*[299] made it clear that it is the arbitrary deprivation of liberty (rather than prevention of physical attack or the adequacy of social welfare benefits) that is in issue under Article 5. Furthermore, Article 5 does not impose a positive obligation[300] on the state to provide physical protection against the threat to personal safety by private individuals.[301] As a result, Article 5 affords protection exclusively against deprivation of liberty and not against other interferences with the physical liberty of a person.[302] **10.85**

---

[290] See para 8.39ff above.

[291] *Cyprus v Turkey (First and Second Application)* (1976) 4 EHHR 482, EComm HR; *Freda v Italy* (1980) 21 DR 250, EComm HR.

[292] *Altmann v France* (1984) 37 DR 225, EComm HR; *Reinette v France* (1989) 63 DR 189, EComm HR; *Freda v Italy* (n 291 above).

[293] S Trechsel, 'The Right to Liberty and Security of the Person—Article 5 of the European Convention on Human Rights in the Strasbourg Case Law' (1980) 1 HRLJ 88; J Fawcett, *The Application of the European Convention on Human Rights* (2nd edn, Clarendon Press, 1987), 69.

[294] Save for the early Commission decision of *Kamma v Netherlands* (1974) 18 YB 300.

[295] *East African Asians v United Kingdom* (1981) 3 EHRR 76, 89, ECommHR.

[296] *X v Germany* (1972) 1 DR 288, EComm HR.

[297] *Dyer v United Kingdom* (1984) 39 DR 246, EComm HR.

[298] J Murdoch, 'Safeguarding the Liberty of the Person: Recent Strasbourg Jurisprudence' (1993) 42 ICLQ 494.

[299] (1986) 9 EHRR 297.

[300] See generally, para 6.97 above.

[301] *X v Ireland* (1973) 16 YB 388, EComm HR.

[302] *Engel and others v Netherlands (No 1)* (1976) 1 EHRR 647; *Winterwerp v Netherlands* (1979) 2 EHRR 387; *Guzzardi v Italy* (1980) 3 EHRR 333; *Bozano v France* (1986) 9 EHRR 297.

10.86 The deprivation of liberty can be distinguished from the 'control of movement'[303] or 'restriction of movement' which is governed by Article 2 of Protocol 4 to the Convention. This Article provides:

> (1) Everyone lawfully within the territory of as State shall, within that territory, have the right to liberty of movement and freedom to choose his residence.
> (2) Everyone shall be free to leave any country, including his own.
> (3) No restrictions shall be placed on the exercise of these rights other than such as are in accordance with law and necessary in a democratic society in the interests of national security or public safety, for the maintenance of public order, for the prevention of crime, for the protection of health or morals, or for the protection of the rights and freedoms of others.
> (4) The rights set forth in paragraph 1 may also be subject, in particular areas, to restrictions imposed in accordance with law and justified by the public interest in a democratic society.

The Article (which has not been enacted as a Convention right under the Human Rights Act) deals with freedom of movement within national territory. It may take the form of limitation of residence to a particular town or district, or prohibition of visits to or residence in certain places, or of journeys for certain purposes.[304] However, the dividing lines between the two provisions are by no means clear-cut; the distinction between deprivations of liberty and other restrictions of liberty is one of degree or intensity, and not one of nature or substance.[305] If personal liberty is freedom of movement, then arrest or detention is an 'extreme form' of the restriction upon freedom of movement generally protected by Article 2 of the Fourth Protocol to the Convention.[306]

10.87 Whether a deprivation of liberty has occurred in a particular case will depend on the individual situation of the person concerned as well as on the circumstances in which he has been placed. In *Guzzardi v Italy*[307] the Court held that

303 Control of movement contemplates the use of passports, systems of identity cards or papers, the registration of aliens or other controls which have an indirect effect on freedom of movement; such requirements will not generally be inconsistent with the rights and freedoms guaranteed in the Convention.

304 S Trechsel, 'The Right to Liberty and Security of the Person—Article 5 of the European Convention on Human Rights in the Strasbourg Case Law', (1980) 1 HRLJ 88, 92 argues that Art 5 does not protect against mere restrictions on the liberty of movement, on the basis that the Fourth Protocol to the Convention was added specifically to do just that, and would have been unnecessary if Art 5 had been considered to cover restrictions on the liberty of movement.

305 *Guzzardi v Italy* (1980) 3 EHRR 333 para 33; *Ashingdane v United Kingdom* (1985) 7 EHRR 528 para 19; but see Murdoch's suggestion that in *Ashingdane*, 'the Court held that confinement in an ordinary psychiatric hospital after detention in a secure establishment did not terminate detention since the patient's transfer merely substituted one regime for another, albeit one less harsh: the suggestion is that substance rather than intensity matters': J Murdoch, 'Safeguarding the Liberty of the Person: Recent Strasbourg Jurisprudence' (1993) 42 ICLQ 494, 495.

306 Cf the discussion in D Harris, M O'Boyle and C Warbrick, *Law of the European Convention on Human Rights* (Butterworths, 1995) 97–99.

307 (1980) 3 EHRR 333.

living on a 2.5 sq km portion of a small island amounted to 'deprivation of liberty' and gave some general guidance about whether restrictions upon freedom of movement are so serious as to fall within the scope of Article 5 (as opposed to the Fourth Protocol). The Court had regard to a whole range of criteria, including type, duration, effects and manner of implementation of the measure in question.[308]

As a result, very short periods of detention are deprivations of liberty where there has been close confinement or arrest by the police or other authorities.[309] Whether or not an individual is detained may depend on the intention of the state; in *X v Germany*[310] a young girl who was questioned for two hours without being arrested, placed in a cell or formally detained was not held in breach of Article 5. **10.88**

In determining whether a deprivation of liberty has occurred, the Court also considers the circumstances of the particular individual in question. The Court has held that a person in a mental hospital under a compulsory detention order who is in an open ward and could sometimes leave the hospital unaccompanied had been deprived his liberty.[311] On the other hand, in *Engel v Netherlands*,[312] restrictions on the liberty of movement of soldiers (such as the obligation to be present in barracks at stated times and during leisure, which would constitute a deprivation of liberty for civilians) were permitted because they were 'not beyond the exigencies of normal military service'. Similarly, in *Nielsen v Denmark*,[313] the Court found no deprivation of liberty when a 12-year old boy was admitted to a psychiatric ward at a state hospital against his will, but with the consent of his mother, the sole holder of parental rights. However, the fact that a person has surrendered to detention does not mean that there is no 'deprivation of liberty' under Article 5.[314] The Commission has taken the view that where a mentally handicapped person is subject to compulsory detention order but is provisionally released, he no longer has Article 5 rights;[315] and also that an individual who is prevented from leaving a particular area by a curfew or order has not been **10.89**

[308] *Guzzardi v Italy* (n 307 above) para 92, adopting the language of *Engel and others v Netherlands (No 1)* (1976) 1 EHRR 647 para 59; but see *Raimondo v Italy* (1994) 18 EHRR 237; person placed under police supervision including a curfew suffered only a 'restriction of liberty'.

[309] *X and Y v Sweden* (1976) 7 DR 123, EComm HR: detention for less than two hours for the purpose of deportation fell under Art 5; *X v Austria* (1979) 18 DR 154, EComm HR: restraint for the length of time required to carry out a blood test constituted a deprivation.

[310] (1981) 24 DR 158, EComm HR.

[311] *Ashingdale v United Kingdom* (1985) 7 EHRR 528 para 42.

[312] (1976) 1 EHRR 647.

[313] (1988) 11 EHRR 175.

[314] See *De Wilde, Ooms and Versyp v Belgium* (1971) 1 EHRR 373 para 36.

[315] *W v Sweden* (1988) 59 DR 158, EComm HR.

deprived of his liberty.[316] The state will be responsible for detention by third parties if public officials transfer a person into the custody of the third party knowing that the person was going to be detained.[316a]

(3) Permissible deprivation of liberty

(a) Introduction

10.90 The justifications for restricting liberty under Article 5 are given a narrow construction.[317] Deprivation of liberty is justifiable if three conditions are satisfied:

- where the procedure in question is prescribed by law;
- where detention can be justified on a substantive legal basis; and
- where one of the specific grounds set out in Article 5(1)(a) to (f) is met.

The second sentence in Article 5(1) which reads: 'No one shall be deprived of his liberty save in the following cases and in accordance with a procedure prescribed by law' sets out the requirement of procedural legality for all the following sub-paragraphs. In addition, each of the justifications in sub-paragraphs (a) through (f) in addition requires that the detention be in substance 'lawful'.

(b) 'In accordance with a procedure prescribed by law'.

10.91 The notion of a 'procedure prescribed by law' is not limited to judicial process. It also covers administrative action and includes rules governing the making of arrests[318] as well as procedures followed by a court when ordering detention.[319] In *Winterwerp v Netherlands*[320] the Court said that 'procedure prescribed by law' means that the procedure followed must not be 'arbitrary', and must conform to municipal law and the Convention. It does not, however, extend to the conditions of the detention itself or (subject to Article 5(3)), its duration.

(c) Substantive law of detention

10.92 Under Article 5(1)(a) to (f) the state must show that the detention is lawful on substantive and procedural grounds and that it is not arbitrary. The two requirements are complementary; and in practice, the Court sometimes merges the two, asking only whether a deprivation has been 'lawful'. In relation to Article 5(1)(f),

[316] *Greek case* (1969) 12 YB 1.
[316a] *Riera Blume v Spain*, Judgment of 14 Oct 1999 (police transferring 'cult' members to their families for 'deprogramming' were responsible for subsequent detention).
[317] *Winterwerp v Netherlands* (1979) 2 EHRR 387 paras 37; *Guzzardi v Italy* (1980) 3 EHRR 333 paras 98 and 100; *Quinn v France* (1995) 21 EHRR 529 para 42.
[318] *Fox, Campbell and Hartley v United Kingdom* (1990) 13 EHRR 157.
[319] *Van der Leer v Netherlands* (1990) 12 EHRR 567.
[320] (1979) 2 EHRR 387 para 45.

the Commission has suggested that 'lawfulness' also requires that the domestic law supporting the detention must be 'accessible and foreseeable' in its application.[321] It is a matter for the national courts to determine whether a deprivation of liberty has occurred.[322]

The second requirement, that the deprivation not be arbitrary, means that it must conform with the purpose of the particular sub-paragraph concerned, and with Article 5 generally.[323] With respect to some, but not all sub-paragraphs of Article 5(1), a detention will also be arbitrary if, even though it is properly motivated, it is not proportionate[324] to the sub-paragraph's purpose.[325] The different treatment of the various sub-paragraphs appears to reflect different approaches of the Commission and the Court. The application of the arbitrariness prohibition to an Article 5 deprivation of liberty is similar to that applied in assessing whether limitations on freedoms under Articles 8 to 11 are 'necessary in a democratic society'.[326] **10.93**

Article 5(1)(a): Detention after conviction. Article 5(1)(a) permits deprivation of liberty which is in accordance with a procedure prescribed by law[327] where a person has been lawfully detained after conviction by a competent court. In order to be lawful, the detention must comply with municipal law and the Convention and must not be arbitrary. Because 'lawfulness' is a condition of 'detention', but not of 'conviction' under Article 5(1)(a), it has been held that the Article does not permit the Commission or Court to review the legality of a conviction[328] or sentence[329] imposed by a national court.[330] Where a conviction or sentence is overturned on appeal, detention will not be rendered retroactively 'unlawful'.[331] If detention is not to be arbitrary, its purpose must be the execution of the sentence **10.94**

[321] *Zamir v United Kingdom* (1983) 40 DR 42, EComm HR; there is no apparent contextual reason why this requirement should not be applied to all sub-paras of Art 5(1); for a discussion of the requirement that the law must be accessible and foreseeable in order to be prescribed by law, see para 10.91 above and see generally, para 6.126ff above.

[322] *Winterwerp v Netherlands* (1979) 2 EHRR 387; *Bozano v France* (1986) 9 EHRR 297.

[323] *Winterwerp v Netherlands* (n 322 above) para 39; *Bouamar v Belgium* (1988) 11 EHRR 1 para 50; in *Bozano v France* (1986) 9 EHRR 297 detention ostensibly for the purpose of deportation allowed under Art 5(1)(f), but in fact an illegal extradition, was 'arbitrary'.

[324] See generally, para 6.40 above.

[325] *Winterwerp v Netherlands* (n 322 above) in relation to Art 5(1)(e).

[326] J Murdoch, 'Safeguarding the Liberty of the Person: Recent Strasbourg Jurisprudence' (1993) 2 ICLQ 494, 499; see generally, para 6.146ff above.

[327] See para 10.91 above and see generally, para 6.126ff above.

[328] *Krzycki v Germany* (1978) 13 DR 57, EComm HR.

[329] *Weeks v United Kingdom* (1987) 10 EHRR 293 para 26: the length and appropriateness of the sentence of life imprisonment in that case was reviewed under Art 3 and not Art 5.

[330] It has been suggested that the better approach would be for the Court to assert the power to review decisions of the municipal courts, while holding to its usual policy of doing so only where clear cases of illegality have occurred: D Harris, M O'Boyle and C Warbrick, *Law of the European Convention on Human Rights* (Butterworths, 1995) 107.

[331] *Krzycki v Germany* (1978) 13 DR 57, EComm HR.

imposed by the court.[332] However, where a domestic court blatantly ignores domestic law, a conviction may be regarded as having no basis in domestic law and will be arbitrary.[333]

10.95 Under Article 5(1)(a) 'conviction' means a finding of guilt, and therefore it does not justify detention that is used merely as a preventive or security measure.[334] It does, however, include situations where the sentence following conviction requires treatment in a mental institution rather than imprisonment.[335] Detention under Article 5(1)(a) is justified following a conviction at a trial. It applies to detention pending a decision by an appeal court.[336] Article 5(1)(c), which governs detention on remand, only applies before a conviction.[337] A conviction for the purposes of Article 5(1)(a) includes one imposed by a foreign court[338] (even if the state concerned is not a party to the European Convention) unless the conviction resulted from a flagrant denial of justice.[339]

10.96 The element in Article 5(1)(a) that has caused the greatest difficulty is the requirement that the detention must be 'after' a conviction. This implies more than a chronological link: there must be a causal connection between the detention and the conviction. This is clear cut where the sentence is a term of imprisonment imposed on a person after conviction. However, it is less straightforward where an indeterminate sentence is imposed: a term of imprisonment followed by a possible further term of detention at the discretion of an administrative body. Article 5 will apply to the administrative decision if it has a sufficiently close connection with the original court sentence.[340] Thus, in *Weeks v United Kingdom*[341] the Court held that the connection between the recall of a prisoner given a discretionary life sentence and the original sentence had not been broken; the intention of the Home Secretary in recalling the applicant was consistent with the original purpose of social protection and rehabilitation of the offender and was justifiably based on the aggressive behaviour of the applicant.

---

[332] Detention pending extradition to another state to serve a sentence in prison following escape was not rendered arbitrary where that period of detention was not taken into account in the sentence: *C v United Kingdom* (1985) 43 DR 177, EComm HR.

[333] *Tsirlis and Kouloumpas v Greece* (1997) 25 EHRR 198.

[334] *Guzzardi v Italy* (1980) 3 EHRR 333.

[335] In regard to psychiatric patients, there may be some overlap between the application of subsections (a) and (e) of Art 5(1): (e) applies to the detention of a mentally ill person, whether or not he or she has been convicted of an offence.

[336] *Wemhoff v Germany* (1968) 1 EHRR 55 para 23.

[337] A conviction exists even though the judgment supplying reasons for it has not yet been delivered: *Crociani v Italy* (1981) 22 DR 147, EComm HR.

[338] *X v Germany* (1963) 6 YB 494, 516, EComm HR.

[339] *Drozd and Janousek v France and Spain* (1992) 14 EHRR 745 para 110.

[340] *Van Droogenbroeck v Belgium* (1982) 4 EHRR 443.

[341] (1987) 10 EHRR 293.

Causation was also an issue in *Monnell and Morris v United Kingdom*[342] where the Court held that the statutory power of the Court of Appeal to order that detention prior to an appeal should not count towards sentence was intended to prevent abuse of the right of appeal (an aim that could be pursued under Article 5(1)(a)) and that there was a sufficient causal connection between the convictions of the applicants and their detention, which was justifiable in the circumstances.[343] **10.97**

The conviction must be by a 'competent' court which has jurisdiction to try the case.[344] 'Court' is a term which appears frequently in the Convention[345] and requires consistent interpretation. It denotes 'bodies which exhibit not only common fundamental features, of which the most important is independence of the executive and of the parties to the case',[346] but also the guarantees of judicial procedure.[347] The forms of the procedure required by the Convention are not necessarily identical in each of the cases where the intervention of a court is required. The adequacy of the guarantees provided in proceedings can only be determined in the particular circumstances in which the proceeding takes place.[348] While it has been presumed that a 'guarantee of judicial procedure' under Article 5(1)(a) implies that the conviction must follow a fair trial within the conditions laid down by Article 6,[349] the procedural requirements under Article 5(1)(a) are not always co-extensive with those of Article 6.[350] Where they overlap, a breach of the right to a fair trial might also mean that detention is unjustified. However, the Court has upheld detention as a result of a foreign **10.98**

[342] (1987) 10 EHRR 205.

[343] It has been suggested that the decision of the Court is influenced by the fact that in many European countries party to the Convention, detention pending appeal is a continuation of detention on remand and the convicted person does not start to serve his sentence until the appeal proceedings are over. The disposition in *Monnell v Morris,* which was unusual for a United Kingdom court, was in conformity with the other European systems (see Harris, O'Boyle and Warbrick, (n 330 above) 109–110).

[344] *X v Austria* (1968) 11 YB 322, 348, EComm HR; *X v Austria* (1970) 13 YB 798, 804, EComm HR.

[345] 'Court' appears in Arts 2(1), 5(1)(a) and (b) and 5(4): (see para 10.149 below); the term 'tribunal' appears in Art 6(1).

[346] *Eggs v Switzerland* (1978) 15 DR 35, 62, EComm HR: the chief military prosecutor was not a court.

[347] *De Wilde, Ooms and Versyp v Belgium* (1971) 1 EHRR 373 para 78; *Engel and others v Netherlands (No 1)* (1976) 1 EHRR 647 para 68.

[348] *De Wilde, Ooms and Versyp v Belgium* n 347 above para 78; eg the criminal case of *Wemhoff v Germany* (1968) 1 EHRR 55 required a public hearing, while the same was not required of military disciplinary proceedings in *Engel and others v Netherlands (No 1)* (1976) 1 EHRR 647.

[349] R Beddard, *Human Rights and Europe* (3rd ed, Cambridge University Press, Grotius Publications) 134.

[350] Harris, O'Boyle and Warbrick (n 330 above) 111.

conviction even though it infringed Article 6 requirements where the state was not a party to the Convention.[351]

10.99 **Article 5(1)(b): Non-compliance with obligations.** Article 5(1)(b) permits deprivation of liberty which is in accordance with a procedure prescribed by law[352] for the lawful arrest or detention of a person for non-compliance with the lawful order of a court, or in order to secure the fulfilment of an obligation prescribed by law. It applies to arrest and detention *both* for offences of a criminal nature and for breaches of the civil law such as failure to comply with an injunction or contempt proceedings The first part of Article 5(1)(b) authorises the detention of a person who has failed to comply with a court order already made against him, while the second justifies detention where there is no order outstanding, to secure fulfilment of a 'specific and concrete obligation which he has until then failed to satisfy'.[353] In relation to both, the detention must be 'lawful' in that it must be consistent with municipal law and the Convention and must not be arbitrary.[354]

10.100 Detention on the ground of inability to pay money in compliance with an order for the enforcement of a contractual obligation is prohibited by Article 1 of the Fourth Protocol[355] but not by Article 5. However, because the justification of detention under Article 5(1)(b) is to secure fulfilment of an obligation, detention will not be justified where it constitutes punishment for the breach of the obligation,[356] nor where the detention occurs before the obligation arises.[357] It has been held that an order for the detention of a person who had not paid his Poll Tax was

[351] In the case of *Drozd and Janousek v France and Spain* (1992) 14 EHRR 745 the applicants, in accordance with a long tradition, served their sentence in a French prison after having been convicted by a court of Andorra. The majority of the Court (12 judges) said that even though the trial in Andorra had infringed Art 6 in more than one respect, the detention did not constitute a breach of Art 5(1)(a) because the parties to the Convention were not entitled to impose the standards of the Convention on non-contracting states; it found that the detention was justified unless the conviction in Andorra was a result of a 'flagrant denial of justice'. The 11 dissenting judges relied on an explanatory report to the European Convention on the International Validity of Criminal Judgments, 1970, which affirmed that it is a condition of the enforcement of foreign criminal judgments that the decision be rendered in accordance with Art 6 of the European Convention.

[352] See para 10.91 above and see generally, para 6.126ff above.

[353] *Engel and others v Netherlands (No 1)* (1976) 1 EHRR 647 para 69.

[354] In *K v Austria* (1993) Series A No 255-B, there was a breach of Art 5(1)(b) in regard to the imprisonment of the applicant for failure to comply with a court order requiring him to give evidence at trial, because the order offended his Art 10 right to freedom of expression.

[355] Art 1 of the Fourth Protocol has not been ratified by the United Kingdom or enacted as a Convention right under the Human Rights Act; for the jurisprudence in other jurisdictions see *Chinamora v Angwa Furnishers (Private) Ltd* (1997) 1 BHRC 460 and the cases there cited, see para 10.270 below.

[356] *Eggs v Switzerland* (1978) 15 DR 35, EComm HR; *Johansen v Norway* (1985) 44 DR 155, EComm HR.

[357] *Ciulla v Italy* (1989) 13 EHRR 346 para 36; but see the comment in relation to the *McVeigh* case (see para 10.102 below), which defines limited circumstances in which detention may be justified at the very point in time at which the obligation arises, in order to ensure its fulfilment.

in accordance with Article 5(1)(b) because the purpose of the detention was to 'secure the fulfilment' of his legal obligations.[358]

The following obligations have been held to be 'specific and concrete' enough to justify detention under the second branch of the sub-paragraph: an obligation to do military or substitute civilian service,[359] to carry an identity card and submit to an identity check,[360] to make a customs or tax return,[361] to live in a designated locality[362] and to 'keep the peace' under a bind over.[363] **10.101**

The Commission have held that a person can be detained for the purposes of enforcing an obligation under the general criminal law. In *McVeigh, O'Neill and Evans v United Kingdom*[364] the applicants were obliged to submit to 'further examination' upon entry into Great Britain from Ireland because of an order made under the Prevention of Terrorism Act.[365] It is difficult to see how this case can be reconciled with *Ireland v United Kingdom* in which a general requirement to submit to interrogation[366] was found to be contrary to Article 5(1)(b). The Court said on that occasion that in certain limited circumstances Article 5(1)(b) will apply to justify short-term detention, even though there has been no prior non-compliance with an obligation, where it is necessary to make the execution of an obligation effective at the time that it arises. It was held that: **10.102**

> In considering whether such circumstances exist, account must be taken . . . of the nature of the obligation. It is necessary to consider whether its fulfilment is a matter of immediate necessity and whether the circumstances are such that no other means of securing fulfilment is reasonably practicable. A balance must be drawn between the importance in a democratic society of securing the immediate fulfilment of the obligation in question, and the importance of the right to liberty. The duration of the period of detention is also a relevant factor in drawing such a balance.

It has been held that Article 5(1)(b) did not justify detention where the obligation imposed on a mafia suspect was a general admonition to change his behaviour.[367] Furthermore, this provision does not justify deprivation of liberty for non-compliance **10.103**

[358] See *Benham v United Kingdom* (1996) 22 EHRR 293.

[359] *Johansen v Norway* (1985) 44 DR 155, EComm HR; presumably, any work that may be required of a person under Art 4(3) of the Convention qualifies.

[360] *Reyntjens (Filip) v Belgium* (Application 16810/90) (1992) unreported, EComm HR; *B v France* (1987) 52 DR 111, EComm HR.

[361] *McVeigh, O'Neill and Evans v United Kingdom* (1981) 25 DR 15, EComm HR.

[362] *Ciulla v Italy* (1989) 13 EHRR 346 para 36.

[363] *Steel v United Kingdom* (1998) 28 EHRR 603.

[364] *McVeigh, O'Neill and Evans v United Kingdom* (1981) 25 DR 15, EComm HR.

[365] Prevention of Terrorism (Supplemental Temporary Provisions) Order 1976.

[366] Ibid reg 10, pursuant to the Civil Authorities (Special Powers) Act (NI) 1922.

[367] *Ciulla v Italy*, n 362 above.

with the general obligation to abide by the law[368] or preventive detention imposed in an emergency situation.[369]

10.104 **Article 5(1)(c): arrest on suspicion of criminal offence.** Article 5(1)(c) permits deprivation of liberty which is in accordance with a procedure prescribed by law[370] for the lawful arrest or detention for bringing a person before a competent legal authority on reasonable suspicion of having committed a criminal offence or when it is reasonably considered necessary to prevent him from committing an offence or fleeing having done so. In other words, Article 5(1)(c) contemplates pre-trial detention[371] or 'detention on remand'. It permits the lawful arrest or detention of a person for the purpose of bringing him before the competent legal authority in three sets of circumstances:

- where there is reasonable suspicion that he has committed an offence;
- when it is reasonably considered necessary to prevent his committing an offence, or
- when it is reasonably considered necessary to prevent his fleeing after having committed an offence.

10.105 This provision, read in conjunction with Articles 5(3)[372] and 6,[373] is part of an overall scheme for the investigation and prosecution of a person for a criminal offence, and is clearly limited to the arrest or detention of persons for the purpose of enforcing the criminal law.[374] The interpretation of these Articles is difficult both because of unclear wording of Article 5(1)(c) and (3) and because of the differences between the systems of criminal procedure in common law and civil law jurisdictions in Europe: the Court has to balance the need for a common European standard of procedure against respect for national approaches.

10.106 Arrest or detention of a person under Article 5(1)(c) is justified if it is 'lawful'[375] and is effected for the purpose of bringing him before a 'competent legal

[368] The possibility would be inconsistent with the rule of law: *Engel and others v Netherlands (No 1)* (1976) 1 EHRR 647 para 69.

[369] *Lawless v Ireland (No 3)* (1961) 1 EHRR 15 para 51; *Guzzardi v Italy* (1980) 3 EHRR 333 para 101.

[370] See para 10.91 above and see generally, para 6.126ff above.

[371] See S Grosz, A McNulty and P Duffy, 'Pre-Trial Detention in Western Europe', (1979) 23 International Commission of Jurists Rev 35; D Harris, 'Recent Cases on Pre-Trial Detention and Delay in Criminal Proceedings in the European Court of Human Rights' (1970) 44 BYIL 87.

[372] Art 5(3), which sets out the rights of persons detained on remand is closely connected with Art 5(1)(a) and is the source of most of the case law generated on the subject.

[373] Art 6 establishes the right to a fair trial, see Chap 11, below.

[374] In *Ciulla v Italy* (1989) 13 EHRR 346 the Court said that the detention for the purpose of bringing a suspected offender before a competent legal authority in order to obtain a compulsory residence order was contrary to Art 5(1)(a) because it could not lead to conviction for a criminal offence.

[375] The detention must be lawful under applicable municipal law, in conformity with the Convention, and must not be arbitrary; it must be consistent with the purpose of Art 5(1)(c).

authority'.[376] Provided that there are reasonable grounds for suspecting that an offence has or will be committed, a person may be arrested in good faith for questioning in order to obtain evidence, even though the detention does not result in that evidence being obtained or in charges.[377]

'Offence', which means an offence under criminal law,[378] has an automonous meaning;[379] it includes military criminal proceedings (but not necessarily disciplinary or regulatory action),[380] prosecution for failing to pay poll tax[381] and breach of the peace.[382] Thus, Article 5(1)(c) does not create a general power of preventative detention.[383] It has been suggested that there is a need to define the limits of the seriousness of the offence which might justify detention, and that this could be accomplished through interpretation of either of the terms 'lawful' or 'offence';[384] but, so far, no such guidelines are to be found in the jurisprudence. In *Brogan v United Kingdom*[385] the term 'offence' was interpreted in connection with a statutory power to arrest any person concerned with the 'commission, preparation or instigation of acts of terrorism'. Even though such involvement was not itself a criminal offence, the concept of terrorism, defined as 'the use of violence for political ends', was considered to be well in keeping with the idea of an 'offence'[386] and, in light of the fact that upon arrest the applicants had been immediately questioned about specific offences of which they were suspected, the power of arrest was held to be justified. **10.107**

The scope of the second and third grounds for detention under Article 5(1)(c) is unclear. The second ground (permitting an arrest when it is considered necessary to prevent committing an offence) could be read as permitting a preventive detention. However, this interpretation was rejected in *Lawless v Ireland*[387] on the basis that it would lead to 'conclusions repugnant to the fundamental principles of the Convention'. In that case, the internment[388] of a suspected IRA activist **10.108**

---

376 The meaning of this term is the same as that of 'judge or other officer authorised to exercise judicial power' in Art 5(3): *Schiesser v Switzerland* (1979) 2 EHRR 417 para 29.

377 *Brogan v United Kingdom* (1988) 11 EHRR 117; *Murray v United Kingdom* (1994) 19 EHRR 193.

378 *Ciulla v Italy* (1989) 13 EHRR 346 (detention motivated by the fear that the applicant might 'avoid possible security measures' not within Art 5(1)(c)).

379 See generally, para 6.17 above and see also para 11.174ff below.

380 *De Jong, Baljet and Van Der Brink v Netherlands* (1984) 8 EHRR 20; disciplinary proceedings, while they do not normally do so, may commence with an arrest, and result in convictions.

381 *Benham v United Kingdom* (1996) 22 EHRR 293 para 56.

382 *Steel v United Kingdom* (1998) 28 EHRR 603.

383 *Lawless v Ireland (No 3)* (1961) 1 EHRR 15 para 14.

384 D Harris, M O'Boyle and C Warbrick, *Law of the European Convention on Human Rights* (Butterworths, 1995) 116.

385 (1988) 11 EHRR 117.

386 Ibid para 51; cf *Ireland v United Kingdom* (1978) 2 EHRR 25 para 196.

387 *Lawless v Ireland (No 3)* (1961) 1 EHRR 15.

388 The statutory power concerned permitted internment of persons 'engaged in activities . . . prejudicial to the . . . security of the state'.

could not be justified as detention 'to prevent the commission of an offence' because it was not effected with the purpose of initiating a criminal prosecution.[389] As a result of the judgment and the fact that in English law an attempt to carry out an offence is in itself an offence, there seems to be no *separate* scope for the second ground of detention: because an arrest could be effected on the first ground of Article 5(1)(c).[389a] The third ground, which contemplates that the fleeing suspect has committed an offence, also appears to be redundant.

10.109 *'Reasonable suspicion'*: The overlap of the three grounds for detention means that only the first ground has been considered in detail. The requirement of reasonable suspicion is an essential safeguard against arbitrary arrest and detention.[390] There can be a 'reasonable suspicion' that an individual has committed an offence, whether or not it can be shown that an offence has been committed at all, or if it has, that the arrested person has committed it.[391] A reasonable suspicion will be present if there are 'facts or information that would satisfy an objective observer that the person concerned may have committed the offence'.[392]

10.110 What is 'reasonable' depends on all of the circumstances[393] known at the time of the arrest.[394] A confession might give rise to a reasonable suspicion,[395] and the fact that the case involves the investigation of terrorist activities will affect how much information is reasonably required by police before an arrest is made. In *Fox, Campbell and Hartley v United Kingdom*[396] suspected terrorists were detained under a statutory police power providing for arrest on a subjective basis,[397] of anyone that the officer suspected of being a terrorist. The issue before the Court was not whether the legislation itself breached the Convention, but whether there was sufficient evidence to amount to a 'reasonable suspicion' in accordance with Article 5(1)(c). The Court concluded that there was not.[398] However, in another terrorism case, *Murray v United Kingdom*[399] it was held that there was enough evidence to satisfy the 'reasonable suspicion' test. Similarly, in *K-F v Germany*[400] the applicants had been arrested on suspicion of fraud after their landlady had

[389] Cf *Ireland v United Kingdom* (1978) 2 EHRR 25 and *Guzzardi v Italy* (1980) 3 EHRR 333.
[389a] Cf *Eriksen v Norway* (2000) 29 EHRR 328.
[390] *Fox, Campbell and Hartley v United Kingdom* (1990) 13 EHRR 157, para 32.
[391] *X v Austria* (1987) 11 EHRR 112, EComm HR.
[392] *Fox, Campbell and Hartley v United Kingdom* n 390, above para 32.
[393] Ibid.
[394] *Nielsen v Denmark* (1961) 1 DR 388, EComm HR.
[395] *Vampel v Austria* (1970) 38 CD 58, EComm HR.
[396] n 390 above.
[397] The House of Lords had held that the words 'any person whom he suspects of being a terrorist' incorporated a subjective test, so that the arrest was acceptable if the police officer had only an 'honestly held', as opposed to a 'reasonable', suspicion.
[398] See also *Loukanov v Bulgaria* (1997) 24 EHRR 121.
[399] (1994) 19 EHRR 193.
[400] (1997) 26 EHRR 390.

informed the police that they were about to make off without paying rent which was due. Police inquiries revealed that their address was a post office box and that one of the applicants had previously been under investigation for fraud. This was held to be sufficient for 'reasonable suspicion'.[401]

Article 5(1)(d): Detention of minors. Article 5(1)(d) permits deprivation of liberty which is in accordance with a procedure prescribed by law[402] for minors. A minor can be detained either by lawful order for the purpose of educational supervision, or for the purpose of bringing him before the competent legal authority. The autonomous[403] Convention meaning of 'minor' is anyone under the age of 18.[404] As elsewhere in Article 5(1), the detention on either ground must be 'lawful'.[405] **10.111**

The most important case in relation to detention for educational supervision is *Bouamar v Belgium.*[406] In that case a seriously disturbed and delinquent 16-year-old was detained in a remand prison for periods totalling 119 days because the only reformatories available were either unwilling to take him or had inappropriate facilities. The Court accepted that, in principle, a minor may be held briefly in a remand prison as a preliminary to his transfer 'speedily' to a reformatory for the purpose of educational supervision; but held that, on the facts, the prison detention was too long and not for the permitted purpose. The Court took the view that the state was required to provide the appropriate educational facilities[407] to comply with Article 5(1)(d), regardless of the cost. **10.112**

The second ground for detention of a minor, to bring him before the competent legal authority, was not intended to duplicate Article 5(1)(c), under which a person may be detained on a criminal charge, but 'to secure his removal from harmful surroundings'.[408] Thus, it has been held that the detention of a minor accused of a crime for an eight-month period whilst a psychiatric report was being prepared did not breach Article 5(1)(d).[409] Detention pending the making of a court order placing a child in care was also justified under this provision.[410] **10.113**

[401] Ibid paras 57–62.
[402] See para 10.91 above and see generally, para 6.126ff above.
[403] *X v Switzerland* (1979) 18 DR 238, EComm HR.
[404] The Committee of Ministers of the Council of Europe recommended that member states reduce the age of majority to 18: CM Res (72) 29.
[405] For detention to be 'lawful' it must comply with municipal law and the Convention and must be in keeping with the purpose of Art 5, to protect the individual from arbitrariness: see *Bouamar v Belgium* (1988) 11 EHRR 1 para 47.
[406] (1988) 11 EHRR 1.
[407] It is not clear exactly what facilities would be sufficiently comprehensive for the required educational regime, but it must be in a 'setting (open or closed) designed and with sufficient resources for the purpose': (1988) 11 EHRR 1 para 50.
[408] 3 *Travaux Préparatoires* 724.
[409] *X v Switzerland* (1979) 18 DR 238, EComm HR.
[410] *Bouamar v Belgium* (1988) 1 EHRR 1 para 46.

10.114 **Article 5(1)(e): Detention of persons in special circumstances.** Article 5(1)(e) permits deprivation of liberty which is in accordance with a procedure prescribed by law[411] for the lawful detention of persons for the prevention of the spreading of infectious diseases, of persons of unsound mind, alcoholics or drug addicts or vagrants. It has been said that the reason why the Convention allows the detention of persons in these categories is not only because they are considered as potentially dangerous for public safety but also because their own interests may necessitate their detention.[412] However, this is difficult to justify unless the person in question is mentally incompetent to make decisions on his own behalf. It is submitted that the only grounds on which an alcoholic, vagrant or person with an infectious disease should be deprived of his liberty is a breach of civil or criminal law, or to protect public safety. The provision has been applied in cases dealing with the detention of psychiatric patients[413] and vagrants[414] but there are no reported cases in which the terms 'drug addicts', 'alcoholics' or 'infectious diseases' have been considered.

10.115 Vagrants are 'persons who have no fixed abode, no means of subsistence and no regular trade or profession'. This is the definition found in the Belgian Criminal Code and applied by the Court in *The Vagrancy Cases*.[415] The Court has rejected the argument that suspected mafia members who had no identifiable sources of income were vagrants.[416]

10.116 'Persons of unsound mind' is not capable of a definitive interpretation because of the lack of clear boundaries to mental illness; but it is clear that detention under Article 5(1)(e) cannot be justified 'simply because his views or behaviour deviate from the norms prevailing in a particular society'.[417] Reference to the relevant municipal law and its application to the case in light of the current psychiatric knowledge are the only other guidelines that have been provided by the Court.[418]

10.117 As in the other subsections of Article 5(1), the detention must be 'lawful'. In other words, it must conform to municipal law (both on substantive and procedural grounds), and with the Convention, and must not be arbitrary. These criteria have been fleshed out in relation to detaining those who are mentally handicapped. The Court has found that the detention of a mentally ill woman without giving her a personal hearing in accordance with Dutch law was 'unlawful'.[419] However, the Court's primary focus has been on the development of the concept of

---

[411] See para 10.91 above and see generally, para 6.126ff above.
[412] *Guzzardi v Italy* (1980) 3 EHRR 333 para 98.
[413] *Winterwerp v Netherlands* (1979) 2 EHRR 387.
[414] *De Wilde, Ooms and Versyp v Belgium* (1971) 1 EHRR 373 ('the Vagrancy Cases').
[415] Ibid.
[416] *Guzzardi v Italy* (1980) 3 EHRR 333 para 98.
[417] *Winterwerp v Netherlands* (1979) 2 EHRR 387 para 37.
[418] Ibid para 38.
[419] *Van der Leer v Netherlands* (1990) 12 EHRR 567.

arbitrariness. In *Winterwerp v Netherlands*[420] the Court held that 'arbitrary' detention arises where a person is detained in breach of the restrictions permitted by Article 5(1)(e) or where the detention is unwarranted on the facts of the case. The Court went on to identify three minimum conditions for detaining the mentally handicapped:

- there must be reliable medical evidence of a mental disorder;
- the mental disorder must be of a kind or degree warranting compulsory confinement; and,
- the mental condition must persist throughout the period of confinement.[421]

The first requirement, that there be reliable medical evidence of a disorder, may be dispensed with in case of an emergency, if it is impractical. In *Winterwerp*, the Court had to consider the decision of an authority to commit the applicant to a psychiatric hospital when he was found lying naked in a police cell after an arrest for theft. The applicant was detained on the emergency basis for six weeks before there was even provisional confirmation by a psychiatrist of the need for detention. However, there was eventually a diagnosis of mental illness; and the complaint was dismissed. Detention without medical confirmation of mental disorder was again held to be lawful in an emergency situation in *X v United Kingdom*.[422] The authorities recalled the applicant, who had been out for three years on provisional release from his detention as a 'restricted patient offender' at Broadmoor special hospital. Even though he was re-arrested on an unconfirmed report by his wife that he was likely to be violent as a result of his mental state, the Court found the action appropriate under Article 5(1)(e) as an emergency case: an individual subject to restricted patient offender orders might be a person who has in the past been dangerous to the public on the basis of medical evidence. A rather different approach was taken in *Kay v United Kingdom*[423] where the applicant was convicted of manslaughter and made subject to a hospital order and restriction order. Following his release from hospital he was sentenced and imprisoned for other offences; while in prison his application for discharge of the hospital/restriction order was refused, even though he was found not to be suffering from any mental disorder. An application for judicial review of the decision was unsuccessful, as was his appeal to the Court of Appeal.[424] Immediately prior to his release from prison he was recalled to hospital, and a medical opinion that he was psychopathic was subsequently obtained. The Commission found the decision to recall the applicant without recourse to current medical information to be a violation of Article 5(1)(e). **10.118**

[420] (1979) 2 EHRR 387.
[421] (1979) 2 EHRR 387 para 39.
[422] (1981) 4 EHRR 188.
[423] (1998) 40 BMLR 20.
[424] *R v Merseyside Mental Health Review Tribunal, ex p K* [1990] 1 All ER 694.

10.119 The third *Winterwerp* principle requires that the patient be released upon cessation of mental illness. Although the lawfulness of continued confinement is dependent on a subsisting mental disorder, it is not unlawful for authorities to attach conditions to the release of the patient or to defer release pending location of suitable accommodation. However, where the conditions and difficulties in placement result in an indefinite deferral of release, the Court may find a breach of Article 5(1)(e).[425]

10.120 In general, the conditions in which the patient is detained and the availability of suitable treatment are not relevant to the question of lawfulness of the detention under Article 5(1)(e). But there will be an arbitrary and unlawful deprivation of liberty if the patient is not detained in a 'hospital, clinic or other appropriate institution' authorised for the detention of such persons.[426] Furthermore, the Court in *Winterwerp* found that the detention of mentally disordered persons under Article 5(1)(e) must be for the protection of the public or the individual, rejecting the argument that it implied a 'right to treatment' appropriate for the mental state of the person, during detention.[427]

10.121 **Article 5(1)(f): Detention pending deportation or extradition or to prevent unlawful entry.** Article 5(1)(f) permits deprivation of liberty which is in accordance with a procedure prescribed by law[428] for the lawful arrest or detention of a person to prevent his effecting an unauthorised entry into the country or of a person against whom action is being taken with a view to deportation or extradition. Most of the cases involve detention pending deportation or extradition of persons already in the contracting state, rather than illegal immigrants seeking to enter. Detention may be justified under Article 5(1)(f) on the basis of enquiries as to possible extradition.[429] Detention may also be justified even though the person in question is never, in fact, extradited or deported.[430]

10.122 As in other sub-paragraphs, Article 5(1)(f) requires that detention be 'lawful': it must comply with municipal law and not be arbitrary. The leading case on lawfulness is *Bozano v France*.[431] A French court refused to order the extradition of an

[425] See *Johnson v United Kingdom* (1999) 27 EHRR 296, where the absence of any means by which the Mental Health Review Tribunal could overcome the problems encountered in securing a hostel place, together with the lack of any procedure, other than at the annual reviews, by which the patient could challenge the condition of release (that he live in a hostel and receive psychiatric supervision), resulted in an indefinite deferral of his release.

[426] *Ashingdane v United Kingdom* (1985) 7 EHRR 528 para 44; *Aerts v Belgium* (1999) 5 BHRC 382 para 46.

[427] However, it is arguable that failure to provide medical treatment under Art 5(1)(e) could amount to 'inhuman treatment' under Art 3, see para 8.48 above.

[428] See para 10.91 above and see generally, para 6.126ff above.

[429] Enquiries constitute 'action', the term substituted for 'proceedings' because of the diversity of types of extradition and deportation proceedings: *X v Switzerland* (1980) 40 DR 42.

[430] *X v Germany* (1983) 5 EHRR 499, EComm HR.

[431] (1986) 9 EHRR 297.

Italian national who had been convicted *in absentia* of murder under Italian law; and the French government attempted to obtain the same result by a deportation order under which it forcefully delivered the applicant into Swiss police custody. The applicant was given no time to contest the order or opportunity to nominate a country of deportation. Shortly afterwards he was extradited by Switzerland following a request by Italy initiated prior to the applicant's deportation from France. The deportation order was subsequently declared invalid as an abuse of power under French law because it was a disguised form of extradition order. The Court found that the detention was unlawful on the ground that it did not comply with domestic law and that it was arbitrary.

The lawfulness of confining aliens who are seeking asylum depends on a number of factors. Although the state undoubtedly has the right to control the entry and residence of aliens in its territory, this right must be exercised in accordance with Article 5(1). Article 5(1)(f) authorises detention with a' view to deportation or extradition': but the wording does not create an obligation to show that detention is necessary to prevent an offence being committed or to prevent absconding.[432] The type, duration, effects and manner of implementation of the measures employed must be taken into account in determining whether an inevitable 'restriction' upon liberty is a 'deprivation' in violation of Article 5.[433] When four Somali asylum seekers with falsified passports were confined to a French hotel for 20 days before being deported to Syria, the Court reversed the decision of the Commission and found the detention to be a deprivation of liberty contrary to Article 5. The four applicants had been detained for 15 days before being permitted to contact a lawyer, to obtain legal aid and to bring an application before an 'urgent applications judge' for release from their confinement.[434] In *Chahal v United Kingdom*,[435] on the other hand, the Court decided that the view of the Secretary of State that national security considerations arose together with the limited way in which detention was reviewed (by the immigration advisory panel procedure) was sufficient to prevent detention from being arbitrary. 10.123

The inquiry under Article 5(1)(f) concerns the legal basis for the detention and whether the deprivation of liberty was arbitrary in its purpose. The Court will not go further and question the decision of the state, on the facts, to deport or 10.124

432 *Bozano v France* (1986) 9 EHRR 297 para 60.

433 *Amuur v France* (1996) 22 EHRR 533, citing *Guzzardi v Italy* (1980) 3 EHRR 333 as saying that the difference between deprivation of and restriction upon liberty is merely one of degree or intensity, and not one of nature or substance. Confinement of aliens, if prolonged excessively, will risk turning into a deprivation of liberty.

434 *Amuur v France* (n 433 above).

435 (1996) 23 EHRR 413 paras 113–117.

extradite.[436] However, this limited inquiry has been expanded by a requirement, either under the heading of non-arbitrariness[437] or as an addition to the lawfulness requirement,[438] that extradition or deportation proceedings be conducted with 'requisite diligence'.[439] Whether this condition has been met will be determined on the basis of the conduct of both the applicant and the authorities, the length of and delay in the proceedings being the pivotal issues. There is no absolute limit as to the time that proceedings may last; the test is one of diligence appropriate in the circumstances.[440]

10.125 In addition to the other elements necessary to the lawfulness of detention under Article 5(1)(f), the Court may also require that the law underpinning the detention for deportation or extradition purposes is accessible and foreseeable to the applicant (in the sense that the term 'law' has been interpreted in connection with 'prescribed by law'[441] in Article 10(2) of the Convention). The Commission applied this requirement in *Zamir v United Kingdom*,[442] but did not discuss it in *Bozano v France*.[443]

[436] In *Zamir v United Kingdom* (1983) 40 DR 42, EComm HR the Commission distinguished the cases such as *Winterwerp* (1979) 2 EHRR 387, concerning mentally disordered persons under Art 5(1)(e), in which the Court was prepared to examine the facts upon which the detention was based, from those under Art 5(1)(f), in which the Commission felt that it was precluded from doing so. The decision in *Bozano v France* (1986) 9 EHRR 297 is consistent with that view, in that the arbitrariness of the detention there was founded not on a review of the facts but of its purpose, which was (illegal) extradition rather than the purported deportation.

[437] Initially the 'requisite diligence' element was regarded as an element of the lawfulness requirement, and in particular, goes to the existence of proportionality, which is necessary if detention is not to be arbitrary: see *Lynas v Switzerland* (1976) 6 DR 141, EComm HR; the approach of the Commission in *Lynas* was endorsed by the Court in *Kolompar v Belgium* (1992) 16 EHRR 197; and referred to in connection with proportionality in *Caprino v United Kingdom* (1980) 22 DR 5, EComm HR.

[438] Subsequent cases appear to treat 'requisite diligence' as a separate, implied requirement.

[439] See *Lynas v Switzerland* (n 437 above) in relation to extradition; deportation cases include *X v United Kingdom* (1977) 12 DR 207, EComm HR and *Z v Netherlands* (1984) 38 DR 145, EComm HR; approved in *Quinn v France* (1995) 21 EHRR 529 para 19.

[440] See *X v Germany* (1983) 5 EHRR 499, EComm HR (22-months' detention during extradition proceedings was considered justifiable while the German government attempted with all diligence to obtain assurances from Turkey that the applicant would not receive the death penalty if extradited); cf *X v United Kingdom* (1977) 12 DR 207, EComm HR where 11-months' delay was attributable to need to obtain evidence and the applicant's own conduct; neither was there a breach of Art 5(1)(f) in *Kolompar v Belgium* (1992) 16 EHRR 197 when the applicant delayed or impliedly consented to prolongation of the proceedings for almost three years; in *Osman v United Kingdom* (Application 15933/89) (1991), unreported, EComm HR over five-years' detention was justified given the applicant's conduct and determination not to be extradited; in *Quinn v France* (1995) 21 EHRR 529 it was held that a period of one year six months was too long.

[441] For a general discussion of the doctrine of 'prescribed by law', see para 10.91 above and see generally, para 6.126ff above.

[442] (1983) 40 DR 42, EComm HR: on the basis of *Sunday Times v United Kingdom* (1979) 2 EHRR 245 the Court rejected the applicant's claim that he could not have reasonably foreseen the consequences, under United Kingdom immigration law, of failing to reveal upon entry into the country the fact that he was married.

[443] n 432, above.

(4) The rights of a person arrested or detained

(a) Introduction

Articles 5(2) and (4) allow any detained person, whether held on suspicion of criminal offence or otherwise, to challenge the deprivation of his liberty and, if successful, to obtain compensation for wrongful detention under Article 5(5). Article 5(2) provides for prompt notification of the reasons for the arrest and of any charge against him, in order that he might bring proceedings, under Article 5(4), to have the lawfulness of the detention decided quickly and his release secured if appropriate. **10.126**

(b) Information as to reasons for arrest (Article 5(2))

Article 5(2) provides that everyone who has been arrested has the right to be informed promptly, in a language which he understands, of the reasons for his arrest and of any charge against him. Article 5(2) is not restricted to criminal cases and applies to the compulsory detention of a mental patient.[444] If Article 5(2) is breached, the detention is unlawful regardless of whether it falls into one of the categories set out in Article 5(1). The rationale of the section comes from the theory underlying Article 5 itself: the liberty of the individual is guaranteed, subject only to encroachments on the basis of the law. A detainee must be given adequate information to discern both the fact of detention[445] and whether the conditions justifying the deprivation of liberty have been met: so that he might make a decision about challenging the detention in court. **10.127**

In criminal cases, Article 5(2) may overlap with both Article 5(4),[446] (to the extent that it also requires that a person be told 'promptly' of the reasons for his detention),[447] and with the requirement in Article 6(3)(a)[448] that an accused be informed promptly of the nature and cause of the accusation against him. Article 5(2) differs from 6(3)(a) in purpose: while Article 5(2) is intended to enable the detainee to challenge the lawfulness of the detention, Article 6 facilitates the preparation by the accused of his defence. **10.128**

The information must be communicated to the detainee in a language known to **10.129**

[444] The application of Art 5(2) is not restricted to criminal cases under Art 5(1)(c) by the wording 'and of any charge': see *Van der Leer v Netherlands* (1990) 12 EHRR 567. The obligation to give reasons arises not only where someone is initially detained but where he is recalled after conditional release, even if the legal basis of the detention has not changed: see *X v United Kingdom* (1981) 4 EHRR 188 para 66.

[445] In *Van der Leer v Netherlands* (n 444 above) the applicant discovered only by accident, 10 days after an order had been issued, that her status had been changed from a voluntary mental health patient to compulsory detainee.

[446] See para 10.145ff below.

[447] *X v United Kingdom* (1981) 4 EHRR 188: the Court applied Art 5(4) only.

[448] See para 11.241 below.

him;[449] and where the capacity of the individual to appreciate the notification is impaired (as, for example, in cases of minors or the mentally handicapped), the information must nevertheless be communicated to his representative, legal agent or guardian.

10.130 What is sufficient information is a matter for determination on the facts of each case. The detainee must be made aware of the legal and factual grounds for his arrest.[450] Article 5(2) does not require that any particular form of communication be used, such as a warrant or other documentation;[451] there need be no writing at all.[452] In cases arising under Article 5(1)(c), it is unnecessary to indicate all of the charges that might later be brought against an arrested person, so long as the information provided justifies the detention.[453] However, once a person has been charged, Article 6(3)(a)[454] then requires that he be informed in detail of the nature and cause of the accusation against him.

10.131 In *Fox, Campbell and Hartley v United Kingdom*,[455] suspected terrorists were initially given only minimal information[456] for the basis of detention. Nevertheless, the Court found that the requirements of Article 5(2) had been met because the factual basis for detention was inferred by the applicants from questions put to them during interrogations shortly after arrest. The case appears to indicate that Article 5(2) does not require the detainee to be expressly informed of the reasons for his arrest, as long as they can be inferred from the circumstances.[457] It is submitted that this is an unacceptable dilution of a basic guarantee.

10.132 The obligation to give information about the arrest or charge 'promptly' does not mean that the information must be given in its entirety immediately upon arrest.[458] The detained person must be informed of the legal and factual grounds for his arrest (whether at one time or over an interval) within a sufficient period following the arrest in order that Article 5(2) is complied with.[459] All the facts of the

[449] But note that in *Delcourt v Belgium* (1967) 10 YB 238, EComm HR even though a French-speaking person received a Dutch arrest warrant, Art 5(2) was not violated because the subsequent interrogations during which the reasons for detention were disclosed, were conducted in French.

[450] *Fox, Campbell and Hartley v United Kingdom* (1990) 13 EHRR 157 para 40.

[451] *X v Netherlands* (1966) 9 YB 474, EComm HR.

[452] *X v Netherlands* (1962) 5 YB 224, EComm HR.

[453] *X v United Kingdom* (1971) 14 YB 250, EComm HR; cf Art 6(3)(a) which requires that the information be more specific and detailed than that called for under Art 5(2) as a result of the nature of its purpose: *Nielsen v Denmark* (1959) 2 YB 412, EComm HR.

[454] See para 11.241 below.

[455] (1990) 13 EHRR 157.

[456] The applicants were informed only of the statutory provision under which they were being arrested.

[457] Contrast the position under s 28 of PACE, see para 10.42 above.

[458] Contrast the position under s 28, PACE, see para 10.42 above.

[459] *Fox, Campbell and Hartley v United Kingdom* (n 455 above).

particular case must be taken into account; and periods of seven hours,[460] 24 hours[461] and even two days[462] between arrest and information were acceptable. However, a delay of 10 days[463] was held to be a breach.

(c) Rights of those on remand

Scope of the rights. Article 5(3) is specifically concerned with persons arrested or detained in accordance with Article 5(1)(c),[464] in other words those who are detained for the purpose of being brought before a competent legal authority on reasonable suspicion of having committed an offence, or when it is reasonably considered necessary to prevent their committing an offence, or fleeing after having done so. Its purpose is to 'minimise the risk of arbitrariness' by providing judicial control over the executive's interference with the right to liberty[465] in the criminal process. Consequently, although reasonable suspicion must continue in order to justify detention under Article 5(1)(c), Article 5(3) requires in addition[466] that there be 'relevant and sufficient' public interest reasons to justify interfering with the liberty of a person presumed to be innocent.[467] In these cases, the detainee has two distinct rights: **10.133**

- he must be 'brought promptly before a judge or other officer authorised to exercise judicial power'; and
- he is 'entitled to trial within a reasonable time or to release pending trial' with the added caveat that 'release may be conditioned by guarantees to appear for trial'.

Right to be brought promptly before a judge. Article 5(3) requires the state to take the initiative[468] to ensure that the police bring an arrested person before a judge or judicial officer. The importance of this right arises from the objective and purpose of Article 5 itself: to protect the individual against arbitrary interferences by the state with his right to liberty.[469] The right to be brought promptly before a judge differs from the right to fair trial governed by Article 6[470] and from the right to challenge the lawfulness of detention under Article 5(4).[471] It emphasises the **10.134**

460 Ibid.
461 *X v Denmark* (1975) 1 Digest 457, EComm HR.
462 *Skoogstrom v Sweden* (1981) 1 Dig Supp para 5.2.2.1, EComm HR.
463 *Van der Leer v Netherlands* (1990) 12 EHRR 567.
464 See para 10.104ff above; the two provisions must be read together, see *Schiesser v Switzerland* (1979) 2 EHRR 417 para 29.
465 *Brogan v United Kingdom* (1988) 11 EHRR 117.
466 It appears that Art 5(1)(c) and (3) are to be read together and that the legal basis for detention does not shift entirely from Art 5(1)(c) to (3) once the latter applies, but the question has been left open by the Court: *Letellier v France* (1991) 14 EHRR 83.
467 *Stögmüller v Austria* (1969) 1 EHRR 155 and *Letellier v France* (1991) 14 EHRR 83.
468 *McGoff v Sweden* (1982) 31 DR 72, EComm HR.
469 *Bozano v France* (1986) 9 EHRR 297 para 54; *Brogan v United Kingdom* (1988) 11 EHHR 117 para 58; *Assenov v Bulgaria* (1999) 28 EHRR 652 para 146.
470 See para 11.150ff below.
471 See para 10.145ff below.

state's duty to have the accused's detention approved by a judge at an early stage, in order to avoid prolonged police detention. The judicial control of detention must be automatic: it cannot be made to depend on a previous application by the detained person.[471a] 'Judge or other judicial officer authorised by law' has the same meaning as 'competent legal authority' in Article 5(1)(c),[472] in other words that it is independent of the executive and is impartial[473] in relation to the parties.

10.135 'Promptness' has only a limited degree of flexibility attached to it.[474] In *Brogan v United Kingdom*[475] the Court said that:

> Whereas promptness is to be assessed in each case according to its special features, the significance to be attached to those features can never be taken to the point of impairing the very essence of the right guaranteed by Article 5(3).

The Court found that:

> the context of terrorism in Northern Ireland has the effect of prolonging the period during which the authorities may, without violating Article 5(3), keep a person suspected of serious terrorist offences in custody before taking him before a judge or other judicial officer.[476]

However, 'promptness' could not be stretched to a period of four days and six hours or more.[477]

10.136 This restrictive approach clearly contemplates that beyond a certain limited period of time the state must make an emergency derogation under Article 15.[478] In ordinary criminal cases 15 days detention is unacceptable;[479] but a delay of four days was acceptable.[480] It is arguable that the minimum period of detention prior to appearance ought to be even less. The Court in *Brogan* said that it was not deciding whether any given period, such as four days, would as a *general* rule be found compatible with Article 5(3).[481]

10.137 On its face, the right to 'trial within a reasonable time, or release pending trial' might be interpreted to mean that a state has the option of releasing an accused if

[471a] *T W v Malta* (1999) 29 EHRR 185 para 43.

[472] *Schiesser v Switzerland* (1979) 2 EHRR 417 para 29; and see 10.106 above.

[473] Impartiality of an officer involves an objective as well as a subjective element: *Huber v Switzerland* (1990) Series A No 188.

[474] *Brogan v United Kingdom* (1988) 11 EHRR 117 para 59.

[475] Ibid.

[476] Ibid para 60.

[477] Ibid para 62; the Commission has established, as a rule of thumb, that ordinarily the period should not be longer than four days: see *Brogan v United Kingdom* (Application 11209/84), 14 May 1987 para 103.

[478] As occurred in *Brannigan and McBride v United Kingdom* (1993) 17 EHRR 539; and see Human Rights Act 1998, ss 14, 15 and 16 and Sch 2.

[479] *Skoogström v Sweden* (1984) 7 EHRR 263.

[480] *X v Netherlands* (1966) 9 YB 564, EComm HR.

[481] *Brogan v United Kingdom* (1988) 11 EHRR 117 para 60.

it does not try him within a reasonable time. That construction has, however, been rejected; it violates the right to 'trial within a reasonable time' for *all* accused persons, whether detained or not, provided by Article 6(1).[482] In other words, Article 5(3) confers a right to trial within a reasonable time and a qualified right to bail.

Right to bail. Although Article 5(3) does not guarantee an absolute right to bail,[483] a person must be released pending trial unless the state can show that there are 'relevant and sufficient reasons' to justify his continued detention.[484] The Court has decided that there are five grounds on which bail may be refused: **10.138**

- the risk of the defendant absconding;
- the risk of the defendant interfering with the course of justice;
- preventing crime;
- preserving public order; and
- detention is necessary for the defendant's own protection.

However, the mere fact that there are reasonable grounds for suspecting that a person has committed an offence is not sufficient ground for justifying detention after a certain period of time. The courts must ensure that pre-trial detention does not exceed a reasonable time:

> To this end they must examine all the circumstances arguing for or against the existence of a requirement of public interest, justifying with due regard to the principle of the presumption of innocence, a departure from the rule of respect for individual liberty and set them out in their decisions on the application for release.[485]

The reason for refusing bail must not be 'abstract or stereotyped'.[485a]

Absconding. Most of the cases regarding bail concern the fear that the accused will abscond. The fear of absconding must be assessed by reference to a number of factors: **10.139**

> there must be a whole set of circumstances, particularly, the heavy sentence to be expected or the accused's particular distaste of detention, or the lack of well-established ties in the country, which give reason to suppose that the consequences and hazards of flight will seem to him to be a lesser evil than continued imprisonment.[486]

However, the severity of the sentence is the most important of the circumstances

---

[482] *Wemhoff v Germany* (1968) 1 EHRR 55 para 5 (the concern of the provision was to minimise the period of provisional detention of the accused rather than to avoid prolongation of the trial).

[483] *X v United Kingdom*, (Application 8097/77), unreported, EComm HR.

[484] *Wemhoff v Germany* (1968) 1 EHRR 55.

[485] *Letellier v France* (1991) 14 EHRR 83 para 35.

[485a] See *Yagci and Sargan v Turkey* (1995) 20 EHRR 505 para 52; *IA v France* 1998-VII RJD 2951 para 104.

[486] *Stögmüller v Austria* (1969) 1 EHRR 15 para 15; see *Letellier v France* (1991) 14 EHRR 83 para 43.

to be taken into account.[487] Where the penalty is expected to be imprisonment, its significance is reduced as the period of detention on remand increases: since this is to be included as part of the sentence.[488] Other factors include: the probable civil liability of the accused if convicted,[489] the threat of further proceedings,[490] the likelihood of absconding itself, the character of the accused, his morals, his home, his occupation, his assets, his family ties, all kinds of links with the country in which he is being prosecuted;[491] and indications that he has links with another country or that he is planning to escape.[492]

10.140 **Interfering with the course of justice and preventing crime.** Bail may also be refused where there is evidence[493] that release of the accused will result in interference with the course of justice[494] by his destruction of documents,[495] collusion with other possible suspects[496] or interference with witnesses.[497] In *Matznetter v Austria*[498] the Court suggested that in 'special circumstances' a person presumed innocent may still be detained in the belief that, if released, the accused will commit another serious offence of the kind with which he is already charged. The risk of committing another offence cannot, without more, be inferred from the fact that he has a criminal record.[498a]

10.141 **Preserving public order and protection of defendant.** The Court has recognised that in the interests of public order an accused may have to be refused bail.[499] The test propounded in *Letellier v France*[500] is whether municipal law recognises the ground and there is evidence that the accused's release 'will actually disturb public order'. The Court acknowledged that, in exceptional circumstances,

> by reason of their particular gravity and public reaction to them, certain offences may give rise to a social disturbance capable of justifying pre-trial detention, at least for a time.[501]

---

[487] Nevertheless, it cannot in itself form a separate basis for refusing bail: *Letellier v France* (1991) 14 EHRR 83 para 43.

[488] *Neumeister v Austria (No 1)* (1968) 1 EHRR 91.

[489] *Neumeister v Austria (No 1)* (n 488 above).

[490] *X v Switzerland* (1980) 21 DR 241, EComm HR.

[491] *Neumeister v Austria (No 1)* (n 488 above) para 10.

[492] *Matznetter v Austria* (1969) 1 EHRR 198.

[493] *Clooth v Belgium* (1991) 14 EHRR 717 para 44.

[494] *Wemhoff v Germany* (1968) 1 EHRR 55 para 25.

[495] Ibid.

[496] Ibid; see also *Clooth v Belgium* (n 493 above) paras 41–46.

[497] *Letellier v France* (1991) 14 EHRR 83.

[498] (1969) 1 EHRR 198 para 9; *Clooth v Belgium* (n 493 above) paras 38–40.

[498a] *Muller v France* 1997-II RJD 374 para 44.

[499] *Letellier v France* (n 497 above).

[500] Ibid.

[501] Threat to public order that justifies detention at the outset may cease with time: *Tomasi v France* (1992) 15 EHRR 1 para 91.

A defendant may also be detained before trial if such detention is necessary for his own protection, at least for a time.[501a] However, there can only be detention on this ground 'in exceptional circumstances having to do with the nature of the offences concerned, the conditions in which they were committed and the context in which they took place'.[501b]

Conditional bail. Article 5(3) states that release may be conditioned by guarantees to appear for trial. It has been held to be permissible to impose conditions such as surrendering travel and driving documents,[502] requiring a surety[503] and imposing a residence requirement.[504] Where a financial condition is imposed, the figure should be calculated by reference to the means of the accused or the person standing surety.[505] **10.142**

The right to a trial within a reasonable time. Even if continued detention is otherwise justified, Article 5(3) will be violated if the proceedings are not conducted expeditiously and with 'special' diligence.[506] This guarantee overlaps with that provided in Article 6(1)[507] in relation to all accused persons, whether detained or not. The strict standard of diligence will also be applied under Article 6(1).[508] In practice, wherever 'reasonable time' claims are made in relation to the period up to trial covered by Article 5(3),[509] they will only be considered under that position. **10.143**

The factors that are relevant when determining whether the trial has occurred within a reasonable time are the same as those under Article 6(1): the complexity of the case, the conduct of the accused and the efficiency of the national authorities.[510] There is no maximum length of pre-trial detention[511] as long as there remain 'relevant and sufficient circumstances'; the reasonableness of the length of proceedings depends on the facts of the case. In *Van der Tang v Spain*[512] a Dutch lorry driver was arrested in Spain in May 1989 with 1,300 kg of hashish and a pistol in his vehicle. His detention was ordered pending trial, but he was released on bail in July 1992; he breached his bail conditions and travelled to the Netherlands, **10.144**

[501a] *I A v France* (n 485a above) para 108.

[501b] Ibid.

[502] *Stögmüller v Austria* (1969) 1 EHHR 155 para 15.

[503] *Wemhoff v Germany* (1968) 1 EHRR 55.

[504] *Schmid v Austria* (1985) 44 DR 195, EComm HR.

[505] *Neumeister v Austria (No 1)* (1968) 1 EHRR 91 para 14.

[506] *Herczegfalvy v Austria* (1992) 15 EHRR 437 para 71.

[507] See para 11.219 below.

[508] The case of *Abdoella v Netherlands* (1992) 20 EHRR 585 overrules earlier statements by the Court that Art 5(3) imposed a stricter 'reasonable time' standard than Art 6 in detention cases.

[509] From arrest to decision by a trial court.

[510] See para 11.220 below.

[511] *W v Switzerland* (1993) 17 EHRR 60, rejecting the contrary view of the Commission and affirming the position established in 1968 in *Wemhoff v Germany* (1968) 1 EHRR 55 para 24.

[512] (1993) 22 EHRR 363.

failing to appear for the trial in Spain in 1993–94. At trial another individual was found to be the leading role in a nationwide drug operation and the applicant was cleared from involvement beyond transporting the goods. His application based on a breach of Article 5(3) was dismissed. Similarly, in *Contrada v Italy*[513] the Court held that detention for a period of two years and seven months to enable complex investigations to be carried out did not breach Article 5(3); the right of an accused person to have his case considered with particular expedition should not hinder the efforts of the courts to carry out their tasks with proper care. In *W v Switzerland*[514] a total of four and a half years pre-trial detention was considered acceptable because there were good grounds for refusing bail and the complexity of the case, rather than any delays attributable to the authorities, was the cause of the extended proceedings. However, Judge Pettiti dissented, suggesting that there ought to be an absolute limit to the length of proceedings and that strong evidence should be necessary to justify both refusing bail and extending proceedings for more than four years.

(d) Right to contest the lawfulness of detention (Article 5(4))

10.145 **Introduction.** Article 5(4) provides that:

> everyone who is deprived of his liberty by arrest or detention shall be entitled to take proceedings by which the lawfulness of his detention shall be decided speedily by a court and his release ordered if the detention is not lawful.

This is the 'habeas corpus' provision of the Convention, enabling a person in detention to test the validity of his detention and obtain his release if unlawful. It applies *whatever* the basis of the detention and whether or not it is justified under Article 5(1). This right must be available even though a detention is 'lawful' under the Convention.[515] However, once an infringement of one of the provisions has been found, the Court will not necessarily rule on compliance with Article 5(4).[516]

10.146 The question as to whether a person's right under Article 5(4) has been respected has to be determined in the light of the circumstances of each case.[517] The issues that have arisen under Article 5(4) have concerned: the nature of the review; the judicial character of the court and the procedural guarantees required of it; the time taken to obtain the remedy; and the continuing nature of the obligation.

[513] RJD 1998-V 2166.

[514] (1993) 17 EHRR 60.

[515] For example, in *De Wilde, Ooms and Versyp v Belgium* (1971) 1 EHRR 373 para 73, Art 5(4) was found to be infringed while Art 5(1) was not.

[516] *Van der Leer v Netherlands* (1990) 12 EHRR 567; *Koendjbiharie v Netherlands* (1990) 13 EHRR 820.

[517] See *RMD v Switzerland* (1997) 28 EHRR 224 para 42.

The nature of the review. The burden of proof lies on the state to show that detention is lawful.[518] The Court will not substitute its discretion for that of the decision-making authority; but must conduct a review which is wide enough to bear on all the conditions which are essential to the lawfulness of the detention.[519] **10.147**

The adequacy of habeas corpus and judicial review proceedings under Article 5(4) has been considered on a number of occasions. In *X v United Kingdom*[520] habeas corpus was inadequate because it did not enable a challenge on medical grounds to detaining an individual on mental health grounds. In *Weeks v United Kingdom*[521] it was held that the limited grounds of challenge in judicial review proceedings did not provide a sufficient means of testing the lawfulness of the recall of a discretionary life prisoner. In *Chahal v United Kingdom*[522] neither judicial review nor habeas corpus provided an adequate basis for challenging a deportation on national security grounds. On the other hand, in *Brogan v United Kingdom*[523] habeas corpus was sufficient to challenge detention under Article 5(1)(c); and in *Zamir v United Kingdom*[524] judicial review was sufficient to establish whether the applicant was an illegal immigrant under Article 5(1)(f) (where no national security issues arose). **10.148**

The 'court'. The detained person must have access to a 'court'. Thus, where the detention is the result of an administrative decision, its legality will require further review by a court. Where the detention was effected by the decision of a competent 'court', whether under Article 5(1)(a) or otherwise,[525] the necessary 'review procedures' are said to have been 'incorporated' in the trial procedures, and normally nothing further is required.[526] A 'court' need not be of the kind that is a part of the standard judicial machinery of the country;[527] but must be a body that has 'judicial character' and which provides 'guarantees of procedure appropriate to the kind of deprivation of liberty in question'.[528] **10.149**

To be of judicial character, a court must be 'independent both of the executive and the parties to the case'[529] and be competent to take a legally binding decision **10.150**

[518] *Zamir v United Kingdom* (1983) 40 DR 42 para 58, EComm HR.
[519] *E v Norway* (1990) 17 EHRR 30 para 50.
[520] (1981) 4 EHRR 188 paras 58–61.
[521] (1987) 10 EHRR 293 para 69.
[522] (1996) 23 EHRR 413 para 130.
[523] (1988) 11 EHRR 117 para 65.
[524] (1983) 40 DR 42, EComm HR.
[525] See *Winterwerp v Netherlands* (1979) 2 EHRR 387.
[526] *De Wilde, Ooms and Versyp v Belgium* (1971) 1 EHRR 373 para 76; cf *Engel and others v Netherlands (No 1)* (1976) 1 EHRR 647 para 77; see also *Iribarne Pérez v France* (1995) 22 EHRR 153.
[527] *Weeks v United Kingdom* (1987) 10 EHRR 293 para 61.
[528] *De Wilde, Ooms and Versyp v Belgium* (n 526 above) para 76.
[529] Ibid para 77.

leading to the person's release.[530] Those held not to have such judicial character include: a public prosecutor,[531] the medical officer of a person of unsound mind[532] and a government minister.[533] The principle of independence was refined in *Weeks v United Kingdom*[534] to require impartiality of the court toward the parties, as well as independence from the executive. A parole board was found to be both independent of the executive and impartial as between the parties[535] but Article 5(4) was violated when a judge who made the decision to detain for non-payment of a fine was the same judge that had originally imposed the fine. In *Chahal v United Kingdom*[536] the Home Office advisory panel on national security cases failed to meet the requirements of a 'court' and resulted in the enactment of the Special Immigration Appeals Commission Act 1997. In *Hood v United Kingdom*[537] the Court took the view that a commanding officer who authorised detention prior to a court martial was not impartial for the purposes of Article 5(4).

10.151 **Procedural requirement.** A 'court' must provide guarantees of judicial procedure,[538] although their adequacy is to be assessed by reference to particular circumstances of the proceedings.[539] In general, the guarantees to be provided in cases of lengthy detention correspond to those in the criminal courts of Council of Europe member states,[540] or the equivalent of the guarantee of the right to a fair trial under Article 6 of the Convention.

10.152 It is not clear whether a detained person has a right to participate in the hearing and argue for his release. Minors[541] and persons of unsound mind[542] are entitled to an oral hearing and, where necessary, to be provided with some form of representation. The

530 In *X v United Kingdom* (1981) 4 EHRR 188 a mental health review tribunal did not qualify as a court because it could make only advisory recommendations to the Home Secretary for release of detainees; the English Parole Board in *Weeks v United Kingdom* (1987) 10 EHRR 293, on the other hand, qualified as a court insofar as it had statutory power to 'direct' the Home Secretary by its recommendations as to the release of recalled life sentence of life prisoners, but not with respect to other of its powers which did not result in binding recommendations.

531 *Winterwerp v Netherlands* (1979) 2 EHRR 387 para 64.

532 *X v United Kingdom* (n 530 above) para 61.

533 Ibid; see also *Keus v Netherlands* (1990) 13 EHRR 700.

534 (1987) 10 EHRR 293 para 61.

535 Ibid para 61; but see *Hussain and Singh v United Kingdom* (1996) 22 EHRR 1, in which a hearing before a Parole Board was found to be in contravention of Art 5(4) as not being a review of detention by a court. A court was required because the sentence in question was akin to a discretionary life sentence rather than a mandatory one.

536 (1996) 23 EHRR 413 para 130.

537 (2000) 29 EHRR 365 paras 57–58.

538 *De Wilde, Ooms and Versyp v Belgium* (1971) 1 EHRR 373 para 78; the earlier decision in *Neumeister v Austria (No 1)* (1968) 1 EHRR 91 that the judicial character of the court in no way related to the procedure to be followed, was reversed.

539 Ibid.

540 Ibid para 79.

541 *Bouamar v Belgium* (1988) 11 EHRR 1 para 60.

542 *Winterwerp v Netherlands* (1979) 2 EHRR 387 para 60.

Court has 'tended to acknowledge the need for a hearing before a judicial authority' in cases under Article 5(1)(c).[543] But in *Sanchez-Reisse v Switzerland*[544] the Court found that written submissions were sufficient in relation to the proceedings under Article 5(1)(f). There was no reason, in retrospect, to believe that the presence of the applicant would have made any difference to the outcome of the hearing. Nevertheless, as a general rule, even in the context of Article 5(1)(f), Article 5(4) will require the detained person or his representative to participate in the hearing.[545] The question of whether the proceedings should take place in public is also unclear.[546]

Procedural guarantees required by Article 5(4) include the provision of legal advice prior to the hearing, as well as representation at it, wherever it is necessary to render the application effective.[547] The guarantee extends to minors,[548] the mentally disabled[549] and those detained under Article 5(1)(c).[550] It involves the provision of free legal aid for a national where it is necessary in order to make the remedy effective.[551] **10.153**

The principle of adversarial proceedings,[552] has been incorporated into Article 5(4). Article 5(4) cases have dealt largely with the narrower issue of whether there was 'equality of arms'. Article 5(4) was found to be infringed on this ground when: the prosecutor, but not the applicant, was present at an appeal regarding the detention,[553] when an accused detained under Article 5(1)(c) was not given the same access as Crown counsel to his official file,[554] and where the prisoner was not given full disclosure of adverse material in the possession of the parole board. Furthermore, it has been held that 'equality of arms' means that the court should give the applicant the opportunity to appear at the same time as the prosecutor.[555] On the **10.154**

543 *Sanchez-Reisse v Switzerland* (1986) 9 EHRR 71 para 51.

544 Ibid.

545 *Farmakopoulos v Belgium* (1992) 16 EHRR 187 Com Rep para 46; see also *Kampanis v Greece* (1996) 21 EHRR 43 in which it was held that the applicant, having not been given the opportunity to see the written submissions of the prosecutor, ought to have been allowed to appear and reply.

546 In *Neumeister v Austria (No 1)* (1968) 1 EHRR 91 para 23 the Court indicated that publicity was not in the interest of the applicant whereas in *De Wilde, Ooms and Versyp v Belgium* (1971) 1 EHRR 373 para 79 it was suggested that a public hearing and public pronouncement of judgment were judicial features required by Art 5(4).

547 *Woukam Moudefo v France* (1988) 13 EHRR 549 paras 86–91.

548 *Bouamar v Belgium* (1988) 11 EHRR 1.

549 *Megyeri v Germany* (1992) 15 EHRR 584.

550 *Woukam Moudefo v France* (1988) 13 EHRR 549; see also *K v Austria* (1993) Series A No 255-B and *S v Switzerland* (1991) 14 EHRR 650.

551 In *Zamir v United Kingdom* (1983) 40 DR 42, EComm HR the Commission went as far as to accept that an illegal immigrant detained pending deportation required free legal aid.

552 Which was developed under Art 6(1) to ensure that all evidence is provided. For the right see para 11.206 below.

553 *Toth v Austria* (1991) 14 EHRR 551.

554 *Lamy v Belgium* (1989) 11 EHRR 529.

555 *Kampanis v Greece* (1995) 21 EHRR 43 para 46ff.

other hand, it was sufficient that an applicant's adviser was given access to a summary, rather than full transcripts, of statements given by a witness to a judge over the telephone, in relation to the state of the applicant's mental health.[556] A detained person must be given time and facilities to prepare his case.[557] The time must be reasonable, meaning that it 'must not be so short as to restrict the availability and tangibility of the remedy'.[558]

10.155 **Speedy determination.** Article 5(4) provides that the lawfulness of the detention shall be decided 'speedily'[559] by a court. This is a lesser degree of urgency than 'promptly'[560] as used in Article 5(3).[561] For purposes of determining the length of the proceedings, the clock normally starts to run when Article 5(4) proceedings are instituted;[562] and ends, not when the person is released, but when the final decision[563] is made as to the legality of the detention.[564] The jurisprudence indicates that there are two distinct requirements as to the speediness of the remedy: that the remedy be exercised immediately upon or 'speedily' after the detention,[565] and that once exercised, it must proceed 'speedily' to completion. The approach taken by the Court is similar to that taken in relation to guarantees in Articles 5(3)[566] and 6(1)[567] of a 'trial within a reasonable time': there must be consideration of the circumstances of each case,[568] including the diligence of the national authorities, and delays introduced by the applicant.

10.156 Where it appears, prima facie, that there has been a delay, the onus is on the state to show that the proceedings have in fact been conducted speedily.[569] It is the

556 *Wassink v Netherlands* (1990) Series A No 185-A.

557 *K v Austria* (1993) Series A No 255-B.

558 *Farmakopolous v Belgium* (1992) 16 EHRR 187: 24 hours was considered an unreasonably short time period.

559 French 'aussitôt'.

560 French 'à bref délai'.

561 See *E v Norway* (1990) 17 EHRR 30 para 28.

562 *Van der Leer v Netherlands* (1990) 12 EHRR 567; however, where there is an administrative decision prior to access to a court under Art 5(4), the length of the proceedings is calculated from the time when the administrative tribunal is seized of the case: *Sanchez-Reisse v Switzerland* (1986) 9 EHRR 71.

563 A decision on appeal, where it is available, will be the final decision, and the time prior to the appeal will be taken into account in the calculation of the length of the proceedings.

564 *Luberti v Italy* (1984) 6 EHRR 440; in that case there was an 11-day gap between the final decision and the release.

565 A breach of Art 5(4) was found when a soldier was detained for six days on a charge of a penal offence before being brought before a military court: *De Jong, Baljet and Van Den Brink v Netherlands* (1984) 8 EHRR 20; a remedy available to a mental patient only after he had been recalled for six months was also a violation: *X v United Kingdom* (1981) 4 EHRR 188.

566 See para 10.133 above.

567 See para 11.219ff below.

568 *Sanchez-Reisse v Switzerland* (1986) 9 EHRR 71.

569 *Luberti v Italy* (1984) 6 EHRR 440; delay as a result of disappearance of the detained person; *Navarra v France* (1993) 17 EHRR 594: delay of applicant in filing an appeal.

obligation of the state to organise its court system efficiently:[570] so that neither judges' holidays[571] nor the extent of their workload[572] is a justifiable excuse for delay where the right to liberty is at stake.[573] Proceedings over periods of five and a half months during detention on remand,[574] five months in relation to a minor,[575] four months for a person of unsound mind,[576] and periods of 31 and 46 days pending extradition[577] were held to violate Article 5(4) requirements. On the other hand, seven months was found acceptable in *Navarra v France,* which included delays by the applicant and the possibility of other appeals. In *Egue v France,*[578] five days was considered 'speedy',[579] as was 16 days to decide on the continued long-term detention of an habitual offender under Article 5(1)(a).[580]

The right under Article 5(4) is not confined to a single occasion. The review must be repeated when the basis of a person's detention is subject to change. Where, for example, the applicant's mental health might improve so as no longer to require detention,[581] or new issues affecting the lawfulness of the detention might subsequently arise,[582] it will be necessary to provide the detained person with 'automatic periodic review of a judicial character' or the 'opportunity for him to take proceedings at reasonable intervals before a court'.[583] What is meant by a 'reasonable interval' depends on the nature of the case: one month is a reasonable interval in the context of detention on remand,[584] while a longer interval, though not in excess of one year,[585] may be acceptable in relation to the mentally ill, unless clear evidence of a change in the mental state of the detainee warrants a hearing **10.157**

570 *Bezicheri v Italy* (1989) 12 EHRR 210 para 24.
571 *E v Norway* (1990) 17 EHRR 30.
572 *Bezicheri v Italy* (n 570 above).
573 *E v Norway* (n 571 above).
574 *Bezicheri v Italy* (n 570 above) para 24.
575 *Bouamar v Belgium* (1988) 11 EHRR 1.
576 *Koendjbiahrie v Netherlands* (1990) 13 EHRR 820; see also *Musial v Poland* Judgment, 25 Mar 1999 where a period of 20 months was incompatible with speediness as required by Art 5(4).
577 *Sanchez-Reisse v Switzerland* (1986) 9 EHRR 71 para 57.
578 (1988) 57 DR 47, EComm HR.
579 See n 565 above to contrast with the *De Jong*, military proceedings case.
580 *Christinet v Switzerland* (1979) 17 DR 35, EComm HR.
581 *X v United Kingdom* (1981) 4 EHRR 188.
582 Ibid para 51.
583 In *X v United Kingdom* (n 581 above) the applicant required either 'automatic periodic review of a judicial character' or the 'opportunity for him to take proceedings at reasonable intervals before a court' to challenge the lawfulness of his continued detention; see also cases involving a continuing remedy in relation to the preventive detention of recidivists: *Van Droogenbroeck v Belgium* (1982) 4 EHRR 443 and *E v Norway* (1990) 17 EHRR 30; detention of minors: *Bouamar v Belgium* (1988) 11 EHRR 1; and the refusal of bail to an accused person: *Bezicheri v Italy* (1989) 12 EHRR 210.
584 The nature of detention on remand calls for review at 'short intervals': *Bezicheri v Italy* (1989) 12 EHRR 210.
585 *Herczegfalvy v Austria* (1992) 15 EHRR 437.

within a shorter period.[586] Arrangements for automatic periodic review are governed by the same standards.[587]

10.158 **Preventative detention.** In general, Article 5(4) does not apply to detention following a conviction.[588] However, preventative detention requires a review of the lawfulness of detention at regular intervals.[589] Thus, the Court has held that there should be periodic reviews of detention where a person is detained in a mental institution,[590] for discretionary life prisoners whose continued detention is justified on grounds of public safety[591] and where juveniles are convicted of murder and detained during Her Majesty's pleasure.[592] However, the Court decided there is no right to a periodic review of detention for mandatory life prisoners;[593] and the Commission took the same view in relation to a 'longer than normal' sentence under section 2(2)(b) of the Criminal Justice Act 1991.[594]

(e) Compensation for wrongful detention (Article 5(5))

10.159 Article 5(5) provides that everyone who has been a victim of arrest or detention in contravention of the provisions of Article 5[595] shall have an enforceable right to compensation. This requires a remedy 'before a court'[596] leading to a legally binding award of compensation[597] to a person who has been arrested or detained contrary to Article 5.[598] The right applies to any detention in breach of Article 5, whether or not the detention was unlawful under national law.[599] However, Article 5(5) does not prevent states from making an award of compensation dependent on the ability of the applicant to show damage resulting from the breach.[600] Article 3 of Protocol 7 of the Convention also provides for a right of compensation for

586 *M v Germany* (1984) 38 DR 104, EComm HR.

587 *Keus v Netherlands* (1990) 13 EHRR 700 para 24.

588 *De Wilde, Ooms and Versyp v Belgium* (1971) 1 EHRR 373 para 76; *Winterwerp v Netherlands* (1979) 2 EHRR 387 para 55.

589 *Winterwerp v Netherlands* (n 588 above) para 55.

590 *X v United Kingdom* (1981) 4 EHRR 188.

591 *Thynne, Wilson and Gunnell v United Kingdom* (1990) 13 EHRR 666.

592 *Hussain v United Kingdom* (1996) 22 EHRR 1.

593 *Wynne v United Kingdom* (1994) 19 EHRR 333.

594 *Mansell v United Kingdom* [1997] EHRLR 666, EComm HR.

595 This includes a breach of any of the sub-paras (1) to (4) of Art 5: *Wassink v Netherlands* (1990) Series A No 185-A.

596 There is no jurisprudence as to the meaning of court specifically in Art 5(4).

597 In practice, it is likely to be financial compensation, but even where it is broader in scope will not include the detained person's release, since that is already provided for in Art 5(4): *Bozano v France* (1984) 39 DR 119, EComm HR. Damage giving rise to compensation may be pecuniary or non-pecuniary, including moral damage such as pain and emotional distress: *Wassink v Netherlands* (1990) Series A No 185-A; *Tsirilis and Kouloumpas v Greece* (1997) 25 EHRR 198: both pecuniary and non-pecuniary awards made.

598 *Brogan v United Kingdom* (1988) 11 EHRR 117; *Fox, Campbell and Hartley v United Kingdom* (1990) 13 EHRR 157.

599 See *Brogan v United Kingdom* (n 598 above) para 34.

600 *Wassink v Netherlands* (1990) Series A No 185-A para 38.

miscarriages of justice; however, this provision has not been ratified by the United Kingdom or enacted under the Human Rights Act.

D. The Impact of the Human Rights Act

(1) Introduction

The 'right to liberty' in Article 5 already finds substantial expression in English law. As we have seen, any interference with liberty is unlawful unless justified and the burden of justifying detention lies on the person responsible for it.[601] However, English law does allow for the deprivation of liberty in a wide range of situations. A number of these derive from the common law, but the large majority depend on statute. Although a statutory provision which interferes with liberty is construed strictly against the person who relies on it,[602] the common law 'right to liberty' must give way to clear statutory provision. As a result, there are a number of areas in which English law may be in conflict with the Convention.[603] Article 5 is likely to have a potential impact in the fields of criminal law, immigration law, mental health law, prison law and police law. It may also have significant repercussions on remedies for wrongful detention. **10.160**

(2) UK cases prior to the Human Rights Act

(a) Introduction

A large number of UK applications based on Article 5 have come before the Commission and the Court. The United Kingdom has been found to be in breach on eleven occasions.[604] The majority of complaints against the UK fall into three **10.161**

[601] See para 10.20ff above.

[602] See *Inland Revenue Commissioners v Rossminster Ltd* [1980] AC 952, 1008 *per* Lord Diplock; *Hill v Chief Constable of South Yorkshire* [1990] 1 WLR 946, 952 *per* Purchas LJ.

[603] See generally, F Klug, K Starmer, S Weir, *The Three Pillars of Liberty* (Routledge, 1996), 252–257.

[604] *X v United Kingdom* (1981) 4 EHRR 188 (habeas corpus proceedings did not secure Art 5(4) rights of mental patients); *Weeks v United Kingdom* (1987) 10 EHRR 293 (breach of Art 5(4) as Parole Board only had an advisory role when reviewing the release of discretionary lifers); *Brogan v United Kingdom* (1988) 11 EHRR 117 (violation of Art 5(3) when terrorist suspects held for periods from four to six days); *Fox, Campbell and Hartley v United Kingdom* (1990) 13 EHRR 157 (arrest of terrorist suspects breached Art 5(1)(c)); *Thynne, Wilson and Gunnell v United Kingdom* (1990) 13 EHRR 666 (violation of Art 5(4) due to lack of regular judicial scrutiny of lawfulness of detention of discretionary lifers); *Hussain and Singh v United Kingdom* (1996) 22 EHRR 1 (sentences of detention at Her Majesty's pleasure breached Art 5(4)); *Johnson v United Kingdom* (1999) 27 EHRR 296 (breach of Art 5(1) in relation to a mental patient); *Hood v United Kingdom* (2000) 29 EHRR 365; *Caballero v United Kingdom* Judgment of 8 Feb 2000 (breach of Art 5(3) due to automatic refusal of bail); *Jordan v United Kingdom*, Judgment of 14 Mar 2000 (breach of Art 5(3) and (5) in relation to suspect who was a soldier); *Curley v United K ingdom* Judgment of 28 Mar 2000 (breach of Arts 5(4) and (5) due to failure to review detention of prisoner detained at Her Majesty's pleasure).

general categories: applications concerning arrest and detention under legislation for the prevention of terrorism, the detention of mental patients and the release of discretionary life prisoners. However, a number of other important issues relating to Article 5 have also been considered in the UK cases.

(b) Terrorism cases

10.162 Detention for the purpose of preventing offences against public order or state security is not authorised by any sub-paragraph of Article 5(1). Consequently, a number of applications involving the arrest of suspected terrorists in Northern Ireland have come before the Commission and Court. Other terrorist cases concerning the questioning, arrest and detention of suspects have also been considered, with varying degrees of success for the applicants. In an early case before the Commission, a challenge to detention for 'examination' for 45 hours was unsuccessful on the basis that it was justified under Article 5(1)(b).[605] However, in *Fox, Campbell and Hartley v United Kingdom*,[606] arrests under the Northern Ireland (Emergency Provisions) Act 1978, which did not require reasonable grounds for suspicion, were in breach of Article 5(1)(c). Although the arrests were based on *bona fide* suspicion, the Government had furnished no information which would satisfy the objective standard in Article 5(1)(c). There was, nonetheless, no breach of Article 5(2) because the reasons for the arrest were brought to the attention of the applicants during their interrogation.[607] Furthermore, a subsequent challenge to an arrest under the same legislation failed as the Court took the view that there were, in fact, reasonable grounds for suspecting that the applicant had committed terrorist offences.[608]

10.163 In *Brogan v United Kingdom*[609] the applicants had been detained for periods of between four and six days under the Prevention of Terrorism Act. This was held to be a breach of Article 5(3); and led to the United Kingdom lodging a 'derogation' under Article 15 on the grounds of emergency.[610] In *Brannigan and McBride v United Kingdom*,[611] the applicants were detained for six days and four days respectively and the Court again held that there had been a breach of Article 5(3), but went on to hold that the derogation was a valid one. In view of the position taken by the United Kingdom Government in the *Brogan* case, considerable

[605] See *McVeigh, O'Neill and Evans v United Kingdom* (1981) 25 DR 15, EComm HR; see para 10.102 above.
[606] (1990) 13 EHRR 157.
[607] Note, this would have been insufficient under PACE, s 28, and the arrest would, therefore, have been unlawful.
[608] *Murray v United Kingdom* (1994) 19 EHRR 193; see para 10.110 above.
[609] (1988) 11 EHRR 117; see para 10.135ff above.
[610] See para 6.93 above; this is preserved by the Human Rights Act, see ss 14, 15 and 16 and Sch 2.
[611] (1993) 17 EHRR 539; see para 10.136 above.

doubts have been expressed as to the correctness of the approach taken by the Court in the later case.[612]

(c) Detention of mental patients

The Convention has had a substantial impact on mental health law in the United Kingdom. In *X v United Kingdom*[613] the applicant had been recalled to a secure mental hospital after discharge. He complained, *inter alia*, of a breach of Article 5(4). The Court rejected the argument of the Government that habeas corpus proceedings satisfied the requirements of the Article: they did not allow examination of the lawfulness of the detention. A breach of Article 5(4) was established. This led to the amendment of the legislation providing Mental Health Review Tribunals with power to direct the discharge of restricted patients.[614] **10.164**

In *Ashingdane v United Kingdom*[615] the applicant was a restricted patient whose transfer from Broadmoor to a local psychiatric hospital had been agreed. As a result of industrial action, however, he could not be transferred and no suitable alternative accommodation could be found. The applicant contended that his detention was, therefore, unlawful. The Court held that, while in principle the detention of a person as a mental patient will only be lawful if effected in a hospital, clinic or other appropriate institution, Article 5(1)(e) was not primarily concerned with suitable treatment or conditions.[616] The failure to effect the transfer of the applicant was therefore not a breach of Article 5. **10.165**

A violation of Article 5 was, however, established in *Johnson v United Kingdom*.[617] In that case, a Mental Health Review Tribunal had decided to make the discharge of the applicant conditional on, *inter alia*, his undergoing a period of rehabilitation in a suitable hostel. However, for a period of three and a half years, no suitable hostel place could be found. This was held to be a breach of Article 5(1) on the basis that neither the Tribunal nor the authorities possessed the necessary powers to ensure that the condition could be implemented within a reasonable time. **10.166**

(d) Life prisoners

A number of cases concerning life prisoners have come before the Court. In *Weeks*[618] the Court held that there was a breach of Article 5(4) in relation to the review of the detention of a recalled discretionary life prisoner. In *Thynne, Wilson* **10.167**

[612] See P van Dijk and G van Hoof, *Theory and Practice of the European Convention on Human Rights* (3rd edn, Kluwer, 1998) 743–747.
[613] (1981) 4 EHRR 188.
[614] Mental Health Act 1983, ss 72 and 73; see also *Ashingdane v United Kingdom* (1985) 7 EHRR 528 para 19.
[615] n 614 above.
[616] Para 44.
[617] (1999) 27 EHRR 296.
[618] (1987) 10 EHRR 293.

and Gunnell[619] it was held that the regime under which discretionary lifers were subject to recall was in breach of Article 5(4), in that it failed to provide for a court rather than a minister to consider at reasonable intervals the lawfulness of the continued detention of discretionary lifers. These decisions led to the enactment of section 34 of the Criminal Justice Act 1991.[620] However, in *Wynne v United Kingdom*[621] it was held that recall provisions relating to mandatory lifers were not in breach of Article 5(4). The Court accepted the argument of the government that as mandatory life sentences are imposed by law, they are essentially 'punitive' in nature, with no element of discretion.

10.168 The position of prisoners detained 'during Her Majesty's pleasure' was considered by the Court in *Hussain and Singh v United Kingdom*.[622] Both applicants complained of a breach of Article 5(4) in that the lawfulness of their detention had not been reviewed by the court at reasonable intervals. The Court took the view that, as the sentence of detention during Her Majesty's pleasure was imposed on young persons, it differed significantly from mandatory life sentences and was not wholly punitive in character: sentence was similar to the discretionary life sentence. As a result, the Court decided that there was a breach of Article 5(4). The Government then enacted section 28 of the Crime (Sentences) Act 1997 to allow a review of the continuing detention of prisoners detained 'during Her Majesty's pleasure'. A similar result was reached in the case of *Curley v United Kingdom*.[622a]

(e) Other applications

10.169 A number of other applications under Article 5 have been considered by the Commission and the Court. In *Benham v United Kingdom*,[623] the Divisional Court had quashed an order for the imprisonment of the applicant for default in payment of a Community Charge, but the applicant was not, as a result of section 45 of the Justices of the Peace Act 1979,[624] entitled to compensation. The Court held that there was no violation of Article 5(1) or 5(5), as it had not been established that the detention was unlawful under English law.

10.170 In *Chahal v United Kingdom*,[625] the Court rejected the complaint of the applicant that his three and a half year period of detention, 'with a view for deportation' on national security grounds, was a breach of Article 5(1).[626] In *Zamir v United*

[619] (1990) 13 EHRR 666.
[620] See the discussion in *R v Secretary of State for the Home Department, ex p H* [1995] QB 43.
[621] (1994) 19 EHRR 333.
[622] (1996) 22 EHRR 1.
[622a] Judgment of 28 Mar 2000.
[623] (1996) 22 EHRR 293 see para 10.175 below.
[624] As amended by Courts and Legal Services Act 1990, s 108.
[625] (1997) 23 EHRR 413.
[626] See also *Caprino v United Kingdom* (1982) 4 EHRR 97, EComm HR; and *Osman v United Kingdom* (Application 15933/89), (1991), EComm HR unreported: over five-years' detention pending extradition was acceptable, given the conduct of the applicant in seeking to avoid extradition.

Kingdom[627] the Commission suggested that the national law authorising the detention under Article 5(1)(f) must be accessible and foreseeable. Dismissing the application and holding that the Immigration Rules[628] contained a procedure prescribed by law, the Commission rejected the claim of the applicant that he could not reasonably have foreseen the consequences under English immigration law of failing to disclose, upon entry, that he was married. A number of difficult questions concerning the compatibility of breach of the peace with Article 5 were addressed in *Steel v United Kingdom*.[629] It was held that arrests for breach of the peace was 'in accordance with a procedure prescribed by law'.

In *Cabellero v United Kingdom*[629a] it was held that the automatic refusal of bail under section 25 of the Criminal Justice and Public Order Act 1994 was a breach of Article 5(3). The point was conceded by the Government. In *Hood v United Kingdom*[629b] the Court upheld a complaint by a soldier that his commanding officer was not an impartial tribunal for the review of his pre-trial detention. A similar result was reached in the case of *Jordan v United Kingdom*[629c] where the United Kingdom did not contest the point. **10.170a**

(3) The impact on remedies for wrongful detention

(a) Habeas corpus

Article 5(4) of the Convention protects the right of a person deprived of liberty to 'take proceedings by which the lawfulness of his detention shall be decided speedily by a court'. The lawfulness of detention for Convention purposes depends on whether the three substantive requirements established by the Court in *Winterwerp v Netherlands*[630] have been met. **10.171**

The traditional remedy in English law of habeas corpus[631] permits the court to enquire whether the detention complies with the relevant statutory requirements and with the applicable principles of the common law. It is clear, however, that the domestic habeas corpus procedure is not adequate to comply with Article 5(4), because it permits the court to examine only the *formal* lawfulness of the decision of the administrative authority, and not its grounds or merits.[632] Thus, whenever a statute confers a discretion, the court in habeas corpus proceedings will confine **10.172**

[627] (1983) 40 DR 42, 55, EComm HR.
[628] Statement of Immigration Rules for Control on Entry: EEC and Other Non-Commonwealth Nationals; HC paper (1972–73) No 81.
[629] (1998) 28 EHRR 603; see para 10.193 below.
[629a] Judgment of 8 Feb 2000.
[629b] (2000) 29 EHRR 365.
[629c] Judgment of 14 Mar 2000.
[630] (1979) 2 EHRR 387; see para 10.117 above.
[631] See para 10.07ff above.
[632] See *X v United Kingdom* (1981) 4 EHRR 188 paras 56–59.

itself to whether the discretion has been exercised in accordance with the empowering statute.[633] Access to a court by which to obtain a ruling that detention is 'lawful' in English law cannot, therefore, save in exceptional circumstances,[634] be decisive as to whether there is sufficient review of 'lawfulness' for the purposes of Article 5(4) of the Convention.

10.173 Furthermore, Article 5(4) of the Convention requires that the review be conducted on the principle of adversarial proceedings developed under Article 6(1); this necessitates the exchange of evidence with a view to adversarial argument and 'equality of arms' of the parties.[635] The right of the parties to equal access to facilities for the presentation of their case is a distinct procedural right which is absent from domestic habeas corpus proceedings.

(b) Compensation for wrongful detention

10.174 Article 5(5) provides that victims of arrest or detention in contravention of the Article must have 'an enforceable right to compensation'. In general, English law is in conformity with this provision, in that anyone who is wrongfully detained has a right to damages for false imprisonment. There are, however, at least two areas of potential difficulty.

10.175 First, those who are imprisoned pursuant to court orders which are made without jurisdiction have a right to compensation in only very limited circumstances.[636] This provision was considered by the European Court of Human Rights in *Benham v United Kingdom,*[637] a case concerning the unlawful committal to prison of a poll tax defaulter. The order for detention had been quashed by the Divisional Court which had not dealt with the question as to whether the magistrates had acted within their jurisdiction.[638] The Court held, therefore, that as it had not been established that the magistrates had acted in excess of jurisdiction, the detention was justified under Article 5(1)(b). There were strong dissents from Judges Bernhardt and Foighel in relation to this highly unsatisfactory decision.

---

633 Ibid.

634 *X v United Kingdom* (n 632 above) paras 56–59: the remedy of habeas corpus can on occasion constitute an effective check against arbitrariness; for example the discretion of authorities in regard to using emergency procedures for the detention of persons of unsound mind must inevitably reduce the role of the courts, and such measures, provided they are of short duration are capable of being 'lawful' even though they are not attended by all of the usual guarantees . . .

635 See *Sanchez-Reisse v Switzerland* (1986) 9 EHRR 71; *Lamy v Belgium* (1989) 11 EHRR 529; *Toth v Austria* (1991) 14 EHRR 551; in *Weeks v United Kingdom* (1987) 10 EHRR 293 para 66 the Court found that Art 5(4) had not been complied with because the applicant seeking release had not been apprised of the full contents of adverse material in the possession of the Parole Board; see para 10.96 above.

636 See para 10.77ff above.

637 (1996) 22 EHRR 293.

638 In accordance with the test laid down in *Re McC (A Minor)* [1985] 1 AC 528; see *R v Manchester City Magistrates' Court, ex p Davies* [1989] QB 631.

There are pending a number of other applications in which there were specific findings of unlawfulness.[639]

The scope for obtaining damages where judicial decisions are made in breach of Article 5 has been widened by the Human Rights Act. Section 9 of the Act is designed in general terms to limit the circumstances in which judicial acts can be subject to challenge.[639a] However, section 9(3) states that: **10.175A**

> In proceedings under this Act in respect of a judicial act done in good faith, damages may not be awarded otherwise than to compensate a person to the extent required by Article 5(5) of the Convention.

It appears that the language of section 9(3) is sufficient to reverse the long established common law doctrine that superior judges are not liable for damages where they make a court order which is *ultra vires* (such as where a Crown Court judge passes an unlawful sentence). Its impact on the liability of magistrates is more uncertain. The statutory immunity of magistrates for *ultra vires* acts (except where they act in *bad faith*) is expressed in these terms:

> an action shall lie against any justice of the peace . . . with respect to a matter which is within his jurisdiction, if but only if, it is proved that he acted in good faith.[639b]

Because the statute prohibits an 'action' being taken, it is difficult to see how the provision could be 'read down' under section 3 of the Human Rights Act[639c] in a way which imposed liability on magistrates who had acted in good faith when making an *ultra vires* act or omission.[639d]

Secondly, the Mental Health Act 1983[640] protects those involved in the detention of mental patients from actions for damages. It provides that: **10.176**

> No person shall be liable, whether on the ground of want of jurisdiction or on any other ground, to any civil or criminal proceedings to which he would have been liable apart from this section in respect of any act purporting to be done in pursuance of this Act or any regulations or rules made under this Act . . . unless the act was done in bad faith or without reasonable care.

This provision does not exclude applications for judicial review[641] but it does impact on actions for damages. It means that a person who is unlawfully detained under the Mental Health Act, in circumstances in which there is no bad faith or

[639] See the commentary at [1996] EHRLR 548.
[639a] See para 5.110ff above.
[639b] Justices of the Peace Act 1997, s 52.
[639c] See para 4.17ff above.
[639d] However, in S Grosz, J Beatson and P Duffy, *Human Rights: The 1998 Act and the European Convention* (Sweet & Maxwell, 2000) para 6–18, it is suggested that s 9(3) impliedly repeals s 52.
[640] s 139.
[641] See *Ex p Waldron* [1986] QB 824.

want of reasonable care, has no right to compensation. This is a clear breach of Article 5(5) and, as result, a declaration of incompatibility should be available.[642]

(4) Specific areas of impact

(a) Criminal law

10.177 The general presumption in favour of bail in the Bail Act 1976 is consistent with the approach required by Article 5(3).[643] In 1994, the Act was amended to include an absolute prohibition of bail for defendants who have previous convictions for serious offences,[644] a provision which relieved the state of the usual burden of establishing 'relevant and justified' reasons for continued detention.[645] A number of applications in relation to this section were declared admissible by the Commission[646] and the absolute bar was removed in 1998.[647] In *Caballero v United Kingdom*[647a] the Court found that the absolute prohibition on bail was a breach of Article 5(3). Under the amended provision, a person with previous convictions for serious offences will now be granted bail only if a constable or court is satisfied that 'there are exceptional circumstances which justify it'. It is arguable that the provision, even as amended, fails to satisfy Article 5(3) in that it places the burden of establishing an entitlement to bail on the detained person rather than on the state.[648]

10.178 There are a number of other areas in which the present law relating to bail may not be compatible with the Convention:

- The provision in paragraph 2A of Schedule 1 to the Bail Act 1976 which permits the court to refuse bail if the offence charged is indictable and the defendant was on bail when he is alleged to have committed it appears to be incompatible with Article 5(3) in that it appears to create a 'presumption' against bail in such cases.[648a]
- The provision in paragraph 6 of Part I of Schedule 1 which permits the court to refuse bail where a defendant has been arrested for 'breach of bail' under section 7 also appears to be incompatible with Article 5(3) for similar reasons.[648b]

---

[642] Cf D Feldman, *Civil Liberties and Human Rights in England and Wales* (Clarendon Press, 1993) 312.
[643] See para 10.133ff above; for a comprehensive discussion of the relationship between the Bail Act 1976 and Art 5 see Law Commission, *Bail and the Human Rights Act*, Consultation Paper No 157 (The Stationery Office, 1999).
[644] Criminal Justice and Public Order Act 1994, s 25.
[645] See para 10.57 above.
[646] See *B H v United Kingdom* (1998) 25 EHRR CD 136; and *C C v United Kingdom* [1998] EHRLR 335, EComm HR.
[647] Crime and Disorder Act 1998, s 56.
[647a] Judgment, 8 Feb 2000.
[648] See para 10.138 above; and see Law Commission (n 643 above) Pt IX; and cf the discussion of similar issues under the South African Constitution in *State v Dlamini* 1999 (7) BCLR 771.
[648a] See Law Commision (n 643 above) Pt VI.
[648b] Ibid Pt VIII.

- The use of 'conditional bail' by the English courts also gives rise to issues of compatibility with Article 5(3).[649] The only conditions expressly mentioned in the Convention are 'guarantees to appear for trial'. It is arguable that no other conditions are permissible[650] although it seems likely that the conditions designed to prevent interference with the course of justice, the commission of crime and the preservation of public order would be consistent with Article 5.[651]
- The approach of the English courts to the refusal of bail due to the risk of offending could lead to a breach of Article 5(3) because the English courts are not required to ensure that the feared offence is 'serious', and the risk of commission is 'real' before refusing bail on this ground.[651a] However, the present law could be applied in a manner which is compatible with the Convention and the Law Commission have recommended that the issue be dealt with by way of guidance to courts.[651b]
- The approach of the English courts to the refusal of bail for a suspect's own protection may also be incompatible with the Convention. The English courts are not required to ensure that bail is refused on this ground only in exceptional circumstances. Once again, the present law could be applied in a manner which is compatible with the Convention and the Law Commission have recommended that the issue be dealt with by way of guidance to courts.[652]
- The practice of the police and courts to impose conditions such as curfew and geographical restrictions as a matter of course may well be called into question.
- The use of bail conditions to restrict the activities of protestors[653] may also be in breach of Article 5.

(b) Immigration

There are a number of ways in which the Convention may affect English immigration law.[654] The statutory regime for the exercise of the power of detention of asylum seekers in the United Kingdom appears to be in broad compliance with Article 5(1).[655] Article 5(1)(f) permits detention in only two circumstances: to **10.179**

[649] See F Klug, K Starmer and S Weir, *The Three Pillars of Liberty* (Routledge, 1996) 202.

[650] See D Harris, M O'Boyle and C Warbrick, *Law of the European Convention on Human Rights* (Butterworths, 1995) 142.

[651] These being permissible grounds for refusal of bail, see para 10.138 above; cf *Schmidt v Austria* (1985) 44 DR 195, EComm HR (surrender of documents and residence requirement).

[651a] See Law Commission (n 643 above) Pt V.

[651b] Ibid para 5.17, p 56.

[652] Ibid Pt VII; for the recommendation, see para 7.6, p 62.

[653] See para 10.58 above.

[654] For a detailed discussion, see I Macdonald and N Blake, *Immigration Law and Practice in the United Kingdom* (4th edn, Butterworths, 1995) 439ff; N Blake and L Fransman, *Immigration, Nationality and Asylum: Under the Human Rights Act 1998* (Butterworths, 1999) 42–44.

[655] See N Blake QC, 'Opinion for Justice on the International Principles Governing Detention of Asylum Seekers', 27 May 1998.

prevent unauthorised entry into the country or where action is being taken with a view to deportation or extradition. The case law under the Immigration Act 1971[656] is consistent with the Convention. An asylum seeker who presents himself to the immigration authorities on arrival at UK customs, and does not present a forged document or otherwise seek to deceive the immigration officer, is not attempting illegal entry. He cannot, therefore, be detained under Article 5(1)(f).[657] If it is reasonably suspected, however, that the person is guilty of an immigration offence, then the detention could be justified under Article 5(1)(c).[658]

10.180 The present procedures for the review of a decision to detain asylum seekers probably do not comply with Article 5. There is no right to a review, at reasonable intervals, of the lawfulness of the detention.[659] There is no right to apply for bail within the first seven days of detention. The absence of frequent assessment of the lawfulness of a detention decision could, arguably, render the decision arbitrary and hence unlawful. It has been suggested that compliance with the requirements of Article 5 would require the imposition of a duty on the state to bring a detainee before a court within 48 hours of his arrest and at regular intervals while he is on remand pending a decision.[660] Similar considerations apply in relation to a person who is detained in order to be removed as an illegal immigrant or to be deported.[661] The lack of provision for assessment of the lawfulness of the detention is arguably in breach of Article 5(4).

(c) Local government law

10.181 The power to detain a person in need of care and assistance[662] is unlikely to survive the Human Rights Act since it is a power of arrest which cannot be justified under any of the grounds in Article 5.

(d) Mental health law

10.182 The provisions of Article 5 have already had a very important impact on mental health law in the United Kingdom.[663] There are, however, a number of areas in which the present law may be incompatible with Article 5.[664] It is clear that the

[656] See para 10.51ff above.
[657] *R v Naillie* [1992] 1 WLR 1099, affirmed [1993] AC 674.
[658] Ibid; in *R v Naillie,* the respondent was justifiably suspected of facilitating the illegal entry of others into the United Kingdom by providing them with forged passports, in spite of the fact that the other parties involved sought political asylum and were admitted without proffering the falsified documentation to immigration officers.
[659] See para 10.145ff above.
[660] See generally, N Blake (n 655 above) para 18 ff.
[661] D Feldman (n 642 above) 336.
[662] National Assistance Act 1948, s 47(1): see para 10.54 above.
[663] See para 10.164 above.
[664] See generally, O Thorold, 'Implications of the Convention for UK Mental Health Legislation'[1996] EHRLR 619.

detention of a mental patient can only be justified under Article 5(1)(e) if three minimum conditions are satisfied:

- the patient is reliably shown to be of unsound mind, on the basis of objective medical assessment;
- the mental disorder is of a kind or degree warranting compulsory confinement; and
- the continuance of confinement is predicated solely on the persistence of such mental disorder.[665]

These conditions are relaxed in emergency cases.[666] It appears, therefore, that the power to detain persons in public places who are apparently suffering from mental disorder[667] which does not require medical assessment, does not breach Article 5(1)(e). It also seems mental patients who are informally admitted and lack the capacity to consent to their detention will nevertheless be detained in accordance with Article 5(1)(e).[668] **10.183**

The Home Secretary does, however, retain the power to recall conditionally released patients at any time.[669] There is no requirement for medical assessment before a recall is made. It is difficult to see how this power is compatible with the Convention.[670] **10.184**

Under Article 5(1)(e), the period of detention of a mental patient must not extend beyond the persistence of the mental disorder.[671] In relation to unrestricted patients, the responsible medical officer[672] can discharge a patient on the basis of his own decision that the disorder no longer persists.[673] Restricted patients,[674] however, can only be discharged after a decision of the Home Secretary or a Tribunal.[675] As a result, a patient whose medical condition no longer justifies detention may be held pending a 'discharge decision'. It appears that, at present, it is the view of the Home Secretary that he has a right to withhold consent to discharge notwithstanding favourable assessment by a responsible medical officer and the absence of a contradictory psychiatric opinion.[676] Such an approach would also appear to be a breach of Article 5. **10.185**

[665] See *Winterwerp v Netherlands* (1979) 2 EHRR 387 para 40; *Luberti v Italy* (1984) 6 EHRR 440 para 27; *Johnson v United Kingdom* (1997) 27 EHRR 296 para 60; and see para 10.117 above.

[666] See *X v United Kingdom* (1981) 4 EHRR 188 para 40; see para 10.118 above.

[667] Mental Health Act 1983, s 136.

[668] *R v Bournewood Community and Mental Health NHS Trust, ex p L* [1998] 3 WLR 107.

[669] Under s 42(3) where the patient was conditionally discharged by the Home Secretary and under s 73 where he was discharged by the Mental Health Review Tribunal.

[670] Cf *Kay v United Kingdom* (1998) 40 BMLR 20.

[671] See para 10.119 above.

[672] That is, the medical practitioner in charge of his treatment.

[673] s 23.

[674] That is, patients in respect of which a hospital order is made by the Crown Court, s 41.

[675] Under s 42(2) or s 73.

[676] See O Thorold (n 664 above) 623.

10.186 A mental patient must have access to a judicial body that is independent of the executive.[677] In general, the right of access to Mental Health Review Tribunals will satisfy this requirement. However, when a conditionally discharged restricted patient is re-admitted for treatment,[678] there is no entitlement to apply to a tribunal until there has been a formal recall by the Home Secretary under section 42(3).[679] This is an anomaly which again gives rise to a breach of Article 5(4).[680] The inability of a person detained in a secure hospital following a conviction to obtain a review of his detention may also violate Article 5(4); and the Commission[681] has admitted to a complaint to this effect.

10.187 Under Article 5(4), a person who is detained is entitled to have the lawfulness of his detention 'decided speedily by a court'. The period of time allowed for review depends on the circumstances.[682] It has been held, though, that eight weeks was a breach in relation to the assessment of the lawfulness of the initial detention[683] and four months was unreasonable in the case of a periodic review.[684] The time limits established by the Mental Health Review Tribunal Rules suggest that a hearing is unlikely to be achieved within an eight-week period. It has therefore been suggested that compliance with Article 5(4)[685] will require the imposition of tighter time limits.

10.188 A Mental Health Review Tribunal is authorised to discharge restricted patients upon the imposition of conditions which allow it to retain residual control over them.[686] This power is compatible with Article 5(1)(e).[687] However, the unfettered power to defer conditional discharge pending the making of arrangements to accommodate the patient[688] is, in the absence of any assurance that the decision could be implemented within a reasonable time, in breach of Article 5.[689]

(e) Police law

10.189 **Stop and search powers.** It has been suggested that police powers of detention for the purposes of 'stop and search' may constitute a breach of Article 5.[690] The

677 See para 10.150 above.
678 Under s 3.
679 See s 41(3)(b).
680 Cf *Lines v United Kingdom* [1997] EHRLR 297.
681 *Benjamin and Wilson v United Kingdom* Application 28212/95 23 Oct 1997.
682 See para 10.155ff above.
683 *E v Norway* (1994) 17 EHRR 30.
684 *Koendjbiharie v Netherlands* (1990) 13 EHRR 820.
685 See Thorold (n 664 above) 626.
686 s 72(3); and see *R v Merseyside Mental Health Review Tribunal, ex p K* [1990] 1 All ER 694, 699.
687 See *Johnson v United Kingdom* (1997) 27 EHRR 296 para 55.
688 s 72(7); *Secretary of State for the Home Department v Oxford Regional Mental Health Review Tribunal* [1988] AC 120.
689 See *Johnson v United Kingdom* (n 687 above) para 66.
690 See F Klug, K Starmer and S Weir, *The Three Pillars of Liberty* (Routledge, 1996) 250–1.

grounds on which deprivation of liberty is permissible under Article 5(1) are exhaustive,[691] and do not include 'stop and search'.

10.190 However, there appear to be a number of possible counter-arguments. First, it might be said that the short period of detention involved in a 'stop and search' is insufficient to constitute a 'deprivation of liberty' for the purposes of Article 5,[692] an argument that appears, however, to be inconsistent with the jurisprudence.[693] Secondly, it could be argued[694] that such detention is lawful under Article 5(1)(b).[695] This reasoning was accepted in *McVeigh, O'Neill and Evans v United Kingdom*[696] but that decision seems to be inconsistent with the view expressed in some of the other cases that this sub-paragraph only permits detention to fulfil a 'specific and concrete obligation' which the person detained has failed to satisfy.[697] Thirdly, it might be argued that stop and search is justified under Article 5(1)(c). The difficulty with this argument is that this sub-paragraph only permits a deprivation of liberty for the purpose of bringing the detained person before the competent judicial authority.[698]

10.191 Although the stop and search powers under PACE[699] and the Misuse of Drugs Act 1971[700] are exercisable on the basis of 'reasonable grounds',[701] no such qualification applies to the power under section 60 of the Criminal Justice and Public Order Act 1994. Once the senior police officer has authorised the use of the power[702] a constable is entitled to stop and search pedestrians or vehicles 'whether or not he has any grounds for suspecting that the person or vehicle is carrying weapons or articles of that kind'.[703] If a person fails to stop when required to do so, then he commits an offence punishable by imprisonment for up to one month.[704] Although it appears difficult to reconcile these powers with Article 5 they may be

[691] See *Ireland v United Kingdom* (1978) 2 EHRR 25 para 194.

[692] See R Reiner and L Leigh, 'Police Powers' in C McCrudden and G Chambers (eds), *Individual Rights and the Law in Britain* (Oxford University Press, 1994) 93–94.

[693] See *X v Austria* (1979) 18 DR 154, EComm HR (restraint for the length of time required to carry out a blood test constituted a deprivation of liberty).

[694] Cf D Cheney, L Dickson, J Fitzpatrick and S Uglow, *Criminal Justice and the Human Rights Act 1998* (Jordans, 1999) para 3.2.

[695] See also *Ruth (Toivo) v Sweden* (1985) 42 DR 127, EComm HR: detention for the purpose of verifying the ownership of a vehicle.

[696] (1981) 25 DR 15, EComm HR.

[697] See *Engel and others v Netherlands (No 1)* (1976) 1 EHRR 647 para 69; and see *Guzzardi v Italy* (1980) 3 EHRR 333 para 101; but see *Steel v United Kingdom* (1998) 28 EHRR 603 and see generally, para 10.101 above.

[698] See *Lawless v Ireland (No 3)* (1961) 1 EHRR 15 para 14; and see generally, para 10.103 above.

[699] s 1.

[700] s 23(2).

[701] See para 10.26 above.

[702] On the ground that 'incidents involving serious violence' may take place, not the ground that he believes that they *will* take place: see s 60(1).

[703] s 60(5).

[704] s 60(8).

justifiable under Article 5(1)(b): it might be argued that the detention is in relation to an obligation imposed in connection with the enforcement of an obligation under the criminal law which is 'specific and concrete'.[705]

10.192 **Breach of the peace.** A number of questions arise as to the compatibility of breach of the peace with Article 5. Several commentators have drawn attention to the curious status of 'breach of the peace' in English law and the resulting difficulties of justifying arrest and detention by the police on this ground.[706] Breach of the peace is not the subject of any statutory definition and it is not a criminal offence under English law.[707] It covers situations in which there has already been a breach of the peace and situations in which a breach is threatened. The power of arrest appears to be unnecessary, in that all or most of the situations in which it can be exercised are covered by statutory powers of arrest for ordinary criminal offences.[708]

10.193 Any deprivation of liberty must, under Article 5(1), be 'in accordance with a procedure prescribed by law'. In the context of other Articles of the Convention, this phrase has been held to entail a 'foreseeability' principle: the law must be formulated with sufficient precision to enable a citizen to foresee the consequences of a given action.[709] The uncertainty as to the parameters of a 'breach of the peace' might imply a contravention of this principle.[710] Nevertheless, in *Steel v United Kingdom*[711] the Court took the view that the English law on the concept of breach of the peace provided sufficient guidance and was formulated with sufficient precision to be 'in accordance with the law'.

10.194 Even if an arrest for breach of the peace is 'in accordance with a procedure prescribed by law', it must be justified under one of the specific categories in Article 5(1). There are two possibilities. The first is an arrest to 'secure the fulfilment of an obligation prescribed' by law in accordance with Article 5(1)(b). Such an obligation must, however, be 'specific and concrete'[712] as opposed to the general obligation to keep the peace.[713] In any event, this provision does not authorise preventative arrest or detention.[714]

[705] See para 10.99ff above.

[706] See Law Commission, *Binding Over* (Law Com No 222); Nicolson and Reid, 'Arrest for Breach of the Peace and the European Convention on Human Rights' [1996] Crim L Rev 764.

[707] See *R v County of London Quarter Sessions Appeals Committee, ex p Metropolitan Police Commissioner* [1948] 1 KB 670.

[708] For example, the power to arrest for 'disorderly conduct' in the Public Order Act 1986, s 5.

[709] See *Sunday Times v United Kingdom (No 1)* (1979) 2 EHRR 245 para 49; see para 6.133 above.

[710] See the detailed argument on this point in Nicolson and Reid (n 706 above) 766–770.

[711] (1998) 28 EHRR 603, paras 25–28 and 55.

[712] See *Engel and others v Netherlands (No 1)* [1976] 1 EHRR 647; and see para 10.99ff above.

[713] Cf *Guzzardi v Italy* (1980) 3 EHRR 333 para 101.

[714] *Lawless v Ireland (No 3)* (1961) 1 EHRR 15 para 51.

The Court in *Steel* held that breach of the peace was a specific and concrete obligation prescribed by law. However, it did not provide detailed reasoning for its conclusion; and the question might require further argument if it were considered under the Human Rights Act. **10.195**

The second possible justification for making an arrest for breach of the peace is under Article 5(1)(c). But it would be difficult to rationalise an arrest under Article 5(1)(c) since such an arrest must be for the purpose of investigating an offence under the criminal law.[715] By contrast, the Convention case law suggests that detention under Article 5(1)(c) should have as its objective the initiation of a prosecution.[716] As a matter of English law, however, a breach of the peace is not an offence and no 'prosecution' can result.[717] **10.196**

A person who has committed or threatened to commit a breach of the peace may be 'bound over' by a magistrates' or Crown Court.[718] It could be argued that the power to imprison for refusal to accept a 'bind over' is inconsistent with the 'prescribed by law' requirement in Article 5(1)(b).[719] However, in *Steel*[720] the Court held that the national law was formulated with sufficient precision to allow the applicants to foresee the consequences of their actions in refusing a bind over. This decision should be contrasted with *Hashman and Harrup v United Kingdom*[720a] where the Court took the view that a bind over to be of good behaviour was too imprecise to be 'prescribed by law'. **10.197**

Arrest and detention under PACE. The provisions of the Police and Criminal Evidence Act 1984 in relation to arrest and detention appear to meet and (in most cases are stricter than) the standards laid down by Article 5.[721] It has been suggested that the powers of arrest in section 24(4), (5) and (7), are exercisable when someone is 'in the act of committing', 'is guilty of' or 'is about to commit' an arrestable offence, and are in breach of Article 5(1)(c) because of the absence of a 'reasonable grounds' requirement.[722] It is submitted that this conclusion is unfounded because these powers will not be lawfully exercised if the suspect has not **10.198**

[715] *Ciulla v Italy* (1989) 13 EHRR 346.

[716] See para 10.106 above.

[717] F Klug, K Starmer, S Weir, *The Three Pillars of Liberty* (Routledge, 1996) 251–252.

[718] See para 10.61 above.

[719] See D Feldman, *Civil Liberties and Human Rights in England and Wales* (Clarendon Press, 1993) 841.

[720] (1998) 28 EHRR 603 para 75.

[720a] Judgment of 25 Nov 1999 paras 29–41.

[720b] The obligation of behaviour *contra bonos mores* has been described as 'conduct which has the property of being wrong rather than right in the judgment of the majority of contemporary fellow citizens': *per* Glidewell LJ in *Hughes v Holley* (1988) 86 Crim App Rep 130.

[721] For example, in relation to 'reasons on arrest', s 28 is more strict than Art 5(2) as interpreted in *Fox, Campbell and Hartley v United Kingdom* (1990) 13 EHRR 157.

[722] See R Reiner and L Leigh, 'Police Powers' in C McCrudden and G Chambers (eds), *Individual Rights and the Law in Britain* (Oxford University Press, 1994) 94.

actually committed, attempted to commit or is in the act of committing the offence: the arrestor acts at his own risk.[723]

10.199 Article 5(3) guarantees a right to be brought 'promptly' before a judge or judicial officer. The Court has not laid down any strict time limits but, it seems likely that the 'detention' provisions of Part IV of PACE are compatible with Article 5. It has been suggested that:

> The extensive rules set out in PACE are sufficient to satisfy international requirements that detention should not be arbitrary and that a person arrested should be brought before a judge or other officer authorised by law to exercise judicial power.[724]

10.200 **Terrorism cases.** It is clear that the 'detention' provisions of the UK legislation for the prevention of terrorism breach Article 5. The 'derogation' under Article 15 is, by its nature, temporary and, in situations where there are paramilitary ceasefires, may no longer be justifiable. If the ceasefires continue, there are strong grounds for believing that a 'declaration of incompatibility' under section 4 of the Human Rights Act would be available. Despite the decision of the Commission in *McVeigh, O'Neill and Evans*[725] it is arguable that powers of detention for 'examination',[726] which validate detention for a period of up to 12 hours without need for reasonable suspicion, are incompatible with Article 5.[727]

(f) Prison law

10.201 Article 5 is concerned solely with the deprivation of liberty; it does not deal with issues concerning prison conditions. But Article 5(4) does apply in relation to the discretionary release and recall of prisoners.[728] As a direct result of the *Weeks* and *Thynne, Wilson and Gunnell* decisions,[729] the position of discretionary lifers was clarified by the Criminal Justice Act 1991. There are, however, still a number of issues which remain in relation to life prisoners and those detained at Her Majesty's pleasure.

10.202 First, there is the question as to whether the 'tariff fixing' exercise for these types of prisoner attracts the safeguards of Article 5(4). Tariffs are presently fixed by the Home Secretary after consultation with the trial judge and the Lord Chief Justice.[730] The process appears secretive and potentially unfair. As such, it could

---

[723] See *Walters v W H Smith* [1914] 1 KB 595.

[724] Klug, Starmer and Weir (n 717 above) 255: the authors go on to draw attention to evidence that these requirements are not always observed in practice.

[725] See para 10.102 above.

[726] Under Sch 5 of the Prevention of Terrorism Act 1989.

[727] See Klug, Starmer and Weir (n 717 above) 252.

[728] See generally, S Livingstone and T Owen, *Prison Law* (2nd edn, Oxford University Press, 1999) paras 13.20ff (mandatory lifers) and 14.08ff (on discretionary lifers).

[729] See para 10.167 above.

[730] See generally, para 10.67 above.

amount to a violation of liberty, but could equally and perhaps more naturally, be regarded as a matter of 'due process rights' under Article 6.[731] In *Watson v United Kingdom*,[732] an application by a discretionary lifer in relation to tariff fixing was declared admissible under both Articles 5 and 6. Similar issues arise in relation to prisoners sentenced to detention 'during Her Majesty's pleasure'.[733]

Secondly, there is the issue of delays in relation to the reviews of detention by the Parole Board.[734] In *R v Secretary of State for Home Department, ex p Norney*,[735] Dyson J took Article 5(4) into account in declaring unlawful the policy of the Home Secretary of not referring discretionary lifer cases to the Parole Board until the 'tariff' had expired. He relied on the decision in *E v Norway*,[736] in which an eight-week delay in a review of detention was held to be too long. The review system continues to be subject to delays and a number of applications on this point have been declared admissible by the Commission.[737] **10.203**

Thirdly, it is unclear whether the sentences of mandatory lifers should be subjected to the same 'review' as those of discretionary lifers. Even though the argument of the Government in *Wynne v United Kingdom*,[738] that they should not be so treated was accepted, the point remains open for decision by an English court following incorporation. The English courts have shown themselves willing to review decisions of the Home Secretary in relation to 'tariff' for mandatory life prisoners.[739] It is arguable that mandatory life sentences include 'punitive' and 'preventive' elements and that, as a result, Article 5(4) must apply.[740] **10.204**

Appendix 1: The Canadian Charter of Rights

(1) Introduction

The Canadian Charter of Rights and Freedoms does not deal with personal liberty and security, justification for deprivation of liberty and the rights of a detained person all under one discrete head. The substantive guarantee of liberty and security and grounds for interference with liberty are dealt with in section 7. Section 8 provides protection against unreasonable search or seizure and section 9 contains a guarantee of freedom from arbitrary detention or imprisonment. The rights of a person upon arrest or detention are found in section 10. Section 11, which applies once charges are laid, provides assurance of a presumption of innocence, right to bail and a fair trial process. **10.205**

731 See para 11.150ff above.
732 [1997] EHRLR 181.
733 Cf commentary on *Hussain and Singh v United Kingdom* [1996] EHRLR 331.
734 *AT v United Kingdom* [1996] EHRLR 92, EComm HR: admissible.
735 (1995) 7 Admin LR 861; see generally, para 2.36 above.
736 (1990) 17 EHRR 30.
737 See eg *Watson v United Kingdom* [1997] EHRLR 181.
738 (1994) 19 EHRR 333.
739 See eg *R v Secretary of State for the Home Department, ex p Pierson* [1998] AC 539.
740 See generally, Livingston and Owen (n 728 above) paras 13.21–13.23.

(2) Liberty and security

(a) Introduction

10.206 Section 7 of the Charter states :

> Everyone has the right to life, liberty and security of the person and the right not to be deprived thereof except in accordance with the principles of fundamental justice.

This applies only to individuals: as an artificial person such as a corporation is incapable of possessing the 'life, liberty or security of persons' attributable only to natural persons.[741] 'Liberty' and 'security of the person' have often been treated separately. In general, 'liberty' has been treated as a right to freedom from physical restraint, such as arrest or detention, while security of the person has been connected with a right to freedom from interference with bodily integrity.

10.207 Section 7 of the Charter does not set out any exceptions to the right of liberty and security. It expresses only the general requirement that any deprivations must be 'in accordance with principles of fundamental justice'.[742] The courts have, therefore, been left to define the parameters of the justifiable exceptions and, in doing so, they have focused on the concept of fundamental justice rather than on the meaning of liberty and security.[743]

(b) 'Liberty'

10.208 'Liberty' means freedom from interference with physical or mental integrity. It does not include interference with one's good name or reputation.[744] Any law that provides for a penalty of imprisonment (whether the sentence is mandatory[745] or discretionary)[746] is a deprivation of liberty, and must comply with the principles of fundamental justice. Statutes requiring fingerprinting,[747] production of documents[748] and presentation of oral testimony[749] also constitute a deprivation of physical liberty requiring conformity to the principles of fundamental justice.

10.209 In general, the Supreme Court has refused to extend liberty beyond freedom from physical

---

[741] *Irwin Toy v Quebec (A-G)* [1989] 1 SCR 927, 1004; *Dywidag Systems v Zutphen Bros* [1990] 1 SCR 705, 709.

[742] See Chap 7 'Right to Life', see para 7.76ff above.

[743] See generally, P W Hogg, *Constitutional Law of Canada* (4th edn, Carswell, 1997) Chap 44 'Fundamental Justice'.

[744] *MacBain v Canadian Human Rights Commission* [1984] 1 FC 696; appeal allowed on other grounds: (1985) 22 DLR (4th) 119, FCA; *Elliott v Canadian Broadcasting Corporation* (1994) 108 DLR (4th) 385, appeal dismissed (1995) 25 OR (3d) 302; leave to appeal refused, SCC 7 Mar 1996.

[745] *Re BC Motor Vehicle Act* [1985] 2 SCR 486 (a mandatory term of imprisonment was found to be a denial of liberty); *R v Swain* [1991] 1 SCR 933; 63 CCC (3rd) 41 (the automatic detention of a person acquitted on the ground of insanity was also a denial of liberty).

[746] *In Re ss 193 and 195.1 of the Criminal Code (Manitoba) ('Prostitution Reference')* [1990] 1 SCR 1123; 56 CCC (3rd) 1990, 65: even the 'possibility of imprisonment' was a denial of liberty.

[747] *R v Beare* [1988] 2 SCR 387.

[748] *Thomson Newspapers Ltd v Canada (Director of Investigation and Research, Restrictive Trade Practices Commission)* [1990] 1 SCR 425.

[749] Ibid and see *Stelco v Canada* [1990] 1 SCR 617.

restraint.[750] However, a broader view has gained some support. Thus, in *B(R) v Children's Aid Society*[751] the issue was whether the provincial Child Welfare Act denied parents the right to choose medical treatment for their infants, contrary to section 7 of the Charter. It was argued that such parental rights constituted 'liberty'. However, the Court held that 'liberty' was not merely freedom from physical restraint and that a free and democratic society required that the individual must be left room for personal autonomy and to make decisions that are of fundamental personal importance. Such personal 'liberty' included the right to nurture and care for a child and to make decisions for it in such matters as medical care. Nevertheless, interference by the state for the protection of the health or autonomy of the child was found on the facts to be justified in accordance with principles of fundamental justice.[752]

It is clear that 'liberty' does not include 'economic liberties' such as the right to property or freedom of contract.[753] The drafters of the Canadian constitution specifically omitted any mention of property or any guarantee of the obligation of contracts, in order to avoid the pitfalls of the US experience in the wake of *Lochner v New York*.[754] **10.210**

(c) 'Security of the person'

Introduction. 'Security of the person' includes freedom from the threat of physical punishment or suffering as well as freedom from such punishment itself.[755] It will be sufficient if the threat is to 'psychological integrity'.[756] However, emotional stress falls outside Article 7. Thus, there was no infringement to the security of a child who was required to accompany his father who was being deported.[757] **10.211**

In *R v Chatham*[758] it was said that if the element of compulsion in a demand for a breath sample leads to involuntary deprivation of liberty (as the Supreme Court of Canada held in *R v Therens*),[759] then taking a blood sample in the same circumstances must lead to an involuntary deprivation of the right to security of the person. **10.212**

---

[750] See eg *Re ss 193 and 195.1 of the Criminal Code (Manitoba) ('Prostitution Reference')* [1990] 1 SCR 1123 and see generally, P W Hogg, *Constitutional Law of Canada* (4th edn, Carswell, 1997) s 44.7(b).

[751] [1995] 1 SCR 315, SCC; and see *R v O'Connor* [1995] 4 SCR 411 para 111 (liberty includes privacy).

[752] Other members of the Court reached the same conclusion, on the basis of different reasons: Lamer J suggested that it was not the intention of the framers of the Charter to protect 'liberty' in its broadest sense; Cory, Iacobucci and Major, JJ found that an exercise of parental beliefs that grossly invades the best interests of the child falls completely outside the protection of the right to liberty in section 7.

[753] *Re ss 193 and 195.1 of the Criminal Code (Manitoba) ('Prostitution Reference')* (n 750 above) 1163–1166 *per* Lamer J; also *Edward Books and Art Ltd v R* [1986] 2 SCR 713.

[754] (1905) 198 US 45 (the US Supreme Court struck down a law providing for maximum hours of work, the decision was overturned in *West Coast Hotel v Parrish* (1937) 300 US 379); see generally, L Tribe, *American Constitutional Law* (2nd edn, Foundation Press, 1986) Chap 8, A Cox, *The Court and the Constitution* (Houghton Miffin, 1987) Chaps 6 and 8.

[755] *Singh v Canada (Minister of Employment and Immigration)* [1985] 1 SCR 177.

[756] *R v Morgentaler (No 2)* (1988) 44 DLR (4th) 385; and most recently *New Brunswick (Minister of Health and Community Services) v G (J)* (1995) 131 DLR (4th) 273; leave to appeal to SC granted 150 DLR (4th) vii; 10 Sept 1999.

[757] *Downes v MEI* (1986) 4 FTR 215.

[758] (1985) 23 CRR 344.

[759] [1985] 1 SCR 613.

10.213 **Physical apprehension.** In *R v Wilson*[760] it was decided that a security guard had used excessive force in the apprehension and arrest of a thief in violation of the security interest under section 7. Having followed the accused, who was carrying stolen meat from the store to his car, the security guard, without identifying himself as such, asked the man to stop and climbed into the passenger side of the vehicle as he began to drive away. A struggle ensued and the guard eventually applied a carotid throat hold to the thief, rendering him unconscious. When the accused had regained consciousness the guard arrested him. The actions of the security guard had deprived the accused of the security of his person contrary to the principles of fundamental justice and the degree of force used was not reasonable and proportionate to the seriousness of the offence. The Supreme Court treated the section 7 issue as one of security of the person.

10.214 **Abortion.** The right to security of the person has also been addressed in the context of the abortion debate. While the right to life of the foetus is not constitutionally protected until birth,[761] the right of a pregnant woman to security of the person under section 7 has formed the basis for rejecting restrictions on the availability of abortion. Thus, in *R v Morgentaler (No 2)*,[762] the Court struck down the federal Criminal Code restrictions on abortion on the ground that they constituted a denial of the right of the pregnant woman to 'security of the person', other than in accordance with the principles of fundamental justice. As a result of *Morgentaler*, there are no longer any legal restrictions on abortion in Canada. but it is recognised that the state nevertheless has a legitimate interest in regulating abortion.[763]

10.215 **Physician-assisted suicide.** The *Rodriguez*[764] case dealt with a request for physician-assisted suicide by a terminally ill patient. Ms Rodriguez sought to have a Criminal Code prohibition on aiding and abetting suicide struck down so that, at her direction, a physician might lawfully administer a lethal dose of medication to end her life in the later stages of her progressive and terminal motor neurone disease. The Court found that the Criminal Code provision did infringe the security interest of the appellant within the meaning of section 7 although it did not deprive her of security in breach of the principles of fundamental justice. It constituted a justifiable limitation on the right of the individual to autonomy over her person. The legislation fulfilled the Government's objectives of preserving life and protecting the vulnerable. The blanket prohibition on assisted suicide was considered neither arbitrary nor unfair as it reflected the policy of the state that human life should not be depreciated by allowing life to be taken.

10.216 **Medical treatment: mental health.** In *Fleming v Reid*[765] the Ontario Court of Appeal found that provisions of the Mental Health Act deprived the appellants of their right to security of the person in contravention of section 7 of the Charter. The legislation authorised a review board to override the competent refusal of an involuntary patient to consent to the administration of anti-psychotic drugs in the event of his incompetence. The provision was found contrary to the common law doctrine of informed consent by which every competent adult has a right to freedom from unwanted medical treatment.

---

760 *R v Wilson* (1994) 29 CR (4th) 302.

761 *Borowski v A-G (Canada)* (1987) 57 DLR (4th) 231.

762 [1988] 1 SCR 30.

763 The Government introduced a less restrictive bill to re-criminalise abortion (Bill C-43) which was passed by the House of Commons but defeated by the Senate on a tied vote in 1991.

764 *Rodriguez v British Columbia (A-G)* (1993) 107 DLR (4th) 342.

765 (1991) 82 DLR (4th) 298.

(3) Protection from arbitrary detention or imprisonment

Section 9 of the Charter provides that: 10.217

> Everyone has the right not to be arbitrarily detained or imprisoned.

'Detained' is broader in scope than 'imprisoned' and its meaning is critical to the application of this section. 'Detained' in section 9 has the same meaning as 'detention' in section 10 and will be addressed in connection with that section.[766]

'Arbitrariness' implies a discretion characterised by a lack of criteria, express or implied, which govern its exercise.[767] Random spot checks of motorists was an arbitrary exercise of police discretion under section 9 (although such checks were upheld as a reasonable contribution to highway safety under section 1).[768] An accused acquitted of a criminal charge by reason of insanity successfully challenged the Criminal Code provision requiring automatic detention in a psychiatric institution on such grounds:[769] the duty of the trial judge was unqualified by 'any standards whatsoever'.[770] 10.218

Furthermore, the standards applied must be rationally related to the purpose of the power of detention. Thus, in *R v Lyons*[771] the dangerous offender provisions of the Criminal Code were upheld because they supplied criteria for the classification of an offender as dangerous which were carefully designed to carry out the purposes of the legislation. 10.219

In order to comply with section 9, detention must also meet the legal requirements of other sections of the Charter. These standards comprise, in part, the criteria that govern arbitrariness. But in some situations detention is unlawful even though a discretion is exercised in good faith because it falls short of a standard such as 'reasonable and probable cause' for arrest without a warrant. In these circumstances it is not clear whether an unlawful detention is, for that reason alone, arbitrary under section 9.[772] 10.220

(4) Rights on arrest or detention

(a) The rights

Section 10 of the Charter states: 10.221

> Everyone has the right on arrest or detention:
> (a) to be informed promptly of the reasons therefor;
> (b) to retain and instruct counsel without delay and to be informed of that right; and
> (c) to have the validity of the detention determined by way of *habeas corpus* and to be released if the detention is not lawful.

[766] See para 10.221 below.
[767] *R v Hufsky* [1988] 1 SCR 621, 633 *per* Le Dain J.
[768] *R v Hufsky* (n 767 above).
[769] *R v Swain* [1991] 1 SCR 933.
[770] Ibid 1012; the position is now governed by s 672.54 of the Criminal Code which has been found to be in accordance with s 7 of the Charter, see *Winko v British Columbia (Forensic Psychiatry Institute)* [1999] 2 SCR 625.
[771] [1987] SCR 309.
[772] Cf *dicta* in *R v Duguay* [1985] 50 OR (2d) 375, 382, CA; SCC decision at 56 DLR (4th) 46.

The rights protected by section 10 depend on there being an arrest or detention, which involves 'some form of compulsion or coercion'.[773] The right to reasons for detention, counsel and habeas corpus are not available if, for example, a person cooperates with the police by voluntarily answering questions or voluntarily accompanying the police to the police station to provide information.

10.222 The meaning of detention has been extended considerably, on an arguably 'insecure foundation'[774] to include situations in which:

> a police officer or other agent of the state assumes control over the movements of a person by a demand or direction which may have significant legal consequences and which prevents or impedes access to counsel.[775]

In *Therens*[776] the accused supplied police with a breath sample upon request. However, failing to inform him of his right to counsel was a breach of section 10: since the demand for the breath sample amounted to a 'detention'. The fact that the demand was made at a police station distinguishes the case from that of a road-side detention, which is governed by a different Criminal Code provision requiring that the request for a sample must be complied with 'forthwith'. At the road-side, the possibility of consulting counsel prior to submission is excluded, but such a limitation on section 10 rights was found to be a reasonable one under section 1 of the Charter.[777]

10.223 In *R v Hufsky*[778] it was held that police random checks on vehicles constituted arbitrary detention under section 9, and that 'detained' there has the same meaning as 'detention' in section 10. It follows that every brief or routine restraint between the police and the public ought to be accompanied by a warning of the right to counsel. Thus, a restraint at an international border crossing may result in a detention: in *R v Simmons*[779] the Supreme Court of Canada said that the decision by a customs officer to order a strip search of a suspected drug smuggler constituted legally sanctioned control over the traveller that required that she be warned of her rights.

10.224 In *R v Debot*[780] the accused was 'frisked' in accordance with the federal Food and Drug Act and a seizure of illegal drugs was made. It was held that there was a detention in accordance with the *Therens* doctrine but the search could proceed without waiting for the detained person to exercise his right to counsel. Sopinka J, who concurred with the result, said that it was better to hold simply that there was no right to counsel in such circumstances.

(b) The right to reasons

10.225 Section 10(a) provides the right, on arrest or detention, 'to be informed promptly of the reasons therefor'. A breach of the section was found when an accused was questioned in relation to a shooting incident, but was not informed until after he had made a statement that the victim had died. He was then charged with murder.[781] There will also be a breach

---

773 *R v Therens* [1985] 1 SCR 613.
774 See P W Hogg, *Constitutional Law of Canada* (4th edn, Carswell, 1997) s 47.2(b).
775 *R v Therens* (n 773 above).
776 Ibid.
777 *R v Thomsen* [1988] 1 SCR 640.
778 [1988] 1 SCR 621.
779 [1988] 2 SCR 495.
780 [1989] 2 SCR 1140; 52 CCC (3rd) 193.
781 *R v Smith* [1991] 1 SCR 714.

when a person, who is under arrest for one offence, is not told he is under suspicion for another.[782] However, there was no breach when, during interrogation, the police became suspicious that the detained person suspected of a drug offence was implicated in a murder.[783]

(c) The right to counsel

Section 10(b) of the Charter confers the right on arrest or detention 'to retain and instruct counsel without delay and to be informed of that right'. To be effective, the warning must be given 'without delay',[784] upon or before[785] 'arrest or detention', and must be understood by the detained person.[786] The accused must understand the full 'extent of his jeopardy', because an informed decision as to the need for counsel cannot be made if he does not appreciate the seriousness of his situation. Thus, in *R v Greffe*[787] the accused was informed that he was being arrested on charges of traffic violations. In fact, the police suspected him of (and later charged him with) drug importation. This was a breach of the right to counsel.[788] The police were under a duty to advise the accused of the change of the extent of his jeopardy and to repeat the warning about his right to counsel once they had changed the focus of their investigation to the accused's involvement in a murder during the course of their interrogation. **10.226**

The duty to warn of the right to counsel does not require that the authorities offer an individual assistance in contacting counsel.[789] However, if a detained person indicates that he wishes to exercise the right to retain counsel, then the police must refrain from (or cease) questioning him;[790] and provide him with a 'reasonable opportunity to retain and instruct counsel without delay'.[791] Such an opportunity is denied if the accused is not offered the use of a telephone,[792] or if the police, who are questioning him,[793] demand a **10.227**

---

782 *R v Borden* [1994] 3 SCR 145.

783 *R v Evans* [1991] 1 SCR 869.

784 *R v Schmautz* [1990] 1 SCR 398, 416.

785 Ibid (although the words 'on arrest or detention' do not contemplate a warning before an arrest takes place, a prior warning will be valid if there is 'a close factual connection relating the warning to the detention and the reasons therefor'. A warning given 10 minutes before detention in the form of a demand for a breath test was therefore upheld as part of a single act of communication of the accused's rights).

786 In *R v Evans* [1991] 1 SCR 869; 63 CCC (3rd) 289, a violation of the right to counsel occurred when the police failed to make further explanation to a detainee of low intelligence who said that he did not understand what the warning meant.

787 [1990] 1 SCR 755.

788 See also, *R v Black* [1989] 2 SCR 138, where the charge of attempted murder was changed to murder when the victim subsequently died, it was required that the accused not only be informed of the death but also re-warned of his right to counsel.

789 *R v Baig* [1987] 2 SCR 537.

790 In *R v Manninen* [1987] 1 SCR 1233 (the accused's voluntary and incriminating statement made after he had indicated that he wished to consult counsel was excluded on the ground that there had been a breach of s 10(b)); not every incriminating statement made by the accused before he has had reasonable opportunity to seek counsel will be excluded: statements to another prisoner, a visitor or even directly to the police will be admissible so long as the police did nothing to elicit the information: *R v Logan* [1990] 2 SCR 731; *R v Graham* (1990) 1 OR (3d) 499.

791 *R v Manninen* (n 790 above) 1241.

792 Ibid.

793 Ibid.

breath sample[794] or place him on an identity parade[795] before he has had enough time to make contact with counsel. In *R v Bartle*[796] it was held that there was a breach of section 10(b) as a result of a police officer failing to give a suspect a telephone number to contact free counsel at night. However, where there is no 24-hour duty lawyer service, the section 10(b) duty will be discharged by providing home numbers of legal aid lawyers[797] and, if there is no free after hours legal advice service there is no obligation to give telephone numbers.[798]

10.228 If the accused is unable to obtain counsel on his own, there is probably a constitutional obligation on the authorities to assist him to find a lawyer. If the accused does not make a 'reasonably diligent' effort to contact counsel,[799] or he clearly and unequivocally waives[800] the right to retain and instruct counsel the police are free to proceed to question him.

10.229 Each province has a statutory legal aid plan and a duty counsel program for the assistance of those who cannot afford a lawyer although, in some provinces, this is not a 24-hour service.[801] It is now clear that there is no obligation on the state under section 10(b) to provide the free 24-hour duty legal services.[802] It is not clear whether there is a constitutional right to free legal aid at trial.[803]

10.230 In deciding whether evidence obtained in breach of section 10(d) should be excluded, the court will consider the nature of the evidence, the nature of the conduct by which the evidence was obtained and the effect on the system of justice of excluding the evidence.[804] The courts have refused to exclude evidence where the accused was using his right to counsel as a 'delaying tactic'[805] or where the breach had not been deliberate.[806]

(d) Habeas corpus

10.231 Section 10(c) provides for the right, on arrest or detention, 'to have the validity of the detention determined by way of habeas corpus and to be released if the detention is not lawful'. This paragraph does not expand the common law remedy of habeas corpus.[807] The

794 *R v Tremblay* [1987] 2 SCR 435.

795 *R v Ross* [1989] 1 SCR 3.

796 [1994] 3 SCR 173; see also *R v Pozniak* [1994] 3 SCR 310, *R v Harper* [1994] 3 SCR 343 and *R v Cobham* [1994] 3 SCR 360, all to the same effect.

797 *R v Prosper* [1994] 3 SCR 236.

798 *R v Matheson* [1994] 3 SCR 328.

799 *R v Smith* [1989] 2 SCR 368.

800 R v*Clarkson* [1986] 1 SCR 383; *R v Brydges* [1990] 1 SCR 190: waiver was not unequivocal where the accused said that he did not want counsel because he could not afford to pay, and the police did not explain that legal aid or duty counsel was available; waiver must be based on full knowledge of the extent of his jeopardy: *R v Smith* [1991] 1 SCR 714, for waiver in general see para 6.159 above.

801 *R v Brydges* (n 800 above).

802 *R v Prosper* [1994] 3 SCR 236; for a general discussion of the issue, see P W Hogg, *Constitutional Law of Canada* (4th edn, Carswell, 1997) s 47.4(k).

803 Cf *R v Rowbotham* (1988) 63 CR (3d) 113 (accused denied legal aid for 12-month trial, because just outside income limits, held that this was a breach of s 7 and s 11(d).

804 *R v Collins* [1987] 1 SCR 265, 284–286; for a full discussion, see P W Hogg (n 802 above) s 38.8 and see generally, para 21.128ff below.

805 *R v Tremblay* [1987] 2 SCR 435.

806 *R v Simmons* [1988] 2 SCR 495.

807 *Re Reimer and the Queen* (1987) 47 Man R (2d) 156.

right under this section can be used to review the jurisdiction of a provincial parole board, despite broad exclusive jurisdiction clauses.[808]

(5) Rights on being charged: section 11

(a) Introduction

The rights of a person on being charged with an offence are contained in section 11 of the Charter; they include not only the right to bail but extend to all aspects of the right to fair trial. Only the right to bail will be considered in this section.[809] For Charter purposes, 'offence' means any breach of law, whether federal or provincial, to which a penal sanction is attached.[810] **10.232**

(b) Bail

Section 11(e) of the Charter states that any person charged with an offence has the right not to be denied reasonable bail without just cause.[811] Pre-trial release from custody, now called 'judicial interim release',[812] must be 'reasonable' in its terms and conditions and must not be denied 'without just cause'. The Criminal Code provisions which establish grounds for pre-trial detention[813] have been found to provide 'just cause' for denial of bail.[814] Section 11(e) applies to bail pending extradition hearings[815] and to bail pending a re-trial[816] but does not apply in relation to applications for bail pending appeal.[817] **10.233**

The only substantial issue that has arisen under section 11(e) of the Charter is whether the shift of onus from prosecution to accused[818] in relation to a few Criminal Code offences, including murder, constituted a denial of bail without just cause. Such provisions are to be regarded as denials of bail and must, therefore, meet the 'just cause' standard. A reverse onus provision did meet this standard where an accused was charged with having **10.234**

---

808 *Re Cadeddu* (1982) 146 DLR (3d) 629.

809 For fair trial see para 11.392ff below.

810 *R v Wigglesworth* [1987] 2 SCR 541; for a full discussion of the status of proceedings before disciplinary or regulatory bodies, see P W Hogg (n 802 above) s 48.1.

811 For discussion of the right to bail under s 2(f) of the Canadian Bill of Rights, see W S Tarnopolsky, *The Canadian Bill of Rights* (2nd edn, McClelland and Stewart, 1975) 276; in *R v Bray* (1983) 40 OR (2d) 766 the Court said that the language of s 11(e) of the Charter is virtually identical to that of s 2(f) and has the same meaning.

812 Criminal Code, RSC 1985, c C-46, ss 515–526; the word 'bail' in s 11(e) refers to all forms of judicial interim release; see *R v Pearson* [1992] 3 SCR 665, 690.

813 Pre-trial detention is justified on only two grounds: either (1) that the accused's detention is necessary to ensure his attendance in court, or (2) that his detention is necessary for the protection of safety of the public, having regard to the likelihood that he would commit further crimes pending his trial; a third ground 'necessary in the public interest' was held to be void for vagueness in *R v Morales* [1992] 3 SCR 711, 728.

814 *R v Bray* (1983) 40 OR (2d) 766, 769.

815 *Re Global Communications Ltd and A-G of Canada* (1984) 10 CCC (3d) 97.

816 *R v Sutherland* (1994) 90 CCC (3d) 376.

817 *R v Branco* (1993) 87 CCC (3d) 71.

818 Whereas, in general, the Criminal Code places the onus on the prosecution to establish one of the two grounds for denial of interim judicial release, an amendment in 1976 reversed the presumption in a few instances, so that with respect to those offences an accused is required to prove that bail was warranted.

committed an indictable offence whilst awaiting trial on an earlier indictable offence.[819] The courts have also upheld 'reverse onus' provisions in relation to persons charged with drug trafficking[820] and with murder.[821]

10.235 The bail imposed must be 'reasonable' and to impose a condition which the accused is unable to meet is to deny him his section 11(e) right.[822] It is contrary to section 11(e) to deny bail to an accused who has no previous convictions or charges pending, no pattern of criminal behaviour and where there is no concern that he will not appear at trial, simply because of the seriousness of the offences with which he is charged.[823]

Appendix 2: The New Zealand Bill of Rights Act

(1) Introduction

10.236 The New Zealand Bill of Rights Act contains a number of provisions relating to liberty and security of the person:

> 22. **Liberty of the person**—Everyone has the right not to be arbitrarily arrested or detained.
>
> 23. **Rights of person arrested or detained**—
>
> (1) Everyone who is arrested or who is detained under any enactment—
> (a) shall be informed at the time of the arrest or detention of the reason for it; and
> (b) shall have the right to consult and instruct a lawyer without delay and to be informed of that right; and
> (c) shall have the right to have the validity of arrest or detention determined without delay by way of habeas corpus and to be released if the arrest or detention is not lawful.
>
> (2) Everyone who is arrested for an offence has the right to be charged promptly or to be released.
>
> (3) Everyone who is arrested for an offence and is not released shall be brought as soon as possible before a court or competent tribunal.
>
> (4) Everyone who is—
> (a) arrested; or
> (b) detained under any enactment
> for any offence or suspected offence shall have the right to refrain from making any statement and to be informed of that right.
>
> (5) Everyone deprived of liberty shall be treated with humanity and with respect for the inherent dignity of the person.

The rights in section 22 and section 23(1), (2) and (3) cover similar grounds as the 'right to liberty'. Section 23(4) deals with the 'privilege against self-incrimination of a person under arrest' and is considered in relation to Article 6 of the Convention[824] and section 23(5) does not appear to have been considered by the New Zealand Courts.[825]

---

[819] *R v Morales* (n 813 above).
[820] *R v Pearson* [1992] 3 SCR 665.
[821] *R v Sylvester* (1994) 23 WCB (2d) 380.
[822] *R v Fraser* (1982) 38 OR (2d) 172.
[823] *R v Dellacio* [1988] RJQ 425.
[824] See para 11.445 below.
[825] It derives from Art 10(1) of the ICCPR, the text of which is reproduced at App J in Vol 2.

Sections 22 and 23 are closely related to sections 9, 10 and 11 of the Canadian Charter. However, whilst the latter establishes 'two tiers' of rights: rights of arrested persons and fair trial rights,[826] the Bill of Rights Act separates the rights of a charged person from the right to fair trial.[827] **10.237**

(2) Liberty of the person

Section 22 contains the right 'not to be arbitrarily arrested or detained'. There has been some difference of judicial opinion as to what makes an arrest or detention 'arbitrary'. In general, any unlawful arrest or detention will be 'arbitrary'.[828] However, in exceptional circumstances a detention which is unlawful may escape arbitrariness, for example, if there were some grounds for an arrest, falling just short of 'reasonable cause'.[828a] Evidence obtained during unlawful detention for questioning will be excluded.[829] **10.238**

The question as to what constitutes 'detention' has been considered in a number of cases. It does not depend on the subjective intentions of the police or the perceptions of the suspect.[830] The test is whether the accused formed a reasonably held belief, induced by police conduct, that he was not free to leave. The reasonableness of the belief could relate to the abilities of the accused to understand what was taking place.[831] In determining whether there was a detention the court considers factors such as the language used by the police in requesting the suspect to come to the police station, the nature of the questions asked and whether the suspect was told in clear terms that he was free to go.[831a] **10.239**

Detention for the purposes of section 22 has been held to have taken place in the following situations: **10.240**

- where there is a deprivation of liberty by physical means;[832]
- where there is a statutory restraint upon the person accompanied by a penalty for failure to comply;[833] and
- where it is made clear by words or conduct that the person is not free to leave.[834]

---

826 See *R v Kalanj* [1989] 1 SCR 1594; 70 CR (3d) 260.

827 Which are contained in s 25 of the Bill of Rights Act; see generally, *R v Gibbons* [1997] 3 NZLR 585.

828 See *R v Goodwin (No 2)* [1993] 2 NZLR 390, 394; and see generally, A Shaw and A Butler, 'Arbitrary Arrest and Detention Under the New Zealand Bill of Rights' [1993] NZLJ 139.

828a See generally, *R v Dacombe*, unreported, 1 Apr 1999, *per* Fisher J at 21.

829 See *R v Goodwin (No 2)* (n 828 above) 394; also *R v Edwards* (n 828 above).

830 See *R v M* [1995] 1 NZLR 242, 244.

831 Ibid 246 (limited ability to understand English taken into account).

831a See generally, *R v Dacombe*, unreported, 1 April 1999 *per* Fisher J at 19; see also A Butler, 'Regulatory Offences and the Bill of Rights' in G Huscroft and P Rishworth, *Rights and Freedoms* (Brookers, 1995) 376ff.

832 *R v Kirifi* [1992] 2 NZLR 8: handcuffing to a fence.

833 As in the 'drink driving' cases: *Ministry of Transport v Noort* [1992] 3 NZLR 260; *Police v Smith and Herewini* [1994] 2 NZLR 306.

834 *R v Goodwin* [1993] 2 NZLR 153: suspect was directed to remain at the police station; for factors in determination as to whether a person is detained at the time of being questioned, see *R v Moran* (1987) 36 CCC (3d) 225; Ont CA.

(3) Rights of a person arrested

10.241 An arrest only takes place for the purposes of section 23 if there has been a communication or manifestation by the police of an intention to apprehend or hold the person concerned in the exercise of authority to do so; or the arrestor, acting or purporting to act under legal authority, had made it plain that the subject has been deprived of the liberty to go where he pleases. A citizen who is constrained to remain for questioning where no claim to exercise any legal authority was made cannot rely on section 23(1).[835]

10.242 The nature of the right to consult and instruct a solicitor before questioning under section 23(1)(b) must be brought home to the suspect.[835a] Thus, there was a breach when the record of interview suggested that an inexperienced 17-year-old might not have understood the nature of the right.[836] However, it is not necessary for a police officer, in advising a person of his right to consult and instruct a lawyer without delay to add expressly that he was entitled to do so in private.[837]

10.243 The right to be 'charged' promptly in section 23(2) does not mean that the formal charge process must be commenced by the swearing of an information or laying of an indictment. It is sufficient for the arrested person to be formally advised that he is to be prosecuted and to be given particulars of the charges he will face.[838] When considering this right, it must be borne in mind that charging will not always immediately follow arrest but may be made after a brief period of investigation.[839]

10.244 The right under section 23(3) is to be brought before a court 'as soon as possible'. This imports a concept of reasonableness.[840] The reasonableness of the time lapse is governed by the 'practicalities of the process'.[841]

Appendix 3: Human Rights Cases in Other Jurisdictions

(1) Australia

10.245 The Australian Constitution contains no Bill of Rights. However, the High Court has identified a number of 'implied constitutional rights'.[842] In *Kable v DPP*[843] the High Court struck down a statute directed specifically at the preventive detention of one named person. The appellant was nearing the end of a prison sentence for murder when the New South Wales State Government became concerned about his use of threatening correspondence. The Government accordingly passed the Community Protection Act 1994, expressed to apply only to the appellant. A court order was initially made that the

835 See *R v Goodwin* [1993] 2 NZLR 153; *R v P* [1996] 3 NZLR 132, 136.
835a *R v Mallinson* [1993] 1 NZLR 528.
836 See *R v Schriek* [1997] 2 NZLR 139, 158–59.
837 *R v Piper* [1995] 3 NZLR 540.
838 See *R v Gibbons* [1997] 2 NZLR 585, 594, preferring the view of the minority of the Supreme Court of Canada in *R v Kalanj* [1989] 1 SCR 1594; 70 CR (3d) 260.
839 See *R v Barlow* (1995) 14 CRNZ 9, 28.
840 See *Whithair v A-G* [1996] 2 NZLR 45, 54; see also *R v Schriek* [1997] 2 NZLR 139, 153.
841 See *R v Te Kira* [1993] 3 NZLR 257, 263.
842 See generally, para 1.39 above.
843 (1996) 138 ALR 577.

appellant be detained in prison following the expiry of his sentence, being satisfied on the balance of probabilities that he was more likely than not to commit a serious act of violence. That order, together with the parent statute, was struck down. Gaudron J stated that a central tenet of the judicial process was the protection of an individual's liberty from arbitrary punishment and derogation of rights. The making of preventive detention orders under the statute offended this tenet. The Court also found that the statute breached the separation of powers doctrine.

(2) Hong Kong

Articles 5 and 6 of the Hong Kong Bill of Rights Ordinance are in the same terms as Articles 9 and 10 of the International Covenant on Civil and Political Rights.[844] These provisions have only been considered by the courts on a small number of occasions. In *Ex p Lee Kwok Hung*[845] it was held that the powers of Securities and Finance Commission investigators to require a person to attend in order to give information were not inconsistent with the guarantee of 'liberty and security' in Article 5. The Court of Appeal said that it would be 'wholly contrived and artificial to categorise the compulsion exercised by an investigator over an interviewee as an "arrest" or "detention" ' as the investigator had no power physically to detain an interviewee who chose to walk out.[846] **10.246**

In *R v Leung Tak Choi*[847] the defendant had been found to be under a mental disability, and therefore not fit to be tried. This finding triggered a statutory mechanism whereby the defendant was detained in a mental hospital for treatment. The defendant could be tried later if he was deemed fit to be tried. This statute was found to be in conformity with Articles 5 and 6, in that the detention was established by law, and not arbitrary. **10.247**

(3) Human Rights Committee

Article 9 of the International Covenant on Civil and Political Rights provides for the right to liberty and security of the person.[848] In *Kulomin v Hungary*,[849] the UN Human Rights Committee found the pre-trial detention of the applicant to be a violation of Article 9(3) and (7) of the International Covenant on Civil and Political Rights. The applicant had been arrested, charged with murder and detained for three days before being given a form to sign; he remained in police custody for five months before being moved to a prison; 18 months after arrest he was tried and found guilty of homicide, sentenced to 10 years and subsequent expulsion from Hungary. In *Hugo Van Alphen v The Netherlands*[850] the Committee found that it was arbitrary to arrest and detain a lawyer to force him to waive his professional obligation of secrecy. **10.248**

(4) India

Article 21 of the Indian Constitution provides that: **10.249**

844 See App J below.
845 [1994] 1 LRC 150.
846 Ibid 157 c–d.
847 [1995] 2 HKCLR 32.
848 See App J in Vol 2.
849 (1996) 1 BHRC 217, UNHCR.
850 305/1988.

> No person shall be deprived of his life or personal liberty except according to procedure established by law.[851]

Such procedures must be reasonable, fair and just.[852] The phrase 'personal liberty' has been given a wide interpretation, and includes the right to travel abroad.[853] In *Khedat Mazdoor Chetna Sangath v State of MP*,[854] the Supreme Court stated that fettering a prisoner's limbs was repugnant to Article 21.[855] If extreme circumstances necessitated such fettering, the reasons for doing so should be recorded in writing so that the court could issue any necessary directions. In *Joginda Kumar v State of UP* the Court set out a number of principles in regard to the exercise of the power of arrest and the rights of a detainee.[856]

10.250 Article 22 of the Indian Constitution provides that:

> (1) No person who is arrested shall be detained in custody without being informed, as soon as may be, of the grounds for such arrest nor shall he be denied the right to consult, and to be defended by, a legal practitioner of his choice.
>
> (2) Every person who is arrested and detained in custody shall be produced before the nearest magistrate within a period of 24 hours of such arrest excluding the time necessary for the journey from the place of arrest to the court of the magistrate and no such person shall be detained in custody beyond the said period without the authority of a magistrate.
>
> (3) Nothing in clauses (1), or (2) shall apply—
>
> (a) to any person who for the time being is an enemy alien; or
> (b) to any person who is arrested or detained under any law providing for preventive detention;
>
> (4) No law providing for preventive detention shall authorise the detention of a person for a longer period than three months unless—
>
> (a) an Advisory Board consisting of persons who are, or have been, or are qualified to be appointed as, Judges of a High Court, has reported before the expiration of the said period of three months that there is in its opinion sufficient cause for such detention;
>
> Provided that nothing in this sub-clause shall authorise the detention of any person beyond the maximum period prescribed by any law made by Parliament. . . .
>
> (7) Parliament may by law prescribe—
>
> (a) the circumstances under which, and the class or classes of cases in which, a person may be detained for a period longer than three months under any law providing for preventive detention without obtaining the opinion of an Advisory Board . . .

10.251 The words 'arrest and detention' have been interpreted to exclude civil detention, such as removal of persons from a brothel under a statute designed to suppress immoral traffic,[857]

---

[851] See generally, N Jaswal, *Role of the Supreme Court with Regard to the Life and Personal Liberty* (Ashish, 1990).

[852] *Maneka v Union of India* AIR 1978 SC 597; *Mullin v Administrator, Union Territory of Delhi* AIR 1981 SC 746 para 3.

[853] *Satwant v Assistant Passport Officer* A 1967 SC 1836,1844–1845.

[854] (1994) 6 SCC 260.

[855] See also *Citizens for Democracy v State* [1995] 3 SCR 943 (placing of detainees in handcuffs while they were in a closed ward with security guards was unlawful; if necessary to prevent escape, extra armed guards could be utilised).

[856] 1994 4 SCC 260.

[857] *Raj Bahadur v Legal Remembrancer* A 1953 Cal 522.

and deportation of an alien.[858] 'Preventive detention' means the detention without trial in such circumstances that the evidence is insufficient to charge or convict the detainee.[859] The object of preventive detention is to prevent an individual from acting contrary to public order or national or state or security. An order for preventive detention may be made in anticipation of a prosecution, or after discharge or acquittal in a criminal proceeding.[860]

(5) Ireland

Article 40.4.1 of the Irish Constitution provides that: **10.252**

> No citizen shall be deprived of his personal liberty save in accordance with the law.

Statutes which cut down personal liberty are scrutinised on general constitutional principles rather than being automatically treated as being 'in accordance with the law'. As was said in *King v Attorney-General*:[861]

> . . . no citizen shall be deprived of personal liberty save in accordance with law—which means without stooping to methods which ignore the fundamental norms of the legal order postulated by the Constitution.

In *The People (DPP) v Coffey*[862] the accused had voluntarily accompanied the police to the police station, but had not been informed that he was at all times free to leave. Hamilton J found that this detention was unlawful.

In *Brennan v Governor of Portlaoise Prison*[863] a prisoner sought an absolute order of habeas corpus, on the basis that he was being forced to mix with drug addicts and people suffering from contagious diseases, which was threatening to both his physical and mental health. He also claimed that 'slopping out' and inadequate sanitation facilities further endangered his health. The court refused his application, stating that an order directing the release of a convicted prisoner should only be made in exceptional circumstances: such as where his constitutional rights were being consciously and deliberately violated; where the prisoner is being subject to cruel and degrading treatment; or where the conditions of detention were such as to seriously threaten the life or health of the prisoner and the authorities were unwilling or unable to rectify those conditions. The failure to comply with prison rules did not of itself entitle the applicant to be released. The applicant failed to show that the departure from the rules had in fact seriously endangered his health, or subjected him to inhuman or degrading treatment. However, the court noted that segregation of prisoners with diseases such as AIDS and HIV, and hepatitis B and C, would serve no useful purpose where the diseases in question could only be spread through bodily fluids. Furthermore, a policy of segregation would involve compulsory testing which might conflict with a prisoner's right to bodily integrity and medical confidentiality.[864] **10.253**

---

[858] *State of UP v Abdus Samad* A 1962 SC 1506.

[859] *Sasthi v State of WB* (1973) 1 SCR 468, 470.

[860] *Haradhon v State of WB* 1974 SC 2154, CB; *Ram Bali v State of WB* A 1975 SC 623; *Babulal v State of WB* A 1975 SC 606.

[861] [1981] IR 233.

[862] [1987] ILRM 727.

[863] [1999] 1 ILRM 190.

[864] Cf *Stephen Walsh v Governor of Limerick Prison* [1995] 2 ILRM 158 (the proposition that a breach of prison rules would in some way render detention unconstitutional and entitle the prisoner to be released was startling and certainly never contemplated by the Constitution).

10.254 Where a child is being detained in a certified reformatory school under a ministerial statutory power, because he exercised an 'evil influence' over other children, the investigative process leading to such detention had to be carried out constitutionally and in accordance with natural justice.[865]

(6) Kenya

10.255 Section 72(5) of the Constitution of Kenya, provides that:

> If a person arrested or detained . . . is not tried within a reasonable time, then without prejudice to any further proceedings that may be brought against him, he shall be released either unconditionally or upon reasonable conditions including in particular such conditions as are reasonably necessary to ensure he appears at a later date for trial or for proceedings preliminary to trial.

The High Court held that a provision which purported to remove the right of the court to grant bail in cases of murder, treason or robbery with violence was inconsistent with this provision and thus void.[866] However, on the facts, the court refused to grant bail to a person accused of robbery with violence. A provision that suspects held on suspicion of murder or treason could be held in custody indefinitely has also been declared void.[867]

10.256 In common with a number of Commonwealth countries, the Constitution of Kenya contains provisions allowing for administrative detention of persons under 'public security' regulations.[868] A person who is detained must be:

> furnished with a statement in writing in a language that he understands specifying in detail the grounds upon which he is detained.[869]

It has been held that the statement must furnish sufficient information to enable the detainee to know what is being alleged against him so that he can make adequate representations to a review tribunal.[870]

(7) South Africa

10.257 The right to freedom and security of the person, guaranteed in both the interim Constitution and the 1996 Constitution, has been considered in a number of cases by the Constitutional Court. Section 35(1) spells out the rights of arrested persons: the right to remain silent; to be informed of the right and of the consequences of waiving it; and the right not to be compelled to make an admission or confession. The section gives a suspect the right to be brought before a court as soon as reasonably possible, but within 48 hours of arrest, and at that first appearance to be charged, or told the reason for further

[865] *In the Matter of an Enquiry pursuant to Art 40.4 of the Constitution 1937* [1995] 2 ILRM 546.

[866] *Ngui v Republic of Kenya* [1986] LRC (Const) 308, 311 d–f.

[867] See *Kihoro v A-G of Kenya* [1993] 3 LRC 390 (detention for 74 days in police custody before being served with a detention order unlawful and amounting to mental torture, compensatory damages of Shs 400,000 awarded, no punitive damages).

[868] Constitution, s 83; and Preservation of Public Security Act, Cap 57.

[869] Constitution, s 83(2)(a).

[870] *Republic of Kenya v Commissioner of Prisons* [1985] LRC (Const) 624, relying on decisions on similar provisions in St Christopher, Nevis and Anguilla (*Herbert v Phillips and Sealey* (1967) 10 WIR 435) and Zambia (*Mutale v A-G of Zambia* (1976) ZR 139); and see also *A-G v Jones* [1985] LRC (Const) 635, Zam SC.

detention, or released. Section 35(2) likewise makes detailed provision for the protection of the interests of detainees, assuming that detention is constitutionally acceptable.[871] The Court has held that physical integrity of the person is the primary object of the guarantee.[872]

The case of *De Lange v Smuts NO*[873] concerned insolvency legislation which gave a power to a presiding officer to commit to prison where a person summoned to appear before a meeting of creditors refused to be sworn by the presiding officer at the meeting, failed to produce any book or document required to be produced, or refused to answer any question lawfully put to him. A majority of the Constitutional Court held that the provision permitting imprisonment was unconstitutional to the extent that it permitted a presiding officer who was not a magistrate[874] to issue a warrant committing an examinee at a creditors' meeting to prison. The Court noted that the right to freedom and security of the person has both a substantive and a procedural aspect. The substantive aspect required consideration of whether there was just cause for the power to commit to prison. It concluded that the power to commit recalcitrant witnesses at insolvency hearings served an important public objective, namely to ensure that bankrupts and other persons in a position to give important information relating to an insolvency do not evade supplying it: which constituted just cause for the deprivation of freedom. With regard to the procedural aspect of the right to freedom, Ackermann J noted that in several foreign countries government personnel other than judicial officers were not permitted to imprison a reluctant witness in an insolvency proceeding. Ackermann J concluded that because non-judicial government officers lack the independence of the judiciary, non-judicial officers cannot commit uncooperative witnesses to prison. However, magistrates who commit uncooperative witnesses in aid of an insolvency inquiry do so in a judicial and not an administrative capacity. Accordingly, committal by a magistrate presiding at creditors' meetings is constitutionally permissible.[875] **10.258**

That decision should be contrasted with the decision in *Nel v Le Roux NO*.[876] The applicant in that case was summoned under statutory powers to appear before a magistrate to provide relevant information in connection with alleged offences committed by his associate. Failure to answer questions without 'just excuse' made an examinee liable to summary imprisonment. The applicant's challenge based on the right not to be detained without trial failed. Summary proceedings before a judicial officer which could lead to **10.259**

[871] See App S in Vol 2.

[872] See *Ferreira v Levin* (1996) (1) BCLR 1, in which the majority rejected the broader approach of Ackermann J. Ackermann J's judgment provides a useful survey of comparative jurisprudence in this area.

[873] 1998 (3) SA 785.

[874] A meeting of creditors could be presided over by a magistrate, a Master or an officer in the public service designated by the Master of the High Court by a magistrate.

[875] It should be noted that Didcott J held that committal by non-judicial officers was constitutional; Mokgoro J and O'Regan J held that the entire provision was unconstitutional. O'Regan J stated that a magistrate presiding at a creditors' meeting was not acting in a judicial capacity, but rather fulfilling an administrative or quasi-judicial function. Powers of coercive imprisonment were seldom conferred on administrative or quasi-judicial bodies. Coercive imprisonment was a deprivation of personal liberty requiring thorough procedural safeguards of the type ordinarily found in a court of law. It also demanded impartiality and independence not only of the presiding officer but of the institution exercising those powers.

[876] 1996 (3) SA 562.

imprisonment were not inconsistent with the right not to be detained without trial, as they complied with the requirement that an impartial entity, independent of the executive and the legislature, act as arbiter between the individual and the state.

10.260 The imprisonment of judgment debtors for failure to pay judgment debts was struck down by the Constitutional Court in *Coetzee v Government of the Republic of South Africa.*[877] The Court found that while the goal of providing a mechanism for the enforcement of judgment debts was both legitimate and reasonable, the means chosen to achieve this goal were unreasonable. The statutory provisions in issue allowed persons to be imprisoned without actual notice of either the original judgement or of the hearing, placed a punitive burden of proof on the debtor without any express obligation on the magistrate to explain the rights and duties to an undefended lay person and failed to distinguish between those who cannot and those who will not pay.

(8) Sri Lanka

10.261 Article 13(1) of the Sri Lankan Constitution requires arrest according to a procedure laid down by law. Wanasundera J noted in *Joseph Perera v A-G*[878] that 'the Court has to take cognizance of the fact that a state of terrorism amounting to civil war is raging in the northern and eastern provinces of this country'.[879] Article 13(2) of the Constitution provides that:

> Every person held in custody, detained or otherwise deprived of personal liberty shall be brought before the judge of the nearest competent court according to procedure established by law, and shall not be further held in custody, detained or deprived of personal liberty except upon and in terms of the order of such judge made in accordance with procedure established by law.

Article 15(7) of the Constitution permits Article 13(1) and 13(2) rights to be restricted on a number of grounds, including the interests of national security and public order. In *Kumaratunga v Samarasinghe*[880] the Supreme Court stated that where an authority has power to arrest, the arrest is lawful even if the authority purports to carry out the arrest with reference to a wrong provision of law.

10.262 The Supreme Court declined to find that the petitioner in *Mahinda Rajapakse v Kudahetti*[881] had been detained when he was required to be searched before leaving the country. The petitioner in that case sought to board an airplane bound for Geneva, where he was due to attend a human rights conference. A police officer at the airport searched the petitioner's baggage for fabricated documents likely to be prejudicial to the interests of national security or to promote anti-government feeling, an offence under emergency regulations. The officer seized papers belonging to the petitioner containing information on missing persons, and photographs, and issued a receipt for them. The petitioner was then permitted to board the aircraft. It was held that there was no restriction of liberty. The petitioner was under no threat of being imprisoned if he did not permit search, but instead would not have been allowed to go to Geneva. The Court noted that the facts could potentially give rise to claims based on freedom of expression and freedom of movement.

[877] 1995 (4) SA 631.
[878] [1992] 1 Sri LR 199.
[879] Ibid 235.
[880] FRD (2) 347; see also *Edirisuriya v Navaratnam* [1985] 1 Sri LR 100.
[881] [1992] 2 Sri LR 223.

While Sri Lanka was under emergency rule from 1983 to 1993, a regulation permitted the Secretary to the Ministry of Defence to order a person to be detained when he was of the opinion that it was necessary to prevent that person from, *inter alia,* acting in a manner prejudicial to national security, public order, and the maintenance of essential services. This regulation was challenged in *Wickremabandhu v Herath*,[882] on the basis of the absence of a limit to the period of detention. The Supreme Court held that the question did not arise because the validity of the detention could be questioned on its merits if it is shown that a continued detention is manifestly unwarranted or excessive. The subjective satisfaction of the Secretary is required as to the necessity of the order.[883] However, the relevant question was whether it would be reasonable for the authority on whom the power is conferred to be satisfied of the existence of facts, the existence of which empowered him to make the order.[884] **10.263**

In *Wickremabandhu*'s case, emergency regulations which enabled the Secretary to the Ministry of Defence to deprive a detainee of the right to make representations to the President or the Advisory Committee set up for that purpose were held to be unconstitutional. The total exclusion of the right to seek review through the executive was unreasonable, in the national conditions then prevailing. The Supreme Court also held that a provision which stated that preventive detention should not be called in question in any court or on any ground whatsoever did not affect the fundamental rights jurisdiction of the Supreme Court. **10.264**

(9) Tanzania

Article 15 of the Tanzanian Constitution provides that: **10.265**

> (1) Man's freedom is inviolable and every person is entitled to his personal freedom.
> (2) For the purpose of protecting the right to personal freedom, no person shall be subject to arrest, restriction or detention, exile or deprivation of his liberty in any other manner save in the following cases:
>
> (a) in certain circumstances, and subject to a procedure prescribed by law; or
> (b) in the execution of the sentence or order of a court in respect of which he has been convicted.

In *DPP v Pete*[885] the Tanzanian Court of Appeal held that Article 15(2)(a) allowed for the deprivation of personal liberty through the prohibition of bail. However, the importance of the right to personal liberty was such that it could only be denied by a procedure which was fair and reasonable.[886] As the statutory bail provisions for bail contained no procedural safeguards, they were held to be in violation of the Constitution.

(10) Trinidad and Tobago

The appellants in *Phillip v Director of Public Prosecutions of Trinidad and Tobago*[887] were **10.266**

[882] [1990] 2 Sri LR 348.
[883] *Hirdramani v Ratnavel* [1973] 75 NLR 67; *Gunasekera v Ratnavel* [1974] 76 NLR 316; applying *Liversedge v Anderson* [1942] AC 206; but see also *Wickremabandhu v Herath* (n 882 above).
[884] *Janatha Finance v Liyanage* FRD (2) 373, 384, 387; *Shanthi Chandrasekaran v D B Wijetunge* [1992] 2 Sri LR 293, 301.
[885] [1991] LRC (Const) 553.
[886] Following *Maneka Ghandi v Union of India* AIR 1978 SC 597.
[887] [1993] 1 LRC 589.

insurrectionists who were granted a pardon by the acting President in exchange for release of hostages. The appellants were subsequently arrested, detained and charged with offences encompassed by the pardon. The Privy Council held that the applicants had established *prima facie* that they were the beneficiaries of a valid pardon which would render their detention unlawful. The applicants were accordingly entitled to a writ of habeas corpus as of right so that the lawfulness of their imprisonment could be immediately determined.

(11) Zimbabwe

10.267 By section 13(1) of the Constitution it is provided that:

> No person shall be deprived of his personal liberty save as may be authorised by law in any of the situations specified in subsection (2).[888]

By subsection 2(e), a person may be detained on reasonable suspicion of his having committed a criminal offence. It has been said:

> This standard represents a necessary accommodation between the individual's fundamental right to the protection of his personal liberty and the state's duty to control crime . . . The criterion of reasonable suspicion is a practical, non-technical concept which affords the best compromise for reconciling these often opposing interest.[889]

10.268 The Constitution preserved the power to detain without trial.[890] Schedule 2(1) provides safeguards for persons detained under any law providing for preventive detention. Such persons are entitled to be informed as soon as reasonably practicable after the commencement of the detention, and in any event not later than seven days thereafter, of the reasons for their detention; to obtain and instruct without delay (but at their own expense), and communicate with, a legal representative of their own choice. Preventive detention must be submitted to a review tribunal not more than 30 days (if this is during a period of public emergency) after the commencement of detention. The tribunal must review the case forthwith, and thereafter at intervals of 180 days (if this is during a period of public emergencies). The tribunal has the power to recommend release, but such recommendations are not binding.

10.269 The reasons given to detainees for their detention must 'furnish sufficient information to enable the detained person to know what is being alleged against him and to bring his mind to bear upon it.'[891] Thus, in *Paweni v Minister of State (Security)*[892] an allegation that the applicant was engaged in 'acts of economic sabotage against the State and People of Zimbabwe' and that 'It is considered that your activities pose a threat to the economic security of Zimbabwe' were held not to be sufficient. The detainee must receive the basic facts and material particulars which form the foundation of detention. Although it has been stated that adequate reasons are given when details of the date, time, place and material particulars of the alleged conduct are provided, the mere failure to give a specific date

[888] See The Zimbabwe Constitution Order (1979) 3 EHRR 418, 419.

[889] *A-G v Blumears* 1991 (1) ZLR 118, 122; see also *Smyth v Ushewokunze* [1998] 4 LRC 120.

[890] See Constitution, Sch 2 and see generally, J Hatchard, *Individual Freedoms and State Security in the African Context: The Case of Zimbabwe* (James Currey, 1993) Chap 6.

[891] This test was originally formulated in the Zambian case of *Kapwepwe and Kaenga* [1972] ZR 248, 262.

[892] [1985] LRC (Const) 612.

or to spell out the nature of the force being planned against the State do not render the reasons inadequate, unless failure to inform the detainee of the specific date hinders the preparation of his defence.[893] An allegation that a person is a 'South African espionage agent and a threat to the security of Zimbabwe' is too vague.[894] Where possible, the reasons must set out an assessment by the detaining body as to the reliability of the information upon which detention is based with such particularity as is consistent with security.[895] The violation of the safeguards relating to continued detention after the making of a detention order does not, without more, invalidate the detention, but must, initially be remedied by way of an order to ensure that the safeguard is afforded to the detainee.[896]

The civil imprisonment of debtors was considered by the Supreme Court of Zimbabwe in *Chinamora v Angwa Furnishers (Private) Ltd*.[897] It was held that this was an imprisonment for an obligation imposed by law within the words of section 13(1).[898] The Court also rejected the argument that the procedure for civil imprisonment was 'tainted' because the possibility existed of a judgment creditor being deprived of his liberty on account of total inability to pay.[899] This was because the procedure was fair and distinguished between debtors that were unable to pay and those who were unwilling to pay. **10.270**

893 *Austin and Harper v Minister of State* 1986 (2) ZLR 28.
894 Ibid.
895 Ibid.
896 *York v Minister of Home Affairs* 1982 (4) SA 496.
897 (1997) 1 BHRC 460.
898 Ibid 472–473.
899 Distinguishing *Coetzee v The Government of South Africa* 1995 (4) SA 631.

11

FAIR TRIAL RIGHTS

A. The Nature of the Rights

11.01 The closely related principles of 'due process' and 'the rule of law' are fundamental to the proection of human rights. Such rights can only be protected and enforced if the citizen has recourse to courts and tribunals which are independent of the state and which resolve disputes in accordance with fair procedures. The fairness of the legal process has a particular significance in criminal cases but 'fair trial rights' must also be applied in other proceedings which deal with disputes between citizen and state. The protection of procedural due process is not, in itself, suficient to protect against human rights abuses but it is the foundation stone for 'substantive protection' against state power. The protection of human rights therefore begins but does not end with fair trial rights.

11.02 One of the earliest and most well known provisions is to be found in the 'Bill of Rights' comprising the first ten amendments to the United States Constitution.[1] The Fifth Amendment[2] provides that:

[1] For a discussion of American due process rights, see generally, L Tribe, *American Constitutional Law* (2nd edn, Foundation Press, 1988) Chap 10 in relation to procedural due process rights and at Chap 8 in relation to substantive due process rights.

[2] The Fifth Amendment applies to the laws and actions of the federal government; however, due process rights are extended to the states under the Fourteenth Amendment.

> No person shall . . . be deprived of life, liberty, or property, without due process of law.

The Sixth Amendment includes the provision that:

> In all criminal prosecutions, the accused shall enjoy the right to a speedy and public trial, by an impartial jury . . .

Over 150 years later the need for 'fair trial' or 'due process' rights was recognised by the drafters of the Universal Declaration. Article 10 provides:

> Everyone is entitled in full equality to a fair and public hearing by an independent and impartial tribunal, in the determination of his rights and obligations and of any criminal charge against him.

The Convention was the first international human rights instrument to set out detailed protection for fair trial rights.[3] The rights were dealt with under four headings (which have been followed in many other international instruments): **11.03**

- general rights to procedural fairness, including a public hearing before an independent and impartial tribunal which gives a reasoned judgment;[4]
- the presumption of innocence in criminal proceedings;[5]
- specific rights for those accused of criminal offences, including rights to be informed of the charge, to trial within a reasonable time, to legal assistance and to cross-examine witnesses;[6]
- the right to be free from retrospective criminal laws.[7]

Other 'legal process' rights were added by the Seventh Protocol to the Convention and have also been recognised by other instruments:

- the right of appeal in criminal matters;[8]
- the right to compensation for wrongful conviction;[9]
- the right not to be tried or punished twice for the same offence.[10]

[3] Art 6, see para 11.150 below, and Art 7, see para 11.152 below.

[4] Convention, Art 6(1); Covenant, Art 14(1); American Convention on Human Rights, Art 6(1).

[5] Convention, Art 6(2); Covenant, Art 14(2), American Convention on Human Rights, Art 6(2); African Charter, Art 7(1)(b).

[6] Convention, Art 6(3); Covenant, Article 14(3); American Convention on Human Rights, Art 14(2).

[7] Convention, Art 7; Covenant, Article 15; American Convention on Human Rights, Art 9; African Charter, Art 7(2).

[8] Seventh Protocol, Art 2; Covenant, Art 14(5); American Convention on Human Rights, Art 7(2)(h).

[9] Seventh Protocol, Art 3; Covenant, Art 14(6); American Convention on Human Rights, Art 10.

[10] Seventh Protocol, Art 4; Covenant, Art 14(7); American Convention on Human Rights, Art 8(4).

Although the Seventh Protocol has not been ratified by the United Kingdom, it has ratified the Covenant and is, therefore, obliged to give effect to these additional rights as a matter of international law.[11]

11.04 'Fair trial rights' give rise to a large number of difficult issues. The following can be highlighted:

The extent of the right of access to the courts. It is always necessary to prescribe some limits on access to the courts, for example, in relation to stale or vexatious claims. The state has, traditionally, sought to restrict access to the courts by, for example, 'ouster clauses', and the use of special procedures and immunities; and this requires examination of the extent to which 'fair trial rights' include a right of access to the courts for the resolution of disputes.

The types of dispute subject to 'fair trial rights'. Although it is generally accepted that 'fair trial rights' should apply in the ordinary criminal courts, there is no clear consensus as to which other 'determinations' should attract protection. The extension of procedural rights into the area of 'administrative' decision-making is controversial and its limits have been worked out in varying ways in different contexts.

The nature of the tribunal. It is clearly established that a fair tribunal should be independent of the parties and impartial; but there has been considerable debate concerning the content of these notions and there is no generally accepted definition of either. 'Independence' gives rise to problems when the members of the tribunal are appointed on a temporary basis or can be removed by the executive. A variety of tests for 'impartiality' have been suggested—including 'real likelihood', 'real danger' or 'reasonable suspicion'. Their application continues to give rise to practical difficulties.

The content of due process rights. The principle of 'natural justice', *audi alteram partem* (hear the other side) is generally accepted but there is no consensus as to what this entails. Questions arise, for example, as to whether there should be advance disclosure of evidence, a public oral hearing, legal representation, cross-examination of witnesses and a reasoned judgment.

Restrictions on fair trial rights. In criminal cases, it is often necessary to balance the rights of the individual defendant against the wider interest. When considering fair trial provisions, courts are repeatedly faced with decisions as the extent to which the rights of defendants should be modified or restricted in the wider interest. Three examples can be given of areas which have caused particular controversy: first, the use of statutory provisions which place the burden of proving a defence on the accused; secondly, the circumstances in which the courts should admit evidence obtained by the exercise of state powers of 'compulsion'; and thirdly, the extent to which the courts should exclude evidence or

[11] See para 2.09ff above.

stay proceedings when the human rights of suspects have been violated. In all three examples the courts have been called on to balance the interests of the individual suspect against those of the community generally with differing results in different jurisdictions.

These and similar issues have, of course, been explored in the English case law, but usually without reference to broader 'fair trial' principles. They have also been considered in other common law jurisdictions; and on many occasions by English judges in the Privy Council. Fair trial rights will be an area in which the case law in other jurisdictions is likely to be of particular assistance in dealing with issues which arise under the Human Rights Act. **11.05**

B. The Rights in English Law Before the Human Rights Act

(1) Introduction

English law provides no explicit general statement of rights in relation to the conduct of legal process. Nevertheless, it is possible to identify a number of elements which are conventionally regarded as 'fair trial' rights. These have been most thoroughly explored in the context of administrative law but have been increasingly recognised as being of general application. **11.06**

The right of access to the court in order to have disputes determined in accordance with the law is deeply rooted in the common law. Blackstone viewed the right of access to the courts as one of the 'outworks or barriers, to protect and maintain inviolate the three great and primary rights, of personal security, personal liberty and private property'. He described it in these terms: **11.07**

> A third subordinate right of every Englishman is that of applying to the courts of justice for redress of injuries. Since the law is in England the supreme arbiter of every man's life, liberty and property, courts of justice must at all times be open to the subject and the law be duly administered therein.[12]

The constitutional importance of the rights of the citizen to use the courts has been consistently emphasised. As Lord Diplock said: **11.08**

> Every civilised system of government requires that the state should make available to all its citizens a means for the just and peaceful settlement of disputes between them as to their respective legal rights. The means provided are courts of justice to which *every citizen has a constitutional right of access* in the role of plaintiff to obtain the remedy to which he claims to be entitled . . .'[13]

---

[12] R Kerr (ed), *Blackstone's Commentaries on the Laws of England* (4th edn, John Murray, 1876) 111.

[13] *Bremer Vulkan Schiffbau und Maschinenfabrik v South India Shipping Corporation Ltd* [1981] AC 909, 917.

11.09 More generally, although the phrase 'due process of law' is most familiar in the context of the United States Constitution,[14] it has its origins in the early history of English law. Thus, the right to trial by due process of law is sometimes traced back to clause 39 of the Magna Carta of 1215 which states that:

> No freeman shall be taken and imprisoned or disseised of any tenement or of his liberties or free customs . . . except by lawful judgment of his peers or by the law of the land (*per legem terrae*).[15]

This interpretation has been doubted[16] but the term 'due process' appears in a number of medieval statutes. The most well-known example is the Statute of Edward III which provides that:

> no man of what estate or condition that he be, shall be put out of land or tenement, nor taken, nor imprisoned, nor disinherited, nor put to death, without being brought in answer by due process of the law.[17]

11.10 The doctrine of 'due process of law' was revived in the early seventeenth century by Sir Edward Coke who interpreted the words '*per legem terrae*' as meaning, 'Without being brought in to answer but by due process of the common law'.[18] Coke's view of the importance of 'due process' was extremely influential.[19] Limited statutory provision for 'due process rights' was made by Articles 10 and 11 of the Bill of Rights of 1689 which provided:

> That excessive bail ought not to be required nor excessive fines imposed nor cruel and unusual punishments inflicted.
>
> That jurors ought to be duly impanelled and returned . . .[20]

The independence of the judges was finally confirmed in the Act of Settlement of 1701. During this period, it was emphasised that there must be no punishment except as prescribed by a previously existing law, that all statutes must have only prospective (and not retrospective) operation and that the discretion of magistrates should be strictly circumscribed by law.

11.11 Since the late nineteenth century, procedural forms of justice have been inextricably linked to the concept of the rule of law. The Privy Council has said that the phrase 'due process of law' invokes the concept of the rule of law itself and the universally accepted standards of justice observed by civilised nations.[20a] In Dicey's

[14] See generally, H Abraham and B Perry, *Freedom and the Court* (7th edn, Oxford University Press, 1998) Chap 4 'The Fascinating World of Due Process of Law'.

[15] See *Halsbury's Statutes* (4th edn, Butterworths, 1995) Vol 10, 15–16.

[16] See generally, D Galligan, *Due Process and Fair Procedures* (Clarendon Press, 1996) 171–3.

[17] 28 Edw II Ch 3 (1354); *Halsbury's Statutes* (n 15 above) Vol 10, 21.

[18] *Coke's Institutes*, Chap 29, 51; see generally, D Galligan (n 16 above) 188ff.

[19] See D Galligan (n 16 above) 174ff.

[20] *Halsbury's Statutes* (n 15 above) Vol 10, 46; Art 10 is reproduced as the Ninth Amendment to the US Constitution.

[20a] *Thomas v Baptiste* [1999] 3 WLR 249, 259 dealing with the 'due process clause' in the Constitution of Trinidad and Tobago.

exposition, the 'rule of law' involved the supremacy of regular law as opposed to arbitrary power and equality before the law.[21] The concept of the rule of law involves a number of ideas which are now seen as part of the 'fair trial' or 'due process' rights. However, as Galligan has pointed out, the notion of 'due process' is not mentioned in Dicey's *Introduction to the Study of the Law of the Constitution*.[22] The procedural aspects of 'due process' were treated as being contained in the procedures of the ordinary courts which were not further analysed.

Over the past 200 years, common law 'due process rights' have received their most sustained development not in relation to the procedure of the superior courts, but in connection with inferior tribunals and administrative bodies.[23] The principles of 'natural justice' were developed in cases involving proceedings before justices and the deprivation of public office. By a series of nineteenth century cases, they were applied to 'every tribunal or body of persons invested with authority to adjudicate upon matters involving civil consequences to individuals'.[24] The approach of the courts was classically expressed in *Cooper v Wandsworth Board of Works*[25] in which it was held that a power to demolish buildings was subject to an implied right to be heard. As Willes J said: **11.12**

> a tribunal which is by law invested with power to affect the property of one of Her Majesty's subjects, is bound to give such subject an opportunity of being heard before it proceeds: and that the rule is of universal application and founded on the plainest principles of justice.[26]

However, in the first third of the twentieth century, the courts drew back from the broader application of 'natural justice' principles.[27] In the *Venicoff* case[28] it was held that the Home Secretary's power of deportation was a purely executive function and the deportee had no right to be heard. 'Natural justice' principles were taken to be restricted to decision-makers who were under a duty to 'act judicially', a category which was understood to exclude most administrative decisions.[29] In a **11.13**

[21] A Dicey, *An Introduction to the Study of the Law of the Constitution* (10th edn, Macmillan, 1961), 202–203.

[22] D Galligan, (n 16 above) 178–9.

[23] See generally, H Wade and C Forsyth, *Administrative Law* (7th edn, Clarendon Press, 1994) Chap 15; Lord Woolf and J Jowell, *De Smith, Woolf and Jowell, Judicial Review of Administrative Action* (5th edn, Sweet & Maxwell, 1995), Chap 17 and M Beloff, 'Natural Justice—(The Audi Alteram Partem Rule) and Fairness', in M Supperstone and J Goudie, *Judicial Review* (2nd edn, Butterworths, 1997) paras 8.1–8.72.

[24] *Wood v Woad* (1874) LR Ex 190, 196; see generally, *De Smith, Woolf and Jowell* (n 23 above) para 7-012; M Beloff, (n 23 above) paras 8.6–8.10.

[25] (1863) 14 CB (NS) 180.

[26] Ibid 190, see also, Byles J at 194.

[27] See *De Smith, Woolf and Jowell* (n 23 above) para 7–015ff.

[28] *R v Leman Street Police Station Inspector, ex p Venicoff* [1920] 3 KB 72.

[29] *R v Electricity Commissioners, ex p London Electricity Joint Committee Company (1920) Ltd* [1924] 1 KB 171, 205.

series of cases over a period of 40 years, the courts consistently denied 'fair hearing' rights to those affected by administrative decisions.[30]

11.14 The older more vigorous approach was re-asserted by the House of Lords in *Ridge v Baldwin*[31] in which they held that a Chief Constable had an implied entitlement to prior notice of the charge against him and a proper opportunity of meeting it. The House of Lords recognised that any decision which affected a person's rights or interest was subject to the principles of natural justice: any person exercising such power had to act 'judicially'. Over the next three decades, the principles of 'fair hearing' were extended to almost the entire range of public decisions, including decisions under prerogative powers.[32] The scope and extent of the requirements to act fairly in any particular situation depends on the character of the decision-maker, the nature of the decision and the statutory framework.[33] These principles have, increasingly, been applied to the operation of the ordinary courts as the English law has come to recognise the central importance of 'fair trial rights'.

(2) Right of access to the courts

(a) Introduction

11.15 There is a well-established common law presumption of legislative intent that access to the courts in respect of justiciable issues is not to be denied save by clear words in a statute.[34] There is, thus, a 'right' of access to the courts which is, in the familiar way, subject to express or implied statutory provision to the contrary. It is unclear whether the right can be overidden by 'necessary implication'. In *R v Lord Chancellor, ex p Witham*[35] Laws J said he found:

> great difficulty in conceiving of a form of words capable of making it plain beyond all doubt to the statute's reader that the provision in question prevents him from going to court (for that is, what would be required), save in a case where that is expressly stated. The class of cases where it could be done by necessary implication is, I venture to think, a class with no members.[36]

---

[30] See *De Smith, Woolf and Jowell* (n 23 above) paras 7-028–7-030.

[31] [1964] AC 40.

[32] *Council of Civil Service Unions v Minister for the Civil Service* [1985] AC 374 but not to those relating to matters such as the making of treaties, the defence of the realm, the grant of honours, the dissolution of parliament and the appointment of Ministers, *per* Lord Roskill at 415.

[33] *Lloyd v McMahon* [1987] 1 AC 625.

[34] *Pyx Granite Company Ltd v Ministry of Housing and Local Government* [1960] AC 260, 286; and see F Bennion, *Statutory Interpretation* (3rd edn, Butterworths, 1997) s 281, 658ff and *De Smith, Woolf and Jowell* (n 23 above) para 5-017; and, see para 1.34 above.

[35] [1998] QB 575, 586.

[36] Similar views were expressed by Lord Browne-Wilkinson in *R v Secretary of State for the Home Office, ex p Pierson* [1998] AC 539, 575, but see *R v Secretary of State for the Home Office, ex p Leech (No 2)* [1994] QB 198, CA and see also M Supperstone and J Coppel, 'Judicial Review after the Human Rights Act' [1999] EHRLR 301 (in which it is argued that the views of Laws J are inconsistent with the *dicta* in *ex p Leech* and of Lord Reid in *Westminster Bank Ltd v Beverley Borough Council* [1971] AC 508, 529; and see *R v Lord Chancellor ex p Lightfoot* [2000] 2 WLR 318.

This 'right' has been invoked in a number of contexts in order to limit the circumstances in which the 'access to justice' of individual litigants can be restricted. In *R v Boaler* the right was applied to the institution of criminal proceedings.[37] The issue was whether the then statutory provisions relating to vexatious litigants prevented the commencement of a private prosecution. The court held by a majority that they did not. Scrutton J said that: **11.16**

> One of the valuable rights of every subject of the King is to appeal to the King in his Courts if he alleges that a civil wrong has been done to him, or if he alleges that a wrong punishable criminally has been done to him, or has been committed by another subject of the King. This right is sometimes abused and it is, of course, quite competent for Parliament to deprive any subject of the King of it either absolutely or in part. But the language of any such statute should be jealously watched by the Courts, and should not be extended beyond its least onerous meaning unless clear words are used to justify such extension . . . I approach the consideration of a statute which is said to have this meaning with the feeling that unless its language clearly convinces me that this was the intention of the Legislature I should be slow to give effect to what is a most serious interference with the liberties of the subject.

The ability of a citizen to bring a private prosecution has been recognised to be an 'important constitutional right'.[38]

The right of access to the courts was invoked by a prisoner who complained that correspondence with his solicitor concerning litigation was being censored by the prison authorities under the prison rules. The Court of Appeal held that the general 'rule making power' in section 47(1) of the Prison Act 1952 did not extend to the making of rules which created an impediment to the free flow of communication between solicitor and client about contemplated legal proceedings. Steyn LJ said: **11.17**

> It is a principle of our law that every citizen has a right of unimpeded access to a court, In *Raymond v Honey* ([1983] 1 AC 1, 13), Lord Wilberforce described it as a 'basic right'. Even in our unwritten constitution it must rank as a constitutional right.[39]

The impact of this 'constitutional right' on the ability of the executive to make secondary legislation arose in *R v Lord Chancellor, ex p Witham*[40] in which it was held that rules requiring litigants on income support to pay a minimum Writ fee were *ultra vires*. Laws J said that: **11.18**

> the right to a fair trial, which of necessity imports the right of access to the court, is as near to an absolute right as any which I can envisage.[41]

---

[37] [1915] 1 KB 21.

[38] *R v Leeds Magistrates' Court, ex p Serif Systems Ltd* [1997] CLY 1373.

[39] *R v Secretary State for the Home Department, ex p Leech (No 2)* [1994] QB 198, 210A-D; see also *R v Secretary of State, ex p Quaquah*, *The Times*, 21 Jan 2000.

[40] [1998] QB 575; see also *R v Lord Chancellor, ex p Lightfoot* (n 36 above).

[41] Ibid 585.

He went on to express the view that:

> the executive cannot in law abrogate the right of access to justice, unless it is specifically so permitted by Parliament; and this is the meaning of the constitutional right.[42]

11.19 Nevertheless, the right of access to the court cannot be absolute. It has long been accepted that it must be regulated and restricted for the benefit of all litigants. As Sullivan J said in *R v Immigration Appeal Tribunal, ex p* S:[43]

> A right to a hearing is rarely unconditional, even where matters of life and liberty are at stake. One may have to appeal within a certain time, appear at a certain time, not be abusive or disruptive, file certain documents in support of the appeal and so forth. Having an opportunity for a hearing does not mean that one may not disentitle oneself from taking up that opportunity if one behaves in a certain manner. I do not consider that it offends any fundamental principle to say that certain breaches of procedural rules may mean that an Appellant loses his right to a hearing in certain circumstances. The more serious the issues . . . the more serious the breaches would have to be in order to justify depriving an Appellant of his right to a hearing.

There are a number of ways in which the right of access to the courts is restricted: a 'leave requirement' for the commencement of proceedings, the granting of 'immunities' to certain litigants, the imposition of time limits and other restrictions such as those relating to costs.

(b) 'Ouster' provisions

11.20 The attitude of the courts towards restrictions on access to justice is illustrated by the long line of cases dealing with 'ouster' or 'finality' clauses. Such clauses seek to prevent access to the courts for the purposes of judicial review.[44] It has been consistently held that such clauses do not prevent access to the courts in cases where decisions are taken without jurisdiction.[45] As Sir John Laws has said:

> The rigour of the court's approach to ouster clauses is a function of the rule of law; the vindication of the rule of law is the constitutional right of every citizen. So if it is to be breached by Parliament or Parliament's permission, the High Court will require express words to be used.[46]

11.21 It is often said that contracts which oust the jurisdiction of the courts are illegal and contrary to public policy.[47] Arbitration agreements were, however, not treated

---

[42] *R v Lord Chancellor, ex p Witham* [1998] 8 QB 57.

[43] [1998] Imm AR 252.

[44] See generally, Lord Woolf and J Jowell, *De Smith, Woolf and Jowell, Judicial Review of Administrative Action* (5th edn, Sweet & Maxwell, 1995) paras 5-015–5-027; Bennion, *Statutory Interpretation* 74ff.

[45] The leading case is *Anisminic Ltd v Foreign Compensation Commission* [1969] 2 AC 147.

[46] J Laws, 'Illegality: The problem of jurisdiction', in M Supperstone and J Goudie, *Judicial Review* (2nd edn, London: Butterworths, 1997) para 4.23.

[47] *Doleman and Sons v Ossett Corporation* [1912] 3 KB 257.

as offending this principle because the courts retained wide powers to review arbitration awards.[48] Nevertheless, the courts would not recognise provisions which sought to exclude this review jurisdiction, because 'There must be no Alsatia in England where the King's writ does not run'.[49] The position is now governed by the Arbitration Act 1996 which binds parties to arbitration agreement and prevents recourse to the courts save in limited circumstances.[50] The courts have recognised the international policy exemplified in this legislation, that the consent of the parties should be honoured by the courts.[51]

(c) Leave to commence proceedings

In a number of cases the access of litigants to the court is restricted by requirements of 'leave', 'permission' or 'prior authorisation'. Such a requirement applies to special categories of litigant and to special types of proceedings. Special types of litigants who require leave or permission include mental patients, minors and vexatious litigants. Permission is required for applications for judicial review of the decisions of public bodies. **11.22**

Under the Civil Procedure Rules,[52] infants and mental patients cannot bring proceedings without a 'litigation friend'. The proceedings may be stayed if a claim is brought without the participation of a 'litigation friend'. A person may act as a litigation friend without a court order provided that he can fairly and competently conduct the proceedings, has no adverse interest and, when a claim is being brought, undertakes to pay the costs.[53] An authorisation and certificate of suitability must be filed.[54] Otherwise, a litigation friend can be appointed by the court.[55] **11.23**

A 'leave' requirement is imposed on mental patients by section 139(2) of the Mental Health Act 1983. This provides that: **11.24**

> No civil proceedings shall be brought against any person in any court in respect of any [act done in pursuance of the Act] . . . without the leave of the High Court; and no criminal proceedings shall be brought against any person in any court in respect of any such act except by or with the consent of the Director of Public Prosecutions.

48 *Scott v Avery* (1856) 5 HLC 811; *Hallen v Spaeth* [1923] AC 684.

49 Per Scrutton LJ, *Czarnikow v Roth Schmidt and Company* [1922] 2 KB 478, 488 ('Alsatia' being the common name for the Whitefriars area which, until 1697 had certain privileges and was a sanctuary for debtors).

50 See generally, D Sutton, J Kendall and J Gill, *Russell on Arbitration*, (21st edn, Sweet & Maxwell, 1997).

51 See eg *Halki Shipping Corporation v Sopex Oils Ltd* [1998] 1 WLR 726.

52 CPR, Pt 21; formerly, RSC Ord 80.

53 CPR, r 21.4.

54 CPR, r 21.5.

55 CPR, r. 21.6.

Proceedings issued without leave are a nullity.[56] This provision is designed to prevent harassment by 'clearly hopeless actions' so leave should be granted if the case deserves further investigation, even if it is unlikely to succeed.[57] However, leave will be refused if the point is 'virtually unarguable'.[58] The section does not cover applications for judicial review to quash admission decisions.[59] More generally, the court has jurisdiction in all types of case to prevent further applications being made without leave in proceedings which are before the court.[60] It also has jurisdiction to restrain the issue of proceedings which are manifestly vexatious.[61]

11.25 There is also a statutory jurisdiction restricting access to the courts by so-called 'vexatious litigants'. The Attorney-General can apply for an order that a person cannot institute or continue civil or criminal proceedings without the leave of the High Court.[62] This application must be made to the Divisional Court[63] and an order can only be made, if the court is satisfied that the person has 'habitually and persistently and without any reasonable ground' instituted vexatious civil proceedings, made vexatious applications or instituted vexatious prosecutions.[64] Once an order is made against a person then he requires leave to commence proceedings. Leave shall not be given unless the High Court is satisfied:

> that the proceedings or application are not an abuse of the process of the court in question and that there are reasonable grounds for the proceeding or application.[65]

This provision does not, therefore, entirely exclude the vexatious litigant's access to the courts. It is noteworthy that the analogous provision in South Africa has recently been held to be consistent with the 'fair trial' provisions of the Constitution.[66]

11.26 Proceedings to challenge the decisions of public bodies must be brought by way of 'judicial review' applications under CPR Sch 1 R 53.[67] These are subject to a 'permission requirement' under Sch 1 R 53.3(1). The applicant makes an application without notice for permission which will only be granted if the applicant has an

---

56 *Pountney v Griffiths* [1976] AC 314.
57 *Winch v Jones* [1986] QB 296.
58 See eg *James v London Borough of Havering* (1992) 15 BMLR 1.
59 *ex p Waldron* [1986] QB 824.
60 *Grepe v Loam* (1887) 37 Ch D 168.
61 *Ebert v Venvil* [1999] 3 WLR 670.
62 Supreme Court Act 1981, s 42(1A).
63 *In Re Vernazza* [1960] 1 QB 197.
64 s 42(1).
65 s 42(3).
66 *Beinash v Ernst and Young* 1999 (2) BCLR 125.
67 Order 53 was preserved under Sch 1 of the CPR but is being replaced by new rules which take effect on 2 Oct 2000.

'arguable case on the merits'.[68] If permission is refused, the applicant may renew his application at an oral hearing.[69]

(d) Immunities

Introduction. The English law confers a number of immunities from suit on public authorities and private individuals. These can be considered under six heads: **11.27**

- crown immunity;
- parliamentary immunity;
- judicial immunity;
- proceedings immunity;
- negligence immunity; and
- statutory immunities.

Crown immunity. The Sovereign can act either in a personal capacity or in a public capacity. In her personal capacity, the Sovereign is not subject to legal process because no court can have jurisdiction over her.[70] This is sometimes described as an application of the maxim 'the king can do no wrong'.[71] Until 1947 it was possible to bring a claim in contract (but not in tort) against the sovereign personally by the petition of right procedure. It seems that the abolition of the petition of right by the Crown Proceedings Act[72] means that it is no longer possible to bring a contractual claim against the Sovereign.[73] **11.28**

The Crown is the Sovereign in her public capacity and is a 'corporation sole'.[74] The Crown Proceedings Act 1947 removed most of the Crown's immunities against ordinary legal process. For the first time it was possible to sue the Crown in tort.[75] It is now clear that injunctions can be granted against the Crown and that the Crown is subject to the ordinary contempt jurisdiction.[76] **11.29**

After 1947, the Crown retained a statutory immunity in relation to tort actions **11.30**

[68] *R v Legal Aid Board, ex p Hughes* (1992) 24 HLR 698 and generally, R Clayton and H Tomlinson, *Judicial Review Procedure* (Wiley, 1997) Chap 5; *De Smith, Woolf and Jowell* (n 44 above) para 15–011ff.

[69] Clayton and Tomlinson (n 68 above) 127–129 (the precise procedure depends on whether or not the application relates to a 'civil' or a 'criminal' matter).

[70] *Blackstone's Criminal Practice* (Blackstone Press, 1999) Vol 1, 242.

[71] See generally, H Wade and C Forsyth, *Administrative Law*, 7th edn, Clarendon Press, 1994) Chap 21.

[72] s 13 and Sch 1; cf *Franklin v A-G* [1974] 1 QB 185, 201.

[73] See Wade and Forsyth (n 71 above) 833–834.

[74] Wade and Forsyth (n 71 above) 819.

[75] s 2(1).

[76] *M v Home Office* [1994] 1 AC 377; and see Sir Stephen Sedley, 'The Crown In Its Own Courts', in C Forsyth and I Hare, *The Golden Metwand and the Crooked Cord* (Clarendon Press, 1998) 253–66.

arising out of the acts or omissions of members of the armed forces brought by other members of the armed forces.[77] This extended to claims for medical negligence by military doctors.[78] This immunity has now been removed by statute[79] but can be revived by the Secretary of State if it appears to him necessary to do so by reason of 'imminent national danger or great emergency' or 'for the purposes of warlike operations'.[80]

11.31 **Parliamentary immunity.** Parliament and its members have a number of ancient but important immunities and privileges.[81] The most important of these privileges derives from Article 9 of the Bill of Rights 1689 which provides that:

> the freedom of speech and debates or proceedings in parliament ought not to be impeached or questioned in any court or place out of Parliament.

This is a provision of high constitutional importance and ought not to be narrowly construed.[82] 'Proceedings in parliament' extend to everything said or done in the House in the transaction of parliamentary business, the giving of evidence before either House or a committe, the presentation or submission of a document to either House or a committee, the preparation of a document for the purposes of such business, the publication of a document including a report by order of either House and ancillary matters.[83] Article 9 goes only to prohibit:

- the attachment by the courts of any form of legal penalty to a member of Parliament (or any person taking part in proceedings in Parliament) for anything said in Parliament. This means that a member cannot be sued for defamation in relation to any statement made in parliament, nor prosecuted for any offence relating to these statements;[84]
- the direct criticism by the courts of anything said or done in the course of Parliamentary proceedings.[85]

11.32 Furthermore, Article 9 is a manifestation of the wider principle that the courts and Parliament are both astute to recognise their respective constitutional roles. This means that the courts will not allow any challenge to be made to what is said or done within the walls of Parliament in performance of its legislative functions

---

[77] Crown Proceedings Act 1947, s 10.

[78] See *Derry v Ministry of Defence* (1999) 49 BMLR 62; see also *Pearce v Secretary of State for Defence* [1988] AC 755.

[79] Crown Proceedings (Armed Forces) Act 1987, s 1.

[80] Ibid s 2(2).

[81] See generally, D Limon and W McKay (eds), *Erskine May, Parliamentary Practice* (22nd edn, Butterworths, 1997); I Loveland, *Constitutional Law: A Critical Introduction* (Butterworths, 1996) Chap 8, see also *In Re Parliamentary Privilege Act 1770* [1958] AC 331.

[82] See *per* Lord Browne-Wilkinson, *Pepper v Hart* [1993] 1 AC 593, 638D.

[83] See, in relation to defamation proceedings, Defamation Act 1996, s 13; and generally, *Halsburys Laws of England* (4th edn, Butterworths, 1997) Vol 34, 'Parliament', para 1008, and see *A-G of Ceylon v De Livera* [1963] AC 103, 121.

[84] *Ex p Wason* (1869) LR 4 QB 573, 576; *Dillon v Balfour* (1887) 20 LR Ir 600.

[85] See *Hamilton v Al Fayed* [1999] 1 WLR 1569.

and protection of its established privileges.[86] Thus, in *Prebble v Television New Zealand*[87] Lord Browne-Wilkinson approved Blackstone's statement that:

> the whole of the law and custom of Parliament has its original from this one maxim, 'that whatever matter arises concerning either House of Parliament ought to be examined, discussed, and adjudged in that House to which it relates, and not elsewhere'.[88]

As a result, it is a breach of parliamentary privilege to allow what is said in Parliament to be the subject matter of investigation or submission.[89] It is not permissible to bring into question anything said or done in Parliament by suggesting (whether by direct evidence, cross-examination, inference or submission) that the actions or words were inspired by improper motives.[90] Although it is legitimate to prove as a matter of history by reference to *Hansard* what happened in Parliament, it is not acceptable to go beyond history so as to suggest impropriety. Witnesses may not be cross-examined by reference to earlier evidence given to a parliamentary Select Committee.[91] **11.33**

If the exclusion of material on the ground of parliamentary privilege makes it quite impossible fairly to determine the issues between the parties, the court must stay proceedings altogether. The grant of such a stay in *Hamilton v Guardian Newspapers*[92] led to the enactment of section 13 of the Defamation Act 1996 which provides that, where the conduct of a person in or in relation to proceedings in Parliament is in issue in defamation proceedings, he may waive the privilege for the purposes of those proceedings.[93] This waiver is of the privilege of the member alone,[94] and gives rise to potential problems if there is relevant evidence arising out of the conduct of other members who have not waived their privilege.[95] The fact that Parliament has found an MP guilty of misconduct will not prevent the MP taking advantage of the Defamation Act 1996 to sue his accuser for repeating the allegations of misconduct in the media. This will not be a 'questioning of proceedings in parliament'.[96] **11.34**

---

[86] *Burdett v Abbot* (1811) 14 East 1; *Stockdale v Hansard* (1839) 9 Ad & El 1; *Bradlaugh v Gossett* (1884) 12 QBD 271; *Pickin v British Railways Board* [1974] AC 765; *Pepper v Hart* [1993] 1 AC 593; *Hamilton v Al Fayed* [2000] 2 WLR 609.

[87] [1995] 1 AC 321.

[88] *Commentaries on the Laws of England* (17th edn, 1830), Vol 1, 163.

[89] *Church of Scientology of California v Johnson-Smith* [1972] 1 QB 522; approved in *Pepper v Hart* [1993] 1 AC 593.

[90] See *Prebble v Television New Zealand* [1995] 1 AC 321, 333.

[91] See generally, *Hamilton v Guardian Newspapers Financial Times*, 22 Jul 1995, May J.

[92] n 91 above and also in *Allason v Haines The Times*, 25 Jul 1995, *per* Owen J.

[93] For s 13, see generally, P Milmo and W Rogers (eds), *Gatley on Libel and Slander* (9th edn, Sweet & Maxwell, 1998) para 13.30; for the history of the *Hamilton v Guardian, Financial Times*, 22 Jul 1995 litigation (which was discontinued on the first day of the trial).

[94] s 13(3).

[95] See *Hamilton v Al Fayed (No 2)* [2000] 2 WLR 609.

[96] Ibid.

11.35 **Judicial immunity.** The Crown is not liable in respect of actions done by any person 'while discharging or purporting to discharge any responsibility of a judicial nature'.[97] Judges of the superior courts[98] have special immunity against actions in tort even where they are acting outside their jurisdiction.[99] If such a judge acts in bad faith then an action will only lie if he is acting outside his jurisdiction.[100] A similar immunity applies in relation to properly empanelled jurors who are immune from action arising out of anything said or done in their capacity as jurors.[101]

11.36 However, in relation to other judges and magistrates, the common law rule was that they are liable for acts done outside their jurisdiction.[102] The meaning of 'jurisdiction' in this context caused considerable difficulty. Four categories of case have been distinguished:[103] cases in which there is no 'jurisdiction of cause', cases in which magistrates do 'something quite exceptional' in the course of a summary trial, cases in which there is no proper foundation of law for the sentence or order made and cases where, as a result of a technical defect, a magistrate who would otherwise have jurisdiction to try the case and sentence the defendant, acts without juridiction. In the fourth class of case, the magistrate was not liable in damages. Thus, a magistrate who issued a warrant without jurisdiction in the course of properly constituted proceedings was not liable.[104] The common law rule in relation to justices was subsequently reversed by a statute. The Justices of the Peace Act 1997 now makes it clear that no action lies against a justice in relation to any matter within his jurisdiction[105] and, in relation to matters not within his jurisdiction, an action will only lie 'only if, it is proved that he acted in bad faith'.[106] The impact of the Human Rights Act on judicial immunity and claims for damages is discussed in Chapter 5.[106a]

11.37 **'Proceedings immunity'.** There is also an immunity from civil action attaching to preparing a witness statement or giving evidence in court proceedings.[107] It has long been established that no action lies against parties or witnesses for anything said or done, even if falsely and maliciously and without any reasonable and probable cause, in the ordinary course of any proceeding in a court of justice.[108] This

[97] Crown Proceedings Act 1947, s 2(5).

[98] The High Court, Court of Appeal and House of Lords.

[99] See generally, A Olowofoyeku, *Suing Judges: A Study of Judicial Immunity* (Clarendon Press, 1993); and 'State Liability for the Exercise of Judicial Power' [1998] PL 444.

[100] See *Anderson v Gorrie* [1895] 1 QB 668, 670; *Re McC (A Minor)* [1985] AC 528, 540–541.

[101] See *Bushell's* case (1670) 6 State Tr 999; *Henderson v Broomhead* (1859) 4 H&N 569, 579.

[102] *Re McC* (n 100 above) 541B-H.

[103] *R v Manchester City Magistrates' Court ex p Davies* [1989] QB 631.

[104] *R v Waltham Forest Justices, ex p Solanke* [1986] QB 479.

[105] s 51.

[106] s 52.

[106a] See para 5.110ff above and see also para 10.175ff above.

[107] See generally, *Docker v Chief Constable of West Midlands Police*, *The Times*, 1 Aug 2000 (HL).

[108] *Dawkins v Lord Rokeby* (1873) LR 8 QB 255; *Watson v McEwen* [1905] AC 480.

immunity extends to the preparation of evidence to be given in court[109] including the preparation of expert reports.[110] However, in *Docker v Chief Constable of West Midlands Police*[111] the House of Lords distinguished between what a witness said in court or in a witness statement and fabricating evidence (such as a police officer writing down a false confession). It went on to hold that the immunity did not extend to fabricating evidence. Furthermore, it does not apply to proceedings for malicious prosecution,[112] malicious process or malicious arrest.[113] It seems that the immunity does apply to actions for misfeasance in a public office.[114]

It has been said that the test as to whether the immunity should be extended to new situations is a strict one: 'necessity must be shown'.[115] However, in recent times the immunity has been extended to publications in documents prepared in the investigation of crime[116] and to the supply of information by the official receiver in bankruptcy in the ordinary course of his duties.[117] It is difficult to see in some cases how the test of 'necessity' is satisfied and there are powerful arguments in support of the more limited immunity which can be displaced on proof of malice.[118] The approach is also difficult to reconcile with *Docker*. **11.38**

There was formerly a closely related immunity applied to advocates in respect of their conduct and management of a case in court. This applied to any claim for damages for negligence arising out of what is done or omitted in the course of conducting a case in court.[119] This immunity was to be based on public policy and to be part of the general immunity which attaches to judges, witnesses and others participating in trials.[120] It applied to work 'intimately connected with the conduct of the cause in court'.[121] However, the House of Lords in *Arthur J S Hall v Simons*[122] decided that it was no longer in the public interest in the administration of justice for advocates to be immune from suit in civil or criminal litigation. **11.39**

[109] *Marrinan v Vibert* [1963] 1 QB 528.

[110] *Palmer v Durnford Ford (a firm)*[1992] QB 483; *Stanton v Callaghan* [1998] PNLR 116.

[111] See n 107 above.

[112] *Martin v Watson* [1996] 1 AC 74.

[113] *Roy v Prior* [1971] AC 470; *Gizzonio v Chief Constable of Derbyshire*, *The Times*, 29 Apr 1998.

[114] See *Silcott* (n 107 above); *Docker* (n 107 above), but see *Bennett v Commissioner of Police* (1997) 10 Admin LR 245, cf *Taylor v Director of the Serious Fraud Office* [1998] 1 WLR 1040, 1053H.

[115] *Per* Lord Hoffmann, *Taylor* (n 114 above) 1052F, citing *Mann v O'Neill* (1997) 71 ALJR 903.

[116] *Taylor v Director of the Serious Fraud Office* (n 114 above).

[117] *Mond v Hyde* [1998] 2 WLR 499.

[118] See Lord Lloyd dissenting in *Taylor* (n 114 above).

[119] *Rondel v Worsley* [1969] 1 AC 191; see generally, *Arthur J S Hall v Simons* [1999] 3 WLR 873 (an appeal to the House of Lords is pending).

[120] *Saif Ali v Sydney Mitchell and Company* [1980] AC 198.

[121] *Rees v Sinclair* [1974] 1 NZLR 180.

[122] See n 119 above.

Nevertheless, it will normally be an abuse of process[123] for a civil court to hold that a subsisting conviction is wrong whereas, in general, it will not be an abuse to make a collateral challenge in a claim arising from civil proceedings.

However, a litigant does not owe a duty of care to the opposite party in relation to the manner in which the litigation is conducted.[124]

11.40 **Negligence immunity.** Public authorities have immunity from negligence claims in a number of different contexts. A claim in the tort of negligence depends on the existence of a 'duty of care' owed by the defendant to the claimant. Where a claimant can show foreseeability of damage and a relationship of proximity with the defendant, a duty of care will be imposed *provided* the court is satisfied that it is 'just and reasonable' to impose such a duty.[125] This requirement involves considerations of 'public policy'. In a range of cases, the courts have held that it is not 'just and reasonable' to impose a duty of care on public authorities. These authorities have, as a result, been granted immunity from actions in negligence. It has been suggested that a general approach underlies the immunity cases namely:

> a recognition that such a duty [of care] would be inconsistent with some wider object of the law or interest of the particular parties. Thus, if the existence of a duty of care would impede the careful performance of the relevant function, or if investigation of the allegedly negligent conduct would itself be undesirable and open to abuse by those bearing grudges, the law will not impose a duty'.[126]

11.41 At least two difficulties arise from the approach taken by the courts. First, despite some suggestions to the contrary,[127] the language used in the cases suggest that the courts are applying a blanket rule of policy which has the effect of preventing access to the court.[128] Secondly, in reaching policy conclusions, the courts make factual *assumptions* about the practical impact of imposing liability in negligence. The difficulty about applying a priori reasoning to these situations was illustrated by the views expressed in the Court of Appeal in *X (Minors) v Bedfordshire County Council*[129] concerning the impact of imposing a duty of care on psychiatrists; whereas Sir Thomas Bingham MR took the view that imposing a duty of care

[123] See *Hunter v Chief Constable of West Midlands Police* [1982] AC 529.
[124] *Business Computers International Ltd v Registrar of Companies* [1988] Ch 229.
[125] *Caparo Industries plc v Dickman* [1990] 2 AC 605, 617H, *per* Lord Bridge.
[126] *Capital and Counties plc v Hampshire County Council* [1997] QB 1004, 1040D-E, *per* Stuart-Smith LJ.
[127] See eg *per* Lord Browne-Wilkinson in *Barrett v Enfield LBC* [1999] 3 WLR 79; see para 11.44 below.
[128] Although the Court of Appeal struck out a negligence claim on this basis in *Osman v Ferguson* [1993] 4 All ER 344, the European Court of Human Rights in *Osman v United Kingdom* (1998) 5 BHRC 293 decided that this breached the right of access to the Court under Art 6. The principles applied by the Court are discussed at para 11.195 below and its impact under the Human Rights Act are discussed at para 11.307 below.
[129] [1995] 2 AC 633.

would maintain high standards,[130] Staughton LJ said[131] that it would result in overkill and defensive practices. Unfortunately, the courts have not received evidence as to the practical impact of imposing duties of care and have relied on judicial 'hunches'. This has led to highly unsatisfactory (and inconsistent) conclusions as to the existence of immunities.[132] The force of this argument was accepted by Lord Slynn in *Phelps v Hillingdon London Borough Council*[132a] where he said that it must *not* be presumed that the imposing liability will interfere with the performance of a public body's duties. The allegation must be proved and will only be established in exceptional circumstances.

One of the first areas in which such an immunity was recognised was in relation to police investigations. In *Hill v Chief Constable of West Yorkshire*[133] the House of Lords held that, as a matter of public policy, actions for damages for negligence would not lie against the police 'so far as concerns their function in the investigation and suppression of crime'. It was suggested that there was no need to impose a duty of care on the police because 'the general sense of public duty which motivates police forces is unlikely to be appreciably reinforced by the imposition of such liability'. A number of reasons were suggested as to why, as a matter of public policy, the police should be immune from negligence liability: **11.42**

- the imposition of liability may lead to the exercise of a function being carried on in a detrimental fashion;
- negligence actions against the police might require an elaborate investigation of the facts with a consequent diversion of police manpower and resources.

This reasoning depends on a number of factual assumptions about which no evidence had been adduced. Nevertheless, the immunity is now well established. It has been held to apply even in cases in which the negligence alleged related to failures to take care in specific high risk factual situations: **11.43**

- where there was an identified suspect, known to be a threat to named individuals;[134]
- where burglars were present at premises when the police had been called to the scene by an alarm;[135]
- where the police knew about road hazards and had taken no steps to warn road users about them;[136]

---

[130] Ibid 662.

[131] Ibid 675.

[132] See eg the first instance cases discussed in *Capital and Counties plc v Hampshire County Council* [1997] QB 1004, 1022–1024.

[132a] *The Times*, 28 Jul 2000.

[133] [1989] 1 AC 53.

[134] *Osman v Ferguson* [1993] 4 All ER 344, but see *Osman* v *United Kingdom* (1998) 5 BHRC 293; and see para 11.307 below.

[135] *Alexandrou v Oxford* [1993] 4 All ER 328.

[136] *Ancell v McDermott* [1993] 4 All ER 355.

- where a person has been exposed to psychological harm whilst acting as an 'appropriate adult' in police interviews under Code of Practice C;[137]
- where the police negligently damage property when searching a suspect's home.[138]

Similar reasoning has been employed to grant immunity to other public authorities in related situations:

- to the Crown Prosecution Service[139] and the police[140] in the conduct of criminal prosecutions;
- to the immigration service in relation to the provision of information;[141]
- to the Home Office in relation to the provision of information to the Parole Board concerning prisoners.[142]

11.44 There is also an immunity from negligence claims for local authorities in relation to the performance of their statutory duties to protect children and deal with special educational needs. In *X (Minors) v Bedfordshire County Council*[143] the House of Lords held that it would not be 'just and reasonable' to impose a common law duty of care on a local authority in relation to the performance of its statutory duties to protect children. Three reasons were advanced for this. First, that such a duty would 'cut across the whole statutory system set up for the protection of children at risk'. Secondly, because the task of the local authority in dealing with children at risk is extraordinarily delicate. Thirdly, if liability in damages were to be imposed 'it might well be that local authorities would adopt a more cautious and defensive approach to their duties'. Analogous reasoning was applied in holding that local education authorities were immune from claims in negligence arising out of the provision for children with special needs.[144] A similar immunity has been held to apply in relation to claims against local authorities for negligence in relation to foster parents.[145] In addition, it has been held that the immunity extends to the individual educational psychologists employed by local authorities to give advice in relation to children with learning difficulties.[146] The same policy reasons which led the House of Lords to hold that the local authority had immunity applied to claims against the individuals. These included the risk of late and vexatious claims, the difficulties of establishing causation and the risk of 'defensive

[137] *Leach v Chief Constable of Gloucestershire* [1999] 1 WLR 1421 (but it was held that there was a duty to provide counselling afterwards).

[138] *Kinsella v Chief Constable of Nottinghamshire, The Times*, 24 Aug1999.

[139] *Elguzouli-Daf v Commissioner of Police of the Matropolis* [1995] QB 335.

[140] *Kumar v Metropolitan Police Commissioner*, unreported, 31 Jan 1995.

[141] *W v Home Office, The Times*, unreported 14 Mar 1997 CA.

[142] *Dixon v Home Office*, unreported 30 Nov 1998 CA.

[143] [1995] 2 AC 633.

[144] Ibid 761–762; for US cases in which claims for 'educational malpractice' were struck out, see *Phelps v Hillingdon London Borough Council* [1999] 1 All ER 421, 435j–436f.

[145] *W v Essex County Council* [1999] Fam 90.

[146] *Phelps v Hillingdon LBC* [1999] 1 All ER 421.

education'.[147] On the other hand, in *Barrett v Enfield LBC*[148] the House of Lords held that the public policy considerations which meant that it would not be fair, just and reasonable to impose a common law duty of care on a local authority when deciding whether or not to take action in respect of a suspected case of child abuse did not have the same force in respect of decisions taken once the child was in care.

However, there has been a shift of emphasis in recent cases, partly under the influence of the decision of the Court of Human Rights in *Osman v United Kingdom*.[148a] The courts have made it clear that local authority defendants are unlikely to establish a defence which relies on a 'blanket immunity': there must be a proper examination of the facts in each case.[148b] This approach does not, however, preclude the court from making a summary determination of the 'duty of care' issue under the CPR.[148c] **11.44A**

Recent cases have suggested that the police are not immune from liability in negligence if there is 'some form of assumption of responsibility' by them for the plaintiff.[149] Furthermore, there are some cases in which other considerations of public policy, such as the need to protect informers, may prevail.[150] The authorities were reviewed by the Court of Appeal in *Costello v Chief Constable of Northumbria*:[151] **11.45**

> For public policy reasons, the police are under no general duty of care to members of the public for their activities in the investigation and suppression of crime (*Hill's* case). But this is not an absolute blanket immunity and circumstances may exceptionally arise when the police assume a responsibility, giving rise to a duty of care to a particular member of the public (*Hill's* case and *Swinney's* case). The public policy considerations which prevailed in *Hill's* case may not always be the only relevant public policy considerations (*Swinney's* case).[152]

In that case, the police were found liable in negligence as the result of a failure of a police officer to assist a colleague who was being attacked by a prisoner.

It seems that this type of 'policy immunity' does not extend to negligence claims against fire fighters. In *Capital and Counties plc v Hampshire County Council*[153] the **11.46**

[147] Ibid 441h–442h.

[148] [1999] 3 WLR 79; the views expressed by Lord Browne-Wilkinson concerning the decision in *Osman v United Kingdom* (1998) 5 BHRC 293, 84 and their impact on the development of negligence are discussed at para 11.307 below.

[148a] (1998) 5 BHRC 293, see para 11.307 below.

[148b] See, in particular, *Barrett v Enfield London Borough Council* (n 148 above).

[148c] *Kent v Griffiths* [2000] 2 WLR 1158 paras 37–38 (*per* Lord Woolf).

[149] *Elguzouli-Daf v Commissioner of Police of the Metropolis* (n 139 above) 349.

[150] *Swinney v Chief Constable of Northumbria Police Force* [1997] QB 464, 481H–482B.

[151] [1999] 1 All 550.

[152] Ibid 563f–g.

[153] [1997] QB 1004; see also *OLL Ltd v Secretary of State for Transport* [1997] 3 All ER 897 in which a similar approach was taken to the duties of coastguards answering a call at sea.

Court of Appeal considered and dismissed a range of arguments in favour of the imposition of such an immunity including the risk of encouraging 'defensive fire fighting' and the risk of opening the 'floodgates' of litigation.[154] However, fire fighters owe no duty of care in answering calls for help or merely by attending at the scene of the fire and fighting it. A duty of care only arises if the fire fighters themselves create the danger which causes injury. The ambulance service has no immunity and, once a call is accepted, it owes the person on whose behalf the ambulance has been called a duty to attend within a reasonable time.[154a]

11.47 **Statutory immunities.** The Mental Health Act 1983 gives a limited immunity from suit to those involved in dealing with mental patients.[155] By section 139(1) it is provided that:

> No person shall be liable, whether on the ground of want of jurisdiction or on any other ground, to any civil or criminal proceedings to which he would have been liable apart from this section in respect of any act purporting to be done in pursuance of this Act or any regulations or rules made under this Act, or in, or in pursuance of anything done in discharge of functions conferred by any other enactment on the authority having jurisdiction under Part VII of this Act, unless the act was done in bad faith or without reasonable care.

This provision does not create a 'personal immunity' but imposes a fetter on the court's jurisdiction to act in such cases.[156]

(e) Restrictions arising in the course of proceedings

11.48 The courts have, in some circumstances, refused to allow litigants who are in contempt of court to take further steps in the action until the contempt was 'purged'.[157] However, the fact that a party has disobeyed a court order is not now of itself a bar to his being heard.[158] It is only actions of the party which impeded the course of justice in the cause which gave the court a discretion to refuse to hear him until the impediment was removed or good reason shown why it should not be. In *Re Swaptronics*[159] it was said that:

> were the courts to refuse to allow those in contempt access to the courts simply on the grounds that they are in contempt, they could well be acting in breach of the provisions of Article 6.1 of the European Convention on Human Rights which entitles everyone to the determination of his civil rights by means of a fair and public

[154] Ibid 1043D-1044F.

[154a] *Kent v Griffiths* [2000] 2 WLR 1158 (however, the court recognised that, if what was being attacked was the allocation of resources the position might have been different, see para 47, *per* Lord Woolf).

[155] For consideration of these points under the Convention see para 11.191 below.

[156] *Pountney v Griffiths* [1976] AC 314.

[157] *Hadkinson v Hadkinson* [1952] 2 All ER 567, *per* Romer and Somervell LJJ; *Re Jokai Tea Holdings Ltd* [1992] 1 WLR 1196.

[158] *X Ltd v Morgan-Grampian (Publishers) Ltd* [1991] 1 AC 1.

[159] *The Times*, 17 Aug 1998.

> hearing before an independent and impartial tribunal. The 'everyone' in that Article is not subject to an exception in respect of people who are guilty of serious offences or contempt of court.

It has been held that, in the light of Article 6 of the Convention, it is not a proper exercise of the court's power to strike out a case where there has been a breach of the rules or a court order if it can be shown that, notwithstanding the party's conduct, there is no substantial risk that there cannot be a fair trial.[159a]

(f) Limitation periods

The Limitation Act 1980 places a range of time limits on access to the courts. These range from a limit of one year for defamation actions[160] to 30 years for actions for recovery of land brought by the Crown.[161] Actions for personal injury are subject to a limitation period of three years.[162] Other actions in tort and actions in contract are subject to a limitation period of six years.[163] In general, the right of a person from whom goods are stolen to bring an action in respect of the theft is not subject to any limitation period.[164] In relation to persons under a disability,[165] the limitation period is six years from the date when the person ceased to be under a disability.[166] The limitation period may be postponed in cases of fraud, concealment or mistake.[167] **11.49**

Limitation periods are subject to extension in a number of different circumstances. The limitation period for defamation is subject to discretionary extension under section 32A.[168] The limitation period in personal injuries actions is subject to a discretionary extension.[169] Time limits in actions for negligence are subject to extension where relevant facts are not known at the date of accrual, up to a maximum of 15 years.[170] No similar extension applies in contract cases. **11.50**

(g) Financial restrictions on access to the courts

There are, of course, practical and financial limitations on access to justice in English law. Any person wishing to institute proceedings must pay court fees. These fees may be so high as to prevent effective 'access' to the courts. In *R v Lord Chancellor, ex p Witham*[171] the court considered regulations for the imposition of new **11.51**

159a *Arrow Nominees v Blackledge*, *The Times*, 8 Dec 1999 (Evans-Lombe J); see also *Annodeous Entertainment v Gibson*, *The Times*, 3 Mar 2000 (Neuberger J).

160 Limitation Act 1980, s 2A (as substituted by Defamation Act 1996, s 5(2)).

161 The period is 12 years in respect of actions brought by other litigants, s 15.

162 Limitation Act 1980, s 11.

163 ss 2 and 5.

164 s 4.

165 That is, infants and persons of unsound mind, s 38(2).

166 s 28.

167 s 32.

168 See *Oyston v Blaker* [1996] 1 WLR 1326.

169 s 33.

170 s 14A.

171 [1998] QB 575.

fees for the issue of writs in the High Court. The applicant was unemployed, had no savings and was in receipt of income support. He wished to bring proceedings for malicious falsehood and libel as a litigant in person since legal aid was not available for actions in respect of defamation. The Supreme Court Fees (Amendment) Order 1996 provided for a minimum fee of £120 and repealed provisions under the terms of which those in receipt of income support were not obliged to pay fees. As a result, the applicant was unable to issue proceedings and successfully applied for a declaration that the order was *ultra vires*. However, litigants who are not in receipt of income support are still obliged to pay fees for the issue of court process which can be substantial and seem likely to deter litigants of modest means.

11.52 The high level of legal costs prevents or restricts access by most private individuals using their own resources. The recognition of this led to the introduction of legal aid by the state under the provisions of the Legal Aid and Advice Act 1949.[172] The position has until recently been governed by the provisions of the Legal Aid Act 1988. In 1997-98 the sum of £1,526 million was spent on Legal Aid, £597 million of which was spent on criminal cases. Radical changes have been brought about by the Access to Justice Act 1999. This replaces the Legal Aid system with two new schemes: the Community Legal Service for civil cases[173] and the Criminal Defence Service for criminal cases.[174] The Community Legal Service funded by the 'Community Legal Service Fund' has been given a fixed annual budget.[175] This is divided into two main budgets: family and other civil cases. Certain categories of case are excluded from the fund:[176]

- disputes involving negligent damage to person or property —these are generally considered suitable for conditional fees;
- allegations of defamation or malicious falsehood;
- disputes arising in the course of business;
- matters concerned with the law relating to companies or partnerships, the law of trusts and boundary disputes.

Under the Access to Justice Act there is a controlled contracting scheme for legal service providers. It has been held that this scheme is not an unlawful restriction on the common law right of access to the courts.[176a] In contrast, the Criminal Defence Service is a 'demand led' service.[177]

[172] For the background, see Lord Bingham's unpublished Barnett Lecture, 11 Jun 1998, and for criminal legal aid see T Goriely, 'The Development of Criminal Legal Aid in England and Wales', in R Young and D Wall (eds), *Access to Criminal Justice: Legal Aid, Lawyers and the Defence of Liberty* (Blackstone, 1996).

[173] s 1.

[174] s 12.

[175] s 5.

[176] Sch 2.

[176a] See *R v Legal Aid Board, ex p Duncan* (2000) 150 NLJ 276.

[177] s 10.

In some circumstances, litigants can be required to give security for costs before proceeding.[178] There is a discretion to order security if the claimant is ordinarily resident out of the jurisdiction, is a nominal claimant, the claimant's address is not stated in the claim form or the claimant has changed his address with a view to evading the consequences of the litigation.[179] **11.53**

(h) Rights of appeal

Civil cases. In all but three types of civil appeal it is now necessary to obtain permission to appeal from the judge or the Court of Appeal.[180] The only cases in which permission is not required are appeals against: **11.54**

- the making of a committal order;
- a refusal to grant habeas corpus;
- a secure accommodation order made under section 25 of the Children Act 1989.

Appeals from the Court of Appeal to the House of Lords can only be brought with leave of either court.

Criminal cases. A person who is convicted in the magistrates' court following a plea of not guilty may appeal against conviction and/or his sentence to the Crown Court. A person who pleads guilty can only appeal against sentence.[181] The Crown Court may confirm, reverse or vary any part of the decision appealed against.[182] Furthermore, any party to proceedings in the magistrates' court may question the proceedings on the ground that the decision is wrong in law or in excess of jurisdiction by applying for the magistrates to 'state a case for the opinion of the High Court'.[183] **11.55**

In relation to trials on indictment, an appeal against conviction[184] or sentence[185] can only be brought with the leave of the Court of Appeal or if the trial judge certifies that the case is fit for appeal. If it appears to the Registrar of Criminal Appeals that an application for leave or a notice of appeal does not show any substantial ground of appeal, he may refer the appeal or application to the court for summary determination.[186] An unsuccessful applicant for leave to appeal is at risk for a direction for 'loss of time', that is that time spent in custody since the commencement of the appeal proceedings shall not count towards any custodial **11.56**

178 CPR, Sch 1 R 23.1.
179 Ibid.
180 CPR, Sch 1 R 52.3(1).
181 Magistrates' Court Act 1980, s 108.
182 Supreme Court Act 1981, s 48.
183 Magistrates' Court Act 1980, s 111(1).
184 Criminal Appeal Act 1968, s 1.
185 Ibid, s 11.
186 Ibid, s 20.

sentence.[187] However, there will be no direction for loss of time if the appeal is advised by counsel in writing and the grounds were settled and signed by him[188] and, in practice, a direction for loss of time on an unsuccessful leave application is very unusual. A notice of appeal must be served within 28 days of conviction or sentence although there is a discretion to extend time.[188a]

11.57 If an appeal is unsuccessful, the appellant cannot bring a second appeal on the same matter.[189] But the Criminal Cases Review Commission may refer a conviction or sentence to the Court of Appeal[190] if there is a 'real possibility' that the verdict or sentence would not be upheld if the reference were to be made.[191] The Attorney-General can refer to the Court of Appeal any point of law which arose in a case which resulted in an acquittal[192] or a sentence which he considers to be unduly lenient.[193]

(3) Fair trial rights in general

(a) Introduction

11.58 English law provides a number of general rights in relation to the actual conduct of 'legal process'. The common law provides the parties to both criminal or civil proceedings with a number of protections and safeguards which, taken together, form the framework of a common law 'right to a fair trial'. Many of these rights are familiar to public lawyers but it is only in recent years that they have begun to be articulated as part of ordinary court procedures. The common law has long recognised two minimum 'fair trial' principles: *nemo judex in causa sua* (nobody can be a judge in his own cause) and *audi alteram partem* (hear the other side). These are often known as the principles of 'natural justice' and have been developed over the years in relation to all forms of decision-making;[194] they have evolved as the standards of administrative law when the court is reviewing the decision-making of inferior tribunals and public bodies. It has been said that a decision which offends against the principles of natural justice is outside the juris-

---

[187] Ibid, s 29; in practice, such directions are now extremely rare.

[188] *Practice Direction (Crime: Sentence, Loss of Time)* [1980] 1 WLR 270; see also *Monnell and Morris v United Kingdom* (1987) 10 EHRR 205.

[188a] Criminal Appeal Act 1968, s 18(2) and (3).

[189] *R v Pinfold* [1988] QB 462; even if the House of Lords restores a quashed conviction, *R v Berry* [1991] 1 WLR 125.

[190] Criminal Appeal Act 1995, s 9.

[191] Ibid, s 13.

[192] Criminal Justice Act 1972, s 36.

[193] Criminal Justice Act 1988, ss 35 and 36.

[194] See generally, H Wade and C Forsyth, *Administrative Law* (7th edn, Clarendon Press, 1994) Chap 15; Lord Woolf and J Jowell, *De Smith, Woolf and Jowell, Judicial Review of Administrative Action* (5th edn, Sweet & Maxwell, 1995) Chap 17 and M Beloff, 'Natural justice—(The *audi alteram partem* rule) and fairness', in M Supperstone and J Goudie, *Judicial Review* (2nd edn, Butterworths, 1997) paras 8.1–8.72.

diction of the decision-making authority,[195] and that the 'duty to act fairly . . . lies upon everyone who decides anything'.[196] However, the right to a fair trial comprises a number of elements and the right will be considered under five headings: independent and impartial tribunal, fair hearing, public hearing, hearing within a reasonable time and reasoned judgment.

(b) Independent and impartial tribunal

Independence. The nature of the 'tribunal' which considers legal disputes in England and Wales depends on the nature of the right in question. Criminal cases are dealt with either by magistrates or by a judge and jury in the Crown Court. The civil courts still deal with a large proportion of civil disputes and the High Court retains a supervisory jurisdiction over other tribunals. Many civil disputes are now dealt with by statutory tribunals. **11.59**

The large majority of criminal case are tried by magistrates courts, most of which consist of benches of lay magistrates. Magistrates are appointed by the Lord Chancellor to the 'commission of the peace'.[197] They can be removed at the discretion of the Lord Chancellor in circumstances which are not clearly defined.[198] In 1946, the Royal Commission on Justices of the Peace were told that justices were removed: **11.60**

> Where, for any reason, the Lord Chancellor decided that it is inexpedient or contrary to the public interest that the justice should continue to act in any way as such.

The removal is effected by deletion of the justice's name from the commission of the peace to which he is assigned. It has been suggested that, by constitutional usage, the power of removal must be exercised in a judicial manner and the Lord Chancellor must show cause for the removal.[199]

Serious criminal cases are dealt with by judge and jury at the Crown Court. The judges are Circuit judges or High Court judges, appointed by the Queen on the recommendation of the Lord Chancellor. High Court Judges and Circuit judges also deal with civil cases. High Court judges hold office 'during good behaviour, subject to a power of removal by Her Majesty on an address presented to Her by both Houses of Parliament'.[200] No High Court judge in England or Wales has ever been removed under this provision. It cannot be circumvented by the court **11.61**

---

[195] *A-G v Ryan* [1980] AC 718.

[196] *Board of Education v Rice* [1911] AC 179.

[197] Justice of the Peace Act 1997, s 5 (lay magistrates), s 11 (stipendiary magistrates), s 15 (metropolitan stipendiary magistrates).

[198] See generally, A Bradley and K Ewing, *Constitutional Law* (12th edn, Longman, 1997) 419.

[199] See generally, T Skyrme, *History of the Justices of the Peace* (Barry Rose, 1994) App VI 'The Power to Remove Justices of the Peace'.

[200] Supreme Court Act 1981; s 11(3).

administration refusing to assign cases to a judge.[201] Circuit judges can be removed by the Lord Chancellor, if he thinks fit, for incapacity or misbehaviour.[202] Part-time judges, known as 'Recorders' may be appointed[203] for a specified term[204] to act as judges of the Crown Court and carry out such other judicial functions as may be conferred on them. The appointment of a Recorder may be terminated on the ground of incapacity or misbehaviour or of a failure to comply with the terms of his appointment concerning availability.[205] As a temporary measure, the Lord Chancellor may appoint deputy High Court Judges,[206] deputy Circuit judges, deputy District judges, deputy Masters or Registrars of the Supreme Court and retired Law Lords, Lords Justices and High Court Judges to carry out judicial functions. In April 2000 it was announced[207] that, in the light of the Scots decision in *Starrs v Procurator Fiscal, Linlithgow*[207a] and in order to comply with Article 6 of the Convention, the arrangements for part time judicial appointments would be as follows:

- appointments to be for a minimum period of five years;
- appointments to be renewed automatically, except for limited and specific grounds such as misbehaviour, incapacity, or failure to comply with sitting and training requirements;
- removal from office to be only on limited and specific grounds similar to those for non-renewal;
- wherever administratively possible, the offer of a minimum number of sitting days would be guaranteed.

11.62 Appeals in both criminal and civil cases are heard by the Court of Appeal and, in a few cases, by the House of Lords. Lords of Appeal and members of the Court of Appeal are appointed, in the name of the Queen, by the Prime Minister[208] and have the same 'security of tenure' as High Court Judges.

11.63 Statutory tribunals[209] now adjudicate on a large range of rights including such important areas as employment rights and discrimination claims,[210] the rights of

[201] Cf *Rees v Crane* [1994] 2 AC 173 (the decision of Chief Justice of Trinidad and Tobago to exclude a judge from the roster of judges sitting for the following term was quashed as a judge could only be suspended or removed in accordance with the Constitutional procedure).

[202] Courts Act 1971, s 17(4); see *Ex p Ramshay* (1852) 18 QB 173.

[203] Courts Act 1971, s 21; as from Apr 2000, the separate office of Assistant Recorder is no longer retained.

[204] As from Apr 2000, for a period of not less than five years.

[205] Courts Act 1971, s 21(6)

[206] Supreme Court Act 1981, s 9(4).

[207] Lord Chancellor's Department, Press Release, 12 Apr 2000.

[207a] [2000] 1 LRC 718, see para 11.310 below.

[208] Supreme Court Act 1981, s 10.

[209] See generally, Wade and Forsyth (n 23 above) Chap 23.

[210] Employment Tribunals and the Employment Appeal Tribunal.

immigrants and asylum seekers,[211] the detention of mental patients,[212] income tax assessments,[213] and a wide range of disputes concerning land.[214] Most of these tribunals are now governed by the provisions of the Tribunals and Inquiries Act 1992.[215] The Council on Tribunals has overall responsibility for tribunals covered by the Act:[216] of which there are now 78.[217] Some tribunals deal with only a few cases a year and some deal with tens or hundreds of thousands.[218]

Statutory tribunals are intended to be quick and informal and to bring specialist expertise to the resolution of disputes. There are no fixed rules for the composition of tribunals.[219] One form commonly adopted is the 'balanced tribunal' comprising a legally qualified chairman and two expert lay members. The chairman is selected by the appropriate authority from a panel appointed by the Lord Chancellor.[220] The other members are often appointed from panels nominated by the Lord Chancellor or the relevant ministry. Although the legally qualified chairman are usually permanent appointments, the lay members are usually appointed by Government Ministers on terms specified by the Minister. The remuneration, fees and allowances are determined by the Minister. **11.64**

Criminal offences by members of the armed forces or members of their families are dealt with by 'Courts-martial'. Depending on their gravity, charges against army law can be tried by district, field or general court-martial. A court-martial is not a standing court: it comes into existence in order to try a single offence or group of offences. The 'higher authority', who is a senior officer, will decide whether any case referred to him by the accused's commanding officer should be dealt with summarily, referred to the 'prosecuting authority', or dropped. Once the higher authority has taken this decision, he or she will have no further involvement in the case. The 'prosecuting authority' is the Services' legal branch. Following the higher authority's decision to refer a case to them, the prosecuting authority has absolute discretion, applying similar criteria as those applied in civilian cases by the Crown Prosecution Service to decide whether or not to prosecute, what type of court-martial would be appropriate and precisely what charges **11.65**

[211] Immigration adjudicators and the Immigration Appeals Tribunal, Immigration Act 1971, Sch 5.

[212] Mental Health Review Tribunals, Mental Health Act 1983, s 65.

[213] The Commissioners for Income Tax.

[214] Lands Tribunal, Lands Tribunal Act 1949, s 1.

[215] The predecessor of which was enacted to implement the recommendations of the *Report of the Committee of Administrative Tribunals and Enquiries* (1957) Cmnd 218—The Franks Report.

[216] s 1; this has 10 to 15 members, appointed by the Lord Chancellor and makes annual reports.

[217] Sch 1.

[218] Many tribunals have no cases in a particular year, while the Traffic and General Income Tax Commissioners each deal with several hundred thousand, see Annual Report of Council on Tribunals, 1997–98.

[219] See generally, Wade and Forsyth (n 194 above) 912ff.

[220] Tribunal and Inquiries Act 1992, s 6.

should be brought. They will then conduct the prosecution.[221] Court administration officers are appointed in each Service and will be independent of both the higher and the prosecuting authorities. They are responsible for making the arrangements for courts-martial, including arranging venue and timing, ensuring that a judge advocate and any court officials required will be available, securing the attendance of witnesses and selection of members. Officers under the command of the higher authority will not be selected as members of the court-martial.[222] Each court-martial includes a judge advocate as a member. His advice on points of law are rulings binding on the court and he will have a vote on sentence (but not on conviction). The casting vote, if needed, will rest with the president of the court-martial, who will also give reasons for the sentence in open court. Findings by a court-martial are no longer subject to confirmation or revision by a confirming officer (whose role has been abolished). A reviewing authority has been established in each Service to conduct a single review of each case. Reasons will be given for the decision of the reviewing authority. As part of this process, post-trial advice received by the reviewing authority from a judge advocate (who will be different from the one who officiated at the court-martial) will be disclosed to the accused. There is a right of appeal against conviction and sentence to the civilian Courts-Martial Appeal Court.

11.66 **Impartiality.** English law permits parties to any form of dispute to challenge the tribunal on the grounds of actual or apparent bias.[223] This is one of the fundamental principles of 'natural justice' and has been clearly recognised since the seventeenth century. [224] It is rare that actual bias, in the sense of actual partiality is established. The case law is largely concerned with 'apparent bias'.

11.67 The starting point for challenging the appearance of bias is that 'justice should not only be done but should manifestly and undoubtedly be seen to be done'.[225] This principle has two closely related but not identical, applications. First, if a judge or member of a tribunal is a party to litigation or has any direct financial[226] or other interest[227] in a matter in dispute, he is automatically disqualified. The question in each case is 'whether the outcome could, realistically, affect the judge's interest'.[228]

---

[221] See Armed Forces Act 1996, Sch I.

[222] Sch I, Pt III, para 19.

[223] See generally, *De Smith, Woolf and Jowell* (n 194 above) Chap 12; J Goudie, 'Interest and Favour' in M Supperstone and J Goudie, *Judicial Review* (2nd edn, Butterworths, 1997) paras 9.1–9.26; and see P Havers and O Thomas, 'Bias Post-*Pinochet* and Under the ECHR' [1999] JR 111.

[224] For the history, see *De Smith, Woolf and Jowell* (n 194 above) paras 12-001–12-005.

[225] *R v Sussex Justices ex p McCarthy* [1924] 1 KB 256, 259.

[226] See *Dimes v Proprietors of Grand Junction Canal* (1852) 3 HL Cas 759; *Leeson v General Council of Medical Education and Registration* (1889) 43 Ch D 366.

[227] *R v Bow Street Metropolitan Stipendiary Magistrate, ex p Pinochet Ugarte (No 2)* [1999] 2 WLR 272 (promotion of a cause in which Lord Hoffman was involved with one of the parties as a director of a company controlled by Amnesty which was a party to the proceedings).

[228] *Locabail (UK) v Bayfield Properties Ltd* [2000] 2 WLR 870, 881D.

It has been said that the size of the financial interest is irrelevant;[229] however more recent authorities have recognised a *de minimis* exception.[230] In any case giving rise to automatic disqualification a judge should recuse himself from the case before any objection is raised.[231]

Secondly, if the judge's conduct or behaviour gives rise to an appearance of bias then he may be disqualified. There has been considerable uncertainty on the authorities on the appropriate test for ascertaining whether there is bias in this sense.[232] In some instances it has been said that the test for disqualification is whether there is a real likelihood of bias.[233] On other occasions it is said that the appearance of bias is made out if a reasonable person acquainted with the position had reasonable grounds for suspecting bias.[234] In *R v Gough*[235] (a case concerned with the apparent bias of a juror) the House of Lords decided that the correct test for bias was whether there was a real danger of bias. The court should ascertain the circumstances and then: **11.68**

> the court should ask itself whether, having regard to those circumstances, there was a real danger of bias on the part of the relevant member of the tribunal in question, in the sense that he might unfairly regard (or have unfairly regarded) with favour, or disfavour, the case of a party to the issue under consideration.[236]

The perspective from which the matter must be viewed is that of the 'informed observer' and it will very often be appropriate to enquire whether the judge knew of the matter relied on as appearing to undermine his impartiality.[237] The *Gough* test has been adopted in relation to bias issues in a number of different areas.[238] If

229 *R v Hammond* (1863) 9 LT (NS) 423, 'The interest to each shareholder may be 1/4d but it is still an interest' (shareholders in a railway company disqualified from hearing charges of travelling without a ticket); *R v Camborne Justices, ex p Pearce* [1955] 1 QB 41.

230 *Locabail (UK) v Bayfield Properties Ltd* (n 228 above), 881, 882 and the cases there cited.

231 Ibid, 886.

232 See *R v St Edmundsbury Borough Council, ex p Investors in Industry Commercial Properties Ltd* [1985] 1 WLR 1168.

233 See eg *R v Rand* (1866) LR 1 QB 230; *Rv Barnsley Licensing Justices ex p Barnsley and District Licensed Victuallers' Association* [1960] 2 QB 167.

234 *R v Sussex Justices, ex p McCarthy* (n 225 above) 259; *Metropolitan Properties Company (FGC) Ltd v Lannon* [1969] 1 QB 577, 599.

235 [1993] AC 646.

236 Ibid 670; this approach has, however, not been followed in Australia, *Webb and Hay v The Queen* (1994) 181 CLR 41; and see *Rv S (RD)* (1997) 151 DLR (4th) 193 and *BOC New Zealand v Trans Tasman Properties* [1997] NZAR 49; see also *Ex parte Pinochet Ugarte (No 2)* (n 227, above) 284D–G, (Lord Browne-Wilkinson), 289H–290G (Lord Hope) and *Roylance v GMC (No 2)* [1999] 3 WLR 541, 545E–546H, see also *Locabail (UK) v Bayfield Properties Ltd* (n 228 above), 884–885.

237 See *Locabail (UK) Ltd v Bayfield Properties* (n 228 above), 885.

238 *R v Inner West London Coroner, ex p Dallaglio* [1994] 4 All ER 139 (coroner); *Rv Secretary of State for the Environment, ex p Kirkstall Valley Campaign* [1996] 3 All ER 304 (Urban Development Corporation) *AT & T Corporation v Saudi Cable, The Times*, 23 May 2000 (arbitrators); for recent example see Goudie, (n 223 above) para 9.11.

the judge becomes aware of any matter which could arguably be said to give rise to a real danger of bias, disclosure should generally be made in advance of the hearing.[239]

(c) Fair hearing

11.69 **Introduction.** The right to a 'fair hearing' has been extensively analysed in the administrative law context.[240] This right has been said to arise by way of 'statutory implication' so that,

> it is to be implied, unless the contrary appears, that Parliament does not authorise . . . the exercise of powers in breach of the principles of natural justice, and that Parliament does . . . require in the particular procedures, compliance with those principles.[241]

Two general points should be noted about the 'duty to act fairly' in English public law. First, it is a flexible standard. As the House of Lords made clear in *R v Secretary of State for the Home Department, ex p Doody*[242] the standards of fairness are not immutable and change over time, both in general and in their application to particular cases. Furthermore, principles of fairness cannot be applied by rote but depend on the context of the decision in question.[243] Second, the duty goes beyond the areas normally covered by constitutional 'due process rights': the duty does not just lie on those charged with the 'determination of civil rights and obligations or of any criminal charges'[244] but extends to all decisions made by public bodies. In the present context the aim is to examine the common law 'fair hearing rights' which apply to what English public law regards as 'judicial' or 'quasi-judicial' decisions.

11.70 A number of aspects of 'procedural fairness' have been recognised in the cases. Whether or not a particular element applies in a given case will depend on the precise circumstances. There is no established list of the elements of procedural fairness but they include the following: prior notice of the case, adequate time to prepare, disclosure of the material on which the decision is to be based, a hearing, legal representation, calling and cross-examination of witnesses, consideration of evidence and submissions. Procedural fairness may also entail an obligation to give reasons for the decision.[245]

---

239 *Locabail (UK) v Bayfield Properties Ltd* (n 228 above), 886.

240 See generally, Lord Woolf and J Jowell, *De Smith, Woolf and Jowell, Judicial Review of Administrative Action* (5th edn, Sweet & Maxwell, 1995) Chap 9; and M Beloff, 'Natural justice—(The audi alteram partem rule) and Fairness' in M Supperstone and J Goudie, *Judicial Review* (2nd edn, Butterworths, 1997); H Wade and C Forsyth, *Administrative Law* (7th edn, Clarendon Press, 1994) Chap 15.

241 *Fairmount Investments Ltd v Secretary of State for the Environment* [1976] 1 WLR 1255, 1263.

242 [1994] 1 AC 531.

243 See also *Lloyd v McMahon* [1987] 1 AC 625.

244 Contrast Art 6(1) of the Convention.

245 Contrast para 11.89 below.

However, the duty to act fairly can be waived by an applicant where he chooses not to complain about a breach of his rights.[246] Furthermore, a breach of the duty at a hearing can be cured or remedied at a properly conducted appeal hearing. In *Calvin v Carr*[247] the Privy Council distinguished three types of cases: (i) those where the rules for a re-hearing made it possible to treat the appeal as superseding the initial hearing; (ii) those where the hearing structure required a fair hearing at both the initial and appeal hearing; and (iii) those where the court should not intervene because the parties accepted that a fair result had been achieved by fair methods. **11.71**

Prior notice of the case. It has been said that: **11.72**

> One of the principles of natural justice is that a person is entitled to adequate notice and opportunity to be heard before any judicial order is pronounced against him, so that he, or someone acting on his behalf, may make such representations, if any, as he sees fit.[248]

As a result, an individual who is likely to be directly affected by the outcome of a decision should be given prior notification of the action to be taken and be given sufficient particulars of the case against him so he is able to prepare his case to meet them.[249]

Adequate time to prepare. A party must be allowed sufficient time to prepare a case and must not be taken by surprise. Where an adjournment is reasonably needed it must be granted.[250] In criminal cases, this applies to both prosecution and defence.[251] **11.73**

Duty of disclosure. Parties are entitled to proper notice of material which is to **11.74**

[246] See eg *R v Comptroller-General of Patents and Designs, ex p Parke, Davies and Company* [1953] 1 All ER 862; *R v British Broadcasting Corporation, ex p Lavelle* [1983] 1 WLR 23, 29; and see generally, Beloff (n 240 above), and Wade and Forsyth (n 240 above) 8.60.

[247] [1980] AC 574 which was concerned with contractual rights of appeal; and in relation to statutory appeals: see *McMahon v Lloyd* [1987] AC 625; and see, generally, *De Smith, Woolf and Jowell* (n 240 above) paras 10-20–10-24.

[248] *Forrest v Brighton Justices* [1981] AC 1038, 1045; see also *Mahon v Air New Zealand Ltd* [1984] AC 808, 821.

[249] See eg *Kanda v Government of Malaya* [1962] AC 322; *Chief Constable of North Wales Police v Evans* [1982] 1 WLR 1155 (police probationer should be given notice of allegations about private life); *R v Secretary of State for the Home Department, ex p Hickey (No 2)* [1995] 1 WLR 734 (a convicted prisoner seeking reference to Court of Appeal should be given notice of material before Home Secretary); *R v Secretary of State for the Home Department, ex p Fayed* [1998] 1 WLR 763 (freestanding obligation to disclose areas of concern in advance of decision in respect of nationality so that representations can be made even though the statute precluded the requirement to give reasons for the decision); see generally, *De Smith, Woolf and Jowell* (n 240 above) paras 9-004–9-011; Wade and Forsyth, (n 240 above) 531ff; Beloff (n 240 above) paras 8.41–8.42.

[250] *R v Thames Magistrates' Court, ex p Polemis* [1974] 1 WLR 1371; see also, *R v Panel on Take-Overs and Mergers, ex p Guinness plc* [1990] 1 QB 146; Beloff (n 240 above) paras 8.43–8.44.

[251] See *R v Barnet Magistrates, ex p DPP, The Times*, 8 Apr 1994.

be put before the tribunal for their consideration. In ordinary civil litigation, this is done by the process of disclosure and the exchange of witness statements.[252] In other cases, the decision-maker must disclose relevant evidence on which he intends to rely and give access to all material relevant to the case[253] including reports and expert evidence supplied to the tribunal.[254]

11.75 **A hearing.** The body determining a dispute must give each party a fair opportunity to put his own case. The obligation to conduct a hearing does not necessarily mean there should be an oral hearing. For example, in *Lloyd v McMahon*[255] Liverpool councillors who were surcharged by the district auditor for wilful misconduct were given full particulars of the misconduct alleged and offered them the opportunity to make written representations. However, the councillors never asked for and were never offered an oral hearing. The Court of Appeal ruled that the procedure adopted was unfair, but the House of Lords decided that the procedure was fair and suitable in all the circumstances.[256]

11.76 **Legal representation.** It has sometimes been held that there is a right to legal representation in formal tribunal or investigatory hearings.[257] However, it seems that the better view is that there is no right to legal representation but only a discretion depending on the circumstances, and, in particular, the nature of the allegations being made.[258] The House of Lords have taken the view that the existence of discretion to grant legal representation rather than the absolute right is consistent with Article 6(3)(c) of the Convention.[259]

11.77 **Calling and cross-examination of witnesses.** When there is an oral hearing, the tribunal should usually allow witnesses to be questioned.[260] However, this right may be limited in more informal hearings[261] such as an investigation carried out

[252] CPR, Pts 31 and 32.

[253] *R v Army Board of the Defence Council, ex p Anderson* [1992] QB 169; *De Smith, Woolf and Jowell* (n 240 above) paras 9-018–9-020; Wade and Forsyth (n 240 above) 534; Beloff (n 240 above) paras 8.46–8.47.

[254] *R v Kent Police Authority, ex p Godden* [1971] 2 QB 662.

[255] [1987] 1 AC 625.

[256] See also *R v Army Board of Defence, ex p Anderson* [1992] QB 169; *De Smith, Woolf and Jowell* (n 240 above) paras 9-012–9-017 and 9-023–9-025; Wade and Forsyth, (n 240 above) 537; Beloff, (n 240 above) paras 8.48–8.49.

[257] *De Smith, Woolf and Jowell*, (n 240 above) paras 9-029–9-034; Wade and Forsyth (n 240 above) 540.

[258] *R v Secretary of State for the Home Department, ex p Tarrant* [1985] QB 251.

[259] *Hone v Maze Prison Board of Visitors* [1988] 1 AC 379.

[260] *R v Newmarket Assessment Committee ex parte Allen Newport* [1945] 2 All ER 371, 373; *R v Deputy Industrial Injuries Commissioner, ex p Moore* [1965] 1 QB 456, 490; *Nicholson v Secretary of State for Energy* (1977) 76 LGR 693 (failure to allow objectors questions led to the decision being quashed); *De Smith, Woolf and Jowell* (n 240 above) paras 9-026–9-028 and 9-035–9-038; Wade and Forsyth (n 240 above) 538–9; Beloff (n 240 above) para 8.49.

[261] Cf *Bushell v Secretary of State for the Environment* [1981] AC 75, 97.

by the Commission for Racial Equality.[262] Nevertheless, a person who is entitled to be heard orally will normally be given an opportunity to put his own case, particularly where there are important factual disputes or where oral argument will assist the decision-maker.[263]

Consideration of evidence and submissions. However, where there is an oral hearing it seems that a tribunal must consider all the relevant evidence submitted, inform the parties of the evidence taken into account, allow witnesses to be questioned and allow comment on the whole case.[264] A tribunal should make clear its views on any material construction of relevant statutes and rules so that the parties could properly decide whether to give or call evidence.[265] The decision-makers must take into account the material submitted to them and must not rely on points not argued or private inquiries.[266] **11.78**

(d) Public hearing[267]

In relation to court proceedings, the general principle, subject to rare exceptions, is that the court must sit in public.[268] It has been said: **11.79**

> Open justice promotes the rule of law. Citizens of all ranks in a democracy must be subject to transparent legal restraint, especially those holding judicial or executive offices. Publicity whether in the courts, the press or both, is a powerful deterrent to abuse of power and improper behaviour.[269]

In *R v Legal Aid Board, ex p Kaim Todner (a firm)*[270] Lord Woolf MR gave four reasons for the principle of open justice: it deters inappropriate behaviour on the part of the court, it maintains public confidence in the administration of justice and enables the public to know that justice is being administered fairly, it may result in new evidence becoming available, and it makes uninformed and inaccurate comment about court proceedings less likely. Nevertheless, the court has an inherent

[262] *R v Commission for Racial Equality ex p Cottrell and Rothon* [1980] 1 WLR 1580.

[263] See, eg *R v Criminal Injuries Compensation Board, ex p Dickson* [1997] 1 WLR 58 (no entitlement to an oral hearing where there was no dispute as to the primary facts); *R v Criminal Injuries Compensation Board, ex p Cook* [1996] 1 WLR 1037; *R v Secretary of State for Wales, ex p Emery* [1996] 4 All ER 1 (conflict of documentary evidence concerning footpath should have been tested at public inquiry).

[264] *R v Deputy Industrial Injuries Commissioner, ex p Moore* [1965] 1 QB 456, 490.

[265] *Dennis v United Kingdom Central Council for Nursing, The Times*, 2 Apr 1993

[266] *R v Mental Health Review Tribunal, ex p Clatworthy* [1985] 3 All ER 699, 704.

[267] For a general discussion, see *Arlidge, Eady and Smith on Contempt* (2nd edn, Sweet & Maxwell, Chap 7.

[268] *R v Felixstowe Justices ex p Leigh* [1987] QB 582, 592; *A-G v Leveller Magazine Ltd* [1979] AC 440, 449–450.

[269] *Ex Parte Guardian Newspapers* [1999] 1 All ER 65, 79, 82.

[270] [1998] 3 WLR 925, 934; and see *Hodgson v Imperial Tobacco Ltd* [1998] 1 WLR 1056.

power to exclude the public where a public hearing would defeat the ends of the justice.[271] There are a number of grounds on which such an order may be made including:[272]

- the fact that the case involves the maintenance and upbringing of minors;[273]
- the need to preserve secret technical processes or other commercial confidences;
- the need to avoid the possibility of disorde;[274]
- the fact that a witness refuses to testify publicly;[275]
- the fact that a public hearing might deter future prosecutions.[276]

However, considerations of public decency[277] or national security will not, of themselves, be sufficient to allow a hearing in private.[278]

11.80 An order for a hearing in private is a most exceptional step in civil litigation. The position is now governed by CPR Part 39. By rule 39.2(1), the general rule is that a hearing is to be in public. However, this rule 'does not require the court to make special arrangements for accommodating members of the public'.[279] The hearing may be in private if:[280]

- publicity would defeat the object of the hearing;
- it involves matters relating to national security;
- it involves confidential information and publicity would damage that confidentiality;[281]
- a private hearing is necessary to protect the interests of any child or patient;
- it is a hearing of a without notice application and it would be unjust to the respondent for there to be a public hearing;
- it involves uncontentious matters arising in the administration of trusts or in the administration of a deceased's person's estate; or
- the court considers this to be necessary in the interests of justice.

---

[271] *Scott v Scott* [1913] AC 417, 438; *R v Governor of Lewes Prison, ex p Doyle* [1917] 2 KB 254, 271; *A-G v Leveller Magazine Ltd* [1979] AC 440, 449H–450D; *Rv Chief Registrar of Friendly Societies, ex p New Cross Building Society* [1984] QB 227, 235.

[272] Cf Administration of Justice Act 1960 s 12, which deals which the publication of information in relation to proceedings in private and which gives recognition to the first two categories (see also para 15.67ff below).

[273] See *Scott v Scott* (n 271 above) 437, 483; *Re R (Wardship: Restrictions on Publication)* [1994] Fam 254, 271.

[274] *Scott v Scott* (n 271 above) 445–6.

[275] Ibid 439, but this exception must be treated cautiously, the witness can be protected in other ways, such as the grant of anonymity, see para 11.127 below.

[276] *A-G v Leveller Magazine Ltd* (n 271 above) 471C-D.

[277] *Scott v Scott* (n 271 above) 439.

[278] *A-G v Leveller Magazine Ltd* (n 271 above) 471C-D.

[279] CPR, r 39.2(2).

[280] CPR, r 39.3.

[281] PD39 para 1.5 gives a list of hearings which, in the first instance, shall be listed as hearings in private under this rule.

If a hearing is held in private a non-party can seek the leave of the judge to obtain a transcript.[282]

The position is different in criminal cases. Applications for hearings in camera are regularly made in sensitive cases: for example, those involving terrorism or where criminal investigations have been carried out by members of the security services. A judge can order a criminal trial to be held in private if the case involves issues of national security[283] and the public, but not the press, can be excluded when a child is testifying in a case of alleged indecency.[284] The prosecution can apply for a witness to give evidence from behind a screen.[285] An application for an order that all or part of a Crown Court trial should be held in camera for reasons of national security or for the protection of the identity of a witness must be made on seven-days' notice, and a copy of the notice must be displayed in the court building.[286] The notice must be dated and should usually specify the ground relied on.[287] The rule applies to any part of the trial process, including a pre-trial application to stay the proceedings as an abuse of the process.[288] Although the rule is expressed in mandatory terms, it is often not complied with when the need for a hearing in camera is said to arise 'urgently'. In such cases Crown Court judges often proceed on the basis that they have inherent power to order a hearing in camera.[289] A judge should not be left to infer, in the absence of relevant evidence from the Crown, that national security will be at risk if the hearing is not held in camera.[290] **11.81**

There is inherent jurisdiction to exclude the public but not the press if the interests of justice require it. Thus, in *R v Richards*[291] it was held that the judge had acted properly (and in accordance with Article 6 of the Convention) in excluding the public because an 18-year-old witness felt intimidated by their presence. In addition, as part of its inherent power to control proceedings, the court can permit the names of witnesses to be withheld in both civil and criminal proceedings.[292] This power is rarely used in civil proceedings but is commonly invoked in criminal cases, particularly in blackmail cases and in cases involving 'terrorism' and national security.[293] **11.82**

Under the former procedure, if a civil hearing was held in 'chambers' although the **11.83**

282 PD39 para 1.12.
283 Official Secrets Act 1920, s 8(4).
284 Children and Young Persons Act 1933, s 37.
285 See para 11.127 below.
286 Crown Court Rules 1982, r 24A; cf *Rv Crook* (1991) 93 Cr App R 17.
287 *Ex p Guardian Newspapers* [1999] 1 All ER 65.
288 Ibid.
289 Cf *Rv Godwin* [1991] Crim LR 302.
290 *Ex p Guardian Newspapers* (n 287 above).
291 (1999) 163 JP 246.
292 See *A-G v Leveller Magazine Ltd* [1979] AC 440, 458; see generally, para 15.65 above.
293 See para 15.67 above.

public had no right to attend subject to specific statutory exceptions involving children, national security and trade secrets,[294] the proceedings were not 'secret'. As a result, members of the public who wished to attend were, if practicable, given permission.[295] Judgments given in chambers were, subject to the statutory exceptions mentioned, public documents and it was not a breach of confidence to disclose what occurred in chambers.[296]

(e) Hearing within a reasonable time

11.84 The English civil justice system has long been notorious for its delays.[297] However, the past two decades have seen a fundamental change in the attitude of the English courts towards the conduct of litigation. There has been a progressive move away from a 'reactive' system, moving at the pace of the parties, to a 'proactive' system of 'case management'.

11.85 The 'overriding objective' of the Civil Procedure Rules is to deal with cases justly.[298] This entails, dealing with cases, so far as practicable, 'expeditiously and fairly'.[299] The court must further the overriding objective 'by actively managing cases'.[300] The courts have been given extensive powers of management over all proceedings.[301] 'Fast track' cases should be allocated timetables of no more than 30 weeks between commencement and trial.[302]

11.86 Under the former procedural rules the court sought to prevent delay after the commencement of proceedings either by striking out the case for 'want of prosecution'[303] or striking it out under its inherent jurisdiction. However, Lord Woolf MR indicated in *Biguzzi v Rank Leisure*[304] that under the self-contained CPR, the earlier authorities were no longer relevant. He stressed that under the CPR time limits were more important than formerly and that the court now has much broader powers to consider alternatives to striking out the case such as making costs orders (including ordering costs on an indemnity basis), making orders in relation to interest or ordering that money be paid into court.[305] It has, however, been emphasised that the sanction to be invoked by the court to deal with a

[294] Administration of Justice Act 1960, s 12.
[295] *Hodgson v Imperial Tobacco Ltd* [1998] 1 WLR 1056, 1072A-C.
[296] Ibid.
[297] For a general discussion, see Lord Woolf, *Access to Justice* (The Stationery Office, 1996), Chap 3, paras 29–42.
[298] CPR, r 1.1(1).
[299] CPR, r 1.1(2)(d).
[300] CPR, r 1.4(1).
[301] CPR, Pt 3.
[302] CPR, r 28.2(4).
[303] See *Birkett v James* [1978] AC 297; there is a large body of case law dealing with these principles, see the survey in *Shtun v Zalejska* [1996] 1 WLR 1270.
[304] [1999] 1 WLR 1926, 1934; see also *Purdy v Cambran* [1999] CPLR 843.
[305] Ibid 1932, 1933.

particular case of delay should be proportionate and that the court should hesitate before striking out an apparently meritorious claim.[305a]

Criminal cases. In criminal cases, there is no general right to a trial within a reasonable time. However, it has been said that constitutional provisions in relation to trial within a reasonable time 'do no more than codify in writing the requirements of the common law which ensure that an accused person receives a fair trial'.[306] There is no general limit on the length of time that can elapse between charge and trial but certain time limits have been laid down under the Prosecution of Offences Act 1985:[307] **11.87**

- 70 days between first appearance in the magistrates' court and committal proceedings;
- 56 days from first appearance in the magistrates court to the opening day of the trial;
- 112 days between committal for trial and arraignment.

Furthermore, the courts have an inherent jurisdiction to stay prosecutions on the ground of prejudice resulting from delay even though that delay has not been occasioned by fault on the part of the prosecution.[308] However, a stay should not be imposed on the ground of delay unless the defendant shows, on the balance of probabilities that he will suffer serious prejudice to the extent that no fair trial can be held.[309] In cases involving constitutional rights to a speedy trial it has been suggested that the court should look at four factors: the length of delay; the reasons given by the prosecution to justify the delay, the responsibility of the accused for asserting his rights and the prejudice to the accused.[310] In general, this right should be asserted on an application to stay for an abuse of the process to the trial judge.[311] **11.88**

(f) Reasoned judgment

A judge determining an issue of law or fact is under a common law duty to give reasons for his decision. This is a function of 'due process and justice' and has a **11.89**

305a See *Annodeous Entertainment v Gibson*, *The Times*, 3 Mar 2000.

306 *Per* Lord Woolf, *Vincent v The Queen* [1993] 1 WLR 862, 867, PC, Jamaica; but see *DPP v Tokai (Jaikaran)* [1996] AC 856, 158; PC, Trinidad and Tobago).

307 s 22; see Prosecution of Offences (Custody Times Limits) Regulations, 1987, SI 1987/698; see also para 10.60 above.

308 *R v Telford Justices, ex p Badhan* [1991] 2 QB 78; *A-G's Reference (No 1 of 1990)* [1992] QB 630 for a general discussion of the jurisdiction to stay for abuse of the process see para 11.141ff below.

309 *A-G's Ref (No 1 of 1990)* (n 308, above) 644; see also *Jago v District Court of New South Wales* (1989) 168 CLR 23, High Court of Australia and *Tan v Cameron* [1992] 2 AC 205, PC, and generally, *Archbold: Criminal Pleading, Practice and Evidence* (Sweet & Maxwell, 1999), 4–64.

310 *Bell v DPP of Jamaica* [1985] AC 937; referring to *Barker v Wingo* (1972) 407 US 514 ; see also *US v Von Neumann* (1986) 474 US 242; and *Re Mlambo* [1993] 2 LRC 28.

311 See *DPP v Tokai (Jaikaran)* [1996] AC 856.

two-fold rationale: the parties should be in no doubt why they have won or lost and a fully reasoned judgment is more likely to be soundly based on the evidence.[312] A judgment given after the trial should display:

> the building blocks of the reasoned judicial process, where the evidence on each issue is marshalled, the weight of the evidence analysed, all tested against the probabilities based on the evidence as a whole, with clear findings of fact and all reasons given.[313]

11.90 There is no common law rule that non-judicial decision-makers must always give reasons for their decisions.[314] However, the duty to act fairly will often imply an obligation to provide reasons.[315] In *R v Civil Service Appeal Board, ex p Cunningham*[316] Lord Donaldson took the view that implying an obligation to provide reasons depended on:

- the character of the decision-making body;
- the framework within which the body operates; and
- whether additional procedural safeguards are needed to attain fairness.

In *R v Higher Education Funding Council, ex p Institute of Dental Surgery*[317] the Divisional Court took the position further. Sedley J held that there was an implied duty to provide reasons for a decision where (1) the subject matter is of an interest so highly regarded by the law (for example, personal liberty) that fairness requires reasons as of right or (2) the decision appears aberrant (so that fairness requires reasons so that the recipient can see if the aberration is real and challengeable). In *R v Mayor of City of London, ex p Matson*[318] the Court of Appeal suggested that even where a decision was not aberrant, fairness might require that reasons should be given in appropriate circumstances. The Court of Appeal therefore quashed a decision of the Court of Aldermen refusing to confirm the election of the applicant on the ground that no reasons for its conclusion had been given.

11.91 The Privy Council in *Stefan v General Medical Council*[319] recently summarised the position as follows:

[312] *Flannery v Halifax Estate Agencies* [2000] 1 WLR 377.

[313] *Heffer v Tiffin Green, The Times*, 28 Dec 1998.

[314] *R v Secretary of State for the Home Department, ex p Doody* [1994] 1 AC 531, 564 *per* Lord Mustill; *R v Kensington London Borough Council, ex p Grillo* (1996) 28 HLR 94, 105 *per* Neill LJ; *R v Ministry of Defence, ex p Murray* [1998] COD 134.

[315] See generally, Lord Woolf and J Jowell, *De Smith, Woolf and Jowell, Judicial Review of Administrative Action* (5th edn, Sweet & Maxwell, 1995) paras 9-039–9-053; H Wade and C Forsyth, *Administrative Law* (7th edn, Clarendon Press, 1994) 541–5; M Beloff, 'Natural Justice—(The audi alteram partem rule) and Fairness' in M Supperstone and J Goudie, *Judicial Review* (2nd edn, Butterworths, 1997) paras 8.54–8.57; D Toube, *Requiring Reasons at Common Law* [1997] JR 68; and see *Stefan v General Medical Council* [1999] 1 WLR 1293.

[316] [1992] 2 ICR 816; see also *R v Secretary of State for the Home Department, ex p Doody* [1994] AC 531.

[317] [1994] 1 WLR 242.

[318] [1996] 8 Admin LR 49.

[319] [1999] 1 WLR 1293.

> The trend of the law has been towards an increased recognition of the duty upon decision-makers of many kinds to give reasons. This trend is consistent with current developments towards an increased openness in matters of government and administration. But the trend is proceeding on a case by case basis (*R v Royal Borough of Kensington and Chelsea, Ex parte Grillo* (1996) 28 HLR 94), and has not lost sight of the established position of the common law that there is no general duty, universally imposed on all decision-makers. . . . There is certainly a strong argument for the view that what were once seen as exceptions to a rule may now be becoming examples of the norm, and the cases where reasons are not required may be taking on the appearance of exceptions.[320]

Lord Clyde went on to say that a review of the general principles should take place in the context of a case arising out of the Human Rights Act.[321]

The duty to act fairly obliges the Crown Court to give reasons where it is dealing with appeals from the magistrates' courts, identifying the main issues in dispute and how each of them was resolved[322] including appeals in licensing applications.[323] The reasons given must be intelligible and adequate so that the reader knows what conclusions the decision-maker came to on the principal controversial issues.[324] However, this principle is not always applied in criminal cases. It is clear that the decisions of magistrates, even professional stipendiary magistrates, do not call for reasons.[325] A jury does not give reasons for its decisions and Crown Court judges often do not give reasons for decisions made in the course of trials. **11.92**

(4) Fair trial rights in criminal cases

(a) Introduction

It is a fundamental principle of criminal law that 'the court is under the duty to ensure the accused a fair trial'.[326] This is an 'elementary right of every defendant'[327] and is properly described as a 'constitutional right'.[328] The right to fair trial of an accused in criminal cases has a number of components: the right to legal advice, the right to pre-trial disclosure of evidence, the right to a speedy trial, the right to **11.93**

[320] Ibid, 1300F–1301B.

[321] Ibid 1301.

[322] *R v Harrow Crown Court, ex p Dave* [1994] 1 WLR 98; *DPP v Pullum* unreported, 17 Apr 2000.

[323] *R v Snaresbrook Crown Court, ex p Lea, The Times*, 5 Apr 1994.

[324] See *Save Britain's Heritage v Number 1 Poultry Ltd* [1991] 1 WLR 153, 166, 167.

[325] *R v Civil Service Appeal Board; ex p Cunningham* [1992] ICR 816; *Rey v Government of Switzerland* [1998] 3 WLR 1, 10C-H (no implied duty on magistrates to give reasons in extradition proceedings).

[326] *R v Sang* [1980] AC 402.

[327] *Per* Lord Hope, *R v Brown (Winston)* [1998] AC 367, 374F.

[328] *Per* Steyn LJ, *Rv Brown (Winston)* [1994] 1 WLR 1599,1606E; see generally, Lord Steyn, 'The Role of the Bar, the Judge and the Jury' [1999] Public Law 51, 55; and also *Dodd v Chief Constable of Cheshire*, unreported, 22 Oct 1997 ('the plaintiff's constitutional right is for a fair trial . . .'.

silence and presumption of innocence. These rights can be protected by the power of the court to stay proceedings which are an abuse of its process:[328a] serious breaches of such rights may lead to the court ordering a stay. In addition, the court has a general power to exclude evidence whose admission would result in unfairness.

(b) Right to legal advice

11.94 At common law, a person in custody was entitled to consult a solicitor at an early stage of the investigation unless this would caused unreasonable delay or hindrance to the investigation or the administration of justice.[329] This has been described as a 'fundamental right'[330] but its precise ambit at common law was unclear. In relation to individuals held in police custody,[331] the right is now to be found in section 58 of the Police and Criminal Evidence Act 1984 which provides that:

> A person arrested and held in custody in a police station or other premises shall be entitled, if he so requests, to consult a solicitor privately at any time.[332]

This is subject to statutory exceptions, most importantly, if this will lead to harm or interference with evidence or the alerting of other suspects.[333] As was pointed out in *R v Samuel*[334] the officer:

> must believe that a solicitor will, if allowed to consult with a detained person, thereafter commit a criminal offence. Solicitors are officers of the court. We think that the number of times that a police officer could genuinely be in that state of belief will be rare.

There is, however, no established common law right to have a solicitor present at a police interview although it is possible that such a right could be developed.[335] Under paragraph 6.8 of the Code of Practice C (Detention, Treatment and Questioning of Persons), if a suspect has exercised his statutory right to legal advice at a police station and the solicitor is available, the solicitor must be allowed to be present at the interview. The fact that an accused is denied legal advice in a police station, in breach of section 58, does not, necessarily, mean that the

[328a] See para 11.141ff below.

[329] *R v Lemsatef* [1977] 1 WLR 812; *R v Chief Constable of South Wales, ex p Merrick* [1994] 1 WLR 663.

[330] Cf *R v Samuel* [1988] QB 615, in relation to the statutory provision.

[331] That is, whose custody has been authorised by a custody officer, see *R v Kerawalla* [1991] Crim LR 451.

[332] s 58(1).

[333] s 58(8); see also s 58(8A) in relation to 'drug trafficking' offences and s 58(13) in relation to 'terrorism provisions'.

[334] [1988] QB 615; see also *R v Silcott, The Times*, 9 Dec 1991.

[335] *R v Chief Constable of the Royal Ulster Constabulary, ex p Begley* [1997] 1 WLR 1475.

evidence obtained in interview will be excluded.[336] The court will consider whether to exclude the confession under the provisions of the Police and Criminal Evidence Act 1984.[337]

There was no 'right to legal assistance' in criminal cases at common law.[338] Nevertheless, legal advice has been provided for a considerable period under various statutory schemes. Assistance in criminal cases was first made available, in very limited terms, by the Poor Prisoner's Defence Act 1903. It was slightly improved by the Poor Prisoner's Defence Act 1930. Legal aid was granted by magistrates and was paid by local ratepayers. Its availability was gradually increased.[339] The position now is governed by Part I of the Access to Justice Act 1999.[340] The competent authority to grant legal aid is generally the court before which the proceedings take place.[341] A right to representation shall always be granted in such circumstances as may be prescribed.[342] Any question as to whether a right to representation should be granted shall be determined according to the interests of justice.[343] The factors to be taken into account include the following:[344] **11.95**

- whether the individual would, if any matter arising in the proceedings is decided against him, be likely to lose his liberty or livelihood or suffer serious damage to his reputation;
- whether the determination of any matter arising in the proceedings may involve consideration of a substantial question of law;
- whether the individual may be unable to understand the proceedings or to state his own case;
- whether the proceedings may involve the tracing, interviewing or expert cross-examination of witnesses on behalf of the individual;
- it is in the interests of someone other than the accused that the accused be represented.

The general rule is that an individual for whom services are funded by the Commission as part of the Criminal Defence Service shall not be required to make any payment in respect of the services.[345] However, where representation for an

---

336 *R v Alladice* (1988) 87 Cr App R 380 (defendant aware of rights and able to cope with interview), see generally, *Archbold: Criminal Pleading, Practice and Evidence* (Sweet & Maxwell, 1999) para 15–218ff.

337 See para 11.111 below.

338 But see *Dietrich v R* (1992) 177 CLR 292.

339 See T Goriely, 'The Development of Criminal Legal Aid in England and Wales', in R Young and D Wall (eds), *Access to Criminal Justice: Legal Aid, Lawyers and the Defence of Liberty* (Blackstone Press, 1996) 26–54.

340 Replacing Part V of the Legal Aid Act 1988.

341 Access to Justice Act 1999, Sch 3, para 2.

342 Ibid Sch 3, para 5(4).

343 Ibid Sch 3, para 5(1).

344 Ibid Sch 3, para 5(2).

345 Access to Justice Act 1999, s 17(1).

individual in respect of criminal proceedings in any court other than a magistrates' court is funded the court may make an order requiring him to pay some or all of the costs of representation.[346]

(c) Pre-trial disclosure

11.96 The prosecution owe a duty to the courts to ensure that all relevant evidence which assists an accused is either led by them or made available to the defence.[347] This right is part of the more general right to a 'fair trial':

> The rules of disclosure which have been developed by the common law owe their origin to the elementary right of every defendant to a fair trial. If a defendant is to have a fair trial he must have adequate notice of the case which is to be made against him. Fairness requires that the rules of natural justice must be observed.[348]

The prosecution was under a common law duty to provide material which had or might have some bearing on the offences charged. All 'material' evidence was discloseable. This was defined as the evidence:

> which can be seen on a sensible appraisal by the prosecution (1) to be relevant or possibly relevant to an issue in the case; (2) to raise or possibly raise a new issue whose existence is not apparent from the evidence which the prosecution proposes to use; (3) to hold out a real (as opposed to fanciful) prospect of providing a lead on evidence which goes to (1) or (2).[349]

There was a duty to provide all statements which have been taken, whether or not the witnesses were apparently credible.[350] This includes material relevant to the credibility of prosecution witnesses[351] but not material which relates only to the credibility of defence witnesses. This is because:

> Fairness, so far as the preparation of the defence case and the selection of the defence witnesses are concerned is preserved by the existing rules of disclosure and by ensuring that the defendant has adequate time and facilities for the preparation of his defence. That right, which is to be found also in article 6.3(b) of [the Convention] has for long been part of our law relating to the conduct of criminal trials.[352]

11.97 The position has now been modified by the complex provisions of the Criminal Procedure and Investigations Act 1996 ('the CPIA') and the Code of Practice issued under it. These replace the common law rules in relation to prosecution disclosure.[353] The effect of these provisions is, in summary:[354]

---

[346] Ibid s 17(2), this is subject to regulations made under s 17(3).

[347] *R v Ward (Judith)* [1993] 1 WLR 619, 645.

[348] *Per* Lord Hope, *R v Brown (Winston)* [1998] AC 367, 374F.

[349] *R v Keane* [1994] 1 WLR 746.

[350] *R v Mills* [1998] AC 382; cf *Rv Stinchcombe* (1991) 68 CCC (3d) 1.

[351] Cf *Wilson v Police* [1992] 2 NZLR 533.

[352] *R v Brown (Winston)* [1998] AC 367, 381A-B.

[353] CPIA, s 21(1).

[354] For a full account, see *Archbold: Criminal Pleading, Practice and Evidence* (Sweet & Maxwell, 1999) para 12–52ff; P Murphy (ed), *Blackstone's Criminal Practice 1999* (Blackstone Press, 1999) D6.

- the person investigating the offence must record and retain information or material gathered or generated during the investigation;[355]
- the prosecution must disclose the material on which it intends to rely at trial;
- in addition, the prosecution must make 'primary disclosure' of the other material which, 'in the prosecutor's opinion might undermine the case for the prosecution against the accused';[356]
- the defence must then provide a 'defence statement' setting out 'in general terms the nature of the accused's defence' and 'indicating the matters on which he takes issue with the prosecution' and why;[357]
- the prosecution then comes under a duty to make 'secondary disclosure' of any previously undisclosed material 'which might reasonably be expected to assist the accused's defence' as disclosed by the defence statement;[358]
- the prosecutor is under a continuing duty to review questions of disclosure.[359]

Although the disclosure provisions do not apply until after committal, it is envisaged that some disclosure may be required before then although this would not normally exceed primary disclosure.[360]

The prosecutor may, at any time, make an application to the court for an order that material should not be disclosed on the grounds that 'it is not in the public interest to disclose it'.[361] The common law rules as to whether disclosure is in the public interest continue to apply.[362] A number of categories of documents are covered: **11.98**

- documents which would tend to disclose the identity of informers;[363]
- documents which might reveal the location of police observation posts;[364]
- police reports[365] or manuals.[366]

The procedure to be followed was established in *R v Davis*[367] in which the following principles were set out:

---

[355] Code of Practice, para 5.1, see *Archbold: Criminal Pleading, Practice and Evidence* (Sweet & Maxwell, 1999) para 12–105.
[356] CPIA, s 3(1).
[357] CPIA, s 5.
[358] CPIA, s 7.
[359] CPIA, s 9.
[360] See *R v Director of Public Prosecutions, ex p Lee* [1999] 2 All ER 737.
[361] CPIA, s 8.
[362] CPIA, s 21(2).
[363] *Marks v Beyfus* (1890) 25 QBD 494 and see *Savage v Chief Constable of Hampshire* [1997] 1 WLR 1061.
[364] *R v Rankine* [1986] QB 861; *R v Johnson (Kenneth)* [1989] 1 All ER 121.
[365] *Evans v Chief Constable of Surrey* [1988] QB 588; *Taylor v Anderton (Police Complaints Authority Intervening)* [1995] 1 WLR 447.
[366] *Gill and Goodwin v Chief Constable of Lancashire, The Times*, 3 Nov 1992.
[367] [1993] 1 WLR 613.

- in general, the prosecution has a duty to make disclosure voluntarily;
- if the prosecution wishes to rely on public interest immunity it should, wherever possible, notify the defence that it will be applying for a court ruling and indicate the category of material in question, so that the defence has the opportunity of making representations to the court;
- where the disclosure of the category of material would itself reveal the information which the prosecution does not wish to reveal, the prosecution should notify the defence of the application but this will be made *ex parte*;[368]
- in highly exceptional cases, the prosecution may apply to the court *ex parte*, without any notice to the defence.

The procedure now is set out in rules made under the CPIA.[369] The court should study the material before making an order.[370]

11.99 The test to be applied by the court on an application for an order for 'non-disclosure' is unclear. In the leading case of *Marks v Beyfus*[371] it was said that:

> if upon the trial of a prisoner, the judge should be of the opinion that the disclosure of the name of the informant is necessary or right to shew the prisoner's innocence, then one public policy is in conflict with another public policy and that which says that an innocent man is not to be condemned when his innocence can be proved is the policy that must prevail.

This suggests that material which assists the defence should always be disclosed. However, in *R v Keane*[372] the Court of Appeal held that the court must carry out a balancing exercise: between the public interest in the non-disclosure of the documents and the public interest in the proper administration of justice. It is clear that public interest immunity may be overridden

> in order to prevent the possibility that a man may, by reason of the exclusion, be deprived of the opportunity of casting doubt upon the case against him.[373]

Disclosure should always be ordered if the withholding of the information 'may prove the defendant's innocence or avoid a miscarriage of justice'.[374]

11.100 The obligation to make pre-trial disclosure does not apply to trials in the magistrates' court. The absence of such disclosure does not affect the fairness of any

---

368 No *ex parte* application should be made where there is nothing that cannot be said in the presence of defence counsel: *R v Smith (David)* [1998] 2 Cr App R 1.

369 Crown Court (Criminal Procedure and Investigations Act 1996) (Disclosure) Rules 1997, *Archbold: Criminal Pleading, Practice and Evidence* (Sweet & Maxwell, 1999), para 12–77.

370 *R v Brown (Winston)* [1994] 1 WLR 1599; but see *Balfour v Foreign and Commonwealth Office* [1994] 1 WLR 681.

371 (1890) 25 QBD 494, 498; see also *R v Governor of Brixton Prison, ex p Osman* [1991] 1 WLR 281, 290.

372 [1994] 1 WLR 746.

373 *R v Agar* (1990) 90 Cr App R 318.

374 *R v Keane* [1994] 1 WLR 746, 484; see also *R v Turner (Paul)* [1995] 1 WLR 264; and generally, *Archbold: Criminal Pleading, Practice and Evidence* (Sweet & Maxwell, 1999) para 12–44e.

trial, provided that justices appreciate the need to grant reasonable adjournments to enable the defendant to deal with the evidence.[375] Nevertheless, such disclosure ought to be given if requested unless there are good reasons for a refusal, such as protection of a witness (at least where the offences charged could possibly lead to imprisonment).[376] The disclosure position is not affected by the provisions of the CPIA.[377] It has been held that this approach is consistent with Article 6 of the Convention.[378]

(d) The right to silence and the privilege against self-incrimination

Introduction. The 'right to silence' and the 'privilege against self-incrimination' are closely related rights which are deeply embedded in the common law.[379] The right to silence has been analysed by the House of Lords as including the following: **11.101**

> (1) A general immunity, possessed by all persons and bodies, from being compelled on pain of punishment to answer questions posed by other persons or bodies.
> (2) A general immunity, possessed by all persons and bodies, from being compelled on pain of punishment to answer questions the answers to which may incriminate them.
> (3) A specific immunity, possessed by all persons under suspicion of criminal responsibility whilst being interviewed by police officers or others in similar positions of authority, from being compelled on pain of punishment to answer questions of any kind.
> (4) A specific immunity, possessed by accused persons undergoing trial, from being compelled to give evidence, and from being compelled to answer questions put to them in the dock.
> (5) A specific immunity, possessed by persons who have been charged with a criminal offence, from having questions material to the offence addressed to them by police officers or persons in a similar position of authority.
> (6) A specific immunity . . . possessed by accused persons undergoing trial, from having adverse comment made on any failure (a) to answer questions before the trial, or (b) to give evidence at the trial.[380]

In addition, there is a specific immunity from answering questions or providing evidence in the course of an action which might expose the party to contempt proceedings in that action.[380a]

---

[375] *R v Kingston-upon-Hull Justices, ex p McCann* (1991) 155 JP 569.
[376] Ibid 573E–574B; *R v Stratford Justices, ex p Imbert* (1999) 2 Cr App R 276.
[377] See *R v Stratford Justices ex p Imbert* (n 376 above).
[378] Ibid.
[379] See generally, I Dennis, 'Instrumental Protection, Human Right or Functional Necessity? Reassessing the Privilege Against Self-incrimination' (1995) 52 CLJ 342.
[380] *Per* Lord Mustill, *R v Director of Serious Fraud Office, ex p Smith* [1993] AC 1, 30F–31B; see also *Bishopsgate Investment Management v Maxwell* [1993] Ch 1.
[380a] *Memory Corporation v Sidhu* [2000] 2 WLR 1106.

11.102 **The right to refuse to answer questions.** The first aspect of the right to silence has been subject to substantial statutory encroachment over recent years.[381] Witnesses can now be compelled to give evidence in a number of situations where financial irregularity and fraud are being investigated. The Director of the Serious Fraud Office ('SFO') has the power to require a person under investigation or any other person who he has reason to believe has relevant information to produce documents and to provide an explanation of them.[382] The powers can be exercised at any time.[383] SFO do not have to provide the person being interviewed with advance information as to the subject matter of the interview.[384] Legal professional privilege provides a ground for refusing to produce.[385] It was held that the effect of these statutory provisions was to override the privilege against self-incrimination.[386] The privilege has now been restored by statute.[386a]

11.103 Inspectors appointed by the Department of Trade and Industry have powers to compel witnesses to give them assistance, to attend before them and to answer questions on oath.[387] Such inspections are conducted in private and information disclosed to the inspectors is not generally to be made public.[388] A witness cannot refuse to answer such questions on the grounds of self-incrimination.[389] By section 434(5):

> An answer given by a person to a question put to him in exercise of powers conferred [by section 434] . . . may be used in evidence against him.

It was held that such evidence could not be excluded under section 78 of the Police and Criminal Evidence Act 1984[390] simply because the statute overrode the principles against self-incrimination.[391] The privilege has now been restored by statute.[391a] The evidence obtained by inspectors can be used in directors disqualification proceedings.[392] Any refusal to comply with the requirement of an inspector is a contempt of court.[393]

---

[381] See generally, O Davies, 'Self-Incrimination, Fair Trials and the Pursuit of Corporate and Financial Wrongdoing' in B Markesinis (ed), *The Impact of the Human Rights Bill in English Law* (Oxford University Press, 1998) 31.

[382] Criminal Justice Act 1987, s 2.

[383] *R v Turner, The Times*, 2 Jul 1993 (after service of defence statement).

[384] *R v Serious Fraud Office, ex p Maxwell, The Independent*, 7 Oct 1992.

[385] *In Re Barlow Clowes Gilt Managers Ltd* [1992] Ch 208.

[386] *R v Director of Serious Fraud Office, ex p Smith* [1993] AC 1.

[386a] See para 11.107 below.

[387] Companies Act 1985, s 434(2), and (3); and generally, *Re Pergamon Press Ltd* [1971] Ch 388.

[388] See *Hearts of Oak Assurance Co v A-G*[1932] AC 392.

[389] *Re London United Investments plc* [1992] Ch 578.

[390] See para 11.132 below.

[391] *R v Saunders (Ernest)*[1996] 1 Cr App Re 463, 475–477.

[391a] See para 11.107 below.

[392] *R v Secretary of State for Trade and Industry, ex p McCormick* [1998] BCC 379; *Official Receiver v Stern* [2000] UKHRR 332.

[393] s 434.

Comparable powers of compulsion are found in the Insolvency Act 1986.[394] By section 433 it is provided that: **11.104**

> In any proceedings (whether or not under this Act) . . .
>
> (b) any . . . statement made in pursuance of a requirement imposed by or under any [provision of this Act] or by any rules made under this Act;
>
> may be used in evidence against any person making or concurring in making the statement.

As a result, the witness cannot rely on the privilege against self-incrimination to refuse to answer questions[395] and it was possible to use the written record of the examination in criminal proceedings.[396] The common law position has now been restored by statute.[396a]

The Financial Services Act 1986 gives similar powers of compulsion to inspectors investigating insider dealing.[397] It is expressly provided that a statement made by a person in compliance with a requirement imposed on him by an inspector 'may be used in evidence against him'.[398] It was held that there is no power to exclude such evidence.[399] The position has, however, been reversed by statute.[399a] **11.105**

There are similar powers of compulsion in relation to insurance,[400] banking,[401] financial services,[402] planning enforcement[403] and the regulation of waste on land.[404] It has been held that the power to require the provision of information in relation to the supply of waste was conferred not merely for the purposes of obtaining evidence but also for the broad public purpose of protecting public health and the environment and that, as a result, those questioned should not be entitled to rely on the privilege against self-incrimination.[404a] The question of exclusion of potentially incriminating answers on the ground of prejudice was a matter for the discretion of the trial judge. **11.106**

[394] For example, s 236 (provision of information to liquidators by officers of companies in liquidation); s 290 (public examination of a bankrupt), s 366, (examination of bankrupt by receiver).
[395] *Bishopgate Investment Management Ltd v Maxwell* [1993] Ch 1.
[396] *R v Kansal* [1993] QB 244.
[396a] See para 11.107 below.
[397] s 177.
[398] s 177(6).
[399] *R v Morisey* (1997) 2 Cr App R 426 (despite the fact that the provision is incompatible with Art 6 of the Convention).
[399a] See para 11.107 below.
[400] Insurance Companies Act 1982, s 43A.
[401] Banking Act 1987 ss 41 and 42, see *Riley v Bank of England* [1992] Ch 475.
[402] Financial Services Act 1986, ss 94 and 105.
[403] Town and Country Planning Act 1990, ss 171C and 171D.
[404] Environmental Protection Act 1990, ss 34(5) and 71.
[404a] *R v Hertfordshire County Council, ex p Green Environmental Industries* [2000] 2 WLR 373 (HL).

11.107 **Privilege against self-incrimination by provision of evidence.** The 'privilege against self-incrimination' has been described as one of the 'basic freedoms secured by English law'.[405] The privilege entitles a party to civil litigation to refuse to give discovery of documents which may incriminate him[406] and may entitle an individual to refuse to provide documents to comply with a production order made under section 9 of the Police and Criminal Evidence Act 1984.[406a] However, as has been indicated, privilege can be overridden by a wide range of statutory provisions. Thus the use of evidence obtained by compulsion by DTI Inspectors in a subsequent criminal trial was held by the European Court of Human Rights to be a violation of Article 6.[407] As a result, the Attorney-General issued guidance to prosecuting authorities making it clear that the prosecution

> should not normally use in evidence as part of its case or in cross-examination answers obtained under compulsory powers.[408]

All the statutory provisions allowing for the use of compelled evidence in criminal proceedings[408a] have now been amended by section 58 and Schedule 3 of the Youth Justice and Criminal Evidence Act 1999. These amendments have inserted into each statute provisions to the effect that, in relation to completed statements:

(a) no evidence relating to the statement may be adduced, and
(b) no question relating to it may be asked, by or on behalf of the prosecution, unless evidence relating to it is adduced, or a question relating to it is asked, in the proceedings by or on behalf of that person.

In each case an exception is made for prosecutions for perjury or for failure to answer questions.

11.108 **Adverse inferences from silence.** Until 1994, the prosecution in a criminal trial was not permitted to comment on the defendant's failure to give evidence[409] or on his decision to remain silent in the police station.[410] Any comment by the judge had to be measured and the jury had to be warned that guilt must not be assumed on the basis of silence.[411] The position has now been radically altered by sections 34 to 37 of the Criminal Justice and Public Order Act 1994 ('the 1994 Act'),

---

[405] *In Re Arrows Ltd (No 4)* [1995] 2 AC 75.

[406] *Rank Film Distributors Ltd v Video Information Centre* [1982] AC 380; *A T & T Istel Ltd v Tully* [1993] AC 45.

[406a] See *R v Central Criminal Court ex p Bright, The Times*, 26 Jul 2000; and in relation to production orders, see para 15.123ff below.

[407] See *Saunders v United Kingdom* (1996) 23 EHRR 313.

[408] Attorney-General's Chambers *News Release*, 3 Feb 1998.

[408a] The following English provisions have been amended: Insurance Companies Act 1982, s 43A and s 44; Companies Act 1985, s 434; Insolvency Act 1986, s 433; Company Directors Disqualification Act 1986, s 20; Financial Services Act 1986, s 105; Banking Act 1987, s 39; Criminal Justice Act 1987, s 2; Companies Act 1989, s 83; Friendly Societies Act 1992, s 67.

[409] Criminal Evidence Act 1898, s 1(b).

[410] *Hall v R* [1971] 1 WLR 298.

[411] *R v Bathurst* [1968] 2 QB 99.

Section 34 deals with the effect of an accused's failure to mention facts when questioned or charged. Where evidence is given that the accused: **11.109**

(a) at any time before he was charged with the offence, on being questioned under caution by a constable trying to discover whether or by whom the offence had been committed, failed to mention any fact relied on in his defence in those proceedings; or
(b) on being charged with the offence or officially informed that he might be prosecuted for it, failed to mention any such fact[412]

then, if the fact is one which the accused might reasonably have been expected to mention, the court may, in specified circumstances, including at the trial, 'draw such inferences from the failure as appear proper'.[413] However, these provisions do not apply if the accused had not been allowed an opportunity to consult a solicitor prior to being questioned, charged or informed.[413a] The Court of Human Rights has rejected the argument that the caution administered under the 1994 Act is ambiguous or unclear about the effect of a refusal to answer police questions.[413b]

Section 35, deals with the effect of an accused's silence at trial. Subject to narrow exceptions, **11.109A**

> the court or jury, in determining whether the accused is guilty of the offence charged, may draw such inferences as appear proper from the failure of the accused to give evidence or his refusal, without good cause, to answer any question.[414]

The section does not, however, render the accused a compellable witness[415] and he will have 'good cause' to refuse to answer a question if he relies on privilege.[416] Section 36 provides that inferences may be drawn from an accused's failure or refusal to account for 'objects, substances or marks' on his person, clothing or in his possession or in any place in which he is arrested. Section 37 provides that inferences may be drawn from an accused's failure or refusal to account for his presence at a particular place. The various statutory conditions must be fulfilled before these sections can operate.[417] Section 34 only applies to 'facts', not theories, possibilities or speculations advanced by the accused.[418] It is reasonable for the defendant to ask for details of the charge before answering, but the police are not required to reveal their whole case before interview.[419] The defendant is now entitled to have the opportunity to consult counsel or a solicitor before adverse inferences can be drawn from his

412 The 1994 Act, s 34(1).
413 Ibid s 34(2).
413a s 34(2A), added by Youth Justice and Criminal Evidence Act 1999, s 58.
413b *Condron v United Kingdom, The Times*, 9 May 2000, para 59.
414 Ibid s 34(3).
415 Ibid s 34(4).
416 Ibid s 34(5).
417 See *R v Argent* [1997] 2 Cr App R 27, 32–33.
418 *R v N, The Times*, 13 Feb 1998.
419 *R v Imran and Hussain* [1997] Crim LR 754.

silence.[419a] Legal advice to remain silent cannot prevent an adverse inference being drawn.[420] However, if the defendant leads evidence as to the solicitor's reasons for giving such advice, this will be a waiver of legal professional privilege in respect of communications between solicitor and client at the time of the interview.[421] The fact that the privilege is waived in this situation is not inconsistent with Article 6.[421a]

11.110 The 1994 Act provides that a person cannot be found to have a case to answer or be convicted of an offence solely on the basis of inferences drawn from failures or refusals to mention facts, testify or provide explanations.[422] It has been suggested that inferences of guilt should not be drawn from a failure to give evidence to contradict a prosecution case of 'little evidential value'.[423] However, the Court of Appeal have refused to restrict the impact of section 35 and have said that the judge should only direct or advise the jury against drawing an adverse inference where there is some evidential basis for doing so or some exceptional factors.[424]

(e) The admissibility of confessions

11.111 The common law rule that a confession was only admissible in evidence if the prosecution proved beyond reasonable doubt that it was freely and voluntarily given is closely related to the privilege against self-incrimination:

> That privilege aims to protect all citizens against being compelled to condemn themselves. But the law has never set out to protect a subject who condemns himself whilst acting of his own free will. Its only concern has been to ensure that he really does so act, by the general rule which excludes from evidence any confession which is not proved to have been voluntary.[425]

This rule appears to have derived from a determination to eradicate the oppressive and often barbaric methods of interrogation employed by the Star Chamber to extract confessions from accused persons. From the abhorrence of those methods there developed the privilege against self-incrimination, and the right of silence, one aspect of which is the exclusion of compelled confessions, with the onus placed on the prosecution to prove beyond reasonable doubt that any confession relied on was voluntary. The law relating to proof of the voluntariness of confessions was particularly important at a time when an accused was not entitled to give evidence on his own behalf—a disability removed in England only in 1898.[426]

[419a] s 34(2A), s 36(4A) and s 37(3A) of the 1994 Act, inserted by Youth Justice and Criminal Evidence Act 1999, s 58.

[420] *R v Condron (William)* [1997] 1 WLR 827.

[421] *R v Bowden* [1999] 1 WLR 823.

[421a] *Condron v United Kingdom*, *The Times*, 9 May 2000, para 60.

[422] The 1994 Act, s 38(3).

[423] *Murray v DPP* [1994] 1 WLR 1 (on the comparable Northern Ireland provisions); see also *Waugh v The King* [1950] AC 203.

[424] *R v Cowan* [1996] QB 373.

[425] *Per* Lord Mustill, *R v Director of Serious Fraud Office, ex p Smith* [1993] AC 1, 42.

[426] Ibid 34; and see generally, A Zuckerman, *The Principles of Criminal Evidence* (Clarendon Press, 1989) 311ff.

The principle that a confession was only admissible if voluntary was formulated by the Privy Council in *Ibrahim v R*[427] and became Principle (e) of the Judges Rules.[428] Its importance was emphasised in a number of cases. For example, in *Lam Chi-ming v R*[429] Lord Griffiths said that the English cases established: **11.112**

> that the rejection of an improperly obtained confession is not dependent only upon possible unreliability but also upon the principle that a man cannot be compelled to incriminate himself and upon the importance that attaches in a civilised society to proper behaviour by the police towards those in their custody. All three of these factors have combined to produce the rule of law . . . that a confession is not admissible in evidence unless the prosecution establish that it was voluntary.

Nevertheless, the practical application of this principle caused difficulty and it was criticised by the Phillips Commission on Criminal Procedure in 1981.[430]

The position as to the admissibility of confessions is now governed by the Police and Criminal Evidence Act 1984.[431] Section 76(2) provides that: **11.113**

> If, in any proceedings where the prosecution proposes to give in evidence a confession made by an accused person, it is represented to the court that the confession was or may have been obtained—
>
> (a) by oppression of the person who made it;
> (b) in consequence of anything said or done which was likely, in the circumstances existing at the time, to render unreliable any confession which might be made by him in consequence thereof,
>
> the court shall not allow the confession to be given in evidence against him except in so far as the prosecution proves to the court beyond reasonable doubt that the confession (notwithstanding that it may be true) was not obtained as aforesaid.

The Court may, of its own motion, require the prosecution to prove that the confession was not obtained in this way.[432] A 'confession' includes any statement wholly or partly adverse to the person who made it, whether or not it is in words.[433]

'Oppression' includes 'torture, inhuman and degrading treatment and the use or threat of violence'.[434] In general, it must involve the exercise of authority in a 'burdensome, harsh or wrongful manner'[435] and will almost always involve impropriety **11.114**

427 [1914] AC 599, 610.

428 See *Practice Note (Judges' Rules)* [1964] 1 WLR 152).

429 [1991] 2 AC 212, 220; PC; see also *Wong Kam-ming v R*[1980] AC 247, 261, *per* Lord Hailsham.

430 *Royal Commission on Criminal Procedure* (1981), Cmnd 8092 para 4.73.

431 For a full discussion, see *Archbold: Criminal Pleading, Practice and Evidence* (Sweet & Maxwell, 1999), para 15–337ff; *Blackstone's Criminal Practice, 1999* (Blackstone Press, 1999) s F17.1ff; M Zander, *The Police and Criminal Evidence Act 1984* (3rd edn, Sweet & Maxwell, 1995) 217ff.

432 PACE, s 76(3).

433 Ibid, s 82(1); but it does not exclude statements which were initially self-serving but are, later, the accused's detriment (*Rv Sat-Bhambra* (1988) 88 Cr App R 55).

434 PACE, s 76(8).

435 *R v Fulling* [1987] QB 426; see also *R v Emmerson* (1991) 92 Cr App R 284.

on the part of the interrogator.[436] However, not every breach of the Codes of Practice in relation to detention and questioning will be oppressive.[437] Confessions have been excluded under this head where there has been hectoring and bullying questioning[438] or where the evidence has been misrepresented. A wide range of matters have been held to be likely to render a confession unreliable including an offer of bail[439] and minimising the significance of the offence.[440]

(f) The presumption of innocence

11.115 The principle that the prosecution must prove the prisoner's guilt has been said to be the 'golden thread' running through the web of English criminal law:

> the principle that the prosecution must prove the guilt of the prisoner is part of the common law of England and no attempt to whittle it down can be entertained.[441]

This has been described as an 'undoubted fundamental rule of natural justice'.[442] The prosecution has to prove all the elements of the offence, including proving 'negatives', such as the absence of consent on a charge of rape. If a defendant raises defence such as provocation, self-defence or duress then, provided there is some evidence of such a defence, the prosecution must prove that there is no such defence. The only common law exception is the defence of insanity. If a defendant raises this defence he must prove it on the balance of probabilities.[443] This exception has not been extended to the defence of automatism.[444]

11.116 However, the general common law principle is subject to statutory exceptions, whether these are express or implied.[445] A distinction must be drawn between provisions which place an 'evidential burden' on the accused and those which place him under a 'persuasive burden'. [446] Statutory provisions which place only an 'evidential burden' on the accused, requiring him to raise a reasonable doubt, do not breach the presumption of innocence and are likely to be compatible with Article

[436] *R v Fulling* (n 435 above) 432.

[437] *R v Parker* [1995] Crim LR 233, and the commentary by D J Birch.

[438] *R v Paris* (1993) 97 Cr App R 99.

[439] *R v Barry* (1992) 95 Cr App R 384.

[440] *R v Delaney* (1988) 88 Cr App R 338.

[441] *Woolmington v DPP* [1935] AC 462, 481, *per* Lord Sankey; see also *Mancini v DPP* [1942] AC 1, 11; and see generally, P Roberts, 'Taking the Burden of Proof Seriously' [1995] Crim LR 783; Ashworth and Blake, 'The Presumption of Innocence in English Criminal Law' [1996] Crim LR 306.

[442] *Haw Tua Tau v Public Prosecutor* [1982] AC 136.

[443] *Sodeman v The King* (1936) 55 CLR 192.

[444] See *Hill v Baxter* [1958] 1 QB 277, 285; the position is the same in Scotland (*Ross v HM Advocate* 1991 SLT 564 and Northern Ireland (*Bratty v A-G for Northern Ireland* [1963] AC 386).

[445] *R v Hunt (Richard)* [1987] AC 352.

[446] See the general discussion by Lord Hope in *R v DPP, ex p Kebilene* [1999] 3 WLR 972, 991–993.

6(2) of the Convention.[447] Statutory provisions which place a 'persuasive' burden on the accused can be divided into three types:[448]

- provisions which place the burden on the accused to show that he has the benefit of an exemption or proviso;
- presumption of guilt as to an essential element of the offence which is 'discretionary' in the sense that the tribunal of fact may or may not rely on the presumption;
- 'mandatory' presumption of guilt as to an essential element of the offence, based on proof of a particular fact.

In such cases, the burden is on the defence to prove the requisite fact or knowledge 'on the balance of probabilities'.[449]

The first class of case often involves an implied statutory reversal of the burden of proof. In relation to summary trials the matter is governed by section 101 of the Magistrates' Court Act 1980 which provides that, in such a case: **11.117**

> the burden of proving the exception, exemption, proviso, excuse or qualification shall be on [the defendant] . . . notwithstanding that the information or complaint contains an allegation negativing the exception, exemption, proviso, excuse or qualification.

This sets out the common law rule, established in the case of *R v Edwards*[450] However, the presumption is against an inference that the burden was to be placed on the defendant and the courts should be slow to draw such inference from the language of a statute.[451]

In the second class of case the court has a discretion as to whether or not to rely on the presumption. In *R v Killen*[452] the Northern Ireland Court of Appeal held that such provisions should not be used unless, having done so, the court would be left satisfied beyond reasonable doubt of the guilt of the accused. It has been suggested that a similar approach should be applied in England.[453] **11.118**

The third class of case involves a clear breach of the presumption of innocence. There are a number of statutory provisions in this category including:[454] **11.119**

447 Ibid.
448 Ibid.
449 *R v Carr-Briant* [1943] KB 607.
450 [1975] QB 27; see also *Rv Hunt (Richard)* [1987] AC 352.
451 *R v Hunt* (n 450 above) 374.
452 [1974] NI 220.
453 See *R v DPP, ex p Kebilene* [1999] 3 WLR 972, 995 *per* Lord Hope; in relation to s 16A(4) of the Prevention of Terrorism (Temporary Provisions) Act 1989.
454 For a full list, see *R v DPP, ex p Kebilene* (n 453 above) 995H–996B.

- a defence that a person did not believe or suspect that a substance in his possession was a controlled drug;[455]
- that a person in possession of articles in circumstances giving rise to a reasonable suspicion that this is for a purpose connected with terrorism does not have them in his possession for this purpose;[456]
- that a person in possession of information which is likely to be useful to terrorists has a lawful authority or reasonable excuse for the possession of the information.[457]

It is arguable that such provisions are in breach of Article 6(2) of the Convention. This was the view of the Divisional Court in *R v DPP, ex p Kebilene*[458] in relation to the offences under sections 16A and 16B of the Prevention of Terrorism (Temporary Provisions) Act 1989.[459] The House of Lords, in overruling the decision on other grounds, declined to express a view on this point. However, Lord Hope suggested that, in order to decide whether a particular statutory provision was in breach of the presumption of innocence it was necessary to consider, in each case, the balance between the interests of the individual and those of society as a whole. This, in turn, involved the consideration of three questions:

- what does the prosecution have to prove in order to transfer the onus to the defence?
- what is the burden on the accused, does it relate to something which is likely to be difficult for him to prove or something likely to be within his own knowledge?
- what is the nature of the threat faced by society which the provision is designed to combat?[460]

Lord Hope declined to express a concluded view on the facts of that case. It seems likely that this approach will be adopted to 'reverse onus' provisions under the Human Rights Act.[461]

(g) The right to jury trial

11.120 The right to trial by jury is often regarded as central to the rights of criminal

[455] Misuse of Drugs Act 1971, s 28.
[456] Prevention of Terrorism (Temporary Provisions) Act 1989, s 16A (as inserted by CJPOA 1994, s 82(1)).
[457] Prevention of Terrorism (Temporary Provisions) Act 1989, s 16B (as inserted by CJPOA 1994, s 82(1)).
[458] n 453 above.
[459] See para 11.118 above.
[460] *R v DPP, ex p Kebilene* (n 453 above) 998–999.
[461] See para 11.347 below.

defendants[462] and has been described as a 'constitutional right'.[463] To many commentators it is the most important fair trial right of all. In Lord Devlin's well known words:

> trial by jury is more than an instrument of justice and more than one wheel of the constitution: it is the lamp that shows that freedom lives.[464]

The adoption of the institution of the jury reflected 'a fundamental decision about the exercise of official power'.[465] As Deane J put it in the High Court of Australia:

> The institution of trial by jury also serves the function of protecting both the administration of justice and the accused from the rash judgment and prejudices of the community itself. The nature of the jury as a body of ordinary citizens called from the community to try the particular case offers some assurance that the community as a whole will be more likely to accept a jury's verdict than it would be to accept the judgment of a judge or magistrate who might be, or be portrayed as being, over-responsive to authority or remote from the affairs and concerns of ordinary people. The random selection of a jury panel, the empanelment of a jury to try the particular case, the public anonymity of individual jurors, the ordinary confidentiality of the jury's deliberative processes, the jury's isolation (at least at the time of decision) from external influences and the insistence upon its function of determining the particular charge according to the evidence combine, for so long as they can be preserved or observed, to offer some assurance that the accused will not be judged by reference to sensational or self-righteous pre-trial publicity or the passions of the mob.[466]

However, this right is only available for prosecutions for certain classes of offences. **11.121** Criminal offences are divided into three categories: summary only, triable either way and indictable. Offences in the first category are tried in the magistrates' courts. Offences in the second category are tried either in the magistrates' court or in the Crown Court on indictment. Offences in the third category can only be tried on indictment. Trial on indictment is, in all cases, by a judge and jury.

In relation to a wide range of conduct, the prosecution can, therefore, control **11.122** whether or not a defendant has a right to jury trial by the selection of the charge. For example, the same conduct may constitute both assault occasioning actual

[462] See P Devlin, *Trial by Jury* (Stevens, 1966); and *The Judge*, (Oxford University Press, 1979), Chap 5, 'The Judge and the Jury'; see also R Kerr (ed), *Blackstone's Commentaries on the Laws of England*, (4th edn, John Murray, 1876) Vol IV, 360.

[463] see *Rv Islington North Juvenile Court ex p Daley* [1983] AC 347; and see *per* Lord Denning MR in *Rothermere v Times Newspapers* [1973] 1 WLR 448, 452, 'Every defendant has a constitutional right to have his guilty or innocence determined by a jury' (said in the context of defamation proceedings).

[464] Devlin Trial by Jury (n 462 above) 164.

[465] See *Duncan v Louisiana* (1968) 391 US 145, 156; and generally, A Amar, *The Constitution and Criminal Procedure: First Principles* (Yale University Press, 1997) 120–124.

[466] *Per* Deane J, *Kingswell v The Queen* (1985) 62 ALR 161, 188 (in a dissenting judgment); see also *Brown v The Queen* (1986) 160 CLR 171.

bodily harm and assaulting a police officer in the execution of his duty but only the former charge carries the right to jury trial. It is not an abuse of the process for the prosecution to present a lesser summary only charge appropriate to the nature of the offence when they could have charged an offence which would have carried a right to jury trial.[467] This is so even where the prosecution make it clear that they are substituting a lesser charge because it carries no right to jury trial.[468]

11.123 Juries are now selected at random from all the names appearing on the electoral register. In order to be eligible for jury service, a person must be between the ages of 18 and 70,[469] must have been ordinarily resident in the United Kingdom for a total period of at least five years since the age of 13 and must not be ineligible or disqualified.[470] The judiciary, those concerned with the administration of justice, the clergy and the mentally ill are ineligible.[471] A person is disqualified if he has ever been sentenced to a period of imprisonment of five years or more or if he has served any part of a sentence of imprisonment or detention within the past 10 years.[472] However, the fact that a juror was disqualified, ineligible or unfit to serve cannot be a ground of appeal against a jury verdict.[473] A number of persons, including peers, serving members of the armed forces and various medical professionals are excusable from jury service as of right.[474]

11.124 The police can, in appropriate circumstances, check the criminal convictions of potential jurors.[475] In two classes of case, additional checks may be carried out:[476]

- cases in which national security is involved and part of the evidence is likely to be heard in camera;
- terrorist cases.

Such 'jury vetting' should only be carried out on the personal authority of the Attorney-General. Only in the most exceptional cases is the defence permitted to put questions to potential jurors concerning matters which might lead to prejudice or bias.[477]

---

[467] See *Rv Canterbury and St Augustine Justices, ex p Klisiak* [1982] 1 QB 398.

[468] See *Rv Liverpool Stipendiary Magistrate, ex p Ellison* [1990] RTR 220.

[469] Juries Act 1974, s 1(a) and Criminal Justice Act 1988, s 119.

[470] Juries Act 1974, s 1 and Sch 1.

[471] Juries Act 1974, Sch 1, Pt I.

[472] Juries Act 1974, Sch 1, Pt II.

[473] Juries Act 1974, s 18, and see *R v Chapman (William)* (1976) Cr App R 75.

[474] Juries Act 1974, Sch 1, Pt III.

[475] *R v Mason* [1981] QB 881; and see *A-G's Guidelines on Jury Checks* (1978) 88 Cr App R 123.

[476] See *A-G's Guidelines* (n 475 above) paras 3 and 4.

[477] See generally, *R v Andrews (Tracey)* [1999] Crim LR 156; a case in which this was done was *Rv Kray* (1969) 53 Cr App R 412; see also *Murphy v The Queen* (1989) 167 CLR 94, 103.

(h) Other rights in relation to the trial

11.125 There is no specific 'right' to the assistance of an interpreter under English law. However, it has often been said that the accused should be 'capable of understanding the proceedings' which implies a right to an interpreter if a defendant is unrepresented.[478] A trial is a nullity if the accused cannot comprehend the charges and instruct his lawyers.[479] The Crown Court has a discretion to order an accused to pay the costs of an interpreter.[480]

11.126 In general, a criminal trial must take place in the presence of the accused.[481] As a result, no part of the trial should take place in camera in the absence of the accused.[482] However, there is jurisdiction, in exceptional circumstances, to proceed with a trial in the absence of an accused who has entered a plea. These circumstances include misbehaviour by the accused[483] and the voluntary absence of the accused.[484] If the accused is absent for reasons beyond his control then the trial cannot continue in his absence unless he consents.[485]

11.127 There is a fundamental right of a defendant to see and to know the identity of his accusers, including witnesses for the prosecution brought against him.[486] This is a right which should only be denied in rare and exceptional circumstances. Whether or not these circumstances exist is a matter for the discretion of the trial judge. The following factors are relevant:[487]

- there must be real grounds for being fearful of the consequences if the evidence is given and the identity of the witness is revealed;
- the evidence must be sufficiently relevant and important to make it unfair to the prosecution to compel them to proceed without it;
- the prosecution must satisfy the court that the creditworthiness of the witness has been fully investigated and the results of that enquiry disclosed to the defence so far as is consistent with the anonymity sought;
- the court must be satisfied that no undue prejudice is caused to the defendant;
- the court can balance the need for protection, including the extent of any necessary protection, against the unfairness or appearance of unfairness in the particular case.

---

478 *R v Lee Kun* [1916] KB 337; *Kunnath v The State* [1993] 1 WLR 1315.

479 *R v Iqbal Begum* (1991) 93 Cr App R 96.

480 *Practice Direction (Crime Costs)* [1991] 1 WLR 498.

481 *R v Lee Kun* [1916] KB 337.

482 *R v Preston* [1994] 2 AC 130.

483 *R v Lee Kun* (n 481 above).

484 *R v Jones (Robert) (No 2)* [1972] 1 WLR 887; *R v O'Nione* [1986] Crim LR 342; see generally, *Blackstone's Criminal Practice, 1999* (Blackstone Press, 1999) s D12.25.

485 *R v Jones (No 2)* (n 484 above); see also, *R v Howson* (1981) 74 Cr App R 172.

486 See *R v Taylor and Crabb* [1995] Crim LR 253; and also *R v Watford Magistrates' Court, ex p Lenman* [1993] Crim LR 388; see also *Arlidge, Eady and Smith on Contempt* (2nd edn, Sweet & Maxwell, 1999) para 7–45, n 80 and the cases there cited.

487 See *Rv Taylor and Crabb* (n 486 above).

Furthermore, in exceptional circumstances, screens may be used to protect the anonymity of witnesses.[488]

11.128 The criminal courts have power, under the Criminal Justice Act 1988, to receive evidence in the form of written statements from witnesses who do not attend court[489] if:

- the witness is dead, unfit to attend court, abroad or cannot be found;[490]
- the witness does not give oral evidence through fear or because he is kept out of the way (provided that the statement was made to a police officer or other investigator.[491]

The prosecution must prove beyond reasonable doubt that one of these grounds applies.[492] In relation to a witness who does not give oral evidence 'through fear', the prosecution does not have to show that the fear is reasonable,[493] but the 'fear' must be proved by admissible evidence.[494] The court must consider whether it is in the interests of justice that such a statement be admitted,[495] and must have regard to the following factors: the nature and source of the document containing the statement and its likely authenticity, the extent to which the statement appears to supply evidence which would otherwise not be readily available, the relevance of the evidence and to any risk that its admission or exclusion will result in unfairness to the accused.[496] Where a statement has been prepared for the purposes of pending or contemplated criminal proceedings or a criminal investigation, then the statement shall not be given in evidence without the leave of the court, 'unless it is of the opinion that the statement ought to be admitted in the interests of justice'.[497]

11.129 The courts have considered the exercise of the statutory discretion on a number of occasions.[498] The cases establish that:

- the fact that the accused loses his right to cross-examine is not, of itself, unfair;

[488] *R v DJX* (1990) 91 Cr App R 36; *R v Schaub and Cooper*, *The Times*, 3 Dec 1993; see also *Rv Murphy and Maguire* [1990] NI 306 and *Doherty v Ministry of Defence* [1991] 1 NIJB 68 and generally, B Dickson, 'The European Convention in Northern Irish Courts' [1996] EHRLR 496, 508–509.

[489] See also 1988 Act, s 26 which deals with evidence contained in documents.

[490] Ibid s 23(2).

[491] Ibid s 23(3).

[492] See *R v Acton Justices, ex p McMullen* (1990) 92 Cr App R 98.

[493] Ibid *R v Martin* [1996] Crim LR 589.

[494] See *Neill v North Antrim Magistrates' Court* [1992] 1 WLR 1220.

[495] 1988 Act, s 25(1).

[496] Ibid s 25(2).

[497] Ibid s 26.

[498] See most recently, *R v Radak (Jason)* [1999] 1 Cr App R 187 and see generally, *Rv Cole* [1990] 1 WLR 866; and P Murphy (ed), *Blackstone's Criminal Practice 1999* (Blackstone Press, 1999) F16.17.

- an important factor is the quality of the evidence contained in the statement;[499]
- there is no general rule that a statement which is 'crucial' to the case must be excluded;[500]
- there is no general rule against admitting a statement which will force the accused to testify in order to 'controvert' it.[501]

It has been held that the provisions of sections 23 to 26 of the Criminal Justice Act 1988 are consistent with the right to a fair trial[502] under Article 6 of the Convention. In *R v Gokal*[503] the Court of Appeal concluded that:

> Since the whole basis of the discretion conferred by section 26 is to assess the interests of justice by reference to the risk of unfairness to the accused, our procedures appear to us to accord fully with [Article 6].

This decision was followed by the Court of Appeal in *R v Thomas*.[504] Roch LJ pointed out that the European Court of Human Rights had made clear that its task was 'to ascertain whether the proceedings considered as a whole, including the way in which evidence was taken, were fair'.[505] He concluded that:

> the narrow ground which the trial judge has to be sure exists before he can allow a statement to be read to the jury coupled with the balancing exercise that he has to perform and the requirement that having performed that exercise he should be of the opinion that it is in the interest of justice to admit the statement having paid due regard to the risk of unfairness to the accused means that the provisions of sections 23 to 26 of the 1988 Act are not in themselves contrary to Article 6 of the Convention.[506]

The Law Commission has also concluded that Article 6 of the Convention does not require direct supporting evidence where it is sought to prove a particular element of the offence by hearsay.[507]

A statement tendered at committal may, 'without further proof be read as evidence on the trial of the accused'.[508] If the accused objects the statement cannot be read,[509] but the court may order that the objection shall have no effect 'if it **11.130**

[499] *R v Cole*, (n 498 above), *Scott v Queen* [1989] AC 1242.

[500] See *R v Patel (Sabhas)* (1993) 97 Cr App R 294, *R v Setz-Dempsey* (1993) 98 Cr App R 23; this may be a factor in favour of receiving the evidence, *R v Batt* [1995] Crim LR 240.

[501] *R v Moore* [1992] Crim LR 882.

[502] See para 11.204ff below.

[503] [1997] 2 Cr App R 266.

[504] [1998] Crim LR 887.

[505] Citing, *Kostovski v Netherlands* (1989) 12 EHRR 434.

[506] It was pointed out that the Commission had taken the same view in *Trivedi v United Kingdom* (1997) 89 DR 136, EComm HR.

[507] Law Commission, *Report on Evidence in Criminal Proceedings: Hearsay and Related Topics* (Law Com No 245, 1997) (the Law Commission was persuaded to reverse the contrary view taken in its Consultation Paper); see also *McKenna v Her Majesty's Advocate* 2000 SCCR 159.

[508] Criminal Procedure and Investigations Act 1996, Sch 2, para 1(2).

[509] Ibid Sch 2, para 1(3)(c).

considers it to be in the interests of justice'.[510] No statutory criteria are laid down for the exercise of this discretion.[511] A defendant may not examine, in person, a child who is the victim of or a witness to a violent or sexual offence.[512]

11.130A The trial of children and young persons in the Crown Court gives rise to potential difficulties in relation to the right of an accused to participate effectively in his trial. The Court of Human Rights has held that a trial of a ten-year-old for murder violated this right.[512a] As a result, a *Practice Direction* was issued[512b] making it clear that the overriding principle was that all possible steps should be taken to assist the young defendant to understand and participate in the proceedings. These steps include matters such as all the participants being on the same level, the young defendant being free to sit with members of his family, full explanation of the proceedings, no wigs or robes and restricted attendance.

(i) Exclusion of illegally obtained evidence

11.131 The position at common law was that a judge had no discretion to refuse to admit relevant evidence on the ground that it was obtained by improper or unfair means. As Lord Diplock said *R v Sang*:[513]

> (1) A trial judge in a criminal trial has always a discretion to refuse to admit evidence if in his opinion its prejudicial effect outweighs its probative value.
> (2) Save with regard to admissions and confessions and generally with regard to evidence obtained from the accused after commission of the offence, he has no discretion to refuse to admit relevant admissible evidence on the ground that it was obtained by improper or unfair means. The court is not concerned with how it was obtained.

As a result, evidence is admissible even if obtained by theft,[514] unlawful search[515] or the use of agent provocateurs.[516] Even though evidence has been unlawfully obtained from the accused after the commission of the offence, the evidence will not be excluded where it was obtained by someone acting in good faith.[517] It may, however, be excluded if the persons who obtained the evidence used trickery or deception.[518]

---

[510] Ibid Sch 2, para 1(4).
[511] During parliamentary debate on this provision, the Government indicated that it was anticipated that the courts would turn to s 26 of the Criminal Justice Act 1988 for guidance, *per* Baroness Blatch, *Hansard*, HL, 26 Jun 1996, cols 951–952.
[512] Criminal Justice Act 1988, s 34A.
[512a] *T v United Kingdom* (2000) 7 BHRC 659, see para 11.293 below.
[512b] *Practice Note (Trial of Children and Young Persons: Procedure)* [2000] 2 All ER 285.
[513] [1980] AC 402, 437; see also *Kuruma v The Queen* [1955] AC 197.
[514] *R v Leathem* (1861) 8 Cox CC 498, 501.
[515] *Jeffrey v Black* [1978] QB 490.
[516] *R v Sang* [1980] AC 402.
[517] *R v Fox* [1986] AC 281; *Rv Trump* [1980] RTR 274.
[518] See for example *Rv Mason (Carl)* [1988] 1 WLR 139.

The position is now governed by section 78(1) of the Police and Criminal Evidence 1984 which provides: **11.132**

> In any proceedings the court may refuse to allow evidence on which the prosecution proposes to rely to be given if it appears to the court that, having regard to all the circumstances, including the circumstances in which the evidence was obtained, the admission of the evidence would have such an adverse effect on the fairness of the proceedings that the court ought not to admit it.

In exercising this discretion, the court will look at all the circumstances, including unlawful searches, questioning or detention.[519] The approach of the courts has been summarised in the following terms:

> . . . proceedings may become unfair if, for example, one side is allowed to adduce relevant evidence which, for one reason or another, the other side cannot properly challenge or meet, or where there has been an abuse of process, eg because evidence has been obtained in deliberate breach of procedures laid down in an official code of practice.[520]

The fact that conduct is 'unlawful' or 'oppressive' does not necessarily mean that evidence obtained thereby should be excluded. The sole test is fairness.[521] Unlike abuse of process applications, no 'balancing exercise' is involved:

> The exercise for the judge under section 78 is not the marking of his disapproval of the prosecution's breach, if any, of the law in the conduct of the investigation or the proceedings by a discretionary decision to stay them, but an examination of the question whether it would be unfair to the defendant to admit that evidence.[522]

In considering fairness the court looks both at the trial and at the fairness of pre-trial proceedings.[523] The English courts have taken the view that this approach is consistent with the right to a fair trial[524] under Article 6 of the Convention. As Lord Nicholls said in *R v Khan*:[525]

> the discretionary powers of the trial judge to exclude evidence march hand in hand with Article 6(1) of the European Convention on Human Rights. Both are concerned to ensure that those facing criminal charges receive a fair hearing. Accordingly, when considering the common law and statutory discretionary powers under English law, the jurisprudence on Article 6 can have a valuable role to play.

This approach was approved by the European Court of Human Rights in *Khan v United Kingdom*.[525a]

---

[519] For an analysis of the substantial case law, see R Stone, 'Exclusion of Evidence Under Section 78 of the Police and Criminal Evidence Act: Practice and Principles' [1995] 3 Web JCLI.

[520] *R v Quinn* [1990] Crim LR 581.

[521] *R v Chalkley* [1998] QB 848.

[522] Ibid at 876C.

[523] See *Matto v Wolverhampton Crown Court* [1987] RTR 337.

[524] See para 11.204ff below.

[525] [1997] AC 558, 583B-D.

[525a] *The Times* 23 May 2000.

11.133 The relevant factors to be taken into account include apparent breaches of the Convention or the law of a foreign country[526] and the extent to which evidence was obtained as the result of the activities of an agent provocateur.[527] Evidence from 'interviews' is likely to be excluded if the defendant has been detrimentally deprived of legal advice[528] or if the provisions of the Code of Practice relating to interviews have not been complied with.[529] The exclusionary discretion can be exercised even if there has been no bad faith.[530] The fact that evidence has been obtained by a trick[531] or by agent provocateurs[532] will not, of itself, render it inadmissible. In *Nottingham City Council v Amin*[532a] police officers had flagged down a taxi which was not licensed for use in the area and the driver picked them up and carried them to their destination for a fare. The Divisional Court accepted that the officers had 'given the defendant the opportunity' to break the law. Lord Bingham CJ considered the Convention authorities and went on to hold that the proper test was whether or not the effect of admitting the evidence was to deny the respondent a fair trial. On the facts this was not the case and the evidence was admitted.

11.134 The court does not use section 78 to 'discipline' the police or prosecuting authorities.[533] English judges have consistently refused to countenance an approach whereby evidence obtained in breach of fundamental rights of the suspect should always be excluded.[534] The Privy Council has recently rejected a *prima facie* rule against admitting confessions obtained in breach of basic rights whilst accepting that the breach of a constitutional right is a cogent factor militating in favour of exclusion.[535] It is arguable that the courts should adopt a somewhat stricter approach in relation to breaches of the Human Rights Act.[536]

(j) Rule against double jeopardy

11.135 A person cannot, at common law, be prosecuted twice for the same offence. If

[526] *R v Khan* [1997] AC 558.

[527] *R v Smurthwaite* [1994] 1 All ER 898.

[528] See para 11.94ff above; and see R Kirk [1999] 4 All ER 698 (interview excluded when defendant who was being interviewed for theft was not told he was suspected of robbery and manslaughter arising out of the same incident).

[529] *R v Absalom* (1988) 88 Cr App R 332.

[530] *R v Alladice* (1988) 87 Cr App R 380; *DPP v McGladrigan* [1991] RTR 297.

[531] *R v Bailey* [1993] 3 All ER 513 (co-accused placed in same cell and conversation 'bugged').

[532] *R v Christou* [1992] QB 979 (Police 'shop' staffed by undercover officers bought stolen goods); see also *Williams v DPP* [1993] 3 All ER 365 (insecure unattended van containing cigarettes left in busy street, accused seen removing them); *LB of Ealing v Woolworths* [1995] Crim LR 58 (purchase of video by underage child acting on instructions of prosecutor); and see *Rv Maclean* [1993] Crim LR 687.

[532a] [2000] 1 WLR 1071; see generally, para 21.142ff below.

[533] *R v Mason (Carl)* [1988] 1 WLR 139.

[534] The approach of the US Supreme Court, see *Miranda v Arizona* (1966) 384 US 436.

[535] *Mohammed (Allie) v The State* [1999] 2 WLR 552, 561B-563A (Trinidad and Tobago).

[536] See para 21.144ff below.

such a prosecution takes place, the accused can raise the plea of *autrefois acquit* or *autrefois convict*.[537] The principles were restated by the House of Lords in *Connelly v DPP*[538] in which it was made clear that, in order for the rule to apply, the offence charged in the second indictment must have been committed at the time of the first charge and that there must have been an adjudication of guilt or innocence, resulting from a valid process in a court of competent jurisdiction.[539] Where a conviction has been quashed on appeal without an order for re-trial, the accused 'is in the same position for all purposes as if he had actually been acquitted'.[540] Civil contempt proceedings do not constitute a conviction for these purposes.[541] The verdict of a foreign court will generally be sufficient for a plea of *autrefois*, but not if the accused was convicted in his absence abroad and has not served any sentence.[542]

The doctrine applies where the crime charged in the second indictment is the same as that previously adjudicated upon, where he could have been convicted by way of a verdict of guilty of a lesser offence, where proof of the second crime would necessarily entail proof of the crime for which he was acquitted.[543] Furthermore, a person cannot be tried for a crime which is substantially the same as one of which he was acquitted. It appears that this last power does not fall within the strict doctrine of *autrefois* but involves the use of a discretionary power to prevent abuses of the process.[544] **11.136**

There is, however, a statutory exception in the case when a person is convicted of an administration of justice offence involving interference with or intimidation of a juror or a witness[545] in the proceedings which led to an acquittal. In that case, if it appears to the convicting court that: **11.137**

> there is a real possibility that, but for the interference or intimidation, the acquitted person would not have been acquitted[546]

and it is not contrary to the interests of justice to bring fresh proceedings[547] then it must certify that this applies and an application can be made to the High Court

[537] See generally, *Archbold: Criminal Pleading, Practice and Evidence* (Sweet & Maxwell, 1999) para 4–116ff.
[538] [1964] AC 1254.
[539] See *R v West* [1964] 1 QB 15.
[540] *R v Barron* [1914] 2 KB 570; see also *Sambasivam v Public Prosecutor, Federation of Malaya* [1950] AC 458, 479.
[541] *R v Green* [1993] Crim LR 46.
[542] *R v Thomas (Keith)* [1985] QB 604.
[543] *Connelly v DPP* [1964] AC 1254, 1332.
[544] Ibid 1340, 1358, 1364; see also *R v Moxon-Tritsch* [1988] Crim LR 46.
[545] As defined by CPIA, s 54(6).
[546] CPIA, s 54(2)(a).
[547] CPIA s 54(2)(b) and (5).

for an order quashing the acquittal. The High Court must make such an order if it is satisfied that four conditions are fulfilled,[548] namely:

- it is likely that, but for the interference or intimidation, the acquitted person would not have been acquitted;
- it does not appear that it would be contrary to the interests of justice to take fresh proceedings;
- the acquitted person has been given a reasonable opportunity to make written representations to the court;
- it appears likely that the conviction for the administration of justice offence will stand.

(k) Compensation for miscarriages of justice

11.138 There is no general right to compensation for those who have been mistakenly prosecuted or convicted. For a number of years, compensation was awarded under a non-statutory *ex gratia* scheme. In a written Answer to a Commons Question on 29 November 1985[549] the Home Secretary, Mr Douglas Hurd MP, stated the principles governing the non-statutory scheme:

> For many years . . . it has been the Practice for the Home Secretary, in exceptional circumstances, to authorize on application ex gratia payments from public funds to persons who have been detained in custody as a result of a wrongful conviction . . .
>
> I remain prepared to pay compensation to people . . . who have spent a period in custody following a wrongful conviction or charge, where I am satisfied that it has resulted from serious default on the part of a member of the police force or of some other public authority.
>
> There may be exceptional circumstances that justify compensation in cases outside these categories.

A payment under this provision is made under the royal prerogative and the Secretary of State is not obliged to give reasons for refusing to make a payment.[550]

11.139 In 1988, the scheme under the Statement was partially replaced (but not superseded) by section 133 of the Criminal Justice Act 1988[551] which provides that:

> when a person has by a final decision been convicted of a criminal offence and when subsequently his conviction has been reversed, or he has been pardoned, on the ground that a new or newly discovered fact shows beyond reasonable doubt that there has been a miscarriage of justice, the Secretary of State shall pay compensation for miscarriage of justice to the person who has suffered punishment as a result of such conviction . . . unless the non-disclosure of the unknown fact was wholly or partly attributable to the person convicted.

---

548 CPIA, s 55.

549 See *Hansard*, HC, Vol 87, col 689

550 *R v Secretary of State for the Home Department, ex p Harrison* [1988] 3 All ER 86.

551 Which gives statutory effect to Art 14, para 6 of the International Covenant on Civil and Political Rights, see App J in Vol 2.

The question whether there is a right to compensation under the section is determined by the Secretary of State.[552] By section 133(4):

> If the Secretary of State determines that there is a right to such compensation, the amount of the compensation shall be assessed by an assessor appointed by the Secretary of State.

Schedule 12 makes provision as to the appointment and qualifications of the assessor. Section 133 does not give any guidance as to the principles to be applied by the assessor in assessing the amount of compensation.

A case in which a person has been wrongly convicted as a result of judicial error does not fall within section 133. Furthermore, it cannot be dealt with under the second paragraph of the Statement as a judge is not a 'public authority' whose serious default can give rise to a claim for compensation.[553] However, judicial conduct can be of such quality as to give rise to exceptional circumstances under the second limb of the Statement.[554] **11.140**

(l) Protection of fair trial rights: abuse of the process

The English courts now recognise a wide jurisdiction to halt criminal proceedings on the ground that there has been an abuse of the process. In *Connelly v DPP*[555] Lord Devlin said: **11.141**

> Are the courts to rely on the executive to protect their processes from abuse? Have they not themselves an inescapable duty to secure fair treatment for those who come or are brought before them? . . . The courts cannot contemplate for a moment the transference to the executive of the responsibility for seeing that the process of law is not abused.

The power of the court to prevent a prosecution which amounts to an abuse of its processes is 'of great constitutional importance and should be jealously preserved'.[556] An abuse of process is something so unfair and wrong that the court should not allow a prosecutor to proceed with what is in all other respects a regular proceeding.[557] However, common law fair trial rights must give way to statutory provision to the contrary. Thus, it could not be an abuse of the process to try the 17-year-son of a soldier by court-martial because this procedure was authorised by the Army Act 1996.[558]

552 s 133(3).

553 See eg *R v Secretary of State for the Home Department, ex p Harrison* [1988] 3 All ER 86, 89e; *R v Secretary of State for the Home Department, ex p Bateman*, *The Times*, 10 May 1993.

554 *R v Secretary of State for the Home Department, ex p Garner*, (1999) 11 Admin LR 595.

555 [1964] AC 1254, 1354.

556 *Per* Lord Salmon, *R v Humphrys* [1977] AC 1, 46.

557 See *Hui Chi-ming v The Queen* [1992] 1 AC 34, 57B.

558 See *R v Martin (Alan)* [1998] AC 917.

11.142 The court has jurisdiction to stay a prosecution as an abuse of the process if either

- the defendant cannot receive a fair trial; or
- it would not be fair to try the defendant.[559]

The jurisdiction can be exercised if adverse publicity has made a fair trial impossible.[560] or the conviction can be quashed on this ground.[561] The court has jurisdiction to halt a criminal trial as an abuse of the process if the prosecution has deliberately manipulated the criminal process to take unfair advantage of the defendant.[562] This includes matters such as a breach of an undertaking or representation that a person would not be prosecuted if he co-operated.[563] In considering whether a prosecution should be stayed as an abuse of process because it is suggested that the accused cannot have a fair trial the court could, prior to the coming into force of the Human Rights Act, have regard to Article 6 of the Convention.[564]

11.143 The broad basis of the jurisdiction to stay proceedings for abuse of the process was confirmed by the House of Lords in the case of *R v Horseferry Road Magistrates' Court, ex p Bennett*.[565] The defendant was a citizen of New Zealand who claimed to have been brought forcibly to England from South Africa in order to stand trial for certain criminal offences, in disregard of the ordinary procedures for securing his lawful extradition, and in breach of international law. The House of Lords held that the High Court has a wide responsibility for upholding the rule of law where, on the assumed facts, there had been a deliberate abuse of extradition procedures.[566] Lord Griffiths said:

> In the present case there is no suggestion that the appellant cannot have a fair trial, nor could it be suggested that it would have been unfair to try him if he had been returned to this country though extradition procedures. If the court is to have the power to interfere with the prosecution in the present circumstances it must be because the judiciary accept a responsibility for the maintenance of the rule of law that embraces a willingness to oversee executive action and to refuse to countenance

---

559 See *Rv Horseferry Road Magistrates' Court ex p Bennett* [1994] 1 AC 42.

560 *R v Magee*, 23 Jan 1997, Kay J (see *Arlidge, Eady and Smith, On Contempt* (2nd edn, Sweet & Maxwell 1999) para 2–100, n 69).

561 *R v McCann* (1991) 92 Cr App R 239 (Winchester Three convictions quashed in the light of publicity given to comments by the Secretary of State on right to silence); *R v Taylor (Michelle)* (1993) 98 Cr App R 361.

562 *R v Derby Crown Court, ex p Brooks* (1984) 80 Cr App R 164; *Rv Willesden Justices, ex p Clemmings* (1987) 87 Cr App R 280.

563 *R v Croydon Justices, ex p Dean* [1993] QB 769; *Rv Liverpool Stipendiary Magistrates' Court, ex p Slade* [1998] 1 WLR 531.

564 See *R v Stratford Justices, ex p Imbert* (1999) 2 Cr App R 276.

565 [1994] 1 AC 42; see also *R v Mullen (Nicholas Robert Neil)* [1999] 3 WLR 777 (conviction quashed due to fact that police and security services had procured defendants's unlawful deportation from Zimbabwe).

566 Following *Rv Hartley* [1978] 2 NZLR 199; *Sv Ebrahim* 1991 (2) SA 553.

> behaviour that threatens either basic human rights or the rule of law. . . . In my view your Lordships should now declare that where process of law is available to return an accused to this country through extradition procedures our courts will refuse to try him if he has been forcibly brought within our jurisdiction in disregard of those procedures by a process to which our own police, prosecuting or other executive authorities have been a knowing party.[567]

Lord Lowry took the view that it was

> essential to the rule of law that the court should not have to make available its process and thereby indorse (on what I am confident will be a very few occasions) unworthy conduct when it is proved against the executive or its agents, however humble in rank.[568]

The Divisional Court subsequently held that there had, on the facts been an abuse[569] but on further investigation of the facts a similar application was refused in Scotland.[570] The Court of Appeal can quash a conviction as being 'unsafe' if it finds that the prosecution was an abuse of the process, even if the point was not taken before the trial judge.[571]

The categories of 'abuse' are not closed but include the following: **11.143A**

- unjustifiable delay which results in the defendant suffering serious prejudice to the extent that no fair trial can be held;[571a]
- the prosecution of a defendant the police having given a promise, undertaking or representation that he would not prosecuted;[571b]
- the prosecution of a defendant who has already faced criminal charges arising out of the same facts;[571c]
- the trial of a defendant after there has been substantial prejudicial pre-trial publicity;[571d]
- the trial of a defendant after the loss or destruction of relevant material by the prosecution;[571e]
- where it would be contrary to the public interest in the integrity of the criminal justice system that a trial should take place because the prosecution have been

[567] At 61H–62A and 62G.
[568] See n 566 above.
[569] See *R v Horseferry Road Magistrates' Court, ex p Bennett (No 2)* [1995] 1 Cr App R 147.
[570] See *Bennett v HM Advocate* 1995 SLT 510.
[571] See *Rv Mullen (Nicholas Robert Neil)* [1999] 3 WLR 777.
[571a] *A-G's Reference (No. 1 of 1990)* [1992] QB 630; see generally, D Corker and D Young, *Abuse of Process and Fairness in Criminal Proceedings* (Butterworths, 2000) Chap 1.
[571b] R *v Croydon JJ, ex p Dean* (1993) 98 Cr App Rep 76; see generally, Corker and Young (n 571a above) Chap 2.
[571c] *DPP v Humphrys* [1977] AC 1; see generally, Corker and Young (n 571a above) Chap 3.
[571d] *R v Taylor and Taylor* (1993) 98 Cr App Rep 361; see generally, Corker and Young (n 571a above) Chap 4.
[571e] *R v Beckford* [1996] 1 Cr App Rep 94; see generally, Corker and Young (n 571a above) Chap 5.

guilty of 'investigative impropriety'.[571f] This category is often known as '*Bennett* type abuse'.

- where the prosecution have otherwise been guilty of manipulation or misuse of the process of the court.[571g]

The principles to be applied for granting a stay under the Human Rights Act are considered in Chapter 22.[571h]

(5) Retrospective criminal laws

11.144 The common law presumes that statutes are not intended to have retrospective effect.[572] As Blackstone[573] observed, if:

> after an action (indifferent in itself) is committed, the legislator then for the first time declares it to have been a crime, and inflicts a punishment upon the person who has committed it. Here it is impossible that the party could foresee that an action, innocent when it was done, should be afterwards converted to guilt by a subsequent law: he had therefore no cause to abstain from it; and all punishment for not abstaining must of consequence be cruel and unjust. All laws should be therefore made to commence in futuro, and be notified before their commencement; which is implied in the term 'prescribed'.

It has therefore been said that:

> It is a fundamental rule of English law that no statute shall be construed to have a retrospective operation unless such a construction appears very clearly in the terms of the Act, or arises by necessary or distinct implication.[574]

This principle is often said to rest on the idea of 'fairness'. As Staughton LJ stressed in a case involving recovery of overpaid social security benefits:

> the true principle is that Parliament is presumed not to have intended to alter the law applicable to past events and transactions in a manner which is unfair to those concerned in them, unless a contrary intention appears.[575]

It has been suggested that the presumption against retrospectivity is an aspect of the 'principle against doubtful penalisation': a person should not be penalised except under clear law.[576]

[571f] *R v Horseferry Road Magistrates' Court, ex p Bennett* [1994] AC 42; see generally, Corker and Young (n 571a above) Chap 6.

[571g] See generally, Corker and Young (n 571a above) Chap 7.

[571h] See para 21.117ff.

[572] See eg *Yew Bon Tew v Kenderaan Bas Mara* [1983] 1 AC 553, 558; and see generally, F Bennion, *Statutory Interpretation* (3rd edn, Butterworths, 1997) 235ff.

[573] See *Commentaries on the Laws of England*, (1830), Vol I, 45–46.

[574] P Maxwell, *Maxwell on the Interpretation of Statutes* (12th edn Sweet & Maxwell, 1969), 215.

[575] *Secretary of State for Social Security v Tunnicliffe* [1991] 2 All ER 712, 724f (in that case the statute was held to have retrospective effect).

[576] See Bennion *Statutory Interpretation* (3rd edn, Butterworths, 1997) 236 and generally, Pt XVII, 637ff.

The cases give some support to the argument that the presumption against retrospectivity is of no application to 'matters of procedure'[577] and that an enactment fixing the penalty or maximum penalty for a criminal offence is procedural for this purpose.[578] A different approach was taken by the Northern Ireland Court of Appeal in *R v Deery*[579] in which it was held that the maximum sentence should be that prevailing at the time the offence was committed. **11.145**

The confiscation provisions in the Drug Trafficking Offences Act 1986 apply in relation to offences committed before the Act came into force. This led to an adverse finding in the Court of Human Rights.[580] However, in *R v Taylor*[581] it was held that a confiscation order could be made on a conviction in 1994 in respect of 'benefits' gained between 1970 and 1979. The offences for which the appellant was tried in 1994 were committed in the early 1990s and 1993 at which time the 1986 Act was fully in force. As a result, the Court of Appeal held that: **11.146**

> he must therefore be deemed to have committed them with his eyes open as to the possible consequences which were no more severe at the time when he was sentenced than at the time when he offended.[582]

The Court therefore concluded that the confiscation orders did not breach Article 7 of the European Convention on Human Rights.

There remain a number of criminal offences which are not defined by statute but arise under the common law. The most well known of these is murder. The courts have, until recently, retained the power to devise new common law offences.[583] Thus, in *Shaw v DPP*[584] the House of Lords upheld a conviction for conspiracy to corrupt public morals and did not disapprove the Court of Appeal's view that there was a substantive offence of corrupting public morals. Lord Simonds said that: **11.147**

> In the sphere of criminal law I entertain no doubt that there remains in the courts of law a residual power to enforce the supreme and fundamental purpose of the law, to conserve not only the safety and order but also the moral welfare of the State, and that it is their duty to guard it against attacks which may be the more insidious because they are novel and unprepared for.[585]

577 *Re Athlumney* [1898] 2 QB 547, 551; see generally, Bennion (n 572 above) s 98, 238–240.
578 *DPP v Lamb* [1941] 2 KB 89; *R v Oliver* [1944] KB 68.
579 [1977] NI 164; see also *R v Penrith Justices ex p Hay* (1979) 1 Cr App Rep (S) 265.
580 *Welch v United Kingdom* (1995) 20 EHRR 247.
581 [1996] 2 Cr App R 64.
582 Ibid 70.
583 See generally, A T H Smith, 'Judicial Law-Making in the Criminal Law' (1984) 100 LQR 46.
584 [1962] AC 220; for criticism see A Goodhart, 'The Show Case: The Law of Public Morals' (1961) 77 LQR 560; J Hall Williams, 'The Ladies Directory and Criminal Conspiracy. The Judge Custos Morum' (1961) 24 MLR 626.
585 *Shaw v DPP* (n 584 above) 267.

However, in the subsequent case of *Knuller (Publishing, Printing and Promotions) Ltd v DPP*[586] the House of Lords held that there was no residual power to create new common law offences. The task of the courts is limited to recognising 'the applicability of established offences to new circumstances in which they are relevant'.

11.148 The essence of judge made law is that it applies retrospectively. As Lord Woolf MR said in a recent case:

> any authoritative decision of the courts stating what is the law operates retrospectively. The decision does not only state what the law is from the date of the decision, it states what it has always been. This is the position even if in setting out the law the court overrules an earlier decision which took a totally different view of the law.[587]

This 'fiction' applies as much in the field of criminal law as in civil law. Thus, if the courts take a different view of the common law or of statutory interpretation, conduct which was previously lawful may become unlawful and attract criminal penalties. An important recent illustration of this principle involved the so-called 'marital rape exemption'. It had long been understood that a husband could not be guilty of raping his wife because of the 'matrimonial consent'.[588] However, this was challenged in a number of cases[589] culminating in the decision of the House of Lords in *R v R*[590] which made it clear that 'a rapist is a rapist . . . irrespective of his relationship with his victim'. They agreed with the Court of Appeal's view that:

> This is not the creation of a new offence, it is the removal of a common law fiction which has become anachronistic and offensive.[591]

11.149 Article 7 of the Convention strengthens the presumption against judge made retrospectivity since it requires that an individual can, to a reasonable degree, foresee from the wording of a provision what acts or omissions will make him liable of a criminal offence.[592] As Brooke LJ observed in relation to a conviction for a criminal offence based on a breach of a rule by Westminster Council that the licensee shall maintain good order in the premises:

> The Council could do well, in my judgment, to tighten up the language of Rule 9 if it wishes to be able to prohibit activities like these on the licensed premises after the Human Rights Act 1998 comes into force. The extension of the very vague concept of the maintenance of good order to the control of the activities of the prostitutes

586 [1973] AC 435.

587 *R v Governor Brockhill Prison, ex p Evans (No 2)* [1999] 2 WLR 103, 107E-F.

588 The proposition deriving from Hale's *Pleas of the Crown*, 1736 and being confirmed by subsequent case law, *R v Clarence* (1888) 22 QBD 23; *R v Roberts* [1986] Crim LR 188.

589 *R v C (Rape: Marital Exemption)* [1991] 1 All ER 755 (exemption misconceived), *R v J (Rape: Marital Exemption)* [1991] 1 All ER 759 (exemption upheld).

590 [1992] 1 AC 599.

591 [1991] 2 All ER 257, 266.

592 *Kokkinakis v Greece* (1993) 17 EHRR 397 para 52; see generally, para 11.260ff below.

> may have passed muster in the days when the English common law offences did not receive critical scrutiny from national judicial guarantees of a rights-based jurisprudence, but these days will soon be over. English judges will then be applying a Human Rights Convention which has the effect of prescribing that a criminal offence must be clearly defined in law. I do not accept [Counsel's] submission that it is impossible to define the kind of conduct his clients wish to prohibit with greater precision, or that it is satisfactory to leave it to individual magistrates to decide, assisted only by some arcane case-law, whether or not activities of the type which the Council complains in this case amounts to a breach of good order so as to render the licensees liable to criminal penalties.[593]

C. The Law Under the European Convention

(1) Introduction

Article 6 of the Convention provides that: **11.150**

> (1) In the determination of his civil rights and obligations or of any criminal charge against him, everyone is entitled to a fair and public hearing within a reasonable time by an independent and impartial tribunal established by law. Judgment shall be pronounced publicly but the press and public may be excluded from all or part of the trial in the interest of morals, public order or national security in a democratic society, where the interests of juveniles or the protection of the private life of the parties so require, or to the extent strictly necessary in the opinion of the court in special circumstances where publicity would prejudice the interests of justice.
>
> (2) Everyone charged with a criminal offence shall be presumed innocent until proved guilty according to law.
>
> (3) Everyone charged with a criminal offence has the following minimum rights:
>
> (a) to be informed promptly, in a language which he understands and in detail, of the nature and cause of the accusation against him;
> (b) to have adequate time and facilities for the preparation of his defence;
> (c) to defend himself in person or through legal assistance of his own choosing or, if he has not sufficient means to pay for legal assistance, to be given it free when the interests of justice so require;
> (d) to examine or have examined witnesses against him and to obtain the attendance and examination of witnesses on his behalf under the same conditions as witnesses against him;
> (e) to have the free assistance of an interpreter if he cannot understand or speak the language used in court.

In the most general terms, Article 6 applies to proceedings which constitute a determination of criminal charges or the civil rights and obligations of accused persons. As the Convention provides no definition of 'criminal charge', 'civil rights and obligations' or 'determination', the interpretation of those phrases has fallen **11.151**

[593] *Westminster City Council v Blenheim Leisure* (1999) 163 JP 401.

to the Commission and Court. They have affirmed the centrality of the rights of due process and an expansive view of Article 6 as fundamental to the consideration of these issues:

> In a democratic society within the meaning of the Convention, the right to a fair administration of justice holds such a prominent place that a restrictive interpretation of Article 6(1) would not correspond to the aim and the purpose of that provision.[594]

11.152 Article 7 of the Convention provides:

> (1) No one shall be held guilty of any criminal offence on account of any act or omission which did not constitute a criminal offence under national or international law at the time when it was committed. Nor shall a heavier penalty be imposed than the one that was applicable at the time the criminal offence was committed.
>
> (2) This article shall not prejudice the trial and punishment of any person for any act or omission which, at the time when it was committed, was criminal according to the general principles of law recognised by civilised nations.

This article not only embodies the principle against retrospectivity but also the principle that only the law can define a crime and prescribe a penalty.[595] No derogations from this Article are permitted.[596]

11.153 In this section we will begin by considering the scope of Article 6. The nature of the 'guarantees' in Article 6(1) will then be considered. Articles 6(2) and (3) deal with matters which are specific to those charged with criminal offences and are considered together. Finally, we will consider the effect of the prohibition in Article 7.

(2) Proceedings covered by Article 6

(a) Introduction

11.154 Article 6 applies to the determination of 'civil rights and obligations' and 'criminal charges'. Both terms have autonomous meanings under the Convention.[597] These are considered in the next two sections. In order for the guarantees to apply there must be a right, obligation or charge in play and the proceedings must involve its *determination*.

11.155 As a result, Article 6 does not apply to proceedings subsequent to the conviction of an offence of an individual, as they cannot be determinative of the charge. Nei-

594 *Delcourt v Belgium* (1970) 1 EHRR 355 para 25; see also *Moreira de Azevedo v Portugal* (1990) 13 EHRR 721.

595 *Kokkinakis v Greece* (1993) 17 EHRR 397 para 52.

596 See Art 15(2).

597 See generally, para 6.17 above, and see paras 11.163ff and 11.174ff below.

ther are proceedings determinative where they relate to the appointment of a legal aid lawyer,[598] assessment of costs,[599] revocation of a suspended sentence,[600] application for clemency[601] or conditional release,[602] classification of a prisoner,[603] payment for prison work[604] or the recording of an offence.[605]

Proceedings are determinative in relation to civil rights and obligations when the outcome of the proceedings is *decisive* for them, whether or not such determination is the primary purpose of the proceedings.[606] Thus, administrative tribunals that primarily determine questions of purely public concern may also 'determine' civil rights and obligations for the purposes of Article 6.[607] However, the proceedings must be *directly* decisive for civil rights and obligations and a 'tenuous connection or remote consequences do not suffice'.[608] Thus, a decision to deport an alien, which was also decisive for the applicant's private rights pursuant to an employment contract in the deporting state, was not protected by Article 6, because the connection between the deportation and the employment contract was too remote.[609] **11.156**

Determination or 'decisiveness' in relation to civil rights and obligations refers to the decision on the merits of a case and its finality. Proceedings which are not determinative are not subject to Article 6 guarantees. It has been held that the following are not 'determinative': applications for interim relief ,[610] enforcement proceedings,[611] awards of costs,[612] the re-opening of a case,[613] application for leave to appeal[614] and an official report of an investigation into facts relating to the civil **11.157**

598 *X v United Kingdom* (1982) 5 EHRR 273, EComm HR.
599 *X v Germany* (1971) 39 CD 20, EComm HR.
600 *X v Germany* (1967) 25 CD 1, EComm HR.
601 *X v Austria* (1961) 8 CD 9, EComm HR.
602 *X v Austria* (1966) 9 YB 112; *Aldrian v Austria* (1990) 65 DR 337, EComm HR.
603 *X v United Kingdom* (1979) 20 DR 202, EComm HR.
604 *Detained Persons v Germany* (1968) 11 YB 528, EComm HR.
605 *X v Germany* (1960) 3 YB 254, EComm HR.
606 *Ringeisen v Austria (No 1)* (1971) 1 EHRR 455 (this case greatly expanded the scope of Art 6 in this context).
607 In particular, *Benthem v Netherlands* (1985) 8 EHRR 1.
608 *Le Compte, Van Leuven and De Meyere v Belgium* (1982) 5 EHRR 183 para 47.
609 Ibid.
610 *X v United Kingdom* (1981) 24 DR 57; *Alsterlund v Sweden* (1988) 56 DR 229, EComm HR.
611 Art 6 will apply, though, where the proceedings raise new issues in connection with the applicant's rights: *K v Sweden* (1991) 71 DR 94 EComm HR and *Jensen v Denmark* (1991) 68 DR 177, EComm HR.
612 *Asterlund v Sweden* (1988) 56 DR 229 EComm HR; but the position will be different where the costs proceedings are the continuation of a substantive dispute: see *Robins v United Kingdom* (1997) 26 EHRR 527 EComm HR paras 25–29.
613 *X v Austria* (1978) 14 DR 200, EComm HR.
614 *Porter v United Kingdom* (1987) 54 DR 207, EComm HR.

rights and obligations of the applicant.[615] However, Article 6 has been found to apply where a point of constitutionality[616] or a preliminary decision in the case[617] is crucial to the applicant's claim and to separate court proceedings for the assessment of damages.[618]

11.158 **Stage at which Article 6 applies.** There is no strictly defined point in the criminal process at which Article 6 guarantees must be in place. The protections apply as soon as a person is the subject of a criminal charge and continue to apply until the charge is finally determined or discontinued.[619] Furthermore, Article 6 guarantees cover applications for leave to appeal,[620] appeal proceedings themselves[621] and any sentencing hearing that may follow trial or appeal.[622]

11.159 In relation to the determination of civil rights and obligations, Article 6 guarantees will normally apply from the point at which proceedings are commenced. In some circumstances, however, they may be applicable before the claim form is filed.[623] For example, Article 6 was held to apply where compliance with an administrative procedure was required before a public decision could be appealed to a court;[624] and where the dispute arose upon objection by the applicant to a draft land consolidation plan that would substantially affect his real property rights.[625] Where civil rights and obligations are decided by an administrative, executive or professional disciplinary body that is not a tribunal for the purposes of Article 6, the guarantees need not be applied at the initial decision stage, so long as the decision-making body is ultimately subject to a judicial body that meets the Article 6 requirements.[626] Article 6 continues to apply through appeal and judicial review proceedings[627] and the assessment of damages relevant to the applicant's

---

615 In *Fayed v United Kingdom* (1994) 18 EHRR 393 para 61 the Court found that Art 6 did not apply because the findings in the report were not 'dispositive of anything' but established evidence for use in any legal proceedings that might later be brought.

616 *Deumeland v Germany* (1986) 8 EHRR 448; *Ruiz-Mateos v Spain* (1993) 16 EHRR 505; *Kraska v Switzerland* (1993) 18 EHRR 188; *Lombardo v Italy* (1992) 21 EHRR 188.

617 See *Obermeier v Austria* (1990) 13 EHRR 290 (the preliminary question of the validity of the applicant's dismissal from his employment was pivotal to his claim and thus Art 6 applied).

618 *Silva Pontes v Portugal* (1994) 18 EHRR 156 para 33.

619 *Eckle v Germany* (1982) 5 EHRR 1 para 78; *Orchin v United Kingdom* (1983) 6 EHRR 391, EComm HR.

620 *Monnell and Morris v UK* (1987) 10 EHRR 205.

621 This whether the appeal is based on the law or the facts: *Delcourt v Belgium* (1970) 1 EHRR 355; or against conviction or sentence.

622 *Eckle v Germany* (1982) 5 EHRR 1; *Ringeisen v Austria (No 1)* (1971) 1 EHRR 455.

623 *Golder v United Kingdom* (1975) 1 EHRR 524.

624 *König v Germany* (1978) 2 EHRR 170; *Schouten and Meldrum v Netherlands* (1994) 19 EHRR 432 para 62 (the Court held that if the procedure was required it should be carried out expeditiously).

625 *Erkner and Hofauer v Austria* (1987) 9 EHRR 464 para 64.

626 *LeCompte, Van Leuven and De Meyere v Belgium* (1981) 4 EHRR 1.

627 *Konig v Germany* (n 624 above) para 98; *Pretto v Italy* (1983) 6 EHRR 182 para 30; but see para 11.197 below.

claim. The guarantees only cease to apply when the civil rights and obligations have been fully determined, the time for an appeal by the parties expires and the judgment is finalised.[628]

(b) Civil rights and obligations

Introduction. The guarantees in Article 6(1) apply to the determination of civil rights and obligations. The position is complicated by a material difference between the French and English texts of the Article. The French text refers to '*contestations* sur ses droits et obligations de caractère civil'. The word 'contestations' (disputes) has no equivalent in the English text. In this section we will consider the following issues: **11.160**

- the extent to which it is necessary that there be a 'dispute' before Article 6(1) applies;
- the nature of civil rights and obligations to which Article 6(1) applies;
- the rights and obligations to which Article 6(1) does not apply.

Disputes. Despite the absence of the word 'dispute' from the English text of Article 6(1), it is clear that the guarantees are only applicable if there is a dispute in domestic law. The applicable principles have been summarised as follows:[629] **11.161**

- the term 'dispute' must be given a substantive, rather than a formal or technical meaning;[630]
- the dispute may be one which relates not only to the existence but also to the scope or manner of exercise of a right[631] it may also relate to questions both of fact and law;[632]
- the dispute must be genuine and serious;[633]
- there must be a direct link between the dispute and the right in question.[634]

To benefit from Article 6, the applicant must have an arguable right under domestic law. Article 6(1) does not guarantee any particular substantive content for **11.162**

[628] *Pugliese v Italy (No 2)* (1991) Series A No 206; *Lorenzi, Bernardini and Gritti v Italy* (1992) Series A No 231-G.

[629] *Benthem v Netherlands* (1985) 8 EHRR 1 para 32.

[630] See also *Le Compte, Van Leuven and De Meyere v Belgium* (1981) 4 EHRR 1 para 45; the burden of the requirement is not seen to be great because there is no English counterpart to the French term, leading to questions as to its importance: *Moreira de Azevedo v Portugal* (1990) 13 EHRR 721 para 66 expressed doubt as to whether it exists at all.

[631] *Le Compte, Van Leuven and De Meyere v Belgium* (n 630 above).

[632] *Albert and Le Compte v Belgium* (1983) 5 EHRR 533.

[633] 'Genuine' might exclude hypothetical or moot cases; 'serious' may exclude cases of minimal interference with the civil right, but does not require that damages be claimed: *Helmers v Sweden* (1991) 15 EHRR 285; see also *Oerlemans v Netherlands* (1991) 15 EHRR 561.

[634] The dispute must be justiciable: see D Harris, M O'Boyle and C Warbrick, *Law of the European Convention on Human Rights* (Butterworths, 1995) 188; and *Van Marle v Netherlands* (1986) 8 EHRR 483 (applicants' registration as accountants is not a dispute that inherently lends itself to judicial resolution).

civil rights and obligations in national law,[635] but provides only the procedural guarantees for the determination of tenable rights.[636] Although Article 6(1) cannot be used to create a substantive civil right which has no legal basis in the state, it may apply in cases where domestic law contains immunities or procedural bars which limit the possibility of bringing potential claims to court.[637] In such cases, the Convention provides a degree of 'constraint or control' on states' abilities to remove civil rights from the jurisdiction of the courts or to provide immunity to particular groups of persons.

11.163 **The nature of 'civil rights and obligations'.** It is well established that 'civil' does not mean merely 'non-criminal': not all of the rights and obligations that might arguably be claimed by an individual in national law attract the protection of Article 6. The word 'civil' has an autonomous Convention meaning so that the classification of a right in domestic law is not decisive.[638]

11.164 The basic problem in defining the scope of the phrase 'civil rights and obligations' is whether it is also intended to cover certain rights which, under some continental systems of law, fall under administrative law rather than private law.[639] Although the Court initially adopted the distinction between private and public law as the basis for its definition, with civil rights and obligations corresponding to rights and obligations in private law,[640] it is strongly arguable, in the light of the 'drafting history' of the provision, that this approach is misconceived.[641] Subsequent cases show a willingness to extend the scope of Article 6 to include many rights and obligations in a manner that is not easy to explain by reference to the distinction between private and public law. It is widely acknowledged that no clear principles can be derived from the case law; and it has been suggested that the Court should adopt a new approach to the problem.[642] At least three options are available:

- the reclassification of some rights and obligations (such as Convention rights) as 'private law' rights, receiving the benefit of Article 6;

[635] *H v Belgium* (1987) 10 EHRR 339.

[636] *James v United Kingdom* (1986) 8 EHRR 123, para 81; *Powell and Rayner v United Kingdom* (1990) 12 EHRR 288.

[637] *Fayed v United Kingdom* (1994) 18 EHRR 393; *Osman v United Kingdom* (1998) 5 BHRC 293 (but see the criticism of this case in *Barrett v LB Enfield* [1999] 3 WLR 79, 84A–85F (*per* Lord Browne-Wilkinson).

[638] *König v Germany* (1978) 2 EHRR 170 para 89.

[639] F Jacobs and R White, *The European Convention on Human Rights* (2nd edn. Clarendon Press, 1996) 128; F Jacobs, 'The Right to a Fair Trial in European Law' [1999] EHRLR 141.

[640] *Ringeisen v Austria (No 1)* (1971) 1 EHRR 455, para 94; *König v Germany* (n 638 above) para 95.

[641] See P van Dijk, 'Access to the Court' in R St J Macdonald, F Matscher and H Petzold (eds), *The European System for the Protection of Human Rights* (Kluwer, 1983) 347–351.

[642] See Harris, O'Boyle and Warbrick (n 634 above) 184ff; P van Dijk and G van Hoof, *Theory and Practice of the European Convention on Human Rights* (3rd edn, Kluwer, 1998) 404–406.

- the abandonment of the private/public distinction and formulation of a new definition of 'civil rights and obligations';
- the extension of the application of Article 6 to 'all cases in which a determination by a public authority of the legal position of a private party is at stake, regardless of whether the rights and obligations involved are of a private character'.[643]

The last approach is supported by the drafting history[644] and has the merit of simplicity.

The Court has, nevertheless, consistently held that the basis for the definition of civil rights and obligations is the distinction between public and private law. The meaning attributed to 'civil rights and obligations' is autonomous from that used in national law.[645] The Court has not advanced its own definition of 'civil rights and obligations'. It is sufficient, for the application of Article 6, that the outcome of the proceedings should be *decisive for private rights and obligations.*[646] In deciding whether a 'civil right or obligation' is in issue, it is necessary to consider:[647] **11.165**

- the character of the right or obligation in issue;[648]
- any consensus that can be gleaned from national law of European states[649] in connection with the classification of the matter as public or private;
- the classification of the right or obligation in domestic law.[650]

Private law. Proceedings which determine rights and obligations as between private persons are governed by private law and will therefore, in every case, deal with 'civil rights and obligations' requiring the safeguards of a fair trial. Thus it has been held that disputes concerning competition law,[651] insurance law,[652] tort law,[653] the law of succession,[654] family law (including both divorce[655] and cases involving the **11.166**

[643] van Dijk and van Hoof (n 642 above) 406.

[644] See P van Dijk, 'Access to the Court', in Macdonald, Matscher and Petzold (n 641 above) 347–351.

[645] *König v Germany* (1978) 2 EHRR 170.

[646] See the formulation in *H v France* (1989) 12 EHRR 74 para 47.

[647] See generally, Harris, O'Boyle and Warbrick (n 634 above) 176ff.

[648] *Konig v Germany* (1978) 2 EHRR 170 para 90; see also the Commission decision in *Muyldermans v Belgium* (1991) 15 EHRR 204 (which was subject to a friendly settlement) and *Schouten and Meldrum v Netherlands* (1994) 19 EHRR 432.

[649] *Feldbrugge v Netherlands* (1986) 8 EHRR 425 and *Deumeland v Germany* (1986) 8 EHRR 448 refer to any 'uniform European notion' where the Court had to choose how to characterise social security rights.

[650] See *König v Germany* (n 648 above) para 89.

[651] *Barthold v Germany* (1981) 26 DR 145, EComm HR.

[652] *Feldbrugge v Netherlands* (1986) 8 EHRR 425.

[653] *Axen v Germany* (1983) 6 EHRR 195 (negligence).

[654] *X v Switzerland* (1976) 7 DR 104, EComm HR.

[655] *Airey v Ireland* (1979) 2 EHRR 305.

care of,[656] adoption[657] or access[658] to children) and employment law[659] involve the determination of civil rights and obligations. The position is the same if the features of private law are 'predominant'.[660]

11.167 *Disciplinary proceedings.* It has been said that disciplinary proceedings do not ordinarily involve disputes over civil rights and obligations.[661] However, the right to continue in professional practice is a civil right and Article 6 will, therefore, apply when the disciplinary tribunal could suspend a person from professional practice.[662] As a result, Article 6(1) has been applied to disciplinary proceedings involving:

- temporarily suspending a doctor from practice[663] or preventing a doctor from running a clinic;[664]
- removing an avocate from the roll,[665] or disbarring a barrister;[665a]
- a refusal to allow a person to enrol as a pupil advocate;[665b]
- an application to be reinstated as an advocate after suspension;[665c]
- suspending an architect from practice for a period of one year.[665d]

However, Article 6 will not apply if the professional is not at risk of being prevented from practising[666] or if the nature of the 'proceedings' is confined to the assessment of professional ability.[667]

11.168 *Private individuals and the state.* The position is less clear cut when there are proceedings that involve relations *between* the private individual and the state. Not every action or claim involving rights as against a public authority is 'public' in nature so as to be excluded from the fair trial requirements of Article 6. This was made clear by the Court in *Ringeisen v Austria*[668] in which it was held that proceedings before the Regional Land Commission, an administrative tribunal, were

---

656 *Olsson v Sweden (No 1)* (1988) 11 EHRR 259.

657 *Keegan v Ireland* (1994) 18 EHRR 342 (adoption); *Eriksson v Sweden* (1989) 12 EHRR 183 (fostering).

658 *W v United Kingdom* (1987) 10 EHRR 29; *Eriksson v Sweden* (n 657 above).

659 *Bucholz v Germany* (1981) 3 EHRR 597 (unfair dismissal).

660 *Feldbrugge v Netherlands* (1986) 8 EHRR 425 para 18 (statutory sickness benefit).

661 *Albert and Le Compte v Belgium* (1983) 5 EHRR 533 para 25.

662 Ibid para 28; *Le Compte, Van Leuven and De Meyere v Belgium* (1981) 4 EHRR 1 para 48.

663 *Albert and Le Compte v Belgium* (n 661 above) para 28.

664 *König v Germany* (1978) 2 EHRR 170.

665 *H v Belgium* (1987) 10 EHRR 339.

655a *Ginikanwa v United Kingdom* (1988) 55 DR 251.

665b *De Moor v Belgium* (1994) 18 EHRR 372.

665c *H v Belgium* (1987) 10 EHRR 339.

665d *Guchez v Belgium* (1984) 40 DR 100.

666 *X v United Kingdom* (1983) 6 EHRR 583, EComm HR (barrister reprimanded, Art 6 inapplicable).

667 *Van Marle v Netherlands* (1986) 8 EHRR 483.

668 (1971) 1 EHRR 455.

subject to Article 6. It found that it was not necessary to a characterisation of 'private rights and obligations' that both parties to the proceedings should be private persons, and held the determinative factor to be whether the result of the proceedings was 'decisive for private rights and obligations'.

The basic principle is that public law matters are not excluded from being 'civil rights and obligations' if they are directly decisive[669] of private law rights. The most important consideration is whether the applicant has a *financial* interest at stake, in relation to which the action of the state is directly decisive:[670] the existence of such an interest is usually determinative (although in a limited class of cases it may be held to have a 'public law' nature).[671] The following have been held to be 'civil rights': the right to real[672] and personal[673] property rights arising in the context of planning,[673a] the right to engage in commercial activity,[674] to practice a profession[675] and to obtain compensation for monetary loss resulting from illegal state acts.[676] 11.169

However, if compensation is payable on a *purely* discretionary basis, then the applicant will have no 'right' which brings him within the scope of Article 6(1). Thus, it has been held that Article 6 does not apply to a criminal injuries compensation scheme which is discretionary[676a] or which is only *ex gratia*;[676b] similarly, Article 6 could not be invoked in relation to a non statutory disaster fund[676c] or to a discretionary hardship award.[676d] Where, on the other hand, a statute defines in clear 11.169A

[669] See para 11.156 above.

[670] See *Le Compte, Van Leuven and De Meyere v Belgium* (1981) 4 EHRR 1 para 45.

[671] See *Schouten and Meldrum v Netherlands* (1994) 19 EHRR 432 para 50 (the examples of 'public law' pecuniary obligations are criminal fines and tax obligations) and *Pierre-Bloch v France* (1997) 26 EHRR 202 para 51 (forfeiture of national assembly seat because the applicant had exceeded the permitted level of election expenditure).

[672] See eg *Ringeisen v Austria (No 1)* (1971) 1 EHRR 455; *Håkansson and Sturesson v Sweden* (1990) 13 EHRR 1 (permission to own land); *Zander v Sweden* (1993) 18 EHRR 175 (extraction of water); *Sporrong and Lonnroth v Sweden* (1982) 5 EHRR 35 (expropriation of land).

[673] See eg *RR and GR v Netherlands* (1991) 69 DR 219, EComm HR (withdrawal of goods from circulation); *Anca v Belgium* (1984) 40 DR 170, EComm HR (bankruptcy); *Lithgow v United Kingdom* (1986) 8 EHRR 329 (expropriation of shares).

[673a] *Bryan v United Kingdom* (1995) 21 EHRR 342.

[674] See eg *Tre Traktörer Aktiebolag v Sweden* (1989) 13 EHRR 309 (restaurant liquor licence) *Pudas v Sweden* (1987) 10 EHRR 380 (public service licence for private passenger carrier); *Axelsson v Sweden* (1989) 65 DR 99, EComm HR (taxi licence); *Benthem v Netherlands* (1985) 8 EHRR 1 (licence to operate a liquid petroleum gas installation).

[675] See eg *König v Germany* (1978) 2 EHRR 170 (medicine); *H v Belgium* (1987) 10 EHRR 339 (law); *Guchez v Belgium* (1984) 40 DR 100, EComm HR (architecture).

[676] See eg *X v France* (1992) 14 EHRR 483 (claim for damages for negligence of the government authority in the administration of a blood transfusion resulting in contraction of AIDS came within Art6); *Editions Periscope v France* (1992) 14 EHRR 597 (losses resulting from a wrongful refusal of a tax concession).

[676a] *Masson and van Zon v Netherlands* (1996) 22 EHRR 491.

[676b] *B v Netherlands* (1985) 43 DR 198.

[676c] *Nordh v Sweden* (1990) 69 DR 223.

[676d] *Machatova v Sweden* (1997) 24 EHRR CD 44.

terms the pre-conditions for entitlement, an applicant who arguably fulfills those conditions has a right to compensation; and falls within the ambit of Article 6(1).[676e]

11.170 *Social security cases.* The nature of social security and social assistance claims has caused considerable difficulties. In two pivotal cases,[677] the Court found that social security benefits were predominantly private in nature. These benefits were statutory, funded in part by employee contributions, linked to a private employment contract, and had significant consequences for the economic well-being of the applicant. A strong dissenting view in each of the cases, emphasising the limited private law connections, strong collective benefit and diversity of approach across Europe, said that the Court ought not to extend the application of Article 6 to include judicial procedures to determine disputes about social security matters.

11.171 Nevertheless, it is now clear that there is a 'general rule'[678] that Article 6(1) will apply to all welfare benefits (whether contributory[679] or noncontributory).[680] The test with respect to each is whether the grant of the benefit is statutorily required rather than with the discretion of the state.[681] If the former, Article 6 will apply and the Court will not resort to the public and private law balancing process, even in relation to the obligation to pay social security contributions.[682]

11.172 **Cases outside Article 6.** The most obvious examples of disputes considered outside of the reach of Article 6 concern employment in the public sector[683] (although Article 6 *does* apply where a public employee works under a contract of

676e *Gustafson v Sweden* (1998) 25 EHRR 623.

677 In *Feldbrugge v Netherlands* (1986) 8 EHRR 425 the applicant's sick pay under a Dutch health benefits scheme was found by a 10 to 7 majority to be a private law matter; in *Deumeland v Germany* (1986) 8 EHRR 448 the Court held 9 to 8 that industrial injuries benefits under German social security law were private law rights.

678 *Schuler-Zgraggen v Switzerland* (1993) 16 EHRR 405 para 46.

679 *Lombardo v Italy* (1992) 21 EHRR 188 (a police officer's public service pension not associated with a private employment contract); *Nibbio v Italy* (1992) Series A No 228-A (a disability pension); *McGinley and Egan v United Kingdom* (1998) 27 EHRR 1 (an invalidity pension).

680 See *Salesi v Italy* (1993) 26 EHRR 187 para 19.

681 *Lombardo v Italy* (1992) 21 EHRR 188 and *Salesi v Italy* (1993) 26 EHRR 187 were each cases of statutorily-defined rights.

682 In *Schouten and Meldrum v Netherlands* (1994) 19 EHRR 432 the Court, balancing the public and private law nature of an employer's obligation to pay contributions on behalf of his employees, categorized it as private law.

683 A large number of claims by public employees in civil law systems have been rejected at the admissibility stage eg *X v Portugal* (1981) 26 DR 262 (members of armed forces); *Leander v Sweden* (1983) 34 DR 78, EComm HR (civil servants); *X v Portugal* (1983) 32 DR 258, EComm HR (judges); *X v Italy* (1980) 21 DR 208, EComm HR (state school teachers); *X v Belgium* (1969) 32 CD 61, EComm HR (employees of public corporations); *X v. United Kingdom* (1980) 21 DR 168 (police officers); *Neigel v France* RJD 1997-II 399 (local authority employee).

employment),[684] the liability of individuals for payment of tax[685] and eligibility for fiscal advantages.[686] Nevertheless, even in this area the position is not clear cut, thus Article 6 does apply:

- to a judge's right to a statutory pension;[687]
- to a claim for compensation for loss of a fiscal benefit (as the result of a refusal to allow a tax exemption).[688]

Other kinds of disputes excluded from the requirements of Article 6 include: immigration and nationality,[689] liability for military service,[690] legal aid in civil cases,[691] court reporting,[692] government funding for research,[693] state education benefits,[694] tax assessments[695] (but not compensation for the refusal to grant tax concessions[696] or restitution for overpaid tax[697] which fall within the scope of Article 6), patent applications,[698] discipline of prisoners,[699] rights of tenants associations,[700] public compensation funds,[701] state medical treatment,[702] hereditary peerages,[703] right to stand for public office[704] and the validity of parliamentary elections.[705] **11.173**

[684] *Darnell v United Kingdom* (1993) 18 EHRR 205 (doctor employed by the NHS); *C v United Kingdom* (1987) 54 DR 162, EComm HR (janitor at state school).

[685] *X v France* (1983) 32 DR 266, EComm HR; see also *S and T v Sweden* (1986) 50 DR 121, EComm HR (tax on corporate benefits).

[686] *X v Austria* (1980) 21 DR 246, EComm HR (export incentive tax exemption).

[687] See *Lombardo v Italy* (1992) 21 EHRR 188 — even though employment matters in relation to the judiciary are generally considered outside the purview of Art 6, see also *Scuderi v Italy* (1993) 19 EHRR 187.

[688] *Editions Periscope v France* (1992) 14 EHRR 597.

[689] See eg *X, Y, Z, V and W v United Kingdom* (1967) 10 YB 528 (entry); *P v United Kingdom* (1987) 54 DR 211, EComm HR (asylum); *Agee v United Kingdom* (1976) DR 164, EComm HR (deportation); *S v Switzerland* (1988) 59 DR 256, EComm HR (nationality).

[690] *Nicolussi v Austria* (1987) 52 DR 266, EComm HR.

[691] *X v Germany* (1970) 32 CD 56, EComm HR.

[692] *Atkinson Crook and The Independent v United Kingdom* (1990) 67 DR 244, EComm HR.

[693] *X v Sweden* (1974) 2 DR 123, EComm HR.

[694] *Simpson v United Kingdom* (1989) 64 DR 188, EComm HR; *X . Germany* (1984) 7 EHRR 141, EComm HR.

[695] *X v France* (1983) 32 DR 266.

[696] *Editions Periscope v France* (1992) 14 EHRR 597.

[697] *National and Provincial Building Society v United Kingdom* (1997) 25 EHRR 127.

[698] *X v Austria* (1978) 14 DR 200, EComm HR; note that disputes with respect to existing patents are protected by Art 6.

[699] *McFeeley v United Kingdom* (1980) 20 DR 44, EComm HR; note that disciplining of prisoners may also involve a 'criminal charge'.

[700] *X v Sweden* (1983) 6 EHRR 323, EComm HR; *K Association v Sweden* (1983) 33 DR 276, EComm HR.

[701] *Berler v Germany* (1989) 62 DR 207, EComm HR (compensation for Nazi persecution); *B v Netherlands* (1985) 43 DR 198, EComm HR (criminal injuries); *Nordh v Sweden* (1990) 69 DR 223, EComm HR (natural disaster compensation).

[702] *L v Sweden* (1988) 61 DR 62, EComm HR.

[703] *X v United Kingdom* (1978) 16 DR 162, EComm HR (a claim to enter the House of Lords).

[704] *Habsburg-Lothringen v Austria* (1989) 64 DR 210, EComm HR (office of head of state).

[705] *Priorello v Italy* (1985) 43 DR 195, EComm HR; *I Z v Greece* (1994) 76-A DR 65.

(c) Criminal charges

11.174 **'Criminal'.** Article 6(1) also applies to the determination of criminal charges. As a result of the lack of uniformity in the classification of offences in different national legal systems, this phrase has been given a meaning autonomous[706] from that used in domestic jurisdictions. The Court has set out three criteria in order to assess wheher the allegation made is in fact of a criminal nature:

- the categorisation of the allegation in domestic law;
- whether the offence applies to a specific group or is of a generally binding character;
- the severity of the penalty attached to it.[707]

The classification of the offence by the respondent state is a relevant starting point for the assessment, but is not decisive of the nature of the allegation. In practice, if an offence has been treated by the national court as criminal, the Court will, in light of the sanctions and stigma attributable to criminal charges, subject it to the requirements of a fair trial under Article 6.

11.175 If an allegation is not criminalised in national law, the Court must determine whether it is nevertheless criminal in character and subject to the protection of Article 6 by assessing the two 'more important' criteria: the nature of the offence and the severity of the penalty attached to it.[708] These criteria are alternative, not cumulative, although the cumulative approach may be adopted where the analysis of each criterion does not lead to a clear conclusion.[709]

11.176 The second criterion involves consideration of whether or not the 'offence' applies to a specific group or is of a general binding character. In *Oztürk,*[710] the regulatory offence of careless driving was found to be criminal, despite its decriminalisation in German law. This was because the offence was of general application to the public. The Court was apparently unconcerned that the penalty, though punitive and deterrent, was relatively modest: a fine, rather than imprisonment. The failure of Germany to provide the accused with an interpreter was held to be a violation of Article 6. However, in that case several dissenting judges asserted that decriminalisation of 'minor offences' is in the general interests of individuals and ought to be recognised as legitimate. More recently Austrian

[706] *Engel v Netherlands (No 1)* (1976) 1 EHRR 647 para 81.

[707] See *Engel v Netherlands (No 1)* (n 706 above) para 82; *Oztürk v Germany* (1984) 6 EHRR 409; *Campbell and Fell v United Kingdom* (1985) 7 EHRR 165; *Weber v Switzerland* (1990) 12 EHRR 508.

[708] *Engel v Netherlands (No 1)* (n 706 above) para 82.

[709] See *Garyfallou AEBE v Greece* (1999) 28 EHRR 344 para 33; see also *Lauko v Slovakia* [1999] EHRLR 105 para 56.

[710] *Öztürk v Germany* (1984) 6 EHRR 409.

'administrative criminal proceedings' for matters such as breach of planning permission and road traffic offences have been held to fall within Article 6.[711]

Other examples of 'regulatory' offences which have been found to be 'criminal' for the purposes of Article 6 are price-fixing regulations,[712] rules governing competition for contracts,[713] police regulations governing demonstrations[714] and customs codes.[715] Cases dealing with parliamentary privilege[716] and tax evasion[717] have also been treated as 'criminal', for the purposes of Article 6. However, in general, 'disciplinary proceedings' will not be 'criminal' on the basis of this criterion because professional disciplinary matters are essentially matters concerning the relationship between professional associations and individuals rather than a law of general application.[718] Similar reasoning applies to 'regulatory proceedings'.[719] **11.177**

The third criterion concerns the severity of the penalty. The Court has placed great emphasis on the seriousness of the penalty or imprisonment attached to the offence in matters otherwise considered disciplinary in nature. In *Engel* it stated that criminal matters are those characterised by: **11.178**

> deprivations of liberty liable to be imposed as punishment, except those which by their nature, duration or manner of execution cannot be appreciably detrimental.[720]

In that case the proceedings were applicable to armed forces personnel alone, and therefore, in principle, disciplinary rather than criminal. However, the Court's emphasis on the severity of the impending penalty resulted in a finding that a 'criminal charge' was involved. In the disciplinary context, if violations place the accused at risk of 'light arrest' without deprivation of liberty, or confinement of short duration, the offence will not belong to criminal law.[721] A more serious form of punishment involving deprivation of liberty will, however, generally mean that the proceedings are 'criminal' and that the authorities are obliged to afford

---

711 *Schmautzer v Austria* (1995) 21 EHRR 511; *Umlauft v Austria* (1995) 22 EHRR 76; *Pfarrmaier v Austria* (1995) 22 EHRR 175; Noted [1996] EHRLR 181; see also *Lauko v Slovakia* RJD 1998–VI 2492.

712 *Deweer v Belgium* (1980) 2 EHRR 239.

713 *Société Stenuit v France* (1992) 14 EHRR 509.

714 *Belilos v Switzerland* (1988) 10 EHRR 466.

715 *Salabiaku v France* (1988) 13 EHRR 379.

716 See *Demicoli v Malta* (1991) 14 EHRR 47 (journalist was convicted of the non-criminal offence of breach of parliamentary privilege for criticising Members of Parliament; the offence was of general application and generated a penalty of fine or imprisonment).

717 *Bendenoun v France* (1994) 18 EHRR 54.

718 *Wickramsinghe v United Kingdom* [1998] EHRLR 338, EComm HR.

719 See eg *APB Ltd, APP and AEB v United Kingdom*, (1998) 25 EHRR CD 14; *X v United Kingdom* (1998) 25 EHRR CD 88.

720 (1976) 1 EHRR 647, 679 para 82; see also, *Benham v United Kingdom* (1996) 22 EHRR 293 and *Parks v United Kingdom* Judgment, 12 Oct 1999 which held that proceedings to recover community charge involved a criminal charge: see para 11.284 below.

721 See for example *Eggs v Switzerland* (1978) 15 DR 35, 65, EComm HR (five days of strict arrest in a civil prison).

Article 6 guarantees. This approach was followed in *Campbell and Fell v United Kingdom*[722] in relation to disciplinary proceedings in an English prison where the Court declined to decide whether other types of punishment such as loss of privileges, might in some circumstances render an offence 'criminal'. However, the imposition of a substantial fine in disciplinary proceedings will not render the charges 'criminal' in nature.[722a]

11.179 Nevertheless, the definition of 'criminal' remains unclear. This is illustrated by a series of 'contempt of court' cases. In *Weber v Switzerland*[723] the applicant was convicted of a non-criminal offence under Swiss law for revealing confidential information relating to a criminal investigation that had resulted from his complaint. This was held to be a 'criminal charge'.[724] In contrast, in *Ravensborg v Sweden*[725] the applicant was fined, without a hearing three times for making improper statements in written observations to the court. It was held that no 'criminal charge' was involved and the 'criminal charge' provisions of Article 6 did not apply.[726] On the basis of *Engel* and *Campbell and Fell*, it is possible that only military or prison disciplinary sentences will meet the test of severity of sentence. Other types of disciplinary proceedings, such as the liberal professions or civil service are unlikely to carry a penalty of imprisonment[727] and will not be covered by Article 6.[728]

11.180 **The nature of a 'charge'.** The 'criminal provisions' of Article 6 only apply if the allegation is both criminal in nature and constitutes a 'charge'. This is an issue that only becomes relevant in connection with the requirement of 'trial within a reasonable time' and the question of access to a criminal court.[729] The word 'charge' has also been given an autonomous meaning under the Convention[730] determined by reference to substance rather than form.[731] 'Charge' has been defined in general terms as 'the official notification given to an individual by the competent

[722] (1984) 7 EHRR 165.

[722a] *Brown v United Kingdom* (1998) 28 EHRR CD 233 — the fact that a £10,000 fine was imposed by Solicitors Complaints Tribunal did not render the proceedings 'criminal'.

[723] (1990) 12 EHRR 508.

[724] Ibid paras 31–35.

[725] (1994) 18 EHRR 38.

[726] Ibid para 34; see also, to the same effect, *Putz v Austria*, RJD 1996-I 312 paras 34-38.

[727] See *X v United Kingdom* (1980), 21 DR 168, EComm HR and *Dimitriadis v Greece* (1990) 65 DR 279, EComm HR (where the penalty was dismissal); *Saraiva de Carvalho v Portugal* (1981) 26 DR 262, EComm HR (involving transfer of soldier to a reserve) and *Kremzow v Austria* (1990) 67 DR 307 (a risk of loss of pension by way of disciplinary sanction).

[728] However, they may be protected by Art 6(1) on the basis that there is a determination of 'civil rights and obligations'.

[729] *Deweer v Belgium* (1980) 2 EHRR 439.

[730] Ibid.

[731] It is necessary for the Commission or Court to look beyond what is apparent and investigate the realities: *Deweer* (n 729 above) para 44.

authority of an allegation that he has committed a criminal offence',[732] but it may also take the form of other measures which imply such an allegation and substantially affect the suspect's situation.[733] Whether the proceedings resulting in criminal prosecution are initiated by an individual or by public authorities is irrelevant for the purposes of the applicability of Article 6.[734]

Most of the case law relates to civil law systems. A person is charged when he is first notified or affected by an investigation: a 'charge' has been found to exist when there is arrest,[735] official information as to prosecution[736] or knowledge of an investigation,[737] a request for production of evidence,[738] the freezing of a bank account[739] or closing of a shop pending payment or the outcome of criminal proceedings,[740] and the applicant's retention of a defence lawyer following a police report against him.[741] The Commission has, on a number of occasions, found that the mere fact that police are investigating an offence or that a preliminary enquiry has been made by a judicial body is not tantamount to the existence of a criminal charge.[742] On the other hand, the negotiation of a friendly settlement may imply that a criminal charge is already in issue.[743] **11.181**

In relation to the position in England, a person has been found to be charged when he is arrested[744] or has police charges laid against him;[745] but because the test of substance over formality applies here too, the point at which an accused is 'substantially affected' may not always be so obvious. For example, an applicant serving a prison sentence for a separate offence was found to be charged with another from the time of conviction on the first, as it was then that he became aware that further charges were imminent.[746] Given the anxiety and uncertainty potentially caused, it is possible that police questioning or investigation of an individual prior **11.182**

[732] *Deweer* (n 729 above) para 46; see also *Eckle v Germany* (1982) 5 EHRR 1; *Serves v France* (1997) 28 EHRR 265 para 42.

[733] *Foti v Italy* (1982) 5 EHRR 313; *Deweer v Belgium* (1980) 2 EHRR 439; *Adolf v Austria* (1982) 4 EHRR 313; and see *Re Mlambo* [1993] 2 LRC 28 which reaches a similar result from a 'common law' perspective, see para 11.520 below.

[734] *Minelli v Switzerland* (1983) 5 EHRR 554 para 26ff.

[735] *Wemhoff v Germany* (1968) 1 EHRR 55; *Foti v Italy* (1982) 5 EHRR 313.

[736] *Neumeister v Austria (No 1)* (1968) 1 EHRR 91.

[737] *Eckle v Germany* (1982) 5 EHRR 1.

[738] *Funke v France* (1993) 16 EHRR 297.

[739] Ibid.

[740] *Deweer v Belgium* (1980) 2 EHRR 439.

[741] *Angelucci v Italy* Series A No 196-C (1991); see also *P v Austria* (1989) 71 DR 52, EComm HR.

[742] See eg *X v Germany* (1972) 38 CD 77, EComm HR; *X v Germany* (1974) 46 CD 1, EComm HR.

[743] *Deweer v Belgium* (1980) 2 EHRR 439.

[744] *X v United Kingdom* (1979) 17 DR 122, EComm HR.

[745] *Ewing v United Kingdom* (1986) 10 EHRR 141.

[746] *X v United Kingdom* (1978) 14 DR 26, EComm HR.

to his arrest or formal charge could constitute a 'charge' in substance for the purposes of Article 6.[747]

(3) Article 6(1) guarantees

(a) Introduction

11.183 Article 6 provides a general right to a 'fair hearing' and a number of specific rights and elaborates further rights in relation to those facing criminal charges. The fair trial rights guaranteed by Article 6 can usefully be divided into two categories: express and implied rights. Article 6 contains the following specific *express* rights:

- the right to a hearing within a reasonable time;[748]
- the right to a independent and impartial tribunal established by law;[749]
- the right to a public hearing unless it is necessary to exclude the press and public from all or part of the trial in the interest of morals, public order, national security, to protect juveniles or private life or where publicity would prejudice the interests of justice;
- the right to the public pronouncement of judgment;[750]
- the right to minimum standards of fairness in *criminal* proceedings which consist of
  - (i) the presumption of innocence;[751]
  - (ii) the right to information as to the accusation;[752]
  - (iii) the right to adequate time and facilities to prepare a defence;[753]
  - (iv) the right of the accused to defend himself in person or through legal assistance;[754]
  - (v) the right to examine witnesses;[755]
  - (vi) the right to assistance from an interpreter.[756]

These rights are 'absolute' in the sense that it will always be unfair if a person is deprived of them.

11.184 In addition, the Strasbourg authorities have interpreted Article 6 as providing, as aspects of the general right to a fair hearing, the following *implied* rights:

---

[747] See D Harris, M O'Boyle and C Warbrick, *Law of the European Convention on Human Rights* (Butterworths, 1995) 172–73; and see *Re Mlambo* [1993] 2 LRC 28 (Zim SC).
[748] See para 11.219ff below.
[749] See para 11.222ff below.
[750] See para 11.230ff below.
[751] See para 11.236ff below.
[752] See para 11.241ff below.
[753] See para 11.243ff below.
[754] See para 11.245ff below.
[755] See para 11.252ff below.
[756] See para 11.255ff below.

- the right of access to the courts;[757]
- the right to be present at an adversarial hearing;[758]
- the right to equality of arms;[759]
- the right to fair presentation of the evidence;[760]
- the right to cross examine;[761] and
- the right to a reasoned judgment.[762]

These rights are subject to inherent limitations in the sense that a breach of any one of them does not always mean that there has been a violation of Article 6. The fairness of the proceedings as a whole can be considered[763] and it is often necessary to carry out a 'balancing exercise' between the interests of the individual and those of society as a whole.[764] Although the point has not been fully developed in the case law it is often helpful to consider, in each case of apparent violation, whether it is necessary and proportionate in pursuit of a legitimate aim.

(b) Right of access to the courts[765]

General. In one of its most important early decisions, *Golder v United Kingdom,*[766] the Court recognised the existence of an implied right of access to the court. This right was recognised because: 11.185

> It would be inconceivable . . . that Article 6, paragraph 1 should describe in detail the procedural guarantees afforded to parties in a pending lawsuit and should not first protect that which alone makes it in fact possible to benefit from such guarantees, that is, access to the court. The fair, public and expeditious characteristics of judicial proceedings are of no value at all if there are no judicial proceedings . . . it follows that the right of access constitutes an element which is inherent in the right stated by Article 6, paragraph 1.[767]

The right of access to a court is most significant in the context of the determination of private law claims, but also arises in criminal proceedings[768] and in claims 11.186

757 See para 11.185ff below.
758 See para 11.205ff below.
759 See para 11.208ff below.
760 See para 11.214ff below.
761 See para 11.217ff below.
762 See para 11.218 below.
763 See para 11.204 below.
764 See generally, para 6.124 above.
765 For a general discussion of recent cases, see S Phillips, 'The Court v the Executive: Old Battles on New Battlegrounds?' [1996] EHRLR 45; for the English law, see para 11.15 above.
766 (1975) 1 EHRR 524; for comments on this case, see R Lawson and H Schermers, *Leading Cases of the European Court of Human Rights* (Ars Aequi Libri, 1997) 24–27.
767 (1975) 1 EHRR 524, 536; see also *Kaplan v United Kingdom* (1980) 4 EHRR 64, EComm HR.
768 *Deweer v Belgium* (1980) 2 EHRR 439 paras 48, 49.

against the state, including claims arising out of executive decisions.[769] The right overlaps with the Article 13 right to an effective national remedy if the Convention right in question is also a 'civil' right under Article 6.[770]

11.187 Waiver of the right of access to court is possible,[771] but must be 'subjected to careful review'.[772] Whereas voluntary arbitration agreements do not fall within the scope of Article 6, the position is different for compulsory arbitration where the parties have no choice but to refer their dispute to arbitration.[773] However, the Commission has taken a sceptical approach where one party alleges that an arbitration was not voluntary because of duress.[774]

11.188 Settlements of a claim may amount both to a waiver of the right of access to the court and prevent the applicant from proving he is a victim.[775] Three conditions must be satisfied to ensure that a settlement is valid for the purposes of depriving the applicant of his rights under the Convention:

- the waiver must be established in an unequivocal manner; and in relation to procedural rights, a waiver to be effective must provide minimum guarantees commensurate with its importance;[776]
- the settlement will not prevent a claim against the state in proceedings which are based on a complaint that the law is inadequate in regulating the subject area;[777] and
- the settlement does not offend the fundamental principles of the Convention.[778]

11.189 **Effectiveness.** The right of access must be an effective one. In *Golder*, even though the prisoner was not denied a legal right to sue in libel, a failure to allow him contact with a solicitor hindered initiation of proceedings to such an extent that the Court found that he had been precluded access to a court. An effective

[769] *Sporrong and Lonnroth v Sweden* (1982) 5 EHRR 35; *Keegan v Ireland* (1994) 18 EHRR 342.

[770] Cases that speak to the interrelationship between the two guarantees are: *Golder v United Kingdom* (1975) 1 EHRR 524 para 33; *Powell and Rayner v United Kingdom* (1990) 12 EHRR 355; and *W v United Kingdom* (1987) 10 EHRR 29: see the separate opinions of Judges Pinheiro Farinha and De Meyer.

[771] See *Deweer v Belgium* (1980) 2 EHRR 439 para 49 (in which the parties contracted out of their access to court by agreeing to an arbitration provision); see also *R v Switzerland* (1987) 51 DR 83; and for the doctrine of waiver generally, see para 6.148ff above.

[772] *Deweer v Belgium* (n 771 above) para 49; cf the requirement that a waiver be 'unequivocal' in relation to other Art 6 rights.

[773] *Bramelid and Malmstrom v Sweden* (1986) 8 EHRR 116 Com Rep paras 30 and 32.

[774] *R v Switzerland* (1987) 51 DR 83.

[775] See generally, para 22.14ff below for a discussion of *locus standi* under the Convention (and the Human Rights Act).

[776] *Pfeifer and Plankl v Austria* (1992) 14 EHRR 692 para 37; *Oberschlick v Austria (No 1)* (1995) 19 EHRR 389.

[777] See eg *Inze v Austria* (1987) 10 EHRR 394 para 33.

[778] See eg *Donnelly v United Kingdom* (1975) 4 DR 4, 78, EComm HR.

right of access might also require that the state provide legal aid, at least where the nature of the proceedings, if they are to be successful, requires legal representation. In *Airey v Ireland*[779] legal aid was refused to a woman who wished to bring proceedings for judicial separation from her husband in the Irish High Court. The Court held that in light of the complexity of the proceedings, the need to examine expert witnesses and the emotional involvement of the parties, a right of access to the court would be ineffective if she were not legally represented. However, the Court has emphasised that, whilst Article 6(1) guarantees an effective right of access to the courts for the determination of their civil rights and obligations

> it leaves to the state a free choice of the means to be used towards this end. The institution of a legal aid scheme constitutes one of those means but there are others.

It has been said that legal aid will usually be required in civil cases involving family separation or parental rights,[779a] the commission of a person to a psychiatric institution[779b] or the right to liberty.[779c] However in a number of cases it has been found that applicants who have been refused legal aid have not been denied their rights of access[780] and Article 6(1) will not provide a full right of legal aid in civil litigation proceedings comparable to that provided by Article 6(3) for criminal proceedings.[781] The question as to whether the cost associated with litigation might itself infringe the right of effective access to a court has yet to be resolved.[782] Sufficient time is also necessary if the right of access to court is to be effective. A person must receive personal and reasonable notice of a decision interfering with his civil rights and obligations to enable him to challenge it in a court.[783]

Restrictions on access. The Court has developed implied limitations to the right as a corollary to implying the right in the first place. The right of access to the court is not absolute, and states' margin of appreciation in its regulation will vary **11.190**

[779] (1979) 2 EHRR 305; cf *M L B v S L J* (1997) 3 BHRC 47; US Sup Ct (court fees preventing an appeal against a decision removing parental rights, unconstitutional).

[779a] See *Munro v United Kingdom* (1987) 52 DR 158.

[779b] *Megyeri v Germany* (1992) 15 EHRR 584 para 23.

[779c] *Aerts v Belgium* [1998] EHRLR 777.

[780] *Munro v United Kingdom* (1987) 52 DR 158, EComm HR (defamation proceedings); *X v United Kingdom* (1980) 21 DR 95, EComm HR (denial of legal aid where there was 'no reasonable prospect of success' would not be considered a denial of access to court unless the decision was an arbitrary one); *Andronicou and Constantiou v Cyprus* (1997) 25EHRR 491 (offer of *ex gratia* assistance by the state defendant was sufficient); *X v Germany* (1986) 45 DR 291.

[781] See para 11.245ff below.

[782] Cf *X and Y v Netherlands* (1975) 1 DR 66, 71, EComm HR; *X v United Kingdom* (1981) 2 Digest 333, EComm HR; *X v Sweden* (1979) 17 DR 74.

[783] See *De Geouffre de la Pradelle v France* (1992) Series No A 253-B para 33 (the national publication of a decree issued as a result of environmental protection proceedings in relation to the applicant's land was not sufficient communication where the time for appeal had expired before the applicant was directly informed of the decision); *Pérez de Rada Cavanilles v Spain* RJD 1998–VIII 3242 (violation of right of access when applicant allowed only three days for an appeal).

depending on the 'needs and resources of the community and individuals'.[784] Restrictions must not, however, impair the essence of the right of access: they must have a legitimate aim, and the means used must be reasonably proportionate to the aim sought to be achieved.[785] The test for assessing the acceptability of limitation on the right of access is to a large extent similar to the basic requirements when justifying restrictions on interferences with the qualified rights defined under Articles 8 to 11.[786] In a concurring judgment in *De Geoffre de la Pradelle v France*[787] Judge Martens argued that the two tests should be the same; and this appears to be the approach adopted by the Court in *Fayed v United Kingdom*.[788]

11.191 In *Ashingdane v United Kingdom*,[789] the applicant was precluded from challenging an administrative decision to continue his detention in a mental institution. The legislative requirement was leave of the court on a finding of 'substantial grounds' for believing that either bad faith or absence of reasonable care on the part of the administrative authority were present. The Court found that these limitations had the 'legitimate aim' of protecting carers from being unduly targeted by the claims of psychiatric patients, while leaving intact the essence of the right of access, and so were not a violation of Article 6. Restrictions on the access to court of other types of litigants have been justified on the same grounds: these include minors,[790] 'vexatious litigants',[791] prisoners[792] and bankrupts.[793] Various measures to prevent abuses of the right of access, such as the imposition of reasonable time limits on proceedings,[794] the requirement that legal representation be obtained for the lodging of an appeal[795] and payment of security for costs[796] have been held to be permissible. The Court has also held that where the general procedures for telephone tapping comply with Article 8,[797] the lack of a court

[784] *Golder v United Kingdom* (1975) 1 EHRR 524.

[785] *Ashingdane v UK* (1985) 7 EHRR 528 para 57; *Lithgow v United Kingdom* (1986) 8 EHHR 329 para 194; *Tolstoy Miloslavsky v United Kingdom* (1995) 20 EHRR 442 para 59; *Tinnelly & Sons and McElduff and others v United Kingdom* (1998) 27 EHRR 249 para 72.

[786] R A Lawson and H Schermers, *Leading Cases of the European Court of Human Rights* (Ars Aequi Libri, 1997) 26.

[787] (1992) Series A No 253-B para 4.

[788] (1994) 18 EHRR 393 para 67.

[789] (1985) 7 EHRR 528

[790] *Golder v United Kingdom* (1975) 1 EHRR 524 para 39.

[791] *H v United Kingdom* (1985) 45 DR 281, EComm HR.

[792] *Campbell and Fell v United Kingdom* (1984) 7 EHRR 165.

[793] *M v United Kingdom* (1987) 52 DR 269, EComm HR.

[794] *X v Sweden* (1982) 31 DR 223, EComm HR.

[795] *Grepne v United Kingdom* (1990) 66 DR 268, EComm HR.

[796] *Tolstoy Miloslavsky v United Kingdom* (1995) 20 EHRR 442 (order for security for costs of defamation appeal, no violation); but see *Aït-Mouhoub v France* RJD 1998–VIII 3214 (requirement of security for costs of 80,000FF infringed right of access to court).

[797] See para 12.105 below.

remedy to question the legality of telephone tapping in a particular case can be justified in order to ensure the effectiveness of the system.[798]

In contrast, a regulation which precluded a professional person from suing a client for fees by requiring that he leave the claim in the hands of his professional organisation deprived him of the 'essence' of his personal right to access to court.[799] Similarly, a law that precluded monasteries from suing in relation to their property rights except through the Greek Church was a violation of their right to access, even though the Church itself had an interest in the actions.[800] **11.192**

Although limitation periods for proceedings restrict access to the court they serve important purposes and will, generally, not impair the essence of the right. Thus, in *Stubbings v United Kingdom*[800a] the Court held that the limitation periods applicable under English law in sex abuse cases pursued a legitimate aim and were proportionate. There was, therefore, no violation of Article 6. There may, however, be a breach of the right of access to the court if limitation periods are unduly short and rigidly enforced. As a result the Court has found breaches where a three-month time limit had expired before the applicant was effectively notified of the decision,[800b] and where the time limit for lodging an appeal was three days.[800c] **11.192A**

A defence of privilege or immunity raised by states has been treated as a restriction on the right of the claimant's access to court, rather than going to the substance of the claim and the existence of a 'contestation' or dispute under Article 6. The Court has stressed in a number of cases that total restrictions on access will be carefully scrutinised because: **11.193**

> The right guaranteed to an applicant under art 6(1) of the convention to submit a dispute to a court or tribunal in order to have a determination on questions of both fact and law cannot be displaced by the *ipse dixit* of the executive.[801]

Thus, it has been held that the right of access will not be displaced by a certificate that matters of national security are involved.[802]

The privilege or immunity defences have been upheld in a number of cases on the basis of the *Ashingdane* test. Thus, the Court has upheld the immunity from suit **11.194**

---

[798] *Klass v Germany* (1978) 2 EHRR 214 para 56.

[799] *Philis v Greece* (1991) 13 EHRR 741.

[800] *Holy Monasteries v Greece* (1994) (1994) 20 EHRR 1.

[800a] (1996) 23 EHRR 213 paras 53–55, see also para 11.277 below.

[800b] *De Geoffre de la Pradelle v France* (1992) A 253 (notification by publication in *Official Journal* insufficient).

[800c] *Perez de Rada Cavanilles v Spain* [1999] EHRLR 208.

[801] *Tinnelly and Sons Ltd and McElduff and others v United Kingdom* (1998) 27 EHRR 249 para 77.

[802] *Tinnelly and Sons Ltd* (n 801 above) see para 11.301 below (the Court took the view that it was possible to modify judicial procedures to safeguard national security and yet accord the individual a substantial degree of procedural justice, para 78).

of an international institution.[803] In *Fayed v United Kingdom*[804] a defence of privilege in relation to a claim that the Government had promulgated a false inspection report was acceptable because it facilitated the investigation of public companies, a matter of public interest which warranted the means used for its protection. The applicants had themselves attempted to bring the contentious subject matter of the report into the public forum and the remedy of judicial review was available to them in relation to the inspector's activities. The *Ashingdane* approach could equally be used to justify parliamentary privilege[805] or diplomatic and state immunity[805a] from suit.

11.195 However, the public policy immunity from liability in negligence[806] was held to be in breach of the right of access to the court in the important case of *Osman v United Kingdom.*[807] The plaintiff had brought proceedings which had been struck out[808] on the basis of the police immunity for actions in negligence arising out of the 'investigation and suppression of crime'[809] The Court rejected the Government's argument that Article 6 had no application. It accepted that the 'immunity' pursued the legitimate aim of the avoidance of defensive policing and the diversion of police manpower but held that it was not proportionate: the applicant's claim had been struck out without any consideration of the different policy considerations at issue. The Court said that:

> the application of the rule in this manner without further enquiry into the existence of competing public interest considerations only serves to confer a blanket immunity on the police for their acts and omissions during the investigation and suppression of crime and amounts to an unjustifiable restriction on an applicant's right to have a determination on the merits of his or her claim against the police in deserving cases . . . it must be open to a domestic court to have regard to the presence of other public interest considerations which pull in the opposite direction to the application of the rule.[810]

As a result, the Court held that there was a violation of Article 6. Other applications are pending; and the Commission has ruled as admissible an application in relation to public authorities' immunities from actions in negligence by children and has found for the applicants on the merits.[811]

---

[803] See *Beer and Regan v Germany* Judgment of 18 Feb 1999 (European Space Agency).

[804] (1994) 18 EHRR 393.

[805] *X v Austria* (1969) 12 YB 246, EComm HR; *Young v Ireland* [1996] EHRLR 326.

[805a] A number of cases relating to state immunity have been found to be admissible: *McElhinney v Ireland* Application 31253/96, 9 Feb 2000; *Al-Adsani v United Kingdom* Application 35763/97, 1 Mar 2000; and *Fogarty v United Kingdom* Application 37112/97, 1 Mar 2000.

[806] See generally, para 11.40ff above.

[807] (1998) 5 BHRC 293; the English decision was *Osman v Ferguson* [1993] 4 All ER 344; for criticism see Lord Hoffmann, 'Human Rights and the House of Lords' (1999) 62 MLR 159 and *Barrett v Enfield LB* [1999] 3 WLR 79, 84–85.

[808] *Osman v Ferguson* [1993] 4 All ER 344.

[809] See para 11.42 above.

[810] (1998) 5 BHRC 293 para 151.

[811] *T P and K M v United Kingdom* Application 28945/95 26 May 1998 (admissibility), 10 Sep 1999 (merits), EComm HR.

11.196 The decision in *Osman* has attracted considerable criticism.[812] Article 6(1) does not guarantee any particular substantive content for civil rights and obligations in national law;[813] it simply gives procedural guarantees for the determination of *tenable* rights.[814] It has therefore been strongly argued that the Court have unjustifiably extended the scope of Article 6 by interfering in the substantive law of a domestic state. This objection, in turn, depends on whether the policy immunities can properly be characterised as blanket immunities, a view which was sharply criticised by Lord Browne-Wilkinson in *Barrett v Enfield LBC*.[815]

11.197 **Access following administrative decisions.** When decisions are taken by administrative bodies which affect a person's civil rights, he is entitled to a hearing which satisfies the conditions of Article 6. This can be done in two ways:[816]

- the decision-making body must itself comply with the requirements of Article 6 (internal Article 6 compliance) or
- the decision-making body must be subject to control by a judicial body which provides Article 6 guarantees (external Article 6 compliance).

There will be sufficient 'access to the court' where the decision-making body does not comply with Article 6(1) in some respects *provided* that the body exercising judicial control 'has full jurisdiction and does provide the guarantees of Article 6(1)'.[817] In assessing the sufficiency of the review, it is necessary to have regard to matters such as the subject matter of the decision appealed against, the manner in which it was arrived at and the content of the dispute.[818]

11.198 However, the difficult question is whether it is necessary for an appeal to consider *both* issues of fact and law or whether it is sufficient to satisfy Article 6 if only issues of law can be canvassed. In *Bryan v United Kingdom*[819] the Court held that a

812 See eg T Weir 'Downhill—All the Way' [1999] 1 FLR 193; Lord Hoffmann, 'Human Rights and the House of Lords' (1999) 62 MLR 159; Sir Richard Buxton, 'The Human Rights Act and Private Law' (2000) 116 LQR 48.

813 *H v Belgium* (1987) 10 EHRR 339.

814 *James v United Kingdom* (1986) 8 EHRR 123 para 81; *Powell and Rayner v United Kingdom* (1990) 12 EHRR 355; see para 11.162 above.

815 [1999] 3 WLR 79; see para 11.44 above.

816 See *Albert and Le Compte v Belgium* (1983) 5 EHRR 533 para 29.

817 Ibid; *Bryan v United Kingdom* (1995) 21 EHRR 342 para 40; this only applies to decisions of an administrative or disciplinary nature, not to ordinary civil and criminal cases: see *De Cubber v Belgium* (1984) 7 EHRR 236 para 32.

818 *Bryan v United Kingdom*, (n 817 above) para 45; *Zumtobel v Austria* (1993) 17 EHRR 116 para 32.

819 n 817 above; see also *ISKCON v United Kingdom* (1994) 76-A DR 90, EComm HR which also concerned an enforcement notice where the only remedy available to the applicant was judicial review; the Commission said it is 'not the role of Article 6 to give access to a level of jurisdiction which can substitute its opinion for that of the administrative authorities on questions of expediency and where the courts do not refuse to examine any of the points raised'.

planning appeal (which is confined to appealing on a question of law)[820] was sufficient to ensure that a planning inspector's decision[821] complied with Article 6. In addition to attaching significance to the procedural safeguards in the planning procedure[822] the Court stressed:

> In the present case there was no dispute as to the primary facts. . . .. [However, even if there was such a challenge], the Court notes that while the High Court could not have substituted its own findings of fact for those of the inspector, it would have the power to satisfy itself that the inspector's findings of fact or the inferences based on them were neither perverse nor irrational.
>
> Such an approach by an appeal tribunal on questions of fact can reasonably be expected in specialist areas of law such as the one at issue, particularly where the facts have already been established in the course of a quasi-judicial procedure governed by many of the safeguards required by Article 6(1). It is also a feature in the systems of judicial control of administrative decisions found throughout the Council of Europe Member States. Indeed, in the instant case, the subject matter of the contested decision by the inspector was a typical example of the exercise of discretionary judgment in the regulation of citizens's conduct in the sphere of town and country planning.
>
> The scope of review of the High Court was therefore sufficient to comply with Article 6(1)

It appears that the decision in *Bryan* is a narrow one, turning primarily on the question of whether the applicant disputes the primary facts.[823]

11.199 The Commission has, nevertheless, rejected several recent complaints that recourse to judicial review is insufficient to meet the requirements of Article 6(1): where proceedings were brought following a determination by the Secretary of State that the applicant was not a fit and proper person to be the managing director of an insurance company;[824] and, again, following a finding by the Investment Managers Regulatory Organisation that the applicants were not fit and proper persons to carry on investment business.[825] The Commission also took the same approach about the effect of the availability of an appeal to the Privy Council from a decision of the health committee of the General Medical Council.[826]

---

[820] Under s 289(1) of the Town and Country Planning Act 1990.

[821] *Bryan v United Kingdom* (n 817 above); see also *Oerlermans v Netherlands* (1991) 15 EHRR 561.

[822] *Bryan v United Kingdom* (n 817 above) para 46; the Court referred to uncontested safeguards at the procedure before the planning inspector; the quasi judicial character of the decision-making process; the duty on the inspector to exercise independent judgment, the requirement that the inspector must not be subject to improper influence; the stated mission of the Inspectorate to uphold the principles of openness, fairness and impartiality; and the fact that any alleged shortcomings were subject to review by the High Court.

[823] See eg *Fischer v Austria* (1995) 20 EHRR 349 paras 33, 34.

[824] *X v United Kingdom* (1998) 25 EHRR CD 88.

[825] *APB Ltd, APP and AEB v United Kingdom* (1998) 25 EHRR CD 141.

[826] *Stefan v United Kingdom* (1997) 25 EHHR CD 130; *Wickramsinghe v United Kingdom* [1998] EHRLR 338.

In contrast, there have been several occasions where administrative decisions followed by an appeal on a point of law (rather than an appeal on the merits) have resulted in breaches of Article 6: on the ground that decisions of administrative bodies that do not satisfy the requirements of Article 6 must be subject to subsequent control by a 'judicial body which has full jurisdiction'. In *Albert and Le Compte v Belgium*[827] doctors challenging disciplinary decisions against them succeeded in arguing that failure of the appeals procedure to comply with Article 6 guarantees (and, in particular, an appeal confined to points of law) breached the right of access to the court. The Court has held that judicial review does not provide sufficient scope to examine the merits of the case in relation to a local authority's decision as to access to a child;[828] and has reached the same conclusion in a number of other cases.[829] **11.200**

The question of whether a particular administrative decision-maker (which is subject to judicial review) breaches Article 6 will depend on the extent to which the administrative body *itself* meets the procedural safeguards achieved by a quasi-judicial procedure.[830] A number of administrative decisions are made through tribunal procedures (such as planning inquiries) which give an applicant and interested parties extensive opportunities to dispute the facts in issue. Some administrative decisions, on the other hand, have only very rudimentary procedures for allowing the applicant to put his case. The procedural guarantees conferred by Article 6 are comprehensive; and include the right to be present at an adversarial hearing;[831] the right to equality of arms;[832] the right to fair presentation of the evidence;[833] the right to cross examine;[834] the right to a reasoned judgment;[835] the right to a hearing within a reasonable time;[836] the right to an independent and impartial tribunal established by law;[837] and the right to a public hearing and the public pronouncement of judgment.[838] The critical issue in **11.201**

[827] (1983) 5 EHRR 533 para 36.
[828] *W v United Kingdom* (1987) 10 EHRR 29 paras 80-83.
[829] See *Obermeier v Austria* (1990) 13 EHRR 290 para 70 (inadequate as no appeal on merits against dismissal decision); *Schmautzer v Austria* (1995) 21 EHHR 511 para 34 and *Umlauft v Austria* (1995) 22 EHRR 76 para 37 (road traffic conviction followed by appeal to Constitutional Court which can only consider whether conviction conformed to constitution was insufficient to satisfy Art 6).
[830] Cf Sir Stephen Richards;' The Impact of Article 6 of the ECHR on Judicial Review' [1999] JR 106.
[831] See para 11.206 below.
[832] See para 11.208ff below.
[833] See para 11.214 below.
[834] See para 11.217 below.
[835] See para 11.218 below.
[836] See para 11.219ff below.
[837] See para 11.222ff below.
[838] See para 11.230ff below.

every case will be whether an administrative procedure provides the applicant with a fair opportunity which is sufficient to dispute the primary facts.[839]

11.202 **Criminal charges.** In criminal proceedings, the right to access to a court means that the accused has a right to be tried on the charge against him in a court.[840] As the right is not absolute, it does not imply that a victim can himself lay a criminal charge,[841] or that every criminal charge must end in a judicial decision. In some instances, such as a decision by the prosecution to discontinue the proceedings, a criminal matter will not be submitted to a court and Article 6 will be irrelevant so long as no factual or formal 'determination' takes place. Article 6 does not give an accused grounds for demanding continuation of judicial proceedings, but requires only that when he is convicted it is done by a court.[842] Nevertheless, there may be a violation of Article 6 when the dismissal of a charge upon an agreement between the accused and the prosecution amounts to a settlement under duress and de facto denial of access.[843] Similarly, if after withdrawal of a charge there remains some suggestion of guilt on the part of the accused, then there is an arguable breach of Article 6, in light of the presumption of innocence in Article 6(2).[844]

11.203 **Access to appeals.** Under Article 6(1) there is no right of appeal from determinations of civil rights or obligations or criminal charges.[845] However, the guarantees apply to any appeal which does take place.[846]

(c) Right to a fair hearing

11.204 **Introduction.** The concept of fairness in Article 6(1) applies to both criminal hearings and to proceedings in which the determination of civil rights and obligations is involved. A decision as to the fairness of a hearing is based on an assessment of the course of the proceedings *as a whole*.[847] This approach was recently confirmed in *Khan v United Kingdom*[847a] where the Court rejected the argument that Article 6(1) was breached because the only evidence against the applicant was

---

839 See also Lord Clyde's analysis of the position in *Stefan v General Medical Council* [1999] 1 WLR 1293,1299, 1300 discussed at para 11.91 above.

840 *Deweer v Belgium* (1980) 2 EHRR 439.

841 *Kiss v United Kingdom* (1977) 20 YB 156, EComm HR.

842 It does not require an ordinary court or a trial by jury, but only that the court is established by law and meets the other criteria of Art 6: *X v Ireland* (1981) 22 DR 51; *Crociani v Italy* (1981) 22 DR 147, EComm HR.

843 In *Deweer v Belgium* (1980) 2 EHRR 439 the applicant was threatened with the closure of his shop if he did not accept the settlement offered by the public prosecutor.

844 *Adolf v Austria* (1982) 4 EHRR 313.

845 *Delcourt v Belgium* (1970) 1 EHRR 355; in criminal cases, this is guaranteed by Art 2, Seventh Protocol (which has not been ratified by the United Kingdom).

846 *Monnell & Morris v United Kingdom* (1987) 10 EHRR 205.

847 See eg *Kraska v Switzerland* (1993) 18 EHRR 188 para 30; *Barberà, Messegué and Jabardo v Spain* (1988) 11 EHRR 360 para 68; contrast *Stanford v United Kingdom* (1994) Series A No 280-A see also *Khan v United Kingdom The Times*, 23 May 2000.

847a n 847 above.

obtained by a secret listening device in breach of Article 8(1). The Court instead held that the domestic courts had considered whether the admission of the evidence created a substantial unfairness so that its admission did not conflict with the requirements of fairness under Article 6(1). However, a particular aspect of a case may contravene the notion of fairness in such a way that it is possible to draw a conclusion without regard to the rest of the proceedings.[848] In criminal cases, all three paragraphs of Article 6 must be read *together*, as the general provision in Article 6(1) supplements the specific guarantees of Article 6(2) and 6(3). Although Article 6 rights are applicable to both civil and criminal cases, in applying them Contracting States have a greater latitude when dealing with civil cases than they have when dealing with criminal cases.[849]

Article 6 does not give any indication of the content of the right to a fair hearing. A number of principles has been developed by the Commission and the Court including: **11.205**

- the right to be present when evidence is being heard;
- the right to enter into adversarial argument and to present his case to the court under conditions that do not place him at substantial disadvantage in relation to his opponent;
- the right to be provided with reasons for judgment that have sufficient clarity to enable him to exercise a right of appeal available to him.

Right to be present at an adversarial oral hearing. The notion of a 'fair hearing' in a criminal case includes the right of the accused to be present at and to take part in an oral hearing[850] which is adversarial.[851] This means that each party must have the opportunity to comment on all evidence adduced, including experts report.[851a] The right does not extend to appeals unless the appeal court is dealing with the facts as well as the law.[852] The waiver of this right must be established in an unequivocal manner.[853] If it is waived, the accused must have **11.206**

[848] *Crociani v Italy* (1981) 24 YB 222, EComm HR.

[849] *Dombo Beheer BV v Netherlands* (1993) 18 EHRR 213 para 32.

[850] See *Collozza and Rubinat v Italy* (1985) 7 EHRR 516 para 27; *Monnell and Morris v United Kingdom* (1987) 10 EHRR 205 para 58, *Zana v Turkey* (1998) 4 BHRC 241para 68.

[851] *Brandstetter v Austria* (1991) 15 EHRR 378 para 66; *Ruiz-Mateos v Spain* (1993) 16 EHRR 505 para 63.

[851a] See *Mantovanelli v France* (1997) 24 EHRR 370 (applicant denied opportunity to attend interviews of witnesses by court appointed expert and not shown the documents he took into account).

[852] *Monnell v United Kingdom* (n 880 above); *Ekbatani v Sweden* (1988) 13 EHRR 504; contrast the cases where the appeal could be decided on documents alone: see eg *Monnell and Morris v United Kingdom* (1987) 10 EHRR 205; *Andersson v Sweden* (1991) 15 EHRR 218; *Kremzow v Austria* (1993) 17 EHRR 322.

[853] *Colozza and Rubinat v Italy*, (n 880 above) para 28; *Albert and Le Compte v Belgium* (1983) 5 EHRR 533 para 35; *Poitrimol v France* (1993) 18 EHRR 130 para 31; see generally, para 6.149 above.

legal representation.[854] As result, there will be a violation if the accused is not aware of the proceedings and the attempts to trace him are inadequate.[855] The presence of the accused's lawyers will not be sufficient when a person faces a serious criminal charge and has not waived his right to be present.[856] However, a trial in absentia is acceptable if the state has diligently but unsuccessfully given the accused notice of the hearing.[857] In some circumstances it is also permissable to proceed where the applicant is absent through illness.[858]

11.207 In civil cases, there is only a right to be present at an oral hearing in cases in which the 'personal character'[859] or conduct[860] of the applicant is relevant. This right can be waived impliedly by, for example, not attending the hearing after receiving effective notice of it.[861] There may be a right to be present at the hearing of appeals in such cases which consider both the facts and the law.[862]

11.208 **Right to equality of arms.** In both criminal and civil cases, every party to the proceedings must have a 'reasonable opportunity of presenting his case to the court under conditions which do not place him at substantial disadvantage vis-a-vis his opponent'.[863] This right is particularly important in criminal cases where it overlaps with the specific guarantees in Article 6(3) but, in some respects, goes further. In this context, importance is attached to appearances as well as to the increased sensitivity to the fair administration of justice.[864]

11.209 The right to equality of arms means that all parties must have access to the records and documents which are relied on by the court.[865] It appears that the parties should have the opportunity to make copies of the relevant documents from the court file.[866] The parties must be able to cross-examine witnesses.[867] Thus, breaches have been found where:

[854] *Lala v Netherlands* (1994) 18 EHRR 586.

[855] See *Colloza and Rubinat v Italy* (n 850, above) paras 28–29.

[856] See *Zana v Turkey* (n 850 above) para 71 (applicant tried and convicted in his absence because he refused to defend himself in Turkish).

[857] *Colozzo and Rubinat v Italy* (n 850 above).

[858] See eg *Ensslin, Baader and Raspe v Germany* (1978) 14 DR 64, EComm HR where the applicants were on hunger strike.

[859] See eg cases involving access to children: *X v Austria* (1983) 31 DR 66, EComm HR; see also *Xv Germany* (1963) 6 YB 520, 572, EComm HR.

[860] *Muyldermans v Belgium* (1991) 15 EHRR 204 para 64, Com Rep.

[861] See *Cv Italy* (1988) 56 DR 40, EComm HR.

[862] See para 11.198 above.

[863] See eg *De Haes and Gijsels v Belgium* (1997) 25 EHRR 1 para 53; *Delcourt v Belgium* (1970) 1 EHRR 355 para 28.

[864] *Bulut v Austria* (1996) 24 EHRR 84 para 47.

[865] *Lynas v Switzerland* (1977) 10 YB 412, 445–446, EComm HR; *Lobo Machado v Portugal* (1996) 23 EHRR 79 para 31.

[866] See P van Dijk and G van Hoof, *Theory and Practice of the European Convention on Human Rights* (3rd edn, Kluwer, 1998) pp.430–431; relying on *Schuler-Zgraggen v Switzerland* (1993) 16 EHRR 405.

[867] *X v Austria* (1972) 42 CD 145, EComm HR.

- only one of two witnesses to an oral agreement was allowed to be called;[868]
- the applicant was denied a reply to written submissions by counsel for the state;[869]
- the applicant was not given the opportunity to comment on a medical report.[870]

The provision of legal aid could also be seen as a matter of 'equality of arms' with the other party, but has generally been dealt with in terms of the right of access to court.[871]

The right is especially significant in criminal cases. The Commission have held that it means that the prosecution must disclose any material in their possession which 'may assist the accused in exonerating himself or obtaining a reduction in sentence'.[872] Any defence expert must be afforded the same facilities as one appointed by the prosecution.[873] **11.210**

Freedom from self-incrimination. The right of a person charged to remain silent and not to incriminate himself is **11.211**

> generally recognised international standards which lie at the heart of the notion of fair procedure under Art 6 of the Convention. Their rationale lies, inter alia, in protecting the 'person charged' against improper compulsion by the authorities and thereby contributing to the avoidance of miscarriages of justice and to the fulfilment of the aims of Art 6. The right not to incriminate oneself, in particular, presupposes that the prosecution in a criminal case seek to prove their case without resort to evidence obtained through methods of coercion or oppression in defiance of the will of the 'person charged'.[874]

It is incompatible with these immunities to base a conviction solely or mainly on an accused's silence or his failure to answer questions or give evidence.[875] The right has been successfully invoked where the applicant failed to cooperate with authorities in the pre-trial production of documents[876] or refused to answer questions required by law on pain of criminal sanction.[877] In *Funke v France*,[877a] the Court found that the applicant's conviction of the offence of failing to produce bank statements relevant to customs investigations amounted to a compulsion to

[868] *Dombo Beheer BV v Netherlands* (1993) 18 EHRR 213.
[869] *Ruiz-Mateos v Spain* (1993) 16 EHRR 505.
[870] *Feldbrugge v Netherlands* (1986) 8 EHRR 425.
[871] See para 11.185 above.
[872] *Jespers v Belgium* (1981) 27 DR 61 para 54, EComm HR; see also *Edwards v United Kingdom* (1992) 15 EHRR 417; *Bendenoun v France* (1994) 18 EHRR 54 (no breach by failure to disclose a bulky file whose contents the applicant was aware of and which was not relied on by the court).
[873] *Bonisch v Austria* (1985) 9 EHRR 191.
[874] *Serves v France* (1997) 28 EHRR 265 para 47; and see *Funke v France* (1993) 16 EHRR 297para 44, *Murray v United Kingdom* (1996) 22 EHRR 29 para 45, *Saunders v United Kingdom* (1996) 23 EHRR 313 para 68.
[875] *Murray* (n 874 above) para 47.
[876] *Funke v France* (n 874 above).
[877] *Saunders v United Kingdom* (n 874 above).
[877a] n 874 above.

produce incriminating evidence that violated his right to remain silent. In *Saunders v United Kingdom*, where the coercion was the threat of a criminal penalty, the Court stated that the freedom was necessary to safeguard the accused from oppression and coercion during criminal proceedings and was closely linked to the presumption of innocence. It also said that it was necessary to assess the impact of the infringement on the fairness of the trial as a whole before concluding that there had been a breach of Article 6. On the facts, the applicant was convicted of commercial fraud charges and sentenced to imprisonment on the basis of information that he was required to provide to Department of Trade and Industry inspectors and, as a result, there was a breach.

11.212 However, the right to silence is not absolute. It is clear that:

> it cannot and should not prevent that the accused's silence, in situations which clearly call for an explanation from him, be taken into account in assessing the persuasiveness of the evidence adduced by the prosecution.[878]

Whether the drawing of adverse inferences from an accused's silence infringes Article 6 is to be determined in light of all the circumstances of the case, having regard to the situations where inferences may be drawn, the weight attached to them by the national courts in the assessment of the evidence and the degree of compulsion.[879] Following the *Murray* case, the Commission have rejected a series of United Kingdom complaints involving 'inferences from silence' on the basis that there was other evidence and sufficient 'judicial protection' for the accused.[880] However, in *Condron v United Kingdom*[880a] the Court upheld a claim where the judge failed to give adequate directions to the jury about the proper inferences it could draw.

11.213 **Right to legal assistance.** Legal assistance in criminal cases is guaranteed by Article 6(3)(c).[881] In civil cases, the right to a fair hearing includes a right to legal assistance, albeit a less extensive one.[882] Cases can be selected for legal aid on merit with financial contributions being required.[883] The blanket exclusion of legal aid in defamation cases is not a breach.[884] However, the Court has decided in *Benham*

---

[878] *Murray v United Kingdom* (1996) 22 EHRR 29, para 47.

[879] See *Quinn v United Kingdom (Merits)* [1997] EHRLR 167, EComm HR.

[880] See *Quinn* (n 879 above); *Hamill v United Kingdom (Merits)* (Application 22656/93), 2 Dec 1997 and *Murray v United Kingdom* Application 22384/93, 2 Dec 1997.

[880a] *The Times*, 9 May 2000; see para 11.287 below.

[881] See para 11.245ff below.

[882] See *Airey v Ireland* (1979) 2 EHRR 305; and generally, para 11.189 above.

[883] *X v United Kingdom* (1981) 21 DR 95, 101, EComm HR; *Thaw v United Kingdom* (1996) 22 EHRR CD 100.

[884] *Winer v United Kingdom* (1986) 48 DR 154, EComm HR; *Munro v United Kingdom* (1987) 52 DR 158, EComm HR; *S and M v United Kingdom* (1993) 18 EHRR CD 172 (the 'McLibel' case).

v United Kingdom[885] and *Perks v United Kingdom*[886] that the risk of imprisonment and the complexity of the law in community charge cases meant the interests of justice required legal representation before the magistrates.

Right to fair presentation of evidence. As a result of the wide variation in rules of evidence followed in different European legal systems, the Court has not laid down any specific set of evidential rules as a requirement of the guarantee of the right to a fair trial under Article 6. The Court has, nonetheless, provided some guidelines as to the rules that may be applied and a breach of one of these rules may, on the facts of a case, render a trial unfair. The Court will examine the proceedings as a whole.[887] **11.214**

Illegally obtained evidence. The admission of illegally obtained evidence will not contravene Article 6[888] unless it was obtained by an abuse of police powers. Confessions and statements by the accused during investigation must be obtained in the presence of the accused's lawyer, or adequate trial procedures must be available to ensure that they have not been extracted under duress.[889] Thus, in *Khan v United Kingdom*[889a] the admission of evidence obtained by a secret listening device in breach of Article 8 did not of *itself* render the trial unfair since the domestic courts had the discretion to refuse to admit the evidence if it was unfair to do so under section 78 of the Police and Criminal Evidence Act. **11.215**

Agents provocateur.[890] The fact that evidence has been obtained by agent provocateurs will not, of itself, lead to its exclusion in a criminal trial. But the Court has made it clear that: **11.216**

> A distinction had to be drawn between cases where the undercover agent's actions created a criminal intent that had previously been absent and those in which the offender had already been predisposed to commit the offence.[891]

Thus, criminal proceedings will be unfair if the offence was wholly incited by

[885] (1996) 22 EHRR 293 para 61.
[886] Application 25277/94, 12 Oct 1999 para 76.
[887] *Miailhe v France (No 2)* (1996) 23 EHRR 491 para 43.
[888] *Schenk v Switzerland* (1988) 13 EHRR 242 (no breach where illegally obtained tape recording incriminating the accused admitted in evidence); *X v Germany* (1989) 11 EHRR 84, EComm HR (no breach where evidence of conversations overheard by undercover police officer in prison setting was admitted); *X v United Kingdom* (1976) 7 DR 115, EComm HR (admission of evidence of an accomplice who has been promised immunity is acceptable if the jury is aware of the circumstances).
[889] *G v United Kingdom* (1983) 35 DR 75, EComm HR (*voire dire* proceedings and burden on the prosecution to prove voluntariness of the statement were sufficient safeguards where accused had been questioned without his lawyer present).
[889a] *The Times*, 23 May 2000.
[890] See generally, O Davies, 'The Fruit of the Poisoned Tree — Entrapment and the Human Rights Act 1998' (1999) 163 JP 84; and see para 11.353 below.
[891] See *Teixeira de Castro v Portugal* (1998) 28 EHRR 101 para 32; Noted [1998] Crim LR 751.

agent provocateurs[892] rather than being detected by undercover agents.[893] The Court has made it clear that, while the rise in organised crime requires appropriate measures, 'the public interest cannot justify the use of evidence obtained as a result of police incitement'.[894]

11.217 *Cross-examination of witnesses.* In criminal trials witnesses must generally be made available for cross-examination by the accused regardless of the form in which their evidence originally comes before the court. For example, in *Unterpertinger v Austria*[895] family members who were allegedly assaulted by the applicant exercised their right under Austrian law not to give oral testimony, and the prosecution obtained a conviction of the accused 'mainly' on the basis of their sworn statements to the police. The Court found a breach of Article 6(1) as the right of the accused to a defence was 'appreciably restricted'. The decision was followed in *Kostovski v Netherlands*[896] where the conviction was 'to a decisive extent' based on the statements of two witnesses who failed to give evidence at trial and remained anonymous out of fear that their testimony would lead to reprisals by organised crime in which the accused had been involved. These cases suggest that an infringement of Article 6 will occur where the evidence of the missing witness is the 'main' or 'decisive' evidence before the Court. However, in *Asch v Austria*[897] the Court appeared to relax the general rule: holding that there would be no breach where the evidence is absolutely uncorroborated unless it is the 'only' piece of evidence on which the conviction was based. However, the defence must be given an 'adequate and proper opportunity to question a witness against him' at some stage of the proceedings.[898] Where there are potential threats to the life, liberty or security of witnesses, it is permissible for them to remain anonymous[899] and to give evidence from behind a screen.[900] The defence must be able to question the witness, in order to test his credibility and the reliability of the evidence.

11.218 **Right to a reasoned judgment.** A court must give reasons for its judgment so that any party with an interest in the case is informed of the basis of the decision,

---

[892] As in the *Teixeira de Castro* case (n 891 above)

[893] As in *Lüdi v Switzerland* (1992) 15 EHRR 173.

[894] *Teixeira de Castro* (n 891 above) para 36.

[895] (1986) 13 EHRR 175.

[896] *Kostovski v Netherlands* (1989) 12 EHRR 434; see also *Lüdi v Switzerland* (1992) 15 EHRR 173 (breach was found where the evidence was not the sole evidence, but had 'played a part in' the conviction).

[897] *Asch v Austria* (1991) 15 EHRR 597 (no breach was found where other corroborating evidence was present); see also *Artner v Austria* (1992) Series A No 242-A.

[898] *Asch v Austria* (n 897 above) para 27; it is difficult to reconcile this statement of principle with the decision in the case, see the dissenting opinions of Judges Sir Vincent Evans and Bernhardt, see also *Ferantelli and Santangelo v Italy* (1996) 23 EHRR 288 and see generally, O Harris, M O'Boyle and C Warbrick, *Law of the European Convention on Human Rights* (Butterworths, 1995) 212.

[899] *Doorsen v Netherlands* (1996) 22 EHRR 330 paras 68–71.

[900] See *X v United Kingdom* (1992) 15 EHRR CD 113.

so that the public in a democratic society may know the reasons for judicial decisions, and to enable the accused in a criminal trial to exercise the right of appeal available to him.[901] Courts in national jurisdictions are given a great deal of discretion as to the content and structure of their judgments, and a reasoned judgment does not have to deal with every argument raised[902] provided that it indicates the grounds on which the decision is based with 'sufficient clarity'.[903] However, if a point would be *decisive* for the case if accepted, it should be addressed specifically and expressly by the court.[904]

(d) A hearing within a reasonable time

This express right applies to both civil and criminal cases. In a civil case, time begins to run when proceedings are instituted.[905] If, prior to the commencement of proceedings, the applicant has sought to have a right determined by an administrative decision, any delays in such decision will be taken into account.[906] In criminal cases, time runs from the date on which the defendant is subject to a 'charge', which is the date when he is 'officially notified' or 'substantially affected' by proceedings.[907] This will usually be the date on which a person is charged with a criminal offence.[908] In a civil case, the time will stop running when the final appeal decision has been made or the time for appealing has expired.[909] In criminal cases, the period covers the whole of the proceedings, including any appeal[910] but not periods spent unlawfully at large.[911] **11.219**

The reasonableness of the length of proceedings must be assessed in each case taking into account all the circumstances including:[912] **11.220**

- *the complexity of the case*, including matters such as the number of witnesses,[913] the intervention of other parties[914] or the need to obtain expert evidence;[915]

901 *Hadjianastassiou v Greece* (1992) 16 EHRR 219 para 33.
902 *Van der Hurk v Netherlands* (1994) 18 EHRR 481, para 61.
903 *Hadjianastassiou v Greece* (n 901 above) para 33.
904 *Hiro Balani v Spain* (1994) 19 EHRR 565 para 28; and *Ruiz Torija v Spain* (1994) 19 EHRR 542 para 30.
905 *Scopelliti v Italy* (1993) 17 EHRR 493 para 18.
906 *Schouten and Meldrum v Netherlands* (1994) 19 EHRR 432 (delay in confirmation of a decision).
907 *Eckle v Germany* (1982) 5 EHRR 1 para 73.
908 Cf *Ewing v United Kingdom* (1986) 10 EHRR 141, Comm.
909 *Vocaturo v Italy* (1992) A 245-D.
910 *Eckle* (n 907 above) para 76.
911 *Girolami v Italy* (1991) Series A No 196-E.
912 See, for example *Yagci and Sargin v Turkey* (1995) 20 EHRR 505 paras 59–70 and see generally, P van Dijk and G van Hoof, *Theory and Practice of the European Convention on Human Rights* (3rd edn, Kluwer, 1998) 446–7; Harris, O'Boyle and Warbrick (n 898 above) 222ff.
913 *Andreucci v Italy* (1992) Series A No 228-G.
914 *Manieri v Italy* (1992) Series A No 229-D.
915 *Wemhoff v Germany* (1968) 1 EHRR 55.

- *The conduct of the applicant and the conduct of the judicial authorities.*[916] Although an accused person is not required to cooperate in criminal proceedings and is entitled to make full use of his remedies, delay resulting from such conduct is not attributable to the state.[917] Procedural rules that provide for the parties to take the initiative with regard to the progress of civil proceedings does not excuse the courts from ensuring compliance with the requirements of Article 6 in relation to time;[918]
- *The conduct of the relevant authorities,*[919] including matters such as delays in commencing proceedings[920] or in transferring proceedings.[921] The mere fact that the state does not comply with the time-limits which are laid down is not, in itself, contrary to Article 6.[922]

The fact that a defendant in a criminal case is detained in custody is a factor to be considered in assessing reasonableness.[923] The personal circumstances of an applicant in a civil case may be taken into account. Thus, claims for compensation by HIV infected haemophiliacs required 'exceptional diligence' on the part of the authorities.[924] Factors such as the workload of the court and a shortage of resources are not a sufficient justification for delays in a trial because Contracting States are under a duty 'to organise their legal systems so as to allow the courts to comply with the requirements of Article 6(1)'.[925] However, the state is not liable for delays resulting from a backlog caused by an exceptional situation when reasonably prompt remedial action has been taken.[926]

11.221 No general guidelines have been laid down for what constitutes a 'reasonable time' in either civil or criminal proceedings. It is submitted that the proper approach is to decide whether the overall delay is 'unreasonable' and then to consider whether the state is able to justify each period of delay.[927] In civil cases, violations on the grounds of delay have included the following periods of delay:

- four years for a personal injury case;[928]

[916] *Eckle* (n 907 above) para 80.
[917] *Eckle* (n 907 above) para 82.
[918] *Scopelliti v Italy* (1993) 17 EHRR 493 para 25; *Unión Alimentaria Sanders SA v Spain* (1989) 12 EHRR 24.
[919] *König v Germany* (1978) 2 EHRR 170.
[920] *Eckle v Germany* (1982) 5 EHRR 1.
[921] *Foti v Italy* (1982) 5 EHRR 313 para 61.
[922] *G v Italy* (1992) Series A No 228-F.
[923] *Abdoella v Netherlands* (1992) 20 EHRR 585.
[924] *X v France* (1992) 14 EHRR 483.
[925] *Zimmerman and Steiner v Switzerland* (1983) 6 EHRR 17 para 29; *Muti v Italy* (1994) Series A No 281-C para 15.
[926] *Buchholz v Germany* (1981) 3 EHRR 597 para 51.
[927] See Harris, O'Boyle and Warbrick (n 898 above) 229.
[928] *Guincho v Portugal* (1984) 7 EHRR 223.

- nearly nine years for a claim for unfair dismissal;[929]
- four years for the determination of a dispute about costs;[930]
- 14 years for compulsory purchase proceedings;[931]
- over six years for the determination of a dispute concerning the applicant's pension.[932]

In criminal cases, violations have included the following periods of delay:

- 16 years in complex proceedings;[933]
- five years for relatively simple proceedings.[934]

(e) Independent and impartial tribunal established by law

Introduction. The express right to a tribunal which is 'independent', 'impartial' and established by law applies to all types of case. A tribunal includes not only ordinary courts, but also disciplinary or other specialised tribunals that have a judicial function and otherwise meet the requirements of Article 6. Most importantly, a tribunal must be competent to take legally binding rather than merely recommendatory decisions.[935] The three requirements will be considered in turn. **11.222**

Independent. 'Independent' means 'independent of the executive and also of the parties'.[936] A court that takes instructions for the determination of the dispute from a member of the executive is not independent.[937] Neither can a decision-making member of the executive be an independent tribunal for the purposes of Article 6, even though the decision may be essentially judicial in nature.[938] **11.223**

In order to determine whether a tribunal can be considered to be independent regard must be had to factors such as the manner of appointment of members, their term of office, the existence of guarantees against outside pressures and whether the body presents an appearance of independence.[939] Questions as to appropriateness **11.224**

---

929 *Darnell v United Kingdom* (1993) 18 EHRR 205; see also *Obermeier v Austria* (1990) 13 EHRR 290 (claim arising out of a dismissal, nine years).

930 *Robins v United Kingdom* (1997) 26 EHRR 527.

931 *Guillemin v France* (1997) 25 EHRR 435.

932 *Ausiello v Italy* (1996) 24 EHRR 568.

933 *Ferrantelli and Santangelo v Italy* (1996) 23 EHRR 33; see also *Mitap and Müftüoglu v Turkey* (1996) 22 EHRR 209 (16 years in complex criminal proceedings).

934 *Philis v Greece (No 2)* (1997) 25 EHRR 417.

935 *Benthem v Netherlands* (1985) 8 EHRR 1 para 40; *Van der Hurk v Netherlands* (1994) 18 EHRR 481 para 45; other functions do not prevent a tribunal from exercising a judicial one: *Campbell and Fell v United Kingdom* (1984) 7 EHRR 165 para 81.

936 *Ringeisen v Austria (No 1)* (1971) 1 EHRR 455 para 95.

937 See *Beaumartin v France* (1994) 19 EHRR 485 para 38 (where a court accepted as binding Foreign Office advice as to the interpretation of a treaty for application in the case).

938 *Benthem v Netherlands* (1985) 8 EHRR 1 para 42.

939 See *Bryan v United Kingdom* (1995) 21 EHRR 342 para 37, Noted [1996] EHRLR 184.

of the manner of appointment or election of judges[940] and the criteria upon which appointments are made[941] have been decided both in terms of 'impartiality' and 'independence'. Judges' terms of office are not required to be fixed[942] or of any particular duration, although shorter appointments seem to be more acceptable for members of administrative or disciplinary tribunals[943] than for judges in ordinary courts.[944] A lengthy fixed term would assist with reduction of outside pressures on judges, but that has been accomplished instead by the requirement that tribunal members be protected from dismissal during their term of office, either in law or in practice.[945] Other guarantees against outside pressure include prevention of subjection to instructions from the executive,[946] scrutiny of the use of amnesty or pardon by the executive to guard against abuse that would undermine the judicial function,[947] and provision for secrecy of the tribunal's deliberations.[948] In *Campbell and Fell* the Court formulated an objective test for the 'appearance of independence':[949] were the applicants reasonsably entitled to think that the tribunal was dependent on the executive? On the basis of this test, the Board of Visitors was held to be independent in that case. However, in *Sramek v Austria*[950] and *Belilos v Switzerland* it was held that, applying this test, the tribunals were not 'independent'.[951]

[940] It is permissible and usual for judges to be appointed by the executive: *Campbell and Fell v United Kingdom* (1984) 7 EHRR 165, or elected by Parliament: *Crociani v Italy* (1981) 22 DR 147, EComm HR.

[941] Arrangements for appointment or substitution of judges in a particular case may be challengeable if there is an indication of improper motives of attempting to influence the outcome of the case: *Zand v Austria* (1978) 15 DR 70, EComm HR; *Crociani v Italy* (1981) 22 DR 147, EComm HR (appointment by reference to judges' political views); *Barberà, Messegué and Jabardo v Spain* (1988) 11 EHRR 360.

[942] *Engel v Netherlands (No1)* (1976) 1 EHRR 647.

[943] *Campbell and Fell v United Kingdom* (1984) 7 EHRR 165 (three-year term of Board of Visitors was acceptable given the difficulty of securing unpaid members for longer duration).

[944] Even in ordinary courts, judges are not necessarily appointed for life: *Zand v Austria* (1978) 15 DR 70, EComm HR.

[945] *Zand v Austria* (1978) 15 DR 70; see also *Campbell and Fell v United Kingdom* (n 943 above) in which the Court was satisfied that the irremovability of a Board of Visitors member during his term of office was recognised in fact, though not formally in law; and *Eccles, McPhillips and McShane v Ireland* (1988) 59 DR 212, EComm HR (the *Campbell* test was applied to judges on the Irish Special Criminal Court; although they could be dismissed at will and have their salaries reduced, the Commission found that in reality the executive was not attempting to undermine the functioning of the Court and that the ordinary courts had the power of review of its independence).

[946] *Sramek v Austria* (1984) 7 EHRR 351: requirement in law; *Campbell and Fell v United Kingdom* (1984) 7 EHRR 165: required only in practice; *The Greek Case* (1969) 12 YB 1, EComm HR: courts-martial found not to be independent because members were to exercise their discretion 'in accordance with the decisions of the Minister of National Defence'.

[947] *The Greek Case* (n 946 above).

[948] *Sutter v Switzerland* (1979) 16 DR 166.

[949] para 81; note that this is different from the objective test applied in relation to impartiality of a tribunal.

[950] (1984) 7 EHRR 351 (immediate superior to the civil servant member of a tribunal was representing the government party to the case).

[951] (1988) 10 EHRR 466 (a Police Board that convicted the accused of a minor criminal offence was composed of one member who was a lawyer from police headquarters and a municipal civil servant).

Impartial. For the purposes of Article 6(1), the existence of impartiality[952] must be determined according to two tests: 11.225

> a subjective test, that is on the basis of the personal conviction of a particular judge in a given case, and also according to an objective test, that is ascertaining whether the judge offered guarantees sufficient to exclude any legitimate doubt in this respect.[953]

In order to satisfy the subjective test, the applicant must show that the tribunal in fact had personal bias against him.[954] The objective test requires a finding, not of actual bias, but of 'legitimate doubt' as to impartiality that can be 'objectively justified'.[955] The accused's apprehensions are not decisive unless they are objectively justified.[955a] The higher objective standard is necessary to inspire the confidence of the public, and the criminally accused, in the courts and ensures that justice is not only done, but is seen to be done as what is at stake is 'the confidence which the courts in a democratic society must inspire in the public'.[956]

In criminal cases, a judge will not necessarily be partial because he has made pre- 11.226
trial decisions. It is necessary to consider the nature and the extent of such decisions.[957] There is likely to be a 'legitimate doubt' about impartiality where the judge's previous involvement in the case might have facilitated the formation of a considered opinion as to the guilt of the applicant. This is most likely to occur where the pre-trial decisions were made in the context of investigation or prosecution of the case,[958] whereas, in cases in which pre-trial involvement relates to the usual ancillary matters such as bail applications there will be no breach unless some special circumstances are established.[959] A court will not be partial because it hears cases involving different parties arising out of the same set of facts[960] or two different cases involving the same accused.[961] A financial interest in the case

---

952 That is, prejudice or bias, *Piersack v Belgium* (1982) 5 EHRR 169 para 30.

953 *Fey v Austria* (1993) 16 EHRR 387 para 28; see also *Pullar v United Kingdom* (1996) 22 EHRR 391 para 30.

954 The tribunal is presumed to be impartial until the contrary is proved, *Le Compte, Van Leuven and De Meyere v Belgium* (1981) 4 EHRR 1; *Albert and Le Compte v Belgium* (1983) 5 EHRR 533; *Debled v Belgium* (1994) 19 EHRR 506.

955 *Hauschildt v Denmark* (1989) 12 EHRR 266; *Gautrin v France* (1998) 28 EHRR 196; *Incal v Turkey* RJD 1998–IV 1547.

955a *Nortier v Netherlando* (1993) 17 EHRR 273 para 33.

956 *Ferrantelli and Santangelo v Italy* (1996) 23 EHRR 33 para 58.

957 *Fey v Austria* (1993) 16 EHRR 387 para 30.

958 *De Cubber v Belgium* (1984) 7 EHRR 236 (breach where a trial judge was previously an investigating judge on the case though in that role he had been quite independent of the prosecution).

959 See, eg *Sainte-Marie v France* (1992) 16 EHRR 116 (no special circumstances and no breach of Art 6 where two appeal judges who sentenced an accused convicted of weapons possession had earlier sat on the bench that refused his bail application in proceedings arising out of the same facts).

960 *Gillow v United Kingdom* (1986) 11 EHRR 335, EComm HR.

961 *Schmid v Austria* (1987) 54 DR 144; *Brown v United Kingdom* (1985) 8 EHRR 272 (one of the judges in the Court of Appeal Criminal Division had previously granted an injunction freezing the applicant's bank account).

will disqualify a judge, unless the interest is disclosed and no objection made by the applicant,[962] as will non-financial interests in some circumstances.[963] The objective test of impartiality has also been applied in the context of jury trials,[964] where links between members of the jury and the defendants may constitute a breach of impartiality, and to the rules for appointment of arbitrators in compulsory arbitration proceedings.[965]

11.227 There is an obligation on every court to check whether it is an 'impartial tribunal' in accordance with Article 6(1) where the point is raised. Thus, a violation was found when a court refused to investigate the accused's allegation that a juror had made a racist remark.[966]

11.228 There have been findings of violation of Article 6(1) due to failure to meet the objective test of impartiality in a large number of cases, including:

- where the prosecuting officer in a court-martial appointed the members of the court-martial and also had the responsibility of confirming the decision;[967]
- where the Secretary of State was entitled to revoke the power of a planning inspector to hear an appeal at any time;[968]
- where the Bailiff of Guernsey who had presided over the legislature when it had adopted a development plan had subsequently been president of the court which had refused the applicant's planning appeal;[968a]
- where the majority of members of a civil jury were active members of a political party which had close links with the defendant;[969]
- where a trial judge's decision dealt with an allegation of racial bias in a jury trying an Asian defendant by giving directions rather than discharging them;[969a]

[962] *D v Ireland* (1986) 51 DR 117, EComm HR.

[963] *Demicoli v Malta* (1991) 14 EHRR 47 (partiality where two members of the tribunal that tried the applicant for breach of parliamentary privilege were the Members of Parliament that had been criticised in the publication that was the subject of the alleged offence); *Langborger v Sweden* (1989) 12 EHRR 416 (breach where lay members of a tribunal adjudicating upon a tenancy agreement had been nominated by and had connections with associations holding partisan interests in the outcome).

[964] *Holm v Sweden* (1993) 18 EHRR 79; *X v Norway* (1970) 35 CD 37, EComm HR (challenges to jury successful and applications admissible).

[965] *Bramelid and Malmström v Sweden* (1983) 38 DR 18, EComm HR.

[966] *Remli v France* (1996) 22 EHRR 253 para 48; contrast *Gregory v United Kingdom* (1997) 25 EHRR 577 (no violation of Art 6 was found because the judge had considered an allegation of racism by a juror and given a clear direction to the jury to decide the case free of prejudice).

[967] *Findlay v United Kingdom* (1997) 24 EHRR 221, see para 11.296 below.

[968] *Bryan v United Kingdom* (1995) 21 EHRR 342 (there was no breach of Art 6(1) because of the availability of judicial review, see para 11.198 above.

[968a] *McGonnell v United Kingdom* (2000) 8 BHRC 56 (the case was decided on a narrow ground based on the Bailiff's actual involvement in the relevant legislative decision and the Court did not consider the broader issue as to whether it was appropriate for the Bailiff to have judicial, legislative and executive functions), see para 11–283 below.

[969] *Holm v Sweden* (1993) 18 EHRR 79.

[969a] *Sander v United Kingdom* Judgment of 9 May 2000; and see para 11.290 below.

- where a trial court judge was previously the head of the public prosecutor's department that investigated and instituted proceedings against the applicant, even though he had no personal knowledge of the investigation;[970]
- where the trial judge had decided, on a bail application, that there was a 'confirmed suspicion of guilt' against the defendant;[971]
- where a judge who had taken part in a decision quashing an order dismissing criminal proceedings subsequently sat in the hearing of an appeal against the applicant's conviction.[972]

A tribunal 'established by law'. The tribunal should be independent of the executive and should be regulated by law emanating from Parliament.[973] But parts of the judicial organisation may be delegated to the executive, provided that there are sufficient guarantees against arbitrariness.[974] Not only the establishment but also the organisation and functioning of the tribunal must have a basis in law.[975] **11.229**

(f) Right to a public hearing and the public pronouncement of judgment

Public hearing. The holding of court hearings in public is a fundamental principle enshrined in Article 6(1). The public character of hearings protects litigants against the administration of justice in secret without public scrutiny, and is also one of the means whereby confidence in the courts can be maintained.[976] It is implicit in the requirement of publicity that the hearing at the trial court level should be an oral one.[977] As the press plays an important role in publicising the hearing, Article 6(1) requires that it should not, as a general rule, be excluded,[978] but there is no positive obligation on the state to advertise the hearing or to otherwise extend an invitation to the media to attend.[979] **11.230**

However, Article 6(1) provides for a number of express restrictions on this right, allowing for the exclusion of the press and public 'in the interests of morals, public order or national security in a democratic society, where the interests of juveniles or the private life of the parties so require, or to the extent strictly necessary in the opinion of the court in special circumstances where publicity **11.231**

970 *Piersack v Belgium* (1982) 5 EHRR 169.
971 *Hauschildt v Denmark* (1989) 12 EHRR 266.
972 *Oberschlick v Austria (No 1)* (1991) 19 EHRR 389; see also *Castillo Algar v Spain* RJD 1988-VIII 3103 (violation when trial judges had previously sat in chamber hearing appeal against order of investigating judge).
973 *Zand v Austria* (1978) 15 DR 70, 80, EComm HR.
974 Ibid.
975 *Piersack v Belgium* (1986) B 47 23.
976 *Diennet v France* (1995) 21 EHRR 554 para 33.
977 *Fischer v Austria* (1995) 20 EHRR 349 para 44.
978 *Axen v Germany* (1983) 6 EHRR 195.
979 *X v United Kingdom* (1979) 2 Digest 444, EComm HR.

would prejudice the interests of justice'.[980] These provisions have not received detailed consideration in the case law.

11.232 The exclusion of the public has been permitted in cases involving sexual offences against children;[981] in divorce,[982] and medical[983] and prison[984] disciplinary proceedings for the 'protection of the parties'; and to ensure the safety of witnesses in appropriate situations.[985] It was not permitted for the sole purpose of reducing the Court's workload.[986] In relation to appeals there is no general right to a public hearing, even where the court has the jurisdiction to review the case on the facts as well as on the law.[987] The position is assessed on a case-by-case basis, with respect to the 'special features of the proceedings'[988] concerned.

11.233 Apart from the restrictions on a public hearing which are expressly permitted, a public trial will not be necessary if the accused has unequivocally waived the right in a situation in which there is no important public interest consideration which calls for the public to be present.[989] If there is a practice that hearings will not be held in public unless one of the parties expressly requests one, then a failure to make the application is deemed to be an unequivocal waiver.[990] In particular, the practice may be justified where the subject matter of the dispute does not raise issues of public importance, is highly technical and of a private nature.[991]

11.234 Public pronouncement of judgment. The right to public pronouncement of a judgment, unlike the publicity of the hearing, is not subject to any express restriction or principle of waiver under Article 6(1). It has been restricted only in the sense that the language 'pronounced publicly', which implies an oral presentation in open court, has been interpreted to permit the publication of judgments in

---

980 These reservations apply to administrative proceedings as well as civil and criminal cases, *Ringeisen v Austria (No 1)* (1971) 1 EHRR 455 para 98.

981 *X v Austria* (1965) 2 Digest 438, EComm HR (several grounds including 'interests of juveniles' could have applied).

982 *X v United Kingdom* (1977) 2 Digest 452, EComm HR.

983 *Guenoun v France* (1990) 66 DR 181, EComm HR.

984 *Campbell and Fell v United Kingdom* (1984) 7 EHRR 165 para 90.

985 *X v United Kingdom* (1980) 2 Digest 456, EComm HR; *X v Norway* (1970) 35 CD 37, EComm HR.

986 *Axen v Germany* (1983) 6 EHRR 195, EComm HR.

987 *Andersson v Sweden* (1991) 15 EHRR 218 para 27.

988 *Sutter v Switzerland* (1984) 6 EHRR 272.

989 *Håkansson and Sturesson v Sweden* (1990) 13 EHRR 1 para 66 (where the applicant failed to ask for a public hearing before a court which conducted itself in private unless it considered a public hearing to be 'necessary'); *Pauger v Austria* (1997) 25 EHRR 105 para 58; cf *H v Belgium* (1987) 10 EHRR 339 para 54 (no waiver to be implied from a failure to demand a public hearing when, as a matter of practice, the hearings were conducted in camera); and see generally, para 6.149 above.

990 *Zumtobel v Austria* (1993) 17 EHRR 116 para 34.

991 *Schuler-Zgraggen v Switzerland* (1993) 16 EHRR 405 para 58 (complaint concerning lack of oral hearing to determine invalidity benefit).

some proceedings by filing in the court registry.[992] The form of publicity to be given to the judgment is to be assessed in the light of the special features of the case and by reference to the object and purpose of Article 6(1).[993]

(4) Minimum standards of fairness in criminal proceedings

(a) Introduction

Articles 6(2) and 6(3) provide for specific rights in relation to criminal proceedings. These guarantees are specific aspects of the right to fair trial in Article 6(1).[994] These provisions must be read with those of Article 6(1). A criminal trial could be 'unfair' even if the minimum rights guaranteed by Article 6(3) are respected.[995] In addition, Article 6, read as a whole, guarantees the right of an accused to participate effectively in his trial.[995a] This right was violated when two ten-year-olds were tried for the murder of a young boy in a highly publicised trial in the Crown Court.[995b] It should be noted that the provisions of Article 6 do not, of themselves, create any right to compensation for miscarriage of justice.[996] **11.235**

(b) Presumption of innocence

Article 6(2) provides that a person 'charged with a criminal offence shall be presumed innocent until proved guilty according to law'. This applies to persons subject to a 'criminal charge', which has the same autonomous Convention meaning as it does under Article 6(1).[997] As a result, Article 6(2) is not relevant where a person is merely suspected of a crime, or detained for a purpose, such as extradition[998] or deportation[999] that does not involve criminal prosecution. It has not been applied to practices such as blood tests,[1000] medical examinations[1001] or production of documents.[1002] **11.236**

Article 6(2) requires: **11.237**

> that when carrying out their duties, the members of a court should not start with

[992] *Preto v Italy* (1983) 6 EHRR 182; *Axen v Germany* (1983) 6 EHRR 195 (Court of Appeal proceedings).
[993] *Preto v Italy* (n 992 above).
[994] *Edwards v United Kingdom* (1992) 15 EHRR 417 para 33.
[995] *Jespers v Belgium* (1981) 27 DR 61 para 54, EComm HR, cf, P van Dijk and G van Hoof, *Theory and Practice of the European Convention on Human Rights* (3rd edn, Kluwer, 1998) 463.
[995a] *Stanford v United Kingdom* (1994) A 282-A para 26; *T v United Kingdom* (2000) 7 BHRC 659.
[995b] *T v United Kingdom* (n 995a above) paras 97–98 (concurring opinion of Lord Reed).
[996] *Masson and Van Zon v Netherlands* (1995) 22 EHRR 491; this right is provided for in Protocol 7, Art 3 (not ratified by the United Kingdom); for the English law, see para 11.138 above.
[997] *Adolf v Austria* (1982) 4 EHRR 313 para 30; and see para 11.174 above.
[998] *X v Austria* (1963) 6 YB 484, EComm HR.
[999] *X v Netherlands* (1965) 8 YB 228, EComm HR.
[1000] *X v Netherlands* (1978) 16 DR 184, EComm HR.
[1001] *X v Germany* (1962) 5 YB 192, EComm HR.
[1002] *Funke v France* (1993) 16 EHRR 297.

> the preconceived idea that the accused has committed the offence charged; the burden of proof is on the prosecution and any doubt should benefit the accused.[1003]

This also implies that it is for the prosecution to inform the accused of the nature of the case against him.[1004] The presumption will be violated if a judicial decision concerning a person charged with a criminal offence reflects an opinion that he is guilty before he has been proved guilty.[1005] It is not necessary for there to be a formal finding if there is some reasoning suggesting that the Court regards the accused as guilty.[1006]

11.238 Article 6(2) does not prohibit presumptions of fact and law but the State must

> confine them within reasonable limits which take into account the importance of what is at stake and maintain the rights of the defence.[1007]

Thus, it has been held that the following do not violate Article 6(2):

- the requirement that a person charged with criminal libel prove the truth of the statement;[1008]
- the presumption that a person, having come through customs in possession of prohibited goods, had smuggled them;[1009]
- the presumption that a man living with a prostitute was knowingly living off immoral earnings;[1010]
- a presumption that a dog was a member of a specified breed;[1011]
- the burden on the accused to establish the defence of insanity.[1011a]

Furthermore, strict liability offences, which require no mens rea element, will not be a violation of Article 6(2).[1012] The presumption of innocence does not require that guilt be proved 'beyond a reasonable doubt': Article 6(2) simply requires evidence 'sufficiently strong in the eyes of the law to establish . . . guilt'.[1013]

1003 *Barberà Messegué and Jabardo v Spain* (1988) 11 EHRR 360 para 77; *Austria v Italy* (1963) 6 YB 740.

1004 Ibid.

1005 *Allenet de Ribemont v France* (1995) 20 EHRR 557 para 35.

1006 *Minelli v Switzerland* (1983) 5 EHRR 554 para 37 (acquitted defendant ordered to pay the costs on the basis that he would, 'very probably' have been convicted had he not had the advantage of a limitation defence).

1007 *Salabiaku v France* (1988) 13 EHRR 379 para 28.

1008 *Lingens and Leitgens v Austria* (1982) 4 EHRR 373, 290–291, EComm HR.

1009 *Salabiaku v France* (n 1007 above) para 30.

1010 *X v United Kingdom* (1972) 42 CD 135, EComm HR.

1011 *Bates v United Kingdom* [1996] EHRLR 312, EComm HR; (the presumption was held to be within reasonable limits because the accused had an opportunity to rebut it).

1011a *H v United Kingdom* Application 15023/89, 4 Apr 1990, contrast the position in Canada, see para 11.405A below.

1012 *Salabiaku v France* (n 1007 above).

1013 *Austria v Italy* (1963) 6 YB 740, EComm HR.

11.239 Other obligations with respect to evidence under Article 6(2) overlap with the general 'fair hearing' requirement of Article 6(1), as well as with Article 6(3)(d). The presumption of innocence means that the accused must be able to rebut evidence brought against him.[1014] Article 6(2) was not violated by: the admission of a statement made when the accused was not informed of his right to silence,[1015] disclosure of the accused's criminal record to the court prior to conviction,[1016] the arrest of a defence witness for perjury immediately after his testimony,[1017] re-trial of the accused by the court that heard his bail application,[1018] or procedure providing for a guilty plea.[1019]

11.240 Article 6(2) also protects the accused from prejudicial statements by public officials which disclose the view that the applicant is guilty before he has been tried and convicted. In *Krause v Switzerland*,[1020] the Swiss Minister of Justice stated on public television that the applicant, who had been held on remand pending trial for aircraft hijacking, had 'committed common law offences for which she must take responsibility', adding later that he did not know whether she would be convicted. In *Allenet de Ribemont v France*,[1021] a senior police officer, supported by other officials, stated at a press conference that the applicant, who had been arrested and hence 'charged ' under Article 6(2), was one of the 'instigators' of a murder. However, Article 6(2) does not preclude the authorities from providing factual information to the public about criminal investigations, as long as this does not amount to a declaration of guilt.[1022]

(c) Information as to the accusation (Article 6(3)(a))

11.241 Article 6(3)(a) provides that a person charged with a criminal offence be 'informed promptly, in a language which he understands and in detail, of the nature and cause of the accusation against him'. It is arguable that the guarantee will apply as soon as the accused is 'charged' in accordance with Article 6[1023] and is certainly applicable no later than at the point of indictment in a civil law system.[1024]

1014 *Albert and Le Compte v Belgium* (1983) 5 EHRR 533; *Schenk v Switzerland* (1988) 13 EHRR 242.
1015 *X v Germany* (1971) 38 CD 77, EComm HR.
1016 *X v Austria* (1966) 9 YB 550, EComm HR.
1017 *X v Germany* (1983) 5 EHRR 499, EComm HR.
1018 *X v Germany* (1966) 9 YB 484, EComm HR.
1019 *X v United Kingdom* (1972) 40 CD 69, EComm HR.
1020 *Krause v Switzerland* (1980) 13 DR 213.
1021 (1995) 20 EHRR 557.
1022 *Krause v Switzerland* (1978) 13 DR 73, EComm HR.
1023 D Harris, M O'Boyle and C Warbrick, *Law of the European Convention on Human Rights* (Butterworths, 1995) 250–251; the Commission expressly left the question open in *X v Netherlands* (1981) 27 DR 37, EComm HR.
1024 *Kamasinki v Austria* (1989) 13 EHRR 36; in *Brozicek v Italy* (1989) 12 EHRR 371, neither Commission nor Court made a clear finding that Art 6(3)(a) had to be complied with upon commencement of a preliminary investigation, but held, nevertheless, that judicial notification of the investigation complied with it.

Once an accused has been arrested, the exact point at which Article 6(3)(a) starts to run is less relevant because reasons will also be available to him under Article 5(2).[1025]

11.242 What needs to be communicated to the accused is the 'nature' of the accusation or offence with which he is charged and the 'cause' or relevant facts giving rise to the allegation. This will depend, in part, on what he can be taken to have learned during the investigation process and other circumstances of the case[1026] as well as what he might have gleaned had he taken advantage of existing opportunities to learn of the accusation before him.[1027] The words 'in detail'[1028] imply that the information to be provided under Article 6 is to be 'more specific and more detailed' than that which is provided under Article 5(2).[1029] However, it is not necessary that the accused even be informed as to the evidence on which the charge is based: it is sufficient for the accused to be informed of the offences with which he is charged together with the date and place of their alleged commission.[1030] There is no requirement that the information be provided in writing; Article 6(3)(a) will be complied with where the accused has been given sufficient communication orally. It must, however, be provided in a language understandable to either the accused or his lawyer,[1031] failing which the state must provide an appropriate translation[1032] of key documents or statements in order to meet the information requirements.

(d) Adequate time and facilities to prepare a defence (Article 6(3)(b))

11.243 Article 6(3)(b) provides that a person charged with a criminal offence shall be provided with adequate time and facilities for the preparation of his defence. The time element of this guarantee acts as a safeguard to protect the accused against a hasty trial.[1033] Like the other guarantees as to timeliness under the Convention, Article 6(3)(b) applies from the moment the accused is arrested or is otherwise substantially affected[1034] or when he is given notice of charges against him,[1035] and

[1025] See para 10.127ff above.

[1026] *Ofner v Austria* (1960) 3 YB 322.

[1027] *Campbell and Fell v United Kingdom* (1984) 7 EHRR 165: fact that a prisoner failed to attend a preliminary hearing was detrimental to his claim that he had not been adequately informed of the accusation against him.

[1028] Which are not present in Art 5(2).

[1029] *Nielsen v Denmark* (1959) 2 YB 412, EComm HR.

[1030] *Brozicek v Italy* (1989) 12 EHRR 371 para 42.; see also *X v Belgium* (1962) 5 YB 168 ('you are accused of corruption' was sufficient); and see *X v Belgium* (1977) 9 DR 169, EComm HR.

[1031] *X v Austria* (1975) 2 DR 68, EComm HR.

[1032] *Brozicek v Italy* (1989) 12 EHRR 371.

[1033] *Kröcher and Möller v Switzerland* (1981) 26 DR 24, EComm HR.

[1034] *X and Y v Austria* (1978) 15 DR 160, EComm HR.

[1035] *Campbell and Fell v United Kingdom* (1984) 7 EHRR 165.

the adequacy of the time allocation depends on all circumstances of the case.[1036] The right to adequate facilities means that the accused must have the opportunity to organise his defence appropriately, with the view to enabling him to put all relevant arguments before the trial court.[1037] The accused must be allowed to acquaint himself with the results of police or preliminary investigations in the case.[1038] The role of Article 6(3)(b) in this regard is to achieve equality of arms between the prosecution and the defence, a principle also considered an element of fairness under the general fair trial guarantee of Article 6(1).

The most important issue considered under this head is the right to communications with a lawyer. This is of particular significance to those persons in detention on remand pending trial. A prisoner must be allowed to receive a visit from his lawyer in private in order to convey instructions or to pass or receive confidential information relating to the preparation of his defence.[1039] Restrictions on lawyer's visits must be justified in public interests such as prevention of escape or prevention of the obstruction of justice. It may be permissible for a lawyer to be restricted from discussing with his client information about the case that would disclose the name of an informer.[1040] **11.244**

(e) Defence in person or through legal assistance (Article 6(3)(c))

Article 6(3)(c) provides that a person charged with a criminal offence is guaranteed the right to 'defend himself in person or through legal assistance of his own choosing or, if he has not sufficient means to pay for legal assistance, to be given it free when the interests of justice so require'. The purpose of the guarantee is to ensure adequate representation in the case, equality of arms to the accused and vigilance by the defence over procedural regularity on behalf of his client and of public interests generally. Its scope does not extend to proceedings concerning detention on remand, which are covered by Article 5(4),[1041] but otherwise applies at the pretrial stage,[1042] during trial[1043] and, subject to special considerations, to appeal proceedings[1044] following conviction. Although this provision does not expressly **11.245**

1036 Relevant factors include the complexity of the case: *Albert and Le Compte v Belgium* (1983) 5 EHRR 533; defence lawyer's workload: *X and Y v Austria* (1978) 15 DR 160, EComm HR; the stage of proceedings: *Huber v Austria* (1974) 46 CD 99; accused's representation of himself: *X v Austria* (1967) 22 CD 96, EComm HR.

1037 *Can v Austria* (1985) 8 EHRR 121; see also *Twalib v Greece* RJD 1998–IV 1415.

1038 *Kamasinski v Austria* (1989) 13 EHRR 36; *Kremzow v Austria* (1993) 17 EHRR 322; *Jespers v Belgium* (1981) 27 DR 61, EComm HR.

1039 *Campbell and Fell v United Kingdom* (1984) 7 EHRR 165; *Can v Austria* (1985) 8 EHRR 121.

1040 *Kurup v Denmark* (1985) 42 DR 287, EComm HR.

1041 *Woukam Moudefo v France* (1989) 51 DR 62.

1042 *S v Switzerland* (1991) 14 EHRR 670.

1043 *Quaranta v Switzerland* (1991) Series A No 205.

1044 *Monnell and Morris v United Kingdom* (1987) 10 EHRR 205; *Quaranta v Switzerland* (1991) Series A No 205.

guarantee the freedom to communicate with a defence lawyer 'without hindrance', it has been held that:

> an accused's right to communicate with his advocate out of the hearing of a third person is one of the basic requirements of a fair trial in a democratic society.[1045]

This is because, without confidentiality the lawyer's assistance would lose much of its usefulness, whereas the Convention is intended to guarantee rights which are practical and effective.

11.246 The right of everyone under Article 6(3)(c) to be effectively defended by a lawyer, assigned officially if need be, is one of the fundamental features of a fair trial.[1046] This provision does not provide an absolute right to choose between defending oneself and obtaining legal counsel but it does preclude a state from forcing a person to defend himself in person.[1047] The law of some states precludes the person charged from acting on his own behalf, requiring that a lawyer assist him with his defence at the trial stage[1048] or on appeal.[1049] This is not incompatible with Article 6(3)(c).

11.247 An accused person who lawfully chooses to defend himself in person waives his right to be represented by a lawyer,[1050] and, as a result, the state is entitled to expect that he will exhibit a degree of diligence, failing which the state will not be responsible for any resulting deficiencies in the proceedings.[1051] If the accused does not wish to defend himself in person he is entitled to legal representation by his own lawyer or, subject to certain conditions, by a legal aid lawyer.[1052] He cannot be deprived of the right to legal representation on grounds of his failure to appear in court,[1053] though a state may find such denial to be an effective means of discouraging the unjustified absence of the accused.[1054]

11.248 If an accused person chooses legal assistance, Article 6(3)(c) does not provide him with an absolute right to decide which particular lawyer will be appointed to act

[1045] *S v Switzerland* (1991) 14 EHRR 670 para 48.

[1046] *Poitrimol v France* (1993) 18 EHRR 130 para 34.

[1047] *Pakelli v Germany* (1983) 6 EHRR 1.

[1048] *Croissant v Germany* (1992) 16 EHRR 135.

[1049] *Philis v Greece* (1990) 66 DR 260, EComm HR.

[1050] *Melin v France* (1993) 17 EHRR 1.

[1051] Ibid.

[1052] *Poitrimol v France* (1993) 18 EHRR 130.

[1053] Art 6(3)(c) guarantees the accused's right to be present at the trial: *FCB v Italy* (1991) 14 EHRR 909; in *Campbell and Fell v United Kingdom* (1984) 7 EHRR 165 a rule generally denying legal representation before a prison disciplinary body was found to be a breach of Art 6(3)(c), quite apart from the fact that the accused had refused to appear; the absentia of the accused, even without excuse, will not justify depriving him of his right to be defended by counsel under Art 6(3)(c): *Lala v Netherlands* (1994) 18 EHRR 586.

[1054] Denial of legal assistance as a penalty or coercive tactic to ensure the appearance and arrest under warrant of an accused who has absconded after conviction is also an infringement of Art 6(3)(c), on the basis it is not proportionate: *Poitrimol v France* (1993) 18 EHRR 130.

as counsel in the case. The general rule is that the accused's choice of lawyer should be respected.[1055] However, this is not absolute and is subject to limitations where free legal aid is concerned and where the court appoints defence lawyers.[1056] The right is also subject to the regulatory powers of the state, by which it governs qualifications and standards of professional conduct of lawyers.[1057] It is permissible for states to restrict the number of lawyers the accused may appoint, as long as the presentation of the defence is not disadvantaged in relation to the prosecution.[1058]

The right to legal aid under Article 6(3)(c) is subject to two conditions: it will only be provided if the accused lacks 'sufficient means to pay' for the legal assistance and 'where the interests of justice so require'. There is no definition of 'sufficient means' in the Convention and no case law as to the factors to be taken into account in the means test to determine an award of legal aid: the onus is on the applicant to demonstrate at least 'some indications'[1059] that he lacks sufficient means to retain his own counsel. For example, the test was met where the applicant had spent two years in custody prior to the case, had delivered a statement of means upon which the Commission had awarded him legal aid to bring an application under another Article of the Convention, and had proposed to make a similar submission to the German Federal Court.[1060] An accused who is subsequently able to pay for the costs of the free legal assistance may then be required to do so.[1061] **11.249**

Whatever the means of the applicant, the state is not required to provide legal aid lawyers unless it is in the interests of justice to do so. The Court has made its own assessment on the facts.[1062] The test as to whether provision of legal aid is in the 'interests of justice' is not that the presentation of the defence must have sustained actual prejudice, but whether it appears 'plausible in the particular circumstances' that a lawyer would be of assistance on the facts[1063] of the case. The following circumstances are relevant: **11.250**

[1055] *Pakelli v United Kingdom* (1983) 6 EHRR 1; *Goddi v Italy* (1982) 6 EHRR 457.

[1056] *Croissant v Germany* (1992) 16 EHRR 135 para 29.

[1057] *Ensslin, Baader and Raspe v Germany* (1978) 14 DR 64, EComm HR (professional ethics); *X and Y Germany* (1972) 42 CD 139, EComm HR (refusal to wear gown); *X v United Kingdom* (1975) 2 Digest 831, EComm HR (lack of respect for the court); *K v Denmark* Application 19524/92, (1993) unreported (barrister appearing as a witness for the defence); *X v United Kingdom* (1978) 15 DR 242, EComm HR (personal interests involved in barrister son's representation of father).

[1058] *Ensslin, Baader and Raspe v. Germany* (n 1057 above).

[1059] It is not necessary that the lack of sufficient means be shown beyond a reasonable doubt: *Pakelli v Germany* (1983) 6 EHRR 1.

[1060] Ibid.

[1061] *Croissant v Germany* (1992) 16 EHRR 135.

[1062] *Quaranta v Switzerland* (1991) Series A No 205.

[1063] *Artico v Italy* (1980) 3 EHRR 1.

- the complexity of the case;[1064]
- the contribution that the particular accused could make if he defended himself;[1065]
- the seriousness of the offence with which the accused is charged and the potential sentence involved.[1066]

Where deprivation of liberty is at stake, 'the interests of justice in principle call for legal representation'.[1067] Where the effective exercise of a right of appeal under national law requires legal assistance, legal aid must be provided, no matter how slight the accused's chances of success.[1068]

11.251 The legal assistance guaranteed by Article 6(3)(c), whether chosen by the accused himself or provided through legal aid, must be effective. It must actually be delivered[1069] and counsel must be qualified to represent the accused at the particular stage of the proceedings for which the assistance is sought.[1070] If legal assistance is effective it may not have been provided by a qualified lawyer.[1071] A state 'cannot be held responsible for every shortcoming on the part of a lawyer appointed for legal aid purposes'[1072] and will not be obliged to intervene unless inadequacy in the representation is apparent or is sufficiently brought to its attention.[1073] There may be a breach of Article 6(3)(c) where defence lawyers are frequently changed,[1074] inadequate time is allowed for their preparation of the case,[1075] or where the accused is not represented at a hearing because of the failure of the state to notify the correct lawyer.[1076]

[1064] *Granger v United Kingdom* (1990) 12 EHRR 469; *Quaranta v Switzerland* (1991) Series A No 205; *Pham Hoang v France* (1992) Series A No 243.

[1065] *Granger v United Kingdom* (n 1064 above) para 47.

[1066] *Boner v United Kingdom* (1994) 19 EHRR 246; *Maxwell v United Kingdom* (1994) 19 EHRR 97. Where the potential sentence is imprisonment this factor alone may require that legal aid be granted.

[1067] *Quaranta* (n 1064 above) paras 32-38; *Benham v United Kingdom* (1996) 22 EHRR 293 para 61.

[1068] *Boner v United Kingdom* (1994) 19 EHRR 246.

[1069] In *Artico v Italy* (1980) 3 EHRR 1 (violation when the state nominated a lawyer to act for the applicant, but claiming other commitments and sickness, he never met with the accused and the Italian Court of Cassation refused to appoint another lawyer).

[1070] *Biondo v Italy* (1983) 64 DR 5, EComm HR.

[1071] *X v Germany* (1960) 3 YB 174, EComm HR (assistance from a probationary lawyer training in the West German criminal system was satisfactory).

[1072] *Kamasinski v Austria* (1989) 13 EHRR 36 para 65.

[1073] Ibid, *Artico v Italy* (1980) 3 EHRR 1; *Stanford v United Kingdom* (1994) Series A No 280-A; *Tripodi v Italy* (1994) 18 EHRR 295; *Daud v Portugal* RJD 1998-II 739; see also *Imbrioscia v Switzerland* (1993) 17 EHRR 441 para 41.

[1074] *Koplinger v Austria* (1966) 9 YB 240, EComm HR.

[1075] These have also been treated under Art 6(3)(b) (right to adequate facilities): see *X v United Kingdom* (1970) 32 CD 76, EComm HR; *Murphy v United Kingdom* (1972) 43 CD 1, EComm HR.

[1076] *Goddi v Italy* (1984) 6 EHRR 457.

(f) Examination of witnesses (Article 6(3)(d))

Article 6(3)(d) guarantees an accused person the right to examine witnesses for the prosecution and to call and examine witnesses on his behalf under the same conditions as witnesses against him.[1077] The right applies during trial and appeal proceedings, but not at the pre-trial stage.[1078] 'Witness' includes expert witnesses called by the prosecution or the defence[1079] as well as those persons whose statements are produced as evidence before a court even though they may not give oral evidence.[1080] **11.252**

Neither the right of the accused to cross-examine witnesses against him nor to call and examine his own witnesses is absolute; but limitations must not contravene the principle of equality of arms, which is the essential aim of Article 6(3)(d).[1081] Where witnesses against the accused are excused from giving oral testimony[1082] the accused must have the opportunity to confront the person providing the statement during the preceding investigation,[1083] although statements taken from witnesses abroad[1084] or evidence from foreign court proceedings against the accused[1085] are admissible. The court will consider the importance of hearsay evidence in the context of the proceedings as a whole.[1086] The exclusion of the accused himself may be permissible under Article 6(3)(d) to ensure a candid statement by the witness, if his lawyer is allowed to remain and conduct a cross-examination.[1087] **11.253**

The national courts have a wide discretion in the determination as to which defence witnesses are appropriate to be called,[1088] and in control over the accused's questioning of them.[1089] A court must give reasons for not summoning a defence witness expressly requested by the accused,[1090] and found that if properly called by the defence, a court must take all steps within its control[1091] to ensure that **11.254**

[1077] See also, para 11.217 above.

[1078] In particular an accused cannot examine a witness being questioned by the police: *X v Germany* (1979) 17 DR 231, EComm HR; or an investigating judge: *Ferraro-Bravo v Italy* (1984) 37 DR 15, EComm HR.

[1079] *Bönisch v Austria* (1985) 9 EHRR 191, EComm HR.

[1080] *Kostovski v Netherlands* (1989) 12 EHRR 434.

[1081] *Engel and others v Netherlands (No 1)* (1976) 1 EHRR 647 para 91; see also *Brandstetter v Austria* (1991) 15 EHRR 378 para 45.

[1082] For example, a police informer (cf *Kostovski v Netherlands* (1989) 12 EHRR 434).

[1083] See *Ferantelli and Santangelo v Italy* (1996) 23 EHRR 288; and see para 11.217 above.

[1084] *X v Germany* (1987) 10 EHRR 521, EComm HR.

[1085] *S v Germany* (1983) 39 DR 43, EComm HR.

[1086] See para 11.204 above; and cf the analysis of Art 6(3)(d) by the English courts, para 11.129 above.

[1087] *Kurup v Denmark* (1985) 42 DR 287, EComm HR.

[1088] *Vidal v Belgium* (1992) Series A No 235-B.

[1089] *Engel and others v Netherlands* (1976) 1 EHRR 647, 706.

[1090] *Bricmont v Belgium* (1989) 12 EHRR 217; *Vidal v Belgium* (1992) Series A No 235-E.

[1091] There is,however, no liability if a defence witness fails to appear for reasons beyond the court's control or at a time other than that requested by the accused, unless the presentation of the defence is affected.

witnesses appear.[1092] The state is not liable for the failure of defence counsel to call a particular witness.[1093]

(g) Assistance of an interpreter (Article 6(3)(e))

11.255 Article 6(3)(e) guarantees the right of a person charged with a criminal offence to have the free assistance of an interpreter if he cannot understand or speak the language used in court. The guarantee applies once the individual is 'charged' for the purposes of Article 6, and to the pre-trial,[1094] trial and appeal proceedings. The guarantee is intended to enable the accused to understand the language of the court, and does not entitle him to insist on the services of a translator to enable him to conduct his defence in his language of choice.[1095] Whether the accused is incapable of understanding the language is a determination of fact for the state to make, and the onus is on the accused to show the inaccuracy of its assessment.[1096] Article 6(3)(e) provides an unqualified 'exemption or exoneration'[1097] from any requirement on the part of the accused to pay the cost of providing the interpreter, whether or not his means would allow it, or he is ultimately convicted.[1098] The state must make free interpretation a part of criminal justice facilities so that the financial cost of an interpreter does not deter the accused from obtaining such assistance and thus prejudice the fairness of the trial.

11.256 The substance of the 'assistance' required by Article 6(3)(e) extends beyond provision of an interpreter at the hearing to include translations of 'all statements which it is necessary for him to understand in order to have a fair trial'.[1099] This will not require a written translation of every official document,[1100] but it implies that communications between the accused and his legal aid lawyer must be translated[1101] and that, where a lawyer (but not the accused) understands the language in which the hearing is conducted, that the accused be given a personal translation of the proceedings in order to enable him to properly instruct his lawyer.[1102]

1092 *X v Germany* Application 3566/68 (1969) 31 CD 31; *X v Germany* Application 4078/69 (1970) 35 CD 125.

1093 *F v United Kingdom* (1992) 15 EHRR CD 32.

1094 Police questioning prior to a 'charge' is not covered by Article 6(3)(e), but following the charge an accused is entitled to an interpreter during questioning or preliminary investigations prior to trial: *Kamasinski v Austria* (1989) 13 EHRR 36.

1095 *K v France* (1983) 35 DR 203; *Bideault v France* (1986) 48 DR 232, EComm HR.

1096 *X v Germany* (1967) 24 CD 50; *X v United Kingdom* (1978) 2 Digest 916.

1097 *Luedicke, Belkacem and Koç v Germany* (1978) 2 EHRR 149 para 40.

1098 See also in *Öztürk v Germany* (1984) 6 EHRR 409.

1099 *Kamasinski v Austria* (1989) 13 EHRR 36 para 74.

1100 This may depend on the amount of oral information as to its contents given to the accused; see *Kamasinski v Austria* (n 1099 above), where failure to translate either indictment or judgment was a breach.

1101 If the accused appoints his own lawyer he must choose one that can communicate with him if such a lawyer is available: *X v Germany* (1983) 6 EHRR 353, EComm HR.

1102 The Court in *Kamasinski v Austria* (1989) 13 EHRR 36 did not clearly rule on the point, but considered the arguments of the accused as to interpretation at trial, even though his English-speaking lawyer was in attendance.

(5) The provisions of Article 7

(a) Introduction

Article 7 establishes the right to freedom from retroactive penal provisions. More generally, it embodies: **11.257**

> the principle that only the law can define a crime and prescribe a penalty (*nullum crimen, nulla poena sine lege)* and the principle that the criminal law must not be extensively construed to an accused's detriment, for instance by analogy.[1103]

It follows that:

> an offence must be clearly defined in law. This condition is satisfied where the individual can know from the wording of the relevant provision and, if need be, with the assistance of the court's interpretation of it, what acts and omissions will make him liable.[1104]

In this context, 'law' includes judge made law as well as statute law.[1105] Article 7 does not prohibit a second trial for the same offence.[1106]

The Article applies to convictions for criminal offences and to penalties. Both terms have 'autonomous meanings' under the Convention.[1107] The word 'criminal' in Article 7 must have the same meaning as in Article 6.[1108] In assessing whether or not there has been a 'penalty' it is necessary to consider whether the measure in question is imposed following conviction for a criminal offence, the nature and purpose of the measure, its characterisation under national law, the procedures involved in its making and implementation and its severity.[1109] However, Article 7 does not apply to 'preventive measures',[1110] deportation orders[1111] or to matters of extradition law.[1112] The Convention does not prevent the retrospective application of the criminal law in the accused's favour[1113] and does not guarantee that the accused has the benefit of changes in the law between the offence and trial.[1114] **11.258**

1103 *S W and C R v United Kingdom* (1995) 21 EHRR 363 para 35-33; *Kokkinakis v Greece* (1993) 17 EHRR 397 para 52 and see generally, P van Dijk and G van Hoof, *Theory and Practice of the European Convention on Human Rights* (3rd edn, Kluwer, 1998) 480ff.
1104 *Kokkinakis v Greece* (n 1103, above) para 52.
1105 *X Ltd and Y v United Kingdom* (1982) 28 DR 77, 80–81, EComm HR.
1106 This is dealt with by Art 4 of Protocol 7 (not ratified by the United Kingdom).
1107 As to 'penalty', see *Jamil v France* (1995) 21 EHRR 65 para 30.
1108 See para 11.174ff above; and see *Brown v United Kingdom* (1998) 28 EHRR 233.
1109 *Welch v United Kingdom* (1995) 20 EHRR 247 paras 27–28.
1110 *Lawless v Ireland (No 1)* (1960) 1 EHRR 1.
1111 *Moustaquim v Belgium* (1991) 13 EHRR 802 para 34.
1112 *X v Netherlands* (1976) 6 DR 184, 186, EComm HR.
1113 *Kokkinakis v Greece* (1993) 17 EHRR 397; *G v France* (1995) 21 EHRR 288.
1114 *X v Germany* (1978) 13 DR 70, EComm HR.

(b) Retrospective offences

11.259 It is clear that any legislation which criminalises conduct which, at the time it was committed was lawful, will be in breach of Article 7. Examples of such legislation are extremely rare.[1115] The same approach applies to legislation which seeks to impose 'retrospective penalties'. Thus, in *Welch v UK*[1116] a confiscation order made under the Drug Trafficking Offences Act 1986 in respect of offences before the Act came into force was held to constitute a 'retrospective penalty' in breach of Article 7.

(c) Interpretation of criminal law

11.260 Article 7 requires that the interpretation of the law must operate so as to conform with the principle of reasonable certainty. This means that:

> constituent elements of an offence such as, e.g. the particular form of culpability required for its completion may not be essentially changed at least not to the detriment of the accused, by the case law of the courts.[1117]

However, this does not prevent the clarification or adaptation of the existing law. Thus, in the case of *S W & C R v UK*[1118] it was held that the removal of the 'marital rape exemption by the House of Lords[1119] did not amount to a retrospective criminalisation of conduct as it was foreseeable continuation of a line of case law. The 'gradual clarification' of common law offences was consistent with Article 7. Similarly, a conviction for 'unnatural indecency' under Austrian law which involved an 'extensive interpretation' of the statutory provision was not a breach of Article 7 because this interpretation was generally accepted at the time that the acts were committed.[1120]

11.261 The criminal law must be sufficiently accessible and precise to enable an individual to know in advance whether his conduct is criminal[1121] but the fact that legal advice is necessary to elucidate the precise scope of the offence does not necessarily mean that it is not 'reasonably certain' for the purposes of Article 7.[1122] The crucial point is that an offence must be clearly defined in law[1123] so that an individual can know from the wording of the relevant provision (and, if need be, with the

[1115] For an example under EC law, the European Court of Justice applied the same principle embodied in Art 7, see *R v Kirk* [1984] ECR 2689.

[1116] (1995) 20 EHRR 247; but see *Taylor v United Kingdom* [1998] EHRLR 90, EComm HR (no breach of Art 7 when 1994 order made in respect of drug trafficking going back to 1974 because the applicant was aware of the possibility that such an order could be made at the time of conviction).

[1117] *X Ltd and Y v United Kingdom* (1982) 28 DR 77, para 9, EComm HR.

[1118] (1995) 21 EHRR 363, see para 11.299 below.

[1119] See para 11.148 above.

[1120] *X v Austria* (1970) 13 YB 798 (mutual masturbation), EComm HR.

[1121] *G v France* (1995) 21 EHRR 288, 295 Com Rep para 32.

[1122] See *Cantoni v France*, RJD 1996–V 1614.

[1123] *Kokkinakis v Greece* (1993) 17 EHRR 397 para 52.

assistance of the court's interpretation of it), what acts and omissions will make him liable.

(d) Impact of international law

Article 7(1) makes express reference to acts or omissions which constitute criminal offences under international law. The provisions of the Article have no application to such offences. Although the point has not been explored in the case law it is possible that this refers only to breaches of the laws of war and crimes against humanity.[1124] However, it is arguable that a wider range of offences is contemplated, namely those over which states have adopted jurisdiction to try non-nationals.[1125] Such crimes include torture, piracy, hijacking and drug trafficking.[1126] **11.262**

(e) The exception in Article 7(2)

Article 7(2) provides that the Article shall not prejudice the trial and punishment of any person **11.263**

> for any act or omission which, at the time when it was committed, was criminal according to the general principles of law recognised by civilised nations.

The purpose of this exception appears to be to allow the retrospective application of national and international 'war crimes' legislation.[1127] It is arguably inconsistent with Article 15(2) which provides that there shall be no derogation from Article 7 in times of war.[1128]

The words 'the general principles of law recognised by civilised nations' are taken from Article 38 of the Statute of the International Court of Justice.[1129] The nature of conduct which is 'criminal according to the general principles of law recognised by civilised nations' is not clear. It appears to cover the offences described in the Charter of the International Military Tribunal annexed to the Agreement for the Prosecution and Punishment of the Major War Criminals of the European Axis:[1130] that is 'crimes against peace', 'war crimes', and 'crimes against humanity'. It has also been suggested that the words will also cover criminal violations of human rights outside the 'war crimes' context.[1131] **11.264**

[1124] See I Brownlie, *Principles of Public International Law* (5th edn, Oxford University Press), 308 and 565ff.

[1125] D Harris, M O'Boyle and C Warbrick, *Law of the European Convention on Human Rights* (Butterworths, 1995) 277.

[1126] Ibid. see also, Brownlie, (n 1124 above) 307–308; and cf *Rv Bow Street Stipendiary Magistrate, ex p Pinochet Ugarte (No 3)* [1999] 2 WLR 672.

[1127] *X v Belgium* (1961) 4 YB 324, EComm HR.

[1128] See para 6.92ff above; see generally, van Dijk and van Hoof (n 1103 above) 487.

[1129] Art 38.1(c); see generally, Brownlie (n 1124 above) 15ff.

[1130] 8 Aug 1945, 39 AJ (1945), Suppl, 258; see generally, Brownlie, (n 1124 above) 565ff.

[1131] See van Dijk and van Hoof (n 1103 above) 488.

D. The Impact of the Human Rights Act

(1) Introduction

11.265 The Human Rights Act will give further impetus to the increasing focus of the English courts on 'fair trial rights'. Article 6 has already been the subject of detailed discussion in a number of criminal cases.[1132] Its impact on the practice of the criminal courts is likely to be considerable. The complex and frequently changing rules of criminal procedure and sentencing will be subject to re-assessment in the light of Convention 'fair trial' principles. Although it seems unlikely that many criminal statutes will be found to be incompatible with Article 6, the approach of the criminal courts will change in a number of areas.[1133]

11.266 The likely impact of Article 6 on civil cases is less clear. The rules governing civil procedure in the English courts have recently undergone their most substantial overhaul for over a century. Following the Woolf Report on *Access to Justice*, the new Civil Procedure Rules were drafted with Article 6 in mind. Nevertheless, the drive to efficient case management which lies behind many of the new rules does, potentially, generate conflict with Article 6 in a number of areas.[1134]

11.267 The field of regulatory and disciplinary regulation is likely to be a more fertile source of Article 6 challenges. Regulators and disciplinary bodies are of increasing importance, particularly in the area of financial services. At present hearings are often in private without a full range of procedural safeguards. Regulatory and disciplinary bodies will usually be 'functional public authorities' under section 6 of the Human Rights Act.[1135] The many and varied procedural rules of regulatory bodies and disciplinary tribunals are likely to require substantial revision to ensure Article 6 compliance.[1136]

11.268 In addition, there are a number of other areas of substantive law in which English law may be in conflict with the Convention. Articles 6 and 7 are likely to have an impact in the fields of commercial law, education law, employment and discrimination, family, immigration, local government law, planning and environment, police law, prison law and social security law. These are discussed in section (4) below.

[1132] See para 11.93 above.
[1133] See para 11.338ff below.
[1134] See para 11.313ff below.
[1135] See para 5.16ff above.
[1136] See para 11.330ff below.

(2) United Kingdom cases prior to the Human Rights Act

(a) Introduction

More United Kingdom applications to Strasbourg have been based on Article 6 than on any other provision of the Convention. United Kingdom Article 6 complaints have been substantively considered by the Court on more than 60 occasions. This is partly a consequence of the central importance of 'fair trial rights' in the Convention, and partly the result of the failure of public authorities to give proper weight to such rights. The Court has found the United Kingdom to be in violation of Article 6 on 26 occasions[1137] and in violation of Article 7 on one occasion.[1138] The United Kingdom has entered into one friendly settlement on the basis of undertakings to take steps to rectify a breach of Article 6.[1138a] However, a large number of areas of criminal and civil procedure have survived scrutiny by the Commission and the Court. Many of the United Kingdom applications which have been made under Article 6 fall into four general categories: rights of access to the courts, the conduct of civil proceedings, the conduct of criminal proceedings and the rights of prisoners. **11.269**

(b) Access to the courts

One of the most important decisions of the Court concerning access was made in the early United Kingdom prisoner case of *Golder.*[1139] The applicant was a prisoner who wished to bring defamation proceedings against a prison officer but was refused permission to consult a solicitor. The Court held that Article 6 contained an implied right of access to the courts[1140] which had been violated by this refusal.[1141] A violation was found in *Silver v United Kingdom*[1142] on similar facts. **11.270**

[1137] *Golder v United Kingdom* (1975) 1 EHRR 524; *Silver v United Kingdom* (1983) 5 EHRR 347; *Campbell and Fell v United Kingdom* (1984) 7 EHRR 165; *W, B, O, B and H v United Kingdom* (1987) 10 EHRR 29; *Granger v United Kingdom* (1990) 12 EHRR 469 (Scotland); *Darnell v United Kingdom* (1993) 18 EHRR 205; *Boner v United Kingdom* (1994) 19 EHRR 246 (Scotland); *Maxwell v United Kingdom* (1994) 19 EHRR 97 (Scotland); *McMichael v United Kingdom* (1995) 20 EHRR 205; *Benham v United Kingdom* (1996) 22 EHRR 293; *Murray v United Kingdom* (1996) 22 EHRR 29 (Northern Ireland); *Saunders v United Kingdom* (1996) 23 EHRR 313; *Findlay v United Kingdom* (1997) 24 EHRR 221; *Robins v United Kingdom* (1997) 26 EHRR 527; *Coyne v United Kingdom* RJD 1997–V 1842; *Tinnelly and Sons and McElduff v United Kingdom* (1998) 4 BHRC 393 (Northern Ireland); *Osman v United Kingdom* (1998) 5 BHRC 293; *Hood v United Kingdom* (2000) 29 EHRR 365; *Cable v United Kingdom, The Times*, 11 Mar 1999; *Scarth v United Kingdom*, 22 Jul 1999; *T and V v United Kingdom* (2000) 7 BHRC 659; *McGonnell v United Kingdom* (2000) 8 BHRC 56; *Rowe and Davis v United Kingdom, The Times*, 1 Mar 2000; *Condron, The Times*, 9 May 2000; *Magee v United Kingdom, The Times*, 20 Jun 2000, *Averill v United Kingdom, The Times*, 20 Jun 2000.

[1138] *Welch v United Kingdom* (1995) 20 EHRR 247.

[1138a] *Faulkner v United Kingdom, The Times*, 11 Jan 2000.

[1139] (1975) 1 EHRR 524.

[1140] Ibid paras 35-36; see para 11.185 above.

[1141] See also the Commission decisions in *Kiss v United Kingdom* (1977) 19 EHRR CD 17 and *Hilton v United Kingdom* (1978) 3 EHRR 104.

[1142] (1983) 5 EHRR 347.

11.271 However, Article 6 only provides a right of access in relation to the 'determination' of civil rights and obligations and criminal charges. In a number of cases it has been decided that proceedings of a 'preparatory' or 'investigatory' nature are not subject to Article 6 because no 'determination' is involved. The most important case on this point is *Fayed v United Kingdom*[1143] in which the applicants complained that they had been criticised in a report by DTI inspectors[1144] and that, as a result, their reputations had been damaged. As they could make no effective challenge to the conclusions of the report under English law, they contended that they had been denied effective access to the courts. The Court held that the functions of the inspectors was essentially 'investigative'[1145] and were not 'determinative' of any civil right. The Court went on to hold that the defence of absolute or qualified privilege which was available to DTI Inspectors was in pursuit of a legitimate aim and was proportionate.[1146]

11.272 A number of other types of decision have been held not to involve 'determination' of civil rights and obligations. These include:

- decisions as to the classification of prisoners;[1147]
- deportation decisions;[1148]
- decisions in relation to the right to elementary education;[1149]
- applications for interim relief;[1150]
- orders requiring a person to give evidence;[1151]
- decisions by the Secretary of State as to whether someone was a 'fit and proper person' to conduct insurance business;[1152]
- a decision refusing leave to appeal to the House of Lords.[1153]

11.273 The question as to whether care proceedings are within Article 6 has been considered by the Court in several UK cases. In the linked cases of *W, R, O, B and H v United Kingdom*[1154] the applicants made various complaints about care proceedings which restricted their rights of access to their children. It was held that was a

---

1143 (1994) 18 EHRR 393.
1144 Under Companies Act 1985, s 432(2).
1145 Referring to the analysis of the functions of the US Federal Civil Rights Commission in *Hannah v Larche* (1960) 363 US 420; see *Golder* (n 1139 above) para 61.
1146 See also, *Tee v United Kingdom* (1996) 21 EHRR CD 108 (investigation by LAUTRO did not involve 'determination' of a civil right).
1147 *Brady v United Kingdom* (1981) 3 EHRR 297.
1148 *Uppal v United Kingdom (No 1)* (1979) 3 EHRR 391, EComm HR.
1149 *Simpson v United Kingdom* Application 14688/89, (1989) 64 DR 188, EComm HR.
1150 *X v United Kingdom* (1981) 24 DR 57, EComm HR.
1151 *British Broadcasting Corporation v United Kingdom* (1996) 21 EHRR CD 93 (witness summons re video material).
1152 Because this did not involve the determination of any 'dispute'. *Kaplan v United Kingdom* (1980) 4 EHRR 64.
1153 *Porter v United Kingdom* (1987) 54 DR 207, EComm HR.
1154 (1987) 10 EHRR 29.

dispute between the applicant and local authority which concerned the 'civil' right of access. Article 6(1) did not require that all access decisions had to be taken to the courts but only that they should have power to determine any substantial disputes that arose. Applications for judicial review or the institution of wardship proceedings enabled the courts to examine local authorities' decisions concerning access. However, the Court held that there was

> no possibility of a 'determination' in accordance with the requirements of Article 6(1) of the parent's right in regard to access . . . unless he or she can have the local authority's decision reviewed by a tribunal having jurisdiction to examine the merits of the matter.[1155]

The powers of the English courts did not satisfy this requirement and, as a result, there was a violation of Article 6(1). Furthermore, proceedings for access to a child in care which took two years seven months were not concluded within a reasonable time and, as a result, there was a further violation of Article 6(1).[1156] In *McMichael v United Kingdom*[1157] the applicants complained about the procedures at a 'children's hearing' the purpose of which was to consider care orders. The Court accepted that:

> in this sensitive domain of family law there may be good reasons for opting for an adjudicatory body that does not have the composition or procedures of a court of law of the classic kind.[1158]

Nevertheless, the right to fair trial meant the opportunity to have knowledge of and comment on the observations of the other party and the lack of disclosure of such vital documents as social reports meant there had not been a fair hearing.

Proceedings to challenge a planning enforcement notice involve the determination of 'civil rights'.[1159] Because the Secretary of State could revoke the power of the planning Inspector to hear an appeal, the Inspector was not an 'independent and impartial tribunal'. However, since the Inspector was subject to a statutory appeal on a point of law[1160] there was, in the circumstances, no violation of Article 6. It was important that there were no disputes about the primary facts or the factual inferences drawn by the Inspector. **11.274**

The access of a litigant to the courts can be restricted in many different ways. One possibility is the granting of 'immunity' to particular categories of litigants. This has been considered in a number of cases. In *Ashingdane v United Kingdom*[1161] the **11.275**

1155 *W v United Kingdom* (1987) 10 EHRR 29 para 82.
1156 *H v United Kingdom* (1987) A 120, 10 EHRR 95.
1157 (1995) 20 EHRR 205.
1158 Ibid para 80.
1159 *Bryan v United Kingdom* (1995) 21 EHRR 342.
1160 Under the Town and Country Planning Act 1990, s 289.
1161 (1985) 7 EHRR 528.

applicant was a mental patient who complained, inter alia, that he was unable to challenge the lawfulness of a refusal to transfer him from a secure hospital. He had brought an action which had been stayed, the Secretary of State successfully invoking the 'statutory immunity' under the Mental Health Act 1959.[1162]Under this provision, an action could only be brought if there was an allegation of bad faith or want of reasonable care. It was held that there was no violation of Article 6 because the immunity 'did not impair the very essence of Mr Ashingdane's "right to a court" or transgress the principle of proportionality'.[1163]

11.276 The case of *Osman v United Kingdom*[1164] concerned police immunity for actions in negligence arising out of the 'investigation and suppression of crime'.[1165] The Court rejected the government's argument that Article 6 was of no application[1166] and held that the negligence immunity for police acts and omissions during the investigation and suppression of crime amounted to an unjustifiable restriction on an applicant's right to have a determination on the merits of his or her claim. Other applications are pending in relation to public authorities' immunities from actions and the Commission has ruled admissible a complaint concerning negligence of a local authority in taking a child into care .[1167]

11.277 The Commission have held that the imposition of such requirements on 'vexatious litigants'[1168] and bankrupts[1169] is not a breach of Article 6. The requirement of a two-year qualifying period before an employee can bring a claim for unfair dismissal is not a breach of Article 6(1) because it serves a legitimate aim.[1170] The effect of limitation periods on access to the courts was considered in *Stubbings v United Kingdom.*[1171] The applicants' claims for damages for alleged sex abuse in childhood were statute barred under English law and they claimed that they had been denied access to the court under Article 6. The Court pointed out that the right to access to the court was not absolute and that limitation periods in personal

---

[1162] s 141; see now Mental Health Act 1983, s 139(1); see para 11.47 above.

[1163] n 1161 above para 59.

[1164] (1998) 5 BHRC 293; the English decision was *Osman v Ferguson* [1993] 4 All ER 344.

[1165] See para 11.42 above.

[1166] See para 11.195 above.

[1167] *T P and K M v United Kingdom* Application 28945/95, 26 May 1998, EComm HR (admissibility); 10 Sep1999 (merits) the application is the claim against Newham which was struck out in *X (Minors) v Bedfordshire County Council* [1995] 2 AC 633.

[1168] *H v United Kingdom* (1985) 45 DR 281, EComm HR.

[1169] *M v United Kingdom* (1987) 52 DR 269, EComm HR.

[1170] *Stedman v United Kingdom* (1997) 23 EHRR CD 168.

[1171] (1996) 23 EHRR 213; the English decision was *Stubbings v Webb* [1993] AC 498; see generally, E Palmer, 'Limitation Periods in Cases of Sexual Abuse: A Response Under the European Convention' [1996] EHRLR 111; see also *I B v United Kingdom* [1996] EHRLR 524 and *Dobie v United Kingdom* [1997] EHRLR 166.

injury cases were a common feature of the legal systems of Contracting States.[1172] Limitation periods served important purposes and the periods applied were not unduly short. As a result, the very essence of the applicants' right of access were not impaired and the restrictions pursued a legitimate aim and were proportionate. There was, therefore, no violation of Article 6.[1173]

In *Tolstoy Miloslavsky v United Kingdom*[1174] one of the applicant's complaints was that his right of access to the court had been violated by a requirement that he provide substantial security for the costs of an appeal against a jury verdict in a libel action. The Court accepted that, the fundamental guarantees of Article 6 did apply to an appeal system but that the whole of the proceedings had to be considered. It was held that the security for costs order pursued the legitimate aim of protecting the plaintiff in the libel action from an irrecoverable bill for costs and was not disproportionate.[1175] **11.278**

(c) The conduct of civil proceedings

The case of *Robins v United Kingdom*[1176] involved a dispute as to costs following a civil action between neighbours over a question of sewerage. The costs proceedings, although separately decided, were to be seen as a continuation of the substantive litigation, to which Article 6 undoubtedly applied. The Court found that four years from the date of judgment to the final appeal was an unreasonable length of time for the resolution of a relatively straightforward dispute over costs. While state authorities could not be held responsible for all of the delays, periods of 10 months and 16 months in which the courts were totally inactive warranted the finding of breach. **11.279**

In *Darnell v United Kingdom*[1177] the applicant had been dismissed from his health authority post in 1984 after disciplinary proceedings. After a successful judicial review application, the Secretary of State reconsidered his decision and, in 1988 affirmed it. In 1990 the Industrial Tribunal dismissed the applicant's claim for unfair dismissal. His appeal against that decision was dismissed in 1993. It was accepted by the Government that there had been a violation of Article 6(1) because the applicant's civil rights and obligations had not been determined within a reasonable time. **11.280**

Article 6 does not provide for any right to legal aid for civil proceedings and cases may be selected for legal aid on merit with financial contributions being **11.281**

[1172] Ibid paras 48–49.
[1173] Ibid paras 53–55.
[1174] (1995) 20 EHRR 442; see generally, para 15.228 above.
[1175] Ibid paras 61–67.
[1176] (1997) 26 EHRR 527.
[1177] (1993) 18 EHRR 205.

required.[1178] The blanket exclusion of legal aid in defamation cases is not a breach.[1179] However, the Commission has found that the lack of a civil legal aid system in Guernsey was a violation of the right of access to the courts.[1180] A friendly settlement was reached on the Government's undertakings to introduce such a system.[1180a]

11.282 The Commission has found that hearings in private are permissible if they are interlocutory[1181] or if they are renewable in open court.[1182] However, in *Scarth v United Kingdom*[1183] the Court held that the denial of a public hearing in a county court arbitration case was a breach of Article 6(1).[1184]

11.283 The case of *McGonnell v United Kingdom*[1185] involved a challenge to the legal system of Guernsey, where the Royal Court is presided over by the Bailiff, who is also the President of the State of Deliberation (the legislature) and of four States Committees (which are part of the executive). The applicant's challenge to a planning decision had been refused by the Royal Court on the basis that it was consistent with the relevant development plan. The Commission[1185a] found that there was a violation of Article 6 as it was incompatible with the requisite appearances of independence and impartiality for a judge to have substantial legislative and executive functions. It was suggested by some commentators that this could have significant repercussions for the position of the Lord Chancellor. However, the Court found a violation on a narrower basis, namely that the Bailiff had presided over the legislature when the relevant development plan had been adopted.[1185b] This narrower ground for decision left open the question as to whether the Lord Chancellor's combination of legislative, executive and judicial roles is incompatible with Article 6.

(d) The conduct of criminal proceedings

11.284 Many UK applications have dealt with the rights of defendants in criminal proceedings. The first issue to be considered is whether the proceedings are 'criminal'

[1178] *X v United Kingdom* (1980) 21 DR 95, 101, EComm HR; see also *Stewart-Brady v United Kingdom* (1997) 24 EHRR CD 38 and *Thaw v United Kingdom* (1996) 22 EHRR CD 100.
[1179] *Winer v United Kingdom* (1986) 48 DR 154, EComm HR; *Munro v United Kingdom* (1987) 52 DR 158, EComm HR; *S and M v United Kingdom* (1993) 18 EHRR CD 172 (the 'McLibel' case).
[1180] *Faulkner v United Kingdom* Application 30308/96, 30 Nov1996, EComm HR.
[1180a] *Faulkner v United Kingdom, The Times* 11 Jan 2000.
[1181] *X v United Kingdom* (1969) 30 CD 70, EComm HR.
[1182] Cf *Monnell and Morris v United Kingdom* (1987) 10 EHRR 205 (application for leave to appeal in criminal cases).
[1183] Application 33745/96, 22 Jul 1999.
[1184] The point had been conceded by the UK Government, see ibid para 24; the hearing would now be held in public under the CPR, see para 11.80 above.
[1185] (2000) 8 BHRC 56.
[1185a] [1999] EHRLR 335, see para 61 of the full decision.
[1185b] Ibid para 57 and see the concurring opinion of Sir John Laws.

in nature, bearing in mind the 'autonomous' Convention meaning of this term.[1186] In *Benham v United Kingdom*[1187] the applicant was imprisoned by magistrates for non-payment of community charge. He complained, *inter alia*, that full legal aid was not available to him for the committal hearing. The Court found that there was a breach of Article 6(1) and 6(3)(c) taken together because:

> where a deprivation of liberty is at stake, the interests of justice in principle call for legal representation.[1188]

In *Perks v United Kingdom*[1189] the applicants were also imprisoned for non-payment of community charge. The Court again decided that the refusal to give the applicants legal aid breached Article 6. The Court said that:

> Having regard to the severity of the penalty risked by the applicants and the complexity of the applicable law, the interests of justice demanded that, in order to receive a fair hearing, the applicants ought to have benefited from free legal representation before the magistrates.[1189a]

The case of *Air Canada v United Kingdom*[1190] was the other side of the line. This involved the seizure of an aircraft by the Customs as liable to forfeiture because a consignment of drugs had been found on board. The Court held that, although there was, in effect, a fine, the proceedings were not criminal in nature as the criminal courts were not involved and there was no threat of criminal proceedings.[1191]There was a dispute about civil rights but Article 6 was satisfied because the Customs had to take 'condemnation proceedings' before forfeiting the aircraft. It has been held that the following do not constitute 'criminal charges' for the purposes of Article 6: **11.285**

- misconduct proceedings before the Solicitors Disciplinary Tribunal;[1191a]
- company directors disqualification proceedings;[1191b]
- proceedings before the General Medical Council involving allegations of indecent behaviour towards a patient.[1191c]

The 'right to silence' of criminal defendants has given rise to several applications. **11.286**

[1186] See para 11.174ff above.
[1187] (1996) 22 EHRR 293.
[1188] At para 61.
[1189] Application 25277/94, 12 Oct 1999.
[1189a] Ibid para 76.
[1190] (1995) 20 EHRR 150; the English decision was *Customs and Excise Commissioners v Air Canada* [1991] 2 QB 446, CA.
[1191] Ibid paras 50–55.
[1191a] *Brown v United Kingdom* (1998) 28 EHRR CD 233.
[1191b] *D C, H S and A D v United Kingdom* Application 39031/97, 14 Sep 1999 (admissibility decision).
[1191c] *Wickramsinghe v United Kingdom* [1998] EHRLR 338.

The applicant in *Murray v United Kingdom*[1192] had been arrested under the Prevention of Terrorism Act and denied legal advice for 48 hours. He had been tried in Northern Ireland under provisions which allowed the judge to draw adverse inferences from his silence. The Court accepted that, despite the fact that they were not specifically mentioned in Article 6:

> there can be no doubt that the right to remain silent under police questioning and the privilege against self-incrimination are generally recognised international standards which lie at the heart of the notion of fair procedure under Article 6.[1193]

However, it was held that the right to silence was not absolute and, as a result it could not be said that:

> an accused's decision to remain silent throughout criminal proceedings should necessarily have no implications when the trial court seeks to evaluate the evidence against him.[1194]

The question as to whether the drawing of adverse inferences from silence infringes Article 6 was a matter to be determined in all the circumstances in each case. On the facts of the case, there had been no breach. However, because such inferences could be drawn, the concept of fairness enshrined in Article 6 required that the accused had the benefit of a lawyer at the initial stages of police interrogation.[1195] As a result, there had been a breach of Article 6(1) in conjunction with 6(3)(c). Breaches of these provisions were also found in the caes of *Averill v United Kingdom*[1195a] and *Magee v United Kingdom*.[1195b]

11.287 The Commission reached a similar view in *Quinn v United Kingdom*[1196] in which the applicant had been convicted of attempted murder and possession of firearms on the basis of forensic evidence, hearsay evidence and inferences drawn from silence in the absence of a solicitor. The Commission concluded that:

> the forensic evidence relating to gunpowder traces and linking him to the car used in the offence could be regarded, on a common sense basis, as a situation attracting considerable suspicion and reasonably allowing inferences to be drawn in light of the nature and extent of any explanations provided by the applicant. The inference drawn from the applicant's silence was thus only one of the elements upon which the judge found the charge proven beyond reasonable doubt. The Commission

[1192] (1996) 22 EHRR 29; see R Munday, 'Inferences from Silence and European Human Rights Law' [1996] Crim L Rev 370.

[1193] Ibid para 45.

[1194] Ibid para 47.

[1195] Ibid para 66.

[1195a] *The Times*, 20 Jun 2000 (denial of access to a solicitor fo the first 24 hours of questioning).

[1195b] *The Times*, 20 Jun 2000 (denial of access to a solicitor for 48 hours).

[1196] 17 Dec 1997 (Merits) see also (1996) 23 EHRR CD 41, the original case was *Rv Dermot Quinn* (1993) 10 NIJB 70; see also *Hamill v United Kingdom* (Merits) Application 22656/93, 2 Dec 1997 and *Murray v United Kingdom* Application 22384/93, 2 Dec 1997—no violation in relation to adverse inferences on admissibility hearing.

> considers that by taking this element into account the judge did not go beyond the limits of fairness in his appreciation of the evidence in the case.[1197]

In *Condron v United Kingdom*[1197a] the applicants had remained silent on the advice of their solicitor who believed, contrary to the view of the police doctor, that they were not fit to be interviewed. The Court accepted that it was proper to draw adverse inferences from their silence in this situation and to waive privilege on the advice given. There was, however, a breach of Article 6 as a result of an inadequate direction by the trial judge:

> the jury should have been directed that if it was satisfied that the applicants' silence at the police interview could not sensibly be attributed to their having no answer or none that would stand up to cross-examination it should not draw an adverse inference.[1197b]

The Court also expressed concern that the Court of Appeal (Criminal Division) made its decision on the basis of the 'safety' of the applicants' conviction rather than considering whether they received a fair trial:

> the question whether or not the rights of the defence guaranteed to an accused under Article 6 of the Convention were secured in any given case cannot be assimilated to a finding that his conviction was safe in the absence of any enquiry into the issue of fairness.[1197c]

11.288 In the well-known case of *Saunders v United Kingdom*[1198] the applicant complained that he was denied a fair hearing because of the use made at his criminal trial of statements obtained by DTI Inspectors under statutory powers of compulsion.[1199] The trial judge and the Court of Appeal had held these statements were admissible[1200] The issue was whether the use of the statements was an unjustifiable infringement of the right to silence which lay at the heart of 'fair procedure' under Article 6.[1201] The Court rejected the Government's argument that the vital public interest in the prosecution of corporate fraud could justify departure from the principles of fair procedure. It concluded that there had been an infringement of the right of a person not to incriminate himself.[1202]

11.289 The burden of proof in criminal proceedings must, in general, rest on the prosecution. Nevertheless, this does not prevent the law from relying on 'presumptions'.

1197 n 1196 above para 63; there was no violation in relation to the admission of hearsay evidence but there was in relation to lack of access to a solicitor.

1197a *The Times*, 9 May 2000; see *Averill v United Kingdom, The Times*, 20 Jun 2000 (permisible to draw adverse inferences from silence despite the absence of legal advice).

1197b *Condron v United Kingdom* (n 1197a above) para 61.

1197c Ibid para 65.

1198 (1996) 23 EHRR 313.

1199 Under Companies Act 1985, s 432; see generally, para 11.103 above.

1200 *R v Seelig* [1992] 1 WLR 148.

1201 *Saunders* (n 1198 above) para 68.

1202 But see the dissenting judgment of Judges Martens and Kuris.

Thus, the presumptions of fact in the Dangerous Dogs Act 1991 do not breach Article 6.[1203]

11.290 Complaints of 'jury bias' have been unsuccessful in most cases. In *Pullar v United Kingdom*[1204] the applicant complained that the jury trial was unfair because an employee of a key prosecution witness had been a member of the jury. The Court of Appeal had relied on the witness's written statement as to the juror's impartiality. The question was whether or not the jury could be regarded as an 'independent and impartial tribunal' under Article 6(1). The Court held that:

> it does not necessarily follow from the fact that a member of a tribunal has some personal knowledge of one of the witnesses in a case that he will be prejudiced in favour of that person's testimony.[1205]

As a result, it was held that the applicant's misgivings about the impartiality of the jury could not be regarded as being 'objectively justified'. In *Gregory v United Kingdom*[1206] the applicant, who was black, was being tried on an offence of robbery when, after the jury had retired, they handed a note to the judge saying that 'Jury are showing racial overtones'. After consultation with counsel, the judge decided not to discharge the jury but directed them to put thoughts of prejudice out of their minds. It appeared that defence counsel had agreed to this course. The Court found that there was no violation of Article 6.[1207] By contrast, in *Sander v United Kingdom*[1207a] a complaint of bias was upheld in a case involving an Asian defendant. A juror handed up a note anonymously indicating that another juror had made racist jokes; and he was then separated from the other jurors. The judge declined to discharge the jury but recalled them to ask whether they felt able to try the case. The next day the judge received two letters: one from all the jurors rejecting the allegation of bias and another from the juror who had made the jokes, saying that he was sorry that he had given offence and denying that he was racially biased. The judge again declined to discharge the jury but gave them a further direction. The Court took the view that the disclosure of the identity of the juror who had made the complaint had prejudiced his position; and that the admission by a juror that he had made racist jokes should have alerted the judge to the fact that there was something fundamentally wrong with the jury. The Court therefore held the jury should have been discharged on grounds of bias.

11.291 The Commission and Court have also considered complaints concerning the non-disclosure of evidence to defendants in criminal trials. In *Edwards v United*

[1203] *Bates v United Kingdom* [1996] EHRLR 312, EComm HR.
[1204] (1996) 22 EHRR 391 (a Scottish case).
[1205] Ibid para 38.
[1206] (1997) 25 EHRR 577.
[1207] See also, *Hardiman v United Kingdom* [1996] EHRLR 425.
[1207a] Judgment of 9 May 2000.

Kingdom[1208] the applicant complained that evidence which had not been disclosed by the prosecution in the course of his trial rendered the trial unfair. The Court said that its task is to ascertain whether the proceedings in their entirety were fair.[1209] It held that the defects of the original trial were remedied by the subsequent procedure before the Court of Appeal and that, as a result, there had been no breach of Article 6.

Where it is claimed that the material which is not disclosed is subject to 'public interest immunity', the prosecution must make an application to the trial judge, if necessary, without notice.[1210] In *Jasper and Fitt v United Kingdom*[1211] the Court accepted that, in some cases it might be necessary to withhold certain evidence from the defence so as to preserve the fundamental rights of another individual or to safeguard an important public interest. Only such measures restricting the rights of the defence that were strictly necessary were permissible. The Court held that, where the defence had been told of the application for non-disclosure and had been able to outline its position, there was no breach of Article 6(1). However, in *Rowe and Davis v United Kingdom*[1212] the Court held that the failure of the prosecution to make an application to the trial judge to withhold material was a breach of Article 6. The fact that the material had been subsequently reviewed by the Court of Appeal was not sufficient to remedy the unfairness caused at the trial by the absence of any scrutiny of the withheld material by the trial judge.[1213] **11.292**

The reception by a court of the evidence of an accomplice with immunity from prosecution will not be a breach of Article 6.[1214]

In the cases of *T and V v United Kingdom*[1215] the applicants were 10-year-old boys who were convicted of murdering a young boy; they were sentenced to detention at Her Majesty's pleasure. The Court found that there had been violations of Article 6 in respect of the trial because, bearing in mind their age, the application of the full rigours of an adult trial denied them the opportunity to participate effectively in the proceedings. Furthermore, the role of the Home Secretary in fixing the periods for which the applicants should be detained was a breach of Article 6(1). This was because the fixing of the tariff amounted to a sentencing exercise and the Home Secretary was clearly not an 'independent tribunal'. **11.293**

The availability of legal aid in criminal appeals has been considered in several cases **11.294**

1208 (1992) 15 EHRR 417.
1209 Ibid, paras 33–34.
1210 See para 11.98 above.
1211 *The Times*, 1 Mar 2000.
1212 *The Times*, 1 Mar 2000.
1213 Ibid para 79.
1214 See also *X v United Kingdom* (1976) 7 DR 115, EComm HR.
1215 See *T v United Kingdom* [2000] 7 BHRC 659 for the English case, see *R v Secretary of State for the Home Department, ex p Venables* [1998] AC 407.

from Scotland. In *Granger v United Kingdom*[1216] the applicant was refused legal aid in an appeal against his conviction for perjury. The Court held that it would have been in the interests of justice for free legal assistance to have been given to the applicant. As a result, there was a violation of Article 6(3)(c). The same point arose in *Boner v United Kingdom*[1217] and *Maxwell v United Kingdom*[1218] in which the Court followed *Granger* and held that there had been a violation of Article 6.

11.295 The protection of Article 6 continues to apply until the charge is finally determined or discontinuance of the proceedings occurs before trial.[1219] In *Monnell and Morris v United Kingdom*[1220] the applicants had unsuccessfully applied for leave to appeal against conviction and sentence. In dismissing these applications in their absence, the Court of Appeal directed that part of the time spent in custody should not count towards their sentences. The Court accepted the applicants' contention that Article 6 applied to such an application but held that there had been no violation. Article 6 also applies to the referral of a case to the Court of Appeal by the Home Secretary many years after conviction.[1221]

11.296 Over recent years, the Court has considered several cases arising out of the operation of the Court Martial procedure in the armed forces.[1222] In *Findlay v United Kingdom*[1223] the Court had to consider whether the court martial was independent and impartial. The convening officer decided which charges should be brought, convened the court martial and appointed its members and the prosecuting and defending officers. The members of the court martial were subordinate in rank to the convening officer and fell within his chain of command.[1224] In these circumstances, the applicant's doubts about the independence and impartiality of the tribunal could be objectively justified and there was a violation of Article 6(1). The Court followed this case and found violations of Article 6 in relation to court-martial proceedings in the cases of *Coyne v United Kingdom*,[1225] *Hood v United Kingdom*[1226] and *Cable v United Kingdom*.[1227]

11.297 The costs orders made at the conclusion of criminal proceedings have been

---

1216 (1990) 12 EHRR 469.
1217 (1994) 19 EHRR 246.
1218 (1994) 19 EHRR 97.
1219 *Orchin v United Kingdom* (1983) 6 EHRR 391.
1220 (1987) 10 EHRR 205.
1221 *Callaghan v United Kingdom* (1989) 60 DR 296, EComm HR, the referral would now be by the Criminal Cases Review Commission.
1222 See para 11.228 above, the cases concern the former procedure under the Army Act 1955.
1223 (1997) 24 EHRR 221.
1224 Ibid paras 74–76.
1225 RJD 1997–V 1842.
1226 *The Times*, 11 Mar 1999.
1227 *The Times*, 11 Mar1999.

challenged. A violation was found by the Commission in two cases in which the judge refused to allow the defendant's costs for a failed prosecution and made comments implying guilt.[1228] However, there was no violation where the judge refused costs on the basis that the applicant had been greedy and brought the case on himself, as this did not imply guilt.[1229]

(e) Rights of prisoners

In *Campbell and Fell v United Kingdom*[1230] the applicants were prisoners who had been subjected to disciplinary proceedings by the Board of Visitors resulting in the loss of remission and of privileges. Both sought permission to consult a lawyer but, when this was finally granted, consultations had to take place in the presence of a prison officer. It was held that, in the light of the character of the offences, the proceedings before the Board of Visitors were subject to Article 6. The Board of Visitors were an independent and impartial tribunal.[1231] The hearings could proceed in private, because **11.298**

> To require that disciplinary proceedings concerning convicted prisoners should be held in public would impose a disproportionate burden on the authorities of the State.[1232]

However, there was a breach of Article 6 because the decision had not been made public[1233] and legal assistance and representation had been refused.[1234] Furthermore, the delay in allowing the applicants to take legal advice was a denial of access to justice. Finally, the condition that legal consultation had to be in the presence of a prison officer was a breach of Article 6(1).[1235]

(f) Other applications

The applicants in the joined cases of *S W v United Kingdom* and *C R v United Kingdom*[1236]complained that they had been convicted of rape of their spouses as a result of a change in the law removing the 'marital rape exemption'. The Court held that this was the foreseeable continuation of a line of case law. Furthermore, it was held that: **11.299**

> The essentially debasing character of rape is so manifest that the result . . . that the applicant could be convicted of attempted rape irrespective of his relationship with

[1228] *Moody v United Kingdom* Application 22613/93, 16 Jan 1996; *Lochrie v United Kingdom* Application 22614/93, 18 Jan 1996.
[1229] *D F v United Kingdom* Application 22401/93, 24 Oct 1995.
[1230] (1984) 7 EHRR 165.
[1231] Ibid paras 77– 85.
[1232] Ibid para 87.
[1233] Ibid para 89–92.
[1234] Ibid paras 97–99.
[1235] Ibid paras 111–113.
[1236] (1995) 21 EHRR 363; see C Osborne, 'Does the End Justify the Means? Retrospectivity, Article 7 and the Marital Rape Exemption' [1996] EHRLR 406.

> the victim—cannot be said to be at variance with the object and purpose of Article 7 of the Convention, namely to ensure that no-one should be subjected to arbitrary prosecution, conviction or punishment.[1237]

No breach of Article 7 was established in relation to the reporting provisions of the Sex Offenders Act 1997 which required the applicant to inform the police of any change of name or address.[1238] The Commission rejected the argument that this involved a 'retrospective penalty' on the ground that the measure was preventative and operated independently of the ordinary sentencing process.

11.300 The Court did, however, find a violation of Article 7 in the case of *Welch v United Kingdom*[1239] This case concerned a confiscation order made under the Drug Trafficking Offences Act 1986. These provisions came into force in 1987 and an order was made against the applicant when he was convicted in 1988 of offences committed in 1986. The Court took the view that the order was a 'penalty' within the meaning of Article 7 and that, looking at the realities of the situation

> the applicant faced more far-reaching detriment as a result of the order than that to which he was exposed at the time of the commission of the offences from which he was convicted.[1240]

11.301 In *Tinnelly and Sons and McElduff v United Kingdom*[1241] the applicants were contractors who had been refused contracts in Northern Ireland on the ground that their employees were security risks. Complaints of discrimination made under the Fair Employment (Northern Ireland) Act 1976 were met by a ministerial certificate which, by section 43 were conclusive evidence that the contracts had been refused 'for the purpose of safeguarding national security'. The Court observed that:

> The right guaranteed to an applicant under Article 6 §1 of the Convention to submit a dispute to a court or tribunal in order to have a determination of questions of both fact and law cannot be displaced by the *ipse dixit* of the executive.[1242]

There was no proportionality between the protection of national security and the impact which the ministerial certificates had and they constituted a disproportionate restriction on the applicants' right of access to the court. It was pointed out

1237 n 1235 above para 44/42.

1238 *Ibbotson v United Kingdom* [1999] EHRLR 218, 21 Oct 1998; see also *Adamson v United Kingdom* Application 42293/98, 26 Jan 1999.

1239 (1995) EHRR 247; for criticism of this decision see D Thomas, 'Incorporating the European Convention on Human Rights its Impact on Sentencing Laws', in J Beatson, C Forsyth and I Hare (eds), *The Human Rights Act and the Criminal Justice and Regulatory Process* (Hart Publishing, 1999) 84–85.

1240 Ibid para 34.

1241 (1998) 27 EHRR 249.

1242 Ibid para 77.

that it was possible to modify judicial procedures in such a way as to safeguard national security concerns while still according the individual 'a substantial degree of procedural justice'.[1243]

A number of cases have established breaches of the Convention in the context of European Community law. In *Johnston v Chief Constable of the Royal Ulster Constabulary*[1244] the European Court of Justice took Articles 6 and 13 of the Convention into account in determining that the applicant did not have an effective remedy in pursuing a claim for sex discrimination. The relevant legislation provided for a certificate of 'conclusive evidence' which, in effect, excluded the exercise of a power of review by the courts. In *R v Kent Kirk*[1245] it was held a Council Regulation validating the UK ban on Danish vessels fishing within a 12-mile limit could not have retrospective effect. **11.302**

(3) General impact issues

(a) Introduction

Article 6 expressly confers fair hearing rights in broad and unqualified terms. In addition, the Court has recognised an 'implied right' of access to the courts and a series of other 'implied' fair trial rights (such as 'equality of arms' and the right to an adversarial hearing). It has taken the view that implied Article 6 rights can only be restricted in furtherance of a legitimate aim and where the measures taken are necessary for the achievement of this aim and are proportionate. Special additional rights are conferred on those facing 'criminal charges'. There are, therefore, five questions to be asked when considering whether a public body has violated Article 6: **11.303**

- Is the body engaged in a determination of 'civil rights and obligations' or a 'criminal charge'?
- In the case of a 'criminal charge', has there been any breach of the 'minimum guarantees' in Article 6(2) and 6(3)?
- Has there been an infringement of the express rights to an independent and impartial tribunal, a hearing within a reasonable time, a public hearing and public pronouncement of judgment?
- Has there been an apparent infringement of the applicable implied 'fair trial' rights? if so, was this infringement for a legitimate aim, necessary and proportionate?
- Has the applicant waived the right in question?[1245a]

[1243] Ibid para 78.
[1244] [1987] QB 129.
[1245] [1985] 1 All ER 453.
[1245a] See generally, para 6.148ff above.

In relation to the first question, it is clear that any court dealing with a private law or criminal case will be engaged in such a determination.[1246] In relation to other tribunals or decision-makers, the answer to the first question may not be clear cut although the only decisions likely to be excluded are those relating to purely 'administrative' entitlements.[1247]

11.304 There is one general point which arises concerning the impact of Article 6 on administrative decision-makers. Frequently, a public authority cannot show that its internal procedures are 'independent' because (for example, councillors decide entitlements to council benefits). It is submitted that in such circumstances a public authority under the Human Rights Act[1248] will not be acting *incompatibly* with Article 6 under section 6 of the Act[1249] *even though* a decision-maker himself does not meet the guarantees required by Article 6(1) in some respects: *provided* that decision maker is subject to a body exercising judicial control which has full jurisdiction and does provide the guarantees of Article 6(1).[1250] The position has certain parallels with the question of whether an appeal can cure an unfair procedure as a matter of general administrative law;[1251] and reflects the general approach taken when Article 6 is considered before the Court of Human Rights.[1251a] An alternative view is that the public authority has breached the Article 6 obligation placed on it; but it would not be 'just and appropriate' under section 8 of the Human Rights Act to grant relief.[1251b] It would be surprising if relief was granted against a public authority for breach of Article 6 where the complaint was satisfied by a court hearing itself; and where no breach would be found had the case been heard before the Court of Human Rights.

11.304A However, where a public authority relies on a subsequent court hearing to argue that it has acted compatibly with Article 6, the position under the Human Rights Act will depend on:

[1246] Although, as a result of the 'autonomous meaning' of 'criminal charge', the boundaries will not necessarily be in the same place in English law as they are under the Convention, see para 11.174 above.

[1247] Such as claims in relation to education or housing, see para 11.173 above.

[1248] See generally, para 5.03ff above.

[1249] It will be unlawful for a public authority to act in a way which is not compatible with Convention rights; see, generally, para 5.120ff above.

[1250] *Albert and Le Compte v Belgium* (1983) 5 EHRR 533, para 29; *Bryan v United Kingdom* (1995) 21 EHRR 342 para 40; this only applies to decisions of an administrative or disciplinary nature, not to ordinary civil and criminal cases: see *De Cubber v Belgium* (1984) 7 EHRR 236, para 32.

[1251] See para 11.71 above.

[1251a] See para 11.197ff above.

[1251b] See para 21.01ff below.

- the extent to which the decision-maker has himself satisfied the relevant Article 6 rights;[1252] and
- whether the applicant has been given a sufficient opportunity fairly to put his case where the primary facts are at issue.[1253]

The approach taken in Convention law to Article 6(1) and rights of appeal was considered in *Stefan v General Medical Council*[1254] where Lord Clyde identified the principle as being whether the existence of a right of appeal would enable the requirement of fairness embodied in Article 6(1) to be met.

In particular, difficulties may arise where administrative decisions are subject to judicial review or appeals confined to questions of law. Where the important issues of fact are disputed, it may be argued that the applicant has not been given a proper opportunity to contest them.[1255] It may also be said that because the *Wednesbury* test[1256] is such a high one to overcome,[1257] the applicant has not been given an effective opportunity to challenge a public authority's decision.[1258] **11.305**

(b) Access to the courts and immunities

The right of access to the court which is implied into Article 6[1259] is limited by the various 'immunities' available to public authorities.[1260] Such immunities will only be acceptable under the Human Rights Act if they are necessary and proportionate: the court will, in each case, have to strike a balance between the hardship suffered by the claimant and the damage to be done to the public interest.[1261] This could mean that some blanket public policy immunities can no longer be maintained, for example: **11.306**

[1252] The Art 6 rights are stricter than the standards imposed by general administrative law (see, generally, para 11.69ff above) and comprise the right to be present at an adversarial oral hearing (see para 11.206 above); the right to equality of arms (see para 11.208ff above); the right to fair presentation of the evidence (see para 11.214 above); the right to cross examine (see para 11.217 above); the right to a reasoned judgment (see para 11.218 above); the right to a hearing within a reasonable time (see para 11.219ff above); the right to an independent and impartial tribunal established by law (see para 11.222ff above); and the right to a public hearing and the public pronouncement of judgment (see para 11.230ff above).

[1253] See, generally, para 11.198 above.

[1254] [1999] 1 WLR 1293, 1299, 1300 where he discussed *Bryan v United Kingdom* (1995) 21 EHRR 342; *Wickramsinghe v United Kingdom* [1998] EHRLR 338, EComm HR; and the case brought by the applicant himself, *Stefan v United Kingdom* (1997) 25 EHHR CD 130.

[1255] See para 11.198 above.

[1256] See generally, paras 5.123 above.

[1257] See generally, para 5.126 above.

[1258] See *Smith and Grady v United Kingdom*, 27 Sep 1999 paras 138, 139; and see para 21.178 below.

[1259] See para 11.185ff above.

[1260] See para 11.27ff above.

[1261] Cf *Barrett v Enfield LBC* [1999] 3 WLR 79, 84G–85H.

- 'crown immunity' as applied to the Sovereign in her personal capacity in the event it was challenged;[1262]
- 'negligence immunity' of the police and Crown Prosecution Service in relation to the prevention or investigation of crime;[1263] and related immunities;[1264]
- 'negligence immunity' of local authorities in relation to the performance of their statutory duties to protect children;[1265]
- 'proceedings immunity' in relation to negligence claims against legal advisors;[1266]
- 'judicial immunity' in relation to claims against judges or magistrates for actions outside their jurisdiction.[1267]

However, it seems likely that parliamentary immunity would be held to be compatible with Article 6.[1268]

11.307 The question of whether, and to what extent, negligence immunities can survive the Human Rights Act is highly controversial and uncertain. The European Court of Human Rights held in *Osman v United Kingdom*[1269] that the immunity of the police from actions in negligence[1270] breached the right of access to the courts. The Court's decision has been vigorously criticised. It is claimed that the Court has unjustifiably extended the scope of Article 6 as a procedural guarantee by reformulating the substantive law of a domestic state.[1271] It has also been said that the Court misunderstood the English law of negligence. In *Barrett v Enfield LBC*[1272] Lord Browne-Wilkinson described the decision as 'difficult to understand'[1273] because, on a proper analysis of the position in English law, there was no 'immunity from claims' but, rather, no right to make a claim at all. It is submitted that these concerns are misplaced: although, strictly speaking, an element of the

---

[1262] See para 11.28 above.
[1263] Cf *Osman v United Kingdom* (1998) 5 BHRC 293; and see para 11.40 above.
[1264] See para 11.43 above.
[1265] See para 11.41 above; cf *Barrett v Enfield LBC* (n 1261above).
[1266] See para 11.37 above; and see *Docker v Chief Constable of West Midlands Police, The Times*, 1 Aug 2000.
[1267] See para 11.35 above.
[1268] See para 11.31ff above.
[1269] (1998) 5 BHRC 293.
[1270] The Court of Appeal struck out the claim as disclosing no reasonable cause of action: see *Osman v Ferguson* [1993] 4 All ER 344; and generally, para 11.42ff above.
[1271] See para 11.196 above.
[1272] [1999] 3 WLR 79; the views expressed by Lord Browne-Wilkinson concerning the decision in *Osman v United Kingdom* (1998) 5 BHRC 293 at 84 and their impact on the development of negligence are discussed at para 11.196 above.
[1273] *Barrett v Enfield LBC* (n 1272 above) 84B; see also see Lord Hoffmann, 'Human Rights and the House of Lords' (1999) 62 MLR 159; T Weir, 'Downhill—All the Way' [1999] 1 FLR 193; Sir Richard Buxton, 'The Human Rights Act and Private Law' (2000) 116 LQR 48.

tort is not present[1274] the substance of the position (recognised by the frequent use of the term 'immunity' by the courts)[1275] is that a right to claim in negligence is being removed by a 'policy immunity'. This does constitute a restriction on access to the courts in cases involving public authorities and Article 6 is, therefore, brought into play. Lord Browne-Wilkinson also suggested[1276] that the decision in *Osman* makes it inappropriate[1277] to deal with the issue by applying to strike out the case;[1278] and it will be necessary for the court to carry out a detailed factual inquiry into whether the interference can be justified as being a proportionate and legitimate restriction on the right of access.[1279] The Commission has also ruled in favour of the applicants in a case arising out of one[1280] of the claims which had been struck out in the *X (Minors) v Bedfordshire County Council* litigation;[1281] and there are other cases pending. It therefore seems that all of the public policy based negligence immunities will require close examination as a result of the Human Rights Act.

It is submitted that the courts will take a similar approach to other types of 'negligence immunity' and to 'proceedings immunity' and 'judicial immunity'. A defendant will no longer be able to rely on a broad brush justification for immunity which is not specific to the particular case; and will now need to adduce factual evidence to show that the interference with the implied right of access to the Court under Article 6 is justified. As Lord Slynn emphasised in *Phelps v Hillingdon London Borough Council*[1281a] it must not be presumed that imposing liability will interfere with the performance of a public body's duties. The allegations must be proved and will only be established in exceptional circumstances. Nevertheless, in an appropriate case summary determination may be possible.[1281b] **11.308**

(c) Independence and impartiality

Independence. Judges who determine ordinary civil and criminal cases must be independent of the executive.[1282] The full time judiciary in England and Wales are **11.309**

[1274] Namely, the requirement that it is 'just and reasonable' to impose a duty of care.
[1275] See para 11.42ff above.
[1276] *Barrett v Enfield LBC* (n 1272 above) 198.
[1277] Although s 2(1) of the Human Rights Act ensures a court is not bound to follow the decision of the Court of Human Rights (see generally, para 3.46ff above), it would almost inevitably result in an application to Strasbourg.
[1278] Under CPR, r 3.4; but see *Kinsella v Chief Constable of Nottinghamshire*, *The Times*, 24 Aug 1999 and *Kent v Griffiths* [2000] 2 WLR 1 158 123 paras 37–38 (*per* Lord Woolf).
[1279] See generally, para 11.190 above.
[1280] *T P and K M v United Kingdom* Application 28945/95, 26 May 1998 (admissibility), EComm HR.
[1281] [1995] 2 AC 633.
[1281a] *The Times*, 28 Jul 2000.
[1281b] *Kent v Griffiths* (n 1278 above) paras 37–38 (*per* Lord Woolf).
[1282] In such cases, lack of independence cannot be cured by an appeal to an 'independent tribunal', see *De Cubber v Belgium* (1984) 7 EHRR 236 para 32; the position is different in relation to disciplinary and administrative decisions, see para 11.197 above.

clearly independent of the executive for the purposes of Article 6. The position is less clear in relation to part-time judges and lay magistrates.

11.310 The position of temporary judges in Scotland was considered by the High Court of Justiciary in the case of *Starrs v Procurator Fiscal, Linlithgow*.[1283] It was held that temporary sheriffs who were appointed for a period of one year and were subject to a power of recall were not 'independent' for the purposes of Article 6. A number of factors pointed strongly away from independence including:

- the short fixed term of office with the possibility of renewal at the discretion of the executive;
- the fact that temporary sheriffs were very often persons hoping for a permanent appointment and thus had a relationship of dependency with the executive;
- the absence of guarantees against outside pressures, including the power to recall an appointment, to decline to renew it or to fail to provide judicial work.

The court accepted that, in practice, the system was operated with careful regard for judicial independence however the absence of an objective guarantee of security of tenure was fatal. Lord Reed made it clear that protection of independence by convention was not sufficient:

> It is fundamental . . . that human rights are no longer dependent solely on conventions, by which I mean values, customs and practices of the constitution which are not legally enforceable. Although the Convention protects rights which reflect democratic values and underpin democratic institutions, the Convention guarantees the protection of those rights through legal processes, rather than political processes. It is for that reason that Article 6 guarantees access to independent courts. It would be inconsistent with the whole approach of the Convention if the independence of those courts itself rested upon convention rather than law.[1283a]

11.311 If this approach had been followed by the English courts, there would have been strong arguments that assistant recorders, Deputy High Court Judges and various other part time appointees to judicial office would not have constituted 'independent tribunals' for the purposes of Article 6. These potential difficulties were removed by a decision announced on 12 April 2000 that such appointments would, in future, be made for a minimum period of at least five years with various other safeguards.[1284] The position remains unclear in relation to lay magistrates who are subject to removal in circumstances which are not defined by statute.[1285] It is also

[1283] [2000] 1 LRC 718; see also *Clancy v Caird, The Times*, 9 May 2000 (Inner House) in which it was held that temporary judges of the Court of Session, appointed for period of three years were 'independent' for the purposes of Art 6.

[1283a] *Starrs v Procurator Fiscal* (n 1283 above) at 771a–c.

[1284] See para 11.61 above.

[1285] Ibid; note that the Canadian courts have rejected an analogous challenge under the Charter, see *Reference re Justices of the Peace Act* (1984) 16 CCC (3d) 193 and see, generally, para 11.409, below.

strongly arguable that 'statutory tribunals' are not 'independent': the lay members having no security of tenure.[1286] If a challenge were made to magistrates or statutory tribunals on the basis they were not independent or impartial, the objection should be taken immediately; otherwise the court may hold the applicant has waived the Article 6 objection which was the approach taken in Scotland by the Court of Session in *Clancy v Caird*.[1286a]

Impartiality. In English law a tribunal is only disqualified by apparent bias if there is a 'real danger of bias'.[1287] This is a less stringent test than that under Article 6 which requires only a 'reasonable suspicion' or 'reasonable apprehension' of bias.[1288] It is submitted that the result of the Human Rights Act is that the English courts will be obliged to apply the 'reasonable suspicion' test. In the majority of cases the two tests are likely to lead to the same result[1289] but, in some borderline cases, the stricter Article 6 test may affect the outcome. In Scotland it has been held that a judge who made public criticism of the Convention was disqualified from sitting on an appeal in which Convention issues were to be raised.[1289a] **11.312**

(d) Impact on civil proceedings

In general, the rules of English civil court procedure have been found to be in compliance with Article 6.[1290] The common law has generally recognised fair trial rights such as: **11.313**

- the right of access to the courts;[1291]
- the right to trial within a reasonable time;[1292]
- the right to a public, oral hearing, with the cross-examination of witnesses;[1293]
- the right to a reasoned judgment.[1294]

Although these rights can, under English constitutional law, be expressly limited by statute,[1295] such limitations have been rare.

In 1999, English civil procedure was subject to the most radical revision for over **11.314**

[1286] See *Smith v Secretary of State for Trade and Industry* [2000] ICR 69 on this point.
[1286a] *The Times*, 9 May 2000.
[1287] *R v Gough* [1993] AC 646, see para 11.68 above.
[1288] See para 11.225ff above; and see *Locabail (UK) Ltd v Bayfield Properties Ltd* [2000] 2 WLR 870, 884–885 (where this difference is noted); and see P Havers and O Thomas 'Bias Post Pinochet and Under the ECHR' [1999] JR 111.
[1289] Ibid.
[1289a] *Hoekstra v Her Majesty's Advocate (No 3)* (2000) GWD 12–417, High Court of Justiciary.
[1290] Cf Sir Robert Walker, 'Impact of European Standards on the Right to a Fair Trial in Civil Proceedings in English Domestic Law' [1999] EHRLR 4.
[1291] See para 11.15ff above.
[1292] See para 11.84ff above.
[1293] See paras 11.77 and 11.79 above.
[1294] See para 11.89 above.
[1295] See para 1.21 above.

a century. The Civil Procedure Rules give the courts a large range of summary powers over the conduct of civil proceedings with a view to achieving more efficient 'case management'.[1296] Many of these powers can be exercised by the court of its own motion, without a hearing taking place.[1297] The effect of such orders can be to place restrictions on the 'access to justice' of litigants:

- the court can order a party to pay a sum of money into court 'if that party has, without good reason, failed to comply with a rule, practice direction or a relevant pre-action protocol'[1298]—this could prevent an impecunious party from proceeding;
- the 'striking out' of statements of case—which means that cases may be disposed of without a full hearing;[1299]
- the 'summary disposal of claims' on the application of either the claimant or the defendant, which also means that cases may be disposed of without a full hearing;[1300]
- the 'summary assessment of costs' on final hearings—which, in practice, means that substantial financial liabilities are determined without substantial investigation.[1301]

In some circumstances, such orders might be regarded as being incompatible with Article 6: particularly if inflexible rules of practice were developed which prevented the court from considering the merits of a particular case.

11.315 Article 6 issues may also arise where the court exercises its power to decide promptly which issues need full investigation and which can be disposed of summarily,[1302] where the court directs that evidence is given by a single joint expert[1303] (particularly, if it results in an inequality of arms[1304] because the forensic issues are complex and one of the parties has insufficient resources and so is unable to formulate his own case effectively) or where the court limits cross examination.[1305] It should, however, be noted that Article 6 does not apply to 'interim' applications or determinations.[1306] Furthermore, the flexibility which is central to the Civil Procedure Rules means that the Courts will have ample opportunity to adjust

[1296] See CPR, Pt 3.
[1297] The general power is contained in CPR, r 3.3.
[1298] CPR, r 3.1(5).
[1299] CPR, r 3.4.
[1300] CPR, Pt 24.
[1301] In accordance with CPR, r 44.7; a determination of costs which is the continuation of a substantive dispute is subject to Art 6 guarantees: see *Robins v United Kingdom* (1997) 26 EHRR 527 paras 25–29.
[1302] CPR, r 1.4(2)(c).
[1303] CPR, r 37.5; but see *Daniels v Walker, The Times*, 17 May 2000 where Lord Woolf MR strongly discouraged reliance on Art 6 in a dispute arising from the joint instruction of an expert; however, the Court of Appeal decided that the parties were entitled to instruct their own expert.
[1304] See para 11.208ff above.
[1305] CPR, r 32.1(3).
[1306] See *X v United Kingdom* (1981) 24 DR 57, EComm HR, and see para 11.157 above.

their procedures so as to conform with Article 6 as they are required to do by section 6(3) of the Human Rights Act.[1307] In relation to case management issues Lord Woolf MR stressed in *Daniels v Walker*[1307a] that:

> It would be highly undesirable if consideration of these issues was made more complex by the injection into them of Article 6 style arguments. I hope that judges will be robust in resisting any attempt to introduce these arguments.

Where it is claimed that the Rules are being applied in breach of Article 6 rights, it may be appropriate to seek a ruling on that question at an early stage.

The practice of granting freezing injunctions[1307b] in relation to alleged trust monies which contain no proviso allowing payment for legal advice will be affected by Article 6. Where the court is exercising its discretion about whether it is just to refuse to include such a proviso[1307c] the applicant's right to have effective access to the court[1307d] will be an important factor to weigh in the balance. **11.315A**

The new general rule that hearings should be in public[1308] brings English civil proceedings into line with Article 6(1). Nevertheless, the fact that no special arrangements have to be made for accommodating members of the public[1309] could, arguably, lead to a breach of Article 6 as many court premises are arranged in such a way that practical public access to 'chambers' is extremely difficult. **11.316**

The power to order disclosure of privileged documents may breach Article 6 because the right to confidentiality is a fundamental condition for the adminstration of justice.[1310] Thus, the power of the court to require disclosure of privileged material in child care proceedings under Part IV of the Children Act may require further consideration[1311] because legal representatives are obliged to make full and frank disclosure even where it harms their clients' case.[1312] **11.317**

Limitation periods do not breach Article 6 provided they can be justified as a proportionate interference with access to the court.[1312a] It may therefore be difficult **11.317A**

[1307] See generally, para 5.38ff above.
[1307a] Above n 1303.
[1307b] Under CPR r 25.1(1)(f): formerly, Mareva injunctions.
[1307c] See *Fitzgerald v Williams* [1996] QB 657 *per* Sir Thomas Bingham at 669; *United Mizrahi Bank v Docherty* [1998] 1 WLR 435.
[1307d] See in particular, *Airey v Ireland* (1979) 2 EHRR 305; and see para 11.189 above.
[1308] CPR, r 39.2(1); see para 11.80 above.
[1309] CPR, r 39.2(2).
[1310] See eg *General Mediterranean v Patel* [1999] 3 All ER 673.
[1311] See *In re L (A Minor) (Police Investigation Privilege)* [1997] AC 16; see, in particular, the dissenting judgment of Lord Nicholls at 34.
[1312] See eg *Oxfordshire County Council v P* [1995] Fam 161; *Essex County Council v R* [1994] Fam 167; *Re D H (A Minor) (Child Abuse)* [1994] 1 FLR 679.
[1312a] See para 11.190ff above.

to justify under Article 6 limitation periods which cannot be extended for good cause or where the power to extend is very limited in scope;[1312b] potential areas of dispute include the power to extend time to refer disputes to arbitration under section 12(3) of the Arbitration Act 1996,[1312c] the strict approach towards extending time for statutory appeals under CPR Sch 1 R 55,[1312d] appeals against the local authority's decisions in homelessness cases to the county court[1312e] and appeals to the Employment Appeal Tribunal.[1312f]

11.317B Article 6 may call into question the enforceability of certain arbitration agreements. Arbitrators will not be a 'court' or 'tribunal' under section 6(3) of the Human Rights Act.[1312g] and will not be prohibited from acting incompatibly with Convention rights under Section 6(1). It is well established under Convention case law that the right of access to the courts under Article 6 may be waived by a voluntary arbitration agreement.[1312h] However, a waiver will only be effective if it is clear and unequivocal, made in the absence of constraint and made in the full knowledge of the nature and extent of the right.[1312i] It is therefore arguable that an arbitration clause will not be effective if, for example, the applicant was effectively compelled to agree an arbitration clause[1312j] or where the arbitration clause was not expressly agreed.[1312k]

11.318 It is possible that 'self-help' remedies such as distress for rent, forfeiture by re-entry or the power of a mortgagee to obtain possession without a court order[1313] will be held to be contrary to Article 6. It is arguable that self help is 'inimical to a society in which the rule of law prevails'[1314] as it prevents access to the courts for the adjudication of disputes. The power of a mortgagee to take possession of a dwelling house without a court order[1315] appears to be a particularly clear breach of Article 6, bearing in mind the importance of the right to occupy the home which is brought to an end by such a step[1316] and the fact that such a procedure allows the

[1312b] N Giffen, 'Judicial Supervision of Human Rights: Practice and Procedure', Administrative Law Bar seminar, 5 Feb 2000.

[1312c] See *Harbour and General Works v Environment Agency* [2000] 1 All ER 50.

[1312d] *Regalbourne v East Lyndsey District Council* [1994] RA 1.

[1312e] Housing Act 1996, s 204.

[1312f] See eg *Aziz v Bethnal Green City Challenge* [2000] IRLR 111.

[1312g] See para 5.42ff above.

[1312h] See para 6.149ff above.

[1312i] See para 6.160ff above.

[1312j] Because, for example, all traders in a particular area trade on standard terms including such a clause.

[1312k] Because, for example, it was included in 'small print' or 'incorporated by reference' to standard terms, see eg *Zambia Steel and Building Supplies v James Clark and Eaton Ltd* [1986] 2 Lloyd's Rep 225.

[1313] See *Ropaigealach v Barclays Bank* [1999] 3 WLR 17.

[1314] Cf the South African case of *Lesapo v North West Agricultural Bank*, 1999 (12) BCLR 1420; see para 11.494 below.

[1315] See *Ropaigealach v Barclays Bank*, (n 1313 above).

[1316] The right to respect for home under Art 8, see generally, Chap 12 below.

mortgagee to avoid the statutory procedure for suspension of possession orders in residential mortgagees actions.[1317]

(e) Impact on judicial review proceedings

Introduction. The Human Rights Act will, of course, have a substantial impact on judicial review proceedings: incompatibility with Convention rights will, in effect, be an additional basis for seeking judicial review on the ground of illegality[1318] and, when Convention rights are in issue, the range of 'public authorities' amenable to review may be broadened.[1319] There are three situations in which Article 6 itself could have an impact on judicial review proceedings:[1320] **11.319**

- in relation to the court's own procedure for judicial review applications;[1321]
- where the decision under review is alleged to interfere with Article 6 rights;
- where the decision under review itself constitutes a determination of civil rights and obligations or a criminal charge.

Judicial review procedure. The requirement for permission in judicial review applications is consistent with Article 6.[1322] The test to be applied on applications[1323] under the Human Rights Act is unclear: although it might be said that once a *prima facie* violation has been shown, the burden is on the public authority to justify the interference at the substantive stage, the more realistic view is that a claimant will need to show at the permission stage an arguable absence of justification for the interference.[1324] **11.320**

A number of statutes contain time limits restricting the period within which statutory appeals can be made.[1325] In some circumstances, such time limits could constitute unjustifiable restrictions on the right of access to the courts under Article 6 although this is unlikely.[1326] **11.321**

[1317] Under Administration of Justice Act 1970, s 36.

[1318] Which was defined by Lord Diplock in the *GCHQ* case (*Council of Civil Service Unions v Minister for the Civil Service* [1985] AC 374, 410) as 'I mean that the decision-maker must correctly understand the law that regulates his decision-making powers and gives effect to it'; and see generally, Lord Woolf and J Jowell, *De Smith, Woolf and Jowell, Judicial Review of Administrative Action* (5th edn, Sweet & Maxwell, 1995) III-01–III-04.

[1319] See generally, M Supperstone and J Coppel, 'Judicial Review After the Human Rights Act' [1999] EHRLR 301.

[1320] See generally, Sir Stephen Richards, 'The Impact of Article 6 of the ECHR on Judicial Review' [1999] JR 106.

[1321] See generally, para 22.93ff below.

[1322] See para 11.22ff above.

[1323] See R Clayton and H Tomlinson, *Judicial Review Procedure* (2nd edn, Wiley Chancery Law, 1997) 122ff.

[1324] Cf Richards (n 1320 above) 109–110, para 17.

[1325] See for example Town and Country Planning Act 1990, s 288(3) (six weeks); for a fuller list, see R Gordon, *Judicial Review and Crown Office Practice* (Sweet & Maxwell, 1999), appeals by way of re-hearing (paras 5-094–5-103); tribunals to which the Tribunal and Inquiries Act 1992 (paras 5-104–5-113) and other tribunals (paras 114–119).

[1326] See para 11.191 above.

11.321A The question as to whether an application for judicial review should be refused because of a failure to use an alternative remedy[1326a] may require reconsideration where the case involves the applicant's 'civil rights and obligations'.[1326b] If the alternative remedy does not involve a determination by an 'independent and impartial tribunal'[1326c] such as a local authority's complaints procedure, then the court may be acting in breach of its own obligations under section 6(1) if it refuses to grant relief in such circumstances.[1326d]

11.322 The limited availability of disclosure of documents[1327] and cross examination of deponents[1328] in judicial review proceedings are unlikely to satisfy the requirements of Article 6 where the applicant disputes the underlying facts of the dispute in a case involving 'civil rights, and obligations'[1328a] or a 'criminal charge'.[1328b] It is possible that the courts may differentiate between judicial review cases in general and cases under the Human Rights Act. Although the court must ensure it is not acting incompatibly with Article 6 when considering an application for discovery or cross examination, the application will have particular force where the judicial review application is based on Article 6 itself.

11.323 **Review of decisions interfering with Article 6 rights.** Although the English law already recognises a 'constitutional right' of access to the court,[1329] this right is subject to a large number of exceptions. These will be subject to close scrutiny under the Human Rights Act. Any statute which authorises them will be 'read down' under section 3 of the Act to ensure compliance with Article 6.[1330] Other areas of potential challenge include:

- decisions concerning the grant of legal aid in civil and criminal proceedings;[1331]
- decisions concerning the organisation and resourcing of the court system.

11.324 **Review of decisions determining Article 6 rights.** The Human Rights Act does not impose an obligation on all administrative decision-makers or tribunals to comply with Article 6. Although section 6(3) of the Act states that tribunals (as

[1326a] See eg *R v Chief Constable of Merseyside, ex p Calveley* [1986] QB 424; and see generally, *De Smith, Woolf and Jowell, Judicial Review of Administrative Action*, para 18–032ff.

[1326b] See para 11.160ff above.

[1326c] See para 11.222ff above.

[1326d] N Giffen, 'Judicial Supervision of Human Rights: Practice and Procedure', Administrative Law Bar Association seminar, 5 Feb 2000.

[1327] See eg R Clayton and H Tomlinson (n 1323 above) para 7.2.4; R Gordon (n 1325 above) paras 3-658–3-66; and see para 22.102 below.

[1328] See eg Clayton and Tomlinson (n 1323 above) para 7.2.7; R Gordon (n1325 above) paras 3-653–3-657.

[1328a] See para 11.160ff above.

[1328b] See para 11.174ff above.

[1329] *R v Lord Chancellor, ex p Witham* [1998] QB 575; see generally para 11.15ff above.

[1330] For s 3, see, in particular, para 4.27ff above.

[1331] For the position under Art 6, see para 11.189 above.

well as courts) must not act incompatibly with Convention rights, a tribunal is defined in section 21(1) of the Act as any tribunal in which legal proceedings may be brought.[1332] A decision-maker must not act incompatibly with Article 6 if he is determining 'civil rights and obligations'.[1333] Complying with Article 6 may be achieved by a combination of the primary decision-maker and the High Court carrying out judicial review functions.[1334] However, in cases where there are disputes as to the primary facts, it may be necessary for these factual issues to be investigated by disclosure and cross examination in judicial review proceedings[1335] (contrary to the normal practice).

Furthermore, Article 6 will itself provide a number of additional grounds for judicial review of decisions by inferior tribunals and administrative decision-makers. The Convention case law imposes more demanding standards than those which arise under administrative law principles in many situations including complaints concerning: **11.325**

- lack of independence from the executive;[1336]
- a failure of the tribunal to be impartial;[1337]
- failure to hold oral public hearings;[1338]
- failure to allow the cross-examination of witnesses;[1339]
- failure to provide for the 'equality of arms';[1340]
- failure to give any sufficient reasons.[1341]

[1332] See generally, para 5.43 above.

[1333] See para 11.154ff above.

[1334] See *Stefan v General Medical Council* [1999] 1 WLR 1293, 1299E; and see para 11.91 above.

[1335] See para 22.102ff below.

[1336] Contrast the Convention principles (see para 11.223ff above) with those of administrative law (see para 11.53ff above).

[1337] Contrast the Convention principles (see para 11.225ff above) with those of administrative law (see para 11.66ff above); and see P Havers and O Thomas, 'Bias Post-Pinochet and Under the ECHR' [1999] JR 111.

[1338] Contrast the Convention principles (see 11.206 above) with those of administrative law (see para 11.75 above).

[1339] Contrast the Convention principles (see para 11.217 above) with those of administrative law (see para 11.77 above).

[1340] Contrast the Convention principles (see para 11.208 above) with those of administrative law (see para 11.72ff above).

[1341] Contrast the Convention principles (see para 11.218 above) with those of administrative law (see 11.90 above); and see *Stefan v General Medical Council* (n 1334 above) at 1301 where Lord Clyde reviews developments in the duty to give reasons and goes on to express the view that: 'There is certainly a strong argument for the view that what was once seen as exceptions to a rule may now be becoming the norm, and the cases where the reasons are not required may be taking the appearance of being exceptions. But the general rule has not been departed from and their Lordships do not consider the present case provides an appropriate opportunity to explore the possibility of such a departure. They are conscious of a possible re-appraisal of the whole position which the passage of the Human Rights Act 1998 will bring about. The provisions of article 6(1) of the Convention on Human Rights, which is now about to become directly accessible in the national courts, will require closer attention to be paid to the duty to give reasons, at least in relation to those cases where a person's civil rights and obligations are being determined. But it is in the context of the application of that Act that any wide ranging review of the position at common law should take place.'

(f) Impact on ombudsman procedures

11.326 The use of complaints procedures directed to ombudsmen is now well established administrative remedy.[1342] It can be invoked against a diverse range of public bodies including Parliament, local government, the health service, the insurance and banking industry, the legal services and the prison service. It is intended to be an informal mechanism for investigating and resolving complaints. However, there is often no mechanism for bringing a complaint before the court, although judicial review will be available. Where an ombudsman makes binding awards of compensation against public bodies, he is making a determination of 'civil rights and obligations' and the decision-making process must be in accordance with the Article 6 fair trial guarantees.[1343] There are a number of potential difficulties which arise because the 'ombudsman' procedure is often inquisitorial rather than adversarial and there is no disclosure of documents to the complainant or cross-examination of witnesses. It is difficult to see how the guarantees of Article 6 can be provided by judicial review proceedings.[1343a]

(4) Specific areas of impact

(a) Commercial law

11.327 **Introduction.** In the field of commercial law, the most important area of impact concerns regulatory and disciplinary hearings.[1344] A large range of statutory and non-statutory bodies are now responsible for the regulation of financial and commercial activities.[1345] There are, at present, no general rules governing the operation of such bodies although they are generally subject to judicial review[1346] and must, therefore, conduct themselves in accordance with the flexible standards of fairness which have been laid down by the courts on a case-by-case basis.[1347] Article 6 will provide a much stricter and more uniform framework within which the activities of such bodies must be carried out.[1348]

[1342] See, generally, H W R Wade and C Forsyth, *Administrative Law* (7th edn, Clarendon Press, 1994) 79–105.

[1343] See para 11.183ff above.

[1343a] See Tim Lowe; 'Financial Services: Parliamentary Anatomy of Human Rights' in Wilberforce Chambers, *The Essential Human Rights Act 1998* (Wilberforce Chambers, 2000) 152–156.

[1344] See para 11.267 above.

[1345] Financial services are now subject to regulation by the Financial Services Authority under the provisions of the Financial Services and Markets Act 1999, see generally, B Harris, *The Law and Practice of Disciplinary and Regulatory Proceedings* (2nd edn, Barry Rose, 1999).

[1346] See generally, para 5.23ff above.

[1347] See para 11.69ff above.

[1348] See generally, P Davies, 'Self Incrimination, Fair Trials and the Pursuit of Corporate and Financial Wrongdoing' and N Jordan 'The Implications for Commercial Lawyers in Practice' in B Markesinis (ed), *The Impact of the Human Rights Bill on English Law* (Oxford University Press, 1998); J Beatson 'Which Regulatory Bodies are Subject to the Human Rights Act?', N Jordan, 'Im-

The first issue in relation to regulatory hearings is whether they involve 'determination of civil rights and obligations' or criminal charges.[1349] Such bodies will be subject to Article 6 safeguards if they involve determination of matters such as fitness to remain in business or awards of compensation.[1350] **11.328**

Where a regulatory offence is equivalent to a 'criminal charge' the person charged is entitled to a first instance hearing which fully meets the requirements of Article 6.[1351] However, where no criminal charge is involved, regulatory bodies can meet the requirements of Article 6 in one of two ways: either the bodies themselves can comply with the requirements or they are subject to subsequent control by a judicial body which has full jurisdiction and does provide Article 6 guarantees:[1352] **11.329**

> In cases involving applications for judicial review under English law, the sufficiency of the review exercised by the High Court must be assessed having regard to matters such as the subject matter of the decision appealed against, the manner in which that decision was arrived at, and the content of the dispute including the desired and actual grounds of appeal.[1353]

Regulatory proceedings involving 'criminal charges'. In a limited range of cases, a 'regulatory' offence may be treated as a 'criminal charge' under Article 6 and the applicant is entitled to procedural safeguards such as the presumption of innocence,[1354] the right to be informed promptly and in detail of the nature and cause of the accusations against him,[1355] the right to have adequate time and facilities for the preparation of his defence,[1356] the right to defend himself in person or through legal assistance of his own choosing (and, if he does not have the means to pay, to be given free legal assistance when the interests of justice require it)[1357]and to examine the witnesses against him and to obtain the attendance and examination of witnesses on his own behalf.[1358] **11.330**

---

pact of the Human Rights Act upon Compliance: the Taxation Viewpoint', R Nolan 'Human Rights and Corporate Wrongs: the impact of the Human Rights Act 1998 on Section 236 of the Insolvency Act 1986', G Staple, 'Financial Services and the Human Rights Act', M Blair, 'Human Rights and Market Abuse' and Counsels' Opinions on the impact of the ECHR on the Draft Financial and Markets Bill' in J Beatson, C Forsyth and I Hare (eds), *The Human Rights Act and the Criminal Justice and Regulatory Process* (Hart Publishing, 1999); Tim Lowe, 'Financial Services: Parliamentary Anatomy of Human Rights' in Wilberforce Chambers, *The Essential Human Rights Act 1998* (Wilberforce Chambers, 2000).

1349 For 'civil obligation' see para 11.163ff above and for 'criminal charge' see para 11.174ff above.

1350 See eg *Editions Periscope v France* (1992) 14 EHRR 597, 613 para 40.

1351 See *De Cubber v Belgium* (1984) 7 EHRR 236 paras 31–32; *Findlay v United Kingdom* (1997) 24 EHRR 221 para 79.

1352 See *Albert and le Compte v Belgium* (1983) 5 EHRR 533 para 29; and para 11.197 above.

1353 *A P B Ltd, APP and AEB v United Kingdom*, (1998) 25 EHRR CD 141 (admissibility decision); and see *Bryan v United Kingdom* (1995) 21 EHRR 342, 359 para 40, 360–361 paras 44–47.

1354 Art 6(2); see generally, para 11.236ff above.

1355 Art 6(3)(a); see generally, para 11.241ff above.

1356 Art 6(3)(b); see generally, para 11.243ff above.

1357 Art 6(3)(c); see para 11.245ff above.

1358 Art 6(3)(d); see para 11.252ff above.

11.331 In a number of recent cases the Commission has held that regulatory proceedings taken to discipline and disqualify certain individuals did not constitute 'criminal proceedings' for the purposes of Article 6. Thus, consideration of whether the applicant was a fit and proper person to carry on investment business,[1359] to be the managing director of an insurance company[1360] or to practice medicine[1361] were treated as determinations of 'civil rights and obligations' rather than as 'criminal charges'. Nevertheless, it is arguable that some types of disciplinary proceedings under the Financial Services and Markets Bill may be characterised as 'criminal' for the purposes of Article 6: in particular, the disciplinary offences which may be committed by a very wide range of persons and may involve substantial financial penalties.[1361a]

11.332 The Government has recognised that 'market abuse' under Part VII of the Financial Services and Markets Bill may be a 'criminal charge' as it is of a generally binding character and has a high degree of overlap with criminal offences of 'insider trading'.[1362] As a result, the Bill has been modified in part to reflect a perceived need to provide the 'criminal charge' guarantees of Article 6(2) and (3) to those charged with market abuse. For example, the Bill now imposes certain limitations on the use of statements made by a person in compliance with a requirement imposed by a regulator;[1363] the Government has indicated that financial support will be provided to defend market abuse proceedings in appropriate cases and a warning notice or decision notice will be taken by a person who is not directly involved in establishing the evidence on which the decision is based.[1364]

11.333 Directors' disqualification proceedings under the terms of the Company Directors Disqualification Act 1986 are also subject to the provisions of Article 6.[1365] It has been suggested that such proceedings should be treated as 'criminal' for the purposes of Article 6[1366] on the basis of the nature of the penalty.[1367] This issue was considered by the Court of Appeal in *R v Secretary of State for Trade and Industry,*

[1359] *A P B Ltd, APP and AEB v United Kingdom* (1998) 25 EHRR CD 141.

[1360] *X v United Kingdom* (1998) 25 EHRR CD 88.

[1361] *Wickramsinghe v United Kingdom* [1998] EHRLR 338.

[1361a] See Tim Lowe, 'Financial Services: Parliamentary Anatomy of Human Rights' in Wilberforce Chambers, *The Essential Human Rights Act 1998* (Wilberforce Chambers, 2000) 140–145.

[1362] See generally, G Staple, 'Financial Services and the Human Rights Act' and 'Counsels' opinions on the impact of the ECHR on the Draft Financial and Markets Bill' in J Beatson, C Forsyth and I Hare (eds), *The Human Rights Act and the Criminal Justice and Regulatory Process* (Hart Publishing, 1999).

[1363] Cl 144.

[1364] Cl 340.

[1365] See *E D C v United Kingdom* [1996] EHRLR 189 (the applicant's complaint of over four years' delay in such proceedings was held to be admissible by the Commission).

[1366] See generally, para 11.174ff above.

[1367] See A Mithani, *Directors' Disqualification*, (Butterworths, 1998) VIII, 65 (where the arguments in favour of this contention are conveniently summarised).

ex p McCormick.[1368] The Court pointed out that not every deprivation of liberty or fine necessarily belonged to the criminal law;[1369] and that the Commission had held that proceedings concerning a prohibition on acting as a business agent were not 'criminal'.[1370] It relied on the fact that:

> The disqualification order does not prevent the person subject to its terms carrying on any commercial activity in his own name (save those of a receiver, liquidator or company promoter, etc.); its effect is to remove the privilege of doing so through a company with limited liability. The consequences of the order are serious for the individual concerned and have been described as penal but they do not involve a deprivation of liberty, livelihood or property'.[1371]

As a result, it was held that the Secretary of State was not bound to treat the proceedings as criminal.[1372] This conclusion was confirmed by the Court of Human Rights in *D C, H S and A D v United Kingdom*.[1372a] It has therefore been held that the use of statements obtained under section 235 of the Insolvency Act 1986 in disqualification proceedings did not necessarily involve a breach of Article 6. The issue of fair trial had to be determined by having regard to relevant factors by the trial judge.[1372b]

Regulatory proceedings involving 'civil rights and obligations'. If the regulatory proceedings are within the scope of Article 6 because they concern 'civil rights and obligations', the 'tribunal' must be independent and impartial. It must, therefore, be independent of the parties[1373] and should have a proportion of lay members. The tribunal should not contain members who have been involved in previous informal or conciliatory stages of the case.[1374] However, the procedure does not have to be formal and the tribunal can, in regulating its own procedure, limit the extent of oral argument and questioning. **11.334**

Furthermore, there must be an open and public hearing with judgment being pronounced publicly. This is a fundamental principle which is designed to maintain public confidence in the administration of justice.[1375] However, the 'publicity' requirement is flexible and depends on all the circumstances, including the nature of the proceedings and the other interests protected by a private hearing.[1376] For **11.335**

1368 [1998] BCC 379.
1369 Relying on *Société Stenuit v France* (1992) 14 EHRR 509.
1370 *Jaxel v France* (1987) 54 DR 70, EComm HR.
1371 See n 1368 above.
1372 Mithani reaches the same conclusion, (n 1367 above) VIII, 81–83.
1372a Application 39031/97, 14 Sep 1999 (admissibility decision).
1372b *Official Receiver v Stern* [2000] UKHRR 332.
1373 *Re S (A Barrister)* [1981] QB 683; B Harris, *Law and Practice of Disciplinary and Regulatory Proceedings* (2nd edn, Barry Rose, 1999) 181ff.
1374 Cf *Procola v Luxembourg* (1995) 22 EHRR 193.
1375 *Diennet v France* (1995) 21 EHRR 554 para 33.
1376 *Axen v Germany* (1983) 6 EHRR 195.

example, prison[1377] or medical[1378]disciplinary proceedings can be conducted in private for reasons of 'public order and security' or the 'protection of private life' respectively.

11.336 The right to a public hearing can be waived unless there is some clear public interest to the contrary.[1379] In cases where the issues are technical and no issues of public importance are involved it may be appropriate not to hold oral hearings unless a party requests it.[1380]

11.337 **The use of evidence obtained under compulsory powers.** The use of evidence in criminal proceedings which is obtained under powers to compel witnesses to give evidence to regulators[1381] is unlikely to result in breaches of Article 6[1382] following the amendments to the relevant statutory powers made in 1999.[1383] Evidence acquired under a regulator's compulsory powers could be used in civil proceedings. However, it has been argued that admitting such evidence in civil proceedings would breach Article 6(1) because it would infringe the principle of equality of arms[1384] by giving one party to litigation an unfair advantage over the other.[1385]

(b) Criminal law

11.338 **Introduction.** There are a large number of areas of potential impact in the field of criminal law.[1386] In this section, the potential impact is considered under 12 headings: definition of criminal charge, public hearings, hearings within a reasonable time, right to silence, presumption of innocence, information as to charge, disclosure and public interest immunity, legal advice, conduct of trial, agent provocateurs, interpreters, the giving of reasons and sentencing.

1377 See *Campbell and Fell v United Kingdom* (1984) 7 EHRR 165, para 11.178 above.

1378 *Guenuon v France* (1990) 66 DR 181, EComm HR.

1379 *Håkansson and Sturesson v Sweden* (1990) 13 EHRR 1 para 66; see generally, K Reid, *A Practitioner's Guide to the European Convention on Human Rights* (Sweet & Maxerll, 1998) 124.

1380 *Schuler-Zgraggen v Switzerland* (1993) 16 EHRR 405, 433 para 58.

1381 See para 11.101 above.

1382 See para 11.211ff above.

1383 See para 11.107 above.

1384 See para 11.208ff above.

1385 See R Nolan, 'Human Rights and Corporate Wrongs: the impact of the Human Rights Act on Section 236 of the Insolvency Act 1986' in J Beatson, C Forsyth and I Hare (eds), *The Human Rights Act and the Criminal Justice and Regulatory Process* (Hart Publishing, 1999).

1386 For general discussions, see D Cheney, L Dickson, J Fitzpatric and S Uglow, *Criminal Justice and the Human Rights Act 1998* (Jordans, 1999); C Baker (ed), *The Human Rights Act 1998: A Practitioners Guide* (Sweet & Maxwell, 1998), Chap 4, Pt I (Richardson) and A Ashworth, 'Article 6 and the Fairness of Trials' [1999] Crim LR 261; S Sharpe, 'Article 6 and the Disclosure of Evidence in Criminal Trials' [1999] Crim LR 273; A Ashworth 'The European Convention and Criminal Law', Rt Hon Lord Justice Buxton, 'The Convention and the English Law of Criminal Evidence', J Spencer, 'The European Convention and the Rules of Criminal Procedure', D Kyle, 'The Human Rights Act: Post Trial and Hearing' in J Beatson, C Forsyth and I Hare (eds), *The Human Rights Act and the Criminal Justice and Regulatory Process* (Hart Publishing, 1999); for a useful summary of the relevant Convention law, see *Archbold Criminal Pleading, Evidence and Practice* (Sweet and Maxwell, 1999) Chap 15 (Emmerson).

Definition of 'Criminal Charge'. Article 6 provides additional protection to those subject to criminal charges and the term has an 'autonomous Convention meaning'.[1387] In such circumstances the applicant is entitled to procedural safeguards such as the presumption of innocence,[1388] the right to be informed promptly and in detail of the nature and cause of the accusations against him,[1389] the right to have adequate time and facilities for the preparation of his defence,[1390] the right to defend himself in person or through legal assistance of his own choosing (and, if he does not have the means to pay), to be given free legal assistance when the interests of justice require it[1391] and to examine the witnesses against him and to obtain the attendance and examination of witnesses on his own behalf.[1392] **11.339**

There are some cases which come before the courts which, although not 'criminal' in English law will be treated as criminal for Convention purposes and which will, therefore, attract the full protection of Article 6(2) and (3). There are a number of possible candidates: **11.340**

- *'Anti-social behaviour orders'*:[1393] Such orders are made by magistrates on complaint to prohibit the conduct described in the order.[1394] The proceedings are subject to the civil burden of proof but any breach of such an order attracts a potential sentence of imprisonment or a fine[1395] and the court cannot impose a conditional discharge.[1396]
- *'Sex offender orders'*:[1397] Once again, such orders are made by magistrates to prohibit specified conduct.[1398] The orders are made by magistrates on complaint and are subject to the civil burden of proof. Once again, the sanctions for breach are a fine or imprisonment and no conditional discharge can be imposed.[1399]
- *Fine enforcement proceedings*: It is uncertain whether, as a matter of English law, these proceedings are civil or criminal[1400] but the respondent does face the risk of a sentence of imprisonment,[1401] and there is a strong argument that they should be treated as 'criminal' for Article 6 purposes.

1387 See para 11.174ff above; see also the cases under the Canadian Charter of Rights and Freedoms at para 11.394ff below.
1388 Art 6(2); see generally, para 11.236ff above.
1389 Art 6(3)(a); see generally, para 11.241ff above.
1390 Art 6(3)(b); see generally, para 11.243ff above.
1391 Art 6(3)(c); see para 11.245ff above.
1392 Art 6(3)(d); see para 11.252ff above.
1393 Crime and Disorder Act 1998, s 1, see Baker (n 1386 above) para 4–47.
1394 s 1(4).
1395 s 1(10).
1396 s 1(11).
1397 Crime and Disorder Act 1998, s 2.
1398 s 1(3).
1399 s 1(8) and (9).
1400 See *Rv Corby Justices, ex p Mort The Times*, 13 Mar 1998.
1401 See generally, *Benham v United Kingdom* (1996) 22 EHRR 293.

- *Council tax enforcement*: Applications by local authorities to imprison for non-payment of Council tax are likely to be regarded as a criminal charge under Article 6.[1401a]

It seems likely that all these types of proceedings will be regarded as criminal for the purposes of Article 6 and will, therefore, attract the additional protections of Article 6(2) and (3) including the right to legal assistance. In addition, in relation to any charge which is 'criminal' for the purposes of the Convention it may be possible to argue that there has been a breach of Article 7 on the ground that the offence is too vague to allow an individual to foresee to a reasonable degree from the wording of a relevant provision that he is liable to a criminal offence.[1402]

11.341 **Disclosure and public interest immunity.** It has been suggested that the provisions of the Criminal Procedure and Investigations Act 1994[1403] may be in breach of Article 6 for a number of reasons:[1404]

- *There is no independent assessment of the relevance of material*: The initial assessment for 'primary disclosure' is made by the prosecutor on the basis of schedules prepared by the police. If there is no defence statement there is no right to apply to the court for scrutiny of the adequacy of this disclosure. It is arguable that this could render the trial unfair.[1405]
- *Disclosure is 'conditional' on the service of a 'defence statement'*: It is arguable that this is a breach of the privilege against self-incrimination because the defendant is compelled to provide details of his case.[1406] A failure to serve a defence statement allows the court to draw 'such inferences as appear proper'.[1407]
- *There is no obligation to disclose material obtained in other investigations or held by other people*: It seems that the duty of disclosure under Article 6 extends to material 'to which the prosecution or the police could gain access'.[1408] As a result, the narrower statutory obligation could be a breach of Article 6.
- *There is no obligation to provide disclosure in the case of summary trials*: This would appear to be in breach of the 'equality of arms' obligation under Article 6(1). However, it should be noted that, after a review of the Convention case law, the Divisional Court have held that this practice is compatible with the Convention.[1409]

[1401a] Ibid; and see para 11.282 above.
[1402] *Kokkinakis v Greece* (1993) 17 EHRR 397 para 52; see para 11.257 above.
[1403] See para 11.97ff above.
[1404] See, Baker (n 1386 above) 4–52ff; and see generally, S Sharpe, 'Article 6 and the Disclosure of Evidence in Criminal Trials' [1999] Crim L Rev 273.
[1405] But see Sharpe (n 1404 above) 279–281.
[1406] Cf *Williams v Florida* (1970) 399 US 78 *per* Black J.
[1407] Criminal Procedure and Investigation Act 1994, s 11(3)(b).
[1408] See *Jespers v Belgium* (1981) 27 DR 61, EComm HR.
[1409] *R v Stratford Justices, ex p Imbert* (1999) 2 Cr App R 276.

In addition, there is no obligation to provide disclosure of material relevant to the credibility of defence witnesses.[1410]

11.342 The exclusion of evidence on the ground of public interest immunity may, in some circumstances, be incompatible with Article 6. If material is withheld without judicial scrutiny this will, almost certainly, be a breach of Article 6(1).[1411] However, the *ex parte* procedure which is now in place[1412] satisfies Article 6. In *Jasper and Fitt v United Kingdom*[1413] the Court held that where this procedure was followed there was no breach of Article 6(1).

11.343 **Public hearings.** Criminal cases are, in general, heard in public. Hearings are held in camera for reasons such as 'national security' or the need to protect informers.[1414] Bearing in mind the approach taken by the English courts in such cases, it seems unlikely that there will be a breach of Article 6 in this regard. During jury trials, reporting restrictions are imposed as a matter of course on the legal argument. It seems unlikely this will be a breach of Article 6.[1415] However, these questions may be considered as raising issues about freedom of expression.[1415a]

11.344 **Hearing within a reasonable time.**[1416] At present, under English law a prosecution can only be stayed on the ground of delay if the defendant has been prejudiced.[1417] This is not necessary under Article 6 which requires the court to consider the full period between charge and the final disposal of any appeal in order to ascertain whether there has been a determination within a reasonable time.[1418] It may also be of assistance to refer to the extensive case law that has developed in relation to comparable provisions in other jurisdictions.[1419] Under the Convention, the prosecution cannot rely on arguments about administrative difficulties.[1420] Although the complexity of the investigation can be taken into account, it seems likely that some long running prosecutions will be in breach of Article 6 even where no prejudice can be established. There have been a large number of Human Rights Act cases in Scotland where it is said that delays have breached Article 6(1).[1420a] In *McNab v Her Majesty's Advocate*[1420b] the High Court

[1410] See para 11.96 above.
[1411] In *Rowe and Davis v United Kingdom*, *The Times*, 1 Mar 2000.
[1412] See para 11.292 above.
[1413] *The Times*, 1 Mar 2000.
[1414] See para 11.81 above.
[1415] But see Baker (n 1404 above), para 4–72.
[1415a] See para 15.59ff below.
[1416] See Baker (n 1404 above) para 4–75ff.
[1417] See *A-G's Reference (No 1 of 1990)* [1992] QB 630; see generally para 11.88 above.
[1418] See para 11.219ff above.
[1419] See eg the approach taken by the courts in Canada (para 11.397ff below), New Zealand (para 11.438ff below), South Africa (para 11.502ff below); Trinidad and Tobago (para 11.516ff below) and Zimbabwe (para 11.520 below).
[1420] See para 11.220 above.
[1420a] See generally, para 11.219ff above.
[1420b] 2 Sep 1999.

of Justiciary stressed that there is no universally applicable norm and that a 'reasonable time' must be assessed by reference to the particular circumstances in every case. In *Her Majesty's Advocate v Hynd*[1420c] it was said that in a straightforward case, a delay of 10 months was unacceptable. An application based on unreasonable delay under Article 6(1) does not require the applicant to show that the delay has caused serious prejudice whereas this must be proved to obtain a stay under the court's inherent jurisdiction.[1420d]

11.345 **Right to silence and self incrimination.** The statutory provisions allowing adverse inferences to be drawn from silence[1421] may be incompatible with Article 6. Although the drawing of adverse inference from silence will not, of itself, be incompatible, proper safeguards must be in place.[1422] It seems unlikely that these provisions will be regarded as constituting 'coercion' to give evidence within the principle in *Funke*.[1423] The Court of Appeal have warned of the need for the judge to give careful directions to the jury to avoid breaches of Article 6.[1424] The amendment of the statute to ensure that adverse inferences will not be drawn when the accused has not had the benefit of legal advice[1425] is, however, likely to ensure that, in ordinary circumstances, there will be no incompatibility with Convention rights.

11.346 The use of evidence obtained from a person under compulsory powers in a subsequent criminal prosecution of that person is a breach of Article 6.[1426] However, following the amendment of certain statutory provisions such evidence is no longer used in practice unless it is introduced by the defence or the prosecution for perjury in relation to the investigation.[1427] There are, however, a number of compulsory powers which are not covered by the new legislation (such as requiring information in relation to planning enforcement proceedings). Where these powers are exercised, there will be strong Article 6 arguments against the admission of evidence obtained as a result although the question of exclusion on grounds of prejudice is a matter of discretion for the trial judge.[1427a] The courts are likely to give

[1420c] 9 May 2000.
[1420d] See para 11.88 above.
[1421] See para 11.108ff above.
[1422] See *Murray v United Kingdom* (1996) 22 EHRR 29 (but note, this decision related to a trial by a judge alone, in circumstances in which the other evidence was overwhelming, the position in relation to weaker cases before juries could be different, see A Ashworth, 'Article 6 and the Fairness of Trials' [1999] Crim LR 261, 267).
[1423] See *Funke v France* (1993) 16 EHRR 297; but see D Cheney, L Dickson, J Fitzpatrick and S Uglow, *Criminal Justice and the Human Rights Act 1998* (Jordans, 1999) for a contrary view.
[1424] See *R v Birchall*, *The Times*, 10 Feb 1998, *per* Lord Bingham CJ; and see *Condron v United Kingdom*, *The Times*, 9 May 2000 and para 11.287 above.
[1425] See para 11.109 above.
[1426] *Saunders v United Kingdom* (1996) 23 EHRR 313, see para 11.211ff above ; see generally, P Davies, 'Self-Incrimination, Fair Trials and the Pursuit of Corporate and Financial Wrongdoing,' in B Markesinis (ed), *The Impact of the Human Rights Bill on English Law* (Clarendon Press, 1999), 31–62.
[1427] See para 11.107 above.
[1427a] *R v Hertfordshire County Council ex p Green Environment* [2000] 2 WLR 373 (HL).

considerable weight to the approach taken in the Scots case of *Brown v Procurator Fiscal*[1427b] in which it was held that the prosecution could not lead evidence of an admission made to the police exercising the compulsory powers to question motorists under section 172 of the Road Traffic Act 1988. There is a strong argument in favour of this section being 'read down' in a similar way by the English courts.

Presumption of innocence. The common law has a strong presumption of innocence. The issue of reversal of the burden of proof has been considered in a number of jurisdictions.[1428] There are two basic categories of case in which this onus is reversed:[1429] the 'exemption cases' (where the accused bears the burden of proving that he has the benefit of an 'exception, exemption, proviso or excuse') and the 'presumption' cases (in which statute reverses the onus of proof). It seems likely that the reverse onus provisions in 'exemption cases' will not be in breach of Article 6.[1430] In 'presumption cases', the reverse onus provisions must be considered on a case-by-case basis: balancing the rights of the individual against those of society as a whole.[1431] **11.347**

The courts have power to make costs orders in favour of acquitted defendants.[1432] Such orders are usually made unless there are positive reasons for not doing so. Under the former Practice Direction, a defendant's costs order could be refused if the defendant had been acquitted on a technicality.[1433] It was strongly arguable that this offended against Article 6(2) and the Practice Direction has now been amended to remove this provision.[1434] **11.348**

Information as to charge. In general, the provisions as to the information to be given in charges or indictments[1435] are in accordance with the requirements of Article 6. However, if the prosecution are to rely on particular aggravating features of the offence on a plea of guilty then these features should be undisputed or the accused should be clearly 'charged' with them.[1436] It is, therefore, arguable that the prosecution is under a duty to give the defence formal notice of 'aggravating **11.349**

1427b 4 Feb 2000; see para 4.28A (under appeal to the Privy Council).

1428 In addition to the Convention jurisprudence (para 11.236ff above), the issue has been considered, for example, in Canada (para 11.402 below), Hong Kong, in particular the Privy Council case of *A-G of Hong Kong v Lee Kwong-kut* [1993] AC 951 (para 11.471ff below), South Africa (para 11.496ff below) and Zimbabwe (para 11.521 below).

1429 See para 11.116 above.

1430 C Baker (ed), *The Human Rights Act 1998: A Practitioners Guide* (Sweet & Maxwell, 1998) paras 4-80– 4-81.

1431 See *R v DPP, ex p Kebeline* [1999] 3 WLR 972, discussed at para 11.116 above; and see *R v Lambert* [2000] 2 All ER (D) 1135.

1432 Prosecution of Offenders Act 1985, s 16(2); a costs decision is not subject to judicial review, *Re Sampson* [1987] 1 WLR 194.

1433 *Practice Direction (Costs in Criminal Proceedings)* (1991) 93 Cr App R 89 para 2.2.

1434 See *Practice Direction (Crime: Costs in Criminal Proceedings) (No 2)*, *The Times*, 6 Oct 1999.

1435 Indictments Act 1915, s 3.

1436 Cf *De Salvador Torres v Spain* (1996) 23 EHRR 601.

features' which might be relevant to sentencing and which the defence may wish to have resolved at a 'Newton' hearing.[1437]

11.350 **Legal advice.** The common law and statutory right to legal advice appears to comply with Article 6 requirements. However, two areas of potential conflict have been suggested. First, in the light of the importance of the right to communicate with a lawyer without hindrance,[1438] there will be breaches if, as sometimes happens in practice, police officers seek to eavesdrop on telephone calls between persons in detention and their lawyers.

11.351 Secondly, the right to consult with a lawyer is of paramount importance in cases in which the courts can draw adverse inferences from silence.[1439] Until recently, under English law, a person could, in theory, be denied access to legal advice and then be subject to adverse inferences. Adverse inferences could also be drawn from silence prior to the arrival at the police station, when legal advice was not available. It is submitted that these were breaches of Article 6.[1440] The recent amendments to the Criminal Justice and Public Order Act 1994[1440a] are designed to ensure that such inferences cannot now be drawn where there has been no opportunity to obtain legal advice.

11.352 **Conduct of trial.** There are a number of areas in which the English practice at trial may be inconsistent with Article 6:

- The court is, at present, entitled to grant anonymity to witnesses in 'exceptional circumstances'.[1441] A stricter approach is taken under Article 6 where it has been held that granting anonymity to a witness whose evidence is 'decisive' renders the whole proceedings unfair.[1442] It seems, therefore, that the present practice may be inconsistent with Article 6.[1443]
- A conviction can, at present, be based on contested hearsay admitted under the provisions of sections 23 to 26 of the Criminal Justice Act 1988.[1444] The English courts have held that this will not be a breach of Article 6[1445] and this is

[1437] For 'Newton' hearings (*R v Newton* (1982) 77 Cr App R 13) see P Murphy (ed), *Blackstone's Criminal Practice 1999* (Blackstone Press, 1999) D17.2ff; and see Baker (n 1430 above) 4–91.

[1438] *S v Switzerland* (1991) 14 EHRR 670 para 48.

[1439] See para 11.108ff above.

[1440] See *Murray v United Kingdom* (1996) 22 EHRR 29 para 67; and cf *Archbold: Criminal Pleading, Practice and Evidence (*Sweet & Maxwell, 1999) 15–401 and *Condron v United Kingdom, The Times*, 9 May 2000, and see para 11.286ff above.

[1440a] See para 11.109 above.

[1441] See para 11.127 above.

[1442] *Kostovski v Netherlands* (1989) 12 EHRR 434; and *Doorsen v Netherlands* (1996) 22 EHRR 330; see para 11.217 above and see also, the discussion of witness anonymity in a 'war crimes' context, A Cassesse, 'The International Criminal Tribunal for the Former Yugoslavia and Human Rights' [1997] EHRLR 329, 339-342.

[1443] See D Cheney, L Dickson, J Fitzpatrick and S Uglow, *Criminal Justice and the Human Rights Act 1998* (Jordans, 1999) 97.

[1444] See para 11.128ff above.

[1445] See para 11.129 above.

supported by a number of decisions of the Commission and the Scots courts.[1446] However, if the conviction is based 'solely or to a decisive extent' on the evidence of witnesses who the accused has not had an effective opportunity to challenge (which would be permitted under the Act), there may be a violation of Article 6.[1447]

- The hearsay rule means that the confession of a third party is not admissible in evidence at a criminal trial.[1448] It is arguable that this would render the trial of an accused unfair.[1449]
- The anonymity of the complainant in rape cases[1450] may require reconsideration;[1451]
- The power to clear the court when a child gives evidence[1452] may breach the obligation for proceedings to be heard in public.[1453]

Agents provocateurs. Under English law, the fact that evidence has been obtained by an *agent provocateur* will not, of itself, lead to its exclusion in a criminal trial.[1454] It is arguable that this is inconsistent with Article 6. In particular, it is likely that prosecution for any offence which has been 'instigated' by undercover agents of the investigating authority would be a breach of Article 6.[1455] The test to be applied is whether the effect of the evidence of an *agent provocateur* would be to deny the defendant a fair trial. The evidence of undercover police officers who give the defendant an opportunity to commit the offence but who do not 'persuade, pressure, instigate or incite' him to commit it is unlikely to have this effect.[1455a] It has been suggested that, in order to comply with Article 6, it will be necessary to put legal safeguards in place to provide proper regulation of the activities of undercover police agents, perhaps including supervision by an independent third party.[1456] This argument seems to have been accepted by the **11.353**

[1446] *Trivedi v United Kingdom* (1997) 89 DR 136; *Quinn v United Kingdom* Application 23496/94, 11 Dec 1997 (Merits) para 80ff; see also two cases in the High Court of Justiciary *McKenna v Her Majesty's Advocate* 2000 SCCR 159 and *Her Majesty's Advocate v Nulty*, 2000 GWD 11–385.

[1447] See *Quinn*, (n 1446 above) para 80; and generally Cheney, Dickson, Fitzpatrick and Uglow, (n 444, above) 103–104; R Buxton, 'The Convention and the English law of Criminal Evidence' and J Spencer, 'European Convention and the Rules of Criminal Procedure and Evidence in England' in J Beatson, C Forsyth and I Hare, (eds), *The Human Rights Act and the Criminal Justice and Regulatory Process* (Hart Publishing, 1999).

[1448] *R v Blastland* [1986] AC 41; unlike the confession of a co-accused see *Rv Myers* [1998] AC 124.

[1449] See Cheney, Dickson, Fitzpatrick and Uglow (n 1443 above) 104; and see the decision of the US Supreme Court in *Chambers v Mississippi* (1973) 410 US 295; but see the contrary view of the Commission in *Blastland v United Kingdom* (1988) 10 EHRR 528, EComm HR.

[1450] Under Sexual Offences (Amendment) Act 1976, s 4.

[1451] See the Canadian decision in *R v Seaboyer* [1991] 2 SCR 577; and see para 11.406 below.

[1452] Under Children and Young Persons Act 1933, s 37.

[1453] See the Canadian case of *Edmonton Journal v Alberta (A-G)* (1983) 146 DLR (3d) 673; QB.

[1454] See para 11.131 above.

[1455] See generally, *Teixiera de Castro v Portugal* (1998) 28 EHRR 101, see para 11.216 above.

[1455a] *Nottingham City Council v Amin* [2000] 1 WLR 1071.

[1456] See generally, O Davies, 'The Fruit of the Poisoned Tree—Entrapment and the Human Rights Act 1998' (1999) 163 JP 84.

Government and a framework for regulation is contained in Part II of the Regulation of Investigatory Powers Bill.

11.354 **Interpreters.** There is no general right to an interpreter in English law although, in practice, one will be provided where necessary at public expense.[1457] However, the Crown Court has a discretion to order an accused to pay the costs of an interpreter.[1458] It is submitted that this is a breach of Article 6(3)(e) because such costs should always be met by the State.[1459] In addition, there is a strong argument that an accused should have a right to translations of statements and of documents relied on by the prosecution.[1459a]

11.354A **The giving of reasons.** The implied Article 6 right to a 'reasoned judgment'[1459b] may give rise to difficulties in criminal cases. There is a strong argument that Crown Court judges and stipendiary magistrates should, in future, give reasons for all decisions which are 'determinative' of rights.[1459c] The position is more difficult in relation to lay magistrates and juries. It is submitted that it is likely to be held that the absence of reasons for their decisions is a justified limitation on the implied right to reasons: lay participation serves the interests of justice and the decisions are reviewable by other courts.

11.355 **Sentencing.** English law now contains a number of provisions for the confiscation of the proceeds of crime.[1460] These provisions entitle the Court to presume that property which has been in the possession of an offender prior to proceedings is the benefit of a crime. It appears that such a presumption does not breach Article 6(2). In *Welch v United Kingdom*[1461] the Court described the presumption as 'essential to the preventive scheme' and made it clear that it did not 'in any respect' call into question the powers of confiscation conferred on the court as a weapon in the fight against the scourge of drug trafficking.[1461a]

11.356 **Appeals.** An order 'relating to a trial on indictment' in a Crown Court is not susceptible to judicial review.[1462] This means that certain orders made in the course of criminal trials may not be subject to challenge. It has been suggested that this may lead to a breach of Article 6.[1463] However, the absence of an Article 6

1457 See para 11.125 above.

1458 *Practice Direction (Crime Costs)* [1991] 1 WLR 498.

1459 See *Luedicke, Belkacem and Koç v Germany* (1978) 2 EHRR 149 para 40.

1459a Cf the New Zealand case of *Alwen Industries Ltd and Kar Wong v Collector of Customs* [1996] 1 HRNZ 574, see para 11.432 below.

1459b See para 11.218 above.

1459c For the present practice, see para 11.92 above.

1460 Criminal Justice Act 1988, Pt IV; Proceeds of Crime Act 1995; Drug Trafficking Act 1994.

1461 (1995) 20 EHRR 247 para 33.

1461a Ibid para 36.

1462 Supreme Court Act 1981, s 29(3), see generally R Clayton and H Tomlinson, *Judicial Review Procedure* (Wiley Chancery Law, 1997), 19–21.

1463 See *R v Manchester Crown Court, ex p H & M*, 30 Jul 1999, Div Ct, *per* Forbes J.

'right to appeal' means that, provided that the order was made at a hearing complying with Article 6, there is unlikely to be a breach.

The Court of Appeal (Criminal Division) has the power to allow an appeal where a conviction is unsafe.[1464] This means that the Court could decline to quash a conviction for breach of a Convention right if it took the view that the conviction itself was safe.[1465] It is arguable that this approach is not compatible with Article 6 which requires the court to consider the issue of fairness rather than that of safety,[1465a] but the Court of Appeal held in *R v Davis and Rowe*[1465b] that the two issues of 'fairness' and 'safety' should be kept separate. It is also arguable that the Court of Appeal's approach when receiving new evidence[1466] will breach the requirement of fairness under Article 6 if the court determines the question of whether evidence is capable of being believed as a preliminary to receiving the evidence itself.[1467] **11.357**

(c) Education

The Commission has held that the right not to be denied an elementary education falls squarely within the domain of public law, having no private law analogy or repercussions on private rights or obligations;[1468] and it is difficult to see how the right to education might fall within the scope of 'civil rights and obligations'.[1469] Some commentators have, nevertheless, argued that the procedure for school admissions and expulsion are subject to Article 6 and are not compatible with it.[1470] There may be a stronger argument that Article 6 applies in relation to independent schools where it is alleged that the school acted in breach of contract. The inability of a child (as opposed to his parent) to pursue the statutory right of appeal from the special educational needs tribunal[1471] could be a breach of his right of access to the court. **11.358**

[1464] Criminal Appeal Act 1968, s 2(1) as substituted by the Criminal Appeal Act 1995; on this power, see generally *Rv Mullen (Nicholas Robert Neil)* [1999] 3 WLR 777.

[1465] See R Buxton, 'The Convention and the English law of Criminal Evidence' and D Kyle, 'The Human Rights Act: post trial and hearing' in J Beatson, C Forsyth and I Hare (eds), *The Human Rights Act and the Criminal Justice and Regulatory Process* (Hart Publishing, 1999).

[1465a] See *Condron v United Kingdom*, *The Times*, 9 May 2000 para 65, see para 11.287 above.

[1465b] *The Times*, 25 Jul 2000.

[1466] Under the Criminal Appeals Act 1968, s 23 as amended by the Criminal Appeals Act 1995.

[1467] D Kyle, 'The Human Rights Act: post trial and hearing' in J Beatson, C Forsyth and I Hare (eds), *The Human Rights Act and the Criminal Justice and Regulatory Process* (Hart Publishing, 1999).

[1468] *Simpson v United Kingdom* Application 14688/89, (1989) 64 DR 188, EComm HR.

[1469] See para 11.163ff above.

[1470] J Friel and D Hay, 'Education' in C Baker (ed), *The Human Rights Act 1998: A Practitioner's Guide* (Sweet & Maxwell, 1998), para 11–17; A Bradley, 'Scope for Review: the Convention Right to Education and the Human Rights Act 1988' [1999] EHRLR 395; M Supperstone, J Goudie and J Coppel, *Local Authorities and the Human Rights Act 1998* (Butterworths, 1999) 55.

[1471] *S v The Special Educational Needs Tribunal* [1996] 1 WLR 382.

(d) Employment, discrimination and disciplinary bodies

11.359 It is clear that private law employment rights are subject to Article 6 'fair hearing' protection.[1472] The position in relation to public employees is less clear cut. The Convention case law suggests that disputes concerning the recruitment, careers and termination of service of civil servants are outside the scope of Article 6 because, in many civil law jurisdictions such disputes are regarded as matters of public rather than private law.[1473] The position is different if the public employees work under contracts of employment.[1474] Since it is now generally recognised that civil servants are employed under contracts of employment;[1475] their employment rights will attract the protection of Article 6 insofar as they affect their financial interests.[1476] However, this does not mean that public employer's disciplinary procedures must provide the full range of 'fair hearing' protections for employees. Disciplinary proceedings which do not affect an employee's pay or position will not involve the determination of 'civil rights' at all.[1477] As a result, even though public employees have contractual rights in English law,[1478] it is strongly arguable[1479] that disciplinary proceedings are not ordinarily covered by Article 6.[1480]

11.360 In any event, there will be no violation of Article 6 if an employee who is dissatisfied with the result of disciplinary proceedings has recourse to the courts. The availablity of the court procedure will satisfy Article 6.[1481] The way in which unfair dismissal claims are decided under the Employment Tribunals Act 1996 will be compatible with Article 6, but the arbitration scheme for unfair dismissal disputes under the Employment Rights (Disputes Resolution) Act 1998 could raise issues about its compatibility with Article 6.[1482]

11.361 Employment tribunals are paid for, largely appointed and administered by the employment tribunal service, a Department of Trade and Industry agency. The lay members of the tribunals do not have security of tenure. As a result, it is

---

[1472] See para 11.169 above.

[1473] See *Neigel v France* RJD 1997-II 399; and see para 11.172 above.

[1474] *Darnell v United Kingdom* (1993) 18 EHRR 205.

[1475] *R v Lord Chancellor's Department, ex p Nangle* [1991] ICR 743.

[1476] See also G Morris, 'The European Convention on Human Rights and Employment: to Which Acts Does it Apply?' [1999] EHRLR 498; and the decision of the Commission in *Balfour v United Kingdom* [1997] EHRLR 665 to the contrary and the commentary at [1997] EHRLR 666.

[1477] See, generally, M Supperstone, J Goudie and J Coppel (n 1470 above) 46–48.

[1478] By contrast to public employees in Convention countries such as France.

[1479] However, disciplinary proceedings by professional bodies which affect the ability to practise the profession are within the scope of Art 6: see para 11.167 above.

[1480] See eg *Le Compte v Belgium* [1985] 5 EHRR 533 para 25; *De Compte v European Parliament* [1991] ECR II-781.

[1481] See para 11.197 above.

[1482] See B Hepple, 'The Impact on Labour Law', in B Markesinis (ed), *The Impact of the Human Rights Bill on English Law* (Clarendon Press, 1999), 71.

arguable that the Employment Tribunals are not 'independent' for the purposes of Article 6.[1482a] The lack of independence is particularly clear when Employment Tribunals are considering claims for redundancy payments from the Secretary of State for Trade and Industry.[1483]

The inability of an applicant to obtain legal aid to pursue a claim before the employment tribunal (such as a lengthy and complex discrimination case) might breach the right of access to the court under Article 6.[1484] **11.362**

It is well established that Article 6 applies to disciplinary procedures affecting the professions when the right to practice is in issue.[485] Where the internal procedures fail to comply with Article 6, the critical issue is whether any subsequent judicial control does so. The Commission has recently held that the General Medical Council procedure complies with Article 6;[1486] however, the position may be different where it is necessary to investigate issues of fact and the challenge is by way of judicial review.[1487] **11.363**

(e) Family law

Rights dealt with in family law cases are 'civil rights' under Article 6.[1488] The development of English family law has been strongly influenced by decisions under Article 6.[1489] Nevertheless, there are a number of areas of family law where the present English law or practice may be in breach of fair hearing rights. **11.364**

The right of access to the courts may be breached by the provisions of section 91(14) of the Children Act 1989 which allows the court to refuse to hear an application if there is no need for renewed judicial investigation.[1490] The test is 'does the application demonstrate that there is any need for renewed judicial investigation?'[1490a] Bearing in mind the fact that the bar is not an absolute one, it seems that section 91(14) will be found to be compatible with the Convention. The child **11.365**

[1482a] See para 11.223ff above.

[1483] *Smith v Secretary of State for Trade and Industry* [2000] ICR 69.

[1484] See para 11.189 above.

[1485] See for example *König v Germany* (1978) 2 EHRR 170 (medicine); *H v Belgium* (1987) 10 EHRR 339 (law); *Guchez v Belgium* (1984) 40 DR 100, EComm HR (architecture); and see, generally, para 11.167 above.

[1486] *Stefan v United Kingdom* (1997) 25 EHHR CD 130; *Wickramsinghe v United Kingdom* [1998] EHRLR 338.

[1487] See para 11.198 above.

[1488] But not the obligation to pay assessments worked out by the Child Support Agency which are public rights outside Art 6: *Logan v United Kingdom* (1996) 22 EHRR CD 178.

[1489] In particular, the Children Act 1989 was, in part, a response to the decision in *R v United Kingdom* (1987) 10 EHRR 74, see para 11.273 above.

[1490] *Re A (Application for Leave)* [1998] 1 FLR 1, CA.

[1490a] See generally, H Swindells *et al*, *Family Law and the Human Rights Act 1998* (Family Law, 1999) para 7.20ff.

himself has no absolute right to make an application under the Children Act; but this appears to be in accordance with the European Convention on the Exercise of Children's Rights.[1491] It is arguable that the length and complexity of public law child proceedings means that they would attract a right to legal assistance under the principle identified in the *Airey* case.[1492] Such legal aid is available at present[1493] but any restriction could be a breach of the right of access to the court.

11.366 Ancillary relief proceedings involve the determination of civil rights and obligations but are held in chambers.[1493a] It is strongly arguable that this is a breach of Article 6(1).[1494] In addition, the present practice in all family proceedings of giving judgment in private appears to be a breach of the express rights in Article 6(1).[1494a] A number of Article 6 issues arise in relation to proceedings under the Child Abduction and Custody Act 1985 which are, by their nature, summary.[1495]

(f) Health care

11.367 Reliance on Article 6 may assist in clarifying the approach to be taken when declarations are sought in relation to medical treatment for mentally handicapped patients.[1496] Although the court must consider the patient's best interests, it often deals with this question by deciding whether the proposed action is in accordance with an accepted body of medical opinion, in accordance with the '*Bolam* test'.[1497] However, it is arguable that the obligation to ensure effective access to the court means that the court will have to address the issue of the patient's best interests directly.

(g) Housing

11.368 Although Article 6 applies to property rights[1498] (and would apply for example, to compulsory purchase orders), the term 'civil rights and obligations'[1499] does not extend to housing management decisions or issues concerning homelessness. At present disputes about admission to and exclusion from the Housing Register are

---

[1491] See generally, M Horowitz, G Kingscote and M Nicholls, *Rayden and Jackson on Divorce and Family Matters: The Human Rights Act 1998, A Special Bulletin for Family Lawyers* (Butterworths, 1999) para 5.10.

[1492] *Airey v Ireland* (1979) 2 EHRR 305; see para 11.189 above.

[1493] Legal Aid Act 1988, s 15(3)(c).

[1493a] For a discussion of the circumstances in which there should be a public hearing in family cases see *Re B (Minors) (Contact)* [1994] 2 FLR 1.

[1494] Cf Horowitz, Kingscote and Nicholls (n 1491 above) para 6.04.

[1494a] See *Re P B (Hearings in Open Court)* [1996] 2 FLR 765 and generally Swindells, *et al* (n 1490a above) para 8.182ff above.

[1495] See *R B (Minors)(Abduction)(No 2)* [1993] 1 FLR 993; see generally, Horowitz, Kingscote and Nicholls (n 1491above), para 6.47ff.

[1496] See generally, I Kennedy and A Grubb, *Principles of Medical Law* (Oxford University Press, 1998) paras 4.133–4.136.

[1497] See *Bolam v Friern Hospital Management Committee* [1957] 1 WLR 582, 586.

[1498] See para 11.166 above.

[1499] See para 11.163ff above.

decided under a local authority's own review procedures without any right of appeal to the court.[1499a] It has been suggested that this may be a breach of Article 6.[1499b] Difficulties also may arise in relation to the procedure for terminating introductory tenancies created under the Housing Act 1996.[1499c] Under section 127(2) of the Act the court is obliged to make a possession order provided the local authority or registered social landlord has served notice of proceedings under section 128. The only way a tenant can protect his position is to request the landlord to review his decision to seek possession under section 129; and that decision may ultimately be challenged in judicial review proceedings.[1499d] However, it is strongly arguable that the procedure breaches the tenant's civil right determined by an 'independent and impartial' tribunal.[1499e] The practice of obtaining a warrant of possession when there has been a breach of a suspended order without a hearing or notice has also been said to breach Article 6.[1499f]

On the other hand, it is well established that Article 6 covers social welfare benefits.[1500] The determination of housing benefit and its review by housing benefit boards does not comply with the obligation to ensure an independent and impartial tribunal.[1501] However, the boards' decision is subject to judicial review; and it can be argued that this is sufficient to ensure compliance with Article 6.[1502] **11.369**

(h) Local government law

Article 6 is likely to have considerable implications over a number of local authority activities. Many of these will involve the determination of what the Convention regards as 'civil rights and obligations'. However, because administrative procedures are involved, it is not necessary to ensure full 'internal Article 6 compliance': the availability of judicial review will usually be sufficient to ensure that, overall, the procedures adopted are 'fair'.[1502a] The following areas are considered: licensing, community care and child protection. **11.370**

Licensing. Local Authorities have extensive licensing powers.[1503] Since a licence to engage in commercial activity is a civil right for the purpose of Article 6,[1504] **11.371**

[1499a] See Housing Act 1996, s 164.
[1499b] J Luba, 'Acting on Rights—The Housing Implications of the Human Rights Act', Lecture, Sep 1999.
[1499c] Housing Act 1996, ss 124–133.
[1499d] *Manchester City Council v Cochrane* (1996) 31 HLR 810.
[1499e] See para 11.222ff above.
[1499f] See Luba (n 1499b above).
[1500] See para 11.170 above.
[1501] See para 11.222ff above.
[1502] See para 11.198 above.
[1502a] See para 11.304ff above.
[1503] For example, taxis, theatres, street trading. For a list of their principal licensing and registration functions, see App D to S Bailey (ed), *Cross on Local Government Law* (9th edn, Sweet & Maxwell, 1996).
[1504] *Tre Traktörer Aktiebolag v Sweden* (1989) 13 EHRR 309 (withdrawal of alcohol licence; *Axelson v Sweden* (1989) 65 DR 99, EComm HR (refusal to grant taxi licence).

there is a strong argument that 'fair hearing rights' will apply to the grant or withdrawal of licences, including the right to a public oral hearing[1505] before an independent[1506] and impartial[1507] tribunal with a reasoned judgment.[1508] The internal procedures for considering licences are most unlikely to comply with Article 6 guarantees. However, in many instances an applicant will have a right of appeal to the magistrates' or Crown Court. If, on the other hand, the applicant is limited to a judicial review challenge, then compliance with Article 6 will depend on whether he has had a sufficient opportunity to dispute the primary issues of fact.

11.372 A theatre licence may be granted at the discretion of the licensing authority.[1509] The applicant has a right of appeal against a refusal to grant a licence (or to impose conditions and restrictions) to the magistrates' court[1510] which has the power to consider all disputes of fact and law. The licensing authority for cinemas in Greater London is the appropriate borough council;[1511] elsewhere it is the district council.[1512] A person aggrieved by the refusal, revocation or with conditions or restrictions can apply to the Crown Court.[1513] Music and dance licences in Greater London are granted by the appropriate borough council[1514] and a right of appeal to the magistrates' court.[1515] Outside Greater London it is the responsibility, for granting dance and music licences, of the district council.[1516] There are again rights of appeal against the refusal of a licence or against its terms.[1517] In principle, third parties who can show that the 'civil rights and obligations' are affected by granting the licence may have a right to make representations under Article 6.

11.373 The control of licensing sex establishments in Greater London is the responsibility of the relevant borough council (or Common Council of the City of London) and outside Greater London the district councils.[1518] There are some restrictions on the right of appeal to the magistrates[1519] so that the only remedy available is an application for judicial review. In those cases, it may be strongly arguable that

[1505] See para 11.206 above.
[1506] See para 11.223ff above.
[1507] See para 11.225ff above.
[1508] See para 11.218 above.
[1509] Theatre Act 1968, Sch 1, para 1.
[1510] Ibid s 14(1).
[1511] Including the Common Council of the City: see Cinema Act 1985, ss 3(1), 21(1).
[1512] Ibid ss 3(10), 21(1).
[1513] Ibid s 16.
[1514] Or Common Council of the City: see London Local Government Act 1963, s 52(3), Sch 12; Local Government Act 1985, s 16, Sch 7, para 1. Under the Local Government (Miscellaneous Provisions) Act 1982, s 1(1), the Act does not extend to Greater London.
[1515] Local Government Act 1963, Sch 12, para 19.
[1516] Local Government (Miscellaneous Provisions) Act 1982, s 1, Sch 1, para 22; for the Scilly Isles, it is the Council of the Isles.
[1517] Local Government (Miscellaneous Provisions) Act 1982, Sch 1, para 17(1)(2).
[1518] Local Government (Miscellaneous Provisions) Act 1982, s 2.
[1519] Ibid Sch 3, para 17.

Article 6 has been breached. The regime for licensing taxis is different in the Metropolitan police area and the City of London[1520] from that which applies for outside those areas.[1521] Inside the Metropolitan area the refusal, suspension and revocation of a licence can be appealed to the magistrates.[1522] Outside the Metropolitan area the refusal of a district council to grant a licence can be appealed to the Crown Court.[1523] A number of local authorities licence the employment of 'bouncers' at night clubs by operating doorman licensing schemes. These procedures are non statutory and might appear to breach the Article 6 requirement that a tribunal must be 'established by law'. However, if such schemes were challenged, the proceedings themselves would be heard before an independent tribunal and it is submitted that these schemes are not incompatible with Article 6.

Community care. Article 6 may affect a range of decisions in relation to community care. It is well established that social security benefits fall within the scope of Article 6[1524] and it is arguable that where an applicant's circumstances are so severe as to require some level of service provision,[1525] decisions about the level and nature of his provision under the Chronically Sick and Disabled Persons Act 1970 must be made in accordance with the fair trial guarantees under Article 6.[1526] Charging decisions[1527] may also be subject to Article 6 in the same way as decisions concerning social security contributions[1528] although the position is not clear cut.[1529] **11.374**

Article 6 may also require local authorities to take a different approach when considering the cancellation of registration under the Registered Homes Act 1984. It has been suggested that the 'without notice' procedure to cancel registration urgently[1530] may be vulnerable under Article 6.[1531] The practice of many authorities to hear applications to cancel registrations[1532] in private hearings may also be questionable, not least because they are obliged to inform residents and relatives **11.375**

1520 Metropolitan Police Carriage Act 1969, s 9, the London Cab Order 1934 (SR & O 1934 No 1346).
1521 Town Police Clauses Act 1847 ss 37–68, the Town Police Clauses Act 1889, s 76 Public Health Act 1925, the Local Government (Miscellaneous Provisions) Act 1976, Pt II and ss 10–17.
1522 Transport Act 1985, s 17.
1523 Public Health Act 1975, s 171(4); Public Health Acts Amendment Act 1980, ss 2(1), 7(1)(b).
1524 See para 11.170 above.
1525 *R v Gloucestershire County Council, ex p Barry* [1997] 2 AC 584.
1526 M Supperstone, J Goudie and J Coppel, *Local Authorities and the Human Rights Act 1998* (Butterworths, 1999) 74.
1527 Under eg s 22 of the National Assistance Act 1948 or s 17 of the Health and Social Security Adjudications Act 1993.
1528 *Schouten and Meldrum v Netherlands* (1994) 19 EHRR 432.
1529 Contrast the views expressed in Supperstone, Goudie and Coppel, (n 1526 above) 74, relying on the decisions holding that tax assessments are not subject to Art 6: see para 11.173 above.
1530 Registered Homes Act 1984, s 11.
1531 R McCarthy, 'The Human Rights Act and Social Services Functions', lecture 10 May 1999.
1532 Registered Homes Act 1984, s 10.

of their intention.[1533] The critical question in any particular case is whether the procedure as a whole breaches Article 6.

11.376 **Child protection register.** It has been argued that entering a child on the child protection register attracts Article 6 protection. A similar argument could be directed to decisions to place a person on the consultancy service index as being unsuitable to work with children.[1533a] However, it is likely that it will be held that such a step does not involve the determination of civil rights but should be characterised as an interim protective measure.[1534]

(i) Planning and environmental law

11.377 **Introduction.** The fair trial rights under Article 6 have been held to apply to a wide variety of situations including any decision granting or refusing planning permission and to any decisions in relation to enforcement proceedings.[1535] The Court has held that Article 6 applies to a decision to grant permission to extract water from a well,[1536] the application of nature conservation laws,[1537]a permit to build a house,[1538] long term planning blight[1539] and enforcement proceedings under the Town and Country Planning Act.[1540] The existing planning appeal procedures were held by the Court in *Bryan v United Kingdom*[1541] to meet the requirements of Article 6(1). However, it should be noted that in that case there was no dispute regarding the primary facts and the position may be different where the underlying factual position is contested.[1542]

11.378 **Third party rights.** The Court has also held that a third party whose property value is adversely affected by the grant of planning permission has Article 6(1) rights.[1543] Under the English planning system a third party has no right of appeal to the Secretary of State and can only challenge planning permission by taking judicial review proceedings. The absence of the ability to challenge a decision on its merits may breach Article 6(1) particularly, where the primary facts are disputed

[1533] See eg Ombudsman Complaint No 94/13/1323.

[1533a] See now, Protection of Children Act 1999 (s 4 provides for an appeal to a Tribunal against a decision to include a person on the list).

[1534] Supperstone, Goudie and Coppel, (n 1526 above) 86; and see *R v Secretary of State for Health, ex p C, The Times*, 1 Mar 2000 in which it was held that inclusion on the consultancy index was not 'determinative' of any right.

[1535] See generally, T Corner, 'Planning, Environment and the European Convention on Human Rights' [1998] JPL 301.

[1536] *Zander v Sweden* (1990) 18 EHRR 175.

[1537] *Oerlemans v Netherlands* (1991) 15 EHRR 561.

[1538] *Skärby v Sweden* (1990) 13 EHRR 90.

[1539] *Sporrong and Lönnroth v Sweden* (1982) 5 EHRR 35.

[1540] *Bryan v United Kingdom* (1995) 21 EHRR 342.

[1541] (1995) 21 EHRR 342; see also *ISKCON v United Kingdom* (1994) 76-A DR 90, EComm HR.

[1542] See para 11.198 above.

[1543] *Ortenberg v Austria* (1994) 19 EHRR 524.

although it is again arguable that recourse to judicial review is sufficient for these purposes. Nevertheless, the right to Article 6(1) protection will make it easier to pressurise the Secretary of State to call in controversial planning applications.[1544] Some authorities allow third parties to make representations to planning committees; this practice will go some way to prevent a finding that Article 6(1) has been breached.

Where a person is refused permission to be heard at a public hearing concerning a structure plan,[1545] he is a person aggrieved for the purposes of applying to the High Court to challenge its validity.[1546] However, it may be difficult in these circumstances to demonstrate that the applicant has had access to the court on the factual merits. **11.379**

Plan making powers. The powers of local authorities to make plans will also be affected by Article 6. Decisions on structure plans, local plans or waste plans may in some circumstances affect 'civil rights and obligations'[1547] because of their impact on property or commercial activities. It has been argued that the current procedures for hearing and determining local plan objections may well be in breach of Article 6(1).[1548] A local planning authority makes a final decision on its own proposals so that it is neither independent[1549] nor impartial.[1550] The local planning inspector cannot satisfy Article 6 since his function is not to make a determination but to report with recommendations and the power of the Secretary of State is not sufficient to meet Article 6. It is unclear whether the position is saved by the right of a statutory appeal,[1551] especially if the local authority rejects the inspector's recommendations. **11.380**

It has been suggested that a number of difficulties may also arise for authorities in making development plans.[1552] A planning authority must consult in relation to proposed structure plan policies and to consider representations[1553] and must give adequate reasons when dealing with objections to structure plan policies.[1554] It may be criticised because there is no right of hearing at an examination in public of a structure plan[1555] and it must adequately consult on a proposed local plan or **11.381**

[1544] See generally, T Corner, 'Planning, Environment and the European Convention on Human Rights' [1998] JPL 301.
[1545] Under the Town and Country Planning Act, s 35B(4).
[1546] Under the Town and Country Planning Act, s 287.
[1547] See para 11.163ff above.
[1548] T Kitson, 'The European Convention on Human Rights and Local Plans' [1998] JPL 321.
[1549] See para 11.223ff above.
[1550] See para 11.225ff above.
[1551] On the principles of *Bryan v United Kingdom* (n 1540 above).
[1552] M Supperstone, J Goudie and J Coppel, *Local Authorities and the Human Rights Act 1998* (Butterworths, 1999) 113.
[1553] Town and Country Planning Act 1990, s 33.
[1554] See eg *Modern Homes (Whitworth) v Lancaster County Council* [1998] EGCS 73.
[1555] Town and Country Planning Act 1990, s 35B(4).

urban development plan and consider the objections made.[1556] It must give proper consideration to the inspector's recommendations and give adequate reasons for departing from them[1557] and it may be subject to proceedings for failing to hold a second public inquiry if it accepts changes to the plan which prejudice third parties.[1558]

11.381A **Land development.** There are potential conflicts of interest where a local authority seeks to develop land which it owns and is the relevant planning authority which is empowered to grant planning permission. In such circumstances its decisions will be vulnerable to challenge by persons who are affected on the ground that the decision was not made by an 'independent and impartial tribunal'.[1558a]

11.382 **Evidence under compulsory powers.** The use of evidence in criminal proceedings which is obtained under powers to compel witnesses to give evidence in relation to breaches of planning enforcement[1559] and the regulation of waste on land[1560] could result in breaches of Article 6.[1561] The question of exclusion of potentially incriminating answers on the ground of prejudice is a matter for the discretion of the trial judge.[1562] However, there are likely to be challenges to prosecutions on the basis of evidence obtained by use of these powers. If the evidence is obtained in the course of a criminal investigation it is likely to be excluded but it may be admissible if it was initially obtained by compulsion for non-criminal 'regulatory' purposes.[1562a]

(j) Police law

11.383 Article 6(1) rights apply to those 'charged' with criminal offences in accordance with the special Convention meaning of this term which would cover a person under arrest.[1563] However, the manner in which Article 6 is to be applied during the preliminary investigation depends on the circumstances of the case.[1564] For example, Article 6 does not give an accused the right to examine a witness being questioned by the police.[1565] It seems unlikely that Article 6 will provide arrested suspects with any additional rights.

[1556] See eg *Stirk v Bridgnorth District Council* [1996] 73 P & CR 439; *Miller v Wycombe District Council* [1997] JPL 951; *Tyler v Avon County Council* [1996] 73 P & CR 335.

[1557] See eg *Drexfine Holdings v Cherwell District Council* [1998] JPL 361.

[1558] See eg *R v Teeside District Council* [1998] JPL 23.

[1558a] See para 11.222 above.

[1559] Town and Country Planning Act 1990, s 171C and D.

[1560] Environmental Protection Act 1990, ss 71 and 34(5); and see *R v Hertfordshire County Council, ex p Green Environmental Industries* [2000] 2 WLR 373.

[1561] See para 11.346 above.

[1562] See *R v Hertfordshire County Council, ex p Green Environmental Industries* (n 1560 above).

[1562a] See generally, *Brown v Procurator Fiscal* 4 Feb 2000; see para 11.346 above.

[1563] See para 11.180 above.

[1564] *Imbrioscia v Switzerland* (1993) 17 EHRR 441, 38.

[1565] *X v Germany* (1979) 17 DR 231, EComm HR.

(k) Prison law

The right of access to the courts under Article 6 was, of course, first established in a case involving the rights of prisoners in the United Kingdom.[1566] The question arises as to whether all prison disciplinary hearings fall within the scope of Article 6(3).[1567] It could be argued that the threat of loss of remission means that disciplinary allegations are 'criminal charges'.[1568] If so, prisoners would be entitled to Article 6(3) rights, including the right to legal representation.[1569] **11.384**

(l) Social security

It is clear that social security benefits come within the scope of 'civil rights and obligations'.[1570] Nevertheless, it is unlikely that Article 6 will have a substantial impact on English social security law.[1571] Four areas of potential impact have been identified. The first concerns the length of time taken to reach determinations of social security entitlements, particularly where the Social Security Commissioner has set aside a decision and remitted it for a fresh hearing. The delays are often considerable and may breach the requirement to a hearing within a reasonable time.[1572] Secondly, it is arguable[1573] that the approach taken by the Commissioner to refusing an oral hearing where he is satisfied that it can be determined without one may be in breach of Article 6(1).[1574] Thirdly, it might be said that the failure to extend legal aid to appeals before the Commissioner breaches the effective right of access to the court.[1575] Finally, it is arguable that the system for challenging national insurance contributions, which makes no provision for a hearing, contravenes Article 6.[1576] **11.385**

[1566] *Campbell and Fell v United Kingdom* (1984) 7 EHRR 165.

[1567] See generally, S Livingstone and T Owen, *Prison Law* (2nd edn, Oxford University Press, 1999) para 9.25.

[1568] See V Treacey, 'Prisoners' Rights Lost in Semantics' (1989) 28 Howard J of Criminal Law 27, but see *Pelle v France* (1986) 50 DR 263, EComm HR (potential loss of 18-days' remission, not sufficient), C Kidd, 'Disciplinary Proceedings and the Right to a Fair Criminal Trial Under the European Convention on Human Rights' (1987) 36 ICLQ 856.

[1569] Livingstone and Owen (n 1567 above) paras 9.35–9.42; this would reverse the decision in *Hone v Maze Prison Board of Visitors* [1988] 1 AC 379.

[1570] *Feldbrugge v Netherlands* (1986) 8 EHRR 425 (sickness benefit); *Deumeland v Germany* (1986) EHRR 448 (industrial injury pensions); in *Salesi v Italy* (1993) 26 EHRR 187 para 19 the Court extended Art 6 from social insurance benefits to welfare assistance where there was no entitlement to insurance based benefits; see also *Schuler-Zgraggen v Switzerland* (1993) 16 EHRR 405; *Schouten and Meldrum v Switzerland* (1994) 19 EHRR 432; and see generally, para 11.170 above.

[1571] See generally R White, 'Social Security' in C Baker (ed), *The Human Rights Act 1998: A Practitioner's Guide* (Sweet & Maxwell, 1998) paras 12-21–12-24.

[1572] See para 11.219ff above.

[1573] For the right to an oral hearing see para 11.206 above.

[1574] Under the Social Security Commissioner Procedure Regulations 1987, SI 1987 214 (as amended).

[1575] See para 11.185ff above.

[1576] J Peacock and F Fitzpatrick, 'Tax Law' in Baker (n 1571 above) para 14–29.

Appendix 1: The Canadian Charter of Rights

(1) Introduction

11.386 A number of sections of the Canadian Charter of Rights and Freedoms deal with 'legal process rights'. The most important of these is the right to 'fundamental justice' to be found in section 7 which provides:

> Everyone has the right to life, liberty and security of the person and the right not to be deprived thereof except in accordance with the principles of fundamental justice

Specific guarantees in relation to 'Proceedings in criminal and penal matters' are set out in section 11 which provides:

> Any person charged with an offence has the right
> (a) to be informed without unreasonable delay of the specific offence.
> (b) to be tried within a reasonable time.
> (c) not to be compelled to be a witness in proceedings against that person in respect of the offence.
> (d) to be presumed innocent until proven guilty according to law in a fair and public hearing by an independent and impartial tribunal.
> (e) not to be denied reasonable bail without just cause.
> (f) except in the case of an offence under military law tried before a military tribunal, to the benefit of trial by jury where the maximum punishment for the offence is imprisonment for five years or a more severe punishment.
> (g) not to be found guilty on account of any act or omission unless, at the time of the act or omission, it constituted an offence under Canadian or international law or was criminal according to the general principles of law recognized by the community of nations.
> (h) if finally acquitted of the offence, not to be tried for it again and if finally found guilty and punished for the offence, not to be tried or punished for it again.
> (i) if found guilty of the offence and if the punishment for the offence has been varied between the time of commission and the time of sentencing, to the benefit of the lesser punishment.

The right in subsection (e) (right to reasonable bail), has been considered in relation to the right to liberty and security of the person[1577] and will not be addressed here.

11.387 Three other sections of the Charter provide 'fair trial rights'. Section 13 is headed 'Self-incrimination' and provides:

> A witness who testifies in any proceedings has the right not to have any incriminating evidence so given used to incriminate that witness in any other proceedings, except in a prosecution of perjury or for the giving of contradictory evidence.

Section 14 deals with interpreters and provides:

> A party or witness in any proceedings who does not understand or speak the language in which the proceedings are conducted or who is deaf has the right to the assistance of an interpreter.

[1577] See para 10.233 above.

(2) The scope of the rights

(a) Fundamental justice

The 'principles of fundamental justice' is not a phrase which had an established meaning in pre-Charter case law; nor is it further defined in the Charter. It did appear in the Canadian Bill of Rights of 1960,[1578] but because it is used there in connection with a reference to a 'fair hearing', the phrase 'fundamental justice' was regarded as equivalent to the well-defined notion of 'natural justice'. By comparison, the phrase 'fundamental justice' is used in section 7 independently of any reference to 'fair hearing' or other concept that might imply a purely procedural content. **11.388**

If, as the legislative history of the Charter suggests 'fundamental justice' means simply 'natural justice',[1579] the courts are entitled to review only the appropriateness and fairness of the procedures enacted for a deprivation of life, liberty or security of the person, and may not review the substantive justice of the deprivation. However, it is now clear that while the principles of fundamental justice do include a requirement of procedural fairness[1580] which may vary depending on the context,[1581] section 7 also has substantive content.[1582] **11.389**

In *B C Motor Vehicle Reference*[1583] the Supreme Court of Canada did not follow the legislative history of the Charter, but decided that 'fundamental justice' included *both* substantive and procedural justice. On the assumption that sections 8 to 14 are merely illustrative of the deprivations of fundamental justice caught by section 7, and that they expressly extend beyond procedural guarantees, Lamer J concluded that section 7 must provide something more than procedural protection.[1584] The Supreme Court went on to hold that a strict liability criminal offence which provided for imprisonment in the absence of proving *mens rea* facilitated a deprivation of liberty which was not in accordance with the principles of fundamental justice; the offence created a substantive injustice in violation of section 7.[1585] However, none of the judgments in *B C Motor Vehicle Reference* defines the principles of fundamental justice beyond the assertion that they are to be found **11.390**

[1578] The Canadian Bill of Rights guarantees the right to a fair hearing in accordance with the principles of fundamental justice for the determination of his rights and obligations.

[1579] The drafters of the Charter sought to avoid the importation into Canada of the American 'due process' doctrine established in *US v Lochner* (1905) 198 US 45, by which the US Supreme Court had struck down substantive federal and state labour laws during 1905 to 1937; see P Hogg, *Constitutional Law of Canada*, (4th edn, Carswell, 1997), para 44.10.

[1580] See *Singh v Minister of Employment and Immigration* [1985] 1 SCR 177; *Pearlman v Manitoba Law Society* [1991] 2 SCR 869, 882; 'The Principles of Fundamental Justice' (1991) 29 Osgoode Hall Law Journal 51; *R v Lyons* [1987] 2 SCR 309.

[1581] *R v Lyons* (n 1580 above) 361.

[1582] In *R v Fisher* (1985) 39 MVR 287, Scollin J said that 'the protection of basic rights by the principles of fundamental justice must mean more than a mere guarantee of a scenic route to the prison-camp', and that 'life, liberty and security of the person are illusory if they can be unjustly taken away with impunity'; see generally, *Singh v Minister of Employment and Immigration* [1985] 1 SCR 177; *Pearlman v Manitoba Law Society* [1991] 2 SCR 869, 882.

[1583] *Reference Re Section 94(2) of Motor Vehicle Act (British Columbia)* [1985] 2 SCR 486.

[1584] Ibid 502-503; this is problematic, as was pointed out by Wilson J in dissent, as ss 8 through 14 are in fact drafted as free-standing provisions rather than as examples of deprivations under s 7.

[1585] See also, *R v Pontes (A-G of Canada intervening)* [1996] 1 LRC 134 (no violation of Art 7 when offence of absolute liability punishable only by a fine).

'in the basic tenets of the legal system'.[1586] Subsequent decisions have not clarified the meaning of 'fundamental justice'.[1587]

11.391 A number of 'principles of fundamental justice' have been suggested in the cases:

- the right to silence;[1588]
- the principle that the law should be fixed, predetermined, accessible and understandable to the public;[1589]
- the right to present full answer and defence;[1590]
- the right to cross-examine witnesses.[1591]

(b) Rights in criminal proceedings: introduction

11.392 Section 11 of the Charter provides constitutional protection for proceedings which relate to the determination of offences that are criminal in nature. In contrast to the Convention, section 11 of the Charter does not provide any such protection for civil proceedings. It does not apply to 'private domestic or disciplinary matters which are regulatory, protective or corrective',[1592] to persons whose conduct is the subject of a public inquiry,[1593] or to proceedings before securities commissions with power to issue cease-trading orders.[1594] Sections 13 and 14, in relation to freedom from incrimination and the right to an interpreter, applies to a witness (and in the case of section 14 a party) who testifies in 'any proceedings', not just criminal proceedings. Section 14 is further limited to situations in which the party or witness is deaf or does not understand or speak the language.

(c) 'Person charged with an offence'

11.393 Section 11 applies to every 'person', whether a natural person or corporation,[1595] who is charged with an offence. A person is 'charged' within the meaning of section 11 either when an information is sworn alleging an offence against him or, in the absence of an information, a direct indictment is laid against him.[1596] It is not sufficient that the person is merely suspected of the offence, or that the impact of the criminal process is felt by him.[1597] An accused is not 'charged' by reason of an application that he be designated a

[1586] Lamer J, [1985] 2 SCR 486, at 503 and 512; Wilson J accepts this definition, referring, at 530 to 'a fundamental tenet of our justice system'.

[1587] See *Thomson Newspapers Ltd v Canada (Director of Investigation and Research, Resrictive Trade Practices Commission)* [1990] 1 SCR 425, in which five judges gave five different opinions as to the applicable basic tenet of the legal system; see the criticism in Hogg, (n 1579 above) 1079ff.

[1588] see para 11.419ff below.

[1589] *United Nurses of Alberta v Alberta (A-G)* [1992] 1 SCR 901.

[1590] *R v Seaboyer* [1991] 2 SCR 577.

[1591] *R v Osolin* [1993] 4 SCR 595.

[1592] *R v Wigglesworth* [1987] 2 SCR 541; and see *Re James and Law Society of B C* (1982) 143 DLR (3d) 379; see also *Trumbley and Pugh v Metropolitan Toronto Police* [1987] 2 SCR 577.

[1593] *Starr v Houlden* [1990] 1 SCR 1366.

[1594] *Holoboff v Alberta* (1991) 80 DLR (4th) 603.

[1595] See *R v CIP* [1992] 1 SCR 843 (s 11(b) applies to a corporation) and generally, P Hogg, (n 1579 above) para 34.1(b), 835-837.

[1596] See *R v Kalanj* [1989] 1 SCR 1594 *per* MacIntyre J at 1607; also *R v Chabot* [1980] 2 SCR 985 where the term 'charge' in the Criminal Code was interpreted to mean that 'a formal written complaint has been made against the accused and a prosecution initiated'.

[1597] Ibid; the view of dissenting judges Lamer and Wilson JJ was that the accused had been 'charged' upon his initial arrest, as that was the point at which he 'felt the impact of the criminal justice system', even though he was released and an information was not sworn until eight-months later, contrast the position under the Convention, see para 11.182 above.

'dangerous offender',[1598] by the making of an injunction against him for picketing in contempt of court,[1599] or by extradition proceedings to determine whether there is sufficient evidence to warrant his surrender to a foreign jurisdiction.[1600] As a result, section 11 has no application to any of these cases.

(d) 'Offence'

Section 11 rights apply if a person has been charged with an 'offence', meaning any provincial or federal law to which a penal sanction attaches. Two alternative tests as to what constitutes an offence were promulgated in *R v Wigglesworth*:[1601] the matter must either be 'by its very nature' a criminal proceeding,[1602] or lead to a true penal consequence.[1603] In *Wigglesworth*, a police officer, was tried and found guilty by a police tribunal of assaulting a prisoner in the course of interrogation, and was fined $300. Under the first test, the violation was found to constitute an internal and disciplinary matter for regulation within a limited private sphere and was not by nature a criminal proceeding. Nevertheless, because the offence carried the risk of imprisonment of up to one year, it satisfied the second test of attaching a true penal consequence. The Court said that a fine might also constitute a 'true penal consequence' if its magnitude indicated that the purpose of imposing it was to redress a wrong done to society at large. **11.394**

In *R v Genereux*[1604] the Supreme Court found that a member of the armed forces faced with court martial proceedings for breach of the Code of Service was charged with an offence under section 11. Because the Code designated as a 'service offence' any act punishable under the federal Criminal Code or other Act of Parliament and substituted service tribunals for ordinary courts where the offence was committed by a member of the armed forces, proceedings were by 'nature' criminal. In addition, the court martial's power to impose imprisonment met the 'true penal consequence' test. In contrast, in *R v Shubley*[1604a] it was held that prison disciplinary proceedings did not constitute a trial for an offence for the purposes of section 11. **11.395**

(3) Criminal trial guarantees

(a) Section 11(a): specific information

The section 11(a) right to be informed without unreasonable delay of the specific offence entrenches the right that existed prior to the Charter under the Criminal Code, provincial **11.396**

[1598] *R v Lyons* [1987] 2 SCR 309: dangerous-offender designation has been found to be a part of the sentencing process and not a new 'charge' subject to the protections of s 11.

[1599] *BCGEU v British Columbia* [1988] 2 SCR 214: s 11 rights would only apply in the case of a breach of the injunction, upon initiation of proceedings against the individual.

[1600] *R v Schmidt* [1987] 1 SCR 500.

[1601] *R v Wigglesworth* [1987] 2 SCR 541.

[1602] The Court found that a law sanctioned by a penalty would by its very nature be an offence if it was 'intended to promote public order and welfare within a public sphere of activity', but the test would not be satisfied by 'private, domestic or disciplinary matters which are regulatory, protective or corrective and which are primarily intended to maintain discipline, professional integrity and professional standards or to regulate conduct within a limited private sphere of activity'.

[1603] Contrast the position under Art 6(1) of the Convention; see para 11.174 above.

[1604] [1992] 1 SCR 259.

[1604a] [1990] 1 SCR 3; see D Stuart, *Charter Justice in Canadian Criminal Law* (Carswell, 1991) 220, 221.

laws and the common law. This paragraph offers no protection to a person not yet charged.[1605] In considering whether there has been unreasonable delay under this provision, the court should consider: (1) the length of the delay; (2) the waiver of time periods; (3) the reasons for the delay, and (4) prejudice to the accused.[1606] The degree of detail required by the term 'specific' is not entirely clear. It is sufficient if the indictment identifies the relevant time period of the offence, the place of commission, the parties to the offence and its subject matter.[1607] Challenges to the particularity of charges under section 11(a) are very rarely successful.[1607a]

(b) Section 11(b): trial within a reasonable time

11.397 Section 11(b) created a new Charter right:[1608] any person charged with an offence has the right to be tried within a reasonable time. It has been invoked more frequently than any other section of the Charter, because the appropriate remedy for its breach, according to the Supreme Court of Canada, is a stay of proceedings rather than an early trial.[1609]

11.398 The purpose of the right to a reasonable trial is to minimise three detrimental effects of pre-trial detention: time spent by an accused in custody or under restrictive bail conditions; anxiety of the accused awaiting trial; and deterioration of evidence necessary to the accused's defence.[1610] Because the third of these purposes extends equally to corporations as to natural persons, section 11(b) may be invoked by a corporation;[1611] but it can provide no benefit that is not already guaranteed under section 11(d), the right to fair trial. As a corporation can suffer neither imprisonment nor anxiety, the usual presumption of prejudice in the event of unreasonable delay is not applicable and must affirmatively establish prejudice on the sole basis of an impairment of its ability to make full answer and defence.

11.399 The period of time to be considered is that which begins with the charge.[1611a] As mentioned above, the reasonableness of the delay is determined by a process of weighing and balancing four factors:

- the length of the delay;
- waivers of time periods;
- reasons for the delay; and
- prejudice to the accused.[1611b]

The length of the delay is calculated from the point at which the information is laid or the

[1605] *R v Heit* [1984] 3 WWR 614.
[1606] *R v Delaronde* [1997] 1 SCR 213.
[1607] *R v Finta* (1989) 61 D R (4th) 85.
[1607a] See Stuart (n 1604a above) 223–224.
[1608] Right to trial within a reasonable time was not previously known to the common law, statute, or the Canadian Bill of Rights.
[1609] *R v Rahey* [1987] 1 SCR 588; *R v Askov* [1990] 2 SCR 1199; 74 DLR (4th) 355.
[1610] *R v CIP* [1992] 1 SCR 843; previously, the third of these purposes was disputed by Lamer J: see *R v Rahey* (n 1609 above).
[1611] *R v CIP* [1992] 1 SCR 843.
[1611a] *R v Kalanj* [1989] 1 SCR 1594, see generally, D Stuart, *Charter Justice in Canadian Criminal Law* (Carswell, 1991) 226–228.
[1611b] See generally, Stuart (n 1611a above) 228–246; P Hogg, *Constitutional Law of Canada* (4th edn, Carswell, 1997) Chap 49.

indictment is preferred[1612] to the final disposition of the case.[1613] Periods of time that are clearly and unequivocally waived[1614] by the accused are not taken into account in computing the length of the delay under section 11(b).[1615] Various reasons for delay have been addressed by the Supreme Court of Canada, most of which fall into one of four categories: delay inherent to the proceedings; delay attributable to the Crown; delay attributable to the accused; delay that is institutional or systemic to the court system. Of these, delay inherent to the case[1616] and delays attributable to the accused[1617] are considered to be reasonably incurred, while delay attributable to the Crown and delay systemic to the legal system[1618] are not. The last of the four factors to be weighed is that of prejudice to the accused. Where there are actual sources of prejudice, such as the impairment of defence evidence or the continuing deprivation of liberty of the accused, the period of time from charge to trial considered reasonable will be short. Even if there are no such apparent sources, the person awaiting trial is nevertheless presumed to be in 'exquisite agony',[1619] resulting in a presumption of prejudice to the accused as a result of the passage of time. On the other hand, a later case has recognised that often the accused is not interested in a speedy trial and delay works to the advantage of the accused,[1620] a conclusion that appears to contradict the presumption of prejudice established in *Askov*.[1621]

(c) Section 11(c): non-compellability

Section 11(c) of the Charter provides that the accused has the right not to be compelled to **11.400**
be a witness in proceedings against him in respect of the offence. Originally Canadian common law provided that the accused was not a compellable witness for the Crown, and was not competent to testify in his own defence. In 1893 the accused became competent as a witness in either case,[1622] though he remains non-compellable as a witness for the

1612 There is no remedy for delay in laying the charge: *R v L (W K)* [1991] 1 SCR 1091.

1613 Final disposition includes all retrials and appeals; such proceedings will be taken into account in the determination of the question as to reasonableness: in *R v Conway* [1989] 1 SCR 1659 a delay of five years from the charge to commencement of the accused's third trial was not unreasonable.

1614 Such as a delay explicitly incurred in order to secure an adjournment or late trial date. Waiver must be made with full knowledge of the rights that the procedure was enacted to protect and the effect of the waiver on those rights: *R v Morin* [1992] 1 SCR 771. A defence consent to adjournment or a late trial date will not be a waiver unless counsel is alive to the issue of waiver; mere acquiesence in the inevitable may constitute action that falls short of waiver and reasonably extends the proceedings.

1615 *R v Morin* (n 1614 above).

1616 Time for preparation of the case, pre-trial procedures, and processing of a case by the court will vary with the complexity and nature of the case.

1617 Not including the periods explicitly waived by the accused.

1618 This includes delay caused by court congestion resulting from too few judges or courtrooms and inadequate case management procedures to handle the volume of criminal charges; see *R v Askov* [1990] 2 SCR 1199 in which the SCC stayed proceedings against four accused for unreasonable delays in bringing them to trial. The time elapsed from charge to trial had been two years and ten months, but the court drew the line at six to eight months maximum from committal to trial due to systemic delay.

1619 *R v Askov* (n 1618 above).

1620 *R v Morin* (n 1614 above).

1621 In *R v Morin* (n 1614 above), Sopinka J for the majority implied that delay alone might not support the inference of sufficient prejudice to justify a stay of proceedings. Lamer J dissented on the basis that the decision was a fundamental change from the decision in *Askov*, which the Court ought not to depart from.

1622 See now Canada Evidence Act, RSC 1985, c c-5.

Crown.[1623] As a result of the Charter provision, any statute which purports to compel a witness to testify against himself would be invalid. The guarantee is a privilege against testimonial compulsion, and not against compulsion generally, so that the accused must, for example, comply with an order to provide a breath test or with a 'reverse onus' provision which could be discharged by calling witnesses other than himself. Oral examinations for discovery in civil proceedings against a party who is charged with an offence arising out of the same facts does not breach this provision.[1624]

11.401 Section 11(c) prohibits only rules that impose a legal obligation on the accused to testify.[1625] If he chooses to testify, he cannot refuse to answer any question on the grounds that it might incriminate him. Instead, Article 13 applies to ensure that the incriminating answer is not used against the witness in other proceedings. If the accused chooses not to testify on his own behalf, the judge is required[1626] to refrain from making any comment to a jury as to an adverse inference that might be drawn from such failure to testify.

(d) Section 11(d): presumption of innocence

11.402 The first part of section 11(d) provides that 'any person charged with an offence has the right to be presumed innocent. . .'.[1626a] The presumption of innocence at common law is found in the rule that the Crown has the burden of proving the guilt of the accused beyond a reasonable doubt. Under the Charter the law is now reinforced and entrenched and capable of overturning legislative provisions that would reverse the common law onus of proof. The Court in *R v Oakes*[1627] held that legislation requiring that the accused disprove, on a balance of probabilities an 'essential element of the offence'[1628] was a breach of section 11(d) because it meant that a conviction was possible, despite the existence of a reasonable doubt as to the accused's guilt. The accused might adduce enough evidence to raise a reasonable doubt as to the purpose of the possession of illegal drugs, but not enough to prove his innocence on a balance of probabilities of the intention of trafficking. The Court found that the lower standard of proof on the reverse onus did not make such a provision constitutional, because it still contravened the requirement that the Crown prove all elements of an offence beyond a reasonable doubt.

11.403 For a reverse onus provision to be reasonable and hence constitutional, the connection between the proved fact and the presumed fact must at least be such that the existence of the proved fact rationally tends to prove that the presumed fact also exists.[1629]

[1623] Pursuant to the Canada Evidence Act and provincial statutes, the accused is now a competent witness for the defence.

[1624] *Saccomanno v Swanson* (1987) 34 DLR (4th) 462; *Municipal Enterprises v Rowlings* (1990) 107 NSR (2d) 88.

[16256] *R v Boss* (1988) 46 CCC (3d) 523.

[1626] Canada Evidence Act, s 4(6).

[1626a] See generally, D Stuart, *Charter Justice in Canadian Criminal Law* (Carswell 1991) 249–267.

[1627] [1986] 1 SCR 103.

[1628] In that case, the Narcotic Control Act required that, once the Crown had proved possession of an illegal drug beyond a reasonable doubt, the onus shifted to the accused to overturn, on a balance of probabilities, the mandatory presumption that the possession was for the purpose of trafficking.

[1629] See *R v Oakes* (n 1627 above); see also, *R v Bray* (1983) 144 DLR (3d) 305, 309; *R v Dubois (No 2)* (1983) 8 CCC (3d) 344, 346-347; *R v Frankforth* (1982) 70 CCC (2d) 488, 491; and see *Leary v United States* (1969) 395 US 6.

The same reasoning was applied in *R v Whyte,*[1630] even though the reverse onus required the accused to prove a 'fact collateral to the substantive offence' rather than an essential element of the offence. The offence was 'care and control of a motor vehicle while intoxicated'; if the accused occupied the driver's seat of a vehicle while drunk, he was deemed to have the care and control of the vehicle unless he could prove on the balance of probabilities that he did not enter it with the intention to set it in motion. The Court said that a reverse onus clause which required an accused to prove anything in order to avoid conviction, whether an element of the offence, a collateral fact, an excuse or a defence,[1631] violated the accused's right to presumption of innocence, but in *Whyte* the provision was saved by section 1 as a measure to prevent drunken driving. **11.404**

In *R v Downey*[1632] the Supreme Court dealt with a statutory presumption that a person who lives with or is habitually in the company of prostitutes, is, in the absence of evidence to the contrary, committing the offence of living on the proceeds of prostitution. This presumption was also held to infringe the presumption of innocence (although it was held by a majority to be in all the circumstances a justifiable infringement). Cory J summarised the principles derived from the authorities in seven propositions:[1633] **11.405**

> I. The presumption of innocence is infringed whenever the accused is liable to be convicted despite the existence of a reasonable doubt.
> II. If, by the provisions of a statutory presumption, an accused is required to establish, that is to say to prove or disprove, on a balance of probabilities either an element of an offence or an excuse, then it contravenes s 11(d). Such a provision would permit a conviction in spite of a reasonable doubt.
> III. Even if a rational connection exists between the established fact and the fact to be presumed, this would be insufficient to make valid a presumption requiring the accused to disprove an element of the offence.
> IV. Legislation which substitutes proof of one element for proof of an essential element will not infringe the presumption of innocence if, as a result of the proof of the substituted element, it would be unreasonable for the trier of fact not to be satisfied beyond a reasonable doubt of the existence of the other element. To put it another way, the statutory presumption will be valid if the proof of the substituted fact leads inexorably to the proof of the other. However, the statutory presumption will infringe s 11(d) if it requires the trier of fact to convict in spite of a reasonable doubt.
> V. A permissive assumption from which a trier of fact may, but not must, draw an inference of guilt will not infringe s 11(d).
> VI. A provision that might have been intended to play a minor role in providing relief from conviction will nonetheless contravene the Charter if the provision (such as the truth of a statement) must be established by the accused . . .
> VII. It must of course be remembered that statutory presumptions which infringe s 11(d) may still be justified pursuant to s 1 of the Charter.

The following provisions have been held to violate the presumption of innocence in section 11(d) and were not justifiable under section 1: **11.405A**

[1630] [1988] 2 SCR 3.

[1631] But in *R v Holmes* [1988] 1 SCR 914, a majority of the Court held that an excusing provision was not a reverse onus clause.

[1632] [1992] 2 SCR 10; see also *R v Fisher* (1994) 111 DLR (4th) 415 (burden of proving written consent of employee to receipt of commission a violation); *R v Laba* [1994] 3 SCR 965 (burden of proving lawful authority for sale or purchase of ore containing precious metal a violation).

[1633] Ibid at 461.

- a provision requiring an accused to prove insanity;[1633a]
- a provision placing a burden of proving truth on a person charged with wilfully promoting hatred;[1633b]
- a provision requiring the accused to prove ownership, agency or lawful authority for the sale or purchase of ore containing precious metal;[1633c]

In a number of other cases, reverse onus provisions have been held to be justifiable under section 1:

- a 'due diligence' defence to a misleading advertising offence;[1633d]
- the burden on the accused to prove that he had a reasonable excuse for a failure to provide a breath sample;[1633e]
- a requirement that a representation made to the public concerning a product was based on reasonable grounds.[1633f]

(e) Section 11(d): fair and public hearing

11.406 The second part of section 11(d) provides that a person charged with an offence is entitled to a 'fair and public hearing'. The requirement of 'fairness', which is explicitly provided for in section 11(d), has also been found to be implicit in the concept of 'fundamental justice' in section 7 as it applies to the life, liberty and security of the person.[1634] In *R v Seaboyer*,[1635] the Supreme Court of Canada held that both sections 7 and 11(d) guaranteed the 'right to present full answer and defence'. That case overturned the 'rape-shield' provision of the Criminal Code, which restricted the right of a person charged with sexual assault to cross-examine the complainant about her past sexual activity, on grounds that it might exclude relevant evidence that was required to enable the accused to make a full answer and defence. This right has two aspects: the right of the accused to have before him the 'full case to meet' before answering the Crown's case and the right of the accused to defend himself against all the State's efforts to achieve a conviction.[1636] Pre-trial disclosure by the Crown of all information relevant to the offence, once only a voluntary practice, has also been made a constitutional obligation as a result of the accused's right to make full answer and defence,[1637] although the Court referred to section 7 rather than section 11(d).

11.407 The right to a public hearing meant that there was no justification for a requirement that all trials of juveniles should be held in camera.[1638]A complete public trial should be the rule and exceptions should be established on a case-by-case basis.[1639]

1633a *R v Chaulk* [1990] 3 SCR 1303.
1633b *R v Keegstra* [1990] 3 SCR 697.
1633c *R v Laba* [1994] 3 SCR 965.
1633d *R v Wholesale Travel Group Inc* [1991] 3 SCR 154.
1633e *R v Peck* [1994] 21 CPR (2d) 175.
1633f *R v Envirosoft Water Inc* [1995] 61 CPR (3d) 207.
1634 See para 11.388ff above.
1635 [1991] 2 SCR 577.
1636 *R* v *Rose* (1998) 166 DLR (4th) 385.
1637 *R v Stinchcombe* (1991) 68 CCC (3d) 1.
1638 *Edmonton Journal v Alberta (A-G)* (1983) 146 DLR (3d) 673.
1639 *R v Lefevre* (1984) 17 CC (3d) 277.

(f) Section 11(d): Independent and impartial tribunal

Section 11(d) also provides for a public hearing 'by an independent and impartial tribunal'. In *R v Valente*[1640] it was argued that provincially-appointed judges of Ontario's Provincial Court (Criminal Division) would be biased in favour of the Crown as a result of the degree of control exercised by the Attorney-General over their conditions of employment, salaries, pensions and leave. The Supreme Court of Canada held that the three conditions of judicial independence, were security of tenure, financial security and 'the institutional independence of the tribunal with respect to matters of administration bearing directly on the exercise of its judicial function'. On the facts the three conditions had been met and the Provincial Court was therefore capable of trying criminal cases without violating section 11(d) of the Charter. Neither were part-time municipal court judges who maintained private law practices in Montreal found to be inconsistent with section 11(d) as a result of the judges' oath of office, code of ethics and statutory rules requiring their disqualification to avoid conflicts of interest.[1641] Governments do not infringe the principle of judicial independence by reducing the salaries of Provincial Court judges but they are constitutionally obliged to submit proposed changes to an independent, objective and effective body which depoliticises the process.[1642] Justices of the peace were held to be independent for the purposes of section 11(d).[1642a] **11.408**

A jury, however, has been found lacking in impartiality where the ability of the Crown to 'stand by' up to 48 jurors gave the prosecution an undue advantage in the composition of the jury.[1643] The accused's statutory right to challenge potential jurors for cause based on partiality is the only direct means he has to secure an impartial jury.[1644] The trial judge should permit challenges for cause where there is a realistic potential of a racially biased jury.[1645] **11.409**

(g) Section 11(f): trial by jury

Although the term 'tribunal' in section 11(d) does not require a jury as an element of 'fairness', section 11(f) creates the independent right to a jury trial, which has never before been recognised in Canada.[1646] A person charged with an offence is entitled, unless the offence is one under military law triable before a military tribunal, to the benefit of a jury trial where the maximum punishment for the offence is imprisonment for five years or a more severe punishment. The threshold level of potential punishment required by the section was not met by the sentence of compulsory confinement of a young offender in an **11.410**

[1640] [1985] 2 SCR 673.

[1641] *R v Lippé* [1990] 2 SCR 114, SCC; see also *Reference re: Public Sector Pay Reduction Act (PEI) section 10* (1997) 150 DLR (4th) 577 and *Reference re: Territorial Court Act (NWT) section 6(2)* (1997) 152 DLR (4th) 132.

[1642] *R v Wickman* (1997) 150 DLR (4th) 577; see also *R v Campbell* (1995) 150 DLR (4th) 577.

[1642a] *Reference re Justices of the Peace Act* (1984) 16 CCC (3d) 193.

[1643] See *R v Bain* [1992] 1 SCR 91.

[1644] *R v Parks* (1993) 84 CCC (3d) 353, 362; see also *R v Sherratt* [1991] 1 SCR 509.

[1645] *R v Williams* [1998] 1 SCR 1128.

[1646] The Canadian Bill of Rights does not refer to the right to a jury trial; the drafters of the Canadian Charter appear to have been influenced by the provisions of the Sixth amendment to the US Constitution which provides for trial by an 'impartial jury of the state and district wherein the crime shall have been committed'.

'industrial school' for more than five years;[1647] nor where the offender was a corporation, as it could not be 'imprisoned'.[1648]

11.411 Because section 11(f) grants a right to 'the benefit' of a jury, it is apparent that the right can be waived.[1649] It is also clear that the section does not confer a constitutional right to elect a mode of trial other than by jury. In *R v Turpin,*[1650] the Supreme Court of Canada held that an application by two accused murderers to be tried by judge alone constituted a waiver of their right to a jury trial, and it rejected their attempts to invoke section 11(f) in support of the application. Such a waiver, like waivers of other constitutional rights, must be 'clear and unequivocal' and carried out with full awareness of the consequences.[1651] The failure of an accused to appear at his hearing after having opted for a jury was held not to be an unequivocal indication of waiver. However the Criminal Code legislation provided for trial by judge alone in these circumstances, the provision was therefore upheld under section 1 on grounds that it was appropriate to deny a jury where an accused had abused the system in the first instance.

11.412 Section 11(f) does not apply to military offences to be tried before a military tribunal. Because the National Defence Act[1652] includes in its definition of 'service offences' not only breaches of military law, but violations of the Criminal Code and other statutes applicable to the public at large, it has been suggested that for the purposes of the Charter, 'military offences' should be limited to National Defence Act offences that have a connection with military service.[1653]

(h) Section 11(g): retroactive offences

11.413 Under section 11(g) a person charged with a criminal offence has the right not to be found guilty 'on account of any act or omission unless, at the time of the act or omission, it constituted an offence under Canadian or international law or was criminal according to the general principles of law recognised by the community of nations'. The section limits the power of federal or provincial parliaments to create retroactive criminal offences; other types of laws may still be made retroactive, subject to the interpretative presumption that an ambiguous provision shall not be given retroactive effect. Furthermore, even a criminal law that is clearly intended to be applied retroactively may be in conformity with section 11(g) if it was an offence under international law or was considered criminal under principles of law recognised by the community of nations. This provision does not prohibit uncodified common law crimes.[1654]

[1647] *R v S B* (1983) 146 DLR (3d) 69; as the confinement was intended to treat rather than punish him, the sentence was not 'punishment' for the purposes of entitling him to a jury under s 11(f). The decision has been criticised on the basis that if there are sound policy reasons for denying young offenders a jury trial the limitation of s 11(f) ought to be justified by way of s 1 of the Charter: see P W Hogg, *Constitutional Law of Canada* (4th edn, Carswell, 1999), 1188.

[1648] As the maximum penalty an incorporation can receive is a fine, it is disentitled from a trial by a jury, in spite of the fact that a corporation would have benefited from it. The view of the dissent was that the benefit of the right to a jury in relation to the most serious offences is as relevant to a corporation as to an individual.

[1649] *R v Turpin* [1989] 1 SCR 1296, 1314-1316.

[1650] Ibid.

[1651] *R v Lee* [1989] 2 SCR 1384, 1411.

[1652] RSC 1985, c N-5.

[1653] *R v Macdonald* (1983) 150 DLR (3d) 620: 'military nexus'; see also the pre-Charter case of *R v Mackay* [1980] 2 SCR 370, 380, *per* MacIntyre J.

[1654] *United Nurses of Alberta v Alberta (A-G)* [1992] 1 SCR 901.

(i) Section 11(h): double jeopardy

The common law rules against double jeopardy[1655] are now embodied in the Charter under section 11(h) which provides that a person charged with an offence has the right, 'if finally acquitted of the offence, not to be tried for it again and if finally found guilty and punished for the offence, not to be tried or punished for it again'. The section applies only where both proceedings are in relation to an 'offence', and the latter is substantially identical to or included in the offence of which the accused was convicted. So, for example, where an attack by one prison inmate on another was dealt with first by way of disciplinary hearing and punishment, the accused was not in a position to resist, on grounds of section 11(f), trial for subsequent Criminal Code charges of assault.[1656] Similarly, in *R v Wigglesworth,*[1657] the conviction of a police officer for a 'service offence' under the Royal Canadian Mounted Police Act did not preclude a subsequent trial for assault under the Criminal Code. **11.414**

In order for attempted 'second' proceedings to trigger section 11(h) protection, the first must result in a final disposition of the charges: where the original proceedings ended in a stay[1658] or mistrial, the accused could be tried again in relation to the same offence. 'Final' disposition is not rendered until all appeal proceedings are complete; an appeal from a trial verdict is not therefore a retrial of the same offence. Where an appeal process took the form of a 'trial *de novo*',[1659] however, the Supreme Court of Canada held that it was not in fact an appeal but a disguised retrial in violation of section 11(h). **11.415**

(j) Section 11(i): variation in penalty

Under section 11(i), any person charged with an offence has the right if found guilty of the offence and if the punishment for the offence has been varied between the time of commission and the time of sentencing, to the benefit of the lesser punishment. The section applies where the penalty for the offence has been varied after an accused has committed an offence but before he has been sentenced.[1660] Where the penalty is not strictly a 'punishment', as in the case of the suspension of a driver's licence,[1661] the section will not apply, but if it is applicable, the accused must have the benefit of the lesser, rather than merely the latter, of the two penalties in question. **11.416**

[1655] See *Kienapple v The Queen* [1975] 1 SCR 729 in regard to *res judicata*; special pleas of autrefois acquit and autrefois convict; issue estoppel; possibly abuse of process: *R v Van Rassel* [1990] 1 SCR 225, 233-239.

[1656] *R v Shubley* [1990] 1 SCR 3; see also *R v Schmidt* [1987] 1 SCR 500 where the accused, who had been convicted of a federal offence in the US, tried to invoke s 11(f) to avoid Canadian extradition proceedings to return him to the US for a trial on what he claimed was the same offence. The extradition proceedings, being not determinative of guilt or innocence, did not constitute a trial in relation to an 'offence' and so the Court left it to the foreign court to deal with the objections of the accused.

[1657] *R v Wigglesworth* [1987] 2 SCR 541.

[1658] *Re Burrows* (1983) 150 DLR (3d) 317.

[1659] In *Corporation Professionnelle des Médecins v Thibault* [1988] 1 SCR 1033, Quebec legislation enabled a prosecutor to appeal from an acquittal by trial *de novo* which allowed evidence to be re-adduced and supplemented as necessary.

[1660] But see *R v Gamble* [1988] 2 SCR 595, where the Court found a breach of s 7 rather than s 11 when an accused mistakenly tried and sentenced under law enacted after the commission of the offence.

[1661] In *Re Bulmer* (1987) 36 DLR (4th) 688 the suspension was a 'civil consequence' rather than a punishment.

(k) Section 14: right to an interpreter

11.417 This section reflects the common law right to an interpreter which itself derives from the principles of 'natural justice'.[1662] It is the duty of the judge to determine whether the need for an interpreter has been established.[1663] The right applies to all proceedings, civil as well as criminal.[1664] The interpretation must meet the standard of 'continuity, precision, impartiality, competence and contemporaneousness'.[1665] Thus, there was a breach of section 14 when, at the trial of a Vietnamese speaker, a witness testified in English and then gave a brief summary of his testimony in Vietnamese at the end of his evidence in chief and his cross-examination.[1666] Although the accused had suffered no prejudice, the fact that he was unable to follow part of the proceedings meant that his right under section 14 had been infringed. A new trial was ordered.

(4) Freedom from self-incrimination.

11.418 Section 13 of the Charter gives a witness the right not to have incriminating evidence he gives used to incriminate him in any other proceedings.[1667] The rights of an accused under section 13 were infringed when he was cross-examined by prosecuting counsel on testimony he had given on his prior trial for the same offence, a re-trial having been ordered.[1668] However the section does not prohibit cross-examination as to credit.[1669] The section provides no basis for the assertion of a right to remain silent in civil proceedings arising out of the same facts as a criminal charge.[1670]

11.419 The principles of 'fundamental justice' in section 7 of the Charter include the right to silence which is a 'basic tenet of the legal system'.[1671] The essence of the right is the notion that the person whose freedom is placed in question by the judicial process must be given the choice of whether or not to speak to the authorities.[1672] Thus, a confession obtained by disguising a police officer as a fellow prisoner was held to be a breach of this right.[1673] The right can be violated not only by undercover police officers but by any agent of the state.[1674] A statement arising from a prior inadmissible confession cannot be used even for the limited purpose of undermining the credibility of the accused.[1675]

11.420 However, the right to silence is not an absolute one and there must be a careful balance between the interests of the individual and those of the state:[1676] the principle must be considered in the factual circumstances of each particular case.[1677] If a witness is compelled to

[1662] *R v Tran* [1994] 2 SCR 361.
[1663] Ibid 979.
[1664] See P W Hogg, *Constitutional Law of Canada* (4th edn, Carswell, 1997), s 53.5(e).
[1665] *R v Tran* (n 1662 above).
[1666] *R v Tran* (n 1662 above) (the witness was the person who had interpreted for the rest of the trial who was called by the defence).
[1667] See generally, Hogg (n 1664 above) Chap 51.
[1668] *R v Mannion* [1986] 2 SCR 272.
[1669] *R v Johnstone and Law Society of British Columbia* (1987) 40 DLR (4th) 550.
[1670] *Caisse Populaire Laurier d'Ottawa Ltée v Guertin* (1983) 150 DLR (3d) 541.
[1671] *R v Hebert* [1990] 2 SCR 151.
[1672] Ibid.
[1673] Ibid; see also *R v Broyles* [1991] 3 SCR 595.
[1674] *R v Broyles* (n 1673 above).
[1675] *R v G* (1999) 6 BHRC 97.
[1676] *R v S (RJ)* [1995] 1 SCR 451.
[1677] *R v Fitzpatrick* [1995] 4 SCR 154, 166-169.

testify he will be entitled to claim effective subsequent derivative-use immunity or other appropriate protection with respect to the compelled testimony.[1678] In *Thomson Newspapers v Director of Investigations and Research*[1679] the Supreme Court considered the relation between the right to silence and compulsory investigative powers.[1680] Although witnesses could be compelled to give evidence, this evidence could not be used in subsequent proceedings. Section 13 was not applicable because the investigation was the first proceeding. The majority held that this 'subsequent use immunity' meant that there had been no infringement of the right to silence. In *R v Fitzpatrick*[1681] the use in evidence of the daily fishing reports made by the accused under the applicable fishery regulations was not a breach of the privilege. The Court relied on the lack of real coercion, the lack of an 'adversarial relationship' at the time the reports were made, the absence of an increased risk of unreliable confessions as a result of statutory compulsion and the absence of an increased risk of abuses of power by the state. In contrast, in *R v White*[1682] the Supreme Court held that the admission in evidence of an accident report made under a statutory requirement was a breach of section 7. In that case there was a potential adversarial relationship between the driver and the police officer taking the statement, a prospect of unreliable confessions and the possibility of abusive conduct by the state.

Appendix 2: The New Zealand Bill of Rights Act

(1) Introduction

The New Zealand Bill of Rights Act 1990 contains a number of provisions granting rights in relation to legal process: **11.421**

> 24. **Rights of persons charged**—
>
> Everyone who is charged with an offence—
>
> (a) shall be informed promptly and in detail of the nature and cause of the charge; and
> (b) shall be released on reasonable terms and conditions unless there is just cause for continued detention; and
> (c) shall have the right to consult and instruct a lawyer; and
> (d) shall have the right to adequate time and facilities to prepare a defence; and
> (e) shall have the right, except in the case of an offence under military law tried before a military tribunal, to the benefit of a trial by jury when the penalty for the offence is or includes imprisonment for more than three months.
> (f) shall have the right to receive legal assistance without cost if the interests of justice so require and the person does not have sufficient means to provide for that assistance; and
> (g) shall have the right to have the free assistance of an interpreter if the person cannot understand or speak the language used in court.

[1678] *British Columbia (Securities Commission) v Branch* [1995] 2 SCR 3.
[1679] [1990] 1 SCR 425, see the discussion in Hogg (n 1664 above) 44.10(b).
[1680] Under the Combines Investigation Act 1970—investigations designed to determine whether there had been a breach of competition law.
[1681] [1995] 4 SCR 154.
[1682] (1999) 6 BHRC 120, the case contains a useful survey of the present state of the Canadian law on self-incrimination.

25. Minimum standards of criminal procedure—

Everyone who is charged with an offence, has, in relation to the determination of the charge, the following minimum rights:

(a) the right to a fair and public hearing by an independent and impartial court:
(b) the right to be tried without undue delay:
(c) the right to be presumed innocent until proved guilty according to law:
(d) the right not to be compelled to be a witness or to confess guilt:
(e) the right to be present at the trial and to present a defence:
(f) the right to examine the witnesses for the prosecution and to obtain the attendance and examination of witnesses for the defence under the same conditions as the prosecution:
(g) the right, if convicted of an offence in respect of which the penalty has been varied between the commission of the offence and sentencing, to the benefit of the lesser penalty:
(h) the right, if convicted of the offence, to appeal according to law to a higher court against the conviction or against the sentence or against both:
(i) the right, in the case of a child, to be dealt with in a manner that takes account of the child's age.

26. Retroactive penalties and double jeopardy—

(1) No one shall be liable to conviction of any offence on account of any act or omission which did not constitute an offence by such person under the law of New Zealand at the time it occurred.

(2) No one who has been finally acquitted or convicted of, or pardoned for, an offence shall be tried or punished for it again.

27. Right to justice—

(1) Every person has the right to the observance of the principles of natural justice by any tribunal or other public authority which has the power to make a determination in respect of that person's right, obligations, or interests protected or recognised by law.

(2) Every person whose rights, obligations, or interests protected or recognized by law have been affected by a determination of any tribunal or other public authority has the right to apply in accordance with law, for judicial review of that determination.

(3) Every person has the right to bring civil proceedings against, and to defend civil proceedings brought by the Crown, and to have those proceedings heard, according to law, in the same way as civil proceedings between individuals.

11.422 The scope of these provisions differ from the Convention in a number of respects. First, the Bill of Rights Act provides for an express right to a fair and public hearing only in the context of minimum standards of criminal procedure. The principle of open justice and its exceptions in the civil law in New Zealand therefore remain governed by the common law[1683] and by section 27 which reflects the general right of every person to 'the observance of the principles of natural justice' whenever their interests or obligations are to be determined before a competent tribunal or other public authority. In practice, the Bill of Rights Act is not viewed as the definitive statement on issues of public administration of justice, access to justice or the principles of fairness, but is given consideration in conjunction with other relevant statutory provisions and the common law. It has been suggested that the Bill of Rights Act may be minimised or disregarded altogether as a measure of fairness of criminal and civil proceedings in New Zealand.[1684]

[1683] M McDowell, 'The Principle of Open Justice in a Civil Context' [1995] NZLR 214.

[1684] Cf C Baylis, 'Justice Done and Justice Seen to be Done—The Public Administration of Justice' (1991) 21 Victoria University of Wellington L Rev 177.

There are, however, some signs that the New Zealand courts are taking a 'rights centred' approach which emphasises the primacy of the individual rights and freedoms affirmed in the Bill of Rights.[1685] This would mean that the Bill of Rights Act is given constitutional status. The argument is that the fundamental nature of the affirmed rights is more important than the legal form in which they are declared and that consequently, the reasoning of foreign courts interpreting constitutionally entrenched human rights is applicable to the New Zealand Bill of Rights Act: **11.423**

> Enjoyment of the basic human rights are the entitlement of every citizen, and their protection the obligation of every civilized state. They are inherent in and essential to the structure of society. They do not depend on the legal or constitutional form in which they are declared. The reasoning that has led the Privy Council and the Courts of Ireland and India to the conclusions reached in the cases to which I have referred . . . is in my opinion equally valid to the New Zealand Bill of Rights Act if it is to have life and meaning.[1686]

The result in *Baigent's Case*[1687] was that the majority of the Court established an independent civil claim directly against the Crown for infringement of the section 21 freedom from unreasonable search and seizure. As Crown liability is direct liability in public law rather than a vicarious liability in tort for the acts of Crown servants, the usual Crown immunities do not apply. However, this application of the purposive approach to interpretation of the Bill of Rights Act has not escaped criticism.[1688] **11.424**

Nevertheless, this approach has far-reaching implications which will potentially affect the right to observance of principles of natural justice and to a fair and public hearing in New Zealand. The New Zealand courts have the power to award damages where 'fair trial rights have been denied'. An award was made in the recent case of *Upton v Green (No 2)*[1689] arising out of a failure by a District Judge to hear a defendant who had pleaded guilty before sentence. Compensation in the sum of NZ$15,000[1690] was awarded for this breach. **11.425**

(2) The guarantees

(a) Access to the courts

The New Zealand Bill of Rights Act does not contain any general principle of access to the courts, though a fundamental right to access to justice has been derived from various provisions for access in particular contexts. Whether access to the courts can or needs to be differentiated from the right to access to justice is not clear. Several sections of the Act may be construed to imply a right of access to the courts. They either provide a right of access in a specific criminal context, or appear to assume a right of access to the courts. Section 24(f) recognises the principle of access in its guarantee of a right to legal assistance without cost if the interests of justice so require and the person does not have sufficient means to provide for that assistance. Section 27 is entitled 'access to justice' and establishes that compliance with the rules of natural justice by public decision makers, judicial review and the right to take action in civil proceedings against the Crown must be provided in particular contexts that go beyond criminal law. **11.426**

1685 See in particular, *Simpson v Attorney-General (Baigent's Case)* [1994] 3 NZLR 667.
1686 Ibid 702.
1687 Ibid.
1688 See J Smillie, 'The Allure of "Rights Talk"' (1994) 8:2 Otago L Rev 188.
1689 (1996) 3 HRNZ 179, affd *sub nom A-G v Upton* (1998) 5 HRNZ 54.
1690 Approx £4,700.

It is not clear whether the Bill of Rights Act adds anything to the common law in facilitating access to the judicial process. Sir Robin Cooke has gone so far as to suggest, *obiter*, that even at common law the Court of Appeal

> has reservations as to the extent to which in New Zealand even an Act of Parliament can take away the rights of citizens to resort to the ordinary Courts of law for the determination of their rights.[1691]

This is difficult to reconcile with parliamentary sovereignty, which ensures that, if it does so in sufficiently clear language, Parliament can deny access to the courts.

(b) Fairness: sections 24 and 25

11.428 In contrast to the Convention, the right to a fair (and public) hearing is expressly provided for only in relation to an accused person 'charged with a criminal offence'. In the non-criminal context, persons charged with an offence are guaranteed the specific rights set out in section 24, and the protection of the general principles of 'natural justice' under section 27, including the right to apply for judicial review, or bring a suit against the public authorities. The concept of fairness runs throughout the jurisprudence in relation to both sections 24 and 25. All of the rights specified in subsections of those provisions are treated as elements of a fair trial, with occasional reference to the 'minimum' standards to be afforded in the criminal context when it is section 25 rights that are in issue. There is no reference to another standard of fairness applicable with respect to the determination of civil obligations, as most of the jurisprudence involves determination of criminal charges.

11.429 **The right to be informed promptly of the charge.** Section 24(a) provides that everyone charged with an offence has the right to be informed promptly and in detail of the nature and cause of the charge. This does not oblige the police authorities to provide the accused with an opportunity to deny charges for the police record and so avoid having to testify in court,[1692] nor to put all the potential charges revealed by his statements to him in an interview, nor to interview the accused at all, if they have sufficient evidence upon which to proceed without doing so.[1693] The 'detail' required by the subsection does not extend to the exact dates of sexual offences that allegedly took place over a period of several years.[1694] The power to amend an information does not conflict with this provision.[1695]

11.430 **Adequate time and facilities to prepare.** The right in section 24(d) to adequate time and facilities to prepare a defence is an important element of a fair trial designed to put the defence on an equal footing with the prosecution in preparation for trial.[1696] It does not oblige the Crown to call all its witnesses at a preliminary hearing, if the accused will have a chance to cross-examine them at trial,[1697] but it does include the right to adequate access to evidence which the accused requires to present his or her case,[1698] such as the opportunity to obtain evidence that might have an exculpatory effect. In *R v Donaldson,*[1699]

[1691] *New Zealand Drivers' Association v New Zealand Road Carriers* [1982] 1 NZLR 374, 390.
[1692] *R v K* [1995] 2 NZLR 440.
[1693] Ibid.
[1694] *W v A-G* [1993] 1 NZLR 1.
[1695] *Jones v Police* [1998] 1 NZLR 447.
[1696] See Richardson J in *R v Accused* (1994) 12 CRNZ 417.
[1697] See *R v Haig* [1996] 1 NZLR 184.
[1698] Ibid.
[1699] [1995] 3 NZLR 641.

section 24(d) was breached when the appellant, who was arrested on suspicion of driving under the influence of a drug, was denied the right to have a blood sample taken, in spite of the fact that the alcohol breath test conducted at the scene proved negative and a qualified doctor was in attendance at police headquarters. The refusal was considered, in the circumstances, to be an obstruction of the preparation of a defence, implying that the police are required not to obstruct, an obligation narrowly distinguishable in practice from an affirmative duty to assist in the collection of evidence useful for the defence. The Court in *Donaldson* took the view that a breach of section 24(d) could result from a variety of factors, including:

- 'bad faith' on the part of the police which would point towards obstruction;
- the degree and foreseeability or materiality of the lost evidence; and
- the existence and extent of any practical difficulties in obtaining or preserving that evidence.

Where the accused, charged with sexual offences, sought an order that the complainant undergo a medical examination,[1700] the Court was faced with the problem of the competing interests of the complainant who had a right to refuse the examination. The Judge found that the test in determining whether a fair trial has been prevented is whether the evidence denied (in this case, the medical examination) might have provided a reasonable prospect of exculpating the accused. A 'working expression of the test' could be found in the *obiter dictum* of Cooke P: 'there must be a compelling need for the evidence; the Court must be satisfied that justice could not be done without it'.[1701] **11.431**

In another section 24 case,[1702] the court ordered that a Chinese-speaking defendant charged with illegal importation of goods must be provided with written translations of volumes of documentary evidence briefs delivered by the prosecution prior to the hearing. Using a purposive approach to the interpretation of section 24(g),[1703] and in light of the common law principles,[1704] the phrases 'assistance of an interpreter' and 'language used' were considered broad enough to include both written and spoken language; written interpretation as well as oral translation. Once it is determined that the accused person is incapable of understanding or speaking the language used in Court, section 24(g) is applicable, which in this case meant that the onus was on the court to provide pre-trial translations, at no expense to the accused, in a timely fashion. **11.432**

The right to a jury. In two cases,[1705] the right to elect trial by jury in section 24(e) has been held to be overridden by section 43 of the Summary Offences Act. Section 43 was clearly intended, with respect to certain specified offences, to abrogate the right to elect a jury trial which was normally afforded in connection with offences punishable by prison **11.433**

1700 *R v B (No 2)* [1995] 2 NZLR 752; the first appeal failed in *R v B* [1995] 2 NZLR 172 because the Court of Appeal held that it had no jurisdiction to deal with the matter on an interlocutory appeal.

1701 *R v B* [1995] 2 NZLR 172, 177.

1702 *Alwen Industries Ltd and Kar Wong v Collector of Customs* [1996] 1 HRNZ 574.

1703 The Court found that the aim of the right is to ensure that the defendant receives a fair trial; specifically that he understands the proceedings, and is able to instruct counsel fully and prepare a defence.

1704 The Court referred to the common law right of the defendant to an interpreter which is an aspect of the fundamental right to a fair trial.

1705 *Reille v Police* [1993] 1 NZLR 587; *Dreliozis v Wellington District Court* [1994] 2 NZLR 198.

sentences in excess of three months. The offences included assaults involving a police officer[1706] in the execution of his duty which carried a penalty of six-months' imprisonment or a fine of $2,000. There was no meaning consistent with the Bill of Rights Act that could be given the provision; to grant the accused a jury trial would be to impliedly repeal[1707] section 43 or to render it ineffective in relation to such offences, contrary to section 4, an argument decisively rejected by the Court.

11.434 **Section 25: introduction.** The general heading of section 25, which indicates that its provisions are 'minimum standards of criminal procedure' has been referred to in recent cases. In *R v L*,[1708] the court emphasised that the right to a fair trial[1709] and to cross-examine witnesses[1710] are 'minimum rights', affirmed by the parallel provisions of the International Covenant on Civil and Political Rights. Where judicial powers of adjournment or remand in contempt proceedings were challenged because they were not addressed in section 206 of the Summary Proceedings Act,[1711] it was held that they were nevertheless consistent with and 'enhanced' the various 'rights of minimum standards of criminal procedure' in section 25 of the New Zealand Bill of Rights Act 1990. Lastly, 'minimum standards' does not limit the number of retrials that an accused may be subjected to if the jury cannot come to an agreement.[1712]

11.435 **Section 25(a): fair and public hearing before an independent and impartial court.** The right to a fair and public hearing by an independent and impartial court under subsection 25(a) is typically invoked in Bill of Rights cases wherever a challenge under the general category of abuse of process or unfairness is made. All of the subsections of section 25 are, in effect, elements of 'fairness'.[1713] It has been emphasised that, in the absence of compelling reasons to the contrary, criminal justice must be public justice.[1713a] The trial should be disposed of as near as possible to where the crimes occur but, where there is a risk of unfairness, it will be moved to another venue.[1713b] The judge who deals with a 'settlement type' hearing should not preside over the trial.[1713c] A District Court judge sitting with a jury is an independent and impartial Court.[1714] In reaching this conclusion, the Court of Appeal relied heavily on Article 6 of the Convention. The case of *R v L*[1715] emphasised the role of

---

[1706] In *Reille*, a police constable was charged with assaulting a complainant in the course of her arrest under s 9 of the Summary Offences Act; *Dreliozis* involved a charge of assault against a police officer in the execution of his duty under s 10 of the same Act.

[1707] In *Dreliozis v Wellington District Court* [1994] 2 NZLR 198, the Court rejected a further argument that the Bill of Rights Act, while not impliedly repealing s 43, did so expressly, in an indirect fashion.

[1708] *R v L* [1994] 2 NZLR 54.

[1709] s 25(a).

[1710] s 25(f).

[1711] s 206 was alleged to be a codification of the rules of contempt of court.

[1712] *R v Barlow* [1996] 2 NZLR 116.

[1713] See, however, *Martin v Tauranga District Court* [1995] 1 NZLR 491, in which the Court made an express distinction between the right to trial without undue delay under s 25(b) and the right to a fair trial.

[1713a] *R v Bain* [1996] 3 HRNZ 108.

[1713b] *R v Lory* [1996] 3 HRNZ 99.

[1713c] *Pickering v Police* [1999] 5 HRNZ 154.

[1714] See *A-G v McNally* [1993] 1 NZLR 550 (it was also held that there was nothing contrary to the Bill of Rights Act in the fact that only those accused persons to be tried in the High Court can apply for trial by Judge alone).

[1715] [1994] 2 NZLR 54.

cross-examination of witnesses in ensuring a fair trial. In *R v Haig,*[1716] the fairness of the proceedings was unsuccessfully challenged in connection with allegations that a failure of the Crown to call all of its witnesses at a preliminary hearing breached the accused's right to cross-examination of prosecution witnesses under 25(f) and prejudiced the defence preparation for trial under 24(d). A challenge under the same three grounds was successful in *R v B (No 2),*[1717] in which the complainant refused to undergo a medical examination following her allegations of sexual assault. The test for establishing whether a denial of the opportunity to obtain further evidence prevents the accused from having a fair trial is whether the evidence might have provided a reasonable prospect of exculpating him. There was no unfairness made out when a decision to retry a criminal case for the third time was challenged on the grounds of undue delay and infringement of presumption of innocence.[1718]

A number of grounds were considered together in *R v Coghill,*[1719] where the issue was pretrial publicity with the complicity of the police. The Court held that the quashing of a trial on the basis of deprivation of fairness requires a 'fatal defect', which on the facts had not been proved. The length of time that had elapsed (which was not 'undue' under section 25(b)) had eradicated any substantial risk that the publicity would be prejudicial to the accused's right to be assumed innocent until proven guilty (section 25(c)). **11.436**

It has been said in several cases that section 25(a) adds nothing to the arguments made under the common law. The case of *R v Ellis,*[1720] which involved inflammatory media attention given to an accused charged with sexual assault of children in his care, emphasised the need to consider and balance all relevant factors. The Court found that section 25(a) (insofar as it related to fairness) added nothing to the court's inherent jurisdiction to deal with the matter. Similarly in *R v Accused,*[1721] the general submission alleging contravention of the right to a fair trial was said to add nothing to the common law arguments in relation to the admissibility of evidence. However, in *Upton v Green (No 2)*[1721a] it was held that a failure by a District Judge to hear a defendant who had pleaded guilty before sentence was a breach of his rights under section 25(a). Compensation in the sum of NZ$15,000[1721b] was awarded for this breach. **11.437**

Section 25(b): undue delay. The case of *Martin v Tauranga District Court*[1722] provides a comprehensive overview of principles to be applied in relation to undue delay under section 25(b). On the facts, a period of 17 months from the laying of charges to end of trial, including a period of five months of systemic or institutional delay, was not of such magnitude to be categorised as 'undue'. The Court said that wherever the length of time taken to complete a trial had gone beyond the time in which most cases were able to be disposed of and the accused then raised the issue of undue delay, it is for the Crown to prove on a balance of probabilities that the delay had not become 'undue delay'. It was not appropriate to specify a guideline period as has been done in other jurisdictions.[1723] The Court must **11.438**

[1716] [1996] 1 NZLR 184.
[1717] [1995] 2 NZLR 752.
[1718] *R v Barlow* [1996] 2 NZLR 116.
[1719] [1995] 3 NZLR 651.
[1720] [1993] 3 NZLR 317.
[1721] [1991] 2 NZLR 187.
[1721a] (1996) 3 HRNZ 179, affd *sub nom A-G v Upton* (1998) 5 HRNZ 54.
[1721b] Approx £4,700.
[1722] [1995] 1 NZLR 491.
[1723] See para 11.399 above.

assess the situation in light of the accused's right to be presumed innocent, taking into account:

- the overall length of delay, calculated from the laying of the charge to the end of the trial;
- the reasons for the delay including the inherent time requirements of the case, actions of the accused, actions of the prosecution, actions of judicial officers, limits on institutional resources, and other reasons;
- any prejudice to the accused arising from the delay; and
- any informed waiver by the accused of the section 25(b) right.

The Court also found that prejudice to the accused was relevant only to the extent that it arose from the delay in bringing charges to trial, not from the delay in laying of the charges, or prejudice in relation to the trial itself. Prejudice might, however, be presumed where there had been an exceptionally long delay. The Court expressed the view that the protection against undue delay under section 25(b) is a guarantee distinct and apart from that which guarantees the right to a fair trial.

11.439 The case of *R v B*[1724] involved two appeals relating to jury trials in a District Court that had been experiencing serious backlogs. Neither case was particularly complex or difficult and in each case the court rejected the complaint that section 25(b) was breached.

11.440 In *Hughes v Police,*[1725] the Court was prepared to dismiss or order a stay of prosecution on the basis that delays in the criminal process, while outside of the scope of application of section 25(b), may nevertheless result in unfairness prejudicial to the accused. Hughes had been the object of a series of investigations for fraud over a period of six years. On the basis of the final investigation, which was completed within 8 months, he was charged with 14 counts of misappropriation of moneys and committed to trial. The Court considered that, even though the specific application of the Act is to the period between initiation of the prosecution and trial, section 25(b) ought to have some significance for the person who is aware that he is under investigation; the pressures imposed are just as real before the formal initiation of the prosecution where the potential accused is aware that it is in contemplation. It found that prejudice could be considered in 'wider terms than merely whether or not ultimately a fair trial in the ordinary sense could take place'; and held that the reopening of the case on the basis of the last investigation involved an 'unfairness' that constituted a 'prejudice' justifying the intervention of the Court.

11.441 In other cases, a decision to go ahead with a second retrial after 19 months of prior proceedings did not constitute 'undue delay', where every effort had been made to expedite the charges against the accused.[1726] A period of 12 months from arrest to the end of a murder trial was not undue delay, in light of the large number of witnesses, the complexity of the case and problems of Court resources.[1727] Neither was a period of three years from police enquiries to sentencing offensive, given that the case had progressed steadily in spite of a history of complexity and difficulties.[1728]

[1724] [1996] 1 NZLR 386.
[1725] [1995] 3 NZLR 443.
[1726] *R v Barlow* [1996] 2 NZLR 116.
[1727] *R v Haig* [1996] 1 NZLR 184.
[1728] *R v Coghill* [1995] 3 NZLR 651.

Subsection 25(c): presumption of innocence until proven guilty. Section 25(c) ensures that everyone charged with an offence has, as a minimum right, the right to be presumed innocent until proved guilty according to law. This reflects the basic principle of the criminal law that the onus of proof beyond a reasonable doubt will lie with the Crown on a criminal or quasi-criminal allegation unless Parliament gives a reasonably clear indication that it should be otherwise.[1729] In *R v Rangi,*[1730] the accused successfully appealed against his conviction of having a sheath knife in a public place where the judge had instructed the jury that once the Crown had proved possession of the knife, it was for the accused to establish the authority or excuse for the possession on a balance of probabilities. It was held that the offence of 'having a knife in a public place without lawful authority or reasonable excuse' indicated no clear legislative intention that the onus was to shift to the accused to disprove any element of the offence. If the issue of authority or excuse was raised on the evidence, it was incumbent on the Crown to prove beyond a reasonable doubt that no such defence existed. 11.442

In relation to the possession of a cannabis plant for the purpose of sale,[1731] on the other hand, the legislative intent was clearly to shift the burden of proof. Where the Crown had proved possession of a certain amount of the substance beyond a reasonable doubt, such possession was deemed to be for a proscribed purpose (in this case sale) 'until the contrary is proved'. On appeal against conviction of the accused, the defence argued that by application of section 6 of the Bill of Rights Act, an interpretation consistent with subsection 25(c) of that Act would render 'until the contrary is proved' to mean that the defence had only to raise sufficient evidence to cast a reasonable doubt on the guilt of the accused and that it remained for the Crown to prove that sale was the purpose of the possession beyond a reasonable doubt. The Court rejected the argument, finding it 'strained and unnatural' and held that the trial judge was correct in his direction to the jury that the onus of proof shifted to the accused to overturn the presumption as to purpose on a balance of probabilities. 11.443

In *R v Coghill,*[1732] the court considered the connection between an offence against the accused's presumption of innocence and the fairness of the trial itself as a result of alleged complicity by the police in pretrial publicity. However, the Court failed to address the question of a separate remedy for a violation of 25(c) and found that the pretrial violation did not affect the fairness of the trial. 11.444

Subsection 25(d): self-incrimination. The right of an accused not to be compelled to be a witness in his own case has been asserted in situations in which, had pretrial procedures been conducted in a different manner, the accused may have chosen not to testify at trial. In *R v K,*[1733] the question was whether the police ought to have interviewed the accused in regard to the specific charge of rape, and thus provide him with the opportunity to have his denial entered on the police record that would be submitted as evidence at trial. The Court found that there was no such obligation on the police and that the accused was not in law compelled to testify. 'Compelled' means 'can be mandatorily required' and though it should not be unduly refined, it cannot be stretched to mean compelled 'in fact', 11.445

1729 *R v Rangi* [1992] 1 NZLR 385.
1730 Ibid.
1731 *R v Phillips* [1991] 3 NZLR 175.
1732 [1995] 3 NZLR 651.
1733 *R v K* [1995] 2 NZLR 440.

just because a disadvantageous inference might be drawn from a failure of the accused to testify. In light of *R v K*, the reasoning, if not the decision of the earlier case of *Reille v Police*[1734] is difficult to support.

11.446 **Subsection 25(e): the right to be present at the trial and to present a defence.** The right to be present at the trial was considered in *R v Duval*[1735] where the accused sought a stay of proceedings on the ground that his chronic back pain made it impossible for him to sit through a trial or if he did, to obtain a fair one. The Court found that section 25(e) affirms the requirement of the criminal justice system that an accused must be fit to stand trial. The Court stated that 'the notion that a person must be able to plead and stand trial is not just a matter of procedural fairness . . . , but a substantive requirement firmly rooted in an accused's constitutional rights to a fair trial'; 'a trial would not be fair if the accused suffers a disability which prevents him from effectively defending him or herself, and the section 25(e) right to be present and present a defence would be rendered ineffectual unless the accused is capable of comprehending the case against him and presenting a defence to that case'.

11.447 The second part of subsection 25(e), the right to present a defence, has been asserted in connection with the right to adequate facilities in order to prepare a defence[1736] where the complainant refused to undergo a medical examination which might have provided evidence helpful to the accused's case.[1737]

11.448 **Sub-section 25(f): right to examine prosecution witnesses.** The purpose of subsection 25(f) is to ensure that the accused has an adequate and proper opportunity to challenge and question witnesses against him at some stage in the proceedings. It does not appear to be necessary that this opportunity is always afforded at trial,[1738] or at a preliminary stage if the accused has the right to examine witnesses at trial.[1739] Where the witness is not available for cross-examination at all, the potential significance of cross-examination ought to be calculated as far as possible,[1740] but will not always be a mandatory element of a fair trial. Where the issue is one of admissibility of evidence, it is a matter of discretion as to the circumstances in which it will be proper to exclude.[1741] The jurisdiction of the Court is 'wide', going beyond the immediate question as to whether the prejudicial effect of the evidence outweighs its probative value, to questions as to overall unfairness to the accused.[1742]

11.449 In *R v Petaera*, the Court excluded a video-taped statement of a witness who had since died, because lack of opportunity to cross-examine would seriously impede a fair trial.[1743] On the other hand, *R v L*[1744] was a 'perhaps rare case' in which the court confidently

1734 [1993] 1 NZLR 587, 593-594.
1735 [1995] 3 NZLR 202.
1736 Bill of Rights Act, s 24(d).
1737 See *R v B* [1995] 2 NZLR 172; *R v B (No 2)* [1995] 2 NZLR 752.
1738 *R v Haig* [1996] 1 NZLR 184, 192: this can be 'either at the time of the making of the statement or at some later stage of the proceeding'.
1739 In *R v Haig* [1996] 1 NZLR 184, it was not a breach of s 25(f) that the Crown failed to call all of its potential witnesses at the depositions stage.
1740 *R v Haig* [1996] 1 NZLR 184.
1741 In *R v L* [1994] 2 NZLR 54, the Court considered ten principles governing the discretion to exclude otherwise admissible evidence in a series of steps. The last two concerned the applicability of standards of criminal justice under provisions of the New Zealand Bill of Rights Act 1990.
1742 *R v Petaera* [1994] 3 NZLR 763.
1743 Ibid.
1744 [1994] 2 NZLR 54.

concluded that there was no basis for giving any substantial weight to the absence of any practical opportunity to cross-examine the complainant at the preliminary hearing.

In *R v B*[1745] and *R v B (No 2)*[1746] the right to cross-examine prosecution witnesses was one of the grounds put forward for justifying the refusal of the complainant to obtain a medical examination anticipated to provide evidence in support of the position of the accused. The connection between such refusal and the right to cross-examination is tenuous, and the decision does not elaborate on the application of section 25(f) specifically. **11.450**

Sub-section 25(g): benefit of a lesser penalty. This protects the right, if convicted of an offence in respect of which the penalty has been varied between the commission of the offence and sentencing, to the benefit of the lesser penalty. In *Norton-Bennett v Attorney General,*[1747] an increase in the period of ineligibility for parole from seven to ten years,[1748] following conviction of the accused, did not constitute a variation in 'penalty' and the prisoner was not entitled to parole upon serving the lesser period. **11.451**

Sub-section 25(h): right of appeal. This does not guarantee an appeal from a pre-trial interlocutory application that does not lead to conviction. The issue was raised when the Court of Appeal denied jurisdiction to hear an appeal from an unsuccessful application for an order that the complainant undergo a medical examination.[1749] It held that the Bill of Rights Act conferred no jurisdiction in relation to appeals from pre-trial applications where there was none granted under the terms of the Judicature Act.[1750] **11.452**

(c) Freedom from retroactive penalties and double jeopardy: section 26.

Section 26(1) guarantees that no person shall be liable to conviction of any offence on account of any act or omission which did not constitute an offence by such person under the law of New Zealand at the time it occurred. The provision recognises the fundamental principle of substantive criminal law that the law should not take effect retrospectively. Where a statutory amendment had broadened the scope of a serious sexual violation following an alleged commission of the offence, the judge, citing subsection 26(1) of the New Zealand Bill of Rights Act, instructed the jury not to apply it to the case before them.[1751] **11.453**

Subsection 26(2) which prohibits 'double jeopardy', provides that no one who has been finally acquitted or convicted of, or pardoned for, an offence shall be tried or punished for it again. This section applies only to criminal proceedings.[1752] In *Bracanov v Moss,*[1753] **11.454**

1745 [1995] 2 NZLR 172.

1746 [1995] 2 NZLR 752.

1747 [1995] 3 NZLR 712.

1748 The statute was unambiguous in that it stated clearly that the new minimum non-parole period was to apply to sentences imposed after a specific date, regardless of when the offence had been committed.

1749 *R v B* [1995] 2 NZLR 172.

1750 The Court did allow that s 6 of the Bill of Rights Act provides for a liberal interpretation of the Judicature Act and may enable appeals to be brought in habeas corpus proceedings, but those are not proceedings subject to the same appellate limitations as criminal proceedings.

1751 In *R v King* [1995] 3 NZLR 409 (amendment to the Crimes Act definition of 'sexual violation of a female child' from penetration of the 'vagina' to penetration of the 'genitalia' had the effect of expanding the crime to include acts that had previously been considered indecency).

1752 *Daniels v Thompson* [1998] 3 NZLR 22.

1753 *Bracanov v Moss* [1996] 1 NZLR 445.

Mr Bracanov was ordered to enter into a bond of $9000 on his own recognisance to keep the peace, in anticipation of a repeat of his expressions of anti-royalist sentiment that had led to his conviction for breach of the peace on eight previous occasions. The court, rejecting the argument of the accused, held that the peace bond order is not a conviction or an acquittal, so that a breach of the bond together with the conviction for the offence resulting in the breach could not amount to double jeopardy.

(d) Natural justice: section 27

11.455 Section 27 provides that every person has the right to the observance of the principles of natural justice by any tribunal or other public authority which has the power to make a determination in respect of that person's rights, obligations, or interests protected or recognised by law. Wherever those rights have been affected by such a determination a person may apply for judicial review of the decision; in addition, everyone has the right to bring or defend civil proceedings against or by the Crown and to have them heard in the same way as civil proceedings between individuals. A prosecutor is not a 'public authority' within the scope of section 27; the principles of natural justice had no application where a decision was made to transfer proceedings to the High Court to enable the Crown to proceed by way of indictment.[1754]

11.456 The remedy of judicial review in New Zealand, as defined by the Judicature Act, lies only in relation to a refusal to exercise a statutory power; it does not apply in relation to the exercise of a prerogative power where the subject of the decision is not justiciable. In *Burt v Governor-General,*[1755] the prerogative of mercy was said to be a matter of a value or conceptual judgment which had become a (non-reviewable) constitutional safeguard against mistakes in the criminal justice system.

11.457 **'Principles of natural justice'.** Section 27 requires that any tribunal or other public authority which has the power to make a determination in respect of a person's rights, obligations or interests protected or recognised by law observes the principles of natural justice. It is not clear, however, what 'principles of natural justice' are and how they differ from minimum considerations of fairness protected by section 25 of the Bill of Rights Act. Principles of natural justice provide that the applicant must have an opportunity to place before the decision-maker information relevant to his decision. In order to do so effectively, he must also have a fair opportunity to comprehend the conditions upon which the decision is to be made.[1756] In *Ankers,*[1757] the decision of the authorities in relation to an application for social welfare benefits was in breach of section 27 because the applicant had not been informed as to the principal criteria bearing on his eligibility.

11.458 It is apparent from the case law that the principles of natural justice are to some degree intertwined with the essential elements of a fair trial in criminal cases.[1758] In several cases the

---

1754 *R v K* [1995] 2 NZLR 440.

1755 [1992] 3 NZLR 672 (when Mr Burt's application for leave to appeal his murder conviction was refused, he applied to the Governor-General for exercise of the prerogative of mercy and grant of full pardon. When it was declined, he commenced a judicial review proceeding of that decision, alleging that the Justice Department had failed to act fairly and reasonably in dealing with the application. The proceeding was dismissed on the basis that no reasonable cause of action was disclosed, and the applicant appealed).

1756 *Ankers v A-G* [1995] NZAR 241.

1757 Ibid.

1758 Ibid.

overlap between the minimum standards of criminal justice and 'natural justice' is also apparent. It has been found that the section 25(e) right to be present and present a defence would be rendered ineffectual where the accused is not capable of comprehending the case against him as required by the principles of natural justice.[1759] In *W v A-G; P v Wellington District Court,*[1760] a refusal of leave to cross-examine the complainant at a preliminary hearing was found not contrary to the principles of 'natural justice', because there would be an opportunity to cross-examine at trial as required by section 25(f). Compliance with section 27 rested on the existence of one of the minimum elements of fairness required by section 25.

Appendix 3: Human Rights Cases in Other Jurisdictions

(1) Introduction

Over the past 50 years, 'fair trial' issues have been considered by the courts in many jurisdictions. However, the most developed 'due process' jurisprudence remains that decided under the US Constitution. Despite its idiosyncrasies, this jurisprudence continues to influence the development of the law throughout the common law world. There are two specific areas: general 'due process' and 'criminal due process' rights. **11.459**

The general 'due process' rights in the US Constitution are to be found in the Fifth Amendment which provides that: **11.460**

> No person shall . . . be deprived of life, liberty, or property, without due process of law.

The Fourteenth Amendment extends this protection to the States: its 'due process' clause was the means by which provisions of the Bill of Rights were made applicable to the States. A distinction has been drawn between substantive and procedural due process: substantive due process deals with what public authorities can do and procedural due process deals with the way in which the public authorities act.[1761] The due process clauses apply only to deprivations of 'life, liberty or property' and these notions have all been subject to extensive analysis[1762] which is not directly relevant to the subject matter of the present chapter.[1763]

The fair trial rights as dealt with by Article 6 of the Convention, find their equivalent in the US doctrine of procedural due process with its general requirements of prior notice and the right to be heard.[1764] The more significant the interest involved, the stricter the requirement for effective notice.[1765] The right to be heard generally includes the right to **11.461**

[1759] *R v Duval* [1995] 3 NZLR 202.

[1760] [1993] 1 NZLR 1.

[1761] See generally, H Abraham and B Perry, *Freedom and the Court* (7th edn, Oxford Universitgy Press, 1998), Chap 4, 'The Fascinating World of Due Process of Law'; and see also D Galligan, *Due Process and Fair Procedures* (Clarendon Press, 1996), Chap 6 'The American Doctrine of Procedural Due Process'.

[1762] See generally, L Tribe, *American Constitutional Law* (2nd edn, Foundation Press, 1988) 663ff; Galligan (n 1761 above) 192-197.

[1763] But see para 18.116ff below (in relation to the deprivation of 'property').

[1764] See Tribe (n 1762 above) 732ff.

[1765] See for example *Memphis Light, Gas and Water Division v Craft* (1978) 436 US 1 (notice threatening cutting off of utilities must indicate the procedures for challenging the decision); *Greene* v *Lindsey* (1982) 456 US 444 (statute allowing notice of possession proceedings by attachment to door after one attempt at personal service violated due process rights).

present evidence and to cross-examine witnesses.[1765a] However, these rights may be limited or denied in exceptional circumstances.[1766] In determining whether particular procedures satisfy the procedural due process requirements, three factors are considered:[1767]

- the nature of the private interest affected;
- the risk of mistaken deprivation of that interest and the probable value of the additional procedural safeguards;
- the government's interest, including the function involved and fiscal and administrative burden of the additional procedural safeguards.[1767a]

These factors have sometimes led the US courts to deny the right to a hearing: for example, in relation to prison[1768] discipline or dismissal of students for failure to meet academic standards,[1769] the suspension of employees facing criminal charges,[1770] the termination of social security disability benefits[1770a] or issues relating to academic evaluation.[1771] Public employees who have tenure or fixed term contracts have a right to due process in dismissal proceedings.[1771a] The due process clause limits the use of government agents to seize property from one private individual to convey it to another. This covers matters such as prejudgment garnishee orders[1771b] and prejudgment seizure of property.[1771c]

11.462 Other provisions of the US Bill of Rights provide 'fair trial' rights to those charged with criminal offences. These cover protection against unreasonable search and seizure,[1772] self-incrimination,[1773] cruel and unusual punishment,[1774] double jeopardy,[1775] and excessive bail[1776] as well as the Sixth Amendment rights to counsel, to be confronted with witnesses, to trial by jury and to a speedy trial. In a series of well known cases in the 1960s, the Supreme Court considered the effect of violations of these rights on the admissibility of evidence, holding that evidence was inadmissible in both state and federal courts if obtained

- by searches and seizures in violation of the Fourth Amendment;[1777]
- by secretly taping conversations with a suspect after indictment;[1778]

[1765a] See generally, C Antieau and W Rich, *Modern Constitutional Law* (2nd edn, West Group, 1997) Vol 2, para 35.00ff.
[1766] See generally, Tribe (n 1762 above) 736ff.
[1767] See *Mathews v Eldridge* (1976) 424 US 315.
[1767a] *United States v James Daniel Good Property* (1993) 510 US 43.
[1768] *Wolff v McDonnell* (1974) 418 US 539.
[1769] *Board of Curators v Horowtiz* (1978) 435 US 78; but there will be due process rights in cases of suspension for misconduct: see *Goss v Lopez* (1975) 419 US 565.
[1770] *Gilbert v Homar* (1997) 520 US 924 (state university policeman arrested on drugs charges).
[1770a] *Mathews v Eldridge* (1976) 424 US 319.
[1771] *Board of Curators v Horowitz* (1978) 435 US 78.
[1771a] *Cleveland Board of Education v Loudermill* (1985) 470 US 532.
[1771b] *Sniadach v Family Finance Corporation* (1969) 395 US 377.
[1771c] *Fuentes v Shevin* (1972) 407 US 67.
[1772] Fourth Amendment.
[1773] Fifth Amendment.
[1774] Eighth Amendment.
[1775] Fifth Amendment.
[1776] Eighth Amendment.
[1777] *Mapp v Ohio* (1961) 367 US 643.
[1778] *Massiah v United States* (1964) 377 US 201.

- by the interrogation of a suspect in custody, without his consent, unless a defence lawyer is present;[1779]
- by eavesdropping on or bugging a suspect without a warrant.[1780]

However, the Supreme Court has retreated from strictness of this approach in a number of cases over the past three decades. For example,

- a suspect's confession in the absence of his lawyer can be used to attack his credit;[1781]
- a compulsory blood sample[1782] or videotape of drunk driving suspects[1783] does not violate the self-incrimination rule;
- evidence obtained on a search when the police act in an 'objectively reasonable' reliance on a warrant which turns out to be defective.[1784]

The approach of the US courts to criminal due process issues can be characterised 'pragmatic', on a case-by-case basis.

There is now a substantial body of international human rights 'fair trials' jurisprudence in relation to criminal cases. This is helpfully summarised in the *Fair Trials Manual* published by Amnesty International.[1784a] A wide range of 'international standards' have been suggested including the following: **11.462A**

- the right not to be compelled to testify or confess guilt, which includes a prohibition against any form of coercion;[1784b]
- the exclusion of evidence elicited as a result of torture or other coercion (including violence, threats or methods of interrogation which impairs the judgment of detainees);[1784c]
- the right to call and examine witnesses (including a right to know the identity of prosecution witnesses).[1784d]

(2) Australia

Section 80 of the Australian Constitution guarantees that: **11.463**

> The trial on indictment of any offence against any law of the Commonwealth shall be by jury.[1785]

This section has been interpreted narrowly. The federal Parliament can itself determine whether a trial is to be on indictment and, as a result, whether there will be a jury trial.[1786]

1779 *Miranda v Arizona* (1966) 384 US 436.
1780 *Katz v United States* (1967) 389 US 347.
1781 *Harris v New York* (1971) 401 US 222; see also *Michigan v Harvey* (1990) 494 US 344.
1782 *Schmerber v California* (1966) 384 US 757.
1783 *Pennsylvania v Muniz* (1990) 496 US 582.
1784 *Massachusetts v Sheppard* (1984) 468 US 981.
1784a Amnesty International, 1998.
1784b Ibid para 16.1.
1784c Ibid Chap 17.
1784d Ibid Chap 22.
1785 See generally, G Williams, *Human Rights Under the Australian Constitution* (Oxford Univeristy Press, 1999) 103-110.
1786 See *R v Archdall and Roskruge, ex p Carrigan and Brown* (1928) 41 CLR 128 and *R v Federal Court of Bankruptcy, ex p Lowenstein* (1939) 59 CLR 556.

This point has, however, been the subject of a number of powerful dissenting judgments[1787] in which it has been argued that section 80 should be given substantive meaning. However, it has been held that once an accused has a right to trial by jury this right cannot be waived[1788] and the verdict must be unanimous.[1789]

11.464 In addition, the High Court has recognised an 'implied constitutional right'[1790] to a 'fair trial'.[1791] This is recognised as the 'central thesis of the administration of criminal justice' in Australia.[1792] In *Dietrich v The Queen*[1793] it was held that lack of legal representation could mean that an accused is unable to receive a fair trial. In that case where a person charged with a serious offence was, through no fault of his own, without legal representation, the court ordered that the trial should be stayed until representation was available.

11.465 The privilege against self-incrimination is not a constitutionally protected right[1794] and is not available to corporations.[1795] The courts have considered the role that the privilege plays in ensuring a fair trial. The fact that evidence is obtained by deception or trickery does not mean that it should be excluded at trial.[1796] However in *R v Swaffield, Pavic v R*[1797] the High Court held that covertly recorded confession evidence could be excluded if the police tactics caused unfairness to the accused.[1798]

11.466 The High Court has also recognised a limited form of procedural due process guarantee. Thus,

> to cause a court to act in a manner contrary to natural justice would impose a non-judicial requirement inconsistent with the exercise of judicial power[1799]

Some support has also been expressed for an implied constitutional right to equality before the law.[1800] but such an approach was rejected by the majority of the High Court in *Kruger v The Commonwealth*[1801] The Court rejected the argument that a statute which allowed the removal of Aboriginal children from their families was invalid because it was discriminatory.

[1787] See eg *per* Dixon and Evatt JJ in *R v Federal Court of Bankruptcy, ex p Lowenstein* (n 1786 above); Deane J in *Kingswell v The Queen* (1985) 159 CLR 264.

[1788] *Brown v The Queen* (1986) 160 CLR 171.

[1789] *Cheatle v The Queen* (1993) 177 CLR 541.

[1790] See generally, para 1.39 above.

[1791] See *Jago v District Court of New South Wales* (1989) 168 CLR 23; this right has been recognised for many years, see *R v Macfarlane, ex p O'Flanagan and O'Kelly* (1923) 32 CLR 518, 541-2; see generally, J Hope, 'A Constitutional Right to a Fair Trial? Implications for the Reform of the Australian Criminal Justice System' (1996) 24 FLR 173; and G Williams (n 1786 above) 214-225.

[1792] *McInnis v R* (1979) 143 CLR 575.

[1793] (1992) 177 CLR 292.

[1794] *Sorby v Commonwealth of Australia* (1983) 152 CLR 281.

[1795] *Environment Protection Authority v Caltex Refining Pty Ltd* (1993) 178 CLR 477.

[1796] *Ridgeway v The Queen* (1995) 129 ALR 41, 53; see the discussion in Williams (n 1785 above) 218-219.

[1797] (1998) 151 ALR 98.

[1798] Referring to *R v Hebert* [1990] 2 SCR 151 (SCC) and *R v Broyles* [1991] 3 SCR 595.

[1799] *Leeth v Commonwealth* (1992) 174 CLR 455, 470 (Mason CJ, Dawson and McHugh JJ).

[1800] Ibid, *per* Deane and Toohey JJ (dissenting).

[1801] (1997) 190 CLR 1.

(3) Bermuda

The Supreme Court of Bermuda held in *Fubler v A-G*,[1802] that the constitutional right to a fair trial included legal professional privilege. That case concerned a police search of a lawyer's office under a lawful warrant. The police also made a back-up tape of the office's word-processing system. The lawyer objected that the tape contained confidential information. The court noted that privilege in documents on a word-processing system was not breached until those documents were reviewed. The police were accordingly permitted to sort documents on the back-up tape in the same way that hard-copies were sorted. **11.467**

(4) Hong Kong

(a) Introduction

Articles 10, 11 and 12 of the Hong Kong Bill of Rights contain the 'fair trial rights' in the terms of Articles 14 and 15 of the International Covenant on Civil and Political Rights.[1803] It has been held that an arrested person cannot rely on Articles 10 and 11 to challenge the evidence gathering process of the prosecuting authorities.[1804] This was because these articles relate to the determination of a criminal trial whereas the process of evidence gathering did not form part of the trial. At that stage, the rights and liberty of a suspected person were not at stake or in jeopardy. **11.468**

(b) Scope of the rights

The rights in Article 10 come into play with respect to 'suits at law'. Accordingly, the rights do not apply to an administrative hearing which is part of a planning process;[1805] an initial classification of an article by the Obscene Articles Tribunal, without the institution of criminal proceedings;[1806] a tax assessment by the Commissioner of Inland Revenue;[1807] or extradition proceedings.[1808] However, Article 10 has been successfully utilised in some administrative law contexts. In *Re Otis Elevator Co (HK) Ltd*,[1809] for example, the court found that Article 10 was breached when a Director of Electrical and Mechanical Services brought charges against a lift contractor for negligence or misconduct, and then sat as a member of the disciplinary board. This was a clear case of a person sitting as a judge in his own cause. However, the court issued a warning in *R v The Town Planning Board, ex p The Real Estate Developers Association of Hong Kong*[1810] that an argument based on the rules of natural justice which would not succeed on the basis of the common law was unlikely to be improved by the invocation of the Bill of Rights. **11.469**

In *Chan Po Ming v Chow Tat Ming; Re Lau San Ching; Fung Chan Ki v Chow Tat Ming*[1811] **11.470**

[1802] [1996] 2 CHRLD 268.
[1803] See App J in Vol 2.
[1804] *A-G v Osman* [1992] 1 HKCLR 35.
[1805] *Kwan Kong Co Ltd v Town Planning Board* 11 Jul 1996, CA, *Hong Kong Law Digest*, Jul 1996, G 168; see also *Auburntown Ltd v Town Planning Board* [1994] 2 HKLR 272.
[1806] *Re Loui Wai Po* [1994] HKLY 200.
[1807] *Commissioner of Inland Revenue, Hong Kong v Lee Lai Ping* [1993] HKLY 178.
[1808] *Re Suthipong Smittachartch* [1993] 1 HKLR 93.
[1809] [1995] 2 HKLR 1.
[1810] 8 Jun 1996, *Hong Kong Law Digest*, Jul 1996 G8.
[1811] [1995] 2 HKLR 14.

legislation which restricted the remedies available to electoral candidates to election petitions, as opposed to judicial review, was upheld as being in conformity with Article 10, even though a candidate would be unable to assert his rights until the outcome of the election. One of the most important considerations under the legislation was to preserve the integrity of the electoral process. The procedure laid down for election petitions was designed to protect this in an orderly manner. Having regard to the tight timetable for each of the successive steps in an election, it would be most unsatisfactory if interested parties were able to resort to the courts during the currency of the election and perhaps cause confusion and uncertainty.

(c) The presumption of innocence

11.471 A large number of cases concerning whether reverse onus clauses contravene the presumption of innocence have been considered under the Hong Kong Bill of Rights. The leading decision in this area is *A-G of Hong Kong v Lee Kwong-kut*.[1812] The Privy Council stated in that case that it would be difficult to justify a criminal law presumption unless it can be said with substantial assurance that the presumed fact is more likely than not to flow from the proved fact on which it is made to depend. There is also a requirement of proportionality, in that the presumption must go no further than necessary having regard to the evil that it was aimed at and the difficulty the Crown would have in combatting it without the aid of the presumption.[1813]

11.472 The following presumptions have been struck down by Hong Kong courts:

- That a person who possessed a certain quantity of drugs was trafficking in them (the quantity which triggered that presumption was very low, and failed the test of rationality and proportionality);[1814] and
- That any person who obtained property by means of a cheque which is dishonoured would, until the contrary is proved, be deemed to have obtained the property with knowledge that the cheque would be dishonoured.[1815] Further, the court refused to interpret the provision as imposing an evidential burden only on the accused.

The courts have, however, upheld the presumption that a person present in a gambling establishment was taking part in the gambling;[1816] the presumption that a person proved to be in physical possession of dangerous drugs knew what the drugs were, a presumption which could be rebutted on the balance of probabilities;[1817] the presumption that a Crown servant maintaining a standard of living above that which was commensurate with his official emoluments was involved in bribery.[1818]

[1812] [1993] AC 951.
[1813] *R v Sin Yau Ming* [1992] 1 HKCLR 127.
[1814] *R v Sin Yau Ming* [1992] 1 HKCLR 127.
[1815] *R v Lau Shiu Wah* [1992] HKDCLR 11.
[1816] *R v Choi Kai On* [1995] 1 HKCLR 79.
[1817] *R v Sin Yau Ming* [1992] 1 HKCLR 127.
[1818] *A-G v Hui Kin Hong* [1995] 1 HKCLR 227. See also: *R v Chong Ah Choi* 1994 3 HKC 68 (presumption concerning possession of offensive weapons); In *R v Chan Chak Fan* 1994 3 HKC 145; *R v Lai Yiu Pui* [1994] 2 HKCLR 17 (presumption relating to ships smuggling unauthorised entrants); *R v Wong Hiu Chor* [1993] 1 HKCLR 107 (if it was proved that a person possessed a restricted article in circumstances that gave rise to a reasonable suspicion that there is an intent to evade a restriction it would be presumed that a person had the requisite intent in the absence of evidence to the contrary; presumption upheld, particularly as the burden on the accused was evidential only).

The presumption of innocence was held not to apply to presumptions in drug trafficking legislation that sums received by a person convicted of drug trafficking were the proceeds of such drug trafficking. That was because those presumptions were not being used to penalise drug traffickers, but instead to disgorge drug traffickers of their ill gotten gains. When a prison term in default was fixed, it was not to punish the drug trafficker for trafficking, but rather to enforce the court's order for payment. In any event, the presumptions were rational and realistic, and proportionate to the grave danger to society of leaving drug traffickers rich and to that extent powerful even when behind bars.[1819] This approach can be contrasted to that taken in *R v Chan Suen Hay*,[1820] in which a discretionary disqualification order under companies legislation was found to be a 'penalty' within the meaning of Article 12 (ban on retrospective penalties). **11.473**

(d) The right to legal assistance

Article 11(2)(d) provides that a person facing a criminal charge has the right 'to have legal assistance assigned to him, in any case where the interests of justice so require, and without payment by him in any such case if he does not have sufficient means to pay for it'. This provision was considered in *R v Wong Cheung Bun*,[1821] in which a defendant charged with robbery was refused legal aid because his assets exceeded the maximum specified in the relevant legal aid rules. The reason for this decision was the defendant's ownership of a village house. The defendant succeeded in obtaining a stay of the prosecution based on a breach of Article 11(2)(d). The defendant required legal representation, and could not realistically pay for it. Reasonable but unsuccessful efforts had been made to mortgage the property. Further, it was clear that sale was not a practical possibility because of the nature of the property and the family circumstances. **11.474**

(e) Double jeopardy

The court considered the prohibition on double jeopardy in Article 11(6) in *R v Wan Kit Man*.[1822] That case concerned a driver's disqualification based on the accumulation of fixed penalty offences. The driver argued that he should not have been disqualified after he had duly paid all the fixed penalties. The court held that disqualification was not a punishment but the civil consequence of an offence. Even if disqualification was a punishment, it did not constitute double punishment. A single act (namely, the final fixed penalty offence which resulted in disqualification) could have more than one consequence. **11.475**

(5) India

Article 20 of the Indian Constitution provides that: **11.476**

> (1) No person shall be convicted of any offence except for the violation of a law in force at the time of the commission of the act charged as an offence, nor be subjected to a penalty greater than that which might have been inflicted under the law in force at the time of the commission of the offence.
> (2) No person shall be prosecuted and punished for the same offence more than once.
> (3) No person accused of any offence shall be compelled to be a witness against himself.

[1819] *R v Ko Chi Yuen* [1994] 2 HKCLR 65.
[1820] [1995] HKLY 205.
[1821] [1992] 1 HKCLR 240.
[1822] [1992] 1 HKCLR 224.

The prohibition in Article 20(1) of conviction under *ex post facto* law does not apply to a trial under procedural rules enacted after the commission of an offence;[1823] sanctions by a civil or revenue authority, to enforce a civil liability;[1824] preventive detention;[1825] or the retrospective creation of a new rule of evidence or presumption relating to an existing offence.[1826] The privilege against self-incrimination in Clause 3 extends to production of documentary evidence, but does not extend to giving thumb impressions, specimen writing or showing parts of the body by way of identification.[1827]

(6) Ireland

11.478 Article 38.1 of the Irish Constitution provides that:

> No person shall be tried on any criminal charge save in due course of law.[1828]

In *Goodman International v Hamilson (No 1)*,[1829] the Supreme Court held that the establishment of a tribunal to investigate alleged criminal (or potentially criminal) conduct could not 'in any circumstances' amount to a trial of a criminal charge. That was because the tribunal's findings could not form the basis of a conviction or an acquittal, nor could the tribunal impose penalties on any person.

11.479 The question of what constitutes a 'criminal charge' under Article 38 has been considered in a number of customs and excise cases. The indicia of a criminal offence are:

- its character as an offence against the community at large rather than an individual;
- the punitive nature of the sanction; and
- the requirement of *mens rea*.[1830]

Thus, in *McLoughlin v Tuite*,[1831] the imposition of a penalty under a tax statute was held to be a civil matter. Although the penalty was payable to the community at large, there was no imprisonment if the penalty was not paid; and the fact that liability to pay the penalty did not cease on death but continued against the estate of the deceased indicated that *mens rea* was not an essential ingredient.[1832]

11.480 The phrase 'in due course of law' has been described as:

> a phrase of very wide import which includes within its scope not merely matters of statutory and constitutional jurisdiction, the range of legislation with respect of criminal offences, and matters of practice and procedure, but also the application of basic principles of justice which are inherent in the proper course of the exercise of the judicial function.[1833]

[1823] *Shiv Bahadur v State of U P* A 1953 SC 394.
[1824] *Brij Bhukan v S D O* A 1955 Pat 1, SB; *State of W B v S K Ghose* 1963 SC 255; *Shiv Dutt v Union of India* A 1984 SC 1194.
[1825] *Prahlad v State of Bombay* A 1952 Bom 1.
[1826] *Sajjan Singh v State of Punjab* A1964 SC 464, 468.
[1827] *State of Bombay v Kathi Kalu* A 1961 SC 1808, 1816.
[1828] See generally, J M Kelly, *The Irish Constitution* (3rd edn, Butterworths Ireland, 1994) 572–623.
[1829] [1992] 2 IR 542.
[1830] *Melling v Mathghamhna* [1962] IR 1.
[1831] [1986] IR 235.
[1832] See also: *DPP v Downes* [1987] IR 139 (fixed mandatory revenue penalty where there had been failure to comply with statutory requirements created a non-criminal liability: statutory language was not criminal); cf *DPP v Boyle* [1993] ILRM 128 (statutory provisions which referred to 'excise penalties', 'offence' and 'summary conviction' created a criminal offence).
[1833] *The State (Healy) v Donoghue* [1976] IR 325.

The requirement of 'in due course of law' encompasses both procedural and substantive rights. Thus, a defendant who was convicted by a judge after a summary trial on a charge of robbery, not having been informed of his right to be tried by jury for that offence, had not been tried 'in due course of law';[1834] a statutory provision which made certain conduct an offence if committed by a 'suspected person or reputed thief' was held not to be 'in due course of law', because of vagueness.[1835] The concept incorporates traditional common law principles of criminal law, such as the prohibition against double jeopardy and retroactivity;[1836] and the principle that sentences must not be arbitrary or disproportionate.[1837] Finally, the phrase 'in due course of law' has been relied upon to overturn convictions where there has been a delay in the trial. An important factor in such cases is the prejudice to the defence.[1838]

Legal process rights have also been considered in the context of Article 40.3.1 of the Irish Constitution, which provides that: **11.481**

> The State guarantees in its laws to respect, and, as far as is practicable, by its laws to defend and vindicate the personal rights of the citizen.

The right to have access to the courts is an unenumerated right under Article 40.3.1.[1839] In *Macauley v Minister for Posts and Telegraphs*[1840] it was decided that the requirement for the Attorney-General's consent in order to bring actions against government ministers was an infringement of that right. Common law immunities may be vulnerable to the right to litigate. The Supreme Court stated in *Ryan v Ireland*[1841] that the state's immunity from suit in respect of negligence occurring during armed conflicts would be inconsistent with Article 40.3.1. However, the state is not obliged to assist litigants financially in order to bring claims.[1842]

The right of access to the courts has had an impact on civil procedure. Thus, litigants should not be denied access to a court by fixing security of costs at too high a level.[1843] In *Bula v Tara Mines Ltd*[1844] the court stated that the right of access to courts gave rise to a right to inspect property which was part of the subject matter of a claim, and also to inspect documents, without having to prove a *prima facie* case. **11.482**

In the context of criminal cases, where a constitutional breach is committed 'for the purpose of securing a confession', the confession must be excluded, 'on that ground alone'.[1845] The Supreme Court held in *Cahalane v Murphy*[1846] that delay in charging the defendant **11.483**

1834 *The State (Vozza) v O'Floinn* [1957] IR 227.
1835 *King v A-G* [1981] IR 233.
1836 Kelly (n 1828 above) 577–585.
1837 *Cox v Ireland* [1992] 2 IR 503.
1838 See *State (O'Connell) v Fawsitt* [1986] IR 362 (applicant tried in 1985 for alleged assault in 1981; delay had led to unavailability of important defence witnesses).
1839 *Macauley v Minister for Posts and Telegraphs* [1996] IR 345.
1840 Ibid.
1841 [1989] IR 177.
1842 See eg *M C v Legal Aid Board* [1991] 2 IR 43. But see *The State (O'Healy) v Landy* High Court, 10 Feb 1993 (legal aid required for mother to contest wardship proceedings which, like criminal proceedings, pitted a litigant against the power of the state, and had very serious consequences).
1843 *Fallon v An Bord Pleanála* [1992] 2 IR 380.
1844 [1987] IR 85.
1845 See *People (The) (DPP) v Lynch* [1982] IR 64, 79, following *People (The) (A-G) v O'Brien* [1965] IR 142; *People (The) (DPP) v Kenny* [1990] 2 IR 110.
1846 [1994] 2 ILRM 383.

can be taken into account when assessing whether a defendant has been tried within a reasonable time.[1847]

(7) Jamaica

11.484 By section 20 of the Constitution of Jamaica it is provided that:

> Whenever any person is charged with a criminal offence he shall, unless the charge is withdrawn, be afforded a fair hearing within a reasonable time by an independent and impartial court established by law

It has been held that the accused did not have to show any specific prejudice before being entitled to have charges against him dismissed because of unreasonable delay.[1848] In determining whether the accused had been deprived of a fair trial by reason of delay, factors which are relevant are the length of the delay, the reasons given by the prosecution to justify it, the efforts made by the accused to assert his rights and the prejudice to the accused.[1849]

11.485 The issue of bias in criminal appellate proceedings was considered in *Berry v DPP (No 2)*.[1850] In that case, the appellant appealed against his conviction for murder to the Court of Appeal of Jamaica. The Court dismissed his appeal, finding his version of facts to be 'incredible'. As a result of prosecution and trial irregularities, the Privy Council allowed the appellant's further appeal and remitted the case to the Jamaican Court of Appeal with a direction to quash the conviction and either enter a verdict of acquittal or order a new trial. The Court of Appeal, which included two of the same judges who had earlier dismissed the appellants' appeal, ordered a new trial. The appellant brought proceedings claiming there was a reasonable suspicion that he had not received a fair hearing by reason of the judges' participation in the earlier decision. The Privy Council rejected that argument. The Court's task on remission was to balance competing considerations in order to determine whether the interests of justice required a new trial. The Court of Appeal was best equipped to perform this balancing. The fact that two judges participated in an earlier judgment which expressed strong views about the guilt of the appellant in light of the evidence before them did not mean there was any danger of bias in the Court of Appeal's decision to order a new trial. Further, the scrupulous care the judges took in weighing the relevant considerations in their judgment on the issue of a new trial confirms that there is no reason to believe that they were not wholly impartial.

11.486 In *Robinson v the Queen*[1851] the Privy Council held that the right to legal representation of choice was not an absolute right, in that it was not necessary for an adjournment to be granted to ensure than any defendant in a criminal matter who desired legal representation was duly represented.[1852] In exercising its discretion whether to grant an adjournment the court had to consider matters such as present and future availability of witnesses. As the absence of legal representation in this case was caused by the conduct of the

1847 See also *EO'R v DPP* [1996] 2 IR 128 (prosecution prohibited for sexual offences committed several years prior to charge).
1848 *Bell* v *DPP of Jamaica* [1985] AC 937.
1849 Following *Barker v Wingo* (1972) 407 US 514.
1850 [1996] 3 LRC 697.
1851 [1985] 1 AC 956.
1852 It should be noted that Lord Scarman and Lord Edmund-Davies dissented.

defendant's counsel and also by the defendant's failure to ensure that his counsel were paid or otherwise to apply in advance for legal aid, the judge's failure to adjourn the trial in order to instruct an alternative legal representative did not deprive the defendant of his right to be represented by an advocate of his own choice. It should be noted that the judge's failure in this case to adjourn led to the defendant being unrepresented in a capital case.[1853]

The case of *Huntley v A-G for Jamaica*[1854] concerned a statutory provision whereby every person under a sentence of death for murder was to be reviewed by a judge of the Jamaica Court of Appeal with a view to determining whether the murder was to be treated as capital or non-capital. There was no provision for prior notice of the judge's classification to be given to the convicted person but a person whose case had been classified as capital murder had the right to have that classification reviewed, and the right to be represented at that review. The appellant argued that the classification process was unconstitutional because it denied a person charged with a criminal offence the opportunity to be heard. That challenge was rejected by the Privy Council. The classification was a limited exercise whereby a judge would review the trial record and ask whether a properly directed jury could have reached any conclusion other than that the murder had been capital murder. That process did not involve the determination of guilt or innocence. **11.487**

(8) Mauritius

Section 10(1) of the Constitution of Mauritius provides that: **11.488**

> Where any person is charged with a criminal offence, then, unless the charge is withdrawn, the case shall be afforded a fair hearing within a reasonable time by an independent and impartial court established by law.

The effect of this provision is that a trial must take place within a reasonable time after arrest and, in some cases, it may be proper to take into account the period before the arrest.[1855] This provision:

> injects the need for urgency and efficiency into the prosecution of offenders and demands the provision of adequate resources for the administration of justice but, in determining whether the constitutional rights of an individual have been infringed, the courts must have regard to the constraints imposed by harsh economic reality and local conditions.[1856]

It is a fundamental requirement of justices that those required to deliver the verdict must have heard all the evidence and a conviction was quashed when one of the convicting magistrates had not heard all the evidence.[1857]

(9) Namibia

In *Mwellie v Ministry of Works*[1858] the High Court of Namibia upheld a limitation period of 12 months for bringing wrongful dismissal proceedings against the State. The Court **11.489**

[1853] For an example of a case where a court's refusal to adjourn following withdrawal of counsel led the Privy Council to quash a conviction, see *Dunkley v R* [1995] 1 AC 419.
[1854] [1995] 2 AC 1.
[1855] *Mungroo v R* [1992] LRC (Const) 591, 594.
[1856] Ibid, 594-595 (four-years' delay from arrest to hearing, no breach).
[1857] *Curpen v R* [1992] LRC (Crim) 120; see also *Ng (alias Wong) v R* [1987] 1 WLR 1356.
[1858] 1995 (9) BCLR 1118.

stated that different limitation periods were not unconstitutional provided parties had a reasonable time to bring actions, and they were based on a reasonable classification. The distinction between state and non-state employees was reasonable and rationally connected to a legitimate objective, considering factors such as the size and geographical spread of the public service, the number of individual ministries and departments, staff turnover, budgetary constraints and the need for detailed and urgent investigations of challenges to dismissals.

11.490 In *State v Scholtz*[1859] the Supreme Court considered the information to which a criminal defendant is entitled. The court held that, upon service of an indictment, an accused person should ordinarily be entitled to the information contained in the police docket relating to the case prepared by the prosecution against the accused (including copies of witness statements) whether or not the prosecution intended to call those witnesses at trial. The state would be entitled to withhold any information, however, if it satisfied the court on the balance of probabilities that it had reasonable grounds for believing that disclosure might reasonably impede the ends of justice or otherwise be against the public interest. The time at which such disclosure should occur would depend on the circumstances of the case, but the overriding principle should be to give the accused reasonable time to prepare his case thoroughly. The duty of disclosure did not apply to the defence. In magistrates' courts, disclosure is not always necessary: it will be required in cases involving any complexity of fact or law.[1860] The right to 'adequate facilities' for the defence includes the opportunity to view and listen to material video and audio recordings.[1861]

11.491 Article 12(1)(d) provides that:

> All persons charged with an offence shall be presumed innocent until proven guilty according to law, after having had the opportunity of calling witnesses and cross-examining those called against them.

The Namibian courts have considered reverse onus provisions in a number of cases. A provision to the effect that a person who had rights in a forfeited article had to prove that he had taken all reasonable steps to prevent the use of the article in connection with the offence has been held to be unconstitutional.[1862]

(10) Pakistan

11.492 In *Al-Jehad Trust v Federation of Pakistan*[1863] certain judicial appointments, and non-appointments and transfers were challenged. It was alleged that those actions had been politically motivated. The Supreme Court of Pakistan upheld the challenges. The court noted that the right to an independent judiciary was a fundamental right. The constitutional consultation requirements concerning judicial appointments required effective, meaningful, purposive and consensus-oriented consultation. The opinion of the Chief Justice of Pakistan and the Chief Justice of a High Court as to the suitability of a candidate for judicial office should be accepted in the absence of very sound reasons, which should

1859 [1997] 1 LRC 67.
1860 *State v Angula* [1998] 1 LRC 14.
1861 *State v Nassar* [1994] 3 LRC 295, 328.
1862 *Freiremar SA v Prosecutor-General of Namibia* [1994] 2 LRC 251; see also *State* v *Van den Berg* [1995] 2 LRC 619.
1863 PLD 1996 SC 324; [1996] PLR 394.

be recorded, and are justiciable. Political affiliation was not a sufficient ground in itself for disqualifying a candidate, if the candidate had unimpeachable integrity, sound legal knowledge, and had been recommended by the Chief Justice of the High Court concerned and the Chief Justice of Pakistan. Although judges will normally sever their political connections, it was not desirable to appoint strong political activists, as it might not be possible for them to avoid unconscious favouritism. Finally, the court added that it is contrary to the principle of independence of the judiciary to appoint acting judges when permanent vacancies existed, as acting judges had no security of tenure.

(11) Singapore

In *Balasundaram v Public Prosecutor*[1864] the High Court of Singapore held that the right of the accused to be defended by a legal practitioner of his choice applied only if counsel was willing and able to represent the accused. If counsel failed to attend or was not willing or able to act for the accused, he could not, by reason of that fact alone, claim that his constitutional right had been violated. There was no miscarriage of justice when the trial judge refused the appellant's application for an adjournment in order to let the accused's preferred counsel represent him, when the preferred counsel had made it clear that he would not be available for the trial date, and another counsel was willing to represent the accused. **11.493**

(12) South Africa

(a) Introduction

Section 34 of the South African Constitution provides that: **11.494**

> Everyone has the right to have any dispute that can be resolved by the application of law decided in a fair public hearing in a court or, where appropriate, another independent and impartial forum.

The rights of arrested, detained and accused persons are dealt with in detail in section 35.[1865] It has been said that the right of access to the courts is 'foundational to the stability of society'.[1866] The Constitutional Court has held that 'self-help' remedies are inimical to the rule of law and contrary to Section 34.[1867] The rule against self-help is necessary to protect individuals against 'arbitrary and subjective decisions and conduct of an adversary'. In view of the importance of access to the court, statutory self-help remedies were not a justifiable limitation on Section 34 rights.

Fair trial rights were held not to apply in the case of *Nel v Le Roux NO*,[1868] as the applicant was not an 'accused'. The applicant was summoned under statutory powers to appear before a magistrate to provide relevant information in connection with alleged offences committed by his associate. Failure to answer questions without 'just excuse' made an examinee liable to summary imprisonment. The applicant challenged the provision on **11.495**

[1864] [1996] 4 LRC 597.

[1865] See generally, M Chaskalson, J Kentridge, J Klaaren, G Marcus, D Spitz and S Woolman (eds), *Constitutional Law of South Africa* (Juta, 1996) Chaps 26–28.

[1866] *Concorde Plastics (Pty)* v *NUMSA* 1997 (11) BCLR 1624; *Lesapo v North West Agricultural Bank* 1999 (12) BCLR 1420.

[1867] *Lesapo v North West Agricultural Bank* (n 1866 above).

[1868] [1996] 4 LRC 126.

the grounds that it infringed his right not to be detained without trial, the right to personal privacy, the right to freedom of expression, the right to procedural fairness in administrative matters, and the right to a fair trial. Those challenges failed. A 'just excuse' not to answer questions at an examination included situations where to do so would infringe any of a person's fundamental constitutional rights. Further, the fair trial rights were not applicable because the applicant was not, at that stage, 'an accused person'. The examinee was, however, entitled under the Constitution to have proceedings conducted with procedural fairness. It held further that the summary proceedings before a judicial officer which could lead to imprisonment were not inconsistent with the right not to be detained without trial, as they complied with the requirement that an impartial entity, independent of the executive and the legislature, act as arbiter between the individual and the state.

(b) The presumption of innocence

11.496 There have been a number of decisions by the Constitutional Court concerning reverse onus clauses. The basic approach of the Court is the same as that of the Canadian Supreme Court. In other words, the presumption of innocence is breached where a person can be convicted despite the existence of reasonable doubt as to his guilt. If the reverse onus provision is reasonable, however, it may be upheld under the general limitations clause. The decision in *Osman v A-G, Transvaal*[1869] contains a useful discussion of when onus in a criminal case is regarded as having shifted to the accused. That case concerned a provision that any person found in possession of any goods in regard to which there is a reasonable suspicion that they have been stolen and is unable to give a satisfactory account of such possession shall be guilty of an offence. The Court stated that it was the inability and not the failure or unwillingness to give a satisfactory account of possession that constituted the offence in section 36. The inability to give a satisfactory account of possession was an element of the offence, and the burden of proving it remained with the state. At no point did the onus of proof shift, nor did the accused ever lose the protection of the presumption of innocence. Accordingly, there was no violation of the presumption of innocence.[1870]

11.497 The Court has struck down reverse onus clauses on a number of occasions. The case of *S v Zuma*[1871] concerned a statutory rebuttable presumption that confessions recorded in writing by a magistrate were free and voluntary. The applicant successfully argued that the presumption violated his right to a free trial because it required him to prove, on the balance of probabilities, that such a confession was not free and voluntary. The fact that an accused could be required to prove on a balance of probabilities that a confession was not voluntary would permit a conviction in spite of a reasonable doubt as to its voluntariness. This was contrary to the constitutional rights to be presumed innocent, in addition to the rights to remain silent, not to be compelled to make confession and not to be a compellable witness against himself. The claim that the presumption acted to discourage

[1869] 1998 (11) BCLR 1362.

[1870] The Court also held that there was no breach of the right to silence, or not to be compelled into making a confession. The provision neither compelled an arrested or detained person to do anything, nor constituted pressure being applied on such person to make a statement. Such persons had a choice as to whether or not to provide an explanation for the possession of the goods. Arrested or detained persons suffered no prejudice at trial stage in the absence of a prior explanation, because they retained the express right to furnish an explanation at trial if no explanation had previously been given.

[1871] 1995 (4) BCLR 401.

dishonest retractions of confessions and thus shortened trials did not justify such a substantial infringement of fundamental rights. Therefore the breach of fair trial rights was not justified under section 33.

In *S v Bhulwana; S v Gwadiso*[1872] the Constitutional Court declared contrary to the presumption of innocence the inference of drug dealing from possession of a specified quantity of drugs, unless the accused could prove the contrary, on a balance of probabilities. The court noted that the possible penalties for drug dealing were very high. Langa J stated, at para 23: **11.498**

> It does not appear to be logical to presume that a person found in possession of 115g of dagga [cannabis]is more likely than not to have been dealing in dagga . . . [the state] conceded that it would not be unreasonable for a regular user of dagga to possess that quantity of dagga . . . No explanation was proffered by the State as to why this particular quantity was selected. It appears to be an arbitrary figure, nowadays, whatever sense, if any, it may have made in the socio-economic environment that prevailed when it was originally introduced.[1873]

The case of *Scagell v A-G*[1874] concerned two presumptions in a gambling statute. The first was that where gambling devices, or other items capable of being used in gambling, were found at any place, it shall be prima facie evidence that the person in control of that place permitted gambling at that place, and that any person found on the place was visiting with the intention of gambling. The second presumption was that where a police officer was authorised to enter any particular place, but was refused entry, it was to be presumed that the person in charge of the place permitted gambling at that place. Those presumptions were declared to be unconstitutional. **11.499**

In *S v Mbatha; S v Prinsloo*[1875] the presumption relating to the offence of unlawful possession of arms and ammunition was declared unconstitutional. That presumption was that where it was proved that arms and ammunition had been on any premises at any time, any person who was at that time in charge of or present at those premises, or any part thereof, would be presumed to have been in possession of the arms or ammunition, until the contrary was proved. The Court also found that the breach was not justified under the limitations clause. Although South Africa had high levels of crime, the presumption was widely phrased, and included within its reach many categories of potentially innocent people. **11.500**

The reverse onus clauses challenged in *S v Coetzee*[1876] were struck down. The first clause provided that, where in criminal proceedings an accused is charged with an offence of which false representation is an element and it is proved that a false representation was made by the accused, the accused shall be presumed to have made the representation **11.501**

[1872] 1995 (12) BCLR 1579.

[1873] See also following cases concerning drug related presumptions: *S v Julies* 1996 (4) SA 313 (Court declared unconstitutional presumption that a person found in possession of any quantity of an undesirable dependence producing substance was presumed to be dealing in that substance); *S v Ntsele* 1998 (11) BCLR 1543 (Court declared unconstitutional presumption that anyone in charge of cultivated land which has dagga [cannabis] plants growing on it is dealing in dagga); *S v Mello; S v Van Nell* 1988 (3) SA 712 (Court declared unconstitutional presumption that person found in immediate vicinity of drug would be presumed unless the contrary was proved to be in possession of drug).

[1874] 1996 (11) BCLR 1446, CC.

[1875] 1996 (3) BCLR 263.

[1876] 1997 (4) BCLR 437.

knowing it to be false, unless the contrary is proved. The second presumption was that where a corporate body has committed an offence, a servant or director of the corporate body is deemed to be guilty of that offence and personally liable to punishment unless the accused can show on a balance of probabilities that he did not participate in the offence and could not have prevented it. As regards the latter clause, although the Court recognised that directors bear a special responsibility to society, the presumption was too wide ranging in that it applied to any possible offence, and any type of liability. In *S v Baloyi*[1876a] the Constitutional Court adopted a construction of a statute relating to domestic violence which did not impose a reverse onus on the accused: although this involved some erosion of the right to silence it was a constitutionally appropriate balancing of the rights of all concerned.

(c) Trial within a reasonable time

11.502 A person charged with a criminal offence is entitled to a trial 'within a reasonable time'. The Constitutional Court considered the meaning of that phrase in *Sanderson v A-G.*[1877] In that case, the appellant teacher had been charged with committing sexual offences against two female pupils at a school at which he had previously taught. The appellant's first court appearance was in December 1994, but he had still not been brought to trial almost two years later. He applied for a permanent stay of prosecution, alleging that the delay had infringed his constitutional right to a trial within a reasonable time. The Court stated that in deciding what a reasonable time is, a court must make a value judgment, considering such factors as the kind of prejudice suffered by the accused, the nature and complexity of the case and lack of state resources which might hamper the investigation or prosecution of the case. The only prejudice suffered by the appellant had been social embarrassment. Because this social prejudice had not been seriously aggravated by the delay, the right in question had not been infringed. The right to be tried within a reasonable time was designed to protect both trial related prejudice, such as impairment to the accused's defence, and other forms of prejudice such a pre-trial incarceration, restrictive bail conditions, anxiety and stress, loss of income and social ostracism.[1878]

11.503 Delays in appellate proceedings were considered in *S v Pennington.*[1879] In that case, it held that appellate delays were materially different from trial delays. In the former, there could be no question of prejudice because the appeal is settled on the record, and when the appeal fails, the trial court's finding of guilt is merely confirmed. The Court left open the question of whether an appeal delay might, in some circumstances, constitute a violation of this or some other right.

(d) Access to the court

11.504 The right of access to courts for the settlement of justiciable disputes was considered in *AZAPO v President of RSA.*[1880] That case concerned the amnesty granted to people who had committed offences for political offences, and made a full disclosure to the Truth and

[1876a] 2000 (1) BCLR 86.
[1877] 1997 (12) BCLR 1675
[1878] See also *Wild v Hoffert NO* 1998 (6) BCLR 656 (stay of prosecution was not an ordinarily appropriate form of relief for failure to be tried within a reasonable time, unless there was trial related prejudice).
[1879] 1997 (12) BCLR 1413.
[1880] 1996 (4) SA 672.

Reconciliation Commission, from criminal and civil prosecution. The applicants argued that the amnesty was unconstitutional because it limited their rights under section 22 of the interim Constitution to have justiciable disputes settled by a court of law or other independent or impartial forum. The Court accepted that the amnesty limited rights to have justiciable disputes settled by a court of law but held that the limitation was sanctioned by the epilogue to the interim Constitution. Further, the Court noted that the amnesty was a crucial component of the negotiated transition to democracy, without which the Constitution would not have come into being. The amnesty provisions were not inconsistent with international norms and did not breach any of the country's obligations in terms of public international law instruments.

The right of access to civil courts was also considered in *Mohlomi v Minister of Defence.*[1881] **11.505** The applicant in that case challenged a provision whereby any civil action against the state or any person arising from the conduct of armed forces be instituted within six months of the cause of action arising. Further, notice in writing of such civil action had to be given to the defendant at least one month before its commencement. The basis of the challenge was that the provision challenged the applicant's right to have justiciable disputes settled by a court of law or, where appropriate, another independent and impartial forum. The Court struck down that provision, stating that its overall effect was to require that notice be given no later than five months after the cause of action arose. Each particular limitation period must be scrutinised to see whether its terms were compatible with the rights embodied in section 22. The key question was whether there was, in all the circumstances characterising the class of case in question, a real and fair initial opportunity available to exercise the right. This limitation period was too short. The Court's finding was made against the background of conditions prevailing in South Africa, namely poverty, illiteracy, cultural and language differences and the inaccessibility of legal assistance.

(c) Other issues

The right of an accused not to be compelled to give testimony was considered in *Ferreira v Levin NO.*[1882] **11.506** That case concerned a provision in companies legislation which stated that the Master of the Court may require any person to answer questions in winding up proceedings notwithstanding that the response might tend to incriminate that person and that the answer may thereafter be used as evidence against him. Failure to answer was an offence. It was held that use of such evidence in criminal proceedings was a breach of the privilege against self-incrimination, and therefore was not admissible at criminal proceedings. As regards the use in a subsequent criminal trial of evidence derived from compelled testimony, as distinct from the compelled testimony itself, the fairness of admitting or excluding such 'derivative evidence' was a matter to be decided by the judge or other officer presiding over the criminal trial.

The accessibility of police dockets to the defence was considered in *Shabalala v A-G of the* **11.507** *Transvaal.*[1883] The accused in that case, charged with murder, applied before the trial for copies of the relevant police dockets, containing witness statements, and lists of exhibits in the possession of the state. Their application was refused at first instance because the trial court was not satisfied that the accused required the documents in order to exercise

[1881] 1996 (12) BCLR 1559.
[1882] 1996 (1) BCLR 1.
[1883] 1995 (12) BCLR 1593.

his rights to a fair trial. A related application for an order directing the state to make state witnesses available to the defence legal representatives for the purposes of consultation was also refused by the trial court, on the ground that the court was unable to conclude that the applicants would not be given a fair trial unless the court departed from the practice that the accused or his legal representatives could only consult with a state witness with the consent of the prosecutor. The Court stated that whether the right to a fair trial includes the right to have access to a police docket depends on the particular circumstances of each case, and is in the discretion of the court. The accused normally should have access to documents in the police docket, including statements of witnesses, unless the state can justify the denial of such access on the ground it is not required for the exercise of a fair trial. The claim to consult state witnesses can only be justified in circumstances where the accused's right to a fair trial would, in the special circumstances of the case, be impaired if the opportunity to consult is denied. The discretion to direct access to state witnesses rests with the court, which may refuse it where the prosecution is able to establish a reasonable risk of intimidation or of other prejudice to the proper ends of justice. Further, no state witness could be compelled to such consultation.

11.508 The right to appeal in criminal cases was considered in *S v Ntuli.*[1884] That case concerned a challenge to a criminal statute whereby convicted prisoners who lacked legal representation and who were convicted in a magistrates' court did not have an automatic right of appeal to the Supreme Court. Such prisoners could only appeal against their convictions or sentences if a Supreme Court judge certified that there were reasonable grounds for appeal. All other types of convicted prisoners did not require such permission to appeal from a decision of the magistrates' court to the Supreme Court. Didcott J stated, in a judgment with which all the other justices concurred, that the constitutional right to have recourse by way of appeal or review to a higher court at the minimum implied the opportunity to have an adequate reappraisal of every case and an informed decision on it. The relevant statute made no provision for such reappraisal. The decision on whether a certificate should be granted was generally made by a judge in chambers, without the benefit of oral argument. Moreover, there was no requirement or practice that the judge obtain a full copy of the criminal record from below. The requirement to obtain a judge's certificate also breached the equality rights in section 8(1) of the interim Constitution. The scheme impermissibly differentiated between appellants who were legally unrepresented, and those who were represented.

11.509 However, in *S v Rens*[1885] the requirement for leave to appeal in criminal cases was upheld. That leave could be obtained from the judge before whom conviction occurred, or the Chief Justice by way of a petition procedure. As stated by Langa J, with whom the other members of Constitutional Court concurred:

> It cannot be in the interests of justice and fairness to allow unmeritorious and vexatious issues of procedure, law or fact to be placed before three judges of the appellate tribunal sitting in open court to re-hear oral argument. The rolls would be clogged by hopeless cases, thus prejudicing the speedy resolution of those cases where there is sufficient substance to justify an appeal.
>
> In my view the petition procedure which is available to every accused whose application for leave to appeal has been refused [by the trial judge] allows such accused recourse to a higher court to review, in a broad and not a technical sense, the judgment of a trial court. The

[1884] 1996 (1) BCLR 141.
[1885] 1996 (2) BCLR 155.

> procedure involves a re-assessment of the disputed issues by two judges of the higher court, and provides a framework for that assessment, which ensures that an informed decision is made by them as to the prospects of success. In this respect the procedure is materially different to the procedure for judges' certificates which we found to be inconsistent with the Constitution in . . . *S v Ntuli*.[1886]

The right of appeal in civil cases was challenged in *Besserglik v Minister of Trade, Industry and Tourism*[1887] as in breach of the right of access to courts. The Court expressed some doubt as to whether the right of access to courts included a right to appeal. Even if such a right were included, a screening process excluding unmeritorious appeals was not a denial of a right of access to a court. In *Beinash v Ernst and Young*[1888] the Constitutional Court held that the procedure whereby a person is declared a vexatious litigant and may not institute legal proceedings without first obtaining court permission limited that person's right of access to the courts, but was reasonable and justifiable. **11.510**

(13) Sri Lanka

Article 13(4) of the Constitution provides that: **11.511**

> No person shall be punished with death or imprisonment except by order of a competent court, made in accordance with procedure established by law. The arrest, holding in custody, detention or other deprivation of personal liberty of a person, pending investigation or trial, shall not constitute punishment.[1889]

Preventive detention under emergency regulations is not punishment within the terms of this article, as such detention is a precautionary rather than punitive measure.[1890]

Article 13(6) prohibits retrospective criminal legislation, but with a proviso for the trial and punishment of any person for any act or omission which at the time when it was committed was criminal, according to the general principles of law recognised by the community of nations, even though it was not an offence under local law. That proviso was applied by the Supreme Court in a decision concerning the constitutionality of the Offences Against Aircraft Bill of 1982. That Bill sought to give effect to certain conventions relating to the safety of aircraft. The Supreme Court held that the offences referred to in the Bill were all criminal according to the general principles of law recognised by the community of nations. **11.512**

(14) Trinidad and Tobago

Section 5 of the Constitution of Trinidad and Tobago protects a number of fair trial rights. By section 5(2), Parliament may not, subject to limited exceptions, **11.513**

> (c) deprive a person who has been arrested or detained—
>
> (i) of the right to be informed promptly and with sufficient particularity of the reason for his arrest or detention;

[1886] Paras 25–26.
[1887] 1996 (6) BCLR 745.
[1888] 1999 (2) BCLR 125.
[1889] See generally, J Wickramaratne, *Fundamental Rights in Sri Lanka* (Navrang, 1996) Chap 6; S Sharvananda, *Fundamental Rights in Sri Lanka* (Arnold's International Printing House Private Ltd, 1993) Chap XI.
[1890] *Kumaratunga v Samarasinghe* FRD (2) 347.

(ii) of the right to retain and instruct without delay a legal adviser of his own choice and hold communication with him;
(iii) of the right to be brought promptly before an appropriate judicial authority;
(iv) of the remedy by way of habeas corpus for the determination of the validity of his detention and for his release if the detention is not lawful;

(d) authorise a court, tribunal, commission, board or other authority to compel a person to give evidence unless he is afforded protection against self-incrimination and, where necessary to ensure such protection, the right to legal representation;
(e) deprive a person of the right to a fair hearing in accordance with the principles of fundamental justice for the determination of his rights and obligations;
(f) deprive a person charged with a criminal offence of the right

(i) to be presumed innocent until proved guilty according to law, but this shall not invalidate any law by reason only that the law imposes on any such person the burden of proving particular facts;
(ii) to a fair and public hearing by an independent and impartial tribunal; or
(iii) to reasonable bail without just cause;

(g) to deprive a person of the right to the assistance of an interpreter in any proceedings in which he is involved or in which he is a party or a witness before a court, commission, board or other tribunal if he does not understand or speak English; or
(h) deprive a person of the right to such procedural provisions as are necessary for the purpose of giving effect and protection to the aforesaid rights and freedoms.

11.514 The Privy Council has held that section 5(2)(c)(ii) conferred a right to communicate with a legal adviser. Furthermore, since that right would be ineffective without a procedure whereby the person should be informed of it, a person arrested or detained had a constitutional right to be informed of his right to communicate with a legal adviser as soon as possible.[1891] A confession obtained in breach of this right is *prima facie* (but not automatically) inadmissible.[1892]

(a) Pre-trial publicity

11.515 In *Boodram v A-G of Trinidad and Tobago*[1893] the appellant was charged with murder. In the time up to his trial, there were several newspaper articles about the appellant, which he claimed were calculated and intended to create prejudice in the mind of potential jurors, and would deny him the right to receive a fair trial by an independent and impartial tribunal. The appellant sought a stay of the trial in order for the prejudice to dissipate. He sought further a declaration that the DPP had done nothing to stem the tide of adverse and hostile publicity, in particular by instituting contempt of court proceedings. The Court of Appeal of Trinidad and Tobago rejected the appellant's claim. The state did not guarantee in advance that a person charged would receive a fair trial. If the trial judge failed to ensure that the appellant obtained a fair trial, resulting in clear prejudice and amounting to a miscarriage of justice, his action would be corrected on appeal. As regards the alleged prejudice of the newspaper articles, it is insufficient to establish that the articles were likely to have a prejudicial effect on the minds of potential jurors. It had to be further established that the prejudice was so widespread and so indelibly impressed in the minds of potential jurors that it was unlikely that an impartial jury would be empanelled.

[1891] *A-G of Trinidad and Tobago v Whiteman* [1991] 2 AC 240; see also *Thornhill v A-G of Trinidad and Tobago* [1981] AC 61 (on the identical provision under the 1962 Constitution).
[1892] *Mohammed (Allie) v The State* [1999] 2 WLR 552.
[1893] [1996] AC 842.

(b) Trial within a reasonable time

11.516 The Privy Council dealt with pre-trial delay in *DPP v Jaikaran Tokai.*[1894] The Privy Council noted that the Constitution of Trinidad and Tobago did not include a right to a speedy trial or trial within a reasonable time. It did however, include a right to a fair trial. That right to a fair trial was primarily secured by the traditional procedures available to the criminal trial judge, including, in an exceptional case of delay, the power to grant a stay. Where a stay is not granted, the trial judge must direct the jury as to all matters arising from the delay which tell in favour of the accused. It is only possible to claim constitutional relief in advance of the trial where the procedures available to the trial judge are obviously and inevitably going to be insufficient to secure a fair trial.

11.517 The case of *Sookermany v DPP*[1895] also concerned the issue of pre-trial delay. The Court of Appeal of Trinidad and Tobago noted that the framers of the Constitution had omitted to include a right to trial within a reasonable time and no such right could be inferred from pre-constitutional common law or statutory sources. Further, any infringement of the right to liberty and security of the person caused by long pre-trial detention could be remedied by granting bail. Fairness was the touchstone in determining whether an accused's constitutional rights had been infringed by undue delay. An accused is constitutionally entitled to a stay of prosecution if the delay was not attributable to the accused and the case of the accused had suffered significant impairment which could not be remedied by the powers of the trial judge, for example in jury directions or the exclusion of evidence. Privy Council decisions from jurisdictions whose constitutions expressly protect the right to be tried within a reasonable time provide important guidelines which apply to cases based on common law rights. The right of the accused to be tried within a reasonable time should be balanced against the public interest in having the accused tried and, in performing this balancing exercise, the court is entitled to take into account the prevailing system of legal administration and the economic, social and cultural conditions of the country.[1896] The right at common law was more extensive than that formulated constitutionally, as it could take into account time elapsed from the commission of the offence, as opposed to time elapsed from charge. There is a difference in approach to the common law right and the constitutional right. For example, the question of whether the accused has suffered actual prejudice is more important in a common law case, whereas damage to an accused's security interest is given a greater weighting in cases based on express constitutional provisions. Also, the trial judge's powers to remedy prejudice, while highly relevant for the common law right, may be disregarded in enforcing an explicit written right. Similarly, systemic delays can only be used in a very limited extent to deny an explicitly given right but may be more relevant in a common law situation. The appellant had not suffered any actual prejudice in his case other than his and his witnesses' fading memories. However, that disadvantage was shared with the prosecution. Nor was it a case where the appellant had spent a long time in prison pending trial. The appellant had, however, suffered the stigma, anxiety and uncertainty of being charged with a serious criminal offence for much longer than was reasonable. He had, therefore, suffered damage to his security interest. A stay, if granted in this case, would have far reaching effects in pending cases as it would affect the

[1894] [1996] AC 856.

[1895] [1996] 2 LRC 292.

[1896] See *Bell v DPP* [1985] 1 AC 937.

safety of citizens, leave victims with no recourse, and provoke resentment against and loss of confidence in the law and administration. Moreover, persons already convicted after similar delays might bring claims to be released and for compensation. The interest of society in requiring the appellant to stand trial outweighed any injury to the appellant. The court noted that the same result would be reached even if the court had adopted the more stringent approach to delays required by an express constitutional provision.

(15) Zimbabwe

(a) Introduction

11.518 The Constitution of Zimbabwe contains extensive 'fair trial' rights for those charged with criminal offences and in relation to the determination of 'civil rights and obligations'.[1897] A statutory provision which allows a minister to determine civil rights and obligations without according a hearing in accordance with the principles of natural justice is unconstitutional and will be struck down.[1898]

11.519 Section 18(2) provides that:

> If any person is charged with a criminal offence, then, unless the charge is withdrawn, the case shall be afforded a fair hearing within a reasonable time by an independent and impartial court established by law.

This section embodies a 'constitutional value of supreme importance' and must be interpreted in a 'broad and creative manner'.[1899] As a result, it covers not only the impartiality of the decision-making body but also:

> the absolute impartiality of the prosecutor himself whose function as an officer of the court, forms an indispensable part of the judicial process. His conduct must, of necessity reflect on the impartiality or otherwise of the court.[1900]

(b) The right to a hearing within a reasonable time

11.520 In *Re Mlambo*[1901] the Supreme Court considered the right to a hearing 'within a reasonable time' contained in section 18(2). The Court followed the US Supreme Court[1902] in holding that the purpose of this right was to minimise the adverse effects of a charge:

> Trials held within a reasonable time have an intrinsic value. If innocent, the accused should be acquitted with a minimum disruption to his social and family relationships. If guilty, he should be convicted and an appropriate sentence imposed without unreasonable delay.[1903]

In addition, the Court emphasised the important practical advantages arising from the expeditious resolution of the charges.[1904] It was held that, for the purposes of 'fair trial

[1897] See Zimbabwe Declaration of Rights, s 18 (1979) 3 EHRR 418.
[1898] See *Holland v Minister of the Public Service, Labour and Social Welfare* [1998] 1 LRC 78 (provision allowing minister a discretion to suspend members of the executive committee of a registered private voluntary organisation struck down).
[1899] See *Smyth v Uhsewokunze* [1998] 4 LRC 120, 129b.
[1900] Ibid 129b-c.
[1901] [1993] 2 LRC 28; see also *Smyth v Uhsewokunze* (n 1899 above).
[1902] See eg *US v Loud Hawk* (1986) 474 US 302, 311.
[1903] *Re Mlambo* (n 1901 above) 34e–f.
[1904] Cf *R v Askov* [1990] 2 SCR 119.

rights', the 'charge' was not the formal charge but 'the start of the impairment of the individual's interests in the liberty and security of his person'.[1905] In considering the factors to be taken into account in determining whether the hearing was within a 'reasonable time' the Court adopted the analysis of Powell J in *Barker v Wingo*.[1906] The applicant had been arrested in October 1986 and his trial was not listed to take place until April 1991. In the circumstances, there was a breach of the right to a fair trial and the prosecution was stayed.

(c) The presumption of innocence

By section 18(3)(a) a person charged with a criminal offence is presumed to be innocent until proved guilty. However, by section 18(3)(b) there will be no breach of this presumption if a law imposes the burden of proving particular facts on the person charged. It has been held that this cannot place the entire onus on the accused and that reverse onus provision must be in accordance with guidelines developed by the common law.[1907] In *State v Chogugudza*[1908] it was held that statutory presumption in the Prevention of Corruption Act that an action by a public officer showing favour or disfavour was done for that purpose was not a breach of the constitutional presumption of innocence. **11.521**

(d) Other cases

The case of *Mutasa v Makombe*[1909] concerned disciplinary proceedings within Parliament. A Member of Parliament, while addressing a seminar of senior public servants, voiced the opinion as to the low calibre and intelligence of MPs. The Speaker of Parliament ruled that the MP's statements were a breach of parliamentary privilege, and a Select Committee was appointed to look at the matter. The committee took evidence in the MP's absence, and also questioned the MP himself, though he was not permitted to engage legal counsel or to recall for further examination witnesses who had testified. The committee reported its findings to the House, which resulted in the MP being severely reprimanded. The MP challenged proceedings based on a lack of fair trial, and breach of freedom of expression. The Speaker issued a certificate which the presiding judge deemed to be conclusive of the matter and thereafter proceedings were stayed. The Supreme Court upheld that stay, stating that proceedings in Parliament for contempt were not a trial for a criminal offence. Further, the right to freedom of expression did not assist the MP, as that was limited for the purpose of maintaining the authority and independence of Parliament. **11.522**

In *Banana v A-G*[1910] the Supreme Court considered an application for a stay of proceedings on the ground that widespread hostile pre-trial publicity had made a fair trial impossible. The Court accepted that, in exceptional circumstances, media reporting could be so irresponsible and prejudicial as to make unfairness irreparable and the administration of justice impossible. The test was whether the accused person had established 'that there was a real or substantial risk that . . . he could not obtain a fair trial'.[1911] The Court noted that although the English courts had recently granted a stay of proceedings on the ground of a **11.523**

[1905] *Re Mlambo* (n 1901 above) 36c; relying on *Foti v Italy* (1982) 5 EHRR 313 and *United States v Marion* (1971) 404 US 307.
[1906] (1972) 407 US 514, 530–532; see para 11.88 above.
[1907] See *State v Chogugudza* [1996] 3 LRC 683, 690b.
[1908] [1996] 3 LRC 683, afer considering the Canadian and European law.
[1909] (1997) 2 BHRC 325.
[1910] 1999 (1) BCLR 27.
[1911] Ibid 34.

real or substantial risk of jurors being influenced by what they had read in the newspapers, a stronger line appeared to have been taken in Canada and Australia.[1912] The application was refused.

11.524 In *Lees Import and Export (Pvt) Ltd v Zimbabwe Banking Corp Ltd*[1913] the applicant company argued that the rule that a company had to be represented by a lawyer infringed its right to access to justice. The Supreme Court held that this rule breached the right to a fair hearing: the right given to 'every person' included a corporate body appearing through its alter ego. This was an exception to the general rule and did not permit a corporation to appear through a mere director, officer or servant.

[1912] Ibid 39, relying on *R v Vermette* (1989) 34 CRR 218 and *The Queen v Glennon* (1991–1992) 173 CLR 592.
[1913] (2000) 7 BHRC 647.

12

THE RIGHT TO RESPECT FOR PRIVACY AND THE HOME

A. The Nature of the Rights

12.01 The rights to privacy and respect for the home are less well established in human rights jurisprudence than traditional civil rights such as life, liberty or freedom from slavery. Although the right of persons to be secure in their homes from unreasonable searches has long been acknowledged,[1] a more general right to privacy and respect for the home was only clearly recognised in the twentieth century.[2] Most modern international human rights instruments now protect the right of the individual to 'privacy' or 'private life', but the limits of the right are still not clearly defined. Article 12 of the Universal Declaration provides that:

> No one shall be subjected to arbitrary interference with his privacy, family, home, or correspondence, nor to attacks upon his honour and reputation. Everyone has the right to protection of the law against such interference or attacks.

Article 17 of the International Covenant on Civil and Political Rights describes it in similar terms.[3] Article 8 of the Convention refers to 'respect for private and family life, home and correspondence'.

12.02 At the heart of the right to privacy lies the notion of personal liberty and autonomy.[4] There is an enormous literature on 'privacy rights'[5] in which a variety of different definitions of the scope of the rights have been suggested. In addition to the

[1] See, eg Fourth Amendment, US Constitution which reflected the English common law, cf A Amar, *The Bill of Rights* (Yale University Press, 1998) 65ff and see para 12.10 below; for a recent discussion of the position under the Fourth Amendment, see *Minnesota v Carter* (1998) 5 BHRC 457.

[2] It has been suggested that the need to recognise privacy did not arise earlier because, in small rural communities, there was less distinction between 'private' and 'public' life, see F Schoeman, *Privacy and Social Freedom* (Cambridge University Press, 1992) Chap 7.

[3] See App J in Vol 2, Art 17 refers to 'arbitrary *or unlawful* interference . . .'. For the effect of the latter term, see Human Rights Committee, General Comment 16, Doc A 43/40, 181–3.

[4] See generally, D Feldman, *Civil Liberties and Human Rights in England and Wales* (Clarendon Press, 1993) Chap 8; see also E Barendt, 'Privacy as a Constitutional Right and Value' in B Markesinis (ed), *Protecting Privacy* (Oxford University Press, 1999).

[5] See eg A Westin, *Privacy and Freedom* (Bodley Head, 1967); JUSTICE Report, *Privacy and the Law* (Stevens, 1970); R Wacks, *The Protection of Privacy* (Sweet & Maxwell, 1980); R Wacks *Privacy and Press Freedom* (Blackstone, 1995). For a full discussion of privacy in the human rights context, see D Feldman, (n 4 above) Pt III.

'right to be let alone',[6] privacy rights have been said to cover matters as diverse as an individual's dignity or moral integrity,[7] the unauthorised circulation of portraits,[8] the control of personal information,[9] the establishment and development of emotional relationships with others[10] and the freedom from media intrusion.[11] The wide range of areas in which the right has been invoked have led to scepticism as to whether it is helpful to speak of a general 'right to privacy' at all.[12] However, in analysing privacy rights it is important to distinguish between the 'human right' to privacy as against the state and the right to privacy as against private individuals or organisations.[13] Although the two are closely connected, the range of the former has been greater than that of the latter because of the greater power of the state over all aspects of private life as compared to private organisations.

The right to respect for private life in human rights instruments has its origin in traditional human rights concerns about state interference with the individual. Thus, the constitutional right to privacy in American law arises as an 'emanation'[14] derived from liberty rights enshrined in the Bill of Rights.[15] The protection of the home from unreasonable searches has expanded to protection from surveillance and interception of telephones.[16] More generally, the constitutional right to privacy has been invoked in cases concerning state interference with private decisions relating to birth control[17] and abortion,[18] clothing and appearance[19] and sexual conduct.[20] **12.03**

In the private law sphere, the right to privacy has been more limited. It was first suggested at the end of the nineteenth century in the United States,[21] where it has **12.04**

---

[6] S Warren and L Brandeis, 'The Right to Privacy' (1890) 4 Harv LR 193.

[7] See eg J C Inness; *Privacy, Intimacy and Isolation* (Oxford University Press, 1992); S Stoljar, 'A Re-examination of Privacy' (1984) 4 LS 67; D Feldman, 'Secrecy, Dignity or Autonomy? Views of Privacy as a Social Value' (1994) 47 CLP 41.

[8] See Warren and Brandeis (n 6 above) 195.

[9] See eg Westin, (n 5 above); R Wacks, *The Protection of Privacy* (Sweet & Maxwell, 1980).

[10] *X v Iceland* (1976) 5 DR 86, EComm HR.

[11] See eg *Kaye v Robertson* [1991] FSR 62.

[12] See eg R Wacks, 'The Poverty of "Privacy" ' (1980) 96 LQR 73.

[13] For a discussion about the debate between proponents of the vertical as against the horizontal approach towards human rights, see para 5.39ff above.

[14] Or a 'penumbra' or 'shadow'; see *Whalen v Roe* (1977) 429 US 589.

[15] The right has evolved, for example, from due process clauses of the Fifth and Fourteenth Amendments (see *Roe v Wade* (1973) 410 US 113, 153), the Ninth Amendment (see *Griswold v Connecticut* (1965) 381 US 479, 486–499) (Goldberg J concurring); see generally, L Tribe, *American Constitutional Law* (2nd edn, Foundation Press, 1988) 15–03.

[16] See eg the Convention cases, para 12.138ff below.

[17] *Griswold v Connecticut* (1965) 381 US 479.

[18] *Roe v Wade* (1973) 410 US 113, see para 12.259 below.

[19] See eg *Kelley v Johnson* (1976) 425 US 238 (police department regulations on officers' hair styles).

[20] See eg *Dudgeon v United Kingdom* (1981) 4 EHRR 149.

[21] See S Warren and L Brandeis, 'The Right to Privacy', (1890) 4 Harv L Rev 193.

been extensively analysed and developed in the case law.[22] It has, however, usually been restricted to the four areas summarised in the *Restatement of the Law of Torts*[23] which states that:

> The right to privacy is invaded by
> (a) the unreasonable intrusion upon the seclusion of another;
> (b) the appropriation of the other's name or likeness;
> (c) unreasonable publicity given to the other's private life;
> (d) publicity that unreasonably places the other in a false light before the public.

Private law privacy issues most commonly arise in the context of media intrusion into a person's private life. This can take a wide variety of forms including intrusive photography, the publication of personal information and 'harassment' by journalists and photographers. Such activities may give rise to causes of action in private law. However, they also indirectly bring the 'human right' to privacy into play as a result of the state's positive obligations to ensure that the private lives of its citizens are protected. The extent to which these obligations require the courts, as emanations of state to provide the individual with private law remedies for 'breach of privacy' is of fundamental importance in English law because of its failure to provide full protection for private law privacy rights.[24]

12.05 The issues arising in relation to the right to privacy in the context of human rights law can be conveniently considered under four heads:

Misuse of personal information: A right to restrict the use of 'personal' or 'private' information about an individual is central to the right to privacy. A large volume of such information is held by public bodies and is, potentially, open to misuse. The extent to which the use of this information is controlled or restricted is one of the most important 'privacy' issues.

Intrusion into the home: The right of the individual to respect for his home is fundamental to any notion of privacy. The issues which arise under this head include, in particular, protection of the citizen against unreasonable entries, searches and seizures by public officials.

Photography, surveillance and telephone tapping: The 'private sphere' is not only invaded by physical intrusion into the home. The right of privacy is generally understood to extend to private 'correspondence'. Modern technology provides a wide range of means of surveillance including telephone tapping, 'bugging' and photography of various forms. When surveillance is carried out by public officials there is potentially a 'direct' infringement of privacy rights.

[22] See *Restatement of the Law of Torts*, 2nd edn, para 625A ff.

[23] Ibid 2nd edn, para 625A; save for the right in para 2(b), an action for invasion of privacy can be maintained only by a living individual whose privacy is invaded (ibid para 652I).

[24] See para 12.06ff below.

However, surveillance may also be carried out by private organisations, in particular, the media. This gives rise to difficult issues as to the applicability of human rights instruments in the private sphere.[25]

The extent of other privacy rights: Finally, there are a range of other 'privacy rights' to be considered. These cover all forms of interference in the 'private sphere' including appropriation of a person's image, interference with private sexual behaviour and questions of the sexual identity of transsexuals.

Difficulties arise in each of these areas as to the extent to which interference with the privacy rights of the individual can be justified by the interests of society as a whole in, for example, the investigation of suspected criminal offences or the exposing of wrongdoing. The English courts already have to strike a balance in such cases.[26] After the Human Rights Act comes into force, the policy issues will have to be confronted in a wide range of cases.

B. The Rights in English Law Before the Human Rights Act

(1) Introduction

It is well established that English law does not recognise a right to privacy as such.[27] The point was considered by the Court of Appeal in *Kaye v Robertson*.[28] In that case, a well known actor had undergone extensive surgery and was in hospital when he was photographed and allegedly interviewed by a tabloid newspaper. He sought an injunction to restrain publication of the interview. The case was argued on a number of bases, the most straightforward of which was infringement of privacy. In rejecting this head of claim, Glidewell LJ remarked that the case was **12.06**

> a graphic example of the desirability of Parliament considering whether and in what circumstances statutory provision should be made to protect the privacy of individuals.[29]

The House of Lords considered the issue in *R v Khan*[30] in the course of deciding whether surveillance evidence obtained in breach of Article 8 of the Convention was admissible in a criminal trial; Lord Nolan[31] (with whom Lord Keith concurred)

---

[25] See generally, para 5.40ff above.

[26] See eg the cases concerning the disclosure of allegations of sex abuse, para 12.38 below.

[27] See the remarks of Lord Denning MR in *Re X (A Minor)* [1975] Fam 47, 58; *Malone v Metropolitan Police Commissioner* [1979] Ch 344, 372; for a useful collection of material on all aspects of this topic see S Bailey, D Harris and B Jones, *Civil Liberties: Cases and Materials* (4th edn. Butterworths, 1995) Chap 8.

[28] [1991] FSR 62.

[29] Ibid 66; an injunction was granted on the basis of a potential claim in malicious falsehood.

[30] [1997] AC 558, see also *Khan v United Kingdom*, Application 35394/97, 20 April 1999 (Commission admissibility decision).

[31] *R v Khan* (n 30 above) 577.

expressed the view that there was no right to privacy but Lord Browne-Wilkinson,[32] Lord Slynn[33] and Lord Nicholls[34] preferred to leave the question open.

12.07 Despite the absence of a developed 'right of privacy', the courts have taken 'privacy interests' into account in a number of cases. Thus, in *Derby v Weldon (No 2)*[35] Sir Nicholas Browne-Wilkinson recognised that:

> discovery[36] in the course of an action is an interference with the right of privacy which an individual would otherwise enjoy to his own documents. As a result of the public interest in ensuring that all relevant information is before the court in adjudicating on the claim in the action that right of privacy is invaded and the litigant is forced, under compulsion by the process of discovery, to disclose his private documents. But such invasion of privacy being only for the purpose enabling a proper trial of the action in which the discovery is given, the court is astute to prevent a document so obtained from being used for any other purpose.

However, such recognition has been sporadic. The consequences of the refusal of the courts to recognise a right of privacy was vividly illustrated by the case of *R v Brentwood Borough Council, ex p Peck*[37] in which it was held that a local authority had lawfully released to the media the closed-circuit television footage of the applicant's attempted suicide.[38]

12.08 The question of reform of the English law in this area has received considerable attention over the last thirty years.[39] The impetus for reform has come largely from the perceived need to curb the excesses of the tabloid press. In response to a 1969 private members bill on the subject, the Younger Committee on Privacy was established. In 1972, the Committee decided, by a majority, against creating a 'general right to privacy', primarily because it would confer upon the courts an exceedingly wide discretion to enforce the law.[40] An attempt to introduce a Protection of Privacy Bill in the 1988–89 session of Parliament failed to achieve a Third Reading. In 1990, the Calcutt Committee on Privacy concluded that no tort of infringement of privacy should be introduced.[41] The Committee recommended the establishment of a Press Complaints Commission. This Commission

---

[32] Ibid 571.

[33] Ibid 571.

[34] Ibid 582, 583.

[35] *The Times*, 20 Oct 1988; for a recent example, see *Haig v Aitken* [2000] 3 All ER 80 (sale of bankrupt's private correspondence would be an infringement of his right of privacy).

[36] Now 'disclosure' under CPR, Pt 31.

[37] *The Times*, 18 Dec1997.

[38] See also *M v BBC* [1997] 1 FLR 51; but see *Marcel v Commissioner of Police of the Metropolis* [1992] Ch 225, 234C–D, taking into account the 'fundamental human right' of privacy in relation to disclosure of documents.

[39] For recent general discussions, see D Eady, 'A Statutory Right to Privacy' [1996] EHRLR 243; Lord Bingham, 'Should there be a Law to Protect Rights of Personal Privacy?' [1996] EHRLR 450.

[40] *Report of the Committee on Privacy*, Cmnd 5012 (1972) paras 33–44 and 661–666.

[41] See *Report of the Committee on Privacy and Related Matters*, Cmnd 1102 (1990).

was established but attracted considerable criticism, and in his 1993 Review of Press Self-Regulation Sir David Calcutt QC recommended that further consideration be given to the introduction of a tort of infringement of privacy.[42] The debate still continues.[43] Increasing numbers of senior judges have, however, expressed the view that it is open to the courts to develop a privacy law. As Lord Irvine LC said in the course of debates on the Human Rights Bill:

> I believe that the true view is that the courts will be able to adapt and develop the common law by relying on existing domestic principles in the laws of trespass, nuisance, copyright, confidence and the like to fashion a common law right to privacy.[44]

Despite the absence of a general 'right of privacy' in English law, such rights do receive a degree of *indirect* protection from a number of sources.[45] The torts of trespass to land and goods protect individuals against direct intrusions into their homes. The law of breach of confidence provides some protection against the disclosure of information and possibly against some forms of surveillance. There is limited statutory protection in relation to police surveillance and the use of information held on computer. These protections will be considered in the next four sections. **12.09**

(2) Intrusion into the home: entry, search and seizure

(a) Introduction

The common law has always treated the right to freedom from interference with personal property[46] as fundamental.[47] It has given rise to perhaps the most well-known of all maxims of the English law: **12.10**

> 'An Englishman's home is his castle' is one of the few principles of law known to every citizen . . . The rule is, of course, subject to exceptions, but they are few . . .[48]

In fact, the principle has always been subject to numerous limitations: by 1604 it

---

42 (1993) Cm 2315, para 17; see also the House of Commons, National Heritage Committee, Fourth Report on Privacy and Media Intrusion, Mar 1993, (1992–93) HC Papers 294; and Lord Chancellor's Consultation Paper, *Infringement of Privacy* (Jul 1993).

43 See eg the debate in House of Lords on the Human Rights Bill, *Hansard*, HL cols 771–787 (24 Nov 1997).

44 Ibid col 785; see also Lord Bingham, 'Should there be a Law to Protect Rights of Personal Privacy?' [1996] EHRLR 450.

45 See generally, B Neill, 'Privacy: A Challenge for the Next Century', in B Markesinis (ed), *Protecting Privacy* (Oxford University Press, 1999).

46 For a fuller treatment, see eg D Feldman, *The Law relating to Entry, Seizure and Search* (Butterworths, 1986); R Clayton and H Tomlinson, *Civil Actions Against the Police* (3rd edn, Sweet & Maxwell, 2001) Chap 7.

47 R Kerr (ed), *Blackstone's Commentaries on the Laws of England* (4th edn, John Murray, 1876) 100 ff.

48 *McLorie v Oxford* [1982] 1 QB 1290 *per* Donaldson LJ.

provided protection only against the forcible entry of outer doors of dwelling houses, and gave way to legal process in the name of the King.[49] Nevertheless, it remains the case that the police or other public officials can enter premises only in the limited situations defined by statute or common law and that the burden is on them to justify the entry.

12.11 In the famous constitutional case of *Entick v Carrington*,[50] an entry and seizure by the King's messengers was said to be justified by a warrant issued by one of the four principal secretaries of state. Lord Camden CJ dismissed this defence in stirring words:

> The great end, for which men entered into society was to secure their property. That right is preserved sacred and incommunicable in all instances, where it has not been taken away or abridged by some public law for the good of the whole. . . . By the laws of England every invasion of private property, be it ever so minute, is a trespass.

This approach, which applies both to searches of property and seizures of goods has been applied, somewhat unevenly, ever since. Search, seizure and retention by public officials will be unlawful unless justified by some common law or statutory power.[51]

12.12 However, the idea of 'respect for the home' under Article 8(1)[52] has rather broader implications in the public law field; and has been successfully utilised in some recent judicial review cases. For example, in *R v North and East Devon District Health Authority, ex p Coughlan*[53] the Court of Appeal held that moving a disabled person out of a long stay residence after giving her an express assurance that she could remain there for life constituted an interference with the right to her home which required the public body to comply with its duty to act fairly.

(b) Interference with land and goods

12.13 Any unjustified direct physical intrusion onto land in possession of another is a trespass at common law. The slightest entry, such as putting a foot in the door or a microphone on a window, is sufficient. The person who enters must justify the entry. Honest belief in a right to enter is not a defence.[54] A public official who enters under an authority given by law becomes a trespasser *ab initio* if he abuses that

---

[49] See D Feldman, *Civil Liberties and Human Rights in England and Wales* (Clarendon Press, 1993) 403–4.

[50] (1765) 2 Wils 275; 19 State Trials 1029.

[51] For an illuminating general discussion see Feldman (n 46 above).

[52] See para 12.95ff below.

[53] [2000] 2 WLR 622.

[54] *Hewlitt v Bickerton* (1947) 150 EG 421; and see *Entick v Carrington* (n 50 above) 1066G: 'No man can set his foot upon my ground without my licence, but he is liable to an action, though the damage be nothing'.

authority.[55] This means that the occupier of the land can recover damages for the whole period that the wrongdoer is on the land and not just for the period after the abuse.[56]

Any interference with a person's goods is also, *prima facie*, tortious. An unjustified direct physical interference with goods in the possession of a person will be sufficient to constitute a trespass to goods.[57] If the person interfering with the goods acts in a manner inconsistent with the rights of the person in possession, he will be guilty of conversion. Conversion covers actions such as keeping and refusing to return, using, destroying, and returning the goods to a third party. Proceedings can be brought for trespass to goods when goods are removed, damaged or even touched. Conversion will be more appropriate if the plaintiff is prevented from gaining access to his goods, if lawfully seized goods are lost or damaged, or if there is a refusal to return goods which are no longer needed for the purpose for which they were seized. **12.14**

(c) Powers of entry under warrant

A warrant is a legal authority to carry out acts which would, otherwise, be unlawful.[58] A large number of statutes empower justices of the peace to issue search warrants to police officers and other public officials.[59] Constables who act 'in obedience' to such a warrant are protected from claims in trespass if the warrant is issued without jurisdiction.[60] However, where police officers have acted maliciously in procuring the search warrant, they will be liable in damages.[61] **12.15**

Applications for search warrants by police officers must be made in accordance with the procedure laid down in section 15 of the Police and Criminal Evidence Act 1984 ('PACE'). An application must be supported by an 'information' in writing.[62] The warrant must specify the name of the person who applies for it, the date on which it is issued, the enactment under which it is issued, the premises to be searched[63] and the articles or persons to be sought.[64] The execution of warrants **12.16**

55 *Six Carpenters Case* (1610) 8 Co Rep 146a; and see *Cinnamond v British Airports Authority* [1980] 1 WLR 582, 588; and generally, Clayton and Tomlinson (n 46 above) Chap 6.

56 See *Shorland v Govett* (1826) 5 B & C 485.

57 *Fouldes v Willoughby* (1841) 8 M & W 540, 549.

58 For a comprehensive discussion, see D Feldman, *The Law Relating to Entry Search and Seizure* (Butterworths, 1986).

59 For a comprehensive list of statutory police powers to enter and search premises, see H Levenson, F Fairweather and E Cape, *Police Powers: A Practitioner's Guide* (3rd ed, Legal Action Group, 1996), App 6.

60 Constables Protection Act 1750, s 6; see generally, R Clayton and H Tomlinson, *Civil Actions Against the Police* (3rd edn Sweet & Maxwell, 2001) Chap 7.

61 See, most recently, *Gibbs v Rea* [1998] AC 786 and see generally, Clayton and Tomlinson (n 60 above) Chap 8.

62 s 15(3).

63 *R v Southwestern Magistrates' Court, ex p Cofie* [1997] 1 WLR 885.

64 s 15(6).

by police officers is governed by section 16 of PACE. The constable must, if the occupier is present, identify himself, produce the warrant and supply a copy.[65] If the occupier is not present, a copy of the warrant must be left at the premises.[66] A warrant does not permit a 'general search' of the premises:[67] a search under a warrant may only be a search 'to the extent required for the purpose for which the warrant was issued'.[68] The warrant must be endorsed, stating whether the articles which were sought were found and what other articles were seized.[69] The safeguards imposed by sections 15 and 16 of PACE are 'stringent in effect'.[70] Any search which is not carried out in accordance with these provisions will be unlawful.[71] Thus, searches have been held to be unlawful where copies of the schedules to the warrants were not supplied to the applicant at the time of the search[72] and where the enactment under which the warrant was issued was not specified.[73]

12.17 Special provisions apply to 'items subject to legal privilege',[74] 'excluded material'[75] and 'special procedure material'.[76] A provision of any enactment, passed prior to PACE, which permits searches for any of these three types of material, is of no effect.[77] A constable can, however, obtain access to excluded material or special procedure material by obtaining an appropriate order from a circuit judge if a number of special access conditions are fulfilled.[78] It has been emphasised that this procedure is 'a serious inroad upon the liberty of the subject' and that 'it is of cardinal importance that circuit judges should be scrupulous in discharging that responsibility'.[79] There is no power to search for or seize items subject to legal privilege. PACE provides, however, that this privilege is lost if the material is held 'with the intention of furthering a criminal purpose'.[80] The relevant provision[81] was given a very broad interpretation by the House of Lords in *R v Central Criminal Court, ex p*

[65] s 16(5).
[66] s 16(7).
[67] See eg *R v Chief Constable of Warwick Constabulary, ex p Fitzpatrick* [1999] 1 WLR 564.
[68] s 16(8).
[69] s 16(9).
[70] *R v Central Criminal Court, ex p A J D Holdings* [1992] Crim LR 669.
[71] s 15(1) which covers the composite process of entering and searching; *R v Chief Constable of Lancashire, ex p Parker* [1993] QB 577.
[72] Ibid.
[73] *R v Reading Justices, ex p South West Meats* (1992) 4 Admin LR 401.
[74] As defined in s 10(1).
[75] That is personal records, human tissue or journalistic material held in confidence: see s 11(1).
[76] That is, non-confidential journalistic material and confidential business material, s 14(1); for the impact of freedom of expression under Art 10 on these applications, see para 15.126 below.
[77] s 9(2).
[78] s 9 and Sch 1.
[79] *R v Maidstone Crown Court, ex p Waitt* [1988] CLR 384; as a result, there is an implied obligation to give reasons for the decision: see *R v Southampton Crown Court, ex p J and P* [1993] Crim LR 962.
[80] s 10(2).
[81] Ibid.

Francis and Francis[82] in which it was found that, although the material was held innocently, the privilege was lost as a result of the 'criminal purpose' of a third party.[83]

In cases involving the use of warrants, the courts have emphasised the need to carry out a balancing exercise between, the public interest in the effective investigation and prosecution of crime and the public interest in protecting the personal and property rights of citizens against infringement and invasion:[84] **12.18**

> [PACE] . . . seeks to effect a carefully judged balance between these interests and that it why it is a detailed and complex Act. If the scheme intended by Parliament is to be implemented it is important that the provisions laid down in the Act should be fully and fairly enforced.[85]

This approach has led to warrants being quashed in a number of cases.[86] However, there is no obligation on magistrates to give reasons for the grant of a warrant[87] and no record of the proceedings. As a result, it remains extremely difficult, in practice, to mount a successful challenge to a search warrant.[88]

(d) Powers of entry without warrant

A police officer has a common law power of entry into premises 'to deal with or prevent a breach of the peace'.[89] The power allows police officers to enter whether the breach is actually in progress or merely apprehended.[90] They may also enter in the fresh pursuit of someone suspected of a breach of the peace committed elsewhere. When the pursuit ends, however, and there is no likelihood of the breach recurring, the common law power to enter is terminated.[91] **12.19**

PACE provides police officers with a number of statutory powers of entry. Officers may enter to: **12.20**

---

82 [1989] AC 346.

83 The dispute arose when solicitors were ordered to produce material, comprising advice to a client, to assist in the tracing of proceeds of crime; the police argued that the material was held by the solicitors as a result of the plan of suspected drug traffickers for laundering their criminal gains. This decision has been subject to considerable criticism: see A Newbold, 'The Crime/Fraud Exception to Legal Professional Privilege' (1990) 53 MLR 472; and see generally, D Feldman, *Civil Liberties and Human Rights in England and Wales* (Clarendon Press, 1993), 448–450.

84 *R v Crown Court at Lewes, ex p Hill* (1990) 93 Cr App R 60, 65.

85 Ibid *per* Bingham LJ.

86 See eg *R v Lewes Crown Court, ex p Nigel Weller & Co*, unreported, 12 May 1999.

87 Although it is desirable, see *R v Marylebone Magistrates' Court, ex p Amdrell Ltd (trading as 'Get Stuffed')* (1998) 162 JP 719.

88 See eg *ex p Amdrell* (n 87 above) in that case, the fact that the police did not disclose an intention to invite the media to attend the execution of a warrant did not invalidate its issue or execution.

89 PACE, s 17(6); for a discussion of the meaning of breach of the peace, see para 16.13 below.

90 See *Thomas v Sawkins* [1935] 2 KB 249; and see *McLeod v Commissioner of Police of the Metropolis* [1994] 4 All ER 553.

91 *R v Marsden* (1868) LR 1 CCR 131.

- execute an arrest warrant;[92]
- arrest for an arrestable offence;[93]
- arrest for certain specified offences;[94]
- recapture a person unlawfully at large;[95]
- save life, limb or property;[96]
- search the premises of a person under arrest for evidence;[97] and
- search premises attended by a person immediately prior to or at the time of his arrest.[98]

The first four powers are only exercisable if the constable has reasonable grounds to believe that the person sought is on the premises.[99] The last requires reasonable grounds for believing that evidence which would justify the search is located on the premises.

(e) Powers of seizure and retention of goods

12.21 Police officers have a common law power to seize the 'fruits', 'evidence' or 'instruments' of serious crime from anyone 'implicated' in the crime or who unreasonably refuses to hand them over.[100] These powers have been superseded, but not replaced, by powers of seizure under PACE which are 'in addition to any power otherwise conferred'.[101]

12.22 Police officers have powers to enter premises and seize goods under a wide range of statutes. PACE provides for seven powers of seizure without warrant. The police may seize:

- items obtained through crime which may be disposed of;[102]
- evidence of crime which may be disposed of;[103]
- information on a computer which may be disposed of;[104]
- evidence found on the premises of a person under arrest;[105]

---

92 PACE, s 17(1)(a).
93 PACE, s 17(1)(b).
94 PACE, s 17(1)(c).
95 PACE, s 17(1)(d).
96 PACE, s 17(1)(e).
97 PACE, s 18(1).
98 PACE, s 32(2)(b).
99 PACE, s 17(2)(a).
100 *Ghani v Jones* [1970] 1 QB 693, 708–709; the last category was added by Lord Denning MR when revising the judgment and is of dubious authority: see Jackson [1970] CLJ 1; and see generally, D Feldman, *The Law Relating to Entry Search and Seizure* (Butterworths, 1986), 409–416.
101 PACE, s 19(5).
102 PACE, s 19(2).
103 PACE, s 19(3).
104 PACE, s 19(4).
105 PACE, s 18(1).

- evidence obtained through a stop and search procedure;[106]
- evidence found after arrest;[107]
- property located on a person brought to a police station.[108]

When the police seize large quantities of goods they must consider each item separately and decide whether or not there are reasonable grounds for believing that it is seizable. If proper consideration is not given to each item, a trespass to goods will result.[109] Where the search or seizure is unlawful, the goods must be returned.[110] As the Divisional Court stressed in *R v Chesterfield Justices, ex p Bramley*,[111] it is not unlawful to seize documents which are legally privileged if the police officer who did so did not have reasonable grounds for believing they were. However, the police are not entitled to remove documents to carry out a preliminary sift to investigate the position and must return documents immediately as soon as they have reasonable grounds for believing the documents are privileged.

Even if goods have been lawfully seized, the police will be guilty of wrongful interference with goods if they cannot justify the continued retention of them. When the police seize an item under their common law powers they must not keep it for longer than is reasonably necessary for their investigations.[112] The property must be returned when charges are dropped or the proceedings have been disposed of. **12.23**

The common law position is confirmed by section 22 of PACE, under which any material seized may be retained for 'so long as is necessary in all the circumstances'. Goods may be retained if there are reasonable grounds for believing they are the fruits of crime.[113] If goods are seized from a person in custody, on grounds that they might be used to cause injury, damage to property, interfere with evidence or assist in escape, they must be returned when the person is released from custody.[114] No goods can be retained for use as evidence at a trial or for investigation if a photograph or a copy would be sufficient.[115] Section 21 of PACE provides that the owner of documents has rights of access and copying. There is also a right of access to anything retained for the purpose of investigation of an offence, unless the police have reasonable grounds for believing that to give access would prejudice the investigation.[116] Owners of documents nevertheless often experience considerable practical difficulty in obtaining access or copies. **12.24**

106 PACE, s 1(6).
107 PACE, s 32(2)(a).
108 PACE, s 54(1) and (3).
109 *Reynolds v Commissioner of Police of the Metropolis* [1985] QB 881.
110 See *R v Chief Constable of Lancashire, ex p Parker* [1993] QB 577.
111 [2000] 1 All ER 411.
112 *Ghani v Jones* [1970] 1 QB 693.
113 PACE, s 22(2)(b).
114 PACE, s 22(3).
115 PACE, s 22(4).
116 PACE, s 21(8).

12.25 The powers to seize and retain documents are conferred for the performance of public functions and cannot be used to make information available to private individuals for private purposes. This is because

> Search and seizure under statutory powers constitute fundamental infringements of the individual's immunity from interference by the state with his property and privacy—fundamental human rights.[117]

The police must nevertheless respond to a subpoena to produce documents to the court for the purposes of a civil action.[118]

(3) The misuse of personal information

(a) Introduction

12.26 The English law in relation to the protection of rights in personal information can be considered under two headings. First, there are the common law rights to protect the dissemination of information which is 'confidential'.[119] Although much of the earlier case law relates to trade secrets, these rights now also extend to many categories of 'personal' information. Secondly, there are a number of statutory rights of access to inaccurate information held in confidential files by public authorities and to correct inaccurate information which they may contain.

(b) Breach of confidence

12.27 **Introduction.** The nineteenth century case law on 'breach of confidence' was the inspiration for the development of the right of privacy in the United States. The doctrine derives from a case in which Prince Albert obtained an injunction on the basis of breach of confidence to prevent an exhibition of etchings by himself and Queen Victoria: the injunction was granted against a defendant who had acquired copies without their consent.[120] The doctrine has proved to be extremely flexible and protects not merely trade secrets, but also confidential information about an individual's private life such as marital secrets,[121] sexual relationships,[122] a medical condition (such as having AIDS)[123] as well as artistic confidences.[124] The approach

---

[117] See *Marcel v Commissioner of Police of the Metropolis* [1992] Ch 225, 235D–E *per* Browne-Wilkinson J; approved by the Court of Appeal, 256D; and see also *Taylor v Director of the Serious Fraud Office* [1998] 3 WLR 1040.

[118] See *Marcel v Commissioner of Police* (n 117 above) 257D, 265D–G (the Court of Appeal overruling Browne-Wilkinson J on this point).

[119] For a fuller treatment, see eg R Toulson and C Phipps, *Confidentiality* (Sweet & Maxwell, 1996).

[120] *Prince Albert v Strange* (1848) 2 De G & Sm 652; the decision was heavily relied on by Warren and Brandeis (n 6 above).

[121] *Argyll (Duchess) v Argyll (Duke)* [1967] 1 Ch 302.

[122] *Stephens v Avery* [1988] Ch 449; *Barrymore v News Group* [1997] FSR 600.

[123] *X v Y* [1990] 1 QB 220.

[124] See eg *Gilbert v Star Newspapers* (1894) 11 TLR 4.

of the courts has been pragmatic and breach of confidence has developed into an adaptable remedy for the protection of privacy in an important class of cases.[125]

In order to establish a breach of confidence a claimant must show: **12.28**

- that the information was confidential;
- that it was imparted in circumstances of confidence and
- that there has been or will be a misuse of that information.[126]

All three elements have been the subject of detailed consideration by the courts.

The nature of the information. First it must be shown that the information in question has the 'necessary quality of confidentiality'. This will not attach to 'trivial or useless information'[127] or to 'tittle tattle or gossip'.[128] More importantly, it will not attach to information which is already in the public domain. As Megarry J said in *Coco v A N Clarke (Engineerings) Ltd*:[129] **12.29**

> something which is public property and public knowledge cannot *per se* provide any foundation for proceedings for breach of confidence. However confidential the circumstances of the communication, there can be no breach of confidence in revealing to others something which is already common knowledge.

Whether the publication of information has been so extensive as to destroy confidentiality is 'a question of degree depending on the facts of the particular case'.[130] Where marital secrets had been discussed by both parties in a number of newspaper articles, they were no longer 'confidential information'.[131] Furthermore, the confidentiality of information may be lost by the passage of time or change of circumstances.[132]

The fact that a matter has once been in the public domain cannot, however, prevent its resurrection, possibly many years later, from being an infringement of privacy; the determination is matter of fact and degree.[133] It has been held that **12.30**

125 See generally, F Gurry, *Breach of Confidence* (Oxford University Press, 1984), and Toulson and Phipps (n 119 above).

126 See generally, *Saltman Engineering Co Ltd v Campbell Engineering Co Ltd* [1963] 3 All ER 413; and Toulson and Phipps (n 119 above) Chap III.

127 See *McNicol v Sportsman's Books* (1930) McG CC 116.

128 Cf *Stephens v Avery* [1988] Ch 449.

129 [1969] RPC 41, 47.

130 *Franchi v Franchi* [1967] RPC 149, 153; for a discussion as to the effect of foreign publication see *A-G v Guardian Newspapers Ltd (No 2)* [1990] 1 AC 109; and see Toulson and Phipps (n 119 above) Chap IV.

131 *Lennon v News Group Newspapers* [1978] FSR 573, CA.

132 See eg *A-G v Jonathan Cape Ltd* [1976] 1 QB 752 regarding the confidentiality of Cabinet discussions lost after 10 years; publication of 'Crossman Diaries' not restrained.

133 *R v Broadcasting Complaints Commission, ex p Granada TV* [1995] EMLR 163, 168; see also *R v Chief Constable of North Wales Police, ex p Thorpe* [1999] QB 396, 429A.

previous convictions and sentences cannot be confidential information,[134] but this may be an overstatement of the position.[135]

12.31 **'Circumstances of confidence'.** In order to be 'confidential', the information must have been imparted in circumstances importing an obligation of confidence. In many cases, the obligation will arise from the nature of the relationship between the persons giving and receiving the information. Thus, a relationship of confidence exists between doctor and patient,[136] journalist and source,[137] husband and wife[138] and between the parties to any sexual relationship.[139] Questions of confidentiality will, of course, only arise if the information being imparted is confidential in nature.

12.32 The general test is whether or not a reasonable man in the position of the recipient 'would have realised, upon reasonable grounds, that the information was being given to him in confidence'.[140] However, in the *Spycatcher* case,[141] Lord Goff suggested that the notion of a 'confidential relationship' could have a wider meaning. He accepted:

> the broad general principle . . . that a duty of confidence arises when confidential information comes to the knowledge of a person (the confidant) in circumstances where he has notice, or is held to have agreed, that the information is confidential, with the effect that it would be just in all the circumstances that he should be precluded form disclosing the information to others.[142]

He went on to state that the majority of cases in which a duty of confidence arises are those in which there is a pre-existing relationship between confider and confidant. Nevertheless, he said:

> It is well settled that a duty of confidence may arise in equity independently of such cases; and I have expressed the circumstances in which the duty arises in broad terms, not merely to embrace those cases where a third party receives information from a person who is under a duty of confidence in respect of it, knowing that it has been disclosed by that person to him in breach of his duty of confidence, but also to include certain situations, beloved of law teachers—where an obviously confidential document is wafted by an electric fan out of a window into a crowded street, or

[134] *Elliott v Chief Constable of Wiltshire The Times*, 5 Dec 1996.

[135] Cf *Melvin v Reid* (1931) 112 Cal App 285 (a film identifying the plaintiff as a prostitute who, seven years earlier, had been acquitted of murder was a breach of privacy after she had 'abandoned her life of shame, had rehabilitated herself'); and see W Prosser, 'Privacy', (1960) 48 Calif Rev 383, 396.

[136] *W v Edgell* [1990] 1 Ch 359.

[137] *A-G v Mulholland* [1963] 2 QB 477, and see *In re an Inquiry under the Company Securities (Insider Dealing) Act 1985* [1988] AC 660.

[138] *Argyll (Duchess) v Argyll (Duke)* [1967] 1 Ch 302.

[139] *Barrymore v News Group Newspapers* [1997] FSR 600.

[140] *Coco v A N Clarke (Engineerings) Ltd* [1969] RPC 41, 48.

[141] *A-G v Guardian Newspapers Ltd (No 2)* [1990] 1 AC 109.

[142] Ibid 281.

where an obviously confidential document, such as a private diary, is dropped in a public place, and is then picked up by a passer by.

Interesting and difficult questions have arisen as to the extent to which a court can 'impute' an obligation of confidence in circumstances in which no actual 'passing of information' takes place. These are considered below in relation to surveillance.[143]

Misuse of the information. In order to maintain an action for breach of confidence, the information must have been disclosed to, or come into the hands of, a third party without the authorisation of the 'confider', or been used for a purpose other than that for which it was imparted to the confidant.[144] Thus, information obtained by the police from an interview under caution[145] or documents seized by the police when performing public functions (such as investigating and prosecuting crime) cannot be disclosed to private individuals for their private purposes;[146] and documents disclosed during the course of civil[147] or criminal[148] proceedings are likewise subject to an implied undertaking that they cannot be used for a collateral purpose. It is not clear whether it is necessary for the claimant to show 'detriment'. The better view, at least in relation to 'personal information', appears to be that this is not necessary.[149] It has been suggested that the test for determining whether there has been a misuse is whether a reasonable confidant's conscience would be affected by the disclosure.[149a] Applying this test, it has been held that the disclosure by doctors and pharmacists of anonymised information about prescribing habits was not a breach of confidence.[149b] **12.33**

The defence of 'public interest'. The English courts have recognised that the duty of confidence can be a restriction on the freedom of expression and that there may be occasions on which the public interest in the preserving of confidence is outweighed by other public interests. This is sometimes known as the defence of 'public interest'.[150] One aspect of this defence is the refusal of the courts to intervene to protect disclosure of information regarding 'wrongdoing'. This is because 'there is no confidence as to the disclosure of iniquity'.[151] This defence **12.34**

---

143 See para 12.52ff below.

144 See generally, *Coco v A N Clark (Engineers) Ltd* [1969] RPC 41.

145 *Bunn v British Broadcasting Corporation* [1998] 3 All ER 552.

146 *Marcel v Commissioner of Police of the Metropolis* [1992] Ch 225, 255, 256 *per* Dillon LJ.

147 *Home Office v Harman* [1983] AC 280; and see *Crest Homes plc v Marks* [1987] AC 829; and *Sybron Corporation v Barclays Bank plc* [1985] Ch 299.

148 *Taylor v Director of the Serious Fraud Office* [1998] 1 WLR 1040.

149 Cf Lord Keith's example of the 'anonymous donor' in *A-G v Guardian Newspapers Ltd (No 2)* [1990] 1 AC 109, 255–6.

149a See *R v The Department of Health ex p Source Informatics Ltd* [2000] 1 All ER 786.

149b Ibid.

150 See *Beloff v Pressdram Ltd* [1973] 1 All ER 241, 260; but see *Price Waterhouse v BCCI* [1992] BCLC 583; and R Toulson and C Phipps *Confidentiality* (Sweet & Maxwell, 1996) 81–83.

151 *Gartside v Outram* (1857) 26 LJ Ch 113.

> extends to any misconduct of such a nature that it ought to be in the public interest to disclose it to others . . . The exception should extend to crimes, frauds, misdeeds, both those actually committed as well as those in contemplation provided always—and this is essential—that the disclosure is justified in the public interest. The reason is because 'no private obligation can dispense with that universal one which lies on every member of society to discover every design which be formed contrary to the laws of society, to destroy the public welfare'.[152]

12.35 This principle has been held to justify disclosure of suspected criminal conduct,[153] disclosure by the police of a photograph of a suspect where they make reasonable use of it for the purpose of the prevention and detection of crime and the apprehension of suspects or persons unlawfully at large,[154] disclosure of fraudulent business practices,[155] alleged miscarriages of justice and corrupt and disgraceful police practices,[156] alleged corruption by a local authority,[156a] dangerous medical practices which endanger the public,[157] dangerous medical hazards[158] and information about 'cults'.[159] It has also been held to justify the voluntary disclosure of confidential information to an inquiry set up under the Banking Act[160] and to regulators[161] (including disclosure of information acquired from police interview).[162] In matters of sexual conduct, however, the court will not refuse to enforce a duty of confidence simply because some people might regard the conduct as immoral.[163]

12.36 It is important to note that the defence of public interest does not depend upon proof of the iniquity of the person claiming breach of confidence; it involves balancing the public interest in favour of publication against the public interest in maintaining the right of confidentiality.[164] It has been extended to situations in which entertainers have sought to restrain revelations by their former

---

152 *Initial Services v Putterill* [1968] 1 QB 398, 405.

153 *Malone v Metropolitan Police Commissioner* [1979] Ch 344.

154 *Hellewell v Chief Constable of Derbyshire* [1995] 1 WLR 804.

155 *Gartside v Outram* (1857) 26 LJ Ch 113.

156 *Cork v McVicar The Times*, 31 Oct 1984.

156a *Preston Borough Council v McGrath The Times*, 19 May 2000.

157 *Schering Chemicals Ltd v Falkman Ltd* [1982] 1 QB 1.

158 *W v Egdell* [1990] 1 Ch 359.

159 *Hubbard v Vosper* [1972] 2 QB 84 (in relation to a book about Scientology).

160 See *Price Waterhouse v BCCI* [1992] BCLC 583; cf the criticism of this decision in Toulson and Phipps (n 150 above) 81–83.

161 See *Re A Company's Application* [1989] Ch 477.

162 *Woolgar v Chief Constable of Sussex The Times*, 28 May 1999.

163 *Stephens v Avery* [1988] Ch 449 (a married woman's lesbian relationship).

164 *Lion Laboratories Ltd v Evans* [1985] QB 526: injunction refused in relation to information suggesting doubts about the accuracy of a breathalyser device; see also *X v Y* [1988] 2 All ER 648: injunction granted to restrain publication of information from medical records that two doctors were suffering from AIDS.

press agents.[165] The broad ambit of the 'public interest' defence has been criticised[166] and the defence has not been recognised in Australia.[167]

(c) Disclosure of information by public bodies

It appears that the obligations of public bodies in relation to the disclosure of confidential information may be different from those imposed in private law. In *R v Chief Constable of North Wales Police, ex p Thorpe*[168] the applicants were convicted sex offenders who sought judicial review of a decision to inform the owner of a caravan site where they were living of their convictions. Lord Bingham CJ held that where a public body acquires information relating to a member of the public which is not generally available and is potentially damaging: **12.37**

> the body ought not to disclose such information save for the purpose of and to the extent necessary for performance of its public duty or enabling some other public body to perform its public duty.[169]

He went on to hold that this principle did not rest on a duty of confidence but on a 'fundamental rule of good administration'.[170] Buxton J was of the view that, because of the overriding obligation of police officers to enforce the law and prevent crime, they did 'not have power or *vires* to acquire information on terms that preclude their using that information in a case where their public duty demands such use'.[171] This approach was approved by the Court of Appeal who said that:

> The issue here is not the same as it would be in private law. The fact that the convictions of the applicants had been in the public domain did not mean that the police as a public authority were free to publish information about their previous offending absent any public interest in this being done.[172]

The Court went on to say that both under Article 8 of the European Convention on Human Rights and under English administrative law, the police were entitled to use information when they reasonably conclude that this is what is required in order to protect the public.

---

165 *Woodward v Hutchins* [1977] 1 WLR 760; see also *Khasshogi v Smith* (1980) 130 NLJ 168.

166 See Toulson and Phipps (n 150 above) 81.

167 See *Castrol Australia v Emtech Associates* (1980) 33 ALR 31, 54; and *Corrs Pavey Whiting and Byrne v Collector of Customs* (1987) 74 ALR 428, 445–50.

168 [1999] QB 396.

169 Ibid 409H.

170 Ibid 410.

171 Ibid 415B; this analysis gives rise to a number of difficulties which have not been explored in the case law which have proceeded on the basis that public bodies have the same obligations in relation to confidential information as private ones, see Toulson and Phipps (n 150 above) Chap V 'Public Sector Confidentiality'.

172 [1999] QB 396, 429A–B, *per* Lord Woolf MR.

12.38 The general principle appears to be that a public body should not disclose information which is confidential or of a confidential character[173] unless there is a 'pressing need'[174] for disclosure in the interests of public health or safety,[175] corruption[175a] or similar purposes.[175b] Such disclosure could be made without a request from the third party but should be on the basis that the confidentiality of the information should be maintained save insofar as the third party needs to use the material for the purpose for which it was disclosed.[176] The balance has to be struck between the competing public interests and, in a case involving disclosure of information by the police concerning a past investigation it was said that:

> In order to safeguard the interests of the individual, it is . . . desirable that where the police are minded to disclose, they should . . . inform the person affected of what they propose to do in such time as to enable that person, if so advised, to seek assistance from the court.[177]

(d) Confidential files

12.39 Public bodies hold on file very large quantities of personal information about individuals. This is often, but not always, stored on computer. Until the enactment of the Data Protection Act, the only potential remedy for misuse of this information would be a finding of breach of confidence: the claimant had to show that the information concerned was originally acquired 'in confidence' and that the recipient had notice of its confidential nature.

12.40 The Younger Committee on Privacy[178] recommended legislation to keep under review the techniques of collecting and processing personal information on computer. In 1975, a white paper was published proposing a permanent statutory agency to protect data subjects and the Lindop Committee on Data Protection was appointed the following year. In 1978, this Committee recommended the establishment of a Data Protection Authority.[179] The proposal was not accepted. In 1984, however, the Data Protection Act 1984 was passed in order to comply with

---

[173] For example, information which has been in the public domain at some earlier date and which may not, therefore, attract the protection of the private law: see R Toulson and C Phipps, *Confidentiality* (Sweet & Maxwell, 1996) para 3–08ff.

[174] *Re L (Sexual Abuse: Disclosure)* [1999] 1 WLR 307, 306A (in that case, the Court of Appeal quashed the decision to disclose findings made in care proceedings because there were no pending investigations); *R v A Police Authority, ex p LM*, 6 Sep 1999 (decision to disclose past unproven allegations of sex abuse quashed).

[175] See *Woolgar v Chief Constable of Sussex Police* [1999] 3 All ER 604.

[175a] *Preston Borough Council v McGrath The Times*, 19 May 2000.

[175b] See also *R v Secretary of the State for the Home Department, ex p Amnesty International*, 15 Feb 2000, unreported where the Divisional Court held that fairness required that medical reports concerning General Pinochet be disclosed to the states who had requested his extradition.

[176] Ibid, 615.

[177] Ibid.

[178] *Report of the Committee on Privacy*, Cmnd 5012 (1972) para 621.

[179] *Report of the Committee on Data Protection* (1978) Cmnd 7341.

the provisions of the European Convention for the Protection of the Individual With Regard to the Automatic Processing of Personal Data.[180] The Act has now been replaced by the Data Protection Act 1998, which gave effect to the European directive[181] on the processing and free movement of personal data.

The purpose of the Data Protection Act is to protect personal data. 'Personal' does not, however, mean 'private'. Whereas the 1984 Act only applied to automatically processed data, the definition of data under the 1998 Act includes information which is recorded as part of a relevant filing system (or with the intention of forming a relevant filing system) or part of an accessible record.[182] The Act applies to data which relates to a living individual who can be identified from the data or from the data and other information which is in the possession (or is likely to come into the possession) of the data controller[183] and includes expressions of personal opinion.[184] **12.41**

An individual who is the subject of personal data is entitled[185] if he makes a request in writing to a data controller[186] to be promptly informed of whether there is any personal data which is being processed.[187] The data controller may charge a fee for the service. Where the processing of personal data is causing (or is likely to cause) unwarranted and substantial damage to the data subject[188] or another, the data subject is entitled to require the data controller, after the expiry of a reasonable period, to cease processing[189] (or not to begin processing) unless one of several specified exceptions apply.[190] He may also apply to the court[191] to rectify, block, erase or destroy personal data if the court is satisfied[192] that the data processed by the data controller is incorrect or misleading as to any matter of fact.[193] Any individual who suffers damage as a result of a data controller contravening the Act is entitled to compensation.[194] **12.42**

The Act provides that data must be used in accordance with the data protection principles. Part I of Schedule I of the Act lists these principles; guidance concerning their interpretation is contained in Part II of the Schedule. The data protection principles are as follows: **12.43**

---

180 See R Austin, 'The Data Protection Act 1984: The Public Law Implications' [1984] PL 618.
181 EC Directive (EC) 95/46.
182 s 1(1) of the 1998 Act.
183 As defined by s 1(1) of the 1998 Act.
184 Ibid s 1(3).
185 Under s 7 of the 1998 Act.
186 As defined by s 1(1) of the 1998 Act.
187 As defined by s 1(1) of the 1998 Act.
188 As defined by s 1(1) of the 1998 Act.
189 As defined by s 1(1) of the 1998 Act.
190 s 10 of the 1998 Act.
191 See s 15 of the 1998 Act.
192 Under s 14 of the 1998 Act.
193 s 70(2) of the 1998 Act.
194 Ibid s 13.

- personal data shall be processed fairly and lawfully and, in particular, shall not be processed unless at least one of the conditions in Schedule 2 is met and, in the case of sensitive personal data,[195] at least one of the conditions in Schedule 3 is met;[196]
- personal data shall be obtained only for one or more specified and lawful purposes, and shall not be processed in any manner incompatible with that purpose or those purposes;
- personal data held shall be adequate, relevant and not excessive in relation to the purpose or purposes for which they are processed;
- personal data shall be accurate and, where necessary, kept up to date;
- personal data processed for any purpose or purposes shall not be kept longer than is necessary for that purpose or those purposes;
- personal data shall be processed in accordance with the rights of data subjects under the Act;
- appropriate technical and organisational measures shall be taken against unauthorised or unlawful processing of personal data and against accidental loss or destruction of, or damage to, personal data; and
- personal data shall not be transferred to a country or territory outside the European Economic Area unless that country or territory ensures an adequate level of protection for the rights and freedoms of data subjects in relation to the processing of personal data.

12.44 However, the Data Protection Act contains exemptions in the following areas:

- national security;[197]
- crime and taxation;[198]
- health education and social work;[199]
- regulatory activity;[200]
- journalism, literature and art;[201]
- research, history and statistics;[202]

---

[195] As defined by s 2 of the 1998 Act.

[196] The data subject must give his consent (para 1); the processing must be necessary for the purposes of exercising rights or obligations conferred by law on the date controller in connection with his employment (para 2); the processing must be necessary to protect the vital interests of the data subject (para 3); the processing is carried out by a non profit making body (para 4); the information is public as a result of steps deliberately taken by the data subject (para 5); the processing is necessary in connection with legal proceedings or advice (para 6), the administration of justice, statutory functions or governmental functions (para 7) or medical purposes (para 8); the processing consists of information relating to racial or ethnic origin (para 9) or is processed in circumstances specified by the Secretary of State (para 10).

[197] See s 28.

[198] See s 29.

[199] See s 30.

[200] See s 31.

[201] See s 32.

[202] See s 33.

- information available to the public by or under any enactment;[203]
- disclosures required by law or made in connection with legal proceedings;[204]
- domestic purposes;[205] and
- miscellaneous exemptions.[206]

The Secretary of State also has power to make further orders for exemptions.[207]

The Data Protection Commissioner has power to ensure that data controllers comply with the Act by using the enforcement procedures in Part V of the Act. The Act also creates a number of criminal offences,[208] prosecutions for which cannot be instituted except by the Commissioner or Director of Public Prosecutions. **12.45**

(e) Access to personal information

There are a number of statutory provisions which give individuals a right of access to personal information. These rights should be distinguished from obligations on public bodies to provide freedom of information which are discussed in Chapter 15.[209] The Labour Government elected in 1997 is committed to a Freedom of Information Act and a draft Bill was published in 1999. A Freedom of Information Act is likely to become law in the course of 2000. **12.46**

Files which are held manually are subject to the provisions of the Access to Personal Files Act 1987. There is no equivalent of the Data Protection Commissioner and the Act is not of general application. The authority holding such records has such obligations with regard to access and accuracy 'as are imposed by the regulations'.[210] The only files which are covered are those held by social services[211] and housing departments.[212] There are a wide range of exemptions and the Act has proved of limited value.[213] **12.47**

There is a right of access to personal information in the following areas: **12.48**

[203] See s 34.
[204] See s 35.
[205] See s 36.
[206] See s 37 and Sch 7.
[207] See s 38.
[208] Such as unlawfully obtaining or disclosing personal data and selling or offering to sell personal data: see s 55.
[209] See para 15.133ff below.
[210] s 1(1).
[211] Access to Personal Files (Social Services) Regulations 1989, SI 1989/206, as amended by SI 1991/1587.
[212] Access to Personal Files (Housing) Regulations 1989, SI 1989/503.
[213] See generally, P Birkinshaw, *Freedom of Information: The Law, the Practice and the Ideal*, (2nd edn, Butterworths, 1996), 259ff.

- social services files;[214]
- housing files;[215]
- health records after 1 November 1989 under the Access to Health Records Act 1990;
- information concerning physical or mental health collected by or on behalf of health professionals under the Access to Medical Reports Act 1988;[216]
- special educational needs in England[217] and Wales;[218] and
- environmental information.[219]

(4) Photography, surveillance and telephone tapping

(a) Introduction

12.49 One important way in which privacy may be invaded is by the taking of unauthorised photographs or film of a person or his home.[220] A person may be photographed or filmed in a 'private setting', such as while sunbathing at home, or in a public place. The photographs or films may be taken by public officials such as police officers or by third parties such as journalists or private investigators.

12.50 Closely related is the invasion of privacy by means of 'listening devices'. Devices can be placed in the home or fixed to a telephone line; they can also take the form of 'long range' listening devices which record conversation in a building without any form of physical intrusion. Such surveillance may, again, be carried out by public officials or third parties.

(b) Photography

12.51 The traditional view is that the English law gives a person no 'right to his own image'[221] or to an image of his home.[222] The law has, however, undergone considerable development in recent years, and privacy rights in relation to photographs may now find some protection in the law of confidentiality.

12.52 Prior to *Spycatcher*, it had been assumed that the requirement of a pre-existing relationship between the 'confider' and 'confidant' prevented the law of breach of confidence from providing protection against unauthorised photography. On the

[214] Access to Personal Files (Social Services) Regulations 1989, SI 1989/206, as amended by SI 1991/1587.

[215] Access to Personal Files (Housing) Regulations 1989, SI 1989/503.

[216] See also, Access to Health Records (Control of Access) Regulations 1993, SI 1993/746.

[217] Education (Special Educational Needs)(Information) Regulations 1994, SI 1994/1048.

[218] Education (Special Educational Needs)(Information) Regulations 1999, SI 1999/1442.

[219] Environment Information Regulations 1992, SI 1992/1711, as amended by SI 1998/1447.

[220] This was one of the areas of mischief mentioned by S Warren and L Brandeis in 'The Right to Privacy' (1890) 4 Harv Law Rev 193.

[221] See *Sports Press Agency v Our Dogs* [1916] 2 KB 880.

[222] *Baron Bernstein of Leigh v Skyways View and General Ltd* [1978] 1 QB 479.

basis of an 'imputed confidential relationship' suggested by *Spycatcher*,[223] however, it has been held that a breach of an express or implied obligation not to take photographs may give rise to action for breach of confidence. Thus, in *Shelley Films v Rex Features*,[224] the defendant was restrained from using photographs of a mask and a film-set which had been taken in spite of clear signs which banned entry by non-authorised persons and prohibited photography. In finding a relationship of confidentiality, the judge relied on both *Spycatcher* and the Australian case of *Franklin v Gliddins*,[225] in which a thief was held to be under a duty of confidentiality.[226]

The position was put more generally in *Hellewell v The Chief Constable of Derbyshire*,[227] which dealt with the use which police officers could make of photographs taken of persons in custody. Laws J held that there was undoubtedly an obligation of confidence between the plaintiff and police, as the photograph was not a 'public fact' and could be described as a 'piece of confidential information'. Nevertheless, the public interest in the prevention of crime outweighed the public interest in maintaining confidentiality. Laws J said, *obiter*, that: **12.53**

> If someone with a telephoto lens were to take from a distance, and with no authority, a picture of another engaged in some private act, his subsequent disclosure of the photograph would in my judgment as surely amount to a breach of confidence as if he had found or stolen a letter or diary in which the act was recounted, and proceeded to publish it. In such a case the law would protect what might reasonably be called a right of privacy, though the name accorded to the cause of action would be breach of confidence.[228]

It may be that a relationship of confidentiality would be found if unauthorised listening devices were used to monitor a person's conversations;[229] these points have not yet been given direct consideration in the cases. The potential availability of a claim for breach of confidence in relation to photographs taken with telephoto lenses has led the European Commission on Human Rights to reject a claim under Article 8 on the ground that the applicant had failed to exhaust domestic remedies.[230]

(c) Surveillance

The common law provides very limited protection to the victims of visual or aural surveillance. If an individual is kept under constant observation he might have a **12.54**

223 See *A-G v Guardian Newspapers Ltd (No 2)* [1990] 1 AC 109; see para 12.32 above.
224 [1994] EMLR 134.
225 [1977] QR 72.
226 See also *Creation Records v News Group Newspapers The Times*, 29 Apr 1997.
227 [1995] 1 WLR 804.
228 Ibid 807.
229 See *Francome v Mirror Group Newspapers Ltd* [1984] 1 WLR 892.
230 See *Earl and Countess Spencer v United Kingdom* [1998] EHRLR 348, EComm HR.

claim for harassment.[231] If his conversation is recorded by surveillance devices, he may have an action for breach of confidence on the basis of an 'imputed relationship of confidentiality'.[232] The most obvious remedies are found in nuisance and trespass to land but these suffer from important limitations.

12.55 If any person enters onto another's land to observe him or to plant a listening device, he will be guilty of trespass. Damages have accordingly been awarded for trespass where a defendant secretly installed a microphone in the flat of the plaintiff[233] and under a marital bed.[234] The significance of an action in trespass has, however, been undermined by the highly sophisticated nature of surveillance devices. Such technology has made it a simple matter to eavesdrop on a home without entering the premises to install the device.

12.56 A nuisance will be committed if an act or omission of one person unreasonably interferes with the enjoyment of land of another. In *Victoria Park Racing v Taylor*,[235] however, the High Court of Australia held that spying is not an actionable nuisance. It refused to prevent racing broadcasts from a high platform built to gain an unimpeded view over the race track of the plaintiff, since the activities of the defendant neither interfered with nor were intended to interfere with the land of the plaintiff, but merely rendered his business less profitable. Another action in nuisance failed in a case in which a dentist in Balham sought an injunction against neighbours who installed large mirrors to observe his study and surgery.[236]

12.57 In *Bernstein v Skyways*[237] it was held that aerial photography over the plaintiff's land did not constitute a trespass because the rights of the landowner in the airspace above his property are limited to such a height as is necessary for the ordinary use and enjoyment of the land. However, Griffiths J went on to say that:

> if the circumstances were such that the plaintiff was subjected to the harassment of constant surveillance of his house, accompanied by the photographing of his every activity, I am far from saying that the court would not regard such a monstrous invasion of his privacy as an actionable nuisance for which they would give relief.

In *Khorasandjian v Bush*,[238] it was held that persistent and protracted harassment by telephone constituted a nuisance. This attempt to extend the tort of nuisance to cover interference with privacy rights was, however, criticised by the House of Lords in *Hunter v Canary Wharf*[239] on the basis that the essence of the tort is injury

231 See now Protection from Harassment Act 1997.
232 See para 12.31ff above.
233 *Greig v Greig* [1966] VR 376.
234 *Sheen v Clegg The Daily Telegraph*, 22 Jun 1961.
235 (1937) 58 CLR 479.
236 C Kenny, *Cases on Tort* (4th edn, 1926) 367.
237 [1978] 1 QB 479.
238 [1993] QB 727.
239 [1997] AC 655, 691G–692B, *per* Lord Goff; 706B–7–7E, *per* Lord Hoffmann.

to land. Harassment is now a statutory offence,[240] but a tort of harassment might have developed independently on the basis of an extension of the tort in *Wilkinson v Downton*[241] to cover cases in which the claimant only suffers distress or discomfort.[242]

The surveillance of citizens by the security services or the police was, until recently, entirely unregulated by statute. Police surveillance was regulated by Home Office Guidelines[243] which did not provide a lawful authority for the placing of listening devices on private premises. This constituted an actionable trespass. On a number of occasions, the courts have described the position as unsatisfactory. In *R v Khan*[244] the defendant sought to exclude evidence obtained by the use of a listening device on the basis that the device had been illegally installed. Even though it was accepted that the surveillance had been illegal, the evidence was admitted as the result of an exercise of judicial discretion in accordance with section 78 of PACE. **12.58**

A number of the judges in *R v Khan* expressed the view that it was highly desirable that police surveillance be given a statutory foundation. Counsel for the prosecution indicated that the Government intended to introduce such legislation.[245] The position is now governed by Part III of the Police Act 1997, entitled 'Authorisation of Action in Respect of Property'. This legislation deals only with those forms of police surveillance which involve 'interference with property'. It does not provide a general scheme to regulate the use of listening devices by the police. **12.59**

Section 92 of the Police Act 1997 provides that: **12.60**

> No entry on or interference with property or with wireless telegraphy shall be unlawful if it is authorised by an authorisation having effect under this Act.

Authorisation may be given in cases where the authorising officer believes:

> (a) that it is necessary for the action specified to be taken on the ground that it is likely to be of substantial value in the prevention or detection of serious crime, and
> (b) that what the action seeks to achieve cannot reasonably be achieved by other means.[246]

---

240 See Protection from Harassment Act 1997.
241 [1897] 2 QB 57.
242 At present, the tort requires the claimant to have suffered nervous shock, see *Hunter v Canary Wharf* (n 239 above) 707E–G, *per* Lord Hoffmann; and see the discussion of the tort in R Wacks, *Privacy and Press Freedom* (Blackstone, 1995), 80–89.
243 The Guidelines on the Use of Equipment in Police Surveillance Operations, 19 Dec 1984, Dep NS 1579.
244 [1997] AC 558; see para 11.132 above.
245 See *R v Khan* (n 244 above) 582, *per* Lord Nolan.
246 s 93(2).

Conduct shall be regarded as 'serious crime' if:

(a) it involves the use of violence, results in substantial financial gain or is conduct by a large number of people in pursuance of a common purpose; or
(b) the offence . . . is an offence for which a person who has attained the age of twenty-one and has no previous convictions could reasonably be expected to be sentenced to imprisonment for a term of three years or more.[247]

The authorisation may be given by a chief officer of police or equivalent senior officer[248] or, if that is not reasonably practicable, by a designated deputy.[249] The authorisation should, save in an urgent case, be provided in writing.[250]

12.61 In some cases an authorisation is not permitted to take effect until it has been approved by a Commissioner[251] appointed under the provisions of the Act.[252] Such approval is required where the property to which the authorisation relates is a dwelling house, hotel bedroom or office or in which:

it is likely to result in any person acquiring knowledge of
(i) matters subject to legal privilege;[253]
(ii) confidential personal information;[254] or
(iii) confidential journalistic material.[255]

These provisions do not, however, apply to an authorisation 'where the person who gives it believes that the case is one of urgency'.[256] The Act provides for the Secretary of State to issue a Code of Practice in relation to the issuing of authorisations. It also provides for a 'complaints procedure'. Such complaints are to be investigated by a Commissioner.[257] A Commissioner who is satisfied that there are no reasonable grounds for believing the specified matters may quash the authorisation or renewal.[258] Wide-ranging changes to the statutory regime governing surveillance are proposed by the Regulation of Investigatory Powers Bill which, for the first time, provides a legal framework for non-intrusive surveillance and the use of 'covert human intelligence sources' such as informants and undercover police officers.[258a]

247 s 93(4).
248 s 93(5).
249 s 94.
250 s 95.
251 s 97(1).
252 See s 91.
253 Defined in s 98.
254 Defined in s 99.
255 Defined in s 100; s 97(2).
256 s 97(3).
257 s 107 and Sch 7.
258 s 103.
258a See para 12.215 below.

Surveillance by the security and intelligence services is also governed by statute. In *Hewitt and Harman v United Kingdom*[259] the Commission on Human Rights declared admissible a complaint by two former officials of Liberty who had allegedly been under surveillance by MI5. This resulted in the enactment of the Security Services Act 1989. which establishes MI5 as a statutory body and defines its functions.[260] By section 5, the Home Secretary is authorised to issue warrants for entry onto or interference with property or for interference with wireless telegraphy. Similar provisions relating to MI6 and GCHQ are to be found in the Intelligence Services Act 1994. Both regimes will be supplemented by the provisions of the Regulation of Investigatory Powers Bill. **12.62**

The Security Service Act 1996 extended the function of the Security Service to allow it to **12.63**

> act in support of the activities of police forces and other law enforcement agencies in the prevention and detection of serious crime.[261]

The Act also extends the power of the Home Secretary to issue warrants authorising entry onto or interference with property or interference with wireless telegraphy for the purposes of this function. These warrants may relate to property in the British Islands if either:

(a) the conduct concerned involves the use of violence, results in substantial financial gain or is conduct by a large number of persons in pursuit of a common purpose, or
(b) the offence or one of the offences is an offence for which a person who has attained the age of 21 and has no previous convictions could reasonably be expected to be sentenced to imprisonment of three years or more.[262]

These provisions involve an executive power to issue warrants which is not controlled by the courts.[263]

(d) Intercepting letters and telephone tapping

The interception of a letter does not constitute a trespass unless the letter is actually touched in an unauthorised manner: 'the eye cannot by the laws of England be guilty of a trespass'.[264] Nevertheless, the interception of letters by warrant of the Home Secretary is a practice of long standing, in spite of the absence of clear authority for it.[265] The lawfulness of telephone tapping was unsuccessfully challenged **12.64**

259 (1989) 67 DR 88, EComm HR.
260 s 1(1).
261 s 1(1), amending s 1 of the Security Service Act 1989.
262 s 2, adding s 5(3B) to the Intelligence Services Act 1994.
263 See P Duffy and M Hunt, 'Goodbye Entick v Carrington: the Security Service Act 1996', [1997] EHRLR 11.
264 *Entick v Carrington* (1765); 19 St Tr 1029, 1066.
265 See *Report of Committee of Privy Councillors* (1957) Cmnd 283, 'the Birkett Committee'.

in *Malone v Commissioner of Police for the Metropolis*.[266] Sir Robert Megarry V-C rejected a number of arguments based on a 'right to privacy'[267] and the 'direct effect of the Convention'.[268] The European Court of Human Rights subsequently found a violation of Article 8 in this case.[269]

12.65 The lawfulness of the power of the Home Secretary to authorise telephone tapping was the subject of review in slightly different circumstances in *R v Secretary of State for Home Affairs, ex p Ruddock*.[270] An official of the Campaign for Nuclear Disarmament unsuccessfully alleged that the Home Secretary had acted unlawfully by authorising MI5 to tap her telephone for party political purposes. Taylor J accepted that the court had jurisdiction to hear the case. He held that, as the Home Secretary was under a duty to act fairly, the official must act in accordance with the published criteria governing the issuance of warrants. He was not prepared, however, to infer from the evidence that the Home Secretary had issued a warrant in breach of his criteria.

12.66 In response to the decision of the European Court of Human Rights in the *Malone* case the Government published a White Paper[271] and the Interception of Communications Act 1985 was the result. The Act regulates the interception of post as well as telephone tapping and covers any communication sent by a public telecommunications system.[272] The Secretary of State cannot issue a warrant unless

> he considers the warrant is necessary:
> (a) in the interests of national security;
> (b) for the purpose of preventing or detecting serious crime;
> (c) for the purpose of safeguarding the economic well-being of the United Kingdom.[273]

Serious crime has the same broad definition as that used subsequently in the Police Act 1997.[274] When considering whether to issue a warrant, the Secretary of State must specifically address whether the information could be reasonably obtained by other means.[275]

12.67 A warrant permits the interception of communications sent to or from one or more specific addresses. The addresses specified are those to or from which

---

266 [1979] Ch 344.
267 See para 12.06 above.
268 See para 2.09ff above.
269 *Malone v United Kingdom* (1984) 7 EHRR 14.
270 [1987] 1 WLR 1482.
271 *The Interception of Communications in the United Kingdom* (1985) Cmnd 9438.
272 s 1.
273 s 2(2).
274 See s 93(4) and see para 12.59 above.
275 s 2(3).

communications are likely to be made by the persons identified in the warrant. The interception of other communications is, however, permissible as necessary to intercept the communications described in the warrant.[276] A warrant issued by the Home Secretary is normally valid for a period of two months.[277] Warrants issued on the grounds of national security or economic well-being may be renewed for up to six months if they are endorsed to this effect; other warrants only benefit from a one-month renewal period.[278] The warrant may be modified by the Home Secretary at any time.[279]

There are a number of types of telephone tapping which are not covered by the 1985 Act.[280] It does not extend to non-public networks.[281] Furthermore, the public network ends at the socket in the wall and, as a result, interceptions of cordless phones are not covered by the Act.[282] It is also unclear whether the interception of mobile telephones falls within the Act.[283] In addition, no authorisation is required if one of the participants in a telephone conversation consents to the interception.[284] Telephone metering, that is the recording of information about the use of a telephone but not the actual conversation does not require any warrant but is permitted under section 45 of the Telecommunications Act 1985 for 'the prevention and detection of crime or the purposes of criminal proceedings'.[285] **12.68**

The Interception of Communications Act is designed to prohibit allegations of telephone tapping or interception of post being made in any court proceedings. Thus, section 9(1) provides that: **12.69**

> In any proceedings before any court or tribunal no evidence shall be adduced and no questions shall be asked which, in either case, tends to suggest

that an offence under section 1 was committed or a warrant issued. The Act provides that a tribunal will hear the application of any person who believes that his communications have been intercepted.[286] The issues which such a tribunal may consider are, however, extremely limited. Unless the complaint is frivolous or vexatious, the investigation of the tribunal is restricted to an assessment as to whether a warrant (or certificate) was issued in accordance with the authorisation requirements. The role of the tribunal is limited to the investigation of whether there is a

[276] s 3(1).
[277] s 4.
[278] s 4(6)(c).
[279] s 5.
[280] See generally, JUSTICE, *Under Surveillance: Covert Policing and Human Rights Standards* (Justice 1998), 16–18.
[281] Cf *Halford v United Kingdom* (1997) 24 EHRR 523.
[282] See *R v Effik* [1995] 1 AC 309.
[283] See JUSTICE (n 280 above).
[284] See eg *R v Rasool* [1987] Crim LR 448.
[285] Cf JUSTICE (n 280 above) 17.
[286] s 7 and Sch 1.

formally valid warrant, rather than the question of whether there were proper grounds for the issue of the warrant in the first place.

12.70 Even if the warrant is found to have been properly authorised, the tribunal is not at liberty to concern itself with the way in which the material intercepted is subsequently handled. There is therefore no remedy under the Act for improper disclosure of material following its interception. Furthermore, by section 7(8):

> The decision of the Tribunal (including any decision as to its jurisdiction) shall not be subject to appeal or liable to be reviewed in any court.

If the tribunal finds that there has been a contravention of the Act, it may quash the relevant warrant (or certificate), direct that copies of the intercepted material be destroyed and direct that the Secretary of State pay compensation in a specified sum.[287]

12.70A The statutory regime governing the interception of communications is to be reformed to ensure that investigatory powers are used in accordance with human rights. The Regulation of Investigatory Powers Bill 2000 envisages the repeal of the above provisions of the Interception of Communications Act 1985. Part I deals with the interception of communications and extends to all types of telecommunications systems. Part IV of the Bill provides for increased scrutiny of Secretary of States powers to authorise interception of communications by an Interception of Communications Commissioner and the establishment of a Tribunal to consider complaints. The Tribunal will also be the appropriate tribunal for actions under section 7 of the Human Rights Act 1998 in relation to the interception of communications. It will apply the same principles for making a determination as would be applied by a court on an application for judicial review.

(5) Privacy and the media

(a) Introduction

12.71 A large proportion of all complaints of invasion of privacy relate to the activities of the media.[288] As noted above,[289] many advocates of a tort of invasion of privacy have been motivated by the perceived need to curb the excesses of the tabloid press. Some protection against invasion of privacy by the press is contained in the Code of Practice adopted by the Press Complaints Commissions. Invasion of privacy by radio or television broadcasters is regulated by the Broadcasting Act 1996.

---

[287] s 7(5).

[288] For a fuller treatment, see eg G Robertson and A Nicol, *Media Law* (3rd edn, Penguin Books, 1992).

[289] See para 12.07 above.

(b) Press regulation

The Press Complaints Commission ('PCC') was established in 1991 on the recommendation of the Calcutt Committee.[290] It is a non-statutory body established by the press. The Commission has 16 members, the majority of whom are from outside the industry. One of the most important functions of the Commission is the enforcing of a Code of Practice for newspapers and periodicals. This was adopted in April 1994 and has been amended on two occasions since.[291] **12.72**

The Code of Conduct contains a number of provisions dealing with privacy issues. Paragraph 3 is headed 'Privacy' and provides: **12.73**

> (i) Everyone is entitled to respect for his or her private and family life, home, health and correspondence. A publication will be expected to justify intrusions into any individual's private life without consent.
> (ii) The use of long lens photography to take pictures of people in private places without their consent is unacceptable.
>
> Note—Private places are public or private property where there is a reasonable expectation of privacy.

Paragraph 4 is headed 'Harassment' and provides:

> (i) Journalists and photographers must neither obtain nor seek to obtain information or pictures through intimidation, harassment or persistent pursuit.
> (ii) They must not photograph individuals in private places (as defined by the note to clause 3) without their consent, must not persist in telephoning, questioning, pursuing or photographing individuals after having been asked to desist, must not remain on their property after having been asked to leave and must not follow them.

Paragraph 5 states that, enquiries in cases involving grief or shock should be made with sympathy and discretion. Paragraph 8 deals with listening devices and states:

> Journalists must not obtain or publish material obtained by using clandestine istening devices or by intercepting private telephone conversations.

The Code provides that exceptions may be made to all of these clauses 'where they can be demonstrated to be in the public interest'. The public interest is not exhaustively defined but is said to include:

> (i) Detecting or exposing crime or a serious misdemeanour;
> (ii) Protecting public health and safety;
> (iii Preventing the public from being misled by some statement or action of an individual or organisation.

If a complaint of breach of the Code is brought to the PCC, the Commission will make an adjudication. Any publication which is criticised by the PCC is required **12.74**

---

290 *Report of the Committee on Privacy and Related Matters* (1990) Cm 1102.
291 The latest version is dated 26 Nov1997.

to print the adjudication in full and with due prominence. The PCC has no power to award compensation. There is no procedure for appeal from a decision of the PCC. However, the PCC is arguably a 'public authority' and as such susceptible to judicial review.[292] The PCC has attracted considerable public criticism. In his second report on self-regulation, Sir David Calcutt concluded that the press freedom had been emphasised by the PCC to the detriment of fairness to the individual.[293]

(c) Regulation of broadcasting

12.75 Radio and television broadcasting has long been subject to statutory control in relation to standards and complaints. Part V of the Broadcasting Act 1996 establishes a Broadcasting Standards Commission ('BSC').[294] The BSC is an amalgam of the Broadcasting Complaints Commission[295] and the Broadcasting Standards Council.[296] The functions of the BSC are applicable to all television and radio services provided by the BBC and other television and radio companies in the United Kingdom. The BSC has a duty to

> draw up and from time to time review, a code giving guidance as to the principles to be observed and the practices to be followed in connection with the avoidance of—
> (a) unjust or unfair treatment in programmes . . .
> (b) unwarranted infringement of privacy in or in connection with the obtaining of material contained in such programmes.[297]

In addition, it has a duty to draw up a code giving guidance as to the practices to be followed in connection with the portrayal of violence and sexual conduct.[298]

12.76 The Act establishes a complaints procedure.[299] When the BSC has adjudicated upon a complaint involving allegations of infringement of privacy concerning a programme that has been broadcast,[300] it is under a duty to send a statement of findings to the complainant.[301] It may also give directions for the publication of

---

[292] The point was accepted as being 'at least arguable' in *R v Press Complaints Authority, ex p Stewart-Brady* (1997) 9 Admin LR 274; see the debate in House of Lords on the Human Rights Bill, *Hansard*, HL cols 771–787 (24 Nov 1997) in which Lord Irvine LC expressed the view that the PCC might well be a 'public authority' under the Human Rights Act.

[293] See *Review of Press Self-Regulation* (1993) Cm 2315.

[294] s 106.

[295] Established by the Broadcasting Act 1980, s 17 and continued by the Broadcasting Act 1981, s 53 and the Broadcasting Act 1990, s 142.

[296] See the Broadcasting Act 1990, s 151.

[297] 1996 Act, s 107.

[298] s 108.

[299] ss 110–20.

[300] *R v Broadcasting Complaints Commission, ex p Barclay* (1997) 9 Admin LR 265.

[301] s 115(8) and see, *R v Broadcasting Complaints Commission, ex p British Broadcasting Corporation The Times*, 24 Feb 1995; and *R v Broadcasting Complaints, ex p Channel Four Television* [1995] EMLR 170.

its findings.[302] The BSC has no power to award compensation to a person whose privacy has been infringed. The Act extends to unwarranted interference with the privacy of companies which do have activities of a private nature which need protection from unwarranted intrusion.[303]

There is no right of appeal against findings of the BSC, but it is a 'functional public authority'[304] and its decisions are susceptible to judicial review. It is unlikely however, that a court will be quick to interfere with findings of the BSC in relation to privacy: the BSC is a specialist body, has members with experience of broadcasting and is authorised to determine difficult questions of fact, degree and value judgment.[305] **12.77**

(6) Other privacy rights

(a) Introduction

English law gives little clear recognition to privacy rights outside the fields of misuse of information, surveillance and intrusion. Two particular areas give rise to concern: 'false light' claims in which the name or likeness of an individual is misappropriated by a third party, and restrictions relating to sexual preferences. **12.78**

(b) 'False light' and related claims

English law provides a limited range of remedies in relation to publications which cast a person in a 'false light'.[306] A defamatory publication will give rise to an action for damages.[307] A publication is defamatory if the image of a person is used in such a way that the estimation of him by others is lowered. Thus, in *Tolley v Fry*,[308] the use of a caricature of a well known amateur golfer in an advertisement for chocolate was held to be defamatory, on grounds that it suggested that he had prostituted his amateur status. The *Tolley* case may be contrasted with that of *Correlli v Wall*,[309] in which the plaintiff author failed to restrain the publication of postcards depicting imaginary scenes from her private life, as the cards were not libellous. Even if photographs which present a person in a 'false light' are defamatory, no action will **12.79**

302 s 119.

303 *R v Broadcasting Standards Commission, ex p BBC The Times*, 12 Apr 2000.

304 See para 5.16ff above; for the purposes of judicial review, it is well established that the Broadcasting Complaints Commission is a public authority (see eg *R v Broadcasting Complaints Commission, ex p Owen* [1985] QB 1153.

305 See *R v Broadcasting Complaints Commission, ex p Granada Television Ltd* [1995] EMLR 163, 167, Div Ct.

306 On the appropriation of personality: T Frazer, 'Appropriation of Personality—A New Tort?' (1983) 99 LQR 281.

307 See para 15.24ff below.

308 [1931] AC 33.

309 (1906) 22 TLR 532; see also *Monson v Tussauds* [1894] 1 QB 671: no injunction to restrain exhibition of waxwork model of a person accused of murder but acquitted.

lie in English law if the publication, read as a whole, makes the true position clear. Thus, no action lay against a newspaper which published 'doctored' photographs showing the plaintiffs' faces on bodies in pornographic poses because the article made it clear that the photographs had been produced without the knowledge of the plaintiffs.[310] There is no action open to a non-trader by which he might restrain the unauthorised use of his name in an advertisement.[311] The position is different if the defendant makes a false attribution of authorship, even in the context of a piece which many readers will read as a caricature.[312]

(c) Privacy and sexual identity

12.80 It has been suggested that a person has a right to his or her own sexual preferences and to determine his or her sexual identity and that this is an aspect of privacy rights. No such right is recognised in the law of the United Kingdom. Thus, attempts by transsexuals to have their birth certificates changed to reflect their new sexual identities have been rejected by the English courts.[313]

C. The Law Under the European Convention

(1) The scope of the right

(a) Introduction

12.81 Article 8 of the Convention provides:

> (1) Everyone has the right to respect for his private and family life, his home and his correspondence.
>
> (2) There shall be no interference by a public authority with the exercise of this right except such as is in accordance with the law and is necessary in a democratic society in the interests of national security, public safety or the economic well-being of the country, for the prevention of disorder or crime, for the protection of health or morals, or for the protection of the rights and freedoms of others.

The issues raised by Article 8(1) concern the scope and content of 'private life', home and correspondence and the obligation of the state to 'respect' those interests. They also address the lengths to which the state must go to ensure that the private life, home and correspondence of individuals are respected.[314]

---

[310] See *Charleston v News Group Newspapers Ltd* [1995] 2 AC 65.

[311] See *Dockerell v Dougall* (1899) 80 LT 556, 557.

[312] *Clark v Associated Newspapers Ltd* [1998] 1 WLR 1558.

[313] See *Re P and G (Transsexuals)* [1996] 2 FLR 90; the applicants have also failed before the European Court of Human Rights, see *Rees v United Kingdom* (1986) 9 EHRR 56; *Cossey v United Kingdom* (1990) 13 EHRR 622; *Sheffield and Horsham v United Kingdom* (1998) 27 EHRR 163.

[314] See eg D Feldman, 'The Developing Scope of Article 8 of the European Convention on Human Rights' [1997] EHRLR 265.

Article 8(2) provides the grounds for justifying an interference with the right to privacy and the home. In each case, it is necessary to consider two questions: first, has the state failed to provide 'respect' for the privacy of individuals, and, if so, secondly, is that failure justified as being in accordance with the law, for a legitimate aim; and necessary in a democratic society? **12.82**

Although Article 8 states that everyone has the right to respect for his private and family life, home and correspondence, it is arguable that a company has no rights to privacy under Convention case law.[315] The right to 'family life' in Article 8 will be dealt with in conjunction with Article 12: the right to marry and found a family in Chapter 13. The meaning of 'respect' and the elements of 'private life', 'home' and 'correspondence' are examined in this chapter. **12.83**

(b) 'Private life'

Introduction. The Court has given some guidance about the meaning of 'private life' and has indicated that it extends beyond the Anglo-American idea of privacy with its stress on secrecy of personal information and seclusion.[316] In *Niemetz v Germany*[317] it said that: **12.84**

> The Court does not consider it possible or necessary to attempt an exhaustive definition of the notion of 'private life'. However, it would be too restrictive to limit the notion to an 'inner circle' in which an individual may choose to live his personal life as he chooses and to exclude entirely the outside world not encompassed within that circle. Respect for private life must also comprise to a certain degree the right to establish and develop relationships with other human beings.
>
> There appears, furthermore, to be no reason in principle why this understanding of the notion of 'private life' should be taken to exclude the activities of a professional or business nature since it is, after all, in the course of their working lives that the majority of people have a significant, if not the greatest opportunity of developing relationships with the outside world.

The right to respect for private life and home must not be looked at in isolation. Article 8 must be read in conjunction with freedom of religion under Article 9,[318] the right to receive and impart information and ideas under Article 10[319] and the right to education under Article 2 of the First Protocol.[320]

315 See para 22.21 below and see also *R v Broadcasting Standards Commission, ex p BBC The Times*, 12 Apr 2000 in which it was held that, under the Broadcasting Act 1996, a company did have privacy rights.

316 *X v Iceland*, (1976) 5 DR 86, EComm HR.

317 (1992) 16 EHRR 97 para 29.

318 See para 14.36ff below.

319 *Kjeldsen, Busk Madsen and Pedersen v Denmark* (1976) 1 EHRR 711; and see para 15.137ff below.

320 See *Belgian Linguistics case (No 2)* (1968) 1 EHRR 252 para 7 which states that 'measures taken in the field of education may affect the right to respect for private and family life or derogate from it'; and see para 19.34ff below.

12.85 The following areas have been considered by the Court to form part of 'private life' within the terms of Article 8:

- moral and physical integrity;
- personal identity;
- personal information;
- personal sexuality; and
- personal or private space.

12.86 **Physical and moral integrity.** 'Private life' covers the physical and moral integrity of the person. It therefore includes physical or sexual assault,[321] corporal punishment[322] and a compulsory blood[323] and urine[324] test. However, not all interferences with moral or physical integrity of an individual will violate private life. Thus, in *Costello-Roberts*,[325] the Court indicated that Article 8 could in some circumstances provide protection against school discipline; but found that the punishment 'did not entail adverse effects sufficient to bring it within the scope of the prohibition contained in Article 8'. It is difficult to reconcile these views with other cases of slight physical intervention: except, perhaps, because the incident took place at school. On the other hand, the Court stressed in *Raninen v Finland*[326] that the right to physical and moral integrity guaranteed by Article 8 comes into play even though it is not so severe as to amount to inhuman treatment under Article 3.[327]

12.87 **Personal identity.** At the heart of private life is the capacity of the individual to formulate a perception of himself and to choose his personal identity. An individual therefore has the right to choose his own name,[328] how he should dress[329] and how to determine his own sexual identity. He may also be entitled to information about his identity, such as the records of his upbringing in public foster care[330] or his paternity[331] if it is significant to the development or determination of his personal identity. Identity also involves the manner in which an individual presents himself to the state and to others.[332]

---

321 *X and Y v Netherlands* (1985) 8 EHRR 235, involved a sexual assault by a man on a mentally handicapped young woman: at para 22, the Court found that the facts concerned a matter of 'private life'.

322 *Costello-Roberts v United Kingdom* (1993) 19 EHRR 112, Com Rep para 49.

323 *X v Austria* (1979) 18 DR 154, EComm HR.

324 *Peters v Netherlands* (1994) 77–A DR 75, EComm HR.

325 (n 322 above).

326 (1997) 26 EHHR 563.

327 See para 8.15ff above.

328 *Burghartz v Switzerland* (1994) 18 EHRR 101; *Stjerna v Finland* (1994) 24 EHRR 194; *Konstandinis v Stadt Altensteigstandsamt* [1993] ECR-I 1191, ECJ.

329 See *McFeeley v United Kingdom* (1980) 20 DR 44, 91, EComm HR (prison dress).

330 *Gaskin v United Kingdom* (1989) 12 EHRR 36 paras 36–37.

331 *Rasmussen v Denmark* (1984) 7 EHRR 371 para 33; *M B v United Kingdom* (1994) 77–A DR 108, 114–116, EComm HR.

332 Cf the discussion of the transsexual cases at para 12.93 below.

Personal information. The collection of personal information by state authorities without consent is a violation of private life. This is most obvious where the collection is surreptitious, by activities such as telephone tapping or interception of post. In *Z v Finland*[333] the Court emphasised that the protection of personal data, not least medical data, is of fundamental importance to a person's enjoyment of his right to respect for privacy and family life; and that there must be appropriate safeguards to prevent communication or disclosure of personal health data. **12.88**

There is also a *prima facie* breach of the right to respect for private life where personal information is collated by an official census,[334] fingerprinting and photography by the police,[335] a compulsory medical examination[336] and the maintenance of medical records;[337] in contrast, the Commission held that an obligation to carry an identity card and to show it on request was not a breach of private life.[338] A security check on a potential employee is not of itself a violation of private life unless it involves the collection of information about his private affairs.[339] Proof that the information is used to the detriment of the applicant is unnecessary, so long as the compilation and retention of such a dossier is adequately shown.[340] **12.89**

In some circumstances Article 8 can give rise to a right of access to personal information. In *Gaskin v United Kingdom*[341] the Court declined to express an opinion on whether a general right of access to personal data and information could be derived from Article 8. However, it took the view that information concerning highly personal aspects of the applicant's childhood, development and history related to his private and family life in such a way that the question of access to it came within the scope of Article 8. In *Guerra v Italy*[341a] the Court held that the state's positive obligations to ensure effective protection of the right to respect for private and family life included the provision of information which would have enabled the applicants to assess the environmental dangers of living near a factory where an accident might occur. Similarly, in *McGinley and Egan v United Kingdom*[342] it decided that withholding documents about the exposure of the applicants to radiation at Christmas Island was a breach of Article 8. **12.90**

---

333 (1997) 25 EHRR 371.
334 *X v United Kingdom* (1982) 30 DR 239, EComm HR.
335 *Murray v United Kingdom* (1994) 19 EHRR 193 para 85; *McVeigh v United Kingdom* (1981) 25 DR 15, 49.
336 *X v Austria* (1979) 18 DR 154.
337 *Chare nee Jullien v France* (1991) 71 DR 141, 155, EComm HR.
338 *Filip Reyntjens v Belgium* (1992) 73 DR 136.
339 *Hilton v United Kingdom* (1988) 57 DR 108, 117.
340 Ibid 118.
341 (1989) 12 EHRR 36.
341a (1998) 26 EHRR 357.
342 (1998) 27 EHRR 1; but contrast *LCB v United Kingdom* (1998) 27 EHRR 212 where no positive obligation to provide information arose on the facts.

12.91 It is unclear whether the state has a positive obligation to control intrusive activities by private bodies (such as the press) when they acquire personal information.[343] However, the Commission has taken the view that the range of English remedies protecting privacy rights (and, in particular, a claim for breach of confidence)[344] provides sufficient protection for the purposes of Article 8.[345]

12.92 **Personal sexuality.** Private life also encompasses choice about personal relationships with others: in particular, social and sexual activities.[346] Sexual activity is clearly part of 'private life'. In *Dudgeon v United Kingdom*[347] the Court described sexual activity as 'a most intimate aspect of private life'; and the Commission acknowledged, in an abortion case, the importance of 'untroubled sexual relations' as a part of private life.[348] Most of the cases in this area deal with homosexuality. It is clear that adult, consenting homosexual activity is now universally accepted in Member states.[349] In the recent cases of *Lustig-Prean v United Kingdom*[350] and *Smith v United Kingdom*,[351] the Court confirmed that only weighty and convincing evidence could justify interfering with private life by investigating and dismissing members of the armed forces on grounds of their homosexuality.

12.93 A number of cases have considered the position of transsexuals. The Court has rejected a number of cases brought because the United Kingdom has failed to amend a birth certificate to reflect the applicant's change of identity, most recently in *Sheffield and Horsham v United Kingdom*.[352] However, a similar complaint succeeded in *B v France*,[353] primarily because of its greater impact on the applicant's social and professional life. The Court also found there was no breach of Article 8 where the United Kingdom failed to recognise a transsexual as the father of a child born after artificial insemination from a donor.[354]

---

[343] The Court rejected the government's argument in *A v France* (1993) 17 EHRR 462 that telephone tapping was not undertaken on behalf of the state; see para 12.105 below.

[344] See para 12.27ff above.

[345] See, *Winer v United Kingdom* (1986) 48 DR 154, EComm HR; *Earl Spencer and Countess Spencer v United Kingdom* (1998) 25 EHRR CD 105.

[346] Some aspects of relations with others will be treated under other Convention heads, whether they are strictly private or not: see Art 11 (freedom of association) and Art 8 (in relation to family life).

[347] (1981) 4 EHRR 149 para 52.

[348] *Brüggemann and Scheuten v Germany* (1978) 10 DR 100, EComm HR.

[349] *Dudgeon v United Kingdom* (1981) 4 EHRR 149 para 52; consensual homosexual acts between adult men in private; also *Norris v Ireland* (1988) 13 EHRR 186; *Modinos v Cyprus* (1993) 16 EHRR 485.

[350] (1999) 7 BHRC 65.

[351] *The Times*, 11 Oct 1999.

[352] (1998) 27 EHRR 163; see, also *Rees v United Kingdom* (1986) 9 EHRR 56 and *Cossey v United Kingdom* (1990) 13 EHRR 622.

[353] (1993) 16 EHRR 1 paras 55–62.

[354] *X, Y and Z v United Kingdom* (1997) 24 EHRR 143.

Personal or private space. The noise nuisance cases[355] can be explained on the basis of the infringement of private space, which is to be enjoyed free from unwelcome interference, whether apparent or covert.[356] The difficult question is whether 'private space' includes anything beyond those places in which the applicant has exclusive rights of occupancy. In *Friedl v Austria*[357] the Commission took the view that police photography of the applicant participating in a 'sit-in' as part of a political demonstration did not violate Article 8. By comparison, in *Murray v United Kingdom*[358] a photograph which was taken at an army centre was held to be an interference with her right to privacy. Some assistance can be derived from the Court's approach in *Halford v United Kingdom*;[359] it decided that a telephone call made from a private telephone line in an office came within the scope of Article 8(1) because the applicant had a *reasonable expectation* of privacy.[360] 12.94

(c) 'Home'

In addition to protecting 'private life', Article 8 requires respect for the home and correspondence of individuals. These concepts clearly overlap; and some actions, such as searches and seizures or interference with telephone conversations in the home, may constitute an invasion of privacy on two or more senses. In *Miailhe v France*,[361] for example, the Court found it unnecessary to examine whether the searches involved the 'home', as it was sufficient to base the interference on the 'private life' and 'correspondence' provisions. 12.95

Article 8 creates a right of 'respect for the home'. It does not establish a right to the home as such; and the Commission has held that the failure to provide a refugee with a decent home did not breach Article 8.[362] It emphasised in *Burton v United Kingdom*[362a] that: 12.96

> the Commission does not consider that Article 8 can be interpreted in such a way as to extend a positive obligation to provide alternative accommodation of an applicant's choosing.

The Court takes the view that respect for 'home' involves more than the integrity of home life; what is at stake is the physical security of a person's living quarters

355 In *Powell and Rayner v United Kingdom* (1990) 12 EHRR 355, the complaint was directed at the noise generated by the operation of four major airports; see also *Arrondelle v United Kingdom* (1982) 26 DR 5 (F Sett), EComm HR and *Baggs v United Kingdom* (1987) 52 DR 29, EComm HR.

356 D Harris, M O'Boyle and C Warbrick, *Law of the European Convention on Human Rights* (Butterworths, 1995) 308.

357 (1995) 21 EHRR 83, Com Rep paras 48 and 51; and see, generally, S Naismith, 'Photographs, Privacy and Freedom of Expression' [1996] EHRLR 150.

358 (1994) 19 EHRR 193.

359 (1997) 24 EHRR 523.

360 Ibid para 45.

361 (1993) 16 EHRR 332.

362 *X v Germany* (1956) 1 YB 202.

362a (1996) 22 EHRR CD 135.

and possessions.[363] It includes the ability (facilitated by the state) to live freely in the home and to enjoy it, not merely as a property right.[364] In *Buckley v United Kingdom*[365] the Court rejected the argument that Article 8 only protected a home which was lawfully established; and went on to find that a gypsy who had continuously occupied land for five years without planning permission was nevertheless entitled to respect for the home. The negotiation of a lease by a Tenants' Union, on the other hand, did not fall within the scope of Article 8; thus, the Court in *Langborger*[366] rejected the argument that the rights and obligations derived from a lease are rooted in the concept of 'home' and are protected by Article 8.

12.97 'Home' has been given a broad interpretation.[367] In general, the term is taken to mean the place where a person lives on a settled basis.[368] However, it might also include a caravan site where a gypsy and her family lived for several years in breach of planning permission[369] a holiday home,[370] or a place of intended, rather than actual, residence.[371] It does not, on the other hand, extend to a home which is to be built in the future.[372] The 'home' of a professional person also includes his business premises; since these activities can be conducted from a private residence and those which are not so related can be carried on in a business or commercial premises, it may be difficult to draw a clear distinction between the two. This approach is consistent with the use of 'domicile' in the French text of the Convention.[373] Premises used wholly for work purposes, however, are not likely to be protected under the right to respect for one's home.[374] A person may have more than one 'home'.

12.98 An interference with the home arises where there is a direct infringement (such as a forcible search by executing a seizure order[375] or searching of a lawyer's

[363] Ibid, *Gillow v United Kingdom* (1986) 11 EHRR 335; see also *Selcuk and Asker v Turkey* (1998) 26 EHRR 477 in which the burning of the property of the applicant constituted grave and unjustified interference.

[364] *Howard v United Kingdom* (1987) 52 DR 198, EComm HR.

[365] (1996) 23 EHHR 101 paras 52–55.

[366] *Langborger v Sweden* (1989) 12 EHRR 416.

[367] *Niemetz v Germany* (1992) 16 EHRR 97.

[368] *Murray v United Kingdom* (1994) 19 EHRR 193 paras 84–96.

[369] *Buckley v United Kingdom* (1996) 23 EHRR 101.

[370] *Kanthak v Germany* (1988) 58 DR 94, EComm HR, for example, raises the question as to whether a camper van could be 'home'.

[371] *Gillow v United Kingdom* (1986) 11 EHRR 335; the applicants had lived in several places around the world and had houses in England and Guernsey; the Court accepted that although they had been long absent from it, they had always intended to return to Guernsey and held that they had a right to re-establish home life in that particular house.

[372] *Loizidou v Turkey* (1996) 23 EHRR 513 para 66.

[373] *Niemetz v Germany* (1992) 16 EHRR 97 para 30.

[374] D Harris, M O'Boyle and C Warbrick, *Law of the European Convention on Human Rights* (Butterworths, 1995) 318–319.

[375] *Chappell v United Kingdom* (1989) 12 EHRR 1.

office)[376] or where the home itself is threatened (by, for example, a compulsory purchase order).[377] The protection of 'respect for home' implies a right of access and occupation,[378] and a right not to be displaced or prevented from the physical possibility of returning to the home.[379] This may be difficult to distinguish from the right to enjoyment of property protected by Article 1 of Protocol 1, and certain government measures might interfere with both Article 8 and the Protocol. In *Cyprus and Turkey*,[380] the Commission found that the failure to allow Greek Cypriots to return to their homes in the north of Cyprus was a breach of Article 8, while the taking and occupation of their houses and land by Cypriot and mainland Turks, both civilian and military, was held to be a continuing violation of Article 1 of Protocol 1. Physical removal of persons from their homes and the taking, occupation or destruction of possessions[381] might each be considered a violation of the Article 8 right to respect for the home.

Interference with the home also includes blights on the environment such as the noise generated by aircraft,[382] and serious pollution.[383] Severe environmental pollution may affect individuals' well-being and prevent them from enjoying their homes in such a way as would affect their private and family life adversely, without, however, seriously endangering their health.[384] In *Powell and Rayner v United Kingdom*[385] the Court rejected a complaint that the noise disturbance created by Heathrow Airport breached Article 8. It stressed that a fair balance had to be struck between the competing interests of the individual and the community as a whole; and held that the operation of a major international airport pursued a legitimate aim and that the steps taken by the Government to control, abate and compensate for airport noise did not exceed its margin of appreciation. In *Lopez Ostra v Spain*[386] the applicant complained about the failure of the local authority to use its powers to prevent a waste treatment plant releasing fumes and smells. The Court again stated that regard must be had to the fair balance to be struck between the competing interests of the individual and the community as a whole; **12.99**

[376] *Niemetz v Germany* (n 373 above).

[377] *Howard v United Kingdom* (1987) 52 DR 198, EComm HR.

[378] *Wiggins v United Kingdom* (1978) 13 DR 40, EComm HR; *Gillow v United Kingdom* (1986) 11 EHRR 335.

[379] *Cyprus v Turkey* (1976) 4 EHRR 482, 519–20, EComm HR; *Cyprus v Turkey* (1983) 72 DR 5, 41–43, EComm HR.

[380] (1983) 72 DR 5, 41–43, EComm HR.

[381] See also *Mentes v Turkey* (1997) 26 EHRR 595 where the homes of the applicants were burnt down.

[382] *Powell and Rayner v United Kingdom* (1990) 12 EHRR 355.

[383] *Guerra v Italy* (1998) 26 EHRR 375.

[384] See *Lopez-Ostra v Spain* (1994) 20 EHRR 277; and *Guerra v Italy* (1998) 26 EHRR 375.

[385] (1990) 12 EHRR 355; see also *Arrondelle v United Kingdom* (1982) 26 DR 5 (F Sett), EComm HR and *Baggs v United Kingdom* (1987) 52 DR 29, EComm HR.

[386] (1994) 20 EHRR 277; and see generally, P Sands, 'Human Rights, Environment and the *Lopez-Ostra* Case' [1996] EHRLR 597.

and decided that Article 8 had been breached. More recently, in *Guerra v Italy*,[387] the Court also ruled that a failure of the authorities to reduce the risk of pollution from a chemical factory violated Article 8.

(d) 'Correspondence'

12.100 **Introduction.** The right to respect for correspondence in Article 8 has been considered in relation to interference with postal delivery, search and seizures of written documents and the interception of telephone conversations.

12.101 **Interference with postal correspondence.** The cases concerning interference with correspondence have primarily been brought by prisoners. Control over prisoners' correspondence is not of itself incompatible with the Convention.[388] It is not clear whether this implies a threshold of permissible control that does not violate Article 8 or that some supervision of correspondence, while an interference, is justifiable under the second paragraph. The nature and extent of the interference, including the existence of a rule or regime of control, will be taken into account.

12.102 Preventing a prisoner from initiating correspondence with his solicitor was held to be the most far-reaching form of interference with the exercise of the right to respect for correspondence.[389] However, in *Campbell v United Kingdom*[390] correspondence between the applicant and his solicitor was opened and read in accordance with the Prison rules. The Court held in favour of the applicant who alleged that he was restricted from communications with his solicitor 'because he knew his letters would be read'.[391] Similarly, in *Campbell and Fell v United Kingdom*,[392] in which only one letter from the adviser to the applicant was stopped, the 'prior ventilation rule' was found to amount to an interference of Article 8 because it, in effect, prevented all correspondence between the applicants and their advisers concerning proposed litigation until the internal inquiry in question had been completed. Thus, the practice of a psychiatric hospital forwarding the applicant's correspondence to a curator for screening prior to delivery was conceded by the Government to be an interference.[393] Even supervision of correspondence 'to a certain extent' during detention of the applicant has been found by the Court

[387] (1998) 26 EHHR 375.

[388] See *Silver v United Kingdom* (1983) 5 EHRR 347; also *Boyle and Rice v United Kingdom* (1988) 10 EHRR 425: although the prisoner had previously benefited from a more liberal regime, he was nevertheless required to serve his time at his then current place of detention on the same terms and conditions as the other prisoners there.

[389] *Golder v United Kingdom* (1975) 1 EHRR 524.

[390] (1992) 15 EHRR 137.

[391] The Court rejected the Government's argument that the applicant had not made out his claim because he had not proved that a specific letter related to the pending proceedings had been opened.

[392] (1984) 7 EHRR 165.

[393] *Herczegfalvy v Austria* (1992) 15 EHRR 437.

unquestionably to constitute an 'interference by a public authority with the exercise of the right enshrined in paragraph 1 of Article 8'.[394]

The Court has found interference with respect for correspondence in a number of situations: where 64 letters were stopped or delayed;[395] where the investigating judge deleted certain passages from the applicant's letter;[396] and where the authorities failed to forward the applicant's letter to the addressee.[397] In *McCallum v United Kingdom*[398] the Court held that stopping letters, withholding copies of letters and a 28-day restriction on correspondence imposed by a prison disciplinary award violated Article 8. In *Messina v Italy*[399] there was a factual dispute as whether there had been an interference. The applicant claimed that he had not received his correspondence while the Government contended that the letters, postcard and telegram in question had been delivered. The Commission held that the onus was on the authorities to show that they had discharged their obligations, and that provision by the state of a record of a prisoner's incoming mail was not sufficient proof that the items reached their destination. **12.103**

Searches and seizures. The Court has taken the view that house searches and seizures raise issues in connection with all the rights secured in Article 8(1), with the exception of the right to respect for family life.[400] Searches and seizures are not restricted to certain types of 'correspondence'.[401] Where a warrant issued by a court ordered a search and seizure of 'documents' resulting in the examination of four cabinets containing client data and six individual files, the operations were found to be covered by 'correspondence' and the material was regarded as such for Article 8 purposes.[402] Furthermore, correspondence does not have to be 'personal' in nature; no mention was made in *Niemetz*[403] of the possibility that Article 8 might be inapplicable on the ground that correspondence with a lawyer was of a professional nature.[404] **12.104**

Telephone tapping. Although telephone conversations are not expressly mentioned in Article 8(1), the Court has made it clear that they are covered by the **12.105**

394 *De Wilde, Ooms and Versyp v Belgium (No 1)* (1971) 1 EHRR 373.
395 *Silver v United Kingdom* (1983) 5 EHRR 347.
396 *Pfeifer and Plankl v Austria* (1992) 14 EHRR 692.
397 *Schönenberger and Durmaz v Switzerland* (1988) 11 EHRR 202.
398 (1990) 13 EHRR 596.
399 Series A No 257–H (1993).
400 *Funke v France* (1993) 16 EHRR 297; *Crémieux v France* (1993) 16 EHRR 357; *Miailhe v France* (1993) 16 EHRR 332.
401 *Niemetz v Germany* (1992) 16 EHRR 97
402 Ibid.
403 (1992) 16 EHRR 97.
404 Ibid.

notion of 'private life', 'family life' and 'correspondence'.[405] As a result, telephone surveillance of individuals constitutes an 'interference' with Article 8 rights by a public authority.[406] The mere existence of legislation permitting surveillance constitutes an interference that:

> strikes at the freedom of communication between users of the . . . telecommunication services and . . . with the exercise of the applicants' right to respect for private and family life and correspondence.[407]

In *Malone v United Kingdom*[408] interception of only one call could be proved.[409] Nevertheless, the Court found that, because the system established in England and Wales for the surveillance of communications itself amounted to an 'interference', it was unnecessary to inquire into the claims of the applicant that the interceptions had spanned a number of years.[410] The broad approach taken by the Court was confirmed in *Halford v United Kingdom*,[411] where it held that respect for correspondence extended to private telephone calls at work on a personal line.

(e) 'Respect'

12.106 Article 8 does not protect privacy or family or home or correspondence *as such*. It guarantees a '*respect*' for these rights. In view of the diversity of circumstances and practices in the contracting states, the notion of 'respect' (and its requirements) are not clear-cut; they vary considerably from case to case.[412]

12.107 The main issue concerning the scope of 'respect' is whether the obligation on the public authority under Article 8(1) is a purely *negative* one or whether it also has a positive component. On the one hand, the state might be required to simply

405 Telephone conversations between family members are covered by both 'family life' and 'correspondence' under Art 8: *Andersson v Sweden* (1992) 14 EHRR 615; see also *Kopp v Switzerland* (1998) 27 EHRR 91, in which it was undisputed that telephone calls to and from business premises may be covered by notions of 'private life' and 'correspondence' within the meaning of Art 8(1). The interception of the telephone conversations of the applicant constituted an interference with private life and correspondence: *Lüdi v Switzerland* (1992) 15 EHRR 173.

406 But see *A v France* (1993) 17 EHRR 462: where two parties conceived and carried out a plan to make a recording of telephone conversations, it was conceded that the actions constituted an interference with 'correspondence' of the applicant. The issue was whether the actions involved a public authority so as to invoke the responsibility of the state under the Convention.

407 *Klass v Germany* (1978) 2 EHRR 214.

408 (1984) 7 EHRR 14.

409 The Government declined to disclose to what extent, if at all, the telephone calls of the applicant had been otherwise intercepted on behalf of the police.

410 See also *Huvig v France* (1990) 12 EHRR 528; which followed *Klass* and *Malone* in holding that telephone-tapping amounted to an 'interference by a public authority' with the exercise of the right to respect for 'correspondence' and 'private life'; *Kruslin v France* (1990) 12 EHRR 547: where a police wire-tap of a telephone line of one party resulted in the recording of several conversations of the applicant, leading to proceedings taken against him, the Government did not deny that there had been an 'interference'; and see *Valenzuela Contreras v Spain* (1998) 28 EHRR 483.

411 (1997) 24 EHRR 523 paras 53–58.

412 *Abdulaziz, Cabales and Balkandali v United Kingdom* (1985) 7 EHRR 471 para 67.

refrain from doing anything that might unduly infringe the right to private life. On the other hand, the state might be obliged to take positive action to protect individuals from the adverse consequences of its inaction: which might imply a further obligation to prevent acts; or even to require positive action by third parties (such as newspaper journalists) where there is a potential interference with private life. This important distinction between negative and positive obligations which flow from Convention rights was examined in Chapter 6.[413]

The Court has repeatedly stressed that the object of Article 8 is essentially that of **12.108**
protecting the individual against arbitrary interference by the public authorities:[414] this is a 'primarily negative' undertaking. Nevertheless, it has stressed that there may, in addition, be positive obligations upon states[415] that are inherent in an effective 'respect' for Article 8 rights.

Two further points should be made. First, the Court has allowed a certain margin **12.109**
of appreciation[416] to states to determine whether 'respect' for Article 8 rights demands positive action in the circumstances.[417] Secondly, there is a distinction to be made between the assessment of the content of the right under Article 8(1) and the justification process under Article 8(2). Under Article 8(1), 'in determining whether a positive obligation exists, a fair balance must be struck between the general interest of the community and the interests of the individual'.[418] In justifying an interference under subsection 8(2), the interests of the state are balanced against a right which has already been established and which has therefore, at least formally, some degree of weight attached to it.

In practice, the Court has treated the distinction rather casually.[419] It has found **12.110**
the applicable principles to be broadly similar, regardless of whether the issue is formulated as a 'positive duty on the state to take reasonable measures to secure

413 See para 6.95ff above.

414 *Belgian Linguistic (No 2)* (1968) 1 EHRR 252 para 7; cited in *Marckx v Belgium* (1979) 2 EHRR 330; *X and Y v Netherlands* (1985) 8 EHRR 235; *Abdulaziz, Cabales and Balkandali v United Kingdom* (1985) 7 EHRR 471; *Rees v United Kingdom* (1986) 9 EHRR 56; *Keegan v Ireland* (1994) 18 EHRR 342; *Hokkanen v Finland* (1994) 19 EHRR 139; *Kroon v Netherlands* (1994) 19 EHRR 263.

415 *Marckx v Belgium* (1979) 2 EHRR 330 para 31; *Airey v Ireland* (1979) 2 EHRR 305 para 32; *X and Y v Netherlands* (1985) 8 EHRR 235 para 23; see also *Johnston v Ireland* (1986) 9 EHRR 203 para 55); *Powell and Rayner v United Kingdom* (1986) 47 DR 5, 12, EComm HR. All of these cases affirm or reaffirm that 'Article 8 does not merely compel the state to abstain from interference: in addition to this, there may be positive obligations inherent in an effective respect for private and family life even in the sphere of the relations of individuals between themselves'

416 See generally, para 6.31ff above.

417 *Lopez-Ostra v Spain* (1994) 20 EHRR 277 para 51; see also *Cossey v United Kingdom* (1990) 13 EHRR 622.

418 *Cossey v United Kingdom* (n 417 above) para 37: 'the search for which balance is inherent in the whole of the Convention'.

419 See eg C Warbrick, 'The Structure of Article 8' [1998] EHRLR 32.

the rights of the applicant under Article 8(1)', or as an 'interference by a public authority to be justified in accordance with paragraph 2'. The Court has stated that in both contexts regard must be had to the fair balance between the competing interests of the individual and of the community as a whole.[420] In striking the required balance in relation to the positive obligations flowing from Article 8(1), the aims under Article 8(2) will have some relevance.[421]

12.111 **Positive action where the applicant suffers directly from inaction.** In some circumstances, the state will be required to provide positive protection where the applicant stands to suffer directly from its inaction.[422] The transsexual cases are an illustration of this approach. In none of these cases was the physical transformation of the individuals in issue; no state had prevented the treatment, and in the United Kingdom the public health system had provided it. The complaint was that the Government had failed to respect the private life of the applicants by refusing to alter their birth certificates to reflect the change in gender once the physical procedure had been undergone. In *Van Oosterwijk v Belgium*[423] the Commission said that the state 'had refused to recognise an essential element of his personality' and the effect was to 'restrict the applicant to a sex which can scarcely be considered his own'. In the four cases which have come before it, the Court has regarded the interest at stake to be the right to keep private the applicant's original sex by ensuring it would not be revealed whenever they were required to rely upon their birth certificates. In the United Kingdom cases, *Rees*,[423a] *Cossey*[423b] and *Sheffield and Horsham*,[423c] the Court weighed the fact that the certificate was intended to register the position at birth and the burden on the state if it altered the system, against the applicant's interest to have the certificate amended. In each case it held there was no failure of the state to respect the

420 *Powell and Rayner v United Kingdom* (1990) 12 EHRR 355 paras 37–46; also *Lopez-Ostra v Spain* (n 417 above) paras 47–58: 'Whether the question is analysed in terms of a positive duty on the state—to take reasonable and appropriate measures to secure the applicant's rights under para 1 of Article 8— . . . or in terms of an "interference by a public authority" to be justified in accordance with para 2, the applicable principles are broadly similar. In both contexts regard must be had to the fair balance between the competing interests of the individual and of the community as a whole, and in any case the state enjoys a certain margin of appreciation'.

421 *Powell and Rayner v United Kingdom* (n 420 above) paras 37–46 (there was 'no violation of the Convention, however the claim was framed'); *Rees v United Kingdom* (1986) 9 EHRR 56 para 37.

422 This was contemplated in *Stjerna v Finland* (1994) 24 EHRR 194, even though the applicant was unable to show that state refusal to allow registration of change of name was either a failure to respect his private life or an 'interference' requiring justification under Art 8(2). In *Gaskin v United Kingdom* (1989) 12 EHRR 36 the Court required that authorities take steps to release records of the applicant's foster care which were held to be of special importance to his private life.

423 (1979) B 36 Com Rep para 52, EComm HR.

423a (1986) 9 EHRR 56.

423b (1990) 13 EHRR 622.

423c (1998) 27 EHRR 163.

applicant's private life. In *B v France*,[424] on the other hand, the applicant succeeded because the French administrative system could be more easily changed than that of the British, and the need to rely frequently in practice on the certificate meant that a failure to rectify it would have more serious consequences for the applicants.

In *McGinley and Egan v United Kingdom*[425] a complaint was made about the withholding of documents concerning the exposure of the applicants to radiation at Christmas Island. The Court took the view that where the government engages in hazardous activities with hidden consequences for health, respect for private and family life requires an effective and accessible procedure to ensure that all relevant and appropriate information is made available. **12.112**

Positive action to prevent interference by a private individual. States might also be obliged to take positive action to prevent or stop another *individual* from interfering with private life. The argument that Article 8(2) refers only to justification of interference by a 'public authority' has been rejected by the Court as irrelevant to the question as to what rights are protected by Article 8(1). It is clear that in appropriate cases **12.113**

> there may be positive obligations inherent in effective respect for private or family life. These obligations may involve the adoption of measures designed to secure respect for private life even in the sphere of the relations of individuals between themselves . . . In order to determine whether such obligations exist, regard must be had to the fair balance that has to be struck between the general interest and the interests of the individual.[426]

Thus, a failure to provide essential information concerning severe environmental pollution was a breach of Article 8.[427] However, the limits of this approach were illustrated by *Botta v Italy*[428] where the Court held that respect for private life did not extend to giving a disabled person a right of access to the beach and sea which was distant from his normal holiday residence. Similarly, in *Barreto v Portugal*[429] the Court held that respect for private and family life did not require the existence in national law of legal protection enabling each family to have a home for themselves or giving the landlord a right to recover possession of a rented house in any circumstances.

In *Winer v United Kingdom*[430] the Commission found that the government had **12.114**

[424] (1992) 16 EHRR 1.
[425] (1998) 27 EHRR 1.
[426] *Botta v Italy* (1998) 26 EHRR 241 para 33.
[427] See *Guerra v Italy* (1998) 26 EHRR 357, para 58; see also *Lopez-Ostra v Spain* (1994) 20 EHRR 277 para 51 where the court referred to a positive duty to take 'reasonable and appropriate measures' to secure Art 8 rights.
[428] n 426 above para 34ff.
[429] [1996] EHRLR 214.
[430] (1986) 48 DR 154, EComm HR.

not failed to respect the private life of the applicant where the only remedies for protection of reputation were those available in defamation in respect of untrue statements. The Commission's reluctance to require a direct remedy for invading privacy was because this would infringe another Convention right, the freedom of expression. A similar conclusion was reached in *Earl and Countess Spencer v United Kingdom*[431] where the Commission decided that the failure to take proceedings for breach of confidence meant that the applicant had failed to exhaust his domestic remedies. The position concerning the invasion of privacy by photographs is uncertain.[432] However, it seems there is no interference with respect for privacy where the photograph is obtained in a public place.[433]

12.115 Whether or in what circumstances the positive obligation will extend to the criminalisation of private acts remains unresolved. In one instance the state was held to have a duty to provide an effective criminal remedy to ensure deterrence in relation to sexual assault,[434] but given the special facts of that case, it is unlikely to create a precedent for a wide obligation on the state to criminalise private activities. There may be cases which attract this type of obligation but it is difficult to predict whether there will be a duty to criminalise such activities as private surveillance, data collection or publication of true statements about matters of private life.

12.116 An issue arises as to whether the margin of appreciation will be different according to whether the dispute is a conflict between individual and state or one in which the state is exercising a duty of positive action in an essentially private dispute. Clapham has argued[435] that there should be a wider margin in the latter case, reflecting the greater complexity of questions which arise when the state is found to have a positive duty to intervene between individuals for the protection of human rights.

12.117 **Positive obligation to require positive action by private persons.** The obligation to provide 'respect' may impose a duty on the state to require positive action by private persons. States might be obliged to require that private data collection firms grant access to individuals to records kept about them or that the parent with custody of children allow access to the other parent or other relatives like grandparents.[436]

---

[431] (1998) 25 EHRR CD 105.

[432] See eg S Naismith, 'Photographs, Privacy and Freedom of Expression' [1996] EHRLR 150.

[433] See *Friedl v Austria* (1995) 21 EHRR 83, Com Rep paras 48 and 51.

[434] *X and Y v Netherlands* (1985) 8 EHRR 235 (failure to prosecute a sexual assault on a mentally defective girl of 16).

[435] A Clapham, *Human Rights in the Private Sphere* (Clarendon Press, 1993) 211–22.

[436] See *Hokkanen v Finland* (1994) 19 EHRR 139, Com Rep paras 129–146 which relates to family life.

(2) Justification under Article 8(2)

(a) Introduction

Under Article 8(2) interference by a public authority must be justified as being in accordance with the law and necessary in a democratic society in support of one of the following legitimate aims: **12.118**

- national security;
- public safety;
- the economic well-being of the country;
- the prevention of disorder or crime;
- the protection of health or morals; and
- the protection of the rights and freedoms of others.

(b) 'Interference by a public authority'

In order to make out his claim, the applicant must establish the fact of interference.[437] The question of whether a governmental act constitutes an interference is not usually contested by the state. The Court has therefore placed little emphasis on defining interference, focusing instead on its justification once it is determined that there is a protected right. Government acts which have been found to constitute interference include 'supervision' of correspondence,[438] stopping, delaying or failing to forward letters to the applicant,[439] impeding a person from even initiating correspondence,[440] 'secret surveillance' measures[441] including interception of telephone conversations,[442] house searches and seizures,[443] the imposition of a fine on the applicant for failing to obtain a licence to live in his own home,[444] the generation of airport noise pollution[445] and the storage and release of personal information on the applicant.[446] **12.119**

---

[437] *Campbell v United Kingdom* (1992) 15 EHRR 137 para 32; and see generally, para 6.100 above.

[438] *De Wilde, Ooms and Versyp v Belgium (No 1)* (1971) 1 EHRR 373.

[439] *Silver v United Kingdom* (1983) 5 EHRR 347; *Campbell and Fell v United Kingdom* (1984) 7 EHRR 165; *Schönenberger and Durmaz v Switzerland* (1988) 11 EHRR 202; *McCallum v United Kingdom* (1990) 13 EHRR 596; *Herczegfalvy v Austria* (1992) 15 EHRR 437.

[440] *Golder v United Kingdom* (1975) 1 EHRR 524.

[441] *Klass v Germany* (1978) 2 EHRR 214.

[442] *Malone v United Kingdom* (1984) 7 EHRR 14; *Huvig v France* (1990) 12 EHRR 528; *Kruslin v France* (1990) 12 EHRR 547; *Lüdi v Switzerland* (1992) 15 EHRR 173; *A v France* (1993) 17 EHRR 462.

[443] *Funke v France* (1993) 16 EHRR 297; *Crémieux v France* (1993) 16 EHRR 297; *Miailhe v France* (1993) 16 EHRR 332; *Murray v United Kingdom* (1994) 19 EHRR 193; *Chappell v United Kingdom* (1989) 12 EHRR 1; *Niemetz v Germany* (1992) 16 EHRR 97.

[444] *Gillow v United Kingdom* (1986) 11 EHRR 335.

[445] In *Powell and Rayner v United Kingdom* (1990) 12 EHRR 355, the Court stated that the quality of the private life of the applicant and enjoyment of amenities of his home were 'adversely affected'; see also *Lopez Ostra v Spain* (1994) 20 EHRR 277.

[446] *Leander v Sweden* (1987) 9 EHRR 433, where the storage and release of information was coupled with a refusal to allow the complainant to refute the information.

12.120 In addition, two issues have been addressed by the Court. First, it has considered whether a failure to act can be called an 'interference' requiring justification under Article 8(2). This question has been answered in the negative.[447] Where the substance of the complaint is not that the state has acted, but has failed or refused to act, it cannot be said to have 'interfered'.[448]

12.121 Secondly, the Court has considered whether an interference might be established in the absence of measures directly affecting the complainant. In these circumstances a 'victim' test has been employed: in other words, even when the alleged government acts cannot be proved the Court might nevertheless make a finding of interference on grounds that the existence of a legislative or administrative system may be sufficient in itself to constitute an interference with the Article 8 rights of the applicant. In several different contexts, the Court has held that a complainant may be victimised by an established system or legal regime if it is one which facilitates infringement, and which *might* be applied to him, whether or not an intrusion can be proven on the facts.[449] The 'victim' test[450] means that the applicant need only establish a sufficient threat or risk to the effective enjoyment of his rights, whether the potential impact is a material one or has only a psychological effect.

12.122 Thus, legislation which criminalised homosexual activity was found to be a 'continuing interference' with private life, even though the risk of proceedings against consenting adult male homosexuals was not great.[451] The applicant had, however, been investigated and the threat of prosecution was found not to be 'illusory or theoretical'. In this context it was held that the legislation affected the private life of male homosexuals, including the applicant. Similar reasoning was used by the Court in *Norris v Ireland*,[452] although there had been no criminal investigation into the homosexual activities of the applicant and in spite of arguments that the existence of the legislation posed no threat to his lifestyle.

12.123 In other areas of 'private life' and 'correspondence', a system which facilitates surreptitious interception of telephone conversations has been found to create a 'menace of surveillance', even where applicants could not prove actual interception.[453] The existence in England and Wales of laws and practices which permitted and

[447] See the discussion at para 6.100 above.

[448] *Airey v Ireland* (1979) 2 EHRR 305; however, the Court's approach to failures to carry out positive obligations has, in practice, been very similar; see, generally, para 6.100 above.

[449] Ibid; *Campbell* was a prison case involving intervention with the prisoner's correspondence; prison rules allowed for letters to be opened and read even though the applicant could not show that any particular letter had been opened.

[450] For comment on this see P Duffy, 'The Protection of Privacy, Family Life and Other Rights Under Article 8 of the European Convention on Human Rights' (1982) 2 YEL 191.

[451] *Dudgeon v United Kingdom* (1981) 4 EHRR 149 para 40.

[452] A 142 (1988) para 37.

[453] *Klass v Germany* (1978) 2 EHRR 214.

established a system for effecting secret surveillance of communications amounted in itself to an 'interference', whether or not any measures were actually taken against the applicant.[454] It was enough in the *Malone* case that the complainant, who was suspected of receiving stolen goods, was a member of a class of persons against whom measures of postal and telephone interception were liable to be employed.

A similar approach has been taken where there was a general policy of supervision of correspondence of prisoners,[455] whether or not correspondence is actually interfered with. Although in *Campbell and Fell v United Kingdom*[456] it was proved that one letter had been stopped, the Court noted that the effect of the established 'prior ventilation rule' was to prevent all correspondence between the applicants and their advisers concerning the proposed litigation until an internal inquiry had been completed. **12.124**

(c) 'In accordance with the law'

Justification of an interference under Article 8(2) requires that the measures in question be imposed 'in accordance with law'. The Court has identified a number of requirements as flowing from that phrase[457] and these are examined in detail in Chapter 6.[458] **12.125**

First, the acts being challenged must have a basis in domestic law.[459] Clearly 'in accordance with law' refers to national law,[460] which includes statute,[461] other non-statutory enactments[462] and common law,[463] as the Court has interpreted 'law' in its substantive rather than its formal sense.[464] It does not, however, merely **12.126**

454 *Malone v United Kingdom* (1984) 7 EHRR 14.

455 Supervision has been held to be 'unquestionably' an interference by a public authority with the exercise of Art 8 rights: *De Wilde, Ooms and Versyp v Belgium (No 1)* (1971) 1 EHRR 373; *Silver v United Kingdom* (1983) 5 EHRR 347 in which 64 letters were stopped or delayed.

456 (1984) 7 EHRR 165.

457 See *Olsson v Sweden (No 1)* (1988) 11 EHRR 259 in which the Court itemises them.

458 See para 6.126ff above.

459 *Leander v Sweden* (1987) 9 EHRR 433 para 50; *Chappell v United Kingdom* (1989) 12 EHRR 1 para 52; *Margareta and Roger Andersson v Sweden* (1992) 14 EHRR 615; *A v France* (1993) 17 EHRR 462 para 38; *Murray v United Kingdom* (1994) 19 EHRR 193 para 88.

460 *Campbell and Fell v United Kingdom* (1984) 7 EHRR 165 para 37.

461 *Norris v Ireland* (1988) 13 EHRR 186 para 40: the interference was plainly 'in accordance with the law' since it arose from the very existence of the impugned legislation.

462 *De Wilde, Ooms and Versyp v Belgium (No 1)* (1971) 1 EHRR 373 para 93; *Golder v United Kingdom* (1975) 1 EHRR 524 para 45 involving Prison Rules 1964.

463 See *Dudgeon v United Kingdom* (1981) 4 EHRR 149 para 44; *Kruslin v France* (1990) 12 EHRR 547 para 29; *Huvig v France* (1990) 12 EHRR 528 para 28; *Herczegfalvy v Austria* (1992) 15 EHRR 437 para 91: the provisions in question did not offer the minimum degree of protection against arbitrariness required by the rule of law and there was no case law to remedy the situation; *Murray v United Kingdom* (1994) 19 EHRR 193: the taking and retention of a photograph of the applicant without her consent had no statutory basis but was lawful under the common law.

464 *Kruslin v France* (1990) 12 EHRR 547 para 29; *Huvig v France* (1990) 12 EHRR 258 para 28.

refer to the existence of domestic law, but to the quality of the law, requiring it to be compatible with the rule of law, which is expressly mentioned in the preamble to the Convention.[465] 'In accordance with law' thus implies that the interfering measures must be accompanied by adequate and effective safeguards in the domestic law to protect against arbitrary interferences by authorities with the rights guaranteed by Article 8(1).[466] In light of the necessity of determining that measures are rooted in national law, the Court has reiterated on several occasions that its role is not to interpret and apply domestic law: this is primarily the task of the national courts.[467] The role of the Court in reviewing compliance with domestic law is relatively limited.[468]

12.127 Secondly, the law must be accessible and foreseeable. It must be accessible to the persons concerned, and formulated with sufficient precision to enable the citizen to foresee, to a reasonable degree, the consequences which a given action may entail.[469] In determining whether this criterion has been met, the Court must take into account that absolute precision is unattainable and that, in order to avoid excessive rigidity and to keep pace with changing circumstances, many laws will inevitably be couched in terms which are to some extent vague.[470] The degree of precision required of the 'law' will depend upon the particular subject matter.[471] Thus, a prisoner who was unable to read unpublished regulations succeeded in establishing that the procedure was not in accordance with the law.[472]

12.128 In the special context of secret surveillance,[473] the Convention requirement of

---

465 *Malone v United Kingdom* (1984) 7 EHRR 14 para 67; *Silver v United Kingdom* (1983) 5 EHRR 347 para 90; *Golder v United Kingdom* (1975) 1 EHRR 524 para 34.

466 *Malone v United Kingdom* (n 465 above) para 67; *Herczegfalvy v Austria* (1992) 15 EHRR 437 para 91; *Rieme v Sweden* (1992) 16 EHRR 155 para 60: although a basis in Swedish law was undisputed, the applicant argued (unsuccessfully) that the law in question did not afford him adequate protection against arbitrary interference; *Chappell v United Kingdom* (1989) 12 EHRR 1 para 56 discusses Anton Piller orders in United Kingdom law and their associated dangers which necessitate accompanying provisions safeguarding against arbitrary interference and abuse; see also *Eriksson v Sweden* (1989) 12 EHRR 183 para 60 and *Olsson v Sweden (No 1)* (1988) 11 EHRR 259 para 62 which discuss safeguards in relation to taking children into public care: 'preparatory work' providing guidance as to the exercise of the discretion conferred, and administrative review at several levels.

467 *Olsson v Sweden (No 2)* (1992) 17 EHRR 134 para 79; *Andersson v Sweden* (1992) 14 EHRR 615 para 82; *Kruslin v France* (1990) 12 EHRR 547 para 29; *Eriksson v Sweden* (1989) 12 EHRR 183 para 62; *Chappell v United Kingdom* (1989) 12 EHRR 1 para 54; *Campbell v United Kingdom* (1992) 15 EHRR 137 para 37: it is not for the Court to examine the validity of secondary legislation.

468 *Eriksson v Sweden* (1989) 12 EHRR 183 para 62.

469 *Olsson v Sweden (No 1)* (1988) 11 EHRR 259 para 61.

470 *Silver v United Kingdom* (1983) 5 EHRR 347 para 88; *Olsson v Sweden (No 1)* (n 469 above); see also *Sunday Times v United Kingdom (No 1)* (1979) 2 EHRR 245 para 49.

471 *Sunday Times v United Kingdom* (n 470 above) para 49; *Malone v United Kingdom* (1984) 7 EHRR 14 para 67.

472 *Silver v United Kingdom* (n 470 above); *Petra v Roumania* RJD 1998–VII 2844.

473 *Malone v United Kingdom* (n 471 above) para 79; *Hewitt and Harman v United Kingdom* (1989) 67 DR 88, 99, EComm HR; *N v United Kingdom* (1989) 67 DR 123, 132, EComm HR; *Kruslin v France* (1990) 12 EHRR 547 para 17.

foreseeability cannot be exactly the same as it is where the law seeks to restrict the conduct of individuals. It obviously does not require the authorities to give the applicant advance warning of the surveillance: it is enough that he knows whether he might be subject to surveillance. Nevertheless, Article 8 requires that the law must be sufficiently clear in its terms to:

> give citizens an adequate indication as to the circumstances in which and the conditions on which public authorities are empowered to resort to this secret and potentially dangerous interference with the right to respect for private life and correspondence.[474]

It is essential to have clear, detailed rules on the subject.[475] The Court has made it clear that the following minimum safeguards should be set out in the statute in order to avoid abuse of power:

> a definition of the categories of people liable to have their telephones tapped by judicial order, the nature of the offences which may give rise to such an order, a limit on the duration of the telephone tapping, the procedure for drawing up the summary reports containing intercepted conversations, the precautions to be taken in order to communicate the recordings intact and in their entirety for possible inspection by the judge and by the defence and the circumstances in which recordings may or must be erased or the tapes destroyed, in particular where an accused has been discharged by an investigating judge or acquitted by a court.[476]

Thirdly, a law which confers a discretion is not in itself inconsistent with the requirement of foreseeability, provided that the scope of the discretion and the manner of its exercise are indicated with sufficient clarity, having regard to the legitimate aim of the measure in question, to give the individual adequate protection against arbitrary interference.[477] A related issue is the extent to which the necessary detail must itself be contained in the substantive law, as opposed to accompanying administrative practice and associated directives.[478] This point was considered in the *Silver*[479] case in which the Court stated that although the scope of the discretion must be indicated in the law, it is not necessary that the detailed procedures be contained in rules of substantive law. In that case administrative directives nonetheless constituted an established practice that was to be followed save in exceptional circumstances, rather than one that varied with each individual case. **12.129**

474 *Malone v United Kingdom* (n 471 above) para 67.

475 See *Valenzuela Contreras v Spain* (1998) 28 EHRR 483 para 46, Principle (iii).

476 Ibid para 46, Principle (iv), relying on *Kruslin v France* (1990) 12 EHRR 547 para 35 and *Huvig v France* (1990) 12 EHRR 528 para 34.

477 *Malone v United Kingdom* (1984) 7 EHRR 14 para 67; *Gillow v United Kingdom* (1986) 11 EHRR 335 para 51; *Olsson v Sweden (No 1)* (1988) 11 EHRR 259 para 61; *Kruslin v France* (1990) 12 EHRR 547; *Andersson v Sweden* (1992) 14 EHRR 615; *Eriksson v Sweden* (1989) 12 EHRR 183 para 60.

478 *Malone v United Kingdom* (n 477 above) para 68; *Silver v United Kingdom* (1983) 5 EHRR 347 paras 88–90.

479 (1983) 5 EHRR 347.

On the other hand, where the practice applied in a particular case conflicted with the administrative safeguards in place, the applicant succeeded in proving that the authorities had not acted in accordance with the law.[480]

12.130 Following the decision in *Malone v United Kingdom*[481] that there was no legal basis in the United Kingdom for the interception of telephone conversations,[482] Parliament enacted the Interception of Communications Act 1985 which now provides a statutory foundation for telephone-tapping which meets the substantive as well as formal requirements of 'law'.[483] Similarly, the Security Services Act of 1989 remedied the lack of foundation for secret surveillance indicated in *Hewitt and Harman v United Kingdom.*[484] In France, the law that 'the investigating judge shall, in accordance with the law, take all investigative measures which he deems useful for establishing the truth',[485] and case law to the effect that such measures included telephone-tapping did not provide sufficient safeguards against abuse of the power to render it in accordance with 'law' under Article 8. Furthermore, where a court rejected a complaint about illegal surveillance on the ground that the telephone line that was tapped belonged to a third party, the Court held there was a breach of Article 8.[486] The law of telephone-tapping in Luxembourg, on the other hand, exhibited the necessary detail and provision for control of the use of the discretion so as to be in accordance with 'law.'[487]

(d) 'Necessary in a democratic society' for a legitimate aim

12.131 Article 8(2) provides that:

> there shall be no interference by a public authority with the exercise of this right except such as is in accordance with the law and is necessary in a democratic society in the interests of
>
> (a) national security,
> (b) public safety, or
> (c) the economic well-being of the country;
> (d) for the prevention of disorder or crime,

[480] *Kopp v Switzerland* (1998) 27 EHRR 91.
[481] (1984) 7 EHRR 14.
[482] (1984) 7 EHRR 14.
[483] *Christie v United Kingdom* (1993) 78–A DR 119, 133, EComm HR: the Commission declared inadmissible an application claiming that the legislation was not sufficient protection against abuse of the power to issue warrants, see generally, para 12.66ff above.
[484] (1989) 67 DR 88: for comment see I Leigh and L Lustgarten (1989) 52 MLR 801. The enactment of the Intelligence Services Act 1994 provides further statutory foundation for secret surveillance procedures: for comment see J Wadham, 'The Intelligence Services Act 1994' (1994) 57 MLR 916.
[485] Code of Criminal Procedure, Art 81.
[486] *Lambert v France* RJD 1998-V 2230.
[487] *Mersch v Luxembourg* (1985) 43 DR 34, 94, 114, EComm HR (the Commission acknowledged the presence of the ultimate safeguard: the Convention was directly applicable in Luxembourg law).

(e) for the protection of health or morals, or
(f) for the protection of the rights and freedoms of others.

The state must identify at least one of these objectives as a basis for its claim that its interference with privacy is necessary in a democratic society. The legitimate aims are similar to those set out in Articles 9 to 11 of the Convention, with the distinction that Article 8(2) permits interference in the interests of 'the economic well-being of the country'.[488]

The Court has dealt with the meaning of the phrase 'necessary in a democratic society', the nature of the functions of the Court in the examination of issues turning on that phrase, and the manner in which it performs those functions on a number of occasions.[489] The relevant principles are discussed in Chapter 6.[490] The following general points can be made. First, the term 'necessary' is not synonymous with 'indispensable' but does not have the flexibility of such expressions as 'admissible', 'ordinary', 'useful', 'reasonable' or 'desirable'.[491] Secondly, 'necessary in a democratic society', in the context of Article 8, as in connection with other Convention interests, requires the state to demonstrate that the interference corresponds to a 'pressing social need' and that it is 'proportionate' to the legitimate aim.[492] Thirdly, it is for the authorities of Member States to make the initial assessment as to necessity: a certain margin of appreciation[493] is left to them, subject to review by the Court. Fourthly, in search and seizure cases it is necessary to show that there are procedures in place which provide adequate and effective safeguards against abuse.[493a] Thus, in *Camenzind v Switzerland*[493b] the Court emphasised that if individuals are to be protected from arbitrary interference by the authorities with Article 8 rights, there must be a legal framework and very strict limits on the powers it confers. **12.132**

It is well established that the exceptions under Article 8(2) are to be interpreted narrowly and the need for them in a given case must be convincingly **12.133**

488 See generally, para 6.144 above.
489 See *Dudgeon v United Kingdom* (1981) 4 EHRR 149 paras 50–54, 60; *Silver v United Kingdom* (1983) 5 EHRR 347 paras 97–98.
490 See para 6.146ff above.
491 *Handyside v United Kingdom* (1976) 1 EHRR 737 para 48; cited in *Silver v United Kingdom* (1983) 5 EHRR 347 para 97; and see generally, para 6.148 above.
492 *Handyside v United Kingdom* (1976) 1 EHRR 737 para 48; *Dudgeon v United Kingdom* (1981) 4 EHRR 149, para 51; *Silver v United Kingdom* (1983) 5 EHRR 347 para 97; *Gillow v United Kingdom* (1986) 11 EHRR 335 para 55; *Leander v Sweden* (1987) 9 EHRR 433 para 58; *Olsson v Sweden (No 1)* (1988) 11 EHRR 259, para 67; *Schönenberger and Durmaz v Switzerland* (1988) 11 EHRR 202 para 27; *Berrehab v Netherlands* (1988) 11 EHRR 322 para 28; *Moustaquim v Belgium* (1991) 13 EHRR 802 para 43 (as to family life); *Campbell v United Kingdom* (1992) 15 EHRR 137 paras 44, 53; *Beldjoudi v France* (1992) 14 EHRR 801 para 74; and see generally, para 6.147 above.
493 See generally, para 6.31ff above.
493a See eg *Funke v France* (1993) 16 EHRR 297 para 56; *Miailhe v France* (1993) 16 EHRR 332 para 37; *Crémieux v France* (1993) A 256-B para 39.
493b RJD 1997–III 2880 para 45.

established.[494] There is no scope for implying limitations to Article 8.[495] Furthermore, as the Court emphasised in *Dudgeon v United Kingdom*,[496] where the restrictions concern a most intimate part of an individual's private life, there must be particularly serious reasons to satisfy the requirements of justifying Article 8(2). The detailed factual analysis which should be undertaken is illustrated in the recent cases of *Lustig-Prean v United Kingdom*[497] and *Smith and Grady v United Kingdom*;[498] the Government failed to show that the investigations into the applicant's sexual orientation (once they had confirmed their homosexuality) and subsequent dismissal were sufficiently convincing and weighty to comply with Article 8(2).

12.134 **National security and public safety.** Justification that has as its objective the protection of national security and public safety is readilyestablished. This is particularly true in the context of secret surveillance. While in most cases search and seizure procedures will be carried out under criminal law procedures and require at least judicial authorisation by warrant,[499] where the state can show that there are 'exceptional conditions', surreptitious measures of surveillance will be justified. For example, sophisticated techniques of foreign espionage in *Klass v Germany*[500] justified exceptional telephone tapping counteraction measures, and internal terrorist activity in *Leander* amounted to a serious threat to national security which justified the collection of information and maintenance of secret files on candidates for sensitive employment positions.[501]

12.135 **The economic well-being of the country.** The unusual ground of the economic well-being of the country has been found to justify a wide variety of government activities: a licensing scheme for the occupation of premises;[502] immigration control policy;[503] the operation of an international airport;[504] customs investigation

494 See eg *Klass v Germany* (1978) 2 EHRR 214 para 42; *Silver v United Kingdom* (1983) 5 EHRR 347 para 97; *Funke v France* (1993) 16 EHRR 297 para 55.

495 See *Golder v United Kingdom* (1975) 1 EHRR 524 para 44; and see para 6.116 above.

496 (1981) 4 EHRR 149 para 52.

497 (1999) 7 BHRC 65 paras 83–104.

498 (2000) 29 EHRR 493 paras 90–111.

499 See eg *Funke v France* (1993) 16 EHRR 297, in which the lack of prior judicial authorisation was determinative in regard to a search of the applicant's house resulting in seizure of documents and collection of information as to his foreign assets; even a warrant may not be sufficient: see *Niemetz v Germany* (1992) 16 EHRR 97 where a search for documents was found disproportionate to the aim of prevention of crime and protection of rights of others, even though a warrant had been procured.

500 A 28 (1978) para 56: the aim of the G10 is to safeguard national security and/or prevent disorder or crime.

501 *Leander v Sweden* (1987) 9 EHRR 433 para 60 in regard to the Swedish personnel control system.

502 *Gillow v United Kingdom* (1986) 11 EHRR 335.

503 *Berrehab v Netherlands* (1988) 11 EHRR 322.

504 *Powell and Rayner v United Kingdom* (1990) 12 EHRR 355.

procedures;[505] and disclosure of medical records for the purpose of assessing a social security claim.[506]

In *Gillow v United Kingdom*,[507] as a consequence of a change in the law the applicants, who had lost their 'residence qualifications' and were refused the required licence to live in their house in Guernsey, were convicted and fined for unlawful occupation of the premises. The Court held that it was legitimate for the authorities to try to maintain the population within limits that would permit the balanced economic development of the island. It was also legitimate for them to discriminate in the granting of licences in favour of persons who had strong attachments to the island, or who were engaged in an employment essential to the community. However, there was a breach in the application of the legislation of the facts. **12.136**

The existence of large international airports, even in densely populated urban areas, and the increasing use of jet aircraft have also become necessary in the interests of a country's economic well-being. The Court in *Powell and Rayner*[508] found that Heathrow Airport occupies a position of central importance in international trade and communications and in the economy of the United Kingdom. The applicants conceded that the Government had pursued a legitimate aim, and that the negative impact on the environment which resulted could not be entirely eliminated. **12.137**

Customs investigations leading to seizure of information about assets abroad and documents concerning foreign bank accounts in connection with customs offences under French law, though 'perhaps also for the prevention of crime' as held by the Commission, were primarily in the interests of the economic well-being of the country.[509] **12.138**

In *M S v Sweden*[510] the applicant had injured her back in an accident while at work. When, a number of years later, she made a claim for compensation under the Industrial Injury Insurance Act, it was discovered that copies of her confidential medical records had been submitted by the clinic to the Social Insurance Office, in breach of professional secrecy contrary to the Secrecy Act 1980. The Court decided that the interference was justified as all the information disclosed was necessary and relevant for the determination of the applicant's claim for compensation; and it was necessary for the economic well-being of the country to ensure that public funds were only allocated to deserving claimants. **12.139**

505 *Funke v France* (1993) 16 EHRR 297.
506 *M S v Sweden* RJD 1997–IV 1437.
507 (1986) 11 EHRR 335.
508 *Powell and Rayner v United Kingdom* (1990) 12 EHRR 355.
509 *Funke v France* (1993) 16 EHRR 297; also *Crémieux v France* (1993) 16 EHRR 357; and *Miailhe v France* (1993) 16 EHRR 332.
510 RJD 1997–IV 1437.

12.140 **For the prevention of disorder or crime.** Measures interfering with Article 8(1) rights which have been found to be for the legitimate aim of the prevention of disorder and crime include the supervision of prisoners' correspondence,[511] telephone interception and other forms of secret surveillance,[512] immigration control policy[513] and searches for and seizure of documents and other physical evidence in connection with alleged offences.

12.141 When considering whether searches and seizures for the prevention of disorder and crime are necessary, the Court will look at the seriousness of the interference, the nature of the crime involved and the presence or absence of judicial warrant. The search of the office of a lawyer who was accused of insulting and imposing pressure on a judge was found to be disproportionate to its aim[514] on grounds that the warrant was a broadly framed order for seizure of 'documents' without limitation, and unduly infringed professional secrecy. In *Funke v France*[515] the Court agreed that measures including house searches and seizures (which 'might' be for the prevention of crime but were undoubtedly in the interests of the economic well-being of the country) were necessary in order to obtain physical evidence of exchange-control offences and to prevent outflow of capital and tax evasion, but nevertheless held that the legislation did not provide adequate safeguards against abuse of the wide powers available to customs authorities. The Court also emphasised that in the absence of the requirement of a judicial warrant, conditions and restrictions on the law were too lax to ensure that interferences with the rights of the applicant were proportionate to the aim pursued.[516] In *McLeod v United Kingdom*[517] the entry of police officers into the applicant's home to prevent a breach of the peace was disproportionate to the legitimate aim of the prevention of disorder. On the other hand, in *Camenzind v Switzerland*[517a] the specific procedures in place and the limited scope of the search were a proportionate interference with the right of respect for the home. Similarly, in *Murray v United Kingdom*[518] entry and search of the Murray family home by military authorities in Northern Ireland was not disproportionate to the aim of arresting Mrs Murray, who was reasonably

---

511 *De Wilde, Ooms and Versyp v Belgium (No 1)* (1971) 1 EHRR 373; *Schönenberger and Durmaz v Switzerland* (1988) 11 EHRR 202; *Pfeifer and Plankl v Austria* (1992) 14 EHRR 692; *Campbell v United Kingdom* (1992) 15 EHRR 137.

512 *Lüdi v Switzerland* (1992) 15 EHRR 173; *Klass v Germany* (1978) 2 EHRR 214.

513 *Beldjoudi v France* (1992) 14 EHRR 801.

514 *Niemetz v Germany* (1992) 16 EHRR 97; (the interference pursued aims that were legitimate under Act 8(2), namely the prevention of crime and protection of the rights of others, that is the honour of the judge).

515 (1993) 16 EHRR 297; *Miailhe v France* (1993) 16 EHRR 332; *Crémieux v France* (1993) A 256-B.

516 See also *Crémieux v France* (n 515 above); and *Miailhe v France* (n 515 above).

517 (1998) 27 EHRR 493; for the decision in English law see *McLeod v Commissioner of Police of the Metropolis* [1994] 4 All ER 553, see para 12.19 above.

517a RJD 1997–III 2880 paras 45–47.

518 (1994) 19 EHRR 193.

suspected of terrorist-linked crime. The Court noted that special precautions were justified as a means to that end, given the 'conditions of extreme tension' under which such arrests in Northern Ireland had to be carried out.

The significance of the particular applicant's interest emerges clearly from the cases involving interference with prisoners' correspondence. Although some measure of control of prisoners' correspondence is not incompatible with the Convention,[519] the Court has given high priority in this context to protecting the right of prisoners to communicate with their legal advisers. In *Golder v United Kingdom*[520] the Court rejected the Government's argument that a refusal of the authorities to transmit a letter from prisoner to solicitor regarding the prospect of action against a prison official, was necessary to prevent disorder. In *Campbell v United Kingdom*[521] the introduction of Standing Orders for English and Scottish prisons which allowed the opening and reading of letters regarding prospective legal proceedings, but not those already in progress, was held to infringe Article 8. Clearly no useful distinction could be made between instituted and contemplated proceedings and the privilege attached to all such letters was upheld, requiring that the government must at least show reasonable cause for suspecting that the correspondence contains illicit material before opening it. **12.142**

Correspondence in general does not require the same degree of confidentiality as lawyer-client communications, but powers of supervision,[522] interception and scrutiny must not be exercised under general terms which would expose the contents of unobjectionable letters, but must relate to some specific objection. However, in *Schönenberger and Durmaz v Switzerland*[523] the Court accepted that preventing disorder or crime may justify wider measures of interference for convicted prisoners than individuals who are at liberty. Nevertheless, measures such as stopping letters which hold the prison authorities up to contempt, or deleting passages of private letters may be disproportionate to the aim of ensuring the protection of the rights of others or the prevention of crime.[524] Telephone surveillance measures have been justified on grounds of prevention of disorder and crime as well as national security. In *Z v Finland*[525] the Court had to consider balancing the confidentiality of information about a person's HIV infection against the interests of the public in investigating and prosecuting crime and having public court proceedings; and stressed that interference with Article 8 could only be justified by an overriding requirement of the public interest. **12.143**

519 See eg *Pfeifer and Plankl v Austria* (1992) 14 EHRR 692 para 46.
520 (1975) 1 EHRR 524 para 45.
521 (1992) 15 EHRR 137 see also *Foxley v United Kingdom, The Times*, 4 Jul 2000.
522 See *De Wilde, Ooms and Versyp v Belgium (No 1)* (1971) 1 EHRR 373.
523 (1988) 11 EHRR 202.
524 *Pfeifer and Plankl v Austria* (1992) 14 EHRR 692.
525 (1997) 25 EHRR 371.

12.144 **For the protection of health or morals.** Interferences justified on grounds of the protection of health alone usually involve the taking of children into care by public authorities[526] and impact not on private life, home or correspondence but on family life.[527] The 'protection of morals and of the rights and freedoms of others'[528] or the 'protection of health and morals'[529] have been claimed as the basis for interference with prisoners' correspondence; and the 'protection of morals' alone has been asserted most often in conjunction with restrictions on sexual activity. This is an area in which the Court has required particularly substantial reasons to justify the interference. So, for example, the existence of legislation in Northern Ireland dating back to 1861 and 1885[530] nevertheless contravened the Article 8 rights of the applicant to his private life.[531] The decision of the Court was taken in the face of a contrary assessment by the United Kingdom and wide support for the existing position in Northern Ireland; it relied instead on the developing European consensus towards eliminating criminal sanctions and the absence of evidence to show that the failure of Northern Ireland authorities to implement the law had reduced moral standards. The Court affirmed the qualities of broad-mindedness and tolerance as features of a democratic society and held that the shock factor of homosexual practices was not sufficient justification for criminalising them.[532]

12.145 **For the protection of the rights and freedoms of others.** The protection of rights and freedoms of others is generally coupled with other bases for justification under Article 8(2) and has most often been cited in connection with cases involving 'family'[533] rather than 'private' life. In the *Vagrancy* case[534] the aim of restrictions in connection with the supervision of prisoners' correspondence was not discussed or questioned before the Court, but the Commission had considered whether each interference was necessary for one of the purposes pleaded by the

526 See *W v United Kingdom* (1987) 10 EHRR 29; *B v United Kingdom* (1987) 10 EHRR 87; *R v United Kingdom* (1987) 10 EHRR 74.

527 See para 13.119 below.

528 *Silver v United Kingdom* (1983) 5 EHRR 347.

529 *De Wilde, Ooms and Versyp v Belgium (No 1)* (1971) 1 EHRR 373.

530 The scope of the legislation had been restricted in England, Scotland and Wales, but remained unchanged in Northern Ireland.

531 *Dudgeon v United Kingdom* (1981) 4 EHRR 149.

532 *Norris v Ireland* (1988) 13 EHRR 186.

533 *W v United Kingdom* (1987) 10 EHRR 29; *B v United Kingdom* (1987) 10 EHRR 87; *R v United Kingdom* (1987) 10 EHRR 74; *Olsson v Sweden (No 1)* (1988) 11 EHRR 259: a decision to take children into care had legitimate aims of protecting health and morals and protecting the rights and freedoms of others; see also *Olsson v Sweden (No 2)* (1992) 17 EHRR 134; *Andersson v Sweden* (1992) 14 EHRR 615; *Keegan v Ireland* (1994) 18 EHRR 342; *Hokkanen v Finland* (1994) 19 EHRR 139; *Eriksson v Sweden* (1989) 12 EHRR 183: legislation was clearly designed to protect the rights of children on the lifting of a care order. Though restrictions had no basis in domestic law, the Court was convinced that they were imposed with the legitimate aim of protecting the health and rights of the child.

534 *De Wilde, Ooms and Versyp v Belgium (No 1)* (1971) 1 EHRR 373.

Government: protection of morals or protection of the rights and freedoms of others.

In other contexts, the protection of the 'honour' of a judge, coupled with prevention of crime, was not sufficient justification for a blanket warrant to search a lawyer's office for 'documents'.[535] A search of the home of a video dealer being sued in breach of copyright was, however, justified as a legitimate means of protecting the rights of others in that it served to defend the plaintiffs' copyright against unauthorised infringement.[536] The proceedings were civil and a seizure order (formerly an *Anton Piller* order) was employed in order to keep the evidence from 'disappearing'; even though the invasion of privacy was 'disturbing, unfortunate and regrettable' the order was not disproportionate to that end.[537] **12.146**

Finally, the retention and use of personal information collected about an individual may require justification separate and apart from that of the collection itself. If information is used for a purpose other than that for which it was legitimately collected, this may constitute an interference. For example, in *T V v Finland*[538] the fact that a prisoner was HIV-positive was disclosed to prison staff directly involved in his custody; they were themselves subject to rules of confidentiality and the disclosure of the information was found to be justified in 'the interests of others'. **12.147**

D. The Impact of the Human Rights Act

(1) Introduction

The absence of a right to privacy in English law demonstrates the limited capacity of the common law to evolve new ways of protecting human rights. As Sir Robert Megarry V-C emphasised in *Malone v Metropolitan Police Commissioner*[539] when rejecting a claim that telephone tapping breached the 'right to privacy': **12.148**

> it is no function of the courts to legislate in a new field. The extension of the existing laws and principles is one thing, the creation of an altogether new right is another. At times judges must, and do, legislate; but as Holmes J once said, they do so only interstitially, and with molecular rather than molar motion: see *Southern Pacific Co v Jensen* (1917) 244 US 205, 221, in a dissenting judgment. Anything beyond that must be left for legislation. No new right in law, fully-fledged with all the appropriate safeguards, can spring from the head of a judge deciding a particular case; only Parliament can create such a right.

535 *Niemetz v Germany* (1992) 16 EHRR 97.
536 *Chappell v United Kingdom* (1989) 12 EHRR 1.
537 Ibid para 65–66.
538 (1994) 76A DR 140, EComm HR.
539 [1979] Ch 344, 372; see also *Kaye v Robertson* [1991] FSR 62.

The bundle of rights which the English law provides[540] gives only patchy and incomplete protection for the citizen. However, the position will radically alter as a result of the Human Rights Act. Public authorities[541] will be required to respect privacy rights, reversing the decision in *Malone v Metropolitan Police Commissioner*. Furthermore, the fact that section 6(3) of the Act requires a court (or tribunal) in private litigation to act in a way which is not incompatible with privacy rights[542] may have a substantial impact on 'privacy' rights in the context of private litigation.

12.149 The obligation to 'respect for the home' will also have important ramifications for public authorities. Where an administrative decision interferes with the right,[543] the starting point will be that the decision–maker must not act incompatibly with Convention rights; although the public authority can justify the interference under Article 8(2), the exceptions are to be interpreted narrowly and the need for them in a given case must be convincingly established.[544]

12.150 The incorporation of Article 8 will therefore lead to some of the most important developments which result from the Human Rights Act. It will have an important impact on employment rights, on public bodies regulating the media and on police powers of search and surveillance. It will also have some effect on the areas of civil litigation, commercial and criminal law, freedom of information, local government, mental health and planning and environmental law.

12.151 The potential impact of the Human Rights Act on the media generated considerable concern during the passage of the Bill and led to the inclusion of section 12 which was designed to provide stricter tests for the granting of interlocutory injunctions to restrain interference with privacy.[545] These issues are considered in Chapter 15.[546] The impact of the Act on the 'privacy rights' of citizens against private bodies depends on the extent to which it has 'horizontal effect'. In accordance with the approach to 'horizontality' outlined above,[547] the Human Rights Act is likely to have a significant impact on the development of the common law in relation to privacy.

(2) United Kingdom cases prior to the Human Rights Act

(a) Introduction

12.152 A large number of applications based on Article 8 have come before the Commission and the Court. The United Kingdom has been found to have violated the

540 See para 12.09ff above.
541 See para 5.03ff above.
542 See generally, para 5.38ff above.
543 See para 12.95ff above.
544 *Funke v France* (1993) 16 EHRR 297 para 55.
545 See *Hansard*, HC col 535 (2 Jul 1998) (Home Secretary introducing s 12).
546 See para 15.237ff below.
547 See Chap 4 above.

right to respect for private life, home and correspondence on 17 occasions.[548] The majority of Article 8 cases under these had fallen into three general categories: prisoners' privacy rights, telephone tapping and surveillance and complaints concerning privacy and sexual relationships. However, several other important issues have also been considered.

(b) Prisoners' rights

Prisoners have successfully challenged the interference with their correspondence on several occasions. In *Golder v United Kingdom*[549] the letters of the applicant to his MP were stopped and he was refused permission to consult a solicitor. The Court held that these constituted the most far-reaching interference with the applicant's right to respect for correspondence. In *Silver v United Kingdom*[550] the applicants complained of letters being stopped because of a 'prior ventilation' rule and the Court found that the majority of them had not been legitimately stopped.[551] The case of *Campbell v United Kingdom*[552] concerned the regular opening and screening of a prisoner's letters to his solicitor. This was again held to be an unjustified interference with his Article 8 rights. However, it has been made clear that prisoners' rights to correspondence can be legitimately restricted in accordance with Article 8(2). Thus, the practices of reading prisoners' letters[553] and restricting the numbers of letters which prisoners may send[554] have been upheld. In *Galloway v United Kingdom*[554a] the Commission rejected a complaint that mandatory drug tests in prisons breached Article 8. **12.153**

(c) Telephone tapping and surveillance

In *Malone v United Kingdom*[555] the applicant complained that his telephone had been tapped by the police. The Court held that the regulation of telephone tapping by administrative practice was not regulation 'in accordance with the law'. This case resulted in the enactment of the Interception of Communications Act **12.154**

548 *Golder v United Kingdom* (1975) 1 EHRR 524; *Dudgeon v United Kingdom* (1981) 4 EHRR 149; *Silver v United Kingdom* (1983) 5 EHRR 347; *Campbell and Fell v United Kingdom* (1984) 7 EHRR 165; *Malone v United Kingdom* (1984) 7 EHRR 14; *Gillow v United Kingdom* (1986) 11 EHRR 335; *Boyle and Rice v United Kingdom* (1988) 10 EHRR 425; *Gaskin v United Kingdom* (1989) 12 EHRR 36; *McCallum v United Kingdom* (1990) 13 EHRR 596; *Campbell v United Kingdom* (1992) 15 EHRR 137; *Halford v United Kingdom* (1997) 24 EHRR 523; *McLeod v United Kingdom* (1998) 27 EHRR 493; *Lustig-Prean v United Kingdom* (1999) 7 BHRC 65; *Smith and Grady v United Kingdom*, (2000) 29 EHRR 493; *Khan v United Kingdom*, *The Times*, 23 May 2000; *Foxley v United Kingdom*, *The Times*, 4 Jul 2000; *ADT v United Kingdom*, Judgment, 31 Jul 2000.

549 (1975) 1 EHRR 524.

550 (1983) 5 EHRR 347; and see also *McCallum v United Kingdom* (1990) 13 EHRR 596.

551 See also *Campbell and Fell v United Kingdom* (1984) 7 EHRR 165.

552 (1992) 15 EHRR 137.

553 *Boyle and Rice v United Kingdom* (1988) 10 EHRR 425.

554 See *Chester v United Kingdom* (1990) 60 DR 65.

554a (1998) 27 EHRR CD 241.

555 (1984) 7 EHRR 14.

1985. The Act itself has been held to satisfy the requirements of Article 8.[556] However, the Act does not apply to tapping of calls on internal communications systems operated by public authorities. As a result, the interception of office telephone calls was held in *Halford v United Kingdom*[557] to constitute a breach of Article 8. Complaints have also been made about other forms of surveillance by the police. In *Govell v United Kingdom*[558] the Commission declared admissible an application relating to the lack of legal authority for intrusive police surveillance. In *Khan v United Kingdom*[558a] the Court held that, in the absence of a scheme of statutory regulation,[558b] the use of a secret listening device was not 'in accordance with the law'. As a result, the interference with the applicant's rights under Article 8 could not be justified.

12.155 Applications have also been brought in relation to surveillance by the security service. The Commission held that a security check was not, of itself, objectionable; but could be where it was based on information about a person's private life.[559] In *Hewitt and Harman (No 1) v United Kingdom*[560] the applicants were both employed by the National Council for Civil Liberties and complained that they had been placed under secret surveillance by the security service. The Commission ruled the complaint to be admissible on the basis that the interference with the private life of the applicant was not 'in accordance with the law'. A friendly settlement was reached with the applicants and the Security Service was placed on a statutory basis by the Security Services Act 1989.[561] In *Esbester v United Kingdom*[562] the Commission held that the Security Services Act meant that secret surveillance by the Security Service was 'in accordance with the law'. A similar challenge to the activities of the security services was rejected by the Commission in *Hewitt and Harman (No 2) v United Kingdom*[563] in which the Commission dismissed the application as 'manifestly ill-founded'.

(d) Privacy and sexual relationships

12.156 Complaints about interference with private life by legislation regulating sexual orientation have frequently been made. In *X v United Kingdom*[564] the applicant

556 *Christie v United Kingdom* (1994) 78–A DR 119, EComm HR.
557 (1997) 24 EHRR 523.
558 (1996) 23 EHRR CD 101 (admissibility), [1999] EHRLR 191 (merits: the Commission found violations of Arts 8 and 13); see also *Khan v United Kingdom* Application 35394/97, 20 Apr 1999 (ECtHR: admissibility decision arising out of *R v Khan* [1997] AC 558).
558a *The Times*, 23 May 2000.
558b The use of such devices is now regarded by the Police Act 1997, see para 12.59ff above.
559 *Hilton v United Kingdom* (1988) 57 DR 108, EComm HR; and *N v United Kingdom* (1989) 67 DR 123, EComm HR.
560 (1991) 14 EHRR 657.
561 See para 12.62ff above.
562 (1994) 18 EHRR CD 72.
563 (1991) 47 DR 88, EComm HR.
564 (1978) 3 EHRR 63.

had been found guilty of buggery of two 18-year-old males. The Commission took the view that the age of consent of 21 for homosexuals was an interference with the applicant's private life under Article 8 but was 'justified as being necessary in a democratic society for the protection of the rights of others'.

The most important case in this area is the Northern Ireland case of *Dudgeon v United Kingdom*.[565] The applicant complained that the laws restricting homosexual conduct were an interference with his private life. The Court agreed, holding that, even though the applicant had not in fact been prosecuted, the very existence of the legislation continuously and directly affected his private life. It also rejected the Government's contention that the legislation was 'necessary in a democratic society', noting that it differed from the position in the large majority of Council of Europe states. This case led to the Homosexual Offences (NI) Order 1982 which brought the law in Northern Ireland into line with the rest of the United Kingdom. It was followed in cases relating to Ireland[566] and Cyprus[567] and it is now clear that legislation criminalising any type of homosexual activity is contrary to Article 8.[568] **12.157**

Transsexuals have contended that the refusal of the United Kingdom authorities to change the sex indicated on the register of births constituted a breach of their rights under Article 8. Such a claim by a female to male transsexual was rejected by the Court in *Rees v United Kingdom*.[569] It was held that the mere refusal to alter the register of births could not constitute an 'interference' under Article 8 and that the positive obligations to protect privacy rights did not extend as far as making arrangements to assist transsexuals. A similar result was reached in the male to female transsexual case of *Cossey v United Kingdom*;[570] and again in the cases of *X, Y and Z v United Kingdom*[571] and *Sheffield and Horsham v United Kingdom*.[572] **12.158**

In *Laskey, Jaggard and Brown v United Kingdom*[573] the applicants had engaged in sado-masochistic acts and were convicted of assault occasioning actual bodily harm. The applicants' argument that this constituted an unjustified interference with their right to private life was rejected by the Court. It was common ground that the interference pursued the legitimate aim of the 'protection of health or morals' and the Court held that the interference was 'necessary in a democratic **12.159**

565 (1981) 4 EHRR 149.
566 *Norris v Ireland* (1988) 13 EHRR 186.
567 *Modinos v Cyprus* (1993) 16 EHRR 485.
568 See generally, R Wintemute, *Sexual Orientation and Human Rights* (Clarendon Press, 1995) Chap 4.
569 (1986) 9 EHRR 56.
570 (1990) 13 EHRR 622.
571 (1997) 24 EHRR 143.
572 (1998) 27 EHRR 163.
573 (1997) 24 EHRR 39.

society'. The case of *Sutherland v United Kingdom*[574] on the age of consent is pending before the Court. In *ADT v United Kingdom*[575] the Court decided that the offence of gross indecency between men in private was a violation of Article 8.

(e) Other applications

12.160 **Personal information.** The Court has considered two important cases involving the right to obtain personal information. In *Gaskin v United Kingdom*[576] it held that personal information about the applicant's childhood, development and history related to his private and personal life to such an extent that access to it came within the scope of Article 8. In *McGinley and Egan v United Kingdom*[577] it held that withholding documents concerning the exposure of the applicants to radiation at Christmas Island was a breach of Article 8.

12.161 However, the Commission has dismissed a number of recent applications where individuals have claimed access to personal information. In *Martin v United Kingdom*[578] the Commission decided that a fair balance had been struck between the applicant and the state where access to medical records was denied to a person suffering from catatonic schizophrenia on the ground that it protected his medical health. In *Wiltshire v United Kingdom*[579] the Commission held that there was no breach of Article 8 where the applicant's files were edited to protect third parties.

12.162 **Right to respect for home.** In *Gillow v United Kingdom*,[580] the applicants complained about the refusal of the Guernsey authorities to allow them to occupy their house. It was held that the refusal of a licence to occupy was disproportionate to the legitimate aim of promoting the economic well being of the island; and constituted a violation of Article 8. In *Buckley v United Kingdom*,[581] however, the refusal to grant the applicant gypsy planning permission to keep caravans on her own land did not breach Article 8. The planning restrictions in question pursued the legitimate aims of public safety, economic well-being, the protection of health and the protection of the rights of others. In *McLeod*[582] the applicant complained that the police had entered her house at the request of her ex-husband. The Court held that the power to enter premises to prevent a breach of the peace was 'in

574 [1997] EHRLR 117 (the Commission held by 14 votes to 4 that the fixing of a minimum age for lawful homosexual activities at 18 rather than 16 was in violation of Art 8 of the Convention).
575 Judgment, 31 Jul 2000.
576 (1989) 12 EHRR 36.
577 (1998) 27 EHRR 1.
578 (1996) 21 EHRR CD 112.
579 (1997) 23 EHRR CD 188.
580 (1986) 11 EHRR 335.
581 (1996) 23 EHRR 101; see also two Commission decisions involving gypsies: *Turner v United Kingdom* (1997) 23 EHRR (CD) 181 and *Webb v United Kingdom* [1997] EHRLR 680.
582 (1998) 27 EHRR 493.

accordance with the law'[583] and was for the legitimate aim of 'the prevention of crime or disorder'. However, on the facts, the entry of the police into the applicant's home was disproportionate as it did not strike a fair balance between her right to respect for home and the prevention of crime and disorder.[584]

Environmental cases. The case of *Powell and Rayner v United Kingdom*[585] concerned a complaint by applicants living near Heathrow Airport that excessive aircraft noise was interfering with their private life and home. Such interference was established in one case but was held to be 'necessary in the interests of the economic well-being of the country'. In a number of other cases involving aircraft noise, friendly settlements have been reached following Commission admissibility decisions in favour of the applicants.[586] **12.163**

Personal privacy. In *Winer v United Kingdom*[587] the Commission found that there had been no failure to respect the private life of the applicant because the only remedies for protection of reputation were those available in defamation in respect of untrue statements. In *Earl and Countess Spencer v United Kingdom*[588] the Commission rejected a claim that the absence of a right to privacy in English law breached Article 8 on the basis that the applicant failed to bring a claim for breach of confidence. Similarly, in *Steward-Brady v United Kingdom*[588a] the Commission rejected the allegation that the state had breached its positive obligations under Article 8 because the Press Complaints Commission had dismissed the applicant's complaint that the publication of his photograph in the *Sun* newspaper breached his right to privacy under its Code of Practice. **12.164**

(3) General impact issues

(a) Privacy and the common law

Although thc Human Rights Act creates privacy rights against public authorities, we argued earlier that the Human Rights Act does not, in general, entitle the court to create new causes of action between *private* parties in litigation.[589] As a result, it **12.165**

[583] Ibid paras 38–45.
[584] Ibid paras 49–58.
[585] (1990) 12 EHRR 355.
[586] *Arrondelle v United Kingdom* (1980) 19 DR 186; (1982) 26 DR 5, EComm HR: payment of £7,500 made re noise at Gatwick; *Baggs v United Kingdom* (1985) 44 DR 13; (1987) 52 DR 29, EComm HR: noise at Heathrow; see also *Vearncombe v United Kingdom and Germany* (1989) 59 DR 186, EComm HR: noise from a military shooting range not intolerable; application inadmissible.
[587] (1986) 48 DR 154, 170–1, EComm HR.
[588] (1998) 25 EHRR CD 105.
[588a] (1998) 27 EHRR CD 284.
[589] See para 5.95ff above.

will not result in the immediate establishment of a general 'private law' right to privacy. Furthermore, the rationale for a right to privacy is very different where the individual seeks protection from intrusion by the state rather than from a private person. For example, the constitutional rights to privacy in American law arise as 'emanations', 'penumbras' or 'shadows'[590] derived from liberty rights enshrined in the Bill of Rights.[591] The reasons for requiring protection from unjustified coercion by the state to a person's 'inner life' on issues such as abortion or personal sexuality are therefore not the same as those which warrant a court placing restrictions on the excesses of the tabloid press.

12.166 Nevertheless, the Human Rights Act may encourage development of the common law based on existing causes of action,[592] particularly breach of confidence.[593] Furthermore, the Act may justify the formulation of a new cause of action where the court is under a positive duty to ensure respect for privacy.[594] It seems likely, however, that, whatever view the English courts take of 'horizontality issues', the incorporation of Article 8 will lead to a decisive impetus towards the establishment of a common law tort of infringement of privacy.[595] The Convention case law may provide the English courts with considerable assistance in defining the limits of the tort and the defences available.[596]

12.167 Two general issues will arise in relation to such a tort: what constitutes an 'infringement of privacy'? and what defences should be available to a person who has infringed another's privacy? In relation to the first, the English Courts will doubtless draw some inspiration from the highly developed United States case law. A useful starting point is the US *Restatement on Torts* which suggests that the tort of infringement of privacy is committed, *inter alia*, by:

> One who gives publicity to a matter concerning the private life of another . . . if the matter publicized is of a kind that:
>
> (a) would be highly offensive to a reasonable person.[597]

---

590 *Whalen v Roe* (1977) 429 US 589.

591 The right has evolved, for example, from due process clauses of the Fifth and Fourteenth Amendments (see *Roe v Wade* (1973) 410 US 113, 153, the Ninth Amendment (see *Griswold v Connecticut* (1965) 381 US 479, 486 to 499 (Goldberg J concurring); see generally, L Tribe, *American Constitutional Law* (2nd edn, Foundation Press, 1988) 15–03.

592 See para 5.91ff above.

593 See para 12.27ff above.

594 See para 12.111ff above.

595 Cf Lord Bingham, 'Should There be a Law to Protect Rights of Personal Privacy?' [1996] EHRLR 450; and 'The Way we Live Now: Human Rights in the New Millennium' [1998] 1 Web J of Current Legal Issues; and contrast for example D Eady, 'A Statutory Right to Privacy' [1996] EHRLR 243.

596 Cf R Mullender, 'Privacy, Paedophilia and the European Convention on Human Rights' [1998] PL 384.

597 *Restatement of Torts*, 2d, §625D.

The Convention case law may provide some assistance in defining the limits of 'infringement'. This approach may mean that, unlike the present position in relation to breach of confidence,[598] the fact that information has, at one time, been in the public domain will not, of itself, prevent it from being private. Nevertheless, it is arguable that under Convention case law there will be no infringement of privacy by filming activities which take place in public in the absence of special circumstances.[599] This is, however, a controversial issue, as it has been held in a number of jurisdictions that the 'right to one's image' is included in the right to respect for private life.[600] It may also depend on whether the applicant has in the particular circumstances in question a reasonable expectation of privacy.[601]

12.168 By far the most important defence is likely to be 'public interest'.[602] The limits of that defence have been the subject of considerable debate; and the specific issues that arise concerning the conflict between the right to privacy and freedom of expression are considered in Chapter 15.[603] The Article 8 jurisprudence may again provide some assistance in two respects. First, the 'legitimate purposes' listed in Article 8(2) provide potential guidance as to the limits of a 'public interest' defence. Thus, it might be argued that the defence should not be available unless it can be shown that the infringement of privacy rights is necessary in the interests of national security, public safety or the economic well-being of the country, the prevention of disorder or crime, the protection of health or morals or the protection of the rights and freedoms of others.[604]

12.169 Secondly, the analysis of the 'public interest' defence may be assisted by the concept of 'proportionality'. Thus, even if an infringement of privacy is 'legitimate', its effects may be disproportionate to the legitimate aim to be achieved. This would give a 'sliding scale' for the application of the defence: the more substantial the interference with privacy, the more important the justification must be.

---

598 See para 12.29ff above.

599 See *Friedl v Austria* (1995) 21 EHRR 83, Com Rep paras 48, 51, but contrast *R v Broadcasting Standards Commision, ex p BBC, The Times*, 12 Apr 2000; see generally, para 12.114 above.

600 For a general discussion, see *Aubry v Les Editions Vice-Versa* [1998] 1 SCR 591; and for the position in Germany see H Stoll, 'General Rights to Personality in German Law' in B Markesinis (ed), *Protecting Privacy* (Oxford University Press, 1999).

601 See eg *Halford v United Kingdom* (1997) 24 EHRR 523 at para 12.94 above; and the Canadian cases at para 12.223ff below.

602 In addition, to 'public interest', defences of 'innocent infringement', consent, privilege, legal authority and protection of property and legitimate business interests have also been suggested: see JUSTICE, *Privacy and the Law*, (Justice, 1970) 36–8. It may be that the last three of these would be subsumed under a broad 'public interest' defence.

603 See para 15.245ff below.

604 For a discussion of the effect of such limitations in the context of s 10 of the Contempt of Court Act 1981, see *X Ltd v Morgan-Grampian (Publishers) Ltd* [1991] 1 AC 1; discussed at para 15.76ff below.

12.170 A 'public interest' defence which is developed on these lines may be narrower than that which is presently available in breach of confidence cases. In particular, the broad 'iniquity' defence[605] might well be cut down by considerations of 'legitimate purpose' and 'proportionality'. The Convention can, in this area, provide a helpful guide to the development of the common law.

(b) The impact on civil procedure

12.171 For the purposes of litigation one of the parties may use surveillance or tape telephone discussions in order to assist its case; this is not uncommon where a defendant in personal injury cases wishes to challenge a claim that the claimant is unable to return to work or where an employer seeks to discover if an employee is breaching restrictive covenants. If the litigant in question is a standard public authority[606] or a functional authority which fails to show the nature of the act is private,[607] the surveillance will breach Article 8(1). However, the public authority is likely to succeed in justifying the interference under Article 8(2) on the basis that it is necessary for the protection of the rights of others.

12.172 Under section 6(3) of the Act, the court must not act in a way which is incompatible with Convention rights.[608] The admission of evidence which is obtained in breach of Article 8(1) can be justified under Article 8(2). In *Chappell v United Kingdom*[609] the Court held that an *Anton Piller* order (now a seizure order) was a proportionate interference which had a legitimate aim; and this decision provides useful general guidance under the Human Rights Act. The court will have to consider, in each case, whether the measure which inteferes with Article 8 rights is 'accompanied by safeguards calculated to keep its impact within reasonable bounds'.[610]

12.173 A number of issues arise concerning the impact of Article 8 on powers under the Civil Procedure Rules to order disclosure of legally privileged material. The power to order disclosure of privileged documents in applications for wasted costs under CPR 48.7.3 has been held to be *ultra vires* by Toulson J in *General Mediterranean Holdings v Patel*.[611] A similar argument may be advanced concerning the power to

[605] See paras 12.036–12.038 above.
[606] See para 5.14ff above.
[607] Under s 6(5): see para 5.28ff above.
[608] See para 5.120 above.
[609] (1989) 12 EHRR 1.
[610] Ibid para 60.
[611] [1999] 3 All ER 673 where Toulson J also took account of Art 6; see also the prisoner cases concerning the *vires* of prison rules which permitted inspection of legally privileged documents. In *R v Secretary of State for the Home Department, ex p Leech (No 2)* [1994] QB 198 the Court of Appeal declared the inspection of legally privileged correspondence unlawful. However, in *R v Secretary of State for the Home Department, ex p Simms* [1999] QB 349 the Court of Appeal accepted that the inspection of documents on security grounds in closed prisons was lawful; the decision was not subject to the appeal made to the House of Lords.

order experts to disclose the substance of their instructions under CPR, rule 35.10(3)(4).[612] It is unlikely that the Human Rights Act will add any additional arguments on these questions.

(c) The right of access to personal information

Article 8 may create a right of access to personal information held by public authorities. The right of access to personal information can be distinguished from the right to freedom of information which may arise under Article 10 because of the obligation on a public authority to impart information. Article 10 basically prohibits a government from restricting a person from receiving information that others wish or may be willing to impart to him.[613] Although the Court declined to express a view in *Gaskin v United Kingdom*[614] on whether a general right of access to personal data and information could be derived from Article 8, it held that information concerning highly personal aspects of the applicant's childhood, development and history created a right of access to that information. In *McGinley and Egan v United Kingdom*[615] the Court said that where the government engages in hazardous activities with hidden consequences for health, respect for private and family life requires an effective and accessible procedure to ensure that all relevant and appropriate information is made available. Nevertheless, Article 8 may also supplement the current statutory provisions which enable access to information[616] by, for example, reversing the effect of *R v Mid-Glamorgan Family Health Services Authority, ex p Martin*[617] in relation to older records which are not subject to these provisons. **12.174**

(4) Specific areas of impact

(a) Commercial law

The 'horizontal impact' of Article 8 on the law relating to business may be very substantial. If the courts develop a tort of infringement of privacy, this will have a significant impact on employment practices.[618] It will also impact on the storage and use of information by business. The 'vertical' effect is likely to be most important in the 'media' and 'planning' areas.[619] **12.175**

612 Although Toulson J expressed the view in *General Mediterranean v Patel* (n 611 above) 693 that these rules did not infringe the substantive right to legal confidentiality.
613 See *Leander v Sweden* (1987) 9 EHRR 433 para 74; *Guerra v Italy* (1998) 26 EHRR 357 para 53; and see, generally, para 15.253 below.
614 (1989) 12 EHRR 36.
615 (1998) 27 EHRR 1.
616 See para 12.46ff above.
617 [1995] 1 WLR 110.
618 See para 12.181 below.
619 See paras 12.190 and 12.193 below.

12.176 The privacy rights in Article 8 may, however, provide business with limited protection against the activities of regulatory bodies. The right to 'private life and home' in Article 8(1) covers office premises[620] of professionals and searches and removal of documents are subject to the 'justification' provisions of Article 8(2).[621] On the other hand, under the Convention jurisprudence it is arguable that a company is not entitled to privacy rights.[622]

(b) Criminal law

12.177 The impact of Article 8 on criminal proceedings seems likely to be limited. However, there are many instances where surveillance techniques breach Article 8.[623] Furthermore, the use of non-statutory guidelines to regulate the activities of informers or undercover police officers where they intrude into a suspect's home or private life may breach the requirement that interferences with Article 8 rights must be 'in accordance with the law'.[624]

12.178 One important question that arises is whether evidence obtained in breach of Article 8 would be inadmissible in criminal proceedings. This issue was considered by the House of Lords in the *Khan* case where it was said that:

> if evidence has been obtained in circumstances which involve an apparent breach of article 8 . . . that is a matter which may be relevant to the exercise of the section 78 power.[625]

In that case, the evidence was held to be admissible and it is unlikely that a breach of Article 8 would, of *itself*, be sufficient to exclude evidence.[626] The *Schenk*[627] case shows that challenges to admissibility must be considered in the broader context of Article 6 rights; and that was the approach taken by the Court in *Khan v United Kingdom*.[627a] On the other hand, it might be argued that the Human Rights Act creates constitutional rights so that a stricter test must be overcome to justify admitting evidence obtained in breach of Article 8.[628]

---

620 See *Niemetz v Germany* (1992) 16 EHRR 97.

621 Cf M Smyth, 'The United Kingdom's Incorporation of the European Convention and its Implications for Business' [1998] EHRLR 273, 276.

622 See para 22.21 below but see *R v Broadcasting Standards Commission, ex p BBC The Times*, Apr 2000.

623 See para 12.105 above.

624 M Colvin, 'Surveillance and the Human Rights Act' in Centre for Public Law at the University of Cambridge, *The Human Rights Act and the Criminal Justice and Regulatory Process* (Hart Publishing, 1999).

625 See *R v Khan* [1997] AC 558, 581.

626 See generally, Chap 21.

627 *Schenk v Switzerland* (1988) 13 EHRR 242.

627a *The Times*, 23 May 2000.

628 See generally, para 21.142ff above.

In deciding issues such as the publicity to be given to private information about defendants or witnesses, a court must take Article 8 into account. Thus, criminal courts may be required to make orders prohibiting the publication of information about HIV positive witnesses if such publication would infringe their right to privacy.[629] In spite of the decriminalisation of sexual activity between men in 1967, the criminal law currently maintains a discrepancy between heterosexuals and homosexuals in regard to the lawful age of consent which appears to be contrary to Article 8.[630] It may also be arguable that the offence of *possessing* indecent photographs of children under section 160 of the Criminal Justice Act 1988[631] is in breach of the right to privacy, impinging, as it does, on the 'private sphere'.[632] 12.179

It is possible that Article 8 will have an impact on sentencing practice in the criminal courts. In *Laskey, Jaggard and Brown*[633] the European Court of Human Rights took the length of the sentences imposed into account in determining whether the measures taken were 'proportionate'. It has been suggested that a longer sentence might have led the Court to take a different view on whether there had been a breach of Article 8.[634] While any sentence of community service or imprisonment involves interference with the private and family life of a convicted person, it is submitted that Article 8 does not have the general consequence that the sentencing court must consider the proportionality of this impact in every case. 12.180

(c) Education

Children with special educational needs may become subject to a statement of educational needs (which a local educational authority has accepted or which has been imposed by a special educational needs tribunal).[635] It has been strongly argued that Article 8 (together with the right to education)[636] imposes obligations to take sufficient or appropriate steps to protect the physical or psychological integrity of a child and members of his family and that these will be breached where the authority fails to deliver the obligations contained in the statement of special education needs.[637] 12.181

---

629 See *Z v Finland* (1997) 25 EHRR 371: an order to make public in 2002 the transcripts of evidence given by the medical advisers of the applicant was a violation of Art 8.

630 See para 12.188 below in relation to discrimination on the grounds of sexual orientation.

631 As opposed to the offence of distributing such photographs under the Protection of Children Act 1978, see para 15.90 below.

632 See the South African decision of *Case v Minister of Safety and Security* (1997) 1 BHRC 541 at para 12.168 below.

633 (1997) 24 EHRR 39, 60 para 49.

634 D Cheney, L Dickson, J Fitzpatrick and S Uglow, *Criminal Justice and the Human Rights Act 1998* (Jordans, 1999) 138.

635 See generally, para 19.26 below.

636 See para 19.34ff below.

637 M Supperstone, J Goudie and J Coppel, *Local Authorities and the Human Rights Act 1998* (Butterworths, 1999) 64; it is also argued that the authority has breached the right to education: see, generally para 19.92 below.

(d) Employment and discrimination

12.182 **Introduction.** The Human Rights Act means that employees of standard public authorities will, in effect, have a 'right of privacy' against their employer. They will also have a right to respect for family life under Article 8: this is discussed in Chapter 13.[638] There are several important areas in which violations of Article 8 might take place: the monitoring of the activities of employees at work, the regulation of 'private aspects' of employees' conduct, the collection of personal data on employees and sexual orientation discrimination.

12.183 **Monitoring employees.** In relation to this area the important question is whether an employee has a 'reasonable expectation of privacy'[639] in relation to a particular work activity. In *Halford v United Kingdom*[640] the applicant had a reasonable expectation of privacy in using a 'private telephone line' in her own office because her employers had given her permission to use it in connection with the sex discrimination claim she had brought against them. However, if employers expressly warn employees that they will monitor telephone calls, then surveillance is unlikely to breach Article 8. There is a strong argument that an expectation of privacy would also arise in relation to telephones in employee rest rooms or staff canteens, regardless of whether the employers give a warning. On the other hand, considerable difficulty may arise in establishing a reasonable expectation of privacy concerning the use of telephones in shared offices or in circumstances in which private use is forbidden. Violations of Article 8 may also occur if a public authority employer monitors private e-mail messages or monitors rest rooms or toilets by closed-circuit television.

12.184 Employers may be entitled to monitor the activities of employees if Article 8 rights are waived in the contract of employment. In principle, Convention rights can be waived[641] and employees can sign away Convention rights in their contract of employment.[642] However, it is well established under Convention case law that any waiver of a Convention right must be established in an unequivocal manner.[643] It seems that simply signing a contract may not be sufficient to amount to a waiver.[644] It is submitted that in order to rely on a waiver of Convention rights, an employer will be obliged to draw the provision specifically to the attention of the employees. It has been suggested that the Court should take a different

[638] See para 13.148ff below.

[639] See para. 12.94 above for a discussion of the Canadian case law considering this phrase, see para 12.226 below.

[640] (1997) 24 EHRR 523.

[641] *Deweer v Belgium* (1980) 2 EHRR 439 para 49; see generally, para 6.148ff above.

[642] See eg *Vereinigung Rechtswinkels Utrecht v Netherlands* (1986) 46 DR 200, EComm HR.

[643] See para 6.153 above.

[644] See eg *Rommelfanger v Germany* (1989) 62 DR 151, EComm HR.

approach towards prospective rather than existing employees.[645] In the Convention cases a distinction has been made between employees who have the choice of whether or not to accept a job[646] and employees in post who are put at risk of losing their jobs if they refuse to sign a waiver.[647]

Regulation of 'private aspects' of employees' conduct. The Human Rights Act may also affect the ability of public authority employers to restrict private areas of conduct by means of provisions such as dress codes. The EAT has held that a dress code preventing male employees from wearing their hair in pony tails did not constitute sex discrimination.[648] However, it could be argued that such codes constitute interference with the 'private life' of the employees.[649] The right to privacy will also have an impact on the scope of the implied term of mutual trust and confidence[650] and may be relevant to issues such as random drug tests.[651] Furthermore it may be a breach of Article 8 for health checks to be carried out on an employee without 'informed consent' having been given.[652] **12.185**

When deciding whether a dismissal is unfair, section 6(3) of the Human Rights Act requires that employment tribunals must not act incompatibly with Convention rights.[653] Privacy rights[654] must be taken into account when a tribunal decides **12.186**

645 J Carter, 'Employment and Labour Relations Law' in C Baker (ed), *Human Rights Act 1998: A Practitioner's Guide* (Sweet & Maxwell, 1998) para 13–47.

646 See eg *Glasenapp v Germany* (1986) 9 EHRR 25; *Kosiek v Germany* (1986) 9 EHRR 328.

647 See eg *Knudsen v Norway* (1985) 42 DR 247, EComm HR.

648 *Smith v Safeway plc* [1996] ICR 686; see also *Schmidt v Austicks Bookshops Ltd* [1978] ICR 85. It has been forcefully argued that *Safeway* is inconsistent with the reasoning in *Jones v Eastleigh Borough Council* [1990] 2 AC 751 (see R Wintemute, 'Recognising New Kinds of Direct Sex Discrimination: Transsexualism, Sexual Orientation and Dress Codes' (1997) 60 MLR 334, 353ff); and see G Clayton and G Pitt, 'Dress Codes and Freedom of Expression' [1997] EHRLR 54.

649 Cf *McFeeley v United Kingdom* (1980) 20 DR 44, 91, EComm HR (a case concerning prison dress); *Kara v United Kingdom* (1998) 27 EHRR CD 272 (a bisexual male transvestite who wore female clothes to express his identity established that restrictions placed on his dress breached the right to private life; however, the Commission took the view that the interference was legitimate and proportionate); there has been considerable litigation in the United States on the question as to whether the control of dress or grooming is unconstitutional: see L Tribe, *American Constitutional Law*, (2nd edn, Foundation Press, 1988) para 15–15 (he points to over 200 cases in the two decades up to 1988).

650 *Mahmud v Bank of Credit and Commerce International SA* [1998] AC 20.

651 J Wadham and H Mountfield, *Blackstone's Guide to the Human Rights Act* (Blackstone, 1999) para 9.8.6.

652 See *X v Commission* [1995] IRLR 320 and generally, B Watt, 'The Legal Protection of HIV and Health Care Workers and the Human Rights Jurisprudence of the European Court of Justice' [1998] EHRLR 301.

653 Employment Tribunals are 'public authorities' under s 6 of the Human Rights Act, see generally, para 5.05ff above.

654 For an instructive article on the approach of the American courts to privacy in the employment relationship, see eg M Finkin, 'Employee Privacy, American Values and the Law' (1996–97) 72 Chicago-Kent LR 222.

cases involving, for example, dress regulations,[655] no smoking rules, private conduct outside the workplace which is alleged to affect working relationships (such as homosexuality[656] and mental illness)[657] or medical (including HIV and psychological) testing. However, the positive duty on public authorities to take 'reasonable and appropriate measures' to secure Article 8 rights[657a] does not oblige the courts to create a general right to privacy.[657b] The tribunal is not obliged to apply strict Article 8(2) tests to the acts of private employers. It seems likely that it will be sufficient for the tribunal to continue to decide unfair dismissal cases by applying the well established 'reasonable responses test' for determining whether a dismissal is unfair.[657c]

12.187 **Collection and use of personal data on employees.** Employers hold and collect substantial amounts of personal data on employees which may be subject to misuse. The International Labour Organisation has expressed concern about the need to protect such data from misuse.[658] Security checks on employees which involve the collection of information about their private affairs would be a breach of Article 8.[659]

12.188 **Sexual orientation discrimination.** Discrimination by public employers in connection with sexual orientation is also likely to breach Article 8.[660] In *Lustig-Prean v United Kingdom*[661] and *Smith and Grady v United Kingdom*[662] the Court held that the investigation and dismissal of homosexuals from the armed forces was a breach of Article 8. Public authorities will violate the right to private life if they conduct intrusive investigations into the sexuality of employees; and, in practice, they will be acting unlawfully by dismissing employees on the grounds of their sexual orientation. It may also be arguable that the principle of statutory horizontality[663] will mean that the Sex Discrimination Act[664] must be read to

[655] See eg *Boychuk v Symons Holdings* [1977] IRLR 395; see Clayton and Pitt (n 648 above) which relies on *Stevens v United Kingdom* (1986) DR 245, EComm HR to argue that the right of dress and appeareance is a manifestation of the right of freedom of expression (see, generally, para 15.271 below); cf Carter (n 645 above) paras 13-22–13-24.

[656] See eg *Saunders v Scottish National Camps Association* [1980] IRLR 174.

[657] See eg *O'Brien v Prudential Assurance* [1979] IRLR 140.

[657a] See para 12.113ff above.

[657b] See para 12.165ff above.

[657c] See eg *British Leyland v Swift* [1981] IRLR 91 and *Iceland Frozen Foods v Jones* [1982] IRLR 439. But note that this test is now open to question as a result of the decisions in *Haddon v Van den Bergh Foods* [1999] IRLR 672 and *Midland Bank v Madden* [2000] IRLR 288; see now, CA decision, 31 Jul 2000 which confirms the reasonable responses test.

[658] For the concerns expressed by the ILO see: *Protection of Workers' Personal Data: An ILO Code of Practice* (ILO, 1997).

[659] See *Hilton v United Kingdom* (1998) 57 DR, EComm HR.

[660] See generally, R Wintemute, *Sexual Orientation and Human Rights* (Clarendon Press, 1995) Chap 4; and see R Wintemute, 'Lesbian and Gay Britons, the Two Europes and the Bill of Rights Debate' [1997] EHRLR 466.

[661] (1999) 7 BHRC 65.

[662] (2000) 29 EHRR 493.

[663] See para 5.84ff above.

[664] Cf *Smith v Gardner Merchant Ltd* [1998] IRLR 510.

include sexual orientation discrimination: so that private employers will also be prohibited from dismissing or subjecting employees to a detriment because they are homosexual. Although the Court in *Lustig-Prean v United Kingdom*[665] and *Smith v United Kingdom*[666] did not make any separate ruling on the complaint of discrimination under Article 14[667] in conjuction with Article 8, it could nevertheless be argued that the obligation to construe the Sex Discrimination Act in accordance with Article 14 means that discrimination will now cover sexual orientation discrimination.[668]

Although the dismissal of a public employee on the grounds of sexual orientation will constitute a breach of Article 8, the public authority can justify such dismissal under Article 8(2). This may be straightforward in the police or armed forces[669] but the justification may be more difficult in other areas of employment. **12.189**

(e) Family law

The Article 8 issues which arise concerning the right of respect for family life are discussed in Chapter 13.[670] However, the power of the court to require disclosure of privileged material in child care proceedings under Part IV of the Children Act 1989 may require further consideration;[671] there is a duty on legal representatives to make full and frank disclosure even where it harms their clients' case.[672] When making interim care or supervision orders, the court has the power to give directions for the medical or psychiatric examination or other assesment of a child.[673] When making such an order, the court must not act incompatibly with the child's right to privacy. **12.190**

(f) Health care

It is arguable that a right to personal automony which can be derived from Article 8;[674] is relevant to the validity of a patient's consent to medical treatment which **12.191**

[665] n 661 above, paras 108–109.

[666] *The Times*, 11 Oct 1999 (paras 115–116 in the full judgment).

[667] See generally, para 17.130ff below.

[668] Contrast *Smith v Gardner Merchant Ltd* (n 664 above) under the Act; and under European Community law, *Grant v South-West Trains Ltd* [1998] ECR I–621; *R v Secretary of State of Defence, ex p Perkins (No 2)* [1998] IRLR 508.

[669] See *Boitteloup v France* (1988) 58 DR 127; also *Bruce v United Kingdom* (1983) 34 DR 68: dismissal of a gay soldier for engaging in sexual activity with a 20-year-old soldier was justified. However, under the Human Rights Act there will be no blanket exclusion for acts done to ensure the combat effectiveness of the armed forces as there is under s 85(4) of the Sex Discrimination Act as amended.

[670] See para 13.150ff below.

[671] See *In re L (A Minor) (Police Investigation Privilege)* [1997] AC 16; see, in particular, the dissenting judgment of Lord Nicholls at 34.

[672] See eg *Oxfordshire County Council v P* [1995] Fam 161; *Essex County Council v R* [1994] Fam 167; *Re D H (A Minor) (Child Abuse)* [1994] 1 FLR 679.

[673] Children Act 1989, s 38(6); and see *Re C (A Minor) (Interim Care Order: Residential Assessment)* [1997] AC 489.

[674] See para 12.84ff above.

would otherwise amount to a battery.[675] At common law the patient must understand in broad terms the nature of the procedure he is agreeing to[676] and the doctor is obliged to disclose the risks inherent in and the alternatives to the procedure. It is arguable, however, Article 8 may impose a stricter duty on doctors to provide more detailed information to patients.

12.192 The right to personal automony may also affect the controversial question of whether a parent can overule the refusal of a '*Gillick* competent'[677] child or a 16- or 17-year-old child[678] to have medical treatment.[679] At common law the court is not bound to implement the wishes of a *Gillick* competent[680] child or of the 16- or 17-year-old child.[681] However, under the Human Rights Act it will be arguable that the child's wishes should prevail over its parents.

(g) Housing law

12.193 Article 8 does not create a right to a home as such:[681a] the right is to respect for a home. This may affect a number of areas in the field of housing law. The Human Rights Act will apply directly to local authorities. It is likely that registered social landlords under the Housing Act 1996 (formerly housing associations) are functional public authorities.[682] Article 8 will therefore have an important impact on housing management questions. The implications of a right of respect for the home and private life are discussed below. The impact of the right to respect for the family are examined in Chapter 13.[683]

12.194 Article 8 may affect the housing allocation policies of some local authorities. It would be a breach of the right of respect for private life, for example, to give

---

675 See generally, I Kennedy and A Grubb, *Principles of Medical Law* (Oxford University Press, 1998) paras 3.86–3.100.

676 *Chatterton v Gerson* [1981] QB 432, 443; *Sidaway v Board of Governors of the Bethlem Royal Hospital and the Maudsley Hospital* [1984] 1 All ER 1018, 1026, CA *per* Sir John Donaldson MR and 1029 *per* Dunn LJ.

677 A child can validly consent to medical treatment where he has sufficient understanding and intelligence to understand fully what is proposed: see *Gillick v West Norfolk and Wisbech Area Health Authority* [1986] AC 112, 169m 186, 188–189, 195, 201.

678 Family Law Reform Act 1969, s 8.

679 See, generally, Kennedy and Grubb (n 675 above) para 4.62–68.

680 *In re R (A Minor)(Wardship: Consent to Treatment)* [1992] Fam 11; *In re W (A Minor)(Medical Treatment: Court's Jurisdiction)* [1993] Fam 64.

681 *In re R (A Minor)(Wardship: Consent to Treatment)* (n 680 above); *In re W (A minor)(Medical Treatment: Court's Jurisdiction)* (n 680 above).

681a See para 12.96 above.

682 The decision in *Peabody Housing Association v Green* (1978) 38 P & CR 633 deciding that a housing association is not amenable to judicial review does not require a court to hold it is a public authority and is unlikely to be applied to the Human Rights Act; see *Hoyle v Castlemilk East Housing Co-operative, The Times*, 16 May 1997; and see, generally, para 5–16ff above; and C Hunter and A Dymond; 'Housing Law' in C Baker (ed), *The Human Rights Act 1998: A Practitioner's Guide* (Sweet & Maxwell, 1998) para 7–08 and see also, *R v Servite Homes, ex p Goldsmith*, 12 May 2000, Div Ct, unreported.

683 See 13.161 below.

preference to housing married couples; and it may well breach Article 8 to require applicants for council housing to disclose their criminal convictions, particularly if those convictions are spent under the Rehabilitation of Offenders Act.[684] It will also require local authority landlords to justify standard conditions in tenancy agreements such as the prohibition on tenants having pets[684a] by demonstrating, for example, that the condition is favoured by tenants and tenants' associations.

It is increasingly common for local authorities and housing associations to install closed circuit television cameras to monitor the common parts of housing estates to discourage and prevent crime and anti-social behaviour. It seems likely that, in some circumstances at least, these cameras will record 'private events' and their use will, therefore, constitute a *prima facie* interference with the right to respect for private life. Nevertheless, it is submitted that provided the public authority can adduce proper evidence that the use of such cameras is necessary for one of these legitimate purposes, these measures are a justifiable interference with the right to private life. **12.194A**

Local authority landlords may be obliged to take positive steps[685] to protect their own tenants from noise,[686] fumes,[687] pollution[688] (which might extend to matters such as vermin and cockroaches) and anti-social neighbours.[689] These positive obligations may mean that a local authority will be liable, for example, if it fails to take proper steps to protect its tenants from nuisance caused by other local authority tenants[690] or to sound-proof local authority flats.[691] Article 8 may also be breached by the failure of the local authority to take action under Parts VI and IX of the Housing Act 1985 in relation to unfit housing for private tenants as well as local authority tenants.[692] The question of whether a positive obligation arises in these cases will depend on the balance struck by the court between the general interest of the community and the rights of the individual.[692a] **12.195**

[684] s 1(1), s 4(1)(2) and s 5 of the Act.
[684a] See J Luba, 'Acting on Rights—The Housing Implications of the Human Rights Act', Lecture, Sep 1999.
[685] See para 12.108 above.
[686] *Arrondelle v United Kingdom* (1982) 26 DR 5, EComm HR; *Powell and Rayner v United Kingdom* (1990) 12 EHRR 394; contrast the position in domestic law where a tenant cannot make a claim for breach of the covenant of quiet enjoyment or nuisance: see *Southwark London Borough Council v Mills* [1999] 3 WLR 939.
[687] *Lopez Ostra v Spain* (1994) 20 EHRR 277.
[688] *Guerra v Italy* (1998) 26 EHRR 357.
[689] There is no implied covenant on a landlord to enforce a covenant not to commit a nuisance against a neighbour (see *O'Leary v Islington London Borough Council* (1983) 9 HLR 81); nor can the landlord be liable for the acts of the neighbour in nuisance: see *Smith v Scott* [1973] Ch 314; *Hussein v Lancaster City Council* [1999] 4 All ER 125.
[690] Requiring reconsideration of *Hussain v Lancaster City Council* (n 689 above).
[691] Requiring reconsideration of *Southwark London Borough Council v Mills* (n 686 above).
[692] A local authority cannot use the enforcement provisions of the Housing Act against itself: see *R v Cardiff City Council ex p Cross* (1981) 6 HLR 6.
[692a] See para 6.99ff above.

12.196 Under section 6(3) of the Act, the court must not act in a way which is incompatible with Convention rights.[693] It will therefore be necessary to consider the impact of Article 8 when the court considers whether to make a discretionary possession order in relation to an assured tenancy,[694] when considering whether it is reasonable to make a possession order in relation to a secure tenancy[695] and when considering mortgagee possesssion orders. It may, for example, be argued that, in a case involving modest rent arrears, it would be disproportionate to make a possession order.

12.197 **Private nuisance.** The definition of 'private nuisance' in English law may have to be revised in the light of Article 8. In *Hunter v Canary Wharf Ltd*[696] the plaintiffs' claims for nuisance based on interference with television reception by large buildings were dismissed by the House of Lords. It is arguable that the Article 8 'respect for home' would require the courts to take a broader view of what types of 'interference' should be regarded as constituting an actionable nuisance and to develop the common law accordingly.[697]

(h) Immigration law

12.198 It seems likely that the law relating to immigration and deportation will be significantly affected by Article 8 of the Convention. Deportations have been subject to challenge on a number of occasions on the ground of interference with Article 8 rights.[698] However, these challenges have almost always been based on interference with 'family life' rather than 'private life' and are dealt with in Chapter 13.[699]

(i) Local government law

12.199 The obligation to respect the home may have a significant effect on a wide range of administrative decisions; the implications of the right of respect for family life (in particular, in relation to public law child care cases)[700] are discussed in Chapter 13.[701] In community care cases a failure to respect the home when moving disabled adults and children in residential accomodation will provide an additional ground for challenge in judicial review proceedings.[702]

[693] See para 5.120ff above.
[694] Under Housing Act 1988, Pt II, Sch 2.
[695] Cases 1 to 8 and 12 to 16 in Sch 2 of the Housing Act 1985 are subject to s 84(2).
[695a] See Luba (n 684a above).
[696] [1997] AC 655.
[697] See the dissenting judgment of Lord Cooke in *Hunter v Canary Wharf Ltd* (n 696 above); and see para 5.93 above.
[698] See para 13.142 below; and see A Sherlock, 'Deportation of Aliens and Article 8 ECHR' (1998) 23 ELR Checklist No 1, HR 62.
[699] But see, *C v Belgium* RJD 1996–III 915.
[700] See para 13.30ff below.
[701] See para 13.175 below.
[702] See eg *R v North and East Devon District Health Authority, ex p Coughlan* [2000] 2 WLR 622; see para 12.12 above.

The power to inspect small residential homes under the Residential Homes (Amendment) Act 1991 must not be used in an instrusive way so as to comply with the right of respect for private life. Although a failure to register such homes is a criminal offence, it would be a *prima facie* breach of Article 8 if a prosecution was brought where the arrangement was made out of friendship or in return for companionship.[703] **12.200**

Article 8 will affect the use local authorities may make of information gathered in the course of carrying out their functions. It may facilitate the general right to freedom of information[704] by providing a right of access to personal information.[705] It is also difficult to see how the release to the media by a local authority of video material from closed-circuit television could be lawful after the coming into force of the Human Rights Act.[706] **12.201**

(j) Media law

Even in the absence of 'horizontal' application, it is likely that the Human Rights Act will have considerable impact on media law. It is clear that there are many situations in which the media infringes the private life and home of individuals. Although the press is not subject to direct state regulation, it is strongly arguable that the Press Complaints Commission is a functional public authority[707] and, as result, must act in conformity with Article 8. The Broadcasting Standards Commission is a body established by statute and is also a functional public authority.[708] As a result, if the Press Complaints Commission and Broadcasting Standards Commission fail to establish and effectively police a regulatory regime which provides proper protection for Article 8 rights then their actions may be unlawful under section 6 of the Human Rights Act. A 'victim' may be entitled to damages or injunctive relief. The effect of 'privacy rights' in the media law context, however, gives rise to complex issues of balancing of rights under the Convention.[709] These issues are considered in relation to freedom of expression in Chapter 15.[710] **12.202**

(k) Mental health law

Article 8 of the Convention will be relevant to mental health law insofar as it protects the right of persons detained under the Mental Health Act to 'respect for **12.203**

[703] L Clements, *Community Care and the Law* (Legal Action Group, 1996) 82, 83.
[704] See para 15.253 below.
[705] See para 12.46 above.
[706] Reversing *R v Brentwood Borough Council, ex p Peck The Times*, 18 Dec 1997.
[707] See para 5.16ff above and *R v Press Complaints Authority, ex p Stewart-Brady* (1997) 9 Admin LR 274; and see para 12.74 above, n 292.
[708] See para 5.16ff above.
[709] See eg R Singh, 'Privacy and the Media After the Human Rights Act' [1998] EHRLR 712.
[710] See para 15.245ff below.

home and correspondence'. It seems likely that the present position in relation to the interception of correspondence is compatible with Article 8(2).[711]

12.204 Another matter raised by Article 8 is that of state-imposed controls in connection with the care and housing of conditionally discharged patients in the community. Under Article 8 the state will be required to demonstrate a social need for restrictions on home or private life such as a mandatory period of residence in monitored accommodation. This could amount to a significant departure from existing practice, under which many post-discharge restrictions are established on a relatively automatic basis.

12.205 When a person is in involuntary detention in a psychiatric institution important functions are exercised by the person designated as their 'nearest relative' under section 26 of the Mental Health Act 1983. The 'nearest relative' is privy to private information concerning the patient. In limited circumstances an application may be made to the County Court to change the person exercising the functions of the 'nearest relative'.[712] However, such a change cannot be made on the ground that the patient has concerns about the identity of the nearest relative and does not wish this person to have access to private information. The Commission took the view that this gives rise to a breach of Article 8[713] and a friendly settlement was reached involving an agreement to amend the legislation.[713a]

(l) Planning and environment law

12.206 **Introduction.** The right to respect for 'home' in Article 8 has a potential impact on planning law. Thus the refusal of planning permission to allow a person to continue to live in a particular place is a *prima facie* breach of Article 8.[714] However, Article 8 will only apply if the 'home' is already established. The right does not extend to land on which a person plans to build a house.[715]

12.207 More importantly, after the Human Rights Act comes into force planning authorities will have to take into account the potential impact of their decisions on the Article 8 rights of individuals. It is well established that personal circumstances are only relevant to planning decisions in exceptional circumstances.[716] However, the general approach of the Convention is that personal circumstances

[711] See O Thorold, 'The Implications of the European Convention on Human Rights for United Kingdom Mental Health Legislation' [1996] EHRLR, 619, 633.
[712] Mental Health Act 1983 s 29.
[713] See *J T v United Kingdom* [1999] EHRLR 443 (merits).
[713a] *JT v United Kingdom*, Judgment, 30 Mar 2000.
[714] Cf *Buckley v United Kingdom* (1996) 23 EHRR 101; and see *Chesterfield Properties v Secretary of State for the Environment* [1998] JPL 568 where Laws J dealt with a *Wednesbury* challenge to a compulsory purchase order on the basis it involved a fundamental human right.
[715] See *Loizidou v Turkey* (1996) 23 EHRR 513.
[716] *Great Portland Estate v City of Westminster Council* [1985] AC 661.

are put first[717] and any interference with those rights must be justified as 'necessary in a democratic society'. It has been suggested that this might require a fundamental change of approach:

> . . . the approach under the Convention is that interference with individual rights is unjustified unless public interest reasons are adduced which are of sufficient importance. In current planning policy, decisions are made in accordance with the public interest, with affected private rights being subsidiary.[718]

If such a change is implemented, planning authorities will have to make clear, in the reasons for their decisions that they have not acted incompatibly with Article 8 rights.[719] If the reasons given do not demonstrate that there is a 'Convention justification' for the interference, then the decision will be unlawful and liable to be quashed.

Enforcement powers. An authority must not use its powers to enforce compliance with planning controls under Part VII of the Town and Country Planning Act 1990 by evicting trespassing gypsies in a way which is incompatible with the right to respect for the home. Even before the enactment of the Human Rights Act, the courts have taken account of the fundamental right to shelter when considering local authority decisions to evict gypsies;[720] and gypsies will be able to rely directly on Article 8 as a defence to possession proceedings.[721] In *Buckley v United Kingdom*[722] the Court held that the refusal to grant a gypsy planning permission and the institution of criminal proceedings for failing to comply with an enforcement notice was a proportionate interference with Article 8 which had a legitimate aim. However, there are a number of similar applications before the Commission by gypsies alleging violation of Article 8 which have been ruled admissible.[723] It may also **12.208**

[717] See the approach taken in *Britton v Secretary of State for the Environment* [1997] JPL 617.

[718] See T Corner, 'Planning, Environment and the European Convention on Human Rights' [1998] JPL 301, 312.

[719] See *Britton v Secretary of State for the Environment* [1997] JPL 617; and contrast *R v Leicestershire County Council, ex p Blackfordby and Boothorope Action Group* (unreported) 15 Mar 2000.

[720] See eg *R v Lincolnshire County Council, ex p Atkinson* [1996] 160 JPLCL 580 and *R v Wolverhampton Metropolitan Borough Council, ex p Dunne* (1997) 29 HLR 754 in relation to the powers to deal with unauthorised encampments under the Criminal Justice and Public Order Act 1994; and *R v Kerrier District Council, ex p Uzell* [1996] 71 P & CR 566 in relation to a decision of a planning authority to take enforcement action against gypsies occupying a site in breach of planning control; and contrast the approach taken where a local authority commences summary proceedings for possession in *R v Brighton and Hove Council, ex p Marman* [1998] 2 PLR 48 and *R v Hillingdon Borough Council, ex p McDonagh, The Times*, 9 Nov 1998.

[721] Until the Human Rights Act comes into force, gypsies have been obliged to apply to adjourn the possession proceedings so that judicial review proceedings can be brought to challenge the decision to commence the possession proceedings: see *Avon County Council v Buscott* [1988] QB 656.

[722] (1996) 23 EHHR 101; see also *Turner v United Kingdom* (1997) 23 EHRR CD 181.

[723] *Coster v United Kingdom* (1998) 25 EHRR CD 24; *Beard v United Kingdom* (1998) 25 EHRR CD 28; *Smith v United Kingdom* (1998) 25 EHRR CD 42; *Lee v United Kingdom* (1998) 25 EHRR CD 46; *Varey v United Kingdom* (1998) 25 EHRR CD 49; *Chapman v United Kingdom* (1998) 25 EHRR CD 64.

be argued that an authority discriminates against gypsies when taking possession proceedings against them.[724]

12.209 **Statutory nuisance.** The Human Rights Act may also have an impact on the extent to which local authorities are obliged to exercise their powers to require the abatement of statutory nuisances.[725] A failure to exercise these powers in circumstances in which noise,[726] fumes,[727] pollution[728] affect individuals' enjoyment of their homes could constitute a breach of Article 8.[729] It is also arguable that compulsory purchase orders must comply with Article 8 and the right to the enjoyment of possessions under Article 1 of the First Protocol. The issues they raise are considered in Chapter 18.[730]

(m) Police law

12.210 **Introduction.** Police powers of surveillance constitute an 'interference' with the rights guaranteed by Article 8 and must, therefore, be 'in accordance with the law' and 'necessary in a democratic society' for one of the specified purposes.[731] This does not necessarily mean that the machinery of supervision should be in the hands of a judge[732] but there must be adequate and effective safeguards against abuse and sufficient independence.

12.211 **The Interception of Communications Act.** The Interception of Communications Act 1985 was enacted as a direct result of the decision of the Court in *Malone v United Kingdom.*[733] Since the Act came into force, the Commission have held[734] that the 'review machinery' which it establishes (and the similar machinery relating to the security and intelligence services)[735] are sufficient to satisfy Article 8. Nevertheless, these decisions are not binding on the English courts and there are powerful arguments to the contrary. The Tribunal does not consider the merits of the issue of a warrant, does not conduct oral hearings and does not give

[724] See para 17.165 below.
[725] Environmental Protection Act 1990, ss 79, 80.
[726] *Arrondelle v United Kingdom* (1982) 26 DR 5, EComm HR; *Powell and Rayner v United Kingdom* (1990) 12 EHRR 394.
[727] *Lopez Ostra v Spain* (1994) 20 EHRR 277.
[728] *Guerra v Italy* (1998) 26 EHRR 357.
[729] See generally, Corner (n 718 above) 313 and P Sands, 'Human Rights, Environment and the *Lopez Ostra* Case' [1996] EHRLR 597.
[730] See para 18.103 below.
[731] See generally, the Rt Hon Lord Justice Auld, 'Investigations and Surveillance' and M Colvin, 'Surveillance and the Human Rights Act' in Centre for Public Law at the University of Cambridge, *The Human Rights Act and the Criminal Justice and Regulatory Process* (Hart Publishing, 1999).
[732] See para 12.125ff above.
[733] (1984) 7 EHRR 14.
[734] See para 12.154 above.
[735] See para 12.155 above.

reasons. Although there are about 50 complaints a year, the Tribunal has not yet found a breach of the Act. As Klug, Starmer and Weir point out:

> it is imperative that the tribunals set up to investigate surveillance by the secret services have power to question whether the surveillance complained about was justified; and to report their findings either way. Otherwise, whether they provide an adequate safeguard is unknowable. Equally the fact that the tribunal cannot 'go behind' a decision of the secret services to target an individual because he or she belonged to a group or category of people regarded by them as requiring investigation presents the tribunal with a circular obstacle . . .[736]

Furthermore, there are limitations on the impact of the Interception of Communications Act which mean that certain types of police surveillance is likely to be a breach of Article 8.[737] The 1985 Act does not apply to private telecommunications networks and does not, for example, cover interceptions of radio signals from cordless telephones[738] or of e-mails whilst travelling on internet service providers on the private network. The 1985 Act also does not apply to any inteception carried out with the consent of one of the parties to the communication.[739] However, the regime governing the interception of communications will be radically recast when the Regulation of Investigatory Powers Bill becomes law. This extends the statutory regime to all forms of telecommunication and makes provision for a new Tribunal to deal with complaints concerning interception. This Tribunal will conduct hearings and allow legal representation and will meet some of the criticisms of the Interception of Communications Act 1985.[740] 12.212

The Security Services Act. The Security Service Act 1996 extended the functions of the Security Service to acting in support of the activities of the police force and other law enforcement agencies in the prevention and detection of serious crime.[741] By section 2, the Act extends the power of the Secretary of State to issue warrants[742] to cover applications in relation to the new function. These warrants may relate to property in the British Islands if they are in relation to 'serious crime'. It has been forcefully argued that this new power to issue warrants may be in breach of Article 8 because the Secretary of State is given a broad discretion which does not satisfy the requirements of 'foreseeability' and 'precision'.[743] In addition, there is a 12.213

[736] F Klug, K Starmer, S Weir, *The Three Pillars of Liberty* (Routledge, 1996) 230; also, JUSTICE, *Under Surveillance: Covert Policing and Human Rights Standards* (Justice, 1998) 24–27.
[737] See generally, Colvin (n 731 above).
[738] *R v Effik* (1994) 99 Crim App R 312.
[739] Interception of Communications Act 1985, s 1(2).
[740] For the background to the Bill see the Consultation Paper *Interception of Communications in the United Kingdom* (HMSO, 1999), CM 4368.
[741] Security Service Act 1996, s 1(1), amending Security Service Act 1989, s 1.
[742] Intelligence Services Act 1994, s 5.
[743] See P Duffy and M Hunt, 'Goodbye Entick v Carrington: the Security Service Act 1996' [1997] EHRLR 11, 15–16.

lack of effective judicial supervision. The various bodies established under the Security Service and Intelligence Service Acts are immune from judicial review. Duffy and Hunt argue that, in cases in which the purpose of the surveillance is not the protection of national security, these bodies do not provide an adequate substitute for judicial supervision.[744]

12.214 **Regulation of other forms of surveillance.** Other surveillance by public authorities in the United Kingdom has, traditionally, been unregulated by statute. In *Govell v United Kingdom*[745] the Commission declared admissible an application relating to the lack of legal authority for intrusive police surveillance. The concerns raised by the House of Lords in *R v Khan*[746] led to the enactment of the Police Act 1997. This brought in a system of review in relation to intrusive surveillance. In *Khan v United Kingdom*[746a] the Court confirmed that the system which had existed prior to the Police Act 1997 was not 'in accordance with law' and, as a result, constituted a breach of Article 8.

12.215 There are a number of serious issues concerning the compatibility of police surveillance with Article 8.[747] First, although it seems likely that the regime under the Police Act 1997, in general, satisfies Convention standards, there remain areas of concern. In particular, although the police now have to obtain prior approval of a Commissioner where surveillance would involve intrusion which could infringe privacy, this does not apply to an authorisation 'where the person who gives it believes that the case is one of urgency'.[748] It is arguable that authorisation of this type lacks the safeguards which the Court of Human Rights has identified as being necessary to ensure that interferences were proportionate.[749] Secondly, the Police Act 1997 does not cover 'non-intrusive' surveillance such as the tape recording of conversations using long range microphones, video surveillance and so on. These are also 'interferences' with Article 8 rights and remain unregulated by law in the United Kingdom. This is a plain breach of the Convention[750] and the Government is seeking to rectify the position by the provisions of Part II of the Regulation of Investigatory Powers Bill. This Bill applies to

---

[744] Ibid 18–19.

[745] (1996) 23 EHRR CD 101.

[746] [1997] AC 558; see generally, para 12.54ff above.

[746a] *The Times*, 23 May 2000.

[747] For a general discussion, see M Colvin, 'Surveillance and the Human Rights Act' in Centre for Public Law at the University of Cambridge, *The Human Rights Act and the Criminal Justice and Regulatory Process* (Hart Publishing, 1999).

[748] Police Act 1997, s 97(3).

[749] See eg *Funke v France* (1993) 16 EHRR 297 para 54ff; and contrast *Camenzind v Switzerland* RJD 1998–III 2880 paras 45–47.

[750] But see *Hutcheon v United Kingdom* [1997] EHRLR 195 (visual surveillance of applicant's home by 75 ft observation tower held to be within the normal duties of RUC and thus 'in accordance with the law', for a legitimate aim).

any surveillance which is 'intrusive',[750a] or 'directed'.[750b] It will also apply to the 'conduct and use of covert human intelligence sources' that is informants and undercover police officers. The Bill proposes an 'authorisation regime' similar to that in the Police Act 1997 with additional safeguards in the form of a Covert Investigations Commissioner and a Tribunal. The Tribunal will also be the appropriate tribunal for actions under section 7 of the Human Rights Act 1998 in relation to surveillance.[750c] The Tribunal will apply the same principles for making a determination as would be applied by a court on an application for judicial review.

Search warrants. Police powers of search and seizure are largely regulated by the provisions of the Police and Criminal Evidence Act 1984 and appear, in general, to be in conformity with the Convention. However, an issue may arise as to whether the procedure for the issue of search warrants by magistrates[751] conforms with Article 8. This is because the procedure appears, in practice, to be little more than a 'rubber stamping exercise', with refusals being exceedingly rare.[752] A warrant does not show the grounds on which it was issued and the 'information in writing' is usually formal in nature. Justices have no obligation to give reasons for the grant of a warrant and no record is kept of proceedings.[753] This makes legal challenges extremely difficult. If a warrant is issued without proper grounds, then the person whose property is searched has no remedy against the police. The issuing justices are only liable if malice can be shown. No such action has been successful in modern times.[754] These factors lead Feldman to conclude: **12.216**

> one is left with an impression that justices of the peace do not provide the independent judicial scrutiny of proposed entries and searches under warrants which is needed to ensure that interferences with the right to respect for a person's private life and home are justified . . . The formal trappings of scrutiny are there, but the substance is sadly lacking in most cases.[755]

As a result, it is arguable that the procedure for the grant of search warrants is in breach of Article 8. It should be noted, however, that a challenge to the issue of a

[750a] That is surveillance involving the presence of an individual or device on residential premises or private vehicle or which is carried out in relation to anything taking place on such premises or in such vehicle, clause 25(3).

[750b] That is surveillance undertaken for a specific operation which is likely to result in the obtaining of personal information, clause 25(2).

[750c] See clause 56 and generally, Part IV.

[751] See para 12.08 above.

[752] See K Lidstone and C Palmer, *Bevan and Lidstone's: The Investigation of Crime* (2nd edn, Butterworths, 1996) para 4.10; D Dixon, C Coleman and K Bottomley 'PACE in Practice' (1991) 141 NLJ 1586.

[753] *R v Marylebone Magistrates Court, ex p Amdrell Ltd (trading as 'Get Stuffed')* (1998) 162 JP 719, although giving reasons is desireable.

[754] See generally, R Clayton and H Tomlinson, *Civil Actions Against the Police* (3rd edn, Sweet & Maxwell, 2000) Chap 7.

[755] D Feldman, *Civil Liberties and Human Rights in England and Wales* (Clarendon Press, 1993), 414.

warrant under Article 8 was unsuccessful in the Scots case of *Birse v HM Advocate*.[755a] The evidence of the Justice was that his 'invariable practice' was to question the requesting officer as to the reason for applying for the warrant and the source of any information relied on. The Court also rejected the argument that there was a breach of Article 8 because no record had been kept of the proceedings because the complainer was deprived of a proper basis for ensuring that the application had been considered properly. There was no consideration of the extent to which the Justice's 'invariable procedure' provided an effective scrutiny of the warrant[755b] and the impact of the Article 8 requirement for 'procedural safeguards'.[755c]

12.217 There is increasing concern about the execution of search warrants in the presence of the media. A search warrant involves a serious interference with a person's home and private life. Media involvement and the publication of material relating to the search, including films of police entry, means that there is a much greater degree of interference. Although the Divisional Court has stated that any general practice of inviting the media to attend on the execution of warrants is deplorable[756] it refused to quash a warrant on the ground that television cameras had been invited to attend. In the United States, in contrast, the practice of inviting the media to attend the execution of a warrant, known as 'ride-along', has been held to be unconstitutional.[757] The Supreme Court held that media 'ride-alongs' could not be justified by matters such as the need to publicise law enforcement activities, minimise police abuses and protect suspects and officers: the right to the privacy of the home prevailed. It is strongly arguable that a similar approach will be taken under Article 8.

12.218 Another area of potential impact concerns police powers to seize material which is subject to legal professional privilege. Although there is no statutory power to search for or seize such material, privilege is lost if the material is held 'with the intention of furthering a criminal purpose'.[758] Case law establishes that the privilege is lost when the material was held innocently for a third party's 'criminal purpose'.[759] This can be contrasted with the approach taken by the European Court of Human Rights in *Niemetz v Germany*[760] in which a search of a lawyer's office was held to be a breach of Article 8, as disproportionate to the aim of prevention of crime and protection of rights of others. There is a good argument that the

---

755a Unreported, 13 Apr 2000.

755b No consideration was given to the question as to how often the Justice refused applications for warrants.

755c See para 12.132 above.

756 *R v Marylebone Magistrates Court, ex p Amdrell Ltd (trading as 'Get Stuffed')* (1998) 162 JP 719.

757 See *Wilson v Layne* (1999) 7 BHRC 274, SC, there was violation of Fourth Amendment rights.

758 PACE, s 10(2).

759 See *R v Central Criminal Court, ex p Francis and Francis* [1989] AC 346; see para 12.17 above.

760 (1992) 16 EHRR 97; cf D Harris, M O'Boyle and C Warbrick, *Law of the European Convention on Human Rights* (Butterworths, 1995) 345.

Niemetz approach is to be preferred. An interference with legal professional privilege will be disproportionate unless it can be shown that the solicitor, or perhaps his client, was intending to further a criminal purpose.[761]

(n) Prison law

The United Kingdom Government has been found to be in violation of Article 8 on three occasions in cases relating to prisoners' correspondence.[762] The relevant standing orders were modified to take account of these decisions.[763] However, the Human Rights Act may have an impact in a number of other areas.[764] Any impact of the privacy aspects of Article 8[765] would be on matters relating to access to the outside world.[766] It appears that the present regime dealing with correspondence and family visits is in conformity with Article 8 requirements. The restrictions on visits by journalists and communication with the media are considered under Article 10.[767] **12.219**

Appendix 1: The Canadian Charter of Rights

(1) Introduction

The Canadian Charter of Rights and Freedoms makes no special provision for the constitutional protection of privacy. However, the Federal Privacy Act provides extensive protection for this right in ordinary domestic law and some provinces have also enacted legislation.[768] **12.220**

Two important cases have considered the impact of the right to privacy under section 5 of the Quebec Charter of Human Rights and Freedoms. This provides that every person has the right to respect for his private life. **12.221**

In *Godbout v Longueil*[769] the Supreme Court of Canada took a liberal view of the concept of privacy and said that its purpose was to protect a sphere of individual autonomy for all decisions relating to choices which are of fundamentally private or inherently personal nature. The city of Longueil had adopted a resolution which required all permanent employees to reside within its boundaries; and the plaintiff had signed a declaration agreeing that her employment would be terminated if she moved outside the city. She moved out of the city, was dismissed and brought an action for damages and reinstatement. The **12.222**

[761] See Feldman (n 755, above) 447–51.
[762] See para 12.153 above.
[763] See S Livingstone and T Owen *Prison Law* (2nd edn, Oxford University Press, 1999) para 7.23.
[764] See the general discussion in Livingstone and Owen (n 763 above) para 16.42ff.
[765] For the 'family law' aspects, see para 13.78 below.
[766] For the present position, see Livingstone and Owen (n 763 above) Chap 7.
[767] See para 15.286 below.
[768] For a survey, see J Craig and N Nolte, 'Privacy and Free Speech in Germany and Canada: Lessons for an English Privacy Tort' [1998] EHRLR 162.
[769] [1997] 3 SCR 844.

Supreme Court decided that the residence requirement deprived the plaintiff of the right to privacy: it deprived the plaintiff of the ability to choose where to establish her home.

12.223 In *Aubry v Les Editions Vice-Versa*[770] the Supreme Court had to consider the extent to which 'privacy' rights would protect material gathered in a public place. A photograph was taken of a young woman sitting on a step in front of a building and was published without her consent by a magazine. She then brought proceedings against the magazine. The Supreme Court took the view that the right to individual autonomy included the ability to control the use made of one's image; and that this right was infringed when the image was published without consent, enabling an individual to be identified. However, the right to privacy had to be balanced against the right to freedom of expression. The Supreme Court held that the balance depends both on the nature of the information and the situation of those concerned and concluded that the plaintiff's right to protection of her image was more important than the artist's right to publish a photograph without first obtaining her consent.

12.224 The conflict between privacy and freedom of expression has been considered in a number of other cases.[771] In *Silber v BCTV*[772] a televison company decided to make a film about a long and bitter strike at the plaintiff's company. A television crew were attempting to film from the car park because the plaintiff had been uncooperative and a violent struggle ensued which was broadcast on television. When damages were sought under the provincial privacy legislation, the television company relied on a public interest defence; and succeeded on the ground that the filming of the struggle took place in a parking lot which was open to the public, that both the plaintiff and the strike were newsworthy and that the television company was motivated by a desire to inform the public about a serious issue in the community. By comparison, in *Valiquette v The Gazette*[773] a teacher recovered damages when a newspaper disclosed the fact he had AIDs. The public interest defence was rejected because the plaintiff was not himself a public figure, the newspaper was motivated primarily by commercial interests and the revelations seriously affected his health.

12.225 The right to privacy has also been embraced by the Supreme Court of Canada as the rationale for the guarantee against unreasonable search and seizure under section 8 of the Charter.[774] Under the common law, police and government authorities were precluded from entering private property without authorisation to search for evidence of crime, subject to two exceptions: they could search for and seize evidence without warrant if it was incidental to a lawful arrest, and they could obtain a judicial warrant on sworn evidence of a strong basis for belief that the goods are concealed in the place to be searched. The common law against unreasonable search and seizure was founded on the protection of property rights rather than privacy. Entry onto private premises was trespass and removal of goods or paper amounted to conversion. Outside of the law regarding invasion of property rights, there

---

770 [1998] 1 SCR 591.

771 See eg in relation to Quebec, *Field v United Amusements* [1971] SC 283; *Rebeiro v Shawningan Chemicals* [1973] SC 389; and in relation to British Columbia, *Pierre v Pacific Press* [1994] 7 WWR 759, BCCA; *Hollinsworth v BCTV* (1996) 34 CCLT (2d) 95; and see generally, Craig and Nolte (n 768 above).

772 (1986) 69 BCLR 34.

773 (1992) 8 CCLT (2n) 302; the case was unsuccessfully appealed on 10 Dec 1996 unreported.

774 Section 8 of the Charter guarantees the right to be secure against unreasonable search and seizure.

was no prohibition against evidence derived from what state officials might see or hear. Moreover, some of the common law safeguards, such as warrants, have been overridden in Canadian jurisdictions by enactment of statutory powers of search and seizure which omit them. However, where the police took hair samples, buccal swabs, and teeth impressions from a 17-year-old arrested for a brutal murder but failed to seize them in accordance with the Criminal Code or under common law powers, the seizure was held to be highly intrusive and in breach of section 8.[775]

The value protected by the law of search and seizure has now shifted from property rights to privacy. The Supreme Court of Canada in its interpretation of section 8 in *Hunter v Southam*[776] held that the Charter guaranteed against unreasonable search and seizure protected a 'reasonable expectation of privacy'. In doing so, it followed the American decision in *Katz v United States*[777] which involved police placement of an electronic listening device on the outside of a public telephone booth to record the accused's end of a telephone conversation. In the absence of police trespass onto private property, the US Supreme Court found that the 'bug' was an infringement of the Fourth Amendment which prohibits 'unreasonable searches and seizures', on grounds that there had been an invasion of the 'reasonable expectation of privacy' relied upon by the accused in using the telephone booth. The Supreme Court of Canada in *Hunter v Southam* adopted the 'reasonable expectation of privacy' basis even though that case involved actual entry onto the premises of a corporation for the purposes of a combines investigation. It found that a corporation has the same constitutionally protected expectation of privacy as an individual, and, because the purpose of section 8 is to 'protect individuals from unjustified state intrusions upon their privacy', that an *ex post facto* determination as to reasonableness of the search would not suffice. It said that the purpose of the section 'requires a means of preventing unjustifiable searches before they happen, not simply of determining, after the fact, whether they ought to have occurred in the first place'. **12.226**

(2) Section 8 principles[778]

The basic principles which apply to the right to be secure against unreasonable search or seizure under section 8 were summarised in *R v Edwards*:[779] **12.227**

- A claim for relief under section 24(2) of the Charter can be made only by the person whose Charter rights have been infringed.[780]
- Like all Charter rights, section 8 is a personal right; it protects people, not places.[781]
- The right to challenge the legality of a search depends upon the accused establishing that his personal rights to privacy have been violated.[782]

[775] *R v Stillman* [1997] 1 SCR 607.
[776] *Hunter v Southam* [1984] 2 SCR 145.
[777] *Katz v United States* (1967) 389 US 347; cf *Minnesota v Carter* (1998) 5 BHRC 457 (in which the majority of the US Supreme Court took a restrictive approach to this case).
[778] See generally, J Fontana, *The Law of Search and Seizure in Canada* (3rd edn, Butterwoth-Heinemann 1992) and P Hogg, *Constitutional Law of Canada* (4th edn, Carswell, 1997) para 45.5.
[779] [1996] 1 SCR 128.
[780] *R v Rahey* [1987] 1 SCR 588, 619.
[781] *Hunter v Southam* [1984] 2 SCR 145; citing Stewart J in *Katz v United States* (1967) 389 US 347.
[782] *R v Pugliese* (1992) 71 CCC (3d) 295.

- As a general rule, two distinct inquiries must be made in relation to section 8. The first is whether the accused had a reasonable expectation of privacy; the second, if such an expectation is present, is whether the police search was conducted reasonably.
- A reasonable expectation of privacy is to be determined on the basis of the totality of the circumstances.[783]
- The factors to be considered in assessing the totality of the circumstances may include, but are not restricted to, the following:
  - (a) presence at the time of the search;
  - (b) possession or control of the property or place searched;
  - (c) ownership of the property or place;
  - (d) historical use of the property or item;
  - (e) the ability to regulate access, including the right to admit or exclude others from the place;
  - (f) the existence of a subjective expectation of privacy; and
  - (g) the objective reasonableness of the expectation.

(3) A personal right

12.228 The essence of section 8 protection is the existence of a personal privacy right.[784] The right allegedly infringed will, therefore, be that of the person, most often the accused, who makes the challenge.

12.229 A personal right of privacy is not coterminous with a possessory or property interest in premises or articles,[785] although possession or ownership might properly be considered evidence of that personal right.[786] For example, as the applicant in *Pugliese*[787] was unable to advance any ground for privacy beyond ownership of the building in question, the Court concluded that he had no expectation of privacy in a leased apartment in the building or the portion of it from which drugs were seized. Neither did possession of a driver's licence in *Hufsky* give its owner any right to withhold it from the authorities. Instead, the courts have indicated that a key element in privacy is the right to be free from intrusion or interference,[788] an element which could not be established in *Edwards* in which the accused had been no more than a 'privileged guest' in the home of his girlfriend. Particularly relevant was the fact that it was not the accused but his girlfriend who had the authority to regulate access to, and exclude others from, the premises.

12.230 It is possible, in some circumstances, to establish an expectation of privacy in goods themselves.[789] Such was the case in relation to the records of a business proprietorship in *Thomson Newspapers*[790] which were subject to an order for production under the federal

783 *R v Colarusso* (1984) 13 DLR (4th) 680.

784 *R v Edwards* [1996] 45 CR (4th) 307, 318, SCC; *R v Pugliese* (1992) 71 CCC (3d) 295.

785 Dickson J in *Hunter v Southam* [1984] 2 SCR 145 emphatically rejected any requirement of a connection between the section 8 right and a property interest in the premises searched.

786 *R v Edwards* [1996] 45 CR (4th) 307, 318 quoting Finlayson JA in *R v Pugliese* (1992) 71 CCC (3d) 295.

787 Ibid.

788 *R v Edwards* (n 786 above) 321.

789 *R v Edwards* (n 786 above) 319: the appellant sought unsuccessfully to assert a right in the drugs seized, after having maintained in the Court of Appeal that they did not belong to him. The SCC precluded him from changing his position so as to raise a fresh defence.

790 *Thomson Newspapers Ltd v Canada* [1990] (*Director of Investigation and Research, Restrictive Trade Practices Commission*) 1 SCR 425.

Combines Investigation Act. The accused in *R v Plant*,[791] on the other hand, failed to establish a right of privacy in his electricity bills. The accused in *Edwards* was also unsuccessful in arguing that an interest in seized drugs[792] created a reasonable expectation of privacy.

The expectation of privacy by third parties is not relevant to the disposition of an application under section 8. In *R v Edwards*, the police conducted a drug search of the premises of the girlfriend of the accused, who was persuaded to allow them access without a warrant, in the absence of her boyfriend. The majority held the search to be constitutional as the accused had no reasonable expectation of privacy in the apartment. The rights of his girlfriend were not in issue before the Court, although it was acknowledged that the intrusion of the search on third parties might have been relevant to the reasonableness of the search in the second stage of the analysis, had it been necessary to go that far.[793] Contrary to the view of the majority, Judge La Forest felt that section 8 protects a public interest in security from intrusion by unwarranted police searches and that the expectation of privacy of the girlfriend ought to have been taken into account in the first stage. **12.231**

(4) Section 8 analysis: a two-step process

(a) Introduction

The determination as to whether section 8 has been infringed is a two stage process.[794] The expectation of privacy is relevant to each stage. First, the presence (or absence) of a reasonable expectation of privacy is relevant to whether the activity in question constitutes a search or seizure. Secondly, once a search or seizure has been established, the court must assess its reasonableness; and presumes the search or seizure is reasonable unless the contrary is proved. Where a reasonable expectation exists, but in a diminished form, the threshold will be lowered and the presumption of unreasonableness more easily rebutted. Whether a reasonable expectation of privacy exists is to be ascertained without reference to the police conduct during the search[795] or to the seriousness of the alleged offences.[796] Whether the search constitutes an unreasonable intrusion on that right to privacy is a separate question. **12.232**

(b) 'Reasonable expectation of privacy'

The existence of a 'search' or 'seizure'. The Supreme Court of Canada has followed the American decision in *Katz*[797] to hold that electronic surveillance is a search or seizure under section 8 of the Charter.[798] A reasonable expectation of privacy is violated when a telephone conversation is intercepted without the knowledge or consent of the participants.[799] **12.233**

[791] *R v Plant* [1993] 3 SCR 281.

[792] *R v Edwards* (n 786 above) 319; see also *R v Sandhu* (1993) 82 CCC (3d) 236 in which the question of ownership of a suitcase for drug delivery arose.

[793] *R v Edwards* (n 786 above) 316 for the two stages see para 12.232 below.

[794] *R v Edwards* [1996] 45 CR (4th) 307, 316 *per* Cory J.

[795] Ibid.

[796] *R v Plant* [1993] 3 SCR 281.

[797] *Katz v United States* (1967) 389 US 347.

[798] *R v Duarte* [1990] 1 SCR 30.

[799] *R v Thompson* [1990] 2 SCR 1111.

12.234 The Supreme Court has, however, refused to distinquish between 'participant electronic surveillance', in which one party to a conversation or interaction consents to its surreptitious electronic recording, and 'third-party electronic surveillance', in which none of the parties consents. In *Duarte*[800] the police obtained the cooperation of an informer to enable them to instal audio visual equipment on his premises and to record his drug transaction with the accused; in *R v Wiggins*[801] the informer consented to wear a microphone which transmitted his conversations with the accused about the drug dealings to the police. In each of these cases, the surreptitious recording was found to invade a reasonable expectation of privacy. The difficulty with this approach is that the breaching of confidence is not an invasion of privacy and disclosure of a private conversation by one of the parties is therefore admissible evidence. As a result, evidence from informers is admissible whereas electronic recordings of a conversation is not.[802] Another problem is that if the recording is an invasion of privacy, it is so whether or not it is tendered as evidence, and thus police are prohibited from using recording devices even as a means of protection of undercover officers or informers.

12.235 In spite of these difficulties, the Supreme Court of Canada has maintained the view that a participant does not accept the risk of disclosure by another participant. It has extended the finding of reasonable expectation of privacy from private telephone conversations to the video-taping of an illegal gambling operation in a crowded hotel room. In *R v Wong*[803] the hotel consented to the installation of a hidden camera, and although few of the guests knew one another, the Court found that the recording of events in the room invaded their reasonable expectation of privacy, in violation of the Charter.

12.236 As a result, the police in Canada can lawfully use electronic surveillance techniques only where there is no reasonable expectation of privacy, such as a conversation or transaction taking place on the street or in a public venue. The Charter would not apply to a recording initiated by a private individual, but if, for example a shop proprietor installed a video camera at the suggestion of the police, he might be deemed an agent of the police.[804]

12.237 The collection of evidence, even in the absence of a search, might also amount to a 'seizure' on the basis of reasonable expectation of privacy. In *R v Dyment*[805] a doctor collected blood from the wound of an unconscious traffic accident victim for medical purposes, but then delivered it to a police officer for analysis, resulting in charges of impaired driving against the victim. Although section 8 did not apply to the private act of collection of the sample by the doctor, the Court found that the receipt of the sample by the police officer, without warrant and without the consent, was an unreasonable 'seizure' violating the expectation of privacy of the accused. The Court also used the expectation of privacy to distinguish the 'gathering' of evidence from that of an unconstitutional taking, citing the example of police collection of blood from the seat of a car, rather than that flowing from

800 *R v Duarte* [1990] 1 SCR 30.
801 *R v Wiggins* [1990] 1 SCR 62.
802 Evidence obtained in breach of the Charter is not admissible, unless it can be shown that the police were unaware that they had violated the Charter and were acting in good faith.
803 *R v Wong* [1990] 3 SCR 36.
804 *R v Broyles* [1991] 3 SCR 595 where a friend of a suspect visiting the suspect in prison at the suggestion of the police, and recording their conversation, was a police agent.
805 [1988] 2 SCR 417.

a wound. The individual in the former case would be considered to have 'abandoned' the blood, retaining no reasonable expectation of privacy in regard to it.

Where there is a reasonable expectation of privacy in relation to documents, an order for their production also constitutes a 'search' or 'seizure' under section 8. In *R v Hufsky*[806] a demand by a police officer that a driver produce a driver's licence and vehicle insurance certificate was found not to be a 'search' under the section because it did not intrude on a reasonable expectation of privacy. It was clear that there could be no such intrusion by way of a request for evidence of compliance with a requirement that is a lawful condition of the exercise of a right or privilege.[807] While there is no reasonable expectation of privacy in regard to a motor vehicle licence, such expectation does exist in regard to business records. **12.238**

In order for constitutional protection to be extended to commercial documents, the information seized must be of a 'personal and confidential nature';[808] this would include information revealing intimate details of the lifestyle of its owner. The computerised records of electricity consumption were found in *Plant*[809] to reflect a purely commercial relationship between appellant and utility, because they revealed little personal information of the occupant of the residence, and were available to the public. By contrast, in *Thomson Newspapers v Canada*[810] the records of a business proprietor were characterised as confidential communications. There, the order under the federal Combines Investigation Act to produce the documents was found to be a 'seizure', even though there was no entry or search of premises[811] on grounds that there was 'little difference between taking a thing and forcing a person to give it up'.[812] **12.239**

The reasonableness of the search or seizure. The expectation of privacy will also, to some extent, be relevant in the assessment of the reasonableness of the search or seizure. The test of reasonableness was established by unanimous decision of the Supreme Court of Canada in *Hunter v Southam*;[813] the power of search and seizure in the Combines Investigation Act was found to infringe section 8 of the Charter because it authorised 'unreasonable' searches and seizures. The Court decided that a search or seizure is presumed to be unreasonable; and acknowledged that it would not always be feasible to satisfy the prescribed criteria. Nevertheless, a search without a warrant might be justified if a presumption of unreasonableness could be rebutted. **12.240**

In relation to electronic surveillance, provided the requirements of the Criminal Code for 'wiretaps' have been met,[814] the search or seizure will be not only lawful, but will not be **12.241**

806 [1988] 1 SCR 621; followed by *R v Ladouceur* [1990] 1 SCR 1257.
807 *R v Hufsky* [1988] 1 SCR 621, 638.
808 *R v Plant* [1993] 3 SCR 281.
809 Ibid.
810 [1990] 1 SCR 425.
811 *Thomson Newspapers v Canada* [1990] 1 SCR 425.
812 Note, though, that ultimately the seizure was found to be a reasonable one, in spite of the fact that it had been authorised by the investigating agency, rather than a court, on grounds that a demand to produce is far less intrusive upon privacy than an actual search of premises.
813 *Hunter v Southam* [1984] 2 SCR 145: the Court said that a search was reasonable only if it was authorised by statute which stipulated three conditions: a prior warrant or other authorisation; issued by a person 'capable of acting judicially'; and on oath that there are 'reasonable and probable grounds' for believing that an offence has been committed and that evidence is located in the place to be searched.
814 The Criminal Code requires a judicial warrant obtained on reasonable and probable grounds to authorise the electronic interception of telephone conversations.

'unreasonable' under section 8 of the Charter.[815] In subsequent cases, the Court has held the presumption of unreasonableness to be rebutted where the search or seizure is not significantly intrusive, or where the expectation of privacy itself is diminished, or both.[816]

12.242 The order for production of documents in *Thomson Newspapers*, for example, was considered minimally intrusive, in comparison with the imposition of an actual search, upon the undiminished expectation of privacy in the documents. As a result, the order for production, though issued under non-judicial authorisation, resulted in a reasonable 'seizure' when held up to a reduced standard or threshold of reasonableness in the circumstances. In *Plant*, on the other hand, the lower court decision that a perimeter search of premises was not unreasonable, given its minimal level of intrusion, was overturned by the Supreme Court of Canada which found that it could not be justified without warrant.

12.243 A lower expectation of privacy will also reduce the standard of reasonableness so as not to require fulfilment of the warrant requirements of *Hunter v Southam*. This will occur, for example, where prison inmates, while having some expectation of privacy, might be subject to random or routine searches of their person or cells;[817] in a school context, where it has been held reasonable for a teacher to search a student without warrant for possession of drugs;[818] at an international border, where the absence of a warrant requirement in the Customs Act was reasonable;[819] or during travel in an automobile.[820] The expectation of privacy will also be less if the activity in question is regulated: administrative inspections of commercial premises, or even private homes in order to check for compliance with building standards, zoning rules, public health and safety requirements are not unreasonable searches[821] and confiscation of an illegal or dangerous or diseased thing without a warrant in such circumstances is not an unreasonable seizure.[822]

815 See also *R v Garafoli* [1990] 2 SCR 1421; *R v Lachance* [1990] 2 SCR 1490; *Dersch v Can* [1990] 2 SCR 1505; *R v Zito* [1990] 2 SCR 1520.

816 See *R v Wise* [1992] 11 CR (4th) 253 which held that the expectation of privacy in a motor vehicle is reduced in comparison to that in a home or office and that installation of an unsophisticated tracking device in the interior of the motor vehicle was only minimally intrusive.

817 *Weatherall v Canada* [1991] 1 FC 85.

818 *R v JMG* (1986) 56 OR (2d) 705.

819 *R v Simmons* [1988] 2 SCR 495.

820 *R v Wise* [1992] 11 CR (4th) 253: the expectation of privacy in automobile travel is markedly decreased relative to the expectation of privacy in one's home or office; in *R v Belnais* [1997] 3 SCR 341 the Supreme Court held that the reasonable expectation depends on the totality of the circumstances.

821 See *Re Belgoma Transportation* (1985) 51 OR (2d) 509: employment standards; *R v Quesnel* (1985) 53 OR (2d) 338: marketing board inspection; *R v Bichel* (1986) 33 DLR (4th) 254: building inspection of private home; *Ontario Chrysler (1997) Ltd v Ontario* (1990) 72 OR (2d) 106: business practices inspection.

822 *R v Bertram S Miller* [1986] 3 FC 291: (confiscation and destruction of diseased plants); *Re Ozubko* (1986) 33 DLR (4th) 714 Man CA: (confiscation of illegal syringe); *Re Milton* (1986) 37 DLR (4th) 694: (confiscation of illegal fishing nets).

Appendix 2: The New Zealand Bill of Rights Act

(1) Introduction

Like the Canadian Charter of Rights and Freedoms, the New Zealand Bill of Rights Act 1990 makes no express provision for the guarantee of respect to privacy. Section 21 of the New Zealand Bill of Rights Act provides that: **12.244**

> **Unreasonable search and seizure**
>
> Everyone has the right to be secure against unreasonable search or seizure, whether of the person, property or correspondence or otherwise.

The final words reflect the Fourth Amendment in the American Bill of Rights and have some similarity to the privacy provision of the European Convention. The New Zealand courts have followed the Canadian example and have dealt with the concept of privacy under the heading of the section 21 guarantee against unreasonable search and seizure.

(2) The interpretation of section 21

The New Zealand approach to reasonableness of search and seizure places less emphasis on the protection of privacy than does that of the Canadian courts. Whether a search or seizure has been unreasonable and evidence unfairly or improperly obtained is determined by balancing all of the relevant interests in the circumstances, including, but not focusing exclusively on an 'expectation of privacy'. **12.245**

The Court of Appeal first considered the relationship of privacy to search and seizure in *R v Jeffries*,[823] in which the police, believing the accused and his companions to be fleeing an armed robbery, stopped and searched the vehicle they were driving for weapons and stolen goods. The search, conducted without warrant, would have been lawful under the Arms Act had they identified themselves properly and advised the suspects of the section of the Act under which the search was to take place; they did not so comply with the statute and the search of the boot of the car revealed not arms but $30,000 worth of cannabis. The issue before the Court of Appeal was whether the search was reasonable under the New Zealand Bill of Rights Act. Five of the seven judges agreed that a search may be 'unlawful' and yet reasonable under the Bill of Rights Act; four found that although the search was unlawful it had not been rendered unreasonable. Two judges held that the search was lawful and reasonable; one judge in dissent held the unlawful search was *ipso facto* unreasonable. The cannabis was admitted as evidence in the trial of the accused. **12.246**

After consideration of the Canadian position on the relationship of privacy to the reasonableness of a search,[824] Richardson J stated that: an analysis of section 21 would emphasise four considerations: **12.247**

(i) rights of the citizen reflect an amalgam of values: property, personal freedom, privacy and dignity. A search of premises or the person is an invasion of property rights, a restraint on individual liberty, an intrusion on privacy and an affront to dignity.

[823] [1994] 1 NZLR 290.

[824] In particular *Hunter v Southam* (1984) 14 CCC 3d 97 and the US case of *Katz v United States* 389 US 347.

(ii) neither the Bill of Rights Act nor the International Covenant provides a general guarantee of privacy, and New Zealand did not have a general privacy law. There is no one privacy value that applies in all cases; rather, the nature and significance of a privacy value depends on the circumstances in which it arises.

(iii) a section 21 inquiry is an exercise in balancing competing values and interests; in particular, the legitimate state interests in detection and prosecution of offending against the immunity of citizens from arbitrary and unlawful searches of their property and persons. Whether the intrusion is 'unreasonable' involves weighing all relevant public interest considerations and their application in the particular case.

(iv) protection against unreasonable search or seizure must be distinguished from a 'reasonable expectation of privacy'. The two would be the same if one could ignore the interests of society as a whole or the interests of anyone other than the person whose privacy is affected, but rights are never absolute and individual freedoms are necessarily limited by membership of society.

A section 21 assessment must start with the presumption that any search is a significant invasion of individual freedom. How significant it is will depend on the particular circumstances and the other values and interests including law enforcement considerations which weigh in the particular case.

The intrusiveness of the search and the extent of the violation of individual rights vary according to the subject-matter of the search and the manner in which it is carried out. Thus, frisking an individual is less intrusive than a search of body cavities; the home is more a sanctuary than the office. Reasonable expectations of privacy are lower in public places than within private property. While in a mobile society the privacy of one's motor vehicle is highly valued and may be perceived as a projection of the privacy of the home, road safety and the legitimate protection of other users of the roads justify extensive rules governing the use of vehicles and allowing surveillance and supervision of vehicles, drivers and passengers. The expectation of privacy may be less where the property searched belongs to a third party, particularly where that person purports to consent to the search, and the complainant is a guest or family member or shares the use of the property. The manner in which a search is carried out will also affect the degree of any intrusion on private rights. It follows that in assessing the reasonableness of a search or seizure it is important to consider 'both the subject-matter and the time, place and circumstance'.

12.248 Since 1994, the New Zealand Court of Appeal has been inundated with section 21 cases.[825] The Court has preferred the 'amalgam of values' approach taken in *Jeffries* to the 'expectation of privacy' perspective of the American and Canadian jurisprudence. The test of unreasonableness of a search or seizure involves an assessment of all of the circumstances: the relevant values and public interest considerations and their application in the particular case.[826]

[825] See eg *R v A* [1994] 1 NZLR 429; *R v H* [1994] 2 NZLR 143; *R v Ririnui* [1994] 2 NZLR 439; *R v Pratt* [1994] 3 NZLR 21; *Simpson v A-G (Baigent's case)* [1994] 3 NZLR 667; *Auckland Unemployed Workers' Rights Centre Inc v A-G* [1994] 3 NZLR 720; *R v McNicol* [1995] 1 NZLR 576; *R v Kahu* [1995] 2 NZLR 3; *R v Stockdale* [1995] 2 NZLR 129; *Television New Zealand Ltd v A-G* [1995] 2 NZLR 641; *R v Reuben* [1995] 3 NZLR 165; *R v Wojcik* (1994) 11 CRNZ 463; *Campbell v Police* [1994] 3 NZLR 260; *R v Wong-Tung* (1995) 13 CRNZ 422; *R v Smith* (1996) 13 CRNZ 481; *R v Barlow* (1995) 14 CRNZ 9; *R v Faasipa* (1995) 2 HRNZ 50; *Queen Street Backpackers Ltd v Commerce Commission* (1994) 2 HRNZ 94; *R v Dodgson* (1995) 2 HRNZ 300.

[826] *R v A* [1994] 1 NZLR 429; *R v Pratt* [1994] 3 NZLR 21, 24: the test 'whether the circumstances giving rise to it make the search itself unreasonable or if a search that is otherwise reasonable is carried out in an unreasonable manner'.

While *Jeffries* established that lawfulness does not always determine reasonableness, or vice versa, the unlawfulness of a search and seizure is highly relevant to reasonableness.[827] If a warrant is readily obtainable, that will tell strongly against the reasonableness of an unauthorised search.[828] Only in rare cases will an unlawful search and seizure be reasonable.[829] So for example, in *R v H* where the police deliberately decided to refrain from obtaining a search warrant readily available under the Summary Proceedings Act, the search of the premises of an accountant and seizure of the company records was found to be unreasonable. The principles were restated by the Court of Appeal in *R v Grayson and Taylor*.[830] In that case, the police observed suspicious activity, including the construction of an electric fence and erection of shadecloth on the appellants' kiwi fruit orchard. Believing that they did not have enough evidence to obtain a search warrant, the police entered the property for the purposes of corroborating the information they had received. The entry involved negotiating electric fences and thick underbrush, but was not forceful. During their five minutes on the property, the officers observed rows of cannabis plants growing between the kiwifruit vines. A search warrant was subsequently obtained and surveillance videos taken, plants seized and appellants charged with cultivation of cannabis. The trial judge found the initial search unlawful but not unreasonable. The Court of Appeal dismissed the appeal and held that in all the circumstances, entry onto the property was reasonable and the evidence admissible.

The Court of Appeal in *Grayson* has set out a number of statutory and common law principles relevant to a challenge to the admissibility of evidence on grounds of breach of section 21. It was pointed out that entry and search of private property by state officials, without permission, is an actionable trespass,[831] but that evidence obtained by illegal searches is admissible, subject only to a discretion to exclude it on the ground of unfairness to the accused.[832] This basis for a challenge to admissibility is not affected by section 21. The Court noted that section 21 is a restraint on governmental action that does not confer any positive power[833] on the state to conduct a 'reasonable search'. **12.250**

The Court of Appeal went on to hold that: **12.251**

> A search is unreasonable if the circumstances giving rise to it make the search itself unreasonable or if a search which would otherwise be reasonable is carried out in an unreasonable manner. So too seizure. Whether a police search or seizure is unreasonable depends on both the subject-matter and the particular time, place and circumstance.[834]

A prime purpose of section 21 is to ensure that governmental power is not exercised unreasonably. A section 21 enquiry is an exercise in balancing legitimate state interests against any intrusions on individual interests. It requires weighing relevant values and public interests.[835] The guarantee under section 21 to be free from unreasonable search and seizure reflects an amalgam of values. A search of premises is an invasion of property rights and an intrusion on privacy. It may also involve a restraint on individual liberty and

[827] See *R v H* [1994] 2 NZLR 143, 148.
[828] Ibid 148.
[829] *R v Pratt* [1994] 3 NZLR 21, 24.
[830] [1997] 1 NZLR 399.
[831] Ibid Principle 1, 406.
[832] Ibid Principle 2, 407.
[833] Ibid Principle 3, 407.
[834] Ibid Principle 4.
[835] Ibid Principle 5.

an affront to dignity. Any search is a significant invasion of individual freedom. How significant it will be depends on the circumstances.[836]

12.252 The Court gave express consideration to the role of 'privacy' in connection with the reasonableness of searches under section 21:

> Contemporary society attaches a high value to privacy and to the security of personal privacy against arbitrary intrusions by those in authority. Privacy values underlying the section 21 guarantee are those held by the community at large. They are not merely the subjective expectations of privacy which a particular owner or occupier may have and may demonstrate by signs or barricades. Reasonable expectations of privacy are lower in public places than on private property. They are higher for the home than for the surrounding land and for land not used for residential purposes. And the nature of the activities carried on, particularly if involving public engagement or governmental oversight, may affect reasonable expectations of privacy. An assessment of the seriousness of the particular intrusion involves considerations of fact and degree, not taking absolutist stances. In that regard, and unlike the thrust of the American Fourth Amendment jurisprudence, the object of section 21 is vindication of individual rights rather than deterrence and disciplining of police misconduct.[837]

Taking these matters into account, illegality was not the touchstone of unreasonableness. In terms of section 21, what is unlawful is not necessarily unreasonable. The lawfulness or unlawfulness of a search will always be highly relevant but will not be determinative either way.[838]

12.253 After considering the specific provisions of New Zealand law in relation to search warrants, the Court summarised the position in relation to the Bill of Rights Act as follows:

> The Bill of Rights is not a technical document. It has to be applied in our society in a realistic way. The application and interpretation of the Bill must also be true to its purposes as set out in its title of affirming, protecting and promoting human rights and fundamental freedoms in New Zealand, and affirming New Zealand's commitment to the International Covenant on Civil and Political Rights. The crucial question is whether what was done constituted an unreasonable search or seizure in the particular circumstances. Anyone complaining of a breach must invest the complaint with an air of reality and must lay a foundation for the complaint before the trial Court by explicit challenge or cross-examination or evidence.[839]

12.254 There are a large number of the decisions dealing with admissibility of evidence obtained under unlawful searches. A minor non-compliance with statutory procedural requirements was not sufficient to render a search 'unreasonable'.[840] The 'close surveillance' of a prisoner, involving collection and examination of bowel motions, was not unreasonable where authorities believed that he had controlled drugs secreted within his body for an unlawful purpose. The heroin packets recovered were admissible and the procedures, although 'draconian' were reasonable in the interests of the health of the prisoner and for prison safety.[841] However, evidence has been excluded in a number of search cases. In *R v*

[836] Ibid Principle 6.
[837] Ibid Principle 6.
[838] Ibid Principle 7.
[839] Ibid Principle 10, 409.
[840] *R v Jeffries* [1994] 1 NZLR 290.
[841] *R v Stockdale* [1995] 2 NZLR 129.

Pratt[842] the defendant had been strip searched in the street. The police had found keys in his pocket which were used to gain access to a building in which a quantity of cocaine was discovered. The evidence of the finding of the keys and what the police did with them was excluded. In *Frost v Police*[842a] the use of dogs and other forceful measures by police after two noise complaints were not reasonable, given that the intent was to conduct a warrantless search for drugs under the auspices of noise control legislation at premises where drug dealing was suspected, police had had ample time to obtain a search warrant. The courts have also excluded evidence from the warrantless search of bags in the back of the accused's car[842b] and of a car boot.[842c] When property was thrown away by an accused in the course of an unlawful and unreasonable search this was sufficiently linked to breaches of section 21 to require its exclusion.[842d]

(3) Electronic surveillance

(a) Non-participant surveillance

In *R v Fraser*[843] the police video-taped an accused drug dealer apparently concealing items in the garden of an address where he was not a resident. The surveillance took place from outside the private property without a warrant. Under the Summary Proceedings Act, the police could have obtained a warrant to 'enter' and search for 'things', but the Court found that no such warrant was necessary to conduct a video-recording in the open area outside a private residence. The search was lawful, as there was no statutory or common law prohibition against observing or video-taping the open area surrounding a residential property. **12.255**

Nevertheless, the search was not necessarily reasonable under the Bill of Rights Act; this depended on what the accused might reasonably be subjected to in the circumstances, having regard to standards of the community concerning respect for privacy. It was necessary to consider all the circumstances prevailing at the time the search was undertaken and to balance the legitimate interests of the individual to a reasonable expectation of privacy with those of the state in the detection and prosecution of criminal activities. The Court found no evidence that the accused could have expected not to be observed in the area covered by the video camera. A similar result was reached in *R* v *Peita*[843a] where cannabis was discovered growing on the appellant's farm by a police spotter plane. It was held that the conduct of the aerial surveillance was not unreasonable and that evidence discovered as a result of that activity was admissible. **12.256**

(b) Participant recording

In relation to 'participant recording' or 'participant surveillance' the New Zealand Court has followed the United States rather than the Canadian approach and held that such surveillance is not unreasonable under the Act. The Court in *R v A*[844] provided four reasons for this position: **12.257**

---

[842] [1994] 3 NZLR 21; see also *R v McNicol* [1995] 1 NZLR 576; *R v Kahu* [1995] 2 NZLR 3; *Campbell v Police* [1994] 3 NZLR 260.
[842a] [1996] 2 NZLR 716.
[842b] *Longley v Police* [1995] 1 NZLR 87.
[842c] *R v Brainbridge* (1999) 5 HRNZ 317.
[842d] Ibid, distinguishing *R v Reuben* [1995] 3 NZLR 165.
[843] [1997] 2 NZLR 442.
[843a] (1999) 5 HRNZ 250.
[844] [1994] 1 NZLR 429.

- It is not unlawful for any participant in a conversation to record a discussion surreptitiously. There is no basis in parliamentary consideration of electronic surveillance for the courts to conclude that public policy requires treatment of participant recording as inherently destructive of basic values.
- Advances in information technology have advantages as well as risks. The social answer to the problem turns on an examination of all of the circumstances rather than on an impossible quest for universally agreed moral absolutes. It is a matter of time, place and circumstance.
- The expectation of privacy, while important, is not the only consideration in determining whether a search or seizure is unreasonable.
- Characterising participant recording as always constituting unreasonable search and seizure would have significant consequences contrary to the public interest. First, if such recording is a breach of section 21 it would, *prima facie*, be excluded from evidence, while the intrusion on privacy would have occurred in any event. Secondly, it would necessarily inhibit the police from wiring a police officer for safety reasons.

Appendix 3: Human Rights Cases in Other Jurisdictions

(1) Introduction

12.258 The right to privacy is protected under the civil and criminal law of most European states. In France, Article 9 of the Civil Code was introduced in 1970 and provides for the right to 'respect for privacy'. This has now been recognised as a 'constitutional right'.[845] The German courts have developed a general 'right to personality' which has enabled them to protect a range of privacy rights.[846] The protection of privacy rights in Italy has also been a matter for judge made law.[847]

12.259 In many common law jurisdictions the right to privacy is now the subject of statutory protection.[848] The right has, however, been the subject of sustained consideration in the constitutional context in the American courts where the right has been recognised as covering both the interest in avoiding the disclosure of personal information and the 'interest in independence in making certain kinds of important decisions'.[849] This right has been used to provide constitutional protection for the use of contraception,[850] the distribution of

[845] See generally, E Picard, 'The Right to Privacy in French Law', in B Markesinis (ed), *Protecting Privacy* (Oxford University Press, 1999).

[846] See generally, P Quint, 'Free Speech and Private Law in German Constitutional Theory' (1989) 48 Maryland L Rev 247–346; B Markesinis, 'Privacy, Freedom of Expression and the Horizontal Effect of the Human Rights Bill: Lessons from Germany' [1999] 115 LQR 47; H Stoll, 'General Rights to Personality in German Law' in Markesinis (n 845 above); and see, J Craig and N Nolte, 'Privacy and Free Speech in Germany and Canada: Lessons for an English Privacy Tort' [1998] EHRLR 162.

[847] See G Alpa, 'Protection of Privacy in Italian Law' in Markesinis (n 845 above).

[848] See for example the Privacy Act 1988 (Australia).

[849] *Whalen v Roe* (1977) 429 US 589, 599–600 *per* Stevens J; a full discussion is outside the scope of this book but see generally, L Tribe, *American Constitutional Law* (2nd edn, Foundation Press, 1988) Chap 15 and also D Anderson, 'The Failure of American Privacy Law' in Markesinis (n 846 above).

[850] *Griswold v Connecticut* (1965) 381 US 479 (criminal law prohibiting the use of contraceptive unconstitutional).

contraceptives to unmarried persons[851] and abortion.[852] The right has not, however, been extended to sexual privacy generally, the Supreme Court refusing to strike down statutes criminalising sodomy.[853] Furthermore, the right to privacy is subject to freedom of expression rights, and the publication of false private information will only be actionable if malicious.[854]

The Fourth Amendment to the US Constitution affirms the right of the people to be secure 'in their persons, houses, papers and effects, against unreasonable searches and seizures'. This provision embodies the principle of respect for privacy of the home,[854a] but not a general right of privacy.[854b] It also protects persons on office premises[854c] overnight guests in hostels[854d] or houses[854e] but does not extend to 'open fields'[854f] or to a visitor to a house.[854g] It also covers the use of hidden microphones and telephone tapping,[854h] but not aerial inspection of a garden.[854i] Government officials are not permitted to undertake searches or seizures without an 'individualised suspicion' unless it was based on 'special needs' beyond the normal requirements of law enforcement.[854j] **12.259A**

(2) Human Rights Committee[855]

Article 17 of the International Covenant on Civil and Political Rights provides that: **12.260**

> (1) No one shall be subjected to arbitrary or unlawful interference with his privacy home or correspondence, nor to unlawful attacks on his honour and reputation.
>
> (2) Everyone has the right to the protection of the law against such interferences or attacks.

---

851 *Eisenstad v Baird* (1972) 405 US 438.

852 *Roe v Wade* (1973) 410 US 113 (law prohibiting abortion unconstitutional); this was, of course, one of the most controversial decisions of modern times, see generally, Tribe (n 849 above) para 15–10 and also *Planned Parenthood v Casey* (1992) 505 US 833.

853 *Bowers v Hardwick* (1986) 478 US 186; but see *Romer v Evans* (1996) 517 US 620 (Colorado constitutional amendment prohibiting action designed to protect homosexuals from discrimination unconstitutional under Fourteenth Amendment 'Equal Protection' provisions); see generally, Tribe (n 849 above) para 15–21 and R Wintemute, *Sexual Orientation and Human Rights* (Clarendon Press, 1995) Chaps 2 and 3.

854 *Time Inc v Hill* (1967) 385 US 374.

854a *Wilson v Layne* (1999) 7 BHRC 274 ('media ride alongs' unconstitutional).

854b *Katz v United States* (1967) 389 US 347, 350.

854c *Gouled v United States* (1921) 255 US 298.

854d *Lustig v United States* (1949) 338 US 74.

854e *Minnesota v Olson* (1990) 495 US 91.

854f *Oliver v United States* (1984) 466 US 170.

854g *Minnesotav v Carter* (1998) 5 BHRC 457.

854h *Katz v United States* (n 854b above; *United States v United States District Court for Eastern District of Michegan* (1972) 407 US 297.

854i *California v Ciraolo* (1986) 476 US 207; *Florida v Riley* (1989) 488 US 445.

854j *Chandler v Miller* (1997) 3 BHRC 234 (drug testing programme for candidates for state office unconstitutional); contrast the drug testing programmes approved in *National Treasury Employees Union v Von Raab* (1989) 489 US 109 (customs officials) and *Vernonia School District 47J v Acton* (1995) 515 US 646 (high school students engaged in athletic competitions).

855 See generally, J Michael, 'Privacy' in D Harris and S Joseph (eds), *The International Covenant on Civil and Political Rights and United Kingdom Law* (Clarendon Press, 1995) 333–354.

This provision does not, unlike other Articles, specify the grounds on which a state party may interfere with privacy.

12.261 An interference will be 'unlawful' unless it is authorised by a domestic law which itself complies with 'the provisions, aims and objectives of the Covenant'.[856] An interference can be arbitrary even if it is lawful. The concept of arbitrariness is intended to guarantee that an interference is 'reasonable' in the circumstances.[857] Article 17 is the subject matter of General Comment 16, in which it was stated that:

> the competent public authorities should only be able to call for such information relating to an individual's private life the knowledge of which is essential in the interests of society as understood under the Covenant.[858]

12.262 In *Toonen v Australia*[859] the Committee took the view that the requirement of 'reasonableness' implied that 'any interference with privacy must be proportional to the end sought and be necessary in the circumstances of any given case'. It was held that laws in Tasmania prohibiting sex between men were an arbitrary interference with privacy.[860]

(3) India

12.263 Article 21 of the Constitution of India provides that:

> No person shall be deprived of his life or personal liberty except according to procedure established by law.

The Supreme Court has held that a right to privacy is implicit in this provision.[861] In *Rajagopal v State of Tamil Nadu*[862] B P Jeevan Reddy J summarised the position in relation to this implicit right as follows:

> This is a 'right to be let alone'. A citizen has a right to safeguard the privacy of his own, his family, marriage, procreation, motherhood, child-bearing and education among other matters. None can publish anything concerning the above matters without his consent—whether truthful or otherwise or whether laudatory or critical. If he did so, he would be violating the right to privacy of the person concerned . . .[863]

There are, however, exceptions in relation to the publication of information based on public records and the right to privacy is not available if public officials are acting in the course of their official duties unless, in the latter case, the publication is made with reckless disregard for the truth.[864]

---

856 General Comment 16 para 3.
857 Ibid paras 4 and 8.3.
858 Ibid para 7.
859 488/1992, 31 Mar 1994, UNHRC.
860 Cf the discussion in R Wintemute, *Sexual Orientation and Human Rights* (Clarendon Press, 1995) 143–149.
861 *Kharak Singh v State of UP* [1964] 1 SCR 332; *Gobind v State of MP* (1975) 2 SCC 148; *Rajagopal v State of Tamil Nadu* [1995] 3 LRC 566.
862 Ibid 581e.
863 Ibid 581d–f.
864 Ibid 581f–582b.

In *People's Union for Civil Liberties v Union of India*[865] it was held that telephone tapping infringed Article 21 which had to be interpreted in accordance with Article 17 of the International Covenant on Civil and Political Rights.[866] Although there were statutory restrictions on the power to intercept messages or conversations, these had to be backed by procedural safeguards to ensure that the power was exercised in a fair and reasonable manner.[867] It was held that, as the Government had laid down no procedural safeguards it was necessary for the Court to do so. The Court specified who should authorise telephone tapping, the duration and scope of authorisations, the records which should be maintained and the limits on the use of intercepted material. 12.264

(4) Ireland[868]

The Irish Constitution does not make express provision for any right to privacy. In the 1980s the courts rejected a number of attempts to establish such a right.[869] However, the right was finally recognised in the 'telephone tapping' case of *Kennedy v Ireland*.[870] It was held that: 12.265

> although not specifically guaranteed by the Constitution, the right to privacy is one of the fundamental personal rights of the citizen which flow from the Christian and democratic nature of the State. It is not an unqualified right. Its exercise may be restricted by the constitutional rights of others, or by the requirements of the common good, and it is subject to the requirements of public order and morality.

As a result, it was held that the unjustifiable tapping of the plaintiffs' telephones by the state was a breach of their rights to privacy. In one case,[871] the Supreme Court was prepared to assume, for the purpose of argument, that there might be a right to privacy in a public street. However, police surveillance was justified in that case and in a case in which a person in police custody was kept under observation.[872] In *Redmond v Mr Justice Flood*[873] the applicant complained that public hearings of a statutory tribunal relating to certain planning matters were an interference with his right to privacy. The Supreme Court dismissed the application holding that the constitutional right to privacy was not an absolute one and could be outweighed by the exigencies of the common good. The inquiry in question had to be held in public for the purpose of allaying the public disquiet that led to its appointment.

(5) South Africa

The Constitution of South Africa provides: 12.266

> (14) Everyone has the right to privacy, which includes the right not to have—

---

[865] [1999] 2 LRC 1.

[866] See App J in Vol 2. It was also held that telephone tapping infringed rights of freedom of expression under Art 19 of the Constitution, see para 15.362 below.

[867] Applying *Maneka Ghandi v Union of India* (1978) 1 SCC 248.

[868] See generally, J M Kelly, *The Irish Constitution* (3rd edn, Butterworths, 1994) 767–770.

[869] *Norris v A-G* [1984] IR 36 (in relation to criminal laws penalising homosexuality); *Madigan v A-G* [1986] IRLM 136 (in relation to laws requiring disclosure of income).

[870] [1987] IR 587.

[871] *Kane v Governor of Mountjoy Prison* [1988] IR 757.

[872] *DPP v Kenny* [1992] 2 IR 141.

[873] [1999] 1 IRLM 241.

(a) their person or home searched;
(b) their property searched;
(c) their possessions seized; or
(d) the privacy of their communications infringed.

This is subject to the 'limitations' set out in section 36 'to the extent that the limitation is reasonable and justifiable in an open and democratic society based on human dignity, equality and freedom'. The South African Constitutional Court has considered this provision on a number of occasions.

12.267 In *Bernstein v Bester*[874] the applicants challenged the constitutionality of provisions of the Companies Acts[875] providing for the summoning and examination of persons in relation to the affairs of a company being wound up. It was contended that the examination mechanism infringed, *inter alia*, rights to privacy. These argument were rejected by the Court. Ackermann J said that:

> The truism that no right is to be considered absolute, implies that from the outset of interpretation each right is always already limited by every other right accruing to another citizen. In the context of privacy this would mean that it is only the inner sanctum of a person, such as his/her family life, sexual preference and home environment, which is shielded from erosion by conflicting rights of the community. This implies that community rights and the rights of fellow members place a corresponding obligation on a citizen, thereby shaping the abstract notion of individualism towards identifying a concrete member of civil society. Privacy is acknowledged in the truly personal realm, but as a person moves into communal relations and activities such as business and social interaction, the scope of personal space shrinks accordingly.[876]

12.268 The right to privacy was considered in the 'obscene publications' context in *Case v Minister of Safety and Security*.[877] It was held that a statutory provision forbidding the possession of 'indecent or obscene photographic matter' was a violation of the 'right to privacy'. Didcott J stated that:

> what erotic material I may choose to keep within the privacy of my home, and only for my personal use there, is nobody's business but mine.[878]

However, the majority took a more restrictive view, holding that the possession of such material could be subjected to limitation even in the privacy of one's own home.[879]

12.269 In *National Council for Gay and Lesbian Equality v Ministry of Justice*[880] the Constitutional Court held that the common law offence of sodomy and number of related statutory offences were unconstitutional and invalid. The applicants' arguments were based on the right to equality[881] but the Court stressed that the right to privacy was also infringed:

[874] 1996 (4) BCLR 449, CC paras 65 and 67.
[875] ss 417 and 418; analogous to Insolvency Act 1986, s 236.
[876] Ibid para 67; cf the discussion of the South African common law of privacy at paras 68ff.
[877] (1997) 1 BHRC 541 (the Court was dealing with the Interim Constitution, s 13 of which is in materially identical terms).
[878] *Case v Minister of Safety* (n 877 above) para 91, 575e–f.
[879] See Langa J, para 99, 578b–d; Madala J paras 103–107, 579a–580f.
[880] 9 Oct 1998; upholding Heher J (1998) (6) BCLR 726 (W).
[881] s 9 of the Constitution.

> Privacy recognises that we all have a right to a sphere of private intimacy and autonomy which allows us to establish and nurture human relationships without interference from the outside community. The way in which we give expression to our sexuality is at the core of this area of private intimacy. . . . The fact that a law prohibiting forms of sexual conduct is discriminatory, does not, however, prevent it at the same time being an improper invasion of the intimate sphere of human life to which protection is given by the Constitution in section 14. We should not deny the importance of a right to privacy in our new constitutional order, even while we acknowledge the importance of equality.[882]

There will, however, be no invasion of the constitutional right of privacy if information is communicated in a situation analogous to a 'privileged occasion' at common law.[883] Thus, in *Mistry v Interim National Medical and Dental Council of South Africa*[884] the Constitutional Court held that there was no breach of the right to privacy when one medicines control inspector communicated information to another for the purpose of planning a search of premises for a regulatory inspection. The Court took into account, *inter alia*, the fact that the information had not been obtained in an intrusive manner, it did not concern intimate aspects of the applicant's life and it was communicated only to a person who had statutory regulatory responsibilities. **12.270**

[882] *Per* Ackermann J at para 32; see also Sachs J concurring at paras 108 to 119 for an important analysis of the relationship between equality and privacy rights.

[883] M Chaskalson, J Kentridge, J Klaaren, G Marcus, D Spitz and S Woolman (eds), *Constitutional Law of South Africa* (Juta, 1996) para 18–12.

[884] 1998 (7) BCLR 880.

13

THE RIGHT TO MARRY AND TO FAMILY LIFE

A. The Nature of the Rights

13.01 Rights in relation to marriage and the family go beyond classical 'civil liberties'. Such rights are, nevertheless, firmly established in international human rights law; and the duty on states to protect the rights of persons freely to marry and to raise a family is well recognised. The rights are dealt with in varying ways in different human rights instruments. The first formulation is found in Article 16 of the Universal Declaration which provides that:

> (1) Men and women of full age, without any limitation due to race, nationality or religion, have the right to marry and found a family. They are entitled to equal rights as to marriage, during marriage and at its dissolution.
> (2) Marriage shall be entered into only with the free and full consent of the intending spouses.
> (3) The family is the natural and fundamental group unit of society and is entitled to protection by society and the State

Similar protection is afforded by Article 23 of the International Covenant on Civil and Political Rights. However, other instruments take a different approach and there 'has not been universal acceptance of the need to recognise the rights to marriage and to family life as being fundamental in the sense that they require express constitutional protection'.[1]

13.02 The family law rights recognised by international rights instruments cover five different areas:[2]

- the right to marry and to found a family;
- the right not to marry without full and free consent;
- equal rights in and after marriage;
- the right of the family to protection; and
- the right of children to protection.

[1] *In re Certification of the Constitution of RSA 1996* [1996] 4 SA 744 para 98; see para 13.197 below.

[2] See generally, P Sieghart, *The International Law of Human Rights* (Clarendon Press, 1983) 201–202.

In relation to this last area, the civil, political, economic and social rights of the child are comprehensively protected by the United Nations Convention on the Rights of the Child.[3] This gives children a number of rights which enhance their ability to enjoy family life: the right to an identity,[4] the right of a child not to be separated from his parents against his will except when a court determines it is necessary in the best interests of the child,[5] the right to maintain personal relations and direct contact with both parents except if this is contrary to the child's best interests,[6] the right of the child to express views,[7] the obligation to ensure that both parents have common responsibilities for the upbringing and development of the child[8] and the obligation to protect children from violence and neglect.[9] However, the European Convention on Human Rights does *not* confer any specific rights to the child[9a] (although children may successfully complain that they are victims[10] of breaches of the Convention rights).[11]

A number of controversial issues arise concerning family and marriage rights including: **13.03**

> **The rights of same sex couples:** The extent to which the right to marry[12] and other family law rights extend to same sex couples remains a contentious issue.[13]
>
> **The rights of parents vs the rights of children:** The relationship between the right of parents to family life and the rights of children is difficult to reconcile, particularly where the parents are subject to the test of the 'best interests of the child' in child residence and contact disputes. The rights of parents and children also clash where the state intervenes in public law care cases.
>
> **Family rights and administrative decisions:** The extent to which the right to family life should be taken into account in administrative decisions has

---

[3] See generally, D McGoldrick, 'The United Nations Convention on the Rights of the Child' (1991) 5 IJLF 132; B Walsh, 'The United Nations Convention on Human Rights: A British View' (1991) 5 IJLF 170; P Alston, S Parker and J Seymour, *Children Rights and the Law* (Oxford University Press, 1992).

[4] Arts 7 and 8.

[5] Art 9(1).

[6] Art 9(1).

[7] Art 12(1).

[8] Art 18(1).

[9] Art 19.

[9a] See eg J Fortin, 'Rights Brought Home For Children' [1999] 62 MLR 350.

[10] See para 22.20ff below.

[11] For example, corporal punishment (*Tyrer v United Kingdom* (1978) 2 EHHR 1; *A v United Kingdom* (1998) 27 EHRR 611); the right to education (*Campbell and Cosans v United Kingdom* (1982) 4 EHHR 293).

[12] For a general discussion, see *Quilter v A-G of New Zealand* (1997) 3 BHRC 461, see para 13.186 below.

[13] Ibid.

important implications, such as where the expulsion of immigrants has a disruptive effect on the family life of those affected.

B. The Rights in English Law Before the Human Rights Act

(1) Introduction

13.04 English law provides no general right to family life. However, as a matter of legal policy, the law seeks to uphold the validity of marriage[14] and to safeguard the foundations of family life.[15] The 'patriarchal' approach of the common law to marriage and child cases has gradually been replaced by statutory provisions providing for equality within marriage and the 'paramountcy' of the interests of the child. In this process, there has been no place for 'family rights' as such. It has been suggested, with considerable justification, that English family law appears to be

> little more than a jumble of procedures, couched almost entirely in terms of remedies rather than rights, moving directly from the formation of marriage to divorce or death, pausing only to give the parties the right to apply to the court for protection from violence.[16]

In this section we summarise those aspects of family law which may be relevant from a human rights perspective.

(2) Marriage and divorce

(a) Introduction

13.05 Marriage in English law[17] is the voluntary union for life of one man and one woman to the exclusion of others.[18] In *J v S T (formerly J) (Transsexual: Ancillary Relief)*[19] the Court of Appeal confirmed that the fundamental essence of matrimony was the union between people of the opposite sex. The parties must be at least 16; if a party to the marriage is less than 18, he or she must obtain consent under the Children Act 1989. This age restriction has been justified on the basis that early marriage and childbirth is 'socially and morally wrong'.[20] Marriages in which one or both of the parties are under 16 will be recognised provided that

---

[14] *Lawrence v Lawrence* [1985] Fam 106, 134.

[15] See F Bennion, *Statutory Interpretation* (3rd edn, Butterworths, 1997) s 274 'Statutory Interference with Family Rights', 648–649.

[16] S M Cretney, 'The Codification of Family Law' (1981) 44 MLR 1, 9 (the words are put into the mouth of a foreign enquirer).

[17] For a fuller treatment see eg M Booth, G Maple, A Biggs and N Wall (eds), *Rayden and Jackson on Divorce and Family Matters* (17th edn, Butterworths, 1997) Chap 4.

[18] *Hyde v Hyde and Woodmansee* (1866) LR 1 P&D 130, 133 *per* Lord Penzance.

[19] [1997] 1 FLR 402.

[20] *Pugh v Pugh* [1951] P 482.

neither party is domiciled in the United Kingdom and the marriage is recognised by the law of the parties' country of domicile.[21] In addition, marriage is not permitted if the parties have certain blood relationships.[22] However, the English courts will recognise foreign marriages within the prohibited relationships provided that the marriage is not 'offensive to the conscience of the English court'.[23] The English courts will not recognise a polygamous marriage celebrated in the United Kingdom.[24]

In order for a marriage to be valid in English law all the parties must observe the necessary formalities under the Marriage Acts.[25] A marriage may be solemnised according to the rites of the Church of England[26] or under a superintendent registrar's certificate.[27] A civil marriage can be solemnised on any premises approved by the local authority.[28] A non-Anglican religious ceremony which takes place without any civil formalities is not effective as a solemnisation of marriage.[29] **13.06**

(b) The position of transsexuals and homosexuals

The basic principle expressed by Ormrod J in *Corbett v Corbett*[30] is that a person's sex is determined at birth and cannot be changed by gender reassignment. Consequently, a marriage made between parties who are not male and female at birth is void.[31] Similarly, a man born as a male remains a male for the purposes of the Sexual Offences Act[32] and the Registrar of Birth and Deaths is entitled to refuse to amend the Registrar of Births and Deaths to correct the birth entry of a transsexual.[33] **13.07**

The European Court of Justice has also expressed similar views concerning homosexual relationships and marriage. In *Grant v South-West Trains Ltd*[34] it was said that: **13.08**

[21] *Alhaji Mohamed v Knott* [1969] 1 QB 1.

[22] See Marriage Act 1949, Sch 1.

[23] *Cheni v Cheni* [1965] P 85.

[24] The US Supreme Court has held that such a ban does not interfere with freedom of religion, *Reynolds v US* (1878) 98 US 145.

[25] Marriage Act 1949 as amended by the Marriage Act 1949 (Amendment) Act 1954, the Marriage Acts Amendment Act 1958, the Marriage (Enabling) Act 1960, Marriage (Wales and Monmouthshire) Act 1962, Marriage (Registrar General's Licence) Act 1970, Marriage Act 1983, Marriage (Wales) Act 1986, Marriage (Prohibited Degree of Relationship) Act 1986, Marriage Act 1994.

[26] Marriage Act 1949, Pt II.

[27] Ibid Pt III.

[28] Marriage Act 1994.

[29] Cf *R v Bham* [1966] 1 QB 159.

[30] [1971] P 83; see also *S-T (formerly J) v J* [1998] Fam 103.

[31] Matrimonial Causes Act 1973, s 11(c).

[32] *R v Tan* [1983] QB 1053.

[33] *Re P and G (Transsexuals)* [1996] 2 FLR 90.

[34] [1998] ICR 449, 478.

> in the present state of the law within the Community, stable relationships between two persons of the same sex are not to be treated as equivalent to marriage or stable relationships outside marriage between persons of the opposite sex.

Furthermore, in *Fitzpatrick v Sterling Housing Association*[35] the House of Lords held that a person could not live with someone of the same sex as 'his husband or wife' under the Rent Act 1977.

(c) The right to divorce

13.09 The right to obtain a divorce[36] is contained in the Matrimonial Causes Act 1973.[37] The court has jurisdiction to entertain proceedings for divorce or separation[38] provided one of the parties meets the requirements for domicile or residence in England and Wales.[39] Since the Divorce Reform Act 1969, a petition for divorce is presented 'on the ground that the marriage has broken down irretrievably'.[40] In order to establish irretrievable breakdown the petitioner must show one or more of five 'facts':[41]

- that the respondent has committed adultery and the petitioner finds it intolerable to live with the respondent;
- that the respondent has behaved in such a way that the petitioner could not reasonably be expected to live with the respondent;
- that the respondent has deserted the petitioner for a continuous period of at least two years immediately preceding the presentation of the petition;
- that the parties to the marriage have lived apart for a continuous period of at least two years and the respondent consents;
- that the parties to the marriage have lived apart for a continuous period of five years.

If one of these facts cannot be established, the court cannot grant a divorce, even though the marriage has irretrievably broken down.[42]

13.10 A report from the Law Commission,[43] led to the enactment of the Family Law Act 1996 which introduced fundamental reform of the law of divorce. Under the Act a party (or parties) initiating a divorce will have to attend an information

[35] [1999] 3 WLR 1113.

[36] For a fuller treatment see eg M Booth, G Maple, A Biggs and N Wall (eds), *Rayden and Jackson on Divorce and Family Matters* (17th edn, Butterworths, 1997) Chap 6.

[37] The date when the 1973 Act is to be replaced by Part II of the Family Law Act 1996 has yet to be announced.

[38] Matrimonial Causes Act 1973, s 17; and Family Law Act 1996, s 20.

[39] See Domicile and Matrimonial Proceedings Act 1973, s 5; to be replaced by Family Law Act 1996, s 19(2).

[40] See now Matrimonial Causes Act 1973, s 1(1).

[41] Matrimonial Causes Act 1973, s 1(2).

[42] *Buffery v Buffery* [1988] 2 FLR 365.

[43] *Grounds for Divorce* (Law Com No 190, 1990).

meeting;[44] after waiting a further three months, he (or they) may then make a statement of marital breakdown.[45] The statement of marital breakdown will indicate that the marriage has broken down, that he (or they) are aware of the purpose of the period of reflection and consideration and wish to make arrangements for the future.[46] However, a statement made before the first anniversary of a marriage will be ineffective for the purposes of obtaining a divorce.[47] The irretrievable breakdown of a marriage will be established by the time taken when the period for reflection and consideration passes. The period begins 14 days after the court receives the statement of marital breakdown and, as a general rule, lasts for nine months.[48] Either or both of the parties may apply for a divorce under section 3[49] which will require the following to be proved. First, it is necessary to show that the marriage has broken down irretrievably by showing that a statement of marital breakdown has been made in accordance with section 6. Secondly, the requirements for an information meeting must be satisfied. Finally, it must be demonstrated that the parties' arrangements have been satisfied in relation to the family's finances and property, any religious usages concerning divorce and the arrangements for the welfare of the children.[50]

(3) **Rights of children**

(a) Introduction

At common law the father had the right to custody of children to the exclusion of any claims of the mother. Fathers were regarded as having a natural right to their children whose interests were best served by upholding the rights of the father.[51] The sole concern in custody matters was for the rights of the father with little regard for the effect of such decisions on the child. Over the past 150 years there has been a shift from the rights of the parents to those of the child. In 1839 Talfourd's Act[52] allowed courts to make an order of access to the mother, and to award her the custody of children under the age of seven. The best interests of the child gradually became the focus of custody decisions. The equitable *parens patriae* jurisdiction of the Courts of Chancery gradually extended the notion of the 'best interests of the child' to include the emotional, physical and spiritual welfare of the child. The importance of welfare of the child was recognised by the Guardianship of **13.11**

44 Family Law Act 1996, s 8(2).
45 Ibid s 20(1).
46 Ibid s 6(2), (3).
47 Ibid s 7(6).
48 See generally, ibid s 7.
49 The party applying for divorce need not be the party who made the initial statement of marital breakdown: see ibid s 5(2).
50 See generally ibid s 9.
51 See *R v De Manneville* (1804) 5 East 221; *In re Taylor* (1876) 4 Ch D 157.
52 An Act to amend the Law relating to the Custody of Infants 2 & 3 Vict, c 54.

Infants Act, 1886 and by the Guardianship of Infants Act 1925 became 'the first and paramount consideration' and women were granted equal custody rights.

13.12 Over the past 100 years English law has seen a gradual erosion of the notion of 'parental rights' over children. The law has moved from the Victorian notion which was close to the child being treated as a form of property[53] to a position where parents are seen as having responsibilities rather than power. The rights of parents over children 'yield to the child's right to make his own decisions when he reaches sufficient understanding and intelligence'.[54] In *Gillick v West Norfolk and Wisbech Area Health Authority*[55] the House of Lords held that a doctor could lawfully prescribe contraceptives for a girl under 16 without the consent of the parents. Lord Fraser and Lord Scarman both expressed the view that parental rights existed for the protection and benefit of the child and yielded to the child's right to make his own decisions when he reached sufficient understanding.[56]

13.13 The High Court has, traditionally, had a jurisdiction[57] to protect children from injury. This was exercised through 'wardship' proceedings. The practical significance of this jurisdiction in respect of children has been significantly reduced by the Children Act. Its principal effect has been in public law cases because the Children Act makes wardship and local authority care incompatible.[58] It is now clear that wardship proceedings do not create any advantages which are not available in ordinary family proceedings.[59]

13.14 The court's inherent discretion can be invoked where there are no statutory means of seeking a court order and the decision in question may create significant harm; this may arise, for example, where the local authority seeks to override the refusal of medical treatment by a 16-year-old in care[60] or where leave is sought to allow sterilisation[61] or life saving treatment.[62]

---

[53] J Montgomery, 'Children as Property?' (1988) 51 MLR 323.

[54] *Hewer v Bryant* [1970] 1 QB 357, 369.

[55] [1986] AC 112; see generally, J Eekelaar, 'The Eclipse of Parental Rights' (1986) 102 LQR 4.

[56] But see *In re R (A Minor) (Wardship: Consent to Treatment)* [1992] Fam 11 in which it was held that the parent retained the right to consent for a child over 16; see also In *re W (A Minor) (Medical Treatment: Court's Jurisdictian)* [1993] Fam 64.

[57] '*Parens patriae*' (father of the nation).

[58] If a care order is made under s 31 in relation to a ward of court, the wardship ceases under s 91(4); if, on the other hand, a child is in care, he cannot be made a ward of court under s 100(2)(c) and s 41(2A) of the Supreme Court Act.

[59] *In re T (A Minor) (Child: Representation)* [1994] Fam 49.

[60] *Re W (A Minor) (Medical Treatment: Court's Jurisdiction)* [1993] Fam 64.

[61] *Practice Note (Sterilisation: Minors and Mental Health Patients)* [1993] 3 All ER 222.

[62] See eg *Re C (Medical Treatment)* [1998] 1 FLR 384.

(b) The Children Act 1989: introduction

The Children Act 1989[63] represented a fundamental reform and reorganisation of child law in the United Kingdom. It placed private and public law on child care under one statutory regime, changed the court structure effectively to create a specialist division dealing with children at every level and introduced a number of important changes to procedure and evidence. **13.15**

In particular, the Children Act lays down a number of principles of very wide application. For example, section 1(5) of the Children Act requires that wherever a court is considering whether to make an order under the Act, it shall not do so unless it considers that doing so is better for the child than not making any order (the 'no order' principle). **13.16**

The paramountcy principle. Section 1(1) enacts the principle that a child's welfare is the court's paramount consideration wherever the court determines any question concerning a child's upbringing or the administration of the child's property or income. The principle is relevant to *any* court proceedings including, for example, wardship[64] or a parental responsibility order[65] as well as in care proceedings[66] and decisions about contact orders under section 34.[67] On the other hand, the paramountcy principle does not apply outside litigation; nor does it apply to decisions by the local authority where they are providing services to children and their families under Part III of the Children Act[68] or to issues which only indirectly concern a child's upbringing.[69] **13.17**

The statutory checklist for identifying welfare. The Children Act does not define what is meant by a child's welfare. However, section 1(3) of the Act sets out a checklist which requires the court to consider the following factors: the ascertainable wishes and feelings of the child (considered in the light of the child's age and understanding); the child's physical, emotional and educational needs; the likely effect on the child of any change in circumstances; the child's age, sex, background and any characteristics of the child which the court considers relevant; any harm **13.18**

[63] For a fuller treatment see eg A Bainham, *Children: The Modern Law* (2nd edn, Jordans 1998), Chap 2.

[64] *J v C* [1970] AC 668.

[65] Under s 4 of the Children Act: see *Re H (Parental Responsibility)* [1998] 1 FLR 855; 859 *per* Butler Sloss LJ and contrast the views in *Re G (A Minor) (Parental Responsibility Order)* [1994] 1 FLR 504 and *Re E (Parental Responsibility)* [1994] 2 FLR 709, 715.

[66] *Humberside County Council v B* [1993] 1 FLR 257 approved by the Court of Appeal in *F v Leeds Council* [1994] 2 FLR 60.

[67] *In re T (Minors) (Termination of Contact: Discharge of Order)* [1997] 1 WLR 393; *In re B (Minors) (Termination of Contact: Paramount Consideration)* [1993] Fam 301.

[68] *Re M (A Minor) (Secure Accommodation Order)* [1995] Fam 108, 115 *per* Butler Sloss LJ.

[69] For example, where the court sanctions a blood test (*S v S, W v Official Solicitor* [1972] AC 24) or applications to exclude a husband from the matrimonial home (*Richards v Richards* [1984] AC 174).

the child has suffered or is at risk of suffering; how capable each of the child's parents, and any other person in relation to whom the court considers the question to be relevant, is of meeting the child's needs; and the range of powers available to the court under the Act in the proceedings in question.

13.19 Section 1(4) of the Children Act states that the section 1(3) checklist must be considered in a contested proceedings under section 8 for a contact order, prohibited steps order, residence order and specific issue order. The checklist must also be taken into account in all proceedings under Part IV of the Children Act[70] including those relating to care and supervision orders. However, the court is entitled[71] to consider the checklist in other proceedings. Thus, in *Re B (Minors: Change of Surname)*[72] Wilson J said that although he did not have to apply the checklist when deciding an application for leave to change a child's surname, the list remained a useful aide memoire of the factors that might impinge on a child's welfare.

13.20 **Delay.** Section 1(2) of the Children Act requires the court to take account of the general principle that any delay in determining the question is likely to prejudice the welfare of the child in any proceedings where a question of a child's upbringing arises. The principle applies not only to proceedings under the Children Act but also to adoption proceedings and proceedings under the High Court's inherent jurisdiction. Section 1(2) places the onus on the court to ensure that any proceedings involving children are conducted as expeditiously as possible.

(c) Parental responsibility orders

13.21 At present an unmarried father[73] does not have parental responsibility unless he has acquired it under the Children Act.[74] He has to apply for a parental responsibility order[75] unless the mother agrees to him having parental responsibility and they enter into a formal agreement. An unmarried father can have a parental responsibility order revoked by further order of the court,[76] is not required to consent to his child's adoption[77] or freeing for adoption, need not be informed of adoption applications unless maintaining the child[78] and may not be consulted by adoption agencies about his wishes and feelings if it is not practicable.

---

[70] See s 1(4)(b).

[71] *Southwark London Borough Council v B* [1993] 2 FLR 559; *In re W (A Minor) (Medical Treatment: Court's Jurisdiction)* [1993] Fam 64.

[72] [1996] 1 FLR 791.

[73] As defined by s 105(1).

[74] Children Act 1989, s 2(2).

[75] Ibid s 4(1)(a).

[76] Ibid s 4(3).

[77] *Re M (An Infant)* [1955] 2 QB 489; *Re L (A Minor)(Adoption: Procedure)* [1991] 1 FLR 171; *Re C (Adoption: Parties)* [1995] 2 FLR 483.

[78] When he must be joined under the Adoption Rules 1984, r 15(2)(h).

(d) Private law children proceedings

Introduction. The principles affecting private law family proceedings are set out in Part II of the Children Act 1989.[79] The courts are empowered to make a range of orders under section 8 of the Act. Parents and guardians are entitled to seek section 8 orders as of right whereas others such as relatives require the permission of the court. Under section 10(1) the court[80] may make a section 8 order in any family proceedings[81] where a question arises about the welfare of a child. **13.22**

The power to make section 8 orders. Section 8(1) permits the court to make a contact order, a prohibited steps order, a residence order and a specific issue order. The court can achieve further flexibility by using its supplementary powers.[82] A residence order means an order settling the arrangements to be made concerning the person with whom a child is to live;[83] although a court can make a joint residence order it will only do so if there is a positive benefit in making an unconventional order.[84] The extent to which the non-residential parent has the right to be consulted by the residential parent is uncertain.[85] **13.23**

A contact order requires the person with whom a child lives to allow the child to visit, stay with or have contact with a named person.[86] Although a contact order can be made prohibiting any contact,[87] it is only appropriate to do so if it relates to the person with whom the child lives. If the order of no contact is against some other person, then a prohibited steps order must be obtained.[88] **13.24**

A prohibited steps order means that no step which could be taken by a parent in meeting his parental responsibilities[89] of a kind specified in the order shall be taken by that person without the court's consent.[90] A specific issue order[91] means an order giving directions for the purpose of determining a specific question which has arisen (or may arise) in connection with any aspect of parental responsibility.[92] **13.25**

---

[79] For a fuller treatment see eg M Booth, G Maple, A Biggs and N Wall (eds), *Rayden and Jackson on Divorce and Family Matters* (17th edn, Butterworths 1997) pra 40.11–40.62.

[80] ie the High Court, county court or magistrates' court: s 92(7).

[81] As defined in s 8(3) or in the statutes listed in s 8(4).

[82] Children Act 1989, s 11(7).

[83] Ibid s 8(1).

[84] *A v A (Shared Residence Order)* [1994] 1 FLR 669.

[85] Contrast *Re G (Parental Responsibility: Education)* [1994] 2 FLR 694 with *Re P (A Minor) (Parental Responsibility)* [1994] 1 FLR 578.

[86] s 8(1).

[87] *Nottingham City Council v P* [1994] Fam 18, 38, 39 *per* Sir Stephen Brown P.

[88] *Re H (Minors) (Prohibited Steps Order)* [1995] 1 WLR 667.

[89] Which is defined under s 3(1) as all rights, duties, powers, responsibility and authority which by law a parent of a child has in relation to the child and his property.

[90] 1989 Act, s 8(1).

[91] Ibid.

[92] Which is defined under s 3(1) as all rights, duties, powers, responsibility and authority which by law a parent of a child has in relation to the child and his property.

13.26 There are a number of restrictions that prevent section 8 orders from being made. No section 8 order shall be made after a child has attained 16[93] or have effect beyond the age of 16[94] unless there are exceptional circumstances.[95] Where a child is already subject to a local authority care order,[96] a section 8 order cannot be made (except a residence order which will discharge the care order).[97] Section 9(2) prevents a local authority applying for (and a court granting) a residence or contact order and prevents a local authority from obtaining parental responsibility[98] other than through a care order under section 31.[99] Although a local authority is entitled to seek leave to apply for a prohibited steps order or specific issue order in relation to a child which is not under its care, it must instead take direct action by initiating care proceedings[100] where intervention is thought necessary to protect children from significant harm.[101]

13.27 Parents,[102] guardians, those who have obtained a residence order and certain defined individuals[103] may apply for a section 8 order without seeking leave.[104] Everyone else[105] including children[106] as well as any body, authority or organisation concerned with the child must seek leave.

13.28 **The principles to be applied in making section 8 orders.** Where a court has to consider making a section 8 order, the paramount consideration is the welfare of the child;[107] and the court is obliged to apply the statutory checklist.[108] Whilst the child's views are the first factor identified in the statutory checklist as a matter to be considered, they are not determinative[109] of the question; but the views of an

[93] s 9(7).
[94] s 9(6).
[95] See eg *Re M (A Minor) (Immigration: Residence Order)* [1993] 2 FLR 858.
[96] See para 13.33 below.
[97] s 9(1).
[98] Which is defined under s 3(1) as all rights, duties, powers, responsibility and authority which by law a parent of a child has in relation to the child and his property.
[99] See para 13.35 below.
[100] See para 13.33ff below.
[101] *Nottingham County Council v P* [1994] Fam 18; *F v Cambridge County Council* [1995] 1 FLR 516.
[102] As a result of the Family Law Reform Act 1987 parent includes an unmarried father but not the former parents of a child who has been adopted: *Re C (Minors) (Adoption: Residence Order)* [1994] Fam 1.
[103] Under s 10(5).
[104] s 10(4).
[105] Any person who has in the preceding six months been a local authority foster home must in addition seek the consent of the local authority unless he is a relative or has lived with the child for three years: s 9(3).
[106] Provided the court is satisfied that the child is of sufficient age and understanding: *Re S (A Minor) (Independent Representation)* [1993] Fam 263, 276 *per* Sir Thomas Bingham MR.
[107] See para 13.17 above.
[108] See para 13.18ff above.
[109] *Re W (Minors) (Residence Order)* [1992] 2 FCR 461; *Re W (A Minor) (Residence Order)* [1993] 2 FLR 625.

older child may tip the balance where the other factors are evenly balanced.[110] The other factors to be taken into account are: a child's physical needs (which includes accommodation[111] and the time a parent can devote to child care);[112] his emotional needs (such as ideally that a young child should live with his mother[113] or that it is in the best interests of the child to live with his natural parents);[114] his educational and other needs; the likely effect of the child of a change of circumstances; the child's age, sex, background and any characteristics that the court considers relevant such as religion,[115] cultural background,[116] any harm which the child has suffered or is likely to suffer; and the capability of the parents and any other person the court considers relevant in meeting a child's needs.[117]

The court will also take account of the statutory checklist[118] when deciding **13.29** whether or not to make a contact order. The welfare of the child is paramount[119] and there is no legal presumption that a parent should be permitted contact.[120] Nevertheless, it is almost always in the interests of the child to have contact with the parent with whom he is not living,[121] not least[122] because Article 9(3) of the United Nations Convention on the Rights of the Child imposes a duty on the state to respect the right of a child to maintain personal relations and direct contact with both parents on a regular basis except if it is contrary to the child's best interest. It seems that a contact order will be refused if the fundamental need of every child to have an enduring relationship with his parents is outweighed by the harm he would suffer by virtue of the order.[123]

(e) Public law children proceedings

Introduction. The services which local authorities[124] must provide to children **13.30** and their families are contained in Part III of the Children Act.[125] Section 17

[110] See eg *Re F (Minors) (Denial of Contact)* [1993] 2 FLR 677.

[111] See eg *Re F (An Infant)* [1969] 2 Ch 238.

[112] See eg *Re K (Minors) (Children: Care and Control)* [1977] Fam 179.

[113] See the views of Lord Jauncey in *Brixey v Lynas* [1996] 2 FLR 499, 505.

[114] See *Re W (A Minor) (Residence Order)* [1993] 2 FLR 625 at 633 *per* Balcombe LJ; and see eg *Re M (Child's Upbringing)* [1996] 2 FLR 44.

[115] See eg *Re R (A Minor) (Residence: Religion)* [1993] 2 FLR 163.

[116] See eg *Re M (Child's Upbringing)* [1996] 2 FLR 44.

[117] eg, the court can therefore take account of the fact that a mother is a lesbian but cannot regard that fact as meaning that she is unfit to look after the child; see eg *C v C (Custody of Child)* [1991] 1 FLR 174; *B v B (Custody Care and Control)* [1991] Fam Law 174.

[118] See para 13.18 above.

[119] See para 13.17 above.

[120] *S v S (Access Order)* [1997] 1 FLR 980.

[121] See generally, the approach set out by Wall J in *Re P (Contact: Supervision)* [1996] 2 FLR 314, 328.

[122] *Re R (A Minor) (Contact)* [1993] 2 FLR 762, 767 *per* Butler Sloss LJ.

[123] *Re M (Contact: Welfare Test)* [1995] 1 FLR 274.

[124] As defined by s 105(1).

[125] For a fuller treatment see eg M Booth, G Maple, A Biggs and N Wall (eds), *Rayden and Jackson on Divorce and Family Matters* (17th edn, Butterworths, 1997) Chap 41.

places the local authority under a general duty to safeguard and promote the welfare of children in their area who are in need[126] and, so far as is consistent with that duty, to promote the upbringing of such children by their families by providing a range and level of services appropriate to those needs. Local authorities also have a number of specific duties and powers under Schedule 2 Part I of the Act including, for example, promoting the upbringing of children by their family.

13.31 **The provision of accommodation.** Local authorities have both an obligation[127] and a discretion[128] to provide accommodation for a child to live away from home with foster parents, relatives or in a community, voluntary or registered children's home. However, any person with parental responsibility[129] who is willing and able to arrange accommodation can object.[130]

13.32 The Children Act imposes a number of specific duties on local authorities who look after children who have been provided with accommodation[131] or who are in care as a result of a care order:[132] to safeguard and promote his welfare and to make such use of services available for children cared for by their own parents as appears to the authority reasonable in the case of a particular child;[133] to ascertain as far as practicable the wishes and feelings of the child, his parents, any other person who has parental responsibility[134] and any other person who the local authority thinks relevant;[135] to give due consideration,[136] having regard to his age and understanding, to such wishes and feelings of the child as the authority has been able to ascertain, to his religious persuasion, racial origin and cultural and linguistic background and to the wishes and feelings of any other person;[137] and to advise, assist and befriend him with a view to promoting his welfare when he ceases to be looked after by the authority.[138]

---

[126] As defined by s 17(10).

[127] Under s 20(1).

[128] Under s 20(4) for *any* child if it considers that to do so would safeguard or promote his welfare; and under s 20(5) for any person aged 16 to 21 if it considers that to do so would safeguard or promote his welfare.

[129] Which is defined under s 3(1) as all rights, duties, powers, responsibility and authority which by law a parent of a child has in relation to the child and his property.

[130] s 20(7) (unless the exceptions in s 20(9) apply).

[131] As defined by s 22(2).

[132] Under s 22(1).

[133] s 22(3).

[134] Which is defined under s 3(1) as all rights, duties, powers, responsibility and authority which by law a parent of a child has in relation to the child and his property.

[135] s 22(4).

[136] Under s 22(5).

[137] As defined by s 22(4).

[138] s 24(1).

The power to make care and supervision orders. Only a local authority or authorised person[139] may apply to the court for a care or supervision order.[140] The local authority has a statutory duty[141] to investigate all cases where it reasonably believes that a child who lives in its area is suffering (or is likely to suffer) significant harm and to decide whether to bring proceedings. In deciding what action to take in individual cases, a local authority utilises child protection conferences in order to disseminate information about a child to various agencies and to co-ordinate the work of those agencies. The failure to invite parents to a child protection conference may be held to be unlawful as a breach of natural justice.[142] A blanket ban on solicitors attending child protection conferences is also unlawful.[143] **13.33**

No care or supervision orders may be made in relation to a child who has reached 17 (or is 16 and married).[144] The child and any person with parental responsibility[145] are automatically parties in any care proceedings. An unmarried father must seek leave to be joined as a party. Care proceedings are normally brought in the family proceedings court[146] although they may be transferred to the county court or High Court under the Children (Allocation of Proceedings) Order 1991.[147] **13.34**

A court may only make a care or supervision order if it finds that the threshold criteria under section 31(2) apply. The court must be satisfied that the child concerned is suffering[148] significant harm or is likely[149] to suffer significant harm and the harm or likelihood of harm is attributable to the care given or likely to be given to the child, not being what it would be reasonable to expect a parent to give him or alternatively because the child is beyond parental control. Harm is ill treatment or impairment of health or development.[150] Where the question of whether harm suffered by a child is significant in terms of his health or development, his health or development should be compared to that which can be reasonably expected of a similar child.[151] **13.35**

---

139 As defined by s 31(9).

140 s 31(1).

141 Under s 47.

142 See eg *R v Harrow London Borough Council, ex p D* [1990] Fam 133; *R v East Sussex County Council, ex p R* [1991] 2 FLR 358; *R v Devon County Council ex p L* [1991] FLR 541.

143 *R v Cornwall County Council, ex p L, The Times*, 25 Nov 1999.

144 s 31(3).

145 Which is defined under s 3(1) as all rights, duties, powers, responsibility and authority which by law a parent of a child has in relation to the child and his property.

146 That is, a specially constituted magistrates' court, see Magistrates' Courts Act 1980, s 67.

147 1991/1677 Art 3.

148 *Re M (A Minor) (Care Order: Threshold Conditions)* [1994] 2 AC 424.

149 *Re H (Minors) (Sexual Abuse: Standard of Proof)* [1996] AC 563.

150 As defined by s 31(9).

151 s 31(10).

13.36 If the threshold criteria are satisfied, the court then considers the welfare stage,[152] applying the general principles of section 1.[153] As Booth J stressed in *Humberside County Council v B*,[154] the threshold and welfare stages are quite separate, with only the latter governed by section 1. The court must regard the welfare of the child as the paramount consideration,[155] is bound[156] to take account of the statutory checklist[157] and must consider whether to make a section 8 order[158] (regardless of whether it has been applied for[159] and even if the threshold requirements are not met). Although there is no statutory requirement to do so, the local authority normally[160] submits a care plan to the court. At the welfare stage the court has a wide discretion about the orders it can make including making no order at all[161] or making a section 8 order[162] (with or without a supervision order), a supervision order or a care order. The court may also grant interim care and interim supervision orders[163] as well as residence orders and section 8 orders for a limited period.

13.37 **Care orders.** A care order requires a designated local authority[164] to receive the child into its care and keep him in its care while the order is in force[165] and vests parental responsibility[166] in the authority[167]. A care order lasts until the child is 18[168] unless it is brought to an end earlier. An application to discharge a care order may be made by any person with parental responsibility,[169] the child himself and the designated authority.[170]

13.38 Once a care order has been made, the responsibility for the child vests in the local authority. The court has no general power to review the case[171] and the court cannot fetter the local authority's discretion by, for example, imposing any conditions

---

152 *Re M and R (Child Abuse: Evidence)* [1996] 2 FLR 195, 202 *per* Butler Sloss LJ.
153 See para 13.17ff above.
154 [1993] 1 FLR 257, 261; approved in *F v Leeds City Council* [1994] 2 FLR 60.
155 See para 13.17 above.
156 s 1(4)(b).
157 See para 13.18 above.
158 See para 13.28ff above.
159 Under s 10(1)(b).
160 See eg *Manchester City Council v F* [1993] 1 FLR 419; *Re J (Minors) (Care: Care Plan)* [1994] 1 FLR 253.
161 See para 13.16 above.
162 See para 13.23ff above.
163 Under s 38.
164 Under s 31(1)(a).
165 s 33(1).
166 Which is defined under s 3(1) as all rights, duties, powers, responsibility and authority which by law a parent of a child has in relation to the child and his property.
167 s 33(3)(a).
168 s 91(12).
169 Which is defined under s 3(1) as all rights, duties, powers, responsibility and authority which by law a parent of a child has in relation to the child and his property.
170 s 39(1).
171 *Re B (Minors) (Care:Contact:Local Authority's Plans)* [1993] 1 FLR 543.

on the care order.[172] Challenges to the decisions of a local authority concerning a child in care must be brought by judicial review; and the applicant can only quash a decision on its merits if it is *Wednesbury* unreasonable.[173] However, the court still has the power to consider issues of contact[174] and whether to make an adoption order.[175]

Furthermore, section 34 imposes a duty on the local authority requiring it normally to allow reasonable[176] contact between a child in care and his parents[177] which can only be departed from by agreement or a court order. At the time a court makes a care order or subsequently, the court[178] may make such order as it considers appropriate as to the contact to be allowed[179] or to refuse contact with a named person[180] or to impose conditions.[181] The court must apply the principle that the welfare of the child is paramount,[182] must consider the statutory checklist[183] and may make an order only if it would be better for the child than making no order at all.[184] The local authority, child and any person named in the order can apply to vary or discharge a section 34 order.[185] **13.39**

Supervision orders. A supervision order places the child under the supervision of a designated local authority or a probation officer.[186] The child is then under the supervision of a supervisor.[187] A supervision order initially lasts for a year[188] and can be extended by the supervisor for up to three years.[189] **13.40**

Short term orders. Part V of the Children Act creates a number of powers to ensure that the short term interests of a child are protected. The court can make a child assessment order[190] to ensure a multi disciplined assessment of the child. **13.41**

---

[172] *Re T (A Minor) (Care Order: Conditions)* 1994 2 FLR 423.

[173] See eg *R v Bedfordshire County Council, ex p C* [1987] 1 FLR 239; *R v Hertfordshire County Council, ex p B* [1987] 1 FLR 358.

[174] Under s 34.

[175] See para 13.44ff below.

[176] See eg *Re P (Minors) (Contact with Children in Care)* [1993] 2 FLR 156, 161 *per* Ewbank J; *L v London Borough of Bromley* [1998] 1 FLR 709.

[177] Or any other person as defined by s 34(1).

[178] As Butler Sloss LJ emphasised in *In re B (Minors) (Termination of Contact: Paramount Consideration)* [1993] Fam 301, 311 the court and not the local authority has the duty to decide on contact; approved by Simon Brown LJ in *Re E (A Minor) (Care Order: Contact)* [1994] 1 FLR 146.

[179] s 34(2).

[180] s 34(4).

[181] s 34(7).

[182] See para 13.17 above.

[183] See para 13.18ff above.

[184] See para 13.16 above.

[185] s 34(9).

[186] s 31(1)(b).

[187] s 105(1) whose duties are defined by s 35(1) as amplified by Sch 3.

[188] Sch 3, para 6(1).

[189] Sch 3, para 6(3), (4).

[190] s 43(1).

The magistrates can grant an emergency protection order[191] for the immediate removal or retention of a child in an emergency. The police have limited powers to protect children under section 46.

(f) Guardianship

13.42 The law of guardianship[192] is contained in section 5 and section 6 of the Children Act. Any parent[193] with parental responsibility[194] and any guardian of a child may appoint an individual as a child's guardian.[195] An appointment of a guardian normally takes effect on the death of the sole remaining parent with parental responsibility.[196] The High Court, county court and magistrates' court can appoint a guardian if a child has no parents with parental responsibility or a current residence order has been made in favour of the parent or guardian who has died.[197] The revocation of guardianship must be undertaken in accordance with section 6.

13.43 The legal position of a guardian is similar to parents with parental responsibilities.[198] However, a guardian, unlike a parent, cannot become obliged to maintain a child as a 'liable relative' under the Social Security Administration Act 1992[199] or as an 'absent parent' under the Child Support Act 1991.[200] No court may order a guardian to make financial provision for or transfer property to a child under the Children Act.[201] The duties of a guardian end if a child dies or attains the age of 18.[202] The court may order an appointment to end under section 6(7) and will be guided by the welfare principle in section 1(1) of the Children Act.[203]

(g) Adoption

13.44 **Introduction.** Where the adopters are a married couple, an adopted child is treated in law[204] as if he had been born as a child of the marriage. This applies whether or not he was in fact born after the marriage was solemnised. In any other case, the adopted child is treated as if he was born to the adopter in wedlock (but

---

191 Under s 44(1).

192 For a fuller treatment see eg M Booth, G Maple, A Biggs and N Wall (eds), *Rayden and Jackson on Divorce and Family Matters* (17th edn, Butterworths, 1997) paras 40.1–40.10.

193 Thereby excluding a person who is an unmarried father without parental responsibility.

194 Which is defined under s 3(1) as all rights, duties, powers, responsibility and authority which by law a parent of a child has in relation to the child and his property.

195 s 5(3), (4).

196 s 5(8).

197 s 5(1).

198 Which is defined under s 3(1) as all rights, duties, powers, responsibility and authority which by law a parent of a child has in relation to the child and his property.

199 See ss 78(6) and s 105(3).

200 s 3.

201 s 15 and Sch 1.

202 Children Act 1989, s 91(7), (8).

203 See para 13.17 above.

204 For a fuller treatment see eg *Rayden and Jackson on Divorce and Family Matters* (n 192 above) Chap 47.

not as a child of any marriage of the adopters).[205] A minor of any nationality who is adopted under a court order will become a British citizen if one of his adopters is British.[206]

In reaching any decision relating to the adoption of a child, the court or adoption agency must consider all the circumstances, the first consideration being the need to safeguard and promote the welfare of the child; and shall, so far as is practicable, ascertain the wishes and feelings of the child and give due consideration to them, having regard to his age and understanding.[207] **13.45**

The power to make adoption orders. Before an adoption order can be made, the parent with parental responsibility or guardian must agree to the order or have his agreement dispensed with.[208] The court will dispense with an agreement where a parent (but not an unmarried father)[209] or guardian unreasonably[210] withholds his agreement, where he persistently fails without reasonable cause[211] to discharge his parental duties, where he abandons or neglects the child or where he has persistently ill-treated the child. The child must live with the applicants for a period before an order is made.[212] **13.46**

The applicants can apply to the High Court, county court or family proceedings court. The court must be satisfied that the order, if made, will be for the child's welfare,[213] that every parent or guardian, freely and with full understanding agrees unconditionally to the making of the order (unless his agreement has been dispensed with and that no unauthorised payments have been made).[214] The adoption order may contain such terms and conditions as the court thinks fit.[215] On an application for adoption, the first consideration for the court is the welfare of the child throughout his childhood; this can include for a non-British child, the benefits from the acquisition of British nationality and the right of abode.[216] **13.47**

In adoption proceedings[217] the court may also grant section 8 orders[218] and cannot properly consider adoption without considering the other alternatives.[219] **13.48**

205 Adoption Act 1976, s 39.
206 British Nationality Act 1981, s 1(5).
207 Adoption Act 1976, s 6.
208 Ibid s 16(1)(b).
209 *Re M (An Infant)* [1955] 2 QB 489; *Re L (A Minor) (Adoption: Procedure)* [1991] 1 FLR 171; *Re C (Adoption: Parties)* [1995] 2 FLR 483.
210 *Re W (An Infant)* [1971] AC 682.
211 *Re D (Minors) (Adoption by Parent)* [1973] Fam 209, 214 *per* Baker P.
212 Adoption Act 1976, s 13(1), (2).
213 s 6.
214 s 24(2).
215 s 12(6).
216 *In re B (A Minor) (Adoption Order: Nationality), The Times*, 15 Mar 1999.
217 Which are designated family proceedings under the Children Act: see s 8(4)(d).
218 See para 3.23ff above.
219 See eg *Re M (Adoption or Residence Order)* [1998] 1 FLR 570.

Thus, in an exceptional case the court can make a contact order imposing conditions in favour of a child's natural family despite the objections of the adopting parents.[220]

(4) Family rights in other areas

(a) Medically assisted reproduction and surrogacy arrangements

13.49 The Human Fertilisation and Embryology Act 1990 regulates infertility treatment that involves the use of donated genetic material or involves the creation of an embryo outside the body. Section 13(5) of the 1990 Act affects access to treatment by stating that a woman shall not be provided with treatment services unless account is taken of the welfare of the child who may be born as a result of the treatment (including the need of that child for a father) and of any other child who may be affected by the birth.

13.50 The 1990 Act only deals with treatment services within the United Kingdom. However, section 24(4) allows the Human Fertilisation and Embryology Authority to permit a licence holder to export sperm. In *R v Human Fertilisation and Embryology Authority, ex p Blood*[221] the Court of Appeal held that where the applicant was prevented from taking her dead husband's semen abroad to obtain treatment, the denial of access to medical treatment abroad breached European Community law since it could only be justified if it were absolutely necessary. In *U v W*[222] Waite LJ took a less strict view of the scope for restricting the freedom to provide services under Article 49[223] of the Treaty; because artificial insemination involves such complex medical, legal and ethical issues, he said that the state has a wide margin of appreciation in defining and protecting family life.

13.51 It is an offence for third parties to assist on a commercial basis in making surrogacy arrangements[224] where a woman agrees to bear a child for another and hand it over at birth; and surrogacy arrangements are not enforceable.[225] However, the court has jurisdiction to decide on the basis of the paramountcy principle[226] who should take care of the child[227] and can make an adoption order where the surrogacy arrangements break down.[228] The Human Fertilisation and Embryology Act also allows a parental order to be made in prescribed circumstances.[229]

---

[220] See eg *Re C (A Minor) (Adoption Order: Conditions)* [1989] AC 1.
[221] [1997] 2 WLR 806.
[222] [1997] 2 FLR 282.
[223] Formerly Art 59.
[224] Surrogacy Arrangements Act 1986, s 2(1), (2).
[225] Surrogacy Arrangements Act 1986, s 1A; Human Fertilisation and Embryology Act 1990, s 36(1).
[226] See para 3.17 above.
[227] See eg *Re C (A Minor) (Wardship: Surrogacy)* [1985] FLR 846.
[228] See eg *Re M W (Adoption: Surrogacy)* [1995] 2 FLR 789.
[229] s 30.

There is no right of access to artificial insemination facilities under domestic or Convention law. As a result a prisoner's application to quash the Home Secretary's refusal to arrange for artificial insemination of the prisoner's wife was dismissed.[229a] **13.51A**

(b) Immigration

Section 1(1) of the Immigration Act 1971 states that anyone who is expressed to have the right of abode[230] in the United Kingdom shall be free to live in and to come and go into and from the United Kingdom without let or hindrance. Prior to 1 January 1983 the right of abode depended on whether or not a person was a patrial under section 2 of the Immigration Act 1971.[231] In broad terms patrials were citizens of the United Kingdom and Colonies by birth,[232] adoption,[233] naturalisation[234] or registration in the United Kingdom;[235] citizens of the United Kingdom and Colonies with similar connections to the United Kingdom through a parent or grandparent;[236] Commonwealth citizens with a parent born in the United Kingdom;[237] and women who became patrial through marriage.[238] **13.52**

The definition of right of abode was changed by the British Nationality Act 1981.[239] A person is a patrial in broad terms if he is a British citizen;[240] a Commonwealth citizen with a parent born in the United Kingdom;[241] and Commonwealth women who became patrial through marriage.[242] However, obligations under the European Community[243] law significantly benefit European Community citizens. Article 8a(1) of the Treaty of European Union states that every citizen of the European Community has the right to move freely within the territory of the Member States subject to the limitations of the Treaty and the measures adopted to give it effect. Under the Treaty there are the rights of free movement of workers,[244] **13.53**

[229a] *R v Secretary of State for the Home Department ex p Mellor* [2000] All ER (D) 1136.

[230] For a fuller treatment see I MacDonald and N Blake, *Immigration Law and Practice in the United Kingdom* (4th edn, Butterworths, 1995) Chap 6.

[231] Now repealed and replaced by the British Nationality Act 1981.

[232] Those born before January 1949 qualified under the Nationality Act 1948, s 12 whereas those born after must qualify under the Nationality Act 1948, s 14.

[233] Adoption Act 1976, s 40.

[234] Nationality Act 1948, s 10.

[235] Immigration Act 1971, s 2(1)(a) (now repealed).

[236] Ibid s 2(1)(b) (now repealed).

[237] Ibid s 2(1)(d) (now repealed).

[238] Ibid s 2(2) (now repealed).

[239] Amending Immigration Act 1971, s 2.

[240] Which included all old citizens of the United Kingdom and Colonies who were patrials who had been born, adopted, registered, or naturalised in the United Kingdom; those with similar connections to the United Kingdom through a parent or grandparent and those who had been ordinarily resident in the United Kingdom for five years free of immigration control.

[241] Under the Immigration Act 1971, s 2(1)(d) (now repealed).

[242] Ibid s 2(2) (now repealed).

[243] For a fuller treatment see MacDonald and Blake (n 230 above) Chap 8.

[244] Arts 39–42 (formerly Arts 48–51).

freedom of establishment[245] and freedom to provide services.[246] A person is entitled to free movement rights if he is a national (or a family member)[247] of the European Economic Area who undertakes the activities of a worker, self employed person, provider of services, recipient of services, a self sufficient person, a retired person or a student.[248]

13.54 The regulation of admission to the United Kingdom of family members[249] of British citizens is governed by the Immigration Rules unless the family members have travelled and worked elsewhere in the European Community when they can benefit from the more generous provisions of European Community law.[250] In particular, an estranged parent can apply for the entry clearance of a UK resident child where he has a court order in his favour.[251]

13.55 Anyone who wishes to enter the United Kingdom to settle with a family member must first obtain an entry clearance certificate.[25] The entry clearance officer will have to be satisfied of the ability of the family member to be maintained without recourse to public funds and in appropriate accommodation.[253] In order to obtain admission as a spouse, the applicant must satisfy the entry clearance officer that the marriage is lawful and in accordance with the Immigration Rules. Under the primary purpose rule[254] the applicant[255] must show that the primary purpose of the marriage was not settlement. The immigration rules no longer provide for the admission of co-habitees.[256] There is a practice of allowing admission to some partners in 'common law relationships' as a matter of discretion.[257] However, this only applies if the parties are 'legally unable to marry under United Kingdom law' and have been living in a relationship which has existed for at least four years. It does not, therefore, cover heterosexual cohabitants who could marry.

---

[245] Arts 43–48 (formerly Arts 52–58).

[246] Arts 49–55 (formerly Arts 59–66).

[247] *Gul v Regierungspräisdent Dusseldorf* [1986] ECR 1573; members of the family are defined as: the spouse, children under 21 (or dependents on their parents), dependent grandchildren, non dependent grandchildren under 21 (in the case of workers only) and dependent relatives in the ascending line (for example, parents and grandchildren): see Art 10 of Regulation 1612/68; Art 1 of Directive 68/360 and Art 1(1) of Directive 73/148.

[248] Arts 2 and 6 of the European Economic Area Order 1994, SI 1994/1895.

[249] For a fuller treatment see MacDonald and Blake (n 230 above) Chap 11.

[250] See para 13.53 above and for a fuller treatment see MacDonald and Blake (n 230 above) Chap 8.

[251] Immigration Rules (HC 395) paras 246–248.

[252] Immigration Rules (HC 395) spouse, para 281(vii); fiancé, 290(viii); children, 297(v), 301(vi), 310(ix), 314(xii); other dependant relatives, 317(vi).

[253] Immigration Rules (HC 395) spouses, para 281(v)(vi), 284(viii)(ix); fiancées, 290(vi)(vii), 293(iv); children, 297(iv), 298(iv), 301(iv), 310(iv); other dependants, 317(iv).

[254] Immigration Rules (HC 395) para 281, 290.

[255] *R v Immigration Appeal Tribunal, ex p Hoque and Singh* [1988] Imm AR 216.

[256] The rules were changed in 1985.

[257] 'Common Law and Same-sex Relationships (Unmarried partners)', Immigration Directorate Instructions, Chap 8, Section 7.

Children under 18 may be admitted to the United Kingdom under the Immigration Rules. The meaning of parents is restrictively defined under the Rules[258] and includes, for example, both parents of an illegitimate child if paternity is proved. A child with a right of abode is dealt with in the same way as any other British citizen. Non British citizens born in the United Kingdom can apply for registration as a British citizen[259] and require leave to enter if they travel and seek readmission.[260] Children of parents who are settled in the United Kingdom qualify for entry clearance and will be given indefinite leave on arrival[261] whereas a child of a single parent must show that the parent in the United Kingdom has sole responsibility for him.[262] Furthermore, a child may qualify on the ground that there are serious and compelling family or other reasons which make his exclusion from the United Kingdom undesirable so that arrangements have to be made for his care.[263] **13.56**

Where a child is adopted under a court order in the United Kingdom[264] or is subject to a recognised[265] overseas adoption, he is treated in law as if he was a legitimate child of the adoptive parents.[266] A person who became a United Kingdom citizen by adoption is a patrial as is a Commonwealth citizen legally adopted by an overseas adoption by a parent born in the United Kingdom.[267] This general definition of adopted children does not apply to the admission of children for settlement[268] who are subject to different rules.[269] Under the Immigration Rules a child cannot be brought to the United Kingdom for adoption although there is an established practice of doing so.[270] **13.57**

Difficulties arise where the effect of a deportation order is to separate a parent and child or to remove a child and the Home Office apply guidance[271] which is expressed to take into account the effect of the European Convention on Human Rights. The guidance records the fact that: **13.58**

> Article 8 of the Convention guarantees the right to respect for family life and recent European Court cases have demonstrated that, however unmeritorious the applicant's immigration history, the Court is strongly disposed to find a breach of Article

---

258 Immigration Rules (HC 395) para 6.
259 British Nationality Act 1981, s 1(3), (4).
260 Immigration Rules (HC 395) paras 304–306.
261 Immigration Rules (HC 395) paras 297, 299.
262 Immigration Rules (HC 395) para 297(1)(e).
263 Immigration Rules (HC 395) para 297(i)(f).
264 See para 13.46ff above.
265 Where the adoption is in a country designated under the Adoption (Designation of Overseas Adoption) Order 1973, SI 1973/19.
266 Adoption Act 1976, s 39.
267 Immigration Act 1971, s 1(2)(b) as amended by the British Nationality Act 1981.
268 Immigration Rules (HC 395) para 6.
269 Immigration Rules (HC 395) para 310.
270 The RON 117 procedure.
271 DP/2/93, see M Hunt, *Using Human Rights in the English Courts* (Hart Publishing, 1997) App VI, 415–419.

8 where the effect of an immigration decision is to separate an applicant from his/her spouse or child.[272]

It has been held that, under this guidance, the Home Secretary conducts a balancing exercise in which the considerations of the interests of the child and immigration policy are both weighed and that this approach is consistent with the approach of the Court and Commission under Article 8.[273]

13.59 There are substantial restrictions under the Immigration Rules on the ability of grandparents to join their children in the United Kingdom.[274] Parents, grandparents and other exceptional relatives must obtain entry clearance before seeking leave to enter.[275]

13.60 **Deportation.** Deportation[276] is the process by which a non British citizen can be compulsorily removed from the United Kingdom and prevented from returning unless the order is revoked.[277] A person may be liable to be deported by his failure to observe conditions relating to the right to enter for a limited period or breach of conditions such as a restriction on employment,[278] because the Home Secretary deems that deportation is conducive to the public good[279] (which, in practice, is most frequently used against convicted criminals) or if another person in his family has been ordered to be deported.[280] Furthermore, if a decision[281] is made to deport a man, there is a power also to deport his wife and any children.[282] However, if a man or woman ordered to be deported actually leaves and eight weeks elapse, no family deportation order can be made.[283]

13.61 Furthermore, where a non citizen over 17[284] is convicted of an offence punishable with imprisonment, the magistrates' or Crown Court may make a recommendation for deportation.[285] In considering whether to make a recommendation for deportation, the court will take account of a number of factors including the impact on the family;[286] the court will weigh up the balance of the potential detriment of

[272] DP/2/93, Introduction, para 1.
[273] *R v Secretary of State for the Home Department, ex p Gangadeen and Khan* [1998] 1 FLR 762.
[274] Immigration Rules (HC 395) para 317.
[275] Immigration Rules (HC 395) para 317(iii).
[276] For a fuller treatment see I MacDonald and N Blake, *Immigration Law and Practice* (4th edn, Butterworths, 1995) Chap 15.
[277] Immigration Act 1971, s 5(1), (2).
[278] Ibid s 3(5)(a).
[279] Ibid s 3(5)(b).
[280] Ibid s 3(5)(c).
[281] No deportation order is necessary: *Ibrahim v Immigration Appeals Tribunal* [1989] Imm AR 111.
[282] Immigration Act 1971, s 5(4)(a); if, on the other hand, the wife is subject to an order for deportation, the children but not the husband may be deported under s 5(4)(b).
[283] Ibid s 5(3).
[284] Ibid s 6(3)(a).
[285] Immigration Act 1971, s 3(6).
[286] *R v Nazari* [1980] 1 WLR 1366.

the offender's continued presence in the United Kingdom with the harm to dependants who are resident in the United Kingdom if he is deported.[287]

When deciding whether to deport an individual, the Home Secretary considers the right course on its merits and balances the public interest in favour of deportation against any compassionate circumstances in the case; the Home Secretary will take account of all relevant factors known to him including a number of prescribed factors.[288] In particular, the Home Office now applies a policy on deportation[289] which takes a very restrictive approach to its impact on spouse and children. The decision to deport members of the family must be taken independently and considered on its merits rather than following as a matter of course.[290] The Home Secretary will not deport a wife who has qualified for settlement in her own right or where she lives apart from the deportee;[291] children will not normally be considered for deportation.[292] **13.62**

Removal. The Home Secretary has an administrative power to remove immigrants summarily[293] in a wide variety of circumstances. The power of removal is a purely administrative measure which is very different from deportation. Removal is used where someone has no legal status because he has not been given leave to enter or entered illegally; and in general[294] can only challenge the decision by taking proceedings for judicial review. In contrast, deportation is a legal process where there is a statutory right of appeal.[295] **13.63**

Where a passenger arriving in the United Kingdom is refused leave to enter, the immigration officer has two months to arrange for his removal by the owners (or agents) of the ship or aircraft which brought him in;[296] after the two months have expired, the Home Secretary still has the power of removal[297] and must make the necessary arrangements to do so.[298] Illegal immigrants[299] are subject to the same procedures.[300] The Home Secretary can make arrangements to remove a deportee on broadly the same basis.[301] **13.64**

[287] See eg *R v Cravioto* (1990) 12 Cr App Rep (S) 71.
[288] Immigration Rules (HC 395) para 364.
[289] DP/3/96; DP/4/96; DP/5/96.
[290] *Yau Yau v Home Office* [1982] Imm AR 16.
[291] Immigration Rules (HC 395) para 365.
[292] Immigration Rules (HC 395) para 366.
[293] For a fuller treatment see MacDonald and Blake (n 276 above) Chap 17.
[294] Other than a person with a visa who is refused entry or whose appeal right is exercisable from abroad under s 13(3) of the Immigration Act.
[295] Immigration Act 1971, s 5.
[296] Ibid Sch 2, para 8(1), (2).
[297] Ibid Sch 2 para 10(1)(b).
[298] Ibid Sch 2 para 10(3.
[299] For a fuller treatment of the issue, see I MacDonald and N Blake, *Immigration Law and Practice* (4th edn, Butterworths, 1995) Chap 16.
[300] Immigration Act 1971, Sch 2, para 9.
[301] Ibid Sch 3, para 1.

(c) Prisoners

13.65 A convicted prisoner is entitled to two visits every four weeks.[302] Closed visits will be imposed where required by security or control[303] and the Court of Appeal has upheld a policy which restricts any physical contact between prisoners and their children as not being *Wednesbury* unreasonable.[304] Prisoners are not entitled to conjugal visits under the Prison Rules.[305]

13.66 The Home Secretary is entitled to determine the prison to which a prisoner is committed and to direct the removal of a prisoner from one prison to another.[306] Relatives of prisoners are often given very little notice of a prison transfer. In *R v Secretary of State for the Home Department, ex p McAvoy*[307] Webster J held that the difficulties caused by ill health of parents making a prison visit were relevant considerations to any transfer decision but that it was inappropriate for the court to interfere in a decision taken by the Home Secretary on operational and security grounds. The Home Secretary also has broad powers under the Criminal (Sentences) Act 1997[308] to transfer prisoners between various United Kingdom penal jurisdictions. The discretion to transfer does not require the Home Secretary to regard the maintenance of family unity as being the overriding criterion in making his decision.[309]

13.67 The Prison Rules recognise the medical needs of women in relation to pregnancy and child care. Where a prisoner is pregnant and likely to give birth shortly before release, arrangements will be made for her early release or transfer to a local hospital to give birth. All restraints placed on a pregnant prisoner should be removed when she attends an ante natal clinic unless there is a high escape risk.[310] A prisoner can also apply to keep her baby with her in a mother and baby unit after the birth.[311]

13.68 A prisoner may be granted a temporary licence[312] where there are exceptional personal reasons such as visits to dying relatives or other tragic circumstances or a resettlement licence towards the end of his sentence for the purpose of maintaining family ties.

---

302 Prison Rules 1964, SI 388/1964, r 34(2)(b) as amended.
303 Ibid, r 5A(24)(2).
304 *R v Secretary of State for the Home Department, ex p O'Dhuibhir* [1997] COD 315.
305 See S Livingstone and T Owen, *Prison Law* (2nd edn, Oxford University Press, 1999) para 7.40.
306 Prison Act 1952, s 12(2); see generally, Livingstone and Owen (n 305 above) para 8.05ff.
307 [1984] 1 WLR 1408.
308 Sch 1, Pt I.
309 *R v Secretary of State for the Home Department, ex p McComb*, *The Times*, 15 Apr 1991.
310 PSI 05/97 amending Security Manual 60.25.
311 Prison Rules 1964, SI 388/1964, r 9(3) as amended.
312 Ibid r 6.

(d) 'Family' and statutory rights

A 'family' is entitled to rights in many different statutory contexts, particularly in the social welfare field. Often the legislation itself will provide a definition of the term 'family'. However, in some statutes the word is left undefined. In the important case of *Fitzpatrick v Sterling Housing Association Ltd*[313] the House of Lords had to construe the phrase 'member of the original tenant's family' when considering whether a person in a longstanding, loving and monogamous homosexual relationship could succeed his partner to the tenancy under the Rent Act 1977. By a bare majority, the House of Lords held that the same sex partner of a tenant was now to be recognised as capable of being a member of the tenant's family. As Lord Clyde put it: **13.69**

> The concept of the family has undergone significant development during recent years both in the United Kingdom and overseas . . . Social groupings have come to take a number of different forms. The form of the single parent family has been long recognised. A more open acceptance of differences in sexuality allows a greater recognition of the possibility of domestic groupings of partners of the same sex. The formal bond of marriage is now far from being a significant criterion for the existence of a family unit. While it remains as a particular formalisation of the relationship between heterosexual couples, family units may now be recognised to exist both where the principal members are in a heterosexual relationship and where they are in a homosexual or lesbian relationship.[314]

C. The Law Under the European Convention

(1) Introduction

The rights to family life in the Convention are to be found in Articles 8 and 12.[315] Article 8[316] states that: **13.70**

> 1. Everyone has the right to respect for his private and family life, his home and his correspondence.
>
> 2. There shall be no interference by a public authority with the exercise of this right except such as is in accordance with the law and is necessary in a democratic society in the interests of national security, public safety or the economic well-being of the country, for the prevention of disorder or crime, for the protection of health or morals, or for the protection of the rights and freedoms of others.

313 [1999] 3 WLR 1113.

314 Ibid 1135E-G; see also 1123B-1124F (Lord Slynn) and 1129C–1130f (Lord Nicholls).

315 Art 5 of the Seventh Protocol deals with equality between spouses. It has not been ratified by the United Kingdom and will not be considered further.

316 For a discussion on the right to respect for privacy, the home and correspondence see para 12.81ff above.

Article 8 also protects the right to private life and many complaints about breaches of the right to family life can overlap with alleged violations of the right to private life.[317]

13.71 Article 12, on the other hand, is confined to the right to 'marriage' and 'to found a family'. Article 12 states that:

> Men and women of marriageable age have the right to marry and to found a family, according to the national laws governing the exercise of this right.

Article 12 means that the Convention confers preferential status to the traditional marriage. Married couples are, therefore, not treated as being in an analogous position with unmarried couples in relation to their right to found a family[318] or where complaints of discrimination[319] are made concerning differential tax regimes[320] or differences in their parental rights.[321]

13.72 The dividing line between Article 8 and Article 12 is sometimes obscure. The essence of the right to marry under Article 12 is the right to formation of a legally binding association between a man and a woman.[322] By contrast, Article 8 protects individuals from intrusion into family life *once* marriage has been established. Thus, a claim that legal restrictions preclude a couple from marrying will come under Article 12 whereas complaints concerning the state's failure to provide the material circumstances which make marriage effective will engage Article 8.

13.73 Although Article 8 has been interpreted very broadly by the Court and Commission, the Strasbourg case law[323] has not taken an expansive approach to Article 12. In particular, Article 12 expressly states that it creates a right 'according to national law'. This means that the state has a wide margin of appreciation[324] to establish rules governing capacity and formal requirements for marriage.

(2) The right to marry and to found a family

(a) The scope of the right

13.74 Article 12 refers both to a right to marry and to a right to found a family. The text of the Article in referring to 'this right' implies that the intention of the drafters

---

[317] See para 12.84 above.
[318] See para 13.74 above.
[319] See Chap 17.
[320] *Lindsay v United Kingdom* (1986) 49 DR 181, EComm HR.
[321] *McMichael v United Kingdom* (1995) 20 EHRR 205.
[322] *Draper v United Kingdom* (1980) 24 DR 72, 81, EComm HR; *Hamer v. United Kingdom* (1979) 24 DR 5, 16, EComm HR.
[323] See *Marckx v Belgium* (1979) 2 EHRR 330 para 31; *B R and J v Germany* (1984) 36 DR 130, 140, EComm HR.
[324] See para 6.31ff above.

was to define a single right. Nevertheless, Article 12 has been described as a 'close conjunction between two distinct rights'[325] and the Court has taken the view that there are two parts of Article 12 which are closely related.[326] Although the Commission has found that a prisoner has the right to marry irrespective of any possibility of procreation,[327] neither the Commission nor the Court have yet affirmed the right to found a family in the *absence* of marriage.[328] On the contrary, in *Marckx v Belgium*,[329] the Court rejected the claim of a mother of an illegitimate child that a right 'not to marry' would be an equivalent basis for the right to found a family. It held that whatever disadvantages a woman would suffer by not marrying the father of her child, they were not a barrier to the exercise of her freedom to marry or remain single under Article 12.

The conjunctive nature of the rights to marry and to found a family suggests that the unmarried individuals do not have the same right to found a family as that afforded a married couple. Jacobs and White point out that if Article 12 had been worded as 'everyone has the right to marry and to found a family', it might have been easier to infer that unmarried people also have the right to found a family.[330] **13.75**

Furthermore, the Court in *Marckx v Belgium*[331] left open the question of whether the right not to marry could be derived from Article 12. It therefore seems that the state is entitled to treat married families more favourably than unmarried families when founding a family in relation to custody rights[332] or adoption[333] and in relation to social programmes and artificial reproductive techniques[334] (provided the treatment of unmarried family does not breach Article 8). Harris, O'Boyle and Warbrick argue[335] that any claim to the effect that such differential treatment amounts to discrimination under Article 14[336] is bound to fail because Article 12 itself authorises the difference in treatment. **13.76**

325 J Fawcett, *The Application of the European Convention on Human Rights* (2nd edn, Clarendon Press, 1987) 285.

326 *Rees v United Kingdom* (1986) 9 EHRR 56 paras 49–50; and *Cossey v United Kingdom* (1990) 13 EHRR 622 para 43.

327 *Hamer v United Kingdom* (1979) 24 DR 5, 16, EComm HR.

328 See *Rees v United Kingdom* (1986) 9 EHRR 56 para 49, although the issue there was the right to marry rather than the right to found a family.

329 (1979) 2 EHRR 330.

330 F Jacobs and R White, *The European Convention on Human Rights* (2nd edn, Clarendon Press, 1996) 117.

331 (1979) 2 EHRR 330 para 67.

332 *B R & J v Germany* (1984) 36 DR 130, EComm HR.

333 *X v Belgium and Netherlands* (1975) 7 DR 75, EComm HR.

334 See the discussion in D Harris, M O'Boyle and C Warbrick, *The Law of the European Convention on Human Rights* (Butterwoths, 1995), 441.

335 Ibid 435.

336 See para 17.89ff below.

13.77 The fact that the right to marry under Article 12 is 'according to the national law' entails that the legal framework for marriage is a question for the state *itself* to determine. The state may establish criteria for marriage such as capacity, marriageable age, form, and prohibited degrees of consanguinity; and it is entitled to decide on the principles it wishes to apply where there are conflicts of law such as the question of whether an individual is already married[337] or whether he is of marriageable age.[338] Furthermore, the state is not under a duty to allow marriages in a particular form (such as polygamous unions or particular religious ceremonies).[339]

13.78 However, the language of Article 12 does not authorise a state to go so far as to 'completely deprive a person or a category of persons of the right to marry.'[340] The state's freedom to determine the legal framework of marriage will be restricted where the standards applied are arbitrary or where they completely empty the right of its content.[341] Because the right to marry guaranteed by Article 12 refers to the traditional marriage between persons of the opposite biological sex,[342] Article 12 has not been extended to transsexuals or homosexuals.[343]

13.79 Furthermore, Article 12 makes no express reference to divorce. In *Johnston v Ireland*[344] the Court rejected the complaint that impediments on the right to divorce breached Article 12, taking the view that it could not by creative interpretation derive from the Convention a right that was not originally granted. However, Harris, O'Boyle and Warbrick[345] suggest that the reasoning in *Johnston v Ireland*[346] is difficult to reconcile with *F v Switzerland*.[347] In that case the Court emphasised that divorced persons should not be unduly restricted from remarrying, so as to protect children from illegitimacy and the subsequent spouse from abuse.

(d) The relationship between Article 12 and Article 8

13.80 Cases under Article 12 often raise the issue of whether the state, having established the legal vehicle of marriage, has any *further* duty to provide the material circumstances which will make the right to marry effective. A number of points arise.

---

337 *X v United Kingdom* (1970) 35 CD 102, EComm HR; *X v Switzerland* (1981) 26 DR 207, EComm HR.

338 *Khan v United Kingdom* (1986) 48 DR 253, EComm HR.

339 *X v Germany* (1974) 1 DR 64, EComm HR.

340 *Van Oosterwick v Belgium* (1980) 3 EHRR 557, Com Rep para 56.

341 *Rees v United Kingdom* (1986) 9 EHRR 56 para 50.

342 *Rees v United Kingdom* (n 341 above) para 49; *Cossey v United Kingdom* (1990) 13 EHRR 622 para 46; *Sheffield and Horsham v United Kingdom* (1998) 27 EHRR 163 para 66.

343 See para 13.87ff below.

344 (1986) 9 EHRR 203 para 53; the Commission considered that according to the *travaux préparatoires* the omission was deliberate: see Com Rep paras 92-102.

345 n 335 above 440.

346 Ibid.

347 (1987) 10 EHRR 411 para 36.

First, since marriage is a consensual union, the state has no obligation to ensure that the event is in fact celebrated. Secondly, where circumstances prevent willing parties from entering into a lawful marriage, the state may become obliged to mitigate or eliminate these obstacles. In *Hamer v United Kingdom*[348] and *Draper v United Kingdom*[349] prisoners complained that Article 12 was breached because the Marriage Act of 1949 required that the celebration of marriage take place at locations outside prisons. The failure of the prison authorities to approve temporary release for this purpose caused delays to such an extent[350] that it violated the right to marry. Similarly, in *F v Switzerland*[351] the Court decided that a divorced person is entitled to remarry without being subject to unreasonable restrictions which were disproportionate to the legitimate aim pursued. **13.81**

Thirdly, the right to marry does not impose on the state any duty to ensure cohabitation or consummation is feasible after the marriage has been solemnised. A couple have a right to marry even in the absence of prospects of cohabitation; however, if they choose to marry in such circumstances the state has no duty under Article 12 to facilitate their life together to ensure that they may found a family.[352] **13.82**

Fourthly, it appears that the question of whether there is a duty on the state to facilitate married life is more appropriately decided under Article 8 as a matter of 'respect for family life'[353] rather than Article 12. Article 12 does not guarantee a right to sufficient living accommodation or subsistence to keep a family.[354] Article 8, rather than Article 12, is the source of any available remedy where a couple are separated by reason of a deportation or immigration order[355] or by the application of conflicts of laws to matters of recognition of foreign marriages. Nonetheless, van Dijk and van Hoof[356] have suggested that the right to marry and found a family entails a prohibition on the state from imposing a sanction based on marital or parental status (such as a public authority dismissing an employee). **13.83**

---

[348] (1979) 24 DR 5, EComm HR.

[349] (1980) 24 DR 72, EComm HR.

[350] In *Hamer v United Kingdom* (n 348 above) the opportunity to marry would have been delayed until the prisoner obtained parole; in *Draper v United Kingdom* (n 349 above) a prisoner serving a life sentence had virtually no foreseeable date of release when he might marry.

[351] (1987) 10 EHRR 411.

[352] *Hamer v United Kingdom* (n 348 above); *Draper v United Kingdom* (n 349 above).

[353] See para 13.113ff below.

[354] *Andersson and Kullman v Sweden* (1986) 46 DR 251, EComm HR.

[355] See para 13.121 below.

[356] *Theory and Practice of the European Convention on Human Rights* (3rd edn, Kluwer, 1998) 602; D Harris, M O'Boyle and C Warbrick, *Law of the European Convention on Human Rights* (Butterworths, 1995) 438 argue that this suggestion should be treated with circumspection.

(c) The position of transsexuals

13.84 The right to marry guaranteed by Article 12 refers to the traditional marriage between persons of the opposite biological sex.[357] The question of marriage for transsexuals under Article 12[358] depends on whether the change in sexual status is *recognised*. If the sex change were acknowledged, then to deny the transsexual the right to marry a person of the (now) opposite sex would be contrary to Article 12. Some states take the view, however, that the original gender is retained regardless of the physical treatment undergone; and that a marriage between a transsexual and a person of the transsexual's original sex is essentially a homosexual union.

13.85 In *Rees v United Kingdom*[359] the Commission split evenly over the issue, although it unanimously denied the claimant transsexual the right to marry. Half of the Commission found the union contrary to Article 12 only because the state had not given legal recognition to the sexual transformation; the failure to do so was a violation of Article 8 which, when rectified, would make marriage accessible to the claimant. The other half held that the substance of marriage included the physical capacity to procreate, a requirement which excludes transsexuals from marrying. However, the Court decided in *Rees v United Kingdom*[360] that:

> the right to marry guaranteed by Article 12 refers to the traditional marriage between persons of the opposite biological sex.

13.86 On the same question in *Cossey v United Kingdom*[361] the Commission by a 10:6 majority held that a denial of marriage to transsexuals did violate Article 12; but the Court overturned the decision to uphold again the traditional concept of marriage which it had asserted in *Rees v United Kingdom*. Although the Court[362] accepted that some states did accept marriages between transsexuals, the Court did not consider it open to it to take a new approach to the interpretation of Article 12. The Court recently returned to these issues in *Sheffield and Horsham v United Kingdom*.[363] It concluded that the right to marriage under Article 12 refers to the traditional marriage between persons of the opposite sex and that it was open to the state to use biological criteria to determine a person's sex for the purpose of marriage.

---

[357] *Rees v United Kingdom* (1986) 9 EHRR 56 para 49; Com Rep paras 52-55; *Cossey v United Kingdom* (1990) 13 EHRR 622 para 46.

[358] It could be argued that the refusal to allow transsexual marriages breaches the right of respect for privacy (see para 12.106 above) or constitutes discrimination (see para 17.89ff below).

[359] *Rees v United Kingdom* (1986) 9 EHRR 56.

[360] Ibid para 49.

[361] (1990) 13 EHRR 622.

[362] Ibid para 46.

[363] (1998) 27 EHRR 163 paras 66–68.

(d) The position of homosexuals

Homosexual marriages have not been recognised by the Strasbourg authorities as being protected by Article 12. As a result, refusal by a state to recognise homosexual marriages does not constitute a violation of Article 12.[364] This is not, perhaps, surprising, since the Commission has found that homosexual unions do not constitute 'family life' under Article 8;[365] and the recognition of homosexual marriages would go beyond even the affirmation of transsexual marriages which can be construed as being between a man and a woman. There is some support for the idea that homosexual unions should be recognised on the basis of substance, rather than by the character of the partners,[366] so that for example a 'registered partnership' such as that allowed by Danish law might have some of the legal effects of marriage without being marriage.[367] **13.87**

(e) The right to found a family

Article 12 protects couples from interference with their right to found a family and has been described by the Commission as an absolute right.[368] However, the Commission has held that Article 12 does not guarantee the right of adoption.[369] It also seems that Article 12 does not impose a positive obligation on the state to provide programmes to encourage the legitimate family.[370] Whether it confers a right to artificial reproduction has not yet been addressed. **13.88**

(3) The meaning of family life under Article 8

(a) The scope of 'family life'

Article 8 provides a guarantee of 'respect for family life'. It does not protect a right to establish family life by marriage or to found a family: that right is embodied in Article 12.[371] Neither does Article 8 provide an automatic right to terminate family life, although in certain circumstances it might be found necessary to terminate **13.89**

---

[364] It could, however, be argued that the refusal to allow homosexual marriages breaches the right of respect for privacy (see para 12.106ff above) or constitutes discrimination (see para 17.189ff below); for same-sex marriages generally, see *Quilter v A-G of New Zealand* (1997) 3 BHRC 461, para 13.186 below.

[365] See para 13.107 below.

[366] See the dissent of Mr Schermers in *W v United Kingdom* (1989) 63 DR 34, 48.

[367] See L Nielsen, Family Rights and the Registered Partnership in Denmark (1990) 4 IJL Fam 297.

[368] *X v United Kingdom* (1975) 2 DR 105 106, EComm HR.

[369] See *X and Y v United Kingdom* (1977) 12 DR 32, EComm HR; *X v Netherlands* (1981) 24 DR 176, EComm HR.

[370] See the discussion of the issues which arise in relation to artificial insemination by Harris O'Boyle and Warbrick (n 356 above) 441.

[371] It may however require that the state acknowledge the existence of a *de facto* family already established.

some family obligations in order to protect the interests of other members of the family. The absence of a 'family life' connection between particular individuals does not mean that their family relationship is excluded from Article 8 protection. For example, where parents divorce, it is possible that a familial relationship between the non-custodial parent and his child may survive,[372] if real contact is maintained between them.

13.90 There is no precise definition of 'family life' in the Convention case law.[373] The existence of family life does not depend on a close analysis of the complainant's circumstances but depends on proving there is a sufficiently close factual tie.[374] The fundamental element of family life is the right to live together so that family relationships can develop naturally[375] and that members of the family can enjoy one another's company.[376]

13.91 The 'existence or non-existence of "family life" is essentially a question of fact depending upon the real existence in practice of close personal ties'.[377] However, cohabitation between the parents[378] or between parents and young children[379] is not essential to prove the existence of a family. As the Court said in *Boughanemi v France*:[379a]

> The concept of family life on which Article 8 is based embraces, even when there is no cohabitation, the tie between a parent and his or her child, regardless of whether or not the latter is legitimate. Although that tie may be broken by subsequent events, this can only happen in exceptional circumstances.

13.92 In *X, Y and Z v United Kingdom*[380] the Court emphasised that the notion of family life is not confined to families based on marriage and may encompass other *de facto* relationships; whether a relationship amounts to family life depends on a number of factors including whether the couple lived together, whether they demonstrated the commitment to each other by having children together or by any other means. Sometimes the fact of prolonged voluntary separations results in a finding that the individuals concerned do not feel the need for close family ties.[381] However, in *Moustaquim v Belgium*[382] the Court accepted that an applicant

[372] *Berrehab v Netherlands* (1988) 11 EHRR 322.

[373] See generally, J Liddy, 'The Concept of Family Life Under the ECHR' [1998] EHRLR 15; and see U Kilkelly, *The Child and the European Convention on Human Rights* (Ashgate, 1999) Chap 9.

[374] See eg *Marckx v Belgium* (1979) 2 EHRR 330 para 31.

[375] Ibid.

[376] *Olsson v Sweden (No 1)* (1988) 11 EHRR 259 para 59.

[377] *K v United Kingdom* (1986) 50 DR 199, 207, EComm HR.

[378] *Kroon v Netherlands* (1994) 19 EHRR 263.

[379] *Berrehab v Netherlands* (n 372 above).

[379a] (1996) 22 EHRR 228 para 35.

[380] (1997) 24 EHRR 143 para 36.

[381] See generally, P van Dijk and G van Hoof, *Theory and Practice of the European Convention on Human Rights* (3rd edn, Kluwer, 1998) 507.

[382] (1991) 13 EHRR 802.

who ran away and had been imprisoned had nevertheless not terminated his family relationships. Van Dijk and van Hoof[383] argue that in such cases the following factors should be considered: who took the initiative for the separation in the past, the nature of the continued ties, the family traditions within the religious, ethnic and cultural community and the degree of dependency between the applicant and his parents or relatives.[384]

(b) Marriages: formal and informal

The scope of 'family life' under the Convention extends far beyond formal relationships and legitimate arrangements.[385] The relationship between a co-habiting husband and wife obviously falls within the concept of 'family life';[386] and where there is a legal marriage, there is a presumption that Article 8 applies to married couples even if they have not yet established a family relationship.[387] **13.93**

In *Abdulaziz, Cabales and Balkandali v United Kingdom*[388] the Court took the view that Article 8 extended to those seeking admission into a country in order to marry. However, sham marriages entered into solely for purposes of immigration status or nationality[389] (as well as other legitimate family relationships)[390] may lack enough substance to come under Article 8. **13.94**

Article 8 applies equally to an 'informal marriage',[391] at least when there is a child involved.[392] Where marital relationships are not legally formalised, the existence of family life will depend on all of the circumstances of the relationship in question: in particular its intensity and duration.[393] *De facto* family ties will normally be evidenced by a relationship of sufficient constancy that the man and woman have lived together for a significant period of time,[394] but cohabitation is not essential. **13.95**

[383] n 381 above, 508.

[384] Contrast *X v United Kingdom* (1973) 43 CD 119, EComm HR and *X and F v United Kingdom* (1972) YB 564, EComm HR.

[385] *Johnston v Ireland* (1986) 9 EHRR 203; *Marckx v Belgium* (1979) 2 EHRR 330.

[386] *Abdulaziz, Cabales and Balkandali v United Kingdom* (1985) 7 EHRR 471.

[387] Ibid para 62.

[388] Ibid paras 59, 60.

[389] See *Benes v Austria* (1992) 72 DR 271, EComm HR where annulment of a marriage entered into solely to establish spouse's nationality was justified under Art 8(2).

[390] See eg *Moustaquim v Belgium* (1991) 13 EHRR 802, Comm Rep para 51: the Government initially questioned whether a couple had asserted 'family life' with their teen-aged son solely for Convention purposes.

[391] *Marckx v Belgium* (1979) 2 EHRR 330.

[392] *Keegan v Ireland* (1994) 18 EHRR 342 para 44; *Kroon v Netherlands* (1994) 19 EHRR 263 para 30.

[393] The context may also be relevant to the assessment: see P Duffy, 'The Protection of Privacy, Family Life and Other Rights Under Article 8 of the European Convention on Human Rights' (1982) 2 YEL 191 in which he draws a distinction between domestic and immigration cases.

[394] *Keegan v Ireland* (n 392 above); in *Kroon v Netherlands* (n 392 above), a bond of 'family life' was found between the couple on the basis that they had produced four children, regardless of the contribution of the father to his son's upbringing.

The stability of the relationship over time and the intentions of the parties are the significant factors.[395]

(c) The relationship between parents and children

13.96 Article 8 covers the mutual enjoyment by a parent and child of one another's company which is a fundamental element of family life.[396] Natural relationships between parents and young children will normally amount to substantive family relationships. It is implicit in the concept of family life that parents have some authority over their young children.[397] It is not necessary that the parent continues to live with the child[398] or that the child is 'legitimate',[399] so long as there exists regular contacts and a certain dependency on the parent.

13.97 Article 8 also embraces within the concept of 'family life' adoptive parent-child relationships.[400] The position concerning foster parents and their children has yet to be determined by the Court; but van Dijk and van Hoof[401] suggest that they should be treated as part of the family on the same basis as the children of adoptive parents.[401a]

13.98 Many complaints about breaches of the right to family life arise out of divorce cases. The fundamental concern is the predominant interest of the child.[402] However, Article 8 does not have any specific impact on the question of which parent should be awarded custody of the children following a divorce;[403] this is a question for the national authorities to decide on the basis of national law.[404] On the other hand, the right to family life does entitle a non-custodial parent to visit and contact his child and the state is only entitled to interfere if there are serious reasons for doing so under Article 8(2).[405]

[395] *Kroon v Netherlands* (n 392 above); contrast *M B v United Kingdom* (1994) 77-A DR 108, EComm HR where a relationship of six months with a non-cohabiting woman who later gave birth to an unplanned child was insufficient to come within the scope of family life.

[396] *Andersson v Sweden* (1992) 14 EHRR 615.

[397] *R v United Kingdom* (1987) 10 EHRR 74 para 64; *Nielsen v Denmark* (1988) 11 EHRR 175 para 61.

[398] *Hendriks v Netherlands* (1982) 29 DR 5, EComm HR; *A and A v Netherlands* (1992) 72 DR 118.

[399] *Boughanemi v France* (1996) 22 EHRR 228; followed by the Commission in *McCullough v United Kingdom* (1988) 25 EHRR CD 34.

[400] *X v Belgium and Netherlands* (1975) 7 DR 75, EComm HR; *X v France* (1982) 31 DR 241, EComm HR; *Gaskin v United Kingdom* (1989) 12 EHRR 36 (in relation to foster arrangement).

[401] n 383 above 506.

[401a] The Commission has found that such a relationship amounts to 'private life' only: *X v Switzerland* (1978) 13 DR 248.

[402] *X v Germany* (1979) 14 DR 175.

[403] *X v Netherlands* (1963) 6 YB 262; *X v Germany* (1979) 14 DR 175.

[404] *X v Netherlands* (1963) 6 YB 262; *X v Sweden* (1973) 44 CD 128.

[405] *X v Germany* (1979) 14 DR 175.

13.99 Where a parent still has genuine ties with a child but has not been awarded residence, Article 8 generally requires that he is given the right of contact.[406] However, depriving a parent of the right of contact may be justified under Article 8(2).[407] The same principles apply to the termination of contact between a parent and an illegitimate child.[408]

13.100 The Court has consistently expressed the view that the natural connection between a mother and child at birth amounts to 'family life', whatever degree of contact she might have with the father; where the child is born into a marital union, it is 'ipso facto' part of that relationship and, as such, there exists a bond amounting to 'family life' which subsequent events cannot break, save in exceptional circumstances.[409] Attempts to keep in communication and to arrange contact may be sufficient to maintain the continuation of family life.[410] However, separating a mother from her baby while she is in prison may violate Article 8.[411]

13.101 On the other hand, the Commission has emphasised that the natural bond between a father and child does not itself necessarily amount to 'family life', even if the father is married to the mother, if he has minimal or no contact with the mother and child. The existence of family life between father and child therefore remains more likely than the relationship of mother and child to depend on some degree of constancy and commitment between the parents,[412] as well as contact with the child.[413] However, the Commission has rejected the claim by the father of a foetus that family life existed between them, at least where the question was his right to be consulted as to whether the mother should have an abortion.[414]

13.102 It has been argued[415] that there ought to be a presumption that a blood tie will always result in 'family life' but the idea has not been well-received in light of technological advances in artificial fertilisation which enable the biological parent to be completely removed from the child. For example, the Commission found that

[406] *X v Sweden* (1955-1957) YB 211; *X v Sweden* (1977) 12 DR 192, EComm HR; *Hendriks v Netherlands* (1982) 29 DR 5, EComm HR.

[407] *X v United Kingdom* (1973) 44 Coll 66; *X v Sweden* (1978) 12 DR 192; *Hendriks* (1982) 29 DR 5 EComm HR.

[408] *X v Denmark* (1978) 15 DR 128, EComm HR.

[409] *Berrehab v Netherlands* (1988) 11 EHRR 322 and *Gul v Switzerland* (1996) 22 EHRR 93.

[410] *Gul v Switzerland* (n 409 above).

[411] *Togher v United Kingdom* (1998) 25 EHRR CD 99.

[412] It has been suggested that there is no reason why the same test ought not to be applied equally to a mother and her child born outside of marriage (see J Liddy, 'The Concept of Family Life under the ECHR' [1998] EHRLR 15), but the rationale for the test in regard to the father is probably based on an assumption that the mother has residence in relation to the young child; if so, her bond to the child will be less substantially affected by her ties to the father.

[413] See *M B v United Kingdom* (1994) 77-A DR 108, EComm HR, in which a man's six-month relationship with a woman which produced a child outside of wedlock and cohabitation did not come under the umbrella of 'family life'.

[414] *X v United Kingdom,* (1980) 19 DR 244, EComm HR.

[415] See the opinion of Mr Schermers in *Kroon v Netherlands* (1994) 19 EHRR 263, Com Rep.

the relationship between the applicant father and a child born to a lesbian to whom he had donated his sperm did not amount to 'family life', even though he baby sat weekly during the child's infancy.[416] Furthermore, the complex scientific, legal, moral and social issues raised by transsexuality means that Article 8 does not imply an obligation on the state to recognise as the father of a child a person who is not the biological father of the child.[417]

13.103 Issues concerning paternity raise difficult questions about proof of a familial relationship. A legal presumption that a husband has fathered the child of his wife is not itself contrary to the Convention, although such a presumption must be subject to rebuttal in order to establish the biological and social reality of the situation.[418] However, issues arising in relation to compulsory and voluntary testing by a husband to disprove paternity are considered to be questions of 'private life' rather than family life.[419]

13.104 Relationships between parents and their adult children require close consideration; and the Commission and the Court have taken different approaches. The Commission has been cautious in its acceptance of the idea of continuance of family life between adult children and parents, evidencing the need for real and close factual links. As a child grows older, a continuing substantive connection amounting to 'family life' rather than just a family relationship will have to be demonstrated.[420] The Commission has placed the onus on the applicant to show that there are particularly close links, such as financial dependency, which go beyond normal emotional ties.[421]

13.105 By comparison, in *Boughanemi v France*[422] the Court has applied to parental relationships with adult children its presumption that there is a bond of 'family life' which exists from birth and which may be broken only in exceptional circumstances; the 33-year-old deported applicant successfully argued that the separation from his parents and seven brothers and sisters, all of whom resided lawfully in France amounted to an interference with his 'family life'.

(a) Non-traditional family units

13.106 'Non-traditional families' include a range of family units such as homosexual or transsexual couples and their children, which can, for example, result from sperm

[416] *M v Netherlands* (1993) 74 DR 120, EComm HR.
[417] *X, Y and Z v United Kingdom* (1997) EHRR 143 para 52.
[418] *Kroon v Netherlands* (n 415 above).
[419] *Rasmussen v Denmark* (1984) 7 EHRR 371.
[420] *Singh v United Kingdom* (1967) 10 YB 478, EComm HR.
[421] *S and S v United Kingdom* (1984) 40 DR 196, EComm HR.
[422] (1996) 22 EHRR 228; citing *Berrehab v Netherlands* (1989) 11 EHRR 322 and *Gül v Switzerland* (1996) 22 EHRR 93.

donation and artificial insemination of one of the partners or a surrogate mother. The extent to which the concept of 'family life' extends to such arrangements has not been fully considered by the Court.

A stable homosexual or lesbian relationship does not itself receive the protection of 'family life' under Article 8,[423] even where there is a shared parenting role[424] (although there may be arguments about the breaches of the right of respect for private life).[425] In *X Y and Z v United Kingdom*[426] a female-male transsexual complained about the lack of recognition as the father of a child born into his stable relationship with a woman. The transsexual partner had been involved in the process of seeking and obtaining artificial insemination by donation, and had acted as the father to the child since its birth, but because the law deemed him to be a female, he was denied the right to registration as the father. The Commission found an interference with 'family life' in relation to lack of recognition of his role; the distinction between this and the lesbian cases is in the willingness of the Commission to view the unit as indistinguishable from a traditional family and to be influenced by the fact that the relationships of the parties were in effect a creation of English legislation. The Court, however, held that the United Kingdom law did not amount to a failure of respect for family life. The absence of consensus among the Member States of the Council of Europe concerning issues arising from the technology of medically assisted procreation (and filiation, in particular) led the Court to take the view[427] that: **13.107**

> the community as a whole has an interest in maintaining a coherent system of family law which places the best interests of the child at the forefront..(and) whilst it has not been suggested that the amendment to the law would be harmful to the interests of the child or of children conceived by AID in general, it is not clear that it would necessarily be to the advantage of such children.

Even though the meaning of 'family life' may have been extended beyond relationships of blood, marriage or adoption into *de facto* relationships of a certain duration and commitment, the measures applicable to ensure respect for family life may be different depending on whether one has reference to a biological parent or a non-biological parent-figure. This is particularly true in the areas of inheritance and measures designed to give a degree of legal security to father-figures in custody matters. **13.108**

---

423 *S v United Kingdom* (1986) 47 DR 274, EComm HR; *B v United Kingdom* (1990) 64 DR 278, EComm HR; *X and Y v United Kingdom* (1983) DR 32, 220, EComm HR; cf *Grant v South-West Trains Ltd* (1998) 3 BHRC 578 para 33 (ECJ's comments on position under Art 8).

424 *Kerkhoven v Netherlands* Application 15666/89, 19 May 1992 unreported discussed by D Harris, M O'Boyle and C Warbrick, *Law of the European Convention on Human Rights* (Butterworths, 1995) 442.

425 See para 12.92 above and see also para 17.121 below (sexual orientation discrimination).

426 (1997) 24 EHRR 143.

427 Ibid para 47.

(e) The extended family

13.109 The meaning of 'family life' has been expanded to include the ties between near relatives since such relatives play a considerable part in family life.[428] Although a child may have a family relationship with an aunt[429] and uncle,[430] the Commission has been reluctant to extend family life to uncles and nephews[431] except in exceptional circumstances.[432] Furthermore, in several recent cases[433] the Court has relaxed its earlier attitude that a 'sufficiently close link' between adult siblings[434] was necessary to support 'family life', or it may be that special circumstances beyond the sibling relationship supported the findings.[435]

13.110 In *Marckx v Belgium*[436] the Court indicated that family life could extend to grandparents and grandchildren. 'Family life' of the social, moral and cultural sort envisaged by *Marckx v Belgium*[437] will depend on whether 'real' *de facto* family relations exist between them,[438] a matter which is usually evidenced by the care given by the grandparents to the grandchildren. Convention law reflects the fact that in relation to interests of a more material kind, such as rights of inheritance on intestacy and ownership of property, it is quite acceptable for states to impose formal rules which do not depend on the determination of prior *de facto* relationships between the parties.[439] The Commission has interpreted the *dicta* in *Marckx v Belgium*[440] narrowly and held that Article 8 does not automatically apply to grandparents and grandchildren. The same approach has been taken toward adoptive grandparent-grandchildren relationships.[441]

---

[428] *Marckx v Belgium* (1979) 2 EHRR 330 para 45.

[429] Ibid.

[430] *Boyle v United Kingdom* (1994) 19 EHRR 179.

[431] *X and Y v United Kingdom* (1971) 12 DR 32, EComm HR.

[432] *Boyle v United Kingdom* (n 430 above).

[433] *Moustaquim v Belgium* (1991) 13 EHRR 802; *Boughanemi v France* (1996) 22 EHRR 228; see also *Nasri v France* (1995) 21 EHRR 458.

[434] *Family X v United Kingdom* (1982) 30 DR 232, EComm HR.

[435] See *Nasri v France* (n 433 above) where the applicant was a deaf mute: his deportation was found to infringe on respect for family life; in *Boughanemi v France* (n 433 above) Judge Pettiti said that it was not enough to establish family life that a person has brothers and sisters; the Court noted that there was no evidence before the Commission of an absence of ties of the applicant to his extended family, but this would be insufficient to support an application to the Commission in the first instance.

[436] *Marckx v Belgium* (n 428 above).

[437] Ibid.

[438] *X v Switzerland* (1981) DR 24, 183; *Lawlor v United Kingdom* (1988) 57 DR 216, EComm HR.

[439] *Marckx v Belgium* (n 428 above); *Vermeire v Belgium* (1993) 15 EHRR 488.

[440] n 428, above.

[441] *Price v United Kingdom* (1988) 55 DR 224.

(4) Interference with family life

The essential purpose of Article 8 is to protect the individual against arbitrary interference by the public authorities.[442] A complainant must establish there has been an interference and in practice has little difficulty in doing so. For example, the mutual enjoyment by a parent and child of each other's company constitutes a fundamental element of family life and the natural family relationship is not terminated by the fact of taking the child into public care; therefore, removing the child from its parents is a plain interference with its family life.[443] **13.111**

However, a restrictive view has been taken of the meaning of 'interference'. For example, in *Rees v United Kingdom*[444] the Court said that the mere refusal to alter the sex of transsexuals in the register of births or to issue birth certificates different from the register did not constitute interferences but raised questions about the nature and scope of the positive obligation to respect the family. Similarly, the refusal to allow an applicant to adopt a new surname did not amount to an interference with family life as it would have if it required him to change his surname; it could only violate Article 8 if it amounted to a breach of the obligation to respect the family.[445] On the other hand, the statutory requirements that formerly applied to amending a birth certificate did breach the right to respect for family life.[446] **13.112**

(5) The right of respect for family life

(a) Introduction

The right[447] of respect for family life, in essence, protects the right of family members to live together, so that the family relationships may develop 'normally' and that they may enjoy one another's company. The Court emphasised in *Abdulaziz, Cabales and Balkandali v United Kingdom* that:[448] **13.113**

> so far as those positive obligations are concerned [which are inherent in an effective 'respect' for family life], the notion of 'respect' is not clear cut: having regard to the diversity of the practices followed and the situations obtaining in the Contracting States, the notion's requirements will vary considerably from case to case. Accordingly, this is an area in which the Contracting Parties enjoy a wide margin of appreciation in determining the steps to be taken to ensure compliance with the Convention with due regard to the needs and resources of the community and of individuals.

442 *Hokkanen v Finland* (1994) 19 EHRR 139 para 35.
443 See eg *Olsson v Sweden (No 1)* (1988) 11 EHRR 259 para 59.
444 (1986) 9 EHRR 56 para 36; *Cossey v United Kingdom* (1990) 13 EHRR 622.
445 *Stjerna v Finland* (1994) 24 EHRR 194 para 38.
446 *A V v United Kingdom* [1998] EHRLR 650.
447 For a general introduction to the meaning of 'respect' under Art 8(1), see para 12.111 above.
448 (1985) 7 EHRR 471 para 67.

13.114 The obligation to respect family life requires a fair balance that has to be struck between the general interest of the community and the interests of the individual; and the state has a wide margin of appreciation in striking the balance.[449] In *Stjerna v Finland*[450] the Court expressed the view that:

> The boundaries between the State's positive and negative obligations under Article 8 do not lend themselves to precise definition. The applicable principles are nonetheless similar. In both contexts regard must be had to the fair balance between the competing interests of the individual and of the community as a whole.

It is often said that the broad approach taken towards respect for family life results in incoherence and arbitrariness. It has been argued that these difficulties would be removed if the Court adopted a narrower concept of 'respect' for family life.[451]

(b) The obligations imposed on the state to respect family life

13.115 The obligation of the state to have 'respect for family life' requires it to do more than abstain from interference. In addition to this primarily negative undertaking, there are also positive obligations inherent in an effective 'respect for family life'.[452] This concept has been interpreted broadly by the Commission who said in *Z and E v Austria*[453] that:

> in shaping the domestic law, the state must act in a manner calculated to allow those concerned to lead a normal family life . . . The Commission is of the opinion that this consideration applies not only to legislation regulating family relationships, but also to legislation regulating the use of property insofar as it interferes with the possibility to use this property for family purposes.

13.116 However, the roles of different family members are not identical and the assertion of the collective right of respect for family life may conflict with the autonomous rights of individual members. In particular, parental authority over children may be offset by the rights of the child, even where he is too young to express his wishes, given the responsibility on the state to act in his 'best interests'. The exercise of parental rights is recognised to be fundamental to 'family life' and Convention jurisprudence allows parents to make decisions in regard to the upbringing, education, religious teaching,[454] personal relationships and sexual activities[455] of the child. Article 2 of the First Protocol expressly entitles parents to

---

[449] *Rees v United Kingdom* (1986) 9 EHRR 56 para 37; *Cossey v United Kingdom* (1990) 13 EHHR 622 para 37; *Sheffield and Horsham v United Kingdom* (1998) 27 EHRR 163 para 52.

[450] (1994) 24 EHHR 194 para 38.

[451] See C Warbrick, 'The Structure of Article 8' [1998] EHRLR 32.

[452] *Marckx v Belgium* (1979) 2 EHRR 330 para 31; *Airey v Ireland* (1979) 2 EHRR 305 para 32.

[453] *Z and E v Austria* (1986) 49 DR 67, EComm HR.

[453a] *Hokkanen v Finland* (1994) 19 EHRR 139 para 58.

[454] *Hoffmann v Austria* (1993) 17 EHRR 293 implies that parents are entitled to bring up their children in their own religious tradition.

[455] *X v Netherlands* (1974) 2 DR 118, EComm HR.

educate their children in accordance with their own religious and philosophical convictions.[456] But the right of the child to respect for his private life or to exercise freedom of thought, conscience and religion in a manner which is at variance with the directives of his parents, has been receiving increased attention, so that the weight given to parental authority may be reduced.[457]

The balancing of the rights of parents and children in 'family life' is most obvious in cases of removal of children into public care. Even though the state must protect the 'interests of the child' the importance of family life requires that it prove the necessity of the removal; efforts to facilitate contact of parents to children in care, or to reunite them are also taken into account by the Court.[458] The determination of the rights of children and the content of family life is most complicated where divorced or separated parents are involved. **13.117**

Thus, the Court has extensively developed the range of positive obligations which the state must meet: to require it to take positive steps to establish a system which would facilitate the integration of an illegitimate child into the family;[459] to relieve the parties to a marriage from the obligation to live with one another;[460] to provide an effective and accessible remedy for protection of one family member from the threats of violence of another;[461] to ensure that contact proceedings are decided sufficiently speedily so that delay did not in fact decide the question;[462] to provide a mechanism for resolution of questions concerning paternity;[463] to take measures in dealing with a child in public care so as to reunite him with his parents;[464] to enforce a father's right of contact with his daughter;[465] to consult with the natural father before placing a child for adoption;[466] to enable the tie to be established and the legal safeguards to be in place to ensure a child's integration with his biological father;[467] to refuse to allow changes of name;[468] and to admit relatives of settled immigrants in order to develop family life.[469] **13.118**

456 See para 19.53ff below.

457 See *X v Denmark* (1976) 7 DR 81, EComm HR; *Rieme v Sweden* (1992) 16 EHRR 155, where decisions of public authorities based predominantly on the wishes of the child rather than those of the parents, were not contrary to the Convention; *Hokkanen v Finland* (1994) 19 EHRR 139.

458 *Eriksson v Sweden* (1989) 12 EHRR 183; *Andersson v Sweden* (1992) 14 EHRR 615.

459 *Marckx v Belgium* (1979) 2 EHRR 330.

460 *Johnston v Ireland* (1986) 9 EHRR 203 para 57.

461 *Airey v Ireland* (1979) 2 EHRR 305.

462 *H v United Kingdom* (1987) 10 EHRR 95.

463 See *Rasmussen v Denmark* (1984) 7 EHRR 371.

464 *Eriksson v Sweden* (1989) 12 EHRR 183.

465 *Hokkanen v Finland* (1994) 19 EHRR 139 paras 58-62.

466 *Keegan v Ireland* (1994) 18 EHRR 342.

467 *Kroon v Netherlands* (1994) 19 EHRR 263.

468 *Stjerna v Finland* (1994) 24 EHRR 194; *Burghartz v Switzerland* (1994) 18 EHRR 101; *Guillot v France* [1997] EHRLR 196.

469 See eg *Gül v Switzerland* (1996) 22 EHRR 93.

(c) Respect for family life in care cases

13.119 Where public authorities must make decisions to interfere with family life, such as those to take children into care or place children for adoption, there will be procedural obligations on the state. In addition to the procedural safeguards imposed by Article 6(1) in relation to the determination of 'civil rights',[470] Article 8(1) requires that the procedure be sufficient to protect the family members. In *W v United Kingdom*[471] the Court took the view that:

> what has to be determined is whether, having regard to the particular circumstances of the case, and notably the serious nature of the decisions to be taken, the parents have been involved in the decision making process, seen as a whole, to a degree sufficient to provide them with the requisite protection of their interests. If they have not, there will have been a failure to respect their family life and the interference resulting from the decision will not be capable of being regarded as 'necessary' within the meaning of Article 8.

In *McMichael v United Kingdom*[472] the Court explained the rationale for the procedural safeguards by stating that Article 6(1):

> affords a procedural safeguard, namely the 'right to a court' in the determination of one's civil rights and obligations . . .; whereas not only does the procedural requirement inherent in Article 8 cover administrative procedures as well as judicial proceedings, but is ancillary to the wider purpose of ensuring proper respect for, *inter alia*, family life.

However, in *McCullough v United Kingdom*[473] the Commission decided that where an exclusion order under the Prevention of Terrorism Act had an indirect effect on family relationships, the lack of guarantees of independence and procedural safeguards in the procedures used did not violate Article 8.

13.120 The positive obligations on the state to respect family life will rarely go so far as to require financial or other practical support.[473a] The state is, for example, not required to provide financial assistance to enable one parent to stay at home with children, when free daycare was made available to enable them both to work.[474] On the other hand, it has been suggested that minimum welfare provision ought to be necessary to achieve an effective respect for family life.[475] However, the Commission has

[470] See para 11.183ff above.

[471] (1987) 10 EHRR 29 para 64.

[472] (1995) 20 EHRR 205 para 91.

[473] (1988) 25 EHRR CD 34.

[473a] See U Kilkelly, *The Child and the European Convention on Human Rights* (Ashgate, 1999) 210–212.

[474] *Andersson and Kullman v Sweden* (1986) 46 DR 251, EComm HR; see also *Petrovic v Austria* Judgment of 27 Mar 1998 (no sex discrimination in refusing to grant parental leave allowance to fathers), see para 17.114. below.

[475] See P Duffy 'The Protection of Privacy, Family Life and Other Rights Under Article 8 of the European Convention on Human Rights' (1982) 2 YEL 191, 199, who argues that welfare benefits probably come under Art 8.

taken the view that the assessment of maintenance payments from absent parents under the Child Support Act 1991 does not disclose a lack of respect for family life.[476]

(d) Respect for family life in immigration cases

The positive obligation on states to respect family life has considerable implications for immigration and deportation questions, particularly in relation to a family member who has no legal right to enter or live in the Convention state where other family members reside.[476a] Under Article 8 there is no general obligation on a state to allow married couples an unrestricted choice of residence requiring admittance of a non-national spouse for settlement in that country.[477] **13.121**

In *Gül v Switzerland*[478] the Court described the general principles as follows: **13.122**

- the extent of a state's obligation to admit relatives into its territory will vary according to the particular circumstances of the persons involved and the general interest;
- as a matter of well-established international law and subject to its treaty obligations, a state has the right to control the entry of non nationals into its territories; and
- where immigration is concerned, Article 8 cannot be considered to impose on the state a general obligation to respect the immigrant's choice of the country of matrimonial residence and to authorise family reunion within its territory.

At one stage the Commission took the view that the ordinary place of residence of a couple was where the husband or father had a right to reside.[479] It has subsequently accepted that this test could not be used as an absolute criterion due to its discriminatory nature and the fact that the impact of the expulsion of the husband on family members besides his spouse might also adversely affect family life.[480] **13.123**

Article 8 may require that a Convention state admit an alien, who would otherwise have no legal right to enter and establish family life or to join his or her family members there, if the applicant can show that there are substantial obstacles to the establishment of family life elsewhere.[481] If, for example, it is possible to **13.124**

---

[476] *Logan (Henry) v United Kingdom* (1996) 22 EHRR CD 178.

[476a] For a general discussion of Art 8 and immigrant and refugee children see U Kilkelly, n 473a above, Chap 10.

[477] *Abdulaziz, Cabales and Balkandali v United Kingdom* (1985) 7 EHRR 471 para 68.

[478] (1996) 22 EHRR 93 para 38; see also *Ahmut v Netherlands* (1996) 24 EHRR 62.

[479] *Agee v United Kingdom* (1976) 7 DR 164, EComm HR: in that case the husband had no right to reside in the United Kingdom and there were no demonstrable obstacles to his wife accompanying him if he were deported from the UK.

[480] *Uppal v United Kingdom (No 1)* (1979) 17 DR 149, EComm HR.

[481] In *Abdulaziz, Cabales and Balkandali v United Kingdom* (1985) 7 EHRR 471 para 68, no such obstacles were shown and the applicants were unsuccessful.

reunite the family abroad as in *Gül v Switzerland*,[482] then there is no breach of the obligation to respect family life. The critical issue is whether it is reasonable to require the family unit to be kept abroad, having weighed up the disadvantages of the applicants against the immigration policy of the state. Thus, economic and cultural disadvantages to family life outside the Convention state do not constitute sufficient obstacles to establishing family life elsewhere.[483] A variety of factors will be examined such as the links with the other country,[484] the possibility of jointly residing in the state where the family was founded[485] and the economic impact of removal.[486] However, there will be a breach of respect for family life if the state refuses to admit family members to join the individual expelled or where the alien is a refugee and therefore unable to return to his home.

13.125 Recent case law indicates that where a non-national resident in the Convention state can show a long and established family life, the right to respect for family life may require the state to allow him to remain. The obligation to allow family life to continue where it has been enjoyed is apparently not dependent on circumstances in the state to which removal is proposed.[487] In *Berrehab v Netherlands*[488] the Court held that expulsion under Dutch law of a Moroccan national following his divorce would fail to respect his family ties with his daughter. The principle was extended in *Moustaquim v Belgium*[489] in which a second generation Belgian immigrant who had been taken there by his parents from Morocco as an infant demonstrated strong family attachments in Belgium; the state deportation order evidenced a lack of respect for his family life. In *Beldjoudi v France*[490] the Court gave special protection to aliens; Judge Martens going so far as to suggest that 'integrated aliens' should be no more liable to expulsion than nationals.[491] The Court again found that the deportation of a long term resident Algerian, would fail to respect the family life which the applicant enjoyed in France with his French wife.

---

482 (1996) 22 EHRR 93 para 39: the Court distinguished the position from *Berrehab v Netherlands* (1988) 11 EHRR 322, where a daughter born and raised in the Netherlands could not reasonably be required to live in Morocco.

483 See *Beldjoudi v France* (1992) 14 EHRR 801 para 79 where requiring that the wife follow her husband 'might imperil the unity or even the very existence of the marriage'.

484 See eg *Moustaguim v Belgium* (1991) 13 EHRR 802 para 45; *Beldjoudi v France* (1992) 14 EHRR 801 para 77.

485 See eg *X and Y v United Kingdom* (1973) 43 CD 82; *X v United Kingdom* (1978) DR 42; *Jasmine Sorabjee v United Kingdom* [1996] EHRLR 216.

486 See eg *X and Y v United Kingdom* 5269/71 (1972) 15 YB 564; *Family X v United Kingdom* (1983) 30 DR 232.

487 Note though that while the obligation to allow established family life to continue may be independent of conditions in the state of destination, such conditions will be relevant to the separate question as to whether removal is a justifiable interference under Art 8(2).

488 *Berrehab v Netherlands* (1988) 11 EHRR 322.

489 *Moustaquim v Belgium* (1991) 13 EHRR 802.

490 (1992) 14 EHHR 801.

491 Ibid in his concurring judgment at para 2.

Similarly, in *Lamguindaz v United Kingdom*[492] the Commission found a breach of Article 8 where a 19-year-old Moroccan who had lived in the United Kingdom since age seven was being deported to Morocco where he had difficulties speaking Arabic and had no social support.

(e) Respect for family life in prisoner cases

Article 8 requires the state to assist prisoners so far as possible to create and sustain ties with people outside prison in order to facilitate their social rehabilitation.[493] It seems that the distress caused to prisoners by placing general restrictions on prison visits does not breach Article 8[494] and that a prisoner must show that the restrictions go beyond what is normally acceptable.[495] For example, Article 8 is not breached by a refusal to allow prisoners to attend family funerals[496] or conjugal visits.[497] The state does, however, have an obligation to help prisoners to maintain contact with their families,[498] although that will only rarely compel a transfer to a different prison.[499] The obligation to maintain contact with the family is more onerous in relation to the prisoner's contact with his children than with his spouse, who is presumed to be able to travel to visit him.[500] **13.126**

However, it has been argued that it is contrary to modern penological standards to restrict unnecessarily the family life of prisoners: if prisoners are to be able to take their positions again in society, they should have the greatest contact with the outside world that is consistent with the fact of detention.[501] It is pointed out that restrictions on prisoners which were once justified may cease to be permissible as standards improve in the light of the practices of the Contracting Parties. It is possible that, in the future, Article 8 may be of more importance in prisoner cases. **13.127**

---

492 (1994) 17 EHRR 213; a friendly settlement was reached with the result that the deportation order was revoked, he was granted indefinite leave to remain and the Secretary of State agreed to consider his claim for naturalisation.

493 *McCotter v United Kingdom* (1993) 15 EHRR CD 98.

494 *X v United Kingdom* (1983) 30 DR 113.

495 *X v United Kingdom* (1974) 46 CD 112.

496 See eg *X v United Kingdom* (1972)15 YB 370; *X v United Kingdom* (1973) 42 CD 140.

497 *X v Germany* (1970) 12 YB 332; *X and Y v Switzerland* (1978) 13 DR 241, EComm HR.

498 *X v United Kingdom* (1982) 30 DR 113, EComm HR; *McCotter v United Kingdom* (1993) 15 EHRR CD 98.

499 *Campbell v United Kingdom* Application 7819/77, unreported, 6 May 1978 (discussed in D Harris, M O'Boyle and C Warbrick, *Law of the European Convention on Human Rights* (Butterworths, 1995) 331); *S v United Kingdom* (1993) 15 EHRR CD 106; *Kavanagh v United Kingdom* Application 19085/91, 9 Dec 1992 (application by Northern Irish prisoner inadmissible, only in 'exceptional circumstances' would the detention of a prisoner a long way from home violate Art 8).

500 *Ouinas v France* (1990) 65 DR 265; *Wakefield v United Kingdom* (1990) 66 DR 251, EComm HR.

501 Ibid.

(6) Justification for interference with family life

(a) Introduction

13.128 Where a public authority seeks to justify an interference with family life, it can only do so on the grounds contained under Article 8(2). A public authority must therefore show that it has acted in accordance with the law,[502] that it has interfered with the right on a legitimate ground as defined by Article 8(2)[503] and that the interference was 'necessary in a democratic society'[504] and proportionate to the aim to be achieved. In the context of family life the 'necessity' of an interference by a public authority has required particularly careful scrutiny where family life has been disrupted by taking children into public care or deporting members of the family.

(b) The public care cases

13.129 The removal of a child into public care is an interference with respect for family life which requires justification under Article 8(2). Similarly, any order denying or regulating parental contact with children in care will also be an interference requiring justificaion. In each case, the interference will require justification by reference to the 'best interests of the child.[504a] There is a positive obligation on the state to provide procedural safeguards against arbitrary treatment in order to justify interference with family life.[505] This means that there must be an administrative and legal process which, taken as a whole, involves the parents to a degree sufficient to protect their interests. The need for protection against arbitrary interferences is even greater because the decisions may prove to be irreversible.[506] Thus, in *W, B, O and R v United Kingdom*[507] the Court held that there was a breach of Article 8 because the exclusion of the parents from the process coupled with the delays in court proceedings were not necessary for the protection of the child.

13.130 In the *Olsson v Sweden* cases[508] the Court put forward a two part test for justification for interfering with family life:

---

502 As in *Eriksson v Sweden* (1989) 12 EHRR 183 para 67 and *Olsson v Sweden (No 2)* (1992) 17 EHRR 134 para 76 (breach because the national child care law gave no legal basis for the conditions imposed by the social workers restricting access to their children while they were in public care).

503 The interference must be in the interests of national security, public safety or the economic well-being of the country, for the prevention of disorder or crime, for the protection of health or morals, or for the protection of the rights and freedoms of others.

504 See para 6.146 above.

504a See generally, U Kilkelly *The Child and the European Convention on Human Rights* (Ashgate, 1999), Chap 12.

505 See para 13.111ff above.

506 *W v United Kingdom* (1987) 10 EHHR 29.

507 Ibid; *H v United Kingdom* (1987) 10 EHRR 95; *O v United Kingdom* (1987) 10 EHRR 82; *B v United Kingdom* (1987) 10 EHRR 87; *R v United Kingdom* (1987) 10 EHRR 74.

508 *Olsson v Sweden (No 1)* (1988) 11 EHRR 259; *Olsson v Sweden (No 2)* (1992) 17 EHRR 134.

- First, in the light of the national policy in place, the authorities must show 'relevant and sufficient reasons' for acting as they did in removing children and/or deciding to continue the arrangements.
- Secondly, there is a positive obligation on the state to involve the parents in any decision that is made, regardless of the difficulty that may pose for the authorities.

The Court went on to find that the state had breached Article 8 in one respect since the ultimate aim of taking the child into care was to reunite the parents and two children had been placed a great distance away from their family members. When the case was again considered by the Court four years later, the goal of reunification still having not been achieved, the Court found that there was a positive but not absolute duty on the state to take such steps toward reuniting the family, subject to a margin of appreciation, 'as could reasonably be demanded in the circumstances of each case'.[509]

In *Eriksson v Sweden*[510] the Court held that Article 8 was violated as a result of the failure to implement as quickly as possible a decision to return a child to her natural parents. In *Andersson v Sweden*[511] the Court had to consider restrictions on contact and communication between parents and children in care and held that there were not 'strong' enough reasons to justify them. In *Johansen v Norway*[512] the Court again decided the refusal to allow contact with a child in care and the deprivation of parental responsibilities breached Article 8. In *Keegan v Ireland*[513] the secret placement of an illegitimate child by the state for adoption failed to respect the father's family life and could not be justified. In *Kroon v Netherlands*[514] legislation which prevented a biological father from recognising his child as long as the mother was married to another man failed to respect the biological father's right to family life. In *Soderback v Sweden*[515] the Commission found that the decision to allow the applicant's daughter to be adopted without his consent totally deprived him of his family life and was outside the margin of appreciation. On the other hand, in *Bronda v Italy*[516] the Court accepted that the best interests of the child are always a crucial consideration but went on to decide that the national authority had not acted outside its margin of appreciation. **13.131**

509 Ibid, para 90.
510 (1989) 12 EHRR 183.
511 *Andersson v Sweden* (1992) 14 EHRR 615.
512 (1996) 23 EHRR 33.
513 (1994) 18 EHRR 342.
514 (1994) 19 EHRR 263.
515 [1998] EHRLR 342.
516 [1998] EHRLR 756.

(c) The deportation of non-national family members

13.132 The Convention does not guarantee any right of entry or residence to a Contracting State.[517] The question in every case is whether the refusal or entry constitutes an interference with (or breach of respect for) the right of the family. Some of the case law concerning the expulsion of aliens from Convention states has been discussed in the context of whether such conduct constitutes a failure to respect family life.[518] Where expulsion breaches Article 8(1), the public authority must then attempt to justify the removal of a non-national family member on the grounds provided in Article 8(2) such as the protection of the economic well-being of the country, the protection of public order or the prevention of crime. It will also be necessary to show that the interference with family life was 'necessary in a democratic society'. In considering this last requirement the following factors are particularly important:

- whether family life can be resumed elsewhere;
- the strength of the 'general interest' in the deportation.

13.132A A number of factors are taken into account when considering whether family life can be resumed elsewhere after deportation. The Court will consider whether there are legal or practical obstacles to this taking place.[518a] Factors such as the age and nationality of the children and the family links with the destination country are taken into account.[518b]

13.133 The Court has recognised the right of states to control entry and residence.[518c] However, the exercise of that right in circumstances in which there is a serious interference with family life and no strong countervailing public interest is likely to be disproportionate. Thus in *Berrehab v Netherlands*[519] the Court rejected the justification for expelling an alien following his divorce from a Dutch national because of the ties with his daughter which would be seriously disrupted by deportation. The Court's decision in *Moustaquim v Belgium*[520] was more controversial; the Court found that the criminal activity exhibited by the applicant did not warrant his deportation and consequent interference with his family life on grounds of prevention of crime. Similarly, in *Beldjoudi v France*[521] the Court held

---

[517] *X and Y v United Kingdom* (1973) 42 Coll 146; *Abdulaziz, Cabales and Balkandali v United Kingdom* (1985) 7 EHRR 471 paras 59–60.

[518] See para 13.121ff above.

[518a] *Beljoudi v France* (1992) 14 EHRR 801 para 78; see also *Maikoe and Baboelal v Netherlands* Application 22791/93, 30 Nov 1994.

[518b] See para 13.124 above; and generally, U Kilkelly, *The Child and the European Convention on Human Rights* (Ashgate, 1999) 223–226 (where it is suggested that the 'elsewhere' approach may, itself, be incompatible with the Convention).

[518c] *Boulchelkia v France* (1997) 25 EHRR 686 para 48.

[519] (1988) 11 EHRR 322 para 29.

[520] (1991) 13 EHRR 802.

[521] (1992) 14 EHRR 801.

that deportation of a professional criminal who had spent half his adult life in prison, was unjustified as being disproportionate to the aim of preventing crime. The Court found that removal of the applicant would jeopardise the unity or even the existence of his 20-year marriage to a French national who would have encountered obstacles to prevent her from accompanying her husband to Algeria. It should be noted, however, that *Beldjoudi v France*[522] concerned an 'integrated alien' who had lived in France for his whole life and had no connection with Algeria save for nationality. In his concurring opinion Judge Martens suggested that the Court should recognise that 'integrated aliens' should be no more liable to expulsion than nationals.[523] Harris, O'Boyle and Warbrick[524] suggest that in relation to 'integrated aliens' serious crime may not be sufficient justification for disruption of family life and that the state may need to show some further impact on public order, such as may be involved in terrorism or drug trafficking before prevention of crime will outweigh the right to respect for family life.

Nevertheless, the court does give considerable weight to considerations of 'public order' when considering the impact of deportation on family life. In a number of cases involving the deportation of parents involved in serious crime, it has been held that deportation strikes a fair balance between respect for family life and the prevention of crime and disorder. In *Boughanemi v France*[525] the factors that counted against the applicant included the seriousness of his criminal offences and the fact that he had retained some links with Tunisia; and the Court took a similar approach in *C v Belgium*.[526] In *Bouchelkia v France*[527] the Court attached great importance to the gravity of the crime even though the applicant was a minor at the time it was committed. **13.134**

D. The Impact of the Human Rights Act

(1) Introduction

The absence of a clearly articulated 'right to family life' in English law means that Article 8 has a potential impact across the whole range of family law cases (both private and public law). However, its greatest impact is likely to be in the field of administrative law. Many decisions of public authorities impinge on family life; and it is likely that challenges will be made on the ground that they have to respect family life. This will be of particular importance in immigration law cases, where **13.135**

522 Ibid.
523 Ibid 840–841.
524 (n 499 above) 352.
525 (1996) 22 EHRR 228.
526 RJD 1996-III 915.
527 (1997) EHRR 886.

deportation and asylum decisions often have a direct effect on the family life of those involved.

(2) United Kingdom cases prior to the Human Rights Act

(a) Introduction

13.136 Both the right to marry and the right of respect for family life have provoked a large number of applications against the United Kingdom, particularly in relation to family law issues. A number of unsuccessful complaints have also been made by prisoners alleging violations of their right to family life.[528] The United Kingdom has been found to be in breach of the right to respect for family life on six occasions.[529] The United Kingdom has not been found to be in breach of Article 12.[530]

(b) The right to marry

13.137 Some of the most important cases about the scope of Article 12 have been brought against the United Kingdom. In *Rees v United Kingdom*[531] and again in *Cossey v United Kingdom*[532] transsexuals challenged the prohibition against marriage. The Court held that Article 12 is confined to the traditional marriage between persons of the opposite sex and the state is entitled to use biological criteria to determine a person's sex for the purpose of marriage.[533] When the issue was recently canvassed in *Sheffield and Horsham v United Kingdom*[534] the Court continued to maintain that view.

13.138 On the other hand, in *Hamer v United Kingdom*[535] and *Draper v United Kingdom*[536] prisoners successfully complained that Article 12 was breached because the Marriage Act 1949 required the celebration of marriage take place at locations outside prisons. The United Kingdom Government informed the Committee of Ministers that it accepted the Commission's report and had changed its practice with regard to the marriage of prisoners.[537]

---

[528] See para 13.144 below.

[529] *Abdulaziz, Cabales and Balkandali v United Kingdom* (1985) 7 EHRR 471; *W v United Kingdom* (1987) EHRR 29; *R v United Kingdom* (1987) 10 EHRR 74, *O v United Kingdom* (1987) 10 EHRR 82; *B v United Kingdom* (1987) 10 EHRR 87; *McMichael v United Kingdom* (1995) 20 EHRR 205 (also a violation of Art 6); in *Boyle v United Kingdom* (1994) 19 EHHR 179 and *Lamguindaz v United Kingdom* (1994) 17 EHRR 213 friendly settlements were reached after the Commission found a breach.

[530] In *Draper v United Kingdom* (1980) 24 DR 72, EComm HR and *Hamer v United Kingdom* (1979) 24 DR 5, EComm HR the UK Government accepted the Commission's report that there were violations of Art 12.

[531] (1986) 9 EHRR 56 para 49.

[532] (1990) 13 EHRR 622.

[533] See para 13.86 above.

[534] (1998) 27 EHRR 163 paras 66–68.

[535] (1979) 24 DR 5, Ecomm HR.

[536] (1980) 24 DR 72, EComm HR.

[537] See Resolution DH (81) 5, 2 Apr1981, in which the Committee of Ministerrs declared that it was satisfied with the United Kingdom's response.

(c) Children cases

One of the major factors leading to the enactment of the Children Act 1989 was a series of adverse decisions in Strasbourg against the United Kingdom. In *W v United Kingdom*,[538] *R v United Kingdom*,[539] *O v United Kingdom*[540] and *B v United Kingdom*[541] the Court held that the decision-making process when taking children into care must be of a nature to ensure that the views and interests of parents are made known and are taken into account by the local authority and that they are able to exercise in due time any remedies available to them. In *H v United Kingdom*[542] the Court decided that respect for family life required the question of a parent's relationship with her child to be determined solely by the relevant circumstances and not merely by effluxion of time. **13.139**

The absence of a right by an uncle to apply for contact with a nephew for whom he was a father figure was held by the Commission to be a breach of Article 8 in *Boyle v United Kingdom*[543] and was then subject to a friendly settlement. In *McMichael v United Kingdom*[544] the Court regarded the failure to provide proper procedural safeguards in proceedings which decided custody and contact arrangements as resulting in a breach of Article 8 since the applicants had not had sight of certain relevant documents. **13.140**

The denial of contact to a parent, in the best interests of the child, was justified for the protection of the health of the child under Article 8(2).[545] In *Whitear v United Kingdom*[546] the Commission took the view that there should be stricter scrutiny of restrictions on contact than in relation to decisions to place a child in care. Nevertheless, the applicant's complaint that his contact had been severely restricted was inadmissible on the basis that the restriction was in the best interests of the child. **13.141**

(d) Immigration

Complaints alleging that a refusal to admit the decision to expel family members breaches Article 8 have usually been unsuccessful. However, in *Lamguindaz v United Kingdom*[547] a decision to deport a 19-year-old Moroccan who had lived in **13.142**

538 (1987) 10 EHRR 29.
539 (1987) 10 EHRR 74.
540 (1987) 10 EHRR 82.
541 (1987) EHRR 87.
542 (1987) 10 EHRR 95.
543 (1994) 19 EHHR 179.
544 (1995) 20 EHRR 205.
545 *Gribler v United Kingdom* (1988) 10 EHRR 546.
546 [1997] EHRLR 291.
547 (1993) 17 EHRR 213; a friendly settlement was reached with the result that the deportation order was revoked, he was granted indefinite leave to remain and the Secretary of State agreed to consider his claim for naturalisation.

the United Kingdom since the age of seven to Morocco where he had difficulties speaking Arabic and had no social support breached Article 8. In *Abdulaziz, Cabales and Balkandali v United Kingdom*[548] the applicants were women who had settled in the United Kingdom and complained that the Immigration Rules prevented their husbands from remaining in the United Kingdom. Although the Court held that there might be positive obligations to respect the family,[549] it took the view that a state had a wide margin of appreciation in deciding what steps should be taken to comply with the Convention in a case which involved family and immigration issues. However, the Court went on to decide that the United Kingdom entry controls discriminated against women because it was easier for men to bring their wives to join them than for women to bring their partners.[550]

13.143 In *Poku v United Kingdom*[551] Ms Poku was a Ghanian who was an unlawful overstayer. However, her husband had a permanent residence in the United Kingdom, they had a young child and Ms Poku had a child by an earlier marriage to a British citizen. It was said that her deportation would interfere with the Article 8 rights of her husband, former husband and children. The Commission held that the application was manifestly ill-founded. It pointed out that Article 8 did not impose a general obligation on States to respect the choice of residence of a married couple or to accept the non-national spouse for settlement in the country and that:

> Whether removal or exclusion of a family member from a Contracting State is incompatible with the requirements of Article 8 will depend on a number of factors: the extent to which family life is effectively ruptured, whether there are insurmountable obstacles in the way of the family living in the country of origin of one or more of them, whether there are factors of immigration control (eg history of breaches of immigration law) or considerations of public order (eg serious or persistent offences) weighing in favour of exclusion.[552]

On the facts, there were no elements concerning respect for family life which outweighed the valid considerations relating to the proper enforcement of immigration controls.

(e) Other cases

13.144 Article 8 challenges by prisoners have not, in general, been successful. The Commission has found claims involving refusals to allow prisoners to attend family funerals,[553] or to arrange transfers to be close to families[554] to be inadmissible.

[548] (1985) 7 EHRR 471.
[549] See para 13.115 above.
[550] See para 17.111 below.
[551] (1996) 22 EHRR CD 94.
[552] Ibid 97.
[553] *X v United Kingdom* (1972) 15 YB 370; *X v United Kingdom* (1973) 42 CD 140.
[554] *McCotter v United Kingdom* (1993) 15 EHRR CD 98; *Kavanagh v United Kingdom* Application 19085/91, 9 Dec 1992.

However, separating a mother from her baby while she is in prison may violate Article 8.[555]

In *Paton v United Kingdom*[556] the Commission found that the Article 8 rights of a potential father did not include a right to be consulted about a proposed abortion. In *X, Y and Z v United Kingdom*[557] an unsuccessful challenge was made against the refusal to register a transsexual as the father of a child born to his partner as a result of artificial insemination from a donor. 13.145

(3) General impact issues

Public authorities are required to consult with individuals on issues which affect family life in a large range of situations. Fair consultation in the context of public law decision-making involves four elements:[558] 13.146

- consultations when proposals are still at a formative stage;
- adequate information on which to respond;
- adequate time in which to respond;
- conscientious consideration by the authority of the response to the consultation.

It is submitted, by comparison, the degree of consultation required as a result of the obligation to respect family life is more onerous. This reflects the context in terms of the serious (and sometime irreparable) impact of the decisions taken. The obligation to respect family life requires procedural safeguards which are *sufficient* to protect the interests of the family.[559]

(4) Specific areas of impact

(a) Criminal law

The power of a court to make a recommendation for deportation[560] when sentencing an offender with family ties must be exercised in a way which is proportionate to the aim of preventing disorder or crime; and should take account of the approach taken in the case law which has developed when making deportation orders.[561] 13.147

---

555 *Togher v United Kingdom* (1988) 25 EHRR CD 99.

556 (1980) 19 DR 244, EComm HR.

557 (1997) 24 EHRR 143.

558 See *R v Brent London Borough Council ex p Gunning* (1985) 84 LGR 168; *R v Gwent County Council, ex p Bryant* [1988] COD 19; *R v Governors of Haberdashers' Ase Hatcham Schools, ex p ILEA* [1989] COD 435; *R v Rochdale Health Authority, ex p Rochdale Borough Council* (1992) 8 BMLR 137; *R v British Coal Corporation, ex p Price* [1994] IRLR 72; *R v Secretary of State for Trade and Industry, ex p Unison* [1996] ICR 1003.

559 See para 13.119 above.

560 Immigration Act 1971, s 3(6); para 13.61 above.

561 See para 13.121ff above.

(b) Employment and discrimination

13.148 The right to respect for family life may have implications for cases concerning pregnancy and maternity leave.[562] The implications of the right of respect for private life are discussed in Chapter 12.[563]

13.149 The right of respect for family life will also be relevant where employees of standard public authorities[563a] seek time off (or are absent) because of child responsibilities or where there are complaints about working unsocial hours. It may be arguable that the rights under the Employment Relations Act 1999 to time off for maternity and parental leave[564] and time off for domestic incidents[565] must give effect to Article 8 in accordance with the principle of statutory construction contained in the Human Rights Act.[566]

(c) Family law

13.150 At first sight there are fundamental differences between Article 8 and the principles of English family law. The failure of English law to recognise a general right to family life appears to suggest a basic incompatibility with the Convention. The 'paramountcy principle'[566a] must be replaced by a 'balancing exercise' in which the rights to family life of parents and child must be assessed. Under the Convention, the weight to be given to the considerations on each side of the balance is to be assessed according to the individual circumstances of the case.[566b]

13.151 Under the Human Rights Act public authorities have to avoid acting in a way which is incompatible with Article 8. This will apply to local authorities in care proceedings and to the Courts as public authorities in both public and private law cases. In all cases which impact on the family it will be necessary to undertake the two stage Article 8 reasoning process:

- has the applicant has an Article 8 right which has been interfered with?
- is the interference justified under Article 8(2)?

13.152 In children cases, Article 8 includes a right for the parent to 'have measures taken with a view to his or her being reunited with the child' and an obligation on public authorities to take action to promote this right.[567] The question of the welfare

[562] See generally, B Perrins, P Elias and B Napier (eds), Harvey on *Industrial Relations and Employment Law* (Butterworths, 2000 [looseleaf]) Div J.

[563] See para 12.182ff above.

[563a] The meaning of standard authorities is discussed at para 5.14ff and of functional authorities at para 5.16ff. The question of whether employees of functional authorities have Convention rights is complex: see para 5.32 ff above.

[564] s 7 and Sch 4, Pt I of the 1999 Act amending Pt VIII of the Employment Rights Act 1996.

[565] s 8 and Sch 4, Pt II of the 1999 Act.

[566] See, generally, para 4.04ff above.

[566a] See para 3.17 above.

[566b] Cf *R v Secretary of State for the Home Department, ex p Gangadeen and Kahn* [1998] 1 FLR 762.

[567] See eg *Hokkanen v Finland* (1994) 19 EHRR 139 para 55.

of the child will only arise at the stage of justifying a *prima facie* interference.[568] This contrasts with the present attitude of the courts in which contact is regarded as a right of the child and not the parents.

In other words, in all children cases, the court will have to have regard to the rights of the parents as well as the interests of the child. This is a fundamental change of approach. It remains to been seen, however, whether it will make a significant difference in practice. In *Re K D (A Minor) (Termination of Access)*[569] the House of Lords expressed the view that there was no conflict between the English law requiring the paramount consideration of the child's welfare and Article 8 which regarded a parent as having a right of contact with a child which would be overborne if the child's interest so dictated.[570] **13.153**

The principles the courts now apply to applications to remove children permanently from the jurisdiction conflict with the right to respect family life as developed by the Court in relation to expulsion of aliens.[571] At present, whether or not a child should be permanently removed depends on the welfare of the child; and leave will not be withheld unless the interests of the child and those of the custodial parent are clearly incompatible.[572] The failure of the court to take into account the Article 8 rights of the non-residential parent may itself be a breach of Article 8. **13.154**

Private law cases.[572a] The Article 8 'right to contact' with children contrasts with the present position in English law. The courts will have to operate on the basis that there must be a 'fair balance' between the rights of parent and child.[573] This is, however, subject to the proviso that a parent is not entitled to have such measures taken as would harm the child's health and development.[574] The principles to be applied to public law care cases are discussed below.[575] **13.155**

Adoption. The right to respect for family life may have a greater effect on adoption. It is clearly established[576] that decisions concerning adoption will breach the right to family life unless interim steps are taken to preserve the possibility of the child returning to his natural parents up to the point that a decision is made to effect a permanent separation. There is a strong argument that current practice does **13.156**

568 *Johansen v Norway* (1996) 23 EHRR 33.
569 [1988] AC 806.
570 See also, *Dawson v Wearmouth* [1999] 2 WLR 960 (a case involving the change of name) in which Lord Hobhouse said that there was nothing in Art 8 which required the courts 'to act otherwise than in accordance with the interests of the child'.
571 See para 13.121ff above.
572 *M H v G P (Child: Emigration)* [1995] 2 FLR 106.
572a For a general discussion see H Swindells *et al*, *Family Law and the Human Rights Act 1998* (Family Law, 1999) Chap 7.
573 *Johansen v Norway* (1996) 23 EHRR 33.
574 Ibid para 78.
575 See para 13.175 below.
576 See para 13.129ff above.

not give proper weight to the rights of the natural parents.[576a] The right to found a family under Article 12 can include founding a family by adoption[576b] and the operation of the adoption system, including the conditions placed on adoptions, may be subject to challenge by potential adoptive parents.

13.157 **Artificial reproduction.** It is arguable that the right to found a family under Article 12 might create positive obligations in relation to artificial reproduction although there is no Convention case law on this issue.[576c] It is possible that the lack of consistency in NHS practice in relation to artificial reproduction will constitute a breach of such obligations.[576d]

13.158 **Transsexuals and the right to marry.** The right of transsexuals to marry has consistently been rejected by both the English courts[577] and the Court of Human Rights.[578] Nevertheless, since the Convention should be interpreted as a living instrument,[579] the issue is bound to be argued under the Human Rights Act. Although the Court in *Sheffield and Horsham v United Kingdom*[580] was not satisfied that there was a common European approach towards transsexuals, transsexuals have the right to marry in Sweden, Germany, Italy, the Netherlands, Australia, New Zealand and certain parts of the United States.[581]

13.159 **Same sex marriage.** It is not clear whether prohibition against same sex marriages will breach Article 8. The issue was directly considered in New Zealand in *Quilter v A-G of New Zealand*[582] where the Court of Appeal held that 'marriage' meant the traditional common law concept of union between a man and a woman. The Strasbourg case law[583] suggests that the same approach would prevail under the Human Rights Act. There is, however, a developing international consensus in favour of more formal recognition of same sex relationships[583a] and it is arguable that the 'traditional common law concept' of marriage is discriminatory. It is, therefore, possible that Article 8 will ultimately lead to a radical redefinition of the concept of marriage.

[576a] Cf *Clark v United Kingdom* Application 23387/94, 5 Dec 1995 (Application relating to adoption struck out after ex gratia payment by United Kingdom) and see generally, Swindells (n 572a above) para 6.99.

[576b] *X and Y v United Kingdom* (1977) 12 DR 32.

[576c] But see *R v Secretary of State for the Home Department ex p Mellor* [2000] All ER (D) 1136; and see para 13.51A above.

[576d] Cf Swindells (n 572a above) para 11.29.

[577] See para 13.07 above.

[578] See para 13.78 above.

[579] See para 6.23ff above.

[580] (1998) 27 EHRR 163 para 57; see also *X, Y and Z v United Kingdom* (1997) 24 EHRR 143 para 44.

[581] *S-T (formerly J) v J* [1998] Fam 103, 120.

[582] (1997) 3 BHRC 461; see para 13.186 below.

[583] See para 13.84ff above.

[583a] See the discussion in A Barlow *et al*, *Advising Gay and Lesbian Clients* (Butterworths, 1999) para 8.33ff.

Unmarried fathers. The limited nature of the rights of an unmarried father[584] may breach Article 8 where the father has not acquired parental responsibility under the Children Act 1989.[585] However, this issue was fully considered by Hale J in *Re W; Re B (Child Abduction: Unmarried Fathers)*[586] who concluded that Article 8 did not mean that parents should have completely equal parental responsibility and authority as long as there were 'sufficient opportunities of developing the relationship between father and child'. It has been suggested[587] that where the mother unilaterally takes the child to another country, an unmarried father's lack of a remedy[588] under the Hague Convention on Civil Aspects of International Child Abduction may breach his right to family life.[589] **13.160**

(d) Housing

The effect of the right of respect for the home or private life under Article 8 was examined in Chapter 12.[590] The Human Rights Act will apply directly to local authorities. It is likely that registered social landlords under the Housing Act 1996 (formerly housing associations) will be regarded as functional public authorities.[591] **13.161**

The obligation to respect family life will significantly affect housing management decisions on issues such as transfers or succession of tenancies. As a result of *Fitzpatrick v Sterling Housing Association Ltd*[592] it will be necessary to consider homosexual relationships when making such management decisions. Decisions to treat a family as intentionally homeless where this results in the breakup of a family may breach Article 8. The prohibition against children making homelessness **13.162**

---

584 See paras 13.21, and 13.34 above; and see generally, H Swindells *et al*, *Family Law and the Human Rights Act 1998* (Family Law, 1999) para 3.119ff.

585 See para 13.21 above.

586 [1998] 2 FLR 146, 163-168.

587 See I Karsten, 'Atypical Families and the Human Rights Act: The Rights of Unmarried Fathers, Same Sex Couples and Transsexuals' [1999] EHRLR 195, 202, see also Swindells (n 584 above) para 11.34ff.

588 Although *Re J (A Minor) (Abduction: Custody Rights)* [1990] 2 AC 562 decided that an unmarried father lacks 'rights of custody' within the meaning of the Convention, this decision has led to the development of 'inchoate' rights of custody: see *Re B (A Minor) (Abduction)* [1994] 2 FLR 249; *Re O (Child Abduction: Custody Rights)* [1997] 2 FLR 702; and see also *Re W, Re B (Child Abduction: Unmarried Father)* [1998] 2 FLR 146.

589 I Karsten, 'Atypical Families and the Human Rights Act: The Rights of Unmarried Fathers, Same Sex Couples and Transsexuals' (n 587 above).

590 See para 12.193ff above.

591 The decision in *Peabody Housing Association v Green* (1978) 38 P & CR 633 deciding that a housing association is not amenable to judicial review does not require a court to hold it is a public authority and is unlikely to be applied to the Human Rights Act; see *Hoyle v Castlemilk East Housing Co-operative*, *The Times*, 16 May 1997; and see, generally, para 5.16ff above; and see eg C Hunter and A Dymond, 'Housing Law' in C Baker (ed) *The Human Rights Act 1998: A Practitioner's Guide* (Sweet & Maxwell, 1998) para 7–08; see also *R v Servite Homes ex p Goldsmith*, 12 May 2000 unreported.

592 [1999] 3 WLR 1113.

applications may also have to be reconsidered;[593] and a local authority must ensure that local connection referrals in homelessness cases must not be incompatible with Article 8.

13.163 Under section 6(3) of the Human Rights Act, the court must not act in a way which is incompatible with Convention rights.[594] It will therefore be necessary to consider the impact of Article 8 when the court considers whether to make a discretionary possession order in relation to an assured tenancy[595] or whether it is reasonable to make a possession order in relation to a secure tenancy;[596] and the court must not act incompatibly with Article 8 in mortgagee possession proceedings. It could be argued, for example, that it is inappropriate to order possession which destroys the unity of family life except in very clear cases. Thus, in *Albany Homes Ltd v Massey*[597] the Court of Appeal considered the impact of Article 8 in mortgagee possession proceedings; and took the view that a possession order should not be made against a husband in relation to the family home before the wife's defence had finally been determined.

(e) Immigration

13.164 There are a number of respects in which the system of immigration control breaches Article 8 and the Human Rights Act will inspire a large number of judicial review applications.

13.165 The failure to make provision for unmarried co-habitees[598] to obtain entry may violate the right of respect for the family[599] as well as amounting to discrimination contrary to Article 14.[600]

13.166 A 'parent' has been defined in very restrictive terms[601] which means that the procedure where a child under 18 seeks leave to enter probably breaches Article 8. MacDonald and Blake[602] suggest that the fact an estranged parent must apply for entry clearance of a UK resident child where he has a court order in his favour[603] breaches the right of respect for family life. They also argue[604] that the restrictive definition of parent under the Immigration Rules may be in breach of Article 8.

---

[593] *R v Oldham Metropolitan Borough Council ex p Garlick* [1993] AC 509.
[594] See para 5.120 above.
[595] Under Housing Act 1988, Sch 2, Pt II.
[596] Cases 1–8 and 12–16 in Sch 2 of the Housing Act 1985 are subject to s 84(2).
[597] (1997) 29 HLR 902.
[598] See para 13.55 above.
[599] Cf N Blake and L Fransman, *Immigration, Nationality and Asylum under the Human Rights Act 1998* (Butterworths, 1999).101.
[600] See para 17.79ff below.
[601] Immigration Rules (HC 395) para 6.
[602] I MacDonald and N Blake, *Immigration Law and Practice* (4th edn, Butterworths, 1995) para 11.4.
[603] Immigration Rules (HC 395) paras 246–248.
[604] MacDonald and Blake, (n 602 above) para 11.77; and see Blake and Fransman (n 599 above) 103.

The Court of Appeal has held that the Home Secretary's policy on the expulsion of illegal entrants with family connections in the United Kingdom is compatible with Article 8: there has to be a balancing between the interests of the child and immigration policy.[605] However, the current regime which regulates contact between parents and their children under the Immigration Rules[606] and Government guidelines[607] appears to contravene Article 8.[608] The guidelines indicate that a parent can exercise a right of contact from abroad so that this is not a factor to take account on expulsion.[609] Furthermore, the Immigration Rules are narrowly defined and exclude, for example, parents who have never been married or who are widowed. **13.167**

The current Home Office guidelines for immigration and deportation decisions make no specific reference to Article 8[610] and do not comply with the requirements for removing immigrants as developed in the Convention jurisprudence.[611] Furthermore, the right of respect for family life will also affect disputes where the effect of a deportation order is to separate a parent and child. **13.168**

(f) Local government law

Introduction. The obligation to respect family life will significantly affect local government decision-making in many areas. For example, local authorities must not act incompatibly with the right of respect for family life when granting music and dance licences. The impact of the Article 8 right of respect for private life and the home is discussed in Chapter 12.[612] **13.169**

Access to information. In some circumstances, Article 8 could give rise to increased rights of access to information helf by public authorities.[612a] In *Gaskin v United Kingdom*[613] the applicant successfully argued that he was entitled under Article 8 to access to his social services files. These issues are examined in Chapter 12.[614] **13.170**

---

[605] See *R v Secretary of State for the Home Department, ex p Gangadeen and Khan* [1998] 1 FLR 762, see para 13.58 above.

[606] Immigration Rules, HC 395, paras 246–248.

[607] DP/4/96 para 6.

[608] Cf J Carter, 'Immigration and Asylum', in C Baker (ed), *The Human Rights Act 1998: A Practitioner's Guide* (Sweet & Maxwell, 1998) para 5–53 .

[609] Contrast the position under Art 8, see para 13.124ff above.

[610] In contrast to DP/2/93, see para 13.58 above.

[611] See para 13.121 above.

[612] See para 12.199ff above.

[612a] See generally, H Swindells *et al*, *Family Law and the Human Rights Act 1998* (Family Law, 1999) Chap 9.

[613] (1989) 12 EHRR 36.

[614] See para 12.90 above.

13.171 **Community care.** The right of respect for family life may have important consequences for local authorities where they are discharging social services functions in the community care field.

13.172 Local authorities must act in a way which is compatible with the obligation to respect family life where they make arrangements for the elderly to travel to and from residential homes,[615] where they exercise the power to provide welfare services to the elderly,[616] where they exercise the power to provide welfare services to the disabled,[617] where they are under a duty to the disabled to make arrangements for services[618] and where they are under a duty to provide welfare services to those with mental disorders.[619]

13.173 It is arguable that the right of respect for family life requires an authority to provide domicillary care services to a disabled person unless there are overwhelming arguments to the contrary.[620]

13.174 In assessing the level of community care services to provide for individuals, a local authority is under a duty to consider the position of carers who are family members and should take account of the policy guidance in *Community Care in the Next Decade and Beyond.*[621] A local authority must act in a way which is compatible with respect for family life when seeking to involve the service user in the assessment procedure,[622] when assessing the ability of a carer to continue providing care to a disabled person living at home[623] and when assessing the preferences of the user and carer in relation to a care package.[624]

13.175 **Public law child cases.** The right to family life under the Human Rights Act will radically affect the approach local authorities must take to children in care. First and foremost, a local authority will no longer be able to make decisions about children in its care on the basis that they *cannot* be directly challenged on their merits

[615] Under the Department of Health Circular No LAC (93) 10 approvals and directions for arrangements made under the National Health Act 1977, Sch 8 and the National Assistance Act 1948, ss 21, 29.

[616] Health Services and Public Health Act 1968, s 45(1).

[617] National Assistance Act 1948, s 29(1).

[618] Chronically Sick and Disabled Act 1970, s 2.

[619] National Assistance Act 1948, s 29(1) as amended by Mental Health Act 1983, s 8(2).

[620] M Supperstone, J Goudie and J Coppel, *Local Authorities and the Human Rights Act 1998* (Butterworths, 1999) 73.

[621] HMSO 1990; a failure to take account of the guidelines may make the decision unlawful: see *R v North Yorkshire County Council, ex p Hargreaves* (1997) 96 LGR 39; *R v Islington Borough Council, ex p Rixon* [1998] 1 CCLR 119; *R v Sutton Borough Council, ex p Tucker* [1998] 1 CCLR 251.

[622] Community Care in the Next Decade and Beyond (n 621 above) para 3.16.

[623] Disabled Persons (Services, Consultation and Representation) Act 1986, s 8(1).

[624] *Community Care in the Next Decade and Beyond* (n 621 above) para 3.25.

by parents in the courts.[625] A local authority will, for example, breach its duty to respect family life[626] under Article 8(1) by failing to ensure that parents attend child care conferences.[627] It will be obliged to listen and act on the views of parents on day-to-day questions as well as more strategic issues such as any questions concerning whether the child should be adopted. Although an interim care order gives control of the child to a local authority,[628] the authority must nevertheless take steps to ensure it continues to respect family life[629] during this period; and must carry on doing so even after a final order is made.

The obligation to respect family life will have an important influence on the court's approach when dealing with applications by parents (or relatives) for contact with children in care.[630] Article 8 will reinforce the obligation on the court to ensure that parental contact is maintained while a child is in care.[631] It may also assist grandparents and other relatives where they seek leave to apply for a contact order.[632] **13.176**

The court as a public authority will also be required to intervene to respect family life. It will no longer examine the lawfulness of local authority decisions on narrow judicial review grounds;[633] but will make primary judgments about whether Article 8 is breached. For example, the right to family life will 'trump' the inability of the court to examine a care plan.[634] **13.177**

(g) Prison law

The lack of success of prisoners in obtaining a redress under Article 8[635] suggests that the Human Rights Act will have very little impact in this area. For example, it appears the ordinary and reasonable requirement of prisons mean that it is not a breach of Article 8 to restrict convicted prisoners (including those in the lowest security category) to 12 visits a year of one hour in length.[636] It is most unlikely that Article 8 will give rise to a right to congugal visits.[637] **13.178**

625 At present a local authority's decision can only be indirectly tested on judicial review grounds; and can only be contested on the merits if the decision is *Wednesbury* unreasonable.

626 See para 13.119 above.

627 See para 13.33 above.

628 Children Act 1989, s 38.

629 See para 13.119 above.

630 Children Act 1989, s 34; see para 13.39 above.

631 See eg *Berkshire County Council v B* [1997] 1 FLR 171.

632 Children Act 1989, s 34(3)(b); see *Re M (Care: Contact: Grandmother's Application)* [1995] 2 FLR 86.

633 Of illegality, irrationality or breach of the duty to act fairly.

634 See para 13.36 above; and see Swindells *et al*, *Family Law and the Human Rights Act 1998* (Family Law, 1999) para 6.101ff.

635 See para 13.144 above.

636 *Boyle and Rice v United Kingdom* (1988) 10 EHRR 425 para 74; cf S Livingstone and T Owen, *Prison Law* (2nd edn, Oxford University Press, 1999) paras 8.16–8.17.

637 Ibid paras 7.40–7.41; the refusal of such visits do not constitute a violation of the constitutional right to privacy in the United States, see *Lyons v Gilligan* (1974) 382 F Supp 198.

Appendix 1: The Canadian Charter of Rights

(1) Introduction

13.179 The Canadian Charter of Rights contains no express rights to marry or to family life. Nevertheless, 'right to family' issues have arisen in a number of Charter cases. In particular, the courts have considered the following: the extent to which children have Charter rights, the impact of freedom of thought, conscience and religion under section 2,[638] child custody disputes and the definition of 'spouse' in the context of the anti-discrimination provisions of section 15.[639]

(2) The Charter rights of children

13.180 In the case of *B (R) v Children's Aid Society of Metropolitan Toronto*[640] the Supreme Court had to consider the impact of the Charter on an order permitting a child to be given a blood transfusion against the wishes of her parents. It was held that the right to nurture a child, to care for its development and to make decisions for it in fundamental matters such as medical care are part of the liberty interest of a parent. Although children had the benefit of Charter rights to life and to the security of their person, they are unable to assert these rights. It is assumed that parents will exercise their freedom of choice in a manner that does not breach their childrens' rights. The state can properly intervene in situations where parental conduct falls below the socially acceptable threshold. In doing so it is limiting the constitutional rights of parents rather than vindicating the constitutional rights of children. The protection of a child's right to life and to health was said to be a basic tenet of the legal system, and legislation to that end accorded with the principles of fundamental justice, so long as it also meets the requirements of fair procedure.

(3) Custody disputes

13.181 In *New Brunswick (Minister of Health and Community Services) v G (J)*[641] the Supreme Court considered whether parents have a consitutional right to legal assistance when a public authority seeks an order suspending custody of their children. It was held that such an order restricted the parents' right to 'security of the person' under section 7 of the Charter. This right protected both 'physical and psychological integrity'[642] and the removal of a child from parental custody constituted a serious interference with the psychological integrity of the person. As a result, the restriction had to be in accordance with the principles of fundamental justice. The parent had to be able to participate in the hearing adequately and effectively. If the judge was not satisfied that the parent would receive a fair hearing without a lawyer, he should order the Government to provide the parent with state-funded counsel.[643]

---

[638] See generally, para 14.99ff below.

[639] See para 17.173ff below.

[640] [1995] 1 SCR 315.

[641] 10 Sep 1999.

[642] *R v Morgentaler (No 2)* (1988) 44 DLR (4th) 385.

[643] See also, *M L B v S L J* (1997) 3 BHRC 47, (in child custody case state required to provide access to court even if party could not pay fees).

The constitutionality of the 'best interests of the child' test in custody and access disputes has been attacked in a number of cases involving Jehovah's Witnesses. In *Young v Young*[644] a parent involved in a custody and access dispute contended that the test infringed his right to freedom of thought, conscience and religion. This argument was rejected by the Supreme Court which held that 'the best interests of the child standard' did not offend Charter values, but was consonant with the underlying objectives of the Charter. A similar result was reached in *P (D) v S (C)*.[645] **13.182**

(4) The definition of 'spouse'

In *Miron v Trudel*[646] the Supreme Court considered the failure of the statutory standard form car insurance policy to include a 'common law' spouse within the definition of a spouse entitled to accidental benefits. By a 5-4 majority it held that this infringed section 15(1) of the Charter. The freedom to live with a mate of one's choice in the manner of one's choice was of defining importance and it was wrong to distinguish between co-habiting couples on the basis of whether they were married. **13.183**

However, in *Egan v Canada*[647] the majority of the Supreme Court held that statutory provisions for the payment of spouse's allowance to low-income spouses of old age pensioners did not contravene the Charter by defining the term 'spouse' to cover only those in heterosexual unions. Parliament was entitled to give special support to the institution of marriage which is fundamental to the stability and well-being of the family and to extend this support to common law heterosexual relationships. Four members of the majority held that there had been no discrimination. The fifth agreed with the dissenting judges that there had been discrimination on the basis of sexual orientation but held that the infringement was justified under the 'general limitation' provision in section 1 of the Charter. **13.184**

This case was distinguished by the Supreme Court in the important case of *M v H*.[648] The issue was whether the exclusion of same-sex couples from the definition of 'spouse' under legislation providing rights for co-habiting couples was discriminatory. This differential treatment violates the human dignity of individuals in same-sex relationships. The exclusion of same-sex partners from the benefits of the spousal support scheme implies that they are judged to be incapable of forming intimate relationships of economic interdependence, without regard to their actual circumstances. Several members of the Court took into consideration the fact that, in contrast to the position in *Egan*, the decision would place no additional burden on public funds. **13.185**

---

[644] [1993] 4 SCR 3.

[645] [1993] 4 SCR 141.

[646] [1995] 2 SCR 418.

[647] [1995] 2 SCR 513.

[648] (1999) 171 DLR (4th) 577; see also *Rosenberg v Canada (A-G)* (1998) 158 DLR (4th) 664: statutory provision in breach of s15 by only permitting registration of pension plans if survivor benefits restricted to spouses of the opposite sex.

Appendix 2: The New Zealand Bill of Rights Act

13.186 The New Zealand Bill of Rights Act 1990 contains no express rights to marry or to family life. However, the New Zealand Courts have considered the question as to whether the New Zealand Bill of Rights Act has affected the extent of the common law right to marry. In *Quilter v A-G of New Zealand*[649] the applicants were three same-sex couples whose applications for marriage licences were refused. They contended that the Bill of Rights Act required a new approach to the interpretation of the legislation governing marriages so as to permit same-sex marriages. The Court of Appeal held that 'marriage' meant the traditional common law concept of union between a man and a woman and could not be given the meaning sought by the applicants. By 4-1 majority the Court also rejected the argument that there was discrimination against the applicants under section 19 of the Act.

Appendix 3: Human Rights Cases in Other Jurisdictions

(1) Australia

13.187 The Australian Constitution 'does not reveal anything amounting to . . . a right to marry and to found a family'.[650] However, the courts have considered the domestic impact of international conventions affecting family rights. In *Murray v Director Family Services, ACT*[651] the Family Court held that such conventions could not only be used to resolve ambiguity in domestic legislation but also to 'fill lacunae in such legislation'.

13.188 In *Minister for Immigration and Ethnic Affairs v Teoh*[652] the High Court held that ratification of an international treaty was a positive statement by the Government to the world and to the Australian people that the Government and its agencies would act in accordance with that treaty. Accordingly a non-Australian national threatened with deportation was entitled to a stay of deportation until the Government had reconsidered his application for permanent residency on the ground that Australia's ratification of the Convention on the Rights of the Child created a legitimate expectation that the Government would act in accordance with the provisions of the treaty.[653]

(2) Ireland

13.189 Article 41 of the Irish Constitution provides that:

> 1. The State recognises the Family as the natural primary and fundamental unit group of Society, and as a moral institution possessing inalienable and imprescriptible rights, antecedent and superior to all positive law.

---

[649] (1997) 3 BHRC 461; see A Butler, 'Same Sex Marriage and Freedom From Discrimination in New Zealand' [1998] PL 396; P Rishworth, 'Reflections on the Bill of Rights After Quilter v Attorney-General' [1998] NZLR 683.

[650] G Williams, *Human Rights Under the Australian Constitution* (Oxford University Press, 1999), 61.

[651] (1993) FLC 92–416 (an international child abduction case); see also *B and B (Family Law Reform Act 1995)* (1997) FLC 92–755.

[652] (1995) 128 ALR 353.

[653] For the consideration of this point by the English courts, see para 2.38ff above.

2. The State, therefore, guarantees to protect the Family in its constitution and authority, as the necessary basis of social order and as indispensable to the welfare of the Nation and the State.

1. In particular, the State recognises that by her life within the home, woman gives to the State a support without which the common good cannot be achieved.
2. The State shall, therefore, endeavour to ensure that mothers shall not be obliged by economic necessity to engage in labour to the neglect of their duties in the home.

    1. The State pledges itself to guard with special care the institution of Marriage, on which the family is founded and to protect itself against attack.
    2. No law shall be enacted providing for the grant of a dissolution of marriage.
    3. No person whose marriage has been dissolved under the civil law of any other State but is a subsisting valid marriage under the law for the time being in force within the jurisdiction of the Government and Parliament established by this Constitution shall be capable of contracting a valid marriage within that jurisdiction during the lifetime of the other party to the marriage so dissolved.[654]

'Marriage' has been defined as being derived from the Christian notion of 'a partnership based on an irrevocable personal consent given by both spouses which establishes a unique and very special life-long relationship'.[655] Such an approach would appear to deprive non-marital families of the protection of Article 41.[656] However, a non-marital child: **13.190**

> has the same 'natural and imprescriptible rights' (under Article 42) as a child born in wedlock to religious and moral, intellectual, physical and social education.[657]

There is some support for the view that Article 41.2 applies to non-married mothers.[658] The family's right to protection covers deliberate acts only, not negligent acts.[659]

Article 41 has been used in immigration contexts. The courts have held that Article 41 is applicable to residency rights of aliens married to Irish citizens, or whose children are Irish citizens. However, Article 41 is not absolute. In *Pok Sun Shum v Ireland*[660] it was held that the residency of an alien husband of an Irish citizen could be controlled by the Minister of Justice. Likewise in *Fajujonu v Minister of Justice*[661] it was held that while Irish children of alien parents had the constitutional right to the company, care and parentage of their parents within the family unit, that right was subject to the exigencies of the common good. **13.191**

The case of *Murray v Ireland*[662]concerned the right to family life during imprisonment. In that case, married prisoners claimed they had a right to found a family; and that they were entitled to facilities in prison for its exercise. The Supreme Court stated that many constitutional rights arising from marriage were suspended during imprisonment: **13.192**

[654] See generally, J M Kelly, *The Irish Constitution* (3rd edn, Butterworths 1994) 989–1052.

[655] *Murray v Ireland* [1985] IR 532, *per* Costello J.

[656] See *O'B v S* [1984] IR 316 (legislation which precluded non-marital children from succeeding on intestacy to their father's estate was permissible).

[657] *In re M an Infant* [1946] IR 334.

[658] Kelly (n 654 above) 1012.

[659] *Hosford v J Murphy and Sons Ltd* [1987] IR 621.

[660] [1986] ILRM 593.

[661] [1990] 2 IR 151.

[662] [1985] IR 532.

> Of the [marital rights] which I have outlined it is possible to say that only a right of communication, and that without privacy, and a right by communication to take some part in the education of children of the marriage would ordinarily survive a sentence of imprisonment as a convicted prisoner.

13.193 In *Murphy v Attorney-General*[663] a married couple successfully attacked income tax legislation which treated their two incomes as a single income, thus pushing them into a higher tax bracket than if they had been unmarried and singly assessed. The Supreme Court held that the tax legislation was:

> a breach of the pledge by the State to guard with special care the institution of marriage and to protect it against attack. Such a breach is, in the view of the Court, not compensated for or justified by such advantages and privileges [that are accorded to married couples].

13.194 Article 41 has also been applied in the criminal context. In *The People (Director of Public Prosecutions) v T*[664] the Court of Criminal Appeal ruled that the duty to protect the family in Article 41 must be applied against family members guilty of injuring other members of the family. Accordingly, a wife could give evidence against her husband accused of sexual offences against their daughter.

13.195 An attempt by the Government to alter family property arrangements failed in *In the Matter of the Matrimonial Home Bill 1993.*[665] The Bill in question provided that where a dwelling was occupied by a married couple and either or both of the spouses had an interest in that dwelling, the equitable interest in that dwelling was to vest in both spouses as joint tenants. That vesting did not apply to a dwelling already vested in the spouses as joint tenants or tenants in common in equal shares. A spouse in whose favour the vesting operated could, after independent legal advice, make a declaration that the vesting would not operate in her case. Further, the other spouse could seek a court order that the vesting should not operate in his case. The Bill was struck down by the Supreme Court, as an interference with the authority of the family. The Bill's application of automatic ownership as joint tenants interfered with decisions which may have been jointly made in relation to the ownership of the matrimonial home. The application was universal and did not depend on the decision being injurious or oppressive in respect of a spouse or members of the family, or a spouse having failed to discharge his or her family obligations.

13.196 Family rights have also been considered in the context of Article 40.3.1 of the Irish Constitution, which provides that:

> The State guarantees in its laws to respect, and, as far as is practicable, by its laws to defend and vindicate the personal rights of the citizen.

In *C M v T M*[666] a married woman's right to a domicile independent of her husband was recognized as a fundamental right within Article 40.3.1. The court noted that failure to protect independent domicile would lead to hardship to the married woman under the relevant maintenance legislation. Article 40.3.1 has been interpreted to include a right to

---

663 [1982] IR 241.
664 (1988) 3 Frewen 141.
665 [1994] 1 ILRM 241.
666 [1991] IRLM 268.

marry,[667] the right to procreate[668] and the rights of an unmarried mother in relation to the custody and care of her child.[669] However, Article 40.3.1 does not include any constitutional right to guardianship of children on the part of unmarried fathers.[670] A non-marital child has the right under Article 40.3.1 'to be fed and to live, to be reared and educated, to have the opportunity of working and of realising his or her full personality and dignity as a human being'.[671]

(3) South Africa

The South African Constitution does not contain any general 'right to family life'. At the Certification Hearing it was argued that such a right should be included in the new Constitution. However, the Constitutional Court pointed out that: **13.197**

> A survey of national constitutions in Asia, Europe, North America and Africa shows that the duty on the states to protect marriage and family rights has been interpreted in a multitude of different ways. There has by no means been universal acceptance of the need to recognise the rights to marriage and to family life as being fundamental in the sense that they require express constitutional protection.[672]

They went on to draw attention to the fact that:

> Families are constituted, function and are dissolved in such a variety of ways, and the possible outcomes of constitutionalising family rights are so uncertain, that constitution-makers appear frequently to prefer not to regard the right to marry or to pursue family life as a fundamental right that is appropriate for definition in constitutionalised terms. They thereby avoid disagreements over whether the family to be protected is a nuclear family or an extended family, or over which ceremonies, rites or practices would constitute a marriage deserving of constitutional protection.[673]

However, the Constitution does provide express recognition for the rights of children. Section 28(1) provides, *inter alia*:

> Every child has the right—
> (a) to a name and a nationality from birth;
> (b) to family care, parental care, or appropriate alternative care when removed from the family environment.

Despite the absence of express recognition for 'family rights' the Constitutional Court has recognised that 'family life' is one of the rights protected under the heading of privacy.[674] In *Fraser v Children's Court, Pretoria North*[675] it was held that a statutory provision which had the effect that an unmarried father's consent was not required for adoption was unconstitutional because it discriminated against fathers. **13.198**

---

667 See eg *Ryan v A-G* [1965] IR 294; but note *Donovan v Minister for Justice* (1951) 85 ILTR 134 (upheld requirement for police force to obtain prior permission from the Commissioner before marrying).

668 *Murray v Ireland* [1985] IR 532.

669 See eg *The State (Nicolaou) v An Bord Uchtála* [1966] IR 567.

670 *In re S W, an infant, K v W* [1990] 2 IR 437.

671 *G v An Bord Uchtála* [1980] IR 32.

672 *In re Certification of the Constitution of RSA 1996* 1996 4 SA 744, CC para 98.

673 Ibid para 99.

674 *Bernstein v Bester* 1996 4 BCLR 449 para 67.

675 (1997) 2 BCLR 153.

(4) **Zimbabwe**

13.199 In *Rattigan v Chief Immigration Officer*[676] the Supreme Court of Zimbabwe found that an alien spouse married to a citizen was entitled to be granted a residence permit. The applicants succeeded on the basis of the freedom of movement and rights to privacy. The Court stated that the right to freedom of movement had to be viewed in the light of the institution of marriage, the most fundamental institution known to man. Marriage embodied the obligation to found a home, to cohabit, to have children and to live together as a family unit. Adopting a generous and purposive approach, and taking the right to protection for the privacy of the home together with the freedom of movement, the prohibition of husbands from residing in Zimbabwe, and thereby disabling them from living with their wives in the country of which the wives are citizens, was to undermine and devalue the protection of the right to freedom of movement accorded to wives as a member of a family unit. In *Salem v Chief Immigration Officer*[677] the Supreme Court added that alien spouses of citizens were entitled to seek employment. The Constitution of Zimbabwe was subsequently amended to provide that restrictions could be imposed on the movement or residence of a person or the person could be expelled 'whether or not he is married or related to another person who is a citizen of or permanently resident in Zimbabwe'.[678] However, in *Kohlhaas v Chief Immigration Officer*[679] the Supreme Court held that the effect of the amendment was merely to restate the law in relation to the rights of non-citizens and left untouched the rights of a citizen spouse to freedom of movement.[680]

[676] [1994] 1 LRC 343.
[677] [1994] 1 LRC 355.
[678] Constitution of Zimbabwe Amendment (No 14) Act 1996.
[679] 1998 (6) BCLR 757.
[680] See also, *Hambly v Chief Immigration Officer* 1999 (9) BCLR 966.

14

FREEDOM OF THOUGHT, CONSCIENCE AND RELIGION

A. The Nature of the Rights

14.01 The struggle for religious freedom has a long history.[1] The right to the 'free exercise of religion' formed part of the First Amendment to the United States Constitution.[2] Article 18 of the Universal Declaration of Human Rights states that:

> Everyone has the right to freedom of thought, conscience and religion; this right includes freedom to change his religion[3] or belief, and freedom, either alone or in community with others and in public or private, to manifest his religions or belief in teaching, practice, worship and observance.

A right in similar terms is found in all other international human rights instruments.[4] In 1981 the United Nations adopted a 'Declaration on the Elimination of all Forms of Intolerance and Discrimination Based on Religion and Belief'.[5]

14.02 The right to hold religious or other beliefs is itself not controversial. However, difficult questions arise concerning how individuals may communicate or act upon their beliefs; and the extent to which such communication should be facilitated by the state and tolerated by other members of society. The main issues fall into three areas:

The scope of the right: The critical issue is the extent to which the *manifestation* of belief warrants protection. Freedom of thought, conscience and religion includes a right to express or manifest beliefs in society but the expression of beliefs, particularly those of a political or religious nature, leads to conflict, requiring that competing public interests be balanced against one another. Thus, freedom of thought, conscience and religion overlap with questions involving freedom of expression or discriminating between different groups. A broad view would protect manifestations of belief, perhaps subject only to the limits imposed by the criminal law. A more restrictive approach distinguishes motivation from expression, excluding acts which are *motivated* by belief and protecting only those expressions that communicate what the belief is.

The obligation to protect the freedom: A second area of contention arises in relation to the positive steps the state must take to protect an individual's right

---

[1] See generally, N Lerner, 'Religious Human Rights Under the United Nations' in J van der Vyer and J Witte Jr (eds), *Religious Human Rights in the Global Perspective: Legal Perspectives* (Nijhoff, 1996).

[2] See para 14.106ff below.

[3] This provision was controversial, Muslim states being concerned about missionaries, see J Walkate, 'The Right of Everyone to Change His Religion or Belief' (1983) 2 Neth Intl L Rev 146.

[4] See Art 9, European Convention on Human Rights; Art 18, ICCPR; Art 12, American Convention on Human Rights 1965; Art 8, African Charter on Human and Peoples Rights 1981 (omitting the right to 'change religion').

[5] See I Brownlie (ed), *Basic Documents on Human Rights* (3rd edn, Oxford University Press, 1992).

to his beliefs. Is the duty of the state limited to refraining from imposing unnecessary public constraints, or does it extend to protection of individuals from infringement by other private persons? A duty of positive intervention raises the difficulty of providing equal protection of the rights which conflict with one another; the protection of one individual is therefore likely to restrict the rights of another.

Legitimate restrictions on the freedom: Complex problems also emerge when interference with religious or other beliefs has to be justified. The need to balance the freedom of an individual against the interests of public order, health and safety or to accommodate conscientious objectors continues to generate vigorous debates.

B. The Rights in English Law Before the Human Rights Act

(1) The scope of the rights

The common law has not developed any comprehensive definition of 'religion'. It has been suggested that two of the essential attributes of religion are 'faith in god and worship of god'[6] with the result that an organisation promoting belief in 'ethical qualities' or 'secularism' is, in itself, not a religion.[7] However, this definition excludes religions such as Buddhism and Taoism and broader definitions have been adopted in other common law jurisdictions.[8] No attempt has been made to define the limits of 'freedom of conscience'. **14.03**

At common law, punishment for 'erroneous opinions concerning rites or modes of worship' could only be made on the basis of some positive law.[9] There were, however, a number of such laws in the seventeenth and eighteenth century.[10] In particular, the Corporation Act 1661 required all holders of civic office to be communicants of the Church of England. This was reinforced by the Test Act 1673 requiring holders of civil or military office to denounce the doctrine of transubstantiation and to take oaths of Supremacy and allegiance. These Acts were both repealed in 1828, the same year in which an Act for the Relief of Roman Catholics admitted Catholics into the legal profession and allowed Catholic schools and places of worship. Jews were not admitted into Parliament until 1858.[11] **14.04**

---

[6] *Re South Place Ethical Society* [1980] 1 WLR 1565; *R v Registrar General, ex p Segerdal* [1970] 2 QB 697.

[7] *Re South Place Ethical Society*, (n 6 above); *Bowman v Secular Society* [1917] AC 406.

[8] See para 14.105ff below.

[9] *Harrison v Evans* (1767) 3 Bro Parl Cas 465.

[10] For a short history of the development of religious freedom in England see C Hamilton, *Family, Law and Religion* (Sweet & Maxwell, 1995) 1-11.

[11] Under the terms of the Jewish Relief Act 1858.

14.05 Although the Church of England is the 'established church' and has certain privileges in law[12] the promotion of anti-Christian views is no longer regarded as illegal and the phrase 'Christianity is part of the law of England' is not law but rhetoric.[13] There is now, in effect, unrestricted freedom of worship under English law. Particular religious beliefs (or lack of them) are no longer a formal barrier to employment or office. However, there is no legal restriction on general discrimination on the grounds of religion.[14]

14.06 The common law now clearly recognises the importance of religious toleration. The position has been described as follows:

> The common law, like the European Convention on Human Rights, recognises the freedom of individuals to adopt, practise and (relevantly) to change their religion. Any administrative decision which impinges on this right would be justified by a sufficiently weighty competing interest.[15]

In general, the common law has provided no positive protection for the freedom of thought, conscience or religion. It has, nevertheless, recognised the importance of the toleration of the expression of religious beliefs. Thus, in *Redmond-Bate v DPP*[16] the Divisional Court quashed convictions for obstructing the police where three Christian fundamentalists were preaching on the steps of Wakefield Cathedral.[17] Sedley LJ said:

> the Crown Court was right to be alert to the fact that ours is a society of many faiths and none, and of many opinions. If the public promotion of one faith or opinion is conducted in such a way as to insult or provoke others in breach of statute or common law, then the fact that it is done in the name of religious manifestation or freedom of expression will not necessarily save it. It may forfeit the protection of Article 9[18] or Article 10[19] by reason of the limitations permitted in both Articles (provided they are necessary and proportionate) in the interests of public order and the protection of the rights of others.

14.07 There is no statutory or common law restriction on the freedom of expression of religious views, provided that they do not give rise to a breach of the peace[20] or

[12] For example, 26 bishops are, *ex officio*, members of the House of Lords. The ecclesiastical law of the Church of England is part of the law of the land.

[13] See *Bowman v Secular Society* [1917] AC 406.

[14] Although there may be indirect protection via the Race Relations Act 1976, see para 14.17ff below.

[15] *Per* Sedley J, *R v the Secretary of State of Home Department, ex p Moon* (1995) 8 Admin LR 477, 480.

[16] (1999) 7 BHRC 375.

[17] The crowd was becoming hostile. A police officer requested the women to stop preaching; and when they refused, arrested them for breach of the peace. The Divisional Court held that because the threat of violence came from the crowd and not the preachers, it was they (and not the preachers) who should be asked to desist and arrested if they would not.

[18] That is, freedom of religion under the Convention, see para 14.36ff below.

[19] That is, freedom of expression under the Convention, see para 14.137ff below.

[20] Cf *Redmond-Bate v DPP* (n 16 above).

incite racial hatred.[21] The most significant limitation on the expression of religious views is the common law offence of blasphemy which only restricts speech denying the truth of the doctrines of the Church of England.[22] There is no similar common law restriction on speech concerning other religions.[23]

Parliament has, on a number of occasions, legislated to forbid religious practices which are regarded as harmful. For example, the Prohibition of Female Circumcision Act 1985 makes it an offence to perform circumcision on a female.[24] Acting in accordance with religious beliefs is, in general, no defence to a criminal charge. Thus, a parent who refuses, for religious reasons, to obtain medical treatment for a child will have no defence to a charge of child neglect.[25] **14.08**

(2) Rights and privileges of religions

Under English law religious organisations can obtain charitable status and tax exemptions. These privileges are not limited to the Church of England: any association which is properly described as a 'religion' qualifies for charitable status and thus tax exemption. For the purposes of the law of charities, 'religion' ordinarily involves the 'worship of a deity'; sincere belief in ethical qualities is not enough.[26] Buddhism, however, may be an exception to this general approach.[27] This approach has led to a refusal to recognise certain groups, such as the Scientologists, as being 'religions'.[28] However, it has been held that the Exclusive Bretheren are entitled to be registered as a charity, despite arguments that the practice of their religion was not 'beneficial to the community'.[29] **14.09**

(3) Religious worship and education in schools

Education was, historically, largely provided by religious bodies.[30] This led to serious political controversy in the nineteenth century. The Elementary Education **14.10**

[21] See para 15.120 below.

[22] See para 14.07ff above.

[23] See *R v Chief Metropolitan Stipendiary Magistrate, ex p Choudhury* [1991] 1 QB 429; see para 14.15 below.

[24] Female circumcision might be regarded as a 'cultural' rather than a 'religious' custom.

[25] See eg *R v Senior* [1899] 1 QB 283 (member of 'Peculiar People' sect found guilty of manslaughter).

[26] See *Re South Place Ethical Society* [1980] 1 WLR 1565.

[27] See *R v Registrar General, ex p Segerdal* [1970] 2 QB 697, 704.

[28] See *Ex p Segerdal* (n 27, above); but see *Church of the New Faith v Commissioner of Pay-Roll Tax (Victoria)* (1983) 154 CLR 120 in which the Australian High Court held that Scientology is a religion.

[29] *Holmes v Attorney-General, The Times*, 12 Feb 1981; not following a report for the Charity Commissioners which concluded that the Exclusive Bretheren could not be regarded as charitable, Charity Commissioners Report, 1976-77, HC 389, 35.

[30] For a short history of the development of religious education in England see C Hamilton, *Family, Law and Religion* (Sweet & Maxwell, 1995) 242–249.

Act 1870 required the separation of secular and religious subjects in the new publicly funded 'board' schools. Under the Act, public funding was only to be provided for secular education[31] and under a 'conscience clause', a parent was allowed to withdraw a child from religious instruction in any school which received a grant from public funds.[32] In the new board schools, it was provided that 'no religious catechism or religious formulary which is distinctive of any particular denomination should be taught'.[33] The Education Act 1944 provided, for the first time, that there should be a compulsory daily act of 'corporate worship' and religious instruction.[34] However, the right of withdrawal was preserved.[35]

14.11 The position is now governed by the provisions of the School Standards and Framework Act 1998.[36] In all schools maintained by local authorities[37] the local authority, governing body and headteacher shall secure that religious education is given in accordance with the provision for such education included in the school's basic curriculum.[38] Religious education in community schools[39] or foundation[40] or voluntary schools[41] which do not have a religious character must provide religious education in accordance with the agreed syllabus adopted for the school or for the pupils.[42] Voluntary schools or voluntary schools with a religious character must provide religious education in accordance with its trust deed.[43] Voluntary aided schools which have a religious character must provide religious education in accordance with their trust deeds or its specified[44] religious denomination.[45]

14.12 The 1998 Act also states that each pupil in attendance at a local authority maintained school 'shall on each school day take part in an act of collective worship'.[46] Religious worship at community,[47] foundation[48] or voluntary schools[49] in a

---

31 s 97.
32 s 74(2).
33 s 14(2), the 'Cowper-Temple' clause.
34 s 26.
35 s 25(4).
36 For earlier provisions in similar terms see S Bailey, D Harris and B Jones, *Civil Liberties: Cases and Materials* (4th edn, Butterworths, 1995) 587–591.
37 Now divided into three categories: 'community schools', 'foundation schools' and 'voluntary schools', School Standards and Framework Act 1998, s 20.
38 Ibid s 69; Sch 19 determines the provision for religious education which is to be included in the basic curriculum of schools of different types.
39 s 20.
40 Ibid.
41 Ibid.
42 Sch 19, para 2.
43 Sch 19, para 3.
44 s 69(4).
45 Sch 19, para 4.
46 s 70(1).
47 s 20.
48 Ibid.
49 Ibid.

school which does not have a religious character shall be made by the head teacher after consulting the governing body or, if the school is a foundation school with a religious character or a voluntary school, the arrangements shall be made by the governing body after consulting the head teacher.[50] The collective worship[51] at a community school or foundation school which does not have a religious character shall be[52] wholly or mainly of a broadly Christian character (although it does not need to be distinctive of any particular Christian denomination).[53]

However, if the parent of a pupil at such a school requests, he shall be excused from receiving religious education, from attendance at religious worship in the school or from both.[54] Arrangements may be made for the pupil to receive religious education elsewhere.[55] The statutory provisions affecting employees at religious schools are discussed below.[56] **14.13**

(4) Religious expression and blasphemy

Any denial of the truth of Christian doctrine (or its essential precepts) expressed so as to shock or outrage ordinary Christians[57] constitutes blasphemy. Protection from blasphemy is given solely to members of the Church of England (and other Christian denominations sharing its central tenets). This reflects the constitutionally dominant position of the Anglican Church. Blasphemy is rooted in the ecclesiastical offence of heresy; and perpetuates the significant political and cultural role that the Church once enjoyed in British society. Although the offence is now generally regarded as protecting individual believers rather than the state, the connection with the state Church has persisted and the law remains relevant only to the established form of the Christian religion. There has been no change in this since Alderson B, in *R v Gathercole*,[58] said: **14.14**

> . . . a person may, without being liable to prosecution for it, attack Judaism, or Mahomedanism, or even any sect of the Christian Religion (save the established religion of the country); and the only reason why the latter is in a different situation from the others is, because it is the form established by law, and is therefore a part of the constitution of the country.

---

[50] Sch 20, para 2.
[51] *R v Secretary of State of Education, ex p R and D* [1994] ELR 495.
[52] Unless a standing advisory council on religious education disapplied the requirement under Sch 20, para 4.
[53] Sch 20, para 3.
[54] s 71(1).
[55] s 71(3)–(5).
[56] See para 14.24 below.
[57] See J Smith and B Hogan, *Criminal Law* (7th edn, Butterworths, 1999) 723; S Robilliard, *Religion and the Law: Religious Liberty in Modern English Law* (Manchester University Press, 1984) Chap 2; *R v Taylor* (1676) 1 Vent 293; *R v Hetherington* (1841) 9 St Tr (NS) 563; *R v Lemon* [1979] AC 617.
[58] (1838) 2 Lew CC 237, 254.

14.15 The extent of the protection that the law provides to its small group of beneficiaries is uncertain. The *actus reus* of the crime is defined in many different ways,[59] and a clear formulation of the necessary *mens rea* is equally difficult to identify. It might be necessary to show an intention to subvert the Church of England by 'scurrilous vilification';[60] this has been distinguished from rational discussion or mere difference of opinion on the basis of 'tone and spirit' suggesting 'offence, insult and ridicule'.[61] However, the case of *R v Lemon*[62] suggests that actual intention to shock or offend is not necessary; and that 'an intention to publish material' will suffice, so long as the jury finds that the material is 'likely to shock or arouse resentment among believing Christians'.[63]

14.16 The common law offence of blasphemous libel criminalises conduct or expression that is sufficiently offensive to Christians. However, the shift from homogeneity to pluralism of religious belief makes justification of the narrow scope of the law of blasphemy difficult to defend.[64] Various options for reform have been suggested, including abolition of the criminal offence; and, conversely, its expansion to protect the whole range of religious and non-religious beliefs. The current debate concentrates on whether any justification can be found for retaining the offence of blasphemous libel in a pluralistic society as an alternative to its complete abolition.[65] There appears to be a wide consensus in favour of the abolition of the present offence of blasphemy, but the Law Commission is undecided as to what, if anything, should replace it.[66]

(5) Religious discrimination

(a) Introduction

14.17 Almost all of the disabilities imposed by public authorities on non-members of

[59] *R v Taylor* (n 57 above): any 'aspersion' on the Church of England; *R v Hetherington* (n 57 above): an attack on the Old Testament; *R v Lemon* (n 57 above); publications which 'shock and arouse resentment among believing Christians' (Lord Diplock); or any publication 'which contains any contemptuous, reviling, scurrilous or ludicrous matter relating to God, Jesus Christ, or the Bible, or the formularies of the Church of England as by law established' (Lord Scarman).

[60] *R v Chief Metropolitan Stipendiary Magistrate, ex p Choudhury* [1991] 1 QB 429.

[61] *R v Hetherington* (1841) 4 St Tr (NS) 563, 590.

[62] [1979] AC 617.

[63] Ibid 900.

[64] See A Bradney, 'Taking Sides: Religion, Law and Politics' (1993) 143 NLJ 434 for a discussion of the position of Muslims and Salman Rushdie in Britain.

[65] For arguments in support of each position, see D Feldman, *Civil Liberties and Human Rights in England and Wales* (Clarendon Press, 1993) 695–698; S Poulter, 'Towards Legislative Reform of the Blasphemy and Racial Hatred Laws' [1991] PL 371; J Feinberg, *Offense to Others* (Oxford University Press, 1985); J Raz, *The Morality of Freedom* (Clarendon Press, 1986); J Finnis, *Natural Law and Natural Rights* (Clarendon Press, 1980); Law Commission, *Offences against Religion and Public Worship* (Law Cm No 145, 1985); S Robilliard, *Religion and the Law: Religious Liberty in Modern English Law* (Manchester University Press, 1984).

[66] Law Commission Report No 145 (n 65 above).

the Church of England have now been removed.[67] There is, however, no general protection against private religious discrimination.[68] Discrimination on religious or political grounds is not covered by the Race Relations Act 1976.[69] An attempt to include religious discrimination in the Act failed.[70]

Nevertheless, religious discrimination is caught by the Race Relations Act if it falls within the scope of discrimination on grounds of 'colour, race, nationality or ethnic or national origins'.[71] Thus, the refusal of a private school to admit a Sikh because it would be contrary to school rules for him to wear a turban was held to be indirect racial discrimination on the grounds that Sikhs constitute a community recognisable by ethnic origins.[72] The House of Lords set out criteria for identifying a group on the basis of 'ethnic origins'. It is essential that the group has a 'long shared history' and a 'cultural tradition of its own'.[73] Jews are also treated as a 'racial group' within the Race Relations Act.[74] Muslims do not constitute a racial group but an employer's refusal to allow Muslim employees time off work to celebrate a religious festival has been held to justify an award of compensation on the basis it constitutes indirect racial discrimination.[75] **14.18**

The provisions of the Race Relations Act do not assist new religious groups which have not had time to develop a 'long shared history' and 'cultural tradition'. Thus, it has been held that Rastafarians are not a racial group as they have existed for only 60 years.[76] This means that a 'No Hindus' rule would be unlawful but a 'No Catholics' rule, if applied to an English Catholic, would not.[77] **14.19**

[67] Toleration Act 1688 (non-conformist protestants); Roman Catholic Relief Acts 1791 and 1829 and Religious Disabilities Act 1846 (Jews); however the Sovereign must be a member of the Church of England (Act of Settlement 1700, section 3) and his or her consort shall not be a Roman Catholic (ibid s 2).

[68] See generally, A Bradney, *Religions, Rights and Laws* (Leicester University Press, 1993).

[69] See *Ealing LBC v Race Relations Board* [1972] AC 342; *Mandla (Sewa Singh) v Dowell Lee* [1983] 2 AC 548.

[70] HC, Standing Committee A, 29 Apr 1976 and 4 May 1976, cols 84–118.

[71] Race Relations Act 1976, s 3(1).

[72] *Mandla (Sewa Singh) v Dowell Lee* [1983] 2 AC 548.

[73] Ibid *per* Lord Fraser.

[74] See *Mandla v Dowell Lee* (n 72 above); *Seide v Gillette Industries Ltd* [1980] IRLR 427; *Tower Hamlets London Borough Council v Rabin* [1989] ICR 693; in *Simon v Brimham Associates* [1987] ICR 596 the Court of Appeal found that inquiry by an executive of an employment agency into the religious faith of a job applicant which discouraged the (Jewish) applicant from continuing with an application for employment in the Middle East could have amounted to unlawful discrimination under the Race Relations Act 1976. On the facts, however, it was held that the words and acts were not discriminatory and that whether the interviewer had had the religion of the applicant disclosed to him was not determinative.

[75] See *J H Walker Ltd v Hussain* [1996] ICR 291.

[76] *Crown Suppliers (Property Services Agency) v Dawkins* [1991] IRLR 327, [1993] IRLR 284.

[77] See S Bailey, D Harris and B Jones, *Civil Liberties: Cases and Materials* (4th edn, Butterworths, 1995) 638.

(b) Employment

14.20 **Time off for religious observances.** The English courts have, on several occasions, considered whether it is unlawful for an employer to refuse time off to an employee for religious observance. In *Ahmad v Inner London Education Authority*[78] the appellant was a devout Muslim schoolteacher who had been employed at a school which was so far from the mosque that he was not required to attend Friday prayers. He was then transferred to a school close to the mosque; he attended Friday prayers and missed 45 minutes of teaching time. The ILEA informed him that, if he continued to go to the Mosque, he would have to give up his full-time post for a part-time one at a lower salary; so he resigned and brought a claim for unfair dismissal. The Court of Appeal held that he was bound by his contract to be in school on Friday afternoons. Lord Denning MR considered the appellant's rights to freedom of religion; but said that any such rights were subject to the ILEA's rights under the contract. In his dissenting judgment Scarman LJ took into account the rights to freedom of religion in Article 9 of the Convention; and held that there was no breach of contract.[79]

14.21 A similar result was reached by an unfair dismissal case where a bus company dismissed an employee who had converted to the Seventh Day Adventist faith and then, in breach of contract, refused to work on Saturdays.[80] However, in another case, an industrial tribunal held that a Muslim who had been dropped from a sales representative training course because he wished to have time off for Friday prayers was a victim of race discrimination.[81]

14.22 **Sunday working.** When the Sunday Trading Act was enacted in 1994, limited protection was given to shop workers[82] and betting workers[83] in relation to Sunday working. A protected shop or betting worker must have commenced employment on the relevant date[84] and must have been employed either not to work only on Sunday[85] or not to be required to work on Sunday.[86] Furthermore,

[78] [1978] QB 36.

[79] Mr Ahmad's claim was rejected by the Commission (*Ahmad v United Kingdom* (1982) 4 EHRR 126). The Commission appear to have been heavily influenced by the fact that Mr Ahmad had not raised the question of his potential need for time off during school hours during the first six years of his employment or at his interview. They took the view that the school authorities had not arbitrarily disregarded his freedom of religion.

[80] *Esson v United Transport Executive* [1975] IRLR 48; see also *Storey v Allied Breweries* (1976) 84 IRLIB 9 (chambermaid refusing to work Sundays fairly dismissed).

[81] *Yassin v Northwest Homecare* 1993 CRE Rep 21 (compensation of £3,000 was awarded); see also *Azam v J H Walker Ltd* 1993 CRE Rep 20 (race discrimination to refuse to allow Muslim employees to continue to take time off for a religious holiday).

[82] As defined by s 232 Employment Rights Act 1996, s 232.

[83] As defined by ibid s 233.

[84] For shop workers the date is 26 Aug 1994 and for betting workers 3 Jan 1995.

[85] Employment Rights Act 1996, s 36(2).

[86] Ibid s 36(3).

provided a shop or betting worker is not employed only to work on Sunday,[87] he is entitled to give a written notice opting out of Sunday working.[88] A protected worker may also serve an opting-in notice.[89] A protected worker who has opted out has a right not to be subjected to a detriment where he refuses to work on Sundays[90] and a dismissal for refusing to work on Sunday is automatically unfair[91] irrespective of whether the employee has worked for one year.[92]

Religious discrimination. As discussed earlier[93] the Race Relations Act does not extend to discrimination on grounds of religion. However, the Northern Ireland courts have considered religious discrimination as a result of the Fair Employment (Northern Ireland) Act 1976 (which has no equivalent in England and Wales). These have included, for example, cases where employers have discriminated by refusing to appoint Catholics,[94] a failure by an employer to take positive steps where a Catholic barman received a threat to his life[95] and the failure to take positive action to combat religious discrimination.[96] **14.23**

Teachers in denominational schools. The School Standards and Framework Act 1998 contains specific provisions concerning teachers in relation to a number of religious issues. Foundation[97] and voluntary controlled schools[98] which have a religious character are obliged to appoint staff selected for their fitness and competence to give religious education and to permit the dismissal of such teachers because they have failed to give religious education efficiently and suitably.[99] Staff and prospective staff at community,[100] secular foundation,[101] voluntary[102] or special schools[103] are not disqualified from being a teacher because of their religious **14.24**

87 Ibid s 40(3).
88 Ibid s 40(1).
89 Ibid s 35.
90 Ibid s 45(1); however, it is subject to limited exceptions in s 45(5) and s 45(7).
91 Ibid s 101(1).
92 Ibid s 108, 109.
93 See para 14.18 above.
94 See eg *Fair Employment Agency v Craigavon BC* [1986] IRLR 316; *Duffy v Eastern Health and Social Services Board* [1992] IRLR 251 (where a tribunal awarded £25,000 for a failure to appoint a Catholic); *McConnell v Police Authority for Northern Ireland* [1997] IRLR 627 (where the Court of Appeal said that the tribunal should apply the same principles when awarding compensation for hurt feelings as apply in sex and race discrimination cases); *Kelly v Northern Ireland Housing Executive* [1998] 3 WLR 735 (discrimination when selecting solicitors to panel for undertaking public liability work).
95 *Smyth v Crofts Inn* [1996] IRLR 84, CA.
96 *New York City Employees' Retirement System v American Brands Inc* [1986] IRLR 239.
97 s 20.
98 Ibid.
99 s 58.
100 s 20.
101 Ibid.
102 Ibid.
103 Ibid.

opinions or attending (or omitting to attend) religious worship, shall not be required to give religious education and shall not receive less remuneration (or be deprived of promotion or some other advantage) because they do not give religious education or because of their religious opinions or by attending (or omitting to attend) religious worship.[104] Staff at foundation or voluntary schools with religious characters can appoint a headmaster by taking account of his ability and fitness to preserve and develop the religious character of the school; if the school is a voluntary aided school, preference can be given in connection with the appointment, remuneration or promotion of teachers and regard can be had when dismissing them to religious opinions, attending religious worship or giving religious education in accordance with the tenets of the specified[105] religion of the school.[106]

(c) Immigration and extradition

14.25 Arguments based on religious discrimination have also been deployed in extradition cases. In *Re Ramda*[107] an Algerian Muslim suspected of a 1995 bombing campaign in France sought a writ of *habeas corpus* following an extradition request by the French Government. He argued that a trial by special assize court would be prejudiced as a result of discriminatory comments by the Minister of Justice and press reports unfavourable to Algerian Muslims. The Divisional Court disagreed, finding that the special judges were capable of ensuring a fair trial in spite of the media and the personal views of the Minister.

(d) Planning and administrative law

14.26 It is clear that religious considerations are irrelevant in the context of planning decisions. Thus, in *Cherwell District Council v Vadivale*[108] the planning authority refused the applicant permission to continue the use of his outhouse as a family temple which was arguably fundamental to his Hindu way of life. The decision was upheld on appeal on the ground that there was no evidence that the appellant had been treated less favourably than persons practising another religion: the material change of use of the property, increased activity and nuisance to neighbours all went beyond the bounds of planning prudence. The Commission set up to licence Jewish ritual slaughterers can make a licence conditional on geographical limitation if this reasonably meets a requirement of the Jewish religion.[109]

---

[104] s 59.
[105] s 69(4).
[106] s 60.
[107] Independent, 27 Jun 1997.
[108] (1991) 6 PAD 433.
[109] *R v Rabbinical Commission for the Licensing of Shochetim, ex p Cohen The Times*, 22 Dec 1987.

(6) Family law

(a) Marriage

At common law, marriages could be solemnised in various ways, which did not necessarily involve religious ceremonies.[110] The position was regularised by Lord Hardwicke's Marriage Act 1753 which required that, to be valid, a marriage had to take place according to the rites of the Church of England. Only Jews and Quakers were exempt from this requirement. The restrictions were not relaxed until the Marriage Act 1836 allowed marriage by civil ceremony and also allowed marriage according to the religious rites of denominations other than the Church of England. Such marriages had to take place in a 'registered building'. **14.27**

It remains the law that all religious marriages, save for those taking place according to Anglican, Quaker or Jewish rites, must take place in a registered building or approved premises.[111] Very few non-Christian religious marriages in fact take place in registered buildings.[112] It appears that most non-Christian marriages involve a civil ceremony and subsequent religious ceremony at a non-registered building. **14.28**

Polygamous marriages in accordance with the rites of religions which allow them have never been permitted in England.[113] Such a marriage contracted in England or by a person domiciled in England is void.[114] However, the courts will recognise potentially polygamous marriages solemnised abroad.[115] **14.29**

(b) Divorce

English law does not recognise extra-judicial religious divorces.[116] It will, however, recognise such divorces in relation to parties not domiciled in England,[117] even if the 'formalities' take place in England.[118] The position is now governed by the provisions of the Family Law Act 1986. Divorce obtained outside the United Kingdom in 'judicial or other proceedings' is valid if obtained in a country where **14.30**

[110] For a full discussion of marriage and religions see C Hamilton, *Family, Law and Religion* (Sweet & Maxwell, 1995) Chap 2.

[111] Marriage Act 1949, s 26(1)(b), (bb) and s 46A (as amended by Marriage Act 1994).

[112] See C Hamilton (n 110 above) 47–48.

[113] See *Hyde v Hyde and Woodmansee* (1866) 1 LR 1 P&D 130; the US Supreme Court has held that the ban on polygamous marriages does not interfere with freedom of religion, *Reynolds v United States* (1878) 98 US 145.

[114] *Hussain v Hussain* [1982] 1 All ER 369.

[115] *Srini Vasan v Srini Vasan* [1946] P 67 (Hindu marriage in India).

[116] See generally, Hamilton (n 110 above) Chap 3.

[117] *Sasson v Sasson* [1924] AC 1007 ('*get*' obtained by a Jewish couple domiciled in Egypt).

[118] *Har-Shefi v Har-Shefi* [1953] 1 All ER 783 ('*get*' in London recognised because valid by law of husband's domicile).

either spouse is domiciled or habitually resident.[119] An informal divorce, such as Muslim '*talaq*', is only recognised if it is effective under the laws of the country in which it was obtained, each party is domiciled in that country and neither party was habitually resident in the United Kingdom throughout the period of one year immediately preceding the date of divorce.

(c) The upbringing of children

14.31 The right of parents to control the religious upbringing of children is an important aspect of religious freedom.[120] At common law, the rule was that children had to be brought up in the religion of their father.[121] This rule was abolished by the Guardianship of Minors Act 1925. The Children Act 1989 does not impose obligations on parents in respect of religious upbringing or instruction but parental responsibility includes the right to bring up children in a particular religion, or none.[122]

14.32 When applying the paramountcy of welfare test in section 1 of the Children Act 1989,[123] the religious beliefs and practices of the parents are relevant factors to be taken into account. The approach has been summarised as follows:

> It is no part of the court's function to comment upon the tenets, doctrines or rules of any particular section of society provided that these are legally and socially acceptable . . .
>
> The impact of the tenets, doctrines and rules of a society upon a child's future welfare must be one of the relevant factors to be taken into account by the court . . .[124]

As a result, it is open to the court to decide that a child should be brought up in a religion not practised by the parent with whom he resides although this would be unusual.[125] Considerations of the religious views of parents have featured in cases dealing with the care and custody of children: foster care,[126]

---

[119] s 46(1).

[120] See generally, Hamilton (n 110 below) Chap 4.

[121] See eg *Hawksworth v Hawksworth* (1871) LR Ch App 539.

[122] See generally, *Re J (A Minor)* [1999] 2 FCR 145.

[123] See generally, para 13.17ff below.

[124] *Re R (A Minor) (Residence: Religion)* [1993] 2 FLR 163, 171.

[125] *Re J (A Minor)* (n 122, above).

[126] *C v Salford City Council* [1994] 2 FLR 926; *Re K (A Minor)* [1991] 1 FLR 57 in which an Irish Catholic mother became unexpectedly pregnant at a time of great stress and gave her child to a middle-aged Greek Orthodox couple. When she wanted it back later the couple applied for wardship with a view to adoption, which was awarded them in a decision which was subsequently overturned by the Court of Appeal.

adoption,[127] custody and access,[128] abduction[129] and the residence of minors.[130]

The courts intervene in the upbringing of children and act against the religious views of the parents in a number of situations.[131] If the child is suffering from a life threatening condition and the parents' religious beliefs interfere with proper medical treatment, the court will intervene. As was said in *Jane v Jane*:[132] **14.33**

> If there is a conflict between honouring the mother's religious belief and the interest of the child in continuing life, it is perfectly plain that in such a conflict the interests of the child and its welfare are paramount and the mother's religious beliefs have to be overridden in order to save the child.

It is clear that even in the face of religious objection the test remains the welfare of the child.[133]

(7) Religious freedom in other areas

It has been held that whether the oath of a witness who is neither a Christian nor a Jew is lawfully sworn depends upon whether both the court and the witness consider his conscience to be bound.[134] **14.34**

An issue which has arisen in employment cases is the contractual position of ministers of religion. A clergyman is not an employee because of the essentially spiritual nature of the work.[135] In *President of the Methodist Conference v Parfitt*[136] the Court of Appeal stated that a court (or tribunal) must approach this issue by **14.35**

---

[127] See *C v Salford City Council* (n 126 above); *Re K (A Minor)* (n 126 above).

[128] *Re S (Minors) (Access: Religious Upbringing)* [1992] 2 FLR 313: a strong Roman Catholic and father of children ages 13 and 11 sought access to his children after his divorce from their mother as a result of his 'religious obsession'. The children had ceased religious education of their own volition. It was found that while active steps should be taken to promote access, no one should dictate to children of such age.

[129] *H v H (Minors) (No 3)* [1994] Fam Law (143) 13: the applicant father, a fundamentalist Christian, retained his children in the United States at the end of a visit; in response to his application for custody it was found that the children would be better equipped for life in a more liberal environment in England.

[130] In *Re R (A Minor)* [1993] 2 FLR 163, the Court of Appeal dismissed an appeal by members of the fellowship of Exclusive Brethren for a residence order for a 10-year-old boy whose father had been ostracised from the community. The Court dismissed the application and made the order in favour of rehabilitating the relationship of the boy with his father. The impact of the beliefs had to be considered in relation to the application of the Children Act 1989 and the conviction of the child himself was only one factor to be considered.

[131] See generally, C Hamilton, *Family, Law and Religion* (Sweet & Maxwell, 1995) 156–169.

[132] (1983) 4 FLR 712.

[133] *Re S* [1993] 1 FLR 376; for the position in Canada, see para 13.180 below.

[134] *R v Kemble* [1990] 1 WLR 1111.

[135] *President of the Methodist Conference v Parfitt* [1984] QB 368; *Davies v Presbyterian Church of Wales* [1986] 1 WLR 323; *Santokh Singh v Guru Nanak Gurdwara* [1990] ICR 309; *Birmingham Mosque Trust Ltd v Alavi* [1992] ICR 435; *Diocese of Southwark v Coker* [1998] ICR 140.

[136] n 135 above.

considering: first, whether there is a contract at all (that is, whether the parties are *ad idem* and intend to create legal relations) and secondly, whether the contract is a contract of service (where the religious nature of the duties is important).

C. The Law Under the Convention

(1) The scope of the right

(a) Introduction

14.36 Article 9 of the Convention states:

> (1) Everyone has the right to freedom of thought, conscience and religion; this right includes freedom to change his religion or belief and freedom, either alone or in community with others and in public or private, to manifest his religion or belief, in worship, teaching, practice and observance.
> (2) Freedom to manifest one's religion or beliefs shall be subject only to such limitations as are prescribed by law and are necessary in a democratic society in the interests of public safety, for the protection of public order, health or morals, or for the protection of the rights and freedoms of others.

14.37 It is clear from the wording of the first paragraph that the right encompasses *both* the right to hold beliefs[137] and the right to manifest those beliefs. As the Commission has said:

> Article 9 primarily protects the sphere of personal beliefs and religious creeds, i.e. the area which is sometimes called the *forum internum*. In addition, it protects acts which are intimately linked to these attitudes, such as acts of worship or devotion which are aspects of the practice of a religion or belief in a generally recognised form.[138]

14.38 It is not entirely clear whether Article 9 rights are confined to natural persons. It appears that a distinction is drawn between 'freedom of conscience' and 'freedom of religion'. Because only individuals can have 'thoughts' or 'conscience', these freedoms cannot be relied on by corporations[139] or associations.[140] However, a church body or an association with religious and philosophical objects is capable of possessing and exercising the rights contained in Article 9.[141]

[137] Protecting what is sometimes called the '*forum internum*', see P van Dijk and G van Hoof, *Theory and Practice of the European Convention on Human Rights* (3rd edn, Kluwer, 1998) 541.
[138] See *Van den Dungen v Netherlands* (1995) 80-A DR 147, 150; see generally, van Dijk and van Hoof (n 137 above) 543–544.
[139] *Company X v Switzerland* (1981) 16 DR 85, EComm HR.
[140] *Verein 'Kontakt-Information-Therapie' v Austria* (1988) 57 DR 81.
[141] *X and Church of Scientology v Sweden* (1979) 16 DR 68; EComm HR; *Chappell v United Kingdom* (1987) 53 DR 241, EComm HR.

The freedom of thought, conscience and religion under Article 9 will in many cases be associated with other Convention rights. Manifestation of belief may involve the right to freedom of expression, discrimination in the treatment of different religions will raise issues under Article 14, and there is a clear relationship between Article 9 rights and freedom of assembly and association under Article 11.[142] In determining priorities between the competing rights, the Court has attached great significance to religious beliefs and Article 9 rights to the detriment of other freedoms.[143] On the other hand, when considering cases involving several different Convention rights, the Strasbourg authorities have often chosen not to develop the Article 9 points: for example, they have disregarded complaints under Article 9 when addressing questions concerning the right to marriage under Article 12[144] or disputes concerning the custody and education of children.[145] **14.39**

(b) 'Thought, conscience and religion'

The case law provides no comprehensive definition of the words 'thought, conscience and religion'. In the majority of cases, the Court has avoided making any express determination as to whether the subject matter comes within the scope of Article 9.[146] In other cases, the Court has either assumed the existence of a religious belief without question,[147] or has found against the existence of a manifestation of religious belief without determining whether there was a religion in issue.[148] The Commission has been prepared to assume that the Divine Light Zentrum,[149] Druidism,[150] and the Church of Scientology[151] were religions. However, Article 9 does not cover religions with no clear structure and belief systems.[152] **14.40**

Article 9 does not oblige the state to ensure that churches within its jurisdiction grant religious freedom to their members and servants.[153] The freedom of religion **14.41**

[142] *Young, James and Webster v United Kingdom* (1981) 4 EHRR 38.

[143] *Otto-Preminger-Institute v Austria* (1994) 19 EHRR 34.

[144] *Khan v United Kingdom* (1986) 48 DR 253, EComm HR.

[145] *Hoffmann v Austria* (1993) 17 EHRR 293.

[146] See eg *X v Italy* (1976) 5 DR 83, EComm HR in which the applicant who had been convicted of re-organising the Fascist Party complained of a violation of his rights and freedoms under Art 9, 10 and 11. Without addressing which of the rights had been violated, or whether the establishment of a political party constituted a manifestation of religious or other beliefs, the Commission found the legislative restrictions necessary in a democratic society.

[147] *Hoffman v Austria* (1993) 17 EHRR 293 (the refusal of blood transfusions by a Jehovah's Witness was based upon a religious belief).

[148] *X and Church of Scientology v Sweden* (1979) 16 DR 68, EComm HR: having found that an advertisement for commercial purposes precluded a manifestation of religion, the Commission did not address whether Scientology was a religion.

[149] *Omkaranda and the Divine Light Zentrum v Switzerland* (1981) 25 DR 105.

[150] *Chappell v United Kingdom* (1987) 53 DR 241.

[151] *X and Church of Scientology v Sweden* (1979) 16 DR 68, EComm HR.

[152] *X v United Kingdom* (1977) 11 DR 55 (Wicca religion).

[153] See *Karlsson v Sweden* (1988) 57 DR 172, EComm HR (a minister has no claim to be protected against his church in a dispute about doctrine as he is free to leave the church).

of servants of a State church 'is exercised at the moment they accept or refuse employment as clergymen, and their right to leave the church guarantees their freedom of religion in case they oppose its teachings'.[154] It is, however, possible that the dismissal of a church employee for refusal to change his views could raise an issue under Article 9.[155]

14.42 In spite of a lack of positive definition, it is clear that Article 9 protects beliefs apart from those founded in religion. The freedom of thought, conscience and religion is:

> . . . in its religious dimension, one of the most vital elements that go to make up the identity of believers and their conception of life, but it is also a precious asset for atheists, agnostics, sceptics and the unconcerned.[156]

In *Angeleni v Sweden*,[157] the Commission examined whether the atheistic views of Ms Angeleni and her daughter had been violated when a school denied the child exemption from religious education classes. The decision turned on whether the child had been subjected to religious indoctrination, against which Article 9 was found to provide protection.

14.43 Freedom of thought under Article 9 extends to pacificism[158] and veganism[159] It is not clear whether any specific type of thought or belief is excluded from protection.[160] However, Article 9 did not cover protest by IRA prisoners about their 'special category status'.[161] Other cases have considered political opinions or personal convictions not based on religion in the context of trade union membership, conscientious objection to military service[162] or non-payment of taxes.[163]

(c) 'Manifestation'

14.44 Article 9(1) establishes the right to manifest belief alone (or with others) and in public (or private), through 'worship, teaching, practice and observance'. This protects rites and acts of worship as well as teaching, which includes, subject to certain limitations, the freedom to attempt to convert others to one's beliefs. In the case of freedom of religion:

---

[154] *X v Denmark* (1976) 5 DR 157, EComm HR (a Danish clergyman had been required by his church to abandon a certain practice of christening, no breach of Art 9).

[155] See *obiter dicta* in *Knudsen v Norway* (1985) 42 DR 247, 258, EComm HR.

[156] *Kokkinakis v Greece* (1993) 17 EHRR 397 para 31.

[157] (1987) 51 DR 41, EComm HR.

[158] *Arrowsmith v United Kingdom* (1980) 19 DR 5, EComm HR.

[159] *X v United Kingdom* (Application 18187/91), (1993) (unpublished) referred to by K Reid, *A Practitioner's Guide to the European Convention on Human Rights* (Sweet & Maxwell, 1998) 344.

[160] D Harris, M O'Boyle and C Warbrick, *Law of the European Convention on Human Rights* (Butterworths, 1995) 357; P van Dijk and G van Hoof, *Theory and Practice of the European Convention on Human Rights* (3rd edn, Kluwer, 1998) 543-544.

[161] Cf *McFeeley v United Kingdom* (1980) 20 DR 44, EComm HR (refusal to wear prison uniform).

[162] See eg *Grandrath v Germany* (1967) 16 CD 41, EComm HR.

[163] See *C v United Kingdom* (1983) 37 DR 142, EComm HR.

> While religious freedom is primarily a matter of individual conscience, it also implies, inter alia, freedom to 'manifest one's religion'. Bearing witness in words and deeds is bound up with the existence of religious convictions.[164]

The freedom to manifest religion includes the 'right to try to convince one's neighbour'.[165]

14.45 As a matter of principle, it might be thought that the question as to whether or not a particular activity was a 'manifestation' of a particular religion or belief or offensive to it, should be a matter which was determined by the sincere convictions of the adherent. If not, the court must engage in the activity of 'scriptural interpretation'.[166] However, the Court has itself sought to interpret religious beliefs, holding that participation in a National Day parade should not have offended the applicant's pacifist convictions.[167]

14.46 Article 9 does not protect every act motivated or inspired by religion or belief and, in exercising his freedom to manifest religion, an individual may need to take his specific situation into account.[168] Thus, the compulsory retirement of a military officer who had adopted fundamentalist opinions on the basis of his 'conduct and attitude' was not an interference with his rights under Article 9. It is difficult to see how this conclusion can be justified: it is strongly arguable that the Court should have found an interference and then gone on to consider 'justification' under Article 9(2).[169]

14.47 The freedom to 'practice' a belief or religion does not always guarantee the right to behave in the public sphere in a way which is dictated by the belief.[170] Article 9 only protects those manifestations which communicate the *substance* of the belief. In the leading case of *Arrowsmith v United Kingdom*[171] a pacifist distributed a leaflet attempting to discourage soldiers from serving in Northern Ireland. The Commission held that the leaflet was not provided in order to further pacifist views; and did not, therefore, constitute a 'manifestation' of belief.[172] This

[164] *Kokkinakis v Greece* (1993) 17 EHRR 397 para 31.

[165] Ibid.

[166] An approach which has been rejected by the American Courts, see *United States v Lee* (1982) 455 US 252.

[167] See *Valsamis v Greece* (1996) 24 EHRR 294, paras 31–33 (Judges Thór Vilhjálmsson and Jambrek dissenting); see generally, S Stavros, 'Freedom of Religion and Claims for Exemption from generally Applicable, Neutral Laws: Lessons from Across the Pond?' [1997] EHRLR 607.

[168] *Kalaç v Turkey* (1997) 27 EHRR 552 para 27.

[169] Cf the note on the case [1997] EHRLR 691.

[170] *C v United Kingdom* (1983) 37 DR 142, 147, EComm HR.

[171] (1980) 19 DR 5, EComm HR.

[172] Note the separate opinion of Mr Opsahl and dissent of Mr Klecker who criticised the distinction drawn by the Commission between manifestation and motivation. While Mr Opsahl found the distinction necessary in principle, in his opinion it was not clear where the line was to be drawn. Mr Klecker felt that the distribution of the leaflets by the applicant was not merely an extension but an integral part of her belief and disagreed with the Commission's finding for being too narrow on the facts.

approach has been applied in a number of cases. Thus, refusal to perform functions required by the state Church,[173] and to participate in a pension scheme[174] have been treated as actions which are motivated by, but do not expressly communicate, belief.

14.48 A further distinction has been drawn between expression of belief and communications that are commercial in nature. Advertisements which use religious content to promote sales of goods are commercial, as opposed to 'informational' or 'descriptive', and the assertions in them will not be protected by Article 9. On this principle, there was no breach when an injunction was obtained against advertisements for the 'E-meter', an electronic instrument purportedly capable of measuring the 'electrical characteristics of the "static field" surrounding the body and believed to reflect or indicate whether or not the confessing person has been relieved of the spiritual impediment of his sins'.[175] Although the Church of Scientology alleged the meter to be a 'religious artifact' the Court held that the promotional material did not constitute a practice which manifested belief.

(2) The nature of the protection

(a) Negative protection

14.49 The protection afforded by Article 9 has two aspects. First, it provides negative protection. It therefore embraces freedom from any compulsion to express thoughts, to change an opinion, or to divulge convictions. This freedom of the '*forum internum*' is not subject to any justification under Article 9(2). Freedom of thought will also be violated if the State imposes any type of penalty for holding a particular belief or interferes with worship, teaching, practice and observance. Any such compulsion or interference will be a breach of Article 9(1) which must be justified under Article 9(2).[176]

14.50 There will be no 'interference' with rights under Article 9 if it is the result of a restriction imposed by a law of *general* application. Thus, in *Stedman v United Kingdom*[177] the Commission rejected an application from a shop worker who had been dismissed as a result of her refusal to work on Sundays. The Commission said that:

> the applicant was dismissed for failing to agree to work certain hours rather than her religious belief as such and was free to resign and did in effect resign from her employment.

[173] *Knudsen v Norway* (1985) 42 DR 247, EComm HR: the refusal was motivated by, but did not express the views of the applicant contrary to the Church.

[174] *V v The Netherlands* (1984) 39 DR 267, EComm HR (the refusal to join a pension scheme did not express the applicant's anthroposophical beliefs).

[175] *X and Church of Scientology v Sweden* (1979) 16 DR 68, EComm HR.

[176] See para 14.54 below.

[177] (1997) 23 EHRR CD 168 see also *X v Finland* Application 24949/94, 3 Dec1996 (Seventh Day Adventist dismissed for a refusal to work on Friday, no violation of Art 9).

The reasoning in this case is difficult to follow and is inconsistent with the approach taken in indirect discrimination cases.[178] In *C v United Kingdom*[179] the Commission rejected an application by a Quaker based on his religious objection to the payment of taxes for defence expenditure, holding that:

> Article 9 does not confer on the applicant the right to refuse, on the basis of his convictions to abide by legislation, the operation of which is provided for by the Convention, and which applies neutrally and generally in the public sphere, without impinging on the freedoms guaranteed by Article 9.[180]

Criminal law is also law of general application which does not constitute an interference even though it affects manifestations of conscience or religion. For example, a law which prohibited corporal punishment of children did not infringe the Article 9 rights of the parents, even though the applicants maintained that their religious convictions required some such discipline in the form of light physical chastisement.[181] However, laws prohibiting proselytism do constitute an interference with Article 9 rights and require justification under Article 9(2).[182] **14.51**

The difficulties raised by interference with religious beliefs arising from laws of general application may be circumvented if the applicant makes a complaint of religious discrimination under Article 14. In *Thlimmenos v Greece*[182a] the applicant was a Jehovah's witness who was convicted of insubordination for refusing to wear a military uniform at a time of general mobilisation. Some years later he was refused an appointment to the Greek Institute of Chartered Accountants because he had been convicted of a felony. He alleged discrimination on the ground of his religious beliefs and the government responded by arguing that the claim was not 'within the ambit' of Article 9[182b] because the Institute's rules were a law of general application. However, the court found there was discrimination since the Government had failed to treat a conviction which arose out of religious principles differently from an ordinary criminal conviction. This line of reasoning could be extended by imposing a positive duty on the state to protect Article 9 rights by creating exceptions to laws of general application in favour of religious groups. **14.51A**

---

[178] See para 17.18 below; cf the US jurisprudence on the same issue, para 14.108 below; and see generally, S Stavros, 'Freedom of Religion and Claims for Exemption from Generally Applicable, Neutral Laws: Lessons from Across the Pond?' [1997] EHRLR 607, EComm HR.

[179] (1983) 37 DR 142.

[180] Ibid 147; see also *Bouessel du Bourg v France* (1993) 16 EHRR CD 49; and *V v Netherlands* (1984) 39 DR 267, EComm HR.

[181] *Seven Individuals v Sweden* (1982) 29 DR 104, EComm HR.

[182] *Kokkinakis v Greece* (1993) 17 EHRR 397, see para 14.57 below.

[182a] Judgment of 6 Apr 2000.

[182b] See para 17.86ff below.

(b) Positive protection

14.52 The state also has a positive obligation to ensure the peaceful enjoyment of the rights guaranteed by Article 9.[183] This may, in some circumstances, involve the state taking measures to repress conduct which is incompatible with the respect for the freedom of thought, conscience and religion of others.[184] It has been held that blasphemy laws are an appropriate means to prevent attacks on the religious beliefs of its citizens[185] but that Article 9 did not compel the state to have such laws covering all religions.[186]

14.53 The difficulties of this approach are illustrated by the unsatisfactory decision in *Otto-Preminger-Institute v Austria*[187] The applicant was a non-profit making organisation which advertised the film 'Council of Love' by a bulletin distributed to its members and posted in public. The film, which was to be open to all over the age of 17 years, was described as 'targeting trivial imagery and absurdities of the Christian creed in a caricatural mode . . .'. Prior to the showings, at the instigation of the Catholic church, the manager of the applicant was charged with the offence of 'disparaging religious doctrines' and the film was seized and eventually forfeited under media legislation. The applicant's claim under Article 10 was rejected.[188] However, the Court made some general comments about Article 9, suggesting that when religious beliefs were opposed or denied in an extreme way, this could be regarded as a 'malicious violation of the spirit of tolerance',[189] with the result that the state had a positive duty to repress such opposition. The case gives rise to obvious difficulties, particularly in relation to non-majority religions and non-religious beliefs generally.[190]

(3) Justifiable limitations

(a) Absolute right to believe

14.54 The right to think, formulate ideas and opinions and to hold personal convictions is an absolute right. However, the expression of those beliefs may legitimately be restricted on the grounds contained in Article 9(2). This means that any conduct intended to change a thinking process, change an opinion, or force divulgence of convictions, precludes the imposition of any sanction or penalty on the holding of

[183] *Otto-Preminger-Institute v Austria* (1994) 19 EHRR 34 para 47; cf *R v Lemon* [1979] AC 617, 658 where Lord Scarman suggested that, by necessary implication, Art 9 'imposes a duty on all of us to refrain from insulting or outraging the religious feelings of others'.
[184] *Otto-Preminger-Institute v Austria* (n 183 above) (1993) 17 EHRR 397 para 48.
[185] *Gay News Ltd v United Kingdom* (1982) 5 EHRR 123.
[186] *Choudhury v United Kingdom* (1991) 12 HRLJ 172, EComm HR.
[187] (n 183 above).
[188] See para 15.170 below.
[189] n 183 above para 47.
[190] For criticism, see D Pannick, 'Religious Feelings and the European Court' [1995] PL 7.

any view whatever or on the change of a religion or conviction.[191] Arrest on the basis of membership in a particular political party[192] therefore violates Article 9; but 'compulsory voting' does not, as it requires only attendance at the polls, rather than actual registration of a vote.[193]

The establishment of a state church system does not in itself violate Article 9, as long as it does not compel individuals to belong to or to leave the Church.[194] The imposition of a specific Church tax may constitute compulsory involvement in religious activities when it is applied to non-members,[195] but is not an unlawful interference when applied to members, as long as the law allows individuals to leave the Church.[196] **14.55**

(b) Restrictions upon manifestation of belief

Interferences with the manifestation of belief must be 'prescribed by law',[197] and be 'necessary in a democratic society'[198] in pursuit of one of the 'legitimate aims' set out in Article 9(2). There are only five of these: the interests of public safety, and the protection of public order, health, morals or the rights and freedoms of others. **14.56**

The justification of interferences with rights under Article 9 has been considered by the Court in a number of recent cases. In *Kokkinakis v Greece*[199] the Court held that the conviction of a Jehovah's Witness under a national law which prohibited proselytism[200] was incompatible with Article 9. The conviction could not be justified as necessary in a democratic society for the protection of the beliefs of others. The facts available to the national courts were found not sufficiently specific as to the impropriety of the actions of the applicant to support his conviction. In *Larissis v Greece*[201] the Court stressed the need to convictions in the context in which the communications occurred. The applicants were members of the armed **14.57**

[191] P van Dijk and G van Hoof, *Theory and Practice of the European Convention on Human Rights* (3rd edn, Kluwer, 1998) 541–542.

[192] See *Hazar, Hazar and Acik v Turkey* (1992) 72 DR 200, EComm HR (involving three members of the Communist party in Turkey).

[193] *X v Austria* (1972) 15 YB 498.

[194] *Darby v Sweden* (1990) 13 EHRR 774 para 45.

[195] Ibid.

[196] *Gottesmann v Switzerland* (1984) 40 DR 284, EComm HR; see also *E and G R v Austria* (1984) 37 DR 42.

[197] See generally, para 6.126ff above.

[198] See generally, para 6.146ff above.

[199] (1993) 17 EHRR 397 para 48.

[200] The Greek criminal law defined proselytism as: '. . . any direct or indirect attempt to intrude on the religious beliefs of a person of a different religious persuasion, with the aim of undermining those beliefs, either by any kind of inducement or promise of an inducement or moral support or material assistance, or by fraudulent means or by taking advantage of his inexperience, trust, need, low intellect or naivety'. The Constitution protected freedom of all religions and prohibited proselytism in general (not merely that directed against the dominant religion).

[201] (1998) 27 EHRR 329.

forces: their convictions for proselytisation of subordinate airmen did not violate Article 9 as special measures were justified to protect subordinates from risk of harassment.[202] However, the Court concluded that the convictions for proselytisation of civilians did violate Article 9. There was no evidence that the civilians had been subjected to improper pressure.

14.58 The Court also found a breach in *Manoussakis v Greece*.[203] The applicants had applied for prior authorisation to use a building as a place of public worship in accordance with the domestic law but waited 18 months without receiving a decision from the Ministry of Education and Religious Affairs. They were then convicted of operating an unauthorised place of worship. The Government contended that the penalty imposed served to protect public order. The Court accepted that the need for 'authorisation' pursued a legitimate aim under Article 9(2); however, the conviction was not proportionate to the legitimate aim pursued nor necessary in a democratic society. A similar result was reached in *Serif v Greece*[203a] in which the applicant's conviction for usurping the functions of a minister of a known religion could not be justified as being 'necessary in a democratic society'. In *Buscarini v San Marino*[204] the Court decided that requiring the applicants to the General Council to take an oath on the Gospels was a violation of Article 9 which was not 'necessary in a democratic society'.

14.59 The Commission has upheld a number of restrictions under Article 9(2) including: compulsory automobile insurance,[205] a compulsory health scheme designed to prevent tuberculosis among cattle,[206] the compulsory use of crash helmets or seat belts,[207] the refusal to provide a prisoner with a book containing a chapter on martial arts,[208] the refusal to allow a Buddhist prisoner to grow a beard[209] and the refusal of planning permission for religious use of property.[210]

---

[202] Ibid paras 53–55.

[203] (1996) 23 EHRR 387.

[203a] Judgment of 14 Dec 1999.

[204] (1999) 6 BHRC 638.

[205] *X v The Netherlands* (1967) 10 YB, 472, EComm HR: the Commission found the insurance 'necessary for the protection of the rights and freedoms of others' and upheld the conviction of the applicant for driving without coverage, in spite of his objections to insurance on religious grounds.

[206] *X v The Netherlands* (1962) 5 YB 278, EComm HR: the Commission found that the scheme was necessary as a matter of 'protection of health' and held that the conviction of a Dutch dairy farmer who refused on religious grounds to participate in the scheme did not violate Art 9.

[207] *X v United Kingdom* (1978) 14 DR 234, EComm HR.

[208] *X v United Kingdom* (1976) 5 DR 100, EComm HR: the book was refused on the basis of a possible threat to public order.

[209] *X v Austria* (1965) 8 YB 174; see also *X v United Kingdom* (1972) 1 DR 41 (refusal of permission to a Buddhist prisoner to send articles to the editor of a Buddhist magazine); and *X v United Kingdom* (1976) 5 DR 8, EComm HR.

[210] *ISKCON v United Kingdom* (1994) 76-A DR 90, EComm HR (proportionate to the legitimate aims of the protection of public order, health and the rights and freedoms of others).

(c) Conscientious objection

Although there is no automatic right to conscientious objection in the Convention, the state may in some circumstances be required to accommodate differences of conscience by exempting a person from the operation of a general law or requirement where he objects to it on the grounds of religion or beliefs. **14.60**

The issue has been raised in conjunction with religious education in schools and claims by parents that their children be exempt from attending religious lessons, practices or school events that are offensive to their religious convictions. In *Valsamis v Greece*,[211] for example, the applicants claimed, unsuccessfully, that the refusal of the school authorities to exempt their child from participation in a school parade violated both Article 9 and the right to education under Article 2 of the First Protocol.[212] **14.61**

The Convention does contemplate conscientious objection in relation to military service. Article 4 provides that service exacted instead of military service is acceptable for conscientious objectors '. . . in countries where they are recognised'.[213] The Commission has taken this to mean that a state may, but need not, recognise conscientious objectors, and only if it does so must it provide an alternative obligation for them to the ordinary conscripted service.[214] Where such substitute civilian service is available, the question as to whether it is itself objectionable on conscientious or religious grounds[215] may be a question of fact. However, this approach is contrary to a resolution of the Parliamentary Assembly and a recommendation of the Committee of Ministers which have recognised a right of conscientious objection to military service 'deriving logically' from Article 9.[216] **14.62**

Apart from military service, a wide variety of claims on the basis of conscientious objection have been refused by the Commission.[217] The refusal of an education authority to allow a Muslim school teacher to breach his employment contract in order to attend prayers at the mosque was not a violation of his rights under **14.63**

[211] (1996) 24 EHRR 294.

[212] See generally, para 19.59 below.

[213] See *Tsirilis and Kouloumpas v Greece* (1997) 25 EHRR 198 and *Georgiadis v Greece* (1997) 24 EHRR 606. In each of these cases, Greek law provided for exemption from military service to ministers of 'all known religions' and the applicant Jehovah's Witnesses were detained, charged and in one case convicted of insubordination for refusal to provide military service. Eventually the Supreme Administrative Court delivered a judgment in which Jehovah's Witnesses were found to be a 'known religion' and their right of exemption upheld; the central issue on each of the appeals was compensation and assessment of damages.

[214] *Grandrath v Germany* (1967) 16 CD 41, EComm HR.

[215] Ibid.

[216] See P van Dijk and G van Hoof, *Theory and Practice of the European Convention on Human Rights* (3rd edn, Kluwer, 1998) 544.

[217] For a general review of case law in this area see Vermeulen, 'Scope and Limits of Conscientious Objections', in *Proceedings of the Council of Europe: Seminar on Freedom of Conscience* (Council of Europe Press, 1992).

Article 9.[218] The Commission has held that exemption from religious education classes may be required if they amount to indoctrination of religion contrary to the conscience of parent and child; but exemption was not granted where what was provided was merely instruction about religion.[219] In *Prais v Council*[220] the European Court of Justice held that there was a violation of the right to religious freedom of a Jewish job applicant where she was required to take examinations on a Saturday; as a result of her religious obligations, she was precluded from applying for a week-day job.

(d) Margin of appreciation

14.64 The doctrine of the margin of appreciation[221] is particularly important under Article 9. The *Otto-Preminger-Institut* case[222] shows that the Court will defer to the national authorities in cases where there is no uniform view concerning the significance of religion in society,[223] or any comprehensive definition of 'permissible interference'. In those circumstances the national authorities are better placed than the international judge to assess the need for restrictions in the local situation, and, within the limits of their jurisdiction, to consider the interests of society as a whole.

D. The Impact of the Human Rights Act

(1) Introduction

14.65 The failure of English law to recognise a positive right to freedom of thought and religion means that the Human Rights Act may affect a number of areas. In fact, the extensive debates about religious freedom during the passage of the Human Rights Bill assumed that religious rights were threatened by other Convention rights. This led to the enactment of section 13, which requires the court to attach particular significance to freedom of thought, conscience and religion.[223a]

14.66 However, any interference with freedom of thought and religion by a public body must be justified under Article 9(2). The burden of doing so will be placed on the public authority . As a result of the Human Rights Act the right to thought and religion will impinge on several fields including education, employment, immigration, family, police powers and prison law.

[218] *X v United Kingdom* (1981) 22 DR 27, EComm HR.
[219] *Angeleni v Sweden* (1987) 51 DR 41, EComm HR; see also *Trimble and Cosans v United Kingdom* (1982) 4 EHRR 293.
[220] [1976] ECR 1589, ECJ.
[221] See generally, para 6.31ff above.
[222] *Otto-Preminger-Institute v Austria* (1994) 19 EHRR 34.
[223] The Court referred to a similar conclusion in regard to morals in *Müller v Switzerland* (1988) 13 EHRR 212.
[223a] See generally P Cumper.

On the other hand, Article 9 does not prohibit the state from preferring one particular religious group.[224] Consequently, if a public authority assists a particular religious group, the decision may only be challenged under Article 9 on the ground that it constitutes an unacceptable restriction on the rights of others or that it constitutes discrimination under Article 14[225] which cannot be justified.[226] 14.67

(2) United Kingdom cases prior to the Human Rights Act

(a) Introduction

A relatively small number of Article 9 cases have been brought against the United Kingdom prior to the Human Rights Act. They fall into three general categories: the scope of the right and definition of 'religion' under Article 9, whether restrictions on the freedom of religion are justifiable and the extent to which the state is obliged to take positive steps to protect believers from attack. The United Kingdom has not been the subject of any finding of violation of Article 9.[227] 14.68

(b) Scope of the right

The right to manifest religious beliefs only protects activity which expresses religious views.[228] Thus, the Commission in *Arrowsmith v United Kingdom*[229] rejected the applicant's argument that the distribution of pacifist leaflets to troops was a manifestation of her religious conviction protected by Article 9 because this distribution did not articulate what the belief was. In *Khan v United Kingdom*[230] the Commission held that a refusal to allow a Buddhist prisoner to submit writings to a Buddhist magazine may have been motivated by religion; but was not a manifestation for the purposes of Article 9. Such communications with other members of the religion were not required by the tenets of the faith and did not therefore constitute a protected manifestation of belief.[231] In *Chappell v United Kingdom*,[232] on the other hand, the Commission was prepared to assume that Druidism is a religion but decided that restricting access to Stonehenge was justified under Article 9(2). 14.69

[224] By contrast, the 'establishment clause' of the First Amendment to the US Constitution requires a 'wall of separation between Church and state' (*Reynolds v United States* (1879) 98 US 145, 164); and, for example, prohibits prayers in state schools (*Engele v Vitale* (1962) 370 US 421); in relation to the First Amendment generally, see para 14.106ff below.

[225] See para 17.92ff below.

[226] See para 17.100ff below.

[227] The court has only made such findings in five cases: *Kokkinakis v Greece* (1993) 17 EHRR 397; *Manonssakis v Greece* (1996) 23 EHRR 387; *Larissis v Greece* (1998) 27 EHRR 329; *Buscarini v San Marino* (1999) 6 BHRC 638; *Serif v Greece* Jugment, 14 Dec 1999.

[228] See para 14.47 above.

[229] (1980) 19 DR 5, EComm HR

[230] (1986), 48 DR 253, EComm HR.

[231] *X v United Kingdom* (1972) 1 DR 41, EComm HR.

[232] (1987) 53 DR 241, EComm HR.

(c) Justifiability of restrictions

14.70 Justifiable restrictions imposed on religious freedom in the United Kingdom include a refusal to grant a Muslim school teacher leave of absence to attend Friday prayers,[233] compulsory use of crash helmets or seat belts,[234] the enforcement of planning legislation to restrict the use of a place of worship in accordance with the original permit for the protection of the rights of others, public order and health[235] and Government use of general tax revenues for procurement of arms, contrary to conscientious objections.[236]

(d) Positive obligations of the state

14.71 In *Gay News Ltd v United Kingdom*[237] the Commission decided that Article 9 does not preclude the state taking positive action such as penalising attacks on religious views. The publishers of 'Gay News' claimed that their conviction for blasphemous libel for publishing a poem breached their freedom of expression under Article 10. They had been privately prosecuted because the poem vilified Christ by attributing to him promiscuous homosexual practices. The Commission found that the conviction for blasphemy did constitute a restriction on expression and freedom of thought, but was justified primarily to protect the rights of the private prosecutor and ruled the application inadmissible.

14.72 The case of *Choudhury v United Kingdom*[238] confirmed that there is no *obligation* on the state to protect its citizens from offence caused by other private individuals. The applicant alleged that the United Kingdom had failed to protect the Moslem religion from attack by the publication of Salmon Rushdie's 'Satanic Verses' and that the law of blasphemy violated Article 14 of the Convention.[239] The Commission found there had been no direct interference by the state with the applicant's freedom to manifest his religion or belief; and held that Article 9 did not create a right to bring a specific form of proceedings against private individuals whose writing offended the sensitivities of other individuals.

14.73 In *Wingrove v United Kingdom*,[240] the Court found that Article 9 had not been breached where a film depicting a nun involved in erotic activity with the crucified Christ was refused UK classification for distribution. The refusal was expressly made on the ground it was blasphemous. The Court in *Wingrove* justified the limitation on expression under Article 10 because it protected the rights of

233 *Ahmad v United Kingdom* (1982) 4 EHRR 126, EComm HR.
234 *X v United Kingdom* (1978) 14 DR 234, EComm HR.
235 *ISKCON v United Kingdom* (1991) 76-A DR 90, EComm HR.
236 *C v United Kingdom* (1983) 37 DR 142, EComm HR.
237 (1983) 5 EHRR 123.
238 (1991) 12 HRLJ 172.
239 The prohibition against discrimination; see generally, para 17.146 below.
240 (1996) 24 EHRR 1.

others in relation to seriously offensive attacks on Christianity. The Court also held the legitimacy of the objective was not jeopardised by the fact that the law of blasphemy extends only to the Christian faith. These cases imply that in certain circumstances a state may have a responsibility to take active measures to repress forms of conduct incompatible with respect for the religious views of others.

(3) General impact

It seems that the narrow definition of 'religion' in English law may itself be inconsistent with Article 9. The view that 'religion' must involve the 'worship of a deity'[241] is inconsistent with the approach taken by the Commission[242] and with case law in other jurisdictions.[243] It might be argued that the tax privileges accorded to 'deistic' religions[244] constituted indirect restriction on the freedom of observance of the adherents of non-deistic religions. **14.74**

During parliamentary debates on the Human Rights Bill, concerns were expressed about the risks of human rights intruding on religious beliefs and practices. It was suggested, for example, that priests might be forced to marry divorced or homosexual couples and that churches might be forced to employ staff with different religious beliefs. A number of amendments were passed by the House of Lords. These were overturned by the House of Commons which inserted what became section 13(1) in the following terms: **14.75**

> If a court's determination of any question arising under this Act might affect the exercise by a religious organisation (itself or its members collectively) of the Convention right to freedom of thought, conscience and religion, it must have particular regard to the importance of that right.

The intention of this section was to give protection to churches as well as individuals.[245] The Home Secretary, Jack Straw MP, said that its purpose:

> is to focus the courts' attention in any proceedings on the view generally held by the Church in question, and on its interest in protecting the integrity of the common faith of its members against attack, whether by outsiders or individual dissidents.[246]

However, the section does not seek to provide 'absolute protection to the churches'; and the Government rejected an amendment designed to give absolute priority to Article 9.[247] It is difficult to see what practical purpose is served by this section.[248] It has been justly described as a provision that 'has no logical or legal **14.76**

[241] See para 14.09 above.
[242] See para 14.40 above.
[243] See eg para 14.109ff below in relation to Australia.
[244] See para 14.09 above.
[245] Home Secretary (Jack Straw MP), Committee Stage, *Hansard* HC col 1020 (20 May 1998).
[246] Ibid.
[247] Home Secretary (Jack Straw MP), *Hansard* HC col 1340 (21 Oct 1998).
[248] For a critique see Lord Lester and D Pannick, *Human Rights Law and Practice* (Butterworths, 1999) para 2.13, n 2, 50–52.

justification [but] . . . is simply a sop to those who supported the amendments in the House of Lords because of misguided concern about the impact of the Convention'.[249] Sedley LJ has suggested that the priority given to Article 9 rights in section 13[250] may itself breach the prohibition in Article 17 against limiting Convention rights to a greater extent than the Convention provides.[251] However, Article 9 is subject to Article 17;[252] and it is submitted that the Convention right of thought, conscience and religion in section 13 must therefore be read under section 3(1) of the Human Rights Act[253] so as to ensure that it does limit other Convention rights. In other words, section 3(1) prohibits section 13 from being interpreted in a way which gives freedom of religion a priority over other Convention rights.

(4) Specific areas of impact

(a) Criminal law

14.77 It seems likely that the offence of blasphemy will be challenged on the basis that it is confined to the Christian religion. The argument would be that this limitation is a breach of the state's obligation to provide positive protection for all religions equally.[254] In light of recent cases in the Court,[255] it is arguable an English court might not follow the Commission's view in *Choudhury v United Kingdom*[256] that no active steps were required. If this is right, the offence will require transformation in both nature and extent to ensure that protection is made available for the religious feelings of all.[257] It would also require that the recipients of the protection enjoy a right of prosecution previously denied them. Nevertheless, the point remains a controversial one and it has been argued that, rather than extend the offence to cover other religions, it ought to be abolished altogether.[258]

(b) Education

14.78 The provisions allowing children to be withdrawn from religious education and worship mean that the content of education is compatible with Article 9, but

---

[249] Ibid 52.

[250] See para 14.75 above, see also para 3.59 above.

[251] See *Redmond Bate v DPP* (1999) 7 BHRC 375, 380e.

[252] The general obligation under Convention law to read Convention Articles subject to Art 17 is an express obligation under s 1(1) of the Human Rights Act.

[253] See generally, para 4.04 above.

[254] See *Otto-Preminger-Institute v Austria* (1994) 19 EHRR 34 para 13.

[255] See para 14.73 above.

[256] (1991) 12 HRLJ 172.

[257] As suggested by Lord Scarman in *R v Lemon* [1979] AC 617, 658–9.

[258] See S Ghandhi and J James, 'The English Law of Blasphemy and the European Convention on Human Rights' [1998] EHRLR 430; for a general discussion, see D Feldman, *Civil Liberties and Human Rights in England and Wales* (Clarendon Press, 1993) 684–698.

there may be practices which amount to discrimination in breach of Article 14.[259] Article 9 may make it unlawful for schools to make rules which had the effect of preventing adherents of a particular religion from engaging in religious observance such as prayers,[260] wearing garments required by their religion[261] or styling their hair in a particular fashion.[262]

It is not clear whether Article 9 gives religious parents a right to withdraw their children from secular education or courses involving the use of computers where it offends religious sensibilities. Such a right has not been recognised in the United States[263] and it seems unlikely that such a right can be derived from Article 9.[264] **14.79**

Article 9 may provide further assistance to denominational schools in preserving their religious character in relation to their staff when the schools are relying on their rights under the School Standards and Framework Act.[265] Furthermore, the schools can also, if necessary, rely on section 13 of the Human Rights Act.[266] **14.80**

(c) Employment and discrimination

The most immediate issue in this area is whether Article 9 prohibits a standard public authority[266a] from discriminating against religious employees on the grounds of their religious observances by, for example, refusing to give them time off. The Convention case law suggests that laws of general application do not breach Article 9; and that Article 9 is not breached where a religious employee was dismissed for refusing to work on Sunday.[267] However, the American courts have **14.81**

---

[259] See generally, P Cumper, 'School Worship: Praying for Guidance' [1998] EHRLR 45; and see para 17.153 below.

[260] For example, a person in the position of the applicant in *Ahmad v Inner London Education Authority* [1978] QB 36; *Ahmed v United Kingdom* (1982) 4 EHRR 126 who had made his need for religious observance clear from the outset; *Valsamis v Greece* (1996) 24 EHRR 294 in which a girl of a Jehovah's Witness family was exempt from religious education and the Orthodox mass but was required to take part in a school parade.

[261] For example, a refusal to allow Muslim women to wear the 'hijab' (headscarf) (cf the 'race discrimination case' mentioned by S Bailey, D Harris and B Jones, *Civil Liberties: Cases and Materials* (4th edn, Butterworths, 1995) 643).

[262] For example, the wearing of 'dreadlocks' by a Rastafarian (cf the Zimbabwe case of *Re Chikweche* [1995] 2 LRC 93 see para 14.133 below).

[263] See *Davis v Page* (1974) 385 F Supp 395 (Apostolic Lutherans refused exemption from classes in which television was used); see generally C Hamilton, *Family, Law and Religion* (Sweet & Maxwell, 1995) Chap 8.

[264] Cf *Kjeldsen, Busk, Madsen and Pedersen v Denmark* (1976) 1 EHRR 711 in which the Court held that obligatory sex education was not a breach of Art 2, First Protocol to the Convention, see also, para 19.63 below.

[265] See para 14.25 above.

[266] See para 14.75 above.

[266a] The meaning of standard public authorities is discussed at para 5.14ff above, and of functional authorities at para 5.16ff above. The question of whether employees of functional authorities have Convention rights is complex: see para 5.32ff above.

[267] See para 14.50 above.

taken the opposite view;[268] and it is submitted that Article 9 will be breached where general laws have a disparate impact on religious employees on the same principle as that which makes indirect discrimination on grounds of race or sex unlawful.[269] It may also be possible to frame a complaint as a failure to promote positive discrimination under Article 14; this approach succeeded in the recent case of *Thlimmenos v Greece*.[269a]

14.82 Discrimination on religious grounds against employees who work for private employers may be unlawful under the Human Rights Act. The principle of statutory horizontality[270] may require that the definition of 'racial grounds' under the Race Relations Act 1976[271] be read so as to include discrimination on religious grounds.

(d) Family law

14.83 It is arguable that the refusal of the courts to recognise polygamous Muslim marriages celebrated in England[272] and the lack of recognition afforded to Muslim divorce by '*talaq*' which takes place in England is a breach of Article 9 rights. However, such interferences may be justified under Article 9(2) as being for the protection of the rights and freedoms of women.[273] The right of a parent to bring a child up in the religion of parental choice is usually regarded as an aspect of the parent's right to freedom of religion.[274] However, this right of the parent is given no special weight in English law. Article 9 may give a non-custodial parent a greater role in decisions as to a child's religion.[275] It could be argued that limits to the non-custodial parent's involvement in the religious upbringing of the child should not be accepted unless there is clear evidence that access without restrictions would pose a substantial threat of present or future harm to the child.[276]

---

268 See para 14.108 below.

269 See *Griggs v Duke Power* (1971) 401 US 424 which is the discrimination case which is said to have provided the model for statutory indirect discrimination under the Sex Discrimination Act 1975, s 1(1) and the Race Relations Act 1976, s 1(1).

269a Judgment of 6 Apr 2000; see para 14.51A.

270 See para 5.84 above.

271 See para 14.18 above.

272 This is particularly so in light of the fact that parties to a marriage solemnised abroad may seek relief under the Matrimonial Causes Act 1973, s 47.

273 Cf *Kalla v The Master* 1995 (1) SA 261 (T) in which van Dijkhorst J expressed the view *obiter* that polygamous marriages offended against principles of gender equality, see generally, *Bill of Rights Compendium* (Butterworths, South Africa, 1996) para 3C7.

274 See Convention on Rights of the Child 1989, Art 14(2) in I Brownlie (ed), *Basic Documents on Human Rights* (3rd edn, Oxford University Press, 1992) 187.

275 Cf *Re S (Minor) (Access: Religious Upbringing)* [1992] 2 FLR 313.

276 This was the approach of the Pennsylvania Superior Court in *Zummo v Zummo* (1990) 574 A.2d 1130 (Pa) in relation to the 'free exercise clause' (see para 14.106ff below).

(e) Planning and environment

Article 9 does not prohibit a public authority from preferring one particular religious group to another. Thus, in *ISKCON v United Kingston*[277] enforcement proceedings taken against the Krishna society because the influx of pilgrims to a religious centre caused a nuisance was held by the Commission to be a proportionate restriction on the rights of others. **14.84**

(f) Police law

The tolerance which the police must give to religious activities in public order situations (as illustrated by *Redmond-Bate v DPP)*[278] is likely to be enhanced by the Human Rights Act. The powers under the Public Order Act 1986 may well be extended to religious groups. The Act creates a number of offences relating to the incitement of racial hatred: threatening or abusive or insulting words or behaviour,[279] intentionally causing a person harassment, alarm or distress[280] and threatening, abusive or insulting behaviour which provokes fear or violence.[281] The definition of racial group[282] is the same as that in the Race Relations Act 1976;[283] and it is arguable that the principle of statutory horizontality[284] will require that these powers are also applied to activities that are offensive to religious groups. **14.85**

(g) Prison law

It is arguable that in certain circumstances Article 9 might oblige prison authorities to provide facilities for the expression of religious beliefs. Thus, a failure to provide religious services in prisons might be a breach of Article 9. However, these rights will be restricted by considerations of reasonableness: facilities for every type of religious worship do not have to be provided in every institution. It is noteworthy that, in the United States, the Supreme Court has held that the fact that prison policies had the effect of preventing inmates from attending religious services was reasonably related to legitimate penological interests and did not, therefore, violate the inmates' right to religious freedom.[285] **14.86**

---

277 (1994) 76-A DR 90, EComm HR.
278 (1999) 7 BHRC 375; for a discussion of the case see para 14.06 above.
279 Ibid.
280 Public Order Act 1986, s 4A.
281 Ibid, s 4.
282 Ibid, s 17.
283 See para 14.18 above.
284 See para 5.84 above.
285 See *O'Lone v Estate of Shabazz* (1987) 482 US 342 (however, the decision was by a 5:4 majority and turned on the restricted scope of constitutional review in prisoner cases, cf *Bell v Wolfish* (1979) 441 US 520, 562).

Appendix 1: The Canadian Charter of Rights

(1) Scope of the Right

14.87 Section 2(a) of the Charter provides that:

> Everyone has the following fundamental freedoms:
> (a) freedom of conscience and religion . . .

This right cannot apply to a corporation because it has no conscience or religion. However, a corporation can rely on section 2 as a defence to a criminal charge under a law which affects the freedom of religion of individuals as well as corporations.[286]

14.88 The reference to 'conscience' in section 2 means that it is intended to protect non-religious systems of belief and morality.[287] But there are limits to what is properly described as a matter of 'conscience'. Thus, the question of whether there should be public access to videotapes of children or coerced pornography does not raise issues of freedom of conscience.[288]

14.89 The meaning of 'freedom of religion' was examined by Dickson J in *Big M Drug Mart*:[289]

> A truly free society is one which can accommodate a wide variety of beliefs, diversity of tastes and pursuits, customs and codes of conduct. . . . The essence of the concept of freedom of religion is the right to entertain such religious beliefs as a person chooses, the right to declare religious beliefs openly and without fear of hindrance or reprisal, and the right to manifest belief by worship and practice or by teaching and dissemination. But the concept means more than that.
>
> . . . Freedom in a broad sense embraces both the absence of coercion and constraint, and the right to manifest beliefs and practices. Freedom means that, subject to such limitations as are necessary to protect public safety, order, health, or morals or the fundamental rights and freedoms of others, no one is to be forced to act in a way contrary to his beliefs or his conscience.[290]

Freedom of religion under the Charter requires the Government to refrain from coercion to impose religious beliefs or practices for a sectarian purpose. In addition, the Charter protects both religious beliefs and the manifestation of them in worship, practice and teaching or dissemination.

14.90 However, the scope of freedom of religion does not include a *prima facie* privilege for religious communications. The Ontario Court of Appeal in *Church of Scientology et al v R*[291] found that any such 'priest and penitent' privilege may be afforded on a case-by-case basis, and constitutes an exception to the common law rule that all relevant evidence is admissible.

---

[286] *R v Big M Food Mart Ltd* [1985] 1 SCR 295 (charge of selling goods on a Sunday in violation of the federal Lord's Day Act).

[287] See P W Hogg, *Constitutional Law of Canada* (4th edn, Carswell, 1997) 979, citing *R v Morgentaler (No 2)* [1988] 1 SCR 30, 1765-176 *per* Wilson J (regulation of abortion a denial of freedom of conscience, which is 'personal morality which is not founded in religion', and 'conscientious beliefs which are not religiously motivated').

[288] *French Estate v Ontario (A-G)* (1998) 157 DLR (4th) 144.

[289] [1985] 1 SCR 295.

[290] Ibid 353–4.

[291] (1987) 31 CCC (3d) 449.

In *R v Gruenke*[292] the crucial element of an expectation of confidentiality of communication was missing. The Court of Appeal found, on the basis of the statements and actions of the parties that the communications were more for the relief of the emotional stress of the accused than a religious or spiritual purpose; while the existence of a formal practice of 'confession' in the church could be a strong indication of an expectation of confidentiality, it was not necessarily a determinative consideration.

(2) Justifiable limitations

(a) Introduction

14.91 All Charter rights are subject to 'such reasonable limits as can be demonstrably justified in a free and democratic society'.[293] When determining the legitimacy of impugned legislation, it is necessary to look at its purpose and effects, either separately or in conjunction with the application of the section 1 test of 'reasonableness'. In *R v Big M Drug Mart*[294] the Supreme Court held that the test of constitutional validity of legislation is its purpose,[295] while its effects are to be considered only in the event that the purpose infringes the freedom of religion.[296] The test of proportionality[297] has been addressed in two areas: Sunday closing laws and religious education in public or denominational schools.

(b) Sunday closing

14.92 In *R v Big M Drug Mart*[298] the Supreme Court held that Sunday closing laws with an avowedly religious purpose were not considered reasonable limits on religious freedom; they constituted coercion.[299] Furthermore, even though the purpose of the Lord's Day Act violated the Charter, the Court went on to consider whether the means used to achieve the policy objective impaired as little as possible the right or freedom in question.

14.93 The test was elaborated in *R v Edward Books and Art Ltd*[300] where there were again convictions under provincial legislation for carrying on business on Sunday. Although the Supreme Court took the view that the legislation had the secular purpose of establishing a 'pause day', it nevertheless decided that an exemption granted to those who observed Saturday closures, which was limited to 'small' retailers, was a disproportionate restriction. The critical issue was whether the Act abridged the freedom of religion of Saturday

292 [1991] 3 SCR 263.

293 s 1.

294 [1985] 1 SCR 295.

295 The purpose of the legislation is to be determined by reference to four elements: the character and the larger objects of the Charter, the language chosen to articulate the right or freedom, the historical origins of the concepts enshrined and, where applicable, the meaning or purposes of the other specific rights and freedoms with which it is associated within the text of the Charter.

296 In that case, all the judges agreed that the purpose of the Lord's Day Act was to compel observance of the Christian Sabbath, and was therefore in itself contrary to the Charter freedom of religion.

297 For a discussion of the Canadian approach, see para 6.62ff above.

298 *R v Big M Drug Mart Ltd* [1985] 1 SCR 295; 18 DLR (4th) 321.

299 It was held that the Lord's Day Act could not be justified. Rejection of the argument that a day of rest was universally supported was based on the *ultra vires* nature of the secular purpose asserted by the argument, and recognition that such purpose was not primarily intended. Such a secular purpose would have been *ultra vires* the competence of federal Parliament for protection of religion.

300 [1986] 2 SCR 713.

observers as little as reasonably possible. Given the alternatives, it was held that the exemption for small Saturday-closing retailers was justified. It substantially reduced the negative impact of the Act, while avoiding the disruptive effect that a full 'sabbatarian exemption' (for all Saturday-observing retailers) would have on the scope and quality of the pause day objective. The legislation did not necessitate an enquiry into religion in order to establish qualification for the exemption; and it was reasonable for the legislature to protect employees over the interests of employers.

14.94 Following *Edward Books*, the Ontario Act was amended by removing the size limits on the exemption. When the amended Act was challenged in *Peel (Regional Municipality) v Great Atlantic and Pacific Company of Canada Ltd*,[301] the Court held that the opening up of the exemption to all Saturday observing retailers had eliminated the 'competitive pressures on non-Christians' that had been found to be an infringement in *Edward Books* and the Act was valid without reference to the limitation clause.[302]

(c) Religious education

14.95 The justification for limiting freedom of religion has also been addressed in education cases. In *Zylberberg v Sudbury Board of Education*[303] the Court of Appeal considered a provincial legislation requiring daily religious observances; however, participation by students was not mandatory. Even though it was wide enough to allow non-Christian prayers and readings, the regulation was unconstitutional because it authorised a school board to prescribe only Christian 'religious exercises'.

14.96 In *Canadian Civil Liberties Association v Ontario*[304] provincial legislation compelling a public school provide two periods per week of 'religious education' was also struck down. On the basis of the legislative history of the regulation and the curricula that were offered, the Court of Appeal concluded that the purpose of the regulation was the indoctrination of Christian belief, rather than education about a variety of religions. The case followed *Zylberberg* in holding that the regulation imposed the views of the majority on all school children, in spite of an exemption provision.

14.97 The provincial authorities may be required by section 2(a) of the Charter to permit children to be educated outside the secular school system. This conclusion is supported by the reasoning in *R v Jones*[305] where it was held that the provincial requirement of an application for approval of a private school or a certificate to teach at home did not violate section 2(a).

14.98 The question of state funding for denominational schools was considered in *Adler*.[306] Parents challenged the absence of public funding on the grounds that it violated their rights to freedom of religion and equality under the Charter. Their claim failed, because section 93(1) of the Constitution Act provided a 'comprehensive code' of denominational school rights and could not be further extended under section 2(a).

---

[301] (1991) 78 DLR (4th) 333.

[302] See also *London Drugs Ltd v Red Deer (City)* (1988) 52 DLR (4th) 203 and *R v Westfair Foods Ltd* (1989) 65 DLR (4th) 56 regarding Sunday closing laws and sabbatarian exemptions.

[303] (1988) 52 DLR (4th) 577.

[304] (1990) 71 OR (2d) 341.

[305] [1986] 2 SCR 284.

[306] *Adler v The Queen in right of Ontario; Elgersma v A-G for Ontario* [1996] 140 DLR (4th) 385.

(d) Other issues

The courts have also considered issues arising from the toleration of the religious practices of minority groups.[307] The case of *Young v Young*[308] concerned a Jehovah's witness who challenged an access order preventing him from discussing religion with his children. The Supreme Court concluded that the restriction should not remain. Three of the four majority judges took the view that the restriction was not in the best interests of the children. Only Sopinka J based his decision on section 2(a): holding that a restriction on religious communication was a breach unless it could be shown that it was needed to avoid 'substantial harm' to the children. **14.99**

In *B (R) v Children's Aid Society Metropolitan Toronto*[309] the Supreme Court rejected a claim by Jehovah's Witnesses that administering a blood transfusion to their child against their wishes contravened their freedom of religion. It was held that the interference with the rights of the parents was justified to protect the right to life and health of the child. **14.100**

Even if an activity is potentially damaging and offensive it may be protected by section 2(a). The case of *Ross v New Brunswick School District No 15*[310] concerned a teacher who publicly disseminated the view that Christian civilization was being destroyed by a Jewish conspiracy. The Supreme Court held that his dismissal from a teaching position was a breach of section 2(a) but could be justified under section 1. However, section 1 did not justify an order that he would be dismissed from a non-teaching position if he continued with anti-semitic activity. **14.101**

Ontario legislation providing for school holidays at Christmas and Easter but not during Muslim holy days did not infringe rights under section 2(a).[311] The regulation did not create school holidays for religious purposes. It also seems that there is no constitutional obligation on the state to fund religious schools.[312] However, a challenge to school worship succeeded on the ground that social pressures coerced children of religious minorities into conforming with majority religious practices.[313] **14.102**

Appendix 2: The New Zealand Bill of Rights Act

The New Zealand Bill of Rights Act 1990 provides: **14.103**

> 13. **Freedom of thought, conscience, and religion**—Everyone has the right to freedom

---

[307] Pre-Charter cases provide a few examples of practices that have a religious compulsion for a minority religion. See *Donald v Hamilton Board of Education* [1945] OR 518, CA, in which Jehovah's Witnesses refused to salute the flag or sing the anthem; *Saumur v City of Quebec* [1953] 2 SCR 299, in which Jehovah's Witnesses were held exempt from municipal street bylaw; *R v Harrold* (1971) 19 DLR (3d) 471, in which Hare Krishnas were bound by municipal anti-noise bylaw.

[308] [1993] 4 SCR 3; see also *P (D) v S (C)* [1993] 4 SCR 141 (prohibition on parent indoctrinating a child with Jehovah's Witness religion justified).

[309] [1995] 1 SCR 315.

[310] [1996] 1 SCR 825.

[311] *Islamic Schools Federation of Ontario v Ottawa Board of Education* (1997) 145 DLR (4th) 659.

[312] *Bal v Ontario (A-G)* (1997) 151 DLR (4th) 761.

[313] *Zylberberg v Sudbury Board of Education* (1988) OR (2d) 641.

> of thought, conscience, religion, and belief, including the right to adopt and to hold opinions without interference.
>
> 15. **Manifestation of religion and belief**—Every person has the right to manifest that person's religion or belief in worship, observance, practice, or teaching, either individually or in community with others, and either in public or in private.

Freedom of conscience and religion have not been major isues in New Zealand.[313a] It has been held that these provisions do not impose any positive duty on the state to protect freedom of religion: the duty is limited to a negative one not to interfere unreasonably with the individual's right to religious freedom.[314]

14.104 The extent of the right under section 15 was considered in *Re J*.[315] In that case, a three-year-old child required a blood transfusion but his parents, who were Jehovah's Witnesses, refused to consent. High Court orders permitting a transfusion were challenged by the parents, *inter alia*, on the ground that they were contrary to the rights granted by section 15.[316] The Court of Appeal noted that the right to manifest religion and belief could not be an absolute one and drew attention to the conflict which arose between the rights of the parents under section 15 and the child's right to life.[317] The Court approached this conflict by considering the scope of the right under section 15 rather than by considering the issue of 'limitations' on rights under section 5:

> . . . we prefer to approach the potential conflicts of rights assured under the Bill of Rights Act on the basis that the rights are to be defined so as to be given effect compatibly. The scope of one right is not to be taken as so broad as to impinge upon and limit others.[318]

The Court was then able to:

> define the scope of the parental right under s 15 of the Bill of Rights Act to manifest their religion in practice so as to exclude doing or omitting anything likely to place at risk the life, health or welfare of their children.[319]

As a result, the making of an order, which allowed a blood transfusion in response to a threat to the life of a child, was not a breach of parental rights under section 15. The Court pointed out that the parents themselves enjoyed a personal right to refuse to undergo medical treatment under section 11 of the Bill of Rights Act.

313a See generally, P Rishworth, 'Coming Conflicts Over Freedom of Religion' in G Huscroft and P Rishworth (eds), *Rights and Freedoms* (Brookers, 1995).

314 See *Mendelsshon v A-G* (1999) 5 HRNZ 1.

315 *Re J (An Infant)* [1995] 3 NZLR 73; *Re J, B and B v Director-General of Social Welfare* [1996] 2 NZLR 134.

316 Relying on the decision of the Supreme Court of Canada in *B(R) v Children's Aid Society of Metropolitan Toronto* [1995] 1 SCR 315.

317 Under s 8 of the Act.

318 [1996] 2 NZLR 134, 146 line 32.

319 [1996] 2 NZLR 134, 146 line 40.

Appendix 3: Human Rights Cases in Other Jurisdictions

(1) Introduction

The protection of freedom of religion was an early feature of constitutional instruments. The earliest Commonwealth constitutions contained some protection in respect of freedom of religion.[320] There has been extensive consideration of 'religious freedom' issues in a number of jurisdictions outside the Commonwealth. **14.105**

The most important and developed body of case law is in the United States. The First Amendment to the United States Constitution provides that: **14.106**

> Congress shall make no law respecting an establishing of religion, or prohibiting the free exercise thereof . . .

This has two elements : the so-called 'establishment' and 'free exercise' clauses which frequently overlap but have often been in conflict.[321] The 'establishment' clause has few equivalents in other human rights instruments.[322]

The 'free exercise' clause gives special protection to the exercise of religion.[323] The case law is not wholly consistent[324] but it is clear that non-theistic beliefs can qualify.[325] The claimant does not have to be a member of an organised religion or sect;[326] and once a belief is found to be religious, it does not have to be 'acceptable, logical, consistent or comprehensible'.[327] On the other hand, the free exercise clause does not protect personal standards of matters of conduct[328] or, apparently, a belief system which amounts to a revolutionary political organisation.[329] **14.107**

The question of whether laws of general application interfere with the exercise of religion **14.108**

---

320 See generally, N Jayawickrama, 'The Bill of Rights', in R Wacks (ed), *Human Rights in Hong Kong* (Oxford University Press, 1992) 39–40.

321 See generally, L Tribe, *American Constitutional Law* (2nd edn, Freedom Press, 1988) 1157–1189.

322 Its purpose has been described as maintaining Jefferson's concept of the 'wall of separation between Church and State': see eg *Everson v Board of Education for the Township of Ewing* (1947) 330 US 1.

323 *Thomas v Review Board* (1981) 450 US 707, 173.

324 See generally, Tribe (n 321 above), §14–6, 1179ff; for a Table of 'Free Exercise' cases decided for and against the individual, see H J Abraham and B A Perry, *Freedom and the Court* (7th edn, Oxford University Press, 1998) Tables 6.1 and 6.2.

325 *United States v Seeger* (1965) 380 US 163 (requirement for conscientious objection of belief in relation to a Supreme Being included any sincere belief that occupied 'a place in the life of its possessor parallel to that filled by the orthodox belief in God of one who clearly qualifies for the exemption'); see also *Welsh v United States* (1970) 398 US 333 (religious opposition to war included someone whose deeply held moral, ethical or religious beliefs would give them no rest or peace if they became an instrument of war).

326 *Frazee v Illinois Department of Employment Security* (1989) 489 US 829.

327 *Thomas v Review Board of Indiana Employment Security Divison* (1981) 450 US 707, 714.

328 *Wisconsin v Yoder* (1972) 406 US 205, 216.

329 *Africa v Pennsylvania* (1981) 662 F 2d 1025 (3rd Circ); *Theriault v Carlson* (1974) 495 F 2d 390 (5th Circ).

has been a source of continuing difficulty.[330] In the nineteenth century it was held that, in such cases, there was no interference with 'free exercise'. It was said that although religious beliefs were protected absolutely, religious practices only received qualified protection.[331] However, where an individual is required to engage in conduct which violates his religious beliefs he will have First Amendment protection.[332] The Supreme Court then developed a two stage test when considering whether or not laws of general application violate the free exercise clause.[333] The questions to be asked are:

- did the law impose a significant burden on the free exercise of religion? if so
- could this burden be justified on the basis that comprehensive coverage was essential to achieve an overriding or compelling government interest? (the so called 'strict scrutiny' test).

This meant that, for example, the state had to make unemployment benefit available to a Seventh Day Adventist who, for religious reasons, refused to work on Saturdays.[334] Nevertheless, exemptions from such general laws were rarely granted.[335] More recently, the Supreme Court has refused to apply the strict scrutiny test at all[336] and it is possible that laws of general application will not be a violation of the free exercise clause if their interference with religion is only 'incidental'.

(2) Australia

14.109 Section 116 of the Commonwealth Constitution provides that:[337]

> The Commonwealth shall not make any law for establishing any religion, or for imposing any religious observance, or for prohibiting the free exercise of any religion, and no religious test shall be required as a qualification for any office or public trust under the Commonwealth.[338]

[330] For a general discussion in the context of Art 9, see S Stavros, 'Freedom of Religion and Claims for Exemption from Generally Applicable, Neutral Laws: Lessons from Across the Pond?' [1997] EHRLR 607.

[331] *Reynolds v United States* (1878) 98 US 145 (statutory ban on polygamy applied to a person whose religious beliefs required him to take more than one wife upheld).

[332] See eg *West Virginia State Board of Education v Barnette* (1943) 319 US 624 (Jehovah's Witness successfully challenged a law requiring him to salute the flag).

[333] *Sherbert v Verner* (n 333 above); *Wisconsin v Yoder* (1972) 406 US 205 and see generally Tribe (n 321, above) §14.7, 1193ff.

[334] *Sherbert v Verner* (1963) 374 US 398; see also *Hobbie v Unemployment Appeals Commission* (1987) 107 S Ct 1046 (same result in relation to recent convert); contrast the Convention cases, para 14.50 above.

[335] See eg *United States v Lee* (1982) 455 US 252 (refusal to exempt Amish employers from social security taxes); *Goldman v Weinberger* (1986) 106 S Ct 1310 (refusal to allow an Orthodox Jew in the military to wear a yarmulke).

[336] *Lyng v Northwest Indian Cemetry Protection Association* (1988) 485 US 439; *Employment Division, Department of Human Resources of Oregon v Smith* (1990) 494 US 872 (members of Native American Church dismissed for using peyote, which was taken for sacramental purposes, free exercise claims rejected 5–4); for the consequences of these decisions see L Tribe, *American Constitutional Law* (3rd edn, Foundation Press, 2000) §5–16, 947.

[337–338] See generally, P Hanks, *Constitutional Law in Australia* (2nd edn, Butterworths, 1996) 536–540 and G Williams, *Human Rights Under the Australian Constitution* (Oxford University Press, 1999) 110–119.

This section is concerned with both the toleration of all religions and the toleration of the absence of religion.[339] The following have been held to be indicia of religion: a collection of ideas involving belief in the supernatural; ideas relating to the individual's nature and place in the universe; ideas prescribing a code of conduct of practices having supernatural significance; and the adherents to those ideas constituting an identifiable group or groups. The number of adherents was irrelevant, as were the financial motives of the adherents.[340]

The anti-establishment clause does not prohibit the federal Government from providing financial assistance to schools operated by religious organisations on the same basis as assistance is provided to other schools.[341] A law would establish religion only if its express and single purpose was to do so; religion could not be established incidental to some other purpose. Further, while section 116 prohibits the Government from constituting a particular religion or religious body as a state religion or state body, it does not prevent the Government from supporting religion generally.[342] A person who had religious objections to military service is not allowed to rely on section 116.[343] **14.110**

The freedom of religion in section 116 is qualified by public interest. In *Adelaide Company of Jehovah's Witnesses v Commonwealth*[344] a Jehovah's Witness organisation was declared to be an organisation prejudicial to national security and to the efficient prosecution of the Second World War, and its property was seized. The Government succeeded in justifying its actions on the basis that the organisation publicly discouraged its members from participating in the government's defence efforts. As stated by the High Court in *Church of New Faith v Commissioner of Pay-Roll Tax (Victoria)*:[345] **14.111**

> The freedom to act in accordance with one's religious beliefs is not as inviolate as the freedom to believe . . . Conduct in which a person engages in giving effect to his faith in the supernatural is religious, but it is excluded from the area of legal immunity marked out by the concept of religion if it offends against the ordinary laws, i.e. if it offends against laws which do not discriminate against religion generally or against particular religions or against conduct of a kind which is characteristic only of a religion.

In *Grace Bible Church v Reedman*[346] the South Australian Supreme Court held that the South Australian Parliament was not constrained, in the exercise of its legislative powers, by a common law right of religious freedom.

(3) Bermuda

By section 8, the Constitution of Bermuda provides for freedom of conscience, which is said to include freedom of thought and religion. The appellant in *Attride-Stirling v A-G*[347] had conscientious objections to military service. A tribunal concluded that the role of the **14.112**

---

339 *Adelaide Company of Jehovah's Witnesses v Commonwealth* (1943) 67 CLR 116.

340 *Church of New Faith v Commissioner of Pay-Roll Tax (Vic)* (1983) 154 CLR 120.

341 *A-G (Victoria); Ex rel Black v Commonwealth* (1981) 146 CLR 559 (cf Murphy J's dissent, based on *Everson v Board of Education for the Township of Ewing* (1947) 330 US 1.

342 *Ex rel Black* (n 341 above).

343 *Krygger v Williams* (1912) 15 CLR 366; cf *Judd v McKeon* (1926) 38 CLR 380 (religious duty to abstain from voting would be a sufficient reason to refuse to vote).

344 (1943) 67 CLR 116.

345 (1983) 154 CLR 120, 135–6.

346 (1984) 54 ALR 571.

347 [1995] 1 LRC 234.

Bermuda Regiment was mainly to assist the police in civil disorder in times of national emergency such as hurricanes, and that assistance in external defence was a minor role which was unlikely to be exercised in the appellant's lifetime. The appellant was therefore recommended for a non-combatant role. The Court of Appeal of Bermuda allowed the appellant's appeal, noting that because the relevant legislation exempted only those who genuinely objected to being required to do combatant duty, it hindered the freedom of conscience of those whose objection extended to serving in a military organisation in any capacity whatsoever. Furthermore, to force conscientious objectors to serve as members of a military organisation could not be regarded as reasonably required in the interests of defence, public safety or public order as a constitutionally permitted restriction. The Government itself had conceded that the effect on defence would be small.

(4) Human Rights Committee

14.113 Article 18 of the International Covenant on Civil and Political Rights provides for freedom of thought, conscience and religion.[348] The Human Rights Committee has suggested that Article 18 should be broadly construed.[349] Although it is not confined to established religions, it does not extend to a belief consisting primarily in the worship of a narcotic drug.[350] The conviction of a person for involvement in the organisation of a banned fascist party violated his right to profess political beliefs under this Article;[351] but was justifiable under Article 18(3). It is now established that conscientious objection to military service is protected by Article 18.[352] Worship covers 'ritual and ceremonial acts giving direct expression to belief as well as various practices integral to such acts'.[353]

(5) India

14.114 The freedom of religion is dealt with in four Articles of the Indian Constitution. Article 25 provides:

> (1) Subject to public order, morality and health and to the other provisions of this Part, all persons are equally entitled to freedom of conscience and the right freely to profess, practice and propagate religion.
>
> (2) Nothing in this article shall affect the operation of any existing law or prevent the State from making any law—
>
> (a) regulating or restricting any economic, financial, political or other secular activity which may be associated with any religious practice;
>
> (b) providing for social welfare and reform or the throwing open of Hindu religious institutions of a public character to all classes and sections of Hindus.

There are two 'Explanations' to this Article:

> Explanation I. The wearing and carrying of *kirpans* shall be deemed to be included in the profession of the Sikh religion.
>
> Explanation II. In sub-clause (b) of clause (2), the reference to Hindus shall be construed as

[348] See App J in Vol 2.

[349] General Comment 22, UN Doc No A/48/40, Annex VI (1983), para 2.

[350] *M A D, W A T and J-A Y T v Canada* (570/1993) UNHRC.

[351] *M A v Italy* (117/1981)UNHRC

[352] See *J P v Canada* (446/1991) UNHRC; *J and K v Netherlands* (483/1991) UNHRC; General Comment 22, para 11.

[353] General Comment 22, para 4.

including a reference to persons professing the Sikh, Jaina or Buddhist religion, and the reference to Hindu religious institutions shall be construed accordingly.

Article 26 provides that:

Subject to public order, morality and health, every religious denomination or any section thereof shall have the right—
(a) to establish and maintain institutions for religious and charitable purposes;
(b) to manage its own affairs in matters of religion;
(c) to own and acquire movable and immovable property; and
(d) to administer such property in accordance with law.

Article 27 provides that—

No person shall be compelled to pay any taxes, the proceeds of which are specifically appropriated in payment of expenses for the promotion or maintenance of any particular religion or religious denomination.

Article 28 provides that—

(1) No religious instruction shall be provided in any educational institution wholly maintained out of State funds.

(2) Nothing in clause (1) shall apply to any educational institution which is administered by the State but has been established under any endowment or trust which requires that religious instruction shall be imparted in such institution.

(3) No person attending any educational institution recognised by the State or receiving aid out of State funds shall be required to take part in any religious instruction that may be imparted in such institution or to attend any religious worship that may be conducted in such institution or in any premises attached thereto unless such person or, if such person is a minor, his guardian has given his consent thereto.[354]

The term 'denomination' in Article 26 has been defined to mean 'a collection of individuals classed together under the same name; a religious sect or body having a common faith and organisation and designated by a distinctive name'.[355] Article 26 contemplates not only a denomination, but also a section thereof.[356] **14.115**

Freedom of religion includes the freedom to practise rituals and ceremonies which are 'integral parts' of a religion.[357] In deciding whether a particular practice is an 'integral part' of a religion, the test is whether it is regarded as such by the adherents to the religion.[358] Thus, the right to elect members of a Committee for the administration of temple property is not a matter of religion for the Sikhs;[359] marrying a second wife during the lifetime of the first is not a integral part of the Hindu or Muslim religion;[360] and the management of an institution to promote international understanding, as distinguished from the propagation of any religious doctrine, is not a matter of religion, but may be a secular activity associated with religion.[361] **14.116**

[354] See generally, H M Seervai, *Constitutional Law of India* (4th edn, N M Tripathi Ltd, 1991) Chap XII.
[355] *Commr HRE v Lakshmindra* (1954) SCR 1005.
[356] Ibid.
[357] *Ramanuja v State of TN* 1972 SC 1586.
[358] *Govindlalji v State of Rajasthan* A1963 SC 1638, 1660.
[359] *Sarup v State of Punjab* A 1959 SC 860, 866.
[360] *Ramprasad v State of UP* A 1957 All 411; *Badruddin v Aisha* (1957) ALJ 300.
[361] *Sarwar v Addl Judge* A 1983 All 252.

14.117 There are special rules relating to religious processions. Once a community has established its right to take out a religious procession, that right cannot be interfered with on the ground that it offends against the sentiments of another community.[362] Procession music, as such, cannot operate as a nuisance.[363] The state cannot establish a particular religion, nor can it identify itself with, or favour any particular religion.[364]

14.118 Article 28 prohibits religious instruction at an educational institution wholly maintained out of state funds. That prohibition has been interpreted as prohibiting religious education, but not moral education dissociated from any denominational doctrines.[365] Academic study of the teaching and philosophy of any great saint of India and its impact on Indian and world civilisations cannot be considered as 'religious' instruction.[366]

14.119 The freedom of religion of one person cannot encroach upon a similar freedom of another. The punishment of forcible or fraudulent conversion therefore does not breach the right.[367] The right is also subject to public interest, so a person who deliberately outraged the religious feelings of a class of people could not shelter under the right.[368]

(6) Ireland

14.120 Article 44 of the Irish Constitution provides that:

> 1. The State acknowledges that the homage of public worship is due to almighty God. It shall hold His Name in reverence, and shall respect and honour religion.
>
> 2. 1. Freedom of conscience and the free profession and practice of religion are, subject to public order and morality, guaranteed to every citizen.
>   2. The State guarantees not to endow any religion.
>   3. The State shall not impose any disabilities or make any discrimination on the ground of religious profession, belief or status.
>   4. Legislation providing State aid for schools shall not discriminate between schools under the management of different religious denominations, nor be such as to affect prejudicially the right of any child to attend a school receiving public money without intending religious instruction at that school.
>   5. Every religious denomination shall have the right to manage its own affairs, own acquire and administer property, movable and immovable, and maintain institutions for religious or charitable purposes.
>   6. The property of any religious denomination or any educational institution shall not be diverted save for necessary works of public utility and on payment of compensation.[369]

14.121 The phrase 'freedom of conscience' does not permit a person to use contraception in accordance with their conscience. In *McGee v Attorney-General*,[370] FitzGerald CJ stated that:

---

[362] *Gulam v State of UP* A 1981 SC 2198.
[363] *Chandu v Nihalchand* A 1950 Bom 193 (para 3) Chagla, CJ.
[364] *Bommai v Union of India* 1994 SC 1918.
[365] *Nambudripad v State of Madras* A 1954 Mad 335.
[366] *D A V College v State of Punjab (II)* A 1971 SC 1737.
[367] *Stainislaus v State* A 1975 MP 163 (166).
[368] *Ramji Lal v State of UP* 1957 SC 620.
[369] See generally, J M Kelly, *The Irish Constitution* (3rd edn, Butterworths, 1994)1092–1112.
[370] [1974] IR 284.

> the freedom of conscience [in Article 44.2.1] relates to the choice and profession of a religion, and to it alone; . . . Because a person feels free, or even obliged, in conscience to pursue some popular activity which is not in itself a religious practice, it does not follow that such activity is guaranteed protection . . . What the Article guarantees is the right not to be compelled or coerced into living in a way which is contrary to one's conscience and, in the context of the Article, that means contrary to one's conscience so far as the exercise, practice or profession of religion is concerned.

Article 44.2.2 provides that 'the State guarantees not to endow any religion'. The word 'endow' has been interpreted to require enrichment with property, or to provide a permanent income.[371] It should be noted that Articles 42.4 and 44.2.4(4) provide that the state can finance educational activities of religious bodies, provided there is no discrimination on grounds of religious profession, belief or status. **14.122**

The prohibition of religious discrimination did not prevent a landlord from refusing to consent to the assignment by a tenant of the tenant's interest to a Jewish assignee.[372] Such action was viewed by the court as being motivated by race rather than religion. In *Quinn's Supermarket v AG*,[373] delegated legislation restricted opening hours for Dublin meat shops on weekdays, but exempted kosher butchers. The plaintiff was prosecuted for breaching the legislation, and he argued that the legislation was unconstitutional because it discriminated in favour of kosher shops. The Supreme Court invalidated the legislation. Although in principle, differential treatment for one religion could be permitted (and may even be required) where uniform treatment would inhibit the free exercise of a particular religion, the differential treatment was disproportionate in that it applied to all weekdays, and not merely Saturdays. **14.123**

(7) Singapore

The appellants in *Chan Hiang Leng Colin v Public Prosecutor*[374] were convicted for possession of Jehovah's Witnesses literature. All such literature had been banned, and the Jehovah's Witnesses society de-registered, because they discouraged military service. The appellants failed in their claim that their rights to freedom of religion had been breached. The High Court of Singapore noted that religious beliefs must conform with the general law relating to public order and social protection and, where the state perceives the possibility of public disorder, it need not be shown that there is a clear and immediate threat. It was not for the court to substitute its view as to whether the Jehovah's Witnesses or the banned literature were a threat to national security. **14.124**

The Court of Appeal in that case also confirmed that the appellants' right to freedom of religion had not been breached.[375] The Court stated that the right to practise, profess, and propagate the beliefs of Jehovah's Witnesses was not interfered with. The ban only rendered unlawful the practise of Jehovah's Witnesses by resort to the prohibited publication, or through membership of the Congregation. **14.125**

---

[371] *McGrath and O'Ruairc v Trustees of Monmouth College* [1979] ILRM 166.

[372] *Schlegel v Corcoran and Gross* [1942] IR 19.

[373] [1972] IR 1.

[374] [1994] 3 SLR 662.

[375] [1997] 1 LRC 107.

(8) South Africa

14.126 Section 14(1) of the interim South African Constitution provided that:

> Every person shall have the right to freedom of conscience, religion, thought, belief and opinion, which shall include academic freedom in institutions of higher learning.

The Constitutional Court considered section 14 in *S v Lawrence; S v Negal; S v Solberg*,[376] a case which concerned, *inter alia*, the prohibition on the sale of wine by grocery stores on 'closed days'. 'Closed days' were statutorily defined as Sundays, Good Friday, and Christmas Day. A majority of the Court held that the prohibition was a breach of religion, but a differently constituted majority upheld the legislation as justified under the general limitations clause, based on the Government's interest in reducing liquor consumption. As regards breach, the majority held that explicit state endorsement of one religion over others constituted indirect coercion of non-adherents. The choice of 'closed days', which included Christian public holidays but not other public holidays gave a legislative endorsement to Christianity. The minority considered that while there may be circumstances in which endorsement of a religion would be directly or indirectly coercive, such coercion would need to be proved. In this case, the link between Christianity and the restriction against grocers selling wine on Sundays at a time when their shops were open for other business was too tenuous for the restriction to be characterised an infringement of religious freedom.

14.127 The case of *Prince v President of the Law Society, Cape of Good Hope*[376a] concerned a Rastafarian who had been refused admission to a professional body because of previous convictions for the possession of cannabis and his intention to continue to use cannabis for religious purposes. The court accepted that there was a limitation on the applicant's freedom to practise his religion but held that this was a justifiable limitation, concluding that:

> Balancing the right religious freedom against the evils which the legislature sought to combat through the enactment of [legislation criminalising the use of cannabis] the applicant's right to practise his religion must . . . be subordinate to the provisions of [the anti-drug legislation].[376b]

(9) Sri Lanka

14.128 Article 9 of the Sri Lankan Constitution provides that:

> The Republic of Sri Lanka shall give to Buddhism the foremost place and accordingly it shall be the duty of the State to protect and foster the Buddha Sasana while assuring to all religions the rights granted by Articles 10 and 14(1)(e).

Article 10 provides:

> Every person is entitled to freedom of thought, conscience and religion, including the freedom to have or to adopt a religion or belief of his choice.

Article 14(1)(e) provides that a citizen is entitled to:

---

[376] 1997 (4) SA 1176.
[376a] 1998 (8) BCLR 976.
[376b] Ibid 988I.

the freedom, either by himself or in association with others, and either in public or in private, to manifest his religion or belief in worship, observance, practice and teaching.

While Article 10 is an absolute freedom, Article 14(1)(e) may be subject to such restrictions as may be prescribed by law or emergency regulations in the interests of national security, public order and the protection of public health or morality or for the purpose of securing due recognition and respect for the rights and freedoms of others or of meeting the just requirements of the general welfare of a democratic society (Article 15(7)).[377] **14.129**

The Places and Objects of Worship Bill 1973 sought to prohibit the construction of conversion of any building for the purpose of being used as a place or object of public religious worship except under the authority of a licence issued by the Director of Cultural Affairs. It was held that every citizen has a fundamental right, individually or in community with others, to worship in a building either in private or public and to erect a building for this purpose or to erect a statue or other object or to convert any building for this purpose. The court decided, however, that the Bill was justified under the general limitations clause contained in Article 18(2) of the 1972 Constitution. **14.130**

The case of *Premalal Perera v Weerasuriya*[378] concerned the deduction of a day's salary from railway employees, as contributions to the National Security Fund. Employees could opt out of the scheme without incurring any penalties. An employee challenged the scheme, on the basis that the contributions would be used for violence, which was contrary to his Buddhist faith. Furthermore, by making employees part of the scheme unless they chose to opt out, he would be forced to make his pacifist opinions public, thereby exposing him to harassment. The Supreme Court accepted that the employee could not, in keeping with his faith, contribute to causes which could destroy life. However, there was no sanction attached to failure to make a contribution, and no evidence had been presented that the employee would be harassed for failing to do so. **14.131**

(10) Trinidad and Tobago

A Muslim schoolgirl who was not permitted to modify her school uniform to conform with her faith challenged that decision in *Sumayyah Mohamed (A Minor) v Lucia Moraine*.[379] The High Court stated that the Constitution only recognised pre-existing rights, and did not create new ones. The school would have been permitted to enforce its uniform regulations prior to the coming into force of the Constitution. Accordingly, the school's decision did not violate the applicants' constitutional right to freedom of religion. Further, the schoolgirl had not been discriminated against on the basis of her religious persuasion, contrary to the Education Act, as that prohibition applied to her faith in general rather than to aspects of her observance of that faith. **14.132**

[377] See generally; J Wickramaratne, *Fundamental Rights in Sri Lanka* (Navrang, 1996) Chap 3; S Sharvananda, *Fundamental Rights in Sri Lanka* (Arnold's International Printing House, 1993) Chap VII.

[378] (1985) 2 Sri L R 177.

[379] [1996] 3 LRC 475.

(11) Zimbabwe

14.133 The applicant in *Re Chikweche*[380] had not been permitted to take the oath of office to be legal practitioner because of his dreadlocks hairstyle. The Supreme Court of Zimbabwe directed that the applicant be permitted to take the oaths. The court considered the US and Canadian case law and concluded that Rastafarianism had the status of a religion and, in event freedom of conscience was intended to protect belief systems even if not religiously motivated. Dreadlocks were a symbolic expression of Rastafarian religious beliefs, and the role of the Court was not to consider the validity or attraction of religious beliefs, but simply their sincerity.

[380] 1995 (4) BCLR 533.

15

FREEDOM OF EXPRESSION

A. The Nature of the Right

15.01 Freedom of expression is often said to be essential to the operation of democracy.[1] It is sometimes claimed that freedom of expression establishes a market place of ideas[2] which promotes the search for truth;[3] or that free speech ensures individual development and self fulfilment[4] and is, for example, to be derived from the right to human dignity and to equality of concern and respect.[5] However, the most persuasive vindication of freedom of expression is that it secures the right of the citizen to participate in the democratic process.[6] Both the House of Lords[7] and the Supreme Court of Canada[8] have said that expression enjoys special protection on all three grounds.

---

[1] The philosophical underpinnings of the right have been much discussed. See E Barendt, *Freedom of Speech* (Clarendon Press, 1985); D Harris, M O'Boyle, and C Warbrick, *Law of the European Convention on Human Rights* (Butterworths, 1995) 373; F Schauer, *Free Speech: A Philosophical Enquiry* (Cambridge University Press, 1982).

[2] See eg the famous dissenting judgment of Holmes J in *Abrams v United States* 250 US 616 (1919) at 630; see para 15.344 below.

[3] See eg J Milton, 'Areopagitica: A Speech for Licensed Printing' in *Prose Writings* (Everyman, 1958); J S Mill, *On Liberty* (Cambridge University Press, 1989) Chap 2.

[4] Schauer (n 1 above) Chaps 4 and 5; and see the justification for freedom of expression recently reaffirmed by the European Court of Human Rights in *Zana v Turkey* (1997) 27 EHRR 667 para 51: see para 15.139 below.

[5] R Dworkin, *Taking Rights Seriously* (Duckworth, 1977) Chap 12.

[6] See eg Brandeis J in *Whitney v California* (1927) 274 US 357, 375; see para 15.344 below.

[7] *R v Secretary of State for the Home Department, ex p Simms* [1999] 3 All ER 400, 408 *per* Lord Steyn: see para 15.07 below.

[8] *Irwin Toy v Quebec* [1989] 1 SCR 927, 976 *per* Dickson CJ, Lamer and Wilson J; *R v Keegstra* [1990] 3 SCR 697, 762, 763 *per* Dickson CJ.

One of the earliest and most well-known constitutional rights provisions is the First Amendment to the Constitution of the United States which provides that: 15.02

> Congress shall make no law . . . abridging the freedom of speech, or of the press . . .

This has given rise to one of the most highly developed areas of human rights jurisprudence in the world.[9] All of the major international human rights instruments protect the right to freedom of expression. Article 19 of the International Covenant on Civil and Political Rights, for example, states:

> (1) Everyone has the right to freedom of opinion and
> (2) Everyone shall have the right to freedom of expression; this right shall include freedom to seek, receive and impart information and ideas of all kinds, regardless of frontiers, either orally, in writing or in print, in the form of art, or through any other media of his choice.
> (3) The exercise of the right provided for in paragraph 2 of this Article carries with it special duties and responsibilities. It may, therefore, be subject to certain restrictions, but these shall only be
> (a) For respect of the rights or reputations of others;
> (b) For the protection of national security or of public order, or public health or morals.[10]

The major rights instruments and constitutions nevertheless treat the right of expression very differently. Some, like the First Amendment, express it in unqualified terms.[11] Typically, however, human rights instruments expressly define the limitations on freedom of expression.[12] Article 10 of the Convention defines the right in language which is weaker than that of Article 19 of the Covenant and circumscribes the right by provision of a full list of exceptions.[13] 15.03

The freedom of expression must be weighed against other public and private interests. Expressions of opinion and the publication of information in the mass media can violate other rights and freedoms and have a clear and direct impact on the political process. As a result, they are subject to close governmental scrutiny. Regulation of the press and broadcasting raises questions as to the extent of control that national authorities ought to maintain over the production and distribution of information, and the justifiable bases for such interference. 15.04

[9] For an overview, see Barendt (n 1 above); see generally, eg, L Tribe, *American Constitutional Law* (2nd edn, Foundation Press, 1988) Chap 12; and for a general discussion of the relationship between US and European approaches see I Loveland (ed), *Importing the First Amendment* (Hart Publishing, 1998); and see para 15.344ff below.

[10] See also Universal Declaration, Art 19; the text is reproduced at App H in Vol 2.

[11] For a fuller treatment, see eg Tribe (n 9 above) Chap 12.

[12] See eg the Inter-American Convention, Art 13(2), which excludes from protection prior censorship.

[13] See generally, A Lester, 'Freedom of Expression', in R St J Macdonald, F Matscher and H Petzold (eds), *The European System for the Protection of Human Rights* (Kluwer, 1983) 465–68.

15.05 The relationship between freedom of expression and the various limitations to which it may be subject is the subject of serious debate in a number of areas. Five areas can be highlighted:

Prior restraint: an issue of immediate importance concerns the circumstances in which injunctions will be granted by the courts to restrain publication of material which is allegedly defamatory, or otherwise in breach of private or public law. Such injunctions are severely restrictive of freedom of expression but their refusal may lead to irreparable damage to more important interests.

Reputation and privacy: the restriction of expression in order to protect reputation and privacy involves complex questions of the 'balancing' of competing rights particularly where public figures are involved.

Comment on court proceedings: the curtailment of expression in the interests of the administration of justice has been particularly controversial in England where there are strict rules concerning the reporting of pending proceedings.

Blasphemy, obscenity and hate speech: the censorship and regulation of media content on grounds of public morality is an area in which the balance has to be struck between freedom of expression and other important rights and values such as respect for religion and the protection of children. The regulation of 'hate speech' involves a particularly direct conflict of values and has been intensely disputed over recent decades.

Regulation of the media: government regulation of the mass media has also been a focus of 'freedom of expression' debates in a number of jurisdictions.[14] These issues have been given new impetus by the growth of new media such as the Internet which are outside the traditional regulatory regimes.[14a]

B. The Right in English Law Before the Human Rights Act

(1) Introduction

15.06 Freedom of speech, like other fundamental freedoms in the common law, has traditionally been considered to be merely residual in character.[15] Now, however, 'freedom of expression' is increasingly being recognised as a common law, or even

[14] For the position in the United States see E Barendt, 'The First Amendment and the Media' in I Loveland (ed), *Importing the First Amendment* (Hart Publishing 1998); and see generally, T Gibbons, *Regulating the Media* (2nd edn, Sweet 8 Maxwell, 1998).

[14a] Cf *Reno v ACLU* (1997) 2 BHRC 405 (provisions regulating publication of indecent material on the Internet struck down by Supreme Court).

[15] Dicey did not refer to freedom of expression in his discussion of personal liberties, describing it instead in the context of wrongs and libel: see A Dicey, *An Introduction to the Study of the Law of the Constitution* (8th edn, (Macmillan, 1915) Chap 6 'The Right to Freedom of Discussion'; and see also A Boyle, 'Freedom of Expression as a Public Interest in English Law' [1992] PL 574.

'quasi-constitutional' principle[16] to be invoked by the judiciary in the interpretation of statutes, to limit or balance other public interests[17] and as a basis for refusing some types of relief.[18] This shift in the common law has been influenced by judicial consideration of Article 10 of the European Convention, so that to some extent domestic law already conforms to the requirements of the Convention.[19]

15.07 The justifications for the importance of the right of freedom of expression have been summarised by Lord Steyn as follows:

> Freedom of expression is, of course, intrinsically important: it is value for its own sake. But it is well recognised that it is also instrumentally important. It serves a number of broad objectives. First it promotes the self-fulfilment of individuals in society. Secondly, in the famous words of Holmes J (echoing John Stuart Mill), 'the best test of truth is the power of the thought to get itself accepted in the competition of the market'[20] Thirdly, freedom of speech is the lifeblood of democracy. The free flow of information and ideas informs political debate. It is a safety valve: people are more ready to accept decisions that go against them if they can in principle seek to influence them. It acts as a brake on the abuse of power by public officials. It facilitates the exposure of errors in the governance and administration of justice of the country.[21]

15.08 Some types of speech in English law enjoy protection in positive terms. Debate and proceedings in Parliament are absolutely privileged against impeachment or question in any court or place out of Parliament.[22] Media and journalists reporting on parliamentary proceedings are subject to absolute privilege. Reports of court[23] proceedings are also privileged against actions in defamation, so long as their publication is fair, accurate and not actuated by malice. Parliamentary papers and their publishers also receive statutory protection.

---

[16] See E Barendt, 'Libel and Freedom of Expression in English Law' [1993] PL 449, 450; at 459-60, Barendt suggests that freedom of expression may be a positive right. Boyle (n 15, above), suggests that freedom of expression as a public interest exists in addition to the residual categorisation which remains an important sense in which 'rights' exist in English law; see also T Allan, *Law, Liberty and Justice* (Clarendon Press, 1993) Chap 6; and for a discussion of positive rights in English law, see para 1.33ff above.

[17] See in regard to defamation: *Derbyshire County Council v Times Newspapers Ltd* [1993] AC 534; in connection with contempt of court and the defence of public interest disclosure to actions for breach of confidence: *A-G v Guardian Newspapers Ltd (No 2)* [1990] 1 AC 109.

[18] The prior restraint approach is exemplified by the rule in *Bonnard v Perryman* [1891] 2 Ch 269 which precluded an interim injunction in a libel action, where the defendant raised a defence of justification or fair comment; see generally, P Milmo and W Rogers (eds), *Gatley on Libel and Slander* (9th edn, Sweet & Maxwell, 1998) Chap 25.

[19] See para 2.18ff above.

[20] *Abrams v United States* (1919) 250 US 616, 630 *per* Holmes J (dissenting); see para 15.334 below.

[21] *R v Secretary of State for the Home Department, ex p Simms* [1999] 3 WLR 328, 337.

[22] Bill of Rights 1689, Art 9.

[23] See the Defamation Act 1952, s 7, extending heads of qualified privilege; also the Contempt of Court Act 1981, ss 5 and 10.

15.09 English law also imposes statutory duties on certain public bodies to facilitate freedom of speech. For example, free postal communications and broadcast time must be made available prior to parliamentary or European Assembly elections,[24] educational institutions must ensure freedom of speech for members, students, employees and visiting speakers,[25] and individuals who make disclosures of information about their employers are given a limited degree of protection.[26] The Monopolies and Mergers Commission is also required to consider 'the need for accurate presentation of news and free expression of opinion' in reporting on the impact of a newspaper merger upon public interests.[27] Outside these clearly defined areas, the protection of freedom of expression has traditionally been limited to preventing prior restraint of damaging material.[28] In particular, reputation was given greater importance than the right to freedom of expression.[29]

15.10 However, in recent years freedom of expression has gradually assumed a more important positive role. In 1994 the position was summarised by Hoffmann LJ in the following terms:

> There are in the law reports many impressive and emphatic statements about the importance of freedom of speech and the press. But they are often followed by a paragraph which begins with the word 'nevertheless'. The judge then goes on to explain that there are other interests which have to be balanced against press freedom. And in deciding upon the importance of press freedom in the particular case, he is likely to distinguish between what he thinks deserves publication in the public interest and things in which the public are merely interested . . . But a freedom which is restricted to what judges think to be responsible or in the public interest is no freedom. Freedom means the right to publish things which government and judges, however well motivated, think should not be published. It means the right to say things which 'right-thinking people' regard as dangerous or irresponsible. This freedom is subject only to clearly defined exceptions as laid down by common law and statute . . . It cannot be too strongly emphasised that outside the established exceptions . . . there is no question of balancing freedom of speech against other interests. It is a trump card which always wins.[30]

---

[24] Representation of the People Act 1983, ss 95-97, as amended by the Representation of the People Act 1985.

[25] Education (No 2) Act 1986, s 43; E Barendt, 'Freedom of Speech in the Universities' [1987] PL 344 refers to these as 'bizarre' provisions.

[26] Public Interest Disclosure Act 1998 amending the Employment Rights Act 1996.

[27] Fair Trading Act, 1973, s 59(3).

[28] See para 15.24ff below.

[29] It is regarded by Blackstone as part of the 'right of personal security', the first of the 'absolute rights of man', *Blackstone's Commentaries* (17th edn, 1830) Book I, Chap 1.

[30] *R v Central Independent Television plc* [1994] Fam 192; it should, however, be noted that this comment was made in the context of proceedings to restrain the publication of information about children, an area in which the courts have often been ready to place severe restraints on freedom of speech, see para 15.68ff below.

The importance of protecting unpopular speech has been emphasised by Sedley LJ who observed:

> Free speech includes not only the inoffensive but the irritating, the contentious, the eccentric, the heretical, the unwelcome and the provocative provided it does not provoke violence. Freedom only to speak inoffensively is not worth having.[31]

The 'established exceptions' to the freedom of expression are, however, widely drawn and often not clearly defined. The following are the most important: **15.11**

- the law of *defamation* which restricts expression which damages individual reputations or provokes public disorder;
- the law of *contempt of court* which requires that certain expression be curtailed in the interests of the administration of justice;
- the law of *obscenity and indecency* which gives rise to censorship and the regulation of media content on grounds of public morality;
- the *criminal law* which also prohibits certain forms of expression as likely to provoke public disorder or racial hatred, be offensive to the Christian religion or incite persons to violence against the state;
- the law relating to the *regulation and censorship* of broadcast media, film and video;
- civil and criminal law restraints on speech which disclose Government secrets or confidential information, in the interests of *national security*.

In practice, the rules governing the lawfulness of a particular 'item of expression' can be extremely complex. It may be made by one of a number of public or private parties, through a variety of media and may be challenged under more than one head, each subject to various defences. The position is further confused because 'freedom of the press' is not treated consistently: sometimes the press are in the same position as ordinary 'publishers' and sometimes they are given special protection. As a result, the role which any positive principle of 'freedom of expression' will play in a decision is difficult to predict. **15.12**

(2) Prior restraint

(a) Introduction

The power of the courts to *prevent* publication is the most stringent form of restriction upon freedom of expression. Prior restraint has always been approached with particular caution; as Blackstone said: **15.13**

> The liberty of the press is indeed essential to the nature of a free state; but this consists in laying no *previous* restraints upon publications and not in freedom from

[31] *Redmond-Bate v DPP* (1999) 7 BHRC 375, 382, 383; and see *Silkin v Beaverbrook Newspapers Ltd* [1958] 1 WLR 743 in which Diplock J described freedom of speech as 'the right of the crank to say what he likes'.

> censure for criminal matter when published. Every freeman has an undoubted right to lay what sentiments he pleases before the public: to forbid this, is to destroy the freedom of the press; but if he publishes what is improper, mischievous or illegal, he must take the consequence of his own temerity.[32]

This statement of principle appears to have had a significant influence on the development of the law in the United States.[33] The basic principle and its affinity with the provisions of Article 10 of the Convention has been acknowledged in a number of cases. As Laws J put it:

> there is a general principle in our law that the expression of opinion and the conveyance of information will not be restrained by the courts save on pressing grounds. Freedom of expression is as much a sinew of the common law as it is of the European Convention . . .[34]

(b) Defamation cases

15.14 It has long been recognised that freedom of expression is an important consideration in determining whether an interim injunction ought to be granted to restrain the publication of material which is alleged to be defamatory. In such cases, an injunction will not be granted if the defendant asserts a defence of justification on grounds that the words complained of are *true*. The fundamental approach was described in *Bonnard v Perryman*:[35]

> The right of free speech is one which it is for the public interest that individuals should possess and, indeed, that they should exercise without impediment, so long as no wrongful act is done; and unless an alleged libel is untrue there is no wrong committed . . .

This principle has been affirmed in a large number of cases.[36] Provided that the defendant advances some evidence to support a proposed plea of justification, an injunction will be granted only in the extremely rare case in which the claimant can satisfy the court than the plea of justification is bound to fail.[37] Furthermore, the rule in *Bonnard v Perryman* applies, irrespective of motive or the manner in which publication is threatened. A court refused an injunction,

---

[32] *Blackstone's Commentaries*, (17th edn, 1830) Book IV, 151-2; quoted in *Holley v Smyth* [1998] 2 WLR 742, 751D-H.

[33] See *Schering Chemicals Ltd v Falkman Ltd* [1982] 1 QB 1, 17C-H; see generally, L Levy, *The Emergence of a Free Press* (Oxford University Press, 1985); and see also L Tribe, *American Constitutional Law* (2nd edn, Foundation Press, 1988), 785ff.

[34] *R v Advertising Standards Authority Ltd, ex p Vernons Organisation Ltd* [1992] 1 WLR 1289, 1293A.

[35] [1891] 2 Ch 269, 284.

[36] See eg *Fraser v Evans* [1969] 1 QB 349, 360; *Bestobell Paints v Bigg* [1975] FSR 421; *Crest Homes v Ascott* [1980] FSR 396; *Khasshoggi v IPC Magazines Ltd* [1986] 1 WLR 1412.

[37] See generally, P Milmo and W Rogers (eds), *Gatley on Libel and Slander* (9th edn, Sweet & Maxwell, 1998) para 25.6.

for example, even where a defendant sought to extract money from the plaintiffs on threat of publication of what he said were damaging but true allegations about them.[38]

(c) Breach of confidence and other claims

The rule in *Bonnard v Perryman* preventing prior restraint in defamation cases also extends to trade libel, injurious falsehood and related claims.[39] It does not, however, provide a defence against the imposition of interim injunctions sought on the basis of *other* causes of action. **15.15**

A claimant attempting to restrain the publication of material which he believes to be damaging will therefore often seek to do so on other grounds: conspiracy to injure, breach of copyright, trade mark infringement[40] and, most importantly, breach of confidence. A claim for an interlocutory injunction on the basis of an alleged conspiracy to injure was, for example, successful in *Gulf Oil (Great Britain) Ltd v Page*,[41] where the plaintiff obtained an injunction to restrain the defendant from displaying a defamatory airborne sign. **15.16**

Attempts to obtain an injunction on grounds which would avoid the *Bonnard v Perryman* defence may nevertheless be refused. The application for injunction in *Femis-Bank (Anguilla) Ltd v Lazar*[42] was unsuccessful on the basis that, whatever the cause of action, freedom of speech was an important factor to be taken into account in the exercise of the discretion of the court. Even though the rule in *Bonnard v Perryman* does not apply to trademark infringement or breach of copyright, the courts will not allow such a claim to be used as a 'vehicle' for what is, in essence, a claim for defamation.[43] In a claim for breach of a contract 'not to publish', demonstration by the claimant of a good arguable case will not be sufficient grounds for a grant of interim injunction: the court should be able to assess the relative strengths of the parties' cases.[44] **15.17**

The most important basis upon which a claimant may obtain 'prior restraint' of publication is that of a claim of *breach of confidence*. The rule in *Bonnard v Perryman* does not apply to prevent interim injunctions from being granted. Proceedings for confidential information are in a special category, because **15.18**

> if, pending the trial, the court allows publication, there is no point in having a trial since the cloak of confidentiality can never be restored. Confidential information is

[38] See *Holley v Smyth* [1998] QB 726.
[39] *Lord Brabourne v Hough* [1981] FSR 79, 85.
[40] *Gallup Organization v Gallup International*, 29 Nov1995.
[41] [1987] Ch 327.
[42] [1991] Ch 391.
[43] Cf *Service Corporation v Channel Four Television*, unreported, 12 May 1998, Lightman J.
[44] See *Cambridge Nutrition Ltd v British Broadcasting Corporation* [1990] 3 All ER 523.

> like an ice cube . . . Give it to the party who has no refrigerator or will not agree to keep it in one, and by the time of the trial you just have a pool of water.[45]

As a result, the claimant need show only an arguable claim and that the 'balance of convenience' is in favour of granting the order.[46]

15.19 The availability of interim injunctions to restrain breaches of confidence is a serious threat to freedom of expression.[47] The most important example of such restraint was in the *Spycatcher* litigation, in which the British Government sought to restrain the publication of a book by a former intelligence officer, Peter Wright. The book had been written in breach of the Official Secrets Act and of the duty of confidentiality of the author. In June 1986, a number of British newspapers published articles containing allegations made by Mr Wright concerning the Security Service which the British Government was seeking to restrain in court proceedings in Australia.[48] On 27 June 1986, the Attorney-General obtained *ex parte* injunctions to restrain further publication. On 11 July 1986 these injunctions were continued in modified form by Millett J. The injunctions were upheld by the Court of Appeal.

15.20 The application for an injunction before the Australian courts by the British Government was unsuccessful. On 11 July 1987, the book was published in the United States. As a result, after hearing a preliminary issue in July 1987, Sir Nicholas Browne-Wilkinson V-C discharged the interlocutory injunctions.[49] Although the Judge accepted that the 'ice cube' of the confidential information needed to be preserved, he took the view that:

> It has been put in the refrigerator, but the American publication is as though somebody had turned off the refrigerator . . .[50]

The Court of Appeal nevertheless allowed in part the Attorney-General's appeal and granted a modified interlocutory injunction. This injunction was upheld by the House of Lords on 30 July 1987 on the ground that there was an arguable case for the protection of an important public interest, namely the maintenance of the secrecy of the Security Service.[51] However, Lords Bridge and Oliver dissented; and Lord Bridge was particularly critical: [52]

---

[45] *Per* Sir John Donaldson MR in *A-G v Newspaper Publishing plc* [1988] Ch 333, quoted in *A-G v Guardian Newspapers Ltd (No 1)* [1987] 1 WLR 1248, 1259F-H.

[46] In accordance with the principles in *American Cyanamid Company v Ethicon Ltd* [1975] AC 396; however it must be possible to frame an interlocutory injunction in clear terms: cf *Times Newspapers Ltd v MGN Ltd* [1993] EMLR 442 in which an injunction was refused on this ground.

[47] Concerns in relation to this were one reason for the addition of s 12 of the Human Rights Act; see para 15.238ff below.

[48] Mr Wright was resident in Australia and was proposing to publish a book there.

[49] *A-G v Guardian Newspapers Ltd (No 1)* [1987] 1 WLR 1248.

[50] Ibid 1268B-C.

[51] Ibid.

[52] The majority comprised Lords Brandon, Templeman and Ackner.

> I have had confidence in the capacity of the common law to safeguard the fundamental freedoms essential to a free society including the right to freedom of speech which is specifically safeguarded by Article 10 of the Convention. My confidence is seriously undermined by your Lordships' decision . . . The maintenance of the ban, as more and more copies of the book *Spycatcher* enter this country and circulate here, will seem more and more ridiculous. If the Government are determined to fight to maintain the ban to the end, they will face inevitable condemnation and humiliation by the European Court of Human Rights in Strasbourg. Long before that they will have been condemned at the bar of public opinion in the free world.[53]

Lord Templeman took the view that the restraints imposed were necessary in accordance with Article 10 of the Convention.[54]

The newspapers applied to the European Court of Human Rights. In the *Observer and The Guardian v United Kingdom*[55] the Court accepted the argument of the Government that the injunctions had the legitimate aim of 'maintaining the authority of the judiciary' and safeguarding the operation of the security services. Nevertheless, the majority took the view that, the confidentiality of the material having been destroyed by its publication, there was no sufficient reason for the continuation of the injunction after 30 July 1987.[56] **15.21**

(d) Contempt proceedings

The position concerning prior restraint is different for contempt proceedings. The court has jurisdiction to grant an injunction to restrain the publication of any material which may constitute a 'criminal' contempt.[57] Although only the Attorney-General may institute proceedings for criminal contempt[58] it appears that anyone with a sufficiently proximate interest may also apply.[59] **15.22**

Because the prior restraint of a publication is a very serious interference with press freedom, an injunction on grounds of contempt will only be granted where the publication would, manifestly, be a contempt of court.[60] As a result, applications for injunction have been refused in a number of cases.[61] It is clear, however, that **15.23**

---

[53] At 1286C-H; when the case was heard before the Court of Human Rights, it held the injunction breached freedom of expression under Art 10: see *The Observer and The Guardian v United Kingdom* (1991) 14 EHRR 153.

[54] At 1296F-1299G.

[55] n 53 above.

[56] Ibid para 68.

[57] For the distinction between 'civil' and 'criminal' contempts see para 15.42 below.

[58] Contempt of Court Act 1981, s 7.

[59] See *Peacock v London Weekend Television* (1985) 150 JP 71 (Police Federation granted injunction to restrain TV programme on grounds that it would prejudice a pending inquest) and *Leary v BBC*, unreported, 29 Sep1989, CA; but see *Pickering v Liverpool Daily Post and Echo Newspapers plc* [1991] 2 AC 370, 425 where Lord Bridge expressed doubt on this point; see generally, *Arlidge, Eady and Smith on Contempt* (2nd edn, Sweet & Maxwell, 1999) paras 6-9–6-16.

[60] *A-G v British Broadcasting Corporation* [1981] AC 303, 311, 362.

[61] See eg *Schering Chemicals Ltd v Falkman Ltd* [1982] 1 QB 1, but an injunction was granted to restrain breach of confidence; *A-G v News Group Newspapers Ltd* (Botham libel case) [1987] QB 1.

an application to restrain a manifestly contemptuous publication will not be refused simply because the defendant seeks to justify. The position was summarised by Sir John Donaldson MR as follows:

> In practice, I think that the rule in *Bonnard v Perryman* will be decisive unless and until the strict liability rule is invoked. Once it is invoked it will prevail, because, in the form in which it survives in 1981, if strictly construed and applied, the balance must always come down on the side of protecting the right to justice.[62]

It was, however, emphasised that section 5 of the Contempt Act would protect general discussion of topics with which forthcoming trials were incidentally concerned.[63] The result of these matters is that a 'gagging writ' will only be effective after the action becomes 'active' and will not limit discussion on matters of general public interest.[64]

(3) Protection of reputation: defamation

(a) Introduction

15.24 The English law of defamation protects the reputation of every person from defamatory statements about him made to third parties without lawful justification. Although many defamation cases refer to the importance of freedom of expression, the common law has always placed great emphasis on the right to reputation. As the Court of Appeal said in *Kiam v Neill*:[65]

> The right to protection of the law against attacks on honour and reputation are as important in a democratic society as the right to freedom of the press. History discloses examples which show that undermining the reputation of a political opponent of an arbitrary domineering or oppressive regime can be one of the first weapons deployed by the despot.

The effect of this emphasis is that the common law provides no special protection or defence to the press: press publications are subject to the same rules of law as apply to publications by private individuals.[66]

(b) The nature of the claim

15.25 A statement is defamatory if it tends to lower the claimant in the estimation of right thinking members of society generally.[67] The statement does not have to

---

62 *A-G v News Group Newspapers Ltd* (n 61 above) 14.

63 Ibid 14–15.

64 See generally, N Lowe and B Sufrin, *Borrie and Lowe: The Law of Contempt* (3rd edn, Butterworths, 1996) 191–6; *Arlidge, Eady and Smith on Contempt* (n 59 above) para 6-1–6-27.

65 *The Times*, 29 Jul 1996; see also *Reynolds v Times Newspapers Ltd* [1999] 3 WLR 1010, 1023E-H (*per* Lord Nicholls).

66 See P Milmo and W Rogers (eds), *Gatley on Libel and Slander* (9th edn, Sweet & Maxwell, 1998) para 1.9.

67 *Per* Lord Atkin, *Sim v Stretch* (1936) 52 TLR 669; generally, *Gatley on Libel and Slander* (n 66 above) Chap 2.

have any actual effect on reputation: the law looks at its 'tendency'.[68] The court considers the 'natural and ordinary meaning' of the words used rather than the literal meaning: it can include any implication or inference which a reasonable reader would draw from the words.[68a] In addition, a statement may be defamatory on the basis of extrinsic facts known to some readers: this is known as an innuendo.[68b] The meaning of a particular statement and whether or not it is defamatory are matters for a jury[69] but the question of whether the words are 'capable' of being defamatory is decided by the judge.[70] The prominent role of the jury introduces a considerable degree of uncertainty: it is often difficult to predict with any accuracy whether a jury is likely to find particular words defamatory.

The law of defamation presumes that defamatory imputations are false[71] and that the person defamed is of good reputation. The claimant is not required to prove actual damage to reputation or any other loss. The burden of establishing the truth of the words used, or any other defences, is on the publisher of the words. This burden is, inevitably, a considerable restriction on freedom of expression. When a defamatory statement is published in permanent form, the tort of *libel* is committed, and: **15.26**

> the law presumes that *some* damage will flow in the ordinary course of things from the mere invasion of his absolute right to reputation.[72]

Defamation that is expressed orally or in a less than permanent form constitutes the tort of *slander*. Slander is, in general, only actionable at common law if actual damage can be proved. There are, however, a number of forms of slander which are actionable without proof of damage.[73] Once a cause of action in slander is established, damages are 'at large'. **15.27**

(c) Who can bring a defamation action?

An action for defamation can be brought by a natural person or by a company. A trading corporation can sue for damage to its trading reputation[74] and a **15.28**

---

68 See *Hough v London Express Newspapers Ltd* [1940] 2 KB 507, 515.

68a *Lewis v Daily Telegraph* [1964] AC 234, 258; *Jones v Skelton* [1963] 1 WLR 1362, 1370; *Gatley on Libel and Slander* (n 66 above) para 3.14ff. Note that an 'inferred' imputation is sometimes called a 'popular' or 'false' innuendo (*Lewis*, 280).

68b This is a 'true innuendo', see generally, *Gatley on Libel and Slander* (n 66 above) para 31.8ff.

69 There remains a right to trial by jury in libel actions under the Supreme Court Act 1981, s 69(1). This right may be lost if the case involves prolonged examination of documents or accounts: see *Aitken v Guardian Newspapers*, *The Times*, 21 May 1997.

70 See eg *Gillick v BBC* [1996] EMLR 267; and *Gatley on Libel and Slander* (n 66 above) para 30.2ff.

71 *Gatley on Libel and Slander* (n 66 above) para 11.3.

72 *Ratcliffe v Evans* [1892] 2 QB 524, 528.

73 These are: an imputation of a criminal offence punishable by imprisonment, an imputation of a contagious disease, an imputation of unchastity against a woman under the Slander of Women Act 1891, and words calculated to disparage a person in any office, calling, trade or business.

74 *Gatley on Libel and Slander* (n 66 above) para 2.16.

non-trading corporation can bring an action in respect of imputations which are damaging to its property or finances.[75] A trade union cannot, however, sue for libel because it is not a body corporate.[76]

15.29 It is now clear that a local government corporation cannot sue for libel. The point arose in *Derbyshire County Council v Times Newspapers*,[77] in which the Court of Appeal, placing considerable reliance on Article 10 of the Convention,[78] denied a local authority the right to sue for libel. This decision was upheld by the House of Lords on the basis of the common law, without any reliance upon the Convention. Lord Keith was of the view that it was:

> of the highest public importance that a democratically elected governmental body, or indeed any governmental body, should be open to uninhibited public criticism.[79]

As a result, he concluded that:

> not only is there no public interest favouring the right of organs of government whether central or local, to sue for libel, but . . . it is contrary to the public interest that they should have it. It is contrary to the public interest because to admit such actions would place an undesirable fetter on freedom of speech.[80]

This principle has been applied to governmental bodies[81] and to political parties.[82] It does not, however, extend to individually elected officials, public employees or members of political parties.

(d) Defences to an action for defamation

15.30 **Introduction.** The most important defences[83] to actions for defamation are 'justification' on grounds of truth, fair comment on a matter of public interest, absolute privilege and qualified privilege. The 1996 Defamation Act has also introduced a defence of an offer to make amends[84] where a defendant is prepared to pay damages assessed by a judge.

15.31 **Justification.** 'Justification' or proof of the substantial truth of a defamatory imputation is a complete defence. The defendant carries the burden of proving the truth of the defamatory imputations which the words bear:

---

[75] Ibid para 2.19.

[76] *Electrical, Electronic, Telecommunications and Plumbing Union v Times Newspapers Ltd* [1980] QB 585.

[77] [1992] QB 770, CA; [1993] AC 534, HL.

[78] See para 2.19 above.

[79] Ibid 547F–G.

[80] Ibid 549.

[81] *British Coal Corporation v NUM*, unreported, 28 Jun 1996.

[82] *Goldsmith v Bhoyrul* [1998] QB 459.

[83] See generally, P Milmo and W Rogers (eds), *Gatley on Libel and Slander* (9th edn, Sweet & Maxwell, 1998) Pt 2.

[84] See s 3(5); the defence of 'offer to make amends' replaces the statutory defence of unintentional defamation contained in the 1952 Act, s 4.

> When a plea of justification is pleaded, it involves the justification of every injurious imputation which a jury may think is to be found in the alleged libel.[85]

The operation of the defence of justification in the modern law of libel is highly technical. The following points should be noted:

- the claimant must set out the 'sting' of the libel on which he relies;[86]
- the claimant can 'pick and choose' from a publication containing more than one defamatory imputation, basing his claim on only some of the imputations;[87]
- the defendant must justify either the 'sting' relied on by the claimant or a 'lesser' defamatory meaning which he says the words bear;[88]
- if the claimant picks one defamatory imputation, the defendant cannot justify another separate and distinct imputation in the same publication;[89]
- if the claimant complains that the publication contains several defamatory imputations, the defence of justification does not fail only because the truth of every charge is not proved, *if* the untrue words 'do not materially injure the claimant's reputation' having regard to the remaining charges.[90]

The burden on a defendant is a high one. Uncertainty results from the fact that the jury determines the meaning of the words used and is obliged to find a single meaning.[91] The result is that a defendant who can prove the truth of almost everything in a long publication could still be successfully sued if the jury finds that the publication contains one defamatory imputation the truth of which the defendant cannot prove.

Fair comment. Another defence that may be established by the defendant to an action in defamation is that the words used were fair comment[92] on a matter of public interest.[93] There are three stages in proving fair comment. First, the defendant must show that the words used were 'comment', rather than assertions of fact. The test is 'how the words would be understood by an ordinary reader'.[94] In practice, the line between comment and factual assertion is difficult to draw.[95] **15.32**

---

[85] *Digby v Financial News* [1907] 1 KB 502.

[86] See *Lucas-Box v News Group Newspapers Ltd* [1986] 1 WLR 147, 151-152.

[87] *Cruise v Express Newspapers* [1999] 2 WLR 327.

[88] This must be specifically set out in the defence and is known as a 'Lucas-Box' meaning, see *Lucas-Box v News Group Newspapers Ltd* (n 86 above).

[89] *Cruise v Express Newspapers* (n 89 above); *Polly Peck (Holdings) plc v Trelford* [1986] QB 1000.

[90] Defamation Act 1952, s 5.

[91] See *Charleston v News Group Newspapers Ltd* [1995] 2 AC 65.

[92] The defence is, more accurately described as 'honest comment', *per* Lord Nicholls, *Reynolds v Times Newspapers Ltd* [1999] 3 WLR 1010, 1061A.

[93] 'Public interest' in this sense is not confined within narrow limits: see *London Artists Ltd v Littler* [1969] QB 375.

[94] *Slim v Daily Telegraph Ltd* [1968] 2 QB 157.

[95] See generally, *Gatley on Libel and Slander* (n 83 above) para 12.6ff.

Secondly, the facts on which the comment is based must be shown to be true.[96] The defence will not fail, however, solely for lack of proof of the truth of every allegation of fact, if the defendant can show that the expression of opinion is fair comment, having regard to the facts which are proved.[97] Thirdly, the defendant must show that the comment was 'fair'. This is the least onerous requirement because 'fair', in this context, simply means 'capable of being honestly held'. As Diplock J said to the jury in *Silkin v Beaverbrook Newspapers Ltd*:[98]

> do not apply the test of whether you agree with it. If juries did that, freedom of speech, the right of the crank to say what he likes, would go. Would a fair minded man holding strong views, obstinate views, prejudiced views, have been capable of making this comment? If the answer to that is yes then [the defence succeeds].

The defence of fair comment can be rebutted by proof that the defendant was actuated by malice.[99]

15.33 **Absolute privilege.** The public interest requires that individuals be permitted in certain circumstances to express themselves with complete freedom. Certain speech is therefore privileged, which may be absolute or qualified. Absolute privilege is a complete defence, no matter how damaging or defamatory the statements may be, precluding a court from any jurisdiction to hear an action in defamation. The most important heads of 'absolute privilege' are:

- Statements made by witnesses, advocates or judges in the course of litigation.[100] This privilege extends to witness statements,[101] court documents and to any statement made as part of the process of investigating crime.[102] It does not, however, extend to fabricating evidence.[102a]
- Statements made in the debates or proceedings in Parliament, and evidence given by witnesses to select committees.[103] The fact that proceedings in Parliament cannot be 'questioned' means that a party cannot rely, in an action, on anything said in Parliament.[104] A member of Parliament may, however, waive the privilege for the purposes of defamation proceedings.[105]

---

[96] See *Broadway Approvals Ltd v Odhams Press Ltd* [1964] 2 QB 683.
[97] Defamation Act 1952, s 6.
[98] [1958] 1 WLR 743.
[99] For malice, see para 15.37 below.
[100] *Munster v Lamb* (1883) 11 QBD 588, 607; see *Gatley on Libel and Slander* (n 83 above) para 13.3–13.14.
[101] *Watson v M'Ewan* [1905] AC 480.
[102] *Taylor v Director of the Serious Fraud Office* [1998] 1 WLR 1040.
[102a] *Docker v Chief Constable of West Midlands Police*, *The Times*, 1 Aug 2000 (HL).
[103] Bill of Rights 1688, Art 9.
[104] *Prebble v Television New Zealand* [1995] 1 AC 321.
[105] Defamation Act 1996, s 13(1); *Gatley on Libel and Slander* (n 83 above) para13.29–13.30; and see *Hamilton v Al-Fayed* [1999] 1 WLR 1569.

- Fair and accurate reports of court proceedings if they are published contemporaneously with the proceedings.[106]

The courts are cautious about extending the categories of absolute privilege,[107] but the categories are not closed.[108]

Qualified privilege. Words spoken in good faith on other occasions may also be subject to privilege, albeit of a qualified nature. There is now statutory provision for qualified privilege which protects the publication of reports or statements from across a wide range of subject matter,[109] so long as they are 'fair and accurate'.[110] These include fair and accurate reports of the proceedings of foreign legislatures, courts, public commission inquiries, public meetings and local authorities or local authority committees.[111] **15.34**

Qualified privilege protects expression at common law on the premise that there exists a legal, moral, or social duty on the person to communicate a statement, and a corresponding interest or duty on the person who receives the publication. It covers matters such as 'reply to attack'[112] and ordinary business communications. The categories of qualified privilege are not closed: they are no more than applications, in particular circumstances, of an underlying principle of public policy to the effect that both the maker and the recipient of the statement must have a 'duty or interest' in making or receiving it.[113] However: **15.35**

> The essence of this defence lies in the law's recognition of the need, in the public interest, for a particular recipient to receive frank and uninhibited communication of particular information from a particular source.[114]

In determining whether an occasion is subject to qualified privilege, the court has regard to all the circumstances.[115] The question in each case is whether the public was entitled to know the particular information: this 'duty interest' or 'right to know' test cannot be carried out in isolation from factors such as the nature,

[106] Defamation Act 1996, s 14: the privilege extends to reports of proceedings before the European Court of Justice, the European Court of Human Rights, and defined international criminal tribunals.
[107] *Royal Aquarium and Summer and Winter Garden Society Ltd v Parkinson* [1892] 1 QB 431, 451.
[108] See *Merricks v Nott-Bower* [1965] 1 QB 57, 73; and cf *Hasselblad (GB) Ltd v Orbinson* [1985] QB 475.
[109] See Defamation Act 1996, s 15 and Sch 1.
[110] For the case law on this phrase, see P Milmo and W Rogers (eds), *Gatley on Libel and Slander* (9th edn, Sweet & Maxwell, 1998) para 15.4.
[111] See Ibid Chap 15.
[112] *Adam v Ward* [1917] AC 309.
[113] Ibid 334.
[114] *Per* Lord Nicholls, *Reynolds v Times Newspapers Ltd* [1999] 3 WLR 1010, 1017F–G.
[115] *London Association for the Protection of Trade v Greenlands Ltd* [1916] 2 AC 15, 23.

status and source of the material and the circumstances of the publication[116] but there is no separate 'circumstantial test'.[117]

15.36 One important issue that arises is the extent to which qualified privilege protects media reports. Qualified privilege might apply because the media arguably have a duty to supply and the public have an interest in receiving information as to issues of contemporary importance. In *Reynolds v Times Newspapers Ltd*[118] the House of Lords rejected the argument that there should be a new category of qualified privilege for 'political information'[119] on the basis that such a privilege would not provide adequate protection for reputation and that it would be unsound in principle to distinguish 'political expression' from other matters of serious public concern. Lord Hobhouse commented that, to allow for such a privilege:

> would be handing to what are essentially commercial entities a power which would deprive the subjects of such publications of the protection against damaging misinformation. Such persons and the public are entitled to the disinterested and objective involvement of the law. It is for the publisher to establish to the satisfaction of the law that the publication was privileged.[120]

Nevertheless, it was recognised that the 'powerful arguments in favour of the constitutional right of free speech' meant that, 'where politicians are involved, the interest and duty tests are likely to be satisfied in most cases without too much difficulty'.[121] Subsequent case law suggests that, in practice, the 'right to know' test may be easy to satisfy[121a] and that, as a result, media reports on a wide range of matters of 'public interest' may be protected by qualified privilege. This is a rapidly developing area of the law which will be strongly influenced by the Human Rights Act.[121b]

15.37 Once the defendant has established qualified privilege, his good faith is presumed. The onus then shifts to the claimant to rebut the defence by showing that the publication was actuated by express malice. 'Express malice' entails either that the

---

[116] For a list of 'illustrative' circumstances, see *per* Lord Nicholls, *Reynolds v Times Newspapers Ltd* (n 114 above).

[117] See n 114 above, disapproving the approach of the Court of Appeal [1998] 3 WLR 862, 899E–H.

[118] [1999] 3 WLR 1010.

[119] The House of Lords were not persuaded to follow US and Commonwealth cases which recognised, in various degrees, a 'public figure' defence: see *Sullivan v New York Times* (1964) 376 US 254; *Rajagopal v State of Tamil Nadu JT* 1994 6 SC 524; *Lange v Australian Broadcasting Corporation* (1997) 189 CLR 520; *Lange v Atkinson and Australian Consolidated Press NZ Ltd* [1998] 3 NZLR 424.

[120] [1999] 3 WLR 1010, 1061A–B.

[121] Ibid 1056E, *per* Lord Hope.

[121a] See *GKR Karate v Yorkshire Post Newspapers*, unreported, 17 Jan 2000 (Sir Oliver Popplewell)—test satisfied in relation to an article relating to 'dodgy karate lessons' despite the fact that the local newspaper had not given the claimant a reasonable opportunity to respond and had inaccurately quoted the source.

[121b] See para 15.247ff below.

defendant had some improper motive for publication, such as injuring the claimant, or that he knew the words were false or was reckless as to whether they were true or false.[122] The burden imposed is a heavy one, and, if the evidence at trial is equally consistent with malice or its absence, there will be no case for the defendant to answer and the claim may be dismissed without hearing the defendant's evidence.[123]

(e) Remedies

The primary remedy for defamation is damages. The value of the award has traditionally been in the sole province of the jury; judges and counsel were not permitted to influence the decision of the jury by mentioning specific figures that might be appropriate.[124] The powers of intervention of the Court of Appeal were limited to ordering a re-trial if the award was 'divorced from reality'.[125] As a result, jury awards varied over an enormous range. Jury awards were first scrutinised in Convention terms by the Court of Appeal in *Rantzen v Mirror Group Newspapers*[126] which held that the power of the Court to order a new trial or to substitute a different damage award[127] should be applied consistently with Article 10. **15.38**

More recently, in *John v MGN Ltd*,[128] it was held that the reasonableness of jury awards could be tempered by directing the jury to the level of damages in personal injury cases. In practice, both the judiciary and counsel are now permitted to mention figures to the jury. The effect of *Rantzen* and of *John* has been to depress the value of damages awards and settlements in libel cases although a 'tariff' of Court of Appeal approved awards has been slow to develop.[129] The value of settlements in cases against newspapers, in particular, has been substantially reduced. **15.39**

The courts also have power to award permanent injunctions if a claim in defamation is established at trial. An injunction will be granted if there is any reason to believe that the defendant is likely to publish the same or similar defamatory words. Such injunction may also affect the position of third parties who publish the defamatory imputations. It is clear that, where an interim injunction has been granted, a third party will be in contempt of court if his publication is likely to **15.40**

[122] See *Horrocks v Lowe* [1975] AC 135; and P Milmo and W Rogers (eds), *Gatley on Libel and Slander* (9th edn, Sweet & Maxwell, 1998) Chap 16.

[123] See *Telnikoff v Matusevitch* [1991] 1 QB 102, 121: overruled, but not on this point [1992] 2 AC 343; and *Gatley on Libel and Slander* (n 122 above) para 32.28ff.

[124] See *Ward v James* [1966] 1 QB 273; see also *Sutcliffe v Pressdram Ltd* [1991] QB 153.

[125] See *McCarey v Associated Newspapers (No 2)* [1965] 2 QB 86, 111; see generally, *Gatley on Libel and Slander* (n 122 above) para 36.26.

[126] [1994] QB 670.

[127] Under the Courts and Legal Services Act 1990, s 8.

[128] [1997] QB 586.

[129] For such awards, see the Appendix of Court of Appeal 'Approved Libel Awards' in *Gatley on Libel and Slander* (n 122 above) A3.1–A3.6.

interfere with the course of justice between the claimant and the defendant.[130] It is not clear whether the same is true in the case of permanent injunctions.[131] It seems unlikely that, in the absence of a specific intention to interfere with the course of justice, the publication of the libel by a third party would constitute a breach of either an interim or final injunction against a defendant.[132]

(4) Comment on court proceedings: contempt of court

(a) Introduction

15.41 'Contempt of court' means interference with the due administration of justice.[133] Its purpose is to ensure respect for the administration of justice as a whole and for the remedies ordered by the court.[134] Nevertheless, the law of contempt appears to be unduly restrictive of freedom of expression, which the courts have traditionally treated as having secondary importance. It is also open to criticism in its summary trial procedures,[135] absence of maximum sentences[136] and, in particular, its uncertain scope.[137]

15.42 The classification of contempt at common law is not straightforward. 'Civil' contempts such as non-compliance with court orders or undertakings[138] in civil proceedings are generally[139] distinguished from 'criminal'[140] contempts. Criminal contempts can be divided into at least three categories:

- 'contempt in the face of the court' (which refers to conduct of persons in the courtroom);

---

[130] *A-G v News Group Newspapers Ltd* [1987] QB 1.

[131] See *Gatley on Libel and Slander* (n 122 above) para 9.31.

[132] In contrast to the position in breach of confidence, where the purpose of the injunction is to restrain the publication of particular items of confidential information.

[133] See eg *A-G v Times Newspapers Ltd* [1974] AC 273, 322.

[134] See eg *Morris v Crown Office* [1970] 2 QB 114.

[135] The summary trial procedures used in contempt cases may lack the elements of procedural fairness that are normally required for criminal trials, see generally *Arlidge Eady and Smith on Contempt* (2nd edn, Sweet & Maxwell, 1999) paras 2-17–2-25.

[136] With limited exceptions where statutes have intervened, no maximum sentences are prescribed, leaving the court free to impose whatever form of punishment it feels is appropriate, including coercive sanctions for civil contempts.

[137] The substantive criteria for contempt are vague and uncertain in spite of the fact that liability attracts potentially heavy penal sanctions.

[138] These can include injunctions or orders restricting or postponing reporting of trials when the administration of justice may be affected. Such restrictions may be imposed when trials are held in private, when reporting might prejudice the fairness of proceedings, when children, rape or blackmail are involved, or in regard to material disclosed on discovery.

[139] Except in Scotland.

[140] For discussion of the technical distinction between civil and criminal contempt see N Lowe and B Sufrin, *Borrie and Lowe: The Law of Contempt* (3rd edn, Butterworths, 1996) Chap 2; *Arlidge, Eady and Smith on Contempt* (2nd edn, Sweet and Maxwell, 1999) Chap 3; see also the judgments of the Australian High Court in *Witham v Holloway* (1995) 183 CLR 525, 530-49.

- 'scandalising the court' (which involves publications which undermine public confidence in the judicial system or otherwise interfere with the course of justice as a continuing process); and
- 'prejudicing active legal proceedings' under the '*sub judice* rule' (which prohibits publication of material tending to prejudice or impede specific civil or criminal proceedings before the courts).

The law of contempt applies only to 'courts of justice properly so-called'.[141] These include Mental Health Tribunals[142] and Employment Tribunals.[143] The authorities were reviewed by the Court of Appeal in *General Medical Council v British Broadcasting Corporation*[144] which decided that the Professional Conduct Committee of the General Medical Council is not a 'court' for the purposes of the law of contempt. There may be jurisdiction to restrain grave and obvious interference with proceedings before non-curial tribunals but no such order has ever been made.[145] **15.43**

The contempts most likely to be committed by the press or broadcasting media are the criminal contempts of publication of material which prejudices active proceedings or scandalises the court and breaches of civil undertakings or court orders which prohibit media publication. **15.44**

(b) Prejudicing or impeding proceedings

At common law, this type of contempt restricted the media from discussing or reporting on issues being addressed in civil and criminal proceedings on the basis that those proceedings might be prejudiced. The time before and after the trial when a publication was *sub judice* started from the point at which proceedings were 'imminent'.[146] However, the test was criticised for being broad and vague. The *actus reus* involved creating a *real risk* of prejudice to proceedings even if no detriment was suffered. Although it was essential to prove *intent to publish*[147] it was not necessary to show that the contemnor intended that the publication should interfere with the course of justice and, as a result, liability was strict. **15.45**

The House of Lords in the *Sunday Times* case[148] held that a risk of prejudice to proceedings might be brought about by a publication which 'prejudged' the matter at trial, on the basis of policy arguments against 'trial by newspaper' or 'trial by **15.46**

141 *Badry v DPP* [1983] 2 AC 297, 307; cf Contempt of Court Act 1981, s 19: 'court' includes 'any tribunal or body exercising the judicial power of the state'.

142 *Pickering v Liverpool Daily Post and Echo Newspapers plc* [1991] 2 AC 270.

143 *Peach Grey and Company v Sommers* [1995] 1 ICR 549.

144 [1998] 1 WLR 1573.

145 *A-G v British Broadcasting Corporation* [1981] AC 303, 344; see *General Medical Council v British Broadcasting Corporation* (n 144 above).

146 *R v Savundranayagan* [1968] 1 WLR 1761; [1968] 3 All ER 439.

147 *R v Thompson Newspapers Ltd, ex p A-G* [1968] 1 WLR 1.

148 *A-G v Times Newspapers Ltd* [1974] AC 273.

television'. The case involved an attempt to prevent the publication of an article in the *Sunday Times* newspaper which was potentially prejudicial to civil proceedings against the manufacturer of the drug thalidomide. Distillers Limited had manufactured and marketed the drug in the United Kingdom from 1958 to 1961 which, when prescribed to treat nausea in pregnant women, resulted in appalling deformities in hundreds of babies. During Distillers' negotiations to establish a trust fund for the children, the *Sunday Times* ran an article[149] which criticised the company's proposals and announced that a further article, in relation to the history of the tragedy, would be forthcoming. Distillers' complaint to the Attorney-General resulted in an injunction, which was later quashed by the Court of Appeal, to prevent publication of the second article. The House of Lords reinstated it on the basis that the proposed article would 'prejudge' the negligence issue and thereby interfere with the administration of justice. In effect, the House of Lords held that any 'prejudgment' would amount to contempt, whether or not it had a direct effect on the litigant. Previously, only a 'real risk' of influence upon the tribunal, witnesses or parties would amount to contempt, and it had been assumed that this would not normally be found in the absence of a jury trial.[150] The decision imposed greater limitations on the media without any greater certainty as to what was publishable.

15.47 In 1974, in light of the *Sunday Times* case, the Phillimore Committee was established to address the need for reform. Although the Committee stressed the desirability of avoiding trial by media, it criticised the prejudgment test of the House of Lords.[151] It is difficult to distinguish between balanced comment (which would be permissible) and prejudgment (which would not): judicious comment and expressions of opinion may often be difficult to distinguish from prejudgment. Furthermore, the prejudgment test was little different from the requirement to cause a risk of prejudice to the due administration of justice; but its uncertainty made it an unsatisfactory basis for creating a strict liability offence which significantly restricted freedom of expression.

15.48 The Phillimore Committee recommended that this type of contempt remain governed by strict liability.[152] Its report, together with the decision of the European Court of Human Rights in the *Sunday Times* case,[153] prompted the UK Government to enact the Contempt of Court Act 1981.

[149] 24 Sep 1972.

[150] In the *Sunday Times* case the Divisional Court applied the principle that a deliberate attempt to influence the settlement of pending proceedings by bringing public pressure to bear on a party amounted to a contempt of court: see [1973] QB 710.

[151] See S Bailey, D Harris, and B Jones, *Civil Liberties: Cases and Materials* (4th edn, Butterworths, 1995) 409.

[152] This is now reflected in the Contempt of Court Act 1981, ss 1 and 2.

[153] *Sunday Times v United Kingdom* (1979) 2 EHRR 245. The ECHR disagreed with the prejudgment test, and found that the restriction on freedom of expression was not founded on a sufficiently pressing social need to justify it in a democratic society.

Contempt of Court Act 1981. The Act does not codify the common law of contempt: it addresses only publications which may prejudice active legal proceedings, with the aim of bringing the law into line with the European Convention. The Act was intended to be a 'liberalising measure'.[154] It establishes a rule of strict liability, as recommended by the Phillimore Committee, which changes the common law on three important respects: it defines contempt more narrowly, it requires active proceedings and it provides for a public interest defence. Any ambiguity in the Act is presumed to have been intended to avoid future conflict between the law of contempt of court and the obligations of the United Kingdom under the Convention.[155] The statutory purpose of the Act **15.49**

> was to effect a permanent shift in the balance of public interest away from the protection of the administration of justice and in favour of freedom of speech.[156]

When considering whether or not a particular publication is in contempt, the court will, in each case, look at the 'localised balance' between freedom of speech and the right to a fair trial, looking at the significance of the interference in each case.[157]

First, publications[158] which tend to interfere with the course of justice generally (and legal proceedings in particular), are subject to strict liability,[159] regardless of intent. The principles were summarised in *A-G v MGN Ltd*.[160] The test is whether the publication will create a 'substantial risk'[161] that the course of justice in the 'proceedings in question'[162] will be seriously impeded or prejudiced.[163] This test is difficult to apply in practice. Concern has been expressed that the courts have taken a robust attitude when considering applications for the stay of criminal proceedings or appeals based on prejudicial publicity but have been more sensitive when dealing with contempt.[164] It has been suggested that this is because section 2(2) postulates a lesser degree of prejudice than is required to make good an **15.50**

---

[154] See *Arlidge, Eady and Smith on Contempt*, (2nd edn, Sweet & Maxwell, 1999) para 1–114.

[155] *Re Lonrho plc* [1990] 2 AC 154, 208.

[156] *Per* Lloyd LJ, *A-G v Newspaper Publishing plc* [1988] Ch 333, 382.

[157] *Per* Sedley LJ, *A-G v Guardian Newspapers* [1999] EMLR 904.

[158] Defined to include speech or writing or whatever form addressed to the public at large or any section of the public: see s 2(1).

[159] s 1.

[160] [1997] 1 All ER 456; see generally, *Arlidge, Eady and Smith on Contempt* (n 154 above) para 4–79ff and also A Nicol and H Rogers, 'Contempt of Court, Reporting Restrictions and Disclosure of Sources' in *Yearbook of Media and Entertainment Law, 1999* (Oxford University Press, 1999).

[161] Contempt of Court Act 1981, s 2(2); *A-G v MGN Ltd* (n 160 above) 461, Principle 4; 'substantial' means that the risk of influence is 'more than remote', for any risk that is more than remote must be 'substantial' (see *A-G v English* [1983] 1 AC 116, 141F–G).

[162] *A-G v MGN Ltd* (n 160 above) 461, Principle 5; it is noteworthy that the provision does not protect the administration of justice generally.

[163] See also *A-G v Independent Television News Ltd* [1995] 2 All ER 370.

[164] *A-G v Birmingham Post and Mail* [1999] 1 WLR 361 DC; *A-G v Unger* [1998] 1 Cr App Rep 308.

appeal against conviction.[165] However, the better view appears to be that there is a single standard which operates differently in the two contexts.[166]

15.51 Secondly, this rule of strict liability applies only to proceedings which are 'active' at the time of publication, as defined by the Act. Criminal proceedings are considered to be active from the time of arrest without warrant or the issue of warrant or summons.[167] Civil proceedings, on the other hand, are active from the time that 'arrangements for trial are made'.[168] This was the date of 'setting down' but, under the CPR, is likely to be an earlier date.[169] The Act creates a defence of 'innocent publication and distribution'.[170] This is available to a publisher who, having taken all reasonable care, either:

- does not know and has no reason to suspect that relevant legal proceedings are active;[171] or
- does not know and has no reason to suspect that the publication contains matter to which the strict liability rule applies.[172]

The innocent publication defence is only available in respect of prosecutions under the 'strict liability' rule.[173] Furthermore, it does not alter the general common law principle that publishing offending material by mistake is no defence.[174]

15.52 Thirdly, section 5 of the Act states that:

> A publication made as or as part of a discussion in good faith of public affairs, or other matters of general public interest is not to be treated as a contempt of court under the strict liability rule if the risk of impediment or prejudice to particular legal proceedings is merely incidental to the discussion.

Strictly speaking, the provision of section 5 is not a 'defence' at all: the burden is on the prosecution to show that the publication does not fall within the section.[175] The House of Lords in *A-G v English*[176] held that the only question raised by

[165] As was suggested by Simon Brown LJ in *A-G v Birmingham Post and Mail* [1999] 1 WLR 361, 369H.

[166] See *A-G v Guardian Newspapers*, 23 Jul 1999, DC.

[167] Sch I para 4.

[168] Sch I para 13. Under the CPR, there is no procedure for 'setting down'.

[169] The date on which the trial date is fixed under CPR, r 29.2(2).

[170] Contrast the common law position: neither ignorance of the proceedings (*R v Odhams Press Ltd, ex p A-G* [1957] 1 QB 73) nor the content of imported publications (*R v Griffiths, ex p A-G* [1957] 2 QB 192) was a defence.

[171] s 3(1).

[172] s 3(2).

[173] N Lowe and B Sufrin, *Borrie and Lowe: The Law of Contempt* (3rd edn, Butterworths, 1996) 398–400.

[174] See *R v Evening Standard Company Ltd* [1954] 1 QB 578: editor had every reason to believe that the case report was accurate; *R v Thomson Newspapers Ltd, ex p A-G* [1968] 1 WLR 1: editor had established a proper system to avoid prejudicial publication.

[175] *A-G v English* [1983] 1 AC 116.

[176] Ibid.

section 5 is whether the risk of prejudice is 'merely incidental' to the main theme of the publication. The publication complained of in *English* did not refer to any actual proceedings, but it would seem that even if an accused is mentioned by name, section 5 may apply.[177]

Intentional contempt. Since the enactment of the Contempt of Court Act, it has been uncertain whether publications that intentionally threaten to prejudice pending proceedings[178] might be prosecuted at common law to circumvent the more stringent requirements of the Act. The 1981 Act itself, in section 6(c), preserves liability for intentional contempt at common law.[179] **15.53**

Lord Donaldson suggested in the *Spycatcher* case[180] that 'intention' requires a 'specific intent to interfere with the administration of justice'; and that 'recklessness' is therefore not a sufficient basis for liability under section 6. The necessary intent might, however, be inferred from the foreseeability of the consequences of the conduct. In that case, foresight on the part of the editor of the *Independent* that publication would prejudice the action of the Attorney-General against the *Guardian* and the *Observer* could support an inference of intention to prejudice the administration of justice amounting to contempt under the common law. The decision was followed in *A-G v Observer Ltd*[181] which found that libraries which innocently made copies of *Spycatcher* available to the public pending the trial of the action must have had sufficient knowledge of the circumstances to infer intention for the purposes of contempt. **15.54**

Intention to prejudice proceedings was also established where the defendants sought to bring improper pressure to bear on the other party.[182] In *A-G v Hislop*[182a] the defendants published material in *Private Eye* which, it was held, was intended to persuade Sonia Sutcliffe, the wife of the 'Yorkshire Ripper,' to discontinue her defamation action[183] against the publication. There was a substantial risk that the articles might have prejudiced the course of justice because Mrs Sutcliffe might have been deterred from having her complaint tried before a court. **15.55**

[177] See *A-G v Times Newspapers Ltd* (the *Fagan* case), *The Times*, 12 Feb 1983; also *A-G v Guardian Newspapers* [1992] 3 All ER 38; see also *A-G v Guardian Newspapers*, 23 Jul 1999, DC.

[178] Among other reforms, the Report of the Phillimore Committee, at Cmnd 5794, published Dec 1974, recommended that intentional contempt should be dealt with through proper criminal rather than summary procedures, and that contempt in the absence of intention ought to be more narrowly defined.

[179] s 6(3) states that nothing in the previous sections of the Act 'restricts liability for contempt of court in respect of conduct *intended* to impede or prejudice the administration of justice'.

[180] See *A-G v Guardian Newspapers Ltd (No 2)* [1988] Ch 333, 374-5.

[181] [1988] 1 All ER 385; see also *A-G v News Group Newspapers plc* [1989] QB 110.

[182] *A-G v Hislop* [1991] 1 QB 514.

[182a] Ibid.

[183] The magazine was also guilty of statutory contempt.

(c) Scandalising the court

15.56 'Scandalising the court' is a form of contempt that developed to protect the judicial system from media criticism. It has been defined as 'any act done or writing published calculated to bring a court or a judge into contempt or to lower his authority . . .'[184] Scandalising the court is not affected by the Contempt of Court Act 1981, as there are generally no active proceedings which might be prejudiced. Even if the publication occurred when proceedings were active, the effect of any abuse of a court or judge is likely to create a risk of prejudice to the administration of justice in general rather than a risk to particular proceedings. The *actus reus* of the offence may be fulfilled in two ways: by a scurrilous attack on a court or judge, or by an attempt to impute bias to a judge.

15.57 The leading case is *R v Gray*,[185] in which Darling J, in an obscenity trial, directed the press to refrain from publishing an account of the trial, lest they too be prosecuted for obscenity. Following the trial, Gray published a newspaper article attacking Darling J in a vitriolic fashion, insulting him personally and decrying his warning to the media and his capacity to act as a judge of the court. The article was held to be a grave contempt. Other cases have since stressed that criticism consisting of 'respectful, even though outspoken, comments of ordinary men' must not be considered to be contempt.[186] No offence is committed in such cases provided there is no imputation of improper motives to the judge.[187]

15.58 However, a publication which imputes bias to a judge, even if expressed moderately may scandalise the court. The last successful prosecution of a contempt of this type was in the *Colsey* case[188] where an article implied that a judge might have been biased when construing a statute because he had earlier been involved in initiating the legislation as Solicitor General. Prosecutions for scandalising the court only take place in the most serious cases and are very rare.[189] Critics have suggested that the offence should be abolished, since the notion of undermining public confidence in the administration of justice is so vague.[190] They argue that it is not the comment but the

[184] *R v Gray* [1900] 2 QB 36, 40 *per* Lord Russell; see generally, *Arlidge, Eady and Smith on Contempt* (2nd edn, Sweet & Maxwell, 1999) paras 5-208– 5-269.

[185] n 184 above.

[186] *R v Metropolitan Police Commissioner, ex p Blackburn (No 2)* [1968] QB 150; see also *Ambard v A-G for Trinidad and Tobago* [1936] AC 322.

[187] *Ambard v A-G for Trinidad and Tobago* (n 186 above) 335.

[188] *The Times*, 9 May 1931; see also *R v Editor of New Statesman, ex p DPP* (1928) 44 TLR 301; Arlidge, Eady and Smith point out that judges have brought a number of successful libel actions against newspapers in recent years in relation to allegations of incompetence or bias (n 184 above) para 5-209, n 98.

[189] One was, however, instituted in 1999.

[190] See N Lowe and B Sufrin, *Borrie and Lowe: The Law of Contempt* (3rd, edn, Butterworths, 1996) 243; Law Commission, *Offences Relating to Interference with the Course of Justice* (Law Com No 96) 67-8.

conduct which attracts comment which undermines public confidence in the justice system; and that suppressing expression is likely to cause resentment and suspicion.[191] However, it is generally recognised that there is a residual need for the protection afforded by this offence and the Law Commission has recommended a statutory offence of knowingly publishing false allegations that a court is corrupt.[192]

(b) Breach of undertakings or orders that restrict court reporting

There are a number of types of orders a court might make to restrict the media from reporting upon court proceedings. The three most important are: **15.59**

- the power to 'postpone' the reporting of proceedings;
- the power to prevent the publication of the names of parties; and
- restrictions on the publication of information relating to children.[193]

Courts are also permitted to restrict reporting of: indecent matters,[194] the identity of the victims of rape and certain other sexual offences[195] and committal proceedings before magistrates' courts.[196]

A person aggrieved by orders under section 4(2) or section 11 and other orders restricting or preventing reports or restricting public access in relation to a trial in the Crown Court can appeal to the Court of Appeal.[197] This right of appeal is subject to a requirement of permission being granted.[198] There is no further appeal to the House of Lords. Where orders are made by magistrates' courts they can be challenged in applications for judicial review. **15.60**

Orders for postponement of trial reporting. Under section 4(2) of the 1981 Act, a court may order the postponement of the publication of material until the conclusion of a trial or series of trials[199] in order to avoid a risk of prejudice to the **15.61**

---

[191] Cf the American position where this form of contempt is almost extinct following the case of *Bridges v California* (1941), 314 US 252 in which it was held that a display of disrespect for the judiciary should not be averted by enforced silence.

[192] *Offences Relating to Interference with the Court of Justice* (n 190 above) 213.

[193] For a full discussion of these and other powers see *Arlidge, Eady and Smith* (n 184 above) Chaps 6–8.

[194] Judicial Proceedings (Regulation of Reports) Act 1926.

[195] Sexual Offences (Amendment) Act 1976.

[196] Magistrates' Court Act 1980, s 8.

[197] Criminal Justice Act 1981, s 159; after the decision in *R v Central Criminal Court, ex p Crook, The Times,* 8 Nov 1984 and following the application of the journalist to the European Court of Human Rights; see also G Robertson and A Nicol, *Media Law* (3rd edn, Penguin Books, 1992) 347.

[198] Which is determined without a hearing, this provision was held to be *intra vires* in *R v Guardian Newspapers Ltd* [1994] Crim LR 912, see generally, *Arlidge, Eady and Smith on Contempt* (2nd edn, Sweet & Maxwell, 1999) para 7–231ff.

[199] N Lowe and B Sufrin, *Borrie and Lowe: The Law of Contempt* (3rd edn, Butterworths, 1996) 284 ff; *Arlidge, Eady and Smith on Contempt* (n 198 above) paras 7-82–7-231; Robertson and Nicol (n 197 above) 341–350.

administration of justice in those proceedings. The section provides that in any legal proceedings held in public:

> the court may, where it appears to be necessary for avoiding a substantial risk of prejudice to the administration of the justice in those proceedings, or in any other proceedings pending or imminent, order that the publication or any report of the proceedings, or any part of the proceedings, be postponed for such period as the court thinks necessary for that purpose.

The risk to the administration of justice must be 'substantial', and the courts have determined that 'blanket bans' on reporting are likely to be inappropriate.[200]

15.62 In assessing the necessity of such an order, the court must consider the alternatives and should not lightly interfere with the freedom of the press.[201] The test is a three stage one:[202]

- is there a substantial risk of prejudice[203] to the administration of justice?
- is an order necessary?
- should the court exercise its discretion in favour of making an order?

The operation of these tests is illustrated by the case of *Ex parte Central Television plc*.[204] A jury was required to stay overnight in a hotel and the judge, in order to insulate the jurors from the media, ordered that reporting of the trial be postponed until the next day. The Court of Appeal held that there was little evidence that reports would have been anything but fair and accurate and that the risk to the administration of justice was therefore minimal. Even if there had been a substantial risk, the order would not have been automatic, as alternative methods of preventing exposure of the jurors to the media may have been available.[205]

15.63 Orders made under section 4(2) must be formulated in precise terms and committed to writing.[206] It has been suggested that copies of all section 4 orders should be faxed by the court to the Press Association.[207] Unless the order is varied or set aside on appeal, a breach will render the press liable to be committed for contempt.[208]

---

[200] *R v Horsham Justices, ex p Farquarhson* [1982] QB 762; [1982] 2 All ER 269.

[201] *Ex p Central Television plc* [1991] 1 WLR 4; see generally, *Arlidge, Eady and Smith on Contempt* (n 198 above) paras 7-132–7-193.

[202] *MGN Pension Trustees Ltd v Bank of America National Trust and Savings Association* [1995] 2 All ER 355.

[203] Note that, in contrast to the position under the Contempt of Court Act 1981, s 2(2) (see para 15.50 above) there is no requirement that the prejudice be 'serious'.

[204] [1991] 1 WLR 4.

[205] See also *A-G v Guardian Newspapers (No 3)* [1992] 1 WLR 874; *Ex parte The Telegraph plc* [1993] 2 All ER 971; *R v Beck, ex p Daily Telegraph plc* [1993] 2 All ER 177.

[206] *Practice Direction (Contempt: Reporting Restrictions)* [1982] 1 WLR 1475.

[207] *A-G v Guardian Newspapers Ltd (No.3)* (n 205 above).

[208] Ibid 884H–885A.

An employment tribunal also has a power to make a restricted reporting order at any stage until its decision is promulgated in any cases involving allegations of sexual misconduct[209] or in a disability discrimination case where evidence of a personal nature is likely to be heard.[210] In *R v London (North) Industrial Tribunal, ex p Associated Newspapers Ltd*[211] it was emphasised that because of the principle of the freedom of the press to report court hearings fully and contemporaneously, the power to make an order should be interpreted narrowly. **15.64**

Orders to prevent publication of the names of parties. A number of statutory provisions allow certain persons involved in the proceedings to remain anonymous.[212] Under section 11 of the Contempt of Court Act 1981, the court has limited powers to restrict the publication of material in relation to hearings which are held in private[213] and to prohibit the reporting of material, including names of participants, mentioned in open court. The section provides that: **15.65**

> In any case where a court (having power to do so) allows a name or other matter to be withheld from the public in proceedings before the court, the court may give such directions prohibiting the publication of that name or matter in connection with the proceedings as appear to the court to be necessary for the purpose for which it was so withheld.

Section 11 does not confer any additional powers on the court, but simply regulates the exercise of existing powers[214] such as the well-established common law power to withhold the identity of witnesses in blackmail cases since their disclosure would prejudice the administration of justice by discouraging witnesses from coming forward in the future.[215] These policy considerations apply whether or not the accused is subsequently acquitted. Once section 11 orders are made they appear to be binding on everyone who is aware of them.[216] 'Publication' in this section is not understood in the broad sense in which it is used in the law of libel but in its ordinary sense of 'made available to the public'.[217]

An order under section 11 is a draconian measure and should only be used when failure to grant anonymity would render the attainment of justice really doubtful **15.66**

---

[209] Employment Tribunal Act 1996, s 11.

[210] Ibid s 12.

[211] [1998] ICR 1212; see also *Leicester University v A* [1999] IRLR 352.

[212] In addition to the Contempt of Court Act 1981, s 11, see: Sexual Offences (Amendment) Act 1976, s 4, in relation to complainants in rape cases and the Children and Young Persons Act 1933, s 39(1), for children.

[213] *Scott v Scott* [1913] AC 417.

[214] See N Lowe and B Sufrin, *Borrie and Lowe: The Law of Contempt* (3rd edn, Butterworths, 1996) 299; G Robertson and A Nicol, *Media Law* (3rd edn, Penguin Books, 1992) 338–41.

[215] See *R v Socialist Worker Printers and Publishers Ltd, ex p A-G* [1975] QB 637.

[216] *A-G v Leveller Magazine Ltd* [1979] AC 440.

[217] *Borrie and Lowe* (n 214 above) 85.

or, in effect, impracticable.[218] Such orders should not be made to protect the 'comfort and feelings' of parties[219] or to protect businesses from potential loss.[220] In *R v Legal Aid Board, ex p Kaim Todner (a firm)*[221] the Court of Appeal emphasised that, in principle, proceedings should be conducted in public, and that section 11 orders which prevent publication of names or require conduct of proceedings in private require objective justification.

15.67 The general rule is now that hearings are to be in public.[222] Thus, the decision to hold in private an inquiry following the convictions of Dr Shipman for 15 murders was held to be irrational.[222a] However, this general rule does not require the court to make special arrangements for accommodating members of the public.[223] A hearing, or any part of it, may be in private if:

- publicity would defeat the object of the hearing;
- it involves matters relating to national security;
- it involves confidential information and publicity would damage that confidentiality;
- a private hearing is necessary to protect the interest of any child or patient;
- it is a hearing without notice and it would be unjust to any respondent for there to be a public hearing;
- it involves uncontentious matters arising out of the administration of trusts or estates; or
- the court considers it necessary in the interests of justice.[224]

The court may order that the identity of a party or witnesss must not be disclosed if it considers non-disclosure necessary in order to protect the interests of that party or witness.[225] The fact that proceedings are held in private does not mean that they are secret. Other than in exceptional cases, disclosure of judgments or orders made in private and comments on what happened during proceedings in private is not improper. The court should make arrangements, so far as this is practical, for members of the public to attend hearings in private if this is requested.[226]

[218] *R v Westminster City Council, ex p Castelli* [1995] 7 Admin LR 840: no order to conceal the identity of HIV positive applicant; but see *R v Somerset Health Authority, ex p S* [1996] COD 244 where an order for anonymity was made on behalf of a transsexual; and see *R v Criminal Injuries Compensation Board ex p A* [1992] COD 379 (anonymity of applicant seeking compensation for sexual abuse).

[219] *R v Evesham Justices, ex p McDonagh* [1988] 1 QB 553: order banning publication of address of former MP revoked.

[220] *R v Dover JJ, ex p Dover District Council* (1991) 156 JP 433: order banning reporting of name of restaurateur being prosecuted for public health offences.

[221] [1998] 3 WLR 925.

[222] CPR, r 39.2(1).

[222a] *R v Secretary of State for Health ex p Wagstaffe* [2000] 1 All ER (D) 1021.

[223] CPR, r 39.2(2).

[224] CPR, r 39.2(3).

[225] CPR, r 39.2(4).

[226] See *Hodgson v Imperial Tobacco Ltd* [1998] 1 WLR 1056.

Restriction of publication of information concerning children.[226a] The court has a general power to restrict publication of information concerning children. Although a child does not have any special right of privacy or confidentiality,[227] the court will restrain publication to protect the effective administration of justice. The court must balance the protection of the child against the right of freedom of expression. In this balancing exercise the welfare of the child is not paramount.[228] It has been recognised that the court will attach great importance to safeguarding the freedom of the press and will take account of Article 10 of the Convention. The need to protect the child will be weighed against the right of the press to comment on matters of genuine public interest.[229] Where an injunction is sought to restrain the freedom of the press the case should be transferred to the High Court and the Official Solicitor invited to represent the child.[230] **15.68**

Restrictions on publications which identify children may be effected by way of an order under section 39 of the Children and Young Persons Act 1933. That section provides: **15.69**

> (1) In relation to any proceedings in any court . . . the court may direct that . . .
>
> (a) no newspaper report of the proceedings shall reveal the name, address, or school, or include any particulars calculated to lead to the identification of any child or young person concerned in the proceedings, either as being the person [by or against] or in respect of whom the proceedings are taken, or being a witness therein;
>
> (b) no picture shall be published in any newspaper as being or including a picture of any child or young person so concerned in the proceedings as aforesaid;
>
> except in so far (if at all) as may be permitted by the direction of the court.

Such orders, although discretionary, are routinely made in family cases[231] and education cases; they normally should be if a child or young person is before the court.[232] If the child is a defendant in a criminal case and is convicted then the conviction may lead to the order being discharged, although this is not automatic.[233]

Section 39 does not confer an express power to order that publication of the name of the defendant is to be restricted.[234] Nevertheless, the provision is wide enough **15.70**

[226a] Some important changes are envisaged under the Youth and Criminal Evidence Act 1999, but at the time of writing these are not yet in force.

[227] *R v Independent Television* [1994] Fam 192, 207A.

[228] See *Re M and N (Wards) (Publication of Information)* [1990] 1 FLR 149; and see *Re Z (A Minor) (Identification: Restrictions on Publication)* [1997] Fam 1.

[229] See the 'guidelines' set out in *Re W (A Minor) (Wardship: Restrictions on Publication)* [1992] 1 WLR 100, 103.

[230] *Re H–S (Minors) (Protection of Identity)* [1994] 1 WLR 1141.

[231] See *Re X County Council v A* (the Mary Bell case) [1985] 1 All ER 53.

[232] *R v Leicester Crown Court, ex p S (A Minor)* [1992] 2 All ER 659, 662.

[233] See *R v Inner London Crown Court, ex p B* [1996] COD 17; *R v Central Criminal Court, ex p S and P* [1999] Crim LR 159.

[234] *R v Crown Court at Southwark, ex p Godwin* [1991] 3 All ER 818.

to enable the court to prevent the publication of everything concerning the proceedings, including the fact that the order has been made. The Court of Appeal has, however, recognised difficulties with orders of this type and has approved the practice of the release of a summary of the court decision by the Official Solicitor.[235]

15.71 **Restrictions on reporting material made available on disclosure.** Documents which are the subject of disclosure between parties to proceedings cannot be used for any purpose other than the conduct of the litigation and cannot be supplied to the media. This is because disclosure constitutes a serious invasion of privacy and confidentiality.[236] The obligation is imposed by law[237] and applies in criminal proceedings as well as civil.[238]

15.72 The issue has arisen as to whether, once a disclosed document has been read in court, the parties are entitled to supply copies of it to journalists. In *Home Office v Harman*[239] the House of Lords held that they were not. In that case, 800 pages of documents relating to Home Office prison policy had been read in open court and copies were subsequently supplied by the plaintiffs' solicitor to a journalist. It was held that this constituted a contempt of court. The European Commission on Human Rights held that there had been a violation of Article 10.[240] A friendly settlement was reached and as a result the Rules of the Supreme Court were changed.[241] The rule provides that the implied undertaking of confidentiality ceases to apply after a document has been 'read to or by the court or referred to in open court'. This includes documents pre-read by the court, referred to in a skeleton argument or referred to in open court by counsel or the court but not read.[242] However, this rule has been given a restrictive interpretation, allowing the party to make the contents of the document known, but to use it for no other purpose.[243]

(e) Protection of journalistic sources

15.73 The common law provided limited protection for journalistic sources. In libel

[235] *Re G (Minors) (Celebrities: Publicity), The Times*, 28 Oct 1998; and see also *Re R (A Minor)(Wardship: Restrictions on Publication)* [1994] Fam 254 (if order relates to criminal proceedings it should be made by the judge hearing those proceedings, not in wardship proceedings).

[236] *Home Office v Harman* [1983] 1 AC 280, 308.

[237] *Prudential Assurance v Fountain Page Ltd* [1991] 1 WLR 756, 764.

[238] *Taylor v Director of the Serious Fraud Office* [1998] 1 WLR 1040.

[239] Ibid; see generally, I Eagles, 'Disclosure of Material Obtained on Discovery' (1984) 47 MLR 284; N Lowe and B Sufrin *Borrie and Lowe: The Law of Contempt* (3rd edn, Butterworths, 1996) 594–6; G Robertson and A Nicol, *Media Law* (3rd edn, Penguin Books, 1992) 356–358.

[240] *Harman v United Kingdom* (1985) 7 EHRR 146, EComm HR.

[241] RSC Ord 24, r 14A was introduced (and is now CPR, r 31.22).

[242] *Derby v Weldon (No 2) The Times*, 19 Oct1988; *Smithkline Beecham Biologicals SA v Connaught Laboratories Inc* [1999] 4 All ER 498; and see also *GIO Personal Investment Services v Liverpool and London Steamship Protection and Indemnity Association* [1999] 1 WLR 984.

[243] *Singh v Christie, The Times*, 11 Nov 1993; see also the comments of Lord Hoffmann in *Taylor v Director of the Serious Fraud Office* [1998] 1 WLR 1040, 1051.

cases, disclosure of sources was governed by the so-called 'newspaper rule' which meant that newspapers could not be forced to disclose sources of information before trial.[244] In other cases, however, the 'newspaper rule' did not apply.[245] The perceived need to protect journalistic sources more generally led to the enactment of section 10 of the Contempt of Court Act.[246] That section provides:

> No court may require a person to disclose, nor is any person guilty of contempt of court for refusing to disclose, the source of information contained in a publication for which he is responsible,[247] unless it be established to the satisfaction of the court that disclosure is necessary in the interests of justice or national security or for the prevention of disorder or crime.

Section 10 recognises that the protection of sources is a matter of 'high public importance'[248] and effectively creates a presumption in favour of journalists who wish to protect their sources. The presumption is, however, subject to four wide exceptions where disclosure of the source is a matter of necessity: **15.74**

- in the interests of justice;
- in the interests of national security;
- for the prevention of disorder; or
- for the prevention of crime.

The word 'necessary' has a meaning somewhere between 'indispensable' and 'useful' or expedient, the nearest paraphrase being 'really needed'.[249]

In relation to 'national security' and 'the prevention of disorder or crime', the courts have said that: **15.75**

> These two public interests are of such overriding importance that once it is shown that disclosure will serve one of those interests, the necessity of disclosure follows almost automatically.[250]

In *Secretary of State for Defence v Guardian Newspapers Ltd*[251] the House of Lords decided that the *Guardian* should disclose a photocopy of a memorandum, dealing with the arrival in the United Kingdom of cruise missiles, which had been

[244] P Milmo and W Rogers (eds), *Gatley on Libel and Slander* (9th edn, Sweet & Maxwell, 1998) para 30.112.
[245] *British Steel Corporation v Granada Television Ltd* [1981] AC 1096.
[246] *Arlidge, Eady and Smith on Contempt* (2nd edn, Sweet & Maxwell, 1999) Chap 9.
[247] The section applies to information received for the purposes of publication, even though it is never in fact published: see *X Ltd v Morgan-Grampian (Publishers) Ltd* [1991] 1 AC 1, 40F, in which the point was conceded.
[248] Ibid 41E.
[249] *In re An Inquiry under the Company Securities (Insider Dealing) Act 1985* [1988] AC 660, 704.
[250] *X Ltd v Morgan-Grampian (Publishers) Ltd* (n 247 above) 43B, although not if the crime was of a 'trivial nature'.
[251] [1985] AC 339.

supplied by an anonymous source, despite the absence of clear evidence of the sensitivity and urgency of the subject matter.[252] A similar result was reached in *In re An Inquiry under the Company Securities (Insider Dealing) Act 1985*[253] in which it was held to be sufficient to show that disclosure could assist in the prosecution of a crime already committed.[254] Such an application was, however, refused where a health authority sought disclosure of the identity of doctors who were practising despite having contracted AIDS: the prevention of crime was not the task of the plaintiff health authority and criminal investigation was unlikely.[255]

15.76 The question as to whether disclosure is 'necessary in the interests of justice' has given rise to considerable difficulty. The courts have construed 'interests of justice' as being wider than 'the administration of justice'. It covers the interest of the public

> in the maintenance of the system of law, within the framework of which every citizen has the ability and the freedom to exercise his legal right to remedy a wrong done to him or to prevent it being done . . .[256]

In the *Morgan-Grampian* case Lord Bridge set out a number of factors which were relevant when balancing the interests of justice against the policy of protection from disclosure underlying section 10, stating that:

> if it appears that the information was obtained illegally, this will diminish the importance of protecting the source unless, of course, this factor is counter-balanced by a clear public interest in publication of the information.[257]

15.77 In the case itself it was found 'necessary in the interests of justice' that the court should order the disclosure of the source of financial confidential information concerning the claimant's business even though the dissemination of the confidential information had been restrained by injunction. The journalist applied to the European Court of Human Rights. In *Goodwin v United Kingdom*[258] the Court held that, insofar as the disclosure order served to reinforce the injunction, the additional restriction on freedom of expression was not justified under Article 10(2). Furthermore, the Court took the view that the interest of the plaintiff in eliminating the residual threat of damage through dissemination of confidential information and in unmasking a disloyal employee was not sufficient to outweigh the public interest in protecting the journalist's source.

---

[252] *Borrie and Lowe* (n 239 above) 54; G Robertson and A Nicol (n 239 above) 202.

[253] [1988] AC 660.

[254] Rejecting the view of Hoffmann J that it was necessary to show that, in the absence of disclosure, it was likely that further crimes would be committed.

[255] *X v Y* [1988] 2 All ER 648; and see *Handmade Films v Express Newspapers* [1986] FSR 463: no order for disclosure of source of photographs taken on a film set as no serious damage threatened.

[256] *X Ltd v Morgan-Grampian (Publishers) Ltd* (n 247 above) 54C.

[257] n 247 above, 44.

[258] (1996) 22 EHRR 123 (by an 11:7 majority).

When the issue again arose before the English courts in *Camelot Group plc v Centaur Communications Ltd*[259] the Court of Appeal said that 'the tests which the ECHR and the House of Lords applied were substantially the same'. There was no public interest in protecting the source of the draft accounts of the plaintiff and the Court upheld an order for disclosure. This decision can be contrasted with that in *Saunders v Punch Ltd*[260] where Lindsay J refused to order the disclosure of sources of information concerning a DTI inquiry,[261] despite the fact that some of the disclosed information appears to have been protected by legal professional privilege. He said that an injunction already granted to restrain the use of the information meant that the interests of justice were not so pressing as to require that the ban on 'statutory privilege against disclosure' be overridden.[262] This approach was approved by the Court of Appeal in *John v Express Newspapers*[262a] which held that before overriding the public interest in protecting confidential sources, the minimum requirement was that other ways of obtaining the information had to have been explored. **15.78**

(5) **Obscenity and indecency**

(a) Introduction

English law restricts freedom of expression by regulating content and prohibiting the publication of obscene, blasphemous or racially offensive matter.[263] The extent to which the display or publication of such material ought to be criminalised and the content of film, theatre and telecommunications broadcasts ought to be suppressed or regulated, remains highly contentious. **15.79**

(b) The Obscene Publications Acts

Introduction. The moral and legal debate concerning obscenity focuses on whether obscenity falls within the realm of protected expression at all;[264] and if so, whether there are justifiable bases for its restriction.[265] In practice, Parliament and the courts have had difficulty devising a test of obscenity which adequately **15.80**

---

[259] [1999] QB 124; see also *O'Mara Books Ltd v Express Newspapers plc*, 3 Mar 1998, Neuberger J: following *Camelot*, disclosure ordered.

[260] [1998] 1 WLR 986; see also *Chief Constable of Leicestershire v Garavelli* [1997] EMLR 543: disclosure not necessary.

[261] The DTI inquiry concerned Mr Ernest Saunders who was ultimately convicted for his role in the Guinness take over.

[262] At 250b–d.

[262a] *The Times*, 26 Apr 2000.

[263] For a fuller discussion, see G Robertson and A Nicol, *Media Law* (3rd edn, Penguin Books, 1992) Chap 3.

[264] See discussion in E Barendt, *Freedom of Speech* (Clarendon Press, 1985) 247ff.

[265] See J Bakan, [1984] Ottawa L Re, 1; E Barendt, *Freedom of Speech* (n 264 above) 254–279 discusses the three main grounds: specific harm to individuals, impact on the moral tone of society (community standards) and the offensiveness principle.

distinguishes between expression which is defensible and expression which is not.[266]

15.81 The Obscene Publications Acts of 1959 and 1964[267] supersede but do not abolish the common law. They were a response to a number of prosecutions of serious literature during the 1950s followed by deliberations of a Parliamentary Committee and the recommendations of the 'Society of Authors' chaired by Sir Alan Herbert.[268] The Acts prohibit anyone from publishing an obscene article, whether for gain or not, unless it can be shown that the publication is justified as being for the common good[269] or that it can be shown that the publisher was ignorant of the nature of the article.[270] The legislation also provides powers of search and seizure, and for forfeiture of obscene articles upon conviction.

15.82 **Definition of obscenity.** The statutory definition of obscenity provides that an article is 'obscene' if its effect tends to:

> deprave and corrupt persons who are likely, having regard to all relevant circumstances, to read, see or hear the matter contained or embodied in it.[271]

This is the common law *Hicklin*[272] test, modified (to redefine the class of persons liable to be depraved) so as to include those to whom the material is likely to be distributed, circulated or offered for sale.[273] The result is that, for example, material intended for adults will not be 'obscene' merely because it would tend to

[266] See eg proposals in *Pornography: The Longford Report* (1972); *The Pollution of the Mind; New Proposals to Control Public Indecency and Obscenity*, The Society of Conservative Lawyers (1972); *The Obscenity Laws: Report of Arts Council Working Party* (1969); also proposals put forward by the Defence of Literature and the Arts Society (1978) 12 NLJ 423.

[267] See also: Children and Young Persons (Harmful Publications) Act 1955; Indecent Displays (Control) Act 1981; Criminal Justice Act 1988, s 160 in relation to offence of possession of indecent photograph of child; Theatres Act 1968; Post Office Act 1953, s 11; Customs Consolidation Act 1876, s 42 in relation to controls on importation of indecent or obscene articles; Judicial Proceedings (Regulation of Reports) Act 1926, s 1(1)(a) in relation to indecent details of legal proceedings.

[268] See C H Rolph, *Books in the Dock* (Andre Deutsch, 1969) 93; G Robertson, *Obscenity* (Weidenfeld and Nicholson, 1979) Chap 2; Robertson and Nicol (n 263 above) 108–110; also *R v Martin Secker and Warburg Ltd* [1954] 1 WLR 1178, *per* Stable, J.

[269] s 4 of the 1959 Act provides that there should be no conviction or forfeiture if it is proved that the article in question is justified as being for the common good on the ground that it is in the interests of science, literature, art or learning.

[270] s 2(5) of the 1959 Act provides that 'a person shall not be convicted of an offence against this section if he proves that he had not examined the article in respect of which he is charged and had no reasonable cause to suspect that it was such that *his publication* of it would make him liable to be convicted of an offence against this section'. The 1964 Act, s 1(3), amends the 1959 reference to 'his publication' of the article to read 'his having of it'.

[271] Obscene Publications Act 1959, s 1(1).

[272] *R v Hicklin* (1868) LR 3 QB 360, 371. The old test was 'whether the tendency of the matter charged as obscenity is to deprave and corrupt those whose minds are open to such immoral influences and into whose hands such a publication might fall'.

[273] As suggested by *R v Martin Secker and Warburg Ltd* [1954] 1 WLR 1138.

corrupt a young person, to whom it would not normally be made available. In addition, there is authority for the suggestion that 'persons' means a 'significant proportion' of the likely readers,[274] and that 'likely readers' will only be excluded from consideration if they are negligible in number.[275] The provision protects not only the innocent, but also those whose morals are already in a state of corruption because it is fallacious to assume that they cannot be further depraved.[276]

The phrase 'deprave and corrupt' refers to the mental and moral corruption originally propounded by Lord Cockburn CJ in *R v Hicklin*.[277] Depravity is not confined to sexual matters;[278] and sexual explicitness does not necessarily amount to obscenity.[279] Even the fact that an article is 'filthy' or 'lewd' may not be sufficient: it is a defence to assert that the article is so disgusting that, far from corrupting the individual, it would cause him to revolt from the activity it describes.[280] The decision in *R v Calder and Boyars Ltd*[281] suggests that the number of readers susceptible, the strength of the tendency to corrupt and deprave, and the nature of the corruption or depravity are all elements which should be considered.[282] The purpose or intention of the publisher is, however, irrelevant, for the test for obscenity depends on the article itself.[283] **15.83**

Obscene Publications Act 1964. Two loopholes in the 1959 Act's definition of 'publication'[284] were filled by the 1964 Act. The first involved the display of a priced article in a shop which was found not to be an 'offer for sale' so as to constitute publication.[285] The second problem arose because it was said that in a sale to a particular individual, it was necessary to show publication of the article to a **15.84**

[274] *R v Calder and Boyars Ltd* [1969] 1 QB 151.

[275] *DPP v Whyte* [1972] AC 849.

[276] Ibid.

[277] (1868) LR 3 QB 360.

[278] *John Calder (Publications) Ltd v Powell* [1965] 1 QB 509.

[279] *R v Stanley* [1965] 2 QB 327; *Darbo v DPP* [1992] Crim LR 56.

[280] *R v Anderson* [1972] 1 QB 304.

[281] [1969] 1 QB 151.

[282] See also *Hoare v United Kingdom* [1997] EHRLR 678 in which the applicant had engaged in publication and distribution of pornographic videotapes by post: a brochure describing the contents of the videos was provided to those who responded to an advertisement in a Sunday paper, and the videos distributed thereafter, upon request. The applicant was convicted, and given a 30-month prison sentence. His argument that the videos could not deprave or corrupt since only those who shared his interests would have purchased them from the brochure was rejected by the Commission on Human Rights.

[283] *R v Shaw* [1962] AC 220: affirmed on other grounds, [1962] AC 237; followed in *Knuller (Publishing, Printing and Promotions) Ltd v DPP* [1973] AC 435.

[284] The 1959 Act, s 1(3), provides that a person publishes an article who distributes, circulates, sells, lets on hire, gives, lends, offers for sale or for hire an obscene article; and in the case of an article containing matter to be looked at, shows, plays or projects it.

[285] *Mella v Monahan* [1961] Crim LR 175; see also *R v Taylor (Alan)* [1995] Cr App R 131, where the Court of Appeal held that the sale by photographic developing-processing outlets of prints to the owners of developed film constituted a 'publication'.

person who was liable to be corrupted by it.[286] A person is now deemed to have an article for publication for gain if, with a 'view to publication', he has it in his ownership, possession or control.[287]

15.85 **The offences.** By section 2 of the Obscene Publications Act 1959 it is an offence to publish an obscene article or to have an obscene article for publication for gain. The maximum penalty is three-years' imprisonment on trial on indictment. An 'article' includes anything 'containing or embodying matter to be read or looked at or both, any sound record and any film or other record of a picture or pictures'.[288] This includes photographic negatives[289] video cassettes[290] and images on computer disc in digitised form.[291] 'Publication' is given a wide definition[292] and includes giving or lending. It is committed by a photographic developer who develops film sent by customers depicting obsence acts, makes prints and sends them to the customers.[293]

15.86 **Seizure and forfeiture.** By section 3 of the Obscene Publications Act 1959 a justice of the peace can issue a warrant for the search and seizure of obscene articles kept for publication for gain. The articles must be brought before the justice who may issue a summons to the occupier to show cause why the articles should not be forfeited.[294] This provision also applies to articles kept for publication abroad.[295] This procedure is often used by the police to avoid having to prove obscenity offences at a jury trial.[296]

15.87 **Defence of public good.** Section 4 of the Obscene Publications Act 1959 provides that there should be no conviction or forfeiture:

> if it is proved that publication of the article in question is justified as being for the common good on the ground that it is in the interests of science, literature, art or learning or of other objects of general concern.

The defence will only be considered once it is established that an article is obscene,[297] and may be assisted by expert evidence concerning the literary or other

---

[286] See *R v Clayton and Halsey* [1963] 1 QB 163 (where the particular persons to whom the articles were sold were police officers experienced in dealing with obscene articles and who were said to be uncorrupted by it).

[287] Obscene Publications Act 1964, s 1(2).

[288] Obscene Publications Act 1959, s 1(2).

[289] Obsence Publications Act 1964, s 2(1).

[290] *A-G's Reference (No 5 of 1980)* [1981] 1 WLR 88.

[291] *R v Fellows* [1997] 2 All ER 548.

[292] Obscene Publications Act 1959, s 1(3).

[293] *R v Taylor (Alan)* [1995] 1 Cr App R 131.

[294] See *Olympia Press v Hollis* [1973] 1 WLR 1520, see also R Stone, 'Obscene Publications: The Problems Persist' [1986] Crim PR 139.

[295] *Gold Star Publications Ltd v DPP* [1981] 1 WLR 732.

[296] See the criticism by Robertson and Nicol (n 263 above) 134–135.

[297] *R v Calder and Boyars Ltd* [1969] 1 QB 151; *DPP v Jordan* [1977] AC 699.

merits[298] of the material in question.[299] 'Learning' means the 'product of scholarship'[300] and, as a result, a publication used for the purposes of teaching cannot be defended under section 4.

(c) Other obscenity and indecency offences

The Obscene Publications Act 1959 was intended to protect defendants against the prosecution of obscene libel. Thus, section 2(4) provides that an article shall not be proceeded against at common law 'where it is of the essence of the offence that the matter is obscene'. However, this does not prevent prosecutions being brought at common law on the basis that the essence of the offence is 'indecency'.[301] The result is that the defence of 'public good' is not available. Moreover, the common law offences of conspiracy to corrupt public morals[302] and of outraging public decency[303] are unaffected by the legislation. **15.88**

It is an offence publicly to display 'indecent matter'.[304] It appears that material can be 'indecent' for these purposes without being obscene.[305] A public place does not include a place to which the public only have access on payment or a shop to which the public can only gain acess by passing a warning sign.[306] **15.89**

Under the Protection of Children Act 1978 it is an offence to take or permit to be taken any indecent photograph of a child (that is, a person under 16),[307] to distribute or show such photographs,[308] to possess them with a view to distribution,[309] or to publish an advertisement likely to be understood as conveying that the advertiser distributes or shows such indecent photographs.[310] 'Indecent photographs' include films, film negatives and video recordings. The only defence to the offence of taking a photograph is that it is not 'indecent'. The motive for **15.90**

[298] In *John Calder Publications v Powell* [1965] 1 QB 509 it was held that a court is entitled to reject even favourable evidence and hold that the publication is not justified as being for the public good.

[299] s 4(2).

[300] *A-G's Reference (No 3 of 1977)* [1978] 1 WLR 1123.

[301] See Robertson and Nicol (n 263 above) 158–160.

[302] This would not entail the publication of the obscenity, but an agreement to do an act of a kind that may corrupt. See *Shaw v DPP* [1962] AC 220, regarding publication of a magazine offering the services of prostitutes; *Knuller (Publishing, Printing and Promotions) Ltd v DPP* [1973] AC 435.

[303] See *R v Gibson* [1991] 1 All ER 439; the criminal offence of outraging public decency, which prohibits the public display of offensive material, is aimed at protecting individuals from the shock or offence of exposure to certain material, rather than protecting public morals; see also cases on conspiracy to corrupt public morals: *Shaw v DPP* and *Knuller (Publishing, Printing and Promotions Ltd v DPP* (n 302 above).

[304] Indecent Displays (Control) Act 1981, s 1.

[305] Cf *R v Stanley* [1965] 2 QB 327.

[306] Indecent Displays (Control) Act 1981, s 1(3).

[307] s 1(1)(a).

[308] s 1(1)(b).

[309] s 1(1)(c).

[310] s 1(1)(d).

taking the photograph is irrelevant.[311] This means that, for example, taking a photograph for medical purposes would involve the commission of the offence. It is also an offence to possess an indecent picture of a child.[312] It is a defence to show a legitimate reason for possessing the photograph.

15.91 The import into the United Kingdom of 'indecent or obscene prints, paintings, photographs, books, cards, lithographic or other engravings or any other indecent or obsence articles' is prohibited.[313] The test of 'indecency' is much less strict than that under the Obscene Publications Act. However, it was held that insofar as this prohibition related to indecent articles imported from the EC it was in breach of Article 36[314] of the Treaty of European Union[315] and the Customs no longer seize material solely on the ground that it is 'indecent'. When considering a claim for forfeiture by the Customs, the court can order forfeiture if the material is 'obscene' within the definition in section 1 of the Obscene Publications Act 1959. The court does not have to go on to consider whether a section 4 'public good' defence might be available.[316]

(6) Media regulation and censorship

(a) Introduction[317]

15.92 The regulation of broadcasting, theatre, film and video has evolved in Britain over a long period of time and reflects an ambiguous attitude towards the media, which has been seen as both providing important public benefits and as a source of potential harm. It raises issues concerning the independence of radio and television from government, political impartiality and the standards to be applied when regulating the content of broadcasts.

(b) Broadcasting regulation[318]

15.93 **Introduction.** In the 1950s, there was a movement from regulation by means of

[311] *R v Graham-Kerr* [1988] 1 WLR 1098.

[312] Criminal Justice Act 1988, s 160.

[313] Customs Consolidation Act 1876, s 42; see generally, G Robertson and A Nicol, *Media Law* (3rd edn, Penguin Books, 1992), 153–155.

[314] Formerly, Art 30 of the Treaty of Rome.

[315] *Conegate Ltd v HM Customs and Excise* [1987] QB 254.

[316] *R v Bow Street Metropolitan Stipendiary Magistrates, ex p Noncyp Ltd* [1990] 1 QB 123.

[317] For a fuller treatment, see for example T Gibbons, *Regulating the Media* (2nd edn, Sweet & Maxwell, 1998); R Craufurd Smith, *Broadcasting Law and Fundamental Rights* (Clarendon Press, 1997).

[318] See eg A Briggs, *The History of Broadcasting in the UK, Vol I: The Birth of Broadcasting* (Oxford University Press 1961); *Vol II: The Golden Age of Wireless* (Oxford University Press 1965); *Vol IV: Sound and Vision* (1979); B Sendall, *Independent Television in Britain; Origin and Foundations 1946–62* (Macmillan, 1982); R Negrine (ed), *Cable Television and the Future of Broadcasting* (Croom Helm, 1985); T Hollins, *Beyond Broadcasting to the Cable Age* (BFI, 1984).

the criminal law to direct statutory regulation. This change coincided with the introduction of commercial television. In contrast to the absence of direct government regulation of newspapers, there was a perceived need for careful monitoring of television by a public body.

The Independent Broadcasting Authority ('IBA') was established in 1954 to ensure that nothing in independent television programming would offend against good taste, decency or public feeling or would be likely to encourage or incite to crime or to lead to disorder; that news was presented with accuracy and impartiality; and that impartiality of presentation was preserved with respect to matters of political or industrial controversy or relating to current public policy.[319] The Board of Governors of the British Broadcasting Corporation ('BBC') in 1964 voluntarily undertook[320] to comply in general terms with the statutory duties imposed on independent television, so that in effect all broadcasting, both public and independent, was subjected to the same standards. **15.94**

Public broadcasting. Public broadcasting is currently governed by the Royal Charter of the BBC comprising in part a Licence Agreement[321] with the Home Secretary. The 1964 undertaking as to standards has been reaffirmed and is now annexed to the BBC Licence:[322] it is the responsibility of the Governors of the BBC under these instruments to produce a code of content and scheduling requirements for the guidance of programme-makers including standards to be observed for the preservation of good taste, decency, the protection of children and political impartiality. Although the undertaking is not legally enforceable against the Corporation, BBC programming is also monitored by the Broadcasting Standards Commission ('BSC') established by the Broadcasting Act 1996.[323] Manifestly inappropriate material may be subject to injunction under the code of standards elaborated by that body. **15.95**

Independent broadcasting. Independent broadcasting is now governed by the Broadcasting Acts of 1990 and 1996. In an attempt to 'deregulate' independent television, these Acts replaced the IBA with the Independent Television Commission ('ITC') and the Independent Radio Authority, endowing them with licensing and regulatory powers. By section 6(1), the 1990 Act requires that the ITC **15.96**

---

[319] See Broadcasting Act 1981, s 4.

[320] Letter from Lord Normanbrook, Chairman of the BBC to the Postmaster-General 19 Jun 1964: 'The Board accept that so far as possible the programmes for which they are responsible should not offend against good taste or decency, or be likely to encourage crime or disorder, or be offensive to public feeling. In judging what is suitable for inclusion in programmes, they will pay special regard to the need to ensure that broadcasts designed to stimulate thought do not so far depart from their intention as to give general offence.'

[321] See Cmnd 8313 and 8233.

[322] The contents of the letter are noted in the prescribing memorandum under the BBC Licence and Agreement, cl 13(4).

[323] See para 15.99 below.

publish a Code to require that programmes containing politically sensitive material are balanced[324] in order to maintain impartiality.[325] Furthermore, although the Act does not impose a censorship role,[326] it establishes programme guidelines for good taste, decency and portrayal of violence.[327] A similar function is performed by the Independent Radio Authority in relation to monitoring independent radio stations.

15.97 **Satellite television.** The ITC Code only applies to broadcasters who hold an ITC licence. The Broadcasting Act 1990 requires that 'domestic' satellite services and 'non-domestic' satellite services hold an ITC licence. As defined, the two categories together do not represent comprehensive coverage of conceivable satellite services. A domestic service provides direct satellite broadcasting on one of five frequencies allocated to the United Kingdom at the World Administrative Radio Conference of 1977. Non-domestic service refers to satellite re-transmission of programmes either from within the United Kingdom, or into the United Kingdom from outside the territory if the service is nevertheless being dictated by a UK supplier. Any satellite transmission that does not qualify as either a 'domestic' or a 'non-domestic' service is not regulated by the Act.

15.98 Section 89 of the Broadcasting Act 1996, amending section 45 of the 1990 Act, permits immediate suspension of non-domestic satellite transmissions that do not meet the taste and decency standards of section 6(1)(a) of the Act. This UK legislation has been held to be contrary to the EC Directive on Transfrontier Television,[328] which requires that a service licensed from within any EC member state must be given freedom of reception within other member states. No clear exception is created for obscene material, which may create a difficulty for prosecution of satellite material beamed from other EC states.[329] No such difficulty will arise in relation to obscene publications transmitted from non-EC states.

---

[324] 'Balancing' must occur within a programme or series of programmes produced by a particular broadcasting company: it is not sufficient that the company assert that programming by another company will balance the bias exhibited by its production.

[325] The ITC published its Programme Code in 1991.

[326] This is in contrast to its predecessor, the Independent Broadcasting Authority, which previewed and approved scheduled programming; for cases unsuccessfully challenging these powers see: *A-G, ex rel McWhirter v Independent Broadcasting Authority* [1973] QB 629; *R v Independent Broadcasting Authority, ex p Whitehouse, The Times*, 4 Apr 1985.

[327] See *Broadcasting in the 90s: Competition, Choice and Quality* (1988) 517 (White Paper).

[328] 89/552/EEC; in Case 222/94 *Commission v United Kingdom* [1996] ECR-I 4025, it was found that the extraterritorial reach of the Broadcasting Act 1990, s 43 to broadcasters who fell under the regulatory jurisdiction of other member states was a violation of the Directive, Arts 2(1)(2) and 3(2).

[329] There have been a number of proscriptive orders issued under the Broadcasting Act 1990, s 177, against EC satellite channels that transmit hard core pornography: so far these have not been challenged in the European Court of Justice.

Broadcasting Standards Commission. Part V of the Broadcasting Act 1996 establishes a Broadcasting Standards Commission ('BSC').[330] The BSC is an amalgam of the Broadcasting Complaints Commission[331] and the Broadcasting Standards Council.[332] The functions of the BSC are applicable to all television and radio services provided by the BBC and other television and radio companies in the United Kingdom. The BSC has a duty to: 15.99

> draw up, and from time to time review, a code giving guidance as to the principles to be observed and the practices to be followed in connection with the avoidance of—
>
> (a) unjust or unfair treatment in programmes . . .
> (b) unwarranted infringement of privacy in or in connection with the obtaining of material contained in such programmes.[333]

In addition, it is required to draw up a code giving guidance as to the practices to be followed in connection with the portrayal of violence and sexual conduct.[334]

Government powers. The Broadcasting Act confers important powers on the Government over radio and television. Powers of censorship over the BBC are contained in sections 13(4) and 19 of the Licence Agreement: section 19 enables the Home Secretary, in an 'emergency' and when he thinks it 'expedient', to send in the troops to take possession of the BBC in the name of and on behalf of Her Majesty.[335] More significant is the power under section 13(4), by which he may ban transmission of any BBC item or programme at any time, subject to the minimal safeguard that the BBC 'may' tell the public that it has received a section 13(4) order from the Government.[336] 15.100

A parallel power in relation to independent television entitles the Government under section 10(3) of the 1990 Act to order the ITC to refrain from transmitting 15.101

[330] s 106.

[331] Established by the Broadcasting Act 1980, s 17 and continued by the Broadcasting Act 1981, s 53 and the Broadcasting Act 1990, s 142.

[332] See the Broadcasting Act 1990, s 151.

[333] s 107.

[334] s 108. For an example of the BSC's exercise of its powers, see the discussion of its handling of the satellite broadcast channel 'Red Hot Dutch' in S Bailey, D Harris and B Jones *Civil Liberties: Cases and Materials* (4th edn, Butterworths, 1995) 345; also F Coleman and S McMurtrie, 'Too Hot to Handle' [1993] NLJ 10; and see also *R v Secretary of State for the Natural Heritage ex p Continental Television* [1993] 2 CMLR 333.

[335] This provision was established during the General Strike when the Government under Winston Churchill wanted to control the BBC; although it has never been used for that purpose, it was contemplated by Sir Anthony Eden as a basis for broadcasting propaganda during the Suez crisis and was used as such to beam propaganda to Argentina during the Falklands war.

[336] Home Secretary Reginald Maudling tried to use this power to stop BBC broadcasts of a debate about Government action in Ulster, but the safeguard was invoked by Lord Hill, Director-General of the BBC, who threatened to make public the Government's attempts to keep the matter quiet.

any 'matter or classes of matter' on commercial television. Although the veto has been little used, it was recently applied in an attempt to deprive terrorists of publicity by imposing a ban on the broadcast of words as spoken by representatives of specified organisations.[337] A challenge was unsuccessful when the House of Lords, in *R v Secretary of State for the Home Department, ex p Brind*[338] held that Ministers and public bodies were not obliged to exercise their powers in accordance with Convention rights. The ban was lifted in September 1994, following the IRA declaration of ceasefire.

15.102 **DA Notice system.**[339] The Defence Press and Broadcasting Advisory Committee ('DPBAC') is a joint committee of the Ministry of Defence, publishers and broadcasters. It offers informal advice to the press on the content of proposed publications and broadcasts, in the interests of and for the protection of national security. The DPBAC acts as a cooperative consultative and negotiating body between the media and the Ministry: it has no judicial function and participation by the press in the DA Notice system is entirely voluntary.

15.103 The function of the DPBAC, as broadly defined by the Ministry of Defence, is to review proposed publications to identify information that the Government considers it necessary to keep secret. There are eight specific categories of information with which the Committee is concerned:

- defence plans, operational capability, state of readiness and training;
- defence equipment;
- nuclear weapons and equipment;
- radio and radar transmissions;
- cyphers and communications;
- British security and intelligence services;
- war precautions and civil defence; and
- photography etc of defence establishments and installations.

There are six 'standing' DA Notices covering highly classified information about future military operations, defence equipment, nuclear weapons installations, codes and ciphers, details of sites for the use of Government in times of crisis nad information about security and intelligence services.[340]

15.104 A publisher or broadcaster may itself approach the Committee to ask its advice on a proposed publication. The Committee may on, the other hand, initiate

[337] The organisations included, in addition to those identified in the Northern Ireland (Emergency Provisions) Act 1978, Sinn Fein, Republican Sinn Fein, and the Ulster Defence Association.

[338] *R v Secretary of State for the Home Department, ex p Brind* [1991] 1 AC 696.

[339] See D Fairley, 'D Notices, Official Secrets and the Law' (1990) 10 OJLS 430–40. 'D Notices' were renamed 'DA Notices' (Defence Advisory Notices) in 1993.

[340] *The Defence Advisory Notices, A Review of the D Notice System* (Ministry of Defence Open Government Document No 93/06).

contact.[341] If the DPBAC concludes that the contents of a publication threaten national security in one of its areas of responsibility, it will suggest that changes are made. If the advice is not accepted, it will issue a DA Notice.

The DA Notice serves solely as a warning device. The fact that a DA Notice has no legal force has both positive and negative implications: the media can be assured that it will not be prosecuted merely for defying the advice of the Committee; on the other hand, the DPBAC has no power to provide security clearance and provides a publisher with no defence or justification should the Government seek to restrain the publication under the Official Secrets Act[342] or on grounds of breach of confidence.[343] **15.105**

(c) Theatre, film and video censorship

The Theatres Act 1968 removed the official censorship of theatrical productions so that theatre performances are now only subject to the criminal law. Film censorship, on the other hand, continues to be governed by the Cinemas Act 1985 which establishes a licensing requirement for premises used for film exhibitions. The Act also imposes a duty on the licensing authority[344] to define regulations and conditions for the admission of children to such exhibitions. Furthermore, the Act authorises the licensing body to make regulations for the 'safety', 'health', and 'welfare' of children attending film exhibitions. **15.106**

In 1912, the British Board of Film Censors was established by the film industry to provide guidance to local authorities which had been given licensing powers under the Cinematograph Act 1909.[345] The decisions and classification criteria of the non-statutory body were well accepted and the objective of the BBFC largely achieved. Although there has been controversy over specific films, most councils have generally been happy to rely upon the judgment of the BBFC. The Board, renamed the British Board of Film Classification, is also the authority designated by **15.107**

[341] If a publisher does not normally participate in the DA Notice system, the DPBAC will send it a copy of the relevant DA Notice and a guide to the system called the *General Introduction to the D Notice System*: for a copy of this document, see S Bailey, D Harris and B Jones, *Civil Liberties: Cases and Materials* (4th edn, Butterworths, 1995) 470–471.

[342] There is, however, substantial overlap between the contents of a DA Notice and the relevant Government legislation in the area. DA Notice 6 in relation to British Security and Intelligence Services, for example, requests that the media refrain from publishing references to an extensive list of specific matters that comes close to comprehensive coverage of the matters that could be caught by the Official Secrets Act.

[343] For example, when the BBC approached the DPBAC in regard to a radio series exploring aspects of national security in the wake of the *Spycatcher* litigation, it was told that advice was not necessary: nevertheless, the Government sought and obtained injunctions restraining the broadcasts on grounds of breach of confidence. Although the Government eventually acknowledged that the programmes were not a threat and the injunctions were lifted, the BBC delayed their broadcast and in certain instances, declined to deliver altogether.

[344] The licensing authorities are now London boroughs and district councils across the country: see Cinema Act 1985 ss 3(10), 21.

[345] See G Robertson and A Nicol, *Media Law* (3rd edn, Penguin Books, 1992) 566ff.

the Home Secretary to deal with the arrangements for certifying videos under section 4(1) of the Video Recordings Act 1984 as:

> the authority responsible for making arrangements
>
> (a) for determining, for the purposes of [the] Act whether or not video works are suitable for classification certificates to be issued in respect of them, having special regard to the likelihood of video works in respect of which such certificates have been issued being viewed in the home,
>
> (b) in the case of works which are determined in accordance with the arrangements to be so suitable
>
> (i) for making such other determinations as are required for the issue of classification certificates, and
>
> (ii) for issuing such certificates . . .

15.108 The Video Recordings Act 1984 gives rise to a number of problems. First, it requires classification of almost all video recordings,[346] whether or not they have already been broadcast on television. The BBFC will censor videos containing a wide range of material including cruelty to animals, drug use, violence, sexual violence and blasphemy.[347] Decisions regarding classification may be appealed to the Video Appeals Committee,[347a] which is selected by the BBFC. The decision of the Video Appeals Committee to certify the film, called 'Visions of Ecstasy', on the ground of blasphemy resulted in an unsuccessful application to the European Court of Human Rights in *Wingrove v United Kingdom*.[348]

15.109 The BBFC now classifies films and videos in accordance with its published guidelines.[349] It often makes distribution under a particular classification conditional upon cuts being made to the film.

15.110 The power of local authorities to license cinemas is contained in the Cinemas Act 1985. It is an offence to use unlicensed premises for film exhibition.[350] Conditions, which usually require compliance with BBFC classifications, may be attached to licences.[351] Local authorities can, however, prohibit the showing of films which the BBFC have certified for viewing.[352] Local authorities also have licensing powers under which they regulate sex cinemas.[353]

---

[346] For exemptions, see s 2.

[347] See Robertson and Nicol (n 354 above) 584–590.

[347a] See, eg, *R v Video Appeals Committee of the British Board of Film Classification ex p British Board of Film Classification*, 16 May 2000 (unreported).

[348] (1996) 24 EHRR 1.

[349] U (universal); Uc (universal and suitable for young children); PG (parental guidance required); 12 (passed only for persons 12 years and over); 15 (passed only for persons 15 years and over); 18 (passed only for persons 18 years and over); R18 (restricted 18: passed only for distribution through specially licensed cinemas or sex shops to which no one under 18 is admitted)

[350] s 10; licences are not required for exhibitions which are not for private gain.

[351] s 1(3).

[352] Notorious examples include 'Ulysses' and 'The Life of Brian' which were banned in many local authority areas; see generally, Robertson and Nicol (n 345 above) 569–572.

[353] Local Government (Miscellaneous Provisions) Act 1982, Sch 3.

(7) Freedom of expression and the criminal law

(a) Introduction

The criminal law has traditionally placed significant restrictions on freedom of expression. At common law, there were four related offences: obscene libel, blasphemous libel, seditious libel and defamatory libel. Only the first of these has been codified by statute. This is dealt with in section 5 above.[353a] There are also a number of other statutory offences which affect expression. Finally, there are statutory restrictions on police powers to seize 'journalistic material' for the purposes of investigation of criminal offences. **15.111**

(b) Blasphemous libel

It is an offence to publish material which is likely to shock and outrage the feelings of believers[354] in the established religion.[355] The only mental element required is an intention to publish the offending words.[356] This offence is considered in detail in Chapter 14.[357] **15.112**

Prosecutions for blasphemous libel are very rare;[358] and the Law Commission has recommended its abolition.[359] Nevertheless, it currently remains a potential restriction on freedom of expression; and may take on greater importance if the Human Rights Act results in the offence becoming extended to other religions.[360] **15.113**

(c) Seditious libel

It is a common law offence to publish words with a seditious intention. The words may be written or spoken. In *R v Chief Metropolitan Stipendiary Magistrate, ex p Choudhury*[361] the offence was confined to **15.114**

> an intention to incite to violence or create public disturbance or disorder against His Majesty or the institutions of government. Proof of an intention to promote feelings of ill-will and hostility between different classes of subjects does not alone establish a seditious intention. Not only must there be proof of an incitement to violence in this connection but it must be violence or resistance or defiance for the purpose of disturbing constituted authority.[362]

Seditious libel involves demonstration of a more restrictive 'mental element' than other common law libel offences. It seems, however, that the Divisional Court has

---

[353a] See para 15.88 above.
[354] See *Whitehouse v Gay News* [1979] AC 617.
[355] *R v Gathercole* (1838) 2 Lew CC 237, 254; 168 ER 1140, 1145.
[356] See *Whitehouse v Gay News* (n 354 above).
[357] See para 14.14ff above.
[358] The *Gay News* case is the first to have been brought in this area in over 60 years.
[359] See Law Commission, *Offences against Religion and Public Worship* (Law Com No 145, 1985).
[360] See para 14.77 above.
[361] [1991] 1 QB 429.
[362] Ibid 453.

extended the offence by the reference to the 'disturbance of constituted authority'[363] but the precise scope of the offence is uncertain.

15.115 Prosecutions for seditious libel are also very rare, with only one prosecution in the past 80 years. This was the 1947 case of *R v Caunt*[364] which concerned an article attacking British Jews. The editor was acquitted. On the analysis of the offence put forward in *Ex parte Choudhury*,[364a] it would appear that the judge was wrong to hold that the offence could extend to the stirring up of racial hatred or class violence.

(d) Defamatory or criminal libel[365]

15.116 The common law offence of 'defamatory' libel is the most common of the common law libel offences and is often known as 'criminal libel'. The publication must be in permanent form and the words must tend to vilify a person and to bring them into hatred, contempt and ridicule.[366] Furthermore, the words must constitute a 'serious' and not a trivial libel.[367] It is no longer necessary, however, that the libel relate to a public figure or that it should have a tendency to provoke the person defamed to commit a breach of the peace.[368] The mental element of the offence is not clear. It may be that all that is required is an intention to publish the words[369] or perhaps to prove an intention to defame.[370]

15.117 Although the principles of law applicable to civil and criminal libels are for the most part similar, there are several important exceptions. First, while a civil action requires publication of the statement to a third person, it appears that publication to the defamed person alone will sustain a prosecution in criminal libel.[371] Secondly, no civil action lies against a dead person, but if the libel was intended or tends to damage living persons or to cause a breach of the peace, it may be criminally prosecuted. Thirdly, no civil action for libel can be aimed at a group or class of people; but such defamation will be subject to the criminal law if it tends to excite public hatred against the class.[372] Finally, the truth of a defamatory statement

---

[363] See D Feldman, *Civil Liberties and Human Rights in England and Wales* (Clarendon Press, 1993) 679.

[364] Noted in (1947) 64 LQR 203.

[364a] See n 361 above.

[365] See Law Commission, *Report on Criminal Libel* (Law Com No 149, Cmnd 9618, 1985).

[366] This is the traditional definition of libel and continues to apply in the criminal law: see *Goldsmith v Pressdram* [1977] QB 83, 87.

[367] See *Gleaves v Deakin* [1980] AC 477, 487, 495; see generally, P Milmo and W Rogers (eds), *Gatley on Libel and Slander* (9th edn, Sweet & Maxwell, 1998) para 22.2.

[368] *R v Wicks* [1936] 1 All ER 384, 386; *Gleaves v Deakin* (n 367 above) 498g.

[369] *R v Wicks* (n 368 above).

[370] See J Smith and B Hogan, *Criminal Law* (7th edn, Butterworths, 1999) 729 and *Gatley on Libel and Slander* (n 367 above) para 22.3.

[371] Although *Gatley on Libel and Slander* (n 367 above) suggests that this is no longer the case, see para 22.5.

[372] See *R v Williams* (1822) 5 B & Ald 595.

has always been an absolute defence to an action under the civil law; while in the criminal law this was not so at common law. There is, however, a statutory defence of truth to an action in criminal libel, if publication is for the public benefit.[373]

Section 8 of the Law of Libel Amendment Act 1888 requires that leave must be obtained before bringing a prosecution for criminal libel against a proprietor, publisher, editor or any other person responsible for publishing a newspaper. Section 8 does not, however, apply to prosecutions of individual journalists.[374] A judge should not give leave unless there is a clear *prima facie* case and the public interest requires the institution of criminal proceedings.[375] **15.118**

(e) Other criminal offences

Racial hatred. Incitement to racial hatred was first criminalised under the Race Relations Act of 1965. Part III of the Public Order Act 1986 contains a number of offences which restrict freedom of expression. The 1986 Act defines racial hatred as: **15.119**

> hatred against a group of persons in Great Britain defined by reference to colour, race, nationality (including citizenship) or ethnic or national origins.[376]

It therefore does not include hatred based on grounds of religion.[377]

The Public Order Act 1986 creates three main offences relating to the incitement of racial hatred. Each requires that the accused acts either with the intention of stirring up racial hatred, or in circumstances in which there is a likelihood that racial hatred will be stirred up.[378] First, it is an offence to use threatening or abusive or insulting words or behaviour[379] or to display abusive or insulting written material. The same prohibition applies to the publication or distribution of written material,[380] the presentation or direction of public performances of plays,[381] the distribution or presentation of visual images or sounds[382] and the provision or production of a programme or programme service containing such material.[383] Finally, it is an offence to be in possession of written material or recordings of images or sounds which is threatening, abusive or insulting with a view to its being displayed or published.[384] **15.120**

[373] Libel Act 1843, s 6.
[374] See *Desmond v Thorne* [1983] 1 WLR 163; and see *Gatley on Libel and Slander* (n 367 above) para 22.10.
[375] See *Goldsmith v Pressdram* [1977] QB 83, 89; and *Desmond v Thorne* (n 374 above).
[376] s 17.
[377] Cf the discussion of the phrase 'racial grounds' under the Race Relations Act 1976, at para 17.56 below.
[378] s 18.
[379] Ibid.
[380] s 19.
[381] s 20.
[382] s 21.
[383] s 22.
[384] s 23.

15.121 The Public Order Act 1986 also criminalises the use of threatening, abusive or insulting words or behaviour which is likely to cause, in general terms, public disorder. In some circumstances these provisions may be applicable to racially motivated actions. Section 4 provides that it is an offence to use threatening, abusive or insulting words or behaviour or to distribute or display such writing, signs or other visible representation, with intent to cause a person to believe that immediate unlawful violence will be used against him or to provoke him to use violence. Section 5 prohibits disorderly behaviour which is intended to harass. A criminal offence will be committed under that section if words or behaviour that are threatening, abusive or insulting are used or any such material displayed 'within the hearing of a person likely to be caused harassment, alarm or distress'.[385]

15.122 The racial hatred provisions of the Public Order Act 1986 have been criticised as not providing a solution to the problem of racially motivated demonstrations or marches. Although section 18 is likely to be applied in relation to processions and assemblies, it may be ineffective in protecting racial groups against intimidatory marches, which are not intended to stir up racial hatred; furthermore, public or private meetings held in a 'dwelling' are not covered.[386] Behaviour which is not an incitement to racial hatred under sections 18 through 23 may breach sections 4 and 5 if it is threatening to a particular racial group.

(f) Police powers to seize journalistic material

15.123 Material which is acquired or created for the purposes of journalism is specially protected against search and seizure by the police. By section 8 of the Police and Criminal Evidence Act 1984, a Justice of the Peace can authorise entry and search only where the material sought does not consist of or include 'journalistic material'.[387] A constable who wishes to obtain access to excluded material or special procedure material for the purposes of a criminal investigation may make an application to the circuit judge under section 9 of the Police and Criminal Evidence Act 1984 for a production order or a search warrant under and in accordance with Schedule 1. No order can be made for the production of journalistic material held in confidence[388] unless such an order could have been made under the previous law.[389]

385 Animal rights demonstrators using signs designed to shock have been charged with these offences.

386 s 18(2); hence there is no protection against attacks on racial groups meeting in the context of a pub or restaurant.

387 Defined by Police and Criminal Evidence Act 1984, s 13.

388 As defined by ibid s 11(3).

389 This covers a limited range of circumstances, for example, if the material was stolen.

A circuit judge can only make a production order for other journalistic material if he is satisfied that a number of 'access conditions' are fulfilled.[390] There must be reasonable grounds for believing that: **15.124**

- a serious arrestable offence has been committed;
- the material is likely to be of substantial value to the investigation and is likely to be relevant evidence; and
- other methods of obtaining the material have failed or appear to be bound to fail.

More importantly, it must be in the public interest to make an order, having regard to the benefit likely to accrue to the investigation if the material is obtained and to the circumstances under which the person in possession of the material holds it.[391]

The effect of these provisions in relation to journalistic material was considered in *Chief Constable of Avon and Somerset Constabulary v Bristol United Press*.[392] The judge ordered the production of photographs of public disorders taken for 'journalistic purposes.' Although the mere assertion that the material would be of substantial value was insufficient, the court was entitled to draw inferences; but the respondent could produce evidence to the court, without the police seeing it, to show that the material was not of substantial value. It was held that, to fulfil paragraph 2(a) of the access conditions in Schedule 1, it was not necessary for the material sought to relate to some particular criminal offence. The judge was prepared to draw the inference, in the absence of contrary evidence, that photographers would take pictures of assaults and acts of violence and that their material would, therefore, be likely to provide evidence of 'serious arrestable offences'. The judge was of the view that the public interest in the 'impartiality and independence of the press' would not be undermined by making the order. Even if it was undermined in some people's eyes 'that could not outweigh the great public interest in the conviction of those guilty of serious crime'. An application for judicial review of this decision was refused.[393] **15.125**

The court in the *Bristol United Press* case did not directly consider the impact of 'freedom of expression'. However, in *Re an application under Police and Criminal Evidence Act*[394] it was held that the 'public interest' condition was not satisfied. The judge held that interference with the public interest in press freedom had to be 'convincingly established'. The assertion that the material was needed for the detection and prosecution of crime was not, of itself, sufficient for this purpose and the police had to avoid treating these applications as routine. **15.126**

[390] Police and Criminal Evidence Act 1984, Sch 1, para 1.

[391] Ibid Sch 1, para 2(c).

[392] *The Independent,* 4 Nov 1986 (Stuart-Smith J, sitting as a circuit judge).

[393] *R v Bristol Crown Court, ex p Bristol Press and Picture Agency Ltd* (1986) 85 Cr App R 190.

[394] 2 Jul 1999, Central Criminal Court, HHJ Pownall; see also *R v Central Criminal Court ex p Bright, The Times,* 26 Jul 2000 (not reported on this point).

(8) Expression and government secrecy

(a) Introduction

15.127 Restrictions upon freedom of expression are often justified because they protect the national security interests of the state. The laws safeguarding secrecy include the law of confidence[395] and the Official Secrets Acts of 1911 to 1989. The Official Secrets Acts cover everything from serious national security offences to unauthorised releases of public information.

(b) Official secrets and the criminal law

15.128 The Official Secrets Act 1911 was passed through Parliament in one day in an atmosphere of panic and was subjected to intensive criticism over many years.[396] The catch-all provision of section 2 has now been repealed, but the 'espionage' provision of section 1 remains in force.

15.129 Section 1 of the Official Secrets Act 1911 provides that an offence is committed where

> any person for any purpose prejudicial to the safety or interests of the State . . . communicates to any other person any secret official code word, or pass word, or any sketch plan, model, article, note, or other document or information which is calculated to be or might be or is intended to be directly useful to an enemy.[397]

'Enemy' in this section includes 'potential enemy'.[398] In *Chandler v DPP*[399] the House of Lords held that 'the interests of the state' meant such interests according to the policies of the state as they in fact were, not as it might be argued they ought to be.

15.130 Section 2 of the Official Secrets Act 1911 created a very wide offence of 'disclosure of any official information, without authority'. The disclosure of the information did not have to be harmful.[400] This section was repealed by the Official Secrets Act 1989 and replaced by a number of more specific restrictions on various types of disclosure of information. These include:

- disclosure of information relating to security or intelligence by members and former members of the security and intelligence services;[401]

---

[395] See para 12.27ff above.
[396] See eg *Report of the Franks Committee on Section 2 of the Official Secrets Act 1911* (1972) Cmnd 5104; and see P Birkinshaw, *Reforming the Secret State* (Hull University Press, 1990).
[397] s 1(1).
[398] *R v Parrott* (1913) 8 Cr App R 186.
[399] [1964] AC 763.
[400] See *R v Crisp and Homewood* (1919) 83 JP 121: army clothing contracts.
[401] s 1(1), there is no requirement under this subsection that the information is 'damaging'. The House of Lords held in *A-G v Blake, The Times*, 3 Aug 2000, that where an intelligence officer published an autobiography which breached s 1, the Crown was entitled to confiscate his profits by obtaining an order for an account based upon his breach of contract.

- damaging disclosure[402] of security or intelligence information by other Crown servants or Government contractors;[403]
- damaging disclosure[404] of information relating to defence by Crown servants or Government contractors;[405]
- damaging disclosure[406] of information relating to international relations or confidential information obtained from another state by Crown servants or Government contractors;[407]
- disclosure of information obtained as a result of warrants issued under the Interception of Communications Act 1985 or the Security Service Act 1989.[408]

It is also an offence to disclose information which has been disclosed by Crown servants or Government contractors without lawful authority or on terms requiring it to be held in confidence.[409] The Act makes no provision of a defence of 'public interest' or 'prior publication' in relation to any type of disclosure.

(c) Official secrets and breach of confidence

In recent years the Government has increasingly relied on civil remedies against the media to prevent publication of allegedly secret material, particularly breach of confidence.[410] In the 'Crossman Diaries' case[411] the Attorney-General sought an injunction to restrain publication of the diaries, on the ground that disclosure of Cabinet discussions was contrary to the public interest. The defendants' argument that the private law doctrine of 'breach of confidence' did not apply to Cabinet discussions was rejected; Lord Widgery CJ denied that the courts should be powerless to restrain the publication of public secrets.[412] He held, however, that, in order to obtain an injunction, the Attorney-General had to show: **15.131**

(a) that such publication would be a breach of confidence;
(b) that the public interest requires that publication be restrained; and
(c) that there are no other facets of the public interest contradictory to and more compelling than that relied upon. Moreover, the court, when asked to restrain a publication, must examine the extent to which relief is necessary to ensure that restrictions are not imposed beyond the strict requirement of public need.[413]

[402] As defined by s 1(4).
[403] s 1(3).
[404] As defined by s 2(2).
[405] s 2(1).
[406] As defined by s 3(2).
[407] s 3(1).
[408] s 4(1), (3); there is no requirement under this subsection that the information is 'damaging'.
[409] s 5.
[410] See generally, para 12.27ff above.
[411] *A-G v Jonathan Cape Ltd* [1976] 1 QB 752.
[412] Ibid 769G–H.
[413] Ibid 770G–771A.

As much of the material was 10-years-old and three general elections had since been held, there was, on the facts no sufficient public interest in restraining publication and an injunction was refused.[414]

15.132 This principle was invoked most significantly in the *Spycatcher* litigation.[415] The House of Lords in *A-G v Guardian Newspapers Ltd (No 2)*[416] held that members and former members of the security service owed a lifelong duty of confidence to the Crown. Lord Goff, however, made clear that, in the case of Government secrets:

> it is incumbent on the Crown, in order to restrain disclosure of Government secrets, not only to show that the information is confidential, but also to show that it is not in the public interest that it should be published.[417]

(9) Freedom of information

15.133 The Government has always sought to exercise strict control over information concerning the operation of the administration.[418] In recent years, partly under the influence of 'freedom of information' legislation abroad,[419] there has been increasing pressure for greater disclosure of governmental information.[420] In 1994, the Government issued the *Code of Practice on Access to Government Information* (which applies to Government departments and public bodies under the jurisdiction of the Parliamentary Ombudsman).[421] A Freedom of Information Bill was published in 1999.[422]

15.134 There are limited rights to freedom of information from local government.[423] Part VA of the Local Government Act 1972[424] enables any member of the public to inspect and take copies of local authority minutes, reports and background papers. The minutes of decisions by the full council, committee or sub-committee are available for inspection by members of the public.[425] Members of the public are

---

[414] See also *Commonwealth of Australia v John Fairfax and Sons Ltd* (1980) 147 CLR 39.

[415] See para 15.19ff above.

[416] [1990] 1 AC 109

[417] *Per* Lord Goff, *A-G v Guardian Newspapers Ltd (No 2)* (n 416 above); see also *Lord Advocate v The Scotsman Publications Ltd* [1990] 1 AC 812.

[418] For a history see P Birkinshaw, *Freedom of Information: The Law, the Practice and the Ideal* (2nd edn, Butterworths, 1996) Chap 3 'Government and Information: An Historical Development'.

[419] Ibid Chap 2 'Freedom of Information: Overseas Experience'.

[420] See, ibid Chap 8 and also G Robertson and A Nichol, *Media Law* (3rd edn, Penguin, 1992) 412ff.

[421] Ibid 201–213.

[422] For criticism of its contents see P Birkinshaw and N Parry, 'Every Trick in the Book: the Freedom of Information Bill 1999' [1999] EHRLR 373.

[423] See Birkinshaw (n 418 above) 138ff.

[424] Introduced by the Local Government (Access to Information) Act 1985.

[425] Local Government Act 1972, s 100C.

also entitled to inspect the reports considered by officers[426] and background papers.[427] Furthermore, the *Good Administrative Guide* issued by the Local Government Ombudsman contains principles of good administration including information on policies, procedures and complaints.

However, the Local Governmment Act is subject to two significant limitations. First, certain types of information are exempt from access to information[428] such as: **15.135**

- information concerning a particular employee or office holder or former employee or office holder or applicant;
- information concerning a particular occupant or former occupant or applicant for council accommodation;
- information concerning a particular applicant, recipient or former recipient of financial assistance;
- the amount of expenditure incurred by the authority under a particular contract to buy property, goods or services;
- information about consultations or negotiations or contemplated consultations or negotiations concerning labour relations;
- instructions to and advice from counsel regarding any proceedings or determining any matter affecting the authority.

Secondly, Part VA of the Local Government Act does not apply to council working parties. Whether a particular body is a committee or a working party depends primarily on the subjective intention of the local authority; its manifest intention is decisive unless something unlawful lies behind it.[429]

There are also statutory rights to certain information from educational institutions. The following must be made available on request: **15.136**

- the agenda, draft minutes, signed minutes and reports, documents and papers considered at meetings of the governing bodies of schools (subject to certain exceptions);[430]
- a school's statement of its policy concerning secular curiculum;[431]
- information about school admissions procedures and public examination results in England[432] and Wales.[433]

---

[426] Ibid ss 100C, 100E.
[427] Ibid ss 100D, 100E.
[428] Local Government Act 1972, s 100I, Sch 12A.
[429] *R v Warwickshire CC, ex p Bailey* [1991] COD 284.
[430] Education (School Government) Regulations 1989, SI 1989/1503 as modified by Education (School Government) (Transition to New Framework) Regulations 1998, SI 1998/2763.
[431] Education (School Curriculum and Related Information) Regulations 1989, SI 1989/954).
[432] Education (School Information) (England) Regulations 1998, SI 1998/2526.
[433] Education (School Information) (Wales) Regulations 1998, SI 1998/1832.

C. The Law Under the European Convention

(1) Introduction

15.137 Article 10 of the Convention provides:

> (1) Everyone has the right to freedom of expression. This right shall include freedom to hold opinions and to receive and impart information and ideas without interference by public authority and regardless of frontiers. This Article shall not prevent States from requiring the licensing of broadcasting, television or cinema enterprises.
> (2) The exercise of these freedoms, since it carries with it duties and responsibilities, may be subject to such formalities, conditions, restrictions or penalties as are prescribed by law and are necessary in a democratic society, in the interests of national security, territorial integrity or public safety, for the prevention of disorder or crime, for the protection of health or morals, for the protection of the reputation or rights of others, for preventing the disclosure of information received in confidence, or for maintaining the authority and impartiality of the judiciary.

15.138 The Convention was the first human rights instrument to make express provision for limitations on the freedom of expression.[434] Article 10 expressly acknowledges that freedom of expression has the potential to damage the interests of others or the public interest. The tension between the right of expression and the need to protect other rights has been at the heart of the Convention jurisprudence under Article 10.

15.139 The right to freedom of expression has been consistently recognised as being an 'essential foundation of a democratic society' and a 'basic condition for its progress and for the development of every man'.[435] In the recent case of *Zana v Turkey*[436] the Court summarised and reaffirmed the fundamental principles in the following terms:

> The Court reiterates the fundamental principles which emerge from its judgments relating to Article 10:
>
> (1) Freedom of expression constitutes one of the essential foundations of a democratic society and one of the basic conditions for its progress and for each individual's self fulfilment. Subject to Article 10(2), it is applicable not only to 'information' or 'ideas' that are favourably received or regarded as inoffensive or as a matter of indifference, but also to those that offend, shock or disturb the State or any sector of the population. Such are the demands of that pluralism, tolerance and broadmindedness without which there is no 'democratic society'. As set forth in Article 10, this freedom is subject to exceptions which must, however, be construed strictly, and the need for any restrictions must be established convincingly.[437]

[434] Contrast Art 19 of the Universal Declaration, see App H in Vol 2.

[435] Similar formulations are used in cases from *Handyside v United Kingdom* (1976) 1 EHRR 737 para 49 to *Zana v Turkey* (1997) 27 EHRR 667 para 51.

[436] (1997) 27 EHRR 667 para 51.

[437] *Handyside v United Kingdom* (1976) 1 EHRR 737 para 49; *Lingens v Austria* (1986) 8 EHRR 103 para 31; *Jersild v Denmark* (1994) 19 EHRR 1 para 37.

(2) The adjective 'necessary' within the meaning of Article 10 implies the existence of a 'pressing social need'. The Contracting States have a certain margin of appreciation in assessing whether such a need exists, but it goes hand in hand with European supervision, embracing both the legislation and the decisions relating to it, even those given by an independent court. The Court is therefore empowered to give the final ruling on whether a 'restriction' is reconcilable with freedom of expression as protected by Article 10.[438]

(3) In exercising its supervisory jurisdiction, the Court must look at the whole, including the content of the remarks held against the applicant and context in which he made them. In particular, it must determine whether the interference in issue is 'proportionate to the legitimate aim pursued' and whether the reasons adduced by the national authorities are 'relevant and sufficient'.[439] In so doing the Court has to satisfy itself that the national authorities applied standards which are in conformity with the principles embodied in Article 10 and, moreover, that they based themselves on an acceptable assessment of the relevant facts.[440]

(2) Scope of the right

(a) Introduction

'Expression' has been interpreted broadly to include communications of any kind or subject matter: spoken or written words, television programmes[441] and broadcasting,[442] film,[443] video,[444] pictures,[445] dress,[446] images[447] and probably electronic information systems where they are used to express ideas or to convey information. Furthermore, the concept of 'expression' covers conduct such as acts of protest (even where they involve physically interfering with the activity protested against)[448] and the physical expression of feelings.[449] However, it does not extend to linguistic freedom[450] or the right to vote or stand for election.[451] **15.140**

---

[438] *Lingens v Austria* (n 437 above) para 39.

[439] Ibid para 40; and *Barfod v Denmark* (1989) 13 EHRR 493 para 28.

[440] *Jersild v Denmark* (n 437 above) para 31.

[441] See eg *Hodgson v United Kingdom* (1987) 51 DR 136, EComm HR.

[442] See eg *Autronic AG v Switzerland* (1990) 12 EHRR 485 where the Court acknowledged that the public have a right to receive broadcasts.

[443] See eg *Otto-Preminger-Institute v Austria* (1994) 19 EHRR 34.

[444] See eg *Wingrove v United Kingdom* (1996) 24 EHRR 1.

[445] *Müller v Switzerland* (1988) 13 EHRR 212.

[446] *Stevens v United Kingdom* (1986) 46 DR 245, EComm HR.

[447] *Chorherr v Austria* (1993) 17 EHRR 358.

[448] *Steel v United Kingdom* (1998) 5 BHRC 339 para 92; *Chorherr v Austria* (n 447 above); and see para 15.146 below.

[449] *X v United Kingdom* (1978) 3 EHRR 63, EComm HR (homosexual activity).

[450] See the Belgian linguistics cases: *23 Inhabitants of Alsemberg and Beersel v Belgium* (1963) 6 YB 332; *X v Belgium*, (1963) 6 YB 444, in which it was held that the applicant had no freedom of choice as to the language of instruction for his children.

[451] *Liberal Party, Mrs R and Mr P v United Kingdom* (1982) 4 EHRR 106.

15.141 Statements directed against the Convention's underlying values, such as the justification of a pro-Nazi policy, do not enjoy the protection of Article 10.[452] With this exception, there is probably no form of expression that is excluded from the protection of Article 10 on the basis of its *content*[453] (although the Court has occasionally suggested that 'valueless' expression might not be protected).[454] This means, for example, that 'expression' is applicable to ideas that 'offend, shock or disturb'.[455] Thus, in *Jersild v Denmark*[456] the Court held that convicting a journalist for aiding and abetting racist insults in a television programme was disproportionate to the need to protect those whom he had insulted. Similarly, in *Lehideux v France*[457] the Court held that convictions for portraying Marshall Petain positively in a false light were disproportionate interferences with freedom of expression. However, the Commission has applied a low standard of review when considering whether Article 10 has been violated in cases arising from racist literature[458] or support for terrorist activities.[459]

15.142 The distinction in Article 10 between information and ideas makes it clear that 'expression' is not restricted to statements of fact.[460] It encompasses opinions, criticism and speculation, whether or not they are objectively 'true'. In *Thorgeirson v Iceland*[461] the Court considered that an obligation on the applicant to prove the truth of his opinions was an interference with freedom of expression.

15.143 Furthermore, the fact that views are expressed in polemical language does not take them outside the scope of Article 10. Thus, in *De Haes and Gijsels v Belgium*,[462] journalists who personally insulted certain members of the judiciary for their handling of child abuse and incest proceedings when writing critical articles nevertheless were entitled to rely on Article 10.

---

452 See *Lehideux and Isornia v France* (1998) 5 BHRC 540, 558 para 53.

453 D Harris, M O'Boyle, and C Warbrick, *Law of the European Convention on Human Rights* (Butterworths, 1995) 336–374; P van Dijk and G van Hoof, *Theory and Practice of the European Convention on Human Rights* (3rd edn, Kluwer, 1998) 559.

454 *Otto-Preminger-Institute v Austria* (1994) 19 EHRR 34 para 49 addressed 'abusive or inflammatory words'; *Groppera Radio AG v Switzerland* (1990) 12 EHRR 321, *per* Judge Matscher and Judge Valticos, found that light music was mere entertainment and not 'information and ideas'.

455 See *Lehideux and Isornia v France* (n 452 above) 558 para 55.

456 (1994) 19 EHRR 1.

457 (1998) 5 BHRC 540.

458 See eg *Glimmerveen and Hagenbeek v Netherlands* (1979) 18 DR 187, EComm HR (racist leaflets); *X v Germany* (1982) 29 DR 194, EComm HR (Nazi leaflets); *T v Belgium* (1983) 34 DR 158 (Nazi leaflet); *Kuhnen v Germany* (1988) 56 DR 205, EComm HR (Nazi leaflet); *H, W, P and K v Austria* (1989) 62 DR 216, EComm HR (Nazi activities).

459 See eg *Purcell v Ireland* (1991) 70 DR 262, EComm HR (political support for terrorists); *Brind v United Kingdom* (1994) 18 EHRR CD 76, EComm HR (restrictions on broadcasting interviews with supporters of terrorism); *Gerry Adams v United Kingdom* [1997] EHRLR 293 (exclusion order preventing Gerry Adams speaking at House of Commons).

460 *Lingens v Austria* (1986) 8 EHRR 103.

461 (1992) 14 EHRR 843.

462 (1997) 25 EHRR 1; *Jersild v Denmark* (1994) 19 EHRR 1.

Article 10 extends to expression by employees but is subject to restriction under Article 10(2).[463] However, there are some types of employment which, by their nature, involve restrictions on freedom of expression.[464] Furthermore, it is sometimes said that an employee can contract out of his right to freedom of expression, but this is open to question.[465] **15.144**

(b) The relationship with Article 10 and other Convention rights

Article 10 is often invoked in conjunction with complaints about breaches of other Convention rights. In *K v Austria*[466] the Commission decided that passing a sentence of imprisonment on the applicant for refusing to testify against himself was a breach of Article 10 and did not require further consideration as a breach of Article 6.[467] Freedom of expression (and, in particular, the right to hold an opinion) is also closely connected to freedom of thought under Article 9.[468] However, it seems that Article 10 has wider scope than Article 9. Whereas Article 9 only applies if the opinion reflects the conviction of the person who puts it forward,[469] Article 10 contemplates the protection of *any* expression of opinion. **15.145**

Complaints about freedom of expression frequently involve violations of freedom of assembly under Article 11.[470] In *Ezelin v France*[471] the Court said that a disciplinary penalty against a lawyer for participating in a demonstration should be examined as a potential breach of freedom of association under Article 11. However, in *Steel v United Kingdom*[472] the Court accepted that arrests for breach of the peace when exercising a right of protest (even where the protests were not peaceful) could amount to an interference with Article 10(1).[473] In *Vogt v Germany*[474] a teacher was dismissed because of her political activities as a Communist and alleged that both Article 10 and 11 had been breached. The Court based its decision on Article 11 by examining the arguments put forward under Article 10. **15.146**

463 See generally, *Vogt v Germany* (1995) 21 EHRR 205.

464 See eg *Morissens v Belgium* (1988) 56 DR 127, EComm HR (no breach by disciplining a teacher for criticising her superiors in a TV broadcast); see also *Ahmed v United Kingdom* (1998) 5 BHRC 111; *Rekvényi v Hungary* (1996) 6 BHRC 554 (police officers); *Wille v Liechtenstein* (2000) 8 BHRC 69 (members of the judiciary).

465 *Vereiniging Rechtswinkels Utrecht v Netherlands* (1986) 46 DR 200, EComm HR; *Rommelfanger v Germany* (1989) 62 DR 151, EComm HR; and see generally, para 6.149ff above.

466 (1993) Series A No 255–B.

467 That is, of the privilege against self incrimination: see para 11.211ff above.

468 See para 14.39 above.

469 *Arrowsmith v United Kingdom* (1980) 19 DR 5, EComm HR.

470 See generally, para 16.57ff below.

471 (1991) 14 EHRR 362.

472 (1998) 5 BHRC 339.

473 Ibid para 92.

474 (1995) 21 EHRR 205.

15.147 On the other hand, where restrictions on expression are an unintended consequence of a state's decision, the Court has been reluctant to consider the complaint under Article 10. For example, where interference with freedom of expression was incidental to the expulsion of an alien, no violation was found.[475]

15.148 The Court has taken a similar (and more controversial) approach[476] where public service employees protest about restrictions on their freedom of expression. In *Glasenapp v Germany*[477] the applicant was dismissed from his post for expressing views contrary to the German Constitution. He alleged that his Article 10 rights had been breached. The Court took the view that the claimant, who held only a temporary position, was seeking access to public employment (rather than freedom of expression); and that access to public employment was not a right protected by the Convention.[477a] By contrast, in *Vogt v Germany*[478] the Court decided that the dismissal of a teacher because of her membership of the Communist Party violated Article 10. The Court distinguished *Glasenapp v Germany*[479] and *Kosiek v Germany*[480] on the basis that in the earlier cases, the authorities had refused to grant temporary employees access to the civil service because they lacked one of the necessary qualifications.[481] Public officials serving in the judiciary are expected to show restraint in exercising freedom of expression in cases where the authority and impartiality of the judiciary are likely to be called into question.[481a] However, an interference with the freedom of expression of a judge calls for close scrutiny.[481b] A statement by the Head of State that a judge would not be reappointed to public office as a result of views expressed in a lecture violated his freedom of expression.[481c]

[475] *Agee v United Kingdom* (1976) 7 DR 164, EComm HR; but not if the purpose of the expulsion is the restriction of freedom of expression, *Piermont v France* (1995) 20 EHRR 301.

[476] Contrast with the Commission who decided in *Glasenapp* and *Kosiek* that legislation which required an obligation of loyalty and allegiance to the Constitution as a condition of employment directly interfered with freedom of expression under Art 10(1). Van Dijk and Van Hoof (n 453 above) 564 argue that the Court should have followed the opinion of the Commission. Lester suggests that the dissenting Court judgment of Judge Spielam in *Glasenapp v Germany* (1986) 9 EHRR 25 is to be preferred; Judge Spielam holds that the restriction is disproportionate to the aim pursued: see A Lester, 'Freedom of Expression' in R St John Macdonald, F Matscher and H Petzold (eds), *The European System for the Protection of Human Rights* (Kluwer, 1993).

[477] n 476 above; see also *Kosiek v Germany* (1986) 9 EHRR 328; but see *Vogt v Germany* (1995) 21 EHRR 205.

[477a] See also *Wille v Liechtenstein* (2000) 8 BHRC 69 para 41.

[478] (1995) 21 EHRR 205.

[479] n 476 above.

[480] n 477 above.

[481] Ibid para 44.

[481a] *Wille v Liechtenstein* (n 477a above) para 64.

[481b] Ibid.

[481c] Ibid paras 67–70.

(c) The right to hold opinions and to impart information

Article 10 expressly includes the right to 'impart information and ideas'. The freedoms to 'receive' and 'impart' information and ideas are not mere corollaries of one another: they are two independent rights.[482] Thus, a speaker has a right to express opinions and a willing hearer has the right to receive the communication. The state must not stand between the speaker and his audience and thus defeat the purpose for which the protection of expression is realised.[483] In *Groppera Radio AG v Switzerland*[484] the Court declined to give a precise definition of 'information and ideas'. Nonetheless, a right to impart ideas means, for example, that organising an exhibition of paintings was an exercise of freedom of expression on the part of the organisers.[485] **15.149**

However, the right to receive information under Article 10 does *not* entail a corresponding right of access to information (or an obligation on the Government to provide it), even when it is necessary for the purposes of forming an opinion or effectively exercising other freedoms. In *Leander v Sweden*[486] the applicant sought confidential Government information so he could bring a claim arising out of an unsuccessful job application. In dismissing the Article 10 claim, it was said:[487] **15.150**

> The Court observes that the right of freedom to receive information basically prohibits a Government from restricting a person from receiving information that others wish or may be willing to impart to them. Article 10 does not, in the circumstances such as those of the present case, confer on an individual a right of access to a register containing information about his personal position, nor does it embody an obligation on the Government to impart such information to the individual.

In *Open Door Counselling v Ireland*[487a] the court found that an injunction restraining the imparting of information to pregnant women by abortion clinics was a breach of both the clinic's right to impart information and the women's right to receive it. However, in the cases where the Court has accepted that there is a right of access to information, it has done so by reference to Article 8. Thus, in *Gaskin v United Kingdom*,[488] the Court decided the case under Article 8 and expressly denied that Article 10 embodied an obligation on the state to impart the information in question to the individual.

---

482 *Sunday Times v United Kingdom (No 1)* (1979) 2 EHRR 245 paras 65-66.

483 *Groppera Radio AG v Switzerland* (1990) 12 EHRR 321 para 53; *Casado Coca v Spain* (1994) 18 EHRR 1 para 59.

484 n 483 above para 55.

485 *Müller v Switzerland* (1988) 13 EHRR 212.

486 (1987) 9 EHRR 433.

487 Ibid para 74.

487a (1992) 15 EHRR 244.

488 (1989) 12 EHRR 36 paras 37, 52; see also *McGinley and Egan v United Kingdom* (1998) 27 EHRR 1; and see generally, para 12.90 above.

15.151 It should, however, be noted that the Consultative (Parliamentary) Assembly of the Council of Europe has resolved that the right to freedom of expression involves a:

> corresponding duty for the public authorities to make available information on matters of public interest within reasonable limits and a duty for mass communication media to give complete and general information on public affairs.[489]

Although this resolution does not have binding effect, it indicates a trend in legal opinion within Contracting States.[490]

15.152 Similarly, Article 10 does not provide a general right to broadcast time or to advertise on television.[491] However, it may in exceptional circumstances create a right to 'access to broadcast time' such as where one political party is excluded from broadcasting when others are not.[492] But the inability of an independent candidate to make a party political broadcast did not breach Article 10.[493] Nor does Article 10 create a right to be granted a commercial radio licence.[494] However, where the state provides assistance to particular information providers, this must be done in an even-handed way.[495]

15.153 Where the information is otherwise available the state must not obstruct access to it. [496] In *Autronic v Switzerland*[497] the Court held that the refusal of the Swiss authorities to allow a company to receive, without Soviet consent, a satellite broadcast of a Soviet television programme for showing at an exhibition in Zurich, amounted to a violation of its right to receive information 'without interference by public authority and regardless of frontiers'.

(d) Freedom of the press and mass media

15.154 The Court has attached great importance to freedom of the press and of the mass media.[498] There is an obligation on the press to impart information and ideas on political issues and on other areas of public interest;[499] and the public have a right

---

[489] Res 428 (1970), 21st Ordinary Session (Third Part), 22-30 Jan 1970, *Texts Adopted.*

[490] See P van Dijk and G van Hoof, *Theory and Practice of the European Convention on Human Rights* (3rd edn, Kluwer, 1998) 565–566.

[491] *X and Association Z v United Kingdom* (1971) 38 CD 86, EComm HR.

[492] *Haider v Austria* (1995) 85 DR 66, EComm HR.

[493] *Huggett v United Kingdom* [1996] ERHLR 84.

[494] *X v United Kingdom* (1972) 40 CD 29, EComm HR.

[495] *Vereinigung Demokratischer Soldaten Osterreichs and Gubi v Austria* (1994) 20 EHRR 55.

[496] *Z v Austria* (1988) 56 DR 13, EComm HR.

[497] *Autronic AG v Switzerland* (1990) 12 EHRR 485.

[498] See *Bladet Tromsø and Stensaas v Norway* (1999) 6 BHRC 599, 624 para 59 and *Bergens Tidende v Norway* Judgment of 2 May 2000 para 48; for a general discussion from the point of view of English defamation law, see P Milmo and W Rogers (eds), *Gatley on Libel and Slander* (9th edn, Sweet & Maxwell, 1998) para 23.20.

[499] *Lingens v Austria* (1986) 8 EHRR 103 para 26; *Oberschlick v Austria (No 1)* (1991) 19 EHRR 389 para 58; *Castells v Spain* (1992) 14 EHRR 445 para 43; *Thorgeirson v Iceland* (1992) 14 EHRR 843 para 63; *Jersild v Denmark* (1994) 19 EHRR 1 para 31.

to receive them.[500] Journalistic freedom means that the media can have recourse to exaggeration or even provocation.[501] Otherwise the press is not able 'to play its vital role of public watchdog'.[502] The Court has emphasised that:

> Where . . . measures taken by the national authorities are capable of discouraging the press from disseminating information on matters of legitimate public concern, careful scrutiny of the proportionality of the measures on the part of the Court is called for.[502a]

Article 10 provides a safeguard to journalists in relation to reporting on issues of general interest, provided that they are acting in good faith in order to provide accurate and reliable information in accordance with the ethics of journalism.[502b]

The Court has held that prior restraint on publication in the media is not *as such* incompatible with Article 10. However, it requires very close scrutiny: even if the restraints are temporary, they may deprive the information of interest because news is a perishable commodity.[503] **15.155**

The Court has consistently upheld the press where they have criticised politicians in strong or hostile terms.[504] The importance of press freedom also influenced the Court's approach in *Bladet Tromsø and Stensaas v Norway*[505] where it concluded that the vital interest in ensuring an informed public debate over a matter of local and national interest outweighed the interests of those who issued defamation proceedings in protecting their reputation. The Court has also stressed that it should provide very strong protection for journalistic sources which has been described as 'one of the basic conditions for press freedom'.[506] Similarly, in *Bergens Tidende v Norway*[506a] the public interest in dealing with allegations of unacceptable healthcare meant that an award of substantial damages against a newspaper on the basis of the 'natural and ordinary meaning' of the **15.156**

[500] *Sunday Times v United Kingdom* (1979) 2 EHRR 245 para 65; *Fressoz and Roire v France* (1999) 5 BHRC 654 para 51.

[501] *Prager and Oberschlick v Austria* (1995) 21 EHRR 1 para 38.

[502] *The Observer and The Guardian v United Kingdom* (1991) 14 EHRR 153 para 59; *Goodwin v United Kingdom* (1996) 22 EHRR 123 para 39.

[502a] *Bergens Tidende* (n 498 above) para 52.

[502b] Ibid para 53.

[503] *The Observer and The Guardian v United Kingdom* (n 502 above) para 60; *Sunday Times v United Kingdom (No 2)* (1991) 14 EHRR 229 para 51.

[504] See cases such as *Lingens v Austria* (n 499 above); *Oberschlick v Austria* (n 499 above), and *Castells v Spain* (n 499 above).

[505] (1999) 6 BHRC 599; and see also *Dalban v Romania* (2000) 8 BHRC 91 (breach consisted of conviction for defamation as a result of an article concerning criminal activity by a director of a public enterprise and a senator).

[506] *Goodwin v United Kingdom* (n 502 above) para 39: disclosure order and fine for refusing to disclose source a violation of Art 10; see para 15.73ff above for the English cases; see also *K v Austria* (1993) Series A No 255–B.

[506a] Judgment of 2 May 2000, see also para15.204 below.

words used[506b] was disproportionate. In contrast, the Court in *Worm v Austria*[507] decided that restrictions on pre-trial criticism of a politician were justified 'for maintaining the authority and impartiality of the judiciary'.[508]

15.157 Unfortunately, the Court has not taken a consistent approach in press freedom cases.[509] Protection has sometimes been based on the identity of the person defamed with, for example, discussion of politicians receiving the highest degree of protection.[510] In other cases, the Court has focused on the 'public interest content' of the publication itself.[511] The failure of the Court to reconcile these approaches means that the degree of protection afforded to the press remains uncertain.

(e) The licensing power

15.158 Article 10(1) states that it does not prevent states from requiring the licensing of broadcasting, television or cinema enterprises. The Court in *Groppera Radio AG v Switzerland*[512] said:

> . . . the purpose of the third sentence of Article 10(1) of the Convention is to make it clear that states are permitted to control by a licensing system the way in which broadcasting is organised in their territories, particularly in its technical aspects. It does not, however, provide that licensing measures shall not otherwise be subject to the requirements of Article 10(2), for that would lead to a result contrary to the object and purpose of Article 10 taken as a whole.

This view curtails the licensing power substantially, confining it to restrictions that can be construed as part of the licensing function as such.

15.159 The scope of the 'licensing power' is not clear. It entitles a state to establish technical and financial criteria for issuing licences to operate radio, television or cinematic facilities; and permits the taking of enforcement action against unlicensed operators (as in the *Groppera Radio AG* case)[513] provided the proceedings do not include interference with reception of programmes.[514]

15.160 The question of whether a state monopoly on broadcasting breaches Article 10

[506b] There was an 'inferred' meaning that the claimant had been reckless which the newspaper could not justify although the 'underlying facts' were true. For the English approach to meaning see para 15.25 above.

[507] (1997) 25 EHRR 454.

[508] See para 15.212ff below.

[509] See eg S Tierney, 'Press Freedom and Public Interest: The Developing Jurisprudence of the European Court of Human Rights' [1998] EHRLR 419.

[510] See eg *Castells v Spain* (1992) 14 EHRR 445.

[511] See eg *Thorgeirson v Iceland* (1992) 14 EHRR 843.

[512] (1990) 12 EHRR 321 para 61.

[513] (1990) 12 EHRR 321.

[514] *Radio X, S, W and A v Switzerland* (1984) 37 DR 236, EComm HR; *Groppera Radio AG v Switzerland* (n 513 above) para 61.

has to be considered under Article 10(2) rather than 10(1).[515] At one time the maintenance of public monopolies on broadcasting was considered by the Commission to be compatible with the Convention.[516] However, the Commission subsequently changed its view.[517] It is now clear that a public broadcasting monopoly is a breach of Article 10 as it involves a restriction which cannot be justified as being 'necessary in a democratic society'.[518]

The 'licensing power' in Article 10(1) has not been used to review the licensing process although there is scope to do so under the discrimination provisions of Article 14.[519] Nor has the 'licensing power' been invoked to regulate the content of broadcasts. Complaints about the contents of broadcast material have to be justified as interferences with freedom of expression under Article 10(2).[520] **15.161**

(3) Types of expression

(a) Introduction

The Court has distinguished three kinds of expression:[521] **15.162**

- political expression;
- artistic expression; and
- commercial expression.

The Court consistently attaches great importance to political expression; and applies rather less rigorous principles to artistic and commercial expression.

(b) Political expression

Political expression is central to a democratic system which requires that even ideas that 'offend, shock and disturb' be published.[522] Freedom of political debate and the press gives the public one of the best means of discovering and forming an opinion about the ideas and attitudes of political leaders and is a core concept of a democratic society.[523] While the electoral process is not itself protected by Article 10, expression during the course of an election is given specific protection.[524] **15.163**

---

515 *Informationsverein Lentia v Austria* (1993) 17 EHRR 93.

516 See *X v Sweden* (1968) 26 CD 71, EComm HR; *Sacchi v Italy* (1976) 5 DR 435, EComm HR.

517 See *Nydahl v Sweden* (1993) 16 EHRR CD 15.

518 See *Informationsverein Lentia v Austria* (n 515 above) and more recently *Radio ABC v Austria* (1997) 25 EHRR 185.

519 *Verein Alternatives Lokalradio Bern v Switzerland* (1986) 49 DR 126, EComm HR where the Commission discussed this possibility.

520 See eg *Purcell v Ireland* (1991) 70 DR 262, EComm HR; *Brind and McLaughlin v United Kingdom* (1994) 77-A DR 42, EComm HR.

521 See generally, D Harris, M O'Boyle and C Warbrick, *Law of the European Convention on Human Rights* (Butterworths, 1995) 397–406.

522 *Handyside v United Kingdom* (1976) 1 EHRR 737 para 49.

523 *Lingens v Austria* (1986) 8 EHRR 103 para 42.

524 See *Bowman v United Kingdom* (1998) 26 EHRR 1 para 42 (restrictions on election expenses a violation of Art 10).

15.164 As a result, there is little scope for restricting political speech or debate on matters of public interest.[525] Interference with the expression of politicians and, in particular, the views of the opposition, must be given the 'closest scrutiny'.[526] Politicians must be tolerant of sharp criticism of themselves, in the same democratic interest.[527] In particular, the Court has distinguished between facts and value judgments when considering the validity of criticisms made against politicians. Value judgments are not susceptible to proof and, consequently, a requirement that a publisher must prove the truth of an opinion is impossible and is therefore unjustifiable under Article 10(2).[528]

15.165 The concept of political expression is broadly interpreted. In *Thorgeirson v Iceland*[529] the Court considered a complaint about defamation of the police; and said that its jurisprudence did not warrant a distinction between political discussion and discussion of other matters of public concern. A journalist's allegations of bias against a court where two of its lay judges were employed by local government was party to proceedings before it was treated as political expression.[530] Press statements made by a veterinary surgeon about the inadequacies of an emergency veterinary service[531] have also been treated as political expression.

15.166 In a number of cases proceedings for criminal libel in relation to statements about politicians have been found to be in breach of Article 10. Vigorous criticism of a political figure is justified, so that convicting a journalist for criminal libel for failing to prove the truth of an opinion breaches Article 10. In *Lingens v Austria* the conviction of a journalist for making allegations concerning Chancellor Kreisky's views on Nazism was held to have breached Article 10.[532] Similarly, in *Castells v Spain*[533] a member of the Basque nationalist party alleged that the police were responsible for murdering Basque activists and had been protected from prosecution. He was convicted of serious insults to the Government. The Court found that the national courts had denied him the opportunity to prove the truth of his allegations, and that it was not necessary to punish him for the publication of factual assertions which were or might be true. One concurring judge regarded Castell's claims as 'matters of opinion' which were not susceptible to being proved, while another said that as his comments were of 'general interest' the truth of them

[525] *Wingrove v United Kingdom* (1996) 24 EHRR 1 para 58.
[526] *Castells v Spain* (1992) 14 EHRR 445 para 42.
[527] *Lingens v Austria* (1986) 8 EHRR 103; *Oberschlick v Austria (No 1)* (1991) 19 EHRR 389; *Schwabe v Austria* (1992) Series A No 242–B.
[528] *Lingens v Austria* (n 527 above) para 46.
[529] *Thorgeirson v Iceland* (1992) 14 EHRR 843 para 62.
[530] *Barfod v Denmark* (1989) 13 EHRR 493.
[531] *Barthold v Germany* (1985) 7 EHRR 383.
[532] (1986) 8 EHRR 407.
[533] (1992) 14 EHHR 445.

was irrelevant. The same approach was taken in *Oberschlick v Austria (No 1)*,[534] *Thorgeirson v Iceland*[535] and *Schwabe v Austria*[536] where criminal convictions were also held to have violated Article 10. The Court has, however, criticised journalists for not carrying out adequate research and suggested that, in the case of serious allegations, the journalist may be obliged to give the person concerned a right to comment.[537]

Furthermore, the Court has recognised that criticism of other public figures may attract some additional protection under Article 10: **15.167**

> the limits of acceptable criticism are wider with regard to businessmen actively involved in the affairs of large public companies than with regard to private individuals.[538]

When statements are published as part of a 'general interest' debate concerning matters such as public health they may also be accorded greater protection.[539]

On the present state of the Convention case law it cannot be said that Article 10 requires the courts to allow for a 'public figure' defence in defamation actions.[540] Although Article 10 does require the courts to give special scrutiny to restrictions on political expression, the right to reputation of politicians is still acknowledged and protected. The precise balance between the two remains to be worked out. **15.168**

(c) Artistic expression

Artistic expression (such as painting, exhibiting and giving an artist the opportunity to show his works in public) is an indisputable exercise of freedom of expression under Article 10.[541] However, where artistic expression offends or shocks, the Court has taken a cautious position. In *Müller v Switzerland*[542] paintings depicting activities involving homosexuality and bestiality were on public display without warnings. The Court held that the duties and responsibilities of the artist imposed on him special considerations of restraint rather than opportunities of freedom. **15.169**

534 (1991) 19 EHRR 389 para 63 (conviction for publishing complaint that politician's views on immigration reflected philosophy and aims of Nazis).

535 (1992) 14 EHRR 843 para 65 (defamation of the police).

536 (1992) Series A No 242–B (conviction of politician for publishing spent conviction of another politician).

537 *Prager and Oberschlick v Austria* (1995) 21 EHRR 1, para 37.

538 *Fayed v United Kingdom* (1994) 18 EHRR 393 para 75.

539 See *Hertel v Switzerland* (1998) 5 BHRC 260.

540 For the 'public figure' defence, see para 15.247ff below; and cf the discussion of the Convention case law in *Reynolds v Times Newspapers Ltd* [1998] 3 WLR 862 (CA) and [1999] 3 WLR 1010 (HL).

541 See *Müller v Switzerland* (1988) 13 EHRR 212 para 27.

542 Ibid.

15.170 The *Müller* case was applied in *Otto-Preminger-Institute v Austria*.[543] A film was seized and forfeited because its showing created 'justified indignation' among a local population on religious grounds. However, the Court's decision has been much criticised. The reasoning adopted was very broad; the outrage of people who knew the nature of the film but had not seen it justified state interference with expression; and the reaction of persons in a small geographic area was a sufficient justification for a national ban on the film. The decision of the Court was by a majority (6:3), the majority having had to rely on their own assessment of the lack of merit of the film, an approach which was inconsistent with basic principles of freedom of expression. It is difficult to avoid David Pannick's conclusion that:

> To prohibit a film from being seen in private because the ideas which it contains may offend the religious beliefs of others is impossible to reconcile with a developed concept of free speech.[544]

This case should therefore be viewed as limited to its own particular facts and should not be treated as being of general application.

(d) Commercial expression

15.171 Commercial speech has been protected on grounds that Article 10 did not apply 'solely to certain types of information or ideas or forms of expression'.[545] In *Markt Intern and Beermann v Germany*[546] the applicant published a trade magazine which contained an article describing the experience of a chemist who was dissatisfied with a mail order firm and sought a refund; the article also described the response of the firm to its own inquiries. Although the statements in the article were true, an injunction was granted, restraining '*Markt Intern*' from repeating the allegations on the basis that it had acted contrary to honest practices in breach of the Unfair Competition Act. The Court regarded the article as information of a commercial nature which was protected under Article 10, although on the facts the interference was justified. Similarly, in *Casado Coca v Spain*[547] the Court rejected an argument that professional advertising was not protected by Article 10.

15.172 However, as the Court emphasised in *Jacubowski v Germany*,[548] not all expression of commercial value is protected: Article 10 only covers commercial expressions which are directed to furthering the economic interests of individuals and enterprises through advertising (or some other means of providing information to consumers).

[543] (1994) 19 EHRR 34; note though that Judge Spielmann's dissent in *Müller* has been favoured in later cases of the Commission.

[544] See D Pannick, 'Religious Feelings and the European Court', [1995] PL 7.

[545] (1989) 12 EHRR 161 paras 25–26.

[546] Ibid.

[547] (1994) 18 EHRR 1 paras 35–36.

[548] (1994) 19 EHRR 64.

In *Barthold v Germany*[549] the Court distinguished commercial advertising from public discussion of a matter of general interest when considering the conviction of a veterinary surgeon who made comments to the press about the lack of public provision in his field. His conviction in proceedings brought by fellow vets for 'instigating or tolerating publicity on his own behalf' was unjustified; the newspaper article in question was not viewed by the Court as commercial expression but as involving political expression. **15.173**

Commercial expression is treated as being of less importance than either political or artistic expression. Statements made for the purpose of competition fall outside the basic nucleus protected by freedom of expression and receive a lower standard of protection than other ideas or information.[550] Thus, in the *Markt Intern* case[551] the Court upheld an injunction against a trade magazine which prohibited it from publishing. The Court took the view that, as commercial speech, the magazine was subject to different standards. Even if statements in the publication were true, they could, nevertheless, be prohibited because of a duty to respect the privacy of others or the confidentiality of certain commercial information. However, the decisive factor in the Court's reasoning was the wide margin of appreciation it gave to the national courts.[552] By contrast, in *Hertel v Switzerland*[553] where the submission of a research paper to a scientific journal resulted in a criminal conviction, the Court took a much more restrictive approach to the margin of appreciation. It held that the conviction was a disproportionate interference with freedom of expression. **15.174**

The close regulation of advertising in some European countries has resulted in decisions holding that the national authorities have a wide margin of appreciation when interfering with an advertiser's expression. In *Colman v United Kingdom*,[554] the Commission decided that restrictions on advertising by doctors was justified. This approach was followed in *Casado Coca v Spain*[555] where it was held that, in the absence of a common European standard, the regulation of advertising by barristers did not fall outside the wide margin of appreciation which states had on the matter. **15.175**

Cases such as *Markt Intern and Beermann v Germany*[556] and *Jacubowski v Germany*[557] therefore represent a retreat from the fundamental principle established **15.176**

549 (1985) 7 EHRR 383 para 50.
550 *Markt Intern and Beermann v Germany* (1989) 12 EHRR 161 para 32.
551 Ibid, the Court was split 9–9 and the case was decided on the casting vote of the President.
552 Ibid paras 33–38.
553 (1999) 28 EHRR 534; see para 15.207 below.
554 (1993) 18 EHRR 119; the case was the subject of a friendly settlement.
555 (1994) 18 EHRR 1.
556 (1989) 12 EHRR 161.
557 (1994) 19 EHRR 64.

by *Handyside v United Kingdom*[558] and *Sunday Times v United Kingdom (No 1)*[559] that an interference with expression is necessary only if the state presents convincing evidence of a pressing social need for it.[560] As Judge Pettiti observed in his dissenting judgment in *Markt Intern*:

> only in the rarest cases can censorship or prohibition of publication be accepted . . . This is particularly true in relation to commercial advertising or questions of economic or commercial policy. The protection of the interests of users and consumers in the face of dominant positions depends on the freedom to publish even the harshest criticisms of products.[561]

(4) **Justifying limits on expression**

(a) Introduction

15.177 Where there has been an interference with freedom of expression, it will be justified under Article 10(2) if:

- the interference is prescribed by law;
- the interference furthers a 'legitimate aim' (as there set out); and
- the interference is necessary in a democratic society.

The 'legitimate aims' which can, potentially justify restrictions on the freedom of expression are:

- the interests of national security;
- the interests of territorial integrity or public safety;
- for the prevention of disorder or crime;
- for the protection of health or morals;
- for the protection of the reputation or the rights of others;
- for preventing the disclosure of information received in confidence; or
- for maintaining the authority and impartiality of the judiciary.

When the Court (or Commission) assesses the question of justification under Article 10(2), it is essential to be clear whether its decision is based on the ground
15.178 that the interference is a disproportionate restriction which is not 'necessary in a democratic society'; or whether it has decided that the interference is within a state's margin of appreciation. These doctrines are discussed in detail in Chapter 6. The principle of proportionality is a standard of judicial review.[562] On the other

---

[558] (1976) 1 EHRR 737.
[559] (1979) 2 EHRR 245.
[560] D Harris, M O'Boyle and C Warbrick, *Law of the European Convention on Human Rights* (Butterworths, 1995) 404.
[561] Judge Pettiti (n 556 above) 178.
[562] See generally, para 6.43ff above.

hand, the doctrine of the 'margin of appreciation' involves an interpretative obligation on an international human rights court to respect domestic cultural traditions and values.[563]

15.179 The potential justifications for interfering with freedom of expression under Article 10(2) must be narrowly interpreted: the 'necessity' for any restrictions must be 'convincingly established'.[564] The necessity of a restriction depends on the character of the expression, the duties and responsibilities of those exercising freedom of expression, the means of the communication, the audience to which it is directed, the significance of the interference and the purpose for which the restraint is imposed.

15.180 The doctrine of margin of appreciation will therefore have no direct application to the Human Rights Act.[565] Nevertheless, it has played an important and controversial role in the Article 10 jurisprudence. The Court has used a number of different approaches when applying the margin of appreciation to freedom of expression cases;[566]; and it is strongly arguable that excessive use of the concept has seriously eroded the protection given by Article 10.[567]

(b) Interferences

15.181 Prior restraint is not in principle incompatible with Article 10. However, such interference must be subject to strict scrutiny; it prevents transmission of ideas and information to those who wish to assess them for themselves and even temporary interference may be disastrous since information is a perishable commodity.[568] The burden of establishing the necessity of pre-publication measures, such as licensing schemes or court-ordered injunctions, is therefore a heavy one.[569]

15.182 The right to freedom of expression under Article 10 does not cease once information has been placed in the public domain. Post-publication sanctions such as civil and criminal actions, forfeiture of property,[570] the denial of a licence[571] or

---

563 See para 6.31ff above.

564 See generally, the principles restated in *Zana v Turkey* (1997) 27 EHRR 667 para 51, see para 15.139 above.

565 See para 6.37ff above.

566 N Lavender, 'The Problem of the Margin of Appreciation' [1997] EHRLR 380.

567 See for example A Lester 'Freedom of Expression' in R St J Macdonald, F Matscher and H Petzold (eds), *The European System for the Protection of Human Rights* (1993, Kluwer); and see P Mahoney, 'Universiality Versus Subsidiarity in the Strasbourg Case Law on Free Speech: Explaining Some Recent Judgments' [1997] EHRLR 364 and Lord Lester, 'Universiality Versus Subsidiarity: A Reply' [1998] EHRLR 73.

568 *The Observer and The Guardian Newspapers v United Kingdom* (1991) 14 EHRR 153 para 60; but see *Wingrove v United Kingdom* (1997) 24 EHRR 1.

569 *The Observer and The Guardian Newspapers v United Kingdom* (n 568 above) para 60; and see *De Becker v Belgium* (1962) 1 EHRR 43 regarding licensing of outlets or journalists.

570 See eg *Müller v Switzerland* (1988) 13 EHRR 212.

571 See eg *Autronic AG v Switzerland* (1990) 12 EHRR 485; *Radio ABC v Austria* (1997) 25 EHRR 185.

disciplinary penalties[572] will also be carefully scrutinised. The impact of the interference will depend on the kind and degree of consequences for the applicant. Criminal penalties are the most difficult interferences to justify; but high levels of damages in defamation proceedings may pose comparable dangers.[573] The seizure of original works of art also poses difficult problems;[574] and the Commission in *Otto-Preminger-Institute v Austria* expressed the view that very stringent reasons were needed to justify the seizure of a film, thus excluding any chance to discuss its message.[575] Post publication sanctions may also have a 'chilling effect' by acting as a deterrent to future publication of other information and materials.[576]

15.183 In some circumstances Article 10 creates positive obligations[577] on the state to take action to protect the freedom of expression of private individuals. In *Özgür Gündem v Turkey*[578] the Court held that genuine effective exercise of freedom of expression:

> does not depend merely on the State's duty not to interfere, but may require positive measures of protection, even in the sphere of relations between individuals.

In determining whether or not a positive obligation exists, regard must be had to the fair balance that has to be struck between the general interest of the community and the interests of the indiviudal. The obligation must not be interpreted in such a way as to impose an impossible or disproportionate burden on the state.[578a] In the *Özgür Gündem* case the state was found to be in breach of this positive obligation.

(c) Duties and responsibilities

15.184 Article 10(2) states that the exercise of the freedoms in Article 10(1) carries with it 'duties and responsibilities'. The phrase implies that, in determining the necessity of restrictions, these duties and responsibilities must not be overlooked.[579] This consideration might legitimise discriminatory distinctions between people in different positions; and could also serve to justify restrictions upon 'irresponsible' expression. It is, however, unclear how the notion of 'duties and responsibilities' is to be applied. In some cases it has justified a broad interpretation of a

[572] See eg *Casado Coco v Spain* (1994) 18 EHRR 1.

[573] See *Tolstoy Miloslavsky v United Kingdom* (1995) 20 EHRR 442 where the level of damages in English libel law was challenged when the award was £1.5 million; and *Markt Intern and Beermann v Germany* (1989) 12 EHRR 161 where the publisher faced a 500,000 DM fine for failure to comply with an injunction.

[574] *Müller v Switzerland* (1988) 13 EHRR 212 para 43.

[575] (1994) 19 EHRR 34 Com Rep para 77.

[576] *Barthold v Germany* (1985) 7 EHRR 383 para 58; *Lingens v Austria* (1986) 8 EHRR 103 para 44; *Jersild v Denmark* (1994) 19 EHRR 1 para 44.

[577] For the distinction between negative and positive obligations, see para 6.95ff above.

[578] Judgment of 16 Mar 2000 para 43.

[578a] Ibid.

[579] *Handyside v United Kingdom* (1976) 1 EHRR 737 para 49.

limitation, while in other cases it has had the opposite effect.[580] In *Handyside*,[581] which concerned an obscene publication intended for children, the Court emphasised the responsibilities of publishers and upheld a restriction. In *Lingens*,[582] on the other hand, the right of a journalist to criticise a politician was upheld when the press was found to have a duty and responsibility in a democratic society to 'impart information and ideas on political issues'; and in *Castells v Spain*[583] a politician enjoyed the advantage of protection of his special position.

In particular, the phrase has been used to justify interfering with freedom of expression on grounds of status. Thus, the duties and responsibilities of soldiers,[584] civil servants[585] or teachers[586] were said to justify interferences with Article 10. However, the phrase has not played a prominent role in recent cases[587] and it appears to have only minor significance as a further source of justification for interference with freedom of expression. **15.185**

(d) 'Prescribed by law'

An interference with freedom of expression will be prescribed by law where: **15.186**

- the interference in question has some basis in domestic law;
- the law is adequately accessible; and
- the law is formulated so that it is sufficiently foreseeable.

The principle applies to a number of qualified Convention rights and is examined in detail in Chapter 6.[588] There have, however, been a number of important cases which have considered its impact on Article 10.

Restrictions on the freedom of expression must be authorised by national law. Identification of the law or rule[589] in question has not been a source of difficulty. **15.187**

[580] See A Robertson and J Merrills, *Human Rights in Europe: A Study of the European Convention on Human Rights* (Manchester University Press, 1993) 151.

[581] *Handyside v Uunited Kingdom* (n 579 above) para 49.

[582] *Lingens v Austria* (1986) 8 EHRR 103; but a more restrictive view of 'duties and responsibilities' was taken in *Prager and Oberschlick v Austria* (1995) 21 EHRR 1 where it was found that a journalist had failed to prove that he had applied the necessary diligence in his research.

[583] (1992) 14 EHHR 445.

[584] *Engel v Netherlands (No 2)* (1976) 1 EHRR 706 para 100; but see *Vereinigung Demokratischer Solidaten Osterreichs and Gubi v Austria* (1994) 20 EHRR 55 para 27 where the Court expressed the view that freedom of expression under Art 10(1) applies to servicemen just as much as to others.

[585] *B v United Kingdom* (1985) 45 DR 41, EComm HR.

[586] *X v United Kingdom* (1979) 16 DR 101, EComm HR; *Morissens v Belgium* (1988) 56 DR 127, EComm HR.

[587] Cf *Otto-Preminger-Institute v Austria* (1994) 19 EHRR 34 para 49 where the Court suggested that those who criticised the religious views of others had an obligation to avoid so far as possible remarks which were gratuitously offensive.

[588] See para 6.123ff above.

[589] It is accepted that rules made by professional or other bodies constitute 'laws' where rule-making power has been delegated to those authorities; see *Barthold v Germany* (1985) 7 EHRR 383; *Casado Coca v Spain* (1994) 18 EHRR 1.

Whether or not the law is adequately accessible is equally straightforward. However, whether a law regulating freedom of expression is sufficiently foreseeable has been challenged in a variety of applications: in the commercial area,[590] in contempt of court proceedings,[591] in licensing cases[592] and in relation to obscenity law,[593] defamation awards by juries[594] and the disclosure of journalistic sources.[595]

15.188 The law must be formulated with sufficient precision to enable the citizen to regulate his conduct. He must be able—if need be with appropriate advice—to foresee, to a degree that is reasonable in the circumstances, the consequences which a given action may entail.[596] Absolute precision is not achievable, however, and flexibility is necessary where the circumstances are constantly changing.[597]

15.189 The Court has considered on several occasions whether the common law is sufficiently foreseeable. In *Sunday Times v United Kingdom*[598] the Court accepted that a reformulation of the principles of contempt of court by the House of Lords[599] was still sufficiently foreseeable. In *Tolstoy Miloslavsky v United Kingdom*[600] it held that libel awards by juries were not too uncertain to be sufficiently foreseeable. The Court decided in *Steel v United Kingdom*[601] that breach of the peace was formulated with sufficient precision to be sufficiently foreseeable. In *Goodwin v United Kingdom*[602–603] the Court held that section 10 of the Contempt of Court

[590] *Markt Intern and Beermann v Germany* (1989) 12 EHRR 161; *Barthold v Germany* (n 589 above).

[591] *Sunday Times v United Kingdom* (1979) 2 EHRR 245.

[592] *Groppera Radio AG v Switzerland* (1990) 12 EHRR 321; *Autronic AG v Switzerland* (1990) 12 EHRR 485.

[593] *Müller v Switzerland* (1988) 13 EHRR 212.

[594] *Tolstoy Miloslavsky v United Kingdom* (1995) 20 EHRR 442.

[595] *Goodwin v United Kingdom* (1996) 22 EHRR 123.

[596] *Sunday Times v United Kingdom* (1979) 2 EHRR 245 para 48, 49; see also *Grigoriades v Greece* (1997) 27 EHRR 464 para 37.

[597] In *Markt Intern and Beermann v Germany* (1989) 12 EHRR 161, a law requiring 'honest practices' was sufficiently foreseeable in the sphere of competition where changes in the market and in communication precluded absolute precision; see also *Müller v Switzerland* (1988) 13 EHRR 212 in which the Court referred to 'the need to avoid excessive rigidity and to keep pace with changing circumstances'; the language comes from *Sunday Times v United Kingdom* (n 596 above) in which the Court held that a development in the common law of contempt of court was an application of a general principle which might have been anticipated by the applicants and was thus 'reasonable in the circumstances'.

[598] (1979) 2 EHRR 245.

[599] Whereas in *A-G v Times Newspapers Ltd* [1973] QB 710 the Divisional Court applied the principle that a deliberate attempt to influence the settlement of pending proceedings by bringing public pressure to bear on a party amounted to a contempt of court, the House of Lords seemed to prefer the view that it is a contempt to publish material which prejudges pending litigation: see [1974] AC 273.

[600] (1995) 20 EHRR 442.

[601] (1998) 5 BHRC 339 paras 25–28, 55.

[602–603] (1997) 22 EHRR 123.

Act 1981 was sufficiently precise to be foreseeable. On the other hand, in *Hashman and Harrup v United Kingdom*[604] the Court took the view that ordering a bind over on the basis that the applicant's conduct was *contra bonos mores* (that is, 'conduct which is wrong rather than right in the judgment of the majority of contemporary fellow citizens')[605] did not provide sufficient guidance about what sort of conduct would breach the order.

The Court has taken a broad view of the accessibility requirement in commercial expression cases. In *Barthold v Germany*[606] the Court acknowledged a wide discretion to control unfair competition and said that absolute precision is especially difficult in regulating competition. In *Markt Intern and Beermann v Germany*[607] the requirement of honest practices in German competition law was acceptable because absolute precision could not be achieved in a competitive environment which was constantly changing because of developments in the market and in the communications field. The state was entitled to rely on the norms of public international law to prove that its domestic law was sufficiently accessible in *Groppera Radio AG v Switzerland*[608] and in *Autronic AG v Switzerland*.[609] **15.190**

(e) 'Necessary in a democratic society'

The general principles which the Court applies when deciding whether an interference is proportionate[610] and necessary in a democratic society[611] are discussed in Chapter 6. A number of early cases such as *Handyside*,[612] *Sunday Times*,[613] *Barthold*[614] and *Lingens*[615] sought to give expression a preferred status over other protected interests. They also placed the burden on public authorities to show that there is a 'pressing social need' to interfere with the freedom and that the grounds for doing so are not only 'relevant and sufficient', but 'convincingly established'.[616] Although these principles were recently reaffirmed in *Zana v Turkey*,[617] in practice the Court considers a variety of factors including the value of the type of expression,[618] its medium and other circumstances of the communication, its **15.191**

[604] (2000) 8 BHRC 104 paras 36–41.
[605] *Hughes v Holley* (1986) 86 Cr App R 130.
[606] (1985) 7 EHRR 383 para 47.
[607] (1989) 12 EHHR 161 para 30.
[608] (1990) 12 EHRR 321.
[609] (1990) 12 EHRR 485.
[610] See para 6.42ff above.
[611] See para 6.146ff above.
[612] *Handyside v United Kingdom* (1976) 1 EHRR 737.
[613] *Sunday Times v United Kingdom (No 1)* (1979) 2 EHRR 245.
[614] *Barthold v Germany* (1985) 7 EHRR 383.
[615] *Lingens v Austria* (1986) 8 EHRR 103.
[616] *The Observer and The Guardian Newspapers v United Kingdom* (1991) 14 EHRR 153.
[617] (1997) 27 EHRR 667 para 51; see para 15.139 above.
[618] See para 15.162ff above.

audience or target, the objective of the interference and its impact on the applicant.

15.192 Restrictions on freedom of expression may be difficult to justify where directed to a willing adult audience.[619] However, a different approach is taken where children are the target audience. Thus, interference was justified in *Handyside v United Kingdom*[620] on the grounds that the offensive subject matter was marketed specifically to appeal to children. The degree of access given to consumers, particularly unwilling consumers and those in need of protection, may also be decisive. A factor in the *Müller*[621] decision was that the exhibition, at which a shocking painting was observed by a young girl, was open to the public, without warning as to the subject matter of the art. In *Otto-Preminger-Institute v Austria*[622] the Commission held that access to an offensive film was limited because of a public warning about its contents and by the specialised nature of the cinema owned by the applicant. Nevertheless, the Court found that the state interference was justified because, even though no innocent viewer was likely to attend, the warnings themselves and the knowledge that the film was going to be shown, incited community outrage.

15.193 The tolerant and broadminded approach emphasised in *Handyside v United Kingdom*[623] (and recently re-iterated in *Zana v Turkey*)[624] has not prevailed in cases brought by political protesters. In *Arrowsmith v United Kingdom*[625] the Commission held that the conviction and imprisonment which resulted from distributing leaflets advising soldiers not to serve in Northern Ireland was necessary to protect national security. In *Chorherr v Austria*[626] the Court upheld the right of the state to interfere with protesters by suggesting that the commotion they created had brought the interference on themselves. The Commission has also adopted a restrictive approach when considering complaints about interferences with racist expression or support for terrorists.[627]

(f) Objective of the interference

15.194 The necessity of the public interference in a democratic society also requires that an interference furthers one of the aims set out in Article 10(2). In practice, very few disputes arise about whether an interference falls within their broad scope.

---

[619] See eg *Jersild v Denmark* (1994) 19 EHRR 1 where the expression was part of a serious news programme intended for an informed audience; note however, *Otto-Preminger-Institute v Austria* (1994) 19 EHRR 34 where willing viewers were precluded by community standards from seeing a film.

[620] (1976) 1 EHRR 737.

[621] (1988) 13 EHRR 212.

[622] n 619 above.

[623] n 620 above, see para 15.163 above.

[624] (1997) 27 EHRR 667 para 51; see para 15.139 above.

[625] (1980) 19 DR 5, EComm HR.

[626] (1993) 17 EHRR 358 para 33.

[627] See para 15.141 above.

National security, territorial integrity or public safety. The national security restriction featured prominently in the 'Spycatcher' cases which considered the legitimacy of injunctions granted to restrain newspapers from publishing information about the British security services which was derived from the manuscript of a proposed book, *Spycatcher*, written by the former secret intelligence officer, Peter Wright.[628] **15.195**

The main issue facing the Court in *The Observer and The Guardian v United Kingdom*[629] and *Sunday Times v United Kingdom (No 2)*[630] was the compatibility of injunctions issued, modified and extended and finally discharged by the House of Lords, with Article 10. Although the book had been published in the United States, the interlocutory injunctions were continued[631] until the main proceedings were complete. The House of Lords[632] had refused to restrain the newspapers on grounds that the American publication had destroyed any justification for granting the permanent injunctions. The Commission found that the injunctions had violated Article 10. However, the Court decided that the interlocutory injunctions were not a breach, holding that only their continuation by the House of Lords infringed freedom of expression. Initially, the Government had identified several aims to support the ban. National security was indirectly in issue; it was said that Mr Wright's information was protected as it had been received in confidence; and the injunction was necessary to preserve the Attorney-General's claim to confidentiality, thus maintaining the authority of the judiciary.[633] The Court found that, prior to the American publication, revelation of the material could be damaging to the Security Service; and that the objectives of protection of national security and of preserving the Attorney-General's claim were legitimate ones, justifying interference in a democratic society. Once the book had been published,[634] however, this substantially eradicated any justification for continuing the interim injunction to preserve the case of the Attorney-General until trial.[635] Before the Court of Human Rights, the Government argued that protection of national security required the maintenance of the morale and reputation of the Security Service and that others should be discouraged from breaches of confidentiality such as the publishing of memoirs.[636] **15.196**

[628] For the history of the English litigation, see para 15.19ff above.
[629] (1991) 14 EHRR 153.
[630] (1991) 14 EHRR 229.
[631] *A-G v Guardian Newspapers Ltd* [1987] 1 WLR 1248.
[632] Ibid.
[633] Protecting the rights of litigants is recognised as an aspect of maintenance of the authority of the judiciary under Art 10(2): *Sunday Times v United Kingdom* (1979) 2 EHRR 245; see para 15.213 below.
[634] Publication took place in the United States just prior to the continuation of the interlocutory injunctions by the House of Lords.
[635] See the earlier decision of the Court in *Weber v Switzerland* (1990) 12 EHRR 508, where it held that the defence of prior publication might limit the scope of the restrictions on Article 10.
[636] *The Observer and The Guardian Newspapers v United Kingdom* (n 629 above) para 69.

The Court did not directly assess these issues, but decided that the continuation of the injunction had a negative impact on the third party newspapers which was disproportionate to any need to protect the confidence interest.[637] Judge Walsh, dissenting, pointed out[638] that the authorities had not established any threat to national security and ought not to invoke this exception on the basis of opinion alone.

15.197 The Commission has also held that restrictions on broadcasting news material about organisations which support terrorism does not contravene Article 10.[639] On the other hand, there was an unjustified interference with the freedom of expression of soldiers[640] where they were disciplined for distributing a satirical journal within military barracks in breach of military regulations.[641] A number of cases have examined whether restrictions on national security grounds to prevent insults to the armed forces,[642] or statements of support for a terrorist separatist organisation[643] could be justified on national security grounds. In *Grigoriades v Greece*[644] a conviction violated Article 10 because the insults to the armed forces were contained in a letter to a commanding officer without wider publication, did not attack the recipient or any other individual and had little impact on military discipline.

15.198 In *Zana v Turkey*[645] a prosecution for the applicant's outspoken support for the PKK was justified on national security and public safety grounds as part of the fight against terrorism. However, in *Incal v Turkey*[646] a conviction for 'inciting the people to hatred' violated Article 10 where a leaflet was distributed containing virulent remarks about Government policy but no incitement to violence, hostility or hatred. The Court distinguished the *Zana* case on grounds that the applicant could not be regarded as being in any way responsible for problems caused by terrorism in the province of Izmir. The Court has recently considered a number of Turkish cases where convictions on terrorist or public safety grounds were said to be disproportionate restrictions on freedom of expression. Most of the

[637] For an analysis of the *Spycatcher* litigation at Strasbourg see I Leigh, 'Spycatcher in Strasbourg' [1992] PL 200.

[638] *The Observer and the Guardian Newspapers v United Kingdom* (n 629 above) 205 para 4.

[639] *Purcell v Ireland* (1991) 70 DR 262, EComm HR; *Brind and McLaughlin v United Kingdom* (1994) 77–A DR 42, EComm HR.

[640] The Court emphasised in *Hadjianastassiou v Greece* (1992) 16 EHRR 219 that freedom of expression under Art 10(1) extended to soldiers just as much as to civilians.

[641] *Vereinigung Demokratischer Soldaten Österreichs and Bethold Gubi v Austria* (1994) 20 EHRR 55; *Vereniging Weekblad 'Bluf' v Netherlands* (1995) 20 EHRR 189.

[642] *Grigoriades v Greece* (1997) 27 EHRR 464.

[643] *Zana v Turkey* (1997) 27 EHRR 667.

[644] (1997) 27 EHRR 464.

[645] (1997) 27 EHRR 667.

[646] RJD 1998–IV 1547.

applications were held to breach Article 10[647] although two convictions were justified.[648]

The justification for interfering with expression to maintain 'territorial integrity' has been considered less frequently. In *Piermont v France*[649] the applicant had been excluded from French Polynesia after making a speech supporting anti-nuclear and independence demands of local political parties. Although the interference with her freedom of expression was to prevent disorder and maintain territorial integrity, the interference was disproportionate as the demonstration was non-violent and there was a strong interest in protecting political speech. **15.199**

Prevention of disorder or crime. The prevention of disorder or crime includes (but is not limited to) public disorder. The need to protect public order in the face of terrorist threats is a significant justification for restricting freedom of expression[650] or international telecommunications.[651] Prevention of disorder within the armed forces has also been found to be a legitimate aim.[652] **15.200**

Restrictions on political expression, however, are likely to be difficult to justify. Although freedom of political debate is not absolute, the Government must react proportionately and without excess to criticisms made of it.[653] Thus, in *Steel v United Kingdom*[654] arresting protesters for breach of the peace was a legitimate restriction on the right of expression because the arrests were intended to prevent **15.201**

[647] *Karatas v Turkey* Application 23168/94, 8 Jul 1999 (convictions under Prevention of Terrorism Act for poems concerning Kurdish discontent); *Arslan v Turkey* Application 23462/94, 8 Jul 1999 (conviction of author for book maintaining that Kurds were victims of oppression); *Polat v Turkey* Application 23500/94, 8 Jul 1999 (conviction for historical epic concerning Kurdish rebel movement); *Ceylan v Turkey* Application 23556/94, 8 Jul 1999 (conviction of union leader for Marxist explanation for Kurdish movement); *Okçuoglu v Turkey* Application 24246/94, 8 Jul 1999 (conviction for interview expressing views about Kurdish situation); *Gerger v Turkey* Application 24919/94, 8 Jul 1999 (conviction for polemic given at funeral of political activists) *Erdogdu and Ince v Turkey* Application 25067/94, 8 Jul 1999 (conviction for interview of sociologist in monthly review expressing views about Kurds); *Surek v Turkey (No 2)* Application 24762/94, 8 Jul 1999 (conviction for news report identifying officials which were alleged to be terrorist targets); *Surek v Turkey (No 4)* Application 24762/94, 8 Jul 1999 (conviction for news commentary about Kurdistan).

[648] *Surek v Turkey (No 1)* Application 26682/95, 8 Jul 1999 (conviction for polemic about Kurdistan); *Surek v Turkey (No 4)* (conviction for polemic about Kurdistan).

[649] (1995) 20 EHRR 301.

[650] *Chorherr v Austria* (1993) 17 EHRR 358.

[651] *Groppera Radio AG v Switzerland* (1990) 12 EHRR 321 and *Autronic AG v Switzerland* (1990) 12 EHRR 485.

[652] *Engel v Netherlands (No 1)* (1976) 1 EHRR 647; *Vereinigung Demokratischer Soldaten Österreichs and Gubi v Austria* (1994) 20 EHRR 55.

[653] *Incal v Turkey* (1998) 4 BHRC 476, 491–492 paras 52–59: prosecution for publication of a leaflet urging Kurdish population to band together was a violation; see also *Janowski v Poland* (1999) 5 BHRC 672 in which the Court held that conviction of the applicant, for using offensive words to criticise civil servants acting in an official capacity, was justified.

[654] (1998) 28 EHRR 603.

disorder and to protect the rights of others. However, the restrictions were disproportionate since the police could not justify the arrests on the basis that they had reasonable grounds to apprehend a breach of the peace.[655]

15.202 **Protection of health or morals.** Because the Court regards 'morals' as having no objective content, and there is no European consensus to assist in a definition,[656] the Court has given national courts a wide margin of appreciation, both in deciding the content of 'morals' and in what measures are necessary to protect morals.[657] While 'morals' may attract strong local feelings,[658] it is not self evident that local considerations should govern the determination of national standards for protecting morals. On the other hand, in the *Open Door* case[659] the Court found Government interference unjustifiable. While it is primarily for the state to determine the content of 'morals', the very broad and perpetual injunction to restrain anyone (regardless of age, health reasons or necessity) from seeking advice about abortion was not necessary in a democratic society.

15.203 **Protection of the reputation or the rights of others.** The protection of the reputation or rights of others provides the entitlement for an individual to pursue defamation proceedings. The Court has frequently stressed that the limits of acceptable criticism are wider for a politician than a private citizen. A politician lays himself open to close scrutiny of his every word and deed by both journalists and the general public and must display a greater degree of tolerance.[660] The bounds of permissible criticism of the Government is even wider.[661]

15.204 Even where there is substantial damage to reputation, a successful claim in defamation may violate Article 10. In *Bladet Tromsø and Stensaas v Norway*[662] the Court, in a long and detailed analysis of the facts, held that the vital interest in ensuring an informed public debate over seal hunting was a matter of local and national interest which was sufficient to outweigh the interests of those who issued defamation proceedings to protect their reputation. Similarly, in *Nilsen and Johnsen v Norway*[663] the Court again carefully examined the factual issues and concluded that defamation proceedings breached freedom of expression. The

655 Ibid para 110.
656 *Handyside v United Kingdom* (1976) 1 EHRR 737.
657 See eg ibid (the sale of the Little Red Schoolbook); and *Müller v Switzerland* (1988) 13 EHHR 212.
658 In *Handyside v United Kingdom* (n 656 above) and *Müller v Switzerland* (n 657 above) the Court accepted that a 'pressing social need' was necessary to punish expression for the protection of the morals of relatively small areas of the population.
659 *Open Door and Dublin Well Woman v Ireland* (1992) 15 EHRR 244.
660 See eg *Lingens v Austria* (1986) 8 EHRR 103 para 42; and see, generally, para 15.166 above.
661 *Castells v Spain* (1992) 14 EHHR 445 para 46.
662 (1999) 6 BHRC 599 paras 62–73.
663 Judgment, 25 Nov 1999.

Court also took the view in *Tolstoy Miloslavsky v United Kingdom*[664] that the unpredictable nature of jury awards in libel cases was a disproportionate restriction on freedom of expression. In *Bergens Tidende v Norway*[664a] the applicant newspaper had published an article containing critical accounts given by the patients of a cosmetic surgeon, Dr R. Although the accounts were factually accurate, the Supreme Court had held that the 'natural and ordinary' meaning of the words used was that Dr R performed his activities in a reckless way—which was false. As a result, Dr R had been awarded substantial damages.[664b] The Court held that this was a violation of Article 10. It said:

> the Court cannot find that the undoubted interest of Dr R in protecting his professional reputation was sufficient to outweigh the important public interest in the freedom of the press to impart information on matters of legitimate public concern.[664c]

Where the religious beliefs of others are offended, interferences with freedom of expression may be justified. In *Otto-Preminger-Institute v Austria*[665] it justified the nation-wide seizure and forfeiture of a film which offended the rights of a local population on religious grounds. The Court found that, as with 'morals', the lack of a uniform conception of religion in European society gave a wide margin of appreciation to the state to determine the necessity of the ban for the protection of the rights of the local people. However, the case differs from the 'morals' cases because the Court accepted the application of 'local' standards to a national level, finding that the nation-wide ban did not exceed the state's margin of appreciation. Similarly, in *Wingrove v United Kingdom*[666] the refusal of the British Board of Film Classification to grant a licence for the distribution of the film 'Visions of Christ' was justified to protect the rights of Christians. **15.205**

The protection of the rights of others also permits an interference to ensure 'effective political democracy'. Such interferences are not limited to circumstances in which the stability of the constitutional or political order is threatened.[667] Thus, in *Ahmed v United Kingdom*[668] regulations restricting the political activity of local authority employees were a proportionate restriction on freedom of expression. In the special circumstances of the former Eastern bloc countries, restriction on the freedom of police officers to engage in political debate was proportionate.[669] **15.206**

[664] (1995) 20 EHRR 442.
[664a] Judgment of 2 May 2000.
[664b] 930,000 krone, or approximately £75,000.
[664c] *Bergens Tidende* (n 664a above) para 60.
[665] (1994) 19 EHRR 34.
[666] (1996) 24 EHRR 1.
[667] *Ahmed v United Kingdom* (1998) 5 BHRC 111, para 52.
[668] Ibid paras 52-54; for the unsuccessful challenge to these regulations in the English courts, see *R v Secretary of State for the Environment, ex p NALGO* [1993] Admin LR 785.
[669] *Rekvényi v Hungary* (1999) 6 BHRC 554 paras 44–49.

15.207 Interference with commercial expression may also be justified because of its impact on the rights of others. In *Hertel v Switzerland*[670] the applicant was convicted[671] for submitting to a scientific journal a research paper on the possible detrimental effects of the use of microwave ovens. Although the legislation, which was 'intended to guarantee, in the interests of all parties concerned, fair, undistorted competition', had the legitimate aim of the protection of the rights of others, the conviction could not be justified as being necessary in a democratic society. The Court emphasised that the wide margin of appreciation given to states in relation to commercial and competition areas must be reduced when the statement of an individual is not made as a matter of purely 'commercial' interest, but is part of a more general debate.

15.208 Protection of the rights of others was also claimed to justify interfering with freedom of expression in *Lehideux and Isorni v France*.[672] The applicant was convicted of the 'public defence of war crimes or the crimes of collaboration' after publishing an advertisement seeking to present in a positive light information concerning Marshall Petain to secure a retrial of his case. The interference pursued several legitimate aims including the protection of rights of others and the prevention of disorder or crime but was a disproportionate restriction.[673] On the other hand, in *Janowski v Poland*[674] a conviction for using insulting words to criticise the actions of municipal guards in a public setting was justifiable as protecting the reputation and rights of the civil servants. Similarly, in *Peree v Netherlands*[674a] the Commission held that the convictions of the applicant for 'insult and slander' for comparing an anti-discrimination organisation to the Nazi SA were justifiable.

15.209 In *Fressoz and Roire v France*[675] one of the legitimate aims for the conviction of applicants for publishing a press article was the protection of the reputation of M Calvert, the chairman of the French car manufacturer, Peugot. Although the article was intended to contribute to a wider debate, it disclosed details of M Calvert's personal income and tax assessments. The applicants were found guilty of 'the handling of photocopies of tax returns obtained through a breach of professional confidence by an unidentified tax official' and sentenced to substantial fines and damages. The convictions were held to be a disproportionate interference with freedom of expression.

[670] (1999) 28 EHRR 534.

[671] The Federal Unfair Competition Act included in its definition of 'unfair acts' the denigration 'of others or the goods, work, services, prices or business of others by making inaccurate, misleading or unnecessarily wounding statements'.

[672] (1998) 5 BHRC 540.

[673] Ibid paras 51–58.

[674] (1999) 5 BHRC 672.

[674a] (1998) 28 EHRR CD 158.

[675] (1999) 5 BHRC 654.

Preventing the disclosure of information received in confidence. Justification on grounds of prevention of disclosure of information received in confidence overlaps with other legitimate aims. For example, the protection of confidential governmental information may be required 'in the interests of national security' whilst disclosure of private information may be restricted for 'protection of the rights of others'. However, this aim may be relevant in cases concerning confidential Government information which does not affect national security.[676] **15.210**

The Court has considered justification on this basis on a number of occasions. In *Goodwin v United Kingdom*[677] an order for the disclosure of a journalistic source on the ground that it would enable an employer to identify a disloyal employee was not justified by an 'overriding requirement in the public interest'. In *Fressoz v France*[678] the objective of protecting fiscal confidentiality was legitimate but the conviction of journalists for handling documents obtained in breach of professional confidence was disproportionate. **15.211**

Maintaining the authority and impartiality of the judiciary. The need to maintain the authority and impartiality of the judiciary is a ground of justification for interference and overlaps with the right of an individual to a fair trial 'where publicity would prejudice the interests of justice' under Article 6(1).[679] Article 10(2) is broader in scope and pre-trial comments are potentially legitimate under this head. However, in this context the Court has recognised that account must be taken of the central position occupied by Article 6.[680] **15.212**

In the *Sunday Times* case[681] an injunction had been granted restraining the publication of a newspaper article about the merits of pending Thalidomide litigation, on grounds that it would prejudice the trial. The Court decided that there was no 'pressing social need' for the injunction, that there was substantial public interest in the case, that the article used moderate language and that the injunction was broadly framed. The Court took the view that the 'authority and impartiality of the judiciary' were 'objectively determinable' interests; and that the margin of appreciation afforded to the state to take measures to protect them was therefore a narrow one.[682] **15.213**

The impact of criticising the judiciary has also been considered. In *Barfod v Denmark*[683] the applicant was convicted of defaming two lay judges. This conviction was justified despite his arguments that the comments were aimed at the tribunal rather than the individual judges, and that they were part of a wider political tax **15.214**

676 See *X v Germany* (1970) 13 YB, 888, EComm HR.
677 (1996) 22 EHRR 123, see generally, para 15.77ff above.
678 (1999) 5 BHRC 654.
679 Art 6(1); see para 11.231ff above.
680 *Sunday Times v United Kingdom* (1979) 2 EHRR 245 para 55.
681 Ibid.
682 But see *Weber v Switzerland* (1990) 12 EHRR 508.
683 (1989) 13 EHRR 493.

debate. In *Schöpfer v Switzerland*[684] the disciplinary punishment of the applicant lawyer was also justifiable where a lawyer publicly criticised the administration of justice in his jurisdiction in criminal proceedings which were then pending before the courts. In *De Haes and Gijsels v Belgium*[685] journalists argued that the articles, which personally insulted certain members of the judiciary for their handling of child abuse and incest proceedings, were to be seen against the background of the public debate on incest in the region. They argued that the research upon which they were based constituted objective evidence; and that it was only to protect their sources that it had not been presented in court. The Court held that, although the comments were severely critical, they were not disproportionate to the indignation caused by the subject matter of the articles.

15.215 The restriction of pre-trial comment in criminal cases was addressed in *Worm v Austria*[686] where the Court upheld the conviction of a journalist who had written an article which was critical of a former Minister in advance of his trial on charges of tax evasion. The Court held that states were not entitled to restrict all forms of public discussion on matters pending before the courts. It said:

> There is general recognition of the fact that courts cannot operate in a vacuum . . . Provided that it does not overstep the bounds imposed in the interests of the proper administration of justice, reporting, including comment on court proceedings contributes to their publicity and is thus perfectly consonant with the requirements under article 6(1) of the convention that hearings be public.[687]

The Court drew attention to the role of the media in imparting information, particularly where a public figure is involved. However:

> public figures are entitled to the enjoyment of the guarantees of a fair trial set out in art 6 . . . the limits of permissible comment may not extend to statements which are likely to prejudice, whether intentionally or not, the chances of a person receiving a fair trial or to undermine the confidence of the public in the role of the courts in the administration of criminal justice.[688]

The conviction was upheld despite the absence of a requirement in domestic law of actual influence on court proceedings. The Commission took a similar view of a pre-hearing restriction in *Channel Four v United Kingdom*[689] where it held that the broadcasting of contemporaneous reconstructions of the criminal appeal would have an impact both on the right to fair trial and on the reputation of the court.

---

684 [1998] EHRLR 646.
685 (1997) 25 EHRR 1.
686 (1997) 25 EHRR 454.
687 Ibid para 50.
688 Ibid.
689 (1989) 61 DR 285, EComm HR; see also *Hodgson v United Kingdom* (1987) 51 DR 136, EComm HR; *Atkinson Crook and The Independent v United Kingdom* (1990) 67 DR 244, EComm HR (jury trial).

D. The Impact of the Human Rights Act

(1) Introduction

The Human Rights Act will require the courts to give new weight to the freedom of expression which, in the past, has often been subordinated to other interests. There was considerable debate when the Bill was enacted concerning the effect of incorporating Article 10, and its relationship to other Convention rights. The existence of a right to freedom of expression which is subject to narrowly defined limits which must be justified as proportionate[690] will have a significant impact on the English law in a large number of different areas. Nevertheless, during the passage of the Bill the media expressed concerns about the effect of the right of privacy on freedom of expression. As a result, the Government introduced section 12 of the Act which was 'specifically designed to safeguard press freedom'.[691] **15.216**

The Human Rights Act is likely to have important repercussions on private law remedies which restrict expression. In particular, it will give impetus to further developments in the law of defamation. In addition, Article 10 is likely to have an impact in the fields of commercial law, criminal law, education, employment and discrimination, family law, local government, media law, and prison law. **15.217**

(2) United Kingdom cases prior to the Human Rights Act

(a) Introduction

A large number of United Kingdom applications based on Article 10 have come before the Commission and the Court. Many of these were unsuccessful, but the Court has on eight occasions found the United Kingdom to be in violation of Article 10.[692] Most of the Article 10 applications out of the United Kingdom fall into one of four general categories: obscenity and blasphemy, contempt of court, defamation and national security. **15.218**

However, before considering the cases brought in Strasbourg, it is necessary to consider the impact that Article 10 has had on the development of domestic law. Although, in general, Convention rights only affect domestic law indirectly[693] the stance the courts have taken to Article 10 has been rather different. **15.219**

[690] See generally, para 6.40ff above.

[691] See *Hansard*, HC col 538 ff (2 Jul 1998).

[692] *Sunday Times v United Kingdom* (1979) 2 EHRR 245; *Sunday Times v United Kingdom (No 2)* (1991) 14 EHRR 229; *The Observer and The Guardian v United Kingdom* (1991) 14 EHRR 153; *Tolstoy Miloslavsky v United Kingdom* (1995) 20 EHRR 442; *Goodwin v United Kingdom* (1996) 22 EHRR 123; *Bowman v United Kingdom* (1998) 26 EHRR 1; *Steel v United Kingdom* (1998) 28 EHRR 603 (the Art 10 violation incidental to an Art 5 violation); *Hashman and Harrup v United Kingdom* (2000) 8 BHRC 104.

[693] See para 2.09ff above.

(b) The impact of Article 10 on the common law

15.220 Before the Human Rights Act came into force, Article 10 of the Convention had already had a substantial impact on the development of the common law. In the well known passage in *Derbyshire County Council v Times Newspapers Ltd*,[694] Lord Keith said:

> Lord Goff of Chieveley in *A-G v Guardian Newspapers Ltd (No 2)*[695] expressed the opinion that in the field of freedom of speech there was no difference in principle between English law on the subject and article 10 of the Convention. I agree and can only add that I find it satisfactory to be able to conclude that the common law of England is consistent with the obligations assumed by the Crown under the Treaty in this particular field.

15.221 The courts have taken Article 10 into account in refusing local authorities and political parties the right to sue in defamation,[696] in determining the extent of the defence of 'qualified privilege'[697] and in deciding how libel damages should be assessed.[698] Article 10 has had an important influence on the law of contempt[699] and, in particular, on decisions concerning disclosure of journalistic sources under section 10 of the Contempt of Court Act 1981.[700] It has also been considered when the court decides whether to exercise discretion to restrain freedom of expression[701] and as a relevant factor to be taken into account where a public body implements measures which restrain expression.[702] The Human Rights Act can only reinforce the importance of freedom of expression as a fundamental legal value in English law.

(c) Obscenity and blasphemy

15.222 None of the United Kingdom applications under Article 10 in relation to obscenity and blasphemy have been successful. Where there has been doubt as to the 'necessity' of the measures used, the Government has consistently been given the benefit of a 'margin of appreciation'. This is because:

> a wider margin of appreciation is generally available to the contracting states when regulating freedom of expression in relation to matters liable to offend intimate personal convictions within the sphere of morals or, especially, religion.[703]

---

694 [1993] AC 534, 553F.

695 [1990] 1 AC 109, 283–284.

696 Ibid; see para 15.29 above.

697 *Reynolds v Times Newspapers Ltd* [1998] 3 WLR 862, [1999] 3 WLR 1010, see para 15.29 above.

698 *Rantzen v Mirror Group Newspapers (1986) Ltd* [1994] QB 670, see para 15.38 above.

699 See para 15.48ff above.

700 See para 15.73ff above.

701 See *A-G v Guardian Newspapers Ltd (No 1)* [1987] 1 WLR 1248, 1296-7; *R v Advertising Standards Authority Ltd, ex p Vernons Organisation Ltd* [1992] 1 WLR 1289; *Middlebrook Mushrooms Ltd v Transport and General Workers' Union* [1993] IRLR 232, 235.

702 *R v Secretary of State for the Environment, ex p NALGO* [1993] Admin LR 785, 795;

703 See *Wingrove v United Kingdom* (1996) 24 EHRR 1 para 58.

The fact that the margin of appreciation given to national authorities has been determinative in these cases means that the Strasbourg jurisprudence will provide less than reliable guidance to the UK judiciary when such matters arise in the national courts, where 'margin of appreciation' is not relevant.[704]

The leading case of *Handyside v United Kingdom*[705] concerned the Little Red Schoolbook, a publication which was written for schoolchildren and included a chapter on explicitly sexual topics. The applicant was convicted of an offence under the Obscene Publications Act. The issue for the Court was whether the undoubted interference with freedom of expression of the applicant was 'necessary in a democratic society for the protection of morals'. The Court referred to the 'national margin of appreciation' and said that: **15.223**

> The Contracting States have each fashioned their approach in the light of the situation obtaining in their respective territories; they have had regard, *inter alia*, to the different views prevailing there about the demands of the protection of morals in a democratic society.[706]

On this basis, the Court found that the conviction of the applicant on grounds of obscenity was not a violation of Article 10.[707] In *Hoare v United Kingdom*[708] the applicant complained of a breach of Article 10 as a result of his conviction for publishing obscene articles[709] under section 2 of the Obscene Publications Act 1959 and his sentence of 30-months' imprisonment. The Commission took the view that the restriction on the applicant's freedom of expression was for a legitimate aim, namely the protection of morals and was not disproportionate.

The case of *Gay News and Lemon v United Kingdom*[710] concerned the convictions of the applicant for blasphemous libel. The Commission found that this offence restricted freedom of expression for a legitimate purpose, namely 'the protection of the rights of citizens not to be offended in their religious feelings by publications'.[711] The Commission also took the view that the offence of blasphemous libel satisfied the test of 'proportionality' inherent in Article 10(2). As a result, the Commission found that the complaint was manifestly ill-founded. **15.224**

704 See para 6.31ff above.
705 (1976) 1 EHRR 737.
706 Ibid para 57.
707 For a discussion of the case, see R Lawson and H Schermers (eds), *Leading Cases of the European Court of Human Rights* (Ars Aequi Libri, 1997) 37–42; and see A Lester, 'Freedom of Expression' and R St J Macdonald, 'The Margin of Appreciation' in R St J Macdonald, F Matscher and H Petzold (eds), *The European System for the Protection of Human Rights* (Nijhoff, 1993).
708 [1997] EHRLR 678.
709 The articles were hardcore pornographic video tapes distributed by post.
710 (1982) 5 EHRR 123.
711 Ibid para 11.

15.225 Blasphemy was again at issue in *Wingrove v United Kingdom*.[712] A video entitled 'Visions of Ecstasy' depicted St Teresa of Avila in erotic scenes. The British Board of Film Classification had refused the video a distribution certificate. The admitted interference with freedom of expression was held by the Court to be 'prescribed by law', despite the fact that the offence of blasphemy lacked precise legal definition: it took the view that the applicant, with appropriate legal advice, could reasonably have foreseen that the film might fall within the scope of the offence of blasphemy.[713] The interference was also found to have the legitimate aim of protecting the rights of others: more specifically, 'to provide protection against seriously offensive attacks on matters regarded as sacred by Christians'.[714] In holding that the restrictions were 'necessary', the Court took into account the fact that:

> there is as yet not sufficient common ground in the legal and social orders of the Member States of the Council of Europe to conclude that a system whereby a State can impose restrictions on the propagation of material on the basis that it is blasphemous is, in itself, unnecessary in a democratic society and thus incompatible with the Convention.[715]

The Court took into account the wide margin of appreciation for states in relation to matters which are liable to offend intimate personal convictions.[716]

(d) Contempt of court

15.226 One of the best known decisions of the Court is that of *Sunday Times v United Kingdom*[717] which arose out of the Thalidomide litigation. The Attorney-General obtained an injunction restraining publication of an article commenting on the drug 'Thalidomide' as a contempt of court.[718] The Court accepted that the rules relating to contempt of court were 'prescribed by law' and had the legitimate aim, under Article 10(2), of 'maintaining the authority . . . of the judiciary'.[719] However, the Court went on to consider whether the interference by injunction was 'necessary in a democratic society' and concluded that:

> the interference complained of did not correspond to a social need sufficiently pressing to outweigh the public interest in freedom of expression within the meaning of the Convention.[720]

---

[712] (1996) 24 EHRR 1.
[713] Ibid para 43.
[714] Ibid para 48.
[715] Ibid para 57.
[716] For a general discussion, see S Ghandi and J James, 'The English Law of Blasphemy and the European Convention on Human Rights', [1998] EHRLR 430.
[717] (1979) 2 EHRR 245.
[718] The injunction had been granted at first instance, discharged by the Court of Appeal and restored by the House of Lords: see *A-G v Times Newspapers Ltd* [1974] AC 273.
[719] *Sunday Times v United Kingdom* (n 717 above) para 57.
[720] Ibid para 67.

The restraint was therefore a violation of Article 10. This decision resulted in the Contempt of Court Act 1981. In *Channel Four v United Kingdom*,[721] on the other hand, a restraint was acceptable where the Commission found that the broadcasting of contemporaneous reconstructions of a criminal appeal would have an impact on both the right to fair trial and the reputation of the court.

The effect of section 10 of the Contempt of Court Act 1981 was considered by the Court in *Goodwin v United Kingdom*.[722] Section 10 introduced a presumption against the disclosure of journalists' sources, subject only to a 'legitimate aim' and a 'necessity' test, requirements which mirror Article 10(2) of the Convention. The House of Lords had ordered disclosure of the identity of the source of confidential financial documents stolen from the plaintiff company.[723] In contrast, the Court decided that the order breached Article 10; it was not 'necessary in a democratic society' because there was no reasonable relationship of proportionality between the order and the legitimate aim of the protection of the rights of the company. **15.227**

(e) Defamation

The English law of defamation has generated a steady stream of applications under the Convention. The case of *Tolstoy Miloslavsky v United Kingdom*[724] was brought following the notorious libel proceedings in which the jury had awarded Lord Aldington a record £1,500,000 damages because he was alleged to have been involved in war crimes. Article 10 had been infringed as the size of the award could not be justified as being 'necessary in a democratic society'. The Court of Appeal now gives guidance to juries when they consider making awards of damages.[725] **15.228**

The applicants in *Steel and Morris v United Kingdom*[726] complained that restrictions on their expression were unjustified because the state failed to provide legal aid funding for defamation proceedings, simplified legal procedures and restrictions which would limit damage awards. The Commission declared the complaint inadmissible, commenting that the freedom of expression under Article 10 is not absolute; and does not authorise the publication of defamatory material: **15.229**

[721] *Channel Four v United Kingdom* (1989) 61 DR 285, EComm HR; see also *Hodgson v United Kingdom* (1987) 51 DR 136, EComm HR; *Atkinson Crook and The Independent v United Kingdom* (1990) 67 DR 244, EComm HR.
[722] (1996) 22 EHRR 123.
[723] *X Ltd v Morgan-Grampian (Publishers) Ltd* [1991] 1 AC 1; see para 15.76 above.
[724] (1995) Series A No 316–B ; see also *Times Newspapers v United Kingdom* (1990) 65 DR 307, EComm HR: similar argument could not be raised by *The Times* because it was not a victim.
[725] See para 15.39 above.
[726] (1993) 18 EHRR CD 172.

> They have published their views, upon which there was no prior restraint, and, if those views are subsequently found to be libellous, any ensuing sanctions would in principle be justified for the protection of the reputation and rights, within the meaning of Article 10.[727]

In *Times Newspapers v United Kingdom*[728] the Commission rejected the applicant's contention that an apology published in a newspaper gave rise to the defence of qualified privilege.

(f) National security

15.230 The well-known *Spycatcher* litigation[729] led two newspapers to bring applications under Article 10.[730] The *Observer* and *Guardian* newspapers complained about interlocutory injunctions, granted by Millett J and continued by the House of Lords, which banned publication of excerpts from the book, *Spycatcher*,[731] on grounds of national security. By the time of the House of Lords decision, the book had been published in the United States and was obtainable in the United Kingdom. In the related cases of *The Observer and The Guardian v United Kingdom* and *Sunday Times v United Kingdom*[732] the Court held that the continuation of the injunctions after confidentiality had been lost contravened Article 10. It was accepted, on the other hand, that, until publication in the United States, confidentiality was justified; and it was, therefore, proportionate to find that publication in breach of the injunctions was a contempt.[733]

15.231 The applicants in *Brind and McLaughlin v United Kingdom*[734] challenged the Government 'broadcasting ban' on terrorists.[735] The Commission found that the interference was for the legitimate aim of protecting the interests of national security, and, bearing in mind the margin of appreciation in relation to measures against terrorism, took the view that the ban was not disproportionate.[736]

(g) Other applications

15.232 The limits of the concept of 'expression' have been tested in a number of United Kingdom applications. Expression has been held to include television

[727] Ibid para 2; cf the discussion of the Art 10 position by the Court of Appeal in *McDonalds v Steel* unreported, 31 Mar 1999.

[728] [1997] EHRLR 430; arising out of the case of *Watts v Times Newspapers Ltd* [1997] QB 650.

[729] For a general discussion, see para 15.19ff above.

[730] For the history of the litigation see *Sunday Times v United Kingdom (No 2)* (1992) 14 EHRR 153, 156–73.

[731] *A-G v Guardian Newspapers Ltd (No 1)* [1987] 1 WLR 1428.

[732] (1991) 14 EHRR 153, 229.

[733] See *Times Newspapers and Neill v United Kingdom* (1992) 15 EHRR CD 49.

[734] (1994) 18 EHRR CD 76.

[735] See para 15.135 above.

[736] See also *Brind and McLaughlin v United Kingdom* (1994) 18 EHRR CD 76.

programmes[737] but not the physical expression of feelings[738] or the right to vote or stand for election.[739] In *Arrowsmith v United Kingdom*[740] there was a challenge to the applicant's conviction for distributing leaflets inciting soldiers to disaffection. Article 10 was not breached, as the prosecution served the legitimate purpose of protecting disorder in the army.

In *Bowman v United Kingdom*[741] the Court had to consider restrictions on freedom of expression in the context of elections. The applicant anti-abortion campaigner in that case had been prosecuted under section 75 of the Representation of the People Act 1983 for her third party expenditure in excess of £5, 'with a view to promoting or procuring the election of a candidate' during an election period. The applicant had distributed a leaflet setting out the candidates' respective views on abortion. She was acquitted on technical grounds. The Court held that the provisions of section 75 were a restriction on freedom of expression. They were not 'necessary in a democratic society' as they were disproportionate to the legitimate aim of securing equality between candidates. As a result, there had been a violation of Article 10. **15.233**

In *B v United Kingdom*[742] a civil servant was reprimanded by his employers for his participation in a television programme about safety at a nuclear weapons establishment. The reprimand was found to be a justified interference with his freedom of expression. This approach was confirmed in *Ahmed v United Kingdom,*[743] in which local government employees unsuccessfully challenged restrictions placed on their political activities by the Local Government (Political Restrictions) Regulations 1990. Although it was accepted that there had been an interference with the expression of the applicant, one of the 'rights of others' which can justify interference with expression is the right to 'effective political democracy'. Interferences on this ground are not limited to circumstances in which there is a threat to the stability of the constitutional or political order.[744] The Court took the view that the Government had identificd a 'pressing social need' to maintain the political neutrality of local government officers and that the interference was not disproportionate.[745] **15.234**

---

737 See eg *Hodgson v United Kingdom* (1987) 51 DR 136, EComm HR.

738 *X v United Kingdom* (1978) 3 EHRR 63, EComm HR (public displays of affection by homosexuals).

739 *Liberal Party, Mrs R and Mr P v United Kingdom* (1982) 4 EHRR 106, EComm HR.

740 (1980) 19 DR 5, EComm HR.

741 (1998) 26 EHRR 1.

742 (1985) 45 DR 41, EComm HR.

743 (1998) 5 BHRC 111.

744 Ibid para 52.

745 Ibid paras 61–65; the Court also took into account the fact that whenever the right to freedom of expression of public servants was in issue, it had to have regard to the 'duties and responsibilities' referred to in Article 10(2): see para 15.184 above.

15.235 The case of *Colman v United Kingdom*[746] arose out of the advertising restrictions of the General Medical Council. The Commission found that there was an interference with the freedom of expression of the applicant, but that it had been carried out in pursuit of legitimate aims, namely the protection of the health of patients and the rights of other doctors. The restrictions were held to be necessary.[747]

15.236 In *Steel v United Kingdom*[748] the five applicants had been arrested and detained to prevent a breach of the peace while participating in various protests.[749] It was found that the arrest and detention of the first and second applicants conformed to English law, but that that of the third, fourth and fifth applicants had been unlawful.[750] The Court considered that the protests of the applicants constituted expressions of opinion and that the measures taken against them were accordingly violations of Article 10,[751] albeit in pursuit of the legitimate aims of prevention of disorder and protection of the rights of others. In relation to the first and second applicants, taking into account the seriousness of their conduct, the apprehensions were 'necessary in a democratic society'. Interference with the other applicants was, however, unlawful and disproportionate, in violation of Article 10.[752] In *Hashman and Harrup v United Kingdom*[753] the Court again considered the impact of a bind over on protesters. The Court held that a bind over made to prevent behaviour *contra bonos mores*[754] was not sufficiently precise to be forseeable in accordance with the law under Article 10(2).

15.236A The case of *A and Byrne and Twenty-Twenty Television v United Kingdom*[754a] concerned a challenge to an injunction which prevented the transmission of a television programme concerning the illegitimate child of a politician. The Commission held that this was a justifiable interference with freedom of expression: the interference was proportionate to the aim of protecting the welfare of the child. It was justifiable to favour the child's welfare over any public interest in the programme.

---

[746] (1993) 18 EHRR 119.

[747] The restrictions were later relaxed and a friendly settlement reached.

[748] (1998) 28 EHRR 603.

[749] For the facts, see ibid paras 6–38.

[750] These applicants were, therefore, successful in Art 5 claims, ibid para 64.

[751] Ibid paras 92– 93.

[752] Ibid para 110.

[753] (2000) 8 BHRC 104.

[754] Conduct which is wrong rather than right in the judgment of the majority of contemporary citizens: see *Hughes v Holley* (1986) 86 Cr App R 130.

[754a] (1997) 25 EHRR CD 159; for the English case see *Re Z (A Minor) (Identification and Restrictions on Publication)* [1997] Fam 1.

(3) General impact issues

(a) Section 12 of the Human Rights Act

Section 12 of the Human Rights Act is headed 'Freedom of Expression'. It was introduced at the Committee stage by the Government to meet concerns raised about press freedom and the conflict with the right to privacy.[755] The Home Secretary, Jack Straw MP,[756] explained the purpose of section 12 during the Committee stage: **15.237**

> So far as we are able in a manner consistent with the Convention and its jurisprudence, we are saying to the court that wherever there is a clash between article 8 and article 10 rights, they must pay particular attention to the article 10 rights.

In fact, it appears that section 12 has rather broader implications.

Section 12 provides as follows: **15.238**

> (1) This section applies if a court is considering whether to grant any relief which, if granted, might affect the exercise of the Convention right to freedom of expression.
>
> (2) If the person against whom the application for relief is made ('the respondent') is neither present nor represented, no such relief is to be granted unless the court is satisfied—
>
> (a) that the applicant has taken all practicable steps to notify the respondent; or
> (b) that there are compelling reasons why the respondent should not be notified.
>
> (3) No such relief is to be granted so as to restrain publication before trial unless the court is satisfied that the applicant is likely to establish that publication should not be allowed.
>
> (4) The court must have particular regard to the importance of the Convention right to freedom of expression and, where the proceedings relate to material which the respondent claims, or which appears to the court, to be journalistic, literary or artistic material (or to conduct connected with such material), to—
>
> (a) the extent to which—
> (i) the material has, or is about to, become available to the public; or
> (ii) it is, or would be, in the public interest for the material to be published;
> (b) any relevant privacy code.
>
> (5) In this section—
>
> 'court' includes tribunal;
> 'relief' includes any remedy or order (other than in criminal proceedings).

---

755 See HC Deb, 2 Jul 1998, Col 538 ff: The Home Secretary. For *Hansard* extracts on s 12, see J Wadham and H Mountfield, *Blackstone's Guide to the Human Rights Act 1998* (Blackstone, 1999) 227–230.

756 *Hansard* HC 2 Jul 1998, col 543.

It is submitted that these provisions should be construed 'generously'[757] and in accordance with the principle of 'practical effectiveness'.[758] Each sub-section merits specific consideration.

15.239 Section 12(1) establishes the scope of application of the section. First, it is clear that what is being protected is not any English law right, but 'the Convention right to freedom of expression'. This means that the section encompasses the same wide range of 'forms of expression' as that covered by Article 10 of the Convention.[759]

15.240 Secondly, section 12 will apply with respect to 'any relief' which, if granted, 'might affect' the exercise of the Convention right. Therefore, although the section was contemplated to 'safeguard press freedom',[760] it clearly extends beyond court orders which might affect publication of material by the media. Injunctions granted, for example, in actions for breach of confidence, contract or copyright 'might affect' the exercise of the right to freedom of expression. An injunction in a matter of private and public nuisance might similarly be affected if its purpose was to restrain demonstrations.[761] Furthermore, the distinction between 'speech' and 'conduct' is not a clear one[762] and section 12 may have a wider impact than is initially apparent.

15.241 Furthermore, the words 'any relief' are not restricted to 'injunctive' relief. Relief which 'might affect' the exercise of the freedom must include awards of damages in civil actions.[763] As a result of section 12(5), tribunals[764] as well as courts must apply its principles. However, it is clear from section 12(5) that the criminal courts are outside the scope of the section. This means that the provision will not need to be considered when, for example, the court is making reporting restrictions during criminal trials.[765]

15.242 Section 12(2) restricts the circumstances in which an injunction may be granted in the absence of the defendant. It resembles the statutory restrictions on granting interim injunctions in industrial relations disputes;[766] and would appear to apply whenever it is genuinely claimed that relief might affect the right to expression

757 See generally, para 3.23 above.

758 See para 6.28ff above.

759 See para 15.140 above.

760 See n 755 above.

761 Thus, Barendt suggests that no injunction would have been granted in *Hubbard v Pitt* [1976] 1 QB 142 if US freedom of expression analysis had been applied: (see E Barendt, *Freedom of Speech* (Clarendon Press, 1985) 43).

762 See Barendt (n 761 above) 41–48; see para 15.140 above.

763 See *Tolstoy Miloslavsky v United Kingdom* (1995) 20 EHRR 442.

764 Defined in s 21(1) of the Human Rights Act as 'any tribunal in which legal proceedings may be brought'; the meaning of the phrase is discussed at para 5.43 above.

765 See para 15.59 above.

766 Trade Union and Labour Relations (Consolidation) Act 1992, s 222(1).

regardless of whether the claim might succeed.[767] Section 12 gives no indication that it does not also apply to final orders. If the defendant is not present at the trial, the court can only grant a final injunction or award of damages if the claimant shows that he has taken 'all practicable steps to notify the respondent'. This is a stronger test than that presently applied but is likely to be of limited practical importance.

The effect of **section 12(3)** is to raise the threshold test for the restraint of expression: to require the claimant to establish a stronger *prima facie* case.[768] As a result, the standard *American Cyanamid* test[769] for interim injunctions will no longer be applicable in any application to restrain 'expression'. Instead, the claimant will only be entitled to an injunction if he can show that he is 'likely' to succeed at trial.[770] This test does not appear to be as stringent as the rule in *Bonnard v Perryman*,[771] but its scope is much broader. The stricter test must be applied to claims for injunctions to restrain breaches of confidence, copyright or contract. **15.243**

Section 12(4) provides that the court 'must have particular regard to' the importance of the right to freedom of expression when granting relief. Where the proceedings relate to material which the respondent claims, or which appears to the court, to be journalistic, literary or artistic material (or to conduct connected with such material), the court must also have regard to the extent of the current or pending availability of the material to the public; or interest of the public in having it published; and to any relevant privacy code. The reference to 'conduct connected with such material' appears to be intended to cover journalistic enquiries which suggest the presence of a story without the support of existing material.[772] It appears that this sub-section is intended to 'tip the balance' in favour of expression in applications for injunctions to restrain breaches of privacy. Although the rights of the claimant under Article 8 will have to be weighed in the balance, the section makes clear that the Court must pay particular regard to the Article 10 rights of the respondent. **15.244**

The approach the Court will take when resolving conflicts between the freedom of expression and the right to privacy under section 12 is not entirely clear.[773] Although the Strasbourg authorities have stressed the important role of the **15.245**

[767] See *Gouriet v Union of Post Office Workers* [1978] AC 435 in relation to s 221(1).

[768] See *Hansard* HC 2 Jul 1998, col 562.

[769] *American Cyanamid Company v Ethicon Ltd* [1975] AC 396.

[770] s 12(3); this is also the position in New Zealand: see *A-G for England and Wales v Television New Zealand* 2 Dec 1998, CA. The guidance suggested by the House of Lords in *NWL Ltd v Nelson* [1979] ICR 867 in relation to injunctions in industrial relations disputes may provide assistance when applications are made under s 12(3).

[771] [1891] 2 Ch 269, see para 15.14 above.

[772] See *Hansard* HC 2 Jul 1998, col 540 (Jack Straw MP).

[773] See generally, R Singh, 'Privacy and the Media after the Human Rights Act' [1998] EHRLR 712.

media,[774] little guidance has been given about balancing the freedom of the press against the right to respect for private life.[775] The recent case law[776] suggests that the strong public interest in informed public debate about matters of legitimate public concern will outweigh the interest of individuals in reputation, and similar reasoning may well be applied to cases involving 'privacy rights'. The balance between privacy and freedom of expression has also recently been considered by the Supreme Court of Canada[777] which decided that this depends on the nature of the information which is subject to privacy and the factual context of publication.

15.246 It has been suggested that the English courts should adopt the approach taken in Canada and Germany and take into account the following factors[778] when considering privacy:

- the nature of the information at stake;
- the public (or private) status of the claimant; and
- the nature of the place where the invasion of privacy occurred.

When weighing the right to privacy against freedom of expression, the court should examine the extent to which the information contributes to public debate, whether the motivation for publication is commercial or is informed by a desire to inform the public about a serious issue and whether there were alternatives available to the publisher which could have reduced the impact on privacy. The approach that must be taken is not different in principle from the type of public figure defence in defamation considered by the House of Lords in *Reynolds v Times Newspapers Ltd.*[779] Whether freedom of expression should prevail over the right to privacy must ultimately depend on whether the circumstances show that the restriction in question is a disproportionate interference with freedom of expression.

(b) Defamation

15.247 Article 10 has already had a significant impact in this area of law.[780] It is likely that the Human Rights Act will have further repercussions. A number of possibilities have been suggested, the most important being the potential in English law for

[774] See para 15.154 above.

[775] For a general discussion of the balance between press freedom and other public interests see S Tierney, 'Press Freedom and Public Interest: the Developing Jurisprudence of the European Court of Human Rights' [1998] EHRLR 419.

[776] *Bladet Tromsø v Norway* (1999) 6 BHRC 599; *Nilsen and Johnsen v Norway* Judgment of 25 Nov 1999; *Bergens Tidende v Norway* Judgment of 2 May 2000, see para 15.204 above.

[777] *Aubrey v Les Editions Vice-Versa* [1998] 1 SCR 591; see para 12.223 above.

[778] J Craig and N Nolte, 'Privacy and Free Speech in Germany and Canada: Lessons for an English Privacy Tort' [1998] EHRLR 162.

[779] [1999] 3 WLR 1010.

[780] See para 15.220ff above; for a recent discussion of Art 10 and the law of defamation, see *McDonalds v Steel* unreported, 31 Mar 1999 (CA).

recognition of a full-blown 'public figure' defence.[781] Such a defence derives from US case law and, in particular, the decision of the Supreme Court in *New York Times v Sullivan*.[782] In that case the Supreme Court held that a public official could not recover damages for defamation relating to his official conduct unless he proved 'actual malice'.[783] The defence has been extended to defamation against 'public persons'[784] and also to private persons who are defamed in relation to matters of 'public interest'.[785]

The question as to the availability of a 'public figure' defence in libel actions has been considered in several common law jurisdictions. In some, the protection of publishers has taken the form of a defence of privilege or qualified privilege against suit where the impugned statements are matters of political or public interest. The present position can be summarised as follows: **15.248**

Australia: The High Court has held that qualified privilege applies to publications concerning 'government and political matters that affect the people of Australia', provided that the publisher acts reasonably as well as honestly.[786]

Canada: The 'public figure' defence has been rejected by the Supreme Court.[787]

India: The 'public figure' defence has been recognised by the Supreme Court.[788]

New Zealand: The Court of Appeal has held that the defence of 'qualified privilege' applies to generally published statements made about politicians in relation to matters affecting their capacity to meet their public responsibilities.[789]

---

[781] Cf P Milmo and W Rogers (eds), *Gatley on Libel and Slander* (9th edn, Sweet & Maxwell, 1998) para 23.20.

[782] (1964) 376 US 254.

[783] For general discussions, see I Loveland, 'Privacy and Political Speech: An Agenda for the "Constitutionalisation" of the Law of Libel', in P Birks (ed), *Privacy and Loyalty* (Clarendon Press, 1997) 51–92; and L Leigh, 'Of Free Speech and Individual Reputation' in I Loveland (ed), *Importing the First Amendment* (Hart Publishing, 1998), 51. The case grew out of the struggle against segregation in the American south and the plaintiff, who was not mentioned by name, had recovered damages of $500,000 despite the fact that only 35 copies of the newspaper were circulated in the town in which he was a police commissioner. In the light of this extraordinary factual background, it is not surprising that the Court appeared to be anxious to reach a result favourable to the defendant newspaper. The reasoning behind the decision has attracted considerable judicial and academic criticism: see R A Epstein, 'Was New York Times v Sullivan Wrong?' (1986) 53 U Chi L Rev 782, 787; *Dun and Bradstreet Inc v Greenmoss Builders Inc* (1985) 472 US 749, 767; see generally, *Hill v Church of Scientology* [1995] 2 SCR 1130.

[784] *Gertz v Welch* (1974) 418 US 323.

[785] *Milkovich v Lorain Journal Co* (1986) 497 US 1.

[786] *Lange v Australian Broadcasting Corp* (1997) 145 ALR 96; see para 15.353 below.

[787] See *Hill v Church of Scientology* [1995] 2 SCR 1130; see para 15.297 below.

[788] *Rajagopal v State of Tamil Nadu* 1994 6 SCC 632; see para 15.364 below.

[789] *Lange v Atkinson and Australian Consoldiated Press NZ Ltd* [1998] 3 NZLR 424, see para 15.333 below.

There is no requirement that the defendant must have acted reasonably: the defence can only be rebutted by proving 'malice'.

South Africa: It has been held that a defamatory statement in the media will not be unlawful provided that the defendant can show that he acted reasonably.[790] In deciding reasonableness, all the circumstances are taken into account but greater latitude is allowed in respect of political discussion.

However, in *Reynolds v Times Newspapers Ltd*[791] the House of Lords refused to recognise a new category of qualified privilege for 'political information' but accepted that qualified privilege could apply to a publication to the world at large if the media could establish that there was a 'right to know'.[792] Although it was recognised that that, where politicians are involved, it was likely to be relatively easy for the media to establish a defence of qualified privilege,[793] the burden of establishing the privilege remains on the media in each case.

15.249 It is not clear whether this approach will be sufficient to satisfy Article 10 tests. The Convention case law does not make express provision for a 'public figure' or 'political discussion' defence in favour of publishers of potentially defamatory material. Politicians are entitled to have their reputations protected when acting in their public capacity. Nevertheless:

> the requirements of that protection have to be weighed against the interests of open discussion of political issues, since exceptions to freedom of expression must be interpreted narrowly.[794]

The Convention now recognises a species of 'qualified privilege' (described as a 'safeguard to journalists') when 'matters of legitimate public concern' are being discussed by the press.[794a] The *Reynolds* approach does not provide full recognition of this right. Furthermore, it leaves the law of defamation in a state of uncertainty in relation to media discussion of matters of public interest. In the absence of a developed body of case law, a responsible media organisation publishing material relating to matters of 'public interest' will be unable to determine whether a defence is available. It seems that the full background to the publication will have to be investigated in each case in order to satisfy the court that there is a 'right to know'. It is arguable that this uncertainty, *of itself*, constitutes an unacceptable restriction on freedom of expression.

790 *National Media v Bogoshi* 1998 (4) SA 1196, 1212.

791 [1999] 3 WLR 1010, see para 15.36ff above.

792 Ibid.

793 Ibid *per* Lord Hope.

794 *Oberschlick v Austria (No 2)* (1997) 25 EHRR 357 para 29.

794a See, in particular, *Bergens Tidende v Norway* Judgment of 2 May 2000, especially paras 53 and 60.

It is submitted that the Human Rights Act, whether through positive rights horizontality[795] or aiding the development of the common law,[796] will bring about further developments on qualified privilege where it relates to public interest or political discussion. The case law from other jurisdictions shows that there are a number of ways in which the balance can be achieved between 'freedom of expression' and 'right to reputation'. Although a defence of qualified privilege applicable to all 'public interest discussion' seems to go too far towards the 'freedom of expression interest', the present position in English law is unduly favourable to the 'reputation interest'. At present the law of defamation either provides the defendant with a complete defence (for example, qualified privilege) or renders him liable in substantial damages (whether or not actual damage can be proved). There are a number of ways in which a better balance could be struck between freedom of expression and the right to reputation. One possible approach would be to reverse the burden of proof as to truth in cases brought by elected public officials or those seeking elected public office. Another approach would be to provide a person who is defamed with a limited right to an apology or a declaration of falsity, while at the same time providing the media defendant with a 'public figure' defence to an action in damages.[797] **15.250**

Where defamation actions are brought by public bodies, Article 10 will be of direct application. In such cases, it is likely that the courts will recognise a 'public interest defence'. The potential for such actions is, however, greatly reduced because of the restrictions on public bodies bringing proceedings.[798] **15.251**

Article 10 is likely to affect the law of defamation in other respects. For example, it is possible that the right to impart information under Article 10 will, in some circumstances, entitle the court to make an interim order requiring a defendant to publish a correction of a defamatory statement.[799] **15.252**

(c) Freedom of information

Article 10 requires that everyone has the right to 'receive and impart information'. The Court in *Leander v Sweden*[800] took a cautious approach in defining the scope of the obligation although the Consultative (Parliamentary) Assembly of the Council of Europe took a broader view.[801] However, in New Zealand it was held that the right to impart information provided the court with jurisidiction to order **15.253**

---

795 See, generally, para 5.87 above.

796 See para 5.88ff above.

797 See eg the proposal of the New South Wales Law Reform Commission, *Report No 75, Defamation* (Oct 1995) para 6.2ff on a proposed 'declaration of falsity' procedure in which affirmative defences to actions for damages cannot be raised (save for absolute privilege).

798 *Derbyshire County Council v Times Newspapers Ltd* [1993] AC 534; and see para 15.29 above.

799 See eg *TV3 Network v Eveready New Zealand Ltd* [1993] 3 NZLR 435: see para 15.331 below.

800 (1987) 9 EHRR 433; see para 15.331 below.

801 See para 15.151 above.

a mandatory interlocutory injunction to require a correction of a defamatory television programme[802] and the Supreme Court of Canada has developed a constitutional right to use public property for freedom of expression.[803] It is therefore uncertain whether Article 10 will affect any rights to freedom of information by, for example, creating a right to know[804] and widening the exemptions against disclosure in the Freedom of Information Bill or in the Local Government Act 1972.[805]

(4) The potential impact

(a) Commercial law

15.254 Although Article 10 is unlikely to have an immediate substantial impact on commercial law outside the media field, it may have some impact on regulation of advertising. This will depend on the extent to which the courts will defer to the discretion of those responsible for the regulation of commercial expression.[806] For example, in Canada[807] the Supreme Court has ruled that prohibitions on advertising tobacco[808] breached the right to freedom of expression whereas restrictions on advertising directed at children[809] did not. Article 10 may also affect the restrictions on advertising in the professions. Controls on lawyers[810] and doctors[811] have been held to comply with Article 10; however, in Canada the strict regime for advertising dental services breached freedom of expression.[812]

(b) Criminal law

15.255 The various criminal offences which restrict freedom of expression may well be affected by the Human Rights Act. Applications to quash summons or indictments for common law offences such as criminal libel may be made under the Act, or an application could be made for a stay of the proceedings.[813] The following offences

[802] *TV3 Network v Eveready New Zealand Ltd* [1993] 3 NZLR 435; see para 15.331 below.
[803] See para 15.314 below.
[804] Cf *Reynolds v Times Newspapers* [1999] 3 WLR 1010, 1020A–C *per* Lord Nicholls, indicating that the 'right to know' test is preferable to the traditional 'duty and interest' test for qualified privilege.
[805] See para 15.134ff above.
[806] The Convention case law gives a wide margin of appreciation to commercial expression: see para 15.171ff above. Although the margin of appreciation is not directly applicable to the Human Rights Act (see para 6.82ff above), the courts may nevertheless take a broad approach when considering commercial speech: see C McCrudden 'The Impact of Freedom of Speech' in B Markesinis (ed), *The Impact of the Human Rights Bill on English Law* (Oxford University Press, 1998).
[807] See para 15.310ff below.
[808] *R J R-MacDonald v A-G of Canada* [1995] 3 SCR 199.
[809] *Irwin Toy v Quebec* [1989] 1 SCR 927.
[810] *Casado Coca v Spain* (1994) 18 EHRR 1.
[811] *Colman v United Kingdom* (1993) 18 EHRR 119.
[812] *Rocket v Royal College of Dental Surgeons* [1990] 1 SCR 232.
[813] See generally, para 21.110ff below.

will be considered: criminal, blasphemous and seditious libel, obscenity and Official Secrets Act offences.

Criminal libel. The offence of criminal (or defamatory) libel has often been criticised as unduly restrictive of freedom of expression. The problem is not with the offence itself,[814] but with the anomalies and obscurity of elements of the offence at common law. The fact that truth is not a defence and that the burden of proving public interest rests with the defendant means that the offence potentially places undue restriction on expression. The elements of the offence are unclear: the 'seriousness' element is vague and the requisite mental element is obscure.[815] As Lord Diplock said in *Gleaves v Deakin*:[816] **15.256**

> The examination of the legal characteristics of the criminal offence of defamatory libel as it survives today . . . has left me with the conviction that this particular offence has retained anomalies which involved serious departures from accepted principles upon which the modern criminal law of England is based and are difficult to reconcile with international obligations which this country has undertaken by becoming party to the European Convention.

He drew attention, in particular, to the fact that there is no onus on the prosecution to demonstrate that it is 'necessary in a democratic society to suppress or penalise' the defamatory material in order to protect the public interest. Instead, the defendant must prove that the publication was for the public benefit. Lord Diplock castigated the 'sorry state of the law of criminal libel'. These criticisms remain valid. It is therefore open to any person prosecuted for the offence to seek a remedy under the Human Rights Act.[817]

Blasphemous and seditious libel. It is not clear whether blasphemous libel satisfies Convention standards on restrictions of expression. Blasphemy legislation is still in force in a number of European countries, although prosecutions appear to be rare.[818] The Commission and the Court have accepted that the restriction of expression entailed by the offence has the legitimate purpose of protecting the rights of others 'not to be offended in their religious feelings' and can be considered 'necessary in a democratic society'.[819] These decisions have, however, all been based on the 'wide margin of appreciation in relation to morals and religion'.[820] **15.257**

814 Cf *Thorgeirson v Iceland* (1992) 14 EHRR 843 para 59.
815 Cf Law Commission, *Report on Criminal Libel* (Law Com No 149, Cmnd 9618, 1985).
816 [1980] AC 477, 482.
817 See para 21.110ff below.
818 See *Wingrove v United Kingdom* (1996) 24 EHRR 1 para 57.
819 *Gay News and Lemon v United Kingdom* (1982) 5 EHRR 123, 130; and *Wingrove* (n 818 above).
820 *Wingrove* (n 818 above) para 58.

Under the Human Rights Act, the English courts will be able to give direct application to their own assessment of what is 'necessary in a democratic society'.[821] The obscure and discriminatory nature[822] of this offence might be incompatible with Article 10.

15.258 The scope of 'seditious libel' is uncertain and it is possible that the offence could be committed by a person who promotes a campaign of peaceful civil disobedience. This might contravene Article 10, as limitation of such campaigns by use of the criminal law may not be 'necessary in a democratic society'.[823]

15.259 **Obscenity and indecency.** The criminal law relating to obscenity and indecency places substantial restrictions on freedom of expression. The Convention case law recognises a wide 'margin of appreciation' in obscenity cases[824] so that the Convention cases are an uncertain guide to the approach to be taken by the English courts. Article 10(2) recognises 'the protection of morals' as a legitimate aim for an interference with expression. The interference for this purpose must, however, be 'necessary' and 'proportionate'.[825] It is arguable that the law governing obscenity and indecency is incompatible with Article 10 in a number of respects:

- there is a lack of clarity as to the definition of obscenity;[826]
- in relation to the common law offences[827] there is no defence of 'public good' and no requirement that the publications 'deprave and corrupt';[828]
- the use of the 'forfeiture' provisions in section 3 of the Obscene Publications Act 1959[829] arguably provides a disproportionate restraint on freedom of expression.

15.260 **Official secrets.** Section 1 of the Official Secrets Act 1911 is likely to be regarded as an acceptable restriction on freedom of speech to the extent that it is concerned with espionage. However, an offence could be committed by, for example, a journalist publishing information about incompetence in the armed forces. It is submitted that this would be a breach of Article 10 since the restrictions on freedom of expression in section 1 may go beyond 'what is necessary in a democratic society'.

---

[821] See para 6.146ff above.

[822] The fact that the offence does not extend to non Christians may breach Art 9; see para 14.77 above.

[823] See *Steel v United Kingdom* (1998) 28 EHRR 603 discussed at para 15.201 above; and see generally, D Feldman, *Civil Liberties and Human Rights in England and Wales* (Clarendon Press, 1993) 680.

[824] See *Handyside v United Kingdom* (1976) 1 EHRR 737.

[825] See para 15.191 above.

[826] Cf F Klug, K Starmer and S Weir, *The Three Pillars of Liberty* (Routledge, 1996) 174.

[827] See para 15.88 above.

[828] See Klug, Starmer and Weir (n 826 above) 174–175.

[829] See para 15.80 above.

The Official Secrets Act 1989 is also difficult to reconcile with Article 10.[830] In particular, where restrictions on freedom of expression are permissible without the need to prove damage, it is arguable that such restrictions are unnecessary. Under section 1 the defendant could be liable for disclosing information which is already in the public domain. **15.261**

The 1989 Act does not include a 'public interest defence'. This contrasts with proceedings for breach of confidence in which such a defence is available.[831] As Feldman points out, this means that: **15.262**

> under all provisions of the 1989 Act criminal liability may be imposed in circumstances when no injunction could have been obtained to restrain publication.[832]

The result of these considerations is that:

> It seems likely . . . that . . . the restraints on freedom of expression resulting from the [Official Secrets Act 1989 go] . . . further than is necessary in a democratic society.[833]

Public order. English law has increasingly accepted a right to protest when considering public order offences such as obstructing the highway[834] or trespassory assembly.[835] However, Article 10 will give explicit recognition to the right to protest. Where, for example, an individual is bound over, he must be able to foresee with sufficient precision what sort of conduct will breach the order;[836] and Article 10 will require the prosecution to justify any interference with freedom of expression as being a proportionate restriction. The decision in *Steel v United Kingdom*[837] suggests that interferences with peaceful protests will breach Article 10.[838] However, in many cases it will be argued that peaceful protest engages the right to assemble under Article 11[839] rather than freedom of expression issues under Article 10. **15.263**

Racist speech. The criminal law substantially restricts expression which exhibits an intent to stir up racial hatred.[840] In general, such interference will be for a legitimate aim and will be necessary.[841] Where the offences apply to media reporting of racist speech, it is possible that there could be a breach of Article 10.[842] **15.264**

---

[830] See generally, Feldman, (n 823 above) 668–73.
[831] See para 12.34ff above.
[832] Feldman, (n 823 above) 669.
[833] R Stone, *Textbook on Civil Liberties* (2nd edn, Blackstone, 1997) 184.
[834] See eg *Hirst v Chief Constable of West Yorkshire* (1986) 85 Cr App R 143.
[835] *DPP v Jones* [1999] 2 AC 240.
[836] *Hashman and Harrup v United Kingdom* (2000) 8 BHRC 104; see para 15.189 above.
[837] (1998) 5 BHRC 339, see para 15.146 above.
[838] See also *Levy v Victoria* (1997) 146 ALR 248; see para 15.354 above.
[839] See para 16.57ff below.
[840] See Public Order Act 1996, Pt III.
[841] The Commission has applied a low standard of review when examining whether restrictions on racist expression breach Art 10: see para 15.141 above.
[842] See eg *Jersild v Denmark* (1994) 19 EHRR 1.

15.265 **Other offences restricting expression.** By section 5 of the Public Order Act 1986 it is an offence, *inter alia*, to use words or to 'display any writing, sign or other visible representation' which is 'threatening or abusive or insulting' within the hearing or sight of a person 'likely to cause harassment, alarm or distress thereby'. This offence is often used to arrest demonstrators displaying placards which police officers believe to be offensive.[843] The operation of the restrictions on expression contained in this section may be a breach of Article 10.[844]

15.266 By section 1 of the Public Order Act 1936 it is an offence for a person to wear a uniform:

> signifying his association with any political organisation or with the promotion of any political object.

It is possible that the wearing of a uniform might be treated as a form of 'expression';[845] as such, it is difficult to see how this offence, given its broad scope, could be justified under Article 10.[846]

(c) Education

15.267 There are a number of restrictions on freedom of expression in the field of education.[847] Local Education Authorities, governing bodies and head teachers of state schools must, for example, forbid pupils under the age of 12 to pursue partisan political activities.[848] This is a clear breach of Article 10.[849] Furthermore, those responsible for state schools are obliged to forbid the promotion of partisan political views in the teaching of any subject.[850] There is no statutory definition of 'promotion' in this context and the statute may be held to place undue restrictions on the Article 10 rights of both pupils and teachers.

(d) Employment and discrimination

15.268 It is clear that Article 10 rights extend to the workplace[851] and will affect standard

[843] See F Klug, K Starmer and S Weir, *The Three Pillars of Liberty* (Routledge, 1996) 178 for other examples.

[844] Cf the American cases on symbolic speech such as *Cohen v California* (1971) 403 US 15 (jacket with insignia 'Fuck the draft' protected speech under the First Amendment).

[845] Cf Barendt's suggestion that the wearing of a uniform would be 'speech' in the United States (E Barendt, *Freedom of Speech* (Clarendon Press, 1985) 44.

[846] Cf the American cases which treat symbolic speech as protected under the First Amendment such as *Cohen v California* (1971) 403 US 15.

[847] See generally, D Feldman, *Civil Liberties and Human Rights in England and Wales* (Oxford University Press, 1993) 568–571.

[848] Education Act 1996, s 406(1)(a).

[849] It is also a breach of the right of freedom of expression in the UN Convention on the Rights of the Child, 1989 (Art 13).

[850] Education Act 1996, s 406(1)(b). Regarding the 'promotion' of homosexuality, see para 15.276 below.

[851] *Vogt v Germany* (1995) 21 EHRR 205, see para 15.144 above.

public authorities[851a] in their capacity as employers. An employee also owes duties of loyalty and confidentiality to his employers, however, and restrictions designed to enforce these duties may be justified under Article 10(2). There are a number of potential areas of impact on the rights of employees, including restrictions on political activity, workplace dress codes and the rights of whistleblowers.

The Convention case law indicates that the actions of an employer in dismissing[852] or disciplining[853] employees who are exercising freedom of expression are within the scope of Article 10. However, a refusal to appoint probationary employees to the civil service is not.[854] The justification for this distinction is not persuasive[855] and contrasts sharply with the American approach which has rejected the idea that public employment can be made conditional on surrendering constitutional rights.[856] It is submitted that where a standard public authority interferes with freedom of expression in appointing staff, this will be unlawful under the Human Rights Act. **15.269**

However, the current restrictions on the political activities of local government employees will be lawful under Article 10, provided these serve the proper public interest of preserving the impartiality of officials.[857] **15.270**

It has been argued that the right to freedom of expression includes a right to choose styles of dress.[858] It appears, however, that the protection will be limited to a 'right to express ideas or opinions' by dressing in a particular way.[859] On this basis, 'dress or grooming codes' imposed by public authority employers will constitute violations of Article 10 only if the employee can show that his appearance is intended to express some idea or opinion.[860] Such a violation may be justified by the employer if it can be shown that a 'legitimate interest' was served by the **15.271**

[851a] The meaning of 'standard public authorities' is discussed at para 5.14ff above; they are to be distinguished from 'functional public authorities' which are discussed at para 5.16ff. The question of whether employees of functional public authorities have Convention rights is complex; see para 5.32ff.

[852] *Vogt v Germany* (1995) 21 EHRR 205.

[853] See eg *Morrissens v Belgium* (1988) 56 DR 127, EComm HR.

[854] See *Glasenapp v Germany* (1986) 9 EHRR 25; *Kosiek v Germany* (1986) 9 EHRR 328.

[855] See para 15.148 above.

[856] See eg *Perry v Sinermann* (1972) 408 US 593, 597 and *Rutan v Republican Party of Illinois* (1990) 497 US 62; and see, generally, G Morris, 'The European Convention on Human Rights and Employment: To Which Acts Does it Apply?' [1999] EHRLR 498.

[857] See *Ahmed v United Kingdom* (1998) 5 BHRC 111, and para 15.234 above; and the unsuccessful domestic challenge in *R v Secretary of State for the Environment, ex p NALGO* [1993] Admin LR 785; and see generally, G Morris, 'Political Activities of Public Servants and Freedom of Expression' in I Loveland (ed) *Importing the First Amendment* (Hart Publishing, 1998) 99.

[858] See G Clayton and G Pitt, 'Dress Codes and Freedom of Expression' [1997] EHRLR 54.

[859] See *Stevens v United Kingdom* (1986) 46 DR 245 para 2, EComm HR.

[860] For example, wearing of black armbands as an anti-war protest: see *Tinker v Des Moines School District* (1969) 393 US 503; cf *Boychuk v Symons Holdings* [1977] IRLR 395: dismissal for wearing a 'Gay Liberation' badge at work, held to be fair.

restriction and that it was 'necessary'. Dress or grooming which does not relate to the expression of ideas is unlikely to attract Article 10 protection.[861] The issue of dress codes also raises questions about an employee's right to personal autonomy; these are addressed in Chapter 12.[862]

15.272 It has also been argued that the failure of English law in the past to protect 'whistle blowers' from disciplinary action could violate Article 10.[863] However, it is unlikely that Article 10 will have an impact on this area in the light of the Public Interest Disclosure Act 1998.[864] Although the Court[865] has not directly considered the issue, it is clear that the restriction on the ability of employees to publish information about their employers is justifiable under Article 10(2). In any case, the limitations contained in a contract of employment on maintaining confidentiality may waive any right of an employee to rely on Article 10.[866]

15.273 It is likely that peaceful picketing will be protected as expression under Article 10 as it is in Canada[867] and the United States.[868] If peaceful picketing is within the scope of Article 10, the court would have to apply section 12 of the Human Rights Act[869] when an application is made seeking an injunction; and would proceed on the basis that a peaceful picket was *prima facie* lawful unless a restriction on the right was justified as proportionate.[870] On the other hand, it is arguable that it is

[861] Cf *New Rider v Board of Education* (1974) 414 US 1097: suspension of school students for having long hair not reviewed.

[862] See para 12.185 above.

[863] See J Bowers and J Lewis, 'Whistleblowing: Freedom of Expression in the Workplace' [1996] EHRLR 637; L Vickers, 'Whistleblowing in the Public Sector and the ECHR' [1997] PL 594; Sir Gavin Lightman and J Bowers, 'Incorporation of the ECHR and its Impact on Employment Law' [1998] EHRLR 560.

[864] The Act prevents an employee within its scope from being subject to a detriment (Employment Rights Act 1996, s 47B); nor can he be dismissed (s 103A) even if he has not worked for one year (s 108(3)(ff)) or is above the upper age limit (s 109(2)(ff)). However, an employee must show that the nature of the information revealed makes it a 'protected disclosure' under s 43A. If the disclosure is a 'qualifying disclosure' under s 43B, the question of whether the disclosure is *actually* covered by the Act depends on the circumstances in which the information is revealed which are strictly and narrowly defined in ss 43C–H.

[865] But see the Commission decision in *B v United Kingdom* (1985) 45 DR 41, EComm HR where the reprimand of a civil servant for participating in a television programme about safety at a nuclear weapons establishment was a justified interference with his freedom of expression.

[866] See *Vereiniging Rechtswinkels Utrecht v Netherlands* (1986) 46 DR 200, EComm HR; and see generally, para 6.148ff above.

[867] See *Retail, Wholesale and Department Store Union v Dolphin Delivery* [1986] 2 SCR 573; *BCGEU v BC* [1988] 2 SCR 214; *Union Food and Commercial Workers v K Mart Canada*, [1999] 2 SCR 1083; see para 15.318 below.

[868] *Thornhill v Alabama* (1940) 310 US 88; however, it is not protected as free speech where the picketing is for a legal purpose; see, for example, *Teamsters Local 695 v Vogt* 354 US 284 (1957).

[869] See para 15.237ff above.

[870] Cf *DPP v Jones* [1999] AC 240 at 254, 255 where Lord Irvine held that the common law recognised that the public had the right to use the highway for any reasonable purpose provided the activity was not a public or private nuisance and did not unreasonably interfere with the rights of others to pass and repass.

more appropriate for picketing to be considered in relation to freedom of assembly.[871]

(e) Family law

It seems unlikely that the jurisdiction of the court to restrict the publication of information relating to children will be in breach of Article 10.[872] The general policy of conducting in private those trials which relate to children is also likely to be held to be consistent with the Convention.[873] **15.274**

(f) Local government law

Any regulation of the use of local authority property which circumscribes the type of meetings which may be held or material which may be distributed thereon could potentially breach Article 10. A right of access to public property has been derived from the right to freedom of expression in Canada[874] and in the United States.[875] The implications of Article 10 on the freedom of information provisions of the Local Government Act 1972 are discussed above.[876] **15.275**

Section 28 of the Local Government Act 1988 makes it unlawful for local authorities to 'promote homosexuality'.[877] This constitutes a restriction on freedom of expression. It is difficult to see how it can be justified under Article 10. The Government proposes to repeal it shortly.[878] **15.276**

(g) Media law

Introduction. The impact of the Human Rights Act on the law relating to the media is likely to be substantial. The impact on the law of defamation has already been considered.[879] In addition, the Act will affect contempt, the regulation of broadcasting and the certification of films and videos. **15.277**

Contempt. It is arguable that the Contempt of Court Act 1981, which was intended to bring the law into line with the Convention, fails to do so. While the new strict liability rule supersedes the 'prejudgment' test applied by the House of Lords in the *Sunday Times* case,[880] its scope does not encompass unintentionally **15.278**

871 For the position in English Law, see para 16.31 below.

872 Cf *Re H–S (Minors) (Protection of Identity)* [1994] 1 WLR 1141; and *Arlidge, Eady and Smith on Contempt* (2nd edn, Sweet & Maxwell, 1999), para 6–37.

873 *Re P-B (A Minor) (Child Cases: Hearings in Open Court)* [1997] 1 All ER 58; *Official Solicitor v News Group Newspapers* [1994] 2 FLR 174 and see *Arlidge Eady and Smith* (n 872 above) para 7-42–7-43, 8–91.

874 *Committee for the Commonwealth of Canada v Canada* [1991] 1 SCR 139; *Ramsden v Peterborough* [1993] 2 SCR 1084; see para 15.291 below.

875 Cf *Martin v City of Struthers* (1943) 319 US 141: restrictions on leafleting.

876 See para 15.253 above.

877 Cf F Klug, K Starmer and S Weir, *The Three Pillars of Liberty* (Routledge, 1996) 178.

878 See *Hansard* HL 5 Jun 1998, col 654 (Lady Blackstone).

879 See para 15.247ff above.

880 *A-G v Times Newspapers Ltd* [1974] AC 273; see para 15.46 above.

prejudicial conduct apart from publications[881] and all forms of contempt which deliberately impede or prejudice the administration of justice.[882] In these instances, the restrictive common law approach might still be applied, a possibility contemplated by the Act itself,[883] at least in relation to intentional contempts. It should not be assumed, therefore, that the facts of the *Sunday Times* case, should they arise again, could not be successfully prosecuted a second time: this time as an intentional contempt.[884]

15.279 It is arguable, furthermore, that the 'exception' for the 'discussion of public affairs' contained in section 5[885] does not accord with the proper approach under Article 10. The exception does not require the courts to engage in any 'balancing exercise' and does not recognise the importance of the protection of freedom of expression. The application of the exception would not have assisted in the *Sunday Times* Thalidomide case,[886] and the approach adopted by the courts in relation to the affairs of Robert Maxwell[887] suggests that the exception will be of limited value in protecting freedom of expression.

15.280 Section 10 of the Contempt of Court Act has led to a finding by the Court of a violation of Article 10 of the Convention.[888] The section is expressed in the language of Article 10: disclosure will not be ordered unless it is necessary in the interests of justice or national security or for the prevention of disorder or crime. The English courts have, however, been prepared to give a broad construction to the listed 'exceptions'. The interpretation given to 'prevention of crime' extends its ambit beyond specific crimes to include prevention of future crime,[889] and the 'interests of justice' have been held to cover the freedom of private individuals to exercise their legal rights.[890] The difference of approach between the English courts and the European Court of Human Rights is illustrated by the decisions in the *Goodwin* case: while the House of Lords ordered the disclosure of the journalist's sources,[891] the Court of Human Rights held this to be a violation of Article 10.[892] The Human Rights Act may require the English courts to reconsider their approach.

15.281 The maintenance of the authority of the judiciary is a 'legitimate aim' under Article 10(2). It has been suggested that the common law offence of 'scandalising

[881] This exempts private conduct including questions such as payments to witnesses and other forms of pressure on individuals which might be unintentionally prejudicial.
[882] s 6(c).
[883] s 6(c).
[884] See Lord Diplock's comments to this effect in *A-G v English* [1983] 1 AC 116, 143.
[885] See para 15.52 above.
[886] See n 880 above; cf *A-G v English* (n 884 above) 144.
[887] See *Arlidge, Eady and Smith on Contempt* (2nd edn, Sweet & Maxwell, 1999) para 4–296.
[888] *Goodwin v United Kingdom* (1996) 22 EHRR 123.
[889] *In re An Inquiry under the Company Securities (Insider Dealing) Act 1985* [1988] AC 660.
[890] See *X Ltd v Morgan-Grampian (Publishers) Ltd* [1991] 1 AC 1, 54C.
[891] Ibid.
[892] *Goodwin v United Kingdom* (1996) 22 EHRR 123.

the court'[893] is not compatible with Convention rights.[894] However, the Convention case law shows a recognition of the need to protect the judiciary from unfounded attacks[895] and the offence has been accepted as being consistent with freedom of expression in a number of Commonwealth jurisdictions.[896] It seems unlikely that it will be affected by the Human Rights Act.

Reporting restrictions. The Human Rights Act will require that greater emphasis is placed on freedom of expression[896a] as opposed to the right to a fair trial. The case law on the Canadian Charter may be particularly pertinent;[897] and, in particular, the decision of the Supreme Court in *Dagenais v Canadian Broadcasting Corporation*[898] which took a robust view about the value of adopting alternatives where the court is asked to impose a restriction on freedom of expression. 15.282

The police and the media. The right to freedom of expression will significantly alter the principles to be applied when the police seek orders which affect the media. The court must not act incompatibly with Article 10; and the starting point is that interferences with expression must be justified as proportionate where the police seek journalistic material[899] or apply for search warrants to be executed on the premises of the media.[900] 15.283

Regulation of broadcasting. The Human Rights Act will mean that the approach of the courts in *R v Secretary of State for the Home Department, ex p Brind*[901] will be radically transformed. That case upheld the Sinn Fein broadcasting ban on the ground that Ministers and public bodies were not then required by law to exercise their powers in accordance with the Convention. The Government veto power on broadcasts has until now been subject only to the threshold test for judicial review at common law. The effect of the Human Rights Act is to require that such Government action be measured, instead, against the European standard of proportionality. 15.284

Whether the change in perspective will affect the outcome in any particular case is unclear. In the *Brind* case,[902] considered by the Commission, it held that, given the importance of measures against terrorism and the margin of appreciation to be 15.285

[893] See para 15.56 above.
[894] See D Feldman, *Civil Liberties and Human Rights in England and Wales* (Clarendon Press, 1993) 747; and cf *R v Kopyto* (1987) 62 OR (2d) 449 (see para 15.300 below); and contrast *Secretary of Justice v The Oriental Press Group* [1993] HKLY 49 (see para 15.360 below).
[895] See eg *De Haes and Gijesels v Belgium* (1997) 25 EHRR 1; see para 15.143 above.
[896] See *Arlidge, Eady and Smith on Contempt* (n 887 above) paras 5-259–5-269.
[896a] See, eg, *R v Secretary of State for Health ex p Wagstaffe* [2000] 1 All ER (D) 1021; and see para 15.67 above.
[897] See para 15.301ff below.
[898] [1994] 3 SCR 835; see para 15.303 below.
[899] See para 12.17 above.
[900] See cases under the Canadian Charter of Rights at para 15.309 below.
[901] [1991] 1 AC 696.
[902] (1994) 18 EHRR CD 82.

afforded states, the interference occasioned by the Sinn Fein ban was not disproportionate to the aims pursued.

(h) Prison law

15.286 The freedom of expression of prisoners is, of course, restricted by the fact of their imprisonment. These restrictions must now be justified under Article 10. Any restriction which cannot be so justified will be unlawful and the courts will have power to strike down Prison Rules and other secondary legislation which contain them.

15.287 The Prison Rules allow Governors to impose conditions upon prison visitation. Under paragraph 37 of Standing Order 5A, for example,[903] a journalist or author permitted to visit a prison must give a written undertaking to, *inter alia*, ensure that material is not used for professional purposes, in the absence of permission of the Governor.[904] In *R v Secretary of State for the Home Department, ex p Simms*[905] the prison authorities had refused to allow interviews with journalists to take place unless they signed written undertakings not to publish such material. The House of Lords[906] held that although oral interviews with prisoners required careful control, a blanket ban was unlawful. The provisions of the prison standing orders did not affect the prisoners' fundamental right to freedom to communicate with journalists with the object of obtaining a review of their convictions. This right could only be defeated by demonstrating a 'pressing social need'[907] which the Home Secretary had failed to do. The House of Lords refused to follow US cases to the opposite effect.[908]

Appendix 1: The Canadian Charter of Rights

(1) Introduction

15.288 The Canadian Charter of Rights and Freedoms, section 2(b) states:

> (2) Everyone has the following fundamental freedoms: . . .
>
> (b) the freedom of thought, belief, opinion and expression, including freedom of the press and other media of communication.

[903] Made by the Home Secretary pursuant to rule 33 of the Prison Rules 1964, under the authority of the Prison Act 1952, s 47(1).

[904] For a general discussion, see S Livingstone and T Owen, *Prison Law* (Oxford University Press, 1999) para 7.34.

[905] [1999] 2 WLR 730.

[906] Reversing the Court of Appeal, [1999] QB 349.

[907] *Per* Lord Steyn, at 411.

[908] See eg *Pell v Procunier* (1974) 417 US 817, partly based on judicial deference to the views of prison authorities which 'does not accord with the approach under English law', for a general discussion of the US case law on news media interviews, see J Palmer and S Palmer, *The Constitutional Rights of Prisoners* (6th edn, Anderson Publishing, 1999) 43–46.

The Supreme Court in *Irwin Toy v Quebec*[909] expressed the view that freedom of expression is to be valued because: **15.289**

> (1) seeking and attaining the truth is an inherently good activity; (2) participation in social and political decision-making is to be fostered and encouraged; (3) the diversity in forms of individual self-fulfilment and human flourishing ought to be cultivated.

In *Libman v A-G of Quebec*[910] the Supreme Court said that:

> It is difficult to imagine a guaranteed right which is more important to a democratic society than freedom of expression. Indeed, a democracy cannot exist without that freedom to express new ideas and to put forward opinions about the functioning of public institutions. The concept of free and uninhibited speech permeates all truly democratic societies. The vital importance of the concept cannot be over-emphasised. No doubt that is the reason why the framers of the constitution set forth s 2(b) in absolute terms which distinguishes it, for example, from s 8 of the Charter which guarantees the qualified right to be secure from unreasonable search. It seems that the rights enshrined in s 2(b) should only be restricted in the *clearest* of circumstances.

Nevertheless, restrictions on the right of expression may be justified under section 1 of the Charter as being such reasonable limits prescribed by law as can be demonstrably justified in a free and democratic society.

The Supreme Court of Canada has defined 'expression' as activity which attempts to convey meaning.[911] It therefore includes all forms of art,[912] commercial expression[913] and could even extend to parking a car as part of a protest against parking regulations.[914] Freedom of expression is content neutral so that a statement cannot be deprived of constitutional protection no matter how offensive it is.[915] Thus, it includes communicating for the purpose of prostitution,[916] promoting hatred against the Jews (or other racial group),[917] threats of violence[918] and a conviction for the offence of publishing false news by denying the Holocaust.[919] **15.290**

(2) Justifiable limitations

(a) The limitation clause

The limitation provision in section 1 of the Charter applies equally to the freedom of expression as to other Charter rights. 'Prescribed by law'[920] requires that a law must not be **15.291**

[909] [1989] 1 SCR 927 , 976 *per* Dickson CJ, Larmer and Wilson J; *R v Keegstra* [1990] 3 SCR 697, 762, 763 *per* Dickson CJ.

[910] [1997] 3 SCR 569, 581; see also *UFCW Local 1518 v K Mart Canada Ltd* [1999] 2 SCR 1083 para 21.

[911] *Irwin Toy v Quebec* [1989] 1 SCR 927, 968; *Re ss 193 and 195.1 of the Criminal Code (Prostitution Reference)* [1990] 1 SCR 1123, 1180; *Rocket v College of Dental Surgeons* [1990] 2 SCR 232, 244; *R v Keegstra* [1990] 3 SCR 697, 729, 826.

[912] *Re ss 193 and 195.1 of the Criminal Code (Prostitution Reference)* (n 911 above) 1182.

[913] See para 15.171ff above.

[914] *Irwin Toy v Quebec* (n 911 above) 969.

[915] *R v Keegstra* (n 911 above) 828.

[916] *Re ss 193 and 195.1 of the Criminal Code (Prostitution Reference)* (n 911 above).

[917] *R v Keegstra* (n 911 above) 828.

[918] Ibid 733 *per* Dickson CJ for the majority.

[919] *R v Zundel* [1992] 2 SCR 731.

[920] See generally, para 6.146ff above.

excessively vague,[921] and the two-stage *Oakes*[922] test dictates that: first that the legislative objective of the limitation must be justifiable on the grounds of pressing and substantial concerns, and, secondly, that the specific means adopted to implement the objective are proportionate. The principle of proportionality[923] ensures that the means be rationally connected with the legislative objective, that the means result in as little impairment of the right or freedom as possible, and that the effects of the measure be proportional to the objective. It is more difficult to justify a complete ban on a form of expression than a partial ban.[924]

15.292 An application of the proportionality test to expression is exemplified in *Butler*,[925] where the criminal prohibition of pornographic material breached section 2(b) of the Charter by restricting pornography on the basis of its content.[926] The prohibition was, nevertheless, justified because it was no wider than was necessary to accomplish the goal of preventing harm to society: it did not prohibit sexually explicit material that was neither violent nor degrading; neither did it attack private possession or viewing of the obscene materials or prohibit material that was required by the internal necessities of serious artistic work.

(b) The value of expression

15.293 The Canadian courts do not treat all types of expression as being of equal worth.[927] Political speech is considered indispensable,[928] while artistic and commercial speech are less so. Under the Charter the value of the expression becomes relevant only at the stage of the section 1 assessment of the necessity of limitations on it and has nothing to do, in the first instance, with its protection under section 2(b). The approach taken does not, for example, apply special tests to restrictions on commercial expression; instead, the court considers a conflict between expression and the other values said to justify a restriction on expression by examining its social and factual context while taking account of the special features of the expression in question.[929]

(c) Types of restrictions on expression

15.294 The expansive definition of expression and the very general terms in which interferences can be justified under section 1[930] mean that the freedom of expression cases have been argued in a wide variety of contexts.

[921] In *Ontario Film and Video Appreciation Society v Ontario Board of Censors* (1984) 45 OR (2d) 80n a film censorship law was held invalid for failure to supply standards of censorship; *R v Butler* [1992] 1 SCR 452, 491: the Criminal Code prohibition of obscenity was construed not merely as moral disapprobation but as 'the avoidance of harm to society', which gave it sufficient precision to be considered an intelligible standard.

[922] *R v Oakes* [1986] 1 SCR 103.

[923] See generally, para 6.42ff above.

[924] See *Ramsden v Peterborough* [1993] 2 SCR 1085, 1105, 1106; *Ford v Quebec* [1988] 2 SCR 712, 772, 773.

[925] Ibid.

[926] *R v Butler* [1992] 1 SCR 452.

[927] *R v Keegstra* [1990] 3 SCR 697, 760.

[928] *Re Alberta Statutes* (1938) SCR 100, 133 *per* Duff J; *Samur v City of Quebec* [1953] 2 SCR 299.

[929] *Rocket v Royal College of Dental Surgeons* [1990] 2 SCR 232, 246, 247 *per* McLachlin J.

[930] See para 15.291 above.

Prior restraint. The Courts have struck down a variety of prior restraints under section 2. These include: legislation authorising film censorship where there were no statutory standards laid down;[930a] an injunction to prohibit peaceful picketing,[930b] restrictions on the importation of books of an immoral or indecent character.[930c] Before ordering a ban on publication the judge must be convinced that there are no reasonable alternatives less restrictive of freedom of expression, that the ban is as limited as possible in time and scope and that the value of the right protected by the ban outweighs the harm caused to freedom of expression.[930d] **15.295**

Defamation. The most controversial issue that has arisen is whether the Charter provides constitutional protection to public officials by entitling them to a defence of qualified privilege along the lines of *New York Times v Sullivan*.[931] In that case the American Supreme Court held that a defendant had a complete defence where statements made concerned the plaintiff's official conduct unless the defendant was guilty of express malice. At common law the mere existence of a public interest in the subject matter of a publication was insufficient to provide a defence of qualified privilege.[932] There was therefore considerable debate about whether the Charter might affect this principle.[933] **15.296**

The question was addressed by the Supreme Court in *Hill v Church of Scientology of Toronto*.[934] The action was brought by a Crown Attorney in relation to allegations of criminal contempt made by the defendant. The defendant argued that the common law of defamation was contrary to section 2(b) of the Charter. However, the Supreme Court held that the Charter did not have any direct application to non-governmental action.[935] Nevertheless, it went on to consider how the common law should be interpreted in accordance with Charter values[936] and concluded that the common law of defamation did so. The Court acknowledged the criticism which the 'actual malice' rule in *New York Times v Sullivan* had attracted[937] and said *per* Cory J that: **15.297**

> The *New York Times v Sullivan* decision has been criticised by judges and academic writers in the United States and elsewhere. It has not been followed in the United Kingdom or Australia. I can see no reason for adopting it in Canada in an action between private litigants. The law of defamation is essentially aimed at the prohibition of the publication of injurious false

930a *Ontario Film and Video Appreciation Society v Ontario Board of Censors* (1983) 147 DLR (4th) 766.

930b *Halifax Antiques v Hildebrand* (1985) 22 DLR (4th) 289.

930c *Luscher v Canada* (1985) 17 DLR (4th) 503.

930d *Dagenais v CBC* [1994] 3 SCR 835.

931 *New York Times v Sullivan* (1964) 376 US 254.

932 *Banks v Globe and Mail* (1961) 28 DLR (2d) 343, SCC.

933 See M Doody, 'Freedom of the Press, the Canadian Charter of Rights and Freedoms, and a New Category of Qualified Privilege' (1983) 61 Canadian Bar Rev 126; also D Madott, 'Libel Law, Fiction, and the Charter' (1983) 21:4 Osgoode Hall LJ, 741 786 where she suggests that the time is ripe for an expanded defence of qualified privilege.

934 [1995] 2 SCR 1130.

935 For a discussion about the application of the Canadian Charter to private litigation, see para 5.64ff above.

936 For a discussion of indirect horizontality under the Canadian Charter, see para 5.66 above.

937 Citing academic criticism such as: R A Epstein, 'Was New York Times v Sullivan Wrong?' (1986) 53 U Chi L Rev 782, R P Bezanson, 'Libel Law and the Realities of Litigation: Setting the Record Straight' (1985) 71 Iowa L Rev 226; P N Leval, 'The No-Money, No-Fault Libel Suit: Keeping Sullivan in its Proper Place' (1988) 101 Harv L Rev 1287.

> statements. It is the means by which the individual may protect his or her reputation which may well be the most distinguishing feature of his or her character, personality and, perhaps, identity. I simply cannot see that the law of defamation is unduly restrictive or inhibiting. Surely it is not requiring too much of individuals that they ascertain the truth of the allegations they publish. The law of defamation provides for the defences of fair comment and of qualified privilege in appropriate cases. Those who publish statements should assume a reasonable level of responsibility.[938]

15.298 The impact of the right to freedom of expression on criminal libel was examined in *R v Lucas*.[939] The Supreme Court took the view that the protection of reputation was a pressing and substantial objective; and that the negligible value of defamatory expression significantly reduced the burden on the prosecution to demonstrate that the offence minimally impaired expression.

15.299 **Contempt of court.** The law of contempt of court in Canada is broadly similar to that of Britain. Contempt can be either civil[940] or criminal in nature. Criminal contempt is a common law offence[941] and may be 'direct'[942] or 'indirect';[943] it commonly takes the form of a statement prejudicial to the merits of a case. 'Scandalising' of the Court, in which slanderous or insulting remarks are directed at a judge in his official capacity, or impugning his impartiality, is a form of contempt which has been long recognised but rarely invoked.

15.300 In Canada the law of contempt of court has generally favoured the administration of justice over freedom of expression through the press.[944] Obviously, reasonable criticism of the court is not a contempt at common law.[945] However, in *R v Kopyto*[946] the Ontario Court of Appeal found that the contempt of scandalising the court did not survive the adoption of the Charter (although it may be significant that the statement in question was made by the defendant after the trial ended). On the other hand, the Supreme Court has held that an injunction prohibiting a union from picketing the courthouses on the ground that it was a contempt amounted to a restriction on the right of freedom of expression; but it was justified under section 1 in order to ensure unimpeded access to the courts.[947]

15.301 **Reporting restrictions.** Freedom of expression includes freedom of the press to publish proceedings in court. In *Edmonton Journal v Alberta (A-G)*[948] the Supreme Court held

[938] At para 139, *per* Cory J; see generally, L Leigh, 'Of Free Speech and Individual Reputation' in I Loveland (ed), *Importing the First Amendment* (Hart Publishing, 1998) 51–68.

[939] [1998] 1 SCR 439.

[940] The Charter will have no application to civil contempt proceedings where the order in question resolves a dispute between private parties based on the common law. See *Retail, Wholesale and Department Store Union v Dolphin Delivery* [1986] 2 SCR 573.

[941] The offence was preserved by s 8 of the Canadian Criminal Code. The absence of a statutory definition of contempt was not a breach of fundamental justice under s 7 (see generally, para 11.386ff above) of the Charter: see *UNA v Alberta* (1992) 89 DLR (4th) 609.

[942] A direct contempt is committed in the face of the court by words or acts in the courtroom which are intended to disrupt proceedings.

[943] An indirect contempt is committed by words or acts outside the courtroom that are intended to obstruct the administration of justice.

[944] For a review of the area of contempt and freedom of expression, see J Watson, 'Badmouthing the Bench: Is There a Clear and Present Danger? To What?' (1992) 56 Saskatchewan L Rev 113.

[945] *Hebert v A-G Quebec* [1967] 2 CCC 111.

[946] (1987) 62 OR (2d) 449.

[947] *BCGEU v BC* [1988] 2 SCR 214.

[948] (1983) 146 DLR (3d) 673.

that provincial legislation prohibiting press reports of matrimonial cases (with some exceptions) violated freedom of expression because the courts must be open to public scrutiny and to public criticism.[949] It went on to decide that the restriction was wider than necessary to safeguard the privacy of litigants.

A provision in the Criminal Code which prohibited disclosure of the identity of the complainant in a sexual assault was challenged in *Canadian Newspapers Company Ltd v Canada (A-G)*.[950] The Supreme Court took the view that the limitation on expression was justified to foster the victims who needed such an assurance. **15.302**

In *Dagenais v Canadian Broadcasting Corporation*[951] a fictional television programme concerning sexual abuse of children at a Catholic home was restrained from being broadcast. An injunction had been granted in favour of several priests who were charged with offences in circumstances which were very similar to those depicted in the programme. The injunctions were to continue until the last of four trials took place: on the basis of a common law power to prevent a real and substantial risk of interference with the fairness of a trial. However, the Supreme Court took the view that the common law gave too much weight to a fair trial and too little to freedom of expression; the limit on expression was disproportionate since alternative measures could be taken falling short of an injunction: such as adjourning the trial, changing venues, sequestering jurors, allowing challenges for cause and providing strong judicial directions to the jury.[952] The Supreme Court therefore concluded that the restriction on expression could not be justified under section 1. **15.303**

Prohibiting the press from having access to juvenile trials has also been tested under the Charter. In *Re Southam and the Queen (No 1)*[953] the Ontario Court of Appeal held that an absolute bar on access could not be justified as using the least restrictive means of protecting the interests of a child. The legislation was then changed to require juvenile trials to be held in public with the trial judge having a discretion to order a hearing in private. That provision was regarded as a justifiable restriction on expression in *Re Southam and the Queen (No 2)*.[954] **15.304**

In *Canadian Broadcasting Corporation v New Brunswick (A-G)*[955] the press was excluded from part of a sentencing hearing where the offences committed by a sex offender against young girls were being detailed. Although the power to exclude the press was unconstitutional as a breach of freedom of expression, the Supreme Court took the view that the legislation pursued an important purpose by permitting an exclusion order to be made where openness was inimical to the proper administration of justice; furthermore, La Forest J went on to identify the principles to be applied when the court is requested to exericise its discretion to make reporting restrictions. **15.305**

Obscenity and pornography. In *R v Butler*[956] the Supreme Court held that the prohibitions on obscenity breached freedom of expression because they restricted communication **15.306**

949 Ibid 1337.
950 [1988] SCR 122.
951 [1994] 3 SCR 835.
952 Ibid 881.
953 (1983) 41 OR (2nd) 113.
954 (1986) 53 OR (2nd) 663.
955 [1996] 3 SCR 480.
956 [1992] 1 SCR 452.

on the basis of its content.[957] However, the restriction was justified to prevent the 'harm associated with the dissemination of pornography';[958] the justification was therefore 'sufficiently pressing and substantial to warrant some restriction on full exercise of the right to freedom of expression'.[959] Sopinka J said that pornography was not unacceptable because it offended morals; they were perceived by public opinion as being harmful to society, particularly women.[960]

15.307 The *Butler* case has attracted feminist criticism,[961] on the basis that the harm done to women by pornography was misunderstood by the Court: its offensiveness lay in the search for a causal link between pornography and violence towards women, and in the fact that the decision requires censorship of sexually explicit material. A similar debate has occurred in relation to prostitution following the *Prostitution Reference*,[962] in which the Court found that it is legitimate to criminalise public communication for the purpose of prostitution, despite the fact that prostitution itself is clearly legal. While all judges agreed that the criminal provisions did not violate the Charter, there was divergence over whether they could be justified as a limitation under section 1.[963]

15.308 **Racial hatred.** In *R v Keegstra*[964] the Supreme Court stated that the objective of the hate propaganda provisions of the Criminal Code was to 'prevent the pain suffered by target group members and to reduce racial, ethnic and religious tension in Canada'.[965] This was a justified restriction on expression. Similarly, in *Ross v New Brunswick School District No 15*[966] a decision by a human rights tribunal which required a teacher to be removed from his post for disseminating anti semitic literature was held to be a justified restriction on freedom of expression. However, in *R v Zundel*[967] the Supreme Court struck down the conviction for 'spreading false news' of a defendant who had claimed that the Holocaust was a fraud invented by an international Jewish conspiracy. The offence was an unjustified restriction on freedom of expression as the restriction was not confined to any particular type of statement or statements which caused any particular type of injury.

---

957 Ibid 489.

958 See J Cameron, 'Abstract Principle v Contextual Conceptions of Harm: A Comment on *R v Butler*' (1992) 37 McGill LJ 1135.

959 *R v Butler* (n 956 above) 449; see V Ramraj, 'Keegstra, Butler and Positive Liberty: A Glimmer of Hope for the Faithful' 51:2 University of Toronto Faculty of Law Rev, 304, 305.

960 Ibid 479.

961 See eg 'Pornography, Harm and Censorship: A Feminist (Re)Vision of the Right to Freedom of Expression' 52:1 University of Toronto Faculty of Law Rev, 132; R Moon, 'R v Butler: The Limits of the Supreme Court's Feminist Re-Interpretation of Section 163' (1993) 25:2 Ottawa L Rev 361.

962 *Re ss 193 and 195.1 of the Criminal Code* [1990] 1 SCR 1123.

963 For a discussion of the reasoning of the judges, their construction of the legislative objectives, and imposition of legal moralism generally see D Dyzenhaus, 'Regulating Free Speech' (1991) 23:2 Ottawa L Rev, 289; also *Ontario Film and Video Appreciation Society v Ontario Board of Censors* (1984) 45 OR (2d) 80n.

964 [1990] 3 SCR 697; see also *R v Keegstra (No 2)* [1995] 2 SCR 381 and *R v Keegstra (No 3)* [1996] 1 SCR 458.

965 *R v Keegstra* (n 964 above).

966 [1992] 2 SCR 731.

967 [1992] 2 SCR 731; For a discussion of the distinction between *Keegstra* and *Zundel* see P W Hogg, *Constitutional Law of Canada* (4th edn, Carswell, 1997) para 40.9.

Police powers. The Supreme Court has considered the use of search warrants to obtain film taken by television crews of a crime in progress in *Canadian Broadcasting Corporation v Lessard*[968] and *Canadian Broadcasting Corporation v New Brunswick (A-G).*[969] It was argued that the search warrants breached freedom of expression because of their 'chilling' effect on newsgathering. The Court said that the constitutional protection of freedom of expression provides a backdrop against which the reasonableness of a search had to be evaluated: the justice should give careful consideration not only to whether a warrant should issue but also to the conditions which might properly be imposed upon any search of media premises. A warrant would impede the media from fulfilling its news gathering functions and should only be issued where there is a compelling state interest. This could only be demonstrated by showing that there was no reasonable alternative source for the information or if the offence was a grave one and there was an urgent need to obtain the information. On the facts, the warrants were upheld, although the majority stressed that the film had already been shown. **15.309**

Commercial expression. The need to regulate commercial expression such as the advertisement is well recognised under the Charter. The American jurisprudence on commercial expression was analysed by the Supreme Court in *Ford v Quebec (A-G)*[970] where it held that provincial legislation requiring commercial signs to be in French only was unconstitutional. **15.310**

There have been a number of cases which have considered restrictions on advertising. In *Irwin Toy v Quebec*[971] the issue concerned provincial legislation aimed at advertising for children. The legislation did not ban advertising absolutely; but required, for example, that advertisement of toys and breakfast cereals did not use cartoons. The Supreme Court accepted that a ban directed at children was a sufficiently important purpose to limit expression; and upheld the legislation. **15.311**

The acceptability of restricting advertisements by professionals arose in *Rocket v Royal College of Dental Surgeons.*[972] The Supreme Court concluded that the regulations on dentists were unjustified because they had an impact far broader than was needed to ensure high standards of professional conduct; and prevented advertising information which would be genuinely useful if it was made available to the public. **15.312**

The important case of *RJR-McDonald v A-G of Canada*[973] considered the constitutionality of federal legislation banning the advertisement of tobacco and other tobacco products. The Supreme Court struck down the legislation because the restrictions imposed were not carefully tailored to ensure expression was impaired no more than was reasonably necessary. **15.313**

Access to public property. Because the Charter does not apply to private individuals,[974] it cannot create a right to use private property for the purposes of expression.[975] However, **15.314**

968 [1991] 3 SCR 421.
969 [1991] 3 SCR 459.
970 [1988] 2 SCR 712.
971 [1989] 1 SCR 927.
972 [1990] 1 SCR 232.
973 [1995] 3 SCR 199.
974 See generally, para 5.64ff above.
975 *Committee for the Commonwealth of Canada v Canada* [1991] 1 SCR 139, 228 *per* McLachlin J.

in *Committee for the Commonwealth of Canada v Canada*[976] the Supreme Court decided that there is a constitutional right to use public property for freedom of expression although the reasoning of different members of the Court varied significantly. Nevertheless, it held that a manager of a Montreal airport had acted unconstitutionally by prohibiting political leaflets from being distributed at the airport.

15.315 The issue was again considered in *Ramsden v Peterborough*.[977] In that case a musician advertised performances of his band by placing posters on public property in contravention of a bye-law which forbade posters on public property. The Supreme Court did not attempt to reconcile the different approaches taken in *Committee for the Commonwealth of Canada v Canada*;[978] instead, it said that, applying any of the views expressed in the earlier decision, postering on public property was protected by the Charter. The Court also concluded that the limit on expression was not justified under section 1 because it was broader than necessary to accomplish its objective of reducing litter and blight.

15.316 **Picketing.** The Supreme Court has accepted that picketing is entitled to constitutional protection as 'expression' under the Charter. In the *Dolphin Delivery* case[979] a union challenged the constitutionality of an injunction on secondary picketing where the union had induced a breach of contract. The Court decided that the Charter did not apply to the common law in private litigation.[980] However, McIntyre J said *obiter* that picketing came within the scope of 'expression' under the Charter;[981] but went on to decide that secondary picketing could be justified under section 1 in order to prevent industrial conflict spreading beyond the parties in dispute.

15.317 After seeing a picket line outside the Vancouver court house, the Chief Justice of British Columbia of his own motion and without notifying the union issued an injunction restraining the picket. The Supreme Court in *BCGEU v BC*[982] held that the injunction on the picket restricted freedom of expression; but that limitation on expression was justified so as to ensure unimpeded access to the court.

15.318 Peaceful leafleting of customers by pickets at secondary sites was restrained by an order of the Industrial Relations Council which the union then claimed was a restriction on freedom of expression. The Supreme Court in *Union of Food and Commercial Workers v K Mart Canada*[983] held that:

> workers, particularly those who are vulnerable, must be able to speak freely on matters that relate to their working conditions. For employees, freedom of expression becomes not only an important but an essential component of labour relations. It is through free expression that vulnerable workers are able to enlist the support of the public in their quest for better conditions of work. Thus their expression can often function as a means of achieving their goals.[983a]

---

[976] [1991] 1 SCR 139.
[977] [1993] 2 SCR 1084.
[978] Ibid.
[979] *Retail, Wholesale and Department Store Union v Dolphin Delivery* [1986] 2 SCR 573.
[980] See generally, para 5.66ff above.
[981] *Dolphin Delivery* (n 979 above) 105.
[982] [1988] 2 SCR 214.
[983] [1999] 2 SCR 1083.
[983a] Ibid para 25.

The Court decided that leafleting did not have the same coercive effect as a picket and that, in the circumstances, leafleting was lawful.

Political restrictions on public employees. The restrictions preventing federal civil servants from engaging in work for a Parliamentary candidate or for a federal political party were challenged in *Osborne v Canada*.[984] The Supreme Court ruled that the restrictions limited freedom of expression and could not be justified under section 1. The objective of maintaining a neutral public service could justify imposing limits; but the legislation did not adopt the least restrictive means of achieving that objective since the range of activities prohibited and employees covered was wider than needed to accomplish the objective. **15.319**

Restrictions on the political process. In *Libman v A-G of Quebec*[985] the Supreme Court considered a challenge to the constitutional validity of spending limits which had been placed on political groups in the campaign periods for referenda. The restrictions on expression were justified to prevent political debate being dominated by the most affluent. However, the limits did not meet the minimum impairment test required under the proportionality principle; the ceiling was so restrictive that it amounted to a total ban on spending by groups who did not meet the criteria in the legislation which authorised campaign spending. **15.320**

The prohibition on disseminating information about opinion polls during the last three days of a federal election was examined in *Thomson Newspapers v Canada*.[986] The Supreme Court held that a total ban was wider than necessary to guard against the influence of inaccurate polls late in an election campaign; and that the benefits of the ban were outweighed by its detrimental effects. **15.321**

Appendix 2: The New Zealand Bill of Rights Act

(1) Introduction

Section 14 of the New Zealand Bill of Rights Act 1990 provides: **15.322**

> 14. **Freedom of expression**—Everyone has the right to freedom of expression, including the freedom to seek, receive, and impart information and opinions of any kind in any form.

The White Paper which explained the proposed bill described this provision as being of 'central importance' but did not give any detailed analysis and suggested that most laws which were found to infringe freedom of expression would 'no doubt' be held to establish reasonable limitations on the freedom.[986a]

Section 14 has had an impact in several areas: defamation, contempt of court, reporting restrictions, obscenity, racial hatred and police powers. However, section 14 does not impose any positive duties on the state to ensure freedom of expression.[987] **15.323**

---

[984] [1991] 2 SCR 69.
[985] [1997] 3 SCR 569.
[986] [1998] 1 SCR 877.
[986a] *A Bill of Rights for New Zealand: A White Paper* (Government Printer, 1985) 79–80; see generally G Huscroft, 'Defamation, Racial Disharmony and Freedom of Expression' in G Huscroft and P Rishworth (eds) *Rights and Freedoms* (Brooker's, 1995).
[987] *Mendelsson v A-G* [1999] 1 NZLR 268.

15.324 The New Zealand courts have drawn heavily on the case law of the Canadian Charter of Rights and Freedoms.[988] In *Solicitor-General v Radio NZ Ltd*[989] the Canadian approach to the scope of the right was adopted, the court stressing that the Bill of Rights protects all expression that conveys or attempts to convey meaning except threats of violence.[990]

15.325 Freedom of expression under section 14 includes the right to impart information, a feature that it shares with Article 10(1) of the European Convention.[991] This right provides jurisdiction in an exceptional case for the court to grant a mandatory injunction before trial compelling a defendant to broadcast a correction where he has clearly established that he has been defamed.[992]

15.326 There is a public interest in freedom of expression which exists over and above the rights of the individual. In *Police v O'Connor*[993] it was said:

> While the right in section 25(a) (right to fair and public hearing) is couched in terms of an individual right as is Article 14 of the ICCPR, the right to freedom of expression as expressed in section 14 of the NZ Bill of Rights is not. The latter is to be perceived as a public right. While, therefore, the position adopted by the particular defendant will no doubt be significant, it is not a right which he or she can automatically waive. The public interest in freedom of expression is to be recognised apart from the interests of the individual.

(2) Justifiable limitations

(a) Introduction

15.327 The freedoms set out in the New Zealand Bill of Rights Act are subject to such reasonable limits prescribed by law as may be justified in a free and democratic society.[994]

15.328 The basic principles to be applied when deciding whether a limitation on a right is justified under section 5 were described in *Ministry of Transport v Noort*.[995] First, the New Zealand courts have applied the Canadian authorities both on the meaning of 'prescribed by law'[996] and the general approach to justifying limitations on rights.[997] Secondly, the

---

988 For a comparison of the general features of the New Zealand Bill and the Canadian Charter, see *Solicitor-General v Radio NZ Ltd* [1994] 1 NZLR 48, 60, 61.

989 [1994] 1 NZLR 48, 59.

990 *Solicitor-General v Radio NZ Ltd* (n 988 above) 59 relying on *Irwin Toy Ltd v Quebec* [1989] 1 SCR 927, 970: 'a murderer or rapist cannot invoke freedom of expression in justification of the form of expression he has chosen'; also McIntyre J in *Retail, Wholesale and Department Store Union v Dolphin Delivery* [1986] 2 SCR 573, 588 who said 'that freedom of course, would not extend to protect threats of violence or acts of violence'. However, in *R v Keegstra* [1990] 3 SCR 697, 733 the Supreme Court reversed its views and now accepts that threats of violence are within the scope of expression under the Charter.

991 Also with the Universal Declaration of Human Rights, Art 19, and the ICCPR 1966, Art 19(2). Cf the Canadian Charter, s 2(b), and the US First Amendment, which do not specify the right to impart information.

992 *TV3 Network Ltd v Eveready New Zealand Ltd* [1993] 3 NZLR 435.

993 [1992] 1 NZLR 87.

994 ss 4, 5 and 6 of the New Zealand Bill of Rights Act.

995 [1992] 3 NZLR 260, 282-283.

996 See generally, para 6.146ff above.

997 The general approach of the Canadian courts, 'modified to New Zealand conditions', was adopted by the Court of Appeal in *Solicitor-General v Radio New Zealand* [1994] 1 NZLR 48 (reviewing *R v Oakes* [1986] 1 SCR 103 and *Irwin Toy Ltd v Quebec* [1989] 1 SCR 927); see also *Ministry of Transport v Noort* (n 995 above).

burden of proof rests with those seeking to rely on section 5 to demonstrate the reasonableness of the limit and that it can be justified in a free and democratic society. Thirdly, the Court of Appeal defined the process of the inquiry under section 5: it should use the Canadian approach in *R v Oakes*[998] as a starting point;[999] and consider all economic, administrative and social implications, taking into account the following factors:

- the significance of values underlying the Bill of Rights;
- the importance of the public interest in the intrusion;
- the limits sought to be placed on the protected freedom; and
- the effectiveness of the restriction in protecting the interests put forward to justify those limits.

The means used must have a rational relationship with the objective and there must be as little interference as possible with the right or freedom affected:

> Ultimately, whether the limitation in issue can or cannot be demonstrably justified in a free and democratic society is a matter of judgment which the Court is obliged to make on behalf of the society which it serves.[999a]

(b) Restrictions on expression

Prior restraint. The New Zealand courts have recognised that the principle of freedom of expression means that any applicant seeking an injunction to prevent a legitimate publication faces an uphill task.[999b] Nevertheless, such an injunction was granted to restrain the broadcast of a television programme about student suicides on the highly speculative ground that it was possible the programme might trigger a young person to commit suicide.[999c] **15.329**

Defamation. In the field of defamation the Bill of Rights Act has been invoked largely in support of decisions favouring expression. However, its impact has been explained in terms of providing assistance in areas of uncertainty where the law is developing[1000] and to reinforce long established principles.[1001] **15.330**

Thus, in *Quinn v Television New Zealand Ltd*[1002] it was observed that section 14 did not extend the boundaries of the right of expression, affirming the historic common law right of a person to protect his reputation. In particular, it drew attention to section 28 of the Bill of Rights Act which requires that an existing right or freedom should not be abrogated or restricted by reason only that it was not included in the Bill of Rights. On the other hand, in *TV3 Network v Eveready New Zealand Ltd*[1003] a manufacturer which alleged that a television broadcast libelled its produce applied for a mandatory interlocutory injunction to require the television company to broadcast a correction. It held that section 14 did **15.331**

---

998 [1986] 1 SCR 103.

999 See generally, para 15.291 above.

999a *Moonen v Film and Literature Board of Review* (1999) 5 HRNZ 224 para 18.

999b *Board of Trustees of Tuakau College v TVNZ* (1996) 3 HRNZ 87, 96.

999c Ibid.

1000 *TV3 Network Ltd v Eveready New Zealand Ltd* [1993] 3 NZLR 435.

1001 *Auckland Area Health Board v A-G* [1992] 3 NZLR 406 (the jurisdiction to grant interlocutory injunctions to restrain publication of defamatory statements); see also *Quinn v Television New Zealand Ltd* [1995] 3 NZLR 216 which affirmed of historic right to reputation.

1002 [1995] 3 NZLR 216.

1003 n 1000 above; see also *TV3 Network Services v Fahey* [1999] 2 NZLR 129 (no injunction to restrain publication of defamatory material where the defendant announced an intention to justify).

not preclude the court in an exceptional case from providing mandatory injunctive relief; in fact, the statutory definition of expression created a right to impart information and supported the claim for an injunction.

15.332 The question of parliamentary privilege was the subject of the Privy Council decision in *Prebble v Television New Zealand*.[1004] The case arose out of an investigative television programme of a former Government by one of its MPs. When the defendant pleaded particulars of speeches and other statements made by the plaintiff in 'proceedings of Parliament' by way of defence, the plaintiff was successful in having them struck out on grounds of parliamentary privilege. The Court of Appeal ordered a stay of proceedings unless and until parliamentary privilege was waived by both the House and the MP, a solution which precludes both action in defamation by persons maligned by statements in the House and suit by an MP to protect his reputation. The Privy Council held that where the exclusion of privileged material makes it impossible fairly to determine the issue between the parties, a stay of proceedings may be required; but allowed the appeal on the facts because the allegations related to statements which were made outside of the House. However, there has been criticism of the broad approach taken in view of the right to freedom of expression under the Bill of Rights Act.[1005]

15.333 In *Lange v Atkinson and Australian Consolidated Press NZ Ltd*[1006] the Court of Appeal considered section 14 in the context of a claim to qualified privilege in respect of 'political expression' based on *New York Times v Sullivan*.[1007] It took the view that a newspaper report on a matter of public interest could, of itself, give rise to a 'common interest' between the newspaper and the general public in the publication of the report. In particular, it was stressed that:

> a proper interest does exist in respect of statements made about the actions and qualities of those currently or formerly elected to Parliament and those with immediate aspirations to such office, so far as those actions and qualities directly affect or affected their capacity . . . to meet their public responsibilities.[1008]

The Court of Appeal refused to follow the Australian approach[1009] and held that whether or not the defendant had acted reasonably was irrelevant.[1010] However, the plaintiff's appeal was allowed by the Privy Council[1011] which remitted the case back to the New Zealand Court of Appeal to reconsider in the light of the decision of the House of Lords in *Reynolds v Times Newspapers*.[1012]

15.334 **Contempt.** Freedom of expression may be restricted by competing fundamental freedoms such as the right of an accused to a fair hearing[1013] and by the law of contempt of

1004 [1995] 1 AC 321, 332.

1005 See eg R Best, 'Freedom of Speech in Parliament: Constitutional Safeguard or Sword of Oppression?' (1994) 24 VUWLR 91, 97; and see also the comment of Cooke P in his judgment [1993] 3 NZLR 513, 522; and his subsequent analysis of the case in 'A Sketch From the Blue Train. Non-discrimination and Freedom of Expression: The New Zealand Contribution' (1994) NZLJ 10, 13.

1006 [1998] 3 NZLR 424 approving [1997] 2 NZLR 22; see also the discussion of this case in *Reynolds v Times Newspapers Ltd* [1998] 3 WLR 862.

1007 (1964) 376 US 254.

1008 *Lange v Atkinson* (n 1006 above) 613g–h.

1009 See para 15.232ff above.

1010 *Lange v Atkinson and Australian Consolidated Press NZ Ltd* (n 1006 above) 615a-f; 619e-620c.

1011 [2000] 2 LRC 802.

1012 [1999] 3 WLR 1010.

1013 New Zealand Bill of Rights Act 1990, s 25.

court. The conflict between expression in the media and the due administration of justice has traditionally been resolved in favour of the right to a fair trial. The protection of the justice system is considered a substantial and pressing concern;[1014] and the sanction of contempt in achieving this objective has been regarded as being reasonable and demonstrably justified.[1015]

Prior restraints have been imposed on publication in several cases to ensure a fair trial.[1016] **15.335**
The approach in the past has been to impose restraints very readily. More recently, the courts have shifted markedly towards favouring freedom of the media in both law and practice.[1017] *R v Chignell and Walker*[1018] involved an attempt by the Crown to invoke the inherent jurisdiction of the court to restrain a threatened contempt by preventing further public comment concerning an unnamed witness pending a retrial of the accused homicide suspect. The court declined, citing section 14 of the Bill of Rights Act in support of freedom of expression. It held that a mere risk of activity which could undermine a fair trial was insufficient to outweigh the competing considerations of freedom of expression and information; there must be a real likelihood of prejudice to the accused.[1019]

The court in *Police v O'Connor*[1020] went further and said that the English cases:[1021] **15.336**

> fairly read, suggest a balancing exercise in which the interests of justice will prevail over freedom of expression only where the publication of the material will seriously prejudice the conduct of the litigation. Any lingering notion that, where a conflict is found to exist, freedom of expression is to be at once subordinated to the interests of justice is now laid to rest with the enactment of section 14.

However, in *Gisborne Herald v Solicitor-General*[1022]the Court of Appeal held that, in cases in which it was not possible to assure both freedom of expression and fair trial rights:

> it is appropriate in our free and democratic society to temporarily curtail freedom of media expression so as to guarantee a fair trial.[1023]

[1014] *Solicitor-General v Radio NZ Ltd* [1991] 1 NZLR 48: the protection of the due administration of justice, the impartiality and the freedom of deliberation of a jury, the finality of its verdict and preservation of the juror's anonymity are all substantial and pressing concerns of a free and democratic society.

[1015] Ibid 64.

[1016] See *Duff v Communicado Ltd* [1996] 2 NZLR 89; *Greenpeace New Zealand v Minister of Fisheries* [1995] 2 NZLR 463; *R v H* [1996] 2 NZLR 487.

[1017] R E Harrison, 'Mass Media and the Criminal Process: Public Service or Public Circus?' (1992) NZLJ 271; for the media response to Harrison see K Hill, 'Freedom of the Media and the Criminal Law' (1992) NZLJ 278; see the pre-Bill of Rights cases cited in support of the changing style of media coverage: *R v Harawira* [1989] 2 NZLR 714; *The Queen v Tamihere* CA 428/90, 21 May 1992; *Solicitor-General v BCNZ* [1987] 2 NZLR 100; *TV New Zealand Ltd v Solicitor-General* [1989] 1 NZLR 1.

[1018] (1990) 6 CRNZ 476.

[1019] The Court viewed the requested action, which was equivalent to an injunction against the world prohibiting publication of information about the witness, as an unwarranted overreaction to the need for responsibility and restraint to ensure that there was a fair and proper retrial.

[1020] [1992] 1 NZLR, 87, 98-99.

[1021] *A-G v Times Newspapers Ltd* [1974] AC 273; *A-G v British Broadcasting Corporation* [1981] AC 303.

[1022] [1995] 3 NZLR 563.

[1023] At 575, *per* Richardson J.

In *Duff v Communicado*[1024] it was stressed that the relationship between section 14 and contempt is best approached by balancing freedom of expression against the benefits of protecting the administration of justice by examining the facts of each case to see if the particular interference was so serious as to override freedom of expression. The Court went on to hold that remarks made on radio to put pressure on another litigant in proceedings amounted to a contempt.

15.337 **Reporting restrictions.** It is a responsibility of the state to ensure that the administration of justice is carried out in public, so as to safeguard against judicial arbitrariness or idiosyncrasy and to maintain public confidence in the system.[1025] This entails not only the admission of the public to judicial proceedings, but also the publication of fair and accurate press reports so that the public can scrutinise the workings of the courts. The right of the public should not be readily restricted,[1026] reflecting the fact that section 14 provides for the news media to publish information and a public right to receive that information; and in the right of an accused, under section 25, to be given a hearing that is public as well as fair. In *R v H*[1027] a prosecution of an adult for gross indecencies against a child was withdrawn. He subsequently sought an order permanently suppressing his identity. The interference on expression was justified; there was no relevant public interest or need to know that the accused had been charged.

15.338 By contrast, the issue in *Television New Zealand v R*[1028] arose out of a trial where the defendant who had murdered his parents, brother and two sisters wished to adduce certain evidence. An order was made prohibiting publication of the witness and the evidence which was confirmed by the Court of Appeal; however, a television company then applied to rescind the order. The Court of Appeal emphasised that in the absence of compelling evidence to the contrary, criminal justice is public justice; and held that the right to information to the public outweighed the family right to privacy.

15.339 The decision in *National Newspaper Association v Family Court*[1029] considered reporting restrictions in relation to a child suffering from cancer whose parents objected to chemotherapy treatment. The child was taken into hiding and there was widespread public and media interest when the Family Court approved a news release so he could be found. An order was then made suppressing any information relating to the child or the case. The High Court said that great significance should be attached to freedom of the press but that it must bend to the extent necessary to protect the child; and it was necessary to distinguish between mere curiosity and matters of public interest. As a result, any suppression order had to be tailored to intrude only to the extent necessary to ensure that the child's welfare was protected.

15.340 **Obscenity and pornography.** The Bill of Rights Act 1990 appears to have had minimal impact on the regulation of obscenity and pornography. The New Zealand Indecent Publications Act has a statutory definition of indecent[1030] and establishes a tribunal[1031] to

---

1024 (1995) 2 HRNZ 370.
1025 See *Police v O'Connor* [1992] 1 NZLR 87, 95.
1026 Ibid.
1027 [1994] 2 NZLR 143.
1028 [1996] 3 NZLR 393.
1029 [1999] 2 NZLR 344.
1030 Under s 2.
1031 The Indecent Publications Tribunal: see s 11(1) of the Act.

classify or determine the character of any book or magazine, to consider the dominant effect of the magazine as a whole and the persons, classes of persons or age groups to or amongst whom the magazine might be made available. The limitations on expression required under the Act were demonstrably justified in a free and democratic society.[1032] In the important case of *Moonen v Film and Literature Board of Review*[1032a] the Court of Appeal considered the relationship between section 14 and the 'censorship provisions' of The Films, Video and Publications Classification Act 1993. It was held that these provisions must be given a meaning that impinges as little as possible on freedom of expression.[1032b]

Racial hatred. In *Zdrahal v Wellington City Council*[1033] the appellant painted swastikas on the exterior wall and a window of his house, attracting complaints from two neighbours. The Planning Tribunal under the Resource Management Act issued an abatement order, on grounds that the symbols were offensive and objectionable. The Act in question authorised the prohibition of 'anything . . . that in the opinion of the enforcement officer, was likely to be noxious, dangerous, offensive, or objectionable to such an extent that it has or is likely to have an adverse effect on the environment'. The court accepted that the Tribunal was entitled to find that the ordinary person, members of the public, would find the swastikas offensive. The order had been made for a legitimate legislative objective and the means used were proportionate.[1034] **15.341**

Police powers. The restrictions on expression resulting from the imposition of a bind over were considered in *Bracanov v Moss.*[1035] In that case an anti royalist was ordered to enter into a bond to keep the peace because of a royal visit. The court held that any limitations on freedom of expression were justified to ensure a citizen respects the rights and freedoms of others in the community. **15.342**

Appendix 3: Human Rights Cases From Other Jurisdictions

(1) Introduction

The right to freedom of expression is firmly established as a constitutional right in many European countries.[1035a] However, the principles of freedom of expression have been most extensively developed in the United States. American authorities have already had a significant impact on the evolution of the common law on defamation[1036] and, although **15.343**

[1032] *Society for Promotion of Community Standards Inc v Waverley International (1988) Ltd* [1993] 2 NZLR 709.

[1032a] (1999) 5 HRNZ 224.

[1032b] Overruling *Re News Media Ltd v Film and Literature Review Board* (1997) 4 HRNZ 410.

[1033] [1995] 1 NZLR 700.

[1034] Applying s 5 as analysed in *MOT v Noort* [1992] 3 NZLR 260.

[1035] [1996] 1 NZLR 445.

[1035a] See eg S Micahelowski and L Woods, *German Constitutional Law* (Dartmouth, 199) Chap 12.

[1036] See eg *Derbyshire County Council v Times Newspapers Ltd* [1993] AC 534; *Reynolds v Times Newspapers Ltd* [1999] 3 WLR 1010.

the point is not uncontroversial,[1037] it seems likely that American constitutional principles will provide important guidance on the development of freedom of expression under the Human Rights Act.[1038]

15.344 In particular, the American courts have accorded a high priority to political speech. Freedom of expression is said to create a market place of ideas. As Holmes J said in his famous dissenting judgment in *Abrams v United States*:[1039]

> when men have realised that time has upset many fighting faiths, they may come to believe even more than they believe the very foundations of their own conduct that the ultimate good desired is better reached by a free trade in ideas—that the best of truth is the power of the thought to get itself accepted in the competition of the market, and that truth is the only ground upon which their wishes can be safely carried out.

As a result, free speech promotes the search for truth. It also secures the right of the citizen to participate in the democratic process:

> Those who won our independence believed that the final end of the State was to make men develop their faculties, and that in its government the deliberate forces should prevail over the arbitrary . . . They believed the freedom to think as you will and to speak as you think are means indefensible to the discovery and spread of political truth; that without free speech and assembly, discussion would be futile; that with them, discussion affords ordinarily adequate protection against the dissemination of noxious doctrine; that the greatest menace to freedom is the inert people; that public discussion is a political duty; and that this should be the fundamental principle of American government.[1040]

Thus, Meiklejohn argued that the purpose of freedom of expression is to ensure that self government guaranteed under the American constitution is achieved by self education.[1041]

15.345 Nevertheless, it must be borne in mind that there are important differences in philosophy and the political culture between England and the United States which limit the value of directly transposing expression principles.[1042] Furthermore, the drafting of the First Amendment is very unlike Article 10 since it prohibits interference with freedom of speech in absolute terms.[1043] A literal interpretation of the First Amendment would per-

---

[1037] Sir Stephen Sedley takes a more sceptical view about the value of borrowing ideas from the First Amendment, arguing that freedom of expression is at the head of the queue for judicial protection because the media has the funds to underwrite litigation and that it places no sanctions on the mass media to act responsibly: see Sir Stephen Sedley, 'The First Amendment: A Case for Import Controls?' in I Loveland (ed), *Importing the First Amendment* (Hart Publishing, 1998).

[1038] See eg E Barendt, 'The Importance of United States Free Speech Jurisprudence' and I Loveland, 'The criminalisation of Racial Violence' in I Loveland (ed), *A Special Relationship* (Clarendon Press, 1995); R Singh, *The Future of Human Rights in the United Kingdom* (Hart Publishing, 1997) Chap 4; I Loveland (ed), *Importing the First Amendment* (Hart Publishing, 1998).

[1039] (1919) 250 US 616, 630.

[1040] Brandeis J in *Whitney v California* (1927) 274 US 357, 375.

[1041] See A Meiklejohn, *Free Speech and its Relation to Self Government* (Harper & Sons, 1948); 'The First Amendment is an Absolute' [1961] Sup Ct Rev 245; and see, eg W J Brennan, 'The Supreme Court and the Meiklejohn Interpretation of the First Amendment' (1965) 79 Harv L Rev 1; and Sir John Laws, 'Meiklejohn, the First Amendment and Free Speech in English Law' in I Loveland (ed), *Importing the First Amendment* (Hart Publishing, 1998).

[1042] C McCrudden, 'The Impact on Freedom of Expression' in B Markesinis, *The Impact of the Human Rights Bill in English Law* (Oxford University Press, 1998).

[1043] The case law has developed important implied limitations to free speech; some of the basic principles are summarised at para 15.346 below.

mit no interference with freedom of speech. The absolutist approach to the First Amendment is most closely associated with Black J. Thus, in his dissenting judgment in the obscenity case of *Ginzburg v United States*[1044] he said:

> I believe that the Federal Government is without power under the Constitution to put any burden on speech or expression of any kind (as distingusihed from conduct).

He later explained the position, writing extra-judicially in the following terms:

> Some people regard the prohibitions of the Constitution, even its most unequivocal commands as mere admonitions . . . and that all constitutional problems are questions of reasonableness, proximity and review. I cannot accept this approach to the Bill of Rights. It is my belief that there *are* 'absolutes' in our Bill of Rights and that they were put there on purpose by men who knew what the words meant and meant their prohibitions to be 'absolutes' . . . I am discussing here whether liberties *admittedly* covered by the Bill of Rights can nevertheless be abridged on the ground that a superior public interest justifies the abridgement. I think the Bill of Rights makes its safeguards superior.[1045]

However, under the First Amendment even political speech is curtailed where there is a clear and present danger of harm.[1045a] Its regulation is subject to strict scrutiny which must be 'narrowly tailored' to serve a 'compelling governmental interest';[1045b] this means, for example, that First Amendment protection covers lewd epithets[1046] and extends to symbolic speech such as flag burning[1047] or to demonstrators in Nazi uniforms marching through a Jewish community.[1048] In practice, the case law of the American Supreme Court has developed a complex system for justifying limitations on freedom of expression: **15.346**

- by imposing content based restrictions where certain types of speech are singled out as not being sufficiently worthy to attract First Amendment protection[1049] (such as speech which is not essential to the exposition of any idea, libel,[1050] obscenity[1051] and insulting or 'fighting' words)[1052]

[1044] (1966) 383 US 463.

[1045] H L Black, *A Constitutional Faith* (Knopf, 1968); see also, H L Black, 'Bill of Rights' (1960) 35 New York University L Rev 865.

[1045a] The test was formulated by Holmes J in *Schenck v United States* (1919) 249 US 47 52; see *Brandenburg v Ohio* (1969) 395 US 444.

[1045b] The starting point for the strict scrutiny doctrine is the famous passage from the judgment of Stone J in *United States v Carolene Products* (1938) 304 US 144 footnote 4 which he said that: 'there may be narrower scope for the operation of the presumption of constitutionality when legislation appears on its face to be within a *specific prohibition of the Constitution*, such as those of the first ten amendments'.

[1046] See eg *Cohen v California* (1973) 403 US 15 where the Supreme Court held that wearing a badge on a jacket saying 'Fuck the draft' in the corridor of a Los Angelos courtroom could not amount to a criminal offence because it was protected as free speech.

[1047] See eg *Texas v Johnson* (1989) 491 US 397; *United States v Eichman* (1990) 496 US 310.

[1048] *Smith v Collins* (1978) 436 US 953.

[1049] The principles set out in *Chaplinsky v Hampshire* (1942) 315 US 568 268, 269 should now, however, be treated with caution.

[1050] The scope of First Amendment protection depends on whether the plaintiff is a political figure (see *New York Times v Sullivan* (1964) 376 US 254 or a private citizen (see *Gertz v Robert Welch* (1974) 418 US 323).

[1051] Which is confined to hard core pornography: see *Roth v United States* (1957) 354 US 476 and *Miller v California* (1973) 413 US 15.

[1052] The doctrine was radically changed in the controversial decision in *RAV v City of St Paul, Minnesota* (1992) 505 US 377 where a city ordinance against hate crime laws breached the First Amendment because it selectively silenced free speech on the basis of its content; it now seems that only inflammatory words intended to bring about imminent violence are unprotected.

- by regulating conduct which only incidentally affects speech;[1053] or
- by permitting restrictions on the time, place or manner of expression provided they are 'content neutral'.[1054]

15.347 Nevertheless, there are numerous expression issues which the American case law illuminates including: the distinction between speech and conduct[1055] (and in particular, the protection of symbolic speech such as flag burning);[1056] the degree of protection given to extreme political views[1057] or to commercial speech;[1058] and whether restrictions on expression require greater justification because they apply in a public place.[1059]

(2) Antigua and Barbuda

15.348 Section 12(1) of the Constitution of Antigua and Barbuda provides that:

> Except with his own consent, no person shall be hindered in the enjoyment of his freedom of expression.

Restrictions on this freedom must be reasonably required for various stated objectives and must also be 'reasonably required in a democratic society'.

15.349 In *Hector v Attorney-General of Antigua and Barbuda*[1060] the applicant newspaper editor had been charged with printing a false statement which was 'likely to cause fear or alarm in or to the public, or to disturb the public peace, or to undermine public confidence in the conduct of public affairs'. The Privy Council accepted his argument that his rights

---

[1053] The distinction between conduct and speech originates in *Thornhill v Alabama* (1940) 310 US 88 where a state law prohibiting all union picketing was constitutionally protected free speech; the principle means that conduct such as a demonstration is characterised as 'speech plus' and is entitled to a lesser degree of First Amendment protection than 'pure speech': see *Cox v Louisiana* (1965) 379 US 559 *per* Goldberg J at 563. However, the speech/conduct dichotomy is very difficult to maintain: see eg L Tribe, *American Constitutional Law* (2nd edn, Foundation Press, 1988) 12–7.

[1054] See eg *Lloyd Corp v Tanner* (1972) 407 US 551 (rejecting First Amendment protection to distributing antiwar leaflets in a shopping centre).

[1055] See eg *United States v O'Brien* (1968) 391 US 367 (burning a draft card); and see, generally, Tribe (n 1053 above) 12–6, 12–7; E Barendt, *Freedom of Speech* (Clarendon Press, 1985) 41–48.

[1056] See eg *Texas v Johnson* (1989) 491 US 397; *United States v Eichman* (1990) 496 US 310.

[1057] Unless they are directed at inciting (or producing) imminent lawless action and are likely to incite (or produce) such action; see *Brandenburg v Ohio* (1969) 395 US 444; and see generally, Tribe (n 1053 above) 12–9.

[1058] See the seminal case of *Virginia State Board of Pharmacy v Virginia Citizens Consumer Council* (1976) 425 US 748 which struck down legislation preventing a pharmacist advertising the price of prescription drugs in order to protect the interest of the consumer in the flow of information about prices); and includes the right of professionals to advertise fees on a limited factual basis (see eg *Bates v Arizona Bar Association* (1977) 435 US 350; *Shapero v Kentucky Bar Association* (1989) 486 US 466); a prohibition against bans on advertising (see eg *Central Hudson Gas v New York Public Service Commission* (1980) 447 US 557); the right to use the mail to send unsolicited contraceptives (*Bolger v Youngs Drug Products* (1983) 463 US 60); the right to solicit door-to-door within reasonable hours (see eg *Linmark Associates v Willingboro* (1977) 431 US 85; and see generally, Tribe (n 1053 above) 12–16.

[1059] See eg *Hague v CIO* (1939) 307 US 496 (leafleting, parades and other speech related uses of street and parks cannot be banned or subjected to a discretionary licence); *Police Department of City of Chicago v Mosley* (1992) 408 US 92 (city cannot enforce ordinance prohibiting picketing within 150 feet of schools); see generally, Tribe (n 1053 above) 12–24.

[1060] [1990] 2 AC 312.

under section 12 of the Constitution had been contravened by this prosecution. Lord Bridge said:

> In a free democratic society it is almost too obvious to need stating that those who hold office in government and who are responsible for public administration must always be open to criticism. Any attempt to stifle or fetter such criticism amounts to political censorship of the most insidious and objectional kind. At the same time it is no less obvious that the very purpose of the criticism levelled at those who have the conduct of public affairs by their political opponents is to undermine public confidence in their stewardship and to persuade the electorate that the opponents would make a better job of it than those presently holding office. In the light of these considerations their Lordships cannot help viewing a statutory provision which criminalises statements likely to undermine public confidence in the conduct of public affairs with the utmost suspicion.[1061]

The case of *de Freitas v Permanent Secretary of Ministry of Agriculture, Fisheries, Lands and Housing*[1062] concerned a provision of the Civil Service Act restricting the freedom of expression of civil servants. All civil servants were forbidden to communicate 'any information or expressions of opinion on matters of national or international political controversy'. The Privy Council held that a blanket restraint which imposed the same restrictions on all categories of civil servants was not reasonably required for the proper performance of their functions. In addition, the restriction was not reasonably justifiable in a democratic society. **15.350**

(3) Australia

The Constitution Act 1900 does not contain a Bill of Rights but, over recent years, the High Court has implied a number of rights into it.[1063] In two judgments delivered on 30 September 1992, the High Court found that the system of representative government gave rise to an implied constitutional guarantee of freedom of communication in relation to the political and electoral processes.[1064] The right of the electorate to choose members of the legislature carried with it: **15.351**

> the right to convey and receive information, opinions and arguments concerning such elections and the candidates who are involved in them.[1065]

Breaches of this 'implied freedom' rendered statutes invalid. Thus, in *Nationwide News*[1066] the High Court held that a statute making it an offence to use words calculated to bring a member of the Industrial Relations Commission into disrepute was invalid.[1067]

1061 At 318 B–D.

1062 [1998] 3 WLR 675.

1063 See generally, G Williams, *Human Rights Under the Australian Constitution* (Oxford University Press, 1999) Chap 7.

1064 *Nationwide News Pty Ltd v Wills* (1992) 177 CLR 1 and *Australian Capital Television Pty Ltd v The Commonwealth of Australia* (1992) 177 CLR 106 (relying heavily on Canadian authority, see generally Williams (n 1063 above) 171–173).

1065 *Australian Capital Television v Commonwealth of Australia* (n 1064 above) 232.

1066 n 1064 above.

1067 Mason CJ, Dawson and McHugh JJ held that it was invalid because, applying a proportionality test, it was not within the implied incidental power to legislate on industrial relations matters. Brennan, Deane, Toohey and Gaudron JJ held that it was invalid because it breached the implied freedom of political communication.

In *Australian Capital Television Pty Ltd v The Commonwealth of Australia*[1068] the High Court held that a statute prohibiting political advertising during federal elections (coupled with 'free time' for established parties) was invalid because it infringed the implied freedom.

15.352 This approach led the High Court in *Theophanus v Herald and Weekly Times Ltd*[1069] to conclude that the law of defamation raised constitutional issues and unduly limited freedom of communication in political matters. They took the view that the defendant who published material relevant to 'political discussion' should have a defence of qualified privilege if he could show that he had acted reasonably. The same principles were applied by the High Court in *Stephens v West Australian Newspapers Ltd.*[1070]

15.353 The decisions in *Theophanus* and *Stephens* were unsuccessfully challenged by the plaintiff in *Lange v Australian Broadcasting Corp*[1071] In that case, the High Court held that:

> each member of the Australian community has an interest in disseminating and receiving information, opinions and arguments concerning government and political matters that affect the people of Australia. The duty to disseminate such information is simply the correlative of the interest in receiving it.[1072]

As a result, a defence of qualified privilege was available to anyone disseminating such information. However, because the damage from publication to the whole world was potentially very great, the privilege could only be relied on if the defendant was reasonable as well as honest.[1073] In relation to the 'reasonableness requirement', this must depend upon all the circumstances of the case:

> But, as a general rule, a defendant's conduct in publishing material giving rise to a defamatory imputation will not be reasonable unless the defendant had reasonable grounds for believing that the imputation was true, took proper steps, so far as they were reasonably open, to verify the accuracy of the material and did not believe the imputation to be untrue. Furthermore, the defendant's conduct will not be reasonable unless the defendant has sought a response from the person defamed and published the response made (if any) except in cases where the seeking or publication of a response was not practicable or it was unnecessary to give the plaintiff an opportunity to respond.[1074]

15.354 This implied constitutional freedom does not, however, cover all types of discussion which could be described as 'political'. Its purpose is to 'contribute to protecting and reinforcing the system of representative government provided for by the Australian Constitution'.[1075] The freedom has been held to be applicable in relation to criticism of the conduct of members of the Parliament,[1076] the operation of electoral law,[1077] legislation restricting

[1068] n 1064 above.
[1069] (1994) 182 CLR 104.
[1070] (1994) 182 CLR 211; for general discussions of these cases see, I Loveland, '*Sullivan v The New York Times* Goes Down Under' [1996] PL 126; L Leigh, 'Of Free Speech and Individual Reputation' in I Loveland (ed), *Importing the First Amendment* (Hart Publishing, 1998) 62–65.
[1071] (1997) 145 ALR 96; see also *Kruger v Commonwealth* (1997) 146 ALR 126.
[1072] *Lange v Australian Broadcasting Corp* (n 1071 above) at 115.
[1073] Ibid 116–118.
[1074] Ibid 118.
[1075] *Levy v Victoria* (1997) 146 ALR 248, 273, 291.
[1076] *Lange v Australian Broadcasting* (n 1071 above) (the New Zealand Parliament).
[1077] *Australian Capital Television Pty Ltd v The Commonwealth of Australia* (1992) 177 CLR 106; *Muldowney v South Australia (State of)* (1996) 186 CLR 352.

criticism of a public body,[1078] the administration of a Commonwealth ordinance,[1079] and to campaigns for legislative change.[1080] The freedom extends to conduct as well as to speech.[1081]

However, the freedom does not extend to advocacy of law breaking. Thus, in *Brown v Classification Review Board*[1082] the Federal Court upheld a decision of the Classification Review Board refusing classification of a publication containing an 'Art of Shoplifting'.[1083] The Classification Code was enacted for the legitimate aim of preventing crime and was compatible with the maintenance of representative and responsible government, was reasonably appropriate and adapted to achieving the legitimate end.[1084] **15.355**

(4) Hong Kong

(a) Introduction

Article 16 of the Hong Kong Bill of Rights Ordinance gives effect to the right to freedom of expression contained in Article 19 of the International Covenant on Civil and Political Rights.[1085] **15.356**

A number of challenges based on the freedom of expression have been unsuccessful in the courts. In *Ming Pao Newspapers v A-G of Hong Kong*[1086] the Privy Council held that the Prevention of Bribery Ordinance, which prohibited the disclosure of details of investigations into bribery offences, was necessary to preserve the integrity of investigations into corruption. Great weight was given to the fact that the Legislative Council and the Hong Kong Court of Appeal had recognised such a need.[1087] In *Chim Sing Chung* v *Commissioner of Correctional Services*[1088] the Hong Kong Court of Appeal held that the prison authorities decision to remove racing supplements from newspapers did not violate the applicant's right to receive information under Article 16 because the restriction was 'authorised by law'. **15.357**

In *Hong Kong Polytechnic University v Next Magazine Publishing Ltd*[1089] the Hong Kong Court of Appeal rejected an attempt to argue that a university was a 'public authority' which cannot maintain an action in defamation. It was held that the university was entitled to bring an action for defamation to protect its reputation.[1090] In *Re Lee Kwok Hung*[1091] a challenge was brought to a notice issued by the Securities and Futures Commission Ordinance requiring the applicant to attend an interview with an inspector. The challenge based on breach of **15.358**

[1078] *Nationwide News Pty v Wills* (1992) 177 CLR 1.
[1079] *Kruger v Commonwealth* (1997) 146 ALR 126.
[1080] *Levy v Victoria* (n 1075 above).
[1081] Ibid (the entry of protestors into an area in which duck hunting was taking place).
[1082] (1998) 5 BHRC 619, the issues of the limits of the implied constitutional freedom of expression are comprehensively discussed in this case.
[1083] Rendering the publication, sale or distribution of the article an offence.
[1084] Ibid, 631f-g.
[1085] See App J in Vol 2.
[1086] [1996] AC 907.
[1087] The appeal was in fact allowed on the ground that s 30 did not apply when no specific suspect was being investigated.
[1088] (1997) 1 BHRC 394.
[1089] [1996] 2 HKLR 260..
[1090] See generally, Sze Ping-fat, 'Freedom of the Press' (1996) 16 Lit 291; and 'Freedom of the Press Revisited' (1997) 17 Lit 50.
[1091] [1993] HKLR 49.

rights to freedom of expression was rejected. Article 16 was concerned with the right of freedom of opinion and expression, not with providing an immunity from the disclosure of information. In *HKSAR v Ng Kung Siu*[1092] the Court of Appeal held that a law prohibiting the desecration of the national flag was contrary to Article 19 of the ICCPR because it could not be justified as being 'necessary for the protection of public order'.[1093]

(b) Defamation

15.359 In *Cheung Ng Sheong v Eastweek Publisher Ltd*[1094] the unsuccessful defendant in a libel case challenged the award of damages made by the jury. The Court of Appeal held that excessive awards in defamation cases could constitute an impediment to freedom of expression and opinion as guaranteed in Article 16. The Court noted that, although the Bill of Rights did not apply directly to the case as both parties were private individuals, the Court could nevertheless take into account the Bill of Rights when interpreting the common law. The Court of Appeal took a similar approach to that of the English Court of Appeal in *Rantzen v Mirror Group Newspapers (1986) Ltd.*[1095]

(c) Contempt of court

15.360 In *Secretary for Justice v The Oriental Press Group*[1096] it was held that the offence of scandalising the court was compatible with freedom of expression. That case concerned a newspaper group which, after some unfavourable judicial decisions concerning copyright and obscenity, published a series of articles designed to vilify the judiciary. The articles contained abuse and racist slurs. The staff members of the newspaper group also conducted a 'paparazzi' type pursuit of a senior judge, with 24 hour surveillance of the judge, and reports and photographs being published in the paper. The articles and pursuit led to proceedings for scandalising the court. The court found the newspaper guilty of scandalising the court. The court observed that the offence of scandalising the court existed not only for the benefit of the judiciary, but also to maintain public confidence in the legal system. Permissible criticism had to be distinguished from scurrilous abuse, which might have an effect on the administration of justice. The court stated there was a strong argument that the offence of scandalising the court had been developed to preserve the rule of law. The offence was not a restriction of freedom of expression since conduct which jeopardised the rule of law could not be said to be an exercise of the right of freedom of expression at all. Even if there was a breach of freedom of expression, the breach was justified with reference to the need for public order.

(5) **Human Rights Committee**

15.361 Article 19 of the International Covenant on Civil and Political Rights sets out the right to freedom of expression.[1097] In *Faurisson v France*[1098] the Human Rights Committee con-

---

[1092] (1999) 6 BHRC 591.

[1093] The Court relied on the US 'flag burning' cases, *Texas v Johnson* (1989) 491 US 397 (US SC) and *United States v Eichman* (1990) 496 US 310, US SC; see generally, J Nowak and R Rotunda, *Constitutional Law* (5th edn, West Publishing, 1995) 1170–1172.

[1094] [1996] 1 LRC 168.

[1095] [1994] QB 670.

[1096] [1998] 2 HKLRD 123.

[1097] See App J in Vol 2 for the text.

[1098] (1997) 2 BHRC 1.

sidered a communication which contested the provisions of a French statute making it an offence to deny the existence of Nazi war crimes. The Committee took the view that restrictions on freedom of expression under Art 19(3) of the Covenant[1099] could relate to the interests of the 'community as a whole'. As the statements made were such as to raise or strengthen anti-semitic feelings, the restriction on the author's freedom of expression were permissible under Art 19(3)(a) and were necessary to serve the struggle against racism.[1100]

(6) India

By Article 19 the Constitution of India provides: 15.362

> (1) All citizens shall have the right—
>
> (a) to freedom of speech and expression . . .
>
> (2) Nothing in sub-clause (a) of clause (1) shall affect the operation of any existing law, or prevent the State from making any law, in so far as such law imposes reasonable restrictions on the exercise of the right conferred by the said sub-clause in the interests of the sovereignty and integrity of India, the security of the State, friendly relations with foreign States, public order, decency or morality, or in relation to contempt of court, defamation or incitement to an offence.[1101]

Freedom of expression is a 'preferred right which is always very zealously guarded by the court'.[1102] In the context of Article 19(2), 'reasonableness' is applied to each individual statute impugned and no abstract standard can be laid down: 15.363

> The nature of the right alleged to have been infringed, the underlying purpose of the restrictions imposed, the extent and urgency of the evil sought to be remedied thereby, the disproportion of the imposition, the prevailing conditions at the time, should all enter into the judicial verdict.[1103]

Any law which prohibits the circulation of a newspaper in a particular area[1104]or seeks to control the size of a newspaper[1105] will be contrary to Article 19. In *Rajagopal v State of Tamil Nadu JT*[1106] the Supreme Court held that under Article 19 the state had no authority in law to impose prior restraint on publishing which defamed its officials. They went on to hold that: 15.364

> government, local authority and other organs and institutions exercising governmental powers . . . cannot maintain a suit for damages for defaming them.[1107]

1099 See App J in Vol 2.

1100 See also *X v Germany* (1982) 29 DR 194, E Comm HR (in which the Commission declared inadmissible a complaint under Art 10 of the Convention against a prohibition on the display and sale of brochures arguing that the Holocaust was a Zionist fabrication).

1101 See generally H M Seervai, *Constitutional Law of India* (4th edn N M Tripathi Ltd, 1991) Chap 10; and S Kulshreshtha, *Fundamental Rights and the Supreme Court* (Rawat Publications, 1995), 119–131.

1102 *Odyssey Communication Pvt Lted v Lokvidyavan Sansthan* (1988) 3 SCC 410, 414 para 5; see also *Ramesh Thappar v State of Madras* AIR 1950 SC 124.

1103 *Madras v V G Row* [1952] SCR 597, 607.

1104 *Ramesh Thappar v State of Madras* AIR 1950 SC 124.

1105 *Benett Coleman & Co v Union of India* AIR 1973 SC 106.

1106 1994 6 SCC 632.

1107 Ibid 582c.

15.365 The Indian courts have relied on Article 19(2) to uphold a provision which prohibited an election candidate from advocating voting (or not voting) for any person on the ground of his religion or community.[1108] The Court held that the words 'decency' and 'morality' in Article 19(2), which permits the freedom of expression to be limited, should not be confined to sexual morality alone. The Indian Constitution was explicitly secular. Further, promoting hatred between different classes of citizens tended to create public unrest and disturb public order. Given their influence, politicians had a particular duty to be circumspect in their language.

(7) Ireland

15.366 Article 40.6.1 of the Irish Constitution provides that:

> The State guarantees liberty for the exercise, subject to public order and morality, of . . .
>
> i. The right of the citizen to express freely their convictions and opinions.
>
> The education of public opinion being, however, a matter of such grave import to the common good, the State shall endeavour to ensure that organs of public opinion, such as the radio, the press, the cinema while preserving their rightful liberty of expression, including criticism of Government policy, shall not be used to undermine public order or morality or the authority of the State.
>
> The publication or utterance of blasphemous, seditious, or indecent matter is an offence, which shall be punishable in accordance with law.

The precise scope of the protections to be found in this article is controversial.[1109]

15.367 A number of 'limitations' on freedom of expression for reasons of 'public order and morality' have been recognised. It is clear that there is a restriction in the interests of 'state security'[1101] and the protection of official secrets.[1111] This extends to protection of the authority of the courts from the publication of 'scandalous' material and from material tending to obstruct the course of justice.

15.368 Freedom of expression is also restricted in the interest of an individual's right to reputation.[1112] In *Hynes-O'Sullivan v O'Driscoll*[1113] the Supreme Court rejected the argument that the constitutional guarantee of freedom of speech meant that qualified privilege should be recognised in a situation in which the defendant honestly but wrongly believed that the person to whom the communication was made had a right to receive it.[1114] The 'public figure' defence in defamation actions does not appear to have been considered in an Irish case.[1115]

1108 *Dr Ramesh Yeshwant Prabhoo v Prabhakar Kashinath* (1996) 1 SCC 130.

1109 See J M Kelly, *The Irish Constitution* (3rd edn, Butterworths Ireland, 1994) 923–926.

1110 Although not to the interest of other states, see *A-G for England and Wales v Brandon Book Publishers* [1986] IR 597.

1111 See generally, Kelly (n 1109 above) 926–933.

1112 Protected by Art 40.3.2.

1113 [1988] IR 436.

1114 For criticism of this decision see Mcdonald, 'Towards a Constitutional Analysis of Non-Media Qualified Privilege' (1989) 11 DULJ (ns) 94; and generally, Kelly (n 1109 above) 942–943.

1115 A Lexis search in Nov 1998 disclosed no references to *New York Times v Sullivan* in the Irish cases on that database.

A broadcasting ban on advertisements with a religious or political aim, or in relation to any industrial dispute, was upheld in *Murphy v IRTC*.[1116] In relation to the challenge based on freedom of religion, the court observed that the ban did not constitute discrimination on the ground of religious belief: as it operated regardless of the particular religion involved. Moreover, to the extent that the ban was a breach of freedom of expression, it was justified. Irish people with religious beliefs tended to belong to different churches, and religious advertising from a different church could be regarded as proselytising or offensive.[1117] **15.369**

Freedom of expression issues have arisen in the context of Article 40.3.1 of the Irish Constitution, which provides that: **15.370**

> The State guarantees in its laws to respect, and, as far as is practicable, by its laws to defend and vindicate the personal rights of the citizen.

That Article has been held to include the right to communicate.[1118] The courts have held that it is a justifiable restriction on that right for prisoners' letters to be read by prison staff, but the non-delivery of mail to prisoners as a result of a strike by the prison staff was a breach of that right.[1119]

(8) Namibia

By Article 21(1)(a) of the Constitution of Namibia, all persons have the right to 'freedom of speech and expression, which shall include freedom of the press and other media'. In *Kauesa v Minister of Home Affairs*[1120] the Supreme Court struck down a police regulation that prevented police officers from publicly criticising the Government. That regulation had been used to penalise a police officer for publicly commenting unfavourably about the affirmative action policies of the police force. The court noted that the police have the same rights of freedom of speech as ordinary citizens; but accepted that that right had to be balanced against the interest of the police in maintaining discipline. However, there was no rational connection between the impugned regulation and that aim. The Court also noted that the fact that some of the appellant's comments were insulting or defamatory or rendered him criminally liable did not automatically deprive him of his right to free speech. **15.371**

(9) South Africa

(a) Introduction

Section 16 of the South African Constitution provides that: **15.372**

> 16.(1) Everyone has the right to freedom of expression, which includes—
> (a) freedom of the press and other media;
> (b) freedom to receive and impart information and ideas;
> (c) freedom of artistic creativity; and
> (d) academic freedom and freedom of scientific research.

1116 [1997] 2 ILRM 467.

1117 See also *Colgan v IRTC* [1999] 1 ILRM (broadcasting ban applied to group lobbying for change in abortion laws).

1118 *Attorney-General v Paperlink Ltd* [1984] ILRM 343.

1119 *Kearney v Minister for Justice* [1986] IR 116.

1120 [1995] 3 LRC 528.

(2) The right in subsection (1) does not extend to—
(a) propaganda for war;
(b) incitement of imminent violence; or
(c) advocacy of hatred that is based on race, ethnicity, gender or religion, and that constitutes incitement to cause harm.[1121]

It has been held by the Constitutional Court that constitutional provisions as to freedom of expression do not have direct 'horizontal' effect in private law actions in defamation.[1122] However, constitutional considerations are taken into account when considering the development of the common law.

(b) Defamation

15.373 The South African courts have taken the constitutional guarantee of freedom of speech into account in reforming the common law of defamation.[1123] In *Gardener v Whitaker*[1124] it was held that the constitutional guarantee of freedom of expression meant that the plaintiff should now bear the onus of proving the falsity of a defamatory statement and the absence of defences.[1125] In *Holomisa v Argus Newspapers*[1126] the judge held that a defamatory statement regarding 'free and fair' political activity is constitutionally protected even if false, unless a plaintiff can establish that the defendant acted unreasonably. However, in *Buthelezi v South African Broadcasting Corporation*[1127] this approach was criticised on the grounds that it led to the right to freedom of expression being given precedence over the right to reputation. It was suggested that it would be preferable to develop the common law of defamation by expanding the concept of 'public interest' and placing a burden on the defendant to show that he had acted reasonably. This conflict of approach was resolved by the Supreme Court of Appeal in *National Media v Bogoshi*.[1128] It was held that:

> the publication in the press of false defamatory allegations of fact will not be regarded as unlawful if, upon a consideration of all the circumstances of the case, it is found to have been reasonable to publish the particular facts in a particular way and at a particular time.[1129]

In considering reasonableness, account had to be taken of the nature, extent and tone of the allegations.[1130] Greater latitude is allowed in cases of political discussion. The Court held that the burden of establishing that the publication was reasonable was on the defendant, in accordance with the decision in *Buthelezi*. This approach was held to be in conformity with constitutional values.

1121 See generally, M Chaskalson, J Kentridge, J Klaaren, G Marcus, D Spitz and S Woolman (eds), *Constitutional Law of South Africa* (Juta, 1996) Chap 20.
1122 *Du Plessis v De Klerk* 1996 (3) SA 850, in relation to the Interim Constitution see generally, para 5.71ff above .
1123 See generally, Chaskalson (n 1121 above) 20–34.
1124 1994 (5) BCLR 19; the Constitutional Court refused leave to appeal on the grounds that no constitutional issue was raised, 15 May 1996.
1125 Ibid 37D-H.
1126 1996 (6) BCLR 836 (W), Cameron J; see also *Hall v Welz* 1996 (4) SA 1070; *Rivett-Carnac v Wiggins* 1997 (4) BCLR 562.
1127 (1997) (12) BCLR 1733.
1128 1998 (4) SA 1196.
1129 Ibid 632e-f.
1130 Ibid 632f.

(c) Obscenity

In *Case v Ministry of Safety and Security*[1131] the majority dealt with the law of obscenity in terms of the right to personal privacy. However, two of the judges[1132] held that the protection of section 15 extended to sexually explicit material and the criminal law on obscenity unjustifiably violated that right. 15.374

(d) Political restrictions on employees

The case of *South African National Defence Force Union v Minister of Defence*[1133] concerned a law which prohibited members of the armed forces from participating in public protest actions and from joining trade unions. The Court decided that prohibiting participation in acts of public protest violated the right to freedom of expression of Defence Force members. Their rights to receive and express opinions on a wide range of issues, whether in public or private gatherings, was a grave infringement on the fundamental rights of soldiers. Furthermore, such an infringement was unjustifiable, although the Court indicated that a different, narrower legislative provision might be constitutionally justified. 15.375

(e) Privilege

The issue of parliamentary privilege was considered in *De Lille v Speaker of the National Assembly*.[1134] The applicant had named in parliamentary debate eight senior members of the ANC as spies for the apartheid government. The applicant was formally charged with abusing her privilege of freedom of speech, and the House recommended her suspension from the House for 15 days. The applicant succeed in setting aside that recommendation. The court found that the investigation into the applicant's conduct had been flawed and in breach of natural justice. The court held that the nature and exercise of Parliamentary privilege had to be consonant with the Constitution. The court recognised that the principle of separation of powers and the proper exercise of parliamentary privilege was a matter for Parliament alone. Nevertheless, the court could interfere where Parliament improperly exercised that privilege. Furthermore, the suspension of the member was in breach of her freedom of expression. 15.376

(10) Sri Lanka

(a) Introduction

Article 14(1)(a) of the Constitution of Sri Lanka provides that: 15.377

> Every citizen is entitled to the freedom of speech and expression including publication.[1135]

Article 15(7) permits such restrictions to the right as may be prescribed by law, in the interests of national security, public order and the protection of public health or morality, or for the purpose of securing due recognition and respect for the rights and freedoms of

[1131] 1996 (5) BCLR 609.

[1132] Mokgoro and Sachs JJ.

[1133] (1999) 6 BHRC 574.

[1134] 1998 (3) SA 430, CPD.

[1135] See generally, J Wickramaratne, *Fundamental Rights in Sri Lanka* (Navrang, 1996) Chap 7; S Sharvananda, *Fundamental Rights in Sri Lanka* (Arnold's International Printing House, 1993) Chap XII.

others, or of meeting the just requirements of general welfare in a democratic society. There must be proximate and reasonable nexus between the restriction and the object sought to be achieved by the restriction. Article 15(2) also permits such restrictions as may be prescribed by law in the interests of racial and religious harmony or in relation to parliamentary privilege, contempt of court, defamation or incitement to offence. Freedom of the recipient is included within the freedom of speech and expression. Thus, regular readers of a newspaper which had been banned by emergency regulations had standing to seek relief.[1136]

(b) Public order

15.378 A number of cases have been brought raising issues about freedom of expression. In *Joseph Perera's* case,[1137] a regulation which provided that nobody could distribute leaflets or handbills without police permission was struck down, as giving unguided and unfettered discretion to police. The police regulation of a public meeting was held to be a breach of freedom of expression in *Mohottige v Gunatilleke*.[1138] The organisers of the meeting applied for a police permit to use loudspeakers at the public meeting. The police asked for the names of the speakers, and then issued a permit subject to two conditions, that only the named speakers would be permitted to speak, and that the speakers should refrain from criticising the Government, any organisation, or any individual. The Supreme Court held that both conditions violated the freedom of speech and expression. The Court noted that demanding the names of people beforehand can have the effect of silencing people who may otherwise wish to contribute to proceedings by participating.

(c) Defamation

15.379 The case of *A-G v Siriwardana*[1139] arose out of a defamation case where a newspaper criticised the speech of an MP in Parliament, likening MPs in general to bulls and donkeys. The Supreme Court found the remarks to be defamatory, and rejected the newspaper's defence of fair comment. The Supreme Court did not decide the question of whether the defence of fair comment was available, as the newspaper had not engaged in fair criticism. Likewise, a newspaper which contained a false statement concerning a Supreme Court trial, was penalised.[1140] The Court held that the publication was deliberate and wilful, holding the Court to odium and an undue interference with the administration of justice.[1141]

(d) Media regulation

15.380 In *Siriwardena v Liyanage*[1142] the closure of a newspaper was upheld on the basis that its contents were likely to inflame sections of the community to violence and breaches of the

1136 *Visvalingam v Liyanage* [1985] LRC Const 909.
1137 *Perera v A-G* [1992] 1 Sri LR 199.
1138 (1992) 2 Sri LR 246.
1139 (1978-79-80) 1 Sri LR 377.
1140 *In the matter of a rule on De Souza* [1916] 18 NLR 41.
1141 See also *Hulugalle's Case* [1937–39] 39–40 NLR 294 (article which imputed to Supreme Court judge serious breach of duty by taking an unauthorised holiday for the purposes of going to race meetings was disrespectful; press criticism of administration of justice should be honest and in good faith, and not step beyond its bounds).
1142 [1985] LRC Const 909.

peace, and thereby endanger the maintenance of law and order.[1143] The constitutionality of the establishment of a Sri Lankan Broadcasting Authority was considered in *Athukorale v A-G of Sri Lanka*.[1144] It decided that the existence of such an authority was not, of itself, a breach of Article 14.[1145] However, it was held that such an authority had to be independent of the Government. Since the proposed authority lacked independence and was susceptible to ministerial interference, the right of freedom of speech was placed in jeopardy.

(e) Other cases

The Sri Lankan Supreme Court held in *Karunaratne v Bandarnaike*[1146] that a member of **15.381**
a political party has freedom of expression, and cannot be expelled from the party for voicing unpopular views. An MP had urged the party leadership to hold internal party elections for various party committees. When that course of action failed, he made a statement to a newspaper expressing concerns at the non-holding of elections by a party committed to democracy. The petitioner was expelled by the party after a disciplinary enquiry to which he refused to submit. The Supreme Court held that the petitioner's expulsion was unlawful. While the Court accepted that freedom of speech may be limited by voluntarily joining a political association, the petitioner in this case had made every effort to obtain internal party change, before making a public statement. In the circumstances, his public statement was justified as having been made under the exercise of his freedom of speech and therefore guaranteed under the Constitution. His expulsion was therefore invalid.

(11) Zimbabwe

(a) Introduction

Section 20 of the Constitution of Zimbabwe provides, *inter alia*, that: **15.382**

> (1) Except with his own consent or by way of parental discipline, no person shall be hindered in the enjoyment of his freedom of expression, that is to say, freedom to hold opinions and to receive and impart ideas and information without interference and freedom from interference with his correspondence.
>
> (2) Nothing containing in or done under the authority of any law shall be held to be in contravention of subsection (1) to the extent that the law in question makes provision:
>
> (a) in the interests of defence, public safety, public order, the economic interests of the State, public morality or public health;
>
> (b) for the purpose of:
>
> (i) protecting the reputations, rights and freedoms of other persons or the private lives of persons concerned in legal proceedings;
>
> (ii) preventing the disclosure of information received in confidence;
>
> (iii) maintaining the authority and independence of the courts or tribunals or Parliament;
>
> (iv) regulating the technical administration, technical operation or general efficiency or telephony, telegraphy, posts, wireless broadcasting or television or creating or regulating any monopoly in these fields;

[1143] See also *Visvalingam v Liayanage* FRD (2) 310.

[1144] (1997) 2 BHRC 610.

[1145] Relying, *inter alia*, on *Groppera Radio AG v Switzerland* (1990) 12 EHRR 321 and *Informationseverein Lentia v Austria* (1993) 17 EHRR 93.

[1146] [1993] 2 Sri LR 90.

(v) in the case of correspondence, preventing the unlawful dispatch therewith or other matter;

or

(c) that imposes restrictions upon public officers;

except so far as that provision, or, as the case may be, the thing done under the authority thereof is shown not to be reasonably justifiable in a democratic society.

The Supreme Court has held that freedom of expression is a 'core value' of society.[1147] The Zimbabwe courts have taken a generous approach to the meaning of freedom of expression.

(b) State funding of political parties

15.383 In *United Parties v Minister of Justice*[1148] the Supreme Court considered the provision of state funding to political parties. The practical effect of the provision was that only the ruling party, ZANU(PF), qualified for funding. The applicant political party complained that this provision infringed its rights to freedom of expression. The Court considered the systems for the public funding of political parties in a number of jurisdictions. It was held that, as political effectual communication required the expenditure of money, restrictions on state funding caused a reduction in effective political expression. As a result, the statutory provisions for party funding were struck down.

(c) Media regulation

15.384 A generous approach was also taken in *Retrofit (Private) Ltd v Posts and Telecommunications Corp*,[1149] in which the Supreme Court held that a telecommunications monopoly was in breach of freedom of expression. The application was brought by a company which had unsuccessfully applied for a licence to provide a mobile telephone network. The respondent was a public corporation which had a monopoly on the provision of telecommunications services in Zimbabwe. The Court considered the four broad purposes of freedom of expression: assisting the individual to obtain self-fulfilment, assisting in the discovery of truth, strengthening the capacity of the individual to participate in decision-making and providing a mechanism to balance stability and change.[1150] The Court stated that protection of freedom of expression involved protecting the means of expression as well as its content. It went on to hold that for the respondent to monopolise telecommunications services in Zimbabwe and then to furnish a public network of notoriously poor quality:

> manifestly interferes with the constitutional right of every person in the country to receive and impart ideas and information by means of this 'pervasive two-way communications system.[1151]

This monopoly was not 'reasonably justifiable in a democratic society'. Further, the constitutional right to free expression applied to corporations as well as individuals.

[1147] See *Retrofit (Pvt) Ltd v Posts and Telecommunications Corp* [1996] 4 LRC 489, 499–501.

[1148] (1997) 3 BHRC 16.

[1149] n 1147 above.

[1150] Ibid 500f-501f.

[1151] Ibid 505f.

(d) Prisoners

In *Woods v Minister of Justice*[1152] the Supreme Court considered restrictions on the letters which could be sent and received by prisoners. It was held that while the restriction addressed the legitimate objective of public order and safety, the extent of the restrictions were not reasonably justifiable in a democratic society. **15.385**

(e) Other cases

The case of *Mutasa v Makombe*[1153] concerned a finding of contempt of Parliament against a member of Parliament. The Supreme Court held that this was a justifiable interference with his freedom of expression in accordance with section 20(2)(b)(iii) of the Constitution.[1154] Furthermore, the power of Parliament to commit its members for contempt was 'reasonably justifiable in a democratic society'. **15.386**

[1152] [1994] 1 LRC 359.
[1153] (1997) 2 BHRC 325.
[1154] See also *Smith v Mutasa NO* (1990) (3) SA 756.

16

FREEDOM OF ASSEMBLY AND ASSOCIATION

A. The Nature of the Rights

16.01 The rights of individuals to gather together and to form associations for the common pursuit of their interests are now regarded as fundamental to the democratic process. In fact, these rights only became firmly established in the twentieth century. Thus, the right to assemble was originally ancillary to the ancient right to petition the King;[1] and the First Amendment to the US Constitution provided that:

> Congress shall make no law . . . abridging . . . the right of the people peaceably to assemble and to petition the Government for a redress of grievances.

However, the idea that citizens should meet peaceably to consult one another about public affairs and to petition for redress of grievances is now part of the very idea of democratic government.[2]

16.02 Freedom of assembly is closely connected to freedom of political expression. Effective advocacy of political views requires organisation; and freedom of association is another aspect of the right to assemble and petition for redress of grievances. These rights are equally important in the promotion of economic, social and cultural interests, particularly for trade unions, which are protected from interference by the state and by employers. The International Labour Organisation, established in 1919 by the Treaty of Versailles,[3] has as one of its central principles the protection of freedom of association in the context of labour law.[4]

16.03 The rights of assembly and association merge in the industrial relations field which covers both association (the formation of trade unions) and assembly (picketing). The two rights were first combined in a human rights instrument by Article 20 of the Universal Declaration which states:

> (1) Everyone has the right to freedom of peaceful assembly and association.
> (2) No one may be compelled to belong to an association.

---

[1] Asserted by Art 5 of the Bill of Rights 1688.

[2] See *United States v Cruikshank* (1876) 92 US 542.

[3] For a general discussion of the ILO see A Robertson and J Merrills, *Human Rights in the World* (4th edn, Manchester University Press, 1996) 282–288.

[4] See Art I, 'Declaration Concerning the Aims and Purposes of the International Labour Organisation, 1944' in I Brownlie, *Basic Documents on Human Rights* (3rd edn, Oxford University Press, 1992) 243ff; and see also 'Freedom of Association and Protection of the Right to Organize Convention, 1948' in Brownlie ibid 260ff.

The International Covenant on Civil and Political Rights deals with both rights at more length. Article 21 provides:

> The right of peaceful assembly shall be recognised. No restrictions may be placed on the exercise of this right other than those imposed in conformity with the law and which are necessary in a democratic society in the interests of national security or public safety, public order, the protection of public health or morals or the protection of the rights and freedoms of others.

Article 22(1) provides that:

> Everyone shall have the right to freedom of association with others, including the right to form and join trade unions for the protection of his interests.

Article 22(2) prescribes restrictions on this right in the same terms as Article 21, with the addition of a final sentence stating that the Article shall not prevent lawful restrictions on the exercise of the right by members of the armed forces and the police.

The issues which arise concerning freedom of assembly and association can be considered separately. In relation to freedom of assembly, the following areas must be considered: **16.04**

The scope of the right: The debates have centred on the question of what types of assemblies are protected and, in particular, what constitutes a 'peaceful' assembly for these purposes.

The nature of the protection the state must provide: The critical question is the extent to which the state is obliged to intervene positively to protect assemblies from the hostile actions of other groups or persons who oppose them. Difficult problems occur, for example, where peaceful demonstrators provoke violent responses from others, and where employers attempt to quash lawful picketing by trade union members.

Restrictions on assemblies: The need to regulate public assemblies to ensure public order requires consideration of whether the state is entitled to 'license' assemblies or ban them in advance. A licensing power can be a severe restriction on the right and has been subject to particularly careful scrutiny.

Different concerns are important to freedom of association: **16.05**

The scope of the right: Three questions can be identified: the extent to which the right extends beyond 'organised groupings' and protects 'personal association', the freedom of an association to deal with its own internal affairs and whether the right encompasses a negative right of 'non-association'.

The nature of the protection the state must provide: To what extent the state is obliged to take positive steps to provide the conditions in which associations can develop or to protect associations from the hostile actions of opponents.

Restrictions on the activities of associations: It is generally accepted that the state can place restrictions on the formation and activities of associations 'in the interests of the community'. However, the basis for such restrictions is often contentious.

B. The Rights in English Law Before the Human Rights Act[5]

(1) The scope of the right to freedom of assembly

(a) Introduction

16.06 The traditional view is that, in English law, freedom of assembly is a 'residual right' with no positive content.[6] As was said in the well known case of *Duncan v Jones*:[7]

> English law does not recognise any special right of public meeting for political or any other purposes. The right of assembly is nothing more than a view, taken by the court, of the individual liberty of the subject.[8]

On this view, freedom of assembly is a 'right' which individuals are free to exercise unless they are precluded by law from doing so. In the past the right was severely restricted; for example, Chartist leaders were prosecuted for unlawfully meeting for the purpose of exciting discontent and disaffection.[9]

16.07 A more positive articulation of the right is found in other cases.[10] The most famous of these is, perhaps, the dissenting judgment of Lord Denning MR in *Hubbard v Pitt;*[11] he spoke of the right to demonstrate and the right to protest on matters of public concern as being rights 'which it is in the public interest that individuals should possess'. In a subsequent case he stressed that:

> Freedom of assembly is another of our precious freedoms. Everyone is entitled to meet and assemble with his fellows to discuss their affairs and to promote their views; so long as it is not done to propagate violence or do anything unlawful.[12]

This general approach is supported by the decision of the House of Lords in *DPP*

---

[5] See S Bailey, D Harris and B Jones, *Civil Liberties: Cases and Materials* (4th edn, Butterworths, 1995) Chap 3, 'Public Order'; D Feldman, *Civil Liberties and Human Rights in England and Wales* (Clarendon Press, 1993) Chap 17, 'Protest and Public Order'.

[6] For a general discussion of this traditional view of civil liberties, see para 1.20ff above.

[7] [1936] 1 KB 218.

[8] Ibid 249; echoing A Dicey, *An Introduction to the Study of the Law of the Constitution* (8th edn, Macmillan, 1915) App Note V, 351.

[9] *R v Hunt* (1820) 3 B & Ald 566.

[10] See *Beatty v Gillbanks* (1882) 9 QBD 308; *Verrall v Great Yarmouth Borough Council* [1981] 1 QB 202; *Hirst v Chief Constable of West Yorkshire* (1986) 85 Cr App R 143, 151.

[11] [1976] 1 QB 142, 178.

[12] *Verrall v Great Yarmouth Borough Council* (n 10 above).

v Jones;[13] and it now appears that there is a positive common law right to freedom of assembly. Nevertheless, with the exception of the statutory right to picket,[14] the law provides no express protection for this right.

(b) Freedom of assembly and the highway

The use of the highway for protest is central to the right of freedom of assembly. The traditional view is that public rights of use of the highway are limited to 'passage and re-passage' and any uses ancillary thereto which are usual and reasonable.[15] The Divisional Court has indicated that the use of the highway for a peaceful assembly is 'not unlawful'.[16] However, the position was clarified by the House of Lords in the 1999 case of *DPP v Jones*.[17] The House of Lords held that the public had the right to use the highway for peaceful assembly, provided that this was consistent with the primary right to use it for passage and re-passage. Lord Irvine LC expressed the view that: **16.08**

> the public highway is a public place which the public may enjoy for any reasonable purpose, provided the activity in question does not amount to a public or private nuisance and does not obstruct the highway by unreasonably impeding the primary right of the public to pass and repass: within these qualifications there is a public right of peaceful assembly on the highway.[18]

He also stated that, if the common law had been uncertain, he would have invoked Article 11 of the Convention to clarify or develop the common law.[19] Lord Hutton based his decision, in part, on a common law right to freedom of assembly, holding that:

> the common law recognises that there is a right for members of the public to assemble together to express views on matters of public concern and I consider that the common law should now recognise that this right, which is one of the fundamental rights of citizens in a democracy, is unduly restricted unless it can be exercised in some circumstances on the public highway.[20]

Nevertheless, there are no public rights to hold meetings in public buildings or on public land. Thus, in a case concerning the validity of regulations prohibiting public addresses in Hyde Park, it was held that there was no 'right' to hold public **16.09**

[13] [1999] 2 AC 240, see para 16.08 below and see eg G Clayton, 'Reclaiming Public Ground: The Right to Peaceful Assembly' [2000] 63 MLR 252.

[14] The Trade Union and Labour Relations (Consolidation) Act 1992, s 220; the Employment Code of Practice (Picketing) Order 1992, SI 1992/476.

[15] See *Harrison v Duke of Rutland* [1893] 1 QB 142, 154; *Hickman v Maisey* [1900] 1 QB 752; and generally, Bailey, Harris and Jones (n 5 above) 182–189.

[16] See *Hirst v Chief Constable of West Yorkshire* (1986) 85 Cr App Rep 143.

[17] n 13 above (by a 3:2 majority) and see eg Clayton (n 14 above).

[18] Ibid 257.

[19] Ibid 259.

[20] Ibid 287; citing *Hubbard v Pitt* [1976] 1 QB 142, 178 *per* Lord Denning MR, dissenting.

meetings in the park.[21] Similarly, the courts have held that there is no right to hold public meetings in Trafalgar Square.[22] Furthermore, it is clear that the owners of 'quasi public spaces'[23] such as shopping malls, are entitled to exclude members of the public;[24] consequently, they have no right to meet or demonstrate in such spaces.

16.10 There is, however, a right for candidates in parliamentary and local government elections to hold meetings in schools and meeting rooms maintained out of public funds.[25] This right will be upheld even where it is being abused by extremist political parties.[26] It is an offence to use disorderly conduct to break up lawful public election meetings.[27] A meeting is not unlawful merely because it is held on the highway.[28] When a local authority sought to terminate a political party's licence to use a hall for its annual conference, the Court of Appeal took into account the right to freedom of assembly in granting specific performance of the licence.[29]

16.11 Certain meetings are given additional protection by the criminal law. Disorderly conduct which aims to prevent transacting business at a public meeting[30] is subject to fine or imprisonment upon summary conviction, and a fine may be incurred by anyone refusing or falsifying personal details during a police enquiry into such incidents. Obstruction or assault of a minister in the discharge of his duties in a place of worship[31] is also prohibited, as is behaviour of a riotous, violent or indecent nature in an ecclesiastical setting.[32]

(2) Restrictions on assembly

(a) Introduction

16.12 The freedom of assembly in English law is subject to substantial restrictions on 'public order' grounds. These restrictions are rooted in the common law duty to

---

21 See *Bailey v Williamson* (1873) LR 8 QB 118.

22 See *R v Cunninghame Graham and Burns* (1888) 16 Cox CC 420; *Ex p Lewis* (1888) 21 QBD 191; *De Morgan v Metropolitan Board of Works* (1880) 5 QBD 155 and also generally, S Bailey, D Harris and B Jones, Civil Liberties: Cases and Materials (4th edn, Butterworths, 1995) 189–190.

23 See generally, K Gray and S Gray, 'Civil Rights, Civil Wrongs and Quasi-Public Spaces' [1999] EHRLR 46.

24 *CIN Properties v Rawlins* [1995] 2 EGLR 130.

25 Representation of the People Act 1983, s 95.

26 Cf *Webster v Southwark London Borough Council* [1983] QB 698 (National Front could not be denied statutory right to meet).

27 Representation of the People Act 1983, s 97.

28 *Burden v Rigler* [1911] 1 KB 337.

29 *Verrall v Great Yarmouth Borough Council* [1981] 1 QB 202.

30 Public Meetings Act 1908, s 1.

31 Offences Against the Person Act 1861, s 36.

32 Ecclesiastical Courts Jurisdiction Act 1860, s 2.

preserve the 'Queen's peace'[33] and serve both to regulate and to prohibit assemblies. There are a number of criminal offences involving disorder and regulatory powers for the prevention or termination of breaches of the peace. The same provisions cover all types of gatherings of groups of people for whatever purpose.[34] Some special venues such as parks and national heritage sites are governed by specific legislation.

(b) Public order and breach of the peace

The notion of a 'breach of the peace' is central to the regulation of public assemblies. A breach of the peace takes place when there is violence or threat of violence that results in actual or likely harm to a person or his property, or a fear that such harm will occur.[35] The violence or threatened violence must be unlawful if it is to give rise to a breach of the peace. [36] As a result 'public alarm and excitement', 'noise alone' or 'being a nuisance and keeping one's neighbours awake' did not constitute a breach of the peace.[37] A breach of the peace is not limited to violence in public, but may also occur in private.[38] **16.13**

At common law every citizen in whose presence a breach of the peace is being committed (or reasonably appears to be about to be committed) may take reasonable steps to prevent the person who is breaching (or threatening to breach) the peace from doing so.[39] In order to justify any preventive action the possibility of a breach of the peace must be real. The imminence or immediacy of the threat to the peace determines what action is reasonable.[40] This means that police officers may justify the arrest of demonstrators who insist on travelling to a demonstration where violence is feared, even if the arrest takes place a considerable distance from the demonstration.[41] **16.14**

Difficult questions arise where an assembly provokes (or may provoke) third parties **16.15**

---

33 The 'Queen's (or King's) peace' is the freedom from violence which all citizens have a duty to maintain: see J Weber, 'The King's Peace: A Comparative Study' (1989) 10 J of Legal History 135–60; Sir Carleton Kemp Allen, *The Queen's Peace* (Stevens & Son, 1953) 23–66; D Feldman, 'The King's Peace, the Royal Prerogative and Public Order: The Roots and Early Development of Binding Over Powers' [1988] CLJ 101–128.

34 See *R v Caird* (1970) 54 Cr App Rep 499: 'where there is wanton and vicious violence of gross degree, the Court is not concerned with whether it originates from gang rivalry or from political motives. It is the degree of mob violence that matters and the extent to which the public peace is being broken'.

35 *R v Howell (Errol)* [1982] QB 416, 426; *Percy v DPP* [1995] 1 WLR 1382.

36 *McBean v Parker* [1983] Crim LR 399 (owner of property using reasonable force to expel a trespassing constable, no breach of the peace).

37 *Lewis v Chief Constable of Greater Manchester*, *The Times*, 22 Oct 1991.

38 *McConnell v Chief Constable of Greater Manchester Police* [1990] 1 WLR 364.

39 *Albert v Lavin* [1982] AC 546.

40 See *Moss v McLachlan* [1985] IRLR 76.

41 See ibid in which the arrests took place several miles away.

into using violence. In *Beatty v Gillbanks*[42] it was held that a peaceful protest could not be prevented simply on the ground that it provoked others to use unlawful violence.[43] However, it is clear from subsequent cases that if the persons holding the assembly act in a way which is calculated to provoke third parties to use violence, they will be guilty of breach of the peace and liable to be bound over.[44] In other words, an assembly can be prevented on the 'breach of the peace' grounds if the natural consequence of the assembly taking place is the provocation of violence by others.[45] Nevertheless, there will not be a breach of the peace if:

> . . . any violence likely to have been provoked on the part of others would be not merely unlawful but wholly unreasonable - as of course, it would be if the . . . conduct was not merely lawful but such as in no material way interfered with others' rights. *A fortiori*, if the defendant was properly exercising his own basic rights, whether of assembly, demonstration or free speech.[46]

In *Redmond-Bate v DPP*[47] the Divisional Court held that this approach was in conformity with the Convention.

(c) Criminal offences

16.16 Part I of the Public Order Act 1986[48] provides for three crimes of disorder: riot,[49] violent disorder[50] and affray.[51] These offences replaced the common law offences of riot, rout, unlawful assembly and affray. In addition, individual participants in an assembly will be guilty of an offence if their conduct causes fear of or provokes violence[52] or harassment, alarm or distress.[53] All these crimes may be committed by the participants in assemblies. Prosecutions for riot, violent disorder and affray require the prosecution to prove the use or threat of unlawful violence.[54] The

---

[42] (1882) 9 QBD 308; see also *R v Londonderry JJ* (1891) 28 LR Ir 440, 450: 'If danger arises from the exercise of lawful rights resulting in a breach of the peace, the remedy is the presence of sufficient force to prevent the result, not the legal condemnation of those who exercise the right'.

[43] Members of the Salvation Army could not be bound over to keep the peace simply because their procession had provoked violent opposition.

[44] See eg *O'Kelly v Harvey* (1883) 15 Cox CC 435, 445-446; *Wise v Dunning* [1902] 1 KB 167; *Lansbury v Riley* [1914] 3 KB 229.

[45] See *R v Morpeth Justices, ex p Ward* (1992) 95 Cr App R 215 (bind over upheld in relation to people who had noisily and turbulently disrupted a pheasant shoot); contrast *Percy v DPP* [1995] 1 WLR 1382 (no bind over of person who climbed into military bases because no likelihood of trained personnel being provoked to violence).

[46] *Nicol v DPP* (1995) 160 JP 155, 163.

[47] (1999) 7 BHRC 375, 381c.

[48] For a general discussion see: A T H Smith, 'The Public Order Act 1986 Part I: The New Offences' [1987] Crim L Rev 156.

[49] Public Order Act 1986, s 1.

[50] Ibid s 2.

[51] Ibid s 3.

[52] Ibid s 4.

[53] Ibid s 5.

[54] 'Riot' requires the use of such violence for a common purpose (s 1), 'violent disorder' requires the use or threat of violence by persons present together (s 2) and 'affray' simply requires the use or threat of violence towards another (s 3).

offence of 'fear of provocation of violence' requires conduct which causes a person to believe that immediate unlawful violence will be used or which provokes such violence or causes a person to believe that such violence will be provoked.[55] However, the violence must be 'immediate', that is within a relatively short period of time without any intervening occurrence.[56]

The offence of 'causes harassment, alarm or distress' can be committed in a wide range of circumstances in which no use, threat or provocation of violence is present. The offence may be committed where a person uses 'abusive or insulting words or behaviour' or 'displays any writing sign or visible representation which is threatening, abusive or insulting'.[57] The offence can, therefore, be committed by the chanting of slogans or the display of placards at demonstrations.[58] Whether or not words or conduct are 'insulting or abusive' is a question of fact for the magistrates[59] who may take widely divergent views in relation to particular conduct. It should, however, be noted that the offence can only be committed if the defendant intends the thing displayed to be abusive or insulting or was aware that it might be.[60] **16.17**

The holding of assemblies on private land has, traditionally, been the province of the civil law. However, the Criminal Justice and Public Order Act 1994 creates a new offence in relation to trespassers on private land.[61] If the participants in an assembly on private land are trespassing then a number of criminal offences may be committed. The offence of 'aggravated trespass' is committed if trespassers do anything intended to intimidate persons engaged in lawful activity to deter them from engaging in that activity, or obstruct or disrupt that activity.[62] **16.18**

Protestors who seek to persuade a person to abstain from doing any act which he has a right to do by 'watching and besetting' the person's house or place or business or do anything which 'hinders' him in his work may be guilty of an offence under section 241 of the Trade Union and Labour Relations (Consolidation) Act 1992.[63] The prosecution must prove that the protestors were acting 'with a view **16.19**

[55] Public Order Act 1986, s 4.

[56] *R v Horseferry Road Metropolitan Stipendiary Magistrate, ex p Siadatan* [1991] 1 QB 260 (offence not committed by publishers of *The Satanic Verses* when it was alleged that violence would be provoked at some unspecified time in the future).

[57] Public Order Act 1986, s 5(1)(a), (b).

[58] See eg *Morrow v DPP* [1994] Crim LR 58 and *Lewis v DPP* unreported 7 Mar 1995, DC (both cases concerned the display of anti-abortion placards outside abortion clinics).

[59] *Brutus v Cozens* [1973] AC 854.

[60] Public Order Act 1986, s 6(4) and *DPP v Clarke* (1991) 94 Cr App R 359.

[61] This was one of a group of offences designed to deal with perceived threats from 'travellers', 'hunt saboteurs' and the organisers of 'raves'.

[62] Criminal Justice and Public Order Act 1994 s 68(1), this offence has been widely interpreted, see *Winder v DPP*, *The Times*, 14 Aug 1996.

[63] Formerly Conspiracy and Protection of Property Act 1875, s 7.

to compel' the other person to do something.[64] Anti-roads protestors who have sought to 'get in the way' of work on site have been prosecuted under this provision.[65]

16.20 Meetings and assemblies for the purposes of training or drilling in the use of arms or of practising 'military exercise, movements or evolution' without lawful authority are prohibited and all participants are guilty of an offence.[66] Such meetings may be dispersed by justices of the peace or constables and the participants arrested.[67] Drilling for the purpose of 'going to a meeting with ease and regularity' is lawful but, if the purpose is to 'overawe' the Government or to 'give confidence by an appearance of strength to disaffected persons' an offence is committed.[68]

(d) Regulatory powers

16.21 **Introduction.** The regulation of meetings, processions and demonstrations is subject to the general police powers for the prevention of breaches of the peace. The powers, which are both common law[69] and statutory in origin, govern the location and the conduct of assemblies, and are reinforced by the offence of 'obstructing a police officer in the execution of his duty'.[70] If participants in an assembly refuse a reasonable request to disperse[71] from an officer acting in the execution of his duty, they will be committing an offence. An officer will be acting in the execution of his duty if he makes such a request in relation to an assembly which he reasonably believes may lead to a breach of the peace.[72] If a participant refuses to comply with the request, he will be liable to arrest.[73]

16.22 **Location.** At common law the police may reroute the course of a procession or relocate a public gathering in order to prevent an imminent breach of the peace. For example, in *Duncan v Jones*[74] the defendant was intending to address a street

[64] *DPP v Fidler* [1992] 1 WLR 91 (no offence committed by anti-abortion protestors because dissuasion did not amount to compulsion).

[65] See eg *DPP v Todd* unreported, 4 May 1995.

[66] Unlawful Drilling Act 1819, s 1.

[67] Ibid s 2.

[68] *R v Hunt* (1820) 3 B & Ald 566.

[69] See W Birtles, 'The Common Law Power of the Police to Control Public Meetings' (1973) 36 MLR 587; D G Barnum, 'Freedom of Assembly and the Hostile Audience in Anglo-American Law' (1981) 29 American J of Comparative L 59.

[70] Police Act 1996, s 89(2).

[71] 'Reasonableness' is an objective question: see *Redmond-Bate v DPP* (1999) 7 BHRC 375, 377d–e.

[72] See the discussion in *Redmond-Bate v DPP* (n 71 above); and for breach of the peace see para 16.29 below.

[73] But note that 'obstructing an officer in the execution of his duty' is not an arrestable offence and, as a result, a police officer cannot arrest a person he suspects of committing it unless the 'general arrest conditions' in the Police and Criminal Evidence Act 1984, s 25 have been complied with.

[74] [1936] 1 KB 218; in *R v Coventry City Council, ex p Phoenix Aviation* [1995] 3 All ER 37, 59 Simon Brown LJ took the view that the decision did not involve 'any penetrating analysis of the legal principles in play'; and see T Daintith, 'Disobeying a Constable: A Fresh Look at Duncan v Jones'

meeting in front of an unemployed workers' centre and was ordered to desist by a police officer. When she refused, she was arrested and convicted of obstructing a police officer. In *Re Atkinson*[75] the police directed that members of an Orange band with a reputation for being disorderly be prevented from taking their instruments to the venue of a procession in a Northern Ireland town dominated by Nationalists. It was held that stopping the bus before it reached the town was lawful and did not breach Article 11 of the European Convention on Human Rights.

The regulation of the route of a procession and location of an assembly is now largely codified by statute. The Highways Act 1980 does not prohibit street processions or assemblies on highways, as long as they do not wilfully[76] obstruct free passage along it[77] without lawful excuse. Obstruction has been broadly interpreted to mean: **16.23**

> any occupation of part of a road . . . interfering with people having the use of the whole of the road.[78]

However, a person will have a 'lawful excuse' if his use of the highway amounts to a 'reasonable use' in the circumstances.[79] The court will take the right of freedom of assembly into account when considering reasonableness.[80] A moving procession will therefore, *prima facie*, be lawful, in contrast to sitting down in the road in front of traffic[81] or compelling vehicles to stop whilst picketing.[82] It is no defence to a charge of obstruction that the defendant is seeking to block access to premises where, he believes, unlawful activity is taking place.[83]

Conduct of processions and assemblies. Assemblies and processions on the highway are subject to the requirements of Part II of the Public Order Act 1986 which authorises the prohibition or imposing of conditions on both processions and assemblies.[84] A 'public assembly' is defined as: **16.24**

[1966] PL 248; M Supperstone, *Brownlie's Law of Public Order and National Security* (2nd edn, Butterworths, 1981), 111–113; G Robertson, *Freedom the Individual and the Law* (7th edn, Penguin, 1993) 87 describes it as a miserable decision for civil liberties, all the more so because the judges purported to find no difficulty in principle in achieving the result; and see D Feldman, *Civil Liberties and Human Rights in England and Wales* (Clarendon Press, 1993) 801–802.

75 [1987] 8 NIJB 6.

76 In this context, wilfully means 'deliberately' or 'intentionally': *Arrowsmith v Jenkins* [1963] 2 QB 561.

77 Highways Act 1980, s 137.

78 *Nagy v Weston* [1965] 1 WLR 280, 284.

79 *Nagy v Weston* (n 78 above); see also *Lowdens v Keaveney* [1903] 2 IR 82; *R v Clark (No 2)* [1964] 2 QB 315 (anti-nuclear weapons demonstration blocking several streets in London was not necessarily unreasonable), and *Hirst v Chief Constable of West Yorkshire* (1986) 85 Cr App 143, DC.

80 See *Hirst v Chief Constable of West Yorkshire* (n 79 above).

81 *Birch v DPP* [2000] Crim LR 301.

82 *Broome v DPP* [1974] AC 587.

83 *Birch v DPP* (n 81 above).

84 For a general discussion see H Fenwick, *Civil Liberties* (2nd edn, Cavendish Publishing, 1998) 290–299.

an assembly of 20 or more persons in a public place which is wholly or partly open to the air.

A 'public place' is any highway or place to which the public (or any section thereof) has access, on payment or otherwise.[85] A 'public procession' means a procession in a public place.[86]

16.25 The organisers of a public procession[87] are required to give six clear days notice of a proposed public procession which is intended:

(a) to demonstrate support for or opposition to the views or actions of any person or body of persons;
(b) to publicise a cause or campaign; or
(c) to mark or commemorate an event

unless it is not reasonably practicable to give such notice.[88] This notice must set out the date, start time, proposed route and names and addresses of the organisers.[89] On the basis of this information, the police may assess whether imposing conditions is necessary in the circumstances, to avoid not only disorder, but property damage, disruption to community life or the intimidation of others.[90] The conditions laid down may relate to the route of the procession and may include a prohibition on entering any public place specified.[91]

16.26 If, at any time, the chief officer of police reasonably believes that, as a result of special circumstances, the powers to impose conditions will not be sufficient to prevent a public procession from resulting in serious public disorder, he can apply to the local authority for an order banning all public processions for up to three months.[92] In order to obtain a banning order, the Chief Constable must apply to the district council. In London, the order may be made by the Commissioner of Police. In each case, the consent of the Home Secretary is required.[93] In London, there is a further power[94] by which the Commissioners for the Metropolitan or City of London police may make regulations governing 'public processions, public rejoicings or illuminations' which can include orders banning assemblies.

[85] Public Order Act 1986, s 16.

[86] Ibid.

[87] A person may organise a procession by indicating a route, a previously prepared plan is not required and a spontaneous assuming of leadership is sufficient: *Flockhart v Robinson* [1950] 2 KB 498.

[88] Public Order Act 1986, s 11(1); this requirement does not apply to processions 'customarily held' or to processions organised by funeral directors.

[89] Ibid s 11(3).

[90] Ibid s 12(1).

[91] Ibid.

[92] Ibid s 13(1). A similar order under the Public Order Act 1936, s 3 was unsuccessfully challenged in *Kent v Metropolitan Police Commissioner The Times*, 15 May 1981.

[93] Ibid s 13(2), (4).

[94] Metropolitan Police Act 1839, s 52.

However, such regulations cannot be used to ban assemblies which cause no disorder or obstruction.[95]

Although there is no notice requirement or power of prohibition in relation to static assemblies, police may nevertheless impose conditions[96] on them when there is a reasonable belief that disorder, damage, disruption or intimidation may result. It has been held that the mere fact that an assembly may cause discomfort is not sufficient to constitute 'intimidation', some element of compulsion is required.[97] **16.27**

Under section 14A of the Public Order Act 1986[98] banning orders may be made in relation to 'trespassory assemblies', that is gatherings about to take place on land to which the public has no right of access or only a limited right of access and which do not have full permission of the occupier.[99] A Chief Constable can apply for an order to the local authority if he reasonably believes that the assembly may result in serious disruption to the life of the community or damage to land, buildings or monuments.[100] A constable may stop any person he reasonably believes to be on his way to a prohibited assembly and direct him not to proceed in the direction of the assembly.[101] **16.28**

Common law powers continue to apply to the regulation of the conduct of processions and other assemblies for the avoidance of reasonably anticipated and 'imminent'[102] breaches of the peace. The questions that must be considered are: **16.29**

- whether the anticipated violence would (if it occurred) amount to a breach of the peace;[103]
- whether such breach is 'imminent'.

This is, in practice, a 'flexible' guide and is interpreted liberally. In *Duncan v Jones*[104] imminence was wholly absent and the case has been criticised as being unduly restrictive of the freedom of expression and assembly.[105]

A reasonable apprehension of a breach of the peace will justify various measures to prevent or control an assembly. Acts may be justifiable even if they would otherwise **16.30**

95 *Papworth v Coventry* [1967] 1 WLR 663.
96 Public Order Act 1986, s 14.
97 *Police v Reid* [1987] Crim LR 702.
98 Inserted by the Criminal Justice and Public Order Act 1994, s 70.
99 Public Order Act 1986, s 14A(1).
100 Ibid s 14A(1)(b).
101 Ibid s 14C.
102 See *Thomas v Sawkins* [1935] 2 KB 249; *R v Howell (Errol)* [1982] QB 416; *Lewis v Chief Constable of Greater Manchester*, *Independent*, 23 Oct 1991.
103 See para 16.13 above.
104 [1936] 1 KB 218.
105 See eg D Feldman, *Civil Liberties and Human Rights in England and Wales* (Clarendon Press, 1993) 801–802.

constitute an assault or trespass against person or property[106] and whether they are asserted against persons threatening or threatened with violence. Preventive measures include the dispersal of an assembly, attempts to alter its proceedings in such a way as to diffuse tensions, or the arrest and detention of individual offenders. The arrest and binding over of a person to keep the peace,[107] even if he has neither threatened violence nor committed an offence[108] is also justified if that behaviour might provoke others to violence. A reasonable apprehension of breach will also entitle the police to enter or remain on private premises for the purpose of exercising their powers of arrest and detention.[109]

16.31 **Industrial action.** Assemblies in the form of industrial action are governed by special statutory rules.[110] Peaceful picketing is protected from actions in trespass,[111] breaches of contract, or criminal liability for an act which is reasonably necessary to communicate information. Pickets may not, however, unreasonably obstruct highways or access to premises, or attend in excessively large numbers.[112] Injunctions have been granted to limit the number of pickets at a particular location to six.[113] If police officers reasonably believe that there is a real possibility of breach of the peace, they may limit the number of pickets which are present.[114] A picket who stands in front of a vehicle urging the driver not to proceed can properly be convicted of obstructing the highway.[115]

---

106 See *Humphries v Connor* (1864) 17 Ir CLR 1 (police officer removing provocative symbol from the dress of a Protestant Unionist walking through a Catholic area of Northern Ireland); *O'Kelly v Harvey* (1883) 15 Cox CC 435 (magistrate laying a hand on a man while dispersing a meeting of a Catholic organisation being threatened with disruption by Orangemen).

107 See: G Williams, 'Preventive Justice and the Rule of Law' (1953) 16 MLR 417; Law Commission, *Binding Over* (Law Comm No 222 Cm 2439, 1994); D Feldman, 'The King's Peace, the Royal Prerogative and Public Order: The Roots and Early Development of Binding Over Powers' [1988] CLJ 101.

108 See also Law Commission Working Paper No 103, *Criminal Law: Binding Over—the Issues* (HMSO, 1987).

109 In *Thomas v Sawkins* [1935] 2 KB 249; *McLeod v Commissioner of Police of the Metropolis* [1994] 4 All ER 553.

110 See Trade Union and Labour Relations (Consolidation) Act 1992, ss 220–221. Revised Employment Code of Practice on Picketing issued by the Secretary of State under the Employment Act 1980 s 3 (now repealed) and brought into force by the Employment Code of Practice (Picketing) Order 1992, SI 1992/476 is accepted as a statement of good industrial relations practice, although not legally binding.

111 But s 220 does not confer a right to attend on land without the consent of its owner: *British Airports Authority v Ashton* [1983] 1 WLR 1079.

112 *Thomas v National Union of Mineworkers (South Wales Area)* [1986] Ch 20 refers to gatherings in such numbers that the picketers cannot be said to be peacefully obtaining or communicating information (see also *Tynan v Balmer* [1967] 1 QB 91 and *Kavanagh v Hiscock* [1974] QB 600).

113 *Thomas v National Union of Mineworkers (South Wales Area)* (n 112 above); *News Group Newspapers Ltd v Society of Graphical and Allied Trades 1982* [1986] ICR 716.

114 *Piddington v Bates* [1961] 1 WLR 162 (arrest for breach of the peace for refusal to limit number of pickets to two); *Kavanagh v Hiscock* (n 112 above).

115 *Broome v DPP* [1974] AC 587.

Powers in relation to assemblies on private land. The Criminal Justice and Public Order 1994 contains a number of police powers to give directions to groups gathered on private land.[116] The failure to obey such directions is an offence. The powers are as follows: 16.32

- *Powers to remove trespassers*: Police officers who reasonably believe that two or more persons are trespassing on land with a common purpose, that reasonable steps have been taken by the occupier to remove them and those persons have caused damage or using threatening behaviour may direct them to leave.[117]
- *Powers in relation to raves*: Police officers have extensive powers to deal with gatherings in the open air of 100 or more persons (whether or not they are trespassers).[118] Directions may be given to participants to leave the land and remove property.[119]
- *Powers in relation to aggravated trespass*: A senior police officer who reasonably believes that a person is committing, has committed or intends to commit the offence of aggravated trespass[120] or that persons are trespassing with the common purpose of intimidating persons to deter, obstruct or disrupt lawful activity may direct that person or persons to leave.[121] It is an offence to fail to leave or to return to the land as a trespasser within a period of three months from the day on which the direction was given.[122]

Special venues. Open spaces, parks and recreation areas are usually vested in the Crown, or in a local authority, and they may be subject to regulation under a variety of statutory authorities which confer government powers for the use of specific venues.[123] The Local Government Act 1972 also gives district and London borough councils power to provide for the 'good rule and government' and the 'prevention of nuisances' in the whole or any part of their area.[124] Such powers are subject to judicial review if exercised outside of the ambit of the enabling legislation.[125] If a regulation under this provision is in force, the local authority may 16.33

[116] These were designed to deal with perceived threats from 'travellers', 'hunt saboteurs' and the organisers of events such as 'raves'.

[117] Criminal Justice and Public Order Act 1994, s 61 replacing Public Order Act 1986, s 39.

[118] Criminal Justice and Public Order Act 1994, s 63(1).

[119] Ibid s 63(2).

[120] See para 16.18 above.

[121] Criminal Justice and Public Order Act 1994, s 69.

[122] Ibid s 69(3).

[123] For example, Trafalgar Square is vested in the Secretary of State for National Heritage under the Trafalgar Square Act 1844; by the Parks Regulation (Amendment) Act 1926, regulations may be made by the Secretary of State; and under the Trafalgar Square Regulations 1952, no assembly, procession or public speech may take place in Trafalgar Square without permission: see S Bailey, D Harris and B Jones, *Civil Liberties: Cases and Materials* (4th edn, Butterworths, 1995) 190.

[124] s 235.

[125] See *Rai, Allmond and 'Negotiate Now' v United Kingdom* (1995) 19 EHRR CD 93 in which the European Commission found that the regulation of assemblies in the Square was sufficiently prescribed by law.

obtain an injunction to restrain threatened breaches by 'assemblies' of a prohibited type.[126]

16.34 **Protection from harassment.** It has been suggested that unreasonable harassment may be unlawful as a tort where pickets using the highway unreasonably harassed workers who were entering their workplace[127] or where a person makes persistent telephone calls;[128] and the concept has been applied in family law to justify granting injunctions.[129] Nevertheless, it seems that harassment short of physical coercion[130] is not tortious at common law[131] and the House of Lords in *Hunter v Canary Wharf*[132] disapproved of extending the law of nuisance.

16.35 The area is now covered by the Protection from Harassment Act 1997 which makes it a criminal offence to pursue a course of conduct which amounts to harassment of another.[133] The Act does not contain a comprehensive definition of 'harassment': it includes alarming a person or causing a person distress and a course of conduct with this consequence must involve conduct on at least two occasions.[134] It is a defence to show that the course of conduct was reasonable.[135] It is clear that:

> Whatever may have been the purpose behind the Act, its words are clear, and it can cover harassment of any sort. Thus, there may, perhaps in many instances there will be a need for the court to balance the interests of the victim of the harassment against the rights of the person carrying out the course of conduct which amounts to harassment. Those rights will include, in any appropriate case, the right to protest peacefully.[136]

The Act has been used to prosecute protestors on a number of occasions.

---

126 *Burnley Borough Council v England* (1977) 76 LGR 393 and (1978) 77 LGR 227 (interim and permanent injunction to prevent a procession of dog owners in parks protesting against a bye-law banning dogs from parks).

127 See *Thomas v National Union of Miner Workers (South Wales Area)* [1986] Ch 20, 63 *per* Scott J which discussed the position in relation to picketing (which was explained as being based on nuisance by Stuart Smith J in *News Group Newspapers Ltd v Society of Graphical and Allied Trades 1982 (No2)* [1987] ICR 181, 205.

128 *Khorasandjian v Bush* [1993] QB 727. The decision was overruled in *Hunter v Canary Wharf* [1997] AC 655.

129 See eg *Burris v Azdani* [1995] 1 WLR 1372, 1377 *per* Lord Bingham MR; *McCann v Wright* [1995] 1 WLR 1556; *Johnson v Walton* [1990] 1 FLR 350.

130 *Davey v Chief Constable of RUC* [1988] NILR 139.

131 See eg *Patel v Patel* [1988] 2 FLR 179 at 182 *per* Waterhouse J.

132 [1997] AC 655.

133 Protection from Harassment Act 1997, s 2, the Act also gives rise to civil remedies, see s 1 and s 3.

134 Ibid s 7.

135 Ibid s 1(3)(c).

136 *DPP v Moseley, The Times,* 23 Jun 1999; see also *Huntingdom Life Sciences v Curtin, The Times,* 11 Dec 1997 per Eady J (the Act was not intended to be used to restrict those who were exercising their right to protest about a matter of public interest).

(3) The scope of the right to freedom of association

There is no positive right of association in English law. However, the common law has consistently recognised the autonomy of associations in controlling their membership.[137] English law does not place any general limits on freedom of association; and there are no general requirements for registration of political parties or other associations. The courts have not addressed the question of whether freedom of association extends to a right of 'non-association'. It has, however, been acknowledged that freedom of association is a 'mutual right', so 'there can be no right of an individual to associate with other individuals who are not willing to associate with him'.[138] **16.36**

In some cases, a common law freedom of private association with others has been recognised. Thus, in *Re V*[139] an 18-year-old cerebral palsy sufferer obtained a declaration that at the age of majority he would be entitled to choose where he was to live and with whom he would associate as well as an injunction restraining his mother from interfering with those rights. **16.37**

A political party which wishes its name to appear on the ballot paper or to make party political broadcasts must now register.[140] Trade unions have long been subject to legislative regulation and are now governed by a complex legislative code.[141] Other restrictions are imposed on the freedom of association for political purposes for the protection of public order and national security. **16.38**

(4) Trade unions and the right to strike

(a) Introduction

The courts in the nineteenth and early twentieth centuries regarded the agreement of association between members of a trade union with considerable suspicion.[142] In 1834 the 'Tolpuddle Martyrs' were convicted of being members of an illegal society simply because members had taken oaths of mutual fidelity.[143] In *Hornby v Close*[144] it was held that the United Order of Boilermakers was an association **16.39**

---

[137] See eg *Cheall v Association of Professional Executive Clerical and Computer Staff* [1983] 2 AC 180 (a trade union can determine who it will admit to membership).

[138] Ibid 191.

[139] [1995] 2 FLR 1003; see *Cambridgeshire CC v R* [1994] 2 FCR 973 and see generally, K Ewing, 'Freedom of Association', in C McCrudden and G Chambers (eds), *Individual Rights and the Law in Britain* (Oxford University Press, 1994) 239–263.

[140] Registration of Political Parties Act 1998, see para 20.09 below.

[141] See para 16.46 below.

[142] For a general history see W Wedderburn, *The Worker and the Law* (3rd edn, Penguin, 1986) Chap 7.

[143] *R v Lovelass* (1834) 6 C & P 596.

[144] (1867) LR 2 QB 153.

whose main objects were illegal as being in restraint of trade. This decision was reversed by the Trade Union Act 1871 which provided that the purposes of a trade union would not, merely by reason of the fact that they were in restraint of trade, be unlawful.[145] Unions were granted a limited 'statutory immunity' against liability in economic torts.[146] In the early part of the twentieth century legislation was subsequently needed to reverse a House of Lords decision that trade unions could not use their funds to finance political parties.[147] The rights of workers to membership of a trade union was first recognised by statute in 1971.[148]

16.40 The statutory framework governing the rights and responsibilities of trade unions is now found in the Trade Union and Labour Relations (Consolidation) Act 1992. Trade unions are defined as organisations of workers whose principal purposes include the regulation of relations between those workers and employers or employers' associations.[149] Such an organisation must have some degree of formal structure: it cannot be a casual grouping of workers.[150]

16.41 The right to belong to a trade union[151] protects a job applicant from discrimination on the basis of his union status[152] and provides an employee who has been terminated or otherwise aggrieved by reason of his union involvement, with a claim for unfair dismissal[153] or unlawful victimisation.[154] A trade unionist cannot be subjected to any detriment short of dismissal by any act or deliberate failure to act by his employer.[155] Furthermore, the Secretary of State has power to make regulations about cases where a worker is subjected to detriment or dismissed because he refuses to enter into a contract which would differ from the terms of a collective agreement which applies to him.[156]

(b) The 'right to strike'

16.42 A 'strike' has been defined as any 'concerted stoppage of work done with a view to

---

[145] Now the Trade Union and Labour Relations (Consolidation) Act 1992, s 244.

[146] See generally, Wedderburn (142 above) 578–623; and see para 16.43 below.

[147] Trade Union Act 1913, reversing *Amalgamated Society of Railway Servants v Osborne* [1910] AC 87.

[148] Industrial Relations Act 1971, s 5.

[149] Trade Union and Labour Relations (Consolidation) Act 1992, s 1(a).

[150] *Midland Cold Storage Ltd v Turner* [1972] ICR 230.

[151] But see *Council of Civil Service Unions v Minister for the Civil Service* [1985] AC 374.

[152] Trade Union and Labour Relations (Consolidation) Act 1992, s 137.

[153] Ibid s 152.

[154] Ibid s 146; see also Employment Relations Act 1999, s 3 (empowering the Secretary of State to make regulations prohibiting the compilation or use of 'blacklists' of trade unionists).

[155] Trade Union and Labour Relations (Consolidation) Act 1992, s 146 (as amended by Employment Relations Act 1999, Sch 2).

[156] Employment Relations Act 1999, s 17; this would have the effect of reversing the decision of *Associated Newspapers Ltd v Wilson* [1994] 2 AC 454; see generally, K Ewing, 'Freedom of Association and the Employment Act 1999' [1999] ILJ 283, 286–288.

improving wages or conditions or giving vent to a grievance or making a protest'.[157] Strike action includes a ban on overtime and rest-day working.[158] 'Industrial action' has been very widely interpreted and includes 'working to rule'[159] and a refusal to work voluntary overtime.[160]

There are some *dicta* which suggest that English law recognises a 'right to strike' which is an 'essential element in collective bargaining'.[161] However, strikes and industrial action give rise to a large range of potential claims in tort against the trade union and its members.[162] There is no 'right to strike' providing general protection against such claims. There is, however, a limited statutory immunity for acts which are done 'in contemplation and furtherance of a trade dispute'.[163] These will not be actionable in specified economic torts[164] provided the union complies with statutory requirements of a ballot[165] and the strike does not constitute 'secondary action'.[166] **16.43**

In some circumstances it is automatically unfair to dismiss an employee from taking part in industrial action. The industrial action must be covered by the 'statutory immunity' and the dismissal must be within eight weeks from the day on which the employee started to take the industrial action.[167] **16.44**

Certain groups of workers are not permitted to engage in strikes or industrial action. It is an offence to do any act calculated to induce any police officer to withhold his services.[168] It is also an offence for a member of the armed forces to participate in industrial action [169] or if a person maliciously and advisedly endeavours to seduce any member of Her Majesty's Armed Forces from his duty or allegiance to Her Majesty.[170] Similarly, it is unlawful for a person to induce a prison officer to withhold his services.[171] **16.45**

---

[157] *Tramp Shipping Corporation v Greenwich Marine Inc* [1975] ICR 261, 266; see also Trade Union and Labour Relations (Consolidation) Act 1992, s 246.

[158] *Connex South Eastern Ltd v National Union of Rail, Maritime and Transport Workers* [1999] IRLR 249.

[159] *Secretary of State for Employment v ASLEF (No 2)* [1972] 2 QB 455.

[160] *Faust v Power Packing Casemakers Ltd* [1983] ICR 292.

[161] *Crofter Hand Woven Harris Tweed Company v Veitch* [1942] AC 435, 463.

[162] See generally, M Brazier (ed), *Clerk and Lindsell on Torts* (18th edn Sweet & Maxwell, 1998) Chap 23.

[163] The golden formula now defined by Trade Union and Labour Relations (Consolidation) Act 1992, s 219; for a fuller treatment, see *Harvey on Industrial Relations and Employment Law* (Butterworths, 2000), Div N, Chap 15.

[164] Trade Union and Labour Relations (Consolidation) Act 1992, s 219.

[165] Ibid s 226.

[166] Ibid s 224.

[167] Ibid s 238A, inserted by Employment Relations Act 1999, Sch 5; see generally, K Ewing, 'Freedom of Association and the Employment Act 1999' [1999] ILJ 283, 291–293.

[168] Police Act 1964, s 53(1).

[169] Army Act 1955, s 29A and ss 31–39; Air Force Act 1955, s 29A and ss 31–39; Naval Discipline Act 1957, ss 7–18.

[170] Incitement to Disaffection Act 1934, s 1; cf *R v Arrowsmith* [1975] QB 678.

[171] Criminal Justice and Public Order Act 1994, s 127.

(c) The regulation of trade unions

16.46 Trade unions are subject to a complex statutory code which regulates their activities.[172] If an organisation is a 'trade union', it is subject to legislative regulation in many areas. In particular, a trade union must:

- compile and maintain a register of the names and addresses of its members;[173]
- appoint an independent scrutineer for certain union elections and other ballots;[174]
- hold elections for the general secretaries and members of the national executive at five-yearly intervals.[175]

16.47 Industrial action only attracts statutory immunity from claims in tort if strike ballots are held.[176] However, trade unions are no longer required to give notice of the names of any employees they propose to ballot.[177]

16.48 Members of trade unions have a number of statutory rights in relation to their unions. Thus, a member of a trade union has a right to require the union to conduct a ballot before inducing its members from taking part in industrial action.[178] In addition, a member has a right not to be 'unjustifiably disciplined' by his union.[179]

(d) The rights to recognition and consultation

16.49 English law provides no general right of trade unions to be consulted[180] by employers. There are rights of consultation for recognised trade unions in relation to health and safety representation,[181] collective redundancies,[182] transfers of undertakings[183] and occupational pension schemes.[184] Limited new rights for trade union recognition based on workplace balloting have been created by the Employment Relations Act 1999.[185]

---

[172] Consolidated in the Trade Union and Labour Relations (Consolidation) Act 1992.
[173] Ibid ss 24–26.
[174] Ibid ss 46–61; ss 73-81, ss 100–100E.
[175] Ibid Pt I.
[176] Ibid s 219 and s 226.
[177] Ibid s 226A (as amended by Employment Relations Act 1999), reversing the effect of *Blackpool and the Fylde College v National Association of Teachers in Further and Higher Education* [1994] ICR 648; for the subsequent unsuccessful Convention application, see para 16.91 below.
[178] Trade Union and Labour Relations (Consolidation) Act 1992, s 62.
[179] Ibid ss 64–65; cf Sir Gavin Lightman and J Bowers, 'Incorporation of the ECHR and its Impact on Employment Law' [1998] EHRLR 560, 573.
[180] See the discussion in J Hendy, 'The Human Rights Act, Article 11 and the Right to Strike' [1998] EHRLR 582, 611-612.
[181] Safety Representatives and Safety Committees Regulations 1977, SI 1977/500.
[182] Trade Union and Labour Relations (Consolidation) Act 1992, s 188.
[183] Transfer of Undertakings (Protection of Employment) Regulations 1981, SI 1981/1794.
[184] Pension Schemes Act 1993.
[185] See now the Trade Union and Labour Relations (Consolidation) Act 1992 ss 70A, 70B and 70C and Sch A1.

(5) Other restrictions on freedom of association

(a) Prohibition of quasi-military associations

The control or management of quasi-military associations is a criminal offence. Section 2 of the Public Order Act 1936 deals with associations which are organised or trained or equipped either for the purpose of enabling them to be employed in 'usurping the functions of the police or of the armed forces'[186] or for the purpose of enabling them to be employed for the use or display of physical force in promoting any political object.[187] Taking part in the control or management of such an organisation is an offence.[188] The organisers of a fascist group known as 'Spearhead' were successfully prosecuted under the second limb of the section.[189] The section has also been used against organisers of IRA units.[190] **16.50**

Other statutory limitations on freedom of association in the public order context are found in section 1 of the Public Order Act 1936. Unless the chief officer of police decides that wearing uniforms during ceremonial (or special) occasions will not cause public disorder, section 1 prohibits the wearing, in a public place, of a uniform signifying association with any political organisation or with the promotion of a political object. The legislative ban was originally introduced as a response to an increase in the wearing of uniforms by political groups in the 1930s, in particular the Fascists.[191] In *O'Moran v DPP*[192] the Divisional Court held that a black beret was a 'uniform' because each member of a group wore a beret to indicate that they were together and in association. **16.51**

(b) National security

The most stringent restrictions on the right of association have been the prohibition, on grounds of national security, of membership or participation in the activities of certain proscribed organisations.[193] At present, only the Irish Republican Army and the Irish National Liberation Army[194] are proscribed, but others may be added at the discretion of the Secretary of State.[195] **16.52**

---

[186] Ibid s 2(1)(a).
[187] Ibid s 2(1)(b).
[188] Ibid s 2.
[189] *R v Jordan and Tyndall* [1963] Crim LR 123.
[190] *R v Fell* [1974] Crim LR 673.
[191] The section resulted in a number of prosecutions: see *R v Wood* (1937) 81 Sol Jo 108; *R v Charnley* (1937) 81 Sol Jo 509; *O'Moran v DPP*; *Whelan v DPP* [1975] QB 864.
[192] [1975] QB 864.
[193] Prevention of Terrorism (Temporary Provisions) Act 1989, s 1, and the Northern Ireland (Emergency Provisions) Act 1991, s 28.
[194] Prevention of Terrorism Act (Temporary Provisions) Act 1989, s 2.
[195] In 1980, the Government rejected the argument that one or other of the National Front and the Socialist Workers Party ought to be banned as a result of the disorder caused by confrontation between them: Home Office 'Review of the Public Order Act 1936 and Related Legislation' (Cmnd 7891) 1981, 11.

16.53 In the same way, fears of communist threats to external security during the Cold War led to 'purge' and 'positive vetting' procedures in the civil service. From 1985, the policy was to remove or exclude from employment, in all posts which are considered vital to the security of the state:

> members of any subversive group . . . whose aims are to undermine or overthrow Parliamentary democracy in the UK and Northern Ireland by political, industrial or violent means.[196]

Positive vetting procedures revised in 1990 require scrutiny of the character and circumstances of a civil servant in order to ensure that members of such subversive organisations are not employed in the first place.[197]

16.54 The restrictions which can lawfully be placed on the freedom of association of Government employees on 'national security' grounds are illustrated by the GCHQ affair. In the early 1980s staff employed in intelligence gathering work at GCHQ engaged in industrial action and caused some disruption to the service. In January 1984 the Government unilaterally decided to remove all trade union membership rights from these staff. This was done by invoking the royal prerogative to vary the terms and conditions of the staff and by issuing a ministerial order to remove statutory protection against dismissal for participating in trade union activity. The House of Lords upheld the Government's decision on the basis that the Government were entitled to rely on considerations of national security.[198]

(c) Conspiracy

16.55 An association for the purpose of committing a crime, to defraud or do acts which tend to corrupt public morals or outrage public decency is itself a criminal offence: conspiracy.[199] The tort of conspiracy is much wider than the crime,[200] making it actionable for two or more persons to agree to do an unlawful act, or to do a lawful act by unlawful means, or to perform acts other than for their own legitimate benefit, with the object of inflicting damage on a third party.[201]

---

[196] 76 HC Debates 621, 3 Apr1985.

[197] 177 HC Debates 159-161 (WA), 24 Jul 1990.

[198] *Council of Civil Service Unions v Minister for the Civil Service* [1985] AC 374; see S Fredman 'Note: Crown Employment, Prerogative Powers, Consultation and National Security' (1985) 14 ILJ 42; for the case brought under the Convention, see para 16.91 below.

[199] Criminal Law Act 1977, Pt I.

[200] However, for the purposes of the tort the plaintiff must prove that he has suffered damage.

[201] See *Hubbard v Pitt* [1976] 1 QB 142; *Lonrho v Shell Petroleum Company Ltd (No 2)* [1982] AC 173; *Lonrho plc v Fayed* [1992] 1 AC 448.

C. The Law Under the European Convention

(1) Introduction

Article 11 of the Convention provides: 16.56

> (1) Everyone has the right to freedom of peaceful assembly and to freedom of association with others, including the right to form and to join trade unions for the protection of his interests.
>
> (2) No restrictions shall be placed on the exercise of these rights other than such as are prescribed by law and are necessary in a democratic society in the interests of national security or public safety, for the prevention of disorder or crime, for the protection of health or morals or for the protection of the rights and freedoms of others. This article shall not prevent the imposition of lawful restrictions on the exercise of these rights by members of the armed forces, of the police or of the administration of the state.

This Article protects the two distinct freedoms of peaceful assembly and association. The right to form and to join trade unions, while specifically mentioned in Article 11(1), is not a separate right, but a facet of the right to freedom of association. The two freedoms overlap in the area of industrial action and picketing which may involve assembly or procession and constitutes a collective right of a trade union. The protection of opinions and the freedom to express them is also one of the objectives enshrined in Article 11.[202] Rights guaranteed by Article 11, like the other rights guaranteed by the Convention, are intended to be practical and effective.[203]

(2) Assembly

(a) The scope of the right

The freedom of assembly is a 'fundamental right in a democracy and . . . is one of 16.57
the foundations of such a society'.[204] As a result, the right should not be interpreted restrictively.[205] In fact, the principles which have evolved have largely been developed in the context of political demonstrations; and protection has been afforded only to 'gatherings for a common purpose'.[206] 'Assembly' has been construed as including all types of gatherings, such as public and private meetings,[207]

---

[202] *Socialist Party v Turkey* (1998) 27 EHRR 51 para 41; *Vogt v Germany* (1995) 21 EHRR 205 para 64.

[203] See *United Communist Party of Turkey v Turkey* (1998) 4 BHRC 1 para 33; for a general discussion of the doctrine, see para 6.28ff below.

[204] *Rassemblement Jurassien Unité Jurassienne v Switzerland* (1979) 17 DR 93, 119, EComm HR.

[205] *G v Germany* (1989) 60 DR 256, 263, EComm HR.

[206] S Lewis-Anthony, 'Case Law of Article 11 of the European Convention on Human Rights' in 'Freedom of Association', Reykjavik Seminar Proceedings, 34A *Yearbook of the European Convention on Human Rights* (Nijhoff, 1993) 30, n 15.

[207] *Rassemblement Jurassien Unité Jurassienne v Switzerland* (1979) (n 204 above).

marches, public processions[208] and 'sit-ins'.[209] However, Article 11 does not guarantee a right to pass and re-pass in public places or to assemble for purely social purposes anywhere one wishes.[210]

16.58 Article 11 protection is confined to 'peaceful' assemblies. A distinction has been drawn in the cases between violence which is 'incidental to' a peaceful assembly and violence which is an intended result of the organisers.[211] Incidental violence will not remove Article 11 protection but intentional disruption will render the assembly 'unpeaceful' and therefore unprotected.[212] Thus, a non-violent 'sit-in' blocking the entrance to American barracks in Germany was considered peaceful,[213] as was a demonstration involving music and rhythmical instruments.[214] Non-violent assemblies will retain their peaceful character notwithstanding the violent response of other demonstrators:[215]

> the possibility of violent counter-demonstrations, or the possibility of extremists with violent intentions, not members of the organising association, joining the demonstration cannot as such take away that right.[216]

The individual involved in an assembly will not cease to enjoy Article 11 rights because there is sporadic violence or because criminal acts are committed by others in the group.[217] Furthermore, a peaceful assembly will be protected under Article 11 even if it is illegal under domestic law.[218]

(b) Limitations on assembly

16.59 Any restriction on peaceful assemblies must be justified under Article 11(2). In common with other qualified rights[219] such restrictions must be:

- prescribed by law;[220]
- for one of the legitimate aims set out in Article 11(2);
- necessary in a democratic society.[221]

16.60 Article 11(2) allows the interferences with the right of assembly in the interests of national security or public safety, for the prevention of disorder or crime, for the

208 *Christians Against Racism and Fascism v United Kingdom* (1980) 21 DR 138.
209 *G v Germany* (1989) 60 DR 256, EComm HR.
210 *Mark Anderson v United Kingdom* [1998] EHRLR 218.
211 *Christians Against Racism and Fascism v United Kingdom* (n 208 above) 150.
212 Ibid.
213 *G v Germany* (n 209 above).
214 *S v Austria* Application 13812/88, 13 Dec 1990.
215 *Christians Against Racism and Fascism v United Kingdom* (n 208 above).
216 Ibid para 4.
217 *Ezelin v France* (1991) 14 EHRR 362.
218 *G v Germany* (n 209 above).
219 See para 6.90ff above.
220 See para 6.12ff above.
221 See para 6.146ff above.

protection of health or morals or for the protection of the rights and freedoms of others. However, the most common ground for restricting assemblies is that it is necessary for the regulation of public order. This is for the legitimate aim of 'prevention of disorder and crime' and 'protection of the rights and freedoms of others'. Once a foreseeable danger of disorder has been identified, the national authorities have a wide margin of appreciation as to the measures necessary to deal with it.[222]

A requirement of prior notification or permission for assemblies is not of *itself* an interference with freedom of assembly.[223] However, bans on assemblies[224] and criminal or disciplinary[225] penalties for participation in them require justification in accordance with Article 11(2). **16.61**

Bans on particular assemblies have also been upheld in a range of cases: for example, because a demonstration was likely to be excessively noisy[226] and because passers-by were disrupted by a protest in a busy square.[227] There are circumstances in which a total ban on demonstrations may be justified under Article 11(2). A ban relating to a small area for a short period of time in order to dispel tension has been found to be acceptable.[228] A blanket ban on processions for a specified time has been found to be justified on the ground that it would prevent disorder resulting from the activities of one group even though it interfered with the freedom of assembly of other groups.[229] **16.62**

A penalty for participating in a prohibited assembly will be justified if the prohibition was justified under Article 11(2). Thus, the Commission took the view that convictions of demonstrators who had set up a tent outside the Norwegian parliament and had refused a police order to move were justified to prevent disorder as 'a demonstration by setting up a tent for several days in an area open to public traffic must necessarily cause disorder'.[230] Furthermore, there is no breach of Article 11 if a participant in a demonstration who incites or provokes others to violence is arrested.[231] However, imposing penalties for participating in a lawful **16.63**

[222] *Rassemblement Jurassien Unité Jurassienne v Switzerland* (1979) 17 DR 93, EComm HR; for a general discussion of the doctrine of 'margin of appreciation', see para 6.31ff above.
[223] Ibid 119.
[224] Ibid *Christians Against Racism and Fascism v United Kingdom* (1980) 21 DR 138, EComm HR.
[225] *Ezelin v France* (1991) 14 EHRR 362 para 41.
[226] *S v Austria* Application 13812/88, 13 Dec 1990.
[227] *Friedl v Austria* Application 15225/89), 30 Nov 1992.
[228] *Rassemblement Jurassien Unité Jurassienne v Switzerland* (n 222 above).
[229] *Christians Against Racism and Fascism v United Kingdom* (n 224 above); see also *The Greek Case* (1969) 12 YB 1, 171, EComm HR (general restrictions on assemblies in Greece not justified under Art 11(2)).
[230] *X v Norway* (1984) 6 EHRR 357.
[231] *Chorherr v Austria* (1993) 17 EHRR 358; see also *Steel v United Kingdom* (1998) 28 EHRR 603 (both of which dealt with the 'protest' issues under Art 10 but held that the same reasoning applied to the Art 11 claims).

assembly will be a breach of Article 11. In *Ezelin v France*[232] the applicant was a lawyer and trade union official who took part in a demonstration which became violent. Although he was not involved in the violence he was disciplined for his 'breach of discretion' in not dissociating himself from the march and failing to co-operate with the police. Even though the penalty was relatively insignificant, the Court found the sanction was disproportionate to the aim pursued (the prevention of disorder) and that a 'just balance' must not discourage people from making their beliefs peaceably known.

(c) Positive protection of the right of assembly

16.64 There is a positive duty on the state to take steps to enable lawful demonstrations to proceed peacefully. In particular, the state must protect individuals exercising their right of freedom of peaceful assembly from violent disturbance by other demonstrators.[233] Rival gatherings in potentially volatile situations may *each* claim to be exercising their freedom of assembly and the state has a wide margin of appreciation[234] in dealing with them.[235] In the *Plattform* case,[236] the Court found that all appropriate measures had been taken when a cordon of riot police was formed to prevent imminent physical violence between two groups, notwithstanding that eggs and clumps of grass were thrown by one group at the other.

16.65 Whether the state is under a positive duty to require private individuals to allow peaceful assemblies by others on their own property is a question which has not been addressed. The increasing private ownership of quasi-public places such as shopping malls will impinge on freedom of assembly if it can be exercised only in a public place.[237] A positive duty under Article 11 could oblige the state to make provision to allow freedom of assembly in such spaces.[238]

(3) Association

(a) The scope of the right

16.66 Article 11 protects the freedom of individuals to form and join a collective entity or 'association' for the furtherance of the common interests of the members of the group.[239] Mere casual contacts are not sufficient to establish an association, it

232 (1991) 14 EHRR 362.

233 *Plattform 'Ärzte für das Leben' v Austria* (1988) 13 EHRR 204 para 34.

234 For a general discussion of the doctrine, see para 6.31ff above.

235 Ibid.

236 n 233 above.

237 See generally, K Gray and S Gray, 'Civil Rights, Civil Wrongs and Quasi-Public Space' [1999] EHRLR 46.

238 Cf D Harris, M O'Boyle and C Warbrick *Law of the European Convention on Human Rights* (Butterworths, 1995) 419 and see *Mark Anderson v United Kingdom* [1998] EHRLR 218.

239 See *Young, James and Webster v United Kingdom* (1984) B 39, 47, ECommHR; see also *Association X v Sweden* (1977) 9 DR 5, EComm HR.

involves a deliberate effort to set up an organisational structure.[240] This is not the same as a general liberty to enjoy the personal company of others. As the Commission said in *McFeeley v United Kingdom*:[241]

> the concept of freedom of association of which the right to form and join trade unions is a special aspect, is concerned with the right to form or be affiliated with a group or organisation pursuing particular aims. It does not concern the right of prisoners to share the company of other prisoners or to 'associate' with other prisoners in this sense.

The right does not, for example, include a right of association with animals.[242]

(b) The meaning of 'association'

The term 'association' has an autonomous Convention meaning and the classification in national law has only 'relative value'.[243] The Article does *not* protect 'public' or 'para-administrative' associations such as professional regulatory authorities.[244] Because they remain outside of the protection of Article 11, a compulsory membership requirement in relation to such an organisation will not violate the freedom of association. However, the Court will inquire whether, in a given case, an association is properly classified as being 'public': **16.67**

> If contracting states were able, at their discretion, by classifying an association as 'public' or 'para-administrative' to remove it from the scope of Art 11, that would give them such latitude that it might lead to results incompatible with the object and purpose of the Convention.[245]

The performance, by a private association, of functions provided for by law does not transform the association into a public law body.[246]

Trade unions will be protected by Article 11, whether or not they are considered 'associations' under national law.[247] Political parties are a form of association essential to the proper functioning of democracy and there is no doubt that they **16.68**

---

[240] See C Tomuschat, 'Freedom of Association' in R St J Macdonald, F Matscher and H Petzold (eds), *The European System for the Protection of Human Rights* (Nijhoff, 1993) 494.

[241] (1980) 20 DR 44 para 14, EComm HR; see also *X v United Kingdom* (1982) 5 EHRR 260 (no right to receive prison visits from an acquaintance).

[242] *Artingsoll v United Kingdom* (1995) 19 EHRR CD 92 (no right to have a pet in sheltered housing).

[243] See *Chassagnou and others v France* (1999) 7 BHRC 151 para 100; and see para 6.17 above for a discussion of 'autonomous meaning'.

[244] See *Le Compte, Van Leuven and De Meyere v Belgium* (1981) 4 EHRR 1 paras 64 to 65; *A v Spain* (1990) 66 DR 188, EComm HR; *Barthold v Federal Republic of Germany* (1981) 26 DR 145, EComm HR; *Revert and Legallis v France* (1989) 62 DR 309, EComm HR.

[245] *Chassagnou and others v France* (n 243 above) para 100.

[246] *Sigurjonsson (Sigurdur A) v Iceland* (1993) 16 EHRR 462.

[247] See P van Dijk and G van Hoof, *Theory and Practice of the European Convention on Human Rights* (3rd edn, Kluwer, 1998) 591.

come within the scope of Article 11.[248] It is not clear whether Article 11 protects associations for the primary purpose of economic gain.[249]

(c) Right not to join associations

16.69 The freedom of association also extends to the right of an individual to refrain from joining an association. The existence of this 'negative right' of association, once problematic, has now been settled in the context of the 'closed shop' cases.[250] The Court in *Young, James and Webster v United Kingdom*[251] was careful not to pass judgment on the closed shop system generally,[252] but found that the requirement on the applicants to join a specified union, imposed after their engagement and upon threat of dismissal, amounted to compulsion that 'strikes at the very substance of the freedom guaranteed by Article 11'.[253] However, in *Sigurjonsson v Iceland*[254] the Court explicitly affirmed that 'Article 11 must be viewed as encompassing a negative right of association', and found that a 'pre-entry' closed shop also constituted compulsion going to the heart of the freedom. In *Chassagnou v France*[255] it was held to be a breach of Article 11 to compel landowners opposed to hunting on ethical grounds to join a hunter's association and to transfer their hunting rights to it. This went beyond what was necessary to ensure that a fair balance was struck between conflicting interests and was not proportionate to the aim pursued.

16.70 However, there will be no breach of 'negative freedom of association' if the applicant is not subject to compulsion. Thus, in *Sibson v United Kingdom*[256] the refusal of the applicant's co-workers to work with him as a result of his non-membership did not amount to an obligation on the applicant to join the union, in light of the absence of a formal closed shop agreement and the employer's offer of alternative work of a similar kind. In *Gustafsson v Sweden*[257] the Court held that a boycott of the applicant's business by a trade union to pressure him into entering a collective agreement did not constitute a compulsion striking at the very substance of the

[248] See *United Communist Party of Turkey v Turkey* (1998) 26 EHRR 121; *Socialist Party v Turkey* (1998) 27 EHRR 51; *Freedom and Democracy Party v Turkey*, Judgment of 8 Dec 1999.

[249] See the discussion in Tomuschat (n 240 above) 495–496.

[250] *Sigurjonsson (Sigurdur A) v Iceland* (n 246 above); *Young, James and Webster v United Kingdom* (1981) 4 EHRR 38.

[251] n 250 above; for discussions of this case, see: M Forde, 'The "Closed Shop" Case' [1982] 11 ILJ 1; A Drzemczewski and F Wooldridge, 'The Closed Shop Case in Strasbourg' [1982] 31 ICLQ 396.

[252] (1981) 4 EHRR 38 paras 53-55, the Court assumed that Art 11 does not guarantee the negative aspect of the freedom of association on the same footing as the positive aspect, and that, accordingly, compulsion to join a particular trade union may not always be contrary to the Convention.

[253] n 250 above para 55.

[254] (1993) 16 EHRR 462.

[255] (1999) 7 BHRC 151.

[256] (1993) 17 EHRR 193.

[257] (1996) 22 EHRR 409.

freedom of association. As a result, the state was not obliged to intervene in relationships between private individuals.

(d) The content of the right

Forming of associations. Article 11 includes a 'right to form' associations. This right does not apply solely to the creation of trade unions, as the wording would imply, but applies to all types of associations,[258] including employers' associations[259] and political parties.[260] **16.71**

Organisation of associations. The protection afforded by Article 11 lasts for the association's entire life and dissolution of an association by the state must satisfy the requirements of Article 11(2).[261] The right to form associations includes the rights of associations to draw up their own rules and administer their own affairs.[262] **16.72**

Joining of associations. Although everyone has the right to form an association, this does not entail a right to join existing associations. An association has no obligation to allow someone to retain membership.[263] **16.73**

The rights of associations. An association has rights of its own to enable it to operate effectively. These include freedom of expression.[264] However, Article 11 does not confer upon associations any right to legal personality.[265] **16.74**

(e) Right to form and join trade unions

The right to form and join trade unions is expressly included in Article 11 and it is clear that: **16.75**

> the Convention safeguards the freedom to protect the occupational interests of trade union members by trade union action, the conduct and development of which the state must both permit and make possible.[266]

However, Article 11 'does not secure any particular treatment of trade unions or their members'[267] and states are only required to protect rights that are 'indispensable' for the effective enjoyment of trade union freedom.[268]

---

[258] *X v Belgium* (1961) 4 YB 324, EComm HR.

[259] See C Tomuschat, 'Freedom of Association' in R St J Macdonald, F Matscher and H Petzold (eds), *The European System for the Protection of Human Rights* (Nijhoff, 1993) 494.

[260] See eg *Socialist Party and others v Turkey* (1998) 27 EHRR 51.

[261] See *United Communist Party of Turkey v Turkey* (1998) 4 BHRC 1 para 33.

[262] *Cheall v United Kingdom* (1985) 8 EHRR 74 (in relation to trade unions); see generally Tomuschat (n 259 above) 499–500.

[263] *Cheall v United Kingdom* (n 262 above).

[264] See Tomuschat (n 259 above) 498.

[265] In *Lavisse v France* (1991) 70 DR 218, EComm HR, the refusal of the authorities to register an association deprived it of legal personality, but did not prevent it from carrying out its activities.

[266] *National Union of Belgian Police v Belgium* (1975) 1 EHRR 578 para 39.

[267] *Swedish Engine Drivers' Union v Sweden* (1976) 1 EHRR 617 para 39.

[268] Ibid.

16.76 The *only* right which has been held to be 'indispensable' is the right to be heard by the employer,[269] and not a right to be consulted,[270] or to be allowed to enter into a collective agreement.[271] Article 11 gives the state a 'free choice of means' as to how it will protect the right to be heard; such means involve the right to bring claims or representations other than those before the Court, including the right to strike.

16.77 The right to strike, while an important tool for ensuring the right of unions to be heard, is *not* protected by Article 11. In *Schmidt and Dahlström v Sweden*[272] the Court said that:

> The grant of a right to strike represents without any doubt one of the most important means [of protecting the occupational interests of trade union members by trade union action] . . . but there are others. Such a right, which is not expressly enshrined in Article 11, may be subject under national law to regulation of a kind that limits its exercise in certain instances.

In *National Association of Teachers in Further and Higher Education v United Kingdom*[273] a statutory obligation to disclose the names of trade union members to an employer before strike action was taken was not a 'significant limitation on the right to take collective action'. However, the Commission did recognise that in certain circumstances, such a requirement could give rise to an unjustified interference under Article 11.

(f) Interference with freedom of association

16.78 The most obvious form of interference is prohibiting the formation of an association. However, interference can take a number of other forms. Preventing a person from joining an association would be an interference, as would putting pressure on a person to leave an association or imposing sanctions because of membership. The following have been held to be interferences with the freedom of association: the intimidation of an employee to make him give up his function in a trade union,[274] the dismissal of a civil servant for refusal to dissociate herself from a political party[275] and the dismissal of an employee because of activity in a particular political party.[276]

---

[269] *National Union of Belgian Police v Belgium* (n 266 above) 39; *Swedish Engine Drivers' Union v Sweden* (n 267 above).

[270] *National Union of Belgian Police v Belgium* (n 266 above).

[271] In *Swedish Engine Drivers' Union v Sweden* (1976) 1 EHRR 617 (although unable to conclude an agreement, the trade union had been permitted to make representations to protect its members interests, see para 41); for justifiable limitations on this right see para 16.79 below.

[272] (1976) 1 EHRR 632 para 36.

[273] (1998) 25 EHRR CD 122; the relevant statutory provision has now been repealed, see para 16.47 above.

[274] *X v Ireland* (1971) 14 YB 198.

[275] *Vogt v Germany* (1995) 21 EHRR 205.

[276] *Van der Heijden v Netherlands* (1985) 41 DR 264, EComm HR.

(g) Restrictions on freedom of association

Any interference on freedom of association must be justified under Article 11(2). In common with the position in relation to other qualified rights[277] the restrictions must be: 16.79

- prescribed by law;[278]
- for one of the legitimate aims set out in Article 11(2);
- necessary in a democratic society.[279]

At least where restrictions on political parties are concerned, the exceptions in Article 11(2) are to be construed strictly and only 'convincing and compelling reasons can justify restrictions on such parties' freedom of association'.[280]

Article 11(2) allows the interferences with the right of association in the interests of national security or public safety, for the prevention of disorder or crime, for the protection of health or morals or for the protection of the rights and freedoms of others. A number of restrictions on freedom of association have been held to the justified under Article 11(2). These include the dismissal of an employee for membership of a political party which had objectives opposed to those of the employer,[281] the prohibition of an association for illegal aims,[282] the prohibition on certain categories of local government officers from holding office within political parties.[283] A refusal to allow trade unions representing less than 10% of the workforce in a particular industrial sector to enter into collective agreements has been held to be a justifiable limitation on the rights of trade unions, having the legitimate aim of guaranteeing the existence of effective unions.[284] 16.80

However, the dismissal of a state-employed school teacher for her membership in the German Communist Party was held to be disproportionate to the aims of protection of national security and prevention of disorder. As a result, there was a violation of Article 11.[285] The banning and dissolution of the Turkish Communist 16.81

[277] See para 6.90ff above.
[278] See para 6.126ff above.
[279] See para 6.146ff above.
[280] *United Communist Party of Turkey v Turkey* (1998) 4 BHRC 1 para 46; *Socialist Party and others v Turkey* (1998) 27 EHRR 51 para 50.
[281] *Van der Heijden v Netherlands* (1985) 41 DR 264, EComm HR (the employer was a foundation concerned with the welfare of immigrants).
[282] *X v Austria* (1981) 26 DR 89; see also *Piperno v Italy* Application 15510/89, 2 Dec 1992, EComm HR (punishment of an applicant who formed a group to further terrorism was a permissible restriction).
[283] *Ahmed v United Kingdom* (1998) 5 BHRC 111 para 70 (the Court did not rely on special provisions relating to public officials in the second sentence of Art 11(2).
[284] *Dev Maden Sen v Turkey*, Application 32980/96, 9 Dec 1999; see also *Trade Union X v Belgium* (1979) 14 DR 40 and *Association A v Germany* (1983) 34 DR 173.
[285] *Vogt v Germany* (1995) 21 EHRR 205.

Party and the Turkish Socialist Party were both disproportionate to the aim of the prevention of crime and disorder and were in breach of Article 11.[286]

(h) Restrictions on public officials

16.82 The second sentence of Article 11(2) expressly permits restrictions on the rights of members of the armed forces, police and administration of the state. In *Council of Civil Service Unions v United Kingdom*[287] a state ban on the workers' right to join a trade union and its substitution of a right to membership in an approved staff association was held by the Commission to be a lawful restriction under Article 11(2). In *Rekvényi v Hungary*[288] the Court found that prohibitions on political activity by police officers were justified under Article 11(2); and did not find it necessary to deal with the question as to whether an interference which fell within the second sentence was subject only to the condition of lawfulness.

(i) Positive protection of freedom of association

16.83 The case law has emphasised the obligations on the state to protect the Article 11(1) right of association. Individuals have the right to form associations and to have these actions recognised by the state.[289] The extent to which there is a positive obligation on the state to interfere in private relationships in the interests of the effective enjoyment of Article 11 rights is unclear. It has been said that 'Article 11 sometimes requires positive measures to be taken, even in the sphere of relations between individuals, if need be'.[290] In *Gustafsson v Sweden*[291] the Court stressed that national authorities may be obliged to intervene in relationships between private individuals by taking reasonable and appropriate measures to secure the effective enjoyment of the negative right to freedom of association. It also observed that the sensitive political and social issues in achieving a proper balance between competing interests, and particularly in assessing the appropriateness of state intervention to restrict trade union action aimed at extending a system of collective bargaining, require that the state should enjoy a wide measure of appreciation in its choice of the means to be employed.[292]

---

[286] *United Communist Party of Turkey v Turkey* (1998) 26 EHRR 21; *Socialist Party and others v Turkey* (1998) 27 EHRR 51; *Freedom and Democracy Party v Turkey*, Judgment of 8 Dec 1999.

[287] (1987) 10 EHRR 269, EComm HR.

[288] (1999) 6 BHRC 554.

[289] See C Tomuschat, 'Freedom of Association', in R St J Macdonald, F Matscher and H Petzold (eds), *The European System for the Protection of Human Rights* (Nijhoff, 1993) 506.

[290] *Plattform 'Ärzte für das Leben' v Austria* (1988) 13 EHRR 204 para 34.

[291] (1996) 22 EHRR 409.

[292] Nevertheless, the Court ultimately found, on the facts, that the failure of the state to intervene to protect the applicant employer from a trade union boycott of his business was justified on the basis that the complaint concerned matters governed by private contractual relationships.

The state must prevent employers from pressurising a union member to relinquish a position held in the union.[293] It must also protect the individual against any abuse of a dominant position by a trade union including, for example, expulsion in breach of union rules or the application of rules which are wholly unreasonable or arbitrary, or where expulsion resulted in exceptional hardship.[294] In *Young, James and Webster v United Kingdom*[295] the positive obligation on the state had not been discharged where domestic law promoted a closed shop agreement between employer and unions. **16.84**

D. The Impact of the Human Rights Act

(1) Introduction

Article 11 is likely to have substantial implications for both assembly and association in English law. The unsatisfactory nature of the legal principles which regulate public assemblies is well known.[296] The Human Rights Act will lead to reconsideration of the limits of many public order offences and regulatory provisions. Most associations are unregulated by the law. However, it is possible that elements of the statutory scheme regulating trade unions will be found to be unjustifiable under Article 11(2). The rights of assembly and association will have to be properly taken into account by public bodies over a broad range of activities from regulating demonstrations to making meeting rooms available. In addition, attempts may be made to extend the right of association into the sphere of 'private association'. If successful, such an extension would have wide ranging consequences. **16.85**

(2) United Kingdom cases prior to the Human Rights Act

(a) Introduction

A number of United Kingdom applications have been brought addressing assembly and association issues. Only a small number of cases have been declared admissible by the Commission and the Court has found a violation of the 'freedom of association' provision in only one case.[297] The cases will be considered under the headings of 'assembly' and 'association'. **16.86**

---

293 *X v Ireland* (1971) 14 YB 188.

294 *Cheall v United Kingdom* (1985) 8 EHRR 74.

295 (1981) 4 EHRR 38.

296 See para 16.93ff below.

297 *Young, James and Webster v United Kingdom* (1981) 4 EHRR 38.

(b) Assembly

16.87 In *Mark Anderson v United Kingdom*[298] the applicants were a group of black youths who had been banned from a shopping centre because of alleged disorderly behaviour. This ban was upheld by the Court of Appeal. The Commission found their complaint to be inadmissible because they were asserting rights to social assembly and association which were not covered by Article 11.

16.88 In *Christians Against Racism and Fascism v United Kingdom*[299] the applicant was prevented from holding a procession in London because of a four-week ban on all processions save those of a religious, educational, festive or ceremonial character. The Commission held that the tense atmosphere in London due to disturbances caused by National Front demonstrations and counter-demonstrations justified a total ban on processions. The case of *Rai, Allmond and 'Negotiate Now' v United Kingdom*[300] concerned an organisation which sought to sponsor a rally in Trafalgar Square for the promotion of peace in Northern Ireland. Refusal of permission to do so was considered by the Commission to be a proportionate and justifiable restriction. The Commission relied, in particular, on the fact that there was no blanket ban and other central London locations were available.

(c) Association

16.89 A number of cases have dealt with complaints of employees in connection with 'association' in trade unions. The most important of these is *Young, James and Webster v United Kingdom*,[301] in which a closed shop arrangement was found to violate Article 11. The Court held that Article 11 conferred a positive right to belong to a trade union and at least some choice as to whether or not to enter into membership. In the subsequent case of *Sibson v United Kingdom*,[302] the Court decided that there was no such violation, distinguishing *Young, James and Webster* on grounds of the absence of a closed shop and because the applicant had been given the option of moving locations as an alternative to union membership or dismissal. Even though the UK courts had made findings of constructive dismissal and loss of livelihood, the Court found that the applicant had not been subjected to treatment striking at the heart of his Article 11 rights.

16.90 In *Cheall v United Kingdom*[303] the expulsion of a union member in accordance with a membership-protection agreement between his current and previous unions did not engage the responsibility of the state. The individual had no

[298] [1998] EHRLR 218 for the English case see *CIN Properties v Rawlins* [1995] 2 EGLR 130.
[299] (1980) 21 DR 138, EComm HR.
[300] (1995) 19 EHRR CD 93.
[301] (1981) 4 EHRR 38.
[302] (1993) 17 EHRR 193.
[303] (1985) 8 EHRR 74.

general right to be either admitted or to retain his membership and the matter was being appropriately dealt with by trade union rules, through the act of a private body exercising its Convention rights under Article 11.

In *Council of Civil Service Unions v United Kingdom*[304] the Commission found that denial of trade union membership to employees of GCHQ was justifiable as falling under the exception in paragraph 2 of Article 11 for the members of the administration of the state. In *National Association of Teachers in Further and Higher Education v United Kingdom*[305] a statutory obligation to disclose the names of trade union members to an employer before strike action was taken was not a 'significant limitation on the right to take collective action'. However, the Commission did recognise that in certain circumstances, such a requirement could give rise to an unjustified interference under Article 11. In *Wilson and National Union of Journalists v United Kingdom*[306] the Commission found that the applicants' complaints concerning a requirement that a trade unionist sign a personal contract in order to obtain a pay rise was admissible.[307] **16.91**

The Commission has rejected a number of complaints by prisoners in relation to social contact with other prisoners and visitors. It has been held that Article 11 does not concern the right of prisoners to 'share the company' of other prisoners or to 'associate' with them.[308] It has also been held that Article 11 has no application to 'association' for purely social purposes[309] or to association with pets.[310] **16.92**

(3) Impact of Article 11 on the law relating to assembly[311]

(a) Introduction

Under the Human Rights Act the starting point is that individuals have a positive right of assembly. It has therefore been argued that Article 11 creates a right to protest although the Strasbourg case law itself does not provide a very firm foundation for such a right.[311a] Until the Act is implemented English law has regulated public assemblies by both administrative powers and the criminal law. A very large **16.93**

304 (1987) 10 EHRR 269, EComm HR; for the English case, see para 16.54 above.

305 (1998) 25 EHRR CD 122; the relevant statutory provision has now been repealed, see para 16.47 above.

306 Application 30668/96, 14 Sep 1995, EComm HR.

307 For the English law, see para 16.47 above.

308 *McFeeley v United Kingdom* (1980) 20 DR 44, para 14, EComm HR; *X v United Kingdom* (1982) 5 EHRR 260; *Delezarus v United Kingdom* Application 17525/90, 16 Feb 1993, EComm HR.

309 *Mark Anderson v United Kingdom* [1998] EHRLR 218.

310 *Artingsoll v United Kingdom* (1995) 19 EHRR CD 92.

311 See generally, F Klug, K Starmer and S Weir, *The Three Pillars of Liberty* (Routledge, 1996) Chap 10 'The Residual Right of Public Protest'.

311a H Fenwick, 'The Right to Protest, the Human Rights Act and the Margin of Appreciation' [1999] 62 MLR 491.

measure of discretion is placed in the hands of the police and the Home Secretary. English law makes available to police officers a wide range of powers to deal with suspected breaches of the peace. These regulatory powers are extensive.[312] They allow an officer, for example, to turn public speech into a criminal offence whenever a breach of the peace is apprehended, simply by telling the speaker to stop. The United States, by comparison, employs a much higher standard for imposing restrictions on public expression: restrictions are only allowed if the speaker is inciting people to unlawful action[313] and the words or behaviour create a clear and present danger of violence.[314]

16.94 These powers of regulation have grown up in a haphazard fashion over the centuries and have given only intermittent recognition to the rights set out in Article 11. It has been suggested that:

> The cumulative effect of the trespass laws, minor criminal offences, common law rules, bye-law regulations and general and specific police powers means that there is no place in which citizens can insist on meeting. They depend at all turns on the 'good grace' or 'common sense' of the authorities. This represents too fragile a base for such an important political right.[315]

The result is that the freedom of assembly has been said to resemble a 'freedom under the police rather than freedom under the law'.[316] It is arguable that, in some circumstances, these discretionary powers are incompatible with Article 11.

(b) Statutory regulation of public assembly

16.95 The regulatory powers in Part II of the Public Order Act 1986 are, in general, likely to be held to be in conformity with Article 11. The Convention allows the state to require advance notice of demonstrations,[317] to impose conditions on demonstrations which may result in disorder or damage to property[318] or to impose conditions on public assemblies.[319]

---

[312] See para 16.21 above.

[313] 'Inciting' does not mean merely saying things which other people might react violently against, nor even advocating or promising violence.

[314] *Schenck v United States* (1919) 249 US 47 *per* Holmes J at 52; and see generally, eg H J Abraham and B A Perry, *Freedom and the Court* (7th edn, Oxford University Press, 1998) 153–174.

[315] Klug, Starmer and Weir (n 311 above) 203; D Feldman reaches a similar conclusion, see *Civil Liberties and Human Rights in England and Wales* (Clarendon Press, 1993) 842.

[316] See C Gearty, 'Freedom of Assembly' in C McCrudden and G Chambers (eds), *Individual Rights and the Law in Britain* (Oxford University Press, 1994) 55.

[317] As provided for by Public Order Act 1986, s 11; for the Convention position, see para 16.61 above.

[318] As provided for by Public Order Act 1986, s 12; for the Convention position, see para 16.60ff above.

[319] As provided for by Public Order Act 1986, s 14; for the Convention position, see para 16.60ff above.

There are, however, a number of areas in which statutory powers of regulation in Part II of the Public Order Act 1986 may be incompatible with Article 11: 16.96

- *Advance notice of 'spontaneous' processions*: Section 11 requires written notice of processions unless it is not reasonably practicable to give *any* notice and failure to give such notice is an offence.[320] Read literally, this section would require notice to be given if, for example, it is decided at a public meeting to hold a demonstration at the conclusion of the meeting. Although prosecutions under section 11 are rare, this requirement appears to be unduly restrictive of Article 11 rights.[321]
- *Imposing conditions on processions in cases of 'serious disruption to the life of the community'*: By section 12(1)(a), conditions may be imposed on processions where a senior police officer reasonably believes that they are likely to result in 'serious disruption to the life of the community'. This condition is vague and appears to be intended to cover situations where there is no risk of serious public order or damage to property. There is some evidence of it having been applied in an unduly restrictive manner in practice.[322] The uncertainty attaching to this condition arguably involves an unjustifiable restriction on Article 11 rights.[323]
- *General prohibitions on processions*: By section 13 there is a power to prohibit the holding of all processions (or all processions of a specified class) if the 'condition imposing power' under section 12 is not sufficient to prevent processions from causing serious public disorder. Although the Commission has taken the view that such general bans are compatible with Article 11,[324] it is clear that they must be subject to strict scrutiny and should only be made if serious disorder cannot be prevented by lesser means. The power to ban marches has, in general, been exercised sparingly,[325] but once in place, a decision to impose a ban may be difficult to overturn. For example, in *Kent v Metropolitan Police Commissioner*[326] the Campaign for Nuclear Disarmament was unsuccessful in a challenge to a decision to prohibit for 28 days virtually all processions within the 786 square miles of the Metropolitan Police District, which had the effect of banning a CND march. It is submitted that such a restriction would now be held to be unlawful as being disproportionate under Article 11.[327]

---

320 s 11(7).

321 See H Fenwick, *Civil Liberties* (2nd edn, Cavendish Publishing, 1998) 290–291.

322 See F Klug, K Starmer and S Weir, *The Three Pillars of Liberty* (Routledge, 1996), 197–198 where the example is given of restrictions on a demonstration by Campaign Against the Arms Trade involving the release of balloons.

323 Ibid, see also Fenwick (n 321 above) 292.

324 See para 16.62 above.

325 Between 1936 and 1980 orders were used on 11 occasions. However, 42 orders were made in 1981 following the riots that summer with 33 over the next three years; see *Review of Public Order Law*, Cmnd 9510, para 4.7.

326 *The Times*, 15 May 1981.

327 See generally, Fenwick (n 321 above) 295–296.

- *Prohibitions on trespassory assemblies*: Section 14A allows an order to be made banning 'trespassory assemblies' in a particular area which, it is reasonably believed, are likely to result in 'serious disruption to the life of the community'. Although it is now clear that this provision does not allow the banning of non-obstructive assemblies on the highway,[328] it does allow the prohibition of non-criminal assemblies on the basis of a vague and uncertain requirement. It is submitted that this is unduly restrictive of freedom of assembly rights.[329]

(c) Criminal offences relating to assembly

16.97 **Breach of the peace.** It has been argued that the Convention will require clarification of the common law definition of 'breach of the peace'. Uncertainty about the elements of breach of the peace and the extent of the powers available to the police for dealing with it have led some writers to suggest:

> The standard international human rights test - that any restriction of freedom of assembly must be 'prescribed by law' - requires that citizens must have an adequate indication of the legal rules that apply to them in the circumstances; and that such rules must be framed with enough clarity to enable them to regulate their conduct. Breach of the peace fails this test; the courts have approved several different definitions of breach of the peace and citizens are held liable not only for their own behaviour but for the likely (or even unlikely) behaviour of others.[330]

Nevertheless, in *Steel v United Kingdom*[331] the Court of Human Rights has concluded that the concept of 'breach of the peace' was formulated with the degree of precision required by the Convention and the English courts may be reluctant to depart from this view.[332]

16.98 The concept of 'breach of the peace' allows the state to place restrictions on the activities of those involved in demonstrations: if there is an actual or threatened breach of the peace, the demonstrators may be arrested and later 'bound over' in relation to future conduct. [333] However, these restrictions cannot be placed on a person solely because third parties react to a demonstration in an unreasonable way. [334] This appears to be an proportionate restriction on Article 11 rights.[335]

16.99 **Obstructing the highway.** The offence of 'obstructing the highway'[336] places substantial limitations on the rights of protestors. The question as to whether or

[328] *DPP v Jones* [1999] 2 AC 240.

[329] See generally, Fenwick (n 321 above) 296–299.

[330] Klug, Starmer and Weir (n 322 above) 201; see also Law Commission, *Binding Over* (Law Com No 222 1994) para 6.27.

[331] (1998) 28 EHRR 603 para 55.

[332] See generally, para 10.107 above.

[333] See para 16.103 above.

[334] See *Nicol v DPP* (1995) 160 JP 155, 162-163.

[335] Cf *Redmond-Bate v DPP* (2000) 7 BRHC 375, 381.

[336] Highways Act 1980, s 137, see para 16.08ff above.

not an assembly is, *prima facie*, a reasonable and hence non-obstructive use of the highway has not been definitively resolved.[337] It is submitted that the effect of Article 11 is that the courts should approach the question as to whether there has been an obstruction on the basis that a peaceful assembly is a reasonable and proper use of the highway and the participants cannot be guilty of the criminal offence of obstruction unless prosecution can be justified under Article 11(2). Such justification will be available if, for example, there is a threat of disorder or undue interference with the rights of others.

Aggravated trespass. The directions which can be given to a person reasonably believed to be committing an aggravated trespass[338] can be unduly restrictive of rights of peaceful assembly.[339] Such a direction can be given to protestors where no offence has in fact been committed and no offence is intended. It is then a criminal offence for the protestors to return to the land as a trespasser within three months. There is no immediately effective way to challenge such a direction.[340] Peaceful protest on private land would be criminalised even if there was no risk of disorder or property damage. It is submitted that this would be inconsistent with Article 11. **16.100**

(d) Other restrictions on freedom of assembly

There are a number of other situations on which English law imposes restrictions on freedom of assembly which may not be compatible with Article 11.[341] The most important of these are those imposed by bail conditions and 'bind overs'. **16.101**

The first restriction involves the imposition of bail conditions on those awaiting trial for public order offences. For example, in *R v Mansfield Justices, ex p Sharkey*[342] the Divisional Court refused to quash bail conditions imposed on striking miners which had the effect of preventing them from picketing and demonstrating. Such conditions are commonly imposed on hunt saboteurs and road protestors and have the effect of restricting the rights of assembly of those who have not been convicted of any offence.[343] It is arguable that such conditions are in breach of Article 11.[344] **16.102**

337 See generally, para 16.23 above.
338 See para 16.32 above.
339 Cf H Fenwick, *Civil Liberties* (2nd edn, Cavendish Publishing, 1998) 313–315.
340 The only possibility would be an application for judicial review.
341 See generally, F Klug, K Starmer and S Weir, *The Three Pillars of Liberty* (Routledge, 1996) 198–200.
342 [1985] QB 613; see D Feldman, *Civil Liberties and Human Rights in England and Wales* (Clarendon Press, 1993) 837-8; Klug, Starmer and Weir (n 341 above) 199–200.
343 See Klug, Starmer and Weir (n 341 above) 202.
344 Cf the approach in *Bradford v Police* (1995) 2 HRNZ 405, see para 16.140 below.

16.103 Secondly, there is the power of the magistrates' court to bind a person over to be of 'good behaviour'.[345] The order is made on the basis that the person has been guilty of a breach of the peace[346] or of behaviour *contra bonos mores*. This has been described as:

> conduct which has the property of being wrong rather than right in the judgment of the majority of contemporary fellow citizens.[347]

A binding-over order requires the person bound over to enter into a 'recognizance' secured by a sum of money fixed by the court, to keep the peace or be of good behaviour for a specified period of time. If he refuses to consent to the order, the court may commit him to prison. This power has been used in relation to those involved in protests as a way of preventing further involvement. The European Court of Human Rights has held[348] that an order by which a person is bound over to be of good behaviour is not 'prescribed by law' as behaviour *contra bonos mores* was not adequately defined. However, such an order remains available. If one were made the court would be acting incompatibly with Convention rights and the order would be liable to be quashed.

(e) Positive protection for freedom of assembly

16.104 Article 11 requires states to take positive steps to protect freedom of assembly. This involves providing protection for demonstrations against violent counter-demonstrations.[349] It is also arguable that the state's positive duties extend to making sufficient public places available to hold assemblies and processions. One particular issue concerns the 'privatisation' of public space in shopping centres and other formerly public places.[350] In circumstances in which the available 'public space' is limited, it is arguable that the state would fall under an obligation to ensure that such quasi-public spaces would be available for the exercise of Article 11 rights. It is noteworthy that, in the only case in which this issue has been considered[351] one of the grounds for the rejection of the complaint was the fact that the applicants had no history of using the 'quasi-public space' for the purposes of organised assembly or association. The position might be different if the private owners of part of a town centre sought to prevent protestors from using well established places of assembly.

---

[345] Magistrates' Court Act 1980, s 115.

[346] See para 16.13 above.

[347] *Hughes v Holley* (1986) 86 Cr App R 130.

[348] *Hashman and Harrap v United Kingdom*, Application 25594/94, 26 Nov 1999, paras 38–41.

[349] See para 16.64 above.

[350] See generally, K Gray and S Gray, 'Civil Rights, Civil Wrongs and Quasi-Public Spaces' [1999] EHRLR 46.

[351] *Anderson v United Kingdom* (1998) 25 EHRR CD 172.

(4) Impact of Article 11 on the law relating to association

(a) Introduction

16.105 In general, despite the absence of a positive freedom of association, English law appears to be consistent with Article 11. The various restrictions imposed on association in the interests of national security and public order seem to comply with the Convention.[352] In the 1980s the Government introduced compulsory ballots for trade union elections and before strike action. However, the Committee of Experts of the International Labour Organisation has accepted that these restrictions do not violate ILO requirements.[353] Article 11 may, however, have some impact on the law in relation to the regulation of trade unions. It could be argued that the English courts should draw on unincorporated conventions made under the ILO, particularly because legislation passed in the last twenty years has frequently failed to meet ILO standards.[353a] In addition, it is possible that the English courts will expand the notion of 'association' beyond the narrow view adopted by the Strasbourg authorities.[354]

(b) Trade unions

16.106 The statutory right not to be dismissed or refused employment because of non-membership of a trade union[355] is consistent with the approach taken in the case of *Young, James and Webster v United Kingdom*.[356] It is, however, possible that compulsory membership of professional associations contravenes Article 11. Thus, a person in the position of the barrister who refused to pay a compulsory subscription to his professional body[357] may be able to rely on his 'right of non-association'.

16.107 The state is only permitted to interfere in the internal affairs of associations in exceptional circumstances. The Trade Union and Labour Relations (Consolidation) Act 1992 provides that a member has the right not to be 'unjustifiably disciplined' by his union.[358] A union may not expel or penalise a member for strike breaking.[359] It is arguable that these provisions are in breach of Article 11.[360] In particular these provisions:

---

[352] Hence the dismissal of the complaint in the GCHQ case: *Council of Civil Service Unions v United Kingdom* (1987) 10 EHRR 269, EComm HR.

[353] See generally, F Klug, K Starmer and S Weir, *The Three Pillars of Liberty* (Routledge, 1996) 215ff.

[353a] See eg S Mills, 'The International Labour Organisation, the United Kingdom and Freedom of Association: An Annual Cycle of Condemnation' [1997] EHRLR 35.

[354] See para 16.66 above.

[355] Trade Union and Labour Relations (Consolidation) Act 1992, ss 137 and 152.

[356] (1981) 4 EHRR 38.

[357] See *Re S, The Guardian*, 9 Oct 1990.

[358] s 64(1).

[359] s 65(2)(a).

[360] See generally, G Lightman and J Bowers, 'Incorporation of the ECHR and its Impact on Employment Law' [1998] EHRLR 560, 573-574.

- involve state interference in a trade union's internal affairs; and
- restrict the rights of non-association of members (as they are compelled to continue to associate with strike breakers).

As a result, they may be incompatible with Article 11 and a 'declaration of incompatibility' may be available.

16.108 The English law in relation to the right to form unions and to be consulted may contravene Article 11.[361] A provision which seeks to make union recognition conditional on the results of a work place ballot may also be in breach of Article 11. The right to form a union and to be consulted does not depend on whether or not those who wish to exercise this right are in a minority.[362]

16.109 Article 11 does not expressly confer the right to strike and it seems unlikely that the English courts will construe it as containing an 'implied right to strike'.[363] The existence of such a right was rejected by the Privy Council when considering a constitutional 'freedom of association' provision.[364]

(c) Other forms of association

16.110 The concept of 'association' can cover a wide range of possibilities including political associations, trade unions, cultural associations, economic associations, social associations and intimate associations.[365] The case law under the Convention has focused on the first two types of association and has not recognised social or intimate associations as attracting Article 11 protection. Although, historically, 'association' has been construed narrowly, the combination of the doctrine of the Convention as a 'living instrument' and the 'effectiveness' principle[366] suggest that the words of Article 11 should be given their natural and ordinary meaning and should be applied to all forms of 'association with others'. The extension of 'freedom of association' to intimate and social associations[367] would reinforce Article 8 protections and would result in relationships between individuals such as cohabitation with relatives,[368] the social activities of prisoners[369] or loose groupings of friends[370] coming within the scope of Article 11 protection.

---

361 See generally, Lightman and Bowers (n 360 above) 571.

362 Cf Lightman and Bowers (n 360 above) 571.

363 For a contrary argument, see J Hendy, 'The Human Rights Act, Article 11, and the Right to Strike' [1999] EHRLR 582.

364 *Collymore v A-G of Trinidad and Tobago* [1970] AC 538.

365 Cf the discussion in M Chaskalson, J Kentridge, J Klaaren, G Marcus, D Spitz and S Woolman (eds), *The Constitutional Law of South Africa* (Juta, 1996) paras 22-8–22-10.

366 See para 6.28 above.

367 See eg the approach taken by the American courts in *Roberts v United States Jaycees* (1984) 468 US 609.

368 See eg *Moore v East Cleveland* (1977) 431 US 494.

369 Cf *X v United Kingdom* (1982) 5 EHRR 260, see para 16.92 above.

370 Cf *Anderson v United Kingdom* (1998) 25 EHRR CD 172, see para 16.87 above.

Appendix 1: The Canadian Charter of Rights

(1) Introduction

Sections 2(c) and (d) of the Canadian Charter of Rights and Freedoms[371] state: **16.111**

> Everyone has the following fundamental freedoms: . . .
>
> (c) freedom of peaceful assembly; and
> (d) freedom of association.

In contrast to the position under the Convention and in the United States, freedom of association in Canada is independent of those of peaceful assembly and expression.

Legislative authority over assembly in Canada is divided between the federal government, which deals with riots and breaches of the peace under the criminal law, and provincial legislatures which have power to regulate 'matters of a merely local or private nature in the province' including meetings, parades and gatherings on parks and streets. Labour law, including picketing, is governed by whichever level of government has authority over the particular industry involved. **16.112**

Authority over association is also divided, depending on the type of association concerned. The provinces regulate clubs, societies, partnerships and unincorporated associations under 'property and civil rights in the province', while the federal government may prohibit conspiracies under its criminal law and regulate mergers and monopolies in restraint of trade under both the criminal law power and its authority over matters of trade and commerce. Regulation of trade unions is carried out by whichever level of government has authority over the industry in question. **16.113**

(2) Assembly

The courts have dealt specifically with the freedom of assembly in Canada under section 2(c) of the Charter on a limited number of occasions. Municipal bye-laws regulating public gatherings are limitations on the freedom of assembly which require justification under section 1. **16.114**

Before the Charter, the freedom of assembly was effectively emasculated by the decision of *A-G v Dupond*[372] which upheld a Montreal bye-law authorising exceptional emergency measures including the prohibition of 'all assemblies, parades and gatherings' for any period of time, in the discretion of the municipal authorities. The holding of assemblies, parades and gatherings was considered to be distinct from the fundamental freedoms, and also viewed as an aggregate of matters governed by both provincial and municipal legislation. The Supreme Court stated that the English, and, thus, the Canadian, common law knew no right to hold public meetings on a highway or in a park and that such an assembly might constitute a trespass against the urban authority vested with ownership. This decision has been criticised in the light of the Charter.[373] **16.115**

---

371 Constitution Act 1982, Pt I.

372 [1978] 2 SCR 770.

373 For critical assessment of the case in light of the Charter, see E Vogt, 'Dupond Reconsidered: or the "Search for The Constitution and the Truth of Things Generally" ' (1982) Charter Edition, UBCLR 141; also R Stoykewych, 'Street Legal: Constitutional Protection of Public Demonstration in Canada' (1985) 43 UTFLR 43, 56–58.

16.116 Prison inmates cannot have unrestricted freedom of assembly or association, but they must be subjected to the necessity of preservation of discipline and security in the institution.[374] In *Re Fraser v A-G of Nova Scotia*[375] the Nova Scotia Supreme Court dealt with the constitutionality of provincial legislation which prohibited civil servants from engaging in partisan work in connection with a provincial or federal election. The legislation precluded government employees from membership in or association with members of any political party, from being candidates, attending meetings or assemblies, participating in development of policies and platforms, public expression of political views, financial contribution and canvassing or campaigning on behalf of any political party. The Court found the provisions contrary to the rights of freedoms of expression, assembly and association. In spite of an acceptable objective, which was to ensure a politically neutral and impartial civil service, the means used to achieve it were excessive in their impairment of the rights and freedoms in issue; accordingly, the measures could not be justified under section 1 of the Charter.

16.117 In *R v Collins* a bail condition preventing the accused from attending a particular demonstration was removed. It was held that the Crown had to show compelling reasons why basic rights of an individual to do what is lawful should be curtailed.[376] However, an interlocutory injunction to restrain an abortion protest activity was held to be a justifiable limitation on the freedom of assembly.[377]

(3) Association

(a) Definition and scope

16.118 The meaning and scope of the Charter guarantee of freedom of association have primarily been considered in trade union cases. The two main issues have been the right to strike and the 'negative' freedom to refrain from association with a trade union.

16.119 Section 2(d) protects the freedom of individuals to associate with one another for their mutual benefit. This means, at the very least, that the constitutional rights of an individual will not lose their fundamental status by reason of the fact that they are exercised in consort with others.[378] But are other lawful actions of individuals elevated to constitutionally protected status simply by reason of being carried out in the association of others? Do the collective activities of an association also receive constitutional protection, even though they may neither constitute an exercise of a separate Charter freedom nor be capable of being carried out by an individual?

16.120 Prior to 1987 two divergent lines of authority addressed these issues in the provincial courts. The first followed a path similar to that in other common law jurisdictions, asserting that the freedom of association is an individual right only, in accordance with the principle in *Collymore v A-G of Trinidad and Tobago*.[379]

---

374 *R v Butler* (1983) 5 CCC (3d) 356.

375 (1986) 30 DLR (4th) 340.

376 (1982) 31 CR (3d) 283.

377 *Ontario (A-G) v Dieleman* (1994) 117 DLR (4th) 449.

378 Cf *Libman v A-G of Quebec* [1997] 3 SCR 569 (inhibition of the free exercise of a Charter right accordingly violated the freedom of association).

379 [1970] AC 538; see *Dolphin Delivery Ltd v Retail, Wholesale and Dept Store Union, Local 580* (1984) 10 DLR (4th) 198; *Reference re Public Service Employee Relations Act* (1985) 16 DLR (4th) 359; *Public Service Alliance of Canada v Canada* (1984) 11 DLR (4th) 337, FCA.

The second line of cases, based on the doctrine that the Charter should be given a large and liberal construction,[380] held that the freedom of association should extend to the protection of activities of organisations. When Ontario legislation[381] deprived workers of the right to choose their own union and the right, through that union, to collective bargaining and the right to strike, the Ontario Divisional Court in *Broadway Manor*[382] found that the Charter guarantee of freedom of association protects those activities essential to the attainment of the lawful objects of an association. Taking into account the drafting history of the provision, the Court described association as a 'barren and useless thing' if workers could not take lawful steps, through bargaining and striking, to advance their common interests.[383] It concluded that the Charter freedom of association includes at least the freedom to organise, to choose a union, to bargain and to strike. A similar conclusion was reached by the Saskatchewan Court of Appeal in *Re Retail, Wholesale & Department Store Union and Saskatchewan*[384] when provincial legislation effectively prohibited employees from striking against their employers. The majority decision was that the right to organise, bargain and strike must be protected by section 2 of the Charter. **16.121**

The issue was considered by the Supreme Court of Canada in 1987 in a 'trilogy' of labour cases.[385] The Supreme Court concluded that the freedom of association does not guarantee the right to bargain collectively or the right to strike. In the leading *Alberta Reference* case, provincial legislation imposed a blanket denial of strike action for government employees, substituting only a limited right to arbitration. In *PSAC* a two-year prohibition on the right of public employees to strike was federally legislated, with arbitration restricted to compensatory matters, while in the *Dairy Workers* case, the legislation completely denied strike action, but substituted full rights to arbitration. In each case the Supreme Court of Canada held by a 4:2 majority that the right to strike is not a fundamental right but is merely created by the legislature.[386] **16.122**

LeDain J, in a brief judgment for three members of the Supreme Court in *Alberta Reference* held that, because the Charter freedom of association is not solely applicable to trade unions, it would be wrong to define it by singling out and protecting a particular activity (such as strike action) of a particular type of association (such as trade unions). He rejected the argument that the freedom of association would be meaningless if the right to strike were not protected, because it would nevertheless protect the 'freedom to work for the establishment of an association, to belong to an association, to maintain it and to participate in its lawful activity without penalty or reprisal'. **16.123**

---

380 *Southam v the Queen (No 1)* (1983) OR (2nd) 113.

381 Inflation Restraint Act 1982, s 13(b).

382 *Re Service Employees' International Union, Local 204 and Broadway Manor Nursing Home* (1983) 44 OR (2d) 392; 48 OR (2d) 225, CA.

383 'I think that freedom of association, if it is to be a meaningful freedom, must include freedom to engage in conduct which is reasonably consonant with the lawful objects of an association. And I think a lawful object is any object which is not prohibited by law.'

384 (1985) 19 DLR (4th) 609, CA.

385 *Reference Re Public Service Employee Relations Act* [1987] 1 SCR 313 (the '*Alberta Reference*'); *Public Service Alliance of Canada v The Queen in Right of Canada* [1987] 1 SCR 424 ('PASC'); *Saskatchewan v Retail, Wholesale and Dept Store Union, Locals 544, 496, 635 and 955* [1987] 1 SCR 460 (the '*Dairy Workers*' case).

386 See also *Dunmore v A-G of Ontario* (1997) 155 DLR (4th) 193 Ont Ct, Gen Div where the exclusion of agricultural workers from a statutory collective bargaining regime was held not to be a denial of individual rights to form associations. The Court found that there was no positive obligation on legislatures to facilitate such associations.

16.124 MacIntyre J dealt with the matter in more detail, identifying and assessing six approaches[387] available to the Court. He rejected as invalid the last three: the 'Kerans' approach of *Black v Law Society of Alberta*,[388] the *Broadway Manor* approach,[389] and that of Bayda CJS, in the *Dairy Workers* case[390] and accepted the others. Clearly, under the *Collymore* principle, individuals may form groups to promote lawful objectives and, in accordance with the American approach, may do collectively those things which they have a constitutional right to do as individuals. MacIntyre J was also prepared to accept the third, 'Raggi', view[391] that individuals may do in combination those acts which they are not prohibited from doing alone. He held, though, that this would not guarantee the right to strike, for two reasons. First, it is not lawful for an individual to withdraw labour during the term of a contract of employment, and secondly, because strike action is inherently collective, there is no analogy between the cessation of work by a single employee and a strike conducted in accordance with modern labour legislation.[392] MacIntyre J also observed that to protect constitutionally one element (the strike) of the inherently dynamic process of collective bargaining would prejudice the development of alternative forms of dispute resolution and would involve the courts as arbiters of every dispute concerning the scope and justification of strike restrictions.

16.125 In his dissent Dickson CJ rejected the *Collymore* and American approaches on the basis that the express Charter protection of freedom of association must be more expansive than that accepted in the United States, where the protection is only implied. Although he also accepted the wider 'Raggi' approach, and agreed with the majority decision that there is no individual equivalent to a strike, he felt that it did not go far enough. In his view, the strike is qualitatively, rather than quantitatively, different from an individual withdrawal of work. He held that the most important consideration was whether legislative enactment or administrative action interferes with freedom of persons to join and act with others in common pursuits. The protection for the right to strike which is advocated by Dickson CJ is not absolute, but is subject to such restrictions as may be justified under section 1.[393]

---

[387] These six approaches are itemised in: T Christian and K Ewing, 'Labouring Under the Canadian Constitution' (1988) 17 ILJ 73, 80; G England, 'Some Thoughts on Constitutionalizing the Right to Strike' [1988] Queen's LJ, 168, 176; S Renouf, ' "One More Battle to Fight": Trade Union Rights and Freedom of Association in Canada' (1989) Vol 27:2 ALR 226, 229.

[388] (1986) 27 DLR (4th) 527: the Court held that the freedom to associate included not only association with others in the exercise of Charter-protected rights but also 'those other rights which in Canada are thought so fundamental as not to need formal expression: to marry, for example, or to establish a home and family, pursue an education or gain a livelihood'.

[389] *Broadway Manor* would have extended protection to all activities which are essential to the lawful goals of an association.

[390] *Retail, Wholesale and Dept Store Union, Local 544 v Government of Saskatchewan* (1986) 19 DR (4th) 609, Sask CA found that 'where an act is by definition incapable of individual performance, the individual is free to perform the act in association provided the mental component of the act is not to inflict harm.'

[391] R Raggi, 'An Independent Right to Freedom of Association' (1977) 12 Harv CR-CLL Rev 1.

[392] (1987) 38 DLR (4th) 161, 229.

[393] For further analyses of this decision and the others in the trilogy, see: T J Christian and K Ewing, 'Labouring Under the Canadian Constitution' [1988] 17 ILJ, 73; G England, 'Some Thoughts on Constitutionalizing the Right to Strike' [1988] Queen's LJ, 168; S Renouf, '"One More Battle to Fight": Trade Union Rights and Freedom of Association in Canada' [1989] Vol 27:2 Alta LR 226; L Harmer, 'The Right to Strike: Charter Implications and Interpretations' [1988] Vol 47:2 UTFLR 420; P Cavalluzzo, 'Freedom of Association - Its Effect Upon Collective Bargaining and Trade Unions' [1988] Queen's LJ, 267.

Although three out of the six judges in *Alberta Reference* and two of the six in *Professional Institute of the Public Service of Canada v Northwest Territories (Commissioner)*[394] held that freedom of association protects any activity in association with others that was permitted to an individual by law, they were not in fact required to decide the question because strike action was not found to be analogous to any individual right. But a parallel is at least arguable,[395] and it is not difficult to conceive of an extension of the right which would draw analogies between collective activity and apparently similar individual activity. **16.126**

(b) Negative freedom

Arrangements such as the 'closed shop', 'union shop' or 'agency shop',[396] which are typically permitted (and sometimes required) by Canadian labour laws, raise the issue as to whether the Charter freedom of association protects a 'negative' freedom of association, a freedom not to associate. In all three arrangements an employee is compelled to either join or pay dues to a union on the threat of losing his job. **16.127**

In *Lavigne v Ontario Public Service Employees*[397] the plaintiff, a teacher at a community college and non-member of the teachers' union, was required, by the terms of a collective agreement between the college and the union, to pay union dues. While Mr Lavigne did not object to paying for the services of the union as his bargaining agent, he claimed that the agency shop provision violated his freedom of association to the extent that the dues were being used by the union to fund political parties and other causes unrelated to the representation of employees. The Supreme Court unanimously upheld the agency shop provision, but divided on its reasons for doing so. A majority of four judges held that the freedom of association included the right not to associate.[398] Three of these found that the use of the dues to support purposes other than employee representation was a violation of the freedom not to associate, but regarded the provision as justifiable under section 1 as a measure to encourage healthy democratic debate. The fourth judge in the majority felt that to compel payment of dues was not a forced association, because payment of dues did not indicate support by the payer for the causes financed by the union. A minority of three held that the freedom of association did not include a right to refrain from association. Ultimately, all judges upheld the agency provision compelling payment, but only a slim majority agreed that the freedom not to associate was constitutionally protected. The existence and scope of freedom to refrain from association under the Charter therefore remains uncertain. **16.128**

The implications of *Lavigne* are not wholly clear. The majority decision in favour of the freedom not to associate implies that the closed shop and union shop arrangements will also constitute potential infringements of section 2(d) of the Charter. Nevertheless, many of these arrangements will not be violations because, firstly, the Charter does not apply at **16.129**

[394] [1990] 2 SCR 367.

[395] P W Hogg, *Constitutional Law of Canada* (4th edn, Carswell, 1997) 1034.

[396] This is the most common arrangement, which does not require that employees be members of the union, but does require that all employees, whether members or non-members, pay dues to the union.

[397] [1991] 2 SCR 211.

[398] But see *Strickland v Ermel* (1992) 91 DLR (4th) 694; appeal dismissed [1994] 1 WWR 417: the Court found that the judges in *Lavigne* who held in favour of a right to disassociate did so on the facts of the case; that they did not assert an absolute negative right, but one conditional on the circumstances.

all to those that are made in collective agreements with private employers, and, secondly, where it does apply, there will be a strong likelihood of justification under section 1 because the closed and union shop arrangements strengthen the bargaining power of employees and prevent non-union employees from taking advantage of the privileges without sharing any of the burdens of collective bargaining.

16.130 In *Strickland v Ermel*,[399] for example, where provincial legislation required that professional engineers employed by the Saskatchewan Institute of Applied Science and Technology join a trade union as a condition of obtaining employment, the Court found that section 36 of the Trade Union Act RSS 1978 did not contravene section 2(d) of the Charter. The Act also required that existing employees who were union members at the time of the certification of the trade union continue their membership; it did not compel existing non-member employees to join a union if they elected not to do so. The judge found that the purpose of the Trade Union Act was to advance the interests of workers by providing for union security and that allowing employees to opt out of membership at any time would create chaos and skew the balancing of interest that had developed over the years; it reflected a decision on the part of the legislature that certain essential safeguards should be in place to protect workers' rights. While the result was that certain employees might belong to an organisation that they may not wish to be in, the fact that employment of new workers was contingent on union membership was not contrary to section 2(d) of the Charter. The individuals were not compelled to associate with union members; they were free to choose not to take a job, but membership in the union was a term of employment.

The decision in *Lavigne* has been criticised as an inequitable result under the Charter, be-
16.131 cause it protects the right to forego collective bargaining rights while the 'labour trilogy' of cases suggests that section 2(d) does not protect collective bargaining rights in the first place.[400]

(c) Public associations

In determining the scope of the freedom of association under the Charter, the Canadian
16.132 courts, unlike the European Court of Human Rights, have placed little emphasis on the distinction between associations established by the private initiative of individuals, which are within the scope of the protection of freedom of association, and 'public' associations which are not. There is no case law in relation to professional associations, other than *Black v Law Society of Alberta*,[401] in which the Alberta Court of Appeal found that Law Society Rules prohibited the formation of an inter-provincial associations of lawyers. The Supreme Court of Canada did not find it necessary to address the question of an infringement of section 2 of the Charter.

Certainly, the freedom of individuals to associate in private clubs is within the scope of the

[399] (1992) 91 DLR (4th) 694; appeal dismissed [1994] 1 WWR 417.

[400] The Supreme Court of Ontario decision at (1986) 29 DLR (4th) 321 concluded that the agency shop provision was offensive to the individual right to freedom of association, but was justifiable under section 1 of the Charter. For analyses of the case prior to the SCC decision, see P Cavalluzzo, 'Freedom of Association—Its Effect Upon Collective Bargaining and Trade Unions' [1988] Queen's LJ, 267, 298; T Christian and K Ewing, 'Labouring Under the Canadian Constitution' [1988] 17 ILJ 73, 85; B Etherington, 'Freedom of Association and Compulsory Union Dues' (1987) 19:1 Ottawa L Rev, 1 and '*Lavigne v OPSEU*: Moving Toward or Away from a Freedom to Not Associate?' (1991) 23 Ottawa L Rev 533.

[401] (1986) 27 DLR (4th) 527.

protection of section 2, but concern over the criteria for membership in such a club[402] re- **16.133**
lates not to the scope of the freedom but to the requirement of positive protection by the state and the application of the Charter to private relationships generally.[403]

(d) Positive protection

Positive protection of freedom of association requires the state to ensure that private parties (such as the other members of an association or the association itself) do not infringe **16.134**
the right of an individual to associate.

Once an association is established, are relationships between the members or between the association and its members subject to scrutiny? Unlike the European Convention where **16.135**
freedom of association protects the individual from interference both by government and other private persons,[404] the Canadian position is that private relationships are not regulated by the Charter.[405]

The *Lavigne* case[406] indicates that under section 32(1) of the Charter, a court has jurisdiction to apply the Charter only in relation to conduct by a legislature or government of **16.136**
Canada or any of the provinces. Similarly, the Supreme Court of Canada in *Dolphin Delivery*[407] emphasised that the purpose of the Charter was to restrain government action in the realm of individual or group rights, and not to regulate relations between private persons.[408] It has been said that the Charter should apply to private parties only where the actions complained of are caused by, compelled by or are closely connected to government.[409]

But 'governmental action' has been construed to include the cabinet, the ministries and the civil service, but also the actions of Crown agencies.[410] However, the acts of **16.137**
private parties including trade unions and corporations may also be subject to Charter scrutiny if either party to a dispute relies on statutory or other governmental authority for its acts and such reliance causes an infringement of a Charter right. Arguably, to apply the Charter to a privately negotiated union security clause, even though it may be permitted by government legislation, defeats its very purpose by extending government scrutiny over private conduct. The situation is complicated and anomalous.[411]

Where an association such as a private club is established, its relationship with its members is a matter for association rules. Its criteria for membership are immune from **16.138**
challenge.[412] Only rights breached by legislation or exercise of authority emanating di-

---

402 J Freeman, 'Justifying Exclusion: A Feminist Analysis of the Conflict between Equality and Association Rights' (1989) 47:2 UTFLR 269.

403 See 16.138 below.

404 See para 16.69 above.

405 *Lavigne v OPSEU* [1991] 2 SCR 211.

406 Ibid.

407 *Retail, Wholesale and Department Store Union, Local 580 v Dolphin Delivery Ltd* [1986] 2 SCR 573.

408 For a discussion of horizontality under the Charter see para 5.65ff above.

409 P Cavalluzzo, 'Freedom of Association - Its Effect Upon Collective Bargaining and Trade Unions' [1988] Queen's LJ, 267, 285.

410 *Lavigne v OPSEU* (1986) 55 OR (2d) 449.

411 Cavalluzzo (n 409 above) 285.

rectly from the Government will be constitutionally protected.

Appendix 2: The New Zealand Bill of Rights Act

(1) Introduction

16.139 The New Zealand Bill of Rights Act 1990 provides as follows:

> 16. **Freedom of peaceful assembly—**
> Everyone has the right to freedom of peaceful assembly.
>
> 17. **Freedom of association—**
> Everyone has the right to freedom of association.

(2) Assembly

16.140 In *Bradford v Police*[413] the applicant had been arrested during a demonstration for obstructing the police and the highway. She was granted bail on the condition that she did not participate in further protest action for a specified period. The judge held that a restriction on the right to protest must be no more than is reasonably necessary. The bail condition was varied to one prohibiting the applicant from participating in unlawful protests of a specific type.

16.141 The case of *Police v Beggs*[414] concerned a protest in the grounds of Parliament. The Speaker had exercised his powers to warn the protestors to leave. It was held that this exercise was a public function and the Speaker should not deny rights of assembly unless such a denial was reasonable in all the circumstances. Relevant considerations included whether the assembly was unduly prolonged, the rights and freedoms of others enjoying the privilege of being on the Parliament grounds, the rights of the occupier and those whose business or duties take them to Parliament, the size of the assembly and the content of what is being expressed.

(3) Association

16.142 This section has received little judicial attention in New Zealand. The case of *Lewis v Real Estate Institute of New Zealand Inc*[415] dealt with section 17 in passing. Although the freedom of association was invoked by the appellants, the argument was firmly rejected by the Court of Appeal. It found that the questions concerning whether a solicitor is entitled to remuneration by commission in relation to dealings with land, and whether the operation of a real estate centre 'in the course of his or her business' breached the licensing rules[416] have nothing to do with freedom of association.

In *Capital Coast Health Ltd v New Zealand Medical Laboratory Workers Union*[417] the issue

[412] See Freeman (n 402 above) for a comprehensive discussion of possible alternatives for regulation of male-dominated clubs.
[413] (1995) 2 HRNZ 405.
[414] (1999) 5 HRNZ 108.
[415] [1995] 3 NZLR 385.
[416] Under the Real Estate Agents Act 1976.

was whether the Employment Court had failed to strike a proper balance between freedom of association under the Employment Contracts Act 1991 and the freedom of expression[418] in granting a union an injunction against an employer to restrain it from communicating directly with employees. However, the Court of Appeal did not rely on section 17 of the Bill of Rights Act in relation to the right of association, but confined itself to the proper construction of the Employment Contracts Act. 16.143

Appendix 3: Human Rights Cases from Other Jurisdictions

(1) Introduction

The right of freedom of assembly and association is protected in all common law jurisdictions which have bills of rights. The protection of this right can be traced back to the First Amendment to the United States Constitution which provides that: 16.144

> Congress shall make no law . . . abridging . . . the right of the people peaceably to assemble . . .

The US Bill of Rights does not, however, contain any express protection for freedom of association.[419]

In the United States the constitutionality of restrictions on assembly depends on where it is taking place. If an assembly takes place in a 'public forum'[420] such as a street, park or other 'traditional' place for assembly and discussion, the court will apply 'strict scrutiny' to restrictive measures.[421] Restrictions must be 'content neutral' and narrowly tailored to protect a significant governmental interest. Thus, in the notorious case of *Skokie v National Socialist Party of America*[422] the court upheld the right of members of a neo-nazi group to march through a predominantly Jewish suburb wearing the National Socialist uniform and displaying their swastika emblem. However, if the assembly is to take place in a non-public place,[423] restrictive measures need only be content neutral with a reasonable relationship to a legitimate government interest.[424] This 'jurisprudence of labels' has been heavily criticised and a 'balancing test' has been proposed.[425] Orderly picketing is protected by the First Amendment.[426] 16.145

The state cannot make it a crime to participate in peaceful assembly.[427] It is permissible to require every parade or procession on a public street to obtain a licence for a

[417] [1996] 1 NZLR 7.

[418] Under the New Zealand Bill of Rights Act 1990, s 14.

[419] Such a right has been recognised as being implied into the Bill of Rights, see para 16.147 below.

[420] See *Hague v Committee for Industrial Organisation* (1938) 307 US 496.

[421] *United States v Grace* (1983) 461 US 171.

[422] (1978) 373 NE 2d 21, Illinois SC.

[423] For example, a military base, (*Greer v Spock* (1976) 424 US 828) or a school classroom (*Bethel School District v Fraser* (1986) 478 US 675).

[424] *Widmar v Vincent* (1981) 454 US 263.

[425] D Farber and J Nowak, 'The Misleading Nature of Public Forum Analysis: Content and Context in First Amendment Analysis' (1984) 70 Va L Rev 1219; C Dienes, 'The Trashing of the Public Forum: Problems in First Amendment Analysis' (1986) 55 Geo Wash L Rev 109.

[426] *Thornhill v Alabama* (1940) 310 US 88; but see *Giboney v Empire Storage Co* (1949) 336 US 490.

16.146 fee.[428] However, the Supreme Court has struck down a law allowing an administrator to charge a higher fee to groups whose procession was likely to require more police protection.[429]

16.147 Freedom of association is not dealt with explicitly in the Bill of Rights. However, in *National Association for the Advancement of Colored People v Alabama, ex rel Patterson*[430] the Supreme Court struck down an Alabama statute requiring production of the membership lists of the NAACP and recognised for the first time a constitutionally protected right of association. The freedom to engage in association for the advancement of beliefs and ideas is an inseparable aspect of 'liberty'.[431] The right of association is more than the right to attend a meeting:

> it includes the right to express one's attitude or philosophies by membership in a group, or affiliation with it or by other lawful means.[432]

In another line of decisions, the Supreme Court has concluded that choices to enter into and maintain certain intimate human relationships must be secured against undue intrusion by the state because of the role of such relationships in safeguarding individual freedom.[433]

(2) Botswana

16.148 In *Student Representative Council of Molepolole College of Education v A-G of Botswana*[434] the College refused to certify its approval of the constitution of the student representative council, thus preventing its registration as an association in accordance with College regulations. When a student council member claimed that his right to freedom of association took precedence over College regulations requiring the registration of the council as an association, the Court of Appeal in effect agreed. It decided that, although section 13 of the Botswana Constitution did not permit persons to disregard laws regulating associations (in particular the requirement for registration under the Societies Act), the College had exercised its powers improperly because its refusal to approve the constitution was motivated by the desire to protect itself from legal action. It was held that the College was either estopped by its conduct from denying approval to the appellant or had granted interim approval.

(3) India

427 *DeJonge v Oregon* (1937) 299 US 353 (participation in a Communist Party meeting cannot be a crime if violence is not incited).

428 *Cox v New Hampshire* (1941) 312 US 596.

429 *Forsyth County v National Movement* (1992) 505 US 123.

430 (1958) 357 US 449; see generally, J Nowak and R Rotunda, *Constitutional Law* (5th edn, West Publishing, 1995) para 16.14.

431 See also *Bates v Little Rock* (1960) 361 US 516 (tax ordinance requiring supply of list of NAACP members struck down) and *Gibson v Florida Legislative Investigative Committee* (1963) 372 US 539.

432 *Griswold v Connecticut* (1965) 381 US 479.

433 See generally, *Roberts v United States Jaycees* (1984) 468 US 609.

434 [1995] 3 LRC 447.

Article 19 of the Indian Constitution provides that:

> (1) All citizens shall have the right - . . . **16.149**
>
> (b) to assemble peaceably and without arms;
>
> (c) to form associations or unions; . . .[435]

These rights may be reasonably restricted in the interest of the sovereignty and integrity of India, public order or morality.[436] There must be a rational relationship between the impugned legislation and any of the relevant specified grounds.[437] The expression 'public order' is to be narrowly construed, and acts which disturb 'public tranquillity' do not necessarily affect 'public order'.[438] A law will breach Article 19 if interference with these rights is its direct or inevitable consequences, or is an effect which could be said to have been in the contemplation of the legislature.[439]

16.150 In the absence of extraordinary circumstances, the exercise of a basic right such as the freedom of association cannot reasonably be made dependent upon the subjective satisfaction of the Government or any of its officers, without offering any standard for guidance.[440]

16.151 The freedom to form unions includes the freedom not to join and to set up rival trade unions.[441] However, the right does not include a right of any particular association to obtain the recognition of the Government.[442] Conditions for the grant or continuance of recognition, however, must be substantively and procedurally reasonable.[443] There is no infringement of the right of association where the services of a government servant are terminated on the ground of his Communist Party membership. The termination does not prevent the person from remaining a member of the Communist Party, but terminates his service which is held at the pleasure of the Government, and to which there is no fundamental right.[444]

(4) Ireland

16.152 Article 40.6.1.ii of the Irish Constitution provides that the state guarantees liberty for the exercise, subject to public order and morality, of:

> The right of the citizens to assemble peaceably and without arms. Provision may be made by law to prevent or control meetings which are determined in accordance with law to be calculated to cause a breach of the peace or to be a danger or nuisance to the general public and to prevent or control meetings in the vicinity of either House of the Oireachtas [ie the legislative assembly].[445]

The provision was considered in the context of a picketing dispute in *Brendon Dunne Ltd*

[435] See generally, H M Seervai, *Constitutional Law of India* (4th edn, N M Tripathi, 1991) Chap X.

[436] Art 19(3) and (4).

[437] Cf *R v Basudev* A 1950 FC 67.

[438] *Madhu Limaye v SDM* A 1971 SC 2486 para 16.

[439] *Express Newspapers v Union of India* A 1958 SC 578.

[440] *Seshadri v DM* A 1954 SC 747; *Harichand v Mizo District Council* A 1967 SC 829.

[441] *KRW Union v Registrar* A 1967 Cal 507, 508.

[442] *Raghubar v Union of India* A 1962 SC 263, 270.

[443] *State of Madras v V G Row* A 1952 SC 196.

[444] *Balakotiah v Union of India* A 1958 SC 232.

[445] See generally, J M Kelly, *The Irish Constitution* (3rd edn, Butterworths, 1994) 959–987.

v Fitzpatrick.[446] Although picketing is lawful where it is in furtherance of a trade dispute, the Supreme Court held that the picket in that case was unlawful. First, the numbers involved in the picket were excessive. Second, some of the picketers' placards invited the public to support concerns other than the picket. The picketers failed in their reliance on Article 40.6.1.ii, as that Article was subject to 'the overriding proviso that in the exercise of such rights public order is not disturbed'.

16.153 The problem of the 'heckler's veto' has been considered in a number of cases. The general position of the Irish courts is that police may restrain the conduct of a person, even though the conduct is lawful, if such conduct is likely to provoke others into violence.[447]

16.154 Freedom of association is dealt with by Article 40.6.1.iii, pursuant to which the state guarantees liberty for the exercise, subject to public order and morality, of:

> The right of the citizens to form associations and unions. Laws, however, may be enacted for the regulation and control in the public interest of the exercise of the foregoing right.

Article 40.6.2 provides that:

> Laws regulating the manner in which the right of forming associations and unions and the right of free assembly may be exercised shall contain no political, religious or class discrimination.

16.155 A challenge to the legislation penalising homosexual conduct based on the freedom of association failed in *Norris v A-G*.[448] The court observed that the right to freedom of association was not absolute, but was subject to public order and morality. There may be statutory regulation of an association's activities without necessarily breaching Article 40.6.1.iii.[449] However, in *NUR v Sullivan*[450] legislation which established a 'Trade Union Tribunal' which had the power to give specified trade unions the exclusive right to represent workers (or employers) of a particular class was held to be in breach of that Article. The Supreme Court stated that:

> to deprive the citizen of the choice of the persons with whom he will associate . . . is not a control of the exercise of the right to association, but a denial of the right altogether. . . . In the opinion of this Court, a law which takes away the right of the citizens, at their choice, to form associations and unions, not contrary to public order or morality, is not a law which can validly be made under the Constitution.

16.156 A person's right to freedom of association does not require that a trade union accept a particular application for membership.[451] Further, freedom of association also involves freedom not to associate, so that employees cannot be forced to join a trade union.[452] It also includes the right to take part in the decision-making procedures of a trade union, although possibly subject to the rules of the trade union.[453]

---

[446] [1958] IR 29.

[447] *Humphries v Connor* 17 Ir CLR 1; *O'Kelly v Harvey* (1883) 15 Cox CC 435; *Coyne v Tweedy* [1898] 2 IR 167.

[448] [1984] IR 36.

[449] *Loftus v A-G* [1979] IR 221; *PMPS v A-G* [1983] IR 339; *Aughey v Ireland* [1989] ILRM 87.

[450] [1947] IR 77.

[451] *Murphy v Stewart* [1973] IR 97.

[452] *Educational Co of Ireland v Fitzpatrick (No 2)* [1961] IR 345; *Crowley v Cleary* [1968] IR 261; *Murtagh Properties v Cleary* [1972] IR 330; *Meskell v Coras Iompair Eireann* [1973] IR 121.

[453] *Rodgers v ITGWU* [1978] ILRM 51; *Doyle v Croke* (1988) 7 JISLL 170.

(5) Lesotho

In *Seeiso v Minister of Home Affairs*[454] the Government sought to ban an assembly on the ground of 'security of the state', 'protection of the public interest' and 'the maintenance of law and order'. The Court of Appeal held that curtailment of a core constitutional right such as freedom of assembly required 'clear and convincing' evidence. As the state had failed to present such evidence, the Court granted the applicant permission to hold the assembly. **16.157**

(6) Nigeria

In the case of *Agbai v Okogbue*[455] the question arose as to the relationship between customary law and the fundamental freedoms of association and religion. According to customary law, residents in the village of the respondent were grouped into age grades and membership in an 'age grade association' was mandatory. The respondent objected to joining such an association on religious grounds. He was a tailor who had his sewing machine seized when he failed to pay a levy imposed by the association. The Supreme Court held that, although it was obliged by statute to apply customary law, a custom was not enforceable as law if it contravened the constitutional rights of freedom of religion and association, or was 'repugnant to natural justice, equity and good conscience'. The customs on which the appellants based their arguments[456] were in breach of these provisions of the Constitution and were invalid and unenforceable as a result. **16.158**

(7) South Africa

Section 17 of the South African Constitution provides that: **16.159**

> Everyone has the right, peacefully and unarmed, to demonstrate, to picket and present petitions

Section 18 provides that:

> Everyone has the right to freedom of association.

There has been little case law dealing with these provisions or with the equivalent provisions of the Interim Constitution.[457]

The case of *South African National Defence Force Union v Minister of Defence*[458] concerned the question as to whether it was constitutional to prohibit members of the armed forces from participating in public protest actions and from joining trade unions. In a majority judgment delivered by O'Regan J, the Constitutional Court decided that the prohibition on joining a trade union was a breach both of the right of 'every worker' to 'form and join a trade union' and a breach of the freedom of association. O'Regan J noted that though the **16.160**

---

454 1998 (6) BCLR 765.

455 [1993] 1 LRC 541.

456 Membership in the age association, even in the absence of consent, and the resort to self-help to secure payment of outstanding levies.

457 Interim Constitution, ss16 and 17; see generally, M Chaskalson, J Kentridge, J Klaaren, G Marcus, D Spitz and S Woolman (eds), *The Constitutional Law of South Africa* (Juta, 1996) Chaps 21 and 22.

458 (1999) 6 BHRC 574.

relationship with the Defence Force was unusual and not identical to an ordinary employment relationship, the conditions of enrolment of members of the armed forces in many respects mirrored those of people employed under a contract of employment.

(8) Sri Lanka

16.161 Freedom of association is guaranteed to every citizen by Article 14(1)(c) of the Constitution. Article 15(4) permits the restriction of this freedom by law, in the interests of racial and religious harmony or national economy. Article 14(1)(d) guarantees the freedom to form and join a trade union. Article 15(7) permits both freedoms to be restricted on a number of grounds, including national security, public order and the rights and freedoms of others.

16.162 Article 157(A) of the Constitution prohibits any political party or other association from having as one of its aims or objects the establishment of a separate state within the territory of Sri Lanka. When the Supreme Court, upon an application made to it, declares that an association has such an aim or object, that association is deemed to be proscribed. Further, emergency regulations empower the President to proscribe an organisation if he is of the opinion that there is a danger of action, or of the utilisation of, such organisation or its adherents for purposes prejudicial to national security, the maintenance of public order or maintenance of essential services or for the purpose of committing certain specified offences. The Supreme Court stated in *Mallikarachchi v Shiva Pasupathi*[459] that an order of proscription so made cannot be challenged as a violation of a fundamental right because of the immunity of the President from suit granted by Article 35(1) of the Constitution. The right to join a trade union was breached in *Gunaratne v People's Bank*,[460] in which the plaintiff was required to resign from his trade union in order to be promoted despite the fact that the plaintiff could have joined another trade union at his promoted grade.

(9) Trinidad and Tobago

16.163 Section 1 of the Constitution guarantees 'freedom of association and assembly'. In *Collymore v A-G of Trinidad and Tobago*[461] the applicant challenged the validity of a statute which prohibited strike action, substituting a compulsory statutory arbitration scheme. The Privy Council held that this provision did not breach the constitutional freedom of association.

(10) Zambia

16.164 In *Mulundika v Zambia*[462] the Supreme Court of Zambia struck down sections 5(4) and 7 of the Public Order Act which required that a permit be obtained to convene an assembly or public meeting, or to form a procession in public, and provided for prosecution for contravention. The plaintiff and seven others had been arrested while taking part in a public gathering for which no permit had been obtained; the High Court found the provisions being challenged to be justifiable in a democratic society in the interests of public order. However, the Supreme Court held that the right to organise and participate in public

[459] (1985) 1 Sri LR 74.
[460] (1986) 1 Sri LR 338.
[461] [1970] AC 538.
[462] (1996) 1 BHRC 199.

gatherings was inherent in the freedom to express and receive ideas and information without interference and that the requirement of prior permission hindered those freedoms by entailing the possibility that the permission might be refused on improper, arbitrary or even unknown grounds. The legislation was found to be objectionable and ultimately unconstitutional because it left an unfettered and uncontrolled subjective discretion to a regulating officer, without guidelines for its exercise or procedural avenue for review. The cumulative effect was that the provisions were not reasonably justifiable in a democratic society.[463]

(11) Zimbabwe

In *Re Munhumeso*[464] the Supreme Court of Zimbabwe struck down legislation which imposed a prior requirement for a permit before an assembly could be held. Taking part in a **16.165** public procession without a permit was a criminal offence. The provision was unlawful because the discretionary power to issue permits was uncontrolled, there being no definition of the criteria to be used in the exercise of the discretion. Further, the holding of a public procession without a permit was criminalised irrespective of the likelihood or occurrence of any threat to public safety or public order.

[463] See also *Pumbun v A-G* [1993] 2 LRC 317 and *Re Munhumeso* [1994] 1 LRC 282 which were applied in *Mulundika.*

[464] [1994] 1 LRC 282.

17

FREEDOM FROM DISCRIMINATION IN RELATION TO CONVENTION RIGHTS

A. The Nature of the Right

17.01 The principle of equality has long been recognised as a fundamental one. Article 1 of the Declaration of Rights of Man of 1789 declares that:

> Men are born and remain free and equal in rights. Social distinctions may be founded only upon the general good.

The American Declaration of Independence proclaimed the 'self-evident truth' that 'all men are created equal'. The principle of 'equality before the law' has been said to be fundamental to the 'rule of law'.[1] However, the abstract principle of equality—that all persons should be uniformly treated, unless there is some valid reason to treat them differently—provides little content to the right. As human conduct is rarely wholly arbitrary, 'reasons' for discriminatory conduct are usually available and the principle of equality will only have an impact if the range of 'valid reasons' for differentiation is limited. It is noteworthy that, despite the provision of the Fourteenth Amendment to the US Constitution requiring 'equal protection of the laws', it was many years before the American courts took serious steps to end racial discrimination, culminating in *Brown v Board of Education of Topeka*.[2]

17.02 It was only in the last half of the twentieth century that the right to equality in the form of non-discrimination came to be firmly established in constitutional law in both international law and domestic jurisdictions. By 1970, protection from racial discrimination had arguably become an international obligation binding on all states with the status of a peremptory norm.[3] There are also international legal principles of non-discrimination on the ground of gender and religious belief.[4] Constitutional and human rights instruments have, increasingly, provided lists of 'prohibited grounds' for discrimination. These now typically include grounds such as race, gender, sex, pregnancy, marital status, ethnic or social origin, colour,

[1] See generally, A Dicey, *Introduction to the Study of the Law of the Constitution* (10th edn, Macmillan, 1965) 202-203.

[2] (1954) 347 US 483 described by the poet Lawrence Ferlinghetti as 'the Supreme Court's decision to desegregate the land of the free'.

[3] *Barcelona Traction Case (Second Phase)* [1970] ICJ 3, 32; see also the well known dissenting judgment of Judge Tanaka in *South West Africa Case (Second Phase)* [1966] ICJ 286-301 and see generally I Brownlie, *Principles of Public International Law* (5th edn, Oxford University Press, 1999) 602.

[4] Brownlie (n 3 above) 603-604.

sexual orientation, age, disability, religion, conscience, belief, culture, language, and birth.[5] Equality before the law requires that differentiation on such grounds be justified by the state.

The right to equality of treatment is now fundamental to the international protection of human rights. The United Nation Charter states that one of its purposes is to promote and encourage human rights 'without distinction as to race, sex, language or religion';[6] and has initiated multilateral human rights agreements[7] fostering non-discrimination and equality as well as treaties which prevent discrimination on specific grounds, particularly sex[8] and race[9] discrimination. Thus, Article 26 of the International Covenant on Civil and Political Rights states that: **17.03**

> All persons are equal before the law and are entitled without discrimination to the equal protection of the law. In this respect the law shall prohibit any discrimination and guarantee to all persons equal and effective protection against discrimination on any ground such as race, colour, sex, language, religion or other opinion, national or social origin, property, birth or other status.

The International Labour Organisation has, in particular, promulgated rights to equal treatment in the employment field by, for example, adopting the Equal Remuneration Convention.[10]

Article 14 of the European Convention is less ambitious. It forbids discrimination by the state *only* in relation to those rights and freedoms contained elsewhere in the Convention. The absence of a free standing right against discrimination justifies the complaint that the European Convention is an outdated human rights instrument.[11] It means that the Human Rights Act has adopted a much more restrictive approach towards equality rights than those contained in a modern human rights instrument such as the Bills of Rights of Canada,[12] New Zealand[13] or South Africa.[14] **17.04**

[5] South African Constitution, s 9 (this list is non-exhaustive), see App S in Vol 2.

[6] UN Charter, Art 1(3).

[7] International Covenant on Civil and Political Rights 1966, 999 UNTS 171, the text is reproduced at App J in Vol 2; and the International Covenant on Economic, Social and Cultural Rights 1966, 993 UNTS 3, the text is reproduced at App K in Vol 2.

[8] Convention on the Political Rights of Women (1952) 193 UNTS 135; International Convention on the Elimination of Discrimination against Women 1979, UKTS 2 (1989) the text is reproduced at App M in Vol 2; Convention (No 100) Equal Remuneration for Men and Women Workers for Work of Equal Value 1951, 165 UNTS 257.

[9] International Covenant on the Elimination of All Forms of Racial Discrimination 1966, 60 UNTS 195; the text is reproduced in App L in Vol 2.

[10] Cmd 100; Art 2 states that 'each member shall . . . ensure that the application to all workers of the principle of equal remuneration for men and women workers for work of equal value'.

[11] See para 3.78ff above.

[12] See para 1.71ff above.

[13] See para 17.194ff below.

[14] See para 17.224ff below.

17.05 Although the need to prevent discrimination is well recognised, there is no consensus about the reasons for doing so. One rationale is the desire to promote equality of opportunity by prohibiting differences of treatment based on morally irrelevant grounds.[15] However, this approach is too individualistic; and fails to address the structural nature of institutionalised discrimination. Another perspective aims to secure equality of outcomes by improving the relative position of disadvantaged social groups. This viewpoint is also open to criticism; it is vague in its formulation, tends to subordinate individuals to social groups and fails to acknowledge that the burden of rectifying discrimination often falls on economically vulnerable groups which have themselves gained no advantage from past discrimination.[16]

17.06 The limitations placed on discrimination are amongst the most controversial of all human rights issues. The extraordinary political upheavals associated with desegregation in the United States are well known.[17] Challenges to gender discrimination continue to excite intense controversy around the world. The prohibition of discrimination on wider grounds is established in few jurisdictions. The areas of debate concerning discrimination rights include the following:

The scope of the right: How far should the 'equal protection of the law' extend? Should it deal only with the provision of public benefits by the state or should it extend to the operation of all laws? To what extent should private citizens be bound?

The extent of the prohibited grounds: What are the grounds on which discrimination should be prohibited? How far should the list extend beyond the well-recognised categories of race or colour, gender, religion, birth and national origin? Grounds such as sexual orientation, disability and social status have caused particular difficulties.

Prohibition of 'indirect discrimination': Discrimination may be 'direct' in the sense that a law may, on its face, treat different groups differently. On the other hand, discrimination can be 'indirect': an apparently neutral law of general application can have a different impact on different groups. The extent to which prohibitions against discrimination should extend to 'indirect' discrimination is contentious.

The justification of discrimination: Although all human rights instruments recognise that different treatment will be appropriate if objectively justified, the

[15] The notion of discrimination applies the Aristotelian maxim that like cases must be treated alike: see S Livingstone, 'Article 14 and the Prevention of Discrimination in the European Convention on Human Rights' [1997] EHRLR 25.

[16] See generally, C McCrudden (ed), *Anti-Discrimination Law* (International Library of Essays in Law and Legal Theory, 1991).

[17] For a survey see H Abraham and B Perry, *Freedom and the Court* (7th edn, Oxford University Press, 1998) Chap 7.

burden and nature of such justification is hotly contested. It has generally been recognised that some types of discrimination require much more powerful justification than others.[18]

Positive discrimination: The legality of programmes of 'positive discrimination' in favour of previously disadvantaged groups raises complex 'discrimination' and 'equality' issues. Rigorous application of 'equal protection' would mean that such programmes would be prohibited as being discriminatory. Although a number of jurisdictions have recognised the need for 'affirmative action' to compensate for past discrimination the justification for and permissible extent of such action remain controversial.

B. The Right in English Law Before the Human Rights Act

(1) Introduction

Dicey argued that the idea of legal equality is fundamental to the rule of law in England; everyone from the Prime Minister to a police constable is under the same responsibility for an illegal act as that of any other citizen.[19] The Privy Council in *Matadeen v Pointu*[20] recently said that: **17.07**

> 'Equality before the law requires that persons should be uniformly treated, unless there is some valid reason to treat them differently'. Their Lordships do not doubt that such a principle is one of the building blocks of democracy and necessarily permeates any democratic constitution. Indeed, their Lordships would go further and say that treating like cases alike and unlike cases differently is a general axiom of rational behaviour.

Nonetheless, the common law has not provided effective protection against discrimination,[21] particularly in race and sex discrimination cases.[22] Despite the famous *dictum* attributed to Lord Mansfield that 'the air of England is too pure for a slave to breathe', the stance of the common law towards slavery was equivocal; and the courts refused, for example, to hold that slavery in the colonies was contrary to public policy.[23] Similarly, when considering complaints of sex discrimination from the last century onwards, the courts consistently held that the word 'person' did **17.08**

[18] Cf the US jurisprudence on the 'three standards of review' in equal protection cases, para 17.203ff below.

[19] A Dicey, *An Introduction to the Study of the Law of the Constitution* (10th edn, Macmillan, 1965) 193.

[20] [1998] 3 WLR 18, 26.

[21] See generally, Lord Woolf and J Jowell, *De Smith, Woolf and Jowell, Judicial Review of Administrative Action* (5th edn, Sweet & Maxwell, 1995) paras 13-036–13-045.

[22] See eg S Sedley, 'Law and Public Life' in M Nolan and S Sedley (eds), *The Making and Remaking of the British Constitution* (Blackstone, 1997).

[23] *Slave Grace's case* (1827) 2 St Tr NS 273.

not cover 'women', obstructing the extension of rights of women to university education,[24] the electoral franchise[25] and entry to the professions.[26]

17.09 On the other hand, in *Constantine v Imperial Hotel*[27] damages of £5 were awarded where hotel accommodation had been refused on grounds of race on the basis that inn keepers had a 'common calling'. More recently, in *Nagle v Fielden*[28] Lord Denning suggested that the Jockey Club's refusal to allow a woman a trainer's licence might be unlawful as being arbitrary or capricious; and in *Edwards v Society of Graphical and Allied Trades*[29] he said that the courts would not allow a power to be exercised arbitrarily or capriciously or with unfair discrimination either in the making of rules or their enforcement. Thus, although the common law does not, in general, make discrimination unlawful, it may indirectly provide a remedy where discrimination is proved.[30]

17.10 Furthermore, there is a well established principle of administrative law that a public body has acted *Wednesbury* irrationally[31] if it has behaved in a discriminatory manner. Lord Russell CJ said in *Kruse v Johnson*[32] that a bye-law might be *ultra vires* and unreasonable if it is manifestly partial and unequal in its operation between different classes. Thus, a local authority's actions were *ultra vires* where it imposed a condition preventing those affiliated to political parties from participating at an event in the local authority's park.[33] The exercise of an administrative discretion may also be *Wednesbury* irrational where a public body fails to exercise its discretion fairly and consistently.[34] For example, planning permission will not

[24] *Jex Blake v Edinburgh University* (1873) 11 M 784.

[25] *Chorlin v Lings* (1868) LR 4 CP 374 (legislative presumption in the Reform Act 1867 that 'man' included 'woman' was displaced by the historical fact that women had never been allowed to vote); and see, also *Nairn v St Andrews and Edinburgh University Courts* 1909 SC (HL) 10 (the legal disability which prevented women from voting was so self evident that it 'is inconceivable that . . . anyone acquainted with our laws or the methods by which they are ascertained can think, if indeed, anyone does think, that there is room for argument on such a point').

[26] See eg *Bebb v Law Society* [1914] 1 Ch 286 which held that women were not entitled as 'persons' under the Solicitors Act 1843 to take articles.

[27] [1944] KB 693.

[28] [1966] 2 QB 433, 647.

[29] [1971] Ch 354, 376; see also *Weinberger v Inglis* [1919] AC 606.

[30] See eg *Scala Ballroom (Wolverhampton) Ltd v Ratcliffe* [1958] 1 WLR 1057 where it was held that it was a legitimate objective for the purposes of the law of conspiracy for the Musicians' Union to destroy a colour bar; and the cases concerning trust instruments eg *In re Dominion Students' Hall Trust* [1947] Ch 183; *Re Mere's Will Trust, The Times*, 4 May 1957 but compare *In re Lysaght, decd* [1966] 1 Ch 191; *Blathwayth v Baron Cawley* [1976] AC 397.

[31] For a discussion of the doctrine, see para 5.126 above.

[32] [1898] 2 QB 91.

[33] *R v Barnet London Borough Council, ex p Johnson* (1990) 89 LGR 581; and see *Ex p Manshoora* [1986] Imm R 385.

[34] *HTV Ltd v Price Commission* [1976] ICR 170, 185, 186; *Ex p Preston* [1985] AC 835, 864–867; *Inland Revenue Commissioners v National Federation of Self Employed and Small Businesses Ltd* [1982] AC 617, 651; *R v Inland Revenue Commissioners, ex p Mead* [1993] 1 All ER 772, 783; J Jowell, 'Is Equality a Constitutional Principle?' (1994) 7 CLP 1, 12–14; K Steyn, 'Consistency—A Principle of Public Law' [1997] JR 22.

be granted if it creates a precedent that would be difficult to depart from without creating the impression of unfairness.[35] On the other hand, 'justification' of different treatment will be straightforward when *Wednesbury* principles are applied: the decision will only be set aside if wholly irrational. Thus, a complaint of *Wednesbury* irrationality failed in the well-known challenge to the policy of the Ministry of Defence of dismissing homosexuals from the armed forces.[36]

In short, before the Race Relations Act 1965 was enacted, English law had little to say about discrimination.[37] Indeed, the common law right to discriminate outside the narrow categories already discussed was held to justify a restrictive interpretation to provisions in the Race Relations Act 1968.[38] Because the common law does not prohibit certain forms of discrimination, Parliament has intervened by enacting legislation such as the Sex Discrimination Act 1975 as amended, the Equal Pay Act 1970, the Race Relations Act 1976 and the Disability Discrimination Act 1995. European Community law has also provided strong protection against sex discrimination. These initiatives have in turn influenced the development of the common law, particularly in the employment field where, for example, it has been held that sexual harassment can breach the implied term of mutual confidence between employer and employee[38a] and that equal opportunity policies may become incorporated into the contract of employment.[38b] **17.11**

(2) Sex discrimination

(a) The meaning of discrimination

The Sex Discrimination Act 1975 was modelled on the legal principles which developed out of the Civil Rights Act 1964 in the United States. The 1975 Act bans overt discrimination where women are treated differently from men because of their sex; and introduced the concept of 'direct discrimination'. However, the legislation in fact went further. It also prohibits *covert* discrimination in line with the decision of the American Supreme Court in *Griggs v Duke Power*.[39] In that case the Supreme Court held that employers discriminated on race grounds by requiring academic qualifications because this employment practice operated to exclude **17.12**

[35] See eg *Collis Radio v Secretary of State for the Environment* (1975) 73 LGR 211; *Tempo Discount v Secretary of State for the Environment* [1979] JPL 97; *Poundstretcher v Secretary of State for the Environment* [1989] JPL 90.

[36] *R v Ministry of Defence, ex p Smith* [1996] QB 517.

[37] J Griffith, *Coloured Immigrants in Britain* (Oxford University Press—Institute of Race Relations, 1961) 171.

[38] *Dockers' Labour Club and Institute Ltd v Race Relations Board* [1976] AC 285 *per* Lord Diplock at 296-297.

[38a] See eg *Reed v Stedman* [1999] IRLR 299.

[38b] See eg *Taylor v Secretary of State for Scotland* [2000] IRLR 502 (HL); and contrast *Grant v South West Trains* [1998] IRLR 188.

[39] (1971) 401 US 424.

blacks, even though the employers had no intention to discriminate. Adopting this approach the Sex Discrimination Act created the principle of 'indirect discrimination' to extend the scope of the legislation to practices which have the *effect* (if not the intention) of discriminating against women.

17.13 **Direct discrimination.** The Sex Discrimination Act[40] prohibits discrimination against women[41] and men[42] on the grounds of their sex, against married persons on the grounds of their marital status[43] or on grounds of their gender reassignment.[44] It also prohibits victimisation, that is, less favourable treatment because a person has brought discrimination proceedings, given evidence in such proceedings or made an allegation of discrimination.[45] The correct approach when making a comparison for the purposes of a victimisation claim is to consider what the applicant is seeking, not the reason for the employer's treatment of the applicant. Thus, in *Khan v Chief Constable of Yorkshire*[45a] a chief constable refused to give a reference to a police officer who had brought a discrimination case: the Court of Appeal held that the applicant had been victimised because the proper comparator was another officer seeking a reference, not an officer who had commenced some other type of claim against the Chief Constable.

17.14 There is direct discrimination against a woman if, on the ground of her sex, she is treated less favourably than a man is treated or would be treated.[46] There is no need to prove that the reason for the treatment was an intention or desire to discriminate.[47] However, direct discrimination does require that the comparison with an actual or hypothetical comparator is made by examining if the circumstances are the same.[48]

17.15 The Act does not directly address sexual harassment. However, it has been defined in the European Commission Code of Practice[49] as unwanted conduct of a sexual

[40] For a fuller treatment see eg *Butterworth's Discrimination Law Handbook* (Butterworths, 2000) Div 1.

[41] Sex Discrimination Act 1975, s 1.

[42] Ibid s 2.

[43] Ibid s 3.

[44] Ibid s 2A as inserted by the Sex Discrimination (Gender Assignment) Regulations 1999, SI 1999/1102.

[45] Sex Discrimination Act 1975, s 4(1) and see Equal Treatment Directive (EEC) 76/207, Art 7.

[45a] [2000] IRLR 324; and see *TNT Expresss Worldwide v Brown*, *The Times*, 18 Apr 2000.

[46] Sex Discrimination Act 1975, s 1(1)(a); for discrimination against men see ibid s 2(1); for discrimination against married persons see ibid s 3(1).

[47] *Birmingham City Council v Equal Opportunities Commission* [1989] AC 1155; *James v Eastleigh Borough Council* [1990] 2 AC 751; and in relation to race discrimination see *R v Commission for Racial Equality, ex p Westminster City Council* [1984] ICR 770 affirmed [1985] ICR 426.

[48] See eg *Bain v Bowles* [1991] IRLR 356.

[49] Commission Recommendation of 27 Nov1991 on the protection of the dignity of women and men at work (EEC) 91/131 and the Commission Code of Practice on Protecting the Dignity of Women and Men at Work.

nature or other conduct based on sex affecting the dignity of men and women and this definition was adopted for the purposes of the 1975 Act in *British Telecommunications v Williams*.[50] Sexual harassment will constitute direct discrimination. It may involve a course of conduct[51] but can arise from a single act.[52]

It is usually necessary for an applicant to prove her direct discrimination case by inference. The basic principles were described by the House of Lords in *Zafar v Glasgow City Council*.[53] The applicant must prove her case on the balance of probabilities but it is important to bear in mind that it is unusual to find direct evidence of discrimination. The outcome of the case will therefore usually depend on what inferences it is proper to draw from the primary facts found by the tribunal. A finding of a difference of treatment and a finding of a difference of sex will often point to the possibility of sex discrimination and in such circumstances, the tribunal will look to the employer for an explanation. If no explanation is then put forward, or if the tribunal considers the explanation to be inadequate or unsatisfactory, it will be legitimate for the tribunal to infer that the discrimination was on grounds of sex. **17.16**

However, when being invited to draw inferences of unlawful discrimination, an employment tribunal should keep well in mind that it does not follow in logic or reason that because a person's behaviour is unfair, unreasonable, incompetent or unjustified, it should be inferred that his behaviour was unlawfully motivated by discrimination.[54] **17.17**

Indirect discrimination. The principle of indirect discrimination is designed to prevent women being excluded from opportunities by a gender neutral condition which they are less likely to meet than men. Indirect discrimination[55] arises where a person applies a requirement or condition[56] which has a disproportionate effect[57] in that it is more difficult, in practice, for the applicant to comply.[58] The applicant must show that the proportion of those with whom she compares herself who can comply[59] with **17.18**

[50] [1997] IRLR 668.

[51] See eg *Porcelli v Strathclyde Regional Council* [1996] ICR 564.

[52] See eg *Bracebridge Engineering v Derby* [1990] IRLR 3.

[53] [1997] 1 WLR 1659.

[54] See eg *Qureshi v London Borough of Newnham* [1991] IRLR 264; *Fire Brigade Union v Fraser* [1997] IRLR 671; *Martins v Marks and Spencer* [1998] IRLR 326.

[55] Sex Discrimination Act 1975, s 1(1)(b) (in relation to women), s 2(1) (in relation to men) and s 3(1)(b) (in relation to married persons).

[56] See *Perera v Civil Service Commission (No 2)* [1983] ICR 428; but see *Falkirk Council v Whyte* [1997] IRLR 560.

[57] To identify the pool for comparison see eg *London Underground v Edwards* [1995] IRLR 355; *London Underground Ltd v Edwards (No 2)* [1998] IRLR 364.

[58] *Mandla (Sewa Singh) v Dowell Lee* [1983] IRLR 209.

[59] *Price v Civil Service Commission* [1978] ICR 27; *Mandla (Sewa Singh) v Dowell Lee* [1983] 2 AC 548.

the relevant requirement is considerably smaller[60] than the proportion of those who are not in the pool.[61] This is an objective question to be decided by looking at the statistical evidence in relation to the appropriate pool of men and women. The applicant must also prove that the requirement operates to her detriment which requires consideration of her personal circumstances.[62] If there is a *prima facie* case that a particular requirement amounts to indirect discrimination, the requirement may nevertheless be justified by objectively balancing the discriminatory effect of the condition against the reasonable needs of the party which applies the condition.[63] However, the burden of proof lies on the applicant to demonstrate there is indirect discrimination.[63a]

17.19 **Pregnancy.** A dismissal[64] or refusal to offer employment[65] or other detriment on grounds of pregnancy or a pregnancy related illness[66] may be unlawful under the Equal Treatment Directive.[67] In *Webb v Emo Air Cargo (No 2)*[68] the House of Lords held that a dismissal of a pregnant employee was contrary to the Sex Discrimination Act. The House of Lords took the view that the dismissal amounted to direct discrimination, but that comparison with a man was inappropriate. The employee must prove that her pregnancy caused her dismissal.[69] A dismissal will also be automatically unfair if the reason is pregnancy or any other reason connected with pregnancy.[70]

17.20 **Sexual orientation discrimination.** Sexual orientation discrimination is not within the scope of the Sex Discrimination Act 1975.[71] Thus, gender specific words of abuse directed at a homosexual do not amount to sex discrimination.[71a] Although the European Court of Justice has held that it is contrary to the Equal Treatment Directive[72] to dismiss a transsexual for undergoing gender

[60] See *R v Secretary of State for Employment, ex p Seymour-Smith* [1999] 3 WLR 460; *R v Secretary of State for Employment, ex p Seymour-Smith (No 2)* [2000] 1 WLR 435.

[61] See eg *London Underground v Edwards (No 2)* [1998] IRLR 364; *R v Secretary of State for Employment ex p Seymour-Smith* (Case C-167/197) [1999] AC 554 460.

[62] *Briggs v North Eastern Education and Library Board* [1990] IRLR 181.

[63] *Webb v Emo Air Cargo UK* [1993] ICR 175 per Lord Keith at 182; *Hampson v Department of Education and Science* [1989] ICR 179.

[63a] *Barry v Midland Bank* [1998] IRLR 138.

[64] *Handels-og Kontorfunkktionaerernes Foribund i Danmark v Dansk Arbejdsgi verforening* [1990] ECR I-3979.

[65] *Dekker v Stichting Vormgscentrum voor Jong Volwassenen* [1990] ECR I-3941.

[66] *Brown v Rentokil* [1998] IRLR 445; *Boyle v Equal Opportunities Commission* [1998] IRLR 717.

[67] Directive (EEC) 76/207, see para 17.52 below.

[68] [1995] 1 WLR 1454.

[69] *O'Neil v Governors of St Thomas More Roman Catholic Voluntarily Aided Upper School* [1997] ICR 33.

[70] Employment Rights Act 1996, s 99.

[71] *Smith v Gardner Merchant Ltd* [1996] ICR 790.

[71a] *Pearce v Governing Body of Mayfield School, The Times*, 7 Apr 2000.

[72] EEC 75/118.

reassignment,[73] the Court has refused to extend its reasoning to prohibit discrimination on grounds of sexual orientation.[74] On the other hand, an intrusive investigation and dismissal of an employee on grounds of his sexual orientation breaches the right of respect for private life under Article 8 of the Convention.[75]

Positive discrimination. Positive discrimination is, in general, unlawful.[76] **17.21**
However, the Sex Discrimination Act permits specially advantageous treatment for certain limited purposes. Vocational training can be offered on a preferential basis where one sex is seriously unrepresented in the workforce[77] and where discrimination is carried out for the protection of women as required by statute,[78] it is lawful to discriminate in favour of women in employment, vocational training and discriminatory practices.[79]

(b) Acts of discrimination

Introduction. Not all sex discrimination is unlawful under the Sex Discrimina- **17.22**
tion Act 1975. In order to bring a successful claim the applicant must show:

- that she has been the victim of an act of direct or indirect sex discrimination; and
- that the act of discrimination in question is one which is made unlawful by the Sex Discrimination Act.

The Act covers discrimination in employment,[80] in education[81] and in relation to the provision of goods, facilities, services and premises.[82] The Act provides for a number of general exclusions from liability[83] including, for example, discriminating when making risk assessments for insurance purposes.

---

[73] Which is now within the Sex Discrimination Act 1975, see s 2A (inserted by the Sex Discrimination (Gender Assignment) Regulations 1999, SI 1999/1102).

[74] *Grant v South-West Trains* [1998] ECR I-621; *R v Secretary of State for Employment ex p Perkins (No 2)* [1998] IRLR 508.

[75] *Lustig-Prean v United Kingdom* (1999) 7 BHRC 65; *Smith and Grady v United Kingdom* [1999] IRLR 734.

[76] *Lambeth London Borough Council v Commission for Racial Equality* [1990] IRLR 231, 234; *Jepson and Dyas-Elliot v Labour Party* [1996] IRLR 116, see also *Kalanake v Freie Hansestadt Bremen* [1995] ECR I-3051.

[77] Sex Discrimination Act 1975, ss 47 and 48.

[78] These exclusions essentially involve health and safety issues.

[79] Sex Discrimination Act 1975, s 51 as substituted by the Employment Act 1989, s 3(1), (3), (4).

[80] Sex Discrimination Act 1975, Pt II.

[81] Ibid Pt III, ss 22–28.

[82] Ibid Pt III, ss 29–35.

[83] See para 17.34 below.

17.23 **Discrimination in employment.** The Sex Discrimination Act has an extended definition of an employee.[84] It covers individuals who are self employed:[85]that is, those who work under a contract to personally execute work.[86] There are also specific provisions protecting contract workers.[87]

17.24 It is unlawful for an employer to discriminate against prospective employees[88] in the arrangements made to determine who should be offered employment,[89] the terms on which employment is offered or the refusal or failure to offer a job. It is also unlawful to discriminate against employees[90] by restricting or denying opportunities for promotion,[91] transfer or training, by restricting or denying access to any other benefits, facilities or services, dismissing the applicant or subjecting her to a detriment[92] (which can include sexual harassment).[93] An employer may be liable for discriminating against an employee after her employment ceased under the Equal Treatment Directive[94] by, for example, failing to provide a reference.[95] In limited and defined circumstances the employer may prove that sex is a genuine occupational qualification.[96]

17.25 An employer may be vicariously liable for the discriminatory acts of an employee acting in the course of his employment;[97] the phrase 'in the course of employment' should be interpreted purposively as it is used in everyday language.[98] An employer may also be liable for the acts of his clients or customers if they harass employees and he fails to take reasonable steps to prevent the harassment.[99]

[84] Sex Discrimination Act 1975, s 82(1).

[85] See eg *Loughran v Northern Ireland Housing Executive* [1998] 3 WLR 735 under the comparable provisions of the Fair Employment (Northern Ireland) Act 1976 regulating religious discrimination.

[86] *Mirror Group Newspapers Ltd v Gunning* [1986] 1 WLR 546.

[87] Sex discirmiiaton Act 1975, s 9; see eg *Harrods Ltd v Remick* [1997] IRLR 583.

[88] Sex Discrimination Act 1975, s 6(1).

[89] The Equal Opportunities Commission Code of Practice for the Elimination of Discrimination on Grounds of Sex contains a series of recommended practices covering recruitment.

[90] Sex Discrimination Act 1975, s 6(2).

[91] See the recommendations in the Equal Opportunities Commission Code of Practice for the Elimination of Discrimination on Grounds of Sex and Marriage.

[92] Sex Discrimination Act 1975, s 6(2)(b); in *Ministry of Defence v Jeremiah* [1980] QB 87 the Court of Appeal held that detriment involved a disadvantage.

[93] See eg *Porcelli v Strathclyde Regional Council* [1985] ICR 177 affirmed [1986] ICR 564; European Commission Recommendation (EEC) 91/131 on the protection and dignity of women and men at work and Code of Practice.

[94] (EEC) 76/207.

[95] *Coote v Granada Hospitality* [1999] IRLR 452; the position appears to be different under the Race Relations Act: see *Adekeye v Post Office (No 2)* [1997] IRLR 105.

[96] Sex Discrimination Act 1975, s 7.

[97] Ibid s 41(1), (2).

[98] *Jones v Tower Boot Company Ltd* [1997] ICR 254; this broad approach extends vicarious liability to incidents that take place as an extension of the workplace such as having a drink at a public house after work: see *Chief Constable of Lincolnshire v Stubbs* [1999] IRLR 81 and contrast *Waters v Commissioner of Police of the Metropolis* [1997] ICR 1073.

[99] *Burton v De Vere Hotels Ltd* [1996] IRLR 596.

However, an employer has a defence to show he took such steps as were reasonably practicable to prevent the employee from doing the acts complained of.[100]

The Sex Discrimination Act applies to differences in retirement ages and to benefits payable on death or retirement.[101] However, it does not cover other provisions in relation to retirement or death.[102] **17.26**

The Sex Discrimination Act also makes discrimination unlawful in partnerships,[103] unions or professional associations,[104] in any authorities or bodies which confer trade or professional qualifications,[105] vocational training,[106] employment agencies[107] and certain training bodies[108] such as the General Medical Council.[109] In addition, the Act makes it unlawful to discriminate in fields other than in employment. **17.27**

Discrimination in education. The Sex Discrimination Act prohibits discrimination by individual educational establishments and by local educational authorities.[110] It is unlawful for an educational establishment to discriminate against a woman in the terms on which she is admitted as a pupil, her application for admission or, if she is a pupil, in the way she is given access to any benefits, facilities, services or refusing her access to them or excluding her from the establishment or subjecting her to some other detriment.[111] **17.28**

It is also unlawful for a local educational authority in carrying out its functions to do anything which constitutes sex discrimination.[112] Thus, it was unlawful for a local educational authority to maintain an educational system where the opportunities for selective education were much less for girls than boys.[113] There is also a general duty in public sector education not to discriminate.[114] **17.29**

[100] Sex Discrimination Act, s 41(3); see eg *Balgobin v London Borough of Tower Hamlets* [1987] ICR 829.

[101] Sex Discrimination Act 1975, s 6(4) inserted by the Sex Discrimination Act 1986, s 2.

[102] Sex Discrimination Act 1975, s 6(4);

[103] Ibid s 11; unlike the Race Relations Act, which is confined under s 10 to firms comprising more than six partners this prohibition applies regardless of the size of the partnership.

[104] Sex Discrimination Act 1975, s 12.

[105] Ibid s 13; see the approach of the House of Lords in *Loughran v Northern Ireland Housing Executive* [1998] 3 WLR 735 to the comparable provisions of the Fair Employment (Northern Ireland) Act 1976; and see *British Judo Association v Petty* [1981] ICR 660; *Sawyer v Asham* [1999] IRLR 609.

[106] Sex Discrimination Act 1975, s 14 as amended by the Employment Act 1989; note that s 47 allows positive discrimination in limited circumstances: see para 17.21 above.

[107] Sex Discrimination Act 1975, ss 15 and 82(1).

[108] Ibid s 16.

[109] *General Medical Council v Goba* [1988] ICR 885.

[110] For a fuller treatment, see eg R McManus, *Education and the Courts* (Sweet & Maxwell, 1998) Chap 2.

[111] Sex Discrimination Act 1975, s 22.

[112] Ibid s 23.

[113] *R v Birmingham City Council, ex p Equal Opportunities Commission* [1989] AC 1155; *R v Birmingham City Council, ex p Equal Opportunities Commission (No 2)* [1994] ELR 282.

[114] Sex Discrimination Act 1975, s 25.

17.30 However, there are special provisions[115] which ensure that single sex education is lawful and not in breach of other provisions under the Act. It is lawful to discriminate in relation to physical education programmes[116] and to a limited extent in relation to vocational training.[117]

17.31 **Discrimination in providing goods, facilities or services.** It is unlawful[118] to discriminate in providing goods, facilities[119] or services[120] to the public.[121] However, where facilities and services are provided by a public authority, the authority will only be acting unlawfully in relation to an act which is similar to one done by a private person, so that the Act would not extend, for example, to an immigration officer who was controlling would-be immigrants.[122]

17.32 It is unlawful to discriminate in relation to premises of which a person has the power to dispose or manage[123] or to discriminate against withholding a licence or consent for the disposal of premises;[124] however, these provisions do not affect individuals concerned in small premises.[125] There are also exceptions for political parties,[126] for voluntary bodies[127] as well as certain other defined exceptions[128] such as where the presence of a man causes serious embarrassment. It is unlawful for barristers or their clerks to discriminate.[129]

17.33 **Other unlawful acts.** Part IV of the Sex Discrimination Act makes the following unlawful: discriminatory practices,[130] discriminatory advertisements,[131] discriminatory instructions[132] or applying pressure to discriminate[133] or aiding discriminatory acts.[134]

---

[115] Ibid ss 26 and 27.
[116] Ibid s 28.
[117] Ibid s 47.
[118] Ibid s 29; and see ibid s 36.
[119] *Kassam v Immigration Appeals Tribunal* [1980] 1 WLR 1037; *Sarjani v Inland Revenue Commissioners* [1981] QB 458.
[120] Service includes assistance by a police officer (*Farah v Commissioner of Police of the Metropolis* [1998] QB 65), tax advice from a tax officer (*Sarjani v Inland Revenue Commissioners* [1981] QB 458) and a hire purchase credit scheme (*Quinn v Williams Furniture* [1981] ICR 328).
[121] Public is to be contrasted with private so that a private members' club is not covered: see *Charter v Race Relations Board* [1973] AC 868; *Dockers' Labour Club and Institute Ltd v Race Relations Board* [1976] AC 285.
[122] *Amin v Entry Clearance Officer, Bombay* [1983] 2 AC 818.
[123] Sex Discrimination Act 1975, s 30.
[124] Ibid s 31.
[125] Ibid s 32.
[126] Ibid s 33.
[127] Ibid s 34.
[128] Ibid s 35.
[129] Ibid s 35A inserted by the Courts and Legal Services Act 1990, s 64(1).
[130] Sex Discrimination Act 1975, s 37.
[131] Ibid s 38.
[132] Ibid s 39.
[133] Ibid s 40.
[134] Ibid s 42.

General exclusions. The Sex Discrimination Act creates general exceptions from liability. Charitable trusts may discriminate on grounds of sex where the provision is contained in a charitable instrument.[135] It is not unlawful to segregate the sexes in any sport, game or other competitive activity where physical strength, stamina or physique of the average woman places her at a disadvantage with the average man.[136] It is not unlawful to discriminate in relation to any annuity, life policy, accident policy or similar matters involving the assessment of risk.[137] Sex discrimination may be lawful in admitting or providing benefits to communal accommodation.[138] It may be lawful to discriminate in training,[139] recruitment drives[140] or in relation to the elections of trade unions, employers' associations and professional associations.[141] **17.34**

Where there is discrimination in access to certain benefits, facilities or services and the employer (or primary defendant) is exempt from liability under some other provision of the Sex Discrimination Act, then the actual provider of the benefit is entitled to take advantage of the same defence.[142] In general, any statutory provisions which are designed to protect women but are discriminatory take precedence over the Sex Discrimination Act.[143] It may be lawful to discriminate in the interests of national security[144] and a ministerial certificate may be conclusive, although not in employment cases.[145] **17.35**

(c) Remedies

No proceedings may be taken against a person for contravention of the Sex Discrimination Act except as prescribed by the Act.[146] The individual complainant may pursue a complaint of an act of discrimination in the employment field[147] or under the provisions concerned with the liability of employers and principals[148] or aiding discriminatory acts[149] (which is to be treated as discriminating against the **17.36**

---

[135] Ibid s 43 as substituted by the Sex Discrimination Act 1975 (Amendment of s 43) Order 1977, SI 1977/528, art 2.

[136] Sex Discrimination Act 1975, s 44.

[137] Ibid s 45.

[138] Ibid s 46.

[139] Ibid s 47: but see *Kalanke v Freie Hansestadt Bremen* [1995] ECR 1-3051.

[140] Sex Discrimination Act 1975, s 48(3).

[141] Ibid s 49(1).

[142] Ibid s 50(1).

[143] Ibid s 51 as substituted by the Employment Act 1989, s 3(3); see also Employmnt Act 1989, s 1.

[144] Sex Discrimination Act 1975, s 52.

[145] Sex Discrimination (Amendment) Order 1988, SI 1988/249.

[146] Sex Discrimination Act 1975, s 62(1).

[147] Ibid s 63(1) the field of employment is discussed at para 17.23ff above.

[148] Ibid s 41.

[149] Ibid s 42. 'Aid' means to help or assist and contemplates a state of affairs where one party sets out to achieve a result and the other helps him do it: see *Anyanwu v South Bank Students' Union* [2000] IRLR 36. The secondary party must know that the principal is treating (or is about to treat) someone less favourably on grounds of race; recklessness or carelessness is not enough: see *Hallam v Avery, The Times*, 7 Feb 2000.

complainant)[150] by presenting a complaint to the employment tribunal within three months of the discriminatory act. The complaint may be heard even though it is out of time if it is just and equitable to do so.[151] Only the Equal Opportunities Commission[152] can bring proceedings[153] in relation to discriminatory advertisements,[154] discriminatory instructions[155] or the application of pressure to discriminate.[156] A complaint of discrimination in other fields may be brought by the complainant in a designated county court[157] within six months which may be considered out of time if it is just and equitable to do so.[158]

(3) Equal Pay

(a) Introduction

17.37 The principle of equal pay was introduced by the Equal Pay Act 1970.[159] The Equal Opportunities Commission has also produced a Code of Practice on Equal Pay which may be taken into account in any proceedings.[160] The Equal Pay Act 1970[161] deems that a woman's contract of employment includes an equality clause which ensures that she receives contractual benefits equal to a man engaged in like work, work rated as equivalent or work of equal value.[162] The equality clause does not operate where the employer proves that the variation of pay is genuinely due to a material factor other than the difference in sex.[163] The Equal Pay Act 1970 is not limited to equal pay and covers *all* contractual provisions.

17.38 However, the Equal Pay Act 1970 does not apply to non-contractual remuneration which falls within the scope of sections 6 and 8 of the Sex Discrimination Act 1975. The precise relationship between the two statutes is complex[164] although the courts now try to construe the legislative provisions harmoniously to provide a unified code for dealing with unlawful sex discrimination.[165] In general, where

[150] Sex Discrimination Act 1975, s 63(1)(b).
[151] Ibid s 76(1), (5).
[152] Whose functions are defined by ibid s 53(1).
[153] Ibid s 72.
[154] Ibid s 38.
[155] Ibid s 39.
[156] Ibid s 40.
[157] Ibid s 66.
[158] Ibid s 76(2), (5).
[159] Which was substantially amended by the Sex Discrimination Act 1975.
[160] Equal Opportunities Commission Code of Practice on Equal Pay (1997). The Code was made under the Sex Discrimination Act 1975, s 56A; and breach of a provision may be taken by a tribunal where relevant: see ibid s 56A(10).
[161] For a fuller treatment, see eg *Butterworths' Discrimination Law Handbook* (Butterworths, 2000) Div 2.
[162] Equal Pay Act 1970, s 1(2).
[163] Ibid s 1(3).
[164] See the principles set out by Philips J in *Peake v Automative Products Ltd* [1977] QB 780.
[165] *Wallace v Strathclyde Regional Council* [1998] IRLR 146.

the comparison is with a hypothetical person, an applicant will use the Sex Discrimination Act 1975.

The Equal Pay Act also operates in conjunction with European Community law, particularly Article 141[166] of the Treaty and the Equal Pay Directive.[167] The Act is often less favourable to an individual than the equivalent provision in Article 141; and in that circumstance European Community law will prevail.[168] **17.39**

Although the Equal Pay Act applies to contractual rights, the Community right under Article 141 only covers pay and remuneration; however, pay under Article 141 has an extended meaning and can include indirect benefits and non-contractual bonuses,[169] pensions[170] or benefits associated with terminations on grounds of redundancy or unfair dismissal.[171] **17.40**

(b) The right to equal pay

The right to equal pay is available to any person employed under a contract for personal services.[172] The Act implies an equality clause into the contract[173] which is defined as a clause which ensures that a woman is given equal treatment: **17.41**

- to a man[174] in the same employment[175] who has engaged in like work;[176]
- to a man who has been rated as equivalent to her[177] in a job evaluation study; or
- to a man who is otherwise of equal value to hers.[178]

Under the Equal Pay Act itself a woman must have a male comparator[179] which she may choose.[180] However, there is no requirement to have a comparator if the employee claims equal pay under Article 141[181] and it now seems that the Equal **17.42**

[166] Formerly Art 119.
[167] (EEC) 75/107.
[168] See eg *Barber v Guardian Royal Exchange Assurance* [1990] ECR I-1189.
[169] *Garland v British Rail Engineering Ltd* [1982] ECR 359.
[170] *Worringham and Humphreys v Lloyd's Bank Ltd* [1981] ECR 767.
[171] *EC Commission v Belgium* [1993] ECR I-673.
[172] Equal Pay Act, s 1(6).
[173] Ibid s 1(1).
[174] Ibid s 1(2)(a).
[175] Ibid s 1(6).
[176] Ibid s 1(4); and in *Waddington v Leicester Council for Voluntary Services* [1977] 1 WLR 541 the EAT indicated that this depended on (i) whether the work was the same or of a broadly similar nature (*Capper Pass Ltd v Lawton* [1977] QB 852; and (ii) whether there were differences in terms and conditions of practical importance in what was actually done by the female worker and her male comparator (*Combes v Shields* [1978] ICR 1159).
[177] Equal Pay Act 1970, s 1(2)(b).
[178] Ibid s 1(2)(c).
[179] *Meeks v National Union of Agricultural and Allied Workers* [1976] IRLR 198.
[180] *Ainsworth v Glass Tubes and Components Ltd* [1977] ICR 347.
[181] *McCarthy's Ltd v Smith* [1980] ECR 1275 which allowed the applicant to make a comparison with her male predecessor; and see *Diocese of Hallam Trustees v Connaughton* [1996] ICR 860 where the comparison was made with the male successor.

Pay Act must be interpreted purposively in line with Article 141.[182] The male comparator must have common terms of employment[183] with the female. If she wishes to show that she and her comparator are engaged in like work,[184] then it is necessary to examine whether the work is of a broadly similar nature[185] and if so, whether any differences in their tasks justify being given different terms and conditions.[186] Alternatively, a woman may wish to claim that her job is rated under a job evaluation scheme as being of equal value to a man[187] or that her work is of equal value.[188]

17.43 It is, however, permissible to discriminate in terms and conditions where employees are affected by compliance with laws relating to the employment of women,[189] where there was special treatment in connection with childbirth or pregnancy[190] or where the terms related to death or retirement.[191]

17.44 An equality clause will operate in favour of a woman unless the employer can prove that the variation in contractual terms is genuinely due to a material difference other than sex.[192] In *Glasgow City Council v Marshall*[192a] the House of Lords stated that the Equal Pay Act creates a rebuttable presumption of sex discrimination once a gender based comparison shows that a woman doing like work is treated less favourably than a man; however, it does not oblige an employer to prove a 'good' reason for a pay disparity. To justify the disparity an employer must show[193] that he is pursuing measures which correspond to a real need and which are appropriate and necessary to meet the need[194] such as market forces,[195] red

[182] See *Albion Shipping Agency v Arnold* [1982] ICR 22; it is now clear from the Court of Appeal decision in *Staffordshire County Council v Barber* [1996] ICR 379 that Art 141 does not create a free standing right to equal pay.

[183] Equal Pay Act 1970, s 1(6); *British Coal Corporation v Smith* [1996] ICR 515.

[184] Equal Pay Act 1970, s 1(4).

[185] *Capper Pass Ltd v Lawton* [1977] QB 852.

[186] *Dorothy Perkins v Dance* [1977] IRLR 226.

[187] Equal Pay Act 1970, s 1(5).

[188] Ibid s 1(2)(c).

[189] Ibid s 6(1)(a).

[190] Ibid s 6(1)(b).

[191] Ibid s 6(1A)(b); any unjustified discrimination in benefits paid under an occupational pension scheme is unlawful: see *Barber v Guardian Royal Exchange Assurance* [1990] ECR I-1189; *Smith v Avdel Systems Ltd* [1994] ECR I-4435; furthermore, the Sex Discrimination Act 1986 makes unlawful the differential retirement ages for the sexes (as opposed to pension ages); the Occupational Pensions Scheme (Equal Access to Membership) Regulations 1976, SI 1976/742 make it unlawful to discriminate on grounds of length of service or age in relation to access to pension schemes.

[192] Sex Discrimination Act 1975, s 1(3).

[192a] [2000] IRLR 272.

[193] See *Wallace v Strathclyde Regional Council* [1998] IRLR 146 where the House of Lords emphasised a three-stage approach.

[194] *Rainey v Greater Glasgow Health Board* [1987] AC 224; *Enderby v Frenchay Health Authority* [1993] ECR 5535.

[195] Ibid.

circling,[196] length of service[197] or different working hours or holidays.[198] However, the defences of length and different working hours may be challenged as being indirect sex discrimination.[199]

If the equality clause is effective, a woman's contract is varied so as to become no less favourable than the man's contract.[199a] The contract must be examined item by item and modified in any particular which is less favourable.[200] **17.45**

(c) Remedies

Any claim for breach of a term modified or included by virtue of an equality clause may be presented to the employment tribunal[201] although it can also be brought as a breach of contract claim in the High Court or county court. No claim can be referred to the tribunal if the applicant has not been employed in the employment within six months preceding the reference.[202] **17.46**

A claim may be brought for arrears of remuneration or damages.[203] Although there is a two-year time limit for making an award of remuneration or damages[204] this time limit breaches European Community law and is unenforceable.[205] **17.47**

(4) European Community law

(a) Introduction

European Community law has had a significant impact on the development of equal pay and sex discrimination law. Domestic courts as authorities of the state are required to take all appropriate measures to give effect to the obligations on the state arising under Directives and to interpret domestic law so as to be consistent with Community law.[206] Furthermore, under Article 13 of the Treaty on European Union, the Council may take appropriate action on a proposal from the Commission to combat discrimination based on sex, racial or ethnic origin, disability, age or sexual orientation. The Commission has recently proposed a Directive establishing a general framework for equal treatment in employment and occupation and a Directive implementing the principle of equal treatment between persons irrespective of racial or ethnic origin. **17.48**

---

196 See, eg *Benveniste v University of Southampton* [1989] ICR 617.
197 See eg *ARW Transformers v Cupples* [1977] IRLR 228.
198 *Leverton v Clwyd County Council* [1989] AC 706.
199 See para 17.18 above.
199a See *Evesham v North Hertfordshire Health Authority* [2000] IRLR 257.
200 *Hayward v Cammell Laird Shipbuilders Ltd (No 2)* [1988] AC 894.
201 Equal Pay Act 1970, s 2(1).
202 Ibid s 2(4); see *Preston v Wolverhampton Health Care NHS Trust* [1998] 1 WLR 280.
203 Equal Pay Act 1970, s 2(1).
204 Ibid s 2(5).
205 *Levez v Jennings* [1999] IRLR 36, ECJ; *Levez v Jennings (No 2)* [1999] IRLR 764.
206 *Von Colson and Kamann v Land Nordrhein-Westfalen* [1984] ECR 1891; *Marleasing SA v La Comercial Internacionale de Alimentación SA* [1990] ECR I-4135.

(b) Equal pay

17.49 Article 141 of the EC Treaty[207] (which is supplemented by the Equal Treatment Directive)[208] states that each Member State shall ensure the principle of equal pay for male and female workers for equal work or work of equal value. It creates[209] a directly enforceable right for an individual employee in relation both to direct and overt as well as indirect and disguised discrimination.[210] However, the Article does not confer a free standing right[211] and a claim for equal pay brought in the United Kingdom must be made under the Equal Pay Act[212] or the Sex Discrimination Act.[213]

17.50 Discrimination can be proved where a provision directly discriminates against an employee or where it has a disparate impact on women rather than men.[214] Where there is a disparate impact, discrimination will be established under Article 141 unless there are objectively justified factors unrelated to any discrimination on grounds of sex.[215] However, where discrimination is justified by a statutory provision, the Court takes a broader approach.[216] On the other hand, national measures which give women priority for promotion where they are under represented do not breach the Equal Treatment Directive provided women are not given automatic and unconditional priority over men and provided the specific personal situations of all candidates are assessed as part of the exercise.[216a]

17.51 Pay under Article 141 is very widely defined.[217] It therefore extends to non financial benefits such as travel concessions,[218] termination payments[219] and unfair dismissal compensation.[220] When considering the application of equal pay to pensions, the European Court of Justice has distinguished between statutory

---

[207] Formerly, Art 119; for a fuller treatment, see eg *Butterworth's Discrimination Law Handbook* (Butterworths, 2000) Div 2, Pt 1.

[208] (EEC) 75/17.

[209] The history of the Article is discussed by the Advocate-General in *Defrenne v Belgium* [1971] ECR 445.

[210] *Defrenne v Sabena* [1976] ECR 455.

[211] *Barber v Staffordshire County Council* [1996] IRLR 209; *Biggs v Somerset County Council* [1996] ICR 364.

[212] See para 17.46ff above.

[213] See para 17.36 above.

[214] See eg *R v Secretary of State for Employment, ex p Seymour-Smith* [1999] AC 554, ECJ.

[215] See generally, *Bilka-Kaufhau v Weber von Hartz* [1986] ECR 1607.

[216] See eg *R v Secretary of State for Employment ex p Seymour-Smith* (n 214 above).

[216a] *Marschall v Land Nordrhein-Westfalen* [1998] IRLR 39; *Application by Badeck, The Times* 31 Mar 2000; and contrast *Kalanke v Freie Hansestadt Brennan* [1996] ICR 314.

[217] Art 141 states that 'Pay means the ordinary basic or minimum wage or salary and any other consideration, whether in cash or in kind, which the worker receives, directly or indirectly, in respect of his employment from his employer'.

[218] *Garland v British Rail Engineering Ltd* [1982] ECR 359.

[219] *Clark v Secretary of State for Employment* [1997] ICR 64.

[220] *R v Secretary of State for Employment, ex p Seymour-Smith* (n 214 above).

social security schemes which are outside the scope of Article 141 and pension schemes which are determined by the employment relationship.[221] However, Article 141 applies to many occupational pension schemes and possibly to public sector pension schemes.[222] It extends to access to membership of pension schemes[223] and to benefits.[224]

Sex discrimination

Several Community Directives are directed at sex discrimination. Directives are not directly enforceable by individuals although they may be invoked against the state or emanations of the state.[225] The Equal Treatment Directive[226] states its purposes as being to put into effect the principle of equal treatment for men and women in relation to access to employment including promotion, vocational training and working conditions. The European Court of Justice has held that transsexuals are protected under the Directive[227] but not homosexuals.[228] The Directive also extends to social security,[229] discrimination in favour of women in relation to pregnancy and maternity[230] and to less favourable treatment of pregnant employees (or prospective employees).[231] Furthermore, a Directive was introduced to protect pregnant women and women who had recently given birth, primarily as a health and safety measure.[232] There is also an Equal Treatment Directive in relation to Social Security matters.[233] A definition of direct and indirect discrimination has been formulated in the Burden of Proof Directive.[234] **17.52**

[221] *Defrenne v Belgium* [1971] ECR 445.
[222] *Bestuur Van Het Algemeen Burgerlijk Pensionenfonds v Beune* [1994] ECR I-4471.
[223] *Vroege v NCIV Instituut voor Volkshuisvesting BV* [1994] ECR I-4541.
[224] *Barber v Guardian Royal Exchange Assurance* [1990] ECR I-1189.
[225] See para 5.11 above.
[226] (EEC) 76/207.
[227] *P v S and Cornwall County Council* [1996] ECR I-2143.
[228] *Grant v South-West Trains Ltd* [1998] ECR I-621; *R v Secretary of State for Employment, ex p Perkins (No 2)* [1998] IRLR 508.
[229] *Meyers v Adjudication Officer* [1995] ECR I-2131.
[230] *Johnston v Chief Constable of the Royal Ulster Constabulary* [1986] ECR 1651.
[231] *Dekker v Stichting Vormingscentrum voor Jonge Volwassener (VJV-Centum)* [1990] ECR I-3941; *Handels-og Kontorfunkionaerernes Foribund i Danmark v Dansk Arbejds giverforsening* [1990] ECR I-3979; *Brown v Rentokil* [1998] IRLR 455; *Mahlburg v Landmecklenburg-Vorpommern* [2000] IRLR 276.
[232] Council Directive (EC) 92/85 on the introduction of measures to encourage improvements in the safety and health of pregnant workers and workers who have recently given birth or are breast feeding (tenth individual Directive within the meaning of Art 16 of Directive 89/391).
[233] Council Directive (EEC) 79/7 on the progressive implementation of the principle of equal treatment for men and women in social security: for a survey of its impact, see R Drabble, 'Sex Discrimination in United Kingdom Social Security Law: The Impact of the European Union' [1997] EHRLR 242.
[234] (EEC) 97/80 which will come into force in Jul 2001.

(5) Racial discrimination

(a) Introduction

17.53 The most significant legislation prohibiting racial discrimination is the Race Relations Act 1976. However, section 18 of the Local Government Act 1988 empowers local authorities to take account of racial discrimination when carrying out certain contract functions. It is a criminal offence to incite racial hatred[235] and to commit a racially aggravated[236] assault,[237] criminal damage,[238] public order offence[239] or harassment.[240]

17.54 European Community law as yet has had no direct impact on racial discrimination law[241] but European legislation will be introduced under Article 13 of the Treaty of the European Union; the Commission recently proposed a Directive implementing the principle of equal treatment between persons irrespective of racial or ethnic origin. Whereas the Sex Discrimination Act must be construed to give effect to, for example, the Equal Treatment Directive,[242] there is no such obligation to construe the Race Relations Act 1976 in accordance with the Directive.[243] Nevertheless, the Race Relations Act must be construed so that it is consistent with other provisions of European Community law.[244]

(b) The meaning of discrimination

17.55 Like the Sex Discrimination Act 1975[245] the Race Relations Act 1976 prohibits direct discrimination,[246] indirect discrimination[247] and statutory victimisation.[248] Racial segregation constitutes racial discrimination.[249] An employee will also be subject to racial discrimination if his ill treatment relates to the race of a third

---

[235] Public Order Act 1996, ss 18, 19 and 23: see para 15.119ff above.

[236] Crime and Disorder Act 1998, s 28(1),(2).

[237] Ibid s 29.

[238] Ibid s 30.

[239] Ibid s 31.

[240] Ibid s 32.

[241] See G Bindman, 'When Will Europe Act Against Racism?' [1996] EHRLR 143.

[242] See para 17.52 above.

[243] *Adekeye v Post Office (No 2)* [1997] ICR 110 *per* Peter Gibson LJ at 119; and compare the position under the Sex Discrimination Act 1975: see *Coote v Granada Hospitality* [1999] IRLR 452.

[244] See eg *Bossa v Nordstress* [1998] ICR 694.

[245] See para 17.12ff above.

[246] Race Relations Act 1976, s 1(1)(a); see the discussion in relation to sex discrimination at para 17.13ff above.

[247] Ibid s 1(1)(b); and see *Tower Hamlets Borough Council v Qayyum* [1987] ICR 729; and see the discussion in relation to sex discrimination at para 17.18 above.

[248] Race Relations Act 1976, s 2; the proper approach to a claim for victimisation is discussed at para 17.13 above.

[249] Race Relations Act 1976, s 1(2).

party so that, for example, he is dismissed for refusing to carry out a racially discriminatory policy.[250]

It is unlawful to discriminate on 'racial grounds' which are defined as grounds of colour, race, nationality or ethnic origins.[251] Ethnic origins can include religious and cultural factors[252] and, accordingly, the Race Relations Act protects Sikhs,[253] Jews,[254] and gypsies[255] but not Rastafarians.[256] Muslims do not constitute a racial group but an employer's refusal to allow Muslim employees time off work to celebrate a religious festival has been held to justify an award of compensation on the basis that it constitutes indirect racial discrimination.[257] **17.56**

In general, the Race Relations Act prohibits positive discrimination.[258] However, like the Sex Discrimination Act, the Race Relations Act permits specially advantageous treatment for certain limited purposes. Vocational training can be offered on a preferential basis where one race is seriously under-represented in the workforce.[259] **17.57**

(c) Acts of discrimination

Not all racial discrimination is unlawful under the Race Relations Act 1976. In order to bring a successful claim the applicant must show: **17.58**

- that he has been the victim of an act of direct or indirect racial discrimination; and
- that the act of discrimination in question is one which is made unlawful by the Race Relations Act.

The Act covers discrimination in employment,[260] discrimination in education,[261] in relation to planning[262] and in relation to the provision of goods, facilities, services and premises.[263] The Act does not cover discrimination in other fields. In addition, there are a number of general exclusions[264] including, for example, discrimination undertaken under a statutory authority.

[250] *Zarczynska v Levy* [1979] 1 WLR 125; *Showboat Entertainment Ltd v Owens* [1984] 1 WLR 384; *Weathersfield v Sargent* [1999] IRLR 94.
[251] Race Relations Act 1976, s 3(1).
[252] *Mandla (Sewa Singh) v Dowell Lee* [1983] 2 AC 548.
[253] Ibid.
[254] *Seide v Gillette Industries* [1980] IRLR 427.
[255] *Commission for Racial Equality v Dutton* [1989] QB 783.
[256] *Crown Suppliers (Property Services Agency) v Dawkins* [1993] ICR 517.
[257] See *J H Walker Ltd v Hussain* [1996] ICR 291, EAT.
[258] *Lambeth London Borough Council v Commission for Racial Equality* [1990] IRLR 231, 234 *per* Balcombe LJ.
[259] Race Relations Act 1976, ss 37, 38.
[260] Ibid Pt II.
[261] Ibid Pt III, ss 4–16.
[262] Ibid s 19A.
[263] Ibid Pt III, ss 20–26.
[264] See para 17.66 below.

17.59 **Discrimination in employment.** The Race Relations Act has an extended definition of an employee.[265] It covers individuals who are self employed,[265a] that is, those who work under a contract to personally execute work.[265b] There are also specific provisions protecting contract workers.[265c] It is unlawful for an employer to discriminate against prospective employees[266] in the arrangements made to determine who should be offered employment, the terms on which employment is offered or the refusal or failure to offer a person a job. It is also unlawful to discriminate against employees[267] by restricting or denying opportunities for promotion, transfer or training, by restricting or denying access to any other benefits, facilities or services, dismissing the applicant or subjecting her to a detriment[268] (which may include racial harassment).[269] However, it seems that an employer cannot be liable for discrimination which occurs after the employee's employment has ceased.[270] In limited and defined circumstances the employer may prove that race is a genuine occupational qualification.[271]

17.60 An employer may be vicariously liable for the discriminatory acts of an employee acting in the course of his employment;[272] the phrase 'in the course of employment' should be interpreted purposively as it is used in everyday language.[273] An employer may also be liable for the acts of his clients or customers if they harass employees and he fails to take reasonable steps to prevent the harassment.[274] However, an employer has a defence to show he took such steps as were reasonably practicable to prevent the employee from doing the acts complained of.[275]

---

[265] Ibid s 78(1); it includes those who contract personally to execute any work or labour, that is the self employed (see *Mirror Group Newspapers Ltd v Gunning* [1986] 1 WLR 546) and contract workers under s 7 (see *Harrods Ltd v Remick* [1997] IRLR 583).

[265a] See eg, *Loughlan v Northern Ireland Housing Executive* [1998] IRLR 598 under the comparable provisions of the Fair Employment (Northern Ireland) Act 1976 regulating religious discrimination.

[265b] *Mirror Group Newspapers v Gunning* [1986] IRLR 27.

[265c] Race Relations Act 1976, s 7: see eg *Harrods v Remick* [1997] IRLR 583.

[266] Race Relations Act 1976, s 4(1).

[267] Ibid s 4(2).

[268] Ibid s 4(2)(b); in *Ministry of Defence v Jeremiah* [1980] QB 87 the Court of Appeal held that detriment involved a disadvantage.

[269] Which must disadvantage the applicant in her employment: *De Souza v Automobile Association* [1986] ICR 514.

[270] See *Adekeye v Post Office (No 2)* [1997] IRLR 105; and contrast the position under the Sex Discrimination Act 1975: see para 17.24 above.

[271] Race Relations Act 1976, s 5.

[272] Ibid s 32(1), (2).

[273] *Jones v Tower Boot Company Ltd* [1997] IRLR 168.

[274] *Burton v De Vere Hotels Ltd* [1996] IRLR 596.

[275] Race Relations Act 1976, s 32(3); see, eg *Balgobin v London Borough of Tower Hamlets* [1987] ICR 829.

It is contrary to the Race Relations Act to discriminate in Government appointments,[276] in partnerships[277] and for unions, trade associations or professional associations[278] or qualifying bodies[279] (such as the General Medical Council)[280] to discriminate. It is also unlawful for organisations which provide vocational training,[281] for employment agencies[282] or for barristers and their clerks[283] to discriminate. **17.61**

Discrimination in education.[284] It is unlawful for individual educational institutions to discriminate in offers it makes to pupils, in refusing or omitting to deal with a person's application for admission to be a pupil,[285] in affording him access to any benefits, facilities or services, by refusing or deliberately omitting to afford him access or by excluding him or subjecting him to some other detriment.[286] A policy of charging higher fees for non nationals constitutes race discrimination.[287] A requirement that pupils wear caps was found to discriminate indirectly against Sikhs.[288] It is also unlawful for a local educational authority to do any act in carrying out any other of its functions which amounts to racial discrimination.[289] A local authority is obliged to consider a parent's preference for admission to a school[290] even though it was made on racial grounds.[291] Local educational authorities and other education bodies in the public sector are under a further general duty not to discriminate.[292] **17.62**

Discrimination in providing goods, facilities or services. It is unlawful[293] to **17.63**

[276] Race Relations Act 1976, s 75.
[277] Ibid s 10 is confined to firms with more than six partners.
[278] Ibid s 11.
[279] Ibid s 12; see the approach of the House of Lords in *Loughran v Northern Ireland Housing Executive* [1998] 3 WLR 735 to the comparable provisions of the Fair Employment (Northern Ireland) Act 1976; and see *Sawyer v Asham* [1999] IRLR 609.
[280] *General Medical Council v Goba* [1988] ICR 885.
[281] Race Relations Act 1976, s 13.
[282] Ibid ss 14 and 76.
[283] Ibid s 26A added by the Courts and Legal Services Act 1992, s 64(2).
[284] For a fuller treatment see eg R McManus, *Education and the Courts* (Sweet & Maxwell, 1998) Chap 2.
[285] See eg *R v Bradford Metropolitan Borough Council, ex p Sikander Ali* [1994] ELR 299 where a claim that the local educational authority discriminated when drawing up school catchment areas failed.
[286] Race Relations Act 1976, s 17.
[287] *Orphonos v Queen Mary College* [1985] AC 761.
[288] *Mandla (Sewa Singh) v Dowell Lee* [1983] 2 AC 548.
[289] Race Relations Act 1976, s 18 as amended by the Education Act 1996.
[290] See para 19.18ff below.
[291] *R v Cleveland County Council, ex p Commission for Racial Equality* [1994] ELR 44.
[292] Race Relations Act 1976, s 19.
[293] Ibid s 20.

discriminate in providing goods, facilities[294] or services[295] to the public[296] although there are certain statutory exceptions.[297] However, where facilities and services are provided by a public authority, the authority will only be acting unlawfully in relation to an act which is similar to one done by a private person, so that the Act would not extend, for example, to an immigration officer who was controlling would be immigrants.[298]

17.64 It is unlawful to discriminate in relation to premises of which a person has the power to dispose or manage[299] or to discriminate against withholding a licence or consent for the disposal of premises.[300] These provisions do not apply to individuals concerned in small premises.[301] It is unlawful for a membership club of 25 or more to discriminate.[302] It is also unlawful for a planning authority to discriminate in its planning functions.[303]

17.65 **Other discriminatory acts.** It is unlawful to operate discriminatory practices,[304] discriminatory advertisements,[305] to give instructions to discriminate,[306] to apply pressure to discriminate,[307] to aid and abet discrimination[308] or to make a discriminatory contract.[309]

17.66 **General exclusions.** Discriminatory provisions in charitable instruments are in general lawful except where they confer benefits by reference to colour.[310] It is not unlawful to afford individuals of a particular racial group access to facilities or services to meet their special needs in relation to their education, training, welfare or

---

294 *Kassam v Immigration Appeals Tribunal* [1980] 1 WLR 1037; *Sarjani v Inland Revenue Commissioners* [1981] QB 458.

295 Service includes assistance by a police officer (*Farah v Commissioner of Police of the Metropolis* [1998] QB 65), tax advice from a tax officer (*Sarjani v Inland Revenue Commissioners* [1981] QB 458) and a hire purchase credit scheme (*Quinn v Williams Furniture* [1981] ICR 328).

296 'Public' is to be contrasted with 'private' so that a private members' club is not covered: see *Charter v Race Relations Board* [1973] AC 868; *Dockers' Labour Club and Institute Ltd v Race Relations Board* [1976] AC 285; Parliament therefore prohibited race discrimination in membership clubs by enacting the Race Relations Act 1976, s 25.

297 Ibid ss 22, 23 and 35.

298 *Amin v Entry Clearance Officer, Bombay* [1983] 2 AC 818.

299 Race Relations Act 1976, s 21.

300 Ibid s 24.

301 Ibid s 22.

302 Ibid s 25 (subject to s 26).

303 Ibid s 19A added by Housing and Planning Act 1986, s 55.

304 Race Relations Act 1976, s 28.

305 Ibid s 29; see *Commission for Racial Equality v Dutton* [1989] QB 783 where a notice in a public house saying 'no travellers' was an advertisement.

306 Race Relations Act 1976, s 30.

307 Ibid.

308 Ibid s 33.

309 Ibid s 72.

310 Ibid s 34.

ancillary benefits.[311] Certain discriminatory acts connected with sports are lawful.[312] Discriminatory acts are not unlawful if done under a statutory authority.[313] This provision effectively rules out challenges to discriminatory action which is taken in relation to immigration legislation;[314] and also ensured that a local educational authority had to comply with a parental preference for admission to a school which was made on racial grounds.[315] Discriminatory acts will not also be unlawful if they are done for the purposes of national security.[316]

(d) Remedies

No proceedings may be taken against a person for contravention of the Race Relations Act 1976 except as prescribed by the Act.[317] The individual complainant may pursue a complaint of an act of discrimination in the employment field[318] or under the provisions concerned with the liability of employers and principals[319] or aiding discriminatory acts[320] (which is to be treated as discriminating against the complainant)[321] by presenting a complaint to the employment tribunal within three months of the discriminatory act. The complaint may be heard out of time if it is just and equitable to do so.[322] Only the Commission for Racial Equality[323] can bring proceedings[324] in relation to discriminatory advertisements,[325] discriminatory instructions[326] or the application of pressure to discrimination.[327] A complaint of discrimination in other fields may be brought by the complainant in a designated county court[328] within six months which may be considered out of time if it is just and equitable to do so.[329] **17.67**

311 Ibid s 35.
312 Ibid s 39.
313 Ibid s 41; see *Hampson v Department of Education and Science* [1991] 1 AC 171.
314 *Amin v Entry Clearance Officer, Bombay* [1983] 2 AC 818.
315 *R v Cleveland County Council, ex p Commission for Racial Equality* [1994] ELR 44.
316 Race Relations Act 1976, s 42; unlike the Sex Discrimination Act 1975 the Minister may sign a certificate which is conclusive under s 69.
317 Race Relations Act 1976, s 53(1).
318 Ibid s 54(1) the field of employment in Pt II is discussed at para 17.59 above.
319 Ibid s 32.
320 Ibid s 33. 'Aid' means to help or assist and contemplates a state of affairs where one party sets out to achieve a result and the other helps him do it: see *Anyanwu v South Bank Students' Union* [2000] IRLR 36. The secondary party must know that the principal is treating (or is about to treat) someone less favourably on grounds of race; recklessness or carelessness is not enough: see *Hallam v Avery The Times*, 7 Feb 2000.
321 Race Relations Act 1976, s 54(1)(b).
322 Ibid s 68(1), (5).
323 Whose functions are defined by ibid s 43(1).
324 Ibid s 63.
325 Ibid s 29.
326 Ibid s 30.
327 Ibid s 31.
328 Ibid s 57.
329 Ibid s 68(2), (5).

(6) Disability discrimination

(a) Introduction

17.68 The Disability Discrimination Act 1995[330] protects disabled persons in relation to employment and access to employment, the supply of goods and services and the purchase or rental of land or property.

17.69 A person has a disability[331] if he has a physical or mental[332] impairment[333] which has a substantial and long term[334] impact on his abilities to carry out normal day-to-day activities.[335] Impairment affects day-to-day activity if, for example, it affects mobility, manual dexterity or physical co-ordination.[336] When considering whether an impairment has a substantial and long term[337] adverse impact on a person's ability to carry out normal day-to-day activities,[338] account must be taken[339] of guidance issued by the Secretary of State. A person who previously had a disability[340] may also bring claims in relation to employment[341] or goods, facilities, services and premises.[342]

(b) The meaning of discrimination

17.70 The statutory definition of discrimination under the Disability Discrimination Act 1995 is different from the Sex Discrimination and Race Relations Acts. Similar language is used in the Disability Discrimination Act in relation to employment,[343] trade unions,[344] goods, services and facilities[345] and premises.[346] It is unlawful for an employer to give to a disabled person less favourable treatment[347]

[330] For a fuller treatment, see eg *Butterworth's Discrimination Law Handbook* (Butterworths, 2000) Div 4.

[331] Disability Discrimination Act 1995, s 1(1), 2 and Sch 2, para 5; and see generally, *Goodwin v Patent Office* [1999] IRLR 4; *Vicary v British Telecommunications* [1999] IRLR 680.

[332] See *Goodwin v Patent Office* (n 331 above).

[333] See Disibility Discrimination Act 1995, Sch 1, para 1(2) and the exclusions contained in the Disability Discrimination (Meaning of Disability) Regulations 1996, SI 1996/455.

[334] Disability Discrimination Act 1995, Sch 1, para 2.

[335] See generally, *Goodwin v Patent Office* (n 331 above).

[336] See generally, Disability Discrimination Act 1995, Sch 4, para 4(1).

[337] The impairment must last at least 12 months or be likely to last at least 12 months: see ibid Sch 1, para 2.

[338] In *Goodwin v Patent Office* (n 331 above) the EAT stressed that the crucial question is the ability of the applicant to do the acts in question.

[339] Disability Discrimination Act 1995, s 3(3).

[340] Ibid s 2.

[341] Under ibid Pt II: see para 17.59ff above.

[342] Under ibid Pt III; see para 17.62ff above.

[343] Ibid s 5.

[344] Ibid s 14.

[345] Ibid s 20.

[346] Ibid s 24.

[347] Ibid s 5(1); *O'Neill v Symm and Company Ltd* [1998] ICR 481; *Clark v Novacold* [1998] ICR 1044, EAT; *British Sugar v Kirker* [1998] IRLR 624.

or to fail to comply with its duty[348] to make reasonable adjustments.[349] The less favourable treatment must 'relate to the disabled person's disability' of which the employer is aware.[350] However, the applicant should not necessarily be compared directly with a non disabled person; for example, if a disabled person is dismissed for a sickness absence which would not have occurred if he had not been disabled, then the dismissal would amount to discrimination under the Act. The Court of Appeal has made it clear that the tribunal must not undertake the same approach as adopted in sex and race discrimination cases. The crucial distinction is the presence of a defence of justification for all disability discrimination.[351]

Direct discrimination on grounds of disability can be justified under the Act.[352] **17.71** In the employment field an employer can put forward any reason for less favourable treatment if it is material to the particular case and substantial.[353] A balancing exercise must be carried out between the interests of the employee and those of the employer.[354] On the other hand, where services or premises are concerned, justification depends on the ability of the person to provide the service. The service provider can prove justification if he believes one of the relevant conditions[355] is satisfied and it is reasonable in all the circumstances for him to hold that opinion.[356]

It is also unlawful to victimise a person on certain specified grounds.[357] Liability **17.72** under the Act extends to a person who aids an unlawful act[358] and to employers and principals.[359] However, the employer may be able to establish that he took all reasonably practicable steps to prevent discrimination occurring.[360]

(c) Acts of discrimination

Discrimination in employment. Certain employees are excluded from the Dis- **17.73** ability Discrimination Act.[361] Furthermore, Part II of the Act does not apply to

[348] Disability Discrimination Act 1995, s 6.
[349] Ibid s 5(2); *Morse v Wiltshire County Council* [1998] ICR 1023; *Ridout v TC Group* [1998] IRLR 628.
[350] *O'Neill v Symm and Company Ltd* (n 347 above).
[351] *Kenny v Hampshire Constabulary* [1999] ICR 27.
[352] See generally, *Clark v Novacold* [1999] IRLR 318.
[353] It will be relevant to consider the Code of Practice for the elimination of discrimination in the field of employment against disabled persons or persons who have had a disability issued under the Disability Discrimination Act 1995, s 53(1): see *Clark v Novacold* [1998] ICR 1044.
[354] *Saurius General Engineers v Baynton* [1999] IRLR 604.
[355] As set out in the Disability Discrimination Act 1995, s 20(4).
[356] Ibid s 20(3)(b); *Rose v Bonchet* [1999] IRLR 463.
[357] Disability Discrimination Act 1995, s 55.
[358] Ibid s 57.
[359] Ibid s 58.
[360] Ibid s 58(5).
[361] Ibid s 64.

employers of less than 15 employees[362] and special recognition is given to charities for the disabled.[363]

17.74 The Act prohibits discrimination by employers against a disabled person in the arrangements made to determine whether to offer employment, the terms of that employment or by refusing to offer or deliberately not offering him employment.[364] It is unlawful for an employer to discriminate against a disabled employee in the terms of employment, opportunities for promotion, transfer, training or other benefit or to refuse him such opportunities or to dismiss him or subject him to a detriment.[365]

17.75 It is also unlawful to discriminate against contract workers[366] or for trade associations[367] to discriminate[368] and they are under a duty to make reasonable adjustments.[369] Occupational pensions schemes[370] and insurance services[371] must also not discriminate against disabled individuals. The complainant may make a complaint to the employment tribunal.[372]

17.76 **Discrimination in other fields.** It is unlawful to discriminate[373] in relation to goods, facilities and services.[374] Providers of services are under a duty to make reasonable adjustments.[375] Educational services are excluded from these provisions.[376] However, information concerning educational services for disabled individuals must be published as disability statements[377] at prescribed intervals by local educational authorities.[378] It is also unlawful to discriminate[379] in relation to premises[380] unless the exemptions for small dwellings[381] apply.

---

362 Ibid s 7(1).
363 Ibid s 10.
364 Ibid s 4.
365 Ibid.
366 Ibid s 12.
367 Ibid s 13.
368 Ibid s 14.
369 Ibid s 15.
370 Ibid s 17.
371 Ibid s 18.
372 Ibid s 8(1).
373 Ibid s 20.
374 Ibid s 19.
375 Ibid s 21.
376 Ibid s 19(5).
377 Educational (Disability Statements for Local Educational Authorities) (England) Regulations 1997, SI 1997/1625; Educational (Disability Statements for Local Educational Authorities) (Wales) Regulations 1997, SI 1997/2353.
378 Education Act 1996, s 528(1).
379 Disability Discrimination Act 1995, s 24.
380 Ibid s 22.
381 Ibid s 23.

(d) Remedies

A complaint against an employer (or for aiding an employer's unlawful acts[382] or concerning acts done in the course of employment)[383] is made to the employment tribunal.[384] An employment tribunal shall not entertain a complaint unless it is made within three months of the act of discrimination although it may consider an application which is out of time if it is just and equitable to do so.[385] **17.77**

A complaint against a service provider (or for aiding his unlawful acts[386] or which is done in the course of his employment)[387] is brought in the county court.[388] It must be brought within six months of the alleged discrimination although the court may consider a claim which is out of time if it considers it just and equitable to do so.[389] **17.78**

C. The Law Under the European Convention

(1) Introduction

Article 14 of the Convention provides that: **17.79**

> The enjoyment of the rights and freedoms set forth in this Convention shall be secured without discrimination on any ground such as sex, race, colour, language, religion, political or other opinion, national or social origin, association with a national minority, property, birth or other status.

This Article[390] is not a *free standing* prohibition against discrimination and has therefore been called a parasitic[391] right. It does not prohibit all discrimination by the state but merely prevents states from being discriminatory in the way in which they guarantee the rights set out in the Convention. The patent inadequacies of Article 14 have therefore led to a proposal for a new Protocol 12 which will create a stronger and freestanding anti-discrimination provision.[391a]

382 Ibid s 57.
383 Ibid s 58.
384 Ibid s 8.
385 Ibid Sch 3, para 3.
386 Ibid s 57.
387 Ibid s 58.
388 Ibid s 25.
389 Ibid Sch 3, para 3.
390 For a survey of its impact see S Livingstone, 'Article 14 and the Prevention of Discrimination in the European Court of Human Rights' [1997] EHRLR 25.
391 See D Harris, M O'Boyle and C Warbrick, *Law of the European Convention on Human Rights* (Butterworths, 1995) 463.
391a See eg G Moon, 'The Draft Discrimination Protocol to the European Convention on Human Rights: A Progresss Report' [2000] EHRLR 49.

17.80 The weakness of the discrimination provision in the Convention can partly be explained because the Council of Europe established its social and economic rights in the European Social Charter. The preamble to the 1961 Charter[392] states that it is the counterpart in the social field to the European Convention on Human Rights, leading Kahn-Freund to describe the Charter as a big footnote to the Convention.[393] Nevertheless, freedom from discrimination is fundamental to the Convention. As the Court emphasised in the *Belgian Linguistic Case (No 2)*[394] the rights guaranteed under the Convention must be read as though Article 14 'formed an integral part of each of the articles laying down rights and freedoms'.

17.81 There are three requirements which must be satisfied in order to establish a violation of Article 14:

- an act of discrimination which falls within the *ambit* of another Convention Article;
- a difference of treatment in comparison to other persons in an analogous or relevantly similar situation; and
- which is not justifiable, in other words that the treatment amounts to illegal discrimination rather than permissible differentiation.

17.82 In practice, where a breach of a substantive Convention right has been established, the Court has often been very reluctant to address the separate question of a breach of Article 14. The test used to decide whether an Article 14 issue should be considered was formulated in *Airey v Ireland*,[395] whether a 'clear inequality of treatment in the enjoyment of the right in question is a fundamental aspect of the case'. Unfortunately, however, the Court has not identified and developed a set of principles when deciding whether discrimination is fundamental to the case. For example, in *Dudgeon v United Kingdom*,[396] in which the criminalisation of homosexual acts was found to be a breach of private life under Article 8, the Court declined to deal with the Article 14 claim on grounds that it comprised the same complaint from a different angle and its treatment would serve no useful legal purpose.[397]

---

392 The revised Social Charter of 1996 (incorporating the Additional Protocols of 1988, 1991 and 1995) has yet to come into force.

393 O Kahn-Freund, 'The European Social Charter' in F Jacobs (ed) *European Law and the Individual* 182.

394 (1968) 1 EHRR 252, 283 para 9.

395 (1979) 2 EHRR 305 para 30.

396 (1981) 4 EHRR 149 para 69; see also eg *Lustig-Prean v United Kingdom* (1999) 6 BHRC 65 paras 108-109 and *Smith and Grady v United Kingdom* [1999] IRLR 747 paras 115-116 in the full judgment.

397 See also *Norris v Ireland* (1988) 13 EHRR 186 where, on facts similar to those of *Dudgeon*, the Art 14 arguments did not even reach the Court.

(2) The scope of the right

The obligation on the state not to discriminate applies not only to rights which it is obliged to protect under the Convention, but also to rights which the state *voluntarily guarantees*. As a result, if a state chooses to make a provision which the Convention does not strictly require, it must do so in a non-discriminatory fashion. For example, in the *Belgian Linguistic Case (No 2)*[398] the Court observed: **17.83**

> Article 6 requires States 'to set up tribunals' to determine civil cases and 'any criminal charge'; it does not, however, require them to set up 'courts of appeal'. A State which does set up such courts would consequently go beyond its positive obligations derived from Article 6; it would, however, be bound by virtue of Article 14 and not Article 6 to make such courts available to all.

The Court went on to consider a complaint concerning access to language-based state education. It found that there was no obligation on the state to provide any system of education,[399] but if it did so, access to the system could not be restricted on a discriminatory basis.

In *Abdulaziz, Cabales and Balkandali v United Kingdom*[400] the issue considered was whether a concession allowing resident alien men to be joined by their wives (despite the fact the women lacked any immigration status) should also be provided to resident alien women in respect of their husbands. The Court decided that the differential treatment was discriminatory. By contrast, in *Family K and W v Netherlands*[401] it was nationality rather than residence that was conferred by the state, this time on alien wives, but not husbands; there the Commission found that Article 14 did not apply to the matter of differential treatment of men and women because nationality did not confer Convention rights. **17.84**

It is arguable[402] that Article 14 imposes a positive duty on the state to take action to protect against private acts of discrimination such as membership of private associations[403] or restrictive covenants on property rights, a positive duty to take action against expression which gratuitously insults religious feelings[404] and possibly to restrain racially inflammatory speech. **17.85**

[398] (1968) 1 EHRR 252.

[399] See para 19.40ff below.

[400] (1985) 7 EHRR 471.

[401] (1985) 43 DR 216, EComm HR.

[402] See D Harris, M O'Boyle and C Warbrick, *Law of The European Convention on Human Rights* (Butterworths, 1995) 484, 485

[403] *Young James and Webster v United Kingdom* (1981) 4 EHRR 38 para 57; *Sigurjonsson (Sigurdur A) v Iceland* (1993) 16 EHRR 462 para 37.

[404] *Otto-Preminger-Institute v Austria* (1994) 19 EHRR 34.

(3) The 'ambit' of a Convention right

17.86 In order for an applicant to show that he has been the victim of discrimination in relation to a Convention right, it is not necessary for him to show that the other Convention right has been breached. Such a restrictive approach would give no independent scope for the right under Article 14 itself. Instead the Court have taken the view that discrimination can arise wherever the complaint falls within the *ambit* of another Convention right.

17.87 The concept of the ambit of a protected Convention right[405] was introduced in *Van De Mussele v Belgium*[406] and elaborated in *Rasmussen v Denmark*[407] where the Court held that discrimination in relation to time limits for paternity proceedings between husband and wife came within the ambit of Articles 6 and 8. The general principles to be applied have been explained as follows:[408]

> Article 14 complements the other substantive provisions of the Convention and the Protocols. It has no independent existence since it has effect solely in relation to the 'enjoyment of the rights and freedoms' safeguarded by those provisions. Although the application of Article 14 does not necessarily presuppose a breach of those provisions—and to this extent it has an autonomous meaning—there can be no room for its application unless the facts at issue fall within the ambit of one or more of the latter.

The Court has used a number of expressions to describe the degree to which a substantive right must be in play before Article 14 is in play:[409] whenever the subject matter of the disadvantages 'constitutes one of the modalities of the exercise of a right guaranteed'[410] or where the measures complained of are 'linked to the exercise of the right guaranteed'.[411]

17.88 The precise nature of the linkage required has not been systematically examined by the Court and remains to be developed. However, the strong international consensus in favour of the prohibition of discrimination,[412] the 'principle of effectiveness'[413] and the nature of the Convention as a 'living instrument'[414] all suggest that the prohibition on discrimination in Article 14 should be given a broad construction to safeguard groups which are discriminated against in a 'real and practical way'. As a result, it is submitted that the 'ambit' test should be a liberal

[405] See eg *Inze v Austria* (1987) 10 EHRR 394; *Van der Mussele v Belgium* (1983) 6 EHRR 163 para 43.
[406] (1983) 6 EHRR 163 para 43.
[407] (1984) 7 EHRR 371.
[408] Ibid para 29.
[409] See eg *Petrovic v Austria* RJD [1998]-II 579.
[410] *National Union of Belgian Police v Belgium* (1975) 1 EHRR 578 para 45.
[411] *Schmidt and Dahlström v Sweden* (1976) 1 EHRR 632 para 39.
[412] See para 17.2 above.
[413] See para 6.28 above.
[414] See para 6.23 above.

and generous one and the question as to whether a Convention right has been affected should be dealt with in a practical and non-technical way.

(4) The meaning of 'discrimination'

In general, the cases alleging discrimination under Article 14 have required the applicant to prove a difference of treatment. Not every difference in treatment will amount to a violation of Article 14. Instead, it must be established that the other persons in an analogous or relevantly similar situation enjoy preferential treatment, and that there is no objective or reasonable justification for the distinction.[415] Contracting States enjoy a margin of appreciation in assessing whether and to what extent differences in otherwise similar situations justify different treatment in law.[416] **17.89**

The question of whether Article 14 prohibits indirect discrimination[417] has not been addressed by the Court.[418] However, it is strongly arguable that rules which are neutral on their face should be susceptible to challenge under the Convention if their impact is discriminatory.[419] It should be noted, however, that in a number of cases involving allegations of 'religious discrimination'[420] the Commission has held that there is no discrimination if a law of general application has a disproportionate impact on a particular group. It is not clear whether the 'indirect discrimination' points were specifically addressed in these cases which, it is submitted, are unlikely to be followed. **17.90**

It also seems that promoting disadvantaged groups through affirmative action is not contrary to Article 14. In the *Belgian Linguistic Case (No 2)*[421] the Court indicated that not all differential treatment is unacceptable since certain legal inequalities correct factual inequalities. Thus, a tax advantage to married women which fell within the ambit of the right to peaceful possessions of property under the Article 1 of the First Protocol[422] had the objective and reasonable justification **17.91**

[415] See eg *Fredin v Sweden* (1991) 13 EHRR 784; *Stubbings v United Kingdom* (1996) 23 EHRR 213 para 72.

[416] *Rasmussen v Denmark* (1984) 7 EHRR 371 para 40; *Stubbings v United Kingdom* (n 415 above).

[417] For a discussion of the relevant principles in sex and race discrimination, see para 17.14 above; and for the position under European Union law, see para 17.50.

[418] See eg the discussion in D Harris, M O'Boyle and C Warbrick, *Law of the European Convention on Human Rights* (Butterworths, 1995) 478-479 on the approach of the Court in *Abdulaziz, Cabalas and Balkandali v United Kingdom* (1985) 7 EHRR 471.

[419] Cf S Livingstone, 'Article 14 and the Prevention of Discrimination in the European Court of Human Rights' [1997] EHRLR 25, 31.

[420] *Stedman v United Kingdom* (1997) 23 EHRR CD 168; *X v Finland*, Application 24949/94, 3 Dec 1996, see generally, para 14.50 above.

[421] (1968) 1 EHRR 252 para 10.

[422] See generally, para 18.26ff below.

of providing positive discrimination to encourage married women back to work.[423]

17.91A In the important recent decision of *Thlimmenos v Greece*[423a] the court has unequivocally adopted the principle of positive discrimination. The applicant was a Jehovah's witness who was convicted for insubordination for refusing to wear on religious grounds a military uniform at the time of general mobilisation. Some years later he was refused an appointment to the Greek Institute of Chartered Accountants because he had been convicted of a felony. His complaint was that the Institute failed to distinguish between criminal offences which were committed exclusively because of religious belief and convictions for other offences. The Court decided that the applicant had been discriminated against in relation to his religious beliefs and said:

> The Court has so far considered the right under Article 14 not to be discriminated against in the enjoyment of the rights guaranteed under the Convention is violated when states treat differently persons in analogous situations without providing an objective and reasonable justification.[423b] However, the Court considers that this is not the only facet of the prohibition of discrimination under Article 14. The right under the Convention is also violated when States without objective and reasonable justification fail to treat differently persons whose situations are significantly different.[423c]

(5) Establishing a difference of treatment

17.92 In order to prove differential treatment under the Convention case law, the applicant must show:

- that he has been treated substantively differently and less favourably than others;
- that the basis of the distinction is a personal characteristic or status which the applicant exhibits; and
- that the others to whom he is comparing himself are in an analogous situation.

17.93 The applicant does not usually have great difficulty in identifying the unfavourable treatment. The discrepancy is usually obvious on the face of the rule or practice which differentiates between two groups on the basis of a particular characteristic.[424] These measures include positive action afforded by the state to

[423] *D G and D W Lindsay v United Kingdom* (1986) 49 DR 181, 190, 191, EComm HR.
[423a] Judgment of 6 Apr 2000.
[423b] *Inze v Austria* (1988) 10 EHRR 394. para 41.
[423c] *Thlimmenos v Greece* (n 423a above) para 44.
[424] See eg *Hoffmann v Austria* (1993) 17 EHRR 293 where the Austrian Act on the Religious Education of Children provided that where parents divorced, their children must be brought up in the religion originally agreed by the parents unless both parents agreed otherwise.

one group to the detriment of the applicant[425] and the denial of opportunities given to others.[426] On the other hand, a difference in treatment may arise from indirect discrimination where it results from a rule which, while neutral on its face, in effect operates to impact upon one group differently than another.[427] However, the Convention case law on indirect discrimination is not well developed.[428]

In order to prove discrimination the applicant must demonstrate that his circumstances and those of his comparator are comparable. The approach of the Court has been to ask whether their respective situations are analogous or relevantly similar. For example, in *Van der Mussele v Belgium*[429] the applicant trainee barrister was required to act in legal aid cases on a *pro bono* basis, while other professionals, including other lawyers, involved in the same cases were paid for their services. The Court rejected his attempts to compare himself with members of other professions and trained legal professionals. In *Johnston v Ireland*[430] the Court rejected a complaint that Article 14 was violated because the applicants could not obtain a divorce in Ireland whereas others who were resident in Ireland but had the means to do so could obtain a divorce. It concluded that the situations were not analogous because under Irish private international law foreign divorces were only recognised where they were domiciled abroad; the situations of foreign domiciles and the applicants were therefore not analogous. **17.94**

The applicant has the best prospect of establishing a difference of treatment if he can argue that he is treated differently than members of his own clearly defined group. For example, in *Pine Valley Developments Ltd v Ireland*[431] two applicant property developers proved that remedial legislation, introduced to correct a misapplication of a planning law, had been drafted so as to exclude them (but not other holders of planning permission in the same category) from its benefit. On the other hand, the Commission rejected complaints of discrimination from prisoners suffering from AIDS because they could not show any analogous situation. The prisoners argued that the failure of the authorities to offer a mitigation of **17.95**

[425] For example, interference with the enjoyment of possessions, criminalisation of sexual activities and provision of free services.

[426] For example, the right to bring civil actions or to be tried by an ordinary criminal court or to exercise the same freedom of expression.

[427] *Marckx v Belgium* (1979) 2 EHRR 330 found that rules whose *object or result* was to discriminate against a particular group would offend Art 14; see also *Verein Alternatives Lokalradio Berne v Switzerland* (1986) 49 DR 126, EComm HR where the Commission found a claim in discrimination in regard to the distribution of broadcast licences to be manifestly ill-founded, but indicated that it would have found differently had the measure in question deprived residents of a particular region from receiving broadcasts in their mother-tongue.

[428] See eg the discussion in D Harris, M O'Boyle & C Warbrick, *Law of the European Convention on Human Rights* (Butterworths, 1995) 478-479 on the approach of the Court in *Abdulaziz, Cabalas and Balkandali v United Kingdom* (1985) 7 EHRR 471.

[429] (1983) 6 EHRR 163.

[430] (1986) 9 EHRR 203 paras 26, 27.

[431] (1991) 14 EHRR 319.

sentence[432] or compassionate release from jail[433] which are given others with comparable medical conditions constituted unjustifiably discriminatory treatment. The Commission disagreed, finding that the applicant in each case was not as ill as those to whom such discretionary treatment is given.

(6) The prohibited grounds for discrimination

17.96 Article 14 prohibits on the basis of a non-exhaustive and open-ended list of grounds the state from acting in a discriminatory fashion. Article 14 prohibits discrimination on:

> any ground such as sex, race, colour, language, religion, political or other opinion, national or social origin, association with national minority, property birth or *other status*.

However, the Court in *Kjeldsen Madsen and Pedesen v Denmark*[434] stressed that in order to fall within Article 14, discrimination must be based on a personal characteristic or 'status'.

17.97 There are several types of discrimination in the Convention jurisprudence which are seen as being especially serious: race,[435] sex,[436] religion,[437] illegitimacy[438] and nationality.[439] They are treated as being equivalent to 'suspect categories' in American constitutional law[440] so that there is a heavy burden on the state to justify the alleged discrimination.

17.98 In principle, discrimination on any ground might be prohibited by the Article since the list of prohibited grounds are not exhaustive[441] and the Strasbourg au-

---

[432] *R M v United Kingdom* (1994) 77-A DR 98.

[433] *Grice v United Kingdom* (1994) 77-A DR 90, EComm HR.

[434] (1976) 1 EHRR 711 para 56.

[435] *East African Asians v United Kingdom* (1973) 3 EHRR 76; *Patel v United Kingdom* (1970) 36 CD 92, EComm HR.

[436] Since the advancement of the equality of sexes is a major goal, very weighty reasons have to be advanced before a difference in treatment on grounds of sex is to be regarded as compatible with the Convention: see *Abdulaziz, Cabales and Balkandali v United Kingdom* (1985) 7 EHRR 471 para 38; *Schuler-Zgraggen v Switzerland* (1993) 16 EHRR 405 para 22; *Burghartz v Switzerland* (1994) 18 EHRR 101 para 22; *Schmidt v Germany* (1994) 18 EHRR 513 paras 32, 33; *Van Raalte v Netherlands* (1997) 24 EHRR 503 para 39.

[437] *Hoffmann v Austria* (1993) 17 EHRR 293 para 60.

[438] *Marckx v Belgium* (1979) 2 EHRR 330 paras 17–27; but contrast *McMichael v United Kingdom* (1995) 20 EHRR 205.

[439] *Gaygusuz v Austria* (1996) 23 EHRR 365 para 42 where the Court said that very weighty reasons had to be put forward before the Court before it would regard a difference of treatment based exclusively on nationality to be compatible with the Convention.

[440] See eg H Abraham and B Perry, *Freedom and the Court* (7th edn, Oxford University Press, 1998) Chap 2; and see para 17.206 below.

[441] *Rasmussen v Denmark* (1984) 7 EHRR 371 para 34; *James v United Kingdom* (1986) 8 EHRR 123 para 74.

thorities have accepted a number of 'other statuses' as coming within the residual category including:

- sexual orientation;[442]
- marital status;[443]
- legitimacy;[444]
- trade union status;[445]
- military status;[446]
- conscientious objection;[447]
- professional status;[448]
- imprisonment.[449]

The question whether there are *any* limits on the list of grounds was raised in *Dudgeon v United Kingdom.*[450] The applicant complained of discrimination because the laws that had criminalised his homosexual behaviour in Northern Ireland had not been imposed in England and Wales. However, the Government maintained that diversity in domestic laws was not a ground of discrimination since Article 14 referred to personal characteristics of the victim. The Court did not deal with the argument, but one of the judges in dissent[451] agreed that Article 14 did not apply. There is, however, doubt about whether one personal characteristic is a prohibited ground under Article 14, discrimination on the basis of financial status. Although Article 14 specifically prohibits discrimination on grounds of 'property', the Court has been reluctant to address claims on this ground;[452] the area is a difficult one because of the wide discrepancies in financial resources that are tolerated in a market based economy. **17.99**

(7) Justification

The literal meaning of Article 14 is that any difference of treatment is unlawful **17.100**

[442] *Salgueiro da Silva Mouta v Portugal* Judgment of 21 Dec 1999.

[443] See eg *Rasmussen v Denmark* (n 441 above); *Adbulaziz, Cabalas and Balkandali v United Kingdom* (1985) 7 EHRR 471.

[444] See eg *Marckx v Belgium* (1979) 2 EHRR 330; *Inze v Austria* (1987) 10 EHRR 394.

[445] See eg *National Union of Belgian Police v Belgium* (1975) 1 EHRR 578.

[446] *Engel v Netherlands (No 1)* (1976) 1 EHRR 647.

[447] See eg *X v Netherlands* (1965) 8 YB 266.

[448] *Van der Mussele v Belgium* (1983) 6 EHRR 163.

[449] See eg *R M v United Kingdom* (1994) 77-A DR 98.

[450] (1981) 4 EHRR 149.

[451] See ibid *per* Judge Matscher *ibid* where he suggested that the diversity of domestic laws which is characteristic of a federal state can never in themselves amount to discrimination. See also *Nelson v United Kingdom* (1986) 49 DR 170, 174, EComm HR where different regimes in Scotland and England were in no way related to the personal status of the applicant and therefore not discrimination.

[452] See *Airey v Ireland* (1979) 2 EHRR 305 in which the Court preferred to deal with the question of violation of a substantive provision; and see Thornberry (1980) 29 ICLQ 250; generally Michelman (1969) 83 Harv L Rev 7.

discrimination. However, it is clearly established that some differential treatment in the way in which states guarantee Convention rights is permissible. In the *Belgian Linguistic Case (No 2)*[453] the Court rejected as absurd an argument based on the French text, which suggested that every difference of treatment in the exercise of Convention amounted to discrimination under Article 14. Nevertheless, if a government does not plead any justification, then the applicant's claim of violation will inevitably succeed.[454]

17.101 Unlike other provisions in the Convention, Article 14 does not contain a clause which expressly sets out grounds of justification. Even so, in the *Belgian Linguistic Case (No 2)*[455] the Court held that the principle of equality of treatment is violated if there is no *reasonable and objective* justification for the distinction.[456] The Court said[457] that 'the existence of such justification must be assessed in relation to the "aim and effects" of the measure under consideration, regard being had to the principles which normally prevail in democratic societies'. In addition to the pursuit of a legitimate aim, differential treatment will violate Article 14 when 'there is no reasonable relationship of proportionality between the means employed and the aim sought to be realised'.[458]

17.102 The *Belgian Linguistic* test therefore sets out two essential elements:

- a rational aim behind the differentiation; and
- proportionality between the interference and the aim pursued.

The aim must be established by the state, but the onus is on the applicant to disprove proportionality. The proportionality requirement is the need to 'strike a fair balance between the protection of the interests of the community and respect for the rights and freedoms safeguarded by the Convention'.[459]

17.103 Whether the balance has been properly struck is subject to the margin of appreciation of the state.[460] The margin of appreciation affords the domestic law-maker power to determine what differential treatment is proportionate to the objective that it has chosen. Nevertheless, the state is not absolved from proving its explanation for the differentiation on a rational basis and an evidential foundation, so as to minimise the risk of government rationalisation of unjustifiable discrimination.

---

[453] (1968) 1 EHRR 252, 284 para 10.

[454] *Darby v Sweden* (1990) 13 EHRR 774 where the Government declined to advance 'administrative convenience' as the basis for the differential tax treatment of the applicant.

[455] n 453 above.

[456] Ibid para 34.

[457] Ibid.

[458] Ibid.

[459] For a discussion of the principle of proportionality in Convention case law, see para 6.42ff above.

[460] For a general discussion of the doctrine, see para 6.31ff above.

In general, it is not difficult for the state to prove the legitimacy of its aim in implementing the measures in question. Thus, in *Marckx v Belgium*[461] the state identified its aim as the support and encouragement of the traditional family; in *Abdulaziz, Cabales and Balkandali v United Kingdom*[462] the aim was to protect the labour market and protect public order; in the *Belgian Linguistic Case (No 2)*[463] the Government sought to develop linguistic unity in the two language regions which made up its country. Since the necssary standard of justification requires showing rationality and that the state is afforded a margin of appreciation, it is not perhaps surprising that governments frequently succeed on this issue. **17.104**

The more contentious issue is whether the differential treatment is proportionate to its aim. A number of grounds of discrimination are sufficiently serious to be considered as immediately suspect: race, sex, illegitimacy, religion and nationality.[464] The criteria for identifying whether a form of discrimination falls into such category are not clear. Reference to an international agreement will not necessarily be sufficient,[465] but clear evidence of a European consensus or developing European standard is likely to be influential. Extension of the list is controversial and unlikely. **17.105**

Moreover, the closer the treatment is to conforming to a common European standard,[466] the less likely it is that it will fall outside the margin of appreciation[467] allowed to states to determine the boundaries of discrimination. In *Rasmussen v Denmark*[468] the Court held that differential time limits for bringing paternity proceedings between men and women was not out of line with the practice in other European states and that the treatment was within Denmark's margin of appreciation. Similarly, in *Petrovic v Austria*[469] discriminating between husbands and wives in relation to parental leave allowance fell within the margin of appreciation as there was no common standard among the Contracting States. **17.106**

In the absence of a suspect category or a European standard, the Court will have to refer solely to the national situation in its assessment of proportionality. The existence of an alternative means of achieving the same goal in these circumstances **17.107**

---

461 (1979) 2 EHRR 330.

462 (1985) 7 EHRR 471.

463 (1968) 1 EHRR 252.

464 For a discussion of the cases, see para 17.111ff below.

465 In *Abdulaziz, Cabales and Balkandali v United Kingdom* (1985) 7 EHRR 471 the Court disregarded the evidence presented by the applicants that the UNGA Declaration on the Elimination of Discrimination against Women (GA Res 2716) supported the concept of a special status for sex discrimination; in *Inze v Austria* (1987) 10 EHRR 394 it referred to the 1977 European Convention on the Legal Status of Children Born out of Wedlock (ETS 85; UKTS 43 (1981)).

466 Helfer, (1990) 65 New York U L Rev 1044, 1075.

467 See generally, para 6.31ff above.

468 (1984) 7 EHRR 371.

469 RJD [1998]-II 579.

might be considered as evidence of the disproportionality of the Government's choice of means,[470] even if it is not determinative.[471] The margin of appreciation is a strong source of protection for actions taken by the state, including the implementation of schemes which impact very differently on individuals, so long as the effect of the overall scheme is tolerable.[472]

17.108 An applicant may challenge the Government concerning its stated aim or the differentiating factor upon which the treatment is based. Because the basis for the distinction is generally apparent on the face of the legislation or decision[473] and the aim expressly asserted, the applicant may seek to establish a *hidden* motive, basis or reason for the distinction. Arguably, if the real reason for the measures was addressed, it would be found incapable of supporting a reasonable and objective justification for the differential treatment. Some of these applications, particularly challenges to the purported characteristic of distinction, are relatively straightforward in nature.[474] Other claims of disguised discrimination are not so easy to establish and, generally, the Court has treated such complaints with scepticism.[475]

(8) Discrimination cases before the Court

(a) Introduction

17.109 Despite the absence of a free standing right against discrimination, the Court has considered a large number of discrimination cases in very different areas. Many of the discrimination complaints have been made by way of 'alternative submissions' where the central issue concerned a breach of a substantive right. Nevertheless, the Court has found violations in a number of cases where there has been no breach of the relevant substantive right. These cases are most usefully considered from the perspective of the ground of discrimination which was invoked by the applicant.

17.110 Findings of discrimination have been made by the Court on the following

---

[470] *Inze v Austria* (1987) 10 EHRR 394 para 44.

[471] The Court in *Rasmussen v Denmark* (1984) 7 EHRR 371 para 41 found that the margin of appreciation extends to choosing between alternatives.

[472] *James v United Kingdom* (1986) 8 EHRR 123 para 77.

[473] This is not the same thing as the Government's aim which undergirds the justification of the differentiation on these grounds.

[474] *Hoffmann v Austria* (1993) 17 EHRR 293 in which the applicant, a Jehovah's Witness, successfully alleged that treatment afforded her 'in the best interests of her child' was in fact undertaken on grounds of religion. The basis for the discrimination was disproportionate.

[475] See eg *Abdulaziz, Cabales and Balkandali v United Kingdom* (1985) 7 EHRR 471; *Handyside v United Kingdom* (1976) 1 EHRR 737.

grounds: sex,[476] religion,[477] sexual orientation,[478] birth,[479] language,[480] residence,[481] property[482] and national origin.[483] These findings have related to discrimination within the ambit of Articles 4, 6, 8 and Articles 1 and 2 of the First Protocol.

(b) Discrimination cases

17.111 **Sex discrimination.** In *Abdulaziz, Cabales and Balkandali v United Kingdom*[484] the Court considered Immigration Rules which resulted in husbands being refused permission to remain or join their wives in the United Kingdom whereas the spouses of men were entitled to remain or join their husbands. It was held that these rules interfered with the applicants' rights to family life and discriminated on the ground of sex. These rules had the legitimate aim of protecting the domestic labour market. Nevertheless, 'very weighty reasons would have to be advanced before a difference of treatment on ground of sex' could be regarded as compatible with the Convention[485] and the difference of treatment was therefore unjustified. However, the Court rejected the complaints based on race discrimination and found that differences based on treatment of husbands who were born in (or whose parents were born in) the United Kingdom and husbands who had merely settled in the United Kingdom were objectively justifiable and reasonable.

17.112 In *Schuler-Zgraggen v Switzerland*[486] the applicant was refused state invalidity pension on the basis that, as a woman with a child, she would not go out to work. The Court found discrimination proved because the court had assumed, without investigating, that women gave up work when they had children. In *Rasmussen v Denmark*[487] the applicant challenged a statutory time limit which applied to husbands taking paternity proceedings whereas no time limits applied to women; and the Court held that the difference in treatment was justifiable, primarily because in most states the positions of mother and father were regulated differently.

---

476 *Abdulaziz, Cabales and Balkandali v United Kingdom* (n 475 above) (Art 8); *Schuler-Zgraggen v Switzerland* (1993) 16 EHRR 405 (Art 8); *Schmidt v Germany* (1994) 18 EHRR 513 (Art 4); *Burghartz v Switzerland* (1994) 18 EHRR 101; *Van Raalte v Netherlands* (1997) 24 EHRR 503; *Rasmussen v Denmark* (1984) 7 EHRR 371.

477 *Hoffmann v Austria* (1993) 17 EHRR 293; *Canea Catholic Church v Greece* (1997) 27 EHRR 521 (Art 6).

478 *Salgueiro da Silva Mouta v Portugal*, Judgment of 21 Dec 1999 (Art 8).

479 *Marckx v Belgium* (1979) 2 EHRR 330 (Art 1, 1st Prot); *Vermeire v Belgium* (1991) 15 EHRR 488 (Art 1, 1st Prot); *Inze v Austria* (1987) 10 EHRR 394 (Art 1, 1st Prot), *Mazurek v France* Judgment of 1 Feb 2000 (Art 1, 1st Prot).

480 *Belgian Linguistic Case (No 2)* (1968) 1 EHRR 252 para 32 (Art 2, 1st Prot).

481 *Darby v Sweden* (1990) 13 EHRR 774 (Art 1, 1st Prot).

482 *Chassagnou v France* (1999) 7 BHRC 151.

483 *Gayguscuz v Austria* (1996) 23 EHRR 365 (Art 1, 1st Prot).

484 (1985) 7 EHRR 471.

485 Ibid para 78.

486 (1993) 16 EHRR 405.

487 (1984) 7 EHRR 371.

17.113 In *Burghartz v Switzerland*[488] Swiss law prevented a husband from putting his own surname before the family name although it gave this right to married women who adopted their husband's name. It was held that a person's name was an aspect of his private and family life. The Court held that this difference in treatment lacked an objective and reasonable justification and, accordingly, contravened Article 8 together with Article 14. In *Van Raalte v Netherlands*[489] discrimination was again proved because an unmarried man over the age of 45 was obliged to pay contributions towards child benefit whereas childless women were not. A similar conclusion was reached in *Schmidt v Germany*;[490] the Court held that the civic obligation on men to serve as firemen amounted to a breach of Article 14 in conjunction with Article 4 since the same obligation was not imposed on women. In practice, the only obligation was to pay a fire service levy in lieu and, in the imposition of a financial burden of this type a difference of treatment on the ground of sex could not be justified.

17.114 However, differential treatment on the ground of sex has been found to be justified in some cases. Thus, in *Petrovic v Austria*[491] a husband was refused parental leave allowance as only women were entitled to it. His discrimination claim failed; there was no common standard among contracting states for parental leave allowances to be paid to men so that the failure to do so could be justified as falling within the margin of appreciation.

17.115 **Religious discrimination.** In *Canea Catholic Church v Greece*[492] the applicant church could not take domestic proceedings to protect its land and buildings because, under Greek law, it did not have legal personality. In contrast, the Orthodox Church and the Jewish synagogues could bring proceedings. The Court held that there was a breach of Article 14 along with Article 6 because no objective and reasonable justification for the difference in treatment had been put forward. In *Hoffmann v Austria*[493] a mother was refused custody of her children because she was a Jehovah's witness when her husband and children were Catholics. Although the protection of the children's rights was a legitimate aim, a distinction based essentially on a difference in religion alone was not acceptable. As a result, the Court found a breach of Article 14 in conjunction with Article 9. In *Thlimmenos v Greece*[493a] the Court upheld a complaint on the ground that the state had failed to treat a Jehovah's witness differently from others who were convicted of criminal offences. Its decision to exclude the applicant from the Greek Institute of Char-

---

488 (1994) 18 EHRR 101.
489 (1997) 24 EHRR 503.
490 (1994) 18 EHRR 513.
491 RJD [1998]-II 579.
492 (1997) 27 EHRR 521.
493 (1993) 17 EHRR 293.
493a Judgment of 6 Apr 2000.

tered Surveyors on the grounds of a criminal conviction which arose out of his religious beliefs was disproportionate; and the Court found that there were no objective and reasonable grounds for not treating the applicant differently from others who had been convicted.

However, no breach was found in *Kjeldsen, Madsen and Pedesen v Denmark.*[494] The applicants complained of discrimination on the ground of religion because pupils could be exempt from religious instruction but not sex education. The Court decided that religious instruction was not comparable to sex education since it disseminates tenets and not merely knowledge. **17.116**

Discrimination on the ground of language. In the *Belgian Linguistic Case (No 2)*[495] the applicants' complaints concerned the provision of education in Belgium. The French speaking residents of certain communes did not have access to French-language schools in other communes whereas the Dutch-speaking residents did have such access. The restrictions were imposed solely on the ground of language and could not be objectively justified. As a result the measure in question was incompatible with the first sentence of Article 2 of the First Protocol, read in conjunction with Article 14.[496] In *Mathieu-Mohin and Clerfayt v Belgium*[497] the applicants failed to prove discrimination where they claimed that French speaking voters could not elect a French speaking representative to the Flemish Council whereas Dutch voters could appoint Dutch speaking representatives. A requirement that linguistic minorities must vote for candidates who were willing to use the language of the region was not disproportionate. **17.117**

Discrimination on the ground of national origin. The preferential treatment given to nationals of the European Community was challenged in *C v Belgium.*[498] The applicant alleged that his deportation discriminated against him on grounds of race and nationality by comparison with criminals who were EC nationals. However, the Court considered that preferential treatment given to an EC national amounted to a reasonable and objective justification. The allegation of violation of Article 14 was also rejected in *Moustaquim v Belgium*[499] in which a deported juvenile who was a Moroccan national complained of discrimination because Belgian juveniles were treated differently. The Court held that the two situations were not comparable because Belgian juveniles could not legally be deported. In *The Observer and The Guardian v United Kingdom*[500] and *Sunday Times* **17.118**

[494] (1976) 1 EHRR 711 para 56.
[495] (1968) 1 EHRR 252.
[496] Ibid para 32.
[497] (1987) 10 EHRR 1.
[498] [1997] EHRLR 98.
[499] (1991) 13 EHRR 802.
[500] (1991) 14 EHRR 153.

v United Kingdom (No 2)[501] it was argued that there was discrimination on the ground of national origin because foreign newspapers were not subject to the same restrictions as English ones. However, the Court took the view that foreign newspapers were not in a similar position because they were not subject to the jurisdiction of the English courts.

17.119 **Discrimination on the ground of property.** In *James v United Kingdom*[502] the trustees of the estate of the Duke of Westminster challenged the transfer of properties where tenants exercised their rights under the Leasehold Reform Act 1967. One of the arguments put forward was that the legislation discriminated on grounds of property since it was a measure which redistributed property and only applied to long leasehold houses. The Court decided that the legislation had a legitimate aim and was not disproportionate. However, in *Chassagnou v France*[503] the Court held that a measure which required small but not large landowners to join approved inter-municipality hunters' associations discriminated on the ground of property. It was held that the Government had not put forward any objective and reasonable justification for this difference in treatment.[504]

17.120 **Discrimination on the ground of birth.** In *Marckx v Belgium*[505] it was held that limitations on a mother's ability to give or bequeath property to illegitimate children discriminated against unmarried mothers and could not be objectively justified. In *Inze v Austria*[506] Austrian intestacy laws discriminated against illegitimate children and had no objective and reasonable justification. A similar result was reached in *Mazurek v France*.[507] In each case there was a breach of Article 14 taken together with Article 1 of the First Protocol.

17.121 **Sexual orientation discrimination.** In *Salgueiro da Silva Mouta v Portugal*[508] the applicant complained that the Portuguese courts had deprived him of the custody of his daughter because of his sexual orientation. He argued that this constituted a discriminatory interference with his right to respect for family life. The Court held that this decision pursued the legitimate aim of protecting the interests of the child but that it was not objectively justified. As a result there was a breach of Article 14 in conjunction with Article 8.

17.122 **Discrimination on other grounds.** The Court has considered cases involving allegations of discrimination on the basis of a wide range of 'other statuses':

---

501 (1991) 14 EHRR 229.
502 (1986) 8 EHRR 123.
503 (1999) 7 BHRC 151.
504 Ibid para 121.
505 (1979) 2 EHRR 330; see also *Vermeire v Belgium* (1991) 15 EHRR 488.
506 (1987) 10 EHRR 394.
507 Judgment of 1 Feb 2000.
508 Judgment of 21 Dec 1999.

Marital status: In *McMichael v United Kingdom*[509] the applicant complained that Scottish legislation automatically conferred parental rights to the father of a child if he was married but required the father of a child born out of wedlock to apply to the court. The Court ruled that the aim of the legislation was legitimate since it provided a mechanism to identify 'meritorious' fathers; and that the conditions it imposed on natural fathers were proportionate.

Military rank: In *Engel v Netherlands (No 1)*[510] the Court held that differences in army disciplinary procedures between officers, non-commissioned officers and ordinary servicemen were justified. This was because differentiation based on rank reflected differing responsibilities, served the legitimate aim of preserving discipline by methods appropriate to different ranks and was not disproportionate.

Minority: In *Bouamar v Belgium*[511] different procedures for dealing with adults and juveniles in detention were held to be justified: the protective (as opposed to punitive) nature of the process reflected the special position of juveniles.

Profession: In *Van der Mussele v Belgium*[512] the Court rejected the complaint that the requirement on pupil advocates to represent clients without payment was discriminatory and within the ambit of Article 4. However, although work which is itself normal might become abnormal if there was discrimination in the choice of groups or individuals bound to perform it, the Court rejected the comparisons the applicant made with doctors, veterinary surgeons, pharmacists and dentists who were not required to give their services for free. In *National Union of Belgian Police v Belgium*[513] the denial of consultation rights to a union representing police officers was held to be for a legitimate aim and was not disproportionate. Similarly, the prohibition which prevents police officers from engaging in political activities or joining a political party was held to be justified in *Rekvényi v Hungary*.[514] The special duties and responsibilities of police officers justified their difference of treatment both in relation to the freedom of expression and freedom of association.

Residence: In *Darby v Sweden*[515] a non resident successfully complained that his taxes in part financed the religious activities of the Church of Sweden whereas residents might obtain an exemption. The case of *Gillow v United*

[509] (1995) 20 EHRR 205; for a recent Commission case see *Saucedo Gomez v Spain* Application No 37784/97, 19 Jan 1998 (no breach of Art 14 as result of failure to make financial provision for a woman who had cohabited for 18 years).
[510] (1976) 1 EHRR 647.
[511] (1988) 11 EHRR 1.
[512] (1983) 6 EHRR 163.
[513] (1975) 1 EHRR 578.
[514] (1999) 6 BHRC 554.
[515] (1990) 13 EHRR 774.

Kingdom[516] concerned preferential treatment based on a residency requirement. The applicants were refused permission to occupy a house in Guernsey and their subsequent prosecution was justified in order to maintain a population with strong attachments to the island; and was not disproportionate. Furthermore, the licensing system which excluded expensive houses from control and constituted discrimination on grounds of wealth was nevertheless justified; it was legitimate for the state to try and ensure adequate housing for the poorer section of the community and the steps taken were not disproportionate.

D. The Impact of the Human Rights Act

(1) Introduction

17.123 Article 14 issues are likely to arise in a wide range of cases under the Human Rights Act. Despite the absence of a 'free standing right', the prohibited grounds of discrimination are wide ranging and open-ended with the result that the Article can, potentially, be invoked in almost every type of case where individuals are subjected to a 'status based' difference in treatment by public authorities. In some areas the effect may be to create entire new categories of discrimination law. For example, Wintemute[517] has argued that almost any kind of discrimination may be challenged on the basis that it violates Article 14 in conjunction with the right to respect for privacy and family life under Article 8.[518] The Convention right against discrimination is likely to inspire some of the most creative developments under the Human Rights Act. Its potential range is illustrated, for example, by the argument that the equitable 'presumption of advancement' in the law of resulting trusts is in breach of Article 14.[518a]

17.124 Article 14 specifically prohibits discrimination in relation to sex, race, colour and national origin. However, it is unlikely that Article 14 will significantly increase the protection afforded under the present sex[519] and race[520] discrimination legislation even though it will now be easier for an individual complainant to bring discrimination cases outside the employment field. Article 14 also forbids discrimination based on religion, political or other opinion, social origin, association with a

[516] (1986) 11 EHRR 335.

[517] R Wintemute, 'Lesbian and Gay Britons, the Two Europes and the Bill of Rights Debate' [1997] EHRLR 466.

[518] See para 12.81ff above and para 13.70ff above respectively.

[518a] J Ayliffe and R Dew, 'The Development of the Comman Law and Equity. An Example: The Presumption of Advancement' in Wilberforce Chambers, *The Essential Human Rights Act 1998* (Wilberforce Chambers, 2000).

[519] For the Sex Discrimination Act, see para 17.12ff above; the Equal Pay Act is discussed at para 17.37ff above and the European Community law at para 17.48ff above.

[520] See para 17.68ff above.

national minority, property birth or *other* status. These additional grounds of discrimination may stimulate case law in unexpected areas.

(2) United Kingdom cases prior to the Human Rights Act

(a) Introduction

The range of cases brought against the United Kingdom under Article 14 shows the breadth of its potential impact. Article 14 has been raised in every conceivable type of case. However, the United Kingdom has been found to be in breach of Article 14 on only one occasion.[521] Several cases arising out of sex discrimination in relation to the payment of widows' benefits have resulted in 'friendly settlements'[522] and a number are pending before the Court.[523] **17.125**

(b) Sex discrimination

In *Abdulaziz, Cabales and Balkandali v United Kingdom*[524] the Court found that the immigration rules which prevented husbands from joining their wives was discriminatory because very weighty reasons have to be advanced to justify differences of treatment based on sex; by comparison, it rejected the complaint that the immigration rules discriminated on race grounds. **17.126**

In *MacGregor v United Kingdom*[525] the Government did not contest the admissibility of an application relating to discriminatory tax provisions. The applicant was not entitled to an additional personal allowance which would have been available to a man in the same position. A number of applications have been held to be admissible in relation to the refusal of the Government to pay 'widow's benefits' to widowers.[526] A friendly settlement has been reached and the government has indicated its intention to abolish widow's benefit.[527] **17.127**

---

521 *Abdulaziz, Cabales and Balkandali v United Kingdom* (1985) 7 EHRR 471 (Arts 8 and 14).

522 *Crossland v United Kingdom* Application 36120/97, 9 Nov 1999 *Cornwell v United Kingdom*, Judgment of 25 Apr 2000; *Leary v United Kingdom*, Judgment of 25 Apr 2000.

523 See eg *Sutherland v United Kingdom* [1997] EHRLR 117 and the gypsy cases: see *Coster v United Kingdom* (1998) 25 EHRR CD 24; *Beard v United Kingdom* (1998) 25 EHRR CD 28; *Smith v United Kingdom* (1998) 25 EHRR CD 42; *Lee v United Kingdom* (1998) 25 EHRR CD 46; *Varey v United Kingdom* (1998) 25 EHRR CD 49; *Chapman v United Kingdom* (1998) 25 EHRR CD 64.

524 (1985) 7 EHRR 741.

525 [1998] EHRLR 354.

526 See *Willis v United Kingdom* [1999] EHRLR 536; the other cases are *Cornwell v United Kingdom* (1999) 27 EHRR CD 62, *Leary v United Kingdom* Application 38890/97; *Crossland v United Kingdom* Application 36120/97, 9 Nov1999; *Fielding v United Kingdom* Application 36940/97 and *Sawden v United Kingdom* Application 38550/97, EComm HR.

527 *Crossland v United Kingdom* Application 36120/97, 9 Nov 1999; *Cornwell v United Kingdom*, Judgment of 25 Apr 2000; *Leary v United Kingdom*, Judgment of 25 Apr 2000.

(c) Racial discrimination

17.128 In the *East African Asians* case[528] the Commission decided that legislation regulating immigration and nationality discriminated on grounds of race and colour. The case did not reach the Court because the Committee of Ministers held that there was no violation, mainly because of the steps taken by the United Kingdom to meet the objections of the Commission

(d) Sexual orientation discrimination

17.129 In its early decisions under this head the Commission did not take a notably liberal stance. In *X v United Kingdom*[529] it held that discrimination against male homosexuals in relation to the age of consent was justified by reason of a tendency of male homosexuals to proselytise adolescents. A similar conclusion was reached in *Johnston v United Kingdom*[530] where the applicant complained that the fact that the criminal law made it an offence where homosexual acts are committed with more than two adult males present was discriminatory because there was no similar provision relating to lesbians or heterosexuals. The Commission held that the difference in treatment had an objective and reasonable justification in the need to protect the young and vulnerable.

17.130 The case of *Sutherland v United Kingdom*[531] signifies an important change of attitude. The Commission considered the difference between the age of consent for homosexuals and heterosexuals. It concluded that there was no objective and reasonable justification for the maintenance of the higher minimum age of consent for male homosexuals. As a result, it held that there had been a violation of Article 8 in conjunction with Article 14. In *A D T v United Kingdom*[532] the Court considered that a complaint concerning discrimination in relation to the prosecution of male homosexuals for gross indecency in private was a breach of Article 8 and declined to make a separate finding under Article 14.

17.131 Similarly, the Court in *Lustig-Prean v United Kingdom*[533] and *Smith and Grady v United Kingdom*[534] decided that investigating and dismissing servicemen and women on grounds of their homosexuality were breaches of their right to privacy under Article 8.[535] The Court declined to make any separate finding under Article 14.

528 (1973) 3 EHRR 76.
529 (1978) 3 EHRR 63, EComm HR.
530 (1987) 9 EHRR 386.
531 [1997] EHRLR 117.
532 Judgment, 31 Jul 2000.
533 (1999) 7 BHRC 65.
534 [1999] IRLR 734.
535 See para 12.92ff above.

(e) Discrimination on other grounds

Criminal conviction. In *Monnell and Morris v United Kingdom*[536] it was held that the power of the Court of Appeal to order loss of time to convicted prisoners in custody who bring unmeritorious appeals was a discriminatory treatment. However, this had an objective and rational justification and there was, therefore, no breach of Article 14. **17.132**

Marital status. In *McMichael v United Kingdom*[537] the Court held that there were objective grounds for discriminating against unmarried fathers who had no legal right to apply for custody or participate in care proceedings. This approach was followed by the Commission in *Smallwood v United Kingdom.*[538] In *Lindsay v United Kingdom*[539] the applicants' complaints concerning the differential tax treatment of married and unmarried couples were rejected on the grounds that this was justified in that it sought to provide positive discrimination in favour of married women who work. **17.133**

National origin. In the *Spycatcher* cases the Court rejected the newspapers' complaints that an injunction against British papers was discriminatory on grounds of national origin because those who were resident outside the United Kingdom could read the book.[540] **17.133A**

Political opinion. In *Liberal Party, Mrs R and Mr P v United Kingdom*[541] the Commission dismissed the applicant's argument that the 'first past the post' electoral system constituted discrimination on the ground of political opinion. A broadcasting ban on Sinn Fein, insofar as it was discriminatory on the ground of political opinion, was held to be justified.[542] **17.134**

Profession and work status. In *Pinder v United Kingdom*[543] the Commission held that a complaint that a former airman could not bring proceedings for medical negligence in relation to treatment at a Royal Air Force Hospital was inadmissible. The fact that such proceedings could not be brought was a difference in treatment between civilians and servicemen but it had an objective and reasonable justification. **17.135**

Property. In *James v United Kingdom*[544] the applicant complained, *inter alia*, **17.136**

[536] (1987) 10 EHRR 205.
[537] (1995) 20 EHRR 205.
[538] (1998) 27 EHRR CD 155, 162.
[539] (1987) 9 EHRR 555, EComm HR.
[540] *The Observer and The Guardian v United Kingdom* (1991) 14 EHRR 153; *Sunday Times v United Kingdom (No 2)* (1991) 14 EHRR 229.
[541] (1980) 4 EHRR 106, EComm HR.
[542] *Brind and McLaughlin v United Kingdom* (1994) 18 EHRR CD 84.
[543] (1985) 7 EHRR 464.
[544] (1986) 8 EHRR 123.

that leasehold reform legislation discriminated between different categories of property owners; but this was properly justified.[545] In *Munro v United Kingdom*[546] a complaint alleging that the lack of legal aid for defamation proceedings was discrimination on the ground of wealth was held to be inadmissible.

17.137 **Residence.** The fact that the Guernsey authorities gave preferential treatment to those with roots in Guernsey and to wealthy individuals was held to be objectively justified and reasonable.[547]

(f) Other claims

17.138 A large number of applications have been found to be inadmissible. Many of these have been found to involve no relevant 'difference in treatment'. Thus, differences between High Court and county court procedure,[548] between victims of negligence and victims of intentional torts[549] between prisoners and those outside prison,[550] between employers and the self employed[551] and between an alleged deserter from the army and a civilian suspected of a criminal offence[552] have not involved any arguable Article 14 issue.

(3) General impact

(a) Introduction

17.139 As we have indicated,[553] it is unlikely that incorporating Article 14 into English law will significantly affect the rights available under existing discrimination legislation. Nevertheless, since the grounds for discrimination are open-ended,[554] Article 14 increases the range of potential discrimination claims well beyond sex, race or disability discrimination. There are, however, a number of important factors which are likely to limit the impact of the Human Rights Act in the discrimination field.

17.140 First, the scope of Article 14 is limited since it only prohibits discrimination in relation to other Convention rights.[555] Any attempt to extend the scope of Article 14 beyond its apparent language is likely to fail. The Privy Council recently

545 Ibid paras 74–77.

546 (1987) 10 EHRR 503, EComm HR; see also *S and M v United Kingdom* (1993) 18 EHRR CD 172.

547 *Gillow v United Kingdom* (1986) 11 EHRR 335.

548 *X v United Kingdom* (1988) 10 EHRR 149.

549 *Stubbings v United Kingdom* (1996) 23 EHRR 213.

550 *Lockwood v United Kingdom* (1993) 15 EHRR CD 48.

551 *X v United Kingdom* (1985) 7 EHRR 135, EComm HR.

552 *X v United Kingdom* (1987) 9 EHRR 369.

553 See para 17.125 above.

554 See para 17.96ff above.

555 See para 17.88ff above.

considered this issue in *Matadeen v Pointu*.[556] Although the equality provisions of the Constitution of Mauritius were in specific and narrow terms (which loosely corresponded to Article 14 of the Convention in confining the protection from discrimination to the rights and freedoms conferred by the Constitution itself), the Supreme Court of Mauritius had implied a general constitutional right that the law should treat everyone equally unless there was sufficient objective justification for not doing so. Lord Hoffmann held that no general right to equality could be implied which would displace the carefully enumerated grounds of unlawful discrimination expressly provided for in the Mauritian Constitution.

Because Article 14 is confined to discrimination in relation to Convention rights (which are, in the main, traditional political and civil rights), the Human Rights Act will only *indirectly* prohibit discrimination in the economic and social sphere. For example, as the Convention contains no 'right to a job' it would not be a breach of Article 14 for a public authority to discriminate against job applicants on the ground of age. However, because social security benefits can be 'possessions' under Article 1 of the First Protocol, it could be a breach of Article 14 if such benefits were denied on the grounds of age. **17.141**

Secondly, the jurisprudence on Article 14 has tended to be cautious and deferential. This has led some commentators to argue that incorporation will only have a significant impact if the English courts give a broader and more purposive construction to Article 14.[557] For example, it is unclear whether the principle of indirect discrimination is accepted by the Strasbourg courts.[557a] Such a narrow approach would be difficult to justify[557b] and is unlikely to be applied by English courts and tribunals which have extensive experience of indirect discrimination cases. However, the Court of Human Rights has recently taken a more robust approach in Article 14 cases. In *Salgueiro da Silva Mouta v Portugal*[557c] it held that the refusal of access to the applicant's daughter on the grounds of his sexual orientation breached Article 14 in conjunction with Article 8. In *Thlimmenos v Greece*[557d] the Court decided that Article 14 imposed an obligation on the state to promote positive discrimination. **17.142**

Thirdly, it is unclear whether Article 14 will impinge upon an individual's *access* to Convention rights; it may be difficult to show that such a complaint is within the **17.143**

[556] [1998] 3 WLR 18.
[557] See eg S Fredman, 'Equality Issues' in B Markesinis (ed), *The Impact of the Human Rights Bill on English Law* (Oxford University Press, 1998).
[557a] See para 17.90 above.
[557b] See S Livingstone, 'Article 14 and the Prevention of Discrimination in the European Court of Human Rights' [1997] EHRLR 25, 31.
[557c] Judgment of 21 Dec 1999.
[557d] Judgment of 6 Apr 2000; for a discussion of the case see para 17.91A above.

ambit[558] of a Convention right. The position may be comparable to the controversial distinction the Court has made between holding that dismissing members of the Communist Party from the civil service breaches freedom of expression whereas refusing to appoint them to the civil service does not.[559]

17.144 Fourthly, since only public authorities[560] must act in a manner which is compatible with Convention rights whether Article 14 can be used to plug some of the gaps in the existing discrimination legislation (like preventing private clubs from discriminating against women)[561] will depend on the principle of statutory horizontality.[561a] It is also possible that the approach taken towards defining discrimination under Article 14 will affect the interpretation of the concept of discrimination under domestic legislation as in Canada.[561b]

17.144A It therefore may be more advantageous for individuals to rely on other Convention rights when bringing discrimination cases. It has, for example, been strongly argued that it may be advantageous to pursue allegations of race discrimination by relying on the right to an effective investigation of inhuman treatment under Article 3.[561c]

(b) Religious discrimination

17.145 Article 14 will introduce the possibility of making complaints of religious discrimination.[562] Such cases will also arise as a result of the right to freedom of religion under Article 9.[563] The impact of Article 9 on criminal law, education, employment, family law, planning and environment and police law is discussed in Chapter 14.[564] Allegations of religious discrimination, particularly where they involve challenges to a law of general application, may meet with greater success if they are brought as complaints under Article 14: this was the approach which the Court recently accepted in *Thlimmenos v Greece*.[564a]

---

558 See para 17.86ff above.

559 See para 15.148 above.

560 See Chap 5 above.

561 The Sex Discrimination Act 1975, s 29 prohibits discrimination in services to the public; and 'public' in this context is to be contrasted with 'private' so that a private members' club is not covered: see *Charter v Race Relations Board* [1973] AC 868; *Dockers' Labour Club and Institute Ltd v Race Relations Board* [1976] AC 285. There is no equivalent under the Sex Discrimination Act to the Race Relations Act 1976, s 25.

561a See para 5.84ff above.

561b See para 17.180A below.

561c J Goldstone, 'Race Discrimination in Europe: Problems and Prospects' [1999] EHRLR 462 discussing *Assenov v Bulgaria* (1998) 28 EHRR 652: see para 8.19 above.

562 S Fredman, 'Equality Issues' in B Markesinis (ed), *The Impact of the Human Rights Bill on English Law* (Oxford University Press, 1998) 122–126.

563 See para 14.36ff above.

564 See para 14.77ff above.

564a Judgment of 6 Apr 2000; see para 17.91 above.

It is probable that the restriction of common law blasphemy to the Christian religion will be challenged as a breach of freedom of religion[565] coupled with Article 14. However, such a challenge is unlikely to succeed in view of the approach taken in *R v Chief Metropolitan Stipendiary Magistrate, ex p Choudhury*[566] and the subsequent unsuccessful application to Strasbourg. [567] The inability of Muslims to secure state funding for Muslim schools is considered below.[568] **17.146**

(c) Sexual orientation discrimination

Until recently, every claim of sexual orientation discrimination based on Article 14 has been unsuccessful.[569] However, *Sutherland v United Kingdom*[570] shows an important change of attitude; the Commission ruled admissible a complaint that fixing the minimum age of consent for homosexual activity at 18 as opposed to 16 violated respect for private life and was discriminatory. It is therefore now clear that 'sexual orientation discrimination' falls within Article 14.[571] **17.147**

In 1999 the Court decided in *Lustig-Prean v United Kingdom*[572] and *Smith and Grady v United Kingdom*[573] that the intrusive investigation and dismissal of homosexuals in the armed forces breached the right of respect for privacy[574] and declined to make a separate finding in relation to the Article 14 claim. The same approach was taken in *ADT v United Kingdom.*[574a] As a result, it is unlikely that such claims alleging sexual orientation discrimination will be significantly strengthened if applicants rely on Article 14 in addition to Article 8. On the other hand, in *Salgueiro da Silva Mouta v Portugal*[574b] the Court relied on Article 14 in holding that the Convention prohibited the refusal of contact to a parent on the ground of his sexual orientation. **17.148**

(4) Specific areas of impact

(a) Criminal law

Article 14 will require the criminal courts to address allegations of discrimination, particularly complaints of sex and race discrimination. Article 14 may be relevant, for example, to any arguments based on the disproportionate sentencing of women and offenders from ethnic minorities.[575] **17.149**

[565] See para 14.14ff above.
[566] [1991] 1 QB 429
[567] *Choudhury v United Kingdom* (1991) 12 HR LJ 172, EComm HR.
[568] See para 17.153 below.
[569] See generally, R Wintemute, *Sexual Orientation and Human Rights* (Clarendon Press, 1995) 119-143; P Duffy, 'A Case for Equality' [1998] EHRLR 134.
[570] [1997] EHRLR 117.
[571] See eg *Salgueiro da Silva Mouta v Portugal* Judgment of 21 Dec 1999.
[572] (1999) 7 BHRC 65.
[573] [1999] IRLR 734.
[574] See See para 12.92ff above.
[574a] Judgment, 31 Jul 2000.
[574b] Judgment of 21 Dec 1999.
[575] See, Liberty, *Getting It Right: Future Issues Under the Human Rights Act 1998* (Liberty, 1998).

(b) Education

17.150 Because there is a substantive right to education under Article 2 of the First Protocol,[576] there will be considerable scope for discrimination cases in the educational field. Article 14 may have an impact on issues involving school admission procedures, school expulsions, special needs education and religious education.

17.151 A number of issues arise concerning the impact of Article 14 on school admission procedures.[577] Admission policies based on catchment areas which discriminate between applicants may become unlawful.[578] Although the Education Act 1996 does not prohibit parental preferences for schools based on racial grounds,[579] such preferences will be unlawful under Article 14. Furthermore, where parental preferences are defeated by arrangements made to preserve the religious character of a school,[580] parents could argue that Article 14 has been breached. However, public authorities may respond by relying on the particular importance to be given to the right to freedom of religion under section 13 of the Human Rights Act[581] and might prove that the preservation of the religious character of the school in *itself* was a reasonable and objective justification[582] of the discrimination in question. If, however, the preservation of the school's religious character resulted in pupils who were almost all, for example, middle class, it might be argued that the admission arrangements discriminated on grounds of 'social origin'.[583]

17.152 Article 14 could also have implications for school expulsions. The disproportionate number of black children who have been disciplined or expelled from schools might be the subject of an indirect discrimination claim. It has also been suggested that disciplining a pupil for failing to comply with dress requirements might discriminate on grounds of 'social origin' if non compliance resulted from poverty or some problematic family circumstance.[584]

17.153 Furthermore, the failure to offer alternative religious worship to minority children may amount to discrimination in breach of Article 14.[585] On the other hand, complaints that the state discriminates in the way it subsidises education have

---

576 See para 18.26ff below.

577 See generally, para 19.18ff below.

578 Cf *R v Bradford Metropolitan Borough Council, ex p Sikander Ali* [1994] ELR 299 where a claim alleging indirect discrimination was dismissed.

579 *R v Cleveland County Council ,ex p Commission for Racial Equality* [1994] ELR 44

580 Under the Education Act 1996, s 91 the governing bodies of a foundation or voluntary aided school may make arrangements to preserve the religious character of the school.

581 See para 14.75ff above.

582 See para 17.100ff above.

583 M Supperstone, J Goudie and J Coppel, *Local Authorities and the Human Rights Act 1998* (Butterworths, 1999) 58.

584 Supperstone, Goudie and Coppel (n 583 above) 59.

585 See, P Cumper, 'School Worship: Praying for Guidance' [1998] EHRLR 44.

been rejected by the Commission.[586] In many cases, however, the adequacy (or surplus) of school places in a particular locality may mean that there is no reasonable and objective justification for subsidising some denominational schools but not others.[587]

(c) Employment and discrimination

Article 14 is unlikely to have any significant repercussions in this area (outside the area of sexual orientation discrimination).[588] The principle of statutory horizontality[589] could limit the scope of some of the statutory exclusions from liability under the sex[590] or race[591] legislation; or might result in declarations of incompatibility[592] with Article 14. If the right to job security could be properly described as a property right under Article 1 of the First Protocol,[593] Article 14 would prohibit all forms of discrimination in employment; however, this contention is most unlikely to succeed. **17.154**

On the other hand, employers who wish to avoid prosecution for employing immigrants who have no entitlement to work in the United Kingdom[594] by carrying out checks on ethnic minorities may be acting in breach of Article 14 in conjunction with the right to privacy under Article 8.[595] **17.155**

(d) Family law

There are likely to be numerous cases alleging that public authorities discriminate in relation to respecting family life.[596] It is probable that the Human Rights Act will provide an impetus to discrimination claims such as the prohibition against single sex marriage[597] or that a homosexual should be entitled to obtain financial provision from his former partner where the relationship has come to an end.[597a] **17.156**

---

586 See eg *X v United Kingdom* (1978) 14 DR 179, EComm HR; *Verein Gemeinsam Lernen v Austria* (1995) 82-A DR 41, ECommm HR. The right to education under Art 2 of the First Protocol does not oblige the state to subsidise education: see para 18.43ff below.

587 Supperstone, Goudie and Coppel (n 583 above) 60.

588 See para 17.121 above.

589 See para 5.84ff above.

590 See para 17.34ff above.

591 See para 17.66 above.

592 See para 4.43ff above.

593 See para 18.33ff above.

594 Asylum and Immigration Act 1996, s 8.

595 See para 12.84ff above.

596 See generally, H Swindells, A Neaves, M Kushner and R Skilbeck, *Family Law and the Human Rights Act 1998* (Family Law, 1999) paras 11.30ff, 12.31 and I Karsten, 'Atypical Families and the Human Rights Act: The Rights of Unmarried Fathers, Same Sex Couples and Transsexuals' [1999] EHRLR 195.

597 The question whether this breached s 19 of the New Zealand Bill of Rights Act was considered by the Court of Appeal in *Quilter v A-G of New Zealand* [1998] 1 NZLR 523; see A Butler, 'Same Sex Marriage and Freedom From Discrimination in New Zealand' [1998] PL 396.

597a See the Canadian case of *A-G v M and H* [1999] 2 SCR 3 which is discussed at para 17.178ff below.

17.157 Unmarried fathers who have not acquired parental responsibility[598] may make discrimination claims based upon their Article 8 rights to privacy and family life in a variety of areas:[599]

- where the court uses its power to revoke a parental responsibility order;[600]
- because the consent of an unmarried father is not required before the court makes an adoption (or freeing for adoption) order;[601]
- because unmarried fathers need not be informed of an adoption agency unless he is maintaining the child nor be consulted by adoption agencies about his wishes if this is not practicable;[602]
- because a child may not be removed from the jurisdiction except with the consent of everyone who has parental responsibility or the leave of the court;[603]
- because an unmarried father may not be able to prove a breach of the right to custody under the meaning of the Hague Convention on child abduction.[604]

It should be noted, however, that the Strasbourg authorities have found discrimination on the ground of marital status to be justified on a number of occasions.[605] In *Re W; Re B (Child Abduction: Unmarried Fathers)*[606] Hale J held that the position of unmarried fathers did not breach Article 14.

17.158 Decisions affecting a parent's right to a residence order or contact must not discriminate between parents by, for example, refusing to make a residence order because the parent is a Jehovah's witness.[607]

17.159 Article 14 may be invoked by individuals denied access to assisted reproduction technology.[608] Applicants who are refused treatment on grounds of their age may succeed in proving discrimination in relation to their right to family life.

17.160 Article 14 may also be breached where there is differential treatment of 16-year-olds compared to 18-year-olds.[609] Consequently, detaining a 16-year-old youth for treatment for anorexia[610] may contravene the Human Rights Act.

598 See para 13.21 above.
599 Swindells, Neaves, Kushner and Skilbeck (n 596 above) para 3.120.
600 Children Act 1989, s 4(3); see *Re P (Terminating Parental Responsibility)* [1995] 1 FLR 1048.
601 Adoption Act 1976, s 72 as amended.
602 *Re L (A Minor)(Adoption, Procedure)* [1991] 1 FLR 171.
603 Children Act 1989, s 13.
604 *Re J (A Minor)(Abduction: Custody Rights)* [1990] 2 AC 562.
605 See eg *McMichael v United Kingdom* (1995) 20 EHRR 205 and see para 17.122 above.
606 [1998] 2 FLR 146, 163-168.
607 *Hoffmann v Austria* (1993) 5 EHRR 293.
608 See para 13.157 above.
609 *Sutherland v United Kingdom*, [1998] EHRLR 117, EComm HR (discrimination in relation to age of consent)
610 *Re C (A Minor) (Detention for Medical Treatment)*, *The Times*, 21 Mar 1997.

(e) Health care

17.161 Regional disparities in the provision of health care could be subject to Article 14 claims. For example, the well known difficulties experienced by women in some areas in England when seeking abortions under the Abortion Act 1967 may amount to discrimination against their right of respect for family life. It is also likely that differences of approach between health authorities or trust hospitals when rationing particular medical treatment might be subject to challenge under Article 14 provided the complaint is within the ambit of another Convention right.

(f) Housing law

17.162 It is arguable that the exemptions from the Rent Act 1977 of the Crown,[611] local authorities[612] and housing associations[613] and the exemption from an assured tenancy regime of the Crown,[614] local authorities[615] and housing associations[616] from legislation that applies to private tenants violates Article 14.[617]

17.163 It will be unlawful for a public authority to discriminate in relation to the right of respect for the home under Article 8.[618] The open ended grounds for claiming discrimination under Article 14 will make housing management decisions vulnerable to challenge in many areas such as allocation policies, tenancy transfers or decisions made to prioritise repair programmes between different estates. For example, Article 14 may be breached where a public authority discriminates in relation to its policies concerning the allocation of ground floor or larger premises to paticular types of occupants. It has also been suggested that the whole scheme for introductory tenancies discriminates on the basis of property status and breaches Article 14.[618a] The justification for the adoption of a scheme will be carefully scrutinised to see wether creating two classes of tenants in the public rented sector is justified.[618b]

(g) Immigration

17.164 Article 14 could have a substantial impact in the field of immigration law and

611 Rent Act 1977, s 13 for the position before 28 Nov 1980; thereafter the position was changed by the Housing Act 1980, s 73(1).

612 Rent Act 1977, s 14.

613 Ibid s 15.

614 Housing Act 1988, Sch 1, para 11.

615 Ibid, Sch 1, para 12.

616 Ibid Sch 1, para 12.

617 *Larkos v Cyprus* Judgment of 19 Feb 1999.

618 See generally, para 12.95ff above.

618a See J Luba, 'Acting on Rights—the Housing Implications of the Human Rights Act', Lecture, Sep 1999.

618b Cf the candaian case of *Dartmouth/Halifax County Regional Housing Authority v Sparks* (1993) 101 DLR (4th) 244.

nationality law.[619] For the purposes of the British Nationality Act 1981, the relationship of father and child only exists between a man and a legitimate child, but the relationship of mother and child exists between a woman and any child born to her.[620] This means that children of unmarried parents cannot acquire British nationality from their fathers, this may be a breach of Article 14 taken together with Article 8.[621] The failure to make provision for 'common law' spouses[622] to obtain entry may violate the right of respect for the family[623] as well as Article 14.

(h) Local government law

17.165 The whole range of local government activity will be susceptible to scrutiny based on Article 14. Some of the applications that may be raised in the housing field are discussed above.[624] The use of enforcement powers against gypsies may be said to be discrimination contrary to Article 14.[625]

(i) Police law

17.166 Article 14 may be particularly relevant to complaints by ethnic minority groups that the police discriminate when exercising police powers which interfere with liberty rights under Article 5.[626] Although it is arguable that stop and search powers do breach Article 5,[627] a complaint of discriminatory use of stop and search powers will fall within the ambit of Article 5.[628] It might be said, for example, that the disproportionate use of stop and search powers[629] against blacks amounts to indirect discrimination.[630]

(j) Prison law

17.167 Differences in treatment between prisoners and persons outside are unlikely to constitute violations of Article 14 because their positions cannot be regarded as analogous.[631] However, discrimination between different categories of prisoners

[619] For a general discussion, see N Blake and L Fransman (eds), *Immigration, Nationality and Asylum Under the Human Rights Act 1998* (Butterworths, 1999) Chap 6 (S Harrison).
[620] British Nationality Act 1981, s 50(9).
[621] Blake and Fransman (n 619 above) 115.
[622] See para 13.65 above.
[623] Cf Blake and Fransman (n 619 above) 101.
[624] See para 17.62ff above.
[625] The Commission has ruled that a number of applications are admissible which allege breaches of Article 14: see *Coster v United Kingdom* (1998) 25 EHRR CD 24; *Beard v United Kingdom* (1998) 25 EHRR CD 28; *Lee v United Kingdom* (1998) 25 EHRR CD 46; *Varey v United Kingdom* (1998) 25 EHRR CD 49; *Chapman v United Kingdom* (1998) 25 EHRR CD 64; however, there was no breach in *Smith v United Kingdom* (1998) 25 EHRR CD 42.
[626] See para 10.80ff above.
[627] See para 10.189ff above.
[628] See para 17.86ff above.
[629] See, generally, para 10.26ff above.
[630] For a discussion of the principle, see para 17.18ff above.
[631] Cf *Lockwood v United Kingdom* (1993) 15 EHRR CD 48.

may be a breach of Article 14 if other Convention rights are in play. For example, it has been suggested that blanket restrictions on visits or home leave (which are within the ambit of Article 8) could constitute discrimination on the ground of sex if based on assumptions as to security which only apply to male prisoners.[632]

(k) Social security law

Article 14 may have a significant impact since it is well established that social security benefits may be property rights under Article 1 of the First Protocol.[633] **17.168**

Sex discrimination in the social security field is likely to generate cases since it is unregulated by the Sex Discrimination Act or European Community law.[634] Under Article 14 applicants will complain that they have been subject to discrimination compared to others in a way which may provoke a wide range of applications.[635] Discrimination may be alleged where there is differential treatment in terms of entitlements to social security benefits between, for example, single and married people, students and non students and between those who are habitually resident and those who are not.[636] **17.169**

(l) Other areas of impact

Tax law. Article 14 may have some application to tax cases.[637] It has been suggested that discriminating between taxpayers on grounds of their residence[638] may be incompatible with the Article. **17.170**

Appendix 1: The Canadian Charter of Rights

(1) The interpretation of section 15

Section 15 of the Charter of Rights provides that: **17.171**

---

632 S Livingstone and T Owen, *Prison Law* (2nd edn, Oxford University Press, 1999) para 11.10.

633 See para 18.38 below.

634 S Fredman, *Women and the Law* (1997) 168–176.

635 See eg *Van Breedam v Belgium* (1989) 62 DR 109 (comparison of painters and sculptors with writers and musicians for the purposes of social security contributions); *Kraft and Rougeot v France* (1990) 65 DR 51, EComm HR (calculation of judicial pensions comparing those appointed to positions from the private sector and those appointed from within the court service).

636 R White, 'Social Security' in C Baker (ed), *The Human Rights Act 1998: A Practitioner's Guide* (Sweet & Maxwell, 1998) para 12-32.

637 See generally, J Peacock and F Fitzpatrick, 'Tax law' in C Baker (ed), *The Human Rights Act 1998: A Practitioner's Guide* (Sweet & Maxwell, 1998) paras 14-16–14-19; and E Campbell, 'Taxation and Human Rights' in Wilberforce Chambers, *The Essential Human Rights Act 1998* (Wilberforce Chambers, 2000) 89, 90.

638 See eg the cases concerning Art 52 (formerly 48) of the Treaty of European Union such as *Finanzamt Köhn-Altstadt v Schmacker* [1995] ECR I-225 and *Wielockx v Inspecteur der Directe Belastingen* [1995] ECR I-2493.

(1) Every individual is equal before and under the law and has the right to the equal protection and equal benefit of the law without discrimination and, in particular, without discrimination based on race, national or ethnic origin, colour, religion, sex, age or mental or physical disability.

(2) Subsection (1) does not preclude any law, program or activity that has as its object the amelioration of conditions of disadvantaged individuals or groups including those that are disadvantaged because of race, national or ethnic origin, colour, religion, sex, age or mental or physical disability.

17.172 The proper interpretation of section 15 has been very controversial. Initially, the Canadian courts took the view that the right to equality was breached where the law subjected the complainant to worse treatment than others who were similarly situated.[639] However, the Supreme Court in *Andrews v Law Society of British Columbia*[640] decided that the test was seriously deficient because it could justify laws discriminating against Jews and blacks. In *Andrews* a lawyer was refused membership to the Law Society of British Columbia because he was not a Canadian citizen. The approach taken by the Supreme Court to section 15 was to consider whether a disadvantage had been imposed on an individual because he had a section 15 (or analogous) characteristic, and if so, whether the discrimination could be justified under section 1 of the Charter as a reasonable limit by law which was demonstrably justified in a free and democratic society.

17.173 However, this straightforward analysis was not accepted in a trilogy of cases that came before the Supreme Court in 1995. In *Miron v Trudel*[641] the plaintiff claimed an accident benefit under his common law wife's insurance policy; and the Court held that the restriction of the policy to a spouse discriminated against him in breach of section 15 and could not be justified under section 1. The meaning of spouse was also in dispute in *Egan v Canada*[642] because the statutory definition stipulated they must be 'of the opposite sex'; and the Supreme Court decided that the refusal of a pension benefit to a spouse of an established couple in a homosexual relationship was justifiable under section 1. In *Thibeaudeau v Canada,*[643] on the other hand, the Supreme Court rejected a complaint by a divorcee that her liability for income tax on child support payments discriminated against separated custodial parents.

17.174 However, the reasoning adopted by the Supreme Court revealed three strands of thought. The first view, espoused by four members of the Court,[644] was the most straightforward; the imposition of a disadvantage based upon the enumerated or analogous grounds constituting discrimination, following the *Andrews* principle. The second view (which was also taken by four members of the Court),[645] was that there is no discrimination where the differentiation is relevant to the functional objectives of the legislation. The third view taken solely by L'Heureux-Dube J was much more flexible. L'Heureux-Dube J considered that the question of discrimination was to be decided with reference to the nature of the group affected, and the nature of the interests affected. The more vulnerable the group, and the more severe the effect on interests, the more likely that there will be discrimination. She

639 See eg *R v Ertel* (1987) 20 OAC 257.
640 [1989] 1 SCR 143 *per* McIntyre J at 166.
641 [1995] 2 SCR 418.
642 [1995] 2 SCR 513.
643 [1995] 2 SCR 627.
644 Mclachlin, Sopinka, Cory and Iacobucci JJ.
645 Gonthier, Lamer CJ, La Forest and Major JJ.

rejected the narrow approach of discrimination based upon enumerated or analogous grounds.

17.175 These different approaches were reconciled in *Law v Canada (Minister of Employment and Immigration)*[646] which is now the leading case on section 15. In *Law* Iacobucci J took the opportunity to lay down guidelines on the section and established a compromise on the doctrinal differences which had emerged in the Supreme Court in 1995. Iacobucci J, writing for a unanimous Court, explained the proper approach to section 15(1) as follows:

> First, does the impugned law (a) draw a formal distinction between the claimant and others on the basis of one or more personal characteristics, or (b) fail to take into account the claimant's already disadvantaged position within Canadian society resulting in substantively differential treatment between the claimant and others on the basis of one or more personal characteristics? If so, there is differential treatment for the purposes of s 15(1). Second, was the claimant subject to differential treatment on the basis of one or more of the enumerated or analogous grounds? And third, does the differential treatment discriminate in a substantive sense, bringing into play the purpose of s 15(1) of the Charter in remedying such ills as prejudice, stereotyping, and historical disadvantage? The second and third inquiries are concerned with whether the differential treatment constitutes discrimination in the substantive sense intended by s 15(1).

17.176 The underlying purpose of section 15(1) is the protection of human dignity. Therefore, differential treatment which does not violate the human dignity of a person or group will *not* constitute discrimination under section 15; and, in particular, will not be discriminatory where the difference in treatment also ameliorates the position of the disadvantaged within Canadian society:[647]

> The equality guarantee in s 15(1) is concerned with the realization of personal autonomy and self-determination. Human dignity means that an individual or group feels self-respect and self-worth. It is concerned with physical and psychological integrity and empowerment. Human dignity is harmed by unfair treatment premised upon personal traits or circumstances which do not relate to individual needs, capacities, or merits.[648]

The test of whether a person's dignity has been harmed is assessed from the standpoint of the complainant, viewed objectively. It is, therefore, concerned with the perspective of a person in circumstances similar to the claimant, who is informed of and rationally takes into account the various contextual factors.[649] Those factors include pre-existing disadvantage, the relationship between the ground of differentiation and the claimant's characteristics and circumstances, the ameliorative purpose or affects of impugned law and the nature of the interest affected.[650]

17.177 The legislation challenged in *Law* provided benefits to widows or widowers according to age. Those less than 35 years of age received nothing, whereas those aged 35-45 received a reduced amount, and those above the age of 45 received the maximum amount. The law was challenged by a 30-year-old widow, on the basis of age discrimination. As stated above, age is one of the grounds listed in section 15(1). However, the Court held that although a distinction was drawn on the basis of age, there was no discrimination. The

646 [1999] 1 SCR 497 para 88.
647 Ibid para 51.
648 Ibid para 53.
649 Ibid para 61.
650 Ibid paras 63–75.

Court observed that, relatively speaking, adults under the age of 45 have not been consistently and routinely subjected to the sorts of discrimination faced by some of Canada's discrete and insular minorities;[651] and that older people find it more difficult to enter the labour market.[652] The aim of the legislation was to provide long term security for Canadians who lose a spouse, and did not undermine the dignity of those under 45. Furthermore, the legislation had a clear ameliorative purpose in assisting older surviving spouses, who were more economically vulnerable:[653]

> The challenged legislation simply reflects the fact that people in the appellant's position are more able to overcome long-term need because of the nature of a human being's life cycle. Those who are younger when they lose a spouse are more able to replace the income lost from the death of a spouse.[654]

17.178 The case of *A-G v M and H*[655] provides an illustration of the application of the *Law* guidelines. That case concerned a challenge to family law legislation which restricted the right to support to spouses and opposite-sex couples who had cohabited for at least three years. The challenge was brought by a woman who wished to obtain support from her former lesbian partner. The Supreme Court held by a majority that the exclusion of same-sex partnerships from that legislation was a breach of equality rights, for the following reasons.[656] The Court observed that the excluded group suffered significant pre-existing disadvantage and vulnerability. Secondly, there was a lack of congruence between the ground upon which the claim was made, and the actual circumstances of the claimant. A same-sex relationship could be a permanent, conjugal relationship. Thirdly, there was no ameliorative purpose to the legislation. Moreover, the ameliorative nature of legislation was only likely to be relevant where the excluded group was more advantaged in a relative sense. Underinclusive ameliorative legislation that excluded from its scope the members of an historically disadvantaged group would rarely escape the charge of discrimination. Fourthly, the nature of the interest involved, namely financial security, was an important one.

17.179 The Court went on to hold that the discrimination was not justified under section 1.[657] The argument that the goal of the legislation was to provide for women in heterosexual partnerships, who were liable to be financially dependent on their partner, was rejected. The legislation was expressed in gender neutral language, and could be used by male partners of heterosexual relationships. Nor was the legislation to protect the position of children, as people could apply for support regardless of whether they had children. Rather, the objectives of the legislation were (a) to provide for the equitable resolution of economic disputes that arose when intimate relationships between individuals who have been financially interdependent broke down; and (b) to alleviate the burden on the public purse by shifting the obligation to provide support for needy persons to those parents and spouses who had the capacity to provide support to these individuals. Excluding same-sex couples from the legislation was not rationally connected to those objectives.

17.180 Gonthier J dissented on the issue of whether there was discrimination. He held that the

[651] Ibid para 95.
[652] Ibid para 101.
[653] Ibid paras 102–103.
[654] Ibid para 104.
[655] [1999] 2 SCR 3.
[656] Ibid paras 65–74.
[657] Ibid paras 82–135.

purpose of legislation under challenge was to redress dependency issues which were specific to opposite-sex relationships:

> 235 The evidence is uncontroverted that women in long-term opposite-sex relationships tend to become economically dependent on their spouses. This dependence arises for several related reasons. First, women as a group are economically disadvantaged by comparison to men. Women, on average, earn less than men do. A woman cohabiting in an opposite-sex relationship is thus likely to earn less than her male partner. This relative economic disadvantage is both the cause and the effect of gender roles. Second, women in long-term opposite-sex relationships commonly—though, I emphasize, not inevitably—waive educational and employment opportunities or prospects for economic advancement in order to bear and raise children and to shoulder a greater share of domestic responsibilities. . . .
>
> 242 The evidence indicates that lesbian relationships are characterized by a more even distribution of labour, a rejection of stereotypical gender roles, and a lower degree of financial interdependence than is prevalent in opposite-sex relationships.[658]

The principles the courts have developed for indentifying discrimination under section 15 of the Charter have also influenced the way in which provincial anti-discrimination legislation has been interpreted. Under section 15 the Supreme Court has attached very little importance to the difference between direct and indirect discrimination[658a] and in the important case of *British Columbia (Public Service Employee Relations Commission v BCGSEU*[658b] this approach was applied to employment discrimination legislation. The Supreme Court held that the traditional distinction between direct and indirect discrimination[658c] should be replaced by a unified approach which requires an employer to justify a standard which is *prima facie* discriminatory by showing: (i) that the standard is rationally connected to the peformance of the job; (ii) that the particular standard has been adopted in the honest and good belief that it was necessary to the fulfilment of that legitimate work-related performance; and (iii) that the standard is reasonably necessary to accomplish that work-related performance. **17.180A**

(2) Analogous grounds

There have been a number of decisions concerning whether certain grounds are 'analogous grounds', that is analogous to the grounds enumerated in section 15. Citizenship was held to be an analogous ground in *Andrews v Law Society of British Columbia*.[659] That case concerned a challenge to the requirement by the Law Society of British Columbia that entrants to the legal profession must be Canadian citizens. The Supreme Court held that the listed grounds focused on personal characteristics, and were generally immutable. La Forest J stated that: **17.181**

> The characteristic of citizenship is one typically not within the control of the individual and, in this sense, is immutable. Citizenship is, at least temporarily, a characteristic of personhood not alterable by conscious action and in some cases not alterable except on the basis of unacceptable costs.[660]

---

658 Ibid.

658a *Andrews v Law Society of British Columbia* [1989] 1 SCR 143,174; and see para 17.186 below.

658b [1999] 3 SCR 3 applied in *British Columbia (Superintendant of Motor Vehicles) v British Columbia (Council of Human Rights)* [1999] 3 SCR 868.

658c The provincial legislation distinguished between direct and adverse effect which resemble in broad terms the principles in English law.

659 [1989] 1 SCR 143.

660 Ibid 195. The Court further held that the discrimination was not saved by s 1 of the Charter.

17.182 The Court was divided in *Miron v Trudel*[661] as to whether marital status is an analogous ground. The plaintiff in that case challenged insurance benefits which, by statute, were available only to spouses of policy holders. The plaintiff, because he was in a common law relationship, was not eligible for those benefits. The Court, by a narrow majority, held that there was a breach of section 15, which was not justified under section 1. McLachlin J said that immutability was not an absolute requirement but merely an indicator of an analogous ground. Other indicators were historical disadvantage and membership of a discrete and insular minority.[662] She noted that marriage may be out of the control of an individual, for example where the other person did not wish to marry, or was not free to marry. Gonthier J on the other hand, with whom three other Justices concurred, held that marital status was not an analogous ground. He noted that the decision to marry was a joint choice, carrying burdens as well as benefits. Those benefits were available to common law couples by entering into a marriage.

17.183 Sexual orientation was accepted in *Egan v Canada*[663] as an analogous ground, and indeed the point was conceded by the Attorney-General of Canada. The Court referred to the deeply personal nature of sexual orientation, and the historic disadvantages suffered by homosexuals. That case concerned a challenge to certain Government pension benefits, which were only available to heterosexual couples. A narrow majority upheld the challenged legislation. Four of them did so on the basis that there was no discrimination. La Forest J[664] stated that the law was designed to support heterosexual couples, because such couples had the unique ability to procreate. The decisive judgment was given by Sopinka J who found a breach of section 15, but decided that it was justifiable under section 1. Sopinka J seemed concerned to avoid intruding into a sphere of legislative competence, and was of the view that Parliament should be permitted to legislate upon same-sex relationships on an incremental basis. He also noted the costs implications of requiring benefits to be paid to same-sex couples.

17.184 Reserve residency for Canadian Indians was held to constitute an analogous ground in *Corbiere v Canada (Minister of Indian and Northern Affairs)*.[665] The Court struck down legislation which confined voting rights for Indian band councils to members of that band who lived on a reserve. Band members who were resident outside the reserve successfully argued that denial of their right to vote constituted a breach of section 15(1). The Court held that reserve residence constituted an analogous ground, for the following reasons:

> [S]everal factors lead to the conclusion that recognizing off-reserve band member status as an analogous ground would accord with the purposes of s 15(1). From the perspective of off-reserve band members, the choice of whether to live on- or off-reserve, if it is available to them, is an important one to their identity and personhood, and is therefore fundamental. It involves choosing whether to live with other members of the band to which they belong, or apart from them. It relates to a community and land that have a particular social and cultural significance to many or most band members. Also critical is the fact that . . . band members living off-reserve have generally experienced disadvantage, stereotyping, and prejudice, and form part of a 'discrete and insular minority' defined by race and place of residence. In addition, because of the lack of opportunities and housing on many reserves, and the fact that

661 [1995] 2 SCR 418.
662 [1995] 2 SCR 418, 498.
663 [1995] 2 SCR 513.
664 Latimer CJ, Gonthier and Major JJ concurring.
665 [1999] 2 SCR 203.

> Indian Act's rules formerly removed band membership from various categories of band members, residence off the reserve has often been forced upon them, or constitutes a choice made reluctantly or at high personal cost.[666]

The Supreme Court has rejected a number of claims on the basis that listed or analogous grounds were not involved. In *Re Workers' Compensation Act 1983 (Nfld)*[667] a statute which prevented injured employees from suing their employers in tort survived a discrimination challenge. The discrimination in that case, between injured employees, and other injured litigants, was not a listed or analogous ground. In *Rudolf Wolff & Co v Canada*[668] the anti-discrimination provisions were held not to apply to a statute which prevented claims against the Crown being brought in provincial courts, but rather required them to be brought in a federal court. The Court held that the common characteristic of persons disadvantaged by this statute, namely those with a claim against the Crown, was not an immutable personal characteristic analogous to those listed in section 15. **17.185**

(3) Indirect discrimination

Indirect discrimination is covered by section 15, and policies which are neutral in their language may be discriminatory if they have an adverse impact on certain groups. In *Vriend v Alberta*[669] a provincial statute which prohibited employment discrimination on prescribed grounds, excluding sexual orientation, was held to constitute discrimination against homosexuals. Although, in theory, the statute failed to protect both heterosexuals and homosexuals from discrimination on the basis of their orientation, in practice homosexuals required that protection far more than heterosexuals. Therefore, the omission of sexual orientation from such legislation had an adverse impact upon homosexuals.[670] **17.186**

The failure of health care providers to pay for sign language interpretation was held to constitute indirect discrimination in *Eldridge v A-G of British Columbia*.[671] The Court noted that: **17.187**

> Adverse effects discrimination is especially relevant in the case of disability. The government will rarely single out disabled persons for discriminatory treatment.[672]

The Court stated that the principle that discrimination can accrue from a failure to take positive steps to ensure that disadvantaged groups benefit equally from services offered to the general public is widely accepted in the human rights field.[673] However, that duty is subject to the principle of reasonable accommodation. The obligation to make reasonable accommodation for those adversely affected by a facially neutral policy extends only to cases of 'undue hardship'.[674] Effective communication was an indispensable component

---

[666] Ibid para 62. The legislation did not survive s 1 analysis, as it was overbroad. Although there was an argument for restricting voting rights to those most directly affected by band councils' decisions, that did not explain the complete denial of voting rights to off-reserve members. Ibid para 21.

[667] [1989] 1 SCR 922.

[668] [1990] 1 SCR 695.

[669] [1998] 1 SCR 493.

[670] Ibid para 82.

[671] [1997] 3 SCR 624.

[672] Ibid para 64.

[673] Ibid para 78.

[674] Ibid para 79.

of the delivery of medical services[675] and failure to provide sign language where it was necessary for such communication was a *prima facie* violation of equality rights:[676]

> That is not to say that sign language interpretation will have to be provided in every medical situation. The effective communication standard is a flexible one, and will take into consideration such factors as the complexity and importance of the information to be communicated, the context in which the communications will take place and the number of people involved.... For deaf persons with limited literacy skills, however, it is probably fair to surmise that sign language interpretation will be required in most cases.[677]

17.188 The Court declined to find that the discrimination was justified by the general limitations clause, particularly in light of the comparatively low cost of providing sign language interpretation:

> the government has manifestly failed to demonstrate that it had reasonable basis for concluding that a total denial of medical interpretation services for the deaf constituted a minimum impairment or rights. . . . [T]he estimated cost of providing sign language interpretation for the whole of British Columbia was only $150,000, or approximately 0.0025 of the provincial health care budget at the time... In these circumstances, the refusal to expend such a relatively insignificant sum to continue and extend the service cannot possibly constitute a minimum impairment of the appellants' constitutional rights.[678]

(4) Existence of disadvantage

17.189 There can be disputes concerning whether a person is disadvantaged or not by the legislation which is being challenged. In *Thibaudeau v Canada*[679] a majority of the Supreme Court held that the claimant was unable to establish disadvantage. The claimant in that case was a divorced woman who received child support payments from her ex-husband. She objected to paying income tax on those child support payments, on the basis that, in an intact family, income tax would be paid by the spouse earning the income. The Court pointed out that the tax paid by the claimant was matched by a tax deduction for her ex-husband. Since spouses paying child support tended to be in a higher tax bracket than spouses receiving child support, there was an overall tax saving. Furthermore, the claimant's tax liability could be taken into account when assessing the level of child support, and the child support could be grossed up accordingly.

17.190 Similarly, in *Weatherall v Canada*[680] a male prisoner complained that he was liable to be frisk searched by female and male guards, whereas female prisoners could only be frisk searched by female guards. The Court declined to find a breach of the male prisoner's equality rights. As explained by La Forest J, an examination of the larger historical, biological, and sociological context made clear that the practices in question had a different, more threatening impact on women, such that it was not discriminatory in a substantive or purposive sense to treat men and women differently in this regard.[681]

[675] Ibid para 72.
[676] Ibid para 80.
[677] Ibid para 82.
[678] Ibid para 87.
[679] [1995] 2 SCR 627.
[680] [1993] 2 SCR 872.
[681] Ibid 877, 888.

Another case concerning the existence of disadvantage is *Eaton v Brant County Board of Education*.[682] In that case, a special educational tribunal had decided that a 12-year-old child with cerebral palsy should be educated in a special class. The child's parents argued that a failure to educate the child in an ordinary class was a breach of equality rights. The Supreme Court rejected that argument. The purpose of placing the child in a special class was to provide for her special educational needs. Given that the tribunal had found that the child's education was best served by education in a special class, the child had not suffered a disadvantage. The Court took the view that the equality rights at stake belonged to the child, not to her parents. Sopinka J made the following comments concerning discrimination on the basis of disability: 17.191

> 67. The principal object of certain of the prohibited grounds is the elimination of discrimination by the attribution of untrue characteristics based on stereotypical attitudes relating to immutable conditions such as race or sex. In the case of disability, this is one of the objectives. The other equally important objective seeks to take into account the true characteristics of this group which act as headwinds to the enjoyment of society's benefits, and to accommodate them. Exclusion from the mainstream of society which results from the construction of society based solely on 'mainstream' attributes to which disabled persons will never be able to gain access. . . . Rather, it is the failure to make reasonable accommodation, to fine-tune society so that its structures and assumptions do not result in the relegation and banishment of disabled persons from participation, which results in discrimination against them. . . .
>
> [69. Disability], as a prohibited ground, differs from other enumerated grounds such as race or sex because there is no individual variation with respect to these grounds. However, with respect to disability, this ground means vastly different things depending upon the individual and the context. This produces, among other things, the 'difference dilemma' . . . whereby segregation can be both protective of equality and violative of equality depending upon the person and the state of disability. . . . While integration should be recognised as the norm of general application because of the benefits it generally provides, a presumption in favour of integrated schooling would work to the disadvantage of pupils who require special education in order to achieve equality.[683]

A person may be able to raise a discrimination complaint if they are the victim of discrimination based on another's gender. The case of *Benner v Canada (Secretary of State)*[684] concerned a challenge by a man who applied for Canadian citizenship on the basis that his mother was Canadian. He was required to go through security clearance for the purposes of his application. However, if his father had been a Canadian citizen, he would have acquired citizenship automatically. The first point considered by the Court was whether the Charter applied to the applicant's case, given that his citizenship rights were determined with reference to when he was born, which was before the Charter came into force (the legislation in question had been changed after the applicant was born, but did not operate retrospectively). Although the Charter was not retroactive or retrospective,[685] a distinction had to be drawn between challenging a discrete act which took place before the Charter came into force, such as a pre-Charter conviction, and a law which imposed an on-going discriminatory effect. The latter would not be insulated from Charter review simply because the law was enacted prior to the Charter.[686] The Court held that there was continuing discrimination in this case: 17.192

682 [1997] 1 SCR 241.
683 Ibid.
684 [1997] 1 SCR 358.
685 Ibid para 40.
686 Ibid para 44.

50. The respondent urged us to find that the key point in the chronology of events was the appellant's birth in 1962. The respondent argued that the focus placed on birth by the impugned citizenship legislation suggests that the rights granted under that legislation 'crystallize' at birth:... Whatever discrimination took place in the appellant's case, therefore, took place when he was born, since that is when his rights were determined under the impugned legislation. To revisit those rights in light of s 15, according to the respondent, is therefore inescapably to go back and alter a distribution of rights which took place years before the Charter.

51. I am uncomfortable with the idea of rights or entitlements crystallizing at birth, particularly in the context of s 15. This suggests that whenever a person born before [the Charter came into force] suffers the discriminatory effects of a piece of legislation, these effects may be immunized from Charter review. Our skin colour is determined at birth—rights or entitlements assigned on the basis of skin colour by a particular law would, by this logic, 'crystallize' then. Under the approach proposed by the respondent, individuals born before s 15 came into effect would therefore be unable to invoke the Charter to challenge even a recent application of such a law...

52. The preferable way, in my opinion, to characterize the appellant's position is in terms of status or on-going condition. From the time of his birth, he has been a child, born outside Canada prior to [the impugned legislation being reformed], of a Canadian mother and a non-Canadian father. This is no less a 'status' than being of a particular skin colour or ethnic or religious background: it is an on going state of affairs. People in the appellant's position continue to this day to be denied the automatic right of citizenship granted to children of Canadian fathers.

17.193 The discrimination in *Benner* was on the basis of gender, albeit on the basis of the appellant's Canadian parent's gender. However, the appellant was held to have standing to challenge the legislation, as the primary target of sex-based discrimination.[687] The Court emphasised that they were not laying down any general doctrine of 'discrimination by association', but that in this case:

The link between child and parent is of a particularly unique and intimate nature. A child has no choice who his or her parents are. Their nationality, skin colour, or race is as personal and immutable to a child as his or her own.[688]

Appendix 2: The New Zealand Bill of Rights Act

17.194 Section 19 of the Bill of Rights Act, as inserted by the Human Rights Act 1993, provides as follows:

19 (1) Everyone has the right to freedom from discrimination on the grounds of discrimination in the Human Rights Act 1993.

(2) Measures taken in good faith for the purpose of assisting or advancing persons or groups of persons disadvantaged because of discrimination that is unlawful by virtue of Part II of the Human Rights Act 1993 do not constitute discrimination.

20. A person who belongs to an ethnic, religious or linguistic minority in New Zealand shall not be denied the right, in community with other members of that minority, to enjoy that culture, to profess and practise the religion, or to use the language of, that minority.[689]

---

[687] Ibid para 77.

[688] Ibid para 82.

[689] See generally, G Huscroft and P Rishworth (eds), *Rights and Freedoms: The New Zealand Bill of Rights Act 1990 and the HumanRights Act 1993*, (Brookers 1995) Chap 7.

The prohibited grounds of discrimination in the Human Rights Act 1993 include sex, marital status, race, disability, beliefs, age, employment and family status and sexual orientation.[690] The Act establishes a Human Rights Commission and sets out an anti-discrimination code. The Act prohibits discrimination in a number of areas.[691] The Act applies to the Crown, and provides for remedies for breach. Indirect discrimination is prohibited, unless there is a good reason for it.[692] **17.195**

The case of *Quilter v A-G of New Zealand*[693] concerned the issue of same-sex marriages. The appellants were three couples in stable long term lesbian relationships, who complained that the Registrar of Marriages unlawfully refused to accept from them notices of intended marriage under section 23 of the Marriage Act 1955. The Registrar's reason was that the relevant legislation did not provide for same-sex marriage. The Court of Appeal upheld the Registrar's position, the majority holding that there was no discrimination, either on the basis of sexual orientation or gender. However, the Court was unanimous in holding that the legislation clearly permitted heterosexual marriages only, and could not be interpreted so as to permit homosexual marriages. **17.196**

Gault J, who found that there was no discrimination, stated as follows:[694] **17.197**

> The Marriage Act is clear and to give it such different meaning would not be to undertake interpretation but to assume the role of lawmaker which is for Parliament. That is particularly so in an area where the law reflects social values and policy . . .
>
> The Registrar did not refuse the notices because of the gender of the appellants nor because of their sexual orientation (if the Registrar knew it). There would have been no different reaction . . . [if the applicants] had been heterosexual and simply seeking a marriage relationship to take advantage of perceived civil benefits. They contend, however, that because of the choice of partner they have made the effect of the law preventing their marriage bears upon them and persons in like situations and not upon others and so is discriminatory. But denial of choice always affects only those who wish to make the choice. It is not for that reason discriminatory. Denial of the choice of marrying a child or someone already married could not be said to be discriminatory just because a homosexual male wants to make such a choice.[695]

Gault J observed that, to the extent that the appellants' complaints were that they were denied rights and privileges available to married persons, there could be a case of discrimination on the basis of marital status.[696]

Thomas J dissented on the principles involved, finding that exclusion of homosexual couples from the status of marriage was discriminatory, and contrary to section 19 of the Bill of Rights. However, he also held that it was not possible to interpret the Marriage Act so as to permit same-sex marriages.[697] Thomas J said that: **17.198**

[690] s 21.
[691] See Pt II generally.
[692] s 65.
[693] [1998] 1 NZLR 523; see A Butler, 'Same sex marriage and freedom from discrimination in New Zealand' [1998] PL 396.
[694] [1998] NZLR 523, 526.
[695] Ibid 526-7.
[696] Ibid 528.
[697] Ibid.

> I do not apprehend that in this day and age the notion that procreation is the sole or major purpose of marriage commands significant support. While procreation, or the capacity to procreate, may be an aspect of marriages, the definition of marriage by reference to that function ignores those facets or qualities that make up the essence of the marriage relationship, such as cohabitation, commitment, intimacy, and financial interdependence.[698]

Thomas J took the view that there was discrimination both on the basis of sex, and sexual orientation. When considering discrimination on the basis of sex, he remarked:

> the effect of the prohibition against same-sex marriages is that the female applicant is discriminated against on the grounds of her sex because, being female, she is by law unable to marry another woman, and the male applicant is discriminated against by reason of his male sex because, being male, he is by law unable to marry a man . . .
>
> [Alternatively] I can see no sound reason why a couple, united in their intention to form an enduring relationship in the nature of marriage, cannot as a couple claim that they are being discriminated against on the ground of their sex or gender.[699]

In relation to discrimination on the basis of sexual orientation, Thomas J said:

> Based upon [their sexual preference], gays and lesbians are denied access to a central social institution and the resulting status of married persons. They lose the rights and privileges, including the manifold legal consequences which marriage conveys. They are denied a basic civil right in that freedom to marry is rightly regarded as a basic civil right. They lose the opportunity to choose the partner of their choice as a marriage partner, again viewing the right to choose as a basic civil right of all citizens. In a real sense, gays and lesbians are effectively excluded from full membership of society.
>
> But the denial of the opportunity for gay and lesbian couples to marry should not be seen solely in terms of a denial of access to an important social institution . . . . It has a personal dimension which is not difficult to understand. With many gay and lesbian couples the inability to marry must impinge on almost all aspects of their lives. It can only add to the stigmatisation of their relationship and have a detrimental effect upon their sense of self-worth. In the United States, the freedom to marry has long been recognised as 'one of the vital personal rights essential to the orderly pursuit of happiness by free people'. . . . Gay and lesbian couples are denied that pursuit.
>
> The argument that gay and lesbian persons are not discriminated against because they are free to marry persons of the opposite sex is unconvincing. Indeed, I believe it is lacking in logic.[700]

Thomas J also held that the discrimination could not be justified:

> By its very nature discrimination on any of the grounds specified in section 21 cannot be open to justification in a free and democratic society . . . Differentiations which are discriminatory cannot be reconciled with the democratic ideal of equality before and under the law.[701]

17.199 Discrimination on the basis of national origin was found in *Northern Regional Health Authority v Human Rights Commission.*[702] That case concerned the manner in which the plaintiff, a regional health authority, purchased health services from medical practitioners. Such health providers could receive subsidies or benefits for patients only if they had a

698 Ibid 534.
699 Ibid 535-6.
700 Ibid 537.
701 Ibid 540.
702 [1998] 2 NZLR 218.

contract for purchase with the plaintiff. The plaintiff decided that purchase contracts would only be entered into with practitioners who had tertiary medical qualifications from a New Zealand university, unless its patient access criteria could not be met from New Zealand graduate medical practitioners. This policy was successfully challenged as constituting indirect discrimination on the grounds of national origins. The court held that in order to justify indirect discrimination, the means chosen must meet a genuine need, be suitable for attaining that need, and necessary for that purpose. In this case there was no good reason for the continuing implementation of the policy, nor had the plaintiff satisfied the Court that there were no non-discriminatory mechanisms that would meet its objectives. The Court adopted the reasoning of the European Court of Justice in *Bilka-Kaufhaus GmbH v Weber von Hartz.*[703] A finding of discrimination was also made in the case of *Wheen v Real Estate Licensing Board*[704] in which the defendant had refused to recognise the plaintiff's English professional qualifications. The absence of a system of recognition of overseas qualifications was indirect discrimination on the grounds of national origin. However, in *Lal v Residence Appeal Authority*[705] it was held that the residence policy of the Minister of Immigration requiring the production of a 'trade certificate' was not discriminatory on the ground of national origin. The inability of the appellant to obtain such a certificate was not due to his national origin but the fact that Fiji did not provide facilities for issuing such a certificate.

Benefits provided under a superannuation scheme were challenged in *Coburn v Human* **17.200** *Rights Commission,*[706] on the basis of marital status discrimination and age discrimination. The complaint on the basis of marital status discrimination was upheld. Members of the scheme made the same contributions regardless of their marital status, yet received greater benefits from the scheme if they were married. The High Court did not make its judgment retrospective because of the practical and financial difficulties that would have been caused thereby.

A radio broadcast containing derogatory references to Asians was found to be 'threatening **17.201** abusive and insulting' under the Human Rights Act 1993. This was a justified limitation to the freedom of expression guaranteed by the Bill of Rights Act.[707] A similar approach was taken in *Re Gay Rights/Special Rights: Inside the Homosexual Agenda*[708] in which two videos attacking gay people were classified as 'objectionable'. It was held that the right to be free from discrimination took precedence over the right to freedom of expression: the videos were injurious to the public good and this classification was a reasonable limit on expression.

Appendix 3: Human Rights Cases in Other Jurisdictions

(1) Introduction

The first constitutional instrument in the common law world to make express provision **17.202**

703 [1986] ECR 1607.
704 (1996) 2 HRNZ 481, Complaints Review Tribunal.
705 (1999) 5 HRNZ 11.
706 [1994] 3 NZLR 323.
707 *Proceedings Commissioner v Archer* (1996) 3 HRNZ 116, Complaints Review Tribunal.
708 (1997) 4 HRNZ 422, Film and Literature Board of Review.

for the prohibition of discrimination was the Fourteenth Amendment to the US Constitution, brought in after the Civil War in the context of attempts to eliminate laws sanctioning slavery. This included a provision that:

> No State shall . . . deny to any person within its jurisdiction the equal protection of the laws.[709]

This provision has given rise to an immense jurisprudence.[710] It was initially used in relation to racial discrimination but has, more recently, been expanded into other fields, notably sex discrimination.[711]

17.203 When the American courts consider whether or not there has been a breach of the equal protection clause they apply three standards of review, depending on the nature of the rights which are in play:[712]

- *The rational relationship test*: 'Does the classification bear a rational relationship to any legitimate interests of government?';[713]
- *Intermediate review*: 'Is the classification substantially related to an important government interest?';[714]
- *Strict scrutiny*: 'Is the classification necessary to a compelling governmental interest with no less onerous alternative available?'

17.204 The 'rational relationship test' is the traditional test. It gives a strong presumption of constitutionality and means that a law will only be struck down if it is totally arbitrary in its impact. This test is applied in relation to economic regulation.[715] The approach is similar to the *Wednesbury* standard of review in English public law[716] and means that it is unlikely that discriminatory laws subject to this test will be found to be unconstitutional.

17.205 Intermediate review applies in certain, 'quasi suspect', categories. It has been applied in gender and illegitimacy cases.[717] In *Mississippi University for Women v Hogan*[718] the Court struck down a women-only admissions policy at a state nursing school. The state argued that the policy compensated for discrimination suffered by women but the court held that it had not been established that the policy was 'substantially and directly related' to this objective. A similar result was reached in *United States v Virginia*[719] in which it was held that no 'exceedingly persuasive justification' had been offered for excluding women from

709 See App T in Vol 2.

710 See eg L Tribe, *American Constitutional Law* (2nd edn, Foundation Press, 1988) Chap 16; J Nowak and R Rotunda, *Constitutional Law* (5th edn, West Group, 1995) Chap 14; C Antieau and W Rich, *Modern Constitutional Law* (2nd edn, West Group, 1997) Vol 2, Chaps 25–33.

711 For a historical perspective on the Fourteenth Amendment see H Abraham and B Perry, *Freedom and the Court* (7th edn, Oxford University Press, 1998) Chaps 7 and 8.

712 See Nowak and Rotunda (n 710 above) para 14.3, 601–660.

713 See eg *Massachusetts Board of Retirement v Murgia* (1976) 427 US 307.

714 See eg *Craig v Boren* (1976) 429 US 190.

715 See eg *Nordlinger v Hahn* (1992) 505 US 1 (Supreme Court upheld California's 'Proposition 13' which limited property taxes to 1% of value based on 1975-76 assessment).

716 See generally, para 5.126ff above.

717 For a list of cases in gender and related discrimination cases see Abraham and Perry (n 711 above) Table 8.1, 416–422.

718 (1982) 458 US 718.

719 (1996) 518 US 515.

the Virginia Military Institute.[720] Affirmative action is acceptable but the Court will scrutinise the law to ascertain whether it is, in fact, compensatory.[721] Illegitimacy classifications are also subject to intermediate review.[722] But the standard of review in such cases is variable. However, other classifications such as homosexuality,[723] age,[724] mental disability[725] or wealth[726] are not 'quasi suspect' and are subject to the rational relationship test rather than intermediate review.

Strict scrutiny is used where the law employs a 'suspect classification' or where the classification significantly burdens the exercise of a fundamental right. Discriminatory laws are likely to be extremely difficult to justify if 'strict scrutiny' is applied. Race is the paradigm 'suspect classification' and when race is used as a factor in allocating public benefits and burdens the law is subject to the most exacting scrutiny.[727] A similar approach is taken in relation to discrimination based on national origin.[728] Strict scrutiny will apply to affirmative action programmes: the standard of scrutiny is not dependent on the face of those affected.[729] Classification on the basis of whether a person is a citizen (referred to as 'alienage') is a 'sometimes suspect' classification: thus, a state requirement of citizenship for admission to the bar was struck down[730] as was a law making citizenship a requirement for any position in the competitive class of the state civil service.[731] However, other cases have employed a standard closer to 'intermediate review' in alienage cases.[732] There is, nevertheless, an important limitation on strict scrutiny in 'suspect classification' cases: before it is applied it must be established that the discrimination is either *de jure* or intentional.[733] **17.206**

Strict scrutiny will also apply when a law discriminates in relation to the right to engage in a protected constitutional activity: for example in relation to the exercise of First Amendment rights. In addition, it applies to implied rights such as marriage and procreation,[734] voting[735] and travel.[736] **17.207**

---

[720] A parallel institution, Virginia Women's Institute for Leadership, had been established but this was a 'pale shadow' of the all male institution.

[721] See *Califano v Goldfarb* (1977) 430 US 199 (presumption that widows but not widowers are dependent based on 'archaic and overbroad generalisation'); *Orr v Orr* (1979) 440 US 268 (state law authorising alimony only to wives struck down).

[722] See eg *Weber v Aetna Casualty and Surety Co* (1972) 406 US 164 (bar on illegitimate children collecting death benefit struck down).

[723] *Bowers v Hardwick* (1986) 478 US 186.

[724] *Massachusetts Board of Retirement v Murgia* (1976) 427 US 307.

[725] *City of Cleburne v Cleburne Living Center* (1985) 473 US 432.

[726] *James v Valtierra* (1971) 402 US 137.

[727] *Palmore v Sidoti* (1984) 466 US 429.

[728] *Hernandez v Texas* (1954) 347 US 475 (discrimination against Mexican Americans in jury selection).

[729] *City of Richmond v J A Croson & Co* (1989) 488 US 469; *Adarand Constructors Co v Pena* (1995) 515 US 200.

[730] *Application of Griffiths* (1969) 394 US 618.

[731] *Sugarman v Dougall* (1973) 413 US 634.

[732] See eg *Foley v Connelie* (1978) 435 US 291; *Ambach v Norwick* (1979) 441 US 68.

[733] *Washington v Davies* (1976) 426 US 229.

[734] *Skinner v Oklahoma* (1942) 316 US 535.

[735] *Harper v Virginia State Board of Elections* (1966) 383 US 663.

[736] *Shapiro v Thompson* (1968) 394 US 618.

17.208 Although other common law jurisdictions have not adopted these distinctions between different types of review, the US case law is nevertheless extremely influential and is a rich source of material in relation to discrimination issues. The combined influence of the US jurisprudence and the Convention has meant that all Commonwealth constitutional instruments of the last 50 years have included 'non-discrimination' and 'equality before the law' provisions in various forms.[737]

(2) Australia

17.209 The Australian Constitution contains no express 'equal protection' or 'anti-discrimination' provisions. However in *Leeth v Commonwealth*[738] the High Court accepted that the Commonwealth Constitution contained an implied constitutional right to equality.[739] The challenge in that case was to federal legislation which provided that a court imposing a term of imprisonment for a federal offence should impose the same non-parole period as that required by the State or Territory in which they had been convicted. While it was accepted that states had different non-parole periods, the challenge failed. The practical ground of distinction between the prisoners was their incarceration in prisons shared with state prisoners. That was a rational and necessary ground of distinction. A similar approach was taken in *Kruger v Commonwealth*[740] in which the majority held that, apart from equality before the courts, the Constitution does not require equality or uniformity in the operation of laws made by Parliament.

(3) Botswana

17.210 Section 3 of the Constitution of Botswana provides that:

> Whereas every person in Botswana is entitled to the fundamental rights and freedoms of the individual . . . whatever his race, place of origin, political opinion, colour, creed or sex. . .

Section 15 provides, that subject to certain specified exceptions, no law shall make any provision which is discriminatory either of itself or in effect. 'Discriminatory' is defined as affording different treatment of different persons attributable mainly or wholly to their race, tribe, place of origin, political opinions, colour or creed. Although sex is not mentioned, the provision has been construed broadly and, in the light of Botswana's adherence to the African Charter of Human and People's Rights, to cover sex discrmination.[741]

17.211 In *Dow v A-G*[742] the Court of Appeal considered a statutory provision which had the effect that a child born in Botswana would be a citizen if, at the time of his birth, his father was a citizen or, in the case born out of wedlock, his mother was a citizen. In wide ranging judgments the majority held that this provision was discriminatory in respect of the married Botswanan mother of children whose husband was not a citizen.

---

[737] For the provisions in Caribbean constitutions see M Demerieux, *Fundamental Rights in Commonwealth Caribbean Constitutions* (Faculty of Law Library, University of West Indies, 1992) Chap 16 'Protection from Discrimination'.

[738] (1992) 174 CLR 455; for a general discussion of this case see G Williams, *Human Rights Under the Australian Constitution* (Oxford University Press, 1999) 220–225.

[739] See generally, P Hanks, *Constitutional Law in Australia* (2nd edn, Butterworths, 1996) Chap 14.5.

[740] (1997) 146 ALR 126.

[741] *Dow v A-G* [1992] LRC (Const) 623, 648-657.

[742] Ibid.

The case of *Molepolole College SRC v A-G*[743] concerned, *inter alia*, college regulations requiring pregnant students to inform the college immediately and to leave for a period of at least a year. Fines were imposed if pregnancy was concealed and a student who became pregnant for a second time was excluded permanently. The Court of Appeal accepted that there might be a need to regulate the one gender in a manner which was inapplicable to the other but that this had to be done in a way which was: **17.212**

> reasonable, fair, made for the benefit of the gender, without prejudice to the other; it must not be punitive to the gender in question.[744]

The Court held that the purpose of the regulation was punitive and was unreasonable and unfair and it was struck down.

(4) Hong Kong

Article 22 of the Hong Kong Bill of Rights provides that: **17.213**

> All persons are equal before the law and are entitled without any discrimination to the equal protection of the law. In this respect, the law shall prohibit any discrimination and guarantee to all persons equal and effective protection against discrimination on any ground such as race, colour, sex, language, religion, political or other opinion, national or social origin, property, birth or other status.

A court should consider whether sensible and fair minded people would recognise the need to treat the two groups differently.[745] In *L v C*[746] a time limit which prevented an illegitimate child obtaining through its mother appropriate financial provision from its father if the mother failed to make a timely application was held to be discriminatory against the child, and inconsistent with Article 22 of the Bill of Rights. The court noted that the legislative history indicated the intention to place an illegitimate child in the same position as a legitimate one. On the other hand, in *R v Crawley*,[747] a complaint that the Crown was treated differently to other car owners in relation to traffic offences was dismissed. The differential treatment challenged in that case was that ordinary car owners had to pay fines themselves, rather than the driver of a vehicle at the relevant time. The court explained that the absence of an exception for vehicles owned by the Crown would result in the Crown having to pay the fixed penalty to itself and then recovering the sums from the driver concerned. That would be administratively inefficient, expensive, and offer no benefit to the community. Moreover, unlike the majority of privately registered vehicles, there would be no difficulty in identifying the driver of a vehicle at the time of the contravention. The difference in treatment was both rational and proportionate to the need which justified it.

Article 21(c) of the Hong Kong Bill of Rights provides that: **17.214**

> Every permanent resident shall have the right and the opportunity, without any of the distinctions mentioned in article 1(1) and without unreasonable restrictions— . . .
>
> (c) to have access, on general terms of equality, to public service in Hong Kong.

---

743 [1995] 3 LRC 447.
744 Ibid 466h-j.
745 *R v Man Wai Keung (No 2)* [1992] 2 HKCLR 207.
746 [1994] 2 HKLR 92.
747 [1994] 1 HKCLR 156.

This provision was considered in *Association of Expatriate Civil Servants of Hong Kong v Secretary of the Civil Service*,[748] which concerned an overhaul of the terms and conditions of the Hong Kong Civil Service. One of the changes challenged was the regard to be given in certain circumstances to the ability to speak Chinese. The Court of Appeal stated that differential treatment on the basis of an officer's ability to speak Chinese must be supported by clear evidence that serious problems would arise if the distinction was not made. In the instant case, there was no evidence to justify the differential treatment. The Court also held that, while it is justifiable to take account of a person's potential for filling a senior post when deciding whether or not to promote him to a post bordering that senior post, fixing ceilings on the numbers of overseas officers who could be appointed to certain senior posts went too far, and was a disproportionate restriction contrary to Art 21(c).

(5) **India**

17.215 Article 14 of the Indian Constitution provides that:

> The State shall not deny to any person equality before the law or the equal protection of the laws within the territory of India.[749]

The purpose of this Article is to prevent arbitrary action, that is to ensure a reasonable basis for differential treatment.[750] Two conditions must be fulfilled:

- the differentiation must be founded on intelligible criteria; and
- the differentiation must have a rational relation to the object sought by the impugned statute.[751]

It is not necessary that the discrimination under consideration is 'intentional and purposeful', the test is objective.[752]

17.216 However, the legislative classification is not required to be scientifically exact.[753] Thus, for example, a tax statute will be struck down where there is differentiation between tax evaders belonging to the same class merely because the evasion was detected by different methods.[754] When a statute divides the objects of tax into groups or categories, so long as there is equality and uniformity within each group, the statute does not violate Article 14 even if due to fortuitous circumstances some included within a group are advantaged, provided they are not deliberately singled out for special treatment.[755] The mere fact that a person is HIV-infected is not a valid ground for the state to discriminate against him in the matter of employment.[756]

---

[748] (1996) 6 HKPLR 333.

[749] For a general discussion, see H M Seervai, *Constitutional Law of India* (4th edn, N M Tripathi Ltd, 1991) Chap IX.

[750] *Ameeroonissa v Mehboob* (1953) SCR 404.

[751] *Budhan v State of Bihar* (1955) 1 SCR 1045.

[752] *W B v Anwar Ali Sarkar* (1952) SCR 284, 311.

[753] *Kedar North v State of WB* (1953) SC 401.

[754] *ITO v Lawrence Singh* (1968) SC 658, at 661.

[755] *Vrinvaban v Union of India* (1986) UJSC 113.

[756] *X v Y Corp* [1999] 1 LRC 688 (this judgment contains a valuable collection of material in relation to HIV infection).

Article 14 applies to procedural as well as substantive rights. For example, if persons who are similarly situated may be subject to a procedure which is substantially different from the ordinary procedure at the option of the executive, that law will be in breach of Article 14 if it offers no guidance to the executive as to when and how one of the methods or procedures will be chosen.[757] There is no discrimination in providing for appeal from only some of the decisions of an administrative authority, unless the absence of appeal from the other decisions makes the whole procedure arbitrary and oppressive.[758] As to the basis upon which offences may be classified reasonably for trial by a procedure substantially different from the ordinary procedure, it has been held that the necessity for a 'speedier trial' is too vague a criterion to form a rational basis for classification, particularly when the legislature itself does not indicate which offences, in its opinion, required a speedier trial.[759] However, speedier trial of specified offences is a rational basis of classification if the speedy trial has a rational relation to the object of the classification, such as public safety, or maintenance of public order in a dangerously disturbed area.[760] Legislation which confers upon the executive an unguided or uncontrolled discretionary power in applying the law breaches Article 14.[761] **17.217**

Article 15 of the Indian Constitution provides that: **17.218**

> (1) The State shall not discriminate against any citizen on grounds only of religion, race, caste, sex, place of birth or any of them.
> (2) No citizen shall, on grounds only of religion, race, caste, sex, place of birth or any of them, be subject to any disability, liability, restriction or condition with regard to—
> (a) access to shops, public restaurants, hotels and places of public entertainment; or
> (b) the use of wells, tanks, bathing ghats, roads and places of public resort maintained wholly or partly out of State funds dedicated to the use of the general public.
> (3) Nothing in this article shall prevent the State from making any special provision for women and children.
> (4) Nothing in this article or in clause (2) of Article 9 shall prevent the State from making any special provision for the advancement of any socially or educationally backward classes of citizens or for the Scheduled Casters and Scheduled Tribes.

This Article forbids discrimination which is based solely on the specified grounds. Discrimination which is based on a specified ground and also on other grounds is not caught by the Article.[762] The specified ground must be the immediate and direct cause of the discrimination.[763] The reservation of a seat for the Sangha (Buddhist-Lamaic religious body) in the Sikkim Legislative Assembly was upheld because the reservation was not for purely religious reasons. The Sangha was not merely a religious institution but also a political and social institution.[764] Likewise, social reform of Hindus only, such as prohibition of bigamy, has been upheld as being based not only on religion (a forbidden ground) but also on the social advancement of Hindus.[765] Discrimination in favour of backward classes is void only if caste is the reason, as opposed to economic or social backwardness.

[757] *Jagdish v State of Punjab* A 1972 SC 2587, 2590.
[758] *State of Mysore v Achiah* A 1969 SC 477.
[759] *State of WB v Anwar Ali* (1952) SCR 284, 314, 328, 352.
[760] *Gopi Chand v Delhi Administration* A 1959 SC 609.
[761] *State of WB v Anwar Ali* (n 759 above); *Suraj Mall v ITI Commr* A 1954 SC 545; *Satwant v APO* A 1967 SC 1836.
[762] *Chitra v Union of India* A 1970 SC 35, 38.
[763] *State of Bombay v Bombay Education Society* (1955) 1 SCR 568, 584.
[764] *R K Jain v Union of India* A 1993 SC 1769.
[765] *State v Narsu* A 1952 Bom 84.

17.219 Affirmative action measures must strike a reasonable balance between relevant considerations and proceed objectively.[766] A general rule of thumb is that reservations (ie quotas) of 50% or less will be upheld, but reservations of more than 50% will be struck down.[767] If a caste, as a whole, is found to be socially and educationally backward, the inclusion of such caste in the list of backward castes would not breach Article 15(4) even though a few individuals in that caste may be socially and educationally above the average.[768]

(6) Ireland

17.220 Article 40.1 of the Irish Constitution provides that:

> All citizens shall, as human persons, be held equal before the law. This shall not be held to mean that the State shall not in its enactments have due regard to differences of capacity, physical and moral, and of social function.[769]

As explained in *Quinn's Supermarket v A-G*:[770]

> This provision is not a guarantee of absolute equality for all citizens in all circumstances but it is a guarantee of equality as human persons and . . . is a guarantee relating to their dignity as human beings and a guarantee against any inequalities grounded upon an assumption, or indeed a belief, that some individual or individuals or classes of individuals, by reason of their human attributes or their ethnic or racial, social or religious background, are to be treated as the inferior or superior of other individuals in the community. This list does not pretend to be complete, but is merely intended to illustrate the view that this guarantee refers to human persons for what they are in themselves rather than to any lawful activities, trades or pursuits which they may engage in or follow. Furthermore, it need scarcely be pointed out that under no possible construction of the constitutional guarantee could a body corporate or any entity but a human being be considered to be a human person for the purpose of this provision.

17.221 In *Murtagh Properties v Cleary*[771] trade unionists were picketing to effect the dismissal of female employees. It was held that the female employees could not rely on Article 40.1 to argue their right to earn a livelihood irrespective of sex was infringed because that Article:

> relates to [the] essential attributes [of citizens] as persons, those features which make them human beings. It has, in my opinion, nothing to do with their trading activities or with the conditions on which they are employed.

A similar result was reached in *Brennan v A-G*,[772] in which differential tax treatment of land owners was held to be outside the ambit of Article 40.1. The Supreme Court stated that:

> The inequality . . . in this case does not concern . . . treatment as human persons. It concerns the manner in which occupiers and owners of land their property is rated and taxed. Each person who owns or occupies the land in question will be treated in exactly the same way because the tax is related not to the person but to the land, which, irrespective of who he may be, he occupies.[773]

---

766 *State of AP v Balaram* A 1972 SC 1375.

767 *Balaji v State of Mysore* AIP (1963) SC 649; *Periakaruppan v State of TN* A 1971 SC 2303.

768 *State of AP v Balaram* (n 766 above).

769 See generally, J M Kelly, *The Irish Constitution* (3rd edn, Butterworths, 1994) 712-743.

770 [1972] IR 1.

771 [1972] IR 330.

772 [1984] ILRM 355.

773 See also *Madigan v A-G* [1986] ILRM 136; *Greene v Minister for Agriculture* [1990] 2 IR 117; *Browne v A-G* [1991] 2 IR 58.

Similar reasoning was expressed in *Dillane v Ireland*,[774] where the court explained that discrimination on the express or implied ground of difference in social function is not in breach of Article 40.1 unless it is arbitrary, capricious, or otherwise not reasonably capable, when objectively viewed in the light of the social function involved, of supporting the selection or classification. Thus, in *Finnegan v An Bord Pleanála*,[775] a requirement to pay a deposit of £10 for a planning appeal did not constitute impermissible discrimination between wealthy and poor. However, discrimination against 'suspected persons or reputed thieves' was in breach of Article 40.1.[776] **17.222**

(7) Malaysia

Article 8 of the Federal Constitution provides that: **17.223**

> (1) All persons are equal before the law and entitled to the equal protection of the law.
> (2) Except as expressly authorised by this Constitution, there shall be no discrimination against citizens on the ground only of religion, race, descent or place of birth in any law ...

The Federal Court has held that the principles to be applied in deciding whether a law is valid under Article 8 include:

> (a) The first question to be asked is, is law discriminatory ... if it is discriminatory ... is it allowed? ...
> (b) Discriminatory law is good law if it is based on 'reasonable' or 'permissible' classification, provided that
> (i) the classification is founded on an intelligible differentia which distinguishes persons that are grouped together from others left out of the group;
> (ii) the differentia has a rational relation to the object sought to be achieved by the law in question. The classification may be founded on different bases such as geographical, or according to objects or occupations and the like. What is necessary is that there must be a nexus between the basis of classification and the object of the law in question.[777]

A statute which prohibited junior members of the Bar from joining the Bar Council and Committees was held to be constitutional because it was rational and permissible.[778]

(8) South Africa

Article 8 of the interim Constitution provided as follows: **17.224**

> (1) Every person shall have the right to equality before the law and to equal protection of the law.
> (2) No person shall be unfairly discriminated against, directly or indirectly, and, without derogating from the generality of this provision, on one or more of the following grounds in particular: race, gender, sex, ethnic or social origin, colour, sexual orientation, age, disability, religion, conscience, belief, culture or language.

[774] [1980] ILRM 167.
[775] [1979] ILRM 134.
[776] *King v A-G* [1981] IR 233.
[777] *Malaysian Bar v Government of Malaysia* [1988] LRC (Const) 428, 437; following *Datuk Haji Harun bin Idris v Public Prosecutor* [1977] 2 MLJ 155.
[778] *Malaysian Bar v Government of Malaysia* (n 777 above).

(3)(a) This section shall not preclude measures designed to achieve the adequate protection and advancement of persons or groups or categories of person disadvantaged by unfair discrimination, in order to achieve their full and equal enjoyment of all rights and freedoms. . . .

(4) *Prima facie* proof of discrimination on any of the grounds specified in subsection (2) shall be presumed to be sufficient proof of unfair discrimination as contemplated in that subsection, unless the contrary is established.

17.225 Section 9 of the Final Constitution provides:

(1) Everyone is equal before the law and has the right to equal protection and benefit of the law.

(2) Equality includes the full and equal enjoyment of all rights and freedoms. To promote the achievement of equality, legislative and other measures designed to protect or advance persons, or categories of persons, disadvantaged by unfair discrimination may be taken.

(3) The state may not unfairly discriminate directly or indirectly against anyone on one or more grounds, including race, gender, sex, pregnancy, marital status, ethnic or social origin, colour, sexual orientation, age, disability, religion, conscience, belief, culture, language, and birth.

(4) No person may unfairly discriminate directly or indirectly against anyone on one or more grounds in terms of subsection (3). National legislation must be enacted to prevent or prohibit unfair discrimination.

(5) Discrimination on one or more of the grounds listed in subsection (3) is unfair unless it is established that the discrimination is fair.[779]

The Constitutional Court has considered these provisions in a number of judgments.

17.226 The leading case is *Harksen v Lane NO*,[780] which formulates the principles as follows:

(a) Does the provision differentiate between people or categories of people? If so, does the differentiation bear a rational connection to a legitimate government purpose? If it does not then there is a violation of section 8(1) [ie, there is no equality before the law]. Even if it does bear a rational connection, it might nevertheless amount to discrimination.

(b) Does the differentiation amount to unfair discrimination? This requires a two stage analysis:

(b)(i) Firstly, does the differentiation amount to 'discrimination'? If it is on a specified ground, then discrimination will have been established. If it is not on a specified ground, then whether or not there is discrimination will depend upon whether, objectively, the ground is based on attributes and characteristics which have the potential to impair the fundamental human dignity of persons as human beings or to affect them adversely in a comparably serious manner.

(b)(ii) If the differentiation amounts to 'discrimination', does it amount to 'unfair discrimination'? If it has been found to have been on a specified ground, then unfairness will be presumed. If on an unspecified ground, unfairness will have to be established by the complainant. The test of unfairness focuses primarily on the impact of the discrimination on the complainant and others in his or her situation.

If, at the end of this stage of the enquiry, the differentiation is found not to be unfair, then there will be no violation of section 8(2).

[779] See generally, M Chaskalson, J Kentridge, J Klaaren, G Marcus, D Spitz and S Woolman (eds), *Constitutional Law of South Africa* (Juta, 1996) Chap 14.

[780] 1998 (1) SA 300.

(c) If the discrimination is found to be unfair then a determination will have to be made as to whether the provision can be justified under the limitations clause (section 33 of the Constitution).[781]

The first stage of section 8 analysis, therefore, is rationality review under section 8(1), namely whether the impugned measure is arbitrary or irrational. That involves considering 'the governmental purpose of the [impugned measure], whether that purpose is a legitimate one and, if so, whether the differentiation does have a rational connection to that purpose'.[782] If there is no legitimate governmental purpose, or rational connection to that purpose, there will be a breach of section 8(1). **17.227**

The Court has found a breach of section 8(1) in a number of cases, although it should be noted that in such cases, a breach of another constitutional right has also been found.[783] Most appellants' arguments based on section 8(1) alone have, however, failed. In *Harksen v Lane NO*[784] the challenged provision was section 21 of the Insolvency Act 24 of 1936, which provided that where an individual becomes insolvent, the property of his or her spouse ('the solvent spouse') vested in the trustee in bankruptcy. The solvent spouse could recover the property if he or she could prove title. The Court held that section 21, which differentiated between spousal relationships and other business and family relationships, was a rational measure to protect creditors by ensuring that all the property of the insolvent vested in the trustee in bankruptcy. The Court noted that that purpose might be frustrated if the trustee were required to prove which property belonged to the solvent spouse and which belonged to the insolvent spouse. **17.228**

In *Prinsloo v Van der Linde*[785] the impugned provision concerned section 84 of the Forest Act 122 of 1984, which provided that 'when in any action by virtue of the provisions of this Act or the common law the question of negligence in respect a veld, forest or mountain fire which occurred on land situated outside a fire control area arises, negligence is presumed, until the contrary is proved'. A challenge to the section, based on the differentiation between landowners in fire control areas, and landowners outside such areas, failed. The device of the reverse onus clause, applicable only to the latter group, was held to be a rational means of achieving the legitimate governmental purpose of preventing veld fires.[786] **17.229**

---

[781] Ibid para 53.

[782] Ibid para 55.

[783] See eg *S v Ntuli* (breach of s 8(1) found when legally unrepresented persons convicted of offences in magistrates' courts required a judge's certificate to appeal, whereas those legally represented required no such certificate);

[784] 1998 (1) SA 300.

[785] 1997 (3) SA 1012, CC.

[786] See also *East Zulu Motors (Proprietary) Ltd v Empangeni/Zgwelezane Transitional Local Council* 1998 (2) SA 61 (minority declined to find that different planning procedures constituted a breach of s 8(1); majority did not deal with s 8 argument); *Jooste v Score Supermarket Trading* 1998 (9) BCLR 1106 (E) (court upheld legislation curtailing rights of employees to bring common law negligence claims against their employers, but allowing no-fault compensation from fund to which employers were obliged to contribute); *New National Party of South Africa v Government of the Republic of South Africa* 1999 (5) BCLR 489 (requirement of bar-coded identity document in order to vote was rationally related to the legitimate governmental purpose of ensuring the effective exercise of the right to vote).

17.230 Where measures are held to pass the rationality review in section 8(1), the next stage is to consider whether, nevertheless, the measures amount to unfair discrimination under section 8(2). The analysis at this stage differs depending on whether there is differentiation on a specified ground or non-specified ground.[787] If a challenge concerns a non-specified ground, it must first be established whether, in the abstract, without regard to the facts of a particular case, that ground is based on attributes and characteristics which have the potential fundamentally to impair a person's dignity, or affect them in some comparably serious manner. Only in that case does differentiation on that ground amount to 'discrimination'. The Court's decisions have provided three examples of unspecified grounds which may found claims of unfair discrimination—marital status,[788] citizenship[789] and marriages conducted according to different religious rites.[790]

17.231 The third stage of analysis is whether the discrimination is unfair. Unfairness is assessed with reference to the impact of impugned measures on a group. That is done by considering the nature of the group involved, the nature of the power exercised and the nature of the interests involved.[791] Unfairness was found in the following cases. First, in *Fraser v Children's Court, Pretoria North*[792] the applicant was an unmarried father who challenged legislation which dispensed with the need for the father's consent for the adoption of his illegitimate child. The Constitutional Court held that the legislation violated section 8 because it impermissibly discriminated between the rights of a father in certain unions and those in other unions. For example, Islamic marriages were not recognised in South African law, therefore fathers married only under Islamic law would not be able to consent or to refuse consent for the adoption of their children whereas fathers of children born of a recognised union would be able to withhold consent to the adoption of their children.

17.232 Secondly, unfairness was found in *Larbi-Odam v MEC for Education (North West Province)*.[793] In this case, the appellants were a group of foreign citizens employed as teachers in the North West Province. National regulations prevented their employment on a permanent basis, and they had, accordingly, been employed on a 'temporary' basis, in many cases for years on end. The Educators' Employment Act 1984 provided that temporary teachers could be dismissed merely on reasonable notice, whereas permanent teachers could only be dismissed for cause. The North West Province relied on the regulations to issue dismissal notices to the foreign teachers in its employ, in order to provide jobs for unemployed South African citizens. The teachers successfully challenged the regulations which barred their permanent employment. The Court noted that the group affected—foreign citizens—is a vulnerable group, and cited specific incidents of xenophobia directed against the applicants. The Court also noted the vitally important nature of the interests involved in that case—foreign citizens were completely denied security of tenure, regardless of the length of 'temporary' employment, and whether or not they were permanent residents of South Africa.

[787] As stated above, the specified grounds are race, gender, sex, ethnic or social origin, colour, sexual orientation, age, disability, religion, conscience, belief, culture or language.

[788] *Harksen v Lane NO* 1998 (1) SA 300.

[789] *Larbi-Odam v MEC for Education (North West Province)* (1998) 3 BHRC 561.

[790] *Fraser v Children's Court, Pretoria North* 1997 (2) SA 97.

[791] *Hugo v President of the RSA* 1997 (4) SA 1 para 43.

[792] 1997 (2) SA 97.

[793] (1998) 3 BHRC 561.

Thirdly, unfairness was found in *Pretoria City Council v Walker*.[794] In that case, Walker, a resident of the formerly white suburb of Pretoria, challenged the constitutionality of certain actions of the Pretoria City Council. The Council was established by the amalgamation of a number of municipalities, including the former black townships of Atteridgeville and Mamelodi. Walker's action was based on three grounds: first, residents in the formerly white areas were being charged for water and electricity on metered (ie consumption) rates, whereas residents in the formerly black areas were being charged at (lower) flat rates, which amounted to a subsidy of the formerly black areas. Secondly, even when meters had been introduced in some black properties, they were still being charged at the flat rate until all the black properties had meters. Finally, ratepayers in the white areas who defaulted were sued by the Council for arrears, whereas defaulters were not sued in the black areas. **17.233**

A majority of the Court held that the Council's actions amounted to indirect discrimination on the basis of race. However, that discrimination was not unfair with regard to the cross-subsidisation and failure to apply metered rates uniformly. In relation to the selective recovery of debts, the majority held that the impact of the policy was an invasion of dignity and was unfair. **17.234**

Fourthly, unfair discrimination was found in *National Coalition for Gay and Lesbian Equality v Minister of Justice*,[795] in which the Constitutional Court considered the criminalisation of homosexual conduct. The Court found that the offences violated the right to equality in that they unfairly discriminated against gay men on the basis of sexual orientation. Such discrimination was presumed to be unfair, as sexual orientation was a specified ground. The Court noted that gay people were a vulnerable minority group in society, and that sodomy laws criminalised their most intimate relationships. That devalued and degraded gay men, and was a violation of their fundamental right to dignity. No legitimate reason could be found why the rights of gay men should be limited. **17.235**

However, the Court declined to find unfairness in *Harksen v Lane NO*.[796] This case concerned a provision of the Insolvency Act 1936, which provided that, if a spouse becomes insolvent, all of his or her spouse's property is vested in the trustee in bankruptcy until the insolvent spouse can prove it is really his or hers. Such discrimination on the basis of marital status was held to be fair. The group affected, namely solvent spouses, was not one which had suffered discrimination in the past, and was not vulnerable. The purpose of the provision—to protect the interests of creditors of insolvent estates—was not inconsistent with the underlying values protected by section 8(2).[797] Finally, the effects of the provision were not especially severe.[798] First, the statutory vesting of the solvent spouse's property did not necessarily mean that the property was removed from the spouse's possession. Rather, 'the hand of the law' was placed on the property, and it could not be alienated or burdened by the solvent spouse before its release. Secondly, the solvent spouse could bring an action to release the property. Although that spouse would bear the onus of showing title to the property, the facts relating to such title would be peculiarly within the knowledge of the spouses themselves. The Court concluded that the effects of the provision amounted to inconvenience and potential embarrassment, rather than an impairment of fundamental human dignity. **17.236**

[794] 1998 (3) BCLR 257.
[795] [1998] 3 LRC 648.
[796] 1998 (1) SA 300.
[797] *Harksen* (n 795 above) paras 63, 64.
[798] Ibid paras 65, 66.

17.237 The Court also declined to find unfairness in *Hugo v President of the RSA*,[799] in which President Mandela granted amnesty to female prisoners who were the mothers of young children, but not to male prisoners who were fathers of young children. The express basis of the amnesty grant was to further the interests of young children, by enabling them to have maternal care. The majority held that there was no unfair discrimination against male prisoners who were fathers of young children. They noted that young mothers were an extremely vulnerable group in society, implying that young fathers were not as vulnerable. The majority also noted that the power to grant pardons was an exceptional one, to which no one had any right. The male prisoners did not suffer great hardship by being required to fulfil the remainder of their sentence for crimes for which they had been duly convicted and sentenced.

17.238 If unfair discrimination is found, the final step of analysis is to consider whether there is justification. This involves 'a proportionality exercise, in which the purpose and effect of the infringing provisions are weighed against the nature and extent of the infringement caused'.[800] One issue not squarely addressed by Constitutional Court is how the limitations clause ties in with unfairness analysis. In other words, can unfair discrimination ever be justified? It has been argued that there is a difference in principle between the two stages of analysis. Unfairness is assessed with reference to the complainant, whereas the focus of the limitations analysis is on broader societal goals.[801] This view is consistent with the decisions of the Constitutional Court. In *Hugo*, Mokgoro J held that the unfair discrimination against male prisoners was justified with reference to the aim of providing parental care for young children. O'Regan J, in *Harksen*, assessed the unfairness of the discrimination against solvent spouses with respect to the aim of preventing fraud on creditors. Finally, in *Larbi-Odam*, the unfair discrimination against foreign citizens was judged against the aim of reducing unemployment among South African citizens.

17.239 The South African Constitution expressly permits affirmative action. The Constitutional Court in *Public Servants Association of South Africa v Minister of Justice*[802] stated that affirmative action measures had to be carefully constructed so as to achieve adequate protection and advancement of disadvantaged groups, and that 'adequate' meant 'sufficient' and no more. Furthermore, the fact that such measures were designed to enable formerly disadvantaged groups to attain equal enjoyment of all rights and freedoms meant that the interests of the target groups were not considered in the abstract, but also in relation to the rights of others, the interests of the community and the possible advantages that the target groups may themselves suffer. Furthermore, the principle of equal representation could not be pursued at the cost of other constitutional requirements such as efficiency in public administration.

(9) Sri Lanka

17.240 Article 12 of the Sri Lankan Constitution provides that:

> (1) All persons are equal before the law and are entitled to equal protection of the law.

[799] 1997 (4) SA 1.

[800] *Brink v Kitsole NO* 1996 (4) SA 197 para 46.

[801] J Kentridge, 'Equality' in M Chaskalson, *Constitutional Law of South Africa* (Juta, 1996) para 14–i, 14–32.

[802] 1997 (5) BCLR 577.

(2) No citizen shall be discriminated against on the ground of race, religion, language, caste, sex, political opinion, place of birth or any one of such grounds:

Provided that it shall be lawful to require a person to acquire within a reasonable time sufficient knowledge of any language as a qualification for any employment or office in the Public, Judicial or Local Government Service or in the service of any public corporation, where such knowledge is reasonably necessary for the discharge of the duties of such employment or office.

Provided further that it shall be lawful to require a person to have sufficient knowledge of any language as a qualification for any such employment or office where no function of that employment or office can be discharged otherwise than with a knowledge of that language.

(3) No person shall, on the grounds of race, religion, language, caste, sex or any one of such grounds, be subject to any disability, liability, restriction or condition with regard to access to shops, public restaurants, hotels, places of entertainment and places of public worship of his own religion.

(4) Nothing in this Article shall prevent special provision being made, by law, subordinate legislation or executive action, for the advancement of women, children or disabled persons.

Classification is permitted under Article 12 provided it is rational and reasonable.[803] The job scheme challenged in *Palihawadana v A-G*[804] was struck down by the Supreme Court as unreasonable. Applicants for the job scheme were chosen by a member of Parliament. It was stipulated that those applicants should have families with no income earner, or inadequate income. Sharvananda J held that discrimination was inevitable in the scheme, as there were no rules for the selection of 1,000 persons from the undoubtedly large number of eligible candidates. The vesting of such naked arbitrary power on an MP contravened the fundamental right to equality. **17.241**

The Supreme Court struck down an administrative classification in *Perera v University Grants Commission*.[805] That case concerned two separate A-level examinations held in April and August 1979, held on two separate syllabuses. The University Grants Commission decided to allocate available university places to students passing the two examinations in proportion to the numbers passing each examination. The Supreme Court held that the students could not be discriminated against by reference to the examination taken. There was no material available to show that one examination was superior. The Court, accordingly, ordered that the admissions be made out of an integrated list. **17.242**

Affirmative action has been held to be permissible for legitimate objects, and where there is proof of special circumstances.[806] Racial quotas cannot be imposed simply for the purpose of 'correcting' an existing racial imbalance, except perhaps where there is serious, chronic, pervasive underrepresentation sufficient to raise a presumption of past discrimination.[807] In *Seneviratne v UGC*[808] the decision to fill 55% of the vacancies in the universities for the year 1980 on the ratio of population figures of residents in 24 administrative districts was upheld as a fair attempt to distribute university places. **17.243**

[803] The Sri Lankan courts have adopted the reasoning of the Indian Supreme Court on this point. See eg *Decision on Associated Newspapers of Ceylon Ltd, (Special Provisions) Bill* (1977) DCCSL Vol 5.

[804] FRD (1) 1.

[805] (1980) FRD (1) 103.

[806] *Ramupillai v Ministre of Public Administration* (1991) 1 Sri LR 11.

[807] Ibid.

[808] (1978) 1 Sri LR 182.

18

RIGHT TO ENJOYMENT OF POSSESSIONS

A. The Nature of The Right

18.01 The right to own property and not to be arbitrarily deprived of it has traditionally been regarded as a 'fundamental right', answering 'a demand of human nature'.[1] The right was recognised by the Magna Carta[2] and came to be seen as a vitally important guarantee of individual liberty. Article 2 of the Declaration of the Rights of Man of 1789 described the right to property as a 'natural and imprescriptible' right of man. Article 17 provided that:

> Since property is an inviolable and sacred right, no one shall be deprived thereof except where public necessity, legally determined, shall clearly demand it, and then only on condition that the owner shall have been previously and equitably indemnified.

The protection of property rights is central to the United States Bill of Rights. The Fifth Amendment states that:

> No person shall . . . be deprived of . . . property, without due process of law; nor shall private property be taken for public use, without just compensation.[3]

The two elements of this provision—due process and compensation for 'takings'—have given rise to an enormous body of case law over two centuries. This case law demonstrates, for better and for worse, the power of such a provision in the hands of an activist judiciary.[4]

18.02 The right to property was included in the Universal Declaration, Article 17 of which provides:

> (1) Everyone has the right to own property alone as well as in association with others.
> (2) No one shall be arbitrarily deprived of his property.

However, the precise extent of this right has been politically controversial. For this reason, it makes no appearance in either of the Covenants.[4a] Other international instruments have placed various qualifications on the right. Thus, Article 23 of the American Declaration of Rights provides that:

---

[1] *Davis v Mills* (1904) 194 US 451, *per* Holmes J.

[2] Clause 39 provides that: 'No man shall be . . . disseised of any tenement . . . except by the lawful judgment of his peers or by the law of the land'.

[3] Although it has been suggested that the second part of this provision, the 'takings' clause, was designed only to restrain the arbitrary and oppressive mode of obtaining supplies for the army, by impressment: see generally, A Amar, *The Bill of Rights* (Yale University Press, 1998) 79–80.

[4] See generally, L Tribe, *American Constitutional Law* (3rd edn, Foundation Press, 1999) Vol 1, Chap 8 and (2nd edn, Foundation Press, 1988) Chap 9.

[4a] The text of the International Covenant on Civil and Political Rights is reproduced at App J in Vol 2, and that of the International Covenant on Economic, Social and Cultural Rights is reproduced at App K in Vol 2.

> Every person has a right to own such private property as meets the essential needs of decent living and helps to maintain the dignity of the individual and his home.[5]

Many constitutions contain no express protection of property in their constitutions or bills of rights.[6] **18.03**

The issues which arise in relation to property rights include the following:

What rights are covered by the protection of 'property'? Does it simply cover land and goods, or does it extend to 'things in action', information, goodwill and similar rights? To what extent does it encompass benefits conferred by the state. The wider the definition, the more likely it is that 'property' will be interfered with by ordinary state regulatory activities.

What actions of the State constitute 'deprivation' or 'interference' with property? The traditional notion of 'expropriation' in the sense of the transfer of ownership to the state or a third party is only one way in which a person can be deprived of property rights. The state can interfere with property rights in a wide range of ways including preventing a person from enjoying property and extinguishing the right (without transferring it).

When is compensation payable and in what amount? Many disputes concerning property rights arise out of attempts by the state to limit the compensation payable for deprivations of property.

B. The Right in English Law Before the Human Rights Act

(1) Introduction

The right to the ownership and enjoyment of private property is of central importance to the common law. In the well known words of *Entick v Carrington*:[7] **18.04**

> The great end for which men entered into society was to secure their property. That right is preserved sacred and incommunicable in all instances where it has not been abridged by some public law for the good of the whole.

According to Blackstone the third 'absolute right inherent in every Englishman'[8] is that of property:

> which consists in the free use, enjoyment and disposal of all his acquisitions, without any control or diminution save only by the laws of the land.[9]

---

[5] See also the American Convention on Human Rights, Art 21; the African Charter on Human and People's Rights, Art 14.

[6] See the discussion in *In re Certification of the Constitution of RSA 1996* 1996 (4) SA 744 paras 72 to 73.

[7] (1765) 19 State Tr 1029, 1060.

[8] The first two being personal security and personal liberty.

[9] R Kerr (ed), *Blackstone's Commentaries on the Laws of England* (4th edn, John Murray, 1876), p.109.

The right is qualified by reference to the 'laws of the land' but Blackstone was of the view that the regard of the law for private property was so great:

> that it will not authorize the least violation of it; not even for the general good of the whole community.[10]

This remains a fundamental principle of the common law.[11]

18.05 Blackstone also expressed the view that, if Parliament does authorise such a restriction, it should do so with caution and for full compensation.[12] It remains the case that the restriction of private property rights is a matter for Parliament alone:[13] as a matter of constitutional law, only Parliament can authorise the taking of property by public authorities.[14] At common law there is a legal right to compensation in respect of the destruction of property in the exercise of the royal prerogative, unless the damage is done in battle.[15] Despite Blackstone's statement of general principle, it has been said that there is no common law right to compensation: this is only payable if authorised by statute.[16]

18.06 It is first necessary to consider the definition of property in English law. We will then consider the ways in which the law recognises and protects the 'right to property'. This is effectively achieved in two ways: first, as a result of the law of tort dealing with interference with land and goods; and secondly, as a result of the principles of statutory interpretation which apply to any legislation which authorises interference with rights to property.

(2) The nature of 'property'

18.07 The paradigm cases of 'property' are land and goods but the concept is much wider. It is, perhaps, not surprising that English law has not attempted to provide any complete definition of 'property'. In *National Provincial Bank Ltd v Ainsworth*[17] Lord Wilberforce said:

> Before a right or an interest can be admitted into the category of property, or of a right affecting property, it must be definable, identifiable by third parties, capable in its nature of assumption by third parties, and have some degree of permanence or stability.

---

[10] Ibid.

[11] See *Monsanto v Tilly* [2000] Env LR 313, CA, *per* Mummery LJ.

[12] *Blackstone's Commentaries* (n 9 above) 110.

[13] Ibid.

[14] See *Burmah Oil Company Ltd v Lord Advocate* [1965] AC 75 and see *A-G v Blake, The Times*, 3 Aug 2000 (HL).

[15] Ibid, the effect of this decision was reversed by the War Damage Act 1965 which gave rise to concerns as to whether the United Kingdom's acceptance of the right to individual petition under the European Convention on Human Rights might lead to difficulties in Strasbourg: see Lord Lester, 'UK Acceptance of the Strasbourg Jurisdiction' [1998] PL 237.

[16] *Sisters of the Charity of Rockingham v The King* [1922] 2 AC 315, 322; and contrast the position in Canada, see para 18.112 below.

[17] [1965] AC 1175, 1247-1248.

Although property is generally assignable it is not always so.[18] A number of statutes contain definitions of 'property' which provide some guidance on the width of the concept. One of the broadest definitions is found in insolvency legislation:

> 'property' includes money, goods, things in action, land and every description of property wherever situated and also obligations and every description of interest, whether present or future or vested or contingent, arising out of, or incidental to property.[19]

However, not all rights which, taken together, constitute 'property' are themselves properly described as 'property'. In *Belfast Corporation v O D Cars*[20] Viscount Simonds said: **18.08**

> anyone using the English language in its ordinary signification would . . . agree that 'property' is a word of very wide import, including tangible and intangible property. But he would surely deny that any one of those rights which in the aggregate constituted ownership of property could itself and by itself be aptly called 'property'.

(3) The legal protection of property rights

A number of property rights are protected by both the criminal and the civil law. The offence of theft is committed by any person who 'dishonestly appropriates' property belonging to another 'with the intention of permanently depriving' the owner of his property.[21] 'Property' is defined as including money and all other property, real or personal, including things in action.[22] However, a person cannot, in general, steal land.[23] The offence is committed if property is 'appropriated' from anyone having possession of it or any proprietary right or interest in it.[24] Any assumption of any right of an owner amounts to an 'appropriation' for the purposes of the Theft Act.[25] There is no need for an assertion of right 'adverse to the owner'. However, a person's appropriation of property will not be dishonest if it is done in the belief that he has a right to do it or would have consent if the owner knew the circumstances.[26] **18.09**

[18] See *Commissioner of Stamp Duties (NSW) v Yeend* (1929) 43 CLR 235, 245, *per* Isaacs J: 'assignability is a consequence, not a test' of a proprietary right; and see *Don King Productions v Warren* [1998] 3 WLR 276 (non-assignable contract 'property' for the purposes of the Partnership Act 1890).

[19] Insolvency Act 1986, s 436.

[20] [1960] AC 490, 517 (a Northern Ireland case concerning the 'right to property' in the Government of Ireland Act 1920, s 5(1) and a restriction on building above a certain height).

[21] Theft Act 1968, s 1.

[22] Ibid s 4(1).

[23] Ibid s 4(2).

[24] Ibid s 5(1).

[25] Ibid s 3; as interpreted in *R v Gomez* [1993] AC 442.

[26] Theft Act 1968, s 2.

18.10 The offence of theft is only committed if the person who appropriates the property is 'dishonest'. This is not, however, a necessary ingredient of tortious liability for interference with property. The torts of 'trespass' to land and goods and conversion are committed whenever there is an intentional interference with the land or goods. They are actionable without any proof of actual damage and there is no defence of 'honest mistake'.

18.11 A trespass to land is any direct physical intrusion by one person onto land in the possession of another which cannot be justified by law. It is important to note that what the law protects is not the 'ownership' of the land but the 'possession' of it. Only the person in possession can bring a trespass action. In the words of Lord Camden CJ:

> by the laws of England every invasion of private property, be it ever so minute, is a trespass. No man can set his foot upon my ground without my licence, but he is liable to an action, though the damage be nothing.[27]

18.12 Trespass to goods can be defined as any wrongful act of direct physical interference with goods which are in the possession of another. It is generally assumed that many of the same rules which apply to trespass to land are equally applicable to trespass to goods. Any direct physical contact will be sufficient. It is not necessary to actually damage someone else's goods to commit a trespass. As Lord Diplock has said, 'the act of handling a man's goods without his permission is prima facie tortious'[28] Thus, moving another's goods will be a trespass.[29] and a mere touch is sufficient to found an action in trespass to goods.[30]

18.13 The tort of conversion protects any 'adoption of rights of ownership'. Conversion covers a wide range of interferences. The essence of someone 'converting goods to his own use' is a denial of the claimant's rights to those goods or the assertion of some other rights which are inconsistent with them. As Atkin LJ put it:

> It appears to me plain that dealing with goods in a manner inconsistent with the right of the true owner amounts to a conversion, providing it is also established that there is an intention on the part of the defendant in so doing to deny the owner's right or to assert a right which is inconsistent with the owner's right. But that intention is conclusively proved if the defendant has taken the goods as his own or used the goods as his own.[31]

The person who is in possession of goods, or the person who has the right to possession, can sue in conversion.[32]

---

[27] *Entick v Carrington* (1765) 19 State Tr 1029, 1060.
[28] *Inland Revenue Commissioners v Rossminster* [1980] AC 952 at 1011.
[29] *Fouldes v Willoughby* (1841) 8 M & W 540, at 544-5.
[30] See *Hesperides Hotels v Sermet, The Times*, 15 Mar 1982.
[31] *Lancashire and Yorkshire Railway Company v MacNicoll* (1918) 88 LJKB 601.
[32] *Winkworth v Christie Manson and Woods Ltd* [1980] Ch 496 at 499.

State interference with property often involves 'regulation' of its use rather than an appropriation. This will not be actionable in trespass or conversion. However, if it can be characterised as a 'taking' it may attract a statutory right to compensation. In general, a restriction on the use of property imposed by regulatory laws does not constitute a 'taking'. This is because: **18.14**

> The give and take of civil society frequently requires that the exercise of private rights should be restricted in the general public interest. The principles which underlie the right of the individual not to be deprived of his property without compensation are, first, that some public interest is necessary to justify the taking of private property for the benefit of the state and, secondly, that when the public interest does so require, the loss should not fall upon the individual whose property has been taken but should be borne by the public as a whole. But these principles do not require the payment of compensation to anyone whose private rights are restricted by legislation of general application which is enacted for the public benefit. This is so even if, as will inevitably be the case, the legislation in general terms affects some people more than others.[32a]

Nevertheless, it is clear that:

> The general rule is . . . that while property may be regulated to a certain extent, if regulation goes too far it will be recognised as a taking.[33]

A statutory prohibition on carrying on a business of a particular type by anyone other than an agency of the state may involve, in substance, the transfer of such businesses to the agency; and may, therefore, be an 'expropriation' by the state attracting compensation.[34] Whether a law or exercise of an administrative power amounts to a deprivation of property rather than a regulation depends on the substance of the matter rather than upon the form in which the law is drafted.[34a]

(4) Construction of statutes authorising interference with property

The absence of any entrenched rights in English law[35] means that even a right as well-established as the right to property can be removed by statute. Nevertheless, there is a clear presumption against the imposition of a statutory detriment to a **18.15**

[32a] *Grape Bay v A-G of Bermuda* [2000] 1 WLR 574, 583, *per* Lord Hoffman.

[33] *Belfast Corporation v O D Cars Ltd* [1960] AC 490, 519, *per* Viscount Simonds and cf the position in the United States, para 18.118 below.

[34] See eg, *Ulster Transport Authority v James Brown and Sons Ltd* [1953] NI 79 and *Manitoba Fisheries Ltd v The Queen* [1979] 1 SCR 101 (the Canadian Freshwater Fish Marketing Act, conferred upon a statutory corporation the monopoly of exporting fish from Manitoba. The applicants had previously been exporting fish and the effect of the Act was to destroy their business, it was held that they had been deprived of their property, namely, the goodwill of the business, even though that goodwill had not been directly transferred to the corporation); but see *Government of Malaysia v Selangor Pilot Association* [1978] AC 337, see para 18.136 below.

[34a] *Grape Bay v A-G of Bermuda* (n 32a above) 584, referring to *Manitoba Fisheries Ltd v The Queen* (n 34 above) see para 18.112 below.

[35] See para 1.24ff above.

person's property without clear words.[36] Any statute which involves an expropriation of property rights is construed strictly in favour of the party whose property is to be taken.[37] It is a well-recognised canon of construction that:

> an intention to take away the property of a subject without giving him a legal right to compensation for the loss of it is not to be imputed to the legislature unless that intention is expressed in unequivocal terms.[38]

18.16 The same principle applies to the statutory restriction of property rights.[39] The position was summarised by Lord Radcliffe in the following terms:

> . . . the general principle, accepted by the legislature and scrupulously defended by the courts, that title to property or the enjoyment of its possession was not to be compulsorily acquired from a subject unless full compensation was afforded in its place.[40]

This principle applies even when property is acquired by one public authority from another.[41]

18.17 In accordance with this principle, the courts have refused to impose liability to tax in the absence of clear words.[42] As Lord Wilberforce said in *Vestey v Inland Revenue Commissioners*:[43]

> Taxes are imposed on subjects by Parliament. A citizen cannot be taxed unless he is designated in clear terms by a taxing Act as a taxpayer and the amount of his liability clearly defined. A proposition that whether a subject is to be taxed or not, or that, if he is, the amount of his liability is to be decided (even though within a limit) by an administrative body represents a radical departure from constitutional principle.

However, the courts have also recognised countervailing policy considerations deriving from the need to collect public revenue.[44]

(5) Compulsory purchase and compensation

18.18 A number of different statutes empower different authorities to acquire land compulsorily for different specific purposes.[45] The statutory procedure which must be

---

[36] See generally, F Bennion, *Statutory Interpretation* (3rd edn, Butterworths, 1997) 652ff.

[37] *Methuen-Campbell v Walters* [1979] QB 525, 542; *Chilton v Telford Development Corporation* [1987] 1 WLR 872.

[38] *Central Control Board (Liquor Traffic) v Cannon Brewery Company Ltd* [1919] AC 744, 752; *Attorney-General v De Keyser's Royal Hotel Ltd* [1920] AC 508, 542.

[39] *London and North Western Rly Co v Evans* [1893] 1 Ch 16, 27.

[40] *Belfast Corporation v O D Cars* [1960] AC 490, 523.

[41] See *R v Secretary of State for the Environment, ex p Newnham London Borough Council* (1985) 84 LGR 639.

[42] *Re Micklethwait* (1855) 11 Ex Ch 452, 456.

[43] [1980] AC 1148, 1171.

[44] See generally, Bennion (n 36 above) 655.

[45] For a detailed survey, see *Halsbury's Laws of England* (4th edn Reissue, Butterworths, 1996) Vol 8(1), 'Compulsory Acquisition of Land'.

followed before a particular compulsory acquisition can be authorised is now set out in the Acquisition of Land Act 1981. When a compulsory purchase order is made and confirmed, notice is given to owners, occupiers and tenants who have a specified time to make objections. If objections are received a public inquiry will be held at which any landowner objecting to the acquisition may be heard. The acquiring authority must then make good its case in support of the acquisition by fully detailed evidence which can be challenged by the landowner. It is at this stage that the merits of the proposed acquisition are examined and assessed and it is normally on the basis of facts found and recorded in a report of such an inquiry that a Ministerial decision to give effective authority for compulsory acquisition must rest. Such a decision is then open to challenge in the courts on the limited grounds, analogous to those of a judicial review, that the compulsory acquisition authorised was *ultra vires* the enabling statute or that the landowner objecting to the acquisition was prejudiced by a failure to follow the prescribed procedures.[46]

Nevertheless, the presumption against the removal of property rights means that compulsory purchase orders must be 'sufficiently justified' by the Secretary of State.[47] It operates with particular force where a provision appears to have the effect of removing property without compensation. **18.19**

Although there is no 'common law right' to compensation for interference with property rights there is a strong presumption in favour the payment of compensation. Lord Denning MR summarised the position as follows: **18.20**

> No citizen is to be deprived of his land by any public authority against his will, unless it is expressly authorised by Parliament and the public interest decisively so demands; and then on condition that proper compensation is paid.[48]

The court has refused to countenance expropriation by a public authority of money or property belonging to an individual for which there is no statutory authority even where the property has been acquired through criminal activity.[48a] However, the presumption in favour of compensation does not apply in cases in which there has been no actual deprivation. Thus, where a person was caused loss by obeying a lawful order of the state no compensation was payable.[49]

---

46 See also Lord Bridge in *Harel Freres Ltd v The Minister of Housing Lands and Town and Country Planning* No 58 of 1986, Privy Council, 15 Dec 1987.

47 *R v Secretary of State for Transport, ex p de Rothschild* [1989] 1 All ER 933; see also *Prest v Secretary of State for Wales* (1982) 81 LGR 193.

48 *Prest v Secretary of State for Wales* (n 47 above) 198.

48a See *Webb v Chief Constable of Merseyside* [2000] 1 All ER 209.

49 *Frances Fenwick & Co v The King* [1927] 1 KB 458 (no compensation when plaintiff was prevented from discharging coal during a coal strike).

18.21 An owner whose land is compulsorily acquired is entitled to compensation equivalent to the loss that he has suffered.[50] No allowance is to be made for the fact that the acquisition is compulsory and the land is to be valued at the price it might be expected to realise if sold by a willing seller.[51] In addition, the owner is entitled to compensation for disturbance. This covers any loss resulting from the compulsory acquisition provided that it was not too remote and that it was a natural, direct and reasonable consequence of dispossession.[52]

(6) The right to property in European Community Law

18.22 The fundamental principle of respect for private property also forms part of English law as a result of a series of decisions of the European Court of Justice. In *Hauer v Land Rheinland-Pfalz*[53] the Court made clear that:

> The right to property is guaranteed in the Community legal order in accordance with the ideas common to the constitutions of Member States, which are also reflected in the First Protocol to the European Convention for the Protection of Human Rights.[54]

This approach has been followed in a number of subsequent cases.[55]

18.23 In accordance with the approach taken under the Convention[56] the European Court of Justice has recognised that restrictions can be placed on the use of property 'in the general interest'.[57] As was said in the *Wachauf* case:

> The fundamental rights recognised by the Court are not absolute, however, but must be considered in relation to their social function. Consequently, restrictions may be imposed on the exercise of those rights, in particular in the context of a common organisation of a market, provided that those restrictions in fact correspond to objectives of general interest pursued by the Community and do not constitute, with regard to the aim pursued, a disproportionate and intolerable interference, impairing the very substance of those rights.[58]

18.24 In practice, the application of the 'general interest' and 'proportionality' tests makes it very difficult to establish a violation of the right to property.[59] The

---

50 *Horn v Sunderland Corporation* [1941] 2 KB 26; and see generally, *Halsbury's Laws of England*, (4th edn Reissue, Butterworths, 1996), Vol 8(1), para 233ff.

51 *Director of Buildings and Lands v Shun Fung Ironworks Ltd* [1995] 2 AC 111, 115.

52 See *Harvey v Crawley Development Corporation* [1957] 1 QB 485.

53 [1979] ECR 3727.

54 Ibid para 17.

55 See eg *Schräder HS Kraftfutter GmbH and Company KG v Hauptzollamt Gronau* [1989] ECR 2237; *Wachauf v Germany* [1989] ECR 2609; *Germany v Council* [1995] ECR 1- 3723; *Bosphorus Hava Yollari Turizm v Minister for Transport* [1996] ECR I-3953.

56 See para 18.68 below.

57 *Hauer* (n 53 above) para 19.

58 *Wachauf* (n 55 above) para 18.

59 See generally, L Betten and N Grief, *EU Law and Human Rights* (Longman, 1998) 107–108.

European Court of Justice has found restrictions on the planting of new vines[60] and removal of milk quotas without compensation to be justified interferences.[61] This approach has been applied in a case referred by the High Court. In *R v Commissioners of Customs and Excise, ex p Faroe Seafood Co Ltd*[62] it was held that post-clearance recovery of import duties did not constitute an infringement of the right to property. The principle of proportionality had not been infringed despite the fact that the imports had been made in good faith and the importer was no longer in a position to recover the duties from the buyer.

The principles of Community law recognise an obligation to pay fair compensation to the expropriated individual.[63] However, a claim for repayment is not property right unless there was a vested right to restitution.[64] Furthermore, advantages allocated under common market organisation, such as agricultural quotas, are not treated as property rights.[65] As a result, there is no obligation to pay compensation on the transfer of agricultural quotas or to pay compensation for the detriment suffered by landowners deriving from the quota system.[66] **18.25**

C. The Law Under the European Convention

(1) Introduction

Article 1 of the First Protocol to the Convention provides: **18.26**

> Every natural or legal person is entitled to the peaceful enjoyment of his possessions. No one shall be deprived of his possessions except in the public interest and subject to the conditions provided for by law and by the general principles of international law.
>
> The preceding provisions shall not, however, in any way impair the right of a state to enforce such laws as it deems necessary to control the use of property in accordance with the general interest or to secure the payment of taxes or other contributions or penalties.

The protection of property was the subject of considerable controversy when the

[60] *Hauer* (n 57 above).

[61] *O'Dwyer v Council* [1995] ECR II-2071.

[62] [1996] ECR I-2465.

[63] See Opinion of Advocate-General in *Hauer* (n 57 above).

[64] *Marks & Spencer v Customs & Excise Commissioners* [1999] STC 205 and see *R v Customs & Excise Commissioners, ex p Lunn Poly Ltd* [1998] STC 649.

[65] See *R v Ministry of Agriculture, Fisheries and Food, ex p Bostock* [1994] ECR I-955; *R v MAFF, ex p Country Landowners Association* [1995] ECR II-3875; and see also *Harries v Barclays Bank* [1997] 2 EGLR 15.

[66] *R v MAFF, ex p Country Landowners Association* (n 65 above).

Convention was drafted.[67] This explains why Article 1 makes no provision for the right to have access to property or the right to compensation.[68] The inclusion of the right was criticised as it was a social and economic right which was at odds with the civil and political rights which the Convention enshrines; and because it is an extremely weak provision which acknowledges the right to enjoy what one owns without acknowledging the right to own it.[69] This background has perhaps influenced the Court and the Commission in taking a narrow view of the restrictions placed on the state by Article 1 and allowing a wide margin of appreciation.[70] The Court has found violations of this Article on only thirteen occasions.[71]

18.27 Over the past two decades, the Court has repeatedly held that the Article in fact comprises 'three distinct rules'. These are contained in the first sentence of the first paragraph, the second sentence of the first paragraph and in the third paragraph respectively:[72]

- the principle of the peaceful enjoyment of property ('the first rule');
- the principle that the deprivation of possession of property must be in the public interest and subject to the conditions provided for by law and by the general principles of international law ('the second rule');
- the principle that states are entitled to control the use of property in accordance with the general interest and to secure the payment of taxes or other contributions or penalties ('the third rule').

However, the three rules are not 'distinct' in the sense of being unconnected. The second and third rules 'are concerned with 'particular instances of interference with the right to peaceful enjoyment of possessions' and must be construed in the

[67] See generally, D Harris, M O'Boyle and C Warbrick, *Law of the European Convention on Human Rights* (Butterworths, 1995) 516; and see R Salgado, 'Protection of Nationals' Rights to Property Under the European Convention on Human Rights: *Lithgow v United Kingdom*' 27 Virginia Journal of International Law 865, 880-890 (an analysis of *Travaux Préparatoires* in relation to Art 1, First Protocol).

[68] See generally, L Condorelli, 'Premier Protocole Additionnel: Article 1' in L-E Pettiti, E Decaux and P-H Imbert (eds), *La Convention Européene des droits de l'homme* (2nd edn, Economica, 1999).

[69] H G Schmerers, 'International Protection of the Right to Property' in F Matscher and H Petzold (eds), *Protecting Human Rights—the European Dimension: Essays in Honour of G H Wiarde* (Koln, 1990).

[70] For a general discussion see J McBride, 'The Right to Property' (1996) 21 ELR Checklist No 1 40.

[71] *Sporrong and Lönnroth v Sweden* (1982) 5 EHRR 35; *Poiss v Austria* (1987) 10 EHRR 231; *Raimondo v Italy* (1994) 18 EHRR 237; *Stran Greek Refineries and Stratis Andreadis v Greece* (1994) 19 EHRR 293; *Scollo v Italy* (1995) 22 EHRR 514; *Loizidou v Turkey* (1996) 23 EHRR 513; *Akkus v Turkey* RJD 1997-IV 1300; *Immobiliare Saffi v Italy* (1999) 7 BHRC 151; *Chassagnou and others v France* (1999) 7 BHRC 151; *Beyeler v Italy* Judgment, 5 Jan 2000; *Belvedere Alberghiera SA v Italy* Judgment, 30 May 2000; *Carbonara and Ventura v Italy* Jugment, 30 May 2000; *AO v Italy* Judgment, 30 May 2000.

[72] This formulation derives from *Sporrong and Lönnroth v Sweden* (1982) 5 EHRR 35 para 61.

light of the general principle in the first sentence of paragraph 1.[73] The second and third rules cover the three great legislative powers of government: the power of 'eminent domain',[74] the 'police power'[75] and the power of taxation.

18.28 All forms of interference with the enjoyment of possessions must be justified by the state. On a literal reading of Article 1, the standard of 'justification' would appear to be different, depending on which of the three powers is being exercised. Whereas the deprivation of property must be justified on the strict grounds prescribed by the second rule, control of the use of property must simply be 'in accordance with the general interest' (as required by the third rule). However, a general test has been evolved to deal with all three: the state can only justify an interference with the enjoyment of possessions if it can show that a 'fair balance' has been kept between community interests and the rights of the person entitled to enjoyment.[76]

18.29 In this section we will begin by considering the nature and scope of the right protected. We will then consider the forms which 'interference' can take and the circumstances in which compensation for interference with property rights becomes payable. We will then deal with the Court's analysis of 'justification', before turning finally to the operation of the 'fair balance' test.

(2) Nature and scope of the right

(a) Introduction

18.30 Article 1 of the First Protocol, in substance, guarantees the right of property.[77] The right to peaceful enjoyment without state interference implies a person has the general right to have or use his possessions; and ensures that he may encumber or dispose of his own possessions (by, for example, sale, rental or inheritance).[78] Article 1 does not guarantee a right to acquire what one does not already have, regardless of the interest of the individual in doing so.[79] Thus, it does not afford a right to have food or to have shelter, whatever the level of destitution of the claimant[80] or a right to peaceful enjoyment of possessions in a pleasant environment.[81]

[73] *James v United Kingdom* (1986) 8 EHRR 123, 140 para 37; *AGOSI v United Kingdom* (1986) 9 EHRR 1 para 48; *Iatridis v Greece* Judgment, 25 Mar 1999 para 55.

[74] That is, the power to take private property for public use.

[75] That is, the power to regulate the use of property.

[76] See para 18.76 below.

[77] *Marckx v Belgium* (1979) 2 EHRR 330 para 63.

[78] Ibid.

[79] Ibid: Art 1 of the First Protocol 'does not guarantee the right to acquire possessions whether on intestacy or through voluntary dispositions'.

[80] Cf A Cassese, 'Can the Notion of Inhuman and Degrading Treatment Be Applied to Socio-Economic Conditions?' (1991) 1 EJIL 141, with discussion of *Van Volsem v Belgium* Application 14641/89, (1990) unreported.

[81] *Powell and Rayner v Unitd Kingdom* (1986) 47 DR 5, 14, EComm HR.

18.31 Article 1 is frequently relied on in defence of financial interests and it is closely related to Article 6. While Article 1 provides substantive protection for 'possessions', Article 6 ensures that they only be removed after a 'fair trial'.[82]

(b) The persons protected

18.32 Article 1 of the First Protocol expressly protects the right of 'every natural or legal person'. This makes it clear that corporations have property rights under the Convention. The applicant must, however, be the real 'victim':[83] the party, whether corporate or individual, whose rights have been affected. The Court will not, in ordinary circumstances, pierce the 'corporate veil' to allow shareholders to bring applications for interference with the rights of companies.[84] Despite the absence of a right to acquire property, it has been held that an illegitimate child who was adversely affected by intestacy rules was a 'victim' for the purpose of Article 1.[85]

(c) 'Possessions'

18.33 The applicant must first establish the existence of a property right and an entitlement to enjoy it.[86] The term 'possessions' is used in the Article but the French word 'biens' is substantially wider, covering all property rights.[87] Although it is primarily for the national legal system to attribute and identify property rights,[88] the Convention meaning of 'possessions' is an autonomous one.[89] As a result, the fact that domestic law does not acknowledge a particular interest to be a legal right, or recognises it as something other than a property right, is not determinative under Article 1 of the First Protocol.

[82] This is, of course, closely related to the Fifth Amendment to the US Constitution, see para 18.115 below.

[83] See para 22.27ff below.

[84] *Agrotexim and others v Greece* (1995) 21 EHRR 250 (majority shareholders in a liquidated brewery not 'victims') but see the dissent of Judge Walsh at 286–7 and see para 22.34ff below.

[85] *Inze v Austria* (1987) 10 EHRR 394; but see the dissenting opinions in the Commission (1986) 8 EHRR 498, 507-510, EComm HR (on the basis that Art 1 does not cover the right to receive property).

[86] *S v United Kingdom* (1986) 47 DR 274, 279, EComm HR (occupation of property without legal right not a 'possession') and *Agneessens v Belgium* (1988) 58 DR 63, EComm HR (claims to a debt rejected by court not a 'possession').

[87] The dictionary definition is 'Chose matérielle susceptible d'appropriation, et tout droit faisant partie du patrimonie' (*Dictionnaire 'Petit Robert'*); see also *Wiggins v United Kingdom* (1978) 13 DR 40, 46, EComm HR.

[88] There are few restrictions upon what a state may regard as capable of being owned: perhaps the only absolute restriction is on the ownership of people (because of the freedom from slavery in Art 4). But the fact that something is capable of being owned in one legal system (for example, human blood or organs) is not a reason why it must be capable of being owned in another.

[89] *Gasus Dösier-und Fördertechnik GmbH v Netherlands* (1995) 20 EHRR 403 para 53; *Beyeler v Italy* 5 Jan 2000 para 100.

The concept of 'possessions' has been given a broad interpretation; it is not synonymous with ownership.[90] It may be sufficient for the purposes of Article 1 that the applicant demonstrates an established interest with economic value. The applicant must demonstrate that he has a legal right to some benefit, even if it be contingent upon satisfaction of certain conditions.[91] There must be an entitlement to some real economic benefit even if its value is not yet ascertained. There will, therefore, be a right to the enjoyment of possessions where ownership is in dispute.[92] Expectations, on the other hand, do not have the necessary degree of certainty to bring them within the concept of 'possessions.'[93] **18.34**

'Possessions' have been held to include immovable and movable property; corporeal and incorporeal interests, such as shares;[94] and intellectual property such as patents,[95] contractual rights[96] (including leases[97] and property which is subject to a retention of title clause),[98] judgment debts,[99] a crystallised debt[100] and the goodwill of a business.[101] **18.35**

A liquor licence[102] has also been held to be a 'possession' in spite of the fact that it conferred no rights in national law. This was because it was essential to the successful conduct of the restaurant owned by the applicant and its withdrawal had adverse effects on the goodwill and value of the business. On the other hand, a licence will not be protected under Article 1 if the licence holder did not have a reasonable and legitimate expectation as to the lasting nature of the licence.[102a] Thus no property rights arise where a provisional licence is withdrawn on the ground that the applicant has failed to comply with the conditions on which it was **18.36**

90 *Matos e Silva LDA and others v Portugal* (1996) 24 EHRR 573 para 75.

91 The applicant may be entitled under Art 6(1) of the Convention to a fair hearing to determine whether the conditions are satisfied. If they are not, the applicant will have no right to the benefit and the state will not be required to justify its failure to confer the benefit.

92 *Iatradis v Greece* Judgment 25 Mar 1999.

93 *Batelaan and Huiges v Netherlands* (1984) 41 DR 170 at 173, EComm HR; *British-American Tobacco Company Ltd v Netherlands* (1995) 21 EHRR 409—Commission expressed the view that the right to apply for a patent was not a possession, the Court preferred to express no view.

94 *Bramelid and Malmström v Sweden* (1982) 29 DR 64, EComm HR.

95 *Smith Kline and French Laboratories Ltd v Netherlands* (1990) 66 DR 70, 79, EComm HR; *Lenzing AG v United Kingdom* [1999] EHRLR 132, EComm HR.

96 *A, B and Company AS v Germany* (1978) 14 DR 146, 168, EComm HR and *Association of General Practitioners v Denmark* (1989) 62 DR 226, 234, EComm HR.

97 *Mellacher v Austria* (1989) 12 EHRR 391 para 43.

98 *Gasus Dösier-under Fördertechnik GmbH v Netherlands* (1995) 20 EHRR 403.

99 *Stran Greek Refineries and Stratis Andreadis v Greece* (1994) 19 EHRR 293 paras 61-62 (arbitral award).

100 *Agneessens v Belgium* (1988) 58 DR 63, EComm HR.

101 *Van Marle v Netherlands* (1986) 8 EHRR 483 para 41 in which a clientele built up by the efforts of the applicant (as opposed to business goodwill) was an asset that qualified as a possession.

102 *Tre Traktörer Aktiebolag v Sweden* (1989) 13 EHRR 309 para 53; see also *Fredin v Sweden (No 1)* (1991) 13 EHRR 784 para 53 (a licence to extract gravel).

102a *Gudmunsson v Iceland* (1996) 21 EHRR CD 89.

granted[103] or where it is withdrawn in accordance with the provisions of the law which were in force when the licence was issued.[104]

18.37 A claim for damages for negligence which constituted an asset under national law was a 'possession'.[105] However, in *National and Provincial Building Society v United Kingdom*[106] the Court took the view that proceedings for restitution which were defeated by retrospective tax legislation were not sufficiently established to amount to a 'possession'.

18.38 Welfare benefits can, in some circumstances, be treated as 'possessions' under Article 1. Thus, in *Gaygusuz v Austria*[107] the Court held that the right to an advance on a state pension by way of emergency assistance was a 'pecuniary right' and was protected by Article 1 of the First Protocol.[108] It has been accepted that statutory widows benefit[109] and unemployment benefit[110] are, in principle, protected. However, the case law is not wholly consistent and it has been said that the Article does not apply to non-contributory state benefits.[111]

18.39 The Convention may also protect rights under a state pension scheme. Although the Convention does not provide a general right to a pension[112] the payment of contributions to a pension fund may create a property right in a portion of such fund.[113] In the case of a state pension scheme, it is unlikely that there will be a right to a particular level of pension. The Commission has recognised that:

> The operation of a social security system is essentially different from the management of a private insurance company. Because of its public importance, the social security system must take account of political considerations, in particular those of

[103] *Pudas v Sweden* (1984) 20 DR 234, EComm HR; *J S v Netherlands* (1995) 20 EHRR CD 42; *Gudmunsson v Iceland* (n 102a above).

[104] *Gudmunsson v Iceland* (n 102a above).

[105] *Pressos Compañía Naviera SA v Belgium* (1995) 21 EHRR 301 para 31; but see *Agneesens v Belgium* (1988) 58 DR 63, EComm HR; *A, B and Company AS v Germany* (1978) 14 DR 146, EComm HR.

[106] (1997) 25 EHRR 127 paras 67–69; see also *Agneesens v Belgium* (n 105 above); *A, B and Company AS v Germany* (n 105 above).

[107] (1996) 23 EHRR 365 para 41.

[108] As a result, the refusal to give an emergency payment to a Turkish national was a violation of Art 1 taken in conjunction with Art 14 (non-discrimination), see para 17.79 above.

[109] *Cornwell v United Kingdom* (1999) 27 EHRR CD 62.

[110] *Claes v Belgium* (1987) 54 DR 88, EComm HR; *Nahon v United Kingdom* Application 34190/96, 23 Oct 1997, EComm HR; see also *Carlin v United Kingdom* (1997), 25 EHRR CD 75 in which the Commission was prepared to assume that Industrial Injuries Invalidity benefit was a 'possession'.

[111] *G v Austria* (1984) 38 DR 84, EComm HR; *Coke v United Kingdom* [1999] EHRLR 130 (no claim in respect of interference with rights of service widows who had not contributed to the Armed Forces Pension Scheme).

[112] *X v Germany* (1966) 23 CD 10; *X v Sweden* (1986) 8 EHRR 269; *J W and E W v United Kingdom* (1983) 34 DR 153.

[113] *Müller v Austria* (1975) 3 DR 25 EComm HR; *C v France* (1988) 56 DR 20 at 34 EComm HR; *Szraber and Clarke v United Kingdom* [1998] EHRLR 230 (interest in State Earnings Related Pension scheme).

financial policy. It is conceivable, for instance, that a deflationary trend may oblige the state to reduce the nominal amount of pensions. Fluctuations of this kind have nothing to do with the guarantee of ownership as a human right.[114]

(d) Positive obligations

The right to enjoyment of possessions may require the state to take positive steps to protect the enjoyment of possessions.[115] Thus, the state may be under a positive obligation to ensure that the owner of real property can obtain access to it.[116] However, where the interference results entirely from relationships of a private contractual nature, Article 1 of the First Protocol is not brought into play.[117] The state has no obligation to act to prevent loss of value as a result of market factors, or to protect against the effects of inflation.[118] **18.40**

(3) 'Interference'

(a) Introduction

The right to enjoy possessions is subject to the state's entitlement to impose limitations where other important interests are at stake. As in the case of other qualified rights[119] any claim of violation must be considered in two stages: **18.41**

- was there an interference?
- was this interference justified?

The Court has sought to distinguish those interferences which amount to deprivation from lesser forms of interference because the conditions for their justification are governed by different provisions. It has therefore also held that the right to peaceful enjoyment extends to controlling the use of property, interfering with the substance of ownership and hindering its peaceful enjoyment.

In addition, the state will be 'responsible' for only those interferences which affect the economic value of property. In other words, enjoyment of qualities other than the economic value of property (such as the aesthetic or environmental qualities of possessions) is not guaranteed under Article 1. As a result, a complaint may be assessed in economic terms: as, for example, in *S v France*[120] where the French court and then the Commission considered the impact of noise pollution on the value of property without considering the loss of its rural amenity occasioned by industrial development nearby. **18.42**

---

114 *Müller v Austria* (n 113 above) 32; see also *X v Netherlands* (1972) 38 CD 9.
115 *James v United Kingdom* (1986) 8 EHRR 123, paras 35-36.
116 Cf *Loizidou v Turkey* (1996) 23 EHRR 513.
117 *Gustafsson v Sweden* (1996) 22 EHRR 409, para 60.
118 *X v Germany* (1980) 20 DR 226, EComm HR.
119 See para 6.86ff above.
120 (1990) 65 DR 250, 261, EComm HR.

(b) 'Deprivation'

18.43 The primary criterion for establishing a deprivation of property is the *extinction* of all of the legal rights of the owner by operation of the law or the exercise of a legal power to the same effect.[121] However, not every such extinction will constitute a deprivation since the Court has treated some seizures of property as an aspect of control of use of property rather than as deprivations.[122] Furthermore, there will also be a deprivation of property if its owner is deprived of all meaningful use of it.[123]

18.44 In the *Holy Monasteries*[124] case the Court rejected the argument of the Greek Government that a statutory presumption in favour of state ownership of the lands in question was a mere procedural device to facilitate the settlement of disputes, rather than an interference with established titles. Even though no steps had been taken to implement legal transfers to the state, the Court decided that the presumption itself effectively transferred title[125] because the monasteries, founding their claims of entitlement upon ancient adverse possession, were not in a position to rebut it. It held the Greek law to be a substantive provision and the lack of implementation at the time no bar to implementation in the future. In the circumstances, the Court found that the applicants had been deprived of their property.[126]

18.45 In the absence of a formal extinction of legal rights, the Court has been cautious in finding that interference might nevertheless amount to 'deprivation' in fact.[127] Such a '*de facto* deprivation' can only be established where there has been a substantial interference with the enjoyment of possessions, contrary to law,[128] without a formal divesting of the owner of title. Such circumstances will arise only rarely: there has been one such finding[129] to date and even then the Court did not expressly refer to it as a 'deprivation'. In *Papamichalopoulos v Greece*[130] the Court concluded that the interference was serious enough to amount to expropriation of the property on the basis of the extent of physical occupation of the land and the

121 See eg *Lithgow v United Kingdom* (1986) 8 EHRR 329 para 107.

122 *Allegemeine Gold-und Silberscheideanstalt (AGOSI) v United Kingdom* (1986) 9 EHRR 1.

123 *Fredin v Sweden (No 1)* (1991) 13 EHRR 784 para 41ff.

124 *Holy Monasteries v Greece* (1994) 20 EHRR 1.

125 Ibid paras 57–61.

126 Ibid paras 55–56.

127 See eg *Stran Greek Refineries and Stratis Andreadis* (1994) 19 EHRR 293; *Sporrong and Lönnroth v Sweden* (1982) 5 EHRR 35.

128 In *Hentrich v France* ((1994) 18 EHRR 440) the Court did not explicitly endorse the applicant's claim that there had been a *de facto* taking, although it did agree that there had been a deprivation of property. Its treatment of the lawfulness of the deprivation entirely in terms of the substantive qualities of French law indicates that the Court regarded the taking as *de jure*.

129 *Papamichalopoulos v Greece* (1993) 16 EHRR 440.

130 (1993) 16 EHRR 440; see also *Vasilescu v Romania* RJD 1998-III 1064.

remoteness of potential dealings with it. It decided that there had been a breach of Article 1, without particular reference to deprivation or the second sentence.

(c) 'Control of use'

The elimination of one of the 'bundle of rights' comprising ownership will not usually be sufficient to deprive a person of ownership: but such an infringement may amount to a *control* of the use of property.[131] Such control may be effected by the state either by requiring positive action of individuals[132] or by imposing restrictions upon their activities. Restrictions include planning controls,[133] environmental orders,[134] a prohibition on construction,[135] rent control,[136] suspension of eviction from residential property,[137] import and export laws,[138] economic regulation of professions,[139] the seizure of property for legal proceedings[140] or inheritance laws,[141] forfeiture provisions for the enforcement of laws relating to the use or possession of property[142] and forfeiture proceedings to seize or confiscate property in criminal proceedings as a preventative[143] or interim[144] measure. A refusal to grant planning permission will not be an interference but a planning enforcement notice will be.[145] **18.46**

The first stage in a procedure which results in the deprivation of property may not be treated as a control of its use. Thus, expropriation permits[146] and the provisional transfer of property under a consolidation plan[147] or in relation to a land use plan imposing a development ban[148] did not constitute violations of Article 1. **18.47**

Article 1 also gives the state a virtually unlimited power to secure the payment of taxes or other contributions or penalties.[149] The power to secure the payment of **18.48**

---

131 *Baner v Sweden* (1989) 60 DR 128, 140, EComm HR.

132 *Denev v Sweden* (1989) 59 DR 127, EComm HR (obligation on landowner to plant trees in interests of environmental protection).

133 See eg *Jacobsson v Sweden* (1989) 12 EHRR 56; *Pine Valley Developments Ltd v Ireland* (1991) 14 EHRR 319.

134 See eg *Fredin v Sweden (No 1)* (1991) 13 EHRR 784.

135 See eg *Sporrong and Lönnroth v Sweden* (1982) 5 EHRR 35; *Jacobsson v Sweden* (n 133 above).

136 See eg *Mellacher v Austria* (1989) 12 EHRR 391.

137 *Spadea and Scalabrino v Italy* (1995) 21 EHRR 482; *Scollo v Italy* (1995) 22 EHRR 514.

138 See eg *Allgemeine Gold-und Silberscheideanstalt v United Kingdom* (1986) 9 EHRR 1.

139 See eg *Karni v Sweden* (1988) 55 DR 157, EComm HR.

140 See eg *G, S and M v Austria* (1983) 34 DR 119, EComm HR.

141 See eg *Inze v Austria* (1987) 10 EHRR 394.

142 Such as was in issue in *Handyside v United Kingdom* (1976) 1 EHRR 737, para 63 and *Allgemeine Gold-und Silberscheideanstalt v United Kingdom* (1986) 9 EHRR 1 para 54.

143 *Raimondo v Italy* (1994) 18 EHRR 237.

144 *Vendittelli v Italy* (1995) 19 EHRR 464.

145 See *ISKCON v United Kingdom* (1994) 76-A DR 90, EComm HR.

146 *Sporrong and Lönnroth v Sweden* (1982) 5 EHRR 35; *Matos e Silva v Portugal* (1996) 24 EHRR 573.

147 See eg *Wiesinger v Austria* (1991) 16 EHRR 258 para 72.

148 *Katte Klitsche de la Grange v Italy* (1994) 19 EHRR 368.

149 *Gasus Dösier-und Fördertechnik GmbH v Netherlands* (1995) 20 EHRR 403 para 59.

taxes is not a separate but a specific aspect of the right of the state to control the use of property. Because the powers of the state under this provision are very wide, it is important to determine whether or not an interference with the enjoyment of possessions falls within it.

(d) Other interferences

18.49 It is possible, in exceptional circumstances, for there to be an interference with the peaceful enjoyment of possessions which is neither a deprivation nor a control of use. In *Sporrong and Lönnroth v Sweden*[150] the applicants' properties were blighted for many years by expropriation permits which permitted proceedings for expropriation at some future date. However, the permits did not deprive the applicants of their property nor control their use of it. The Court therefore described the effect as interference with the substance of ownership of possessions.

18.50 Similarly, in *Stran Greek Refineries*[151] the Court decided that legislative action rendering an arbitral award in favour of the applicant null and void was interference with enjoyment under the first sentence of Article 1 rather than a *de facto*, or even a *de jure*, deprivation under the second sentence as was contended by the applicants.

18.51 However, the need for this residual category is open to question since it has been applied to situations which can more readily be described as deprivations[152] or control of use.[153] It has been described as a kind of catch-all category for any kind of interference which is hard to pin down.[154]

18.52 Nevertheless, the Court has found interferences in this residual category on a number of occasions. The adoption of a land use plan[155] and the provisional transfer of land under a land consolidation plan[156] were held to be interferences. In *Loizidou v Turkey*[157] the applicant, a Greek Cypriot, claimed that Turkey had interfered with her rights under Article 1 of the First Protocol by reason of its occupation of northern Cyprus and the termination of her access to her real property in that region. The Court held that, although the applicant remained the legal owner of the property and her use of it had not been 'controlled', the hindrance of

---

150 (1982) 5 EHRR 35 para 60; see also *Erkner and Hofauer v Austria* (1987) 9 EHRR 464; *Poiss v Austria* (1987) 10 EHRR 231 para 64; *Agrotexim and others v Greece* (1995) 21 EHRR 250.

151 *Stran Greek Refineries and Stratis Andreadis v Greece* (1994) 19 EHRR 293 para 67; see also *Akkus v Turkey* RJD 1997-IV 1300 (violation of Art 1 due to late payment of compensation).

152 See eg *Stran Greek Refineries and Stratis Andreadis v Greece* (n 151 above).

153 See eg *Katte Klitsche de la Grange v Italy* (1994) 19 EHRR 368; *Phocas v France* [1996] RJD II 519 (building restrictions).

154 L Sermet, *The European Convention on Human Rights and Property Rights* (Council of Europe, 1998) 29.

155 *Katte Klitsche de la Grange v Italy* (n 153 above).

156 See eg *Wiesinger v Austria* (1991) 16 EHRR 258.

157 (1996) 23 EHRR 513 para 49.

her access amounted to a violation of the Convention.[158] A compulsory transfer of hunting rights over land has also amounted to an interference with the right.[159]

(4) The right to compensation for interferences with possessions

(a) Introduction

An interference with the right to peaceful enjoyment of possessions may create an entitlement to receive compensation from the state.[160] This entitlement to compensation as part of the right under Article 1 is separate from and unrelated to any remedy a victim may obtain as just satisfaction[161] where his Convention rights have been breached. **18.53**

The right to compensation for deprivation of property belonging to a non national is a general requirement of public international law which has been specifically included as part of the justification for deprivation of property under Article 1.[162] Although any attempt to differentiate between nationals and non nationals in relation to the right to compensation for deprivation of property would appear to contravene the discrimination provision in Article 14,[163] the Court has consistently refused to apply the same test to nationals as non nationals when considering compensation issues.[164] **18.54**

Nevertheless, the need for a 'fair balance' between the public and the private interest when justifying any interference with property rights[165] requires that some compensation[166] is payable where a national has been deprived of his property in all but an exceptional case.[167] However, it seems that lesser interferences with peaceful enjoyment of possessions do not create a right to compensation. **18.55**

(b) Compensation for deprivation of property

Protection under Article 1 would be 'illusory and ineffective' if nationals did not **18.56**

---

158 Ibid para 63.

159 *Chassagnou v France* (1999) 7 BHRC 151.

160 See generally, D Anderson, 'Compensation for Interference with Property' [1999] EHRLR 543.

161 See generally, para 21.30ff below.

162 See para 18.64ff below.

163 See para 17.79ff below.

164 See eg *James v United Kingdom* (1986) 8 EHRR 123 paras 58–66; *Lithgow v United Kingdom* (1986) 8 EHHR 329 para 119.

165 See para 18.41ff below.

166 A state will be vulnerable where there is *no* right to *any* compensation: *Lithgow v United Kingdom* (1986) 8 EHRR 329, para 120; *Katte Klitsche de la Grange v Italy* (1994) 19 EHRR 368.

167 The 'exceptional case' might include the uncompensated seizure of property in time of war under, for example, the War Damage Act 1965. See also *Holy Monasteries* where the Commission (Com Rep paras 78–83) found an uncompensated taking to be justified, but the Court (para 75) disagreed.

benefit from some compensatory principle equivalent to that of general international law. The Court in *Lithgow*[168] said that:

> the taking of property in the public interest without compensation is treated as justifiable only in exceptional circumstances . . . As far as Article 1 is concerned, the protection of the right of property it affords would be largely illusory and ineffective in the absence of any equivalent principle.

It continued:

> the taking of property without payment of an amount 'reasonably related to its value' would normally constitute a disproportionate interference which could not be considered justifiable under Article 1. Article 1 does not, however, guarantee a right to full compensation in all circumstances, since legitimate objectives of 'public interest'; such as pursued in measures of economic reform or measures designed to achieve greater social justice, may call for less than reimbursement of the full market value . . .

18.57 Even interferences based upon strong public interests may require some compensation. In the *Stran Greek Refineries* case,[169] for example, although the challenged measures were taken in pursuit of a policy of rectifying arrangements made by the former military dictatorship in Greece, the Court unanimously held that the legislative cancellation of an arbitration award, representing compensation for the termination of contractual rights of the applicants, was an unjustifiable interference. It deferred to the judgment of the arbitral tribunal as to the appropriate level of compensation and ordered the state to pay the full amount of the award plus interest. There were also strong public interest concerns in the *Holy Monasteries* case,[170] in which the law depriving the monasteries of their lands effectively made no provision for compensation and failed to provide a fair balance between the rights of the applicants and the public interest.

18.58 In fact, the Court has been reluctant to hold that there are exceptional circumstances which entitle a state to deprive a person of property rights without compensation. In the *Holy Monasteries* case the Commission took the view that a refusal to pay compensation because of the close relationship between the Greek church and state was within the state's margin of appreciation[171] but the Court disagreed.

18.59 Compensation for deprivation must be 'reasonably related' to the value of the property taken; however, legitimate objectives of public interest may mean that reimbursement at full market value is not required.[172] The Convention does not

[168] *Lithgow v United Kingdom* (n 166 above).
[169] Ibid paras 80–83.
[170] (1994) 20 EHRR 1 para 74.
[171] Ibid Com Rep para 83.
[172] *Lithgow v United Kingdom* (1986) 8 EHRR 329 para 121.

demand either full compensation or the same level of compensation for every type of deprivation.[173]

Where the calculation of compensation is manifestly without reasonable foundation, this will amount to a breach of Article 1.[174] Thus, in *Papachelas v Greece*[175] an infringement was found because compensation payable for a compulsory purchase was based on a formula which contained an irrebuttable presumption that the applicant's land had increased in value without regard to whether his particular circumstances justified this approach. **18.60**

(c) Compensation and control on the use of property

In contrast to the position in relation to deprivation, the state has frequently succeeded in showing it has struck a fair balance between the interests of the state and the individual when controlling the use of property, even though it has failed to pay compensation to reflect the reduced value of property. Thus, no obligation to pay compensation arose where the Leasehold Reform Act reduced the value of the property owned by the trustees of the Duke of Westminster,[176] where a gravel permit licence was revoked,[177] where planning permission was withdrawn[178] or where an airplane was forfeited because it was used for drugs.[179] It also seems that the fact that compensation has been paid in respect of the control of use generally results in a finding that Article 1 was not violated.[180] **18.61**

The Commission has said that the control of use does not, as a rule, contain a right to compensation.[181] However, it has been suggested that the unsatisfactory way in which the Court and Commission distinguish between the deprivation of property and the control of its use, in part, arises because there is a presumption that compensation must be paid where a person is deprived of property.[182] **18.62**

(d) Compensation for other interferences

There is no general rule that interference with the substance of ownership[183] or hindering the enjoyment of property requires the payment of compensation. **18.63**

---

[173] Ibid, the court rejected the claim that compensation in nationalisation cases should be established on the same basis (market value) as it is in regard to a compulsory purchase of land.

[174] Ibid para 122.

[175] Application 31423/96, Mar 25, 1999.

[176] *James v United Kingdom* (1986) 8 EHRR 123.

[177] *Fredin v Sweden (No 1)* (1991) 13 EHRR 784.

[178] *Pine Valley Developments Ltd v Ireland* (1991) 14 EHRR 319.

[179] *Air Canada v United Kingdom* (1995) 20 EHRR 150.

[180] See eg *Baner v Sweden* (1989) 60 DR 128, EComm HR; *S v France* (1990) 65 DR 250, EComm HR.

[181] *Pinnacle Meat Processors v United Kingdom* Application 33298/96, 21 Oct 1998, EComm HR (Admissibility decision).

[182] D Anderson ,'Compensation for Interference with Property' [1998] EHRLR 543.

[183] Ibid 551–552.

(5) Justification

(a) Introduction

18.64 Interferences with the right to enjoyment of possessions can be justified on one of three separate grounds. First, according to the second sentence, a deprivation of possessions must be 'in the public interest' and 'subject to the conditions provided for by law and by the principles of international law'. Secondly, it appears that state control of the use of possessions must only satisfy the less stringent test of being 'in the general interest'. Finally, on a literal reading of the Article, the state need not justify laws which it deems necessary to 'secure the payment of taxes, contributions and penalties'.

18.65 Although Article 1 deals with three different kinds of 'interference with the peaceful enjoyment of possessions', the second and third rules must be construed in the light of the general principle laid down in the first rule.[184] Furthermore, it is often difficult to determine which sentence of Article 1 is applicable in the particular circumstances.[185] As a result, despite the literal words of the Article, there has been a tendency for the Court to apply a single test when considering the justification of interferences with the peaceful enjoyment of possessions: has a 'fair balance' been struck between the demands of the general interest and the requirements of the protection of the individual's fundamental rights?[186] In applying this test, the state has consistently been allowed a wide margin of appreciation[187] to identify the general interest and determine whether it outweighs the claims of the applicant.[188] This margin is wider in cases falling under the third rule.

(b) Justification for deprivation and the second rule

18.66 **The conditions to be satisfied.** Under the second rule in Article 1[189] a state may deprive an individual of the enjoyment of possessions:

- if it is subject to conditions provided for by law;
- if the deprivation is 'in the public interest'; and
- subject to the general principles of international law.

In practice, however, the Court has also gone on to consider whether a 'fair balance' has been struck between the demands of the general community and the fundamental rights of the individual.

---

[184] *James v United Kingdom* (1986) 8 EHRR 123 para 37; *Lithgow v United Kingdom* (1986) 8 EHRR 329 para 106; *Immobiliare Saffi v Italy* (1999) 7 BHRC 151 para 44.

[185] See eg *Papamichalopoulos v Greece* (1993) 16 EHRR 440 Com Rep.

[186] *Fredin v Sweden (No 1)* (1991) 13 EHRR 784 para 51.

[187] For a general discussion of the doctrine, see para 6.31ff below.

[188] *Fredin v Sweden* (n 186 above) para 51.

[189] See para 18.27 above.

'The conditions provided by law'. The first and most important requirement of Article 1 is that any interference by a public authority with the peaceful enjoyment of possessions should be lawful.[190] A deprivation by the state must have a basis in national law which is accessible, sufficiently certain, and provides protection against arbitrary abuses. The identification of a relevant domestic law of sufficient accessibility and certainty has created few difficulties. Requirements as to safeguards against arbitrariness are determined in each case by the application of the 'fair balance' test. In *Hentrich v France,*[191] for example, a pre-emptive right to take property vested in the tax authorities, but exercised by them according to a policy which was not explained, neither satisfied the requirement of foreseeability nor contained any procedural safeguards to prevent the unfair use of the power. Deprivation on such a basis was unjustified.[192] Similarly, in *Iatradis v Greece*[193] the failure of the state to return a building after an eviction order had been quashed breached Article 1 because the interference was not in accordance with conditions provided by law. **18.67**

The 'public interest condition'. It is primarily for the state to identify the objective of a deprivation and determine whether it is in the 'public interest'.[194] On the basis of the current case law it would be unusual for the Court to challenge these findings; and the Court has not yet rejected any argument put forward by a state that a particular interference was in the public interest. In *James v United Kingdom*[195] legislation designed to transfer property rights from one individual to another for the purpose of enfranchising long lease-holders was determined to be in the public interest, despite the efforts of the applicants to have it characterised as contrary to the narrower notion of a community interest. The Court asserted that the objective of Article 1 was protection against *arbitrary* confiscation of property, and found that, as the taking furthered a policy calculated to enhance social justice within the community, it was 'properly described as being "in the public interest."'[196] **18.68**

Deprivations of property obtained during the course of criminal activity might also be considered to be 'in the public interest'. In such a case, if the confiscation was found to be carried out in the determination of a criminal charge against the applicant, and the requirements of Article 6 were not satisfied, lack of due process is all that might be established.[197] **18.69**

---

190 *Iatridis v Greece*, Judgment, 25 Mar1999, para 58.

191 (1994) 18 EHRR 440 para 42.

192 Ibid para 48. The level of compensation was also found to be inadequate.

193 n 190 above, para 55.

194 In *Lithgow v United Kingdom* (1986) 8 EHRR 329 the applicants unsuccessfully contested the nationalisation of the ship building industry, the Court said that the 'public interest' factor 'relates to the justification and motives for the actual taking'.

195 (1986) 8 EHRR 123 para 11; see also *Holy Monasteries v Greece* (1994) 20 EHRR 1 para 76.

196 *James v United Kingdom* (n 195 above) para 49; *Holy Monasteries v Greece* (n 195 above) paras 67–69.

197 Note that in many cases, deprivations of property will be effected by legislation which obviates any 'civil' right that the applicant may have had determined pursuant to Art 6(1).

18.70 **General principles of international law.** The reference to 'conditions provided for . . . by general principles of international law' in the second sentence of Article 1 raises questions as to the content and scope of application of the relevant principles of international law. International law protects against arbitrary expropriation and provides standards for compensation of individuals in the event of nationalisation of property. But the relevant principles in relation to compensation and methods of valuation of property are controversial and apply only to expropriation of property owned by non-nationals.[198] It is not clear whether nationals have the benefit of the 'general principles of international law'. Under the 'strict interpretation view'[199] the reference applies only to alien property holders as the sole beneficiaries under international law.[200] Accordingly, the Convention protects the entitlement to peaceful enjoyment of possessions, but the mechanisms employed differ according to the party to be protected.[201] This view rejects full compensation for nationals. The result is that the Convention provides a basis on which non-nationals might take action against a nationalising state without the intervention of their governments.[202]

18.71 The alternative 'plain meaning view'[203] interprets the phrase 'general principles of international law' to apply to both nationals and non-nationals, on grounds that the purpose of the Convention is to protect the human rights of all persons who are subject to the jurisdiction of the state.[204] It emphasises that as international law protects non-nationals quite apart from the Convention, the reference to such principles must be intended to ensure that the state compensate fully its own nationals. This perspective incorporates into the Convention the *standards* of general international law for the benefit of all persons protected by the Convention, without regard to nationality, thus establishing a right to compensation which is defined by the 'general principles of international law'.[205]

18.72 The Court, relying on the *travaux préparatoires*, has found that it was not the intention of the parties to the Convention to extend the protection of general international law to nationals.[206] Principles of international law apply only to

[198] L Oppenheim, *International Law* (9th edn, Longman) Vol I, 910.

[199] See R Salgado, 'Protection of Nationals' Rights to Property Under the European Convention on Human Rights: *Lithgow v United Kingdom*' 27 Virginia J of Intl L 865, 879.

[200] See *Beaumartin v France* (1994) 19 EHRR 485.

[201] See R Higgins, 'The Taking of Property by the State: Recent Developments in International Law' (1982) 176 Recueil des Cours 259, 370.

[202] *James v United Kingdom* (1986) 8 EHRR 123 para 62.

[203] Salgado (n 199 above) 877.

[204] E Schwelb, 'The Protection of the Right of Property of Nationals Under the First Protocol to the European Convention on Human Rights' (1964) 13 American J of Comparative L 518.

[205] *James v United Kingdom* (n 202 above).

[206] See the decision of the Commission in *Gudmunsson v Iceland* (1960) YB 394; and the Court in *James v United Kingdom* (1986) 8 EHRR 123; and *Lithgow v United Kingdom* (1986) 8 EHRR 329.

non-nationals for expropriations of their property. The long-standing controversy was resolved in *Lithgow v United Kingdom*[207] when the UK Government proceeded to nationalise the aerospace and shipbuilding industries by subjecting a number of UK companies to public control and paying 'fair compensation' to their owners.[208] The Court decided that the general principles of international law did not apply to nationals. However, it went on to hold that there was, in effect, an implied right to compensation.[209] In the light of this approach, it seems unlikely that application of the 'principles of international law' would make any practical difference in 'deprivation' cases.

(c) Justification for deprivation and the third rule

The third rule appears to give the state a very wide discretion to interfere with property rights. It is provided that the Article shall not: **18.73**

> in any way impair the right of a State to enforce such laws as it deems necessary to control the use of property in accordance with the general interest or to secure the payment of taxes or other contributions or penalties.

Read literally, this provision provides extremely limited grounds of challenge in 'control of use' and 'tax' cases: the state has a 'right' to enforce the laws it 'deems necessary'. In fact, the courts have interpreted these provisions narrowly. Although earlier cases suggested that the states were the sole judge of necessity under this provision[210] it is now clear that the whole of Article 1 must be read in the light of the principle of 'fair balance'.[211] As a result, there must be a reasonable relationship of proportionality between the means employed and the aim pursued.[212]

The Court has taken what has been described as a 'remarkably indulgent' attitude to measures which override the rights of property owners to recover possession from tenants.[213] In *Spadea and Scalabrino v Italy*[214] a number of decrees suspended the enforcement of eviction orders for a year at a time. The applicants had bought flats to live in and gave the tenants notice to quit when their leases expired. The date fixed for eviction was blocked by the decrees. It was decided that this was a control of use, rather than a *de facto* expropriation. The Court held that the **18.74**

207 Ibid.
208 For the full facts see Salgado (n 199 above).
209 See para 18.53ff above.
210 *Handyside v United Kingdom* (1976) 1 EHRR 737 para 62; *Marckx v Belgium* (1979) 2 EHRR 330.
211 See para 18.76ff above.
212 See eg *Mellacher v Austria* (1989) 12 EHRR 391 para 48; *Chassagnou and others v France* (1999) 7 BHRC 151 para 75; *National and Provincial Building Society v United Kingdom* (1997) 25 EHRR 127 para 80.
213 J McBride, 'The Right to Property' (1996) 21 ELR Checklist No 1, 40, 45.
214 (1995) 21 EHRR 482.

suspension of enforcement had the reasonable aim of preventing people becoming homeless and was proportional.[215]

18.75 The Court has stated that it will 'respect the legislature's assessment' in tax matters unless 'it is devoid of reasonable foundation'.[216] The Commission has summarised the position as follows:

> a financial liability arising out of the raising of taxes or contributions may adversely affect the guarantee of ownership if it places an excessive burden on the person concerned or fundamentally interferes with his financial position. However, it is in the first place for the national authorities to decide what kind of taxes or contributions are to be collected. Furthermore the decisions in this area will commonly involve the appreciation of political, economic and social questions which the Convention leaves within the competence of the Contracting States.[217]

In addition, taxation measures may constitute a violation of Convention rights if they are discriminatory in effect.[218] Applying the proportionality test in 'tax cases' the court has held the following measures to be justified: the seizure of property subject to a retention of title clause to pay tax owed by the purchaser,[219] retrospective legislation to remedy technical defects in taxation legislation[220] and 'windfall taxes'.[221] However, in *Hentrich v France*[222] the Court found that the exercise of a right of pre-emption by the Commissioner of Revenue was disproportionate and a breach of Article 1 of the First Protocol.

(d) Justification and the 'fair balance test'

18.76 It is now clear that when considering whether an interference with the peaceful enjoyment of possessions is justified:

> the Court must determine whether a fair balance was struck between the demands of the general interest of the community and the requirements of the protection of the individual's fundamental rights. The search for this balance is inherent in the whole of the Convention and is also reflected in the structure of Article 1.[223]

---

[215] But see *Scollo v Italy* (1995) 22 EHRR 514 in which the interference was disproportionate because of the applicant's personal circumstances.

[216] *Gasus Dösier-und Fördertechnik GmbH v Netherlands* (1995) 20 EHRR 403 para 60.

[217] *S and T v Sweden* (1986) 50 DR 121, EComm HR; see also *Svenska Managementgruppen v Sweden* (1985) 45 DR 211, EComm HR.

[218] See para 17.79ff above.

[219] See *Gasus* (n 216 above); but see the dissenting opinions of Judges Foighel, Russo and Jungwiert, 439-441 and the criticism of this decision in McBride (n 213 above) 44.

[220] *A, B, C, D v United Kingdom* (1981) 23 DR 203; *National and Provincial Building Society v United Kingdom* (1997) 25 EHRR 127.

[221] *Wasa Liv Omsesidigt v Sweden* (1988) 58 DR 163, EComm HR.

[222] (1994) 18 EHRR 440.

[223] *Sporrong and Lönnroth v Sweden* (1982) 5 EHRR 35 para 69; see also *Stran Greek Refineries and Stratis Andreadis v Greece* (1994) 19 EHRR 293 para 69.

This approach is taken whichever of the three rules applies.[224] However, the detailed application of the 'fair balance' test will not be the same in all circumstances.[225]

In order to satisfy the 'fair balance test' two conditions must be fulfilled: **18.77**

- the interference must have a 'legitimate aim';
- there must be a reasonable relationship of proportionality between the means employed and the aim pursued.[226]

In determining whether these requirements are met the Court recognises that states enjoy a wide margin of appreciation.[227] Thus, where the legislature has made a choice by enacting laws which it considers to be in the general interest, the possible existence of other solutions does not render the legislation unjustified since it is not the role of the Court to say whether the legislation represented the best solution.[228]

The leading case is *Sporrong and Lönnroth v Sweden*.[229] The applicant's properties were subject to expropriation permits and prohibitions on construction pending a redevelopment of the business centre by the City of Stockholm. The permits and prohibition orders remained in place for 23 and 25 years in one case and for 8 and 12 years in the other. Even though the Court was prepared to concede a wide margin to the state in the 'complex and difficult' matters of city planning, it found the 'inflexibility' of the Swedish arrangements precluded 'a fair balance'. The interference was unacceptable on grounds that it left the property owners in a position of great uncertainty over a very long period, without any effective remedy. It found that the applicants had borne: **18.78**

> an individual and excessive burden which could have been rendered legitimate only if they had the possibility of seeking a reduction of the time-limits or of claiming compensation.[230]

Two factors are of particular importance in deciding whether there is a 'fair balance'. First, whether the property owner is entitled to compensation for the **18.79**

224 See *Fredin v Sweden (No 1)* (1991) 13 EHRR 784 para 51.

225 See eg in *Gillow v United Kingdom* (1986) 11 EHRR 335 para 148, the Commission suggested that the application of the proportionality principle is different in cases involving deprivation and cases involving control of use.

226 See *Mellacher v Austria* (1989) 12 EHRR 391 para 48; *Chassagnou and others v France* (1999) 7 BHRC 151 para 75; and for a general discussion of the principle of proportionality, see para 6.40ff above.

227 See eg *Fredin v Sweden (No 1)* (n 224 above) para 51; and for a general discussion of the doctrine of proportionality, see para 6.31ff above.

228 *Mellacher v Austria* (n 226 above) para 53; *Panikian v Bulgaria* (1997) 24 EHRR CD 63.

229 (1982) 5 EHRR 35.

230 Ibid para 73.

interference. This was an significant factor in *Sporrong and Lönnroth v Sweden*[231] and has been prominent in other cases. Thus, the administration of a scheme for the consolidation of agricultural holdings in the interest of their economic exploitation was found to be in violation of Article 1: 16 years after the scheme had been implemented it had still to be concluded and no means of redress for interim losses of the applicants had been provided.[232]

18.80 Secondly, the test includes a procedural element. The absence of a 'fair balance' in *Sporrong and Lönnroth* was attributed to the lack of any procedure by which the expropriation permits and prohibition orders might have been challenged, and the failure to provide compensation for the losses that ensued.[233]

18.81 The 'fair balance' test has not been satisfied by the state in a number of cases. In *Chassagnou v France*[234] the applicants were opposed to hunting but the hunting rights over their land had been transferred by statute to an approved hunting association. The Court held that this was for the legitimate aim of improving the technical organisation of hunting but was disproportionate to this aim. As a result, the statute 'upsets the fair balance to be struck between protection of the right of property and the requirements of the general interest'.[235] In *Immobiliare Saffi v Italy*[236] it was held that a system of temporary suspension of possession orders pursued a legitimate aim. However, as this system risked placing an excessive burden on landlords it had to have procedural safeguards to ensure that it operated in a way which was not arbitrary or unforeseeable. The absence of such safeguards meant that, on the facts,[237] the fair balance had been upset.[238] In *Beyeler v Italy*[239] the Court held that a delay of five years in the exercise by the state of a right of preemption led to it obtaining an unjust enrichment which was incompatible with the requirement of 'fair balance'.

D. The Impact of the Human Rights Act

(1) Introduction

18.82 The right to property is well established as a fundamental one in English law. However, the protection available has been limited in two ways. First, it has

[231] (1982) 5 EHRR 35.

[232] See *Poiss v Austria* (1987) 10 EHRR 231.

[233] See also *Katte Klitsche de la Grange v Italy* (1994) 19 EHRR 368 para 46, in which one of the factors which counted against the applicant was that he had not used a procedure available to him.

[234] (1999) 7 BHRC 151.

[235] Ibid para 85.

[236] (1999) 7 BHRC 151; see also *AO v Italy* Judgment, 30 May 2000.

[237] The applicant's possession order was not enforced over a period of 11 years.

[238] Ibid para 59.

[239] Judgment of 5 Jan 2000 para 121.

traditionally only been available for the 'core' cases of deprivation of possession or transfer of title. Regulation of the *use* of property has not, in general, been recognised as giving rise to an interference attracting protection. Secondly and more importantly, like all fundamental rights in English law, the right to property has always been subject to unfettered interference by Parliament. Article 1 of the First Protocol could provide stronger protections in both areas. However, the Strasbourg authorities have been reluctant to depart from the 'public interest' assessment of public authorities and the 'fair balance' has usually come down in favour of the 'general interest'. If this approach is followed by the English courts, the impact of Article 1 of the First Protocol is unlikely to be substantial.

(2) United Kingdom cases prior to the Human Rights Act

(a) Introduction

A large number of UK cases have been brought under Article 1 of the First Protocol. These can be considered under six heads: compulsory acquisition, landlord and tenant cases, seizure and forfeiture, taxation, state benefits and other cases. Only four UK cases have been held to be admissible by the Commission and no violation has been found by the Court. **18.83**

(b) Compulsory acquisition

The case of *Lithgow v United Kingdom*[240] arose out of the nationalisation of the British shipbuilding industry. The applicants claimed that the compensation which they had received was grossly inadequate and discriminatory because it did not take into account increases in the value of the companies. The Court accepted that compensation must normally be reasonably related to the value of the property but there was not a guarantee of full compensation in all circumstances.[241] The Court held that the decisions regarding compensation could not be characterised as 'manifestly without reasonable foundation' and, as a result, were within the United Kingdom's margin of appreciation. **18.84**

In *Maggiulli v United Kingdom*[242] the compulsory acquisition of property by a local authority in circumstances in which the landlord was unable to commence repair work due to the presence of tenants was not a violation of Article 1. The acquisition pursued the legitimate aim of the improvement of housing and the local authority's refusal to adjourn further the implementation of the compulsory purchase order did not infringe the principle of proportionality. **18.85**

---

240 (1986) 8 EHRR 329, see generally, J Andrews, 'Compensation for Nationalisation in the UK' (1986) 12 ELR 65.

241 (1986) 8 EHRR 329 para 121.

242 Application 12736/87, 5 May 1988, EComm HR.

18.86 In *S v United Kingdom*[243] the UK Government had acquired 75 acres of a Highland estate under compulsory purchase powers for the purposes of building a road. The Commission found that the terms of the compulsory purchase did not infringe the principle of proportionality.

(c) Leasehold property cases

18.87 The case of *James v United Kingdom*[244] was an application by the trustees of the estate of the Duke of Westminster in which it was contended that the compulsory transfer of the freehold of properties under the Leasehold Reform Act 1967 was a breach of Article 1 of the First Protocol. It was accepted that there had been a deprivation of property; the issue was whether this was in the 'public interest'. The Court held that:

> a taking of property effected in pursuance of legitimate social, economic or other policies may be 'in the public interest', even if the community at large has no direct use or enjoyment of the property taken.[245]

The Court went on to hold that the legislation pursued a legitimate social objective, namely, the prevention of unjust enrichment of the landlord on reversion of the property.[246] Finally, having regard to the State's wide margin of appreciation it had not been shown that the terms on which compensation was payable to the landlord did not achieve a fair balance between the general interests of society and the landlord's property rights.[247]

18.88 In *Kilbourn v United Kingdom*[248] the Commission took the view that rent control legislation 'pursues a legitimate aim of social policy' and the Rent Acts were an appropriate means of achieving that aim.[249] In *X* v *United Kingdom*[250] the applicant was a tenant whose lease had been the subject of forfeiture. The applicant complained that under the then legislation there was no jurisdiction to grant relief because the order had been obtained in the county court. The Commission held that the state was not responsible under Article 1 of the First Protocol when there is a dispute between private parties about a lease. As a result, the complaint was inadmissible.

(d) Seizure and forfeiture

18.89 In *Handyside v United Kingdom*[251] the applicant's property, copies of the 'Little

---

243 Application 13135/87, 4 Jul 1988, EComm HR.

244 (1986) 8 EHRR 123; see generally, J Andrews, 'Leasehold Enfranchisement and the Public Interest in the UK' (1986) 11 ELR 366.

245 n 244 above para 45.

246 Ibid para 56.

247 Ibid.

248 (1986) 8 EHRR 81.

249 See *Mellacher v Austria* (1989) 12 EHRR 391 para 55, para 18.77 above.

250 (1988) 10 EHRR 149, 155.

251 (1976) 1 EHRR 737.

Red Schoolbook' was seized and subsequently destroyed as obscene. It was held that the destruction was authorised by the second paragraph of Article 1 of the First Protocol as they were items whose use had been lawfully adjudged to be illicit and dangerous to the general interest.[252]

The application in the *AGOSI* case[253] concerned the seizure by customs officials of krugerrands to which the applicant had legal title. Under the general principles of law recognised in all Contracting States, smuggled goods could be the object of confiscation. The Court held that the availability of judicial review was sufficient to satisfy the procedural requirements of the second paragraph of Article 1. In *Air Canada v United Kingdom*[254] the applicants complained about powers of seizure of aircraft used for the carrying of drugs pending the payment of a £50,000 penalty. This amounted to 'control of use' of property. Taking into account the large quantity of drugs seized and the value of the aircraft, the requirement to pay £50,000 was not disproportionate to the aim pursued and there was no violation of Article 1 of the First Protocol. **18.90**

(e) Taxation

In *A, B, C, D v United Kingdom*[255] the Commission found that retrospective legislation to combat a particular form of tax avoidance was justified. The case of *National and Provincial Building Society v United Kingdom*[256] concerned retrospective legislation to remedy technical defects in tax legislation affecting building societies. The Court accepted that the legislation was an interference with the enjoyment of the building societies' 'possessions'. The case was considered under the third paragraph of Article 1. The Court held that the actions taken did not upset the balance between the protection of the societies' rights and the public interest in securing the payment of taxes. **18.91**

In *NAP Holdings UK Ltd v United Kingdom*[257] the applicant was assessed for capital gains tax on the sale of shares on a basis which, although based on the Revenue's understanding of the position, turned out to be incorrect. As a result, the applicant was assessed for tax on a gain of £424m rather than £31m. Amending legislation was subsequently brought in to restore the position as the Revenue understood it to be but was not retroactive. The Commission pointed out that the legislature's assessment in tax matters was to be respected unless devoid of reasonable foundation. The application was held to be inadmissible. **18.92**

[252] Ibid para 62.
[253] *Allegemeine Gold-und Silberscheideanstalt v United Kingdom* (1986) 9 EHRR 1.
[254] (1995) 20 EHRR 150.
[255] (1981) 23 DR 203.
[256] (1997) 25 EHRR 127.
[257] Application 27721/95, 12 Apr 1996.

(f) State benefits

18.93 In *Szrabjer and Clarke v United Kingdom*[258] the applicants were prisoners who were entitled to state pensions. No payments were made whilst they were in prison. The applicants complained that the suspension of payment of the earnings related element of their pensions amounted to a deprivation of property. The Commission held that the state earnings related pension did constitute a 'possession'. However, the terms of the scheme made it clear that payments would be suspended during periods of imprisonment. The prisoner was being kept at state expense and, as a result, it was in the public interest that pension payments be suspended. An application by a prisoner concerning the removal of Industrial Injuries Invalidity benefit was also held to be inadmissible.[259] In *Nahon v United Kingdom*[260] the applicant was refused unemployment benefit because she was in receipt of an occupational pension. The Commission accepted that, because the applicant had contributed to the national insurance fund for a number of years, her claim to benefit fell within Article 1. However, it was held that:

> the 'means testing' of social welfare benefits cannot, of itself, be contrary to Article 1 of Protocol No 1 of the Convention. The aim of social welfare benefits is to provide those in need with financial support, and means testing is no more than a method of assessing need.

18.94 In *Coke v United Kingdom*[261] the Commission held that a number of applications relating to the Armed Forces Pension Scheme were inadmissible under Article 1 of the First Protocol because, amongst other reasons, the widows who brought the claims had made no contributions and did not, therefore, have any right to the enjoyment of possessions. A series of similar applications were all held to be inadmissible on the same day.[262]

18.95 Applications in relation to the non-availability of statutory widow's benefit for widowers have been more successful. In *Cornwell v United Kingdom*[263] the applicant complained that the lack of provision for widower's benefits was a breach of Article 1 of the First Protocol taken together with Article 14 on the basis that it involved sex discrimination. The case was conceded by the Government and a friendly settlement was reached. A friendly settlement was also reached in *Crossland v United Kingdom*[264] involving payment of the widow's bereavement allowance to the applicant, coupled with an announcement that it was to be abolished in April 2000.

258 [1998] EHRLR 230.
259 *Carlin v United Kingdom* (1997) 25 EHRR CD 75.
260 Application 34190/96, 23 Oct 1997, EComm HR.
261 [1999] EHRLR 130.
262 See the Note at [1999] EHRLR 130.
263 (1999) 27 EHRR CD 62.
264 Application 36120/97, 9 Nov 1999.

(g) Other cases

In *X v United Kingdom*[265] the applicant complained that there was a breach of Article 1 of the First Protocol as the result of a judgment under the terms of which it was found liable to pay £40 million as a result of the frustration of contracts for exploitation of oil concessions in Libya.[266] The Commission held that this did not engage the responsibility of the state because there had been no supervening act of administration or legislation affecting the applicant's position.[267] In *S v United Kingdom*[268] the Commission held that a person's occupation of a property without a legal right (the same sex partner of the tenant) did not have a 'possession' for the purposes of Article 1 of the First Protocol. **18.96**

In *Stevens and Knight v United Kingdom*[269] the Commission held that the operation of the Compensation Recovery Scheme did not infringe the applicant's rights to the enjoyment of possessions. It took the view that the principle that social welfare benefits provided by the state could be recovered from a subsequent award of damages could not be said to be incompatible with Article 1 of the First Protocol. The fact that the CRU recovered the full sum of the applicant's damages[270] was not disproportionate.[271] **18.97**

In *Panvert v United Kingdom*[272] the applicant had been required to demolish part of a building constructed without planning permission. This was a control of use of property and a fair balance had been struck between the applicant's interests and the general interest in planning controls. As a result, the application was declared inadmissible. **18.98**

(3) General impact

(a) Property litigation

In the course of property litigation there are a number of situations in which the court refuses to allow a property owner strictly to enforce his rights but grants some 'indulgence' to the defendant in the wider interest. Perhaps the clearest example of this arises in mortgagee's possession actions relating to dwelling houses in which the courts have extensive statutory powers[273] to adjourn the proceedings **18.99**

[265] (1983) 33 DR 247.

[266] *BP Exploration Company (Libya) Ltd v Hunt (No 2)* [1983] 2 AC 352.

[267] See also *X v United Kingdom* (1988) 10 EHRR 149, para 18.40 above.

[268] (1986) 47 DR 274, EComm HR.

[269] [1999] EHRLR 126.

[270] The applicants having agreed settlements for all heads of damage which were less than the sum claimed for loss of earnings.

[271] See also *Kightley v United Kingdom* Application 28778/95, 9 Apr 1997.

[272] Application 26889/95, 12 Apr 1996, EComm HR; see also *Ryder v United Kingdom* (1989) 11 EHRR 80 (enforcement notice in relation to property used for business purposes for over 20 years in general interest).

[273] See Administration of Justice Act 1970, s 36 and Administration of Justice Act 1970, s 8.

and to make a suspended order for possession. The suspension of possession orders is a 'control over the use of property' and such orders could be challenged under Article 1 of the First Protocol. The suspension of possession orders has the reasonable aim of preventing large numbers of people becoming homeless but there will be a breach of the Convention if a 'fair balance' is not struck between mortgagee and mortgagor.[274] If the court were to suspend an order conditional on payments towards the arrears which made full repayment highly unlikely then, it is arguable, that the balance would be upset.

(b) Taxation

18.100 Article 1 of the First Protocol recognises the right of the state to 'enforce such laws as it deems necessary . . . to secure the payment of taxes or other contributions or penalties'. The Strasbourg authorities have taken a conservative approach to this provision and there has been only one finding of violation in a tax case.[275] It is highly unlikely that a tax raising statute would be held to be incompatible with Article 1. There are, however, a number of points on which UK tax law may be susceptible to challenge on the ground of incompatibility with the Convention: these include the present provisions relating to the recovery of overpaid VAT and the operation of windfall taxes.[276]

(c) Compensation for interference with property rights

18.101 Article 1 may affect the obligation of public authorities to pay compensation where there has been a deprivation of property.[277] It has been suggested that the development of a legal framework for the right to compensation would be enhanced by the Court taking into account, in particular, the nature of the interference to the property right, the extent of the interference, the degree of damage caused to the applicant and the question of whether the interference infringes the legitimate expectation of the applicant upon which he has relied.[278]

(4) Specific areas of impact

(a) Commercial law

18.102 Rent control legislation involves the 'control of use' of property. The Rent Acts have a substantial adverse impact on the value of a landlord's interest in a rented property but are not 'targeted' to assist poor tenants; poor landlords and rich tenants also have the burden and benefit respectively of the legislation. Although the

---

[274] See para 18.76ff above.

[275] *Hentrich v France* (1994) 18 EHRR 440.

[276] For a general discussion see J Peacock and F Fitzpatrick, 'Tax Law' in C Baker (ed), *The Human Rights Act 1998: A Practitioner's Guide* (Sweet & Maxwell, 1998) 416–420.

[277] See para 18.43ff above.

[278] D Anderson, 'Compensation for Interference with Property' [1999] EHRLR 543.

Commission has expressed the view that rent control legislation 'pursues a legitimate aim of social policy' and the Rent Acts were an appropriate means of achieving that aim[279] the position is not clear cut. It is noteworthy that similar legislation in Ireland has been held to be a breach of 'property rights' in the Irish Constitution.[280] It is arguable that the Rent Acts do not achieve a 'fair balance' between the public interest in providing cheaper housing and the private interests of landlords. It has already been suggested that 'self-help' remedies such as distress for rent, forfeiture by re-entry or the power of a mortgagee to obtain possession without a court order[280a] will be held to be contrary to Article 6.[280b] It is also aguable that the self-help remedy of 'distress for rent' will breach Article 1 of the First Protocol.[280c]

(b) Local government law

Local authorities have extensive powers of compulsory purchase.[281] These include powers to acquire properties subject to repair notices[282] and powers to acquire land in relation to slum clearance.[283] The exercise of such powers could be challenged by property owners under Article 1 of the First Protocol[284] although it is likely that the 'fair balance' test would be met in all but the most exceptional cases. **18.103**

Under the Housing Act 1996[285] a landlord can seek possession of a property on the ground that the tenant or a visitor has been: (a) guilty of conduct causing or likely to cause a nuisance or annoyance to a person residing, visiting or engaging in lawful activity in the locality, or (b) has been convicted of using the dwelling house or allowing it to be used for immoral or unlawful purposes; or (c) has been convicted of an arrestable offence, committed in or in the locality of the building. The exercise of such powers involves a deprivation of property, namely the tenancy. In some circumstances, this deprivation would take place when the tenant was not in breach of any of the terms of the tenancy. The 'fair balance' test must, therefore, be applied. Although the aim of controlling anti-social behaviour is a **18.104**

---

279 *Kilbourn v United Kingdom* (1986) 8 EHRR 81 (the Commission were influenced by the fact that the applicant had inherited the properties in question and it is possible that a different conclusion might be reached on other facts).

280 *Blake v A-G* [1982] IR 117; see para 18.130 below.

280a See *Ropaigealach v Barclays Bank* [1999] 3 WLR 17.

280b See para 11.318 above.

280c See J Karas, 'Feudal Rights in the 21st Century. Can the Law of Distress Survive the Convention?' in Wilberforce Chambers, *The Essential Human Rights Act* (Wilberforce Chambers, 2000).

281 See generally, S Bailey, *Cross on Principles of Local Government Law* (2nd edn, Sweet & Maxwell, 1997) Chap 5.

282 Housing Act 1985, Pt VI.

283 Ibid Pt IX.

284 Cf M Supperstone and J Goudie, *Local Authorities and the Human Rights Act 1998* (Butterworths, 1999) 99.

285 s 144 relates to secure tenancies and s 148 to assured tenancies.

legitimate one, it is arguable that the means employed are not proportionate.[286] There are a number of reasons for this. First, the power could be exercised where the level of disturbance is low or where there has only been a small number of incidents. Secondly, the statutory language is open-textured and could, potentially, include a range of activities not properly described as 'anti-social behaviour'. Thirdly, there is no requirement that any other, less drastic, means of controlling anti-social behaviour have been tried before possession is sought. It is, therefore, arguable that in some circumstances it will be unlawful for a local authority to seek such an order and for a court to make one.

(c) Planning and environment law

18.105 Planning legislation is aimed at the 'control of use' of property. However, it is also arguable that some kinds of control will constitute a 'deprivation' of property. There are a number of areas in which it is arguable that Article 1 of the First Protocol will be breached.[287] First, under English law there is no right to compensation where planning permission reduces the value of adjoining land. It is arguable that, where a landowner suffers 'abnormal or special prejudice' from such a grant of planning permission, this will constitute a 'deprivation' of property or an interference with enjoyment.[288] The English courts would then have to consider the 'fair balance' issue. A right to compensation may arise if section 10 of the Compulsory Purchase Act 1965 is read so as to be compatible with Article 1 of the First Protocol.[288a]

18.105A Article 1 may also be breached by the current planning procedure. It has been suggested that, read in conjunction with Article 6, Article 1 will alter the burden of proof in enforcement proceedings by placing it on a public authority; and should give the successful appellant at an enforcement notice inquiry and, perhaps, at a planning appeal, a right to claim costs.[288b]

18.106 Under the legislation concerning 'blight notices',[289] some property owners are entitled to require a public authority whose proposed works are 'blighting' their property to acquire the land.[290] However, this procedure only applies to domestic properties or properties which the owner occupies and which have an annual

[286] See J Alder, 'Housing and the Human Rights Act 1998' [1999] HLJ 67, 71.

[287] See T Corner, 'Planning, Environment and the European Convention on Human Rights' [1998] JPL 301; M Barnes, 'Planning and Compensation' and 'Public Authorities and Land Compensation' in Wilberforce Chambers, *The Essential Human Rights Act 1998* (Wilberforce Chambers 2000).

[288] See *S v France* (1990) 65 DR 250, EComm HR.

[288a] M Barnes, 'Public Authorities and Land Compensation' in *The Essential Human Rights Act 1998* (n 287 above).

[288b] M Barnes, 'Public Authorities and Land Compensation' in ibid.

[289] Town and Country Planning Act 1990, Pt VI, Chap II.

[290] For example, where the land is affected by a compulsory purchase order, ibid Sch 13.

value of less than £18,000. It is arguable that the owners of property who do not have such a 'qualifying interest' are suffering a deprivation of property without compensation. If so, the English courts would have to consider whether the present 'blight notice' procedure strikes a 'fair balance'. The statutory regime applying to listed buildings may also require re-examination as a result of Article 1. It is arguable that Article 1 requires a consultation process before a building is listed and the payment of compensation if the building is listed.[290a]

The practice of planning authorities obtaining 'planning gain' by means of section 106 planning obligations[291] may give rise to issues under Article 1 of the First Protocol. Under such an obligation, the owner of the land may be required to dedicate part of the land to public use as a condition of obtaining planning permission. In the United States, such a condition would be regarded as a 'taking' of property attracting a right to compensation.[292] Even under the less stringent regime of the Convention, it might be argued that in some cases a 'fair balance' was not being achieved as the planning authority was 'controlling the use' of property for an ulterior purpose, not directly related to the planning considerations relating to the land for which planning permission was being sought. **18.107**

(d) Social security

The relationship between 'property rights' and benefits conferred by the state is not straightforward. State incentives, subsidies, grants and welfare benefits are, potentially, extremely valuable and, arguably, constitute property.[293] The question arises as to whether they will attract the protection of Article 1 of the First Protocol. The US jurisprudence recognises a very wide range of rights as 'property' attracting the protection of the 'due process clause': an interest in state benefits will be 'property' if there is an 'entitlement' to such benefits.[294] However, courts in the Commonwealth have, in general, taken the more restrictive view that an individual property only exists once the state has assumed the obligation to pay a specified and ascertainable amount.[295] **18.108**

The Court and the Commission have also taken a similar restrictive view holding that, for example, Article 1 applies to contributory state benefits but not to **18.109**

290a See M Barnes, 'Public Authorities and Land Compensation' in *The Essential Human Rights Act 1998* (n 287 above), but see *Penn Central Transportation Co v City of New York* (1978) 438 US 104 (the New York City's Landmarks Preservation Law was a general law passed in the public interest which did not violate the Fifth Amendment prohibition on taking private property without compensation).

291 Under Town and Country Planning Act 1990, s 106 (as amended).

292 See para 18.118 below.

293 See para 18.107ff above.

294 See *Board of Regents of States Colleges v Roth* (1972) 408 US 564; and see para 18.116 below.

295 *Hewlett v Minister of Finance* [1981] ZLR 571, SC Zim; but see the wider definition of property in *Bahadur v A-G* [1989] LRC (Const) 632, para 18.144 below.

non-contributory benefits.[296] What appears to be required 'is that the applicant demonstrate that he has a legal right to some benefit if he satisfies certain conditions, rather than that he seeks to ensure that a discretion is exercised in his favour'.[297] Nevertheless, the line is often difficult to draw and it is likely that those claiming entitlement to a wide range of state benefits will seek to challenge their removal under Article 1 of the First Protocol. Challenges have been brought in recent years in relation to benefits as varied as unemployment benefit,[298] statutory widow's benefit,[299] the Armed Forces Pension Scheme,[300] Industrial Injuries Invalidity benefit,[301] and the State Earnings Related Pension Scheme.[302] It is likely that a wide range of social security decisions will be challenged under the Convention. However, it seems that, in the absence of discrimination,[303] the Government will be able to satisfy the 'fair balance' test in all but the most extreme cases.

Appendix 1: The Canadian Charter of Rights

18.110 The Canadian Bill of Rights of 1960 provides that:

> It is hereby recognised and declared that in Canada there have existed and shall continue to exist . . . the following human rights and fundamental freedoms namely
>
> (a) the right of the individual to . . . enjoyment of property, and the right not to be deprived thereof except by due process of law.[304]

This provision remains in force, despite the adoption of the Charter.[305] It applies to federal, but not provincial, laws.

18.111 An attempt to include a similar provision in the Charter was defeated in the House of Commons on 23 April 1981 and section 7 of the Charter contains no reference to property. It has been held that the intentional exclusion from this section of the right to property leads to the general inference that economic rights are not within section 7.[306] Thus, the section does not cover employment rights[307] or the economic right to social assistance.[308]

[296] See para 18.38 above.

[297] D Harris, M O'Boyle and C Warbrick, *Law of the European Convention on Human Rights* (Butterworths, 1995) 518.

[298] *Nahon v United Kingdom*, Application 34190/96, 23 Oct 1997, EComm HR.

[299] *Cornwell v United Kingdom* (1999) 27 EHRR CD 62.

[300] *Coke v United Kingdom* [1999] EHRLR 130.

[301] *Carlin v United Kingdom* (1997) 25 EHRR CD 75.

[302] *Szrabjer and Clarke v United Kingdom* [1998] EHRLR 230.

[303] See para 17.79ff above.

[304] s 1(a).

[305] See P W Hogg, *Constitutional Law of Canada* (4th edn, Carswell, 1997), para 32.1.

[306] *Irwin Toy Ltd v Quebec (A-G)* [1989] 1 SCR 927.

[307] See eg *Arlington Crane v Ontario* (1988) 56 DLR (4th) 209.

[308] *Conrad (Guardian ad Litem of) v Halifax (County)* (1993) 12 NSR (2d) 251; affirmed on other grounds, 130 NSR (2d) 305, CA.

It is a rule of statutory interpretation in the common law of Canada that a statute which takes private property is to be read as requiring the payment of compensation.[309] The common law right to compensation can only be ousted by express provision.[310] In *Manitoba Fisheries Ltd v The Queen*[310a] the Canadian Freshwater Fish Marketing Act conferred the monopoly of exporting fish from Manitoba on a statutory corporation. The applicants had previously been exporting fish and the effect of the Act was to destroy their business. The Supreme Court held that they had been deprived of their property, namely the goodwill of the business, even though that goodwill had not been directly transferred to the corporation. The substantial effect of the provision was to enable the corporation to acquire their previous customers. In *The Queen in Right of British Columbia v Tener*[311] it was held that a statute which restricted the plaintiffs' ability to exploit their mineral rights over land in a provincial park was a taking of property which had to be compensated. These cases have expanded the class of 'takings' for which compensation is payable.[311a] **18.112**

Appendix 2: The New Zealand Bill of Rights Act

The New Zealand Bill of Right Act contains no right to property. Nevertheless, the protection of the right to property is recognised as an important constitutional consideration and any intended statutory erosion of it should be spelled out in the plainest terms.[312] **18.113**

Appendix 3: Human Rights Cases in Other Jurisdictions

(1) Introduction

The constitutional instruments of most common law jurisdictions contain provisions for the protection of property rights.[313] The most well known of these is contained in the Fifth Amendment to the US Constitution which provides that: **18.114**

> No person shall . . . be deprived of . . . property, without due process of law; nor shall private property be taken for public use, without just compensation.

The political controversy generated by this provision has led to a general suspicion of 'property rights'.[314] Commercial interests sought to use the Constitution to resist state **18.115**

[309] See generally, Hogg (n 305 above) 28.5(d).

[310] *Manitoba Fisheries Ltd v The Queen* [1979] 1 SCR 101.

[310a] Ibid; but see *Home Orderly Services v Manitoba* (1987) 43 DLR (4th) 300 (Government took over health care business, held no goodwill independent of government and no compensation).

[311] [1985] 1 SCR 533; see also *Casamiro Resource Corp v British Columbia* (1991) 80 DLR (4th) 1, BCCA.

[311a] See Hogg (n 305 above) 714.

[312] See eg *Choudry v A-G* [1999] 2 NZLR 582, 593.

[313] For a general survey see T Allan, 'Commonwealth Constitutions and the Right Not to be Deprived of Property' (1993) 42 ICLQ 523.

[314] Thus, the Canadian Charter was framed so as to 'banish *Lochner* from Canada', see *Re BC Motor Vehicle Act* [1985] 2 SCR 486, 504-505.

economic regulation. In the famous case of *Lochner v New York*[315] the Supreme Court struck down a law prohibiting employers from employing bakery workers for more than 10 hours a day and 60 hours a week. This approach held sway for the first three decades of the twentieth century. The Court began to move away from it in the mid 1930s.[316] In the field of economic regulation, the courts now defer to the legislature.[317]

18.116 Nevertheless, a wide range of 'property rights' has been recognised as attracting 'due process protection' in US Constitutional law. In particular, there has been an increasing recognition that rights conferred by the state are a form of property.[318] Such rights include the following:[319] housing payments,[320] the right to remain as a student within the school system,[321] the right to hold a driving licence,[322] and the employment rights of government employees.[323] Such rights can only be terminated if the requirements of 'procedural due process' are satisfied.

18.117 Both federal and state governments have the power to take private property, the power of 'eminent domain'.[324] Although the property can only be taken for 'public use', once the legislature has declared a taking to be for public use, the role of the courts is a narrow one.[325] As long as the Government is willing to pay fair market value for property which is taken, it will be constitutional provided that it is 'rationally related to a conceivable public purpose'.[326] However, the 'takings' clause cannot be avoided by deeming provisions seeking to redefine the extent of property rights.[327]

18.118 The US courts have developed a considerable jurisprudence as to the meaning of 'taking'. The regulation of property rights can, in certain circumstances, be treated as a 'taking', even if the state does not acquire anything.[328] A temporary loss of use of property will be a 'taking' requiring compensation for the period during which use was denied.[329] The imposition of a condition on a grant of planning will amount to a taking unless there is an

[315] (1905) 198 US 45; see eg A Cox, *The Court and the Constitution* (Houghton Mifflin, 1987) 129–137.

[316] See eg *Nebbia v New York* (1934) 291 US 502 (upholding minimum price for milk); *West Coast Hotel v Parrish* (1937) 300 US 379 (upholding minimum wage for women).

[317] See generally, J Nowak and R Rotunda, *Constitutional Law* (5th edn, West Publishing, 1995) paras 11.1–11.4.

[318] See the highly influential article, C Reich, 'The New Property' (1964) 73 Yale LJ 733; and see M Chaskalson, 'The Problem with Property: Thoughts on the Constitutional Protection of Property in the United States and the Commonwealth' (1993) 9 SAJHR 1449.

[319] Nowak and Rotunda (n 317 above) para 13.5.

[320] *Goldberg v Kelly* (1970) 397 US 254.

[321] *Goss v Lopez* (1975) 419 US 565.

[322] *Bell v Burson* (1971) 402 US 535.

[323] *Perry v Sindermann* (1972) 408 US 593.

[324] This concept is discussed in *Burmah Oil Company Ltd v Lord Advocate* [1965] AC 75.

[325] *Berman v Parker* (1954) 348 US 26.

[326] *Hawaii Housing Authority v Midkiff* (1984) 467 US 229 (statute providing for taking residential property from lessors and transferring title to lessee), cf *James v United Kingdom* (1986) 8 EHRR 123, para 18.87 above.

[327] See eg *Webb's Fabulous Pharmacies v Beckwith* (1980) 449 US 155 (interest accruing from money paid into court 'deemed' to be property of the clerk: this was a 'taking').

[328] See *Pennsylvania Coal v Mahon* (1922) 260 US 393; see also *Lucas v South Carolina Coastal Council* (1992) 112 Sup Ct 2886.

[329] *First English Lutheran Church v Los Angeles County* (1987) 482 US 304.

essential nexus between a legitimate state interest and the condition[330] and a rough proportionality between the impact of the proposed measure and the condition imposed.[331] In one recent case, a plurality of the judges were even prepared to treat economic regulation as a form of 'taking'.[332] The due process clause limits the use of government agents to seize property from one private individual in order to convey it to another. For example, a provision allowing for seizure of goods by creditors without notice or hearing was struck down as unconstitutional.[332a]

(2) Australia

The first appearance of the right to property in a Commonwealth Constitution was in the Australian Constitution of 1901. Section 51 authorises the federal Parliament to make laws with respect to: **18.119**

> (xxxi) The acquisition of property on just terms from any State or person in respect of which the Parliament has powers to make laws . . .[333]

This provision is concerned with compulsory acquisition. Where the Government acquires property through negotiation and agreement, it is presumed that the terms agreed by the property owner are 'just terms'.[334] If acquisition of property can be authorised under other sections of the Constitution, such acquisition does not fall within section 51 (xxxi), and therefore does not have to be carried out on just terms.[335] Further, as stated in *Australian Tape Manufacturers Association Ltd v Commonwealth*:[336]

> In a case where an obligation to make a payment is imposed as genuine taxation, as a penalty for proscribed conduct, as compensation for a wrong done or damages for an injury inflicted, or as a genuine adjustment of the competing rights, claims or obligations of persons in a

[330] *Nollan v California Coastal Commission* (1987) 483 US 825 (planning permission to rebuild house made conditional on the grant of a public easement over applicant's land, the condition was a 'taking'); see generally, Nowak and Rotunda (n 317 above) para 11.12, 452.

[331] *Dolan v City of Tigard* (1994) 512 US 374 (planning permission conditional on decidation of a portion of property for flood control and traffic improvements was a 'taking' requiring compensation), see generally, Nowak and Rotunda (n 317 above) para 11.12, 454–455.

[332] *Eastern Enterprises v Apfel* (1998) 118 Sup Ct 2131; the court by a 5-4 majority struck down a requirement that coal mining companies retroactively pay health benefits to miners. Rehnquist CJ, O'Connor, Thomas and Scalia JJ treated this as a 'taking', Kennedy J concurred on the ground that the statute offended substantive due process.

[332a] *North Georgia Finishing v Di-Chem* (1975) 419 US 601; see generally C Antieau and W Rich, *Modern Constitutional Law*, (2nd edn, West Group, 1997), vol 2 para 36.16 and see the cases cited at para 5.50, n 200 above).

[333] See generally, P Hanks, *Constitutional Law in Australia* (2nd edn, Butterworths, 1996) Chap 14.2; G Williams, *Human Rights Under the Australian Constitution* (Oxford University Press, 1999) 141ff.

[334] *Trade Practices Commission v Tooth & Co Ltd* (1979) 142 CLR 397, 417.

[335] See *Mutual Pools & Staff Pty Ltd v Commonwealth* (1994) 179 CLR 155 (legislation limited right of manufacturer to recover moneys paid by the manufacturer by way of an unconstitutional tax; held that legislation fell outside s 51(xxxi)); *Re Director of Public Prosecutions, ex p Lawler* (1994) 179 CLR 270 (legislation authorising forfeiture of an unlicensed boat held to fall outside s 51(xxxi)); *Health Insurance Commission v Peverill* (1994) 179 CLR 226 (removal of medical practitioner's right to claim Medicare benefits in respect of medical services already provided was not an acquisition of property within s 51(xxxi)).

[336] (1993) 179 CLR 226.

particular relationship or area of activity, it is unlikely that there will be any acquisition of property within s 51(xxxi) of the Constitution.

18.120 The decision in *Nintendo Co Ltd v Centronics Pty Ltd*[337] illustrates that approach. In that case, legislation creating a right in the designer of an electronic circuit to restrain the use of that circuit by others was held not to constitute an acquisition of property. Rather, the legislation was a law for the adjustment and regulation of the competing claims, rights and liabilities of the designers or first makers of original circuit layouts and those who take advantage of, or benefit from, their work. The same approach was taken in *WSGAL Pty Ltd v Trade Practices Commission*.[338] That case concerned a provision authorising courts to order a person who had acquired shares in contravention of anti-monopoly legislation to sell those shares. The legislation was in the public interest as it re-established the competition which prevailed in the market before the occurrence of the prohibited acts, and prevented damage to the competition in the relevant markets; and was therefore outside the scope of section 51(xxxi), as it was a genuine adjustment of competing rights in the area of competition.[339]

18.121 The term 'acquisition' has been interpreted to include the assumption of control. In *Bank of New South Wales v Commonwealth*[340] legislation which authorised the Commonwealth Treasurer to assume control of the business of an Australian bank by displacing the bank's director in favour of its own nominee in effect stripped the bank and its shareholders of possession and control of the undertaking. 'Acquisition' also includes the Government's right to enter into possession of privately owned land for an indefinite period;[341] and the extinction of choses in action such as the statutory extinction of an injured worker's common law right to sue his employer.[342] However, a statutory right to payment out of public funds, although accepted as 'property' by a majority of the High Court in *Health Insurance Commission v Peverill*,[343] was a right inherently susceptible to variation, and therefore there was no acquisition of that right when the right was ended retrospectively. The right to exploit a limited resource has also been held to be 'property' within the terms of section 51(xxxi).[344]

18.122 The relevant acquisition of property need not be for the Government, but may be for other entities.[345] However, there must be some transfer of property. In *Trade Practices Commission v Tooth & Co Ltd*[346] a statutory provision prohibited a corporation which was a lessor of land from refusing to renew a lease of that land for the reason that the lessee was doing business with a competitor of the corporation. The High Court was divided as to

[337] (1994) 181 CLR 134.

[338] (1994) 51 FCR 115.

[339] See *Burton v Honan* (1952) 86 CLR 169 (customs legislation authorising forfeiture of illegally imported goods did not amount to an acquisition of property within s 51(xxxi)); *R v Smithers, ex p McMillan* (1982) 152 477 (confiscation of drug trafficking proceeds not an acquisition of property within s 51(xxxi).

[340] (1948) 76 CLR 1.

[341] *Minister of State for the Army v Dalziel* (1994) 68 CLR 261, 276.

[342] *Georgiadis v Australian and Overseas Telecommunications Commission* (1994) 179 CLR 297.

[343] (1994) 179 CLR 226.

[344] *Minister for Primary Industry and Energy v Davey* (1993) 47 FCR 151 (right to fish); *Commonwealth v Western Mining Corporation Ltd* (1996) 136 ALR 353 (right to explore for petroleum).

[345] *P J Magennis Pty Ltd v Commonwealth* (1949) 80 CLR 382.

[346] (1979) 142 CLR 397.

whether this constituted an acquisition of property by the state (albeit to benefit an individual), or whether the provision merely had the effect of deterring or punishing prohibited conduct. In any event, the Court concluded that if there was an acquisition, it was on just terms.

In *Commonwealth v Tasmania*[347] the State of Tasmania argued that certain federal legislation which restricted the State from using land for a wide variety of purposes amounted to an acquisition of property. A majority of the High Court held that while the legislation regulated land use, it did not give the federal government, or anyone else, any proprietary interest in any kind of property, nor was there a vesting of possession in any person.[348] Likewise, in *Australian Tape Manufacturers Association Ltd v Commonwealth*[349] legislation which authorised the private copying of sound recording for private and domestic purposes was not an acquisition of the property of the copyright holder in that recording. Although the legislation reduced the copyright holder's rights, it did not amount to an acquisition of those rights. The mere extinction or diminution of a proprietary right residing in one person does not necessarily result in the acquisition of a proprietary right by another; and the privilege extended to the copier was not proprietary in nature.[350] **18.123**

The acquisition of property must be on 'just terms'. That requires a balance to be drawn between the interests of the individual whose property is acquired and the interest of the community.[351] The general measure of compensation is market value, although replacement costs may be required in certain circumstances, for example when the property is not used for commercial purposes.[352] The decision concerning the level of compensation may be left with an administrative body, provided that the body's decision is amenable to judicial review.[353] **18.124**

(3) The Gambia

Section 18(1) of the Constitution of the Gambia provides that: **18.125**

> No property of any description shall be taken possession of compulsorily and no right over

[347] (1983) 158 CLR 1.

[348] But see dissenting judgement of Deane J (legislation which effectively froze State land until a federal government Minister had consented to development was an acquisition of property within s 51(xxxi)).

[349] (1993) 176 CLR 480.

[350] See also *Minister for Primary Industry and Energy v Davey* (1993) 47 FCR 151 (reduction of fish quotas of licence holders did not effect an acquisition of property, because nobody received the benefit resulting from the reduction as applied to an individual licence holder); *Waterhouse v Minister for the Arts and Territories* (1993) 43 FCR 175 (similar reasoning applied to uphold legislation prohibiting export of certain 'Australian objects'). These cases should be contrasted with *Commonwealth v Western Mining Corporation Ltd* (1996) 136 ALR 353, in which legislation extinguishing rights to explore for petroleum in the Timor Sea was held to be an acquisition of property. The Government received identifiable benefits, in that it was free to deal with the Timor Sea unencumbered by the rights of the former licence holder (in particular, the Government was able to vest rights over petroleum exploration in the Timor Sea in a joint authority established pursuant to a treaty with the Republic of Indonesia).

[351] *Nelungaloo Pty Ltd v Commonwealth of Australia* (1948) 75 CLR 495, 569. But see also *Georgiadis v Australian and Overseas Telecommunications Corporation* (1994) 179 CLR 297 (just terms requires full compensation).

[352] *Nelungaloo v Commonwealth* (n 351 above) 507.

[353] *Australian Apple and Pear Marketing Board v Tonking* (1942) 66 CLR 77, 99.

or interest in any such property shall be acquired compulsorily in any part of the Gambia except by or under the provision of a law that:

(a) requires the payment of adequate compensation therefor; and
(b) gives to any person claiming such compensation a right of access, for the determination of his interest in the property and the amount of compensation to the Supreme Court.

In *A-G of The Gambia v Momodou Jobe*[354] the Privy Council said that the term 'property' in this section should be read in a wide sense and included choses in action such as a debt owed by a banker to his customer. They went on to hold that a statutory provision which conferred a discretion on the executive to prevent a customer from exercising his contractual right to draw on his account would amount to a 'compulsory acquisition' of a right over or interest in the customer's property. However, on a true construction of the relevant legislation, this discretion was subject to the direction of the magistrate; and there was no contravention of section 18.

(4) India

18.126 Article 19 of the Indian Constitution 1949 provided[355] that:

(1) All persons shall have the right—. . .

(f) to acquire, hold and dispose of property.

This did not affect laws which imposed reasonable restrictions on the exercise of the right.[356] Article 31 provided that:

(1) No person shall be deprived of his property save by authority of law.

(2) No property shall be compulsorily acquired or requisitioned save for a public purpose and save by authority of law which provides for acquisition or requisitioning of the property for an amount which may be fixed by such law or which may be determined in accordance with such principles and given in such manner as may be specified in such law; and no such law shall be called in question in any court on the ground that the amount so fixed or determined is not adequate or that the whole or any part of such amount is to be given otherwise that in cash.

These provisions generated considerable case law.[357] They were replaced in controversial circumstances[358] by Article 300A which provides that:

No person shall be deprived of his property save by authority of law.

Under this Article there is no requirement for just compensation or indemnification of a person who has been deprived of property.[359]

18.127 'Property' had to be the subject matter of an acquisition or taking possession.[360]

[354] [1985] LRC (Const) 556, 565.

[355] This was preceded by the Government of India Act 1935, s 299.

[356] Art 19(5).

[357] See generally, H M Seervai, *Constitutional Law of India* (4th edn, N M Tripathi Ltd, 1991) Vol 1, 823ff (Art 19) and Vol 2, Chap XIV.

[358] See ibid 1354ff.

[359] *Khachar v Gujarat*, [1994] Supp 1 SCR 807, 852.

[360] *State of West Bengal v Subodh Gopal Bose* 1954 SCR 587, 673; it applied to abstract and concrete rights, *Swami Motor Transport (P) Ltd v Sankaraswamigal Mutt* (1963) Supp (1) SCR 282, 305.

'Deprivation' is to be distinguished from 'restriction' of ownership rights which falls short of dispossession of those rights.[361] Thus, there is no deprivation of property where an educational institution is temporarily deprived of its right to manage property.[362]

(5) Ireland

Article 40.3.3 of the Irish Constitution provides that: **18.128**

> 1. The State guarantees in its laws to respect, and, as far as practicable, by its laws to defend and vindicate the personal rights of the citizen.
> 2. The State shall, in particular, by its laws protect as best it may from unjust attack and, in the case of injustice done, vindicate the life, person, good name, and property rights of every citizen.'

Article 43 provides that:

> 1. 1. The State acknowledges that man, in virtue of his rational being, has the natural right, antecedent to positive law, to the private ownership of external goods.
>   2. The State accordingly guarantees to pass no law attempting to abolish the right of private ownership or the general right to transfer, bequeath, and inherit property.
> 2. 1. The State recognises, however, that the exercise of the rights mentioned in the foregoing provisions of this Article ought, in civil society, to be regulated by the principles of social justice.
>   2. The State, accordingly, may as occasion requires delimit by law the exercise of the said rights with a view to reconciling their exercise with the exigencies of the common good.

18.129 Both these provisions have been utilised in the courts in defence of property rights.[363] In *Blake v A-G*[364] the Supreme Court stated that Article 43 protects the institution of private property. In other words, the state cannot abolish private property as an institution.

18.130 Article 40.3 deals with a citizen's right to a particular item of property, and protects that right from unjust attack. Examples of restrictions to property rights which have been struck down include the following: rent control legislation which was arbitrary in operation;[365] retrospective changing of rules governing property rights;[366] legislation requiring construction of electricity masks over defendants' land for laying of electric lines, thereby constituting permanent interference with the land, without any compensation for that interference;[367] limitation period of two months without any exception for plaintiffs in ignorance of their rights;[368] and forfeiture of pension, superannuation allowance and gratuities of state employees upon their conviction for certain offences.[369]

---

361 *State of Bombay v Bhanji* (1955) 1 SCR 777, 780.; see also *Thakar Jagannath Baksh Singh v UP* (1946) 73 IA 123 (Privy Council held that regulation of the rights of landlord and tenant was not acquisition of land).

362 *Katra Education Society v State of UP* A 1967 SC 1307, 1312.

363 See generally, J M Kelly, *The Irish Constitution* (3rd edn, Butterworths 1994) 1061–1091.

364 [1982] IR 117.

365 *Blake v A-G* (n 364 above). Follow up legislation was also held to be a breach of property rights: See *In re Article 26 and the Housing (Private Rented Dwellings) Bill, 1981* [1983] IR 181.

366 *Vone Securities v Cooke* [1979] IR 59.

367 *ESB v Gormley* [1985] IR 129.

368 *Brady v Donegal County Council* [1989] ILRM 282.

369 *Cox v Ireland* [1992] 2 IR 503.

18.131 Examples of property legislation which have survived challenge include limitations on the use of land in the interests of protecting national monuments;[370]the levy regime on milk production;[371] and statutory powers to investigate the control of companies.[372] The cases are unclear on whether compensation is required when property rights are interfered with.[373]

18.132 It is uncertain whether shareholders are to be regarded as having rights as property under the Irish Constitution. In *O'Neill v Ryan*[374] the Supreme Court held that a shareholder of a company did not have an action against a person who had damaged the company, and thereby reduced the value of his shareholding. That was because shares were a right to participate in the company, and a reduction in the value of shares did not affect that right of participation. That decision should be contrasted with *Private Motorists v A-G*[375] and *Pine Valley Developments Ltd v Minister for the Environment*,[376] where shareholders were held to have property rights under Article 40.3 which could be protected against unjustified legislative attack.

18.133 In *Hempenstall v Minister for the Environment*[377] the High Court held that a change in the law which reduces property values cannot in itself amount to an infringement of constitutionally protected property rights. In that case, a moratorium on the granting of taxi and private hire vehicle licences was lifted. This decision was challenged by existing licence holders, on the grounds that it would decrease the value of their licences. The Court added that property rights arising in licences created by law are subject to the conditions created by law and to an implied condition that the law may change those conditions. An amendment of the law changing the conditions under which a licence is held and which has the effect of reducing the commercial value of the licence, cannot be regarded as an attack on the property right in the licence. It is the consequence of the implied condition which is an inherent part of the property right in the licence. However, tax legislation which had the effect that 'withholding tax' reduced a person's ability to pay income tax, and led to double payment of tax, was a breach of taxpayer's property rights.[378]

(6) Lesotho

18.134 Section 9 of the Human Rights Act 1983 in Lesotho provides that the right to property is only subject to derogation 'in the interest of public need . . . and in accordance with the provisions of appropriate laws'. This provision was considered in *A-G of Lesotho v Swisbourgh Diamond Mines (Pty) Ltd*.[379] The Government had issued an order purporting to

[370] *O'Callaghan v Commissioner of Public Works* [1985] ILRM 364.
[371] *Lawlor v Minister of Agriculture* [1990] 1 IR 355.
[372] *Hand v Dublin Corporation* [1991] 1 IR 409.
[373] A number of cases have referred to the availability of compensation as a mitigating factor. See eg *Central Dublin Development Association v Attorney-General* (1975) 109 ILTR 69; *ESB v Gormley* [1985] IR 129. Other cases, however, have suggested that compensation is not required. See eg *O'-Callaghan v Commissioners of Public Works* [1985] ILRM 364; *Rooney v Minister for Agriculture and Food* [1991] 2 IR 539.
[374] [1993] ILRM 557.
[375] [1983] IR 339.
[376] [1987] IR 23.
[377] [1993] IRLM 318.
[378] *Daly v Revenue Commissioners* [1996] 1 ILRM 122.
[379] 1997 (8) BCLR 1122.

revoke the respondents' mining leases and had, effectively, expelled them from the leases areas without compensation. The High Court held that the revocation order was inconsistent with section 9 and was not in accordance with the procedures laid down by law. As a result, the revocation was invalid.

(7) Malaysia

Article 13 of the Constitution of Malaysia provides that: **18.135**

> (1) No person shall be deprived of property save in accordance with law.
> (2) No law shall provide for the compulsory acquisition or use of property without adequate compensation.

The High Court has held that, the exercise of rights under a lease by a Government agency will not be a 'deprivation of property' under this provisions.[380]

Article 13 was considered by the Privy Council in the controversial case of *Government of Malaysia v Selangor Pilot Association*.[381] By statute it became an offence for pilots other than those employed by the port authority to provide pilotage services in a particular port. The port authority offered employment to the pilots employed by the plaintiff association and purchased its physical assets. However, it refused to pay compensation for the loss of the goodwill of the business. The Federal Court of Malaysia granted a declaration that the association was entitled to compensation for loss of goodwill. This decision was reversed by the Privy Council. It was held that any deprivation of property was in accordance with law and there had been no 'acquisition or use' of the association's goodwill. Lord Salmon dissented, holding that the result of the statute was the taking over of the association's business by the port authority: **18.136**

> The Act . . . must have been recognised by the legislature as going so far as making it inevitable that the authority would take the [association's] business immediately the Act came into force. If, contrary to my view, the amending Act can properly be characterised as merely regulatory and it does not go far enough to be recognised as a taking, it is impossible to imagine any regulation that could be recognised.[382]

(8) Mauritius

Section 8 of the Constitution is entitled 'Protection from deprivation of property' and provides by sub-section (1) as follows: **18.137**

> No property of any description shall be compulsorily taken possession of, and no interest in or right over property of any description shall be compulsorily acquired, except where—
> (a) the taking of possession or acquisition is necessary or expedient in the interests of defence, public safety, public order, public morality, public health, town and country planning or the development or utilisation of any property in such a manner as to promote the public benefit or the social and economic well-being of the people of Mauritius;
> (b) there is reasonable justification for the causing of any hardship that may result to any person having an interest in or right over the property; and
> (c) provision is made by a law applicable to that taking of possession or acquisition—

380 *Station Hotels Berhad v Malaysian Railway Administration* [1977] MLJ 112.
381 [1978] AC 337.
382 Ibid 358F–G.

(i) for the payment of adequate compensation; and
(ii) securing to any person having an interest in or right over the property a right of access to the Supreme Court, whether direct or on appeal from any other authority, for the determination of his interest or right, the legality of the taking of possession or acquisition of the property, interest or right, and the amount of any compensation to which he is entitled, and for the purpose of obtaining payment of that compensation.

18.138 The case of *Subramanien v Government of Mauritius*[383] concerned an application by teachers in Roman Catholic primary schools that received government grants. A requirement was introduced that primary schools, as a condition of aid, were required not to discriminate on the grounds of race or religion in recruiting staff. The Roman Catholic Education Agency (RCEA) negotiated with the Government that its schools would be exempt from this requirement. In return, RCEA teachers and staff would not continue to be recognised as public officers, and therefore would no longer be eligible for promotion to any public office, nor entitled to benefits to which government teachers had been entitled to by virtue of their public offices. The teachers claimed that the agreement breached their rights to equal protection, and their right not to be deprived of property. The Privy Council dismissed the teachers' appeal. The advantages enjoyed by the teachers were lost opportunities or expectations rather than existing property rights. The agreement between the RCEA and the Government did not therefore result in a deprivation of property.

18.139 The withdrawal of benefits wrongly conferred on teachers in state-aided primary schools did not constitute an interference with property rights. The advantages which the teachers had lost were opportunities or expectations and not property rights.[384]

18.140 The decision of the Privy Council in *Société United Docks v Government of Mauritius*[385] concerned two appeals on the right to compensation for deprivation. In the first case, the construction of a bulk sugar loading terminal by the Government had resulted in a loss of business of sugar docking and loading companies. Those companies argued that the loss of business constituted a deprivation of property in respect of which they were entitled to compensation. The Privy Council, after surveying comparative jurisprudence in that area, rejected that argument. As Lord Templeman said:

> The Constitution does not afford protection against progress or provide compensation for a business which is lost as a result of technological advance.

The right to compensation only arose if the deprivation took place as a result of 'coercive action' by the state.[386] The Privy Council's decision was unaffected by the fact that a monopoly was conferred on the sugar terminal:

> [The monopoly] did not in the event inflict any damage on the companies. The statutory monopoly was unnecessary to prevent competition by the companies with the bulk terminal. The companies business could not compete with the bulk terminal because the business of the companies no longer provides an efficient service for the sugar industry.

The second appeal in *Société United Docks v Government of Mauritius*[387] concerned an

383 [1995] 4 LRC 320, PC.
384 Ibid.
385 [1985] 1 AC 585, PC.
386 Ibid 604.
387 n 385 above.

attempt by the Government to avoid paying sums awarded to the appellants pursuant to an arbitration. The Privy Council found that those attempts were a deprivation of property without compensation, that property being a chose in action.

(9) South Africa

Property rights are dealt with by section 25 of the South African Constitution which provides:[388] **18.141**

> (1) No one may be deprived of property except in terms of law of general application, and no law may permit arbitrary deprivation of property.
> (2) Property may be expropriated only in terms of law of general application—
> (a) for public purposes or in the public interest; and
> (b) subject to compensation, the amount, timing, and manner of payment, of which must be agreed, or decided or approved by a court.
>
> (3) The amount, timing, and manner of payment, of compensation must be just and equitable, reflecting an equitable balance between the public interest and the interests of those affected, having regard to all relevant factors, including—
> (a) the current use of the property;
> (b) the history of the acquisition and use of the property;
> (c) the market value of the property;
> (d) the extent of direct state investment and subsidy in the acquisition and beneficial capital improvement of the property; and
> (e) the purpose of the expropriation.
>
> (4) For the purposes of this section—
> (a) the public interest includes the nation's commitment to land reform, and to reforms to bring about equitable access to all South Africa's natural resources; and
> (b) property is not limited to land.
>
> (5) The state must take reasonable legislative and other measures, within its available resources, to foster conditions which enable citizens to gain access to land on an equitable basis . . .[389]
> (8) No provision of this section may impede the state from taking legislative and other measures to achieve land, water and related reform, in order to redress the results of past racial discrimination, provided that any departure from the provisions of this section is in accordance with the provisions of section 36(1).

Deprivation of property must be by a law of 'general application'. This must be general, non-arbitrary, public and precise. It seems that, in practice, most statutes and regulations will satisfy this test.[390] A measure will be 'arbitrary' if it bears no rational relationship to the legislative goal: this is the same as the standard of minimal scrutiny in US equality law.[391] **18.142**

The case of *Harksen v Lane*[392] concerned insolvency legislation whereby, upon the bankruptcy of a person, the property of the bankrupt's spouse vested in the trustee in **18.143**

---

[388] See generally, M Chaskalson, J Kentridge, J Klaaren, G Marcus, D Spitz and S Woolman (eds), *Constitutional Law of South Africa* (Juta, 1996) Chap 31 'Property'.

[389] Sub-sections (6) and (7) relate to the rights of those whose property rights were adversely affected by 'past racially discriminatory laws or practices'.

[390] See generally, Chaskalson (n 388 above) para 12.5.

[391] See *S v Lawrence, S v Negal, S v Solberg* 1997 (10) BCLR 1348, CC.

[392] 1998 (1) SA 300.

bankruptcy, unless the solvent spouse could prove she really owned the property. A challenge was made to that vesting provision based on the right to property.[393] The Constitutional Court rejected that challenge, observing that even on the assumption that a vesting in terms of this provision had the effect of transferring the property concerned to a trustee, it did not constitute an expropriation, as there was no permanent transfer of ownership. Rather, the vesting was a temporary measure intended to ensure that neither the solvent nor the insolvent estate was deprived of property before it could be determined what rightfully belonged to each estate.

(10) Trinidad and Tobago[394]

18.144 Section 4 of the Constitution of Trinidad and Tobago recognises and declares certain fundamental human rights and freedoms including 'enjoyment of property and the right not to be deprived thereof except by due process of law'. In *Mootoo v A-G of Trinidad and Tobago*[395] the Privy Council rejected an argument that a statute which provided for an unemployment levy from which the Minister could make advances was in breach of section 4. In *Bahadur v A-G*[396] the applicant complained that an order for the surrender of his driving licence after a fatal accident was 'deprivation of property'. The Court of Appeal held that:

> property within the meaning of s 4(a) of the Constitution includes tangible forms of real and personal property, but also less tangible forms such as social welfare benefits, public services and other things to which people are entitled by law and regulations. A drivers licence or permit is not included within this category.[397]

(11) Zimbabwe

18.145 Section 11(c) of the Zimbabwe Constitution provides that every person in Zimbabwe has the right to:

> protection for the privacy of his home and other property and from the compulsory acquisition of property without compensation.

Section 16(1) provides that:

> No property of any description or interest or right therein shall be compulsorily acquired except under the authority of a law that . . .
>
> (c) subject to the provisions of sub-section (2) requires the acquiring authority to pay fair compensation for the acquisition before or within a reasonable time after acquiring the property interest or right.

'Property' is 'indicative and descriptive of every possible interest which a party can have'.[398]

---

393 See generally Chaskalson (n 388 above) Chap 31.

394 See also the discussion of property rights in Commonwealth Caribbean constitutions in M Demerieux, *Fundamental Rights in Commonwealth Caribbean Constitutions* (Faculty of Law Library, University of West Indies, 1992) Chap 15.

395 [1979] 1 WLR 1334, PC.

396 [1989] LRC (Const) 632.

397 Ibid 641.

398 *Zimbabwe Township Developers (Pty) Ltd v Lou's Shoes (Pvt) Ltd* (1983) 2 ZLR 376, 384.

The meaning of 'compulsory acquisition' was considered by the Supreme Court in *Davies v Ministry of Lands, Agriculture and Water Development.*[399] The plaintiffs were commercial farmers whose land had been designated for compulsory purchase. They sought a declaration that the designations were invalid because they themselves amounted to a compulsory acquisition without compensation. It was held that compulsory acquisition meant the transfer of the ownership or possession of property to the state and that no compensation was required for deprivation of rights short of acquisition.[400] In *Chairman of the Public Service Commission v Zimbabwe Teachers Association*[401] it was held that an annual bonus for public servants was not a right protected by section 16(1): the bonus was an *ex gratia* payment which was not a vested right. **18.146**

The applicant in *Nyambirai v National Social Security Authority*[402] alleged that a pension scheme requiring compulsory contributions by employers and employees was a compulsory acquisition of his property without compensation. The state admitted that the scheme was a compulsory acquisition of property but argued that the contributions were saved as constitutionally permissible tax, and were reasonably justifiable in a democratic society. The Supreme Court accepted that the contributions were a tax, despite the fact that the beneficiaries of the pension scheme were the contributing employees or their survivors, and not members of the public in general. The applicant had failed to discharge his onus of proving, on the balance of probabilities, that the tax went further than was reasonably justifiable in a democratic society. **18.147**

[399] [1997] 1 LRC 123.

[400] See also *Hewlett v Minister of Finance* [1981] ZLR 571 (following *Government of Malaysia v Selangor Pilot Association* [1978] AC 337.

[401] 1996 (9) BCLR 1189.

[402] 1995 (9) BCLR 1221.

19

THE RIGHT TO EDUCATION

A. The Nature of the Right

The right to education is a complex right (or bundle of rights) which is not universally recognised as a fundamental human right.[1] It lies at the boundary between 19.01

[1] Cf *In re Certification of Constitution of Republic of South Africa 1996* 1996 (4) SA 744 paras 76–77.

'civil and political' and 'economic and social rights'.[2] At its heart lies the positive obligation of the state to provide schooling for its citizens. However, the right to education is closely linked to liberty rights—the rights of parental choice of education—and to the rights of the child.[3] Furthermore, respect for pluralism in a democratic society entails a commitment to preserving cultural diversity within the educational process. A number of constitutional instruments therefore regard the protection of minority rights, religious beliefs and individual convictions as fundamental to the provision of education.

19.02 The different aspects of the right to educate are illustrated by the formulation in Article 26 of the Universal Declaration of Human Rights which is its first appearance in a major rights instrument. This provides that:

> (1) Everyone has the right to education. Education shall be free, at least in the elementary and fundamental stages. Elementary education shall be compulsory. Technical and professional education shall be made generally available and higher education shall be equally accessible to all on the basis of merit.
>
> (2) Education shall be directed to the full development of the human personality and to the strengthening of respect for human rights and fundamental freedoms. It shall promote understanding, tolerance and friendship among all nations, racial or religious groups, and shall further the activities of the United Nations for the maintenance of peace.
>
> (3) Parents have a prior right to choose the kind of education that shall be given to their children.

Although the right appears in the First Protocol to the Convention, its inclusion was controversial[4] and the right to education does not figure in the European Social Charter.[5]

19.03 The right to education is also recognised by Article 13 of the International Covenant on Economic, Social and Cultural Rights of 1966.[6] This provides for the right to education in broadly similar terms to the Universal Declaration. It requires that primary school education is to be compulsory and available free to all; secondary education, while not necessarily compulsory or free, is to be equally accessible to all and progressively free; whereas higher education is to be made equally accessible to all on the basis of capacity, by every appropriate means, including the progressive introduction of its free provision. Article 13 also recognises the liberty of parents to choose for their children schools, other than those

[2] See para 1.16 above.

[3] See generally, G van Beuren, 'Education: Whose Right is it Anyway?' in L Heffernan (ed), *Human Rights: A European Perspective* (Round Hall Press, 1994).

[4] See para 19.35 below.

[5] See D Gomien, D Harris and L Zwaak, *Law and Practice of the European Convention on Human Rights and the European Social Charter* (Council of Europe Publishing, 1996) 407–408; the Social Charter rights are confined to vocational guidance and vocational training (Arts 9 and 10).

[6] See App K in Vol 2.

established by the public authorities, which conform to minimum educational standards and to ensure the religious and moral education of their children in conformity with their own convictions.

The human rights instruments which recognise the right to education therefore differ about its boundaries and content. Where a right to education has been formulated, two general issues require consideration: **19.04**

The scope of the right: The extent to which the state is obliged to provide access to educational institutions is a central concern: the types of educational institutions which should be provided and the terms on which access should be granted raise difficult questions of economic and social policy concerning the provision of resources.

Respect for parental convictions: The duty of the state to respect a parent's religious or philosophical convictions leads to debates as to the extent to which instruction must be distinguished from indoctrination, the degree to which different educational provision should be made for different groups and about whether resources must be provided to ensure that these individual rights are properly protected.

B. The Right in English Law Before the Human Rights Act

(1) Introduction

The educational rights of pupils (and their parents) are statutory in origin.[7] The foundations of the modern law can be traced to the Education Act 1944. However, the statutory framework has been substantially amended in later legislation and became consolidated in the Education Act 1996. **19.05**

The legislative scheme was significantly altered by the School Standards and Framework Act 1998. In particular, this Act introduced a new classification of schools.[8] On 1 September 1999 the Act abolished grant maintained schools and replaced them with foundation schools (which will receive local authority funding). County schools have been given community school status; and voluntary schools will become voluntary-aided schools and voluntary-controlled schools. There are now two types of special schools: community and foundation schools. **19.06**

A large number of statutory rights and obligations concerning education can be catalogued. The principles that underlie them are, in general, similar to those contained in the Convention.[9] **19.07**

[7] For a fuller treatment of the relevant law see P Leill, J Coleman and K P Poole *The Law of Education* (9th edn, Butterworths, 1998); J McManus, *Education and the Courts* (Sweet & Maxwell, 1998); O Hyams, *Law of Education* (Sweet & Maxwell, 1998).

[8] School Standards and Framework Act, s 20.

[9] See para 19.34ff below.

(2) The right to education

19.08 The 'right' of a child to education can be derived from the statutory duty[10] on the parent of every child of compulsory school age (between 5 and 16)[11] to cause that child to receive efficient, full time education suitable to his age, ability and aptitude and to any special educational needs[12] he may have by regular attendance[13] at school or otherwise.[14] Under the School Standards and Framework Act 1998 the local educational authority[15] is under a duty to secure nursery education for children.[16]

19.09 Education will be suitable if it primarily equips a child for life within the community of which he is a member (rather than the way of life in the country as a whole) provided the education does not foreclose the option in later life of adopting some other form of life if he wishes.[17] Because efficient education probably demands that the requirements of the National Curriculum[18] are met, it will in practice be difficult to provide efficient education where parents choose[19] to educate a child at home.

19.10 A claim concerning the right to education was made in a rather different context in *O'Conner v Chief Adjudication Officer*.[20] The Court of Appeal rejected the argument that denying income support to a student which prevented his return to full time education breached the Convention right to education;[21] and was *Wednesbury* unreasonable because Parliament could not have intended that a full time external student would have to choose between abandoning his course of education or face destitution.

(3) Access to education

19.11 Local educational authorities[22] are under a duty[23] to provide sufficient schools for

[10] Education Act 1996, s 7.

[11] As defined by s 8 of the Education Act 1996 as inserted by s 52(2) of the Education Act 1997 and the Education Act 1997 (Commencement No 3 and Transitional Provisions) Order, SI 1998/386 which defines the date when a child attains five and attains 16.

[12] See para 19.23ff below.

[13] *Hinchley v Rankin* [1961] 1 WLR 421.

[14] The procedures an authority should follow when assessing whether a child educated at home is receiving full time education suitable for his age, ability and aptitude were considered in *R v Gwent County Council, ex p Perry* (1984) 129 Sol Jo 737.

[15] As defined by the School Standards and Framework Act 1998, s 22(8).

[16] School Standards and Framework Act 1998, s 118.

[17] *R v Secretary of State for Education, ex p Talmud Torah Machzikei Hadass School Trust, The Times*, 12 Apr 1985.

[18] Education Act 1996, ss 353–374.

[19] *R v West Riding of Yorkshire Justices, ex p Broadbent* [1910] 2 KB 192.

[20] [1999] ELR 209.

[21] See para 19.40ff.

[22] As defined by the Education Act 1996, ss 12 and 579(1).

[23] Ibid s 14.

their area, in number, character and equipment and to provide all pupils with the opportunity of appropriate education. The duty in question is a broad and general 'target duty' which is intended to benefit the public in general and does not provide individuals with a cause of action to claim damages.[24] The refusal to continue funding a child at private school under the 'assisted places scheme'[25] is not a breach of the duty under the European Convention on Human Rights to provide access to education.[26]

(4) The obligation to attend school

Where a parent fails to perform his statutory duty[27] to ensure that his child receives efficient full time education, the local educational authority[28] may institute a procedure which results in making a school attendance order.[29] The failure to comply with an attendance order is a criminal offence.[30] **19.12**

It is also a criminal offence for a child who is a registered[31] pupil at a school to fail to attend regularly at school.[32] It is a defence where the child is absent:[33] **19.13**

- with leave;
- where the child[34] is prevented from attending because of sickness or any unavoidable cause; and
- where he is absent on a day exclusively set apart by the religious body to which his parent belongs.[35]

A defence will also be available[36] where: **19.14**

- the school at which the child is registered is not within walking distance of the child's home; and
- no suitable arrangements have been made by the authority (or the funding

[24] *R v Inner London Educational Authority, ex p Ali* (1990) 154 LGR 852, 854 *per* Woolf LJ declining to follow the *dicta* of Lord Denning MR in *Meade v Haringey London Borough Council* [1979] 1 WLR 637, 647.

[25] Under the Education Act 1980 and the Education Act 1997, abolished by Education (Schools) Act 1997.

[26] *R v Department of Education and Employment, ex p Begbie* [2000] 1 WLR 1115, 1128, 1129 *per* Peter Gibson LJ

[27] Under the Education Act 1996, s 7.

[28] As defined by ibid ss 12 and 579(1).

[29] Education Act 1996, s 437; there is a procedure to ensure parental choice for the school once a notice as been served (see ss 438–440) except in relation to children with special needs (see s 441).

[30] Ibid s 443.

[31] Ibid s 434(5).

[32] Ibid s 444.

[33] Ibid s 443(3).

[34] *Jenkins v Howells* [1949] 2 KB 218.

[35] See eg *Marshall v Graham* [1907] 2 KB 112 which held it was not necessary for members of the Church of England to take the whole of the school day for religious observance.

[36] Under the Education Act 1996, s 444(4).

authority)[37] for transport to the school,[38] for boarding accommodation for the pupil at or near the school or for attendance at a near school.

Walking distance[39] is two miles for a child under eight years of age and three miles for those over eight. Distance is measured by reference to the nearest available route.[40]

(5) The right to be educated in accordance with parental convictions

19.15 Section 9 of the Education Act 1996 states that the Secretary of State, local educational authorities[41] and funding bodies[42] in exercising their powers and duties under the Education Act must have regard to the general principle that pupils are to be educated in accordance with the wishes of their parents so far as that is compatible with the provision of efficient instruction and training and with the avoidance of unreasonable public expenditure.[43] Since section 9 is only laying down a general principle, an education authority is entitled to take account of other matters and may make exceptions to the general rule.[44]

(6) Religious education and worship[45]

19.16 There is a duty[46] on every local education authority,[47] governing body and head teacher of every community, foundation or voluntary school to ensure that religious education is given in accordance with the national curriculum.[48] Every pupil attending a community, foundation or voluntary school shall participate on each school day in an act of collective worship.[49]

19.17 However, a pupil at a community, foundation or voluntary school is excused from receiving religious education or attending religious worship where his parent requests that he is excused.[50]

---

[37] As defined by the Education Act 1996, s 26.

[38] There is no requirement that the school itself must be suitable for the particular pupil: see *In re S* [1995] ELR 98 overruling *R v Rochdale Borough Council, ex p Schemet* [1994] ELR 89; and see *R v Kent County Council, ex p C* [1998] ELR 108.

[39] Education Act 1996, s 444(5).

[40] See *Essex County Council v Rogers* [1987] AC 66; *George v Devon* [1989] AC 573.

[41] As defined by the Education Act 1996, ss 12 and 579(1).

[42] As defined by ibid s 26.

[43] See eg *R v London Borough of Lambeth, ex p G* [1994] ELR 207.

[44] See *Watt v Kesteven County Council* [1955] 1 QB 408, 424 *per* Denning LJ and 429 *per* Parker LJ; *Cumings v Birkenhead Corporation* [1972] Ch 12, 36.

[45] For a fuller discussion, see para 14.10ff above.

[46] School Standards and Framework Act 1998, s 69 and Sch 19.

[47] As defined by ibid s 22(8).

[48] Education Act 1996, s 352(1)(a).

[49] School Standards and Framework Act 1998, s 70 and Sch 20.

[50] Ibid s 71.

(7) School admissions and parental choice

The Education Act 1980 introduced parental choice for admissions for pupils to school and has been re-enacted in broadly similar terms in section 86 of the School Standards and Framework Act 1998.[51] **19.18**

Section 86(1) of the 1998 Act imposes an obligation on the local educational authority[52] to make arrangements enabling a parent of a child in its area to express a preference[53] and to give reasons for his preference. The local educational authority and the governing body of a maintained school[54] are under a duty to comply with the preference unless it can be shown under section 86(3) that complying with the preference: **19.19**

- would prejudice the provision of efficient education or the efficient use of resources;[55] or
- if the preferred school is a foundation[56] or voluntary aided school,[57] would be incompatible with any special admission arrangements made to preserve the religious character of the school;[58] or
- would be incompatible with any arrangements made in relation to a school where the arrangements for admission are based wholly on selection by reference to ability or aptitude and are so based with a view to admitting only pupils with high ability or aptitude.[59]

Furthermore, there is no duty to comply with the preference where the child in question has been excluded from two or more schools within two years beginning with the date on which the latest exclusion took effect.[60]

The 1998 Act also permits selective admission to maintained schools under section 99 where there is selection by ability under pre-existing arrangements,[61] by pupil banding[62] or where it is in connection with selecting pupils who are over **19.20**

[51] For a fuller treatment, see eg J McManus, *Education and the Courts* (Sweet & Maxwell 1998); O Hyams, *Law of Education* (Sweet & Maxwell, 1998) 307–329.

[52] As defined by the School Standards and Framework Act 1998, s 22(8).

[53] See *R v Rotherham Metropolitan Borough Council, ex p Clark* [1998] ELR 152.

[54] ie a community, foundation or voluntary school: School Standards and Framework Act 1998, s 84(6).

[55] If admitting a child would prejudice the duty of a local educational authority and governing body to comply with the limits on infant class sizes under the School Standards and Framework Act 1998, s 1(6), then prejudice will be deemed to have arisen: ibid s 86(4).

[56] Ibid s 20.

[57] Ibid.

[58] Under ibid s 91.

[59] Education Act 1996, s 411(3) as substituted by the Education Act 1997, s 10.

[60] School Standards and Frameworks Act, s 87.

[61] Ibid s 100.

[62] Ibid s 101.

compulsory school age. It also permits pupils to be selected by aptitude under pre-existing arrangements[63] or by aptitude for a particular subject.[64]

19.21 Children who have statements of special educational needs[65] or attend special schools[66] do not have the right of parental preferences.[67] Parents have rights of appeal against the admissions decisions of local educational authorities[68] and the governing bodies of foundation[69] or voluntary aided[70] schools.[71]

19.22 The decisions of appeals committees on school admissions are binding on local educational authorities and governing bodies.[72] The appeals committee reaches its decision by asking two questions:[73]

- whether the local educational authority[74] has proved that there will be prejudice to efficient education to admit further pupils to the school; and
- whether the prejudice is on balance outweighed in a particular case by the parental preference.

(8) Children with special needs

(a) The meaning of special educational needs

19.23 The Education Act 1996 contains an elaborate scheme giving rights to children with special educational needs.[75] A child has special educational needs if he has a learning difficulty which calls for special educational provision to be made for him.[76] In general,[77] a child has a learning difficulty if he has significantly greater difficulty in learning than a majority of children of his age, if he has a disability which prevents him (or hinders him) from making use of educational facilities of

---

63 Ibid s 100.

64 Ibid s 102.

65 See under the Education Act 1996, s 324; see para 19.24ff below.

66 As defined by the Education Act 1996, ss 6 and 337; see the School Standards and Framework Act 1998, s 142(8).

67 Ibid s 98(7).

68 Which must make arrangements for appeals under ibid s 94(1).

69 Ibid s 20.

70 Ibid s 20.

71 Ibid s 94.

72 Under ibid s 94(6).

73 See *R v Commissioner for Local Administration, ex p Croydon London Borough Council* [1989] 1 All ER 1033 approving the approach of Forbes J in *R v South Glamorgan Appeals Committee, ex p Evans* 10 May 1984; for the difficulties that arise in relation to multiple appeals, see *R v Education Appeal Committee of Leicester County Council, ex p Tarmohamed* [1997] ELR 48.

74 *R v Committee of Brighouse School, ex p G* [1997] ELR 39.

75 For a fuller treatment see eg J McManus, *Education and the Courts* (Sweet & Maxwell 1998) Chap 3; J Friel and D Hay, *Special Educational Needs and the Law* (Sweet & Maxwell 1996); O Hyams, *Law of Education* (Sweet & Maxwell, 1998) Chap 5.

76 Education Act 1996, s 312(1).

77 Ibid s 312(2).

a kind generally provided for children of his age in schools within the area of the local educational authority[78] or if he is under five years of age and is likely to have difficulties when over that age. Language difficulties arising from being taught in a different language than that used at home do not in themselves amount to a learning difficulty.[79] Special educational provision, for a child over two, is educational provision additional to (or otherwise different from) the educational provision made for children of his age in schools maintained by the local educational authority (excluding special schools)[80] or grant maintained schools[81] in the area.[82]

(b) The obligations owed to children with special educational needs

The local educational authority[83] has a general duty of identifying children with special needs to determine the special educational provision which their learning difficulty may call for.[84] If the local educational authority considers that a child has (or probably has) special educational needs and that it is necessary for it to determine his special educational provision,[85] then the authority must use the prescribed procedure to assess the child's needs. After making the assessment the local educational authority may conclude that it is necessary to make a statement of special educational needs.[86] However, the local educational authority is under a duty[87] to educate children with special needs in mainstream schools unless this is incompatible with a child receiving the special educational provision which his learning calls for, with the efficient education of the children with whom the child will be educated and the efficient use of resources.[88] **19.24**

A statement of special educational needs must identify every special need and identify the provision for meeting that need.[89] The appropriateness of any school named in the statement depends on how it meets the needs.[90] **19.25**

However, the local educational authority is not obliged to provide the best possible education but merely to meet the needs of the child.[91] Parental preferences for **19.26**

[78] As defined by ibid ss 12 and 579(1).
[79] Ibid s 312(3).
[80] As defined by ibid ss 6 and 337.
[81] As defined by ibid s 183.
[82] Ibid s 321(4); in relation to children under two, special educational provision is provision of any kind.
[83] As defined by ibid ss 12 and 579(1).
[84] Ibid s 321.
[85] Under ibid 323 and Sch 26.
[86] As specified in ibid s 324 and Sch 27.
[87] Unless the parents object: see *S v SENT* [1995] 1 WLR 1627.
[88] Education Act 1996, s 316.
[89] *R v Secretary of State for Education and Science, ex p E* [1992] 1 FLR 377; but see *Re L* [1994] ELR 16.
[90] *R v Kingston on Thames and Hunter* [1997] ELR 223.
[91] *R v Surrey County Council Education Committee, ex p H* (1984) 83 LGR 219; *R v Cheshire County Council, ex p C* (1997) 95 LGR 299.

state schools are binding on the authority in the absence of a qualifying factor; and a preference for an independent school is to be considered (together with the reasons for it) in the light of section 9[92] of the Education Act 1996.[93] For the purposes of making arrangements to provide suitable education at school,[94] the local educational authority is not entitled to take account of its own lack of resources.[95] The local educational authority is under a duty to review a child's needs[96] and to assess his needs at his parents' request.[97] Where the parents express a preference for a school outside its boundaries, the local educational authority is entitled to override the preference on the ground that it would undermine the efficient use of resources by reference to its own resources.[97a]

19.27 Since 1993 parents have had a right of appeal to the Special Educational Needs Tribunal:

- where the local educational authority[98] refuses to make a statement following a special needs assessment;[99]
- against the contents of the statement of special educational needs;[100]
- where there is a refusal to assess;[101]
- under section 329(2)(b) of the Education Act 1996; and
- against a decision to refuse to maintain a statement of special educational needs.[102]

(c) Negligence and special educational needs

19.28 The failure to diagnose a child's special educational needs or to educate him appropriately has, in recent years, resulted in a large number of claims against local authorities for negligence. In *X (Minors) v Bedfordshire County Council*[103] the House of Lords held that no duty of care was imposed on a local educational authority in relation to its statutory obligations to children with special needs. However, the House of Lords also decided that where an authority offered an educational psychologists' service to the public, it would be liable for their negligence and that an authority might also be liable if head teachers and advisory teachers acted negligently in advising about the educational needs of a pupil.

92 See para 19.15 above.
93 *Catchpole v Buckingham County Council* [1999] ELR 179.
94 Under the Education Act 1996, s 19.
95 *R v East Sussex County Council, ex p Tandy* [1998] AC 714.
96 Education Act 1996, s 328.
97 Ibid s 329.
97a *B v Harrow London Borough Council* [2000] 1 WLR 223.
98 As defined by ibid ss 12 and 579(1).
99 Under ibid s 325.
100 Under ibid s 326.
101 Under ibid s 328(3)(b).
102 Under ibid Sch 27, para 11(2)(b).
103 [1995] 2 AC 633.

The position has now been clarified by the House of Lords in *Phelps v Hillingdon London Borough Council*.[104] A local educational authority may be vicariously liable for the negligence of a head teacher who failed to exercise reasonable skills in relation to a child's special needs, for a special advisory teacher (particularly, if he knew his advice would be communicated to the pupil's parents) and an educational psychologist who was called in to advise in relation to the assessment and provision for a specific child. Furthermore, the House of Lords in *Phelps* took the view that an authority could be directly liable for negligence[105–106] although it was emphasised that such a claim would be rare. **19.29**

(9) The right to free school transport

Under section 509 of the Education Act 1996 a local educational authority[107] must make such arrangements for the provision of transport[108] as it considers necessary[109] or as the Secretary of State directs; the arrangements must ensure that the child reaches school without undue stress, strain or difficulty.[110] However, the local educational authority is under a *duty*[111] to provide free transport where the parents would have a defence to being prosecuted for the non-attendance of their children at school.[112] The local authority must take account of the pupil's age, the nature of the route and alternate routes and the wish of the parent that the child is educated in accordance with his parent's religion.[113] It is not clear[114] whether there is a duty to provide free transport where a child is beyond the statutory walking distance as a result of exercising parental preference.[115] **19.30**

Section 509A[116] confers a power on a local educational authority to provide **19.31**

[104] *The Times*, 28 Jul 2000.

[105–106] Contrary to the views of Lord Browne-Wilkinson in *X (Minors) v Bedfordshire County Council* (n 103 above) 762 .

[107] As defined by the Education Act 1996, ss 12 and 579(1).

[108] For a fuller treatment see eg J McManus, *Education and the Courts* (Sweet & Maxwell, 1998) Chap 4; O Hyams, *Law of Education* (Sweet & Maxwell 133–139.

[109] See *Devon County Council v George* [1989] AC 573 which considered the provision when it was enacted as the Education Act 1944, s 55.

[110] *R v Hereford & Worcester County Council, ex p P*, *The Times*, 13 Mar 1992.

[111] See *Surrey County Council v Minister of Education* [1953] 1 WLR 516; *Rootkin v Kent County Council* [1981] 1 WLR 1186; *Devon County Council v George* (n 109 above) which considered the statutory provision as enacted as the Education Act 1944, s 39.

[112] Under the Education Act 1996, s 444: see para 19.13 above.

[113] Ibid s 509(4).

[114] See *R v East Sussex County Council, ex p D* [1991] COD 374; *R v Essex County Council, ex p C* [1994] ELR 273; *R v Dyfed County Council, ex p S* [1995] ELR 98; *R v Kent County Council, ex p C* [1998] ELR 108.

[115] See para 19.18ff above.

[116] Inserted by the School Standards and Framework Act 1998, s 124.

assistance with transport where it is satisfied that without such assistance, a child would be prevented from attending premises which are not part of a school but which provide nursery education.

(10) Expulsion from schools

19.32 There are a number of statutory restrictions on the right to exclude children from state schools.[117] The power to exclude a pupil for a fixed period or permanently is vested in the head teacher of a maintained school.[118] The head teacher is under a duty to inform the parents of a decision to exclude a pupil[119] and his decision is then considered by the governing body in accordance with a prescribed procedure.[120] If the governing body does not reinstate the pupil, the pupil can appeal to an appeals panel.[121]

19.33 The appeals panel is obliged to take account of the interest of the pupil, other pupils and the school,[122] the relevant policy[123] of the headmaster[124] (unless the pupil is not guilty of the conduct for which the headmaster expelled him)[125] and is entitled to take account of guidance given by the Secretary of State.[126] Where consideration is given to expelling a pupil permanently, he is entitled to know what is being said against him, he must be given access to material which is before the decision-maker[127] and he must be given a fair opportunity to exculpate himself.[128]

19.33A Where the licence permitting a parent to enter school premises is to be terminated, the Court of Appeal have held that the procedure used must be fair in the public law sense and, in particular, must give the parents an opportunity to make representations before the decision is made.[128a]

---

[117] For a fuller treatment see P Leill, J Coleman and K P Poole, *The Law of Education* (9th edn, Butterworths, 1998) J McManus, *Education and the Courts* (Sweet & Maxwell, 1998) Chap 6.

[118] School Standards and Framework Act 1998, s 64.

[119] Ibid s 65.

[120] Ibid s 66.

[121] Ibid s 67 and Sch 18.

[122] Education Act 1996, Sch 16, para 12A as inserted by Education Act 1997, s 7.

[123] Made under the Education Act 1996, s 157.

[124] Under the Education Act 1997, s 7(2).

[125] Ibid s 7(3).

[126] See *Expulsions from School* (DFE Circular 10/94) and see *R v London Borough of Camden, ex p H* [1996] ELR 360.

[127] *R v Governors of Dunraven School, ex p B* [2000] ELR 156.

[128] *R v Roman Catholic Schools, ex p S* [1998] ELR 304.

[128a] *Wandsworth London Borough Council v A* [2000] 1 WLR 1246.

C. The Law Under the European Convention

(1) Introduction

Article 2 of the First Protocol to the Convention provides: 19.34

> No person shall be denied the right to education. In the exercise of any functions which it assumes in relation to education and teaching, the state shall respect the right of parents to ensure such education and teaching in conformity with their own religious and philosophical convictions.

Article 2 therefore contains a primary right to education[129] and a secondary right to be educated in accordance with parental convictions.

The right to education had a stormy genesis.[130] The Convention did not originally contain any rights in this area and it took three years of debate before a compromise emerged. The initial draft stated that 'every person shall have the right to education'; and was changed to the present wording, 'no person shall be denied the right to education' because it was said that expressing the right in positive terms would be unduly onerous on the state.[131] It did not make explicit the level or type of education which must be provided, not least because the Contracting States did not plan to commit themselves either to build new schools or to provide financial support for private or special schools.[132] Article 2 was intended to ensure that the state must respect parental convictions beyond religious beliefs; and must do more than 'have regard to' the wishes of the parents.[133] The state was required to respect parental religious or philosophical convictions in relation to any educational functions it assumed.[134] However, the state was not obliged to allow pupils or students to be educated in a language different from the national language.[135] Although the state can define the kind of education it wanted to communicate, the right was designed to protect pupils against indoctrination and totalitarian propaganda.[136] 19.35

The controversial nature of the right to education is reflected in the large number of states which entered reservations to the right to education when ratifying the 19.36

---

[129] *Kjeldsen, Busk Madsen and Pedersen v Denmark* (1976) 1 EHRR 711 para 52.

[130] A H Robertson, 'The European Convention on Human Rights—Recent Developments' (1951) British Ybk of Intl L 359, 362–364; L Wildhaber, 'Right to Education and Parental Rights' in R St J Macdonald, F Matscher and H Petzold (eds), *The European System for the Protection of Human Rights* (Nijhoff, 1993).

[131] Robertson (n 130 above) 362.

[132] *Travaux préparatoires* 4, 935; 7, 128.

[133] *Travaux préparatoires* 5, 1080, 1084, 1100; 8, 26, 86.

[134] *Travaux préparatoires* 5, 1138, 1145, 1156, 1168, 1174, 1188, 1197, 1233, 1244; 7, 300.

[135] *Travaux préparatoires* 5, 1110–1116, 1138; 7, 300.

[136] *Travaux préparatoires* 1, 128.

First Protocol.[137] Nevertheless, because the right to education is limited in scope, only four cases have come before the Court.[138]

19.37 Even though Article 2 focuses on primary schooling,[139] it also extends to secondary and higher education. However, the right to higher education does not extend to vocational training[140] or specialist advanced studies.[141] But 'education' is not confined to teaching or instruction; it covers the whole social process whereby adults endeavour to transmit their beliefs, culture and other values to the young.[142] Teaching or instruction refers, in particular, to the transmission of knowledge and to intellectual development.[143] This broad definition, therefore, is wide enough to include internal school administration such as disciplinary issues.[144]

19.38 The rights provided by the first sentence of Article 2 are enjoyed by the child[145] or student (although they may, when the child is young, be exercised by the child's parents).[146] The right continues to be exercised by the parents while a child is in care[147] but are assumed by adoptive parents when the child is adopted.[148] If one parent obtains custody of a child, the right ceases for the other parent.[149] However, parents have separate rights to ensure that their child is educated in accordance with their religious and philosophical convictions.

19.39 Article 2 only makes one negative stipulation: that students are not subjected to the indoctrination of a single point of view, either via the school curriculum or the manner in which it is taught.[150]

---

[137] Several states joined with the United Kingdom in entering reservations to the right to education such as Germany, Ireland, Malta, the Netherlands, Portugal and Sweden: see Council of Europe, ECHR *Collected Texts* (1994) 121–131.

[138] *Kjeldsen, Busk Madsen and Pederson v Denmark* (1976) 1 EHRR 711, *Belgian Linguistic Case (No 2)* (1968) 1 EHRR 252, *Campbell and Cosans v United Kingdom* (1982) 4 EHRR 293 and *Valsamis v Greece* (1994) 24 EHRR 294.

[139] *X v United Kingdom* (1975) 2 DR 50, EComm HR and *15 Foreign Students v United Kingdom* (1977) 9 DR 185, EComm HR; *Yanasik v Turkey* (1993) 74 DR 14; *Sulak v Turkey* (1996) 84-A DR 98.

[140] *X v United Kingdom* (1980) 23 DR 228, EComm HR.

[141] *Sulak v Turkey* (1996) 84-A DR 98, EComm HR.

[142] *Campbell and Cosans v United Kingdom* (1982) 4 EHRR 293 para 33.

[143] Ibid.

[144] Ibid; *Valsamis v Greece* (1996) 24 EHRR 294.

[145] *Campbell and Cosans v United Kingdom* (1982) 4 EHRR 293 para 40.

[146] *Kjeldsen, Busk Madsen and Pedersen v Denmark* (1975) Series B No 21 para 50.

[147] *Aminhoff v Sweden* (1985) 43 DR 120, EComm HR; *Olsson v Sweden (No 1)* (1988) 11 EHRR 259.

[148] *X v United Kingdom* (1977) 11 DR 160, EComm HR.

[149] *X v Sweden* (1977) 12 DR 192, EComm HR.

[150] Under the second sentence of Art 2 (see para 19.53ff below): and see *Kjeldsen, Busk Madsen and Pedersen v Denmark* (1976) 1 EHRR 711 para 56.

(2) The right to education

(a) Introduction

The first sentence of Article 2 states that 'no person shall be denied the right to education'. The significance of the negative formulation was analysed in the *Belgian Linguistic Case (No 2)*.[151] Thus, the Court said that: **19.40**

> The negative formulation indicates . . . that the Contracting Parties do not recognise such a right to education as would require them to establish at their expense, or to subsidise, education of any particular type or at any particular level.[152]

Thus, Article 2 does not impose an express obligation on the state to provide educational facilities. It requires that the state ensures that no one is prevented access to the educational institutions existing at a given time[153] (which implies that some educational facilities must be made available).

The primary objective of Article 2 is therefore to guarantee an equal right of access to existing educational facilities.[154] Under Article 2 the state is given control over the organisation of an education system, and the individual has a right not to be excluded from whatever the state, in its discretion, provides. The state therefore has a wide margin of appreciation[155] to administer and finance its own system of education.[156] **19.41**

In *Belgian Linguistic Case (No 2)*[157] the Court held that educational rights under Article 2 comprise the following: **19.42**

- a right to access to existing educational institutions;
- a right to an 'effective' education; and
- a right to official recognition of studies successfully completed (since otherwise the exercise of the right to education would not be effective).

It decided that there is a right to be taught in the national language and there should be official recognition of any qualifications obtained at the completion of studies. However, there is no right for individuals to be taught in the language of their own (or their parent's) choice; nor was there a right of access to a particular school of choice.

---

[151] (1968) 1 EHRR 252, 280 para 3.
[152] Ibid.
[153] Ibid.
[154] Ibid.
[155] See generally, para 6.31ff above.
[156] *S P v United Kingdom* (1997) 23 EHRR 139.
[157] (1968) 1 EHRR 252 para 4.

(b) The right of access to existing educational institutions

19.43 The Court has said that the state must establish a system of state education for all children[158] and has implied that this might include the provision of private schools.[159] However, in the *Belgian Linguistic Case (No 2)*[160] the Court emphasised that the state retains a discretion to determine what sort of educational system is provided; and is not obliged to establish at the state's expense (or subsidise) education of any particular type or at any particular level.

19.44 Thus, the state is not obliged, for example, to provide selective schools[161] or particular types of adult education,[162] to establish or subsidise schools which provide education in a particular language[163] or to guarantee schools in accordance with particular religious convictions.[164] The Commission has also consistently rejected claims that the state is obliged to subsidise education, even where it is said that parental convictions require funding to subsidise single sex grammar schools,[165] schools for children with special educational needs,[166] private schools[167] and non-denominational schools.[168]

19.45 Furthermore, in the *Belgian Linguistic (No.2)* case[169] the Court held that the state may take into account the needs and resources of the community and of individuals, so long as its discretion does not injure the substance of the right to education nor conflict with other rights enshrined in the Convention. The education provided must therefore not be meaningless or ineffective.[170] This negative formulation of the right of education permits the state to defend the alleged inadequacies of its educational provision by relying on the lack of resources.[171]

---

158 *Kjeldsen, Busk Madsen and Pedersen v Denmark* (1976) 1 EHRR 711.

159 Ibid para 50: '. . . the second sentence of Article 2 must be read together with the first which enshrines the right of everyone to education. It is on this fundamental right that is grafted the right of parents to respect for their religious and philosophical convictions, and the first sentence does not distinguish, any more than the second, between state and private teaching'.

160 (1968) 1 EHRR 252 para 3.

161 *W and D M and M and H I v United Kingdom* (1984) 37 DR 96, EComm HR.

162 *X v Belgium* Application 7010/75, (1975) 3 DR 162, EComm HR.

163 *Belgian Linguistic Case (No 2)* (1968) 1 EHRR 252.

164 *X v United Kingdom* (1978) 14 DR 179, EComm HR.

165 *W and D M and M and H I v United Kingdom* (n 161 above).

166 *Simpson v United Kingdom* (1989) 64 DR 188, EComm HR.

167 *W and K L v Sweden* (1985) 45 DR 143, EComm HR; *Vereig Gemeinsam Lernan v Austria* (1995) 20 EHRR CD 78.

168 *X v United Kingdom* (1978) 14 DR 179, EComm HR.

169 (1968) 1 EHRR 252, 281 para 5.

170 D Harris, M O'Boyle and C Warbrick, *Law of the European Convention on Human Rights* (Butterworths, 1995) 542-543.

171 *Simpson v United Kingdom* (1989) 64 DR 188, EComm HR.

(c) *The right to an effective education*

The state has a duty to ensure the effectiveness of the system by imposing standards. Entry requirements which depend on an objective assessment do not violate the right to education.[172] As a result, individual rights may vary in accordance with the standards applied to different educational levels. For example, where the state provides a primary or secondary education system, it may necessarily offer universal access to it; by contrast, for higher education it is acceptable that enrolment is restricted to those who are capable of benefiting from what is provided.[173] **19.46**

The state is also under a duty to regulate educational activities,[174] both public and private, within its boundaries. It may insist that children are educated at primary and secondary level and enforce legislation against the parents to ensure that parents send their children to school or secure adequate provision for them at home.[175] It may also impose entry requirements to post-secondary courses which ensure that students have a capacity to benefit from such higher education.[176] **19.47**

However, the state must not use its regulatory powers to injure the substance of the right to education. The state, therefore, must not make it impossible to establish private schools.[177] In *Campbell and Cosans v United Kingdom*[178] the Court held that suspending a child for refusing to submit to corporal punishment went beyond reasonable regulation of access of education; it violated the right to education itself.[179] By contrast, reasonable disciplinary measures to discipline pupils or to punish cheating do not breach the right to education.[180] Furthermore, where a child is disciplined after giving a promise to behave himself, he will be partly responsible for his temporary lack of education.[181] **19.48**

(d) *The right to private education*

Under Article 2 the state can permit the establishment of a private education system[182] or allow children to be educated by their parents. If it does so, then the state has no obligation to subsidise these alternatives.[183] **19.49**

---

[172] *X v United Kingdom* (1980) 23 DR 228, EComm HR.
[173] Ibid; *Glazewska v Sweden* (1985) 45 DR 300, EComm HR.
[174] *Belgian Linguistic Case (No 2)* (1968) 1 EHRR 252, 281 para 5.
[175] *Family H v United Kingdom* (1984) 37 DR 105, EComm HR.
[176] *X v United Kingdom* (n 172 above); *Glazewska v Sweden* (n 173 above).
[177] *Ingrid Jordebo Foundation of Christian Schools and Ingrid Jordebo v Sweden* (1987) 51 DR 125, EComm HR.
[178] (1982) 4 EHRR 293.
[179] The question of corporal punishment being in conflict with Art 3 is discussed at para 8.36ff below.
[180] *Yanasik v Turkey* (1993) 74 DR 14; and contrast *Sulak v Turkey* (1996) 84-A DR 98, EComm HR.
[181] *Whitman v United Kingdom* Application 13477/87, 4 Oct 1989.
[182] *Kjeldsen, Busk Madsen and Pedersen v Denmark* (1976) 1 EHRR 711 para 50.
[183] *W and K L v Sweden* (1984) 45 DR 105.

19.50 Whether parents have a fundamental right to establish schools outside the state system has been much debated.[184] The dispute generally focuses on the language of the second sentence of Article 2 which guarantees to parents respect for their religious and philosophical convictions for their children's education:[185] on that basis the state will be obliged to permit some alternatives to state education. This requirement is intended to foster pluralism in education[186] and so avoid the dangers of totalitarianism by indoctrination through a state monopoly over education.

19.51 However, the right to establish private schools may not be dependent on the second sentence of Article 2 as this must be read together with the first sentence which enshrines the right of everyone to education and which 'does not distinguish . . . between State and private teaching'.[187]

19.52 Because the state is not, in general,[188] obliged to subsidise education, it is not, for example, required to assist in privately educating a child in accordance with parental wishes[189] or to subsidise a private secular school.[190] Nor was the Government in Northern Ireland obliged to make a grant to a new non-denominational school.[191]

(3) The right to educate children in accordance with parental convictions

(a) Introduction

19.53 The right protected by the second sentence of Article 2 is the right of parents to ensure that their children are educated in conformity with their beliefs. The second sentence of Article 2 must, however, be read in light of the first; the Court views the right of parents to respect for their religious and philosophical convictions as subsidiary to the fundamental right to education set out in the first sentence.[192] Its purpose was described in *Kjeldsen, Busk Madsen and Pedersen v Denmark*[193] as safeguarding the possibility of pluralism in education which was essential to the preservation of a democratic society.

[184] Compare the views of the Commission which said that Art 2 contained the right of establishment and access to private schools, in *Kjeldsen, Busk Madsen and Pedersen v Denmark* (1976) B 21, 44, with the Court which took a more restrictive view: see (1976) 1 EHRR 711 para 50. However, the Commission has maintained its views, in *Ingrid Jordebo Foundation of Christian Schools and Ingrid Jordebo v Sweden* (1987) 51 DR 125, EComm HR; *Verein Gemeinsam Lernan v Austria* (1995) 82-A DR 41, EComm HR.

[185] See para 19.53ff below.

[186] *Kjeldsen, Busk Madsen and Pedersen v Denmark* (1976) 1 EHRR 711 para 50.

[187] Ibid 50.

[188] See para 19.40 above.

[189] *H v United Kingdom* (1984) 38 DR 105.

[190] *Verein Gemeinsam Lernan v Austria* (1995) 20 EHRR CD 78.

[191] *X v United Kingdom* (1978) 14 DR 179, EComm HR.

[192] *Kjeldsen, Busk Madsen and Pedersen v Denmark* (1976) 1 EHRR 711 para 56.

[193] Ibid para 50.

The duty of the state is to respect that right in all of the functions which it assumes in relation to education and teaching. Respect for convictions applies equally to private and public education as well as to all activities of the state concerning education, whether academic or administrative.[194] 19.54

The parental right therefore means that there are three avenues open to parents in relation to the education of their children: 19.55

- they may enrol their child in the state system (whether or not it conflicts with their personal religious or philosophical convictions);
- they may withdraw the child from the state system and educate him by alternative means (either at home or privately, through the establishment of independent schools); or
- they might seek to enforce their right to 'respect' by demonstrating a failure of the state to fulfil its duty.

The second sentence of Article 2 allows a significant parental influence on both educational content and administration. It principally serves to prevent indoctrination of students by the state and teachers,[195] but also covers the choice of means of discipline, and other administrative measures, insofar as they are offensive to the convictions of parents. 19.56

(b) The nature of the conviction

There is a heavy burden on the parent to demonstrate the relevance of his personal convictions to his claim. The parent must show: 19.57

- that his beliefs constitute a religious or philosophical conviction;
- that the conviction is the reason for his objection to the state's actions;[196] and
- that he has informed the state of the reasons for his convictions.[197]

In *Campbell and Cosans v United Kingdom*[198] the Court stressed that 'convictions' in the ordinary sense are not synonymous with 'opinions' or 'ideas' as in freedom of expression in Article 10[199] and were more akin to 'beliefs' in Article 9.[200] Convictions appear to denote 'views that attain a certain level of cogency, seriousness, cohesion and importance'.[201] 19.58

194 *Campbell and Cosans v United Kingdom* (1982) 4 EHRR 293 paras 33–36.
195 See *Kjeldsen, Busk Madsen and Pedersen* (n 192 above) para 50: 'The second sentence of Art 2 aims in short at safeguarding the possibility of pluralism in education, which possibility is essential for the preservation of the "democratic society" as conceived by the Convention'.
196 *Warwick v United Kingdom* (1986) 60 DR 5, EComm HR.
197 *B and D v United Kingdom* (1986) 49 DR 44, EComm HR.
198 (1982) 4 EHRR 293 para 36.
199 See para 15.40ff above.
200 See para 14.40ff above.
201 *Campbell and Cosans v United Kingdom* (n 198 above) para 36; see also *Valsamis v Greece* (1996) 24 EHRR 294 para 25.

19.59 A parent must prove that he holds a well-formulated conviction which has been made known to the authorities. No definition of religious and philosophical convictions has been given but the case law takes a broad, rather than a restrictive,[202] reading of the phrase. Thus, the Court in *Campbell and Cosans*[203] said that religious and philosophical convictions include:

> such convictions as are worthy of respect in a 'democratic society' and are not incompatible with 'human dignity'.

In *Valsamis v Greece*[204] the Court decided that religious convictions covered an objection by a Jehovah's Witness to attending a school parade commemorating a war because pacifism is a fundamental tenet of his religion.

19.60 In *Campbell and Cosans*[205] the Court held that parental objections to corporal punishment in schools were philosophical because they reached a certain level of cogency, seriousness, cohesion and importance. The desirability of sex education,[206] co-education, progressive teaching methods, religious instruction and objections to state education[207] can also constitute religious and philosophical convictions.

19.61 On the other hand, opinions about the language in which instruction is conducted do not constitute religious or philosophical convictions.[208] Parents have also failed in claiming that the state should provide a place at a grammar school because of the negative ethos of a comprehensive school[209] or that a seven-year-old child should be provided with elementary arithmetic rather than modern mathematics.[210] In *Stevens v United Kingdom*[211] the Commission rejected a complaint that enforcing rules about a school uniform breached the right of respect for private life[212] and the right to be educated in accordance with parental convictions.

(c) The extent of the obligation

19.62 The obligation on the state under Article 2 is to *respect* parental convictions. The Court stressed in *Valsamis v Greece*[213] that:

---

[202] D Harris, M O'Boyle and C Warbrick, *Law of the European Convention on Human Rights* (Butterworths, 1995) 544, asserts that 'the convictions which are to be taken into account are to be interpreted narrowly', but A Lester and D Pannick, *A Joint Opinion: Independent Schools and the European Convention on Human Rights* (ISIS 1982), 8, takes the view that the phrase is given a wide interpretation by the Court.
[203] (1982) 4 EHRR 293 para 36.
[204] (1996) 24 EHRR 294
[205] (1982) 4 EHRR 293 para 36.
[206] *Kjeldsen, Busk Madsen and Pedersen v Denmark* (1976) 1 EHRR 711.
[207] *Family H v United Kingdom* (1984) 37 DR 105, EComm HR.
[208] *Belgian Linguistic Case (No 2)* (1968) 1 EHRR 252, 282 para 6.
[209] *W and D M and M and H I v United Kingdom* (1984) 37 DR 96, EComm HR.
[210] *X, Y and Z v Germany* (1982) 29 DR 224, EComm HR.
[211] (1986) DR 245, EComm HR.
[212] See para 12.84ff above.
[213] (1996) 24 EHRR 294 para 27.

> That duty is broad in its extent as it applies not only to the content of education but to the performance of all the 'functions' assumed by the State. The verb 'respect' means more than to 'acknowledge' or 'take account'. In addition to a primarily negative undertaking, it implies some positive obligation on the state.[214]

Thus, provided the state ensures that sensitive subjects such as sex education are taught in an 'objective, pluralistic and critical manner,'[215] a parent is unlikely to prove a lack of 'respect'. However, it has been argued that the mere presentation of certain types of information might violate the rights of the parent.[216]

Where the parents find the curriculum objectionable, special arrangements made by the school authorities (such as excusing the child from class) may be sufficient to establish respect for their parental convictions. The Court in *Kjeldsen, Busk Madsen and Pedersen v Denmark*[217] indicated that the compulsory sex education policy of the state did not violate Article 2 since parents had other avenues open to them for the education of their children. The Court took the view[218] that the Danish state: **19.63**

> . . . preserves an important expedient for parents who in the name of their creed or opinions, wish to dissociate their children from integrated sex education; it allows parents either to entrust their children to private schools, which are bound by less strict obligations and moreover heavily subsidised by the state, or to educate them or have them educated at home, subject to suffering the undeniable sacrifices and inconveniences caused by recourse to one of those alternative solutions.

It is not clear whether equal significance will be attached to appropriate, but unsubsidised, private schools. The state generally has no obligation to finance private institutions,[219] but if the parents are unable to afford that option,[220] and there is no other feasible alternative that might solve the problem, the state's obligation may extend to financing the institution itself. In *Campbell and Cosans v United Kingdom*[221] the Government argued that an objection to corporal punishment in the state school system could only be met by instituting a dual school system, in **19.64**

[214] *Campbell and Cousins v United Kingdom* (1982) 4 EHRR 293 para 37.

[215] *Kjeldsen, Busk Madsen and Pedersen v Denmark* (1976) 1 EHRR 711 para 53.

[216] See the dissent of Judge Verdross in *Kjeldsen, Busk Madsen and Pedersen v Denmark* (n 215 above) 735 para 7 in which he argued that parents could rightly object to the provision of information in regard to sexual practices, as opposed to the biological science of reproduction, even in an objective manner. However, on the facts, Judge Verdross distinguished information about sexual practices from the biological science of reproduction.

[217] n 216 above.

[218] Ibid (n 216 above) para 54.

[219] *W and K L v Sweden* (1985) 45 DR 143, EComm HR.

[220] It is also conceivable that available but inaccessible alternatives might render the state 'respectful' in compliance with Art 2, while what would otherwise be a 'failure to respect' is permitted to continue within the state system; it seems more likely, though, that the Court will first ensure that there is a respectful 'pluralistic' presentation of sensitive material in the state system and only secondarily, if parents remain dissatisfied, address alternative ways of meeting their concerns.

[221] (1982) 4 EHRR 293.

which some schools were subject to the discipline and others were not. It claimed that such an approach was precluded by the United Kingdom's reservation to Article 2 on the basis of unreasonable expenditure.[222] The Court, however, decided that the duty of respect was subsidiary to the obligation to provide education; and that a viable option existed, involving the exemption of individuals.

19.65 The obligation to respect parental convictions is not an onerous one. The ease with which a state can satisfy the obligation is illustrated by *Valsamis v Greece*[223] where the Court decided that suspending a child for one day for refusing to attend a parade which violated her parents' convictions did not breach the obligation to respect parental convictions.

19.66 Furthermore, the duty to respect parental convictions is not absolute; and the state is not obliged to accommodate particular convictions by providing special facilities[224] or setting up and supporting schools.[225] The duty to respect convictions is qualified by the primary duty of the state in the first sentence of Article 2 to determine the provision and financing of education,[226] and by the fact that it is impossible for any one system to satisfy the personal convictions of all parents.

19.67 Thus, the discretion of the state has generally prevailed over the competing interests of the right of the child to education and the right of the parents to ensure such education.[227] For example, parental convictions that a deaf child should not be educated in a school for the hard of hearing did not compel the pupil's admission at an ordinary school which might require the cost of additional staff or be detrimental to other pupils as opposed to placing him at a special school.[228]

D. The Impact of the Human Rights Act

(1) Introduction

19.68 The Human Rights Act has significant implications in the educational field.[229] Educational bodies such as local educational authorities, school governors, head teachers, university teachers and university Visitors will all be public authorities

[222] See para 19.15 above.

[223] (1996) 24 EHRR 294.

[224] *X v United Kingdom* (1978) 14 DR 179, EComm HR; *Graeme v United Kingdom* (1990) 64 DR 158, EComm HR; *Klerks v Netherlands* (1995) 82-A DR 129, EComm HR.

[225] *X v United Kingdom* (n 224 above); *X and Y v United Kingdom* (1982) 31 DR 210.

[226] *Kjeldsen, Busk Madsen and Pedersen v Denmark* (1976) 1 EHRR 711 para 56.

[227] *W and D M and M and H I v United Kingdom* (1984) 37 DR 96, EComm HR; see also cases on respect for convictions of parents of handicapped children: *P D and L D v United Kingdom* (1989) 62 DR 292, EComm HR; *Graeme v United Kingdom* (n 224 above).

[228] *Klerks v Netherlands* (n 224 above).

[229] See generally, A W Bradley, 'Scope for Review: The Convention Right to Education and the Human Rights Act 1998' [1999] EHRLR 395.

under the Human Rights Act. However, it may be unclear in particular cases which institutions are standard public authorities[230] and which ones will be functional public authorities carrying out functions of a public nature.[231] It is submitted that private schools undertaking educational functions will be functional public authorities.[232]

There are a number of Convention articles which will be relevant to education in addition to the right to education itself. It is likely that education cases will arise in relation to fair trial rights under Article 6,[233] private life under Article 8,[234] freedom of religion under Article 9,[235] freedom of expression under Article 10[236] and discrimination rights under Article 14.[237] **19.69**

The principles contained in the Convention right to education are already broadly reflected in the legislative framework that regulates education in England and Wales. In particular, there is an important limitation on the Convention right of parents to educate their children in accordance with their religious and philosophical convictions. The United Kingdom has entered a reservation[238] to the right to education under Article 2 of Protocol 1 that: **19.70**

> in view of certain provisions of the Education Act in force in the United Kingdom, the principle affirmed in the second sentence of Article 2 is accepted by the United Kingdom only so far as it is compatible with the provision of efficient instruction and training and the avoidance of unreasonable expenditure.

The reservation was entered to reflect the principle that children are to be educated in accordance with the wishes of their parents which is now contained in section 9 of the Education Act 1996.[239] Section 15(1)(a) of the Human Rights Act expressly preserves the derogation.

When considering complaints alleging a failure to educate in accordance with parental convictions,[240] the Commission has been influenced by the reservation, particularly in relation to special needs education.[241] On the other hand, in **19.71**

---

230 See para 5.12ff above.

231 See para 5.14ff above.

232 Judicial review is already available where private schools perform public functions, such as a city technology college (see *R v Governors of Haberdashers' Aske's Hatcham College, ex p T* [1995] ELR 350) or where a private school purported to withdraw an assisted place (see *R v Cobham Hall School, ex p S* [1998] ELR 389); cf *R v Fernhill Manor Public School, ex p A* [1993] 1 FLR 620.

233 It is strongly arguable, however, that the right to education is not a 'civil right or obligation' under Art 6: see para 11.160ff above.

234 See para 12.84ff above.

235 See para 14.36ff above.

236 See para 15.137ff above.

237 See para 17.79ff below.

238 Human Rights Act, s 15(5) and Sch 2 Pt II.

239 See para 19.15 above.

240 See para 19.53 above.

241 See generally, para 19.23ff above.

Campbell and Cosans v United Kingdom[242] the Court declined to give weight to the reservation when it was considering a statutory provision which had been originally enacted before the reservation was entered in 1952. Nevertheless, it is submitted that some weight will need to be attached to section 9 in cases under the Human Rights Act even though the Commission[243] has suggested that the reservation may not withstand a challenge under Convention law.[244]

(2) United Kingdom cases prior to the Human Rights Act

(a) Introduction

19.72 There have been a number of cases brought against the United Kingdom alleging violations of Article 2 of the First Protocol. The majority of cases have related to corporal punishment and special needs education. A violation was found in the only United Kingdom Article 2 case to reach the Court.[245]

(b) Corporal punishment

19.73 Complaints about corporal punishment have normally involved alleged breaches of the prohibition against degrading treatment under Article 3.[246] However, in *Campbell and Cosans v United Kingdom*[247] the parents of children who attended schools which used corporal punishment complained that corporal punishment as such violated the right to educate their children in accordance with their convictions. The Court took a broad view of the scope of the right to education; and held that disciplinary procedures were an integral part of the education system.[248] It rejected the government's reliance on the reservation to the Convention right[249] and concluded that the pupil's suspension from school until he accepted punishment breached his right of access to education since regulation must never injure the substance of a Convention right.[250] By contrast, in *Warwick v United Kingdom*[251] the Commission held that there was no breach of the right of respect for parental convictions where a local educational authority failed to give an assurance that the applicant's daughter would not be subject to corporal punishment; nor was the right to education breached where a pupil was suspended as an alternative to corporal punishment to which his parents were opposed.[252]

---

[242] (1982) 4 EHRR 293 para 37.
[243] *S P v United Kingdom* (1997) 23 EHRR CD 139.
[244] See generally, *Belilos v Switzerland* (1988) 10 EHRR 466 paras 52–59.
[245] *Campbell and Cosans v United Kingdom* (1982) 4 EHRR 293.
[246] See para 8.32ff above.
[247] (1982) 4 EHRR 293.
[248] Ibid paras 33–36.
[249] Ibid para 37.
[250] Ibid paras 39–41.
[251] (1986) 60 DR 5, EComm HR.
[252] *Whitman v United Kingdom* Application 13477/87, 4 Oct 1989 EComm HR.

(c) Special needs education

The Commission has considered a number of applications by children with special needs[253] both in relation to the right to education and the right to be educated in accordance with parental convictions. However, every application to date has been rejected as being manifestly ill founded. **19.74**

In *Simpson v United Kingdom*[254] the Commission rejected a complaint where the state had breached the right to education by refusing to pay fees for a dyslexic child at a private school and instead placed the child in a mainstream comprehensive school. The Commission took the view that a child was not denied the right to education where the comprehensive school had special teaching facilities available, emphasising that public authorities had a wide discretion as to how to best use resources in the interests of disabled children. This approach was applied in *Ford v United Kingdom*[255] where the Commission ruled inadmissible a complaint that the local educational authority had breached the applicant's right of access to mainstream education by deciding he should be educated in a special needs school. Similarly, in *McIntyre v United Kingdom*[256] the Commission dismissed an application alleging that the right to education was breached by failing to provide a disabled child with a lift at school so she could freely use school facilities. **19.75**

The Commission has also rejected a complaint that a local educational authority has breached the right to education by failing to assess a dyslexic child under the statutory[257] procedure[258] or by failing to pay transport costs[259] so that a child with special educational needs could attend a school of his parent's choice which was further away from his home.[260] **19.76**

It has also been argued that placing their children in a special school fails to respect a parent's philosophical conviction that disabled children should be educated in an integrated educational environment. However, the Commission has ruled these complaints inadmissible.[261] The Commission has left open the question of whether a parent's disagreement with a local educational authority about the appropriate school for his child constitutes a philosophical conviction under Article 2.[262] Even where such views constitute a philosophical conviction under Article **19.77**

[253] See generally, para 19.23ff above.
[254] (1989) 64 DR 188, EComm HR.
[255] (1996) EHRLR 534.
[256] Application 29046/95, 21 Oct 1998 EComm HR.
[257] See para 19.23ff above.
[258] *S P v United Kingdom* (1997) 23 EHRR CD 139 EComm HR.
[259] See para 19.30ff above.
[260] *Cohen v United Kingdom* (1996) 21 EHRR CD 104 EComm HR.
[261] See eg *P D and L D v United Kingdom* (1989) 62 DR 292, EComm HR; *Graeme v United Kingdom* (1990) 64 DR 158; *Klerks v Netherlands* (1995) 82-A DR 129, EComm HR.
[262] See eg *P D and L D v United Kingdom* EComm HR (n 261 above); *D v United Kingdom* Application 14137/88, 2 Oct 1987.

2,[263] the Convention right does not require the state to provide special educational facilities.[264] Furthermore, as the Commission has pointed out,[265] inferences may be drawn from the fact that the United Kingdom entered a reservation to the Convention right so as to reflect the terms of section 9 of the Education Act 1996;[266] in fact the language of section 9 is very similar to that used in section 316 of the Education Act 1996 to create a duty to educate children with special needs in mainstream schools.[267] The crucial factor stressed by the Commission is that the right to respect for parental convictions is subsidiary to the fundamental right to education.[268] The Commission took a similar approach in rejecting a complaint that requiring a child to attend a boarding school breached his parent's philosophical convictions.[269]

19.78 The Commission's approach to home education has been to allow the state's assessment of a child's right to education to override the parent's particular convictions. In *Family H v United Kingdom*[270] the parents insisted on teaching dyslexic children at home and were convicted of failing to comply with school attendance orders.[271] The Commission considered it was not its task to decide whether the state's or the parents' views were better for children: the state has a responsibility to verify and enforce educational standards and parents were obliged to co-operate in that assessment.

(d) Other cases

19.79 In *Patel v United Kingdom*[272] the applicant complained that he was asked to leave university after failing his first year examination and a re-sit. The Commission expressed the view that:

> where certain, limited, higher education facilities were provided by the state, it was not incompatible with Article 2 of Protocol No 1 to restrict access thereto to those students who have attained the academic level required to most benefit from the courses offered.[273]

The Commission declared the complaint inadmissible.

19.80 In another case, the applicants complained that the failure of the state to provide financial support for the education of their children at a Rudolf Steiner school was

[263] See eg *Family H v United Kingdom* (1984) 37 DR 105, EComm HR.
[264] see *X v United Kingdom* (1978) 14 DR 179 EComm HR.
[265] *P D and L D v United Kingdom* (n 261 above); *Graeme v United Kingdom* (n 261 above).
[266] See para 19.15 above.
[267] See para 19.24ff above.
[268] See para 19.53 above.
[269] *Northcott v United Kingdom* Application 13884/88, 5 May 1989 EComm HR.
[270] (1984) 37 DR 105, EComm HR.
[271] See para 19.12 above.
[272] (1980) 4 EHRR 256, EComm HR; see also *X v United Kingdom* (1980) 4 EHRR 252 EComm HR.
[273] Ibid para 13.

a breach of the right to education. The Commission held that although the state must not prevent parents from exercising the right to education, it had no obligation to set up or support any educational establishment.[274]

Where the applicants' children had been refused places in state grammar schools due to lack of places, there was no breach of Article 2.[275] Although the parents' religious and philosophical convictions had to be respected in the state school system, this was subject to limitations of a practical nature. **19.81**

In the case of *Stevens v United Kingdom*[276] the applicant complained about rules requiring a school uniform to be worn. The Commission held that this was not a breach of either the right to private life[277] or the right to respect for parental convictions in education. **19.82**

The Commission has recently ruled as admissible several cases which include a complaint that the right to education is breached where children are removed as a result of gypsies being evicted for breaches of planning controls[278] or by the deportation of the children's mother.[279] However, in a number of cases[280] the Commission held that the applicant's departure from the United Kingdom following the deportation of his mother in accordance with a legitimate measure of immigration control could not be construed as depriving him of the right to education. Furthermore, foreign students cannot rely on the right to education as providing them with a right to stay in the United Kingdom.[281] **19.83**

(3) The potential impact

(a) Introduction

The Convention right to education creates very limited positive obligations; and the requirement on public authorities to give access to existing educational institutions is already reflected in the existing legislation.[282] Thus, for example, the right to education does not create obligations on public authorities to subsidise particular types of schools.[283] The Convention right to be educated in accordance **19.84**

[274] *X v United Kingdom* (1983) 5 EHRR 480, EComm HR.
[275] *X v United Kingdom* (1985) 7 EHRR 140, EComm HR.
[276] (1986) 46 DR 245, EComm HR.
[277] See para 12.84ff above.
[278] *Coster v United Kingdom* (1998) 25 EHRR CD 24; *Smith v United Kingdom* (1998) 25 EHRR CD 42; *Lee v United Kingdom* (1998) 25 EHRR CD 46
[279] *Johal, Singh and Singh v United Kingdom* Application 27299/95, 4 Mar 1998.
[280] *Jaramillo v United Kingdom* Application 24865/94, 23 Oct 1995; *Sorabjee v United Kingdom* [1996] EHRLR 216; *Dabhi v United Kingdom* Application 28627/95, 17 Jan 1997.
[281] *15 Foreign Students v United Kingdom* (1977) 9 DR 185, EComm HR.
[282] See para 19.08ff above.
[283] See para 19.40 above.

with parental convictions[284] is also heavily qualified. Furthermore, the reservation to the right to education[285] (preserved under the Human Rights Act)[286] will further restrict the impact of the Convention right to education. Nevertheless, the right to education under Article 2 of the First Protocol has implications for the pupils and parents in several areas affecting educational rights including access to education, respect for parental convictions, school attendance, school transport and special educational needs.

(b) Education

19.85 **Access to education.** The right to access to education may be breached if a school fails to take appropriate action where a pupil is subjected to a campaign of bullying.[287] It is also possible that a local educational authority will be in breach of the right to education if it fails to diagnose a child's special needs and therefore fails to give a child appropriate education.[288]

19.86 **Discipline and expulsion.** The Convention case law[289] indicates that educational authorities will have considerable latitude when exercising disciplinary functions before they will be held liable for breaching the right of access to education.

19.87 **Respect for parental convictions.** The current statutory provisions permitting parents to educate their children in accordance with their religious beliefs[290] and entitling children to absent themselves from religious education and worship[291] probably satisfies the Convention right to education.

19.88 However, a parent's belief that his child should not receive individual advice about contraception without his consent and the belief that a monogamous homosexual relationship should be given the same respect as a family relationship as a monogamous heterosexual relationship both amount to a conviction under Article 2 of the First Protocol.[292]

19.89 By contrast, the Commission has taken a very restrictive view about the right of respect for parental convictions when considering home education[293] or whether

[284] See para 19.24ff above.

[285] See para 19.70 above.

[286] See s 15(1)(a).

[287] M Supperstone, J Goudie and J Coppel, *Local Authorities and the Human Rights Act 1998* (Butterworths, 1999) 64.

[288] Ibid. This cause of action would be in addition to any claim that might be based on negligence; see *Phelps v Hillingdon London Borough Council, The Times*, 28 Jul 2000.

[289] See para 19.48 above. The question of whether the pupil has few trial rights under Art 6 is considered at para 11.358 above.

[290] See para 19.16ff above.

[291] See para 14.12ff above.

[292] Supperstone, Goudie and Coppel (n 287 above) 61.

[293] *Family H v United Kingdom* (1984) 37 DR 105, EComm HR.

children with special needs should be educated in an integrated educational environment.[294]

School attendance. At present a pupil who is prosecuted for failing to attend school may have a defence if he is registered at a school not within walking distance and no suitable arrangements have been made regarding his transport.[295] Since parents will now have the right to ensure that a child is educated in accordance with their religious or philosophical convictions,[296] a child who cannot attend school because no suitable arrangements have been made to transport him[297–298] may now have a defence if they are prosecuted. **19.90**

School transport. It could also be argued that, as a result of the right to education, a local educational authority is under a duty to provide transport which reflects parental preferences for schools,[299] in particular, because section 509(4) expressly obliges the authority to take account of their religious views. **19.91**

Special educational needs. It is now clear that a claim in negligence may be brought where a local educational authority, teachers or educational psychologists are alleged to have failed to diagnose special educational needs or failed to provide appropriate education.[300] In addition, where an authority acknowledges its obligation to provide education under a statement of special educational needs, a failure to meet those obligations might entitle the court to award child damages under the Human Rights Act, both for a breach of Article 8[301] and for breach of the right to education.[302] On the other hand, the Commission has consistently rejected applications by children with special needs[303] for breaches of the right to education; and it is unlikely that the Human Rights Act will have a significant impact in this area. **19.92**

Universities. The Convention right to education is unlikely to affect the relationships between students and universities. It may be arguable that the right to education strengthens the contractual obligation that a university has to enrol a student who has accepted an unconditional place,[304] to provide proper tuition to **19.93**

---

294 *P D and L D v United Kingdom* (1989) 62 DR 292, EComm HR; *Graeme v United Kingdom* (1990) 64 DR 158, EComm HR; *Klerks v Netherlands* (1995) 82-A DR 129, EComm HR.

295 See para 19.12ff above.

296 See para 19.53ff above.

297–298 See generally, para 19.30 above.

299 But see *R v East Sussex County Council, ex p D* [1991] COD 374; *R v Essex County Council, ex p C* [1994] ELR 273; *R v Dyfed County Council, ex p S* [1995] ELR 98.

300 See para 19.28ff above.

301 See para 12.84ff above.

302 M Supperstone, J Goudie and J Coppel, *Local Authorities and the Human Rights Act 1998* (Butterworths, 1999) 64.

303 See para 19.74ff above.

304 *Moran v University of Salford (No 2)* [1994] ELR 187; see also *Casson v University of Aston in Birmingham* [1983] 1 All ER 88.

its students,[305] or in relation to universities which do not provide for a visitor where a student alleges that the university has breached its contractual rules.[305a]

(c) Social security

19.94 In general, students in full time education do not qualify for income support and they may remain ineligible when there is a break in their studies. The right to education was unsuccessfully invoked in a *Wednesbury* challenge to a withdrawal of income support in *O'Conner v Chief Adjudication Officer*.[306] Under the Human Rights Act students will be able to rely directly on the right to education in support of their claims for social security. However, the practical limitations on the right to education are likely to mean that such challenges will be unsuccessful.

Appendix 1: The Canadian Charter of Rights

19.95 The Canadian Charter contains a right to education which is very different to the Convention right. Section 23 is designed to protect minority language education and provides that:

> (1) Citizens of Canada
>
> (a) whose first language learned and still understood is that of the English or French linguistic minority population of the province in which they reside, or
> (b) who have received their primary school instruction in Canada in English or French and reside in a province where the language in which they received that instruction is the language of the English or French linguistic minority population of the province,
>
> have the right to have their children receive primary and secondary school instruction in that language in that province.
>
> (2) Citizens of Canada of whom any child has received or is receiving primary or secondary school instruction in English or French in Canada, have the right to have all their children receive primary and secondary school instruction in the same language.
>
> (3) The right of citizens of Canada under subsections (1) and (2) to have their children receive primary and secondary school instruction in the language of the English or French linguistic minority population of a province
>
> (a) applies wherever in the province the number of children of citizens who have such a right is sufficient to warrant the provision to them out of public funds of minority language instruction; and
> (b) includes, where the number of those children so warrants, the right to have them receive that instruction in minority language educational facilities provided out of public funds.

[305] *Sammy v Birkbeck College, The Times*, 3 Nov 1964.
[305a] *Clark v University of Northumbria* [2000] 3 All ER 752.
[306] [1999] ELR 209.

The beneficiaries of section 23 are the parents rather than their children.[307] The right itself is narrowly defined: it guarantees no more than the right of the linguistic (French or English) minority[308] in a province to an education in the minority language.[309] Section 23 therefore does not guarantee the right of the linguistic minority to an education in the language of the majority; it does not impose a duty on the minority to exercise its right to education in its mother tongue; nor does it give members of the linguistic majority any right to education in the minority language. Its purpose is to preserve and promote the two official languages of Canada.[310] **19.96**

The provision creates a general group right of minority education which places positive obligations on the Government to alter or develop major institutional structures. Unless the number of individuals involved is so minimal as to warrant no action at all,[311] the Government is required to do whatever is practical in the situation to promote minority language education in the province. **19.97**

Section 23(3) implies that the establishment of minority language education is on a discretionary basis, and is subject to sufficient demand. The discretion of a school board is not unfettered, but must be based on an 'objective assessment'[312] of whether the number of children of qualified parents is sufficient to warrant the provision of language instruction or facilities. Although the provincial legislature must decide the minimum threshold, a blanket application of the threshold across the province is not easily justified;[313] the decision must be made on a local basis within the province with qualification or exemption as appropriate. Furthermore, although costs are a relevant consideration in deciding the facilities to be provided, the fact that additional public funds are necessary to finance minority language education was contemplated by the framers of the Charter; and cost is therefore not a sufficient justification for denying the minority right to minority language facilities.[314] **19.98**

If minority student numbers warrant provision out of public funds, the minority language education provided must be of a standard equivalent to that provided to majority language students.[315] However, the right to minority language education does not protect other 'minority concerns' (such as religious or philosophical convictions)[316] and does not guarantee minority denominational facilities.[317] **19.99**

[307] *Reference re Education Act of Ontario and Minority Language Education Rights* (1984) 10 DLR (4th) 491.
[308] *Whittington v Board of School Trustees of School District No 63 (Saanich)* (1987) 44 DLR (4th) 128.
[309] *Société des Acadiens du Nouveau-Brunswick Inc v Minority Language School Board No 50* (1983) 48 NBR (2d) 361.
[310] *Mahe v Alberta* [1990] 1 SCR 342.
[311] Ibid.
[312] Ibid.
[313] Ibid.
[314] *Lavoie v Nova Scotia (A-G)* (1988) 50 DLR (4th) 405.
[315] *Quebec (A-G) v Quebec Association of Protestant School Boards (No 2)* [1984] 2 SCR 66.
[316] *Reference re Education Act of Ontario and Minority Language Education Rights* (n 307 above).
[317] *Griffin v Blainville Deux-Montagnes Commission Scolaire Regionale* (1989) 63 DLR (4th) 37.

Appendix 2: Human Rights Cases in Other Jurisdictions

(1) Introduction

19.100 The right to education has received only limited recognition in domestic rights instruments in common law jurisdictions. The US Constitution contains no express or implied right to education. However, in the famous desegregation decision of *Brown v the Board of Education of Topeka*[318] the Supreme Court held that the Fourteenth Amendment forbids states to use governmental powers to bar children from attending public schools on racial grounds. Warren CJ emphasised the importance of education as a state function:

> Today education is perhaps the most important function of the state. Compulsory school attendance laws and the great expenditure for education both demonstrate our recognition of the importance of education to our democratic society. It is required in the performance of most basic public responsibilities . . . It is the very foundation of good. Today it is a principal instrument in awakening the child to cultural values, in preparing him for later professional training, and in helping him to adjust normally to his environment. In these days, it is doubtful that any child may reasonably be expected to succeed in life if he is denied the opportunity of an education. Such an opportunity, where the state has undertaken to provide it, is a right which must be made available to all on equal terms.[319]

Following this decision the US courts blocked state attempts to resist the basic principle of educational desegregation and, in the early 1970s used flexible equitable remedies to ensure a unitary school system.[320] However, in recent years the Supreme Court has effectively ended judicial oversight of school boards.[321]

19.101 The US courts have refused to recognise interests in education as 'fundamental interests' attracting increased judicial scrutiny.[322] But the courts will take into account the interests of children as innocent victims of discrimination in education. Thus, in *Plyler v Doe*[323] the Supreme Court struck down a Texas statute barring the children of undocumented aliens from attending public elementary schools. It held that the state needed a substantial basis to justify denial of public education to a discrete group of children.[324]

19.102 The US courts have considered a number of cases where teaching methods or the secular nature of the curriculum were alleged to be offensive to religious beliefs.[325] Creationists continue to challenge the teaching of Darwinian evolution although the Supreme Court has found that a ban on teaching evolution breaches the provision of the Constitution relating to the 'establishment' and 'free exercise' of religion.[326] Complaints have also been rejected, for example, from Apostolic Lutherans claiming that their children should be

---

[318] (1954) 347 US 483.

[319] Ibid 493.

[320] *Swann v Charlotte-Mecklenburg Board of Education* (1971) 402 US 1; see generally, C Antieau and W Rich, *Modern Constitutional Law* (2nd edn, West Group, 1997) §27.02ff.

[321] Ibid §27.08 and *Missouri v Jenkins (Jenkins III)* (1995) 515 US 70.

[322] *San Antonio Independent School District v Rodriguez* (1973) 411 US 1.

[323] (1982) 457 US 202.

[324] See generally, Antieau and Rich (n 320 above) §30.04.

[325] See generally, C Hamilton, *Family, Law and Religion* (Sweet and Maxwell, 1995) Chap 8.

[326] *Epperson v Arkansas* (1968) 393 US 97; for a discussion of the constitutional rights for the 'establishment' and 'free exercise' of religion, see para 14.106ff above.

excused from class whenever televisions are used because audio visual aids are forbidden by their religion[327] and claiming that children should be withdrawn from parts of the secular curiculuum[328] or sex education[329] on religious grounds.

(2) India

The right to education has been held to be an unenumerated right under Article 19 of the Constitution of India but the state's obligation to provide education is not absolute.[330] Educational rights in India are grouped together with cultural rights, in Articles 29 to 30 of the Constitution. Article 29 provides: **19.103**

> (1) Any section of the citizens residing in the territory of India or any part thereof having a distinct language, script or culture of its own shall have the right to conserve the same.
> (2) No citizen shall be denied admission into any educational institution maintained by the State or receiving aid out of State funds on grounds only of religion, race, caste, language, or any of them.

Article 30 states that:

> (1) All minorities, whether based on religion or language, shall have the right to establish and administer educational institutions of their choice
> (1A) In making any law providing for the compulsory acquisition of any property of an educational institution established and administered by a minority, referred to in clause (1), the State shall ensure that the amount fixed or determined under such law for the acquisition of such property is such as would not restrict or abrogate the right guaranteed under that clause.
> (2) The State shall not, in granting aid to educational institutions, discriminate against any educational institution on the ground that it is under the management of a minority, whether based on religion or language.

The right of a minority to administer educational institutions under Article 30 does not include a right to maladminister.[331] Although the right in Article 30 is subject to reasonable regulation, it must not displace the minority administration or completely take away its autonomy.[332] Minority aided educational institutions are entitled to make reservations (ie quotas) for their own candidates. However, that intake must not exceed 50% of its annual admission. The admission of other community candidates must be done purely on merit.[333] **19.104**

Article 45 provides that: **19.105**

> The state shall endeavour to provide, within a period of ten years from the commencement of this Constitution, for free and compulsory education for all children until they complete the age of fourteen years.

---

327 *Davis v Page* (1974) 385 F Supp 395.
328 *Kidder v Chellis* (1879) 59 NH 473.
329 *Hopkins v Board of Education* (1979) Conn Sup 397.
330 *Mohini Jain v State of Karnataka* A 1992 SC 1858; but see *Unnikrishnan v State of AP* A 1993 SC 2178.
331 *In re Kerala Education Bill 1957* AIR 1958 SC 956.
332 *St Stephen's College v University of Delhi* (1992) 1 SCC 558.
333 Ibid.

In *Unni Krishnan J P v State of Andhra Pradesh*[334] it was held that the failure of the state to provide for universal primary education was contrary to the Constitution.

(3) Ireland

19.106 Article 42 of the Irish Constitution[335] provides that:

> 1. The State acknowledges that the primary and natural educator of the child is the Family and guarantees to respect the inalienable right and duty of parents to provide, according to their means, for the religious and moral, intellectual, physical and social education of their children.
> 2. Parents shall be free to provide this education in their homes or in private schools or in schools recognised or established by the State.
> 3. 1. The State shall not oblige parents in violation of their conscience and lawful preference to send their children to schools established by the State, or to any particular type of school designated by the State.
>   2. The State shall, however, as guardian of the common good, require in view of actual conditions that the children receive a certain minimum education, moral, intellectual and social.
> 4. The State shall provide for free primary education and shall endeavour to supplement and give reasonable aid to private and corporate educational initiative, and, when the public good requires it, provide other educational facilities or institutions with due regard, however, for the rights of parents, especially in the matters of religious and moral formation.
> 5. In exceptional cases, where the parents for physical or moral reasons fail in their duty towards their children, the State as guardian of the common good, by appropriate means shall endeavour to supply the place of the parents, but always with due regard for the natural and imprescriptible rights of the child.

19.107 Parents' rights to choose the schooling of their children may not be dictated by outsiders. Thus, testamentary bequests to children conditional upon the children being brought up as Catholics have been invalidated to the extent of the condition.[336]

19.108 The term 'education' has a limited meaning. As a result the fluoridation of public water did not interfere with the parental right of educating their children as they saw fit.[337]

19.109 The right to free elementary education was considered in *Byrne v Ireland*.[338] A teachers' strike had closed some schools and many children were without schooling for several months. The Supreme Court held that the Government's failure to intervene in the strike was not in breach of its duty, as it was not required 'to provide' free elementary education, but merely 'to provide for' such education. If the Government had intervened directly in the strike, matters could have escalated into a general strike. On the other hand, the children established a cause of action against the teachers' union, which had prevented them from being accepted at neighbouring schools, and thereby deprived them of their constitutional right to free elementary education.

---

[334] 1993 SC 2178.

[335] See generally, J Kelly, *The Irish Constitution*, (3rd edn, Butterworths, 1994) 1052–1060.

[336] *Burke and O'Reilly v Burke and Quail* [1951] IR 216; *In re Blake, deceased* [1955] IR 89.

[337] [1965] IR 294.

[338] [1972] IR 241.

In *O'Donoghue v Minister for Health*[339] an eight-year-old mentally handicapped boy succeeded in establishing a breach of Article 42 because the state provided inadequate schooling for him. **19.110**

(4) South Africa

Section 32(c) of the Interim Constitution provided that everyone has the right: **19.111**

> to establish, where practicable, educational institutions based on a common culture, language or religion, provided that there shall be no discrimination on the ground of race.[340]

In *Dispute Concerning the Constitutionality of Certain Provisions of the Gauteng School Education Bill of 1995*[341] the Constitutional Court considered clause 19 (prohibiting language competence testing as an admission requirement to a public school); clauses 21(2) and (3) (relating to the formulation of a religious policy by a public school aimed at the development of a national democratic culture of respect for the country's diverse cultural and religious traditions) and clause 22(3) (relating to the right of learners at public schools, or at private schools receiving a subsidy, not to attend religious education classes and religious practices at that school). The petitioners contended that section 32(c) of the interim Constitution imposed a positive obligation on the state to establish, where possible, public schools based on a common culture, language or religion. However, the Court held on a proper construction of section 32(c) that there was no positive obligation on the state. **19.112**

[339] High Court, 27 May 1993; Kelly (n 335 above) 1058–59.

[340] See generally, M Chaskalson, J Kentridge, J Klaaren, G Marcus, D Spitz and S Woolman (eds) *Constitutional Law of South Africa* (Juta, 1996) chap 38.

[341] 1996 (4) BCLR 537.

20

ELECTORAL RIGHTS

A. The Nature of the Rights

The right to participate in periodic free and fair elections is fundamental to the modern notion of a democratic society. The US Constitution made detailed provision in relation to the holding of Congressional and Presidential elections.[1] The Supreme Court has developed an implied right to vote which it has recognised as being of central importance: **20.01**

[1] See Art I, s 2; Art II, s 1, modified by a number of amendments, see in particular Amendments XII (1804), XV (1870) and XIX (1920) and XX (1933).

> No right is more precious in a free country than that of having a choice in the election of those who make the laws under which, as good citizens, they must live. Other rights, even the most basic, are illusory if the right to vote is undermined.[2]

20.02 This right was included in the Universal Declaration, Article 21 of which states that:

> The will of the people shall be the basis of the authority of government; this will shall be expressed in periodic and genuine elections which shall be by universal and equal suffrage and shall be held by secret vote or by equivalent voting procedures.[3]

The International Covenant on Civil and Political Rights provides more general rights of political participation including the right and opportunity, without unreasonable restrictions:

> To vote and to be elected at genuine periodic elections which shall be by universal and equal suffrage and shall be held by secret ballot, guaranteeing the free expression of the will of the electors.[4]

The Convention on the Political Rights of Women (1952),[5] the Convention on the Elimination of All Forms of Discrimination against Women (1979)[6] and the Convention on the Elimination of All Forms of Racial Discrimination (1966)[7] all oblige states to secure a right to participate in elections.

20.03 Although all democratic states accept, in general terms, the rights of citizens to vote and stand in free elections, a number of questions arise in relation to the precise content of these rights. These can be grouped under four headings:

The scope of the rights: Do rights to participate in elections extend beyond elections to the 'national' legislature? The existence of indirectly elected or non-elected second chambers and elected provincial and local bodies gives rise to issues as to the extent of the rights.

Voter and candidate qualifications: Although it is clear that electoral rights include the right to vote and to stand in elections, difficult questions arise as to the extent to which individuals or groups can be disqualified from voting in or standing for election. Problems have arisen in a number of jurisdictions in relation to the rights of prisoners and the mentally handicapped.

Electoral boundaries: Most electoral systems have electoral districts or constituencies which will differ in size. Many political systems have been afflicted by the problem of 'gerrymandering': the adjustment of the size of electoral

2 *Wesberry v Saunders* (1964) 376 US 1, 17.

3 As a result it has inspired provisions for electoral rights in numerous jurisdictions.

4 Art 25(b), the text is reproduced at App J in Vol 2.

5 Art 1.

6 Art 7. The text is reproduced at App M in Vol 2.

7 Article 5(c). The text is reproduced at App N in Vol 2.

districts for political advantage. The question arises as to the extent to which the right to free elections carries with it a right to electoral districts of similar size.

Election campaigns and publicity: A 'free election' can only be held if rival candidates are able to campaign and to publicise their programmes. The question is to what extent electoral rights imply a right to equality of opportunity for campaigning and publicity. This covers matters such as access to television broadcast and the press and the closely related issue of electoral expenditure.

B. The Rights in English Law Before the Human Rights Act

(1) Introduction

It has been said that voting rights lie at the root of parliamentary democracy, being regarded by many as a 'basic human right'.[8] In addition, candidates have a common law right to stand at an election not tainted by corrupt practice.[9] These rights are defined by statute. The Representation of the People Act 1983 deals with the franchise for parliamentary and local elections, the election campaign and the legal proceedings which can be used to challenge elections. There is a presumption that voting rights, as part of the 'basic governmental arrangements', can only be altered by express provision.[10] **20.04**

(2) Voter qualifications

A person is entitled to vote in a parliamentary election if he is:[11] **20.05**

- either resident on the qualifying date[12] or a qualified overseas elector;[13]
- not subject to a legal incapacity;
- a citizen of the Commonwealth or the Republic of Ireland;
- of voting age (that is, 18 or over); and
- registered on the register of electors.

Whether a person is resident at a particular place and whether that residence is permanent is a question of fact and degree and it is possible for a person to be 'resident', for example, in a tent.[14] The lawfulness or otherwise of a person's residence is not relevant to the question as to whether the person is eligible to vote.[15]

[8] *Hipperson v Newbury District Electoral Registration Officer* [1985] QB 1060, 1067.

[9] *Spencer v Huggett, The Times,* 12 Jun 1997.

[10] F Bennion, *Statutory Interpretation* (3rd edn, Butterworths, 1997) 813–814.

[11] See Representation of the People Act 1983, s 1.

[12] Subject to special provision as to Northern Ireland, which requires a period of residence of three months: see ibid s 1(2).

[13] Under the provisions of the Representation of the People Act 1985.

[14] *Hipperson v Newbury District Electoral Registration Officer* (n 8 above).

[15] Ibid.

20.06 A number of categories of persons are not entitled to vote. At common law, peers[16] and persons suffering from severe mental illness had no capacity to vote.[17] In addition, the Representation of the People Act 1983 removes the entitlement to vote from any person found guilty of an offence and detained in a penal institution,[18] a person subject to compulsory detention as a mental patient[19] and a person convicted of a 'corrupt or illegal practice' at an election.[20]

(3) Candidate qualifications

20.07 The categories of persons disqualified from being Members of Parliament are not defined by statute. It appears that, at common law, peers, aliens,[21] infants[22] and persons of unsound mind are disqualified.[23] Although the age at which a person is entitled to vote has been lowered to 18, the qualifying age for candidates remains 21.

20.08 The House of Commons Disqualification Act 1975 disqualifies from candidacy holders of judicial office,[24] civil servants,[25] members of the regular armed forces[26] or the police,[27] members of the legislature of any country or territory outside the Commonwealth,[28] and members of various commissions, boards and tribunals.[29] In addition, convicted persons who are sentenced or ordered to be imprisoned for more than one year are disqualified while they are detained.[30] A number of other persons are also subject to statutory disqualification: bankrupts,[31] clergy of the Church of England, the Church of Ireland, the Church of Scotland and the Roman Catholic Church[32] and those convicted of corrupt or illegal practices.[33] A

16 See *Earl Beauchamp v Madresfield* (1872) 8 CP 245; *Re Parliamentary Election for Bristol South East* [1964] 2 QB 257; Peerage Act 1963, ss 5 and 6.

17 See generally, *Halsburys Laws of England* (4th edn reissue, Butterworths, 1996) Vol 15, para 315.

18 s 3.

19 Curiously, this is not expressed to be a 'legal incapacity' but a provision which, in effect, deems such patients not to be resident: see 1983 Act, s 7.

20 See ibid s 160(4).

21 See Act of Settlement 1700, s 3.

22 See Parliamentary Elections Act 1695.

23 See D Limon and W McKay (eds), Erskine May, *Parliamentary Practice* (20th edn, Butterworths, 1997) 39.

24 s 1(1)(a) and Sch 1.

25 s 1(1)(b).

26 s 1(1)(c).

27 s 1(1)(d).

28 s 1(1)(e).

29 s 1(1)(f) and Sch 1.

30 Representation of the People Act 1981, s 1; see C P Walker 'Prisoners in Parliament—Another View' [1982] PL 389.

31 See Insolvency Act 1986, s 247.

32 See House of Commons (Clergy Disqualification) Act 1801; the Clerical Disabilities Act 1870, s 4; but not those who hold office in the Church in Wales: Welsh Church Act 1914, s 2(4).

33 Representation of the People Act 1983, ss 159(2), 160(4).

sitting member who is convicted of corrupt or illegal practices has to vacate his seat but can resume the seat if the conviction is quashed before a fresh election has taken place.[34]

There have, traditionally, been few prohibitions on political parties in English law. However, the Registration of Political Parties Act 1998 now makes provision for the registration of political parties.[35] The registrar can refuse to grant an application if it proposes a registered name which: **20.09**

(a) would be likely to result in the party's being confused by voters with a party which is already registered,
(b) more than six words,
(c) is obscene or offensive,
(d) includes words the publication of which would be likely to amount to the commission of an offence,
(e) includes any script other than Roman script, or
(f) includes any word or expression prohibited by order made by the Secretary of State.[36]

A political party which is not registered cannot use a party name on the ballot paper or make party political broadcasts.[37] The only groups which may not put up candidates for election are those proscribed under prevention of terrorism legislation[38] which, at present are limited to members of the IRA and the INLA. Political parties with avowedly racist policies are not prohibited from putting up candidates.

Candidates in parliamentary elections need not be resident in the constituency in which they wish to stand for election. They must, however, obtain nomination from 10 registered voters and pay a deposit of £500 which is forfeited if they do not gain at least 5% of the votes cast. **20.10**

(4) Electoral boundaries

The boundaries of parliamentary constituencies in the United Kingdom are fixed by the Boundary Commission under the provisions of the Parliamentary Constituencies Act 1986. There are separate Commissions for England, Northern Ireland, Scotland and Wales, each headed by a High Court Judge. At 15 year intervals, local inquiries are held and reports made to the Home Secretary with **20.11**

[34] *A-G v Jones* [1999] 3 All ER 436.

[35] This was introduced to prevent the use of confusing names on the ballot paper: see *Sanders v Chichester*, *The Times*, 2 Dec 1994; see generally, F Klug, K Starmer, S Weir, *The Three Pillars of Liberty* (Routledge, 1996) 281–282.

[36] s 3(1).

[37] s 13 and 14.

[38] Prevention of Terrorism (Temporary Provisions) Act 1989, s 1, and the Northern Ireland (Emergency Provisions) Act 1991, s 28.

recommendations. These are implemented by an Order in Council being laid before parliament for approval. The procedure is open to political manipulation: a party which believes that the old boundaries are advantageous and which commands a parliamentary majority can refuse to approve the Orders in Council. This happened in 1969.[39]

20.12 The Parliamentary Constituencies Act 1986 provides that:

> The validity of any Order in Council purporting to be made under this Act . . . shall not be called in question in any legal proceedings.[40]

This section is intended to remove issues as to the size of parliamentary constituencies from judicial review. In the case of *R v Boundary Commission for England, ex p Foot*[41] leading members of the Labour Party complained that the Commission had failed to give effect to the principle of equal representation for electors; they sought orders prohibiting the Commission from submitting its report to the Home Secretary. The application was dismissed on the ground that the rules relating to 'equal representation' were guidelines only; and that it had not been shown that the recommendations of the Commission were conclusions which no reasonable commission could have reached.

(5) Election campaigns and publicity

20.13 At one time elections in the United Kingdom were characterised by large scale voter corruption. This was effectively ended by the introduction of the secret ballot and the limitations placed on candidate expenditure by the Corrupt Practices Act 1883. The current provisions relating to campaign finance are to be found in the Representation of the People Act 1983. They limit candidate expenditure to £4,642 plus 3.9p per voter (boroughs) or 5.2p per voter (counties).[42]

20.14 The provisions of the Act relate only to expenditure in support of a particular candidate and not to candidates generally.[43] In other words, there is no limit placed on the amount of money which may be spent by a party on its national campaign. Neither are there limits to the expenditure permitted third parties, either to promote a political party or a particular set of policies. However, the Act does prohibit expenditure directed against particular candidates. Thus, it was held that a leaflet which urged voters not to vote for National Front candidates constituted unauthorised expenditure in favour of the other candidates in the constituency.[44]

[39] For a discussion, see I Loveland, *Constitutional Law: A Critical Introduction* (Butterworths, 1996) 265-267.

[40] s 4(7).

[41] [1983] QB 600.

[42] s 76(2).

[43] See *R v Tronoh Mines Ltd* [1952] 1 All ER 697.

[44] *DPP v Luft* [1977] AC 962; as a result, the publishers of the leaflet were guilty of an offence under the Representation of the People Act.

Paid political advertising on television and radio is prohibited by statute.[45] Free time is, however, provided on radio and television for party political broadcasts. The costs of these broadcasts do not form part of the election expenses of the party candidates who appear on them.[46] Only 'registered political parties' are entitled to broadcasts.[47] These arrangements are not subject to any other statutory control.[48] Broadcasting time is allocated by agreement between the BBC, the ITC and the political parties: both the BBC and the ITV companies allocate at least one party political broadcast of five minutes duration to any party fielding at least 50 candidates in a general election and further time is allocated taking into account factors such as performance at the last general election.[49] Although broadcasters have a duty to be impartial, this is not the same as 'parity or balance' between parties of different strengths, popular support and appeal.[50] The court will, however, intervene if the broadcasters act irrationally in allocating broadcasting time.[51] **20.15**

Under the terms of the Broadcasting Act, independent television and radio have a duty to preserve impartiality in political programmes.[52] The BBC is under a similar duty under the terms of its Charter. The courts in Scotland enforced these duties against independent television when Scottish Television proposed to broadcast, immediately before the 1979 devolution referendum, three party political broadcasts in favour of devolution but only one against.[53] **20.16**

(6) Questioning elections

The right to determine questions of disputed elections was claimed by the House of Commons as a matter of privilege and was exercised between 1604 and 1868. This led to disputes with the courts[54] and the jurisdiction was transferred to the courts by statute in 1868. The questioning of elections is now governed by Part III of the Representation of the People Act 1983. This provides that no parliamentary **20.17**

---

[45] Broadcasting Act 1990, s 8(2)(a).

[46] See *Grieve v Douglas-Home* (1965) SC 315.

[47] See Registration of Political Parties Act 1998, s 14.

[48] For a discussion of arrangements in other jurisdictions see *United Parties v Minister of Justice* (1997) 3 BHRC 16, see also *Australian Capital Television Pty Ltd v The Commonwealth of Australia* (1992) 177 CLR 106.

[49] See BBC 'Producers Guidelines', 3rd Edn, Nov 1996, Pt 18, para 2.2; ITC Programme Code, Summer 1995, para 4.

[50] See *R v BBC, ex p Referendum Party* [1997] COD 459; *Lynch v BBC* [1983] NI 193, 202C-E; *Wilson v IBA* [1979] SC 351, 359.

[51] *R v BBC, ex p Referendum Party* (n 50 above); cf *R v BBC, ex p Pro-Life Alliance*, unreported, 24 Mar 1997 (court refused to intervene in a decision by the BBC to refuse to transmit part of a party political broadcast by an anti-abortion party showing offensive pictures of aborted foetuses on the ground of good taste and decency).

[52] See Broadcasting Act 1990, ss 6(1)(b) and 90(1)(b).

[53] *Wilson v IBA* [1979] SC 351.

[54] See eg *Ashby v White* (1703) 2 Ld Raym 938.

election or return to parliament may be questioned except by a 'parliamentary election petition'.[55]

20.18 An election petition can raise a variety of issues such as corrupt or illegal practices, improper conduct of the election[56] or the legal qualification of the successful candidate.[57] The election will not be declared invalid if it appears that it was conducted substantially in accordance with the law and the act or omission complained of did not affect the result.[58]

C. The Law Under the European Convention

(1) Introduction

20.19 Article 3 of the First Protocol states that :

> The High Contracting Parties undertake to hold free elections at reasonable intervals by secret ballot, under conditions which will ensure the free expression of the opinion of the people in the choice of the legislature.

This provision was initially included in the first version of the Convention. However, the representative of the United Kingdom objected on the ground that its electoral system might not be compatible with the proposed clause.[59] The clause was re-drafted but continuing difficulties meant that it was not included in the Convention. However, these difficulties were quickly resolved and the text was approved for inclusion in the First Protocol which was signed on 20 March 1952.

20.20 Although this provision is expressed as an 'undertaking' rather than a 'right' of individuals, the language is intended to reflect the 'solemnity of the commitment undertaken' and the fact that the primary obligation is not one of non-interference but of the adoption of positive measures: the fact that states have taken on a positive obligation.[60] As a result, the Article does confer a right which can be invoked by individuals.[61]

(2) The nature of a 'legislature'

20.21 The Convention refers to the 'choice of legislature'. It does not, either expressly or by implication, provide for any particular type of legislature. Whether the legislature has one or two chambers, and whether the state is federal in nature are

---

55 s 120(1).
56 *Re Kensington North Parliamentary Election* [1960] 2 All ER 150.
57 *Re Parliamentary Election for Bristol South East* [1964] 1 WLR 762.
58 Representation of the People Act 1983, s 23(3).
59 *Travaux Préparatoires*, Vol IV, 141–143.
60 See *Mathieu-Mohin and Clerfayt v Belgium* (1987) 10 EHRR 1 para 50.
61 Ibid.

matters for determination by individual states.[62]

In *Mathieu-Mohin v Belgium*[63] the Court said that Article 3 of the First Protocol applied to elections to the legislature 'or at least one of its chambers if it has two or more . . .'.[64] It seems that the Convention applies to any elected body which has 'original', rather than delegated, power to make laws. Thus, it applies to regional councils in Belgium[65] and to German Lander[66] but does not apply to elected local government bodies in non-federal states.[67] The Commission has taken the view that English Metropolitan County Councils cannot be considered to be the legislature, since their powers are derivative.[68] **20.22**

It is now clear that the European Parliament cannot be excluded from the scope of Article 3 of the First Protocol on the ground that it is a supranational representative organ.[69] The European Parliament is the principal form of democratic political accountability in the Community system and is therefore part of the 'legislature'.[70] **20.23**

The Commission has expressed the opinion that referenda are not within the terms of Article 3 of the First Protocol.[71] The Convention does not apply to elections to a professional body, even if certain legislative power has been given to it,[72] or to the appointment of a Head of State.[73] **20.24**

(3) The content of the right

(a) Introduction

Article 3 enshrines rights of participation: the right to vote and the right to stand for election to the legislature.[74] These rights are not absolute and there is room for implied limitations. States can make the rights subject to conditions and have a wide margin of appreciation.[75] However, the conditions must not impair the very **20.25**

[62] *Moureaux v Belgium* (1983) 33 DR 97, 128, EComm HR.

[63] (1987) 10 EHRR 1 para 53.

[64] But note the concurring opinion of Judge Pinheiro Farinha suggesting that two conditions must be satisfied: that the majority of the membership of the legislature is elected and that the chamber whose members are not elected does not have greater powers than the elected chamber.

[65] See *Mathieu-Mohin and Clerfayt v Belgium* (1987) 10 EHRR 1.

[66] *X v Germany* (1967) 10 YB 336; *Jan Timke v Germany* [1996] EHRLR 74.

[67] Cf *A v United Kingdom* (1970) 13 YB 340, EComm HR: local government elections in Northern Ireland.

[68] *Booth-Clibborn v United Kingdom* (1985) 43 DR 236, EComm HR; *Edwards v United Kingdom* (1986) 8 EHRR 96 (Greater London Council).

[69] See *Matthews v United Kingdom* (1999) 28 EHRR 361 paras 36-44.

[70] Ibid paras 45–54.

[71] *X v Germany* (1975) 3 DR 98, EComm HR and *X v United Kingdom* (1975) 3 DR 165, EComm HR; *Esko Nurminen v Finland* [1997] EHRLR 446 (referendum on accession to EC).

[72] *X v Netherlands* (1983) 32 DR 27 (Royal Society for Cultivation of Flower Bulbs).

[73] *Habsburg-Lothringen v Austria* (1990) 64 DR 210, 219, EComm HR.

[74] *Mathieu-Mohin and Clerfayt v Belgium* (1987) 10 EHRR 1 para 51.

essence of the rights or deprive them of their effectiveness. Furthermore, such conditions must be imposed in pursuit of a legitimate aim and the means employed must be proportionate.[76] In particular, states enjoy considerable latitude to establish in their constitutional order rules governing the status of parliamentarians, including criteria for disqualification.[77]

(b) 'Reasonable intervals'

20.26 The Convention does not lay down any particular interval for holding elections. The question as to whether elections were held at reasonable intervals must be decided by reference to the purpose of parliamentary elections: ensuring that changes in public opinion were reflected in the opinions of the elected representatives.[78] Too short an interval might impede political planning. On the basis of these considerations, an interval of five years between elections was 'reasonable'.[79]

(c) The electoral system

20.27 The Convention does not require any particular system of voting, such as proportional representation.[80] In the case of *Liberal Party, Mrs R and Mr P v United Kingdom*[81] the applicants contended that the 'first past the post' electoral system violated Article 3 of the First Protocol when read together with Article 14, because it tended to favour the two major parties. The Commission said that:

> Article 3 of the First Protocol may not be interpreted as an Article which imposes a particular kind of electoral system which would guarantee that the total number of votes cast for each candidate or group must be reflected in the composition of the legislative assembly. Both the simple majority system and the proportional representation system are, therefore, compatible with this Article.[82]

Furthermore, the Convention does not prohibit compulsory voting.[83] Nor is the right to free elections contravened by the fact that there were only two candidates for a particular office.[84]

(d) Voter and candidate qualifications

---

75 For a general discussion of the doctrine, see para 6.31ff above.

76 *Mathieu-Mohin and Clerfayt v Belgium* (n 74 above) para 52; *Gitonas v Greece* (1997) 26 EHRR 691 para 39; for a general discussion of the doctrine of proportionality, see para 6.42ff above.

77 *Gitonas v Greece* (n 76 above) para 39.

78 *Jan Timke v Germany* [1996] EHLR 74.

79 Ibid.

80 The Secretariat of the Council of Europe had expressed concerned that an earlier draft seemed to require such a system: *Travaux Préparatoires*, Vol VII, 131.

81 (1980) 21 DR 211, EComm HR.

82 Ibid para 4.

83 *X v Austria* (1965) 8 YB 168.

84 *X v Austria* (1972) 40 DR 50 (the Presidency of Austria).

When considering provisions which disqualify voters, it is necessary to ask whether these restrictions affect the 'free expression of the opinion of the peo- **20.28**
ple'.[85] Disqualifications on the basis of post-conviction imprisonment,[86] foreign residence of citizens[87] and failure to meet language requirements[88] have been found to be acceptable.

The imposition of conditions upon candidacy does not infringe Article 3. The Commission has held that the requirement of a requisite number of signatures[89] **20.29**
or a deposit[90] does not breach the Convention. In *Gitonas v Greece*[91] the Court upheld a complex system for disqualification of candidates under the Greek Constitution. In *Ahmed v United Kingdom*[92] the Court rejected the argument that restrictions on political activities by local government officers contravened Article 3. It emphasised that conditions could be imposed on the exercise of such rights; and that restrictions on the right to contest seats at elections were justified as being for the legitimate aim of securing political impartiality by public servants.

(e) Election expenses and contributions

The Convention does not prohibit public financing of parties.[93] It appears that the Convention does not require that states either subsidise parties or impose lim- **20.30**
its on contributions for their support.[94] The issue of limits of electoral expenditure was addressed in the context of freedom of expression under Article 10 in *Bowman v United Kingdom.*[95] Mrs Bowman had been charged with an offence under the Representation of the People Act 1983 when she printed one and a half million leaflets informing voters of the opinions of several candidates with regard to abortion and related issues, for distribution in constituencies throughout the United Kingdom. Section 75(1) of the 1983 Act prohibited expenditure of more than five pounds sterling by anyone other than a candidate or a person authorised by the candidate, with a view to promoting or procuring the election of a candidate at an election. The Court found that the restriction on expenditures amounted to a total barrier to the publication by Mrs Bowman of her material, which was intended to influence voters in favour of an anti-abortion candidate. Such a re-

[85] *X v Federal Republic of Germany* (1967) 10 YB 336, 338.

[86] Ibid; *H v Netherlands* (1979) 33 DR 242, EComm HR.

[87] *X v Belgium* (1961) 4 YB 324, 338, EComm HR: (Belgians resident in the Congo); *X v United Kingdom*, (1979) 15 DR 137.

[88] *Fryske Nasjonale Partij v Netherlands* (1985) 45 DR 240, EComm HR.

[89] *Association X, Y and Z v Germany* (1976) 5 DR 90, EComm HR.

[90] *Desmeules v France* (1991) 67 DR 166.

[91] (1997) 26 EHRR 691.

[92] (1998) 5 BHRC 111.

[93] *Association X, Y and Z v Germany* (1976) 5 DR 90, 94, EComm HR.

[94] See D Harris, M O'Boyle and C Warbrick, *Law of the European Convention on Human Rights* (Butterworths, 1995) 554.

[95] (1998) 26 EHRR 1; see *Pierre-Bloch v France* (1997) 26 EHRR 202.

striction was disproportionate to the proper government aim of securing equality between candidates and as such was unjustified, particularly in light of the freedom of the press to support or oppose the election of any particular candidate. The Court therefore found a violation of Article 10.

20.31 The Convention does not impliedly require that political parties should have equal, or indeed any, media exposure.[96] There is, however, an argument that political parties may be entitled to some protection in respect of radio and television access during election campaigns.[97]

D. The Impact of the Human Rights Act

(1) Introduction

20.32 There are a number of areas in which it might be argued that English law is not consistent with the 'electoral rights' contained in Article 3 of the First Protocol.[98] Although the European Court of Human Rights has taken a cautious attitude to 'electoral rights' the courts in some common law jurisdictions have, in recent decades, been prepared to intervene in the electoral process to ensure fair elections. This intervention has been most important in the United States[99] and Canada[100] but has also been significant in Australia.[101] It remains to be seen whether the English courts will be prepared to take an activist approach.

(2) United Kingdom cases before the Human Rights Act

(a) Introduction

20.33 A number of cases from the United Kingdom under Article 3 of the First Protocol have been brought before the Court and the Commission. The United Kingdom has been held to be in breach on one occasion.[102] The cases have concerned three areas: the nature of a legislature, electoral systems and other applications.

(b) The nature of a legislature

---

[96] *Purcell v Ireland* (1991) 70 DR 262, EComm HR.

[97] Cf *X and Association Z v United Kingdom* (1971) 38 CD 86, EComm HR.

[98] For a general discussion see F Klug, K Starmer, S Weir, *The Three Pillars of Liberty* (Routledge, 1996) Chap 14 'Britain's Missing Voters'.

[99] See para 20.63ff below.

[100] See para 20.44ff below.

[101] See para 20.67ff below.

[102] *Matthews v United Kingdom* (1999) 28 EHRR 361.

The Greater London Council did not form part of the 'legislature' of the United Kingdom and there was no violation of the Convention when it was abolished.[103] 20.34
Similar reasoning applied to English metropolitan county councils,[104] local authorities in Northern Ireland,[105] an English borough council[106] and to a consultative assembly in Northern Ireland.[107]

The applicant in *X v United Kingdom*[108] complained of interference with Convention rights in relation to the conduct of a referendum. The Commission held 20.35
the application was inadmissible because referenda are not within the scope of Article 3 of the First Protocol.

(c) Electoral systems

In *Lindsay v United Kingdom*[109] the complaint was that different voting systems for elections to the European Parliament had been adopted in Northern Ireland 20.36
and the rest of the United Kingdom. The Commission found that there was no breach as Article 3 of the First Protocol did not require any particular electoral system. In *Liberal Party, Mrs R and Mr P v United Kingdom*[110] the applicants complained that the 'simple majority' system adversely affected the Liberal Party and its members. The Commission expressed the view that both the simple majority system and the proportional representation system were compatible with Article 3. Furthermore, although Article 14 protected against discrimination directed at individuals, it did not protect 'equal voting influence for all voters'.

(d) Other applications

In *X v United Kingdom*[111] the applicant was a non-resident national who complained that he was not entitled to vote. The Commission decided that this re- 20.37
striction was in conformity with Article 3. The Commission has held that although voters in Jersey could not vote in elections for the United Kingdom parliament, which had some responsibility for Jersey, there was no breach. Jersey had its own elected legislature; and in ratifying the Convention, the United Kingdom could not have intended to modify the well established constitutional arrangements relating to the Channel Islands.[112]

Restrictions on the political activities of local government officers were upheld in

[103] *Edwards v United Kingdom* (1986) 8 EHRR 96.
[104] *Booth-Clibborn v United Kingdom* (1985) 43 DR 236, EComm HR.
[105] *X v United Kingdom* (1972) 6 DR 13.
[106] *W C, F S and J T v United Kingdom* Appliation 11931/86, 8 Jul 1986.
[107] *Lindsay v United Kingdom* Application 31699/96, 17 Jan 1997.
[108] (1975) 3 DR 165, EComm HR.
[109] (1979) 15 DR 247, EComm HR.
[110] (1980) 21 DR 211, EComm HR.
[111] (1979) 15 DR 137, EComm HR.
[112] *X v United Kingdom* (1982) 28 DR 99.

20,.38 *Ahmed v United Kingdom.*[113] The Court held that restrictions on the right to contest seats at elections were justified as being for the legitimate aim of securing political impartiality by public servants. In *M v United Kingdom*[114] the Commission ruled that the condition that a candidate should not be a member of another legislature was not inconsistent with the Convention.

(3) Potential impact of the Human Rights Act on electoral law

(a) Introduction

20.39 There is no doubt that Article 3 of the First Protocol will apply to decisions concerning elections to the House of Commons. It is arguable that the Scottish Parliament[115] and the Northern Ireland Assembly[116] will be legislatures for the purposes of the Convention.[117] However, it seems unlikely that the National Assembly for Wales and the Greater London Assembly will be held to be legislatures. The potential impact of the Human Rights Act on electoral law will arise in four areas: voter and candidate qualification, fairness of elections, voter equality and implied electoral rights.

(b) Voter and candidate qualifications

20.40 English law, at present, denies the franchise to a wide range of persons including most prisoners, mental health detainees and 'aliens'. It has been suggested that this could be a breach of international human rights standards;[118] it is arguable that 'blanket' voter disqualifications may breach the Convention 'right to vote'.[119] Furthermore, the present English law provides a higher age for candidate qualification than voter qualification. No proper justification has been advanced for this discrimination which, it could be argued, would fall foul of Article 14 of the Convention.[120]

(c) Fairness of elections

20.41 It is arguable that the present English law fails to require that necessary positive steps are taken to ensure the fairness of elections in several fields. The absence of an 'electoral commission' which might have responsibility for overseeing the conduct of national elections has been criticised.[121]

---

[113] (1998) 5 BHRC 111, see para 20.29 above.

[114] (1984) 37 DR 129.

[115] As constituted by the Scotland Act 1998.

[116] As constituted by the Northern Ireland Act 1998.

[117] See generally H Davis, 'Constitutional Reform and the Right to Free and Fair Elections' [1999] EHRLR 411.

[118] See F Klug, K Starmer, S Weir, *The Three Pillars of Liberty* (Routledge, 1996) 275.

[119] The Canadian courts have repeatedly found blanket disqualifications to contravene the Charter: see para 20.53ff below.

[120] See para 17.79ff above.

[121] Klug, Starmer and Weir (n 118 above) 279.

(d) Voter equality

The limited protection which English law provides to ensure 'voter equality' may be the subject of challenge. At present, the relevant legislation contains no requirement that the Boundaries Commissions ensure relative voter equality and seeks to oust all judicial scrutiny[122] of the issue. The statutory regime therefore provides no scope[122a] either for the principle that votes should be counted equally[122b] or the principle of effective representation in Canada and Australia.[122c] The procedures are subject to potential party political interference[123] and could be a breach of Article 3 of the First Protocol. In an appropriate case, a court could make a declaration of incompatibility in relation to these provisions. **20.42**

(e) Implied electoral rights

Finally, there are a number of potential 'implied rights' under Article 3 of the First Protocol which could have a significant impact on English law. There is a strong argument that a system of free elections necessitates that voters and candidates are able to receive and communicate relevant information without restriction. This, in turn, suggests that laws which have the effect of restricting the freedom to communicate such information may contravene 'electoral rights'. Examples of the 'implication' of rights of expression based on 'electoral rights' can be found in the recent case law of the Canadian and Australian courts.[124] It may be possible to advance arguments similar to those presented before the Australian courts, taking into account the different constitutional bases. Such arguments could call into question the restrictions on television and radio broadcasts by political parties and the operation of the 'party political broadcast' system.[125] **20.43**

[122] See Parliamentary Constituencies Act 1986, s 4(7), para 20.12 above.

[122a] See generally, Sir Anthony Mason, 'One Vote, One Value v The Parliamentary Tradition—The Federal Experience' in C Forsyth and I Hare (eds), *The Golden Metwand and the Crooked Cord* (Oxford University Press, 1998).

[122b] As developed in the United States: see *Wesberry v Saunders* (1964) 376 US 1, 8 *per* Black J; and see para 20.64 below.

[122c] See paras 20.47 and 20.67 below respectively.

[123] See para 20.11 above.

[124] See the Canadian case of *Somerville v Canada (A-G)* (1996) 136 DLR (4th) 205: a true right to vote includes as a component the right to access sufficient information to make an informed vote; also two Australian cases: *Australian Capital Television Pty Ltd v The Commonwealth of Australia* (1992) 177 CLR 106: direct election to the legislature required a freedom of communication in regard to the political and electoral processes, including the right to convey and receive information, opinions and arguments concerning such elections and the candidates. The Court held that regulation of television broadcasts during elections was unconstitutional; and the High Court in *Lange v Australian Broadcasting Corporation* (1997) 189 CLR 520 implied a freedom of communication of 'information, opinions and arguments concerning government and political matters' generally.

[125] The available grounds of challenge under Arts 3 and 14 would be wider than the *Wednesbury* grounds relied on in *R v BBC, ex p Referendum Party* [1997] COD 459.

Appendix 1: The Canadian Charter of Rights

(1) Introduction

20.44 Sections 3, 4 and 5 of the Canadian Charter provide as follows:

> 3. Every citizen of Canada has the right to vote in an election of members of the House of Commons or of a legislative assembly and to be qualified for membership therein.
> 4. (1) No House of Commons and no legislative assembly shall continue for longer than five years from the date fixed for the return of the writs at a general election of its members.
> (2) In time of real or apprehended war, invasion or insurrection, a House of Commons may be continued by Parliament and a legislative assembly may be continued by the legislature beyond five years if such continuation is not opposed by the votes of more than one-third of the members of the House of Commons or the legislative assembly, as the case may be.
> 5. There shall be a sitting of Parliament and of each legislature at least once every twelve months.

Section 3 has been subject to judicial consideration in a large number of cases.[126] These can be considered under the following heads: the 'right to vote', limitations on the right to vote and membership of the legislature.

(2) 'Right to vote'

(a) Scope of the right

20.45 This section governs elections to the House of Commons and to legislative assemblies in the provinces. It has been held that section 3 has no application to voting rights in municipal elections.[127] It does not extend to referenda[128] or plebiscites.[129]

20.46 It has been suggested that the right to vote presupposes certain attributes of the voter, including age, residence and mental capacity, which are inherent but not expressed in section 3. These may be considered qualities of the right, rather than limitations on it and may properly be the subject of re-evaluation by lawmakers without resort to section 1.[130]

(b) Effective representation

20.47 The purpose of the right to vote in section 3 is not to guarantee equality of voting power *per se,* but to provide a right to 'effective representation' in the Government. Nevertheless, relative equality of voting power on the basis of population is the fundamental principle underlying the Canadian system of representational democracy.[131] Effective representation did not require absolute parity of voting power, although parity of voting power was of 'prime importance'.[132]

---

[126] See generally, P W Hogg, *Constitutional Law of Canada* (4th edn, Carswell, 1997) Chap 42 'Voting'.

[127] *Barke v Calgary (City)* (1989) 98 AR 157.

[128] *Haig v Canada* [1993] 2 SCR 995.

[129] *Allman v Northwest Territories (Commissioner)* (1983) 144 DLR (3d) 467.

[130] *Badger et al v A-G of Manitoba* (1986) 27 CCC (3d) 158.

[131] *Re Provincial Electoral Boundaries (Sask)* [1991] 2 SCR 158; *Dixon v Bristol Columbia (A-G) (No 2)* (1989) 59 DLR (4th) 247.

[132] *Re Provincial Electoral Boundaries (Sask)* (n 131 above) 184.

The criteria for electoral boundaries have been considered in a number of cases. Electoral districts are essentially determined on the basis of population, and courts have been reluctant to interfere where due weight has been given to the principle of vote parity.[133] However, when the electoral boundaries in British Columbia did not produce relative equality of voting power, they were struck down;[134] and statutory provisions in Prince Edward Island were declared contrary to the Charter when significant variations in population among electoral districts became evident.[135] **20.48**

Nevertheless, the effective representation of a *specific* community may require an electoral division of a below-average population where specific reasons and presentation of specific facts warrant it. The Constitution of Canada is sufficiently flexible to permit disparity to serve geographical and demographic reality. Variation is, however, not permissible without justification. The onus to establish justification lies with those who propose the variation.[136] **20.49**

Equality of voting power is not the only consideration for the assurance of effective representation. Factors such as geography, community history, community interest and representation of minorities may need to be taken into account[137] in order effectively to represent the diversity of Canadian society. The permissible degree of deviation from voter parity in terms of population is to be determined by the legislature, rather than the courts. Not all departures from absolute parity can be countenanced: only those that can be justified on the ground that they contribute to a better government of the populace as a whole, giving due weight to regional issues and geographic factors.[138] It has also been considered appropriate to set limits beyond which voter parity cannot be eroded: a 25% limit has been applied to federal electoral districts.[139] **20.50**

(c) Informed electoral choice

Although section 3 does not expressly provide a right of information, several cases have confirmed that a true right to vote includes as a component the right to access to sufficient information to make an informed vote.[140] The right to vote is not merely the right to cast a ballot: it is the right to make an informed electoral choice, with complete freedom of access to the process of discussion and interplay of ideas by which public opinion is formed.[141] To constitute an infringement of the right to vote, a restriction on the dissemination of political information would have to undermine the guarantee of effective representation.[142] The limitation of the total time for political broadcasting based on the percentage of seats and popular votes does not infringe section 3: the right to sufficient information does not imply a right to full information or to information in any particular **20.51**

[133] See *Reference re Electoral Boundaries Commission Act (Sask)* (1991) 81 DLR (4th) 16; *Reference re Electoral Boundaries Commission Act (Alberta)* (1991) 84 DLR (4th) 447.

[134] *Dixon v British Columbia (A-G)* (1989) 59 DLR (4th) 247.

[135] *MacKinnon v Prince Edward Island* (1993) 101 DLR (4th) 362.

[136] *Reference re Electoral Divisions Statutes Amendment Act 1993 (Alberta)* (1994) 119 DLR (4th) 1.

[137] *Re Provincial Electoral Boundaries (Sask)* [1991] 2 SCR 158, 185.

[138] *Dixon v British Columbia (A-G) (No 2)* (1989) 59 DLR (4th) 247.

[139] Ibid.

[140] *Somerville v Canada (A-G)* (1996) 136 DLR (4th) 205.

[141] *Jolivet and Barker v The Queen* (1983) 7 CCC (3rd) 431.

[142] *Thomson Newspapers v Canada (A-G)* [1998] 1 SCR 877.

form.[143] Legislation limiting reimbursement of one half of total election expenses to those who have obtained at least 15% of the votes cast did not infringe the Charter.[144]

(3) Limitations on the right to vote

20.52 The right to vote in section 3 is not absolute. It may be subject to standard limitations, including the requirement of a reasonable period of prior residency.[145] Creation of an appropriate period of advance residence is consistent with the Charter, based on the legitimate government purposes of ensuring the integrity of the electoral process, and that voters are properly informed of the issues and have sufficient connection with the jurisdiction. The designation of a reasonable period of residence is a matter peculiarly within the competence of the legislature.[146] While the majority of provinces require a six-month residency period,[147] a longer period may be justified: five provinces impose a 12-month requirement.[148]

20.53 Although limitations on the rights of a prisoner to vote may be justifiable,[149] this does not extend to prisoners on remand: prisoners awaiting trial must be provided with a mechanism to exercise their right to vote.[150] Neither is there justification for prohibiting from voting persons who are merely on probation.[151] A blanket disqualification of all prisoners serving sentences of imprisonment cannot be justified: the matter should be considered on a case-by-case basis by the sentencing judge.[152]

20.54 Other standard bases for disqualification of voters, including restrictions as to age, mental capacity and registration,[153] have been considered. Age restrictions on voting are reasonable.[154] Restriction on the basis of mental 'incapacity' is also reasonable, although this will not encompass all forms of mental disease or instability. A statutory provision which disqualified from voting any person who is restrained of his liberty or movement or deprived of the management of property by reason of mental disease infringed section 3 and was of no effect.[155]

20.55 The administrative procedures involved in effecting registration or otherwise implementing the right to vote must not constitute a practical denial of the right to vote.[156] In British

143 *Reform Party of Canada v Canada (A-G)* [1993] 3 WWR 139.

144 *Barrette v Canada (Procureur Général)* (1994) 113 DLR (4th) 623.

145 *Storey v Zazelenchuk* (1984) 36 Sask R 103; *Arnold v Ontario (A-G)* (1987) 43 DLR (4th) 94.

146 *Storey v Zazelenchuk* (n 145 above).

147 See *Arnold v Ontario (A-G)* (n 145 above).

148 See *Reference re Yukon Election Residency Requirement* (1986) 27 DLR (4th) 146 (a period of 12 months was justified).

149 See *Jolivet and Barker v The Queen* (1983) 7 CCC (3d) 431.

150 *Re Maltby and A-G of Saskatchewan* (1982) 2 CCC (3d) 153; appeal dismissed (1984) 10 DLR (4th) 745, Sask CA.

151 *Reynolds v A-G of British Columbia* (1983) 143 DR (3rd) 365; affirmed (1984) 11 DLR (4th) 380.

152 *Sauvé v Canada* [1993] 2 SCR 438.

153 *Scott and British Columbia (A-G)* (1986) 29 DLR (4th) 545; *Weremchuk v Jacobsen* (1986) 36 DLR (4th) 278.

154 *Reid (Next Friend of) v Canada* (1994) 73 FTR 290.

155 *Canadian Disability Rights Council v Canada* [1988] 3 FC 622.

156 *Scott and British Columbia (A-G)* (n 153 above); *Weremchuk v Jacobsen* (n 153 above).

Columbia, the failure to provide a mechanism to enable absentee electors to vote constituted an infringement of their Charter right.[157] Failure to register a person was not, however, considered a breach of section 3 when he did not appear to understand the required oath or affirmation.[158]

(4) Membership of legislature

Under the Charter, it is permissible to impose some restrictions upon the membership of the legislature. Thus, a legislative provision which vacated a seat and imposed a five-year disqualification on any member convicted of corrupt or illegal practice was a justifiable limitation of the appellant's section 3 rights.[159] Section 3 has no application to the historic right of a legislative assembly to expel a member.[160] **20.56**

Although the Charter permits some restriction of the political activities of civil servants, a general prohibition is too great an infringement. The objective of ensuring the impartiality of civil servants can be achieved by less restrictive means.[161] **20.57**

Appendix 2: The New Zealand Bill of Rights Act

Section 12 of the New Zealand Bill of Rights Act[162] provides as follows: **20.58**

> Every New Zealand citizen who is of or over the age of 18 years
> (a) Has the right to vote in genuine periodic elections of members of the House of Representatives, which elections shall be by equal suffrage and by secret ballot; and;
> (b) Is qualified for membership of the House of Representatives.

Section 12 has been judicially considered in two cases. *In the matter of D*[163] concerned a compulsory treatment order under the Mental Health (Compulsory Assessment and Treatment) Act 1992 and dealt with the relationship between that Act and the New Zealand Bill of Rights Act 1990. **20.59**

In *Peters v Collinge,*[164] Winston Peters, a Member of Parliament and long-standing member of the New Zealand National Party, sought an interim injunction against the national executive of the party. The injunction was to prevent the executive from expelling him and from requiring his written agreement that he would not stand as a parliamentary candidate if he failed to be selected as a National Party candidate. Mr Peters also contested the failure of the national executive to approve him as the party candidate for the Tauranga electorate. **20.60**

---

157 *Hoogbruin and Raffa v British Columbia (A-G)* (1985) 24 DLR (4th) 718.
158 *Craig v New Brunswick* (1992) 128 NBR (2d) 344.
159 *Harvey v New Brunswick (A-G)* [1996] 2 SCR 876.
160 *MacLean v Nova Scotia (A-G)* (1987) 35 DLR (4th) 306.
161 *Fraser v Novia Scotia (A-G)* (1986) 30 DLR (4th) 340.
162 Electoral rights are one of the Bill's Democratic and Civil Rights under Part II of the Bill. Other democratic and civil rights included in the New Zealand Bill are freedom of thought, conscience and religion (s 13), freedom of expression (s 14), manifestation of religion and belief (s 15), freedom of peaceful assembly (s 16), freedom of association (s 17) and freedom of movement (s 18).
163 [1995] NZFLR 28.
164 [1993] 2 NZLR 554, HC.

20.61 In 1991, Mr Peters had been dropped from Cabinet following a considerable history of conflict between himself and key party members, including the Prime Minister. Prior to the 1993 general election, a new nomination form had been distributed, clause 6 of which required an undertaking by candidates that they would refuse nomination other than as a candidate for the National Party. The plaintiff objected, *inter alia,* to signing the nomination document in that form and the High Court thus had to decide whether clause 6 was contrary to section 12 of the New Zealand Bill of Rights Act. Fisher J observed:[165]

> The effect of clause 6 of the nomination form would be to preclude an unsuccessful applicant for the National Party candidacy from standing in competition to the National. The non-competition clause forms part of a contract entered into between every applicant and the National Party at the time that the National candidacy is sought. Essentially, the price of being considered for the candidacy is that the applicant relinquishes his right to stand in competition. The question is whether a person can contract out of the right to stand for Parliament in that way.

Without developing the Bill of Rights issue extensively, Fisher J observed that the right to stand for Parliament seemed implicit within section 12: 'On the face of it one would not expect that a citizen could sell the right or qualification conferred by s 12'.[166] Counsel for the defendant argued, unsuccessfully, that a person is free to contract out of his right to stand for election under section 12: that by doing so he is simply declining to exercise that right, just as a person who is offered legal advice in a police station may decline it. Fisher J rejected this analogy in the following terms:[167]

> In my view there is a distinction between contemporaneously declining to exercise a right upon the occasion that it arises and contracting out in advance. I think that a power to contract out in advance would be open to abuse and contrary to the spirit of s 12 of the New Zealand Bill of Rights Act.

20.62 This interpretation of section 12 by the New Zealand court suggests that the right is fundamental and non-derogable. Although the judge held that a contract which purported to preclude a person from standing for Parliament is contrary to public policy and illegal, he noted also that political parties are private bodies with no statutory or public duties. Accordingly, it is necessary to carefully distinguish between the public law relating to electoral processes and the private law relating to the internal activities of unincorporated societies.[168]

---

[165] *Peters v Collinge* [1993] 2 NZLR 554, 562.

[166] Ibid 565.

[167] Fisher J did not, however, indicate the basis on which unenforceability rests, finding it '. . . unnecessary to decide finally whether unenforceability flows directly from an implied legislative intention in [the Bill of Rights Act itself], although I am inclined to favour that view. The matter can be dealt with more broadly on the basis of public policy'. Ibid.

[168] The decision whether the party will support a candidate must therefore be a voluntary one. There can be no general legal principle or legitimate expectation that a political party will continue to support its present Member of Parliament in the next election: ibid 574–5.

Appendix 3: Human Rights Cases in Other Jurisdictions

(1) Introduction

The most developed common law jurisprudence in relation to electoral rights is in the United States.[169] These rights have been derived by implication from a number of provisions of the Constitution including the provisions relating to the elections to Congress,[170] the First Amendment and the 'equal protection' provision of the Fourteenth Amendment. It has been said that the right to vote is a fundamental right which is 'preservative of other basic civil and political rights'.[171] **20.63**

The most important and well known US cases concern the drawing of electoral boundaries. The first case in which the Supreme Court intervened concerned a law which redrew city boundaries to exclude black voters: this was declared unconstitutional.[172] It has been held that all voters should have an opportunity of equal participation in the electoral process.[173] This 'one person one vote' principle is denied if electoral districts are of significantly different sizes. The courts have applied the principle to the determination of the size of congressional districts[174] and to all local government units.[175] Furthermore, the courts will intervene if electoral districts are gerrymandered to the substantial advantage of a particular political party.[176] **20.64**

The US courts have also dealt with the rights of voters and candidates. A variety of restrictions on the franchise have been held to be unconstitutional including state poll taxes,[177] and a one-year residency requirement.[178] However, literacy tests for voters are not unconstitutional provided that they are not used to promote discrimination.[179] The imposition of fees on poor candidates is likely to be unconstitutional.[180] If a law 'affords minority political parties a real and substantially equal opportunity for ballot qualification' it will be upheld.[181] A statutory scheme which has the effect of preventing prison inmates from voting will be unconstitutional.[182] Furthermore, it has been held that a refusal to register homeless persons to vote was a violation of their right to vote.[183] **20.65**

---

[169] For general discussions see J Nowak and R Rotunda, *Constitutional Law*, (5th edn, West Publishing , 1995) para 14.31ff; L Tribe, *American Constitutional Law* (2nd edn, Foundation Press, 1988) Chap 13.

[170] Art I, s 2.

[171] *Reynolds v Sims* (1964) 377 US 533, 562.

[172] *Gomillion v Lightfoot* (1960) 364 US 339.

[173] *Reynolds v Sims* (1964) 377 US 533.

[174] *Wesberry v Sanders* (1964) 376 US 1.

[175] *Hadley v Junior College District* (1970) 397 US 50.

[176] *Davis v Bandemer* (1986) 478 US 109.

[177] *Harper (Annie E) v Virginia State Board of Elections* (1966) 383 US 663; in presidential and congressional elections such taxes are prohibited by the Twenty Fourth Amendment (1964).

[178] *Dunn v Blumstein* (1972) 405 US 330.

[179] *Lassiter v Northampton County Board of Elections* (1959) 360 US 45.

[180] *Lubin v Panish* (1974) 415 US 709.

[181] *American Party of Texas v White* (1974) 415 US 767—petition signed by 1% of voters who had not participated in another party's primary or nominating process.

[182] *Goosby v Osser* (1973) 409 US 512.

[183] *Collier v Menzel* (1985) 176 Cal App 3d 24.

20.66 The US courts apply 'strict scrutiny' when a state regulates the electoral process which involves infringement of First Amendment rights.[184] Thus, in *McIntyre v Ohio Elections Commission*[185] the Supreme Court struck down a law prohibiting the distribution of anonymous electoral materials. In the well-known case of *Buckley v Valeo*[186] the Supreme Court held that a federal law limiting individual contributions to candidates was valid in limiting the actuality and appearance of corruption but a law limiting expenditure by candidates, individuals and groups was unconstitutional. In *Federal Election Commission v National Conservation Political Action Committee*[187] the Court struck down a statutory provision prohibiting political action committees from spending more than $1,000 to further the candidacy of someone who chose to receive public financing. A prohibition on the expenditure of corporate funds in connection with election to public office was held to violate the First Amendment.[188]

(2) Australia

20.67 The Constitution of Australia Act 1900 makes a number of express provisions in relation to elections. For example, section 7 provides that:

> The Senate shall be composed of senators for each State, directly chosen by the people of the State.

Section 24 provides that:

> The House of Representatives shall be composed of members directly chosen by the people of the Commonwealth.

However, these provisions do not appear to guarantee the right to vote.[189] Furthermore, they do not provide constitutional protection for 'equality of voting power'. In *McKinlay's* case[190] a majority of the High Court held that the Constitution did not demand equality in the size of electorates.[191] A similar conclusion was reached in *Ditchburn v Divisional Returning Officer*[192] in which it was held that the requirements that members be 'directly chosen' and that 'each elector shall vote only once' do not preclude Parliament from providing for a compulsory preferential voting system.

20.68 The statutory provisions which make voting compulsory were challenged in *Langer v Commonwealth of Australia*.[193] Mr Langer had been campaigning for a number of years for voters to vote in a fashion that did not give preference to the major parties. In response to his campaigns the Electoral and Referendum Act 1992 introduced a section 329A in the

---

[184] See generally, Nowak and Rotunda (n 169 above) para 16.50ff.

[185] (1995) 514 US 334.

[186] (1976) 424 US 1.

[187] (1985) 470 US 480.

[188] *Federal Election Commission v Massachusetts Citizens for Life* (1986) 479 US 238 (the case related to a non profit corporation publishing a newsletter urging readers to vote 'pro-life').

[189] See generally, P Hanks, *Constitutional Law in Australia* (2nd edn, Butterworths, 1996) 64–69; G Williams, *Human Rights Under the Australian Constitution* (Oxford University Press, 1999) Chap 7.

[190] *A-G (Commonwealth), ex rel McKinlay v Commonwealth* (1975) 135 CLR 1.

[191] See also *McGinty v State of Western Australia* (1996) 134 ALR 289.

[192] [1999] HCA 41 (22 July 1999).

[193] (1996) 186 CLR 302; see also *Soegemeier v Macklin* (1985) 58 ALR 768; see generally, Williams (n 189 above) 159–161.

Commonwealth Electoral Act making it an offence to publish material 'with the intention of encouraging persons voting at the election to fill in a ballot paper otherwise than in accordance with section 240'. Mr Langer sought a declaration that section 329A was constitutionally invalid. The High Court[194] dismissed Mr Langer's application holding that section 240 was consistent with section 31 and 51(xxxvi) of the Constitution.[195]

However, the system of representative government does give rise to some implied rights in relation to the electoral process. In *Australian Capital Television Pty Ltd v The Commonwealth of Australia*[196] the High Court of Australia held that a requirement that there be direct elections to the legislature created an implied constitutional guarantee of freedom of communication in relation to the political and electoral processes. The right of the electorate to choose members of the legislature carried with it: **20.69**

> the right to convey and receive information, opinions and arguments concerning such elections and the candidates who are involved in them.

As a result, it was held that voters had to have access to the information, ideas and arguments which are necessary to make an informed judgment as to how they have been governed and as to what policies are in the interests of themselves, their communities and the nation. Provisions regulating television broadcasts during elections were, accordingly, unconstitutional.

A similar approach was taken in *Lange v Australian Broadcasting Corporation*,[197] in which the High Court of Australia held that a system of representative and responsible government requires a freedom of communication about government and politicians. This freedom was not protected by the common law and, as a result, the High Court extended the law of qualified privilege to cover the communication of 'information, opinions and arguments concerning government and political matters that affect the people of Australia'. **20.70**

(3) Hong Kong

Article 21 of the Hong Kong Bill of Rights provides that: **20.71**

> Every permanent resident shall have the right and the opportunity, without any of the distinctions mentioned in article 1(1) and without unreasonable restrictions—
>
> (a) to taken part in the conduct of public affairs, directly or through freely chosen representatives;
> (b) to vote and be elected at genuine periodic elections which shall be by universal and equal suffrage and shall be held by secret ballot, guaranteeing the free expression of the will of the electors;
> (c) to have access, on general terms of equality, to public service in Hong Kong.

In *Lau San Ching v A Liu, the Returning Officer of Kwai Tsing District*[198] it was held that a requirement to be ordinarily resident in Hong Kong for 10 years prior to being eligible to **20.72**

194 Brennan CJ, Toohey, Gaudron, McHugh and Gummow JJ, Dawson J dissenting.

195 See also *Muldowney v State of South Australia* (1996) 186 CLR 352 (statute which made it criminal to advocate spoiling ballot papers was constitutional, as tending to further the democratic process).

196 (1992) 177 CLR 106; see generally, Williams (n 189 above) 165ff.

197 (1997) 189 CLR 520.

198 [1995] HKLY 556.

stand for election was in breach of Article 21. In order to justify the requirement, the Crown had to show that it was reasonable. To do so, the Crown had to show that there was a legitimate objective, and that the rationality and proportionality tests were satisfied. While there was a legitimate purpose in imposing a residency requirement, the 10-year requirement was neither rational nor proportionate. It was held that residential requirements in other jurisdictions were far shorter.

20.73 The case of *Lee Miu Ling v A-G*[199] concerned a challenge to the dual constituency voting system. Each member of the electorate had a vote in a geographical constituency, but certain members of the electorate had a further vote in a functional constituency. The appellants, who did not have votes in a functional constituency, challenged the scheme as contrary to the guarantee of universal and equal suffrage. They further contended that because each functional constituency sent one member to the Legislative Council irrespective of population, an individual vote in a small constituency had disproportionate weight, contrary to the inherent right to equal voting power. The Hong Kong Court of Appeal dismissed the appeal. It stated that the difference in weight of votes in functional constituencies was a justified departure from the principle of equality, as those constituencies were bound to differ in size. Further, although the dual constituency system was also a departure from equality, was specifically preserved by Article VII(3) of the Letters Patent.

(4) Ireland

20.74 Article 16.1 of the Irish Constitution provides that:

> 2. i. All citizens, and
>   ii. such other persons in the State as may be determined by law,
>
> without distinction of sex who have reached the age of eighteen years who are not disqualified by law and comply with the provisions of the law relating to the election of members of Dáil Éireann, shall have the right to vote at an election for members of Dáil Éireann.
>
> 3. No law shall be enacted placing any citizen under disability or incapacity for membership of the Dáil Éireann on the ground of sex or disqualifying any citizen from voting at an election for members of Dáil Éireann on that ground.
>
> 4. No voter may exercise more than one vote at an election for Dáil Éireann, and the voting shall be by secret ballot.[200]

20.75 In *Reynolds v A-G*[201] the plaintiff could not vote because his name was not on the electoral register, through no fault of his own. His action was dismissed by the Court because the right to vote was conditional on 'complying' with election law, that is by being duly registered.

20.76 The courts have also considered the nature of a secret ballot. The use of ballot papers which could be traced back to the person who had used the papers has been held to be unconstitutional.[202] However, breaches in secrecy which do not affect an election result have not lead to the setting aside of an election, as that would interfere with the constitutional rights of the remaining voters.[203]

---

[199] [1995] 4 LRC 288.
[200] J M Kelly, *The Irish Constitution* (3rd edn, Butterworths Ireland, 1994) 149–160.
[201] High Court, 16 Feb 1973; Kelly (n 200 above) 153.
[202] *McMahon v A-G* [1972] IR 69.
[203] *Dillon-Leetch v Calleary* Supreme Court, 31 Jul 1974, Kelly (n 200 above) 157.

Electoral rights have also been considered in the context of Article 40.3.1 of the Irish Constitution, which provides that: **20.77**

> The State guarantees in its laws to respect, and, as far as is practicable, by its laws to defend and vindicate the personal rights of the citizen.

In *McKenna v An Taoiseach,*[204] the Court rejected the plaintiff's claim that she had a right that the decision of the electorate on the ratification of the Treaty on European Union should be arrived at by fair procedures and scrupulously in accordance with the Constitution. The Court held that the right claimed did not fall within Article 40.3.1.

State regulation of election broadcasting was considered in *The State v Lynch.*[205] In that case, the Supreme Court upheld a ministerial order which prohibited election broadcasts on behalf of Sinn Fein. The ban was challenged as a breach of freedom of expression. The Court stated that the state was under an obligation to prevent broadcasts which were aimed at, or which might have the effect of, promoting or inciting crime or endangering the authority of the state. The Court also upheld the defendants' decision that, irrespective of the topic under discussion, Gerry Adams could not be divorced in the public mind from advancing the cause of Sinn Fein because of his prominent position within the organisation. **20.78**

(5) South Africa

Section 19 of the Constitution is headed 'Political Rights' and provides: **20.79**

> (1) Every citizen is free to make political choices, which includes the right—
> (a) to form a political party;
> (b) to participate in the activities of, or recruit members for, a political party; and
> (c) to campaign for a political party or cause.
>
> (2) Every citizen has the right to free, fair and regular elections for any legislative body established in terms of the Constitution.
>
> (3) Every adult citizen has the right—
> (a) to vote in elections for any legislative body established in terms of the Constitution, and to do so in secret; and
> (b) to stand for public office and, if elected, to hold office.

The case of *New National Party of South Africa v Government of the Republic of South Africa*[206] concerned a challenge to the need for a special bar-coded document in order to vote in the 1999 national elections. That challenge failed both on the equality ground, and on whether the right to vote had been infringed. The New National Party argued that many voters would be deprived of the right to vote because the Department of Home Affairs did not have the capacity to issue the documents in the limited time available prior to the elections. The legislation prescribing the documentary requirements had been passed in October 1998, but there had been publicity for the requirement from April 1998, and by July 1998, 80% of the population already possessed the requisite bar-coded documents. Registration was possible if an applicant either had a bar coded document or had **20.80**

---

[204] High Court, 8 Jun 1992, see Kelly (n 200 above) 748.

[205] [1982] IR 33.

[206] 1999 (5) BCLR 489; see also *Democratic Party v Minister of Home Affairs* 1999 (6) BCLR 607 dealing with similar issues.

applied for such a document. The Court concluded that those who did not possess bar-coded identity documents had six months to make applications and those who wanted to exercise this right and who took reasonable steps in pursuit of this right could have made such applications timeously and registered as voters. The Court found that Parliament is obliged to provide for a scheme that is reasonably capable of achieving the goal of ensuring that all persons who want to vote, and who take reasonable steps in pursuit of that right, are able to do so. An appellant has to establish that the scheme provided for is not reasonably capable of achieving that purpose and the appellants had failed to do this.

20.81 O'Regan J dissented, holding that the requirement for a bar-coded document was an unreasonable infringement on the right to vote. She noted the fundamental importance of the right to vote coupled with the constitutional obligation on the state to enact legislation which enfranchises, rather than disenfranchises. Secondly, the nature of the right to vote was such that relief granted after the date of the elections would rarely be effective, and would require a litigant to show a breach in advance. Finally, the reasonableness of the requirement depended on the circumstances of the case, namely that several surveys showed that many voters were unaware of the requirement; the Independent Electoral Commission's recommendation that such requirement be abandoned; and the capacity of the Government to issue the necessary documents.

20.82 It has been held that, in the absence of a disqualifying legislative provision, prisoners retained their constitutional right to vote and, as a result, that the Independent Electoral Commission is obliged to make all the necessary and reasonable arrangements to enable them to vote.[207]

(6) Tanzania

20.83 Section 74(12) of the Constitution of Tanzania states that:

> No Court shall have jurisdiction to inquire into anything done by the Electoral Commission in the exercise of its functions according to the provisions of this Constitution.

This provision was considered by the Court of Appeal in *A-G v Kabourou*.[208] It was held that it was to be interpreted as protecting from inquiry only acts done according to the Constitution or the relevant law. There was an implied constitutional principle that elections be free and fair. The Court of Appeal upheld the order of the High Court annulling a parliamentary by-election on various grounds including the fact that broadcasts by Radio Tanzania had unfairly influenced the result.

(7) Zimbabwe

20.84 In *United Parties v Minister of Justice*[209] the Supreme Court considered the impact of state funding of political parties on the right to freedom of expression. The Court considered the systems of public funding of political parties or candidates in Germany, Canada and other jurisdictions. It was held that a provision which, in practice, provided finance for only one party was inconsistent with the principle of freedom of expression.

[207] *August v Electoral Commission* 1999 (3) SA 1.
[208] [1995] 2 LRC 757.
[209] (1997) 3 BHRC 16; see also 15.382.

Part IV

REMEDIES AND PROCEDURES

21

REMEDIES UNDER THE HUMAN RIGHTS ACT

A. Introduction: Section 8 of the Human Rights Act

(1) The provisions of section 8

21.01 The Human Rights Act gives the court power to grant an appropriate remedy where it finds that a public authority[1] has acted in a way which is incompatible[2] with Convention rights.[3] This power is contained in section 8 which provides:

> (1) In relation to any act (or proposed act) of a public authority which the court finds (or would be) unlawful, it may grant such relief or remedy, or make such order, within its powers as it considers just and appropriate.
>
> (2) But damages may be awarded only by a court which has the power to award damages, or to order the payment of compensation in civil proceedings.
>
> (3) No award of damages is to be made, unless, taking account of all the circumstances of the case, including–
>
> (a) any other relief or remedy granted, or order made, in relation to the act in question (by that or any other court), and
> (b) the consequences of any decision (of that or any other court) in respect of that act,
>
> the court is satisfied that the award is necessary to afford just satisfaction to the person in whose favour it is made.
>
> (4) In determining–
>
> (a) whether to award damages, or
> (b) the amount of an award,
>
> the court must take account of the principles applied by the European Court of Human Rights in relation to the award of compensation under Article 41 of the Convention.
>
> (5) A public authority against whom damages are awarded is to be treated–
>
> (a) in Scotland for the purposes of section 3 of the Law Reform (Miscella-

[1] See para 5.03ff above.
[2] See para 5.120ff above.
[3] See para 3.43ff above.

neous Provisions) (Scotland) Act 1940 as if the award were made in an action for damages in which the authority has been found liable in respect of loss or damage to the person to whom the award is made;

(b) for the purposes of the Civil Liability (Contribution) Act 1978 as liable in respect of damages suffered by the person to whom the award is made.

(6) In this section–

'court' includes a tribunal;
'damages' means damages for an unlawful act of a public authority; and
'unlawful' means unlawful under section 6(1).

The section is drafted in very wide terms. The Government emphasised its breadth when explaining why the Convention right to an effective remedy under Article 13 of the Convention was excluded from the Human Rights Act.[4] As Lord Irvine LC said during the debates over the Bill: **21.02**

> I cannot conceive of any state of affairs in which an English court, having held an act to be unlawful because of its infringement of a Convention right, would under [section] 8(1) be disabled from giving an effective remedy.[5]

He made it clear that, in the Government's view that, when considering the 'very ample provisions' of section 8, the courts could have regard to Article 13.[6] However, it is submitted that the views expressed concerning the omission of Article 13 by the Home Secretary, Jack Straw MP, in Committee[6a] do not satisfy the requirement under *Pepper v Hart*[6b] that statements of the Minister about the meaning of the Act must be sufficiently clear.

A court with power to grant a remedy under the Human Rights Act has a wide range of options available to it. Many civil cases under the Act will be brought as judicial review proceedings; and it is therefore necessary to examine how the Act will influence the relief which may be granted in such proceedings. Relief for judicial review has always been discretionary; and the power of the court to grant such relief that it considers just and appropriate under section 8(1) ensures that relief will be discretionary in Human Rights Act cases. A more novel development is the power to award damages under section 8(3): when awarding damages the court must take account of the principles developed in the Convention jurisprudence. There will also be scope to grant relief in private law cases under the **21.03**

[4] For discussion of the controversy this omission has created see para 3.82 above.

[5] *Hansard*, HL col 479 (18 Nov 1997).

[6] Ibid col 475; see also Lord Lester's summary of the position in relation to Art 13, ibid cols 476–477; and see also D Feldman, 'Remedies For Violations of Convention Rights under the Human Rights Act' [1998] EHRLR 691.

[6a] Hansard HC 20 May 1998 cols 979–980, 'If we were to include art 13 in the Bill in addition to the remedies provided the question would inevitably arise what the courts would make of the amendment which, on the face of it, contains nothing new. I suggest that the amendment would either cause confusion or prompt the courts to act in ways not intended by the Bill'.

[6b] [1993] AC 593; for a discussion of the doctrine, see para 4.35ff above.

Human Rights Act. Finally, the Act will have an enormous impact on criminal law and practice; and it is important to ascertain the remedies that will be available to ensure that a public authority does not act in a way which is incompatible with Convention rights in the course of a criminal prosecution.

21.04 Issues concerning the remedies available under the Human Rights Act are distinct from those as to the impact of the Act itself on the English law of remedies. The court itself as a public authority[7] must not act in a way which is incompatible with Convention rights;[8] consequently, even when the court is dealing with issues in proceedings between private parties, the Act will still affect the approach that must be taken. This principle of remedial horizontality is discussed in Chapter 5.[9] In this chapter we examine the issues that arise where a party contends that his Convention rights have been breached and seeks an appropriate remedy.

(2) The scope of the power to grant a remedy

21.05 Section 8(1) enables a court to grant any relief or remedy *within* its power if it considers it just and appropriate to do so. The section confers a discretion which must, of course, be exercised judicially. However, section 8(1) does not otherwise restrict how the court's discretion should be exercised. It has been suggested[10] that the notion of 'just' remedy might make it appropriate to consider the sort of factors the courts take into account when deciding whether it is just and reasonable to impose liability in negligence on a public body:[11] these would include matters such as the adverse impact the remedy might have on the statutory regime, whether it might encourage a defensive approach to performing public duties and whether it might distort spending priorities.

21.06 Section 8(1) resembles the remedies provision of the Canadian Charter of Rights; and some assistance about its effect may be obtained by examining the Canadian jurisprudence in relation to remedies.[12] Section 24(1) of the Charter of Rights states:

> Anyone whose rights and freedoms, as guaranteed by this Charter, have been infringed or denied may apply to a court of competent jurisdiction to obtain such remedy as the court considers appropriate and just in the circumstances.

---

[7] Under s 6(3) of the Human Rights Act: see generally, para 5.32ff above.

[8] Under ibid s 6(1): see generally, para 5.01ff above.

[9] See para 5.82ff above.

[10] M Amos 'Damages for breach of the Human Rights Act 1998' [1999] EHRLR 178.

[11] See eg *X (Minors) v Bedfordshire County Council* [1995] 2 AC 633, 749–751 *per* Lord Browne-Wilkinson; *Stovin v Wise* [1996] AC 923, 958 *per* Lord Hoffmann.

[12] See generally, P W Hogg, *Constitutional Law of Canada* (4th Edn, Carswell, 1997) s 37.2; D Stuart, *Charter Justice in Canadian Criminal Law* (Carswell, 1991) Chap 11; K Roach, *Constitutional Remedies in Canada* (Canada Law Book, 1999) Chap 3.

The Canadian courts have developed a number of limitations on the broad statutory language. A court to which a section 24 application is made, can only grant a remedy within its usual jurisdiction.[13] In general, arguments based on the Charter must be raised within existing court procedures. This means that applications concerning the conduct of a trial should be made to the trial judge who is in the best position to decide if it should be delayed or interrupted.[14] The creation of new procedures such as a pre trial application to suppress evidence in a criminal trial have been discouraged.[15] It has been suggested that the court's discretion under section 24(1) of the Charter should be governed by four factors:

- the redress of the wrong suffered by the applicant;
- the encouragement of future compliance with the Constitution;
- the avoidance of unnecessary interference with the exercise of governmental power;
- the ability of the court to administer the remedy awarded.[16]

Further guidance can be obtained from the decision of the South African Constitutional Court in *Fose v Ministry of Safety*.[17] This case concerned section 7(4)(a) of the South African Interim Constitution which entitled a person to apply to a competent court for 'appropriate' relief. Ackermann J took the view that, when deciding appropriate relief, that the interests of the complainant and society ought, so far as possible, to be served.[18] An appropriate remedy must mean an effective remedy: **21.07**

> it is essential that on those occasions when the legal process does establish that an infringement of an entrenched right has occurred, it be effectively vindicated. The courts have a particular responsibility in this regard and are obliged to 'forge new tools' and shape innovative remedies, if needs be, to achieve this goal.[19]

The provisions of section 8 echo those of section 6(1) of the Hong Kong Bill of Rights Ordinance 1991 which provides that, in proceedings where a violation or threatened violation of the Bill of Rights arises: **21.08**

> A court or tribunal . . . may grant such remedy or relief, or make such order, in respect of such violation or threatened violation as it has power to grant or make in those proceedings as it considers appropriate and just in the circumstances.

---

[13] *R v Mills* [1986] 1 SCR 863, 884-887; but there are powerful contrary arguments, see Hogg (n 12 above) 944.
[14] *R v Smith* [1989] 2 SCR 1120, 1129.
[15] *Re Blackwoods Beverages Ltd* (1984) 15 DLR (4th) 231.
[16] See Hogg (n 12 above) 946.
[17] 1997 (3) SA 786.
[18] Ibid para 38.
[19] Ibid para 69.

This provision appears designed to give effect to Article 2(3) of the International Covenant of Civil and Political Rights[20] which embodies the right to an effective remedy. It does not appear to have been the subject of detailed judicial consideration.

(3) The grant of remedies by tribunals

21.09 During the passage of the Human Rights Bill, concerns were expressed about the jurisdiction of the special adjudicator in asylum cases to consider cases or grant relief under the Human Rights Act.[21] As a result sections 7(11) and 7(12) were enacted:[22]

> (11) The Minister who has power to make rules in relation to a particular tribunal may, to the extent he considers it necessary to ensure that the tribunal can provide an appropriate remedy in relation to an act (or proposed act) of a public authority which is (or would be) unlawful as a result of section 6(1), by order add to–
>
> (a) the relief or remedies the tribunal may grant; or
> (b) the grounds on which it may grant any of them.
>
> (12) An order made under subsection (11) may contain such incidental, supplemental, consequential or transitional provision as the Minister making it considers appropriate.

Immigration adjudicators and the Immigration Appeals Tribunal now have statutory jurisdiction to allow appeals on the ground that there has been a breach of human rights[23] and it is not proposed that any rules will be made under this section. It follows that no other tribunals will have jurisdiction to hear free standing claims under the Human Rights Act. This means, for example, that an employment tribunal cannot provide a remedy based solely on a breach of the act in the same way it cannot do so under European Community law.[23a]

B. Damages Under the Human Rights Act

(1) Introduction

21.10 The power to award damages under the Human Rights Act marks a radical departure in English public law. Maladministration by public bodies does not

[20] See AppJ in Vol 2.

[21] For a discussion of the jurisdictional problems, see H Storey, 'Implications of the ECHR in the Immigration and Asylum Context' [1998] EHRLR 452; for the letter from the Home Office Minister (Lord Williams) announcing the new provision see N Blake and L Fransman (eds), *Immigration, Nationality and Asylum Under the Human Rights Act 1998* (Butterworths, 1999) 57–58.

[22] See also s 7(13) relating to Northern Ireland.

[23] Immigration and Asylum Appeals Act 1999, s.65.

[23a] *Biggs v Somerset County Council* [1996] ICR 364; *Barber v Staffordshire County Council* [1996] IRLR 209.

entitle the injured party to compensation[23b]—contrast the position under European Community law—although the Law Commission expressed the view in 1994 that the time was right for a review of damages for unlawful administrative action.[23c] The general power to grant remedies under section 8 includes the award of damages for acts of public authorities which are incompatible with Convention rights.[24] However, the power to award damages is subject to three limitations:

- damages may only be awarded by a court which has the power to award damages;[25]
- in proceedings in respect of judicial acts done in good faith, damages cannot be awarded otherwise than to compensate a person to the extent required by Article 5(5) of the Convention;[26]
- no award of damages is to be made unless the court is satisfied that the award is necessary to afford 'just satisfaction' to the person in whose favour it is made.[27]

Furthermore, when determining whether to award damages and the amount of damages the court must take account of the Convention principles in relation to 'just satisfaction' under Article 41. According to the Government, the aim of these provisions is to ensure:

> that people should receive damages equivalent to what they would have obtained had they taken their case to Strasbourg.[28]

21.11 The power to grant damages under section 8 of the Human Rights Act raises a number of issues. It is first necessary to consider the nature of damages awarded under the Human Rights Act. The limitations in relation to 'jurisdiction' and judicial acts are next considered before turning to the principles relating to the award of 'just satisfaction' under the Convention. Finally, there is an examination of the principles which are likely to be applied when awarding damages under the Human Rights Act.

(2) The nature of damages under the Human Rights Act

(a) Introduction

21.12 It appears that damages under the Human Rights Act cannot be characterised as damages for a breach of statutory duty in the conventional sense.[29] Since the

[23b] See, eg, *R v Deputy Chief Constable of Thames Valley Police ex p Cotton* [1989] COD 318; *R v Metropolitan Borough of Knowsley ex p Maguire* [1992] COD 499; and see Lord Woolf and J Jowell, *De Smith, Woolf and Jowell, Judicial Review of Administrative Action* (3rd edn, Sweet & Maxwell, 1995) para 19-003ff.

[23c] See *Administrative Law: Judicial Review and Statutory Appeals*, LC No 226 (1994) para 2.32.

[24] See generally, M Amos, 'Damages for Breach of the Human Act 1998' [1999] EHRLR 178.

[25] s 8(2).

[26] s 9(3).

[27] s 8(3).

[28] *Hansard*, HL col 1232 (3 Nov 1997), Lord Irvine LC.

[29] For the withdrawal of a proposal to create such a breach under the Human Rights Bill 1995 see Lord Lester, 'The Mouse That Roared: The Human Rights Bill 1995' [1995] PL 198, 200-201.

Human Rights Act is a constitutional statute,[30] questions arise as to whether the Act has created a new public law remedy of constitutional damages or whether it amounts to a constitutional tort. This is not merely a 'categorisation' question as the characterisation of the 'wrong' involved may have important consequences for the way in which damages under the Human Rights Act are understood and developed by the courts.

(b) Public law remedy

21.13 The underlying principle which justifies awarding damages for breaching human rights has been considered in many jurisdictions. Where the right is contained in a constitutional instrument, the damages awarded are normally regarded as a public law remedy of 'constitutional damages'. Thus, the Privy Council in *Maharaj v A-G of Trinidad and Tobago (No 2)*[31] held that where a barrister was wrongly committed for contempt, his constitutional right not to be deprived of his liberty without due process of law was not defeated by the public policy rule that a judge cannot be liable for anything done in the purported exercise of his judicial functions. Lord Diplock stressed:[32]

> The claim for redress under section 6(1) for what has been done by a judge is a claim against the state for what has been done in the exercise of the judicial power of the state. This is not vicarious liability; it is a liability of the state itself. It is not a liability in tort at all; it is a liability in the public law of the state, not of the judge himself...

21.14 A similar approach has been taken in Ireland. In *The State (at the prosecution of Quinn) v Ryan*[33] O Dalaigh CJ stressed that:

> It was not the intention of the Constitution in guaranteeing the fundamental rights of the citizen that these rights should be set at nought or circumvented. The intention was that rights of substance were being assured to the individual and that the Courts were the custodians of these rights. As a necessary corollary, it follows that no one can with impunity set those rights at nought or circumvent them, and that the Courts' powers in this regard are as ample as the Constitution requires.

Similarly, in *Kearney v Minister for Justice*,[34] where prison officers had infringed a prisoner's rights Costello J held:

> The wrong that was committed in this case was an unjustified infringement of a constitutional right, not a tort; and it was committed by the servant of the State and accordingly, Ireland can be sued.

21.15 The Supreme Court of India has reached the same conclusion. In *Nilabati Bahera*

[30] See para 1.90 above.
[31] [1979] AC 385.
[32] Ibid 399.
[33] [1965] IR 70, 122.
[34] [1986] IR 116 at 122; see also *Kennedy v Ireland* [1987] IR 587; *Conway v Irish National Teachers Organisation* [1991] 2 IR 305.

v State of Orissa[35] the Supreme Court awarded damages against the state where a young man had been beaten to death in police custody; Anand J said:[36]

> The old doctrine of only relegating the aggrieved to the remedies available in civil law limits the role of the courts too much as protector and guarantor of the indefeasible rights of the citizen. The courts have the obligation to satisfy the social aspirations of the citizens because the courts and the law are for the people and expected to respond to their aspirations . . . The purpose of public law is not only to civilise public power but to assure the citizen that they live under a legal system which aims to protect their interests and preserve their rights.

The Supreme Court of Sri Lanka has likewise decided[37] that a claim for redress under the Constitution is a new public law right and is not based in tort.

In *Simpson v A-G*[38] the New Zealand Court of Appeal reached the same conclusion when considering the fact that there was no remedies provision in the New Zealand Bill of Rights Act. It took the view that the Bill of Rights Act implied that effective remedies would be available for its breach and held that the action in damages was a public law action directly against the state for which the state was primarily liable. **21.16**

(c) Constitutional tort

On the other hand, a number of jurisdictions have adopted a private law approach and treated breaches of human rights as a constitutional tort. The most developed jurisprudence is in the United States and Canada. **21.17**

Damages for breaching constitutional rights can be awarded in the United States either under section 1983 of the Civil Rights Act 1871[39] or directly under the Constitution. In *Monroe v Pape*[40] the American Supreme Court held that section 1983 gave a federal remedy which supplemented any appropriate state remedy. However, the Supreme Court has stressed that unless actual damage is proved, only nominal damages will be awarded. Thus, in *Carey v Piphus*[41] two students suspended from school in breach of due process rights were awarded $1. In *Memphis Community School District v Stachura*[42] the Supreme Court stated that there was no room for 'non compensatory damages measured by a jury's perception of the abstract "importance" of a constitutional right' and they were not necessary to vindicate the constitutional rights that section 1983 protects. **21.18**

35 (1993) Crim LJ 2899.
36 Ibid 2912.
37 *Saman v Leeladasa* [1989] 1 Sri LR 1.
38 [1994] 3 NZLR 667.
39 Now 42 United States Code s 1983.
40 (1961) 365 US 157.
41 (1978) 435 US 247.
42 (1986) 477 US 299 at 309, 310 *per* Powell J writing for the Court.

21.19 The US Supreme Court has also fashioned a damages remedy against federal officials under the Bill of Rights itself. In *Bivens v Six Unknown Agents of the Federal Bureau of Narcotics*[43] the Supreme Court held that it had power to provide a remedy to compensate for an unlawful search and assault although the Fourth Amendment made no express provision for damages. The Supreme Court has subsequently extended the right of damages to sex discrimination in *Davis v Passman*[44] as a breach of the equal protection of the Fifth Amendment and in *Carlson v Green*[45] to a failure to provide proper medical care in prison.

21.20 It is also well established that damages may be an appropriate remedy under the Canadian Charter of Rights.[46] The Supreme Court of Canada has not considered the issue directly[47] but various appellate courts[48] have found that damages are an appropriate and just remedy under section 24(1) of the Charter. In *R v Crossman*[49] the Federal Court held that a police officer's denial of a suspect's right to legal advice was tortious; and in *Lord v Allison*[50] Murphy LJSC considered this to be the case with any infringement of the Charter. On the other hand, the Ontario Divisional Court[51] and the Federal Court[52] have treated the violation of the Charter as creating a cause of action of its own. The Supreme Court has said that damages under section 49 of the Quebec Charter are 'compensatory in nature' and comply with the fundamental principle of *restitutio in integrum*.[52a] The court stressed that the Quebec Charter did not create a 'parallel compensation system' which could authorise double compensation.[52b]

(d) The position under the Human Rights Act

21.21 It is submitted that section 8 of the Human Rights Act creates a 'public law remedy' rather than a new 'constitutional tort'.[52c] There are a number of reasons for this. First and most importantly, the 'discretionary' nature of section 8 damages is

[43] (1971) 403 US 388.

[44] (1979) 442 US 228.

[45] (1980) 446 US 14.

[46] See eg K Cooper-Stephenson, *Charter Damages Claims* (Carswell, 1990); Whitman, 'Constitutional Torts' (1980) 79 Mich Law Rev 5; Pilkington, 'Damages as a Remedy for the Infringement of the Canadian Charter of Rights and Freedoms' (1984) 62 Can Bar Rev 517; K Cooper-Stephenson, 'Tort Theory for the Charter Damages Remedy' (1988) 52 Sak L Rev 1.

[47] See *McKinney v University of Guelph* [1990] 3 SCR 229.

[48] See eg the Federal Court of Appeal in *Vespoli v The Queen* (1984) 12 CRR 185, 189; the Quebec Court of Appeal in *Patenaude v Roy* (1994) 123 DLR (4th) 78.

[49] (1984) 9 DLR (4th) 588.

[50] (1986) 3 BCLR (2nd) 300.

[51] *Doe v Metropolitan Police (Municipality) Commissioner of Police* (1990) 72 DLR (4th) 580.

[52] *Rollinson v Canada* [1991] 3 FC 111.

[52a] *Beliveau St Jacques v Federation des Employes de Services Public* [1996] 2 SCR 345.

[52b] Ibid para 121.

[52c] Cf Sir Robert Carnwath, 'ECHR Remedies from a Common Law Perspective' [2000] 49 ICLQ 517.

inconsistent with the traditional English approach to damages in tort which are recoverable as of *right*. If a tort is established the court has no discretion to refuse to award damages.[53] In contrast, the 'discretionary nature of remedies' is central to English public law.[54]

Secondly, if the Human Rights Act were to be viewed as giving rise to a cause of action in tort the courts may be restricted in the awards which they can make by way of 'just satisfaction'. Common law principles of causation, remoteness and mitigation may not be appropriate in cases where fundamental rights have been breached. Similarly, the common law distinctions between compensatory, aggravated and exemplary damages will not always be appropriate. If section 8 damages are a form of public law remedy the court can take a flexible approach: applying common law distinctions in suitable cases and taking a different approach if the circumstances require it. **21.22**

Thirdly, the 'public law' analysis is more consistent with the case law relating to other jurisdictions from *Maharaj*[55] to *Baignent's* case.[56] In most jurisdictions damages granted for breaches of fundamental rights are regarded as 'public law remedies'.[57] **21.23**

If damages awarded under the Human Rights Act were to be regarded as a 'public law remedy' this would not mean that the courts could not, in appropriate cases, derive assistance from the principles governing the award of damages in tort cases. The courts could, for example, be guided by the following tortious principles: **21.24**

- that the purpose of damages is to place the claimant, so far as money can, in the position which he would have been had the wrong never happened;
- that, in cases of 'intentional' violations of rights, the claimant should recover all the loss flowing from the violation, but in the case of unintentional violations, only 'reasonably foreseeable' losses will be recoverable;[58]
- that the claimant should not recover loss which could reasonably have been avoided (the so-called 'duty to mitigate').

However, the flexibility of the remedy would mean that these principles would not have to be applied mechanistically and could be departed from in appropriate cases. As the United States Supreme Court has said,[59] it should be borne in mind

---

[53] Thus, for example, damages cannot be reduced to take into account the provocative conduct by the claimant: *Lane v Holloway* [1968] 1 QB 379.

[54] See generally, Lord Woolf and J Jowell, *De Smith, Woolf and Jowell, Judicial Review of Administrative Action* (5th edn, Sweet & Maxwell, 1995) Chap 20; and see Sir Thomas Bingham, 'Should Public Law Remedies be Discretionary?' [1991] PL 64.

[55] *Maharaj v A-G of Trinidad and Tobago (No 2)* [1979] AC 385.

[56] *Simpson v A-G* [1994] 3 NZLR 667.

[57] See the survey in *Fose v Ministry of Safety and Security* 1997 (3) SA 986, paras 46–55.

[58] *The Wagon Mound* [1961] AC 388.

[59] *Memphis Community School District v Stachura* (1986) 477 US 299, 314.

that common law tort rules do not necessarily provide a complete solution to the damages issue. Compensation should be tailored to the interests protected by the particular right in question: the courts should avoid the 'wooden application of common-law damages rules'[59a] as deprivation of a constitutional right can give rise to damages not contemplated by the common law.

(3) Jurisdiction to award damages under the Act

21.25 Under section 8(2) of the Human Rights Act damages may only be awarded by a court (which includes a tribunal)[60] which has *power* to award damages or compensation in civil proceedings. Criminal courts do not generally have a statutory power to award damages (although the Court of Appeal Criminal Division may do so because the Civil Division can award damages).[61] Similarly, most tribunals do not at present have the jurisdiction to award damages. It is likely that new rules of court will make provision to cover the situation where a finding of violation of Convention rights is made by a court which does not have power to make an award of damages. On the other hand, a claimant in judicial review proceedings can specifically claim damages as part of his application[62] and will be able to seek damages for breach of the Human Rights Act.

(4) Damages for judicial acts

21.26 The general power to award damages under section 8 is subject to express limitations under section 9 in relation to judicial acts. This provides that:

> (3) In proceedings under this Act in respect of a judicial act done in good faith, damages may not be awarded otherwise than to compensate a person to the extent required by Article 5(5) of the Convention.
>
> (4) An award of damages permitted by subsection (3) is to be made against the Crown; but no award may be made unless the appropriate person, if not a party to proceedings, is joined.
>
> (5) In this section-
>
> > . . . 'judge' includes a member of a tribunal, a justice of the peace and the clerk or other officer entitled to exercise the jurisdiction of the court;
> > 'judicial act' includes a judicial act of a court and includes an act done on the instructions, or on behalf of a judge.

21.27 The Human Rights Act therefore reflects the general common law principle of

---

[59a] Ibid.

[60] s 8(6); for a discussion about the definition of 'tribunal' under the Human Rights Act, see para 5.43 above.

[61] Lord Irvine LC in Committee: see *Hansard* HL col 855 (24 Nov 1997).

[62] RSC Ord 53, r 7.

judicial immunity against actions for damages.[63] As Lord Irvine LC said, during the passage of the Bill, the purpose of section 9 is to:

> preserve the existing principle of judicial immunity . . . [so that] proceedings against a court or tribunal on convention grounds may be brought only by an appeal or an application for judicial review.[64]

Section 9(5) takes a broad approach to 'judicial acts' and extends the meaning to cover administrative actions by court staff. However, limitations on the court's ability to award damages under section 9(3) do not prevent it from making a declaration in appropriate circumstances.

The only instance where damages are recoverable under the Human Rights Act for judicial acts is where a person is detained in contravention of Article 5(5).[65] The liability falls on the Crown provided it has been joined to the proceedings. Rules of Court will make provision for such joinder. **21.28**

The Human Rights Act does not affect[66] the immunity of magistrates against claims for compensation for actions within their jurisdiction[67] and for actions in good faith outside their jurisdiction.[68] These provisions and the closely related immunities of judges against actions for damages[69] appear to be incompatible with Convention rights under Article 5(5).[70] **21.29**

(5) 'Just satisfaction' under the Convention

(a) Introduction

Section 8(4) of the Human Rights Act states that: **21.30**

> In determining–
>
> (a) whether to award damages, or
>
> (b) the amount of an award,
>
> the court must take account of the principles applied by the European Court of Human Rights in relation to the award of compensation under Article 41 of the Convention.

[63] See eg *Sirros v Moore* [1975] QB 118 *per* Lord Denning MR; and A Olowofoyeku, *Suing Judges* (Clarendon, 1993) and 'State Liability for the Exercise of Judicial Power' [1998] PL 444; but see N Bamforth, 'The Application of the Human Rights Act 1998 to Public Authorities and Private Bodies' [1999] 58 CLJ 159.

[64] *Hansard* HL col 1232 (3 Nov 1997).

[65] See para 10.175ff above.

[66] For a contrary view see S Grosz, J Beatson and P Duffy, *Human Rights: The 1998 Act and the European Convention* (Sweet & Maxwell, 2000) 142, n 63.

[67] Justices of the Peace Act 1997, s 51.

[68] Ibid s 52.

[69] See paras 11.35–11.36 above.

[70] See para 10.80ff above.

This provision is curious because Article 41 is, in terms, directed to a situation in which domestic law fails to make adequate provision. It provides that:

> If the Court finds that there has been a violation of the Convention or the protocols thereto, and if the internal law of the High Contracting Parties allows only partial reparation to be made, the Court shall, if necessary, afford just satisfaction to the injured party.[71]

The European Court of Human Rights explained in the *Vagrancy* case[72] that the Convention's just satisfaction provision originated from arbitration clauses in international treaties. It appears that the purpose of section 8(4) is to place the English court in the same position as the European Court of Human Rights when making 'damages' awards.[73]

21.31 Section 8(4) of the Human Rights Act imposes a duty on the court to take account of Convention case law. This section uses the same language as section 2(1) of the Human Rights Act which imposes a general obligation to take this case law into account.[74] Although the court 'must take account' of the jurisprudence, the principles are not binding.

(b) The Convention principles

21.32 The Court does not routinely award compensation to successful applicants. Between 1972 and 1981 the Court made awards in seven cases[75] and rejected three such claims.[76] Between 1982 and 1991 applicants sought non-pecuniary damages in 51 cases where the Court held that the judgment alone gave just satisfaction. It has been suggested that these cases share certain general characteristics:

---

[71] Art 41 came into force on 1 Nov 1998 when the Eleventh Protocol came into effect and replaced Art 50 which provided that 'If the Court finds a decision or measure taken by a legal authority or any other authority of a High Contracting Party is completely or partially in conflict with the obligations arising under the present Convention, and if the internal law of the said Party allows only partial reparation to be made for the consequences of this decision or measure, the decision of the Court shall, if necessary, afford just satisfaction to the injured party'.

[72] *De Wilde, Ooms and Versyp v Belgium (No 1)* (1971) 1 EHRR 373 para 16.

[73] Cf Grosz, Beatson and Duffy (n 66 above) para 6-19.

[74] s 2(1) requires that a court or tribunal must take account of Strasbourg case law if, in its opinion, it is relevant, see para 3.46ff above.

[75] *Ringeisen v Austria (No 1)* (1971) 1 EHRR 455 (wrongful and excessive detention); *Engel v Netherlands (No 2)* (1976) 1 EHRR 706 (unlawful arrest, excessive detention and military proceedings in camera); *Deweer v Belgium* (1980) 2 EHRR 439 (coercion of applicant to waive his right to a fair hearing); *Konig v Germany* (1978) 2 EHRR 170 (unreasonable proceedings to revoke doctor's licence to practice); *Artico v Italy* (1980) 3 EHRR 1 (distress for denial of legal assistance in fraud trial); *Guzzardi v Italy* (1980) 3 EHRR 333 (Mafia suspect detained on island pending trial); *Airey v Ireland (Art 50)* (1981) 3 EHRR 592 (denial of legal aid to enable wife in judicial separation proceedings).

[76] *Neumeister v Austria (No 1)* (1968) 1 EHRR 91; *Golder v United Kingdom* (1975) 1 EHRR 524; *Marckx v Belgium* (1979) 2 EHRR 330.

- the Court was very divided on the merits;
- a large majority of cases concerned individuals who were accused of (or were guilty of) criminal offences; and
- they often involved procedural errors in civil or administrative hearings.

The same pattern continued from 1992 until the new Court was established in November 1998. The Court found its judgment sufficient to meet the moral injury caused in 79 of the cases.[77]

Although section 8(4) requires the court or tribunal to examine Convention principles, analysis of the case law on just satisfaction is likely to be of limited assistance. There are serious concerns[78] about the lack of consistency in the case law (for example, over the treatment of criminal fines as financial loss[79] and the appropriate methodology for valuing property),[80] about the obscure nature of the basis on which the Court makes awards of specified amounts of compensation[81] and about the moral judgments the Court makes when evaluating different types of applicants (such as the claims of convicted criminals and terrorists to just satisfaction). It has been suggested[82] that the case law lacks coherence and that advocates and judges are in danger of spending time attempting to identify principles that do not exist; this is a view that is shared by some of the judges of the Court itself.[83] Nevertheless, it is possible to identify some broad principles about how the Court awards compensation under Article 41. **21.33**

Compensation is discretionary. First, compensation under the Convention is *discretionary*; Article 41 states that compensation will be awarded only 'if necessary' and the Court has a certain discretion[84] whether or not to award compensation. Consequently, the Court held in *Dudgeon v United Kingdom*[85] that because the applicant had secured his objective of changing the Northern Irish law by **21.34**

[77] See D Shelton, *Remedies in International Human Rights Law* (Oxford University Press, 1999) 204–211.

[78] See generally, A Mowbray, 'The European Court of Human Rights' Approach to Just Satisfaction' [1997] PL 647 (based on a study of case law from 1991 to 1995).

[79] Whereas the Court refused to award compensation paid by an administrative body which exercised a criminal jurisdiction in breach of Art 6 in *Schmautzer v Austria* (1995) 21 EHRR 511, it failed to distinguish earlier cases where it awarded compensation for criminal fines paid on convictions: see *Jersild v Denmark* (1994) 19 EHRR 1; *Oberschlick v Austria (No 1)* (1991) 19 EHRR 389.

[80] Contrast *Papamichalopoulos v Greece* (1995) 21 EHRR 439 where the Court relied on expert valuation evidence with *Hentrich v France* (1995) 21 EHRR 199 where it did not.

[81] See eg *Lopez Ostra v Spain* (1994) EHRR 277; *Schuler-Zgraggen v Switzerland* (1995) 21 EHRR 404.

[82] A Lester and D Pannick, *Human Rights Law and Practice* (Butterworths, 1999) para 2.8.4.

[83] One former judge of the Court is quoted as privately stating 'We have no principles' and another judge responds by saying 'We have principles, we just do not apply them': see Shelton, (n 77 above) 1 but contrast the views of Sir Robert Carnwath in 'ECHR Remedies from a Common Law Perspective' [2000] 49 ICLQ 517.

[84] *Guzzardi v Italy* (1980) 3 EHRR 333 at para 114.

[85] (1981) 4 EHRR 149 para 14.

lowering the age of consent for homosexuals, the judgment itself constituted just satisfaction for the purposes of Article 43. In *Abdulaziz, Cabales and Balkandali v United Kingdom*[86] the Court accepted that because the applicants knew when they married that they were not entitled to live together in the United Kingdom, the finding that their Convention rights were violated constituted sufficient just satisfaction.

21.35 Furthermore, the Court has frequently refused to award just satisfaction to 'undeserving' applicants such as convicted prisoners.[87] Similarly, in *McCann v United Kingdom*[88] the Court expressed the view:

> having regard to the fact that the three terrorist suspects who were killed had been intending to plant a bomb in Gibraltar, the Court does not consider it appropriate to make an award under this head.

The Court also refused to make an award in *Goodwin v United Kingdom*[89] where a journalist had refused to disclose his source. Although the Court found that there was a link between the anxiety and distress suffered by the applicant and the breach of the Convention, it said that:

> this finding constitutes adequate satisfaction in respect of the damage claimed under this head.

On the other hand, substantial compensation for non-pecuniary loss was awarded for ill treatment during detention in *Tomasi v France*[90] and to the developer in *Pine Valley Developments v Ireland*.[91]

21.36 **The principle of compensation is '*restitutio in integrum*'.** The purpose[92] of Article 41 is to ensure a *restiutio in integrum*: so that the claimant is so far as possible put back into the situation in which he would have been but for the breach of his Convention rights.

21.37 **Compensation is payable only to the 'injured party'.** Article 41 provides for compensation to be paid to the 'injured party'. In the *Vagrancy* case[93] the Court stated that the phrase is synonymous with 'victim'[94] for the purposes of Article 34

---

[86] (1985) 7 EHRR 471 paras 95, 96.

[87] See eg *Pelladoah v Netherlands* (1994) 19 EHRR 81; *Maxwell v United Kingdom* (1994) 19 EHRR 97; *Boner v United Kingdom* (1994) 19 EHRR 246; *Jamil v France* (1995) 21 EHRR 65.

[88] (1995) 21 EHRR 97, 178.

[89] (1996) 22 EHRR 123 paras 49, 50.

[90] (1992) 15 EHRR 1 paras 127–130.

[91] (1993) 16 EHRR 379 paras 16 and 17; the Court awarded IR £50,000 to Mr Healey for non pecuniary damages for discrimination under breach of Art 14 in conjunction with Art 1, Prot 1.

[92] *Pine Valley Developments Ltd v Ireland* (n 91 above) para 20; *Papamichalopoulos v Greece* (1995) 21 EHHR 439 para 38.

[93] *De Wilde, Ooms and Versyp v Belgium (No 2)* (1972) 1 EHRR 438 para 23.

[94] See para 22.27ff below.

so that it will be a person directly affected by the act or omission; an 'injured party' will therefore exclude the applicant's lawyer.[95] Damages for financial loss can be awarded to the heirs or estate of a person directly affected; but non pecuniary damages cannot be claimed unless the heirs also suffered damage.[96]

There must be a 'causal link' between compensation and breach. The applicant must prove a causal link between the compensation he seeks and the breach of his Convention right.[97] For example, in *Airey v Ireland*[98] the applicant failed in her claim for the difference in market value when she moved home; the Court concluded that the move arose not from the lack of an effective right of access to the High Court for her marital breakdown but because of her fear of molestation from her husband. 21.38

(c) 'Just satisfaction' in practice

Compensation for financial loss. Compensation for financial loss has been awarded under Article 41 to include:[99] 21.39

- the loss of past and future earnings;[100]
- damage to property;[101]
- depreciation in the value of property through state inaction;[102]
- loss of profits;[103]
- the repayment of fines[104] or court awards[105] against the applicant in breach of Convention rights;
- reduction of business opportunities caused by adverse comments by public officials.[106]

Where the Court has found it difficult to quantify loss, it has frequently resorted to awarding compensation for financial damage on the basis of loss of

---

[95] See eg *Delta v France* (1990) 16 EHRR 574 para 47.

[96] *X v United Kingdom* (1981) 4 EHRR 188 paras 18, 19; *Colozza and Rubinat v Italy* (1985) 7 EHRR 516 para 38; *Deumeland v Germany* (1986) 8 EHRR 448 para 97; *Gillow v United Kingdom* (1986) 11 EHRR 335 para 23.

[97] See eg *Benthem v Netherlands* (1985) EHRR 1 para 45; *Bönisch v Austria* (1985) 9 EHRR 191 para 11; *Pauwels v Belgium* (1988) 11 EHRR 238 para 43; *Berrehab v Netherlands* (1988) 11 EHRR 322 para 33; *Huber v Switzerland* (1990) Series A No 188 para 46.

[98] (1981) 3 EHRR 592 para 12.

[99] For a table of 'Court's Findings of Pecuniary Loss' see K Reid, *A Practitioner's Guide to the European Convention of Human Rights* (Sweet & Maxwell, 1998) 399–401.

[100] *Young James and Webster v United Kingdom* (1981) 4 EHRR 38.

[101] See eg *Hentrich v France* (1995) 21 EHRR 199.

[102] See eg *Lopez Ostra v Spain* (1994) 20 EHRR 277.

[103] See eg *Open Door Counselling and Dublin Well Woman v Ireland* (1992) 15 EHRR 244 paras 85–87.

[104] See eg *Deweer v Belgium* (1980) 2 EHRR 439 paras 59–60; *Lingens v Austria* (1986) 8 EHRR 103 para 50; *Schwabe v Austria* (1992) Series A No 242-B para 37.

[105] See eg *Stran Greek Refineries and Stratis Andreadis v Greece* (1994) 19 EHRR 293 para 81.

[106] *Allenet de Ribemont v France* (1995) 20 EHRR 557.

opportunity.[107] However, the Court does not provide a detailed explanation for its reasoning, even when considering complex claims of financial loss.[108]

21.40 Where there is a breach of procedural obligations under Article 6(1),[109] it is rare for the Court to hold that it caused loss[110] as a result, for example, of a subsequent conviction[111] or adverse decision affecting civil rights or obligations.[112] The Court usually decides that it is unable to speculate as to what the outcome would have been had the breach not occurred.[113] In exceptional cases it may find that there is a real loss of opportunity. For example, in *Barberà Messegué and Jabardo v Spain*[114] the Court decided that breach of various fair trial guarantees in a criminal trial prevented the applicants from defending themselves and caused them loss. On the other hand, fines and costs incurred in the domestic proceedings which are directly linked to the breach of a Convention Article are recoverable. Similarly, in *Tinnelly and Sons Ltd and McElduff v United Kingdom*[115] an award of £10,000 was made to reflect the loss of the opportunity to succeed in discrimination proceedings. In that case the applicants alleged that they had been denied a tender because of the religious or political beliefs of their employees; however, public interest immunity certificates had been issued which prevented the case from proceeding to trial.

21.41 **Compensation for non-financial loss.** If the Court decides to award compensation, then it is guided by the particular circumstances in every case, having regard to what it describes as equitable considerations. The Court has given little guidance[116] about how the discretion should be exercised, the relevant factors appear to be the applicant's conduct and the extent of the breach. Awards are often made in child care cases[117] but not in relation to procedural breaches of Article 6 or in terrorist cases.[118]

---

107 See eg *Goddi v Italy* (1984) 6 EHRR 457 para 35; *Bönisch v Austria* (1985) 9 EHRR 191 para 11; *Lingens v Austria* (1986) 8 EHRR 103 para 51; *Weeks v United Kingdom* (1987) 10 EHRR 293 para 13; *Barberà Messegué and Jabardo v Spain* (1988) 11 EHRR 360 paras 15–20.

108 See eg *Sporrong and Lönnroth v Sweden* (1982) 5 EHRR 35 paras 25–32; *Papamichalopoulos v Greece* (1995) 21 EHRR 439 paras 34–40.

109 These are summarised at para 11.183 above.

110 See eg the revocation of licence cases such as *Tre Traktörer Aktiebolay v Sweden* (1989) 13 EHRR 309; *Håkansson and Sturesson v Sweden* (1990) 13 EHRR 1; *Fredin v Sweden (No 1)* (1991) 13 EHRR 784; and see also *Saunders v United Kingdom* (1996) 23 EHRR 313.

111 As a result of a criminal charge, see para 11.174ff above.

112 See generally, para 1.160ff above.

113 K Reid, *A Practitioner's Guide to the European Convention on Human Rights* (Sweet & Maxwell, 1998) 398.

114 (1988) 11 EHRR 360.

115 (1998) 27 EHRR 249.

116 D Harris, M O'Boyle and C Warbrick, *The Law of the European Convention on Human Rights* (Butterworths, 1995) 685.

117 See eg *Olsson v Sweden (No 2)* (1992) 17 EHRR 134; *Keegan v Ireland* (1994) 18 EHRR 342; *McMichael v United Kingdom* (1995) 20 EHRR 205.

118 Reid (n 113 above) 402.

Compensation for non financial loss has been awarded to cover:[119] **21.42**

- excessive periods of detention; however, damages will be modest if the breach of Convention rights is technical: as where unlawful detention on remand counts towards the sentence ultimately imposed[120] or where Article 6 has been breached because a hearing was held in private;[121]
- the loss of opportunity to serve a lighter sentence (if, for example, the state had provided a practical and effective defence);[122]
- assaults in police custody;[123]
- the impact of prolonged uncertainty on career prospects;[124]
- distress (which can include uncertainty resulting from a failure to ensure a trial within a reasonable time[125] and feelings of frustration[126] or of unequal treatment).[127]

Awards for distress have covered a wide range: £1,000 in *Papamichalopoulos v Greece*[128] for the applicant's helplessness and frustration at the Government's failure to comply with court orders; £5,000 in *Darnell v United Kingdom*[129] to compensate for the strain of fighting legal battles for five years rather than practising medicine and for the serious damage to his professional career; £5,000 for the distress and anxiety in *Gaskin v United Kingdom*[130] resulting from the failure to provide an independent procedure to allow the applicant access to his social services files; £10,000 in *Keegan v Ireland*[131] for the trauma, anxiety and feelings of injustice which resulted in his daughter's adoption with whom he was unlikely to reunite; £12,000 in *Hokkanen v Finland*[132] for a father's inability to enforce his right of access to his daughter; and £25,000 in *Aydin v Turkey*[133] for psychological harm a woman suffered in custody and on account of being raped. **21.43**

---

[119] For a table of 'Court's Findings of Non-Pecuniary Loss' see Reid (n 113 above) 403–420.

[120] *Neumeister v Austria (No 2)* (1974) 1 EHRR 136; however, the subsequent imprisonment does not 'acquire the character of *restitutio in integrum* for no freedom is given in place of freedom unlawfully taken away': see *Ringeisen v Austria (No 2)* (1972) 1 EHRR 504 para 21.

[121] *Engel and others v Netherlands (No 2)* (1976) 1 EHRR 706.

[122] See eg *Goddi v Italy* (1984) 6 EHRR 457 para 36; *Colozza v Italy* (1985) 7 EHRR 516 para 38; *Bönisch v Austria* (1985) 9 EHRR 191 para 11.

[123] See eg *Ribitsch v Austria* (1995) 21 EHRR 573.

[124] *Konig v Germany* (1987) 2 EHRR 170 at para 19

[125] *Guincho v Portugual* (1984) 7 EHRR 223 at para 44.

[126] See eg *O, H, W, B and R v United Kingdom* (1987) 10 EHRR 82 paras 11–14; this is what is known as 'moral damage' in civil law systems, see Handford, 'Moral Damage in Germany' (1978) 27 ICLQ 849.

[127] See eg *Bönisch v Austria* (1985) 9 EHRR 191 para 11.

[128] (1995) 21 EHRR 439.

[129] (1993) 18 EHRR 205 paras 23, 24.

[130] (1989) 12 EHRR 36 para 58.

[131] (1994) 18 EHRR 342 paras 66–68.

[132] (1994) 19 EHRR 139.

[133] (1997) 25 EHHR 251.

21.44 However, the Court, for example, declined to award compensation for interference with prisoners' correspondence in *Silver v United Kingdom*[134] on the ground that the number of letters which were the subject of an adverse finding was small compared to the number of letters they were allowed to send.

21.45 As already emphasised, it is not possible to identify a tariff which the Court applies to damages for non-financial loss. Nevertheless, it may be helpful to identify some of the awards made in order to provide guidance when assessing quantum.[135]

21.46 **The right to life under Article 2.**[136] The Court awarded 6 million pesetas[137] for ill treatment and death in custody in *Díaz Ruano v Spain.*[138] The failure to conduct an effective investigation into a killing has resulted in an award of £10,000 in *Kaya v Turkey*[139] and 50,000FF[140] in *Gülec v Turkey.*[141]

21.47 **Inhuman treatment in breach of Article 3.**[142] Just satisfaction has been awarded in a number of cases in which there have been findings of inhuman treatment, including an award of 100,000 Austrian schillings[143] for an assault in custody in *Ribitsch v Austria*[144] and £10,000 for corporal punishment in *A v United Kingdom.*[145]

21.48 **Unlawful arrest or detention under Article 5.**[146] A number of awards have been made for breach of liberty rights. For example, in *Engel v Netherlands*[147] detention for two days received a token award of 100 guilders,[148] in part because the detention was taken into account in later proceedings. In *Quinn v France*[149] the Court awarded 10,000FF[150] for 11-hours' unlawful detention and 50,000FF[151] for the unlawful detention of almost two years. In *Johnson v United Kingdom*[152] a three-

[134] (1983) 5 EHRR 347 para 10; see also *Campbell and Fell v United Kingdom* (1984) 7 EHRR 165 para 141; and contrast *Boyle and Rice v United Kingdom* (1988) 10 EHRR 425 para 91 where the Court awarded £3,000 for interfering with one letter.

[135] For these purposes we have drawn heavily on the table of the Court's findings of non-pecuniary damage in K Reid, *A Practitioner's Guide to the European Convention of Human Rights* (Sweet & Maxwell, 1998), 403–420.

[136] See generally, para 7.05ff above.

[137] Current value, approx £21,000.

[138] (1994) 19 EHRR 555.

[139] (1998) 28 EHRR 1.

[140] Current value, approx £4,5000.

[141] (1999) 28 EHRR 121.

[142] See para 8.13ff above.

[143] Current value, approx £4,000.

[144] (1995) 21 EHRR 573.

[145] (1998) 27 EHRR 611.

[146] See para 10.84ff above.

[147] (1976) 1 EHRR 647.

[148] Current value, approx £30.

[149] (1995) 21 EHRR 529.

[150] Current value, approx £900.

[151] Current value, approx £4,500.

[152] (1997) 27 EHRR 296.

year delay in releasing the applicant from a mental hospital resulted in an award of £10,000.

Breach of fair trial rights under Article 6.[153] The large number of successful applications under Article 6 means that there are a comparatively large number of cases where compensation has been awarded. In *Funke v France*[154] the applicant was awarded 50,000FF[155] for breach of the right to silence and for a search of his home contrary to Article 8. In *Fredin v Sweden (No 2)*[156] compensation of 15,000 SEK[157] was given for the lack of a public hearing together with a breach of the right of access to the court. Just satisfaction of 150,000FF[158] was made for lack of reasons in *Fouquet v France*[159] because the decision contained a mistake of fact. **21.49**

Awards are regularly made where there is a failure to provide a fair and public hearing within a reasonable time. For example, in *Neves e Silva v Portugal*[160] a delay of over six years in relation to civil proceedings resulted in compensation of 500,000 escudos[161] and in *Mitap and Muftoglu v Turkey*[162] a delay of almost six years in criminal proceedings led to compensation of 80,000FF each.[163] In *X v France*[164] compensation of 150,000FF[165] was given to the parents of an applicant who died of AIDS to reflect the improvement to his life psychologically had the delay of two years been avoided. In recent years there have been a large number of breaches found against Italy; and awards have ranged from 5 million lire[166] for nearly 10-years' delay[167] to 45 million lire[168] for a delay of 15 years.[169] **21.50**

In *Goddi v Italy*[170] the Court ordered compensation of 5 million lira[171] for the loss of the opportunity to make an effective defence since the applicant was denied a lawyer on appeal. In *Granger v United Kingdom*[172] the absence of a lawyer to assist at an appeal hearing on a complex issue which the applicant could not fully-comprehend led to an award of £1,000. **21.51**

153 See para 1.50ff above.
154 (1993) 16 EHRR 297.
155 Current value, approx £4,500.
156 (1994) Series A No 283-A.
157 Current value, approx £1,100.
158 Current value, approx £14,000.
159 (1996) 22 EHRR 279.
160 (1989) 13 EHRR 535.
161 Current value, approx £1,500.
162 (1996) 22 EHRR 209.
163 Current value, approx £7,000.
164 (1992) 14 EHRR 483.
165 Current value, approx £14,000.
166 Current value, approx, £1,500.
167 *Italiano v Italy*, Judgment of 15 Feb 2000.
168 Current value, approx £13,500.
169 *Padalino v Italy*, Judgment of 15 Feb 2000.
170 (1984) 6 EHRR 457.
171 Current value, approx £1,500.
172 (1990) 12 EHRR 469.

21.52 **The right to respect for private[173] and family life,[174] the home[175] and correspondence[176] under Article 8.** There have been a number of cases where compensation has been awarded for breach of the right of respect for family life. The failure of the criminal law to protect a rape victim in *X and Y v Netherlands*[177] resulted in the Court awarding 3,000 guilders.[178] In *Gaskin v United Kingdom*[179] the distress caused by the absence of an independent procedure to obtain access to social service files for a child in care led to damages of £5,000. The Court in *Z v Finland*[180] awarded 200,000FIM[181] where it was disclosed that the applicant was HIV positive.

21.53 Breaches of the right of respect for family life have frequently led to awards of compensation under Article 50.[182] Thus, the breach of Articles 6 and 8 for unreasonable delays in the child care cases of *W v United Kingdom,*[183] *R v United Kingdom,*[184] *B v United Kingdom*[185] and *H v United Kingdom*[186] resulted in compensation of £12,000, £12,000, £12,000 and £8,000 respectively. In *McMichael v United Kingdom*[187] the Court decided to award £8,000 for procedural defects which contravened Articles 6 and 8. In *Eriksson v Sweden*[188] the denial of access to the court contrary to Article 6 and the delay in returning the child in breach of Article 8 led to compensation of 200,000SEK[189] to the mother and 100,000SEK to the child.[190] An award of 50,000SEK[191] to the mother and child was made in *Andersson v Sweden*[192] to reflect the restriction on contact. An award of 100,000BEF[193] was made for an expulsion which breached the right to family life in *Moustaguim v Belgium.*[194]

21.54 Compensation is sometimes awarded where there is a contravention of the right of respect for the home. The refusal to give the applicants a residence permit in

[173] See para 12.84ff above.
[174] See para 13.89ff above.
[175] See para. 12.95ff above.
[176] See para 12.100ff above.
[177] (1985) 8 EHRR 235.
[178] Current value, approx £800.
[179] (1989) 12 EHRR 36.
[180] (1997) 25 EHRR 371.
[181] Current value, approx £19,500.
[182] Or its predecessor, Art 43.
[183] (1987) 10 EHRR 29.
[184] (1987) 10 EHRR 74.
[185] (1987) 10 EHRR 87.
[186] (1987) 10 EHRR 95.
[187] (1995) 20 EHRR 205.
[188] (1989) 12 EHRR 183.
[189] Current value, approx £14,000.
[190] Current value, approx £7,000.
[191] Current value, approx £3,500.
[192] (1992) 14 EHRR 615.
[193] Current value, approx £1,500.
[194] (1991) 13 EHRR 802.

Guernsey in *Gillow v United Kingdom*[195] caused the Court to award £10,000 for stress and anxiety. A search of the home in *Miahlhe v France (No 2)*[196] attracted compensation of 50,000FF[197] for an applicant and 25,000FF[198] for his wife and mother. The environmental blight in *Lopez Ostra v Spain*[199] resulted in an award of 4 million pesetas[200] for distress and anxiety and an award of 10 million lira[201] in *Guerra v Italy*.[202] The tapping of the applicant's telephone by her employer during the course of sex discrimination proceedings in *Halford v United Kingdom*[203] led to an award of £10,000.

Freedom of religion under Article 9.[204] Convictions for proselytising in *Kokkinakis v Greece*[205] led to an award of 400,000 drachma[206] and an award of 500,000 drachma[207] in *Larissis v Greece*.[208] 21.55

Freedom of expression under Article 10.[209] No awards have been made in cases involving sanctions against journalists and politicians. However, in *Incal v Turkey*[210] damages of 30,000FF[211] were given where the applicant was convicted of insulting behaviour in breach of Article 10. 21.56

The prohibition against discrimination under Article 14.[212] There have been several cases where just satisfaction has been awarded. In *Inze v Austria*[213] the lack of inheritance for illegitimate children resulted in an award of 150,000 schillings.[214] In *Pine Valley v Ireland*[215] discrimination in refusing planning permission was compensated by an award of £50,000. 21.57

The right to quiet enjoyment of property under Article 1 of the First Protocol.[216] 21.58

[195] (1987) 13 EHRR 593.
[196] (1996) 23 EHRR 491.
[197] Current value, approx £4,500.
[198] Current value, approx £2,250.
[199] (1994) 20 EHRR 277.
[200] Current value, approx £14,000.
[201] Current value, approx £3,000.
[202] (1998) 26 EHHR 357.
[203] (1997) 24 EHRR 523.
[204] See para 14.36ff above. 21.60
[205] (1993) 17 EHRR 397.
[206] Current value, approx £700.
[207] Current value, approx £900.
[208] (1998) 27 EHRR 329.
[209] See para 15.137ff above.
[210] (1998) 4 BHRC 476.
[211] Current value, approx £2,700.
[212] See para 17.79 above.
[213] (1987) 10 EHRR 394.
[214] Current value, approx £6,250.
[215] (1993) 16 EHRR 379.
[216] See para 18.26 above.

A delay in paying compensation for expropriation in *Akkus v Turkey*[217] led to an award of US$1,000[218] for hardship.

21.59 **The right to education under Article 2 of the First Protocol.**[219] Compensation of £3,000 was paid to the pupil who had been suspended from school in *Campbell and Cosans v United Kingdom*.[220]

(6) Damages under the Human Rights Act

(a) Introduction

21.60 Section 8(3) provides that:

> No award of damages is to be made, unless, taking account of all the circumstances of the case, including–
> (a) any other relief or remedy granted, or order made, in relation to the act in question (by that or any other court), and
> (b) the consequences of any decision (of that or any other court) in respect of that act,
>
> the court is satisfied that the award is necessary to affect just satisfaction to the person in whose favour it is made.

This reflects Article 41 of the Convention. The wording of section 8(3) makes it unlikely that damages will be routinely awarded under the Human Rights Act.

21.61 There are, however, obvious dangers of inconsistency and subjectivity in a loosely formulated 'merits' based discretion of the type which appears to lie behind the Convention 'just satisfaction' jurisprudence.[221] It is submitted that the English courts should seek to evolve clear principles governing the circumstances in which damages under section 8 should be awarded.

21.62 Section 8(3) directs the court to consider a number of specific factors:

- *Any other relief or remedy granted*: It seems that the court should consider the other relief granted in proceedings where damages are given in a private law claim for an assault or trespass: damages under the Human Rights Act should not result in double recovery.[221a] Thus, in *Fose v Ministry of Safety*[222] the South African Constitutional Court took the view that it was unnecessary to award constitutional damages where the claimant would receive sufficient vindication from damages for assaults.

[217] RJD 1997-IV 1300.
[218] Current value, approx £625.
[219] See para 19.34ff above.
[220] (1982) 4 EHRR 293.
[221] See para 21.33 above.
[221a] For the position in Canada see n 52b above.
[222] 1997 (3) SA 786.

- *The consequences of any decision*: The meaning of this phrase is not wholly clear. It has been suggested that this provision requires the courts to consider the implications of opening the 'floodgates' in relation to other cases if an award is made.[223] The wording of section 8(3) also provides for arguing against awarding damages under the Act on public policy grounds: because compensation might create defensive attitudes amongst public authorities when carrying out their public duties.[224]

Although the court must examine all the circumstances in the case, the conduct of the public authority itself will be an important factor. It would be relevant if the breach of Convention rights is inadvertent or arises from a misunderstanding of the legal position on the one hand, or the public authority had made a conscious decision which breaches Convention rights. The response of a public authority after an adverse finding will also be significant. Hurt feelings would be assuaged if the public authority apologised. Action taken to remedy the position following an adverse decision may provide sufficient vindication for a claimant. If, for example, the public authority conducts a rehearing following a breach of Article 6[225] or rescinds a deportation order, then it may not be necessary to afford just satisfaction by awarding compensation. **21.63**

However, damages for non pecuniary loss are likely to be relatively modest. The general principle elaborated in defamation cases[226] or actions against the police[227] may be relevant: that damages should bear a broad similarity to compensation in personal injury cases. Nevertheless, as has been emphasised in discrimination cases[228] awards should not be too low because that would diminish the respect for the policy of protecting human rights[229] through enacting the Human Rights Act. **21.64**

The English courts are likely to take the following approach when considering a claim for damages under section 8: **21.65**

- the burden will be on the claimant to justify why an award is necessary to afford just satisfaction;

---

[223] M Amos, 'Damages for Breach of the Human Rights Act 1998' [1999] EHRLR 178.

[224] These arguments are particularly common where it is denied that public authorities should owe a duty of care in negligence: see, generally para 11.40ff; it seems that Art 6 may have an impact on these issues: see para 3.07ff above.

[225] See para 11.150ff above.

[226] *John v MGN Ltd* [1997] QB 586.

[227] *Thompson v Commissioner of Police of the Metropolis* [1998] QB 498.

[228] It is submitted that the principles are analogous to those expressed by the Court of Appeal in *Alexander v Home Office* [1988] 1 WLR 968 *per* May LJ at 692 in relation to race discrimination where it was said that low awards of damages would diminish respect for the policy of anti discrimination legislation: society has condemned discrimination and awards must ensure that it is seen to be wrong; see also *Prison Service v Johnson* [1997] ICR 275, 283.

[229] The courts under the Human Rights Act will take a generous and purposive approach to construing the Act, see para 3.12ff above.

- the court will take account of *all* the circumstances and, in particular, the specific factors identified in section 8(3) itself;
- damages under the Human Rights Act will be a public law remedy intended to provide 'just satisfaction'.

21.66 In cases of pecuniary loss the courts are likely to follow well established principles of compensation in order to provide *restitutio in integrum* for the victim of the unlawful behaviour. In cases of damages for non pecuniary loss, it is submitted that the following should be taken into account:

- damages should not be grossly disproportionate to those awarded in personal injury cases;
- the court should take into account the degree of culpability of the conduct of the public authority;
- the court should taken into account matters such as injury to the claimant's dignity and his anger at being humiliated;[230]
- awards must be sufficient to demonstrate the seriousness with which the court views breaches of fundamental human rights.

(b) Aggravated and exemplary damages and the Human Rights Act

21.67 The Human Rights Act does not address the issue as to whether aggravated or exemplary damages might be available for breaches of Convention rights.[231] If, however, damages under the Human Rights Act are regarded as a 'public law remedy',[232] they may not be strictly compensatory in nature and the court may be able to award sums to reflect 'aggravation' and its disapproval of the defendant's behaviour. It would, then, not be strictly necessary to consider whether such damages could properly be described as being 'aggravated' or 'exemplary' under conventional tort classifications. On the other hand, if the courts decide that Human Rights Act damages are damages for a 'constitutional tort', it will then be necessary to consider whether an award of damages under section 8 is purely compensatory in nature or whether it can include aggravated and exemplary damages.

21.68 Aggravated damages are 'compensation for the injured feelings of the plaintiff where his sense of injury resulting from the wrongful physical act is justifiably heightened by the manner in which or motive for which the defendant did it'.[233] Exemplary damages[234] are not designed to compensate a claimant for loss but to

[230] See *Thompson v Commissioner of Police of the Metropolis* [1997] 3 WLR 403, 413 *per* Lord Woolf MR; *Rookes v Barnard* [1964] AC 1129; *Alexander v Home Office* [1988] 1 WLR 968.

[231] See para 3.43ff above.

[232] See 21.21ff above.

[233] *Broome v Cassell and Company Ltd* [1972] AC 1027, 1124.

[234] For a fuller treatment, see eg H McGregor *McGregor on Damages* (16th edn, Sweet & Maxwell, 1997) Chap 11.

punish a defendant; thus, Lord Reid in *Broome v Cassell and Company Ltd*[235] described exemplary damages as 'highly anomalous', stressing that:

> It is confusing the function of the civil law, which is to compensate, with the function of criminal law, which is to inflict deterrent and punitive penalties. Some objection has been taken of the word 'fine' to denote the amount by which punitive or exemplary damages exceed anything justly due to the plaintiffs. In my view the word 'fine' is an entirely accurate description of the part of any award which goes beyond anything justly due to the plaintiff and is purely punitive.

On the other hand, Lord Wilberforce said in the same case[236] that it could not be assumed that the criminal law was a better instrument than the civil law for conveying social disapproval or for redressing a wrong; and it is noteworthy that the Law Commission[237] recently concluded that there was a principled case for retaining exemplary damages, taking the view that civil punishment can be adequately distinguished from criminal punishment and that exemplary damages had an important and distinctive role to play on policy grounds.

Nevertheless, the House of Lords in *Rookes v Barnard*[238] decided to restrict exemplary damages to three categories of case: oppressive, arbitrary and unconstitutional action by servants of the Government, wrongdoing which is calculated to make a profit and where it is expressly authorised by statute. In relation to this first category, the phrase 'servant of the Government' is to be very broadly construed; as Lord Reid indicated in *Broome v Cassell and Company Ltd*:[239] **21.69**

> The contrast is between 'the government' and private individuals. Local government is as much government as national government and the police and many others are exercising governmental functions.

The terms 'oppressive, arbitrary and unconstitutional action' are to be read disjunctively.[240]

Several factors limit the availability of exemplary damages; these include whether the compensatory damages are sufficient to mark the court's disapproval of the defendant's conduct, whether the claimant is guilty of punishable behaviour, whether the defendant has already been punished, the claimant's own conduct and whether the defendant has acted in good faith. Consequently, a claimant must show that the sum to be awarded as compensation is inadequate to punish a defendant for his outrageous behaviour[241] or that the amount the defendant **21.70**

[235] [1972] AC 1027, 1086.
[236] Ibid 1114.
[237] *Report on Aggravated, Exemplary and Restitutionary Damages* (Law Com No 247, 1997) para 5.25–5.29.
[238] [1964] AC 1129, 1221, 1226.
[239] [1972] AC 1027, 1088; but see *A B v South West Water Services Ltd* [1993] QB 507.
[240] *Holden v Chief Constable of Lancashire* [1987] QB 380.
[241] *Rookes v Barnard* [1964] AC 1129, 1228 *per* Lord Devlin.

deserves to pay as punishment exceeds the amount the claimant deserves to receive as compensation.[242]

21.71 There are a number of reasons why breaches of Convention rights[243] under the Human Rights Act are unlikely to result in exemplary damages as such. First and foremost, no damages may be awarded under section 8(3) unless 'the court is satisfied that the award is necessary to affect just satisfaction to the person in whose favour it is made'. It is difficult to see how a court would be entitled to find that an award is necessary to affect just satisfaction; and yet conclude that the compensation was so inadequate that it was necessary to make a further award so as to punish the defendant. Secondly, the Court of Appeal held in *A B v South West Water Services Ltd*[244] that the only causes of action for which exemplary damages can be claimed are causes of action for which exemplary damage were awarded before 1964. This has been held to exclude a claim for exemplary damages in an action for misfeasance in a public office.[245] The cause of action test obviously prevents a victim[246] under the Human Rights Act recovering exemplary damages; indeed, the Law Commission's *Report on Aggravated, Exemplary and Restitutionary Damages*[247] suggested that, in the absence of express statutory authorisation, exemplary damages would not be available under any legislation which incorporated the Convention.

21.72 Furthermore, the Convention jurisprudence on Article 41 provides no support for recovering exemplary damages. The Court rejected a claim for punitive damages where it found that the Turkish security forces had destroyed villages and houses in *Selçuk and Asker v Turkey*[248] and a similar claim in *Akdivar v Turkey*,[249] although it did not explain its reasoning in any detail.

21.73 Exemplary damages have been awarded in some cases[250] under the Canadian Charter of Rights but this must be seen against a background where the Supreme Court of Canada[251] has rejected the restrictions on exemplary damages laid down by *Rookes v Barnard*.[252] However, the Supreme Court has taken a restrictive approach to the express power to award punitive damages in section 49 of the Quebec Charter.[252a] The Constitutional Court of South Africa in *Fose v Ministry of*

[242] *Broome v Cassell and Company Ltd* [1972] AC 1027, 1126 *per* Lord Diplock.
[243] See para 3.43ff above.
[244] [1993] QB 507.
[245] *Kuddus v Chief Constable of Leicestershire*, *The Times*, 16 Mar 2000.
[246] See para 22.14ff below.
[247] Law Com No 247 para 4.25.
[248] (1998) 26 EHRR 477 paras 116–118.
[249] RJD 1998-II 711 paras 35–38.
[250] See eg *Collin v Lussier* (1983) 6 CRR 89; *Lord v Allison* (1986) 3 BCLR (2d) 300.
[251] *Vorvis v ICBC* (1989) 58 DLR (4th) 193.
[252] [1964] AC 1129.
[252a] *Quebec (Public Curator) v Syndicat national des employés de l'hôpital St-Ferdinand* [1996] 3 SCR 211; see also *Augustus v Gosset* [1996] 3 SCR 268.

Safety and Security[253] decided, after a full survey of the case law from other jurisdictions, that effective relief for breach of constitutional rights did not entitle the courts to award exemplary damages. However, this decision must also be seen in its context; South African common law does not, in general, recognise exemplary damages.

It is submitted that exemplary damages cannot be awarded under the Human Rights Act and that such damages would only be available under the Act if the Court of Appeal decision in *A B v South West Water Services Ltd*[254] was overruled. **21.74**

(7) **Misfeasance in a public office**

(a) The nature of the tort

A very different basis for awarding damages against a public authority for breaching Convention rights would arise if a claim was made on the basis of the tort of misfeasance in a public office. Misfeasance in a public office is the only tort specifically tailored to compensate for unlawful actions by public officers; and therefore provides an *alternative* basis for recovering damages to section 8 of the Human Rights Act. Although the existence of the tort was described by Lord Diplock as well established in *Dunlop v Woollahra Municipal Council*,[255] its boundaries have been uncertain.[256] However, the House of Lords has recently subjected the tort to an extended analysis in *Three Rivers Council v Governor and Bank of England (No 3)*[256a] Exemplary damages cannot be recovered in an action for misfeasance in a public office.[257] **21.75**

The tort is committed whenever someone holding public office has misconducted himself by purporting to exercise powers which were conferred on him not for his personal advantage but for the benefit of the public or a section of the public, either with the intent to injure another or in the knowledge that he was acting *ultra vires*.[258] In *Three Rivers District Council v Bank of England (No 3)*[259] the House of Lords emphasised that the tort involves an element of bad faith. **21.76**

[253] 1997 (3) SA 786.

[254] [1993] QB 507.

[255] [1982] AC 158; the older cases are reviewed and analysed at length by the Court of Appeal in *Three Rivers v Bank of England* [2000] 2 WLR 15, 43–47.

[256] See eg *Calveley v Chief Constable of Merseyside* [1989] AC 1228, 1240 where Lord Bridge declined to explore or define its precise limits; *Racz v Home Office* [1994] 2 AC 45, 55 *per* Lord Lowry where he referred to 'the apparent uncertainty as to the precise ambit of the tort'; and *Elguzouli-Daf v Commissioner of Police of the Metropolis* [1995] QB 335, 347 where Steyn LJ referred to the possibility of further development under the influence of European Community law; and see also, *Elliott v Chief Constable of Wiltshire*, *The Times*, 5 Dec 1996 where Sir Richard Scott VC said that the boundaries of the tort were not well defined.

[256a] [2000] 2 WLR 1220.

[257] *Kuddus v Chief Constable of Leicestershire*, *The Times*, 16 Mar 2000.

[258] *Jones v Swansea City Council* [1990] 1 WLR 54, 71.

[259] n 256a above.

21.77 The tort is committed by a public officer who is anyone appointed to discharge a public duty and receives compensation in whatever shape, whether from the Crown or otherwise.[260] Other public officials such as local government officers and the police are covered.[261] Malice can be proved in one of two alternative ways:[262]

- by a malicious act which was aimed at the plaintiff; or
- by a deliberate act which the public officer knew that he did not have power to do.

However, in *Three Rivers District Council v Bank of England (No 3)*[263] Lord Steyn expressed the view that although there are underlying common features in the two alternative ways in which the tort can be committed (namely, the special nature of the tort as directed only at the conduct of public officials and the element of an abuse of power in bad faith), there are also differences between the two forms of the tort which it is important to recognise.

(b) 'Targeted malice'

21.78 The first type of misfeasance in a public office can properly be described as 'targeted malice': since the defendant specifically intended to injure the claimant and the claimant has suffered damages as a result. 'Malice' in this context does not mean 'ill will' but covers any 'corrupt or improper motive';[264] however, it does not extend to recklessness.[265] The wrongful motive must be determinative of the act or omission in question.[266] If, for example, it is alleged that the actions of local authority councillors are malicious, proof that the majority of the councillors present, having voted for a resolution, were malicious amounts to proof against the council of malice.[267]

21.79 Under the second limb of the tort, liability can arise from 'actual knowledge' of the *ultra vires* nature of the act: this will be proved if the defendant acted in the knowledge of, or with a reckless indifference to, the probability of causing injury to the claimant (or to persons of the class of which he was a member). Thus, liability for misfeasance can be established if a defendant is subjectively reckless in the sense of not caring whether the act was illegal or where the consequences

[260] *Henly v Lyme Corporation* (1828) 5 Bing 91, 107.

[261] Cf *R v Dytham* [1979] QB 722 (crime of misfeasance in a public office committed by a police officer).

[262] *Bourgoin SA v Ministry of Agriculture, Fisheries and Food* [1986] QB 716; and see *Three Rivers District Council v Bank of England (No 3)*, n 256a above.

[263] n 256a above, at 1231.

[264] *Tozer v Child* (1857) 7 E&B 377, 379.

[265] *Bennett v Commissioner of Police* [1995] 1 WLR 488; see also, *Bennett v Commissioner of Police*, *The Times*, 24 Oct 1997.

[266] See eg *R v Llewellyn-Jones* (1966) 51 Cr App R 4.

[267] *Jones v Swansea City Council* [1990] 1 WLR 1453.

happened; or where there was a deliberate omission which involved an actual decision not to act.[268]

Misfeasance in a public office requires a claimant to prove he has suffered damage: it is, like negligence, an action on the case so that damages is an essential element of the cause of action. The House of Lords in *Three Rivers District Council v Bank of England (No 3)*[269] held that the *ultra vires* limb of the tort should be in harmony with the first limb of targeted malice; and went on to hold that it was necessary for a plaintiff to prove that a defendant had *actual* foresight that damage would result from his actions. **21.80**

Claims for misfeasance in a public office have been pursued in a wide variety of situations, particularly in recent years. Actions have been brought alleging that a local authority and Minister abused their office and intentionally damaged the plaintiff by making a compulsory purchase order in bad faith;[270] that the Premier of Quebec put pressure on the licensing commission to cancel the plaintiff's liquor licence because he was a Jehovah's witness who antagonised the Government by repeatedly standing bail for Jehovah's witnesses accused of public order offences; that a prison officer abused prisoners in his care;[271] and that a police officer disclosed confidential information for an improper purpose in order to prevent a journalist from publishing certain articles by causing him to be dismissed.[272] **21.81**

(c) 'Knowing ultra vires*'*

The complaint that a public official has knowingly acted *ultra vires* is a more difficult claim to prove. Nevertheless, it has been argued where police officers used their statutory powers to close a hotel, knowing they had no power to do so;[273] where the Minister of Agriculture withdrew the general licence to import turkeys from France, knowing that he was infringing Article 30[273a] of the Treaty of Rome[274] and this would injure the plaintiffs in their business;[275] where cattle station owners whose stock had been placed in quarantine claimed that stock inspectors who imposed restrictions had done so in good faith but knowing that it would cause the plaintiffs loss;[276] and where it was a alleged that in failing to regulate the Bank of **21.82**

[268] *Three Rivers District Council v Bank of England (No 3)*, n 256a above.

[269] n 256a above; they rejected the submission that reasonable foreseeability was the appropriate test.

[270] *Smith v East Elloe Rural District Council* [1956] AC 736.

[271] *Racz v Home Office* [1994] 2 AC 45.

[272] *Elliot v Chief Constable of Wiltshire, The Times*, 5 Dec 1996.

[273] *Farrington v Thomson and Bridgland* [1959] VR 286.

[273a] Now Art 36.

[274] Now Art 28 of the EC Treaty.

[275] *Bourgoin SA v Ministry of Agriculture, Fisheries and Food* [1986] QB 716.

[276] *Northern Territory v Mengel* (1995) 69 ALJR 527.

Credit and Commerce International, the Bank of England made an unlawful and dishonest decision knowing it would cause loss to existing or potential depositors.[277]

21.83 It is clear from the *Three Rivers* case[277a] that a public authority will be liable for misfeasance if it acted in the knowledge of (or with reckless indifference to) the fact that it was breaching Convention rights in the knowledge of (or with reckless indifference to) the probability of injuring the claimant (or individuals of a class of which the claimant was a member). The House of Lords took the view that subjective recklessness in the sense of not caring whether the act was illegal or whether the consequences were sufficient to establish liability was misfeasance. Misfeasance will also be proved if there was a deliberate omission involving an actual decision not to act

C. Remedies in Judicial Review Proceedings

(1) Introduction

21.84 Convention rights[278] under the Human Rights Act are public law rights[279] and claims relating to them will often be brought as judicial review proceedings. In an application for judicial review, claims can be made for six different final remedies: *certiorari*, *mandamus*, prohibition, an injunction, a declaration and damages. Under new rules which take effect on 2 October 2000, an order for *mandamus* will become a prohibiting order and *certiorari* will become a quashing order. Under CPR Sch 1, R 53.2 these remedies may be claimed in the alternative or in addition to each other in any application for judicial review. Relief in judicial review proceedings is discretionary and this discretion has been retained by section 8(1) of the Human Rights Act. It may be said the question of whether a statutory provision should be 'read in' or 'read down' so as to ensure that legislation is compatible with Convention rights under section 3 of the Human Rights Act constitutes a remedy under the Act. The principles themselves are discussed in Chapter 4.[280] However, it is clear that the court does not have a discretion concerning whether or not to apply section 3.

21.85 An application for an order of *certiorari*, *mandamus* or prohibition[281] can only be made by way of an application for judicial review.[282] These remedies can only be

[277] *Three Rivers District Council v Bank of England (No 3)* [2000] 2 WLR 1220.

[277a] Ibid.

[278] See para 3.43ff above.

[279] However, it cannot be argued that the exclusivity rule will require all proceedings to be brought by way of judicial review: see para 22.50ff below.

[280] See para 4.17ff above.

[281] For a fuller treatment, see eg Lord Woolf and J Jowell, *De Smith, Woolf and Jowell, Judicial Review of Administrative Action* (5th edn, Sweet & Maxwell, 1995) Chap 16.

[282] CPR Sch 1, R 53.1(1)(a).

granted against public bodies and are known as 'prerogative orders' because they were originally special types of writs which were available only to the Crown, as one of its 'prerogatives'.[283] An order of *certiorari* has the effect of quashing a decision of a public body, prohibition prevents a public body from acting beyond its jurisdiction and *mandamus* compels a public body to do its duty.

Declarations and injunctions have the same effect in applications for judicial review as in private law actions: legal rights are declared or orders made to prevent or compel specified acts. However, in public law matters, the court has a broad discretion as to whether or not to grant a declaration or injunction on an application for judicial review.[284] Damages can only be awarded if the court is satisfied that such damages could have been awarded if the claimant had brought private law proceedings in, for example, negligence.[285] **21.86**

(2) Interim orders

(a) The nature of the orders

The power to grant interim orders[286] is contained in CPR Sch 1, R 53.1(10) which states that: **21.87**

> Where permission to apply for judicial review is granted, then-
> (a) if the relief sought is an order for prohibition or *certiorari* and the Court so directs, the grant shall operate as a stay of the proceedings to which the application relates until the determination of the application or until the Court otherwise orders;
> (b) if any other relief is sought, the Court may at any time grant in the proceedings interim remedies in accordance with CPR Part 25.

The court will order an interim injunction against a public body including the ministers of the Crown[287] to enforce public duties[288] or to prevent it from acting on an unlawful decision.[289] If there is a serious issue to be tried, the fundamental question to be addressed when granting an injunction is the balance of convenience.[290] However, the mere fact that the applicant has been granted permission does not mean there is a serious issue to be tried for the purposes of seeking an interim injunction.[291] The court will take account of the wider *public* interest **21.88**

---

[283] See H W R Wade and C Forsyth, *Administrative Law* (7th edn, Clarendon Press, 1994), 614–616.
[284] CPR Sch 1, R 53.1(2); the issue of discretionary relief is discussed at para 21.102 below.
[285] CPR Sch 1, R 53.7(1)(b).
[286] For a fuller treatment, see eg De Smith, Woolf and Jowell (n 281 above) paras 17-07–17-19.
[287] *M v Home Office* [1994] AC 377.
[288] See eg *R v Cardiff City Council, ex p Barry* (1989) 22 HLR 261.
[289] See eg *R v North Yorkshire County Council, ex p M* [1989] QB 411.
[290] *American Cyanamid Company v Ethicon Ltd* [1975] AC 396.
[291] *R v London Boroughs Transport Committee, ex p Freight Transport Association* [1990] RTR 109.

against granting an injunction;[292] and in *R v Advertising Standards Authority Ltd, ex p Vernons Organisation*[293] Laws J took the view that interim relief should not be granted to restrain the publication of a decision save on pressing grounds where the effects of publication would damage the applicant irrevocably.

21.89 The court will grant an interim injunction in negative terms to hold the ring pending the substantive hearing.[294] When granting an interim injunction in mandatory terms, the court will normally require the applicant to prove a strong *prima facie* case;[295] this is not an inflexible rule since the crucial question in all cases is whether the injustice suffered if the injunction is granted and the plaintiff fails at trial is worse than the injustice to the plaintiff if the injunction is not granted and he succeeds at trial.[296] It is arguable that a cross undertaking for damages is not necessary in a public law context,[297] particularly where the applicant is legally aided.[298]

21.90 Where a stay affects third parties, the question of whether it should be imposed depends on the balance of convenience.[299] The meaning of 'stay' has been the subject of considerable controversy but appears to have a wide meaning extending decisions or judgments of an inferior court to an administrative decision.[300] Although the idea of granting an interim declaration has been vigorously debated,[301] the Civil Procedure Rules now allow for interim declarations.[302]

[292] See eg *De Falco v Crawley Borough Council* [1980] QB 460 (the court considered the financial cost of providing housing and queue jumping over others in the housing list as factors weighing against the grant of an injunction).

[293] [1992] 1 WLR 1289; see also *R v Advertising Standards Authority, ex p Direct Line Financial Services* [1998] COD 20.

[294] *R v Cardiff City Council, ex p Barry* (1989) 22 HLR 261.

[295] *R v Kensington and Chelsea Royal London Borough Council, ex p Hammell* [1989] QB 518, 531.

[296] *Films Rover International Ltd v Cannon Film Scales Ltd* [1987] 1 WLR 670 applied in *Scotia Pharmaceuticals v Health Secretary* [1994] COD 241.

[297] M Fordham, 'Interim Relief and the Cross Undertaking' [1997] JR 136; but see the views expressed by the Court of Appeal in *R v Inspectorate of Pollution, ex p Greenpeace Ltd* [1994] 1 WLR 570 and of Schiemann J in *R v Secretary of State for the Environment, ex p Rose Theatre Trust Company* [1990] COD 47.

[298] *Allen v Jambo Holdings Ltd* [1980] 1 WLR 1252.

[299] *R v Inspectorate of Pollution, ex p Greenpeace Ltd* [1994] 1 WLR 570.

[300] *R v Secretary of State for Education and Science, ex p Avon County Council* [1991] 1 QB 558; *R v Secretary of State for the Home Department ex p Muboyayi* [1992] 1 QB 244; cf *Minister of Foreign Affairs, Trade and Industry v Vehicles and Supplies Ltd* [1991] 1 WLR 550.

[301] Although an interim declaration was described as a contradiction in terms on the basis that it does not make sense to declare a person's rights as 'X' today with the possibility of declaring them 'Y' tomorrow (see eg *R v IRC, ex p Rossminster Ltd* [1980] AC 952, 1014; *Association of Football Clubs v Football Association of Wales* [1995] 2 All ER 87, 92, 93), the House of Lords were prepared to assume in *R v Secretary of State for the Environment, ex p Royal Society for the Protection of Birds (Port of Sheerness Ltd, Inverness)* (1995) 7 Admin LR 434 the existence of interim declaratory relief (although they refused in the circumstances of the case to make an order pending the reference to the European Court of Justice).

[302] See CPR, r 25.1(1)(a).

(b) Interim relief to restrain breach of Convention rights

One important issue that will arise under the Human Rights Act is whether an interim injunction (or stay) should be granted to restrain a public authority from acting incompatibly with Convention rights[303] pending the substantive hearing. The general principles described above will apply where the applicant seeks to restrain administrative decision-making which contravenes Convention rights. However, a different approach will be necessary where the public authority relies on a statute to justify its position. Under the Human Rights Act a court cannot disapply primary legislation;[304] and the issue will therefore only arise where it is said that construing a statutory provision in accordance with section 3[305] deprives the public authority of its statutory defence. **21.91**

Similar problems have been considered where it is alleged that national law is contrary to European Community law and that a reference must be made to the European Court of Justice.[306] In those circumstances interim relief is often sought.[307] A wide range of considerations may be relevant to the consideration of the balance of convenience and the wider public interest so that no particular factor is decisive.[308] However, a court will not normally disapply national legislation unless it is satisfied that the challenge is so firmly based as to justify such a course.[309] **21.92**

The question of whether an interim injunction or stay should be granted which would effectively override statute has been extensively considered in Canada.[309a] In *Morgentaler v Ackroyd*[310] the applicant was operating an illegal abortion clinic and brought proceedings under the Canadian Charter of Rights. When he sought an interim injunction to prevent the police from investigating or acting on the criminal offence, it was held that the balance of convenience dictates that those who challenge the constitutional validity of legislation must obey it until the issue is decided at trial. In *Re A-G of Canada and Gould*[311] a prisoner who was denied the vote sought a declaration that his Charter rights were violated. The Supreme Court of Canada refused to grant him a mandatory interim injunction even though a general election was imminent and the claim would succeed unless the breach of his rights was justified; the injunction was refused because its invalidity **21.93**

[303] The meaning of 'incompatible' is discussed at para 5.120ff above.

[304] If it cannot be construed to be compatible with Convention rights under s 3, the court may make a declaration of incompatibility: see para 4.43ff above.

[305] See para 4.04ff above.

[306] Under Art 234 of the EC Treaty (formerly, Art 177).

[307] See eg *R v Ministry of Agriculture and Fisheries and Food, ex p Monsanto* [1999] 2 WLR 599.

[308] *R v HM Treasury, ex p British Telecommunications plc* [1994] 1 CMLR 621, 647; *R v Secretary of State for Transport, ex p Factortame Ltd (No 2)* [1991] 1 AC 603, 674.

[309] *R v Secretary of State for Transport, ex p Factortame Ltd (No 2)* (n 308 above); *Kirklees Metropolitan Borough Council v Wickes Building Supplies Ltd* [1993] AC 227, 280.

[309a] See K Roach, *Constitutional Remedies in Canada* (Canada Law Book, 1999) para 7.30ff.

[310] (1983) 42 OR (2nd) 59.

[311] [1984] 2 SCR 124.

would affect all other prisoners. The general principles to be applied were discussed at length by the Supreme Court in *Manitoba (A-G) and Metropolitan Stores.*[312] Granting a stay or injunction either suspends the operation of the legislation under challenge or exempts the litigants from its application. The Court expressed the view that in most cases granting relief would frustrate the common good as decided by democratically elected legislators and would deprive the public of the protection or advantage of the legislation whose invalidity remained uncertain. Although interlocutory relief might be appropriate in limited cases where no significant harm would be suffered by the public and where the statutory provision in dispute applied to a relatively limited number of individuals, the public interest would normally favour compliance with the legislation. This approach effectively involves a presumption that existing legislation represents the public interest. Such a presumption has been described an 'unfortunate'[312a] and the Supreme Court has made clear that it is rebuttable and the Attorney-General cannot be treated as the exclusive representative of the public interest.[312b]

21.94 It is submitted that it will only be appropriate in an exceptional case to restrain a public authority (pending the substantive hearing) from breaching Convention rights if the authority raises a triable issue by relying on a statutory provision which justifies its decision.

(3) The nature of prerogative orders

21.95 *Certiorari* has become the primary remedy in judicial review proceedings. It enables the court to control unlawful acts of public bodies by quashing their decisions. Although the court cannot substitute its own decision for that of the public body, once the decision has been set aside, the course which the public body should lawfully take will often be obvious (because, for example, the court will have indicated the correct interpretation of the applicable statute). It may, therefore, be unnecessary for the court to grant any further remedy although the court may link an order of *certiorari* with a declaration or an order for *mandamus* or may make an order remitting the matter to the court, tribunal or authority concerned with a direction to reconsider it and reach a decision in accordance with the findings of the court.[313]

21.96 The remedy of prohibition is granted to prevent public bodies from acting unlawfully in the future. This remedy is complementary to that of *certiorari*. It has

[312] [1987] 1 SCR 110. For cases applying this approach, see Roach (n 309a above) para 7.410ff above.

[312a] K Roach, (n 309a above) para 7.340ff.

[312b] *RJR-Macdonald v Canada (A-G)* [1994] 1 SCR 311; see also *143471 Canada Inc v Quebec (A-G)* (1994) 167 NR 321.

[313] Supreme Court Act 1981, s 31(5); CPR, Sch 1, R 53.9(4).

been said that there is no difference in principle between *certiorari* and prohibition 'except that the latter may be invoked at an earlier stage'.[314]

An order of *mandamus* requires a public body to perform public duties and can be used to compel public bodies to exercise jurisdiction to hear a case or to consider exercising a discretionary power. If there is only one possible decision in the circumstances then *mandamus* can be granted to require a decision to be made in the applicant's favour.[315] However, in most cases, a public body will have a discretion as to how to perform its duties. The court will therefore not substitute its own decision for that of the public body: it must avoid any appearance that the courts are 'assuming the function assigned by Parliament to the public body and exercising the discretion on their behalf';[316] indeed, to do otherwise would be to convert a discretion into a duty.[317] **21.97**

(4) Declarations and injunctions in judicial review proceedings

Declarations and injunctions are, in origin, private law remedies. A declaration can only be granted in relation to rights which are the subject of genuine dispute; and the courts will not grant declarations to deal with theoretical or academic disputes.[318] There must, in general, be someone with a genuine interest in opposing the application, a 'proper contradictor'[318a] and a declaration will not be granted where the respondent agrees with the applicant's claim.[318b] **21.98**

The availability of declarations and injunctions as public law remedies is now governed by CPR Sch 1 R 53.1(2)[319] which states: **21.98A**

> An application for a declaration or an injunction . . . may be made by way of an application for judicial review, and on such an application the Court may grant the declaration or injunction claimed if it considers that, having regard to–
>
> (a) the nature of the matters in respect of which relief may be granted by way of an order of *mandamus*, prohibition or *certiorari*,
> (b) the nature of the persons and bodies against whom relief may be granted by way of such an order, and
> (c) all the circumstances of the case,
>
> it would be just and convenient for the declaration or injunction to be granted on an application for judicial review.

[314] See *per* Atkin LJ, *R v Electricity Commissioners, ex p London Electricity Joint Committee Company (1920) Ltd* [1924] 1 KB 171, 206.
[315] See eg *R v City of London Licensing Justices, ex p Stewart* [1954] 1 WLR 1325.
[316] *R v Barnet London Borough Council, ex p Nilish Shah* [1983] 2 AC 309, 350.
[317] *R v Secretary of State for Trade and Industry, ex p Lonrho* [1989] 1 WLR 525, 538.
[318] *Re Barnato* [1949] Ch 258.
[318a] *Russian Commercial and Industrial Bank v British Bank for Foreign Trade Ltd* [1921] 2 AC 438, 448.
[318b] *Re Canarvon Harbours Acts 1793 to 1903* [1937] 1 Ch 72.
[319] Following the Supreme Court Act 1981, s 31(2).

Under CPR Sch 1 R 53.1(2) any declaration[320] as to public rights which could formerly be obtained in civil proceedings in the High Court can now also be obtained in judicial review proceedings.[321]

21.98B Declarations have been held to be available in the following public law disputes:

- to establish the validity of advice given in a non-statutory circular by a Government department, where the Department of Health gave advice on contraception[322] and on abortion;[323]
- to challenge the reasoning in the decision by a public body (but only when a point of general public importance was involved);[324]
- to determine whether a proposed course of action was within the powers of a public body;[325]
- to determine the lawfulness of recommendations by advisory bodies;[326] and
- to determine, in advance, the validity of proposed regulations or rules.[327]

It is likely that declaratory relief will be an important remedy under the Act.[327a] In appropriate cases, declarations can be granted in relation to future violations of the Convention.

21.99 In an application for judicial review, an injunction can be granted to restrain a public body from acting unlawfully, to restrain the implementation of unlawful decisions or to compel a public authority to comply with its statutory duties. However, injunctions are rarely granted because once a declaration is made, a public authority will act in accordance with it.[328]

21.100 The Human Rights Act may encourage the courts to make extended use of injunctions to protect Convention rights.[328a] The possibility of granting 'structural orders' is discussed below.[329]

---

[320] For a fuller treatment, see eg Zamir and Woolf, *The Declaratory Judgment* (2nd edn, Sweet & Maxwell, 1993); Lord Woolf and J Jowell, *De Smith, Woolf and Jowell, Judicial Review of Administrative Action* (3rd edn, Sweet & Maxwell, 1995) Chap 18.

[321] *R v Secretary of State for Employment, ex p Equal Opportunities Commission* [1995] 1 AC 1, 36 *per* Lord Browne-Wilkinson.

[322] *Gillick v West Norfolk and Wisbech Health Authority* [1986] AC 112.

[323] *Royal College of Nursing v Department of Health and Social Security* [1981] AC 800.

[324] See, eg *R v Secretary of State for Environment, ex p Greater London Council, The Times*, 30 Dec 1985.

[325] See eg *R v London Transport Executive, ex p Greater London Council* [1983] QB 484; *Home Office v Commission for Racial Equality* [1982] QB 385.

[326] See eg *Grunwick Processing Laboratories Ltd v Advisory, Conciliation and Arbitration Service* [1978] AC 655.

[327] See eg *Pharmaceutical Society of Great Britain v Dickson* [1970] AC 403.

[327a] For a general discussion of declarations as a 'constitutional remedy' see K Roach, *Constitutional Remedies in Canada* (Canada Law Book, 1999 Chap 12.

[328] See eg *R v Liverpool City Council, ex p Ferguson and Ferguson* [1985] IRLR 501, 504.

[328a] For a general discussion of injunctions as a 'constitutional remedy' see Roach (n 327a above) Chap 13.

[329] See para 21.152ff below.

(5) Damages in judicial review proceedings

The general principles that apply to damages under section 8 of the Human Rights Act have been discussed.[330] However, CPR Sch 1 R 53.7 states that: 21.101

> (1) On an application for judicial review the Court may, subject to paragraph (2) award damages to the applicant if–
>
> (a) he has included in the statement in support of his application for permission under rule 3 a claim for damages arising from any matter to which the application relates, and
>
> (b) the court is satisfied that, if the claim had been made in an action begun by the applicant at the time of making his application, he could have been awarded damages.
>
> (2) CPR 16 shall apply to a statement relating to a claim for damages as it applies to a statement of case.

This rule enables the applicant to avoid the duplication of proceedings by claiming damages in his judicial review application.

(6) The discretionary nature of remedies in judicial review proceedings

All public law remedies are discretionary.[331] The benefits of retaining the principle of discretionary relief in public law cases[332] may account for the reluctance of the Government to enact Article 13[333] as a Convention right under the Human Rights Act. The incorporation of the right to an effective remedy under Article 13 would have strengthened[334] the argument that the court was obliged to grant a remedy where a public authority has acted illegally by failing to act compatibly with Convention rights. 21.102

In ordinary judicial review proceedings the courts have refused to grant remedies on a number of grounds which often overlap; however, the principal reasons for refusing relief can be summarised as: 21.103

- the availability of alternative remedies or rights of appeal;
- the conduct of the applicant;
- delay; and
- the likely effects of the remedy.

[330] See 21.10ff above.
[331] For a fuller treatment, see De Smith, Woolf and Jowell (n 320 above) Chap 20.
[332] See eg Sir Thomas Bingham, 'Should Public Law Remedies be Discretionary?' [1991] PL 64.
[333] For a discussion of Art 13, see para 21.156ff below.
[334] In fact, the case law on Art 13 provides no direct support for the proposition that breach of the Convention rights compels a court to grant a remedy in judicial review proceedings: see para 21.156ff below.

21.104 The existence of an alternative remedy does not debar an application for judicial review even where there is a default power so that central government could order a local authority to perform its statutory function.[335] If, on the other hand, a claimant fails to exhaust the appeal procedure, the general rule is that other than in the most exceptional cases, the court will refuse to allow the case to proceed by way of judicial review.[336] However, whether the rule is applied depends on looking at the position overall; the court has to consider whether there are any exceptional circumstances which make it more appropriate, in any given case, to grant leave rather than to require the applicant to exhaust statutory remedies;[337] for example, because of urgency[338] or whether the appeal procedure is suitable for deciding a question of law.[339] It is arguable that in cases where an applicant complains that his civil rights and obligations[339a] have been breached in contravention of Article 6 fair trial rights,[339b] a failure to pursue an alternative remedy which is not 'independent and impartial'[339c] such as a local authority complaints procedure would not justify a refusal to grant relief.[339d]

21.105 Relief may be refused where the applicant has misconducted himself by making material nondisclosure[340] or failing to take a point when it was reasonably open.[341] However, relief should not be refused merely because of the alleged dishonesty of the applicant.[342]

21.106 Relief will also not be granted where it has no practical utility. Thus, relief will be refused where the court considers that it is unnecessary[343] or futile.[344] No remedy

---

[335] *R v Brent London Borough Council, ex p Sawyers* [1994] 1 FLR 203; but see *R v Devon County Council, ex p Baker* [1993] 11 BMLR 141.

[336] *R v Epping and Harlow General Commissioners ex p Goldstraw* [1983] 3 All ER 257, 262 *per* Sir John Donaldson MR.

[337] *Re S (A Minor)* [1995] COD 132; *Harley Development Inc v Commissioner of Inland Revenue* [1996] 1 WLR 727.

[338] See eg *R v Chief Constable of the Merseyside Police, ex p Calveley* [1986] QB 424.

[339] Such as the validity of a regulation (eg *Moss (Henry) of London Ltd v Customs and Excise Commissioners* [1981] 2 All ER 86) or a disciplinary rule (eg *Pharmaceutical Society of Great Britain v Dickson* [1970] AC 403).

[339a] See para 11.160ff above.

[339b] These are summarised at para 11.183 above.

[339c] See para 11.222ff above.

[339d] N Giffen, 'Judicial Supervision of Human Rights: Practice and Procedure', Administrative Law Bar Seminar, 5 Feb 2000.

[340] *R v Jockey Club Licensing Committee, ex p Wright* [1991] COD 306.

[341] *R v Williams, ex p Phillips* [1914] 1 KB 608.

[342] Contrast *R v London Borough of Southwark, ex p Davies* (1994) 26 HLR 677 with *R v Brent London Borough Council, ex p Dorot Properties, The Times*, 7 Mar 1990 where the court refused to grant relief to a ratepayer which had overpaid because of its past conduct as bad payers and because the payment made involved no unjust enrichment of the local authority.

[343] See eg *R v Greater London Council, ex p Blackburn* [1976] 1 WLR 550; *R v Secretary of State for Social Services, ex p Association of Metropolitan Authorities* [1986] 1 WLR 1.

[344] See, eg, *R* v *Secretary of State for Social Services, ex.p. Association of Metropolitan Associations* (n 343 above).

will be granted where a court concludes that the decision would have been the same if the public body had not acted unlawfully.[345] Even if a public body has breached its duty to act fairly, the court may refuse to grant relief on this ground;[346] the unpredictable nature of the decision-making process means that relief will rarely be refused on these grounds if there has been unfairness.[347] If it is said[347a] that a public authority has breached Article 6 because it is not 'independent'[347b] or 'established by law,[347c] it could argue that no relief should be granted on these grounds.

The question of undue delay in bringing proceedings and whether there is good reason to extend time is discussed in Chapter 22.[348] Once permission for judicial review has been granted, the substantive challenge can only be dismissed for delay on the statutory grounds permitted by section 31(6).[349] Section 31(6) of the Supreme Court Act 1981 states: **21.107**

> Where the High Court considers that there has been undue delay in making an application for judicial review, the court may refuse to grant–
>
> (a) leave for the making of the application; or
> (b) any relief sought on the application,
>
> if it considers that the granting of the relief would be likely to cause substantial hardship to, or substantially prejudice the rights of, any person or would be detrimental to good administration.

When considering whether the granting of relief would be detrimental to good administration the court will consider the general public interest in good administration which: **21.108**

> lies essentially in a regular flow of consistent decisions, made and published with reasonable dispatch; in citizens knowing where they stand and how they can order their affairs in the light of the relevant decision.[350]

In most cases, substantial delay is likely adversely to affect this interest. However, if the granting of relief would not be detrimental to the rights of others or to good administration then mere delay should not be a barrier to granting relief. There is

[345] See eg *R v CICB, ex p Aston* [1994] COD 500.

[346] See eg *Malloch v Aberdeen Corporation* [1971] 1 WLR 1578, 1595; *Cinnamond v British Airports Authority* [1980] 1 WLR 582, 593.

[347] See the remarks of Bingham LJ in *R v Chief Constable of Thames Valley Police, ex p Cotton* [1990] IRLR 344, 352; and see *John v Rees* [1970] Ch 345 and *R v Governors of Bacon's School, ex p ILEA* [1990] COD 414.

[347a] However, we argue that a public authority has not contravened Art 6 where a fair trial right is cured in subsequent court proceedings: see para 11.304ff above.

[347b] See para 11.223ff above.

[347c] See para 11.229 above.

[348] See para 22.58ff below.

[349] *R v Criminal Injuries Compensation Board, ex p A* [1999] 2 AC 330.

[350] *R v Dairy Produce Quota Tribunal for England and Wales, ex p Caswell* [1990] 2 AC 738, 749H.

no requirement for a causal connection between prejudice and delay, what is required is a connection between prejudice and the grant of relief sought[351] or where the decision adversely affects third parties who relied on it.[352]

21.109 It is unlikely that cases under Human Rights Act will raise special issues when granting relief. It is unlawful[353] for the court as a public authority to act in a way which is incompatible[354] with Convention rights.[355] Thus, if a Human Rights Act claim is successful it will be on the ground of 'illegality'. It may be arguable that the court should be less prepared to refuse relief in illegality cases since otherwise it is allowing a public body to do something which it is not authorised to do.[356] It has, therefore, been suggested that the court will generally be impelled to grant relief in a Human Rights Act case where the illegality challenge succeeds, even if it is only declaratory relief; unless some form of redress is given, the applicant will remain a victim[357] and the court, arguably, remains in breach of its duty not to act incompatibly with Convention rights.[358]

D. Remedies in Criminal Proceedings

(1) Introduction

21.110 A defendant in criminal proceedings who establishes that his Convention rights[359] have been violated will have a number of potential remedies including:

- an order withdrawing the issue of a summons;
- a motion to quash an indictment;
- a stay of the criminal proceedings;
- the dismissal of the prosecution;
- an order excluding the admission of evidence;
- an order requiring the inclusion of evidence;
- an order of the Court of Appeal quashing a conviction;
- an order of the Divisional Court in judicial review (or on a case stated) quashing a conviction.

---

351 See *R v Secretary of State for Health, ex p Furneaux* [1994] 2 All ER 652.
352 See eg *R v Monopolies and Mergers Commission, ex p Argyll Group plc* [1986] 1 WLR 763
353 Under the Human Rights Act, s 6(1); see para 5.01ff above.
354 See para 5.120ff above.
355 See para 3.43ff above.
356 See eg *R v Exeter City Council, ex p J L Thomas and Company Ltd* [1991] 1 QB 471, 484.
357 See para 22.14ff above.
358 M Supperstone and J Coppell, 'Judicial Review After the Human Rights Act' [1999] EHRLR 301.
359 See para 3.43ff above.

These remedies will usually be sought in the course of the proceedings themselves. The last however will be sought in separate judicial review proceedings. It may be said that the question of whether a statutory provision should be 'read in' or 'read down' so as to ensure that legislation is compatible with Convention rights under section 3 of the Human Rights Act constitutes a remedy under the Act. The principles themselves are discussed in Chapter 4.[360] However, it is clear that the court does not have a discretion concerning whether or not to apply section 3.

A defendant wishing to raise Convention points should do so in the course of the criminal proceedings themselves and not by way of collateral judicial review proceedings.[361] The relevant principles to be applied in criminal cases[362] were clarified in the recent decision of *Boddington v British Transport Police*.[363] In *Boddington* the House of Lords held that a defendant in criminal proceedings could raise as part of his defence the claim that the act or measure (on which his prosecution was based) was substantively or procedurally invalid. The one exception to the rule was where the criminal offence does *not* depend upon the act in question being valid. Thus, in *R v Wicks*[364] a defendant who was being prosecuted for failing to obey a planning enforcement notice, wished to contend that the notice itself was invalid; however, the House of Lords took the view that the statutory provisions required such a challenge to be made by using the statutory appeal procedure or judicial review. No special principles will apply to challenges under the Human Rights Act.[365] **21.111**

(2) An order withdrawing the issue of a summons

Criminal proceedings are commenced by the laying of an information before a magistrate or a magistrates' clerk who then decides whether to issue a summons to the defendant. The issue of the summons is a judicial rather than an administrative act.[366] Once a summons has been issued, the magistrates' court has an inherent power, by virtue of its character of a court, to withdraw the summons.[367] An application to quash the summons can be made by way of judicial review but this should only be done in an exceptional case.[368] If a summons is withdrawn, this does not operate as bar to subsequent prosecution of the defendant for the same offence.[369] **21.112**

---

[360] See para 4.04ff above.
[361] *R v DPP, ex p Kebilene* [1999] 3 WLR 972.
[362] See eg C Lewis, *Judicial Remedies in Public Law* (Sweet & Maxwell, 2000) paras 3-049–3-053.
[363] [1998] 2 WLR 639.
[364] [1998] AC 92.
[365] See generally, G Nardell, 'Collateral Thinking: The Human Rights Act and Public Law Defences' [1999] EHRLR 293.
[366] *R v Gateshead Justices, ex p Tesco Stores Ltd* [1981] QB 470; *R v Manchester Stipendiary Magistrate, ex p Hill* [1983] 1 AC 328.
[367] *DPP v Porthouse* [1989] RTR 177.
[368] *R v Bury Justices, ex p Anderson* (1987) 137 NLJ 410.
[369] See eg *R v Bradford JJ, ex p Sykes* unreported 28 Jan 1999.

21.113 When a defendant contends that a summons has been issued in proceedings which are incompatible with Convention rights because, for example, the substantive offence is in breach of Convention rights, he could apply to the magistrates for an order withdrawing the issue of the summons. The magistrates' court would then be entitled to make an order under section 8 of the Human Rights Act withdrawing the summons.

(3) A motion to quash an indictment

21.114 A motion to quash an indictment may be brought where the indictment is bad on its face because, for example, the facts stated do not amount to an offence punishable in law. In general, the judge is not entitled to consider the prosecution evidence.[370] It does not result in an acquittal but rather in the defendant being discharged. The application must be made to the court where the bill of indictment is proferred and signed. An application to quash the indictment could be made if the offence charged was one which was incompatible with Convention rights.[371] The Crown Court would be entitled to make an order quashing the indictment under section 8 of the Human Rights Act where, for example, it is alleged that the substantive offence contravenes a Convention right.

(4) Stay of proceedings

(a) The present position

21.115 The most important remedy in criminal cases is likely to be the order for a stay of proceedings. The criminal courts already have a wide ranging jurisdiction to order a stay of proceedings on the ground of 'abuse of the process'.[372] An abuse of process is something so unfair and wrong that the court should not allow a prosecutor to proceed with what is in all other respects a regular proceeding;[373] a prosecution may be an abuse either because it is not possible to have a fair trial or because it offends the court's sense of justice and propriety to try the accused in the particular circumstances.[374]

21.116 Under the present law the categories of 'abuse' are not closed but include the following:

- unjustifiable delay which results in the defendant suffering serious prejudice to the extent that no fair trial can be held;[375]

---

370 *R v Jones (John)* [1974] ICR 310.

371 The meaning of 'incompatibility is discussed at para 5.120ff above.

372 See generally, D Corker and D Young, *Abuse of Process and Fairness in Criminal Proceedings* (Butterworths, 2000) to which the discussion in this section is indebted.

373 See *Hui Chi-ming v The Queen* [1992] 1 AC 34, 57B.

374 *R v Horseferry Road Magistrates' Court, ex p Bennett* [1994] 1 AC 42.

375 *A-G's Reference (No 1 of 1990)* [1992] QB 630; see generally, Corker and Young (n 372 above) Chap 1.

- the prosecution of a defendant to whom the police have given a promise, undertaking or representation that he would not prosecuted;[376]
- the prosecution of a defendant who has already faced criminal charges arising out of the same facts;[377]
- the trial of a defendant after there has been substantial prejudicial pre-trial publicity;[378]
- the trial of a defendant after the loss or destruction of relevant material by the prosecution;[379]
- where it would be contrary to the public interest in the integrity of the criminal justice system that a trial should take place because the prosecution have been guilty of 'investigative impropriety'.[380] This category is often known as '*Bennett* type abuse';[381]
- where the prosecution have otherwise been guilty of manipulation or misuse of the process of the court.[382]

(b) The position under the Human Rights Act

In a case in which the court finds that the commencement, conduct or continuation of the prosecution involves a violation of Convention rights it could order a stay under section 8 of the Human Rights Act. An application could be made in any case where the prosecution has acted in a way which is incompatible with the defendant's Convention rights. It is submitted that at least four categories of case should be distinguished:[383] **21.117**

- where a charge is incompatible with Convention rights because, for example, it is unduly restrictive of freedom of expression[384] or freedom of assembly;[385] a stay should normally be granted. Such cases are likely to be unusual;
- where the prosecution has acted in bad faith and chosen to commit a deliberate breach of the defendant's Convention rights, a stay should normally be granted. The position is similar to the common law abuse cases involving deliberate wrongdoing by the prosecution;[386]

376 *R v Croydon Justices, ex p Dean* [1993] QB 769; see generally, Corker and Young (n 372 above) Chap 2.

377 *DPP v Humphrys* [1977] AC 1; see generally, Corker and Young (n 372 above) Chap 3.

378 *R v Taylor (Michelle)* (1993) 98 Cr App Rep 361; see generally, Corker and Young (n 372 above) Chap 4.

379 *R v Beckford (Anthony)* [1996] RTR 251; see generally, Corker and Young (n 372 above) Chap 5.

380 *R v Horseferry Road Magistrates' Court, ex p Bennett* [1994] 1 AC 42; see generally, Corker and Young (n 372 above) Chap 6.

381 *R v Mullen (Nicholas Robert Neil)* [1999] 3 WLR 777.

382 See generally, Corker and Young (n 372 above) Chap 7.

383 Cf the discussion of exclusion of evidence at para 21.125ff below.

384 See para 15.137ff above.

385 See para 16.57 above.

386 See *R v Horseferry Road Magistrates' Court, ex p Bennett* [1994] 1 AC 42 and generally, D Corker and D Young, *Abuse of Process and Fairness in Criminal Proceedings* (Butterworths, 2000) para 6.74ff.

- where the prosecution involves a breach of Convention rights other than Article 6 rights, a stay will be a matter of discretion and is likely to be granted only if the defendant can establish prejudice;
- where there has been a breach of Article 6 rights, a stay is likely to be granted only if the defendant can show that a fair trial is no longer possible.

21.118 The third and fourth categories are likely to cause the most difficulty in practice. If the prosecution act in a way which is incompatible with Convention rights section 6 of the Human Rights Act will mean that their conduct will be unlawful.[387] However, it is well established that the fact that the prosecuting authorities act unlawfully does not necessarily mean that the prosecution will be an abuse of the process. Thus, in *R v Latif*[388] the fact that a customs officer who had facilitated the importation of heroin into England by the defendants had committed the drugs offence for which the defendants had been convicted did not mean that the prosecution was an abuse. The conduct of the customs officer was not so unworthy or shameful that it was 'an affront to the public conscience to allow the prosecution to proceed'. The House of Lords took into account the fact that the crime was already in existence, the motives of the customs officer and his 'degree of criminality' compared to the defendants who were major drug smugglers.[389]

21.119 It is submitted that in cases where the prosecution has acted in good faith but has breached Convention rights, the position under the Human Rights Act will be the same as that at common law. The courts will only grant a stay if the defendant can establish:

- that a fair trial is no longer possible; or
- that the continuation of the prosecution would be an affront to public conscience.

A stay under the second of these heads is likely to be unusual in 'good faith' cases.

(c) Procedural considerations

21.120 All criminal courts have common law jurisdiction to stay proceedings on the grounds that abuse of the process has affected the fairness of the proceedings. It has been held that magistrates' courts do not have jurisdiction to deal with *Bennett*-type abuse.[390] It is submitted that this restriction on the jurisdiction of magistrates will not apply to cases involving violation of Convention rights as there will be jurisdiction to grant a stay under section 8 of the Human Rights Act.

[387] The meaning of 'incompatibility' is discussed at para 5.120 above.
[388] [1996] 1 WLR 104.
[389] See generally, Corker and Young (n 386 above) para 6.62ff.
[390] *R v Horseferry Road Magistrates' Court, ex p Bennett* [1994] 1 AC 42; *R v Belmarsh Magistrates' Court, ex p Watts* [1999] 2 Cr App R 288; and see generally, Corker and Young, (n 386 above) paras 8.6–8.22.

An application to stay criminal proceedings as an abuse of the process should, generally, be made at the earliest possible opportunity. It is of the nature of a 'plea in bar' and, if raised, should be dealt with before the defendant enters a plea.[391] Written notice of an application to stay an indictment on the ground of abuse of the process must be given to the prosecution and to any co-defendant not less than 14 days before the date fixed or warned for trial.[391a] When a case is before the Crown Court an application for a stay will usually be made at the Plea and Directions Hearing. The advocate for the applicant must lodge and serve a skeleton argument specifying the propositions of law relied on in support of the application at least five clear working days before the date fixed or warned for trial.[392] **21.121**

The defendant is not, however, debarred from raising an abuse argument at any time in the course of criminal proceedings if new matters come to light. Applications are often made during trials in those circumstances. The court can order the stay of all or only part of the proceedings.[393] When a magistrates' court refuses to stay criminal proceedings as an abuse, the Divisional Court will only intervene in exceptional circumstances.[394] **21.122**

There are no rules of procedure in relation to the conduct of an application for a stay on the ground of abuse. If appropriate, evidence will be heard.[395] It should be noted that, in general, the judge has no duty to conduct an inquiry into an allegation of abuse.[396] If, however, the court suspects that there may have been a breach of Convention rights, it is submitted that it is under a duty to raise the point of its own motion.[397] **21.123**

(5) Quashing a conviction on appeal

The Court of Appeal can only quash a conviction if it thinks that the conviction is 'unsafe'.[398] This approach may not, strictly speaking, be compatible with the Convention which requires a consideration of 'fairness' rather than 'safety'[398a] although this was not the view of the Court of Appeal in *R v Rowe and Davis*.[398b] It is now clear that a conviction will be unsafe if the prosecution was an abuse of the **21.124**

---

[391] *R v Aldershot Youth Court, ex p A* unreported, 19 Feb 1997.
[391a] *Practice Direction (Crown Court: Abuse of the Process* [2000] 1 WLR 1132, para 2.
[392] See generally, Corker and Young (n 386 above) paras 4 and 5.
[393] *R v Munro* (1992) 97 Cr App R 183.
[394] See *R v Liverpool City Justices, ex p Price* (1998) 162 JP 766; and see generally Corker and Young (n 386 above) para 8.43ff.
[395] See generally, Corker and Young (n 386 above) para 8.106ff.
[396] *R v Heston-Francois* [1984] QB 278.
[397] See para 22.10ff below.
[398] Criminal Appeal Act 1968, s 2(1) (as amended by the Criminal Appeal Act 1995).
[398a] See *Khan v United Kingdom The Times*, 23 May 2000.
[389b] *The Times*, 25 Jul 2000.

process, even if the point was not taken before the trial judge.[399] If there were breaches of Convention rights in the course of a prosecution or trial then a defendant could seek to have his conviction quashed on this ground. It is likely that the conviction would only be quashed if the Court is persuaded that the effect of the breaches was that the defendant did not receive a fair trial or that the conviction would be an affront to public conscience.[400]

(6) Exclusion of evidence

(a) Introduction

21.125 One of the most important remedies for defendants whose human rights have been violated is the exclusion of any evidence which was obtained as a result of the violation.[400a] This is an extremely controversial area in which at least five approaches are possible:

- automatic exclusion of evidence obtained in violation of human rights;[401]
- *prima facie* exclusion a rule of such evidence;
- discretionary exclusion of such evidence with breach of a human right being a cogent factor in favour of the exclusion;
- exclusion of such evidence only if its admission would render the proceedings unfair;
- no exclusion of relevant evidence, however it was obtained.[402]

The last is the traditional common law approach. It has now been superseded by the provisions of section 78 of the Police and Criminal Evidence Act 1984.[403] Before considering the relationship between the Human Rights Act and this provision, it may be useful to consider the approaches which have been adopted in other jurisdictions including the European Court of Human Rights.

(b) Exclusion of evidence under the US Bill of Rights

21.126 The most often cited example of an 'automatic exclusionary rule' is that adopted in the United States. The US courts have adopted a strict exclusionary rule in relation to evidence which has been obtained in breach of constitutional rights.[404] Thus, evidence is excluded in both state and federal courts if obtained:

[399] See *R v Mullen (Nicholas Robert Neil)* [1999] 3 WLR 777; and see generally, Corker and Young (n 386 above) para 8.69ff.

[400] As was the case in *Mullen* (n 399 above).

[400a] For a general discussion see K Roach, *Constitutional Remedies in Canada* (Canada Law Book, 1999) Chap 10.

[401] See eg *Miranda v Arizona* (1966) 384 US 436.

[402] *Kuruma v The Queen* [1955] AC 197; *R v Sang* [1980] AC 402, 437.

[403] See para 21.140ff below.

[404] See generally, C Antieau and W Rich, *Modern Constitutional Law* (2nd edn, West Group, 1997) Vol 2, paras 39.36 and 40.68.

- by unreasonable searches and seizures in violation of the Fourth Amendment;[405]
- by secretly taping conversations with a suspect after indictment;[406]
- by the interrogation of a suspect in custody, without his consent, unless a defence lawyer is present;[407]
- by eavesdropping on or bugging a suspect without a warrant.[408]

This rule applies not only to evidence found during illegal searches but also to the 'fruit of the poison tree'.[409] This covers all evidence which has a causal connection to police illegality.[410]

There are, however, a number of important exceptions to this exclusionary rule:[411] **21.127**

- it is limited to the evidence being led by the prosecution[412] so that a confession in the absence of his lawyer[413] or illegally obtained evidence[414] can be used to attack a defendant's credit;
- there is an exception when law enforcement officers believed, on objectively reasonable grounds and in good faith, that they were acting lawfully.[415]

Furthermore, the 'fruits of the poison tree' doctrine does not apply to evidence which would, inevitably, have been discovered by lawful means[416] or which only has a tenuous connection to the illegality.[417]

(c) Exclusion of evidence under the Canadian Charter

The Canadian Charter of Rights was drafted in terms which sought to compromise between the US exclusionary rule and the common law 'inclusionary' approach.[417a] Section 24(2) of the Charter states: **21.128**

> Where . . . a court concludes that evidence was obtained in a manner that infringed or denied any rights or freedoms guaranteed by the Charter, the evidence shall be excluded if it is established that, having regard to all the circumstances, the admission of it in the proceedings would bring the administration of justice into disrepute.

---

[405] *Weeks v United States* (1914) 255 US 285 (federal courts); *Mapp v Ohio* (1961) 367 US 643 (state courts).

[406] *Massiah v United States* (1964) 377 US 201.

[407] *Miranda v Arizona* (1966) 384 US 436.

[408] *Katz v Missouri* (1967) 389 US 347.

[409] *Wong Sun v United States* (1963) 371 US 471.

[410] *United States v Crews* (1980) 445 US 463.

[411] See generally, Antieau and Rich (n 404 above) paras 40.69 and 40.70.

[412] *United States v Havens* (1980) 446 US 620.

[413] *Harris v New York* (1971) 401 US 222; see also *Michigan v Harvey* (1990) 494 US 344.

[414] *Walder v United States* (1954) 347 US 62.

[415] *Michigan v DeFillippo* (1979) 443 US 31; see also *United States v Leon* (1984) 468 US 897.

[416] *Nix v Williams* (1984) 467 US 431, 444.

[417] See eg *United States v Ceccolini* (1978) 435 US 268.

[417a] For the exclusion of unconstitutionally obtained evidence in Canada, see generally, K Roach, *Constitutional Remedies in Canada* (Canada Law Book, 1999) Chap 10.

Although the Canadian case law at one stage seemed to be moving towards an absolute exclusionary rule,[418] the Supreme Court has now changed direction. In *R v Collins*[419] the Supreme Court of Canada stressed that section 24(2) is not a remedy for police misconduct. It held that disrepute fell into two general types: that resulting from the admission of evidence which would deprive the accused of a fair hearing and that resulting from the judicial condonation of unacceptable conduct by the police or the prosecution. It was emphasised that:

> If the admission of the evidence in some way affects the fairness of the trial, then the admission of the evidence would *tend* to bring the admission of justice into disrepute and, subject to a consideration of the other factors, the evidence [generally] should be excluded'.[419a]

The court indicated[420] that the factors to be examined in deciding if the admission of the evidence would bring the administration of justice into disrepute are the nature of the evidence itself, the nature of the conduct by which the evidence was obtained and the effect on the system of justice of excluding the evidence. The test has been refined in a number of subsequent cases. In determining whether unconstitutionally obtained evidence affects the fairness of a trial the court seeks to determine whether the evidence was obtained through a process of unfair self-incrimination.[421] Admission of real evidence can affect the fairness of the trial[421a] if it could not have been found without an unconstitutionally obtained statement from the accused. Evidence will usually only be excluded to prevent judicial condonation of unacceptable conduct if the Charter violation is deliberate, blatant or flagrant.[421b]

(d) Exclusion of evidence under the New Zealand Bill of Rights Act

21.129 The New Zealand courts initially took a 'rights based view' of the New Zealand Bill of Rights Act and in a series of cases[422] adopted a *prima facie* rule excluding evidence obtained in breach of the Act.[423] The rationale for the *prima facie* exclusionary rule was explained by Hardie Boys J in *R v Te Kira*:[424]

[418] See, in particular, *R v Therens* [1985] 1 SCR 613.

[419] *R v Collins* [1987] 1 SCR 265.

[419a] Ibid 281.

[420] Ibid 284–286.

[421] See, in particular, *R v Stillman* [1997] 1 SCR 607; and generally, K Roach (n 417a above), 10.850ff.

[421a] *R v Burlingham* [1995] 2 SCR 206.

[421b] See eg *R v Wise* [1992] 1 SCR 527, contrast *R v Kokesch* [1990] 3 SCR 3 (evidence excluded after a negligent violation).

[422] See eg *R v Kirifi* [1992] 2 NZLR 8; *R v Butcher* [1993] 2 NZLR 390; *R v Goodwin (No 2)* [1993] 2 NZLR 390; *R v H* [1994] 2 NZLR 143.

[423] See generally, R Mahoney, 'Vindicating Rights: Excluding Evidence Obtained in Violation of the Bill of Rights', in G Huscroft and P Rishworth (eds), *Rights and Freedoms* (Brooker's, 1995) 447–498.

[424] [1993] 3 NZLR 257, 276.

> The court's duty to uphold the rights affirmed by the Act requires it to make an appropriate response where there has been a breach. The response is, and should be seen as itself an affirmation, a vindication of a right that is fundamental to all citizens, and not simply as a punishment of the officer for breach or as compensation to the person affected who may be unworthy of much consideration. Often the only effective way in which the court can affirm the right is by refusing to recognise or give effect to what has resulted from it. That may mean rejection or exclusion of a confessional statement. To those who see that as a rogue's charter, one can only say that it is the price of freedom; that had the police observed the law the evidence would not have been obtained anyway; and that if the law is to be changed that is the function of Parliament, not of the court.

In *R v Grayson and Taylor*[425] the Court of Appeal modified its approach and applied a balancing test of weighing individual rights against the public interest in law enforcement. The Court expressed the view that: **21.130**

> The formulation of appropriate remedies should be approached broadly. To settle upon a single remedy to be applied in all cases rather than keeping open the full range of possible remedies risks inflexibility and the rejection of possibly more appropriate remedies in particular cases. Similarly the response to any particular breach arguably should be at the appropriate level. It should be no less an effective remedy because it is fashioned to bear some relationship to the nature and seriousness of the breach. Whether there should be the same response to breaches of rights in the course of activities resulting in the discovery of real evidence as to breaches of rights in the course of obtaining, for example, confessional evidence also requires careful consideration.[426]

As a result, the Court indicated its willingness to reconsider the *prima facie* exclusionary rule. However, the rule has not been specifically disapproved and, in practice, it has continued to be applied by the New Zealand courts.[427]

(e) Exclusion of evidence under the Convention

The European Court of Human Rights has made it clear that Article 6 does not lay down any rules on the admissibility of evidence which are primarily a matter for regulation under national law.[428] The approach of the Court is to consider whether the reception of the evidence rendered the trial as a whole unfair.[429] Evidence which is obtained as a result of maltreatment of the defendant will be excluded as giving rise to a breach of Article 6.[430] **21.131**

---

425 [1997] 1 NZLR 399, see para 12.249 above; for a critical discussion see S Optican, 'Rolling Back s 21 of the Bill of Rights' [1997] NZLJ 42.

426 *R v Grayson and Taylor* (n 425 above) 408–409.

427 See eg *Police v Lord* (1999) 5 HRNZ 92 (warrantless search, not freely consented to, evidence excluded); *R v Ratima and Warren* unreported 14 Dec 1999 (warrantless search after police officer climbed over a gate with 'No Entry' sign, evidence excluded).

428 *Schenk v Switzerland* (1988) 13 EHRR 242 para 46.

429 Ibid.

430 *Austria v Italy* (1963) 6 YB 740, EComm HR.

21.132 It has been held that the admission of evidence obtained by an undercover agent in a prison was not a breach of Article 6.[431] By contrast, in *Teixeira de Castro v Portugal*[432] the Court decided that evidence obtained by undercover agents who were not subject to proper safeguards rendered the criminal trial unfair; but for the intervention of the undercover agents, the crime would not have been committed.

21.133 In *Khan v United Kingdom*[433] the applicant complained that he had been convicted solely on the basis of unlawfully obtained evidence. He submitted that, although Article 6 did not require the automatic exclusion of evidence obtained in breach of Convention rights, three requirements had to be fulfilled:

- there should be an effective procedure during the trial by which the admissibility of evidence could be challenged;
- the trial court should have regard to the nature of the violation; and
- the conviction should not be based solely on evidence obtained in consequence of breach of a Convention right.

However, the Court confirmed that the question of admissibility depended on whether the proceedings as a whole were fair; and rejected the complaint on the basis that the domestic courts had assessed the fairness of admitting the evidence under section 78 of the Police and Criminal Evidence Act 1984 and had decided it was fair to do so. At the same time the Court stressed its limited jurisdiction when considering concerning the admissibility of evidence:

> The Court re-iterates that its duty, according to Article 19 of the Convention, is to ensure that the observances of the engagements undertaken by the Contracting States to the Convention. In particular, it is not its function to deal with errors of fact or of law allegedly committed by a national court unless and in so far as they may have infringed rights and freedoms protected by the Convention. While Article 6 guarantees the right to a fair trial, it does not lay down any rules on the admissibility of evidence as such which is primarily a matter for regulation under national law.

(f) Exclusion of evidence in other jurisdictions

21.134 **Ireland.** The Supreme Court of Ireland takes the view that where evidence has been obtained in a contravention of a constitutional right, there is a strong presumption in favour of exclusion.[434] As it stressed in *People (A-G) v O'Brien*,[435] evidence which is obtained in deliberate breach of a constitutional right is inadmissible except in 'extraordinary excusing circumstances'. The test as to

[431] *X v Germany* (1989) 11 EHRR 84.
[432] (1998) 28 EHRR 101.
[433] *The Times*, 23 May 2000.
[434] See generally, J M Kelly, *The Irish Constitution* (3rd edn, Butterworths, 1994) 603ff.
[435] [1965] IR 142.

whether there is a deliberate breach of a constitutional right is an objective one: there is no 'good faith exception'.[436] In *The People (DPP) v Healy*[437] the Supreme Court made clear that 'a violation of constitutional rights is not to be excused by the ignorance of the violator'. In *The People (DPP) v Kenny*[438] evidence obtained as a result of a search under a warrant which later turned out to be invalid was excluded. The Supreme Court held that, as between two alternative rules governing the exclusion of evidence obtained as a result of the invasion of personal rights of a citizen, it had an obligation to choose the principle which is likely to provide a stronger and more effective defence and vindication of the right concerned. As a result, it rejected a 'good faith exception':

> To exclude only evidence obtained by a person who knows or ought reasonably to know that he is invading a constitutional right is to impose a negative deterrent. It is clearly effective to dissuade a policeman from acting in a manner which he knows is unconstitutional or from acting in a manner reckless as to whether his conduct is or is not unconstitutional.
>
> To apply, on the other hand, the absolute protection rule of exclusion whilst providing also that negative deterrent, incorporates as well a positive encouragement to those in authority over the crime prevention and detection services of the State to consider in detail the personal rights of the citizens as set out in the Constitution and the effect of their powers of arrest, detention, search and questioning in relation to such rights.
>
> It seems to me to be an inescapable conclusion that a principle of exclusion which contains both negative and positive force is likely to protect the constitutional rights in more instances than is a principle with negative consequences only . . .
>
> The detection of crime and the conviction of guilty persons, no matter how important they may be in relation to the ordering of society, cannot, however, in my view, outweigh the unambiguously express constitutional obligation 'as far as practicable to defend and vindicate the personal rights of the citizen'.

There must, however, be a causative link between the breach of constitutional rights and the obtaining of the evidence in question.[439]

Germany. Under German basic law[440] where the question of excluding evidence arises, the court must first consider whether evidence has been obtained in breach of basic law or in breach of due process; if it is in breach, the court will then exclude the evidence to preserve the integrity of the judicial process. On the other **21.135**

[436] But see *The People v Dalfe* [1998] 4 IR 50 where the Court of Criminal Appeal applied less stringent principles and admitted evidence which had been obtained where the police innocently relied on a defective search warrant.

[437] [1990] 2 IR 73.

[438] [1990] 2 IR 110; but see *The People v Dalfe* (n 436 above) (in which the evidence was admitted).

[439] *Walsh v O Buachalla* [1991] 1 IR 56.

[440] See A Ashworth, Joint Submissions of Liberty and Justice to the Court in *Khan v United Kingdom*, *The Times*, 23 May 2000.

hand, where the evidence has not been excluded, then the court must balance on conventional proportionality grounds an individual's rights against the interests of the community in the preservation of all the evidence.

21.136 **The Netherlands.** Article 359a of the Code of Criminal Procedure[441] provides for three different sanctions for unlawful or unconstitutional conduct by the police during the investigative stage: the case may be dismissed, the evidence excluded or the sentence reduced. The first two sanctions are appropriate where material evidence has been obtained as a direct result of violating a defendant's constitutional rights. In *Zwolsman NJ*[442] the Supreme Court held that telephone surveillance which breached the constitutional right to privacy was not in itself sufficient to dismiss the case: the ultimate sanction of dismissal was only appropriate where the police acted wilfully in gross regard for a suspect's rights.

21.137 **South Africa.** Section 35(5) of the South African Constitution provides that:

> Evidence obtained in a manner that violates any right in the Bill of Rights must be excluded if the admission of that evidence would render the trial unfair or otherwise be detrimental to the administration of justice.

The onus is on the accused to show that evidence should be excluded:[443] it is sufficient to establish either that the trial would be rendered unfair or that admission of the evidence would be detrimental to the administration of justice.[444] It has been held that fairness must be decided on the facts of each case.[445] The South African courts have tended to follow the Canadian cases: excluding improperly obtained admissions but admitting real evidence which exists independently of any self-incriminating act of the accused.[446] In considering whether the admission of evidence would be detrimental to the administration of justice the court seeks to balance the public interest in the detection and punishment of crime against the public interest in ensuring that justice is done to all.[447] Evidence will be excluded if obtained in flagrant and deliberate violation of constitutional rights.[448]

21.138 **Trinidad and Tobago.** In the Trinidad and Tobago appeal of *Mohammed (Allie) v the State*[449] the Privy Council were asked to apply a *prima facie* rule against

441 Ibid.
442 1996/249.
443 *S v Naidoo* 1998 (1) BCLR 46, 86F-87D; *S v Gumede* 1998 (5) BCLR 530, 538D.
444 *S v Lottering* 1999 (12) BCLR 1478.
445 *Key v A-G of Cape of Good Hope* 1996 (4) SA 187.
446 See generally, M Chaskalson, *Constitutional Law of South Africa* (Juta, 1996) para 26.4.
447 See *S v Motlousi* 1996 (1) SA 584.
448 *S v Lottering* 1999 (12) BCLR 1478.
449 [1999] 2 WLR 552.

admitting evidence obtained in breach of constitutional rights.[450] The Privy Council examined the case law in Ireland,[451] Canada and the New Zealand in support of the exclusionary rule. However, Lord Steyn expressly rejected the *prima facie* exclusionary rule, stating[452] that:

> the discretion of the trial judge is neither prima facie exclusionary or prima facie inclusionary. It is, however, also not a completely opened textured discretion . . . the judge has to conduct a balancing exercise. On the one hand, the judge has to weigh the interest of the community in securing relevant evidence bearing on the commission of serious crime so that justice can be done. On the other hand, the judge has to weigh the interest of the individual who has been exposed to the alleged invasion of his rights.
>
> . . . It is a matter of fundamental importance that a right has been considered important enough by the people of Trinidad and Tobago through their representatives, to be enshrined in their Constitution. The stamp of constitutionality on a citizen's rights is not meaningless: it is clear testimony that an added value is attached to the protection of the right. . . . On the other hand, it is important to bear in mind the nature of a particular constitutional guarantee and the nature of the particular breach. For example, a breach of a defendant's constitutional right to a fair trial must inevitably result in a conviction being quashed. By contrast, the constitutional protection requiring a suspect to be informed of his right to a lawyer, although of great importance, is a somewhat lesser right and potential breaches can vary greatly in gravity. In such a case not every breach will result in the confession being excluded. But their Lordships make clear that the fact there has been a breach of a constitutional right is a cogent factor militating in favour of the exclusion of the confession. In this way the constitutional character of the infringed right is respected and accorded a high value. Nevertheless, the judge must perform a balancing exercise in the context of all the circumstances of the case. Except for one point their Lordships do not propose to speculate on the varying circumstances which may come before the courts. The qualification is that it would generally not be right to admit a confession where the police have deliberately frustrated a suspect's constitutional rights.

United Nations. The exclusion of illegally obtained evidence is dealt with in a number of United Nations Documents. Principle 27 of the 'Body of Principles for the Protection of all Persons under any Form of Detention or Imprisonment'[453] states that where there has been non-compliance with the principles in obtaining evidence, this shall be taken into account in determining its admissibility.[454] Guideline 16 of the 'Guidelines on the Role of Prosecutors'[455] provides that: **21.139**

[450] Under the Trinidad and Tobago Constitution a defendant has a constitutional right to communicate with his lawyer.

[451] *The People (DPP) v Lynch* [1982] IR 64 at 79; *The People (DPP) v Kenny* [1990] 2 IR 110

[452] n 449 above 562, 563

[453] UN Body of Principles for the Protection of all Persons under any Form of Detention or Imprisonment 1988 (A/RES/43/173).

[454] Cf *R v N (No 2)* (1999) 5 HRNZ 72.

[455] 8th UN Congress on the Prevention of Crime and the Treatment of Offenders, Havana 27 Aug to 7 Sep 1990, UN Doc A/CONF.144/28/Rev at 189.

> When prosecutors come into possession of evidence against suspects that they know or believe on reasonable grounds was obtained through recourse to unlawful methods, which constitute a grave violation of the suspect's human rights, especially involving torture or cruel, inhuman or degrading treatment or punishment or other abuses of human rights, they shall refuse to use such evidence against anyone other than those who used such methods, or inform the Court accordingly . . .

(g) The exclusion of evidence and section 78

21.140 At present, the issue of the admissibility of evidence in the English courts is addressed by applying section 78 of the Police and Criminal Evidence Act 1984. This provides:

> In any proceedings the court may refuse to allow evidence on which the prosecution proposes to rely to be given if it appears to the court, that having regard to all the circumstances, including the circumstances in which the evidence was obtained, the admission of the evidence would have such an adverse effect on the fairness of the proceedings that the court ought not to admit it.

21.141 In exercising this discretion, the court will look at all the circumstances, including unlawful searches, questioning or detention.[456] The sole test is fairness:[457] no 'balancing exercise' is involved:

> The exercise for the judge under section 78 is not the marking of his disapproval of the prosecution's breach, if any, of the law in the conduct of the investigation or the proceedings by a discretionary decision to stay them, but an examination of the question whether it would be unfair to the defendant to admit that evidence.[458]

The English courts have taken the view that this approach is consistent with the right to a fair trial[459] under Article 6 of the Convention. As Lord Nicholls said in *R v Khan*:[460]

> the discretionary powers of the trial judge to exclude evidence march hand in hand with Article 6(1) of the European Convention on Human Rights. Both are concerned to ensure that those facing criminal charges receive a fair hearing. Accordingly, when considering the common law and statutory discretionary powers under English law, the jurisprudence on Article 6 can have a valuable role to play.

The fact that evidence has been obtained by a trick[461] or by agent provocateurs[462]

[456] For an analysis of the substantial case law, see R Stone, 'Exclusion of Evidence under Section 78 of the Police and Criminal Evidence Act: Practice and Principles' [1995] 3 Web JCLI.

[457] *R v Chalkley* [1998] QB 848.

[458] Ibid 876C.

[459] See para 11.150ff above.

[460] [1997] AC 558, 583B-D.

[461] *R v Bailey* [1993] 3 All ER 513 (co-accused placed in same cell and conversation 'bugged').

[462] *R v Christou* [1992] QB 979 (Police 'shop' staffed by undercover officers bought stolen goods); see also *Williams v DPP* [1993] 3 All ER 365 (insecure unattended van containing cigarettes left in busy street, accused seen removing them); *London Borough of Ealing v Woolworths* [1995] Crim LR 58 (purchase of video by underage child acting on instructions of prosecutor); and see *R v Maclean* [1993] Crim LR 687.

will not, of itself, render it inadmissible and the court does not use section 78 to 'discipline' the police or prosecuting authorities.[463]

(h) Exclusion of evidence and the Human Rights Act

In cases where Convention rights have been violated, the English courts may be inclined to adopt the section 78 'fairness' approach to the exclusion of evidence. This was the approach taken by the Divisional Court in *Nottingham City Council v Amin*[464] in refusing to exclude evidence obtained when police officers 'gave the defendant the opportunity' to break the law. Lord Bingham CJ considered the Convention authorities and went on to hold that the proper test was whether or not the effect of admitting the evidence was to deny the respondent a fair trial. On this analysis the Human Rights Act is unlikely to have a substantial impact on the law governing the admissibility of illegally obtained evidence. A breach of a Convention right will be a factor to take into account in determining fairness but will not be the sole or necessarily the determining factor. **21.142**

However, there are strong grounds for arguing that more rigorous standards are necessary. A recent survey of the position in Canada, Ireland, New Zealand, the United States, the Netherlands, Germany and South Africa concludes that the rationale for excluding evidence through a breach of a Convention right ought to be found on two closely related principles:[465] **21.143**

- the exclusion of evidence should be seen as the *vindication* of the right: the individual's right is protected by denying the prosecution the possibility of taking advantage of that violation; and
- the *integrity* of the judicial system ought to be preserved; and it would compromise that integrity if a court were to allow a decision to be based on evidence obtained through the violation of the right.

It is suggested that these factors provide more persuasive reasons for excluding evidence than the notion that excluding evidence deters police misconduct. This approach leads to a presumption in favour of excluding evidence obtained in breach of Convention rights because the fundamental nature of Convention rights should be assigned a special significance. If the court merely uses a balancing exercise by weighing the breach against the broad notion of the 'public interest', there is a danger that the more serious the crime a person is charged with, the less protection will be afforded to fundamental rights.

---

463 *R v Mason (Carl)* [1988] 1 WLR 139.

464 [2000] 1 WLR 1071.

465 A Ashworth, 'Joint Submissions by Justice and Liberty' in relation to *Khan v United Kingdom*, *The Times*, 23 May 2000.

21.144 It is submitted that the constitutional status of the Human Rights Act[466] requires a more stringent approach to the exclusion of evidence than that which has been taken under section 78 of the Police and Criminal Evidence Act. In particular, the need to vindicate constitutional rights requires the court to give effect to *broader* concerns than just the narrow question of whether it is unfair to a particular individual to admit evidence where Convention rights have been breached. It is further submitted that the need to give practical and effective safeguards[467] to Convention rights would be more readily achieved by applying the following principles to the exclusion of evidence:

- evidence procured by a deliberate violation of Convention rights should be automatically excluded;
- evidence obtained by inhuman treatment contrary to Article 3[468] should be automatically excluded;
- evidence secured by contravening other Convention rights (such as illegal surveillance contrary to Article 8)[469] should be presumed to be inadmissible unless there are good reasons to the contrary. This presumption can be rebutted if there are a cogent reasons for concluding that public interest dictates the admission of the evidence; the court in conducting a balancing exercise must take account of the nature of the breach of the Convention right, the evidential value of the evidence obtained (by comparison with the other evidence in the case), the seriousness of the offence alleged and the extent to which the admission of evidence would bring the administration of justice into disrepute in the eyes of a reasonable person (as in Canada);[470]
- evidence acquired by breaching the fair trial guarantees of Article 6[471] should be ruled inadmissible if its admission would compromise the overall fairness of the criminal trial.

(7) The inclusion of evidence

21.145 It is possible that, in some limited circumstances, the Human Rights Act may require the inclusion of evidence which would otherwise be inadmissible. Thus, in the Canadian case of *R v Seaboyer*[472] the Supreme Court struck down a 'rape shield' provision on the ground that it violated the accused's fair trial rights.

---

466 See para 1.90 above.

467 For a general discussion of this principle of Convention law, see para 6.28ff above.

468 See generally, para 8.13ff above.

469 The obligation on a public authority to act in a manner 'prescribed by law' is discussed at para 12.128ff above, the necessity of such interferences to prevent crime is discussed at para 12.140ff above.

470 See para 21.128 above.

471 See generally, para 11.183ff above.

472 [1991] 2 SCR 577.

E. Remedies in Private Law Proceedings

(1) Introduction

If a claimant succeeds in a case against a public authority under the Human Rights Act in private law proceedings,[473] there are a number of remedies which are available to him. First, the claimant may recover damages.[474] Secondly, it may be appropriate to make a declaration.[475] Thirdly, the court will also have the power to grant an injunction. Fourthly, it is possible that, in some circumstances, the Human Rights Act will require the exclusion of evidence in civil proceedings. Finally, there is the possibility that the courts will have to fashion new remedies to deal with Human Rights Act issues. It may be said that the question of whether a statutory provision should be 'read in' or 'read down' so as to ensure that legislation is compatible with Convention rights under section 3 of the Human Rights Act contitutes a remedy under the Act. The principles themselves are discussed in Chapter 4.[476] However, it is clear that the court does not have a discretion concerning whether or not to apply section 3. **21.146**

(2) Injunctions[476a]

An injunction is an equitable remedy and is, therefore, discretionary. Nevertheless, such discretion must be exercised on the basis of established principles. The Judicature Acts gave the High Court the Court of Chancery's former jurisdiction to grant injunctions. The position is now governed by section 37(1) of the Supreme Court Act 1981. **21.147**

The courts have power to grant interim injunctions under CPR Part 25. Interim injunctions can be granted to protect victims of acts rendered unlawful by section 6 of the Human Rights Act. The relevant principles are discussed above.[477] **21.148**

It is well-established that final injunctions are only available in equity to protect recognised legal or equitable rights.[478] Even when there is jurisdiction to grant an injunction the court has a broad discretion whether or not to grant one in a particular case. The most important factor to be taken into account is the adequacy **21.149**

---

[473] The Act does not require claims under the Human Rights Act to be brought as public law proceedings: see para 22.50ff below.

[474] See para 21.10 above.

[475] See para 21.98ff above.

[476] See para 4.17 above.

[476a] For a discussion of injunctions as constitutional remedies, see generally, K Roach, *Constitutional Remedies in Canada* (Canada Law Book, 1999) Chap 13.

[477] See para 21.91ff above.

[478] *Day v Brownrigg* (1878) 10 Ch D 294; *Paton v British Pregnancy Advisory Service Trustees* [1979] QB 276.

of damages because, like all equitable remedies, injunctions are only granted when the common law remedy of damages is inadequate.[479] If damages are inadequate, however, the fact that the plaintiff will only suffer a small amount of damage will not prevent him obtaining an injunction.[480] The defendant will not be allowed to 'buy' an infringement of a plaintiff's rights by paying damages rather than having an injunction granted against him.[481] An injunction will be refused if the defendant can raise one of the general 'equitable defences'. Thus, a plaintiff will be refused an injunction if he has delayed in making his application. Closely related to delay, but distinct from it, is the defence of 'acquiescence'.

21.150 If the court is considering granting an injunction which might affect the exercise of the Convention right to freedom of expression then the position is governed by section 12 of the Human Rights Act.[482] The court must have particular regard to the importance of the Convention right to freedom of expression[483] and must not grant an interim injunction to restrain publication before trial unless it is satisfied that the applicant is likely to establish that publication should not be allowed.[484]

(3) Exclusion of evidence

21.151 The question as to the existence of a right to exclude admissible evidence in civil proceedings is controversial and has never been definitively decided in the English courts.[485] It is arguable that, if evidence is obtained in breach of Convention rights, it should be excluded by the civil courts.[486]

(4) Other remedies

(a) 'Structural orders'

21.152 It has been argued that litigation with a public law element fundamentally differs from adjudicating disputes between private parties. In such litigation, the court can establish a regime which regulates the future interest of the parties (and others) by subjecting them to continuing judicial oversight. It may therefore grant injunctions which seek to adjust future behaviour by formulating the order on

[479] *Beswick v Beswick* [1968] AC 58.

[480] *Woollerton and Wilson Ltd v Richard Costain Ltd* [1970] 1 WLR 411.

[481] *Shelfer v City of London Electric Lighting Company* [1895] 1 Ch 287; *Kennaway v Thompson* [1981] QB 88.

[482] See para 15.237ff above.

[483] s 12(4).

[484] s 12(3).

[485] See eg *Calcraft v Guest* [1898] 1 QB 759; and contrast *ITC Film Distributors Ltd v Video Exchange Ltd* [1982] Ch 431. It is argued in *Phipson on Evidence* (20th edn, Sweet & Maxwell, 2000) para 33–34ff that the court has no discretion to exclude evidence on the ground that it was unlawfully obtained; but see R Toulson and C Phipps, *Confidentiality* (Sweet & Maxwell, 1996) para 20-16 who take a different view.

[486] See generally, M Chaskalson, *Constitutional Law of South Africa* (Juta, 1996), para 26.20A.

flexible and broadly remedial lines: which are negotiated between the parties but are shaped by the trial judge.[487]

Consequently, in some jurisdictions the courts have used what have been called 'structural orders' to attempt to enforce fundamental rights. In such cases, the court takes on the continuing supervision of a public agency in order to ensure that violations of rights are brought to an end.[488] These remedies were originally developed by the American courts to end the segregation of schools.[489] The courts appointed educational experts to develop school plans and ordered their supervised implementation.[490] The main areas where such injunctions have been granted have been in relation to public education, prisons, mental institutions and police.[491] Although the Supreme Court has, in recent years, emphasised the limits of judicial supervision,[492] the remedy remains available in appropriate cases.[492a] **21.153**

Such a remedy may be appropriate in a variety of situations. For example, in *Rizzo v Goode*[493] the US Supreme Court directed the drafting of a comprehensive programme for dealing with complaints about illegal and unconstitutional mistreatment by police officers. In *MC Mehta v Union of India*[494] the Indian Supreme Court allowed a plant which posed serious environmental hazards to re-open on the basis that stringent safety conditions were complied with. These had to be monitored on a continuing basis and the court appointed an expert committee. In *Basu v State of West Bengal*[495] the court found that the Government was liable for two deaths in custody and directed that police badges with names should be worn by all arresting and interviewing police officers; that a memorandum of arrest should be served on the family member of the person arrested; that a member of the family or friend should be informed of the venue of custody; and that the detainee should be medically examined every 48 hours during custody. In *City Council of Pretoria v Walker*[496] the defendant had refused to pay municipal service charges on the ground that the plaintiff council were **21.154**

[487] A Chayes, 'The Role of the Judge in Public Law Litigation' (1976) 89 Harv L Rev 1281.

[488] See generally, O Fiss, *The Civil Rights Injunction* (1978); Chaskalson (n 486 above) para 9.3 (i) (iii) under the heading 'structural interdicts'.

[489] See generally, C Antieau and W Rich, *Modern Constitutional Law* (2nd edn, West Group, 1997) Vol 2, para 27.03.

[490] See eg *Swann v Charlotte-Mecklenburg Board of Education* (1971) 402 US 1.

[491] See eg F Coffin, 'The Frontier of Remedies: A call for Exploration' (1979) 67 Cal L Rev 983.

[492] *Freeman v Pitts* (1992) 503 US 467; *Missouri v Jenkins (Jenkins III)* (1995) 515 US 70.

[492a] For a discussion of structural injunctions in Canada, see K Roach, *Constitutional Remedies in Canada* (Canada Law Book, 1999) para 13.600ff.

[493] (1976) 423 US 362.

[494] AIR 1987 SC 965. For a general discussion of the position in India, see Roach (n 492a above) para 13.300ff.

[495] [1997] 2 LRC 1.

[496] 1998 (2) SA 363.

levying and enforcing those charges in a racially discriminatory manner. The Constitutional Court held that withholding payment was not the appropriate course because it encouraged victims of discrimination to take the law into their own hands. However, it was suggested that the appropriate remedy would have been an order compelling the council to eliminate the unfair discrimination and to report back to the court:

> The court would then have been in a position to give such further ancillary orders or directions as might be necessary to ensure the proper execution of its order.

It is submitted that, in an appropriate case, the English courts would have power to order such a remedy under section 8 of the Human Rights Act.

(b) Other remedies

21.155 It is possible that the courts will fashion other remedies in Human Rights Act cases. The possibilities include the following:

- *Order for a retraction or a right of reply*: An order that a defendant might be ordered to publish a retraction or give a right of reply in a case involving the publication of material which interferes with the claimant's Convention rights.[497] The court now has limited power to order the publication of a correction and apology in summary defamation proceedings[498] and there appears to be no reason why, in an appropriate case, the court should not make a similar order under section 8 of the Human Rights Act.[499]
- *Order for the publication of an apology*: In an appropriate case, the court could order a public authority to make a public statement apologising for its conduct in acting incompatibly with an applicant's Convention rights.
- *Declaration of incompatibility with international obligations*: The 'declaration of incompatibility' procedure under the Human Rights Act[500] concerns incompatibility between statute and Convention rights. The New Zealand Courts have tentatively recognised the possibility of a declaration of incompatibility between statute law and state obligations under international human rights treaties.[501] Such declarations could be made in cases where both Convention rights and rights under other instruments are in play.[502]

---

[497] Cf *TV3 Network Ltd v Eveready NZ Ltd* [1993] 3 NZLR 435 (claim for mandatory order that corrective advertising be published was arguable).

[498] Under the Defamation Act 1996, s 9(1)(b): the parties must agree its content and the time, manner and form of its publication: ibid s 9(2).

[499] See also *Ramabachan v Trinidad and Tobago* (1985) (cited in M Demerieux, *Fundamental Rights in Commonwealth Caribbean Constitutions* (Faculty of Law Library, University of West Indies, 1992) 455) in which the Trinidad and Tobago High Court ordered a radio station to prepare and file a statement of policy regarding political broadcasting.

[500] See para 4.43ff above.

[501] See *Moonen v Film and Literature Board of Review* (1999) 5 HRNZ 224 para 20.

[502] Reversing the approach in *Malone v Metropolitan Police Commissioner* [1979] Ch 344, see para 2.12 above.

- *Stay pending an application to the European Court of Human Rights*: The possibility of obtaining a stay pending an application to the Court has been considered in several cases. In *Sparks v Harland*[502a] the court granted a stay of proceedings where a decision of the Court of Human Rights might result in legislation which removed a limitation obstacle to the claim.[502b] By contrast, in *Locabail (UK) v Waldorf Investment Corporation (No 4)*[502c] the judge refused an application to stay the execution of a judgment where the claimant proposed to apply to Strasbourg. The domestic courts had conclusively determined the claimant's rights and her remedy was to seek just satisfaction from the European Court of Human Rights.

Appendix: Article 13 of the Convention

(1) Introduction

Article 13 of the Convention was modelled on Article 8 of the Universal Declaration of Human Rights[503] and states: **21.156**

> Everyone whose rights and freedoms as set forth in this Convention are violated shall have an effective remedy before a national authority notwithstanding that the violation has been committed by a person acting in an official capacity.

The Committee of Ministers reinforced Article 13 in 1984 with a recommendation that all members of the Council of Europe provide remedies for governmental wrongs.[504]

The right to an effective remedy is the only article of substance in the Convention which was not enacted by the Human Rights Act; and the decision to omit it was highly controversial.[505] Article 13 has played an important role in recent decisions of the Court[506] and has also been prominent in domestic cases where Convention points have been argued.[507] Article 13 is therefore likely to be invoked under the Human Rights Act even though it will have no direct application, unlike other Convention rights.[508] **21.157**

The importance of the right to a remedy has been increasingly recognised in recent **21.158**

502a [1997] 1 WLR 143.

502b Claimant was seeking to bring a claim for damages for sex abuse the limitation period. The Court of Human Rights Case, *Stubbing v United Kingdom* (1996) 23 EHRR 213 was unsuccessful.

502c *The Times*, 13 Jun 2000.

503 Reproduced at App H in Vol 2.

504 Recommendation No R (84) 15 on Public Liability adopted by the Council of Ministers on 18 Sep 1984.

505 See generally, para 3.18 above.

506 See eg *Aksoy v Turkey* (1996) 23 EHRR 553; *Aydin v Turkey* (1997) 25 EHRR 251.

507 See eg *Rantzen v Mirror Group Newspapers (1986) Ltd* [1994] QB 670; *John v MGN Ltd* [1997] QB 586; *R v Khan* [1997] AC 558.

508 The rights which have been enacted as Convention rights in the Act are set out at para 3.43ff above.

years.[509] In *Aksoy v Turkey*[510] the Court took the opportunity to elaborate some general principles:

> Article 13 guarantees the availability at a national level of a remedy to enforce the substance of the Convention rights and freedoms in whatever form they might happen to be secured in the domestic legal order. The effect of this article is thus to require the provision of a domestic remedy allowing the competent national authority both to deal with the substance of the relevant Convention complaint and to grant appropriate relief, although contracting states are afforded some discretion as to the manner in which they conform to their obligations under this provision. The scope of the obligation under Article 13 varies depending on the nature of the applicant's complaint under the Convention. Nevertheless, the remedy under Article 13 must be 'effective' in practice as well as in law, in particular, in the sense that its exercise must not be unjustifiably hindered by the acts or omissions of the authorities of the respondent state.

(2) The scope of the right

21.159 Article 13 is not a *free standing* right. It only arises for consideration if the applicant raises a complaint involving another substantive Convention right. The applicant need not prove a breach of his other Convention rights. Article 13 merely requires that an individual who claims his rights have been infringed is guaranteed an effective remedy before a national authority.[511] In *Silver v United Kingdom*[512] the Court took the view that the complaint in relation to the other Article must be arguable. The approach taken[513] in *Boyle and Rice v United Kingdom*[514] and *Powell and Rayner v United Kingdom*[515] was to regard the question of arguability as being the same as admissibility, in other words no breach of Article 13 can be established if an application based on the other Convention rights would be ruled inadmissible as being 'manifestly ill-founded'.[516]

21.160 However, Article 13 has no application in cases where the applicant can invoke Convention rights which prescribe stricter requirements in terms of remedies. Thus, it is not relevant where the applicant can rely on the habeas corpus remedy under Article 5(4)[517] or where he alleges that his fair trial rights under Article 6(1)[518] have been violated. Thus, in cases involving the determination of civil rights and obligations, the less strict require-

[509] For a recent survey see M Nowicki, 'Prevention and Remedy: New Standards for Domestic Protection of Rights' (1998/9) 12 Interights Bulletin 175. The approach has significantly changed in recent years; Judges Matscher and Farinha pointed out in their partially dissenting judgment in *Malone v United Kingdom* (1984) 7 EHRR 14, 48-49: 'Article 13 constitutes one of the most obscure clauses in the Convention and its application raises extremely complicated problems of interpretation. This is probably the reason why, for approximately two decades, the Convention institutions avoided analysing this provision, for the most part advancing barely convincing reasons'.

[510] (1996) 23 EHRR 553 para 95.

[511] *Klass v Germany* (1978) 2 EHRR 214 para 64; *Silver v United Kingdom* (1983) 5 EHRR 347 para 113; *Leander v Sweden* (1987) 9 EHRR 433 para 77.

[512] n 511 above.

[513] This approach has, however, been criticised, for example, by Hampson (1990) 39 IQLR 891.

[514] (1988) 10 EHRR 425.

[515] (1990) 12 EHRR 288 para 33.

[516] Under Art 35 (formerly Art 27); see para 23.55 below.

[517] See para 10.145ff above.

[518] See para 11.150 above.

ments of Article 13 are absorbed by those of Article 6.[519] However, Article 13 does not guarantee a remedy in connection with a violation of Article 6.[520]

(3) The nature of the remedy required

Article 13 does not oblige a state to incorporate the Convention into its domestic law.[521] It simply imposes a duty on the state to provide the opportunity to test at a national level whether a Convention right has been violated.[522] **21.161**

Thus, the right to an effective remedy does not require that primary legislation be overridden where it is contrary to Convention rights.[523] As a result, the Commission refused to strike down the Representation of the People Act 1949 because it disproportionately favoured the two main political parties;[524] and the Court also declined to strike down the compensation provisions in legislation nationalising the shipbuilding industry.[525] By contrast, the Court rejected the Government's contention in *Abdulaziz, Cabales and Balkandali v United Kingdom*[526] that the Immigration Rules had legislative status which made them immune from an Article 13 challenge. The Court held that the Rules were a hybrid of delegated legislation and administrative guidelines; and that Article 13 was breached because there was no means of challenging the Rules on the ground that they breached Convention rights. **21.162**

The objective of Article 13 is therefore to guarantee in general terms that a suitable national remedy is available which is *capable* of providing a remedy in an appropriate case; it is not intended to ensure that a particular result is secured on the facts of any specific case.[527] The Court held in *Silver v United Kingdom*[528] that the possibility of making a complaint to the Parliamentary Ombudsman was not an effective remedy because it depended on voluntary compliance with a report presented to Parliament. Similarly, in *Chahal v United Kingdom*[529] it decided that a national authority which was advisory only could not satisfy Article 13; an element of compulsion was necessary. **21.163**

On the other hand, a consistent national practice and tradition of respecting pronouncements (although not formally binding) will comply with Article 13.[530] In *Soering v United Kingdom*[531] and *Vilvarajah v United Kingdom*[532] the Court found that the Home Office **21.164**

[519] *Håkansson and Sturesson v Sweden* (1990) 13 EHRR 1 para 69.

[520] This was the view of the majority of the Commission in *Pizzetti v Italy* (1993) Series A No 257-C, the Court did not find it necessary to deal with the point: see paras 20, 21.

[521] *Ireland v United Kingdom* (1978) 2 EHRR 25 para 239.

[522] *Silver v United Kingdom* (1983) 5 EHRR 347 para 113.

[523] *Leander v Sweden* (1987) 9 EHRR 433 para 77; *James v United Kingdom* (1986) 8 EHRR 123 para 85.

[524] *Liberal Party v United Kingdom* (1980) 4 EHRR 106.

[525] *Lithgow v United Kingdom* (1986) 8 EHRR 329.

[526] (1985) 7 EHRR 471.

[527] *Soering v United Kingdom* (1989) 11 EHRR 439 para 120; *Murray v United Kingdom* (1994) 19 EHRR 193 para 100.

[528] (1983) 5 EHRR 347 para 115.

[529] (1996) 23 EHRR 413 para 154.

[530] *Leander v Sweden* (1987) 9 EHRR 433 para 82.

[531] n 527 above para 123.

[532] (1991) 14 EHRR 248 para 153.

practice of refraining from implementing a deportation decision once leave for judicial review had been granted was sufficient to provide an effective remedy, even though it was not then possible to obtain an interim injunction against the Crown.[533]

21.165 Article 13 does not demand that the state provides judicial remedy before the national authority.[534] In general, a judicial remedy will satisfy Article 13, but this was not so in the *Greek* case[535] because the courts following the Greek coup were held not to be independent and impartial.

(4) The 'effectiveness' of the remedy

21.166 The fundamental requirement under Article 13 is that the substance of the Convention complaint is put in the domestic forum.[536] Article 13 will therefore be breached where a civil claim has no realistic prospect of making a Convention challenge;[537] where primary legislation excludes any possible challenge;[538] or where the executive refuses to comply with a court order.[539] Article 13 will also be contravened where the applicant has no right of recourse in the domestic courts, as in *Halford v United Kingdom*;[540] the applicant had no domestic remedy for interception of her office telephone calls since this type of activity was not regulated by the Interception of Communications Act 1985. In *Akdivar v Turkey*[541] the Court found that domestic remedies were inadequate because an administrative tribunal could award compensation, but could not investigate nor attribute responsibility to the Turkish security forces for the destruction of homes and villages.

21.167 However, the extent of this obligation depends on the nature of the Convention right in question. Thus, in *Chahal v United Kingdom*[542] the Court stressed that the right to an effective remedy should be construed generously where it is alleged that deportation will expose the applicant to a real risk of inhuman treatment.

---

[533] The jurisdiction to grant interim relief was upheld in *M v Home Office* [1994] 1 AC 377.

[534] *Leander v Sweden* (1987) 9 EHRR 433 para 77; *Chahal v United Kingdom* (1996) 23 EHRR 413.

[535] (1969) 12 YB 1, EComm HR.

[536] *Soering v United Kingdom* (1989) 11 EHRR 439 para 122; *Vilvarajah v United Kingdom* (1991) 14 EHRR 248 paras 117–127.

[537] See eg *Costello-Roberts v United Kingdom* (1993) 19 EHRR 112 Com Rep para 59 where the Commission said there was no prospect of challenging corporal punishment as amounting to inhuman treatment in breach of Art 3 because of the defence of reasonable chastisement; but see *A v United Kingdom* (1998) 27 EHRR 611 which held that where a stepfather who assaulted a child successfully invoked the defence of reasonable chastisement, the state failed to provide adequate protection for the child contrary to Art 3; see para 8.19ff above.

[538] See eg *Baggs v United Kingdom* (1985) 9 EHRR 235 (where in certain circumstances the Civil Aviation Act 1982 excluded liability in nuisance for aircraft noise) and *Firsoff v United Kingdom* (1993) 15 EHRR CD 111, EComm HR (where the Post Office Act 1969, s 29 gave the Post Office a statutory immunity from liability in tort for interfering with the mail).

[539] *Iatridis v Greece* Application 31107/96, 25 Mar 1999.

[540] (1997) 24 EHRR 523; see also *Valsamis v Greece* (1996) 24 EHRR 294.

[541] RJD 1996-IV 1210.

[542] (1996) 23 EHRR 413.

On the other hand, the right to an effective remedy will be curtailed to reflect the restricted scope for redress inherent in a system of secret surveillance.[543] In *Klass v Germany*[544] the Court rejected the applicants' complaint that unless they were notified that their telephone calls had been intercepted, they would have been denied an effective remedy under Article 13. It took the same approach in *Leander v Sweden* where the applicant alleged he could not gain access to secret information to show that his failure to be appointed to a government post denied him an effective domestic remedy.[545] **21.168**

The effectiveness of a domestic remedy in terms of an Article 13 challenge has been considered in a number of cases. In *M and E F v Switzerland*[546] the Commission decided that a remedy was not ineffective simply because the official who considered the appeal was under the authority of the decision-maker being appealed against; the position would be different if the appeal body did not make an independent examination of the facts. In *Andersson v Sweden*[547] the Court rejected a claim that the remedies in domestic law breached Article 13 because a child could only challenge decisions taking him into public care through proceedings brought by his guardian. In *Vilvarajah v United Kingdom*[548] the Commission decided that the fact that an appeal against a refusal of asylum could only be exercised if the applicant left the United Kingdom was not an effective remedy to test a claim that his return infringed the prohibition against inhuman treatment under Article 3;[549] however, the Court did not consider the point as it decided that the remedy of judicial review was itself sufficient to comply with Article 13. **21.169**

(a) The need for an independent remedy

In *Silver v United Kingdom*[550] the Court said that the national authority which is providing a remedy must be 'sufficiently independent' of the body alleged to have breached Convention rights; and the Court went on to hold that a right to petition the Home Secretary concerning whether censorship of prisoners' correspondence by the prison authorities complied with his directives was nevertheless an effective remedy. However, the Court took the view in *Chahal v United Kingdom*[551] that a real risk of inhuman treatment contrary to Article 3[552] requires an independent scrutiny of the claim. More recently in *Govell v United Kingdom*[553] the Commission decided that the Police Complaints Authority was not sufficiently independent to constitute sufficient protection against abuse of authority for the purposes of Article 13 when investigating a complaint against the police **21.170**

---

543 P Van Dijk and G Van Hoof argue in *Theory and Practice of the European Convention on Human Rights* (3rd edn, Kluwer, 1998) 708–710 that this approach of assessing the requirements of Art 13 by examining the particular circumstances of each case creates a vicious circle because it reduces the necessity of having an effective remedy under Art 13 to the same question of whether another Convention Article has been breached.

544 (1978) 2 EHRR 214 paras 69–72.

545 (1987) 9 EHRR 433 paras 80–84; and see also *Esbester v United Kingdom* (1994) 18 EHRR CD 72; *Christie v United Kingdom* (1994) 78-A DR 119, EComm HR.

546 (1987) 51 DR 283, EComm HR.

547 (1992) 14 EHRR 615 paras 98–103.

548 (1991) 14 EHRR 248 Com Rep para 153.

549 See generally, para 8.13ff above.

550 (1983) 5 EHRR 347 para 116.

551 (1996) 23 EHRR 413 para 151.

552 See para 8.13ff above.

553 (1996) 23 EHRR CD 101.

concerning illegal surveillance. The Commission's approach was upheld by the Court in *Khan v United Kingdom*.[553a]

(b) Effective investigations

21.171 The Court has stressed the need for an effective investigation in a series of cases involving allegations against Turkish security forces. In *Mentes v Turkey*[554] the Court took the view that the remedy must be effective in practice as well as law, in particular its exercise must not be unjustifiably hindered by the acts or omissions of the state. The gravity of the breach of the right of respect for the home under Article 8[555] which resulted from burning the applicants' homes and forcing them to evacuate south-east Turkey required a thorough and effective investigation, capable of leading to the identification and punishment of those responsible and including effective access for the claimant to the investigative process. The Court in *Aksoy v Turkey*[556] again said that the prohibition from torture under Article 3[557] required a thorough and effective investigation to attain the same objectives. It took a similar approach to allegations of rape and ill treatment in custody in *Aydin v Turkey*[558] where it also emphasised that Article 13 required a thorough and effective investigation of the incident.

(c) Cumulative remedies

21.172 The Court in *Silver v United Kingdom*[559] stated that the cumulative effect of different forms of redress should be considered when examining a complaint that Article 13 has been infringed. However, it went on to decide in *Silver* (and in a number of subsequent cases)[560] that Article 13 is satisfied by the aggregate effect of different remedies even though no single remedy amounted in itself to an effective remedy. The justification for this approach is difficult to understand.[561]

(5) *Wednesbury* review as an 'effective remedy'

21.173 Where an administrative decision is challenged on *Wednesbury* grounds, the applicant must show that the decision is so outrageous in its defiance of logic or of accepted moral standards that no sensible person who had applied his mind to the question to be decided could have arrived at it.[562] The limited scope for the court to intervene on *Wednesbury* grounds has been considered as a potential breach of Article 13 on a number of occasions.

21.174 In *Soering v United Kingdom*[563] the applicant claimed that his extradition to the United

---

553a *The Times*, 23 May 2000.
554 (1997) 26 EHRR 595.
555 See generally, para 12.95ff above.
556 (1996) 23 EHRR 553 para 98.
557 See para 8.13ff above.
558 (1997) 25 EHRR 251 para 103.
559 (1983) 5 EHRR 347 para 118.
560 *Leander v Sweden* (1987) 9 EHRR 433 paras 80–82; *Lithgow v United Kingdom* (1986) 8 EHRR 329; *Chahal v United Kingdom* (1996) 23 EHRR 413 para 145.
561 See D Harris, M O'Boyle and C Warbrick, *The Law of the European Convention on Human Rights* (Butterworths, 1995) 457, 458.
562 *Council of the Civil Service Unions v Minister for the Civil Service* [1985] AC 374, 410 *per* Lord Diplock; and see, generally, para 5.12 above.
563 (1989) 11 EHRR 439.

States to face the death penalty amounted to inhuman treatment in breach of Article 3. He also alleged that he could not put the substantive argument before the domestic courts in contravention of Article 13. The Commission held that he had no effective remedy before the English courts;[564] but the Court decided that there was no breach of Article 13 since it was open to a court to decide that it was irrational for the Home Secretary to conclude there was no serious risk of Article 3 being violated.

The Commission and Court again reached different conclusions about Article 13 in *Vilvarajah v United Kingdom*.[565] A number of Tamils from Sri Lanka unsuccessfully applied for refugee status and were deported back to Sri Lanka. The Commission said that a *Wednesbury* challenge to the Home Secretary's decision could not satisfy Article 13; and concluded that the right of appeal was also ineffective since it had to be pursued from Sri Lanka.[566] The Court disagreed and took the view that a national court could have determined that it was irrational of the Home Secretary to remove the applicants on Article 3 grounds. **21.175**

The Court in *Chahal v United Kingdom*[567] distinguished the *Vilvarajah* case. The applicant also unsuccessfully claimed refugee status. His application for judicial review was dismissed on the basis that the Home Secretary had not acted *Wednesbury* unreasonably in balancing the interests of the applicant against the national security implications of allowing him to remain in the United Kingdom. However, the Court upheld his Article 13 complaint. The right to an effective remedy required an independent scrutiny of his Article 3 claim; and such scrutiny had to be carried out without taking into account any perceived national security threat. **21.176**

In *D v United Kingdom*,[568] on the other hand, the Court took the view that Article 13 was satisfied since the Court of Appeal had applied 'the most anxious scrutiny'[569] in holding that the Home Secretary had acted rationally by deciding to deport a AIDS patient who was terminally ill to St Kitts where only limited treatment was available. **21.177**

The issue was again canvassed in cases brought against the United Kingdom arising out of the policy of dismissing homosexuals from the armed forces. In *Smith and Grady v United Kingdom*[570] the Court found there was a breach of Article 13. It pointed out that although the judges in the domestic courts had commented favourably on the applicants' submissions challenging the reasons advanced by the Government in justification of the policy they had concluded that the policy could not be said to be beyond the range of responses open to a reasonable decision-maker and, accordingly, could not be considered to be 'irrational'. As a result, the Court considered it clear that: **21.178**

> . . . the threshold at which the High Court and the Court of Appeal could find the Ministry of Defence policy irrational was placed so high that it effectively excluded any consideration by the domestic courts of the question of whether the interference with the applicants' rights answered a pressing social need or was proportionate to the national security and public order

[564] Ibid Com Rep para 158–168.
[565] (1991) 14 EHRR 248.
[566] Ibid Com Rep paras 114–160.
[567] (1996) 23 EHRR 413 paras 145–155; for a discussion of the case, see para 6.89 above.
[568] (1997) 24 EHRR 423.
[569] See generally, para 1.31 above.
[570] [1999] IRLR 734 para 137.

> aims pursued, principles which lie at the heart of the Court's analysis of complaints under Article 8 of the Convention.[571]

The Court went on to find that:

> the applicants had no effective remedy in relation to the violation of their right to respect for their private lives guaranteed by Article 8 of the Convention. Accordingly, there has been a violation of Article 13 of the Convention.[572]

(6) State liability under Article 13

21.179 The right to an effective remedy exists 'notwithstanding that a violation has been committed by a person acting in an official capacity'. It has been argued that the language imposes an obligation on the state to provide an effective remedy in relation to breaches of Convention rights by private individuals against one another; and that Article 13 provides some support for Convention rights having horizontal effect in disputes between private individuals.[573] However, the better view is that the wording of Article 13 is designed to preclude immunity being extended to public servants acting in an official capacity where they breach Convention rights.

[571] Ibid para 138.
[572] Ibid para 139.
[573] A Clapham, *Human Rights in the Private Sphere* (Clarendon Press, 1993) 240–244.

22

HUMAN RIGHTS ACT PROCEDURE

A. Introduction

(1) The basic approach

22.01 The Human Rights Act has enacted rules of procedure to allow the courts to adjudicate on allegations of violations of Convention rights. They are designed to integrate Convention issues into ordinary proceedings as much as possible; and there is no prescribed procedure which must be followed in all Human Rights Act cases. The basic ground rules are set out in the Act itself.

22.02 The fundamental principle of the Human Rights Act is that it is unlawful for a public authority[1] to act incompatibly with Convention rights[2] in breach of section 6(1).[3] The rules concerning proceedings for breaches of section 6(1) are contained in section 7 of the Act which states:

> (1) A person who claims that a public authority has acted (or proposes to act) in a way which is made unlawful by section 6(1) may:
>
> (a) bring proceedings against the authority under this Act in the appropriate court or tribunal; or
>
> (b) rely on the Convention right or rights concerned in any legal proceedings,
>
> but only if he is (or would be) a victim of the unlawful act.
>
> (2) In subsection 1(a) 'appropriate court or tribunal' means such court or tribunal as may be determined in accordance with rules; and proceedings against an authority include a counterclaim or similar proceeding.
>
> (3) If the proceedings are brought on an application for judicial review, the application is to be taken to have a sufficient interest in relation to the unlawful act only if he is, or would be, a victim of that act.

22.03 This section contemplates two ways in which a person may advance a contention that a public authority has acted in a way which is incompatible with his Convention rights: either by making a *free standing* claim based on a Convention right in accordance with section 7(1)(a) or by *relying* on a Convention right in proceedings in accordance with section 7(1)(b). In practice, Convention rights can be raised in proceedings in a number of other ways including:

- by making a claim against a public authority that indirectly relies on a Convention right (such as arguing that the formulation of a duty of care owed by a public authority must take into account the court's own duties under Article 6);[4]
- by relying on a Convention right in relation to the court itself in the course of

[1] See para 5.03ff above.
[2] See para 5.120ff above.
[3] See para 3.53ff above.
[4] See para 11.306ff above.

proceedings by or against a public authority or private party[5] (by, for example, relying on fair trial rights under Article 6);[6]

- by relying on section 3 to support a contention that a statutory instrument is *ultra vires* the enabling statute;[7]
- by relying on section 3 to support a particular construction of a statute in the course of proceedings for declaratory relief.[8]

(2) The scope of section 7

Section 7 specifies the procedure to be followed where a claim is made that a public authority has acted incompatibly with Convention rights in breach of section 6(1). A number of questions arise about the scope of section 7 including whether a claimant may bring proceedings which raise Human Rights Act issues *outside* section 7 and to what extent collateral challenges are available when a defendant in proceedings brought by a public authority seeks to argue in defence that the underlying act (or decision) relied on is unlawful under the Human Rights Act.[9] **22.04**

The procedural requirements required by section 7 apply to 'legal proceedings' which is a term not defined in the Act. However, section 7(6) states: **22.05**

> In subsection (1)(b) 'legal proceedings' includes—
>
> (a) proceedings brought by or at the instigation of a public authority, and
> (b) an appeal against a decision of a court or tribunal.'

Thus, section 7(1) appears to contemplate that *any* proceedings (including bringing a counterclaim)[10] falls within the scope of section 7(1)(a) whereas section 7(1)(b) appears to apply if a defendant raises a defence involving a Convention right or asks the court to act in a way which is compatible with Convention rights.[11]

It has been suggested[12] that the absence of a definition of 'legal proceedings' will result in difficulties about its meaning. It is unclear, for example, whether a complaint to a statutory ombudsman is 'legal proceedings' (although an ombudsman is a public authority in any event); or whether it covers hearings by non statutory regulatory organisations which have a contractual relationship with their **22.06**

---

[5] See the discussion at para 5.38ff above.

[6] See para 11.183ff above.

[7] See para 22.44 below.

[8] See para 22.47ff below.

[9] See, generally, G Nardell, 'Collateral Thinking: The Human Rights Act and Public Law Defences' [1999] EHRLR 293.

[10] See s 7(2).

[11] Under s 6(3) of the Human Rights Act: see para 5.38ff above.

[12] J Wadham and H Mountfield, *Blackstone's Guide to the Human Rights Act 1998* (Blackstone, 1999) para 5.5.

members.[13] Although a claimant may not have a right under the Human Rights Act to rely on Convention rights at this early stage, he will nevertheless be able to do so if the adjudication is challenged in a court or tribunal.

22.07 Two points of construction may be made about section 7. First it is confined to section 6 claims against a public authority; and does not impinge on applications which can be made on some *other* basis under the Human Rights Act. Thus, for example, it is strongly arguable that the 'standing' rules would not apply to an application for a declaration that a particular statutory instrument or policy was incompatible with Convention rights as this would not be a section 6 claim.[14] Secondly, the section is, in terms, permissive rather than mandatory. The Human Rights Act seems to make careful distinctions between permissive and mandatory provisions.[15] It could be said therefore that section 7(1) is not exhaustive in terms of defining the circumstances in which section 6(1) claims may be made under the Human Rights Act. This argument is not, however, persuasive because it would allow the statutory 'standing' and 'time limit' requirements to be circumvented. It appears that 'may' is permissive in the sense of allowing a person making a section 6 claim to either bring proceedings or rely on the Convention right (as opposed, for example, to raising the matter in Strasbourg); but is not permissive in relation to the *procedure* to be adopted. Thus, on a true construction of section 7, it contemplates a mandatory procedure for bringing section 6(1) claims.[16]

(3) Rules of procedure under the Human Rights Act

22.08 A number of specific procedural rules are contemplated by the Human Rights Act:

- rules under section 2 governing citation of Convention authority;[16a]
- rules under section 5 regulating joinder in cases where a court is considering whether to make a declaration of incompatibility;
- rules under section 7 concerning the question of taking proceedings in the appropriate court;
- rules under section 9 in relation to damages claims against judicial authorities under s 5(5).

[13] These may be functional public authorities: see para 5.27 above.

[14] See para 22.45ff below.

[15] 'I think that great misconception is caused by saying in some cases "may" means "must". It can never mean "must" so long as the English language retains its meaning; but it gives a power, and then it may be a question of what cases, where a judge has the power given by him by the word "may", it becomes his *duty* to exercise that power': *Re Baker, Nichols v Baker* (1890) 44 ChD 262 *per* Cotton LJ at 270.

[16] Cf Government of Wales Act 1998, s 107(2) which provides in the equivalent of s 6(1)(a) (that is, s 107(1)) does not 'enable a person' to bring proceedings or rely on a Convention right 'unless he would be a victim'.

[16a] See para 3.51 above.

At the time of writing, no rules for criminal cases have been published. Draft rules for civil cases under sections 2, 5, 7 and 9 have been published.[16b] **22.09**

(4) The duties of the court in relation to Human Rights Act issues

Section 7 deals with the position where a person claims that a public authority has acted incompatibly with his Convention rights. In ordinary litigation it is usually a matter for the parties to decide what points they wish to put before the court. The position may, however, be different under the Human Rights Act. It might be said that the court itself had an *independent* duty to raise the question of whether a public authority is acting incompatibly with Convention rights. There are two reasons for this: the court's general duty to take notice of 'illegality' and the court's special role as a public authority under the Human Rights Act. **22.10**

First, it is well established that where a transaction is, on its face, illegal the court will take notice of this fact, even though it is not raised by the parties.[17] If it becomes clear in the course of the hearing that the transaction is illegal then the court will refuse to enforce it.[18] The reason behind this principle is that the court must ensure that its processes are not being abused by enforcing transactions contrary to public policy.[19] **22.11**

Secondly, the court is itself a public authority which cannot lawfully act in a way which is incompatible with Convention rights.[20] Thus, it would be unlawful for a court to give effect to any transaction which entails a breach of a party's Convention rights. If, for example, a prosecution violates a defendant's Convention rights the court would itself be acting unlawfully if it proceeded to convict. In a civil case the court would be acting unlawfully if it made an order which violated a party's Convention rights by, for example, restricting freedom of expression in a manner which was not justified under Article 10(2).[21] **22.12**

As a result, it is strongly arguable that the court must itself raise any Human Rights Act issue which is disclosed on the face of the proceedings: whether in the statements of case, the indictment or in any notice of application or evidence put before the court. In such circumstances, the court should give notice to the parties that it requires the question of whether a Human Rights Act issue arises to be considered. The Practice Direction concerning raising 'devolution issues' in **22.13**

[16b] The Draft Rules are in App C in Vol 2.

[17] *Bank of India v Trans Continental Commodity Merchants Ltd* [1982] 1 Lloyd's Rep 427; and see generally *Halsburys Laws of England* (4th edn, Butterworths, 1996) Vol 6, para 838.

[18] See eg *In re Mahmoud and Ispahani* [1921] 2 KB 716; *Snell v Unity Finance Company Ltd* [1964] 2 QB 203.

[19] *Birkett v Acorn Business Machines*, unreported, 16 Jul 1999.

[20] See para 5.38ff above.

[21] For Art 10(2) see para 15.177ff above.

Wales has a provision to this effect;[22] and a similar Practice Direction may be directed to the civil and criminal courts in relation to the Human Rights Act.

B. Standing Under the Human Rights Act

(1) Introduction

22.14 Section 7(1) of the Human Rights Act makes it clear that a person may only rely on an argument that a public authority has acted in a way which is incompatible with a Convention right if he is the 'victim' of the unlawful act. The point is emphasised by section 7(3) which provides that:

> If the proceedings are brought by an application for judicial review, the applicant is to be taken to have a sufficient interest in relation to the unlawful act only if he is, or would be, a victim of that act.

Section 7(7) makes it clear that the word 'victim' must be taken in its Convention sense:

> For the purposes of this section, a person is a victim of an unlawful act only if he would be a victim of Article 34 of the Convention if the proceedings were brought in the European Court of Human Rights in respect of that act.

22.15 Article 34 of the Convention states:

> The Court may receive applications from any person, non-governmental organisations or group of individuals claiming to be the victim of a violation by one of the rights set forth in the Convention or the protocols thereto. The High Contracting Parties undertake not to hinder in any way the effective exercise of this right.

Until the Convention was amended by the Eleventh Protocol[23] the definition of standing was contained in Article 25(1) of the Convention.[24] Article 25 obliged the European Commission on Human Rights to consider as one of the admissibility questions whether a particular complainant had standing to make an application that the Convention had been breached.

22.16 The 'victim' requirement is one of the most controversial issues[25] that emerged

---

[22] *Practice Direction (Supreme Court: Devolution)* [1999] 1 WLR 1592 para 5.2, see para 22.136ff below.

[23] On 1 Nov1998: see App E in Vol 2.

[24] Art 25(1) stated that 'the Commission may receive petitions addressed to the Secretary- General of the Council of Europe from any person, non-governmental body or group of individuals claiming to be a victim of a violation by one of the High Contracting Parties of the rights set forth in the Convention, provided that the High Contracting Party against whom the complaint has been lodged has declared that it recognises the competence of the Commission to receive such petitions. Those of the High Contracting Parties who made such a declaration undertake not to hinder in any way the effective exercise of this right'.

[25] See para 3.84ff above.

during the debates on the Human Rights Bill. The test for standing under the Act is the same as that under the Convention itself. The rationale was given by Lord Irvine LC at the Committee stage who explained:

> The purpose of the [Act] is to give greater effect to our domestic law to Convention rights. It is in keeping with this approach that a person should be able to rely on Convention rights before our courts in precisely the same circumstances as they can rely on them before the Strasbourg institutions. The wording of [section] 7 therefore reflects the terms of the Convention.[26]

However, there is no reason in principle why standing under the Human Rights Act should be modelled on an international human rights instrument. Although a restrictive approach to standing under the Convention might be justified to prevent a supra national court interfering unduly with domestic decision-making this reasoning has no application to domestic human rights legislation.

Section 7(7) of the Human Rights Act appears to contemplate that a different approach should be taken towards the Convention case law when considering questions of standing from that which applies under the Human Rights Act in general. Section 2((1) of the Human Rights Act[27] obliges a court or tribunal *to take account of* the decisions of the Commission, Court of Human Rights or Committee of Ministers when determining a question in connection with a Convention right; but gives the court or tribunal a discretion about the weight to attach to those views.[28] The language of section 7(7) is strikingly different; section 7(7) states that a person is a victim under the Human Rights Act 'if he would be a victim of Article 34 of the Convention if the proceedings were brought in the Court of Human Rights in respect of that act'. **22.17**

It is submitted that section 7(7) enables the standing requirement to be met if but *only if* the claimant would be a 'victim' were proceedings brought in the Court; and that a court or tribunal must attach *weight* to Convention jurisprudence in conducting a hypothetical exercise of ascertaining whether the Court might have found that the complainant was a 'victim'. **22.18**

The importance to be accorded to Convention case law when considering the victim test has one further consequence. Until the Eleventh Protocol abolished the Commission of Human Rights,[29] the Commission had the responsibility to consider whether complaints were admissible under the Convention[30] and routinely ruled applications under the Convention inadmissible on the ground that the complainant failed to satisfy the victim test. Even though the Court has often **22.19**

[26] *Hansard* HL cols 830–831 (24 Nov 1997).
[27] See para 3.46ff above.
[28] See para 3.48 above.
[29] See para 23.06ff below.
[30] See para 23.04 below.

provided authoritative views on the victim requirement, there are a large number of decisions at Commission level on the victim test, many of which are unreported. It is likely that courts and tribunals will be asked to examine some of these Commission decisions whenever there is an issue arising about the victim requirement.

(2) Who can be a 'victim'?

22.20 Article 34 contemplates that victims can be 'persons, non-governmental organisations or group of individuals'. 'Persons' are not defined in the Convention itself. Applications can be made by children and minors[31] and by individuals who have been placed under guardianship.[32] The Court emphasised in *Loizidou v Turkey (Preliminary Objections)*[33] that the victim principle must be interpreted in the light of present day conditions[34] so as to ensure that Convention safeguards are practical and effective.[35]

22.21 It is well established under Convention case law that a 'person' can be a natural or artificial person. However, a company cannot complain of a breach of Convention rights unless it can show it is *itself* directly affected by the breach of Convention rights. A company cannot, for example, prove it is the victim of a violation of the right to life, that it suffers from inhuman treatment or that it has lost its right to liberty. A company failed to prove that it was a victim in *Brüggemann and Scheuten v Germany*[36] when complaining that abortion legislation breached the right to privacy; and the Commission[37] again held in *Open Door Counselling and Dublin Well Woman v Ireland* that the Open Door clinic could not make a privacy complaint on behalf of its clients (although the issue was left open by the Court).[38] The same issue was considered in *R v Broadcasting Standards Commission, ex p BBC*[39] in relation to a complaint by Dixons plc that a secret film made of its staff breached the company's right to privacy. The Court of Appeal took the view that a company could have privacy rights.

22.22 A company can be a victim of infringements of Article 6 due process rights (such as the right of access to the courts[40] and the right of fair trial in relation to

[31] See eg *Marckx v Belgium* (1979) 2 EHRR 330; *Johnston v Ireland* (1986) 9 EHRR 203.

[32] See eg *Winterwerp v Belgium* (1979) 2 EHRR 387.

[33] (1995) 20 EHRR 99 paras 71, 72.

[34] See generally, para 6.23ff above for a discussion of the 'living instrument' principle of construction.

[35] See generally, para 6.28ff above for a discussion of this principle of construction.

[36] (1978) 10 DR 100, EComm HR.

[37] (1992) 15 EHRR 244 Com Rep para 64.

[38] Ibid paras 81–83.

[39] *The Times*, 12 Apr 2000; see also *A-G v Antigua Times Ltd* [1976] AC 16, 25 (use of word 'person' in a constitution includes corporations).

[40] See eg *Stran Greek Refineries and Stratis Andreadis v Greece* (1995) 19 EHRR 293.

criminal charges)[41] as well as breaches of freedom of thought, conscience and religion,[42] freedom of expression,[43] freedom of association,[44] the right to property[45] and the prohibition from discrimination.[46]

22.23 The Human Rights Act also entitles 'a group of individuals' to bring proceedings so that unincorporated associations might have standing without the need to bring a representative action.[47] The Human Rights Act therefore appears to confirm that unincorporated associations have the capacity to bring judicial review applications.[48]

22.24 'Non governmental organisations' are entitled to commence proceedings on their own account. The nature of the organisations which can be termed 'non governmental organisations' was considered by the European Court of Human Rights in *Holy Monasteries v Greece*:[49]

> the Court notes at the outset that the applicant monasteries do not exercise governmental powers. Section 39(1) of the Charter of Greek Churches describes the monasteries as ascetic religious institutions . . . . Their objectives—essentially ecclesiastical and spiritual ones, but also cultural and social ones in some cases—are not such as to enable them to be classed with governmental organisations established for public administration purposes. From the classification of public-law entities it may be inferred only that the legislature—on account of the special links between the monasteries and the State—wished to afford them the same legal protection vis à vis third parties as was accorded to other public-law entities. Furthermore, the monasteries council's only power consists in making rules concerning the organisation and furtherance of spiritual life and the internal administration of each monastery . . . The monasteries come under the spiritual supervision of the local archbishop . . . not under the supervision of the State and they are accordingly entities distinct from the State, of which they are completely independent. The applicant monasteries are therefore to be regarded as non-governmental organisations.

22.25 A professional body or a non governmental organisation must, therefore, establish that it is *itself* directly affected by the measure it is challenging. It can only act on behalf of its members if it can identify its members and provide evidence that it

41 See eg *Société Stenuit v France* (1992) 14 EHHR 509.

42 *Kustannus v Finland* (1996) 85-A DR 29; but see *Company X v Switzerland* (1981) 16 DR 85, EComm HR; *Verein Kontakt Information Therapie v Austria* (1988) 57 DR 81.

43 See eg *Sunday Times v United Kingdom (No 1)* (1979) 2 EHRR 245.

44 See eg *A Association v Austria* (1984) DR 187.

45 See eg *Lithgow v United Kingdom* (1986) 8 EHRR 329.

46 See eg *Pine Valley Developments Ltd v Ireland* (1991) 14 EHRR 319.

47 Under CPR Sch 1, Ord 15, r 12.

48 *R v London Borough of Tower Hamlets, ex p Tower Hamlets Combined Traders Association* [1994] COD 325; *R v Traffic Commissioner for North Western Traffic Authority, ex p BRAKE* [1996] COD 248; but see *R v Darlington BC, ex p Darlington Taxi Drivers* 1994 COD 424; and see K Gledhill, 'Standing, Capacity and Unincorporated Associations' [1996] JR 67.

49 (1994) 20 EHRR 1 para 49.

has authority to act on their behalf.[50] Thus, the Commission held in *Norris v Ireland*[51] that the National Gay Federation was not a victim of the law prohibiting homosexual acts. In *X Union v France*[52] the Commission decided a teaching union was not a victim that could make a claim where an obligation was placed on teachers to live in the town where their school was situated. In *Purcell v Ireland*[53] it concluded that a trade union could not be considered the victim of broadcasting restraints affecting its members; and again took the same view in *Ahmed v United Kingdom*[54] where it was held that individual employees were victims of political restrictions placed on local government employees but that the union was not. Churches,[55] newspapers[56] and trade unions[57] have all succeeded in establishing that they are victims in their own right. Thus, a trade union can be a victim of an alleged breach of Article 11[58] despite the fact it chooses to organise industrial action in breach of the statutory provisions in the Trade Union and Labour Relations Consolidation Act 1992.[59] However, the Commission has failed to give clear guidance about whether a church can exercise the right to religion.[60]

22.26 It is uncertain whether local authorities or public bodies like the BBC[61] can establish they are victims for the purposes of bringing proceedings under the Human Rights Act. The Commission has held that a municipality is not able to bring proceedings as victim by advancing the argument that it is a 'non governmental organisation' or 'group of individuals'.[62] On the other hand, a local authority as a statutory corporation could be a 'person' for the purposes of satisfying the victim

[50] See eg *A v Denmark* (1996) 22 EHHR 458 where the Court held that where an association had acted on behalf of HIV victims, it had to identify the individual applicants to meet the victim requirement.

[51] (1985) 44 DR 132, EComm HR; see also *Associacion de Aviadores de la Republica v Spain* (1988) 41 DR 211, EComm HR; *CFDT v European Communities* (1986) 47 DR 225, EComm HR.

[52] (1983) 32 DR 261.

[53] (1991) 70 DR 262, EComm HR.

[54] RJD 1998-VI 2356.

[55] See eg *X and Church of Scientology v Sweden* (1979) 16 DR 68, EComm HR; *Church of Scientology and 128 Members v Sweden* (1980) 21 DR 109, EComm HR.

[56] See eg *Sunday Times v United Kingdom (No 1)* (1979) 2 EHRR 245.

[57] See eg *Council of Civil Service Unions v United Kingdom* (1987) 50 DR 228.

[58] See para 16.66ff above.

[59] *National Association of Teachers in Further and Higher Education v United Kingdom* (1998) EHRR CD 122, see para 16.91 above.

[60] A church may make a complaint on behalf of its members: see *Pastor X and Church of Scientology v Sweden* (1979) 22 YB 244; *Chappell v Unied Kingdom* (1987) 53 DR 241; *Finska forsamlingen i Stockholm v Sweden* (1996) 85-A DR 94.

[61] The Commission has left open the question of whether the BBC has the necessary status to bring an application: see eg *British Broadcasting Corporation Scotland, McDonald, Rodgers and Donald v United Kingdom* (1997) 25 EHRR CD 179.

[62] *Rothenthurm Commune v Switzerland* (1988) 59 DR 251, EComm HR; *Ayuntamien to de M v Spain* (1991) 68 DR 209, EComm HR.

requirement. In *Austria Municipalities v Austria*[63] the Commission took the view that such a construction is not consistent with the distinction made in Article 34 between 'non governmental organisations' on the one hand, and 'persons' or 'groups of individuals' on the other. These cases suggest that local government institutions or semi-state bodies do not have standing under the Human Rights Act[64] and the Government expressed the same view during the passage of the Bill.[65] Nevertheless, this conclusion may be open to question; and may turn on whether the maxim *expressio unius est exclusio alterus*[66] imposes a restriction on *alternative* means of establishing standing under the Human Rights Act. Even if local authorities and public bodies do not have standing to make section 6(1) claims, they will be able to commence proceedings under section 3 of the Act[67] and where they have standing to raise administrative law or European Community challenges.

(3) The meaning of 'victim'

(a) The basic test

In order to establish the status of 'victim' under the Convention, the complainant must show that he is *directly affected* by the act or omission in issue. The meaning of the victim requirement was extensively discussed in *Klass v Germany*[68] where three lawyers, a judge and a public prosecutor alleged that their post and telephone calls were secretly intercepted; none of the applicants, however, could demonstrate they were *in fact* subject to secret surveillance. The Court took a purposive approach: **22.27**

> While Article [33][69] allows each Contracting State to refer to the Commission 'any alleged breach' of the Convention by another Contracting State, a person, non governmental organisation or group of individuals must, in order to be able to lodge a

[63] (1974) 17 YB 338, 352.

[64] For discussions of this point see C Baker (ed), *The Human Rights Act 1998: A Practitioner's Guide* (Sweet & Maxwell, 1998) paras 1–56 and 2–16; J Wadham and H Mountfield, *Blackstone's Guide to the Human Rights Act 1998* (Blackstone, 1999) para 5.4; J Coppel, *The Human Rights Act: Enforcing the European Convention in the Domestic Courts* (John Wiley & Sons, 1998) para 2.9; Lord Lester and D Pannick, *Human Rights: Law and Practice* (Butterworths, 1999) para 2.7.2; S Grosz, J Beatson and P Duffy, *Human Rights: The 1998 Act and the European Convention* (Sweet & Maxwell, 2000) para 4–26.

[65] The under secretary of state for the Home Office, Mike O'Brien MP, started that 'The intention is that a victim under the Bill should be in the same position as a victim in Strasbourg. A local authority cannot be a victim under [s] 7 because it cannot be a victim in Strasbourg': see *Hansard* HC 24 Jun 1998, col 1084.

[66] 'The mention of one thing is the exclusion of another'.

[67] See para 22.47 below.

[68] (1978) 2 EHRR 214.

[69] Under the Eleventh Protocol Art 33 replaced Art 24 which stated 'Any High Contracting Party may refer to the Commission, through the Secretary General of the Council of Europe, any alleged breach of the provisions of the Convention by another High Contracting Party'. The wording of the Articles is unchanged save that Art 33 makes no reference to the Commission which was abolished as a result of the Eleventh Protocol: see para 23.06ff above.

> petition in pursuance of Article [34] claim 'to be the victim of a violation . . . of the rights set forth in [the] Convention'. Thus, in contrast to the position under Article [33]—where subject to the other conditions laid down, the general interest attaching to the observance of Convention renders admissible an inter-State application—Article [34] requires that an individual applicant should claim to have been actually affected by the violation he alleges.[70] Article [34] does not institute for individuals a kind of *actio popularis* for the interpretation of the Convention; it does not permit individuals to complain against a law *in abstracto* simply because they feel that it contravenes the Convention. In principle, it does not suffice an individual applicant to claim that the mere existence of a law violates his rights under the Convention; it is necessary to show that the law should have been applied to his detriment. Nevertheless, as both the Government and the Commission pointed out, a law may by itself violate the rights of an individual if the individual is directly affected by the law in the absence of any specific measure of implementation . . .

The Court went on to hold that the applicants should not be deprived of the opportunity of lodging an application because of the secrecy of the measures objected to. This was because:

> the effectiveness . . . of the Convention implies in such circumstances some possibility of having access to the Commission. If it were not so, the efficiency of the Convention's enforcement machinery would be materially weakened. The procedural provisions of the Convention must, in view of the fact that the Commission and its institutions were set up to protect the individual, be applied in a manner which serves to make the system of individual applications efficacious.

22.28 The Court has frequently held that it is not necessary for a victim to prove that he has in fact been prejudiced or suffered a detriment where his Convention rights are breached.[71] Thus, in *Campbell and Cosans v United Kingdom*[72] a pupil could show he was a victim when complaining that corporal punishment was inhuman treatment simply on the ground that his attendance at the school put him at *risk* of being exposed to inhuman treatment. In *Eckle v Germany*[73] the applicant alleged that the length of two sets of criminal proceedings breached Article 6.[74] In one instance the prosecution had been discontinued and in the other the sentence had been mitigated. In *Bowman v United Kingdom*[75] the fact that an acquitted defendant might remain liable to prosecution unless she modified her behaviour was sufficient for her to be a victim. The Court takes the view that the existence of

[70] See *Ireland v United Kingdom* (1978) 2 EHRR 25 paras 239–240.

[71] D Harris, M O'Boyle and C Warbrick point out that the view of the Commission was more strict and that its view of the victim status requires the applicant to have been harmed in some way: *The Law of the European Convention on Human Rights* (London, Butterworths, 1995) 636.

[72] (1982) 4 EHHR 293.

[73] (1982) 5 EHRR 1: see also *Lüdi v Switzerland* (1992) 15 EHRR 173 para 34; *Adolf v Austria* (1982) 4 EHRR 313 para 37; *De Jong, Baljet and Van Der Brink v Netherlands* (1984) 8 EHRR 20 paras 40–41; *Duinhof and Duijf v Netherlands* (1984) 13 EHRR 478 paras 36–37; *Groppera Radio AG v Switzerland* (1990) 12 EHRR 321 paras 45–51.

[74] For the right to a hearing within a reasonable time, see para 11.219ff above.

[75] (1998) 26 EHRR 1.

prejudice is not a pre-condition to a finding that the Convention has been breached although the absence of prejudice will be relevant to any question of compensation.[76] A newspaper can be a victim of a breach of Article 10 despite the fact that no defamation proceedings have been brought because the law is vague.[77]

Nevertheless, there is an inconsistency of approach in the cases which has been criticised.[78] For example, the Commission took the somewhat surprising view[79] in *Leigh, Guardian Newspapers and Observer v United Kingdom*[80] that not every newspaper or journalist who might be affected by the House of Lords decision in *Home Office v Harman*[81] could properly be described as a 'victim'; the Commission decided that to be a 'victim', the detriment must be of a less indirect and remote nature. By contrast, a newspaper editor and journalist were victims where they proposed to write an article which might then make them liable for contempt of court.[82] **22.29**

(b) Public interest challenges

The test of standing under the Convention does not permit a pure public interest challenge or *actio popularis*.[83] For example, in *Greenpeace Schweiz v Switzerland*[84] the pressure group failed to establish that it was a victim for the purposes of challenging the grant of a licence to operate a nuclear power station. **22.30**

Nor does making a complaint entitle the Court to review the law in the abstract; and the Court has consistently emphasised in its decisions that it will confine itself to the particular facts of the concrete case before it.[85] Thus, in *Wingrove v* **22.31**

---

[76] See eg *Adolf v Austria* (1992) 4 EHRR 313, para 49; *Eckle v Germany* (1982) 5 EHRR 1 para 66; *Groppera Radio AG v Switzerland* (1990) 12 EHRR 321 para 47; *Lüdi v Switzerland* (1992) 15 EHRR 173 para 34; *Amuur v France* (1996) 22 EHRR 533 para 36; *Balmer-Schafroth v Switzerland* (1997) 25 EHHR 598; for the relevant principles which apply to compensation see para 21.30ff above.

[77] *Times Newspapers v United Kingdom* (1990) 65 DR 307, EComm HR.

[78] Harris, O'Boyle and Warbrick (n 71 above) 633 suggest that these two English decisions together with *Open Door Counselling and Dublin Well Woman v Ireland* (1992) 15 EHRR 244 demonstrate the elasticity of the notion of victim in the Convention case law; and draw attention to the uncertain and shifting boundaries between those who are directly affected and those who are remotely affected.

[79] P van Dijk and G van Hoof describe the reasoning as not very convincing: *Theory and Practice of the European Convention on Human Rights* (3rd edn, Kluwer, 1998) 51.

[80] (1984) 38 DR 74, EComm HR.

[81] [1983] 1 AC 280.

[82] *Times Newspapers Ltd v United Kingdom* (1985) 41 DR 123, EComm HR.

[83] *X v Ireland* (1960) 3 YB 220; *X Association v Sweden* (1982) 28 DR 204; the position may be different for public interest groups under the Human Rights Act, see para 22.44ff below.

[84] (1990) 13 EHRR CD 116; contrast the position for judicial review where Greenpeace has established that it has standing to bring proceedings: see *R v Secretary of State for the Environment, ex p Greenpeace* [1994] 4 All ER 352.

[85] See eg *Golder v United Kingdom* (1975) 1 EHRR 524 para 39; *Young James and Webster v United Kingdom* (1981) 4 EHRR 38 para 53; *Kokkinakis v Greece* (1993) 17 EHRR 397 para 35.

United Kingdom[86] the Court rejected the argument that the law of blasphemy was discriminatory because it only protected Christianity:

> It is true that the English law of blasphemy only extends to the English faith. . . . However, it is not for the European Court to rule *in abstracto* as to the compatibility of the domestic law with the Convention. The extent to which English law protects other beliefs is not an issue before the Court which must confine its attention to the case before it (see *Klass v Germany)*.[87] The uncontested fact that the law of blasphemy does not treat on an equal footing the different religions practised in the United Kingdom does not detract from the legitimacy of the aim pursued in the present context.

Therefore, men in general who have complained that legislation on abortion breaches the Convention have failed to prove they are victims.[88] Furthermore, a complainant will not succeed in proving he is a 'victim' where he lodges a grievance on behalf of others.[89]

(c) Past breaches of Convention rights

22.32 It is sometimes argued that if the Convention violation terminates before the complaint is examined, then the applicant can no longer prove he is a victim. However, the Court has rejected this contention. In *De Jong, Baljet and Van der Brink v Holland*[90] the applicants could not claim they had been unlawfully detained in breach of Article 6(3) since the time spent in custody on remand had been deducted from their final sentence. The Court held that the deduction did not remove the status of victim although the position might have been different if the national courts had acknowledged that the Convention had been violated. Similarly, in *Inze v Austria*[91] the Court ruled that a settlement between the parties did not deprive the complainant of his victim status although the position might be different if the national authorities had acknowledged the breach and given redress. However, in *Guillemin v France*[92] the Court took the view that the applicant remained a victim despite the fact that the Government had acknowledged the principle of compensation for the breach of her property rights; she still remained *dispossessed* of her property without compensation.

[86] (1996) 24 EHRR 1 para 50.

[87] (1978) 2 EHRR 214 para 33.

[88] See eg *X v Norway* (1961) 4 YB 270; *X v Austria* (1977) 7 DR 87; *Webster v United Kingdom* (1978) 12 DR 168; but contrast *Brüggemann and Scheuten v Germany* (1978) 10 DR 100; however, a man is a victim where he complains about abortion in relation to his wife or partner: see *X v United Kingdom* (1980) 19 DR 244, EComm HR; *Hercz v Norway* (1992) 73 DR 155.

[89] *Leigh, Guardian Newspapers and Observer v United Kingdom* (1984) 38 DR 74; *Hodgson, Woolf Productions and National Union of Journalists and Channel 4 Television v United Kingdom* (1987) 10 EHRR 503, EComm HR.

[90] (1984) 8 EHRR 20.

[91] (1987) 10 EHRR 394.

[92] (1997) 25 EHHR 435.

Where an applicant dies during the course of proceedings, his family (such as his spouse[93] or parents)[94] are entitled to be regarded as victims for the purpose of maintaining his claim. However, an heir may not seek to enforce rights which are personal to the deceased.[95] 22.33

(d) Shareholders as victims

The position concerning shareholders who claim they are victims of violations of Convention rights affecting the company they own is complex; and has radically altered following the decision of the Court in *Agrotexim and others v Greece*.[96] The Commission had taken the view in a number of cases that majority shareholders may succeed in claiming they are victims of breaches of Convention rights which belong to the company;[97] and in *Yarrow v United Kingdom*[98] it held that a minority shareholder was not a victim. However, in *Agrotexim Hellis v Greece*[99] the Commission decided that the sole criterion was not whether the applicants were a majority shareholder: it decided to take account of the fact that the shareholders also had a direct interest in the subject matter of the application and the fact that because the company was in liquidation, the company could not reasonably lodge an application on its own behalf. It accepted that where a violation of a company's rights resulted in a fall in value of its shares there was automatically an infringment of the shareholders' rights.[100] 22.34

This approach was rejected by the Court which drew attention to the potential difficulties which might arise if minority shareholders disagreed. The court concluded that: 22.35

> the piercing of the 'corporate veil' will be justified only in exceptional circumstances, in particular, where it is clearly established that it is impossible for the company to apply to the Convention institutions through the organs set up under the articles of incorporation or—in the event of liquidation—through the liquidators.[101]

The Court went on to conclude that the fact the company was in liquidation was no bar to an application being made alleging a breach of Convention rights. The

93 See eg *Deweer v Belgium* (1980) 2 EHRR 439; *Silver v United Kingdom* (1983) 5 EHRR 347; *Colozza v Italy* (1985) 7 EHRR 516; *Vocaturo v Italy* (1991) Series A No 206-C; *Funke v France* (1993) 16 EHRR 297; *Brannigan and McBride v United Kingdom* (1993) 17 EHRR 539; *Raimondo v Italy* (1994) 18 EHRR 237; *Ahmet Sadik v Greece* (1996) 24 EHRR 323.

94 *X v France* (1992) 14 EHRR 483; *Aksoy v Turkey* (1996) 23 EHHR 553.

95 *Kofler v Italy* (1982) 30 DR 5, EComm HR.

96 (1995) 21 EHRR 250.

97 See eg *X v Austria* (1966) 9 YB 112, EComm HR; *Kaplan v United Kingdom* (1980) 21 DR 5, EComm HR; *Agrotexim Hellis v Greece* (1992) 72 DR 148.

98 (1983) 30 DR 155, EComm HR.

99 n 96 above.

100 Ibid para 64.

101 Ibid para 66.

application could have been made through the liquidators and the minority shareholders had no standing as 'victims' to apply to the Court.

22.36 This can be contrasted with the case of *Neves e Silva v Portugal*[102] which concerned a claim by a minority shareholder that his case had not been determined by the national authorities within a reasonable time in breach of Article 6 of the Convention.[103] The Court decided that he was a victim and that his status as a minority shareholder was irrelevant for the purposes of his claim under Article 6.[103a] In *Pine Valley Developments v Ireland*[104] the Court declined to distinguish between an individual and the companies he controlled when applying the victim test on the ground that the companies were no more than a vehicle through which he proposed to implement planning permission.

(4) Potential, future and indirect victims

(a) Potential victims

22.37 Sections 7(1) and section 7(3) of the Human Rights Act both refer to someone who 'is (or would be) a victim'. Section 7(6), on the other hand, refers to a person who 'is a victim'. As a result, it is arguable that the effect of sections 7(1) and (3) is to widen the category of victims under the Human Rights Act to include *potential* victims. In the light of the Convention case law concerning potential victims, this may not matter.

22.38 Both the Commission and the Court have ruled that a complainant may be a victim even though he cannot establish with *certainty* that his Convention rights have been violated. The basic principle was described by the Court in *Markcx v Belgium*:[105]

> Article [34] entitles individuals to contend that a law violates their rights by itself in the absence of an individual measure of implementation if they run the risk of being directly affected by it.

The Court went on to hold that the applicants risked being directly affected by legislation concerning illegitimate children.[106] The Court has also accepted that homosexuals are victims where homosexual acts between consenting adult males are criminal; the very existence of the legislation continuously and directly affects their private life.[107] The same reasoning was applied by the Commission in

---

[102] (1989) 13 EHRR 535.
[103] For the right to a hearing within a reasonable time, see para 11.219ff above.
[103a] *Neves e Silva v Portugal* (n 102 above) para 39.
[104] (1991) 14 EHRR 319.
[105] (1979) 2 EHRR 330 para 27.
[106] See also *Johnston v Ireland* (1986) 9 EHRR 203.
[107] *Dudgeon v United Kingdom* (1981) 4 EHRR 149; *Norris v Ireland* (1988) 13 EHRR 186; *Modinos v Cyprus* (1993) 16 EHRR 485.

relation to women making complaints against abortion legislation[108] and by parents challenging legislation prohibiting corporal punishment of their children.[109]

22.39 However, the broad view taken of victims in *Klass v Germany*[110] in secret surveillance cases has not been applied in subsequent applications. Where legislation requires notification of surveillance to the person concerned, the applicant will not generally be able to establish that he is a victim without showing that he received such notification.[111] Similarly, where an individual claims he has been the subject of security checks, it is necessary for him to show there is a reasonable likelihood that the security forces have compiled and retained personal information.[112]

(b) Future victims

22.40 A person may be a victim if there is a risk that his Convention rights will be breached in the future. In *Soering v United Kingdom*[113] the applicant sought to prevent his extradition to the United States where he was likely to face the death sentence which he claimed was inhuman treatment contrary to Article 3.[114] Even so, at the time of his application he had not been treated in breach of Article 3 nor had he been extradited. Nevertheless, the Court said:[115]

> It is not normal for Convention institutions to pronounce on the existence or otherwise of potential violations of the Convention. However, where an applicant claims that a decision to extradite him would, if implemented, be contrary to Article 3 by reason of its foreseeable consequences in the requesting country, a departure from this principle is necessary in view of the serious and irreparable nature of the alleged suffering risked, in order to ensure the effectiveness of the safeguard provided by that Article . . .

Similarly, the Commission has held that a person whose extradition to the United States, where he would be subject to the death row phenomenon of excessive delay, might be a victim.[116]

22.41 Where an individual is being expelled to a country where he claims he will be inhumanly treated contrary to Article 3,[117] the Commission has held in a number of

108 *Bruggemann and Scheuten v Germany* (1978) 10 DR 100.
109 *Seven individuals v Sweden* (1982) 29 DR 104, EComm HR.
110 (1978) 2 EHRR 214; see para 12.105 above.
111 *Mersch v Luxembourg* (1985) 43 DR 34, EComm HR; *M S and P S v Switzerland* (1985) 44 DR 175, EComm HR.
112 Contrast *N v United Kingdom* (1988) 58 DR 85, EComm HR where the applicant succeeded in showing that he was a victim with *Hilton v United Kingdom* (1988) 57 DR 108, EComm HR.
113 (1989) 11 EHRR 439.
114 See para 8.28 above.
115 (1989) 11 EHRR 439 para 90.
116 *Kirkwood v United Kingdom* (1984) 37 DR 158, EComm HR.
117 See para 8.28 above.

cases that he can claim to be a victim.[118] However, where the applicant is expelled, he will only establish he is a victim if the expulsion order to the country of destination has actually been made.[119]

(c) Indirect victims

22.42 In some circumstances an applicant can claim he is a victim of a breach of a Convention right affecting *another* person. Thus, a spouse has the standing to complain about the treatment of her husband,[120] a brother about his twin brother[121] and a mother about the detention of her son.[122] The Court has held that a widow has a moral interest on her own behalf as an indirect victim where her husband was executed as a result of an alleged miscarriage of justice[123] and the Commission reached the same conclusion in relation to a claim of a widow following the terrorist killing of her husband and unmarried brother.[124] Similarly, in *Paton v United Kingdom*[125] the Commission held that a prospective father was a victim when he claimed that abortion denied the right to life of a foetus.

22.43 The principle of indirect victim was further developed in *Open Door Counselling and Dublin Well Woman v Ireland*[126] where injunctions prevented two women of child bearing age from providing information to pregnant women about the location, identity or method of communication with abortion clinics in England. The Court took the view that the two women were victims because they belong to a class of women which might be adversely affected by the injunctions.

(5) **Public interest challenges under the Human Rights Act**

22.44 One of the most controversial issues during the passage of the Human Rights Act[127] was the question of whether the narrow definition of standing under the Act prevents a public interest applicant in judicial review proceedings from advancing any arguments about breaches of the Human Rights Act: even though it would have *locus standi* to allege that a public body has acted *ultra vires* its statu-

[118] *A v France* (1991) 68 DR 319; *V v France* (1991) 70 DR 298; *Voulfovitch v Sweden* (1993) 74 DR 199.

[119] Contrast *Soering v United Kingdom* (1989) 11 EHRR 439 (where the Home Secretary had signed the warrant of extradition) with *Vijayanathan and Pusparajah v France* (1992) 15 EHRR 62 (where no expulsion order had been made).

[120] See eg *X and Y v Belgium* (1963) 6 YB 590.

[121] See eg *X v Belgium* (1978) 8 DR 220.

[122] See eg *Y v Austria* (1962) 8 CD 136.

[123] *Nölkenbockhoff v Germany* (1987) 10 EHRR 163.

[124] *Mrs W v Ireland* (1983) 32 DR 211, EComm HR; and see eg *Amekrane v United Kingdom* (1973) 16 YB 356, EComm HR; *Wolfgram v Germany* (1986) 49 DR 213, EComm HR; *Stewart v United Kingdom* (1984) 39 DR 162, EComm HR.

[125] (1980) 19 DR 244.

[126] (1992) 15 EHRR 244, EComm HR.

[127] See para 3.84 above.

tory powers by contravening fundamental rights[128] or has acted in a manner which is incompatible with European Community law.

The wording of section 7(3) on its face suggests that a public interest claimant does not have standing to bring judicial review proceedings alleging that a public authority has acted incompatibly with a Convention right under the Human Rights Act. Section 7(3) also appears to preclude a public interest claimant from bringing proceedings to quash subordinate legislation under the Human Rights Act, as in *R v Secretary of State for Social Security, ex p Joint Council for the Welfare of Immigrants*[129] where a pressure group obtained a declaration that subordinate legislation was *ultra vires* the parent legislation because it breached fundamental human rights. **22.45**

However, there may be scope for public interest claimants to bring proceedings on an alternative basis to making a claim under section 7 as a 'victim'. First, it is arguable that a challenge that delegated legislation is *ultra vires* its primary legislation is a conventional application of administrative law principles.[130] During the Committee Stage of the Bill, the Home Secretary, Jack Straw MP said: **22.46**

> the courts already have the power to strike down subordinate legislation . . . If they feel that a statutory instrument has been introduced in a way that is *ultra vires* the primary legislation, they may do so. When we discussed the matter in detail in the Cabinet Ministerial Sub-Committee on Incorporation of the European Convention on Human Rights, it seemed to us that, as that power was already there, it would be very odd not to allow courts to strike down subordinate legislation if it was not compatible with the [Act].

It is submitted that there is no justification for construing section 7(3) so as to preclude a public interest group from pursuing this sort of conventional administrative law claim.

Secondly, it may be[131] open to a public law claimant to seek an advisory declaration[132] that primary (or secondary) legislation must be read and given effect to in **22.47**

---

128 See para 1.20 above.

129 [1997] 1 WLR 275; for a further discussion of the case, see para 5.106 above.

130 This argument is developed by S Grosz, J Beatson and P Duffy, *Human Rights: The 1998 Act and the European Convention* (Sweet & Maxwell, 2000) para 4–44; but see D Feldman, 'Remedies for Violations of Convention Rights Under the Human Rights Act' [1998] EHRLR 691 who argues that such a challenge must fall within s 7 because it is an 'act' for the purposes of s 6(6).

131 See generally Grosz, Beatson and Duffy (n 130 above); for a contrary view, see M Supperstone and J Coppel, 'Judicial Review after the Human Rights Act' [1999] EHRLR 301.

132 See eg *Royal College of Nursing of the United Kingdom v Department of Health and Social Security* [1981] AC 800; *Airedale NHS Trust v Bland* [1993] AC 789; *In re S (Hospital Patient: Court's Jurisdiction)* [1996] Fam 1; and see I Zamir and Lord Woolf, *The Declaratory Judgment* (2nd edn, Sweet & Maxwell, 1993) paras 4.043–4.052; Sir John Laws in 'Judicial Remedies and the Constitution' (1994) 57 MLR 213 argues that declarations may be awarded in relation to hypothetical questions which have a real practical purpose even though there may be no immediate situation where the decision will have a practical effect; and see also, D Kolinsky, 'Advisory Declarations: Recent Developments' [1999] JR 231.

a way which is compatible with Convention rights under section 3 of the Human Rights Act.[133] It is submitted that there is no reason in principle why proceedings based on section 3 should be defeated by the statutory provision which prescribes the procedure for making section 6 claims. Local authorities (and other public bodies) would also benefit if they could obtain a declaration that particular statutory provision or Government guidance required them to act incompatibly with Convention rights.

22.48 The ability of a claimant to seek a section 3 declaration is comparable to the procedure whereby a local authority takes proceedings in order to obtain guidance about the exercise of its statutory functions.[134] It is probable that public bodies cannot be 'victims' for the purposes of section 7[135] and if they could not seek 'advisory declarations' in relation to Human Rights Act issues they would be unable to obtain the guidance of the Court in an important area.

22.49 A liberal approach towards taking proceedings under the Human Rights Act can be justified on the principle that the Human Rights Act should be given a broad and generous meaning.[136] It also receives some support from the safeguard in section 11(b) which states that:

> A person's reliance on a Convention right does not restrict—. . .
> (b) his right to make any claim or bring any proceedings which he could make or bring apart from section 7 to 9.

The possibility of these alternative avenues for taking proceedings does not, however, detract from the criticisms expressed when the bill was being debated.[137] The narrow definition of standing under section 7(3) of the Act is much more restrictive that the generous approach to *locus standi* in judicial review proceedings;[138] and the apparent prohibition on public interest claimants taking section 6 proceedings is difficult to justify.

C. Commencing Proceedings

(1) The appropriate court

(a) The basic principle

22.50 The general rule for identifying the particular court or tribunal in which proceedings should be brought is set out in section 7(1) of the Act. Section 7(1) states:

---

133 See generally para 4.04ff above.

134 See eg *R v Secretary of State for the Environment, ex p Tower Hamlets London Borough Council* [1993] QB 632; *R v Secretary of State for the Environment, ex p Lancashire County Council* [1994] 4 All ER 165.

135 See para 22.14ff above.

136 See para 3.06ff above.

137 See para 3.84ff above.

138 See para 3.85 above.

> A person who claims that a public authority has acted (or proposes to act) in a way which is made unlawful by section 6(1) may—
>
> (a) bring proceedings against the authority under this Act in the appropriate court or tribunal; or
>
> (b) rely on the Convention right or rights concerned in any proceedings
>
> but only if he is (or would be) a victim of an unlawful act.

By section 7(2) it is provided that 'appropriate court or tribunal' means such court or tribunal as may be determined in accordance with the rules.[139]

The Human Rights Act does not make any specific provision as to the court or tribunal in which proceedings should be brought. It seems that these rules will only make provision as to the court in which damages claims should be brought after a finding of section 6 unlawfulness by a court which has no power to award damages. **22.51**

It could be argued that because proceedings brought against a public authority under section 7(1)(a) involve public law rather than private law rights, they should be brought under the 'judicial review procedure'. There is a general procedural rule that public law claims can only be brought by way of judicial review. This rule itself derives from *O'Reilly v Mackman*[140] In that case a number of prisoners alleged that disciplinary decisions of the Boards of Visitors had breached the rules of natural justice and sought declarations that those decisions were a nullity by proceedings brought as writ actions or in some instances by an originating summons. The prison authorities applied to strike out these proceedings as an abuse of process under RSC Order 18, rule 19. The House of Lords unanimously decided that the proceedings should be struck out. As Lord Diplock observed: **22.52**

> it would in my view as a general rule be contrary to public policy, and as such an abuse of the process of the court to permit a person seeking to establish that a decision of a public authority infringed rights to which he is entitled to protection under public law to proceed by way of an ordinary action and by this means to evade the provisions of Order 53 for the protection of such authorities.

In recent years the courts have taken a flexible approach to the exclusivity

[139] As defined by s 7(9), see para 22.56 below.

[140] [1983] 2 AC 236; the decision was described as an unfortunate decision in the Justice/All Souls Review of Administrative Law, *Administrative Justice* (Clarendon, 1988) para 6.18 and as a step backwards towards the old forms of action which were deservedly buried in 1852: see H Wade and C Forsyth, *Administrative Law* (7th edn, Clarendon Press, 1994) 682. However, Lord Woolf and J Jowell, *De Smith, Woolf and Jowell, Judicial Review of Administrative Action* (5th edn, Sweet & Maxwell, 1995) para 3-082 argue that the decision has served administrative law in England well because it has encouraged the judiciary to extend the scope of judicial review; see, generally, C Lewis, *Judicial Remedies in Public Law* (2nd edn, Sweet & Maxwell, 2000) paras 3-01–3-058.

principle.[141] Lord Slynn stressed in *Mercury Communications Ltd v Director General of Telecommunication* :[142]

> It is of particular importance, as I see it, to retain some flexibility as the precise limits of what is called 'public law' and what is called 'private law' are by no means worked out. The experience of other countries seems to show that the working out of this distinction is not always an easy matter. In the absence of a single procedure allowing all remedies—quashing, injunctive and declaratory relief, damages—some flexibility as to the use of different procedures is necessary. It has to be borne in mind that the overriding question is whether the proceedings constitute an abuse of process.

The impact of the Civil Procedure Rules on the exclusivity rule was considered in detail in *Clark v University of Lincolnshire*[142a] where Sedley LJ said that the CPR:

> have given substance to the suggestion[142b] that the mode of commencement of proceedings should not matter, and what should matter is whether the choice of procedure (which is represented by the indentification of the issues) is critical to the outcome. This focuses attention on what in my view is the single important difference between judicial review and civil suit, the differing time limits. To permit what is in substance a public law challenge to be brought as of right six years later if the relationship is also contractual will in many circumstances circumvent the valuable provision . . . that applications for leave must be made promptly and in any event within three months.

22.53 It is submitted that the rule of 'procedural exclusivity' does not apply to proceedings under the Human Rights Act. There are two reasons for this. First, section 7 itself makes no provision for any such exclusivity. The wording of section 7(3) ('If the proceedings are brought on an application for judicial review . . .') strongly implies that the bringing of judicial review proceedings is *optional* rather than compulsory. Secondly, such an exclusivity rule would be inconsistent with the status of the Human Rights Act as a 'constitutional instrument'.[143] In the absence of any statutory restrictions the courts should develop a flexible and non technical approach in order to ensure that the safeguards afforded by Convention rights are 'practical and effective'.[144] This is also consistent with the approach of the Civil Procedure Rules.

[141] See eg *Roy v Kensington and Chelsea and Westminster Family Practitioners' Committee* [1992] 1 AC 624; *Boddington v British Transport Police* [1999] 2 AC 143; *British Steel plc v Customs and Excise Commissioners* [1997] 2 All ER 366; *Trustees of the Dennis Rye Pension Fund v Sheffield County Council* [1998] 1 WLR 840; *Steed v Home Office* [2000] 1 WLR 1169; and see eg Lewis (n 140 above) Chap 3.

[142] [1996] 1 WLR 48, 57.

[142a] [2000] 3 All ER 752, 757.

[142b] The suggestion refers to the discussion in *De Smith, Woolf and Jowell, Judicial Review and Administrative Action* (3rd edn, Sweet & Maxwell, 1995) at para 3-078–3-081.

[143] See para 3.04ff above.

[144] See *Loizidou v Turkey (Preliminary Objections)* (1995) 20 EHRR 99 para 72; for a general discussion of this principle of construction, see para 6.28 above; and cf *Jaundoo v A-G of Guyana* [1971] AC 972 (in the absence of rules governing applications for constitutional redress an application could be made by any form of procedure).

In other words, it is submitted that proceedings under section 7(1)(a) can be brought: 22.54

- in the Chancery Division or Queen's Bench Division of the High Court by either a Claim Form[145] or, if there is unlikely to be a substantial dispute of fact, under the CPR Part 8 procedure;
- in the county court, by issue of a claim form;
- in the Crown Office, by filing a Notice of Application in Form 86A.[146]

It follows from the fact that courts and tribunals[147] are public authorities for the purposes of the Human Rights Act[148] that Convention rights can be 'relied on' in any proceedings before any court or tribunal.[149]

If, however, Human Rights Acts claims are joined to other public or private law claims, then there will be some procedural restrictions on the appropriate court arising out of the practice and procedure governing *non*-Human Rights Act claims: 22.55

- if a Human Rights Act claim is joined to a private law claim falling exclusively within the jurisdiction of a particular court[150] then it should be commenced in that court;
- if a Human Rights Act claim is joined to an application for judicial review of a decision of a public body on grounds other than illegality under section 6, it should be brought by way of judicial review;
- if a Human Rights Act claim involves an application for a 'public law remedy' such as *certiorari*, it should be brought by way of an application for judicial review.

(b) Rules of court

Section 7 makes it clear that the question of identifying the appropriate court in which proceedings must be commenced will depend on the rules of procedure. Section 7(2) states that: 22.56

> In subsection (1)(a) 'an appropriate court or tribunal' means such court or tribunal as may be determined in accordance with the rules; and proceedings against an authority include a counterclaim or similar proceeding.

Section 7(9) states that:

---

145 Under CPR, Pt 7.
146 CPR Sch 1 R 53.
147 For a discussion of these terms see para 5.42ff above.
148 See s 6(3) and the discussion at para 5.38ff above.
149 Although the remedies which can be granted by tribunals may be limited, see para 21.05ff above.
150 For example, a claim for defamation which can only be dealt with by the High Court.

In this section 'rules' means—

(a) in relation to proceedings before a court or tribunal outside Scotland, rules made by the Lord Chancellor, or the Secretary of State for the purpose of this section or rules of court . . .

22.57 The Lord Chancellor's department has suggested[150a] that a free standing case under section 7(1)(a) can be brought *either* by way of judicial review or in the County Court or the High Court where a claim for damages is made and that the normal jurisdictional limits should apply.[150b] Under the proposed rules, any claim in respect of a judicial act which would be heard in the County Court will be transferred to the Crown Office in the High Court.[150c]

(2) Time limits

(a) The 12-month rule

22.58 Section 7(5) of the Human Rights Act sets out the time limits that will apply to any proceedings brought by a claimant against a public authority[151] claiming a breach of section 6(1) under section 7(1)(a)[152] of the Act. If, however, a person simply relies on Convention rights in any legal proceedings under section 7(1)(b),[153] there will be no such time limits. Section 7(5) of the Human Rights Act states:

Proceedings under subsection (1)(a) must be brought before the end of—

(a) the period of one year beginning with the date on which the act complained of took place; or

(b) such longer period as the court or tribunal considers equitable having regard to all the circumstances,

but that is subject to any rule imposing a stricter time limit in relation to the procedure in question.

Section 7(5) does not affect the ordinary limitation periods that apply to *other* causes of action and would not, for example, affect the six-year period for actions in tort such as false imprisonment, trespass, assault or misfeasance in a public office.[154] Similarly, the fact that an applicant alleges a breach of Convention rights does not entitle him to extend time in commencing a statutory appeal outside the 28-day period allowed by CPR, Sch 1 R 55.

[150a] Consultation Paper, *Human Rights Act 1998: Rules*, CP5/00, Mar 2000, para 12.

[150b] Most importantly, proceedings cannot be started in the High Court unless the value of the claim is £15,000 or more, PD 7, para 2.1.

[150c] CPR, r 30.9 and PD 30, para 7.1. These rules are to be inserted under the Human Rights Act, see App C in Vol 2.

[151] See para 5.03ff above.

[152] See para 22.50ff above.

[153] A person may rely on a Convention right in various ways; see generally, para 22.03 above.

[154] See Limitation Act 1980, s 2.

22.59 The 12-month period will be computed from the date of the 'act complained of'. The word 'act' is defined in broad terms in section 6(6) of the Human Rights Act.[155] However, section 6(6) contemplates that an 'act' is a specific event occurring at a particular point in time and means that time will run under the Human Rights Act from the particular date when the specific event takes place. The legislation therefore contains no statutory provision comparable to that in the sex,[156] race[157] or disability[158] discrimination legislation which enables a claimant to extend time by pointing to an act extending over time (such as a policy or regime) which is treated as taking place at the end of that period of time.[159]

(b) The general power to extend time

22.60 Section 7(5)(b) of the Human Rights Act permits a court or tribunal to extend the 12-month period for 'such longer period as the court or tribunal considers equitable having regard to all the circumstances'. The discretion to be invoked is defined in very wide terms. The discretion to extend will only come into play where the complainant is able to identify a fact or circumstance which makes it equitable to *displace* the general rule; if there is such a fact or circumstance, then the court must ascertain the longer period for which it considers time should be extended. Section 7(5)(b) is neutral as to which party has the burden of proof. It seems that the court or tribunal must satisfy itself that it is equitable having regard to all the circumstances to extend time.

22.61 The provision for extending time under the Human Rights Act is similar in language to that contained in the Sex Discrimination Act 1975,[160] the Race Relations Act 1976[161] and the Disability Discrimination Act 1995.[162] It may therefore be of assistance to examine the principles which have evolved when extending time in discrimination cases. The Employment Appeal Tribunal has emphasised that the discretion to be applied is a very wide one and has deprecated the possibility that very simple wide words might become encrusted with the barnacles of authority.[163] It has therefore held that an industrial tribunal had erred in law when examining the authorities on the meaning of 'equitable' under the Limitation Acts.[164]

155 See para 5.100ff above.
156 Sex Discrimination Act 1975, s 76(6)(b).
157 Race Relations Act 1976, s 68(6)(b).
158 Disability Discrimination Act 1995, Sch 3, para 3(3).
159 See, in particular, *Cast v Croyden College* [1998] ICR 500.
160 s 76(5).
161 s 68(6).
162 Sch 3, para 3(2).
163 *Hutchinson v Westward Television Ltd* [1977] ICR 279.
164 *Hawkins v Ball* [1996] IRLR 258.

Furthermore, a tribunal is entitled to extend time where the applicant's advisors have failed to appreciate the true legal position.[165]

(c) The exceptions to the 12-month rule

22.62 Section 7(5) of the Human Rights Act expressly states that the general 12-month rule is subject to any rule imposing a stricter time limit in relation to the procedure in question. In particular, section 7(5) ensures that where claims under the Human Rights Act are to be made in judicial review proceedings, the time limit in judicial review will apply.[166] CPR Sch 1 R 53.4(1) requires that an application for judicial review shall be made promptly and, in any event within three months from the date when grounds[167] for the application first arose, unless the court considers that there is good reason for extending the period within which the application shall be made.

22.63 Whenever there has been undue delay in making an application in accordance with CPR Sch 1 R 53.4(1),[168] the court is entitled under section 31(6) of the Supreme Court Act 1981 to refuse permission to proceed (or to refuse to grant relief at the substantive application) if it considers that granting relief would be likely to cause substantial hardship to (or substantially prejudice the rights of) any person[169] or would be detrimental to good administration.[170] If a public body wishes to challenge an application on the grounds of undue delay, it must do so at the permission stage; the House of Lords held in *R v Criminal Injuries Compensation Board, ex p A*[171] that once permission was granted, the substantive challenge can only be dismissed for delay on the statutory grounds permitted by section 31(6).

22.64 It is now routine for permission to be refused or the court to hold that an applicant is guilty of delay even where he has applied for judicial review within three

165 *British Coal Corporation v Keeble* [1997] IRLR 336.

166 For a fuller treatment, see eg Lord Woolf and J Jowell, *De Smith, Woolf and Jowell, Judicial Review of Administrative Action* (5th edn, Sweet & Maxwell, 1995) paras 15-019–15-023; R Clayton and H Tomlinson, *Judicial Review Procedure* (2nd edn, John Wiley Chancery Law, 1997) Chap 5; M Beloff , 'Time, Time, Time's On My Side, Yes It Is' in C Forsyth and I Hare (eds), *The Golden Metwand and the Crooked Cord* (Clarendon Press, 1998).

167 See *R v Secretary of State for Trade and Industry, ex p Greenpeace* [1998] Env LR 414; and see eg J Beatson, 'Prematurity and Ripeness for Review' in C Forsyth and I Hare (eds), *The Golden Metwand and the Crooked Cord* (n 166 above).

168 *R v Dairy Produce Quota Tribunal for England and Wales, ex p Caswell* [1990] 2 AC 738, 747.

169 There need be no causal connection between the prejudice and undue delay; all that is needed is a causal connection between prejudice and granting relief: see *R v Secretary of State for Health, ex p Furneaux* [1994] 2 All ER 652.

170 Although the House of Lords did not formulate a definition of 'good administration' in *R v Dairy Produce Quota Tribunal for England and Wales, ex p Caswell* [1990] AC 738, the Court of Appeal indicated that a respondent must show that the delay has caused positive harm including positive harm to potential applicants: see [1989] 1 WLR 1089.

171 [1999] 2 AC 330.

months.[172] If, however, an application is out of time, an extension may be granted if the applicant proves[173] there is a good reason for delay although the court may still refuse to grant permission in the exercise of its discretion.[174] No definition of 'good reason' is found in the rules or the case law[175] but time has been extended where the delay is caused by the time taken to obtain a legal aid certificate,[176] by exhausting other administrative remedies[177] or where the matters raised are of general importance.[178] It is unclear whether delay by the applicant's advisors amounts to a good reason for delay.[179] However, the fact that the applicant has been engaged in attempts to obtain political redress does not constitute a good reason for delay.[180]

Although a litigant who delays in making an application is always at risk because of the undue delay in and of itself,[181] Woolf LJ suggested in *R v Commissioner for Local Administration, ex p Croydon London Borough Council*[182] that as long as no prejudice is caused, a litigant will not be deprived of his remedy. This argument may have particular force where an applicant is invoking Convention rights under the Human Rights Act. **22.65**

(d) Time limits and judicial review proceedings

The time limits in ordinary judicial review proceedings are stricter than those for Human Rights Act claims: the application must be brought promptly and in any event within three months.[183] One of the reasons for the 'exclusivity rule'—as a **22.66**

[172] See eg *R v Independent Television Commission, ex p TV NI Ltd*, *The Times*, 30 Dec1991; in *R v Credigion County Council, ex p McKeon* [1998] 2 PLR 1 Laws J took the view that applications in planning cases should be made within six weeks; but see, J Howell, 'Delay and Planning Judicial Review: 6 Weeks or Out?' [1999] JR 9.

[173] *R v Warwickshire County Council, ex p Collymore* [1995] ELR 217, 228.

[174] *R v City of Westminster, ex p Hilditch* [1990] COD 434.

[175] R Leiper, 'What is a "Good Reason" for Extending Time?' [1996] JR 212.

[176] *R v Stratford-on-Avon District Council, ex p Jackson* [1985] 1 WLR 1319, 1324; and see *R v Governors of La Sainte Union Covenant School, ex p T* [1996] ELR 98.

[177] See eg *R v Rochdale Metropolitan Borough Council, ex p Cromer Ring Mill Ltd* [1982] 3 All ER 761; *R v Wareham Magistrates' Court, ex p Seldon* [1988] 1 WLR 825.

[178] See eg *R v Secretary of State for the Home Department, ex p Ruddock* [1987] 1 WLR 1482; *R v Ministry of Agriculure, Fisheries and Food, ex p Dairy Trade Federation* [1995] COD 3; it has been suggested that reliance on a Convention right in itself may be held to amount to a good reason: see T de la Mare, 'The Human Rights Act 1998: The Impact On Judicial Review' [1999] JR 32.

[179] Delay was excused in eg *R v Secretary of State for Home Department, ex p Oyeleye* [1994] Imm AR 268; *R v Newham LBC, ex p Gentle* (1994) 26 HLR 466; but was not acceptable in *R v Isle of Wight County Council, ex p O'Keefe* (1990) 59 P & CR 283; and *R v Tavistock General Commissioners, ex p Worth* [1985] STC 564 where the delay was caused by the applicant's accountant.

[180] See eg *R v London Borough of Bexley, ex p Barnehurst Golf Club Ltd* [1992] COD 382; to seek assistance of Members of Parliament (*R v London Borough of Redbridge, ex p G* [1991] COD 398) or to organise a Parliamentary lobby (*R v Secretary of State for Health, ex p Alcohol Recovery Project* [1993] COD 344).

[181] See, in particular, *R v Criminal Injury Compensation Board, ex p A* [1998] 1 WLR 277.

[182] [1989] 1 ALL ER 1033, 1046.

[183] CPR Sch 1 R 53.4(1).

result of which it was obligatory to bring public law claims in judicial review proceedings[184]—was to prevent 'tardy' attacks on the decisions of public authorities.[185]

22.67 It could be argued that it would be an abuse of the process to raise a Human Rights Act issue in proceedings brought outside the three month time limit for the same reasons as it is an abuse to seek to bring public law claims by ordinary action. It is submitted that this approach is incorrect because the exclusivity rule has no application in relation to Human Rights Act claims.[186] The time limit laid down by section 7(5) is 12 months and it could not be an abuse of the process to bring proceedings within that time period by ordinary action.

22.68 The position will, however, be different in relation to Human Rights Act claims brought in judicial review proceedings. Section 7(5) provides that the 12-month time limit is 'subject to any rule imposing a stricter time limit in relation to the procedure in question'. The stricter time limits in the judicial review procedure will, therefore, apply to Human Rights Act claims brought in judicial review proceedings.

(e) The impact of time limits

22.69 The existence of strict time limits is unlikely to create difficulties where the claim under the Human Rights Act focuses on a specific event such as a decision of a public authority to act or refuse to act in way which is alleged to be incompatible with a Convention right.

22.70 However, complications may ensue where the complaint is directed at a policy of a public authority which is said to violate Convention rights. The grounds for a judicial review application may arise long before a specific decision is made. As Laws J stated in *R v Secretary of State for Trade and Industry, ex p Greenpeace*:[187]

> a judicial review applicant must move against the substantive act or decision which is the real basis of his complaint. If, after the act was done, he takes no steps but merely waits until something consequential and dependant on it takes place and challenges that, he runs the risk of being put out of court for being too late.

Thus, where a public authority formulates a policy which breaches the Human Rights Act, a claimant may be out of time if he seeks to judicially review an adverse decision in line with that policy.

---

[184] See para 22.52 above.

[185] See *O'Reilly v Mackman* [1983] 2 AC 236 *per* Lord Diplock at 284.

[186] See para 22.53 above.

[187] [1998] Env LR 415, 428; see *R v Secretary of State for Trade and Industry ex p Greenpeace*, *The Times*, 19 Jan 2000; and see N Pleming and K Marcus, 'Greenpeace 1 and 2: delay in judicial review' [2000] JR 6.

Claims put forward by potential victims[188] of breaches of Convention rights are also likely to generate arguments that their case has become time barred. If, for example, allegations are made that a policing operation in a particular locality has contravened Convention rights, then time will run from the date the operation began, not the date the applicant became *aware* that he was a potential victim. On the other hand, it is submitted that in such circumstances the court should treat an application to extend time sympathetically.[189] **22.71**

(3) Parties

(a) Introduction

In general, the claimant in Human Rights Act proceedings will be the 'victim' and the defendant will be the relevant public authority. There are, however, two areas where there are special rules concerning the joinder of parties. First, where a court is considering making a declaration of incompatibility on the basis that a statute cannot be construed compatibly with Convention rights under section 3 of the Act, the Crown will be entitled to receive notice. Secondly, the Act is likely to encourage public interest groups to make third party interventions in proceedings, not least because they cannot show that they are victims for the purpose of taking proceedings alleging that a public authority has acted incompatibly with Convention rights in breach of section 6(1) of the Act.[190] **22.72**

(b) Declarations of incompatibility and the Crown

Statutory provisions. Where a court or tribunal has to consider whether a particular statutory provision conflicts with the Human Rights Act, it must[191] in the first instance construe it so far as possible in a way which is compatible with the Convention rights.[192] If, however, a court cannot read and give effect to the statutory provision in a way which is compatible with Convention rights, then it will be open to the court to make a declaration of incompatibility under section 4(2)[193] of the Act. The Court must fall within the scope of section 4(5) which provides that: **22.73**

> In this section 'court' means—
>
> (a) the House of Lords;
> (b) the Judicial Committee of the Privy Council;
> (c) The Courts-Martial Appeal Court;
> (d) . . .

---

188 See para 22.37 above
189 Cf *R v London Borough of Redbridge, ex p G* [1991] COD 398.
190 See para 22.44ff above.
191 Human Rights Act 1998, s 3(1): see para 4.04ff above.
192 As defined by the Human Rights Act 1998, s 1: see para 3.43ff above.
193 See para 4.46ff above.

(e) in England and Wales or Northern Ireland, the High Court or the Court of Appeal.

22.74 Section 5 of the Human Rights Act prescribes the procedure which enables the Crown to intervene where a court is considering whether to make a declaration of incompatibility. Section 5 provides so far as is relevant that:

> (1) Where a court is considering whether to make a declaration of incompatibility, the Crown is entitled to notice in accordance with the rules of court.
>
> (2) In any case where subsection (1) applies—
>
> (a) a Minister of the Crown (or person nominated by him) . . .
>
> is entitled, on giving notice in accordance with the rules of court to be joined as a party to the proceedings.
>
> (3) Notice under subsection (2) may be given at any time during the proceedings.
>
> (4) A person who has been a party to criminal proceedings (other than in Scotland) as a result of a notice under subsection (2) may, with leave, appeal to the House of Lords against any declaration of incompatibility made in proceedings.
>
> (5) In subsection (4)—
>
> 'criminal proceedings' includes all proceedings before the Court-Martials Appeals Court; and
>
> 'leave' means leave granted by the court making the declaration of incompatibility or by the House of Lords.

22.75 **Procedure in civil proceedings.** Where the claimant brings proceedings seeking a declaration of incompatibility, it will be prudent to serve papers on the Treasury Solicitors at the outset. However, section 5(3) expressly provides that notice can be given at any time during the proceedings and it will be open to the court itself to direct that notice is given.

22.76 Where notice is given, a Minister or person nominated by him has the right to be joined as a party to the proceedings by serving notice in accordance with the rules of court. The Minister is entitled to nominate the particular person he believes to be the appropriate party in a particular case. As a party to civil proceedings, the Minister or his nominee can participate in the normal way and will have the right to appeal an adverse determination.

22.77 Under the proposed Rules of Court, where a court begins to consider whether to make a declaration of incompatibility under section 4, it must give notice to the Crown and the Minister or person nominated by him shall be joined as a party on giving notice to the court.[193a] The notice must be sent to the person named in the list published by the Treasury under section 17 of the Crown Proceedings Act 1947 and must contain sufficient details to identify the claim, the parties, the

[193a] CPR, R 19.5(1) and (2). These rules are to be inserted under the Human Rights Act, at App C in Vol 2.

court and the rights under consideration.[193b] The notice must be given even in cases in which the Crown, a Minister or governmental body is already a party.[193c] The court cannot make a declaration of incompatibility until either the Minister or other person has been joined or a period of 21 days from the giving of the notice has expired.[193d]

The procedure in criminal proceedings. Most criminal prosecutions are brought by the Crown Prosecution Service and it seems unlikely that a Minister of the Crown would, in the ordinary course, also wish to be joined if a declaration of incompatibility is being considered. However, a criminal prosecution may also be brought by a local authority or by a private prosecutor. Where notice has been given that the court is considering making a declaration of incompatibility, the Minister can nominate any person, such as the Director of Public Prosecutions, to give notice so that he becomes a party to the proceedings. Section 5(4) expressly confers a right of appeal in criminal proceedings to any person who becomes a party through this procedure. Section 5(5) ensures that criminal proceedings includes all proceedings before the Court-Martials Appeals Court. **22.78**

An appeal against a declaration of incompatibility may be made to the House of Lords by seeking leave. Leave may be granted by the Court of Appeal (Criminal Division) or by the Divisional Court in relation to a criminal judicial review case or a case stated. If leave is refused, the Crown or its nominee is entitled under section 5(5) to seek leave from the House of Lords. **22.79**

At the time of writing no rules of court relating to criminal proceedings have been made under section 5. **22.80**

(c) Third party interventions

Introduction. The Human Rights Act does not introduce any specific rules of procedure which permit public interest representatives to intervene in proceedings under the Act. During the Committee Stage of the Bill the Lord Chancellor, Lord Irvine, stated:[194] **22.81**

> The European Court of Human Rights rules of procedure allow non-parties such as national and international non-governmental bodies to make written submissions in the form of a brief. There is no reason why any change to primary legislation in this [Act] is needed to develop a similar practice in human rights cases . . . This is a development—that is to say, allowing third parties to intervene and be heard—which has already begun in the higher courts of this country in public law cases.

[193b] PD19, para 6.1 (this provision is to be inserted), see App C in Vol 2.

[193c] PD19, para 6.3. This provision is to be inserted, see App C in Vol 2.

[193d] CPR, R 19.5(3). This rule is to be inserted under the Human Rights Act, see the Draft Rules in App C in Vol 2.

[194] *Hansard* HL col 832 (24 Nov 1997).

22.82 There has been a general recognition in recent years that it may assist the court if such interventions were permitted. As Henry LJ pointed out in *R v Ministry of Defence, ex p Smith*:[195]

> if the Convention were to be made (or possibly be held to be) part of our domestic law, then in the exercise of the primary jurisdiction of the court, for it, a relatively novel constitutional position, might well ask for more material than the adversarial system normally provides such as a 'Brandeis brief'. The court would be taking too limited a view if it hypothetically answered a different question on limited evidence.

Similar views were expressed by Lord Woolf MR in *R v Chief Constable of South Wales, ex p A B*[196] in relation to the judicial review application challenging the decision of the police to disclose information about paedophiles when he said:

> the Secretary of State for the Home Office and the National Association for the Care and Resettlement of Offenders (NACRO) were joined as parties at the outset of the proceedings. In view of the conflicting interests as to what was the appropriate policy to adopt, it was valuable to have the benefit of their submissions. Their contribution confirmed the validity of the conclusions of the Justice Public Law Project, chaired by Laws J on *A matter of public interest, Reforming the law and practice on interventions in public interest cases* (1996).

22.83 The benefits of permitting such public interest interventions were elaborated in *A matter of public interest.*[197] The report drew a distinction between third parties who intervene to protect their *own* interests and those where the intervention is based on the *public* interest. The legitimacy of a public interest intervention depends primarily on the court's perception that the public interest requires the intervener to be heard. Its justification arises precisely because there are cases where the court should be able to call upon bodies with special expertise in whatever area of law was under consideration. The report argued that interventions can promote a better informed court which, in turn, enhances the legitimacy of the court's decisions, particularly in those cases raising fundamental social and moral questions. Some public interest intervenors would have a statutory foundation such as English Heritage or the Equal Opportunities Commission whilst others such as the World Development Movement or Greenpeace would not.

22.84 **The current procedure.** In judicial review proceedings the court has a discretion to hear interested parties who desire to be heard in opposition to the motion under CPR Sch 1 R 53.9(1). The court must hear any person who appears to be a proper person to be heard, even if he has not been served with notice of the

---

[195] [1996] QB 517, 564.

[196] [1998] 3 WLR 57, 66.

[197] JUSTICE (1996) Chap 2; and see also R Singh, 'The Future of Public Interest Litigation' in *The Future of Human Rights in the United Kingdom* (Hart Publishing, 1997) Chap 7; however, this approach has disadvantages in terms of delay and costs: see K Schiemann, 'Interventions in Public Interest Cases' [1996] PL 240.

motion and is not 'directly affected'[198] by the decision. However in *Re Pinochet*[198a] the Divisional Court expressed the view that in criminal proceedings there were no overwhelming reasons for those representing the interests of victims or defendants to be joined to the proceedings as interested parties, at least at the level of the Divisional Court or the Court of Appeal (Criminal Division). In *R v Minister of Agriculture, Fisheries and Food ex p Anastasiou*[199] Popplewell J held that the court had an inherent discretion to permit persons to be heard in order that all those affected by the decision in the case had an opportunity to present their case. There is no express provision under the Rules for a person to be heard in support of the application; but it seems that the court may permit this under its inherent jurisdiction.[200]

In private law proceedings there is a general power to add parties if it is desirable to resolve all the matters in dispute in the proceedings.[201] It is not clear whether the court could join 'public interest intervenors' under this provision. Under CPR Sch 1 R 59.8(1) the Court of Appeal can order that papers be served on any person not a party to those proceedings. The House of Lords rules[202] also allow proposed petitioners to petition the Appeals Committee in civil appeals under Standing Order 34.1. However, the Standing Order does not identify any critera as to how such applications are decided. **22.85**

The Court of Appeal has permitted third parties to intervene in a number of cases: **22.86**

- The Law Society and Bar Council were invited to present arguments on the wasted costs jurisdiction in *Ridehalgh v Horsefield*[203] and in *Tolstoy Miloslavsky v Aldington.*[204]
- In *Shields v E Coomes (Holdings) Ltd*[205] it invited the Equal Opportunities Commission to assist the court on questions of European Community discrimination law.
- In *Anyanwu v South Bank Students' Union*[206] the Commission for Racial Equality was invited to intervene.

In *Science Research Council v Nassé*[207] the House of Lords permitted interventions **22.87**

[198] *R v Liverpool City Council, ex p Muldoon* [1996] 1 WLR 1103.
[198a] *The Times*, 16 Feb 2000.
[199] [1994] COD 329.
[200] *R v Independent Television Commission, ex p Virgin Television Ltd* 26 Jan1996 Lexis; reported *The Times*, 17 Feb 1996, but not on this point.
[201] CPR, 19.1(1).
[202] *Practice Directions and Standing Orders applicable to Civil Appeals* (Jan 1996 edition).
[203] [1994] Ch 205.
[204] [1996] 1 WLR 736.
[205] [1978] 1 WLR 1408.
[206] [2000] IRLR 36.
[207] [1980] AC 1028.

from the Equal Opportunities Commission and Commission for Racial Equality when considering discovery of confidential reports in discrimination cases. In *R v Secretary of State for the Home Department, ex p Sivakumaran*[208] counsel for the United Nations High Commission for Refugees was allowed to address the House of Lords on the proper interpretation of the 1951 Geneva Convention relating to the Status of Refugees. On the other hand, in *Gillick v West Norfolk and Wisbech Area Health Authority*[209] the Children's Legal Centre failed in an application to intervene on the question of the lawfulness of Government guidance to doctors concerning contraceptive advice to children under 16 without obtaining parental consent as a result of an objection by Mrs Gillick's counsel.

22.88 **Human rights cases.** Public interest interventions have been permitted in a number of human rights cases in the last few years. The civil liberties organisation, 'Liberty', was permitted to make written submissions in the House of Lords in *R v Khan*;[210] and was also allowed to make written submissions in the Court of Appeal in the recent case of *R v Broadcasting Standards Commission, ex p BBC*.[211] In *R v Chief Constable of South Wales, ex p A B*[212] the Home Secretary and the National Association for the Resettlement of Offenders were joined as respondents to a judicial review application arising out of the release of information about paedophiles by police officers. Amnesty International and a number of other public interest groups were allowed to make oral submissions in several hearings before the House of Lords arising out of the extradition of General Pinochet.[213] The current practice shows that there are no procedural obstacles which will prevent public interest interventions under the Human Rights Act.

D. Relying on Convention Rights in Proceedings

(1) The basic principles

22.89 A person who wishes to 'rely' on Convention rights under section 7(1)(b) must be a 'victim'[214] of the act of the public authority which is alleged to be unlawful. There are no other procedural limitations placed on a person who wishes to 'rely' on a Convention right in legal proceedings. The proposed rules make provision to ensure that no party is taken by surprise by a human rights issue.[215]

[208] [1988] AC 958.

[209] [1986] AC 112.

[210] [1997] AC 558.

[211] *The Times*, 12 Apr 2000.

[212] [1998] 3 WLR 57.

[213] *Ex p Pinochet Ugarte* [1998] 3 WLR 1456; *R v Bow Street Magistrates, ex p Pinochet Ugarte (No 3)* [1999] 3 WLR 827.

[214] See para 22.14ff above.

[215] CPR, r 16.9(3) (to be inserted), see the Draft Rule in App C in Vol 2; cf the discussion in relation to criminal proceedings, para 22.125 below.

Section 7 does not provide an exhaustive definition of 'legal proceedings'. By section 7(6) of the Human Rights Act, 'legal proceedings' for the purposes of section 7(1)(b) *include*: 22.90

(a) proceedings brought by or at the instigation of a public authority;
(b) appeals against the decision of any court or tribunal.

It is submitted that 'legal proceedings' must also include all civil proceedings, criminal prosecutions and proceedings before tribunals subject to the Human Rights Act.[216]

As a result, a party to any proceedings who is a 'victim' can rely on Convention rights in defence or reply without there being any applicable time limit. Subject to the rules of court[217] these issues can be raised at any time during the proceedings. Furthermore, a party who is bringing an appeal against a decision of a court or tribunal can rely on Convention rights in support of his appeal without being subject to time limits. 22.91

(2) Incompatible acts prior to 2 October 2000

The Human Rights Act will come into full force on 2 October 2000.[218] However, a person can rely on Convention rights in legal proceedings under section 7(1)(b) whenever the act of the public authority in question took place.[219] This means that, for example: 22.92

- in a criminal trial which takes place after 2 October 2000[220] a defendant can rely, for example, on breaches of Article 6 by the prosecution before that date;
- a defendant convicted of an offence prior to 2 October 2000 can rely on Convention rights before that date in support of his appeal (subject to obtaining permission to appeal out of time);[220a]
- in a civil trial which takes place after 2 October 2000, a party can rely on violations of Convention rights which took place prior to that date;
- a party to civil proceedings who was subject to an adverse judgment before 2 October 2000 can rely on Convention rights in support of his appeal (subject to obtaining permission to appeal out of time).

216 See para 5.43.
217 Including, in civil proceedings, the ordinary rules of pleading, see para 22.118 below.
218 See para 3.74 above.
219 s 22(4), see generally, para 3.75 above.
220 See para 3.74 above.
220a In *R v DPP, ex p Kebilene* [1999] 3 WLR 972 at 982 Lord Steyn expressed the view that the Act extended to appeals against decisions in trials before 2 Oct 2000.

E. Procedural Issues in Judicial Review Proceedings

(1) Introduction

22.93 Where a claimant confines himself to a free standing Human Rights Act challenge against a public authority, he is likely to do so by making an application for judicial review. The Act has a number of procedural implications for judicial review proceedings.[221] The specific impact of Article 6 has been discussed in Chapter 11;[222] and the implications of the Act on granting relief in judicial review proceedings are discussed in Chapter 21.[223] The Human Rights Act has created a new illegality ground for judicial review: an applicant will now be able to argue that a decision should be quashed because a public authority has acted incompatibly with Convention rights in breach of section 6(1) of the Act.

22.94 The Act is likely to affect the following areas of judicial review procedure:

- the scope for judicial review;
- the contents of the Notice of Application;
- the approach to applications for permission;
- the nature of the respondent's evidence; and
- disclosure and evidence.

22.95 The Act will disturb the established principles in judicial review procedure concerning the treatment of disputes of fact. As Lord Diplock emphasised in *O'Reilly v Mackman*[224] when explaining the rationale for the very restrictive rules on allowing cross examination in judicial review proceedings:

> This is because of the nature of the issues that normally arise upon judicial review. The facts, except where the claim is invalid on grounds that a statutory tribunal or public authority that made the decision failed to comply with the procedure prescribed by the legislation under which it was acting or failed to observe the fundamental rules of natural justice or fairness, can seldom be a matter of relevant dispute upon an application for judicial review, since the tribunal's or authority's decision of fact, as distinguished from the legal consequences of the facts that they have found, are not open to review by the court in the exercise of its supervisory powers except on the principles laid down in *Edwards v Bairstow and Harrison*;[225] and to allow cross examination presents the court with a temptation, not always easily resisted, to substitute its own view of the facts for that of the decision making body upon whom the exclusive jurisdiction to determine facts has been conferred by Parliament.

[221] See eg T de la Mare, 'The Human Rights Act 1998: The Impact on Judicial Review' [1999] JR 32; M Supperstone and J Coppel, 'Judicial Review After the Human Rights Act' [1999] EHRLR 301; K Steyn and D Wolfe, 'Judicial Review and the Human Rights Act: Some Practical Considerations' [1999] EHRLR 614.

[222] See para 11.319ff above.

[223] See para 21.109 above.

[224] [1983] AC 236, 282.

[225] [1956] AC 14, 36.

It is submitted that the Act radically alters the basic approach; and Article 6[226] will require the court to make findings of fact where they are in issue. Such disputes will arise where there is a contest about the underlying facts in a case or where the justification of qualified rights involves conflicts of evidence in cases which involve a breach of 'civil rights and obligations'[226a] or a 'criminal charge'.[226b] **22.96**

(2) The scope of judicial review

The broad approach the court may take towards identifying those bodies which will be public authorities under the Human Rights Act by virtue of carrying out public functions[227] may encourage the extension of judicial review to a wider range of decision-makers in Human Rights cases. For example, many professional and sporting bodies[228] will be public authorities for the purposes of the Human Rights Act; yet regulate members with whom they have a contractual relationship. There is a well established (if controversial) principle that judicial review is not available where an applicant could bring private law proceedings for breach of contract.[229] If contractual relationships continue to remain outside the scope of judicial review, this will enable claimants to bring proceedings under the Human Rights Act in private law proceedings; and would permit them to seek declarations that the authority has acted incompatibly with Convention rights *outside* the time limits prescribed for judicial review applications. It is submitted that a claim for declaratory relief in such circumstances could not be struck out as an abuse of process in accordance with the principles in *O'Reilly v Mackman*.[230] **22.97**

(3) The Notice of Application

CPR Sch 1 R 53.3(2)(a) states that a Notice of Application for judicial review shall state the relief sought and the grounds on which it is sought. In a case in which the applicant contends that a public authority has acted unlawfully because a Convention right has been breached, it will obviously be necessary for the Notice of Application to state: **22.98**

- the Convention right or rights alleged to have been breached;
- the particular respects in which it has been breached;
- the facts and matters which are said to amount to the breach alleged;
- if the right is a qualified one[231] the basis on which the applicant contends that the interference was not 'justified' under the Convention.

226 See para 11.183ff above.
226a See para 11.163ff above.
226b See para 11.174ff above.
227 See para 5.16ff above.
228 See generally, para 5.16ff above.
229 *R v Disciplinary Committee of the Jockey Club, ex p Aga Khan* [1993] 1 WLR 909; and see eg C Lewis, *Judicial Remedies in Public Law* (2nd edn, Sweet & Maxwell, 2000) paras 2-047–2-062.
230 See para 22.52ff above.
231 See para 6.90ff above.

The proposed rules make no provision as to the contents of the Notice of Application but provide that, where proceedings are being brought against a public authority under section 7(1)(a) of the Human Rights Act, the claim form must state that fact and give details of the Convention right which it is alleged has been infringed and of the infringement.[231a]

(4) The application for permission

22.99 The test to be applied for permission in Human Rights Act applications[232] cases is uncertain. In relation to unqualified rights, an arguable interference on the facts put forward by the applicant should be sufficient. The position in relation to qualified rights[233] is less clear. Interference with such rights is usually easy to establish and it might be argued that, in cases involving qualified rights,[234] once a *prima facie* violation has been shown, the burden is on the public authority to justify the interference at the substantive stage. It is more likely, however, that a claimant will need to show at the permission stage an arguable absence of justification for the interference.[235] On the other hand, the need to examine in detail the reasoning process of the public authority and the evidence it puts forward to justify an interference with a qualified right means that, in general, it will not be appropriate to investigate the question of arguability at any length at the permission stage.[236]

(5) The respondent's evidence

22.100 A public authority's evidence in response to an application for judicial review of a decision involving interference with a qualified right will need careful consideration. The public authority must show that the interference is 'prescribed by law',[237] has a legitimate aim (as defined by the specific article in question) and is proportionate and necessary in a democratic society.[238] As Laws J stressed in *R v Ministry of Agriculture, Fisheries and Food, ex p First City Trading Ltd,*[239] in assessing proportionality the court must test the solution arrived at and pass it only if substantial factual considerations are put forward in its justification: considerations which are

---

[231a] See CPR, r 16.9(3). This rule is to be inserted under the Human Rights Act, see App C in Vol 2.
[232] See R Clayton and H Tomlinson, *Judicial Review Procedure* (Wiley Chancery Law, 1997), 122ff.
[233] Those in Arts 8–11 of the Convention, see para 6.123ff above.
[234] Ibid.
[235] Sir Stephen Richards, 'The Impact of Article 6 of the ECHR on Judicial Review' [1999] JR 106.
[236] M Supperstone and J Coppel, 'Judicial Review after the Human Rights Act' [1999] EHRLR 301.
[237] See generally, para 6.126ff above.
[238] See generally, para 6.40ff above.
[239] [1997] 1 CMLR 250, 279.

relevant, reasonable and proportionate to the aim in view. The approach the court is likely to take is discussed below.[240]

The Act will also have an impact on the obligation on a public authority to give full and frank disclosure once permission has been granted.[241] Very often only the respondent will have access to detailed factual information which might justify its stance; and it is submitted that a public authority will be under a positive duty to disclose this material in order to assist the court. **22.101**

(6) Disclosure and further information

The rules governing disclosure in ordinary judicial review proceedings are extremely restrictive. Disclosure will only be ordered in limited circumstances: the applicant cannot obtain disclosure to ascertain whether there are flaws in the decision-making process[242] or to fill in gaps in his own case.[243] In general, it will only be ordered if the applicant has some material to show that the evidence in the respondent's witness statements is not accurate.[244] **22.102**

These principles will significantly alter under the Human Rights Act. As discussed in Chapter 11,[245] the obligation of the court not to act incompatibly with Article 6 will require a more generous approach. Where there are disputes of fact on the central issues in a case involving 'civil rights and obligations'[245a] or a 'criminal charge',[245b] the applicant will be entitled to an order for disclosure. **22.103**

A party to judicial review proceedings can request further information in relation to any matter in dispute in the proceedings under CPR Part 18. This combines the former provisions relating to 'interrogatories'[246] and Requests for Further and Better Particulars.[247] If further information is not provided the court may order a party to provide additional information.[248] Requests for Further Information are rarely made in judicial review proceedings. However, in Human Rights Act cases such requests **22.104**

---

[240] See para 22.110ff below.

[241] See eg *R v Lancashire County Council, ex p Huddleston* [1986] 2 All ER 941, 945 *per* Sir John Donaldson; and at 947 *per* Parker LJ; *R v Civil Service Appeal Board, ex p Cunningham* [1991] 4 All ER 310, 315, 316; and see generally, R Clayton and H Tomlinson, *Judicial Review Procedure* (2nd edn, Wiley Chancery Law, 1997) 151, 152.

[242] See eg *R v Secretary of State for Home Affairs, ex p Harrison* [1988] 3 All ER 86, CA (which is reproduced in [1997] JR 113); *R v Secretary of State for Environment, ex p Islington London Borough Council, The Independent* 6 Sep 1991 (which is reproduced in [1997] JR 121).

[243] See generally, Clayton and Tomlinson (n 241 above) 160–164.

[244] See eg *R v Secretary of State for Foreign and Commonwealth Affairs, ex p World Development Movement Ltd* [1995] 1 WLR 386, 396C–397H.

[245] See para 11.322 above.

[245a] See para 11.163ff above.

[245b] See para 11.174ff above.

[246] Under RSC Ord 26.

[247] Under RSC Ord 18, r 12.

[248] CPR, r 18.1(1).

are likely to be a useful tool for obtaining factual details from public authorities. Where, for example, a public authority seeks to justify interference with a 'qualified right',[249] an applicant may be entitled to further information in relation to all the matters relied on as rendering the interference 'necessary in a democratic society'.

(7) Evidence and the hearing

(a) Introduction

22.105 In a Human Rights Act application the court will be obliged to determine primary facts. This will have a substantial impact on the conventional techniques of judicial review in such cases. The way in which evidence is adduced will also change. The reception into evidence of statistical material in the form of a 'Brandeis brief' will become an important means of determining complex factual disputes where public authorities seek to justify the interferences with qualified rights such as the right to privacy or freedom of expression.

(b) Brandeis briefs

22.106 In cases involving human rights, the court is often obliged to ascertain not only the facts in dispute between the parties (the adjudicative facts) but also the facts which underpin a particular policy or statutory provision which have been applied to the parties (legislative facts).[250] When examining the validity of legislation, there are, in principle, several different methods the courts could use when deciding the underlying disputes of fact: by taking judicial notice of facts, using Brandeis briefs, relying on evidence at trial or by examining the legislative declaration of facts or committee reports.[251] However, where a court proceeds on the basis of judicial notice, there is a risk, as Mr Justice Holmes put it, that 'the decision will depend on a judgment or intuition more subtle than any articulate major premise'.[252]

22.107 The conventional approach in American constitutional cases is to prove legislative facts by utilising a Brandeis brief.[253] This is a brief which normally consists of statistical information which is received by the court on the basis of an expanded notion of judicial notice. The Brandeis brief[254] takes its name from the written

[249] See para 6.123 above.

[250] Facts which arise from questions of law or policy which are to be distinguished from the adjudicative facts concerning the immediate parties to litigation such as what the parties did, what the circumstances were and what the background conditions were: see K C Davis, 'An Approach to Problems of Evidence in the Administrative Process' (1942) 55 Harv L Rev 364.

[251] H W Bikle, 'Judicial Determination of Questions of Fact Affecting the Constitutional Validity of Legislative Action' (1924) 37 Harv L Rev 6.

[252] In his famous dissenting judgment in *Lochner v New York* (1905) 198 US 45, 76.

[253] For a general discussion of the position in the US and Canada see P W Hogg, *Constitutional Law of Canada* (4th edn, Carswell, 1997) para 57.2, 1395–1399.

[254] See generally, A Henderson, 'Brandeis Briefs and the Proof of Legislative Facts in Proceedings Under the Human Rights Act 1998' [1998] PL 563.

submissions presented by Louis Brandeis (who later became a judge of the American Supreme Court)[255] when he acted as counsel in *Muller v Oregon*.[256] The case itself concerned the constitutionality of a statute restricting the hours of work for women. Brandeis submitted a brief to the Supreme Court which contained two pages of legal argument and 100 pages of detailed factual material including social science data collated from books, article and reports. The Brandeis brief has since become common place. Thus, in the famous desegregation case, *Brown v Board of Education of Topeka*[257] the brief before the Supreme Court included a 'Social Science Statement' signed by 32 experts summarising the scientific consensus about the psychological and sociological impact of segregation. The court is able by the use of Brandeis briefs to admit evidence of a highly sophisticated social science type without incurring the costs and inconvenience of hearing expert evidence.

Despite the wide acceptance of 'Brandeis briefs' no clear rules have emerged as to when they should be used, the appropriate procedures for rebuttal or the weight to be given to the 'facts' in the brief.[258] In constitutional cases in Canada the appeal courts[259] will admit material relevant to the issues provided that it is not inherently unreliable or offends against public policy. Appropriate directions are given in relation to the filing of the material and material in rebuttal. Such evidence is sometimes admitted at trials without formal proof.[260] The effect of the Civil Evidence Act 1995 is that such evidence would be admissible at a hearing without a sworn statement or a witness being called. If, however, the evidence included statements of opinion, it would be necessary to obtain permission to put this evidence before the court under CPR Part 35. **22.108**

The English courts have acquired expertise in utilising this type of evidence in discrimination cases, particularly where a justification has been put forward to defend a claim of indirect discrimination.[261] For example, in *R v Secretary of State of Employment, ex p Equal Opportunities Commission*[262] the House of Lords held that the evidence did not prove that the differential qualifying period of employment protection rights was objectively justified. The techniques which are likely to be applied under the Human Rights Act are illustrated by the approach of the House of Lords in *R v Secretary of State for Employment, ex p Seymour-Smith (No 2)*.[263] **22.109**

[255] See eg S Baskerville, *Of Law and Limitations: An Intellectual Portrait of Louis Dembitz Brandeis* (Fairleigh Dickinson, 1994).

[256] (1908) 208 US 412.

[257] (1954) 347 US 483.

[258] See generally, Hogg (n 253 above) 1396.

[259] See *Residential Tenancies Act Reference* [1981] 1 SCR 714, 722-723 (constitutional reference); *Irwin Toy v Quebec* [1989] 1 SCR 927, 983-984.

[260] See *R v Morgentaler (No 2)* [1988] 1 SCR 30; and see generally, Hogg (n 253 above) 1396–1399.

[261] For the concept of indirect discrimination, see para 17.18 above.

[262] [1995] 1 AC 1.

[263] [2000] 1 WLR 435.

The applicants alleged that the two-year qualifying period for unfair dismissal rights indirectly discriminated against women because fewer women than men were able to satisfy the length of service needed to establish their entitlement. The case was referred to the European Court of Justice which held[264] that the question of disparate impact depended on either the statistics showing that a considerably smaller percentage of women rather than men satisfied the condition or showing that there was a lesser but persistent and relatively constant disparity over a long period between men and women. The House of Lords differed on the proper inferences that could be drawn from the statistics. Furthermore, on the question of whether the discrimination could be justified, Lord Nicholls[265] accepted that obtaining hard evidence (including evidence of the employers' perception) was a difficult task but that the Government had not acted on a mere generalised assumption. There was some supporting factual material and it would be unreasonable to condemn the Minister for failing to carry out further research.

(c) Evidence in human rights cases

22.110 There are powerful arguments that the human rights adjudication, and, in particular, the exacting factual inquiries required to test the principle of proportionality, impose burdens on judicial review procedure which it cannot shoulder.[266] It has been suggested, for example, that had the *Factortame* litigation[267] proceeded as judicial review proceedings without discovery and cross examination, the plaintiffs would have failed to discharge the onus of proving their case.[268] It is therefore submitted that the courts should approach the evidential issues in applications concerning the Human Rights Act differently from the general run of cases. The court will be obliged to do so in order to comply with its own obligation not to act incompatibly with Convention rights[269] and to give practical effect to Convention rights.[270] It may be appropriate to make greater use of the power to convert judicial review applications into ordinary proceedings under CPR Sch 1 R 53.9(5).[271]

22.111 The general rule in judicial review proceedings is that cross examination is not

[264] [1999] AC 554, 597 para 59.

[265] *R v Secretary of State for Employment, ex p Seymour-Smith (No 2)* (n 263 above) 451E–F.

[266] I Leigh and L Lustgarten, 'Making Rights Real: The Courts, Remedies and the Human Rights Act' (1999) 58 CLJ 509.

[267] For a discussion of the litigation, see para 1.72 above.

[268] N Green, 'Proportionality and the Supremacy of Parliament in the UK' in E Ellis (ed), *The Principle of Proportionality in the Laws of Europe* (Hart Publishing, 1998).

[269] Under s 6(3); see, generally para 5.38ff above.

[270] See generally, para 6.28ff above.

[271] See generally, R Clayton and H Tomlinson, *Judicial Review Procedure* (2nd edn, Wiley Chancery Law, 1997) 180, 181.

appropriate because the primary facts are not in dispute[272] and where factual disputes arise, respondents often succeed in arguing that the court must proceed on the basis that their evidence must be accepted.[273]

The approach will be very different in Human Rights Act cases. A refusal to permit cross examination of deponents or witnesses where the critical facts are in dispute may contravene Article 6.[274] It is likely that cross examination will become more common at the substantive hearing in a case involving 'civil rights and obligations'[274a] or a 'criminal charge'.[274b] **22.112**

(d) Costs

It is arguable that special principles should apply to the awards of costs in Human Rights Act cases. The court has a general discretion as to whether costs are payable and the amount of those costs.[275] If the court decides to make an order about costs, the general rule is that the unsuccessful party will be ordered to pay the costs of the successful party but the court may make a different order.[276] In deciding what order for costs, if any, to make the court must have regard to all the circumstances, including: **22.113**

- the conduct of the parties;
- whether a party has succeeded on part of his cases, even if he has not been wholly successful.[277]

It is submitted that the fact that a claimant raises a Human Rights Act point of general importance is an important factor to be taken into account in deciding whether or not to make an order for costs. In *Motsepe v IRC*[278] Ackerman J, in giving judgment for the South African Constitutional Court, said: **22.114**

> One should be cautious in awarding costs against litigants who seek to enforce their constitutional rights against the state, particularly where the constitutionality of a statutory provision is attacked, lest such orders have an unduly inhibiting or 'chilling' effect on other potential litigants in this category. This cautious approach cannot, however, be allowed to develop into an inflexible rule so that litigants are induced into believing that they are free to challenge the constitutionality of statutory provisions in this court, no matter how spurious the grounds for doing so may be or how remote the possibility that this court will grant access. This can neither be in the interests of the administration of justice nor fair to those who are forced to oppose such attacks.

[272] See, generally, Clayton and Tomlinson (n 271 above) 165–167; D Abrahams, 'Conflicts of Evidence in Judicial Review Proceedings' [1999] JR 221.

[273] See eg *R v Hull Visitors, ex p St Germain* [1979] 1 WLR 1401, 1410; *R v Reigate Justices, ex p Curl* [1991] COD 66; *R v Camden London Borough Council, ex p Cran* (1996) 94 LGR 8, 12.

[274] See para 11.217 above.

[274a] See para 11.163ff above.

[274b] See para 11.174ff above.

[275] CPR, r 44.3(1).

[276] CPR, r 44.3(2).

[277] CPR, r 44.3(4).

[278] 1997 (6) BCLR 692, 705.

The South African Courts have refused to make costs orders against unsuccessful applicants raising genuine constitutional questions in a number of cases.[279] If, however, a litigant successfully invokes constitutional rights, an order for costs will usually be made against the unsuccessful respondent.[280]

22.115 In appropriate cases, the court has a power to make 'pre-emptive costs orders': that is, orders determining the costs prior to the substantive hearing, for example, that no order as to costs be made against applicants if they are unsuccessful.[281] This power can be exercised in cases involving public interest challenges which raise issues of general importance where the applicant has no private interest in the outcome of the case.[282] Although public interest groups do not have standing to bring claims under the Human Rights Act, the rules of standing are broad enough to allow claims by 'victims' who have little or no 'private interest' in the outcome.[283] However, pre-emptive costs will only be made when:

- the court is satisfied that the issues raised are ones of general public importance;
- the court concludes that it is in the public interest to make the order;
- the court is satisfied the order is appropriate bearing in mind the respective financial resources of the parties.[284]

It is submitted that in Human Rights Act cases involving issues of general public importance the court should give serious consideration to the making of such orders.

F. Procedural Issues in Other Proceedings

(1) Civil proceedings

(a) Introduction

22.116 Under the proposed rules a claimant who is bringing proceedings against a public authority under section 7(1)(a) must state that fact in the claim form and must, in the claim form or particulars of claim:

- give details of the Convention right which it is alleged has been infringed and of the infringement and,
- where the claim is founded on a finding of unlawfulness by another court or tribunal, give deails of that finding.[285]

[279] See eg *Sanderson v A-G, Eastern Cape* 1997 (12) BCLR 1675; *City Council of Pretoria v Walker* 1998 (3) BCLR 257.
[280] See eg *DPP v Lebona* 1998 (5) BCLR 618, 638.
[281] See generally, K Markus and M Westgate, 'Pre-emptive Costs Orders' [1998] JR 76.
[282] See *R v Lord Chancellor, ex p Child Poverty Action Group* [1999] 1 WLR 347, 353G-H.
[283] For the concept of 'victim' see para 22.14ff above.
[284] See *R v Lord Chancellor, ex p Child Poverty Action Group* (n 282 above) 358C–E.
[285] See CPR, r 16.9(3). This rule is to be inserted under the Human Rights Act, see App C in Vol 2.

Where an appellant is adding a claim against a public authority under section 7(1)(a) of the Human Rights Act 1998 in the appeal, the notice of appeal must state that fact and must give details of:

- the Convention right which it is alleged has been infringed and of the infringement; and
- the finding of the court or tribunal, where there is a finding of unlawfulness by another court or tribunal; or
- the judicial act and the court or tribunal which made it, where it is the act of that court or tribunal which is complained of (as provided by section 9 of the Act).[285a]

By section 9(3) of the Human Rigthts Act, damages can only be awarded in proceedings which are brought in respect of a judicial act done in good faith to the extent required by Article 5(5) of the Convention.[286] On any application or appeal concerning a committal order. a refusal to grant habeas corpus or a secure accommodation order under section 25 of the Children Act 1989, the judgment or order must, if the court orders release, state whether or not the original order was made in circumstances which infringed that person's Convention rights.[286a] It is proposed that any claim under this provision which is proceeding in the County Court will be transferred to the Crown Office List.[287] Where a claim under this provision is based on a finding by a Crown Court, the proposed rules provide that the court hearing the claim may reconsider the evidence of the alleged infringement and the finding of the Crown Court.[288] **22.117**

(b) Statements of Case

The Human Rights Act does not impose any specific requirements for pleading cases under the Act. The proposed rules provide that, when a claim is brought under section 7(1)(a) against a public authority, the claimant must, in his claim form or particular of claim: **22.118**

- give details of the Convention right which it is alleged has been infringed and of the infringement; and
- where the claim is founded on a finding of unlawfulness by another court or tribunal, give details of that finding.[288a]

Furthermore, CPR rule 16.4(1)(a) requires that Particulars of Claim include a

---

[285a] PD 52, para 5.8. This provision is to be inserted under the Human Rights Act, see App C in Vol 2.

[286] See para 21.26ff above.

[286a] CPR, r 40.14(4). This rule is to be inserted under the Human Rights Act, see App C in Vol 2.

[287] CPR, r 30.9 contains a power to make such a transfer, PD 30, para 7.1 provides that such transfers will be made. The provisions are to be inserted under the Human Rights Act: see the Draft Rules in App C in Vol 2.

[288] CPR, r 33.9. This rule is to be inserted under the Human Rights Act: see the Draft Rules in App C in Vol 2.

[288a] See CPR, r 16.9(3). This rule is to be inserted under the Human Rights Act, see App C in Vol 2.

concise statement of the facts on which a claimant relies and CPR rule 16.5(2)(a) requires a defendant to state his reasons for denying an allegation. CPR PD 16 paragraph 16.3(a) also states that a party may refer in his statement of case to any point of law on which his claim or defence is based; and under the Human Rights Act it will always be prudent to do so.

22.119 Where a claimant alleges a public authority has acted incompatibly with a Convention right, he should plead in his Particulars of Claim:

- the Convention right alleged to have been breached;
- the particular respects in which it has been breached (for example, that Article 6 has been breached because of the inequality of arms and absence of reasons);
- the particular facts and matters which are said to amount to the breach alleged;
- the particular public authority which is obliged to comply with the section 6(1) duty;
- all facts and matters relied on in support of any case that the court should exercise its discretion to award for damages for under section 8;[289]
- all facts and matters relied on in support of any claim for aggravated or exemplary damages[290] or interest.[291]

22.120 However, a claimant need not plead in the Particulars of Claim any facts or matters in relation to the case a defendant may put forward to justify a breach of a qualified right[292] such as the right to privacy or freedom of expression. The claimant could address these issues in a Reply to set out on any factual contentions he wishes to put forward on whether, for example, the interference with the qualified right is proportionate.[293] On the other hand, it is often prudent to deal with anticipated defence points in the Particulars of Claim. This obliges the defendant to respond to these points and enables the claimant to focus on the real issues in the Reply.

22.121 It has been suggested that a party should make it clear if he intends to rely on section 3 of the Human Rights Act in support of an argument that legislation should be given a particular construction to be compatible with Convention rights. Although the question of construction raises a point of law, the question of compatibility with Convention rights may require a factual investigation.[294]

---

[289] For a discussion of the power of the court to award damages under the Human Rights Act: see para 21.60ff above.

[290] CPR r 16.4(1)(c): for a discussion concerning whether aggravated or exemplary damages are available under the Act, see para 21.67ff above.

[291] CPR, r 16.4(1)(b) and 16(2).

[292] See generally, para 6.123ff above.

[293] See, generally, para 6.42ff above.

[294] N Giffen, 'Judicial Supervision of Human Rights: Practice and Procedure', Administrative Law Bar Association seminar, 5 Feb 2000.

It is suggested that a defendant public authority should plead the following in its defence: 22.122

- whether it admits that in the circumstances it is subject to section 6 of the Human Rights Act;
- the facts and matter it relies on in contending there is no breach;
- if the claimant's version of events is denied, the defendant's own version of events;[295]
- all facts and matters relevant to any positive case it is making about the scope, nature or effect of alleged breach of the Convention right;
- all facts and matters it relies on in relation to a qualified right in maintaining that it has acted 'in accordance with the law'[296] and that the interference with the right is proportionate;
- any facts and matters relevant to whether the court should exercise discretion to award damages, quantum and mitigation, any claim for aggravated or exemplary damages or any claim for interest;
- any facts and matters relevant to any limitation period which is relied on.[297]

(c) Evidence, disclosure and costs

When Human Rights Act claims are made in ordinary civil litigation, the scope of evidence and disclosure may be significantly increased. If, for example, a public authority seeks to justify an interference with the claimant's right to respect for the home under Article 8(2), it will have to lead evidence to show that the interference was for a legitimate aim and was 'necessary in a democratic society'. This may place the whole range of policy alternatives in issue and give rise to an obligation to disclose all the background documents. it may be appropriate for interveners to be joined to make 'public interest' points and for 'Brandeis briefs' to be lodged. The same issues relating to costs which have been discussed in relation to judicial review proceedings[298] will also apply in civil proceedings in which Human Rights Act issues are raised. 22.123

(2) Criminal proceedings

(a) Procedural issues

On the basis of experience in other jurisdictions it seems likely that Human Rights Act issues will be raised in a large proportion of criminal cases. Rules of court are required to ensure that this is done in an orderly way. Such rules need to deal with 22.124

295 CPR, r 16.5(2).

296 See generally, para 6.126ff above.

297 CPR 16 PD para 16.1; for a discussion of limitation under the Human Rights Act, see para 22.58ff above.

298 See para 22.113 above.

the procedure for giving notice of an intention to raise a Human Rights Act issue, the joinder of parties and the reference of issues to other courts.[299]

22.125 In relation to the notice procedure, the rules may provide that a defendant who wishes to raise a Human Rights Act issue should:

- in summary proceedings, give notice of his intention to raise the issue to the clerk of the court before he is called upon to plead;
- in proceedings on indictment, give notice within a specified period of the service of the indictment;
- also give such notice to a specified authority such as the Director of Public Prosecutions.[300]

22.126 The rules may also lay down a procedure whereby the specified authority gives notice of any intention to apply to be joined as a party to the proceedings.

22.127 It will also be necessary to make provision as to the contents of such a notice. For example, it may be required to specify the facts and circumstances and contentions of law on the basis of which it is alleged that a Human Rights Act issue arises in the proceedings in sufficient detail to enable the court to determine whether such an issue does arise.

22.128 It may also be appropriate to provide for a procedure whereby a magistrates' court can refer a Human Rights Act issue to the Divisional Court and, at the same time, give directions.

(b) Time issues in criminal proceedings

22.129 In most criminal cases, Convention rights will be relied on by way of 'defence' and, as a result, the time limit under section 7(5) will be of no application. If, however, a person who successfully relies on a Convention right as a defence in criminal proceedings wishes to bring a subsequent claim for damages against the prosecuting authority, this will be subject to the 12-month limit. In many cases, the relevant 'act' (for example, the decision to prosecute or to rely on evidence obtained in breach of Convention rights) will have taken place a substantial time before the criminal court determines that there has been an act incompatible with Convention rights. As a result, any subsequent civil proceeding is likely to be outside the 12-month time limit. Nevertheless, provided that the civil proceedings are brought within a few months of the conclusion of the criminal proceedings it is likely that an extension of time[301] would be granted in such a case.

[299] In Scotland, these issues are dealt with in The Act of Adjournal (Devolution Issues Rules) 1999 which amends the Act of Adjournal (Criminal Procedure Rules) 1996 by adding a new Chap 40.

[300] Cf Act of Adjournal (Criminal Procedure Rules) 1996 Chap 40.2(1).

[301] See para 22.60 above.

A person can rely on Convention rights in legal proceedings under section 7(1)(b) whenever the act of the public authority in question took place.[302] An appeal is 'legal proceedings' for the purposes of section 7(1)(b). As a result, a defendant can rely on acts prior to the Human Rights Act coming into force at both a criminal trial after 2 October 2000 and in support of an appeal.[303] **22.130**

(3) Family proceedings

The Lord Chancellor has proposed a number of amendments to the Family Proceedings Rules and Practice Directions. These are in substantially the same form as the proposed amendments to the CPR and deal with the following issues: **22.131**

- a new family proceedings practice direction on the citation of human rights material;[304]
- a new FPR rule 10.26 dealing with joining a Minister when a declaration of incompatibility is being considered;[304a]
- a new family proceedings Practice Direction dealing with cases where an appellant is adding a claim under sections 7(1)(a) and 9(3);[304b]
- a new FPR rule 10.10(8) and Practice Direction dealing with the transfer of claims under section 7(1)(a) and 9(3).[304c]

Special considerations apply in family proceedings in which any question regarding the upbringing of a child arises. The court will have to have regard to the general principle that any delay in determining the question is likely to prejudice the welfare of the child.[305] In proceedings to which the Family Proceedings Rules 1991[306] or the Family Proceedings Courts (Children Act 1989) Rules 1991[307] apply the court will have to comply with[305] the rules which provide that: **22.132**

> no document other than a record of an order, held by the court and relating to proceedings . . . shall be disclosed, other than to (a) a party, (b) the legal representative of a party, (c) the guardian ad litem, (d) the Legal Aid Board, or (e) a welfare officer without the leave of [the court].[309]

---

[302] s 22(4), see generally, para 3.75 above.
[303] See para 22.92 above.
[304] This is to be inserted under the Human Rights Act, see App C in Vol 2, for these rules see para 3.51 above.
[304a] See App C in Vol 2 and for the rules in civil cases, see para 22.77 above.
[304b] See App C in Vol 2 and for the rules in civil cases, see para 22.77 above.
[304c] See App C in vol 2 and for the rules in civil cases, see para 22.77 above.
[305] Children Act 1989, s 2; cf *Practice Direction (Supreme Court: Devolution)* (n 304 above) para 15.1.
[306] SI 1991/1247.
[307] SI 1991/1395.
[308] Cf *Practice Direction (Supreme Court: Devolution)* (n 304 above) paras 15.2 and 15.4.
[309] Family Proceedings Rules, r 4.23, Family Proceedings Courts Rules, r 23.

22.133 In family proceedings, the court itself will be obliged under section 6(3) of the Human Rights Act not to act incompatibly with the right of respect for family life[310] in relation to members of the family which are not party to the proceedings.

(4) Other proceedings

(a) Statutory tribunals

22.134 There are no special rules under the Human Rights Act which apply to tribunals. However, it is possible that the rules applicable to specific tribunals will make provision for the timing and manner in which Human Rights Act issues are to be raised and the notice which should be given to other potential parties. In particular, no rules have been made which would confer jurisdiction on a tribunal to grant relief if a free standing claim under the Act were made. As a result, for example, the employment tribunal has no power to adjudicate in such cases.[310a]

(b) Domestic tribunals

22.135 Where a domestic tribunal is not subject to the Human Rights Act[311] (such as the disciplinary bodies of professional or sporting bodies),[312] difficulties will arise where it is alleged that the tribunal is breaching Convention rights; and that the tribunal should not act incompatibly with them. In principle, three different possibilities can be identified:

- the tribunal could nevertheless apply Convention rights even though it is under no obligation to do so. Although this approach is contrary to the intention of the Human Rights Act, it may commend itself where a legal challenge to the adjudication appears inevitable;
- the tribunal could adjourn the hearing in order to allow argument before a court about, for example, the proper procedures to be applied. It is submitted that this approach is not appropriate, not least because the question of whether a Convention right is breached will often depend on the precise factual circumstances of the case;
- the tribunal could decline to comply with section 6(3) as it is strictly entitled to do. It is submitted that it would, however, be of assistance in any subsequent challenge if the tribunal made any relevant findings of fact and expression of views on the Convention right that is alleged to have been violated.

---

[310] See para 13.70ff above.
[310a] See *Biggs v Somerset County Council* [1996] ICR 364 and *Barber v Staffordshire County Council* [1996] IRLR 209.
[311] See para 5.16ff above.
[312] See para 5.35ff above.

(5) Proceedings in Wales

The National Assembly for Wales has no power to make subordinate legislation or do any act which is incompatible with any Convention rights.[313] A question as to whether the Assembly has acted or failed to act in a way which is incompatible with a Convention right is one of the matters known as a 'devolution issue'.[314] The *Practice Direction (Supreme Court: Devolution)*[315] sets out the rules which apply to the raising of devolution issues. **22.136**

If a devolution issue arises in proceedings the court must order notice of it to be given to the Attorney-General and the Assembly if they are not already parties. They have a right to take part as a party in the proceedings so far as they relate to a 'devolution issue'.[316] The court may, of its own motion, require the question of whether a devolution issue arises to be considered, even if the parties have not used the term.[317] **22.137**

The magistrates' court may refer a devolution issue in summary proceedings to the High Court and the Crown Court may refer such an issue arising in proceedings on indictment to the Court of Appeal.[318] A county court and the High Court may refer a devolution issue arising in civil proceedings to the High Court.[319] The Court of Appeal may refer a devolution issue to the Judicial Committee of the Privy Council.[320] **22.138**

313 Government of Wales Act 1998, s 107.
314 Ibid Sch 8.
315 [1999] 1 WLR 1592.
316 Government of Wales Act, Sch 8, para 5; *Practice Direction (Supreme Court: Devolution)* [1999] 1 WLR 1592 para 3.3(1).
317 Ibid para 5.2.
318 Government of Wales Act 1998, Sch 9, paras 6–9.
319 Ibid Sch 8, paras 6 to 9.
320 Ibid Sch 8, para 10 (unless the devolution issue has been referred to it by another court).

23

COURT OF HUMAN RIGHTS PROCEDURE

A. Introduction and Background

(1) Introduction

The Human Rights Act does not remove the right of individual petition to the European Court of Human Rights. This right was established, for citizens of the 23.01

United Kingdom, on 14 January 1966.[1] Applications can only be brought when 'all domestic remedies have been exhausted'.[2] There are a number of areas in which the Human Rights Act does not allow reliance on Convention rights before the English courts such as the 'act' of either House of Parliament.[3] There may also be occasions where a court makes a declaration of incompatiblity[4] in relation to legislation which the Government fails to rectify under the fast track procedure.[5] In addition, applicants who are dissatisfied with the interpretation of the Convention adopted by the English courts will retain their right to apply to the Court for relief.[5a] In such cases, the only available remedy will remain a complaint to Strasbourg. It seems unlikely that the Human Rights Act will lead to a decline in such applications.

23.02 The procedure of the Court is now governed by[6] the Eleventh Protocol to the Convention which implements the Vienna Declaration of the heads of state of the Council of Europe on 9 October 1993.[7] The Protocol was opened for signature in Strasbourg on 11 May 1994 and came into force on 1 November 1998.

(2) Background

23.03 When the Convention was signed in 1950, supervision by an independent supranational body of the powers of governments over persons within their territories was not seriously contemplated. The supervision of the European Convention on Human Rights was entrusted to the Committee of Ministers of the Council of Europe, a diplomatic body composed of the Foreign Affairs Ministers of each state party to the Convention. The Commission merely provided assistance to the Committee of Ministers. It was authorised to do preparatory work, establish the facts, attempt the negotiation of friendly settlements and report back to the Committee of Ministers. The Commission was at that time largely composed of civil servants and members of parliament. Only three of its initial 13 members had legal experience. Submission to the jurisdiction of a European Court of Human Rights for the determination of individual complaints against governments was an optional extra for a few internationally minded states.

[1] For the historical background to this acceptance, see Lord Lester, 'UK Acceptance of the Strasbourg Jurisdiction: What Really went on in Whitehall in 1965' [1998] PL 237.

[2] Art 35(1); see para 23.44ff below.

[3] HRA, s 6(3), see para 5.104ff above.

[4] See generally, para 22.73ff above.

[5] See generally, para 4.57ff above.

[5a] This right will, of course, not be available to 'public authorities' as they do not have standing to make applications to the European Court of Human Rights, see para 22.26 above.

[6] For the procedure which operated until 30 Oct 1998 see D Harris, M O'Boyle and C Warbrick, *Law of the European Convention on Human Rights*, (Butterworths, 1995) Chap 24.

[7] The most comprehensive account in English is in L Clements, N Mole and A Simmons, *European Human Rights: Taking a Case Under the Convention*, (2nd edn, Sweet & Maxwell, 1999) to which the following discussion is indebted.

Over the next four decades the role of the Convention institutions substantially changed. The Commission evolved into a legal body which submitted reasoned opinions for confirmation without discussion by the Committee of Ministers. However, the inability of the Commission to take binding decisions and its closed proceedings came to be seen as inappropriate and outdated. The most acute problem was the backlog of cases and length of proceedings. Only a small fraction of the cases filed each year reach the Court, all others being either inadmissible or containing no new legal question. Between 1981 and 1993 the annual number of applications registered with the Commission increased from 404 to 2,037. The Commission sought to cope with the problem by increasing the number of sessions organised and increasing its staff and productivity. 23.04

The European Court of Human Rights is composed of one judge from every Member State of the Council of Europe and the Commission was composed of one member from every state. As a result of developments in eastern and central Europe, the membership of these organs increased considerably. These problems provided the impetus for a comprehensive reform of the system which became an urgent priority of the Council of Europe in the early 1990s. 23.05

The possibility of a single Court was first suggested by a meeting of a Committee of Experts[8] in an exchange of views with the Commission in 1982. In 1985 it was raised for the first time at a political level at the European Ministerial Conference on Human Rights in Vienna.[9] It was believed that a procedure with one level would be simpler, faster and cheaper than the original two-tier system.[10] Over several years, delegations of the Member States to the Council of Europe negotiated a protocol to facilitate procedures for the supervision of the Convention. Article 19 provides for a European Court of Human Rights which functions on a permanent basis.[11] 23.06

The Eleventh Protocol came into force on 1 November 1998. The full time Court has made some progress in reducing the delays in hearings but has been faced with an increasing case load. In 1999 8,396 applications were registered,[12] compared to 5,981 in 1998. On 31 December 1999 a total of 12,635 applications were 23.07

[8] The Committee of Ministers mandated a Committee of Experts to study the question.

[9] For details as to the initiatives taken in regard to the proposed reform, see the 'Explanatory Report to Protocol No 11 to the European Convention on Human Rights' (1994) 17 EHRR 501, 517.

[10] For a more comprehensive list and discussion of the advantages of the merger of the Court and the Commission see generally, the Neuchatel Colloquy: *Merger of the European Commission and European Court of Human Rights: Second Seminar on International Law and European Law at the University of Neuchatel* 14–15 Mar 1986 (1987) HRLJ 8.

[11] H G Schermers, 'Adaptation of the 11th Protocol to the European Convention on Human Rights' (1995) 20 ELR, 559, 560.

[12] 429 of which were from the United Kingdom, placing it eighth on the list of states from which applications were registered in 1999.

pending. A total of only 3,696 applications were disposed of in 1999 and it is clear that, in the short term, the back log of cases will rise. In the medium term it seems unlikely that the period between the date of application and judgment on the merits in an admissible application will fall below four years.

(3) The procedure in outline

23.08 The basic order of procedure in a case which proceeds to judgment on the merits is now as follows:[13]

- lodging the application;
- preliminary contacts with the Court registry;
- registration of application;
- assignment of application to a Chamber;
- appointment of Judge Rapporteur by a Chamber;
- examination by a three-member committee;
- communication of the application to the government;
- filing of observations and establishment of facts;
- oral hearing;
- admissibility decision by Chamber;
- possibility of friendly settlement negotiations;
- judgment by the Chamber;
- in exceptional cases the matter may be referred to the Grand Chamber which will render judgment after written and possibly oral proceedings.

The Rules of the Court are reproduced at Appendix F in Vol 2.

23.09 The Eleventh Protocol contains a number of transitional provisions.[14] Applications made before 1 November 1998 which had not been declared admissible by that date are dealt with by the Court in accordance with this procedure.[15] Applications which had already been declared admissible by the Commission were dealt with by the members of the Commission for a period of one year.[16] Applications which had not been dealt with by 30 October 1999 were then transmitted to the Court and dealt with as admissible applications under the new procedure.[17]

[13] See 'Explanatory Report to Protocol No 11 to the European Convention on Human Rights' (n 9 above) para 52.

[14] See generally, Clements, Mole and Simmons (n 7 above) paras 4-10–4-11.

[15] Art 5(2), Eleventh Protocol.

[16] Art 5(3), Eleventh Protocol.

[17] Ibid.

(4) The role of precedent

The Commission and Court do not apply the common law doctrine of precedent. The approach of the Strasbourg authorities has been summarised as follows:[17a] **23.09A**

- Decisions of the Commission and the Court are not binding (in the English sense) on the Commission or the Court although, in practice, decisions of the Court on interpreting the Convention are followed by the Commission.
- Decisions of the Court are authoritative interpretations of the Convention under the social and moral conditions and the state of scientific knowledge current at the time of the decision. They are usually followed 'in the interests of legal certainty and the orderly development of the Convention case law'.[17b]
- Nevertheless, the Court may decide that its earlier interpretation was simply erroneous or may have some other 'cogent reasons' for changing the interpretation including the need to 'ensure that the interpretation of the Convention reflects societal change and remains in line with present day conditions.[17c]
- The Court may depart from an earlier decision interpreting a particular Convention right if necessary to take account of a developing state of knowledge or evolving consensus between societies and States as to the proper scope of that right, although the Court tends to be slow and adopts a gradualist approach to such developments following rather than leading the European consensus.
- Decisions of the Court concerning the applicability of rights are more likely to be authorative statements of general practice than are decisions on the applicability of a State's justification for interfering with rights, which tend to depend heavily on facts and are concerned with balancing exercises under the principle of proportionality[17d] and the margin of appreciation.[17e]
- Even after the abolition of the Commission, decisions of the Commission remain 'important indicators as the meaning of the Convention in the absence of a Court's pronouncement'.[17f]
- There is no real distinction drawn by the Court between *ratio decidendi* and *obiter dictum* in its previous pronouncements. All statements are regarded as sources of enlightenment as to the meaning of the Convention.

[17a] See D Feldman, 'Precedent and the European Court of Human Rights', Law Commission, *Bail and the Human Rights Act*, Consultation paper No. 157 (The Stationery Office, 1999) App C.

[17b] *Cossey v United Kingdom* (1990) 13 EHRR 622 para 35; *Sheffield and Horsham v United Kingdom* (1998) 27 EHRR 163 refusing to depart from its earlier decision in *Rees v United Kingdom* (1986) 9 EHRR 56 in relation to the treatment of transsexuals under Art 8: see para 12.158 above.

[17c] *Cossey v United Kingdom* (n 17b above) para 35; the principle of interpretation that the Convention is a living instrument is discussed at para 6.23ff above.

[17d] For a discussion of the principle, see para 6.42ff above.

[17e] For a discussion of the doctrine, see para 6.31ff above.

[17f] See D Harris, M O'Boyle and C Warbrick, *The Law of the European Convention on Human Rights* (3rd edn, Sweet & Maxwell, 1995) 18.

- The Committee of Ministers did not give reasoned decisions until its decision making role was abolished by the Eleventh Protocol. Its decisions on the applicability of the Convention are therefore of no value as precedents.

B. The Organisation of the Court

(1) General

23.10 A single Court has now replaced the two supervisory organs of the Convention: it performs the functions of both the European Commission and the European Court of Human Rights.[18] The Committee of Ministers will retain its role in supervising the execution of judgments[19] but its role in deciding whether or not there had been a violation of the Convention in cases which were not referred to the Court[20] has been abolished.[21]

23.11 The Court is now full-time, with jurisdiction in all matters regarding interpretation and application of the Convention including inter-state cases as well as individual applications. The Court can also give advisory opinions upon the request of the Committee of Ministers. It consists of a number of judges equal to the number of states party to the Convention:[22] at present there are 40. The Judges are elected by the Parliamentary Assembly for each state party. Judges serve six-year terms and may be re-elected.

23.12 Cases are decided by the Court sitting in committees, Chambers and in a Grand Chamber. The national judge of the state concerned will always sit in the Chambers and the Grand Chamber. Organisational matters will be dealt with by the Court in plenary session. Committees consist of three judges, Chambers of seven judges and the Grand Chamber of 17 judges.

(2) The Plenary Court

23.13 The Plenary Court consists of all the judges who are members of the Court. It does not, however, sit in a judicial capacity but serves certain administrative functions. In particular, the Plenary Court elects its President and two Vice-Presidents for three-year terms, subject to re-election. It sets up Chambers which are consti-

---

[18] For a perspective on the legacy which the Commission will bring to the new procedure, see N Bratza and M O'Boyle 'Opinion: The Legacy of the Commission to the New Court Under the Eleventh Protocol' [1997] EHRLR 211.

[19] Former Art 54, now Art 46.

[20] Under the former Art 32.

[21] For the former role of the Committee of Ministers, see Harris, O'Boyle and Warbrick (n 6 above) 691ff.

[22] Art 20.

tuted for a period of three years.[23] At least four Chambers must be set up.[24] The Plenary Court elects the President of each Chamber.[25] It also adopts the rules of the Court; and elects a Registrar and Deputy Registrars.

(3) The Grand Chamber

The Grand Chamber is the highest judicial body under the Convention. It consists of 17 judges and three substitutes.[26] It includes the President and Vice-President of the Court and the Presidents of the Chambers.[27] If the judge appointed by the respondent state is not already a member of the Grand Chamber he sits *ex officio*, replacing one of the appointed judges.[28] **23.14**

The role of the Grand Chamber is two fold: **23.15**

- the determination of complex cases—where a case raises a serious question affecting the interpretation of the Convention or where a decision may be inconsistent with a previous decision a Chamber may relinquish jurisdiction to the Grand Chamber (unless one of the parties objects);[29]
- the determination of appeals from decisions of Chambers.[30]

(4) The Chambers

Chambers of seven judges[31] are set up for a fixed period of time. The Plenary Court determines which judges sit in a Chamber, in accordance with a procedure to be specified in its rules. Subject to specific powers of the Committees and the Grand Chamber, Chambers have inherent competence to examine the admissibility and the merits of all cases.[32] **23.16**

(5) Judge Rapporteurs and Committees

Once the application is registered, it is assigned to a Chamber which designates a 'Judge Rapporteur'[33] who examines the application and decides whether it should be referred to a Committee or a Chamber.[34] The Rapporteur usually requires that the case be examined by a Committee, however all inter-State cases must be **23.17**

23 Rule 25(1).
24 Ibid.
25 Rule 8.
26 Rule 25(4).
27 Rule 24.
28 Ibid.
29 See para 23.69 below.
30 See para 23.70 below.
31 Art 27(1).
32 Art 29(1).
33 Rule 49(1).
34 Rule 49(2)(b).

decided by a Chamber. With the assistance of the Registry and in communication with the parties, the Judge Rapporteur prepares the case. If a case is declared admissible, he also takes steps with a view to a friendly settlement.

23.18 Committees of three judges are set up by Chambers, for a fixed period of time. The appointment of judges to sit on the Committee, which usually includes the Judge Rapporteur, will also be determined by the Chamber. The purpose of the Committee system is to provide a fast track procedure for rejecting obviously inadmissible cases.[35] Committees only have the power to declare individual cases inadmissible or strike cases off the list.[36] This is done by a unanimous vote. If no such decision is taken by a Committee, the application will be referred to a Chamber for a decision as to admissibility and ultimately merits.

(6) The Registry

23.19 The Registry is responsible for the administration of the Court. It is headed by the Registrar who is appointed by the Plenary Court.[37] The Registrar's functions are set out in Rule 17. Each Chamber has its own Registrar and Deputy Registrar. The Registrar is present when the judges deliberate[38] and the Registry prepares the first draft of the judgment. As a result, the position of the Registry is much more powerful than that of court clerks in common law jurisdictions.[39]

(7) The Committee of Ministers

23.20 The Committee of Ministers is made up of the foreign ministers of the Member States of the Council of Europe. It meets in formal session twice a year. Under Article 46 the final judgment of the Court is transmitted to the Committee of Ministers whose role is to supervise its execution.[40]

C. Making an Application

(1) Representation

23.21 An application may be made by a person, non-governmental organisation or group of individuals.[41] The application may be made by the applicants themselves

[35] See L Clements, N Mole and A Simmons, *European Human Rights: Taking a Case Under the Convention* (2nd edn, Sweet & Maxwell, 1999) para 3–21.

[36] Art 28.

[37] Arts 25 and 26(e).

[38] Rule 22(2).

[39] Cf D Jackson, *The United Kingdom Confronts the European Convention on Human Rights* (University of Florida Press, 1997) 14–15.

[40] See para 23.78ff below.

[41] See generally, para 22.27ff above.

or by an appointed representative.[42] The applicant must be represented at any hearing and after the application has been declared admissible unless the President of the Chamber decides otherwise.[43]

The applicant's representative must be an advocate authorised to practice in any of the Contracting States or any other person approved by the President of the Chamber.[44] Where the applicants are represented a power of attorney or written authority to act shall be supplied by the representative.[45] The President may grant leave to the applicant to present his own case, subject if necessary to being assisted by an advocate or other approved representative.[46] **23.22**

(2) The application

The application must be made in writing and signed by the applicant or the applicant's representative.[47] In the case of a non-governmental organisation or a group of individuals, the signatory must be the person competent to represent the organisation or group.[48] The date of introduction of the application will, generally, be the date of the first communication from the applicant setting out, even summarily, the object of the application. The date is that written on the letter.[49] However, the court may, for good cause, decide that a different date shall be considered to be the date of introduction.[50] When the application is introduced this will stop time running for the purpose of the six-month rule.[51] **23.23**

The initial letter should give details of the applicant and a brief outline of the nature of the application. It should set out the essential basis of the complaint and the Articles of the Convention which, it is alleged, have been violated.[52] **23.24**

When the preliminary letter is received the Registry will open a provisional file and assign a case lawyer with knowledge of the language and legal system of the state to which the application relates. The Court will send the applicant a copy of the standard application form and may indicate its initial views on admissibility **23.25**

---

[42] Rule 36(1); following notification of the application to the respondent that the President of the Chamber may direct that the applicant should be represented: r 36(2).
[43] Rule 36(3).
[44] Rule 36(4).
[45] Rule 45(3).
[46] Rule 36(4).
[47] Rule 45.
[48] Rule 45(2).
[49] See K Reid, *A Practitioner's Guide to the European Convention of Human Rights* (Sweet & Maxwell, 1998) 20: if the letter is undated, the date is that of the postmark and, if this is illegible, the date of arrival.
[50] Rule 47(5).
[51] See para 23.51ff below.
[52] For four precedents, see L Clements, N Mole and A Simmons, *European Human Rights: Taking a Case under the Convention* (2nd edn, Sweet & Maxwell, 1999) App 6, 331–342.

and whether it is considering similar applications. The applicant will then usually be given a period of six weeks to return the application form. If, however, there are compelling reasons, the Court may be prepared to accept a longer period of delay.[53]

23.26 The application must be made on the application form provided[54] unless the Court directs otherwise.[55] The form must set out:[56]

- the name, date of birth, nationality, sex, occupation and address of the applicant;
- the name, occupation and address of the representative, if any;
- the name of the Contracting Party or Parties against which the application is made;
- a succinct statement of the facts;
- a succinct statement of the alleged violation(s) of the Convention and the relevant arguments;
- a succinct statement of the applicant's compliance with the admissibility criteria laid down by Article 35.1 (exhaustion of domestic remedies and the six-month rule);
- the object of the application as well as a general indication of any claims for just satisfaction which the applicant may wish to make.

In addition, the application should be accompanied by copies of any relevant documents, including the decisions, relating to the object of the application.

23.27 The applicant must also:[57]

- provide information enabling it to be shown that domestic remedies have been exhausted and the six-month rule complied with; and
- indicate whether the applicant has submitted complaints to any other procedure of international investigation or settlement.

An applicant who does not wish his identity to be disclosed to the public shall so indicate and must submit a statement of the reasons justifying a departure from the normal rule of public access to information in proceedings before the Court. The President of the Chamber may only authorise anonymity in 'exceptional and duly justified circumstances'.[58] Failure to comply with the requirements in Rules 47(1) and (2) may result in the application not being registered.[59] An applicant

53 See Clements, Mole and Simmons (n 52 above) para 2–29, 37.
54 See App F in Vol 2.
55 Rule 47(1).
56 Ibid.
57 Rule 47(2).
58 Rule 47(3).
59 Rule 47(4).

must keep the Court informed of any change of address and relevant circumstances.[60]

The application form must, of course, be completed with considerable care. In particular, the following points must be borne in mind:[61] **23.28**

- **The parties**: are there 'indirect' victims who should be included in addition to the 'direct' victim?[62]
- **The alleged violations**: each Article should be dealt with separately and if there is an arguable point in relation to a particular Article it should be included as the applicant will not be able to rely on the argument later if it is not included.
- **The object of the application**: this should be dealt with under the headings 'non-financial' (for example, a change in domestic law); 'compensation' (divided into pecuniary and non-pecuniary losses), 'costs'.
- **List of documents**: This should be included in a paginated and indexed bundle. Copies of the relevant domestic statutes and case law should also be included in a separate section.

(3) Legal aid

An applicant can request legal aid from the Court. This may be granted from the moment that observations in writing on admissibility are received from the respondent.[63] The Registry will send a declaration of means form to the applicant. The declaration of means form must be certified by the relevant domestic authority:[64] in the United Kingdom this is the DSS which applies the standard of eligibility for civil legal aid. Once the form is received by the Court it sends a copy to the government for comment and then decides the application.[65] Legal aid is granted where the President of the Chamber is satisfied that it is necessary for the proper conduct of the case before the Chamber and that the applicant has insufficient means to meet all or part of the costs.[66] **23.29**

The level of legal aid is modest by comparison to UK professional fees and legal aid rates. The scale of fees from January 1998 was 3,000FF (about £300) for preparation of a case, 2,000FF (about £200) for preparation of written observations and 2,000FF per day (about £200) for court hearings.[67] **23.30**

---

[60] Rule 47(6).
[61] See generally, Clements, Mole and Simmons (n 52 above) paras 3-06–3-14.
[62] For these concepts, see para 22.27ff above.
[63] Rule 91(1).
[64] Rule 93(1).
[65] Rule 93(2).
[66] Rule 92.
[67] See L Clements, N Mole and A Simmons, *European Human Rights: Taking a Case Under the Convention* (2nd edn Sweet & Maxwell, 1999) para 8–03.

23.31 United Kingdom legal aid is not available for proceedings before the Court. However, parties to such proceedings are able to enter into conditional fee agreements with a mark up of up to 100% on costs.[68]

D. Admissibility

(1) Procedure

(a) Judge Rapporteur and Committee

23.32 Once an application is made it is examined by the Judge Rapporteur.[69] The Judge Rapporteur may request the parties to submit, within a specified time, factual information, documents or other relevant material.[70] He then decides whether to refer the case to a Chamber or to a Committee. The Judge Rapporteur prepares a confidential report for use by the Committee or the Chamber. The Committee may decide, by a unanimous vote only, that an application is inadmissible.[71] This decision is not subject to any appeal. If the Committee does not unanimously decide that the application is inadmissible it is referred to a Chamber.

(b) Chamber: initial procedure

23.33 The Chamber must decide on the admissibility and the merits of the application.[72] These decisions are taken separately unless the Court, in exceptional cases, decides otherwise.[73] When an application is referred to a Chamber it may at once declare it inadmissible and strike it out of the list.[74] Otherwise, the Chamber may:[75]

- request the parties to submit any factual information, documents or other material which it considers to be relevant;
- give notice of the application to the respondent state and invite it to submit written observations on the application;
- invite the parties to submit further observations in writing.

23.34 The Chamber will usually ask for the government's observations to be submitted within six weeks, although extensions of time will usually be sought: this is done by letter or fax, setting out the reason why the time is required. Such extensions

68 See Conditional Fee Agreements Order 1995, SI 1995 No 1674, para 2(1)(f).
69 See para 23.17 above.
70 Rule 49(2).
71 Art 28.
72 Art 29(1).
73 Art 29(3).
74 Rule 54(2).
75 Rule 54(3).

are usually given, typically for three weeks. The government's observations on admissibility will usually consist of four sections dealing with the facts, the law and practice, admissibility and merits and conclusion.[76]

The government's reply will then be copied to the applicant for comment within six weeks. The applicant can seek an extension of time. If the government's response raises new issues, the applicant can request further information directly from the government's agent. The applicant's response should adopt the same format as that of the government and should respond to the government's observations point by point. It is suggested that, at this stage, the applicant should provide the fullest and most detailed exposition of his case.[77] **23.35**

(c) Chamber: admissibility hearing and decision

Before making a decision on admissibility the Chamber may decide, either at the request of the parties or of its own motion, to hold a hearing.[78] The notice of the hearing will set out the facts or issues the Chamber wishes to investigate. The parties will be invited to send their final arguments to the Court so that they can be made available to the judges at the hearing. The parties will be asked for how long they will wish to address the Court but, in practice, hearings usually take half a day, with parties being allowed a total of 45 minutes each to make oral submissions. The parties are invited to file a statement setting out their oral submissions at least 14 days before the hearing: these are copied to the other parties. At least 10 days before the hearing, the Court must be notified of the names and functions of the persons who will appear. The Court can summon witnesses for the purposes of giving oral evidence if it deems this appropriate.[79] However, this is unusual. **23.36**

The hearings are usually in public.[80] If a party fails to appear the Court may proceed with the hearing.[81] At the hearing the state representative usually makes the first speech and the applicant's representative the second. These speeches should last 30 minutes each. Questions may then be put by any judge[82] and the hearing is then adjourned for about 20 minutes for responses to be considered. The parties then have 15 minutes each to deliver their responses and final submissions, with the state representative again speaking first. The parties then leave so that the judges can consider their decision. **23.37**

---

[76] For a detailed discussion, see Clements, Mole and Simmons (n 67 above) para 3–18.
[77] See ibid, para 3–19.
[78] Rule 54(4).
[79] Rule 65.
[80] Art 40(1).
[81] Rule 64.
[82] Rule 68(1).

23.38 After the decision is made the Court issues a press release outlining the case. The details are usually agreed by the representatives in advance. The Registry telephones the representative of the state and of the applicant to advise them of the decision. The Court's reasoned decision is sent to the parties about six weeks after the hearing.

(2) Admissibility criteria

23.39 In order to be admissible for consideration by the Court an application must:

- be made by a person, non-governmental organisation or group of individuals claiming to be the victim against a Contracting State (competence *ratione personae*);[83]
- concern a violation by a Contracting State of the rights in the Convention or the protocols; (competence *ratione materiae*);[84]
- be made at a time when the Contracting State was bound by the Convention (competence *ratione temporis*);
- concern a jurisdiction to which the Convention extends (competence *ratione loci*);
- be made within a period of six months after domestic remedies have been exhausted;[85]
- not be 'manifestly ill-founded, or an abuse of the right of application'.[86]

The Court will not deal with petitions which are either anonymous or substantially the same as a matter which has already been examined by the Court or submitted to a procedure of international investigation or settlement and contain no relevant new information.[87]

(3) The person by and against whom the complaint is made

23.40 An application must be made by a person or organisation which is a 'victim' of the violation. This principle of standing has already been discussed.[88] It must be made in respect of actions or failures to act by the state or state bodies. No complaint can be made against the actions of a private person as such:[89] however, the state may be responsible for the actions of private persons as a result of its positive obligations under the Convention.[90] The question as to the extent to which the

83 Art 34.
84 Ibid.
85 Art 35(1).
86 Ibid.
87 Art 35(2).
88 See para 22.27 above.
89 See eg *Nielsen v Denmark* (1988) 11 EHRR 175.
90 See generally, para 5.10ff above.

state has a responsibility for the actions of private persons raises difficult issues of 'horizontality' which are discussed above.[91] It should, however, be borne in mind that the state has a general responsibility to ensure that its legal system effectively guarantees Convention rights.[92]

(4) Subject matter of the complaint

An application will be inadmissible in terms of its subject matter (*ratione materiae*) if it does not relate to an alleged breach of a right contained in the Convention or a Protocol which has been ratified by the respondent state. The Court cannot deal with rights which are not contained in the Convention. Applications relating to a range of 'rights' have been refused on this ground including the following: **23.41**

- the right to a pension;[93]
- the right to adequate housing;[94]
- the right to a job or a minimum wage;[95]
- the right of access to employment in the public service;[95a]
- the right to a driving licence.[96]

(5) Jurisdiction as to time

An application will be inadmissible as to time (*ratione temporis*) if it relates to events which took place at a time at which the Convention was not applicable to the respondent state. There is no jurisdiction to hear a complaint relating to events which took place before the state's acceptance of the right to individual petition.[97] A complaint against the UK Government will, therefore, be inadmissible on this ground if it relates to events which took place before 14 January 1966. An application in respect of the failure of the UK Government to monitor radiation levels at a nuclear test in Christmas Island in 1957 and 1958 was rejected on this ground.[98] **23.42**

[91] See para 5.74ff above.
[92] *Young, James and Webster v United Kingdom* (1981) 4 EHRR 38 para 49.
[93] *X v Sweden* (1986) 8 EHRR 253.
[94] *X v Germany* (1956) 1 YB 202.
[95] *X v Denmark* (1975) 3 DR 153, EComm HR.
[95a] *Kosiek v Germany* (1986) 9 EHRR 328 para 34.
[96] *X v Germany* (1977) 9 DR 112.
[97] For a general discussion of this requirement, see D Harris, M O'Boyle and C Warbrick, *Law of the European Convention on Human Rights* (Butterworths, 1995) 640–641 and L Clements, N Mole and A Simmons, *European Human Rights: Taking a Case under the Convention* (2nd edn, Sweet & Maxwell, 1999) para 2–12.
[98] *LCB v United Kingdom* (1998) 27 EHRR 212 para 35.

(6) Jurisdiction as to place

23.43 An application will be inadmissible as to place (*ratione loci*) if it relates to events in a place for which the state bears no responsibility. An application is not confined to events within the national territory of a state. A state may be responsible for the authorised acts of its agent which produce effects in its own territory[99] or elsewhere.[100] A state is therefore responsible for extradition and expulsion. However, this does not mean that there is any right to diplomatic intervention or protection.[101] A state may also be responsible where it exercises effective control over an area outside its national territory as a consequence of military action.[102]

(7) Exhaustion of domestic remedies

(a) General

23.44 In accordance with the general principles of international law, an applicant must first exhaust his domestic remedies. Article 35 makes it clear that this is in accordance with 'generally recognised rules of international law'.[103] The rationale for the rule is that the state must first be given the opportunity to prevent or put right the violations alleged against it.[104]

23.45 The rule is applied with flexibility and without excessive formalism.[105] It is not absolute nor capable of being applied automatically. However, the rule does not merely require that applications should be made to the domestic courts and that use should be made of available remedies:

> It normally requires also that the complaints intended to be made subsequently in Strasbourg have been made to those same courts, at least in substance and in compliance with the formal requirements and time limits laid down in domestic law and, further that any procedural means which might prevent a breach of the Convention should have been used.[106]

---

[99] *Drozd and Janousek v France and Spain* (1992) 14 EHRR 745 para 91.

[100] *Cyprus v Turkey* (1975) 2 DR 125, 136–137 EComm HR.

[101] *Bertrand Russell Peace Foundation Ltd v United Kingdom* (1978) 14 DR 117, 124, EComm HR (no obligation to intervene diplomatically with the Soviet authorities to protect the applicant's mail).

[102] *Loizidou v Turkey (Preliminary Objection)* (1995) 20 EHRR 99 para 62.

[103] For which see generally, I Brownlie, *Principles of Public International Law* (5th edn, Oxford University Press, 1998) 496–506.

[104] *Guzzardi v Italy* (1981) 3 EHRR 333 para 72; *Aksoy v Turkey* (1996) 23 EHRR 553 para 51.

[105] *Aksoy v Turkey* (n 104 above) para 53.

[106] *Cardot v France* (1991) 13 EHRR 853 para 34; see also *Barberá Messegué and Jabardo v Spain* (1989) 11 EHRR 360 paras 56–59.

(b) Effective remedy

The rule only applies when effective remedies are available in the national system. The existence of the remedies must be sufficiently certain not only in theory but in practice.[107] Moreover, an applicant who has exhausted a remedy that is apparently effective and sufficient cannot be required also to have tried others that were available but probably no more likely to be successful.[108] There is no requirement that ineffective remedies offering no prospect of success are pursued. Under the 'generally recognised rules of international law' there may be special circumstances which absolve the applicant from the obligation to exhaust domestic remedies.[109] **23.46**

Remedies will not be effective if they do not provide redress. Thus, a power to 'recommend' redress will not be sufficient.[110] Similarly, a 'discretionary' remedy such as a request for an *ex gratia* payment or the discretionary re-opening of proceedings will not be sufficient.[111] The mere fact that there are doubts about the prospects of success of national proceedings will not mean that there is no obligation to exhaust the remedies.[112] But Counsel's opinion that a case has no prospect of success may be enough to indicate that a remedy would not be effective.[113] **23.47**

The exhaustion of the local remedies rule is not applicable in cases in which the applicant has shown a *prima facie* case that he is the victim of an administrative practice consisting of a repetition of acts incompatible with the Convention which is tolerated by state authorities to such an extent that proceedings would be futile or ineffective.[114] **23.48**

The burden of proof is on the government to show that the remedy was an effective one in theory and practice and was capable of providing redress in respect of the applicant's complaints and which offered reasonable prospects of success.[115] If the state satisfies this burden, the applicant must then show that this remedy was, in fact, exhausted or was, for some reason, ineffective and inadequate in the circumstances.[116] **23.49**

[107] *Aksoy v Turkey* (1996) 23 EHRR 553 para 52

[108] *TW v Malta* (1999) 29 EHRR 185 para 34.

[109] Ibid para 52.

[110] *Montion v France* (1987) 52 DR 227, EComm HR (ombudsman).

[111] *Agee v United Kingdom* (1976) 7 DR 164, EComm HR.

[112] *Whiteside v United Kingdom* (1994) 76-A DR 80, EComm HR.

[113] *H v United Kingdom* (1983) 33 DR 247; but see *K, F and P v United Kingdom* (1984) 40 DR 298, EComm HR.

[114] *Akdivar v Turkey* (1997) 23 EHRR 143 para 66–67; *Aksoy v Turkey* (1996) 23 EHRR 553 para 52.

[115] *Akdivar v Turkey* (n 114 above) para 68.

[116] Ibid.

23.50 After the Human Rights Act comes into force applicants will be able to raise Convention rights before any court or tribunal.[117] As a result, in the absence of specific statutory provision to the contrary[118] it is difficult to see how a UK applicant could justify a failure to raise Convention rights[119] in domestic proceedings before making an application to Strasbourg.

(8) Six-month time limit

23.51 This rule cannot be waived by the applicant or the Court.[120] Time will run from the day after the final decision or, if the decision is not publicly pronounced, the day on which the applicant was informed.[121] If the applicant was represented, the relevant date will be that on which the lawyer was informed.[122]

23.52 If there is no domestic remedy, time runs from the date when the applicant became aware of the alleged violation.[123] Where the violation complained of is a sequence of events, time will run from the end of the sequence (unless it was practicable to complain earlier). Where the complaint relates to a continuous state of affairs the six-month time limit does not apply.

23.53 There may be very limited circumstances in which *force majeure* will prevent the strict six-month time limit from applying.[124]

(9) 'Substantially the same as a previous application'

23.54 A complaint will not be admissible if it is substantially the same as matters which have already been examined by the Court or another procedure of international investigation or settlement and contains no relevant new information.[125] New information will include:

- further delay in domestic legal proceedings where a previous complaint of unreasonable delay has been found inadmissible;[126]
- exhaustion of domestic remedies, where the complaint was previously dismissed on this ground;
- discovery of new relevant facts which were not previously available.[127]

---

[117] Under s 7 of the Act; see generally, para 22.01ff above.
[118] See para 4.30 above.
[119] See generally, para 3.43ff above.
[120] *X v France* (1982) 29 DR 228, 240, EComm HR; *K v Ireland* (1984) 38 DR 158, EComm HR.
[121] *K, C and M v Netherlands* (1995) 80-A DR 87, 88.
[122] *Aarts (Martinus Godefridus) v Netherlands* (1991) 70 DR 208.
[123] *Hilton v United Kingdom* (1988) 57 DR 108, 113, EComm HR.
[124] See K Reid, *A Practitioner's Guide to the European Convention of Human Rights* (Sweet & Maxwell, 1998) 21.
[125] Art 32(2)(b).
[126] *X v United Kingdom* (1979) 17 DR 122, EComm HR.
[127] *X v United Kingdom* Application 23956/94, 28 Nov 1994.

However, an application cannot be renewed simply because the applicant wants to advance new legal arguments which were not previously put before the Court.[128]

(10) Manifestly ill-founded or an abuse of the right of application

(a) Manifestly ill-founded

The use of the words 'manifestly ill-founded' might be thought to mean that an application should only be rejected on this ground if it does not disclose any possible ground for showing a violation of a Convention right. However, the Commission and the Court have purported to apply a different test: whether or not there is a '*prima facie*' case.[129] In other words, it has been said that if an application is arguable it cannot be 'manifestly ill-founded'.[130] In practice, the reports of decisions made by the former Commission are scattered with arguable cases which have been dismissed as 'manifestly ill-founded'. The test which is applied in practice is more akin to 'strong *prima facie* case'.[131] **23.55**

(b) Abuse of the right of application

The fact that the applicant persistently uses insulting or provocative language might be considered an abuse of the right of application.[132] It will be an abuse to make repeated inadmissible complaints of a similar nature.[133] However, provided the complaint is made bona fide, it will not be an abuse for an applicant to use the procedure as part of a campaign to influence public opinion or to put pressure on the government.[134] **23.56**

E. Interim Procedural Matters

(1) Interim remedies

By Rule 39, the Chamber or its President may, at the request of the parties or of its own motion, indicate to the parties any interim measures which it considers should be adopted. Notice of these measures must be given to the Committee of **23.57**

---

[128] *X v United Kingdom* (1981) 25 DR 147, EComm HR.

[129] *Airey v Ireland* (1979) 3 EHRR 305 para 18.

[130] *Boyle and Rice v United Kingdom* (1988) 10 EHRR 425 para 54.

[131] Cf L Clements, N Mole and A Simmons, *European Human Rights: Taking a Case Under the Convention* (2nd edn, Sweet & Maxwell, 1999) para 2–35 in which it is suggested that the Court rejects cases which it considers 'weak' even if they are arguable.

[132] *Stamoulakatos v United Kingdom* (1997) 23 EHRR CD 113 (this was also the seventeenth application made by the applicant, with another fourteen pending).

[133] *M v United Kingdom* (1987) 54 DR 214, EComm HR; *Philis v Greece* (1996) 23 EHRR CD 147.

[134] *McFeeley v United Kingdom* (1980) 20 DR 44, EComm HR; *Akdivar v Turkey* (1997) 23 EHRR 143 para 54.

Ministers.[135] Requests for interim remedies are most common in deportation and extradition cases[136] but are also made in other cases where life or health are at immediate risk. The Court recently requested Turkey not to carry out a death sentence until it had the opportunity to examine the admissibility of the applicant's complaints.[137]

23.58 An indication under Rule 39 is not binding on the state: the rule only has the status of a rule of procedure.[138] However, in practice, states usually comply with such indications.[139] The United Kingdom has complied with indications on a number of occasions and seems likely to comply in the future.

23.59 A Rule 39 application may be made in advance of the final decision of the domestic court. It should be made in the form of a separate letter, with supporting documentation, to the Registry.[140] The application should be accompanied by clear independent evidence of the harm likely to result if no interim measure is taken. If a Rule 39 application is being made, the applicant's representative should inform the public authority which is holding the applicant.

(2) Expedited procedure

23.60 The Court has a pending caseload of over 5,000 cases. The average time taken for a case to reach judgment is four to five years. Under the previous procedure, the Commission took between nine months and three years to make admissibility decisions and up to four years to give decisions on the merits.[141] The first cases decided by the court in early 2000 related to applications lodged in 1996 and 1997.

23.61 In urgent cases it may be necessary to expedite the procedure to obtain an early hearing date. By Rule 40, in any case of urgency, the Registrar may, with the authority of the President of the Chamber and without prejudice to any other procedural steps, inform the respondent state of the application and its objects. By Rule 41, the Court may decide to give priority to a particular application. In a number of urgent cases, applications have been heard in 12 months.[142]

[135] Rule 39(2).

[136] See eg *Soering v United Kingdom* (1989) 11 EHRR 439.

[137] Rule 39 Request: *Öcalan v Turkey*, 30 Nov 1999.

[138] *Cruz Varas v Sweden* (1991) 14 EHRR 1 paras 94–104.

[139] Ibid para 100.

[140] For a precedent of a Rule 39 application see Clements, Mole and Simmons, (n 131 above) App 6, 342–345.

[141] For the 1998 position see the Table in K Reid, *A Practitioner's Guide to the European Convention of Human Rights* (Sweet & Maxwell, 1998), 17.

[142] See eg *Soering v United Kingdom* (1989) 11 EHRR 439 (application was lodged on 8 Jul 1988 and the final hearing was on 7 Jul 1989); *X v France* (1992) 14 EHRR 483 (application 19 Feb 1991, hearing 23 Mar 1992).

(3) Participation of third parties

In all cases before the Court the state whose national is the applicant has the right to submit written comments and to take part in the hearing.[143] The decision declaring an application admissible must be notified by the Registrar to such a state.[144] The right to submit comments is often exercised by states which commonly support their own nationals.[145] **23.62**

The President of the Court may invite any state which is not a party or any person concerned who is not the applicant to submit written comments or take part in the hearing.[146] Requests for leave under this provision must be 'duly reasoned' and submitted within a reasonable time after the fixing of the written procedure.[147] A grant of leave may be subject to conditions, including time limits set by the President of the Chamber.[148] The parties are entitled, subject to any conditions, including time limits set by the President of the Chamber, to file written observations in reply.[149] It is obviously of assistance to an applicant to obtain support for an application from respected independent third parties.[150] **23.63**

(4) Friendly settlements

When an application is declared admissible, the Registrar must enter into contact with the parties with a view to securing a friendly settlement of the matter.[151] The negotiations for a friendly settlement are confidential and without prejudice.[152] If the Chamber is informed by the Registrar that a friendly settlement has been agreed it shall, 'after verifying that the settlement has been reached on the basis of respect for human rights', strike the case out of the list.[153] **23.64**

(5) Striking out

Under Article 37, the Court may, at any stage of the proceedings, decide to strike an application out of the list if the circumstances lead to the conclusion that: **23.65**

---

[143] Art 36(1).
[144] Rule 61(1).
[145] See eg *Soering v United Kingdom* (1989) 11 EHRR 439 (German government supporting applicant who was a German national in his opposition to extradition).
[146] Art 36(2).
[147] Rule 61(3).
[148] Rule 61(3).
[149] Rule 61(4).
[150] For a general discussion, see L Clements, N Mole and A Simmons, *European Human Rights: Taking a Case under the Convention* (2nd edn, Sweet & Maxwell, 1999) para 4–04.
[151] Rule 62(1).
[152] Rule 62(2).
[153] Rule 62(3).

- the applicant does not intend to pursue his application—because, for example, the applicant has failed to respond to requests for information or to observe time limits;[154]
- the matter has been resolved;
- for any other reason it is no longer justified to continue examining the application—because, for example, the applicant had obtained adequate domestic redress.[155]

The Court has a general power to retain a complaint which raises serious issues even if the applicant no longer wishes to pursue it.[156] This power is rarely invoked.[157]

F. Determination of Merits and Judgments

(1) Determination by a Chamber

23.66 The Chamber has power to obtain evidence which it considers capable of providing clarification of the facts of the case.[158] It may request the parties to provide documents or decide to hear other persons as witnesses of fact or experts. The Chamber may depute one of its members or another judge to conduct an inquiry, carry out an investigation on the spot or take evidence, with or without the assistance of external experts.[159] Such investigations are not often carried out.[160]

23.67 If there has been no oral admissibility hearing, then the Court will usually provide an opportunity for an oral hearing on merits. The state cannot raise issues on admissibility at this hearing if they are not raised at the admissibility stage.[161] The hearing will take a similar form to that on admissibility.[162] After the hearing the Court deliberates in private.[163] The decisions of the Court are taken by a majority and, if there is a tie, the President has the casting vote.[164] After the deliberations, the Registrar sends the representative a verbatim record of their arguments, statements and evidence in order for this to be approved.[165] Once this is done, it

154 See eg *Wardlaw (Peter) v United Kingdom* (1989) 60 DR 71.
155 *Wilde, Greenhal and Parry v United Kingdom* (1995) 80 DR 132.
156 Art 37(1).
157 *Tyrer v United Kingdom* (1978) 2 EHRR 1.
158 Rule 42(1).
159 Rule 42(2).
160 But see eg *Ireland v United Kingdom* (1978) 2 EHRR 25 (evidence taken from 113 witnesses at seven separate hearings in three different countries).
161 Cf Rule 55 and see *Bricmont v Belgium* (1989) 12 EHRR 217.
162 See para 23.32ff above.
163 Rule 22(1).
164 Rule 23.
165 Rule 70.

is supplied to the Court by the Registry together with a draft judgment which it has prepared from the Registrar's record of the deliberations. The judgment is then finalised by a drafting committee and then returned to the full Chamber for approval.

Judgments of the Court follow a standard format which is laid down in Rule 74. If the question of just satisfaction is ready for decision it should be dealt with in the same judgment. If not, it can be reserved in whole or in part.[166] Any judge who has taken part in the consideration of the case is entitled to annex a separate concurring or dissenting opinion.[167] Final judgments of the Court are transmitted to the Committee of Ministers and to the parties.[168] They are published under the authority of the Registrar.[169] The full text of judgments is now available on the Court's web site[170] on the day of publication. **23.68**

(2) Determination by the Grand Chamber

(a) Relinquishment

Where a case raises a serious question affecting the interpretation of the Convention or the Protocols or where the resolution of an issue before a Chamber might have a result inconsistent with a judgment previously delivered by the Court, the Chamber may relinquish jurisdiction to the Grand Chamber at any time prior to judgment.[171] The Registry must notify the parties of the Chamber's intention to relinquish jurisdiction. The parties then have one month from the date of that notification within which to file a duly reasoned objection. **23.69**

(b) Re-hearing

By Article 43 of the Convention, within three months from the date of judgment of a Chamber, any party may, in exceptional cases, request that the case be referred to the Grand Chamber. This request is considered by a panel of five judges of the Grand Chamber which: **23.70**

> shall accept the request if the case raises a serious question affecting the interpretation of the Convention or the protocols thereto, or a serious issue of general importance.[172]

A serious question affecting the *interpretation* of the Convention is raised when an important issue not previously determined by the Court is at stake, or when

166 Rule 75.
167 Rule 74(2).
168 Rule 77.
169 Rule 78.
170 The address of which is http://www.echr.coe.int.
171 Rule 72.
172 Art 43(2).

the decision is of importance for future cases and the development of the jurisprudence of the Court. A serious question of *application* of the Convention will occur when a substantial change to national law or administrative practice is required in the absence of a serious question of interpretation. A serious question of *general importance* might involve a substantial political or policy issue.

23.71 If the panel accepts the request for a re-hearing, the Grand Chamber decides the case by way of further judgment.[173] The purpose of the possibility of re-hearing is to ensure the quality and consistency of the jurisprudence of the Court by allowing a re-examination of the most important cases under certain conditions.

(3) Just satisfaction

23.72 The primary remedy afforded by the Court is a finding of a violation of a Convention right. In addition, the court may afford 'just satisfaction' to the injured party. 'Just satisfaction' will be afforded if the Court finds that there has been a violation of the Convention or the Protocols and if the internal law of the state party concerned allows only a partial reparation to be made.[174] The only remedies which the Court can award by way of 'just satisfaction' are compensation and costs. The Court does not have the power to overrule a judgment of the domestic court or declare it void.[175] The Court cannot annul a domestic administrative decision.[176]

23.73 If the question of just satisfaction is not ready for decision, it will be adjourned. If the applicant and the respondent can agree on the amount payable and if the Court finds the agreement to be equitable, it will strike the case out of the list. [177] If the applicant and the respondent cannot agree on the amount of just satisfaction, the Court may require the applicant to file a further statement quantifying and justifying the losses which are claimed. The respondent will then be asked to reply. The Court may order compensation for both pecuniary and non-pecuniary loss.[178] It will order any sums to be paid within three months.

23.74 Where the claim for just satisfaction includes a claim for costs, a detailed breakdown should be provided to the Court.[179] If there is objection to this breakdown, the Court will consider the claim for costs item by item.[180] If no breakdown is provided, then no payment will be ordered. The Court will order costs in favour

[173] Art 43(3).
[174] Art 41; this is a shortened version of former Art 50.
[175] *Brozicek v Italy* (1989) 12 EHRR 371.
[176] *Nasri v France* (1995) 21 EHRR 458.
[177] Art 75(4).
[178] For a general discussion, see para 21.32ff above.
[179] For precedents see L Clements, N Mole and A Simmons, *European Human Rights: Taking a Case under the Convention* (2nd edn, Sweet & Maxwell, 1999) App 7.
[180] See eg *Sunday Times v United Kingdom (No 2)* (1991) 14 EHRR 229 paras 63–67.

of an applicant even where the applicant is impecunious and would not have been able to pay them himself if he had not succeeded.[181] If, however, the lawyer makes it clear that he is acting without payment, no costs will be recoverable.[182] An analysis of 17 UK cases shows that, on average, the Court has awarded costs of about 45% of the sums claimed by the applicant.[182a]

(4) Finality of judgments

Judgments of the Grand Chamber are final with immediate effect. The judgment of a Chamber will only become final: **23.75**

- when the parties declare that they will not request that the case be referred to the Grand Chamber; or
- three months after the date of the judgment, if reference of the case to the Grand Chamber has not been requested; or
- when the panel of the Grand Chamber rejects the request to refer under Article 43.[183]

(5) Revision of judgments

If a party discovers a fact which might have a decisive influence and which, when a judgment was delivered, was unknown to the Court and could not reasonably have been known to that party, a request may be made to the Court for revision of the judgment.[184] This request must be made within a period of six months after the party acquired knowledge of the fact.[185] The request must mention the judgment, provide information to show that the 'revision conditions' have been complied with and must be accompanied by all supporting documents.[186] **23.76**

Revision is an exceptional procedure and, as a result, requests for revision of judgments are subjected to strict scrutiny.[187] If the party was on notice of the existence of the evidence which is relied on but did not take steps to obtain it the request for revision will be refused.[188] However, requests have been granted in a number of cases.[189] **23.77**

[181] See eg *Pakelli v Germany* (1983) 6 EHRR 1.
[182] See eg *McCann v United Kingdom* (1995) 21 EHRR 97.
[182a] See the Table in K Reid, *A Practitioner's Guide to the European Convention of Human Rights* (Sweet & Maxwell, 1998) 422–425.
[183] Art 44(2).
[184] Rule 80(1).
[185] Ibid.
[186] Rule 80(2).
[187] *McGinley and Egan v United Kingdom (Revision)*, Judgment of 28 Jan 2000, para 30.
[188] Ibid paras 32–35.
[189] See eg *Pardo v France (Revision)* (1996) 25 EHRR 563.

(6) Execution of judgments

23.78 The state parties to the Convention have undertaken to abide by any final judgment of the Court.[190] The execution of judgments is supervised by the Committee of Ministers. The applicant has no standing before the Committee and cannot influence the course it takes. The decision is referred to the next monthly meeting of the Committee and consideration of it cannot be adjourned for more than six months. As a result, the state must report at least twice a year on the steps which it is taking to comply with the decision.

23.79 The Committee requires written confirmation that the payment has been made. It will, however, allow the state to set off sums owed by the applicant to the state.[191] Where the decision requires legislative or administrative action the state reports to the Committee as to the steps which it is taking. When the Committee is satisfied that the decision has been complied with it will pass a resolution to that effect.[192]

[190] Art 46.

[191] See generally, L Clements, N Mole and A Simmons, *European Human Rights: Taking a Case under the Convention* (2nd edn, Sweet & Maxwell, 1999) para 9–02.

[192] See generally, D Harris, M O'Boyle and C Warbrick, *Law of the European Convention on Human Rights* (Butterworths, 1995) 700–705.

APPENDIX A
THE HUMAN RIGHTS ACT 1998

Full Appendices are contained in Volume 2

APPENDIX A

Human Rights Act 1998

1998 CHAPTER 42

ARRANGEMENT OF SECTIONS

Supplemental

SCHEDULES

An Act to give further effect to rights and freedoms guaranteed under the European Convention on Human Rights; to make provision with respect to holders of certain judicial offices who become judges of the European Court of Human Rights; and for connected purposes.

[9th November 1998]

BE IT ENACTED by the Queen's most Excellent Majesty, by and with the advice and consent of the Lords Spiritual and Temporal, and Commons, in this present Parliament assembled, and by the authority of the same, as follows:—

Introduction

The Convention rights

1.—(1) In this Act 'the Convention rights' means the rights and fundamental freedoms set out in—

(a) Articles 2 to 12 and 14 of the Convention,
(b) Articles 1 to 3 of the First Protocol, and
(c) Articles 1 and 2 of the Sixth Protocol,

as read with Articles 16 to 18 of the Convention.

(2) Those Articles are to have effect for the purposes of this Act subject to any designated derogation or reservation (as to which see sections 14 and 15).

(3) The Articles are set out in Schedule 1.

(4) The Secretary of State may by order make such amendments to this Act as he considers appropriate to reflect the effect, in relation to the United Kingdom, of a protocol.

(5) In subsection (4) 'protocol' means a protocol to the Convention—
(a) which the United Kingdom has ratified; or
(b) which the United Kingdom has signed with a view to ratification.

(6) No amendment may be made by an order under subsection (4) so as to come into force before the protocol concerned is in force in relation to the United Kingdom.

Interpretation of Convention rights

2.—(1) A court or tribunal determining a question which has arisen in connection with a Convention right must take into account any—

* Schedule 4 is not included.

(a) judgment, decision, declaration or advisory opinion of the European Court of Human Rights,
(b) opinion of the Commission given in a report adopted under Article 31 of the Convention,
(c) decision of the Commission in connection with Article 26 or 27(2) of the Convention, or
(d) decision of the Committee of Ministers taken under Article 46 of the Convention,

whenever made or given, so far as, in the opinion of the court or tribunal, it is relevant to the proceedings in which that question has arisen.

(2) Evidence of any judgment, decision, declaration or opinion of which account may have to be taken under this section is to be given in proceedings before any court or tribunal in such manner as may be provided by rules.

(3) In this section 'rules' means rules of court or, in the case of proceedings before a tribunal, rules made for the purposes of this section—
(a) by the Lord Chancellor or the Secretary of State, in relation to any proceedings outside Scotland;
(b) by the Secretary of State, in relation to proceedings in Scotland; or
(c) by a Northern Ireland department, in relation to proceedings before a tribunal in Northern Ireland—
(i) which deals with transferred matters; and
(ii) for which no rules made under paragraph (a) are in force.

Legislation

Interpretation of legislation

3.—(1) So far as it is possible to do so, primary legislation and subordinate legislation must be read and given effect in a way which is compatible with the Convention rights.

(2) This section—
(a) applies to primary legislation and subordinate legislation whenever enacted;
(b) does not affect the validity, continuing operation or enforcement of any incompatible primary legislation; and
(c) does not affect the validity, continuing operation or enforcement of any incompatible subordinate legislation if (disregarding any possibility of revocation) primary legislation prevents removal of the incompatibility.

Declaration of incompatibility

4.—(1) Subsection (2) applies in any proceedings in which a court determines whether a provision of primary legislation is compatible with a Convention right.

(2) If the court is satisfied that the provision is incompatible with a Convention right, it may make a declaration of that incompatibility.

(3) Subsection (4) applies in any proceedings in which a court determines whether a provision of subordinate legislation, made in the exercise of a power conferred by primary legislation, is compatible with a Convention right.

(4) If the court is satisfied—
(a) that the provision is incompatible with a Convention right, and
(b) that (disregarding any possibility of revocation) the primary legislation concerned prevents removal of the incompatibility,

it may make a declaration of that incompatibility.

(5) In this section 'court' means—
(a) the House of Lords;

(b) the Judicial Committee of the Privy Council;
(c) the Courts–Martial Appeal Court;
(d) in Scotland, the High Court of Justiciary sitting otherwise than as a trial court or the Court of Session;
(e) in England and Wales or Northern Ireland, the High Court or the Court of Appeal.

(6) A declaration under this section ('a declaration of incompatibility')—
(a) does not affect the validity, continuing operation or enforcement of the provision in respect of which it is given; and
(b) is not binding on the parties to the proceedings in which it is made.

Right of Crown to intervene

5.—(1) Where a court is considering whether to make a declaration of incompatibility, the Crown is entitled to notice in accordance with rules of court.

(2) In any case to which subsection (1) applies—
(a) a Minister of the Crown (or a person nominated by him),
(b) a member of the Scottish Executive,
(c) a Northern Ireland Minister,
(d) a Northern Ireland department,

is entitled, on giving notice in accordance with rules of court, to be joined as a party to the proceedings.

(3) Notice under subsection (2) may be given at any time during the proceedings.

(4) A person who has been made a party to criminal proceedings (other than in Scotland) as the result of a notice under subsection (2) may, with leave, appeal to the House of Lords against any declaration of incompatibility made in the proceedings.

(5) In subsection (4)—
'criminal proceedings' includes all proceedings before the Courts–Martial Appeal Court;
and
'leave' means leave granted by the court making the declaration of incompatibility or by the House of Lords.

Public authorities

Acts of public authorities

6.—(1) It is unlawful for a public authority to act in a way which is incompatible with a Convention right.

(2) Subsection (1) does not apply to an act if—
(a) as the result of one or more provisions of primary legislation, the authority could not have acted differently; or
(b) in the case of one or more provisions of, or made under, primary legislation which cannot be read or given effect in a way which is compatible with the Convention rights, the authority was acting so as to give effect to or enforce those provisions.

(3) In this section 'public authority' includes—
(a) a court or tribunal, and
(b) any person certain of whose functions are functions of a public nature,

but does not include either House of Parliament or a person exercising functions in connection with proceedings in Parliament.

(4) In subsection (3) 'Parliament' does not include the House of Lords in its judicial capacity.

(5) In relation to a particular act, a person is not a public authority by virtue only of subsection (3)(b) if the nature of the act is private.

(6) 'An act' includes a failure to act but does not include a failure to—
(a) introduce in, or lay before, Parliament a proposal for legislation; or
(b) make any primary legislation or remedial order.

Proceedings

7.—(1) A person who claims that a public authority has acted (or proposes to act) in a way which is made unlawful by section 6(1) may—
(a) bring proceedings against the authority under this Act in the appropriate court or tribunal, or
(b) rely on the Convention right or rights concerned in any legal proceedings,

but only if he is (or would be) a victim of the unlawful act.

(2) In subsection (1)(a) 'appropriate court or tribunal' means such court or tribunal as may be determined in accordance with rules; and proceedings against an authority include a counterclaim or similar proceeding.

(3) If the proceedings are brought on an application for judicial review, the applicant is to be taken to have a sufficient interest in relation to the unlawful act only if he is, or would be, a victim of that act.

(4) If the proceedings are made by way of a petition for judicial review in Scotland, the applicant shall be taken to have title and interest to sue in relation to the unlawful act only if he is, or would be, a victim of that act.

(5) Proceedings under subsection (1)(a) must be brought before the end of—
(a) the period of one year beginning with the date on which the act complained of took place; or
(b) such longer period as the court or tribunal considers equitable having regard to all the circumstances,

but that is subject to any rule imposing a stricter time limit in relation to the procedure in question.

(6) In subsection (1)(b) 'legal proceedings' includes—
(a) proceedings brought by or at the instigation of a public authority; and
(b) an appeal against the decision of a court or tribunal.

(7) For the purposes of this section, a person is a victim of an unlawful act only if he would be a victim for the purposes of Article 34 of the Convention if proceedings were brought in the European Court of Human Rights in respect of that act.

(8) Nothing in this Act creates a criminal offence.

(9) In this section 'rules' means—
(a) in relation to proceedings before a court or tribunal outside Scotland, rules made by the Lord Chancellor or the Secretary of State for the purposes of this section or rules of court,
(b) in relation to proceedings before a court or tribunal in Scotland, rules made by the Secretary of State for those purposes,
(c) in relation to proceedings before a tribunal in Northern Ireland—
(i) which deals with transferred matters; and
(ii) for which no rules made under paragraph (a) are in force,
rules made by a Northern Ireland department for those purposes,

and includes provision made by order under section 1 of the Courts and Legal Services Act 1990.

(10) In making rules, regard must be had to section 9.

(11) The Minister who has power to make rules in relation to a particular tribunal may, to the extent he considers it necessary to ensure that the tribunal can provide an appropriate remedy in

relation to an act (or proposed act) of a public authority which is (or would be) unlawful as a result of section 6(1), by order add to—

(a) the relief or remedies which the tribunal may grant; or
(b) the grounds on which it may grant any of them.

(12) An order made under subsection (11) may contain such incidental, supplemental, consequential or transitional provision as the Minister making it considers appropriate.

(13) 'The Minister' includes the Northern Ireland department concerned.

Judicial remedies

8.—(1) In relation to any act (or proposed act) of a public authority which the court finds is (or would be) unlawful, it may grant such relief or remedy, or make such order, within its powers as it considers just and appropriate.

(2) But damages may be awarded only by a court which has power to award damages, or to order the payment of compensation, in civil proceedings.

(3) No award of damages is to be made unless, taking account of all the circumstances of the case, including—

(a) any other relief or remedy granted, or order made, in relation to the act in question (by that or any other court), and
(b) the consequences of any decision (of that or any other court) in respect of that act,

the court is satisfied that the award is necessary to afford just satisfaction to the person in whose favour it is made.

(4) In determining—

(a) whether to award damages, or
(b) the amount of an award,

the court must take into account the principles applied by the European Court of Human Rights in relation to the award of compensation under Article 41 of the Convention.

(5) A public authority against which damages are awarded is to be treated—

(a) in Scotland, for the purposes of section 3 of the Law Reform (Miscellaneous Provisions) (Scotland) Act 1940 as if the award were made in an action of damages in which the authority has been found liable in respect of loss or damage to the person to whom the award is made;
(b) for the purposes of the Civil Liability (Contribution) Act 1978 as liable in respect of damage suffered by the person to whom the award is made.

(6) In this section—

'court' includes a tribunal;
'damages' means damages for an unlawful act of a public authority; and
'unlawful' means unlawful under section 6(1).

Judicial acts

9.—(1) Proceedings under section 7(1)(a) in respect of a judicial act may be brought only—

(a) by exercising a right of appeal;
(b) on an application (in Scotland a petition) for judicial review; or
(c) in such other forum as may be prescribed by rules.

(2) That does not affect any rule of law which prevents a court from being the subject of judicial review.

(3) In proceedings under this Act in respect of a judicial act done in good faith, damages may not be awarded otherwise than to compensate a person to the extent required by Article 5(5) of the Convention.

(4) An award of damages permitted by subsection (3) is to be made against the Crown; but no award may be made unless the appropriate person, if not a party to the proceedings, is joined.

(5) In this section—

'appropriate person' means the Minister responsible for the court concerned, or a person or government department nominated by him;

'court' includes a tribunal;

'judge' includes a member of a tribunal, a justice of the peace and a clerk or other officer entitled to exercise the jurisdiction of a court;

'judicial act' means a judicial act of a court and includes an act done on the instructions, or on behalf, of a judge; and

'rules' has the same meaning as in section 7(9).

Remedial action

Power to take remedial action

10.—(1) This section applies if—

(a) a provision of legislation has been declared under section 4 to be incompatible with a Convention right and, if an appeal lies—

(i) all persons who may appeal have stated in writing that they do not intend to do so;

(ii) the time for bringing an appeal has expired and no appeal has been brought within that time; or

(iii) an appeal brought within that time has been determined or abandoned; or

(b) it appears to a Minister of the Crown or Her Majesty in Council that, having regard to a finding of the European Court of Human Rights made after the coming into force of this section in proceedings against the United Kingdom, a provision of legislation is incompatible with an obligation of the United Kingdom arising from the Convention.

(2) If a Minister of the Crown considers that there are compelling reasons for proceeding under this section, he may by order make such amendments to the legislation as he considers necessary to remove the incompatibility.

(3) If, in the case of subordinate legislation, a Minister of the Crown considers—

(a) that it is necessary to amend the primary legislation under which the subordinate legislation in question was made, in order to enable the incompatibility to be removed, and

(b) that there are compelling reasons for proceeding under this section,

he may by order make such amendments to the primary legislation as he considers necessary.

(4) This section also applies where the provision in question is in subordinate legislation and has been quashed, or declared invalid, by reason of incompatibility with a Convention right and the Minister proposes to proceed under paragraph 2(b) of Schedule 2.

(5) If the legislation is an Order in Council, the power conferred by subsection (2) or (3) is exercisable by Her Majesty in Council.

(6) In this section 'legislation' does not include a Measure of the Church Assembly or of the General Synod of the Church of England.

(7) Schedule 2 makes further provision about remedial orders.

Other rights and proceedings

Safeguard for existing human rights

11. A person's reliance on a Convention right does not restrict—

(a) any other right or freedom conferred on him by or under any law having effect in any part of the United Kingdom; or

(b) his right to make any claim or bring any proceedings which he could make or bring apart from sections 7 to 9.

Freedom of expression

12.—(1) This section applies if a court is considering whether to grant any relief which, if granted, might affect the exercise of the Convention right to freedom of expression.

(2) If the person against whom the application for relief is made ('the respondent') is neither present nor represented, no such relief is to be granted unless the court is satisfied—

(a) that the applicant has taken all practicable steps to notify the respondent; or
(b) that there are compelling reasons why the respondent should not be notified.

(3) No such relief is to be granted so as to restrain publication before trial unless the court is satisfied that the applicant is likely to establish that publication should not be allowed.

(4) The court must have particular regard to the importance of the Convention right to freedom of expression and, where the proceedings relate to material which the respondent claims, or which appears to the court, to be journalistic, literary or artistic material (or to conduct connected with such material), to—

(a) the extent to which—
 (i) the material has, or is about to, become available to the public; or
 (ii) it is, or would be, in the public interest for the material to be published;
(b) any relevant privacy code.

(5) In this section—
'court' includes a tribunal; and
'relief' includes any remedy or order (other than in criminal proceedings).

Freedom of thought, conscience and religion

13.—(1) If a court's determination of any question arising under this Act might affect the exercise by a religious organisation (itself or its members collectively) of the Convention right to freedom of thought, conscience and religion, it must have particular regard to the importance of that right.

(2) In this section 'court' includes a tribunal.

Derogations and reservations

Derogations

14.—(1) In this Act 'designated derogation' means—

(a) the United Kingdom's derogation from Article 5(3) of the Convention; and
(b) any derogation by the United Kingdom from an Article of the Convention, or of any protocol to the Convention, which is designated for the purposes of this Act in an order made by the Secretary of State.

(2) The derogation referred to in subsection (1)(a) is set out in Part I of Schedule 3.

(3) If a designated derogation is amended or replaced it ceases to be a designated derogation.

(4) But subsection (3) does not prevent the Secretary of State from exercising his power under subsection (1)(b) to make a fresh designation order in respect of the Article concerned.

(5) The Secretary of State must by order make such amendments to Schedule 3 as he considers appropriate to reflect—

(a) any designation order; or
(b) the effect of subsection (3).

(6) A designation order may be made in anticipation of the making by the United Kingdom of a proposed derogation.

Reservations

15.—(1) In this Act 'designated reservation' means—

(a) the United Kingdom's reservation to Article 2 of the First Protocol to the Convention; and

(b) any other reservation by the United Kingdom to an Article of the Convention, or of any protocol to the Convention, which is designated for the purposes of this Act in an order made by the Secretary of State.

(2) The text of the reservation referred to in subsection (1)(a) is set out in Part II of Schedule 3.

(3) If a designated reservation is withdrawn wholly or in part it ceases to be a designated reservation.

(4) But subsection (3) does not prevent the Secretary of State from exercising his power under subsection (1)(b) to make a fresh designation order in respect of the Article concerned.

(5) The Secretary of State must by order make such amendments to this Act as he considers appropriate to reflect—

(a) any designation order; or

(b) the effect of subsection (3).

Period for which designated derogations have effect

16.—(1) If it has not already been withdrawn by the United Kingdom, a designated derogation ceases to have effect for the purposes of this Act—

(a) in the case of the derogation referred to in section 14(1)(a), at the end of the period of five years beginning with the date on which section 1(2) came into force;

(b) in the case of any other derogation, at the end of the period of five years beginning with the date on which the order designating it was made.

(2) At any time before the period—

(a) fixed by subsection (1)(a) or (b), or

(b) extended by an order under this subsection,

comes to an end, the Secretary of State may by order extend it by a further period of five years.

(3) An order under section 14(1)(b) ceases to have effect at the end of the period for consideration, unless a resolution has been passed by each House approving the order.

(4) Subsection (3) does not affect—

(a) anything done in reliance on the order; or

(b) the power to make a fresh order under section 14(1)(b).

(5) In subsection (3) 'period for consideration' means the period of forty days beginning with the day on which the order was made.

(6) In calculating the period for consideration, no account is to be taken of any time during which—

(a) Parliament is dissolved or prorogued; or

(b) both Houses are adjourned for more than four days.

(7) If a designated derogation is withdrawn by the United Kingdom, the Secretary of State must by order make such amendments to this Act as he considers are required to reflect that withdrawal.

Periodic review of designated reservations

17.—(1) The appropriate Minister must review the designated reservation referred to in section 15(1)(a)—

(a) before the end of the period of five years beginning with the date on which section 1(2) came into force; and
(b) if that designation is still in force, before the end of the period of five years beginning with the date on which the last report relating to it was laid under subsection (3).

(2) The appropriate Minister must review each of the other designated reservations (if any)—
(a) before the end of the period of five years beginning with the date on which the order designating the reservation first came into force; and
(b) if the designation is still in force, before the end of the period of five years beginning with the date on which the last report relating to it was laid under subsection (3).

(3) The Minister conducting a review under this section must prepare a report on the result of the review and lay a copy of it before each House of Parliament.

Judges of the European Court of Human Rights

Appointment to European Court of Human Rights

18.—(1) In this section 'judicial office' means the office of—
(a) Lord Justice of Appeal, Justice of the High Court or Circuit judge, in England and Wales;
(b) judge of the Court of Session or sheriff, in Scotland;
(c) Lord Justice of Appeal, judge of the High Court or county court judge, in Northern Ireland.

(2) The holder of a judicial office may become a judge of the European Court of Human Rights ('the Court') without being required to relinquish his office.

(3) But he is not required to perform the duties of his judicial office while he is a judge of the Court.

(4) In respect of any period during which he is a judge of the Court—
(a) a Lord Justice of Appeal or Justice of the High Court is not to count as a judge of the relevant court for the purposes of section 2(1) or 4(1) of the Supreme Court Act 1981 (maximum number of judges) nor as a judge of the Supreme Court for the purposes of section 12(1) to (6) of that Act (salaries etc.);
(b) a judge of the Court of Session is not to count as a judge of that court for the purposes of section 1(1) of the Court of Session Act 1988 (maximum number of judges) or of section 9(1)(c) of the Administration of Justice Act 1973 ('the 1973 Act') (salaries etc.);
(c) a Lord Justice of Appeal or judge of the High Court in Northern Ireland is not to count as a judge of the relevant court for the purposes of section 2(1) or 3(1) of the Judicature (Northern Ireland) Act 1978 (maximum number of judges) nor as a judge of the Supreme Court of Northern Ireland for the purposes of section 9(1)(d) of the 1973 Act (salaries etc.);
(d) a Circuit judge is not to count as such for the purposes of section 18 of the Courts Act 1971 (salaries etc.);
(e) a sheriff is not to count as such for the purposes of section 14 of the Sheriff Courts (Scotland) Act 1907 (salaries etc.);
(f) a county court judge of Northern Ireland is not to count as such for the purposes of section 106 of the County Courts Act (Northern Ireland) 1959 (salaries etc.).

(5) If a sheriff principal is appointed a judge of the Court, section 11(1) of the Sheriff Courts (Scotland) Act 1971 (temporary appointment of sheriff principal) applies, while he holds that appointment, as if his office is vacant.

(6) Schedule 4 makes provision about judicial pensions in relation to the holder of a judicial office who serves as a judge of the Court.

(7) The Lord Chancellor or the Secretary of State may by order make such transitional provision (including, in particular, provision for a temporary increase in the maximum number of judges) as he considers appropriate in relation to any holder of a judicial office who has completed his service as a judge of the Court.

Parliamentary procedure

Statements of compatibility

19.—(1) A Minister of the Crown in charge of a Bill in either House of Parliament must, before Second Reading of the Bill—

(a) make a statement to the effect that in his view the provisions of the Bill are compatible with the Convention rights ('a statement of compatibility'); or

(b) make a statement to the effect that although he is unable to make a statement of compatibility the government nevertheless wishes the House to proceed with the Bill.

(2) The statement must be in writing and be published in such manner as the Minister making it considers appropriate.

Supplemental

Orders etc. under this Act

20.—(1) Any power of a Minister of the Crown to make an order under this Act is exercisable by statutory instrument.

(2) The power of the Lord Chancellor or the Secretary of State to make rules (other than rules of court) under section 2(3) or 7(9) is exercisable by statutory instrument.

(3) Any statutory instrument made under section 14, 15 or 16(7) must be laid before Parliament.

(4) No order may be made by the Lord Chancellor or the Secretary of State under section 1(4), 7(11) or 16(2) unless a draft of the order has been laid before, and approved by, each House of Parliament.

(5) Any statutory instrument made under section 18(7) or Schedule 4, or to which subsection (2) applies, shall be subject to annulment in pursuance of a resolution of either House of Parliament.

(6) The power of a Northern Ireland department to make—

(a) rules under section 2(3)(c) or 7(9)(c), or

(b) an order under section 7(11),

is exercisable by statutory rule for the purposes of the Statutory Rules (Northern Ireland) Order 1979.

(7) Any rules made under section 2(3)(c) or 7(9)(c) shall be subject to negative resolution; and section 41(6) of the Interpretation Act (Northern Ireland) 1954 (meaning of 'subject to negative resolution') shall apply as if the power to make the rules were conferred by an Act of the Northern Ireland Assembly.

(8) No order may be made by a Northern Ireland department under section 7(11) unless a draft of the order has been laid before, and approved by, the Northern Ireland Assembly.

Interpretation, etc.

21.—(1) In this Act—

'amend' includes repeal and apply (with or without modifications);

'the appropriate Minister' means the Minister of the Crown having charge of the appropriate authorised government department (within the meaning of the Crown Proceedings Act 1947);

'the Commission' means the European Commission of Human Rights;
'the Convention' means the Convention for the Protection of Human Rights and Fundamental Freedoms, agreed by the Council of Europe at Rome on 4th November 1950 as it has effect for the time being in relation to the United Kingdom;
'declaration of incompatibility' means a declaration under section 4;
'Minister of the Crown' has the same meaning as in the Ministers of the Crown Act 1975;
'Northern Ireland Minister' includes the First Minister and the deputy First Minister in Northern Ireland;
'primary legislation' means any—

(a) public general Act;
(b) local and personal Act;
(c) private Act;
(d) Measure of the Church Assembly;
(e) Measure of the General Synod of the Church of England;
(f) Order in Council—
  (i) made in exercise of Her Majesty's Royal Prerogative;
  (ii) made under section 38(1)(a) of the Northern Ireland Constitution Act 1973 or the corresponding provision of the Northern Ireland Act 1998; or
  (iii) amending an Act of a kind mentioned in paragraph (a), (b) or (c);

and includes an order or other instrument made under primary legislation (otherwise than by the National Assembly for Wales, a member of the Scottish Executive, a Northern Ireland Minister or a Northern Ireland department) to the extent to which it operates to bring one or more provisions of that legislation into force or amends any primary legislation;
'the First Protocol' means the protocol to the Convention agreed at Paris on 20th March 1952;
'the Sixth Protocol' means the protocol to the Convention agreed at Strasbourg on 28th April 1983;
'the Eleventh Protocol' means the protocol to the Convention (restructuring the control machinery established by the Convention) agreed at Strasbourg on 11th May 1994;
'remedial order' means an order under section 10;
'subordinate legislation' means any—

(a) Order in Council other than one—
  (i) made in exercise of Her Majesty's Royal Prerogative;
  (ii) made under section 38(1)(a) of the Northern Ireland Constitution Act 1973 or the corresponding provision of the Northern Ireland Act 1998; or
  (iii) amending an Act of a kind mentioned in the definition of primary legislation;
(b) Act of the Scottish Parliament;
(c) Act of the Parliament of Northern Ireland;
(d) Measure of the Assembly established under section 1 of the Northern Ireland Assembly Act 1973;
(e) Act of the Northern Ireland Assembly;
(f) order, rules, regulations, scheme, warrant, byelaw or other instrument made under primary legislation (except to the extent to which it operates to bring one or more provisions of that legislation into force or amends any primary legislation);
(g) order, rules, regulations, scheme, warrant, byelaw or other instrument made under legislation mentioned in paragraph (b), (c), (d) or (e) or made under an Order in Council applying only to Northern Ireland;
(h) order, rules, regulations, scheme, warrant, byelaw or other instrument made by a member of the Scottish Executive, a Northern Ireland Minister or a Northern Ireland department in exercise of prerogative or other executive functions of Her Majesty which are exercisable by such a person on behalf of Her Majesty;

'transferred matters' has the same meaning as in the Northern Ireland Act 1998; and
'tribunal' means any tribunal in which legal proceedings may be brought.

(2) The references in paragraphs (b) and (c) of section 2(1) to Articles are to Articles of the Convention as they had effect immediately before the coming into force of the Eleventh Protocol.

(3) The reference in paragraph (d) of section 2(1) to Article 46 includes a reference to Articles 32 and 54 of the Convention as they had effect immediately before the coming into force of the Eleventh Protocol.

(4) The references in section 2(1) to a report or decision of the Commission or a decision of the Committee of Ministers include references to a report or decision made as provided by paragraphs 3, 4 and 6 of Article 5 of the Eleventh Protocol (transitional provisions).

(5) Any liability under the Army Act 1955, the Air Force Act 1955 or the Naval Discipline Act 1957 to suffer death for an offence is replaced by a liability to imprisonment for life or any less punishment authorised by those Acts; and those Acts shall accordingly have effect with the necessary modifications.

Short title, commencement, application and extent

22.—(1) This Act may be cited as the Human Rights Act 1998.

(2) Sections 18, 20 and 21(5) and this section come into force on the passing of this Act.

(3) The other provisions of this Act come into force on such day as the Secretary of State may by order appoint; and different days may be appointed for different purposes.

(4) Paragraph (b) of subsection (1) of section 7 applies to proceedings brought by or at the instigation of a public authority whenever the act in question took place; but otherwise that subsection does not apply to an act taking place before the coming into force of that section.

(5) This Act binds the Crown.

(6) This Act extends to Northern Ireland.

(7) Section 21(5), so far as it relates to any provision contained in the Army Act 1955, the Air Force Act 1955 or the Naval Discipline Act 1957, extends to any place to which that provision extends.

SCHEDULES

Schedule 1
The Articles

Part I
The Convention*
Rights and Freedoms

Article 2
Right to Life

1. Everyone's right to life shall be protected by law. No one shall be deprived of his life intentionally save in the execution of a sentence of a court following his conviction of a crime for which this penalty is provided by law.

* The full text of the Convention and its Protocols are reproduced in Appendix E below.

2. Deprivation of life shall not be regarded as inflicted in contravention of this Article when it results from the use of force which is no more than absolutely necessary:
   (a) in defence of any person from unlawful violence;
   (b) in order to effect a lawful arrest or to prevent the escape of a person lawfully detained;
   (c) in action lawfully taken for the purpose of quelling a riot or insurrection.

Article 3
Prohibition of Torture

No one shall be subjected to torture or to inhuman or degrading treatment or punishment.

Article 4
Prohibition of Slavery and Forced Labour

1. No one shall be held in slavery or servitude.
2. No one shall be required to perform forced or compulsory labour.
3. For the purpose of this Article the term 'forced or compulsory labour' shall not include:
   (a) any work required to be done in the ordinary course of detention imposed according to the provisions of Article 5 of this Convention or during conditional release from such detention;
   (b) any service of a military character or, in case of conscientious objectors in countries where they are recognised, service exacted instead of compulsory military service;
   (c) any service exacted in case of an emergency or calamity threatening the life or well-being of the community;
   (d) any work or service which forms part of normal civic obligations.

Article 5
Right to Liberty and Security

1. Everyone has the right to liberty and security of person. No one shall be deprived of his liberty save in the following cases and in accordance with a procedure prescribed by law:
   (a) the lawful detention of a person after conviction by a competent court;
   (b) the lawful arrest or detention of a person for non-compliance with the lawful order of a court or in order to secure the fulfilment of any obligation prescribed by law;
   (c) the lawful arrest or detention of a person effected for the purpose of bringing him before the competent legal authority on reasonable suspicion of having committed an offence or when it is reasonably considered necessary to prevent his committing an offence or fleeing after having done so;
   (d) the detention of a minor by lawful order for the purpose of educational supervision or his lawful detention for the purpose of bringing him before the competent legal authority;
   (e) the lawful detention of persons for the prevention of the spreading of infectious diseases, of persons of unsound mind, alcoholics or drug addicts or vagrants;
   (f) the lawful arrest or detention of a person to prevent his effecting an unauthorised entry into the country or of a person against whom action is being taken with a view to deportation or extradition.
2. Everyone who is arrested shall be informed promptly, in a language which he understands, of the reasons for his arrest and of any charge against him.
3. Everyone arrested or detained in accordance with the provisions of paragraph 1(c) of this Article shall be brought promptly before a judge or other officer authorised by law to exercise

judicial power and shall be entitled to trial within a reasonable time or to release pending trial. Release may be conditioned by guarantees to appear for trial.

4. Everyone who is deprived of his liberty by arrest or detention shall be entitled to take proceedings by which the lawfulness of his detention shall be decided speedily by a court and his release ordered if the detention is not lawful.
5. Everyone who has been the victim of arrest or detention in contravention of the provisions of this Article shall have an enforceable right to compensation.

Article 6
Right to a Fair Trial

1. In the determination of his civil rights and obligations or of any criminal charge against him, everyone is entitled to a fair and public hearing within a reasonable time by an independent and impartial tribunal established by law. Judgment shall be pronounced publicly but the press and public may be excluded from all or part of the trial in the interest of morals, public order or national security in a democratic society, where the interests of juveniles or the protection of the private life of the parties so require, or to the extent strictly necessary in the opinion of the court in special circumstances where publicity would prejudice the interests of justice.
2. Everyone charged with a criminal offence shall be presumed innocent until proved guilty according to law.
3. Everyone charged with a criminal offence has the following minimum rights:
   (a) to be informed promptly, in a language which he understands and in detail, of the nature and cause of the accusation against him;
   (b) to have adequate time and facilities for the preparation of his defence;
   (c) to defend himself in person or through legal assistance of his own choosing or, if he has not sufficient means to pay for legal assistance, to be given it free when the interests of justice so require;
   (d) to examine or have examined witnesses against him and to obtain the attendance and examination of witnesses on his behalf under the same conditions as witnesses against him;
   (e) to have the free assistance of an interpreter if he cannot understand or speak the language used in court.

Article 7
No Punishment Withour Law

1. No one shall be held guilty of any criminal offence on account of any act or omission which did not constitute a criminal offence under national or international law at the time when it was committed. Nor shall a heavier penalty be imposed than the one that was applicable at the time the criminal offence was committed.
2. This Article shall not prejudice the trial and punishment of any person for any act or omission which, at the time when it was committed, was criminal according to the general principles of law recognised by civilised nations.

Article 8
Right to Respect for Private and Family Life

1. Everyone has the right to respect for his private and family life, his home and his correspondence.

2. There shall be no interference by a public authority with the exercise of this right except such as is in accordance with the law and is necessary in a democratic society in the interests of national security, public safety or the economic well-being of the country, for the prevention of disorder or crime, for the protection of health or morals, or for the protection of the rights and freedoms of others.

Article 9
Freedom of Thought, Conscience and Religion

1. Everyone has the right to freedom of thought, conscience and religion; this right includes freedom to change his religion or belief and freedom, either alone or in community with others and in public or private, to manifest his religion or belief, in worship, teaching, practice and observance.
2. Freedom to manifest one's religion or beliefs shall be subject only to such limitations as are prescribed by law and are necessary in a democratic society in the interests of public safety, for the protection of public order, health or morals, or for the protection of the rights and freedoms of others.

Article 10
Freedom of Expression

1. Everyone has the right to freedom of expression. This right shall include freedom to hold opinions and to receive and impart information and ideas without interference by public authority and regardless of frontiers. This Article shall not prevent States from requiring the licensing of broadcasting, television or cinema enterprises.
2. The exercise of these freedoms, since it carries with it duties and responsibilities, may be subject to such formalities, conditions, restrictions or penalties as are prescribed by law and are necessary in a democratic society, in the interests of national security, territorial integrity or public safety, for the prevention of disorder or crime, for the protection of health or morals, for the protection of the reputation or rights of others, for preventing the disclosure of information received in confidence, or for maintaining the authority and impartiality of the judiciary.

Article 11
Freedom of Assembly and Association

1. Everyone has the right to freedom of peaceful assembly and to freedom of association with others, including the right to form and to join trade unions for the protection of his interests.
2. No restrictions shall be placed on the exercise of these rights other than such as are prescribed by law and are necessary in a democratic society in the interests of national security or public safety, for the prevention of disorder or crime, for the protection of health or morals or for the protection of the rights and freedoms of others. This Article shall not prevent the imposition of lawful restrictions on the exercise of these rights by members of the armed forces, of the police or of the administration of the State.

Article 12
Right to Marry

Men and women of marriageable age have the right to marry and to found a family, according to the national laws governing the exercise of this right.

Article 14
Prohibition of Discrimination

The enjoyment of the rights and freedoms set forth in this Convention shall be secured without discrimination on any ground such as sex, race, colour, language, religion, political or other opinion, national or social origin, association with a national minority, property, birth or other status.

Article 16
Restrictions on Political Activity of Aliens

Nothing in Articles 10, 11 and 14 shall be regarded as preventing the High Contracting Parties from imposing restrictions on the political activity of aliens.

Article 17
Prohibition of Abuse of Rights

Nothing in this Convention may be interpreted as implying for any State, group or person any right to engage in any activity or perform any act aimed at the destruction of any of the rights and freedoms set forth herein or at their limitation to a greater extent than is provided for in the Convention.

Article 18
Limitation on Use of Restrictions on Rights

The restrictions permitted under this Convention to the said rights and freedoms shall not be applied for any purpose other than those for which they have been prescribed.

Part II
The First Protocol

Article 1
Protection of Property

Every natural or legal person is entitled to the peaceful enjoyment of his possessions. No one shall be deprived of his possessions except in the public interest and subject to the conditions provided for by law and by the general principles of international law.

The preceding provisions shall not, however, in any way impair the right of a State to enforce such laws as it deems necessary to control the use of property in accordance with the general interest or to secure the payment of taxes or other contributions or penalties.

Article 2
Right to Education

No person shall be denied the right to education. In the exercise of any functions which it assumes in relation to education and to teaching, the State shall respect the right of parents to ensure such education and teaching in conformity with their own religious and philosophical convictions.

Article 3
Right to Free Elections

The High Contracting Parties undertake to hold free elections at reasonable intervals by secret ballot, under conditions which will ensure the free expression of the opinion of the people in the choice of the legislature.

Part III
The Sixth Protocol

Article 1
Abolition of the Death Penalty

The death penalty shall be abolished. No one shall be condemned to such penalty or executed.

Article 2
Death Penalty in Time of War

A State may make provision in its law for the death penalty in respect of acts committed in time of war or of imminent threat of war; such penalty shall be applied only in the instances laid down in the law and in accordance with its provisions. The State shall communicate to the Secretary General of the Council of Europe the relevant provisions of that law.

Schedule 2
Remedial Orders

Orders

1.—(1) A remedial order may—
- (a) contain such incidental, supplemental, consequential or transitional provision as the person making it considers appropriate;
- (b) be made so as to have effect from a date earlier than that on which it is made;
- (c) make provision for the delegation of specific functions;
- (d) make different provision for different cases.

(2) The power conferred by sub-paragraph (1)(a) includes—
- (a) power to amend primary legislation (including primary legislation other than that which contains the incompatible provision); and
- (b) power to amend or revoke subordinate legislation (including subordinate legislation other than that which contains the incompatible provision).

(3) A remedial order may be made so as to have the same extent as the legislation which it affects.

(4) No person is to be guilty of an offence solely as a result of the retrospective effect of a remedial order.

Procedure

2. No remedial order may be made unless—
- (a) a draft of the order has been approved by a resolution of each House of Parliament made after the end of the period of 60 days beginning with the day on which the draft was laid; or
- (b) it is declared in the order that it appears to the person making it that, because of the urgency of the matter, it is necessary to make the order without a draft being so approved.

Orders laid in draft

3.—(1) No draft may be laid under paragraph 2(a) unless—
(a) the person proposing to make the order has laid before Parliament a document which contains a draft of the proposed order and the required information; and
(b) the period of 60 days, beginning with the day on which the document required by this sub-paragraph was laid, has ended.

(2) If representations have been made during that period, the draft laid under paragraph 2(a) must be accompanied by a statement containing—
(a) a summary of the representations; and
(b) if, as a result of the representations, the proposed order has been changed, details of the changes.

Urgent cases

4.—(1) If a remedial order ('the original order') is made without being approved in draft, the person making it must lay it before Parliament, accompanied by the required information, after it is made.

(2) If representations have been made during the period of 60 days beginning with the day on which the original order was made, the person making it must (after the end of that period) lay before Parliament a statement containing—
(a) a summary of the representations; and
(b) if, as a result of the representations, he considers it appropriate to make changes to the original order, details of the changes.

(3) If sub-paragraph (2)(b) applies, the person making the statement must—
(a) make a further remedial order replacing the original order; and
(b) lay the replacement order before Parliament.

(4) If, at the end of the period of 120 days beginning with the day on which the original order was made, a resolution has not been passed by each House approving the original or replacement order, the order ceases to have effect (but without that affecting anything previously done under either order or the power to make a fresh remedial order).

Definitions

5. In this Schedule—
'representations' means representations about a remedial order (or proposed remedial order) made to the person making (or proposing to make) it and includes any relevant Parliamentary report or resolution; and
'required information' means—
(a) an explanation of the incompatibility which the order (or proposed order) seeks to remove, including particulars of the relevant declaration, finding or order; and
(b) a statement of the reasons for proceeding under section 10 and for making an order in those terms.

Calculating periods

6. In calculating any period for the purposes of this Schedule, no account is to be taken of any time during which—
(a) Parliament is dissolved or prorogued; or
(b) both Houses are adjourned for more than four days.

Schedule 3
Derogation and Reservation

Part I
Derogation

The 1988 notification

The United Kingdom Permanent Representative to the Council of Europe presents his compliments to the Secretary General of the Council, and has the honour to convey the following information in order to ensure compliance with the obligations of Her Majesty's Government in the United Kingdom under Article 15(3) of the Convention for the Protection of Human Rights and Fundamental Freedoms signed at Rome on 4 November 1950.

There have been in the United Kingdom in recent years campaigns of organised terrorism connected with the affairs of Northern Ireland which have manifested themselves in activities which have included repeated murder, attempted murder, maiming, intimidation and violent civil disturbance and in bombing and fire raising which have resulted in death, injury and widespread destruction of property. As a result, a public emergency within the meaning of Article 15(1) of the Convention exists in the United Kingdom.

The Government found it necessary in 1974 to introduce and since then, in cases concerning persons reasonably suspected of involvement in terrorism connected with the affairs of Northern Ireland, or of certain offences under the legislation, who have been detained for 48 hours, to exercise powers enabling further detention without charge, for periods of up to five days, on the authority of the Secretary of State. These powers are at present to be found in Section 12 of the Prevention of Terrorism (Temporary Provisions) Act 1984, Article 9 of the Prevention of Terrorism (Supplemental Temporary Provisions) Order 1984 and Article 10 of the Prevention of Terrorism (Supplemental Temporary Provisions) (Northern Ireland) Order 1984.

Section 12 of the Prevention of Terrorism (Temporary Provisions) Act 1984 provides for a person whom a constable has arrested on reasonable grounds of suspecting him to be guilty of an offence under Section 1, 9 or 10 of the Act, or to be or to have been involved in terrorism connected with the affairs of Northern Ireland, to be detained in right of the arrest for up to 48 hours and thereafter, where the Secretary of State extends the detention period, for up to a further five days. Section 12 substantially re-enacted Section 12 of the Prevention of Terrorism (Temporary Provisions) Act 1976 which, in turn, substantially re-enacted Section 7 of the Prevention of Terrorism (Temporary Provisions) Act 1974.

Article 10 of the Prevention of Terrorism (Supplemental Temporary Provisions) (Northern Ireland) Order 1984 (SI 1984/417) and Article 9 of the Prevention of Terrorism (Supplemental Temporary Provisions) Order 1984 (SI 1984/418) were both made under Sections 13 and 14 of and Schedule 3 to the 1984 Act and substantially re-enacted powers of detention in Orders made under the 1974 and 1976 Acts. A person who is being examined under Article 4 of either Order on his arrival in, or on seeking to leave, Northern Ireland or Great Britain for the purpose of determining whether he is or has been involved in terrorism connected with the affairs of Northern Ireland, or whether there are grounds for suspecting that he has committed an offence under Section 9 of the 1984 Act, may be detained under Article 9 or 10, as appropriate, pending the conclusion of his examination. The period of this examination may exceed 12 hours if an examining officer has reasonable grounds for suspecting him to be or to have been involved in acts of terrorism connected with the affairs of Northern Ireland.

Where such a person is detained under the said Article 9 or 10 he may be detained for up to 48 hours on the authority of an examining officer and thereafter, where the Secretary of State extends the detention period, for up to a further five days.

In its judgment of 29 November 1988 in the Case of *Brogan and Others*, the European Court of Human Rights held that there had been a violation of Article 5(3) in respect of each of the applicants, all of whom had been detained under Section 12 of the 1984 Act. The Court held that even the shortest of the four periods of detention concerned, namely four days and six hours, fell outside the constraints as to time permitted by the first part of Article 5(3). In addition, the Court held that there had been a violation of Article 5(5) in the case of each applicant.

Following this judgment, the Secretary of State for the Home Department informed Parliament on 6 December 1988 that, against the background of the terrorist campaign, and the overriding need to bring terrorists to justice, the Government did not believe that the maximum period of detention should be reduced. He informed Parliament that the Government were examining the matter with a view to responding to the judgment. On 22 December 1988, the Secretary of State further informed Parliament that it remained the Government's wish, if it could be achieved, to find a judicial process under which extended detention might be reviewed and where appropriate authorised by a judge or other judicial officer. But a further period of reflection and consultation was necessary before the Government could bring forward a firm and final view.

Since the judgment of 29 November 1988 as well as previously, the Government have found it necessary to continue to exercise, in relation to terrorism connected with the affairs of Northern Ireland, the powers described above enabling further detention without charge for periods of up to 5 days, on the authority of the Secretary of State, to the extent strictly required by the exigencies of the situation to enable necessary enquiries and investigations properly to be completed in order to decide whether criminal proceedings should be instituted. To the extent that the exercise of these powers may be inconsistent with the obligations imposed by the Convention the Government has availed itself of the right of derogation conferred by Article 15(1) of the Convention and will continue to do so until further notice.

Dated 23 December 1988

The 1989 notification

The United Kingdom Permanent Representative to the Council of Europe presents his compliments to the Secretary General of the Council, and has the honour to convey the following information.

In his communication to the Secretary General of 23 December 1988, reference was made to the introduction and exercise of certain powers under section 12 of the Prevention of Terrorism (Temporary Provisions) Act 1984, Article 9 of the Prevention of Terrorism (Supplemental Temporary Provisions) Order 1984 and Article 10 of the Prevention of Terrorism (Supplemental Temporary Provisions) (Northern Ireland) Order 1984.

These provisions have been replaced by section 14 of and paragraph 6 of Schedule 5 to the Prevention of Terrorism (Temporary Provisions) Act 1989, which make comparable provision. They came into force on 22 March 1989. A copy of these provisions is enclosed.

The United Kingdom Permanent Representative avails himself of this opportunity to renew to the Secretary General the assurance of his highest consideration.

Dated 23 March 1989

Part II
Reservation

At the time of signing the present (First) Protocol, I declare that, in view of certain provisions of the Education Acts in the United Kingdom, the principle affirmed in the second sentence of Article 2 is accepted by the United Kingdom only so far as it is compatible with the provision of efficient instruction and training, and the avoidance of unreasonable public expenditure.

Dated 20 March 1952

Made by the United Kingdom Permanent Representative to the Council of Europe.

INDEX